D1093246

International Civil Litigation in United States Courts

ASPEN CASEBOOK SERIES

International Civil Litigation in United States Courts

Fifth Edition

Gary B. Born

Peter B. Rutledge
Professor of Law
University of Gerogla School of Law

Wolters Kluwer
Law & Business

Copyright © 2011 CCH Incorporated.

Published by Wolters Kluwer Law & Business in New York.

Wolters Kluwer Law & Business serves customers worldwide with
CCH, Aspen Publishers, and Kluwer Law International products.
(www.wolterskluwerlb.com)

To contact Customer Service, e-mail customer.service@wolterskluwer.com,
call 1-800-234-1660, fax 1-800-901-9075, or mail correspondence to:

> Wolters Kluwer Law & Business
> Attn: Order Department
> PO Box 990
> Frederick, MD 21705

Printed in the United States of America.

1 2 3 4 5 6 7 8 9 0

ISBN 978-0-7355-0755-5

Library of Congress Cataloging-in-Publication Data

Born, Gary, 1955-
International civil litigation in United States courts / Gary B. Born,
Peter B. Rutledge.—5th ed.
    p. cm.
Includes bibliographical references and index.
ISBN 978-0-7355-0755-5
1. Conflict of laws—Civil procedure—United States—Cases. 2. Conflict of laws—Jurisdiction—
United States—Cases. 3. Civil procedure-United States—Cases. I. Rutledge, Peter B. II. Title.

KF418.C48B67 2011

347.73'5-dc23

2011029530

About Wolters Kluwer Law & Business

Wolters Kluwer Law & Business is a leading global provider of intelligent information and digital solutions for legal and business professionals in key specialty areas, and respected educational resources for professors and law students. Wolters Kluwer Law & Business connects legal and business professionals as well as those in the education market with timely, specialized authoritative content and information-enabled solutions to support success through productivity, accuracy and mobility.

Serving customers worldwide, Wolters Kluwer Law & Business products include those under the Aspen Publishers, CCH, Kluwer Law International, Loislaw, Best Case, ftwilliam.com and MediRegs family of products.

CCH products have been a trusted resource since 1913, and are highly regarded resources for legal, securities, antitrust and trade regulation, government contracting, banking, pension, payroll, employment and labor, and healthcare reimbursement and compliance professionals.

Aspen Publishers products provide essential information to attorneys, business professionals and law students. Written by preeminent authorities, the product line offers analytical and practical information in a range of specialty practice areas from securities law and intellectual property to mergers and acquisitions and pension/benefits. Aspen's trusted legal education resources provide professors and students with high-quality, up-to-date and effective resources for successful instruction and study in all areas of the law.

Kluwer Law International products provide the global business community with reliable international legal information in English. Legal practitioners, corporate counsel and business executives around the world rely on Kluwer Law journals, looseleafs, books, and electronic products for comprehensive information in many areas of international legal practice.

Loislaw is a comprehensive online legal research product providing legal content to law firm practitioners of various specializations. Loislaw provides attorneys with the ability to quickly and efficiently find the necessary legal information they need, when and where they need it, by facilitating access to primary law as well as state-specific law, records, forms and treatises.

Best Case Solutions is the leading bankruptcy software product to the bankruptcy industry. It provides software and workflow tools to flawlessly streamline petition preparation and the electronic filing process, while timely incorporating ever-changing court requirements.

ftwilliam.com offers employee benefits professionals the highest quality plan documents (retirement, welfare and non-qualified) and government forms (5500/PBGC, 1099 and IRS) software at highly competitive prices.

MediRegs products provide integrated health care compliance content and software solutions for professionals in healthcare, higher education and life sciences, including professionals in accounting, law and consulting.

Wolters Kluwer Law & Business, a division of Wolters Kluwer, is headquartered in New York. Wolters Kluwer is a market-leading global information services company focused on professionals.

This book is for Beatrix, Natascha, and Jedidiah
— G.B.B.

This book is for Birgit
—P.B.R.

PREFACE TO THE FOURTH EDITION

When the first edition of this book was completed in 1988, the field of international civil litigation did not exist in the United States. No case book addressed the subject and virtually no course at any major law school dealt with the litigation of international disputes. Today, almost twenty years later, the fourth edition of this book has been joined by nearly a dozen ably-written competing casebooks on the subject of international civil litigation, a course which is taught at law schools around the United States. Practitioners, as well as academics, now regard international civil litigation as a vital, and profoundly challenging, area of the law.

Other changes have been almost as striking. When this book was conceived, the Alien Tort Statute had been the subject of hardly any litigation, the Supreme Court had not yet decided landmark personal jurisdiction cases like *Asahi* and *Helicopteros*, the Foreign Sovereign Immunities Act had only been recently enacted, *Piper*'s *forum non conveniens* analysis was still fresh, *Timberlane* had only recently addressed the extraterritorial application of U.S. statutes, and the United States had only recently ratified the Hague Service Convention, the Hague Evidence Convention, and the New York Convention. Today, while the central themes addressed in the first edition remain unchanged, the legal landscape is vastly different. The Supreme Court has rendered major decisions in many of these areas, new treaties, statutes, new versions of the Federal Rules of Civil Procedure have come into force, and a growing body of European Union law has provided new opportunities for comparison—necessitating for the first time a separate Documentary Supplement to this edition, containing all the appendices referenced within.

The current edition of this book remains true to its original aspiration: to assist students, practitioners, and scholars alike in understanding international civil litigation in U.S. courts. It continues to do so through a deliberate effort to provide extensive discussion and references to authorities—on the premise that detailed answers provoke better, more challenging questions.

Nearly ten years have passed since the release of the third edition, and our efforts at revision would not have been possible without the assistance of countless colleagues, students, competitors, and friends. We cannot hope to acknowledge them all here and will not attempt to do so. That said, Steven Burbank at the University of Pennsylvania Law School, who has used the book for many years, shared very generously of his time and insight; we benefited hugely from his thoughts. Among our colleagues, Jason File, Kenneth Beale, Duncan Speller, Briana DiBari, Barney Ford, Gordon Jimison, and,

ix

especially, Maureen Smith provided invaluable research assistance, while Steve Young, a research librarian at the Columbus School of Law and former librarian at the U.S. Supreme Court, provided constant support tracking down hard-to-find sources. Elke Jenner and Julie Kendrick, our respective assistants, helped with preparation of the manuscript in innumerable ways. Finally, we would like to thank the entire team at Aspen and Kluwer, especially Carol McGeehan, Taylor Kearns, Gwen de Vries, and Bas Kniphorst for their support.

Gary Born
London/Berlin

Peter Rutledge
Washington, D.C.

November 2006

PREFACE TO THE FIFTH EDITION

The law governing international civil litigation has changed dramatically in the five years since the fourth edition was published. Recent decisions of the United States Supreme Court have had a significant impact on fields such as personal jurisdiction, sovereign immunity, and extraterritoriality. This current edition reflects those changes and raises important questions about the broader implications of those decisions.

Of course, the Supreme Court only decides a fraction of cases where review is sought, and the field of international dispute resolution is no exception. Consequently, much of the law in this area (like others) is shaped by the lower federal courts and state courts. This has been especially true in areas such as the Alien Tort Statute, the Torture Victim Protection Act, discovery, and judgment enforcement. The current edition aims to capture those trends, identify emerging splits in authority, and critique the doctrine.

Developments in this field are of course not limited to the United States. While the book still focuses primarily on United States law, the current edition deliberately incorporates more excerpts, more extensive references, and more questions concerning foreign law, especially European law. In part, this reflects an intellectual desire to stimulate comparative thinking. It also reflects an important reality—known to many practitioners but perhaps less well known to the students—that successful practice in this area, even for the United States lawyer, requires a keen understanding of other legal systems. Whether the matter concerns judicial jurisdiction, the enforceability of forum selection or arbitration clauses, the extraterritorial effect of legislation or the enforcement of judgments and arbitration awards, smart transactional lawyers must comprehend those differences even before a transaction is consummated. Moreover, when disputes do arise, savvy litigators must appreciate differences between legal systems in order to develop a sound strategy regarding the forum in which a dispute will be resolved. The additions of foreign material in this current edition are also designed to teach students (and remind practitioners) of these important considerations. The extensively referenced documents—new treaties, statutes, the Federal Rules of Civil Procedure, a growing body of European Union Law—are all contained in a separate Documentary Supplement to this edition.

Once again, this current work would not have been possible without the support of countless individuals. While the complete list would be too numerous to reproduce here, we must once again acknowledge the exceptional support of Steve Burbank, at the University of Pennsylvania Law School, who has used this book for many years; this current edition has benefited greatly from his penetrating insights. Among our colleagues, Halley Espy, Amanda Holcomb, and Tim Robbins provided invaluable assistance. Jennifer Hill, Elke Jenner, Barbara Pitzl, and Cindy Wentworth helped with the preparation of the manuscript in numerous ways. The University of Vienna Law School generously provided an office and secretarial support to Professor Rutledge while he worked on this book during a sabbatical. Finally, we would like to thank the entire team at Aspen Publishers and Wolters Kluwer, especially Carol McGeehan and John Devins, as well as Troy Froebe of The Froebe Group for their support.

Gary Born
London, England

Peter Rutledge
Athens, Georgia

August 2011

Acknowledgment

ABA Model Rules of Professional Conduct, 2006 Edition. © 2006 by the American Bar Association. Reprinted with permission. Copies of ABA Model Rules of Professional Conduct, 2006 Edition, are available from Service Center, American Bar Association, 321 North Clark Street, Chicago, IL 60610, 1-800-285-2221.

Summary of Contents

Contents

2

Jurisdiction of U.S. Courts over Parties to International Disputes   81

3

Foreign Sovereign Immunity and Jurisdiction of U.S. Courts over Foreign States   **231**

8

Choice of Law in International Litigation   645

9

Act of State and Foreign Sovereign Compulsion   797

PART FOUR
INTERNATIONAL JUDICIAL ASSISTANCE

10

Service of U.S. Process on Foreign Persons   867

11

Extraterritorial Discovery and Taking Evidence Abroad   **965**

12

Recognition and Enforcement of Foreign Judgments   **1077**

13

International Commercial Arbitration and U.S. Courts: An Overview   1157

International Civil Litigation in United States Courts

Part One

Judicial Jurisdiction

The courts of many nations will not adjudicate civil disputes unless the parties (or their property) and their claims are subject to the forum's "judicial jurisdiction" or "jurisdiction to adjudicate." As discussed below, judicial jurisdiction includes both (a) the power of a court to render a judgment against particular persons or things, and (b) the power or competence of a court to adjudicate particular categories of claims.[1]

Judicial jurisdiction is distinguished from "legislative" or "prescriptive" jurisdiction, which refers to the authority of a state to make its laws generally applicable to persons or activities.[2] Judicial jurisdiction is also distinguished from "enforcement jurisdiction" — the authority of a state to induce or compel compliance, or punish noncompliance, with its laws.[3]

In the United States, a court cannot hear a dispute unless it possesses both "personal" jurisdiction over the parties and "subject matter" jurisdiction over their claims.[4] Subject matter and personal jurisdiction are distinct concepts under U.S. law. Subject matter jurisdiction is the power of a court to entertain specified classes of cases, such as any action between parties of differing citizenship.[5] Although subject matter and legislative jurisdiction are sometimes confused, there is a fundamental distinction under U.S. law between the two categories. Subject matter jurisdiction deals with a court's power to hear a class of disputes without necessary regard to the substantive rules that are applied.[6]

---

1. *Restatement (Third) Foreign Relations Law* Part IV Intro. Note & §401 (1987); *Restatement (Second) Conflict of Laws* Ch. 3, Intro. Note (1971); Akehurst, *Jurisdiction in International Law*, 46 Brit. Y.B. Int'l L. 145 (1972-1973).

2. *See infra* pp. 589-591; *Restatement (Third) Foreign Relations Law* Part IV Intro. Note & §401 (1987) ("make its law applicable to the activities, relations, or status of persons, or the interests of persons in things, whether by legislation, by executive act or order, by administrative rule or regulation, or by determination of a court"); *Restatement (Second) Conflict of Laws* Ch. 3, Intro. Note (1971); Akehurst, *Jurisdiction in International Law*, 46 Brit. Y.B. Int'l L. 145, 179-212 (1972-1973). Chapters 7 and 8 *infra* provide a detailed examination of legislative jurisdiction in the international context.

3. *Restatement (Third) Foreign Relations Law* Part IV Intro. Note & §401 (1987). Examples of the exercise of jurisdiction to enforce include execution upon property, seizure of goods, and arrest. These materials do not directly address international law limits on national enforcement jurisdiction.

4. *Insurance Corp. of Ireland v. Compagnie des Bauxites de Guinee*, 456 U.S. 694, 701 (1982) ("The validity of an order of a federal court depends upon that court's having jurisdiction over both the subject matter and the parties."); *Still v. Gottlieb*, 305 U.S. 165, 171-172 (1938).

5. *See Verlinden BV v. Central Bank of Nigeria*, 461 U.S. 480 (1983); C. Wright & A. Miller, *Federal Practice and Procedure*, 1350-1351, 3522 (2006 & Supp. 2010); *Restatement (Third) Foreign Relations Law* §401 comment c (1987).

6. For example, the federal district courts enjoy "diversity jurisdiction" and "alienage jurisdiction" over all civil actions between citizens of different states, or suits between U.S. and foreign nationals, where the amount in

In contrast, legislative jurisdiction deals with the power of a state to prescribe substantive law, without necessary regard to the forum in which that law is applied.[7]

There is also a fundamental distinction under U.S. law between subject matter jurisdiction and personal jurisdiction.[8] Personal jurisdiction involves the power of a court to adjudicate a claim against the defendant's person and to render a judgment enforceable against the defendant and any of its assets.[9] In contrast, subject matter jurisdiction refers to a court's power to hear categories of claims, without necessarily considering the relationship of the parties to particular cases to the forum.[10]

Part One considers the judicial jurisdiction of U.S. courts in international civil litigation. Chapter 1 examines the subject matter jurisdiction of federal courts in international disputes. Chapter 2 considers the personal jurisdiction of U.S. courts over parties to international litigation (and particularly non-U.S. parties). Chapter 3 explores the subject matter and personal jurisdiction of U.S. courts over foreign states and their state-related entities.[11]

All three chapters also include comparative materials, which illustrate how selected foreign states address issues of judicial jurisdiction. In particular, we consider how the European Union deals with questions of judicial jurisdiction and how these issues were recently addressed in (abortive) efforts to negotiate an international convention on jurisdiction and judgments under the auspices of the Hague Conference on Private International Law.[12]

Judicial jurisdiction has substantial practical importance in international litigation. That importance derives from the role of judicial jurisdiction in determining the forum (or forums) in which an international dispute can be litigated. As discussed below, forum selection has vital consequences for the resolution of many international disputes, thus giving jurisdictional issues a vital importance in many cases.

For a variety of reasons, the same dispute can often be resolved in significantly different ways in different forums. Procedural, substantive law, and choice of law principles vary

---

controversy exceeds $75,000. *See* 28 U.S.C. §1332(a); U.S. Const. Art. III, §2. In conferring this jurisdiction, Congress did not generally prescribe rules of substantive law, but left federal courts to apply the substantive law that would be applied by a state court in the state where the federal court sits. *Erie R.R. v. Tompkins*, 304 U.S. 64 (1938); *infra* pp. 10-13. Much the same approach was taken with respect to claims against foreign states. *See* Chapter 3 *infra.*

7. *See infra* pp. 589-591; *Restatement (Third) Foreign Relations Law* §401 comment c (1987). Despite this distinction, there is often an important relation in the United States between subject matter and legislative jurisdiction. In many cases, Congress's prescription of a substantive rule of law is accompanied by a grant of subject matter jurisdiction to the federal courts for cases arising under those substantive rules. The federal antitrust and securities laws are prime examples of the simultaneous exercise of prescriptive jurisdiction and grant of subject matter jurisdiction. *See infra* pp. 32, 672-673, 707, 709-711; 15 U.S.C. §§1, 2 & 15 (antitrust); 15 U.S.C. §§77(g), 77l(2), 78aa, 78j (securities).

8. *Insurance Corp. of Ireland v. Compagnie des Bauxites de Guinee*, 456 U.S. 694, 701 (1982); *Verlinden BV v. Central Bank of Nigeria*, 461 U.S. 480 (1983).

9. *See infra* pp. 81-91; *Restatement (Second) Conflict of Laws* Ch. 3, Intro. Note (1971); *Shaffer v. Heitner*, 433 U.S. 186, 199 (1977). U.S. law distinguishes between *in personam* (or personal) jurisdiction, *in rem* jurisdiction, and *quasi in rem* jurisdiction. *In rem* jurisdiction involves the adjudication of preexisting claims of ownership or other rights in specific property (*e.g.*, a ship or a bank deposit); although judgments rendered on the basis of *in rem* jurisdiction extend only to the specific assets that are before the court, they are binding on the interests of all persons in such property. *Quasi in rem* jurisdiction most often involves the exercise of jurisdiction on the basis of property present in the forum where personal jurisdiction over the defendant is lacking; unlike *in rem* jurisdiction, the judgment only affects the rights between persons to the property. *Restatement (Second) Conflict of Laws* Ch. 3, Intro. Note (1971); *Shaffer v. Heitner*, 433 U.S. 186, 199 (1977).

10. *See Insurance Corp. of Ireland v. Compagnie des Bauxites de Guinee*, 456 U.S. 694, 701 (1982). Again, there is sometimes an important practical relation between subject matter and personal jurisdiction. As discussed below, the Foreign Sovereign Immunities Act makes federal court subject matter and personal jurisdiction coextensive. *See infra* Chapter 3 at p. 234.

11. A number of other significant means of influencing forum selection are discussed in Chapters 4, 5 & 6 below, including the *forum non conveniens* doctrine, forum selection agreements, *lis pendens*, and venue.

12. *See infra* pp. 107-108, 485-486, 1080, 1085-1086.

substantially from one forum to another.[13] The identity, character, competence, and neutrality of the tribunal that decides civil disputes can also differ materially depending upon the forum where adjudication occurs. Some forums may be unfavorable to one party to a dispute: for reasons of convenience, local bias, and otherwise, parties are sometimes particularly reluctant to litigate in the courts of their adversary. As one commentator has correctly observed, "[t]he choice of forum has become a key strategic battle fought to increase the chances of prevailing on the merits."[14]

Forum selection is especially important in the international context. Procedural, substantive, and choice of law rules differ far more significantly from country to country than they do from state to state within the United States.[15] Differences in political, economic, social, and other attitudes of courts and lawyers are more pronounced in international matters than domestic ones. Inconvenience, forum bias, and the risk of multiple proceedings will be more important factors in international than in domestic litigation.[16] Obtaining effective enforcement of judgments in foreign countries can also often be unusually difficult, as compared to enforcement issues within a single jurisdiction.[17]

Forum selection for an international dispute can be particularly important where one potential forum is the United States. This is because litigation in U.S. courts often differs dramatically from that in other countries, including with respect to its procedures, risks, expenses, and potential rewards. A number of factors contribute to make U.S. litigation unusual when compared to other countries. In general, as detailed below, these factors make the United States a particularly attractive forum for plaintiffs: "As a moth is drawn to the light, so is a litigant drawn to the United States. If he can only get his case into their courts, he stands to win a fortune."[18]

First, by constitutional guarantee and historical precedent, civil suits in the United States are ordinarily decided by juries of lay men and women, who have very different backgrounds and sympathies from many judges, whether members of U.S. or foreign judiciaries. Although there are regional, economic, social, and other variations, U.S. juries can be remarkably pro-plaintiff, particularly in cases involving individual litigants or small businesses. That is particularly true when compared to jurisdictions where judges are government lawyers or career bureaucrats. As one eminent foreign judge has remarked, "[t]here is in the United States a right to trial by jury. These are prone to award fabulous damages. They are notoriously sympathetic [to plaintiffs]."[19]

Second, several procedural aspects of U.S. litigation tend to favor plaintiffs. Plaintiffs in U.S. courts can enter into contingent fee agreements, which is often forbidden or highly restricted in foreign courts. Unsuccessful U.S. litigants are also not ordinarily liable for their adversary's attorneys' fees, although they are in many foreign jurisdictions.[20] Discovery in U.S. proceedings is extremely broad, by international standards, and provides means for plaintiffs both to prove their substantive claims from the

---

13. *See generally* M. Glendon, M. Gordon & C. Osakwe, *Comparative Legal Traditions* (1985); G. Gloss, *Comparative Law* (1979); J. Merryman, *The Civil Law Tradition: An Introduction to the Legal Systems of Western Europe and Latin America* (2d ed. 1985).

14. Stein, *Forum Non Conveniens and the Redundancy of Court-Access Doctrine*, 133 U. Pa. L. Rev. 781, 794-795 (1985).

15. *See* Born, *Reflections on Judicial Jurisdiction in International Cases*, 17 Ga. J. Int'l & Comp. L. 1, 25 (1987).

16. *See Asahi Metal Industry Co. v. Superior Court*, 480 U.S. 102, 114 (1987) (noting "[t]he unique burdens placed upon one who must defend oneself in a foreign legal system"); Born, *Reflections on Judicial Jurisdiction in International Cases*, 17 Ga. J. Int'l & Comp. L. 1, 24-25 (1987).

17. *See infra* Chapter 12 at pp. 1085-1086.

18. *Smith Kline & French Labs. v. Block* [1983] 2 All E.R. 72, 74 (Denning, J.).

19. *Smith Kline & French Labs. v. Block* [1983] 2 All E.R. 72, 74 (Denning, J.) ("At no cost to himself, and at no risk of having to pay anything to the other side, the lawyers there will conduct the case 'on spec' as we say, or on a 'contingency fee' as they say.").

20. *See* Symposium, *Attorney Fee Shifting*, 47 Law & Contemp. Probs. 1 (1984).

defendants' own files, and to impose unrecoverable litigation costs on a defendant.[21] U.S. pleading requirements, though recently tightened by several Supreme Court decisions, still often permit fairly loosely formulated claims to be advanced, sometimes enabling plaintiffs with weak cases to survive all efforts to obtain summary disposition.[22] At the same time, plaintiffs' attorneys frequently combine litigation in traditional judicial forums with public relations, legislative and other actions directed toward the defendants. The cumulative effect of these procedural features of U.S. litigation is often to improve a plaintiff's prospects of successful recovery (including by providing substantial leverage in negotiating settlement of marginal or unwinnable suits).

Third, and at the bottom line, is the simple fact that U.S. damage awards tend to be dramatically larger than those in other countries.[23] U.S. juries are often both sympathetic and generous, at least from an injured plaintiff's perspective. U.S. substantive laws are sometimes unusually favorable: American product liability and other tort doctrines, and U.S. antitrust and securities fraud statutes often grant plaintiffs very generous avenues of recovery.[24] Moreover, many U.S. state and federal statutes provide for mandatory awards of multiple damages, while state common law often permits jury awards of punitive damages based on vague, discretionary standards.

At the same time, aspects of U.S. litigation can make it distinctly unattractive to some foreign (and domestic) plaintiffs. Few litigants welcome the prospect of participating in any proceeding, far from home, in an unfamiliar forum that may be inconvenient, parochial, or worse. In the United States, legal proceedings can be uniquely expensive and, compared to at least some foreign alternatives, relatively slow. The availability of broad discovery can be a threat to some potential foreign plaintiffs, as is the case with extensive public, press, and governmental access to U.S. judicial proceedings and discovery materials. And the possibility of large damages awards, by potentially unpredictable local lay juries, can be a disincentive to potential foreign plaintiffs where they anticipate that counterclaims are likely.

For all the foregoing reasons, it is critically important in international commercial disputes for a litigant to have its claims adjudicated in the best available forum, especially where one potential forum is the United States. Plaintiffs therefore often devote substantial effort and ingenuity to finding the most advantageous forum in which to proceed with their claims. Chief Justice Rehnquist commented on the "litigation strategy of countless plaintiffs who seek a forum with favorable substantive or procedural rules or sympathetic local populations."[25]

From a practical perspective, the issues of judicial jurisdiction discussed in Part One are vital aspects of these disputes over forum selection. At the same time, these issues of judicial jurisdiction involve basic limitations on the authority and competence of U.S. courts in international matters. For these reasons, these issues warrant careful attention at the beginning of any study of international litigation.

---

21. *Societe Nationale Industrielle Aerospatiale v. U.S. District Court*, 482 U.S. 522 (1987); *Hickman v. Taylor*, 329 U.S. 495, 500-507 (1947). The scope of U.S. pretrial discovery is discussed below at *infra* pp. 965-968, 978-1000.

22. *See* C. Wright & A. Miller, *Federal Practice and Procedure* §§1202, 1215-1225, 1286, 1375 (2006 & Supp. 2010)

23. In one foreign judge's terse summary, "in the United States the scale of damages for injuries of the magnitude sustained by the plaintiff is something in the region of ten times what is regarded as appropriate by . . . the courts of [England]." *Castanho v. Brown & Root (U.K.) Ltd.* [1980] 1 W.L.R. 833, 859, *aff'd*, 1981 A.C. 557 (Shaw, J.).

24. *E.g.*, *British Airways Bd. v. Laker Airways* [1984] W.L.R. 413 (H.L.) (English plaintiff sues English and other European defendants in United States, to take advantage of U.S. antitrust laws, which were more favorable than applicable English law); *Virgin Atlantic Airways Ltd. v. British Airways plc*, 872 F. Supp. 52 (S.D.N.Y. 1994) (same).

25. *Keeton v. Hustler Magazine, Inc.*, 465 U.S. 770, 779 (1984).

1

Jurisdiction of U.S. Courts over Subject Matter in International Disputes

A U.S. court cannot adjudicate a case unless it has "subject matter" jurisdiction over the action. Subject matter jurisdiction (also referred to as "competence") is the power of a court to entertain specified classes of cases, such as any claim in excess of $75,000 and between parties of differing citizenships.[1] This chapter considers the subject matter jurisdiction of U.S. courts in international cases, focusing on the federal courts.

A. Introduction

1. Plenary State Subject Matter and Legislative Jurisdiction

For the most part, there are few restrictions on the subject matter jurisdiction of U.S. state courts: state trial courts ordinarily possess general jurisdiction over all but a few specialized categories of claims. Those exceptions that are of importance to international litigation are relatively scarce.[2] The same generalization is true with respect to state substantive law in the United States. States generally are subject to few significant internal limitations on their powers to exercise legislative jurisdiction.[3]

2. Limited Federal Legislative and Subject Matter Jurisdiction

a. Limited Federal Legislative Authority Under Article I. Article I of the U.S. Constitution endows Congress with only limited legislative powers; those powers not granted to Congress are expressly reserved to the several states.[4] This arrangement reflects the

---

1. *See Verlinden BV v. Central Bank of Nigeria,* 461 U.S. 480 (1983); C. Wright et al., *Federal Practice and Procedure* §1350 (2004 & Supp. 2010); *Restatement (Third) Foreign Relations Law* §401 comment c (1987).
2. Claims under some federal statutes, including the federal securities laws, may be brought exclusively in federal court. *See* 15 U.S.C. §§77l(2) & 78aa. Sometimes, a federal statute not only creates exclusive federal jurisdiction but designates a particular forum. *See* §408(b)(3) of the Air Transportation Safety and System Stabilization Act, 115 Stat. 230, 241 (2001) ("[t]he United States District Court for the Southern District of New York shall have original and exclusive jurisdiction over all actions brought for any claim (including any claim for loss of property, personal injury, or death) resulting from or relating to the terrorist-related aircraft crashes of September 11, 2001").
3. The U.S. Constitution limits the legislative jurisdiction of the several states, *see infra* pp. 612-630, and valid federal statutes or U.S. treaties may preempt state law, *see infra* pp. 5-7, 10-13, 630-644.
4. Article I, §1, provides Congress with only the "legislative [p]owers herein granted." In addition, the Tenth Amendment provides that "The powers not delegated to the United States by the Constitution, nor prohibited by it to the States, are reserved to the States respectively, or to the people."

Framers' judgment that the national government's authority should be restricted, both to prevent abuse of its powers and to avoid invading the prerogatives of the several states.

Congress's principal enumerated powers include the authority to regulate interstate and foreign commerce, to levy taxes, and to appropriate funds.[5] These powers have proved both overwhelmingly important and difficult to restrain. The Supreme Court has interpreted congressional authority expansively in the last four decades and, until recently, had abandoned meaningful judicial efforts to limit Congress's legislative powers over commercial matters.[6] There continue to be few aspects of national commercial matters that Congress cannot regulate.

Congress's powers over U.S. foreign relations are particularly extensive. Among other things, Article I of the Constitution grants Congress the power to declare war, maintain an army and navy, and define and punish piracy and violations of the law of nations,[7] while the Senate is vested with the power to advise on and consent to treaties and the appointment of ambassadors.[8] The Supreme Court has said that the "supremacy of the national power in the general field of foreign affairs . . . is made clear by the Constitution . . . , and has since been given continuous recognition by this Court."[9] The Court has also repeatedly said that the states have only the most limited of roles in international relations, declaring that the Constitution prohibits any "intrusion by the State into the field of foreign affairs which the Constitution entrusts to the President and the Congress."[10] Invoking this constitutional authority, Congress and the President have frequently preempted state laws in the area of foreign relations.[11]

The Constitution also provides for broad federal legislative power over international trade, conferred principally by Article I, §8's "foreign commerce" clause.[12] In the Court's words, "[f]oreign commerce is preeminently a matter of national concern."[13] The Court has held that federal power over foreign commerce is broader than that over interstate commerce, and that the "dormant" foreign commerce clause requires greater scrutiny of state restrictions on foreign commerce than for purely domestic commerce.[14]

Congress has frequently exercised its constitutional authority over foreign commerce, particularly in recent decades. Thus, federal legislation exhaustively regulates the fields of foreign sovereign immunity and international arbitration, as well as international trade

5. U.S. Const. Art. I, §8, cl. 1, 3.

6. *United States v. Morrison*, 529 U.S. 598 (2000); *United States v. Lopez*, 514 U.S. 549 (1995); *South Carolina v. Baker*, 485 U.S. 505 (1988); *Garcia v. San Antonio Metro. Transit Auth.*, 469 U.S. 528 (1985), *overruling National League of Cities v. Usery*, 426 U.S. 833 (1976).

7. U.S. Const. Art. I, §8.

8. U.S. Const. Art. II, §2.

9. *Hines v. Davidowitz*, 312 U.S. 52, 62 (1941).

10. *Zschernig v. Miller*, 389 U.S. 429, 439 (1968). *See also* Henkin, *The Foreign Affairs Power of the Federal Courts: Sabbatino*, 64 Colum. L. Rev. 805 (1964); Moore, *Federalism and Foreign Relations*, 1965 Duke L.J. 248. Or, as the Court remarked elsewhere, "in respect of our foreign relations generally, state lines disappear. As to such purposes the State . . . does not exist." *United States v. Belmont*, 301 U.S. 324, 331 (1937).

11. *E.g.*, *American Ins. Ass'n v. Garamendi*, 539 U.S. 396 (2003); *Crosby v. Nat'l Foreign Trade Council*, 530 U.S. 363 (2000); *Dames & Moore v. Regan*, 453 U.S. 654 (1981); *Hines v. Davidowitz*, 312 U.S. 52 (1941); *United States v. Pink*, 315 U.S. 203 (1942); *United States v. Belmont*, 301 U.S. 324 (1937).

12. *See Container Corp. of America v. Franchise Tax Bd.*, 463 U.S. 159 (1983); *Japan Line, Ltd. v. County of Los Angeles*, 441 U.S. 434, 447 (1979); *Michelin Tire Corp. v. Wages*, 423 U.S. 276 (1976); Abel, *The Commerce Clause in the Constitutional Convention and in Contemporary Comment*, 25 Minn. L. Rev. 432 (1941). Article I also grants Congress the power to impose import and export duties and to regulate immigration. U.S. Const. Art. I, §§8 & 9.

13. *Japan Line, Ltd. v. County of Los Angeles*, 441 U.S. 434, 448 (1979).

14. *Japan Line, Ltd. v. County of Los Angeles*, 441 U.S. 434, 448 & n.12 (1979) ("Although the Constitution, art. I, §8, cl. 3, grants Congress power to regulate commerce 'with foreign Nations' and 'among the several states' in parallel phrases, there is evidence that the founders intended the scope of the foreign commerce power to be the greater."); *see also Dep't of Revenue of Ky. v. Davis*, 552 U.S. 328, 348 n.17 (2008); *National Foreign Trade Council v. Natsios*, 181 F.3d 38, 66-71 (1st Cir. 1999), *aff'd on other grounds sub nom. Crosby v. Nat'l Foreign Trade Council*, 530 U.S. 363 (2000). *See infra* pp. 630-644.

practices, international transportation and telecommunications, tariffs and customs, and export controls. Notwithstanding its broad legislative powers, there remain numerous areas in the international field where Congress has not chosen to exercise its authority. Thus, federal legislation is generally silent in the international context with respect to substantive contract and tort law, as well as with respect to rules regarding agency, damages, contribution, choice of law, and recognition of foreign judgments. In all of these fields, state law usually provides the applicable rule of decision.[15]

b. Limited Federal Judicial Authority Under Article III. Just as the Constitution granted Congress only enumerated powers, the federal judiciary was established with only limited subject matter jurisdiction.[16] A federal court generally cannot exercise subject matter jurisdiction unless both the U.S. Constitution and valid federal legislation grant such jurisdiction.[17] Article III of the U.S. Constitution defines the "judicial Power" — or subject matter jurisdiction — of the federal courts. A federal statute cannot validly confer subject matter jurisdiction on a federal court except within the limits of Article III's grants.[18] Conversely, without a federal statutory grant of jurisdiction, federal courts cannot exercise subject matter jurisdiction contemplated by Article III.[19]

Federal subject matter jurisdiction is generally a nonwaivable requirement, and cannot ordinarily be conferred by the parties' consent.[20] It is permitted — indeed, affirmatively required — for a federal court to raise the lack of subject matter jurisdiction on its own motion.[21] In both respects, subject matter jurisdiction differs from personal jurisdiction.[22]

3. Overview of Federal Subject Matter Jurisdiction in International Cases

a. Article III's Grants of Subject Matter Jurisdiction. Three of Article III's grants of judicial power are especially important for international cases. First, the federal courts are granted "federal question" (or "arising under") jurisdiction over "all Cases, in Law and Equity, arising under this Constitution, the Laws of the United States, and Treaties made

---

15. *See infra* pp. 468-471, 791-796, 1188-1190.

16. *Insurance Corp. of Ireland v. Compagnie des Bauxites de Guinee*, 456 U.S. 694, 701 (1982) ("Federal courts are courts of limited jurisdiction.").

17. *Verlinden BV v. Central Bank of Nigeria*, 461 U.S. 480 (1983); *Hodgson & Thompson v. Bowerbank*, 9 U.S. 303 (1809); C. Wright et al., *Federal Practice and Procedure* §3522 (2008 & Supp. 2010). One exception to this general rule may be the Supreme Court's jurisdiction. The Constitution expressly sets out the original jurisdiction of the Supreme Court over certain matters such as cases "affecting ambassadors." U.S. Const. Art. III, §2. By contrast, the Constitution does not set out the jurisdiction of the lower federal courts or, for that matter, require the creation of such inferior courts. Instead, it leaves the creation of lower courts to Congress's discretion. U.S. Const. Art. III, §1.

18. *Verlinden BV v. Central Bank of Nigeria*, 461 U.S. 480 (1983) ("Congress may not expand the jurisdiction of the federal courts beyond the bounds established by the Constitution").

19. *Argentine Republic v. Amerada Hess Shipping Corp.*, 488 U.S. 428, 433 (1989); *Insurance Corp. of Ireland v. Compagnie des Bauxites de Guinee*, 456 U.S. 694, 701 (1982) (federal subject matter jurisdiction is "limited to those subjects encompassed within the statutory grant of jurisdiction"). Although a federal court cannot exercise subject matter jurisdiction without a statutory grant, Congress's ability to regulate federal courts' jurisdiction is probably subject to some constitutional limitations. *See* Hart, *The Power of Congress to Limit the Jurisdiction of the Federal Courts: An Exercise in Dialectic*, 66 Harv. L. Rev. 1362 (1953).

20. *Arizonans for Official English v. Arizona*, 520 U.S. 43, 73 (1997); *Insurance Corp. of Ireland v. Compagnie des Bauxites de Guinee*, 456 U.S. 694, 702 (1982); *California v. LaRue*, 409 U.S. 109 (1972).

21. *Steel Co. v. Citizens for a Better Environment*, 523 U.S. 83, 94 (1998); *Insurance Corp. of Ireland v. Compagnie des Bauxites de Guinee*, 456 U.S. 694, 702 (1982).

22. *Insurance Corp. of Ireland v. Compagnie des Bauxites de Guinee*, 456 U.S. 694, 702 (1982); *Leroy v. Great W. United Corp.*, 443 U.S. 173, 180 (1979) ("neither personal jurisdiction nor venue is fundamentally preliminary in the sense that subject matter jurisdiction is, for both are personal privileges of the defendant, rather than absolute strictures on the court, and both may be waived by the parties").

or which shall be made, under their Authority."[23] Second, Article III grants so-called "alienage jurisdiction" over all cases "between a State, or the Citizens thereof, and foreign States, Citizens or Subjects."[24] Third, federal jurisdiction extends to a variety of specialized cases that may raise international issues.[25]

It is not coincidental that Article III contains several grants of federal subject matter jurisdiction specifically applicable in international contexts. In drafting the Constitution, one of the Framers' central concerns was to ensure that the federal government would enjoy broad control over the foreign affairs and trade of the new Republic. The Founding Fathers were convinced that, in these matters, the United States must speak with a single voice. As Thomas Jefferson wrote to James Madison in 1786: "The politics of Europe rendered it indispensably necessary that with respect to everything external we be one nation firmly hooped together; interior government is what each State should keep to itself."[26] Thus, the Supreme Court has said that the Federalist Papers demonstrate the "importance of national power in all matters relating to foreign affairs and the inherent danger of state action in this field."[27]

The perceived importance of federal control over matters affecting U.S. foreign relations and commerce shaped Article III's provisions regarding the subject matter jurisdiction of the federal courts. The Framers repeatedly said that it was vital for Article III to grant federal courts jurisdiction over most international disputes. Alexander Hamilton said:

> [T]he peace of the WHOLE ought not to be left at the disposal of a PART. The Union will undoubtedly be answerable to foreign powers for the conduct of its members. And the responsibility for an injury ought ever to be accompanied with the faculty of preventing it. As the denial or perversion of justice by the sentences of courts, as well as in any other manner, is with reason classed among the just causes of war, it will follow that the federal judiciary ought to have cognizance of all causes in which the citizens of other countries are concerned.[28]

This rationale was used by Hamilton to justify Article III's grants of admiralty jurisdiction[29] and federal question jurisdiction,[30] as well as "alienage jurisdiction."[31]

b.   Statutory Grants of Federal Subject Matter Jurisdiction.   Pursuant to these Article III authorizations, Congress has made numerous statutory grants of subject matter jurisdiction to the lower federal courts which are of importance in international civil litigation. Two such statutory authorizations are principally applicable in domestic cases, but are also significant in international disputes: (1) cases involving "federal

---

23. Art. III, §2. *See infra* pp. 30-70.

24. Art. III, §2. *See infra* pp. 21-30.

25. Article III authorizes federal jurisdiction over "all Cases affecting Ambassadors, other public ministers and Consuls," and "all cases of admiralty and maritime jurisdiction." U.S. Const. Art. III, §2. As to the former, Article III grants the Supreme Court original jurisdiction.

26. Letter dated October 1786 (quoted in C. Warren, *The Making of the Constitution* 46 (1937)).

27. *Hines v. Davidowitz*, 312 U.S. 52, 62 n.9 (1941).

28. A. Hamilton, J. Madison & J. Jay, *The Federalist Papers*, No. 80 at 476 (C. Rossiter ed., 1961).

29. Admiralty disputes typically involved foreign parties and transactions. This was cited at the Constitutional Convention as a primary reason justifying federal jurisdiction. 1 M. Farrand, *Records of the Federal Convention of 1787* 124 (1937).

30. In particular, it was thought necessary that federal courts decide cases arising under U.S. treaties. *See infra* pp. 30-31.

31. Frequent comments were made during the debates surrounding the Constitution regarding the importance of federal subject matter jurisdiction in disputes involving foreigners. *See infra* pp. 21-22, 26.

questions" arising under the U.S. Constitution, statutes, and regulations;[32] and (2) diversity of citizenship cases, between citizens of different U.S. states.[33] Several other statutory grants of federal subject matter jurisdiction are generally applicable only in international disputes. These include: (3) alienage jurisdiction, over actions between U.S. and foreign parties;[34] (4) jurisdiction under the Alien Tort Statute;[35] and (5) jurisdiction over actions against foreign states under the Foreign Sovereign Immunities Act (or "FSIA").[36]

c. Removal. If both a constitutional and statutory basis for federal subject matter jurisdiction exists, then a plaintiff can commence an action in U.S. district court.[37] When plaintiffs choose to commence litigation against foreign defendants in state court, federal law may permit the defendant to "remove" the case from state to federal court. Section 1441 of Title 28 permits removal of any action that could originally have been brought in federal court. If diversity of citizenship or alienage provides the basis for federal jurisdiction, the action ordinarily may be removed only if none of the defendants is a citizen of the state where the action was brought.[38] If federal question jurisdiction is asserted, the case is removable "without regard to the citizenship or residence of the parties."[39]

d. Practical Considerations Relevant to Federal Subject Matter Jurisdiction. Although these bases for federal jurisdiction can raise complex legal issues, discussed below, they also involve very important practical considerations. Litigation in federal court can differ in significant ways from litigation in state court, particularly for foreign parties. In some cases, these differences can be outcome-determinative, leading to vigorous disputes over the availability of federal subject matter jurisdiction.

Federal courts are frequently said to possess greater detachment from local political, economic, and social concerns than their state counterparts. Differences in perspective are attributed to the fact that federal judges are appointed with life tenure, while state judges are frequently elected for limited terms, and to the different pools from which federal and state judges and jurors are traditionally drawn.[40] In disputes between a local resident and a foreigner, this detachment may be of considerable significance. Federal judges are also sometimes more experienced in handling complex commercial disputes, particularly involving international matters.

32. 28 U.S.C. §1331. Pursuant to the Constitution's authorization for federal question jurisdiction, Congress has granted the federal courts jurisdiction to hear claims arising under a number of substantive federal statutes, including the antitrust and securities laws. *See infra* pp. 32, 672-673, 707-708, 709-711.

33. 28 U.S.C. §1332(a)(1). Diversity-of-citizenship jurisdiction encompasses disputes between parties from different states where the amount in controversy exceeds $75,000.

34. 28 U.S.C. §1332(a)(2) & (3); *infra* pp. 21-30.

35. 28 U.S.C. §1350; *infra* pp. 33-62.

36. 28 U.S.C. §1330(a); *infra* pp. 70-79 *See Powerex Corp. v. Reliant Energy Servs., Inc.*, 551 U.S. 224, 236-238 (2007) (discussing relationship between FSIA and removal). A separate provision of the diversity statute provides for subject matter jurisdiction over suits brought *by* "a foreign state" (as defined in the FSIA) and *against* "citizens of a State or different states." 28 U.S.C. §1332(a)(4). *See Republic of Ecuador v. ChevronTexaco Corp.*, 376 F. Supp. 2d 334, 346 (S.D.N.Y. 2005).

37. As discussed below, the plaintiff will also be required to establish personal jurisdiction over the defendant, valid service of process, and proper venue. *See infra* pp. 81-91, 458-459, 867-880.

38. 18 U.S.C. §1441(b). *See Lincoln Property Co. v. Roche*, 546 U.S. 81 (2005); C. Wright et al., *Federal Practice and Procedure*, §§3723, 3731.

39. 28 U.S.C. §1441(b). Under these circumstances, the district court may exercise jurisdiction over the entire case or remand "all matters in which State law predominates." 28 U.S.C. §1441(c). *See Carlsbad Tech., Inc. v. HIF Bio, Inc.*, 129 S. Ct. 1862 (2009).

40. *See, e.g., Caperton v. A.T. Massey Coal Co., Inc.*, 129 S. Ct. 2252 (2009) (describing relationship between state supreme court justice and litigant who had contributed $3 million to justice's election campaign).

Equally important, federal courts may apply "procedural" rules that can differ materially from those in state courts.[41] These include the *forum non conveniens* doctrine, principles governing the enforceability of forum selection clauses, *lis pendens*, and discovery rules. Differences between federal and state procedural rules may be dispositive in particular cases.[42]

For these and other reasons, foreign parties facing legal action in the United States often prefer to litigate in federal courts. This preference may be generally sound, but it is wise to consider the actual differences between specific federal and state forums in particular cases. State courts, judges, and procedural rules differ significantly from state to state, and in some cases may be more hospitable to foreign litigants than a federal forum.

4. Relationship Between U.S. State and Federal Law[43]

a. The *Erie* Doctrine.   The relationship between state and federal law in federal courts gives rise to complex issues in both domestic and international cases. These issues are subject to the so-called "*Erie* doctrine."

Until the 1930s, the federal courts had followed the rule of *Swift v. Tyson* and applied a general federal common law in diversity cases.[44] Under *Swift v. Tyson*, federal courts were generally free to apply a general federal common law, while state courts were at liberty to apply state common law (without preemptive effect from inconsistent federal common law decisions).[45] In *Erie Railroad Co. v. Tompkins*, however, the Supreme Court narrowly limited the federal courts' authority to fashion general common law rules.[46] Declaring that "[t]here is no federal *general* common law,"[47] the Court held that, in the absence of valid federal legislation, federal courts must ordinarily apply state substantive law, including state common law rules fashioned by state courts. The Court based its decision in large part on the perceived "mischievous results" that flowed from permitting federal courts to apply federal law, and state courts to apply state law, to the same issues:

> [*Swift v. Tyson*] made rights . . . vary according to whether enforcement was sought in the state or in the federal court; and the privilege of selecting the court in which the right should be determined was conferred upon the noncitizen. Thus, the doctrine rendered impossible equal protection of the law. In attempting to promote uniformity of law throughout the United States, the doctrine had prevented uniformity in the administration of the law of the state.[48]

To redress these perceived defects, *Erie* established fundamentally new principles governing the relationship between state and federal law. It is, of course, fundamental under *Erie*

---

41. For a good recent example of how differences between state and federal procedural rules can affect the course of a case, *see Shady Grove Orthopedic Assocs., P.A. v. Allstate Ins. Co.*, 130 S. Ct. 1431 (2010) (holding that federal court sitting in diversity should apply federal class action standards even where state law precludes availability of class action).

42. *See infra* pp. 10-11, 453-458, 544-546, 791-796. *See especially Dow Chemical Co. v. Castro Alfaro*, 786 S.W.2d 674 (Tex. 1990), *infra* pp. 378-383, and *Sequihua v. Texaco, Inc.*, 847 F. Supp. 61 (S.D. Tex. 1994), *infra* pp. 63-65.

43. *See generally* R. Fallon *et al.*, *Hart & Wechsler's The Federal Courts and the Federal System* 620-673 (5th ed. 2003); C. Wright et al., *Federal Practice and Procedure* §4504-4511 (1996 & Supp. 2010); Westen & Lehman, *Is There Life for* Erie *After the Death of Diversity?*, 78 Mich. L. Rev. 311 (1980).

44. *See Swift v. Tyson*, 41 U.S. 1 (1842); Friendly, *In Praise of* Erie — *And of the New Federal Common Law*, 39 N.Y.U. L. Rev. 383 (1964); R. Fallon et al., *Hart & Wechsler's The Federal Courts and the Federal System* 620-630 (5th ed. 2003).

45. *Swift v. Tyson*, 41 U.S. 1 (1982).

46. 304 U.S. 64 (1938).

47. 304 U.S. at 78 (emphasis added).

48. 304 U.S. at 74-75.

and its progeny that a valid federal statute, treaty, or regulation preempts inconsistent state laws, and must be applied by both state courts and federal diversity and alienage courts.[49] If no valid federal substantive law applies, however, the *Erie* doctrine provides generally that "procedural" issues in federal diversity actions are governed by federal procedural law, while "substantive" issues are governed by state substantive law.[50] Federal "procedural" law applies only in federal courts, not in state courts.[51]

In areas not governed by federal statute or rule of procedure, the Court has generally been reluctant to ignore state law rules. For example, the Court has held that statutes of limitations and choice of law rules are "substantive" and therefore governed by state law.[52] Moreover, as noted earlier, state substantive law provides the basic rules of contract, tort, agency, damages, contribution, and the like.

Conversely, *Erie*'s "procedural" category is limited. It generally includes all subjects dealt with by the Federal Rules of Civil Procedure.[53] In addition, even absent an applicable Federal Rule, a few common law doctrines fashioned by the federal courts are characterized as "procedural," rather than "substantive";[54] these federal procedural rules govern in federal courts, but not in state courts, and they do not preempt state law. In defining the scope of federal procedural law, the Supreme Court has sought to avoid relying exclusively on the "substance" and "procedure" labels. Instead, the Court has categorized issues in order to further what it has described as two central purposes of the *Erie* doctrine: (1) the "discouragement of forum shopping" between state and federal courts that could result from divergent state and federal laws, and (2) "avoidance of inequitable administration of the laws."[55]

b. Substantive Federal Common Law. Although *Erie* made it clear that "there is no federal *general* common law,"[56] the Supreme Court has sanctioned the judicial development of a limited number of substantive rules of "federal common law," even in the absence of a valid federal statute, treaty, or regulation.[57] Unlike federal procedural

---

49. *See* U.S. Const. Art. VI, cl. 2; *Hines v. Davidowitz*, 312 U.S. 52 (1941); *Jones v. Rath Packing Co.*, 430 U.S. 519 (1977); *Stewart Organization, Inc. v. Ricoh Corp.*, 487 U.S. 22 (1988); *Walker v. Armco Steel Corp.*, 446 U.S. 740, 749-752 (1980) ("The first question [is] whether the scope of the federal rule in fact is sufficiently broad to control the issue before the Court.").

50. *Stewart Organization, Inc. v. Ricoh Corp.*, 487 U.S. 22 (1988); *Guaranty Trust Co. v. York*, 326 U.S. 99 (1945); *Erie Railroad Co. v. Tompkins*, 304 U.S. 64, 74 (1938); C. Wright et al., *Federal Practice and Procedure* §4508 (1996 & Supp. 2010). The same general rule applies in federal question cases, although federal substantive law will generally preempt state law in many respects. *See* C. Wright et al., *Federal Practice and Procedure* §4515 (1996 & Supp. 2010).

51. *See American Dredging Co. v. Miller*, 510 U.S. 443 (1994); *Hanna v. Plumer*, 380 U.S. 460 (1965).

52. *Klaxon Co. v. Stentor Elec. Mfg. Co.*, 313 U.S. 487 (1941); *Walker v. Armco Steel Corp.*, 446 U.S. 740 (1980).

53. *Shady Grove Orthopedic Assocs., P.A. v. Allstate Ins. Co.*, 130 S. Ct. 1431 (2010); *Hanna v. Plumer*, 380 U.S. 460 (1965); C. Wright et al., *Federal Practice and Procedure* §4508-4510 (1996 & Supp. 2010). In unusual circumstances, a purportedly "procedural" provision of the Federal Rules of Civil Procedure might be found to exceed either the rulemaking powers delegated to the Supreme Court by the Rules Enabling Act, 28 U.S.C. §2072, or Congress's constitutional authority. *See Walker v. Armco Steel Corp.*, 446 U.S. 740, 752 n.14 (1980); C. Wright et al., *Federal Practice and Procedure* §4505 (1996 & Supp. 2010). While the Federal Rules apply in diversity cases regardless of state procedural law, the Supreme Court has instructed that those Rules should be interpreted "with sensitivity to important state interests and regulatory policies." *Gasperini v. Center for Humanities, Inc.*, 518 U.S. 415, 427 n.7 (1996).

54. *See American Dredging Co. v. Miller*, 510 U.S. 443 (1994) (*forum non conveniens* doctrine in domestic admiralty actions is governed by federal procedural law); *Byrd v. Blue Ridge Rural Electric Coop., Inc.*, 356 U.S. 525 (1958) (federal procedural law determines what issues are to be submitted to jury).

55. *Hanna v. Plumer*, 380 U.S. 460, 468 (1965); *Walker v. Armco Steel Corp.*, 446 U.S. 740, 747 (1980); *Gasperini v. Center for Humanities, Inc.*, 518 U.S. 415, 428 (1996).

56. 304 U.S. at 78 (emphasis added).

57. *Sosa v. Alvarez-Machain*, 542 U.S. 692 (2004); *Boyle v. United Technologies Corp.*, 487 U.S. 500 (1988); *United States v. Little Lake Misere Land Co.*, 412 U.S. 580 (1973).

rules, these federal common law rules are substantive federal law, applicable in both federal and state courts, that preempt inconsistent state law. As the Supreme Court has declared, "a few areas, involving 'uniquely federal interests' . . . are so committed by the Constitution and laws of the United States to federal control that state law is preempted and replaced, where necessary, by federal law of a content prescribed (absent explicit statutory directive) by the courts—so-called 'federal common law.' "[58]

Substantive federal common law rules will be fashioned only in "few and restricted" cases[59] and only if rigorous standards are satisfied. First, the proposed rule must arise in an area involving "uniquely federal interests."[60] Examples of such federal interests have included the division of interstate waters,[61] the conduct of U.S. foreign relations,[62] the immunity of individual government officers,[63] the design and manufacture of U.S. military equipment,[64] the civil liability of federal officials for actions taken in the course of their duty,[65] the rights and duties of the United States under its contracts,[66] and certain rules of preclusion.[67] The mere fact that the U.S. Government is involved in the litigation does not, by itself, present the "unique interests" necessary to justify the crafting of a federal common law rule.[68]

Second, even in such "uniquely federal" areas, federal common law will be fashioned only to prevent "significant conflict" between state laws and federal policies and interests.[69] If state law does not conflict with federal policies, it will not necessarily be preempted and, even if a conflict exists, preemptive federal common law will be fashioned only to the extent necessary to eliminate the conflict.[70]

Federal common law can play a potentially significant role in international litigation. International disputes frequently implicate federal interests in U.S. foreign relations and foreign commerce. As noted above, both fields fall squarely with the constitutional powers of Congress and the President, and can clearly involve uniquely federal interests.[71] Several

---

58. *Boyle v. United Technologies Corp.*, 487 U.S. 500, 504 (1988).

59. *Wheeldin v. Wheeler*, 373 U.S. 647, 651 (1963). *See Atherton v. FDIC*, 519 U.S. 213, 218 (1997) ("'Whether latent federal power should be exercised to displace state law is primarily a decision for Congress,' not the federal courts" (quoting *Wallis v. Pan Am. Petroleum Corp.*, 384 U.S. 63, 68 (1966)); *Texas Industries, Inc. v. Radcliff Materials, Inc.*, 451 U.S. 630, 641 (1981) ("Against some congressional authorization to formulate substantive rules of decision, federal common law exists only in such narrow areas as those concerned with the rights and obligations of the United States, interstate and international disputes implicating conflicting rights of states or our relations with foreign nations, and admiralty cases"); *Milwaukee v. Illinois*, 451 U.S. 304, 312-313 (1981) ("The enactment of a federal rule in an area of national concern, and the decision whether to displace state law in doing so, is generally made not by the federal judiciary, purposefully insulated from democratic pressures but by the people through their elected representatives in Congress").

60. *Danforth v. Minnesota*, 552 U.S. 264, 290 n.24 (2008); *Boyle v. United Technologies Corp.*, 487 U.S. 500, 504 (1988); *United States v. Little Lake Misere Land Co.*, 412 U.S. 580 (1973).

61. *Hinderlider v. La Plata River & Cherry Creek Ditch Co.*, 304 U.S. 92 (1938).

62. *Zschernig v. Miller*, 389 U.S. 429 (1968); *Banco Nacional de Cuba v. Sabbatino*, 376 U.S. 398 (1964).

63. *See Samantar v. Yousuf*, 130 S. Ct. 2278 (2010).

64. *Boyle v. United Technologies Corp.*, 487 U.S. 500, 505-507 (1988).

65. *Westfall v. Erwin*, 484 U.S. 292 (1988); *Howard v. Lyons*, 360 U.S. 593 (1959).

66. *United States v. Little Lake Misere Land Co.*, 412 U.S. 580 (1973); *Priebe & Sons, Inc. v. United States*, 332 U.S. 407 (1947).

67. *Semtek Int'l Inc. v. Lockheed Martin Corp.*, 531 U.S. 497 (2001) (claim-preclusive effect of dismissal of case on state statute-of-limitations grounds by federal court sitting in diversity). *See* Burbank, Semtek, *Forum Shopping, and Federal Common Law*, 77 Notre Dame L. Rev. 1027 (2002).

68. *See Empire Healthchoice Assur., Inc. v. McVeigh*, 547 U.S. 677, 691 (2006).

69. *O'Melveny & Myers v. FDIC*, 512 U.S. 79, 87-88 (1994); *Boyle v. United Technologies Corp.*, 487 U.S. at 507-508.

70. *Boyle v. United Technologies Corp.*, 487 U.S. at 507-508.

71. *See* Bradley & Goldsmith, *Federal Courts and the Incorporation of International Law*, 111 Harv. L. Rev. 2260 (1998); Jessup, *The Doctrine of* Erie Railroad v. Tompkins *Applied to International Law*, 33 Am. J. Int'l L. 740 (1939); Edwards, *The* Erie *Doctrine in Foreign Affairs Cases*, 42 N.Y.U. L. Rev. 674 (1967); Henkin, *The Foreign Affairs Powers of the Federal Courts*: Sabbatino, 64 Colum. L. Rev. 805 (1964); Hill, *The Law Making Power of the Federal Courts*:

Supreme Court decisions, fashioning rules of federal common law in international disputes, are illustrative.

In *Banco Nacional de Cuba v. Sabbatino*,[72] the Supreme Court announced a federal "act of state" doctrine that forbade U.S. courts from adjudicating the validity of certain foreign governmental acts. Relying on federal authority over foreign relations and foreign commerce, the Court declared that the act of state doctrine was a principle of federal common law that was equally binding on both state and federal courts:[73] it is plain that the problems involved are uniquely federal in nature. If federal authority, in this instance this Court, orders the field of judicial competence in this area for the federal courts, and the state courts are left free to formulate their own rules, the purposes behind the doctrine could be as effectively undermined as if there had been no federal pronouncement on the subject. Likewise, in *First National City Bank v. Banco Para El Comercio Exterior de Cuba*[74] the Supreme Court adopted a federal common law standard governing the circumstances in which the separate legal identity of foreign state-related entities will be disregarded. Citing *Sabbatino*, the Court emphasized the need for a uniform federal standard in matters affecting U.S. relations with foreign states.[75]

To much the same effect, in *Zschernig v. Miller*, the Supreme Court held unconstitutional an Oregon statute that forbade foreign heirs or legatees from receiving property from Oregon estates if the property would be confiscated by foreign governments or if U.S. heirs or legatees could not reciprocally receive property from abroad. The Supreme Court held that this "kind of state involvement in foreign affairs and international relations—matters which the Constitution entrusts solely to the Federal Government"—threatens U.S. foreign relations and is unconstitutional.[76]

Finally, in *Sosa v. Alvarez-Machain*, the Supreme Court held that federal courts have a limited power to create common-law causes of action for torts that violate the "law of nations." This federal common law power, though, is not unlimited, warned the *Sosa* Court. Any such judicially created cause of action must rest on a "norm of international character accepted by the civilized world."[77] The cause of action must be "defined with a specificity" comparable to certain paradigmatic, historically accepted violations such as acts of piracy. The Court did not indicate what present-day causes of action satisfy this test. It held only that this "residual common law discretion" did not include the authority to create a claim of short-term "arbitrary" detention.

5. Relationship Between International Law and U.S. Law

International law can play an important role in deciding cases in U.S. courts. In theory, the relationship between domestic U.S. law and international law is simple: "International law is part of our law, and must be ascertained and administered by the courts of justice of appropriate jurisdiction, as often as questions of right depending upon it are duly presented for their determination."[78] In reality, the role of international law in

---

Constitutional Preemption, 67 Colum. L. Rev. 1024 (1967); Moore, *Federalism and Foreign Relations*, 1965 Duke L.J. 248.

72. 376 U.S. 398 (1964). *See infra* pp. 801-817 for a more detailed discussion.

73. 376 U.S. at 424.

74. 462 U.S. 611 (1983). *See infra* pp. 252-253, 257-261, 271-272.

75. 462 U.S. at 623 ("The principles governing this case are common to both international law and federal common law, which in these circumstances is necessarily informed both by international law principles and by articulated congressional policies.").

76. 389 U.S. 429, 436 (1968). *See infra* pp. 630-633, 637-639, for a more detailed discussion.

77. 542 U.S. 692 (2004). *See infra* pp. 35-36, 38-47, 49-53.

78. *The Paquete Habana*, 175 U.S. 677, 700 (1900); *Restatement (Third) Foreign Relations Law* §111(1) (1987).

U.S. litigation is more complex. A brief summary of the applicable principles is all that space permits.[79]

a. International Law. International law scholars and practitioners distinguish between "public" and "private" international law (also sometimes referred to as "conflict of laws").[80] Definitions of "private" international law vary considerably, but they generally refer to the body of national law applicable to disputes between private persons, in domestic courts or private arbitral forums, arising from activities having connections to two or more nations.[81] Topics falling within the private international law category typically include judicial jurisdiction, choice of forum, choice of law, taking evidence abroad, service of process abroad, and recognition of foreign judgments. In the United States, these topics are dealt with by "Conflict of Laws" treatises and the American Law Institute's *Restatement (Second) Conflict of Laws.*[82]

In contrast, "public international law" refers to the international legal principles that govern relations between sovereign nation-states.[83] In the words of the *Restatement (Third) Foreign Relations Law,* "[i]nternational law is the law of the international community of states. It deals with the conduct of nation-states and their relations with other states, and to some extent also with their relations with individuals, business organizations and other legal entities."[84] Subjects traditionally governed by public international law include the law of the sea, the law of treaties, limits on national jurisdiction, the use of force, foreign sovereign immunity, responsibility toward aliens, recognition, and state succession. In the United States, these subjects have in recent decades been dealt with by the ALI's Second and Third *Restatements of Foreign Relations Law* and by public international law treatises.[85]

This distinction between "public" and "private" international law is apparently of recent origin. During the nineteenth century, subjects of transnational concern were generally subject to the "law of nations," which was understood as broadly encompassing legal relations between sovereign states, conflict of laws rules, maritime law, and the law merchant.[86] It was only in the early decades of the twentieth century that "public" and "private" international law came to be regarded as distinct subjects.[87]

---

79. For more detailed discussions, *see* L. Henkin, R. Pugh, O. Schachter & H. Smit, *International Law* (1980); *Restatement (Third) Foreign Relations Law* (1987); Bradley & Goldsmith, *Federal Courts and the Incorporation of International Law,* 111 Harv. L. Rev. 2260 (1998); Bradley & Goldsmith, *Customary International Law as Federal Common Law: A Critique of the Modern Position,* 110 Harv. L. Rev. 815 (1997).

80. Lowenfeld, *Public Law in the International Arena, Conflict of Laws, International Law, and Some Suggestions for Their Interaction,* 163 Recueil des Cours 311 (1979); Starke, *The Relation Between Private and Public International Law,* 207 Law Q. Rev. 395 (1936); Stevenson, *The Relationship of Private International Law to Public International Law,* 52 Colum. L. Rev. 561 (1952).

81. *See Restatement (Second) Conflict of Laws* §2 (1971).

82. Leading U.S. conflict of laws treatises include E. Scoles et al., *Conflict of Laws* (4th ed. 2004); Symeonides, *The American Choice-of-Law Revolution,* 298 Recueil des Cours 1 (2003); Symeonides *et al., Conflict of Laws: American Comparative International* (2d ed. 2003); R. Weintraub, *Commentary on the Conflict of Laws* (4th ed. 2001). *See also* L. Brilmayer & J. Goldsmith, *Conflict of Laws: Cases and Materials* (5th ed. 2002). The *Restatement (First) Conflict of Laws* (1934) also dealt with private international law issues, as well as selected jurisdictional principles of public international law. *See infra* pp. 645-651, 723-791.

83. *See* J. Brierly, *The Law of Nations* 1-3 (6th ed. 1963); W. Bishop, *International Law: Cases and Materials* 3-6 (3d ed. 1971).

84. *Restatement (Third) Foreign Relations Law* Part I, Ch. 1, Intro. Note at 16 & §101 (1987).

85. *See supra* note 79.

86. Dickinson, *The Law of Nations as Part of the National Law of the United States,* 101 U. Pa. L. Rev. 26, 26-29 (1952); Jay, *Origins of Federal Common Law: Part Two,* 133 U. Pa. L. Rev. 1231, 1263-1264 (1985); Rheinstein, *The Constitutional Bases of Jurisdiction,* 22 U. Chi. L. Rev. 775, 805 (1955).

87. Nussbaum, *Rise and Decline of the Law-of-Nations Doctrine in the Conflict of Laws,* 42 Colum. L. Rev. 189 (1942); Cheatham, *Sources of Rules for Conflict of Laws,* 89 U. Pa. L. Rev. 430 (1941); Wortley, *The Interaction of Public and Private International Laws Today,* 85 Recueil des Cours 245 (1954).

Contemporary public international law is generally the creation of sovereign nations: it is fundamental that public international law is based on the consent of the states that comprise the international community. "Modern international law is rooted in acceptance by states which constitute the system."[88] Thus, a state is not ordinarily bound by rules of international law to which it has not expressly or implicitly agreed.[89]

There are several means by which the consent of states to particular rules of international law is expressed: (1) international agreements; (2) customary international law; and (3) general principles of law.[90] In theory, these sources are of equal weight in the formation of public international law. In practice, however, the best-accepted sources of international law are international agreements.[91]

International agreements between states can take many forms, including treaties, conventions, concordats, and exchanges of notes. Whatever their form, international agreements are analogous to contracts between private parties; in general, they deal with whatever matters the parties choose to address and they create law only for the states that are party to the agreements.[92] There are only a very limited number of fundamental norms of international law (*jus cogens*), from which states may not derogate, by agreement or otherwise.[93] A considerable body of international law exists governing the making, interpretation, application, and termination of international agreements.[94]

A second source of international law is customary international law.[95] Customary international law is not based on express agreements among nations, but instead results from the ongoing practice (or "custom") of states. There is no precise formula for determining how many states must follow a particular custom, nor how long the practice must be followed before it crystallizes into law. Most authorities require the existence of a general, consistent practice of substantially all concerned states, followed out of a sense of legal obligation.[96] Evidence of state practice is derived from the actions of states, their official statements (*e.g.*, in diplomatic notes), and the international agreements they enter into. A rule of customary international law is not binding on a state that declares its disagreement during the rule's formation.[97]

Finally, general principles of international law can be derived from the rules prevailing in major legal systems.[98] "General principles of law" are typically regarded as a secondary source of international law, available only interstitially where no international agreement or customary international law exists. General principles are usually based on domestic laws common to nations with well-developed legal systems.

b.   Relationship Between International Agreements and U.S. Law.   International law has a complex relationship to U.S. law. At the outset, it is important to distinguish between

---

88. *Restatement (Third) Foreign Relations Law* Part I, Ch. 1, Intro. Note at 18 (1987).

89. *Restatement (Third) Foreign Relations Law* §102 comment d (1987).

90. *See* Statute of the International Court of Justice Art. 38(1); Parry, *The Sources and Evidences of International Law* (1965); Akehurst, *The Hierarchy of the Sources of International Law*, 47 Brit. Y. B. Int'l L. 273 (1974).

91. For commentary concerning the relative weights of the sources of international law, *see* M. Villiger, *Customary International Law and Treaties* (1985); A. D'Amato, *The Concept of Custom in International Law* (1971); Akehurst, *Custom as a Source of International Law*, 48 Brit. Y.B. Int'l L. 1 (1974-1975).

92. *Restatement (Third) Foreign Relations Law* §321 (1987).

93. *Restatement (Third) Foreign Relations Law* §§102 comment k, 331, & 702 comment n (1987).

94. *See* Vienna Convention on the Law of Treaties, 8 Int'l Leg. Mat. 679 (1969); I. Sinclair, *The Vienna Convention on the Law of Treaties* (2d ed. 1984).

95. *Restatement (Third) Foreign Relations Law* §102(1)(a) (1987).

96. *North Sea Continental Shelf Cases*, [1969] I.C.J. Rep. 3; *Asylum Case* [1950] I.C.J. Rep. 266; A. D'Amato, *The Concept of Custom in International Law* (1971).

97. *Fisheries Case (United Kingdom v. Norway)* [1951] I.C.J. Rep. 116.

98. *Restatement (Third) Foreign Relations Law* §102(1)(c), §102(4), & Reporters' Note 7 (1987).

the status in U.S. courts of: (i) treaties (or other international agreements) and (ii) customary international law.

There is a considerable body of U.S. law dealing with the appropriate domestic mechanism, under the U.S. Constitution, by which the United States enters into international agreements.[99] The U.S. Constitution permits entry by the United States into "treaties," which require the approval of the President and two-thirds of the Senate.[100] In determining the legal effects of a treaty under U.S. law, U.S. courts distinguish sharply between "non-self-executing" and "self-executing" treaties. A self-executing treaty is intended to have immediate legal effects within the contracting states, without the need for implementing legislation or regulations; a non-self-executing treaty is not intended to have direct legal effect, but instead contemplates domestic implementing legislation.[101] Whether a treaty is self-executing or non-self-executing depends on the intentions of the United States in ratifying the treaty.[102]

Article VI of the U.S. Constitution declares that self-executing treaties are the "supreme Law of the Land." Even without implementing legislation, self-executing treaties are federal law that enjoy essentially the same status in U.S. courts as federal statutes.[103] Self-executing treaties may create enforceable rights and remedies in U.S. courts and may preempt inconsistent state law.[104] In the case of conflicts between treaties and federal statutes, a "last-in-time" rule applies: a federal statute supersedes prior inconsistent treaties, and conversely, a treaty supersedes prior inconsistent federal statutes. However, this last-in-time principle is limited by a canon under which courts will not construe ambiguous statutes to abrogate treaties.[105]

In contrast, non-self-executing treaties lack binding force in U.S. courts until implemented by congressional statute.[106] As a result, federal law ordinarily prevails over inconsistent non-self-executing treaties.[107] The same result apparently also applies with respect to state statutes and state common law.[108]

It is common for the United States to enter into international agreements in other forms than "treaties." So-called "Congressional-Executive" agreements must be approved by both the President and a majority of each House of Congress (rather

99. *See generally* L. Henkin, *Foreign Affairs and the Constitution* 173-176 (1972); Treaties and Other International Agreements: The Role of the United States Senate, S. Rep. No. 205, 98th Cong., 2d Sess. (1984).

100. U.S. Const. Art. II, §2.

101. *Asakura v. Seattle,* 265 U.S. 332, 341 (1924); *Fairfax's Devisee v. Hunter's Lessee,* 11 U.S. 603 (1813); *Restatement (Third) Foreign Relations Law* §111(3) & (4) & comment h (1987).

102. *Restatement (Third) Foreign Relations Law* §111(4) & Reporters' Note 5 (1987); *Calderon v. Reno,* 39 F. Supp. 2d 943, 956 (N.D. Ill. 1998); *People of Saipan v. Department of Interior,* 502 F.2d 90, 97 (9th Cir. 1974).

103. *Restatement (Third) Foreign Relations Law* §115(1) & (2) (1987). When interpreting treaties, courts accord "considerable weight" to the views of other signatory nations. *Abbott v. Abbott,* 130 S. Ct. 1983, 1993 (2010); *El Al Israel Airlines v. Tsui Yuan Tsenf,* 525 U.S. 155, 176 (1999); *Air France v. Saks,* 470 U.S. 392, 404 (1985).

104. *See Sanchez-Llamas v. Oregon,* 126 S. Ct. 2669, 2680 (2006); *United States v. Belmont,* 301 U.S. 324, 331 (1937); *Asakura v. Seattle,* 265 U.S. 332, 341 (1924); *Fairfax's Devisee v. Hunter's Lessee,* 11 U.S. 603 (1813); *Ware v. Hylton,* 3 U.S. 199, 244-245 (1796); *Safety Nat. Cas. Corp. v. Certain Underwriters at Lloyd's London,* 587 F.3d 714, 724 (5th Cir. 2009) (*en banc*) (holding that New York Convention superseded state law). Some treaties establish international bodies charged with their enforcement. Such treaties raise a related set of questions about the enforceability of the decisions of those bodies under United States law. *See Medellin v. Texas,* 552 U.S. 491 (2008).

105. *See Trans World Airlines, Inc. v. Franklin Mint Corp.,* 466 U.S. 243, 252 (1984); *Cook v. United States,* 288 U.S. 102, 119-120 (1933).

106. *Restatement (Third) Foreign Relations Law* §111(3) (1987) ("a 'non-self-executing' agreement will not be given effect as law in the absence of necessary implementation").

107. *Foster v. Neilson,* 27 U.S. 253 (1828); *Cameron Septic Tank Co. v. Knoxville,* 227 U.S. 39 (1913). An unresolved question is whether the above-referenced canon—under which ambiguous statutes are not construed to abrogate treaties—applies in the case of a non-self-executing treaty. *See Fund for Animals, Inc. v. Kempthorne,* 472 F.3d 872, 879-882 (D.C. Cir. 2006) (Kavanaugh, J., concurring).

108. *Sei Fujii v. California,* 242 P.2d 617 (Cal. 1952).

than, as for treaties, by the President and two-thirds of the Senate).[109] In general, a valid Congressional-Executive agreement has the same legal effect as a treaty — it is federal law that preempts inconsistent state law, supersedes prior federal statutes, and is superseded by subsequent federal statutes.[110]

Sole Executive agreements, made by the President, are frequently entered into in areas within the President's constitutional powers.[111] Within these fields, an Executive agreement generally has the same legal effects as a treaty.[112]

c. Relationship Between Customary International Law and U.S. Law. The status of customary international law in U.S. courts is less clear than that of treaties and other international agreements. In practice, the direct application of customary international law occurs in relatively few cases, owing principally to the comprehensive character of U.S. law and the fragmentary coverage of international law.[113]

In the absence of any U.S. law on an issue, U.S. courts will generally give effect to customary international law.[114] "In appropriate cases [U.S. courts] apply international law . . . without the need of enactment by Congress or proclamation by the President."[115] As discussed below, customary international law — like international agreements — is often said to be federal law.[116]

If a subsequent federal statute requires a result contrary to preexisting principles of customary international law, then U.S. courts must give Congress's legislation priority.[117] They must do so even though this will place the United States in violation of international law. "Federal courts must give effect to a valid unambiguous congressional mandate, even if such effect would conflict with another nation's laws or violate international law."[118] Moreover, even when a preexisting federal statute is said to be inconsistent with subsequent international practice (but not an international agreement), the prior statute will probably prevail.[119] The same result should apply in conflicts between customary international law and rules of federal common law.

---

109. *See Restatement (Third) Foreign Relations Law* §303 (1987); *United States v. Belmont,* 301 U.S. 324 (1937); *B. Altman Co. v. United States,* 224 U.S. 583 (1912).

110. *Restatement (Third) Foreign Relations Law* §111(3) & comment h (1987). Like treaties, Congressional-Executive agreements can be either self-executing or non-self-executing.

111. *Restatement (Third) Foreign Relations Law* §303(4) (1987); *see, e.g., American Ins. Ass'n v. Garamendi,* 539 U.S. 396 (2003).

112. *Restatement (Third) Foreign Relations Law* §303(4) & Reporters' Note 11 (1987); *United States v. Pink,* 315 U.S. 203 (1942); *American Insurance Ass'n v. Garamendi,* 539 U.S. 396 (2003); *Gross v. German Foundation Indus. Initiative,* 549 F.3d 605, 610-612 (3d Cir. 2008); *United States v. Guy W. Capps, Inc.,* 204 F.2d 655 (4th Cir. 1953), *aff'd on other grounds,* 348 U.S. 296 (1955).

113. Trimble, *A Revisionist View of Customary International Law,* 33 UCLA L. Rev. 665 (1986).

114. *The Paquete Habana,* 175 U.S. 677 (1900); *Restatement (Third) Foreign Relations Law* §115 comment d (1987). *See also* Bradley & Goldsmith, *Federal Courts and the Incorporation of International Law,* 111 Harv. L. Rev. 2260 (1998); Bradley & Goldsmith, *Customary International Law as Federal Common Law: A Critique of the Modern Position,* 110 Harv. L. Rev. 815 (1997).

115. *Restatement (Third) Foreign Relations Law* §111 comment c (1987); *Sosa v. Alvarez-Machain,* 542 U.S. 692 (2004). *See* Paust, *Rediscovering the Relationship Between Congressional Power and International Law: Exceptions to the Last in Time Rule and the Primacy of Custom,* 28 Va. J. Int'l L. 393, 418-443 (1988).

116. *Restatement (Third) Foreign Relations Law* §111 (1987); *infra* pp. 62-70.

117. *See Head Money Cases,* 112 U.S. 580, 598-599 (1884); *Whitney v. Robertson,* 124 U.S. 190, 194 (1888); *T.M.R. Energy, Ltd. v. State Property Fund of Ukraine,* 411 F.3d 296, 302 (D.C. Cir. 2005) ("Customary international law comes into play only where there is no treaty, and no controlling executive or legislative act or judicial decision. . . . Never does customary international law prevail over a contrary federal statute."); *Restatement (Third) Foreign Relations Law* §115(1) & §403 comment g (1987).

118. *CFTC v. Nahas,* 738 F.2d 487, 495 (D.C. Cir. 1984). *See United States v. Alcoa,* 148 F.2d 416, 443 (2d Cir. 1945) ("We are concerned only with whether Congress chose to attach liability to the conduct outside the United States. . . . [A]s a court of the United States, we cannot look beyond our own law.").

119. *See Morrison v. Australian Nat'l Bank,* 130 S. Ct. 2869, 2887 (2010) ("The Solicitor General points out that the "significant and material conduct" test is in accord with prevailing notions of international comity. If so, that

The effect of a conflict between customary international law and state law is less clear. Because customary international law is federal law, it should in principle preempt both prior *and subsequent* state law.[120] Parties have rarely argued that customary international law preempts state law, however, and there is little judicial precedent on the issue.[121]

d. Presumption That Congressional Legislation Is Consistent with International Law. Few cases involve irreconcilable conflict between domestic and international law. Much more common are cases in which a measure of uncertainty surrounds the content of both U.S. law and international law. In these circumstances, U.S. courts have sought to minimize conflict between international law and domestic U.S. law.

U.S. courts generally apply a canon of statutory construction dictating that, in the absence of an express legislative statement to the contrary, Congress will not be assumed to have enacted a statute that violates international law. As the Supreme Court remarked in 1804, "[a]n act of Congress ought never to be construed to violate the law of nations, if any other possible construction remains."[122] The *Restatement (Third) Foreign Relations Law* adopts the same approach: "[w]here fairly possible, a United States statute is to be construed so as not to conflict with international law or with an international agreement of the United States."[123] Not infrequently, the meaning of federal statutes have been significantly affected by this presumption.[124]

6. Separation of Powers Considerations

An essential feature of the constitutional structure of the U.S. federal government is the separation of powers into three distinct branches.[125] This allocation of government authority was motivated by a desire to guard against tyranny and rash decision-making by diffusing power among largely independent legislative, executive, and judicial branches.[126] Nonetheless, the international field has long been thought to raise special separation of powers concerns. As a result, the Framers endowed the national executive and legislative branches with expansive authority in the field of foreign relations.

---

proves that if the United States asserted prescriptive jurisdiction pursuant to the 'significant and material conduct' test it would not violate customary international law; but it in no way tends to prove that that is what Congress has done."). *Cf. Restatement (Third) Foreign Relations Law* §115 Reporters' Note 4 (1987) ("Courts in the United States will hesitate to conclude that a principle has become a rule of customary international law if they are required to give it effect in the face of an earlier inconsistent statute."); Henkin, *International Law and Law in the United States*, 82 Mich. L. Rev. 1555 (1984). *Compare* Goldklang, *Back on Board the Paquete Habana: Resolving the Conflict Between Statutes and Customary International Law*, 25 Va. J. Int'l L. 143 (1984).

120. *Restatement (Third) Foreign Relations Law* §115 comment e (1987).

121. *See infra* pp. 630-632.

122. *Murray v. The Schooner Charming Betsy*, 6 U.S. 64, 118 (1804). *See also Chew Heong v. United States*, 112 U.S. 536, 539-540 (1884); *MacLeod v. United States*, 229 U.S. 416, 434 (1913); *Lauritzen v. Larsen*, 345 U.S. 571, 578 (1953); *McCulloch v. Sociedad Nacional de Marineros de Honduras*, 372 U.S. 10, 20-21 (1963); *Weinberger v. Rossi*, 456 U.S. 25, 32 (1982); *F. Hoffmann-La Roche, Ltd. v. Empagran S.A.*, 542 U.S. 155, 164 (2004); *Spector v. Norwegian Cruise Line, Ltd.*, 545 U.S. 119, 144-145 (2005) (Ginsburg, J., concurring in part and concurring in the judgment).

123. *Restatement (Third) Foreign Relations Law* §114 (1987).

124. *INS v. Cardoza-Fonseca*, 480 U.S. 421 (1987); *Weinberger v. Rossi*, 456 U.S. 25, 32 (1982). The presumption is discussed in greater detail below, *see infra* pp. 646-651, 664-671, 703-706, 898-899.

125. *Free Enterprise Fund v. Public Co. Accounting Oversight Bd.*, 130 S. Ct. 3138 (2010); *Clinton v. City of New York*, 524 U.S. 417 (1998); *Bowsher v. Synar*, 478 U.S. 714 (1986); *INS v. Chadha*, 462 U.S. 919 (1983); L. Henkin, *Foreign Affairs and the Constitution* 31-35 (1972).

126. *Boumediene v. Bush*, 128 S. Ct. 2229, 2246 (2008); *Myers v. United States*, 272 U.S. 52, 293 (1926) (Brandeis, J., dissenting); A. Hamilton, J. Madison & J. Jay, *The Federalist Papers*, Nos. 47 & 51 (C. Rossiter ed., 1961).

The central figure in U.S. foreign relations is the President. Despite fairly modest textual foundation in the Constitution,[127] successive presidents have wielded broad authority over the nation's foreign affairs. Thus, although its expansive formulation has been criticized, the Supreme Court has acknowledged "the very delicate, plenary and exclusive power of the President as the sole organ of the federal government in the field of international relations."[128]

As discussed above, Congress also enjoys substantial "international" powers, particularly in the foreign commerce field.[129] The allocation of authority between the executive and the legislative branches in the foreign affairs field is imprecise and overlapping. As a result, throughout the nation's history the President and Congress have struggled for control over the conduct of U.S. foreign relations.[130] Particularly in recent decades, Congress has become increasingly assertive, enacting legislation that restricts presidential foreign relations authority or furthers congressional policies.[131]

Notwithstanding this legislative-executive competition, it is clear that Congress and President together enjoy largely exclusive control over national foreign affairs. As the Supreme Court remarked in *Oetjen v. Central Leather Co.*, "[t]he conduct of the foreign relations of our Government is committed by the Constitution to the Executive and Legislative — the political — Departments of the Government."[132]

One consequence of the political branches' preeminence in the field of foreign relations has been a marked reluctance on the part of the federal courts to interfere in the conduct of foreign relations.[133] It has long been recognized that international civil litigation can affect foreign governmental and private interests.[134] As a consequence, international cases in U.S.

---

127. The Constitution's grants of foreign affairs authority to the President are not especially impressive at first glance: the chief executive is the "Commander-in-Chief" of the armed forces and is solely responsible for "making treaties" and receiving foreign "Ambassadors and other public Ministers." In addition, the President is obliged to execute the laws of the nation and is arguably vested with an unenumerated "executive" power. U.S. Const. Art. II.

128. *United States v. Curtiss-Wright Export Corp.*, 299 U.S. 304, 320 (1936). *See also Republic of Iraq v. Beaty*, 129 S. Ct. 2183 (2009). More recently, the Court has embraced more restrictive, but nonetheless broad, views of presidential foreign affairs powers. *See American Insurance Ass'n v. Garamendi*, 539 U.S. 396 (2003); *Crosby v. National Foreign Trade Council*, 530 U.S. 363 (2000); *Dames & Moore v. Regan*, 453 U.S. 654, 669 (1981) (presidential authority in foreign affairs field varies depending on legislative approval "along a spectrum running from explicit congressional authorization to explicit congressional prohibition"); *Youngstown Sheet & Tube Co. v. Sawyer*, 343 U.S. 579, 637 (1952) (Jackson, J., concurring). For an exceptional decision limiting the President's foreign affairs power in the context of an executive order designed to override state rules governing postconviction relief, *see Medellin v. Texas*, 552 U.S. 491, 523-532 (2008).

129. *See supra* pp. 5-7, 11-13.

130. *See Goldwater v. Carter*, 444 U.S. 996 (1979); *Youngstown Sheet & Tube Co. v. Sawyer*, 343 U.S. 579 (1952); *Roeder v. Islamic Republic of Iran*, 333 F.3d 228 (D.C. Cir. 2003). *See* Bellia, *Executive Power in Youngstown's Shadows*, 19 Const'l Comm. 87, 114-154 (2002); Yoo, *The Continuation of Politics by Other Means: The Original Understanding of War Powers*, 84 Cal. L. Rev. 167 (1996); Bestor, *Separation of Powers in the Domain of Foreign Affairs: The Intent of the Constitution Historically Examined*, 5 Seton Hall L. Rev. 527, 590 (1974).

131. *See* T. Franck & E. Weisband, *Foreign Policy by Congress* (1979); L. Henkin, *Foreign Affairs and the Constitution* 89-123 (1972). *See, e.g.*, 28 U.S.C. §1605A (stripping state sponsors of terrorism of sovereign immunity); 22 U.S.C. §§6021-6091 (Helms-Burton Act) (subjecting foreign companies that do business with Cuba to legal action).

132. 246 U.S. 297, 302 (1918).

133. For a rare exception, *see Boumediene v. Bush*, 128 S. Ct. 2229 (2008) (invalidating congressional legislation, supported by Executive Branch, that established military commissions for detainees at Guantanamo Bay, Cuba during ongoing military hostilities in the Middle East); *Hamdan v. Rumsfeld*, 548 U.S. 557 (2006) (construing federal statute so as not to preclude Supreme Court jurisdiction over claims by detainee at Guantanamo Bay).

134. *See, e.g.*, *Sosa v. Alvarez-Machain*, 542 U.S. 692, 732-733 n.21 (2004); *Christopher v. Harbury*, 536 U.S. 403, 417 (2002) ("Judicial enquiry [into conduct of foreign relations by United States Government] . . . will raise concerns for the separation of powers in trenching on matters committed to the other branches."); *Verlinden BV v. Central Bank of Nigeria*, 461 U.S. 480, 493 (1983) ("Actions against foreign sovereigns in our courts raise sensitive issues concerning the foreign relations of the United States, and the primacy of federal concerns is evident."); *Asahi Metal Indus. Co. v. Superior Court*, 480 U.S. 102 (1987).

courts have the potential to interfere with U.S. foreign relations and commerce. In the words of *Federalist Paper No. 80*, "the denial or perversion of justice by the sentences of courts . . . is with reason classed among the just causes of war."[135]

In several contexts, U.S. courts have fashioned prudential doctrines designed to forestall judicial disruption of national foreign relations. The classic example is the act of state doctrine, noted above, which precludes U.S. courts from adjudicating the validity of acts of foreign states on their own territory. The Court has attributed the act of state doctrine, at least in part, to "the strong sense of the Judicial Branch that its engagement in the task of passing on the validity of foreign acts of state may hinder rather than further this country's pursuit of goals . . . in the international sphere."[136]

Another classic prudential device is the political question doctrine. That doctrine, not limited to international cases, bars federal courts from resolving cases that raise issues more appropriately committed to other branches of government.[137] Among the factors relevant to determining whether a case presents a political question are a "textually demonstrable commitment" of an issue to the Executive or Legislative Branches, the lack of "judicially discoverable and manageable standards" for resolving an issue, or the existence of prudential considerations counseling for judicial abstention.[138] A number of lower courts have considered the applicability of the political question doctrine in international cases. In general, these decisions weigh the same factors as in domestic political question cases and, in some instances, find the doctrine to bar claims.[139] Other courts find that the doctrine does not bar jurisdiction over international claims.[140] As one judge recently noted, "[t]he political question doctrine has occupied a more limited place in the Supreme Court's jurisprudence than is sometimes assumed. . . . [F]rom the time of John Marshall to the present, the Court has decided many sensitive and controversial cases that had enormous national security or foreign policy ramifications."[141]

---

135. A. Hamilton, J. Madison & J. Jay, *The Federalist Papers* No. 80, at 476 (C. Rossiter ed., 1961).

136. *Banco Nacional de Cuba v. Sabbatino*, 376 U.S. 398, 423 (1964). *See also infra* pp. 801-817.

137. *See Baker v. Carr*, 369 U.S. 186 (1962); *Goldwater v. Carter*, 444 U.S. 996 (1979).

138. *See Goldwater v. Carter*, 444 U.S. at 997-998 (Powell, J., concurring).

139. *E.g., El-Shifa Pharmaceuticals, Inc. v. United States*, 607 F.3d 836 (D.C. Cir. 2010) (*en banc*) (claims by owners of Sudanese pharmaceutical plant following President's decision to launch cruise missile strike on plant); *Harbury v. Hayden*, 522 F.3d 413 (D.C. Cir. 2008) (state law tort claims against CIA officers sued in personal capacities); *Corrie v. Caterpillar*, 503 F.3d 974 (9th Cir. 2007) (claims against U.S. corporation based on use of its bulldozers by Israeli Defense Forces in Palestinian Territories); *Gonzalez-Vera v. Kissinger*, 449 F.3d 1260 (D.C. Cir. 2006) (claims against former U.S. Government officials based on alleged human rights abuses by Chilean governmental officials); *Bancoult v. McNamara*, 445 F.3d 427 (D.C. Cir. 2006) (claims based on alleged forced relocation in order to make way for United States naval base); *Whiteman v. Dorotheum GmbH & Co. KG*, 431 F.3d 57 (2d Cir. 2005) (claims for Nazi-era property deprivations); *Hwang Geum Joo v. Japan*, 413 F.3d 45 (D.C. Cir. 2005) (claims by Japanese "comfort women" against Japanese army present nonjusticiable political question); *Alperin v. Vatican Bank*, 410 F.3d 532 (9th Cir. 2005) (holding some but not all claims against Vatican Bank for alleged activities during World War II to be political question); *Made in the USA Foundation v. United States*, 242 F.3d 1300 (11th Cir. 2001) (whether NAFTA qualifies as Treaty presents nonjusticiable political question); *Occidental of Umm al Qaywayn, Inc. v. A Certain Cargo of Petroleum*, 577 F.2d 1196 (5th Cir. 1978) (dismissing antitrust suit based on charges of bribery and foreign border alterations).

140. *E.g., Sarei v. Rio Tinto plc*, 487 F.3d 1193 (9th Cir. 2007) (doctrine does not bar suit against foreign company for alleged violations of international law in connection with operation of mine); *Doe v. Exxon Mobil Corp.*, 473 F.3d 345 (D.C. Cir. 2007) (refusing mandamus from district court's refusal to dismiss on political question grounds ATS action against multinational corporation for activities in Indonesia); *Gross v. German Found. Indus. Initiative*, 456 F.3d 363 (3d Cir. 2006) (doctrine does not bar interest claims in settlement arising out of slave labor during World War II); *Klinghoffer v. Achille Lauro SNC*, 937 F.2d 44 (2d Cir. 1991) (political question doctrine does not bar suit against PLO for hijacking and murder); *Ramirez de Arellano v. Weinberger*, 745 F.2d 1500, 1511-1515 (D.C. Cir. 1984), *vacated*, 471 U.S. 1113 (1985) (political question doctrine does not bar suit against U.S. Government for occupation of plaintiff's ranch in Honduras by U.S.-backed military forces).

141. *El-Shifa Pharmaceutical Industries Co. v. United States*, 607 F.3d 836, 856 & n.3 (D.C. Cir. 2010) (*en banc*) (Kavanaugh, J., concurring in the judgment).

In addition to the act of state and political question doctrines, other examples of judicial deference to the political branches' handling of international matters include cases that are dismissed on grounds of "comity,"[142] cases involving foreign sovereign or head of state immunity,[143] cases involving the boundaries of foreign states,[144] and cases involving settlement of foreign claims.[145]

B. Alienage Jurisdiction of Federal Courts[146]

1. Introduction and Historical Background

Article III's grant of "alienage jurisdiction" conferred judicial power on the federal courts over cases "between a State, or the Citizens thereof, and foreign States, Citizens or Subjects." This grant of jurisdiction "was of critical importance to the Framers and the members of the First Congress."[147] It was thought vital to ensure that U.S. courts would speak with a single voice on matters affecting foreign parties. Federal courts were also thought less likely than state courts to treat foreign nationals unfairly,[148] thereby prejudicing the Nation's foreign relations and foreign commerce.[149] In explaining why federal subject matter jurisdiction should extend to cases involving aliens, Alexander Hamilton reasoned that "an unjust sentence against a foreigner, where the subject of controversy was wholly relative to the *lex loci,* would . . . if unredressed, be an aggression upon his sovereign, as well as one which violated the stipulations in a treaty or the general laws of nations."[150] At the same time, disputes involving aliens were thought likely to involve legal and other issues of national importance, which the federal courts were best able to decide.[151]

The First Congress immediately implemented the Constitution's grant of alienage jurisdiction in the first Judiciary Act of 1789. Consistent with the broad language used by Alexander Hamilton and others in justifying Article III's grant of alienage jurisdiction, §11 of the Act empowered the federal courts to hear any cases in which "an alien is a party."[152]

142. *E.g., In re Nazi Era Cases Against German Defendants Litig.,* 129 F. Supp. 2d 370, 383 (D.N.J. 2001); *Iwanowa v. Ford Motor Co.,* 67 F. Supp. 2d 424 (D.N.J. 1999); *Sequihua v. Texaco, Inc.,* 847 F. Supp. 61 (S.D. Tex. 1994).

143. *See infra* pp. 272-275; *Ye v. Zemin,* 383 F.3d 620 (7th Cir. 2004); *Weixum v. Xilai,* 568 F. Supp. 2d 35 (D.D.C. 2008; *Lafontant v. Aristide,* 1994 U.S. Dist. LEXIS 641 (E.D.N.Y. Jan. 27, 1994).

144. *See Occidental of Umm al Qaywayn, Inc. v. A Certain Cargo of Petroleum,* 577 F.2d 1196 (5th Cir. 1978).

145. *E.g., Dames & Moore v. Regan,* 453 U.S. 654 (1981); *United States v. Pink,* 315 U.S. 203 (1942); *Whiteman v. Dorotheum GmbH & Co KG,* 431 F.3d 57 (2d Cir. 2005); *Burger-Fischer v. Degussa AG,* 65 F. Supp. 2d 248 (D.N.J. 1999).

146. Commentary on alienage jurisdiction includes, *e.g.,* Bassett, *Statutory Interpretation in the Context of Federal Jurisdiction,* 76 Geo. Wash. L. Rev. 52 (2007); Johnson, *Why Alienage Jurisdiction? Historical Foundations and Modern Justifications for Federal Jurisdiction Over Disputes Involving Noncitizens,* 21 Yale J. Int'l L. 1 (1996); Rubenstein, *Alienage Jurisdiction in the Federal Courts,* 17 Int'l Law. 283 (1983); Mahoney, *A Historical Note on* Hodgson v. Bowerbank, 49 U. Chi. L. Rev. 725 (1982); Note, *Alien Corporations and Federal Diversity Jurisdiction,* 84 Colum. L. Rev. 177 (1984); Note, *Federal Jurisdiction over Suits Between Diverse United States Citizens with Aliens Joined to Both Sides of the Controversy Under 28 U.S.C. §1332(a)(3),* 38 Rutgers L. Rev. 71 (1985).

147. *17th Street Associates, LLP v. Markel Int'l Ins. Co. Ltd.,* 373 F. Supp. 2d 584, 603 (E.D. Va. 2005).

148. *See infra* pp. 26-27; Note, *Diversity Jurisdiction: The Dilemma of Dual Citizenship and Alien Corporations,* 77 Nw. U. L. Rev. 565, 568-575 (1982). *See also* Dickinson, *The Law of United States (Pt. 1),* 101 U. Pa. L. Rev. 26, 34-55 (1952).

149. *See infra* pp. 26-27; A. Hamilton, J. Madison & J. Jay, *The Federalist Papers* No. 80 at 476 (C. Rossiter ed., 1961); 3 Elliot, *The Debates in the Several State Conventions on the Adoption of the Federal Constitution* 533-534, 583 (2d ed. 1941) (James Madison); A. Prescott, *Drafting the Federal Constitution* 673-674 (1941).

150. A. Hamilton, J. Madison & J. Jay, *The Federalist Papers* No. 80, at 476 (C. Rossiter ed., 1961).

151. A. Hamilton, J. Madison & J. Jay, *The Federalist Papers* No. 80, at 476 (C. Rossiter ed., 1961) ("So great a proportion of the cases in which foreigners are parties involve national questions that it is by far most safe and most expedient to refer all those in which they are concerned to the national tribunals.").

152. Judiciary Act of 1789, ch. 20, §11, 1 Stat. 73; Mahoney, *A Historical Note on* Hodgson v. Bowerbank, 49 U. Chi. L. Rev. 725, 731-732 (1982).

Disputes almost immediately arose over the scope of §11: in particular, did the section reach all cases involving foreigners — including those where one alien litigated against another alien — or was it limited to suits where a U.S. citizen litigated against an alien? After some uncertainty,[153] the Supreme Court held in 1809 that the federal courts' Article III alienage jurisdiction was limited to suits involving an alien and a U.S. citizen. Despite the broader terms of the Judiciary Act, the Court concluded in *Hodgson & Thompson v. Bowerbank* that Article III's grant of alienage jurisdiction did not extend to suits solely between aliens; it was confined to cases between a U.S. citizen and an alien.[154] Absent constitutional authorization, the grant of subject matter jurisdiction over suits between aliens in §11 of the Judiciary Act was invalid.

2. Contemporary Statutory Grants of Alienage Jurisdiction

Although federal statutes defining alienage jurisdiction have evolved over time, the basic questions addressed in the early years of the Republic about the scope of alienage jurisdiction continue to arise. At present, statutory provisions dealing with alienage jurisdiction are found in 28 U.S.C. §1332(a)(2) and §1332(a)(3).

a. Section 1332(a)(2). Section 1332(a)(2) provides the district courts with original jurisdiction over civil actions where more than $75,000 is at stake and the controversy is between "citizens of a State and citizens or subjects of a foreign state." Some applications of §1332(a)(2) are straightforward. The clearest case of alienage jurisdiction under §1332(a)(2) is a suit by a single U.S. plaintiff against a single foreign defendant.[155] Similarly, §1332(a)(2) applies if two or more U.S. plaintiffs sue an alien.[156]

Conversely, it is equally clear that alienage jurisdiction under §1332(a)(2) does *not* extend to a suit by one alien against another alien.[157] This is a constitutional requirement, imposed by Article III, as well as a limitation of §1332(a)(2).[158]

Other cases are more difficult, especially in multiparty disputes. The requirement of "complete diversity" between all adverse parties (*e.g.*, Florida and New York versus Arizona and Pennsylvania and *not* Florida and New York versus Florida and Arizona) is well established as a statutory requirement in most domestic diversity of citizenship cases.[159] Particularly with this historical background, the language of §1332(a)(2), requiring a dispute "between . . . citizens of *a State* and citizens or subjects of *a foreign state*," has

---

153. *Mason v. The Ship Blaireau*, 6 U.S. 240 (1804); *Mossman v. Higginson*, 4 U.S. 12 (1800).

154. *Hodgson & Thompson v. Bowerbank*, 9 U.S. 303 (1809).

155. *E.g., Allied Semi-Conductors Int'l Limited v. Pulsar Components Int'l, Inc.*, 842 F. Supp. 653 (E.D.N.Y. 1993); *Maciak v. Olejniczak*, 79 F. Supp. 817 (E.D. Mich. 1948).

156. *E.g., Romero v. International Terminal Operating Co.*, 358 U.S. 354 (1959); *De Korwin v. First Nat'l Bank*, 156 F.2d 858 (7th Cir. 1946); *GE Healthcare v. Orbotech, Ltd.*, 2009 U.S. Dist. LEXIS 72221 (E.D. Wis. July 2, 2009).

157. *E.g., Universal Licensing Corp. v. Paola del Lungo S.p.A.*, 293 F.3d 579 (2d Cir. 2002); *Karazanos v. Madison Two Associates*, 147 F.3d 624, 626-627 (7th Cir. 1998); *Saadeh v. Farouki*, 107 F.3d 52, 58 (D.C. Cir. 1997); *Joseph Muller Corp. v. Société Anonyme de Gerance et d'Armement*, 451 F.2d 727, 729 (2d Cir. 1971); *Koupetoris v. Konkar Intrepid Corp.*, 402 F. Supp. 951 (S.D.N.Y. 1975), *aff'd*, 535 F.2d 1392 (2d Cir. 1976); *Mediterranean Shipping Co. v. Ningbo Toptrade Imp. Exp. Co.*, 2007 U.S. Dist. LEXIS 9628 (C.D. Cal. June 27, 2007); *Gall v. Topcall Int'l, AG*, 2005 WL 664502 (E.D. Pa. Mar. 21, 2005); *Chavez-Organista v. Vanos*, 208 F. Supp. 2d 174, 177 (D.P.R. 2002); *Matsuda v. Wada*, 128 F. Supp. 2d 659, 667 (D. Haw. 2000); *Marcus v. Five J Jewelers Precious Metals Industry Ltd.*, 111 F. Supp. 2d 445, 447 (S.D.N.Y. 2000); *Banci v. Wright*, 44 F. Supp. 2d 1272, 1275-1276 (S.D. Fla. 1999); *Engstrom v. Hornseth*, 959 F. Supp. 545, 547-548 (D.P.R. 1997); *Bergen Shipping Co. v. Japan Marine Serv., Ltd.*, 386 F. Supp. 430, 432 (S.D.N.Y. 1974).

158. *See Verlinden BV v. Central Bank of Nigeria*, 461 U.S. 480, 491-492 & n.18 (1983).

159. *See Strawbridge v. Curtiss*, 7 U.S. 267 (1806) (Marshall, C.J.); *Caterpillar, Inc. v. Lewis*, 519 U.S. 61, 68 (1996); *see also* 28 U.S.C. §1369 (granting subject matter jurisdiction in certain mass accident cases where only minimal diversity exists).

been susceptible of a "complete diversity" reading. This reading has generally precluded alienage jurisdiction under §1332(a)(2) in cases with aliens appearing on both sides of the dispute (*e.g.*, France and New York versus Germany and Pennsylvania).[160] The same result applies in cases where a U.S. citizen, joined by an alien, attempts to litigate against another alien.[161]

b. Section 1332(a)(3). In recent years, the Supreme Court has said that *Strawbridge*'s complete diversity requirement is not constitutionally mandated.[162] It instead flows from the language of Congress's jurisdictional statutes, which could be amended without constitutional obstacle to permit jurisdiction based on minimal diversity.[163] This interpretation of Article III clearly extends to alienage diversity, thus permitting Congress to authorize federal jurisdiction where aliens appear on both sides of a suit that also involves a U.S. party.[164]

In 1948, Congress enacted §1332(a)(3), which authorizes federal jurisdiction in actions between "citizens of different States and in which citizens or subjects of a foreign state are additional parties." The apparent purpose of §1332(a)(3) was to grant jurisdiction where a citizen of one U.S. state and a foreign citizen were aligned against the citizen of a second U.S. state (*e.g.*, New York and France versus Pennsylvania). It was thought that *domestic* diversity existed in these cases (*e.g.*, New York versus Pennsylvania), and that the presence of an alien on one side of the dispute should not deprive a domestic litigant of its federal diversity forum. Section 1332(a)(3) has frequently been applied in cases with this alignment.[165]

The literal language of §1332(a)(3), in contrast to that of §1332(a)(2), arguably also allows jurisdiction where a citizen of a U.S. state and an alien are aligned against the citizen of a second U.S. state and an alien (*e.g.*, Germany and Pennsylvania versus France and New York). Most lower courts have held that §1332(a)(3) grants federal alienage

160. *E.g., Grupo Dataflux v. Atlas Global Group, LP*, 541 U.S. 567 (2004); *Ruhrgas AG v. Marathon Oil Co.*, 526 U.S. 574, 580 n.2 (1999); *Stiftung v. Plains Mktg., L.P.*, 603 F.3d 295, 299 (5th Cir. 2010); *US Motors v. General Motors Europe*, 551 F.3d 420, 422-424 (6th Cir. 2010); *Franceskin v. Credit Suisse*, 214 F.3d 253, 258 (2d Cir. 2000); *Cabulceta v. Standard Fruit Co.*, 883 F.2d 1553, 1557 (11th Cir. 1989); *Faysound Ltd. v. United Coconut Chem. Inc.*, 878 F.2d 290 (9th Cir. 1989); *Cheng v. Boeing Co.*, 708 F.2d 1406 (9th Cir. 1983); *Field v. Volkswagenwerk*, 626 F.2d 293 (3d Cir. 1980); *IIT v. Vencap, Ltd.*, 519 F.2d 1001 (2d Cir. 1975); *Ed & Fred, Inc. v. Puritan Marine Ins. Underwriters Corp.*, 506 F.2d 757 (5th Cir. 1975); *Certain Underwriters at Lloyd's v. Mach. Mgmt. LLC*, 2010 U.S. Dist. LEXIS 49632 (Apr. 26, 2010); *LBA Int'l Ltd v. C.E. Consulting L.L.C.*, 2010 U.S. Dist. LEXIS 6240 (Jan. 26, 2010); *Oteng v. Golden Star Resources, Ltd.*, 615 F. Supp. 2d 1229 (D. Colo. 2009); *Thompson v. Deloitte & Touche LLP*, 503 F. Supp. 2d 1118 (S.D. Iowa 2007); *Krause v. Forex Exchange Market, Inc.*, 356 F. Supp. 2d 332, 337 (S.D.N.Y. 2005); *Rivas v. IMA SRL*, 2004 WL 225051 (E.D. Pa. 2004).

161. *E.g., USHA (India), Ltd. v. Honeywell Int'l, Inc.*, 421 F.3d 129, 133 (2d Cir. 2005); *General Technology Applications, Inc. v. Exro Ltda*, 388 F.3d 114, 120-121 (4th Cir. 2004); *Extra Equipamentos e Exportacao Ltd. v. Case Corp.*, 361 F.3d 359, 361 (7th Cir. 2004); *Universal Licensing Corp. v. Paola del Lungo S.p.A.*, 293 F.3d 579 (2d Cir. 2002); *Karazanos v. Madison Two Associates*, 147 F.3d 624, 627 (7th Cir. 1998); *Saadeh v. Farouki*, 107 F.3d 52, 58 (D.C. Cir. 1997); *Eze v. Yellow Cab Co.*, 782 F.2d 1064 (D.C. Cir. 1986); *Ed & Fred, Inc. v. Puritan Marine Ins. Underwriters Corp.*, 506 F.2d 747 (5th Cir. 1975); *Lindsay v. Toyota Motor Sales, U.S.A., Inc.*, 2005 WL 2030311, at *2 (S.D.N.Y. 2005); *Impuls I.D. Intern., S.L. v. Psion-Teklogix, Inc.*, 234 F. Supp. 2d 1267, 1273 (S.D. Fla. 2002); *Lee v. Trans American Trucking Service, Inc.*, 111 F. Supp. 2d 135, 141 (E.D.N.Y. 1999); *China Nuclear Energy Industry Corp. v. Andersen, LLP*, 11 F. Supp. 2d 1256, 1258-1260 (D. Colo. 1998).

162. *See Caterpillar, Inc. v. Lewis*, 519 U.S. 61, 68 n.3 (1996); *Verlinden BV v. Central Bank of Nigeria*, 461 U.S. 480, 492 n.18 (1983); *Owen Equip. & Erection Co. v. Kroger*, 437 U.S. 365, 373 n.13 (1978).

163. *See* 28 U.S.C. §1369 (authorizing subject matter jurisdiction in certain mass accident cases where only minimal diversity exists).

164. *Verlinden BV v. Central Bank of Nigeria*, 461 U.S. 480, 492 n.18 (1983).

165. *E.g., Tuck v. Pan American Health Org.*, 668 F.2d 547, 550 (D.C. Cir. 1981); *Turton v. Turton*, 644 F.2d 344, 346 n.1 (5th Cir. 1981); *In re Bridgestone/Firestone, Inc., Tires Products Liability Litig.*, 247 F. Supp. 2d 1071, 1073-1076 (S.D. Ind. 2003); *Weight v. Kawasaki Heavy Indus.*, 597 F. Supp. 1082, 1084 (E.D. Va. 1984); *American Nat'l Bank & Tr. Co. v. Hamilton Indus. Int'l*, 583 F. Supp. 164 (N.D. Ill. 1984). *See Karazanos v. Madison Two Associates*, 147 F.3d 624, 627 (7th Cir. 1998).

jurisdiction in these minimally diverse circumstances.[166] These decisions have reasoned that "[i]t would be inconsistent with the intent of the provision to deny a federal forum to diverse [U.S.] citizens because aliens were present on both sides of the controversy."[167] Nevertheless, some authority supports a complete diversity requirement in these circumstances (denying jurisdiction if aliens were both plaintiffs and defendants).[168]

Significant limitations still exist on alienage jurisdiction under §1332(a)(3). Suppose, for example, a New York plaintiff and a German plaintiff sue New York and Spanish defendants. Because §1332(a)(3) requires a suit between "citizens of different States," which means different U.S. sister states, §1332(a)(3) would not apply. Similarly, §1332(a)(3) would appear inapplicable to a suit by an alien plaintiff against a U.S. citizen and another alien.[169] This result follows from the absence of diverse U.S. parties on both sides of the action, which is the necessary predicate for §1332(a)(3) jurisdiction.

It is less clear how §1332(a)(3) should be applied to cases involving adverse foreign parties from the same foreign nation, together with diverse U.S. parties (e.g., Germany and New York versus Germany and New Jersey). Some authorities have concluded that §1332(a)(3) does not reach this situation, even if it does not require complete diversity.[170] Other commentators, and most of the courts that do not require complete diversity under §1332(a)(3), reject this view.[171]

166. See Tango Music, LLC v. DeadQuick Music, Inc., 348 F.3d 244, 245 (7th Cir. 2003) ("We have held in previous cases that the presence of foreigners on both sides of a diversity case does not destroy diversity."); Dresser Indus., Inc. v. Underwriters at Lloyd's of London, 106 F.3d 494 (3d Cir. 1997); Transure, Inc. v. Marsh & McLennan, Inc., 766 F.2d 1297 (9th Cir. 1985) (California and England versus Delaware and South Africa); Zenith Elec. Corp. v. Kimball Int'l Mfg., Inc., 114 F. Supp. 2d 764, 768 (N.D. Ill. 2000) ("virtually every authority that has construed §1332(a)(3) has held that the presence of aliens as additional parties on both sides of the action does not destroy diversity jurisdiction (provided there are diverse domestic citizens on both sides of the action who are legitimately interested parties in the dispute)"); Timco Engineering, Inc. v. Rex & Co., 603 F. Supp. 925 (E.D. Pa. 1985) (Florida and Hong Kong versus Texas and Hong Kong); K&H Business Consultants Ltd. v. Cheltonian, Ltd., 567 F. Supp. 420 (D.N.J. 1983) (England and Delaware versus England and Texas); Samincorp, Inc. v. Southwire Co., 531 F. Supp. 1, 2 (N.D. Ga. 1980) (New York versus Georgia and Venezuela; dicta that "diversity is [not] destroyed if citizens of foreign states are both plaintiffs and defendants").

167. K&H Business Consultants v. Cheltonian, Ltd., 567 F. Supp. 420, 423 (D.N.J. 1983).

168. Hercules Inc. v. Dynamic Export Corp., 71 F.R.D. 101 (S.D.N.Y. 1976). Cf. Cabalceta v. Standard Fruit Co., 883 F.2d 1553, 1557 (11th Cir. 1989) ("[T]he presence of at least one alien on both sides of an action destroys diversity"); Int'l Shipping Co. v. Hydra Offshore, Inc., 875 F.2d 388, 391 (2d Cir. 1989) (complete diversity requirement "[c]learly . . . applies in cases where aliens appear on both sides of a case"); Corporacion Venezolana de Fomento v. Vintero Sales Corp., 629 F.2d 786, 790 (2d Cir. 1980); China Nuclear Energy Industry Corp. v. Andersen, LLP, 11 F. Supp. 2d 1256, 1257 (D. Colo. 1998) ("[T]he presence of at least one alien on both sides of an action precludes diversity jurisdiction."); Simon Holdings PLC Group of Cos. U.K. v. Klenz, 878 F. Supp. 210, 211 (M.D. Fla. 1995) ("Complete diversity does not exist where there are aliens on both sides of the litigation . . . even if the aliens are from different countries.").

169. E.g., Israel Aircraft Indus. Ltd. v. Sanwa Business Credit Corp., 16 F.3d 198, 202 (7th Cir. 1994); Eze v. Yellow Cab Co., 782 F.2d 1064 (D.C. Cir. 1986) (no §1332(a)(2) or (a)(3) jurisdiction in suit by Nigerian plaintiffs against Virginian and Ghanaian defendants); Ed & Fred, Inc. v. Puritan Marine Ins. Underwriters Corp., 506 F.2d 757 (5th Cir. 1975); In re Arrowhead Capital Mgmt. LLC Class Litig., 2010 U.S. Dist. LEXIS 48246 (D. Minn. May 17, 2010); IGY Ocean Bay Props., Ltd. v. Ocean Bay Props. I, Ltd., 534 F. Supp. 2d 446 (S.D.N.Y. 2008).

170. E.g., DeWit v. KLM Royal Dutch Airlines, 570 F. Supp. 613, 617 (S.D.N.Y. 1983); Currie, The Federal Courts and the American Law Institute, 36 U. Chi. L. Rev. 1, 20 (1968).

171. E.g., Tango Music, LLC v. DeadQuick Music, Inc., 348 F.3d 244, 245-246 (7th Cir. 2003); Dresser Indus., Inc. v. Underwriters at Lloyd's of London, 106 F.3d 494 (3d Cir. 1997); Glenn Seed v. Vannet, 2009 U.S. Dist. LEXIS 93739 (W.D. Wis. Oct. 6, 2009); Scotts Co. v. Rhone-Poulenc SA, 347 F. Supp. 2d 543, 545 (S.D. Ohio 2004); Zenith Elec. Corp. v. Kimball Int'l Mfg., Inc., 114 F. Supp. 2d 764 (N.D. Ill. 2000); K&H Business Consultants v. Cheltonian, Ltd., 567 F. Supp. 420 (D.N.J. 1983); Jet Traders Inv. Corp. v. Tekair, Ltd., 89 F.R.D. 560 (D. Del. 1981); Samincorp v. Southwire Co., 531 F. Supp. 1 (N.D. Ga. 1980); 15 Coquillette et al., Moore's Federal Practice §102.72 at 102-140.3 (2009).

3. Selected Materials on Alienage Jurisdiction

Excerpted below is *Hercules Inc. v. Dynamic Export Corp.*, which illustrates some of the complexities that can arise in applying §§1332(a)(2) and 1332(a)(3) in the context of multiparty litigation. It also provides the basis for considering the purposes served by alienage jurisdiction, and the limitations on the scope of such jurisdiction.

HERCULES INC. v. DYNAMIC EXPORT CORP.
71 F.R.D. 101 (S.D.N.Y. 1976)

CANNELLA, DISTRICT JUDGE. [Hercules Inc. ("Hercules"), a Delaware corporation, appointed Dynamic Export Corp. ("Dynamic"), a New York corporation, as its distributor for certain chemical products in Iran. These products were to be sold to Dynamic by HITCO, a Hercules affiliate incorporated in the Bahamas. After disagreements between the parties arose, Hercules and HITCO sued Dynamic for some $200,000 allegedly owed to them by Dynamic for chemical products sold and delivered to Dynamic. Dynamic defended by alleging that it was acting on behalf of H. Mottahedan & Co. ("HMC"), an Iranian company, and joined HMC in a counterclaim seeking damages from Hercules and HITCO for breaching their contract to deliver a larger amount of the chemical involved. The court first concluded that Dynamic could pursue its counterclaims against Hercules and HITCO as agent for HMC, and that HMC could be joined under Federal Rules of Civil Procedure, Rule 20 as a plaintiff on these counterclaims. The court then considered whether the joinder of HMC as a plaintiff on the counterclaims destroyed diversity jurisdiction over the action.]

HMC, counterclaim-plaintiff, and HITCO, counterclaim-defendant, are both aliens. The presence of aliens on both sides of a controversy will defeat diversity jurisdiction. *E.g., Merchants' Cotton Press and Storage Co. v. Ins. Co. of North America*, 151 U.S. 368, 385-86 (1894). In the face of this doctrine, counterclaimants Dynamic and HMC present an ingenious argument. They assert that 28 U.S.C. §1332(c), deeming a corporation "a citizen of any State by which it has been incorporated and of the State where it has its principal place of business," is applicable to foreign corporations which have their principal place of business within the United States. This being the case, HITCO should be considered a citizen of Delaware, where it has its principal place of business, and not the Bahamas, where it is incorporated. The alignment of the parties on the counterclaims would then be an alien, HMC, and a citizen of New York, Dynamic, versus two citizens of Delaware, Hercules and HITCO. Although this argument may have surface appeal, it is neither supported by the case law nor consistent with the purpose of §1332(c).

Prior to 1958 an alien corporation, for purposes of diversity jurisdiction, was considered a citizen solely of the foreign state in which it was incorporated. *E.g., Barrow S.S. Co. v. Kane*, 170 U.S. 100 (1898). Since the enactment of §1332(c) in 1958 most federal courts have held it inapplicable to foreign corporations, leaving the traditional rule in effect. . . . On the other hand, courts confronting the issue more recently have found §1332(c) applicable to foreign corporations whose principal place of business is located in the United States. . . . [These decisions have] applied the section to defeat diversity jurisdiction between a citizen of a state and an alien corporation with its principal place of business in that state. This application of the subsection is in consonance with its avowed purpose, the restriction of diversity jurisdiction. S. Rep. No. 1830, 85th Cong., 2d Sess. (1958). . . .

For the purposes of the case at bar, however, we need not determine whether §1332(c) is, in fact, applicable to a foreign corporation. For even assuming that it is, it cannot be read to deem such a corporation a citizen of either the jurisdiction in which it is incorporated *or* the state in which it has its principal place of business, whichever it may choose. The statute creates a principle of dual citizenship, not one of alternative citizenship. Thus, where a corporation is incorporated in state A and has its principal place of business in state B and the adverse party is a citizen of either A or B, diversity is lacking. Likewise, assuming *arguendo* §1332(c) is applicable to alien corporations, when an alien corporation with its principal place of business in state A is adverse to either an alien or a citizen of state A, diversity would be lacking. . . .

Notes on Hercules v. Dynamic

1. *Historic rationale for alienage jurisdiction.* Consider the rationale for granting federal subject matter jurisdiction over disputes between aliens and Americans. As discussed above, these lawsuits were thought to carry the risk of offending foreign states, and hence of interfering with U.S. foreign relations and foreign commerce; the federal courts were thought to have greater institutional competence to resolve disputes involving aliens in ways that would be fair and internationally acceptable. Recall Alexander Hamilton's words, *supra* p. 8, about the importance of federal court jurisdiction over international disputes.

Many comments made during the debates surrounding the Constitution reflected the importance of alienage jurisdiction, often describing it in broad terms. Letter from James Madison to Edmund Randolph (April 8, 1787), reprinted in 9 *The Papers of James Madison* 368, 370 (R. Rutland & W. Rachal eds., 1975) ("all cases which concern foreigners"); 3 *The Debates in the Several State Conventions on the Adoption of the Federal Constitution* 530 (J. Elliot ed., 1836) (remarks of J. Madison) ("all occasions of having disputes with foreign powers"); *The Federalist Papers*, No. 80, at 501 (A. Hamilton) (C. Rossiter ed., 1961) ("all causes in which the citizens of other countries are concerned. . . .").

2. *Contemporary relevance of historic rationale for alienage jurisdiction.* Is the historic rationale for alienage jurisdiction relevant today?

(a) *Impact of U.S. civil litigation on U.S. foreign relations and commerce.* Is there now really a risk, as Alexander Hamilton could warn, that some European power will regard a U.S. judgment as a "just cause[] for war"? On the other hand, consider the political, diplomatic, and commercial impact of such cases as proceedings against Microsoft, Yahoo, or Google in Europe, the punishments imposed by some foreign tribunals against U.S. nationals, foreign judicial decisions imposing expropriatory penalties on U.S. companies, and the extraterritorial application of various U.S. laws in U.S. civil proceedings. Can judicial decisions in these sorts of cases not have significant impacts upon U.S. foreign relations?

Sophisticated businesses carefully consider the legal environment in nations where they are considering investments. Judicial decisions are an important aspect of this subject. James Madison's observation, 200 years ago, still has a substantial measure of truth: "if foreigners cannot get justice done them in these courts, [this will] prevent[] many wealthy gentlemen from trading or residing among us." 3 Elliot, *The Debates in the Several State Conventions on the Adoption of the Federal Constitution* 533-534, 583 (2d ed. 1941) (James Madison). The quality of U.S. justice in international cases, affecting foreign parties, will have a direct impact upon their willingness to trade with and invest in the United States. It may also affect the quality of justice received by U.S. parties abroad.

In light of the foregoing, consider this explanation of the contemporary importance of alienage jurisdiction:

> The power to create federal courts and confer them with alienage jurisdiction is one of the most important tools that the Constitution affords Congress to safeguard the collective interest of the Union. Its importance extends beyond merely protecting foreign investment and international commercial contracts; it encompasses our security and our relationship with foreign nations. *17th Street Assocs., LLP v. Markel Int'l Ins. Co. Ltd.*, 373 F. Supp. 2d 584, 605 (E.D. Va. 2005).

Do you agree? Or does this exaggerate the contemporary importance of alienage jurisdiction?

(b) Federal courts' relative competence to decide alienage disputes. Even if disputes with aliens can affect U.S. foreign relations and commerce, are federal courts any better suited to resolve such disputes than contemporary state courts? Even determined opponents of diversity jurisdiction generally concede that federal courts should retain jurisdiction over suits involving aliens. In the late Judge Friendly's words: "I would retain two, and only two, pieces of the present diversity jurisdiction. One is for suits between a citizen and foreign states or citizens or subjects thereof." H. Friendly, *Federal Jurisdiction: A General View* 149-150 (1973). Why?

Alienage jurisdiction is a fundamentally radical concept: local judges and jurors (*i.e.*, state courts) may be denied the power to decide disputes, involving local residents, that are otherwise within their jurisdiction. Principally in order to avoid foreign diplomatic displeasure and to attract foreign trade and investment, the state courts are replaced, if one of the litigants chooses, with specialized tribunals that are thought to be more sympathetic to foreign concerns. Is this not an unusual arrangement? Is it any more unusual than domestic diversity jurisdiction?

3. *Constitutional limits on alienage jurisdiction.* Article III grants federal judicial power over cases "between a State, or the Citizens thereof, and foreign States, Citizens or Subjects." The Supreme Court has not read this provision expansively.

(a) No Article III jurisdiction over suits by one alien against another. As noted above, despite the broader terms of the Judiciary Act and expansive comments by the Framers in the Federalist Papers and elsewhere, the Supreme Court concluded long ago that the Constitution's grant of alienage jurisdiction did not extend to suits solely between aliens. *Hodgson & Thompson v. Bowerbank*, 9 U.S. 303 (1809). This continues to be the rule today. *See Verlinden BV v. Central Bank of Nigeria*, 461 U.S. 480, 491-492 & n.18 (1983).

Some commentators have questioned the Court's holding that §11 of the Judiciary Act was unconstitutional, observing that the Judiciary Act of 1789 was enacted largely by those who drafted the Constitution. Warren, *New Light on the History of the Federal Judiciary Act of 1789*, 37 Harv. L. Rev. 49, 57 (1923). Are the purposes of the Constitution's authorization of alienage jurisdiction served by a narrow interpretation of the grant?

Even if *Bowerbank* was rightly decided, what are its implications? Nothing in the decision precludes state courts from exercising jurisdiction over suits exclusively between aliens. Does this make sense? Why should state courts, which play a limited role in foreign affairs, have greater claim to suits between foreign citizens (that are more likely to touch upon foreign affairs) than to suits between U.S. citizens? Might other doctrines constrain state court assertions of judicial jurisdiction in this context? *See infra* pp. 81-83, 84-105, 108-203 (personal jurisdiction) and pp. 365-435, 437-452 (*forum non conveniens*). Does *Bowerbank* entirely preclude federal courts from resolving cases solely between foreign parties? What if a foreign plaintiff brought claims against a foreign defendant that arose under federal law? What would be the basis for federal subject matter jurisdiction in that instance?

(b) Complete diversity. The requirement of "complete diversity" between adverse parties (*e.g.*, Florida and New York versus Arizona and Pennsylvania) is well established as a statutory requirement in most domestic diversity of citizenship cases. *See Strawbridge v. Curtiss*, 7 U.S. 267 (1806). It also appears settled that complete diversity is not constitutionally required in the alienage context. *See supra* pp. 21-24. Should complete diversity be *constitutionally* required in alienage cases? Consider the Framers' purposes.

4. *Alienage jurisdiction under §1332(a)(2).* Section 1332(a)(2) grants federal subject matter jurisdiction over disputes "between . . . citizens of *a State* and citizens or subjects of *a foreign state.*" The "complete diversity" rule has been extended to alienage jurisdiction under 28 U.S.C. §1332(a)(2), where it has precluded alienage jurisdiction in cases with aliens appearing on both sides of the dispute. *See supra* pp. 22-23. Should §1332(a)(2) require complete diversity? That is, should the section reach cases in which there are aliens as both plaintiffs and defendants (*e.g.*, Texas and Tanzania versus Minnesota and Malawi)? Are cases with aliens on both sides less likely to involve the threat of parochial bias and interference with U.S. trade and diplomacy than cases with aliens on one side? Does it matter whether the aliens are from the same foreign state? For a thorough discussion of §1332(a)(2), *see JP Morgan Chase Bank v. Traffic Stream (BVI) Infrastructure Ltd.*, 536 U.S. 88 (2002).

5. *Alienage jurisdiction under §1332(a)(3) and "complete diversity."* In 1948, Congress enacted §1332(a)(3), which grants federal jurisdiction in actions between "citizens of different States and in which citizens or subjects of a foreign state are additional parties." Like §1332(a)(2), the new provision has raised the question whether complete diversity is required. How does *Hercules* answer this question? Is the *Hercules* result consistent with one of the basic purposes underlying alienage jurisdiction — namely, to ensure that state courts are not the only available tribunals in cases where they may be inclined to favor a U.S. litigant over a foreign litigant? Is it consistent with the goal of ensuring a federal forum for disputes that implicate U.S. foreign relations?

Is *Hercules* correct that "complete diversity" is required in alienage cases under §1332(a)(3)? That is, suppose that foreign corporations are present as both plaintiffs and defendants in an action: may alienage jurisdiction exist, or is "complete diversity" required? *See Dresser Indus. v. Underwriters at Lloyds of London*, 106 F.3d 494 (3d Cir. 1997) (§1332(a)(3) abrogated "complete diversity," permitting alien corporations to appear as "additional parties" as both plaintiffs and defendants). Is this result required by the language of §1332(a)(3)? Is it wise? For a recent examination of these issues, *see Caribbean Telecoms, Ltd. v. Guy. Tel. & Tel. Co.*, 594 F. Supp. 2d 522 (D.N.J. 2009).

6. *Citizenship of contemporary multinational corporations.* Section 1332(c) provides that a corporation is "a citizen of any State by which it has been incorporated and of the State where it has its principal place of business." The structure of some companies may complicate application of this rule. Contemporary multinational enterprises often consist of numerous corporate vehicles, each with a different place of incorporation; shareholdings are often diffused among citizens of many different states. Management is also "multinational" in composition. In these circumstances, what should be regarded as a company's citizenship? Do major multinationals — like General Electric, Microsoft, Shell, or DaimlerChrysler — in fact have a "citizenship" in the traditional sense?

How is a court to determine which location supplies the principal place of business? *See Hertz Corp. v. Friend*, 130 S. Ct. 1181 (2010) (where company has its "nerve center").

Hercules addresses the dual citizenship of a foreign corporation with a principal place of business in the United States. *See also Slavchev v. Royal Caribbean Cruises, Ltd.*, 559 F.3d 251 (4th Cir. 2009) (foreign corporation with domestic principal place of business has two citizenships); *Caribbean Telecoms, Ltd v. Guyana Tel. & Tel. Co.*, 594 F. Supp. 2d 522 (D.N.J. 2009) ("The federal diversity statute does not permit domestic corporations to select among their two jurisdictional citizenships in order to preserve or defeat diversity. Diversity must be satisfied by both corporate citizenship designations; otherwise, the corporate citizenship provision would accomplish nothing. The Court sees no reason why alien corporations should be treated any differently."). Does this "dual citizenship" rule apply when the company is incorporated domestically but maintains its principal place of business in a foreign country? *See MAS Capital v. Biodelivery Sciences Int'l Inc.*, 524 F.3d 831 (7th Cir. 2008) (holding that such a company only has citizenship of state of incorporation).

7. *Section 1332 and the permanent resident alien provision.* In 1988, Congress amended the diversity statute to provide that "an alien admitted to the United States for permanent residence shall be deemed a citizen of the State in which such alien is domiciled." 28 U.S.C. §1332(a). Despite its apparent clarity, the amendment has been the source of significant confusion among the lower courts. Specifically, is the effect of this statute to accord a permanent resident alien a single citizenship for purposes of diversity jurisdiction (namely that of the state of domicile), or a second citizenship (namely, the state of domicile and the country of citizenship)? The plain language of the Act suggests the former interpretation whereas the limited legislative history of the amendment suggests the latter. *See* Bassett, *Statutory Interpretation in the Context of Federal Jurisdiction*, 76 Geo. Wash. L. Rev. 52 (2007). Can you see why the answer to this question would be significant in cases of diversity jurisdiction?

While this amendment affects the citizenship determination of individuals, it has at least two implications in cases involving companies. First, a case can arise between a permanent resident and a foreign company. In such cases, jurisdiction might lie under §1332(a)(2) if the 1988 amendment accords the permanent resident a single citizenship. But if the 1988 amendment creates a second citizenship for the permanent resident, then jurisdiction would not lie (can you see why?). Second, cases can arise between certain business entities (like partnerships and limited liability companies) and foreign companies. Business entities like partnerships and limited liability companies assume the citizenship of all their members. So if one partner (or member) is a permanent resident, this alignment has the potential to defeat jurisdiction under §1332(a)(2). Again, do you see why?

8. *Appropriate scope of federal subject matter jurisdiction in international cases.* Given the historic purposes of alienage jurisdiction, is it sufficient to focus strictly on the presence of foreign and U.S. nationals in litigation? Suits only involving aliens can implicate U.S. foreign relations, even if no American is a party and no question of parochial bias is involved. *Cf. Verlinden BV v. Central Bank of Nigeria*, 461 U.S. 480 (1983); *Republic of Philippines v. Marcos*, 806 F.2d 344 (2d Cir. 1986). In these circumstances, the parties' formal citizenship is often not a dispositive indicator of a case's likely impact on U.S. diplomatic or trade relations. Given this, would it be wiser for federal courts to be granted substantially wider subject matter jurisdiction over all "international cases"? Would Article III permit this?

9. *Relationship between alienage jurisdiction and applicable law.* There is a distinction between a court's jurisdiction to adjudicate a specific dispute, and the substantive law that governs that dispute. *See supra* pp. 1-2 and *infra* pp. 589-590. Sections 1332(a)(2) and

1332(a)(3) grant subject matter jurisdiction to federal courts, but do not directly address what substantive law applies in alienage actions.

(a) Application of Erie doctrine in alienage cases. As discussed above, it is fundamental that state substantive law applies in federal diversity actions, except where valid federal statutory or other law preempts state law. *Erie Railroad Co. v. Tompkins*, 304 U.S. 64, 74 (1938); *supra* pp. 10-11. It is orthodox teaching that the same principle generally applies outside the diversity context, including in alienage cases. C. Wright et al., *Federal Practice and Procedure* §4515 (1996 & Supp. 2010). Does that extension of *Erie* make sense?

(b) Arguments for applying federal substantive law in alienage cases. Are the purposes of alienage jurisdiction served merely by granting federal jurisdiction over alienage disputes? Consider the following argument, also made by Alexander Hamilton in support of Article III's grant of alienage jurisdiction: "So great a proportion of the cases in which foreigners are parties involve national questions that it is by far most safe and most expedient to refer all those in which they are concerned to the national tribunals." A. Hamilton, J. Madison & J. Jay, *The Federalist Papers* No. 80, at 476 (C. Rossiter ed. 1961).

Suppose federal substantive law did apply in alienage cases. Consider the problems that would arise from such a proposal. Where would federal substantive common law be derived from, in such fields as contract, tort, agency, and damages? Would it be thinkable for disputes involving foreigners to be subject to a different set of substantive rules than those involving U.S. nationals? Is this any different from subjecting disputes involving foreigners to a different set of courts than those involving most U.S. nationals?

10. *Federal subject matter jurisdiction distinguished from international competence.* As discussed below, both international and U.S. law restrict: (a) the personal jurisdiction of U.S. courts to adjudicate claims against foreign parties that lack meaningful contacts with the United States; and (b) the legislative jurisdiction of Congress (and state legislatures) to make U.S. law applicable to foreign conduct that lacks meaningful connection to the United States. *See infra* pp. 83-101.

International law could also forbid U.S. courts from hearing certain disputes — even where the parties are subject to U.S. personal jurisdiction and even though non-U.S. law is applied. International law could be interpreted to restrict the "competence" or "subject matter jurisdiction" of a nation's courts to resolve certain cases, regardless of personal and legislative jurisdiction, because the subject matter of the dispute lacked any connection to that nation. There is little authority for such a rule in common-law jurisdictions. Would it be sensible for such a doctrine to exist?

C.   Federal Question Jurisdiction in International Cases[172]

The single most significant aspect of the federal courts' subject matter jurisdiction involves actions arising under federal law.[173] This "federal question" jurisdiction derives from Article III's grant of jurisdiction over "[c]ases . . . arising under this Constitution, the Laws of the United States, and Treaties made, or which shall be made, under their authority."[174]

---

172. Commentary on federal question jurisdiction in international cases includes, *e.g.*, Bradley & Goldsmith, *Federal Courts and the Incorporation of International Law*, 111 Harv. L. Rev. 2260 (1998); Bradley & Goldsmith, *Customary International Law as Federal Common Law: A Critique of the Modern Position*, 110 Harv. L. Rev. 815 (1997); Randall, *Federal Jurisdiction over International Law Claims: Inquiries into the Alien Tort Statute*, 18 N.Y.U. J. Int'l L. & Pol'y 1 (1985); Rogers, *The Alien Tort Statute and How Individuals Violate International Law*, 21 Vand. J. Transnat'l L. 47 (1988); Henkin, *International Law as Law in the United States*, 82 Mich. L. Rev. 1555 (1984); Moore, *Federalism and Foreign Relations*, 1965 Duke L.J. 248, 291-297.

173. *See* C. Wright et al., *Federal Practice and Procedure* §3561 (2008 & Supp. 2010).

174. U.S. Const. Art. III, §2.

1. Introduction and Historical Background

a. Article III's Grant of Federal Question Jurisdiction. Article III's grant of federal question jurisdiction was one of the principal reasons that the Framers provided for the establishment of a federal court system.[175] From almost the beginning of the Constitutional Convention, it was accepted that federal courts should have jurisdiction over actions arising under federal statutes.[176] Cases arising under the Constitution and U.S. "Treaties" were added later in the Convention.[177] The Framers explained the constitutional grant of federal question jurisdiction as a safeguard against state court subversion of federal law,[178] a basis for achieving national uniformity of federal law,[179] and a means of obtaining neutral arbiters detached from local prejudice.[180]

Particular importance was attached to Article III's grant of federal question jurisdiction in cases arising under U.S. treaties. The Framers emphasized that such cases have "an evident connection with the preservation of the national peace."[181] The same rationales that justified alienage jurisdiction were advanced for federal question jurisdiction over treaties: because such cases were sensitive, and engaged national obligations toward foreign states, federal courts ought to have responsibility for them.[182]

b. Statutory Grants of Federal Question Jurisdiction. Notwithstanding the importance attributed to it, Article III's grant of federal question jurisdiction was not generally implemented until 1875. Neither the First Judiciary Act, nor any legislation for another 80 years, contained any general authorization for federal courts to hear cases arising under federal statutes.[183] In contrast, however, the First Judiciary Act contained several specialized grants of federal question jurisdiction directed specifically toward international disputes.

First, the Judiciary Act of 1789 included a grant of subject matter jurisdiction to the federal courts over "all causes where an alien sues for a tort only, [committed] in violation of the law of nations or a treaty of the United States."[184] Although no legislative history or other evidence specifically explains the reasons for this grant of federal question jurisdiction — today called the "Alien Tort Statute" — it graphically illustrates the importance

---

175. The first of Article III's jurisdictional grants is federal question jurisdiction. *See The Federalist* No. 16, at 116 (Alexander Hamilton) (Clinton Rossiter ed., 1961) ("The majesty of the national authority must be manifested through the medium of the courts of justice").

176. 1 M. Farrand, *Records of the Federal Convention of 1787* 22, 211-212, 220, 244 (1937); 2 *id.* 46-47, 186-187. After considering the report of the Committee of the whole, Madison proposed that federal "jurisdiction shall extend to all cases arising under the National laws: And to such other questions as may involve the National peace and harmony." 2 M. Farrand, *Records of the Federal Convention of 1787* 46 (1937). The suggestion was agreed.

177. 2 M. Farrand, *Records of the Federal Convention of 1787* 423-424, 430-431 (1937).

178. *The Federalist* No. 80, at 476 (Alexander Hamilton) (Clinton Rossiter ed., 1961) ("No man of sense will believe, that such prohibitions [on state authority] would be scrupulously regarded, without some effectual power in the government to restrain or correct the infractions of them").

179. *Id.* ("The mere necessity of uniformity in the interpretation of the national laws, decides the question").

180. *Id.* at 478 ("Tribunal which, having no local attachments, will be likely to be impartial between the different States and their citizens, and which, owing its official existence to the Union, will never be likely to feel any bias inauspicious to the principles on which it is founded.").

181. *Id.* at 480. The Framers emphasized that the "national peace and harmony" was affected by cases involving "the security of foreigners where treaties are in their favor." 1 M. Farrand, *Records of the Federal Convention of 1787* 238 (1937).

182. *The Federalist* No. 80 (Alexander Hamilton) (Clinton Rossiter ed., 1961).

183. C. Wright et al., *Federal Practice and Procedure* §3561 (2008 & Supp. 2010).

184. Judiciary Act of 1789, ch. 20 §9(b), 1 Stat. 73, 77, codified at 28 U.S.C. §1350 ("[t]he district courts shall have original jurisdiction of any civil action by an alien for a tort only, committed in violation of the law of nations or a treaty of the United States").

that was attributed to international disputes at the time.[185] Although Article III would have permitted jurisdiction in any case arising under the U.S. Constitution, statutes, or Treaties, Congress's implementation of Article III's federal question jurisdiction was limited principally to claims under U.S. Treaties and "the Law of Nations" — presumably those subjects where the legislature deemed federal jurisdiction most necessary.[186]

Second, in 1875, Congress substantially enlarged the federal question jurisdiction of federal courts. With little debate, Congress granted federal district courts original jurisdiction over cases arising under federal laws.[187] That legislation has been preserved substantially unchanged, and is currently codified in 28 U.S.C. §1331: "district courts shall have original jurisdiction of all civil actions arising under the Constitution, laws, or treaties of the United States."[188]

Most actions under §1331 are based on specific federal substantive statutes. Typical examples are cases in which a plaintiff files a complaint in federal court alleging violations of the federal antitrust laws, RICO, or securities laws.[189] These actions "arise under" federal law, and are within the scope of §1331. (They do not raise specifically international issues, and are not further considered here.)

Determining whether an action "arises under" federal law within the meaning of §1331 can present difficult issues in both domestic and international contexts.[190] As a matter of statutory interpretation under §1331, the issue is typically decided by applying the "well-pleaded complaint" rule, which requires examining the plaintiff's complaint to determine whether it asserts claims created by federal, rather than state, law.[191] In general, an action does not arise under federal law for purposes of §1331 if the federal law at issue in a case is merely a defense to a nonfederal claim.[192] Federal question jurisdiction will exist, however, even if state (or foreign) law creates the plaintiff's cause of action, provided that a substantial, disputed issue of federal law is a necessary element of the plaintiff's state claim.[193]

Third, in 1976, Congress enacted the Foreign Sovereign Immunities Act ("FSIA").[194] The FSIA grants federal district courts concurrent jurisdiction over civil actions against foreign states and state-related entities.[195] The FSIA's grant of federal subject matter

---

185. *See infra* pp. 32-33; R. Fallon et al., *Hart and Wechsler's, The Federal Courts and the Federal System* 755-756 (5th ed. 2003).

186. The Alien Tort Statute is discussed in detail below. *See infra* pp. 33-62. The First Congress also granted federal subject matter jurisdiction over admiralty and maritime cases and cases involving foreign consuls. C. Wright et al., *Federal Practice and Procedure* §§3662, 3671, 3675 (1998 & Supp. 2010).

187. Act of March 3, 1875, §1, 18 Stat. 470.

188. In addition, a number of federal substantive statutes (such as the antitrust and securities laws) contain specialized grants of federal subject matter jurisdiction relating to particular federal substantive statutes. *See supra* pp. 8-9 and *infra* pp. 672-673.

189. These exercises of both legislative jurisdiction and subject matter jurisdiction are discussed below at *infra* pp. 707-708, 709-711.

190. *See Franchise Tax Bd. v. Construction Laborers Vacation Tr.*, 463 U.S. 1 (1983); R. Fallon et al., *Hart & Wechsler's The Federal Courts and the Federal System* 856-899 (5th ed. 2003).

191. *Louisville & Nashville R.R. v. Mottley*, 211 U.S. 149 (1908). *See also Empire Healtchoice Assur., Inc. v. McVeigh,* 547 U.S. 677 (2006). As discussed below, Article III's constitutional grant of jurisdiction over claims "arising under" federal law is broader than §1331's statutory grant of jurisdiction "arising under" federal law. *See infra* pp. 62-70. Congress could therefore grant federal courts broader federal question jurisdiction than that permitted under §1331's "well-pleaded complaint" rule. Congress did so in enacting the Foreign Sovereign Immunities Act, and the Court held that Article III had not been overstepped. *Verlinden BV v. Central Bank of Nigeria*, 461 U.S. 480 (1983); *infra* pp. 70-79.

192. *Franchise Tax Bd. v. Construction Laborers Vacation Tr.*, 463 U.S. 1 (1983); *Louisville & Nashville R.R. v. Mottley*, 211 U.S. 149 (1908); C. Wright et al., *Federal Practice and Procedure* §§3522, 3562 (2008 & Supp. 2010). *But see* 28 U.S.C. §2679(d)(2) (permitting removal of cases from state court where Attorney General certifies that federal officer was acting within scope of his employment).

193. *Franchise Tax Bd. v. Construction Laborers Vacation Trust*, 463 U.S. 1 (1983).

194. 28 U.S.C. §§1330, 1601-1611.

195. *See infra* pp. 70-71, 234-235.

jurisdiction is consistent with Congress's history of providing federal jurisdiction over international disputes. Nevertheless, as discussed below, it has given rise to difficult issues under Article III.[196]

The following sections examine each of the foregoing grants of federal question jurisdiction, focusing on the application of these grants in international litigation.

2. Jurisdiction of Federal Courts Under the Alien Tort Statute

a. The Alien Tort Statute. As described above, the First Judiciary Act granted federal courts jurisdiction over "all causes where an alien sues for a tort only, [committed] in violation of the law of nations or a treaty of the United States."[197] The Alien Tort Statute's grant of jurisdiction was[198] and remains concurrent with the state courts.[199]

For much of two centuries, the Alien Tort Statute was largely ignored. Indeed, commenting in 1975 on the statute's allegedly obscure origins, Judge Friendly dubbed the provision a "Legal Lohengrin" (after the mysterious, shadowy character in a Wagner opera), and remarked that "no one seems to know from whence it came."[200] Before 1980, it was also true that no one seemed to care very much where the Alien Tort Statute might go: jurisdiction under the Act had apparently been upheld on only two occasions.[201] In the comparatively small number of other cases where §1350 jurisdiction was claimed, but denied, courts generally concluded that the defendant's alleged conduct did not violate the law of nations.[202]

b. *Filartiga* and *Tel-Oren*. In 1980, the Alien Tort Statute left the shadows and, at least for a time, took center stage. In a controversial opinion titled *Filartiga v. Pena-Irala*,[203] which is excerpted below, the Second Circuit held that the Alien Tort Statute provided the basis for federal jurisdiction in a suit against a former Paraguayan police official for the alleged torture and murder of the plaintiff's deceased Paraguayan relative. According to the court, customary international law prohibits official torture, and §1350 provides a jurisdictional basis for suits in federal courts for violations of this "law of nations" prohibition.

The Second Circuit's decision in *Filartiga v. Pena-Irala* provoked extensive commentary, both approving and disapproving.[204] *Filartiga* also provided the impetus for a flurry of

---

196. *See infra* pp. 70-79, 231-361; *Verlinden BV v. Central Bank of Nigeria*, 461 U.S. 480 (1983).

197. Judiciary Act of 1789, ch. 20 §9(b), 1 Stat. 73, 77.

198. Judiciary Act of 1789, ch. 20 §9, 1 Stat. 73, 77.

199. 28 U.S.C. §1350.

200. *ITT v. Vencap, Ltd.*, 519 F.2d 1001, 1015 (2d Cir. 1975). For analysis of the origins of the Alien Tort Statute, *see* Bradley, *The Alien Tort Statute and Article III*, 42 Va. J. Int'l L. 587 (2002); Sweeney, *A Tort Only in Violation of the Law of Nations*, 18 Hastings Int'l & Comp. L. Rev. 445 (1995); Casto, *The Federal Courts' Protective Jurisdiction Over Torts Committed in Violation of the Law of Nations*, 18 Conn. L. Rev. 467 (1986); Randall, *Federal Jurisdiction Over International Law Claims: Inquiries Into the Alien Tort Statute*, 18 N.Y.U. J. Int'l L. & Pol'y 1 (1985); Rogers, *The Alien Tort Statute and How Individuals Violate International Law*, 21 Vand. J. Transnat'l L. 47 (1988).

201. *See Adra v. Clift*, 195 F. Supp. 857 (D. Md. 1961) (use of passport under false pretenses); *Bolchos v. Darrel*, 3 F. Cas. 810 (D.S.C. 1795) (no. 1607) (seizure of neutral vessel). *See also* 1 Op. Att'y Gen. 57 (1795) (raid on neutral settlement); 26 Op. Att'y Gen. 250 (1907) (diversion of international waterway).

202. *See, e.g., Huynh Thi Anh v. Levi*, 586 F.2d 625 (6th Cir. 1978); *Benjamins v. British European Airways*, 572 F.2d 913 (2d Cir. 1978); *Dreyfus v. Von Finck*, 534 F.2d 24 (2d Cir. 1976); *IIT v. Vencap, Ltd.*, 519 F.2d 1001 (2d Cir. 1975); *Akbar v. New York Magazine Co.*, 490 F. Supp. 60 (D.D.C. 1980) (libel is not violation of law nations); *Valanga v. Metropolitan Life Ins. Co.*, 259 F. Supp. 324 (E.D.N.Y. 1966).

203. 630 F.2d 876 (2d Cir. 1980). Since *Filartiga*, more than 100 cases have been filed under the Alien Tort Statute. *See* Ku, *The Third Wave: The Alien Tort Statute and the War on Terrorism*, 19 Emory Int'l L. Rev. 105, 108-109 & nn.15-16 (2005).

204. For commentary approving the result in *Filartiga*, *see, e.g.*, Burley, *The Alien Tort Statute and the Judiciary Act of 1789: A Badge of Honor*, 83 Am. J. Int'l L. 461 (1989); Cole et al., *Interpreting the Alien Tort Statute: Amicus Curiae Memorandum of International Law Scholars and Practitioners in* Trajano v. Marcos, 12 Hastings Int'l & Comp. L. Rev. 1

litigation under the Alien Tort Statute. In the two decades following *Filartiga*, the decision was often invoked by plaintiffs with human rights grievances against foreign officials.[205] This litigation prompted expressions of concern from both courts and commentators, on the grounds that adjudication of sensitive claims of human rights abuses by U.S. courts will interfere with the conduct of U.S. foreign relations by Congress and the President.[206]

One of the more thoughtful discussions of these issues was in the various opinions in *Tel-Oren v. Libyan Arab Republic*.[207] The *Tel-Oren* plaintiffs' claim arose out of an incident in which members of the Palestine Liberation Organization ("PLO") and other groups murdered a number of civilians during a terrorist attack in Israel. The victims — citizens of Israel, the United States, and the Netherlands — filed an action in federal district court against the PLO and Libya, asserting jurisdiction under the Alien Tort Statute. The district court dismissed, among other things, for lack of subject matter jurisdiction. The Court of Appeals for the D.C. Circuit unanimously affirmed, but all three members of the panel wrote separately.

Two members of the panel, Judges Robb and Bork, rejected the *Filartiga* construction of the Alien Tort Statute, although for different reasons. Judge Robb argued that human rights disputes, such as those in *Filartiga* and *Tel-Oren*, were nonjusticiable political questions, because they involved sensitive matters that touch on American foreign relations.[208] He thought that *Filartiga* failed to "consider the possibility that ad hoc intervention by courts into international affairs may very well redound to the decisive disadvantage of the nation."[209] "[T]he political questions doctrine is designed to prevent just this sort of judicial gambling."[210]

Judge Bork said it was not necessary to determine whether the political question doctrine barred the plaintiffs' claim.[211] But, like Judge Robb, he believed that the *Filartiga* interpretation of the Alien Tort Statute would thrust the judiciary into foreign affairs and he therefore adopted a narrow construction of the Alien Tort Statute.[212] According to Judge Bork, §1350 was merely jurisdictional and did not itself grant plaintiffs a private "cause of action."[213] Judge Bork also reasoned that the separation of powers principles underpinning the act of state and political question doctrines counseled against implying a cause of action. Finally, he would have held that the human rights conventions and principles of customary international law on which the *Tel-Oren* plaintiffs relied did not create a private cause of action.[214]

(1988); Blum & Steinhardt, *Federal Jurisdiction Over International Human Rights Claims: The Alien Tort Claims Act After* Filartiga, 22 Harv. Int'l L.J. 53 (1981); Paust, *Litigating Human Rights: A Commentary on the Comments*, 4 Hous. J. Int'l L. 8 (1981). For criticism of *Filartiga, see, e.g.*, Oliver, *Problems of Cognition and Interpretation in Applying Norms of the Customary International Law of Human Rights in United States Courts*, 4 Hous. J. Int'l L. 59 (1981); Rusk, *A Comment on* Filartiga v. Pena-Irala, 11 Ga. J. Int'l & Comp. L. 311 (1981). For an analysis of academic reactions to *Filartiga, see* Yoo & Ku, *Beyond Formalism in Foreign Affairs: A Functional Approach to the Alien Tort Statute*, 2004 Sup. Ct. Rev. 153, 156-164.

205. *E.g., Abebe-Jira v. Negewo*, 72 F.3d 844 (11th Cir. 1996); *Kadic v. Karadzic*, 70 F.3d 232 (2d Cir. 1995); *In re Estate of Ferdinand E. Marcos Human Rights Litig.*, 978 F.2d 493 (9th Cir. 1992); *Trajano v. Marcos*, 878 F.2d 1439 (9th Cir. 1989); *Siderman de Blake v. Republic of Argentina*, 965 F.2d 699 (9th Cir. 1992); *Tel-Oren v. Libyan Arab Republic*, 726 F.2d 774 (D.C. Cir. 1984). *See generally* Bellinger, *Enforcing Human Rights in U.S. Courts and Abroad: The Alien Tort Statute and Other Approaches*, 42 Vand. J. Transnat'l L. 1 (2009).

206. *E.g., Tel-Oren v. Libyan Arab Republic*, 726 F.2d 774 (D.C. Cir. 1984); *Al Odah v. United States*, 321 F.3d 1134 (D.C. Cir. 2003) (Randolph, J., concurring).

207. 726 F.2d 774 (D.C. Cir. 1984).

208. 726 F.2d at 823.

209. 726 F.2d at 826 n.5.

210. 726 F.2d at 827 n.5.

211. 726 F.2d at 798, 803.

212. 726 F.2d at 803.

213. 726 F.2d at 811.

214. 726 F.2d at 808-819.

Judge Edwards was the only member of the *Tel-Oren* panel to accept the *Filartiga* reading of the Alien Tort Statute. In so doing, he rejected Judge Bork's contention that §1350 plaintiffs were required to show a private right to sue independent of the Alien Tort Statute, apparently concluding that both §1350 and other sources of national law provided a right to sue.[215] Judge Edwards nonetheless rejected Alien Tort Statute jurisdiction over the *Tel-Oren* plaintiffs' claims, because no tort in violation of the "law of nations" had occurred.[216] He observed that the PLO was not a state recognized by the United States, and reasoned that, because the law of nations ordinarily does not impose responsibility or liability on nonstate actors, the PLO could not commit "a tort in violation of the law of the nations."[217]

As discussed below, *Filartiga* considered only the question whether the Alien Tort Statute provided a grant of federal question jurisdiction, not whether the Act also created a private right of action.[218] Subsequently, however, other lower courts concluded that the Alien Tort Statute granted both federal jurisdiction and a private cause of action for torts against aliens in violation of international law.[219] Relying on these authorities, a wide range of human rights claims were asserted in U.S. courts.[220]

c. *Sosa v. Alvarez-Machain.* It was only a matter of time before the Supreme Court sought to clarify the confusion surrounding the Alien Tort Statute. It finally attempted to do so in *Sosa v. Alvarez-Machain*, excerpted below. While *Sosa* resolved some questions regarding the statute, it left many others unresolved, either intentionally or otherwise.[221] The Court's opinion will ensure that the meaning of the Alien Tort Statute remains a topic of abundant litigation for years to come.

Excerpted below are the Second Circuit's decision in *Filartiga* and the Supreme Court's decision in *Sosa*. In reading the decisions, consider the following issues: (1) the precise questions of statutory interpretation before the courts; (2) the question of federal common law making power separating the Court's opinion in *Sosa* and Justice Scalia's separate opinion; (3) whether it is sound policy to grant federal courts jurisdiction over the types of misconduct alleged in the case; and (4) whether the courts adequately take into account separation of powers considerations.

After you read *Sosa*, review the Torture Victim Protection Act (or "TVPA") found in Appendix A. The TVPA, codified as a statutory "note" to the Alien Tort Statute, was enacted to implement the Convention Against Torture and Other Cruel, Inhuman or

---

215. 726 F.2d at 777-782, 782-789.

216. 726 F.2d at 791-796.

217. 726 F.2d at 796. *Compare Kadic v. Karadzic*, 70 F.3d 232 (2d Cir. 1995) (certain forms of conduct violate the law of nations whether undertaken by those acting under the auspices of a state or only as private individuals).

218. *See infra* pp. 47-49.

219. *See Flores v. Southern Peru Copper Corp.*, 414 F.3d 233, 244-247 (2d Cir. 2003) (collecting cases); *Al Odah v. United States*, 321 F.3d 1134, 1145-1146 (D.C. Cir. 2003) (Randolph, J., concurring) (collecting cases), *reversed sub nom. Rasul v. Bush*, 542 U.S. 466 (2004).

220. *E.g.*, *Aldana v. Del Monte Fresh Produce, N.A., Inc.*, 416 F.3d 232 (7th Cir. 2005) (*per curiam*) (torture by owner of banana plantation); *Cabello v. Fernandez-Larios*, 402 F.3d 1148 (11th Cir. 2005) (human rights abuses by former Chilean military officer); *Flores v. Southern Peru Copper Corp.*, 414 F.3d 233, 244-247 (2d Cir. 2003) (environmental offenses); *Wiwa v. Royal Dutch Petroleum Co.*, 226 F.3d 88 (2d Cir. 2000) (human rights abuses perpetrated by Nigerian officials acting in cooperation with multinational corporation); *Abebe-Jira v. Negewo*, 72 F.3d 844 (11th Cir. 1996) (torture and other acts by official of former Ethiopian government); *In re Estate of Ferdinand E. Marcos Human Rights Litigation*, 978 F.2d 493 (9th Cir. 1992) (kidnap, torture, and murder).

221. For analysis of *Sosa*, *see* Yoo & Ku, *Beyond Formalism in Foreign Affairs: A Functional Approach to the Alien Tort Statute*, 2004 Sup. Ct. Rev. 153, 165-176; Kontorovich, *Implementing* Sosa v. Alvarez-Machain: *What Piracy Reveals About the Limits of the Alien Tort Statute*, 80 Notre Dame L. Rev. 111 (2004).

Degrading Treatment or Punishment,[222] which the United States has ratified. Article 14 of the Convention requires member states to adopt measures to ensure that torturers within their territory are held accountable for their acts.[223] Enacted in 1992, the TVPA creates a federal civil action against individuals who, under the actual or apparent authority or color of law of any foreign state, subject a person to torture or extrajudicial killing.[224] According to the TVPA's legislative history, "[t]his legislation will . . . mak[e] sure that torturers and death squads will no longer have a safe haven in the United States."[225] As you read the TVPA, consider how it illuminates the proper meaning of the Alien Tort Statute and, conversely, how the Alien Tort Statute illuminates the proper meaning of the TVPA.

FILARTIGA v. PENA-IRALA
630 F.2d 876 (2d Cir. 1980)

KAUFMAN, CIRCUIT JUDGE. [Plaintiffs are a Paraguayan man and his daughter living in the United States. The son/brother of the plaintiffs was brutally tortured and killed by defendant when the latter was inspector general of police in a Paraguayan city. After unsuccessfully seeking relief from the Paraguayan courts, plaintiffs discovered defendant living in the United States, where he was served with process. The district court dismissed the complaint, ruling that the alleged tort was not in violation of the "law of nations" and therefore that 28 U.S.C. §1350 did not apply. The plaintiffs appealed.]

Appellants rest their principal argument in support of federal jurisdiction upon the Alien Tort Statute, 28 U.S.C. §1350. . . . Since appellants do not contend that their action arises directly under a treaty of the United States, a threshold question on the jurisdictional issue is whether the conduct alleged violates the law of nations. . . . [W]e find that an act of torture committed by a state official against one held in detention violates established norms of the international law of human rights, and hence the law of nations. [The Court initially conducted an exhaustive survey of the public international law treatment of torture, concluding that international law forbids torture by state officials. In doing so, the Court relied heavily on a number of multilateral international documents, including the U.N. Charter and various human rights conventions.]

Having examined the sources from which customary international law is derived — the usage of nations, judicial opinions and the works of jurists — we conclude that official torture is now prohibited by the law of nations. The prohibition is clear and unambiguous, and admits of no distinction between treatment of aliens and citizens. . . . The treaties and accords cited above, as well as the express foreign policy of our own government, all make it clear that international law confers fundamental rights upon all people vis-à-vis their own governments. While the ultimate scope of those rights will be a subject for continuing refinement and elaboration, we hold that the right to be free from torture is now among them.

---

222. G.A. Res. 39/46, 39 U.N. GAOR Supp. No. 51, at 197, U.N. Doc. A/RES/39/708 (1984), *reprinted in* 23 I.L.M. 1027 (1984).

223. *See* S. Rep. No. 249, 102d Cong., 1st Sess. 3 (1991).

224. Torture is defined to include the intentional infliction of severe pain or suffering, whether physical or mental, for the purposes of obtaining a confession, punishment, or coercion. "Extrajudicial killing" is defined as "a deliberate killing not authorized by a previous judgment pronounced by a regularly constituted court affording all judicial guarantees which are recognized as indispensable by civilized peoples." Because of the requirement that the conduct at issue be "under actual or apparent authority, or color of law," plaintiffs are required to demonstrate governmental involvement in the tortious activity underlying the claim.

225. S. Rep. No. 249, 102d Cong., 1st Sess. 3 (1991).

Appellee submits that even if the tort alleged is a violation of modern international law, federal jurisdiction may not be exercised consistent with the dictates of Article III of the Constitution. The claim is without merit. Common law courts of general jurisdiction regularly adjudicate transitory tort claims between individuals over whom they exercise personal jurisdiction, wherever the tort occurred. Moreover, as part of an articulated scheme of federal control over external affairs, Congress provided, in the first Judiciary Act, §9(b), 1 Stat. 73, 77 (1789), for federal jurisdiction over suits by aliens where principles of international law are in issue. The constitutional basis for the Alien Tort Statute is the law of nations, which has always been part of the federal common law.

It is not extraordinary for a court to adjudicate a tort claim arising outside of its territorial jurisdiction. A state or nation has a legitimate interest in the orderly resolution of disputes among those within its borders, and where the *lex loci delicti commissi* is applied, it is an expression of comity to give effect to the laws of the state where the wrong occurred.

. . . Here, where *in personam* jurisdiction has been obtained over the defendant, the parties agree that the acts alleged would violate Paraguayan law, and the policies of the forum are consistent with the foreign law. . . .

[W]e proceed to consider whether the First Congress acted constitutionally in vesting jurisdiction over "foreign suits," alleging torts committed in violation of the law of nations. A case properly "aris[es] under the . . . laws of the United States" for Article III purposes if grounded upon statutes enacted by Congress or upon the common law of the United States. *See Illinois v. City of Milwaukee*, 406 U.S. 91, 99-100 (1972). . . . The law of nations forms an integral part of the common law, and a review of the history surrounding the adoption of the Constitution demonstrates that it became a part of the common law *of the United States* upon the adoption of the Constitution. Therefore, the enactment of the Alien Tort Statute was authorized by Article III.

During the eighteenth century, it was taken for granted on both sides of the Atlantic that the law of nations forms a part of the common law. Under the Articles of Confederation, the Pennsylvania Court of Oyer and Terminer at Philadelphia, *per* McKean, Chief Justice, applied the law of nations to the criminal prosecution of the Chevalier de Longchamps for his assault upon the person of the French Consul-General to the United States, noting that "[t]his law, in its full extent, is a part of the law of this state. . . ." *Respublica v. DeLongchamps*, 1 U.S. 113, 119 (1784). . . . As ratified, the judiciary article contained no express reference to cases arising under the law of nations. Indeed, the only express reference to that body of law is contained in Article I, sec. 8, cl. 10, which grants to the Congress the power to "define and punish . . . offenses against the law of nations." Appellees seize upon this circumstance and advance the proposition that the law of nations forms a part of the laws of the United States only to the extent that Congress has acted to define it. This extravagant claim is amply refuted by the numerous decisions applying rules of international law uncodified in any act of Congress. . . . Thus, it was hardly a radical initiative for Chief Justice Marshall to state in *The Nereide*, 13 U.S. 388, 422 (1815), that in the absence of a congressional enactment, United States courts are "bound by the law of nations, which is a part of the law of the land." These words were echoed in *The Paquete Habana*: "[i]nternational law is part of our law, and must be ascertained and administered by the courts of justice of appropriate jurisdiction, as often as questions of right depending upon it are duly presented for their determination."

The Filartigas urge that 28 U.S.C. §1350 be treated as an exercise of Congress's power to define offenses against the law of nations. While such a reading is possible, *see Lincoln Mills v. Textile Workers*, 353 U.S. 488 (1957) (jurisdictional statute authorizes judicial explication of federal common law), we believe it is sufficient here to construe the Alien Tort Statute, not as granting new rights to aliens, but simply as opening the federal courts for adjudication of the rights already recognized by international law. The statute nonetheless does inform our analysis of Article III, for we recognize that questions of jurisdiction "must be considered part of an organic growth — part of an evolutionary process," and that the history of the judiciary article gives meaning to its pithy phrases. *Romero v. International Terminal Operating Co.*, 358 U.S. 354, 360 (1959). The Framers' overarching concern that control over international affairs be vested in the new national government to safeguard the standing of the United States among the nations of the world therefore reinforces the result we reach today.

Although the Alien Tort Statute has rarely been the basis for jurisdiction during its long history, in light of the foregoing discussion, there can be little doubt that this action is properly brought in federal court.[226] This is undeniably an action by an alien, for a tort only, committed in violation of the law of nations. The paucity of suits successfully maintained under the section is readily attributable to the statute's requirement of alleging a "*violation* of the law of nations" (emphasis supplied) at the jurisdictional threshold. . . .

For example, the statute does not confer jurisdiction over an action by a Luxembourgeois international investment trust's suit for fraud, conversion and corporate waste. *IIT v. Vencap*, 519 F.2d 1001, 1015 (1975). In *IIT*, Judge Friendly astutely noted that the mere fact that every nation's municipal law may prohibit theft does not incorporate "the Eighth Commandment, 'Thou Shalt not steal' . . . [into] the law of nations." It is only where the nations of the world have demonstrated that the wrong is of mutual, and not merely several, concern, by means of express international accords, that a wrong generally recognized becomes an international law violation within the meaning of the statute. . . .

Appellee Pena . . . advances several additional points that lie beyond the scope of our holding on jurisdiction. Both to emphasize the boundaries of our holding, and to clarify some of the issues reserved for the district court on remand, we will address these contentions briefly.

Pena argues that the customary law of nations, as reflected in treaties and declarations that are not self-executing, should not be applied as rules of decision in this case. In doing so, he confuses the question of federal jurisdiction under the Alien Tort Statute, which requires consideration of the law of nations, with the issue of the choice of law to be applied, which will be addressed at a later stage in the proceedings. The two issues are distinct. Our holding on subject matter jurisdiction decides only whether Congress intended to confer judicial power, and whether it is authorized to do so by Article III. The choice of law inquiry is a much broader one, primarily concerned with fairness; consequently, it looks to wholly different considerations. Should the district court decide that [a choice of law] analysis requires it to apply Paraguayan law, our courts will not have occasion to consider what law would govern a suit under the Alien Tort Statute where the challenged conduct is actionable under the law of the forum and the law of nations, but not the law of the jurisdiction in which the tort occurred.

SOSA v. ALVAREZ-MACHAIN
542 U.S. 692 (2004)

SOUTER, JUSTICE delivered the opinion of the Court. [In 1985, a Drug Enforcement Administration (DEA) agent was captured in Mexico, taken to a home, tortured and

---

226. We recognize that our reasoning might also sustain jurisdiction under the general federal question provision, 28 U.S.C. §1331. We prefer, however, to rest our decision upon the Alien Tort Statute, in light of that provision's close coincidence with the jurisdictional facts presented in this case. *See Romero v. International Terminal Operating Co.*, 358 U.S. 354 (1959).

murdered. Federal officials eventually determined that Humberto Alvarez-Machain (Alvarez), a Mexican physician, prolonged the agent's life during the interrogation. A U.S. grand jury later indicted Alvarez. Eventually, a group of Mexicans, including Jose Francisco Sosa (Sosa), abducted Alvarez, held him overnight in a Mexican motel and then brought him by private plane to Texas. Following criminal proceedings, the district court acquitted Alvarez and he returned to Mexico. Subsequently, Alvarez sued Sosa, a DEA operative and others. He sought relief under, among other grounds, the ATS. The District Court granted him summary judgment and awarded him $25,000. On appeal, the Ninth Circuit, initially as a panel and later *en banc*, affirmed the judgment. With respect to the ATS claim, the *en banc* court held "that the ATS not only provides federal courts with subject matter jurisdiction, but also creates a cause of action for an alleged violation of the law of nations." It held that Alvarez's arrest and detention violated a "clear and universally recognized norm prohibiting arbitrary arrest and detention."] . . .

. . . Alvarez says that the ATS was intended not simply as a jurisdictional grant, but as authority for the creation of a new cause of action for torts in violation of international law. We think that reading is implausible. As enacted in 1789, the ATS gave the district courts "cognizance" of certain causes of action, and the term bespoke a grant of jurisdiction, not power to mold substantive law. *See, e.g.*, The Federalist No. 81, pp. 447, 451 (J. Cooke ed. 1961) (A. Hamilton) (using "jurisdiction" interchangeably with "cognizance"). The fact that the ATS was placed in §9 of the Judiciary Act, a statute otherwise exclusively concerned with federal-court jurisdiction, is itself support for its strictly jurisdictional nature. Nor would the distinction between jurisdiction and cause of action have been elided by the drafters of the Act or those who voted on it. As Fisher Ames put it, "there is a substantial difference between the jurisdiction of courts and rules of decision." 1 Annals of Cong. 807 (Gales ed. 1834). In sum, we think the statute was intended as jurisdictional in the sense of addressing the power of the courts to entertain cases concerned with a certain subject. But holding the ATS jurisdictional raises a new question, this one about the interaction between the ATS at the time of its enactment and the ambient law of the era.

"When the United States declared their independence, they were bound to receive the law of nations, in its modern state of purity and refinement." *Ware v. Hylton*, 3 Dall. 199, 281 (1796) (Wilson, J.). In the years of the early Republic, this law of nations comprised two principal elements, the first covering the general norms governing the behavior of national states with each other: "the science which teaches the rights subsisting between nations or states, and the obligations correspondent to those rights," E. de Vattel, *The Law of Nations, Preliminaries* §3 (J. Chitty et al. transl. and ed. 1883) (hereinafter Vattel) (footnote omitted), or "that code of public instruction which defines the rights and prescribes the duties of nations, in their intercourse with each other," 1 James Kent Commentaries *1. This aspect of the law of nations thus occupied the executive and legislative domains, not the judicial. *See* 4 W. Blackstone, *Commentaries on the Laws of England* 68 (1769) (hereinafter Commentaries) ("[O]ffenses against" the law of nations are "principally incident to whole states or nations").

[The Court then reviewed the early history surrounding the Continental Congress's attempts to punish the law of nations and the drafting of Article III and the Judiciary Act described above. Among other things, it cited] the so-called Marbois incident of May 1784, in which a French adventurer, Longchamps, verbally and physically assaulted the Secretary of the French Legion in Philadelphia. *See Respublica v. De Longchamps*, 1 Dall. 111 (O.T. Phila. 1784). . . .

The Framers responded by vesting the Supreme Court with original jurisdiction over "all Cases affecting Ambassadors, other public ministers and Consuls." U.S. Const., Art. III, §2, and the First Congress followed through. The Judiciary Act reinforced this Court's original jurisdiction over suits brought by diplomats, *see* 1 Stat. 80, ch. 20, §13, created alienage jurisdiction, §11 and, of course, included the ATS, §9.

Although Congress modified the draft of what became the Judiciary Act, it made hardly any changes to the provisions on aliens, including what became the ATS. There is no record of congressional discussion about private actions that might be subject to the jurisdictional provision, or about any need for further legislation to create private remedies; there is no record even of debate on the section. . . .

Still, the history does tend to support two propositions. First, there is every reason to suppose that the First Congress did not pass the ATS as a jurisdictional convenience to be placed on the shelf for use by a future Congress or state legislature that might, some day, authorize the creation of causes of action or itself decide to make some element of the law of nations actionable for the benefit of foreigners. The second inference to be drawn from the history is that Congress intended the ATS to furnish jurisdiction for a relatively modest set of actions alleging violations of the law of nations. Uppermost in the legislative mind appears to have been offenses against ambassadors; violations of safe conduct were probably understood to be actionable, and individual actions arising out of prize captures and piracy may well have also been contemplated. But the common law appears to have understood only those three of the hybrid variety as definite and actionable, or at any rate, to have assumed only a very limited set of claims. As Blackstone had put it, "offences against this law [of nations] are principally incident to whole states or nations," and not individuals seeking relief in court. 4 *Commentaries* 68.

[The Court cited] the 1795 opinion of Attorney General William Bradford, who was asked whether criminal prosecution was available against Americans who had taken part in the French plunder of a British slave colony in Sierra Leone. 1 Op. Atty. Gen. 57. Bradford was uncertain, but he made it clear that a federal court was open for the prosecution of a tort action growing out of the episode:

> But there can be no doubt that the company or individuals who have been injured by these acts of hostility have a remedy by a civil suit in the courts of the United States; jurisdiction being expressly given to these courts in all cases where an alien sues for a tort only, in violation of the laws of nations, or a treaty of the United States. . . .

Although it is conceivable that Bradford (who had prosecuted in the Marbois incident) assumed that there had been a violation of a treaty, 1 Op. Atty. Gen., at 58, that is certainly not obvious, and it appears likely that Bradford understood the ATS to provide jurisdiction over what must have amounted to common law causes of action. . . .

In sum, although the ATS is a jurisdictional statute creating no new causes of action, the reasonable inference from the historical materials is that the statute was intended to have practical effect the moment it became law. The jurisdictional grant is best read as having been enacted on the understanding that the common law would provide a cause of action for the modest number of international law violations with a potential for personal liability at the time.

IV. We think it is correct, then, to assume that the First Congress understood that the district courts would recognize private causes of action for certain torts in violation of the law of nations, though we have found no basis to suspect Congress had any examples in mind beyond those torts corresponding to Blackstone's three primary offenses: violation of safe conducts, infringement of the rights of ambassadors, and piracy. We assume, too, that no development in the two centuries from the enactment of §1350 to the birth of the modern line of cases beginning with *Filartiga* . . . has categorically precluded federal courts from recognizing a claim under the law of nations as an element of common law; Congress has not in any relevant way amended §1350 or limited civil common law power by another statute. Still, there are good reasons for a restrained conception of the discretion a federal court should exercise in considering a new cause of action of this kind. Accordingly, we think courts should require any claim based on the present-day law of nations to rest on a norm of international character accepted by the civilized world and defined with a specificity comparable to the features of the 18th-century paradigms we have recognized. This requirement is fatal to Alvarez's claim.

A. A series of reasons argue for judicial caution when considering the kinds of individual claims that might implement the jurisdiction conferred by the early statute. First, . . . a judge deciding in reliance on an international norm will find a substantial element of discretionary judgment in the decision.

Second, along with, and in part driven by, that conceptual development in understanding common law has come an equally significant rethinking of the role of the federal courts in making it. *Erie R. Co. v. Tompkins*, 304 U.S. 64 (1938), was the watershed in which we denied the existence of any federal "general" common law, which largely withdrew to havens of specialty, some of them defined by express congressional authorization to devise a body of law directly. Elsewhere, this Court has thought it was in order to create federal common law rules in interstitial areas of particular federal interest. *E.g., United States v. Kimbell Foods, Inc.*, 440 U.S. 715, 726-727 (1979). And although we have even assumed competence to make judicial rules of decision of particular importance to foreign relations, such as the act of state doctrine, *see Banco Nacional de Cuba v. Sabbatino*, 376 U.S. 398, 427 (1964), the general practice has been to look for legislative guidance before exercising innovative authority over substantive law. It would be remarkable to take a more aggressive role in exercising a jurisdiction that remained largely in shadow for much of the prior two centuries.

Third, this Court has recently and repeatedly said that a decision to create a private right of action is one better left to legislative judgment in the great majority of cases. The creation of a private right of action raises issues beyond the mere consideration whether underlying primary conduct should be allowed or not, entailing, for example, a decision to permit enforcement without the check imposed by prosecutorial discretion. . . . [T]he possible collateral consequences of making international rules privately actionable argue for judicial caution.

Fourth, the subject of those collateral consequences is itself a reason for a high bar to new private causes of action for violating international law, for the potential implications for the foreign relations of the United States of recognizing such causes should make courts particularly wary of impinging on the discretion of the Legislative and Executive Branches in managing foreign affairs. . . .

The fifth reason is particularly important in light of the first four. We have no congressional mandate to seek out and define new and debatable violations of the law of nations, and modern indications of congressional understanding of the judicial role in the field have not affirmatively encouraged greater judicial creativity. It is true that a clear mandate appears in the Torture Victim Protection Act of 1991, 106 Stat. 73, providing authority that "establish[es] an unambiguous and modern basis for" federal claims of torture and extrajudicial killing, H.R. Rep. No. 102-367, pt. 1, p. 3 (1991). But that affirmative authority is confined to specific subject matter, and although the legislative history includes the remark that §1350 should "remain intact to permit suits based on other norms that already exist or may ripen in the future into rules of customary international law," Congress as a body has done nothing to promote such suits. Several times, indeed, the Senate has expressly declined to give the federal courts the task of interpreting and applying international human rights law, as when its ratification of the International Covenant on Civil and Political Rights declared that the substantive provisions of the document were not self-executing. 138 Cong. Rec. 8071 (1992).

B. These reasons argue for great caution in adapting the law of nations to private rights. Justice SCALIA concludes that caution is too hospitable, and a word is in order to summarize where we have come so far and to focus our difference with him on whether some norms of today's law of nations may ever be recognized legitimately by federal courts in the absence of congressional action beyond §1350. All Members of the Court agree that §1350 is only jurisdictional. We also agree, or at least Justice Scalia does not dispute that the jurisdiction was originally understood to be available to enforce a small number of international norms that a federal court could properly recognize as within the common law enforceable without further statutory authority. Justice SCALIA concludes, however, that two subsequent developments should be understood to preclude federal courts from recognizing any further international norms as judicially enforceable today, absent further congressional action. As described before, we now tend to understand common law not as a discoverable reflection of universal reason but, in a positivistic way, as a product of human choice. And we now adhere to a conception of limited judicial power first expressed in reorienting federal diversity jurisdiction, *see Erie R. Co. v. Tompkins*, that federal courts have no authority to derive "general" common law.

Whereas Justice SCALIA sees these developments as sufficient to close the door to further independent judicial recognition of actionable international norms, other considerations persuade us that the judicial power should be exercised on the understanding that the door is still ajar subject to vigilant doorkeeping, and thus open to a narrow class of international norms today. *Erie* did not in terms bar any judicial recognition of new substantive rules, no matter what the circumstances, and post-*Erie* understanding has identified limited enclaves in which federal courts may derive some substantive law in a common law way. For two centuries we have affirmed that the domestic law of the United States recognizes the law of nations. . . . It would take some explaining to say now that federal courts must avert their gaze entirely from any international norm intended to protect individuals.

We think an attempt to justify such a position would be particularly unconvincing in light of what we know about congressional understanding bearing on this issue lying at the intersection of the judicial and legislative powers. The First Congress, which reflected the understanding of the framing generation and included some of the Framers, assumed that federal courts could properly identify some international norms as enforceable in the exercise of §1350 jurisdiction. We think it would be unreasonable to assume that the First Congress would have expected federal courts to lose all capacity to recognize enforceable international norms simply because the common law might lose some metaphysical cachet on the road to modern realism. Later Congresses seem to have shared our view. The position we take today has been assumed by some federal courts for 24 years, ever since the Second Circuit decided *Filartiga,* and for practical purposes the point of today's disagreement has been focused since the exchange between Judge Edwards and Judge Bork in *Tel-Oren.* Congress, however, has not only expressed no disagreement with our view of the proper exercise of the judicial power, but has responded to its most notable instance by enacting legislation supplementing the judicial determination in some detail.

While we agree with Justice SCALIA to the point that we would welcome any congressional guidance in exercising jurisdiction with such obvious potential to affect foreign relations, nothing Congress has done is a reason for us to shut the door to the law of nations entirely. It is enough to say that Congress may do that at any time (explicitly, or implicitly by treaties or statutes that occupy the field) just as it may modify or cancel any judicial decision so far as it rests on recognizing an international norm as such.[227]

C. We must still, however, derive a standard or set of standards for assessing the particular claim Alvarez raises, and for this case it suffices to look to the historical antecedents. Whatever the ultimate criteria for accepting a cause of action subject to jurisdiction under §1350, we are persuaded that federal courts should not recognize private claims under federal common law for violations of any international law norm with less definite content and acceptance among civilized nations than the historical paradigms familiar when §1350 was enacted. This limit upon judicial recognition is generally consistent with the reasoning of many of the courts and judges who faced the issue before it reached this Court. And the determination whether a norm is sufficiently definite to support a cause of action[228] should (and, indeed, inevitably must) involve an element of judgment about the practical consequences of making that cause available to litigants in the federal courts.[229] Thus, Alvarez's detention claim must be gauged against the current state of international law, looking to those sources we have long, albeit cautiously, recognized. "[W]here there is no treaty, and no controlling executive or legislative act or judicial decision, resort must be had to the customs and usages of civilized nations; and, as evidence of these, to the works of jurists and commentators, who by years of labor, research and experience, have made themselves peculiarly well acquainted with the subjects of which they treat. Such works are resorted to by judicial tribunals, not for the speculations of their authors concerning what the law ought to be, but for trustworthy evidence of what the law really is." *The Paquete Habana*, 175 U.S., at 700.

To begin with, Alvarez cites two well-known international agreements that, despite their moral authority, have little utility under the standard set out in this opinion. He says that his abduction by Sosa was an "arbitrary arrest" within the meaning of the Universal Declaration of Human Rights (Declaration), G.A. Res. 217A (III), U.N. Doc. A/810 (1948). And he traces the rule against arbitrary arrest not only to the Declaration, but also to article nine of the International Covenant on Civil and Political Rights (Covenant), Dec. 19, 1996, 999 U.N.T.S. 171, to which the United States is a party, and to various

---

227. Our position does not, as Justice Scalia suggests, imply that every grant of jurisdiction to a federal court carries with it an opportunity to develop common law (so that the grant of federal-question jurisdiction would be equally as good for our purposes as §1350). Section 1350 was enacted on the congressional understanding that courts would exercise jurisdiction by entertaining some common law claims derived from the law of nations; and we know of no reason to think that federal-question jurisdiction was extended subject to any comparable congressional assumption. Further, our holding today is consistent with the division of responsibilities between federal and state courts after *Erie*, as a more expansive common law power related to 28 U.S.C. §1331 might not be.

228. A related consideration is whether international law extends the scope of liability for a violation of a given norm to the perpetrator being sued, if the defendant is a private actor such as a corporation or individual.

229. This requirement of clear definition is not meant to be the only principle limiting the availability of relief in the federal courts for violations of customary international law, though it disposes of this case. For example, the European Commission argues as *amicus curiae* that basic principles of international law require that before asserting a claim in a foreign forum, the claimant must have exhausted any remedies available in the domestic legal system, and perhaps in other fora such as international claims tribunals. We would certainly consider this requirement in an appropriate case. Another possible limitation that we need not apply here is a policy of case-specific deference to the political branches. For example, there are now pending in federal district court several class actions seeking damages from various corporations alleged to have participated in, or abetted, the regime of apartheid that formerly controlled South Africa. The Government of South Africa has said that these cases interfere with the policy embodied by its Truth and Reconciliation Commission, which "deliberately avoided a 'victors' justice' approach to the crimes of apartheid and chose instead one based on confession and absolution, informed by the principles of reconciliation, reconstruction, reparation and goodwill." The United States has agreed. *See* Letter of William H. Taft IV, Legal Adviser, Dept. of State, to Shannen W. Coffin, Deputy Asst. Atty. Gen., Oct. 27, 2003. In such cases, there is a strong argument that federal courts should give serious weight to the Executive Branch's view of the case's impact on foreign policy.

other conventions to which it is not. But the Declaration does not of its own force impose obligations as a matter of international law. And, although the Covenant does bind the United States as a matter of international law, the United States ratified the Covenant on the express understanding that it was not self-executing and so did not itself create obligations enforceable in the federal courts. Accordingly, Alvarez cannot say that the Declaration and Covenant themselves establish the relevant and applicable rule of international law. He instead attempts to show that prohibition of arbitrary arrest has attained the status of binding customary international law.

Here, it is useful to examine Alvarez's complaint in greater detail. As he presently argues it, the claim does not rest on the cross-border feature of his abduction. . . . Instead, it relied on the conclusion that the law of the United States did not authorize Alvarez's arrest, because the DEA lacked extraterritorial authority under 21 U.S.C. §878, and because Federal Rule of Criminal Procedure 4(d)(2) limited the warrant for Alvarez's arrest to "the jurisdiction of the United States." It is this position that Alvarez takes now: that his arrest was arbitrary and as such forbidden by international law not because it infringed the prerogatives of Mexico, but because no applicable law authorized it. . . .

Alvarez thus invokes a general prohibition of "arbitrary" detention defined as officially sanctioned action exceeding positive authorization to detain under the domestic law of some government, regardless of the circumstances. Whether or not this is an accurate reading of the Covenant, Alvarez cites little authority that a rule so broad has the status of a binding customary norm today.[230] He certainly cites nothing to justify the federal courts in taking his broad rule as the predicate for a federal lawsuit, for its implications would be breathtaking. His rule would support a cause of action in federal court for any arrest, anywhere in the world, unauthorized by the law of the jurisdiction in which it took place, and would create a cause of action for any seizure of an alien in violation of the Fourth Amendment, supplanting [more well-known federal civil rights] actions. It would create an action in federal court for arrests by state officers who simply exceed their authority; and for the violation of any limit that the law of any country might place on the authority of its own officers to arrest. And all of this assumes that Alvarez could establish that Sosa was acting on behalf of a government when he made the arrest, for otherwise he would need a rule broader still.

Alvarez's failure to marshal support for his proposed rule is underscored by the *Restatement (Third) of Foreign Relations Law* (1987), which says in its discussion of customary international human rights law that a "state violates international law if, as a matter of state policy, it practices, encourages, or condones . . . prolonged arbitrary detention." *Id.*, §702. Although the *Restatement* [(*Third*)] does not explain its requirements of a "state policy" and of "prolonged" detention, the implication is clear. Any credible invocation of a principle against arbitrary detention that the civilized world accepts as binding customary international law requires a factual basis beyond relatively brief detention in excess of positive authority. . . .

Whatever may be said for the broad principle Alvarez advances, in the present, imperfect world, it expresses an aspiration that exceeds any binding customary rule having the

---

230. Specifically, he relies on a survey of national constitutions, Bassiouni, *Human Rights in the Context of Criminal Justice: Identifying International Procedural Protections and Equivalent Protections in National Constitutions*, 3 Duke J. Comp. & Int'l L. 235, 260-261 (1993); a case from the International Court of Justice, *United States v. Iran*, 1980 I.C.J. 3, 42; and some authority drawn from the federal courts. None of these suffice. The Bassiouni survey does show that many nations recognize a norm against arbitrary detention, but that consensus is at a high level of generality. The *Iran* case, in which the United States sought relief for the taking of its diplomatic and consular staff as hostages, involved a different set of international norms and mentioned the problem of arbitrary detention only in passing; the detention in that case was, moreover, far longer and harsher than Alvarez's. *See* 1980 I.C.J., at 42, 91 ("detention of [United States] staff by a group of armed militants" lasted "many months"). . . .

specificity we require. Creating a private cause of action to further that aspiration would go beyond any residual common law discretion we think it appropriate to exercise. It is enough to hold that a single illegal detention of less than a day, followed by the transfer of custody to lawful authorities and a prompt arraignment, violates no norm of customary international law so well defined as to support the creation of a federal remedy.

JUSTICE SCALIA, concurring in part and concurring in the judgment.[231] There is not much that I would add to the Court's detailed opinion, and only one thing that I would subtract: its reservation of a discretionary power in the Federal Judiciary to create causes of action for the enforcement of international-law-based norms. . . .

At the time of its enactment, the ATS provided a federal forum in which aliens could bring suit to recover for torts committed in "violation of the law of nations." The law of nations that would have been applied in this federal forum was at the time part of the so-called general common law. General common law was not federal law under the Supremacy Clause, which gave that effect only to the Constitution, the laws of the United States, and treaties. U.S. Const., Art. VI, cl. 2. Federal and state courts adjudicating questions of general common law were not adjudicating questions of federal or state law, respectively—the general common law was neither. . . .

This Court's decision in *Erie R. Co. v. Tompkins*, signaled the end of federal-court elaboration and application of the general common law. *Erie* repudiated the holding of *Swift v. Tyson*, that federal courts were free to "express our own opinion" upon "the principles established in the general commercial law." After canvassing the many problems resulting from "the broad province accorded to the so-called 'general law' as to which federal courts exercised an independent judgment," the *Erie* Court extirpated that law with its famous declaration that "[t]here is no federal general common law." *Erie* affected the status of the law of nations in federal courts not merely by the implication of its holding but quite directly, since the question decided in *Swift* turned on the "law merchant," then a subset of the law of nations.

After the death of the old general common law in *Erie* came the birth of a new and different common law pronounced by federal courts. There developed a specifically federal common law (in the sense of judicially pronounced law) for a "few and restricted" areas in which "a federal rule of decision is necessary to protect uniquely federal interests, and those in which Congress has given the courts the power to develop substantive law." Unlike the general common law that preceded it, however, federal common law was self-consciously "made" rather than "discovered," by judges. . . . Because post-*Erie* federal common law is made, not discovered, federal courts must possess some federal-common-law-making authority before undertaking to craft it. "Federal courts, unlike state courts, are not general common-law courts and do not possess a general power to develop and apply their own rules of decision." . . .

The rule against finding a delegation of substantive lawmaking power in a grant of jurisdiction is subject to exceptions, some better established than others. The most firmly entrenched is admiralty law, derived from the grant of admiralty jurisdiction in Article III, §2, cl. 3, of the Constitution. In the exercise of that jurisdiction federal courts develop and apply a body of general maritime law, "the well-known and well-developed venerable law of the sea which arose from the custom among seafaring men."

With these general principles in mind, I turn to the question presented. The Court's detailed exegesis of the ATS conclusively establishes that it is "a jurisdictional statute creating no new causes of action." The Court provides a persuasive explanation of why

---

231. Chief Justice Rehnquist and Justice Thomas joined this opinion in full.

respondent's contrary interpretation, that "the ATS was intended not simply as a jurisdictional grant, but as authority for the creation of a new cause of action for torts in violation of international law," is wrong.

These conclusions are alone enough to dispose of the present case in favor of petitioner Sosa. None of the exceptions to the general rule against finding substantive lawmaking power in a jurisdictional grant apply. . . . In Benthamite terms, creating a federal command (federal common law) out of "international norms," and then constructing a cause of action to enforce that command through the purely jurisdictional grant of the ATS, is nonsense upon stilts.

The analysis in the Court's opinion departs from my own in this respect: After concluding in Part III that "the ATS is a jurisdictional statute creating no new causes of action," the Court addresses at length in Part IV the "good reasons for a restrained conception of the discretion a federal court should exercise in considering a new cause of action" under the ATS. By framing the issue as one of "discretion," the Court skips over the antecedent question of authority. This neglects the "lesson of *Erie*," that "grants of jurisdiction alone" (which the Court has acknowledged the ATS to be) "are not themselves grants of law-making authority." On this point, the Court observes only that no development between the enactment of the ATS (in 1789) and the birth of modern international human rights litigation under that statute (in 1980) "has categorically precluded federal courts from recognizing a claim under the law of nations as an element of common law." This turns our jurisprudence regarding federal common law on its head. The question is not what case or congressional action prevents federal courts from applying the law of nations as part of the general common law; it is what authorizes that peculiar exception from *Erie*'s fundamental holding that a general common law does not exist.

The Court would apparently find authorization in the understanding of the Congress that enacted the ATS, that "district courts would recognize private causes of action for certain torts in violation of the law of nations." But as discussed above, that understanding rested upon a notion of general common law that has been repudiated by *Erie*. The Court recognizes that *Erie* was a "watershed" decision heralding an avulsive change, wrought by "conceptual development in understanding common law . . . [and accompanied by an] equally significant rethinking of the role of the federal courts in making it." The Court's analysis, however, does not follow through on this insight, interchangeably using the unadorned phrase "common law" in Parts III and IV to refer to pre-*Erie* general common law and post-*Erie* federal common law. This lapse is crucial, because the creation of post-*Erie* federal common law is rooted in a positivist mindset utterly foreign to the American common-law tradition of the late 18th century. Post-*Erie* federal common lawmaking (all that is left to the federal courts) is so far removed from that general-common-law adjudication which applied the "law of nations" that it would be anachronistic to find authorization to do the former in a statutory grant of jurisdiction that was thought to enable the latter. Yet that is precisely what the discretion-only analysis in Part IV suggests.

The lack of genuine continuity is thus demonstrated by the fact that today's opinion renders the ATS unnecessary for federal jurisdiction over (so-called) law-of-nations claims. If the law of nations can be transformed into federal law on the basis of (1) a provision that merely grants jurisdiction, combined with (2) some residual judicial power (from whence nobody knows) to create federal causes of action in cases implicating foreign relations, then a grant of federal-question jurisdiction would give rise to a power to create international-law-based federal common law just as effectively as would the ATS. This would mean that the ATS became largely superfluous as of 1875, when Congress granted general federal-question jurisdiction subject to a $500 amount-in-controversy requirement, and entirely superfluous as of 1980, when Congress eliminated the amount-in-controversy requirement.

Because today's federal common law is not our Framers' general common law, the question presented by the suggestion of discretionary authority to enforce the law of nations is not whether to extend old-school general-common-law adjudication. Rather, it is whether to create new federal common law. The Court masks the novelty of its approach when it suggests that the difference between us is that we would "close the door to further independent judicial recognition of actionable international norms," whereas the Court would permit the exercise of judicial power "on the understanding that the door is still ajar subject to vigilant doorkeeping." The general common law was the old door. We do not close that door today, for the deed was done in *Erie.* Federal common law is a new door. The question is not whether that door will be left ajar, but whether this Court will open it. . . .

Though it is not necessary to resolution of the present case, one further consideration deserves mention: Despite the avulsive change of *Erie,* the Framers who included reference to "the Law of Nations" in Article I, §8, cl. 10, of the Constitution would be entirely content with the post-*Erie* system I have described, and quite terrified by the "discretion" endorsed by the Court. That portion of the general common law known as the law of nations was understood to refer to the accepted practices of nations in their dealings with one another (treatment of ambassadors, immunity of foreign sovereigns from suit, etc.) and with actors on the high seas hostile to all nations and beyond all their territorial jurisdictions (pirates). Those accepted practices have for the most part, if not in their entirety, been enacted into United States statutory law, so that insofar as they are concerned the demise of the general common law is inconsequential. The notion that a law of nations, redefined to mean the consensus of states on any subject, can be used by a private citizen to control a sovereign's treatment of its own citizens within its own territory is a 20th-century invention of internationalist law professors and human-rights advocates. The Framers would, I am confident, be appalled by the proposition that, for example, the American peoples' democratic adoption of the death penalty could be judicially nullified because of the disapproving views of foreigners. . . .

We Americans have a method for making the laws that are over us. We elect representatives to two Houses of Congress, each of which must enact the new law and present it for the approval of a President, whom we also elect. For over two decades now, unelected federal judges have been usurping this lawmaking power by converting what they regard as norms of international law into American law. Today's opinion approves that process in principle, though urging the lower courts to be more restrained. This Court seems incapable of admitting that some matters — any matters — are none of its business. In today's latest victory for its Never Say Never Jurisprudence, the Court ignores its own conclusion that the ATS provides only jurisdiction, wags a finger at the lower courts for going too far, and then — repeating the same formula the ambitious lower courts themselves have used — invites them to try again. . . .

TORTURE VICTIM PROTECTION ACT
28 U.S.C. §1350 (note) [excerpted in Appendix A]

Notes on **Filartiga, Sosa,** *and* **TVPA**

1. *Distinction between federal court jurisdiction and substantive cause of action.* Both *Filartiga* and *Sosa* distinguish between the ATS: (a) granting federal court jurisdiction; and (b) creating a substantive cause of action. What exactly is the difference between these two categories? How are they related? Compare the treatment of these issues in the TVPA. How does the TVPA differ from the ATS?

2. Section 1350 creates federal jurisdiction. Both *Sosa* and *Filartiga* hold that the ATS provides a jurisdictional grant over a specified category of actions (for tort claims brought by an alien in violation of the law of nations). The *Sosa* Court reasons: "Congress intended the ATS to furnish jurisdiction for a relatively modest set of actions alleging violations of the law of nations." Is there any question that this conclusion is correct? What else might the ATS mean? Does Justice Scalia agree? What was Judge Bork's view in *Tel-Oren*?

3. Scope of §1350's jurisdictional grant. What is the scope of the ATS's jurisdictional grant? Is federal court jurisdiction co-extensive with the (limited) circumstances in which there is a private cause of action for violations of international law? Or does the ATS's jurisdictional grant extend more broadly? For example, if Mr. Alvarez brought a new action in state court, alleging that U.S. state law or foreign law created a private right of action for the allegedly wrongful temporary detention involved in his arrest, would that action be subject to federal court jurisdiction under the ATS? Or does the existence of federal court jurisdiction depend on the existence of a valid private cause of action under international law? *Compare Bell v. Hood*, 327 U.S. 678 (1946).

4. Section 1350 does not itself create a substantive cause of action. Is there any indication in the ATS's language that the provision was intended to create a substantive cause of action? Compare the TVPA. Although it was often cited for the proposition that the ATS creates a private cause of action, what does *Filartiga* hold with regard to this issue? Where exactly does the *Filartiga* opinion hold that an alien injured by a tort in violation of international law has a substantive right of action in federal courts under the ATS? Note the *Filartiga* Court's comment that questions about the existence of a substantive cause of action are relevant at the stage of resolving choice of law issues. Is that consistent with suggestions that *Filartiga* created a substantive cause of action? Is it necessarily inconsistent?

Sosa specifically rejects the view that the ATS creates a substantive cause of action: "the ATS is a jurisdictional statute creating no new causes of action." Indeed, Justice Scalia uncharitably termed this argument "nonsense upon stilts." Consider the arguments advanced by the *Sosa* Court for rejecting the notion that the ATS created a substantive cause of action. Are they persuasive? Compare the following, which was how the Ninth Circuit, in a pre-*Sosa* case, justified its conclusion:

> The [defendant] argues that the Alien Tort Act is a purely jurisdictional statute which does not provide the plaintiffs a cause of action. The Estate contends that §1350, like the §1331 "arising under" jurisdictional provision, does not grant a cause of action. . . . However, in contrast to §1331, "which requires that an action 'arise under' the laws of the United States, section 1350 does not require that the action 'arise under' the law of nations, but only mandates a 'violation of the law of nations' in order to create a cause of action." *Tel-Oren v. Libyan Arab Republic*, 726 F.2d 774, 779 (D.C. Cir. 1984) (Edwards, J., concurring). It is unnecessary that international law provide a *specific* right to sue. International law "does not require any particular reaction to violations of law. . . . Whether and how the United States wished to react to such violations are domestic questions." *Id.*, at 777-78 (quoting L. Henkin, *Foreign Affairs and the Constitution* 224 (1972)). "[N]othing more than a *violation* of the law of nations is required to invoke §1350." *Id.* at 779. *Hilao v. Estate of Marcos*, 25 F.3d 1467, 1475 (9th Cir. 1994).

Is this explanation coherent? It is well settled (and undisputed) that §1331 does not create a substantive right of action. *See supra* pp. 7-13 and *infra* pp. 62-70. How exactly does §1350 differ from §1331 in this regard? If international law itself does not create a right of action, then what part of §1350 does so?

On the other hand, is it in fact so odd ("nonsense upon stilts") to think that Congress might have wished to create a substantive cause of action, in federal court, for specific violations of the law of nations. Consider the Marbois incident. Against that background, would it have been nonsense for Congress to have wanted to give victims of violations of international law a substantive remedy in federal courts? Would a grant of federal court jurisdiction have done any good to injured foreign nationals without a private cause of action? What argues against this conclusion?

5. *Power of federal courts under §1350 to create, or recognize, common law causes of action based on international law.* Accepting *Sosa*'s holding that the ATS is a jurisdictional statute, and that the ATS does not create a general cause of action for all cases falling within its jurisdictional grant, what power do federal courts have under the ATS to create or, depending on one's view of matters, recognize substantive causes of action under international law? Consider how *Filartiga* answers this question. Does *Sosa*, in the words of one judge, deputize federal courts to serve as a "quasi international[] tribunal" applying a law that "supersed[es] and suppl[ies] the deficiencies of national constitutions and laws"? *In re Agent Orange Product Liability Litig.*, 373 F. Supp. 2d 7, 17 (E.D.N.Y. 2005).

(a) What did Sosa *hold regarding availability of substantive cause of action under §1350?* How does the *Sosa* Court answer the question whether the ATS permits a federal court to create, or recognize, substantive causes of action based on international law? Consider the following statements by the Court in *Sosa*:

> the ATS gave the district courts "cognizance" of certain causes of action, and the term bespoke a grant of jurisdiction, not *power to mold* substantive law.

> We think it is correct, then, to assume that the First Congress understood that the district courts *would recognize* private causes of action for certain torts in violation of the law of nations.

> We think it would be unreasonable to assume that the First Congress would have expected federal courts to lose all capacity *to recognize* enforceable international norms simply because the common law might lose some metaphysical cachet on the road to modern realism.

What exactly does the *Sosa* Court hold with regard to the power of federal courts to make—or to recognize—substantive causes of action under international law? Do federal courts "mold," "make," or "create" a federal common law cause of action, based on their analysis of the content of international law? Or do federal courts only "recognize" existing causes of action that have already been created under international law? Does the Court's opinion clearly explain which approach it takes?

(b) "Making" versus "recognizing" a cause of action under §1350. Why might a distinction between "making" and "recognizing" a substantive cause of action under the ATS matter? If a federal court can only "recognize" (and not "create") a cause of action, mustn't the plaintiff demonstrate that international law *itself* has already created a private cause of action? What institutions define the content of international law? Is a power on the part of federal courts to "recognize" existing international law causes of action less susceptible to Justice Scalia's separation of powers critiques than a power to "make" such claims? Or is this semantics?

What is the source of authority for federal courts to "recognize" private rights of action for international law violations? Is this any different from a federal court applying foreign (or state) law? What would be the authority of federal courts to "make" private rights of action for international law violations? Recall the *Erie* doctrine and the Rules of Decision Act, discussed above. *See supra* pp. 10-11.

(c) Wisdom of Sosa *holding regarding substantive causes of action under §1350.* The *Sosa* Court appears to have affirmed a power, on the part of federal courts, to recognize

(or, arguably, to make) federal common law causes of action based on certain categories of international law principles. Was this a sensible conclusion? Was it warranted by the text and purposes of the ATS? Is this merely a corollary to the principle that the international law forms part of the Nation's common law? Or is it, as Justice Scalia argues in his separate opinion, a gross violation of the *Erie* principle?

Compare the Second Circuit's analysis of, and conclusions about, substantive causes of action in *Filartiga* with the Court's analysis and holding in *Sosa*. Are there any material differences? Compare Justice Scalia's analysis and conclusions.

(d) Role of federal common law under the Alien Tort Statute. Under the *Sosa* Court's analysis, are substantive causes of action based on international law rules of federal common law or are they something else (such as rules of international or foreign law applied by a federal court)? If the ATS creates federal court jurisdiction over tort claims for violations of international law, then must such claims be based on federal common law? Why can't federal courts simply "recognize" those torts claims that exist under international or foreign law?

Consider the Court's opinion in *Sosa* again. Where does it address the nature of the substantive cause of action that Mr. Alvarez (or other aliens) could assert under the ATS? Is the Court's opinion clear on the nature of the claims that can be heard under the ATS? Note that the Court refers in passing to "federal common law" claims, *supra* p. 43, and discusses in a footnote, *supra* note 227, the federal common law-making powers of federal courts. Is that decisive evidence that the Court contemplated the recognition (or creation) of federal common law rules?

(e) Customary international law as federal law — an initial view. Is customary international law properly considered to be federal law or state law? What does *Sosa* suggest? *See generally* Bradley & Goldsmith, *Customary International Law as Federal Common Law: A Critique of the Modern Position*, 110 Harv. L. Rev. 815 (1997). *See also infra* pp. 62-63, 65-70.

6. Permissible causes of action based on international law under §1350. Assuming that it is correct that *Sosa* affirmed the power of federal courts to recognize (or, perhaps, make) causes of action for certain violations of international law, what is the scope of this power? What does §1350 mean when it refers to the "law of nations"? *See supra* p. 33. Is the "law of nations" a clear and specific set of legal rules? How is it ascertained? Putting these questions aside, what sorts of causes of action under the law of nations did the *Sosa* Court recognize? What are the requirements that must be satisfied in order to create, or recognize, a substantive cause of action under *Sosa*'s analysis?

(a) Historic tort claims under international law. Most clearly, *Sosa* recognizes three causes of action based on customary rules of international law which, in the Court's view, have a demonstrated historical pedigree, extant in 1789, when the ATS was enacted — "violations of safe conduct, infringement of the rights of ambassadors and piracy." What falls within these categories? *See Mwani v. bin Laden*, 417 F.3d 1, 14 (D.C. Cir. 2005) (claim based on an attack against American embassy presents "colorable argument" falling within *Sosa* historical examples).

(b) Possibility of additional causes of action under contemporary international law. Prior to *Sosa*, courts and scholars grappled with the question whether §1350 incorporated the "law of nations" as it evolved over time and not simply as it existed when the Alien Tort Statute was enacted in 1789. Most courts answered in the affirmative, holding that the category of international claims that were recognized in 1789 could expand (or, presumably, contract) over time. *See, e.g., Beanal v. Freeport McMoRan*, 197 F.3d 161, 165 (5th Cir. 1999); *Kadic v. Karadzic*, 70 F.3d 232 (2d Cir. 1995); *Tel-Oren v. Libyan Arab Republic*, 726 F.2d 774, 777, 820 (D.C. Cir. 1984).

For example, as noted in *Filartiga*, contemporary international law recognizes broader protections of individuals vis-à-vis foreign states (and in some instances, vis-à-vis their own states) than was historically the case. *See supra* pp. _____. By contrast, some historical scholarship indicates that the "law of nations" has in fact diminished in scope as the distinction between "public" and "private" international law has emerged. Dickinson, *The Law of Nations as Part of the Law of the United States*, 101 U. Pa. L. Rev. 26, 26-29 (1952); Jay, *Origins of Federal Common Law: Part Two*, 133 U. Pa. L. Rev. 1231, 1263-1264 (1985); Nussbaum, *Rise and Decline of the Law-of-Nations Doctrine in the Conflict of Laws*, 42 Colum. L. Rev. 189 (1942); Cheatham, *Sources of Rules for Conflict of Laws*, 89 U. Pa. L. Rev. 430 (1941).

The *Sosa* Court apparently holds that contemporary international law may recognize tort claims that did not exist in 1789. Is that sensible? Would Congress have wanted to create an upended grant of authority to federal courts in this manner? Consider again the purposes of the ATS and the role of customary international law in eighteenth- and nineteenth-century U.S. law.

(c) Standards for contemporary international law claims. What standards does the *Sosa* Court articulate for identifying such contemporary international law claims that may be recognized under §1350? Note the Court's comment in *Sosa* that "federal courts should not recognize private claims under federal common law for violations of any international law norm with less definite content and acceptance among civilized nations than the historical paradigms familiar when §1350 was enacted." What does the Court mean by this phrase? How is this different, if at all, from the Second Circuit's standard (albeit in the context of jurisdictional analysis) in *Filartiga*? Why did the Court impose these "definiteness" and "acceptance" requirements? Are they justified?

How is a court (or a private litigant for that matter) supposed to determine that a particular claim has sufficiently "definite content and acceptance among civilized nations"? As one court has observed, that holding "relegated to the lower federal courts the task of grappling with and determining what offenses against international law fit within that narrow class of offenses." *In re South African Apartheid Litig.*, 346 F. Supp. 2d 538, 547 (S.D.N.Y. 2004), *rev'd sub nom. Khulumani v. Barclay Nat'l Bank Ltd.*, 504 F.3d 254 (2d Cir. 2007). Post-*Sosa* courts have struggled with this task. For a sampling of cases reaching conflicting conclusions on whether various claims satisfy the *Sosa* standard, *see Estate of Amergi v. Palestinian Authority*, 2010 WL 2898991 (11th Cir. July 27, 2010) (concluding that single murder committed by private actors during ongoing armed conflict does not satisfy *Sosa* standard) *and Vietnam Ass'n for Victims of Agent Orange v. Dow Chemical Co.*, 517 F.3d 104, 120 (2d Cir. 2008) ("There is lack of a consensus in the international community with respect to whether the proscription against poison would apply to defoliants that had possible unintended toxic side effects, as opposed to chemicals intended to kill combatants."); *Abdullahi v. Pfizer, Inc.*, 562 F.3d 163 (2d Cir. 2009) (concluding that prohibition on nonconsensual medical experimentation on human beings satisfies *Sosa* standard) *and Sarei v. Rio Tinto plc*, 456 F.3d 1069 (9th Cir. 2006) (concluding that claims of racial discrimination, violation of laws of war, and violation of UN Convention on Law of Seas are actionable under ATS). For an example of two decisions reaching conflicting results on the same question, *compare Enahoro v. Abubakar*, 408 F.3d 877, 883-886 (7th Cir. 2005) (torture and extrajudicial killing not actionable under ATS) *with Aldana v. Del Monte Fresh Produce, NA, Inc.*, 416 F.3d 1242, 1250-1253 (11th Cir. 2005) (torture based on intentionally inflicted emotional pain actionable under ATS).

What sources are relevant to determining whether a particular cause of action is sufficiently well-recognized and definite under international law to provide a jurisdictional base under the ATS? *See, e.g., Al Quraishi v. Nakhla*, 2010 WL 30001986, at *41-45 (D. Md.

July 29, 2010); *Wiwa v. Royal Dutch Petroleum Co.*, 626 F. Supp. 2d 377 (S.D.N.Y. 2009). Note the *Sosa* Court's reference to "the works of jurists and commentators, who by years of labor, research and experience, have made themselves peculiarly well acquainted with the subjects of which they treat," citing *The Paquete Habana*, 175 U.S., at 700 — or perhaps, in Justice Scalia's term, "internationalist law professors." What is the relationship between these "jurists and commentators" and the democratic law-making processes set out in the Constitution?

If "internationalist law professors" unanimously and definitely recognize a particular tort claim under international law (say, aiding and abetting global warming or a right to life), are U.S. courts obliged to give effect to this? What if a decisive majority of foreign states and internationalist law professors were to conclude that international law does not in fact create private rights of action (*e.g.*, for extrajudicial killing or torture)? What is the consequence for jurisdiction under §1350?

(d) Result in Sosa. Why did the *Sosa* Court conclude that brief transboundary kidnapping did *not* have the acceptance necessary for a cause of action under international law? What authorities were relevant to the Court's analysis? Note that some authorities have criticized the *Sosa* Court's application of its standards to the claims at issue. *See* Steinhardt, *Laying One Bankrupt Critique to Rest:* Sosa v. Alvarez-Machain *and the Future of International Human Rights Litigation in U.S. Courts*, 57 Vand. L. Rev. 2241, 2281-2283 (2004).

(e) Sosa *and pleading.* Most claims under the Alien Tort Statute never reach a verdict. Most are either dismissed or settled. Consequently, it is critically important for a plaintiff adequately to plead (and a defendant to scrutinize) an allegation of a claim under the ATS. Technically, the Federal Rules of Civil Procedure only require a short, plain statement of the claim showing that the plaintiff is entitled to relief. Fed. R. Civ. P. 8. Recently, the Supreme Court has begun to demand more detailed pleadings from plaintiffs in order to avoid dismissal of a complaint. *See Bell Atlantic Corp. v. Twombly*, 550 U.S. 544 (2007); *Iqbal v. Ashcroft*, 129 S. Ct. 1937 (2009). Though neither of these cases expressly involved the ATS, lower courts have begun to apply these heightened pleading standards to ATS claims. *See, e.g., Sinaltrainal v. Coca Cola Co.*, 578 F.3d 1252, 1266-1270 (11th Cir. 2009). In light of these developments, what must a plaintiff be able to allege in order to state an actionable claim arising under the Alien Tort Statute?

7. ***Discretionary factors relevant to existence of cause of action under international law after*** **Sosa.** The *Sosa* Court identifies five factors as relevant to the decision whether to recognize (or create) a particular cause of action under international law. *See supra* pp. 41-42. What is the precise purpose of these considerations? *See El-Shifa Pharmaceuticals Indus. Co. v. United States*, 607 F.3d 836, 854-855 (D.C. Cir. 2010). How do these considerations relate to the Court's requirement that any contemporary cause of action be as "definite" and "well-recognized" as Blackstone's three historic categories? Do these considerations permit a federal court to deny the existence of a cause of action even if there is overwhelming support for it under international law?

Apply the Court's five considerations to the torture claim at issue in *Filartiga*. Putting aside the TVPA, would the *Sosa* analysis permit a cause of action based on torture? Apply the Court's considerations to the various cases referred to in the preceding note, where lower courts have permitted federal common law claims for torture, extrajudicial killing, crimes against humanity, and war crimes. Are these holdings consistent with the *Sosa* Court's discretionary considerations?

8. ***Relevance of generally applicable standards for federal common law under §1350.*** Consider the requirements that are typically imposed for the creation of federal common law, including the existence of a uniquely federal field and the conflict with a specific federal interest. *See supra* pp. 11-13 and *infra* pp. 453-459, 529-546, 1110-1114. Is federal common law analysis under §1350 identical to that in other contexts? That is, must the foregoing generally applicable standards be satisfied in particular cases in order to justify recognition (or creation) of a specific cause of action? Or does the *Sosa* Court indicate that Congress granted federal courts some special authority, not present generally, to recognize (or make) rules of federal common law under §1350? Consider *supra* p. 43, note 227. Which approach would be wiser?

Consider Justice Scalia's concurring opinion. Is there any ambiguity in Justice Scalia's view about whether claims can be asserted under the ATS? What does Justice Scalia's opinion make of federal common law causes of action based on international law?

9. *Obligation of state courts to apply* **Sosa** *standards to federal common law claims.* If *Sosa* held that the existence and content of tort claims based on international law is a matter of federal common law, what courts control the recognition of such claims—state or federal? Consider again the definiteness and acceptance requirements and the five factors identified by the *Sosa* Court as relevant to the recognition of a cause of action under international law. Are these factors binding on state courts if they consider international law claims based on federal common law? If they are federal common law rules, mustn't they be?

Could a state court adopt stricter, or more lenient, standards for permitting international law claims based on federal common law? Consider again the purposes of the ATS. Would these be hindered, or furthered, by treating tort claims as matters of federal common law? Suppose that the federal courts refuse to recognize a particular federal common law right of action; could state courts then recognize the claim under federal common law anyway? If a state court cannot recognize the claim, what is a state judge supposed to do if confronted with a claim arising under the ATS? How does your answer to these questions square with the concurrent (*i.e.*, nonexclusive) grant of jurisdiction under the Alien Tort Statute?

10. *Availability of international law claims under state, foreign, or international law.* Assuming that *Sosa* treated international law claims under the ATS as federal common law claims, did the Court hold that such claims could *only* be federal common law claims? Suppose that allegedly tortious conduct occurred entirely in a foreign state, affecting only aliens, and that, under any choice of law analysis, foreign law would apply to the plaintiff's claims; suppose further that the relevant foreign law recognized substantive causes of action for violations of international law. Can a claim based on foreign law be brought under the ATS?

Why does it matter whether claims that are heard under the ATS are federal common law claims or not? As discussed below, *Sosa* imposed significant restrictions on the recognition (or creation) of federal common law substantive causes of action under the ATS—including "definiteness," "acceptance," and five discretionary factors. This requires significantly more demanding showings than the ordinary creation of "non-federal" common law. Suppose that foreign law did not impose similar requirements, recognizing a claim based on international law in circumstances where *Sosa* would not. Can that claim be brought under the ATS? Under alienage jurisdictional grants?

Suppose, for example, that Mexican law provided a cause of action for forced removals of Mexicans from Mexico. Would a claim based on this Mexican law be cognizable under the ATS? Why or why not? What should the answer be? If the answer is in the affirmative, what role, if any, would the five discretionary factors identified in *Sosa* be? What if the Mexican rule of law was an incorporation of rules of international law (like those at issue in *Sosa*)?

If federal courts could recognize and apply foreign law claims, what about state law claims? Suppose that California law recognized a substantive cause of action based on international law, in precisely the circumstances that *Sosa* rejected. Is that possible under *Sosa*? Why not?

11. *Separation of powers and foreign relations considerations in interpreting §1350.* Note the separation of powers and foreign relations concerns which Justice Scalia concluded were relevant to interpreting §1350. Recall the similar concerns voiced by Judge Bork in his *Tel-Oren* opinion. *See supra* pp. 33-35. Are these concerns grounds for a narrow interpretation of either the jurisdictional grant or the scope of federal common law private rights of action under §1350? Note that the *Sosa* Court accepts that foreign relations and separation of powers considerations are relevant to applying §1350, holding that "Since many attempts by federal courts to craft remedies for the violation of new norms of international law would raise risks of adverse foreign policy consequences, they should be undertaken, if at all, with great caution."

What is the thrust of the foregoing concerns — best articulated by Justice Scalia and Judge Bork — about interference with U.S. foreign relations? Is it not that federal courts should not permit "internationalist law professors and human rights advocates" to pursue international law claims under §1350 that will interfere with U.S. foreign relations by the Executive Branch? Suppose that these groups do not persuade *federal* courts to create common law claims based on international law: where will they turn next? Will they not turn to persuading state courts to do so? Does not Justice Scalia's narrow view of federal jurisdiction and common law-making authority in the international arena open the door to this result?

Consider again the purposes of the ATS — and particularly the objective of ensuring that national courts would have the capacity to prevent the serious interference with national foreign relations that can arise when a court considers delicate matters of international law. Are these purposes advanced by leaving state courts free to fashion either very narrow or very broad causes of action based on international law? In the Marbois incident, the concern was that state courts might fashion unduly narrow (or no) causes of action, that did not afford a foreigner adequate remedies for violations of international law; in some contemporary cases, the concern could be that state courts might fashion unduly broad causes of action, that afforded foreigners exorbitant rights. Whatever one's view of the appropriate scope of claims under international law, isn't the basic objective of the ATS to ensure that such issues be resolved by federal courts? How would Justice Scalia reply?

Consider the following comments from the former Legal Advisor to the U.S. State Department:

> The ATS has given rise to friction, sometimes considerable, in our relations with foreign governments, who understandably object to their officials or domestic corporations being subjected to U.S. jurisdiction for activities taking place in foreign countries and having nothing to do with the United States. . . .

Bellinger, *Enforcing Human Rights in U.S. Courts and Abroad: The Alien Tort Statute and Other Approaches*, 42 Vand. J. Transnat'l L. 3 (2009) (citing protests from, among other countries, Canada, the United Kingdom, Australia, and China to ATS suits against officials of those countries or companies organized under their laws).

12. *Foreign relations and separation of powers: an exhaustion requirement under §1350?* One way of addressing the concerns raised by Justice Scalia and Judge Bork would be to require plaintiffs to exhaust their remedies in foreign forums before bringing a suit in the United States. Section 2(b) of the TVPA contains an explicit exhaustion requirement. In *Sosa*, the European Commission urged such a course, which the Court "would certainly consider . . . in an appropriate case." For a recent case summarizing competing viewpoints on the operation and scope of an exhaustion requirement under the ATS, *see Sarei v. Rio Tinto plc*, 550 F.3d 822 (9th Cir. 2008) (*en banc*). For thoughtful commentary, *see* Holtzclaw, *Finding A Balance: Creating an International Exhaustion Requirement for the Alien Tort Statute*, 43 Ga. L. Rev. 1245 (2009).

13. *Foreign relations and separation of powers: Executive Branch views under §1350.* Another way of addressing Justice Scalia and Judge Bork's concern would be to give weight to the view of the Executive Branch. *See* Yoo & Ku, *Beyond Formalism in Foreign Affairs: A Functional Approach to the Alien Tort Statute*, 2004 Sup. Ct. Rev. 153, 181-199 (comparing the institutional competences of courts and the Executive Branch). To express its views, the Executive Branch sometimes files a statement of interest in litigation touching on matters of international affairs. *See* 28 U.S.C. §517. *Sosa* also envisioned this possibility and cited a letter by the Department of State that explained how federal litigation against corporations doing business in South Africa during apartheid interfered with the policies underpinning South Africa's Truth and Reconciliation Commission. In such circumstances, *Sosa* acknowledged there is a "strong argument that federal courts should give serious weight to the Executive Branch's view of the case's impact on foreign policy." Is that "argument" persuasive? If so, on what doctrine(s) should a court rely to give the weight to the Executive Branch's view?

Does this practice safeguard a proper conception of the separation of powers, by protecting the Executive Branch's foreign policy prerogatives? Or does it trench upon the Judicial Branch's prerogatives (and responsibilities) to decide cases presented to the courts in accordance with the law? Out of a concern that deference not become blind acceptance, some courts recently have declined to dismiss cases on justiciability grounds even when the Executive Branch has so urged. *See Sarei v. Rio Tinto plc*, 487 F.3d 1193 (9th Cir. 2007) (refusing to dismiss case on political question grounds despite stated views of Executive Branch); *Doe v. Exxon Mobil Corp.*, 473 F.3d 345 (D.C. Cir. 2007) (refusing mandamus from district court's refusal to dismiss on political question grounds despite stated views of Executive Branch).

What should a court do when the foreign government changes leadership? For a recent example, stemming from the South Africa litigation discussed in *Sosa, see In re South Africa Apartheid Litig.*, 617 F. Supp. 2d 228 (S.D.N.Y. 2009).

What should a court do when the Executive Branch does not file a statement of interest? Does this permit an inference that exercising jurisdiction over a suit does not tread upon separation of powers principles? *See, e.g., Gross v. German Foundation Indus. Initiative*, 456 F.3d at 389-390; *Presbyterian Church of Sudan v. Talisman Energy, Inc.*, 2005 WL 2082846 (S.D.N.Y. 2005). Is this step consistent with separation of powers concerns? Is it wise as a matter of policy? Consider the following comments:

> [C]ase-by-case participation can put the Executive Branch in a difficult spot. Foreign governments will continue to press U.S. administrations to weigh in on their behalf in ATS litigation. If the Executive is expected to weigh in when litigation presents foreign policy concerns, courts may come to infer (wrongly) from its silence in other cases that there are no such concerns. In addition, foreign governments may come to regard the Executive's decisions whether or not to file as a reflection of the United States' view of the bilateral relationship with that government. Domestically, foreign policy submissions will often be read as partisan support for the activities of foreign governments over the deserving interests of plaintiff victims.

Bellinger, *Enforcing Human Rights in U.S. Courts and Abroad: The Alien Tort Statute and Other Approaches*, 42 Vand. J. Transnat'l L. 3, 11 (2009). Do these comments suggest that the *Sosa* Court erred in its belief that case-by-case deference to the views of the Executive Branch can adequately monitor the foreign policy implications of an ATS case? How does this framework compare to other circumstances where courts look to the views of the Executive Branch? *See infra* at 247, 254, 261-275 (official immunity determinations) and 801-808, 838-842 (*Bernstein* exception).

14. *Justiciability limits under §1350.* Judge Robb reasoned in *Tel-Oren* that *Filartiga* failed to "consider the possibility that ad hoc intervention by courts into international affairs may very well redound to the decisive disadvantage of the nation." 726 F.2d at 826 n.5. He would have invoked the "political question" doctrine, discussed *supra* at 20-21, in holding that the case fell outside Article III's grant to federal courts of jurisdiction over "cases" or "controversies." How might this doctrine address some of the separation of powers concerns raised by Justice Scalia and Judge Bork?

How do these justiciability doctrines operate with respect to ATS cases in state court? Such doctrines derive from Article III, which generally applies only to the judicial power of federal courts, not state courts. Does that mean that a state court is free, under the U.S. Constitution, to hear disputes that Article III prevents federal courts from considering because they involve matters committed to the political branches' discretion? *See* Judge Bork's comment above, *supra* p. 34, and the discussion below, *infra* pp. 801-856.

15. *The relationship between "law of nations" and "treaty of the United States."* The Alien Tort Statute provides a forum for torts either committed in violation of the law of nations or in violation of a treaty of the United States. What was the purpose for creating two different classes of cases to which the statute would apply? *See Abagninin v. AMVAC Chemical Corp.*, 545 F.3d 733, 738-740 (9th Cir. 2008). Note that merely because a treaty has been ratified, it does not necessarily follow that an action for damages will be available under the ATS. *See Mora v. New York*, 542 F.3d 183 (2d Cir. 2008).

After *Sosa*, can nonbinding agreements or resolutions of political bodies (such as the United Nations) constitute the "law of nations"? What about treaties that the United States has refused to ratify? Is it reasonable to interpret the "law of nations" to include unratified treaties and other nonbinding documents when another provision of the statute specifies that the forum is available for violations of treaties of the United States? *See Abagninin v. AMVAC Chemical Corp.*, 545 F.3d 733, 738 (9th Cir. 2008) ("A treaty not ratified by the United States at the time of the alleged events cannot form a basis for an ATS claim."); *Flores v. Southern Peru Copper Corp.*, 414 F.3d 233, 256-265 (2d Cir. 2003). To what extent does *Sosa* answer these questions?

16. *"When an alien sues": ATS applies only to suits by an "alien."* If Alvarez had been a U.S. citizen, he could not have sued under §1350, because the Alien Tort Statute only applies to suits by *aliens*. *E.g., Corrie v. Caterpillar, Inc.*, 403 F. Supp. 2d 1019, 1026 (W.D. Wash. 2005); *Freidman v. Bayer Corp.*, 1999 WL 33457825 (E.D.N.Y. Dec. 15, 1999). Why should Congress want federal courts to protect foreign victims, but not U.S. plaintiffs that complain of identical abuses?

Alienage jurisdiction would permit U.S. plaintiffs to bring suits against foreign defendants in federal courts. *See supra* pp. 21-30. Alternatively, the U.S. Government could espouse claims of U.S. citizens against foreign states diplomatically, whereas it could generally not do so on behalf of foreign nationals (who are only entitled to the diplomatic protection of their home state). Finally, §1350 only concerns the jurisdiction of *federal* courts, not *state* courts. Because §1350 does not confer exclusive jurisdiction, U.S. citizens could pursue claims against foreign defendants in state court. Still, why should they not have a federal forum for international law violations?

17. *Liability of private actors under the Alien Tort Statute.* Can private parties be liable under §1350? *Sosa* leaves the question unresolved. A number of lower courts have answered affirmatively, though the precise theory depends on the nature of the claim. *See, e.g., Kadic,* 70 F.3d at 241-243; *Bao Ge v. Li Peng,* 201 F. Supp. 2d 14, 20-22 (D.D.C. 2001) *Iwanowa v. Ford Motor Co.,* 67 F. Supp. 2d 424, 443-446 (D.N.J. 1999). *But see Sanchez-Espinoza v. Reagan,* 770 F.2d 202, 206-207 (D.C. Cir. 1985) (Scalia, J.) (customary international law "does not reach private, non-state conduct of this sort"). What about corporations? Lower courts split on this question. *Compare, e.g., Kiobel v. Royal Dutch Shell Petroleum Co.,* 2010 WL 3611392 (2d Cir. Sept. 17, 2010) (holding that corporations cannot be liable) *with Romero v. Drummond Co., Inc.,* 552 F.3d 1303, 1315 (11th Cir. 2008) (holding that corporations can be liable); *Mohamad v. Rajoub,* 664 F. Supp. 2d 20 (D.D.C. 2009); *Al Quraishi v. Nakhla,* 2010 WL 30001986, at *39-41 (D. Md. July 29, 2010) (collecting cases). For commentary, *see* Dhooge, *Due Diligence as a Defense to Corporate Liability Pursuant to the Alien Tort Statute,* 22 Emory Int'l L. Rev. 455 (2008).

For a few international law violations, private actors can be directly liable; most violations, though, require state action. In this latter set of cases, the private actor's liability is established through some theory that either establishes a close relationship between a state actor and a private defendant or that imputes the state actor's conduct to the private actor. *See Bigio v. Coca-Cola Co.,* 239 F.3d 440, 447-448 (2d Cir. 2001); *Kadic,* 70 F.3d at 239.

Under many legal systems, tort principles extend liability to third parties including co-conspirators and aiders and abettors. Does the Alien Tort Statute incorporate such principles? Prior to *Sosa,* a number of courts embraced this theory. *See, e.g., Presbyterian Church of Sudan v. Talisman Energy, Inc.,* 244 F. Supp. 2d 289, 311 (S.D.N.Y. 2003); *Doe v. Unocal Corp.,* 395 F.3d 932 (9th Cir. 2002), *rehearing en banc granted, appeal dismissed,* 403 F.3d 708 (9th Cir. 2005); *Mehinovic v. Vuckovic,* 198 F. Supp. 2d 1322, 1355-1356 (N.D. Ga. 2002). Since *Sosa,* however, courts have split over the question. For a good set of opinions collecting cases and reaching different conclusions on the issue, *see Khulumani v. Barclay Nat'l Bank Ltd.,* 504 F.3d 254 (2d Cir. 2007). For commentary on the issue, *see* Keitner, *Conceptualizing Complicity in Alien Tort Cases,* 60 Hastings L.J. 61 (2008).

If the Alien Tort Statute does embrace such principles of imputation, this raises a host of questions. For example, are the principles of imputation themselves subject to *Sosa's* strict standard governing new causes of action? Moreover, what source of law supplies the standard for imputation? International law? Federal common law? State law? *See Presbyterian Church of Sudan v. Talisman Energy, Inc.,* 582 F.3d 244, 259 (2d Cir. 2009) ("*Sosa* and our precedents send us to international law to find the standard for accessorial liability."). Compare this to the choice-of-law analysis in other areas. *See infra* at pp. 231-261, 320-324, 343-346 (FSIA) and pp. 791-796 (choice of law and *Erie*).

18. *Alien Tort Statute and immunity.* Many suits under §1350 involve suits against current or former foreign government officials, which raises issues of official immunity. *See infra* pp. 261-265, 272-275 (describing circumstances where foreign state official can qualify for immunity under federal common law). Because the international law rules that §1350 incorporates almost always apply to the actions of nation-states, the availability of an immunity defense under §1350 is significant. As discussed below, the Supreme Court has held that the Alien Tort Statute cannot be used as a jurisdictional base for suits against foreign states: the FSIA provides the exclusive jurisdictional base for such

actions. *Argentine Republic v. Amerada Hess Shipping Corp.*, 488 U.S. 428 (1988); *infra* pp. 70-71, 234-235, 276-277.

Should officers of the United States be treated differently than foreign government officials? While early ATS litigation focused principally on former government officials (or companies allegedly collaborating with them), some more recent ATS (and TVPA) litigation has named U.S. officials (or contractors) as defendants. *See* Ku, *The Third Wave: The Alien Tort Statute and the War on Terrorism*, 19 Emory Int'l L. Rev. 105 (2005). Much of this litigation stems from steps taken by the U.S. Government following the 9/11 terrorist attacks—such as the detention of suspected terrorists at Guantanamo Bay, Cuba or the "extraordinary rendition" of alleged terrorist ringleaders to countries which did not observe the same restraints on interrogation as the United States. Generally, plaintiffs in these suits have not prevailed. *See, e.g., Arar v. Ashcroft*, 585 F.3d 559 (2d Cir. 2009) (*en banc*); *Saleh v. Titan Corp.*, 580 F.3d 1 (D.C. Cir. 2009). *But cf. Rasul v. Bush*, 542 U.S. 466, 484-485 (2004) (appearing to hold that fact of detention abroad in U.S. military facility does not bar jurisdiction under ATS for suit against U.S. officials). Recall that some of the defendants in *Sosa* included federal narcotics enforcement agents. Even if actions against U.S. officials are actionable *and* the standard for creation of a common law cause of action can be satisfied, how is a court supposed to apply the case-specific deference to the Executive Branch when the Executive Branch is itself a defendant? Does this not suggest that the ATS does not extend to suits against U.S. Government officials? On the other hand, wouldn't allowing suits against such officials supply a healthy check upon potential violations of international law by the U.S. Government?

19. *Applying* **Sosa.** Consider the following representative fact patterns based on actual cases filed under the ATS:

- A suit against an American company for selling bulldozers to the Israeli government pursuant to a U.S. military assistance program. The bulldozers are used to raze the homes of Palestinian citizens;
- A suit against an American chemical company for manufacturing chemicals used by the United States military during the Vietnam War;
- A suit against high-ranking officials of the United Arab Emirates for their alleged abuse of underaged camel jockeys;
- A suit against over 100 U.S. and non-U.S. corporations for their corporate activities in South Africa during the apartheid era.

What would you need to know to determine whether any of these fact patterns gives rise to a cause of action under the *Sosa* standard? Even if the alleged tort satisfied the *Sosa* standard, do any of the aforementioned prudential grounds counsel against judicial cognizance of the suit?

20. *Sections 1350 and 1331.* Note that *Filartiga* raised the possibility that an action for a tort in violation of international law might be brought under §1331. *See supra* p. 38, note 226. Suppose that a federal court concludes that a particular rule of international law gives rise to a federal common law cause of action, which may be pursued under §1350. Why isn't that cause of action also capable of being pursued under §1331? Note that this is not of (solely) academic interest: among other things, U.S. plaintiffs, as well as aliens, can pursue claims under §1331.

Consider *supra* p. 43, note 227, where the *Sosa* Court discusses §1350 and §1331. If a court concludes that international law is sufficiently settled and definite, and that the *Sosa* prudential guidelines are sufficiently aligned, to permit recognition of a private right of action under §1350 for (say) extrajudicial killing, then is it really true that no such cause of action lies under §1331? Suppose a group of U.S. and Canadian tourists are murdered by foreign officials in Iran. Can it be that the Canadians can sue in the United States, but the U.S. nationals cannot? Once a rule of federal common law is recognized under one jurisdictional statute, can it be used under others? Or is it like good wine, which can't travel?

21. *Section 1350 and Section 1332.* Recall that both the Alien Tort Statute and the statutory grant of alienage jurisdiction, discussed at pp. 21-62, were both part of the Judiciary Act of 1789, which set forth the initial grant of subject matter jurisdiction to federal courts. Does the simultaneous enactment of these two measures shed light on the purpose that the Alien Tort Statute was designed to serve? The original grant of alienage jurisdiction contained an amount-in-controversy requirement, requiring the suit to involve at least $500. By contrast, the Alien Tort Statute contained no such limitation. This has prompted one commentator to conclude that the Alien Tort Statute simply was designed to authorize federal court jurisdiction in cases between aliens and U.S. citizens that did not otherwise survive the amount-in-controversy requirement. *See* Bradley, *The Alien Tort Statute and Article III*, 42 Va. J. Int'l L. 587 (2002). Federal courts (including the Supreme Court in *Sosa*) have not embraced this construction of the statute.

22. *Torture Victim Protection Act.* Read the TVPA. How does the TVPA differ from the Alien Tort Statute? Does the TVPA create federal subject matter jurisdiction? Does the TVPA create a federal cause of action?

Who may assert claims under the TVPA? Who may be a defendant under the TVPA? If Singapore officials torture Singapore citizens, should that be the concern of U.S. courts? What if they torture Americans? What types of conduct are actionable? How does the conduct prohibited by the TVPA compare with that covered by other statutes? *Compare* 28 U.S.C. §1605A, discussed *infra* at pp. 351-361 (abrogating sovereign immunity for extrajudicial killings, the definition of which draws on the TVPA).

23. *The TVPA's cause of action.* Unlike the ATS, the TVPA expressly provides a federal cause of action for claims of official torture. S. Rep. No. 249, 102d Cong., 1st Sess. 3-4 (1991) (noting that Judge Bork "questioned the existence of a private right of action under the Alien Tort Claims Act," and declaring that "[t]he TVPA would provide such a grant"). Does Congress's creation of a private cause of action for one defined set of international claims — and not others — imply a view about the availability of private causes of action for other violations of international law? Does the legislative history surrounding the TVPA's enactment signify a rejection of Judge Bork's reading of the Alien Tort Statute and the cause of action requirement? *See Abebe-Jira v. Negewo,* 72 F.3d 844, 848 (11th Cir. 1996); *Doe v. Islamic Salvation Front,* 993 F. Supp. 3, 7 (D.D.C. 1998). If so, did the Supreme Court err in *Sosa* by holding that the ATS does not create a cause of action? Or does Congress's *failure* to amend the Alien Tort Statute when it enacted a cause of action under the TVPA suggest that Congress did *not* intend to create a cause of action under the Alien Tort Statute?

24. *Federal subject matter jurisdiction under the TVPA.* Can claims under the TVPA be brought in federal court? How? The TVPA's legislative history says that the Act "specifically provides Federal districts [*sic*] courts with jurisdiction over . . . suits" involving official torture. S. Rep. No. 249, 102d Cong., 1st Sess. 5 n.6 (1991). Is this accurate? What provision of the TVPA grants subject matter jurisdiction? Will the Alien Tort Statute and §1331's general grant of federal question jurisdiction provide jurisdiction in most TVPA cases? *See, e.g., Kadic v. Karadzic,* 70 F.3d 232 (2d Cir. 1995).

25. *The TVPA's exhaustion requirement.* The TVPA requires that a court "decline to hear a claim . . . if the claimant has not exhausted adequate and available remedies" in the place where the relevant conduct occurred. What is this "exhaustion" requirement intended to accomplish? How is a court to determine whether remedies are "adequate" and "available"? *Compare Rojas Mamani v. Sanchez Berzain*, 636 F. Supp. 2d 1326 (S.D. Fla. 1989) (dismissing case for failure to exhaust) *with Doe v. Rafael Saravia*, 348 F. Supp. 2d 1112, 1151 (E.D. Cal. 2004) (exhaustion not required where remedies "unobtainable, ineffective, inadequate, or obviously futile") *and Lizarbe v. Rondon*, 642 F. Supp. 2d 473 (D. Md. 2009) (declining to dismiss case on exhaustion grounds). Should the plaintiff or the defendant bear the burden of proving issues of availability and adequacy? *Compare Sarei v. Rio Tinto plc*, 550 F.3d 822 (9th Cir. 2008) (*en banc*) (placing burden on defendant) *and Jean v. Dorelien*, 431 F.3d 776 (11th Cir. 2005) (same) *with Abiola v. Abubakar*, 2005 WL 3050607 (N.D. Ill. Nov. 8, 2005) (adopting burden-shifting framework).

How should the inclusion of an exhaustion requirement in the TVPA inform a court's view about such a requirement under the ATS? Does the omission of an exhaustion requirement from the ATS imply an intention to dispense generally with such a requirement? Or does the codification of the TVPA as a statutory note to the ATS imply that the TVPA's principles should inform judicial interpretation of the ATS?

26. *Possible defendants under TVPA.* Who may be sued under the TVPA? The TVPA authorizes claims against foreign officials only, not foreign states. *See Sinaltrainal v. Coca-Cola Co.*, 578 F.3d 1252 (11th Cir. 2009); *Matar v. Dichter*, 563 F.3d 9, 15 (2d Cir. 2009); *Belhas v. Ya'alon*, 515 F.3d 1279 (D.C. Cir. 2008). The legislative history makes clear that official immunity will not generally be available as a defense in suits brought against individuals under this Act. *See Arrar v. Ashcroft*, 585 F.3d 559, 568 (2d Cir. 2009) (*en banc*). Nevertheless, diplomatic immunity and head of state immunity may provide a defense to TVPA actions. *E.g., Lafontant v. Aristide*, 844 F. Supp. 128 (E.D.N.Y. 1994). Moreover, in light of the Supreme Court's recent decision in *Samantar, infra* p. 261, the Executive Branch might nonetheless conclude that a government official is entitled to common law immunity. Why did Congress permit actions against individuals, but not states? Why did Congress not permit actions against U.S. officials or citizens? *See Saleh v. Titan Corp.*, 580 F.3d 1 (D.C. Cir. 2009).

27. *Definition of torture.* The TVPA sets out a detailed definition of torture. This borrows heavily from the 1984 United Nations Convention Against Torture and Other Cruel, Inhuman or Degrading Treatment or Punishment. U.N. Doc. A/39/51 (1984). Is the definition too broad? Too narrow? For differing approaches to the definition of torture, *compare Chowdhury v. WorldTel Bangladesh Holding, Ltd.*, 588 F. Supp. 2d 375 (E.D.N.Y. 2008); *Doe v. Qi*, 349 F. Supp. 2d 1258, 1314-1318 (N.D. Cal. 2004); and *Simpson v. Socialist People's Libyan Arab Jamahiriya*, 326 F.3d 230 (D.C. Cir. 2003).

28. *Relationship between TVPA and ATS over actions for torture.* The TVPA sets forth a detailed scheme for causes of action based on claims of torture. As noted above, it differs from the ATS in several important respects — among other things, the proper plaintiffs, proper defendants, availability of a cause of action, possibly an exhaustion requirement, and possibly even the definition of torture. In light of these important differences, may a federal court properly exercise its residual authority under *Sosa* to recognize a federal common law cause of action for torture? Or should the TVPA, as a congressional enactment in the field, be understood to preclude the creation of such a cause of action? *Compare, e.g., Enahoro v. Abubakar*, 408 F.3d 877, 884 (7th Cir. 2005) (holding that the TVPA "occupied the field" for torture claims) *and Mohamad v. Rajoub*, 664 F. Supp. 2d 20, 24 (D.D.C. 2009) ("Surely, caution in developing a cause of action under federal common law is appropriate in situations such as this where Congress has already established a cause of action and explicitly defined its scope in the TVPA.") *with Cabello v. Fernandez-Larios*,

402 F.3d 1148, 1154 (11th Cir. 2005) (holding that the TVPA merely extended to U.S. citizens the right to bring torture claims, a right unavailable to them under the ATS) *and Ali Shafi v. Palestinian Authority*, 686 F. Supp. 2d 23, 28 (D.D.C. 2010) (holding that TVPA does not preclude torture claims under federal common law against non-natural persons). *See generally Bowoto v. Chevron Corp.*, 557 F. Supp. 2d 1080, 1085-1086 (N.D. Cal. 2008) (collecting cases).

29. *International competence revisited.* Recall the suggestion above that international law may limit the "competence" of national courts over foreign disputes — even where the parties are subject to personal jurisdiction and where restrictions on legislative jurisdiction are observed. *See supra* p. 30. Where a dispute lacks any connection to the United States, should international law permit a U.S. court to exercise competence over the action? What if a plaintiff's claims were based on torture, an offense generally regarded as subject to so-called "universal jurisdiction," which any state may punish? *Cf. Restatement (Third) Foreign Relations Law* §423 (1987).

30. *The Alien Tort Statute and Belgium's war crimes law.* The Alien Tort Statute is not the only attempt by a country to create a legal remedy for international law violations. In 1993, Belgium enacted a law providing criminal punishments for certain grave breaches of international humanitarian law. Under the law, a private citizen (regardless of his citizenship or nationality) could file a criminal complaint with Belgian authorities, which would then be investigated by a magistrate who could issue arrest warrants. In its initial form, the law covered violations of the 1949 Geneva Conventions and their accompanying protocols. Later amendments added additional crimes, such as genocide and torture.

Initially, the law was heralded as a success, and, in its initial test, was used to prosecute successfully several Rwandans for genocide. Eventually, however, the law became a favored tool for the international human rights community and a flashpoint for diplomatic conflict. In the years following the law's original enactment and amendment, private citizens filed several dozen lawsuits against current and former world leaders, including claims relating to the two Iraq wars and the hostilities in Afghanistan.

Following these and other lawsuits, diplomatic protests were made to the Belgian government. Current and former foreign leaders objected that the law made travel to Belgium virtually impossible. The United States warned that continued enforcement of the law jeopardized Belgium's status as the seat of NATO and other international institutions. It also threatened to oppose funding for various NATO construction projects until Belgium abandoned the law.

In 2003, the Belgian government substantially revised the law. In its revised form, the law applied only to certain circumstances where either the victim or the suspect has Belgian nationality or residence. Additionally, the amended law accorded immunity to, among other parties, current heads of state and foreign ministers during their term of office. Finally, the amended law vested discretion in the public prosecutor's office, which could decline to refer a case to an examining magistrate where, among other grounds, referral elsewhere is "in compliance with Belgium's international obligations." Following the law's amendment, the Belgian Supreme Court dismissed most of the charges. For a good discussion of the Belgian law and the international reaction to it, *see* Halberstam, *Belgium's Universal Jurisdiction Law: Vindication of International Justice or Pursuit of Politics?*, 25 Cardozo L. Rev. 247 (2003); Ratner, *Belgium's War Crimes Statute: A Postmortem*, 97 Am. J. Int'l L. 888, 984-987 (2003).

How does Belgium's law compare to the Alien Tort Statute? Are there benefits to a criminal remedy (under Belgium's law) as opposed to a civil one (under the Alien Tort Statute)? Should public authorities serve as gatekeepers for the types of claims that may go forward under such laws? *See infra* at pp. 351-361 (discussing the State Department's role in suits under the FSIA's terrorism exception). Is the Belgian model superior to the "vigilant doorkeeping" that *Sosa* promised?

More generally, what business does any country have providing a remedy—whether civil or criminal—for acts that in some cases may have little or no connection with that country's territory? *See infra* at p. 718 (discussing relationship between Supreme Court's jurisprudence on extraterritoriality and the Alien Tort Statute). Brief of the United States as *Amicus Curiae* in support of Petitioners in *American Isuzu Motors, Inc. v. Ntsebeza*, 2008 WL 408389, at *14 (Jan. 10, 2008) ("Concerns for international friction are even greater when domestic courts purport to sit in judgment over the conduct of the foreign state itself, especially in its own territory."); *id.* at *16 ("Enactment of the Alien Tort Statute was motivated in large part by assaults on foreign ambassadors *in the United States* that had caused international incidents.").

On the other hand, what explains the vociferous reaction of foreign nations to laws such as Belgium's where the underlying principles and rights that the laws attempt to advance would seem to be universally embraced? Or does this preceding question build in an assumption about uniform values with which persons in some parts of the world might disagree? Does the experience of the Belgium law suggest that vindicating human rights through the courts is a misguided enterprise? Are such claims better left to diplomatic channels where seasoned foreign diplomats can better navigate the complex issues of foreign relations underpinning such claims? On the other hand, isn't there something fundamentally wrong with the notion that courts cannot be open to claims of violations of such basic rights?

3.   Federal Question Jurisdiction in Cases Arising Under International Law and Federal Common Law

Sosa and *Filartiga* illustrate that U.S. courts often confront issues arising under international law, derived from a variety of different sources, including formal international agreements and customary international law. Even apart from the Alien Tort Statute, many such cases fall within the federal courts' federal question jurisdiction. Jurisdiction in cases arising under international law is based on Article III's grant of jurisdiction over "Cases . . . arising under this Constitution, the Laws of the United States, and Treaties. . . ." In turn, the general federal question statute, 28 U.S.C. §1331, provides federal subject matter jurisdiction over "all civil actions arising under the Constitution, laws, or treaties of the United States."[232] The application of both Article III and §1331 to claims arising under international law is examined below.

a.   International Law Regarded as Federal Law.   Article VI of the U.S. Constitution provides that U.S. "Treaties" (like the Constitution and federal statutes) are federal law—specifically, the "supreme Law of the Land." As discussed above, valid treaties preempt inconsistent state laws, supersede prior federal statutes, and can be superseded by subsequent federal statutes.[233] The same is generally true of international agreements other than treaties and customary international law.[234]

232. 28 U.S.C. §1331; *supra* pp. 7-10.
233. *See supra* pp. 15-18.
234. *See supra* pp. 15-17; *Restatement (Third) Foreign Relations Law* §111(1) & comment d (1987) ("Customary international law is considered to be like common law in the United States, but it is federal law. A determination of international law by the Supreme Court is binding on the States and on State courts."); Henkin, *International*

Article III specifically provides that cases arising under U.S. "Treaties" arise under federal law for the purposes of federal judicial power. Thus, U.S. courts have naturally held that claims arising under U.S. treaties are within the federal question jurisdiction of both §1331 and Article III.[235] The same rule applies to Congressional-Executive and sole Executive agreements.[236] And, because customary international law is regarded as federal law, actions arising under customary international law are also said to "arise under" federal law, and therefore to fall within §1331. Although this view has been controversial among lower federal courts, it has been the holding of several lower court decisions,[237] and it is the rule adopted in the *Restatement (Third) Foreign Relations Law.*[238]

b. Selected Materials on Federal Question Jurisdiction over Claims Based on International Law. Excerpted below are selected materials on the scope of federal question jurisdiction in cases involving international law and federal common law. First, consider §111 of the *Restatement (Third) Foreign Relations Law,* which states the general principles of federal subject matter jurisdiction in the field. Second, in light of these principles, reread *Filartiga.* Finally, the district court's decision in *Sequihua v. Texaco, Inc.,* also excerpted below, illustrates the application of these principles in cases involving international law or federal common law rules.

RESTATEMENT (THIRD) FOREIGN RELATIONS LAW OF THE UNITED STATES
§111 (1987) [excerpted at Appendix AA]

FILARTIGA v. PENA-IRALA
630 F.2d 876 (2d Cir. 1980) [excerpted at supra pp. 36-38]

SEQUIHUA v. TEXACO, INC.
847 F. Supp. 61 (S.D. Tex. 1994)

NORMAN W. BLACK, CHIEF JUDGE. Plaintiffs, residents of Ecuador and a community in that country, filed this action in state court asserting a variety of causes of action arising out of the alleged contamination of the air, ground and water in Ecuador. In addition to

---

Law as Law in the United States, 82 Mich. L. Rev. 1555 (1984); *Sampson v. Federal Republic of Germany,* 250 F.3d 1145, 1152 n.4 (7th Cir. 2001); *Forti v. Suarez-Mason,* 672 F. Supp. 1531, 1543-1544 (N.D. Cal. 1987). For a critique of this position, *see* Bradley & Goldsmith, *Federal Courts and the Incorporation of International Law,* 111 Harv. L. Rev. 2260 (1998); Bradley & Goldsmith, *Customary International Law as Federal Common Law: A Critique of the Modern Position,* 110 Harv. L. Rev. 815 (1997).

235. *International Ins. Co. v. Caja Nacional de Ahorro Seguro,* 293 F.3d 392, 396 (7th Cir. 2002); *In re Air Disaster at Lockerbie, Scotland on Dec. 21, 1988,* 928 F.2d 1267 (2d Cir. 1991); *Boehringer-Mannheim Diagnostics, Inc. v. Pan American World Airways, Inc.,* 737 F.2d 456 (5th Cir. 1984); *Benjamins v. British European Airways,* 572 F.2d 913 (2d Cir. 1978); *Republic of Ecuador v. ChevronTexaco Corp.,* 376 F. Supp. 2d 334, 347 (S.D.N.Y. 2005); *Bobian v. CSA Czech Airlines,* 222 F. Supp. 2d 598, 603 (D.N.J. 2002).

236. *Restatement (Third) Foreign Relations Law* §111(2) & comment e (1987).

237. *Pacheco de Perez v. AT&T,* 139 F.3d 1368 (11th Cir. 1998); *Torres v. Southern Peru Copper Corp.,* 113 F.3d 540, 542 (5th Cir. 1997); *In re Estate of Ferdinand E. Marcos Litig.,* 978 F.2d 493 (9th Cir. 1992); *Filartiga v. Pena-Irala,* 630 F.2d 876 (2d Cir. 1980); *Republic of the Philippines v. Marcos,* 806 F.2d 344 (2d Cir. 1986); *Grynberg v. British Gas plc,* 817 F. Supp. 1338 (E.D. Tex. 1993); *Sequihua v. Texaco, Inc.,* 847 F. Supp. 61 (S.D. Tex. 1994). *But see Patrickson v. Dole Food Co.,* 251 F.3d 795 (9th Cir. 2001), *aff'd in part and cert. dismissed in part,* 538 U.S. 468 (2003); *In re Tobacco/Governmental Health Care Costs Litig.,* 100 F. Supp. 2d 31, 34-38 (D.D.C. 2000), *mandamus denied sub nom. Republic of Venezuela v. Philip Morris, Inc.,* 287 F.3d 192 (D.C. Cir. 2002); *Xuncax v. Gramajo,* 886 F. Supp. 162, 193-194 (D. Mass. 1995).

238. *Restatement (Third) Foreign Relations Law* §111(2) (1987).

monetary relief, Plaintiffs seek an injunction requiring Defendants to return the land to its former condition and the imposition of a "trust fund" to be administered by the Court. The case was removed [and] . . . is before the Court on . . . Plaintiffs' Motion to Remand and Defendants' motions to dismiss or for summary judgment. . . .

Defendants . . . argue that the Court has federal question jurisdiction because the lawsuit "not only raises questions of international law, but threatens to create an international incident." In this regard, the Court notes that the Republic of Ecuador has officially protested this litigation, asserting that it will do "violence" to the international legal system, and has asked that the case be dismissed. Clearly, such issues of international relations are incorporated into federal common law, which presents a federal question under §1331. *See Banco Nacional de Cuba v. Sabbatino* [excerpted at *infra* pp. 801-808]. . . . Plaintiffs in their complaint assert injuries that arose solely in Ecuador to as many as 500,000 Ecuadorans in an area that covers 1/3 of Ecuador. Plaintiffs complain about conduct which is regulated by the government in Ecuador, which is a country with its own environmental laws and regulations, a nation that owns the land at issue, and that treats all petroleum exploration and development as a "public utility" controlled by the government. Such matters affecting international law and the relationship between the United States and foreign governments give rise to federal question jurisdiction. *Texas Industries, Inc. v. Radcliff Materials*, 451 U.S. 630 (1981); *Sabbatino, supra.*

Additionally, there are essential elements of Plaintiffs' claims which, if "well-pleaded," require the application and resolution of the federal common law regarding foreign relations. Plaintiffs' claims of nuisance and for injunctive relief require them as part of their prima facie case to challenge the policies and regulations of Ecuador, as well as the approvals from Ecuador that Defendants received, in order to show that the conduct was improper on land owned by Ecuador. Federal question jurisdiction clearly exists where, as here, the essential elements of Plaintiff's prima facie case necessarily involve federal international relations, such as the international law relating to the control by a foreign country over its own resources.

Lastly, Plaintiffs' request for a trust fund asks this Court to step into the shoes of the Ecuadoran Health Ministry and supervise a medical monitoring scheme of unknown cost, scope or duration for as many as 500,000 Ecuadoran citizens over the protest of the government of Ecuador. It is incomprehensible that Plaintiffs could argue this does not fully and completely involve the relationship between the United States through this Court and the Republic of Ecuador.

Based upon the important foreign policy implications of this case, upon the international legal principle that each country has the right to control its own natural resources, and the strong opposition expressed by the Republic of Ecuador to this litigation, the Court finds without reservation that Plaintiffs' state law claims, if well-pleaded, raise issues of international relations which implicate federal common law. Consequently, this Court has federal question jurisdiction and the motion to remand must be denied.

Defendants have moved to dismiss on a number of grounds. . . . Under the doctrine known as comity of nations, a court should decline to exercise jurisdiction under certain circumstances in deference to the laws and interests of another foreign country. *See Société Nationale Industrielle Aérospatiale v. United States District Court*, 482 U.S. 522, 543 n.27 (1987) [excerpted at *infra* pp. 1033-1040]. . . . Consideration of these factors leads to the inescapable conclusion that the Court should decline to exercise jurisdiction over this case. The challenged activity and the alleged harm occurred entirely in Ecuador; Plaintiffs are all residents of Ecuador; Defendants are not residents of Texas; enforcement in Ecuador of any judgment issued by this Court is questionable at best; the challenged conduct is regulated by the Republic of Ecuador and exercise of jurisdiction by this Court would interfere with Ecuador's sovereign right to control its own environment and resources; and the Republic of Ecuador has expressed its strenuous objection to the exercise of jurisdiction by this Court. Indeed, none of the factors favor the exercise of jurisdiction. Accordingly, the case should be dismissed under the doctrine of comity of nations.

Defendants have also moved to dismiss on the basis of *forum non conveniens*, asserting that the convenience of the parties and the Court and the interests of justice require that the case be tried in Ecuador. *See Piper Aircraft Co. v. Reyno*, 454 U.S. 235 (1981) [excerpted at *infra* pp. 373-378]. . . . The Court finds without reservation that dismissal on the basis of *forum non conveniens* will "best serve the convenience of the parties and the ends of justice."

Notes on Third Restatement §111, Filartiga, *and* Sequihua

1. *Treaties and international agreements as federal law.* Section 111 of the *Restatement* provides that U.S. treaties enjoy the status of federal law—which is the "supreme Law of the Land" and which therefore preempts inconsistent state law. What in Article VI's language and purposes requires that treaties be treated as federal law—beyond the powers of alteration by individual states? Note that federal statutes can override prior U.S. treaties. *See supra* pp. 15-17. Why didn't the Framers permit the individual states to do the same?

Although Article VI deals only with "Treaties," §111 also categorizes "international agreements" as federal law. The reason for according this status to international agreements has been explained as follows:

Complete power over international affairs is in the national government and is not and cannot be subject to any curtailment or interference on the part of the several states. . . . In respect of all international negotiations and compacts, and in respect of our foreign relations generally, state lines disappear. *United States v. Belmont*, 301 U.S. 324, 331 (1937).

Is this rationale entirely persuasive?

2. *Authorities concluding that customary international law is federal law.* Section 111(1), *Filartiga*, and other authorities also declare that customary international law is federal law. The view rests primarily on the oft-cited passage in *The Paquete Habana*, 175 U.S. 677 (1900):

International law is part of our law, and must be ascertained and administered by the courts of justice of appropriate jurisdiction, as often as questions of right depending upon it are duly presented for their determination.

See also Republica v. DeLongchamps, 1 U.S. 113, 119 (1784); *The Nereide*, 13 U.S. 388, 422 (1815). Is it clear that §111(1) is correct that international law is *federal* law? Note that *Paquete Habana* only says "our" law, which presumably does not resolve internal U.S. issues of federalism. Consider the differences between international agreements—made by the federal political branches—and customary international law—"made" by U.S. judges and academics. Do these differences suggest that customary international law should *not* be regarded as federal law? What are the consequences of treating customary international law as federal law?

3. *Authorities concluding that customary international law is not federal law.* Until the second half of the twentieth century, customary international law was *not* regarded as federal law. *York Life Ins. Co. v. Hendren*, 92 U.S. 286 (1875); *Oliver American Trading Co. v. Mexico*, 264 U.S. 440 (1924). Consider also the following excerpt from a case in which a foreign diplomat claimed immunity from service in the United States:

> since the defendant was served while the cause was in the state court, the law of New York determines its validity, and although the courts of that state look to international law as a source of New York law, their interpretation of international law is controlling upon us, and we have to follow them so far as they have declared themselves. Whether an avowed refusal to accept a well-established doctrine of international law, or a plain misapprehension of it, would present a federal question we need not consider, for neither is present here. *Bergman v. De Sieyes*, 170 F.2d 360, 361 (2d Cir. 1948).

Why cannot state courts continue to be left to interpret customary international law? If customary international law is not federal law, then how would inconsistent decisions by U.S. state courts be reviewed? Would it be acceptable for different U.S. states to hold different views of international law (both from each other and from the federal courts)? If international law is not federal law, would it be subject to the *Erie* doctrine — requiring federal courts to follow state court decisions? For a thoughtful article arguing that customary international law should not be considered federal common law, *see* Bradley & Goldsmith, *Customary International Law as Federal Common Law: A Critique of the Modern Position*, 110 Harv. L. Rev. 815 (1997).

   4. Effect of Sosa *on categorization of customary international law claims as federal law*. What does the Court's analysis in *Sosa* indicate about whether international law is federal law? Note the Court's reference to the standards for creating a "federal common law" cause of action. *See supra* pp. 41-42. Does this suggest that international law is generally federal law? Or that only particular international law claims can be recognized (or created) as federal law? Note the Court's discussion, *supra* p. 43, note 227, of §§1331 and 1350. What does this suggest? Compare the Court's reliance on *The Paquete Habana*, *Respublica v. DeLongchamps*, and *The Nereide*. Does this suggest that all issues of international law are issues of federal law?

   What should the result be? Should international law be considered federal law? State law? Something else? What depends on the answer?

   5. *Article III federal question jurisdiction over cases arising under U.S. "Treaties."* Article III grants federal courts subject matter jurisdiction over cases arising under "Treaties made, or which shall be made, under [the] authority [of the United States]." As with alienage jurisdiction, this was a class of disputes thought to require the institutional attributes of the federal courts. Chief Justice Jay explained that, because the "United States were responsible to foreign nations for the conduct of each State, relative to the laws of nations, and the performance of treaties, . . . the inexpediency of referring all such questions to State Courts, and particularly to the Courts of delinquent States became apparent." *Chisholm v. Georgia*, 2 U.S. 419, 474 (1793). Why was it "inexpedient" to refer cases involving treaties to state courts? Is this still true?

   6. *Section 1331 federal question jurisdiction over cases arising under U.S. "Treaties."* Article III's grant of subject matter jurisdiction is implemented by the general grant of federal question jurisdiction in 28 U.S.C. §1331 over "all civil actions arising under the Constitution, laws, or treaties of the United States." If you were drafting §1331 today, would you include treaties? Why?

   7. *Jurisdiction distinguished from cause of action in cases "arising under" treaties*. Recall the distinction between the questions whether jurisdiction lies over cases arising under U.S. treaties and whether a cause of action is available for claims under those treaties. Even if federal question jurisdiction will lie, it does not necessarily follow that a plaintiff can state a cause of action. *See Sanchez-Llamas v. Oregon*, 548 U.S. 331 (2006); *Breard v. Greene*, 523 U.S. 371, 377 (1998) (*per curiam*); *McKesson Corp. v. Islamic Republic of Iran*, 539 F.3d 485, 488-491 (D.C. Cir. 2008) (holding that Treaty of Amity did not create private right of action); *Gross v. German Foundation Indus. Initiative*, 549 F.3d 605 (3d Cir. 2008) (holding that joint statement announcing creation of reparations fund did not create private cause of action); *Stutts v. De Dietrich Group*, 2006 WL 1867060 (E.D.N.Y. June 30, 2006) (holding that Geneva Convention and U.N. Security Council Resolutions do not create private right of action). *Compare Cornejo v. County of San Diego*, 504 F.3d 853, 858-864 (9th Cir. 2007) (holding that federal civil rights statute did not provide vehicle for bringing cause of action under international treaty) *with Jogi v. Voges*, 480 F.3d 822, 827-836 (7th Cir. 2007) (reaching opposite conclusion).

8. *Federal subject matter jurisdiction in cases arising under international agreements other than treaties.* As noted above, the United States frequently enters into international agreements with foreign states in forms other than treaties. In particular, international agreements are often concluded as "Congressional-Executive" agreements (authorized, ratified, or approved by Congress and the President) and "sole Executive" agreements (made solely by the President). *See supra* pp. 14-17. Courts have generally held that cases arising under such international agreements arise under federal law for purposes of Article III and §1331. *E.g., B. Altman & Co. v. United States*, 224 U.S. 583, 601 (1912); *Restatement (Third) Foreign Relations Law* §111(2) (1987). Why is this? Consider the language of both Article III and §1331. Is an international agreement a "treaty" or a "law of the United States"?

9. *Federal subject matter jurisdiction in cases arising under customary international law.* *Filartiga, Sequihua,* and *Restatement (Third) Foreign Relations Law* §111(2) provide that cases arising under international law are within the grant of federal subject matter jurisdiction in Article III and §1331. This view extends to customary international law, and is not limited to actions arising under U.S. treaties or other international agreements. Indeed, *Filartiga* and *Sequihua* involved principles of customary international law: "the modern view is that customary international law in the United States is federal law." *Restatement (Third) Foreign Relations Law* §111 Reporters' Note 3 (1986). "Matters arising under customary international law also arise under 'the laws of the United States,' since international law is 'part of our law.'" *Id.* at Reporters' Note 4 (quoting *The Paquete Habana*). Is this persuasive? Under Article III and §1331, is customary international law categorized as a "Treaty" or a "law of the United States"? Should federal courts have federal question jurisdiction over all cases arising under international law, including customary international law? Consider *Al-Bihani v. Obama*, 590 F.3d 866, 871 (D.C. Cir. 2010) ("The international laws of war as a whole have not been implemented domestically by Congress and are therefore not a source of authority for U.S. courts."). Why should the Texas courts not have been permitted to decide *Sequihua*?

10. *Criticism of decisions considering customary international law claims under §1331.* Some authorities have vigorously criticized decisions like *Sequihua* and *Filartiga*, holding that customary international law claims may be brought under §1331. Consider the following:

> To be sure, cases arising under the federal common law (as well as those arising under federal positive law) have been found to support statutory federal question jurisdiction, and federal common law embraces international law. Nevertheless . . . because international law is not itself a source of private rights of action—as is, for example, the common law of contracts or torts—a plaintiff's claims for violation of human rights cannot ordinarily "arise under" federal-common-law-cum-international-law and consequently, §1331 jurisdiction does not

extend to such claims. In the absence of an express Congressional directive—of the type I have found in §1350 and in the TVPA—providing a private right of action arising under federal law for a violation of a treaty or of international law norms, the federal courts should not imply one. Consequently, §1331 standing alone would not provide plaintiffs with jurisdiction in this Court in these matters. *Xucanax v. Gramajo*, 886 F. Supp. 162, 193 (D. Mass. 1995).

What principles animate the hesitancy of the Court in *Xucanax*? Are they well founded? Does the judge conflate subject matter jurisdiction with a cause of action? Note the comment in *Xucanax* that "international law is not itself a source of private rights of action." Is the judge's analysis viable in light of *Sosa*?

Recall the *Sosa* Court's footnote reference to the differences in federal common law-making power, in international cases, under §1350 and §1331. *See supra* p. 43, note 227. What impact does this have on the correctness of the analysis in *Sequihua*?

11. ***Rules of customary international law that are likely to arise in U.S. civil litigation.*** What rules of customary international law are likely to arise in U.S. litigation? Possibilities include: (a) prohibitions against uncompensated expropriation of property; (b) denials of justice; (c) violation of international boundaries; (d) assertions of jurisdiction beyond the limits permitted by international law; and (e) human rights violations. Should these sorts of international law rules be treated as federal law, subject to federal court jurisdiction?

Recall that international law is generally categorized into two categories—public and private international law. As discussed above, this was not always the case. *See supra* p. 14. Until this century, the "law of nations" and "international" law were generally regarded as encompassing the subjects that are presently divided into public and private international law. *See supra* p. 14. Given this, should actions arising under private international law be subject to federal question jurisdiction? Would this be consistent with the Framers' purposes? What sorts of cases would it extend to?

12. ***Federal question jurisdiction over customary international law claims.*** *Filartiga* suggested that §1331 would provide a basis for actions based on customary international law. *See supra* p. 38, note 226. The rationale for this result is, like §111, that international law is *federal* common law, and therefore that an action based on international law arises under federal law for purpose of §1331.

Recall the footnote in the Court's opinion in *Sosa* indicating that standards for federal common law-making under §1331 differ from those under §1350. *See supra* p. 43, note 227. Consider the Court's analysis in this note. Does it make sense to say that Congress assumed that federal courts could recognize federal common law claims, based on international law, under §1350, but not §1331? Doesn't this confuse issues of jurisdiction with substantive law? What about the apparent argument that it is more acceptable (post-*Erie*) to make federal common law under §1350 than §1331, because the latter is more "expansive"? Isn't the question whether or not the particular rules of federal common law are expansive, regardless what the jurisdictional base?

What does the *Sosa* Court's footnote concerning §1350 and §1331 mean? Does it mean that federal common law rules may not be based on international law under §1331? Or that the generally applicable standards for federal common law must be satisfied?

What obstacles would plaintiffs encounter in pursuing a claim based on international law under §1331? *Compare Tel-Oren v. Libyan Arab Republic*, 726 F.2d 774, 779-780 n.4 (D.C. Cir. 1984) (Edwards, J., concurring) (§1331 requires proof of a private cause of action under international law); *Handel v. Artukovic*, 601 F. Supp. 1412, 1421 (C.D. Cal. 1985) (same) *with Sarei v. Rio Tinto, plc*, 497 F.3d 1193, 1201 n.5 (9th Cir. 2007) (reading *Sosa* to require same jurisdictional showing for claims under Alien Tort Statute and §1331 claims predicated on international law). Recall that *Sosa* requires satisfying a number of discretionary factors, before a substantive cause of action based on international law may be asserted under §1350. Are these same factors applicable under §1331? Is there any reason that they shouldn't be? If international law did not itself provide a cause of action, would a suit arise under international law? Conversely, note that §1331 would permit suit by U.S. citizens as well as by "aliens." In deciding whether there was rule of federal common law permitting a U.S. national to pursue international law claims under §1331, could (and should) a court consider the fact that such a claim has been recognized for aliens under §1350?

A number of lower courts have upheld §1331 jurisdiction in cases based upon international law. *See Deutsch v. Tanner Corp.*, 324 F.3d 692, 718 (9th Cir. 2003); *Kadic v. Karadzic*, 70 F.3d 232 (2d Cir. 1995); *Bodner v. Banque Paribas*, 114 F. Supp. 2d 117, 127 (E.D.N.Y. 2000); *Abebe-Jiri v. Negewo*, 1993 WL 814304 (N.D. Ga. Aug. 20, 1993), *aff'd*, 72 F.3d 844 (11th Cir. 1996); *Forti v. Suarez-Mason*, 672 F. Supp. 1531, 1544 (N.D. Cal. 1987).

13. Federal subject matter jurisdiction in cases arising under substantive federal common law. *Sequihua* held that federal subject matter jurisdiction under Article III and §1331 extends to cases arising under substantive federal common law. Substantial precedent supports this view. In *Illinois v. Milwaukee*, 406 U.S. 91 (1972), the Supreme Court held that "§1331 jurisdiction will support claims founded upon federal common law as well as those of statutory origin." *See also National Farmers Union Ins. Co. v. Crow Tribe of Indians*, 471 U.S. 845, 850 (1985); *Romero v. International Terminal Operating Co.*, 358 U.S. 354, 393 (1959) (Brennan, J., dissenting).

Was *Sequihua* correctly decided? Lower courts are currently divided over the extent to which cases presenting foreign policy implications raise substantial questions of federal common law and, thereby, give rise to federal jurisdiction. *Compare Pacheco de Perez v. AT&T Co.*, 139 F.3d 1368 (11th Cir. 1998) *with Provincial Gov't of Martinique v. Placer Dome, Inc.*, 582 F.3d 1083, 1088-1090 (9th Cir. 2009); *Patrickson v. Dole Food Co.*, 251 F.3d 795 (9th Cir. 2001), *aff'd in part and cert. dismissed in part*, 538 U.S. 468 (2003) *and In re Tobacco/Governmental Health Care Costs Litig.*, 100 F. Supp. 2d 31 (D.D.C. 2000), *mandamus denied sub nom. Republic of Venezuela v. Philip Morris, Inc.*, 287 F.3d 192 (D.C. Cir. 2002).

In *Patrickson v. Dole Food*, the Ninth Circuit declined to follow the analysis in *Sequihua* and, in an opinion by Judge Kozinski, offered the following critique:

> Federal judges, like state judges, are bound to decide cases before them according to the rule of law. If a foreign government finds the litigation offensive, it may lodge a protest with our government; our political branches can then respond in whatever way they deem appropriate — up to and including passing legislation. Our government may, of course, communicate its own views as to the conduct of the litigation, and the court — whether state or federal — can take those views into account. But it is quite a different matter to suggest that courts — state or federal — will tailor their rulings to accommodate the expressed interests of a foreign nation that is not even a party.
>
> Nor do we understand how a court can go about evaluating the foreign policy implications of another government's expression of interest. Assuming that foreign relations are an appropriate consideration at all, the relevant question is not whether the foreign government is pleased or displeased by the litigation, but how the case affects the interests of the United States. That is an inherently political judgment, one that courts — whether state or federal — are not competent to make. If courts were to take the interests of the foreign government into account, they would be conducting foreign policy by deciding whether it serves our national interests to continue with the litigation, dismiss it on some ground such as *forum non conveniens*, or deal with it in some other way. Because such political judgments are not within the

competence of either state or federal courts, we can see no support for the proposition that federal courts are better equipped than state courts to deal with cases raising such concerns. 251 F.3d 795, 803-04 (9th Cir. 2001), *aff'd in part and cert. dismissed in part*, 538 U.S. 468 (2003).

Does the foregoing critique alter your assessment of *Sequihua*? Is Judge Kozinski's critique consistent with the premises underlying the ATS and the grant of alienage jurisdiction to federal courts? Why was it, again, that Congress authorized federal courts to decide the matters raised in such cases? What reasons are there for having federal courts decide questions of federal law under §1331? If international law is, in truth, federal law, then are these reasons not fully applicable?

Note that *Sequihua* appears to go beyond a conclusion that international law questions are matters of federal law. It appears to hold that matters which affect U.S. foreign relations sufficiently directly and intensively involve matters of federal common law. Is that a proper formulation of federal common law? How expansive is its rationale? *See also Torres v. Southern Peru Copper Corp.*, 113 F.3d 540 (5th Cir. 1997) ("plaintiffs' complaint raises substantial questions of federal common law by implicating important foreign policy concerns," arising from the Peruvian Government's interests in the case). What would Justice Scalia say about these results? What reasons would he give?

   14. *"Well-pleaded complaint" requirement.* As discussed above, federal question jurisdiction does not exist under §1331 unless a "well-pleaded complaint" asserts a claim based upon federal law. It is not sufficient that federal law provide a defense to a state claim. *See supra* pp. 31-33. What rule of international law (or federal common law) did the *Sequihua* complaint arise under? Was international law only relevant as a defense? Even if §1331 did not provide a proper jurisdictional base, would §1350 be available? Does the well-pleaded complaint rule apply under §1350? Does it apply to federal common law? How does the court in *Sequihua* answer this question? How would the court in *Patrickson* answer it? Note that the well-pleaded complaint rule is a *statutory* requirement. *Verlinden BV v. Central Bank of Nigeria*, 461 U.S. 480, 494-495 (1983). Would Article III permit the use of §1350 in *Sequihua*?

   15. *Foreign relations and federalism.* If federal courts do not enjoy subject matter jurisdiction in cases where the claims implicate foreign relations of the United States, where precisely will those cases end up? State court is the obvious answer. Is that a sensible outcome? Why should state courts entertain suits that, by all accounts, touch upon matters that are committed to the national government? On the other hand, isn't this precisely the right result in a system that meaningfully allocates power between federal and state authorities? Are state courts bound to apply the various justiciability doctrines discussed in this chapter and elsewhere in this book? If so, what is the precise legal basis for requiring state courts to apply substantive federal common law?

   16. *Practical importance of federal jurisdiction.* Why did the plaintiffs in *Sequihua* want to be in Texas state court? Why did the defendants want to be in federal court? Note the district court's disposition of the case — dismissal on grounds of comity and *forum non conveniens*. Would those grounds be available in a Texas state court? We consider this below. *See infra* pp. 453-459.

4.   Sovereign Immunity and Judicial Jurisdiction Under the Foreign Sovereign Immunities Act

Foreign states have long enjoyed various jurisdictional immunities under international and national law. Foreign sovereign immunity is governed in the United States by the

Foreign Sovereign Immunities Act of 1976 ("FSIA"), discussed in Chapter 3, below. This section examines federal subject matter jurisdiction under the FSIA and Article III.

Section 1604 of the FSIA provides foreign states (as defined) with a basic grant of sovereign immunity from the judicial jurisdiction of U.S. courts (both state and federal).[239] Section 1605 then sets forth a number of significant exceptions to this grant of immunity, specifying in detail the circumstances in which foreign states will not enjoy immunity from U.S. judicial jurisdiction. These include, for example, cases where foreign states have waived their immunity, engaged in commercial conduct having a U.S. nexus, or committed noncommercial torts in the United States.[240]

Under the FSIA, issues of sovereign immunity are inextricably linked with both the personal and subject matter jurisdiction of U.S. courts. Thus, the FSIA affirmatively grants both subject matter and personal jurisdiction to federal district courts in all those cases where a foreign state is denied immunity by §1605. Section 1330(a) grants U.S. district courts

> original jurisdiction without regard to amount in controversy of any nonjury civil action against a foreign state . . . to any claim for relief in personam with respect to which the foreign state is not entitled to immunity either under §§1605-07 of this title or under any applicable international agreement.[241]

Similarly, §1330(b) provides that "[p]ersonal jurisdiction over a foreign state shall exist as to every claim for relief over which the district courts have jurisdiction under [§1330(a)] where service has been made under §1608 of this title."[242]

Excerpted below is the Supreme Court's opinion in *Verlinden BV v. Central Bank of Nigeria.* The decision considers the application of the FSIA's jurisdictional provisions in cases where a foreign plaintiff sues a foreign sovereign, and the extent to which the statute's jurisdictional grant is consistent with Article III.

VERLINDEN BV v. CENTRAL BANK OF NIGERIA
461 U.S. 480 (1983)

CHIEF JUSTICE BURGER. We granted certiorari to consider whether the [FSIA], by authorizing a foreign plaintiff to sue a foreign state in a United States District Court on a non-federal cause of action, violates Article III of the Constitution.

I. [The Federal Republic of Nigeria entered into a contract with Verlinden BV, a Dutch corporation. The contract provided that Nigeria would purchase 240,000 metric tons of cement by Nigeria, that Dutch law would govern and that disputes would be resolved by arbitration in Paris. Nigeria also agreed to establish an irrevocable, confirmed letter of credit for the total purchase price through a Dutch bank (according to Verlinden's complaint, instead Nigeria opened an unconfirmed letter with a New York bank).]

Verlinden subcontracted with a Liechtenstein corporation to purchase the cement. Nigerian ports then became overwhelmed by ships carrying cement sent by other

---

239. *See infra* pp. 234-235, 276-277.
240. *See* 28 U.S.C. §1605(a)(1), (2) & (5); *infra* pp. 276-361. A recent amendment to the FSIA also strips foreign states of the immunity if the state is designated as a state sponsor of terrorism and has supported certain prohibited acts such as aircraft sabotage. 28 U.S.C. §1605A.
241. 28 U.S.C. §1330(a).
242. 28 U.S.C. §1330(b).

suppliers. Thereafter, Nigeria's Central Bank ordered its banks to amend their letters of credit, including the one guaranteeing Verlinden's contract, and informed its suppliers of changes in the payment terms.

[Verlinden then sued Central Bank in U.S. district court, alleging, among other things, breach of the letter of credit. The district court held that it had subject matter jurisdiction under the FSIA and that, even though Verlinden's claim arose under common law, this grant of jurisdiction comported with Article III. It dismissed the complaint on the ground that the Central Bank was entitled to sovereign immunity under the FSIA.]

[The Second Circuit affirmed on the ground that the FSIA, as applied in this case, violated Article III.] In the view of the Court of Appeals, neither the diversity clause nor the "arising under" clause of Article III is broad enough to support jurisdiction over actions by foreign plaintiffs against foreign sovereigns; accordingly it concluded that Congress was without power to grant federal courts jurisdiction in this case, and affirmed the District Court's dismissal of the action. . . .

In 1976, Congress passed the FSIA in order to . . . clarify the governing standards [for foreign sovereign immunity] and to "assur[e] litigants that . . . decisions are made on purely legal grounds and under procedures that insure due process," H.R. Rep. No. 94-1487, p. 7 (1976), *reprinted in* [1976] U.S. Code Cong. & Ad. News 6604. To accomplish these objectives, the Act contains a comprehensive set of legal standards governing claims of immunity in every civil action against a foreign state or its political subdivisions, agencies or instrumentalities.

For the most part, the Act codifies, as a matter of federal law, the restrictive theory of sovereign immunity. A foreign state is normally immune from the jurisdiction of federal and state courts, 28 U.S.C. §1604, subject to a set of exceptions specified in §§1605 and 1607. Those exceptions include actions in which the foreign state has explicitly or impliedly waived its immunity, and actions based upon commercial activities of the foreign sovereign carried on in the United States or causing a direct effect in the United States. When one of these or the other specified exceptions applies, "the foreign state shall be liable in the same manner and to the same extent as a private individual under like circumstances," 28 U.S.C. §1606.[243]

The Act expressly provides that its standards control in "the courts of the United States and of the States," §1604, and thus clearly contemplates that such suits may be brought in either federal or state courts. However, "[i]n view of the potential sensitivity of actions against foreign states and the importance of developing a uniform body of law in this area," H.R. Rep. No. 94-1487, at 32, the Act guarantees foreign states the right to remove any civil action from a state court to a federal court, §1441(d). The Act also provides that any claim permitted under the Act may be brought from the outset in federal court, §1330(a).[244] If one of the specified exceptions to sovereign immunity applies, a federal district court may exercise subject matter jurisdiction under §1330(a); but if the claim does not fall within one of the exceptions, federal courts lack subject matter jurisdiction.[245] In such a case, the foreign state is also ensured immunity from the jurisdiction of state courts by §1604.

---

243. Section 1606 somewhat modifies this standard of liability with respect to punitive damages and wrongful death actions.

244. "[T]o encourage the bringing of actions against foreign states in Federal courts," H.R. Rep. No. 94-1487, at 13, the Act specifies that federal district courts shall have original jurisdiction "without regard to amount in controversy." 28 U.S.C. §1330(a).

245. In such a situation, the federal court will also lack personal jurisdiction.

III. The District Court and the Court of Appeals both held that the FSIA purports to allow a foreign plaintiff to sue a foreign sovereign in the courts of the United States, provided the substantive requirements of the Act are satisfied. We agree.

On its face, the language of the statute is unambiguous. The statute grants jurisdiction over "any non-jury civil action against a foreign state . . . with respect to which the foreign state is not entitled to immunity," 28 U.S.C. §1330(a). The Act contains no indication of any limitation based on the citizenship of the plaintiff. The legislative history is less clear in this regard. The House Report recites that the Act would provide jurisdiction for "*any* claim with respect to which the foreign state is not entitled to immunity under §§1605-1607," H.R. Rep. No. 94-1487, at 13 (emphasis added), and also states that its purpose was "to provide when and how *parties* can maintain a lawsuit against a foreign state or its entities," *id.* at p. 6 (emphasis added). At another point, however, the Report refers to the growing number of disputes between "American citizens" and foreign states, *id.* at 6-7, and expresses the desire to ensure "*our* citizens . . . access to the courts," *id.*, at 6 (emphasis added).

Notwithstanding this reference to "our citizens," we conclude that, when considered as a whole, the legislative history reveals an intent not to limit jurisdiction under the Act to actions brought by American citizens. Congress was aware of concern that "our courts [might be] turned into small 'international courts of claims[,]' . . . open . . . to all comers to litigate any dispute which any private party may have with a foreign state anywhere in the world." Testimony of Bruno A. Ristau, Hearings on H.R. 11315, at 31. As the language of the statute reveals, Congress protected against this danger not by restricting the class of potential plaintiffs, but rather by enacting substantive provisions requiring some form of substantial contact with the United States. If an action satisfies the substantive standards of the Act, it may be brought in federal court regardless of the citizenship of the plaintiff.[246]

IV. We now turn to the core question presented by this case: whether Congress exceeded the scope of Article III of the Constitution by granting federal courts subject matter jurisdiction over certain civil actions by foreign plaintiffs against foreign sovereigns where the rule of decision may be provided by state law. This Court's cases firmly establish that Congress may not expand the jurisdiction of the federal courts beyond the bounds established by the Constitution. *See, e.g., Hodgson v. Bowerbank*, 5 Cranch 303 (1809). Within Article III of the Constitution, we find two sources authorizing the grant of jurisdiction in the FSIA: the diversity clause and the "arising under" clause. The diversity clause, which provides that the judicial power extends to controversies between "a State, or the Citizens thereof, and foreign States," covers actions by citizens of states. Yet diversity jurisdiction is not sufficiently broad to support a grant of jurisdiction over actions by foreign plaintiffs, since a foreign plaintiff is not "a State, or [a] Citize[n] thereof." *See Mossman v. Higginson*, 4 Dall. 12 (1800).[247] We conclude, however, that the "arising under" clause of Article III provides an appropriate basis for the statutory grant of subject matter jurisdiction to actions by foreign plaintiffs under the Act.

---

246. Prior to passage of FSIA, which Congress clearly intended to govern all actions against foreign sovereigns, state courts on occasion had exercised jurisdiction over suits between foreign plaintiffs and foreign sovereigns, *see, e.g., J. Zeevi & Sons v. Grindlays Bank*, 371 N.Y.S.2d 892, *cert. denied*, 423 U.S. 866 (1975). Congress did not prohibit such actions when it enacted the FSIA, but sought to ensure that any action that might be brought against a foreign sovereign in state court could also be brought in or removed to federal court.

247. Since Article III requires only "minimal diversity," *see State Farm Fire & Casualty Co. v. Tashire*, 386 U.S. 523, 530 (1967), diversity jurisdiction would be a sufficient basis for jurisdiction where at least one of the plaintiffs is a citizen of a State.

The controlling decision on the scope of Article III "arising under" jurisdiction is Chief Justice Marshall's opinion for the Court in *Osborn v. Bank of the United States,* 9 Wheat. 738 (1824). In *Osborn,* the Court upheld the constitutionality of a statute that granted the Bank of the United States the right to sue in federal court on causes of action based upon state law. There, the Court concluded that the "judicial department may receive . . . the power of construing every . . . law" that "the Legislature may constitutionally make." The rule was laid down that: "[I]t is a sufficient foundation for jurisdiction, that the title or right set up by the party, may be defeated by one construction of the constitution or laws of the United States, and sustained by the opposite construction."

Osborn thus reflects a broad conception of "arising under" jurisdiction, according to which Congress may confer on the federal courts jurisdiction over any case or controversy that might call for the application of federal law. The breadth of that conclusion has been questioned. It has been observed that, taken at its broadest, *Osborn* might be read as permitting "assertion of original federal jurisdiction on the remote possibility of presentation of a federal question." We need not now resolve that issue or decide the precise boundaries of Article III jurisdiction, however, since the present case does not involve a mere speculative possibility that a federal question may arise at some point in the proceeding. Rather, a suit against a foreign state under this Act necessarily raises questions of substantive federal law at the very outset, and hence clearly "arises under" federal law, as that term is used in Article III.

By reason of its authority over foreign commerce and foreign relations, Congress has the undisputed power to decide, as a matter of federal law, whether and under what circumstances foreign nations should be amenable to suit in the United States. Actions against foreign sovereigns in our courts raise sensitive issues concerning the foreign relations of the United States, and the primacy of federal concerns is evident. *See, e.g., Banco Nacional de Cuba v. Sabbatino; Zschernig v. Miller.* To promote these federal interests, Congress exercised its Article I powers[248] by enacting a statute comprehensively regulating the amenability of foreign nations to suit in the United States. The statute must be applied by the District Courts in every action against a foreign sovereign, since subject matter jurisdiction in any such action depends on the existence of one of the specified exceptions to foreign sovereign immunity, 28 U.S.C. §1330(a).[249] At the threshold of every action in a District Court against a foreign state, therefore, the court must satisfy itself that one of the exceptions applies — and in doing so it must apply the detailed federal law standards set forth in the Act. Accordingly, an action against a foreign sovereign arises under federal law, for purposes of Article III jurisdiction.

In reaching a contrary conclusion, the Court of Appeals relied heavily upon decisions construing 28 U.S.C. §1331, the statute which grants district courts general federal question jurisdiction over any case that "arises under" the laws of the United States. The court placed particular emphasis on the so-called "well-pleaded complaint" rule, which provides, for purposes of statutory "arising under" jurisdiction, that the federal question must appear on the face of a well-pleaded complaint and may not enter in anticipation of a defense. *See, e.g., Louisville & Nashville R. Co. v. Mottley,* 211 U.S. 149

---

248. In enacting the legislation, Congress relied specifically on its powers to prescribe the jurisdiction of Federal courts, Art. I, §8, cl. 9; to define offenses against the "Law of Nations," Art. I, §8, cl. 10; to regulate commerce with foreign nations, Art. I, §8, cl. 3; and to make all laws necessary and proper to execute the Government's powers, Art. I, §8, cl. 18.

249. The House Report on the Act states that "sovereign immunity is an affirmative defense that must be specially pleaded," H.R. Rep. No. 94-1487, at 17. Under the Act, however, subject matter jurisdiction turns on the existence of an exception to foreign sovereign immunity, 28 U.S.C. §1330(a). Accordingly, even if the foreign state does not enter an appearance to assert an immunity defense, a District Court still must determine that immunity is unavailable under the Act.

(1908). In the view of the Court of Appeals, the question of foreign sovereign immunity in this case arose solely as a defense, and not on the face of Verlinden's well-pleaded complaint.

Although the language of §1331 parallels that of the "arising under" clause of Article III, this Court never has held that statutory "arising under" jurisdiction is identical to Article III "arising under" jurisdiction. Quite the contrary is true. §1331, the general federal question statute, although broadly phrased, "has been continuously construed and limited in the light of the history that produced it, the demands of reason and coherence, and the dictates of sound judicial policy which have emerged from the [statute's] function as a provision in the mosaic of federal judiciary legislation. *It is a statute, not a Constitution, we are expounding.*" *Romero v. International Terminal Operating Co.*, 358 U.S. 354, 379 (1959) (emphasis added). In an accompanying footnote, the Court further observed, "Of course the many limitations which have been placed on jurisdiction under §1331 are not limitations on the constitutional power of Congress to confer jurisdiction on the federal courts." As th[is and other] decisions make clear, Article III "arising under" jurisdiction is broader than federal question jurisdiction under §1331, and the Court of Appeals' heavy reliance on decisions construing that statute was misplaced.

In rejecting "arising under" jurisdiction, the Court of Appeals also noted that §2 of the FSIA, 28 U.S.C. §1330, is a jurisdictional provision.[250] Because of this, the court felt its conclusion compelled by prior cases in which this Court has rejected Congressional attempts to confer jurisdiction on federal courts simply by enacting jurisdictional statutes. . . .

From these cases, the Court of Appeals apparently concluded that a jurisdictional statute can never constitute the federal law under which the action arises, for Article III purposes. Yet the statutes at issue in these prior cases sought to do nothing more than grant jurisdiction over a particular class of cases. . . .

In contrast, in enacting the FSIA, Congress expressly exercised its power to regulate foreign commerce, along with other specified Article I powers. [*See supra* p. 74, n. 248.] As the House Report clearly indicates, the primary purpose of the Act was to "se[t] forth comprehensive rules governing sovereign immunity,"; the jurisdictional provisions of the Act are simply one part of this comprehensive scheme. The Act thus does not merely concern access to the federal courts. Rather, it governs the types of actions for which foreign sovereigns may be held liable in a court in the United States, federal or state. The Act codifies the standards governing foreign sovereign immunity as an aspect of substantive federal law, and applying those standards will generally require interpretation of numerous points of federal law. Finally, if a court determines that none of the exceptions to sovereign immunity applies, the plaintiff will be barred from raising his claim in any court in the United States — manifestly, "the title or right set up by the party, may be defeated by one construction of the . . . laws of the United States, and sustained by the opposite construction." *Osborn v. Bank of the United States*, 9 Wheat. at 822. That the inquiry into foreign sovereign immunity is labeled under the Act as a matter of jurisdiction does

250. Although a major function of the Act as a whole is to regulate jurisdiction of federal courts over cases involving foreign states, the Act's purpose is to set forth "comprehensive rules governing sovereign immunity." H.R. Rep. No. 94-1487, at 12. The Act also prescribes procedures for commencing lawsuits against foreign states in federal and state courts and specifies the circumstances under which attachment and execution may be obtained against the property of foreign states. In addition, the Act defines "Extent of Liability," setting out a general rule that the foreign sovereign is "liable in the same manner and to the same extent as a private individual," subject to certain specified exceptions, 28 U.S.C. §1606. In view of our resolution of this case, we need not consider petitioner's claim that §1606 itself renders every claim against a foreign sovereign a federal cause of action.

not affect the constitutionality of Congress' action in granting federal courts jurisdiction over cases calling for application of this comprehensive regulatory statute.

Congress, pursuant to its unquestioned Article I powers, has enacted a broad statutory framework governing assertions of foreign sovereign immunity. In so doing, Congress deliberately sought to channel cases against foreign sovereigns away from the state courts and into federal courts, thereby reducing the potential for a multiplicity of conflicting results among the courts of the 50 states. The resulting jurisdictional grant is within the bounds of Article III, since every action against a foreign sovereign necessarily involves application of a body of substantive federal law, and accordingly "arises under" federal law, within the meaning of Article III. . . .

Notes on Verlinden

1. *Subject matter jurisdiction under the FSIA in cases brought by foreign plaintiffs against foreign states.* All three courts in *Verlinden* concluded that the FSIA's statutory language granted federal courts subject matter jurisdiction over actions brought by foreign plaintiffs against foreign states. Is that correct? Note the numerous references in the legislative history to "U.S. citizens" and "Americans." *See also Verlinden BV v. Central Bank of Nigeria*, 647 F.2d 320, 323-324 (2d Cir. 1981) (citing many other examples). As a consequence, the Second Circuit concluded in *Verlinden* that, "[f]rom this murky and confused legislative history, only one conclusion emerges: Congress formed no clear intent as to the citizenship of plaintiffs under the Act. It probably did not ever consider the question." 647 F.2d at 324. Why should Congress have intended to open U.S. courts, or provide the public resources of those courts, for such actions? Moreover, given the foreign relations and other international implications of suits against foreign states, why should the United States bear the costs of rendering judgments against foreign sovereigns in favor of foreign nationals? In cases of doubt as to Congress's intent to grant jurisdiction over foreign states, should not ambiguity be resolved *against* unintended assertions of jurisdiction? Consider the discretionary factors identified by the Court in *Sosa* and the separation of powers concerns raised by Justice Scalia. *See supra* pp. 41-42, 44-47. Do these argue for narrower — or broader — grants of federal jurisdiction? If a foreign national cannot sue a foreign government in federal court, then where will it pursue its claims?

2. *Foreign states' general right of access to U.S. courts.* U.S. courts have long held that there is no general bar forbidding foreign states from suing in U.S. courts. *See* 28 U.S.C. §1332(a)(4) (authorizing subject matter jurisdiction in action brought by foreign state against citizens of the United States); *United Arab Shipping Co. v. Eagle Sys., Inc.*, 2008 WL 4087121 (S.D. Ga. Sept. 2, 2008) (mag.) (relying on §1332(a)(4) to support subject matter jurisdiction in action brought by foreign state); *Republic of Benin v. Mezel*, 483 F. Supp. 2d 312 (S.D.N.Y. 2007) (same). In reaching this conclusion, courts have frequently relied on principles of international law and comity. Consider the following excerpt from *Pfizer, Inc. v. Government of India*, 434 U.S. 308, 319 (1978):

> [Holding that foreign states may sue for relief under the Sherman Act] does not involve any novel concept of the jurisdiction of the federal courts. This Court has long recognized the rule that a foreign nation is generally entitled to prosecute any civil claim in the courts of the United States upon the same basis as a domestic corporation or individual might do. "To deny him this privilege would manifest a want of comity and friendly feeling." *The Sapphire*, 11 Wall. 164, 167; *Monaco v. Mississippi*, 292 U.S. 313, 323 n.2; *Banco Nacional de Cuba v. Sabbatino*; *see* U.S. Const., Art. III, §2, cl. 1. To allow a foreign sovereign to sue in our courts for treble

damages to the same extent as any other person injured by an antitrust violation is thus no more than a specific application of a long-settled general rule. To exclude foreign nations from the protections of our antitrust laws would, on the other hand, create a conspicuous exception to this rule, an exception that could not be justified in the absence of clear legislative intent.

Pfizer relied on a presumption — derived from international law and comity — that foreign states are entitled to access to U.S. courts. This presumption is an application of the more general presumption, discussed above, that statutes will not be interpreted to violate international law unless they clearly require such a result. *See supra* p. 18 and *infra* pp. 646-651, 664-671, 703-706, 898-899.

3. *Foreign nationals' general right of access to U.S. courts.* It has long been established that neither foreign citizens nor foreign residents are generally barred from access to U.S. courts. Joseph Story explained:

> all foreigners, sui juris, and not otherwise specially disabled by the law of the place where the suit is brought, may there maintain suits to vindicate their rights and redress their wrongs. The same doctrine applies to foreign sovereigns and to foreign corporations. J. Story, *Commentaries on the Conflict of Laws* §565 (2d ed. 1841).

See also Rasul v. Bush, 542 U.S. 466, 484 (2004) ("The courts of the United States have traditionally been open to nonresident aliens."); *Disconto Gesellschaft v. Umbreit*, 208 U.S. 570, 578 (1908) ("Alien citizens, by the policy and practice of the courts of this country, are ordinarily permitted to resort to the courts for the redress of wrongs and the protection of their rights."). This rule rested on international law and the law of nations. It was acknowledged by U.S. and foreign commentators and applied by state and federal U.S. courts. *E.g.*, H. Wheaton, *Elements of International Law* §140-1 (8th ed. 1866); 3 G. Hackworth, *Digest of International Law* 562 (1941); 4 J. Moore, *Digest of International Law* 2 (1906); Wilson, *Access-to-Court Provisions in United States Commercial Treaties*, 47 Am. J. Int'l L. 20, 26, 30 (1953) ("quite apart from treaty provisions, the alien has had, from the beginning of the National Government in the United States, freedom of access to Federal courts on practically the same footing as citizens"). Is this presumption relevant to the FSIA interpretation in *Verlinden*? Compare the reliance in *Pfizer* on the presumption that foreign states have access to national courts.

This principle, however, is not universal and is subject to limitation by Congress. For example, under recent amendments to the FSIA concerning state sponsors of terrorism, Congress has directed courts not to hear a claim if neither the claimant nor the victim was a national of the United States. 28 U.S.C. §1605A(ii). *See also* 18 U.S.C. §2333 (providing civil remedy for victims of international terrorism but limited class of eligible plaintiffs to a "national of the United States"). Why would Congress want to limit the forum for such cases to nationals of the United States?

4. *Constitutional and policy bases for FSIA.* What is the constitutional basis under Article I for Congress's legislative enactment of the FSIA? What are the federal interests in enacting a statute dealing comprehensively with foreign sovereign immunity? Why did Congress deem it advisable to enact the FSIA?

5. *Article III's "arising under" clause.* Even though the FSIA granted federal courts jurisdiction over suits by foreign plaintiffs against foreign states, this authorization would not be effective unless it was within Article III's provisions concerning the judicial power. Article III's alienage clause was inapplicable because *Verlinden* (like *Filartiga*) only involved aliens. *See supra* pp. 21-24, 27-30. Moreover, the applicable law governing the merits of the parties' contract dispute was either state or foreign law—not federal law. Given this, why is it, according to Chief Justice Burger, that suits against foreign states under the FSIA "arise under" federal law? *See Guttierez de Martinez v. Lamagno*, 515 U.S. 417 (1995).

Note that foreign sovereign immunity is immunity from the judicial jurisdiction of U.S. courts. *See supra* pp. 70-71 and *infra* pp. 276-277. Could Congress enact a statute comprehensively granting the federal courts jurisdiction (both subject matter and personal) over all suits against aliens in U.S. courts? Suppose that the statute paralleled the FSIA, permitting state courts concurrent jurisdiction over aliens but forbidding them from hearing claims against aliens not authorized by the federal legislation. Consider the Second Circuit's analysis in *Verlinden*: "There is no intent here [in the FSIA] to create new federal causes of action; the purpose of the Act instead is to provide 'access to the courts in order to resolve ordinary legal disputes.' The House Report states flatly: 'the bill is not intended to affect the substantive law of liability.'" 647 F.2d 325 (quoting House Report at 6605 & 6610). Compare the Court's reply in *Verlinden*:

> The Act does not merely concern access to the federal courts. Rather, it governs the types of actions for which foreign sovereigns may be held liable in a court in the United States, federal or state. The Act codifies the standards governing foreign sovereign immunity as an aspect of substantive federal law; and applying these standards will generally require interpretation of numerous points of federal law.

Does this answer the Second Circuit satisfactorily? Would this observation not also apply to the hypothetical statute governing jurisdiction over alien private defendants described above? Should Congress enact a comprehensive statute of this type?

6. *"Federal question" jurisdiction and the Due Process Clause.* As discussed below, foreign defendants cannot be subject to suit in a U.S. court unless they are within its personal jurisdiction. In most cases, personal jurisdiction over foreign defendants is defined by the Constitution's Due Process Clause. *See infra* pp. 81-83. Assuming that the Due Process Clause does apply to exercises of personal jurisdiction over foreign states, *see infra* pp. 308, 333-334, 343-344, 360, why does it not follow that actions against foreign defendants "arise under" federal law for purposes of Article III and §1331? Recall that the Supreme Court has held that federal question jurisdiction exists under §1331 even if state (or foreign) law creates the plaintiff's cause of action, provided that a substantial disputed issue of federal law is a necessary element of the state law claim. *Grable & Sons Metal Prods., Inc. v. Darue Eng'g & Mfg.*, 545 U.S. 308 (2005); *Franchise Tax Bd. v. Construction Laborers Vacation Trust*, 464 U.S. 1 (1983). *Compare Empire Healthchoice Assur., Inc. v. McVeigh*, 547 U.S. 677, 700-701 (2006) (limiting scope of federal question jurisdiction based on relationship between state-created claim and federal law).

7. *Federal uniformity under the FSIA.* *Verlinden* emphasized that "Congress deliberately sought to channel cases against foreign sovereigns away from the state courts and into federal courts, thereby reducing the potential for a multiplicity of conflicting results among the courts of the 50 States." Why did Congress think that this was appropriate? In most international disputes, state law plays a substantial role in defining both the jurisdiction of U.S. courts and the substantive rules of decision. *See supra* pp. 6-7 and *infra* pp. 528-546, 791-796, 814-816, 1111-1113. Why should cases involving foreign states be treated any differently? If there is a compelling reason for channeling cases against foreign states into federal courts, doesn't that reason also support channeling all international disputes into federal court, regardless of whether a foreign state happens to be a party? Does the logic of this position also apply to suits against foreign government officials (as opposed to the governments themselves)? *See infra* at pp. 261-265, 272-275.

8. ***FSIA's simultaneous grant of personal and subject matter jurisdiction.*** As described above, the FSIA makes issues of sovereign immunity and jurisdiction identical: if there is immunity, there is no subject matter or personal jurisdiction, and if there is no immunity, there is affirmative subject matter and personal jurisdiction. Is it wise to make questions of subject matter and personal jurisdiction identical under the FSIA? *See supra* pp. 70-71. Consider the following remarks:

> In structure, the FSIA is a marvel of compression. Within the bounds of a few tersely-worded sections, it purports to provide answers to three crucial questions in a suit against a foreign state: the availability of sovereign immunity as a defense, the presence of subject matter jurisdiction over the claim, and the propriety of personal jurisdiction over the defendant. . . . Through a series of intricately coordinated provisions, the FSIA seems at first glance to make the answer to one of the questions, subject matter jurisdiction, dispositive of all three. This economy of decision has come, however, at the price of considerable confusion in the district courts. *Texas Trading & Milling Corp. v. Federal Republic of Nigeria,* 647 F.2d 300, 306-07 (2d Cir. 1981).
>
> The effect of this construction is to conceal distinctions that need to be drawn in careful analysis. *Harris v. VAO Intourist,* 481 F. Supp. 1056, 1062 (E.D.N.Y. 1979).

Is such criticism warranted? Are there any practical consequences of treating sovereign immunity as either a matter of subject matter or personal jurisdiction? Note that §1605(a)(1) denies sovereign immunity to foreign states that waive their immunity. As a result, §1330(a) can grant subject matter jurisdiction based on a party's consent; this runs contrary to well-established rules that subject matter jurisdiction cannot be waived or created by agreement.

2

Jurisdiction of U.S. Courts over Parties to International Disputes[1]

A U.S. court cannot adjudicate a case unless it has "personal" jurisdiction over the parties to the action. Personal jurisdiction involves the power of a court to adjudicate a claim against the defendant's person and to render a judgment enforceable against the defendant and any of its assets.[2] This chapter considers the personal jurisdiction of U.S. courts over both foreign and domestic parties to international disputes.[3]

A. Introduction and Historical Background

1. Statutory and Constitutional Requirements for Exercise of Personal Jurisdiction

In determining whether a U.S. court has personal jurisdiction over a party, it is critical to distinguish between two requirements. First, there must be a legislative authorization granting the forum's courts the power to exercise jurisdiction over the defendant.[4] Second, the exercise of jurisdiction pursuant to any such authorization must be consistent

---

1. Commentary on judicial jurisdiction in U.S. international litigation includes, *e.g.,* R. Casad & W. Richman, *Jurisdiction in Civil Actions* (3d ed. 1998 & Supp. 2010); Born, *Reflections on Judicial Jurisdiction in International Cases,* 17 Ga. J. Int'l & Comp. L. 1 (1987); Brilmayer, *How Contacts Count: Due Process Limitations on State Court Jurisdiction,* 1980 Sup. Ct. Rev. 77; Burbank, *The United States' Approach to International Civil Litigation: Recent Developments in Forum Selection,* 19 U. Pa. J. Int'l Econ. L. 1, 13 (1998); Casad, *Jurisdiction in Civil Actions at the End of the Twentieth Century: Forum Conveniens and Forum Non Conveniens,* 7 Tul. J. Int'l & Comp. L. 91 (1999); Dubinsky, *Is Transnational Litigation a Distinct Field? The Persistence of Exceptionalism in American Procedural Law,* 44 Stan. J. Int'l L. 301 (2008); Kurland, *The Supreme Court, the Due Process Clause and the In Personam Jurisdiction of State Courts,* 25 U. Chi. L. Rev. 569 (1958); Lowenfeld, *International Litigation and the Quest for Reasonableness* 46-108 (1996); Michaels, *Two Paradigms of Jurisdiction,* 27 Mich. L. Rev. 1003 (2006); Parrish, *Sovereignty, Not Due Process: Personal Jurisdiction Over Alien Defendants,* 41 Wake Forest L. Rev. 1 (2006); Rhodes, *Clarifying General Jurisdiction,* 34 Seton Hall L. Rev. 807 (2004); Silberman, *Reflections on* Burnham v. Superior Court: *Toward Presumptive Rules of Jurisdiction and Implications for Choice of Law,* 22 Rutgers L.J. 569 (1991); Stein, *Styles of Argument and Interstate Federalism in the Law of Personal Jurisdiction,* 65 Tex. L. Rev. 689 (1987); von Mehren & Trautman, *Jurisdiction to Adjudicate: A Suggested Analysis,* 79 Harv. L. Rev. 1121 (1966).

2. *Restatement (Second) Conflict of Laws* Chap. 3, Intro. Note (1971); *Shaffer v. Heitner,* 433 U.S. 186, 199 (1977).

3. This chapter does not consider subject matter jurisdiction, venue, or service of process. These topics are dealt with in Chapters 1, 4, and 10, respectively.

4. While virtually all contemporary personal jurisdiction cases involve legislative authorizations, in theory a legislative authorization might be unnecessary if the forum permitted court-made rules authorizing the exercise of personal jurisdiction. Even if permitted, any such judicially derived rule for personal jurisdiction still would have to comport with the Due Process Clause.

with the Due Process Clause of the U.S. Constitution. Only if both requirements are satisfied may the forum's courts exercise personal jurisdiction.[5]

a.   Statutory Authorization for the Exercise of Judicial Jurisdiction

(1)   State Long-Arm Statutes.   All the states of the Union have enacted statutes (or rules of court) defining the personal jurisdiction of state courts over nonresident defendants, including foreign defendants.[6] Most such statutes provide for "long-arm" jurisdiction over, and service of process upon, defendants who are located outside of the state's territory but have specified contacts with the state. State long-arm statutes are typically used to obtain jurisdiction over defendants located in other U.S. states, but are also generally applicable to defendants located outside the country.[7]

Although long-arm statutes differ from state to state, there are now two basic legislative approaches. First, some state laws incorporate the due process limits of the Fourteenth Amendment. For example, they may grant jurisdiction to the "fullest extent permitted by the Due Process Clause of the Fourteenth Amendment to the United States Constitution."[8] Slightly different are statutes that authorize jurisdiction to the extent permitted by both federal and state constitutions. Thus, California's long-arm statute provides that "[a] court of this state may exercise jurisdiction on any basis not inconsistent with the constitution of this state or of the United States."[9] The trend among the several states in recent years has been toward long-arm statutes that permit jurisdiction to the Constitution's limits.

Second, a number of states have enacted long-arm statutes that catalogue with greater or lesser detail the circumstances in which state courts may assert personal jurisdiction over foreign defendants.[10] These statutes do not necessarily extend the personal jurisdiction of the state's courts to its constitutional limit. Illinois' long-arm statute was one of the earliest examples of such legislation, although it has been amended to include a catch-all provision authorizing jurisdiction to the limits of the Due Process Clause.[11] New York's current jurisdictional statute provides an example of a "laundry list" approach.[12]

In interpreting state long-arm statutes, decisions of the relevant state's courts are generally dispositive.[13] State courts often interpret long-arm legislation expansively — even when this is not apparent from a statute's language. Many state courts have interpreted their long-arm statutes as conferring jurisdiction to the limits permitted by the U.S. Constitution.[14] In these circumstances, courts have concluded that jurisdiction depends

---

5. *See Asahi Metal Indus. Co., Ltd. v. Superior Court of California, Solano County,* 480 U.S. 102 (1987); *Omni Capital Int'l v. Rudolf Wolff & Co.,* 484 U.S. 97, 104 (1987); C. Wright & A. Miller, *Federal Practice and Procedure* §1064 (3d ed. 1998 & Supp. 2010); *infra* pp. 82-91.

6. *See* 1 R. Casad & W. Richman, *Jurisdiction in Civil Actions* §4-1 (3d ed. 1998 & Supp. 2010) (describing and reproducing state long-arm statutes).

7. In addition, state statutes ordinarily provide for service of process within the state on agents or officers of nonresident defendants, *see infra* pp. 873-874, as well as for jurisdiction over residents or domiciliaries of the state and companies with sufficiently close connections to the state, *see infra* pp. 109-115.

8. *E.g.,* Utah Code Ann. §78B-3-201 (2010).

9. *E.g.,* Cal. Civ. Proc. Code §410.10 (2010).

10. Some state long-arm statutes enumerate the bases for personal jurisdiction over nonresident defendants. *E.g.,* Fla. Stat. Ann. §48.171 (2010); N.Y. Civ. Prac. Law §302(a) (2010). Other state long-arm statutes contain less detailed formulae specifying when jurisdiction may be asserted over nonresidents. *E.g.,* Tex. Civ. Prac. & Rem. Code Ann. §17.043 *et seq.* (2009).

11. 735 ILCS 5/2-209(c) (2010). *See* Currie, *The Growth of the Long Arm: Eight Years of Extended Jurisdiction in Illinois,* 1963 U. Ill. L.F. 533.

12. N.Y. Civ. Prac. Law §302(a) (2010).

13. *E.g., DeMelo v. Toche Marine,* 711 F.2d 1260 (5th Cir. 1983); *Wells Fargo & Co. v. Wells Fargo Express Co.,* 556 F.2d 406 (9th Cir. 1977); *infra* pp. 215, 221-223.

14. 1 R. Casad & W. Richman, *Jurisdiction in Civil Actions* §4-1[1][b] & n.18 (3d ed. 1998 & Supp. 2010) (exhaustively collecting lower state court decisions).

on only a single inquiry—whether a "trial court's exercise of jurisdiction over [a foreign defendant is] . . . consistent with the requirements of due process of law under the Constitution of the United States."[15]

Other courts have rejected this "one-step" approach on the grounds that particular long-arm statutes were intended to confer jurisdiction to the constitutional limits only as to those specific categories listed in the statute, and not as to other categories.[16] In addition, not all state long-arm statutes have been interpreted as extending to the limits of the Due Process Clause, even with respect to specified categories of cases.[17] In these circumstances, it is important to distinguish between statutory interpretation and constitutional analysis.

(2)   Federal Long-Arm Statutes and Rules.   There are important differences between the personal jurisdiction of state courts and of federal courts.[18] In contrast to the universal adoption of state long-arm statutes, Congress has not enacted a general federal long-arm statute.[19] Instead, the jurisdiction of federal courts is governed in the first instance by Federal Rule of Civil Procedure 4.

Rule 4 provides federal courts with three basic grants of jurisdiction. First, it authorizes federal courts to "borrow" the long-arm statute of the state in which the federal court is located.[20] Second, Rule 4 makes it clear that a federal court can exercise grants of personal jurisdiction contained in any applicable federal statute—such as the antitrust and securities laws.[21] Third, Rule 4(k)(2) provides what amounts to a federal long-arm authorization, to the limits of the Due Process Clause, in certain federal question cases.[22]

Although there is no general federal long-arm statute, a number of federal statutes contain specialized provisions for service of process and personal jurisdiction in actions under the statute.[23] When such a statute is applicable, federal courts may generally exercise jurisdiction as authorized by the federal statute (incorporated by Rule 4(k)(1)(d)), as provided for by the long-arm statute of the state where the federal court is located (incorporated by Rule 4(k)(1)(A)), or as provided in Rule 4(k)(2). Like state long-arm statutes, many federal jurisdictional grants have been interpreted as extending to the limits of the Due Process Clause.[24]

Rule 4's provisions regarding personal jurisdiction are generally exclusive. If a borrowed state long-arm statute, federal jurisdictional grant, or Rule 4(k)(2) does not provide a basis for personal jurisdiction, then the federal courts will not fashion a federal common law basis for jurisdiction.[25]

b.   Due Process Limits on Judicial Jurisdiction: Historical Overview and Vocabulary.
The Due Process Clauses of the Fifth and Fourteenth Amendments play a vital role in

---

15. *Hall v. Helicopteros Nacionales de Colombia, SA,* 638 S.W.2d 870, 871 (Tex. 1982), *rev'd on other grounds,* 466 U.S. 408 (1984).

16. *E.g., Deluxe Ice Cream Co. v. R.C.H. Tool Corp.,* 726 F.2d 1209 (7th Cir. 1984); *Brown v. American Broadcasting Co.,* 704 F.2d 1296 (4th Cir. 1983).

17. *E.g., Banco Ambrosiano v. Artoc Bank & Trust, Ltd.,* 476 N.Y.S.2d 64 (1984) (N.Y.C.P.L.R. §302 not intended to extend to due process limits); *Fowler Prods. Co. v. Coca-Cola Bottling Co.,* 413 F. Supp. 1339 (M.D. Ga. 1976); *Bank of Wessington v. Winters Gov't Sec. Corp.,* 361 So. 2d 757 (Fla. Dist. Ct. App. 1978).

18. *See infra* pp. 203-229.

19. *Omni Cap. Int'l v. Rudolf Wolff & Co.,* 484 U.S. 97 (1987); *infra* pp. 203-205.

20. Fed. R. Civ. P. 4(k)(1)(A); *infra* pp. 204-205, 215-216, 221-224.

21. Fed. R. Civ. P. 4(k)(1)(D); *infra* pp. 204-205, 206-213.

22. Fed. R. Civ. P. 4(k)(2); *infra* pp. 216-229.

23. *See supra* p. 32 and *infra* pp. 672-673, 707-708, 709-711; 15 U.S.C. §22 (federal antitrust laws); 15 U.S.C. §77v (federal securities laws); 15 U.S.C. §78aa (federal securities laws).

24. *See infra* pp. 213-214.

25. *Omni Cap. Int'l v. Rudolf Wolff & Co.,* 484 U.S. 97 (1987); *infra* pp. 204-205.

defining the personal jurisdiction of U.S. courts over foreign defendants.[26] First, even if a long-arm statute authorizes jurisdiction over a foreign defendant, there will be circumstances in which due process forbids the assertion of jurisdiction. Second, because most long-arm statutes extend to the Constitution's limits, the Due Process Clause often effectively defines the jurisdiction of U.S. courts.

(1)   Territorial Sovereignty and *Pennoyer v. Neff.*   From the earliest days of the Republic, American courts and commentators relied on principles of territorial sovereignty and international law to limit judicial jurisdiction.[27] Here, as in other contexts, Joseph Story's classic *Commentaries on the Conflict of Laws* were central to American thinking.[28] With respect to judicial jurisdiction, Story offered an uncompromising statement of the territoriality doctrine:

> Considered in an international point of view, jurisdiction, to be rightfully exercised, must be founded either upon the person being within the territory, or upon the thing being within the territory; for, otherwise, there can be no sovereignty exerted, upon the known maxim; *Extra territorium jus dicenti impune non paretur* . . . no sovereignty can extend its process beyond its own territorial limits, to subject either persons or property to its judicial decisions.[29]

Story's views were consistently reflected in nineteenth-century U.S. judicial decisions. In 1808, the Supreme Court refused to recognize a foreign prize court's judgment on the grounds that the court had lacked judicial jurisdiction.[30] The case, *Rose v. Himely,* involved a vessel that had been seized outside of the foreign state's territorial waters. Holding that the foreign court could not have asserted jurisdiction over the vessel consistent with international law, the Court reasoned:

> [if a court] exercises a jurisdiction which, according to the law of nations, its sovereign could not confer . . . [its judgments] are not regarded by foreign courts. . . . [T]he law of nations is the law of all tribunals in the society of nations, and is supposed to be equally understood by all.[31]

Similarly, in 1811, in *Mills v. Duryee,* a dissenting opinion of Justice Johnson cited "certain eternal principles of justice," one of which was "that jurisdiction cannot be justly exercised by a state over property not within the reach of its process, or over persons . . . not subjected to their jurisdiction, by being found within their limits."[32] And in *D'Arcy v. Ketchum,*[33] the Court held that the Full Faith and Credit Clause did not require a state

---

26. The Fourteenth Amendment to the U.S. Constitution provides that no state shall "deprive any person of life, liberty, or property, without due process of law." The Fifth Amendment contains nearly identical language, applicable to the federal government. *See infra* pp. 205, 209-214.

27. *Rose v. Himely,* 8 U.S. 241 (1808). *See also Mason v. The Ship Blaireau,* 6 U.S. 240 (1804); *The Bee,* 3 Fed. Cas. 41, No. 1219 (D. Me. 1836) ("established principles of the jus gentium").

28. *See* de Nova, *The First American Book on Conflict of Laws,* 8 Am. J. Leg. Hist. 135 (1964); Lorenzen, *Selected Articles on the Conflict of Laws* 193-194 (1947) ("Story's *Commentaries* were without question the most remarkable and outstanding work on the conflict of laws which had appeared since the thirteenth century in any country and in any language"); Yntema, *The Historic Bases of Private International Law,* 2 Am. J. Comp. L. 297, 307 (1953).

29. J. Story, *Commentaries on the Conflict of Laws* §539 (2d ed. 1841). Story's territorial view of national jurisdiction also applied to legislative jurisdiction, which is discussed in detail below. *See infra* pp. 591-604.

30. *Rose v. Himely,* 8 U.S. 241, 277 (1808).

31. 8 U.S. at 276-277. Writing for the Court, Chief Justice Marshall also said that a U.S. court must inquire into "the right of the foreign court to take jurisdiction of the thing . . . [under] the law of nations and [any applicable] treaties." 8 U.S. at 271. *See also The Schooner Exchange v. McFaddon,* 11 U.S. 116 (1812) (relying on international law for rule limiting U.S. judicial jurisdiction against foreign states).

32. 11 U.S. 481, 486 (1813) (Johnson, J., dissenting).

33. 52 U.S. 165 (1850).

court to enforce a judgment rendered by another state court that lacked valid personal jurisdiction over the judgment-debtor. Among other things, the Court observed:

> That countries foreign to our own disregard a judgement merely against the person, where he has not been served with process nor had a day in court is the familiar rule; national comity is never thus extended. The proceeding is deemed an illegitimate assumption of power, and resisted as mere abuse. . . . We deem it free from controversy that these adjudications are in conformity to the well-established rules of international law.[34]

The Court went on to hold that the judicial jurisdiction of the several states was restricted by international law, and that the judgment in *D'Arcy* need not be recognized because it was based on a jurisdictional assertion that violated international law.[35]

The Supreme Court's reliance on international law to sustain territorial limits on judicial jurisdiction culminated in its classic decision in *Pennoyer v. Neff.*[36] In *Pennoyer,* the Court relied on what it termed "well-established principles of public law respecting the jurisdiction of an independent State."[37] In ascertaining what international law required, the Court cited leading international law commentaries and particularly Story's *Commentaries on the Conflict of Laws.*[38]

From these authorities *Pennoyer* derived three principles of international law: (1) "every State possesses exclusive jurisdiction and sovereignty over persons and property within its territory";[39] (2) "no State can exercise direct jurisdiction and authority over persons and property without its territory";[40] and (3) "process from the tribunals of one State cannot run into another state."[41] These principles required that the defendant "must be brought within [the forum court's] jurisdiction by service of process within the State" or voluntarily appear.[42] According to the Court in *Pennoyer,* these principles of international law were applicable in domestic American disputes, limiting the jurisdiction of the courts of the several states.[43]

Pennoyer's strict territorial view of judicial jurisdiction found wide support among nineteenth-century American commentators.[44] It paralleled equally strict nineteenth-century territorial limits on legislative jurisdiction.[45] Moreover, Story's conception of territorial sovereignty provided the basis for early American doctrine of foreign sovereign immunity.[46]

---

34. 52 U.S. at 174.

35. 52 U.S. at 175-176 ("[T]he international law as it existed among the States in 1790 was, that a judgment rendered in one State, assuming to bind the person of a citizen of another, was void within the foreign States, when the defendant had not been served with process or voluntarily made defence, because neither the legislative jurisdiction, nor that of courts of justice had binding force.").

36. 95 U.S. 714 (1877).

37. In stating these principles, the Court cited its earlier reliance in *D'Arcy v. Ketchum,* 52 U.S. 165, 175-176 (1850), on "international law as it existed among the states in 1790."

38. 95 U.S. at 722 (citing J. Story, *Commentaries on the Conflict of Laws* [no edition specified]; H. Wheaton, *International Law* [no edition specified]). These treatises relied, in turn, on Ulrich Huber's *De Conflictu Legum. See* Weinstein, *The Dutch Influence on the Conception of Judicial Jurisdiction in 19th Century America,* 38 Am. J. Comp. L. 73 (1990).

39. 95 U.S. at 722.

40. 95 U.S. at 722.

41. 95 U.S. at 727.

42. 95 U.S. at 733.

43. 95 U.S. at 722.

44. J. Story, *Commentaries on the Conflict of Laws* §539 (2d ed. 1841); H. Wheaton, *Elements of International Law* §§77, 111-114, 134-151 (8th ed. 1866); F. Wharton, *Conflict of Laws* §§646, 649, 715 (3d ed. 1905); T. Cooley, *Constitutional Limitations* 447-448 (2d ed. 1871).

45. *See infra* pp. 591-594.

46. *The Schooner Exchange v. McFaddon,* 11 U.S. 116 (1812); *infra* pp. 231-234.

Territorial limits on judicial jurisdiction were also relied upon by the United States in its foreign relations. During the nineteenth century, the United States consistently opposed efforts by more established world powers to assert judicial (and legislative)[47] jurisdiction beyond their borders. The U.S. Department of State lodged numerous diplomatic protests with foreign governments, challenging assertions of jurisdiction over U.S. nationals as inconsistent with public international law.[48] As one U.S. diplomatic note opined, it is the "uniform declaration of writers on public law" that "in an international point of view, either the thing or the person made the subject of jurisdiction must be within the territory, for no sovereignty can extend its process beyond its own territorial limits."[49]

(2)   *International Shoe* and "Minimum Contacts."   *Pennoyer*'s territorial limits on judicial jurisdiction in domestic cases came under growing pressure as the industrial era progressed. Manufacturing and commerce were increasingly operated without regard to interstate and international boundaries. States affected by foreign corporations' conduct sought to regulate those activities, including by way of judicial proceedings. Those efforts inevitably confronted *Pennoyer*'s rule that a state court could exercise jurisdiction only over persons served with process within the state. The perception that state regulatory needs required less rigid limits on personal jurisdiction made change irresistible.

In 1945, after many decisions foreshadowing the change, the Supreme Court modified *Pennoyer*'s territorial approach to jurisdiction. *International Shoe Co. v. Washington* held that the Due Process Clause permitted a state court to exercise personal jurisdiction over persons located outside the state:[50]

> due process requires only that in order to subject a defendant to a judgment *in personam,* if he be not present within the territory of the forum, he have certain minimum contacts with it "such that the maintenance of the suit does not offend 'traditional notions of fair play and substantial justice.' "[51]

Applying this now-classic "minimum contacts" test, the Court concluded that International Shoe, which was headquartered in Missouri, could be subjected to the jurisdiction of Washington's courts in an action to collect contributions to a state unemployment compensation fund. The Court relied on the fact that International Shoe had maintained a dozen commissioned salesmen in Washington to solicit orders for its products. This ongoing solicitation satisfied the "minimum contacts" test, notwithstanding the fact that International Shoe had no office in Washington and had entered into no contracts within the state.[52]

International Shoe did not entirely abandon *Pennoyer*'s emphasis on territorial sovereignty. The Court cited *Pennoyer* with approval for the proposition that the Due Process Clause "does not contemplate that a state may make binding a judgment *in personam* against an individual or corporate defendant with which the state has no contacts, ties, or

---

47. *See infra* pp. 97-101, 591-594, 598-601.

48. *Case of Lund v. Ogden,* 6 Op. Att'y Gen. 75, 76-77 (1853) (holding that exercise of judicial jurisdiction over U.S. resident by Texas would be "in violation of international comity and a usurpation of general sovereignty, in derogation of the rights of co-equal States"); Letters from Secretary of State Fish to General Schenck dated Nov. 8, 1873 and Mar. 12, 1875, *reprinted in Foreign Relations of the United States* 490 (1874) and *id.* at 592, 633 (1875) (protesting that exercise of judicial jurisdiction by British courts over civil disputes arising on high seas between sailors on U.S. vessels violates "rules of comity between nations and the principles of international law").

49. Letter Concerning the Schooner Daylight from Secretary of State Frelinghuyser to Mr. Morgan, dated May 17, 1884, *reprinted in Foreign Relations of the United States* 358 (1884).

50. 326 U.S. 310 (1945).

51. 326 U.S. at 316.

52. 326 U.S. at 321-322.

relations."[53] Rather, *International Shoe*'s minimum contacts test modified the content of the territoriality doctrine: state sovereignty continued to limit judicial jurisdiction, but its constraints were less restrictive than *Pennoyer*'s strict territorial limits.

International Shoe remains a precedent of almost mystical import for due process analysis. Nevertheless, after the Supreme Court modified *Pennoyer*'s territoriality doctrine, it was often unclear what limitations the Due Process Clause imposed. The Court has issued a number of decisions seeking to clarify the "minimum contacts" formula,[54] but without notable success.[55] As the Court has conceded, "few answers [to due process inquiries] will be written 'in black and white. The greys are dominant and even among them the shades are innumerable.' "[56]

(3)   *Hanson v. Denckla* and "Purposeful Availment."   Decisions following *International Shoe* confirmed that *Pennoyer*'s territorial restrictions had been significantly relaxed. In 1957, *McGee v. International Life Ins. Co.*[57] held that nothing in the Constitution precluded a California court from exercising jurisdiction over a Texas insurance company based solely on its use of interstate mail to sell a single insurance policy to a California resident. The Court cited technological changes in transportation and communications, and an increasingly national economy, as justifications for diminished due process restrictions on judicial jurisdiction:

> Today many commercial transactions touch two or more States and may involve parties separated by the full continent. With this increasing nationalization of commerce has come a great increase in the amount of business conducted by mail across state lines. At the same time modern transportation and communication have made it much less burdensome for a party sued to defend himself in a State where he engages in economic activity.[58]

Notwithstanding these developments, the Court soon made it clear that the Due Process Clause continued to impose significant limits on assertions of personal jurisdiction. In *Hanson v. Denckla*,[59] the Court emphasized that, no matter how trivial the burden upon a party of defending in a particular forum, due process required a showing that the defendant had deliberately engaged in activities that created contacts with the forum. Adopting what would become another touchstone of due process analysis, the Court declared that the Constitution requires "some act by which the defendant *purposefully avails* itself of the privilege of conducting activities within the forum state, thus invoking the benefits and protections of its laws."[60]

Beginning in the 1970s, the Court's due process decisions increasingly came to reflect profound doctrinal disagreement. Some members of the Court (notably Justices Brennan

---

53. 326 U.S. at 319.

54. *E.g.*, *Burnham v. Superior Court*, 495 U.S. 604 (1990); *Asahi Metal Indus. v. Superior Court*, 480 U.S. 102 (1987); *Phillips Petroleum Co. v. Shutts*, 472 U.S. 797 (1985); *Burger King Corp. v. Rudzewicz*, 471 U.S. 462 (1985); *Helicopteros Nacionales de Colombia, SA v. Hall*, 466 U.S. 408 (1984); *Calder v. Jones*, 465 U.S. 783 (1984); *Keeton v. Hustler Magazine*, 465 U.S. 770 (1984); *Insurance Corp. of Ireland v. Compagnie des Bauxites de Guinee*, 456 U.S. 694 (1982); *Rush v. Savchuk*, 444 U.S. 320 (1980); *World-Wide Volkswagen Corp. v. Woodson*, 444 U.S. 286 (1980); *Kulko v. Superior Court*, 436 U.S. 84 (1978).

55. A number of authorities have criticized the Court's jurisdictional analysis on the grounds that it provides inadequate guidance for courts, litigants, and businesses. *E.g.*, Abrams, *Power, Convenience and the Elimination of Personal Jurisdiction in the Federal Courts*, 58 Ind. L.J. 1 (1982); Weintraub, *An Objective Basis for Rejecting Transient Jurisdiction*, 22 Rutgers L.J. 611, 625 (1991) ("Jurisdictional doctrine is in chaos."); *Lakeside Bridge & Steel Co. v. Mountain State Constr. Co.*, 445 U.S. 907 (1980) (White, J., dissenting from denial of certiorari).

56. *Kulko v. Superior Court*, 436 U.S. 84, 92 (1978).

57. 355 U.S. 220 (1957).

58. 355 U.S. at 222-223.

59. 357 U.S. 235 (1958).

60. 357 U.S. at 253 (emphasis added).

and Marshall), attached little importance to notions of territorial sovereignty, and emphasized a general "reasonableness" or "fairness" analysis; other members of the Court (notably Justices O'Connor and Scalia) continued to stress the role of state sovereignty in due process analysis.

Opinions for the Court, written by different Justices, reflected this tension. Thus, in *Hanson v. Denckla,* the Court declared that restrictions on state jurisdiction "are more than a guarantee of immunity from inconvenient or distant litigation. They are a consequence of territorial limitations on the power of the respective States."[61] Yet, in *Shaffer v. Heitner,* the Court characterized *Hanson* as "simply mak[ing] the point that the States are defined by their geographical territory," and went on to emphasize the primacy of reasonableness.[62] Moreover, the Court was increasingly unable to produce majority opinions, with important cases decided by sharply divided pluralities.[63]

(4)   *World-Wide Volkswagen* and Contemporary Due Process Analysis: "Purposeful Contacts" and "Reasonableness."   Contemporary due process analysis has been significantly influenced by the Supreme Court's 1980 decision in *World-Wide Volkswagen Corp. v. Woodson.*[64] There, the Due Process Clause was held to preclude an Oklahoma court's exercise of jurisdiction over a regional automobile distributor. Reaffirming the "purposeful availment" requirement, the Court remarked that " 'foreseeability' alone has never been a sufficient benchmark for personal jurisdiction under the Due Process Clause."[65] The Court went on to articulate a two-prong due process analysis. First, the Court required purposefully created minimum contacts between the defendant and the forum[66] — perhaps most accurately characterized as "purposeful contacts." Second, the Court held that jurisdiction could not be exercised unless it would be "reasonable."[67] Justices Brennan and Marshall dissented, concluding that an exercise of jurisdiction need only be fair and foreseeable.[68]

Five years later, in *Burger King Corp. v. Rudzewicz,*[69] the Court revisited this two-prong analysis. It held that due process permitted Burger King, a franchisor based in Florida, to proceed with a Florida suit against a franchisee based in Michigan. Justice Brennan wrote the Court's opinion in *Burger King,* which reflected the ongoing tension between various members of the Court; Justice Brennan treated "reasonableness" as a predominant aspect of due process analysis, in a discussion reminiscent of his dissenting opinions over the preceding decade.[70]

(5)   The Reemergence of Territorial Sovereignty: *Asahi, Burnham,* and *Nicastro.*   The Supreme Court's journey from *Pennoyer*'s strict doctrine of territorial sovereignty toward Justice Brennan's reasonableness analysis appears to have come to at least a pause — and

61. 357 U.S. at 257.

62. 433 U.S. 186, 204 n.20 (1977). *See also* the Court's conflicting comments about territorial sovereignty in *World-Wide Volkswagen Corp. v. Woodson,* 444 U.S. 286 (1980) and *Insurance Corp. of Ireland v. Compagnie des Bauxites de Guinee,* 456 U.S. 694, 702 n.10 (1982), discussed at *infra* pp. 98-99, 209-214.

63. *E.g., Asahi Metal Indus. v. Superior Court,* 480 U.S. 102 (1987); *Burnham v. Superior Court,* 495 U.S. 604 (1990).

64. 444 U.S. 286 (1980) (excerpted below at *infra* pp. 94-96).

65. 444 U.S. at 295.

66. 444 U.S. at 299.

67. 444 U.S. at 292.

68. 444 U.S. at 299, 313.

69. 471 U.S. 462 (1985).

70. Justice Brennan's opinion in *Burger King* purported to apply the two-prong test set forth in *World-Wide Volkswagen.* In fact, his opinion reflected an increasing focus on "reasonableness" considerations. Thus, it defined "purposeful availment" as requiring relatively few contacts with the forum state. 471 U.S. at 473-475. Justice Brennan also commented that considerations of convenience and "fairness" sometimes serve to establish the reasonableness of jurisdiction upon a "lesser showing of minimum contacts than would otherwise be required." 471 U.S. at 477.

perhaps a more permanent reversal. In *Asahi Metal Indus. Co. v. Superior Court*,[71] a plurality of the Court firmly rejected a pure reasonableness approach to jurisdiction, and emphasized the continuing importance of the "purposeful availment" requirement. Justice O'Connor's plurality opinion held that a foreign component manufacturer lacked "minimum contacts" with California because its "awareness that the stream of commerce may or will sweep the product into the forum State does not convert the mere act of placing the product into the stream into an act purposefully directed toward the forum state."[72] Separately, Justice O'Connor also would have denied jurisdiction on reasonableness grounds under *World-Wide Volkswagen*'s two-prong analysis.[73]

Justice Brennan, joined by three other Justices, concurred.[74] He would have held that, by knowingly placing its products in the stream of commerce, the foreign manufacturer had the requisite minimum contacts with the forum. Nonetheless, he agreed with Justice O'Connor that the exercise of jurisdiction would not comport with fair play and substantial justice. While the Court ultimately resolved the case on "reasonableness" grounds, four Justices affirmed the continuing significance of "purposeful availment" and territorial sovereignty.

Subsequently, *Burnham v. Superior Court* unanimously upheld a California court's assertion of jurisdiction based solely on tag service on the defendant while he was present within California.[75] As in *Asahi*, however, the Court divided sharply on the reasons for this result. Justice Scalia's plurality opinion held that the mere fact of tag service within the forum satisfied the Due Process Clause — and that considerations of reasonableness were irrelevant.[76] "Jurisdiction based on physical presence alone constitutes due process," without regard to questions of "fairness" or "reasonableness."[77]

As in *Asahi*, Justice Brennan, joined by three other Justices, concurred. His opinion acknowledged that due process "generally permits a state court to exercise jurisdiction over a defendant if he is served while voluntarily present in the forum State."[78] But, in contrast to Justice Scalia, Justice Brennan demanded that "*every* assertion of state-court jurisdiction . . . must comport with contemporary notions of due process," which incorporated principles of reasonableness and fairness.[79]

Finally, and most recently, in *Nicastro v. J. McIntyre Machinery, Ltd.*, a majority of the Court held that the Due Process Clause did not permit a New Jersey court to exercise personal jurisdiction over a foreign manufacturer whose only contact to New Jersey was the sale of a metal-shearing machine, through a United States based distributor, to a New Jersey company.[80] As in *Asahi*, the Justices divided badly over the reasoning. Justice Kennedy's plurality opinion, joined by three other Justices, articulated a framework for the constitutional limits on judicial jurisdiction that was based substantially on notions of territorial limits to state sovereignty.[81] Justice Breyer's opinion concurring in the

71. 480 U.S. 102 (1987).
72. 480 U.S. at 112.
73. 480 U.S. at 113-116. Seven Justices joined Justice O'Connor's "reasonableness" analysis. Justice Brennan concurred in the judgment, on the grounds that the exercise of jurisdiction would be unreasonable. He wrote separately, however, to reject Justice O'Connor's purposeful availment analysis: "A defendant who has placed goods in the stream of commerce benefits economically from the retail sale of the final product in the forum state." 480 U.S. at 117.
74. 480 U.S. at 116.
75. 495 U.S. 604 (1990).
76. 495 U.S. at 619.
77. 495 U.S. at 610 & 619.
78. 495 U.S. at 628-629.
79. 495 U.S. at 632.
80. 2011 WL 2518811 (U.S. June 27, 2011).
81. *Id.* at *8-9.

judgment, joined by Justice Alito, was unprepared fully to embrace the plurality's theory but seemed at least equally skeptical of the pure "reasonableness" test articulated by Justice Brennan in *Asahi* and embraced by the New Jersey Supreme Court.[82] Justice Ginsburg, joined by two Justices, substantially adopted Justice Brennan's reasonableness approach to judicial jurisdiction.[83] Thus, while *Nicastro* suggests some shift in the approach of the Court to issues of personal jurisdiction — towards a territorially based doctrine and away from a pure reasonableness analysis — its inability to muster a firm majority ensures continued confusion in this important area of law."

    c. "General" and "Specific" Jurisdiction.   The Supreme Court's due process analysis has increasingly come to distinguish between two types of personal jurisdiction: (1) "general" jurisdiction, and (2) "limited" or "specific" jurisdiction.[84] These categories of jurisdiction differ both in the showings required to establish jurisdiction and the consequences of concluding that jurisdiction may be exercised. They are vital to contemporary due process analysis.

    "General jurisdiction" permits a court to adjudicate *any* claim against a defendant.[85] As discussed below, the Due Process Clause allows the exercise of general jurisdiction over a defendant that has any of several relatively close and enduring relationships with the forum — such as nationality, domicile, or incorporation. Once one of these showings has been made, a U.S. court is constitutionally permitted to assert general jurisdiction over the defendant with respect to *all* claims arising from the defendant's activities, including activities unrelated to the forum state.[86]

    In contrast, "specific jurisdiction" permits only the adjudication of claims that are related to or arise out of a defendant's contacts with the forum state.[87] A defendant whose only contacts with the forum were, for example, the advertising and sale of product X within the forum, might be subject to the jurisdiction of the forum's courts with respect to claims arising out of these sales of product X. But if only specific jurisdiction over the defendant existed, the defendant would not be subject to the personal jurisdiction of the forum's courts with respect to claims based on its other activities outside the forum (such as sales of product Y outside the forum).

    Specific jurisdiction may be exercised when the activities of a defendant that relate to the plaintiff's suit have sufficient purposeful contacts with the forum to satisfy the due process standard articulated in *World-Wide Volkswagen* and later cases.[88] The level of contacts required to sustain specific jurisdiction is substantially less than that required for general jurisdiction.[89]

    d. Procedural Posture of Litigation over Personal Jurisdiction.   Jurisdiction ordinarily is tested during the pleading stage before discovery on the merits.[90] This presents a

---

    82. *Id.* at *10-13.
    83. *Id.* at *14-16.
    84. *See Goodyear Dunlop Tires Operations, S.A. v. Brown,* 2011 WL 2518815 at *3, 6 (U.S. June 27, 2011); *Helicopteros Nacionales de Colombia, SA v. Hall,* 466 U.S. 408, 414 (1984); *Calder v. Jones,* 465 U.S. 783, 786 (1984). The terms were first coined by Professors von Mehren and Trautman in von Mehren & Trautman, *Jurisdiction to Adjudicate: A Suggested Analysis,* 79 Harv. L. Rev. 1121, 1136-1164 (1966).
    85. *See infra* pp. 107-109, 109-137. *Compare* Twitchell, *The Myth of General Jurisdiction,* 101 Harv. L. Rev. 610 (1988).
    86. *See infra* pp. 108-109.
    87. *Goodyear Dunlop Tires Operations, S.A. v. Brown,* 2011 WL 2518815 at *3, 6 (U.S. June 27, 2011); *Helicopteros Nacionales de Colombia, SA v. Hall,* 466 U.S. 408, 414-415 & nn.8 & 10 (1984); von Mehren & Trautman, *Jurisdiction to Adjudicate: A Suggested Analysis,* 79 Harv. L. Rev. 1121, 1144-1164 (1966).
    88. *See infra* pp. 137-175.
    89. *E.g., In re Damodar Bulk Carriers, Ltd.,* 903 F.2d 675 (9th Cir. 1990); *Donatelli v. National Hockey League,* 893 F.2d 459, 462-463 (1st Cir. 1990); *Brand v. Menlove Dodge,* 796 F.2d 1070 (9th Cir. 1986); *infra* pp. 137-139.
    90. For a discussion of the role of discovery in U.S. litigation, *see* Chapter 12.

challenge for plaintiffs and an opportunity for defendants. The challenge for plaintiffs is to amass the facts necessary to demonstrate a defendant's contacts before any discovery has occurred. The opportunity for defendants is to achieve an early dismissal of the case before the plaintiff has pursued discovery (which might strengthen the plaintiff's case on the merits or bolster its claim that the court has jurisdiction over the defendant).

Courts resolve this dilemma in different ways. In some cases, courts have addressed the problem by allowing jurisdictional discovery by the plaintiff or a full-fledged evidentiary hearing on jurisdiction. In other cases, courts have ruled on motions to dismiss without any jurisdictional discovery or hearing. In these cases, courts typically lower the plaintiff's burden of proof by requiring simply a *prima facie* showing of jurisdiction.[91] In so doing, they must decide what distinguishes a *prima facie* showing from an ordinary showing.[92] They also must craft standards for (1) when they will grant jurisdictional discovery and (2) how much jurisdictional discovery they will allow.[93]

2. Selected Materials on the Foundations of Personal Jurisdiction

The following materials introduce the fundamental principles of personal jurisdiction in the United States. *Pennoyer v. Neff*, §47 of the *Restatement (First) Conflict of Laws*, and *World-Wide Volkswagen* document the historical development of due process analysis. Section 421 of the ALI's *Restatement (Third) Foreign Relations Law* purports to state, from a U.S. (not international) perspective, the limitations that contemporary international law imposes upon judicial jurisdiction.

PENNOYER v. NEFF
95 U.S. 714 (1878)

MR. JUSTICE FIELD. [The case involved a dispute over ownership of real estate in Oregon. The case turned upon the validity of the defendant's claim to the property. That claim was based on a sheriff's sale of the property, following execution of a default judgment by an Oregon court against the plaintiff. At the time of the proceedings leading to the default judgment, the plaintiff resided outside of Oregon; he was not personally served and did not appear in the proceedings. Constructive service was purportedly made upon him under Oregon law by publication. At issue in the Supreme Court was the validity of that service, and hence of the default judgment against the plaintiff.]

[An Oregon statutory provision] declares that no natural person is subject to the jurisdiction of a court of the State, "unless he appear in the court, or be found within the State, or be a resident thereof, or have property therein; and, in the last case, only to the extent of such property at the time the jurisdiction attached." Construing this latter provision to mean, that, in an action for money or damages where a defendant does not appear in the court, and is not found within the State, and is not a resident thereof, but has property therein, the jurisdiction of the court extends only over such property, the

---

91. *E.g., Nuovo Pignone, SpA v. STORMAN ASIA M/V,* 310 F.3d 374, 378 (5th Cir. 2002); *Glencore Grain Rotterdam BV v. Shivnath Rai Harnarain Co.,* 284 F.3d 1114, 1119 (9th Cir. 2002).

92. *See S.E.C. v. Carillo,* 115 F.3d 1540, 1542 (11th Cir. 1997) (describing standard for *prima facie* case); *AT&T Co. v. Compagnie Bruxelles Lambert,* 94 F.3d 586, 588 (9th Cir. 1996) (same).

93. *E.g., Base Metal Trading, Ltd. v. OJSC Novokuznetsky Aluminum Factory,* 283 F.3d 208, 216 n.3 (4th Cir. 2002) (affirming district court order that denied jurisdictional discovery); *United States v. Swiss American Bank, Ltd.,* 274 F.3d 610, 625-627 (1st Cir. 2002) (prerequisites to jurisdictional discovery include that plaintiff has colorable claim and has been reasonably diligent in pursuing its rights); *Jazini v. Nissan Motor Co., Ltd.,* 148 F.3d 181 (2d Cir. 1998) (describing standards for jurisdictional discovery).

declaration expresses a principle of general, if not universal, law. The authority of every tribunal is necessarily restricted by the territorial limits of the State in which it is established. Any attempt to exercise authority beyond those limits would be deemed in every other forum, as has been said by this court, in illegitimate assumption of power, and be resisted as mere abuse. *D'Arcy v. Ketchum,* 11 How. 165. . . .

[It] is insisted upon here, that the [default] judgment in the State court against the plaintiff was void for want of personal service of process on him, or of his appearance in the action in which it was rendered. . . . If these positions are sound, the ruling of the Circuit Court as to the invalidity of that judgment must be sustained. . . . And that they are sound would seem to follow from two well-established principles of public law respecting the jurisdiction of an independent State over persons and property. The several States of the Union are not, it is true, in every respect independent, many of the right and powers which originally belonged to them being now vested in the government created by the Constitution. But, except as restrained and limited by that instrument, they possess and exercise the authority of independent States, and the principles of public law to which we have referred are applicable to them. One of these principles is, that every State possesses exclusive jurisdiction and sovereignty over persons and property within its territory. As a consequence, every State has the power to determine for itself the civil status and capacities of its inhabitants; to prescribe the subjects upon which they may contract, the forms and solemnities with which their contracts shall be executed, the rights and obligations arising from them, and the mode in which their validity shall be determined and their obligations enforced; and also [to] regulate the manner and conditions upon which property situated within such territory, both personal and real, may be acquired, enjoyed, and transferred. The other principle of public law referred to follows from the one mentioned; that is, that no State can exercise direct jurisdiction and authority over persons or property without its territory. [Joseph] Story, *Conflict of Laws,* c. 2; [Henry] Wheaton, *International Law,* pt. 2, c. 2. The several States are of equal dignity and authority, and the independence of one implies the exclusion of power from all others. And so it is laid down by jurists, as an elementary principle, that the laws of one State have no operation outside of its territory, except so far as is allowed by comity; and that no tribunal established by it can extend its process beyond that territory so as to subject either persons or property to its decisions. "Any exertion of authority of this sort beyond this limit," says Story, "is a mere nullity, and incapable of binding such persons or property in any other tribunals." [Joseph] Story, *Conflict of Laws,* §539.

But as contracts made in one State may be enforceable only in another State, and property may be held by non-residents, the exercise of the jurisdiction which every State is admitted to possess over persons and property within its own territory will often affect persons and property without it. To any influence exerted in this way by a State affecting persons resident or property situated elsewhere, no objection can be justly taken; whilst any direct exertion of authority upon them, in an attempt to give ex-territorial operation to its laws, or to enforce an ex-territorial jurisdiction by its tribunals, would be deemed an encroachment upon the independence of the State in which the persons are domiciled or the property is situated, and be resisted as usurpation.

Thus the State, through its tribunals, may compel persons domiciled within its limits to execute, in pursuance of their contracts respecting property elsewhere situated, instruments in such form and with such solemnities as to transfer the title, so far as such formalities can be complied with; and the exercise of this jurisdiction in no manner interferes with the supreme control over the property by the State within which it is situated. So the State, through its tribunals, may subject property situated within its limits owned by non-residents to the payment of the demand of its own citizens against them. . . .

These views are not new. They have been frequently expressed, with more or less distinctness, in opinions of eminent judges. . . . Thus, in *Picquet v. Swan*, 5 Mass. 35, Mr. Justice Story said:

> Where a party is within a territory, he may justly be subjected to its process, and bound personally by the judgment pronounced on such process against him. Where he is not within such territory, and is not personally subject to its laws, if, on account of his supposed or actual property being within the territory, process by the local laws may, by attachment, go to compel his appearance, and for his default to appear judgment may be pronounced against him, such a judgment must, upon general principles, be deemed only to bind him to the extent of such property, and cannot have the effect of a conclusive judgment in personam, for the plain reason, that, except so far as the property is concerned, it is a judgment coram non judice. . . .

[This] is the only doctrine consistent with proper protection to citizens of other States. If, without personal service, judgments in personam, obtained ex parte against non-residents and absent parties, upon mere publication of process, which, in the great majority of cases, would never be seen by the parties interested, could be upheld and enforced, they would be the constant instruments of fraud and oppression. Judgments for all sorts of claims upon contracts and for torts, real or pretended, would be thus obtained . . . when the evidence of the transactions upon which they were founded, if they ever had any existence, had perished. . . . [Although substituted service may sometimes be effective,] where the entire object of the action is to determine the personal rights and obligations of the defendants, that is, where the suit is merely in personam, constructive service in this form upon a non-resident is ineffectual for any purpose. Process from the tribunals of one State cannot run into another State, and summon parties there domiciled to leave its territory and respond to proceedings against them. . . .

Since the adoption of the Fourteenth Amendment to the Federal Constitution, the validity of such judgments may be directly questioned, and their enforcement in the State resisted, on the ground that proceedings in a court of justice to determine the personal rights and obligations of parties over whom that court has no jurisdiction do not constitute due process of law. . . . [Due process] mean[s] a course of legal proceedings according to those rules and principles which have been established in our systems of jurisprudence for the protection and enforcement of private rights. To give such proceedings any validity, there must be a tribunal competent by its constitution — that is, by the law of its creation — to pass upon the subject-matter of the suit; and, if that involves merely a determination of the personal liability of the defendant, he must be brought within its jurisdiction by service of process within the State, or his voluntary appearance. . . .

[W]e do not mean to assert . . . that a State may not authorize proceedings to determine the status of one of its citizens towards a non-resident, which would be binding within the State, though made without service of process or personal notice to the non-resident. The jurisdiction which every State possesses to determine the civil status and capacities of all its inhabitants involves authority to prescribe the conditions on which proceedings affecting them may be commenced and carried on within its territory. . . . Neither do we mean to assert that a State may not require a non-resident entering into a partnership or association within its limits, or making contracts enforceable there, to appoint an agent or representative in the State to receive service of process and notice in legal proceedings instituted with respect to such partnership, association, or contracts . . . and provide, upon their failure, to make such appointment . . . that service may be made upon a public officer designated for that purpose, or in some other prescribed way, and that judgments rendered upon such service may not be binding upon the non-residents both within and without the State. . . .

RESTATEMENT (FIRST) CONFLICT OF LAWS (1934)
§47 [excerpted in Appendix X]

WORLD-WIDE VOLKSWAGEN CORP. v. WOODSON
444 U.S. 286 (1980)

JUSTICE WHITE. Respondents Harry and Kay Robinson purchased a new Audi automobile from petitioner Seaway Volkswagen, Inc. ("Seaway"), in Massena, N.Y., in 1976. The following year the Robinson family, who resided in New York, left that State for a new home in Arizona. As they passed through the State of Oklahoma, another car struck their Audi in the rear, causing a fire which severely burned Kay Robinson and her two children. The Robinsons subsequently brought a products-liability action in Oklahoma District Court, claiming that their injuries resulted from defective design of the Audi's gas tank. They joined as defendants the automobile's . . . regional distributor, petitioner World-Wide Corp. ("World-Wide"); and its retail dealer, petitioner Seaway. . . . World-Wide is incorporated and has its business office in New York. It distributes vehicles, parts, and accessories to retail dealers in New York, New Jersey, and Connecticut. Seaway, one of these retail dealers, is incorporated and has its place of business in New York. Insofar as the record reveals, Seaway and World-Wide are fully independent corporations whose relations with each other and with [the automobile's manufacturers] are contractual only. Respondents adduced no evidence that either World-Wide or Seaway does any business in Oklahoma, ships or sells any products to or in that State, has an agent to receive process there, or purchases advertisements in any media calculated to reach Oklahoma. . . . Indeed there was no showing that any automobile sold by World-Wide or Seaway has ever entered Oklahoma with the single exception of the vehicle involved in the present case. The Supreme Court of Oklahoma rejected challenges by World-Wide and Seaway to the personal jurisdiction of the Oklahoma courts.

As has long been settled, and as we reaffirm today, a state court may exercise personal jurisdiction over a nonresident defendant only so long as there exist "minimum contacts" between the defendant and the forum State. The concept of minimum contacts, in turn, can be seen to perform two related, but distinguishable, functions. It protects the defendant against the burdens of litigating in a distant or inconvenient forum. And it acts to ensure that the States, through their Courts, do not reach out beyond the limits imposed on them by their status as coequal sovereigns in a federal system.

The protection against inconvenient litigation is typically described in terms of "reasonableness" or "fairness." We have said that the defendant's contacts with the forum State must be such that maintenance of the suit "does not offend 'traditional notions of fair play and substantial justice.'" . . . Implicit in this emphasis on reasonableness is the understanding that the burden on the defendant, while always a primary concern, will in an appropriate case be considered in light of other relevant factors, including the forum State's interest in adjudicating the dispute; the plaintiff's interest in obtaining convenient and effective relief, at least when that interest is not adequately protected by the plaintiff's power to choose the forum; the interstate judicial system's interest in obtaining the most efficient resolution of controversies; and the shared interest of the several States in furthering fundamental substantive social policies.

The limits imposed on state jurisdiction by the Due Process Clause, in its role as a guarantor against inconvenient litigation, have been substantially relaxed over the years. . . . Nevertheless, we have never accepted the proposition that state lines are irrelevant for jurisdictional purposes, nor could we, and remain faithful to the principles of interstate federalism embodied in the Constitution. The economic interdependence of the States was foreseen and desired by the Framers. In the Commerce Clause, they provided that the Nation was to be a common market, a "free trade unit" in which the States are debarred from acting as separable economic entities. But the Framers also intended that the States retain many essential attributes of sovereignty, including, in particular, the sovereign power to try causes in their courts. The sovereignty of each State, in turn, implied a limitation on the sovereignty of all of its sister States — a limitation express or implicit in both the original scheme of the Constitution and the Fourteenth Amendment.

Hence, even while abandoning the shibboleth that "[t]he authority of every tribunal is necessarily restricted by the territorial limits of the State in which it is established," *Pennoyer v. Neff, supra,* we emphasized that the reasonableness of asserting jurisdiction over the defendant must be assessed "in the context of our federal system of government," *International Shoe, supra,* and stressed that the Due Process Clause ensures not only fairness, but also the "orderly administration of the laws." . . . Thus, the Due Process Clause "does not contemplate that a state may make binding a judgment *in personam* against an individual or corporate defendant with which the state has no contacts, ties, or relations." Even if the defendant would suffer minimal or no inconvenience from being forced to litigate before the tribunals of another State; even if the forum State has a strong interest in applying its law to the controversy; even if the forum State is the most convenient location for litigation, the Due Process Clause, acting as an instrument of interstate federalism, may sometimes act to divest the State of its power to render a valid judgment.

Applying these principles to the case at hand, we find . . . a total absence of those affiliating circumstances that are a necessary predicate to any exercise of state-court jurisdiction. Petitioners carry on no activity whatsoever in Oklahoma. They close no sales and perform no services there. They avail themselves of none of the privileges and benefits of Oklahoma law. They solicit no business there either through salespersons or through advertising reasonably calculated to reach the State. Nor does the record show that they regularly sell cars at wholesale or retail to Oklahoma customers or residents or that they indirectly, through others, serve or seek to serve the Oklahoma market. In short, respondents seek to base jurisdiction on one, isolated occurrence and whatever inferences can be drawn therefrom: the fortuitous circumstance that a single Audi automobile, sold in New York to New York residents, happened to suffer an accident while passing through Oklahoma.

It is argued, however, that because an automobile is mobile by its very design and purpose it was "foreseeable" that the Robinsons' Audi would cause injury in Oklahoma. Yet "foreseeability" alone has never been a sufficient benchmark for personal jurisdiction under the Due Process Clause. . . . If foreseeability were the criterion, . . . [e]very seller of chattels would in effect appoint the chattel his agent for service of process. His amenability to suit would travel with the chattel. . . .

This is not to say, of course, that foreseeability is wholly irrelevant. But the foreseeability that is critical to due process analysis is not the mere likelihood that a product will find its way into the forum State. Rather, it is that the defendant's conduct and connection with the forum State are such that he should reasonably anticipate being haled into court there. The Due Process Clause, by ensuring the "orderly administration of the laws," *International Shoe,* gives a degree of predictability to the legal system that allows potential defendants to structure their primary conduct with some minimum assurance as to where that conduct will and will not render them liable to suit.

When a corporation "purposefully avails itself of the privilege of conducting activities within the forum State," *Hanson v. Denckla,* it has clear notice that it is subject to suit there, and can act to alleviate the risk of burdensome litigation by procuring insurance, passing the expected costs on to customers, or, if the risks are too great, severing its connection with the State. Hence if the sale of a product of a manufacturer or distributor such as Audi or Volkswagen is not simply an isolated occurrence, but arises from the efforts of the manufacturer or distributor to serve, directly or indirectly, the market for its product in other States, it is not unreasonable to subject it to suit in one of those States if its allegedly defective merchandise has there been the source of injury to its owner or to others. The forum State does not exceed its power under the Due Process Clause if it asserts personal jurisdiction over a corporation that delivers its products into the stream of commerce with the expectation that they will be purchased by consumers in the forum State. *Cf. Gray v. American Radiator & Standard Sanitary Corp.,* 176 N.E.2d 761 (1961).

But there is no such or similar basis for Oklahoma jurisdiction over World-Wide or Seaway in this case. Seaway's sales are made in Massena, N.Y. World-Wide's market, although substantially larger, is limited to dealers in New York, New Jersey, and Connect-icut. There is no evidence of record that any automobiles distributed by World-Wide are sold to retail customers outside this tristate area. It is foreseeable that the purchasers of automobiles sold by World-Wide and Seaway may take them to Oklahoma. But the mere "unilateral activity of those who claim some relationship with a nonresident defendant cannot satisfy the requirement of contact with the forum State." Because we find that petitioners have no "contacts, ties, or relations" with the State of Oklahoma, *International Shoe Co.,* the judgment of the Supreme Court of Oklahoma is reversed.

RESTATEMENT (THIRD) FOREIGN RELATIONS LAW OF THE UNITED STATES (1987)

§421 *[excerpted in Appendix AA]*

FRENCH CIVIL CODE ARTICLE 14

14. An alien, even not residing in France, may be summoned before the French courts for the fulfilment of obligations contracted by him in France toward a French person; he may be brought before the French courts for obligations contracted by him in a foreign country toward French persons.

EUROPEAN COUNCIL REGULATION 44/2001

[excerpted in Appendix E]

Notes on **Pennoyer, World-Wide Volkswagen,** *and Legislative Materials*

1. *Lack of textual basis for territorial limits on judicial jurisdiction.* The Due Process Clause of the Fourteenth Amendment provides: "nor shall any State deprive any person of life, liberty, or property, without due process of law." That provision does not, as *Pennoyer* appeared to acknowledge, contain express limitations on the judicial jurisdiction of state courts. *See* Redish, *Due Process, Federalism, and Personal Jurisdiction: A Theoretical Evaluation,* 75 Nw. U. L. Rev. 1112, 1136-1137 (1981). How does *Pennoyer* overcome this difficulty?

2. *Role of international law in* **Pennoyer**'s *due process analysis.* In articulating due process limits on jurisdiction, *Pennoyer* invoked principles of international "public law" applicable to independent nation states: "The several States of the Union possess and exercise the authority of independent States, and the principles of public law to which we have

referred are applicable to them." The Court also relied on earlier decisions invoking "well-established rules of international law." *See D'Arcy v. Ketchum*, 52 U.S. 165 (1850); *Rose v. Himely*, 8 U.S. 241 (1808). What is the relevance of international law to the interpretation of the Due Process Clause, particularly as applied in a purely domestic case? Was *Pennoyer* correct in analogizing Oregon-California relations to United States–France relations? Note in particular that Oregon and California are bound by the Full Faith and Credit Clause, and subject to the legislative powers of Congress, while the United States and France are not.

3. *Nineteenth-century territorial limits on judicial jurisdiction.* When they looked to international law, *Pennoyer, D'Arcy,* and similar nineteenth-century decisions perceived what the Court characterized as a universally accepted principle of territorial sovereignty. Under these rules, an attempt "to enforce an ex-territorial jurisdiction by its tribunals . . . would be deemed an encroachment upon the independence of the State in which the persons are domiciled or the property is situated, and be resisted as usurpation."

Territorial sovereignty was central to defining national jurisdiction in nineteenth-century American understandings of international law. It defined U.S. judicial jurisdiction for much of the next century. *See supra* pp. 83-87 and *infra* pp. 98-99. There was also broad consensus among American authorities that international law imposed territorial limits on legislative jurisdiction, *see infra* pp. 591-594, while the territoriality doctrine dominated nineteenth-century American choice of law thinking, *see infra* pp. 723-731, 777-782. Similarly, territorial sovereignty was central to the treatment of sovereign immunity, the act of state doctrine, and recognition of foreign judgments. *See infra* pp. 231-234, 797-801, 832-838 and 1081-1082.

4. *Rationale for territorial limits on judicial jurisdiction.* What was the rationale for nineteenth-century territorial limits on jurisdiction? *Pennoyer* relied on principles of sovereign equality and territorial sovereignty, derived from Joseph Story's *Commentaries on the Conflict of Laws.* Consider:

> The several States are of equal dignity and authority, and the independence of one implies the exclusion of power from all others. And so it is laid down by jurists, as an elementary principle, that the laws of one State have no operation outside of its own territory, except so far as it is allowed by comity; and that no tribunal established by it can extend its process beyond that territory so as to subject either persons or property to its decisions. 95 U.S. at 722.

Why does one state's assertion of jurisdiction over a person in the territory of another state infringe upon the "sovereignty" of the second state? What if jurisdiction is sought to be exercised over a national of the first state? In respect of actions occurring solely within the first state?

What interests were served by *Pennoyer*'s territorial limits on judicial jurisdiction? Were these limits intended only to protect state sovereignty? Or did they also protect individuals from unforeseeable, unreasonable assertions of jurisdiction? Is there any support in *Pennoyer* for the latter purpose?

5. *Early erosion of territorial limits on judicial jurisdiction.* There were difficulties in maintaining a conceptually pure territoriality doctrine even in *Pennoyer*. Note the Court's efforts to explain how a court in one state may "indirectly" affect property located in another state, by means of an *in personam* judgment against the owner of the property. Note also, in the final paragraph of the Court's opinion, that the territoriality doctrine was thought to permit jurisdiction where a party consented, or could be deemed to have consented, to a state's adjudication of its rights. *See supra* pp. 93-94. In the decades following *Pennoyer*, this caveat provided the basis for increasingly broad assertions of jurisdiction over nonresident defendants, on the theory that their in-state conduct had constituted implied consent to jurisdiction. Kurland, *The Supreme Court, the Due Process and the In Personam Jurisdiction of State Courts — From* Pennoyer *to* Denckla: *A Review,* 25 U. Chi. L. Rev. 569, 577-586 (1958). Finally, as discussed below, it was generally accepted that international law permitted a state to exercise jurisdiction over absent nationals. *See infra* pp. 109-113.

6. *Due process analysis in* **World-Wide Volkswagen** *and* **Pennoyer.** Is the analysis in *World-Wide Volkswagen* more clearly rooted in the text of the Due Process Clause (or other provisions of the Constitution) than that in *Pennoyer?* What is the rationale for *World-Wide Volkswagen* — international law, federalism, protection against unfairness, or something else?

(a) Importance of territorial sovereignty. Does *World-Wide Volkswagen* entirely abandon *Pennoyer*'s territorial approach to issues of jurisdiction? What is the continuing role of territoriality sovereignty after *World-Wide Volkswagen?*

(b) Importance of international law and federalism. What are the roles of international law and federalism principles in *Pennoyer* and *World-Wide Volkswagen?* Note Justice White's discussion of principles of federalism in *World-Wide Volkswagen,* including his observation that: "The sovereignty of each State, in turn, implied a limitation on the sovereignty of all its sister States — a limitation express or implicit in both the original scheme of the Constitution and the Fourteenth Amendment." Is it appropriate for the Court to elevate a limitation "implicit" in the "original scheme of the Constitution" into a limitation on state court jurisdiction? Where should one look for guidance on the content of federalism principles? Is there anywhere else, except for international law, that can be consulted? What about the manner in which other federal states — like Canada, Germany, Russia, and India — deal with federalism issues?

(c) Relative significance of "territorial sovereignty" and "reasonableness." Contemporary due process analysis has seen an ongoing debate over the relative significance of "territorial sovereignty" and "reasonableness." *See supra* pp. 86-91. *World-Wide Volkswagen* emphatically concluded that territoriality remained a critical element of due process analysis. Other Supreme Court decisions, like *Burger King Corp. v. Rudzewicz,* 471 U.S. 462 (1985), accorded greater weight to considerations of reasonableness. *See supra* p. 88. What should the respective roles of territoriality and reasonableness be?

(d) Role of territorial sovereignty in Compagnie des Bauxites. Consider whether *World-Wide Volkswagen*'s reliance on territorial sovereignty retains vitality after the following remarks — also by Justice White, the author of *World-Wide Volkswagen* — in *Insurance Corp. v. Compagnie des Bauxites de Guinee,* 456 U.S. 694, 702 n.10 (1982):

> It is true that we have stated that the requirement of personal jurisdiction, as applied to state courts, reflects an element of federalism and the character of state sovereignty vis-à-vis other States. . . . The restriction on sovereign power described in *World-Wide Volkswagen Corp.,* however, must be seen as ultimately a function of the individual liberty interest preserved by the Due Process Clause. The clause is the only source of the personal jurisdiction requirement and the clause itself makes no mention of federalism concerns. Furthermore, if the federalism concept operated as an independent restriction on the sovereign power of the court, it would not be possible to waive the personal jurisdiction requirement: Individual actions cannot change the powers of sovereignty, although the individual can subject himself to powers from which he may otherwise be protected.

Justice Powell, concurring in the same case, said:

> Before today, of course, our cases had linked minimum contacts and fair play as *jointly* defining the "sovereign" limits on state assertions of personal jurisdiction over unconsenting

defendants. . . . The court appears to abandon the rationale of these cases in a footnote. . . . For the first time it defines personal jurisdiction *solely by reference to abstract notions of fair play. Id.* at 714 (emphasis added).

Do the increasing ease of communication and transportation, the volume of international commerce, and expanding notions of jurisdiction under international law undermine the importance of territorial sovereignty? *See Nicastro v. J. McIntyre Machinery, Ltd.*, 2011 WL 2518811at *17 (U.S. June 27, 2011) (Ginsburg, J., dissenting) ("[T]he constitutional limits on a state court's adjudicatory authority derive from considerations of due process, not state sovereignty."). Do these factors argue that territorial sovereignty is *more,* not *less,* important? To provide predictability and order in a more fluid international environment?

    7. *Role of territorial sovereignty in international cases.* Putting aside interstate cases, what role should territorial sovereignty play in international cases? Unlike assertions of jurisdiction over U.S. citizens resident in other states, a state court's assertion of jurisdiction over a foreign defendant, who resides and conducts his affairs abroad, generally does not infringe on the sovereignty of other *U.S.* states. Assertions of jurisdiction over foreign defendants can, however, implicate the sovereignty of *foreign nations. See Asahi Metal Industry Co. v. Superior Court,* 480 U.S. 102, 115 (1987) (due process requires a court to "consider the procedural and substantive policies of other nations whose interests are affected by the assertion of jurisdiction by the [U.S.] court").

    What role should the sovereignty of foreign nations play in due process analysis? Is foreign sovereignty more or less important, for due process purposes, than the sovereignty of a sister state? Put more concretely, should the Court in *World-Wide Volkswagen* have treated the jurisdiction of an Oklahoma court over a New York automobile distributor differently than its jurisdiction over a Mexican automobile distributor?

    8. *Restatement §421 and international law limits on judicial jurisdiction.* Section 421 of the *Third Restatement* purports to state principles of international law from a U.S. perspective. Its authors characterize these as "international rules and guidelines for the exercise of jurisdiction to adjudicate in cases having international implications, applicable to courts both in the United States and in other states." *Restatement (Third) Foreign Relations Law* 305 (1987). As discussed below, authorities from other states have different views about international law limits on jurisdiction. *See infra* pp. 100-101.

    (a) Section 421's "reasonableness requirement." The *Restatement* adopts what its authors describe as a "reasonableness" principle, set forth in §421(1). Section 421(2) particularizes this "reasonableness" requirement, identifying circumstances in which jurisdiction can ordinarily be exercised. Compare these jurisdictional bases with those in Council Regulation No. 44/2001. What are the differences? Similarities? Which is preferable?

    (b) Sources of international law limits on jurisdiction. As discussed above, international law limits on judicial jurisdiction can arise from several sources: (a) international agreements binding on the United States; (b) customary international law; and (c) general principles of law. *See supra* p. 15.

    The United States is party to virtually no treaties dealing even indirectly with judicial jurisdiction. It is a party to certain specialized treaty regimes governing particular industries, such as air transport; some such treaties designate permissible forums for particular claims, thereby affecting judicial jurisdiction. These jurisdictional rules are, however, highly specialized. *See, e.g.,* Convention for the Unification of Certain Rules for International Carriage by Air, S. Treaty Doc. 106-45 (May 28, 1999); Convention for the Unification of Certain Rules Relating to International Transportation by Air (Warsaw Convention), Art. 28, 49 Stat. 3000, T.S. No. 876.

In contrast, other countries have entered into a variety of international agreements dealing with the judicial jurisdiction. These arrangements are either bilateral or regional. The leading examples of regional international agreements dealing with judicial jurisdiction are the Brussels and Lugano Conventions, the former having been replaced in large part by EU Council Regulation 44/2001, discussed below. *See infra* pp. 105-106, 1092. A leading historic example of a bilateral jurisdiction agreement is the Franco-Swiss Convention on Jurisdiction and Execution of Judgments of June 15, 1809; it provides that nationals of each signatory state must be sued in their own country (i.e., a French plaintiff must sue a Swiss defendant in Switzerland, not France).

(c) Evidence of customary international law limits on judicial jurisdiction. Customary international law also arguably limits the jurisdiction of national courts. In defining customary international law, "substantial weight is accorded to (a) judgments and opinions of international judicial and arbitral tribunals; (b) judgments and opinions of national judicial tribunals; (c) the writings of scholars; (d) pronouncements by states that undertake to state a rule of international law, when such pronouncements are not seriously challenged by other states." *Restatement (Third) Foreign Relations Law* §103(2) (1987). *See also Sosa v. Alvarez-Machain,* 542 U.S. 692, 734 (2004), citing *The Paquete Habana,* 175 U.S. at 700 for sources of international law.

Recall the treatment of international law in nineteenth-century U.S. Supreme Court decisions (like *Pennoyer*) and the diplomatic protests made by the United States during the nineteenth and early twentieth centuries. *See supra* pp. 83-86. During the twentieth century, however, there were few judicial decisions or diplomatic protests concerning international law limits on judicial jurisdiction. *See Restatement (Third) Foreign Relations Law* Intro. Note Chap. 2, at 304 (1987) ("The jurisdiction of courts in relation to private controversies was not an important concern of public international law. . . ."). For some exceptions, *see* Note from the United States Department of State to Embassy of Greece, dated June 18, 1973, *reprinted in* Department of State, *Digest of United States Practice in International Law* 197-198 (1973); G. Hackworth, II *Digest of International Law* 172-173 (1941) (U.S. protest that Panama's exercise of judicial jurisdiction over Canal Zone residents violates U.S. sovereignty).

(d) Does international law limit judicial jurisdiction? The *Third Restatement*'s claim that contemporary international law limits judicial jurisdiction is not universally accepted. Some authors have suggested that no mandatory limits are sufficiently widely accepted to achieve the status of international law, particularly as to litigation between private parties. Consider the following conclusions, by an eminent English commentator:

> [W]hen one examines the practice of States . . . one finds that States claim jurisdiction over all sorts of cases and parties having no real connection with them and that this practice has seldom if ever given rise to diplomatic protests. . . . The acid test of the limits of jurisdiction in international law is the presence or absence of diplomatic protests. Protests in civil cases are not as frequent or as well known as they are in criminal cases, but they do exist. However, when they are examined closely it will be seen that some of them are isolated protests against practices which are so general that the law must be taken to follow the general practice rather than the isolated protest. . . . In practice the assumption of jurisdiction by a State does not seem to be subject to any requirement that the defendant or the facts of the case need have any connection with that State; and this practice seems to have met with acquiescence by other States. . . . It is hard to resist the conclusion that . . . customary international law imposes no limits on the jurisdiction of municipal courts in civil trials. Akehurst, *Jurisdiction in International Law,* 46 Brit. Y.B. Int'l L. 145, 174-77, 212-14, 226-27 (1972-73).

Is this persuasive? When long-established jurisdictional limits rest on fundamental principles of national sovereignty, is detailed evidence of state practice necessary? Note also that states generally refuse to enforce foreign judgments that were based upon assertions of judicial jurisdiction in violation of the enforcing state's views of international law. *See infra* pp. 1120-1132. Is this practice not more relevant than the number of diplomatic protests? The weight of authority agrees with the *Third Restatement* in supporting the existence of some international law limits on national assertions of judicial jurisdiction. *E.g.,* Born, *Reflections on Judicial Jurisdiction in International Cases,* 17 Ga. J. Int'l & Comp. L. 1, 18-20 (1987); Mann, *The Doctrine of Jurisdiction in International Law,* 111 Recueil des Cours 1, 73-81 (1964).

(e)   Why should international law limit judicial jurisdiction? Articulate why it is that international law would limit judicial jurisdiction. How does a state's exercise of judicial jurisdiction over an individual infringe the "sovereignty" of foreign states? Is it because jurisdiction is asserted over the national of a foreign state, because jurisdiction is asserted over an individual in respect of its conduct in a foreign state's territory, or for some other reason? Would international law prevent the foreign individual from voluntarily consenting to another state's jurisdiction? Does international law only protect the sovereignty of states, or does it also concern itself with fairness to individuals?

(f)   Does international law impose "reasonableness" limits on judicial jurisdiction? Assuming that international law does limit assertions of judicial jurisdiction, what limits does it impose? Consider §421's "reasonableness" requirement. Does "reasonableness" provide meaningful restraint on assertions of jurisdiction? In a world of 160 independent states, with vastly differing legal, economic, and political traditions, what does "reasonableness" mean? Does it mean anything at all?

9. *Evolution of international law from territoriality to reasonableness.* Contrast U.S. views during the nineteenth century, when the territoriality doctrine was held to limit jurisdiction, with §421's reasonableness requirement. What explains the transformation of U.S. views regarding international law limits on judicial jurisdiction?

Consider the quotation from *McGee v. International Life Insurance Co.,* excerpted at *supra* p. 87. Are technological advances a sufficient explanation for declining importance of territorial sovereignty?

Consider the possible change in U.S. interests internationally between 1850 and 1950. As discussed above, nineteenth-century American diplomats relied on territorial jurisdictional limits against more powerful, expansive European states. After WWII, however, the United States frequently sought to extend U.S. regulatory regimes to international activities, often requiring more expansive assertions of judicial jurisdiction than were historically permitted. Compare the evolution of international law in the context of legislative jurisdiction, *see infra* pp. 591-598.

10. World-Wide Volkswagen — *"purposeful availment" and "reasonableness."* Compare the two-prong approach to judicial jurisdiction adopted in *World-Wide Volkswagen* with the generalized reasonableness requirement adopted in §421 of the *Restatement.* Compare it also with *Pennoyer*'s focus on territorial sovereignty. Which approach is wiser?

11. World-Wide Volkswagen's *"purposeful availment" requirement.* *World-Wide Volkswagen*'s purposeful availment test is unhelpfully circular: the defendant must have purposefully availed himself of the forum's protections in a manner "such that he should reasonably anticipate being haled into Court there." But expectations about jurisdiction will inevitably be determined in significant part by the jurisdictional standards that are announced by the courts. Despite this ambiguity, several principles can be deduced under the "purposeful availment" test.

(a)   No requirement that defendant have been physically present in forum. In *Pennoyer*, jurisdiction required service of process on the defendant within the forum's territory. In contrast, contemporary due process analysis permits jurisdiction even if the defendant has never been on the forum's territory — either at the time of service or before:

> Although territorial presence frequently will enhance a potential defendant's affiliation with a State and reinforce the reasonable foreseeability of suit there, it is an inescapable fact of modern commercial life that a substantial amount of business is transacted solely by mail and wire communication across state lines, [as well as wireless and email communication more recently,] thus obviating the need for physical presence within a State in which business is conducted. *Burger King Corp. v. Rudzewicz*, 471 U.S. 462, 476 (1985).

(b)   Acts outside the forum causing "effects" within the forum. In some circumstances, the Due Process Clause will permit jurisdiction over a foreign defendant based on the effects its conduct has had within the forum. One influential formulation of the "effects" doctrine for purposes of judicial jurisdiction is §37 of the *Restatement (Second) Conflict of Laws* (1971):

> A state has power to exercise judicial jurisdiction over an individual who causes effects in the state by an act done elsewhere with respect to any cause of action arising from these effects unless the nature of the effects and of the individual's relationship to the state make the exercise of such jurisdiction unreasonable.

Compare §37 with §421(2)(j) of the *Third Restatement* and Article 5(3) of Regulation 44/2001. Do either §37 or §421(2)(j) permit jurisdiction based simply on effects, without regard to the actor's objective expectations? Why not?

(c)   "Stream of commerce" doctrine. *World-Wide Volkswagen* appeared to endorse, albeit in dicta, the so-called "stream of commerce" doctrine: "The forum State does not exceed its power under the Due Process Clause if it asserts personal jurisdiction over a corporation that delivers its products into the stream of commerce with the expectation that they will be purchased by consumers in the forum State." 444 U.S. at 298.

Suppose D, a Brazilian manufacturer, sells its products to an unrelated Brazilian distribution company, with title and risk of loss passing in Brazil. The products are then distributed to wholesalers and retailers in a large number of countries (and U.S. states), who in turn sell about 100,000 of D's products each year in Iowa. D is aware that its products are sold in many countries, including the United States, but has no specific knowledge that its products are sold in Iowa; D could obtain this information with minimal effort. D encourages the Brazilian distribution company to maximize sales of its products, particularly in the United States. D has no other contacts with the United States. After *World-Wide Volkswagen*, could an injured customer in Iowa obtain personal jurisdiction over D in Iowa's courts? What result if D does know specifically of the sales in Iowa? In the United States? Suppose D encourages distribution there, for example, by requiring distributors to perform market research or advertising. What result? For more detailed analysis of the stream of commerce doctrine, see *infra* at 102-103, 138-162.

(d)   Mere foreseeability of effects in forum does not constitute minimum contacts. As *World-Wide Volkswagen* illustrates, the mere foreseeability that the defendant's products will have effects in the forum does not establish minimum contacts: " 'foreseeability' alone has never been a sufficient benchmark for personal jurisdiction under the Due Process Clause." Rather, the defendant must "purposefully" engage in conduct that creates minimum contacts with the forum.

What more than foreseeability that one's products or acts will have some consequence within the forum should the "purposeful availment" standard require? *See infra* pp. 137-162.

What purposes are served by requiring "purposeful availment"? Does this safeguard foreign states' territorial sovereignty?

12. World-Wide Volkswagen's "reasonableness" requirement. The second prong of *World-Wide Volkswagen's* analysis requires that any assertion of personal jurisdiction be "reasonable." Deciding whether an assertion of jurisdiction is "reasonable" requires considering a number of factors, set forth above at *supra* pp. 94-95. Compare the role of "reasonableness" in *World-Wide Volkswagen* with that in §421. Which approach is preferable?

13. *Relationship between jurisdiction and enforcement of judgments.* Jurisdictional disputes usually arise at the *outset* of litigation, as in *World-Wide Volkswagen,* when one party resists a court's purported assertion of jurisdiction. In addition, however, jurisdiction can also be relevant at the *end* of litigation — as in *Pennoyer.* Even if a court renders a judgment in the plaintiff's favor, the defendant may continue to resist. If the defendant has assets within the forum, then it will usually be fairly easy for the plaintiff to enforce the judgment against them. But if the defendant's assets are in a foreign forum, jurisdiction may need to be relitigated (depending on foreign preclusion rules) or (in the case of a default judgment) litigated for the first time.

It is important to consider at the outset of litigation possible jurisdictional obstacles to the enforceability of any judgment that might be obtained. Foreign defendants often have only minimal assets within the forum, and enforcement of a judgment will then require litigation in either their home state or another foreign country. As described below, the willingness of foreign states to enforce U.S. judgments is uncertain. Even where a U.S. judgment is, in principle, enforceable, it will often be necessary to satisfy local requirements regarding the jurisdiction of the rendering court. *See infra* pp. 1084-1085. Counsel in international cases must consider these requirements when suing foreign parties against whom it may be necessary to seek enforcement abroad.

14. *Primary importance of defendant's contacts and inconvenience.* As *Pennoyer, World-Wide Volkswagen,* and §421 all reflect, due process analysis focuses on the *defendant's* contacts with the forum and the inconvenience and burden imposed on the *defendant.* The *plaintiff's* contacts with the forum are of little importance (except as one factor in "reasonableness" analysis). *See Goodyear Dunlop Tires Operations, S.A. v. Brown,* 2011 WL 2518815 at *10 n.5 (U.S. June 27, 2011); *Keeton v. Hustler Magazine,* 465 U.S. 770 (1984) (holding that plaintiff's lack of contacts with forum was not a basis for denying jurisdiction under Due Process Clause).

Is this focus on the defendant appropriate? Would it not be more appropriate to look broadly to the relations of both parties, and their conduct, to the potential forum?

Several rationales are advanced for the Due Process Clause's focus on the defendant. Some commentators invoke "the old rule of *dubrio prop reo:* the fault of the defendant has still to be proved." De Winter, *Excessive Jurisdiction in Private International Law,* 17 Int'l & Comp. L.Q. 706, 717 (1968). Others reason that:

> The defendant's jurisdictional preference rests on the advantages that a plaintiff typically enjoys in selecting among several forums and on the proposition that, other things being equal, burdens that must rest on either the challenger or the challenged are to be borne by him who seeks to change the status quo. von Mehren, *Adjudicatory Jurisdiction: General Theories Compared and Evaluated,* 63 B.U. L. Rev. 279, 321-322 (1983).

Finally, by focusing on the defendant's reasonable expectations, due process analysis seeks to provide "a degree of predictability to the legal system that allows potential defendants to structure their primary conduct with some minimum assurance as to where that conduct will and will not render them liable to suit." *World-Wide Volkswagen Corp.,* 444 U.S. at 297. Are these explanations sufficient?

15. *Applicability of Due Process Clause to foreign defendants.* As discussed below, some U.S. courts have queried the soundness of affording foreign defendants due process protection against the exercise of U.S. personal jurisdiction. *See infra* pp. 104-105, 150-152; *Afram Export Corp. v. Metallurgiki Halyps, SA,* 772 F.2d 1358 (7th Cir. 1985); Parrish, *Sovereignty, Not Due Process: Personal Jurisdiction Over Nonresident Alien Defendants,* 41 Wake Forest L. Rev. 1 (2006). Should foreign defendants be entitled to due process protections in the personal jurisdiction context? The same protections as U.S. defendants? Why?

(a) Authorities applying Due Process Clause to aliens. A number of courts and commentators have considered whether due process applies to assertions of jurisdiction over foreigners, concluding it should. *E.g., Asahi Metal Indus. Co. v. Superior Court,* 480 U.S. 102, 108-109, 113 n.*, 114-115 (1987) (excerpted below); *infra* pp. 150-152. As a matter of constitutional interpretation and policy, should the Due Process Clause protect foreigners from U.S. jurisdiction? *World-Wide Volkswagen* focused on safeguarding the territorial sovereignty of U.S. states from jurisdictional claims by their sister states. *See supra* pp. 88, 94-95. What application does this rationale have in international cases? When assertions of jurisdiction arguably infringe the territorial sovereignty of foreign states, is it a matter for U.S. foreign relations? Or for principles of international comity?

World-Wide Volkswagen also sought to protect individuals from unfair jurisdictional claims. Does this rationale not apply in cases involving foreign defendants? Note that several Supreme Court decisions have held that nonresident aliens seeking admittance to the United States may not invoke the procedural protections of the Due Process Clause. *Shaughnessy v. United States ex rel. Mezei,* 345 U.S. 206, 212 (1953); *Fong Yue Ting v. United States,* 149 U.S. 698 (1893).

Nevertheless, would it not "be unfair and ironic to hale an alien into an unfamiliar United States court, forcing him to litigate according to our procedures and laws, yet deny him the protections of the Due Process Clause on the grounds that he is an alien"? Born, *Reflections on Judicial Jurisdiction in International Cases,* 17 Ga. J. Int'l & Comp. L. 1, 22 (1987). *See also Home Insurance Co. v. Dick,* 281 U.S. 397 (1930) (Due Process Clause applies to state court's choice of law in case involving foreign party). The application of due process protections to foreign states is discussed separately below. *See infra* pp. 277, 308, 333-334, 343-344, 360.

(b) Verdugo-Urquidez *'s interpretation of Fourth Amendment. United States v. Verdugo-Urquidez,* 494 U.S. 259 (1990), held that the Fourth Amendment does not apply to searches and seizures of foreign nationals conducted by U.S. Government agents outside of U.S. territory. The Fourth Amendment provides, *inter alia,* that "[t]he right of the people to be secure in their persons, houses, papers, and effects, against unreasonable searches and seizures, shall not be violated. . . ." The Court reasoned that the Fourth Amendment applied only to "the people," a phrase that it interpreted to protect only U.S. citizens and residents. Does this interpretation have any implications for due process analysis? Note that the Due Process Clause does not refer to "the people," but to "persons."

16. *Relevance of defendant's foreign identity to due process analysis.* Assertions of jurisdiction over foreign defendants often raise different issues than assertions of jurisdiction over U.S. defendants from other states of the Union. The inconvenience that results from requiring a defendant (or plaintiff) to litigate in a foreign country is often greater than that resulting from requiring an American to litigate in another part of the United States. Major differences in procedural and substantive rules — such as the scope of discovery, the existence of fee-shifting provisions or contingent fee arrangements, and the right to a jury trial — are also more likely in the international context. Moreover, a state court's assertion of jurisdiction over residents of another U.S. state never provokes retaliatory measures; in contrast, assertions of jurisdiction over *foreign* defendants can result in foreign retaliation. *See* Born, *Reflections on Judicial Jurisdiction in International Cases*, 17 Ga. J. Int'l & Comp. L. 1, 21-34 (1987).

Should these differences between assertions of jurisdiction over foreign, as compared to domestic, defendants produce any differences in due process analysis? *See* Parrish, *Sovereignty, Not Due Process: Personal Jurisdiction over Nonresident Alien Defendants*, 41 Wake Forest L. Rev. 1, 7 (2006) ("[T]he assumption that the same due process considerations apply equally to nonresident, alien defendants as to domestic defendants in the personal jurisdiction context is doctrinally inconsistent with broader notions of American constitutionalism."). Should due process standards make it easier or harder to obtain jurisdiction over a foreigner? *Compare Restatement (Third) Foreign Relations Law* §421, Reporters' Note 1 (1987) ("the criteria for exercise of judicial jurisdiction are basically the same for claims arising out of international transactions or involving a non-resident alien as a party" as the criteria for domestic cases) *and Deutsch v. West Coast Machinery Co.*, 497 P.2d 1311 (Wash. 1972) (rejecting argument that "a different rule must be applied when [taking jurisdiction] involves the manufacturer in a foreign country") *with Asahi Metal Indus. Ltd. v. Superior Court*, 480 U.S. 102 (1987) ("Great care and reserve should be exercised when extending our notions of personal jurisdiction into the international field."). Which of these various approaches is most sensible?

17. *Judicial jurisdiction of foreign courts.* Consider Article 14 of the French Civil Code. French courts have interpreted Article 14 as permitting jurisdiction over a foreign defendant in any case brought by a French plaintiff, including cases based on contract and tort. *See Weiss v. Soc. Atlantic Electric,* Revue Critique de Droit International Privé 113 (1971). Is the French statute consistent with §421 of the *Third Restatement?*

18. *EU Council Regulation 44/2001.* The most important international agreement governing judicial jurisdiction was the Brussels Convention, among the Member States of the European Union ("EU"), which has been largely replaced by Council Regulation 44/2001. The Brussels Convention was a so-called "double convention," which regulated both the recognition of foreign judgments and the permissible bases for judicial jurisdiction in EU Member States. *See infra* p. 1092 for a discussion of the Convention's treatment of foreign judgments. The Brussels Convention (and now, Regulation 44/2001) was designed to produce a high degree of jurisdictional certainty. The Regulation governs jurisdiction in two ways — by prescribing a series of permissible jurisdictional bases and a series of forbidden jurisdictional bases.

(a) Permitted jurisdictional bases under Regulation 44/2001. First, Regulation 44/2001 provides an exclusive list of the permissible ("green") bases for jurisdiction over EU domiciliaries. Article 3(1) of the Regulation states the basic rule that "persons domiciled in a Member State may be sued in the courts of another Member State only by virtue of the rules" set out in the Regulation. Article 2(1) of the Regulation provides the basic rule that persons are subject to suit (on any claim) in the place where they are domiciled, regardless of their nationality: "persons domiciled in a Member State shall, whatever their nationality, be sued in the Courts of that Member State." In addition, Articles 5 and 6 of the Regulation set forth a series of permissible (green) "claim-based" or "activity-based" grounds for jurisdiction, which may also be used against Member State domiciliaries. Among other things, the Regulation provides that contract claims may be brought in "the place of performance of the obligation in question," Article 5(1); that tort claims may be brought in "the place where the harmful event occurred or may occur," Article 5(3); and that, if multiple defendants are involved, "where any one of them is domiciled, provided that the claims are so closely connected that it is expedient to hear and determine them together to avoid the risk of irreconcilable judgments resulting from separate proceedings." Article 6(1).

Note that some of the permitted jurisdictional bases under Regulation 44/2001 are very broad, including Articles 5(3) and 6(1).

   (b)   Forbidden jurisdictional bases under Regulation 44/2001. Second, Article 3(2) of Regulation 44/2001 forbids the use of several exorbitant ("red") jurisdictional bases against persons domiciled in a Member State. As detailed in Annex I of the Regulation, these impermissible (red) jurisdictional bases include Articles 14 and 15 of the French Civil Code (giving French courts jurisdiction over any case involving a French national) and Section 23 of the German Code of Civil Procedure (giving German courts jurisdiction over the owners of property located in Germany). Consistent with the objective of achieving jurisdictional certainty, and with legal regimes in most civil law states, the Regulation does not permit judicial discretion to decline jurisdiction (whether as *forum non conveniens* dismissals or otherwise).

   (c)   Recognition of judgments under Regulation 44/2001. Third, Regulation 44/2001 also provides for recognition of judgments rendered in other EU Member States. See Articles 33-37. In particular, the Regulation provides that, in recognizing of the judgment of another EU Member State, the enforcing court may not consider jurisdictional issues (since these have been regulated at the litigation phase by the Regulation). As a consequence of the Regulation, EU Member State judgments are enforceable freely throughout the EU, in much the same fashion as U.S. judgments are enforceable under the Full Faith and Credit Clause. *See infra* p. 1092.

   (d)   Limitation to EU domiciliaries. The Regulation (like the Convention before it) does not regulate assertions of jurisdiction over non-EU domiciliaries. Under Articles 4(1) and 4(2) of the Regulation, Member States are left free to exercise jurisdiction over non-EU domiciliaries based upon the "exorbitant" jurisdictional bases that are prohibited by Article 3 of the Regulation (such as Article 14 of the French Civil Code).

   (e)   Effect of Regulation 44/2001. Review the provisions of the Regulation that permit and prohibit particular jurisdictional bases. Compare these bases of jurisdiction with those that are permitted by §421 and the Due Process Clause. What are the principal similarities and differences? How does Regulation 44/2001 deal with tag service as a jurisdictional base? With "stream of commerce" or "effects" jurisdiction? With "general jurisdiction" where a foreign defendant engages in substantial business within the forum?

   Recall how the Regulation 44/2001 protects EU domiciliaries from exorbitant assertions of personal jurisdiction by Member State courts. *See supra* p. 105. As noted above, Articles 3 and 4 of the Regulation expressly provide that the foregoing limitations protect *only* persons domiciled in a Member State. Persons domiciled in the United States, or other non-EU nations, are generally not protected, and may be subjected to any available basis of jurisdiction under local law. Indeed, subject to an exception for treaties with non-EU states (which does not apply to the United States), the Regulation requires the EU-wide enforcement of judgments based upon exorbitant jurisdiction against non-domiciliaries. *See also infra* p. 1092. Is this a wise approach? From whose perspective? How would the Due Process Clause apply to a Texas court's assertion of jurisdiction over a French defendant if the United States followed the Regulation's example in its treatment of foreign defendants?

   19. *Applicability of Due Process Clause to foreign defendants revisited.* Consider again the discussion above of due process protections for foreign defendants. *See supra* pp. 103-104. Why should not due process serve only to protect U.S. domiciliaries, the way that Regulation 44/2001 protects only EU domiciliaries? Why should not, for example, Florida be barred from exorbitant jurisdiction over Georgia residents, but not over French or Russian residents? *See* Nadelmann, *Jurisdictionally Improper Fora in Treaties on Recognition of Judgments: The Common Market Draft,* 67 Colum. L. Rev. 1995, 1001 (1967) (Brussels

Convention "challenge[s] the friendly relations between nations built on respect for due process of law"); von Mehren, *Recognition and Enforcement of Foreign Judgments,* 167 Rec. des Cours 13, 101 (1981) (Article 4 of Brussels Convention is the "single most regressive step that has occurred in international recognition and enforcement practice in this century").

Are these criticisms of the Convention (and Regulation) warranted? If they are, what weight should U.S. courts give to the discriminatory features of Regulation 44/2001? Is responding to such discrimination a judicial function, or a political function? Recall the origins of due process analysis in *Pennoyer.* If you were constructing an argument for taking into account foreign jurisdictional regimes, like Regulation 44/2001, what would it be?

20. *Relevance of reciprocity to judicial jurisdiction in international cases.* Recall the role of international law in due process analysis. Why should a U.S. court consider only *U.S.* conceptions of jurisdiction? If France permits French courts to decide all cases brought against U.S. defendants by French plaintiffs, why shouldn't U.S. courts give U.S. plaintiffs the same rights when they sue French defendants? Given the role of international law in due process analysis, is reciprocity not also a component of that analysis? What benefits would such an approach produce? What costs?

21. *Efforts by Hague Conference on Private International Law to negotiate jurisdiction and judgments convention.* In May 1992, the United States proposed that the Hague Conference on Private International Law undertake efforts to negotiate a multilateral treaty on the recognition of foreign judgments. For the next decade, the Member States of the Hague Conference (including the EU Member States, Japan, and the United States) devoted substantial effort to reaching agreement on an acceptable text of a multilateral convention on jurisdiction and judgments. *See* Burbank, *Jurisdictional Equilibrium, the Proposed Hague Convention and Progress in National Law,* 49 Am. J. Comp. L. 203 (2001); Pfund, *Intergovernmental Efforts to Prepare a Convention on Jurisdiction and the Enforcement of Judgments,* 76 A.L.I. Proc. 927 (1999); Silberman, *Comparative Jurisdiction in the International Context: Will the Proposed Hague Judgments Convention Be Saved?,* 52 DePaul L. Rev. 319 (2002).

The Hague Conference negotiations aspired to a convention, like the Brussels and Lugano Conventions, that would have both regulated the exercise of jurisdiction and required the mutual recognition of judgments. In particular, it was hoped that the Hague Conference's Member States could reach agreement, like that in the Brussels Convention, on both permitted (green) and prohibited (red) jurisdictional bases.

By 1999, a draft convention had been drafted and circulated. *See* Hague Conference on Private International Law, Preliminary Draft Convention on Jurisdiction and Foreign Judgments in Civil and Commercial Matters (Amended Version) (1999) (available at http://www.hcch.net and reprinted in *A Global Law of Jurisdiction and Judgments: Lessons from The Hague* App. I (John J. Barcelo III & Kevin M. Clermont eds., 2002)). Ultimately, however, the negotiations failed. Among other things, European states insisted that any proposed convention prohibit (a) tag jurisdiction, where general jurisdiction is based on service of process within the forum state's territory (*see infra* pp. 129-137); and (b) "doing business" jurisdiction, where general jurisdiction is based upon a foreign, nondomiciliary defendant engaging in significant levels of business activities in the forum (*see infra* pp. 116-127). Dubinsky, *Proposals of the Hague Conference and Their Effect on Efforts to Enforce International Human Rights Through Adjudication,* HCPIL Working Doc. 117 (1998); Van Schaack, *In Defense of Civil Redress: The Domestic Enforcement of Human Rights Norms in the Context of the Proposed Hague Judgments Convention,* 42 Harv. Int'l L.J. 141, 176 (2001).

During the negotiations, the United States proposed a compromise, which was to pursue a "mixed convention," rather than a pure "double convention." The mixed convention would have included agreed red and green jurisdictional bases, but added a new category of jurisdictional bases whose use was neither permitted nor prohibited (purple); states would have been left free to use purple jurisdictional bases, but other states would not have been obligated to enforce judgments resting on such bases. In effect, certain jurisdictional bases and resulting judgments would have been left unregulated by the convention. The U.S. proposal failed to attract support within the EU, and negotiations on the convention eventually reached deadlock, where they remain. In the words of one commentator:

> The Europeans, having achieved free movement of judgments among EU member states, and with arguably less reciprocally to gain given the expansive recognition practice in the United States, consider themselves to be running the show and are dictating to a certain extent the terms of the convention. Without a strong bargaining position, the United States is unable to advance its own goals or achieve cooperation on other issues. . . . Many consider the struggle over approved and prohibited jurisdictional bases — namely, the controversy over "doing business" jurisdiction and "tag" jurisdiction — to be potentially incapable of resolution. Miller, *Playground Politics: The Wisdom of Writing a Reciprocity Requirement into U.S. International Recognition and Enforcement Laws*, 35 Geo. J. Int'l L. 239 (2004).

Given the differences between national positions on issues of judicial jurisdiction, it is difficult to see how agreement will be reached in the foreseeable future. *See also* Juenger, *A Hague Judgments Convention*, 24 Brook. J. Int'l L. 111, 121 (1998).

   22. *Hague Conference on Private International Law's Convention on Choice of Court Agreements.* In place of the jurisdiction and judgments convention, the Hague Conference instead proposed the Hague Convention on Choice of Court Agreements. As discussed below, the Convention has been signed by a number of states (including the United States), but not ratified. Among other things, the Convention regulates the enforcement of choice of forum clauses, and judgments based upon such clauses. *See infra* pp. 468, 485-486.

   23. *Possibility of personal jurisdiction in multiple fora.* Both due process and international law permit more than one forum to exercise jurisdiction over a defendant in respect of the same dispute. This was true even under *Pennoyer,* where a defendant could be subject to personal jurisdiction in each forum in which he could be served or to whose jurisdiction he had consented. It is even more likely under *World-Wide Volkswagen* and *Restatement (Third)* §421. Should either the Due Process Clause or international law seek to confine personal jurisdiction to only one forum — for example, by picking the most appropriate of several theoretically available fora in particular cases? If this is not done, won't infringements on territorial sovereignty and unfairness to individual litigants inevitably result? Consider Article 27 of Regulation 44/2001, providing for stays of jurisdiction in all courts of EU Member States that might otherwise have jurisdiction once an action has been filed in a forum within one EU Member State. Is this a sensible approach? Should U.S. courts adopt it in international cases?

B.   General Jurisdiction of U.S. Courts in International Cases

As outlined above, the Due Process Clause has been interpreted to distinguish between "general" and "specific" jurisdiction. General jurisdiction allows a court to adjudicate *any* claim against the defendant, regardless whether the claim has any connection to the forum.[94] Because general jurisdiction is an expansive basis for judicial authority, it can only be exercised in narrow circumstances. Due process typically permits general jurisdiction over defendants only if they have significant, permanent connections with the forum. This section examines the principal bases for general jurisdiction under the Due Process Clause: (1) nationality, domicile, or residence; (2) incorporation or registration to do business; (3) consent; (4) "continuous and systematic" activities within the forum (also termed "presence" or "doing business"); and (5) tag service.

1. General Jurisdiction Based on Nationality, Domicile, or Residence of the Defendant

A natural person who is a citizen or national of a state may generally be subjected to that state's jurisdiction without offending either the Due Process Clause or international law.[95] According to §421 of the *Restatement (Third) Foreign Relations Law:* "In general, a state's exercise of jurisdiction to adjudicate with respect to a person . . . is reasonable if, at the time jurisdiction is asserted, . . . the person, if a natural person, is a national of the state."[96]

Nationality as a basis for personal jurisdiction under the Due Process Clause was approved by the Supreme Court in *Blackmer v. United States,* excerpted below. *Blackmer* arose when a federal court, acting pursuant to the so-called Walsh Act,[97] ordered a U.S. citizen residing in Europe to return to the United States to give testimony in pending U.S. criminal proceedings.

BLACKMER v. UNITED STATES
284 U.S. 421 (1932)

CHIEF JUSTICE HUGHES. [A U.S. federal court issued two subpoenas requiring Blackmer, a U.S. citizen residing in France, to testify at a U.S. criminal trial. The subpoenas were issued under the Walsh Act, described above. Although the subpoenas were served upon Blackmer (in France), he did not respond and was found in contempt. Blackmer challenged the contempt order arguing, among other grounds, that the Walsh Act and the proceedings against him violated the Fifth Amendment's Due Process Clause.]

While it appears that the petitioner removed his residence to France in the year 1924, it is undisputed that he was, and continued to be, a citizen of the United States. He continued to owe allegiance to the United States. By virtue of the obligations of citizenship, the United States retained its authority over him, and he was bound by its laws made applicable to him in a foreign country. Thus, although resident abroad, the petitioner remained subject to the taxing power of the United States. For disobedience to its laws through conduct abroad, he was subject to punishment in the courts of the United States. With respect to such an

---

94. *Goodyear Dunlop Tires Operations, S.A. v. Brown,* 2011 WL 2518815 at *3, 6 (U.S. June 27, 2011); *Helicopteros Nacionales de Colombia, SA v. Hall,* 466 U.S. 408, 414 & n.9 (1984); *Perkins v. Benguet Consol. Mining Co.,* 342 U.S. 437 (1952); Brilmayer, *How Contacts Count: Due Process Limitations on State Court Jurisdiction,* 1980 Sup. Ct. Rev. 77, 81.

95. *Restatement (Second) Conflict of Laws* §31 (1971); *Restatement (First) Conflict of Laws* §47 (1934); *Blackmer v. United States,* 284 U.S. 421 (1932). It is said that "[n]ationality was not generally recognized as a basis of judicial jurisdiction at common law." *Restatement (Second) Conflict of Laws* §31 comment d (1971). As discussed below, however, both Joseph Story's *Commentaries on the Conflict of Laws* and *Pennoyer* recognized the principle, at least to a point. Moreover, when the issue arose, however, U.S. courts often concluded that nationality or citizenship was an adequate jurisdictional basis. *E.g., Henderson v. Staniford,* 105 Mass. 504 (1870); *Matter of Dennick,* 36 N.Y. Supp. 518 (4th Dep't 1895). *Compare Grubel v. Nassauer,* 103 N.E. 1113 (N.Y. 1913) (refusing jurisdiction over German national because he was domiciled in New York, not Germany).

96. *Restatement (Third) Foreign Relations Law* §421(2)(d) (1987).

97. 28 U.S.C. §§1783-1784. The Walsh Act authorizes U.S. courts to issue and serve subpoenas on U.S. citizens, located outside the United States, in limited circumstances. *See infra* pp. 886-887.

exercise of authority, there is no question of international law,[98] but solely of the purport of the municipal law which establishes the duties of the citizen in relation to his own government.[99] While the legislation of the Congress, unless the contrary intent appears, is construed to apply only within the territorial jurisdiction of the United States, the question of its application, so far as citizens of the United States in foreign countries are concerned, is one of construction, not of legislative power. *American Banana Co. v. United Fruit Co.,* 213 U.S. 347, 357 (1909) [excerpted below at pp. 651-653]; *United States v. Bowman.* Nor can it be doubted that the United States possesses the power inherent in sovereignty to require the return to this country of a citizen, resident elsewhere, whenever the public interest requires it, and to penalize him in case of refusal. . . . It is also beyond controversy that one of the duties which the citizen owes to his government is to support the administration of justice by attending its courts and giving his testimony whenever he is properly summoned. . . .

In the present instance, the question concerns only the method of enforcing the obligation. The jurisdiction of the United States over its absent citizen, so far as the binding effect of its legislation is concerned, is a jurisdiction in personam, as he is personally bound to take notice of the laws that are applicable to him and to obey them. But for the exercise of judicial jurisdiction in personam, there must be due process, which requires appropriate notice of the judicial action and an opportunity to be heard. . . . The question of the validity of the provision for actual service of the subpoena in a foreign country is one that arises solely between the government of the United States and the citizen. The mere giving of such a notice to the citizen in the foreign country of the requirement of his government that he shall return is in no sense an invasion of any right of the foreign government and the citizen has no standing to invoke any such supposed right. While consular privileges in foreign countries are the appropriate subjects of treaties, it does not follow that every act of a consul, as, *e.g.,* in communicating with citizens of his own country, must be predicated upon a specific provision of a treaty. The intercourse of friendly nations, permitting travel and residence of the citizens of each in the territory of the other, presupposes and facilitates such communications. . . .

Notes *on* Blackmer

1. *Role of international law analysis in due process analysis.* Consider *Blackmer*'s reliance on principles of international law. Compare this due process analysis with that in *Pennoyer, see supra* pp. 83-84, 91-93.

2. *Nationality principle under international law.* As *Blackmer* suggests, international law has long permitted states to exercise a measure of jurisdiction over their nationals, even when they are outside of national territory. Joseph Story recognized the nationality principle, at least to a point:

as to citizens of a country domiciled abroad, the extent of jurisdiction, which may be lawfully exercised over them *in personam,* is not so clear upon acknowledged principles. It is true, that

---

98. "The law of Nations does not prevent a State from exercising jurisdiction over its subjects travelling or residing abroad, since they remain under its personal supremacy." 1 Oppenheim, *International Law* §145, p. 281 (4th ed.); Story, *Conflict of Laws* §540, p. 755 (8th ed.); 2 *Moore's International Law Digest* 255-256; 1 Hyde, *International Law,* §240, p. 424; Borchard, *Diplomatic Protection of Citizens Abroad,* §13, pp. 21, 22.

99. *Compare The Nereide,* 13 U.S. 388, 422, 423 (1815); *Rose v. Himely,* 8 U.S. 241, 279 (1808); *The Apollon,* 22 U.S. 362, 370 (1824); *Schibsby v. Westenholz,* L.R. 6 Q.R. 155, 161. Illustrations of acts of the Congress applicable to citizens abroad are the provisions found in the chapter of the Criminal Code relating to "Offenses against operations of government" 18 U.S.C.A. §§71-151; *United States v. Bowman,* 260 U.S. 94, 98-102 (1822) and the provisions relating to criminal correspondence with foreign governments, Act of January 30, 1799, 1 Stat. 613, 18 U.S.C. §5.

nations generally assert a claim to regulate the rights, and duties, and obligations, and acts of their own citizens, wherever they may be domiciled. And, so far as these rights, duties, obligations, and acts afterwards come under the cognizance of the tribunals of the sovereign power of their own country, either for enforcement, or for protection, or for remedy, there may be no just ground to exclude this claim. But when such rights, duties, obligations, and acts, come under the consideration of other countries, and specially of the foreign country, where such citizens are domiciled, the duty of recognising and enforcing such a claim of sovereignty, is neither clear, nor generally admitted. J. Story, *Commentaries on the Conflict of Laws* §540 (2d ed. 1841).

For contemporary authority, *see Restatement (Third) Foreign Relations Law* §421(2)(d) (1987). (International law also recognizes nationality as a basis for *legislative* jurisdiction. *See infra* pp. 594, 599.) What is the rationale for nationality as a basis for judicial jurisdiction under international law? Should international law permit jurisdiction based on nationality? Does *Pennoyer*'s territoriality doctrine support (or contradict) judicial jurisdiction based on nationality?

3. *Nationality under long-arm statutes and the Due Process Clause.* U.S. state long-arm statutes do not generally contain specific authorizations for jurisdiction based upon nationality, and it is very rarely invoked in practice. Rather, most long-arm statutes refer to persons "domiciled" or "resident" in the state. *See infra* pp. 112-113. Federal long-arm statutes also generally do not expressly provide for jurisdiction based on nationality. "In actions between private persons, the Congress of the United States has never authorized the federal courts to exercise jurisdiction on the basis of citizenship over citizens of the United States who are domiciled abroad." *Restatement (Second) Conflict of Laws* §31 comment b (1971). The Walsh Act, at issue in *Blackmer,* was a rare exception. *See also SEC v. Home,* 514 F.3d 661 (7th Cir. 2008) (relying on nationality principle to support contempt finding against U.S. citizens residing abroad who violated injunction freezing company's assets).

Suppose that a state or federal long-arm statute provided for personal jurisdiction in civil actions based solely on the defendant's nationality or citizenship. Would due process permit this? Doesn't *Blackmer* suggest that the answer is in the affirmative? Is that sensible? Should a U.S. court have jurisdiction over claims against a U.S. defendant, regardless of the other connections between the defendant and the United States and regardless of the connections between the dispute and the United States? Should a Texas court have jurisdiction over claims against a Texan, regardless of the connections of the defendant and the dispute with Texas? *Compare* Regulation 44/2001, Art. 2(1).

4. *Rationale for general jurisdiction.* What is the rationale for *any* assertion of general jurisdiction? Why should a nation's courts ever consider claims that have nothing to do with that nation? Consider the following:

domicile, place of incorporation, and principal place of business [are] the paradigm bases for general adjudicative jurisdiction. . . . These are relationships so direct that they make fair the assertion of state adjudicative power. . . . They are unique affiliations that an individual or legal entity normally will have with only one state. Brilmayer et al., *A General Look at General Jurisdiction,* 66 Tex. L. Rev. 720, 782 (1988).

Justice requires a certain and predictable place where a person can be reached by those having claims against him. . . . For an individual, the sole community where it is fair to require him to litigate any cause of action is his habitual residence; for a corporation, it is the corporate headquarters—presumably both the place of incorporation and the principal place of business, where these differ. von Mehren & Trautman, *Jurisdiction to Adjudicate: A Suggested Analysis,* 79 Harv. L. Rev. 1121, 1137, 1179 (1966).

Are these explanations persuasive? Consider the two basic purposes of limits on judicial jurisdiction — safeguarding territorial sovereignty and preventing unfairness to individuals. Do the foregoing explanations for general jurisdiction address both purposes?

5. *Role of reasonableness in* Blackmer. What role does the "reasonableness" prong of *World-Wide Volkswagen* play in *Blackmer*? Does the opinion in *Blackmer* leave any room for even a compelling showing of unreasonableness to overcome jurisdiction based on nationality? Suppose that the desired testimony concerned matters occurring wholly outside the United States, that foreign law forbade the defendant's return to the United States to give testimony, and that the defendant had resided outside the United States for 30 years.

6. *Conflicts between jurisdiction based on territoriality and jurisdiction based on nationality.* Nationality-based general jurisdiction makes it inevitable that cases will arise in which two or more fora have personal jurisdiction over a defendant in respect of the same claims. For example, when the national of State A commits a tort in State B, both States A and B will generally be able to assert jurisdiction based on nationality and territoriality bases. Is this desirable? Should the Due Process Clause or international law provide a basis for choosing one of several potential fora? *See supra* p. 108.

7. *Definition of nationality under international law.* If jurisdiction can be based on nationality, then the definition of nationality is critical. International law has been invoked to restrict exorbitant definitions of nationality. Section 211 of the *Third Restatement* provides: "For purposes of international law, an individual has the nationality of a state that confers it, but other states need not accept that nationality when it is not based on a genuine link between the state and the individual." *Restatement (Third) Foreign Relations Law* §211 (1987). *See Nottebohm Case (Liechtenstein v. Guatemala)*, [1955] I.C.J. Rep. 4.

8. *U.S. judicial refusals to recognize foreign assertions of nationality.* Nationality is sometimes invoked as a basis for enforcement of a foreign court's judgment against one of its nationals. U.S. courts did not always accept foreign claims of nationality. *E.g., Grubel v. Nassauer,* 103 N.E. 1113 (N.Y. 1913) (refusing to recognize Bavarian judgment against Bavarian national who had emigrated to the United States before foreign action had begun); *Smith v. Grady,* 31 N.W. 477 (Wis. 1887) (refusing to enforce judgment against Canadian national because of his absence for prolonged period from country of nationality and acquisition of U.S. domicile).

9. *Domicile as a basis for general jurisdiction.* Closely related to nationality as a jurisdictional basis is domicile. It is now widely accepted that an individual may constitutionally be subject to general jurisdiction in the state in which he or she is domiciled. *E.g., Goodyear Dunlop Tires Operations, S.A. v. Brown,* 2011 WL 2518815 at *6 (U.S. June 27, 2011); *Restatement (Second) Conflict of Laws* §29 (1971); *Restatement (Third) Foreign Relations Law of the United States* §421(2)(b) (1987). *See* Regulation 44/2001, Art. 2(1).

Why is it that domicile subjects one to general jurisdiction? The leading precedent is *Milliken v. Meyer,* 311 U.S. 457 (1940), where the Court declared:

> Domicile in the state is alone sufficient to bring an absent defendant within the reach of the state's jurisdiction for purposes of a personal judgment by means of appropriate substituted service. . . . As in case of [*sic*] the authority of the United States over its absent citizens (*Blackmer v. United States*), the authority of a state over one of its citizens is not terminated by the mere fact of his absence from the state. The state which accords him privileges and affords protection to him and his property by virtue of his domicile may also exact reciprocal duties. "Enjoyment of the privileges of residence within the state, and the attendant right to invoke the protection of its laws, are inseparable" from the various incidences of state citizenship. The responsibilities of that citizenship arise out of

the relationship to the state which domicile creates. That relationship is not dissolved by mere absence from the state. The attendant duties, like the rights and privileges incident to domicile, are not dependent on continuous presence in the state. . . . 311 U.S. at 462-463.

Is this persuasive? Does it explain the basis for jurisdiction based on nationality? One's domicile can be different from one's nationality. Is it desirable to have two places in which an individual is subject to general jurisdiction? What are the respective merits and demerits of nationality versus domicile as a jurisdictional base?

   10. *Nationality and domicile under proposed Hague Judgments Convention.* The proposed June 2001 Interim Text, which led to failure of the Hague negotiations, included the "nationality of the defendant" among the "prohibited grounds of jurisdiction" in Article 18(2)(c), while noting that there was "no consensus" on the issue. At the same time, Article 3(1) of the Interim Text provided that: "a defendant may be sued in the courts of [a] [the] State [in which] that defendant is [habitually] resident." (There was disagreement about the definition of "resident" or "habitually resident," but it appeared to include a natural person's principal place of residence and a company's place of incorporation or principal place of business.) What impact, if any, should these views have on U.S. jurisdictional analysis?

   11. *Residence as a basis for general jurisdiction.* Closely related to domicile as a basis for general jurisdiction is the defendant's "residence" at the time an action is commenced. "Residence" is often defined as a place where a person has an abode in which he spends considerable periods of time. *Restatement (Second) Conflict of Laws* §30, comment a (1971). Residence within the forum can provide the basis for general jurisdiction. *Restatement (Third) Foreign Relations Law* §421(2)(c) (1987).

   12. *Service of process in a foreign state—an initial view.* In addition to challenging U.S. jurisdiction, Mr. Blackmer argued that subpoena service on him in France could not properly be effected without infringing French sovereignty. The Court rejected the argument: "The mere giving of such a notice to the citizen in the foreign country of the requirement of his government that he shall return is in no sense an invasion of any right of the foreign government and the citizen has not standing to invoke any such supposed right." Is that persuasive? Why isn't service of U.S. process on a foreign state's territory at least arguably a violation of its territorial sovereignty? *See infra* pp. 880-888.

2.   General Jurisdiction Based on Incorporation or Registration to Do Business

   a.   Incorporation.   Business entities may be subjected to general jurisdiction if they have a sufficiently permanent and substantial connection with the forum. It is widely accepted that a corporation may be subjected to general jurisdiction in the state where it is incorporated.[100] One commentary has explained:

   A corporation is subject to jurisdiction in the state of its incorporation for any cause of action. Being incorporated in a state is a sufficiently substantial connection to support unlimited general jurisdiction. . . .[101]

---

   100. *Restatement (Second) Conflict of Laws* §41 (1971); *Restatement (Third) Foreign Relations Law* §421(2)(e) (1987). In the early 1800s, corporations were treated as artificial persons that could only be sued in the state that created them. *Bank of Augusta v. Earle,* 38 U.S. 519, 588 (1839).
   101. 1 R. Casad & W. Richman, *Jurisdiction in Civil Actions* §3-2[1] (3d ed. 1998 & Supp. 2010).

Although they have not frequently considered the question, lower courts have reached the same result.[102] Similarly, §421(2)(e) of the *Third Restatement* permits a state to exercise jurisdiction over an entity if "the person, if a corporation or comparable juridical person, is organized pursuant to the law of the state."[103]

Recall from the discussion of alienage jurisdiction that corporations sometimes have their "principal place of business" in a state other than the state of incorporation.[104] In such situations, it could be argued that the state of the principal place of business also may assert general jurisdiction over the corporation. Much like the case of citizens of one country or state domiciled in a different state, this possibility gives rise to competing assertions of general jurisdiction by two different sovereigns. Recently, the Supreme Court alluded in dicta to this theory of general jurisdiction over a corporation, although the case did not require resolution of the issue.[105]

b.   Registration or Qualification to Do Business.   Companies incorporated outside of the forum state may be subject to general jurisdiction there if they register or qualify to do business within the forum. Virtually all states require foreign corporations to appoint a registered agent as a condition of "transacting business" or "doing business" within the state.[106] In this context, both "transacting business" and "doing business" are usually defined as requiring substantial, ongoing business relations with the forum.[107]

In some states, such as Delaware, statutory agents are authorized by state law to accept service of process in *any* action, regardless whether it arises from activities within the state.[108] Other states have limited the process that may be served upon statutory agents to suits arising from in-state activities.[109] Where state law authorizes statutory agents to accept *any* service of process, lower courts have been required to consider whether due process permits general jurisdiction based on service on such agents. Lower courts are divided, with some answering affirmatively,[110] and others disagreeing.[111]

---

102. *E.g., Applied Biosystems, Inc. v. Cruachem, Ltd.,* 772 F. Supp. 1458, 1461 (D. Del. 1991) ("Because [defendant] is a Delaware corporation, there is no question that this Court can exercise personal jurisdiction over [it].").

103. Note that Article 3(3) of the June 2001 Interim Text of the proposed Hague Judgments Convention would have conferred general jurisdiction on the courts of the place where a corporate defendant was incorporated.

104. *See supra* pp. 25-26, 28-29.

105. *See Goodyear Dunlop Tires Operations, S.A. v. Brown,* 2011 WL 2518815 at *3 (U.S. June 27, 2011). Among other things, the Court did not explain whether the "nerve center" test for determining a company's principal place of business under the diversity and alienage statutes also governs in the personal jurisdiction context. *See supra* pp. 28-29.

106. *See* 1 R. Casad & W. Richman, *Jurisdiction in Civil Actions* §3-2[2][a] (3d ed. 1998 & Supp. 2010).

107. *See* 1 R. Casad & W. Richman, *Jurisdiction in Civil Actions* §4-2[1] (3d ed. 1998 & Supp. 2010); *Kachemak Seafoods, Inc. v. Century Airlines, Inc.,* 641 P.2d 213 (Alaska 1982).

108. *E.g., Macklowe v. Planet Hollywood, Inc.,* 1994 WL 586838, at *4 (Del. Ch. 1994); *Sternberg v. O'Neill,* 550 A.2d 1105 (Del. 1988).

109. *E.g., Pearrow v. National Life & Accident Ins. Co.,* 703 F.2d 1067, 1069 (8th Cir. 1983) (Arkansas registration statute interpreted "at its broadest, to cover only causes of action arising out of . . . transactions in Arkansas"). *See generally* 1 R. Casad & W. Richman, *Jurisdiction in Civil Actions* §3-2[2][a] at 334 & n.429 (3d ed. 1998 & Supp. 2010).

110. *E.g., Merriman v. Compton Corp.,* 146 P.3d 162, 174 (Kan. 2006); *Sondergard v. Miles, Inc.,* 985 F.2d 1389, 1396-1397 (8th Cir. 1993); *Knowlton v. Allied Van Line, Inc.,* 900 F.2d 1196 (8th Cir. 1990); *Speed v. Pelican Resort NV,* 1992 U.S. Dist. LEXIS 8278 (S.D.N.Y. 1992) ("Both this Court and the New York State courts have consistently held that a foreign corporation which registers [to do business] under BCL §1304 and establishes the Secretary of State as its agent upon whom process may be served under BCL §304, has consented to personal jurisdiction in the State of New York"); *Restatement (Second) Conflict of Laws* §44 (1971) ("A state has power to exercise judicial jurisdiction over a foreign corporation which has authorized an agent or a public official to accept service of process in actions brought against the corporation in the state as to all causes of action to which the authority of the agent or official to accept service extends.").

111. *E.g., Consolidated Development Corp. v. Sherritt, Inc.,* 216 F.3d 1286, 1293 (11th Cir. 2000) (citing *International Shoe* for the proposition that "[t]he casual presence of a corporate agent in the forum is not enough to subject the corporation to suit where the cause of action is unrelated to the agent's activities"); *Siemer v. Learjet Acquisition Corp.,* 966 F.2d 179 (5th Cir. 1992) ("being qualified to do business . . . is of no special weight in

3. General Jurisdiction Based on Consent or Waiver

It is well settled that a private party may consent, or waive its objections, to personal jurisdiction in a U.S. court. *Pennoyer* acknowledged that due process permitted extraterritorial jurisdiction based upon consent.[112] More recently, the Supreme Court said: "Because the requirement of personal jurisdiction represents first of all an individual right, it can, like other such rights, be waived."[113] Consent or waiver can take many forms, both express and implied, and they can be either "general" or limited to "specific" matters. Whatever their form, disputes can arise as to the interpretation and enforceability of purported consents or waivers.

a. Prorogation Agreements or Nonexclusive Forum Selection Agreements. International commercial contracts commonly include a provision in which one or more parties submit a defined set of disputes to the jurisdiction of a designated court.[114] Provisions of this sort are sometimes referred to as "prorogation" agreements, or "nonexclusive" forum selection clauses. Such agreements differ from "exclusive" forum agreements, discussed below, in that they *permit* jurisdiction in the contractual forum without *excluding* litigation in other fora.[115]

In order to provide an effective grant of jurisdiction, a prorogation agreement must satisfy both applicable statutory requirements and the Due Process Clause. In most U.S. states, local law will enforce prorogation agreements as a basis for jurisdiction, even where the parties' transaction has no connection with the forum.[116] There are exceptions, but these are anomalies.[117]

If state law will enforce an express contractual submission to jurisdiction, the Due Process Clause generally will not preclude jurisdiction. The Supreme Court declared, in *National Equipment Rental, Ltd. v. Szukhent,* that "parties to a contract may agree in advance to submit to the jurisdiction of a given court, to permit notice to be served by the opposing party, or even to waive notice altogether."[118] In general, if a submission agreement is the result of fraud, duress, adhesion, or similar circumstances, neither the Due Process Clause nor state law will permit enforcement. We examine these defenses to

---

evaluating general personal jurisdiction"); *Sandstrom v. ChemLawn Corp.,* 904 F.2d 83, 89-90 (1st Cir. 1990) (obtaining license to do business in state, appointment of agent for service of process, and recruitment of personnel by advertisement in state not sufficient to support general jurisdiction); *Jones v. Family Inns, Inc.,* 1989 WL 57130 (E.D. La. 1989) ("defendant's sole contact with the State of Louisiana is an appointed agent for service of process," which does not satisfy *International Shoe*). *See generally* 1 R. Casad & W. Richman, *Jurisdiction in Civil Actions* §3-2[2][a][ii] (3d ed. 1998 & Supp. 2010).

112. 95 U.S. at 735-736.

113. *Insurance Corporation of Ireland v. Compagnie des Bauxites de Guinee,* 456 U.S. 694, 703 (1982). *See also D.H. Overmyer Co. v. Frick Co.,* 405 U.S. 174 (1972); *Nicastro v. J. McIntyre Machinery, Ltd.,* 2011 WL 2518811at *6 (U.S. June 27, 2011) (plurality opinion).

114. Consent to personal jurisdiction in a pending action (for example, by entering a general appearance) is virtually always regarded as satisfying both statutory and constitutional requirements. *See* 1 R. Casad & W. Richman, *Jurisdiction in Civil Actions* §3-1[5][c][i] (3d ed. 1998 & Supp. 2010).

115. *See infra* pp. 462-463.

116. *E.g., Vanier v. Ponsoldt,* 833 P.2d 949 (Kan. 1992); *Transway Shipping Ltd. v. Underwriters at Lloyd's,* 717 F. Supp. 82 (S.D.N.Y. 1989); *Alpa SA v. Acli Int'l, Inc.,* 573 F. Supp. 592 (W.D. Pa. 1983); 1 R. Casad & W. Richman, *Jurisdiction in Civil Actions* §3-1[5][c][iv] (3d ed. 1998 & Supp. 2010).

117. *E.g., McRae v. J.D./M.D., Inc.,* 511 So.2d 540 (Fla. 1987) ("Conspicuously absent from the long arm statute is any provision for submission to in personam jurisdiction merely by contractual agreement."); *Keelean v. Central Bank of the South,* 544 So.2d 153 (Ala. 1989); Mich. Comp. Law. Ann. §600.745(2). *See generally* C. Wright & A. Miller, *Federal Practice and Procedure* §1064 n.19 (3d ed. 1998 & Supp. 2010).

118. 375 U.S. 311, 315-316 (1964). *See also Hoffman v. National Equip. Rental Ltd.,* 643 F.2d 987 (4th Cir. 1981); *Gaskin v. Stumm Handel, GmbH,* 390 F. Supp. 361 (S.D.N.Y. 1975); *Restatement (Third) Foreign Relations Law* §421(2)(g) (1987); *infra* pp. 462-463, 485.

the enforceability of forum selection agreements below.[119] We also discuss the unratified Hague Convention on Choice of Court Agreements.[120]

b. Implied Submissions to Jurisdiction.   Implied submissions to the forum's jurisdiction are common, and generally enforceable, in the United States. As with prorogation agreements, both applicable legislative authorizations and the Due Process Clause must be satisfied before a waiver will confer jurisdiction. The most frequent instances of waiver involve a party's failing to raise jurisdictional defenses at an appropriate time during litigation;[121] in the first instance, the jurisdictional consequences of this are subject to the forum's procedural rules, which differ widely between states.[122]

There is little due process precedent dealing with implied waivers. In *Insurance Corp. v. Compagnie des Bauxites de Guinee,*[123] the Supreme Court held that the Due Process Clause did not preclude finding that a defendant's refusal to make jurisdictional discovery constituted an implied waiver of jurisdictional objections. According to the Court, the defendants' "refusal to produce evidence material to the administration of due process was but an admission of the want of merit in the asserted defense."[124]

4. General Jurisdiction Based on "Presence" or "Continuous and Systematic" Business Activities Within the Forum

Another basis for assertions of general jurisdiction is "continuous and systematic" business activity by the defendant within the forum,[125] also referred to as the "presence" or "doing business" standard.[126] If a defendant is found to have continuously and systematically engaged in business activities within the forum, then many long-arm statutes and the Due Process Clause will expose it to the forum's general jurisdiction.

a. Legislative Authorization.   In order for a court to exercise general jurisdiction based on continuous and systematic contacts, a legislative authorization must exist.[127] Many states recognize this basis for general jurisdiction, often by means of catch-all provisions that have been interpreted as granting jurisdiction to the limits of the Constitution.[128] As discussed below, Rule 4(k)(2) also appears to authorize general jurisdiction based on continuous and systematic contacts.[129]

---

119. *See infra* pp. 468-528.

120. *See infra* pp. 468, 485, 486.

121. *See Qassas v. Daylight Donut Flour Co, LLC,* 2010 WL 1816403 (N.D. Okla. May 3, 2010) (collecting cases).

122. 1 R. Casad & W. Richman, *Jurisdiction in Civil Actions* §3-1[5][b] (3d ed. 1998 & Supp. 2010); C. Wright & A. Miller, *Federal Practice and Procedure* §1064 n.18 (3d ed. 1998 & Supp. 2010); *Restatement (Third) Foreign Relations Law* §421(3) (1987).

123. 456 U.S. 694 (1982).

124. 456 U.S. at 709 (citing *Hammond Packing Co. v. Arkansas,* 212 U.S. 322, 351 (1909)).

125. *See Goodyear Dunlop Tires Operations, S.A. v. Brown,* 2011 WL 2518815 at *3, 8-10 (U.S. June 27, 2011); *Helicopteros Nacionales de Colombia, SA v. Hall,* 466 U.S. 408 (1984); *Perkins v. Benguet Consol. Mining Co.,* 342 U.S. 437 (1952).

126. *See Rosenberg Brothers & Co. v. Curtis Brown Co.,* 260 U.S. 516 (1923); *McGowan v. Smith,* 437 N.Y.S.2d 643, 645 (1981) (general jurisdiction requires showing that defendant is " 'engaged in such a continuous and systematic course of "doing business" here as to warrant a finding of its "presence" in this jurisdiction.' "); *Deluxe Ice Cream Co. v. R.C.H. Tool Corp.,* 726 F.2d 1209 (7th Cir. 1984); *Broadcasting Rights Int'l Corp. v. Societe du Tour de France, SARL,* 675 F. Supp. 1439 (S.D.N.Y. 1987).

127. *E.g., Provident National Bank v. California Federal S. & L. Ass'n,* 819 F.2d 434, 436 (3d Cir. 1987); *Landoil Resources Corp. v. Alexander & Alexander Services,* 918 F.2d 1039 (2d Cir. 1990); *Complaint of Damodar Bulk Carriers Ltd.,* 903 F.2d 675 (9th Cir. 1990).

128. *E.g.,* N.Y.C.P.L.R. §301 ("A court may exercise such jurisdiction over persons, property, or status as might have been exercised" at common law); *Landoil Resources Corp. v. Alexander & Alexander Serv., Inc.,* 918 F.2d 1039 (2d Cir. 1990).

129. *See infra* pp. 228-229.

b. Due Process Clause. General jurisdiction based on "presence" or "continuous and systematic" contacts is a potent litigation tool. As we have seen, general jurisdiction permits a plaintiff to assert any claim against the defendant, including claims that have nothing whatsoever to do with the forum.[130] This gives a plaintiff substantially increased opportunities to select a favorable forum for its claims. Reflecting this, most bases for general jurisdiction are commensurately unique and demanding — such as nationality, domicile, incorporation, and consent. As the following discussion illustrates, however, "presence" is a markedly less precise formula, which permits more expansive assertions of jurisdiction.

Due process has long been interpreted as permitting the assertion of general jurisdiction based on a defendant's continuous and systematic connections with the forum.[131] *Perkins v. Benguet Consolidated Mining Co.* is the leading Supreme Court decision finding jurisdiction based on this rationale.[132] In *Perkins*, a company organized under Philippines law, with its properties in the Philippines, was operated during Japan's World War II occupation of the Philippines, from an office in Ohio. The company's president maintained corporate records in Ohio, held board meetings there, paid salaries from an Ohio bank, and otherwise managed the company from Ohio. While not using the term "general jurisdiction," the Court held that the Philippines company could be sued in Ohio in an action arising out of activities unrelated to Ohio; the Court relied on the fact that the company had been "carrying on in Ohio a continuous and systematic, but limited part of its general business."[133]

Defining what activities will satisfy the "continuous and systematic" contacts or "presence" test is difficult.[134] In one court's words:

> The problem of what contacts with the forum state will suffice to subject a foreign corporation to suit there on an unrelated cause of action is such that the formulation of useful general standards is almost impossible and even an examination of the multitude of decided cases can give little assistance.[135]

It is clear, however, that the "presence" or "doing business" tests require a much more demanding showing than that for specific jurisdiction.[136] Indeed, some courts have concluded that *Perkins* was an unusual case and that general jurisdiction based on the continuous business contacts of a nonresident defendant is seldom available.[137]

---

130. *See supra* pp. 90, 108-109.

131. *International Shoe Co. v. Washington,* 326 U.S. 310, 318 (1945).

132. 342 U.S. 437 (1952). Recently, the Supreme Court described *Perkins* as "[t]he textbook case of general jurisdiction appropriately exercised over a foreign corporation that has not consented to suit in the forum." *Goodyear Dunlop Tires Operations, S.A. v. Brown,* 2011 WL 2518815 at *8 (U.S. June 27, 2011) (quoting *Donahue v. Far Eastern Air Transport Corp.,* 652 F.2d 1032, 1037 (D.C. Cir. 1981)).

133. 342 U.S. at 438.

134. *E.g., Complaint of Damodar Bulk Carriers Ltd.,* 903 F.2d 675 (9th Cir. 1990); *Borg-Warner Acceptance Corp. v. Lovett & Tharpe, Inc.,* 786 F.2d 1055, 1057 (11th Cir. 1986); *Reliance Steel Prods. Co. v. Watson, Ess. Marshall & Enggas,* 675 F.2d 587 (3d Cir. 1982) (" 'continuous and substantial' forum affiliations"). *See infra* pp. 123-128.

135. *Aquascutum of London, Inc. v. SS American Champion,* 426 F.2d 205, 211 (2d Cir. 1970).

136. *E.g., Provident National Bank v. California Federal Savings & Loan Ass'n,* 819 F.2d 434 (3d Cir. 1987); *Romero v. Aerolineas Argentinas,* 834 F. Supp. 673 (D.N.J. 1993) ("General jurisdiction requires a plaintiff to show significantly more than mere minimum contacts"); *Rolls-Royce Motors, Inc. v. Charles Schmitt & Co.,* 657 F. Supp. 1040, 1044 (S.D.N.Y. 1987) (general jurisdiction requires a corporation to be present not merely " 'occasionally or casually, but with a fair measure of permanence and continuity.' "). *Goodyear Dunlop Tires Operations, S.A. v. Brown,* 2011 WL 2518815 at *8 (U.S. June 27, 2011) ("A corporation's continuous activity of some sorts within a state . . . is not enough to support the demand that the corporation be amenable to suits unrelated to that activity.") (citation and internal quotations omitted).

137. *E.g., Congoleum Corp. v. DLW, AG,* 729 F.2d 1240, 1242 (9th Cir. 1984) (*Perkins* is "limited to its unusual facts"); *Cubbage v. Merchent,* 744 F.2d 665, 667-668 (9th Cir. 1984).

c. Selected Materials on "Presence" as a Basis for General Jurisdiction. The Supreme Court considered the "continuous and systematic" business test in *Helicopteros Nacionales de Colombia v. Hall,* excerpted below. Also excerpted below is the Fifth Circuit's decision in *Adams v. Unione Mediterranea di Sicurta,*[138] which applies *Helicopteros* and Federal Rule of Civil Procedure 4(k)(2) in finding general jurisdiction over a foreign defendant.

HELICOPTEROS NACIONALES DE COLOMBIA v. HALL
466 U.S. 408 (1984)

JUSTICE BLACKMUN. [Petitioner Helicopteros Nacionales de Colombia, SA ("Helicol"), is a Colombian corporation that provides helicopter transportation for construction companies in South America. In 1976, a helicopter owned by Helicol crashed in Peru, killing four U.S. citizens. Respondents are the survivors and representatives of the decedents. The four decedents were employed by Consorcio, a Peruvian consortium, which was the alter ego of a joint venture named Williams-Sedco-Horn ("WSH"), headquartered in Houston, Texas. Consorcio was engaged in the construction of a pipeline running from the interior of Peru to the Pacific Ocean.

In 1974, on request of Consorcio/WSH, the chief executive officer of Helicol, Francisco Restrepo, flew to Houston and met with the joint venture about Consorcio/WSH's need for helicopter transportation on the Peruvian pipeline project. At the meeting, Consorcio/WSH accepted a contract for the supply of helicopters proposed by Helicol. When finalized, the contract was written in Spanish on Peruvian government stationery. It provided that the residence of all the parties would be Lima, Peru, and that disputes arising out of the contract would be submitted to the Peruvian courts. The contract also provided that Consorcio/WSH would make payments to Helicol's account in New York.

Helicol had a variety of other contacts with Texas. It purchased approximately 80 percent of its helicopter fleet, as well as spare parts from Bell Helicopter Company in Fort Worth. Helicol also sent pilots and other personnel to Fort Worth for training and to ferry the helicopters it purchased to South America. Helicol received into its New York City and Panama City, Fla., bank accounts over $5 million in payments from Consorcio/WSH drawn on First City National Bank of Houston. Nonetheless, Helicol was never authorized to do business in Texas and never had an agent for the service within the state. It never performed helicopter operations in Texas or sold any product that reached Texas, never solicited business in Texas, never signed any contract in Texas, and never employed or recruited any employee in Texas. In addition, Helicol never owned property in Texas or maintained an office there. Helicol had no records or shareholders in Texas.[139] None of the respondents or their decedents were domiciled in Texas.[140] All of the decedents were hired in Houston by Consorcio/WSH to work on the Peru pipeline project.

---

138. 364 F.3d 646 (5th Cir. 2004).

139. The Colombian national airline, Aerovias Nacionales de Colombia, owns approximately 94 percent of Helicol's capital stock. The remainder is held by Aerovias Corporacion de Viajes and four South American individuals.

140. Respondents' lack of residential or other contacts with Texas of itself does not defeat otherwise proper jurisdiction. *Keeton v. Hustler Magazine, Inc.,* 465 U.S. 770, 780 (1984); *Calder v. Jones,* 465 U.S. 783, 788 (1984). We mention respondents' lack of contacts merely to show that nothing in the nature of the relationship between respondents and Helicol could possibly enhance Helicol's contacts in Texas. The harm suffered by respondents did not occur in Texas. Nor is it alleged that any negligence on the part of Helicol took place in Texas.

Respondents instituted wrongful-death actions in Texas state court against Consorcio/ WSH, Bell Helicopter, and Helicol. Helicol unsuccessfully moved to dismiss for lack of *in personam* jurisdiction. After a jury trial, judgment was entered against Helicol on a jury verdict of $1,141,200 in favor of the respondents. On appeal, the Supreme Court of Texas held that the state's long-arm statute reaches as far as the Due Process Clause permits and that it was consistent with due process for Texas courts to assert *in personam* jurisdiction over Helicol.]

The Due Process Clause of the Fourteenth Amendment [is] satisfied when *in personam* jurisdiction is asserted over a nonresident corporate defendant that has "certain minimum contacts with [the forum] such that the maintenance of the suit does not offend 'traditional notions of fair play and substantial justice.'" When a controversy is related to or "arises out of" a defendant's contacts with the forum, the Court has said that a "relationship among the defendant, the forum, and the litigation" is the essential foundation of *in personam* jurisdiction.[141] Even when the cause of action does not arise out of or relate to the foreign corporation's activities in the forum State,[142] due process is not offended by a State's subjecting the corporation to its *in personam* jurisdiction when there are sufficient contacts between the state and the foreign corporation. *Perkins v. Benguet Consolidated Mining Co.* [discussed *supra* at p. 117]. [In *Perkins,* we held that] the foreign corporation, through its president, "ha[d] been carrying on in Ohio a continuous and systematic, but limited, part of its general business," and the exercise of general jurisdiction over the Philippine corporation by an Ohio court was "reasonable and just."

All parties to the present case concede that respondents' claims against Helicol did not "arise out of," and are not related to, Helicol's activities within Texas.[143] We thus must explore the nature of Helicol's contacts with the State of Texas to determine whether they constitute the kind of continuous and systematic general business contacts the Court found to exist in *Perkins.* We hold that they do not. It is undisputed that Helicol does not have a place of business in Texas and never has been licensed to do business in the State. Basically, Helicol's contacts with Texas consisted of sending its chief executive officer to Houston for a contract negotiation session; accepting into its New York bank account checks drawn on a Houston bank; purchasing helicopters, equipment, and training services from Bell Helicopter for substantial sums; and sending personnel to Bell's facilities in Fort Worth for training. The one trip to Houston by Helicol's chief executive officer for the purpose of negotiating the transportation services contract with Consorcio/WSH cannot be described or regarded as a contact of a "continuous and systematic" nature, as *Perkins* described it, and thus cannot support an assertion of *in personam* jurisdiction over Helicol by a Texas court. Similarly, Helicol's acceptance from Consorcio/ WSH of checks drawn on a Texas bank is of negligible significance for purposes of

141. It has been said that when a State exercises personal jurisdiction over a defendant in a suit arising out of or related to the defendant's contacts with the forum, the State is exercising "specific jurisdiction" over the defendant.

142. When a State exercises personal jurisdiction over a defendant in a suit not arising out of or related to the defendant's contacts with the forum, the State has been said to be exercising "general jurisdiction" over the defendant.

143. . . . Respondents have made no argument that their cause of action either arose out of or is related to Helicol's contacts with the State of Texas. Absent any briefing on the issue, we decline to reach the questions (1) whether the terms "arising out of" and "related to" describe different connections between a cause of action and a defendant's contacts with a forum, and (2) what sort of tie between a cause of action and a defendant's contacts with a forum is necessary to a determination that either connection exists. Nor do we reach the question whether, if the two types of relationship differ, a forum's exercise of personal jurisdiction in a situation where the cause of action "relates to," but does not "arise out of," the defendant's contacts with the forum should be analyzed as an assertion of specific jurisdiction.

determining whether Helicol had sufficient contacts in Texas. There is no indication that Helicol ever requested that the checks be drawn on a Texas bank or that there was any negotiation between Helicol and Consorcio/WSH with respect to the location or identity of the bank on which checks would be drawn. Common sense and everyday experience suggest that, absent unusual circumstances, the bank on which a check is drawn is generally of little consequence to the payee and is a matter left to the discretion of the drawer. Such unilateral activity of another party or a third person is not an appropriate consideration when determining whether a defendant has sufficient contacts with a forum State to justify an assertion of jurisdiction.

The Texas Supreme Court focused on the purchases and the related training trips in finding contacts sufficient to support an assertion of jurisdiction. We do not agree with that assessment, for the Court's opinion in *Rosenberg Bros. & Co. v. Curtis Brown Co.*, 260 U.S. 516 . . . , makes clear that purchases and related trips, standing alone, are not a sufficient basis for a State's assertion of jurisdiction. The defendant in *Rosenberg* was a small retailer in Tulsa, Okla., who dealt in men's clothing and furnishings. . . . Its only connection with New York was that it purchased from New York wholesalers a large portion of the merchandise sold in its Tulsa store. The purchases sometimes were made by correspondence and sometimes through visits to New York by an officer of the defendant. The Court concluded: "Visits on such business, even if occurring at regular intervals, would not warrant the inference that the corporation was present within the jurisdiction of [New York]."

This Court in *International Shoe* acknowledged and did not repudiate its holding in *Rosenberg*. In accordance with *Rosenberg*, we hold that mere purchases, even if occurring at regular intervals, are not enough to warrant a State's assertion of *in personam* jurisdiction over a nonresident corporation in a cause of action not related to those purchase transactions.[144] Nor can we conclude that the fact that Helicol sent personnel into Texas for training in connection with the purchase of helicopters and equipment in that State in any way enhanced the nature of Helicol's contacts with Texas. The training was a part of the package of goods and services purchased by Helicol from Bell Helicopter. The brief presence of Helicol employees in Texas for the purpose of attending the training sessions is no more a significant contact than were the trips to New York made by the buyer for the retail store in *Rosenberg*. . . . We hold that Helicol's contacts with the State of Texas were insufficient to satisfy the requirements of the Due Process Clause of the Fourteenth Amendment. . . .[145]

---

144. This Court in *International Shoe* cited *Rosenberg* for the proposition that "the commission of some single or occasional acts of the corporate agent in a state sufficient to impose an obligation or liability on the corporation has not been thought to confer upon the state authority to enforce it." 326 U.S. at 318. Arguably, therefore, *Rosenberg* also stands for the proposition that mere purchases are not a sufficient basis for either general or specific jurisdiction. Because the case before us is one in which there has been an assertion of general jurisdiction over a foreign defendant, we need not decide the continuing validity of *Rosenberg* with respect to an assertion of specific jurisdiction, *i.e.*, where the cause of action arises out of or relates to the purchases by the defendant in the forum State.

145. As an alternative to traditional minimum-contacts analysis, respondents suggest that the Court hold that the State of Texas had personal jurisdiction over Helicol under a doctrine of "jurisdiction by necessity." *See Shaffer v. Heitner*, 433 U.S. 186, 211 n.37 (1977). We conclude, however, that respondents failed to carry their burden of showing that all three defendants could not be sued together in a single forum. It is not clear from the records, for example, whether suit could have been brought against all three defendants in either Colombia or Peru. We decline to consider adoption of a doctrine of jurisdiction by necessity — a potentially far-reaching modification of existing law — in the absence of a more complete record.

ADAMS v. UNIONE MEDITERRANEA DI SICURTA
364 F.3d 646 (5th Cir. 2004)

DAVIS, W. EUGENE, CIRCUIT JUDGE. On October 16, 1993, while en route from New Orleans to Cincinnati, two Canal Barge Company [("Canal Barge")] barges carrying 158 slabs of steel cargo broke away from their flotilla and sank in the Mississippi river. The loss occurred during the final leg of a carriage of 1,290 steel slabs that began in Italy. The owner of the steel slabs was Duferco SA ("Duferco"), a Swiss company, which had agreed to ship the steel to AK Steel, an Ohio Company. Plaintiff underwriters Steven Henry Adams et al. ("Adams") and [Unione Mediterranea di Sicurta] UMS, an Italian insurer, concurrently insured the steel cargo under separate marine cargo policies. Adams insured the steel through a cargo policy originally issued to Canal Barge, with Duferco named as an additional insured. Duferco was separately insured under an open cargo policy issued by UMS. . . . [After the accident,] a professional salvage company, American Eagle Marine, Inc. ("American Eagle") attempted to salvage the lost cargo believing it to have been abandoned in its entirety. American Eagle successfully salvaged 127 of the sunken steel slabs and sold them to AK Steel for a net profit of $190,975.68.

Plaintiff Adams . . . brought this action in June 1994 seeking a declaratory judgment: (1) identifying whom it should pay for the loss of the cargo under their cargo policy with Canal Barge; (2) that UMS was obligated under its open cargo policy with Duferco to contribute to payment for the loss; and (3) that Plaintiffs were obligated to pay only their proportionate share of the loss. Plaintiffs named as defendants, among others, Canal Barge, UMS, and Duferco. [The district court denied UMS's motion to dismiss for lack of personal jurisdiction. In the excerpted passage, the Court of Appeals considered whether jurisdiction lay under Rule 4(k)(2).]

Rule 4(k)(2)[, excerpted in Appendix C,] provides for service of process and personal jurisdiction in any district court for cases arising under federal law where the defendant has contacts with the United States as a whole sufficient to satisfy due process concerns and the defendant is not subject to jurisdiction in any particular state. The Rule was enacted to fill an important gap in the jurisdiction of federal courts in cases arising under federal law:

> Thus, there was gap in the courts' jurisdiction: while a defendant may have sufficient contacts with the United States as a whole to satisfy due process concerns, if she had insufficient contacts with any single state, she would not be amenable to service by a federal court sitting in that state. . . . Rule 4(k)(2) was adopted in response to this problem of a gap in the courts' jurisdiction. . . . *World Tanker Carriers Corp. v. MV Ya Mawlaya*, 99 F.3d 717, 721-22 (5th Cir. 1996).

[The Court first concluded that UMS was not subject to the jurisdiction of any state and that Adams's claim arose under federal law. It then considered whether, under Rule 4(k)(2), jurisdiction over UMS would be "consistent with the Constitution and laws of the United States."] In applying Rule 4(k)(2) the Court must determine whether [UMS] has sufficient ties to the United States as a whole to satisfy constitutional due process concerns. . . .

UMS has paid claims to numerous U.S. companies, 155 in all from 1991 to 1994. The defendant insurer has covered numerous other U.S. companies which made no claims. UMS has insured hundreds of shipments to the United States. Specifically, records produced by UMS and Duferco show that UMS insured approximately 260 shipments to the United States between 1989 and 1995 for Duferco alone; 138 of these Duferco shipments to the United States made between 1991 and 1994 were valued at over $130 million. Moreover, UMS used and paid a number of individuals in the United States as claims adjusters, surveyors, investigators and other representatives to enable it to conduct business in this country. Given the volume of activity, we have no difficulty concluding that UMS has continuous and systematic contacts with the United States as a whole. *See Helicopteros Nacionales de Colombia, supra.* It was foreseeable that suit in U.S. courts would result from these business contacts. Defendant was well aware of the shipments to the United States and in fact enabled the prosecution of claims in the United States by providing claims agents and surveyors here. Thus, subjecting UMS to suit here does not offend notions of fair play and substantial justice.

Notes on Helicopteros Nacionales and Adams

1. *Practical significance of a U.S. forum.* The four plaintiffs in *Helicopteros* were awarded approximately $1.1 million by a Texas jury. That figure is not unusual by U.S. standards. But in Bogota, Lima, and many other places, a recovery of this magnitude would be inconceivable. Mrs. Hall could realistically have expected no more than 5 percent of her Texas verdict had she proceeded in Colombia or Peru; and that amount would have been subject to local taxes, foreign exchange controls, and other restrictions. What significance should such factors have in due process analysis? Is it relevant to the "purposeful availment" prong? To the "reasonableness" prong? To neither?

2. *Relevance of defendant's foreign identity in* Helicopteros. As described above, jurisdiction over foreign defendants differs in important ways from jurisdiction over U.S. defendants. What importance did *Helicopteros* assign to the fact that the defendant was a Colombian corporation? Suppose that Helicol had been a Californian corporation, operating in Arizona, and the fatal crash had occurred in Arizona. Would Helicol have been subject to suit in Texas? Is the argument for Texas jurisdiction stronger or weaker in the California-Arizona hypothetical, or in the actual *Helicopteros* case? Why? What relevance should be assigned to the unusual hardships a U.S. plaintiff may encounter in a Colombian forum (as compared to a Californian one)? *See supra* pp. 3-4 & *infra* pp. 397-399. What is the relevance of the burdens that a foreign defendant may face in a U.S. forum?

3. *Relevance of plaintiff's U.S. identity in* Helicopteros. What relevance should the plaintiff's nationality have for due process analysis? Note that in *Helicopteros,* the plaintiffs were U.S. citizens. Does that make for a stronger due process argument than would have been the case if the plaintiffs were Colombian or Peruvian nationals?

4. *"Continuous and systematic" presence in* Helicopteros. *Helicopteros* held that general jurisdiction requires "the kind of continuous and systematic general business contacts . . . found to exist in *Perkins*" Why didn't Helicol have this sort of contacts with Texas? It is clear that the "continuous and systematic" contacts test imposes a substantially more rigorous standard than the "minimum contacts" test applicable in the specific jurisdiction context. *See supra* pp. 88-90. Consider, however, the following excerpt from the dissenting opinion in *Helicopteros:*

> As a foreign corporation that has actively and purposefully engaged in numerous and frequent commercial transactions in the State of Texas, Helicol clearly falls within the category of nonresident defendants that may be subject to that forum's general jurisdiction. Helicol not only purchased helicopters and other equipment in the State for many years, but also sent pilots and management personnel into Texas to be trained in the use of this equipment and

to consult with the seller on technical matters. Moreover, negotiations for the contract under which Helicol provided transportation services to the joint venture that employed the respondents' decedents also took place in the State of Texas. 466 U.S. at 423-424.

Are you persuaded? If so, would Texas courts have jurisdiction over a suit by a Peruvian bank to recover money loaned to Helicol in Peru? A suit by a Peruvian secretary for unfair dismissal from her position at Helicol's Peruvian office? A tort suit by a Peruvian oil pipeline worker injured in rural Peru—for example, in the same helicopter accident that killed the U.S. plaintiffs in *Helicopteros*?

5. *"Continuous and systematic" presence in* **Adams.** What facts led the *Adams* Court to say that there was "no difficulty" in concluding that UMS was subject to general jurisdiction in the United States? Consider that UMS probably insures hundreds of thousands of companies, and pays tens of thousands of claims annually. Is it not extraordinary that a foreign insurance company would be subject to U.S. general jurisdiction because it insured a few hundred U.S. companies and paid a few hundred U.S.-related claims over several years? Will decisions like *Adams* have an impact on the availability and cost of insurance for U.S. companies? Is *Adams* consistent with the rigorous standard for general jurisdiction in *Helicopteros*?

6. Perkins *and general jurisdiction. Perkins* is the only contemporary Supreme Court decision affirming an assertion of general jurisdiction (other than *Burnham*, a "tag" jurisdiction case which is excerpted and discussed at *infra* pp. 129-137). Should the "continuous and systematic" contacts test for general jurisdiction be confined to cases like *Perkins*, where the defendant cannot be sued in its place of incorporation? Is *Perkins* even a general jurisdiction case? Or did the claim "arise from" the defendant corporation's Ohio contacts?

7. *Factors relevant to application of "continuous and systematic" contacts test.* A variety of factors can be relevant to the "doing business" test:

(a) Solicitation. Lower courts have frequently held that "mere solicitation" by a foreign corporation does not constitute "doing business." *E.g., Fraser v. Smith*, 594 F.3d 842, 847 (11th Cir. 2010); *United States v. Swiss American Bank, Ltd.*, 274 F.3d 610, 620 (1st Cir. 2001) (advertisements insufficient for general jurisdiction); *Pizarro v. Hoteles Concorde Int'l CA*, 907 F.2d 1256 (1st Cir. 1990) (placing nine ads in forum newspaper does not sustain general jurisdiction over foreign hotel). On the other hand, some courts have suggested that solicitation provides a substantial basis for general jurisdiction, provided that some other forum contacts also exist. *E.g., H. Heller & Co. v. Novacor Chem. Ltd.*, 726 F. Supp. 49 (S.D.N.Y. 1988) ("once solicitation is found in any substantial degree courts have required very little more to support a conclusion of 'doing business'"). Is this appropriate? If taken seriously, does it not permit general jurisdiction in a broad range of cases?

(b) Shipment of products into the forum. The shipment of products into the forum, without more, will not ordinarily permit general jurisdiction. *E.g., Johnston v. Multidata Sys. Int'l Corp.*, 523 F.3d 602, 611-614 (5th Cir. 2008); *Glencore Grain Rotterdam BV v. Shivnath Rai Harnarain Co.*, 284 F.3d 1114, 1124-1125 (9th Cir. 2002) (multiple shipments into forum insufficient to establish general jurisdiction); *Associated Transport Line, Inc. v. Productos Fitosanitarios Proficol El Carmen, SA*, 197 F.3d 1070, 1075 (11th Cir. 1999) (multiple sales over four-year period held insufficient to support general jurisdiction); *Bearry v. Beech Aircraft Corp.*, 818 F.2d 370 (5th Cir. 1987) ($50 million in annual sales, over a number of years, to 17 distributors within forum not sufficient for general jurisdiction); *Ahern v. Pacific Gulf Marine*, 2008 WL 706501 (M.D. Fla. Mar. 14, 2008); *In re New Motor Vehicles Canadian Export Antitrust Litig.*, 307 F. Supp. 2d 145, 151 (D. Me. 2004); *In re Ski Train Fire in Kaprun, Austria on Nov. 11, 2000*, 257 F. Supp. 2d 717, 732-733 (S.D.N.Y. 2003); *Delta Brands, Inc. v. Danieli Corp.*, 2002 WL 31875560, at *5 (N.D. Tex. 2002).

However, in a few cases, general jurisdiction has been found by lower courts based on substantial sales to forum purchasers. *E.g., Metcalfe v. Renaissance Marine, Inc.*, 566 F.3d 324, 335 (3d Cir. 2009) (product sales coupled with ten-year warranty); *Howse v. Zimmer Mfg. Co.*, 757 F.2d 448 (1st Cir. 1985) (out-of-state manufacturer subject to general jurisdiction because it frequently sent agents into forum, had "sizeable sales volume" in forum, and received payments directly from forum customers); *Paradise Motors, Inc. v. Toyota de Puerto Rico Corp.*, 314 F. Supp. 2d 495, 499 (D.V.I. 2004) (out-of-state manufacturer subject to general jurisdiction based on regular annual volume of automobile sales to forum coupled with visits by defendant's representatives).

Supreme Court precedent has cast doubt on this latter line of authority. In *Keeton v. Hustler Magazine, Inc.*, 465 U.S. 770, 779-780 & n.11 (1984), the Court strongly suggested that the monthly distribution of 10,000 to 15,000 magazines by defendant to forum residents was not "so substantial as to support jurisdiction over a cause of action unrelated to those activities." The Court distinguished *Perkins* on the grounds that there "Ohio was the corporation's principal, if temporary, place of business." 465 U.S. at 780 n.11. More recently, in *Goodyear Dunlop Tires Operations, S.A. v. Brown*, 2011 WL 2518815 (U.S. June 27, 2011), the Court held that foreign companies' sporadic sale of products, via intermediaries, into the forum state did not give rise to general jurisdiction. The Court in *Goodyear* found such sporadic sales indistinguishable from the sporadic purchases in *Helicopteros* and distinguished *Perkins* on the ground that it involved a company "whose sole wartime business activity was conducted in Ohio." *Id.* at *9-10. Is it appropriate to impose such a demanding standard for general jurisdiction?

(c) *Purchase of products from forum.* The Supreme Court held in *Rosenberg*, and reaffirmed in *Helicopteros*, that the purchase of products from the forum usually does not confer general jurisdiction. Lower courts have virtually never upheld general jurisdiction based on purchases from the forum. *E.g., Associated Transport Line, Inc. v. Productos Fitosanitarios Proficol El Carmen, SA*, 197 F.3d 1070, 1075 (11th Cir. 1999) ("[A] party's purchases in the United States are never enough to justify jurisdiction."); *Rolls-Royce Motors, Inc. v. Charles Schmitt & Co.*, 657 F. Supp. 1040, 1046 (S.D.N.Y. 1987) (foreign corporation's purchase of a "major share of the merchandise to be sold at its place of business outside the state, even if systematic and made upon visits occurring at regular intervals, do not warrant a finding that the defendant was present" in New York); *BMC Software Belgium, NV v. Marchand*, 83 S.W.3d 789, 797-798 (Tex. 2000). *Compare In re Ocean Ranger Sinking*, 589 F. Supp. 302, 312 (E.D. La. 1984) (general jurisdiction upheld based on $124 million in purchases from forum vendors over four-year period). Why are purchases of products not a basis for general jurisdiction?

The U.S. Government submitted an *amicus curiae* brief in *Helicopteros* arguing that general jurisdiction should not ordinarily be based on a foreign defendant's *purchase* of goods in the United States.

[T]o the extent that the decision below relies on Helicol's purchase of its helicopter fleet in Texas, coupled with the presence of Helicol employees in Texas to receive training on the operation and maintenance of the helicopters, it has a significant potential for discouraging foreign firms from purchasing American products. This would thwart positive efforts of Congress and the Executive Branch to make American firms and products more competitive internationally. Brief for the United States as Amicus Curiae at 6, 9-12 *Helicopteros Nacionales de Colombia, SA v. Hall*, 466 U.S. 408 (1984).

Are these factors properly relevant to due process analysis?

Helicopteros held that a foreign purchaser's contacts with the forum were less significant for general jurisdiction than a foreign seller's contacts. Should this reasoning also apply to specific jurisdiction? Note that the Supreme Court leaves the issue unresolved. 466 U.S. at 418 n.12. Many lower courts have also been unwilling to base personal jurisdiction on an out-of-state person's purchase of products from the forum state. *E.g., Revlon, Inc. v. United Overseas Ltd.*, 1994 WL 9657 (S.D.N.Y. 1994) ("well-settled distinction between sales activity and purchasing activity"). What is the rationale for distinguishing between sales and purchases?

(d) *Ownership of property in forum.* In most cases, a foreign corporation's ownership of property in the forum is not a sufficient basis for general jurisdiction. Most of the cases to consider this point have involved bank accounts. *E.g., Landoil Resources Corp. v. Alexander & Alexander Services, Inc.*, 563 N.Y.S.2d 739 (1990) (foreign company's $9 billion trust fund not a basis for general jurisdiction); *Vendetti v. Fiat Auto SpA*, 802 F. Supp. 886 (W.D.N.Y. 1992) (foreign auto maker's maintenance of incidental bank accounts in New York, plus making of payments to New York marketing entities and communications with dealers not sufficient for general jurisdiction). However, if a foreign corporation makes sufficiently continuous and substantial use of a forum bank account, that may provide an independent basis for general jurisdiction. *E.g., Provident National Bank v. California Federal Savings & Loan Ass'n*, 819 F.2d 434 (3d Cir. 1987) (maintaining bank account, used on a daily basis as a "central" part of defendant's business, is sufficient basis for general jurisdiction); *United Rope Distributors, Inc. v. Kim-Sail, Ltd.*, 770 F. Supp. 128 (S.D.N.Y. 1991).

(e) *Visits to forum by employees or agents.* Lower courts have generally held that visits to the forum by a company's employees or agents do not create general jurisdiction. *E.g., Johnston v. Multidata Sys. Int'l Corp.*, 523 F.3d 602, 614 (5th Cir. 2008); *Purdue Research Foundation v. Sanofi-Synthelabo, SA*, 338 F.3d 773, 788 (7th Cir. 2003); *Marathon Oil Co. v. A.G. Ruhrgas*, 182 F.3d 291, 295 (5th Cir. 1999); *Complaint of Damodar Bulk Carriers, Ltd.*, 903 F.2d 675 (9th Cir. 1990) (several bunkering calls by defendant's vessel to forum do not permit general jurisdiction); *BBC Chartering & Logistic GmbH & Co. KG v. Usiminas Mecanica S/A*, 2009 WL 259618 (S.D.N.Y. Feb. 4, 2009) (several meetings in forum state over two-year period held insufficient); *Isood v. Diagem Res. Corp.*, 2006 WL 1788374 (D. Nev. June 26, 2006) (telephone calls and visit by defendant's executive to forum held insufficient). *Cf. Porina v. Marward Shipping Co.*, 521 F.3d 122, 129 (2d Cir. 2008) (vessel's visits to forum at request of charterers insufficient to establish continuous and systematic contacts).

(f) *Unincorporated branch office.* The presence of an unincorporated branch office within the forum will ordinarily permit general jurisdiction. *E.g., Trabucco v. Intesa Sanpaolo, S.p.A.*, 695 F. Supp. 2d 98 (S.D.N.Y. 2010) (branch office in forum coupled with regular business there held sufficient); *Donnelly Corp. v. Reitter & Schefenacker GmbH & Co.*, 189 F. Supp. 2d 696, 712-714 (W.D. Mich. 2002) (presence of three employees in forum state coupled with other contacts such as purchases, sales and solicitation gave rise to general jurisdiction); *Goss Graphic Systems v. Man Roland Druckmaschinen Aktiengesellschaft*, 139 F. Supp. 2d 1040, 1068-1069 (N.D. Iowa 2001) (employee presence in forum, correspondence with forum, sales in forum, and advertisement in forum collectively supported general jurisdiction over foreign corporation); *Revlon, Inc. v. United Overseas Ltd.*, 1994 WL 9657 (S.D.N.Y. 1994) ("The maintenance of even a relatively minor office in New York alone justifies an assertion of jurisdiction over a foreign corporation . . ."); *Ciprari v. Servios Aeros Cruzeiro do Sul, SA*, 232 F. Supp. 433 (S.D.N.Y. 1964). *Compare Submersible Systems, Inc. v. Perforadora Central, SA de CV*, 249 F.3d 413, 419 (5th Cir. 2001) (temporary office established in forum during single construction project insufficient to establish general jurisdiction); *Speed v. Pelican Resort NV*, 1992 U.S. Dist. LEXIS 8278 (S.D.N.Y. 1992) ("the maintenance of mere telephone lines and listings does not constitute 'presence' or 'doing business' "). Is this appropriate? Why should jurisdiction not be limited to the activities and business of the branch office?

(g)   *Entering into contracts with forum residents.* Lower courts have usually refused to find general jurisdiction based upon the fact that the defendant has entered into a number of contracts with forum residents over a significant period of time. *E.g., Consolidated Development Corp. v. Sherritt, Inc.*, 216 F.3d 1286, 1292 (11th Cir. 2000) (periodic offer of securities to forum residents held insufficient); *El Fadl v. Central Bank of Jordan*, 75 F.3d 668, 675 (D.C. Cir. 1996) (isolated and sporadic loan agreements insufficient to give rise to general jurisdiction but remanding for jurisdictional discovery); *Golden Gulf Corp. v. Jordache Enterprises, Inc.*, 1994 WL 62384 (S.D.N.Y. 1994) (no general jurisdiction based upon foreign corporation's entry into licensing agreement providing for payment of fees to New York company, provision of materials and information to New York company, and arbitration in New York). In a few cases, however, general jurisdiction has been based principally on contractual arrangements with forum residents, although other factors have also usually been present. *E.g., Elliott v. Faber and Schleicher AG*, 1994 WL 322975 (E.D. Pa. 1994) (asserting general jurisdiction over foreign manufacturer because it appointed exclusive U.S. distributor); *La Nuova D & B, SpA v. Bower Co.*, 513 A.2d 764 (Del. 1986).

(h)   *Maintenance of websites.* The advent of the Internet has added a new set of issues in jurisdictional inquiry — with websites, email, and other Internet activities being claimed to provide a basis for both general and specific jurisdiction. Most courts have rejected the argument that a website accessible from the forum could, without more, provide the basis for general jurisdiction. *E.g., FC Investment Group v. IFX Markets, Ltd.*, 529 F.3d 1087, 1092-1093 (D.C. Cir. 2008); *Soma Med. Int'l v. Standard Chartered Bank*, 196 F.3d 1292, 1297 (10th Cir. 1999); *Bancroft & Masters, Inc. v. Augusta Nat'l Inc.*, 223 F.3d 1082, 1086 (9th Cir. 2000); *Elayyan v.* Melia, 571 F. Supp. 2d 886, 901 (N.D. Ind. 2008); *Autogenomics, Inc. v. Oxford Gene Tech, Ltd.*, 2008 WL 7071464 (C.D. Cal. Jan. 17, 2008), *aff'd*, 566 F.3d 1012 (Fed. Cir. 2009); *Thiring v. Borden*, 2007 WL 1875656 (D. Or. June 27, 2007); *Hy Cite Corp. v. Badbusinessbureau.com, LLC*, 297 F. Supp. 2d 1154, 1161-1162 (W.D. Wis. 2004); *Dagesse v. Plant Hotel NV*, 113 F. Supp. 2d 211, 220-221 (D.N.H. 2000) (collecting cases).

However, a minority view holds that a defendant's maintenance of an interactive website, from which regular commercial transactions can be conducted with residents in the forum, can amount to the "continuous and systematic" contacts necessary to give rise to general jurisdiction. *E.g., Gorman v. Ameritrade Holding Corp.*, 293 F.3d 506, 509-513 (D.C. Cir. 2002) *See* Pielemeier, *Why General Personal Jurisdiction over "Virtual Stores" Is a Bad Idea*, 27 Quinnipiac L. Rev. 625 (2009); Kaye, *Internet Web Site Activities of Nonresident Person or Corporation as Conferring Personal Jurisdiction Under Long-Arm Statutes and Due Process Clause*, 81 A.L.R.5th 41 (2000).

8. Rationale for general jurisdiction based on continuous and systematic contacts. Both *Helicopteros* and *Adams* held that jurisdiction could be asserted against a defendant with respect to claims not "arising out of" the defendant's activities in the forum state, based simply on the fact that the defendant had substantial, continuous contacts with the forum that were unrelated to the dispute. This is a far-reaching and exceptional jurisdictional basis. Consider various factual circumstances in which "continuous and systematic contacts" might justify jurisdiction over a foreign defendant; how far can you push the doctrine's limits?

Is the "continuous and systematic contacts" rule sensible and just? Why should a defendant *ever* be subject to suit in the forum on claims entirely unrelated to activities within the forum? What interest does the forum state have in adjudicating such claims? Does general jurisdiction pose special threats to the territorial sovereignty of foreign states? To the fair treatment of private parties?

Reconsider the justifications for general jurisdiction: the desirability of having one forum where a defendant will clearly be subject to jurisdiction on all claims, without the need for expensive litigation over "minimum contacts" or "reasonableness," and the perception that defendants will be neither inconvenienced nor surprised if subjected to jurisdiction in their "backyard." *See supra* p. 111. Is this persuasive? Does it address due process and international law concerns about infringing on the territorial sovereignty of foreign states or treating private parties unfairly?

Even accepting the foregoing rationale for general jurisdiction, does it not extend only to jurisdiction based on domicile or incorporation, and not to jurisdiction based upon "continuous and systematic" activities? Is general jurisdiction based on "continuous and systematic" contacts necessary in order that the defendant undeniably be subject to jurisdiction in at least one forum? Note that, unlike the place of domicile or incorporation, a defendant can have continuous and systematic contacts with multiple jurisdictions; indeed, for major corporations, one might argue that they have continuous and systematic contacts with almost every jurisdiction conceivable. Is there any serious reason that Volkswagen, Microsoft, or Total should be subject to jurisdiction on any claim in any forum in the world?

Is there a significant risk of unfairness in permitting suit against the defendant at a place where it is continuously and systematically present? Note that permitting general jurisdiction based on comparatively "easy" showings significantly increases a plaintiff's choice of potential forums — and hence its litigation advantages. *See supra* pp. 3-4, 103, 108, 111-112.

9. *General jurisdiction and reasonableness.* Are assertions of general jurisdiction based upon "continuous and systematic" contacts subject to the "reasonableness" requirement of *World-Wide Volkswagen*? Lower courts have not frequently addressed the issue, but, like the court in *Adams*, generally appear to have assumed that they are. *E.g., Fraser v. Smith*, 594 F.3d 842, 850 (11th Cir. 2009); *Johnston v. Multidata Sys. Int'l Corp.*, 523 F.3d 602 (5th Cir. 2008); *Porina v. Marward Shipping Co.*, 521 F.3d 122, 129 (2d Cir. 2008) ; *Metropolitan Life v. Robertson Ceco*, 84 F.3d 560 (2d Cir. 1996); *Amoco Egypt Oil Co. v. Leonis Navigation Co.*, 1 F.3d 848 (9th Cir. 1993) (holding that "reasonableness" test is applicable to general jurisdiction); *de Reyes v. Marine Management & Consulting, Ltd.*, 586 So. 2d 103 (La. 1991) (applying reasonableness in "continuous and systematic" contacts case). *But see Capital Equipment Inc. v. CNH America, LLC*, 394 F. Supp. 2d 1054 (E.D. Ark. 2005) (refusing to apply reasonableness in general jurisdiction case).

Does it make sense to apply reasonableness limitations in the context of general jurisdiction? What impact does the Court's analysis in *Burnham* have on this result? *See infra* pp. 129-137. Compare the Court's analysis in *Blackmer. See supra* pp. 109-113. Do you agree with the "reasonableness" analysis in *Adams*?

10. *General jurisdiction based on "continuous and systematic" contacts and EU Regulation 44/2001.* Does the Regulation 44/2001 permit general jurisdiction based on continuous and systematic contacts? Is that approach wise?

11. *General jurisdiction based on "continuous and systematic" contacts and international law.* Are U.S. assertions of general jurisdiction over foreign companies based upon their "continuous and systematic" activities in the forum consistent with international law? Note that the *Third Restatement* §421(2)(a) & (h) provide for general jurisdiction where a person is "present" in the forum's territory or "regularly carries on business in the state."

As discussed above, the Hague Conference negotiations broke down, in part, over disagreement between U.S. and European negotiators over general jurisdiction based on "doing business" within the forum. Article 18(2)(e) of the June 2001 Interim Text provided that jurisdiction could not be exercised on the basis of "the carrying on of commercial or other activities by the defendant in that State, [whether or not through a branch, agency, or any other establishment of the defendant], except where the dispute is directly related to those activities." *See* http://www.hcch.net. What impact, if any, should European views about "doing business" jurisdiction have on U.S. due process analysis? On U.S. legislative activity?

Consider the result in *Adams* again. Would this result have been permitted under European Council Regulation 44/2001? Under Article 18(2)(e) of the Interim Text? Under the *Restatement (Third)* §421?

Recall the discussion above, *supra* p. 30, concerning the possibility of international law limits on the competence of national courts. Are the limits that specific jurisdiction imposes on the claims that may be asserted against a defendant analogous to limits on competence?

12. ***Relationship between plaintiff's claims and defendant's forum contacts in*** **Helicopteros.** According to *Helicopteros*, the plaintiffs' claims against Helicol did not "arise out of" and were not "related to" Helicol's activities within Texas. The Court relied on the plaintiffs' apparent concession to that effect. 466 U.S. at 415 n.10. The dissent in *Helicopteros* and a number of commentators have urged that the plaintiffs' claims did in fact "relate to" Helicol's activities in Texas because the ill-fated helicopter was purchased in Texas and because training for the helicopter pilots was provided in Texas. Consider the dissenting opinion in *Helicopteros*:

> [A]lthough I agree that the respondent's cause of action did not formally "arise out of" specific activities initiated by Helicol in the State of Texas, I believe that the wrongful-death claim filed by the respondents is significantly related to the undisputed contacts between Helicol and the forum. On that basis, I would conclude that the Due Process Clause allows the Texas courts to assert specific jurisdiction over this particular action. The wrongful-death actions filed by the respondents were premised on a fatal helicopter crash that occurred in Peru. Helicol was joined as a defendant in the lawsuits because it provided transportation services, including the particular helicopter and pilot involved in the crash, to the joint venture that employed the decedents. Viewed in light of these allegations, the contacts between Helicol and the State of Texas are directly and significantly related to the underlying claim filed by the respondents. The negotiations that took place in Texas led to the contract in which Helicol agreed to provide the precise transportation services that were being used at the time of the crash. Moreover, the helicopter involved in the crash was purchased by Helicol in Texas, and the pilot whose negligence was alleged to have caused the crash was actually trained in Texas. This is simply not a case, therefore, in which a state court has asserted jurisdiction over a nonresident defendant on the basis of wholly unrelated contacts with the forum. 466 U.S. at 425-26.

Why might these factors be relevant to the exercise of jurisdiction in *Helicopteros*? Which of these factors would go furthest in arguing against the Court's result in *Helicopteros*? Note that the *Helicopteros* Court refuses to address the dissent's argument that specific jurisdiction can be asserted over all claims "relating to" the defendant's forum contacts and that this is a broader category of claims than those "arising out" of such contacts. The Court also refused to decide whether a hypothetically broader "relating to" category of claims would be treated as an assertion of specific jurisdiction.

As discussed below, some lower courts have adopted a "but for" test for specific jurisdiction, while other courts have adopted more restrictive standards, including "proximate cause" requirements. *See infra* pp. 173-175. How would *Helicopteros* be decided under these tests?

13. ***Defining the territory of the forum in*** **Adams** — *a preliminary look at nationwide* ***contacts.*** In *Adams*, the court exercised general jurisdiction over a foreign defendant based on the defendant's "continuous and systematic" contacts with the United States as a whole. Rule 4(k)(2), discussed in greater detail *infra* pp. 205-206, 209-231, enables this. As *Adams* explains, Rule 4(k)(2) allows federal courts, in certain cases, to aggregate the defendant's nationwide contacts rather than consider only the defendant's contacts with a forum state. Rule 4(k)(2) expands the geographic unit to which contacts are relevant even if the plaintiff's claim is not in any way "related to" the defendant's contacts, resulting in even more far-reaching exercises of general jurisdiction.

5. General Jurisdiction Based on Personal Service During the Transitory Presence of the Defendant Within the Forum

Consistent with nineteenth-century notions of territorial sovereignty, the historic American basis for judicial jurisdiction was the defendant's presence before the court.[146] In Justice Holmes' classic phrase, "the foundation of jurisdiction is physical power."[147] Against this background, U.S. courts long held that service of process on an individual while he was physically within the forum was a sufficient basis for general jurisdiction.[148]

The rule that service during the defendant's transitory presence within the forum provided a basis for general jurisdiction reached its most extreme application in *Grace v. MacArthur*.[149] *Grace* upheld tag service on the defendant while he was a passenger in an aircraft in flight through the airspace of the forum state. The transitory jurisdiction rule, particularly in its more extreme applications, has been the subject of substantial criticism. The *Restatement (Third)* treats it as illegitimate under international law,[150] and many commentators and lower courts rejected it under the Due Process Clause.[151]

Nonetheless, transitory jurisdiction continues to be important in many U.S. states. Moreover, the Supreme Court's divided decision in *Burnham v. Superior Court*,[152] discussed earlier in this chapter and reprised in the excerpt below, made it clear that the Due Process Clause imposes only limited (if any) constraints on tag service as a basis for general jurisdiction. The decisions in *CSB Commodities, Inc. v. Urban Trends (HK) Ltd.* and *Oyuela v. Seacor Marine (Nigeria), Inc.*, excerpted below, illustrates a post-*Burnham* treatment of tag service in international cases.

C.S.B. COMMODITIES, INC. v. URBAN TRENDS (HK) LTD.
626 F. Supp. 2d 837 (N.D. Ill. 2009)

Dow, District Judge: [C.S.B. Commodities, Inc. ("CSB"), a New York corporation, filed suit against Urban Trend, a Hong Kong corporation, and Kushner, an employee of Urban Trend who resided in Hong Kong. While Kushner, who was responsible for selecting the products that Urban Trend manufactures and markets, was in Illinois on company-related

---

146. *Burnham v. Superior Court*, 495 U.S. 604 (1990). *But see* Ehrenzweig, *The Transient Rule of Personal Jurisdiction: The "Power" Myth and Forum Conveniens*, 65 Yale L.J. 289, 292-303 (1956) (arguing that jurisdiction based on mere presence was a "myth" that began with *Pennoyer*).

147. *McDonald v. Mabee*, 243 U.S. 90, 91 (1917).

148. *Restatement (Second) Conflict of Laws* §28 (1971); *Pennoyer v. Neff*, 95 U.S. 714 (1878); *Burnham v. Superior Court*, 495 U.S. 604 (1990).

149. 170 F. Supp. 442 (E.D. Ark. 1959).

150. *Restatement (Third) Foreign Relations Law* §421 Reporters' Note 4 (1987).

151. *E.g.*, Ehrenzweig, *The Transient Rule of Personal Jurisdiction: The "Power" Myth and Forum Conveniens*, 65 Yale L.J. 289 (1956); Weintraub, *An Objective Basis for Rejecting Transient Jurisdiction*, 22 Rutgers L.J. 611 (1991).

152. 495 U.S. 604 (1990); *infra* pp. 133-135.

business, he was served with the complaint in CSB's lawsuit. Both defendants moved to dismiss on, among other grounds, lack of personal jurisdiction. Relying on *Burnham*, CSB argued that personal service on Kushner in Illinois sufficed to establish personal jurisdiction over both Kushner and Urban Trend.]

Plaintiff argues that pursuant to [*Burnham*], personal service of process on Kushner while he was present in the district is sufficient to assert personal jurisdiction over him. While present in Illinois, Kushner clearly was amenable to service of process. "A court may exercise jurisdiction in any action arising within or without this State against any person who is a natural person present within this State when served." 735 ILCS 5/2-209(b)(1). Kushner is a natural person served with process within Illinois and thus jurisdiction is proper under the Illinois long-arm statute. The only issue as to Kushner is whether in-forum service is sufficient to allay due process concerns.[153]

On its face, *Burnham* would appear to foreclose any argument that Kushner might have that defending this lawsuit in this court would violate his due process. However, Defendants note that the Court's decision in *Burnham* lacked a majority opinion and argue that minimum contacts analysis is still required to test due process. The dispute within the Court in *Burnham* arose over the justification for upholding the constitutionality of transitory jurisdiction. Justice Scalia (joined by Justice Kennedy, Chief Justice Rehnquist and largely Justice White) based his opinion on the historical pedigree:

> Among the most firmly established principles of personal jurisdiction in American tradition is that the courts of a State have jurisdiction over nonresidents who are physically present in the State. The view developed early that each State had the power to hale before its courts any individual who could be found within its borders, and that once having acquired jurisdiction over such a person by properly serving him with process, the State could retain jurisdiction to enter judgment against him, no matter how fleeting his visit. *Burnham*, 495 U.S. at 610-611 (Scalia, J.).

According to Justice Scalia, this was the understanding shared by American courts at the crucial time period, adoption of the Fourteenth Amendment. Therefore, he saw no reason to independently analyze other contacts the defendant had with the state. The decline of [*Pennoyer*] and its power theory of jurisdiction, and the concordant rise in *International Shoe* and its progeny, merely permitted "minimum contacts" to replace physical presence as the sole basis for jurisdiction. *International Shoe* made physical presence unnecessary but it did not render presence insufficient. "[J]urisdiction based on physical presence alone constituted due process because it is one of the continuing traditions of our legal system that define the due process standard of 'traditional notions of fair play and substantial justice.' That standard was developed by analogy to 'physical presence,' and it would be perverse to say it could now be turned against that touchstone of jurisdiction." *Burnham*, 495 U.S. at 619.

Justice Brennan (joined by Justice Marshall, Justice Blackmun and Justice O'Connor), while agreeing with the result, would not agree that tradition was "the only factor such that all traditional rules of jurisdiction are, ipso facto, forever constitutional." *Burnham*, 495 U.S. at 629. He stated that "all rules of jurisdiction, even ancient ones, must satisfy contemporary notions of due process." *Id.* Despite Justice Brennan's less bright-line approach, his opinion hints that rare (if ever) would be the situation when transient

---

153. *International Shoe*, its progeny, and *Burnham* were decided in the diversity jurisdiction context while this case pertains to federally created rights. However, the Seventh Circuit has held that there is no operative difference between the concept of due process as applied to the states through the Fourteenth Amendment and due process applied through the Fifth Amendment for federal claims.

jurisdiction would not satisfy due process.[154] "The transient rule is consistent with reasonable expectations and is entitled to a strong presumption that it comports with due process." *Burnham*, 495 U.S. at 637 (Brennan, J.). Justice Brennan noted that an individual travelling to a jurisdiction assumes the risk that the jurisdiction will exercise its power over the individual while there. *Id.* (citing *Shaffer v. Heitner*, 433 U.S. 186, 218 (1977)) (Stevens, J., concurring in judgment).

That the defendant has already journeyed at least once before to the forum — as evidenced by the fact that he was served with process there — is an indication that suit in the forum likely would not be prohibitively inconvenient. Finally, any burdens that do arise can be ameliorated by a variety of procedural devices. "For these reasons, as a rule the exercise of personal jurisdiction over a defendant based on his voluntary presence in the forum will satisfy the requirements of due process." *Id.* at 638-639 (emphasis added).

Defendants have made no argument that their presence in the forum was either involuntary or unknowing. Therefore, even under Justice Brennan's test, service of process would satisfy due process. Since *Burnham* was decided, there does not appear to be a single published opinion in which a court has found jurisdiction lacking where an individual was served in the forum. This court sees no reason to break from that apparently unbroken line of precedent. Finally, and unlike in *Burnham*, Kushner was served while in the forum solely for the activities leading to the complaint. In these circumstances, service alone satisfied due process as to Defendant Kushner. . . .

Kushner not only was served individually, but also as a representative of Urban Trend. Plaintiffs make an initial argument, premised on *Burnham*, that service was sufficient to confer general personal jurisdiction over Urban Trend as well. Although in-state service was sufficient as to Kushner individually, *Burnham* left unresolved whether the same service on corporations satisfies due process. If *Burnham* does not apply, Plaintiff argues in the alternative that Urban Trend is nonetheless amenable to specific personal jurisdiction based on its contacts with the forum. . . .

The only mention of corporations in *Burnham* was in a footnote in Justice Scalia's opinion. He pointed out that corporations "have never fitted comfortably in a jurisdictional regime based primarily upon 'de facto power over the defendant's person.'" *Burnham*, at 610 n. 1 (quoting *International Shoe*). Even that brief aside was made in response to a different question — whether individual defendants can ever be subject to general jurisdiction based on their "continuous and systematic" contacts in a state and in any event Justice Scalia made clear that the Court was expressing no views on the matter. Attempting to resolve this question of first impression in this district, the Court believes application of *Burnham* to corporate defendants to be improper. Even if a representative of the corporation is served with process in forum, minimum contacts with the forum remain necessary for this court to exercise personal jurisdiction.

The problem which first gave rise to the minimum contacts test was determining where corporations were "present" under the power theory of jurisdiction which prevailed under *Pennoyer v. Neff.* In lieu of legal fictions that the states were creating to ensure corporations could be subject to jurisdiction (e.g., registered agents), the Court held in *International Shoe* that "minimum contacts" are the ultimate touchstone. The Court succinctly summarized the problem created by corporations in a jurisdictional framework as follows:

> [I]t is clear that unlike an individual its "presence" without, as well as within, the state of its origin can be manifested only by activities carried on in its behalf by those who are authorized

---

154. In a footnote, Justice Brennan seemingly limited the instances in which service of process would not satisfy due process to instances of a "defendant's involuntary or unknowing presence." *Burnham*, at 637 n. 11.

to act for it. To say that the corporation is so far "present" there as to satisfy due process requirements, for purposes of taxation or the maintenance of suits against it in the courts of the state, is to beg the question to be decided. For the terms "present" or "presence" are used merely to symbolize those activities of the corporation's agent within the state which courts will deem to be sufficient to satisfy the demands of due process. Those demands may be met by such contacts of the corporation with the state of the forum as make it reasonable, in the context of our federal system of government, to require the corporation to defend the particular suit which is brought there. *Int'l Shoe Co.*, 326 U.S. at 316-317 (citing *Hutchinson v. Chase & Gilbert*, 45 F.2d 139, 141 (2d Cir. 1930)) (L. Hand, J.).

Permitting service on any employee or agent of a corporation to create general jurisdiction on the theory that a corporation is therefore "present" would create the same issues minimum contacts hoped to resolve. A traditional minimum contacts analysis removes the necessity of drawing bright but arbitrary lines of where a non-physical entity is present and ensures that due process is satisfied. [The Court went on to conclude that CSB failed to make a prima facie case that Urban Trend had the constitutionally required minimum contacts with Illinois.]

OYUELA v. SEACOR MARINE (NIGERIA), INC.
290 F. Supp. 2d 713 (E.D. La. 2003)

FALLON, DISTRICT JUDGE. Plaintiff Reynaldo Oyuela, a Honduran citizen, worked as a second engineer aboard the M/V SMIT LLOYD 25, an oil field supply vessel that operated off the coast of Nigeria. The M/V SMIT LLOYD 25 was owned by SEACOR Smit Offshore (Worldwide) Ltd., a wholly owned subsidiary of SEACOR SMIT, Inc., and flew the flag of St. Vincent and the Grenadines during the relevant time period. [Plaintiff Oyuela was injured while working on the vessel in the Port of Calabar, Nigeria. Oyuela later filed a civil action in the U.S. district court for the Eastern District of Louisiana.

SEACOR Marine (Bahamas), Inc. is a Bahamian corporation through which SEACOR SMIT, Inc. employed its foreign seaman such as Oyuela. It has corporate offices but owns no tangible assets. Mr. Lenny Dantin, a Vice President of SEACOR SMIT, Inc. also serves as Assistant Secretary of SEACOR Marine (Bahamas), Inc. but does not receive compensation for the position. In his capacity as an officer of SEACOR Marine (Bahamas), Inc., he was personally served with Oyuela's complaint at SEACOR Marine, Inc.'s offices in Louisiana.]

[T]he plaintiff sued SEACOR Marine (Bahamas) Inc. and personally served Mr. Lenny Dantin, one of the company's officers. Jurisdiction achieved through personal service while a defendant is temporarily within the forum is known as transient jurisdiction. The question is whether this is sufficient in and of itself to satisfy due process. . . . [I]n *Burnham*, the Supreme Court concluded that personal service of process while a party is in the forum is a constitutionally valid basis for exercising jurisdiction. *Burnham*, however, lacks a majority opinion, and the Court split over whether traditional bases for exercising jurisdiction (such as service of process within the jurisdiction) always satisfied due process or whether those bases generally satisfied due process subject to the constraint imposed by "contemporary notions of due process" (i.e., some minimal contacts with the forum). Regardless of the Supreme Court's rationale, *Burnham* makes it clear that personal service of process upon an individual who is voluntarily present in the forum is a sufficient basis for jurisdiction. Furthermore, the exercise of transient jurisdiction has been upheld in circumstances where the contacts have been more fleeting than those presented in this case. Wright and Miller note, " '[t]agging' — the practice of serving defendants who are only transitorily present in the forum state — also remains widely accepted, even though it can occur when the defendant's presence in the state is fortuitous or under circumstances in which the minimum contacts test would not be satisfied." 4 Wright & Miller, *Federal Practice and Procedure* §1067.3 (3d ed. 2002). In the present case not only was an officer of SEACOR Marine (Bahamas), Inc. voluntarily within the forum, but he also lives and works within the territorial jurisdiction of this Court. . . .

The defendant argues that *Burnham* is limited to natural persons and not corporations. *Burnham*'s reassertion of the general validity of transient jurisdiction provides no indication that it should only apply to natural persons. Prior case law suggests that service of process upon a corporate agent provides a sufficient basis to assert jurisdiction over nonresident corporations. . . . In the present case, this Court obtained personal jurisdiction over SEACOR Marine (Bahamas) Inc. when the plaintiff personally served Mr. Lenny Dantin, Assistant Secretary of SEACOR Marine (Bahamas), Inc., at SEACOR Marine, Inc.'s offices in Morgan City, Louisiana. Mr. Dantin resides within the forum, and has lived there for several years. Service of process on Mr. Dantin provided SEACOR Marine (Bahamas), Inc. with adequate notice of the litigation and is a sufficient basis to assert personal jurisdiction over the company.

Notes *on* CSB Commodities *and* Oyuela

1. *The Supreme Court's decision in* Burnham. The *Burnham* Court unanimously held that, on the facts before it, the exercise of personal jurisdiction over an individual by virtue of "tag" service comported with the Due Process Clause. What do you make of that result? Consider again the *Restatement (Third)* §421 & Reporters' Note 4 (1987) and its criticisms of tag jurisdiction.

As in other recent personal jurisdiction cases, the Justices divided badly in *Burnham* on the rationale for their result. Consider the two approaches in *Burnham* summarized in *CSB*. Which view of due process—that of Justice Scalia or Justice Brennan—is more consistent with *Pennoyer, World-Wide Volkswagen,* and the Court's other due process decisions? Does Justice Scalia's view that "reasonableness" and "fairness" are irrelevant to due process analysis of tag service find support in the Court's decisions? Should it? Under the two-prong analysis in *World-Wide Volkswagen*, due process forbids unreasonable assertions of jurisdiction even where minimum contacts exist; would the same rationale not preclude jurisdiction in some circumstances, even where service within the forum territory had been effected? How does Justice Scalia reply?

2. *Territorial sovereignty as rationale for transitory presence rule.* Justice Scalia's defense of tag service rests on notions of territorial sovereignty, reminiscent of *Pennoyer*. Are these arguments persuasive? Does a rule of *tag service* inevitably follow from an acknowledgment of *territorial sovereignty*? Why is it that the *act of service* on the defendant within the forum's territory—as opposed, for example, to the act of mailing a complaint within the forum's territory—has such significance? Is that significance logically compelled by the doctrine of territorial sovereignty?

Tag service developed at a time when modes of travel and methods of communication were far different. Does the replacement of the stagecoach by the airplane, and the carrier pigeon by the Internet, affect the rationale for tag service? What about the considerable expansion of judicial jurisdiction during the last century? *See supra* pp. 83-91, 97-103.

3. *Criticism of transitory presence rule.* Consider the following remarks about the tag service rule:

> Sitting in the lounge of his plane on a nonstop flight over New York, a citizen of California is handed a summons. For many years to come, to his great expense and greater annoyance, he

will have to defend a law suit in a New York court three thousand miles away from his home, even though the plaintiff may be a spiteful competitor alleging a fanciful claim dating back many years to a trip abroad. . . . The inadequacy of [the transient presence] rule, and its contrast with the law prevailing elsewhere in the world, have often been stressed. . . . The *Pennoyer* rule is on the way out, having reached the end of its brief usefulness. . . . And pseudomedieval formulas established and perpetuated by nineteenth century conceptualism, which for decades have obstructed the free flow of legal progress, will have been replaced by what may become known as the new and old American common law of interstate venue in the *forum conveniens.* Ehrenzweig, *The Transient Rule of Personal Jurisdiction: The "Power" Myth and Forum Conveniens,* 65 Yale L.J. 289 (1959).

Consider also:

It can hardly be claimed that the interests of our own citizens, or friendly intercourse with other nations, will be served by encouraging the establishment of a sort of international syndicate for promoting the collection of home debts through foreign courts, so that each traveller shall be compelled to run the gauntlet of such litigation under threat of snap judgments, upon which his own government must issue execution on his return. Such a policy would offer premiums to scavengers of sham and stale claims at every center of travel, breeding a class of process servers to lie in wait for their game at docks and railway stations. *Fisher v. Fielding,* 34 A. 714, 729 (Conn. 1895) (Hamersley, J., dissenting).

Are you persuaded by these criticisms of the transient presence rule? Are the alleged injustices and inconveniences cited by Professor Ehrenzweig all that oppressive? Note Justice Brennan's acknowledgment that individuals travelling to a state "assume the risk" that it will exercise jurisdiction over them. Is that why Professor Ehrenzweig has to reach for the odd example of service in the first-class lounge on a transcontinental aircraft flight? *See supra* p. 133.

Criticism of tag jurisdiction is often coupled with doubts about the importance of territoriality in due process analysis. Professor Ehrenzweig derides "pseudomedieval formulas established and perpetuated by nineteenth century conceptualism." Is there any plausible alternative to a territoriality-based approach to jurisdiction? What if states were permitted to exercise jurisdiction over parties to any cases in which the state had an "interest"? How would "interest" be defined?

Other views focus not so much on the unfairness to the unsuspecting defendant or Justice Scalia's constitutional methodology but, instead, on the alleged incompatibilities between transient jurisdiction and international law:

[Justice Scalia argues in *Burnham*] that declaring transient jurisdiction unconstitutional would be "subjective" and "imperious." One way to rebut this argument would be to identify an objective basis for casting transient jurisdiction beyond the pale of civilized procedure. One such objective basis comes from the fact that the use of a defendant's temporary presence in the forum as grounds for personal jurisdiction is contrary to the consensus of civilized nations and, if used against foreigners, may violate international law. Weintraub, *An Objective Basis for Rejecting Transient Jurisdiction,* 22 Rutgers L.J. 611, 612 (1990-1991).

Can international law supply a basis for shaping constitutional norms? Even if it could, how would one go about evaluating the content of international law and the point at which the "consensus" was uniform enough to justify jettisoning transient jurisdiction as a matter of constitutional law?

4. *International law objections to tag jurisdiction.* The *Third Restatement* declared that tag jurisdiction violates international law. "Jurisdiction based on service of process on one only transitorily present in a state is no longer acceptable under international law if that is the only basis for jurisdiction and the action in question is unrelated to that state." *Restatement (Third) Foreign Relations Law* §421 & Reporters' Note 5 (1987). The *Restatement* does not, however, cite any authority for that conclusion — beyond reliance upon the Brussels Convention, the predecessor to Regulation 44/2001. Consider Article 3 and Annex 1 of Regulation 44/2001, which forbid U.K. courts from asserting jurisdiction on EU domiciliaries based solely on tag service. Does that support the *Restatement*'s position? Does it matter that (in an Article not cited by the *Restatement*'s Reporters' Note) the Convention specifically preserves England's right to exercise tag jurisdiction over nondomiciliaries of EU Member States (*e.g.*, U.S. domiciliaries)? *See supra* pp. 105-106.

    5. *Moderation of transitory presence rule.* What is the current status of the transitory presence rule? After *Burnham,* is the service of process within the forum's territory sufficient for general jurisdiction? What would Justice Scalia say? Justice Brennan?

    Consider the lower courts' analysis in *Oyuela* and *CSB.* What did each court conclude about the tag service rule? Why did the court discuss where Mr. Dentin had resided for the past several years? Did it matter that Mr. Kushner was in Illinois engaged in activities in related to the lawsuit? What if he had been there on unrelated business? On vacation? Is that relevant to the transitory presence rule? What if Mr. Dentin did not live in the forum but, instead, had merely been traveling through Louisiana on a business trip? On a family vacation? Would service in those cases have been effective? If not, how do you draw the distinction?

    Recall that *Burnham* was an interstate, not an international case. In light of that distinction (and the fractured alignment of justices), why did the court in *CSB* even feel compelled to follow *Burnham? See Dubinsky, Is Transnational Litigation a Distinct Field? The Persistence of Exceptionalism in American Procedural Law,* 44 Stan. J. Int'l L. 301, 330-331 (1998) (state and federal courts "have upheld transient jurisdiction over foreign defendants, and they have done so with unadorned citations to *Burnham* without explaining why they believe *Burnham* requires this result in a transnational setting.").

    As *CSB* and *Oyuela* illustrate, few lower courts have concluded that the transitory presence rule must be qualified by at least a measure of inquiry into "reasonableness." *See Amusement Equipment, Inc. v. Mordelt,* 779 F.2d 264 (5th Cir. 1985). Most lower court decisions are to the contrary. *See, e.g., In re Edelman,* 295 F.3d 171, 179 (2d Cir. 2002); *First American Corp. v. Price Waterhouse LLP,* 154 F.3d 16, 20-21 (2d Cir. 1998); *Kadic v. Faradic,* 70 F.3d 232, 247 (2d Cir. 1995); *Rutherford v. Rutherford,* 971 P.2d 220, 221 (Ariz. App. 1998) (rejecting reasonableness inquiry in tag jurisdiction case).

    Of course, a reasonableness requirement is not the only means by which a court might moderate the transitory presence rule. Courts might rely on other doctrines such as *forum non conveniens, infra* at 365-459, to accomplish the same result (keeping the defendant out of the foreign forum) albeit by a different doctrine.

    6. *Exceptions to transitory presence rule — fraud, litigation, and settlement negotiations.* The perceived harshness of the transitory presence rule has been mitigated somewhat by judicially fashioned exceptions. In general, tag service will not confer jurisdiction if the defendant's presence was procured by the plaintiff's fraud or force. *See* Annotation, *Attack on Personal Service as Having Been Obtained by Fraud or Trickery,* 98 A.L.R.2d 551 (1964). Another exception has arisen for persons entering a state solely for the purpose of litigation. *Estate of Unger v. Palestinian Authority,* 396 F. Supp. 2d 376, 379-382 (S.D.N.Y. 2005); *Restatement (Second) Conflict of Laws* §83 (1971). A related exception has been recognized for persons who enter the forum to negotiate settlement of a dispute. *Hinkle Corp. v. Edgemont, SA,* 1991 WL 62453 (E.D. Pa. 1991). Are these exceptions consistent with the territoriality principle underlying the rule of transitory jurisdiction? Would Justice Scalia permit jurisdiction where tag service was effected by fraud?

7. *Tag service on corporations.* *CSB* held that services on Kushner did not suffice to establish general jurisdiction over Urban Trend even though he was physically present in the forum state, on company business, engaged in the very activities that related to CSB's complaint. Under the court's view in *CSB*, is transient jurisdiction based on tag service on a corporate agent ever possible?

Compare the result in *CSB* with that in *Oyuela*. Is tag service on a corporate agent grounds for jurisdiction under *Oyuela*'s analysis?

Which approach — that of *CSB* or of *Oyuela* — is wiser? Why? *Burnham*, which involved service on an individual, did not *compel* the result reached in *Oyuela*. Moreover, corporations differ from individuals in material respects. An individual can generally be "tagged" only in one place at any given time. By contrast, the "tag" service exposes a corporation to personal jurisdiction in multiple states (wherever some agent may be present). Additionally, individuals can more easily manage their personal affairs and decide whether to enter a jurisdiction, thereby exposing themselves to the risk of tag service. By contrast, corporations, particularly in an increasingly global marketplace, cannot help but have agents who enter multiple forums in the course of doing business.

Do these differences matter? What would Justice Scalia say? If corporations were exempt from the "tag" rule of *Burnham*, wouldn't such a rule ironically expose corporations to a lower risk of being sued into an unfamiliar forum than individuals, even though the corporate defendant may be better prepared financially and institutionally to defend itself?

8. *Tag service on corporate officers.* Assuming that *CSB* reached the wrong result and that corporations are subject to "tag" service, how exactly may it be effected? What officers may be "tagged" in the name of the corporation? What was the office held by Kushner? What if he had been the chief executive officer? The chairman of the board?

(a)   Lower court decisions dealing with tag service on corporate officers. The few lower courts to have considered whether tag service on a corporate officer provides general jurisdiction over the corporation are divided. In addition to *Oyuela* and *CSB, compare Schulz Research and Development, Inc. v. Kruse*, 720 F. Supp. 710 (N.D. Ill. 1989) (Due Process Clause does not permit jurisdiction over company based upon tag service on corporate officer); *Easterling v. Cooper Motors, Inc.*, 26 F.R.D. 1 (M.D.N.C. 1960) ("the mere fact that there is personal service upon an officer of a foreign corporation who is present in the State is insufficient to subject a foreign corporation to the jurisdiction of the court") *with Northern Light Technology, Inc. v. Northern Lights Club*, 236 F.3d 57, 63 n.10 (1st Cir. 2001); *Aluminal Indus., Inc. v. Newtown Commercial Assoc.*, 89 F.R.D. 326 (S.D.N.Y. 1980) (limited partnership subject to general jurisdiction based solely on tag service on general partner in New York). *See also First American Corp. v. Price Waterhouse LLP*, 988 F. Supp. 353, 361 (S.D.N.Y. 1997) (alternative holding that personal service on partner would not suffice to establish personal jurisdiction over partnership).

*(b)   *Burnham* dicta dealing with tag service on corporate officers.* As the court in *CSB* noted, in *Burnham*, a plurality subscribed to a footnote that purported to explain the result in *Perkins*: "[Our holding] involved 'regular service of summons upon [the corporation's] president while he was in [the forum State] acting in that capacity.' " *Burnham v. Superior Court*, 495 U.S. 604, 610 n.1 (1990) (quoting *Perkins*). The apparent suggestion is that general jurisdiction was appropriate in *Perkins* only (or principally) because the company's president had been served while within the forum. That suggests that tag service on a corporate officer has at least some jurisdictional consequences for his corporation. *Perkins* itself makes clear, however, that tag service was not the basis of (or even a material factor supporting) jurisdiction. Moreover, the Court had earlier held that tag service upon a corporate officer did not provide a constitutionally adequate basis for jurisdiction over the company. *E.g., James-Dickinson Farm Mortgage Co. v. Harry*, 273 U.S. 113 (1927).

(c) Result in Oyuela. Consider again the result in *Oyuela*. What if Mr. Dentin had not resided in the forum, and had merely been served when transitorily present there? Is that sufficient to confer general jurisdiction on the companies in which he is an officer? If so, consider the effect that such a notion of tag service could have on commerce. Given the extensive use of Internet, email, telephone, fax, and other communications to conduct very substantial business, should the personal wanderings of various corporate officers really provide a basis for general jurisdiction? Does that make jurisdiction depend on state sovereignty and history or on random fortuity?

9. *Practical implications of tag service.* Although the transitory presence rule is invoked infrequently, lawyers should be aware of its existence in counseling clients. Personal service within the forum on the defendant, or a proper agent of the defendant, might foreclose or seriously weaken jurisdictional defenses that are otherwise available. Counsel should take care that potential defendants and their agents avoid or minimize travel to the forum in these circumstances.

10. *Treatment of tag service in negotiations for draft Hague jurisdiction and judgments convention.* Recall the discussion above, *supra* pp. 107-108, 136, of European insistence during negotiations at the Hague Conference on a jurisdiction and judgments convention that jurisdiction based on tag service be prohibited. Note that Article 18(2)(f) of the June 2001 Interim Text listed, among the "prohibited bases" for jurisdiction, "the service of a writ upon the defendant in that State." *See* http://www.hcch.net. What relevance, if any, does this have for due process analysis in international cases?

11. *Tag service in human rights litigation.* In recent human rights litigation in U.S. courts, some plaintiffs have relied on the transitory presence rule to effect service on current or former foreign officials. *E.g., Kadic v. Karadzic*, 70 F.3d 232, 246-248 (2d Cir. 1995); *Doe v. Qi*, 349 F. Supp. 2d 1258, 1273 (N.D. Cal. 2004). *See* Dubinsky, *Human Rights Law Meets Private Law Harmonization: The Coming Conflict*, 30 Yale J. Int'l L. 211, 262-265 (2005). What is the wisdom of permitting such service? Are there reasons that tag service might be particularly important in human rights cases?

12. *General jurisdiction in human rights cases.* The June 2001 Interim Text of the abortive Hague judgments convention contained a provision dealing with human rights cases. Article 18(3) provided:

> Nothing in this article shall prevent a court in a Contracting State from exercising jurisdiction under national law in an action claiming damages in respect of conduct which constitutes (a) genocide, a crime against humanity or a war crime; or (b) a serious crime under international law, provided that this State has exercised its criminal jurisdiction over that crime in accordance with an international treaty to which it is a Party and that claim is for civil compensatory damages for death or serious bodily injuries arising from that crime. Sub-paragraph (b) only applies if the party seeking relief is exposed to a risk of a denial of justice because proceedings in another State are not possible or cannot reasonably be required.

Would this provision be wise? What would justify the exceptional treatment of human rights cases?

C. Specific Jurisdiction of U.S. Courts over Foreign Defendants

As described above, contemporary due process analysis distinguishes between general and specific jurisdiction. While general jurisdiction permits adjudication of any claim against a defendant, specific jurisdiction permits the adjudication only of claims that "arise out of" or "relate to" a defendant's activities within the forum state.[155] This section focuses on assertions of specific jurisdiction in international litigation. It begins with tort cases (concentrating on product liability) and then turns to contract cases.

1.   Specific Jurisdiction in International Product Liability and Tort Cases

Vast quantities of products are imported into the United States each day. Inevitably, some of these products cause injury to American individuals or companies, leading to efforts by the injured parties to obtain compensation from those involved in the design, manufacture, and distribution of the products. These efforts have resulted in countless lower court decisions considering the extent to which foreign parties are subject to U.S. jurisdiction in product liability actions. Unfortunately, despite several attempts by the Supreme Court, this litigation has produced few clear rules.

a.   Purposeful Contacts and the Stream of Commerce Doctrine.   The "stream of commerce" doctrine has played a central role in international product liability and tort cases. That theory is generally traced to *Gray v. American Radiator & Standard Sanitary Corp*,[156] a frequently cited 1961 decision of the Illinois Supreme Court. In *Gray*, the court asserted specific jurisdiction in a product liability suit over an out-of-state manufacturer of components that were incorporated by another out-of-state company into water heaters. The water heaters were then distributed on an interstate basis, including into Illinois, where one of them malfunctioned. Apparently relying entirely on the fact that the component manufacturer knowingly placed its product in the interstate "stream of commerce," the Illinois court upheld jurisdiction. *Gray* was widely followed in other states, including in international cases.[157]

The Supreme Court's decision in *World-Wide Volkswagen* provides the contemporary foundation for dealing with specific jurisdiction in international product liability and tort cases.[158] The Court set out a two-part test under which jurisdiction cannot be asserted unless: (a) the defendant has "minimum contacts" with the forum as a result of "purposefully availing" itself of the benefits and protections of the forum's laws; and (b) the exercise of jurisdiction would be "reasonable." *World-Wide Volkswagen* emphasized that the mere "foreseeability" that conduct would have effects within a forum did not satisfy the "purposeful availment" test.[159]

Nevertheless, *World-Wide Volkswagen* also accepted at least some formulations of the stream of commerce doctrine. The Court said that due process does not preclude "personal jurisdiction over a corporation that delivers its products into the stream of commerce with the expectation that they will be purchased by consumers in the forum

---

155. *E.g., Goodyear Dunlop Tires Operations, S.A. v. Brown*, 2011 WL 2518815 at *3, 6 (U.S. June 27, 2011); *Helicopteros Nacionales de Colombia, SA v. Hall*, 466 U.S. 408, 414-415 (1984); *Restatement (Third) Foreign Relations Law* §421(2)(i), (j) & (k) (1987); *supra* p. 90 and *infra* pp. 162, 173-175, 188.

156. 176 N.E.2d 761 (Ill. 1961).

157. *E.g., World-Wide Volkswagen Corp. v. Woodson*, 444 U.S. 286, 297-298 (1980) ("[t]he forum State does not exceed its powers under the Due Process Clause if it asserts personal jurisdiction over a corporation that delivers its products into the stream of commerce with the expectation that they will be purchased by consumers in the forum State"); *Mason v. F. LLI Luigi & Franco dal Maschio FU G.B. s.n.c.*, 832 F.2d 383, 386 & n.4 (7th Cir. 1987); *Oswalt v. Scripto, Inc.*, 616 F.2d 191, 201-202 (5th Cir. 1980); *McCombs v. Cerco Rentals*, 622 S.W.2d 822 (Tenn. Ct. App. 1981). *See also Asahi Metal Indus. Co. v. Superior Court of Cal.*, 480 U.S. 102, 112 (1987) (four Justice plurality opining that in addition to placing a product in the stream of commerce with the expectation that it will be purchased by consumers in the forum State, there must also be a finding the defendant purposefully directed its activities toward the forum State in order to establish personal jurisdiction).

158. *See supra* pp. 88-90, 94-96, 98-104.

159. *See supra* pp. 88-90, 94-96.

State."[160] It also referred to *Gray*'s stream of commerce analysis, but without specifying approval.[161]

In *Asahi Metal Indus. Co. v. Superior Court*, excerpted below, the Court reconsidered the "stream of commerce" theory, producing a splintered decision.[162] Although eight members of the Court agreed that the assertion of jurisdiction would be "unreasonable," the Court split 4-4-1 on whether the Due Process Clause's "purposeful contacts" requirement was satisfied. Four Justices thought that it was not. They joined an opinion by Justice O'Connor reasoning that a defendant's mere awareness that the stream of commerce might carry its product into the forum was not purposeful availment.[163]

Four other Justices thought that purposeful contacts did exist. They joined an opinion by Justice Brennan finding minimum contacts because the defendant had purposefully placed its components in the stream of commerce knowing that they were regularly sold in the forum.[164] As in *Burnham*, Justice Stevens joined neither opinion, but concluded that purposeful contacts existed.[165]

Unsurprisingly, the splintered decision in *Asahi* produced much confusion in the lower courts. Over the next quarter century, lower court disagreed over what conduct satisfied the stream of commerce theory and disagreed even over what opinion of the Supreme Court stated the governing rule. After nearly twenty-five years of lower court confusion, the Supreme Court agreed to decide a case that offered the opportunity to clarify matters. Yet when it finally decided *Nicastro v. J. McIntyre Machinery, Ltd.*, excerpted below, a majority of the Court (as in *Asahi*) was again unable to coalesce around a single opinion. The splintered opinions in *Nicastro*, following the splintered opinions in *Asahi*, ensure that lower courts (and parties) will continue to struggle to comprehend the contours of this theory.

b. Reasonableness. The reasonableness prong of *World-Wide Volkswagen*'s due process analysis also plays a significant role in product liability cases. As described above, "reasonableness" encompasses a range of factors, including the burden on the defendant, the plaintiff's interest, the forum state's interest, and the interests of other states.[166]

The reasonableness analysis raises special issues in international cases. The hardship resulting from U.S. jurisdiction is usually greater for defendants in international cases than in domestic ones. International cases also usually affect both foreign nations and U.S. international relations in ways that domestic cases do not. These factors often pull in different directions, and give rise to difficult questions under the Due Process Clause's reasonableness prong. Some guidance is provided in *Asahi*, which applies the

---

160. 444 U.S. at 297-298.
161. The *World-Wide Volkswagen* Court wrote:

"The forum State does not exceed its power under the Due Process Clause if it asserts personal jurisdiction over a corporation that delivers its products into the stream of commerce with the expectation that they will be purchased by consumers in the forum State. *Cf. Gray v. American Radiator & Standard Sanitary Corp.*,176 N.E.2d 761 (1961)." 444 U.S. at 297-298.

The "*cf.*" citation is capable of ambiguity and ordinarily requires an explanatory parenthetical. According to *The Bluebook*, a "*cf.*" citation meant that the "[c]ited authority supports a proposition different from the main proposition but sufficiently analogous to lend support." *The Bluebook* 55 (19th ed. 2010).

162. 480 U.S. 102 (1987).
163. 480 U.S. at 111.
164. 480 U.S. at 117.
165. 480 U.S. at 111.
166. *See supra* pp. 94-95.

reasonableness requirement to deny jurisdiction. But lower courts continue to have difficulty with these issues, reaching inconsistent results.[167]

c. Defining the Forum "State": A Preliminary View.   Finally, both *Asahi* and *Nicastro* invite reflection upon the relevant geographic unit for purposes of applying the Due Process Clause's "purposeful contacts" test. In *World-Wide Volkswagen* and *Helicopteros*, the issue was whether the defendant had constitutionally sufficient contacts with the particular U.S. state where the forum court was located (*e.g.*, Texas or Louisiana). That is, of course, consistent with the Due Process Clause's focus on state action, as well as the emphasis in *Pennoyer* and *World-Wide Volkswagen* on state sovereignty. Consider, however, whether this makes sense in international cases. For example, should the Due Process Clause force a district court in Pennsylvania to ignore a French defendant's contacts with New Jersey, Delaware, New York, and Maryland? Consider this issue as you read *Kopke*.

ASAHI METAL INDUSTRY CO. v. SUPERIOR COURT OF CALIFORNIA, SOLANO COUNTY
480 U.S. 102 (1987)

Justice O'Connor announced the judgment of the Court and delivered the unanimous opinion of the Court with respect to Part I, the opinion of the Court with respect to Part II-B, in which The Chief Justice, Justice Brennan, Justice White, Justice Marshall, Justice Blackmun, Justice Powell, and Justice Stevens join, and an opinion with respect to Part II-A and III, in which The Chief Justice, Justice Powell, and Justice Scalia join.

This case presents the question whether the mere awareness on the part of a foreign defendant that the components it manufactured, sold, and delivered outside the United States would reach the forum state in the stream of commerce constitutes "minimum contacts" between the defendant and the forum state such that the exercise of jurisdiction "does not offend 'traditional notions of fair play and substantial justice.' "

I.   On September 23, 1978, on Interstate Highway 80 in Solano County, California, Gary Zurcher lost control of his Honda motorcycle and collided with a tractor. Zurcher was severely injured, and his passenger and wife, Ruth Ann Moreno, was killed. In September 1979, Zurcher filed a product liability action in the Superior Court of the State of California in and for the County of Solano. Zurcher alleged that the 1978 accident was caused by a sudden loss of air and an explosion in the rear tire of the motorcycle, and alleged that the motorcycle tire, tube, and sealant were defective. Zurcher's complaint named, *inter alia*, Cheng Shin Rubber Industrial Co., Ltd. ("Cheng Shin"), the Taiwanese manufacturer of the tube. Cheng Shin in turn filed a cross-complaint seeking indemnification from its codefendants and from petitioner, Asahi Metal Industry Co., Ltd., ("Asahi"), the manufacturer of the tube's valve assembly. Zurcher's claims against Cheng Shin and the other defendants were eventually settled and dismissed, leaving only Cheng Shin's indemnity action against Asahi.

California's long-arm statute authorizes the exercise of jurisdiction "on any basis not inconsistent with the Constitution of this state or of the United States." Asahi moved to quash Cheng Shin's service of summons, arguing the State could not exert jurisdiction over it consistent with the Due Process Clause of the Fourteenth Amendment.

Asahi is a Japanese corporation. It manufactures tire valve assemblies in Japan and sells the assemblies to Cheng Shin, and to several other tire manufacturers, for use as

167. *See infra* pp. 156-162.

components in finished tire tubes. Asahi's sales to Cheng Shin took place in Taiwan. The shipments from Asahi to Cheng Shin were sent from Japan to Taiwan. Cheng Shin bought and incorporated into its tire tubes 150,000 Asahi valve assemblies in 1978; 500,000 in 1979; 500,000 in 1980; 100,000 in 1981; and 100,000 in 1982. Sales to Cheng Shin accounted for 1.24 percent of Asahi's income in 1981 and 0.44 percent in 1982. Cheng Shin alleged that approximately 20 percent of its sales in the United States are in California. Cheng Shin purchases valve assemblies from other suppliers as well, and sells finished tubes throughout the world.

In 1983 an attorney for Cheng Shin conducted an informal examination of the valve stems of the tire tubes sold in one cyclery in Solano County. The attorney declared that of the approximately 115 tire tubes in the store, 97 were purportedly manufactured in Japan or Taiwan, and of those 97, 21 valve stems were marked with the circled letters "A," apparently Asahi's trademark. Of the 21 Asahi valve stems, 12 were incorporated into Cheng Shin tire tubes. The store contained 41 other Cheng Shin tubes that incorporated the valve assemblies of other manufacturers. An affidavit of a manager of Cheng Shin whose duties included the purchasing of component parts stated: " 'In discussions with Asahi regarding the purchase of valve stem assemblies the fact that my Company sells tubes throughout the world and specifically the United States has been discussed. I am informed and believe that Asahi was fully aware that valve stem assemblies sold to my Company and to others would end up throughout the United States and in California.' " An affidavit of the president of Asahi, on the other hand, declared that Asahi, " 'had never contemplated that its limited sales of tire valves to Cheng Shin in Taiwan would subject it to lawsuit in California.' " . . .

The Supreme Court of the State of California [held that Asahi was subject to the personal jurisdiction of the California courts]. The court considered Asahi's intentional act of placing its components into the stream of commerce — that is, by delivering the components to Cheng Shin in Taiwan — coupled with Asahi's awareness that some of the components would eventually find their way into California, sufficient to form the basis for state court jurisdiction under the Due Process Clause.

II.A.[168] . . . It had been argued in *World-Wide Volkswagen* that because an automobile retailer and its wholesale distributor sold a product mobile by design and purpose, they could foresee being haled into court in the distant States into which their customers might drive. The Court rejected this concept of foreseeability as an insufficient basis for jurisdiction under the Due Process Clause. The Court disclaimed, however, the idea that "foreseeability is wholly irrelevant" to personal jurisdiction, concluding that "[t]he forum State does not exceed its powers under the Due Process Clause if it asserts personal jurisdiction over a corporation that delivers its products into the stream of commerce with the expectation that they will be purchased by consumers in the forum State." . . .

Since *World-Wide Volkswagen*, lower courts have been confronted with cases in which the defendant acted by placing a product in the stream of commerce, and the stream eventually swept defendant's product into the forum State, but the defendant did nothing else to purposefully avail itself of the market in the forum state. Some courts have understood the Due Process Clause, as interpreted in *World-Wide Volkswagen*, to allow an exercise of personal jurisdiction to be based on no more than the defendant's act placing the product in the stream of commerce. Other courts have understood the Due Process Clause and the above-quoted language in *World-Wide Volkswagen* to require the action of the defendant to be more purposefully directed at the forum State than the mere act of placing a product in the stream of commerce.

---

168. [Only Justices Rehnquist, Powell, and Scalia joined Part II-A of Justice O'Connor's opinion — Eds.]

The reasoning of the Supreme Court of California in the present case illustrates the former interpretation of *World-Wide Volkswagen*. The Supreme Court of California held that . . . Asahi's awareness that its valves would be sold in California was sufficient to permit California to exercise jurisdiction over Asahi consistent with the requirements of the Due Process Clause. The Supreme Court of California's position was consistent with those courts that have held that mere foreseeability or awareness was a constitutionally sufficient basis for personal jurisdiction if the defendant's product made its way into the forum State while still in the stream of commerce. . . .

Other courts, however, have understood the Due Process Clause to require something more than that the defendant was aware of its product's entry into the forum State through the stream of commerce in order for the state to exert jurisdiction over the defendant. In *Humble v. Toyota Motor Co., Ltd.*, 727 F.2d 709 (8th Cir. 1984), an injured passenger brought suit against Arakawa Auto Body Company, a Japanese corporation that manufactured car seats for Toyota. Arakawa did no business in the United States; it had no office, affiliate, subsidiary, or agent in the United States; it manufactured its component parts outside the United States and delivered them to Toyota Motor Company in Japan. The Court of Appeals . . . noted that although it "does not doubt that Arakawa could have foreseen that its product would find its way into the United States," it would be "manifestly unjust" to require Arakawa to defend itself in the United States. . . .

We now find this latter position to be consonant with the requirements of due process. The "substantial connection" between the defendant and the forum State necessary for a finding of minimum contacts must come about by *an action of the defendant purposefully directed toward the forum State*. The placement of a product into the stream of commerce, without more, is not an act of the defendant purposefully directed toward the forum State. Additional conduct of the defendant may indicate an intent or purpose to serve the market in the forum State, for example, designing the product for the market in the forum State, advertising in the forum State, establishing channels for providing regular advice to customers in the forum State, or marketing the product through a distributor who has agreed to serve as the sales agent in the forum State. But a defendant's awareness that the stream of commerce may or will sweep the product into the forum State does not convert the mere act of placing the product into the stream into an act purposefully directed toward the forum State.

Assuming, *arguendo*, that respondents have established Asahi's awareness that some of the valves sold to Cheng Shin would be incorporated into tire tubes sold in California, respondents have not demonstrated any action by Asahi to purposefully avail itself of the California market. Asahi does not do business in California. It has no office, agents, employees, or property in California. It does not advertise or otherwise solicit business in California. It did not create, control, or employ the distribution system that brought its valve to California. . . . On the basis of these facts, the exertion of personal jurisdiction over Asahi by the Superior Court of California exceeds the limits of Due Process.

II.B.   The strictures of the Due Process Clause forbid a state court from exercising personal jurisdiction over Asahi under circumstances that would offend "traditional notions of fair play and substantial justice." We have previously explained that the determination of the reasonableness of the exercise of jurisdiction in each case will depend on the evaluation of several factors. A court must consider the burden on the defendant, the interests of the forum state, and the plaintiff's interest in obtaining relief. It must also weigh in its determination "the interstate judicial system's interest in obtaining the most efficient resolution of controversies; and the shared interest of the several States in furthering fundamental substantive social policies." A consideration of these factors . . . clearly reveals the unreasonableness of the assertion of jurisdiction over Asahi, even apart from the question of the placement of goods in the stream of commerce.

Certainly the burden on the defendant in this case is severe. Asahi has been commanded by the Superior Court of California not only to traverse the distance between Asahi's headquarters in Japan and the Superior Court of California in and for the County of Solano, but also to submit its dispute with Cheng Shin to a foreign nation's judicial system. The unique burdens placed upon one who must defend oneself in a foreign legal system should have significant weight in assessing the reasonableness of stretching the long arm of personal jurisdiction over national borders.

When minimum contacts have been established, often the interests of the plaintiff and the forum in the exercise of jurisdiction will justify even the serious burdens placed on the alien defendant. In the present case, however, the interests of the plaintiff and the forum in California's assertion of jurisdiction over Asahi are slight. All that remains is a claim for indemnification asserted by Cheng Shin, a Taiwanese corporation, against Asahi. The transaction on which the indemnification claim is based took place in Taiwan; Asahi's components were shipped from Japan to Taiwan. Cheng Shin has not demonstrated that it is more convenient for it to litigate its indemnification claim against Asahi in California rather than in Taiwan or Japan.

Because the plaintiff is not a California resident, California's legitimate interests in the dispute have considerably diminished. The Supreme Court of California argued that the State had an interest in "protecting its consumers by ensuring that foreign manufacturers comply with the state's safety standards." [This] definition of California's interest, however, was overly broad. The dispute between Cheng Shin and Asahi is primarily about indemnification rather than safety standards. Moreover, it is not at all clear at this point that California law should govern the question whether a Japanese corporation should indemnify a Taiwanese corporation on the basis of a sale made in Taiwan and a shipment of goods from Japan to Taiwan. . . .

World-Wide Volkswagen also admonished courts to take into consideration the interests of the "several States," in addition to the forum state, in the efficient judicial resolution of the dispute and the advancement of substantive policies. In the present case, this advice calls for a court to consider the procedural and substantive policies of other *nations* whose interests are affected by the assertion of jurisdiction by the California court. The procedural and substantive interests of other nations in a state court's assertion of jurisdiction over an alien defendant will differ from case to case. In every case, however, those interests, as well as the Federal interest in its foreign relations policies, will be best served by a careful inquiry into the reasonableness of the assertion of jurisdiction in the particular case, and an unwillingness to find serious burdens on an alien defendant outweighed by minimal interests on the part of the plaintiff or the forum State. "Great care and reserve should be exercised when extending our notions of personal jurisdiction into the international field." *United States v. First National City Bank*, 379 U.S. 378, 404 (1965) (Harlan, J., dissenting). *See* Born, *Reflections on Judicial Jurisdiction in International Cases*, [17 Ga. J. Int'l & Comp. L. 1 (1987)].

III.   Considering the international context, the heavy burden on the alien defendant, and the slight interests of the plaintiff and the forum State, the exercise of personal jurisdiction by a California court over Asahi in this instance would be unreasonable and unfair.

JUSTICE BRENNAN, with whom JUSTICE WHITE, JUSTICE MARSHALL, and JUSTICE BLACKMUN join, concurring in part and in the judgment. I do not agree with the plurality's interpretation of the stream-of-commerce theory, nor with its conclusion that Asahi did not "purposely avail itself of the California market." I do agree, however, with the Court's conclusion in Part II-B that the exercise of personal jurisdiction over Asahi in this case would not comport with "fair play and substantial justice." This is one of those rare cases in which "minimum requirements inherent in the concept of 'fair play and substantial justice' . . . defeat the reasonableness of jurisdiction even [though] the defendant has purposefully engaged in forum activities." . . .

The plurality states that "a defendant's awareness that the stream of commerce may or will sweep the product into the forum State does not convert the mere act of placing the product into the stream into an act purposefully directed toward the forum State." The plurality would therefore require a plaintiff to show "[a]dditional conduct" directed toward the forum before finding the exercise of jurisdiction over the defendant to be consistent with the Due Process Clause. I see no need for such a showing, however. The stream of commerce refers not to unpredictable currents or eddies, but to the regular and anticipated flow of products from manufacture to distribution to retail sale. As long as a participant in this process is aware that the final product is being marketed in the same forum State, the possibility of a lawsuit there cannot come as a surprise. . . .

In this case, the facts found by the California Supreme Court support its findings of minimum contacts. The Court found that "[a]lthough Asahi did not design or control the system of distribution that carried its valve assemblies into California, Asahi was aware of the distribution system's operation, and it knew that it would benefit economically from the sale in California of products incorporating its components." Accordingly, I cannot join the plurality's determination that Asahi's regular and extensive sales of component parts to a manufacturer it knew was making regular sales of the final product in California is insufficient to establish minimum contacts with California.

JUSTICE STEVENS, with whom JUSTICE WHITE and JUSTICE BLACKMUN join, concurring in part and concurring in the judgment. The judgment of the Supreme Court of California should be reversed for the reasons stated in Part II-B of the Court's opinion. While I join Parts I and II-B, I do not join Part II-A. . . . [E]ven assuming that [a "purposeful direction] test ought to be formulated here, Part II-A misapplies it to the facts of this case. The Court seems to assume that an unwavering line can be drawn between "mere awareness" that a component will find its way into the forum State and "purposeful availment" of the forum's market. Over the course of its dealings with Cheng Shin, Asahi has arguably engaged in a higher quantum of conduct than "[t]he placement of a product into the stream of commerce, without more. . . ." Whether or not this conduct rises to the level of purposeful availment requires a constitutional determination that is affected by the volume, the value, and the hazardous character of the components. In most circumstances I would be inclined to conclude that a regular course of dealing that results in deliveries of over 100,000 units annually over a period of several years would constitute "purposeful availment" even though the item delivered to the forum State was a standard product marketed throughout the world.

J. MCINTYRE MACHINERY, LTD. v. NICASTRO
2011 WL 2518811 (2011)

JUSTICE KENNEDY announced the judgment of the Court and delivered an opinion, in which THE CHIEF JUSTICE, JUSTICE SCALIA, and JUSTICE THOMAS join. [Nicastro, a New Jersey resident, injured his hand at his employer's New Jersey facilities while using a metal-shearing machine manufactured by McIntyre Machinery. The machine was manufactured in England where McIntye Machinery is incorporated and operates. McIntyre sold the machine to a distributor that had the right to resell McIntyre products throughout the United States. The distributor sold the Machine to Nicastro's employer after the employer examined it at a trade show in Nevada. According to the record in the case, no more than four McIntyre machines (and perhaps only one, the one that caused Nicastro's injuries) ever ended up in New Jersey. Apart from the sale of the machines to its United States distributor, the only other facts connecting McIntyre to the United States include attendance of its personnel at various trade shows (but never in New Jersey), the holding of U.S. patents, some direction and guidance to its distributor about how to structure its advertising and sales efforts, and some evidence that the distributor bought some goods on consignment.

The New Jersey Supreme Court held that jurisdiction over McIntyre was proper. Building on Justice Brennan's opinion in *Asahi*, the New Jersey court announced that jurisdiction over a nonresident manufacturer comported with the Due Process Clause when the injury occurred in the forum state; the manufacturer knew or reasonably should have known that its products are distributed through a nationwide distribution system that might lead to those products being sold in any of the fifty states; and where it failed to take some reasonable step to prevent the distribution of its products in this State.]

II. The Due Process Clause protects an individual's right to be deprived of life, liberty, or property only by the exercise of lawful power. This is no less true with respect to the power of a sovereign to resolve disputes through judicial process than with respect to the power of a sovereign to prescribe rules of conduct for those within its sphere. As a general rule, neither statute nor judicial decree may bind strangers to the State. *Cf. Burnham v. Superior Court of Cal.*, 495 U.S. 604, 608-609 (1990) (opinion of Scalia, J.)

A court may subject a defendant to judgment only when the defendant has sufficient contacts with the sovereign such that the maintenance of the suit does not offend traditional notions of fair play and substantial justice. Freeform notions of fundamental fairness divorced from traditional practice cannot transform a judgment rendered in the absence of authority into law. As a general rule, the sovereign's exercise of power requires some act by which the defendant purposefully avails itself of the privilege of conducting activities within the forum State, thus invoking the benefits and protections of its laws, though in some cases, as with an intentional tort, the defendant might well fall within the State's authority by reason of his attempt to obstruct its laws. In products-liability cases like this one, it is the defendant's purposeful availment that makes jurisdiction consistent with "traditional notions of fair play and substantial justice.

[The Court then reviewed the differences between general and specific jurisdiction, described *supra* at p. 90, and described those categories in terms of different ways by which a defendant may subject itself to a sovereign's authority. It then considered the fractured decision in *Asahi*.]

The imprecision arising from *Asahi*, for the most part, results from its statement of the relation between jurisdiction and the "stream of commerce." The stream of commerce, like other metaphors, has its deficiencies as well as its utility. It refers to the movement of goods from manufacturers through distributors to consumers, yet beyond that descriptive purpose its meaning is far from exact. This Court has stated that a defendant's placing goods into the stream of commerce "with the expectation that they will be purchased by consumers within the forum State" may indicate purposeful availment. *World-Wide Volkswagen Corp. v. Woodson*, 444 U.S. 286, 298 (1980) (finding that expectation lacking). But that statement does not amend the general rule of personal jurisdiction. It merely observes that a defendant may in an appropriate case be subject to jurisdiction without entering the forum — itself an unexceptional proposition — as where manufacturers or distributors "seek to serve" a given State's market. The principal inquiry in cases of this sort is whether the defendant's activities manifest an intention to submit to the power of a sovereign. In other words, the defendant must purposefully avail itself of the privilege of conducting activities within the forum State, thus invoking the benefits and protections of its laws. Sometimes a defendant does so by sending its goods rather than its agents. The defendant's transmission of goods permits the exercise of jurisdiction only where the defendant can be said to have targeted the forum; as a general rule, it is not enough that the defendant might have predicted that its goods will reach the forum State. . . .

Since *Asahi* was decided, the courts have sought to reconcile the competing opinions. But Justice Brennan's concurrence, advocating a rule based on general notions of fairness and foreseeability, is inconsistent with the premises of lawful judicial power. This Court's precedents make clear that it is the defendant's actions, not his expectations, that empower a State's courts to subject him to judgment.

The conclusion that jurisdiction is in the first instance a question of authority rather than fairness explains, for example, why the principal opinion in *Burnham* conducted no independent inquiry into the desirability or fairness of the rule that service of process within a State suffices to establish jurisdiction over an otherwise foreign defendant. As that opinion explained, "[t]he view developed early that each State had the power to hale before its courts any individual who could be found within its borders." Furthermore, were general fairness considerations the touchstone of jurisdiction, a lack of purposeful availment might be excused where carefully crafted judicial procedures could otherwise protect the defendant's interests, or where the plaintiff would suffer substantial hardship if forced to litigate in a foreign forum. . . .

Two principles are implicit in the fore-going. First, personal jurisdiction requires a forum-by-forum, or sovereign-by-sovereign, analysis. The question is whether a defendant has followed a course of conduct directed at the society or economy existing within the jurisdiction of a given sovereign, so that the sovereign has the power to subject the defendant to judgment concerning that conduct. Personal jurisdiction, of course, restricts judicial power not as a matter of sovereignty, but as a matter of individual liberty, for due process protects the individual's right to be subject only to lawful power. But whether a judicial judgment is lawful depends on whether the sovereign has authority to render it.

The second principle is a corollary of the first. Because the United States is a distinct sovereign, a defendant may in principle be subject to the jurisdiction of the courts of the United States but not of any particular State. This is consistent with the premises and unique genius of our Constitution. Ours is a legal system unprecedented in form and design, establishing two orders of government, each with its own direct relationship, its own privity, its own set of mutual rights and obligations to the people who sustain it and are governed by it. For jurisdiction, a litigant may have the requisite relationship with the United States Government but not with the government of any individual State. That would be an exceptional case, however. If the defendant is a domestic domiciliary, the courts of its home State are available and can exercise general jurisdiction. And if another State were to assert jurisdiction in an inappropriate case, it would upset the federal balance, which posits that each State has a sovereignty that is not subject to unlawful intrusion by other States. Furthermore, foreign corporations will often target or concentrate on particular States, subjecting them to specific jurisdiction in those forums.

It must be remembered, however, that although this case and *Asahi* both involve foreign manufacturers, the undesirable consequences of Justice Brennan's approach are no less significant for domestic producers. The owner of a small Florida farm might sell crops to a large nearby distributor, for example, who might then distribute them to grocers across the country. If foreseeability were the controlling criterion, the farmer could be sued in Alaska or any number of other States' courts without ever leaving town. And the issue of foreseeability may itself be contested so that significant expenses are incurred just on the preliminary issue of jurisdiction. Jurisdictional rules should avoid these costs whenever possible.

The conclusion that the authority to subject a defendant to judgment depends on purposeful availment, consistent with Justice O'Connor's opinion in *Asahi*, does not by itself resolve many difficult questions of jurisdiction that will arise in particular cases. The defendant's conduct and the economic realities of the market the defendant seeks to serve will differ across cases, and judicial exposition will, in common-law fashion, clarify the contours of that principle.

III. In this case, petitioner directed marketing and sales efforts at the United States. It may be that, assuming it were otherwise empowered to legislate on the subject, the Congress could authorize the exercise of jurisdiction in appropriate courts. That circumstance is not presented in this case, however, and it is neither necessary nor appropriate to address here any constitutional concerns that might be attendant to that exercise of power. *See Asahi*, 480 U.S., at 113 n. *. Nor is it necessary to determine what substantive law might apply were Congress to authorize jurisdiction in a federal court in New Jersey. A sovereign's legislative authority to regulate conduct may present considerations different from those presented by its authority to subject a defendant to judgment in its courts. Here the question concerns the authority of a New Jersey state court to exercise jurisdiction, so it is petitioner's purposeful contacts with New Jersey, not with the United States, that alone are relevant.

[In the brief remainder of its opinion, the plurality concluded that the above-described facts did not suffice to establish that the New Jersey court's exercise of personal jurisdiction over McIntyre satisfied the Due Process Clause.]

Justice Breyer, with whom Justice Alito joins, concurring in the judgment. The Supreme Court of New Jersey adopted a broad understanding of the scope of personal jurisdiction based on its view that "[t]he increasingly fast-paced globalization of the world economy has removed national borders as barriers to trade." I do not doubt that there have been many recent changes in commerce and communication, many of which are not anticipated by our precedents. But this case does not present any of those issues. So I think it unwise to announce a rule of broad applicability without full consideration of the modern-day consequences. . . .

None of our precedents finds that a single isolated sale, even if accompanied by the kind of sales effort indicated here, is sufficient. Rather, this Court's previous holdings suggest the contrary. The Court has held that a single sale to a customer who takes an accident-causing product to a different State (where the accident takes place) is not a sufficient basis for asserting jurisdiction. *See World-Wide Volkswagen Corp. v. Woodson*, 444 U.S. 286 (1980). And the Court, in separate opinions, has strongly suggested that a single sale of a product in a State does not constitute an adequate basis for asserting jurisdiction over an out-of-state defendant, even if that defendant places his goods in the stream of commerce, fully aware (and hoping) that such a sale will take place. *See Asahi Metal Industry Co. v. Superior Court of Cal., Solano Cty.*, 480 U.S. 102, 111, 112 (1987) (opinion of O'Connor, J.) (requiring "something more" than simply placing "a product into the stream of commerce," even if defendant is "awar[e]" that the stream "may or will sweep the product into the forum State"); *id.*, at 117 (Brennan, J., concurring in part and concurring in judgment) (jurisdiction should lie where a sale in a State is part of "the regular and anticipated flow" of commerce into the State, but not where that sale is only an "edd[y]," i.e., an isolated occurrence); *id.*, at 122 (Stevens, J., concurring in part and concurring in judgment) (indicating that "the volume, the value, and the hazardous character" of a good may affect the jurisdictional inquiry and emphasizing Asahi's "regular course of dealing").

Here, the relevant facts found by the New Jersey Supreme Court show no "regular . . . flow" or "regular course" of sales in New Jersey; and there is no "something more," such as special state-related design, advertising, advice, marketing, or anything else. Mr. Nicastro, who here bears the burden of proving jurisdiction, has shown no specific effort by the British Manufacturer to sell in New Jersey. He has introduced no list of potential New Jersey customers who might, for example, have regularly attended trade shows. And he has not otherwise shown that the British Manufacturer "purposefully avail[ed] itself of the privilege of conducting activities" within New Jersey, or that it delivered its goods in the stream of commerce "with the expectation that they will be purchased" by New Jersey users. *World–Wide Volkswagen, supra*, at 297-298. . . .

The plurality seems to state strict rules that limit jurisdiction where a defendant does not "inten[d] to submit to the power of a sovereign" and cannot "be said to have targeted the forum." But what do those standards mean when a company targets the world by selling products from its Web site? And does it matter if, instead of shipping the products directly, a company consigns the products through an intermediary (say, Amazon.com) who then receives and fulfills the orders? And what if the company markets its products through popup advertisements that it knows will be viewed in a forum? Those issues have serious commercial consequences but are totally absent in this case.

But though I do not agree with the plurality's seemingly strict no-jurisdiction rule, I am not persuaded by the absolute approach adopted by the New Jersey Supreme Court. . . . Under that view, a producer is subject to jurisdiction for a products-liability action so long as it "knows or reasonably should know that its products are distributed through a nationwide distribution system that might lead to those products being sold in any of the fifty states." In the context of this case, I cannot agree.

For one thing, to adopt this view would abandon the heretofore accepted inquiry of whether, focusing upon the relationship between "the defendant, the forum, and the litigation," it is fair, in light of the defendant's contacts with *that forum*, to subject the defendant to suit there. *Shaffer v. Heitner*, 433 U.S. 186, 204 (1977) (emphasis added). It would ordinarily rest jurisdiction instead upon no more than the occurrence of a product-based accident in the forum State. But this Court has rejected the notion that a defendant's amenability to suit "travel[s] with the chattel." *World-Wide Volkswagen*, 444 U.S., at 296.

For another, I cannot reconcile so automatic a rule with the constitutional demand for [minimum contacts and purposeful availment]. A rule like the New Jersey Supreme Court's would permit every State to assert jurisdiction in a products-liability suit against any domestic manufacturer who sells its products (made anywhere in the United States) to a national distributor, no matter how large or small the manufacturer, no matter how distant the forum, and no matter how few the number of items that end up in the particular forum at issue. What might appear fair in the case of a large manufacturer which specifically seeks, or expects, an equal-sized distributor to sell its product in a distant State might seem unfair in the case of a small manufacturer (say, an Appalachian potter) who sells his product (cups and saucers) exclusively to a large distributor, who resells a single item (a coffee mug) to a buyer from a distant State (Hawaii). I know too little about the range of these or in-between possibilities to abandon in favor of the more absolute rule what has previously been this Court's less absolute approach.

Further, the fact that the defendant is a foreign, rather than a domestic, manufacturer makes the basic fairness of an absolute rule yet more uncertain. I am again less certain than is the New Jersey Supreme Court that the nature of international commerce has changed so significantly as to require a new approach to personal jurisdiction.

It may be that a larger firm can readily "alleviate the risk of burdensome litigation by procuring insurance, passing the expected costs on to customers, or, if the risks are too great, severing its connection with the State." *World-Wide Volkswagen, supra,* at 297. But manufacturers come in many shapes and sizes. It may be fundamentally unfair to require a small Egyptian shirt maker, a Brazilian manufacturing cooperative, or a Kenyan coffee farmer, selling its products through international distributors, to respond to products-liability tort suits in virtually every State in the United States, even those in respect to which the foreign firm has no connection at all but the sale of a single (allegedly defective) good. And a rule like the New Jersey Supreme Court suggests would require every product manufacturer, large or small, selling to American distributors to understand not only the tort law of every State, but also the wide variance in the way courts within different States apply that law.

Justice Ginsburg, with whom Justice Sotomayor and Justice Kagan join, dissenting.

The modern approach to jurisdiction over corporations and other legal entities, ushered in by *International Shoe,* gave prime place to reason and fairness. Is it not fair and reasonable, given the mode of trading of which this case is an example, to require the international seller to defend at the place its products cause injury? Do not litigational convenience and choice-of-law considerations point in that direction? On what measure of reason and fairness can it be considered undue to require McIntyre UK to defend in New Jersey as an incident of its efforts to develop a market for its industrial machines anywhere and everywhere in the United States? Is not the burden on McIntyre UK to defend in New Jersey fair, i.e., a reasonable cost of transacting business internationally, in comparison to the burden on Nicastro to go to Nottingham, England to gain recompense for an injury he sustained using McIntyre's product at his workplace in Saddle Brook, New Jersey?

McIntyre UK dealt with the United States as a single market. Like most foreign manufacturers, it was concerned not with the prospect of suit in State X as opposed to State Y, but rather with its subjection to suit anywhere in the United States. As a McIntyre UK officer wrote in an e-mail to McIntyre America: "American law—who needs it?!" If McIntyre UK is answerable in the United States at all, is it not "perfectly appropriate to permit the exercise of that jurisdiction . . . at the place of injury"? *See* [] Degnan & Kane, The Exercise of Jurisdiction Over and Enforcement of Judgments Against Alien Defendants, 39 Hastings L.J. 799, 813-815 (1988) (noting that "[i]n the international order," the State that counts is the United States, not its component States,[169] and that the fair place of suit within the United States is essentially a question of venue).

In sum, McIntyre UK, by engaging McIntyre America to promote and sell its machines in the United States, "purposefully availed itself" of the United States market nationwide, not a market in a single State or a discrete collection of States. McIntyre UK thereby availed itself of the market of all States in which its products were sold by its exclusive distributor. "Th[e] 'purposeful availment' requirement," this Court has explained, simply "ensures that a defendant will not be haled into a jurisdiction solely as a result of 'random,' 'fortuitous,' or 'attenuated' contacts." *Burger King,* 471 U.S., at 475. Adjudicatory authority is appropriately exercised where "actions by the defendant himself" give rise to the affiliation with the forum. *Ibid.* How could McIntyre UK not have intended, by

169. "For purposes of international law and foreign relations, the separate identities of individual states of the Union are generally irrelevant." Born, *Reflections on Judicial Jurisdiction in International Cases,* 17 Ga. J. Int'l & Comp. L. 1, 36 (1987). *See also Hines v. Davidowitz,* 312 U.S. 52, 63 (1941) ("For local interests the several States of the Union exist, but for national purposes, embracing our relations with foreign nations, we are but one people, one nation, one power.") (internal quotation marks omitted); Restatement (Third) of Foreign Relations Law of the United States § 421, Comment f, p. 307 (1986) ("International law . . . does not concern itself with the allocation of jurisdiction among domestic courts within a [nation,] for example, between national and local courts in a federal system.").

its actions targeting a national market, to sell products in the fourth largest destination for imports among all States of the United States and the largest scrap metal market?

[The dissent then responded to McIntyre's reliance on *Woodson* and *Asahi*] Notably, the foreign manufacturer of the Audi in [*Woodson*] did not object to the jurisdiction of the Oklahoma courts and the U.S. importer abandoned its initially stated objection. And most relevant here, the Court's opinion indicates that an objection to jurisdiction by the manufacturer or national distributor would have been unavailing. To reiterate, the Court said in [*Woodson*] that, when a manufacturer or distributor aims to sell its product to customers in several States, it is reasonable "to subject it to suit in [any] one of those States if its allegedly defective [product] has there been the source of in-jury." . . .

Asahi, unlike McIntyre, did not itself seek out customers in the United States, it engaged no distributor to promote its wares here, it appeared at no tradeshows in the United States, and, of course, it had no Web site advertising its products to the world. Moreover, Asahi was a component-part manufacturer with little control over the final destination of its products once they were delivered into the stream of commerce. It was important . . . in *Asahi* that "those who use Asahi components in their final products, and sell those products in California, [would be] subject to the application of California tort law." To hold that *Asahi* controls this case would, to put it bluntly, be dead wrong.

The Court's judgment also puts United States plaintiffs at a disadvantage in comparison to similarly situated complainants elsewhere in the world. Of particular note, within the European Union, in which the United Kingdom is a participant, the jurisdiction New Jersey would have exercised is not at all exceptional. The European Regulation on Jurisdiction and the Recognition and Enforcement of Judgments provides for the exercise of specific jurisdiction "in matters relating to tort . . . in the courts for the place where the harmful event occurred." Council Reg. 44/2001, Art. 5, 2001 O.J. (L.12) 4. [For a fuller discussion of Regulation 44/2001, see *supra* pp. 105-107]. The European Court of Justice has interpreted this prescription to authorize jurisdiction either where the harmful act occurred or at the place of injury. *See Handelskwekerij G.J. Bier B.V. v. Mines de Potasse d'Alsace S. A.,* 1976 E.C.R. 1735, 1748-1749.

Notes *on* Asahi *and* Nicastro

1. *Original stream of commerce doctrine.* Prior to *Asahi*, some courts held that due process permits jurisdiction whenever a manufacturer's products are carried by the "stream of commerce" into the forum. These decisions apparently do not consider whether the defendant either purposefully directed its products into the forum or knew or should have known that its products were sold in the forum; rather, the defendant need only purposefully "place its products in the stream of commerce." *See Hedrick v. Daiko Shoji Co.,* 715 F.2d 1355 (9th Cir. 1983); *Swanigan v. Amadeo Rossi, SA,* 617 F. Supp. 66 (E.D. Mich. 1985) What precedential value do these decisions have after *Asahi* and *Nicastro*? Why shouldn't this minimalist stream of commerce analysis be adopted? If the defendant makes a product that malfunctions in the forum, why shouldn't that be an end of analysis? What interests are protected by requiring "purposeful" contacts with the forum? Does this requirement protect the defendant? Or foreign sovereignty?

2. *Stream of commerce in* Asahi. In *Asahi*, the Court again divided sharply over the "stream of commerce" test.

(a) *Justice O'Connor's plurality opinion.* Four Justices concluded in *Asahi* that placing a product into the stream of commerce "without more" is not an act purposefully directed toward the forum State. That is true even where a defendant is "aware[] that the stream of commerce may or will sweep the product into the forum." Rather, the plurality required some additional evidence of "an intent or purpose to serve the market in the forum State," such as designing products for the forum, advertising in the forum, or marketing products through an agent who agreed to serve the forum market.

What does Justice O'Connor's opinion require to demonstrate "purposeful" contacts?

(b)   Justice Brennan's concurring opinion. Justice Brennan and three other Justices rejected the plurality's analysis in *Asahi*. They concluded that "[a]s long as *a participant* in [the distribution of products] *is aware* that the final product is being marketed in the forum State, the possibility of a lawsuit there cannot come as a surprise." These Justices would have held that "Asahi's regular and extensive sales of component parts to a manufacturer it knew was making regular sales of the final product in California" satisfied the Due Process Clause. What is Justice Brennan's test? Is mere "awareness" enough to establish minimum contacts? Is this view consistent with *World-Wide Volkswagen?* Does it remain a valid approach after *Nicastro?*

(c)   Justice Stevens' concurring opinion. Justice Stevens did not join either Justice O'Connor's or Brennan's opinion in *Asahi*. He did, however, predict that "[i]n most circumstances I would be inclined to conclude that a regular course of dealing that results in deliveries of over 100,000 units annually over a period of several years would constitute 'purposeful availment.' " (Note that Justice Stevens' statistics were confused: the number of Asahi's valves that were sold each year in California by Cheng Shin appear to have been no more than 100,000 (in 1979 and 1980) and often only 20,000 — and then only by making the very unlikely assumption that Cheng Shin sold *all* its tire tubes in the United States, with California sales constituting 20 percent of this amount.). Following *Asahi*, most lower courts gave little credit to Justice Stevens' opinion. Does Justice Breyer's opinion in *Nicastro* breathe new life into this view?

(d)   Evaluating Asahi's *stream of commerce opinions.* What are the differences between these three views of the stream of commerce analysis? Which is wiser?

3. *Lower court applications of stream of commerce doctrine after* Asahi. Following *Asahi*, lower courts divided badly over the proper test under the stream of commerce doctrine. As one lower court has observed: "The *Asahi* case left lower courts in a quandary, not knowing what principles they should apply in deciding the minimum contacts issue." *Lister v. Marangoni Meccanica SpA*, 728 F. Supp. 1524, 1527 (D. Utah 1990). *See generally* Moore's Federal Practice-Civil §108.42 n. 35 & 36 (3d ed. 2010) (collecting cases).

(a)   Lower courts holding that Asahi *does not affect due process analysis.* Some courts took the view that the Court's inability to produce a majority opinion in *Asahi* left the stream of commerce doctrine unchanged. In turn, that leaves litigants to contend with local, pre-*Asahi* interpretations of *World-Wide Volkswagen* and the stream of commerce test. *E.g., Ex Parte DBI, Inc.*, 23 So.3d 635, 649 (Ala. 2003) ("[I]n the murky aftermath of the plurality opinions in *Asahi*, the task has not been made any easier. Until more definite direction is given, we revert to the last expressions from the United States Supreme Court in *World-Wide Volkswagen* and *Burger King* that are not hampered by the lack of a majority.").

(b)   Lower courts holding that Justice O'Connor's opinion in Asahi *rejects the stream of commerce doctrine.* Some courts held that Justice O'Connor's opinion indicates that the Court will reject the stream of commerce doctrine. *E.g., Spir Star AG v. Kimich*, 310 S.W.3d 868, 873 (Tex. 2010); *State v. North Atlantic Refining Ltd.*, 2010 WL 1816418 at *6 (N.H. 2010); *CSR, Ltd. v. Taylor*, 983 A.2d 492, 507 (Md. 2009); *Bridgeport Music, Inc. v. Still N The Water Pub.*, 327 F.3d 472, 480 (6th Cir. 2003); *Jarre v. Heidelberger Druckmaschinen AG*, 19 F.3d 1430 (4th Cir. 1994); *Boit v. Gar-Tec Products, Inc.*, 967 F.2d 671, 683 (1st Cir. 1992).

(c)   Lower courts holding that Justice Brennan's opinion in Asahi *reaffirms stream of commerce doctrine.* Other lower courts concluded that *Asahi*'s plurality opinion could not overrule *World-Wide Volkswagen* and other previous Supreme Court decisions purportedly adopting the stream of commerce doctrine; these courts have generally followed Justice Brennan's

opinion. For the most part, the New Jersey Supreme Court followed this approach in *Nicastro. Nicastro v. McIntyre Machinery America, Ltd.*, 987 A.2d 575, 589 (N.J. 2010).

4. Stream of commerce in Nicastro. In light of the sharp divisions among lower courts over such a critical legal question, it is rather remarkable that the Supreme Court allowed nearly twenty-five years to pass before attempting to resolve these conflicts. When it agreed to review *Nicastro,* many observers anticipated that the Court would finally inject some much-needed clarity into this area of law. Regrettably, the Court again divided sharply over the "stream of commerce" test.

(a) Justice Kennedy's plurality opinion. Four Justices concluded in *Nicastro* that the stream of commerce theory did not displace the traditional minimum contacts analysis of *International Shoe,* including the purposeful availment requirement of *Hanson. See supra* pp. 146-147. Accordingly, "it is not enough that the defendant might have predicted that its goods will reach the forum State." Instead, the foreign manufacturer must have "targeted" the forum. What precisely does it mean to "target" the forum? How, according to the *Nicastro* plurality, should a lower court determine whether a foreign manufacturer has "targeted" the forum? What does Justice Kennedy mean when he writes that "the authority to subject a defendant to judgment depends on purposeful availment, consistent with Justice O'Connor's opinion in *Asahi*"? Does this analysis differ from the "additional conduct" required by Justice O'Connor's plurality opinion in *Asahi?*

(b) Justice Breyer's concurring opinion. Justice Breyer and Justice Alito agreed with the *Nicastro* plurality that the New Jersey Supreme Court's decision required reversal but declined to embrace its analysis. What rule does Justice Breyer derive from the Court's precedents to decide that reversal was warranted? Do the precedents actually support Justice Breyer's rule? *Compare McGee v. Int'l Life Ins. Co.,* 355 U.S. 220 (1957) (sale of single insurance policy to resident of forum state sufficient to support exercise of personal jurisdiction under Due Process Clause). What "broad rule of applicability" announced by the plurality does Justice Breyer find "unwise?" The plurality unquestionably rejects Justice Brennan's test from *Asahi.* Does Justice Breyer? Recall that the New Jersey Supreme Court relied principally on Justice Brennan's opinion from *Asahi* to uphold the exercise of jurisdiction. Doesn't Justice Breyer's explicit reject of the "absolute approach adopted by the New Jersey Supreme Court" necessarily imply a rejection of Justice Brennan's opinion. According to Justice Breyer, did the New Jersey Supreme Court misinterpret Justice Brennan's opinion in *Asahi?* Or has Justice Breyer reinterpreted it?

(c) Justice Ginsburg's dissenting opinion. Justice Ginsburg, joined by two other justices, would have upheld the exercise of personal jurisdiction over McIntyre. What rule of law provides the basis for her view? Is it the same view that Justice Brennan expressed in *Asahi?* The view expressed in *World Wide Volkswagen?* If one reads Justice Ginsburg's opinion alongside Justice Breyer's, does a majority of the Court actually *reject* the view expressed by the *Nicastro* plurality? Or does Justice Ginsburg's opinion sweep more broadly? If so, where exactly do Justice Ginsburg's and Justice Breyer's opinions part ways?

(d) Evaluating Nicastro *'s stream of commerce opinions.* What is the law governing the stream of commerce theory after *Nicastro?* Does a majority of the Court now reject Justice Brennan's concurrence from *Asahi?* Does a majority of the Court rejected the rule of "broad applicability" articulated by the *Nicastro* plurality? Does a majority of the Court share the view that a single isolated sale, even if accompanied by the kind of sales effort indicated [in *Nicastro*]" is insufficient? What, if anything, should be inferred from the fact that, unlike the opinions in *Asahi,* none of the opinions in *Nicastro* discussed the "reasonableness" prong of the minimum contacts test?

5. Examples of purposeful availment in international stream of commerce cases. After *Asahi,* numerous lower courts considered whether a foreign manufacturer's conduct satisfied the (unclear) standards of the stream of commerce test. Consider the extent to which these decisions remain valid after *Nicastro*.

(a) *Designing products for forum market*. A common basis for purposeful availment is designing a product specifically for the forum market. *E.g., Chea v. Fette*, 2004 WL 220866 (E.D. Pa. 2004); *In re Perrier Bottled Water Litigation*, 754 F. Supp. 264, 268 (D. Conn. 1990) (holding that Perrier designed its product for U.S. market "which, of course, includes Connecticut and Pennsylvania," because bottles had ounce, rather than metric labels); *Lister v. Marangoui Meccanica SpA*, 728 F. Supp. 1524, 1527 (D. Utah 1990) (upholding jurisdiction where a company in the forum provided the specifications for the custom-built product to the defendant). *Compare Brown v. Abus Kransysteme GmbH*, 11 So. 3d 788 (Ala. 2008) (refusing jurisdiction because product model "was not authorized for sale in the United States"); *Soo Line RR Co. v. Hawker Siddeley Canada, Inc.*, 950 F.2d 526 (8th Cir. 1991) (refusing jurisdiction because "Hawker Siddeley did not design its railcars for use in Minnesota per se; it designed its railcars for use in most of North America"). Does the answer depend on whether the product is a mass-produced one for general use (like an automobile) as opposed to a region-specific one (like a snowblower)? *See Ex Parte DBI, Inc.*, 23 So.3d 635, 655 (Ala. 2003). Should it suffice if the defendant designs its product for a region of the United States, of which the forum state is a part? *See State v. North Atlantic Refining, Ltd.*, 2010 WL 1816418 at *7 (N.H. May 7, 2010).

(b) *Providing literature in or tailored for forum*. Lower courts have found purposeful availment based upon the defendant's supply of promotional or other literature tailored for forum users. *E.g., S.E.C. v. Carillo*, 115 F.3d 1540, 1545-1546 (11th Cir. 1997) (finding purposeful availment in advertising and mailing directed at forum); *Weight v. Kawasaki Motors Corp., U.S.A.*, 604 F. Supp. 968 (E.D. Va. 1985) (foreign manufacturer subject to jurisdiction because, among other things, it provided English owner's manuals); *Van Eeuwen v. Heidelberg Eastern, Inc.*, 306 A.2d 79 (N.J. Super. 1973).

(c) *Sending employees or agents into forum*. Lower courts have cited foreign defendants' dispatch of employees or agents to the forum as evidence of purposeful availment. *Compare Weiss v. La Suisse*, 69 F. Supp. 2d 449, 456 (S.D.N.Y. 1999) (insurance company set up agency relationship with local brokers) *with Brabeau v. SMB Corp.*, 789 F. Supp. 873 (E.D. Mich. 1992) (no jurisdiction where defendant's "technician assist[ed] in the installation of a printing press" in forum which caused no injury to plaintiff).

(d) *Establishing distribution network in forum*. Significant factors in finding purposeful availment have been the defendant's establishment of a distribution system serving the forum and advertising in the forum. *E.g., Spir Star AG v. Kimich*, 310 S.W.3d 868, 875-78 (Tex. 2010); *State ex rel. Edmondson v. Native Wholesale Supply*, 2010 WL 267499 at *9 (Okla. July 6, 2010); *Anderson v. Dassault Aviation*, 361 F.3d 449, 454 (8th Cir. 2004) (relying on fact that foreign corporation purposely directed activities toward United States through distribution system); *Nuovo Pignone, SpA v. STORMAN ASIA M/V*, 310 F.3d 374, 379-381 (5th Cir. 2002) (relying on stream of commerce theory where defendant contracted "with third party intermediaries who brought the crane to [forum state]"); *Mott v. Schelling & Co.*, 966 F.2d 1453 (6th Cir. 1992); *Vermeulen v. Renault, U.S.A. Inc.*, 965 F.2d 1014, 1026 (11th Cir. 1992) (foreign defendant "created and controlled the distribution network that brought its products into the United States and Georgia").

Other authority suggests that the mere establishment of a distribution network, without more, may not establish purposeful availment. *Commissariat A L'Energie Atomique v. Chi Mei Optoelectronics Corp.*, 395 F.3d 1315, 1322 (Fed. Cir. 2005) (declining to decide whether "additional conduct, beyond a showing of use of established distribution channels, is required to meet the demands of due process under the stream of commerce theory of personal jurisdiction").

(e)   *Granting licenses for distribution in forum.* Lower courts have relied on a defendant's grant of a U.S. distribution license as evidence of purposeful availment. *Compare Saia v. Scripto-Tokai Corp.*, 851 N.E.2d 693, 701 (Ill. App. Ct. 2006) (relying on existence of exclusive U.S. distributor to support exercise of personal jurisdiction over foreign manufacturer), *with Maschinenfabrik Seydelmann v. Altman*, 468 So.2d 286 (Fla. App. 1985) (no jurisdiction where German defendant appointed exclusive U.S. distributor and, over 22-year period, sold 23 machines with total value under $1 million).

(f)   *Substantial numbers of units sold.* A few lower courts have relied principally on large numbers of sales in the forum in inferring purposeful availment. *E.g., Oswalt v. Scripto, Inc.*, 616 F.2d 191 (5th Cir. 1980) (relying on 3 to 4 million units in annual sales); *McHugh v. Kenyon*, 547 So.2d 318 (D. Ct. App. Fla. 1989) ("A manufacturer that produces hundreds of thousands of product units [ladders] that are distributed over a five-year period in the United States, of which at least 6,000 were marketed in Florida, should reasonably anticipate being sued" there); *Allen v. Canadian General Electric Co.*, 410 N.Y.S.2d 707 (App. Div. 1978). *Compare* Justice Stevens' observations in *Asahi* as to the unit and dollar sales he thought sufficient for due process purposes, *supra* p. 144. Is it useful, or proper, to rely on the number or value of annual sales? Which represents more significant contacts for Due Process purposes — a one-time large shipment or numerous smaller shipments? How is any of this relevant to the territorial sovereignty of foreign states or the fairness to the defendant? To what extent do *Nicastro* and *Goodyear*, discussed *infra* at pp. 160-161, bear on this mode of analysis?

(g)   *What's in the stream?* "Stream of commerce" analysis can potentially be applied to a wide range of products and services. Early cases such as *McGee* and *Asahi* concerned the sale of component parts (or finished products). Is the stream of commerce theory limited to manufacturers of physical goods. *See Tech. Patents, LLC v. Deutsche Telekom AG*, 573 F. Supp. 2d 903 (D. Md. 2008) (rejecting personal jurisdiction in patent infringement suit and observing that "it is doubtful whether text messages themselves can be considered products in the stream of commerce"). Can labor and other services enter the stream of commerce? *See Kopke v. A. Hartrodt SRL*, 629 N.W.2d 662 (Wis. 2001). What about instrumentalities of commerce like planes and ships? *Compare Fortis Corporate Ins. v. Viken Ship Mgmt.*, 450 F.3d 214, 221-22 (6th Cir. 2006) (rigging vessels for use in forum state found sufficient under stream-of-commerce theory), *with D'Jamoos ex rel. Estate of Weingeroff v. Pilatus Aircraft Ltd.*, 566 F.3d 94, 105-06 (3d Cir. 2009) (declining to find personal jurisdiction over airplane manufacturer in claims arising from crash where airplane, though conforming with federal aviation requirements, merely flew into forum state and, thus, did not enter state *via* stream of commerce). Are there any limits? *See Merriman v. Crompton Corp.*, 146 P.3d 162, 183 (Kan. 2006) (applying stream-of-commerce theory to claim that foreign defendants engaged in price-fixing conspiracy).

6. *Stream of commerce and the Internet.* As discussed above, use of the Internet has raised significant issues in jurisdictional analysis. *See supra* at 126, 154-155. While courts have been reluctant to rely on a website as the basis for establishing general jurisdiction, *see, e.g., Holland America Line Inc. v. Wartsila North America, Inc.*, 485 F.3d 450, 460 (9th Cir. 2007), the law relating to specific jurisdiction is more complex.

At the time the Supreme Court decided *Asahi*, the internet was not a widely used tool for the sale of goods and services (or the marketing of products). As it became a more potent tool, lower courts developed different tests for determining whether the maintenance of a website satisfied the minimum contacts test. Some courts differentiate between interactive websites (which permit a party to order products, enter into contracts, and download material) and passive websites (advertising vehicles); according to this approach, maintenance of an interactive website used by forum residents is more likely to support the exercise of specific jurisdiction. *See Carefirst of Maryland, Inc. v. Carefirst Pregnancy Centers, Inc.*, 334 F.3d 390, 398-401 (4th Cir. 2003); *Toys "R" Us, Inc. v. Step Two, SA*, 318 F.3d 446, 452 (3d Cir. 2003) ("If a defendant web site operator intentionally targets the site to the forum state, and/or knowingly conducts business with forum state residents via the site, then the 'purposeful availment' requirement is satisfied."); *Zippo Mfg. Co. v. Zippo Dot Com, Inc.*, 952 F. Supp. 1119, 1123-1126 (W.D. Pa. 1997) (interactive/ passive distinction). In some cases applying this approach, courts couple the maintenance of the interactive website with other contacts to support the exercise of personal jurisdiction. *E.g., Euromarket Designs, Inc. v. Crate and Barrel Ltd.*, 96 F. Supp. 2d 824 (N.D. Ill. 2000). Others reject this classification and conduct a more traditional minimum contacts analysis. *E.g., Hy Cite Corp. v. Badbusinessbureau.com, LLC*, 297 F. Supp. 2d 1154, 1160-1161 (W.D. Wis. 2004).

Though *Nicastro* did not involve sales over the Internet, briefs in the case clearly made the Court aware that whatever rule it announced could have implications for such sales. While the plurality appeared prepared to announce a rule of general applicability, the narrower approach taken by Justice Breyer seems at least partly attributable to his uncertainty about how stream of commerce principles should be adapted to the internet. Suppose a lower court judge is confronted with the sort of case that worries Justice Breyer — a company targets the world by selling products from its Web site? How should he rule after *Nicastro*? Suppose a case involving Internet sales and the stream of commerce reaches the Supreme Court? Should it modify the general rules governing the constitutional limits on personal jurisdiction to take into account the development of the Internet? Is it even appropriate for courts to shape constitutional doctrines in light of changing social phenomenon?

7. *Importance of foreseeability to stream of commerce analysis.* What is the role of the defendant's ability to foresee, or actual knowledge, that its products would be shipped into the forum state in stream of commerce analysis? How do Justice O'Connor, Brennan, and Stevens answer this question in *Asahi*?

In *Nicastro*, the plurality observed that an approach "based on general notions of fairness and foreseeability" was "inconsistent with the premises of lawful judicial power." Does Justice Ginsburg anchor her proposed rule in considerations of foreseeability? Justice Breyer? Is it fair to say that, after *Nicastro*, jurisdictional approaches grounded on the foreseeability that the goods would enter the forum state are now dead?

8. *Defining the territory of the forum — another preliminary look.* Classic jurisdictional analysis requires a court to consider the defendant's contacts with the "forum." Why should the relevant contacts be so limited? Before *Nicastro*, most lower courts generally did not address the relevance of a foreign defendant's contacts with other U.S. states under the Fourteenth Amendment. Nevertheless, some lower courts, without explanation, apparently attributed jurisdictional significance to a foreign defendant's contacts with the entire United States. *E.g., Vermeulen v. Renault, U.S.A. Inc.*, 965 F.2d 1014 (11th Cir. 1992) ("Although . . . there is no evidence that [defendant] designed the LeCar specifically for the Georgia market, the fact that [defendant] designed its products for the United States generally as part of a nationwide marketing effort . . . " satisfies *Asahi*); *Etchieson v. Central Purchasing LLC*, 232 P.3d 301, 307 (Colo. Ct. App. 2010); *Ensign-Bickford Co. v. ICI Explosives USA Inc.*, 817 F.Supp. 1018 (D. Conn. 1993). By contrast, other lower court decisions apparently accorded no weight to a defendant's contacts with U.S. states other than the forum state. *E.g., CSR v. Taylor, Ltd.*, 983 A.2d 492, 509-10 (Md. 2009); *Jennings v. AC Hydraulic A/S*, 383 F.3d 546, 550-551 (7th Cir. 2004) (rejecting argument that sale of defendant's products in state other than forum state, without more, sufficed to establish minimum contacts); *Pawluczyk v. Global Upholstery Co.*, 854 F. Supp. 364 (E.D. Pa.

1994) (rejecting argument that "the sale of [defendant's products] anywhere in the United States is sufficient to establish personal jurisdiction . . . in Pennsylvania"); *Brabeau v. SMB Corp.,* 789 F. Supp. 873, 878 n.2 (E.D. Mich. 1992) ("contacts with the state in which the district court sits are controlling, not contact with the United States as a whole").

In *Nicastro*, the identity of the forum and the identification of the relevant contacts was a critical point dividing the different opinions. The *Nicastro* plurality believed that the Constitution required a "a forum-by-forum, or sovereign-by-sovereign, analysis." It also observed that the United States was a "distinct sovereign" and, consequently, "a defendant may in principle be subject to the jurisdiction of the courts of the United States but not of any particular State." Justice Breyer's opinion was more hazy. On the one hand, it appeared to believe relevant (if inadequate) that McIntyre had engaged in a "sales effort" elsewhere in the United States. On the other hand, its rejection of the New Jersey Supreme Court's opinion stresses the centrality of the defendant's conduct with "*the forum.*" Finally, Justice Ginsburg's opinion believed that it was entirely appropriate for the New Jersey courts to exercise personal jurisdiction over McIntyre based on its decision to target "the United States market nationwide." After *Nicastro*, may a state court take into account a foreign manufacturer's contacts with other states? May a federal court? Does it depend on the basis for the federal court's subject matter jurisdiction? For a fuller discussion of these issues, *see infra* at pp. 158-160.

9. **Asahi's** *"reasonableness" test. Asahi* is also significant because of its treatment of the "reasonableness" prong. Reconsider Part II-B of Justice O'Connor's opinion. Note that eight Justices agreed that, even if minimum contacts existed, reasonableness would preclude jurisdiction.

Consider the factors cited in *Asahi's* reasonableness analysis. In addition to requiring "great care and reserve" in exercising personal jurisdiction over foreigners, the Court emphasized that "California's interests in the dispute have considerably diminished," because the case involved a fairly unusual indemnification dispute between two *foreign* companies. The Court also remarked that "[w]hen minimum contacts have been established, often the interests of the plaintiff and the forum in the exercise of jurisdiction will justify even the serious burdens placed on the alien defendant." It remains to be seen whether the factual setting of *Asahi* will detract from the admonition to exercise "great care and reserve" in asserting jurisdiction over foreign defendants. *See supra* pp. 150-152.

Consider the Court's conclusion that "the interests of the plaintiff and the forum in California's assertion of jurisdiction over Asahi are slight," because "[a]ll that remains is a claim for indemnification asserted by Cheng Shin, a Taiwanese corporation, against Asahi." Is this sensible? Isn't it obvious that Cheng Shin—like most parties seeking indemnification—would strongly prefer litigating its claims in the same forum where the underlying claims were asserted against it?

Justice O'Connor's opinion in *Asahi* also reasoned that in the international context the reasonableness framework must be modified to take into account "the procedural and substantive policies of other nations whose interested are affected by the assertion of jurisdiction by the California courts." Was this a sensible application of the reasonableness test? What makes it "reasonable" to consider foreign states' substantive policies in due process analysis? Federalism concerns? Fairness concerns?

10. *Lower court applications of reasonableness requirement after* **Asahi**. After *Asahi*, a number of lower courts applied its reasonableness test in international cases.

(a)   *General reluctance to decline jurisdiction where minimum contacts exists.* In general, lower courts have been reluctant to decline jurisdiction over foreign defendants that have minimum contacts with the forum because of reasonableness concerns. *E.g., Spir Star*

AG v. Kimich, 310 S.W.3d 868, 878 (Tex. 2010) ("Only in rare cases, however, will the exercise of jurisdiction not comport with fair play and substantial justice when the nonresident defendant has purposefully established minimum contacts with the forum state."); *Fortis Corporate Ins. v. Viken Ship Management*, 450 F.3d 214, 223 (6th Cir. 2006) (where minimum contacts and relatedness are established, the assertion of jurisdiction will be unreasonable only in an "unusual case"). Nevertheless, a few post-*Asahi* decisions have denied jurisdiction on reasonableness grounds. *E.g.*, *Bunch v. Lancair Int'l, Inc.*, 202 P.2d 784, 799 (Mont. 2009); *Miller v. Nippon Carbon Co., Ltd.*, 528 F.3d 1087, 1092 (8th Cir. 2008); *Johnston v. Multidata Sys. Int'l Corp.*, 523 F.3d 602, 615-18 (5th Cir. 2008); *TH Agriculture & Nutrition, LLC v. Ace European Group Ltd.*, 488 F.3d 1282, 1292-98 (10th Cir. 2007); *Ticketmaster-New York, Inc. v. Alioto*, 26 F.3d 201, 212 (1st Cir. 1994); *Ellicott Machine Corp. v. John Holland Party Ltd.*, 995 F.2d 474, 475-76 (4th Cir.1993).

(b) *Plaintiff's nationality or residence.* In *Asahi*, Justice O'Connor emphasized that "[b]ecause the plaintiff is not a California resident, California's legitimate interests in the dispute have considerably diminished." Suppose that the Court had been considering a Californian court's jurisdiction over Asahi (and Cheng Shin) in Mr. Zurcher's underlying suit. Would Justice O'Connor's reasonableness analysis have produced any different result? Note that Asahi would face the same burdens in defending the action, while California's "interest" in the suit would have been substantially greater. *See Spir Star AG v. Kimich*, 310 S.W.3d 868, 879 (Tex. 2010) ("Texas has a significant interest in exercising jurisdiction over controversies arising from injuries a Texas resident sustains from products that are purposefully brought into the state and purchased by Texas companies."); *Theunissen v. Matthews*, 935 F.2d 1454, 1462 (6th Cir. 1991) ("Michigan has interest in providing a forum for" Michigan citizens). Several lower courts have declined to assert jurisdiction in disputes between two non-U.S. parties. *E.g.*, *Base Metal Trading, Ltd. v. OJSC Novokuznetsky Aluminum Factory*, 283 F.3d 208, 215 (4th Cir. 2002); *Fields v. Sedgwick Assoc. Risks, Ltd.*, 796 F.2d 299, 300 (9th Cir. 1986); *Pacific Atlantic Trading Co. v. M/V Main Express*, 758 F.2d 1325, 1330 (9th Cir. 1985) (forum has only slight interest in dispute between two foreign parties).

In effect, after *Asahi*, it was easier for U.S. citizens than it is for foreign citizens to obtain personal jurisdiction over foreign defendants. To what extent does this view remain good law after *Nicastro*? Even if this approach survives *Nicastro*, is this appropriate? Compare the importance of the plaintiff's nationality in the *forum non conveniens* and choice of law contexts, *infra* pp. 388, 394-408, 669-671, 680, 753-754.

(c) *Situs of injuries.* Other courts have focused on a state's interest in redressing injuries that occur *on its territory* without regard to the nationality of the victim. *E.g.*, *Keeton v. Hustler Magazine, Inc.*, 465 U.S. 770, 779 (1984) ("It is beyond dispute that New Hampshire has a significant interest in redressing injuries that actually occur within the State."); *State v. North Atlantic Refining, Ltd.*, 2010 WL 1816418 at *9 (N.H. May 7, 2010); *Nuovo Pignone, SpA v. STORMAN ASIA M/V*, 310 F.3d 374, 382 (5th Cir. 2002) ("Unlike the situation in *Asahi*, where the underlying tortious conduct giving rise to an indemnification claim occurred in Japan and the Republic of China, this case is one in which the plaintiff alleges the commission of a tort within the forum."). Which factor — the plaintiff's nationality/domicile or the situs of the injury — is more significant for due process analysis? Why? Does *Nicastro* affect the validity of this view?

(d) *Strength of minimum contacts showing.* An important factor in reasonableness analysis has been the strength of any showing of minimum contacts. *Asahi* involved what was at best a marginal minimum contacts showing, even in Justice Brennan's view. Lower courts accorded considerable weight in reasonableness analysis to the quantum and quality of the defendant's minimum contacts. *E.g.*, *Spir Star AG v. Kimich*, 310 S.W.3d 868, 872 (Tex.

2010); *OMI Holdings v. Royal Ins. Co. of Canada*, 149 F.3d 1086, 1092 (10th Cir. 1998); *Ticketmaster-New York, Inc. v. Alioto*, 26 F.3d 201, 210 (1st Cir. 1994); *Core-Vent Corp. v. Nobel Industries AB*, 11 F.3d 1482 (9th Cir. 1993) (reasonableness analysis considers "the extent of interjection" into the forum). To what extent does this view remain good law after *Nicastro*? Note that none of the opinions in *Nicastro* even addressed the reasonableness analysis?

11. *Lower court applications of reasonableness requirement after* **Nicastro.** Reconsider the opinions in *Nicastro*. Did any of them discuss (much less apply) the reasonableness analysis from *Asahi*? What should be understood from the silence among the justices on this point?

The answer may depend on the opinion. In the case of Justice Ginsburg's dissent, it was responding to the plurality's approach and, consequently, did not have occasion to address the reasonableness test. By contrast, the plurality opinion contains strong language, similar to that employed in *Burnham* (*supra* pp. 133-135) suggesting a desire to discard the reasonableness test altogether. ("Freeform notions of fundamental fairness divorced from traditional practice cannot transform a judgment rendered in the absence of authority into law."). It does, however, allude to the "traditional notions of fair play and substantial justice." Finally, Justice Breyer's opinion appears to accord some relevance to the sorts of factors identified in the *Asahi* reasonableness test (like the burden on the defendant) but does not explicitly embrace (or apply) that test precisely.

12. *Other factors relevant to the stream of commerce analysis.* Step back from the doctrinal squabbles for a moment. Instead of debating whether "sovereignty" or "fairness" drives the constitutional analysis, should the Court instead simply take a more practical approach to these questions. Should factors such as the nature of the foreign company, the size of its operations or its nationality matter? Consider the following:

(a)   Component part manufacturers vs. Finished product manufacturers. Recall that the stream of commerce theory originated with an out-of-state manufacturers whose component parts were incorporated into water heaters by another out-of-state company. Similarly, *Asahi* involved a foreign manufacturer of tire valve assemblies whose products were incorporated by another foreign company into finished tire tubes. By contrast, *Nicastro* involved a foreign manufacturer that sold finished goods to a United States-based distributor. Why should these two types of cases (component part vs finished product) be treated equivalently? Does not a manufacturer of finished goods, regardless of its location, have greater control over the markets that its product enters? By contrast, can a component part manufacturer as easily control where and how its products enter the stream of commerce? Or is it reasonable to require a component part manufacturer to exercise some oversight into the products that its market enters?

(b)   Small companies vs large companies. While the purposeful availment prong does not differentiate between defendants of different sizes and economic strengths, the "reasonableness" prong in *Asahi* gives some weight to this issue. Presumably, the "burden on the defendant" will vary depending on whether the defendant is a large multinational company as opposed to a small, family-run operation. Similarly, in *Nicastro*, Justice Breyer observes that "[w]hat might appear fair in the case of a large manufacturer which specifically seeks, or expects, an equal-sized distributor to sell its product in a distant State might seem unfair in the case of a small manufacturer (say, an Appalachian potter) who sells his product (cups and saucers) exclusively to a large distributor, who resells a single item (a coffee mug) to a buyer from a distant State (Hawaii)." Is this an appropriate distinction? Why should the application of constitutional rules vary with the financial power of the defendant? Doesn't this punish large multinational companies for carefully structuring their operations precisely to avoid judicial jurisdiction in certain forums?

Does the relevance (or irrelevance) of this factor turn on whether sovereignty or fairness supplies the animating principle for this constitutional doctrine?

(c) Nationality of the defendant. While the original stream of commerce doctrine involved an out-of-state (but domestic) defendant company, *Asahi* and *Nicastro* demonstrate that the doctrine is increasingly important to foreign companies as well. Should the constitutional analysis differ depending on the nationality of the defendant? *Asahi* instructed U.S. courts to exercise "great care and reserve" in asserting jurisdiction over foreigners? As noted above, one reason *Asahi* gave was the burdens imposed on foreign defendants litigating abroad: Why should this be so? Consider:

> In many international cases one party will be required to follow procedural rules that differ markedly from those in its home jurisdiction. The most important differences involve broad discovery in the United States, greater reliance on the adversary system, trial by jury, different approaches to fee shifting and contingent fee arrangements, the relatively greater size of United States damage awards, and different choice-of-law rules. In addition, one litigant will generally be a significantly greater distance from the forum than in purely domestic cases, and time differences, language barriers, mail delays, transportation difficulties, and other logistical obstacles which impede efficient communications will create further hardships. Furthermore, while the United States is a relatively homogeneous legal, economic, cultural, social and political unit, the domestic institutions and attitudes within this country often differ markedly from those in foreign states. Born, *Reflections on Judicial Jurisdiction in International Cases*, 17 Ga. J. Int'l & Comp. L. 1, 24-25 n.102 (1987).

Are these persuasive reasons for restraining jurisdiction over foreigners? The burdens imposed on a foreign defendant in international litigation are not unique. U.S. plaintiffs will face the reverse difficulties that foreign defendants encounter in this country if jurisdiction is denied and they are required to litigate their claims abroad. How should this "symmetry" of burdens affect the treatment of foreign defendants? Consider the following observations from Justice Ginsburg's dissent in *Nicastro*: "Is not the burden on McIntyre UK to defend in New Jersey fair, i.e., a reasonable cost of transacting business internationally, in comparison to the burden on Nicastro to go to Nottingham, England to gain recompense for an injury he sustained using McIntyre's product at his workplace in Saddle Brook, New Jersey?" Note that personal jurisdiction analysis ordinarily focuses on the burdens that litigation in the forum imposes on the defendant, not the plaintiff. *See supra* pp. 103, 143. Is this a sufficient response? Should it matter whether the plaintiff voluntarily purchased the product or, as in *Nicastro*, was required in connection with his job to use a dangerous piece of machinery purchased by his employer?

Asahi also reasoned that heightened restraint was necessary in evaluating reasonableness because assertions of jurisdiction over foreign defendants affect foreign policies, laws, and interests, as well as U.S. foreign relations. Before *Asahi* was decided, a number of lower courts had considered foreign sovereign interests and concluded that they required a greater showing of reasonableness to justify asserting jurisdiction over a foreign defendant than is required for domestic defendants. *E.g., Pacific Atlantic Trading Co. v. M/V Main Express*, 758 F.2d 1325, 1330 (9th Cir. 1985) ("sovereignty barrier is high"); *Rocke v. Canadian Auto. Sport Club*, 660 F.2d 395, 399 (9th Cir. 1981) ("Where the defendant is a resident of a foreign nation rather than a resident of another state within our federal system, the sovereignty barrier is 'higher.'"). Was *Asahi* correct in indicating that foreign relations concerns should play a role in due process analysis? Or should these "political" concerns be cognizable only by Congress and the President in their conduct of the nation's foreign relations? Recall the U.S. Government's *amicus curiae* brief in *Helicopteros* invoking U.S. export promotion efforts. *See supra* p. 124. Suppose the defendants in *Asahi* had been tube and valve manufacturers that were incorporated and based in the United States (for example, Illinois). Would a California court's assertion of jurisdiction on these facts be any more or less reasonable than in the actual *Asahi* case? Why? Do the differences relate to different "sovereignty" concerns? *See Roth v. Garcia Marquez*, 942 F.2d 617, 623 (9th Cir. 1991) ("higher jurisdictional barrier" "in international cases is not dispositive because, if given controlling weight, it would always prevent suit against a foreign national in a United States Court"); *Saccamani v. Robert Reiser & Co.*, 348 F. Supp. 514 (W.D. Pa. 1972).

Assuming that the nationality of the defendant *should* affect the constitutional analysis, how precisely is such a consideration best incorporated into the doctrine? Should it factor into the *Asahi* reasonableness test? Alternatively, should it factor into the quantity and quality of contacts necessary to satisfy the "purposeful availment" requirement? Consider two possible modifications that might be made to purposeful contacts analysis in international cases: (i) a higher or lower showing of purposeful contacts must be made to obtain specific jurisdiction over a foreign defendant; and (ii) the purposeful contacts inquiry should consider the defendant's contacts with the entire United States, not merely the particular forum state. Are these modifications permissible under the Due Process Clause? To what extent do the various opinions from *Nicastro* address these modifications? Are such modifications desirable?

(d)   Nationality of the plaintiff. Why should not the nationality of the plaintiff determine the constitutionally acceptable Court to hear a case? Does not New Jersey have an overriding interest in providing a forum for its citizens injured in New Jersey by a product that was deliberately sold there? Moreover, why should the Constitution accord more weigh t to the interests of a non-citizen corporation than a citizen of the United States, As Justice Ginsburg noted in her opinion in *Goodyear*, under the French Civil Code, the French nationality of the plaintiff suffices to establish the jurisdiction of the French Courts. 2011 WL 2518811 at *10 n. 5. Why should not the same rule apply in the United States?

13. *Stream of commerce theory and general jurisdiction.* In *Asahi*, the plaintiffs sought to use the stream of commerce theory to support an assertion of specific jurisdiction, that is where the claim bears the necessary relationship with the defendant's contacts. *See supra* at pp. 140-143. After *Asahi*, a disagreement emerged among the lower courts over whether the stream of commerce theory also could support a claim of general jurisdiction. *Compare, e.g., Bearry v. Beech Aircraft Corp.*, 818 F.2d 370, 375 (5th Cir.1987) (rejecting theory), *with Brown v. Meter*, 681 S.E.2d 382 (N.C. App. 2009) (apparently embracing it). As noted above, in *Goodyear Dunlop Tires Operations, S.A. v. Brown*, 2011 WL 2518815 (U.S. June 27, 2011), the Supreme Court held that the stream of commerce theory could not support the exercise of general jurisdiction. Is this a wise decision? If a company incorporates and sets up operations in Mexico, just over the border from California, and regularly sends goods into California, why shouldn't California courts be able to exercise general jurisdiction over that company? What are the countervailing concerns?

14. *Tort jurisdiction under Regulation 44/2001.* Consider the discussion of European law at the end of Justice Ginsburg's dissent in *Nicastro*. Article 5(3) of Regulation 44/2001 permits jurisdiction in tort actions in "the place where the harmful event occurred or may occur." In *Bier v. Mines de Potasse d'Alsace*, Case 21/76 [1976] E.C.R. 1735, the European Court of Justice held that Article 5(3) of the Brussels Convention, the predecessor to Regulation 44/2001, gives the plaintiff a choice of suing either (a) where tortious injury occurred, or (b) where tortious conduct occurred. The case involved claims that the dumping of pollutants in a river in one state caused injury in downstream states. Would the rule in *Bier* be possible under the Due Process Clause? Is *Bier* consistent with *Asahi* and *World-Wide Volkswagen*? With §421 and international law?

When comparing the rule in *Bier* to the Court's judgment in *Nicastro* Justice Ginsburg asserts that the Court's judgment "puts United States plaintiffs at a disadvantage in comparison to similarly situated complainants elsewhere in the world." Is that right? If it is, who cares? Why should the constitutional limits of judicial jurisdiction in the United States be interpreted to place United States plaintiffs on an equal footing as similarly situated complainants elsewhere? Are not the United States and Europe different entities? On the other hand, if American constitutional law should be interpreted to place United States citizens at parity with their foreign counterparts, then wasn't *Goodyear* wrongly decided? Consider the discussion of the French nationality rule, *supra* p. 96. Does not *Goodyear*'s rejection of *that* rule also "put United States plaintiffs at a disadvantage in comparison to similarity situated complainants" in France? Can Justice Ginsburg's dissent in *Nicastro* and her majority opinion in *Goodyear* be reconciled?

15. *International law limits on "stream of commerce" or "effects" doctrine.* Does (and should) international law limit assertions of jurisdiction based on a "stream of commerce" or "effects" doctrine? Consider *Restatement (Third) Foreign Relations Law* §421(2)(j), which provides that jurisdiction is permitted where "the person . . . carried on outside the state an activity having a substantial, direct and foreseeable effect within the state, but only in respect of such activity," but without citing any authority. How does §421's requirement of "foreseeable" effects compare with *Asahi* and *World-Wide Volkswagen*? Note that no foreseeability requirement appears to exist under Regulation 44/2001.

Article 10 of the June 2001 Interim Text of the abortive Hague judgments convention provided the following:

> 1. A plaintiff may bring an action in tort . . . in the courts of the State (a) in which the act or omission that caused injury occurred; or (b) in which the injury arose, unless the defendant established that the person claimed to be responsible could not reasonably foresee that the act or omission could result in an injury of the same nature in that State.
>
> 2. A plaintiff may bring an action in tort in the courts of the State in which the defendant has engaged in frequent or significant activity, or has directed such activity into that State, provided that the claim arises out of that activity and the overall connection of the defendant to that State makes it reasonable that the defendant be subject to suit in that State.
>
> 3. The preceding paragraphs do not apply in situations where the defendant has taken steps to avoid acting in or directing activity into that State.
>
> 4. A plaintiff may also bring an action in accordance with paragraph 1 [where] the act or omission, or the injury may occur.

The sub-paragraphs resulted from European proposals, reflecting tort jurisdiction in Regulation 44/2001. Subparagraphs 3 and 4 were disputed (with the Hague Conference's secretariat noting that there "was no consensus" regarding them). *See* http://www.hcch.net. Suppose that these provisions were accepted. Would "purposeful availment" be required for jurisdiction over a product liability claim? Would foreseeability? Make the best argument that you can that the Due Process Clause would not forbid such exercises of jurisdiction. Recall the origins of limits on jurisdiction in *Pennoyer* and principles of international law.

16. *Proposed federal products liability legislation.* In 2009, members of the House and Senate introduced the Foreign Manufacturers Legal Accountability Act. The Act would require foreign manufacturers of certain products to designate agents for service of process in any state which has a "substantial connection" to the importation, sale or distribution of the products. The law would prohibit the importation of products by foreign manufacturers who have not so designated agents within a certain period of time following its adoption. Would the adoption of this Act largely obviate the need for stream of commerce doctrine? Would the Act violate the due process clause? Why or why not? How would such legislation fare under the various approaches taken by the justices in *Nicastro?*

2.   Specific Jurisdiction in International Contract Disputes

International contract disputes have given rise to difficult issues of jurisdiction in U.S. courts. The two-prong test articulated in *World-Wide Volkswagen* and *Asahi* again provides the foundation for analysis. In addition, the Supreme Court's 1985 decision in *Burger King Corp. v. Rudzewicz* provides more specific guidance in contract disputes.[170]

Burger King, a domestic case, discussed the circumstances in which a contract could support personal jurisdiction under the Due Process Clause. The Court first held that the existence of a contract with a resident of the forum did not necessarily subject the defendant to jurisdiction there:

> [W]e note a continued division among lower courts respecting whether and to what extent a contract can constitute a "contact" for purposes of due process analysis. If the question is whether an individual's contract with an out-of-state party *alone* can automatically establish sufficient minimum contacts in the other party's home forum, we believe the answer clearly is that it cannot. The Court long ago rejected the notion that personal jurisdiction might turn on "mechanical" tests, or on "conceptualistic . . . theories of the place of contracting or of performance."[171]

The Court went on to hold that the existence of a contract was nevertheless highly relevant to due process analysis:

> [W]e have emphasized the need for a "highly realistic" approach that recognizes that a "contract" is "ordinarily but an intermediate step serving to tie up prior business negotiations with future consequences which themselves are the real object of the business transaction." It is these factors — prior negotiations and contemplated future consequences, along with the terms of the contract and the parties' actual course of dealing — that must be evaluated in determining whether the defendant purposefully established minimum contacts. . . .[172]

Applying this analysis, *Burger King* upheld a Florida district court's jurisdiction over an out-of-state franchisee of a Florida franchisor. The Court based its holding upon a long-term franchise agreement between the plaintiff and defendant. The Court emphasized the long-term character of the parties' franchise agreement; the contract's "careful structure," "continuing wide-reaching" character, and "exacting regulation" of the franchisee's conduct; the fact that notices and payments were to be sent to an address in the forum; and the defendants' dealing with plaintiff's representatives located within the forum.[173] The decisions excerpted below, *Afram Export Corp. v. Metallurgiki Halyps, SA*, and *Benton v. Cameco Corp.*, illustrate the application of *Burger King* to international contracts.

170. 471 U.S. 462 (1985).
171. 471 U.S. at 478-479.
172. 471 U.S. at 479.
173. 471 U.S. at 476.

AFRAM EXPORT CORP. v. METALLURGIKI HALYPS, SA
772 F.2d 1358 (7th Cir. 1985)

POSNER, CIRCUIT JUDGE. Afram Export Corporation, the plaintiff, is a Wisconsin corporation that exports scrap metal. Metallurgiki Halyps, SA, the defendant, is a Greek corporation that makes steel. In 1979, after a series of trans-Atlantic telephone and telex communications, the parties made a contract through an exchange of telex messages for the purchase by Metallurgiki of 15,000 tons of clean shredded scrap, at $135 per ton, F.O.B. Milwaukee, delivery to be made by the end of April. . . . Afram agreed to pay the expenses of an agent of Metallurgiki — Shields — to inspect the scrap for cleanliness before it was shipped. . . . Shields arrived to inspect the scrap on April 12. He told Afram that the scrap was clean but that Metallurgiki would not accept it, because the price of the scrap had fallen. Sure enough, Metallurgiki refused to accept it. Afram brought this suit after selling the scrap to other buyers. Metallurgiki unsuccessfully challenged the court's jurisdiction over it, [and] the district judge gave judgment for Afram for $425,149. . . .

Metallurgiki does not argue that international law or the due process clause of the Fifth Amendment places limitations on the district court's power to assert jurisdiction over Metallurgiki beyond those in the due process clause of the Fourteenth Amendment, while Afram does not argue that Metallurgiki, as an alien, has fewer rights to challenge the long-arm statute than a nonresident American firm would have. Countless cases assume that foreign companies have all the rights of U.S. citizens to object to extraterritorial assertions of personal jurisdiction. *See, e.g., Helicopteros Nacionales.* The assumption has never to our knowledge actually been examined, but it probably is too solidly entrenched to be questioned at this late date, and in any event it has not been made an issue in this case.

In arguing against extraterritorial jurisdiction, Metallurgiki points out that it has no office, employees, or assets in Wisconsin and that all the dealings between the parties (apart from Shield's visit of inspection) were conducted by international telephone and telex communications and by face-to-face discussions in New York. Shields, the only representative of Metallurgiki who set foot in Wisconsin, although an agent and former employee of Metallurgiki, was in April 1979 an independent contractor, and he spent only five hours in Wisconsin on the inspection trip and only 20 to 40 minutes (the record is unclear which) in the actual inspection. It is also unclear who initiated the negotiations that led up to the making of the contract.

A state cannot force a nonresident to litigate in its courts unless there is "some act by which the defendant purposefully avails itself of the privilege of conducting activities within the forum State, thus invoking the benefits and protections of its laws." *Hanson v. Denckla*, 357 U.S. 235, 253 (1958). . . . By this criterion, a contract between a resident of a state and a nonresident is not enough by itself to give the courts of the resident's state jurisdiction over the nonresident in the resident's suit for breach of the contract. *See Burger King Corp. v. Rudzewicz.* Imagine that a bank in Atlanta, in response to an advertisement in an Atlanta newspaper, ordered office equipment by mail from a company in California, and the seller arranged for the delivery of the equipment at the bank's office in Atlanta. The bank would be justifiably surprised to find that by doing this it has exposed itself to suit in California should a dispute arise over the sale. What benefit had California conferred on it? No doubt California provided some of the services that enabled the seller to produce and sell the office equipment, but the benefit thereby conferred on the distant buyer is too attenuated to require him to bear the expense of involuntarily litigating in so remote a forum. This would be even clearer if the buyer were an individual rather than a firm and the seller were trying to sue the buyer in a small-claims court in the seller's state. . . . Since the dispute must be litigated somewhere, there is perhaps implicit in the foregoing analysis the idea that the seller can sue more easily in the buyer's jurisdiction than the buyer can defend in the seller's. The seller in our example presumably sells office equipment all over the country and can without much difficulty arrange for local counsel wherever disputes with its buyers arise, while the buyer buys office equipment rarely and may be somewhat at a loss to arrange for an effective defense on the seller's home ground. This is one of several factors that distinguish our case from the hypothetical example. Putting aside the adventitious circumstance that Metallurgiki has an office in New York City and at oral argument (but not before then) expressed willingness to entertain the possibility of being suable in New York, the argument against extraterritorial jurisdiction here amounts to saying that if a foreign company negotiates by phone a large purchase of industrial raw materials from an American company for delivery in America, the American company still must go abroad in order to sue for breach of the contract. Since the buyer's role is not passive as in our mail-order hypothetical, since the buyer is not a one-time or infrequent purchaser of the product in question but a recurrent purchaser of what is a basic raw material used in his business, since performance is technically complete in the United States, and since the alternative forum may represent a substantial hardship to the seller, it is hard to see why it is more reasonable to make the seller go to the buyer's forum to sue (Georgia in our hypothetical example) than to make the buyer defend in the seller's forum. Most though not all courts probably would uphold extraterritorial jurisdiction in such a case. . . .

We do not want to put too much weight on any single one of the distinguishing factors that we have mentioned. If the bank in our hypothetical example had sent its office manager to California to inspect the office equipment before it was shipped, we doubt whether this would be enough to subject the bank to the jurisdiction of the California courts in the event that the seller sued over the contract of sale. Neither would delivery in the seller's state be enough by itself. *Lakeside Bridge & Steel Co. v. Mountain State Construction Co.*, 597 F.2d 596 (7th Cir. 1979), a leading precedent for the rule that a single contract is not enough to confer personal jurisdiction over a nonresident buyer, refused to apply Wisconsin's long-arm statute in a case superficially much like this one: A Wisconsin seller had agreed to deliver the goods called for by the contract in Milwaukee, at the seller's rail siding, for shipment to the buyer, a company in West Virginia, and the contract had been negotiated in person outside of Wisconsin and over the telephone. . . .

Our subsequent cases, however, treat *Lakeside* as standing at the outer limits of the principle that sale and delivery to the nonresident in the resident's state do not establish sufficient contacts with that state to give it jurisdiction over the nonresident in the resident's suit for breach of contract. These cases uphold jurisdiction if there are other contacts with the seller's state besides delivery. Here there is Shields' visit to Wisconsin to inspect the scrap — and thus inspection as well as delivery in the seller's state. The visit was brief, but Shields was the buyer's agent sent to the seller's state to carry out a vital function in the administration of the contract. We are not just mechanically counting contacts; Wisconsin not only provided police and fire protection and perhaps other services for the facilities at which the buyer took possession (as in *Lakeside*), but also provided protection for the visit of the buyer's agent to inspect the goods before shipment.

Another point distinguishes this case from *Lakeside*. The alternative forum for this litigation (for as we have said the suggestion that Afram might have sued Metallurgiki in New York comes too late) would have been Greece; and the fact that Metallurgiki has an office in the United States, but Afram (so far as appears) no office outside the United States, would seem to make the alternative forum more burdensome for Afram than Wisconsin was for Metallurgiki. Metallurgiki could not have been surprised to discover that if it ordered goods in America and went into America (through agents or directly) to inspect the goods and take delivery of them, it might be forced in the event of a contract dispute to litigate in America rather than being able to retreat to Greece.

BENTON v. CAMECO CORP.
375 F.3d 1070 (10th Cir. 2004)

HENRY, CIRCUIT JUDGE. Mr. Benton is a Colorado resident who has been engaged in the business of mining, milling, brokering, and trading uranium for many years. Cameco is a Saskatchewan company organized under the Canada Business Corporations Act with its principal offices in Saskatchewan. Between 1988 and 1996, Mr. Benton's NUEXCO Trading Company ("NTC") and Cameco entered into a series of approximately two dozen transactions concerning the sale of uranium. These transactions typically consisted of Cameco selling uranium to NTC, buying uranium from NTC, or swapping its uranium for a like amount of NTC's uranium. The transactions were "spot market" transactions, meaning that "each transaction involved separate, independent contractual negotiations, as opposed to a series of sales or trades pursuant to a single, longer term contract." Such transactions were made in the ordinary course of business and did not require the approval of Cameco's Board of Directors.

In November 1994, Mr. Benton and Cameco entered into the Memorandum of Understanding ("MOU"), the document at issue in this case. The MOU describes two separate transactions between Mr. Benton and Cameco. First, Cameco would provide Mr. Benton's affiliates with quantities of uranium to satisfy Mr. Benton's sales commitments to eighteen different utility companies around the world. Second, the MOU provided for the creation of a joint venture pursuant to which the parties, under Cameco's control, would conduct future uranium trading activities. The MOU conditioned the agreement to pursue these transactions upon several factors, including (a) a satisfactory due diligence review by Cameco . . . and (b) the approval of Cameco's Board of Directors. After the MOU was signed, members of Cameco's staff spent two days in Colorado conducting the due diligence review of Mr. Benton's eighteen supply contracts. In December 1994, Cameco's Board of Directors met and declined to approve any of the transactions listed in the MOU.

[Benton sued Cameco alleging, *inter alia,* breach of contract. The district court dismissed the case on the ground that Benton had failed to establish that Cameco had minimum contacts with Colorado. An appeal followed. The Court of Appeals first considered Cameco's minimum contacts and then the reasonableness of exercising jurisdiction.]

We note at the outset that this is a very close case. . . . A contract between an out-of-state party and a resident of the forum state cannot, standing alone, establish sufficient minimum contacts with the forum. However, "with respect to interstate contractual obligations . . . parties who reach out beyond one state and create continuing relationships and obligations with citizens of another state are subject to regulation and sanctions in the other State for the consequences of their activities." *Burger King,* 471 U.S. at 473. In a contract case, relevant factors for assessing minimum contacts include "prior negotiations and contemplated future consequences, along with the terms of the contract and the parties' actual course of dealing." *Id.* at 479.

In this case, the parties entered into a "Memorandum of Understanding" that proposed the terms of several uranium transactions and a joint venture to pursue uranium trading activities. The "prior negotiations" and the "contemplated future consequences" of the MOU centered around the continuing business relationship between Cameco and Mr. Benton. Although the uranium transactions themselves would occur in places other than the state of Colorado, the business end of the transactions — the brokering of the deals, the coordination of the parties, the exchange of money and information between the parties, and the decision-making behind the joint venture — would take place partially in Canada, where Cameco has its principal place of business, and partially in Colorado, where Mr. Benton has his principal place of business. Indeed, the instant dispute does not concern the uranium transactions, but the conduct of the parties in redefining their business relationship. By engaging in a business relationship with Mr. Benton, who operates his business from Colorado, Cameco "'purposefully avail[ed] itself of the privilege of conducting activities within the forum State, thus invoking the benefits and protections of its laws.'" *Burger King*, 471 U.S. at 475 (quoting *Hanson*, 357 U.S. at 253).

Although "phone calls and letters are not necessarily sufficient in themselves to establish minimum contacts," the correspondence exchanged between Cameco and Mr. Benton during the negotiation of the MOU provides additional evidence. . . . Even more significant to our minimum contacts analysis, Cameco sent several of its employees to Mr. Benton's office in Colorado to conduct the due diligence review required by the MOU. . . . Although the due diligence review would have not been enough, in isolation, to establish minimum contacts, it represents an additional instance in which Cameco purposefully and knowingly availed itself of a business opportunity in Colorado.

Cameco argues that Mr. Benton's presence in Colorado is a mere coincidence that is inadequate to confer specific jurisdiction over Cameco. . . . This is not a case in which the defendant's only contacts with the forum resulted from "the mere unilateral activity" of the plaintiff. Rather, Cameco voluntarily conducted business with Mr. Benton, whom Cameco knew to be located in Colorado for many years prior to and at the time of the events at issue. Again, Cameco's sending employees to conduct the due diligence review at Mr. Benton's place of business demonstrates Cameco's willingness to engage in bilateral business activity taking place in Colorado.

The touchstone of a minimum contacts analysis is whether "the defendant's conduct and connection with the forum State are such that he should reasonably anticipate being haled into court there." *World-Wide Volkswagen*, 444 U.S. at 297. Cameco has transacted business with Mr. Benton since at least 1988, and at all times Mr. Benton has been located in Colorado. When Cameco negotiated and entered into the MOU in 1994, it voluntarily and knowingly entered into a relationship with a Colorado resident. . . . Over the course of Cameco's negotiations with Mr. Benton, Cameco established several minor contacts with the state of Colorado. Although none of these contacts individually could support a finding of minimum contacts, we find that in the aggregate, Cameco's "conduct and connection with the forum State [were] such that he should reasonably anticipate being haled into court there." . . .

Although we have [thus] found that there are sufficient minimum contacts between Cameco and Colorado, we are also required to "consider whether the exercise of personal jurisdiction over the defendant offends traditional notions of fair play and substantial justice." Therefore, we inquire "whether a district court's exercise of personal jurisdiction over a defendant with minimum contacts is 'reasonable' in light of the circumstances surrounding the case." . . . The analyses of minimum contacts and reasonableness are complementary, such that "[T]he reasonableness prong of the due process inquiry evokes a sliding scale: the weaker the plaintiff's showing on [minimum contacts], the less a defendant need show in terms of unreasonableness to defeat jurisdiction. The reverse is equally true: an especially strong showing of reasonableness may serve to fortify a borderline showing of [minimum contacts]." *OMI*, 149 F.3d at 1092. . . .

In this case, the burden on the defendant is significant. Cameco is a Canadian corporation with principal offices in Saskatchewan, and it has no office or property in Colorado, is not licensed to do business in Colorado, and has no employees in Colorado. Cameco's officers and employees "will not only have to travel outside their home country, they will also be forced to litigate the dispute in a foreign forum unfamiliar with the Canadian law governing the dispute." Therefore, this factor weighs against an exercise of personal jurisdiction over Cameco. . . .

In this case, [the forum's state's interest] favors both Mr. Benton and Cameco. Mr. Benton is a Colorado resident, and the state has an interest in providing him a forum for his suit against Cameco. However, the parties agree that Canadian law will govern the dispute. Therefore, this factor does not weigh heavily in favor of either party. . . .

[Another factor is] whether the Plaintiff may receive convenient and effective relief in another forum. This factor may weigh heavily in cases where a plaintiff's chances of recovery will be greatly diminished by forcing him to litigate in another forum because of that forum's laws or because the burden may be so overwhelming as to practically foreclose pursuit of the lawsuit. Because Canadian law governs the suit and because Mr. Benton has not established that litigating the matter in Canada would cause undue hardship to him, we find that Mr. Benton would be able to receive convenient and effective relief by bringing suit in Canada. Therefore, this factor weighs in Cameco's favor, against an exercise of jurisdiction. . . .

[Another reasonableness factor is] "whether the forum state is the most efficient place to litigate the dispute." "Key to the inquiry are the location of witnesses, where the wrong underlying the lawsuit occurred, what forum's substantive law governs the case, and whether jurisdiction is necessary to prevent piecemeal litigation." . . . [M]any of the witnesses in the dispute would be directors, officers, and employees of Cameco, all of whom are located in Canada. . . . Moreover, Mr. Benton need not litigate the action in Colorado to avoid piecemeal litigation. Therefore, we find that litigating the dispute in Colorado would not be more convenient than in Canada . . .

The fifth factor of the reasonableness inquiry "focuses on whether the exercise of personal jurisdiction by [the forum] affects the substantive social policy interests of other states or foreign nations." "The Supreme Court has cautioned that 'great care and reserve should be exercised when extending our notions of personal jurisdiction into the international field.'" Therefore, we must look closely at the extent to which an exercise of personal jurisdiction by Colorado over Cameco interferes with Canada's sovereignty. Relevant facts include "whether one of the parties is a citizen of the foreign nation, whether the foreign nation's law governs the dispute, and whether the foreign nation's citizen chose to conduct business with a forum resident." Cameco did chose to conduct business with Mr. Benton, a resident of Colorado. However, Cameco is a Canadian corporation, Canadian law will govern the dispute, and we are required to give deference to the international nature of this case. Therefore, we find that an exercise of personal jurisdiction would affect Canada's policy interests.

We have already concluded that Cameco's contacts with Colorado were quite limited, barely satisfying the minimum contacts standard. As a result, Cameco need not make a particularly strong showing in order to defeat jurisdiction under this reasonableness inquiry. Because the majority of the five reasonableness factors weigh in Cameco's favor, we hold that an exercise of personal jurisdiction over Cameco would offend traditional notions of fair play and substantial justice. . . .

HOLLOWAY, CIRCUIT JUDGE, concurring in part and dissenting in part. I [dissent] for two principal reasons: Cameco's contacts with Colorado were not "quite limited" and Cameco failed to proffer the requisite "compelling case" that the exercise of personal jurisdiction in this case is unreasonable. . . .

[First,] Cameco's contacts with Colorado were made as part of a deliberate effort by Cameco to enter into a contract with a known resident of Colorado. As the majority noted, the instant lawsuit arose from an alleged breach of a Memorandum of Understanding ("MOU") between Cameco and Benton. The acts contemplated by the MOU, future purchases of uranium and a joint venture, were to be partly performed in Colorado. In addition, the formation of the MOU involved Cameco negotiating over the telephone and by mail with Colorado residents and Cameco sending two of its employees to Colorado to conduct a due diligence review. These contacts, alone and in the aggregate, are clear manifestations of Cameco's desire to enter into a business relationship with a Colorado resident. And, when Cameco allegedly interrupted this relationship, the resulting damages accrued exactly where expected, in Colorado and borne by Colorado citizens. Under these circumstances, even if Cameco's contacts with Colorado were not numerous, this is a case where upon executing its agreement with Benton, Cameco should "reasonably anticipate being haled into court" in Colorado. . . .

[Second,] the majority's conclusion that the exercise of personal jurisdiction in this case would be unreasonable rests primarily upon what I believe to be an exaggeration of the burden on Cameco to litigate in Colorado. In particular, the majority is concerned that litigation in Colorado will require Cameco employees to "travel outside their home country" and litigate the dispute "in a forum unfamiliar with the Canadian law governing the dispute." Both of these concerns are overwrought. . . . [A]s the Supreme Court noted nearly a half century ago, "modern transportation and communication have made it much less burdensome for a party sued to defend himself in a State where he engages in economic activity." *McGee v. International Life Ins. Co.,* 355 U.S. 220, 223 (1957). Since that time, transportation has become even more convenient. In this case, Cameco's headquarters in Saskatchewan is only a reasonable journey from Colorado and Cameco has already demonstrated its ability to make that trip by sending its employees to Colorado to conduct the due diligence review for the MOU.

In addition, even though Canadian and United States law are not completely congruent, both are "rooted in the same common law traditions." . . . Here, Benton's primary claim is that Cameco breached the implied duty of good faith and fair dealing. This duty of good faith is similar in both United States and Canadian law. Thus, "The unfairness of forcing a foreign party to litigate in an unfamiliar legal system is alleviated here by the fact that the Canadian legal system is similar in many respects to the legal system in the United States." *Ensign-Bickford Co. v. ICI Explosives USA, Inc.,* 817 F. Supp. 1018, 1031 (D. Conn. 1993). . . . In addition to owning a subsidiary based in Nevada, Cameco operates major uranium mines in both Wyoming and Nebraska. Thus, Cameco employees regularly operate in and travel to the United States to conduct economic activity. Accordingly, I am satisfied that forcing Cameco to litigate this dispute in Colorado is not "gravely difficult and inconvenient."

Another factor to be considered . . . is Colorado's interest in providing a forum. The majority concedes that Colorado has an interest but concludes that this interest is attenuated by the fact Canadian rather the Colorado law applies. I disagree. "States have an important interest in providing a forum in which their residents can seek redress for injuries caused by out-of-state actors." *OMI,* 149 F.3d at 1092. This interest is separate from and in addition to the interest a state may have "where resolution of the dispute requires a general application of the forum state's law." Thus, the fact that the plaintiff is a resident of the forum state supports the finding that the exercise of personal jurisdiction is reasonable irrespective of what state's law may apply. In this case, Benton is a resident of the forum state. In addition, he alleges that the injuries inflicted upon him by Cameco exceed 100 million dollars. Thus, Colorado has an "important interest" in providing a forum in which Benton can seek redress. . . .

[With regard to identifying an efficient forum, while] several factors do not favor Colorado as a forum, the location of potential witnesses is ambiguous. Cameco asserts that the majority of the employees involved in the MOU reside in Canada. However, Cameco also admits that some live in Minnesota. Moreover, Benton asserts that there are "approximately one dozen potential witnesses with pertinent relevant knowledge that reside in Colorado." Thus, no matter which forum is selected, Colorado or Canada, a substantial number of witnesses may need to travel. And, given the demonstrated ability of Cameco employees to travel to and from the United States, I do not believe Colorado is materially more inefficient than Canada. . . .

Notes on **Afram Export** *and* **Benton**

1. *A contract does not necessarily sustain specific jurisdiction. Burger King* held that specific jurisdiction could not necessarily be based solely upon a defendant's contract with a forum resident. Like other lower courts, *Afram* and *Benton* repeat that proposition. *See also Dickson Marine Inc. v. Panalpina, Inc.,* 179 F.3d 331, 337 (5th Cir. 1999); *Lehigh Coal & Nav. Co. v. Geko-Mayo, GmbH,* 56 F. Supp. 2d 559, 567 (E.D. Pa. 1999); *Guardian Ins. Co. v. Bain Hogg Int'l Ltd.,* 52 F. Supp. 2d 536, 543 n.6 (D.V.I. 1999).

Why doesn't entering into a contract with a forum resident ordinarily suffice for specific jurisdiction in the forum? Entering into a contract is usually a clearly defined act, universally understood as having binding legal consequences, that could provide notice that the courts of *either* of the parties might assert jurisdiction. Would not jurisdiction in such cases be more readily foreseen than jurisdiction based on the stream of commerce doctrine? Note that jurisdiction is routinely available in multiple forums under the Due Process Clause; what harm would come from permitting the courts of the contracting parties' domiciles to decide disputes concerning their contract? Does it matter whether the forum-state plaintiff or nonresident defendant initiated the contact that eventually resulted in the contractual relationship? *See CFA Institute v. Institute of Chartered Financial Analysts of India,* 551 F.3d 285, 295 n.17 (4th Cir. 2009).

Consider the hypothetical in *Afram* concerning an Atlanta bank that purchases equipment by mail from a California company. Would, in fact, the bank be "justifiably surprised" at being sued in California for failure to pay the purchase price? Why are the benefits that California provides to the buyer "too attenuated" for due process purposes? Are those benefits any different from those that Georgia provides to the seller? If somebody breaks a promise to pay money in the forum, why should not a forum resident be able to seek relief in the forum?

2. *Additional contacts necessary for specific jurisdiction over foreign contracting party. Afram* held that a sales contract with a foreign purchaser, even when delivery will occur in the seller's state, does not independently permit the seller's state to exercise jurisdiction over the purchaser. Instead, "other contacts with the seller's state besides delivery" are required — such as negotiations within the forum, training courses for the purchaser's employees in the forum, and after-purchase requests for and provision of product assistance. Are any of these factors as significant as entering into the purchase contract specifying a place of performance? If service of process within the forum permits general jurisdiction, then why shouldn't agreement to purchase and take title to an item within the forum permit specific jurisdiction?

Was *Afram* correctly decided? If a sales contract, with delivery in the seller's state, does not provide the basis for jurisdiction, what additional factor in *Afram* permits a contrary result — Mr. Shields' inspection, Metallurgiki's New York office, Metallurgiki's role as a "recurrent purchaser" of scrap metal, or the "substantial hardship" that denying juris-diction would have on *Afram*? If a contract alone does not establish minimum contacts, what other contacts are necessary? *See Chloe v. Queen Bee of Beverly Hills, LLC,* 616 F.3d 158 (2d Cir. 2010) (single sale in forum state coupled with seller's other business activities sufficient to support personal jurisdiction); *SunCoke Energy Inc. v. MAN Ferrostaal Aktien-gesellschaft,* 563 F.3d 211, 217 (6th Cir. 2010) (contract plus negotiations in forum state); *TH Agriculture & Nutrition, LLC v. Ace European Group Ltd.,* 488 F.3d 1282, 1288-1291 (10th Cir. 2007) (worldwide territory of coverage clause in insurance contract).

What contacts sufficed for jurisdiction to be upheld in *Benton*? Was *Benton* correctly decided? Both the majority and Judge Holloway conclude that Cameco had minimum contacts with Colorado. Do you agree? What contacts, in addition to the parties' abortive contract, were most important?

   3. *Mail, telephone, and other international communications.* Contemporary international business is frequently conducted by Internet, email, telephone, fax, and mail commu-nications. As the Court observed in *Benton,* much of the parties' negotiation was con-ducted in this fashion, while there was never any face-to-face meeting of the parties themselves in *Afram Export.*

What jurisdictional weight is appropriate for assurances made in international com-munications? Consider the following passage from *Burger King Corp. v. Rudzewicz,* 471 U.S. 462, 476 (1985) ("Although territorial presence frequently will enhance a potential defendant's affiliation with a State and reinforce the reasonable foreseeability of suit there, it is an inescapable fact of modern commercial life that a substantial amount of business is transacted solely by mail and wire communication across state lines, thus obviating the need for physical presence within a State in which business is conducted. So long as a commercial actor's efforts are 'purposefully directed' toward residents of another State, we have consistently rejected the notion that an absence of physical con-tacts can defeat personal jurisdiction there."). What guidance does this provide lower courts about the sufficiency of communications with the forum state? *Compare Moncrief Oil Int'l, Inc. v. OAO Gazprom,* 481 F.3d 309, 312 (5th Cir. 2007) ("An exchange of commu-nications in the course of developing and carrying out a contract also does not, by itself, constitute the required purposeful availment of the benefits and protections of [forum] law. Otherwise, jurisdiction could be exercised based only on the fortuity that one of the parties happens to reside in the forum state.") *and Far W. Capital, Inc. v. Towne,* 46 F.3d 1071, 1077 (10th Cir. 1995) ("It is well-established that phone calls and letters are not necessarily sufficient in themselves to establish minimum contacts.") *with AST Sports Science, Inc. v. CLF Distribution Ltd.,* 514 F.3d 1054, 1059 (10th Cir. 2008) ("Phone calls, letters, facsimiles, and emails provide additional evidence that [the foreign defendant] pursued a continuing business relationship with [the plaintiff].") *and Taylor v. Phelan,* 912 F.2d 429, 433 n.4 (10th Cir. 1990) ("so long as it creates a substantial connection, even a single telephone call into the forum state can support jurisdiction").

   4. *Physical presence of employees/agents in the forum.* Note the considerable weight that *Benton*'s minimum contact analysis gives to the fact that "Cameco sent several of its employees to Mr. Benton's office in Colorado to conduct the due diligence review required by the MOU." Note also the significance that *Afram* gives to the fact that "the buyer's agent was sent to the seller's state" where he received "police and fire protection." Is this emphasis on physical presence sensible, in the light of the use of modern tele-communications in contemporary business? Does physical presence remain necessary both as a consequence of territorial sovereignty (*see* the discussion of *Burnham, supra* pp. 129-137), and as a good proxy for reasonable expectations (*see supra* p. 135)? Suppose Mr. Benton had packed his files up and sent them to Cameco's staff by courier, or as PDF files attached to an email, so that due diligence could have been conducted. Should that have altered the result in the case?

5. *Length, nature, and terms of contract.* The *Benton* Court devoted comparatively little attention to the terms of the parties' agreement. Is that not a little unusual, in a case involving jurisdiction over a breach of contract claim? What aspects of the parties' MOU would you consider most relevant to the question of jurisdiction over Cameco? The fact that the parties entered into a long-term agreement? The fact that the parties' agreement involved a joint venture, requiring close and ongoing cooperation? The fact that no products would be shipped into or from Colorado? Consider Judge Posner's analysis of the nature of the sale contract in *Afram,* as well as his hypotheticals concerning less substantial contractual relations. For lower court decisions considering the impact of contractual relations on due process analysis, *see Pilgrim's Pride Corp. v. ASFI, Inc.,* 2006 WL 984695, at *2 (E.D. Tex. 2006) ("To evaluate purposeful availment, courts look to such factors as the places of negotiation, contracting, performance, delivery and payment, the place where title to any goods would pass, and the contract's choice-of-law clause, if any exists."); *WPI Electronics, Inc. v. Super Vision Intern., Inc.,* 2000 WL 1466118, at *5 (D.N.H. 2000) (contract terms critical to personal jurisdiction inquiry include governing law, place of performance, and place of payment).

6. *Absence of choice of court or arbitration clause.* It is unusual for a significant international contract to lack a choice of forum or arbitration clause. *See* G. Born, *International Arbitration and Forum Selection Agreements: Drafting and Enforcing* 2-13 (3d ed. 2010); *infra* pp. 461-463. These clauses often select a neutral forum for resolving contractual disputes, or specify the home jurisdiction of one of the parties. Can any inferences be drawn from the failure of a defendant to include such a clause in an international contract? Should one conclude that a party that deviates from customary practice, of selecting a neutral or "home-court" forum, assumes the risk of being sued in its counter-party's home jurisdiction?

7. *Reasonableness in contract cases.* How should the reasonableness prong of due process analysis apply in international contract cases? Should the same factors apply in contract cases as in tort cases? Why or why not?

Consider the reasonableness analyses of the majority and the dissenting opinion in *Benton?* Who has the better argument? What role does reasonableness play in the *Afram* opinion?

8. *Effect of defendant's foreign residence on reasonableness analysis.* The *Benton* Court emphasized that the burden on Cameco of litigating in Colorado would be significant, given the fact that Cameco was based in Canada. Do you find that persuasive? Consider how difficult it really is, with international telecommunications and transportation, to litigate abroad. Should this aspect of the reasonableness analysis be modified in light of technological advancements? Consider the following observations (made in the context of a product liability case):

Those who litigated in matters involving international parties in the early and mid 1980s, when the most recent cases on personal jurisdiction over nonresident defendants from the United States Supreme Court were decided, will recall that the airplane was the principal means of conveying people, documents, and objects between the offices of a corporate party in a foreign country and the United States. Telephone calls were plagued by annoying echoes and delays in this era predating submarine fiber-optic cables. Facsimile machines had recently become available, but were a clumsy means of transferring documents of any significant size.

Today, the airplane remains the only practical method of conveying people and bulky objects, but the necessity for travel by lawyers and witnesses is significantly diminished by the availability of video conferencing. Voluminous documents and visual images can be transmitted instantaneously by attachment to e-mails sent over the Internet. The facsimile machine, which had not even been invented when *McGee* was decided in 1957, now has a very limited role. Compact cellular telephones with self-contained batteries relying on satellite signals offer reliable, cost-effective, and high-quality communication between the United States and abroad, technology unavailable when the United States Supreme Court last addressed the issue of personal jurisdiction over a foreign corporation. *Ex parte DBI, Inc.,* 23 So. 3d 635, 657 (Ala. 2009).

Aren't these observations about the developments in technology clearly correct? If so, does this suggest that due process analysis should be modified in light of changing technologies? Why or why not? If your answer is yes, then when will a foreign defendant ever be able successfully to oppose jurisdiction under the "reasonableness" prong? If your answer is no, then was *International Shoe* wrong to jettison the *Pennoyer* framework?

Reconsider the facts in *Benton.* What do you make of the dissent's comments about Cameco's affiliated U.S. operations and experience? Aren't these factors important to an analysis of burdensomeness and reasonableness? Does the majority respond to the dissent? Does the logic of this argument stop simply with which party happens to have a foreign office or foreign connection?

Compare *Afram,* which reasoned that Metallurgiki's foreign residence "would seem to make the alternative forum (*i.e.,* Greece) more burdensome for Afram than Wisconsin was for Metallurgiki." The basis for this conclusion was the fact that Metallurgiki had a New York office, which presumably could oversee litigation in Wisconsin. Why shouldn't the presence of a New York office have permitted Afram to sue in New York, thereby alleviating any alleged hardship of dismissing its Wisconsin suit? (What jurisdictional base would have permitted Afram to sue in New York?) Suppose that Metallurgiki had not had a U.S. office. What effect should its foreign residence (and the foreign location of any alternative forum) have on due process analysis? *Compare Sea Lift, Inc. v. Refinadora Costarricense de Petroleo, SA,* 792 F.2d 989 (11th Cir. 1986) (nonexistence of alternative forum is relevant only to reasonableness inquiry, after a finding of purposeful availment). What if the plaintiff had superior access to the foreign forum? *See Foster v. Arletty 3 Sarl,* 278 F.3d 409, 416 (4th Cir. 2002) (alternative holding that jurisdiction would be unreasonable where litigation in foreign forum would be less burdensome for plaintiff).

In international cases, whether grounded in tort or contract, doesn't the reasonableness analysis boil down, at bottom, to an assessment of the relative burdens of litigating in a foreign forum? *See Enviro Petroleum, Inc. v. Kondur Petroleum,* 79 F. Supp. 2d 720, 725 (S.D. Tex. 1999) ("[I]n light of the fact that Defendants are highly sophisticated international business concerns, with multi-million dollars projects scattered throughout the world, it is hard for this Court to find it too burdensome to Defendants to answer in a Texas forum for their alleged breach of a Texas contract they actively solicited from a Texas corporation."). Are these factors better considered as a matter of personal jurisdiction or of *forum non conveniens, infra* at pp. 377, 386-387.

9. *Relationship between choice of law and personal jurisdiction.* What role should choice of law considerations play in personal jurisdiction analysis? In particular, should due process analysis give controlling weight to the fact that the forum's substantive law will apply? Compare how the *Benton* majority and dissenting opinions analyzed these issues.

(a)   Applicability of forum's substantive law does not necessarily sustain jurisdiction. The Supreme Court has consistently held that application of the forum's substantive law does not necessarily mean that due process permits personal jurisdiction. *See Burger King Corp. v. Rudzewicz,* 471 U.S. 462, 481 (1985) ("choice-of-law analysis — which focuses on all elements

of a transaction, and not simply on the defendant's conduct—is distinct from minimum-contacts jurisdictional analysis—which focuses at the threshold solely on the defendant's purposeful connection to the forum"); *Shaffer v. Heitner,* 433 U.S. 186, 215 (1977). *See infra* p. 464. On the other hand, various authorities have also accorded some weight, in due process analysis, to the fact that the forum's substantive laws would be applicable to a claim. Justice Brennan wrote in dissent in *Shaffer v. Heitner,* 433 U.S. 186, 224-226 (1977):

> I would not compartmentalize thinking in this area quite so rigidly as it seems to me the Court does today, for both inquiries [*i.e.,* personal jurisdiction and choice of law] are often closely related. . . . In either case an important linchpin is the extent of contacts between the controversy, the parties, and the forum state. . . . At a minimum, the decision that it is fair to bind a defendant by a State's laws and rules should prove to be highly relevant to the fairness of permitting that same State to accept jurisdiction for adjudicating the controversy.

What importance should choice of law have for jurisdiction analysis? If a state has a sufficient interest in a dispute to apply its own law, why shouldn't due process permit it to exercise personal jurisdiction? What weight does *Benton* give to the applicability of Canadian law to the dispute? For a good discussion, *see* Burbank, *All the World His Stage,* 52 Am. J. Comp. L. 741 (2004).

   (b)   Jurisdictional significance of choice of law agreement. Parties commonly include choice of law provisions in their contracts. *See infra* pp. 758-776. Lower courts have generally held that a choice of law clause does *not* constitute a submission to the jurisdiction of the courts of specified state. *E.g., Paccar Int'l, Inc. v. Commercial Bank of Kuwait, S.A.K.,* 757 F.2d 1058, 1063 n.6 (9th Cir. 1985) ("The fact that a contract is governed by the law of a particular state does not establish that the parties have purposefully availed themselves of the privilege of conducting business in that state . . . [c]hoice of law provisions . . . are irrelevant to" purposeful availment). Other courts have held that a choice of law provision does have jurisdictional significance. *E.g., Moncrief Oil Int'l Inc. v. OAO Gazprom,* 481 F.3d 309, 313 (5th Cir. 2007); *Purdue Research Foundation v. Sanofi-Synthelabo, SA,* 338 F.3d 773, 785 (7th Cir. 2003); *Sea Lift, Inc. v. Refinadora Costarricense de Petroleo, SA,* 792 F.2d 989, 992 n.2 (11th Cir. 1986) ("choice of English law to govern the agreement is in itself an indication that [defendant] did not avail itself of the benefits and protections of Florida law"); *Harper-Wyman Co. v. In-Bond Contract Mfg.,* 1994 WL 22321 (N.D. Ill. 1994). Is this general approach sensible?

   10. *Jurisdiction in contract cases under EU Regulation 44/2001.* Consider Article 5(1) of Regulation 44/2001. It provides for jurisdiction in "the place of performance of the obligation in question." What result would Article 5(1) require in *Burger King* and *Benton?* Note that the Regulation contains special rules governing consumer and employment cases. *See* Regulation 44/2001, Arts. 15-21.

   11. *The "relatedness" requirement: scope of specific jurisdiction.* Unlike general jurisdiction, specific jurisdiction requires that the defendant's contacts with the forum be "related" to the plaintiff's claim. Where the requisite relation is lacking, a court cannot assert specific jurisdiction over the defendant. No dispute over this requirement arose in *Asahi, Benton,* or *Kopke:* all the defendants' contacts with the forum were clearly related to the plaintiff's claims; the only question was whether these contacts satisfied the Due Process Clause's "purposeful availment" requirement. Nonetheless, *Helicopteros* and other cases have raised the question whether the defendant's contacts with the forum were sufficiently related to the plaintiff's claims to count in assessing "purposeful contacts." Due to the difficulties in establishing general jurisdiction, this "relatedness" requirement is of considerable importance. What does it mean for a claim to be "related" to a defendant's contacts? How closely "related" to the claim must the contacts be?

(a)   Helicopteros' *treatment of the scope of specific jurisdiction.* The Supreme Court has not provided much guidance on the "relatedness" requirement. *Helicopteros* expressly refused to decide "what sort of tie between a cause of action and a defendant's contacts with a forum" will satisfy the requirement. Indeed, the Court declined either to choose between an "arising out of" and a "relating to" standard, or to indicate whether the two formulations differed materially. 466 U.S. at 415 n.10.

(b)   *Lower court treatment of scope of specific jurisdiction.* Absent Supreme Court guidance, lower courts have encountered difficulty applying the "relatedness" requirement. This has led some courts to observe that this is the least developed part of due process inquiry—a fairly harsh criticism. *United States v. Swiss American Bank, Ltd.,* 274 F.3d 610, 621 (1st Cir. 2001). A number of lower courts have applied the "arising out of" criteria without formulating any generally applicable standard. *E.g., Hirsch v. Blue Cross, Blue Shield,* 800 F.2d 1474 (9th Cir. 1986); *Afram Export Corp. v. Metallurgiki Halyps, SA,* 772 F.2d 1358 (7th Cir. 1985). Other courts have struggled to formulate some rule capable of providing guidance to litigants, generally adopting one of three approaches: (1) a but-for test, (2) a proximate cause test, or (3) a substantial connection test. *See Tamburo v. Dworkin,* 601 F.3d 693 (7th Cir. 2010) (collecting cases); *Dudnikov v. Chalk & Vermillion Fine Arts, Inc.,* 514 F.3d 1063, 1078 (10th Cir. 2008) (same).

(c)   *"But for" test for scope of specific jurisdiction.* Some courts have adopted broad "but for" tests for determining whether the plaintiff's claims arise out of the defendant's forum contacts. *See, e.g., Fortis Corporate Ins. v. Viken Ship Management,* 450 F.3d 214, 222-223 (6th Cir. 2006); *Glencore Grain Rotterdam BV v. Shivnath Rai Harnarain Co.,* 284 F.3d 1114, 1123-1124 (9th Cir. 2002); *Theunissen v. Mathews,* 935 F.2d 1454 (6th Cir. 1991) (specific jurisdiction requires only that "the cause of action, of whatever type, have a substantial connection with the defendant's in-state activities"; "arising out of" requirement satisfied if plaintiff's cause of action is "made possible by," "lies in the wake of" or "relates to" the defendant's contacts with the forum). *Shute v. Carnival Cruise Lines,* 863 F.2d 1437 (9th Cir. 1990), is a leading example. *Shute* involved Carnival Cruise Lines, a Panamanian corporation with its principal place of business in Miami, which operated a cruise line. Plaintiff was a Washington resident who purchased a cruise from California to Mexico on a Carnival Cruise vessel. The cruise was purchased through a Washington travel agent, and Carnival Cruise mailed the tickets to the agent. Plaintiff traveled from Washington to California to embark on the cruise. While the vessel was off the coast of Mexico, plaintiff was injured in a slip-and-fall accident, and later filed suit against Carnival Cruise in Washington.

Aside from plaintiff's purchase of her ticket, through her travel agent, Carnival Cruise had few contacts with Washington. It advertised in national publications that were distributed (in limited numbers) in Washington and it had relationships with travel agents in Washington. Nonetheless, the Ninth Circuit held that Carnival Cruise was subject to specific jurisdiction in Washington. It adopted a "but for" test for jurisdiction, and held that but for Carnival's solicitations in Washington, and its mailing of the ticket to a Washington travel agent, plaintiff would not have taken the cruise or suffered her injury.

(d)   *"Proximate cause" test for scope of specific jurisdiction.* In contrast, other courts have adopted less expansive views of specific jurisdiction, sometimes referred to as "proximate cause" analysis. *E.g., Platten v. HG Bermuda Exempted, Ltd.,* 437 F.3d 118, 137 (1st Cir. 2006). Courts adopting a proximate cause approach have, however, carved out a limited exception "[w]hen a foreign corporation directly targets residents in an ongoing effort to further a business relationship, and achieves its purpose." *Nowak v. Tak How Investments, Ltd.,* 94 F.3d 708, 715 (1st Cir. 1996).

(e) *"Substantial connection" test for scope of specific jurisdiction.* Finally, a third set of courts has required a "substantial connection" or "discernible relationship" between the contacts and the claim. *See, e.g., O'Connor v. Sandy Lane Hotel Co.*, 496 F.3d 312, 319 (3d Cir. 2007). Under this approach, the degree of relatedness varies with the extent of the contacts. Where the contacts are extensive, only a tenuous relationship with the claim is necessary for an assertion of personal jurisdiction to comport with the Due Process Clause. *See also Chew v. Dietrich*, 143 F.3d 24, 29 (2d Cir. 1998).

12. *Appropriate scope of specific jurisdiction.* Which of these "relatedness" tests is more appropriate? Is the but-for approach over-inclusive, making any cause of action, no matter how unforeseeable, necessarily "related to" the initial contact? *Oldfield v. Pueblo de Bahia Lora, S.A.*, 558 F.3d 1210, 1223 (11th Cir. 2009). Does the requirement of a substantial connection "blur[] the distinction between specific and general jurisdiction"? *Dudnikov v. Chalk & Vermillion Fine Arts, Inc.*, 514 F.3d 1063, 1078 (10th Cir. 2008).

13. *Pendent personal jurisdiction.* Assume that a plaintiff brings a multi-count complaint asserting several different claims. What if a court concludes that some of the claims are sufficiently related to the defendant's forum contacts but others are not? Consider the following:

> If there is jurisdiction over the tort based on the state's "especial interest" in deterring the specific conduct, then so too will jurisdiction over contract claims arising from that same conduct be proper. This result obtains even though the forum contacts related to the contract claim are, by themselves, insufficient to support jurisdiction. *Anderson v. Century Products Co.*, 943 F. Supp. 137, 144-47 (D.N.H. 1996).

What do you think of the doctrine of pendent personal jurisdiction? How can a claim be *insufficiently* "related to" a defendant's contacts with the forum for jurisdictional purposes yet *sufficiently* related to other claims (over which a court does have personal jurisdiction) in order to be "pendent"? Does this not override the constitutional principles of territorial sovereignty underlying specific jurisdiction? Most courts have nonetheless approved the doctrine. *See Avocent Huntsville Corp. v. Aten Int'l Co., Ltd.*, 552 F.3d 1324, 1339-1340 (Fed. Cir. 2008); *Robinson Eng'g Co. Ltd. v. Pension Plan & Trust v. George*, 223 F.3d 445, 449 (7th Cir. 2000); *ESAB Group, Inc. v. Centricut, Inc.*, 126 F.3d 617, 628-629 (4th Cir. 1997); *IUE AFL-CIO Pension Fund v. Herrman*, 9 F.3d 1049, 1056 (2d Cir. 1993) (pendent personal jurisdiction may be invoked for related state law claims "even if personal jurisdiction is not otherwise available"); *Oetiker v. Jurid Werke, GmbH*, 556 F.2d 1, 4-5 (D.C. Cir. 1977); *Starlight Int'l, Inc. v. Herlihy*, 13 F. Supp. 2d 1178, 1185 (D. Kan. 1998) ("every circuit court confronting the issue has . . . upheld the principle of pendent personal jurisdiction"); Simard, *Exploring the Limits of Specific Personal Jurisdiction*, 62 Ohio St. L.J. 1619, 1622-1627 (2001). *Compare SunCoke Energy Inc. v. MAN Ferrostaal Aktiengesellschaft*, 563 F.3d 211, 221 & n.2 (6th Cir. 2009) (Rogers, J. dissenting) (pendent personal jurisdiction has been used "sparingly" in diversity cases and is "typically found where one or more federal claims for which there is nationwide personal jurisdiction are combined in the same suit with one or more state or federal claims for which there is not nationwide personal jurisdiction").

D. Jurisdiction Based on Corporate Affiliations or Agency Relationships

It is common for international businesses to incorporate separate foreign subsidiaries; to engage agents, distributors, brokers, and other partners; or to enter into joint ventures or strategic alliances. Corporate affiliations can take widely differing forms. At one extreme, a small, privately held company in one country may contract with an existing, unrelated business in another country to perform a specific task for it, such as distributing a product. At the other extreme, national tax regimes and other considerations drive some enterprises to establish corporate structures with complex tiers of 100 percent–owned subsidiaries and other affiliates — some engaging in little actual business, without separate management, and entirely controlled by corporate affiliates.

Most visible are some of today's major multinational groups — like Exxon, IBM, Sony, DaimlerChrysler, Mitsubishi, and Unilever. Such enterprises typically include dozens (or hundreds) of separately incorporated companies, many of which are 100 percent–owned by corporate affiliates.[174] Ordinarily, the ultimate "parent" of the group is a publicly traded company. In many cases, members of the group will have one corporate name and logo (*e.g.,* Coca-Cola or Ford), and will deal in the same products. While each entity belonging to the corporate group will have its own board of directors and management, concerted efforts will be made to articulate a single corporate strategy. Moreover, different members of the corporate group will often engage in business dealings such as purchasing one another's products, providing financing, and supplying services.

For present purposes, these various arrangements are important because they can have significant U.S. jurisdictional consequences. By acting through an agent, subsidiary, or other business partner, a foreign company can avoid direct contacts of its own with the United States: all U.S. contacts can be those of the agent, subsidiary, or distributor. This may permit a finding that the foreign company is not subject to U.S. jurisdiction, because it lacks its own minimum contacts with the relevant U.S. forum under either the applicable long-arm statute or Due Process Clause.[175]

It is clear, however, that the use of an agent, subsidiary, or other business partner does not necessarily insulate a foreign corporation from U.S. jurisdiction.[176] In particular, lower U.S. courts have relied on several related theories to exercise jurisdiction over foreign companies by attributing to them their business partners' contacts with the U.S. forum. This section examines the two most significant ones in detail. First, U.S. courts have asserted jurisdiction when a domestic company is merely the "alter ego" of a foreign parent. Second, jurisdiction may be exercised where a domestic subsidiary is the "agent" of its foreign parent.[177]

1. Personal Jurisdiction Based on Alter Ego Status

a. Law Governing Alter Ego Status.   The starting point for analysis is the basic principle that corporations are distinct legal entities, with a separate identity from

174. "[A]fter World War II . . . the phenomenon of the multinational enterprise, as we now know it, became a major factor in the world scene. Since then tens of thousands of subsidiaries have been created or acquired by parent enterprises located in other countries. . . . After the Second World War investment in the United States by foreign parent companies . . . expanded tremendously. . . . Total assets of foreign-owned affiliates in the United States in 1974 were $174.3 billion, of which more than one-fifth was Japanese-owned. These trends have accelerated. The vehicles of this modern international economic growth were and are the multinational enterprises. Their size is often awesome: the annual sales of General Motors exceeded the gross national products of Switzerland, Pakistan, or South Africa." *Bulova Watch Co. v. Hattori & Co.,* 508 F. Supp. 1322 (E.D.N.Y. 1981).

175. *See supra* pp. 82-90.

176. We have already seen how a foreign manufacturer's use of independent U.S. distributors for its products may not preclude specific jurisdiction in U.S. product liability litigation on a stream of commerce theory. *See supra* p. 153.

177. U.S. courts may exercise personal jurisdiction over nonresidents on several other less common theories, including conspiracy, ratification, and guaranty. *See* 1 R. Casad & W. Richman, *Jurisdiction in Civil Actions* §4-3 (3d ed. 1998 & Supp. 2010).

their shareholders and subsidiaries.[178] Thus, a foreign company's ownership of the shares of a corporation doing business within the forum does not automatically confer liability on or jurisdiction over the parent corporation.[179] In one authority's words, "[j]udicial jurisdiction over a subsidiary corporation does not of itself give a state judicial jurisdiction over the parent corporation. This is true even though the parent owns all of the subsidiary's stock."[180]

Despite this basic rule, there are circumstances in which a parent will be held to be the "alter ego" of its subsidiary, permitting the subsidiary's contacts to be attributed to the parent for purposes of jurisdiction. There is considerable disagreement over the content of "alter ego" standards. In Judge Cardozo's memorable phrase, the effect of parent-subsidiary relations is enveloped in "mists of metaphor."[181]

As in other jurisdictional contexts, two levels of alter ego analysis are necessary—statutory and constitutional. Only if both a legislative grant of jurisdiction exists, and the Due Process Clause permits, may a U.S. court exercise jurisdiction on an alter ego basis.[182] Unfortunately, most decisions dealing with alter ego issues fail to distinguish clearly between statutory and constitutional issues, further thickening the "mists" described by Justice Cardozo.

Virtually all state long-arm statutes are silent concerning the significance of alter ego relations, with state common law providing the only authority on the issue. Regardless of applicable law, state courts have often looked to due process precedents in formulating state alter ego doctrines.[183] Conversely, many due process discussions draw substantially on state common law principles. Given this, we focus on general principles of alter ego analysis, without always distinguishing between constitutional and statutory issues.

It is not settled what substantive law—apart from due process limits—governs whether one company is the alter ego of another. Possible choices include the law of the subsidiary's state of incorporation, the parent's state of incorporation, the state law of the forum, federal common law, and the state with the closest relationship to the transactions at issue. There is no consensus as to which approach should be followed.[184]

178. *E.g., United States v. Bestfoods,* 524 U.S. 51, 61 (1998) ("It is a general principle of corporate law deeply ingrained in our economic and legal systems that a parent corporation (so-called because of control through ownership of another corporation's stock) is not liable for the acts of its subsidiaries") (internal quotations omitted).

179. *See United States v. Bestfoods,* 524 U.S. 51 (1998).

180. *Restatement (Second) Conflict of Laws* §52 comment b (1971). *See* C. Wright & A. Miller, *Federal Practice and Procedure* §1069.4 (3d ed. 1998 & Supp. 2010).

181. *Berkey v. Third Ave. Ry. Co.,* 244 N.Y. 84 (1926) (Cardozo, J.). Justice (then Judge) Cardozo warned against substituting labels for careful analysis: "The whole problem of the relation between parent and subsidiary corporations is one that is still enveloped in the mists of metaphor. Metaphors in law are to be narrowly watched, for starting as devices to liberate thought, they end often by enslaving it." *Id.* at 94.

182. *See Hargrave v. Fibreboard Corp.,* 710 F.2d 1154 (5th Cir. 1983); *Wells Fargo & Co. v. Wells Fargo Express Co.,* 556 F.2d 406 (9th Cir. 1977).

183. *E.g., Hargrave v. Fibreboard Corp.,* 710 F.2d 1154 (5th Cir. 1983); *Omni Exploration, Inc. v. Graham Engineering Corp.,* 562 F. Supp. 449 (E.D. Pa. 1983).

184. *E.g., Southern New England Tel. Co. v. Global NAPs, Inc.,* 2010 WL 3325926 at *10 (2d Cir. Aug. 25, 2010) (avoiding the question); *Jackson v. Tanfoglio Giuseppe S.R.L.,* 2010 WL 3295514 at *8 (5th Cir. Aug. 23, 2010) (same); *Estate of Thomson v. Toyota Motor Corp. Worldwide,* 545 F.3d 357, 362 (6th Cir. 2008) (applying state law); *IDS Life Ins. Co. v. SunAmerica Life Ins. Co.,* 136 F.3d 537, 541 (7th Cir. 1998) (implicitly holding that state law provided substantive standard); *De Castro v. Sanifill, Inc.,* 198 F.3d 282 (1st Cir. 1999) (same); *Pauley Petroleum, Inc. v. Continental Oil Co.,* 231 A.2d 450, 457 (1967), *aff'd,* 239 A.2d 629 (1968) (applying Delaware law to question whether foreign subsidiary was alter ego of Delaware parent); *In re Ski Train Fire in Kaprun, Austria on Nov. 11, 2000,* 257 F. Supp. 2d 717, 730 (S.D.N.Y. 2003) (holding that state law governs jurisdictional veil piercing in diversity cases). *Cf. United States v. Bestfoods,* 524 U.S. 51, 62-63 & n.9 (1998) (discussing choice of state or federal common law in determining liability under federal environmental statute); *Restatement (Second) Conflict of Laws* §302(2) (1971). Alter ego issues in cases involving foreign state-related entities are discussed below. *See infra* pp. 250-270.

The conclusion that a foreign parent is subject to U.S. *jurisdiction* on an alter ego theory does not necessarily mean that the foreign company will be *liable on the merits* on this theory. Corporate veil-piercing standards for jurisdiction and liability differ significantly, and jurisdiction can exist where liability does not.[185] Under most state laws, alter ego liability (as opposed to alter ego jurisdiction) requires that both: (i) corporate formalities were wholly disregarded by a pervasively controlling parent; and (ii) fraud or its equivalent resulted on third parties.[186] As discussed below, similarly rigorous requirements do not always apply to alter ego jurisdiction.

b.   *Cannon Manufacturing*: The Importance of Corporate Formalities.

Discussion of alter ego jurisdiction begins with *Cannon Manufacturing Company v. Cudahy Packing Company*.[187] In *Cannon*, a North Carolina corporation brought a breach of contract suit in North Carolina against a Maine corporation. Service was effected upon the North Carolina agent of an Alabama corporation, which was a wholly owned subsidiary of the Maine corporate defendant. The plaintiff argued that service upon the Alabama subsidiary was effective as to its Maine parent, on the grounds that the two companies were in reality one. The Supreme Court affirmed dismissal of the suit on the grounds that service was invalid.

Cannon conceded that, "[t]hrough ownership of the entire capital stock and otherwise, the defendant dominates the Alabama corporation, immediately and completely," and "that the parent exerts its control both commercially and financially in substantially the same way, and mainly through the same individuals, as it does over those selling branches or departments of its business not separately incorporated."[188] Nevertheless, the Court concluded:

> The existence of the Alabama company as a distinct corporate entity is, however, in all respects observed. Its books are kept separate. All transactions between the two corporations are represented by appropriate entries in their respective books in the same way as if the two were wholly independent corporations.[189]

The Court later added that "[t]he corporate separation, though perhaps merely formal, was real. It was not pure fiction."[190]

Many lower courts have applied *Cannon*, reasoning that the decision permits jurisdiction on alter ego grounds only where a parent wholly disregards its subsidiary's "corporate formalities." This is true regardless whether the parent "controlled" or "dominated" the subsidiary.[191] In one lower court's words, "[t]he test under *Cannon* is not the degree of control over the subsidiary by the parent."[192]

---

185. *E.g., Dakota Indus., Inc. v. Ever Best Ltd.,* 28 F.3d 910, 915 (8th Cir. 1994) ("A determination to pierce the corporate veil does not necessarily answer the question of a court's jurisdiction over the individuals behind the veil.").

186. *See infra* pp. 178-180, 184-188.

187. 267 U.S. 33 (1925).

188. 267 U.S. at 335.

189. 267 U.S. at 335.

190. 267 U.S. at 337.

191. *E.g., Epps v. Stewart Info. Servs. Corp.,* 327 F.3d 642, 649 (8th Cir. 2003); *Schwartz v. Elec. Data Sys., Inc.,* 913 F.2d 279, 282 (6th Cir. 1990); *Topp v. Compare Inc.,* 814 F.2d 830, 835-836 (1st Cir. 1987); *Kramer Motors v. British Leyland,* 628 F.2d 1175 (9th Cir. 1980); *Quarles v. Fugua Indus.,* 504 F.2d 1358 (10th Cir. 1974); *Farkas v. Texas Instruments,* 429 F.2d 849 (1st Cir. 1970); *Peterson v. U-Haul Co.,* 409 F.2d 1174, 1182-1183 (8th Cir. 1969); *Manville Boiler Co. v. Columbia Boiler Co.,* 269 F.2d 600 (4th Cir. 1959) (no alter ego relationship where parent "extensively controlled" subsidiary but separate records were maintained).

192. *Consolidated Engineering Co. v. Southern Steel Co.,* 88 F.R.D. 233, 237-238 (E.D. Va. 1980).

c. Alternative Alter Ego Standards. Notwithstanding its importance, there is a vigorous debate regarding *Cannon*'s original precedential significance. A number of courts and commentators have concluded that *Cannon* was not a due process holding, relying in part on a fairly cryptic comment in Justice Brandeis's opinion, that "[n]o question of the constitutional powers of the State, or of the federal Government, is directly presented."[193] Other courts have concluded that *Cannon* has been superseded by more recent due process holdings.[194] Nevertheless, many authorities continue to apply *Cannon* in determining due process and common law restraints on the alter ego doctrine.[195]

A potentially significant departure from *Cannon* was the Supreme Court's decision in *United States v. Scophony Corp. of America*,[196] considering whether personal jurisdiction existed over a foreign defendant under §12 of the Clayton Act. *Scophony* held that both §12 and due process permitted jurisdiction over the foreign company because its utilization of "complex working arrangements . . . with [American subsidiaries that required] constant supervision and intervention beyond normal exercise of shareholders' rights by the [foreign parent]."[197] The *Scophony* alter ego standard is less stringent than the *Cannon* formula. It allows jurisdiction where a parent exercises a significant degree of direct control over the operations of its subsidiary, going beyond a controlling shareholder's "ordinary" rights. Jurisdiction can be asserted, on this alter ego theory, even where corporate formalities are observed.[198] Some courts have concluded that *Scophony* implicitly overruled *Cannon*, at least in the antitrust context.[199] Other lower courts have disagreed, holding that *Cannon* remains good law.[200]

In recent years, a number of courts have expressly or impliedly modified *Cannon*'s focus on corporate formalities. In one court's words, "multitudinous decisions of state and federal courts . . . [have] changed the older concept of jurisdiction and substantially eroded the stringent jurisdictional test applied in [*Cannon*]."[201] Although there have been many formulations of new alter ego standards, several general rules can be identified.

First, many courts now inquire into the extent and character of a parent corporation's "control" over its subsidiary.[202] A number of courts have held that an alter ego

193. 267 U.S. at 336.

194. *E.g., Topp v. Compare Inc.*, 814 F.2d 830, 835-836 (1st Cir. 1987); *Schwartz v. Elec. Data Sys., Inc.*, 913 F.2d 279, 282 (6th Cir. 1990); *Metro-Goldwyn-Mayer Studios Inc. v. Grokster, Ltd.*, 243 F. Supp. 2d 1073, 1098-1100 (C.D. Cal. 2003) (describing trend away from *Cannon* and development of modern "attribution" and "merger" theories for imputing subsidiary's contacts to parent); *In re Telectronics Pacing Systems, Inc.*, 953 F. Supp. 909, 917-918 (S.D. Ohio 1997) (collecting cases and concluding "that *International Shoe* has supplanted *Cannon* in the context of personal jurisdiction").

195. *See supra* note 194; *Richard v. Bell Atlantic Corp.*, 946 F. Supp. 54, 69 (D.D.C. 1996) ("This Circuit adheres to the formalistic approach announced by the Supreme Court in [*Cannon*]."); *Consolidated Engineering Co. v. Southern Steel Co.*, 88 F.R.D. 233, 237-238 (E.D. Va. 1980).

196. 333 U.S. 795 (1948).

197. 333 U.S. at 816.

198. 333 U.S. at 813-816.

199. *E.g., Omega Homes, Inc. v. Citicorp Acceptance Co.*, 656 F. Supp. 393, 397-398 (W.D. Va. 1987); *Chrysler Corp. v. General Motor Corp.*, 589 F. Supp. 1182 (D.D.C. 1984).

200. *E.g., Allen v. Toshiba Corp.*, 599 F. Supp. 381 (D.N.M. 1984); *Thompson Trading Ltd. v. Allied Lyons plc*, 123 F.R.D. 417 (D.R.I. 1989).

201. *Roorda v. Volkswagenwerk, AG*, 481 F. Supp. 868 (D.S.C. 1979).

202. *E.g., Spir Star AG v. Kimich*, 310 S.W.3d 868, 872 (Tex. 2010); *Central States, Southeast and Southwest Areas Pension Fund v. Reimer Express World Corp.*, 230 F.3d 934, 943 (7th Cir. 2000); *Consolidated Development Corp. v. Sherritt, Inc.*, 216 F.3d 1286, 1293-1294 (11th Cir. 2000) (attribution of subsidiary's contacts to parent requires proof that subsidiary's separate existence was mere formality); *Dickson Marine Inc. v. Panalpina, Inc.*, 179 F.3d 331, 338 (5th Cir. 1999) (requiring control); *Dean v. Motel 6 Operating LP*, 134 F.3d 1269, 1274-1275 (6th Cir. 1998) (requiring control); *In re Genetically Modified Rice Litig.*, 576 F. Supp. 2d 1063 (E.D. Mo. 2008); *In re Ski Train Fire in Kaprun, Austria on November 11, 2000*, 343 F. Supp. 2d 208, 214-215 (S.D.N.Y. 2004); *Goss Graphic Systems v. Man Roland Druckmaschinen AG*, 139 F. Supp. 2d 1040, 1067-1068 (N.D. Iowa 2001); *Smith v. S&S Dundalk Engineering Works, Ltd.*, 139 F. Supp. 2d 610, 621 (D.N.J. 2001); *Clark v. Matsushita Elec. Indus. Co.*, 811 F. Supp. 1061, 1068 (M.D. Pa. 1993).

relationship exists, for jurisdictional purposes, if one entity exercises sufficient "control" over another. Thus, according to the *Restatement (Second) Conflict of Laws* §52, comment b (1971):

> Judicial jurisdiction over a subsidiary corporation will . . . give the state judicial jurisdiction over the parent corporation if the parent so controls and dominates the subsidiary as in effect to disregard the latter's independent corporate existence.

In one court's words, an alter ego relationship will be found if a parent "exercises dominion and control over the subsidiary as demonstrated by its continual supervision of and intervention in the subsidiary's affairs."[203] Or, according to another court, an alter ego relationship exists where the parent "exercises day-to-day control over [subsidiary] so complete as to render [it] a mere department of [the parent]."[204]

Second, other courts depart further from *Cannon,* finding alter ego status where a parent and its subsidiary are sufficiently "integrated."[205] For example, some courts have found alter ego relationships where a parent and subsidiary "function as an integrated whole" and "compete in a worldwide enterprise."[206]

Finally, some lower courts have held that alter ego status requires more than a showing that a parent controls its subsidiary, even if corporate formalities are disregarded. Relying on decisions concerning substantive alter ego liability, these courts have demanded proof that the subsidiary's separate incorporation was used to perpetrate a fraud on the plaintiff.[207] In one court's words, disregarding corporate identities "may be done only in the interest of justice, when such matters as fraud, contravention of law or contract, [or] public wrong . . . are involved."[208]

d. Selected Materials on the Application of Alter Ego Doctrine in International Cases. Alter ego issues frequently arise in international cases. The decision in *In re Telectronics,* excerpted below, illustrates the topic. As you read the excerpt, consider whether you agree with (1) the Court's decision to jettison *Cannon,* and (2) the Court's decision to exercise personal jurisdiction.

---

203. *Omega Homes, Inc. v. Citicorp Acceptance Co.,* 656 F. Supp. 393, 397-398 (W.D. Va. 1987).

204. *Photo Promotions Assocs. v. Household Int'l Inc.,* 584 F. Supp. 227, 237 (D. Del. 1984). *See also Northeastern Power Co. v. Balcke-Durr, Inc.,* 49 F. Supp. 2d 783, 790 (E.D. Pa. 1999).

205. *See Color Systems, Inc. v. Meteor Photo Reprographic Systems, Inc.,* 1987 WL 11085 (D.D.C. 1987) (purporting to conclude that *Cannon* is still "good law" but holding that an alter ego relationship exists because "the two corporations function as an integrated whole" and "compete in a worldwide enterprise"); *Finance Co. of Am. v. Bankamerica Corp.,* 493 F. Supp. 895 (D. Md. 1980) ("operations of the parent and subsidiary are sufficiently integrated to justify piercing the corporate veil").

206. *Jackson v. Tanfoglio Giuseppe S.R.L.,* 2010 WL 3295514, at *8 (5th Cir. Aug. 23, 2010); *In re Chocolate Confectionary Antitrust Litig.,* 674 F. Supp. 2d 580 (M.D. Pa. 2009); *Richard v. Bell Atlantic Corp.,* 946 F. Supp. 54, 70 (D.D.C. 1996).

207. *E.g., BMC Software Belgium, NV v. Marchand,* 83 S.W.3d 789, 799 (Tex. 2002); *Miller v. Honda Motor Co.,* 779 F.2d 769 (1st Cir. 1985) ("there is nothing fraudulent or against public policy in limiting one's liability by the appropriate use of corporate insulation"); *Luckett v. Bethlehem Steel Corp.,* 618 F.2d 1373, 1379 (10th Cir. 1980) ("fraud or illegal or inequitable conduct is the result of the use of the corporate structures"); *In re Western States Wholesale Natural Gas Litig.,* 605 F. Supp. 2d 1118, 1132 (D. Nev. 2009); *Doe v. Unocal Corp.,* 27 F. Supp. 2d 1174, 1187 (C.D. Cal. 1998) (alter ego require proof of unity of interest and proof that failure to disregard corporate form would result in fraud or injustice), *aff'd on reasoning of District Court,* 248 F.3d 915 (9th Cir. 2001); *AT&T Co. v. Compaigne Bruxelles Lambert,* 94 F.3d 586, 591 (9th Cir. 1996) (same). *Cf. United States v. Bestfoods,* 524 U.S. 51, 62 (1998) ("[T]he corporate veil may be pierced and the shareholder held liable for the corporation's conduct when, *inter alia,* the corporate form would otherwise be misused to accomplish certain wrongful purposes, most notably fraud, on the shareholder's behalf.").

208. *Pauley Petroleum Inc. v. Continental Oil Co.,* 239 A.2d 629, 633 (Del. 1968).

IN RE TELECTRONICS PAPER SYSTEMS, INC.

953 F. Supp. 909 (S.D. Ohio 1997), rev'd on other
grounds, 221 F.3d 870 (6th Cir. 2000)

SPIEGEL, SENIOR DISTRICT JUDGE. [The case involves a class-action products liability suit brought against companies involved in the manufacture of pacemakers.] Defendant, TPLC, Inc. ("TPLC"), is a Delaware corporation engaged in the business of designing, manufacturing, and marketing medical devices including the Accufix atrial "J" lead pacemakers at issue in this case. Defendant, Telectronics Pacing Systems, Inc. ("TPSI"), is a corporation organized under the laws of the State of Delaware. TPSI owns 100% of the stock of TPLC. TPSI's sole business is to hold certain industrial property rights, real estate and the equity interest in TPLC.

Nucleus Limited ("Nucleus") is a corporation organized under the laws of Australia. It is a holding company [which] . . . owns a group of companies that design, manufacture and sell pacemakers and defibrillators around the world under the trade name "Telectronics Pacing Systems" or "Telectronics" (collectively referred to as the "Telectronics Companies"). TPLC and TPSI are the two Telectronics Companies that operate in the United States.

Until 1988, Nucleus was a publicly-held Australian company. In 1988, [another Australian company,] Pacific Dunlop Limited ("PDL" or "Pacific Dunlop") purchased Nucleus and thus became beneficial owner of TPLC and TPSI. . . . PDL is organized into five core business areas (automotive, distribution, consumer products, building and construction and health care) consisting of over 225 separate corporate affiliates and subsidiaries with annual sales worldwide of approximately $5.5 billion. Pacific Dunlop is a publicly held corporation. Its shares trade on the NASDAQ. It maintains bank accounts in the United States — New York. Pacific Dunlop also files reports with the Securities and Exchange Commission ("SEC") as the law requires. . . . Four divisions of Pacific Dunlop conduct business in the United States, but none of which conducts business in Ohio. The four divisions have total sales in the United States of $1.1 million, none of which is in Ohio. Nucleus, TPSI and TPLC are all subsidiaries in Pacific Dunlop's health care business. These three Defendants plus the other Telectronics Companies and other Nucleus' owned medical companies make up the "Nucleus Group" which is the medical products group of the Pacific Dunlop Family. The companies of the Nucleus Group are all separately incorporated but operate as part of a "functional organization." . . .

[The Court first concluded that the Australian defendants (Nucleus and Pacific Dunlop) had insufficient contacts with the forum directly to sustain jurisdiction. It then considered whether the Australian defendants were subject to jurisdiction based on their subsidiaries' contacts with the forum.]

A fundamental rule of corporate law is that, normally, shareholders, officers and directors are not liable for the debts of the corporation. The alter ego doctrine was developed as an exception to this general rule in order to protect a corporation's creditors from shareholders who use the corporation's limited liability for fraudulent purposes. Thus, the plaintiff can "pierce the corporate veil" by this doctrine and hold shareholders liable for the debts of the corporation "when it would be unjust to allow the shareholders to hide behind the fiction of the corporate entity." Although the exact conditions which justify piercing the corporate veil vary somewhat from state to state, most courts examine whether the corporate form was used for fraudulent purposes.

The Australian Defendants insist that the Telectronics Companies are not alter egos of PDL or Nucleus. They assert that their involvement with the Telectronics Companies is merely that which is required of any owner of a publicly traded corporation. While the companies of the Nucleus Group "functionally cooperate," PDL argues that does not mean they have disregarded the corporate form in order to justify piercing the corporate veil. PDL argues that all of the companies have separate boards and books. TPLC owns all of its own facilities, develops and manufactures its own products, hires its own employees and does not purchase materials from PDL or Nucleus. . . . PDL further asserts that it has not changed the structure of the companies or replaced the existing officer and directors since the takeover. In addition, only one PDL officer has served on the Board of Directors of a Telectronics Company.

The formalistic approach of the alter ego doctrine, however, is irrelevant to the question whether the exercise of jurisdiction over an absent parent corporation would violate the Due Process Clause. *Energy Reserves Group, Inc. v. Superior Oil Co.*, 460 F. Supp. 483, 506 (D. Kan. 1978). Concededly, a corporation's relationship with an affiliated corporation in the forum is relevant to the due process question in a manner different from that in which it pertains to the corporate law question of alter ego relationships and "veil piercing." For alter ego purposes the nature of the relationship — the identity between the corporations is alone controlling. For jurisdictional purposes, the fact of the existence of the relationship . . . is a minimum "contact, tie or relation" with the forum that may render possible the constitutional exercise of jurisdiction if the relevant factors, including both convenience and the orderly administration of the laws, balance in that direction. The mere existence of the relationship is one relevant factor. The nature of the relationship the degree of control or identity bears upon the weight to be given that one factor, but it does not foreclose reliance on this factor as a legitimate consideration in the due process analysis.

Many courts, however, continue to conflate the requirements of due process and the alter ego doctrine. Much of confusion stems from questions regarding the continuing viability of the Supreme Court's opinion in *Cannon*. . . . Following [*International Shoe,*] it would seem appropriate, for the purpose of determining the amenability to jurisdiction of a foreign corporation which happens to own a subsidiary corporation carrying on local activities, to inquire whether the parent has the requisite minimum contacts with the State of the forum. . . . The court stressed that this minimum contacts test is "an analytical rather than a mechanical or formalistic" inquiry. . . . Several factors are helpful in illustrating why much of *Cannon* is inapplicable to the personal jurisdiction analysis. First, Justice Brandeis insisted that the issue in *Cannon* did not involve "questions of the constitutional powers of the State, or federal Government." *Cannon*, 267 U.S. at 336. Instead, courts and commentators have found that *Cannon* is "limited to an analysis of local service of process on a domestic subsidiary as a means of effecting service on an absent corporate parent." *Consolidated Engineering Co. v. Southern Steel Co.*, 88 F.R.D. 233, 238 (E.D. Va. 1980). . . . The rule in *Cannon* did not turn on constitutional considerations of due process, as in *International Shoe*. Rather, the rule was based on principles of corporate separateness.

Second, and more importantly, even if *Cannon* purported to set a constitutional standard, that standard has undergone drastic changes since 1925. The question before the Court in *Cannon* was whether the "defendant was doing business within the State in such a manner and to such an extent to warrant the inference that *it was present there.*" *Cannon*, 267 U.S. at 334 (emphasis added). In *International Shoe*, the Supreme Court replaced the "presence" test of *Pennoyer v. Neff*, with an inquiry into whether the defendant has such minimum contacts with the forum "to make it reasonable and just, according to our traditional conception of fair play and substantial justice" for the forum to exercise jurisdiction over the defendant. The Supreme Court has not commented directly on the relevance of *Cannon* to the present due process analysis of personal jurisdiction. However, the Court has expressed support for the concept that jurisdiction over an absent corporation may be based upon on the activities of an agent. *See World-Wide Volkswagen, supra.* . . .

Cannon's presumption of form over substance is out-of-step with the modern approach to personal jurisdiction which is based upon fairness and reasonableness. Accordingly, we conclude that the formalistic alter ego principles of *Cannon* are no longer applicable in the analysis of whether the exercise of personal jurisdiction over a foreign corporation is constitutional. Instead, the proper exercise of jurisdiction depends on a "sufficient connection between the defendant and the forum as to make it fair to require defense of the action in the forum." *Energy Reserves,* 460 F. Supp. at 502.

Our next task is to determine what level of interaction between the parent corporation and its in-forum subsidiary is sufficient to find that jurisdiction over the parent comports with traditional notions of fair play and substantial justice. [The Court cited authority holding that the plaintiff must show either "(1) attribution, 'that the absent parent instigated the subsidiary's local activity;' or (2) merger, 'that the absent parent and the subsidiary are in fact a single legal entity.'"] . . .

The attribution test implies that the in-forum subsidiary is acting on behalf of the absent parent. Thus, the Court attributes the subsidiary's contacts to the parent because the parent "purposefully avails" itself of doing business in the forum by accessing the market through a subsidiary. The clearest example of this theory occurs when a foreign manufacturer uses a subsidiary to distribute its products in the forum. . . . Another way to view the attribution theory of jurisdiction is to look to see if the "parent uses the subsidiary to do what it otherwise would have done itself." *Gallagher v. Mazda Motor of America, Inc.,* 781 F. Supp. 1079, 1085 (E.D. Pa. 1992).

Under the merger theory of jurisdiction, the two entities are so closely aligned that it is reasonable for the parent to anticipate being "haled" into court in the forum because of its relationship with its subsidiary. Some factors that might indicate a sufficient relationship with the subsidiary to justify jurisdiction include overlap in board of directors and officers, interchange of personnel between the parent and the corporation, exchange of documents and records between parent and subsidiary, listing subsidiary as a branch, agent or division of the parent, or indicating that subsidiary and parent are part of the same entity, sending technical personnel to subsidiary by parent at its own expense to assist the subsidiary with its operations.

The line between these two theories is not always clear. . . . Thus, some courts have applied a balancing test to determine whether foreign defendant's contacts through a subsidiary are sufficient to satisfy due process. . . . Other factors which help determine whether the defendant's contacts are substantial and therefore justify jurisdiction as reasonable include: (1) the quantity of the contacts; (2) the nature and quality of the contacts; (3) the source of the contacts and their connection with the cause of action; (4) the interests of the forum; and (5) the convenience of the parties. . . .

The relationship between the Australian Defendants and the Telectronics Companies displays the characteristics of the merger theory of jurisdiction rather than attribution. The Australian Defendants purchased the Telectronics Companies as operating companies. The Telectronics Companies design, manufacture and distribute their own product, rather than perform a service for the parent corporation. Thus, the Australian Defendants did not "instigate" the Telectronics Companies' actions in the forum, nor did the Telectronics Companies perform duties which Nucleus and PDL would have performed themselves in the forum.

On the other hand, the Australian Defendants exercised a great deal of control over the Telectronics Companies. The . . . managing director of PDL, or the PDL Board approved all large capital expenditures by the Telectronics Companies. [A Nucleus committee met] monthly to review monthly reports on the Telectronics Companies and provide strategic planning and advice. Mr. Thomas, CEO of the Telectronics Companies and Nucleus, was an employee of PDL and PDL paid his salary. As for day-to-day oversight, he reported to Philip Brass the managing Director of PDL rather than the Board of Nucleus or the Telectronics Companies. A committee of Nucleus and PDL officers oversaw the operations and approved actions of the Telectronics Companies. Thus, the association between the Telectronics Companies and the Australian Defendants is deep and wide-ranging and evidences "undue control" of the Telectronics Companies by the Australian Defendants. . . .

PDL maintained a bank in New York which served as a sort of treasury for the companies of the Nucleus Group. This account acted as a central depository for the cash of the companies of the Nucleus Group. In addition, the Nucleus Group Companies could borrow money at will from PDL's account as long as the money was within budget parameters. Apparently, any money owing to or owed by the individual companies was "reallocated" into a capital contribution or reduction in capital at the end of the fiscal year.

Furthermore, there is evidence that PDL officials maintained that the Telectronics Companies and their products were part of PDL in statements to outsiders. Philip Brass, managing director of PDL, corresponded with officials from the Food and Drug Administration ("FDA") concerning the Accufix "J" lead problem. Nucleus officials portrayed the Telectronics Companies as the "Medical Division of Pacific Dunlop Ltd." In a letter to potential American investors. . . .

Finally, the Court finds PDL's involvement in the Accufix "J" Lead controversy to be especially telling as to the intimate affiliation between the parent and subsidiary. Mr. Brass went to Washington, D.C. to meet with FDA officials to discuss the "J" Leads. He even referred to TPLC as "we" when discussing the "J" Lead recall and patient management program. Essentially, the Telectronics Companies' problems became problems for Nucleus and PDL as well.

The Court finds that these facts create an inference "that the absent parent and the subsidiary are in fact a single legal entity," at least for the purposes of exercising jurisdiction. PDL and Nucleus officials participated in the day-to-day operations of the Telectronics Companies. Collectively, Defendants often treated these institutions as one entity for internal and external purposes. [The Court then applied the "reasonableness" prong of due process analysis, and found it satisfied.]

Notes *on* Telectronics

1. *Lower standard for alter ego jurisdiction than alter ego liability.* Alter ego theories are relevant to both substantive liability and personal jurisdiction issues. Consider the discussion of these issues in *In re Telectronics*. As that discussion indicates, alter ego standards for liability are generally more difficult to satisfy than those for jurisdiction. Is it appropriate to apply a reduced alter ego standard for jurisdiction? For representative lower court decisions dealing with the distinction between jurisdiction and liability, *see Meredith v. Health Care Products, Inc.,* 777 F. Supp. 923, 926 (D. Wyo. 1991) ("Factors which indicate those circumstances under which a subsidiary corporation and its parent or owner may be treated as one for purposes of liability . . . have little relation to those which bear upon the

due process fairness question."); C. Wright & A. Miller, *Federal Practice and Procedure* §1069.4 at 174-185 (3d ed. 1998 & Supp. 2010).

   2. *Legislative authorization and due process limits.* Although state and federal long-arm statutes address many jurisdictional issues, there are virtually no long-arm statutes that provide for jurisdiction on the basis of alter ego status. Assertions of jurisdiction on the basis of alter ego status are common law creatures. Is it appropriate for courts to create a potentially expansive jurisdictional basis in these circumstances?

   In addition to questions of legislative authorization, an assertion of alter ego jurisdiction also raises due process questions. How should due process analysis of alter ego jurisdiction differ from analysis of legislative authorization? Consider the Court's analysis in *Telectronics*. Is the Court addressing questions of legislative authorization or due process limits? Many courts fail to distinguish between these questions. *See supra* notes 183 and 184.

   Recall the due process analysis set forth in *International Shoe, supra* pp. 86-87. Should that same analysis govern assertions of jurisdiction based on alter ego and other theories that impute contacts to a defendant? Many federal courts omit any minimum contacts analysis in alter ego cases and simply recite the following passage: "federal courts have consistently acknowledged that it is compatible with due process for a court to exercise personal jurisdiction over an individual or a corporation that would not ordinarily be subject to personal jurisdiction in that court when the individual or corporation is an alter ego or successor of a corporation that would be subject to personal jurisdiction in that court." *Patin v. Thoroughbred Power Boats Inc.*, 294 F.3d 640, 653 (5th Cir. 2002) (collecting cases). Is this appropriate? Should generally applicable due process protections be considered in alter ego cases?

   3. *Influence of* **Cannon** *on alter ego doctrine.* The Supreme Court's decision in *Cannon* has played a substantial role in the development of alter ego analysis, both as to questions of legislative authorization and due process limits. As described above, *Cannon* held that a parent corporation which "dominated" its subsidiary "immediately and completely" could nonetheless not be subjected to the forum state's personal jurisdiction because the existence of the subsidiary "as a distinct corporate entity [was] in all respects observed." 267 U.S. at 335. The *Cannon* alter ego theory requires showing that the subsidiary is a "pure fiction" and that its separate corporate existence is ignored, for example, by failing to maintain the "formal" trappings of corporate identity. *See* cases cited at *supra* p. 178, note 191. How likely is it that this requirement of proof could be satisfied?

   4. *Criticism of* **Cannon's** *alter ego standard.* Despite its continuing influence, there is considerable question as to the precedential value of *Cannon*. Does *Cannon* adopt a sensible test for due process analysis? Should the Due Process Clause shield someone from jurisdiction merely because they complete routine corporate forms — such as board minutes, shareholders and board resolutions, tax filings, and annual reports? On the other hand, is *Cannon* an appropriate interpretation of "legislative" authorization? Absent statutory guidance, should courts be expansive or cautious in asserting new jurisdictional bases?

   Consider the discussion of *Cannon* in *Telectronics*. What response is there to the argument that Cannon was not really a due process precedent and, even if it were, *International Shoe* and *World-Wide Volkswagen* have superseded it? Recall Justice Scalia's analysis in *Burnham*, discussed *supra* pp. 129-137. How might one appeal to that reasoning in addressing alter ego issues?

   If *Cannon* was not a due process holding, then what constitutional limits *should* be imposed on the alter ego doctrine? Does the Constitution require states to provide for corporations with limited liability? Are states required to "recognize" corporations created as separate legal persons under the laws of sister states? What provision of the Constitution would require this? Would the obligation extend to foreign countries? If *Cannon* was not a due process holding, does that change its authority or value in ascertaining the existence of legislative authorization for alter ego jurisdiction?

5. *Control as a basis for alter ego jurisdiction.* Many courts cite *Cannon*, but apply less stringent tests for alter ego status. *See supra* note 194. Other courts, like *In re Telectronics*, do not follow *Cannon* at all. *See supra* note 194. In both instances, courts frequently look to the extent of a parent corporation's "control" over its subsidiary or other affiliate.

(a)   Control for alter ego purposes does not mean power to elect board of directors. What is meant by the "control" required to establish an alter ego relationship? In one important sense, almost every parent corporation "controls" its majority owned subsidiaries: by virtue of its stock ownership, the parent has the power to remove and elect its subsidiaries' boards of directors. Why is this standard not also applicable in defining alter ego relations? *See Central States, Southeast and Southwest Areas Pension Fund v. Reimer Express World Corp.*, 230 F.3d 934, 943 (7th Cir. 2000) ("[C]onstitutional due process requires that personal jurisdiction cannot be premised on corporate affiliation or stock ownership alone where corporate formalities are substantially observed and the parent does not exercise an unusually high degree of control over the subsidiary."). What standard of control does *Telectronics* apply?

(b)   Authorities holding that control requires showing of continual, day-to-day management. Lower courts have generally said that alter ego status requires a showing that the parent exercises "intimate and complete" or "day-to-day" control of its subsidiary, or that the parent "continually supervises" and "intervenes in" its subsidiary's affairs. For some representative examples, *see Coca-Cola v. Procter & Gamble Co.*, 595 F. Supp. 304, 308 (N.D. Ga. 1983) (alter ego jurisdiction where parent exercised pervasive control through interlocking directorates, common officers, and review and approval of subsidiary actions); *Velandra v. Regie Nationale des Usines Renault*, 336 F.2d 292, 296 (6th Cir. 1962) (whether "the parent has exercised an undue degree of control over the subsidiary"); *Clark v. Matsushita Elec. Indus. Co.*, 811 F. Supp. 1061, 1068 (M.D. Pa. 1993) ("actual day-to-day control . . . required"). The parent's control must ignore the subsidiary's "separate existence," or treat it as a "mere instrumentality" or "pure fiction." *See supra* pp. 179-180.

(c)   Factors relevant to control. The foregoing formulae do little to identify what types of conduct by a parent corporation constitute control for alter ego purposes. Instead, as *Telectronics* illustrates, lower courts have typically relied on unreflective recitations of various "factors." These factors include, among others, the parent's percentage ownership, any overlap in directors and officers, adherence to corporate formalities, how the companies account and pay for goods provided to one another, the subsidiary's capitalization, the interdependence of the parent and subsidiary's businesses and the extent to which the parent (or its officers) approve significant decisions by the subsidiary. *See Dickson Marine Inc. v. Panalpina, Inc.*, 179 F.3d 331, 339 (5th Cir. 1999) (articulating seven-factor control test); *Gundle Lining Const. Corp. v. Adams County Asphalt, Inc.*, 85 F.3d 201, 208-209 (5th Cir. 1996) (articulating 12-factor test); *Volkswagenwerk AG v. Beech Aircraft*, 751 F.2d 117, 120-122 (2d Cir. 1984) (four-factor test). What is the rationale for such lists? How are these various factors to be evaluated?

(d)   What should constitute control for alter ego purposes? What types of acts by a parent corporation should constitute sufficient "control" to create an alter ego relationship? A thoughtful analysis was provided in *United States v. Scophony Corp. of America*, 333 U.S. 795, 816 (1948), where the Court required a showing of "constant supervision and intervention beyond *normal exercise of shareholders' rights.*" This formula contemplates that parent corporations will exercise control over subsidiaries in their capacity as shareholders. If

they leave that role, and directly manage the subsidiary's business as its officers, then an alter ego relation may be found. Is this a sensible distinction? What is a "normal exercise of shareholders' rights"?

(e) Relevance of company's cultural roots. Is it appropriate for a U.S. court to consider the cultural milieu and character of a foreign parent corporation in determining whether the parent "controls" its U.S. subsidiary? The suggestion has been made that some cultures may be more disciplined, or authoritarian, and hence that "control" may more readily be presumed or found. Is this a legitimate line of reasoning? Consider the following excerpt from a lengthy opinion, upholding alter ego jurisdiction over a Japanese parent corporation, principally because of the acts of Japanese managers at the Japanese parent's U.S. subsidiary:

> Japanese subsidiaries in particular may be singularly responsive to the wishes of their parent companies. . . . Significant in terms of cultural considerations that seem to affect real economic power relationships relevant to jurisdiction is the widely-noted hierarchical structure that joins the Japanese subsidiary to its parent, and the Japanese employee to his or her employer. In Japan subsidiaries are commonly referred to as ko-gaisha (child company) in relation to oya-gaisha (parent). "The use of the words 'parent' and 'child' suggests the existence of a familial relationship of control and dependency." K. Haitani, *The Japanese Economic System: An Institutional Overview* 126 (1976). Thus, quite apart from the matter of one hundred percent stock ownership, a Japanese parent may expect to exert control over any of its child companies. The sense of hierarchy is apparently to be found in typical employee-employer relations as well. An inferior in Japanese social organization is "conditioned to attribute authority to the wishes of his superior. . . . The subordinate is extremely conscious of his standing in the group." K. Haitani, *The Japanese Economic System: An Institutional Overview* 92 (1976). *Bulova Watch Co. v. K. Hattori & Co.,* 508 F. Supp. 1322, 1339 (S.D.N.Y. 1981).

Is it helpful to use such stereotypes in analyzing whether one corporate management controlled another? On the other hand, can a court meaningfully evaluate control without understanding the expectations of foreign executives and employees?

6. *Economic integration as basis for alter ego jurisdiction.* As discussed above, a few decisions have departed further from the *Cannon* analysis, instead considering whether a parent and subsidiary are "economically integrated." *See supra* pp. 179-180. A leading example of this approach was *Bulova Watch Co. v. K. Hattori & Co.,* 508 F. Supp. 1322, 1327 (E.D.N.Y. 1981), where the court remarked:

> To any layman it would seem absurd that our courts could not obtain jurisdiction over a billion dollar multinational which is exploiting the critical New York and American markets to keep its home production going at a huge volume and profit. This perception must have a bearing on our evaluation of fairness. The law ignores the common sense of a situation at the peril of becoming irrelevant as an institution. . . .

Most parents are economically integrated with their subsidiaries; they establish those subsidiaries to develop and expand their business into other territories. An economic integration standard would treat many such arrangements as alter ego relations. Is that appropriate?

7. *Fraud or other wrongdoing required.* As noted above, some courts have required that there be some element of fraudulent or otherwise wrongful conduct by the defendant in order for the alter ego theory to be applied. *See supra* pp. 179-180. Was there any indication of such conduct in *Telectronics*? Should fraud or similar misconduct be required in order to establish alter ego jurisdiction? As a legislative matter? As a matter of due process analysis?

8. *Specific jurisdiction based upon a foreign parent's own forum contacts related to its subsidiary's activities in forum.* Even if a U.S. subsidiary is not the alter ego of its foreign parent, the foreign parent's contacts with its subsidiary may still be relevant to establishing specific jurisdiction over it. Numerous courts have taken a foreign parent's dealings with its U.S. subsidiary into account in determining the parent's own forum contacts. *E.g., Laitram Corp. v. Oki Elec. Indus. Co.,* 1994 WL 24241 (E.D. La. 1994) (although foreign parent was not alter ego of U.S. subsidiary, parent's knowledge of subsidiary's marketing activities supported stream of commerce jurisdiction); *Brunswick Corp. v. Suzuki Co.,* 575 F. Supp. 1412 (E.D. Wis. 1983). Note that the Court in *Telectronics* described this as an "attribution" theory of alter ego jurisdiction, as distinguished from a "merger" theory. What exactly is the difference between these two theories?

Consider the following explanation, drawn from a case where the plaintiff sought to establish personal jurisdiction in Georgia over a French car manufacturer, based upon its relations with its wholly owned U.S. marketing subsidiary:

> Although we agree that (1) no "alter ego" relationship existed between [the U.S. subsidiary] and [the French parent], and that (2) to impute the actions of the former to the latter would therefore be improper, the fact that no alter ego relationship existed between the two entities does not mean that [the French parent] could not possess minimum contacts with Georgia as a result of its own independent role in the process that brought [the French parent]'s 1982 Renault LeCar to the United States. The question is not whether the contacts between [the U.S. subsidiary] and Georgia establish minimum contacts between Georgia and [the French parent], but rather whether [the French parent], by virtue of its relationship with [the U.S. subsidiary], purposefully availed itself of the privilege of conducting business in Georgia such that it could reasonably anticipate being haled into court there. That [the French parent] did not exercise sufficient control over [the U.S. subsidiary] to establish an alter ego relationship does not necessarily mean that it had insufficient contacts with Georgia as a result of its own actions and its participation in the decisions that resulted in [the U.S. subsidiary]'s presence and activity in Georgia. *Vermeulen v. Renault, U.S.A. Inc.,* 965 F.2d 1014 (11th Cir. 1992).

Is this analysis convincing?

9. *Specific jurisdiction based upon a foreign parent causing a domestic subsidiary to engage in conduct in the forum.* If a parent corporation causes its subsidiary to engage in certain conduct, it may be subject to jurisdiction in the same manner that the subsidiary would be. According to one court, "[i]f the subsidiary corporation does an act, or causes effects, in the state at the direction of the parent corporation or in the course of the parent corporation's business, the state has judicial jurisdiction over the parent to the same extent that it would have had such jurisdiction if the parent had itself done the act or caused the effects." *Allen v. Toshiba Corp.,* 599 F. Supp. 381, 389 (D.N.M. 1984). Is this an application of the "attribution" theory of alter ego analysis, or something else?

10. *Application of the "relatedness" requirement to alter ego analysis.* Recall the requirement that, in determining whether or not specific jurisdiction exists, only the forum contacts of the defendant that relate to the plaintiff's claim(s) will count. *See supra* pp. 173-175. Is this requirement relevant to alter ego analysis?

Suppose that a parent company exercises intimate, day-to-day control over a generally independent subsidiary with respect to the transactions or activities underlying the plaintiff's claims. Is this more or less relevant than the parent's control over unrelated actions by the subsidiary? Note the comment in *Telectronics* that "the Court finds PDL's involvement in the Accufix 'J' Lead controversy — which was precisely the controversy giving rise to the plaintiff's claims — to be especially telling as to the intimate affiliation between the parent and subsidiary."

Suppose a major foreign company with operations throughout, for example, India and Asia, owns a small subsidiary in Delaware that carries on a modest amount of business relating solely to the United States. Suppose further that the foreign parent exercises complete, day-to-day control over all aspects of the U.S. subsidiary, and also does a poor job observing corporate formalities, satisfying whatever standard of alter ego jurisdiction one might apply. If one of the foreign parent's petrochemical plants suffers a disastrous mishap in Asia, killing numerous local residents and causing vast property damage, will the foreign parent be subject to general jurisdiction in Delaware? Why not? If the Delaware subsidiary "is" the foreign parent, by reason of the alter ego theory, why are not the Delaware subsidiary and the foreign parent subject to general jurisdiction in Delaware? What is wrong with this analysis? *Compare Doe v. Unocal,* 27 F. Supp. 2d 1174, 1186-1188 (C.D. Cal. 1998), *aff'd,* 248 F.3d 915 (9th Cir. 2001).

11. *Presence of "division" within the forum.* It is common for a single corporate entity to divide its operations among several unincorporated "divisions." This is done for both internal administrative and marketing purposes (as when a division does business under a different name than the company of which it is a part). It is well settled that a company can be regarded as doing business in the places where its divisions are present. *E.g., Wells Fargo & Co. v. Wells Fargo Express Co.,* 556 F.2d 406, 425 (9th Cir. 1977) ("Clearly, a corporation may be 'present' in several jurisdictions by operating 'divisions' there so that it may not, in some instances, be unreasonable or unfair to subject the corporation to the general jurisdiction of anyone of those forms regardless of where the cause of action arose or which of the corporation's divisions' activities gave rise to it."). *See also supra* pp. 123-126, discussing general jurisdiction based on presence of an office in the forum.

12. *Critiques of alter ego jurisdiction.* Principles of piercing the corporate veil are well established as rules of substantive liability. As *Telectronics* makes clear, though, those principles do not necessarily carry over into jurisdictional analysis. Some recent scholarship has called into doubt the entire enterprise — arguing both that, as a matter of precedent, lower courts have misread *Cannon* and, as a matter of policy, imputing jurisdictional contacts to a parent corporation is unwise. Consider:

> Contrary to accepted wisdom, the use of veil piercing for jurisdictional purposes is not authorized by Justice Brandeis's decision in *Cannon.* . . . The Court's failure to expressly repudiate *Cannon* has undoubtedly furthered misconceptions regarding the propriety of indirectly measuring state court judicial power. . . . Continued acceptance of the use of veil piercing has had the effect of enshrining *Cannon* as the originating and validating source for invoking the substantive law doctrine in the jurisdictional test. . . .
>
> Beyond the lack of precedential support for it, the use of veil piercing is fundamentally ill-conceived as a doctrinal tool for measuring state court power. There are pragmatic problems with applying veil piercing for jurisdictional purposes that flow directly out of the twin failings of indeterminacy and irrelevance shared by all veil-piercing cases. . . . To the extent that justification is sought for vicarious jurisdiction on equity grounds as an escape hatch for those unsatisfied with the current limits on judicial jurisdiction, the exercise of indirect jurisdiction may run afoul of both the legislative prerogative to limit state court power and the Supreme Court's authority to mark the due process limits of judicial jurisdiction. Hoffman, *The Case Against Vicarious Jurisdiction,* 152 U. Pa. L. Rev. 1023, 1102 (2004).

Consider also EU Council Regulation 44/2001. What does it provide with regard to alter ego jurisdiction?

Note that a basic principle of modern economic enterprise is that of limited liability, which permits investors to limit their exposure to risks for new ventures. Bainbridge, *Abolishing Veil Piercing*, 43 Corp. Prac. Commentator 517, 535 (2001). Limited liability is particularly important to the U.S. economy and to the activities of U.S. corporations around the world. In many instances, U.S. companies are in the position of seeking to defend the principle of limited liability against actions by foreign regulatory authorities and courts. *See* Presser, *Piercing the Corporate Veil* §§5.1-5.6 (1991 & Supp. 2006) (describing foreign countries' approaches to veil piercing). Is it wise for U.S. courts to disregard principles of limited liability in asserting jurisdiction over foreign companies? If foreign courts follow suit, where does this lead?

2. Personal Jurisdiction Based on Agency Relationship

Closely related to the alter ego doctrine is jurisdiction based upon an "agency" relationship. It is well settled that U.S. personal jurisdiction may be exercised over a foreign corporation based on its "agency" relationship with a U.S. corporation or other entity with U.S. contacts:

> Even in the absence of a stock relationship between a local and a foreign corporation, jurisdiction over the foreign corporation has sometimes been exercised on the basis of activities that the local corporation has conducted in the state as the agent of the foreign corporation.[209]

Numerous lower courts have exercised jurisdiction over foreign principals based upon their relations with local agents.[210]

a. Law Governing Agency Relationship for Jurisdictional Purposes. In order for jurisdiction to be exercised based on an agency relationship, both statutory and due process requirements must be satisfied. As in the alter ego context, state and federal jurisdictional grants do not always deal expressly with agency as a basis for jurisdiction. As a result, the circumstances in which jurisdiction may be asserted as a result of an agency relationship is often defined by common law decisions. Lower courts seldom distinguish clearly between state common law requirements and due process limits, apparently assuming that state law extends to the limits of the Constitution. Moreover, in diversity cases, lower courts rarely reflect on the difficult questions concerning what law governs the agency analysis.[211]

b. Agency Standards for Jurisdictional Purposes. There is no clear definition of "agency" for jurisdictional purposes under either most state laws or the Due Process Clause.[212] Courts often say that they have "focused on the realities of the relationship

---

209. *Restatement (Second) Conflict of Laws* §52 comment b (1971).

210. *E.g., Stubbs v. Wyndham Nassau Resort and Crystal Palace Casino,* 447 F.3d 1357, 1361-1362 (11th Cir. 2006); *Chan v. Society Expeditions, Inc.,* 39 F.3d 1398, 1405 (9th Cir. 1994); *Dong AH Tire & Rubber Co., Ltd. v. Glasforms, Inc.,* 2009 WL 975817, at *7-8 (N.D. Cal. Apr. 10, 2009); *In re Lernout & Hauspie Securities Litig.,* 337 F. Supp. 2d 298, 316-317 (D. Mass. 2004); *In re Tamoxifen Citrate Antitrust Litig.,* 262 F. Supp. 2d 17, 24-25 (E.D.N.Y. 2003). Other courts have refused, on particular facts, to find any agency relationship. *E.g., Doe v. Unocal Corp.,* 27 F. Supp. 2d 1174, 1188-1190 (C.D. Cal. 1998), *aff'd on reasoning of District Court,* 248 F.3d 915 (9th Cir. 2001); *Antares Aircraft, LP v. Total C.F.P.,* 1991 U.S. Dist. LEXIS 1511 (S.D.N.Y. 1991).

211. *See, e.g., Patterson v. Home Depot USA, Inc.,* 684 F. Supp. 2d 1170, 1183 (D. Ariz. 2010).

212. Courts have generally held that agency principles differ from alter ego principles for purposes of personal jurisdiction analysis. *See, e.g., In re Lernout & Hauspie Securities Litig.,* 337 F. Supp. 2d 298, 313 (D. Mass. 2004); *SGI Air Holdings II LLC v. Novartis Int'l AG,* 239 F. Supp. 2d 1161, 1166 (D. Colo. 2003); *Dagesse v. Plant Hotel NV,* 113 F. Supp. 2d 211, 216 n.2 (D.N.H. 2000).

in question rather than the formalities of agency law."[213] As with the alter ego doctrine, courts have usually concluded that "a more informal" and "more lenient" definition of agency is appropriate for jurisdictional purposes, than for liability purposes.[214]

Following this rationale, the weight of authority has held that an agency relationship exists if three requirements are satisfied: (a) the alleged agent must have acted for the benefit of the alleged principal; (b) the principal must have had knowledge of, and must have consented to, the agent's actions on its behalf; and (c) the principal must have had sufficient control over the agent's actions.[215]

Other courts have taken subtly different approaches. Some courts have required only "the principal's express or implied authority to perform acts which give rise to submission to jurisdiction."[216] In order for its contacts to be attributed to its principal, an agent must have acted within the scope of its authority.[217]

Other courts have required that the agent have performed services that are "sufficiently important to the foreign corporation"; they have inquired whether, for example, the corporation's own officials would undertake to perform particular actions if the company's agents had not done so.[218] Finally, some courts have abandoned any attempt at articulating a test, opting instead for a "totality of the circumstances" approach.[219]

There is no requirement that a principal have any ownership interest in, or other corporate affiliation with, its agent. Agency relations are routinely found between unaffiliated entities. Nevertheless, the existence of an ownership interest is not irrelevant to the existence of an agency relationship. Courts frequently say that the greater the degree of corporate affiliation, the more likely it is that jurisdiction will be exercised based on an agency theory.[220]

Most courts have required that the alleged principal enjoyed significant "control" over its purported agent.[221] The degree of control required to establish an agency relationship is unclear, with different courts requiring varying levels of control. Some opinions have said that "all that plaintiff need demonstrate is the degree of control required by common law agency rules."[222] Other cases say that "the parent must have actual, participatory and total control of the subsidiary."[223]

c. Selected Materials on Agency as a Basis for Personal Jurisdiction in International Cases. The three following decisions illustrate common applications of the agency doctrine in international cases. Over 40 years ago, in *Frummer v. Hilton Hotels,* the New York Court of Appeals subjected the U.K. parent of a New York subsidiary to general jurisdiction because the subsidiary acted as its agent. More recently, in *Wiwa v. Royal Dutch Shell Petroleum Co.,* the Second Circuit built upon *Frummer* to hold that a foreign corporation is

---

213. *B.E.E. Int'l Ltd. v. Hawes,* 267 F. Supp. 2d 477, 483 (M.D.N.C. 2003) ("The significance of this designation [agent] stems not from the title itself, but rather from any actual conduct that shows purposeful availment by [the defendant]"); *CutCo Indus., Inc. v. Naughton,* 806 F.2d 361, 366 (2d Cir. 1986).

214. *Reiner v. Durand,* 602 F. Supp. 849, 851 (S.D.N.Y. 1985).

215. *McFadin v. Gerber,* 587 F.3d 753, 761-762 (5th Cir. 2009); *Melea, Ltd. v. Jawer SA,* 511 F.3d 1060, 1069 (10th Cir. 2007); *CutCo Indus., Inc. v. Naughton,* 806 F.2d 361, 367 (2d Cir. 1986); *Grove Press, Inc. v. Angleton,* 649 F.2d 121, 122 (2d Cir. 1981).

216. *Boden Products, Inc. v. Novachem, Inc.,* 663 F. Supp. 226, 229 (N.D. Ill. 1987).

217. *E.g., In re Cohen,* 422 B.R. 350 (E.D.N.Y. 2010).

218. *E.g., D'Jamoos v. Pilatus Aircraft, Ltd.,* 566 F.3d 94, 108 (3d Cir. 2009); *Doe v. Unocal Corp.,* 248 F.3d 915, 928 (9th Cir. 2001); *Stutts v. De Dietrich Group,* 465 F. Supp. 2d 156, 162 (E.D.N.Y. 2006); *In re Tamoxifen Citrate Antitrust Litig.,* 262 F. Supp. 2d 17, 23 (E.D.N.Y. 2003).

219. *E.g., Arch v. American Tobacco Co., Inc.,* 984 F. Supp. 830, 837 (E.D. Pa. 1997).

220. *E.g., Doe v. Unocal Corp.,* 248 F.3d 915 (9th Cir. 2001).

221. *Id.,* at 926.

222. *Pennie & Edmonds v. Austad Co.,* 681 F. Supp. 1074, 1078 (S.D.N.Y. 1988)

223. *Akzona Inc. v. E.I. Du Pont De Nemours & Co.,* 607 F. Supp. 227, 237 (D. Del. 1984).

subject to general jurisdiction by virtue of an agent's actions. Finally, in *Cartwright v. Fokker Aircraft*, a district court relied on agency principles to assert jurisdiction in a product liability case. All three decisions reflect an expansive, potentially exorbitant, jurisdictional doctrine.

FRUMMER v. HILTON HOTELS INTERNATIONAL
281 N.Y.S.2d 41 (1967)

FULD, CHIEF JUDGE. This appeal calls upon us to determine whether jurisdiction was validly acquired over one of the defendants, Hilton Hotels (U.K.) Ltd., a British corporation ["Hilton (U.K.)"]. The plaintiff alleges that in 1963 when he was on a visit to England he fell and was injured in his room at the London Hilton Hotel while attempting to take a shower in an "ovular," modernistic type bathtub. He seeks $150,000 in damages not only from . . . Hilton (U.K.) but also from the defendants Hilton Hotels Corporation and Hilton Hotels International, both of which are Delaware corporations doing business in New York. . . . Hilton (U.K.), which is the lessee and operator of the London Hilton Hotel, has moved [to dismiss on personal jurisdiction grounds]. . . .

The plaintiff does not allege that he had any dealings at all with the British corporate defendant or its agents in this State. Therefore, it may not be said that his cause of action arose from the British corporation's transaction of any business here, and he is not entitled to avail himself of C.P.L.R. §302(a)(1) in order to bring the defendant within the jurisdiction of our courts.

Jurisdiction was, however, properly acquired over Hilton (U.K.) because . . . it was "doing business" here in the traditional sense. . . . [A] foreign corporation is amenable to suit in our courts if it is "engaged in such a continuous and systematic course of 'doing business' here as to warrant a finding of its presence in this jurisdiction." Although "mere solicitation" of business for an out-of-state concern is not enough to constitute doing business, due process requirements are satisfied if the defendant foreign corporation has "certain minimum contacts with [the State] such that the maintenance of the suit does not offend 'traditional notions of fair play and substantial justice.'" In *Bryant v. Finnish Nat. Airline*, 15 N.Y.2d 426, 432, the court declared that the "test for 'doing business' . . . should be a simple pragmatic one," and, applying that test, went on to hold that the requisite minimum contacts with New York were made out when it appears that the defendant foreign corporation, an airline, "has a lease on a New York office . . . employs several people and . . . has a bank account here . . . does public relations and publicity work for defendant here including maintaining contacts with other airlines and travel agencies . . . transmits requests for space to defendant in Europe and helps to generate business."

In the case before us, these same services are provided for the defendant Hilton (U.K.) by the Hilton Reservation Service which has a New York office, as well as a New York bank account and telephone number. The Service advertises that it was "established to provide the closest possible liaison with Travel Agents across the country," that lodging "rates for certified wholesalers and/or tour operators [could] be obtained [from the Service] on request" and that it could "confirm availabilities immediately . . . and without charge" at any Hilton hotel including the London Hilton. Thus, it does "public relations and publicity work" for the defendant Hilton (U.K.), including "maintaining contacts with . . . travel agents" and tour directors; and it most certainly "helps to generate business" here for the London Hilton — which, indeed, was the very purpose for which it was established. Moreover, unlike the *Bryant* case, where the defendant's New York office did not make reservations or sell tickets, the Hilton Reservation Service both accepts and confirms room reservations at the London Hilton. In short — and this is the significant and pivotal factor — the Service does all the business which Hilton (U.K.) could do were it here by its own officials.

The defendant's reliance on *Miller v. Surf Properties,* 4 N.Y.2d 475, is misplaced. In that case, we held that the activities of a "travel agency" were not sufficient to give our courts *in personam* jurisdiction over a Florida hotel when the agency's services "amounted to little more than rendering telephone service and mailing brochures" for the hotel and 30 other independent and unassociated Florida establishments. Indeed, in *Bryant,* we found it significant that in the *Miller* case the New York activities were carried on "not [by] an employee of the defendant [Florida hotel] but an independent travel agency representing defendant in New York City." Although, in the case before us, the Hilton Reservation Service is not the "employee" of Hilton (U.K.), the Service and that defendant are owned in common by the other defendants and the Service is concededly run on a "non-profit" basis for the benefit of the London Hilton and other Hilton hotels. . . .

We are not unmindful that litigation in a foreign jurisdiction is a burdensome inconvenience for any company. However, it is part of the price which may properly be demanded of those who extensively engage in international trade. When their activities abroad, either directly or through an agent, become as widespread and energetic as the activities in New York conducted by Hilton (U.K.), they receive considerable benefits from such foreign business and may not be heard to complain about the burdens. Since, then, Hilton (U.K.) was "doing business" in New York in the traditional sense . . . as provided by statute (CPLR §313), our courts acquired personal jurisdiction over the corporation for any cause of action asserted against it, no matter where the events occurred which give rise to the cause of action.

BREITEL, JUDGE, dissenting. The occasion for disagreement in this case is the extension of personal jurisdiction over a foreign corporation simply because of its relationship with subsidiary or affiliated corporations of a parent corporation. Moreover, such jurisdiction is extended in the absence of fraud, misrepresentation, or intermingling of activities of separate corporations. Before considering the particular facts of this case it should be observed that important policy and commercial considerations are involved in preventing or allowing business enterprises to limit liability, suability, and exposure to governmental regulation, by the creation of truly separate corporate entities, with or without separate ownership structures, but especially where the ownership is not identical. These considerations are particularly important for a country engaged in worldwide trade and investment, often in the less developed countries of the world, because of the encouragement or discouragement to risk capital and the exposure to reciprocal treatment of jurisdictional bases in foreign countries. . . .

There is no claim by plaintiff that the Hilton complex or any of its components is used to defraud, deceive, or mislead those who deal with it, or that there has been any failure in the operation and management of the several corporations to keep their internal affairs and management separate and distinct. It is contended and it is undisputed that the advertising and soliciting for business by the Hilton enterprises is done by offering the several respective services of the affiliated hotel corporations, reservations services, and credit card facilities, in common advertising.

The pivotal, but disputed, assertion upon which the present decision depends is that the Hilton Credit Corporation in handling reservations for the British corporation "does all the business which Hilton (U.K.) could do were it here by its own officials." . . . As recognized, the solicitation or mere promotion of business for an out-of-State enterprise does not constitute the doing of business in the State. . . . On the other hand, the maintenance of localized activities in the State has, of course, been the basis for asserting personal jurisdiction. The majority bridges the gap between these two rules by finding that separate but affiliated corporations perform the localized services, albeit local services of the narrowest scope, on behalf of the foreign corporation and, therefore, the foreign corporation is performing the localized services here, thus subjecting it to personal jurisdiction. This, of course, is a *non sequitur*, unless there is no power or privilege on the part of business enterprises to limit and segregate their assets, liabilities, and suability, if done, in fact, and if done without fraud or deception, by the utilization of separate, adequately financed corporations, either subsidiary or affiliated. . . .

On this analysis, the present case extends the "doing business" rule well beyond the existing principles or precedents. And the effect on the flexibility and promotion of world-wide business enterprises would be drastic and unhealthy. It is well established in this country that a foreign parent corporation will not be subjected to the judicial jurisdiction of a State merely because of its ownership of a subsidiary corporation doing business within the State, if the parent diligently maintains the formal separateness of the subsidiary entity (*e.g., Cannon Mfg. Co. v. Cudahy Packing Co.*). Similarly, courts in the United Kingdom evidently will not assert jurisdiction over a foreign corporation merely because it maintains a subsidiary in [the forum]. . . .

While the circumstances in this case are not as serious in their effect in permitting personal jurisdiction, because plaintiff is indeed a New York resident, and the Hilton enterprises looked at in the large as a layman would view them are so much "present," the rules applied will not stay so limited. Under such grossly extended rules nonresidents would also be able to sue in New York, where tort verdicts are regarded as very high; and there are other categories in which jurisdiction might be invoked under circumstances much less appealing than here. Again, it is pointed out that this case does not involve a cause of action which arose here, but one that arose in another country across the seas.

WIWA v. ROYAL DUTCH SHELL PETROLEUM CO.
226 F.3d 88 (2d Cir. 2000)

LEVAL, CIRCUIT JUDGE. Defendant Royal Dutch is a holding company incorporated and headquartered in the Netherlands. Defendant Shell Transport is a holding company incorporated and headquartered in England. The two defendants jointly control and operate the Royal Dutch/Shell Group, a vast, international, vertically integrated network of affiliated but formally independent oil and gas companies. Among these affiliated companies is Shell Petroleum Development Company of Nigeria, Ltd. ("Shell Nigeria"), a wholly-owned Nigerian subsidiary of the defendants that engages in extensive oil exploration and development activity in the Ogoni region of Nigeria. . . . [Plaintiffs are Nigerian émigrés who allege that the defendants directly or indirectly participated in human rights abuses perpetrated against their families and friends in Nigeria by Nigerian authorities.]

Neither of the defendants has extensive direct contacts with New York. Both companies list their shares, either directly or indirectly,[224] on the New York Stock Exchange. They

---

224. Shares of Royal Dutch are traded directly on the New York Stock Exchange. Shell Transport's shares are traded indirectly in the United States; investors may purchase American Depository Receipts (ADR's) for shares of Shell, rather than shares themselves.

conduct activities in New York incident to this listing, including the preparation of filings for the Securities and Exchange Commission ("SEC") and the employment of transfer agents and depositories for their shares. Royal Dutch also maintains an Internet site, accessible in New York. They have participated in at least one lawsuit in New York as defendants, without contesting jurisdiction. They have for many years retained New York counsel.

Defendants own subsidiary companies that do business in the United States, including Shell Petroleum Inc. ("SPI"), a Delaware corporation. SPI in turn owns all the shares of Shell Oil Company ("Shell Oil"). . . . Shell Oil has extensive operations in New York and is undisputedly subject to the jurisdiction of the New York courts.

The defendants also maintain an Investor Relations Office in New York City, administered by James Grapsi, whose title is "Manager of Investor Relations." The office is nominally a part of Shell Oil. However, all of its functions involve facilitating the relations of the parent holding companies, the defendants Royal Dutch and Shell Transport, with the investment community. The expenses of the office (consisting primarily of rent and salaries) are directly paid in the first instance by Shell Oil, but Shell Oil is reimbursed by the defendants, who therefore bear the full expense of the office. Those expenses average about $45,000 per month, or about $500,000 per year. The Investor Relations Office's duties involve fielding inquiries from investors and potential investors in Royal Dutch and Shell Transport, mailing information about the defendants to thousands of individuals and entities throughout the United States, and organizing meetings between officials of the defendants and investors, potential investors, and financial analysts. . . .

[A] court may exercise jurisdiction over any defendant "who could be subjected to the jurisdiction of a court of general jurisdiction in the state in which the district court is located," Fed. R. Civ. P. 4(k)(1)(a), provided of course that such an exercise of jurisdiction comports with the Fifth Amendment's Due Process Clause. The question is therefore whether the defendants may be subjected to the jurisdiction of the courts of the State of New York. . . . Under New York law, a foreign corporation is subject to general personal jurisdiction in New York if it is "doing business" in the state. "[A] corporation is 'doing business' and is therefore 'present' in New York and subject to personal jurisdiction with respect to any cause of action, related or unrelated to the New York contacts, if it does business in New York 'not occasionally or casually, but with a fair measure of permanence and continuity.'" In order to establish that this standard is met, a plaintiff must show that a defendant engaged in "continuous, permanent, and substantial activity in New York." *Landoil Resources Corp. v. Alexander & Alexander Servs., Inc.*, 918 F.2d 1039, 1043 (2d Cir. 1990).

The continuous presence and substantial activities that satisfy the requirement of doing business do not necessarily need to be conducted by the foreign corporation itself. In certain circumstances, jurisdiction has been predicated upon activities performed in New York for a foreign corporation by an agent. Under well-established New York law, a court of New York may assert jurisdiction over a foreign corporation when it affiliates itself with a New York representative entity and that New York representative renders services on behalf of the foreign corporation that go beyond mere solicitation and are sufficiently important to the foreign entity that the corporation itself would perform equivalent services if no agent were available. *See, e.g., Frummer, supra*. To come within the rule, a plaintiff need demonstrate neither a formal agency agreement, nor that the defendant exercised direct control over its putative agent. The agent must be primarily employed by the defendant and not engaged in similar services for other clients. *See, e.g., Miller v. Surf Properties, Inc.*, 4 N.Y.2d 475, 481 (1958) (holding that independent contractors with many clients are not considered agents of their individual clients for jurisdictional purposes).

[The district court] found that Grapsi and the Investor Relations Office were agents of the defendants for jurisdictional purposes. We agree. While nominally a part of Shell Oil, Grapsi and the Investor Relations Office devoted one hundred percent of their time to the defendants' business. Their sole business function was to perform investor relations services on the defendants' behalf. The defendants fully funded the expenses of the Investor Relations Office . . . and Grapsi sought the defendants' approval on important decisions.

The defendants nonetheless argue that the relationship does not meet the *Frummer/ Gelfand* test. They contend the services of the Investor Relations Office were not sufficiently important that the defendants would have performed them if an agent had been unavailable. . . . The defendants are huge publicly-traded companies with a need for access to capital markets. The importance of their need to maintain good relationships with existing investors and potential investors is illustrated by the fact that they pay over half a million dollars per year to maintain the Investors Relations Office. In our view, the amount invested by the defendants in the U.S. investor relations activity substantially establishes the importance of that activity to the defendants.

Defendants also contend that, if they were to perform the Investor Relations services themselves, it would not necessarily be in New York. The argument is extremely weak. While of course it is true, especially given technological advances in communication, that such an office could conceivably be located anywhere in the world, the strongest indications are that the defendants selected New York as the locus of the present office because that is the most logical place for it. Insofar as the office concerns itself with investors in the U.S. capital markets, it makes better sense to have the office in the United States, rather than in another country. . . . It seems most likely that the Investor Relations Office established by Shell Oil for the benefit of its parents and at their insistence was established in New York City because that was the best place for such an office, and that it would most likely be located in New York City regardless whether operated directly by the defendants, by Shell Oil, or by any other agent. . . .

The defendants contend their Investor Relations Office is an activity that is "incidental" to their listing on the New York Stock Exchange. They cite to a long stream of case law reaching back over a century that they argue precludes courts from considering activity "incidental" to stock market listings when evaluating whether a corporation is doing business in the state of New York. We agree that the prevailing case law accords foreign corporations substantial latitude to list their securities on New York-based stock exchanges and to take the steps necessary to facilitate those listings (such as making SEC filings and designating a depository for their shares) without thereby subjecting themselves to New York jurisdiction for unrelated occurrences. However, defendants misread the scope of the existing case law when they argue that all contacts related to stock exchange listings are stripped of jurisdictional significance.

To begin with, it is not that activities necessary to maintain a stock exchange listing do not count, but rather that, without more, they are insufficient to confer jurisdiction. . . . The Investor Relations Office conducts a broader range of activities on the defendants' behalf than those described in the cited cases as merely "incidental" to the stock exchange listing. These activities, which range from fielding inquiries from investors and potential investors to organizing meetings between defendants' officials and investors, potential investors, and financial analysts, do not properly come within the rule upon which the defendants rely. The defendants' Investor Relations program results not from legal or logistical requirements incumbent upon corporations that list their shares on the New York Stock Exchange, but from the defendants' discretionary determination to invest substantial sums of money in cultivating their relationship with the New York capital markets. . . . In summary, the large body of case law the defendants point to at most stands for the proposition that, absent other substantial contacts, a company is not "doing business" in New York merely by taking ancillary steps in support of its listing on a New York exchange. The activities chargeable to the defendants go well beyond this minimum. . . .

The defendants further contend that the activities of the Investor Relations Office are quantitatively insufficient to confer jurisdiction. We find no merit to this contention. Where, as here, plaintiffs' claim is not related to defendants' contacts with New York, so that jurisdiction is properly characterized as "general," plaintiffs must demonstrate "the defendant's 'continuous and systematic general business contacts.'" *Metropolitan Life Ins. Co. v. Robertson-Ceco Corp.*, 84 F.3d 560, 568 (2d Cir. 1996). Defendants' contacts constitute "a continuous and systematic general business" presence in New York and therefore satisfy the minimum contacts portion of a due process analysis.

Citing to a string of cases holding that solicitation of business plus minimal additional contacts satisfies Section 301, [the district judge] characterized the activities of the Investor Relations Office as satisfying the test of "solicitation plus." . . . [T]he central question is whether the defendant (or its agent) behaved in such a way so as to encourage others to spend money (or otherwise act) in a manner that would benefit the defendant. Judge Wood's characterization of the Investor Relations Office's activities as "solicitation" appears to be a sound interpolation of pre-existing precedent into a new factual context.

However, we need not rely upon such a characterization to support general jurisdiction in this case, because even without relying on the "solicitation plus" formulation, the activities of the Investor Relations Office meet the "doing business" standard. In assessing whether jurisdiction lies against a foreign corporation, both this court and the New York courts have focused on a traditional set of indicia: for example, whether the company has an office in the state, whether it has any bank accounts or other property in the state, whether it has a phone listing in the state, whether it does public relations work there, and whether it has individuals permanently located in the state to promote its interests. *See, e.g., Frummer,* 19 N.Y.2d at 537. The Investor Relations Office, whose activities are attributable to the defendants under the *Frummer* analysis, meets each of these tests. . . . It constitutes a substantial "physical corporate presence" in the State, permanently dedicated to promoting the defendants' interests. We agree with [the court below] that the continuous presence of the Investor Relations program in New York City is sufficient to confer jurisdiction.

Finally, the defendants argue that it would violate the fairness requirement of the Due Process Clause for a New York court to exercise jurisdiction over them. Again, we disagree. . . . While it is true that certain factors normally used to assess the reasonableness of subjection to jurisdiction do favor the defendants (they are foreign corporations that face something of a burden if they litigate here, and the events in question did not occur in New York), litigation in New York City would not represent any great inconvenience to the defendants. The defendants control a vast, wealthy, and far-flung business empire which operates in most parts of the globe. They have a physical presence in the forum state, have access to enormous resources, face little or no language barrier, have litigated in this country on previous occasions, have a four-decade long relationship with one of the nation's leading law firms, and are the parent companies of one of America's largest corporations, which has a very significant presence in New York. New York City, furthermore, where the trial would be held, is a major world capital which offers central location, easy access, and extensive facilities of all kinds. We conclude that the inconvenience to the defendants involved in litigating in New York City would not be great and that nothing in the Due Process Clause precludes New York from exercising jurisdiction over the defendants.

CARTWRIGHT v. FOKKER AIRCRAFT U.S.A., INC.
713 F. Supp. 389 (N.D. Ga. 1988)

Horace T. Ward, District Judge. . . . The complaint alleges that plaintiff, who was an airline baggage handler, was injured when he exited the baggage compartment of an airplane. It claims that the cargo compartment was negligently designed and defective and that its defects were the proximate cause of plaintiff's injuries. . . . [I]n order for Fokker Aircraft BV to come within the coverage of the [Georgia long-arm] statute it must have, in person or through an agent, regularly done or solicited business in the state of Georgia, engaged in a persistent course of conduct with Georgia, or derived substantial revenue from sales in Georgia.

The complaint alleged that defendants Fokker Aircraft USA, Fokker Aircraft BV, and Fokker BV designed, manufactured, distributed, and sold the airplane which caused plaintiff's injuries. . . . Fokker Aircraft USA is a wholly-owned subsidiary of Fokker Aircraft BV, Fokker Aircraft USA is licensed to do business in Georgia, and Fokker Aircraft USA provides Fokker Aircraft BV with marketing, sales and support of certain Fokker aircraft in the United States. Fokker Aircraft USA sold the airplane involved to Piedmont Airlines. The contract of sale indicates that Piedmont is obligated to pay certain taxes incurred by Fokker Aircraft BV; work done on the airplane pursuant to the contract is performed by or on behalf of Fokker Aircraft BV at Fokker Aircraft BV's plant; Fokker Aircraft BV provides field service representatives to advise Piedmont on aircraft maintenance and spare parts; and Fokker Aircraft BV provides training courses at its training facilities.

The parties agree that the airplane involved in this matter was manufactured by Fokker Aircraft BV and sold to Piedmont Airlines through Fokker Aircraft USA. The plane was sold by Fokker Aircraft BV to Fokker Aircraft USA in Amsterdam and then Fokker Aircraft USA resold the airplane to Piedmont Airlines. Defendant submitted an affidavit which states that Fokker Aircraft BV is a Dutch corporation, with its principal offices located in Amsterdam, The Netherlands; Fokker Aircraft BV holds title to certain inventory of spare parts which are located in a Georgia warehouse which is operated by Fokker Aircraft USA; all sales of aircraft by Fokker Aircraft BV are made in The Netherlands; Fokker Aircraft BV transacts no business within Georgia; Fokker Aircraft BV advertises in some national trade magazines but does not do or solicit business in Georgia; Fokker Aircraft BV does not derive any revenue from goods used or consumed or services rendered in Georgia; Fokker Aircraft BV does not own, use, or possess any real property situated within Georgia; Fokker Aircraft BV does not maintain an office in Georgia, nor does it have any employees or agents in Georgia; and Fokker Aircraft BV is not and never has been licensed to do business in Georgia. . . .

[P]laintiff has made a prima facie showing that defendant Fokker Aircraft BV committed a tortious injury in this state which was caused by an act or omission outside the state. He has also made a prima facie showing that Fokker Aircraft BV, through its subsidiary Fokker Aircraft USA, engages in a persistent course of conduct with the state. Fokker Aircraft BV not only advertised in national trade publications and held title to certain spare parts kept in Georgia, it also utilized a subsidiary distributor who regularly does and solicits business in Georgia. The court finds that although Fokker Aircraft BV and Fokker Aircraft USA have separate corporate identities, it is appropriate in these circumstances to consider Fokker Aircraft USA the "agent" of Fokker Aircraft BV in the context of the Georgia long arm statute. . . .

[As for due process,] defendant Fokker Aircraft BV has taken actions which were purposefully directed toward the forum state. It has advertised in national publications, some of whose audience is presumably in Georgia. More importantly, it markets its product through a distributor which services its products exclusively and is licensed to do business in Georgia. These facts establish the requisite "substantial connection" between defendant and the forum state which make the exercise of jurisdiction over defendant consistent with "traditional notions of fair play and substantial justice."

Notes on Hilton Hotels, Wiwa, and Fokker

1. *What does "agency" mean for jurisdictional purposes?* At common law, "[a]gency is the fiduciary relation which results from the manifestation of consent by one person to another that the other shall act on his behalf and subject to his control, and consent by the other so to act." *Restatement (Second) Agency* §1 (1958). *Hilton Hotels, Wiwa,* and *Fokker* do not devote much attention to the terms (or even existence) of an agency relationship between the defendant parties.

Wiwa notes only that no formal agreement is required to demonstrate an agency relationship for jurisdictional purposes. *See supra* pp. 195-196. Other lower courts have specifically disclaimed any obligation to consider the terms of agreements between an alleged principal and agent. *E.g., First American Corp. v. Price Waterhouse LLP,* 988 F. Supp. 353, 363 (S.D.N.Y. 1997) ("[T]he domestic agent need not be an official agent or even legally related to the foreign corporation to establish an agency function sufficient to support jurisdiction."); *East New York Sav. Bank v. Republic Realty Mtg. Corp.,* 402 N.Y.S.2d 639, 641 (App. Div. 1978). Why are not the terms of the agency relationship relevant to jurisdiction? These decisions suggest that, in the context of jurisdiction, agency means something less demanding than what it means for substantive purposes. *See supra* pp. 190-191. Is a "less stringent" agency standard appropriate? What exactly do *Hilton Hotels, Wiwa,* and *Fokker* require to establish an agency relationship?

2. *Long-arm statutes authorizing jurisdiction based on agency relationship.* Unlike alter ego jurisdiction, a number of state long-arm statutes authorize jurisdiction on the basis of actions by an agent. *See, e.g.,* Idaho Code §5-514 ("Any person . . . or corporation, whether or not a citizen or resident of this state, who . . . through an agent does any of the acts hereinafter enumerated, thereby submits said person . . . or corporation to the jurisdiction of the courts of this state as to any cause of action arising from the doing of any of said acts"); Mass. Gen. Laws ch. 223A, §3(a) ("A court may exercise personal jurisdiction over a person, who acts directly or by an agent, as to a cause of action in law or equity arising from the person's . . . transacting any business in this commonwealth."); Va. Code Ann. §8.01-328.1(A)(1) ("A court may exercise personal jurisdiction over a person, who acts directly or by an agent, as to a cause of action arising from the person's . . . [t]ransacting any business in this Commonwealth."). How does this affect analysis?

3. *Agency as a basis for specific jurisdiction.* Agency can provide the basis for subjecting a foreign principal to specific jurisdiction. In such cases, the plaintiff's claims must arise out of the agent's actions in the forum in its capacity as the principal's agent. *Hilton Hotels* was not a specific jurisdiction case because "[t]he plaintiff does not allege that he had any

dealings at all with the British corporate defendant or its agents in this case." *Wiwa* also was not a specific jurisdiction case (although the Court is not quite so direct about this as that in *Hilton Hotels*).

Suppose that the plaintiff in *Hilton Hotels* had contacted Hilton Reservation Service in New York and that it had reserved a room with Hilton (U.K.) for the plaintiff. Would specific jurisdiction have been proper?

Was *Fokker* a specific jurisdiction case? Note that Fokker BV manufactured the allegedly defective aircraft, which it sold to its alleged agent, Fokker USA. Note also that jurisdiction was based upon a provision of the Georgia long-arm statute applicable when "tortious injury" is caused within the state by an act committed outside the state. What if Fokker BV had manufactured the allegedly defective aircraft, but that it was *not* sold to or distributed by Fokker USA? Would jurisdiction still be permitted?

4. *Agency as basis for general jurisdiction.* Both *Hilton Hotels* and *Wiwa* exercised jurisdiction over foreign defendants based on activities within New York by their agents that were unrelated to the plaintiffs' claims. Other courts have also relied on agency theories to assert general jurisdiction over foreign defendants. *E.g., Stubbs v. Wyndham Nassau Resort and Crystal Palace Casino,* 447 F.3d 1357, 1361-1362 (11th Cir. 2006); *SGI Air Holdings II LLC v. Novartis Int'l AG,* 239 F. Supp. 2d 1161 (D. Colo. 2003); *Presbyterian Church of Sudan v. Talisman Energy, Inc.,* 244 F. Supp. 2d 289, 330-331 (S.D.N.Y. 2003).

Is it appropriate to permit general jurisdiction based on an agency relationship? What are the risks of such a jurisdictional base? If agency is permitted as a basis for general jurisdiction: (a) what kinds of actions should the agent be required to carry out within the forum state; (b) how extensive a set of contacts should the agent be required to have with the forum; and (c) what kind of control should the principal be required to have over the agent?

5. **Hilton Hotels'** *analysis.* Consider the facts in *Hilton Hotels.* What is the legal basis for concluding that the actions of Hilton Hotels Corporation in New York could be attributed to Hilton (U.K.)? Consider Judge Breitel's dissent. Does the majority respond effectively to his critique?

Suppose that Hilton Hotels Corporation had only delivered mail from Hilton (U.K.) to guests at Hilton hotels in the United States. Would this agency relationship have sufficed for jurisdiction under the majority's analysis in *Hilton Hotels*? Suppose that Hilton (U.K.) had a New York accountant, law firm, or investment bank, which provided services relating to Hilton (U.K.)'s activities outside the United States. Would this have sufficed for jurisdiction? Why or why not? Note the Court's comment that an agent who provides services to other parties is different from one who provides services only to the defendant. Why should this matter?

Would the agency relationship in *Fokker* sustain general jurisdiction? Could one of Fokker BV's Dutch suppliers (for example, of seatbelts) sue it in Georgia? Could a Chinese passenger, injured in a domestic Chinese flight on a Fokker aircraft sold to a Chinese airline, sue Fokker BV in Georgia? From the available facts, how different was the *Fokker* relationship from the *Hilton* relationship?

6. *Scope of duties required for general agency relationship.* The showing required for an agency relationship should vary depending on whether specific or general jurisdiction is involved. The existence of a general agency relationship should depend on the breadth and character of the agent's duties. One standard emphasizes that the general agent must "have broad executive responsibilities and that his relationship [must] reflect a degree of continuity." *Gottlieb v. Sandia Am. Corp.,* 452 F.2d 510 (3d Cir. 1971). That is apparently the focus of *Hilton Hotels'* comment that the U.S. subsidiary "does all the business which Hilton (U.K.) could do were it here by its own officials."

Another standard for determining when a company is subject to the forum's general jurisdiction because of an agent's activities was suggested in *Gelfand v. Tanner Motors Tours*, 385 F.2d 116, 121 (2d Cir. 1967):

> [The defendant's] New York representative provides services beyond "mere solicitation" and these services are sufficiently important to the foreign corporation that if it did not have a representative to perform them, the corporation's own officials would undertake to perform substantially similar services.

Consider how these different standards would be applied to various external service providers, such as law firms, accountants, investment banks, travel agencies, courier services, and the like. How are these service providers different from suppliers of products, like offices supplies, clothing, or additives? Should agency relationships, or similar commercial dealings, with these entities provide the basis for general jurisdiction?

Recall that in *Afram*, the Greek buyer sent an agent to Illinois to inspect the relevant goods, and that the Court relied on this. What role should such conduct by agents within the forum have in due process analysis?

7. *Listing of shares on U.S. stock exchange.* As the *Wiwa* opinion concedes, it is well settled that a foreign company's listing of its shares on a U.S. stock exchange (and compliance with related U.S. securities regulations) does not subject the company to general jurisdiction in New York (or the United States). *See Doe v. Unocal Corp.*, 248 F.3d 915, 922 (9th Cir. 2001); *Action Mfg. Co. v. Simon Wrecking Co.*, 375 F. Supp. 2d 411, 425-426 (E.D. Pa. 2005); *Telecordia Technologies, Inc. v. Alcatel SA*, 2005 WL 1268061, at *7 (D. Del. 2005); *Presbyterian Church of Sudan v. Talisman Energy, Inc.*, 244 F. Supp. 2d 289, 330 (S.D.N.Y. 2003). *Wiwa* does not mention it, but the costs of maintaining such registration (in accounting, legal, and other fees) vastly exceed the $500,000 that was spent annually on the Investor Relations Office and involve significantly more effort and personnel.

Why exactly is it that a foreign company's act of listing its shares on a U.S. stock exchange does not constitute continuous and systematic contacts with the U.S. forum? Suppose that U.S. nationals acquire a significant portion of the foreign company's shares (say, 30 percent) on U.S. exchanges — should that provide grounds for general jurisdiction over the foreign company? Why or why not?

8. *Wiwa's analysis.* Consider the facts in *Wiwa*. Note that the alleged wrongdoing occurred in Nigeria, and did not involve the New York Investor Relations Office (or Shell's various U.S. operations) in any way. Note also that the Investor Relations Office was directed only toward a specific category of activities in New York. *Wiwa* nonetheless holds that Royal Dutch Shell, Shell Trading, and Shell Nigeria are all subject to general jurisdiction in New York because of the Investor Relations Office's activities.

Suppose that an aggrieved Nigerian supplier of Shell Nigeria brought an action for unpaid invoices in New York. What does *Wiwa* hold about jurisdiction over Shell Nigeria in that case? Suppose that a class of Nigerian (or Armenian or Zambian) gas consumers sues Shell Nigeria (or Shell Armenia or Zambia) in New York for breaches of warranties or unfair competition. What does *Wiwa* say about jurisdiction over Shell Nigeria (or Shell Armenia)? Can this really be the law?

What does the *Wiwa* Court do with *Hilton Hotels'* requirement that Hilton Hotels Corporation "does all the business which Hilton (U.K.) could do were it here by its own officials"? Could Royal Dutch Shell not conduct a wide range of activities in New York beyond those carried out by the Investor Relations Office? Could Royal Dutch Shell not obtain the investor relations assistance from any number of external suppliers, such as securities firms, independent consultants, and the like? Suppose Royal Dutch Shell had obtained investor relations assistance from an external consultant. Would that provide a basis for general jurisdiction under *Wiwa*? Should it? Suppose Royal Dutch Shell had obtained advertising advice about its worldwide image from an employee at Shell Oil in New York. Would that provide a basis for general jurisdiction under *Wiwa*? Should it?

What did the Investor Relations Office accomplish beyond Royal Dutch Shell's listing on the New York Stock Exchange? Note that the consequences of this listing were vastly more significant—in terms of cost and legal consequences—than establishment of the Investment Relations Office. Is there any serious reason that operation of the Office should have altered Shell's jurisdictional status so dramatically?

How could *Wiwa*'s analytical excesses best be corrected? Should it be by: (a) forbidding any general jurisdiction based on agency relationships; (b) holding that the contacts required by the Due Process Clause for general jurisdiction will not exist unless the activities performed by an agent within the forum are "general," rather than confined to a specific subject matter (such as investor relations); (c) holding that the contacts required by the Due Process Clause for general jurisdiction will not exist unless the foreign defendant is shown to have "continuously and systematically" controlled the activities of the agent; (d) holding that the Due Process Clause's "reasonableness" standard will not ordinarily permit general jurisdiction to be exercised on the basis of an agency relationship; or (e) holding that legislative authorization for alter ego jurisdiction is lacking, under any of points (a) to (d)? Or, do you think *Wiwa* is correctly decided?

9. ***"Control" required to establish agency relationship.*** A critical element in establishing agency for jurisdictional purposes in some states is the principal's "control" over the agent. *See supra* p. 191. Recall that a parent almost always "controls" its subsidiary. Is that enough? What degree of control over the agent should be required? What degree of control existed in *Wiwa*?

10. ***Effect of corporate affiliation on existence of agency relationship.*** The fact that an alleged principal is also the parent of its purported agent is typically a significant consideration in agency analysis. *See supra* p. 191. Note that both *Frummer* and *Fokker* involved parent-subsidiary relations. Suppose that Shell's Investment Relations Office had been run by an independent third-party consultant, wholly owned by local New York residents, not by Shell Oil. Would *Wiwa* still have found jurisdiction? Suppose that Fokker's U.S. distributors were independent companies. Would they still have been "agents" of Fokker BV?

11. ***Wisdom of applying agency standard in international cases.*** Is it wise to assert jurisdiction based on agency relations in international cases? Recall the special role that the concept of limited liability companies plays in countries such as the United States engaged in global trade and investment. *See supra* pp. 189-190. Is it in the interest of U.S. (and international) commerce for U.S. courts to make expansive jurisdictional claims based upon agency relations? Note Judge Brietel's concern about the "important policy and commercial considerations" that attach to limited liability incorporation, particularly for a country, like the United States, "engaged in worldwide trade and investment." Are these relevant concerns for U.S. jurisdictional analysis?

12. ***Conspiracy as basis for personal jurisdiction.*** Some courts have wed principles of personal jurisdiction to principles of conspiracy. This theory, like the agency theory, imputes one entity's jurisdictional contacts to another entity. *See generally* 1 R. Casad & W. Richman, *Jurisdiction in Civil Actions* §4-3[1] at 476-483 (3d ed. 1998 & Supp. 2006). While conceptually similar to the agency theory, conspiracy is analytically distinct, requiring different elements and forms of proof. Generally speaking, the conspiracy theory requires a plaintiff to prove that a member of the conspiracy undertook substantial acts in furtherance of conspiracy in the forum state and that the co-conspirator (to whom the plaintiff seeks to impute the contacts) was aware or should have been aware of these acts. *See id.* §4-3[1] at 481.

The propriety of conspiracy as a jurisdictional base is hotly disputed and a number of courts have refused to recognize it. For international cases recognizing the conspiracy theory of personal jurisdiction, *see, e.g., Melea Ltd. v. Jawaer SA*, 511 F.3d 1060, 1069 (10th Cir. 2007) (recognizing theory but finding that plaintiff had failed to allege sufficient facts); *Lolavar v. de Santibanes*, 430 F.3d 221, 229 (4th Cir. 2005) (same); *World Wide Minerals, Ltd. v. Republic of Kazakhstan*, 296 F.3d 1154, 1168-1169 (D.C. Cir. 2002) (recognizing theory but remanding for further factfinding); *Simon v. Philip Morris, Inc.*, 86 F. Supp. 2d 95 (E.D.N.Y. 2000) (applying theory). For courts rejecting the conspiracy theory, *see, e.g., In re New Motor Vehicles Canadian Export Antitrust Litig.*, 307 F. Supp. 2d 148, 157-158 (D. Me. 2004); *Insolia v. Philip Morris Inc.*, 31 F. Supp. 2d 660, 672 (W.D. Wis. 1998).

The conspiracy theory of jurisdiction raises a number of issues. First, does the theory comport with due process? For a skeptical view, *see* Althouse, *The Use of Conspiracy to Establish Personal Jurisdiction: A Due Process Analysis*, 52 Fordham L. Rev. 234 (1983). Second, assuming no constitutional impediment, how does a plaintiff go about proving the conspiracy at the pleading stage? Recall the discussion of jurisdictional discovery, *supra* pp. 90-91. Note that the jurisdictional inquiry into conspiracy can be tied closely to the underlying merits: conspiracy may not only form the basis of a jurisdictional claim but also the basis for substantive liability. In light of this overlap, how is a court supposed to manage the plaintiff's need to prove jurisdiction with the defendant's desire to avoid a fishing expedition before the court rules on dispositive motions at the pleading stage? Finally, what law should a federal court apply to evaluate a jurisdictional argument rooted in the conspiracy theory? Federal law? State law? Does it depend on the basis for subject matter jurisdiction?

E. Personal Jurisdiction in Federal Courts: Federal Rule of Civil Procedure 4 and the Due Process Clauses

1. Introduction

The personal jurisdiction of federal courts is subject to different rules than those applicable in state courts. Like a state court, a federal court cannot exercise jurisdiction unless two requirements are satisfied: (1) a legislative authorization for jurisdiction must exist;[225] and (2) the Constitution must not prohibit the exercise of jurisdiction.[226] Unlike a state court, however, federal courts have no general federal long-arm statute on which to rely.

Instead, Federal Rule of Civil Procedure 4 directs federal courts to "borrow" either specific federal long-arm statutes or local state long-arm statutes.[227] This approach produces complicated questions about the relationship between Rule 4, borrowed jurisdictional statutes, and the Due Process Clauses of the Fifth and Fourteenth Amendments. In important respects, the law is unsettled with divergent and confused lower court decisions.

225. As noted above, where authority to define the jurisdiction of local courts has been delegated by the legislature (or is assigned otherwise), then the relevant question is whether the body with the power to authorize exercises of judicial jurisdiction has done so. *See supra* p. 81, note 4.

226. *See infra* pp. 204-206. Other requirements exist before a federal court may hear a dispute, including the presence of subject matter jurisdiction, compliance with venue requirements, and valid service. *See supra* pp. 5-10 and *infra* pp. 458-459.

227. *See infra* pp. 204, 215-224.

a. Federal Rule of Civil Procedure 4: Amenability and Manner of Service Distinguished.   The personal jurisdiction of federal courts is defined, in the first instance, by Federal Rule of Civil Procedure 4.[228] Rule 4 was extensively revised in 1993, in part to address issues arising specifically in international cases.[229] Rule 4 deals with both a defendant's *amenability* to personal jurisdiction and the *manner* of effecting service of process on a defendant. These are separate requirements, which both must be satisfied to permit personal jurisdiction.[230]

Amenability refers to the circumstances in which the forum's courts may assert personal jurisdiction over the defendant.[231] Rule 4 does not itself directly define a defendant's amenability to suit. Instead, Rule 4(k) authorizes federal district courts to "borrow" other sources of jurisdictional power—in particular, state and federal long-arm statutes—that themselves define amenability to personal jurisdiction.[232] Rule 4 also prescribes rules regarding the manner of service. Service of process is the mechanism for giving notice to the defendant that an action has been commenced.[233] Most importantly for international litigants, Rule 4(f) provides detailed instructions regarding the modes of serving of process outside the United States (discussed in Chapter 10 below). These provisions deal only with the manner of serving process on foreign defendants and not with the circumstances in which they will be amenable to jurisdiction.

b. Rule 4(k)'s Jurisdictional Grants: An Overview.   Rule 4's provisions dealing with amenability to jurisdiction are contained in Rule 4(k). Rule 4(k) provides three principal jurisdictional authorizations:

1. Rule 4(k)(1)(A) authorizes a district court to borrow the jurisdictional powers of state courts in the state where it is located;
2. Rule 4(k)(1)(D) confirms the availability of any applicable federal statute granting personal jurisdiction; and
3. Rule 4(k)(2) grants district courts personal jurisdiction to the limits of the Due Process Clause in certain federal question cases.

Much of Rule 4(k) is based on Rule 4(e) of the pre-1993 Federal Rules of Civil Procedure.[234] Decisions under Rule 4(e) remain useful in interpreting the new Rule.

c. No Federal Personal Jurisdiction Without Legislative Authorization: *Omni Capital.*   A federal court may not exercise personal jurisdiction without legislative

---

228. *Omni Capital Int'l v. Rudolf Wolff & Co.*, 484 U.S. 97, 104 (1987) ("service of process in a federal action is covered generally by Rule 4"). Special provisions concerning jurisdiction and service of process exist in a few fields, such as condemnation proceedings and admiralty. *See* C. Wright & A. Miller, *Federal Practice and Procedure* §1062 (3d ed. 1998 & Supp. 2010).

229. For commentary on the 1993 revisions to Rule 4, *see* Born & Vollmer, *The Effect of the Revised Federal Rules of Civil Procedure on Personal Jurisdiction, Service, and Discovery in International Cases*, 150 F.R.D. 221 (1993); Burbank, *The United States' Approach to International Civil Litigation: Recent Developments in Forum Selection*, 19 U. Pa. J. Int'l Econ. L. 1 (1998); Kelleher, *The December 1993 Amendments to the Federal Rules of Civil Procedure—A Critical Analysis*, 12 Touro L. Rev. 7, 35 (1995).

230. *Omni Capital Int'l v. Rudolf Wolff & Co.*, 484 U.S. 97, 104-105 (1987).

231. C. Wright & A. Miller, *Federal Practice and Procedure* §1075 (3d ed. 1998 & Supp. 2010); *Arrowsmith v. United Press Int'l*, 320 F.2d 219 (2d Cir. 1963).

232. *See infra* pp. 206-215, 215-224; *Omni Capital Int'l v. Rudolf Wolff & Co.*, 484 U.S. 97, 105 (1987). Rule 4(k)(2), which authorizes jurisdiction in certain federal question cases, is an exception to this general principle (although even it "borrows" the Due Process Clause). *See infra* pp. 215-231.

233. *See infra* pp. 867-880.

234. *See* Advisory Committee Notes, 28 U.S.C.A. Fed. R. Civ. P. 4, 119; D. Siegel, *Supplementary Practice Commentaries*, 28 U.S.C.A. Fed. R. Civ. P. 4, at C4-33 (1994 Supp.).

authorization, generally provided by incorporation through Rule 4. That was reaffirmed in *Omni Capital Int'l v. Rudolf Wolff & Co.*, where the Supreme Court rejected the argument that federal courts should exercise a common law power to create their own bases of personal jurisdiction.[235]

Omni was a suit in federal district court asserting federal claims under the Commodity Exchange Act ("CEA")[236] and pendent state law claims. The defendants, who resided in England, moved to dismiss for lack of personal jurisdiction. The Court of Appeals held that neither the CEA nor the local state long-arm statute, which had been borrowed pursuant to old Federal Rule of Civil Procedure 4(e), conferred jurisdiction. Moreover, the court rejected the suggestion that a common law basis for jurisdiction be judicially fashioned.[237]

The Supreme Court affirmed. It first concluded that no federal or state long-arm statute, and no provision of old Rule 4(e), authorized jurisdiction over the defendant. The Court then considered whether, "even if authorization for service of process . . . cannot be found in a statute or rule, such authorization should be created by fashioning a remedy to fill a gap in the Federal Rules."[238] The Court declined this invitation: "We reject the suggestion that we should create a common-law rule authorizing service of process, since we would consider that action unwise, even were it within our power."[239]

Although *Omni* was decided under old Rule 4(e), nothing in the text or drafting history of new Rule 4(k) suggests any different result under the revised Rule.[240] Moreover, *Omni* rested on a general reluctance by federal courts to fashion their own jurisdictional bases, rather than on a specific interpretation of Rule 4(e).[241] It is fairly clear, therefore, that the rule stated in *Omni* remains operative: a federal court generally cannot exercise jurisdiction over a defendant unless one of Rule 4(k)'s jurisdictional grants (or some other legislative authorization) permits it to do so.

d. Due Process Limits: "State" or "National" Contacts?   Even if personal jurisdiction in a federal court is authorized by Rule 4, the Due Process Clause must also be satisfied. As discussed below, the application of due process standards to international cases in federal courts can raise complex issues not present in state court actions.

A recurrent question concerns what territorial unit is relevant for due process purposes — an individual state or the entire United States. The issue arises most frequently in disputes whether a foreign defendant must have "state contacts" with the particular state where a federal court is located, or whether it is sufficient if the defendant has "national

---

235. 484 U.S. 97 (1987). *See Insurance Corp. of Ireland v. Compagnie des Bauxites de Guinee*, 456 U.S. 694, 711 (1982) (Powell, J., concurring) ("As courts of limited jurisdiction, the federal courts possess no warrant to create jurisdictional law of their own.").

236. 7 U.S.C. §1 *et seq.*

237. *See Point Landing, Inc. v. Omni Capital Int'l, Ltd.*, 795 F.2d 415, 423 (5th Cir. 1986) (citing "the unmalleable principle of law that is unyielding to legal blandishments . . . that federal courts . . . must ground their personal jurisdiction on a federal statute or rule"). A dissenting opinion in the Court of Appeals reasoned that, even if no authorization for personal jurisdiction could be found in old Rule 4(e), the federal courts should act to fill the "interstices in the law inadvertently left by legislative enactment," by fashioning a common law basis for service and personal jurisdiction. 794 F.2d at 431-432.

238. 484 U.S. at 103.

239. 484 U.S. at 111.

240. The Advisory Committee Notes to new Federal Rule of Civil Procedure 4(k) cite *Omni* with approval, and, although they do not directly address the point, are generally supportive of the view that Rule 4(k)'s bases for personal jurisdiction are exclusive. *Advisory Committee Notes*, 28 U.S.C.A. Fed. R. Civ. P. 4, at 118.

241. *See* 484 U.S. at 104-105.

contacts" with the entire United States.[242] The same basic question can arise where jurisdiction is based on tag service in the United States or other jurisdictional bases.[243]

The distinction between national and state contacts can have considerable practical importance.[244] As we have already seen, many foreign defendants have fairly significant contacts with the United States as a whole, but do not have substantial contacts with any particular U.S. state.[245] When this is the case, a national contacts test is of great practical import, because it may provide the only means for *any* U.S. court to exercise jurisdiction over the foreign defendant.[246]

2.   Federal Long-Arm Statutes Granting Jurisdiction Based on a Foreign Defendant's National Contacts

Rule 4(k)(1)(D) of the Federal Rules provides that service of a summons (or filing a waiver of service) is "effective to establish jurisdiction over the person of a defendant . . . (D) when authorized by a statute of the United States." Rule 4(k)(1)(D) is a revised version of the pre-1993 Rule 4(e), which also authorized the borrowing of federal jurisdictional statutes.

A number of federal statutes contain provisions addressing issues of personal jurisdiction and service of process. Some of the federal statutes that contain jurisdictional provisions expressly provide for personal jurisdiction based on the defendant's national contacts. The best example of this is the Foreign Sovereign Immunities Act of 1976 ("FSIA"), discussed in Chapter 3 below. Other federal statutes that address personal jurisdiction and service include the Clayton Act, the Securities Act of 1933, the Securities Exchange Act of 1934, RICO, the Federal Interpleader Act, and the Antiterrorism Act.[247] Many of these statutes permit "world-wide" service of process anywhere that the defendant "transacts business" or "may be found."[248] Other federal statutes are limited to "nation-wide" service within the United States.[249]

Both "nation-wide" and "world-wide" service of process provisions have frequently been applied in domestic cases to allow jurisdiction in any U.S. district where the defendant has been served.[250] In addition, some courts have construed these provisions to authorize the use of national contacts tests for purposes of asserting jurisdiction over foreign defendants.[251] Lower courts have almost uniformly rejected due process challenges to the use of a national contacts test in these circumstances.[252] The following excerpt from *Pinker v. Roche Holdings* illustrates this analysis.

---

242. *See infra* pp. 209-214.

243. *See infra* pp. 225-231.

244. In *Nicastro v. J. McIntyre Machinery, Ltd.*, 2011 WL 2518811at *8 (U.S. June 27, 2011), a four-Justice plurality placed great emphasis on this distinction between an individual state and the United States, but the opinion failed to attract a majority.

245. *McCombs v. Cerco Rentals*, 622 S.W.2d 822 (Tenn. Ct. App. 1981); *Gould v. P.T. Krakatau Steel*, 957 F.2d 573 (8th Cir. 1992). *See* Born, *Reflections on Judicial Jurisdiction in International Cases*, 17 Ga. J. Int'l & Comp. L. 1 (1987).

246. *Advisory Committee Notes*, 28 U.S.C.A. Fed. R. Civ. P. 4, 119.

247. *See* 15 U.S.C. §22 (Clayton Act); 15 U.S.C. §77v (federal securities laws); 15 U.S.C. §78aa (federal securities law); 18 U.S.C. §1965 (RICO); 28 U.S.C. §2361; 18 U.S.C. §2334(a) (ATA); 2 J. Moore et al., *Moore's Federal Practice* §4.33 (2d ed. 1988).

248. *See* 15 U.S.C. §22 (Clayton Act); 15 U.S.C. §§77v, 78aa (securities laws). *See infra* pp. 214-215.

249. *See* 18 U.S.C. §1965 (RICO). *See infra* p. 213-214.

250. *E.g., Mississippi Publishing Corp. v. Murphree*, 326 U.S. 438, 442 (1946); *Robertson v. Railroad Labor Bd.*, 268 U.S. 619, 622 (1925); *FTC v. Jim Walter Corp.*, 651 F.2d 251 (5th Cir. 1981).

251. *E.g., Securities Investor Protection Corp. v. Vigman*, 764 F.2d 1309, 1314-1316 (9th Cir. 1985); *Fitzsimmons v. Barton*, 589 F.2d 330 (7th Cir. 1979); *International Controls Corp. v. Vesco*, 490 F.2d 1334 (2d Cir. 1974); *Leasco Data Processing Equip. Corp. v. Maxwell*, 468 F.2d 1326, 1340 (2d Cir. 1972); *infra* pp. 213-214.

252. *See* cases cited *supra* note 251 and *infra* 209-214.

PINKER v. ROCHE HOLDINGS, LTD.
292 F.3d 361 (3d Cir. 2002)

Becker, Circuit Judge. American Depositary Receipts ("ADRs") are financial instruments that allow investors in the United States to purchase and sell stock in foreign corporations in a simpler and more secure manner than trading in the underlying security in a foreign market. Harold Pinker, the plaintiff in this putative securities fraud class action, invested in ADRs of the defendant, Roche Holdings Ltd. ("Roche"), a Swiss corporation. . . . The gravamen of Pinker's action is that he purchased Roche ADRs at a price that was artificially inflated due to the company's misrepresentations about the competitiveness of the vitamin market when in fact its subsidiaries were engaged in a worldwide conspiracy to fix vitamin prices. As the truth about Roche's collusive activity began to emerge, Pinker alleges, the price of Roche ADRs dropped, and Pinker . . . suffered a loss. As a result, Pinker claims, Roche is liable for securities fraud in violation of Section 10(b) of the Securities Exchange Act, and Rule 10b-5, promulgated thereunder by the Securities and Exchange Commission ("SEC"). . . .

Roche is a Swiss holding company that conducts its operations through a network of subsidiary corporations. . . . Pinker alleges that Roche, acting in concert with its subsidiaries, entered into a worldwide conspiracy with certain competitors in the early 1990s to fix prices and allocate market share for bulk vitamins. Pinker's complaint alleges that at the same time it was engaging in this conspiracy, Roche made material misrepresentations and misleading statements indicating that the vitamin market was competitive. Pinker's complaint points to press releases and annual and semi-annual reports issued by Roche in which it described the competition in the vitamin market as, among other things, "fiercely" and "highly" competitive. In the face of this supposed competition, Pinker avers, Roche's statements portrayed it as a company succeeding and excelling through superior business practices when, in fact, its financial success was due to its participation in a collusive scheme. . . . [Pinker relies on Roche's May 20, 1990 announcement that it had reached a settlement with the U.S. Department of Justice under which it and a former company executive agreed to plead guilty to conspiracy to fix prices and allocate market share and Roche agreed to pay a record $500 million fine for its wrongdoing.] . . .

An ADR is a receipt that is issued by a depositary bank that represents a specified amount of a foreign security that has been deposited with a foreign branch or agent of the depositary, known as the custodian. . . . ADRs are tradable in the same manner as any other registered American security, may be listed on any of the major exchanges in the United States or traded over the counter, and are subject to the Securities Act and the Exchange Act. . . . SEC Form F-6 governs the registration of ADRs. Form F-6 requires that the registrant disclose important information related to the issuance of the ADR [and] a description of the ADRs being registered. . . . ADRs that are traded on American securities exchanges must abide by the Exchange Act's periodic reporting requirements. ADRs that are not traded on exchanges, such as Roche's, are not subject to the Exchange Act's reporting requirements, but under SEC Rule 12g3-2(b) the issuer must furnish such annual reports, shareholder communications, and other materials that are required to be prepared pursuant to regulations in its home country. Pursuant to these requirements, Roche filed a Form F-6 registration statement in June 1992 to register 100 million ADRs, and has since filed its annual and semi-annual reports with the SEC in compliance with Rule 12g3-2(b). It is through these annual and semi-annual reports, as well as through press releases, that Pinker alleges that Roche communicated to the investing public its misrepresentations about the competitiveness of the vitamin market from 1996 to 1999. . . .

In a case such as this, where the plaintiff's claim is based on a federal statute authorizing nationwide service of process, 15 U.S.C. §78aa, . . . the relevant forum for analyzing the extent of the defendant's contacts is the United States as a whole. . . . [The aggregation of the national contacts of an alien defendant is not unfair] under the Fifth Amendment in light of the fact that a federal court sits as a unit of the national government and, therefore, the territorial limitations that apply to the exercise of state court jurisdiction — or, for that matter, federal jurisdiction in diversity cases — are inapposite. Where Congress has spoken by authorizing nationwide service of process, therefore, as it has in the Securities Act, the jurisdiction of a federal court need not be confined by the defendant's contacts with the state in which the federal court sits. Following this reasoning, the district courts within this Circuit have repeatedly held that a "national contacts analysis" is appropriate "when appraising personal jurisdiction in a case arising under a federal statute that contains a nationwide service of process provision." *AlliedSignal, Inc. v. Blue Cross of Cal.*, 924 F. Supp. 34, 36 (D.N.J. 1996). . . . [C]onsistent with several of our sister courts of appeals, [we] hold that a federal court's personal jurisdiction may be assessed on the basis of the defendant's national contacts when the plaintiff's claim rests on a federal statute authorizing nationwide service of process. . . .

Once minimum contacts have been established, we assess whether the exercise of personal jurisdiction is consistent with "traditional notions of fair play and substantial justice." *Int'l Shoe*, 326 U.S. at 316.[253] In the context of state courts, the Supreme Court has stated that this inquiry requires evaluating "the burden on the defendant, the forum State's interest in adjudicating the dispute, the plaintiff's interest in obtaining convenient and effective relief, the interstate judicial system's interest in obtaining the most effective resolution of controversies, and the shared interests of the several States in furthering fundamental substantive social policies." *Burger King*, 471 U.S. at 477. In the federal court context, the inquiry will be slightly different, taking less account of federalism concerns and focusing more on the national interest in furthering the policies of the law(s) under which the plaintiff is suing.

Pinker's complaint alleges that Roche sponsored an ADR facility in the United States in 1992; that these ADRs "were actively traded on the over the counter market;" and that "the average daily trading volume of Roche ADRs during the Class Period was about 25,000 ADRs." . . . The complaint also alleges, as noted above, that Roche made a series of fraudulent statements in various reports and media releases that had the effect of

---

253. To be sure, there has been some debate as to whether this second prong of the *International Shoe* analysis ought to apply in the context of a federal statute authorizing nationwide service of process. *Compare, e.g., Vigman,* 764 F.2d at 1315-1316 (requiring only minimum contacts), *with Republic of Panama,* 119 F.3d at 945 (requiring that the "constitutional notions of fairness and reasonableness" be met). This Court has not issued an authoritative ruling on the matter, although we have hinted that a fairness analysis consisting of more than an assessment of the defendant's national contacts would be appropriate. *See In re Real Estate,* 869 F.2d at 766 n.6. Because the plaintiff has not objected to the application of a "fair play and substantial justice" analysis, we will assume, without deciding, that such an analysis is appropriate in this context.

It is important to note that the application of a "fair play and substantial justice" test has generated the most controversy in cases in which a defendant has contested the jurisdiction of the particular district court in which he was being sued in addition to, or rather than, his contacts with the nation as a whole, on the basis that the forum was a particularly unfair one. Here, by contrast, Roche does not contend that being sued in the District of New Jersey is any more unfair than being sued anywhere else in the United States. Rather, its argument focuses on its lack of sufficient contacts with the United States as a whole. Consequently, our assessment of the "fair play and substantial justice" prong need not concern itself with the propriety of litigating this action in the District Court of New Jersey vis-à-vis other district courts throughout the nation. *Cf. Max Daetwyler,* 762 F.2d at 294 & n.5 ("[A]n alien defendant's preference for a particular state as a more or less convenient forum generally [should not] rise to the level of a constitutional objection.").

artificially inflating its ADR price. Although the complaint does not specify to whom the press releases were addressed, it does allege that the releases "were carried by national newswires," and that "Roche's ADRs were followed by analysts from major brokerages. . . ."

In our view, by sponsoring an ADR facility, Roche "purposefully avail[ed] itself of the privilege of conducting activities" in the American securities market, and thereby established the requisite minimum contacts with the United States. . . . [S]ponsored ADRs such as Roche's require the issuer to deposit shares with an American branch of a depositary and to enter a deposit agreement with the ADR holders defining the rights of ADR holders and the corresponding duties of the issuer. By sponsoring an ADR, therefore, Roche took affirmative steps purposefully directed at the American investing public. The aim of sponsoring an ADR, after all, is to allow American investors to trade equities of a foreign corporation domestically. Roche, therefore, clearly took "action" — sponsoring an ADR in a deliberate attempt to solicit American capital — "purposefully directed toward the [United States]." *Asahi Metal Indus.*, 480 U.S. at 112. . . .

We also conclude that the exercise of personal jurisdiction over Roche comports with "traditional notions of fair play and substantial justice." Roche submits that because unlisted ADRs are subject only to minimal disclosure requirements under federal securities laws, it is therefore unfair to subject Roche to the disclosure requirements of §10(b). Roche argues that it could not have been expected to know that American investors would assume that its disclosures abided by American standards or that American investors might later claim to have been defrauded under a fraud-on-the-market theory. However, even though Roche's ADRs were unlisted, they were still subject to some reporting requirements — namely, whatever requirements Switzerland imposes. Moreover, while the parties have not addressed the issue, it would appear that the alleged fraudulent misstatements of Roche, being affirmative misrepresentations and not simply material omissions, would violate the disclosure requirements of any securities regulatory regime, including Switzerland's.[254]

Notes on Pinker

1. *International law limits on the use of national contacts test.* As we have seen, international law imposes limits on a court's jurisdiction over a foreign defendant who has no meaningful relationship to the forum. *See supra* pp. 99-101. Does international law restrict a U.S. court's power to base jurisdiction on a foreign defendant's national contacts with the entire United States, rather than its state contacts?

For purposes of international law, the individual States of the Union are generally irrelevant. In the Supreme Court's words, "[f]or local interests, the several States of the Union exist, but for national purposes, embracing our relations with foreign nations, we are but one people, one nation, one power." *Chae Chan Ping v. United States*, 130 U.S. 581, 606 (1889). *See Restatement (Third) Foreign Relations Law* §1 Reporters' Note (1987) ("A state of the United States is not a 'state' under international law. . . . The United States

---

254. Even if Roche is correct that the fraud-on-the-market theory is unique to American law and that, as a Swiss corporation, it could not have expected that its misrepresentations would subject it to liability under this theory, this is a problem that can be addressed by choice-of-law doctrine, for it goes to the merits of the case rather than to the question of personal jurisdiction. *See Burger King*, 471 U.S. at 481-482 ("[C]hoice of law analysis — which focuses on all elements of a transaction, and not simply on the defendant's conduct — is distinct from minimum-contacts jurisdictional analysis — which focuses at the threshold solely on the defendant's purposeful connection to the forum.").

alone, not any of its constituent states, enjoys international sovereignty and nation-hood"). As a consequence, foreign states should have "no basis for complaint under international law when a United States court asserts jurisdiction over a national who has a reasonably close relationship to the United States, even if the foreign national has *no* connections with the state of the Union asserting jurisdiction." Born, *Reflections on Judicial Jurisdiction in International Cases*, 17 Ga. J. Int'l & Comp. L. 1, 37 (1987).

Is this conclusion entirely persuasive? What if different U.S. state courts (*e.g.*, Louisiana and Oregon) would apply significantly different substantive laws and procedural rules? What if this national contacts rule would subject foreign nationals to both great inconvenience and many potential forums from which plaintiffs could choose? Suppose that the EU nations that are subject to Regulation 44/2001 adopted a "Community contacts" test, permitting a U.S. company that had contacts with England to be sued in Greece (notwithstanding its lack of Greek contacts).

2. *Supreme Court treatment of national contacts test.* The Supreme Court has expressly reserved the question whether a national contacts test may constitutionally be applied by a federal court in a federal question case. Thus, in *Asahi Metal Indus. v. Superior Court*, the Court noted:

> We have no occasion here to determine whether Congress could, consistent with the Due Process Clause of the Fifth Amendment, authorize federal court personal jurisdiction over alien defendants based on the aggregate of *national* contacts, rather than on the contacts between the defendant and the State in which the federal court sits. 480 U.S. 102, 113 n.* (1987). *See also Omni Capital Int'l v. Rudolf Wolff & Co.*, 484 U.S. 97, 103-104 n.5 (1987).

3. *Due process limits in federal question cases when a federal jurisdictional grant is relied on.* In considering due process limits on federal court jurisdiction, most authorities have distinguished (a) federal question from diversity cases, and (b) cases where federal long-arm statutes are invoked from those where state long-arm statutes are invoked. In *Pinker*, a federal statute provided the cause of action and a federal long-arm statute was the basis for personal jurisdiction.

(a)   Decisions holding that the Fifth Amendment's Due Process Clause permits national contacts test in federal question cases when a federal jurisdictional grant is relied on. Pinker held that the Fifth Amendment's Due Process Clause permits consideration of a defendant's contacts with the entire United States where federal law claims are asserted and a federal jurisdictional statute is relied on. A number of other lower courts and commentators have agreed. *E.g.*, cases cited *supra* p. 206, note 243; *infra* pp. 210-212. Is this result persuasive? Why should issues of minimum contacts and fairness vary so significantly depending upon whether state or federal courts and claims are concerned? Are not the several states sufficiently important in U.S. legal and economic matters that jurisdiction should depend on state contacts? Will not defendants be subject to identical inconvenience and surprise in both federal and state courts?

(b)   Congress's territorial sovereignty over entire United States. The primary rationale supporting the constitutionality of a national contacts test in a federal court is that Congress and the President—which created the federal courts, federal substantive claims, and federal jurisdictional grants—possess sovereignty over the entire United States. This *national* territorial sovereignty is the equivalent of a *state*'s territorial sovereignty under *Pennoyer, International Shoe*, and *Burnham. See supra* pp. 83-86, 96-99. Thus, just as the Constitution requires minimum contacts with a forum state before a state court can exercise judicial jurisdiction, so it should require minimum contacts *with the United States* before a federal court can assert jurisdiction. Considerable authority supports this

analysis. Several Supreme Court decisions expressly recognized Congress's power to authorize nationwide service of process from federal courts, at a time when such service was deemed sufficient to confer personal jurisdiction. For example, in *United States v. Union Pacific Railroad*, 98 U.S. 569, 603-604 (1878), the Court said that a federal statute permitted service in a federal action anywhere in the United States, not merely in the state where the federal court hearing the case was located: "[t]here is . . . nothing in the Constitution which forbids Congress to enact that [any federal court] . . . shall, by process served anywhere in the United States, have the power to bring before it all the parties necessary to its decision." *See Mississippi Publishing Corp. v. Murphee*, 326 U.S. 438, 442 (1946).

(c) *Role of Fifth Amendment's Due Process Clause.* The foregoing analysis is almost always accompanied by observations that the jurisdiction of federal courts is limited by the Fifth, rather than the Fourteenth, Amendment. *E.g., Quick Technologies, Inc. v. Sage Group plc*, 313 F.3d 338, 344 (5th Cir. 2002); *Trans-Asiatic Oil Ltd. SA v. Apex Oil Co.*, 743 F.2d 956 (1st Cir. 1984); *DeJames v. Magnificence Carriers*, 491 F. Supp. 1276, 1284 (D.N.J. 1980), *aff'd*, 654 F.2d 280 (3d Cir.); *Noble Sec., Inc. v. MIZ Engineering, Ltd.*, 611 F. Supp. 2d 513 (E.D. Va. 2009). Consider, for example, the Advisory Committee Notes to the 1993 revision of Rule 4(k):

> constitutional limitations on the exercise of territorial jurisdiction by federal courts over persons outside the United States . . . arise from the Fifth Amendment rather than from the Fourteenth Amendment. . . . The Fifth Amendment requires that any defendant have affiliating contacts with the United States sufficient to justify the exercise of personal jurisdiction. 28 U.S.C.A. Fed. Rule Civ. Proc. 4, at 118.

It is also argued that the Fifth Amendment's Due Process Clause imposes different limits than the Fourteenth Amendment:

> The principal difference [between Fifth and Fourteenth Amendment due process analysis] is that under the Fifth Amendment the court can consider the defendant's contacts throughout the United States, while under the Fourteenth Amendment only the contacts with the forum state may be considered. *Chew v. Dietrich*, 143 F.3d 24, 28 n.4 (2d Cir. 1998).

(d) *Doubts about role of territorial sovereignty in due process analysis.* Does *Pinker* accept the rationales discussed above for a national contacts test? What implications does that have for a "reasonableness" prong to due process analysis?

As discussed above, *supra* pp. 98-99, dicta in *Compagnie des Bauxites de Guinee* arguably abandons territorial sovereignty in due process analysis, in favor of more flexible notions of "reasonableness" and individual liberty. For courts adopting this conclusion, *see Wichita Federal S. & L. Ass'n v. Landmark Group, Inc.*, 657 F. Supp. 1182, 1194 (D. Kan. 1987) (*Bauxite*'s "rejection of sovereignty as a basis for *in personam* jurisdiction means there is no compelling reason for a court to observe sovereign boundaries"); *Bamford v. Hobbs*, 569 F. Supp. 160, 164-165 (S.D. Tex. 1983).

(e) *Fairness considerations supporting national contacts test.* Territorial sovereignty is not the sole justification that has been advanced for a national contacts test under the Due Process Clause in international cases. First, a national contacts test is sometimes the only way that U.S. jurisdiction can be asserted over a foreign defendant that has substantial U.S. contacts spread thinly over a number of individual states. *E.g., Superior Coal Co. v. Ruhrkohle AG*, 83 F.R.D. 414, 418 n.3 (E.D. Pa. 1979) ("a foreign-based corporation may have substantial contacts diffused throughout the nation to the extent that in no one state do these contacts accumulate sufficiently to allow any state to assume jurisdiction"); *Engineered Sports Products v. Brunswick Corp.*, 362 F. Supp. 722, 728 (D. Utah 1973).

Second, foreign defendants will generally regard the United States as a single nation. It is their *U.S.* contacts, not their *state* contacts, that best reflect their reasonable expectations. And a foreign defendant usually will not face greater or lesser inconvenience by defending in one U.S. state instead of another. "[C]orporations . . . headquartered in foreign lands will usually be no more inconvenienced by a trip to one state [of the Union] than another." *Centronics Data Computer Corp. v. Mannesmann AG,* 432 F. Supp. 659, 663 (D.N.H. 1977). *See Afram Export Corp. v. Metallurgiki Halyps, SA,* 772 F.2d 1358 (7th Cir. 1985) (excerpted above *supra* pp. 163-165).

Third, when a U.S. court exercises jurisdiction over a foreign defendant based on national (instead of state) contacts, it does not ordinarily intrude upon the sovereignty of other U.S. states. It may intrude on the sovereignty of foreign states, but international law does not appear to restrict application of a national contacts test. *See Ferree v. Life Ins. Co. of North America,* 2006 WL 2025012, at *10 (N.D. Ga. 2006); *supra* p. 209.

Are these generalizations necessarily accurate in all cases? Suppose that a Canadian defendant has significant contacts with Maine, but none at all with Louisiana. Should the Due Process Clause permit personal jurisdiction based on national contacts in Louisiana? Recall the two-part due process analysis adopted in *World-Wide Volkswagen* and *Asahi,* which considered reasonableness and fairness to the defendant, as well as territorial sovereignty.

(f) *Decisions holding that the Fifth Amendment's Due Process Clause imposes "fairness" limits on national contacts test in federal courts.* Some courts have concluded that the Fifth Amendment imposes "reasonableness" or "fairness" limits on exercises of jurisdiction. *E.g., Republic of Panama v. BCCI Holdings (Luxembourg) SA,* 119 F.3d 935, 945-948 (11th Cir. 1997); *Horne v. Adolph Coors Co.,* 684 F.2d 255 (3d Cir. 1982); *Kinsey v. Nestor Exploration,* 604 F. Supp. 1365 (E.D. Wash. 1985); *Majer v. Sonex Research, Inc.,* 2006 WL 2038604, at *7 (E.D. Pa. July 19, 2006) (discussing fairness considerations). *Cf. ESAB Group, Inc. v. Centricut, Inc.,* 126 F.3d 617, 626-627 (4th Cir. 1997) (appearing to hold that national contacts test is subject to fairness limits). Under these decisions, a defendant's national contacts can be considered, but due process also requires that the location of the federal court hearing the dispute be "fair." Consider the following explanation of the fairness doctrine:

> [T]he U.S. Supreme Court [has] unequivocally rejected sovereignty as the basis for the Due Process Clause's minimum contacts requirement and corresponding limitations of personal jurisdiction. In *Compagnie des Bauxites de Guinee,* the Court stated that "[t]he personal jurisdiction requirement recognizes and protects an individual liberty interest. It represents a restriction on judicial power not as a matter of sovereignty, but as a matter of individual liberty." The minimum contacts requirement is therefore merely a method to establish whether or not the defendant's Due Process liberty interest in fundamental "fair play and substantial justice" is satisfied. There is no impelling reason to equate traditional fair play and substantial justice to minimum contacts with the nation as a whole. Nor, in light of modern communication and transportation and Congress's express authorization of nationwide service, can fair play and substantial justice turn simply upon whether the Andover defendants must cross a state border to get to the Southern District of Texas. For as another district court once observed, a Portland, Maine defendant forced to litigate in Raleigh, North Carolina must cross twelve state borders, yet travels no farther than an El Paso, Texas defendant forced to litigate in Beaumont, Texas. Since the bounds of fairness do not necessarily run along state borders, the Fifth Amendment's Due Process Clause does not go so far as to require that the Andover defendants have minimum contacts with the State of Texas. *GRM v. Equine Inv. & Mgt. Group,* 596 F. Supp. 307, 314 (S.D. Tex. 1984).

Is this persuasive?

Not all courts have agreed that the Fifth Amendment imposes "reasonableness" limits on assertions of jurisdiction. *See In re Lernout & Hauspie Securities Litig.*, 337 F. Supp. 2d 293, 317-318 & n.13 (D. Mass. 2004) (discussing divergent views on the issue). What does *Pinker* conclude about the applicability of a reasonableness analysis under the Fifth Amendment?

Recall that the reasonableness prong of due process analysis developed in state cases where the Fourteenth Amendment's Due Process Clause supplied the relevant constitutional rule. Is there any principled reason for subjecting exercises of jurisdiction in federal question cases such as *Pinker* to less constitutional scrutiny than cases not involving nationwide contacts tests? Aren't reasonableness limits particularly important in international cases in light of the special burdens on the foreign defendant?

(g) *Effect of* Burnham *on national contacts test.* What effect, if any, does *Burnham, supra* pp. 129-137, have on the argument that fairness restricts the importance of territorial sovereignty? Recall Justice Scalia's plurality opinion (discussed in *CSB, supra* at p. 130), concluding that reasonableness considerations are irrelevant if service is made in the forum. Does *Burnham*'s reaffirmation of territorial sovereignty support an unqualified national contacts test? Or is *Burnham* limited to tag service?

(h) *Effect of* Nicastro *on national contacts test.* Recall that, in *Nicastro*, a plurality of the Court sought to restore sovereignty as the centerpiece of due process analysis. Consistent with this approach, the plurality emphasized that "[b]ecause the United States is a distinct sovereign, a defendant may in principle be subject to the jurisdiction of the courts of the United States but not of any particular State." *Nicastro v. J. McIntyre Machinery, Ltd.*, 2011 WL 2518811 at *8 (U.S. June 27, 2011). Much like the *Burnham* plurality, the *Nicastro* plurality disdained "[f]reeform notions of fundamental fairness divorced from traditional practice." *Id.* at *5. Does *Nicastro* suggest that the territoriality approach of *Burnham* remains central to the due process analysis, or does the *Nicastro* plurality's failure to garner a majority cast doubt on the vitality of notions of territorial sovereignty? Note the *Nicastro* majority's explanation of territorial limits on state sovereignty. What exactly is the source of those limits and what is their relationship to the Due Process Clause?

4. *Interpretation of jurisdictional reach of federal statutes.* Under Rule 4(k)(1)(D), as with old Rule 4(e), federal courts can rely on federal jurisdictional grants. When a federal jurisdictional statute is used, it must be interpreted as a matter of federal law.

(a) *Antitrust and securities laws as statutory bases for national contacts test.* The Clayton Act, 15 U.S.C. §22, has been interpreted by a number of lower courts as authorizing both "world-wide" extraterritorial service and use of a national contacts test. *E.g., In re Automotive Refinishing Paint Antitrust Litig.*, 358 F.3d 288, 297 (3d Cir. 2004); *Access Telecom, Inc. v. MCI Telecomm. Corp.*, 197 F.3d 694, 718 (5th Cir. 1999); *Go-Video, Inc. v. Akai Elec. Co.*, 885 F.2d 1406 (9th Cir. 1989); *Stabilisierungsfonds Fuer Wein v. Kaiser Stuhl Wine Distrib.*, 647 F.2d 200, 204 & n.6 (D.C. Cir. 1981); *In re Polyester Staple Antitrust Litig.*, 2008 WL 906331 (W.D.N.C. 2008). *But see Howard Hess Dental Laboratories, Inc. v. Dentsply Int'l Inc.*, 516 F. Supp. 2d 324, 337-338 (D. Del. 2007) (declining to apply nationwide contacts test to domestic defendant in Clayton Act case); *Emerson Elec. Co. v. Le Carbone Lorraine S.A.*, 500 F. Supp. 2d 437, 456 (D.N.J. 2007) (declining to apply nationwide contacts test to foreign individual (as opposed to foreign corporate) defendant). By contrast, other courts require the plaintiff first to establish venue under the Clayton Act before it can invoke a nationwide contacts test under the worldwide service of process provision. *See Daniel v. American Board of Emergency Medicine*, 428 F.3d 408 (2d Cir. 2005). As in *Pinker*, lower federal courts have also held that the federal securities laws, 15 U.S.C. §§77v and 78aa, authorize a national contacts test in determining jurisdiction over foreigners. *E.g., S.E.C. v. Carillo*, 115 F.3d 1540, 1544 (11th Cir. 1997); *Application to Enforce Admin. Subpoena*

Duces Tecum of the SEC v. Knowles, 87 F.3d 413, 417 (10th Cir. 1996); *Securities Investor Protection Corp. v. Vigman*, 764 F.2d 1309 (9th Cir. 1985); *Bersch v. Drexel Firestone*, 519 F.2d 974 (2d Cir. 1975); *In re Parmalat Securities Litigation*, 414 F. Supp. 2d 428, 442 (S.D.N.Y. 2006).

(b)   *Interpretation of federal statutes containing worldwide service of process provisions to permit national contacts tests.* Some statutes such as the Clayton Act authorize worldwide service of process. Lower courts have, almost without exception held that federal courts may employ a nationwide contacts test to exercise personal jurisdiction under such statutes, *supra* at 212-214. Do such authorizations for *service of process* address the proper contacts standard for *jurisdictional* purposes? *See Leasco Data Processing Equipment Corp. v. Maxwell*, 468 F.2d 1326, 1340 (2d Cir. 1972) ("Although the section does not deal specifically with *in personam* jurisdiction, it is reasonable to infer that Congress meant to assert personal jurisdiction over foreigners not present in the United States to but, of course, not beyond the bounds permitted by the dues process clause of the fifth amendment."). Would it not be entirely possible to permit worldwide *service* of process without meaning to disturb the traditional state contacts approach to *jurisdiction*? On the other hand, why would Congress want the enforcement of a federal statute, in federal court, to depend on state borders? Would such borders provide a measure of predictability and be a reasonable proxy for convenience?

(c)   *Interpretation of federal statutes containing nationwide service provisions to permit national contacts test.* Service of process provisions in other statutes have been interpreted as *not* authorizing service of process outside the United States. *See Nordic Bank plc v. Trend Group*, 619 F. Supp. 542 (S.D.N.Y. 1985) (RICO authorizes nationwide but not extraterritorial service); *Soltex Polymer Corp. v. Fortex Indus.*, 590 F. Supp. 1453 (E.D.N.Y. 1984), *aff'd*, 832 F.2d 1325 (2d Cir. 1987) (same); *Nichols Family Invs., LLC v. Hackenberg*, 2006 WL 1549674 (W.D.N.C. June 1, 2006).

On the other hand, some lower courts (including the court in *Pinker*) have interpreted such statutes to authorize a nationwide contacts test. *See* cases cited at *supra* p. 206, notes 250 and 251; *see FC Inv. Group LC v. IFX Markets, Ltd.*, 529 F.3d 1087, 1099 (D.C. Cir. 2008) (collecting cases and declining to hold that RICO authorizes nationwide contacts test in all circumstances). While *Pinker* concludes that a nationwide service of process provision suffices, why should this be so? Again, nothing in the service-of-process language explicitly addresses the scope of jurisdiction or the proper "contacts" analysis. Moreover, almost by definition, such a statute does not extend to the Constitution's limits. So, even if nationwide contacts analysis is an appropriate default rule in statutes authorizing worldwide service of process, why should the same hold true in statutes that merely authorize nationwide service? Do theories of territorial sovereignty help to supply an answer?

(d)   *Interpretation of federal jurisdictional statutes to permit tag service.* Do statutes permitting nationwide or worldwide service authorize jurisdiction based upon tag service anywhere in the United States? If they extend to the limits of due process, isn't the answer yes after *Burnham*?

5. *Use of national contacts test where federal statute does not address service.* A national contacts test cannot be applied where the plaintiff's claim rested on a federal statute, but where the statute did not contain a nationwide or worldwide service of process provision. *See Omni Capital Int'l v. Rudolf Wolff & Co.*, 484 U.S. 97 (1987) (Commodity Exchange Act contains no service or jurisdictional provision and therefore no national contacts test is authorized by federal law); *Chandler v. Barclays Bank plc*, 898 F.2d 1148 (6th Cir. 1990); *DeJames v. Magnificence Carriers*, 654 F.2d 280 (3d Cir. 1981); *Capitol Records LLC v. Video Egg, Inc.*, 611 F. Supp. 2d 349, 357 (S.D.N.Y. 2009); *Pearson*

Education, Inc. v. Shi, 525 F. Supp. 2d 551, 555 (S.D.N.Y. 2007); *Goss Graphic Systems v. Man Roland Druckmaschinen Aktiengesellschaft,* 139 F. Supp. 2d 1040, 1065 (N.D. Iowa 2001). As discussed below, however, state long-arm statutes might arguably provide a basis for application of a national contacts test, even if no federal statute does. *See infra* pp. 221-224. Additionally, Federal Rule of Civil Procedure 4(k)(2) may also provide a basis for a national contacts test in certain circumstances where the claim arises under federal law. *See infra* pp. 216-231.

6. *Appropriateness of relying on service of process provision to determine relevant forum for contacts analysis.* Lower courts consistently hold that a nationwide contacts analysis is appropriate for federal statutes containing a nationwide or worldwide service of process provision. *See supra* p. 206, notes 250 and 251. But why precisely should the two be connected? Except in cases of tag jurisdiction, aren't service of process and personal jurisdiction discrete inquiries serving discrete purposes? Why do "service of process" provisions in federal statutes provide the necessary legislative authorization to stretch a statute's jurisdictional reach to the constitutional limit? Shouldn't Congress be required either to enact a general federal long-arm statute or to specify in the statute the application of a nationwide contacts test? For a skeptical view of the prevailing orthodoxy, *see Bellaire General Hosp. v. Blue Cross Blue Shield of Michigan,* 97 F.3d 822, 826 (5th Cir. 1996).

7. *Transfers and* **forum non conveniens.** Many authorities adopting a national contacts test have also taken a more lenient view of transfers of venue under 28 U.S.C. §1404 and *forum non conveniens,* discussed *infra* at pp. 371-373. The purpose is to avoid significant inconvenience to defendants subject to a national contacts jurisdictional test. *See Fitzsimmons v. Barton,* 589 F.2d 330, 334-335 (7th Cir. 1979). This is particularly important because the Alien Venue Act makes venue over a foreign defendant proper in any judicial district. *See infra* at pp. 458-459. Suppose that a Mexican defendant has minimum contacts with Arizona (and only Arizona), but that a U.S. plaintiff sues it in Maine, just to make defense difficult. Should the Due Process Clause forbid this? Would the *forum non conveniens* doctrine or §1404 transfers provide sufficient protection?

3. Borrowed State Long-Arm Statutes Under Rule 4(k)(1)(A) and the Due Process Clauses

State long-arm statutes have historically played a central role in defining the jurisdiction of federal district courts, both in diversity and federal question cases. That remains the case. This is because of Rule 4(k)(1)(A), which authorizes federal courts to borrow the jurisdictional powers of the state courts in the state where they are located. Rule 4(k)(1)(A) provides that:

> Service of a summons or filing of a waiver of service is effective to establish jurisdiction over the person of a defendant (A) who could be subjected to the jurisdiction of a court of general jurisdiction in the state in which the district court is located. . . .

Rule 4(k)(1)(A) is the revised version of former Rule 4(e), which continued a longstanding federal practice of "borrowing" state long-arm statutes.[255] Rule 4(k)(1)(A)

---

255. The predecessor to new Rule 4(k)(1)(A) was contained in the second sentence of old Rule 4(e), and authorized a federal court, in diversity of citizenship cases, to "borrow" the long-arm statute of the state in which it is located. Old Rule 4(e) provided that "service may . . . be made under the circumstances and in the manner prescribed in [a] statute" of the state in which the district court is held. *See Point Landing, Inc. v. Omni Capital Int'l, Ltd.,* 795 F.2d 415 (5th Cir. 1986), *aff'd,* 484 U.S. 97 (1987); C. Wright & A. Miller, *Federal Practice and Procedure* §1075 (3d ed. 1998 & Supp. 2010).

permits such borrowing in all cases—including diversity of citizenship, alienage, and federal question matters.[256] In federal question cases, a plaintiff may choose to borrow a state long-arm statute either because the applicable substantive federal statute contains no personal jurisdiction provision[257] or because its jurisdictional provisions do not reach the defendant.[258]

4.   Personal Jurisdiction Under Rule 4(k)(2)

In addition to preserving the historic practice of "borrowing" state long-arm statutes, the 1993 revisions to Rule 4 made a fundamental change to the jurisdiction of federal district courts.[259] As discussed above, prior to 1993, federal courts were generally subject to the same due process limits as state courts when jurisdiction was based on borrowed state long-arm statutes under Rule 4(e).[260] As a result, federal courts generally applied "state contacts" tests either under the applicable state long-arm statute or the Fourteenth Amendment's Due Process Clause. Particularly in federal question cases and actions against foreign defendants, this "lock-step" approach was criticized.[261]

Rule 4(k)(2) significantly extended the jurisdiction of federal courts in federal questions cases. It authorizes federal district courts to exercise personal jurisdiction to the limits of the Constitution, in federal question cases, "over the person of any defendant who is not subject to the jurisdiction of the courts of general jurisdiction of any state." As discussed below, Rule 4(k)(2) was specifically designed for international cases.

The following excerpts illustrate the application of Rule 4(k)(1)(A) and Rule 4(k)(2) in international cases. First, read the text of Rule 4(k) and consider the requirements for each of the Rule's parts to apply. Then, read the excerpt from *United States v. Swiss American Bank,* which interprets Rule 4(k)(1)(A) and Rule 4(k)(2). Finally, reread *Adams v. Unione Mediterranea di Sicurta,* excerpted above, and consider how it addresses issues of general jurisdiction under Rule 4(k)(2).

---

256. It was well settled under old Rule 4(e) that state long-arm statutes could be borrowed in both federal question and diversity cases. *E.g., Omni Capital Int'l, Ltd. v. Rudolf Wolff & Co.,* 484 U.S. 97 (1987); C. Wright & A. Miller, *Federal Practice and Procedure* §1075 (3d ed. 1998 & Supp. 2010). Rule 4(k)(1)(A) produces the same result: nothing in the Rule draws any distinction between federal question and diversity actions, or suggests any change from old Rule 4(e). *See* D. Siegel, *Supplementary Practice Commentaries,* 28 U.S.C.A. Fed. R. Civ. P. 4, at C4-33 (1994 Supp.). For recent examples of federal courts borrowing state long-arm statutes in diversity cases, *see, e.g., Melea, Ltd. v. Jawer SA,* 511 F.3d 1060, 1065 (10th Cir. 2007); *Sole Resort, S.A. de C.V. v. Allure Resorts Mgmt., LLC,* 450 F.3d 100 (2d Cir. 2006); *Ellan Corp. v. Dongkwang Int'l Co.,* 2010 U.S. Dist. LEXIS 34458 (S.D.N.Y. 2010).

257. *See, e.g., Gessler v. Sobieski Destylarnia S.A.,* 2010 U.S. Dist. LEXIS 71414 (S.D.N.Y. 2010); *Gucci Am., Inc. v. Frontline Processing Corp.,* 2010 U.S. Dist. LEXIS 62654 (S.D.N.Y. 2010). Many federal statutes that create private causes of action do not address the issue of personal jurisdiction. *See supra* pp. 203-205; *Omni Capital Int'l, Ltd. v. Rudolf Wolff & Co.,* 484 U.S. 97 (1987).

258. *See Delong Equip. Co. v. Washington Mills Abrasive Co.,* 840 F.2d 843 (11th Cir. 1988) (using federal nationwide service provisions of Clayton Act as to corporate defendants and state long-arm statute as to individual defendants (who were not covered by Clayton Act's jurisdictional grant)); *Karsten Mfg. Corp. v. United States Golf Ass'n,* 728 F. Supp. 1429 (D. Ariz. 1990) (same).

259. For commentary on Rule 4(k)(2), *see* Burbank, *The United States' Approach to International Civil Litigation: Recent Developments in Forum Selection,* 19 U. Pa. J. Int'l Econ. L. 1 (1998); Kelleher, *The December 1993 Amendments to the Federal Rules of Civil Procedure—A Critical Analysis,* 12 Touro L. Rev. 7, 35 (1995).

260. *See supra* pp. 203-204, note 255.

261. *See* authorities cited *supra* pp. 121-122.

FEDERAL RULES OF CIVIL PROCEDURE
Rules 4(k)(1)(A) and 4(k)(2) [excerpted in Appendix C]

UNITED STATES v. SWISS AMERICAN BANK, LTD.
191 F.3d 30 (1st Cir. 1999)

SELYA, CIRCUIT JUDGE. [The United States brought a civil forfeiture action against several foreign banks to recover funds it claimed to own under a plea bargain with a criminal defendant. The banks argued that the district court lacked personal jurisdiction over them. The district court agreed and dismissed the action. On appeal, the Government argued, in part, that Rule 4(k)(2) supplied a basis for personal jurisdiction over the banks.]

A court [may not exercise jurisdiction] unless it possesses statutory authorization. . . . This authorization may derive from a federal statute, *see, e.g.*, 15 U.S.C. §22 (providing for worldwide service of process on certain corporate antitrust defendants), or from a state statute of general application, *see, e.g.*, Mass. Gen. Laws ch. 223A, §3 (providing "long-arm" jurisdiction). A state long-arm statute furnishes a mechanism for obtaining personal jurisdiction in federal as well as state courts. *See* Fed. R. Civ. P. 4(k)(1)(A).

[The Court first considered Rule 4(k)(1)(A) and the Massachusetts long-arm statute.] Because the United States sued in the District of Massachusetts, Rule 4(k)(1)(A) permits recourse to the Massachusetts long-arm statute. . . . Section 3(d) of the Massachusetts long-arm statute authorizes personal jurisdiction over one who causes "tortious injury in this commonwealth by an act or omission outside this commonwealth if he regularly does or solicits business, or engages in any other persistent course of conduct, or derives substantial revenue from goods used or consumed or services rendered, in this commonwealth." . . . [T]here is no showing here that the United States suffered tortious injury *in Massachusetts*. The legal injury occasioned by the tort of conversion is deemed to occur where the actual conversion takes place. In this instance, the bank accounts were depleted and the forfeited assets redirected in Antigua, and, thus, the claimed injury occurred there. By like token, since the government's claim of unjust enrichment is essentially a claim for restitution based on the alleged conversion, the legal injury stemming from it also must be presumed to have taken place in Antigua. . . .

[T]he government replies that the forfeiture order was issued in Massachusetts. Fair enough — but this fact at most demonstrates that, upon the occurrence of the alleged conversion and the consequent unjust enrichment, the United States felt the effects of a tortious injury in the forum state. And since §3(d) requires that the injury itself occur in Massachusetts, and does not apply merely because the plaintiff feels the effects of a tortious injury there, these observations effectively end the matter. . . .

[The Court next considered Rule 4(k)(2).] In limited circumstances, the requisite authorization can be provided by Rule 4(k)(2), which functions as a sort of federal long-arm statute. When a plaintiff depends upon this recently adopted rule to serve as the necessary statutory authorization for the exercise of specific personal jurisdiction, the constitutional requirements are the same as those limned above, but the analytic exercises are performed with reference to the United States as a whole, rather than with reference to a particular state. The defendant's national contacts take center stage because the rule applies only to situations in which federal courts draw jurisdictional authority from the federal sovereign (unreinforced by "borrowed" state statutes), and, thus, the applicable constitutional requirements devolve from the Fifth rather than the Fourteenth

Amendment. *See* Born & Vollmer, *The Effect of the Revised Federal Rules of Civil Procedure on Personal Jurisdiction, Service, and Discovery in International Cases,* 150 F.R.D. 221, 225 (1993). . . . [Rule 4(k)(2)'s] fabric contains three strands: (1) the plaintiff's claim must be one arising under federal law; (2) the putative defendant must be beyond the jurisdictional reach of any state court of general jurisdiction; and (3) the federal courts' exercise of personal jurisdiction over the defendant must not offend the Constitution or other federal law. . . .

[First, by] its terms, Rule 4(k)(2) requires that the putative defendant not be subject to jurisdiction in any state court of general jurisdiction. The government argues that this requirement encompasses both subject matter and personal jurisdiction, and that, therefore, it can satisfy the negation requirement simply by showing that the state courts have no subject matter jurisdiction over a particular cause of action. Building on this porous foundation, the government then argues that 28 U.S.C. §1345 — the statute under which it brought this suit — grants exclusive subject matter jurisdiction to the federal courts.[262] We find this reasoning unconvincing. . . . [W]e consider it pellucid that Rule 4(k)(2)'s reference to defendants who are "not subject to the jurisdiction" refers to the absence of personal jurisdiction. . . . Service is the traditional means by which a court establishes personal jurisdiction over a defendant. Section (k) of Rule 4 governs the circumstances in which service (or waiver of service) will suffice to confer personal jurisdiction. The rule's two subsections both speak of the means by which "jurisdiction over the person" of a defendant can be established. In this setting, it strains credulity to suggest that the mention of the unmodified word "jurisdiction" should be construed as anything other than a reference to "personal jurisdiction," when that understanding of the term makes reasonable sense in application (as it does here). . . . *See, e.g., World Tanker Carriers Corp. v. MV Ya Mawlaya,* 99 F.3d 717, 720 (5th Cir. 1996). . . .

The advisory committee's explanation of the rationale behind the adoption of Rule 4(k)(2) cinches matters. The drafters created this proviso to deal with a gap in personal jurisdiction noted by the Supreme Court in *Omni Capital Int'l, Ltd. v. Rudolf Wolff & Co.,* 484 U.S. 97, 111 (1987). Before Rule 4(k)(2) was conceived, federal courts "borrowed" from state law when a federal statute did not otherwise provide a mechanism for service of process (regardless of the state courts' subject matter jurisdiction). Accordingly, foreign defendants who lacked single-state contacts sufficient to bring them within the reach of a given state's long-arm statute (whether by reason of the paucity of the contacts or of limitations built into the statute itself), but who had enough contacts with the United States as a whole to make personal jurisdiction over them in a United States court constitutional, could evade responsibility for civil violations of federal laws that did not provide specifically for service of process. To close this loophole, the drafters designed the new Rule 4(k)(2) to function as a species of federal long-arm statute. The rule's final clause, restricting its application to those cases in which the putative defendant "is not subject to the jurisdiction of the courts of general jurisdiction of any state" works to cabin the rule's sweep and ensure its application only in the relatively narrow range of cases identified by the *Omni* Court (in which the states' personal jurisdiction rules prove impuissant). The government's self-serving interpretation of the term "jurisdiction," as used here, would extend the rule's scope well beyond its intended purpose and, in the bargain, would allow plaintiffs with claims falling within exclusive federal jurisdiction

---

262. The statute reads in pertinent part: "Except as otherwise provided by Act of Congress, the district courts shall have original jurisdiction of all civil actions, suits or proceedings commenced by the United States." 28 U.S.C. §1345.

statutes complete discretion to forum-shop without any regard for concentrated contacts. . . .

The government's better argument is that its case falls within the limits of Rule 4(k)(2) even when the rule is interpreted — as it must be — to require negation of personal jurisdiction over the defendant in any state court. The defendants' rejoinder is that, while the government alleged in its complaint that Rule 4(k)(2) supplied the necessary means for obtaining personal jurisdiction, it failed to plead or prove facts demonstrating the absence of personal jurisdiction over the defendants throughout the fifty states. . . .

The defendants (and the district court) certainly are correct in their insistence that a plaintiff ordinarily must shoulder the burden of proving personal jurisdiction over the defendant. Some district courts, relying on this shibboleth, have assigned outright to plaintiffs the burden of proving the Rule 4(k)(2) negation requirement. This paradigm in effect requires a plaintiff to prove a negative fifty times over — an epistemological quandary which is compounded by the fact that the defendant typically controls much of the information needed to determine the existence and/or magnitude of its contacts with any given jurisdiction. There is a corresponding problem with assigning the burden of proof on the Rule 4(k)(2) negation requirement to defendants: doing so threatens to place a defendant in a "Catch-22" situation, forcing it to choose between conceding its potential amenability to suit in federal court (by denying that any state court has jurisdiction over it) or conceding its potential amenability to suit in some identified state court. . . .

The architects of the rule — and Congress, by adopting it — clearly intended to close the gap identified by the *Omni* Court and to ensure that persons whose contacts with this country exceeded the constitutional minimum could not easily evade civil liability in the American justice system. . . . In our view, this core purpose can be achieved much more salubriously by crafting a special burden-shifting framework. To accomplish the desired end without placing the judicial thumb too heavily on the scale, we will not assign the burden of proof on the negation issue to either party in a monolithic fashion. . . . We hold that a plaintiff who seeks to invoke Rule 4(k)(2) must make a prima facie case for the applicability of the rule. This includes a tripartite showing (1) that the claim asserted arises under federal law, (2) that personal jurisdiction is not available under any situation-specific federal statute, and (3) that the putative defendant's contacts with the nation as a whole suffice to satisfy the applicable constitutional requirements. The plaintiff, moreover, must certify that, based on the information that is readily available to the plaintiff and his counsel, the defendant is not subject to suit in the courts of general jurisdiction of any state. If the plaintiff makes out his prima facie case, the burden shifts to the defendant to produce evidence which, if credited, would show either that one or more specific states exist in which it would be subject to suit or that its contacts with the United States are constitutionally insufficient. *See* Burbank, *The United States' Approach to International Civil Litigation: Recent Developments in Forum Selection*, 19 U. Pa. J. Int'l Econ. L. 1, 13 (1998). Should the defendant default on its burden of production, the trier may infer that personal jurisdiction over the defendant is not available in any state court of general jurisdiction. If, however, the defendant satisfies its second-stage burden of production, then the aforementioned inference drops from the case.

What happens next depends on how the defendant satisfies its burden. If the defendant produces evidence indicating that it is subject to jurisdiction in a particular state, the plaintiff has three choices: he may move for a transfer to a district within that state, or he may discontinue his action (preliminary, perhaps, to the initiation of a suit in the courts of the identified state), or he may contest the defendant's proffer. If the plaintiff elects the last-mentioned course, the defendant will be deemed to have waived any claim that it is not subject to personal jurisdiction in the courts of general jurisdiction of any state other than the state or states which it has identified, and the plaintiff, to fulfill the negation requirement, must prove that the defendant is not subject to suit in the identified forum(s). Of course, the defendant may satisfy its burden of production by maintaining that it cannot constitutionally be subjected to jurisdiction in any state court. In that event, the defendant will be deemed to have conceded the negation issue, and the plaintiff, to succeed in his Rule 4(k)(2) initiative, need only prove that his claim arises under federal law and that the defendant has contacts with the United States as a whole sufficient to permit a federal court constitutionally to exercise personal jurisdiction over it. . . .

[Second, the Court turned to the "arising under" federal law requirement.] We begin with bedrock: a case in which the rule of decision must be drawn from federal common law presents a uniquely federal question, and, thus, comes within the original subject matter jurisdiction of the federal courts. Here, the United States seizes upon this principle in an effort to fulfil Rule 4(k)(2)'s "arising under" requirement. It argues vigorously that its case is founded on, and should be decided according to, federal common law. The defendants demur. They contend that this is a garden-variety tort and/or breach of contract case, governed by state law.

There are good arguments on both sides. On the one hand, it is beyond cavil that federal common law sometimes may be fashioned by federal courts to protect the proprietary interest of the federal sovereign. On the other hand, it is equally true that the power to create federal common law should be used sparingly, so as not to intrude upon areas like tort and contract that are traditionally within the states' bailiwick. . . . [T]he proper mode of analysis for questions of this kind is binary. This two-part approach involves what may be characterized as the source question and the substance question. The former asks: should the source of the controlling law be federal or state? The latter (which comes into play only if the source question is answered in favor of a federal solution) asks: should the court, in defining the substance of the rule to be applied in the particular situation, adopt state law as a proxy for an independent federal common law rule, or alternatively, fashion a uniform federal rule? . . .

[T]he key determinant must be the strength of the relevant federal interest. The government touts the federal interest here as having multiple dimensions, *e.g.*, protecting its property interest in funds forfeited in consequence of a federal criminal prosecution, validating an order of a federal court, and safeguarding federal hegemony in foreign affairs. The most commonplace of these is the government's property interest. That type of federal interest formed the basis for the invocation of a federal source in cases such as *Kimbell Foods*, 440 U.S. at 726-27, and [*Clearfield Trust Co. v. United States*, 318 U.S. 363 (1943)]. This type of interest also led the Court to designate a federal source of law for construing government contracts. . . . *See also Banco Nacional de Cuba v. Sabbatino*, 376 U.S. 398, 425 (1964) (discussing federal government's exclusive power to control the foreign relations of the United States) [excerpted *infra* pp. 801-808]. . . . [W]e hold that, when the United States sues to assert its rights against an alleged converter to recoup assets (or obtain the value of assets) forfeited to it, the rights that it has acquired find their roots in, and must be adjudicated in accordance with, a federal source. . . .

[Third,] the government must make one additional showing to gain access to Rule 4(k)(2): that the defendants have adequate contacts with the United States as a whole to support personal jurisdiction and that an assertion of jurisdiction over them would be reasonable. The government tried to make this showing below, but requested jurisdictional discovery to permit it to marshal the necessary proof. . . . The district court denied the motion for limited discovery on the ground that the government had failed to negate state court jurisdiction. Our holding today . . . undermines the rationale for the district court's decision. We therefore vacate the denial of the government's motion for jurisdictional discovery. On remand, the court must reevaluate the government's request.

ADAMS v. UNIONE MEDITERRANEA DI SICURTA

364 F.3d 646 (5th Cir. 2004) [excerpted above at pp. 121-122]

Notes on Rule 4(k), **Swiss American Bank,** *and* **Adams**

1. *Rule 4(k)(1)(A) in historical perspective.* Prior to the enactment of Rule 4(k)(1)(A), Rule 4(e) governed the borrowing of state long-arm statutes. *See supra* pp. 203-205. Rule 4(e) provided that "service may . . . be made under the circumstances and in the manner prescribed in [a] statute [of the state in which the district court sits.]" Broadly speaking, the jurisdiction of federal district courts was defined by the local long-arm statutes in the states where they were located.

Rule 4(e) was replaced by Rule 4(k) in 1993. As noted above, new Rule 4(k)(1)(A) continued the historic pattern of borrowing state long-arm statutes to provide the basis for personal jurisdiction in federal courts. Like old Rule 4(e), Rule 4(k)(1)(A) permits federal courts to borrow state long-arm statutes in both diversity and federal question cases. Lower courts have routinely applied Rule 4(k)(1)(A) in international cases. *See United States v. Botefuhr,* 309 F.3d 1263, 1271 (10th Cir. 2002); *ALS Scan, Inc. v. Digital Serv. Consultants, Inc.,* 293 F.3d 707, 710 (4th Cir. 2002); *Glencore Grain Rotterdam BV v. Shivnath Rai Harnarain Co.,* 284 F.3d 1114, 1123 (9th Cir. 2002); *Central States, Southeast & Southwest Areas Pension Fund v. Reimer Express World Corp.,* 230 F.3d 934, 940 (7th Cir. 2000).

2. *National contacts standard for personal jurisdiction under old Rule 4(e).* Lower courts divided over whether old Rule 4(e) precluded jurisdiction by a federal court where a state court could not, in identical circumstances, assert jurisdiction because of due process constraints. In diversity actions, virtually all lower courts concluded that it would be "anomalous" for a federal court "to utilize a state long-arm rule to authorize service of process in a manner that the state body enacting the rule could not constitutionally authorize." *DeJames v. Magnificence Carriers, Inc.,* 654 F.2d 280, 284 (3d Cir. 1981).

In federal question cases, however, courts were divided. Some insisted on a "lock-step" approach that limited federal court jurisdiction to precisely that which state courts could exercise. *See In re Damodar Bulk Carriers, Ltd.,* 903 F.2d 675, 679 n.5 (9th Cir. 1990); *DeJames v. Magnificence Carriers, Inc.,* 491 F. Supp. 1276, 1283 & n.3 (D.N.J. 1980) (refusing to permit national contacts based on state long-arm because "[t]he power of the State of New Jersey . . . is still limited by the due process requirements of the fourteenth amendment"); *Amburn v. Harold Forster Indus. Ltd.,* 423 F. Supp. 1302, 1305 (E.D. Mich. 1976) ("It remains, however, a state statute and the power of the State of Michigan is limited by the due process requirements of the Fourteenth Amendment."). Other courts reached opposite conclusions, holding that Rule 4(e) allowed federal courts, if the Fifth Amendment's Due Process Clause permitted, to exercise jurisdiction beyond the limits which a state court could. *See Handley v. Indiana & Michigan Elec. Co.,* 732 F.2d 1265 (6th Cir. 1984); *United Rope Distributors, Inc. v. Seatriumph Marine Corp.,* 930 F.2d 532 (7th Cir. 1991); *Cryomedics, Inc. v. Spembly, Ltd.,* 397 F. Supp. 287, 290 (D. Conn. 1975) ("[w]hen a federal court is asked to exercise personal jurisdiction over an alien defendant sued on a *claim* arising out of a federal law, jurisdiction may appropriately be determined on the basis of the alien's aggregated contacts with the United States as a whole, regardless of whether the contacts with the state in which the district court sits would be sufficient if considered alone"). Keep these decisions in mind as you consider how new Rule 4(k) deals with similar issues.

3. *Interpreting state long-arm statutes that are borrowed under Rule 4.* As *Swiss American Bank* illustrates, a federal court cannot exercise personal jurisdiction under Rule 4(k)(1)(A) unless the "borrowed" state long-arm authorizes an assertion of jurisdiction. That is clear from the language of Rule 4(k)(1)(A), and it was black letter-law under old Rule 4(e). *See Omni Capital Int'l v. Rudolf Wolff & Co.*, 484 U.S. 97 (1987); *supra* pp. 204-205.

(a)   State court interpretations of state long-arm statutes binding on federal court. In interpreting a borrowed state long-arm statute, federal courts are generally bound by the local state courts' statutory interpretations. *See supra* pp. 82-83. In the context of international litigation, however, that statement can conceal significant complexities. In particular, (i) as a matter of statutory interpretation, is a state long-arm statute meant to permit inquiry into a defendant's national contacts, and (ii) as a matter of Fourteenth Amendment due process analysis, can a state long-arm statute permit inquiry into national contacts?

(b)   State long-arm statutes extending to the limits of the U.S. Constitution. Some state long-arm statutes expressly grant jurisdiction to the full extent permitted by the U.S. Constitution. *See supra* pp. 204-205; Gen. Laws. R.I. §9-5-33(a) ("every case not contrary to the provisions of the Constitution or laws of the United States"). Many other state long-arm statutes extend by implication to the limits of the U.S. Constitution. *See supra* pp. 204-205.

Should state long-arm statutes that extend expressly or impliedly to the U.S. Constitution's limits be interpreted as authorizing application of a national contacts test? Some courts have answered this in the affirmative. For example, in *Cryomedics, Inc. v. Spembly, Ltd.*, 397 F. Supp. 287 (D. Conn. 1975), the district court held that Connecticut's long-arm statute permitted use of a national contacts test. Although Connecticut's long-arm statute did not expressly permit a national contacts inquiry, the district court emphasized that the statute had been interpreted by Connecticut courts as authorizing jurisdiction to the fullest extent of the Due Process Clause.

By contrast, in *Wells Fargo & Co. v. Wells Fargo Express Co.*, 556 F.2d 406 (9th Cir. 1977), the court described a provision in California's long-arm statute, authorizing jurisdiction to the limits of the U.S. Constitution, as an example of a statute that would support application of a national contacts test. *Wells Fargo* also held that, in contrast to California's statute, Nevada's long-arm statute did not authorize the use of a national contacts test. The court reached this result even though Nevada courts had interpreted the Nevada long-arm statute as permitting jurisdiction to the limits of the Due Process Clause. *Wells Fargo* specifically rejected *Cryomedics'* interpretation of the similar Connecticut statute.

Which court's analysis of the local long-arm statute is more persuasive — *Cryomedics* or *Wells Fargo*?

4. *"Lock-step" application of state long-arm statutes under Rule 4(k)(1)(A) in diversity actions.* Does the language of Rule 4(k)(1)(A) require a lock-step approach to state long-arm statutes? The Rule provides that a district court may exercise jurisdiction over a defendant "who could be subjected to the jurisdiction of a court of general jurisdiction in the state in which the district court is located." How does this compare with the language of old Rule 4(e)?

Virtually all courts conclude that, in diversity actions, Rule 4(k)(1)(A) requires application of state long-arm statutes in a "lock-step" fashion, with a state contacts standard under the Fourteenth Amendment. *See, e.g., Bank Brussels Lambert v. Fiddler Gonzalez & Rodriguez*, 305 F.3d 120, 124 (2d Cir. 2002); *In re Terrorist Attacks on September 11, 2001*, 349 F. Supp. 2d 765, 804 (S.D.N.Y. 2005); *Kohler Co. v. Titon Indus., Inc.*, 948 F. Supp. 815 (E.D. Wis. 1996) ("A federal court sitting in diversity acts as the state's agent in applying state law. . . . Thus, because a state court's jurisdiction would be limited by the Due Process Clause of the Fourteenth Amendment, the jurisdiction of a federal court sitting in diversity likewise is limited by the Fourteenth Amendment."); *In re Automotive Refinishing Paint Antitrust Litig.*, 229 F.R.D. 482, 487-490 (E.D. Pa. 2005). *See also United Rope Distributors, Inc. v. Seatriumph Marine Corp.*, 930 F.2d 532, 535-536 (7th Cir. 1991) ("Federal courts accordingly absorb the 'whole law' of the states, including limitations on personal jurisdiction"). Indeed, most courts assume without discussion that a state contacts test is applicable. If a *federal* court hears a case, why should *federal due process* analysis be affected by the state law character of the underlying substantive rights or the long-arm statute? Does anything in the rules, the Constitution, or the Supreme Court's jurisprudence support these distinctions? *See Stafford v. Briggs*, 444 U.S. 527, 554 (1980) (Stewart, J., dissenting) ("Due process requires only certain minimum contacts between the defendant and *the sovereign that has created the court*").

5. ***Application of state long-arm statutes under Rule 4(k)(1)(A) in federal question actions.*** As noted above, Rule 4(k)(1)(A) provides for borrowing state long-arm statutes in federal question, as well as diversity, cases. For example, in *Swiss American Bank*, the Government brought its claims under federal common law. *See also Sunward Electronics, Inc. v. McDonald*, 362 F.3d 17, 22 (2d Cir. 2004) (Lanham Act); *Glencore Grain Rotterdam BV v. Shivnath Rai Harnarain Co.*, 284 F.3d 1114, 1123 (9th Cir. 2002) (FAA); *Kohler Co. v. Titon Indus., Inc.*, 948 F. Supp. 815 (E.D. Wis. 1996) (Lanham Act). In such cases, a recurrent issue under Rule 4(k)(1)(A) has been whether a lock-step approach to state long-arm statutes applies in federal question cases, as well as in diversity actions. As discussed below, lower courts have continued to reach divergent conclusions under Rule 4(k)(1)(A) on this issue, just as they did under old Rule 4(e).

(a) *Lock-step approach under Rule 4(k)(1)(A) to state long-arm statutes and Fourteenth Amendment in federal question cases.* Note that the Court in *Swiss American Bank* looks to the terms of the Massachusetts long-arm statute in determining the reach of the federal district court's personal jurisdiction under Rule 4(k)(1)(A). That is an express requirement of Rule 4(k)(1)(A)'s authorization of jurisdiction over any defendant "who could be subjected to the jurisdiction of a court of general jurisdiction in the state in which the district court is located"; unless the state long-arm statute authorizes jurisdiction over a defendant, then Rule 4(k)(1)(A) does nothing to grant jurisdiction. Thus, in *Swiss American Bank*, the fact that the Massachusetts long-arm statute did not grant jurisdiction meant that Rule 4(k)(1)(A) did not authorize the federal district court to exercise jurisdiction. *See also Impact Productions, Inc. v. Impact Productions, LLC*, 341 F. Supp. 2d 1186, 1189 (D. Colo. 2004).

Suppose, however, that a state long-arm statute does purport to grant jurisdiction over a defendant, but that the Due Process Clause of the Fourteenth Amendment forbids the exercise of jurisdiction. Most typically, this will be because the state long-arm statute authorizes jurisdiction over the defendant, but a state contacts test under the Fourteenth Amendment forbids the exercise of jurisdiction. In these circumstances, will the jurisdictional authorization granted to federal courts by Rule 4(k)(1)(A) be limited by the Fourteenth Amendment's state contacts test, or does it extend to the limits permitted by the Fifth Amendment's national contacts test?

Lower courts have reached divergent results in answering the foregoing question. A number of courts have concluded that a state contacts test must be applied, even in federal question cases. *See Red Wing Shoe Co., Inc. v. Hockerson-Halberstadt, Inc.*, 148 F.3d 1355, 1358 n.*. (Fed. Cir. 1998) ("[W]hen a federal court asserts personal jurisdiction based on a state's long-arm statute, as opposed to a federal statute or rule, the Due Process Clause of the Fourteenth Amendment also comes into play. Because the Fourteenth

Amendment constrains the reach of a state's long-arm statute, it also constrains the reach of a federal court that relies on such a statute."); *Kohler Co. v. Titon Indus., Inc.*, 948 F. Supp. 815 (E.D. Wis. 1996); *L.H. Carbide*, 852 F. Supp. at 1431. Consider the following explanations of this result:

> Because Rule 4(k)(1)(A) delimits the scope of effective federal service in terms of the limits on state court jurisdiction, our inquiry into the federal court's jurisdiction pursuant to Rule 4(k)(1)(A) incorporates the Fourteenth Amendment due process standard, even though that Amendment applies of its own force only to states. *ESAB Group, Inc. v. Centricut, Inc.*, 126 F.3d 617, 622-23 (4th Cir. 1997).

Is this persuasive? What language in Rule 4(k)(1)(A) requires that the Fourteenth Amendment be applied to limit the extent of federal court jurisdiction? Is it the fact that Rule 4(k)(1)(A)'s authorization is limited to "the jurisdiction of a court of general jurisdiction in the state" where the federal court is located? When Rule 4(k)(1)(A) refers to "the jurisdiction" of state courts, does it mean the jurisdiction that is legislatively granted, or the jurisdiction that remains after federal constitutional constraints are applied? How much sense does it really make to apply the federal Constitution's constraints on *state* courts to *federal* courts? More fundamentally, how much sense does it make to apply constraints on state court jurisdiction to a federal court in a federal question case? Can the rulemakers and Congress have intended this?

   (b) *Application of national contacts test under Rule 4(k)(1)(A) in federal question cases.* Other lower courts have concluded that federal courts are not obliged to apply state long-arm statutes in a lock-step fashion in federal question cases. Consider the following:

> May a state law, constitutionally insufficient to authorize jurisdiction in state court, supply the necessary basis of jurisdiction in federal court? The apparent oddity of a law being unconstitutional in the state forum and constitutional in the federal one need detain us only briefly. Courts often say that laws are constitutional in one application and unconstitutional in another. "Facial" unconstitutionality (to use the entrenched but maladroit metaphor) is the exception. No one doubts that [the local state long-arm statute] may be applied to some defendants consistent with the Constitution, while the due process clause blocks its application to others. So too [the long-arm statute] may be constitutional to the extent Fed. R. Civ. P. 4(e) absorbs its terms as the fulcrum of federal power, even though the state may not hale the party into its own courts. *United Rope Distributors, Inc. v. Seatriumph Marine Corp.*, 930 F.2d 527 (7th Cir. 1991) (decision predating the 1993 amendments to the Federal Rules).

And

> When exercising the power of the national sovereign, logic suggests that a federal court is not limited by the same constitutional concerns that limit the power of a state sovereign. Of course, a forum state's long-arm statute must still be satisfied. That is the primary means by which a federal court acquires jurisdiction over a defendant. But once the requirements of the long-arm statute are met, the only due process concern should be whether the defendant has sufficient national contacts such that the exercise of jurisdiction by the nation's court under the nation's laws does not offend traditional notions of fair play and substantial justice. *Hayeland v. Jaques*, 847 F. Supp. 630, 634 (E.D. Wis. 1994).

Consider again why Congress would subject federal courts to a constitutional limitation that everyone recognizes does not, as a matter of Fifth Amendment doctrine, apply to them? Do principles of federalism, forum shopping, or fundamental fairness help to supply an answer?

6. Due process limits on national contacts test in state courts. Suppose a *state* court relied on a defendant's national contacts in a case involving substantive state law claims. Would the Fourteenth Amendment forbid this?

(a) Authorities rejecting state court use of national contacts test. No state court appears to have relied expressly on a national contacts test to justify personal jurisdiction over a foreign defendant, in either a federal question or a state law case. Some courts have suggested that the Constitution would forbid this action by a state court. *See United Rope Distributors, Inc. v. Seatriumph Marine Corp.*, 930 F.2d 532 (7th Cir. 1991); *DeJames v. Magnificence Carriers, Inc.*, 654 F.2d 280, 283-284 (3d Cir. 1981). What is the basis for a rule that a state court must apply a state contacts test?

(b) Possible justifications for state court use of national contacts test. Why is it that a state should not be able to take into account a foreigner's contacts with its sister states? Cannot a powerful argument be made that a state court should at most be precluded from considering national contacts in the "purposeful availment" prong of *World-Wide Volkswagen*'s two-prong due process analysis, and not in the "reasonableness" prong? Are not notions of territorial sovereignty relevant only to the minimum contacts prong of due process analysis? If the reasonableness prong permits inquiry into the interests of the "interstate system," can it not look to a defendant's contacts with other U.S. states?

Cannot a substantial argument be made that national contacts are also relevant to the minimum contacts prong? Consider the authorities quoted above declaring that international law would not affect a state's power to apply a national contacts test. Where due process limits — including those reflecting territorial sovereignty — were first derived in *Pennoyer* from international law, should not the absence of any international law limit on application of a national contacts test to foreign defendants be important?

(c) Sub silentio applications of national contacts tests by state courts. Although there are virtually no reported cases in which state courts have expressly applied a national contacts test, that conceals a more complex (and interesting) reality. Courts that apply the Fourteenth Amendment often appear to give at least some weight to the contacts of foreign defendants with other U.S. states. *E.g., Amusement Equip. v. Mordelt*, 779 F.2d 264 (5th Cir. 1985); *Afram Export Corp. v. Metallurgiki Halyps, SA*, 772 F.2d 1358 (7th Cir. 1985). ("Metallurgiki could not have been surprised to discover that if it ordered goods in *America* and went into *America* (through agents or directly) to inspect the goods and take delivery of them, it might be forced in the event of a contract dispute to litigate in *America* rather than being able to retreat to Greece.") (emphasis added); *supra* pp. 128-129, 171-172.

(d) Due process limits on state court use of national contacts test in federal question cases. Many federal causes of action can be brought in either state or federal court. *See supra* pp. 5-9. Suppose that a federal claim is brought in state court and that a federal jurisdictional statute would permit the jurisdiction based on a national contacts test. Could a state court constitutionally apply a national contacts test? Why or why not?

7. Purpose of Rule 4(k)(2). As discussed above, Rule 4(k)(2) was intended to fill a perceived gap in federal authorizations for personal jurisdiction, existing where a foreign defendant might avoid suit in any U.S. forum, because its contacts with the United States were sufficiently dispersed to fall below the "minimum contacts" standard in any particular state, while nonetheless satisfying due process standards for the entire United States. *See supra* p. 216. Thus, the Advisory Committee Notes for Rule 4(k)(2) explain that the provision was intended to "correct[] a gap in the enforcement of federal law":

Under the former rule, a problem was presented when the defendant was a non-resident of the United States having contacts with the United States sufficient to justify the application of United States law and to satisfy federal standards of forum selection, but having insufficient contact with any single state to support jurisdiction under state long-arm legislation or meet the requirements of the Fourteenth Amendment limitation on state court territorial jurisdiction. 28 U.S.C.A. Fed. Rule Civ. Proc. 4, at 118.

Was it appropriate to "fill" this perceived gap? Would there be any legislative reason not to do so?

8. *Requirements of Rule 4(k)(2).* *Swiss American Bank* identifies three requirements of Rule 4(k)(2): (1) a claim arising under federal law; (2) that the defendant not be subject to personal jurisdiction in the courts of general jurisdiction of any state; and (3) that the exercise of jurisdiction comport with due process. Other authorities concur. *Saudi v. Northrop Grumman Corp.*, 427 F.3d 271 (4th Cir. 2005); *Glencore Grain Rotterdam BV v. Shivnath Rai Harnarain Co.*, 284 F.3d 1114 (9th Cir. 2002); *Purdue Research Found. v. Sanofi-Synthelabo, SA*, 338 F.3d 773, 783 n.12 (7th Cir. 2003).

Does the language of Rule 4(k)(2) impose any other requirements? What about the requirement for service? Could that requirement have any independent significance?

(a) *"Claims arising under federal law" for Rule 4(k)(2) purposes.* The first requirement identified in *Swiss American Bank* and other lower courts is that Rule 4(k)(2) is only available "with respect to claims arising under federal law." In many cases, it is clear that particular claims arise under federal law—such as claims under the federal antitrust or securities laws. However, as *Swiss American Bank* demonstrates, particular claims also may arise under federal law even where they are not grounded in federal statutes. *See also De Leon v. Shih Wei Nav. Co., Ltd.*, 269 Fed. Appx. 487 (5th Cir. 2008); *World Tanker Carriers Corp. v. MV Ya Mawlaya*, 99 F.3d 717, 723 (5th Cir. 1996) (holding that Rule 4(k)(2) applies to admiralty claims). What about claims arising under international law and foreign law? *See supra* pp. 62-70 for a discussion of jurisdiction under §1331.

(b) *Requirement under Rule 4(k)(2) that defendant not be subject to jurisdiction elsewhere in the United States.* The second requirement identified by *Swiss American Bank*, and other lower courts, is that Rule 4(k)(2) applies only if the defendant is subject to personal jurisdiction in no other U.S. state. The pertinent part of Rule 4(k)(2) provides that a defendant must not be "subject to the jurisdiction of the courts of general jurisdiction of any state." What does it mean for a defendant to be "subject to the jurisdiction" of a state court? One possibility, suggested by the Government in *Swiss American Bank*, is that "jurisdiction" means subject matter jurisdiction. How serious an argument is that?

There are several other possibilities for interpreting the requirement that a defendant be "subject to the jurisdiction" of a state court: (a) the defendant must be subject to jurisdiction in a state court on the claims at issue in the plaintiff's case; (b) the defendant need only be subject to jurisdiction in a state court on *some* claim; or (c) the defendant must be subject to general jurisdiction in a state court. The purpose underlying Rule 4(k)(2), as described in the Advisory Committee Notes, suggests that possibility (a) is the sensible alternative (although language in the Notes also points toward possibility (b)). Is inquiry under Rule 4(k)(2) confined to what state long-arm statutes provide? Or are due process limits also relevant? What about state door-closing statutes and *forum non conveniens* rules? How does *Swiss American Bank* address these issues?

Assuming that the quoted language means personal jurisdiction in state court (however precisely defined), does this imply that a federal court must first determine whether jurisdiction lies under Rule 4(k)(1)(A) before it can conduct an analysis under Rule 4(k)(2)? Some courts hold that Rule 4(k)(2) becomes relevant only to the extent that jurisdiction is absent under Rule 4(k)(1)(A) and will assess personal jurisdiction under the state long-arm statute before addressing Rule 4(k)(2). *See CFA Institute v. Institute of Chartered Financial Analysts of India*, 551 F.3d 285 (4th Cir. 2009); *Oldfield v. Pueblo de*

Bahia Lora, S.A., 558 F.3d 1210, 1219-1220 n.22 (11th Cir. 2009); *Fortis Corporate Ins. v. Viken Ship Management*, 450 F.3d 214, 218 (6th Cir. 2006).

As *Swiss American Bank* illustrates, Rule 4(k)(2) also raises burden of proof issues, and may lead to anomalous litigation positions. Typically, a defendant is obliged to raise personal jurisdiction defenses, after which the plaintiff continues to have the burden of persuasion. *See Mellon Bank (East) PSFS, NA v. DiVeronica Bros., Inc.*, 983 F.2d 551 (3d Cir. 1993). But this approach fits awkwardly with Rule 4(k)(2), where a plaintiff would be required to prove a negative (*i.e.*, no jurisdiction), under more than 50 different state and other long-arm statutes, as applied to facts that are generally within the defendant's possession. Conversely, defendants resisting jurisdiction under Rule 4(k)(2) will face a dilemma: if they cite a U.S. state as permitting jurisdiction, they may well be found later to have consented to jurisdiction there.

To resolve this dilemma, *Swiss American Bank* adopted a burden-shifting framework. How does the *Swiss American Bank* framework function? Does it effectively allocate burdens to the parties most able to advance the information necessary to support its position? Even if it does so, is this a fair allocation of burdens, particularly where, by definition, a foreign defendant is being haled into a potentially unfamiliar forum and being confronted with the choice of either conceding jurisdiction in a state or, alternatively, subjecting itself to jurisdictional discovery in order to test its nationwide contacts? How does the *Swiss American Bank* test deal with the possibility that defendants will to engage in reverse forum shopping — by conceding that they *are* subject to jurisdiction in another forum, whose procedural or substantive laws might be more favorable to the defendant. *See, e.g., Richards v. Tsunami Goods, Inc.*, 239 F. Supp. 2d 80, 87 (D. Me. 2003) (rejecting personal jurisdiction under Rule 4(k)(2) because defendant conceded that it was subject to personal jurisdiction in another state).

Not all courts adopt an explicit burden-shifting framework. The Seventh Circuit puts the choice to the defendant very starkly:

> A defendant who wants to preclude use of Rule 4(k)(2) has only to name some other state in which the suit could proceed. Naming a more appropriate state would amount to a consent to personal jurisdiction there. . . . If, however, the defendant contends that he cannot be sued in the forum state and refuses to identify any other where suit is possible, then the federal court is entitled to use Rule 4(k)(2). *ISI Int'l, Inc. v. Borden Ladner Gervais LLP*, 256 F.3d 548, 552 (7th Cir. 2001).

Is this approach appropriate? Does it not save time and money, by cutting straight to the dispositive issue? *See Touchcom, Inc. v. Bereskin & Parr*, 574 F.3d 1403, 1415 (Fed. Cir. 2009); *Oldfield v. Pueblo de Bahia Lora, S.A.*, 558 F.3d 1210 (11th Cir. 2009); *Mwani v. bin Laden*, 417 F.3d 1, 11 (D.C. Cir. 2005); *Adams v. Unione Mediterrenea di Sicurta*, 364 F.3d 646, 651 (5th Cir. 2004).

What is the effect of the Seventh Circuit's approach in the foregoing excerpt? If a foreign defendant acknowledges that it is subject to jurisdiction in one of the 50 states, then Rule 4(k)(2) can become a useful forum selection tool for defendants. By contrast, if a foreign defendant refuses to acknowledge its amenability to jurisdiction in any of the 50 states, then the Seventh Circuit's rule effectively reads the requirement out of the statute (by relieving the plaintiff of any burden of proving the foreign defendant's nonamenability to any state forum). Shouldn't a court instead require some record development before deciding whether a defendant is subject to jurisdiction in the courts of some state? *See Base Metal Trading, Ltd. v. OJSC Novokuznetsky Aluminum Factory*, 283 F.3d 208, 215 (4th Cir. 2002) (implicitly putting burden on plaintiff to establish that defendant is not subject to jurisdiction in a state); *Goss Graphic Systems v. Man Roland Druckmaschinen AG*, 139 F. Supp. 2d 1040, 1066 (N.D. Iowa 2001) (same); *Smith v. S&S Dundalk Engineering Works, Ltd.*, 139 F. Supp. 2d 610, 622-623 (D.N.J. 2001) (same).

In *Nicastro v. J. McIntyre Machinery, Ltd.*, the plurality briefly addressed the possibility of a defendant subject to the judicial jurisdiction of the United States but not any particular state:

> For jurisdiction, a litigant may have the requisite relationship with the United States Government but not with the government of any individual State. That would be an exceptional case, however. If the defendant is a domestic domiciliary, the courts of its home State are available and can exercise general jurisdiction. And if another State were to assert jurisdiction in an inappropriate case, it would upset the federal balance, which posits that each State has a sovereignty that is not subject to unlawful intrusion by other States. Furthermore, foreign corporations will often target or concentrate on particular States, subjecting them to specific jurisdiction in those forums.

2011 WL 2518811 at *9 (U.S. June 27, 2011). Does this view shed any light on how a lower court should conduct the 4(k)(2) analysis? Does it lend support to the approach taken in *Swiss American Bank*? In *ISI*? Based on the readings in this section, do you agree with the *Nicastro* plurality that cases of defendant not subject to the jurisdiction of any state are "exceptional?"

(c) *Rule 4(k)(2)'s requirement that jurisdiction be "consistent with the laws and Constitution of the United States."*   The third requirement imposed by Rule 4(k)(2) is that the exercise of jurisdiction be "consistent with" the Constitution and laws of the United States. What does this mean? Obviously, at a minimum, this imports notions of minimum contacts and the Fifth Amendment's due process rules. *See Son v. Kim*, 2007 WL 950085 (D.D.C. 2007). That requires application of the Fifth Amendment's national contacts test — which was one of the major reforms contemplated by the drafters of Rule 4(k)(2). Lower courts have given effect to this intention, applying national contacts tests under Rule 4(k)(2). *See Touchcom, Inc. v. Bereskin & Parr*, 574 F.3d 1403 (Fed. Cir. 2009); *Synthes (U.S.A.) v. G.M. Dos Reis Jr. Ind. Com de Equip. Medico*, 563 F.3d 1285 (Fed. Cir. 2009); *Porina v. Marward Shipping Co.*, 521 F.3d 122, 129 (2d Cir. 2008); *Holland America Line Inc. v. Wartsila North America, Inc.*, 485 F.3d 450 (9th Cir. 2007); *Glencore Grain Rotterdam BV v. Shivnath Rai Harnarain Co.*, 284 F.3d 1114, 1126-1127 (9th Cir. 2002); *Associated Transport Line, Inc. v. Productos Fitosanitarios Proficol El Carmen, SA*, 197 F.3d 1070, 1074 (11th Cir. 1999); *World Tanker Carriers Corp. v. M/V Ya Mawlaya*, 99 F.3d 717, 720-721 (5th Cir. 1996).

9. *Applications of Rule 4(k)(2).* Consider how new Rule 4(k)(2) would have applied in *Asahi, Benton, Wiwa,* and *Afram Export*. In which cases, if any, would Rule 4(k)(2) have permitted jurisdiction that was otherwise lacking? In which cases would Rule 4(k)(2) have provided a more straightforward basis for exercising jurisdiction?

10. *General jurisdiction under Rule 4(k)(2) based on continuous and systematic contacts.* As the *Adams* decision illustrates, Rule 4(k)(2) is not applicable only in specific jurisdiction cases; it also affects a federal court's general jurisdiction based upon "continuous and systematic" business contacts or "presence." As discussed above, federal courts have historically been confined to application of local state standards for defining the level of "presence" or "continuous and systematic" necessary for general jurisdiction. *See supra* pp. 116-129; *Arrowsmith v. United Press Int'l*, 320 F.2d 219 (2d Cir. 1963); C. Wright & A. Miller, *Federal Practice and Procedure* §1075 (3d ed. 1998 & Supp. 2010). That arguably continues to be the case under Rule 4(k)(1)(A). *See supra* pp. 223-224. Under Rule 4(k)(2), however, a federal court is now authorized to exercise personal jurisdiction in federal question cases to the limits of the Due Process Clause. Thus, if a foreign corporation has sufficient contacts with New York (or any other State) to permit general jurisdiction under the Due Process Clause, then a federal court in New York arguably may exercise general jurisdiction — provided of course that no state court has jurisdiction over the defendant. *See supra* pp. 226-228.

Indeed, Rule 4(k)(2) arguably goes further: all of the defendant's contacts with the entire United States can be considered in determining whether it is subject to general jurisdiction. "[F]inding a corporation present in any individual state, could permit the federal court to entertain any federal claim at all against the corporation, even if the claim itself does not arise out of the aggregate national activities of the defendant." D. Siegel, *Supplementary Practice Commentaries, 28 U.S.C.A. Fed. Rules Civ. Proc. Rule 4*, C4-36 (1994 Supp.). *See Adams v. Unione Mediterranea di Sicurta*, 364 F.3d 646, 651-652 (5th Cir. 2004) (relying on defendant's systematic and continuous contacts "with the United States as a whole" to establish general jurisdiction under Rule 4(k)(2)); *Submersible Systems, Inc. v. Perforadoru Central, SA de CV*, 249 F.3d 413, 420-421 (5th Cir. 2001) (analyzing defendant's nationwide contacts in Rule 4(k)(2) analysis); *Consolidated Development Corp. v. Sherritt, Inc.*, 216 F.3d 1286, 1292-1293 (11th Cir. 2000) (same). That would be a significant change from the law under old Rule 4(e). *See supra* pp. 223-225.

Recall that in *Goodyear Dunlop Tires Operations, S.A. v. Brown*, 2011 WL 2518815 (U.S. June 27, 2011), the Supreme Court re-emphasized the high bar set by the "continuous and systematic contacts" test. To what extent do these decisions, finding general jurisdiction based upon "continuous and systematic contacts" with the United States, remain good law after *Goodyear*?

11. *General jurisdiction based on tag service under Rule 4(k)(2).* Does Rule 4(k)(2) authorize personal jurisdiction based solely on tag service? Rule 4(k)(2) grants federal courts the power to exercise personal jurisdiction whenever "consistent with the Constitution and laws of the United States." After *Burnham, supra* pp. 129-137, tag service appears to be permitted under the Fourteenth Amendment. Assuming the same general rule under the Fifth Amendment, it seems likely that Congress could constitutionally authorize personal jurisdiction to any U.S. district based upon tag service anywhere in the United States. That is because the relevant territorial unit for purposes of federal jurisdictional grants is the entire United States. *See supra* pp. 83-85, 96-99, 210-211; *United States v. Union Pacific Railroad*, 98 U.S. 569, 603-604 (1878). Would Rule 4(k)(2) be available to a district court in one state when tag service was made in a different state that permitted it as a jurisdictional base? Or would that run afoul of Rule 4(k)(2)'s requirement that jurisdiction not otherwise exist in "any state"? Would it be wise to permit nationwide tag service on foreign defendants?

12. *General jurisdiction based on nationality, domicile, and incorporation under Rule 4(k)(2).* As described above, the Due Process Clause permits general jurisdiction based upon nationality, domicile, and incorporation within the forum. *See supra* pp. 109-114. Does the same rationale that arguably supports jurisdiction based on tag service under Rule 4(k)(2) also extend to jurisdiction based upon U.S. nationality, domicile, and incorporation?

13. *Legislative approaches to U.S. judicial jurisdiction in international cases.* Recall EU Council Regulation 44/2001 and its discriminatory provisions with regard to non-EU domiciliaries. *See supra* pp. 105-106. Recall the abortive Hague Conference negotiations on a jurisdiction and judgments convention. *See supra* pp. 107-108. If you were a U.S. legislator, what legislative amendments would you consider to improve the international position of U.S. companies and domiciliaries? What carrots would you envisage? What sticks? What role would notions of reciprocity play in your thinking? Would the Constitution stand in the way of any of your ideas?

3

Foreign Sovereign Immunity and Jurisdiction of U.S. Courts over Foreign States[1]

In most nations, including the United States, foreign states and state-related entities enjoy important immunities from the judicial jurisdiction of national courts. Issues of foreign sovereign immunity arise with considerable frequency in contemporary international litigation. This is because of the extensive involvement of foreign governments and their agencies — including airlines, banks, shipping lines, and other "commercial" entities — in international trade and finance. This chapter examines the circumstances in which foreign states and related entities are subject to the judicial jurisdiction of U.S. courts.

A. Introduction

1. Historical Background

Foreign sovereign immunity is a well-established feature of U.S. law.[2] An early statement of the doctrine in the United States was the Supreme Court's opinion in *The Schooner Exchange v. McFaddon*,[3] where the Court held a French naval vessel immune from the jurisdiction of U.S. courts. Although no statutory or constitutional provision granted jurisdictional immunity to foreign sovereigns,[4] Chief Justice Marshall relied on principles of international law and territorial sovereignty in concluding that U.S. courts lacked

---

1. Commentary on foreign sovereign immunity includes, *e.g.,* J. Dellapenna, *Suing Foreign Governments and Their Corporations* (2d ed. 2003); Dellapenna, *Refining the Foreign Sovereign Immunities Act,* 9 Willamette J. Int'l L. & Dis. Res. 57 (2001); Feldman, *The United States Foreign Sovereign Immunities Act of 1976 in Perspective: A Founder's View,* 35 Int'l & Comp. L.Q. 302 (1986); Lauterpacht, *The Problem of Jurisdictional Immunities of Foreign States,* 28 Brit. Y. B. Int'l L. 220 (1951); Singer, *Abandoning Restrictive Sovereign Immunity: An Analysis in Terms of Jurisdiction to Prescribe,* 26 Harv. Int'l L.J. 1 (1985); Kane, *Suing Foreign Sovereigns: A Procedural Compass,* 34 Stan. L. Rev. 385 (1982); Portnoy *et al., The Foreign Sovereign Immunities Act: 2008 Year in Review,* 16 L. & Bus. Rev. Am. 179 (2010); Report of the ABA Working Group, *Reforming the Foreign Sovereign Immunities Act,* 40 Colum. J. Transnat'l L. 489 (2002).
2. *See Republic of Philippines v. Pimentel,* 128 S. Ct. 2180, 2190 (2008) ("The doctrine of foreign sovereign immunity has been recognized since early in the history of our Nation.)*; see generally* E. Allen, *The Position of Foreign States Before National Courts* (1933); T. Guittari, *The American Law of Sovereign Immunity: An Analysis of the Legal Interpretation* 26-42 (1970).
3. 11 U.S. 116 (1812).
4. *Verlinden BV v. Central Bank of Nigeria,* 461 U.S. 480, 486 (1983) ("foreign sovereign immunity is a matter of grace and comity . . . and not a restriction imposed by the Constitution").

judicial jurisdiction over foreign sovereigns.[5] Among other things, Chief Justice Marshall's opinion for the Court reasoned:

> The jurisdiction of the nation within its own territory is necessarily exclusive and absolute. . . . This full and absolute territorial jurisdiction being alike the attribute of every sovereign . . . would not seem to contemplate foreign sovereigns nor their sovereign rights as its objects. . . . This perfect equality and absolute independence of sovereigns, and this common interest impelling them to mutual intercourse, and an interchange of good offices with each other, have given rise to a class of cases in which every sovereign is understood to waive the exercise of a part of that complete exclusive territorial jurisdiction, which has been stated to be the attribute of every nation.[6]

The Court had no difficulty incorporating this international practice into U.S. law, and adopting a common law rule of sovereign immunity. In addition to relying on international law, *Schooner Exchange* also noted that the U.S. executive branch had appeared and argued that immunity would be appropriate.[7]

Schooner Exchange provided the basis for a common law doctrine of sovereign immunity which U.S. courts applied throughout the nineteenth century.[8] In general, U.S. courts applied the so-called "absolute theory" of foreign sovereign immunity, which granted foreign states immunity with respect to all their activities, both governmental and commercial.[9] For example, in *Berizzi Brothers Co. v. The Pesaro*,[10] the Court considered whether a foreign state-owned commercial vessel was subject to the jurisdiction of U.S. courts in a straightforward breach of contract case. The Court affirmed dismissal of the suit on sovereign immunity grounds:

> We think that the principles [of sovereign immunity stated in *Schooner Exchange*] are applicable alike to all ships held and used by a government for a public purpose, and that when, for the purpose of advancing the trade of its people or providing revenues for its Treasury, a government acquires, mans, and operates ships in the carrying of trade, they are public ships in the same sense that warships are.[11]

Pesaro rested entirely on the Supreme Court's understanding of prevailing international law principles. The Court did not consider the views of the Executive Branch regarding U.S. foreign relations.[12]

In subsequent years, however, the U.S. Department of State came to play a central role in the application of the doctrine of foreign sovereign immunity in the United States.

---

5. This analysis paralleled the Court's subsequent reliance on principles of international law to define U.S. judicial jurisdiction in cases like *Rose v. Himely* and *Pennoyer v. Neff. See supra* pp. 83-90.

6. 11 U.S. 116, 137 (1812).

7. 11 U.S. at 132-135.

8. *E.g., Berizzi Bros. Co. v. SS Pesaro*, 271 U.S. 562 (1926); *United States v. Diekelman*, 92 U.S. 520, 524 (1875). *See* T. Guittari, *The American Law of Sovereign Immunity: An Analysis of the Legal Interpretation* 26-42 (1970).

9. *E.g., Compania Espanola de Navegacion Maritima, SA v. The Navemar*, 303 U.S. 68 (1938). In this respect, U.S. law continued to parallel international practice, which saw widespread acceptance of absolute immunity. *See* Harvard Research in International Law, *Draft Convention and Comment on Competence of Courts in Regard to Foreign States*, 26 Am. J. Int'l L. Supp. 451, 527 (1932).

10. 271 U.S. 562 (1926).

11. 271 U.S. at 574.

12. Indeed, in *Pesaro*, the U.S. Department of State had concluded that sovereign immunity should not be accorded, because of its view that the vessel was a commercial one (not a public one) and the dispute was purely commercial. The Department of Justice disagreed, however, and refused to submit the Department of State's views to the Court. *The Pesaro*, 277 F. 473, 479-480 n.3 (1921); 2 Hackworth, *Digest of International Law* 429-430, 438-439 (1941).

In *Ex parte Peru*,[13] the Court held that a Peruvian state-owned commercial vessel was immune from U.S. jurisdiction even in a purely commercial case. In contrast to *Pesaro,* however, the Court placed central reliance on the views of the Department of State, which had formally recognized the Peruvian government's claim of immunity. According to *Ex parte Peru*, a State Department certificate of immunity "must be accepted by the courts as a conclusive determination by the political arm of the government that the continued retention of the vessel interferes with the proper conduct of our foreign relations."[14]

Two years later, in *Republic of Mexico v. Hoffman*,[15] the Supreme Court denied immunity to a Mexican state-owned commercial vessel. The Court justified its result (which, on the facts, appeared directly contrary to the results in *Pesaro* and *Ex parte Peru*) by reference to the State Department's refusal to suggest immunity. According to Chief Justice Stone: "It is . . . not for the courts to deny an immunity which our government has seen fit to allow, or to allow an immunity on new grounds which the government has not seen fit to recognize."[16]

After the Court's decisions in *Ex parte Peru* and *Republic of Mexico,* the State Department adopted a procedure by which it would make initial determinations of immunity based on submissions by foreign states wishing to claim immunity from U.S. jurisdiction. If the State Department concluded that a foreign state was entitled to immunity, it would make a "suggestion" of immunity to the court in which claims against the foreign state were pending. The courts, in turn, treated State Department suggestions as binding.[17]

During the early twentieth century, a number of foreign states abandoned the absolute theory of immunity in favor of the so-called "restrictive theory." Under the restrictive theory, states do not enjoy sovereign immunity with respect to their private or commercial activities (*jure gestionis*), although immunity is retained for sovereign or public acts (*jure imperii*).[18] In 1952, the Department of State embraced the restrictive theory of immunity in a frequently cited letter by Jack Tate, the State Department's Legal Adviser. The "Tate Letter" noted the growing international acceptance of the restrictive theory and the increasing involvement of state-owned enterprises in commercial dealings with private parties.[19] Relying on these developments, the Tate Letter declared that future suggestions of immunity would be made in accordance with the restrictive theory.[20]

Following release of the Tate Letter in 1952, the State Department routinely decided whether or not a foreign state's conduct or property was "sovereign," and hence entitled to immunity.[21] Application of the restrictive theory by the Department of State encountered difficulties.[22] Although it is a political institution, the Tate Letter required the State

---

13. 318 U.S. 578 (1943).

14. 318 U.S. at 589.

15. 324 U.S. 30 (1945).

16. 324 U.S. at 35-36.

17. *E.g., Republic of Mexico v. Hoffman,* 324 U.S. 30 (1945); *Ex parte Republic of Peru,* 318 U.S. 578 (1943). *See* T. Guittari, *The American Law of Sovereign Immunity* 111-121, 143-162, 174-187 (1970) (collecting commentary and cases).

18. Letter of Jack B. Tate, Acting Legal Adviser, to Acting Attorney General (1952) (hereinafter the "Tate Letter"), *reprinted in* Appendix 2 to *Alfred Dunhill of London v. Republic of Cuba,* 425 U.S. 682, 711 (1976); Dobrovir, *A Gloss on the Tate Letter's Restrictive Theory of Sovereign Immunity,* 54 Va. L. Rev. 1 (1968); Higgins, *The Death Throes of Absolute Immunity: The Government of Uganda Before the English Courts,* 73 Am. J. Int'l L. 465 (1979).

19. *See* Friedmann, *Changing Social Arrangements in State-Trading States and Their Effect on International Law,* 24 Law & Contemp. Probs. 350 (1959); Tate Letter, *reprinted in* Appendix 2 to *Alfred Dunhill of London v. Republic of Cuba,* 425 U.S. 682, 711 (1976).

20. Tate Letter, *reprinted in* 425 U.S. 682, 711 (1976).

21. *See* H.R. Rep. No. 1487, 94th Cong., 2d Sess. 8-9 (1976), *reprinted in* 1976 U.S. Code Cong. & Admin. News 6604, 6607; *Alfred Dunhill, Inc. v. Cuba,* 425 U.S. 682, 698-705 (1976).

22. *See* H.R. Rep. No. 1487, 94th Cong., 2d Sess. 12, *reprinted in* 1976 U.S. Code Cong. & Admin. News 6604, 6610-6611.

Department to perform a judicial function. The Department lacked the capacity to take factual evidence or afford appellate review. Moreover, the State Department was subjected to diplomatic and political pressures in connection with immunity decisions. This produced unpredictable, sometimes unprincipled, results for private litigants and foreign states.[23]

2.　The Foreign Sovereign Immunities Act of 1976: Overview

Defects in Executive Branch application of the restrictive theory generated pressure for reform. After a lengthy legislative process, Congress enacted the Foreign Sovereign Immunities Act of 1976 (the "FSIA" or "Act"),[24] which is reproduced in Appendix F of the Documentary Supplement accompanying this volume. The FSIA transferred responsibility for sovereign immunity decisions from the State Department to the judiciary.[25] The Act also provided a comprehensive statutory system governing issues of foreign state immunity, as well as procedural issues such as service of process, provisional relief, and the enforcement of judgments.[26] In general, the FSIA implements the restrictive theory of immunity: it provides foreign states immunity for their "sovereign" acts and denies them immunity for their "commercial" or "private" acts.[27]

The FSIA was enacted to provide the "sole and exclusive standards to be used in resolving questions of sovereign immunity raised by foreign states before federal and state courts in the United States."[28] Under the Act, all "foreign states" are presumptively entitled to immunity, and thus cannot be subjected to the jurisdiction of U.S. courts (either state or federal).[29] However, the FSIA also contains important exceptions to this presumptive grant of immunity, which define circumstances in which foreign states will not enjoy immunity in U.S. courts.[30]

The FSIA is fundamentally a *jurisdictional* statute. As discussed elsewhere, where a foreign state does not enjoy immunity, 28 U.S.C. §1330 affirmatively grants federal courts both personal and subject matter jurisdiction involving claims against it.[31] The FSIA does *not* generally deal with issues of substantive liability: §1606 of the Act provides that foreign states are liable "to the same extent as a private individual under like circumstances."[32]

---

23. *E.g., Rich v. Naviera Vacuba SA,* 295 F.2d 24 (4th Cir. 1961) (per curiam) (State Department suggestion of immunity in a clearly commercial case, made as *quid pro quo* to gain release of hijacked airplane). *See* Cardozo, *Judicial Deference to State Department Suggestions,* 48 Corn. L.Q. 461 (1963); Jessup, *Has the Supreme Court Abdicated One of Its Functions?,* 40 Am. J. Int'l L. 168 (1946); H.R. Rep. No. 1487, 94th Cong., 2d Sess. 12, *reprinted in* 1976 U.S. Code Cong. & Admin. News at 6610-6611.

24. 28 U.S.C. §1602.

25. 28 U.S.C. §1602.

26. While the FSIA governs the immunity of foreign states (defined therein), it generally does not govern the immunity of government officials. *See infra* pp. 254, 261-265.

27. *See Verlinden BV v. Central Bank of Nigeria,* 461 U.S. 480 (1983).

28. H.R. Rep. No. 1487, 94th Cong., 2d Sess. 12, *reprinted in* 1976 U.S. Code Cong. & Admin. News at 6610-6611.

29. 28 U.S.C. §§1604, 1330(a) & (b).

30. 28 U.S.C. §1605. These exceptions are subject to international agreements in effect at the time of the FSIA's enactment. Thus, in cases where an existing agreement accorded an immunity greater than the FSIA, the agreement prevails. If the United States entered into an agreement subsequent to the FSIA's enactment that accorded immunity to the foreign state, the agreement would also likely control under the last-in-time principle. For a recent decision discussing the relationship between the FSIA and so-called "treaty exception," *see World Holdings, LLC v. Federal Republic of Germany,* 613 F.3d 1310 (11th Cir. 2010).

31. *See supra* pp. 70-71 & *infra* pp. 276-277.

32. *See First National City Bank v. Banco Para El Comercio Exterior de Cuba,* 462 U.S. 611, 620-621 (1983).

Section 1330(a) limits the FSIA's grant of original jurisdiction to federal courts to "nonjury civil" actions. This provision is applicable only to federal court actions against foreign sovereigns, although it applies whether the action was initiated in federal court or removed from state to federal court.[33] Courts that have addressed the question have noted that §1330(a) was meant to prohibit use of juries when foreign sovereigns are sued even where there would otherwise be alternative grounds for subject matter jurisdiction (such as, alienage jurisdiction) that would permit use of a jury.[34] In addition, lower courts have concluded that §1330's provision for nonjury trials does not violate the Seventh Amendment.[35]

Finally, the FSIA contains a variety of provisions dealing with procedural and quasi-procedural issues. These include sections regarding service of process, time for answering, enforcement of judgments, and other matters.[36] These provisions are generally applicable in both federal and state courts.[37]

3. International Recognition of the Restrictive Theory of Foreign Sovereign Immunity

At the same time that the United States was adopting the restrictive theory of foreign sovereign immunity, other states took similar steps. These steps were reflected in national sovereign immunity legislation and national court decisions, which increasingly denied immunity to foreign states for their commercial and other "non-sovereign" activities. They were also reflected in the 1972 European Convention on State Immunity (which led to reforms of foreign sovereign immunity legislation in leading European states).

Despite these developments, Communist (and some developing) states resisted the evolution of foreign sovereign immunity doctrine. They criticized the basic premises of the restrictive theory, arguing that all conduct by a sovereign state was sovereign and that it was improper and arbitrary to treat states' conduct as "commercial" or "private." These objections increasingly lost appeal following the demise of the Soviet Union and its empire, although some quarters retain their hostility to the restrictive theory's conceptions of foreign sovereign immunity.

In 2004, the United Nations General Assembly adopted the U.N. Convention on Jurisdictional Immunities of States and their Property ("U.N. State Immunities Convention"), excerpted in Appendix G. The U.N. State Immunities Convention marked the culmination of nearly three decades of work by the International Law Commission. It adopts the restrictive theory of immunity, confirming the final demise of the absolute theory and the basic approach of the FSIA. Nevertheless, there are material differences between the U.N. State Immunities Convention and the FSIA, which can be expected to provoke litigation and diplomatic activities in coming years. The Convention will come into force after 30 states ratify it.

33. *See Arango v. Guzman Travel Advisors*, 761 F.2d 1527, 1532 (11th Cir. 1985).
34. *See McKeel v. Islamic Republic of Iran*, 722 F.2d 582 (9th Cir. 1983); *Goar v. Compania Peruana de Vapores*, 688 F.2d 417 (5th Cir. 1982); *Rex v. Cia. Peruana de Vapores*, 660 F.2d 61 (3d Cir. 1981). *But see Icenogle v. Olympic Airways, SA*, 82 F.R.D. 36 (D.D.C. 1979).
35. *Bailey v. Grand Trunk Lines*, 805 F.2d 1097 (2d Cir. 1986); *Arango v. Guzman Travel Advisors Corp.*, 761 F.2d 1527 (11th Cir. 1985); *Goar v. Compania Peruana de Vapores*, 688 F.2d 417 (5th Cir. 1982); *Rex v. Compania Peruana de Vapores*, 660 F.2d 61 (3d Cir. 1981); *Ruggiero v. Compania Peruana de Vapores*, 639 F.2d 872 (2d Cir. 1981).
36. *See infra* pp. 953-964 (service), p. 1023 (discovery) & pp. 348-349, 360-361 (enforcement of judgments).
37. Given the uncertain text of the FSIA, however, questions continue to arise over whether the Act preempts various state rules. *See, e.g., Hyundai Corp. v. Republic of Iraq*, 794 N.Y.S.2d 327 (App. Div. 2005) (divided opinion over whether FSIA preempted state law governing vacatur of default judgments).

4.   Selected Historical Materials Concerning Foreign Sovereign Immunity

The materials excerpted below address the historical origins and evolution of the foreign sovereign immunity doctrine in the United States. The first excerpt is the Supreme Court's opinion in *The Schooner Exchange v. McFaddon*. Consider the rationale adopted by the Court in denying U.S. jurisdiction, and compare the Court's reliance on international law to the reasoning in decisions like *Pennoyer v. Neff*. Also excerpted below are the Court's opinions in *Berizzi Bros. Co. v. SS Pesaro* and *Republic of Mexico v. Hoffman*. In reading these excerpts, recall the separation of powers considerations which were explored in the context of the Alien Tort Statute.[38] Next, consider the Tate Letter and its impact on the doctrine of sovereign immunity. Thereafter, briefly review the text of the FSIA and read the Supreme Court's decision in *Republic of Austria v. Altmann,* which reflects the Court's current views on the origins of the foreign sovereign immunity doctrine.[39] Finally, consider the U.N. Jurisdictional Immunities Convention, generally reflecting prevailing international views regarding the subject.

THE SCHOONER EXCHANGE v. McFADDON
11 U.S. 116 (U.S. 1812)

MARSHALL, CHIEF JUSTICE. [Two U.S. nationals brought a libel against the vessel "the Schooner Exchange." The libellants claimed that the Schooner Exchange was theirs, and that they were entitled to possession of the vessel. They alleged that the vessel had been seized on the high seas in 1810 by French naval forces and that no prize court of competent jurisdiction had pronounced judgment against the vessel. No one appeared for the vessel to reply to the libellants' allegations. The United States Attorney for Pennsylvania appeared on behalf of the U.S. Government to request that the libel be dismissed. He stated that the United States and France were at peace, that a public ship (known as "the Balaou") of the Emperor of France had been forced by storms to enter the port of Philadelphia, and was prevented from leaving by the process of the court. The United States Attorney urged that, even if the vessel had in fact been wrongfully seized, ownership had passed to the Emperor of France. The District Court dismissed the libel, the Circuit Court reversed, and the United States Attorney appealed to the Supreme Court.]

. . . The jurisdiction of the nation within its own territory is necessarily exclusive and absolute. It is susceptible of no limitation not imposed by itself. . . . This full and absolute territorial jurisdiction being alike the attribute of every sovereign . . . would not seem to contemplate foreign sovereigns nor their sovereign rights as its objects. One sovereign being in no respect amenable to another; and being bound by obligations of the highest character not to degrade the dignity of his nation, by placing himself or its sovereign rights within the jurisdiction of another, can be supposed to enter a foreign territory only under an express license, or in the confidence that the immunities belonging to his independent sovereign station, though not expressly stipulated, are reserved by implication, and will be extended to him.

This perfect equality and absolute independence of sovereigns, and this common interest impelling them to mutual intercourse, and an interchange of good offices with each other, have given rise to a class of cases in which every sovereign is understood

---

38. *See supra* pp. 53-56.
39. 541 U.S. 677 (2004).

to waive the exercise of a part of that complete exclusive territorial jurisdiction, which has been stated to be the attribute of every nation.

    1st.   One of these is admitted to be the exemption of the person of the sovereign from arrest or detention within a foreign territory . . .

    2d.   A second case, standing on the same principles with the first, is the immunity which all civilized nations allow to foreign ministers . . .

    3d.   A third case in which a sovereign is understood to cede a portion of his territorial jurisdiction is, where he allows the troops of a foreign prince to pass through his dominions.

[The Court reasoned that a state's permission for foreign armies to enter its territory must be express, and not merely implied, but that a different rule applied in the case of foreign ships.] . . . If there be no prohibition, the ports of a friendly nation are considered as open to the public ships of all powers with whom it is at peace, and they are supposed to enter such ports and to remain in them while allowed to remain, under the protection of the government of the place. . . .

When private individuals of one nation spread themselves through another as business or caprice may direct, mingling indiscriminately with the inhabitants of that other, or when merchant vessels enter for the purposes of trade, it would be obviously inconvenient and dangerous to society, and would subject the laws to continual infraction, and the government to degradation, if such individuals or merchants did not owe temporary and local allegiance, and were not amenable to the jurisdiction of the country. . . . But in all respects different is the situation of a public armed ship. She constitutes a part of the military force of her nation; acts under the immediate and direct command of the sovereign; is employed by him in national objects. He has many and powerful motives for preventing those objects from being defeated by the interference of a foreign state. Such interference cannot take place without affecting his power and his dignity. The implied license therefore under which such vessel enters a friendly port, may reasonably be construed, and it seems to the Court, ought to be construed, as containing an exemption from the jurisdiction of the sovereign, within whose territory she claims the rights of hospitality. Upon these principles, by the unanimous consent of nations, a foreigner is amenable to the laws of the place; but certainly in practice, nations have not yet asserted their jurisdiction over the public armed ships of a foreign sovereign entering a port open for their reception.

Bynkershoek, a jurist of great reputation, has indeed maintained that the property of a foreign sovereign is not distinguishable by any legal exemption from the property of an ordinary individual, and has quoted several cases in which courts have exercised jurisdiction over causes in which a foreign sovereign was made a party defendant. Without indicating any opinion on this question, it may safely be affirmed, that there is a manifest distinction between the private property of the person who happens to be a prince, and that military force which supports the sovereign power, and maintains the dignity and the independence of a nation. A prince, by acquiring private property in a foreign country, may possibly be considered as subjecting that property to the territorial jurisdiction; he may be considered as so far laying down the prince, and assuming the character of a private individual; but this he cannot be presumed to do with respect to any portion of that armed force, which upholds his crown, and the nation he is entrusted to govern. . . .

It seems then to the Court, to be a principle of public law, that national ships of war, entering the port of a friendly power open for their reception, are to be considered as exempted by the consent of that power from its jurisdiction. . . . The arguments in favor of this opinion which have been drawn from the general inability of the judicial power to enforce its decisions in cases of this description, from the consideration, that the sovereign power of the nation is alone competent to avenge wrongs committed by a sovereign, that the questions to which such wrongs give birth are rather questions of policy than of law, that they are for diplomatic, rather than legal discussion, are of great weight, and merit serious attention. But the argument has already been drawn to a length, which forbids a particular examination of these points. . . .

If the preceding reasoning be correct, the Exchange, being a public armed ship, in the service of a foreign sovereign, with whom the government of the United States is at peace, and having entered an American port open for her reception, on the terms on which ships of war are generally permitted to enter the ports of a friendly power, must be considered as having come into the American territory, under an implied promise, that while necessarily within it, and demeaning herself in a friendly manner, she should be exempt from the jurisdiction of the country.

BERIZZI BROS. CO. v. SS PESARO
271 U.S. 562 (1926)

VAN DEVANTER, JUSTICE. [The Pesaro was a merchant vessel owned and operated by Italy. It was engaged in carrying cargo and passengers on a purely commercial basis. A libel was brought against the Pesaro to enforce a claim for cargo damage. The case was considered on agreed facts showing, *inter alia,* that the vessel would not be immune from suit in Italy, and that merchant vessels owned by the United States Government would not be immune in Italian courts. The State Department declined to take a position on the vessel's immunity, but the ship's master objected on jurisdictional grounds. Judge Mack overruled the objections. *The Pesaro,* 277 Fed. 473 (S.D.N.Y. 1921). Among other things, he reasoned:

> To deprive parties injured in the ordinary course of trade of their common and well-established legal remedies would not only work great hardship on them, but in the long run it would operate to the disadvantage and detriment of those in whose favor the immunity might be granted. Shippers would hesitate to trade with government ships, and salvors would run few risks to save the property of friendly sovereigns, if they were denied recourse to our own courts and left to prosecute their claims in foreign tribunals in distant lands. . . . The attachment of public trading vessels, in my judgment, is not incompatible with the public interest of any nation or with the respect and deference due a foreign power. . . . [In] my opinion, a government ship should not be immune from seizure as such, but only by reason of the nature of the service in which she is engaged. And as the Pesaro was employed as an ordinary merchant vessel for commercial purposes at a time when no emergency existed or was declared, she should not be immune from arrest in admiralty, especially as no exemption has been claimed for her, by reason of her sovereign or political character, through the official channels of the United States.
>
> [Even if that were error, the Pesaro would not be entitled to immunity.] I do not base this upon the fact that ships owned and operated for commercial purposes by the United States would not be exempt from ordinary process under Italian law, for retaliation and reprisal are for the executive branches of our government and not for the courts. . . . But the fact that the steamship Pesaro itself is subject to the ordinary processes of the Italian court would seem to be vital and decisive. There is no reason of international comity or courtesy which requires that Italian property not deemed extra commercium in Italy should be treated as res publica and extra commercium in the United States. . . .

Judge Mack was subsequently reversed, and the libellants appealed to the U.S. Supreme Court.] . . .

The single question presented for decision by us is whether a ship owned and possessed by a foreign government, and operated by it in the carriage of merchandise for hire, is immune from arrest under process based on a libel in rem by a private suitor in a federal district court exercising admiralty jurisdiction. The precise question never had been considered by this Court before. . . . The nearest approach to it in this Court's decisions is found in *The Exchange.* . . . It will be perceived that the opinion . . . contains no reference to merchant ships owned and operated by a government. But the omission is not of special significance, for in 1812, when the decision was given, merchant ships were operated only by private owners, and there was little thought of governments engaging in such operations. That came much later.

The decision in *The Exchange* therefore cannot be taken as excluding merchant ships held and used by a government from the principles there announced. On the contrary, if such ships come within those principles, they must be held to have the same immunity as war ships, in the absence of a treaty or statute of the United States evincing a different purpose. No such treaty or statute has been brought to our attention. We think the principles are applicable alike to all ships held and used by a government for a public purpose, and that when, for the purpose of advancing the trade of its people or providing revenue for its treasury, a government acquires, mans and operates ships in the carrying trade, they are public ships in the same sense that war ships are. We know of no international usage which regards the maintenance and advancement of the economic welfare of a people in time of peace as any less a public purpose than the maintenance and training of a naval force. . . .

REPUBLIC OF MEXICO v. HOFFMAN (*THE BAJA CALIFORNIA*)
324 U.S. 30 (1945)

STONE, CHIEF JUSTICE. [The owner of a vessel damaged in a collision filed a libel against the *Baja California,* a Mexican Government-owned merchant vessel operated in freight service by a private Mexican company under a five-year contract. The contract provided for complete control of the vessel by the private company and for a sharing of profits with the state. The Mexican Ambassador filed a suggestion of immunity, and the U.S. District Attorney presented a communication from the U.S. Department of State calling attention to the claim of immunity and accepting as true its statement regarding Mexican Government ownership. The State Department expressed no opinion as to the immunity claimed by the Mexican state.] . . .

It is therefore not for the courts to deny an immunity which our government has seen fit to allow, or to allow an immunity on new grounds which the government has not seen fit to recognize.[40] The judicial seizure of the property of a friendly state may be regarded as such an affront to its dignity and may so affect our relations with it, that it is an accepted rule of substantive law governing the exercise of the jurisdiction of the courts that they will accept and follow the executive determination that the vessel shall be treated as immune. . . . But recognition by the courts of an immunity upon principles which the political department of government has not sanctioned may be equally embarrassing to it in securing the protection of our national interests and their recognition by other nations.

When such a seizure occurs the friendly foreign government may adopt the procedure of asking the State Department to allow it. But the foreign government may also present

---

40. This salutary practice was not followed in *Berizzi Bros. Co. v. SS Pesaro.*

its claim of immunity by appearance in the suit and by way of defense to the libel. In such a case the court will inquire whether the ground of immunity is one which it is the established policy of the department to recognize. . . . Such a policy, long and consistently recognized and often certified by the State Department and for that reason acted upon by the courts even when not so certified, is that of allowing the immunity from suit of a vessel in the possession and service of a foreign government. . . .

The lower Federal courts have consistently refused to allow claims of immunity based on title of the claimant foreign government without possession. . . . More important, and we think controlling in the present circumstances, is the fact that, despite numerous opportunities like the present to recognize immunity from suit of a vessel owned and not possessed by a foreign government, this government has failed to do so. We can only conclude that it is the national policy not to extend the immunity in the manner now suggested, and that it is the duty of the courts, in a matter so intimately associated with our foreign policy and which may profoundly affect it, not to enlarge an immunity to an extent which the government, although often asked, has not seen fit to recognize. . . .

LETTER OF ACTING LEGAL ADVISER, JACK B. TATE, TO DEPARTMENT OF JUSTICE, MAY 19, 1952
26 Department of State Bulletin 984 (1952)

A study of the law of sovereign immunity reveals the existence of two conflicting concepts of sovereign immunity, each widely held and firmly established. According to the classical or absolute theory of sovereign immunity, a sovereign cannot, without his consent, be made a respondent in the courts of another sovereign. According to the newer or restrictive theory of sovereign immunity, the immunity of the sovereign is recognized with regard to sovereign or public acts (*jure imperii*) of a state, but not with respect to private acts (*jure gestionis*). There is agreement by proponents of both theories, supported by practice, that sovereign immunity should not be claimed or granted in actions with respect to real property (diplomatic and perhaps consular property excepted) or with respect to the disposition of the property of a deceased person even though a foreign sovereign is the beneficiary.

The classical or virtually absolute theory of sovereign immunity has generally been followed by the courts of the United States, the British Commonwealth, Czechoslovakia, Estonia, and probably Poland. The decisions of the courts of Brazil, Chile, China, Hungary, Japan, Luxembourg, Norway, and Portugal may be deemed to support the classical theory of immunity if one or at most two old decisions anterior to the development of the restrictive theory may be considered sufficient on which to base a conclusion. . . .

A trend to the restrictive theory is already evident in the Netherlands where the lower courts have started to apply that theory following a Supreme Court decision to the effect that immunity would have been applicable in the case under consideration under either theory. The German courts, after a period of hesitation at the end of the nineteenth century have held to the classical theory, but it should be noted that the refusal of the Supreme Court in 1921 to yield to pressure by the lower courts for the newer theory was based on the view that that theory had not yet developed sufficiently to justify a change. In view of the growth of the restrictive theory since that time the German courts might take a different view today.

The newer or restrictive theory of sovereign immunity has always been supported by the courts of Belgium and Italy. It was adopted in turn by the courts of Egypt and

Switzerland. In addition, the courts of France, Austria, and Greece, which were traditionally supporters of the classical theory, reversed their position in the 20's to embrace the restrictive theory. . . .

Furthermore, it should be observed that in most of the countries still following the classical theory there is a school of influential writers favoring the restrictive theory and the views of writers, at least in civil law countries, are a major factor in the development of the law. Moreover, the leanings of the lower courts in civil law countries are more significant in shaping the law than they are in common law countries where the rule of precedent prevails and the trend in these lower courts is to the restrictive theory. . . .

It is thus evident that with the possible exception of the United Kingdom little support has been found except on the part of the Soviet Union and its satellites for continued full acceptance of the absolute theory of sovereign immunity. There are evidences that British authorities are aware of its deficiencies and ready for a change. The reasons which obviously motivate state trading countries in adhering to the theory with perhaps increasing rigidity are most persuasive that the United States should change its policy. Furthermore, the granting of sovereign immunity to foreign governments in the courts of the United States is most inconsistent with the action of the Government of the United States in subjecting itself to suit in the same courts in both contract and tort and with its long established policy of not claiming immunity in foreign jurisdictions for its merchant vessels. Finally, the Department feels that the widespread and increasing practice on the part of governments of engaging in commercial activities makes necessary a practice which will enable persons doing business with them to have their rights determined in the courts. For these reasons it will hereafter be the Department's policy to follow the restrictive theory of sovereign immunity in the consideration of requests of foreign governments for a grant of sovereign immunity.

It is realized that a shift in policy by the executive cannot control the courts but it is felt that the courts are less likely to allow a plea of sovereign immunity where the executive has declined to do so. There have been indications that at least some Justices of the Supreme Court feel that in this matter courts should follow the branch of the Government charged with responsibility for the conduct of foreign relations.

FOREIGN SOVEREIGN IMMUNITIES ACT OF 1976
28 U.S.C. §§1601-11 [excerpted at Appendix F]

REPUBLIC OF AUSTRIA v. ALTMANN
541 U.S. 677 (2004)

STEVENS, JUSTICE. [In the underlying action, the heiress of the original owner of various famous paintings sued the Austrian Government and related entities for return of those paintings, allegedly seized during the Nazi Era. Austria argued that it was entitled to sovereign immunity and claimed that this immunity was absolute because the underlying conduct took place prior to the issuance of the Tate Letter. Both the district court and the appellate court rejected this argument.]

III. Chief Justice Marshall's opinion in *Schooner Exchange v. McFaddon,* 7 Cranch 116 (1812), is generally viewed as the source of our foreign sovereign immunity jurisprudence. In that case, the libellants claimed to be the rightful owners of a French ship that had taken refuge in the port of Philadelphia. The Court first emphasized that the jurisdiction of the United States over persons and property within its territory "is susceptible of no limitation not imposed by itself," and thus foreign sovereigns have no right to immunity in our courts. Chief Justice Marshall went on to explain, however, that as a matter of comity, members of the international community had implicitly agreed to waive the exercise of jurisdiction over other sovereigns in certain classes of cases, such as those involving foreign ministers or the person of the sovereign. Accepting a suggestion advanced by the Executive Branch, the Chief Justice concluded that the implied waiver theory also served to exempt the Schooner Exchange—"a national armed vessel . . . of the emperor of France"—from United States courts' jurisdiction.

In accordance with Chief Justice Marshall's observation that foreign sovereign immunity is a matter of grace and comity rather than a constitutional requirement, this Court has "consistently . . . deferred to the decisions of the political branches—in particular, those of the Executive Branch—on whether to take jurisdiction" over particular actions against foreign sovereigns and their instrumentalities. *Verlinden BV v. Central Bank of Nigeria, supra* (citing *Ex parte Peru,* 318 U.S. 578, 586 (1943); *Republic of Mexico v. Hoffman, supra*). Until 1952 the Executive Branch followed a policy of requesting immunity in all actions against friendly sovereigns. In that year, however, the State Department concluded that "immunity should no longer be granted in certain types of cases." In a letter to the Attorney General, the Acting Legal Adviser for the Secretary of State, Jack B. Tate, explained that the Department would thereafter apply the "restrictive theory" of sovereign immunity. . . .

As we explained in our unanimous opinion in *Verlinden,* the change in State Department policy wrought by the "Tate Letter" had little, if any, impact on federal courts' approach to immunity analyses: "As in the past, initial responsibility for deciding questions of sovereign immunity fell primarily upon the Executive acting through the State Department," and courts continued to "abid[e] by" that Department's "suggestions of immunity." The change did, however, throw immunity determinations into some disarray, as "foreign nations often placed diplomatic pressure on the State Department," and political considerations sometimes led the Department to file "suggestions of immunity in cases where immunity would not have been available under the restrictive theory." Complicating matters further, when foreign nations failed to request immunity from the State Department:

> [T]he responsibility fell to the courts to determine whether sovereign immunity existed, generally by reference to prior State Department decisions. . . . Thus, sovereign immunity determinations were made in two different branches, subject to a variety of factors, sometimes including diplomatic considerations. Not surprisingly, the governing standards were neither clear nor uniformly applied.

In 1976 Congress sought to remedy these problems by enacting the FSIA, a comprehensive statute containing a "set of legal standards governing claims of immunity in every civil action against a foreign state or its political subdivisions, agencies, or instrumentalities." The Act "codifies, as a matter of federal law, the restrictive theory of sovereign immunity," and transfers primary responsibility for immunity determinations from the Executive to the Judicial Branch. The preamble states that "henceforth" both federal and state courts should decide claims of sovereign immunity in conformity with the Act's principles. 28 U.S.C. §1602.

The Act itself grants federal courts jurisdiction over civil actions against foreign states, §1330(a), and over diversity actions in which a foreign state is the plaintiff, §1332(a)(4); it contains venue and removal provisions, §§1391(f), 1441(d); it prescribes the procedures for obtaining personal jurisdiction over a foreign state, §1330(b); and it governs the extent to which a state's property may be subject to attachment or execution, §§1609-1611. Finally, the Act carves out certain exceptions to its general grant of immunity, including the expropriation exception on which respondent's complaint relies. These exceptions are central to the Act's functioning: "At the threshold of every action in a district court against a foreign state, . . . the court must satisfy itself that one of the exceptions applies," as "subject-matter jurisdiction in any such action depends" on that application. *Verlinden,* 461 U.S. at 493-494. . . .

[A]pplying the FSIA to all pending cases regardless of when the underlying conduct occurred is most consistent with two of the Act's principal purposes: clarifying the rules that judges should apply in resolving sovereign immunity claims and eliminating political participation in the resolution of such claims. We have recognized that, to accomplish these purposes, Congress established a comprehensive framework for resolving any claim of sovereign immunity: "We think that the text and structure of the FSIA demonstrate Congress' intention that the FSIA be the sole basis for obtaining jurisdiction over a foreign state in our courts. . . . As we said in *Verlinden,* the FSIA 'must be applied by the district courts in every action against a foreign sovereign, since subject-matter jurisdiction in any such action depends on the existence of one of the specified exceptions to foreign sovereign immunity.'" *Argentine Republic v. Amerada Hess Shipping Corp.,* 488 U.S. 428, 434-435 (1989) (quoting *Verlinden,* 461 U.S. at 493 (1962)). . . . [O]ur observations about the FSIA's inclusiveness are relevant in this case: Quite obviously, Congress' purposes in enacting such a comprehensive jurisdictional scheme would be frustrated if, in postenactment cases concerning preenactment conduct, courts were to continue to follow the same ambiguous and politically charged "'standards'" that the FSIA replaced. . . .

Finally, while we reject the United States' recommendation to bar application of the FSIA to claims based on preenactment conduct, nothing in our holding prevents the State Department from filing statements of interest suggesting that courts decline to exercise jurisdiction in particular cases implicating foreign sovereign immunity. The issue now before us . . . concerns interpretation of the FSIA's reach — a "pure question of statutory construction . . . well within the province of the Judiciary." *INS v. Cardoza-Fonseca,* 480 U.S. 421, 446, 448 (1987). While the United States' views on such an issue are of considerable interest to the Court, they merit no special deference. In contrast, should the State Department choose to express its opinion on the implications of exercising jurisdiction over particular petitioners in connection with *their* alleged conduct,[41] that opinion might well be entitled to deference as the considered judgment of the Executive on a particular question of foreign policy.[42] *See, e.g., Verlinden,* 461 U.S. at 486; *American Ins. Assn. v. Garamendi,* 539 U.S. 396, 414 (2003) (discussing the President's "'vast share of

---

41. We note that the United States Government has apparently indicated to the Austrian Federal Government that it will not file a statement of interest in this case. The enforceability of that indication, of course, is not before us.

42. Mislabeling this observation a "constitutional conclusion," the dissent suggests that permitting the Executive to comment on a party's assertion of sovereign immunity will result in "[u]ncertain prospective application of our foreign sovereign immunity law." We do not hold, however, that executive intervention could or would trump considered application of the FSIA's more neutral principles; we merely note that the Executive's views on questions within its area of expertise merit greater deference than its opinions regarding the scope of a congressional enactment. Furthermore, we fail to understand how our holding, which requires that courts apply the FSIA's sovereign immunity rules in all cases, somehow injects greater uncertainty into sovereign immunity law than the dissent's approach, which would require, for cases concerning pre-1976 conduct, case-by-case analysis of the status of that law at the time of the offending conduct — including analysis of the existence or nonexistence of any State Department statements on the subject.

responsibility for the conduct of our foreign relations' "). We express no opinion on the question whether such deference should be granted in cases covered by the FSIA.

KENNEDY, JUSTICE, dissenting. . . . The Court's abrupt announcement that the FSIA may well be subject to Executive override undermines the Act's central purpose and structure. As the Court acknowledges, before the Act, "immunity determinations [had been thrown] into some disarray, as 'foreign nations often placed diplomatic pressure on the State Department,' and political considerations sometimes led the Department to file 'suggestions of immunity in cases where immunity would not have been available under the restrictive theory.'" Congress intended the FSIA to replace this old and unsatisfactory methodology of Executive decision-making. The President endorsed the objective in full, recommending the bill upon its introduction in Congress, and signing the bill into law upon its presentment. The majority's surprising constitutional conclusion suggests that the FSIA accomplished none of these aims. The Court states that the statute's directives may well be short-circuited by the sole directive of the Executive.

The Court adds a disclaimer that it "express[es] no opinion on the question whether such deference should be granted [to the Executive] in cases covered by the FSIA." The disclaimer, however, is inadequate to remedy the harm done by the invitation, for it is belied by the Court's own terms: Executive statements "suggesting that courts decline to exercise jurisdiction in particular cases implicating foreign sovereign immunity . . . might well be entitled to deference as the considered judgment of the Executive on a particular question of foreign policy." Taking what the Court says at face value, the Court does express an opinion on the question: Its opinion is that the Executive statement may well be entitled to deference, and so may well supersede federal law that gives courts jurisdiction. . . .

Where post-enactment conduct is at stake, the majority's approach promises unfortunate disruption. It promises to reintroduce Executive intervention in foreign sovereign immunity determinations to an even greater degree than existed before the FSIA's enactment. Before the Act, foreign nations only tended to need the Executive's protection from the courts' jurisdiction in instances involving private acts. The Tate Letter ensured their public acts would remain immune from suit, even without Executive intervention. Now, there is a potential for Executive intervention in a much larger universe of claims. The FSIA has no public act/private act distinction with respect to certain categories of conduct, such as expropriations. Foreign nations now have incentive to seek Executive override of the Act's jurisdictional rules for both public and private acts in those categories of cases.

With the FSIA, Congress tried to settle foreign sovereigns' prospective expectations for being subject to suit in American courts and to ensure fair and evenhanded treatment to our citizens who have claims against foreign sovereigns. This was in keeping with strengthening the Executive's ability to secure negotiated agreements with foreign nations against whom our citizens may have claims. Over time, agreements of this sort have been an important tool for the Executive. *See, e.g.,* Agreement Relating to the Agreement of Oct. 24, 2000, Concerning the Austrian Fund "Reconciliation, Peace and Cooperation," Jan. 23, 2001, U.S.-Aus., 2001 WL 935261 (settling claims with Austria); Claims of U.S. Nationals, Nov. 5, 1964, U.S.-Yugo., 16 U.S.T. 1, T.I.A.S. No. 5750 (same with Yugoslavia); Settlement of Claims of U.S. Nationals, July 16, 1960, U.S.-Pol., 11 U.S.T. 1953, T.I.A.S. No. 4545 (same with Poland). Uncertain prospective application of our foreign sovereign immunity law may weaken the Executive's ability to secure such agreements by compromising foreign sovereigns' ability to predict the liability they face in our courts and so to assess the ultimate costs and benefits of any agreement.

U.N. CONVENTION ON JURISDICTION IMMUNITIES
OF STATES AND THEIR PROPERTY
44 Int'l Legal Mats. 801 (2005) [excerpted at Appendix G]

Notes on Schooner Exchange, Pesaro, Republic of Mexico, *Tate Letter,* FSIA, Altmann, *and U.N. State Immunities Convention*

1. *Sovereign immunity in* **Schooner Exchange.** In *Schooner Exchange,* the French vessel was located firmly within U.S. territory. Under prevailing territorial rules of judicial jurisdiction, the vessel was unambiguously subject to the jurisdiction of U.S. courts. *See supra* p. 236. Nevertheless, Chief Justice Marshall held that the vessel was not subject to U.S. jurisdiction, adopting a rule that "national ships of war, entering the port of a friendly foreign power open for their reception, are to be considered as exempted by the consent of that power from its jurisdiction." What was the basis for this rule? What policies supported the rule? Consider how the Supreme Court appeared to have answered these questions in *Altmann.* Do you agree?

2. *Relationship between international law and U.S. law.* Consider Chief Justice Marshall's reliance on "principles of public law," recognized by "the unanimous consent of nations." These are the same principles of international law that were invoked in *Rose v. Himely* and *Pennoyer* to justify territorial limitations on national jurisdiction. *See supra* pp. 83-86, 129-137. Why did the Court, in *Schooner Exchange* and *Pennoyer,* look to international law in defining the jurisdiction of U.S. courts? In both cases, there were U.S. statutes that defined the jurisdiction of U.S. courts. What made international law relevant?

Consider how Justice Stevens describes the *Schooner Exchange* opinion in *Altmann.* Does Justice Stevens refer to the international law principles, or "principles of public law," discussed by Chief Justice Marshall?

3. *Rationale for* **Schooner Exchange.** Recall how firmly entrenched the territoriality doctrine was in nineteenth-century American law — permitting tag jurisdiction and forbidding the assertion of judicial jurisdiction over persons not served with process within the forum's territory. *See supra* pp. ____. Indeed, *Schooner Exchange* acknowledged that "[t]he jurisdiction of the nation within its own territory is necessarily exclusive and absolute," and that a nation's jurisdiction within its territory "is susceptible of no limitation not imposed by itself." According to the Court in *Schooner Exchange,* what provision of law was sufficiently compelling to overcome this doctrine and deny jurisdiction over a ship in U.S. waters?

(a) Judicial abstention. Consider the Court's brief reference, at the conclusion of its opinion in *Schooner Exchange,* to the arguments concerning the "general inability of the judicial power to enforce its decisions in cases of this description," the consideration that "the sovereign power of the nation is alone competent to avenge wrongs committed by a sovereign," the consideration that "the questions to which such wrongs give birth are rather questions of policy than of law," and the consideration that such questions "are for diplomatic, rather than legal discussion." The Court declines to pass upon these issues, beyond noting that they are of "great weight."

Schooner Exchange might be regarded as a form of abstention; a judicial decision not to exercise jurisdiction granted by Congress because doing so would be contrary to international law and would interfere with U.S. foreign relations. Compare the political question and act of state doctrines. *See supra* pp. 54-56 and *infra* pp. 797-857. Would it be legitimate for a court to refuse to exercise jurisdiction granted by a federal statute on these grounds? In other contexts, the Supreme Court has emphasized that U.S. federal courts are subject to a "virtually unflagging obligation" to exercise jurisdiction that Congress has granted to them. *Colorado River Water Conservation District v. United States,* 424 U.S. 800 (1976) ("virtually unflagging obligation of the federal courts to exercise the jurisdiction given to them"); *W.S. Kirkpatrick & Co. v. Environmental Tectonics Corp.,* 493 U.S. 400 (1990) ("The short of the matter is this: Courts in the United States have the power, and ordinarily the obligation, to decide cases and controversies properly presented to them."); *infra* pp. 549-552. Was *Schooner Exchange* a violation of the federal courts' duty to exercise jurisdiction conferred by Congress?

(b) Due Process Clause and other constitutional limits. In *Pennoyer,* the Supreme Court held that international law was incorporated or inherent in the Constitution, and hence operated directly upon the jurisdiction of state courts. *See supra* pp. 91-94, 96-98. Could the same be said in *Schooner Exchange?* Were international law principles of foreign sovereign immunity incorporated within the Fifth Amendment's Due Process Clause, and hence applicable to the federal courts' assertion of jurisdiction over foreign states? Did the Court suggest anything of the sort? *Compare Verlinden BV v. Central Bank of Nigeria,* 461 U.S. 480, 486 (1983) ("foreign sovereign immunity is a matter of grace and comity . . . and not a restriction imposed by the Constitution"). Note the consequences of the foregoing analysis: Congress would likely be incapable of legislating in a manner inconsistent with prevailing principles of international law. Is that desirable? Is it compelled by accepting that the Due Process Clause incorporates international law limits?

Several Supreme Court decisions have expressed doubt about the theory that the Constitution constrains Congress's ability to regulate foreign sovereign immunity. *See College Sav. Bank v. Florida Prepaid Postsecondary Educ. Expense Bd.,* 527 U.S. 666, 686 n.4 (1999) ("[S]tate sovereign immunity, *unlike foreign sovereign immunity,* is a constitutional doctrine that is meant to be both immutable by Congress and resistant to trends."); *Kiowa Tribe of Oklahoma v. Manufacturing Technologies, Inc.,* 523 U.S. 751, 759 (1998).

(c) U.S. Government's role in Schooner Exchange. As noted above, a U.S. district attorney appeared and argued that the *Schooner Exchange* was immune from the jurisdiction of U.S. courts. What role did this play in the Court's analysis? Did *Schooner Exchange* reason that, since the Executive had taken a position in a matter involving foreign relations, U.S. courts should defer? Consider how the *Altmann* Court describes the role of the Executive Branch in *Schooner Exchange.* Is that description accurate?

(d) Presumption that Congress intends to comply with international law. Would it be appropriate to interpret the Court's opinion in *Schooner Exchange* as an exercise in statutory construction? In other contexts, the Court has applied the presumption that Congress does not intend to violate international law. Under this presumption, a federal statute will not be construed as violating international law unless Congress expressly requires this result. *See supra* pp. 13-18; *infra* pp. 898-901 (service abroad); *infra* pp. 664-671, 685-707 (extraterritorial application of U.S. law). How would this presumption apply to the generally worded jurisdictional statute in *Schooner Exchange?*

4. Schooner Exchange *and absolute immunity.* Was Chief Justice Marshall's opinion in *Schooner Exchange* a statement of the "absolute theory" of sovereign immunity? Consider the Court's discussion of the private property of a "prince." Is that consistent with the notion that all of a foreign state's property — commercial and noncommercial — enjoys sovereign immunity? Note how the Tate Letter describes the historical status of the sovereign immunity doctrine in the United States.

5. *Development of the absolute theory of immunity.* Whatever the intended scope of the rule of immunity in *Schooner Exchange,* the Court subsequently made it clear that foreign states *were* entitled to absolute immunity in U.S. courts. In *Berizzi Bros. Co. v. SS Pesaro,* 271 U.S. 562 (1926), the Court held that a vessel owned and operated by the Italian government, and used for carrying commercial cargo and passengers, was not subject to the jurisdiction of U.S. courts. Is the principle of absolute immunity adopted in *Pesaro* sensible? What is the response to the district court's reasoning that it is both unjust to private parties and, in the long run, disadvantageous to foreign states, to immunize them from jurisdiction for their commercial acts?

6. *Considerations of reciprocity.* The district court had observed in *Pesaro* that "ships owned and operated for commercial purposes by the United States would not be exempt from ordinary process under Italian law." 277 F. 473, 482 (S.D.N.Y. 1921). The district court refused to draw any conclusion from this, noting that "retaliation and reprisal are for the executive branches of our government and not for the courts." Is this the right result? If Italy would not grant sovereign immunity to U.S. Government commercial vessels, why should U.S. courts accord such immunity to Italian government vessels? Is this merely a matter of "retaliation and reprisal"? If it applies the cited rule, Italy presumably does not think international law forbids the exercise of judicial jurisdiction over foreign state-owned commercial vessels. Given that, how would U.S. application of the same rule violate Italy's rights under international law? The district court did, however, consider the fact that Italian courts would also not accord immunity to the Pesaro in concluding that U.S. courts also should not grant immunity. Is this rationale persuasive? Might a nation be more willing to submit itself to its own courts than to foreign courts? Consider *Schooner Exchange*'s basic rationale for sovereign immunity.

7. *The role of Executive Branch "suggestions" of immunity.* Contrast the rationale for immunity in *Republic of Mexico* with that in *Schooner Exchange*. Which rationale is more satisfactory? What are the difficulties with permitting the Executive Branch to make suggestions of immunity, that are binding on the courts? Is such an approach consistent with due process and the rule of law? Does it not permit a political branch of the government—relying on political considerations—to decide individual civil disputes? *See infra* pp. 277, 265-266, discussing the role of the Executive Branch in official immunity determinations and pp. 838-842, discussing the *Bernstein* exception under the act of state doctrine. Consider *Altmann*'s discussion of the problems with Executive Branch "suggestions" of immunity.

8. *Restrictive theory and the Tate Letter.* Consider the restrictive theory of sovereign immunity, articulated in the Tate Letter. Are the justifications advanced for the theory persuasive? Note how the Tate Letter—like *Schooner Exchange*—relies primarily on state practice and evidence of contemporary international law, but that international law had evolved significantly since 1812. Can any meaningful line be drawn between "commercial" or "private" activities, and "sovereign" or "public" ones? What, for example, is a foreign state's purchase of boots, which it intends to use to outfit its army? Is it a routine commercial transaction or a sovereign defense of national interests?

9. *Restrictive immunity vs. absolute immunity.* Compare the rule of absolute immunity reflected in *Berizzi Bros.* with the rule of restrictive immunity reflected in the Tate Letter and FSIA. Which is preferable from a policy perspective? Why? If the primary concern of immunity is to provide courts a clear and workable rule, what was wrong with a system of absolute immunity that sprang from the *Schooner Exchange* case? Absolute immunity provides a clear rule that minimizes any risk of disruption to the foreign relations of the United States. What is wrong with that rule?

What makes "commercial" or "private" actions of a foreign state different from "sovereign" actions? Some critics have reasoned that "[t]he concept of acts *jure gestionis,* of commercial, non-sovereign, or less essential activity, requires value judgments which rest on political assumptions as to the proper sphere of state activity and of priorities in state policies." I. Brownlie, *Principles of Public International Law* 330 (3d ed. 1979). Even if this is true, does the restrictive theory rest only on notions of the "proper sphere of state activity," or does it rest on fairness to private parties and on a desire to facilitate efficient, neutral international dispute resolution? Compare the following views, expressed by Bulgaria and Venezuela during the drafting of the U.N. Convention:

> These principles of contemporary international law function in all spheres of inter-State relations, be they political, economic, trade, social, scientific-technological or cultural ones. Therefore, the State always acts as *imperium*, a purveyor of State authority in its external relations, and no additional circumstances, such as the development of State functions, can undermine the sovereignty and the principle of non-submission of one State to the jurisdictional authority of another.
>
> This requires that the draft articles on jurisdictional immunities of States and their property should be based on the generally acknowledged and traditional tenet of full State immunity, regulating only a limited number of clearly specified exceptions to it which would be acceptable to the overwhelming majority of States. The draft articles under consideration could not serve as a basis for a universally applicable concept in this field, since in their drafting the legislation of only a limited number of developed Western States has been taken into consideration and consulted. The draft articles should reaffirm the concept of immunities of States and their property, rather than undermine it through many exceptions encompassing important spheres of State activity, thus largely reducing it to a mere legal fiction. Jurisdictional Immunities of States and their Property, Comments and Observations Received from Governments, Document A/CN.4/410, Y.B. I.L.C. 1988, Vol. II(1) (Bulgaria comments).
>
> Venezuela also expressed concern at the fact that the Commission had opted for a system which allows numerous exceptions to the sovereign immunity of States and their property. This detracts from the general principle that States are immune among themselves and, in the opinion of Venezuela, is prejudicial to the developing countries, where owing to the lack of private capital the State has to undertake diverse and varied activities related to the international economy and commercial relations. In this connection, it was stressed that the developing countries should endeavor to ensure that, in the final text, the exceptions to or limitations on the sovereign immunity of States and their property are fewer in number or lesser in scope. *Id.* (Venezuela comments).

What other values are at stake that counsel in favor of a more restrictive theory of immunity? What would be the consequences for international trade of an absolute theory of immunity, during an era when foreign states are heavily involved in commercial and financial affairs? *See also infra* pp. 284-288. Would a theory of absolute immunity be consistent with the basic foundations of a community founded on the rule of law? Note that the United States has waived its sovereign immunity in significant respects. *See* 28 U.S.C. §1346. Is it just for foreign states to be absolutely immune from judicial process?

10. *Judicial vs. Executive Branch determinations of foreign sovereign immunity.* Was it wise to replace the practice of *ad hoc* executive determinations of sovereign immunity with the FSIA's legislative solution, applied in judicial proceedings? As the Court in *Altmann* discusses, one purpose of the FSIA was to combat the politicization of immunity determinations and to provide more predictable rules for courts.

Are immunity determinations inherently political judgments? Is there any way that one can really "de-politicize" these decisions? Note that the U.N. State Immunities Convention appears capable of articulating specific legal rules concerning state immunity. Is the political content of foreign sovereign immunity decisions any different from many other decisions that courts must make in international (and domestic) cases?

What were the benefits of Executive Branch determinations of immunity? The costs? If one accepts that there is a principled distinction, derived from public international law doctrine, between "sovereign" and "private" or "commercial" actions, then does it follow that application of this distinction should be a judicial responsibility? Even if sovereign immunity determinations are appropriately for judicial resolution, did the FSIA as drafted succeed in supplying rules that would help to provide more consistent and predictable outcomes? Keep this question in mind as you explore the various aspects of the FSIA in greater detail in the remainder of this chapter, particularly the recent decision in *Samantar* involving determinations about the immunity of foreign government officials. While the FSIA was designed to reallocate power to make foreign sovereign immunity determinations to the judiciary, pre-FSIA practice still informs interpretation of the statute. Specifically, the Supreme Court identified "two well-recognized and related purposes of the FSIA: adoption of the restrictive view of sovereign immunity and codification of international law at the time of the FSIA's enactment." *Permanent Mission of India to the United Nations v. City of New York*, 551 U.S. 193 (2007). This suggests that questions of FSIA interpretation will be resolved, at least in part, by reference to the common law of restrictive immunity against which the FSIA was adopted and by reference to *international law*. Is this explicit reference to international law wise? How does it differ (if at all) from the "law of nations" requirement under the Alien Tort Statute? What should a court do if the pre-FSIA federal common law and the international law standards cut in different directions?

Compare the basic structure and terms of the FSIA and the U.N. State Immunities Convention. What are the advantages and disadvantages of each?

11. *Executive Branch authority under* **Altmann.** Consider the debate between Justice Stevens and Justice Kennedy in *Altmann* over whether the Executive Branch may intervene and urge a court to decline jurisdiction in a particular case with serious foreign relations implications. Do you agree with Justice Kennedy's charge that the Court acknowledges a significant weight to Executive Branch interventions? Why should that sort of political intervention be accorded any weight in a judicial proceeding? Why should it be permissible?

Does the text of the FSIA admit of Executive Branch intervention in foreign sovereign immunity cases? Hasn't Congress already decided whether, and to what extent, courts may hear claims against foreign sovereigns? As Justice Kennedy argues, does Justice Stevens' suggestion concerning Executive Branch interventions undercut the entire congressional scheme of the FSIA? Does the suggestion return this area of the law to an era more akin to that under the Tate Letter? What does Justice Stevens mean when, writing for the majority, he says that the Executive's views do not "trump considered application of the FSIA's more neutral principles" but "merit greater deference" when they touch upon the Executive's "area of expertise"?

Consider your answers to these questions in light of other areas where the Court has addressed the role of the Executive Branch's views on the foreign relations implications of a lawsuit. *See supra* pp. 53-56 (political question doctrine), *infra* pp. 809-812, 831 (official immunity determinations), pp. 838-842 (act of state doctrine), and *infra* pp. 258-275 (the head of state doctrine). How do those doctrines influence this debate? Do they suggest that the views of the Executive Branch can be accommodated in other ways? Or are there peculiar features of lawsuits against foreign sovereigns that make the Executive Branch's views particularly important?

As a matter of practice, the Executive Branch frequently files statements of interest in litigation against foreign sovereigns. *See, e.g., City of New York v. Permanent Mission of India to the United Nations*, 446 F.3d 365, 376 n.17 (2d Cir. 2006); *Flatow v. Islamic Republic of Iran*, 305 F.3d 1249 (D.C. Cir. 2002); *Sea Hunt, Inc. v. Unidentified Shipwrecked Vessel or Vessels*, 221 F.3d 634 (4th Cir. 2000); *McDonald v. Socialist People's Libyan Arab Jamahiriya*, 666 F. Supp.

2d 50, 51-52 (D.D.C. 2009). What weight should be accorded an Executive Branch statement of interest? Is such a statement of interest just like an amicus curiae brief — capable of presenting important facts and law, if such exist? Or is it entitled to some sort of special weight and authority, given its conclusions and judgments? If the latter, how is this consistent with judicial function?

Assuming that they are entitled to some weight, what inference, if any, should a court draw where the Executive Branch has *not* filed a statement of interest? *See Cassirer v. Kingdom of Spain*, 616 F.3d 1019 (9th Cir. 2010) (*en banc*). Does this suggest that the court should feel especially comfortable permitting the suit against the foreign sovereign provided that it has jurisdiction under the FSIA? Or would that be an unreasonable inference? Recall the comments of a former Legal Advisor about the complexities in deciding whether to file a statement of interest, *supra* pp. 55-56.

12. *Retroactivity of the FSIA.* The enactment of the FSIA, like most statutes, gave rise to questions over its retroactive application. Should the Act apply to conduct occurring prior to its enactment? To conduct occurring prior to the formal embrace of the restrictive theory of immunity in the Tate Letter?

Remarkably, nearly 30 years passed following enactment of the FSIA in 1976 before the Supreme Court decided whether the Act was retroactive. When it finally did so, the Court's answer in *Altmann* surprised many observers. What reasons does Justice Stevens give for retroactive application of the FSIA? What do you make of the argument that it would "de-politicize" cases involving pre-1976 conduct to apply the FSIA to such conduct? Doesn't Justice Stevens take away with one hand, what he gave with the first — when he highlights the possibility for Executive Branch intervention? Or are such statements of interest fundamentally different from pre-FSIA Executive Branch determinations?

Doesn't the Court's holding that the FSIA applied to conduct occurring even prior to its enactment upset foreign states' expectations about their absolute immunity when they engaged in that conduct? What protection, if any, does the majority's opinion accord to the foreign states' reliance interests? Compare the treatment of retroactivity in the U.N. State Immunities Convention. Which is wiser?

Do foreign states really have reliance interests in conduct that is decades old? Don't statutes of limitations provide some protection here? To the extent they don't, by the time of *Altmann,* haven't foreign states had nearly three decades' notice that they might be haled into U.S. courts, including for conduct that occurred during an era of absolute immunity?

B. Entities Entitled to Immunity Under the FSIA

Only entities that satisfy the FSIA's definition of "foreign states" are entitled to §1604's presumptive grant of immunity. Conversely, only "foreign states" are subject to the FSIA's grants of personal and subject matter jurisdiction.

Section 1603 of the FSIA contains the basic statutory definition of "foreign state." The provision states, in §1603(a), that:

A "foreign state," except as used in §1608 of this title, includes a political subdivision of a foreign state or an agency or instrumentality of a foreign state as defined in subsection (b).

Thus, §1603(a) defines "foreign state" to include each of three entities: (1) a "*foreign state,*" (2) "a *political subdivision* of a foreign state," and (3) "an *agency or instrumentality* of a foreign state." Section 1603(b) goes on to define an "agency or instrumentality" of a foreign state.

Foreign states frequently establish a wide range of governmental, administrative, geographic, and corporate entities to perform various functions.[43] These entities can range from administrative departments (*e.g.*, Ministry of Defense) to geographic subdivisions (*e.g.*, a state or province) to corporations (*e.g.*, France Telecom), and can possess varying degrees of functional and legal separation from the foreign state that creates them. Some foreign governmental entities are merely *ad hoc* administrative bodies, without separate legal identity under foreign law; other foreign governmental entities are separate juridical persons, with an independent legal status under foreign law.[44]

One of the most frequently encountered forms of organization associated with foreign states is the corporation. Examples include state-owned corporations such as airlines, banks, telecommunications providers, or shipping companies.[45] These corporations can be owned either directly by a foreign state (or political subdivision thereof) or indirectly, through one or more tiers of holding companies.[46]

Application of the FSIA's definition of "foreign state" to this diversity of organizations is often difficult. Although there are many clear answers (*e.g.*, the Republic of Austria is a foreign state) there are also numerous unclear subjects. The following sections examine each of the various categories of §1603(a).

1. Foreign States Proper

The first of the three categories of "foreign state" encompasses "foreign states proper"—that is, nation states such as the Federal Republic of Germany or the United Kingdom. For FSIA purposes, the definition of "foreign state" is generally understood as including any nation recognized by the United States in its diplomatic relations as an independent state. U.S. courts have routinely afforded the FSIA's protections to foreign countries, even when their relations with the United States are acrimonious, provided they enjoy U.S. diplomatic recognition.[47]

International law provides various definitions of "statehood."[48] For purposes of the FSIA, however, the application of these definitions has been left largely to the discretion of the U.S. Executive Branch. Most U.S. courts have said they will defer to the President's decisions regarding the recognition or nonrecognition of foreign states.[49] Nevertheless,

43. *See* Hoffman, *The Separate Entity Rule in International Perspective: Should State Ownership of Corporate Shares Confer Sovereign Status for Immunity Purposes?*, 65 Tulane L. Rev. 535 (1991); Note, *Jurisdiction Over Foreign States for Acts of Their Instrumentalities: A Model for Attributing Liabilities*, 94 Yale L.J. 394 (1984).

44. Friedmann, *Government Enterprise: A Comparative Analysis, in Government Enterprise: A Comparative Study* 306-334 (W. Friedmann & J.F. Garner eds., 1970); United Nations Department of Economic and Social Affairs, Organization, Management and Supervision of Public Enterprises in Developing Countries 63-69 (1974).

45. *See, e.g., Voest-Alpine Trading USA Corp. v. Bank of China*, 142 F.3d 887 (5th Cir. 1998) (state-owned bank); *Filetech SA v. France Telecom, SA*, 212 F. Supp. 2d 183 (S.D.N.Y. 2001), *aff'd*, 304 F.3d 180 (2d Cir. 2002) (state-owned telecommunications company); *LeDonne v. Gulf Air, Inc.*, 700 F. Supp. 1400 (E.D. Va. 1988) (state-owned airline).

46. *Dole Food Co. v. Patrickson*, 538 U.S. 468 (2003) (discussing a corporation owned indirectly by a foreign state and finding that it was not an agent or instrumentality of the foreign state).

47. *E.g., Ministry of Defense and Support for the Armed Forces of the Islamic Republic of Iran v. Elahi*, 128 S. Ct. 1722 (2009); *Ministry of Defense and Support for Armed Forces of Islamic Republic of Iran v. Elahi*, 546 U.S. 450 (2006); *Adler v. Federal Republic of Nigeria*, 107 F.3d 720, 723 (9th Cir. 1997); *Frolova v. USSR*, 761 F.2d 370 (7th Cir. 1985); *Berkovitz v. Islamic Republic of Iran*, 735 F.2d 329 (9th Cir. 1984); *Carey v. National Oil Co.*, 592 F.2d 673 (2d Cir. 1979) (Libya).

48. *E.g., Restatement (Third) Foreign Relations Law* §201 (1987) ("a 'state' is an entity which has a defined territory and permanent population, under the control of its own government, and which engages in, or has the capacity to engage in, formal relations with other such entities.").

49. *See O'Bryan v. Holy See*, 556 F.3d 361, 372 & n.2 (6th Cir. 2009); *Owens v. Republic of Sudan*, 531 F.3d 884, 892-893 (D.C. Cir. 2008); *Klinghoffer v. S.N.C. Achille Lauro*, 937 F.2d 44 (2d Cir. 1991) (PLO is not a foreign state for FSIA purposes); *Estates of Ungar v. Palestinian Authority*, 315 F. Supp. 2d 164, 176-186 (D.R.I. 2004) ("[T]he PA

atypical foreign entities, such as the Trust Territories and other quasi-national entities that are not recognized by the U.S. Executive Branch, have been held by some courts to qualify as foreign states because of their state-like characteristics.[50]

The FSIA generally treats "foreign states" in the same fashion as "agencies and instrumentalities." Nevertheless, it provides differing treatments in some important respects, including the scope of the expropriation exception, service of process, venue, punitive damages, and execution of judgments.[51] Difficulties have occasionally arisen in deciding how to classify, for these purposes, foreign entities that are related to what is concededly a "foreign state," but which also possess a measure of independence from the foreign government. Are such entities: (a) the "foreign state" itself or (b) an "agency" or "instrumentality" of the foreign state? In deciding whether particular foreign entities should be categorized as "foreign states" or "agencies or instrumentalities," courts have generally examined the degree to which the entity is integrated into the foreign government's political and administrative decision-making apparatus.[52]

2.   Foreign State "Political Subdivisions"

The definition of foreign state in §1603(a) of the Act includes "political subdivisions" of foreign states.[53] According to the FSIA's legislative history, "[t]he term "political subdivisions" includes all governmental units beneath the central government, including local governments."[54] Under this definition, the states, provinces, cantons, and other regional subdivisions of foreign nations qualify as "foreign states," while entities established and owned by these subdivisions can qualify as "agencies or instrumentalities of the foreign state."[55] It is not clear how foreign possessions or dependencies of foreign states would be treated under §1603(a).

3.   Agencies and Instrumentalities of Foreign States

Foreign state-related entities that are not a foreign state proper or a foreign state's political subdivision nonetheless may qualify as a "foreign state" under §1603(a). To do so, they must fall within the FSIA's definition of "agency or instrumentality of a foreign state." Section 1603(b) of the Act defines an "agency or instrumentality" as an entity:

> (1) which is a separate legal person, corporate or otherwise, and (2) which is an organ of a foreign state or political subdivision thereof, or a majority of whose shares or other ownership

---

and PLO are not foreign States that are entitled to sovereign immunity."); *Knox v. Palestine Liberation Organization*, 306 F. Supp. 2d 424, 439 (S.D.N.Y. 2004); *Transportes Aereos de Angola v. Ronair, Inc.*, 544 F. Supp. 858 (D. Del. 1982).

50. *Compare Morgan Guaranty Trust Co. v. Republic of Palau*, 639 F. Supp. 706 (S.D.N.Y. 1986) (notwithstanding status as Trust Territory, Palau is "foreign state" because of its de facto exercise of sovereign powers) *with Sablan Constr. Co. v. Government of Trust Territory of Pacific Islands*, 526 F. Supp. 135 (D.N. Mar. C. 1981) (Trust Territory is not a "foreign state").

51. In each of these contexts, foreign states proper receive different (usually more favorable) treatment than foreign state agencies or instrumentalities. *See* 28 U.S.C. §1608 (service); §1391(f) (venue); §1606 (punitive damages); §§1609-10 (enforcement).

52. *See Roeder v. Islamic Republic of Iran*, 333 F.3d 228, 234-235 (D.C. Cir. 2003); *Transaero, Inc. v. La Fuerza Aerea Boliviana*, 30 F.3d 148 (D.C. Cir. 1994); *Hyatt Corp. v. Stanton*, 945 F. Supp. 675, 680-684 (S.D.N.Y. 1996); *Unidyne Corp. v. Aerolineas Argentinas*, 590 F. Supp. 398, 400 (E.D. Va. 1984); *Marlowe v. Argentine Naval Comm'n*, 604 F. Supp. 703 (D.D.C. 1985).

53. 28 U.S.C. §1603(a) (1982).

54. H.R. Rep. No. 1487, 94th Cong., 2d Sess. 15, *reprinted in* 1976 U.S. Code Cong. & Admin. News at 6604, 6613.

55. *Restatement (Third) Foreign Relations Law* §452, comment b (1987).

interest is owned by a foreign state or political subdivision thereof, and (3) which is neither a citizen of a State of the United States . . . nor created under the laws of any third country.

This definition of "agency and instrumentality" has given rise to a number of interpretative questions. In particular, it was unclear for some time whether a company qualified as an "agency or instrumentality" when a foreign state held indirect ownership interests in the company, through an intermediate holding corporation.[56] As discussed below, the Supreme Court has resolved this question, holding that only direct subsidiaries of a foreign state, a foreign state organ, or a foreign state's political subdivision qualify as "agencies or instrumentalities."[57]

It was also unclear at what point in time the §1603(a) tests should be applied — at the time of the underlying activities, at the time an action is filed in U.S. courts, or at the time a decision is to be made. Again, after a period of uncertainty, the Supreme Court resolved this issue. It held that "instrumentality status [must] be determined at the time suit is filed."[58]

There remain important interpretative questions concerning the definition of "foreign state" under the FSIA. In particular, lower courts continue to struggle with the question whether particular entities are foreign states proper or "organs" of foreign states.[59] There is also uncertainty concerning the role of foreign (and international) law in determining when particular entities are "separate legal persons" or "owned" by foreign states, as well as the role of the Executive Branch in judicial determinations as to whether particular entities are entitled to foreign state status.[60]

4. Separate Legal Identities of Foreign Government Entities and Grounds for Disregarding

As discussed above, a foreign state agency or instrumentality that possesses separate legal status is treated as distinct from the "foreign state" proper, by the FSIA.[61] In general, consistent with their approach outside the FSIA context,[62] U.S. courts will recognize the separate legal identity of such agencies and instrumentalities.[63] Nevertheless, there are circumstances in which the actions or liability of one foreign state instrumentality will be attributed to another agency, or to the foreign state itself.

The question of attribution of corporate liability can arise in a variety of circumstances. These include attempts to enforce a judgment made as to one entity against a second entity, attempts to attribute one entity's jurisdictional contacts to a second entity, and assertions of a claim or counterclaim based on the acts of one entity against a different entity. The Supreme Court addressed this question in *First National City Bank v. Banco Para El Comercio Exterior de Cuba ("Bancec")*,[64] which arose after the Cuba's expropriation of Citibank's Cuban assets.

---

56. *Compare Patrickson v. Dole Food Co.,* 251 F.3d 795 (9th Cir. 2001) (holding that an indirectly owned subsidiary was not an instrumentality of a foreign state) *with Delgado v. Shell Oil Co.,* 231 F.3d 165, 176 (5th Cir. 2001) ("The plain language of the statute simply requires 'ownership' by a foreign state. It draws no distinction between direct and indirect ownership; neither does it expressly impose a requirement of direct ownership.").

57. *Dole Food Co. v. Patrickson,* 538 U.S. 468 (2003).

58. *Dole Food Co. v. Patrickson,* 538 U.S. 468 (2003).

59. *See infra* pp. 266-267.

60. *See infra* pp. 267-269.

61. *See supra* pp. 252-253.

62. *See supra* pp. 175-190.

63. *See First National City Bank v. Banco Para El Comercio Exterior de Cuba ("Bancec"),* 462 U.S. 611 (1983).

64. 462 U.S. 611 (1983).

As discussed in greater detail below, the *Bancec* Court reaffirmed the general principle that corporations, including state-owned corporations, are separate legal entities. Nonetheless, the Court also held that, in relatively narrow circumstances, similar to those applicable to private companies, the separate legal identity of a foreign state–owned entity could be disregarded.[65] The Court's decision has been applied, in a variety of contexts, by lower courts.

5. Foreign Heads of State and State Officials

Heads of foreign states and other governmental officials are not expressly accorded immunity under the FSIA. Nonetheless, lower courts have long recognized that foreign heads of state and other governmental officials enjoy a measure of immunity in U.S. courts.[66] Following the FSIA's enactment, lower courts reached a variety of results, often contradictory, concerning both the analytical basis for head-of-state and official immunity and the circumstances in which such immunity applies.[67] The Supreme Court's decision in *Samantar v. Yousuf* clarified that government officials generally do not fall within the FSIA's ambit and, at most, enjoy official immunity under federal common law.[68]

6. Selected Materials on Foreign State Entities

The materials excerpted below illustrate the application of §1603 of the FSIA and its definition of "foreign state." First, read *Dole Food Co. v. Patrickson,* where the Supreme Court attempted to resolve some of the uncertainties surrounding the identities of the entities entitled to protection under the FSIA. Second, read *Bancec,* where the Court considers the separate juridical status of foreign state–related entities and the attribution of liability among such entities. Finally, read *Samantar,* where the Court considers whether the FSIA extends to individual government officials.

DOLE FOOD CO. v. PATRICKSON
538 U.S. 468 (2003)

KENNEDY, JUSTICE. [A group of foreign farmworkers sued the Dole Food Company and other defendants in Hawaii state court, alleging that they had been exposed to toxic chemicals from their use of an agricultural pesticide. Dole impleaded two companies — Dead Sea Bromine Co., Ltd., and Bromine Compounds, Ltd., ("the Dead Sea Companies"), chemical companies formerly owned indirectly by the Israeli government. The Dead Sea Companies sought to remove the case to federal court on the theory that they were "agencies and instrumentalities" of the State of Israel. In relevant part, both the

---

65. 462 U.S. at 629-633.

66. *See Restatement (Second) Foreign Relations Law* §65 (1965); *Chuidian v. Philippine Nat'l Bank,* 912 F.2d 1095, 1103 (9th Cir. 1990); *Republic of the Philippines v. Marcos,* 806 F.2d 344, 360-361 (2d Cir. 1986); *Doe I v. State of Israel,* 400 F. Supp. 2d 86, 111 (D.D.C. 2005); *Lafontant v. Aristide,* 844 F. Supp. 128 (E.D.N.Y. 1994); *Herbage v. Meese,* 747 F. Supp. 60, 65-67 (D.D.C. 1990), *aff'd,* 1991 WL 180053 (D.C. Cir. 1991).

67. *See, e.g., Enahoro v. Abubakar,* 408 F.3d 877, 881 (7th Cir. 2005); *Velasco v. Government of Indonesia,* 370 F.3d 392, 399 (4th Cir. 2004); *Byrd v. Corporacion Forestal y Industrial de Olancho SA,* 182 F.3d 380, 388-389 (5th Cir. 1999); *El-Fadl v. Central Bank of Jordan,* 75 F.3d 668, 671 (D.C. Cir. 1996); *Chuidian v. Philippine Nat'l Bank,* 912 F.2d 1095, 1106 (9th Cir. 1990); *Republic of Philippines v. Marcos,* 806 F.2d 344, 360-361 (2d Cir. 1986); *Bolkiah v. Superior Court,* 74 Cal. App. 4th 984 (Cal. Ct. App. 1999).

68. 130 S. Ct. 2278 (2010).

district court and Court of Appeals held that the Dead Sea Companies were not entitled to removal on this basis.]

The State of Israel did not have direct ownership of shares in either of the Dead Sea Companies at any time pertinent to this suit. Rather, these companies were, at various times, separated from the State of Israel by one or more intermediate corporate tiers. For example, from 1984-1985, Israel wholly owned a company called Israeli Chemicals, Ltd.; which owned a majority of shares in another company called Dead Sea Works, Ltd.; which owned a majority of shares in Dead Sea Bromine Co., Ltd.; which owned a majority of shares in Bromine Compounds, Ltd.

The Dead Sea Companies, as indirect subsidiaries of the State of Israel, were not instrumentalities of Israel under the FSIA at any time. Those companies cannot come within the statutory language which grants status as an instrumentality of a foreign state to an entity a "majority of whose shares or other ownership interest is owned by a foreign state or political subdivision thereof." §1603(b)(2). We hold that only direct ownership of a majority of shares by the foreign state satisfies the statutory requirement. . . .

A basic tenet of American corporate law is that the corporation and its shareholders are distinct entities. *See, e.g., First Nat. City Bank v. Banco Para El Comercio Exterior de Cuba,* 462 U.S. 611, 625 (1983) ("Separate legal personality has been described as 'an almost indispensable aspect of the public corporation'"); *Burnet v. Clark,* 287 U.S. 410, 415 (1932) ("A corporation and its stockholders are generally to be treated as separate entities"). An individual shareholder, by virtue of his ownership of shares, does not own the corporation's assets and, as a result, does not own subsidiary corporations in which the corporation holds an interest. A corporate parent which owns the shares of a subsidiary does not, for that reason alone, own or have legal title to the assets of the subsidiary; and, it follows with even greater force, the parent does not own or have legal title to the subsidiaries of the subsidiary. The fact that the shareholder is a foreign state does not change the analysis. *See First Nat. City Bank,* 462 U.S. at 626-627 ("[G]overnment instrumentalities established as juridical entities distinct and independent from their sovereign should normally be treated as such").

Applying these principles, it follows that Israel did not own a majority of shares in the Dead Sea Companies. The State of Israel owned a majority of shares, at various times, in companies one or more corporate tiers above the Dead Sea Companies, but at no time did Israel own a majority of shares in the Dead Sea Companies. Those companies were subsidiaries of other corporations. . . .

The FSIA's definition of instrumentality refers to a foreign state's majority ownership of "shares or other ownership interest." §1603(b)(2). The Dead Sea Companies would have us read "other ownership interest" to include a state's "interest" in its instrumentality's subsidiary. The better reading of the text, in our view, does not support this argument. The words "other ownership interest," when following the word "shares," should be interpreted to refer to a type of interest other than ownership of stock. The statute had to be written for the contingency of ownership forms in other countries, or even in this country, that depart from conventional corporate structures. The statutory phrase "other ownership interest" is best understood to accomplish this objective. Reading the term to refer to a state's interest in entities lower on the corporate ladder would make the specific reference to "shares" redundant. Absent a statutory text or structure that requires us to depart from normal rules of construction, we should not construe the statute in a manner that is strained and, at the same time, would render a statutory term superfluous.

The Dead Sea Companies say that the State of Israel exercised considerable control over their operations, notwithstanding Israel's indirect relationship to those companies.

They appear to think that, in determining instrumentality status under the Act, control may be substituted for an ownership interest. Control and ownership, however, are distinct concepts. The terms of §1603(b)(2) are explicit and straightforward. Majority ownership by a foreign state, not control, is the benchmark of instrumentality status. We need not delve into Israeli law or examine the extent of Israel's involvement in the Dead Sea Companies' operations. Even if Israel exerted the control the Dead Sea Companies describe, that would not give Israel a "majority of [the companies'] shares or other ownership interest." The statutory language will not support a control test that mandates inquiry in every case into the past details of a foreign nation's relation to a corporate entity in which it does not own a majority of the shares.

The better rule is the one supported by the statutory text and elementary principles of corporate law. A corporation is an instrumentality of a foreign state under the FSIA only if the foreign state itself owns a majority of the corporation's shares.

[The Court then turned to the second question presented by the case — the relevant date for determining whether an entity qualified as an "agency or instrumentality."] [T]he Dead Sea Companies must show that they are entities "a majority of whose shares or other ownership interest is owned by a foreign state." §1603(b)(2). We think the plain text of this provision, because it is expressed in the present tense, requires that instrumentality status be determined at the time suit is filed. Construing §1603(b) so that the present tense has real significance is consistent with the "longstanding principle that 'the jurisdiction of the Court depends upon the state of things at the time of the action brought.'" *Keene Corp. v. United States,* 508 U.S. 200, 207 (1993) (quoting *Mollan v. Torrance,* 9 Wheat. 537, 539 (1824)). . . .

Any relationship recognized under the FSIA between the Dead Sea Companies and Israel had been severed before suit was commenced. As a result, the Dead Sea Companies would not be entitled to instrumentality status even if their theory that instrumentality status could be conferred on a subsidiary were accepted.

BREYER, JUSTICE, dissenting. . . . Does this type of majority-ownership interest count as an example of what the statute calls an "other ownership interest"? The Court says no, holding that the text of the FSIA requires that "only direct ownership of a majority of shares by the foreign state satisfies the statutory requirement." I disagree.

The statute's language, standing alone, cannot answer the question. That is because the words "own" and "ownership" — neither of which is defined in the FSIA — are not technical terms or terms of art but common terms, the precise legal meaning of which depends upon the statutory context in which they appear. *See* J. Cribbet & C. Johnson, *Principles of the Law of Property* 16 (3d ed. 1989) ("Anglo-American law has not made much use of the term ownership in a technical sense"). . . .

The [FSIA] itself makes clear that it seeks: (1) to provide a foreign-state defendant in a legal action the right to have its claim of a sovereign immunity bar decided by the "courts of the United States," *i.e.,* the federal courts, 28 U.S.C. §1604; *see* §1441(d); and (2) to make certain that the merits of unbarred claims against foreign states, say, states engaging in commercial activities, *see* §1605(a)(2), will be decided "in the same manner" as similar claims against "a private individual," §1606; but (3) to guarantee a foreign state defending an unbarred claim certain protections, including a prohibition of punitive damages, the right to removal to federal court, a trial before a judge, and other procedural rights (related to service of process, venue, attachment, and execution of judgments). . . .

As far as this statute is concerned, decisions about how to incorporate, how to structure corporate entities, or whether to act through a single corporate layer or through several corporate layers are matters purely of form, not of substance. . . . The need for federal-court determination of a sovereign immunity claim is no less important where subsidiaries are involved. The need for procedural protections is no less compelling. The risk of adverse foreign policy consequences is no less great. . . .

FIRST NATIONAL CITY BANK v. BANCO PARA EL COMERCIO EXTERIOR DE CUBA
462 U.S. 611 (1983)

JUSTICE O'CONNOR. In 1960 the Government of the Republic of Cuba established respondent Banco Para El Comercio Exterior de Cuba (Bancec) to serve as "[a]n official autonomous credit institution for foreign trade . . . with full juridical capacity . . . of its own. . . ." Law No. 793, Art. 1 (1960). In September 1960 Bancec sought to collect on a letter of credit issued by petitioner First National City Bank (now Citibank) in its favor in support of a contract for delivery of Cuban sugar to a buyer in the United States. Within days after Citibank received the request for collection, all of its assets in Cuba were seized and nationalized by the Cuban Government. When Bancec brought suit on the letter of credit in U.S. District Court, Citibank counterclaimed, asserting a right to set off the value of its seized Cuban assets. The question before us is whether Citibank may obtain such a setoff, notwithstanding the fact that Bancec was established as a separate juridical entity. Applying principles of equity common to international law and federal common law, we conclude that Citibank may apply a setoff.

I. . . . Bancec was established by Law No. 793, of April 25, 1960. . . . Bancec's stated purpose was "to contribute to, and collaborate with the international trade policy of the Government and the application of the measures concerning foreign trade adopted by the 'Banco Nacional de Cuba,' " — Cuba's central bank ("Banco Nacional"). Bancec was empowered to act as the Cuban Government's exclusive agent in foreign trade. The Government supplied all of its capital and owned all of its stock. The General Treasury of the Republic received all of Bancec's profits, after deduction of amounts for capital reserves. A Governing Board consisting of delegates from Cuban governmental ministries governed and managed Bancec. Its president was Ernesto Che Guevara, who also was Minister of State and president of Banco Nacional. . . .

In contracts signed on August 12, 1960, Bancec agreed to purchase a quantity of sugar from [INRA], an instrumentality of the Cuban Government which owned and operated Cuba's nationalized sugar industry, and to sell it to the Cuban Canadian Sugar Company. The latter sale agreement was supported by an irrevocable letter of credit in favor of Bancec issued by Citibank on August 18, 1960, which Bancec assigned to Banco Nacional for collection. Meanwhile, in July 1960 the Cuban Government enacted Law No. 851, which provided for the nationalization of the Cuban properties of United States citizens. By Resolution No. 2 of September 17, 1960, the Government ordered that all of the Cuban property of three U.S. banks, including Citibank, be nationalized through forced expropriation. . . .

On or about September 15, 1960, before the banks were nationalized, Bancec's draft was presented to Citibank for payment by Banco Nacional. The amount sought was $193,280.30 for sugar delivered at Pascagoula, Mississippi. On September 20, 1960, after its branches were nationalized, Citibank credited the requested amount to Banco Nacional's account and applied the balance in Banco Nacional's account as a setoff against the value of its Cuban branches.

On February 1, 1961, Bancec brought this diversity action to recover on the letter of credit in the U.S. District Court for the Southern District of New York. On February 23,

1961, by Law No. 930, Bancec was dissolved and its capital was split between Banco Nacional and "the foreign trade enterprises or houses of the Ministry of Foreign Trade," which was established by Law No. 934 the same day. All of Bancec's rights, claims, and assets "peculiar to the banking business" were vested in Banco Nacional, which also succeeded to its banking obligations. All of Bancec's "trading functions" were to be assumed by "the foreign trade enterprise or houses of the Ministry of Foreign Trade." By Resolution No. 1, dated March 1, 1961, the Ministry of Foreign Trade created [Empresa, a state entity,] which was empowered to conduct all commercial export transactions formerly conducted by Bancec "remaining subrogated in the rights and obligations of said bank [Bancec] as regards the commercial export activities."

. . . Citibank's answer alleged that [Bancec's] suit was "brought by and for the benefit of the Republic of Cuba by and through its agent and wholly-owned instrumentality, [Bancec,] . . . which is in fact and in law and in form and function an integral part of and indistinguishable from the Republic of Cuba." . . . [On appeal, the Second Circuit rejected Citibank's argument, holding that "Bancec was not an alter ego of the Cuban government for the purpose of [Citibank's] counterclaims."]

IIA. As an initial matter, Bancec contends . . . that as a substantive matter the FSIA prohibits holding a foreign instrumentality owned and controlled by a foreign government responsible for actions taken by that government. We disagree. The language and history of the FSIA clearly establish that the Act was not intended to affect the substantive law determining the liability of a foreign state or instrumentality, or the attribution of liability among instrumentalities of a foreign state. Section 1606 of the FSIA provides in relevant part that "[a]s to any claim for relief with respect to which a foreign state is not entitled to immunity . . . , the foreign state shall be liable in the same manner and to the same extent as a private individual under like circumstances. . . ." The House Report on the FSIA states: "The bill is not intended to affect the substantive law of liability. Nor is it intended to affect . . . the attribution of responsibility between or among entities of a foreign state; for example, whether the proper entity of a foreign state has been sued, or whether an entity sued is liable in whole or in part for the claimed wrong." H.R. Rep. No. 94-1487, p. 12 (1976). . . .

B. We must next decide which body of law determines the effect to be given to Bancec's separate juridical status. Bancec contends that internationally recognized conflict-of-law principles require the application of the law of the state that establishes a government instrumentality — here Cuba — to determine whether the instrumentality may be held liable for actions taken by the sovereign. We cannot agree. As a general matter, the law of the state of incorporation normally determines issues relating to the internal affairs of a corporation. Application of that body of law achieves the need for certainty and predictability of result while generally protecting the justified expectations of parties with interests in the corporation. Different conflicts principles apply, however, where the rights of third parties external to the corporation are at issue. *See Restatement (Second) of Conflict of Laws* §301 & §302, Comments a & e (1971). To give conclusive effect to the law of the chartering state in determining whether the separate juridical status of its instrumentality should be respected would permit the state to violate with impunity the rights of third parties under international law while effectively insulating itself from liability in foreign courts. We decline to permit such a result.[69]

---

69. Pointing out that 28 U.S.C. §1606, contains language identical to the Federal Tort Claims Act ("FTCA"), 28 U.S.C. §2674, Bancec also contends alternatively that the FSIA, like the FTCA, requires application of the law of the forum state — here New York — including its conflicts principles. We disagree. Section 1606 provides that

Bancec contends in the alternative that international law must determine the resolution of the question presented. Citibank, on the other hand, suggests that federal common law governs. The expropriation claim against which Bancec seeks to interpose its separate juridical status arises under international law, which, as we have frequently reiterated, "is part of our law. . . ." *The Paquete Habana*, 175 U.S. 677, 700 (1900). As we set forth below, the principles governing this case are common to both international law and federal common law, which in these circumstances is necessarily informed both by international law principles and by articulated congressional policies.

IIIA. . . . Increasingly during this century, governments throughout the world have established separately constituted legal entities to perform a variety of tasks. . . . A typical government instrumentality, if one can be said to exist, is created by an enabling statute that prescribes the powers and duties of the instrumentality, and specifies that it is to be managed by a board selected by the government in a manner consistent with the enabling law. The instrumentality is typically established as a separate juridical entity, with the powers to hold and sell property and to sue and be sued. . . . The instrumentality is run as a distinct economic enterprise; often it is not subject to the same budgetary and personnel requirements with which government agencies must comply. These distinctive features permit government instrumentalities to manage their operations on an enterprise basis while granting them a greater degree of flexibility and independence from close political control than is generally enjoyed by government agencies. . . .

Separate legal personality has been described as "an almost indispensable aspect of the public corporation." . . . [W]hat the Court stated with respect to private corporations in *Anderson v. Abbott*, 321 U.S. 349 (1944), is true also for governmental corporations: "Limited liability is the rule, not the exception; and on that assumption large undertakings are rested, vast enterprises are launched, and huge sums of capital attracted." Freely ignoring the separate status of government instrumentalities would result in substantial uncertainty over whether an instrumentality's assets would be diverted to satisfy a claim against the sovereign, and might thereby cause third parties to hesitate before extending credit to a government instrumentality without the government's guarantee. As a result, the efforts of sovereign nations to structure their governmental activities in a manner deemed necessary to promote economic development and efficient administration would surely be frustrated. Due respect for the actions taken by foreign sovereigns and for principles of comity between nations, *see Hilton v. Guyot*, 159 U.S. 113, 163-164 (1895), leads us to conclude — as the courts of Great Britain have concluded in other circumstances[70] — that government instrumentalities established as juridical entities distinct and independent from their sovereign should normally be treated as such. . . .

"[a]s to any claim for relief with respect to which a foreign state is not entitled to immunity . . . , the foreign state shall be liable in the same manner and to the same extent as a private individual in like circumstances." Thus, where state law provides a rule of liability governing private individuals, the FSIA requires the application of that rule to foreign states in like circumstances. The statute is silent, however, concerning the rule governing the attribution of liability among entities of a foreign state. In *Banco Nacional de Cuba v. Sabbatino*, this Court declined to apply the State of New York's act of state doctrine in a diversity action between a United States national and an instrumentality of a foreign state, concluding that matters bearing on the nation's foreign relations "should not be left to divergent and perhaps parochial state interpretations." When it enacted the FSIA, Congress expressly acknowledged "the importance of developing a uniform body of law" concerning the amenability of a foreign sovereign to suit in United States courts. H.R. Rep. No. 94-1487, p. 32. In our view, these same considerations preclude the application of New York law here.

70. [The Court cited *C. Czarnikow, Ltd. v. Rolimpex*, [1979] A.C. 351, 364; *I Congreso del Partido*, [1983] A.C. 244, 271. — EDS.]

B. In discussing the legal status of private corporations, courts in the United States[71] and abroad,[72] have recognized that an incorporated entity . . . is not to be regarded as legally separate from its owners in all circumstances. Thus, where a corporate entity is so extensively controlled by its owner that a relationship of principal and agent is created, we have held that one may be held liable for the actions of the other. *See NLRB v. Deena Artware, Inc.*, 361 U.S. 398, 402-404 (1960). In addition, our cases have long recognized "the broader equitable principle that the doctrine of corporate entity, recognized generally and for most purposes, will not be regarded when to do so would work fraud or injustice." *Taylor v. Standard Gas Co.*, 306 U.S. 307, 322 (1939). . . . And, in *Bangor Punta Operations, Inc. v. Bangor & Aroostook Railroad Co.*, 417 U.S. 703 (1974), we concluded:

> Although a corporation and its shareholders are deemed separate entities for most purposes, the corporate form may be disregarded in the interests of justice where it is used to defeat an overriding public policy. . . . [W]here equity would preclude the shareholders from maintaining the action in their own right, the corporation would also be precluded. . . . [T]he principal beneficiary of any recovery and itself estopped from complaining of petitioners' alleged wrongs, cannot avoid the command of equity through the guise of proceeding in the name of . . . corporations which it owns and controls.

C. We conclude today that similar equitable principles must be applied here. In *National City Bank v. Republic of China*, 348 U.S. 356 (1955), the Court ruled that when a foreign sovereign asserts a claim in a U.S. court, "the consideration of fair dealing" bars the state from asserting a defense of sovereign immunity to defeat a setoff or counterclaim. *See* 28 U.S.C. §1607(c). As a general matter, therefore, the Cuban Government could not bring suit in a U.S. court without also subjecting itself to its adversary's counterclaim. Here there is apparently no dispute that, . . . "the devolution of [Bancec's] claim, however viewed, brings it into the hands of the Ministry [of Foreign Trade], or Banco Nacional," each a party that may be held liable for the expropriation of Citibank's assets. Bancec was dissolved even before Citibank filed its answer in this case, apparently in order to effect "the consolidation and operation of the economic and social conquests of the Revolution". . . . Thus, the Cuban Government and Banco Nacional, not any third parties that may have relied on Bancec's separate juridical identity, would be the only beneficiaries of any recovery. In our view, this situation is similar to that in the *Republic of China* case. "We have a foreign government invoking our law but resisting a claim against it which fairly would curtail its recovery. It wants our law, like any other litigant, but it wants our law free from the claims of justice."

Giving effect to Bancec's separate juridical status in these circumstances, even though it has long been dissolved, would permit the real beneficiary of such an action, the Government of the Republic of Cuba, to obtain relief in our courts that it could not obtain in its own right without waiving its sovereign immunity and answering for the seizure of

---

71. *See* W.M. Fletcher, *Cyclopedia of the Law of Private Corporations* §41 (rev. perm. ed. 1974): "[A] corporation will be looked upon as a legal entity as a general rule, and until sufficient reason to the contrary appears; but, when the notion of legal entity is used to defeat public convenience, justify wrong, protect fraud, or defend crime, the law will regard the corporation as an association of persons."

72. In *Case Concerning the Barcelona Traction, Light & Power Co.*, 1970 I.C.J. 3, the International Court of Justice acknowledged that, as a matter of international law, the separate status of an incorporated entity may be disregarded in certain exceptional circumstances: ". . . It is in this context that the process of 'lifting the corporate veil' or 'disregarding the legal entity' has been found justified and equitable in certain circumstances or for certain purposes. The wealth of practice already accumulated on the subject in municipal law indicates that the veil is lifted, for instance, to prevent misuse of the privileges of legal personality, as in certain cases of fraud or malfeasance, to protect third persons such as a creditor or purchaser, or to prevent the evasion of legal requirements or of obligations." *Id.* at 38-39.

Citibank's assets—a seizure previously held by the Court of Appeals to have violated international law. We decline to adhere blindly to the corporate form where doing so would cause such an injustice. . . . We therefore hold that Citibank may set off the value of its assets seized by the Cuban Government against the amount sought by Bancec.

IV. Our decision today announces no mechanical formula for determining the circumstances under which the normally separate juridical status of a government instrumentality is to be disregarded.[73] Instead, it is the product of the application of internationally recognized equitable principles to avoid the injustice that would result from permitting a foreign state to reap the benefits of our courts while avoiding the obligations of international law.

SAMANTAR v. YOUSUF
130 S. Ct. 2278 (2010)

JUSTICE STEVENS.[74] [From 1980 until 1990, Samantar held various positions in the government of Somalia, including Minister of Defense and Prime Minister. In 1991, after the Somali Government collapsed, he fled the country and eventually became a resident of Virginia. In 2004, Yousuf and other members of the Isaaq clan in Somalia sued Samantar under the Alien Tort Statute and Torture Victim Protection Act. They alleged that Samantar "exercised command and control over members of the Somali military forces who tortured, killed, or arbitrarily detained them or members of their families; that petitioner knew or should have known of the abuses perpetrated by his subordinates; and that he aided and abetted the commission of these abuses." The district court held that Samantar was entitled to immunity under the FSIA. The court of appeals reversed. It held that the FSIA did not apply to individual government officials.[75]]

II. The doctrine of foreign sovereign immunity developed as a matter of common law long before the FSIA was enacted in 1976 [dating back to the Court's opinion in *Schooner Exchange*, excerpted *supra* pp. 236-238. *Schooner Exchange*, according to *Verlinden*, excerpted *supra* pp. 337-340, was] interpreted as extending virtually absolute immunity to foreign sovereigns as "a matter of grace and comity."

Following *Schooner Exchange*, a two-step procedure developed for resolving a foreign state's claim of sovereign immunity, typically asserted on behalf of seized vessels. Under that procedure, the diplomatic representative of the sovereign could request a "suggestion of immunity" from the State Department. If the request was granted, the district court surrendered its jurisdiction. But "in the absence of recognition of the immunity by the Department of State," a district court "had authority to decide for itself whether all the requisites for such immunity existed." In making that decision, a district court inquired "whether the ground of immunity is one which it is the established policy of the [State Department] to recognize." Although cases involving individual foreign

---

73. The District Court adopted, and both Citibank and the Solicitor General urge upon the Court, a standard in which the determination whether or not to give effect to the separate juridical status of a government instrumentality turns in part on whether the instrumentality in question performed a "governmental function." We decline to adopt such a standard in this case, as our decision is based on other grounds. We do observe that the concept of a "usual" or a "proper" governmental function changes over time and varies from nation to nation. . . .

74. The separate opinions of Justices Alito, Thomas, and Scalia are omitted.

75. As an alternative basis for its decision, the Court of Appeals held that even if a current official is covered by the FSIA, a former official is not. Because we agree with the Court of Appeals on its broader ground that individual officials are not covered by the FSIA, petitioner's status as a former official is irrelevant to our analysis. [This footnote has been relocated. — EDS.]

officials as defendants were rare, the same two-step procedure was typically followed when a foreign official asserted immunity. *See, e.g., Heaney,* 445 F.2d, at 504-505; *Waltier v. Thomson,* 189 F. Supp. 319 (S.D.N.Y. 1960).[76]

[The Court then summarized the history of foreign sovereign immunity, including the development of the restrictive theory of sovereign immunity, the Tate Letter, and the enactment of the FSIA. The Court then framed the issue before it in the following terms:] After the enactment of the FSIA, the Act—and not the pre-existing common law—indisputably governs the determination of whether a foreign state is entitled to sovereign immunity. . . . What we must now decide is whether the Act also covers the immunity claims of foreign officials. We begin with the statute's text and then consider petitioner's reliance on its history and purpose.

III. [Petitioner Samantar advanced two arguments based on the statute's text: (1) that an individual official is an "agency or instrumentality" and (2) that an individual official is a "foreign state."]

We turn first to the term "agency or instrumentality of a foreign state," §1603(b). . . . First, the statute specifies that " 'agency or instrumentality . . .' means any *entity*" matching three specified characteristics, §1603(b) (emphasis added), and "entity" typically refers to an organization, rather than an individual. Furthermore, several of the required characteristics apply awkwardly, if at all, to individuals. The phrase "separate legal person, corporate or otherwise," §1603(b)(1), could conceivably refer to a natural person, solely by virtue of the word "person." But the phrase "separate legal person" typically refers to the legal fiction that allows an entity to hold personhood separate from the natural persons who are its shareholders or officers. *Cf. First Nat. City Bank v. Banco Para El Comercio Exterior de Cuba,* 462 U.S. 611, 625 ("Separate legal personality has been described as 'an almost indispensable aspect of the public corporation' "). It is similarly awkward to refer to a person as an "organ" of the foreign state. See §1603(b)(2). And the third part of the definition could not be applied at all to a natural person. A natural person cannot be a citizen of a State "as defined in section 1332(c) and (e)," §1603(b)(3), because those subsections refer to the citizenship of corporations and estates. Nor can a natural person be "created under the laws of any third country." Thus, the terms Congress chose simply do not evidence the intent to include individual officials within the meaning of "agency or instrumentality."[77]

[The Court then turned to the term "foreign state." Initially, it rejected Samantar's argument that the use of the term "includes" in the definition of foreign state, 28 U.S.C. §1603, meant that the definition provided a non-exhaustive list.] [E]lsewhere in the FSIA Congress expressly mentioned officials when it wished to count their acts as equivalent to those of the foreign state, which suggests that officials are not included within the unadorned term "foreign state." For example, Congress provided an exception from the general grant of immunity for cases in which "money damages are sought against a foreign state" for an injury in the United States "caused by the tortious act or omission

---

76. Diplomatic and consular officers could also claim the "specialized immunities" accorded those officials, Restatement (Second) of Foreign Relations Law of the United States §66, Comment b (1964-1965) (hereinafter Restatement), and officials qualifying as the "head of state" could claim immunity on that basis, *see Schooner Exchange v. McFaddon,* 7 Cranch 116, 137 (1812) (describing "the exemption of the person of the sovereign" from "a jurisdiction incompatible with his dignity").

77. Nor does anything in the legislative history suggest that Congress intended the term "agency or instrumentality" to include individuals. On the contrary, the legislative history, like the statute, speaks in terms of entities. *See, e.g.,* H.R. Rep. No. 94-1487, p. 15 (1976), U.S. Code Cong. & Admin. News 1976, at p. 6614 (hereinafter H.R. Rep.) ("The first criterion, that the entity be a separate legal person, is intended to include a corporation, association, foundation, or any other entity which, under the law of the foreign state where it was created, can sue or be sued in its own name").

of that foreign state or of any official or employee of that foreign state while acting within the scope of his office." §1605(a)(5) (emphasis added) [discussed *infra* pp. 308-324]. . . . If the term "foreign state" by definition includes an individual acting within the scope of his office, the phrase "or of any official or employee . . ." in 28 U.S.C. §1605(a)(5) would be unnecessary. . . .

Furthermore, Congress made specific remedial choices for different types of defendants. See §1606 (allowing punitive damages for an agency or instrumentality but not for a foreign state); §1610 (affording a plaintiff greater rights to attach the property of an agency or instrumentality as compared to the property of a foreign state). By adopting petitioner's reading of "foreign state," we would subject claims against officials to the more limited remedies available in suits against states, without so much as a whisper from Congress on the subject. (And if we were instead to adopt petitioner's other textual argument, we would subject those claims to the different, more expansive, remedial scheme for agencies.) The Act's careful calibration of remedies among the listed types of defendants suggests that Congress did not mean to cover other types of defendants never mentioned in the text.

IV. Petitioner argues that the FSIA is best read to cover his claim to immunity because of its history and purpose. . . . [O]ne of the primary purposes of the FSIA was to codify the restrictive theory of sovereign immunity, which Congress recognized as consistent with extant international law. See §1602. We have observed that a related purpose was "codification of international law at the time of the FSIA's enactment," *Permanent Mission of India to United Nations v. City of New York*, 551 U.S. 193, 199 (2007) and have examined the relevant common law and international practice when interpreting the Act. Because of this relationship between the Act and the common law that it codified, petitioner argues that we should construe the FSIA consistently with the common law regarding individual immunity, which — in petitioner's view — was coextensive with the law of state immunity and always immunized a foreign official for acts taken on behalf of the foreign state. Even reading the Act in light of Congress' purpose of codifying state sovereign immunity, however, we do not think that the Act codified the common law with respect to the immunity of individual officials. . . .

[T]he relationship between a state's immunity and an official's immunity is more complicated than petitioner suggests, although we need not and do not resolve the dispute among the parties as to the precise scope of an official's immunity at common law. The very authority to which petitioner points us, and which we have previously found instructive, *Permanent Mission*, 551 U.S., at 200, states that the immunity of individual officials is subject to a caveat not applicable to any of the other entities or persons[78] to which the foreign state's immunity extends. The Restatement provides that the "immunity of a foreign state . . . extends to . . . any other public minister, official, or agent of the state with respect to acts performed in his official capacity *if the effect of exercising jurisdiction would be to enforce a rule of law against the state*." Restatement §66 (emphasis added). And historically, the Government sometimes suggested immunity under the common law for individual officials even when the foreign state did not qualify. *See, e.g., Greenspan v. Crosbie*, No. 74 Civ. 4734 (GLG), 1976 WL 841 (S.D.N.Y. Nov. 23, 1976). There is therefore little reason to presume that when Congress set out to codify state immunity, it must also have, *sub silentio*, intended to codify official immunity.

---

78. The Restatement does not apply this caveat to the head of state, head of government, or foreign minister. See Restatement §66. Whether petitioner may be entitled to head of state immunity, or any other immunity, under the common law is a question we leave open for remand. We express no view on whether Restatement §66 correctly sets out the scope of the common law immunity applicable to current or former foreign officials.

Petitioner urges that a suit against an official must always be equivalent to a suit against the state because acts taken by a state official on behalf of a state are acts of the state. We have recognized, in the context of the act of state doctrine, that an official's acts can be considered the acts of the foreign state, and that "the courts of one country will not sit in judgment" of those acts when done within the territory of the foreign state. *See Underhill v. Hernandez,* 168 U.S. 250, 252, 254 (1897). Although the act of state doctrine is distinct from immunity, and instead "provides foreign states with a substantive defense on the merits," we do not doubt that in some circumstances the immunity of the foreign state extends to an individual for acts taken in his official capacity. But it does not follow from this premise that Congress intended to codify that immunity in the FSIA. It hardly furthers Congress' purpose of "clarifying the rules that judges should apply in resolving sovereign immunity claims" to lump individual officials in with foreign states without so much as a word spelling out how and when individual officials are covered.[79]

Petitioner would have a stronger case if there were any indication that Congress' intent to enact a comprehensive solution for suits against states extended to suits against individual officials. But to the extent Congress contemplated the Act's effect upon officials at all, the evidence points in the opposite direction. As we have already mentioned, the legislative history points toward an intent to leave official immunity outside the scope of the Act. And although questions of official immunity did arise in the pre-FSIA period, they were few and far between. The immunity of officials simply was not the particular problem to which Congress was responding when it enacted the FSIA. The FSIA was adopted, rather, to address "a modern world where foreign state enterprises are every day participants in commercial activities," and to assure litigants that decisions regarding claims against states and their enterprises "are made on purely legal grounds." H.R. Rep., at 7, U.S. Code Cong. & Admin. News 1976, at p. 6606. We have been given no reason to believe that Congress saw as a problem, or wanted to eliminate, the State Department's role in determinations regarding individual official immunity.[80]

Finally, our reading of the FSIA will not "in effect make the statute optional," as some Courts of Appeals have feared, by allowing litigants through "artful pleading . . . to take advantage of the Act's provisions or, alternatively, choose to proceed under the old common law," *Chuidian v. Philippine Nat. Bank,* 912 F.2d 1095, 1102 (C.A.9 1990). Even if a suit is not governed by the Act, it may still be barred by foreign sovereign immunity under the common law. And not every suit can successfully be pleaded against an individual official alone.[81] Even when a plaintiff names only a foreign official, it may be

---

79. The courts of appeals have had to develop, in the complete absence of any statutory text, rules governing when an official is entitled to immunity under the FSIA. For example, Courts of Appeals have applied the rule that foreign sovereign immunity extends to an individual official "for acts committed in his official capacity" but not to "an official who acts beyond the scope of his authority." *Chuidian [v. Philippine Nat'l Bank,* 912 F.2d 1095, 1103, 1106 (9th Cir. 1990). That may be correct as a matter of common-law principles, but it does not derive from any clarification or codification by Congress. . . .

80. The FSIA was introduced in accordance with the recommendation of the State Department. H.R. Rep., at 6, U.S. Code Cong. & Admin. News 1976, at p. 6605. The Department sought and supported the elimination of its role with respect to claims against foreign states and their agencies or instrumentalities. . . . But the Department has from the time of the FSIA's enactment understood the Act to leave intact the Department's role in official immunity cases. See [Sovereign Immunity Decisions of the Dept. of State, May 1952 to Jan. 1977 (M. Sandler, D. Vagts & B. Ristau eds.), in Digest of U.S. Practice in Int'l Law 1020, 1080 (1977)] 1020.

81. Furthermore, a plaintiff seeking to sue a foreign official will not be able to rely on the Act's service of process and jurisdictional provisions. Thus, a plaintiff will have to establish that the district court has personal jurisdiction over an official without the benefit of the FSIA provision that makes personal jurisdiction over a foreign state automatic when an exception to immunity applies and service of process has been accomplished in accordance with 28 U.S.C. §1608. See §1330(b) ("Personal jurisdiction over a foreign state shall exist as to every claim for relief over which the district courts have jurisdiction under subsection (a)," i.e., claims for which the foreign state is not entitled to immunity, "where service has been made under section 1608 of this title").

the case that the foreign state itself, its political subdivision, or an agency or instrumentality is a required party, because that party has "an interest relating to the subject of the action" and "disposing of the action in the person's absence may . . . as a practical matter impair or impede the person's ability to protect the interest." Fed. Rule Civ. Proc. 19(a)(1)(B). If this is the case, and the entity is immune from suit under the FSIA, the district court may have to dismiss the suit, regardless of whether the official is immune or not under the common law. Or it may be the case that some actions against an official in his official capacity should be treated as actions against the foreign state itself, as the state is the real party in interest. *Cf. Kentucky v. Graham*, 473 U.S. 159, 166 (1985) ("[A]n official-capacity suit is, in all respects other than name, to be treated as a suit against the entity. It is not a suit against the official personally, for the real party in interest is the entity.").

Notes *on* Dole Food, Bancec *and* Samanatar

1. *Differing treatment of foreign states proper and foreign state organs, agencies, or instrumentalities.* Review the FSIA. How are foreign states treated differently from foreign state agencies or instrumentalities? Consider in particular the Act's provisions regarding service of process and enforcement of judgments. Why is there this distinction? Is there any difference in the treatment of foreign states proper and foreign state organs, agencies, or instrumentalities in the U.N. State Immunities Convention?

2. *FSIA does not generally address substantive liability.* The FSIA is generally silent regarding a foreign state's substantive liability. Section 1606 of the FSIA provides that a foreign state will be liable "to the same extent as a private individual under like circumstances." Why was this approach adopted? What were the alternatives? One exception to this general rule is claims arising under the exception for state sponsors of terrorism. Recent amendments to the FSIA provide an express cause of action for certain damages. *See infra* pp. 351-353, 358, 360-361. Was it appropriate for Congress to adopt special rules for these actions? Could Congress enact comprehensive substantive liability standards for foreign states that preempt any state standards?

3. *Foreign states proper generally not liable for punitive damages.* In one exception to the FSIA's general approach of not addressing substantive liability, §1606 generally forbids state or federal courts from awarding punitive damages against a foreign state. Is this appropriate? If foreign states are not above the law, under the FSIA, then why are they treated specially with regard to punitive damages? Are states incapable of outrageous behavior that warrants punitive damages? Recent amendments to the FSIA, concerning state sponsors of terrorism, create a narrow exception allowing claims of punitive damages against foreign states. *See infra* pp. 351-353, 358, 360-361. Is it appropriate that these claims receive special treatment?

In contrast to the general treatment of foreign states proper, §1606 expressly permits punitive damages to be awarded against foreign state agencies or instrumentalities, irrespective of the jurisdictional basis. Such damages are sometimes awarded. *E.g., Saludes v. Republica de Cuba*, 655 F. Supp. 2d 1290, 1297 (S.D. Fla. 2009); *Campuzano v. Islamic Republic of Iran*, 281 F. Supp. 2d 258 (D.D.C. 2003); *Stern v. Islamic Republic of Iran*, 271 F. Supp. 2d 286 (D.D.C. 2003). Is it appropriate to treat "agencies or instrumentalities" differently from foreign states proper? Why?

4. *Foreign states proper.* Is there any question about what constitutes a foreign state proper? Shouldn't this be an easy question? Consider the definition of a state in the *Restatement (Third) of Foreign Relations Law*: "a 'state' is an entity which has a defined territory and permanent population, under the control of its own government, and

which engages in, or has the capacity to engage in, formal relations with other such entities." *Restatement (Third) of Foreign Relations Law* §201 (1987). This category clearly includes nations like the Republic of Ireland, the Islamic Republic of Iran, and the Republic of Argentina. It clearly does not include separate legal entities like the Dead Sea Companies and Bancec, which were involved in the *Dole Food* and *Bancec* cases. Nevertheless, beyond these easy cases, difficult questions have arisen concerning what parts of a foreign state's governmental structure fall within the definition of a foreign state proper. Does the U.N. State Immunities Convention provide any guidance in addressing such questions? *See* U.N. State Immunities Convention, Art. 2(1)(b).

(a) Role of Executive Branch recognition. Is it U.S. courts, or is it the Executive Branch, that is responsible for applying a definition of "foreign state"? What if the United States has not accorded diplomatic recognition to a foreign entity, but that entity claims status as a foreign state in U.S. litigation? Note that the *Restatement (Third)*'s definition of a foreign state imposes no requirement for Executive Branch recognition; note also that it is the Executive Branch that has the constitutional authority for decisions whether or not to recognize a foreign state. *See Restatement (Third) of Foreign Relations Law* §§201, 204 Rptrs. Notes 1-2. Would it unacceptably interfere with U.S. foreign policy if a U.S. court "recognized" a foreign entity as a "foreign state," when the U.S. Executive Branch refused to do so for diplomatic reasons? Consider the cases of Taiwan, the Palestine Liberation Authority, and Tibet. In practice, U.S. courts have virtually always followed the suggestions of the Executive Branch. *See supra* pp. 247, 265-266.

(b) Foreign state proper distinguished from foreign state "organ." When is a foreign entity a foreign state proper and when is it a foreign state's "organ" or "agency or instrumentality" (referred to in §1603(b))? For example, is a foreign state's Ministry of Foreign Affairs, or Ministry of Tourism, a part of the foreign state proper, or an organ or agency or instrumentality of the foreign state? The Supreme Court recently declined to address the question whether a foreign state's governmental ministry was part of the foreign state proper or a separate agency or instrumentality. *See Ministry of Defense and Support for the Armed Forces of the Islamic Republic of Iran v. Elahi,* 546 U.S. 450 (2006). Lacking guidance from the Supreme Court, federal courts take different approaches to this question. Some courts assess the "legal characteristics" of the governmental entity. Other courts consider whether the entity's "core functions" are "predominantly governmental or commercial." For a good decision with conflicting opinions on these various approaches, *see Garb v. Republic of Poland,* 440 F.3d 579, 591-597 (2d Cir. 2006). For caselaw, *see Roeder v. Islamic Republic of Iran,* 333 F.3d 228, 234-235 (D.C. Cir. 2003) (Iranian Ministry of Foreign Affairs was foreign state, not agency or instrumentality); *S & Davis Int'l, Inc. v. Republic of Yemen,* 218 F.3d 1292 (11th Cir. 2000) ("General Corporation for Foreign Trade and Grains" is part of Ministry of Supply & Trade, which was foreign state proper); *Transaero, Inc. v. La Fuerza Aerea Boliviana,* 30 F.3d 148 (D.C. Cir. 1994) (Bolivian Air Force was foreign state, not agency or instrumentality); *Unidyne Corp. v. Aerolineas Argentinas,* 590 F. Supp. 398, 400 (E.D. Va. 1984) (Argentine Naval Commission "is part and parcel of the Argentine Navy thereby qualifying as a foreign state or a political subdivision of the Argentine government").

What distinguishes a foreign state proper from an "organ" of a foreign state under the text of §1603(b)? Note that a foreign state "organ" must be a "separate legal person." What law defines whether or not a foreign entity is a "separate legal person"? The law of the foreign state? International law? The FSIA? Federal common law? What does *Bancec* suggest?

In *Ministry of Defense and Support for the Armed Forces of the Islamic Republic of Iran v. Elahi,* the U.S. Government urged the Court to hold that the Iranian Ministry of Defense was a "foreign state," rather than an "agency or instrumentality," a determination with critical implications for the immunity of certain Ministry property from attachment. No. 04-1095, 2006 WL 386291 (Feb. 21, 2006). The Court declined to consider the issue.

(c) Foreign state "organs" distinguished from foreign state "agencies or instrumentalities." Note that an "organ" of a foreign state can qualify under §1603(b)(2) as an "agency or instrumentality" regardless of the share ownership. What exactly is an "organ" and how is it different from an "agency" or "instrumentality"? Most lower courts have developed some type of multi-factor test. *See, e.g., Bd. of Regents of University of Texas System v. Nippon Tel. & Tel. Corp.*, 478 F.3d 274, 279 (5th Cir. 2007); *Filler v. Hanvit Bank*, 378 F.3d 213, 217 (2d Cir. 2004); *EIE Guam Corp. v. Long Term Credit Bank of Japan, Ltd.*, 322 F.3d 635, 639-642 (9th Cir. 2003). According to one court, the definition of "organ" turns on multiple factors:

> (1) whether the foreign state created the entity for a national purpose; (2) whether the foreign state actively supervises the entity; (3) whether the foreign state requires the hiring of public employees and pays their salaries; (4) whether the entity holds exclusive rights to some right in the [foreign] country; and (5) how the entity is treated under foreign state law. *Filler v. Hanvit Bank*, 378 F.3d 213, 217 (2d Cir. 2004).

Is this the appropriate mix of factors? What others might be appropriate? *Compare California Dep't of Water Resources v. Powerex Corp.*, 533 F.3d 1087, 1098 (9th Cir. 2008) ("organ" decided by reference to "the circumstances surrounding the entity's creation, the purpose of its activities, its independence from the government, the level of government financial support, its employment policies, and its obligations and privileges under state law"). Whatever the proper test, what law determines whether an entity qualifies as an "organ"? Federal common law? Foreign law? International law? State law? Again, what does *Bancec* suggest?

5. Organs and "arms" of a foreign state In the domestic sovereign immunity context, the Supreme Court has held that "arms" of the state (such as public universities) share in the immunity enjoyed by states of the union. *See, e.g., Regents of the University of California v. Doe*, 519 U.S. 425 (1997). Do the standards developed in the domestic sovereign immunity context shed light on the circumstances under which foreign entities qualify as "organs" for purposes of foreign sovereign immunity? To what extent (if at all) can (or should) state sovereign immunity doctrines inform foreign sovereign immunity doctrines? Consider your answer in light of the Supreme Court's statement, *supra* at pp. 263-265, that state sovereign immunity is a matter of constitutional law whereas foreign sovereign immunity is a matter of legislative grace. Does that difference suggest the need for a stricter definition of "organ"? Or a more relaxed one? *See generally* Granne, *Defining "Organ of a Foreign State" Under the Foreign Sovereign Immunities Act of 1976*, 42 U.C. Davis L. Rev. 1 (2008).

6. Foreign state "agency or instrumentality." Many FSIA cases involve foreign state "agencies or instrumentalities." This unhappily cumbersome phrase is defined by §1603(b) as an entity

> (1) which is a separate legal person, corporate or otherwise, and (2) which is an organ of a foreign state or political subdivision thereof, or a majority of whose shares or other ownership interest is owned by a foreign state or political subdivision thereof, and (3) which is neither a citizen of a State of the United States . . . nor created under the laws of any third country.

268 Chapter 3. Foreign Sovereign Immunity and Jurisdiction of U.S. Courts over Foreign States

This definition can cover a wide range of entities, ranging from ordinary business corporations to ad hoc committees to airlines.

Consider the three requirements imposed by §1603(b). What is the reason for each of these? What is the reason for requiring that an agency or instrumentality be a "separate legal person"? Is it to distinguish foreign states proper from foreign state agencies or instrumentalities? What is the reason for requiring majority "ownership" of an entity's shares or other ownership interests? Is not the ability to control a more important factor? Note that many contemporary regulatory regimes (*e.g.*, antitrust, securities regulations, environmental), around the world, focus on control in corporate contexts, rather than mere ownership. Why is a different approach taken in the FSIA?

7. *"Agency or instrumentality": direct ownership interest required by* **Dole.** It is clear under §1603(b) that corporations incorporated and doing business within a foreign country, whose shares or similar ownership interests are wholly and directly owned by that foreign state are ordinarily regarded as foreign state "agenc[ies] or instrumentalit[ies]." *E.g.*, *Alberti v. Empresa Nicaraguense de la Carne,* 705 F.2d 250 (7th Cir. 1983); *S&S Machinery Co. v. Masinexportimport,* 706 F.2d 411 (2d Cir. 1983). Similarly, a company incorporated in a foreign state will be treated as a foreign state instrumentality even if it is less than wholly state-owned, provided that that foreign state directly holds more than 50 percent of the company's ownership interests. *E.g.*, *Carey v. National Oil Co.,* 592 F.2d 673, 676 n.1 (2d Cir. 1979). These are the easy cases.

It is common-place, however, for corporate groups to be structured with multiple subsidiaries, divided into different types of activities and levels of responsibility. *See supra* pp. 250-253. In many cases, as apparently with the Dead Sea Companies in *Dole,* most or all of the members of the corporate group are 100 percent owned by the ultimate parent. As *Dole* reflects, a critical issue under the FSIA was whether second-tier and other indirectly owned subsidiaries qualified as "agencies or instrumentalities" under §1603(b).

The *Dole* Court held that "only direct ownership of a majority of shares by the foreign state satisfies the statutory requirements." Did this conclusion follow from the FSIA's language? Consider again the relevant text of §1603(b), defining an "agency or instrumentality" as an entity "a majority of whose shares or other ownership interest is owned by a foreign state or political subdivision thereof." Is the majority's textual argument so clear? When the statute says "owned," does it mean "directly owned"? Or is that implied? *See Delgado v. Shell Oil Co.,* 231 F.3d 165, 176 (5th Cir. 2000) ("The plain language of the statute simply requires 'ownership' by a foreign state. It draws no distinction between direct and indirect ownership; neither does it expressly impose a requirement of direct ownership.").

Recall the Court's focus in *Altmann* on the purposes of the FSIA. Are the Act's purposes served by *Dole*'s interpretation of "agency or instrumentality"? Consider the discussion of this issue in Justice Breyer's dissent. Justice Breyer stresses the importance of a federal forum and the need for procedural and substantive protections for foreign state–owned entities; he also focuses on the United States' foreign relations interests. In his view, the Court's rule thwarts these purposes, which are as dominant in indirect-ownership cases as in direct-ownership ones. Do you agree with Justice Breyer's characterization of the FSIA's purposes? How does Justice Kennedy respond? Compare the reliance in *Altmann* on the FSIA's purposes to determine the Act's retroactivity.

Does *Dole* foreclose the possibility that an indirectly owned entity may qualify as an "agency or instrumentality"? What if the indirectly held entity satisfied the requirements for the definition of an "organ"?

8. *"Agency or instrumentality": some unanswered questions under the FSIA.* While *Dole* sheds some light on the meaning of "agency or instrumentality," a number of interpretive questions remain. For example, does a foreign company enjoy immunity even if its capital stock is held by an administrative agency of the foreign state? *E.g., O'Connell Mach. Co. v. M.V. Americana,* 734 F.2d 115, 116 (2d Cir. 1984) ("The fact that the Italian Government saw fit to double tier its administrative agencies" does not preclude immunity). Is a foreign company an "agency or instrumentality" where the foreign corporation's principal place of business is in the United States? *E.g., Bailey v. Grand Trunk Lines New England,* 609 F. Supp. 48 (D. Vt. 1984), *vacated in part,* 805 F.2d 1097 (2d Cir. 1986). Is a foreign company entitled to immunity where several foreign states jointly own a company, but no single state owns more than 50 percent? *Compare Mangattu v. M/V Ibn Hayyan,* 35 F.3d 205 (5th Cir. 1994) *with Linton v. Airbus Industrie,* 794 F. Supp. 650 (S.D. Tex. 1992). *See generally Sea Transport Contractors, Ltd. v. Industries Chemiques du Senegal,* 411 F. Supp. 2d 386, 391-392 (S.D.N.Y. 2006) (discussing split).

9. *"Agency or instrumentality"—relevant time for determining status.* In *Dole,* the Court unanimously held "that instrumentality status be determined at the time suit is filed." The Court relied primarily on the use of the present tense in §1603(b) and other decisions holding that subject matter jurisdiction should be determined at filing. Are you persuaded? Recall again the Court's focus in *Altmann* on the purposes of the FSIA. Doesn't a suit against a company owned by a sovereign at the time of the relevant conduct risk offense to the sovereign? *See Belgrade v. Sidex Int'l Furniture Corp.,* 2 F. Supp. 2d 407, 413 (S.D.N.Y. 1998) ("In such a case, the conduct and potential liability of the foreign sovereign are the subject of judicial scrutiny, which implicates the dignity of the foreign sovereign and triggers the policy concerns of the FSIA.").

Doesn't the Court's rule give foreign states an incentive to shield their major national concerns that engage in some conduct potentially giving rise to liability? Suppose that a company engaged in some wrongdoing and, at that time, was privately held? Anticipating a suit, the company seeks the protection of the country where it is located, and the host country proceeds to nationalize the company or, at a minimum, purchase a majority of its shares. Doesn't the rule in *Dole* encourage such structuring? Or do the exceptions to the FSIA such as commercial activity and nondiscretionary tort effectively mitigate that concern because, even if the company restructures itself between the time of its wrongful act and the time litigation commences, an exception to the sovereign immunity likely will apply?

Conversely, doesn't the rule in *Dole* run the risk that previously private foreign entities might now be subject to the jurisdiction of the federal courts if, at the time of filing, they are subject to the FSIA? Depending on whether such state-owned entities are entitled to the protections of the Due Process Clause, *see infra* pp. 308, 334-335, 343-344, 360, *Dole* creates the possibility that those entities could be subject to the jurisdiction of the federal courts even where personal jurisdiction would not lie if they were presently private entities. *See Abrams v. Societe Nationale des Chemins de Fer Francais,* 389 F.3d 61 (2d Cir. 2004). Can it make sense to interpret a federal statute, designed to regulate a sovereign's immunity to suit in light of the sensitive implications for foreign relations, to accord *greater* protection to private entities than public ones?

10. *"Agency or instrumentality"—treatment under U.N. State Immunities Convention.* Consider how the U.N. State Immunities Convention addresses the question of immunity for foreign state agencies and instrumentalities. U.N. State Immunities Convention, Art. 2(1)(b)(iii). Is this not a materially more restrictive grant of immunity than the FSIA? What does it mean when Article 2(1)(b)(iii) says that agencies or instrumentalities are treated as foreign states "to the extent that they are entitled to perform and actually performing acts in the exercise of sovereign authority of the State"? Does this really provide much of an answer?

11. *Role of international law in* **Bancec** *and* **Dole Food.** Consider the role of international law in *Bancec* and *Dole.* Why does the Court consider international law in *Bancec*? Does the Court apply international law directly in the U.S. action; does it look to international law as persuasive, but not binding authority; does it leave open the question of the relationship between international and federal law; or does it do something else?

Compare the role of international law in *Bancec* to that in *Pennoyer, Schooner Exchange, Filartiga,* and *Sosa.* Compare it also to the role of international law in *Dole.* Did Justice Kennedy pay any attention to how foreign states, or international treaties, deal with the definition of foreign states? Recall the role of reciprocity and international law in the formation of the foreign sovereign immunity doctrine. At least where Congress provided little, or ambiguous, guidance in the FSIA, would it not be sensible to consider how other states or the U.N. State Immunities Convention approach questions of foreign sovereign immunity?

12. *Role of federal common law in* **Bancec, Dole** *and* **Samantar.** What was the basis for the rule of law adopted by *Bancec* with respect to the separate legal identity of foreign state entities? Does the FSIA address this issue? Note that the *Bancec* Court expressly claimed that it was adopting rules of "federal common law." If the FSIA did not address the separate legal identity of foreign state entities, then why don't ordinary state (or foreign) law rules on the subject apply? Why doesn't §1606 dictate that state law rules apply? What is the basis for adopting a rule of federal common law in *Bancec*? What makes the separate legal identity of Bancec any different from the separate legal identity of major companies like Citibank? Federal law does not generally govern this issue with respect to private entities; why should it do so with respect to foreign states?

Though it does not squarely address the issue, *Samantar* strongly suggests that federal common law also supplies a source of immunity for individual officials of foreign governments. Why is this an appropriate exercise of federal courts' common law power? Didn't Congress speak comprehensively when it enacted the FSIA?

Consider the standards set forth in *Boyle, supra* pp. 11-13, for the formation of rules of federal common law. Did the veil-piercing issue in *Bancec* involve a "uniquely federal" area? What about the immunity issue in *Samantar*? Did the Courts in those cases consider whether there was a "significant conflict" between federal policies under the FSIA and otherwise applicable law? What if state law provided for a very expansive alter ego theory based solely on "economic integration"? What if state law limited veil-piercing very narrowly? What if state law defined the immunity of foreign government officials more broadly? More narrowly?

Did *Dole* involve any issue of federal common law? Or did it merely involve interpretation of provisions of the FSIA?

13. *Presumption that foreign state's separate legal entity will be respected.* Is *Bancec* correct in concluding that a foreign state entity's separate legal status should presumptively be respected? Bancec was organized under Cuban law — not New York or other U.S. law. Why should a U.S. court give any effect to purported provisions of Cuban law that are said to grant Bancec a separate legal identity? What reasons does *Bancec* give for presumptively deferring to Cuban law?

Is it correct to analogize a foreign state–owned entity (like Bancec) to private companies? Does it matter that the relevant foreign law in *Bancec* was Cuban — the law of a state with a legal and political system which is fundamentally different from that of the United

States? Would it be appropriate to distinguish between the laws of democracies with developed legal systems and the laws of other nations?

What would be the result if Cuban law had also provided that the Cuban state was ultimately responsible for the liabilities of Bancec? Or that Bancec's shareholders were liable for its unsatisfied obligations? Should U.S. courts nevertheless respect its "separate" legal identity?

14. *Standards for ignoring the separate legal identity of a foreign state entity.* In what circumstances does *Bancec* permit a U.S. court to ignore the separate legal identity of a foreign state entity? Although the Court's opinion is not entirely clear, it appears to identify three conceivable bases for ignoring separate legal identity: (a) sufficiently extensive control, *see EM Ltd. v . Republic of Argentina*, 2010 WL 3001777 (2d Cir. 2010); *TMR Energy Ltd. v. State Property Fund of Ukraine*, 411 F.3d 296, 301-302 (D.C. Cir. 2005); (b) to prevent fraud or injustice, *see Bridas S.A.P.I.C. v. Government of Turkmenistan*, 447 F.3d 411 (5th Cir. 2006); and (c) public policy, *see Alejandre v. Telefonica Larga Distancia de Puerto Rico, Inc.*, 183 F.3d 1277, 1286-1287 (11th Cir. 1999). In fashioning these standards, the Court relied principally on its own decisions in the context of private corporations in domestic U.S. cases. *See also* the discussion above of the rules regarding agency and alter ego jurisdiction. *See supra* pp. 175-203. Are these rules an appropriate basis for standards governing foreign *sovereign* entities? Is a foreign state not going to inevitably exercise greater control over the actions of publicly owned companies, typically active in sensitive economic areas with a degree of self-regulatory authority?

How does the U.N. State Immunities Convention deal with the possibility of disregarding the separate legal identity of a foreign state entity? Consider the "understandings" with regard to Article 19 in the Annex to the Convention. Where does that leave matters? Does it acknowledge the possibility of disregarding the separate legal identity of foreign state entities?

15. *Application of* **Bancec** *standards on the facts.* Why did *Bancec* conclude that Citibank could set off against Bancec's affirmative claims Cuba's liabilities to Citibank? What precisely led to the finding that Banccc's separate legal status could be ignored? *See Pravin Banker Associates, Ltd. v. Banco Popular del Peru*, 9 F. Supp. 2d 300 (S.D.N.Y. 1998) ("The central fact relied upon by the Supreme Court in holding that a set-off was fair was that the entities that may be held liable for the expropriation of Citibank's assets are the only beneficiaries of any recovery on the original suit [against Citibank]. . . . The Court ruled that the transfer was a device to gain a litigation advantage and therefore was an abuse of the corporate form.").

16. *Lower court applications of* **Bancec** *on questions of substantive liability.* The *Bancec* decision plays a significant role in a variety of contexts arising in litigation against foreign states. Courts have applied *Bancec*'s holding to determine whether to impute the sovereign's liability to foreign-owned entities. *E.g., General Star Nat'l Ins. Co. v. Administratia Asigurarilor de Stat*, 713 F. Supp. 2d 287 (S.D.N.Y. 2010); *EM Ltd. v. The Republic of Argentina*, 2010 WL 1404110 (S.D.N.Y. Apr. 7, 2010); *Pravin Banker Associates, Ltd. v. Banco Popular del Peru*, 9 F. Supp. 2d 300, 303-307 (S.D.N.Y. 1998). In other cases, courts have considered whether to impute a foreign-owned entity's liability to the state. *See Bayer & Willis Inc. v. Republic of Gambia*, 283 F. Supp. 2d 1 (D.D.C. 2003) (ordering additional discovery in support of this theory); *Greenpeace, Inc. (U.S.A.) v. State of France*, 946 F. Supp. 773, 787 (C.D. Cal. 1996) (implicitly recognizing this theory but holding that plaintiffs failed to meet their burden of proof).

17. *Lower court applications of* **Bancec** *on questions of jurisdiction.* Note that *Bancec* involved questions of substantive liability, rather than of amenability to jurisdiction.

Recall that, in the context of nonstate actors, the standards for substantive alter ego and agency liability differ from jurisdictional standards involving the same concepts. *See supra* pp. 178, 184, 190-191, 199. Is the *Bancec* Court's analysis applicable also to jurisdictional issues under the FSIA? Does the analysis need to be modified in any respect?

Lower courts have used *Bancec*'s principles in determining whether to exercise jurisdiction over the foreign-owned entity (or its agent) under the FSIA. *E.g., Doe v. Holy See*, 557 F.3d 1066, 1077-1078 (9th Cir. 2009); *TMR Energy Ltd. v. State Property Fund of Ukraine*, 411 F.3d 296, 301-302 (D.C. Cir. 2005); *In re Potash Antitrust Litig.*, 686 F. Supp. 2d 816, 821-822 (N.D. Ill. 2010); *Servaas, Inc. v. Republic of Iraq*, 686 F. Supp. 2d 346, 357 (S.D.N.Y. 2010). *See generally Dewhurst v. Telenor Invest AS*, 83 F. Supp. 2d 577, 588 (D. Md. 2000) (collecting cases).

In general, most courts have been reluctant to disregard the foreign sovereign entity's separate status. *E.g., EM Ltd. v. Republic of Argentina*, 473 F.3d 463, 479 (2d Cir. 2007); *California v. NRG Energy Inc.*, 391 F.3d 1011, 1025 (9th Cir. 2004); *Transamerica Leasing, Inc. v. La Republica de Venezuela*, 200 F.3d 843, 847-854 (D.C. Cir. 2000); *Alejandre v. Telefonica Larga Distancia, de Puerto Rico, Inc.*, 183 F.3d 1277, 1284-1289 (11th Cir. 1999); *Federal Ins. Co. v. Richard I. Rubin & Co.*, 1993 U.S. App. LEXIS 33704 (3d Cir. 1993). In a few cases, however, courts have relied on *Bancec* to do so. *E.g., Bridas S.A.P.I.C. v. Government of Turkmenistan*, 447 F.3d 411, 420 (5th Cir. 2006); *TMR Energy Ltd. v. State Property Fund of Ukraine*, 411 F.3d 296, 301-302 (D.C. Cir. 2005); *S & Davis Int'l, Inc. v. Republic of Yemen*, 218 F.3d 1292, 1298-1300 (11th Cir. 2000); *U.S. Fidelity and Guar. Co. v. Braspetro Oil Services Co.*, 199 F.3d 94, 98 (2d Cir. 1999).

18. *Immunity of foreign governmental officials: types of immunity.* While the FSIA unambiguously extends sovereign immunity to foreign states, their subdivisions, and their agencies or instrumentalities, the statute does not expressly address the immunity of government officials. Under these circumstances, what should courts do?

It is important to distinguish between three types of immunity that government officials might enjoy. First, there is an immunity accorded to diplomats and consular officials. As *Samantar* observes in a footnote, that immunity once existed as a matter of common law. Today, treaties largely govern its scope. *See, e.g.*, Vienna Convention on Diplomatic Relations Art. 31; Vienna Convention on Consular Relations, Art. 43. In the United States, federal statutes make clear that these treaties set forth the scope of a diplomat's immunity and, additionally, accord immunity to employees of certain international organizations. *See* Diplomatic Relations Act, 22 U.S.C. §254a *et seq.*; International Organizations Immunities Act, 22 U.S.C. §288a *et seq.*

Second, heads of state enjoy a separate grant of immunity. *See, e.g., Ye v. Zemin*, 383 F.3d 620 (7th Cir. 2004); *Lafontant v. Aristide*, 844 F. Supp. 128 (E.D.N.Y. 1994). That immunity traces its origins to eras where monarchs literally embodied the states that they ruled (captured in Louis XIV's memorable phrase "L'etat c'est moi"). Federal courts recognized head of state immunity as a matter of federal common law and, at least where the Executive Branch filed a suggestion of immunity, relied on it to dismiss actions against heads of state. *See United States v. Noriega*, 117 F.3d 1206, 1212 (11th Cir. 1997) (categorizing caselaw); *see generally* Note, *Ex-Head of State Immunity: A Proposed Statutory Tool of Foreign Policy*, 97 Yale L.J. 299 (1987); Note, *Resolving the Confusion over Head of State Immunity: The Defined Rights of Kings*, 86 Colum. L. Rev. 169 (1986). *Samantar* makes clear that the FSIA's enactment does not affect the continued validity of this immunity.

Third, lower-ranking foreign government officials also enjoyed a form of immunity, sometimes referred to as "official immunity." This immunity, developed as a matter of federal common law, protected foreign government officials from liability for acts taken in their "official capacity"; it did not, however, protect government officials from acts beyond the scope of their authority. *Samantar* makes clear that the FSIA did not displace this immunity, but the decision raises a number of difficult issues.

19. *Immunity of governmental officials.* Does *Samantar* completely foreclose application of the FSIA to suits against government officials? What does the Court mean when it says that it does "not doubt that in some circumstances the immunity of the foreign state extends to an individual for acts taken in his official capacity"? Does this mean that certain suits against individual officers should be recharacterized as suits against foreign states, as suggested in the final passage of the *Samantar* opinion? If so, what standards should a court apply to decide whether such recharacterization is appropriate?

20. *Immunity of governmental officials: federal common law standards.* Assuming that foreign government officials are entitled to immunity as a matter of federal common law, what is its scope? The *Samantar* Court made clear it was not "resolv[ing] the dispute among the parties as to the precise scope of an official's immunity at common law." In a footnote, the Court cites the following standard from an important early post-FSIA appellate decision: "foreign sovereign immunity extends to an individual official 'for acts committed in his official capacity' but not to 'an official who acts beyond the scope of his authority.'" *Chuidian [v. Philippine Nat'l Bank,* 912 F.2d 1095, 1103, 1106 (9th Cir. 1990)]. The Court says the articulation in *Chuidian* "may be correct as a matter of common-law principles." Does *Samantar* suggest any other standards? *See Restatement (Second) of Foreign Relations* §66(f) ("immunity of a foreign state ... extends to ... any other public minister, official, or agent of the state with respect to acts performed in his official capacity *if the effect of exercising jurisdiction would be to enforce a rule of law against the state*") (emphasis added).

Assume that *Chuidian* does supply the proper standard for immunity. What law determines whether the individual was acting in his official capacity? Federal law? State law? The law of the country where the government official served? International law?

Consider the allegations of *Samantar.* What if Samantar, in his capacity as Defense Minister, did in fact order the torture and extrajudicial killings of members of the Isaaq clan? Would such conduct have been taken in his "official capacity"? How does the enactment of the TVPA affect your answer? The ATS? Are there certain acts which, as a matter of international law, cannot be within an individual's official capacity? Can the federal common law of individual officer immunity exceed that accorded to foreign states? What if a federal court held that, as a matter of federal common law, government officials enjoyed immunity even with respect to acts of torture which are otherwise actionable under the Torture Victim Protection Act? *Compare* S. Rep. No. 102-249, at 8 (1991) ("[T]he committee does not intend [FSIA, diplomatic, and head-of-state] immunities to provide former officials with a defense to a lawsuit brought under [the TVPA]. To avoid liability by invoking the FSIA, a former official would have to prove an agency relationship to a state, which would require that the state admit some knowledge or authorization of relevant acts. Because all states are officially opposed to torture and extrajudicial killing, however, the FSIA should normally provide no defense to an action taken under the TVPA against a former official.") *with Sabbithi v. Al Saleh,* 605 F. Supp. 2d 122 (D.D.C. 2009) (TVPA does not override residual immunity of former diplomat).

21. *Immunity of governmental officials: role of the State Department. Samantar* noted that, in the pre-FSIA era, the State Department played a critical role both with respect to the immunity of foreign states and government officials. While recognizing that the State Department had reduced its role with respect to foreign state immunity, the Court observed that it "had been given no reason to believe that Congress saw as a problem, or wanted to eliminate, the State Department's role in determinations regarding individual official immunity." What role, then, does *Samantar* envision for the State Department? *See Matar v. Dichter*, 563 F.3d 9, 14 (2d Cir. 2009) (pre-*Samantar* decision deferring to State Department's suggestion of immunity for former official). Does it differ from the "two-step process" that *Schooner Exchange* established? Is this any different from a court defining "foreign state" by reference to the sovereign countries that the Executive Branch has formally recognized? *See Owens v. Republic of Sudan*, 531 F.3d 884, 892-893 (D.C. Cir. 2008). Reconsider the facts of *Bancec*. After *Samantar*, if the State Department filed a brief requesting the Court to disregard the separate juridical form of a sovereign-owned entity, would the Court be bound to follow this suggestion? How does the Government's role in making suggestions of official immunity compare to its role in other questions of federal common law such as whether to create a cause of action that arises under the Alien Tort Statute? *See supra* pp. 272-273. Whether to dismiss a case on political questions grounds? *See supra* at 20-21, 34.

   22. *Head-of-state immunity.* The defendant in *Samantar* served both as Prime Minister and in various other capacities. The Court consequently noted that, on remand, he may be entitled to head-of-state immunity in addition to the official immunity enjoyed by other government officials. Who precisely enjoys head-of-state immunity? The self-declared head of state? Only the head of state recognized by the Executive Branch? In a country with both a monarch and a prime minister, does it cover merely the monarch? What about members of a royal family? *See Leutwyler v. Office of Her Majesty Queen Rania Al-Abdullah*, 184 F. Supp. 2d 277, 280 (S.D.N.Y. 2001). What about the Prime Minister? *See Saltany v. Reagan*, 702 F. Supp. 319 (D.D.C. 1988), *aff'd in relevant part*, 886 F.2d 438 (1989) (*per curiam*). His or her spouse? *See Howland v. Resteiner*, 2007 WL 4299176 (S.D.N.Y. Dec. 5, 2007). Someone acting as the official representative of the head of state at an official function? *See First American Corp. v. Al-Nahyan*, 948 F. Supp. 1107, 1119 (D.D.C. 1996). What about other cabinet ministers? If these ministers also perform a function indispensable to the work of the head of state, aren't there sound policy reasons for extending head-of-state immunity to them as well? *But see In re Agent Orange Products Liability Litig.*, 373 F. Supp. 2d 7, 110 (E.D.N.Y. 2005) ("The fact that a head of state may not be sued for official activities does not provide authorization for others to act illegally under the cloak of his immunization.").

   The U.S. Government has frequently submitted "suggestions" of immunity with respect to foreign heads of state. *Ye v. Zemin*, 383 F.3d 620, 625-626 (7th Cir. 2004); *Tachiona v. United States*, 386 F.3d 205, 221 (2d Cir. 2004); *Doe I v. Roman Catholic Diocese of Galveston-Houston*, 408 F. Supp. 2d 272 (S.D. Tex. 2005); *Alicog v. Kingdom of Saudi Arabia*, 860 F. Supp. 379 (S.D. Tex. 1994); *Kilroy v. Windsor*, 1978 Digest U.S. Prac. Int'l Law 641-643 (N.D. Ohio 1978); *Psirakis v. Marcos*, 1975 Digest U.S. Prac. Int'l Law 344-345 (N.D. Cal. 1975). It has taken the position that its suggestions are binding on courts, a position that courts routinely accept. *See, e.g., Weixum v. Xi Lai*, 568 F. Supp. 2d 35, 37 (D.D.C. 2008) (collecting cases); *Abiola v. Abubakar*, 267 F. Supp. 2d 907, 915 (N.D. Ill. 2003). Is there any reason why suggestion of head-of-state immunity should be more binding on federal courts than suggestions of official immunity? Could a court accord head-of-state immunity in the face of a contrary suggestion by the Executive Branch? *See Kadic v. Karadzic*, 70 F.3d 232, 248 (2d Cir. 1996). Conversely, could a court entertain jurisdiction, in the face of a suggestion of immunity, where a federal statute like the Torture Victim Protection Act authorized federal jurisdiction and creates a cause of action? Consider this question in light of the legislative history surrounding the enactment of the Torture Victim Protection Act suggesting that Congress did not intend for former officials to be immune from suit, *supra* at 273.

23. *Official immunity and the FSIA.* Consider the features of the FSIA discussed in the preceding section — its jurisdictional grant, its punitive damages bar, its service rules, the retroactivity rule in *Altmann,* and the time-of-filing rule in *Dole.* To what extent (if at all) do these principles operate as part of the federal common law of official immunity? Consider the following problems:

- Suppose members of the Isaaq clan sue both the state of Somalia and its former prime minister for torture. Neither Somalia nor the minister have any contacts with the United States. Both defendants move to dismiss for lack of personal jurisdiction. What result? *Compare infra* p. 360 (foreign states not entitled to due process protections regarding the exercise of personal jurisdiction).
- Suppose the same plaintiffs serve process on both Somalia and the former prime minister. They serve process on Somalia pursuant to the provisions of the FSIA. They serve the former prime minister pursuant to a court order authorizing service by publication (a method not authorized by the FSIA). What result?
- Suppose the same plaintiffs file suit seeking punitive damages against both defendants. What result?
- Suppose a suit is filed against a foreign state and its former justice minister, alleging malicious prosecution, stemming from the justice minister's asserted campaign of frivolous litigation designed to intimidate political opponents. What result? *See infra* pp. 308-319 (discussing noncommercial torts exception).
- Suppose the plaintiffs have filed suit in state court. Can the justice minister remove the suit to federal court? *See supra* p. 242 (discussing removal provisions of FSIA); *Martinez v. Republic of Cuba,* 708 F. Supp. 2d 1298 (S.D. Fla. 2010) (FSIA's removal provision must be construed narrowly and authorizes only foreign states to remove action).
- Finally, suppose that a suit is filed against the justice minister of a foreign state. At the time of the events in question, the justice minister was an attorney in private practice. But at the time the suit was filed, he had become justice minister. Does the official immunity protect the officer during the period while he sits in office, even if it concerns conduct that occurred before he assumed office? Does the time-of-filing rule announced in *Dole* apply? *See Matar v. Dichter,* 563 F.3d 8, 12-13 (2d Cir. 2009) (pre-*Samantar* decision describing split over whether *Dole* principle applies to individual immunity determinations).

24. *Official immunity and the TVPA.* What are *Samantar*'s implications for litigation under the Torture Victim Protection Act, *supra* pp. 273-275? Recall that the legislative history behind that enactment indicates that Congress did not intend for foreign government officials to be immune against claims that they violated the TVPA. *See Arrar v. Ashcroft,* 585 F.3d 559, 568 (2d Cir. 2009) (*en banc*). Assuming that proposition is correct (or if Congress affirmatively amended the TVPA to make that view clear in the text of the statute), how would that rule affect the federal common law of immunity? Would your answer differ if the allegation was that the foreign official violated a *jus cogens* norms, *see supra* at 15, which was not yet codified in a federal statute? What if, despite such a rule, the Executive Branch filed a statement of interest suggesting that a foreign government official were nonetheless entitled to official immunity? Should a court follow that suggestion? Would it be affirmatively obligated to do so?

C.   Bases for Judicial Jurisdiction over Foreign States Under the FSIA

The FSIA's general grant of jurisdictional immunity for "foreign states" is subject to important exceptions, set forth in §§1605 through 1607 of the Act.[82] These exceptions generally implement the restrictive theory of sovereign immunity, granting immunity for many "public" or "sovereign" acts and denying it for "private" or commercial activities. In outline, the Act denies sovereign immunity for nine statutory reasons: (1) commercial activity with a U.S. nexus; (2) noncommercial torts in the United States; (3) taking of property, located in the United States, in violation of international law; (4) waiver; (5) arbitration-related matters; (6) rights to property in the United States that were acquired by succession or gift, or rights to immoveable property situated in the United States; (7) certain admiralty matters; (8) counterclaims; and, most recently (9) involvement in certain acts of terrorism. In addition, §1604 makes it clear that foreign state immunity is subject to variation by international agreement.

The plain language of the FSIA, as well as the Act's legislative history, makes it clear that these exceptions are the *exclusive* circumstances in which a foreign state will be denied immunity in U.S. courts.[83] The Supreme Court so held in *Argentine Republic v. Amerada Hess Shipping Corp.,* where it rejected the argument that the Alien Tort Statute provides an exception to the FSIA for violations of international law.[84]

As discussed above, the FSIA does not merely *deny* immunity when one of these exceptions applies to a foreign state's conduct. In addition, whenever an exception to immunity exists, the Act provides federal courts an *affirmative* grant of both personal and subject matter jurisdiction.[85] In short, the terse formulae of §1605's exceptions simultaneously serve three critical functions in litigation against foreign states: they grant personal jurisdiction, grant subject matter jurisdiction, and deny immunity.[86]

Some lower courts have been critical of both the FSIA's amalgamation of principles of immunity and jurisdiction and its sometimes cryptic language. In one court's view, the FSIA is "remarkably obtuse" and a "statutory labyrinth that, owing to the numerous interpretive questions engendered by its bizarre structure and its many deliberately vague provisions, has during its lifetime been a financial boon for the private bar but a constant bane of the federal judiciary."[87] Although these criticisms may be somewhat overstated,[88] the Act's exceptions are complex and require careful attention.

The following sections examine several of §1605's most significant exceptions to jurisdictional immunity — commercial activity with a nexus to the United States, tortious conduct within the United States, expropriatory actions with a nexus to the United States, and waivers. Thereafter, we consider the 1996 and 2008 amendments to the FSIA — which

---

82. 28 U.S.C. §1604 (1982). The general grant of foreign sovereign immunity from jurisdiction is also subject to any "existing international agreements to which the United States is a party at the time of enactment" of the FSIA. *Id.* For a case interpreting this exception, *see World Holdings LLC v. Federal Republic of Germany,* 2010 WL 3081442 (11th Cir. Aug. 9, 2010).

83. 28 U.S.C. §1602; H.R. Rep. No. 1487, 94th Cong., 2d Sess. 12, *reprinted in* 1976 U.S. Code Cong. & Admin. News at 6610.

84. 488 U.S. 428 (1989).

85. *See supra* pp. 70-71, 234-235; 28 U.S.C. §§1330(a) & (b) (1982).

86. *See Verlinden BV v. Central Bank of Nigeria,* 461 U.S. 480, 488-490 (1983).

87. *Gibbons v. Udaras na Gaeltachta,* 549 F. Supp. 1094, 1105-1106 (S.D.N.Y. 1982). *See also Vencedora Oceanica Navigacion, SA v. Compagnie Nationale Algerienne de Navigation,* 730 F.2d 195 (5th Cir. 1984); *Texas Trading & Milling Corp. v. Federal Republic of Nigeria,* 647 F.2d 300 (2d Cir. 1981).

88. See Feldman, *The United States Foreign Sovereign Immunities Act of 1976 in Perspective: A Founder's View,* 35 Int'l & Comp. L.Q. 302 (1986).

added another exception to immunity for terrorism-related actions and provide a new approach to the immunity of foreign sovereigns.

Application of these exceptions to the FSIA is complicated by the Fifth Amendment's potential due process limitations on assertions of personal jurisdiction authorized by the Act.[89] Because the FSIA grants personal jurisdiction — as well as denies sovereign immunity — the exercises of judicial authority that it authorizes are presumptively subject to the Due Process Clause's limits. Nonetheless, the Supreme Court has thus far refused to decide whether the Due Process Clause applied to assertions of personal jurisdiction over foreign states. Indeed, the Court has raised the possibility that foreign states are not "persons" within the meaning of the Fifth Amendment.[90] This has prompted a division among lower courts over whether exercises of personal jurisdiction under the FSIA must satisfy the Due Process Clause's minimum contacts requirements. While many early courts held that the Due Process Clause must be satisfied, recent decisions have rejected this requirement.[91] This latter view stands in some tension with the FSIA's legislative history. That legislative history confirms the need to satisfy the minimum contacts requirements of the Due Process Clause, although it also indicates that the §1605 exceptions are generally consistent with these requirements.[92]

1. Commercial Activity with a U.S. Nexus

As recounted in the Tate Letter, the increase in the trading activities of foreign governmental entities was central to the development of the restrictive theory of sovereign immunity.[93] Consistent with these developments, §1605(a)(2) of the FSIA denies immunity to certain commercial activities of foreign states. This is the single most important exception to foreign sovereign immunity in the United States. Section 1605(a)(2)'s "commercial activity" exception provides that foreign states will not enjoy immunity in a case:

> (2) in which the action is based upon a commercial activity carried on in the United States by the foreign state; or upon an act performed in the United States in connection with a commercial activity of the foreign state elsewhere; or upon an act outside the territory of the United States in connection with a commercial activity of the foreign state elsewhere and that act causes a direct effect in the United States.

Three related issues of interpretation are critical to understanding §1605(a)(2). First, what types of governmental conduct constitute "commercial activity"? Second, when is an action "based upon" a commercial activity or an "act . . . in connection with" a

---

89. See supra p. 79 & infra pp. 308, 333-334, 343-344, 360. Similarly, questions arise under the Fourteenth Amendment with respect to FSIA actions in the state courts. In particular, questions arise as to whether Congress could constitutionally authorize state courts to exercise jurisdiction over foreign sovereigns under the FSIA even if the foreign sovereign did not have the necessary minimum contacts with the forum state under *International Shoe.*

90. 488 U.S. at 443.

91. *Compare Corzo v. Banco Cent. de Reserva del Peru,* 243 F.3d 519 (9th Cir. 2001) (requiring minimum contacts analysis) *with Price v. Socialist People's Libyan Arab Jamahiriya,* 294 F.3d 82, 86 (D.C. Cir. 2002) (not requiring minimum contacts analysis for foreign state) *and Frontera Resources Azerbaijan Corp. v. State Oil Co. of the Azerbaijani Republic,* 582 F.3d 393 (2d Cir. 2009) (not requiring minimum contacts analysis for agency or instrumentality of foreign state).

92. H.R. Rep. No. 1487, 94th Cong., 2d Sess. 18, reprinted in 1976 U.S. Code Cong. & Admin. News at 6616. *See BP Chemicals Ltd. v. Jiangsu SOPO Corp. (Group),* 420 F.3d 810, 818 & n.6 (8th Cir. 2005) (finding personal jurisdiction and noting that nexus requirement is likely more stringent than minimum contacts standard).

93. See supra pp. 240-241, 247-248.

commercial activity? Third, what "nexus" is required between a foreign state's commercial activity and the United States?

a.   Definition of "Commercial Activity."   The FSIA's definition of "commercial activity" raises difficult issues of interpretation. The general rationale for the commercial activity exception is that when a state enters into "commercial" contracts or engages in profit-making activity, it ceases to act in a "sovereign" capacity and should not enjoy immunity.[94] The difficulty, however, lies in determining what types of conduct are commercial, rather than sovereign. Some commentators have observed that there is no clear dividing line between commercial and public acts and that virtually all activities by states further sovereign purposes.[95] Thus, according to a classic example, even the purchase of boots by a foreign state can serve sovereign objectives when, for example, the boots will be used to equip the purchaser's armed forces.

Against this background, §1603(d) defines "commercial activity" as "either a regular course of commercial conduct or a particular commercial transaction or act." In addition, §1603(d) provides that "[t]he commercial character of an activity shall be determined by reference to the nature of the course of conduct or particular transaction or act, rather than by reference to its purposes."[96] Many have remarked on the circularity of §1603(d), which fails to define the critical term "commercial."[97] In one authority's words, "[s]tart with 'activity,' proceed via 'conduct' or 'transaction' to 'character,' then refer to 'nature,' and then go back to 'commercial,' the term you started out to define in the first place."[98]

Nonetheless, §1603(d)'s emphasis on the "nature," rather than the "purpose," of a foreign state's activity places important limits on the scope of foreign sovereign immunity. The FSIA's legislative history explains that "the fact that goods or services to be procured [by a foreign state] through a contract are to be used for a public purpose is irrelevant; it is the *essentially commercial nature of an activity* or transaction that is critical."[99] By virtue of this gloss, the FSIA resolves the classic hypothetical of a foreign state's purchase of equipment for its armed forces: such purchases are commercial in nature, notwithstanding their public purpose.

The FSIA's legislative history also provides additional explanations of the intended meaning of "commercial activity." Most importantly, the House Report on the Act provides:

> [S]ection 1603 defines the term "commercial activity" as including a broad spectrum of endeavor, from an individual commercial transaction or act to a regular course of commercial conduct. A "regular course of commercial conduct" includes the carrying on of a commercial enterprise such as a mineral extraction company, an airline or a state trading corporation. Certainly, if an activity is customarily carried on for profit, its commercial nature could readily be assumed. At the other end of the spectrum, a single contract, if of the same character as a

---

94. *See supra* pp. 247-248; *Tate Letter, reprinted in* 425 U.S. 711 (1976); H.R. Rep. No. 1487, 94th Cong., 2d Sess. 16-17, *reprinted in* 1976 U.S. Code Cong. & Admin. News at 6614-15.

95. *E.g.,* I. Brownlie, *Principles of Public International Law* 330 (1979) ("The short point is that there is a logical contradiction in seeking to distinguish the 'sovereign' and 'non-sovereign' acts of a state"); Sornarajah, *Problems in Applying the Restrictive Theory of Sovereign Immunity*, 31 Int'l & Comp. L.Q. 661 (1982).

96. 28 U.S.C. §1603(d).

97. *Republic of Argentina v. Weltover, Inc.*, 504 U.S. 607 (1992) (FSIA "leaves the term 'commercial' largely undefined"); *Texas Trading & Milling Corp. v. Federal Republic of Nigeria*, 647 F.2d 300, 308 (2d Cir. 1981).

98. Lowenfeld, *Litigating a Sovereign Immunity Claim—The Haiti Case*, 49 N.Y.U. L. Rev. 377, 435 & n.244 (1974).

99. H.R. Rep. No. 1487, 94th Cong., 2d Sess. 16, *reprinted in* 1976 U.S. Code Cong. & Admin. News at 6615 (emphasis added). *See Restatement (Third) Foreign Relations Law* §453 & comment b (1987); *Republic of Argentina v. Weltover, Inc.*, 504 U.S. 607 (1992).

contract which might be made by a private person, could constitute a "particular transaction or act."

As the definition indicates, the fact that goods or services to be procured through a contract are to be used for a public purpose is irrelevant; it is the essentially commercial nature of an activity or transaction that is critical. Thus, a contract by a foreign government to buy provisions or equipment for its armed forces or to construct a government building constitutes a commercial activity. The same would be true of a contract to make repairs on an embassy building. Such contracts should be considered to be commercial contracts, even if their ultimate object is to further a public function. Activities such as a foreign government's sale of a service or a product, its leasing of property, its borrowing money, its employment or engagement of laborers, clerical staff or public relations or marketing agents, or its investment in a security of an American corporation, would be among those included within the definition.[100]

Despite this gloss, the Act's legislative history abjures any effort to define commercial activity comprehensively. Instead, Congress deliberately left the judiciary freedom to develop a definition on a case-by-case basis: "The courts would have a great deal of latitude in determining what is a 'commercial activity' for purposes of this bill. It has seemed unwise to attempt an excessively precise definition of this term, even if that were practicable."[101] Courts have been less confident about the wisdom of Congress's refusal to define "commercial activity."[102]

The Supreme Court considered the FSIA's definition of "commercial activity" at length in *Republic of Argentina v. Weltover, Inc.,* which is excerpted below. Although the Court's opinion provides guidance, the historic uncertainties that have surrounded the distinction between commercial and sovereign acts can be expected to persist. That is illustrated by *MOL, Inc. v. People's Republic of Bangladesh* excerpted below.

REPUBLIC OF ARGENTINA v. WELTOVER, INC.

504 U.S. 607 (1992) [also partially excerpted below at pp. 300-301]

JUSTICE SCALIA [for a unanimous Court]. This case requires us to decide whether the Republic of Argentina's default on certain bonds issued as part of a plan to stabilize its currency was an act taken "in connection with a commercial activity" that had a "direct effect in the United States" so as to subject Argentina to suit in an American court under [the FSIA].

Since Argentina's currency is not one of the mediums of exchange acceptable on the international market, Argentine businesses engaging in foreign transactions must pay in U.S. dollars or some other internationally accepted currency. In the recent past, it was difficult for Argentine borrowers to obtain such funds, principally because of the instability of the Argentine currency. To address these problems, petitioners, the Republic of Argentina and its central bank, Banco Central (collectively "Argentina"), in 1981 instituted a foreign exchange insurance contract program ("FEIC"), under which Argentina effectively agreed to assume the risk of currency depreciation in cross-border transactions involving Argentine borrowers. This was accomplished by Argentina's agreeing to sell to domestic borrowers, in exchange for a contractually predetermined amount of local

---

100. H.R. Rep. No. 1487, 94th Cong., 2d Sess. 16, *reprinted in* 1976 U.S. Code Cong. & Admin. News at 6614-6615.

101. H.R. Rep. No. 1487, 94th Cong., 2d Sess. 16, *reprinted in* 1976 U.S. Code Cong. & Admin. News at 6615.

102. *See Republic of Argentina v. Weltover, Inc.*, 504 U.S. 607 (1992); *Gibbons v. Udaras na Gaeltachta,* 549 F. Supp. 1094, 1106 (S.D.N.Y. 1982).

currency, the necessary U.S. dollars to repay their foreign debts when they matured, irrespective of intervening devaluations.

Unfortunately, Argentina did not possess sufficient reserves of U.S. dollars to cover the FEIC contracts as they became due in 1982. The Argentine government thereupon adopted certain emergency measures, including refinancing of the FEIC-backed debts by issuing to the creditors government bonds. These bonds, called "Bonods," provide for payment of interest and principal in U.S. dollars; payment may be made through transfer on the London, Frankfurt, Zurich, or New York market, at the election of the creditor. Under this refinancing program, the foreign creditor had the option of either accepting the Bonods in satisfaction of the initial debt, thereby substituting the Argentine government for the private debtor, or maintaining the debtor/creditor relationship with the private borrower and accepting the Argentine government as guarantor.

When the Bonods began to mature in May 1986, Argentina concluded that it lacked sufficient foreign exchange to retire them. Pursuant to a Presidential Decree, Argentina unilaterally extended the time for payment, and offered bondholders substitute instruments as a means of rescheduling the debts. Respondents, two Panamanian corporations and a Swiss bank who hold, collectively, $1.3 million of Bonods, refused to accept the rescheduling, and insisted on full payment, specifying New York as the place where payment should be made. Argentina did not pay, and respondents then brought this breach-of-contract action in the United States District Court for the Southern District of New York, relying on the [FSIA] as the basis for jurisdiction. Petitioners moved to dismiss for lack of subject-matter jurisdiction, lack of personal jurisdiction, and *forum non conveniens.* The District Court denied these motions and the Court of Appeals affirmed. . . .

The [FSIA] establishes a comprehensive framework for determining whether a court in this country, state or federal, may exercise jurisdiction over a foreign state. Under the Act, a "foreign state *shall* be immune from the jurisdiction of the courts of the United States and of the States" unless one of several statutorily defined exceptions applies. §1604 (emphasis added). The FSIA thus provides the "sole basis" for obtaining jurisdiction over a foreign sovereign in the United States. *See Argentine Republic v. Amerada Hess Shipping Corp.* The most significant of the FSIA's exceptions — and the one at issue in this case — is the "commercial" exception of §1605(a)(2). . . .

In the proceedings below, respondents relied only on the third clause of §1605(a)(2) to establish jurisdiction and our analysis is therefore limited to considering whether this lawsuit is (1) "based . . . upon an act outside the territory of the United States"; (2) that was taken "in connection with a commercial activity" of Argentina outside this country; and (3) that "cause[d] a direct effect in the United States." The complaint in this case alleges only one cause of action on behalf of each of the respondents, viz., a breach-of-contract claim based on Argentina's attempt to refinance the Bonods rather than to pay them according to their terms. The fact that the cause of action is in compliance with the first of the three requirements "that it is 'based upon an act outside the territory of the United States' (presumably Argentina's unilateral extension)" is uncontested. The dispute pertains to whether the unilateral refinancing of the Bonods was taken "in connection with a commercial activity" of Argentina, and whether it had a "direct effect in the United States." . . .

Respondents and their *amicus,* the United States, contend that Argentina's issuance of, and continued liability under, the Bonods constitute a "commercial activity" and that the extension of the payment schedules was taken "in connection with" that activity. The latter point is obvious enough, and Argentina does not contest it; the key question is whether the activity is "commercial" under the FSIA.

[The FSIA's] definition [of commercial activity in §1603(d)] leaves the critical term "commercial" largely undefined: The first sentence simply establishes that the commercial nature of an activity does *not* depend upon whether it is a single act or a regular course of conduct, and the second sentence merely specifies what element of the conduct determines commerciality (*i.e.,* nature rather than purpose), but still without saying what "commercial" means. Fortunately, however, the FSIA was not written on a clean slate. As we have noted, *see Verlinden BV v. Central Bank of Nigeria,* the Act (and the commercial exception in particular) largely codifies the so-called "restrictive" theory of foreign sovereign immunity. . . . The meaning of "commercial" is the meaning generally attached to that term under the restrictive theory at the time the statute was enacted.

This Court did not have occasion to discuss the scope or validity of the restrictive theory of sovereign immunity until our 1976 decision in *Alfred Dunhill of London, Inc. v. Republic of Cuba,* 425 U.S. 682. Although the Court there was evenly divided on the question whether the "commercial" exception that applied in the foreign-sovereign-immunity context also limited the availability of an act-of-state defense, there was little disagreement over the general scope of the exception. The plurality noted that, after the State Department endorsed the restrictive theory of foreign sovereign immunity in 1952, the lower courts consistently held that foreign sovereigns were not immune from the jurisdiction of American courts in cases "arising out of purely commercial transactions." The plurality further recognized that the distinction between state sovereign acts, on the one hand, and state commercial and private acts, on the other, was not entirely novel to American law. The plurality stated that the restrictive theory of foreign sovereign immunity would not bar a suit based upon a foreign state's participation in the marketplace in the manner of a private citizen or corporation. A foreign state engaging in commercial activities "do[es] not exercise powers particular to sovereigns"; rather, it "exercise[s] only those powers that can also be exercised by private citizens." The dissenters did not disagree with this general description. Given that the FSIA was enacted less than six months after our decision in *Alfred Dunhill* was announced, we think the plurality's contemporaneous description of the then-prevailing restrictive theory of sovereign immunity is of significant assistance in construing the scope of the Act.

In accord with that description, we conclude that when a foreign government acts, not as regulator of a market, but in the manner of a private player within it, the foreign sovereign's actions are "commercial" within the meaning of the FSIA. Moreover, because the Act provides that the commercial character of an act is to be determined by reference to its "nature" rather than its "purpose," 28 U.S.C. §1603(d), the question is not whether the foreign government is acting with a profit motive or instead with the aim of fulfilling uniquely sovereign objectives. Rather, the issue is whether the particular actions that the foreign state performs (whatever the motive behind them) are the *type* of actions by which a private party engages in "trade and traffic or commerce." Thus, a foreign government's issuance of regulations limiting foreign currency exchange is a sovereign activity, because such authoritative control of commerce cannot be exercised by a private party; whereas a contract to buy army boots or even bullets is a "commercial" activity, because private companies can similarly use sales contracts to acquire goods.

The commercial character of the Bonods is confirmed by the fact that they are in almost all respects garden-variety debt instruments; they may be held by private parties; they are negotiable and may be traded on the international market (except in Argentina); and they promise a future stream of cash income. We recognize that, prior to the enactment of the FSIA, there was authority suggesting that the issuance of public debt instruments did not constitute a commercial activity. [*Victory Transport, Inc. v. Comisaria General,* 336 F.2d 354 (2d Cir. 1964).] There is, however, nothing distinctive about the state's assumption of debt (other than perhaps its purpose) that would cause it always to be classified as *jure imperii,* and in this regard it is significant that *Victory Transport* expressed confusion as to whether the "nature" or the "purpose" of a transaction was controlling in determining commerciality. Because the FSIA has now clearly established that the "nature" governs, we perceive no basis for concluding that the issuance of debt should be treated as categorically different from other activities of foreign states.

Argentina contends that, although the FSIA bars consideration of "purpose," a court must nonetheless fully consider the *context* of a transaction in order to determine whether it is "commercial." Accordingly, Argentina claims that the Court of Appeals erred by defining the relevant conduct in what Argentina considers an overly generalized, acontextual manner and by essentially adopting a *per se* rule that all "issuance of debt instruments" is "commercial." We have no occasion to consider such a *per se* rule, because it seems to us that even in full context, there is nothing about the issuance of these Bonods (except perhaps its purpose) that is not analogous to a private commercial transaction.

Argentina points to the fact that the transactions in which the Bonods were issued did not have the ordinary commercial consequence of raising capital or financing acquisitions. Assuming for the sake of argument that this is not an example of judging the commerciality of a transaction by its purpose, the ready answer is that private parties regularly issue bonds, not just to raise capital or to finance purchases, but also to refinance debt. That is what Argentina did here: by virtue of the earlier FEIC contracts, Argentina was *already* obligated to supply the U.S. dollars needed to retire the FEIC-insured debts; the Bonods simply allowed Argentina to restructure its existing obligations. Argentina further asserts (without proof or even elaboration) that it "received consideration [for the Bonods] in no way commensurate with [their] value." Assuming that to be true, it makes no difference. Engaging in a commercial act does not require the receipt of fair value, or even compliance with the common-law requirements of consideration.

Argentina argues that the Bonods differ from ordinary debt instruments in that they "were created by the Argentine Government to fulfill its obligations under a foreign exchange program designed to address a domestic credit crisis, and as a component of a program designed to control that nation's critical shortage of foreign exchange." In this regard, Argentina relies heavily on *De Sanchez v. Banco Central de Nicaragua,* 770 F.2d 1385 (5th Cir. 1985), in which the Fifth Circuit took the view that "[o]ften, the essence of an act is defined by its purpose"; that unless "we can inquire into the purposes of such acts, we cannot determine their nature"; and that, in light of its purpose to control its reserves of foreign currency, Nicaragua's refusal to honor a check it had issued to cover a private bank debt was a sovereign act entitled to immunity. Indeed, Argentina asserts that the line between "nature" and "purpose" rests upon a "formalistic distinction [that] simply is neither useful nor warranted." We think this line of argument is squarely foreclosed by the language of the FSIA. However difficult it may be in some cases to separate "purpose" (*i.e.,* the *reason* why the foreign state engages in the activity) from "nature" (*i.e.,* the outward form of the conduct that the foreign state performs or agrees to perform), the statute unmistakably commands that to be done. We agree with the Court of Appeals that it is irrelevant *why* Argentina participated in the bond market in the manner of a private actor; it matters only that it did so. We conclude that Argentina's issuance of the Bonods was a "commercial activity" under the FSIA. . . .

MOL, INC. v. PEOPLE'S REPUBLIC OF BANGLADESH
736 F.2d 1326 (9th Cir. 1984)

WRIGHT, CIRCUIT JUDGE. MOL, Inc. sues Bangladesh for termination of a licensing agreement for the export of rhesus monkeys from Bangladesh. Because the granting and revocation of a license to export a natural resource are sovereign acts, we have no jurisdiction over this claim.

In 1977, a division of the Bangladesh Ministry of Agriculture granted MOL, Inc., an Oregon Corporation, a ten-year license to capture and export rhesus monkeys. The licensing agreement specified quantities and prices and required MOL to build in Bangladesh in 1978 a breeding farm for rhesus monkeys. By its terms, the agreement was granted "on the grounds and sole condition that the primates exported by [MOL] from Bangladesh shall be used exclusively for the purposes of medical and other scientific research by highly skilled and competent personnel for the general benefit of all peoples of the world." To enable Bangladesh to monitor uses of the monkeys, it required MOL to keep available records on each monkey and arrange for duplicate records in Bangladesh. The agreement provided for arbitration of disputes, each party selecting one arbitrator. Bangladesh reserved the right to terminate the agreement "without notice if [MOL] has failed to fulfill its obligations under this Agreement."

In November 1977, India banned the export of its rhesus monkeys. As India had been the major exporter of these animals, which are valuable for research because of their anatomical and behavioral similarity to humans, Bangladesh became an important supplier. Although world monkey prices rose while MOL's payments to Bangladesh remained fixed, Bangladesh complied with the licensing agreement through the spring of 1978. Bangladesh threatened to cancel the agreement in May 1978 because MOL had not built the breeding farm or exported agreed quantities. MOL denied any departure from the agreement. In September 1978, it delivered some Bangladesh monkeys to the United States armed services for radiobiological research.

Bangladesh announced on January 3, 1979, that it was terminating the agreement because MOL had not constructed the breeding farm in 1978 and had breached the requirement that the monkeys be used only for humanitarian purposes. It claimed that MOL sold the monkeys to the armed services for "neutron bomb radiation experiments." When MOL sought arbitration, Bangladesh refused, asserting its right to terminate for breach by MOL. Apparently MOL asked the State Department to intervene. Despite these efforts and MOL's reassurances that monkeys would not be used for radiation experiments, Bangladesh did not reinstate the licensing agreement. In 1982, MOL sued Bangladesh for $15 million. Bangladesh did not appear, and MOL moved for default. Amicus curiae, Attorneys for Animal Rights moved to dismiss for lack of jurisdiction under the FSIA. The district court denied the default judgment and dismissed the action, holding it barred [by] the FSIA. . . . [We affirm.]

MOL argues that Bangladesh does not enjoy sovereign immunity because its acts fall under the commercial activity exception of the FSIA. That Act denies immunity in any case in which the action is based "upon an act outside the territory of the United States in connection with a commercial activity of the foreign state elsewhere and that act causes a direct effect in the United States." 28 U.S.C. §1605(a)(2). . . . A crucial step in determining whether the basis of this suit was a commercial activity is defining the "act complained of here." *IAM v. OPEC*, 649 F.2d 1354, at 1357-58. The court must then decide whether that act is commercial or sovereign.

MOL asserts that the activity here relates to Bangladesh's contracting to sell monkeys. It admits that licensing the exploitation of natural resources is a sovereign activity. It argues, however, that this suit arises not from license revocation but from termination of a contract. In essence, Bangladesh lost its sovereign status when it contracted and then terminated pursuant to contract terms. The argument seems persuasive because, in breaking the agreement, Bangladesh itself spoke in commercial terms, basing its termination on MOL's alleged breaches. The true nature of the action, however, does not depend on terminology.

Bangladesh was terminating an agreement that only a sovereign could have made. This was not just a contract for trade of monkeys. It concerned Bangladesh's right to *regulate imports and exports,* a sovereign prerogative. It concerned Bangladesh's *right to regulate its natural resources,* also a uniquely sovereign function. *See IAM v. OPEC,* 477 F. Supp. 553, 567-68 (C.D. Cal. 1979), *aff'd on other grounds,* 649 F.2d 1354 (9th Cir. 1981). A private party could not have made such an agreement. MOL complains that this conclusion relies on the *purpose* of the agreement, in contradiction of the FSIA. *See* 28 U.S.C. §1603(d) (1982). But consideration of the special elements of export license and natural resource looks only to the *nature* of the agreement and does not require examination of the government's motives. In short, the licensing agreement was a sovereign act, not just a commercial transaction. Its revocation was sovereign by nature, not commercial. Bangladesh has sovereign immunity from this suit.

Notes on Weltover and MOL

1. *"Commercial" and "sovereign" acts distinguished.* After you have read various efforts to distinguish between "commercial" and "sovereign" acts, is the restrictive theory's distinction between the categories of conduct either principled or workable? Isn't everything that a state does "sovereign"? Consider again the rationales for the restrictive theory in the Tate Letter and *Pesaro,* and the criticisms of this theory. *See supra* pp. 238-241, 247-248. Is any different approach conceivable? Consider U.N. State Immunities Convention, Arts. 2(1)(c), 2(2) and 10.

2. *"Nature" and "purpose" distinguished.* As noted above, the FSIA expressly requires that the commercial or noncommercial character of a foreign state's activity be determined by reference to the "nature" of the activity, rather than its "purpose." 28 U.S.C. §1603(d) (1982). What does this distinction mean? One commentator has remarked:

> [T]he nature test ignores altogether the fact that one of the parties to the transaction is a sovereign State. Where a foreign sovereign State in pursuance of a newly formulated general policy seeks to change its existing commercial obligations, a political element creeps into the situation and no amount of pretence will make it disappear. Sornarajah, *Problems in Applying the Restrictive Theory of Sovereign Immunity,* 31 Int'l & Comp. L.Q. 661, 669 (1982).

Is this criticism persuasive? Is the distinction between "nature" and "purpose" useful in deciding *Weltover? MOL, Inc.?* Consider again U.N. State Immunities Convention, Art. 2(2).

3. **Weltover's historical approach to commercial activity definition.** Consider *Weltover's* analysis of §1603(d)'s definition of commercial activity. Note that Justice Scalia appears to adopt an historical approach to the issue: "The meaning of 'commercial' is the meaning generally attached to that term under the restrictive theory at the time the statute was enacted." Compare the approach taken by the Court in *Sosa* to the Alien Tort Statute.

See supra pp. 38-45, 47-52. On the other hand, compare Justice Scalia's similar historical approach to the Due Process Clause in *Burnham,* discussed *supra* pp. 129-133.

Recall the significant recent historic evolution of foreign sovereign immunity from the absolute to the restrictive theory. Given this, is Justice Scalia's focus on the restrictive theory in 1976 an appropriate way to define "commercial activity"? Does this mean that post-1976 developments should be ignored? Is that consistent with Congress's instruction that the judiciary develop the definition of commercial activity on a case-by-case basis?

4. *Test for commercial activity after* Weltover. What definition does *Weltover* adopt for "commercial activity"? Consider the following: "when a foreign government acts, not as a regulator of a market, but in the manner of a private player within it, the foreign sovereign's actions are 'commercial' within the meaning of the FSIA." Is this a workable test? What does it mean to act "in the manner of a private player within [a market]"? Does the "market" have to be a private market — or does the market for sovereign debt (or jet fighters) also qualify? For a discussion, *see Mortimer Off Shore Servs., Ltd. v. Federal Republic of Germany,* 2010 WL 2891069 (2d Cir. July 26, 2010). What about the provision of insurance? *See Anglo-Iberia Underwriting Mgmt. v. P.T. Jamsostek,* 600 F.3d 171 (2d Cir. 2010).

How was the Government of Bangladesh in *MOL, Inc.* acting like a private player? What exactly is the "manner of a private player"? How did Argentina act like a private player when it issued billions of dollars of public debt in close coordination with the International Monetary Fund, World Bank, and other public institutions? Is that what private people do? What precisely are the attributes of "private" conduct that led to a finding that the Court's "private player" test was satisfied? Is it because the Bonods are "in almost all respects garden-variety debt instruments"? What made them so ordinary?

5. *Application of the commercial activity definition in* Weltover. Was *Weltover* correct in concluding that the issuance of the Bonods was a commercial activity? What is the answer to Argentina's arguments that the debt was issued as part of a national economic recovery program, and that no private party could issue debt of this character? If you were advising a foreign government on the issuance of public debt, what suggestions would you make to ensure immunity? Is there any question how the transactions at issue in *Weltover* would be treated under the U.N. State Immunities Convention? How does Article 10(1) of the Convention apply?

What if Argentina had enacted foreign exchange control regulations that left the Bonds' terms intact, as a contractual matter, but imposed legislative restrictions that forbid the holders of such instruments from withdrawing their funds from Argentina. Would these actions have been subject to jurisdiction under the FSIA? If you were advising the Republic of Argentina, how would you structure such foreign exchange regulations to maximize the chance that your client would remain immune?

6. *Profit-making enterprise as commercial activity.* The FSIA's legislative history indicates that an important factor in the "commercial activity" definition is whether the activity is carried on for profit: "Certainly, if an activity is customarily carried on for profit, its commercial nature could be readily assumed." *See* H.R. Rep. 1487, 94th Cong., 2d Sess. 16, *reprinted in* 1976 U.S. Code Cong. & Admin. News at 6615. Does this definition look to the actor's purpose (*i.e.,* earn a profit) in engaging in particular conduct? If so, is this consistent with the FSIA's distinction between nature and purpose?

The Bonods were not issued for purposes of earning a profit. Does that suggest that *Weltover* was wrongly decided? Or is profit-making only one indicia of a "commercial" activity — as opposed to a requirement?

7. *Contractual relations as commercial activity.* The FSIA's legislative history also strongly suggests that when a foreign state enters into or breaches a contract, including a contract for the sale or purchase of goods or services, the state is engaged in a commercial activity.

"[A] single contract, if of the same character as a contract which might be made by a private person, could constitute a 'particular transaction or act' and thus fall within the definition of commercial activity." *See* H.R. Rep. 1487, 94th Cong., 2d Sess. 16, *reprinted in* 1976 U.S. Code Cong. & Admin. News at 6615; U.N. State Immunity Convention, Art. 2(1)(c).

Even before *Weltover,* lower courts had concluded that a foreign state's breach of its contractual obligations falls within the commercial exception, even when the breach is motivated by political concerns or public objectives. *E.g., McDonnell Douglas Corp. v. Islamic Republic of Iran,* 758 F.2d 341 (8th Cir. 1985) (plaintiff's action was based on defendant's breach of contract regarding military aircraft, which was a commercial activity notwithstanding political motivations underlying breach); *Texas Trading & Milling Corp. v. Federal Republic of Nigeria,* 647 F.2d 300 (2d Cir. 1981) (plaintiff's claim was based on defendant's breach of cement purchase contracts, which was commercial activity notwithstanding the fact that the cement was for public projects and the decision to breach was made at high levels of government).

Does this mean that *all* contracts of foreign states are "commercial activity"? Foreign states routinely enter into countless forms of agreements, both with private parties and other sovereigns. Are all of these agreements "commercial activities" within the meaning of the FSIA—including treaties and multilateral conventions? *Compare Rush-Presbyterian-St. Luke's Medical Ctr. v. Hellenic Republic,* 877 F.2d 574, 578 (7th Cir. 1989) ("Contracts for the purchase or sale of goods or services are presumptively commercial activities.") *with MCI Telecommunications Corp. v. Alhadhood,* 82 F.3d 658 (5th Cir. 1996) (alleged promise to pay for telephone calls made through diplomatic channels held noncommercial). If only some contracts are "commercial" how does one tell the difference between those that are commercial and those that are not? Does the test adopted in *Weltover* enable one to do so?

8. **MOL, Inc. and the sovereign/commercial distinction.** *MOL, Inc.* illustrates how some U.S. lower courts have been reluctant to assert jurisdiction over foreign states, even when they are engaged in what appear to be commercial activities. What aspects of the *MOL, Inc.* contract with Bangladesh led the court to hold that it was "a sovereign act, not just a commercial transaction"? The fact that Bangladesh agreed to grant export licenses? That the agreement related to natural resources? Would either factor alone have led to a holding of immunity? Suppose the case had involved the export of handicrafts or consumer goods or automobiles pursuant to an agreement that obligated Bangladesh to grant export licenses? Suppose the case had involved Bangladesh's breach of an agreement to use MOL's services to raise rhesus monkeys in Bangladesh, without provisions regarding exports? What if the agreement called for the export of timber, coffee, or oil?

9. *Is MOL, Inc. correctly decided?* Was the result in *MOL, Inc.* consistent with the reasoning and holding in *Weltover*? Did Bangladesh act "in the manner of a private player"? How? How would *MOL, Inc.* be decided under the U.N. State Immunities Convention?

10. *Relevance of exercise of governmental authority to commercial activity.* In addition to suggesting special treatment for activities relating to natural resources, *MOL, Inc.* and several other lower court decisions suggest that contracts are noncommercial if they include undertakings by foreign states or their agencies to exercise sovereign responsibilities (such as granting export licenses, tax benefits, or immigration waivers). *See Honduran Aircraft Registry, Ltd. v. Government of Honduras,* 129 F.3d 543 (11th Cir. 1997); *Drexel Burnham Lambert Group, Inc. v. Committee of Receivers,* 12 F.3d 317, 329 (2d Cir. 1993); *Millen Industries, Inc. v. CCNAA,* 855 F.2d 879 (D.C. Cir. 1988); *Practical Concepts v. Republic of Bolivia,* 811 F.2d 1543 (D.C. Cir. 1987). *Compare Schoenberg v. Exportadora de Sal, SA,* 930 F.2d 777 (9th Cir. 1991) (state-owned company's transportation of Japanese university

representatives, at request of Mexican government, held commercial activity). Is this aspect of *MOL, Inc.* persuasive?

11. *Employment-related actions as commercial activities.* Another area testing the limits of the sovereign/commercial distinction involves employment disputes. *See El-Hadad v. United Arab Emirates,* 216 F.3d 29, 31-32 (D.C. Cir. 2002) ("Our precedent makes clear that the employment of personnel by a foreign state is not per se commercial activity under the FSIA."). Here, relying on the FSIA's legislative history, courts have appeared to reach different results depending on the employee's identity. Where the employee served in a diplomatic, civil service or security function, employment actions have been deemed "sovereign." *See Butters v. Vance Int'l, Inc.,* 225 F.3d 462, 465 (4th Cir. 2000); *Crum v. Kingdom of Saudi Arabia,* 2005 WL 3752271 (E.D. Va. July 13, 2005) (following *Butters*). By contrast, where the employee served in an administrative capacity, employment actions have been deemed commercial. For cases exploring this distinction in employment-related disputes, *see Kato v. Ishihara,* 360 F.3d 106 (2d Cir. 2004) *Holden v. Canadian Consulate,* 92 F.3d 918, 922 (9th Cir. 1996).

What is the basis for the foregoing distinction in the employment context? *See Shih v. Taipei Economic and Cultural Representative Office,* 693 F. Supp. 2d 805 (N.D. Ill. 2010). Is it consistent with the reasoning in *Weltover?*

12. *The "based upon" requirement—an initial look.* The first clause of §1605(a)(2) requires that an action be "based upon" a commercial activity; the second and third clauses of §1605(a)(2) require that an action be "based upon" an act "in connection with" a commercial activity. *See infra* pp. 287-299, 299-308.

What does "based upon" mean? *See Transatlantic Schiffahrtskontor GmbH v. Shanghai Foreign Trade Corp.,* 204 F.3d 384, 390 (2d Cir. 2000) ("based upon" implies some causal relationship at a minimum); *Murphy v. Korea Asset Management Corp.,* 2005 WL 2675110, at *18 (S.D.N.Y. Oct. 19, 2005) (discussing *Transatlantic*). What "commercial activity" or "act" was the claim in *Mol, Inc.* "based upon"? Was the action based upon termination of the licensing agreement, or upon failure to grant export licenses? Does the distinction matter? *See infra* pp. 299-308. Consider how the U.N. State Immunities Convention deals with the "based upon" requirement in Article 10(1).

13. *The FSIA and forum selection.* As discussed in greater detail in Chapters 5 and 13, parties to international commercial agreements routinely utilize forum selection clauses or arbitration clauses. Those clauses channel disputes arising under the contract to the designated forum and, thereby, reduce jurisdictional uncertainty when disputes arise. Such clauses are not automatically enforceable but are subject to various defenses; for example, as detailed in Chapter 5, U.S. courts will consider whether a forum selection clause is valid under generally applicable contract law principles, as well as whether it contravenes some important public policy in the forum. *See infra* pp. 487-499.

Contracts between private parties and sovereign states often also contain forum selection or arbitration clauses. In some cases, the designated forum will be the sovereign's own country. If enforceable, such clauses remove the dispute from U.S. courts, denying the private party the benefits of a neutral forum. If a private party commences suit in the United States under the FSIA against the foreign sovereign and argues that the forum selection clause is unenforceable, should a court apply the same standards applicable to forum selection clauses between private parties? Or do such cases present especially grave risks of "self-dealing" where the sovereign's own courts would be sitting in judgment of its conduct?

Even where private parties have not employed forum selection clauses, defendants may employ a variety of other forum selection tools to channel the case to a foreign forum. For example, they may argue that the case should be dismissed on *forum non conveniens* grounds because another country's courts provide an adequate (and more convenient) forum with a stronger interest in the case. *See infra* pp. 365-459. Alternatively, in cases of parallel litigation, they may argue that the U.S. court should stay the litigation during the pendency of the foreign proceedings. Suppose that, in a case under the FSIA, a foreign sovereign urges a dismissal or stay of litigation on one of these grounds. Should a court employ the standards applicable in disputes between private parties? If the sovereign argues that the case should be dismissed because its own courts provide a more convenient forum, should a U.S. court approach skeptically the argument that the sovereign's own courts are "adequate"? Does it depend on extrinsic evidence of the sovereign's commitment to a rule of law? Is it even appropriate for a U.S. court to be rendering an opinion about the adequacy or fairness of a foreign forum? (Similar issues arise in the context of judgment enforcement, *see infra* at 468, 808.) For cases raising some of these issues of forum selection and the FSIA, *see, e.g., UNC Lear Services Inc. v. Kingdom of Saudi Arabia*, 581 F.3d 210 (5th Cir. 2009); *Northrop Grumman Ship Systems, Inc. v. Ministry of Defense of Republic of Venezuela*, 2010 WL 5058645 (S.D. Miss. Dec. 4, 2010).

b.   The "Based Upon" and "In Connection" Requirements.   Section 1605(a)(2) lifts immunity only from suits that are "based upon" a commercial activity (§1605(a)(2)'s first clause) or that are "based upon" an act "in connection" with a commercial activity (§1605(a)(2)'s second and third clauses). The Act and its legislative history shed little light on the "based upon" or "in connection" requirements,[103] and lower courts have reached divergent results in applying them.[104]

Ascertaining the precise activity of a foreign state that an action is "based upon" has two important consequences.[105] First, this determination provides the basis for defining the conduct of a foreign state that must be examined to determine whether "commercial activity" (discussed immediately above) is involved. Second, it provides the basis for defining the conduct of the foreign defendant that must be examined for purposes of satisfying §1605(a)(2)'s "nexus" requirements (discussed immediately below). In both instances, the scope of the activity on which the plaintiff's claim is "based" can significantly affect the ultimate determination of immunity.

Following enactment of the FSIA, lower courts were not able to agree upon any precise definition of the "based upon" requirement. Two Courts of Appeals said that, in applying the "based upon" requirement, "we must isolate the specific conduct that underlies the suit," rather than looking generally to "the broad program or policy of which the individual transaction is a part."[106] Other decisions took broader views, specifically rejecting a "niggardly construction" of the "based upon" requirement.[107] In *Saudi Arabia v. Nelson*, excerpted below, the Supreme Court resolved this debate. It held that the "based

103. Lowenfeld, *Litigating a Sovereign Immunity Claim — The Haiti Case*, 49 N.Y.U. L. Rev. 377 (1974); Brittenham, *Foreign Sovereign Immunity and Commercial Activity: A Conflicts Approach*, 83 Colum. L. Rev. 1440, 1488-1491 (1983).

104. *See Vencedora Oceanica Navigacion v. Compagnie Nationale Algerienne de Navigation*, 730 F.2d 195 (5th Cir. 1984) (summarizing divergent lower court results). *See also Garb v. Republic of Poland*, 2006 WL 515500, at *6 (2d Cir. Mar. 3, 2006) ("in connection with" is a term of art that should be narrowly construed).

105. *See Callejo v. Bancomer, SA*, 764 F.2d 1101, 1110 (5th Cir. 1985); *Kern v. Oesterreichische Elektrizitaetswirtschaft AG*, 178 F. Supp. 2d 367 (S.D.N.Y. 2001) (illustrating importance of "based upon" requirement); *Nazarian v. Compagnie Nationale Air France*, 989 F. Supp. 504 (S.D.N.Y. 1998).

106. *Weltover, Inc. v. Republic of Argentina*, 941 F.2d 145, 150 (2d Cir. 1991) (quoting *Rush-Presbyterium St. Luke's Medical Center v. Hellenic Republic*, 877 F.2d 574, 580 (7th Cir. 1989, aff'd, 112 S. Ct. 2160 (1992)). *See also Baglab Ltd. v. Johnson Matthey Bankers Ltd.*, 665 F. Supp. 289, 294 (S.D.N.Y. 1987) (must "define with precision"); *Braka v. Bancomer, SA*, 589 F. Supp. 1465, 1469 (S.D.N.Y. 1984), aff'd, 762 F.2d 222 (2d Cir. 1985).

107. *Gemini Shipping, Inc. v. Foreign Trade Org.*, 647 F.2d 317, 319 (2d Cir. 1981). *See also Gilson v. Republic of Ireland*, 682 F.2d 1022, 1027 n.22 (D.C. Cir. 1982).

upon" requirement called for a determination of "those elements of a claim that, if proven, would entitle a plaintiff to relief under his theory of the case."[108]

Relatively few cases have considered the meaning of the "in connection" requirement, as used in the second and third clauses of §1605(a)(2). In *Nelson,* the Court reasoned that the term must have a more expansive meaning than "based upon," but it did not say what that meaning was.[109] Lower courts have been cautious in reading the term broadly.[110]

SAUDI ARABIA v. NELSON
507 U.S. 349 (1993)

JUSTICE SOUTER. The FSIA entitles foreign states to immunity from the jurisdiction of courts in the United States, subject to certain enumerated exceptions. One is that a foreign state shall not be immune in any case "in which the action is based upon a commercial activity carried on in the United States by the foreign state." [28 U.S.C. §1605(a)(2).] We hold that respondents' action alleging personal injury resulting from unlawful detention and torture by the Saudi Government is not "based upon a commercial activity" within the meaning of the Act, which consequently confers no jurisdiction over respondents' suit.

I. Because this case comes to us on a motion to dismiss the complaint, we assume that we have truthful factual allegations before us. . . . Petitioner Kingdom of Saudi Arabia owns and operates petitioner King Faisal Specialist Hospital in Riyadh, as well as petitioner Royspec Purchasing Services, the Hospital's corporate purchasing agent in the United States. The Hospital Corporation of America, Ltd. ("HCA"), an independent corporation existing under the laws of the Cayman Islands, recruits Americans for employment at the Hospital under an agreement signed with Saudi Arabia in 1973.

In its recruitment effort, HCA placed an advertisement in a trade periodical seeking applications for a position as a monitoring systems engineer at the Hospital. The advertisement drew the attention of respondent Scott Nelson in September 1983, while Nelson was in the United States. After interviewing for the position in Saudi Arabia, Nelson returned to the United States, where he signed an employment contract with the Hospital . . . and attended an orientation session that HCA conducted for Hospital employees. . . . HCA identified Royspec as the point of contact in the United States for family members who might wish to reach Nelson in an emergency.

In December 1983, Nelson went to Saudi Arabia and began work at the Hospital, monitoring all "facilities, equipment, utilities and maintenance systems to insure the safety of patients, hospital staff, and others." He did his job without significant incident until March 1984, when he discovered safety defects. . . . Nelson repeatedly advised Hospital officials of the safety defects and reported the defects to a Saudi Government commission as well. Hospital officials instructed Nelson to ignore the problems. The Hospital's response to Nelson's reports changed, however, on September 27, 1984, when certain Hospital employees summoned him to the Hospital's security office where agents of the Saudi Government arrested him.[111] The agents transported Nelson

---

108. 507 U.S. at 357.
109. 507 U.S. at 357.
110. *See infra* pp. 297-298.

111. Petitioners assert that the Saudi Government arrested Nelson because he had falsely represented to the Hospital that he had received a degree from the Massachusetts Institute of Technology and had provided the Hospital with a forged diploma to verify his claim. The Nelsons concede these misrepresentations, but dispute that they occasioned Scott Nelson's arrest.

to a jail cell, in which they "shackled, tortured and bea[t]" him, and kept him four days without food. Although Nelson did not understand Arabic, Government agents forced him to sign a statement written in that language. . . . Two days later, Government agents transferred Nelson to the Al Sijan Prison "to await trial on unknown charges." At the Prison, Nelson was confined in an overcrowded cell area infested with rats, where he had to fight other prisoners for food and from which he was taken only once a week for fresh air and exercise. Although police interrogators repeatedly questioned him in Arabic, Nelson did not learn the nature of the charges, if any, against him. For several days, the Saudi Government failed to advise Nelson's family of his whereabouts, though a Saudi official eventually told Nelson's wife . . . that he could arrange for her husband's release if she provided sexual favors.

Although officials from the United States Embassy visited Nelson twice during his detention, they concluded that his allegations of Saudi mistreatment were "not credible" and made no protest to Saudi authorities. It was only at the personal request of a United States Senator that the Saudi Government released Nelson, 39 days after his arrest, on November 5, 1984. Seven days later, after failing to convince him to return to work at the Hospital, the Saudi Government allowed Nelson to leave the country.

In 1988, Nelson and his wife filed this action against petitioners in the U.S. District Court for the Southern District of Florida seeking damages for personal injury. The Nelsons' complaint sets out 16 causes of action, which fall into three categories[: (i) various intentional torts, including battery, unlawful detainment, wrongful arrest and imprisonment, false imprisonment; (ii) negligently failing to warn Nelson of otherwise undisclosed dangers of his employment, namely, that if he attempted to report safety hazards the Hospital would likely retaliate against him and the Saudi Government might detain and physically abuse him without legal cause; and (iii) claims that Vivian Nelson sustained derivative injury resulting from petitioners' actions]. Presumably because the employment contract provided that Saudi courts would have exclusive jurisdiction over claims for breach of contract, the Nelsons raised no such matters. . . .

II. The [FSIA] "provides the sole basis for obtaining jurisdiction over a foreign state in the courts of this country." *Argentine Republic v. Amerada Hess Shipping Corp., supra.* Under the Act, a foreign state is presumptively immune from the jurisdiction of United States courts; unless a specified exception applies, a federal court lacks subject-matter jurisdiction over a claim against a foreign state.

Only one such exception is said to apply here. The first clause of §1605(a)(2) of the Act provides that a foreign state shall not be immune from the jurisdiction of United States courts in any case "in which the action is based upon a commercial activity carried on in the United States by the foreign state." The Act defines such activity as "commercial activity carried on by such state and having substantial contact with the United States," §1603(e), and provides that a commercial activity may be "either a regular course of commercial conduct or a particular commercial transaction or act," the "commercial character of [which] shall be determined by reference to" its "nature," rather than its "purpose." §1603(d).

There is no dispute here that Saudi Arabia, the Hospital, and Royspec all qualify as "foreign state[s]" within the meaning of the Act. For there to be jurisdiction in this case, therefore, the Nelsons' action must be "based upon" some "commercial activity" by petitioners that had "substantial contact" with the United States within the meaning of the Act. Because we conclude that the suit is not based upon any commercial activity by petitioners, we need not reach the issue of substantial contact with the United States.

We begin our analysis by identifying the particular conduct on which the Nelsons' action is "based" for purposes of the Act. Although the Act contains no definition of the phrase "based upon," and the relatively sparse legislative history offers no assistance, guidance is hardly necessary. In denoting conduct that forms the "basis," or "foundation," for a claim, *see Black's Law Dictionary* 151 (6th ed. 1990) (defining "base"); *Webster's Third New International Dictionary* 180, 181 (1976) (defining "base" and "based"), the phrase is read most naturally to mean those elements of a claim that, if proven, would entitle a plaintiff to relief under his theory of the case.

What the natural meaning of the phrase "based upon" suggests, the context confirms. [Section] 1605(a)(2) contains two clauses following the one at issue here. The second allows for jurisdiction where a suit "is based . . . upon an act performed in the United States in connection with a commercial activity of the foreign state elsewhere," and the third speaks in like terms, allowing for jurisdiction where an action "is based . . . upon an act outside the territory of the United States in connection with a commercial activity of the foreign state elsewhere and that act causes a direct effect in the United States." Distinctions among descriptions juxtaposed against each other are naturally understood to be significant, and Congress manifestly understood there to be a difference between a suit "based upon" commercial activity and one "based upon" acts performed "in connection with" such activity. The only reasonable reading of the former term calls for something more than a mere connection with, or relation to, commercial activity.[112]

In this case, the Nelsons have alleged that petitioners recruited Scott Nelson for work at the Hospital, signed an employment contract with him, and subsequently employed him. While these activities led to the conduct that eventually injured the Nelsons, they are not the basis for the Nelsons' suit. Even taking each of the Nelsons' allegations about Scott Nelson's recruitment and employment as true, those facts alone entitle the Nelsons to nothing under their theory of the case. The Nelsons have not, after all, alleged breach of contract, but personal injuries caused by petitioners' intentional wrongs and by petitioners' negligent failure to warn Scott Nelson that they might commit those wrongs. Those torts, and not the arguably commercial activities that preceded their commission, form the basis for the Nelsons' suit.

Petitioners' tortious conduct itself fails to qualify as "commercial activity" within the meaning of the Act, although the Act is too " 'obtuse' " to be of much help in reaching that conclusion. *Callejo,* 764 F.2d at 1107. We have seen already that the Act defines "commercial activity" as "either a regular course of commercial conduct or a particular commercial transaction or act," and provides that "[t]he commercial character of an activity shall be determined by reference to the nature of the course of conduct or particular transaction or act, rather than by reference to its purpose." 28 U.S.C. §1603(d). If this is a definition, it is one distinguished only by its diffidence; as we observed in our most recent case on the subject, it "leaves the critical term 'commercial' largely undefined." *Republic of Argentina v. Weltover, Inc.*; Lowenfeld, *Litigating a Sovereign Immunity Claim — The Haiti Case,* 49 N.Y.U. L. Rev. 377, 435, n.244 (1974) ("Start with 'activity,' proceed via 'conduct' or 'transaction' to 'character,' then refer to 'nature,' and then go back to 'commercial,' the term you started out to define in the first place"); G. Born & D. Westin, *International Civil Litigation in United States Courts* 479-480 (2d ed. 1992). We do not, however, have the option to throw up our hands. The term has to be given some interpretation, and congressional diffidence necessarily results in judicial responsibility to determine what a "commercial activity" is for purposes of the Act. . . .

---

112. We do not mean to suggest that the first clause of §1605(a)(2) necessarily requires that each and every element of a claim be commercial activity by a foreign state, and we do not address the case where a claim consists of both commercial and sovereign elements. We do conclude, however, that where a claim rests entirely upon activities sovereign in character, as here, jurisdiction will not exist under that clause regardless of any connection the sovereign acts may have with commercial activity.

We explained in *Weltover* that a state engages in commercial activity under the restrictive theory where it exercises "'only those powers that can also be exercised by private citizens,'" as distinct from those "'powers peculiar to sovereigns.'" Put differently, a foreign state engages in commercial activity for purposes of the restrictive theory only where it acts "in the manner of a private player within" the market. . . . Unlike Argentina's activities that we considered in *Weltover*, the intentional conduct alleged here (the Saudi Government's wrongful arrest, imprisonment, and torture of Nelson) could not qualify as commercial under the restrictive theory. The conduct boils down to abuse of the power of its police by the Saudi Government, and however monstrous such abuse undoubtedly may be, a foreign state's exercise of the power of its police has long been understood for purposes of the restrictive theory as peculiarly sovereign in nature. *See Victory Transport Inc. v. Comisaria General de Abastecimientos y Transportes*, 336 F.2d 354, 360 (2d Cir. 1964) (restrictive theory does extend immunity to a foreign state's "internal administrative acts").[113] Exercise of the powers of police and penal officers is not the sort of action by which private parties can engage in commerce. . . .

The Nelsons and their amici urge us to give significance to their assertion that the Saudi Government subjected Nelson to the abuse alleged as retaliation for his persistence in reporting Hospital safety violations, and argue that the character of the mistreatment was consequently commercial. . . . But this argument does not alter the fact that the powers allegedly abused were those of police and penal officers. In any event, the argument is off the point, for it goes to purpose, the very fact the Act renders irrelevant to the question of an activity's commercial character. Whatever may have been the Saudi Government's motivation for its allegedly abusive treatment of Nelson, it remains the case that the Nelsons' action is based upon a sovereign activity. . . .

In addition to the intentionally tortious conduct, the Nelsons claim a separate basis for recovery in petitioners' failure to warn Scott Nelson of the hidden dangers associated with his employment. The Nelsons allege that, at the time petitioners recruited Scott Nelson and thereafter, they failed to warn him of the possibility of severe retaliatory action if he attempted to disclose any safety hazards he might discover on the job. In other words, petitioners bore a duty to warn of their own propensity for tortious conduct. But this is merely a semantic ploy. For aught we can see, a plaintiff could recast virtually any claim of intentional tort committed by sovereign act as a claim of failure to warn, simply by charging the defendant with an obligation to announce its own tortious propensity before indulging it. To give jurisdictional significance to this feint of language would effectively thwart the Act's manifest purpose to codify the restrictive theory of foreign sovereign immunity.

III. The Nelsons' action is not "based upon a commercial activity" within the meaning of the first clause of §1605(a)(2) of the Act, and the judgment of the Court of Appeals is accordingly reversed.

Justice White, with whom Justice Blackmun joins, concurring in the judgment. . . . The majority concludes that petitioners enjoy sovereign immunity because respondents' action is not "based upon a commercial activity." I disagree. I nonetheless concur in the judgment because in my view the commercial conduct upon which respondents base their complaint was not "carried on in the United States."

---

113. The State Department's practice prior to the passage of the Act supports this understanding. Prior to the Act's passage, the State Department would determine in the first instance whether a foreign state was entitled to immunity and make an appropriate recommendation to the courts. A compilation of available materials demonstrates that the Department recognized immunity with respect to claims involving the exercise of the power of the police or military of a foreign state. . . .

As the majority notes, the first step in the analysis is to identify the conduct on which the action is based. Respondents have pointed to two distinct possibilities. The first, seemingly pressed at trial and on appeal, consists of the recruiting and hiring activity in the United States. Although this conduct would undoubtedly qualify as "commercial," I agree with the majority that it is "not the basis for the Nelsons' suit," for it is unrelated to the elements of respondents' complaint.

In a partial change of course, respondents suggest to this Court both in their brief and at oral argument that we focus on the hospital's commercial activity in Saudi Arabia, its employment practices and disciplinary procedures. Under this view, the Court would then work its way back to the recruiting and hiring activity in order to establish that the commercial conduct in fact had "substantial contact" with the United States. The majority never reaches this second stage, finding instead that petitioners' conduct is not commercial because it "is not the sort of action by which private parties can engage in commerce." If by that the majority means that it is not the manner in which private parties ought to engage in commerce, I wholeheartedly agree. That, however, is not the relevant inquiry. Rather, the question we must ask is whether it is the manner in which private parties at times do engage in commerce.

To run and operate a hospital, even a public hospital, is to engage in a commercial enterprise. The majority never concedes this point, but it does not deny it either, and to my mind the matter is self-evident. By the same token, warning an employee when he blows the whistle and taking retaliatory action, such as harassment, involuntary transfer, discharge, or other tortious behavior, although not prototypical commercial acts, are certainly well within the bounds of commercial activity. The House and Senate Reports accompanying the legislation virtually compel this conclusion, explaining as they do that "a foreign government's . . . employment or engagement of laborers, clerical staff or marketing agents . . . would be among those included within" the definition of commercial activity. H.R. Rep. No. 94-1487, 16 (1976) ("House Report"); S.R. Rep. No. 94-1310, p. 16 (1976) ("Senate Report"). Nelson alleges that petitioners harmed him in the course of engaging in their commercial enterprise, as a direct result of their commercial acts. His claim, in other words, is "based upon commercial activity."

Indeed, I am somewhat at a loss as to what exactly the majority believes petitioners have done that a private employer could not. As countless cases attest, retaliation for whistle-blowing is not a practice foreign to the marketplace. Congress passed a statute in response to such behavior, as have numerous States. On occasion, private employers also have been known to retaliate by enlisting the help of police officers to falsely arrest employees. More generally, private parties have been held liable for conspiring with public authorities to effectuate an arrest, and for using private security personnel for the same purposes.

Therefore, had the hospital retaliated against Nelson by hiring thugs to do the job, I assume the majority—no longer able to describe this conduct as "a foreign state's exercise of the power of its police,"—would consent to calling it "commercial." For, in such circumstances, the state-run hospital would be operating as any private participant in the marketplace and respondents' action would be based on the operation by Saudi Arabia's agents of a commercial business.

At the heart of the majority's conclusion, in other words, is the fact that the hospital in this case chose to call in government security forces. I find this fixation on the intervention of police officers, and the ensuing characterization of the conduct as "peculiarly sovereign in nature," to be misguided. To begin, it fails to capture respondents' complaint in full. Far from being directed solely at the activities of the Saudi police, it alleges that agents of the hospital summoned Nelson to its security office because he reported safety concerns and that the hospital played a part in the subsequent beating and imprisonment. Without more, that type of behavior hardly qualifies as sovereign. Thus, even assuming for the sake of argument that the role of the official police somehow affected the nature of petitioners' conduct, the claim cannot be said to "rest[] entirely upon activities sovereign in character." At the very least it "consists of both commercial and sovereign elements," thereby presenting the specific question the majority chooses to elude. . . .

Reliance on the fact that Nelson's employer enlisted the help of public rather than private security personnel is also at odds with Congress' intent. The purpose of the commercial exception being to prevent foreign states from taking refuge behind their sovereignty when they act as market participants, it seems to me that this is precisely the type of distinction we should seek to avoid. Because both the hospital and the police are agents of the state, the case in my mind turns on whether the sovereign is acting in a commercial capacity, not on whether it resorts to thugs or government officers to carry on its business. That, when the hospital calls in security to get even with a whistleblower, it comes clothed in police apparel says more about the state-owned nature of the commercial enterprise than about the noncommercial nature of its tortious conduct. . . .

C. Contrary to the majority's suggestion, this conclusion does not involve inquiring into the purpose of the conduct. Matters would be different, I suppose, if Nelson had been recruited to work in the Saudi police force and, having reported safety violations, suffered retributive punishment, for there the Saudi authorities would be engaged in distinctly sovereign activities. *Cf.* House Report, at 16 ("Also public or governmental and not commercial in nature, would be the employment of diplomatic, civil service, or military personnel"). The same would be true if Nelson was a mere tourist in Saudi Arabia and had been summarily expelled by order of immigration officials. In this instance, however, the state-owned hospital was engaged in ordinary commercial business and "[i]n their commercial capacities, foreign governments do not exercise powers peculiar to sovereigns. Instead, they exercise only those powers that can also be exercised by private citizens." *Alfred Dunhill v. Republic of Cuba,* 425 U.S. 682, 704 (1976) (plurality opinion). . . .

II. Nevertheless, I reach the same conclusion as the majority because petitioners' commercial activity was not "carried on in the United States." The Act defines such conduct as "commercial activity . . . having substantial contact with the United States." 28 U.S.C. §1603(e). Respondents point to the hospital's recruitment efforts in the United States, including advertising in the American media, and the signing of the employment contract in Miami. As I earlier noted, while these may very well qualify as commercial activity in the United States, they do not constitute the commercial activity upon which respondents' action is based. Conversely, petitioners' commercial conduct in Saudi Arabia, though constituting the basis of the Nelsons' suit, lacks a sufficient nexus to the United States. Neither the hospital's employment practices, nor its disciplinary procedures, has any apparent connection to this country. On that basis, I agree that the Act does not grant the Nelsons access to our courts. . . .

JUSTICE KENNEDY, with whom JUSTICE BLACKMUN and JUSTICE STEVENS join as to Parts I-B and II, concurring in part and dissenting in part. I join all of the Court's opinion except the last paragraph of Part II, where, with almost no explanation, the Court rules that, like the intentional tort claim, the claims based on negligent failure to warn are outside the subject-matter jurisdiction of the federal courts. These claims stand on a much different footing from the intentional tort claims for purposes of the FSIA. In my view, they ought to be remanded to the District Court for further consideration.

I agree with the Court's holding that the Nelsons' claims of intentional wrongdoing by the Hospital and the Kingdom of Saudi Arabia are based on sovereign, not commercial, activity, and so fall outside the commercial activity exception to the grant of foreign sovereign immunity contained in 28 U.S.C. §1604. The intentional tort counts of the Nelsons' complaint recite the alleged unlawful arrest, imprisonment, and torture of Mr. Nelson by the Saudi police acting in their official capacities. These are not the sort of activities by which a private party conducts its business affairs; if we classified them as commercial, the commercial activity exception would in large measure swallow the rule of foreign sovereign immunity Congress enacted in the FSIA.

By the same token, however, the Nelsons' claims alleging that the Hospital, the Kingdom, and Royspec were negligent in failing during their recruitment of Nelson to warn him of foreseeable dangers are based upon commercial activity having substantial contact with the United States. As such, they are within the commercial activity exception and the jurisdiction of the federal courts. Unlike the intentional tort counts of the complaint, the failure to warn counts do not complain of a police beating in Saudi Arabia; rather, they complain of a negligent omission made during the recruiting of a hospital employee in the United States. To obtain relief, the Nelsons would be obliged to prove that the Hospital's recruiting agent did not tell Nelson about the foreseeable hazards of his prospective employment in Saudi Arabia. Under the Court's test, this omission is what the negligence counts are "based upon."

Omission of important information during employee recruiting is commercial activity as we have described it. It seems plain that recruiting employees is an activity undertaken by private hospitals in the normal course of business. Locating and hiring employees implicates no power unique to the sovereign. In explaining the terms and conditions of employment, including the risks and rewards of a particular job, a governmental entity acts in "the manner of a private player within" the commercial marketplace. . . .

The recruiting activity alleged in the failure to warn counts of the complaint also satisfies the final requirement for invoking the commercial activity exception: that the claims be based upon commercial activity "having substantial contact with the United States." 28 U.S.C. §1603(e). Nelson's recruitment was performed by Hospital Corporation of America ("HCA"), a wholly owned subsidiary of a U.S. corporation, which, for a period of at least 16 years beginning in 1973, acted as the Kingdom of Saudi Arabia's exclusive agent for recruiting employees for the Hospital. HCA in the regular course of its business seeks employees for the Hospital in the American labor market. HCA advertised in an American magazine, seeking applicants for the position Nelson later filled. Nelson saw the ad in the United States and contacted HCA in Tennessee. After an interview in Saudi Arabia, Nelson returned to Florida, where he signed an employment contract and underwent personnel processing and application procedures. Before leaving to take his job at the Hospital, Nelson attended an orientation session conducted by HCA in Tennessee for new employees. These activities have more than substantial contact with the United States; most of them were "carried on in the United States." 28 U.S.C. §1605(a)(2). In alleging that the petitioners neglected during these activities to tell him what they were bound to under state law, Nelson meets all of the statutory requirements for invoking federal jurisdiction under the commercial activity exception.

Having met the jurisdictional prerequisites of the FSIA, the Nelsons' failure to warn claims should survive petitioners' motion under Federal Rule of Civil Procedure 12(b)(1) to dismiss for want of subject-matter jurisdiction. Yet instead of remanding these claims to the District Court for further proceedings, the majority dismisses them in a single short paragraph. . . . The Court's summary treatment may stem from doubts about the under-lying validity of the negligence cause of action. . . . These doubts, however, are not rele-vant to the analytical task at hand. . . .

JUSTICE STEVENS, dissenting. Under the [FSIA], a foreign state is subject to the jurisdic-tion of American courts if two conditions are met: The action must be "based upon a commercial activity" and that activity must have a "substantial contact with the United States." These two conditions should be separately analyzed because they serve two different purposes. The former excludes commercial activity from the scope of the for-eign sovereign's immunity from suit; the second identifies the contacts with the United States that support the assertion of jurisdiction over the defendant.

In this case, as Justice White has demonstrated, petitioner's operation of the hospital and its employment practices and disciplinary procedures are "commercial activities" within the meaning of the statute, and respondent's claim that he was punished for acts performed in the course of his employment was unquestionably "based upon" those activities. Thus, the first statutory condition is satisfied; petitioner is not entitled to immunity from the claims asserted by respondent.

Unlike Justice White, however, I am also convinced that petitioner's commercial activities—whether defined as the regular course of conduct of operating a hospital or, more specifically, as the commercial transaction of engaging respondent "as an employee with specific responsibilities in that enterprise,"—have sufficient contact with the United States to justify the exercise of federal jurisdiction. Petitioner Royspec maintains an office in Maryland and purchases hospital supplies and equipment in this country. For nearly two decades the Hospital's American agent has maintained an office in the United States and regularly engaged in the recruitment of personnel in this country. Respondent himself was recruited in the United States and entered into his employment contract with the hospital in the United States. Before traveling to Saudi Arabia to assume his position at the hospital, respondent attended an orientation program in Tennessee. The position for which respondent was recruited and ultimately hired was that of a monitoring systems manager, a troubleshooter, and . . . it was precisely respondent's performance of those responsibilities that led to the hospital's retaliatory actions against him.

Whether the first clause of §1605(a)(2) broadly authorizes "general" jurisdiction over foreign entities that engage in substantial commercial activity in this country, or, more narrowly, authorizes only "specific" jurisdiction over particular commercial claims that have a substantial contact with the United States,[114] petitioners' contacts with the United States in this case are, in my view, plainly sufficient to subject petitioners to suit in this country on a claim arising out of its nonimmune commercial activity relating to respondent. If the same activities had been performed by a private business, I have no doubt jurisdiction would be upheld. And that, of course, should be a touchstone of our inquiry; for as Justice White explains, when a foreign nation sheds its uniquely sovereign status and seeks out the benefits of the private marketplace, it must, like any private party, bear the burdens and responsibilities imposed by that marketplace. . . .

---

114. Though this case does not require resolution of that question (because petitioners' contacts with the United States satisfy, in my view, the more narrow requirements of "specific" jurisdiction), I am inclined to agree with the view expressed by Judge Higginbotham in his separate opinion in Vencedora Oceanica Navigacion, SA v. Compagnie Nationale Algerienne de Navigation, 730 F.2d 195, 204-205 (1984) (concurring in part and dissent-ing in part), that the first clause of §1605(a)(2), interpreted in light of the relevant legislative history and the second and third clauses of the provision, does authorize "general" jurisdiction over foreign entities that engage in substantial commercial activities in the United States.

Notes *on* Nelson

1. *Significance of determining what activity an action is "based upon."* A critical issue in *Nelson* was whether the plaintiff's claims were "based upon" one set of activities (*i.e.,* employment relations at a commercial hospital) or another set of activities (*i.e.,* police and detention practices). As *Nelson* illustrates, determining what conduct the plaintiff's action is "based upon" is closely related to determining both whether particular conduct is "commercial activity" and whether that conduct has a sufficient U.S. nexus.

2. *Definition of "based upon" requirement.* Justice Souter's majority opinion in *Nelson* interpreted §1605(a)(2)'s "based upon" requirement as "denoting conduct that forms the 'basis,' or 'foundation,' for a claim." The Court continued: "[T]he phrase is read most naturally to mean those elements of a claim that, if proven, would entitle a plaintiff to relief under his theory of the case." None of the various dissents and concurrences in *Nelson* appear to disagree with this rule. Nevertheless, some lower courts had arrived at somewhat different interpretations of §1605's "based upon" requirement. In *Gilson v. Republic of Ireland,* 682 F.2d 1022, 1027 n.22 (D.C. Cir. 1982), the court rejected a "narrow construction" and held that "[s]ection 1605's 'based upon' standard is satisfied if plaintiff can show a direct causal connection between [the defendant's commercial activity in the United States] and the [acts] giving rise to his claims . . . or if he can show that [the defendant's U.S. commercial activity] is an element of the cause of action under whatever law governs his claims."

Which view of the "based upon" standard is more persuasive? Are any of these tests workable? Are due process precedents defining the scope of specific jurisdiction relevant to the FSIA's "based upon" requirement?

Note Article 10(1) of the U.N. State Immunities Convention, which lifts immunity for "a proceeding arising out of that commercial transaction." Is this not a substantially broader, more readily satisfied nexus standard than the FSIA's "based upon" requirement? Is this standard relevant in interpreting the "based upon" requirement? Would it not be ironic if the United States — which was the impetus for the restrictive theory — were to accord foreign states substantially broader immunity than other states or than international law requires? Would this benefit the United States in any way?

3. *Application of "based upon" standard in* Nelson. Did Justice Souter correctly apply the "based upon" standard in *Nelson*? What conduct was the Nelsons' complaint based upon? Consider the following possibilities: (a) the arrest, detention, and mistreatment of Nelson; (b) the recruitment and hiring of Nelson; (c) the operation of the King Faisal Hospital.

(a) Divergent views in Nelson. What conduct did Justice Souter think the Nelsons' complaint was based upon? Justice White? Justice Kennedy? Did the various Justices apply different definitions of "based upon" in reaching their various different conclusions? What does this suggest about the value and reliability of the "based upon" standard? Which Justice reached the right conclusion in *Nelson* regarding the application of the "based upon" requirement?

(b) Justice Souter's "based upon" analysis. Is Justice Souter guilty of a "single-minded focus on the exercise of police power," as Justice White writes? Or was it the Nelsons' complaint that had a single-minded focus? Consider how Justice Souter disposes of the "failure to warn" claims. Was he concluding that these claims did not fall within the FSIA's jurisdictional grants, or was he in fact saying that these claims were meritless, and could therefore not be pursued? Would it be appropriate to make determinations about the merits of claims at the jurisdictional stage of proceedings? *Cf. Bell v. Hood,* 327 U.S. 678, 682-683

(1946) (clearly frivolous federal claims not subject to general federal subject matter jurisdiction).

(c) Justice White's "based upon" analysis. Consider Justice White's argument that respondents suggested "to *this Court* both in their brief and at oral argument that we focus on the hospital's commercial activity in Saudi Arabia." Is that appropriate? Does not §1605(a)(2) of the FSIA (and sound judicial administration) require focusing on what is in plaintiff's complaint, not what it argues on appeal in the Supreme Court? Suppose that Nelson had complained that the Hospital had unlawfully procured his false arrest and subsequent poor treatment, in an effort to protect its shoddy operating practices. What activity would that claim be "based upon"?

(d) Justice Kennedy's "based upon" analysis. Consider Justice Kennedy's view that the Nelsons' intentional tort claims were "based upon" official police conduct, but that their negligent "failure to warn" claims were based upon the defendants' recruitment and hiring activities in the United States. How does Justice Souter deal with this point? Is Justice Kennedy correct in concluding, under the majority's own test, that the failure to warn claims were "based upon" recruitment in the United States? Or, were those claims ultimately "based upon" the same police practices as to which warnings should have been given?

4. *Mixed sovereign/commercial activities.* A plaintiff's complaint may be "based upon" both commercial and noncommercial activities. If this occurs, can §1605(a)(2) be satisfied? Or must "each and every element of a claim be commercial activity by a foreign state"? Justice Souter writes in a footnote that the Court does not "address the case where a claim consists of both commercial and sovereign elements." *See supra* p. 291, note 112. How should such cases be decided? Does it matter which clause of §1605(a)(2) is involved? Was the claim in *MOL, Inc.* based upon both sovereign and commercial activities? *See also BP Chemicals Ltd. v. Jiangsu Sopo Corp.*, 285 F.3d 677, 682 (8th Cir. 2002) ("We emphasize that only one element of a plaintiff's claim must concern commercial activity carried on in the United States.").

As discussed above, some lower courts have held that promises to perform sovereign acts are not "commercial," even if they are contained in a "commercial" contract. A few of these courts have held that the contract must be dissected to distinguish between commercial and noncommercial obligations: the FSIA permits suits for the former, but not the latter. In the words of one court, considering whether a foreign state was immune from a suit based upon breach of its promise to exempt the plaintiff's products from duty:

> when a transaction partakes of both commercial and sovereign elements, jurisdiction under the FSIA will turn on which element the cause of action is based on. . . . [T]o the extent that the causes of action are based on promises, breaches of promises, and other allegedly actionable conduct involving extending duty-free status . . . these would plainly be sovereign aspects of the transaction over which we lack jurisdiction. *Millen Industries, Inc. v. Coordination Council for North American Affairs*, 855 F.2d 879 (D.C. Cir. 1988).

Is this a sensible line of analysis? Is *Nelson* in fact a case that was based upon both commercial and sovereign acts?

5. *Application of "based upon" requirement under first clause of §1605(a)(2).* Suppose that a foreign state engages in a sovereign act — such as issuing a decree or enacting a law — that cancels both its own commercial contracts and those of private parties. Is an action for breach of contract "based upon" the commercial contract or the sovereign decree? *See Jamini v. Kuwait University*, 1995 WL 19331 (D.C. Cir. 1995) (suit is based on contract's termination, not issuance of decree). What activities was the plaintiff's suit "based upon" in *MOL, Inc.* and *Weltover?*

c. The "Nexus" Requirements. Closely related to §1605(a)(2)'s "based upon" and "in connection" requirements are the section's so-called "nexus" requirements. Even if a plaintiff's action is "based upon" the indisputably "commercial activity" of a foreign state defendant, the defendant may still enjoy immunity from U.S. jurisdiction. In order to establish jurisdiction under §1605(a)(2), a plaintiff must also satisfy one of the section's nexus requirements, which demand that the foreign state's commercial conduct have a sufficiently close relationship to the United States.

Section 1605(a)(2) enumerates three relationships between the defendant's conduct and the United States that will permit an exercise of U.S. jurisdiction:

1. The plaintiff's action is "based upon a commercial activity carried on in the United States by the foreign state";
2. The plaintiff's action is based upon an "act" in the United States "in connection with a commercial activity of the foreign state elsewhere"; or
3. The plaintiff's action is based "upon an act outside the territory of the United States in connection with a commercial activity of the foreign state elsewhere and that act causes a direct effect in the United States."

The Act and its legislative history shed little light on these three clauses. Section 1603(e) defines "a commercial activity carried on in the United States by a foreign state" as "commercial activity carried on by such state and having *substantial contact* with the United States."[115] The legislative history of the first clause of §1605(a)(2) adds that:

> [t]his definition includes cases based on commercial transactions performed in whole or in part in the United States, import-export transactions involving sales to, or purchases from, concerns in the United States, business torts occurring in the United States . . . and an indebtedness incurred by a foreign state which negotiates or executes a loan agreement in the United States, or which receives financing from a private or public lending institution located in the United States.

The FSIA's legislative history also provides a gloss on the second clause of §1605(a)(2), which applies to acts within the United States in connection with commercial activities elsewhere. In the words of the House Report to the Act, the second clause "looks to conduct of the foreign state in the United States which relates either to a regular course of commercial conduct elsewhere or to a particular commercial transaction concluded or carried out in part elsewhere."[116] Examples provided by the legislative history include:

> a representation in the United States by an agent of a foreign state that leads to an action for restitution based on unjust enrichment; an act in the United States that violates U.S. securities laws or regulations; the wrongful discharge in the United States of an employee of the foreign state who has been employed in connection with a commercial activity carried on in some third country.[117]

---

115. H.R. Rep. No. 1487, 94th Cong., 2d Sess. 17, *reprinted in* 1976 U.S. Code Cong. & Admin. News at 6615-6616.
116. H.R. Rep. No. 1487, 94th Cong., 2d Sess. 17, *reprinted in* 1976 U.S. Code Cong. & Admin. News at 6615-6616.
117. H.R. Rep. No. 1487, 94th Cong., 2d Sess. 17, *reprinted in* 1976 U.S. Code Cong. & Admin. News at 6615-6616.

The following cases illustrate how U.S. courts have applied the "U.S. nexus" requirements of §1605(a)(2). *Republic of Argentina v. Weltover, Inc.* applies the "direct effects" standard of the third clause of §1605(a)(2). Also reread *Saudi Arabia v. Nelson,* which examines the first clause of §1605(a)(2), as well as the "based upon" requirement.

REPUBLIC OF ARGENTINA v. WELTOVER, INC.
504 U.S. 607 (1992) [also partially excerpted at supra pp. 279-282]

JUSTICE SCALIA. [In a portion of the Court's unanimous opinion excerpted above, Justice Scalia held that Argentina's issuing of certain debt instruments, named "Bonods," constituted commercial activity within the meaning of §1605(a)(2). The remainder of the Court's opinion, excerpted below, concluded that the rescheduling of the Bonods had a "direct effect" in the United States within the meaning of the third clause of §1605(a)(2).]

The remaining question is whether Argentina's unilateral rescheduling of the Bonods had a "direct effect" in the United States. In addressing this issue, the Court of Appeals rejected the suggestion in the legislative history of the FSIA that an effect is not "direct" unless it is both "substantial" and "foreseeable." That suggestion is found in the House Report, which states that conduct covered by the third clause of §1605(a)(2) would be subject to the jurisdiction of American courts "consistent with principles set forth in §18, *Restatement (Second) Foreign Relations Law* (1965)." H.R. Rep. No. 94-1487, p. 19 (1976). Section 18 states that American laws are not given extraterritorial application except with respect to conduct that has, as a "direct and foreseeable result," a "substantial" effect within the United States. Since this obviously deals with jurisdiction to *legislate* rather than jurisdiction to *adjudicate,* this passage of the House Report has been charitably described as "a bit of a *non sequitur,*" *Texas Trading & Milling Corp. v. Federal Republic of Nigeria,* 647 F.2d 300, 311 (2d Cir. 1981). Of course the generally applicable principle *de minimis non curat lex* ensures that jurisdiction may not be predicated on purely trivial effects in the United States. But we reject the suggestion that §1605(a)(2) contains any unexpressed requirement of "substantiality" or "foreseeability." As the Court of Appeals recognized, an effect is "direct" if it follows "as an immediate consequence of the defendant's . . . activity."

The Court of Appeals concluded that the rescheduling of the maturity dates obviously had a "direct effect" on respondents. It further concluded that that effect was sufficiently "in the United States" for purposes of the FSIA, in part because "Congress would have wanted an American court to entertain this action" in order to preserve New York City's status as "a preeminent commercial center." The question, however, is not what Congress "would have wanted" but what Congress enacted in the FSIA. Although we are happy to endorse the Second Circuit's recognition of "New York's status as a world financial leader," the effect of Argentina's rescheduling in diminishing that status (assuming it is not too speculative to be considered an effect at all) is too remote and attenuated to satisfy the "direct effect" requirement of the FSIA.

We nonetheless have little difficulty concluding that Argentina's unilateral rescheduling of the maturity dates on the Bonods had a "direct effect" in the United States. Respondents had designated their accounts in New York as the place of payment, and Argentina made some interest payments into those accounts before announcing that it was rescheduling the payments. Because New York was thus the place of performance for Argentina's ultimate contractual obligations, the rescheduling of those obligations necessarily had a "direct effect" in the United States: money that was supposed to have been delivered to a New York bank for deposit was not forthcoming. We reject Argentina's suggestion that the "direct effect" requirement cannot be satisfied where the plaintiffs are all foreign corporations with no other connections to the United States. We expressly stated in *Verlinden* that the FSIA permits "a foreign plaintiff to sue a foreign sovereign in the courts of the United States, provided the substantive requirements of the Act are satisfied."

Finally, Argentina argues that a finding of jurisdiction in this case would violate the Due Process Clause of the Fifth Amendment, and that, in order to avoid this difficulty, we must construe the "direct effect" requirement as embodying the "minimum contacts" test of *International Shoe Co.*[118] Assuming, without deciding, that a foreign state is a "person" for purposes of the Due Process Clause, *cf. South Carolina v. Katzenbach,* 383 U.S. 301, 323-324 (1966) (States of the Union are not "persons" for purposes of the Due Process Clause), we find that Argentina possessed "minimum contacts" that would satisfy the constitutional test. By issuing negotiable debt instruments denominated in U.S. dollars and payable in New York and by appointing a financial agent in that city, Argentina "purposefully avail[ed] itself of the privilege of conducting activities within the [United States]," *Burger King Corp.,* quoting *Hanson.* . . .

We conclude that Argentina's issuance of the Bonods was a "commercial activity" under the FSIA; that its rescheduling of the maturity dates on those instruments was taken in connection with that commercial activity and had a "direct effect" in the United States; and that the District Court therefore properly asserted jurisdiction, under the FSIA, over the breach-of-contract claim based on that rescheduling. Accordingly, the judgment of the Court of Appeals is affirmed.

SAUDI ARABIA v. NELSON
507 U.S. 349 (1993) [excerpted above at pp. 289-296]

Notes *on* Weltover *and* Nelson

1. *Section 1605(a)(2)'s three U.S. nexus requirements.* As discussed above, even if the plaintiff's claim is "based upon" a "commercial activity," each of §1605(a)(2)'s three clauses contains a "nexus" requirement: (a) the action must be "based upon a commercial activity carried on in the United States by the foreign state"; (b) the action must be "based . . . upon an act performed in the United States in connection with a commercial activity of the foreign state elsewhere"; or (c) the action must be "based . . . upon an act outside the territory of the United States in connection with a commercial activity of the foreign state elsewhere and that act causes a direct effect in the United States." Each of these three provisions requires a different type of U.S. nexus. For two opinions parsing each of these provisions, *see Orient Mineral Co. v. Bank of China,* 506 F.3d 980 (10th Cir. 2007); *Kensington Int'l, Ltd. v. Itoua,* 505 F.3d 147 (2d Cir. 2007).

What purpose is served by these various U.S. nexus requirements? Note that the various provisions of §1605(a) — and particularly those of §1605(a)(2) — are all broadly similar to state long-arm statutes. Viewing §1605(a) as a federal long-arm statute over foreign states, does it serve the purposes of such jurisdictional grants? Could it be improved? Why didn't Congress merely rely on existing state and federal long-arm statutes (as Rule 4 of

---

118. Argentina concedes that this issue "is before the Court only as an aid in interpreting the direct effect requirement of the Act" and that "[w]hether there is a constitutional basis for personal jurisdiction over [Argentina] is not before the Court as an independent question." Brief for Petitioners 36 n.33.

the Federal Rules of Civil Procedure does)? Alternatively, why didn't Congress merely authorize personal jurisdiction over foreign states to the limits of the Due Process Clause?

2. Section 1605(a)(2)'s first clause — commercial activity "carried on in the United States." The first clause of §1605(a)(2) grants jurisdiction over "commercial activity carried on in the United States by the foreign state." Section 1603(e) then defines "commercial activity carried on in the United States" as "commercial activity . . . having substantial contact with the United States."

(a) Justice Souter's application of the first clause of §1605(a)(2). Justice Souter did not reach the question whether the activity which the Nelsons' claim was "based upon" had a U.S. nexus. He did not need to, because he concluded that the only conduct that the Nelsons' suit was "based upon" was not "commercial activity," and therefore that the question of a U.S. nexus was moot.

(b) Justice White's application of the first clause of §1605(a)(2). Justice White concluded that the operations of the King Faisal Hospital were "commercial activity," but then he held that the activity "lacks a sufficient nexus to the United States," because neither the "hospital's employment practices, nor its disciplinary procedures, has any apparent connection to this country." Is that persuasive? Once it is determined that the Nelsons' claim is "based upon" the Hospital's operations, why is it necessary to single out particular aspects of those operations — namely "employment practices" and "disciplinary procedures"? Why cannot analysis focus generally on the connections between the Hospital and the United States?

(c) Justice Stevens' application of the first clause of §1605(a)(2). Justice Stevens agrees with Justice White that the Hospital's operations were "commercial activity," but goes on to conclude that those operations satisfy the U.S. nexus requirement of §1605(a)(2). Accepting Justice White's view that the Nelsons' complaint is "based upon" the Hospital's operations, which Justice is correct — Justice White or Justice Stevens — in his analysis of the nexus requirement?

(d) Specific and general jurisdiction under the first clause of §1605(a)(2). What rationale does Justice Stevens rely upon in finding a U.S. nexus? Note his willingness to rely on both specific and general jurisdiction in reaching this result. What do these due process standards have to do with the statutory language of §1605(a)(2)? Is it fair to assume that Congress meant to incorporate due process standards?

Would there be specific jurisdiction in a case like that brought by the Nelsons against the Hospital? What are the Hospital's minimum contacts with the United States? Does the Nelsons' claim arise from those contacts? Would there be general jurisdiction, based upon the Hospital's purchasing of supplies? Recall the analysis in *Helicopteros, supra* pp. 118-129. (*See also* the discussion below regarding the availability of general jurisdiction, as a statutory matter, under the FSIA, *infra* pp. 302-303.)

A number of lower courts have considered whether §1605(a)(2) grants general jurisdiction "that is, jurisdiction over claims that do not have any nexus with the United States" over foreign sovereign entities with sufficiently close U.S. contacts. Most lower courts have refused to permit general jurisdiction. *BP Chemicals Ltd. v. Jiangsu Sopo Corp.,* 285 F.3d 677, 682 (8th Cir. 2002); *Haven v. Polska,* 215 F.3d 727, 736 (7th Cir. 2000); *Sun v. Taiwan,* 201 F.3d 1105, 1109 (9th Cir. 2000); *Goodman Holdings v. Rafidain Bank,* 26 F.3d 1143, 1146 (D.C. Cir. 1994); *Santos v. Compagnie Nationale Air France,* 934 F.2d 890, 892 (7th Cir. 1991) (requiring an "identifiable nexus" between plaintiff's claim and defendant's commercial activity in the United States); *Barkanic v. CAAC,* 822 F.2d 11, 13 (2d Cir. 1987) ("a nexus is required between the [defendant's] commercial activity in the United States and the [plaintiff's] cause of action"; tort action against Chinese airline for crash on Nanjing-Peking flight is within U.S. jurisdiction because ticket for flight was sold in

U.S. by nonexclusive sales agent for Chinese airline); *Vencedora Oceanica Navigacion, SA v. Compagnie National Algerienne de Navigation,* 730 F.2d 195 (5th Cir. 1984).

In contrast, some lower courts have held that §1605(a)(2)'s first clause is satisfied so long as the defendant is doing business in the United States, even if the plaintiff's cause of action does not arise directly from the defendant's activities in the United States. *E.g., In re Rio Grande Transp.,* 516 F. Supp. 1155, 1165 (S.D.N.Y. 1981) ("Congress apparently did not intend to require that the specific commercial transaction or act upon which an action is based have occurred in the United States or have had substantial contact with the United States; only the broad course of conduct must be so connected.").

(e) Justice Stevens' view of general jurisdiction.   Consider Justice Stevens' brief analysis of the availability of general jurisdiction in *Nelson:* "I am inclined to agree . . . that the first clause of §1605(a)(2), interpreted in light of the relevant legislative history and the second and third clauses of the provision, does authorize 'general' jurisdiction over foreign entities that engage in substantial commercial activities in the United States." Justice Stevens relied on a concurring opinion in *Vencedora Oceanica Navigacion, SA v. Compagnie Nationale Algerienne de Navigation,* 730 F.2d 195, 206-207 (5th Cir. 1984), which reasoned as follows:

> When the relevant portions of §1603(d) and (e) are inserted into clause one of §1605(a)(2), we are left with the task of construing:
>
>> A foreign state shall not be immune from the jurisdiction of the courts of the United States or of the States in any case in which the action is based upon a regular course of commercial conduct carried on by such state and having substantial contact with the United States.
>
> Because this language cannot be interpreted literally, courts have been driven to substitutions for the words "based upon." The majority's substitution is "having a nexus with." . . . I would expect a search for a nexus to be a search for an act or series of acts that will be part of the conduct of the business without constituting the entire conduct of the business. It follows that allowing only claims with a nexus to the "commercial activity" carried on in the United States would not exhaust the full range of clause one when "commercial activity" is defined as a "regular course of commercial conduct."
>
> The "substantial contact" language of §1603(e) also supports my reading. This language appears to draw upon the "minimum contacts" test of *International Shoe.* That test marks off a "doing business" ground as involving "instances in which the continuous corporate operations within a state [are] thought so substantial and of such a nature as to justify suit against it on causes of action arising from dealings entirely distinct from these activities." The FSIA's "substantial contact" language thus does not signal a congressional intent to enact more stringent a test than the "minimum contacts" necessary for "doing business" jurisdiction. To the contrary, the phrase could be lifted straight from *International Shoe.*
>
> Furthermore, reading clause one to embody a "doing business" jurisdictional ground gives a coherent organizational structure to the three clauses of the "commercial activities" exception. If "doing business" is allowed as a basis for jurisdiction under clause one, then the three clauses of §1605(a)(2) roughly correspond to three jurisdictional categories; personal jurisdiction exists where the defendant (1) does business in the United States, (2) commits an act within the United States but is not "doing business," and (3) does not commit a relevant act in the United States, but causes a direct effect in the United States. These categories reflect the development of jurisdictional principles, from *Pennoyer v. Neff* (doing business) [sic], through *International Shoe* (committing an act can constitute minimum contacts), *McGee v. International Life Insurance Co.* (effects can constitute minimum contacts), and beyond. Given these three historical grounds, it seems reasonable to read clause one as embodying a "doing business" ground in addition to a "nexus" ground when the language can support this construction.

Does *Nelson* resolve the question whether general jurisdiction is available under §1605(a)(2)? How should the question be resolved? Is the foregoing excerpt from *Vencedora* persuasive?

3. Relevance of "based upon" requirement to the second and third clauses of §1605(a)(2). How does *Nelson*'s statement of the "based upon" requirement apply to actions under the second and third clauses of §1605(a)(2)? Consider the specific language of each clause: what must the plaintiff's claim be "based upon" — an "act" or "commercial activity"? Suppose that a foreign state engaged in commercial activity outside the United States but performed a noncommercial act in the United States "in connection" with that commercial activity. Would the second clause of §1605(a)(2) apply? Suppose that a foreign state committed a noncommercial act outside the United States that concededly had a direct effect in the United States, and that the act was "in connection" with commercial activity. Would §1605(a)(2)'s third clause apply?

The "based upon" requirement is relevant to the second and third clauses of §1605(a)(2), but in a different way than under §1605(a)(2)'s first clause. The "based upon" requirement identifies an "act" which must: (a) have a particular U.S. nexus; and (b) have a "connection" to a course of "commercial activity."

4. Section 1605(a)(2)'s "in connection" requirement. What is the meaning of the "in connection" requirement of the second and third clauses of §1605(a)(2)? Note *Nelson*'s contrast between the more expansive "in connection" formulation and the less expansive "based upon" requirement. Justice Souter reasoned that the second two clauses referred to an action being "based upon" acts that were "in connection with" commercial activity; the Court reasoned that these provisions required only "a mere connection with, or relation to, commercial activity," and that the "based upon" requirement of the first clause "calls for something more." Just how expansive is the "in connection" standard? *See Drexel Burnham Lambert Group, Inc. v. Committee of Receivers,* 12 F.3d 317, 329-330 (2d Cir. 1993) ("If the 'connection' language of §1605(a)(2) were read . . . to include tangential commercial activities to which the 'acts' forming the basis of the claim have only an attenuated connection, the 'commercial activity' exception would effectively be rewritten to authorize the exercise of jurisdiction over acts that are essentially sovereign in nature").

5. Second clause of §1605(a)(2) — U.S. acts. The second clause of §1605(a)(2) grants jurisdiction where an action is based upon "an act performed in the United States in connection with a commercial activity of the foreign state elsewhere." Although not invoked in either *Nelson* or *Weltover,* the clause warrants exploration. What must the plaintiff's claim be "based upon" — the "act" or the "commercial activity"? Who must perform the "act" — the foreign state or someone else? Does the "act" have to be "commercial," or can it be sovereign? Does every element of the claim have to be provided by the "act"?

6. Third clause of §1605(a)(2) — direct effects. The third clause of §1605(a)(2) grants jurisdiction where an action is based upon an "act outside the territory of the United States in connection with a commercial activity of the foreign state elsewhere and that act causes a direct effect in the United States." This provision is potentially the most expansive of the three clauses of §1605(a)(2), and it has provoked considerable litigation, which is outlined below. Consider initially some of the interpretative issues arising under the third clause. As with the second clause, must the action be based entirely upon the "act," or can it be based more broadly on the "commercial activity"? Can the act be noncommercial? Must the foreign state commit the act? What is the meaning of the "in connection" requirement?

There has been extensive litigation involving the meaning of the "direct effects" component of §1605(a)(2). For representative lower court decisions, *see Guevara v. Republic of Peru,* 608 F.3d 1297 (11th Cir. 2010); *Guirlando v. T.C. Ziraat Bankasi A.S.,* 602 F.3d 69

(2d Cir. 2010); *Cruise Connections Charter Mgmt. 1, LP v. Attorney General of Canada*, 600 F.3d 661 (D.C. Cir. 2010); *UNC Lear Services v. Kingdom of Saudi Arabia*, 582 F.3d 210 (5th Cir. 2009); *Orient Mineral Co. v. Bank of China*, 506 F.3d 980 (10th Cir. 2007); *Virtual Countries, Inc. v. Republic of South Africa*, 300 F.3d 230, 238-241 (2d Cir. 2002); *Corzo v. Banco Cent. de Reserva del Peru*, 243 F.3d 519, 525-526 (9th Cir. 2001); *Byrd v. Corporacion Forestal y Industrial de Olancho SA*, 182 F.3d 380, 390-391 (5th Cir. 1999).

7. *Direct effects test adopted in* Weltover. What standard was adopted in *Weltover* for the direct effects test in §1605(a)(2)'s third prong? Note the Court's remark that "[b]ecause New York was thus the place of performance for Argentina's ultimate contractual obligations, the rescheduling of those obligations necessarily had a 'direct effect' in the United States; money that was supposed to have been delivered to a New York bank for deposit was not forthcoming." What exactly is the "direct effects" test? Is it appropriate to rely in so conclusive a fashion on the contractual "place of performance"? Note that this will often mean that jurisdiction will turn upon fine details about payment, delivery, or place of performance in contracts. Is that appropriate? What other approaches might have been taken by the Court? What does the Court mean by "ultimate contractual obligations"?

8. *Application of direct effects test in* Weltover. Was the direct effects portion of *Weltover* correctly decided? *Weltover* relied on the fact that the plaintiff Bonod-holders "had designated their accounts in New York as the place of payment, and Argentina made some interest payments into those accounts. . . ." Note that the Bonods did not independently require Argentina to pay money in the United States, and that it was only the Bonod-holders' designation of New York that imposed the obligation. Would the case have been decided differently if the Bonods had been repayable anywhere designated by the holders (as opposed to being repayable at any one of four cities, including New York, designated by the holders)?

Note that the "funds" that were to be paid to the plaintiffs in New York would likely have: (a) been paid by electronic transfers between two U.S. banks (the parties' New York correspondents); and (b) remained in the plaintiffs' bank accounts only briefly (perhaps less than 24 hours) before being remitted to the plaintiffs' home country; and (c) all of these transfers would likely have been accomplished by book-keeping changes to the size of inter-bank accounts. Does this affect the *Weltover* "direct effects" conclusion? What if the Bonods had no place of payment, but were governed by a substantive law, which required that (absent agreement) debts were payable at the lender's place of business? What if the Bonods contained no place of payment provision, but interest on the Bonods had historically been paid in New York? *Compare Pons v. People's Republic of China*, 666 F. Supp. 2d 406 (S.D.N.Y. 2009) (default on bonds lacks direct effect in United States where only connection was sales on secondary market).

9. *"Direct effects" requirement in contract actions.* Prior to *Weltover*, several lower courts found the direct effects test satisfied where a foreign defendant has failed to make a payment that was contractually payable to a *U.S.* company within the United States. *E.g., Gould, Inc. v. Pechiney Ugine Kuhlmann*, 853 F.2d 445 (6th Cir. 1988); *Texas Trading & Milling Corp. v. Federal Republic of Nigeria*, 647 F.2d 300 (2d Cir. 1981) (foreign state breaches obligation payable within the United States); *Schmidt v. Polish People's Republic*, 579 F. Supp. 23 (S.D.N.Y.), *aff'd*, 742 F.2d 67 (2d Cir. 1984) (foreign state breaches obligation negotiated and payable within the United States). As *Weltover* illustrates, the result is the same where the defendant refuses to repay a *foreign* company at a contractually designated location in the United States.

Likewise, several lower courts have held that a foreign state's wrongful request for payment out of funds held by a U.S. company within the United States constitutes a "direct effect" in the United States. *E.g., Transamerican Steamship Corp. v. Somali Democratic*

Republic, 767 F.2d 998 (D.C. Cir. 1985) (foreign state wrongfully requires U.S. company to transfer funds to its U.S. bank account); *Harris Corp. v. National Iranian Radio & Television,* 691 F.2d 1344 (11th Cir. 1982) (wrongful call on letter of credit from U.S. bank).

   10. *"Direct effects" test in contract cases following* **Weltover.** Disagreement among the lower courts over the direct effects test has persisted even after *Weltover.* One disagreement has centered on whether a plaintiff must show that a "legally significant act" occurred in the United States. *See American Telecom Co., L.L.C. v. Republic of Lebanon,* 501 F.3d 534 (6th Cir. 2007) (discussing split); *United World Trade, Inc. v. Mangyshlakneft Oil Production Ass'n,* 33 F.3d 1232, 1237 (10th Cir. 1994) (struggling to "identify objective standards that would aid in determining what does and does not qualify as a 'direct effect in the United States' " because the phrase seemed "hopelessly ambiguous when applied to any particular transaction").

   Does anything in the FSIA or *Weltover* support a requirement that the "effects" in the United States be "legally significant"? *Compare Guirlando v. T.C. Tiraat Bankasi A.S.,* 602 F.3d 69 (2d Cir. 2010) (discussing relationship between *Weltover* and "legally significant act" test) *with Orient Mineral Co. v. Bank of China,* 506 F.3d 980 (10th Cir. 2007) (criticizing the "legally significant act" test). What exactly does it mean for an effect to be "legally significant"? According to some authorities, the "legally significant" standard requires "express provision for payment" in the United States. *Global Index, Inc. v. Mkapa,* 290 F. Supp. 2d 108, 114-115 (D.D.C. 2003). Why would it make sense to require an *"express"* provision for payment in the United States? If the parties' agreement impliedly required — but nonetheless legally required — payment in the United States, why should this not satisfy *Weltover* and the "direct effect" test?

   The alternative standard is the unhappily named "supposed to" test. *See Peterson v. Royal Kingdom of Saudi Arabia,* 416 F.3d 83, 90 (D.C. Cir. 2005); *Goodman Holdings v. Rafidain Bank,* 26 F.3d 1143, 1146 (D.C. Cir. 1994) (finding no direct effect when "[n]either New York nor any other United States location was designated as the 'place of performance' where money was 'supposed' to have been paid"); *Parex Bank v. Russian Savings Bank,* 116 F. Supp. 2d 415 (S.D.N.Y. 2000) ("The parties contracted at a location outside the United States that a monetary deposit would be made by one party into the other party's New York bank account. And, as in both *Weltover* and *Hanil Bank,* '[m]oney that was supposed to have been delivered to a New York bank for deposit was not forthcoming.'"). Lower courts have apparently treated this standard as requiring an agreement — express or implied — or, arguably, a consistent practice to make payments into the United States. *Global Index, Inc. v. Mkapa,* 290 F. Supp. 2d 108, 114-115 (D.D.C. 2003).

   How significant is the difference between these two tests? Is there a genuine conflict? If the difference is between requiring an "express" agreement to make payment in the United States and an implied agreement or a preexisting practice, which is preferable? *Compare I.T. Consultants, Inc. v. Republic of Pakistan,* 351 F.3d 1184, 1190 (D.C. Cir. 2003) (finding direct effect where complaint alleged that payment should occur in United States and finding it irrelevant whether designation of situs was "contemporaneous with the signing of the underlying agreement giving rise to the obligation to pay"); *Hanil Bank v. PT Bank Negara Indonesia (Persero),* 148 F.3d 217, 132-133 (2d Cir. 1998) (finding direct effect where letter of credit authorized holder to designate payment situs), *with United World Trade, Inc. v. Mangyshakneft Oil Product Ass'n,* 33 F.3d 1232 (10th Cir. 1994) (fact that funds relating to European transaction were wired to New York, solely for currency conversion, and then transferred back to Europe held not to be a direct effect: "Congress did not intend to provide jurisdiction whenever the ripples caused by an overseas transaction manage eventually to reach the shores of the United States"). *See generally Agrocomplaect, AD v. Republic of Iraq,* 524 F. Supp. 2d 16 (D.D.C. 2007) (thorough discussion of payment cases under direct effect doctrine).

11. *Relevance of plaintiff's nationality in* **Weltover.** Argentina argued in *Weltover* that the " 'direct effect' requirement cannot be satisfied where the plaintiffs are all foreign corporations with no other connections to the United States." The Court rejected the argument. Was this correct? Why does an "effect" occur in the United States when a Swiss bank is not paid money by an Argentine debtor? Why doesn't the effect occur in Switzerland?

Does the plaintiff's nationality have any relevance in direct effects analysis after *Weltover*? If so, what?

12. *Direct effects in* **Nelson.** Consider the possibility that the defendants in *Nelson* were subject to U.S. jurisdiction under §1605(a)(2)'s direct effects test. Mr. Nelson said he was tortured, by governmental officials who knew he was an American and that he would return to the United States. Did Mr. Nelson's ongoing pain and suffering when he returned to the United States constitute a direct effect there?

Suppose that Mr. Nelson had instead been a patient at the defendant hospital and that he was denied critical treatment because he was black. Suppose further that Mr. Nelson suffered devastating injuries because of the hospital's action and returned to the United States completely paralyzed. *See Martin v. Republic of South Africa*, 836 F.2d 91 (2d Cir. 1987) for a case involving these facts. Why is that not a direct effect in the United States? Note that U.S. taxpayers would be required to support Mr. Nelson in this hypothetical for the remainder of his life. Note also that the defendants would have known that they were dealing with a U.S. national, and that their conduct could cause harm to him in the United States.

13. *Direct effects and personal injuries abroad.* In some cases, the commercial activities of a foreign state can result in personal injuries or other injury, giving rise to tort claims. For example, a foreign state may operate an airline, one of whose aircraft crashes. The resulting tort claims may fall within the noncommercial tort exception of §1605(a)(5), discussed *infra* pp. 308-319. In addition, however, §1605(a)(2)'s commercial activities exception may be available. Generally, U.S. courts have been reluctant to assert "direct effects" jurisdiction under the commercial activities exception in such cases. *E.g., Coyle v. PT Garuda Indonesia*, 363 F.3d 979, 993-994 (9th Cir. 2004) (plane crash where tickets for relevant leg of flight purchased in Indonesia); *Jungquist v. Sheikh Sultan Bin Khalifa Al Nahyan*, 115 F.3d 1020 (D.C. Cir. 1997) (boat accident occurring abroad); *Martin v. Republic of South Africa*, 836 F.2d 91 (2d Cir. 1987) (refusal of state-owned hospital to treat black American plaintiff lacked direct effect in United States, although plaintiff's U.S. nationality was known); *Australian Gov't Aircraft Factories v. Lynn*, 743 F.2d 672 (9th Cir. 1984) (crash in Indonesia of aircraft manufactured in Australia lacked direct effect in the United States, even though not-for-profit organization located in United States owned, operated, and would be forced to replace the aircraft). *But see Kirkham v. Societe Air France*, 429 F.3d 288 (D.C. Cir. 2005) (injury where ticket purchased in United States); *Sun v. Taiwan*, 201 F.3d 1105 (9th Cir. 2000) (remanding for further consideration of whether commercial activity exception could support jurisdiction over tort claim for injuries incurred abroad by U.S. citizen where plaintiff's theory was based on failure to warn in United States).

When a U.S. citizen is injured or killed abroad, isn't it clear that substantial and "direct" economic effects will be felt in this country? Is this fact altered if the defendant is unaware of the nationality of the plaintiff, as appears generally to be true in these tort cases?

14. Nelson *revisited.* Mr. Nelson's alleged mistreatment was torture — a violation of international law. *See Filartiga v. Pena-Irala*, 630 F.2d 876 (2d Cir. 1980). Does that affect "direct effects" analysis? *See Argentine Republic v. Amerada Hess Shipping Corp.*, 488 U.S. 428 (1989); *infra* pp. 313-319, 351-353.

15. *Due process analysis under the FSIA after* Weltover. *Weltover* suggests that a "foreign state" may not be a "person" for purposes of the Due Process Clause. Would this result be consistent with a conclusion that, for purposes of §1603(d), the foreign state had not acted in a sovereign capacity, but had instead acted "in the manner of a private player"? Would foreign state-owned companies also be deemed nonpersons? Should Justice Scalia's suggestion be accepted? Note the Court's suggested analogy to cases holding that states of the Union are not persons for purposes of the Due Process Clause. Are there any relevant differences between foreign states and states of the Union?

If foreign states do not enjoy due process protection, then how far does this rule extend? Would this rule also deny due process protections to an "agency or instrumentality" of a foreign state? Recall that an "agency or instrumentality" must be a "separate legal person" under §1605(b). *See supra* pp. 252-253, 267-268. Would it not be rather peculiar to say that a foreign state-owned company — organized under general legislation as a stock corporation and engaged in commercial activities — was not a "person"? On the other hand, would it not also be peculiar to say that foreign state-owned companies were entitled to due process protection, but their shareholder was not? For further consideration of these issues, *see infra* pp. 335, 343, 359-360; *Frontera Resources Azerbaijan Corp. v. State Oil Co. of the Azerbaijani Republic*, 582 F.3d 393 (2d Cir. 2009) (holding that minimum contacts test does not apply to agencies or instrumentalities of foreign state).

16. *Nexus requirement under U.N. State Immunities Convention.* Consider Article 10(1) of the U.N. State Immunities Convention. How does it deal with the "nexus" requirement? Note its reference to "the rules of private international law" conferring jurisdiction on a national court. Does this provide any guidance at all in interpreting §1605(a)(2)'s nexus requirement?

2.   Noncommercial Torts Occurring Within the United States

The FSIA denies sovereign immunity in certain cases involving tortious injury occurring in the United States. Section 1605(a)(5) provides an exception to immunity where "money damages are sought against a foreign state for personal injury or death, or damage to or loss of property, occurring in the United States and caused by the tortious act or omission of that foreign state," or by the acts or omissions of the foreign state's employees acting within the scope of their employment. Under §1605(a)(5), a foreign state is denied immunity in cases

> not otherwise encompassed in paragraph (2) above, in which money damages are sought against a foreign state for personal injury or death, or damage to or loss of property, occurring in the United States and caused by the tortious act or omissions of that foreign state or of any official or employee of that foreign state while acting within the scope of his office or employment; except this paragraph shall not apply to (A) any claim based upon the exercise or performance or the failure to exercise or perform a discretionary function regardless of whether the discretion be abused; or (B) any claim arising out of malicious prosecution, abuse of process, libel, slander, misrepresentation, deceit, or interference with contract rights.

The FSIA's legislative history explains that §1605(a)(5) is "directed primarily at the problem of traffic accidents" involving embassy automobiles and personnel.[119]

---

119. H.R. Rep. No. 1487, 94th Cong., 2d Sess. 20-21, *reprinted in* 1976 U.S. Code Cong. & Admin. News at 6619. *See also Beato v. Pakistan Embassy*, 754 N.Y.S.2d 633 (App. Div. 2003) (applying noncommercial tort exception to traffic accident).

Nonetheless, the provision is broadly drafted and has been held to reach a much wider range of tort claims.[120] Indeed, the House Report provides that "[a]s used in §1605(a)(5), the phrase 'tortious act or omission' is meant to include causes of action which are based on strict liability as well as on negligence."[121] Section 1605(a)(5) apparently permits recovery for all compensable injuries, intangible as well as tangible.[122]

Section 1605(a)(5) provides a potentially expansive and controversial exception to the sovereign immunity of foreign states.[123] The provision contemplates the application of U.S. (or foreign) tort law principles in cases against foreign sovereigns, which is likely to require more judgmental, policy-laden assessments of foreign governmental conduct by U.S. courts than the application of commercial law in most cases under §1605(a)(2) typically demands. Section 1605(a)(5) is also a potential source of controversy because, at least in the view of those lower courts to consider the issue, it denies immunity to *all* tortious foreign state conduct — without regard to whether the conduct is "commercial," "private," or "sovereign."[124]

Perhaps in recognition of the sensitive inquiries required by §1605(a)(5), the FSIA's drafters provided several important exceptions to the provision. First, the section does not apply to claims based on malicious prosecution, libel, misrepresentation, or other similar torts.[125] Second, §1605(a)(5) applies only to actions based on torts causing damage "occurring in the United States." Finally, §1605(a)(5) is not applicable to claims based on the defendant's "discretionary functions."[126] As the following sections illustrate, disputes over these latter two exceptions have frequently arisen, with both provisions often being at issue in the same case.

---

120. *E.g.*, *O'Bryan v. Holy See*, 556 F.3d 361, 385 (6th Cir. 2009) (abuse by priests); *Blaxland v. Commonwealth Director of Public Prosecutions*, 323 F.3d 1998, 1203 (9th Cir. 2003) (false imprisonment); *Risk v. Halvorsen*, 936 F.2d 393 (9th Cir. 1991) (conspiracy to violate California child custody order); *Liu v. Republic of China*, 892 F.2d 1419 (9th Cir. 1989) (homicide); *Joseph v. Office of Consulate General of Nigeria*, 830 F.2d 1018 (9th Cir. 1987) (destruction of property); *Gerritsen v. de la Madrid Hurtado*, 819 F.2d 1511 (9th Cir. 1987) (kidnap and assault); *Letelier v. Republic of Chile*, 488 F. Supp. 665, 673 (D.D.C. 1980) (murder).

121. H.R. Rep. No. 1487, 94th Cong., 2d Sess. 23-24, *reprinted in* 1976 U.S. Code Cong. & Admin. News at 6621.

122. *See De Sanchez v. Banco Central de Nicaragua*, 770 F.2d 1385, 1400 (5th Cir. 1985) (Rubin, J., concurring) (economic loss); *Persinger v. Republic of Iran*, 729 F.2d 835, 843-844 (D.C. Cir. 1984) (Edwards, J., dissenting) (emotional distress) (1984). One commentator has suggested, however, that §1605(a)(5)'s phrase "damage to or loss of property" only permits recovery for tangible injury. G. Badr, *State Immunity: An Analytic and Prognostic View* 120-124 (1984).

123. A critical feature of §1605(a)(5)'s reach is the question of causation. What does it mean for a foreign sovereign to "cause" personal injury or death? What if the foreign sovereign merely provides money or financial assistance that is eventually linked to the covered injury? For a discussion of the issue of causation in the tort exception, *see Burnett v. Al Baraka Inv. & Development Corp.*, 292 F. Supp. 2d 9, 19-20 (D.D.C. 2003).

124. *E.g.*, *MacArthur Area Citizens Ass'n v. Republic of Peru*, 809 F.2d 918 (D.C. Cir.), *vacated on other grounds*, 823 F.2d 606 (D.C. Cir. 1987); *Olson ex rel. Sheldon v. Mexico*, 729 F.2d 641 (9th Cir. 1984); *Kline v. Republic of El Salvador*, 603 F. Supp. 1313 (D.D.C. 1985); *De Sanchez v. Banco Central de Nicaragua*, 515 F. Supp. 900, 914 (E.D. La. 1981), *aff'd on other grounds*, 770 F.2d 1385, 1399 n.19 (5th Cir. 1985); *Letelier v. Republic of Chile*, 488 F. Supp. 665, 673 (D.D.C. 1980). *But see Frolova v. USSR*, 558 F. Supp. 358, 362-363 (N.D. Ill. 1983), *aff'd on other grounds*, 761 F.2d 370 (7th Cir. 1985).

125. 28 U.S.C. §1605(a)(5)(B) (1982). Some courts have interpreted this exclusion to cover claims not explicitly listed by nonetheless "deriv[ing] from the same corpus of allegations." *O'Bryan v. Holy See*, 556 F.3d 361, 385 (6th Cir. 2009); *Blaxland v. Commonwealth Director of Public Prosecutions*, 323 F.3d 1198, 1203 (9th Cir. 2003); *Cabiri v. Government of Republic of Ghana*, 165 F.3d 193, 200 (2d Cir. 1999). In some tension with this line of cases, other courts have held that this limitation does not preclude jurisdiction over claims that fit under one of the other exceptions in §1605, particularly the commercial activity exception. *See El-Hadad v. United Arab Emirates*, 216 F.3d 29, 35 (D.C. Cir. 2000); *Southway v. Central Bank of Nigeria*, 198 F.3d 1210, 1219 (10th Cir. 1999); *Dale v. Colagiovanni*, 337 F. Supp. 2d 825, 841 (S.D. Miss. 2004); *WMW Machinery, Inc. v. Werkzeugmaschinenhandel GmbH im Aufbau*, 960 F. Supp. 734, 741-742 (S.D.N.Y. 1997). *See generally Leutwyler v. Office of Her Majesty Queen Rania*, 184 F. Supp. 2d 277, 294-295 (S.D.N.Y. 2001) (discussing caselaw); *Southway v. Central Bank of Nigeria*, 994 F. Supp. 1299, 1310 (D. Colo. 1998) (same).

126. 28 U.S.C. §1605(a)(5)(A).

a.   Situs Requirement for Noncommercial Torts.   Much as §1605(a)(2) imposes a nexus requirement for foreign state's commercial activity, §1605(a)(5) contains a "situs" requirement for noncommercial torts. In contrast to §1605(a)(2), however, §1605(a)(5)'s situs requirement is narrowly drafted and demands a much closer connection to the United States than is necessary in the commercial activity context. The two cases excerpted below— *SEDCO* and *Olsen ex rel. Sheldon*—illustrate two differing approaches that have emerged in applying the situs requirement.

IN RE SEDCO, INC.
543 F. Supp. 561 (S.D. Tex. 1982)

O'CONNOR, DISTRICT JUDGE. The 1979 IXTOC I well disaster in the Bay of Campeche has produced a tangle of litigation. . . . Petroleos Mexicanos (Pemex), which is both a direct defendant to certain private and public plaintiffs and a third party defendant to claims asserted by Sedco, has moved to be dismissed from all claims on the basis of the grant of sovereign immunity provided by the FSIA. By asserting this motion, Pemex alleges that this Court lacks jurisdiction to hear claims based upon acts purportedly done in its capacity as a foreign sovereign. . . .

Petroleos Mexicanos was created in 1938 as a decentralized governmental agency charged with the exploration and development of Mexico's hydrocarbon resources. Unlike in the United States, the government of Mexico owns its country's natural resources, in particular, its hydrocarbon deposits. The Regulatory Law passed pursuant to the Mexican Constitution specifically creates a national oil company, Pemex, to implement the National Development Plan for hydrocarbon resources. Pemex is not privately owned and is governed by a council (Consejo de Administracion) composed of Presidential appointees. Decisions made by the governing council are made in furtherance of Mexican National policy concerning its Petroleum resources. Beyond a doubt, Pemex is a "foreign state" as contemplated by §1603(a) of the FSIA. . . .

[I]t is urged that this Court exercise jurisdiction over Pemex under the "noncommercial tort" exception to the FSIA, §1605(a)(5). Section 1605(a)(5) provides that a suit for damages based on an alleged noncommercial tort committed by a foreign state in the United States is actionable in federal court. For jurisdiction to exist, the following must be shown: (1) a noncommercial act by the foreign state; (2) causing personal injury or damages to, or loss of property; and (3) that the claim is not based upon the exercise of a discretionary function, or upon libel, slander, misrepresentation, or interference with contract rights.

Section 1605(a)(5) is silent with respect to where the noncommercial tort must occur for jurisdiction to exist. Plaintiffs argue the tort may occur, in whole or in part, in the United States, and that the tort occurs in the United States if the acts or omissions directly affect this country. This argument may be correct in other circumstances, *see Ohio v. Wyandotte Chemicals Corp.*, 401 U.S. 493 (1971); however, legislative history appears to reject this theory with respect to the FSIA. In describing the purpose of §1605(a)(5), the House Committee Report accompanying the House Bill, which ultimately became the FSIA, states:

> [Section 1605(a)(5)] denies immunity as to claims for personal injury or death, or for damage to or loss of property caused by the tortious act or omission of a foreign state or its officials or employees, acting within the scope of their authority; *the tortious act or omission must occur within the jurisdiction of the United States.* . . . House Report, at p. 6619 (emphasis added).

The primary purpose of this exception is to cover the problem of traffic accidents by embassy and governmental officials in this country. While the exception does extend generally to all noncommercial torts committed in this country, this Court finds that the tort, in whole, must occur in the United States. The alleged acts or omissions made the basis of this lawsuit all took place in Mexico or its territorial waters in the Bay of Campeche, and §1605(a)(5) is, therefore, inapplicable.

Notwithstanding the fact that the tort did not occur wholly within the United States, the acts complained of were discretionary in nature, done in furtherance of Pemex' legal mandate to explore for Mexico's hydrocarbon deposits. Discretionary acts by a sovereign are specifically immunized from suit under the FSIA. 28 U.S.C. §1605(a)(5)(A). The language of this exemption and its legislative history demonstrate that it parallels the discretionary act exception to the Federal Tort Claims Act, 28 U.S.C. §2680(a). House Report, at p. 6620. The scope of this discretionary act exception has troubled courts for years. However, the facts of this case closely resemble those of *Dalehite v. United States,* 346 U.S. 15 (1953), still the leading case on the issue. In *Dalehite,* the Supreme Court found the government's actions in formulating and then directing the execution of a formal plan for a fertilizer export program could not form the basis of a suit under the Federal Tort Claims Act. Such actions were found to be discretionary under §2680(a), even though an alleged abuse of that discretion resulted in the 1947 Texas City disaster.

Pemex, in this case, was executing a national plan formulated at the highest levels of the Mexican government by exploring for Mexico's natural resources. Any act performed by a subordinate of Pemex in furtherance of this exploration plan was still discretionary in nature and immune from suit under the FSIA. To deny immunity to a foreign state for the implementation of its domestic economic policies would be to completely abrogate the doctrine of foreign sovereign immunity by allowing an exception to swallow the grant of immunity preserved by §1604.

OLSEN EX REL. SHELDON v. GOVERNMENT OF MEXICO
729 F.2d 641 (9th Cir. 1984)

Nelson, Circuit Judge. Erin Olsen and Ursula Sanchez appeal from the dismissal of their wrongful death claims for lack of personal jurisdiction. . . . [T]he Government of Mexico ("Mexico") also challenges subject matter jurisdiction under the FSIA. We find that both subject matter jurisdiction and personal jurisdiction exist and therefore reverse.

Appellants Olsen and Sanchez, United States citizens domiciled in California, are minor children claiming the wrongful death of their parents. As prisoners of the Mexican government, the parents of appellants were to be transferred to authorities for incarceration in the United States pursuant to the Prisoner Exchange Treaty between the United States and Mexico. On the night of October 27, 1979, a twin-propeller plane owned and operated by the Mexican government carrying guards, pilots and appellants' parents, departed Monterrey, Mexico for Tijuana, where the transfer was to take place. En route, the pilots, employees of the Mexican Department of Justice, learned of thick fog and diminishing visibility at their destination. They requested an instrument landing which, at Tijuana Airport requires the airplane to enter United States airspace so it can approach the runway from the west. Following procedures established by a Letter of Agreement between aviation authorities of the United States and Mexico, Tijuana air control sought and received permission for the airplane to cross the border. . . .

Because its radar and instrument landing navigational system were inoperative, Tijuana air control asked its counterpart in San Diego to radio direction headings, altitude and location data necessary for an instrument landing to the aircraft. . . . [T]he San Diego air controllers relayed the information via the telephone "hotline" to Tijuana air control which radioed a translation to the pilots. . . . With the continued use of navigational data from San Diego air control, the airplane re-entered United States airspace. The pilots aligned the aircraft with the proper compass heading and descended on course, but failed to maintain the proper altitude. After striking a telephone pole, the airplane crashed three-quarters of a mile inside the United States, killing all on board. . . .

Mexico argues that §1605(a)(5) does not apply and it is therefore immune from suit. First, Mexico contends that Congress, in enacting the FSIA, adopted the restrictive theory of sovereign immunity and that Mexico's conduct was of the public nature held to be immune under that theory. Second, Mexico asserts that the §1605(a)(5) exception to immunity requires all the acts or omissions constituting the tort to occur within the United States. Finally, Mexico characterizes its activities which led to the crash as discretionary functions, thus falling within the exception to jurisdiction set forth in §1605(a)(5)(A). We consider these arguments in turn.

It is clear that the FSIA, for the most part, codifies the restrictive principle of sovereign immunity. Under this principle, the immunity of a foreign state is "restricted" to suits involving that state's public acts (*jure imperii*) and does not extend to suits based on its private or commercial acts (*jure gestionis*). Mexico argues that this public/private distinction applies not only to the FSIA generally, but specifically to §1605(a)(5), the noncommercial torts exception to immunity. According to Mexico's interpretation, foreign states would be immune from jurisdiction for those torts which otherwise come within the bounds of §1605(a)(5) but which are public in nature.

Section 1605(a)(5) cannot be read, however, other than in conjunction with §1605(a)(5)(A), which exempts from the reach of §1605(a)(5) those torts committed in a foreign state's discretionary capacity. Discretionary functions, as discussed below, include those acts or decisions made at the policy making or planning level of government. Those torts involving acts or omissions of a fundamentally governmental nature are not actionable. Thus, despite §1605(a)(5), a foreign state remains largely immunized from torts committed in its governmental capacity. Mexico's position, that governmental acts are automatically read out of §1605(a)(5), would render §1605(a)(5)(A) superfluous. Its argument is therefore untenable.

Section 1605(a)(5) requires the injury complained of to occur in the United States. The provision does not indicate that the conduct causing the tort must also take place in the United States. Ordinarily, this would end our inquiry and there would be no need to consider the location of the tortious conduct. Where, as in the instant case, the injuries occurred in the United States, and all other requirements of §1605(a)(5) are met, the foreign state would not be immune. However, the legislative history to §1605(a)(5) indicates that "the tortious act or omission must occur within the jurisdiction of the United States. . . ." A careful reading of the record in this case suggests that many potentially tortious acts and omissions occurring both in Mexico and the United States caused the crash. Pilot error, the absence of operational radar and navigational aids at Tijuana airport, defective aircraft instruments, the decision to forego a visual landing at another airport, inaccurate data from San Diego air control, and other factors may have contributed causally to the accident.

Mexico, relying on *Matter of SEDCO,* 543 F. Supp. 1561, 1567 (S.D. Tex. 1982), contends that §1605(a)(5) must be construed to require all of the tortious conduct to occur in the

United States before a foreign state will be denied immunity. In *SEDCO*, an exploratory off-shore well operated by Pemex, the Mexican national oil company, exploded in Mexican waters. The resulting oil slick washed up on the shores of Texas. Citizens there sued Pemex and other parties under §1605(a)(5). Citing that section's legislative history requiring the tortious act or omission to occur within the United States, the court held that for the noncommercial tort exception to apply, "the tort, in whole, must occur in the United States." Thus, Mexico argues, because some allegedly tortious acts or omissions took place outside the United States "such as the maintenance of the aircraft and the inoperative radar at Tijuana airport" Mexico should be immune.

The instant case is distinguishable from *SEDCO* in one crucial respect. In *SEDCO, none* of the alleged acts or omissions, only the resultant injury, occurred in the United States. By requiring every aspect of the tortious conduct to occur in the United States, a rule such as in *SEDCO* would encourage foreign states to allege that some tortious conduct occurred outside the United States. The foreign state would thus be able to establish immunity and diminish the rights of injured persons seeking recovery. Such a result contradicts the purpose of FSIA, which is to "serve the interest of justice and . . . protect the rights of both foreign states and litigants in United States courts." 28 U.S.C. §1602. . . . Consequently, we hold that if plaintiffs allege at least one entire tort occurring in the United States, they may claim under §1605(a)(5). In this case, appellants allege conduct constituting a single tort of the negligent piloting of the aircraft which occurred in the United States. We are satisfied that appellants have alleged sufficient conduct occurring in the United States to bring this case within the noncommercial torts exception. . . .

Notes on SEDCO *and* Olsen ex rel. Sheldon

1. *Rationale for noncommercial tort exception.* Why are noncommercial torts excepted from the FSIA's grant of immunity? Is this consistent with the restrictive theory of immunity? Under the FSIA, how would the following hypotheticals be resolved: (a) a Canadian Air Force plane, on military operations, crashes in the United States, killing persons on the ground; (b) an embassy guard at a foreign embassy in Washington D.C. shoots protesters; (c) a foreign state conspires with companies based in its territory to steal trade secrets located in the United States from a U.S. company and to drive the company out of business; (d) a Mexican factory releases toxic waste, which is carried into U.S. rivers and kills numerous U.S. citizens? Consider the tort exception in Article 12 of the U.N. State Immunities Convention.

2. *Situs requirement for noncommercial torts.* *SEDCO* held that, in order for the FSIA's noncommercial tort exception to apply, the tortious act or omission of a foreign state must occur within U.S. territory. This result does not appear to be required by the language of §1605(a)(5), which is ambiguous, but which apparently lifts immunity in cases where *injury* is suffered in the United States from tortious conduct (regardless of where the *conduct* occurred). In the statute's words, the exception covers actions seeking damages "for personal injury or death, or for damage to or loss of property, occurring in the United States and caused by the tortious act or omission of that foreign state."

Both *SEDCO* and *Olson* placed particular emphasis on the Act's legislative history, which tersely comments that "the tortious act or omission must occur within the jurisdiction of the United States." H.R. Rep. No. 1487, 94th Cong., 2d Sess. 21, *reprinted in* 1976 U.S. Code Cong. & Admin. News at 6619. Does this language unambiguously require the result reached in *SEDCO* and *Olsen*? What is meant by "jurisdiction of the United States"? Is this something different from "territory" of the United States? If "jurisdiction" does not mean "territory," then what does it mean? Would principles developed in the judicial or legislative jurisdiction contexts provide guidance on this issue? *See supra* pp. 84-86 and *infra* pp. 646-651 (discussing territoriality presumption).

**3. SEDCO*'s situs requirement.* *SEDCO* held that §1605(a)(5) required that "the tort, *in whole,* must occur in the United States." That apparently means that every element of the tort must have occurred in the United States. Other courts have adopted the same test. *O'Bryan v. Holy See,* 556 F.3d 361, 382 (6th Cir. 2009); *Wolf v. Federal Republic of Germany,* 95 F.3d 536, 542 (7th Cir. 1996). Is this conclusion dictated by either the FSIA, the FSIA's legislative history, or the *Amerada Hess* decision? *See Burnett v. Al Baraka Inv. & Dev. Corp.,* 292 F. Supp. 2d 9, 19 n.4 (D.D.C. 2003) (rejecting the entire tort theory based on the plain language of the text). Is it wise?

**4. Olsen*'s situs requirement.* *Olsen* apparently rejected the reading of the situs requirement adopted in *SEDCO.* What rule did *Olsen* ultimately adopt? Suppose two "entire torts" were alleged in *Olsen*: (1) pilot error wholly within the United States; and (2) negligent maintenance of the ill-fated aircraft wholly within Mexico. Under the *Olsen* rule, could the plaintiffs proceed on both counts, or only on the pilot error claim? As this hypothetical suggests, several possible views of §1605(a)(5)'s situs requirement emerge from *SEDCO* and *Olsen*: (1) only injury must occur within the United States; (2) all tortious conduct and injury must occur within the United States; (3) one "entire tort," including all elements of the tort and the injury, must occur within the United States; or (4) the center of gravity of the tort and injury must be within the United States. Which view is preferable?

5. *Third Restatement's situs requirement.* Section 454 of the ALI's *Restatement (Third) Foreign Relations Law* adopts a less restrictive situs requirement for noncommercial torts than that embraced in *SEDCO.* Comment e to §454 provides that "courts in the United States have jurisdiction over tort claims against a foreign state only if the injury took place in the United States, but the courts have jurisdiction even if the act or omission causing the injury took place elsewhere." *Restatement (Third) Foreign Relations Law* §454, comment e (1987).

6. *U.N. State Immunities Convention.* How does Article 12 of the U.N. State Immunities Convention deal with the noncommercial tort exception's situs requirement? Note Article 12's requirements that (a) the allegedly tortious "act or omission occurred in whole or in part in the territory" of the state exercising jurisdiction, and (b) the "author of the act or omission was present in that territory [of the state exercising jurisdiction] at the time of the act or omission." How does this compare with the FSIA? Which is preferable? Why should the FSIA be interpreted to grant foreign states broader immunity than the United States would receive abroad?

7. *Cross-border torts.* Suppose an industrial accident occurs at a foreign state-owned pesticide factory located near the U.S. border. Toxic fumes escape and kill large numbers of Americans living in the United States. Would §1605(a)(5) provide a jurisdictional basis for claims against the foreign state? What result would *Amerada Hess* suggest? How is this hypothetical different from *SEDCO*? Would §1605(a)(2) apply to this hypothetical? What if the accident occurred at a military research facility? Suppose that decisions are made in a foreign state in connection with tortious conduct by that nation in the United States. Does this decision-making activity constitute part of the tortious conduct, and if so, what effect does this have on the situs requirement? What law governs this question?

b.   The Discretionary Function Exclusion for Noncommercial Torts.   The noncommercial tort exception does not apply to actions arising out of a foreign state's performance of "discretionary functions."[127] Section 1605(a)(5)'s discretionary function exclusion was modelled on the Federal Tort Claims Act ("FTCA"), which sets forth the circumstances in which the U.S. Government may be sued in tort.[128] The language of §1605(a)(5)(A) tracks that of 28 U.S.C. §2680(a), and the FSIA's legislative history refers courts to the FTCA.[129] Thus, lower courts have relied on FTCA precedents in §1605(a)(5) cases.[130]

The Supreme Court's decisions under the FTCA have provided only a measure of guidance. In *Dalehite v. United States,* the Court held that "discretion" meant:

> more than the initiation of programs and activities. It also includes determinations made by executives or administrators in establishing plans, specifications, or schedules or operations. Where there is a room for policy judgment and decision there is discretion.[131]

More recently, in *United States v. Varig Airlines,* the Court held that the United States could not be sued under the FTCA for the alleged negligence of the Federal Aviation Administration in administering air safety standards. The Court reasoned that the FTCA's discretionary function exception was designed to "prevent judicial 'second-guessing' of legislative and administrative decisions grounded in social, economic, and political policy through the medium of an action in tort."[132]

It is difficult to determine when the discretionary function exclusion from the non-commercial tort exception applies. Courts are required to decide whether a particular activity is sufficiently laden with policy-making, judgmental, and political factors to render it a "discretionary function." Some cases have taken a broad view of discretionary functions, apparently regarding all conduct "in furtherance" of an important national policy as discretionary.[133] Other courts have taken narrower views of what constitutes a "discretionary function."[134]

The materials excerpted below explore the discretionary function exclusion. *SEDCO* considers whether a particular course of governmental conduct was "discretionary" or not. Also excerpted below is an opinion in *Letelier v. Republic of Chile.* Unlike *SEDCO,* it was clear in *Letelier* that the defendant's conduct involved high-level foreign policy-making. Nonetheless, *Letelier* invoked basic U.S. public policies in concluding that Chile was not entitled to immunity under the discretionary function exclusion.

---

127. 28 U.S.C. §1605(a)(5)(B).

128. *See Joseph v. Office of Consulate General of Nigeria,* 830 F.2d 1018, 1026 (9th Cir. 1987); *In re SEDCO,* 543 F. Supp. 561 (S.D. Tex. 1982).

129. H.R. Rep. No. 1487, 94th Cong., 2d Sess. 21, *reprinted in* 1976 U.S. Code Cong. & Admin. News 6620.

130. *E.g., Risk v. Halvorsen,* 936 F.2d 393 (9th Cir. 1991); *Joseph v. Office of the Consulate General of Nigeria,* 830 F.2d 1018, 1026 (9th Cir. 1987); *Maalouf v. Swiss Confederation,* 208 F. Supp. 2d 31, 35 (D.D.C. 2002); *In re SEDCO,* 543 F. Supp. 561 (S.D. Tex. 1982).

131. 346 U.S. 15, 35-36 (1953).

132. 467 U.S. 797, 814 (1984).

133. *E.g., In re SEDCO, Inc.,* 543 F. Supp. 561 (S.D. Tex. 1982). *See Risk v. Halvorsen,* 936 F.2d 393 (9th Cir. 1991) (consular officer's assistance to foreign national in leaving United States is discretionary function); *MacArthur Area Citizens Ass'n v. Peru,* 809 F.2d 918, 922 (D.C. Cir. 1987), *vacated on other grounds,* 823 F.2d 606 (1987); *In re Terrorist Attacks on September 11, 2001,* 392 F. Supp. 2d 539, 555-556 (S.D.N.Y. 2005) (allocation of funds to charities); *In re Terrorist Attacks on September 11, 2001,* 349 F. Supp. 2d 765, 802 (S.D.N.Y. 2005); *Alicog v. Kingdom of Saudi Arabia,* 860 F. Supp. 379 (S.D. Tex. 1994) (confiscation of travel documents and forcible confinement held discretionary); *Travel Associates, Inc. v. Kingdom of Swaziland,* 1990 U.S. Dist. LEXIS 11455 (D.D.C. Aug. 30, 1990) (supervision of diplomat is discretionary function); *Anonymous v. Anonymous,* 1990 U.S. App. LEXIS 12353 (7th Cir. 1990) (military attack on Pearl Harbor was discretionary function).

134. *E.g., Olsen ex rel. Sheldon,* 729 F.2d 641 (9th Cir. 1984); *Joseph v. Office of Consulate General of Nigeria,* 830 F.2d 1018 (9th Cir. 1987); *Pulaski v. Republic of India,* 212 F. Supp. 2d 653, 656 (S.D. Tex. 2002).

IN RE SEDCO, INC.
543 F. Supp. 561 (S.D. Tex. 1982) [excerpted above at pp. 310-311]

LETELIER v. REPUBLIC OF CHILE
488 F. Supp. 665 (D.D.C. 1980)

GREEN, DISTRICT JUDGE. [Orlando Letelier and Ronni Moffitt were active in an organization in the United States that was critical of the Republic of Chile. After the violent deaths of Letelier and Moffitt, their survivors filed suit against the Republic of Chile, its intelligence agency (Centro Nacional de Intelligencia or CNI), and various agents of CNI. The suit alleged that the defendants constructed, planted, and detonated a bomb that killed Letelier, the former Chilean foreign minister, and Moffitt. The plaintiffs sought damages under various tort-based causes of action.]

As is made clear both in the [FSIA] and in its legislative history, one of [the Act's] principal purposes was to reduce the foreign policy implications of sovereign immunity determinations and assure litigants that such crucial decisions are made on purely legal grounds, an aim that was to be accomplished by transferring responsibility for such a decision from the executive branch to the judiciary. In addition, the Act itself is designed to codify the restrictive principle of sovereign immunity that makes a foreign state amenable to suit for the consequences of its commercial or private, as opposed to public, acts. . . .

[R]elying on §1605(a)(5) . . . plaintiffs have set forth several tortious causes of action arising under international law, the common law, the Constitution, and legislative enactments, all of which are alleged to spring from the deaths of Orlando Letelier and Ronni Moffitt. The Republic of Chile, while vigorously contending that it was in no way involved in the events that resulted in the two deaths, further asserts that, even if it were, the Court has no subject matter jurisdiction in that it is entitled to immunity under the Act, which does not cover political assassinations because of their public, governmental character. As supportive of its conclusion that political tortious acts of a government are to be excluded, the Republic of Chile makes reference to the reports of the House and Senate Judiciary Committees with regard to the Act, in which it was stated: "Section 1605(a)(5) is directed primarily at the problem of traffic accidents but is cast in general terms as applying to all tort actions for money damages." . . . It is clear from these passages, the Chilean government asserts, that the intent of Congress was to include only private torts like automobile accidents within the exclusion from immunity embodied in §1605(a)(5).

Prominently absent from defendant's analysis, however, is the initial step in any endeavor at statutory interpretation: a consideration of the words of the statute. Subject to the exclusion of these [*sic*] discretionary acts defined in subsection (A) and the specific causes of action enumerated in subsection (B), neither of which have been invoked by the Republic of Chile, by the plain language of §1605(a)(5) a foreign state is not entitled to immunity from an action seeking damages "for personal injury or death . . . caused by the tortious act or omission of that foreign state" or its officials or employees. Nowhere is there an indication that the tortious acts to which the Act makes reference are to only be those formerly classified as "private," thereby engrafting onto the statute . . . the requirement that the character of a given tortious act be judicially analyzed to determine whether it was of the type heretofore denoted as *jure gestionis* or should be classified as *jure imperii*. Indeed, the other provisions of the Act mandate that the Court not do so, for it is made clear that the Act and the principles it sets forth in its specific provisions are henceforth to govern all claims of sovereign immunity by foreign states. 28 U.S.C. §§1602, 1604.

Although the unambiguous language of the Act makes inquiry almost unnecessary, further examination reveals nothing in its legislative history that contradicts or qualifies its plain meaning. The relative frequency of automobile accidents and their potentially grave financial impact may have placed that problem foremost in the minds of Congress, but the applicability of the Act was not so limited, for the committees made it quite clear that the Act "is cast in general terms as applying to all tort actions for money damages" so as to provide recompense for "the victim of a traffic accident or other noncommercial tort." . . .

Examining then the specific terms of §1605(a)(5), despite the Chilean failure to have addressed the issue, the court is called upon to consider whether either of the exceptions to liability for tortious acts found in §1605(a)(5) applies in this instance. It is readily apparent, however, that the claims herein did not arise "out of malicious prosecution, abuse of process, libel, slander, misrepresentation, deceit, or interference with contract rights," 28 U.S.C. §1605(a)(5)(B), and therefore only the exemption for claims "based upon the exercise or performance or the failure to exercise or perform a discretionary function regardless of whether the discretion be abused," §1605(a)(5)(A), can be applicable.

As its language and the legislative history make apparent, the discretionary act exemption of subsection (A) corresponds to the discretionary act exception found in the Federal Tort Claims Act. As defined by the United States Supreme Court in interpreting the Federal Tort Claims Act, an Act that is discretionary is one in which "there is room for policy judgment and decision." *Dalehite v. United States,* 346 U.S. 15, 36 (1953). Applying this definition to the instant action, the question becomes, would the alleged determination of the Chilean Republic to set into motion and assist in the precipitation of those events that culminated in the deaths of Orlando Letelier and Ronni Moffitt be of the kind in which there is "room for policy judgment and decision."

While it seems apparent that a decision calculated to result in injury or death to a particular individual or individuals, made for whatever reason, would be one most assuredly involving policy judgment and decision and thus exempt as a discretionary act under §1605(a)(5)(A), that exception is not applicable to bar this suit. As it has been recognized, there is no discretion to commit, or to have one's officers or agents commit, an illegal act. *Cruikshank v. United States,* 431 F. Supp. 1355, 1359 (D. Hawaii 1977); *see Hatahley v. United States,* 351 U.S. 173, 181 (1956). Whatever policy options may exist for a foreign country, it has no "discretion" to perpetrate conduct designed to result in the assassination of an individual or individuals, action that is clearly contrary to the precepts of humanity as recognized in both national and international law. Accordingly there would be no "discretion" within the meaning of §1605(a)(5)(A) to order or to aid in an assassination and were it to be demonstrated that a foreign state has undertaken any such act in this country, that foreign state could not be accorded sovereign immunity under subsection (A) for any tort claims resulting from its conduct. As a consequence, the Republic of Chile cannot claim sovereign immunity under the FSIA for its alleged involvement in the deaths of Orlando Letelier and Ronni Moffitt.

Notes on SEDCO *and* Letelier

1. *Public or sovereign torts.* Was §1605(a)(5) applicable at all in *Letelier*? Chile argued that its alleged torts arose from "public" or "governmental" acts and that the tort exception contained in §1605(a)(5) should be limited to "private" torts. Put differently, Chile

argued that the restrictive theory lifts immunity with respect only to "private" acts and therefore that its tortious conduct had to be examined to determine whether it was "public" or "private." *Letelier* rejected the argument, on the grounds that it would render §1605(a)(5)(A)'s exceptions for discretionary acts superfluous. Is that persuasive? Recall that the FSIA was intended to codify the restrictive theory. Is there any way to interpret §1605(a)(5) as excluding "public" torts? Recall the presumption that Congress should not be interpreted as violating international law absent a clear statement to that effect. *See supra* p. 18.

2. *Definition of discretionary function.* The FSIA does not define the term "discretionary function." As noted above, some courts have given it an expansive treatment, other courts a narrow one, *supra* p. 315, notes 133-134. In doing so, they have developed different tests to decide whether an official was engaged in a discretionary function. Some courts take two factors into account: (a) whether there was discretion to act or to choose appropriate conduct; and (b) whether the decisions were based upon social, economic, or political policy. *Fagot Rodriguez v. Republic of Costa Rica,* 297 F.3d 1, 9 (1st Cir. 2002); *MacArthur Area Citizens Ass'n v. Peru,* 809 F.2d 918, 922 (D.C. Cir. 1987), *vacated on other grounds,* 823 F.2d 606 (1987); *In re Terrorist Attacks on September 11, 2001,* 392 F. Supp. 2d 539, 554 (S.D.N.Y. 2005). Other courts consider whether the action involves an element of judgment and, if so, whether the judgment is of the kind that the exception was designed to protect. *See, e.g., Doe v. Holy See,* 557 F.3d 1068, 1084-1085 (9th Cir. 2009); *O'Bryan v. Holy See,* 556 F.3d 361, 384 (6th Cir. 2009). Is either definition particularly useful? What was the definition of discretionary function that was used in *SEDCO* and *Letelier?*

3. *Application of discretionary function test in* **SEDCO.** Did the court reach the correct result in *SEDCO?* Was the drilling of an oil well really a "discretionary" function? Is a malfunction on an oil rig not just an ordinary commercial and technical error that has little to do with the broader programs and purposes of Pemex and Mexico's petroleum exploration program?

4. *"Discretionary functions" and illegal acts.* Although *Letelier* apparently conceded that the decision to execute a dissident involves "policy judgment and decision," it avoided applying §1605(a)(5)(A) by invoking the maxim that "there is no discretion to commit . . . an illegal act." The Ninth Circuit reached much the same result in *Liu v. Republic of China,* 892 F.2d 1419 (9th Cir. 1990) (excerpted *infra* at pp. 320-322), where it held that a foreign governmental official had no discretion to order the alleged murder of a dissident in the United States. Is this an appropriate line of analysis? Does the FSIA say anything about an "illegality" exception to the "discretionary function" exclusion? Particularly in sensitive areas like those in *Letelier* and *Liu,* is it desirable for U.S. courts to imply such limits on foreign states' immunity?

5. *Are all illegal acts nondiscretionary?* What is the scope of *Letelier*'s principle that there is no discretion to commit an illegal act? Must the defendant's action merely violate U.S. law before it ceases to be "discretionary"? Must such conduct also violate international law? Won't virtually all noncommercial tort actions involve alleged violations of U.S. tort law? *See Burnett v. Al Baraka Inv. & Development Corp.,* 292 F. Supp. 2d 9, 21 (D.D.C. 2003) (distinguishing *Liu* based on directness of causal connection between sovereign's acts and injury). Note that the FSIA already contains, in §1605(a)(3), an exception for certain international law violations. Does this throw any question onto the *Letelier* rationale? Or did the court instead mean that some (but not all) illegal acts are so contrary to fundamental U.S. public policies that they will not enjoy immunity under the discretionary function exclusion? *Compare* the "public policy" exceptions that exist in the forum

selection, antisuit injunction, choice of law, and enforcement of judgments contexts, *see infra* pp. 511-528, 582, 736-737, 756, 771, 1133-1146. *See also Berkovitz by Berkovitz v. United States,* 486 U.S. 531, 539 (1988) ("The discretionary function exception applies only to conduct that involves the permissible exercise of policy judgment.").

In *Risk v. Halvorsen,* 936 F.2d 393 (9th Cir. 1991), a U.S. national brought suit under the FSIA against Norway and two Norwegian consular officers. The suit charged the officials, and Norway, with tortious interference with a California child custody order and with parent-child relations: the claims arose from assistance allegedly provided by the officials to the plaintiff's wife in removing the couple's children from California to Norway. California law apparently provided a substantial basis for treating the defendant's conduct as a felony. Cal. Penal Code §278.5 (West 1988) ("Intentional violation of a custody order, or of the rights of a parent under such an order, is a felony in California"). Citing *Liu* and *Letelier,* plaintiff argued that the defendants lacked "discretion" to commit felonies under California law, and thus that §1605(a)(5) was applicable. The Ninth Circuit distinguished *Letelier* and *Liu,* reasoning "[a]lthough these acts may constitute a crime under California law, it cannot be said that every conceivable illegal act is outside the scope of the discretionary function exception," apparently because both *Letelier* and *Liu* involved acts that were "clearly contrary to the precepts of humanity." 936 F.2d at 396 (*quoting Letelier,* 488 F. Supp. at 673). What is the legal basis for distinguishing between different types of state law crimes?

6. *Discretionary or sovereign acts under U.N. State Immunities Convention.* How does the U.N. State Immunities Convention deal with sovereign acts or "discretionary functions" in the context of torts? Is this even an issue under the language of Article 12 of the Convention? Doesn't Article 12 apply to any allegedly tortious activity that causes death, bodily injury, or damage to tangible property, regardless whether it was "sovereign" or "discretionary"? What explains this apparent difference between the FSIA and the Convention? Recall the much narrower "situs" requirement under the Convention. *See supra* p. 310. Does that make the absence of any discretionary function exception more understandable? *Compare* Stewart, *Current Developments: The UN Convention on Jurisdictional Immunities of States and Their Property,* 99 Am. J. Int'l L. 194, 202 (2005) ("It is debatable, however, whether the traditional 'public/private' distinction has entirely lost its vitality or its relevance in the area of noncommercial torts.").

7. *Discretionary functions and individual officials.* All of the cases excerpted here were decided prior to the Supreme Court's decision in *Samantar, supra,* which held that the FSIA did not extend to individual government officials. Consider the facts of *Letelier* and focus on the fact that individual agents were sued as well. Does the federal common law of individual officer immunity protect them in the exercise of the discretionary functions? How does this compare to the "official act" standard that some courts developed under the federal common law of individual immunity? *See supra* at p. 274.

c. The "Scope of Employment" Requirement. Unlike other parts of §1605, §1605(a)(5) contains specific language addressing the liability of foreign states for the tortious acts or omissions of their employees and agents. Thus, §1605(a)(5) denies foreign states immunity in cases where money damages are sought:

> for personal injury or death, or damage to or loss of property, occurring in the United States and caused by the tortious act or omission of that foreign state or *of any official or employee of that foreign state while acting within the scope of his office or employment.*

Only a few lower court decisions have considered the "scope of employment" requirement in any detail.[135] The following opinion, in *Liu v. Republic of China,* is one of these decisions.

LIU v. REPUBLIC OF CHINA
892 F.2d 1419 (9th Cir. 1989)

BOOCHEVER, CIRCUIT JUDGE. [The District Court and the Court of Appeals proceeded on the basis of factual findings reached in various ROC tribunals. In summary, these findings showed that one Henry Liu, a journalist and businessman living in California, was shot at his home by two gunmen. The gunmen were members of a criminal racketeering group in the Republic of China ("ROC") called the Bamboo Union Gang. The shootings occurred after leaders of the Bamboo Union Gang had met with one Vice-Admiral Wong—the Director of the ROC "Defense Intelligence Bureau" ("DIB"), a governmental agency within the ROC Ministry of Defense. Wong recruited the Bamboo Union Gang for various activities, including teaching Liu a "lesson" for his apparent hostility to Wong and his outspoken criticism of the ROC government. Wong arranged for the training of two gang members and supplied them with information concerning Liu. The gunmen travelled to the U.S., murdered Liu, and returned to the ROC where they reported to Wong.

Wong and the Gang members were later apprehended by the ROC police. They were tried and convicted for murder and conspiracy. They received sentences of life imprisonment. The ROC courts found that Wong had acted secretly, without the knowledge of his superiors, and in violation of ROC law and DIB regulations. These courts also found that Wong had a "personal grudge" against Liu.]

Liu's allegations were sufficient to bring this suit within the tortious activity exception of 28 U.S.C.A. §1605(a)(5). Liu sued for damages for the wrongful death of her husband which occurred within the United States. Section 1605(a)(5) removes immunity for torts committed either by a foreign state or its agents acting within the scope of their employment. Liu alleged both grounds: 1) that the ROC was involved in the conspiracy to kill Henry Liu; and 2) that Wong acted within the scope of his employment in ordering the assassination.

The district court eventually ruled that the act of state doctrine precluded inquiry into the alleged ROC involvement in the conspiracy and that Wong's act was not committed within the scope of his employment under California law. Consequently the court held that the ROC was not liable under the doctrine of respondeat superior for Liu's damages. This determination constituted a decision that the district court lacked subject matter jurisdiction because §1605(a)(5) requires that acts of agents of a foreign state be within the scope of their employment.

"The 'scope of employment' provision of the tortious activity exception [of the FSIA] essentially requires a finding that the doctrine of respondeat superior applies to the tortious acts of individuals." *Joseph v. Office of Consulate General of Nigeria,* 830 F.2d 1018 1025 (9th Cir. 1987). In *Joseph,* we held that state law, not federal common law, governs whether an employee's action is within the scope of employment in determining the applicability of the FSIA.

135. *E.g., Doe v. Holy See,* 557 F.3d 1066 (9th Cir. 2009); *Randolph v. Budget Rent-A-Car,* 97 F.3d 319, 325-326 (9th Cir. 1999) ("The question of whether Maghrabi was a Saudia employee is governed by California law."); *Republic of China v. Liu,* 892 F.2d 1419 (9th Cir. 1989); *Joseph v. Office of Consulate General of Nigeria,* 830 F.2d 1018, 1025 (9th Cir. 1987); *Howland v. Hertz Corp.,* 431 F. Supp. 2d 1328 (M.D. Fla. 2006); *Skeen v. Federative Republic of Brazil,* 566 F. Supp. 1414, 1417 (D.D.C. 1983).

We have held that there are two choice of law questions that must be resolved prior to determining whether the ROC is liable under respondeat superior. First, we must decide the choice of law rule applicable to the respondeat superior issue determinative of jurisdiction under the FSIA. Second, assuming that we have jurisdiction under that Act, we must ascertain the law to be applied in determining whether the ROC is liable on the merits. . . .

[F]ederal common law provides the choice of law rule applicable to deciding the merits of an action involving a foreign state. *See Harris v. Polskie Linie Lotnicze,* 820 F.2d 1000, 1003-1004 (9th Cir. 1987). In *Harris,* the parents of a passenger killed in an airplane crash in Poland sued the Polish airline in federal court in California. The FSIA applied to the suit because the Polish airline was an instrumentality of the state of Poland. The plaintiffs argued that California's choice of law rules should determine the substantive law of damages because the parties sued in California. We rejected this argument and held that federal common law provided the appropriate choice of law rule in cases arising under the FSIA. We adopted the *Restatement (Second) of Conflicts of Laws* approach, which creates a presumption that "the law of the place where the injury occurred applies" unless another state has a "more significant relationship to the [tort] and to the parties." In *Joseph* . . . [we] held that California's law of respondeat superior, not federal common law, applied to determine whether the tortious acts of Nigeria's employees were within the scope of employment for purposes of the tortious activity exception in the FSIA. . . .

[W]e apply [a] federal choice of law rule to determine the applicable law of respondeat superior on the merits. If a different choice of law rule applied to determine the applicable respondeat superior law for jurisdictional purposes under the FSIA, it would be cumbersome, present grave practical difficulties, and could result in different substantive laws being applied in the same suit. We do not believe that Congress intended different choice of law rules to apply. We therefore hold that the federal choice of law rule controls the applicable law of respondeat superior both for jurisdiction under the FSIA and on the merits.

California is the place where injury occurred, and under the federal choice of law rule, its law will apply to the merits of the action unless the ROC has a more significant relationship to the tort and the parties. Although the ROC has some connection with the tort and the parties, we cannot say that it has the more significant relationship. California and the ROC have offsetting interests in the parties to this suit: Henry Liu was domiciled in California when he was killed, and the ROC and other ROC nationals are parties to the suit. California, however, has a significant interest in ensuring that its residents are compensated for torts committed against them, and in discouraging the commission of such torts within its borders. We conclude that California's relationship to the tort is at least as significant as the ROC's. . . .

[Under California law,] an employer is vicariously liable for the torts of employees committed within the scope of their employment. *See, e.g., Alma W. v. Oakland Unified School Dist.,* 176 Cal. Rptr. 287, 289 (1981). "This includes willful and malicious torts as well as negligence." California follows the "enterprise theory" of liability:

> California has adopted the rationale that the employer's liability should extend beyond his actual or possible control over the employees to include risks inherent in or created by the enterprise because he, rather than the innocent injured party, is best able to spread the risks through prices, rates or liability insurance. *Rodgers v. Kemper Constr. Co.,* 124 Cal. Rptr. 143, 148 (1975).

A country such as the ROC cannot spread risks like a private business by means of the prices it charges for a product. But by means of the public fisc, it similarly can spread risks which would otherwise fall on the individual harmed by the tortious conduct of the country's employees.

California has established a two-prong test to determine whether an employee is acting within the scope of employment. Generally, an employer will be liable for an employee's wrongful act if 1) the act was required or incident to the employee's duties or 2) the act was reasonably foreseeable to the employer. In this case, we find that Liu has established facts sufficient to meet the first prong of the test and therefore do not address the issue of foreseeability. . . .

Wong used the ROC facilities entrusted to him to help [the Bamboo Union] prepare for the assassination. Wong sent [Bamboo Union members] to the DIB training school for four days, and provided them with a dossier on Liu prepared by the DIB. As the ROC correctly states, the mere use of facilities entrusted to the employee is insufficient to impose liability on the employer. Although Wong's use of facilities alone would be insufficient to impute liability to the ROC, this factor combined with Wong's use of his authority to accomplish a task, partly for the benefit of his employer, is sufficient to impose vicarious liability on the ROC. . . .

Last, the ROC contends that it should not be liable for Wong's act because Wong violated ROC internal law prohibiting murder, and none of its other officials knew of or sanctioned his act. First, the mere fact than an employee violated an employer's express rules is not dispositive. If this were a complete defense, then "few employers would ever be held liable." Likewise, the fact that the ROC officials did not sanction Wong's act or were unaware of it is irrelevant because under respondeat superior an employer is held vicariously liable for the risks inherent in his enterprise irrespective of his own personal fault.

We can accept the ROC courts' findings that no other official was aware of or sanctioned Wong's wrongful act and still find that Liu has established as a matter of law that Wong's act was committed within the scope of his employment as Director of the DIB. Consequently, we reverse the district court's denial of Liu's motion for partial summary judgment and its decision that the ROC could not be vicariously liable for Henry Liu's death.

Because we conclude that the ROC is liable under respondeat superior, we also hold that there is subject matter jurisdiction under the FSIA, unless Wong's conduct falls within the discretionary function exception to that Act. 28 U.S.C. §1330(a). [The court held that the exception was not satisfied.]

Notes on Liu v. Republic of China

1. *Federal common law choice of law rule under FSIA.* Issues of substantive liability are generally not governed by the FSIA. Under 28 U.S.C. §1606, a foreign state shall be "liable in the same manner and to the same extent as a private individual under like circumstances." Thus, in determining the liability of a foreign state, a court must choose a body of substantive law. *Liu* held that choice of law questions under the FSIA were governed by federal common law: "federal common law provides the choice of law rule applicable to deciding the merits of an action involving a foreign state." The rationale of *Liu* is that the FSIA was intended to provide a uniform federal statutory framework for questions of jurisdiction over and immunity of foreign states, and that important federal foreign relations interests are served by such uniformity. Is this persuasive? Does not §1606 require application of the same choice of law rules that would apply in private litigation? Under *Erie* and *Klaxon v. Stentor Elec. Mfg. Co.*, would this not be the local choice of law rules of the state in which the federal court was located? *See infra* pp. 791-796. How

compelling is the need for uniform treatment of choice of law questions under the FSIA? Why should not state choice of law rules apply in litigation against foreign states?

2. Standard for determining scope of employment. Applying a federal choice of law rule, *Liu* concluded that California state law governed the question whether Mr. Liu's killers had acted within their "scope of employment" by the Republic of China. Is it appropriate for the meaning of §1605(a)(5)'s jurisdictional provisions to be determined by state law? Note that the phrase "scope of employment" occurs in a federal statute and thus that the meaning of this phrase would presumptively be a matter of federal law. *NLRB v. Hearst Publications, Inc.*, 322 U.S. 111, 123 (1944) ("it is not only proper but necessary for us to assume, 'in the absence of a plain indication to the contrary, that Congress . . . is not making the application of [a] federal act dependant on state law.'") (*quoting Jerome v. United States*, 318 U.S. 101, 104 (1943)). Note also that the FSIA's drafters emphasized their intention of establishing uniform, federal standards governing the immunity of foreign states and the jurisdiction of U.S. courts over those states. 28 U.S.C. §1602; H.R. Rep. No. 1487, 94th Cong., 2d Sess., at 12, *reprinted in* 1976 U.S. Code Cong. & Admin. News 6604, 6610 (FSIA "sets forth the sole and exclusive standard to be used in resolving questions of sovereign immunity"); *Verlinden BV v. Central Bank of Nigeria*, 461 U.S. 480, 488, 493 (1983).

Even if §1605(a)(5) did not provide a specific federal statutory test for "scope of employment" jurisdiction, would this be an appropriate case for formulating a rule of federal common law? Note that in *First National City Bank v. Bancec*, 462 U.S. 611 (1983) [excerpted at *supra* pp. 257-261], the Supreme Court adopted a rule of federal common law defining the circumstances in which U.S. courts could disregard the separate juridical identity of foreign state-owned companies, reasoning that:

> matters bearing on the Nation's foreign relations "should not be left to divergent and perhaps parochial state interpretations." When it enacted the FSIA, Congress expressly acknowledged the "importance of developing a uniform body of law" concerning the amenability of a foreign sovereign to suit in United States courts. *Bancec*, 462 U.S. at 622 n.11 (quoting *Banco Nacional de Cuba v. Sabbatino*, and H.R. Rep. No. 1487, at 32).

Does *Liu* provide an adequate response to these indications that federal law should govern §1605(a)(5)'s "scope of employment" standard? Note that the California standard of enterprise liability is significantly broader than that prevailing elsewhere. *See* 1 S. Speiser, C. Krause & A. Gans, *The American Law on Torts* §4.51 at 740 (1983) ("thus far used only in California"). Is it appropriate for individual states to define the immunity of foreign states through 50 divergent standards for defining "scope of employment"? What if a state broadens the scope of employment test significantly beyond that adopted by California? What if it adopts an especially broad (or narrow) test applicable only to foreign states?

3. Content of scope of employment test. What is the appropriate content of §1605(a)(5)'s scope of employment test? Note that the test adopted by *Liu* does not require any showing that the employer could have foreseen the employee's misconduct, and that it disregards both the fact that the employee committed an outrageous crime and that the employee had personal motivations. Section 228 of the *Restatement (Second) of Agency*, like the laws of most states, generally requires consideration of foreseeability, outrageousness of the employee's act, and personal motivations. Would this standard be more appropriate than California's theory of enterprise liability?

4. Immunity of foreign heads of state and governmental officials revisited. Recall the discussion of the immunity of foreign heads of state and foreign governmental officials. Suppose Admiral Wong had been named a defendant in *Liu,* and that service was effected.

Would he have been entitled to immunity? What about his governmental superiors? What about the governmental officials involved in Letelier's murder? What is the relationship between the scope of employment requirement under §1605(a)(5) and the "official capacity" test suggested by *Samantar*? Are the tests related? Does the same substantive law apply in both cases?

3. Expropriation with a U.S. Nexus

The FSIA also denies foreign states immunity from actions involving takings in violation of international law, provided that there is a close connection to the United States. Section 1605(a)(3) denies immunity in actions involving expropriations where the wrongfully expropriated property (or its proceeds) is present in the United States in connection with a commercial activity carried on by the foreign state in the United States. Section 1605(a)(3) lifts immunity in cases:

> In which rights in property taken in violation of international law are in issue and that property or any property exchanged for such property is present in the United States in connection with a commercial activity carried on in the United States by the foreign state; or that property or any property exchanged for such property is owned or operated by an agency or instrumentality of the foreign state and that agency or instrumentality is engaged in a commercial activity in the United States.

This provision has given rise to uncertainty concerning both the types of actions that constitute takings of property in violation of international law and the necessary U.S. nexus. The decision excerpted below, *Siderman de Blake v. Republic of Argentina*, illustrates these difficulties. In reading the decision, note that the Court's description of the "facts" relies solely on the Sidermans' submissions, because Argentina defaulted during the evidentiary phases of the trial court proceedings.

SIDERMAN DE BLAKE v. REPUBLIC OF ARGENTINA
965 F.2d 699 (9th Cir. 1992)

FLETCHER, CIRCUIT JUDGE. Susana Siderman de Blake and Jose, Lea, and Carlos Siderman (collectively, "the Sidermans") appeal the dismissal of their action against the Republic of Argentina and the Argentine Province of Tucuman (collectively, "Argentina"). The Sidermans' complaint alleged eighteen causes of action arising out of the torture of Jose Siderman and the expropriation of the Sidermans' property by Argentine military officials. The district court dismissed the expropriation claims on the basis of the act of state doctrine, but granted a default judgment to Jose and Lea Siderman on the torture claims. Argentina then entered its first appearance in the case and moved for relief from judgment on the ground that the FSIA rendered it immune from the Sidermans' action. The district court granted the motion and vacated the default judgment. The Sidermans now appeal. We reverse and remand for further proceedings.

The factual record, which consists only of the Sidermans' complaint and numerous declarations they submitted in support of their claims, tells a horrifying tale of the violent and brutal excesses of an anti-Semitic military junta that ruled Argentina. On March 24, 1976, the Argentine military overthrew the government of President Maria Estela Peron and seized the reins of power for itself, installing military leaders of the central government and the provincial governments of Argentina. That night, ten masked men carrying machine guns forcibly entered the home of Jose and Lea Siderman, husband and wife, in Tucuman Province, Argentina. The men, who were acting under the direction of the military governor of Tucuman, ransacked the home and locked Lea in the bathroom. They then blindfolded and shackled 65-year old Jose, dragged him out of his home, tossed him into a waiting car, and drove off to an unknown building. For seven days the men beat and tortured Jose. Among their tools of torture was an electric cattle prod, which they used to shock Jose until he fainted. As they tortured him, the men repeatedly shouted anti-Semitic epithets, calling him a "Jew Bastard" and a "Shitty Jew." They inflicted all of these cruelties upon Jose Siderman because of his Jewish faith.

At the end of this nightmarish week, his body badly bruised and his ribs broken, Jose was taken out of the building and driven to an isolated area, where the masked men tossed him out of the car. The men told Jose that if he and his family did not leave Tucuman and Argentina immediately, they would be killed. On the day of Jose's release, he and Lea fled to Buenos Aires in fear for their lives. Their son Carlos followed shortly thereafter, and the night Carlos left Tucuman, military authorities ransacked his home. In June 1976, Jose, Lea, and Carlos left Argentina for the United States, where they joined Susana Siderman de Blake. She is the daughter of Jose and Lea and is a United States citizen.

Before the hasty flight from Tucuman to Buenos Aires, Jose was forced to raise cash by selling at a steep discount part of his interest in 127,000 acres of land. Prior to their departure for the United States, the Sidermans also made arrangements for someone to oversee their family business, Inmobiliaria del Nor-Oeste, SA ("INOSA"), an Argentine corporation. Susana Siderman de Blake, Carlos Siderman and Lea Siderman each owned 33% of INOSA and Jose owned the remaining one percent. Its assets comprised numerous real estate holdings including a large hotel in Tucuman, the Hotel Gran Corona. The Sidermans granted management powers over INOSA to a certified public accountant in Argentina.

After the Sidermans left Argentina for the United States, Argentine military officers renewed their persecution of Jose. They altered real property records in Tucuman to show that he had owned not 127,000, but 127 acres of land in the province. They then initiated a criminal action against him in Argentina, claiming that since he owned only 127 acres he had sold land that did not belong to him. Argentina sought the assistance of our courts in obtaining jurisdiction over his person, requesting via a letter rogatory that the Los Angeles Superior Court serve him with documents relating to the action. The court, unaware of Argentina's motives, complied with the request.

Soon thereafter, while he was travelling in Italy, Jose was arrested pursuant to an extradition request from Argentina to the Italian government. Argentina charged that Jose had fraudulently obtained the travel documents enabling him to leave Argentina in 1976. Jose was not permitted to leave Cremora, Italy, for seven months, and actually was imprisoned for 27 days, before an Italian Appeals Court finally held that Argentina's extradition request would not be honored, as it was politically motivated and founded on pretextual charges.

The Argentine military also pursued INOSA with vigor. In April 1977, INOSA was seized through a sham "judicial intervention," a proceeding in which property is put into receivership. The purported reasons for the intervention were that INOSA lacked a representative in Argentina and that INOSA had obtained excessive funds from a Tucuman provincial bank. Though these reasons were pretexts for persecuting the Sidermans because of their religion and profiting from their economic success, the Sidermans were unable to oppose the intervention because Argentine officials had imprisoned and killed the accountant to whom they had granted management powers over INOSA. In 1978, the Sidermans retained an attorney in Argentina and brought a derivative action in a

Tucuman court in an effort to end the intervention. The court ordered that the intervention cease, and the order was upheld by the Supreme Court of Tucuman, but the order remains unenforced and the intervention has continued. Argentine military officials and INOSA's appointed receivers have extracted funds from INOSA, purchased various assets owned by INOSA at sharply discounted prices, and diverted INOSA's profits and revenues to themselves.

In 1982, Jose, Lea, and Carlos, who by then had become permanent residents of the United States, and Susana, a United States citizen since 1967, turned to federal court for relief. They filed a complaint asserting eighteen causes of action based on the torture and harassment of Jose by Argentine officials and the expropriation of their property in Argentina. Named defendants included the Republic of Argentina, the Province of Tucuman, INOSA, and numerous individual defendants who participated in the wrongdoing. [Argentina did not answer the Sidermans' complaint and the district court initially entered judgment for the Sidermans on their torture claims, while dismissing their expropriation claims (under §1605(a)(3)). Thereafter, Argentina appeared and successfully moved to vacate the default award and dismiss all of the Sidermans' claims. This appeal by the Sidermans followed.]

Since the district court did not consider jurisdiction under the FSIA with regard to the expropriation claims, it made no findings of fact concerning jurisdiction. The record consists of the complaint and numerous declarations submitted by the Sidermans in support of their contention that certain of the FSIA exceptions apply, but includes no pleadings or evidence from Argentina, which had not yet entered an appearance in the case when the expropriation claims were dismissed. Argentina contends that the Sidermans' complaint and declarations fail to demonstrate that the expropriation claims fall within an FSIA exception, and asks us to affirm the district court's dismissal on that ground. We therefore review the record to determine whether the Sidermans have sustained their initial burden of alleging jurisdiction under the FSIA. If the allegations in the Sidermans' complaint, which we must accept as true, and the uncontroverted evidence presented by the Sidermans bring the claims within an FSIA exception, the burden then shifts to Argentina to prove that any relevant exceptions do not apply. . . .

Where, as here, the plaintiff alleges in his complaint that his claim is based on a foreign state's strictly commercial acts, the defendant must establish a prima facie case that it is a sovereign state and that the plaintiff's claim arises out of a public act. This proof establishes a presumption that the foreign state is protected by immunity. The plaintiff then has the burden of going forward with the evidence by offering proof that one of the FSIA exemptions applies. Once the plaintiff has presented this evidence, the defendant must prove its entitlement to immunity by a preponderance of the evidence. . . .

The Sidermans argue that their claims . . . fall within the international takings exception to the FSIA's rule of immunity. . . . Though few courts have had the opportunity to consider the international takings exception, it is clear that Jose, Lea, and Carlos Siderman cannot assert a claim that comes within this exception. In *Chuidian v. Philippine Nat'l Bank*, 912 F.2d 1095, 1105 (9th Cir. 1990), we held that the exception does not apply where the plaintiff is a citizen of the defendant country at the time of the expropriation, because "[e]xpropriation by a sovereign state of the property of its own nationals does not implicate settled principles of international law." However, Susana Siderman de Blake is eligible to invoke the international takings exception, and the Sidermans' allegations and evidence bring her claims within clause two of that exception.

Under that clause, the property at issue must have been taken in violation of international law. At the jurisdictional stage, we need not decide whether the taking actually violated international law; as long as a "claim is substantial and non-frivolous, it provides a sufficient basis for the exercise of our jurisdiction." *West v. Multibanco Comermex, SA,* 807 F.2d 820, 826 (9th Cir. 1987). In *West,* we described three requisites under international law for a valid taking. First, "[v]alid expropriations must always serve a public purpose." Second, "aliens [must] not be discriminated against or singled out for regulation by the state." Finally, "[a]n otherwise valid taking is illegal without the payment of just compensation." These well-established principles track the *Restatement [(Third)] of Foreign Relations Law,* which provides: "A state is responsible under international law for injury resulting from: (1) a taking by the state of the property of a national of another state that (a) is not for a public purpose, or (b) is discriminatory, or (c) is not accompanied by provision for just compensation." The legislative history of the FSIA reveals a similar understanding of what constitutes a taking in violation of international law. *See* H.R. Rep. No. 1487, 94th Cong., 2d Sess. 19-20, *reprinted in* 1976 U.S. Code Cong. & Admin. News 6604, 6618. If a taking violates any one of the aforementioned proscriptions, it violates international law.

Susana Siderman de Blake's claim that Argentina violated the international law of expropriation is substantial and non-frivolous. The complaint alleges that Argentina officials seized INOSA for their personal profit and not for any public purpose. The complaint also alleges that Argentina seized INOSA because the Siderman family is Jewish — a discriminatory motivation based on ethnicity. *See Restatement [(Third)]* §712 Comment f (noting that "taking that singles out aliens generally, or aliens of a particular nationality, or particular aliens, would violate international law"). Finally, none of the Sidermans has received *any* compensation for the seizure, let alone just compensation. As in *West,* we have no difficulty concluding that the Sidermans' complaint contains "substantial and non-frivolous" allegations that INOSA was taken in violation of international law.

Beyond establishing that property has been taken in violation of international law, Susan Siderman de Blake must demonstrate that the expropriated property, or property exchanged for it, is owned or operated by an agency or instrumentality of Argentina and that the agency or instrumentality is engaged in commercial activity in the United States. The Sidermans' allegations establish that INOSA itself has become an agency or instrumentality of Argentina. As an Argentine corporation, INOSA satisfies the first and third elements of [§1603(b)], and the Sidermans' basic allegation that Argentina has expropriated INOSA suffices as an allegation that INOSA is now an "organ" of Argentina or Tucuman. The Sidermans' allegations thus satisfy the "agency or instrumentality" definition. The final requirement under clause two — that the agency or instrumentality must be engaged in a commercial activity in the United States — is also met. The Sidermans' allegations concerning Argentina's solicitation and entertainment of American guests at the Hotel Gran Corona and the hotel's acceptance of American credit cards and traveler's checks are sufficient at this stage of the proceedings to show that Argentina is engaged in a commercial activity in the United States. The Sidermans' allegations bring Susana Siderman de Blake's expropriation claims within clause two of the international takings exception.

We hold that the Sidermans' complaint and declarations allege sufficient facts to bring their expropriation claims within both the commercial activity and international takings exceptions to the FSIA's grant of foreign sovereign immunity. We emphasize the preliminary nature of our holding; following further development of the factual record on remand, the district court ultimately must determine whether the FSIA exceptions do or do not apply to the expropriation claims. While the Sidermans have sustained their initial burden of alleging applicable exceptions to the FSIA, Argentina will have the opportunity on remand to challenge the evidence presented by the Sidermans and to

present its own. Under the procedures our circuit has developed for considering jurisdiction under the FSIA, Argentina now bears the burden of proving by a preponderance
of the evidence that none of the FSIA exceptions applies to the Sidermans' claims. . . .

Notes *on* Siderman de Blake

1. *"Taken in violation of international law."* Section 1605(a)(3) applies only where property has been "taken in violation of international law." How are U.S. courts to ascertain
and apply principles of international law under §1605(a)(3)? The FSIA's statutory incorporation of principles of international law is similar to the incorporation of the "law of
nations" in the Alien Tort Statute. *See supra* pp. 33-62. Should the principles articulated
in *Sosa* and other ATS authorities be relevant to analysis under §1605(a)(3)? Is it not
obvious that the same sources — international treaties and conventions, decisions by
international tribunals, writings by "internationalist law professors," and national
court decisions — should be considered in determining the content of international
law? Is it obvious that the same restraint should be exercised in recognizing international
law protections against expropriation under §1605(a)(3) as applies in recognizing tort
claims under the ATS? Why or why not? Returning for a moment to the ATS, does Congress's decision to single out expropriation claims for protection under the FSIA suggest
anything about the viability of such claims under the ATS's standards of acceptance and
definiteness? *See supra* pp. 41-43, 49-53.

2. *Standards of expropriation under international law and §1605(a)(3).* A number of
lower courts have considered when expropriation claims, for takings in violation of
international law, will be available. *See, e.g., Cassirer v. Kingdom of Spain*, 616 F.3d 1019
(9th Cir. 2010) (*en banc*); *Agudas Chasidei Chabad v. Russian Fed'n*, 528 F.3d 934 (D.C. Cir.
2008); *Amorrortu v. Republic of Peru*, 570 F. Supp. 2d 916 (D.D.C. 2008); *Altmann v. Republic
of Austria*, 142 F. Supp. 2d 1187 (C.D. Cal. 2001); *Greenpeace, Inc. (U.S.A.) v. France*, 946
F. Supp. 773 (C.D. Cal. 1996).

As *Siderman* illustrates, lower courts frequently look to the *Restatement (Third) Foreign
Relations Law* §712, which provides:

> A state is responsible under international law for injury resulting from (1) a taking by the state
> of the property of a national of another state that (a) is not for a public purpose, or (b) is
> discriminatory or (c) is not accompanied by provision for just compensation.

The FSIA's legislative history reflects similar standards. H.R. Rep. No. 1487, 94th Cong.,
2d Sess., at 19-20, *reprinted in* 1976 U.S. Code Cong. & Admin. News 6604, 6618 ("without
payment of the prompt, adequate and effective compensation required by international
law" or is "arbitrary or discriminatory in nature"). Note the Court's comment in *Siderman*
that "If a taking violates any one of the aforementioned proscriptions [of the *Restatement
(Third)* or House Report], it violates international law."

How does one determine what was a "public purpose" or whether a particular governmental action was "discriminatory" or whether compensation was "just"? Consider
how these standards apply to the Sidermans' allegations. If those allegations were true,
would Argentina's conduct amount to an unlawful taking under international law? What
defenses might Argentina advance? What if Argentina sought to distance itself from
actions by unauthorized local officials?

3. *Relevance of arbitral awards addressing expropriation under bilateral investment treaties
to interpretation of §1605(a)(3).* As discussed below, there are more than 2,000 bilateral

investment treaties ("BITs") in force among a wide range of capital-exporting and capital-importing states. The United States is party to more than 45 such treaties. The centerpiece of most BITs is a broad protection for investors of one state in the other state against expropriatory or similar conduct. *See* C. McLachlan, L. Shore & M. Weiniger, *International Investment Arbitration: Substantive Principles* ¶¶1.24-1.30, 2.20 (2009); A. Newcombe & L. Paradell, *Law and Practice of Investment Treaties: Standards of Treatment* 156-157, 255-261, 332-336 (2009). Many BITs also include standing offers to arbitrate disputes under such expropriation protections. As a consequence, there is a substantial and growing body of arbitral awards addressing the question of what constitutes an unlawful expropriation in the context of such BITs. Should such awards be relevant to the definition of an unlawful taking under §1605(a)(3)?

4. ***Controversy over international law standards of expropriation.*** There was historically substantial controversy over the extent to which international law protected foreign investors against expropriation of their property. Consider the following excerpt from Justice Harlan's opinion in *Banco Nacional de Cuba v. Sabbatino,* 376 U.S. 398, 428-429 (1964):

> There are few if any issues in international law today on which opinion seems to be so divided as the limitations on a State's power to expropriate the property of aliens. There is, of course, authority, in international judicial and arbitral decisions, in the expressions of national governments, and among commentators for the view that a taking is improper under international law if it is not for a public purpose, is discriminatory, or is without provision for prompt, adequate, and effective compensation. However, Communist countries, although they have in fact provided a degree of compensation after diplomatic efforts, commonly recognize no obligation on the part of the taking country. Certain representatives of the newly independent and underdeveloped countries have questioned whether rules of state responsibility towards aliens can bind nations that have not consented to them and it is argued that the traditionally articulated standards governing expropriation of property reflect "imperialist" interests and are inappropriate to the circumstances of emergent states.

Justice Harlan's description of controversy about the content of international law restrictions on expropriation was probably exaggerated even in 1964. It has certainly lost substantial force during the past two decades, as the fall of the Iron Curtain and the widespread acceptance of BITs has undermined suggestions that states are free arbitrarily or discriminatory to take foreigners' property. Nevertheless, there remains substantial controversy over the contents of international law restrictions on expropriatory conduct. *See* A. Akinsanya, *The Expropriation of Multinational Property in the Third World* (1980).

What relevance should this history, and these continuing objections to international law prohibitions against expropriation, have in interpreting the FSIA? Should U.S. courts care what Fidel Castro or Hugo Chavez says about expropriation? About how the government's conduct in *Siderman* should be characterized?

The U.S. Government has consistently espoused strong international law protections against expropriation. *See, e.g., Shanghai Power Co. v. U.S.,* 4 Cl. Ct. 237, 241 & n.3 (1983). Are U.S. courts required to give effect to the standards of international law espoused by the U.S. Executive Branch in applying §1605(a)(3)? Why or why not? *See Freund v. Republic of France,* 592 F. Supp. 2d 540 (S.D.N.Y. 2008).

5. ***Expropriation claims under U.N. State Immunities Convention.*** How does the U.N. State Immunities Convention deal with claims of expropriation? Does it? Consider the following: "The omission of comparable exceptions to immunity in the convention derives from their not enjoying broad acceptance in the international community—by virtue, some would contend, of their still-emergent nature." Stewart,

Current Developments: The UN Convention on Jurisdictional Immunities of States and Their Property, 99 Am. J. Int'l L. 194, 206 (2005).

6. *"Rights in property" under §1605(a)(3)*. What constitutes "rights in property" under §1605(a)(3)? Is there any reason that the term should not be interpreted to encompass any sort of property rights, including tangible property (land, physical assets), intangible property (shares, contract rights, debt obligations, and intellectual property)? Consider the following definition of property: "that which is one's own; the condition of being one's own; a piece of land owned by somebody; right of possessing, employing, etc.; ownership; an asset, something which brings profit or income[.]" Chambers Dictionary 1318 (1998).

The FSIA's legislative history provides little guidance in interpreting the phrase "rights in property." It refers in passing to the so-called Second Hickenlooper Amendment (discussed at *infra* pp. 856-857), which limited application of the Act of State doctrine to expropriatory actions by foreign states. The Second Hickenlooper Amendment was applicable to foreign state actions affecting "rights to property," which arguably is similar to §1605(a)(3)'s reference to "rights in property." Most decisions under the Second Hickenlooper Amendment have interpreted the phrase "rights to property" narrowly, to cases involving in rem claims to specific physical property. *See infra* pp. 856-857. It is doubtful, however, that the legislative history was intended to incorporate the Second Hickenlooper Amendment's definition of property, which ill-serves the Act's purposes. Rather, the FSIA more likely incorporated definitions of "property" under international law, which reflect an expansive conception of the rights protected against expropriatory conduct. *See* Christie, *What Constitutes a Taking of Property Under International Law?*, 38 Brit. Y.B. Int'l L. 307 (1964); *Banco Nacional de Cuba v. Chemical Bank New York Trust Co.*, 822 F.2d 230, 238 (2d Cir. 1987) ("as defined in international law, property commonly includes intangible assets and 'any interest in property if such interest has a reasonably ascertainable value.'").

Consistent with this, some lower courts have interpreted §1605(a)(3)'s reference to "rights in property" broadly. *See, e.g., Nemariam v. Fed. Democratic Republic of Ethiopia*, 491 F.3d 470 (D.C. Cir. 2007); *De Sanchez v. Banco Cent. de Nicaragua*, 770 F.2d 1385, 1395 (5th Cir. 1985); *Kalamazoo Spice Extraction Co. v. Provisional Military Gov't of Socialist Ethiopia*, 616 F. Supp. 660, 663 (W.D. Mich. 1985). For example, *Kalamazoo Spice* involved a claim that a government's taking of a controlling interest in a company's stock amounted to an expropriation vis-à-vis the other shareholders because it represented control over the company's profits and assets. Consider the court's analysis of whether this claim involved a "right in property" under §1605(a)(3):

> The rights in property that are at issue are the assets of [the company]. Although the [foreign entity] purported to seize only fifty-one percent of [the plaintiff-shareholder's] stock, [the shareholder's] complaint alleges that, without majority' ownership and control, its remaining stock ownership is worthless. . . . [S]ection 1605(a)(3) can only logically be interpreted to encompass the property interest seized in this case. It would not make sense to distinguish between the expropriation of the physical assets of a company, which would clearly fall within section 1605(a)(3), and expropriation of a controlling interest in the stock of the company. In either case, the foreign state has expropriated control of the assets and profits of the company. 616 F. Supp. at 663.

By contrast, other courts have interpreted §1605(a)(3)'s reference to "rights in property" narrowly. *IDAS Res. N.V. v. Empresa Nacional de Diamantes de Angola*, 2006 U.S. Dist LEXIS 77928 (D.D.C. 2006); *Intercontinental Dictionary Series v. De Gruyter*, 822 F. Supp. 662

(C.D. Cal. 1993), *disapproved on other grounds, Sun v. Taiwan,* 201 F.3d 1105 (9th Cir. 2000); *Canadian Overseas Ores Ltd. v. Cia. de Acero del Pacifico,* 528 F. Supp. 1337, 1346 (S.D.N.Y. 1982), *aff'd on other grounds,* 727 F.2d 274 (2d Cir. 1984). For example, in *Canadian Overseas,* the court rejected a claim that "right in property" included a contractual right to payment. It relied heavily on the Second Hickenlooper Amendment, discussed *infra* pp. 856-857, which precludes application of the act of state doctrine in certain cases involving a "right to property":

> As the House Report states, the [expropriation exception] "in no way affects existing law on the extent to which, if at all, the 'act of state' doctrine may be applicable." That statement is followed by a reference to [the Second Hickenlooper Amendment]. . . .
>
> The phrase used in the Hickenlooper Amendment "claim of title or other right to property" has been interpreted to apply only to takings of tangible property, not to include intangible interests like the contractual right of payment asserted . . . here. . . . Were the phrase "rights in property taken in violation of international law" in the FSIA interpreted more broadly than the similar phrase utilized in the Hickenlooper Amendment, Congress would have conferred jurisdiction for suits only to have them dismissed in accordance with the act of state doctrine. The legislative history of the FSIA indicates that such an incongruous result was not intended. Rather [the expropriation exception] appears to be intended to match the Act of state doctrine created by the Hickenlooper Amendment just as [§1605(a)(2)] corresponds to the "commercial activities" exception to the act of state doctrine announced in *Alfred Dunhill of London v. Republic of Cuba* [excerpted *infra* pp. 818-819], 528 F. Supp. at 1346.

Which view do you find more persuasive? Can *Kalamazoo Spice* and *Canadian Overseas* be reconciled?

Consider the property rights at issue in *Siderman.* They included 127,000 acres of real estate, cash and bank accounts, shares in INOSA (which in turn owned valuable real estate and businesses), and INOSA's assets and profits. Which of these various property rights should be protected under §1605(a)(3)? Should there be any difference in how they are treated under the FSIA? If one requires that "tangible property" be taken under §1605(a)(3), then doesn't the provision apply only to takings of the 127,000 acres of real estate? Aren't shares in a company intangible rights? What law should determine this question?

7. ***Takings and contract rights.*** Some lower courts (and commentators) have concluded that contractual rights to payment, absent expropriation of real property, do not constitute "property" under the FSIA's takings provision §1605(a)(3). *See Allen v. Russian Fed'n,* 522 F. Supp. 2d 167 (D.D.C. 2007); *Canadian Overseas Ores Ltd. v. Cia. de Acero del Pacifico,* 528 F. Supp. 1337, 1346-1347 (S.D.N.Y. 1982), *aff'd on other grounds,* 727 F.2d 274 (2d Cir. 1984). *See also Brewer v. Socialist People's Republic of Iraq,* 890 F.2d 97, 101 (8th Cir. 1989); *Zappia Middle East Constr. Co. v. Emirate of Abu Dhabi,* 1996 WL 413680, at *8 (S.D.N.Y. July 24, 1996), *aff'd on other grounds,* 215 F.3d 247, 251 (2d Cir. 2000).

8. ***Nationality of plaintiff under §1605(a)(3).*** Who may bring a claim under §1605(a)(3)? Could Jose and Lea Siderman bring claims? Why not? Could Susanna Siderman? Why is that?

9. ***Appropriate level of scrutiny of lawfulness of "taking" at jurisdictional stage under §1605(a)(3).*** Section 1605(a)(3) links a foreign state's immunity to the extent to which it has violated international law: a foreign state is not immune for takings in violation of international law (and that have the requisite U.S. nexus), while it retains its immunity for actions that do not violate international law. This arguably requires a measure of inquiry into the merits of a claim at the jurisdictional phase, because the foreign state's immunity depends on the extent to which the plaintiff's wrongful taking claim is well-founded. How does the *Siderman* Court address this issue? Is this appropriate? Does it not result in foreign states being subject to U.S. jurisdiction — on highly sensitive matters — based simply on the plaintiff's allegations? For other lower court decisions on this issue, *see Zappia Middle East Constr. Co. Ltd. v. Emirate of Abu Dhabi,* 215 F.3d 247, 253 (2d Cir. 2000); *West v. Multibanco Comermex, SA,* 807 F.2d 820, 826 (9th Cir. 1987); *Crist v. Republic of Turkey,* 995 F. Supp. 5, 11-14 (D.D.C. 1998); *Gibbons v. Udaras na Gaeltachta,* 549 F. Supp. 1094, 1107 n.4 (S.D.N.Y. 1982).

10. *U.S. nexus under §1605(a)(3).* Section 1605(a)(3) grants jurisdiction only in cases where one of two nexus requirements is satisfied: (a) the expropriated property (or property exchanged for that property) is present in the United States "in connection with a commercial activity carried on in the United States by the foreign state"; or (b) the expropriated property (or property exchanged for that property) is "owned or operated" by an agency or instrumentality of the foreign state which is "engaged in a commercial activity in the United States." Consider what kinds of scenarios these two nexus requirements encompass. What kinds of scenarios do they exclude?

What nexus requirement was satisfied in *Siderman*? There was no claim, was there, that the expropriated property was present in the United States? What if responsible Argentine officials had sold the Siderman's 127,000 acres of land and deposited the proceeds in New York? What if the deposit had merely been a passive investment, without any accompanying business activity? Note the *Siderman* Court's conclusion that the expropriating company (INOSA) is now an "agency or instrumentality" of a foreign state. Does this conclusion survive *Dole*? What do you need to know to decide? Assuming that INOSA is a foreign state agency or instrumentality, is it really "engaged in a commercial activity in the United States"? Is a provincial hotel in rural Argentina engaged in business in the United States? Does that mean that a family-owned business in Tennessee is engaged in business in London or Hong Kong? Does the solicitation of U.S. customers — in unspecified ways — really amount to engaging in commercial activity in the United States? Recall the role of solicitation in establishing general jurisdiction. *See supra* p. 123-125, 194-198. Did the *Siderman* Court's heart run away with its head? What other potential avenues of relief were available to the Sidermans?

For other lower court decisions dealing with the nexus requirements under §1605(a)(3), *see Agudas Chasidei Chabad v. Russian Fed'n,* 528 F.3d 934 (D.C. Cir. 2008); *Garb v. Republic of Poland,* 440 F.3d 579 (2d Cir. 2006); *Vencedora Oceanica Navigacion v. Compagnie National Algerienne de Navigation,* 730 F.2d 195, 204 (5th Cir. 1984); *Agudas Chasidei Chabad v. Russian Fed'n,* 2010 U.S. Dist. LEXIS 78552 (D.D.C. 2010); *Freund v. Republic of France,* 592 F. Supp. 2d 540 (S.D.N.Y. 2008). Few courts have considered the alternative nexus theory (unique to the expropriation exception) under which an agency or instrumentality "own[s] or operate[s]" the expropriated property (or property exchanged for it) and is "engaged in a commercial activity in the United States." As a textual matter, does this language require that the property itself have a nexus to the United States? Assuming it doesn't, what precisely does it mean for an "agency or instrumentality" to "own or operate" property? Courts have reached conflicting conclusions. According to one court, the term requires that the property be used in a manner to benefit the foreign state:

[S]ection 1605(a)(3) was intended to subject to United States jurisdiction any foreign agency or instrumentality that has nationalized or expropriated property without compensation, or that is using expropriated property taken by another branch of the state. The vessel in this case thus would have been owned or operated under section 1605(a)(3) if . . . some Algerian agency had assumed control of the vessel and had used it to carry oil for the benefit of the Algerian government.

Vencedora Oceanica Navigacion, S.A. v. Compagnie Nationale Algerienne de Navigation, 730 F.2d 195 (5th Cir. 1984). *See also Greenpeace, Inc. v. State of France,* 946 F. Supp. 773 (C.D. Cal. 1996) (following *Vencedora*). In contrast, other courts have rejected the benefit requirement:

> To "own" is to "have or hold as property or appurtenance . . . [possess]," *see* Webster's Third New International Dictionary 1612 (3d ed. 1993), and to "operate" is to "exert power or influence," *id.* at 1580. Moreover, the legislative history the Fifth Circuit cited [in *Vencendora*], H.R. Rep. No. 94-1487, at 19-20, U.S. Code Cong. & Admin. News 1976, at pp. 6604, 6617-19, did not impose such a requirement or even refer to the "owned or operated" language. Rather, the House Report defined the phrase "taken in violation of international law," stating, "The term 'taken in violation of international law' would include the nationalization or expropriation of property without payment of the prompt[,] adequate and effective compensation required by international law." H.R. Rep. No. 94-1487, at 19-20, U.S. Code Cong. & Admin. News 1976, at pp. 6604, 6617-19. Even assuming the Report addressed the "owned or operated" language, the plain meaning of "nationalization or expropriation" dovetails with the plain meaning of "owned or operated" and thus weighs against imposing a benefit requirement. That is, to "expropriate" is to "transfer (the property of another) to one's own possession," Webster's, *supra,* at 803, and to "nationalize" is to "invest in the central government of a nation the control or ownership of" property, *id.* at 1505. "Where . . . the plain language of the statute is clear, the court generally will not inquire further into its meaning, at least in the absence of a clearly expressed legislative intent to the contrary." Accordingly, we decline to add a benefit element to the "owned or operated" requirement and conclude instead that the phrase "owned or operated" means "possessed or exerted control or influence over" the property at issue.

Nemariam v. Federal Democratic Republic of Ethiopia, 491 F.3d 470, 480-481 (D.C. Cir. 2007). Which view is more persuasive? Regardless of which view is correct, what law determines the "ownership" question?

11. *Section 1605(a)(3) and the Act of State doctrine.* As discussed below, the Act of State doctrine is a judicially created rule that results in U.S. courts declining to adjudicate certain claims involving allegations of violations of international law. *See infra* pp. 797-857. The quotation in Note 4 above from Justice Harlan's opinion in *Sabbatino* was one of the seminal statements of the Act of State doctrine. As discussed below, the *Sabbatino* Court held that U.S. courts "will not examine the validity of a taking of property within its own territory by a foreign sovereign government, extant and recognized by this country at the time of suit, in the absence of a treaty or other unambiguous agreement regarding controlling legal principles, even if the complaint alleges that the taking violates customary international law." 376 U.S. at 428. What effect does the Act of State doctrine have on actions under §1605(a)(3)? Does §1605(a)(3) override the Act of State doctrine? Could it? Does §1605(a)(3) suggest that the analytical foundation of *Sabbatino*— that there is no international consensus on standards of expropriation — is out-of-date? *See infra* pp. 805-806, 813, 815-816. For discussions of the relationship between the FSIA and the Act of State doctrine, *see Agudas Chasidei Chabad v. Russian Fed'n,* 528 F.3d 934 (D.C. Cir. 2008); *Nemariam v. Fed. Democratic Republic of Ethiopia,* 491 F.3d 470 (D.C. Cir. 2007).

12. *Section 1605(a)(3) and due process limitations.* Did Argentina have minimum contacts with the United States sufficient to permit the exercise of personal jurisdiction? What is the evidence of such contacts? For other decisions considering the application of due process constraints under §1605(a)(3), *see Altmann v. Republic of Austria*, 317 F.3d 954, 970 (9th Cir. 2002); *Malewicz v. City of Amsterdam*, 517 F. Supp. 2d 322 (D.D.C. 2007); *Zappia Middle East Constr. Co. Ltd. v. Emirate of Abu Dhabi*, 1996 WL 413680, at *6 (S.D.N.Y. 1996), *aff'd on other grounds*, 215 F.3d 247, 251 (2d Cir. 2000); *Kalamazoo Spice Extraction Co. v. Provisional Military Government of Socialist Ethiopia*, 616 F. Supp. 660, 665-666 (W.D. Mich. 1985).

13. **Section 1605(a)(3) and exhaustion.** Suppose a foreign state provides local remedies for takings of private property. Is a plaintiff under §1605(a)(3) required to exhaust those local remedies before suing the foreign state in the United States? *See Cassirer v. Kingdom of Spain*, 616 F.3d 1019 (9th Cir. 2010) (*en banc*); *Agudas Chasidei Chabad v. Russian Fed'n*, 528 F.3d 934 (D.C. Cir. 2008). Does the language of the FSIA require exhaustion? *Compare* the Torture Victim Protection Act, *supra* pp. 59-60. Does the presence of a similar requirement in the terrorism exception (requiring an opportunity to arbitrate), *infra* p. 358, shed light on whether Congress intended plaintiffs to exhaust their remedies with respect to other exceptions? Would an exhaustion requirement promote the objectives that underpin the FSIA? Is it sensible to require exhaustion when any foreign avenue of relief likely will be in the courts or administrative tribunals of the sovereign alleged to have engaged in the expropriation? Absent exhaustion, has the taking occurred "in violation of international law"? Consider the comments of Justice Breyer from *Altmann* (excerpted above at 241-244):

> [A] plaintiff may have to show an absence of remedies in the foreign country sufficient to compensate for any taking. *Cf.* Restatement (3d) §713, Comment f ("Under international law, ordinarily a state is not required to consider a claim by another state for an injury to its national until that person has exhausted domestic remedies, unless such remedies are clearly sham or inadequate, or their application is unreasonably prolonged"); *Monterey v. Del Monte Dunes at Monterey, Ltd.*, 526 U.S. 687, 721 (1999) (requirement of exhausting available post-deprivation remedies under United States law); *Kirby Forest Industries, Inc. v. United States*, 467 U.S. 1, 10 (1984) (same). A plaintiff who chooses to litigate in this country in disregard of the postdeprivation remedies in the "expropriating" state may have trouble showing a "tak[ing] in violation of international law." 28 U.S.C. §1605(a)(3).

541 U.S. at 714. Is this persuasive? Pay close attention to the excerpt from §713 of the *Restatement (Third)*. Does that concern suits by private parties? What about the two Supreme Court decisions? Do those concern international takings? *See Agudas Chasidei Chabad of U.S. v. Russian Fed'n*, 528 F.3d 934, 949 (D.C. Cir. 2008) ("[O]ne may question whether it makes sense to extend such a requirement from the domestic context, in which state courts are already bound by the U.S. Constitution, to the foreign context, in which the courts that a plaintiff would be required to try may observe no such limit."). On the other hand, isn't Justice Breyer's last point — that a "taking" implies a lack of compensation from available remedies — unassailable?

14. **Does §1605(a)(3) apply where the foreign state defendant did not commit the expropriation?** Recall that the FSIA grants subject matter jurisdiction and, generally, does not create a cause of action. Read the text of §1605(a)(3) carefully. Does it actually require the defendant-foreign state to have expropriated the property? What happens if one state expropriates property, and that property later comes into the possession of another state? In those circumstances, does the expropriation exception potentially strip the second state of its immunity? One recent appellate decision held that it could. *See Cassirer v. Kingdom of Spain*, 616 F.3d 1019, 1028-1031 (9th Cir. 2010) (*en banc*). According to the majority:

the plain language of the statute does not require that the foreign state against whom the claim is made be the entity which took the property in violation of international law. Section 1605(a)(3) simply excepts from immunity "a foreign state" in any case "in which *rights in property taken in violation of international law* are in issue." (emphasis added). The text is written in the passive voice, which "focuses on an event that occurs without respect to a specific actor." . . . Our reading of the text is buttressed by the articulated purpose of the FSIA to immunize foreign states for their public, but not for their commercial, acts. As Congress declared: "Under international law, states are not immune from the jurisdiction of foreign courts insofar as their commercial activities are concerned." 28 U.S.C. §1602 (Findings and Declaration of Purpose). Consistent with this purpose, §1605(a)(3) restricts jurisdiction over an entity of a foreign state that owns property taken in violation of international law to those engaged in commercial activity in the United States. No other restriction is manifest.

. . .

Finally, the Foundation posits that bizarre consequences unintended by Congress will occur if §1605(a)(3) is interpreted as granting jurisdiction against foreign entities regardless of who did the expropriating or when, and regardless of whether the defendant was a good faith purchaser. We cannot say whether floodgates might open, but in any event, jurisdictional boundaries are for Congress to set, not for courts to write around.

The dissent responded:

Congress intended the FSIA to be consistent with international law. . . . When customary international law concludes that an act by a foreign state, that is, the taking of property in violation of international law, is no longer a sovereign act, the foreign state is no longer entitled to sovereign immunity. International law therefore supports the exercise of jurisdiction over foreign states that have themselves taken property in violation of international law; it does not support the exercise of jurisdiction over sovereign entities that have legitimately acquired property that was at some other time and by some other foreign state taken in violation of international law. To conclude otherwise would provide U.S. courts with unbridled jurisdiction over any sovereign foreign state that has in its possession property that was at one time taken in violation of international law by another foreign state. It would not matter if the expropriation occurred seventy years ago, as in this case, or seven hundred years ago. Congress would not have intended such a result. . . . [B]ecause Spain is a sovereign with immunity from suit, we should respect that unless we have better reason than merely a deserving victim of Nazi aggression. Equally important, and I think a part of comity, is the common sense notion of the golden rule. We should not do to other nations what we would not want other nations to do to us. I am concerned that by indulging now the sympathetic claim of Cassirer as a Jewish heir with entitlement to priceless art stolen by Nazi Germany, but doing so at the cost of fairness to Spain and disrespect of its sovereignty, we will likely sow the seeds of maltreatment of the United States and its officials in foreign courts. 616 F.3d at 1038-1044 (Gould, J., dissenting).

Which view makes more sense as a matter of statutory construction? As a matter of policy? Is this simply a drafting error that Congress needs to correct? Or are the implications of an erroneous rule sufficiently weighty that the majority should have interpreted the statute to apply only to the country engaging in the expropriation?

4. Waiver of Sovereign Immunity

The FSIA subjects foreign states to jurisdiction in U.S. courts where they have waived, or can be deemed to have waived, their immunity. Section §1605(a)(1) provides that a foreign state will not enjoy immunity if it "has waived its immunity either explicitly or by implication."[136] The Act provides no further guidance regarding what will constitute a waiver under §1605(a)(1), and the FSIA's legislative history is only slightly more illuminating:

> With respect to implicit waivers, the courts have found such waivers in cases where a foreign state has agreed to arbitration in another country or where a foreign state has agreed that the law of a particular country should govern a contract. An implicit waiver would also include a situation where a foreign state has filed a responsive pleading in an action without raising the defense of foreign sovereign immunity.[137]

Although the proposition that a foreign state should be held to a waiver of its sovereign immunity appears straightforward, lower courts have encountered difficulty applying §1605(a)(1). First, it has not always been clear whether particular foreign state acts or agreements constitute implied waivers of immunity under §1605(a)(1). In particular, choice-of-law and choice-of-forum clauses have presented thorny questions of interpretation.

Second, unlike §1605's other exceptions to immunity, neither §1605(a)(1) nor its legislative history appear to require any nexus between a foreign state's waiver and the United States.[138] Read literally, §1605(a)(1) would permit U.S. jurisdiction in all cases involving *any* "waiver" of immunity by a foreign state, even if a case has no connection to the United States and even if the foreign state's waiver was intended to apply only to proceedings in another country's courts. *Verlinden BV v. Central Bank of Nigeria*, excerpted below, illustrates both of these difficulties.

Closely related to §1605(a)(1)'s "waiver" provision is the "arbitration exception," contained in §1605(a)(6). Section 1605(a)(6) was added to the FSIA in 1988, when the Act was amended to deny foreign states immunity for actions to enforce certain arbitration agreements or confirm certain arbitral awards. Section 1605(a)(6) provides that a foreign state shall not be immune in any case:

> in which the action is brought, either to enforce an agreement made by the foreign state with or for the benefit of a private party to submit to arbitration all or any differences which have arisen or which may arise between the parties with respect to a defined legal relationship, whether contractual or not, concerning a subject matter capable of settlement by arbitration under the laws of the United States, or to confirm an award made pursuant to such an agreement to arbitrate, if (A) the arbitration takes place or is intended to take place in the United States, (B) the agreement or award is or may be governed by a treaty or other international agreement in force for the United States calling for the recognition and enforcement of arbitral awards, (C) the underlying claim, save for the agreement to arbitrate, could have been brought in a United States court under this section or section 1607, or (D) paragraph (1) of this subsection is otherwise applicable.

Section 1605(a)(6) expressly preserved the waiver provisions of §1605(a)(1), but went further by making clear that U.S. courts would have jurisdiction over foreign states in actions to enforce international arbitration agreements and awards having minimum

---

136. 28 U.S.C. §1605(a)(1).
137. H.R. Rep. No. 1487, 94th Cong., 2d Sess. 18, *reprinted in* 1976 U.S. Code Cong. & Admin. News at 6617.
138. *Compare 28* U.S.C. §1605(a)(2) ("commercial activity carried on in the United States") and §1605(a)(5) (noncommercial tort "occurring in the United States"). *See Verlinden BV v. Central Bank of Nigeria*, 461 U.S. 480, 490 n.15 (1983).

connections with the United States.[139] The operation of this provision is illustrated by the decision in *Cargill Int'l, SA v. M/T Pavel Dybenko.*[140]

VERLINDEN BV v. CENTRAL BANK OF NIGERIA
488 F. Supp. 1284 (S.D.N.Y. 1980)

WEINFELD, DISTRICT JUDGE. Verlinden BV ("Verlinden"), a Dutch corporation with its principal offices in Amsterdam, The Netherlands, commenced this action for anticipatory breach of an irrevocable documentary letter of credit established in its favor by the defendant Central Bank of Nigeria, and advised and payable by its correspondent bank, Morgan Guaranty Trust Company in New York. The defendant Central Bank of Nigeria ("Central Bank") is the central bank of the Federal Republic of Nigeria ("Nigeria") and is an "agency or instrumentality of a foreign state" within the meaning of the FSIA.

Although the instant action is based upon the alleged breach and repudiation by Central Bank of its obligations with respect to the irrevocable letter of credit, in order to put the matter into proper perspective, it is necessary to refer to events prior and subsequent to its issuance. On April 21, 1975, plaintiff entered into a contract whereby Nigeria agreed to buy from plaintiff, 240,000 metric tons of Portland Cement for the price of $60 per ton, or a total of $14,400,000.[141] The Nigerian government agreed to establish, within 21 days after the contract was signed, "an Irrevocable, Transferable abroad, Divisible and confirmed Letter of Credit in favor of the seller for the total purchase price through Slavenburg's Bank, Amsterdam, Netherlands."[142] . . . The parties also agreed that the contract was to be governed by the Laws of the Netherlands and that disputes arising thereunder would be resolved by arbitration before the International Chamber of Commerce, Paris, France. . . .

[O]n June 23, 1975 the defendant established its Documentary Credit No. CBN/BP/75/145 ("the letter of credit" or "the credit") in favor of plaintiff for the full contract price ($14,400,000); the credit included [as required by Nigeria's cement agreement with plaintiff] an open-ended amount for demurrage, to be paid at the rate of $3,500 per day per vessel. However, contrary to the terms of the cement agreement, the letter of credit was advised by and made payable through Morgan Guaranty Bank in New York, rather than plaintiff's bank (Slavenburg's) in the Netherlands [and, in addition, the credit varied from the terms of the cement agreement in other material respects]. . . .

In August 1975, the ports of Nigeria became bottlenecked with hundreds of ships carrying cargoes of cement, sent by more than 68 other cement suppliers from whom Nigeria had purchased cement. As a result of the increasing congestion in these ports, Central Bank commencing in mid-September 1975 unilaterally directed its correspondent banks, including Morgan, to adopt a series of amendments to all irrevocable letters of credit issued in connection with the cement contracts. In essence, the advising banks were directed to stop demurrage payments against documents unless those documents had been sent to and certified for payment by Central Bank. . . . It can hardly be questioned—and the parties do not seriously dispute the fact—that these unilateral

---

139. 28 U.S.C. §1605(a)(6).

140. 991 F.2d 1012 (2d Cir. 1993); *infra* pp. 340-342.

141. The contract was signed by the "Permanent Secretary, Ministry of Defense, Lagos . . . on behalf of the Federal Military Government of the Federal Republic of Nigeria."

142. The letter of credit was to be governed by the Uniform Customs and Practice for Documentary Credits (The International Chamber of Commerce Brochure No. 222) (1962 Revision). . . .

amendments to the irrevocable letter of credit constitute violations of the Uniform Customs and Practice for Documentary Credits the terms of which, by stipulation of the parties, are applicable.

Plaintiff alleges that, in reliance upon the issuance of an irrevocable letter of credit as agreed upon, it contracted with another European concern, Interbuco Anstalt, Vaduz, Liechtenstein ("Interbuco"), for the purchase of cement and thereby exposed itself to a potential liability in liquidated damages. It seeks to recover damages for payments already made or owing to Interbuco, as well as its own lost profits, counsel fees and expenses in the sum of $4,660,000 as compensatory damages and punitive damages in a like amount. Presently before the Court are the defendant's motion to dismiss the action for, [among other things,] lack of subject matter jurisdiction [and] lack of in personam jurisdiction over Central Bank based upon sovereign immunity. . . .

Foreign states are not immune from the jurisdiction of the courts of the United States in any case "(1) in which the foreign state has waived its immunity either explicitly or by implication, . . . notwithstanding any withdrawal of the waiver which the foreign state may purport to effect except in accordance with the terms of the waiver." . . . There is no assertion in the case at bar that the defendant has explicitly waived its immunity; instead, plaintiff argues that Central Bank has implicitly waived its immunity in two related aspects. The cement contract signed by Nigeria and Verlinden contains the following provision:

> The construction, validity and performance of *this contract* shall be governed by the Laws of the Netherlands and all disputes of any nature whatsoever which may arise under, out of, in connection with, or in relation to *this contract* shall be submitted to the arbitration of the International Chamber of Commerce, Paris, France, in accordance with its Rules at the date thereof. (Emphasis supplied.)

Plaintiff contends that Nigeria's choice of a foreign forum for arbitration and of foreign law precludes it from asserting any immunity, on its own behalf or that of its instrumentalities, with respect to any issue connected with the Verlinden cement contract. Specifically, Verlinden contends that Nigeria's choice of Dutch law and a French tribunal constitutes a waiver of objection to American jurisdiction, and that this waiver is binding as well upon Central Bank, Nigeria's instrumentality charged with the task of making payments under the cement contract. Some support for this view appears in the cryptic language of the Congressional report, which noted:

> With respect to implicit waivers, the courts have found such waivers in cases where a foreign state has agreed to arbitration in another country or where a foreign state has agreed that the law of a particular country should govern a contract. An implicit waiver would also include a situation where a foreign state has filed a responsive pleading in an action without raising the defense of sovereign immunity.

Moreover, at least one court has held, in one of the other cement contract cases, that Nigeria's choice of European laws and a European forum to resolve disputes constituted a waiver of its sovereign immunity in the American courts. Even if that case were correct on the law, it is inapplicable to the facts here.[143]

---

143. *Ipitrade International, SA v. Federal Republic of Nigeria,* 465 F. Supp. 824 (D.D.C. 1978), did not require a decision on the issue of implicit waiver. The Ipitrade action was brought to enforce an arbitration award against Nigeria made by a French tribunal applying Swiss law. The District Court had subject matter jurisdiction of the enforcement action by virtue of a treaty to which the United States, France, Switzerland, and Nigeria all are parties. 9 U.S.C. §§201-208 (Supp. 1980). The treaty explicitly federalizes all such enforcement actions, id.§203,

Here plaintiff, for reasons which are apparent, has decided not to sue upon its cement agreement with Nigeria. Instead it bases its claim upon the Verlinden letter of credit. But that instrument, unlike the contract, is devoid of any provision accepting foreign law for its interpretation, nor does it name any foreign tribunal for arbitration.

Plaintiff seeks to blur the distinctions between two separate obligations binding between different parties. The cement contract was signed by Nigeria's Minister of Defense on behalf of the Nigerian government; Central Bank is not a party to that agreement, which binds only Verlinden and Nigeria. By its very definition, the letter of credit is a separate and distinct obligation;[144] in this case, it bound only Central Bank, and not the Nigerian government. Nigeria's obligation under the contract was "*to establish*" the letter of credit in favor of Verlinden within a specified period of time. Central Bank's obligation under the letter of credit matured upon presentation of appropriate documents. Nigeria undertook no obligations under the letter of credit; nor did Central Bank, under the contract. This is not a hypertechnical distinction. The contract indicates that to whatever extent, if at all, Nigeria waived its immunity by reason of the arbitration provision, it did so only with respect to the contract, not the credit. Plaintiff can hardly have been unaware of these distinctions when it chose to pursue its remedies against Central Bank under the credit, rather than against Nigeria under the contract.

Even if Nigeria's waiver of immunity under one contract were held to bind its instrumentality under a different obligation, we would nevertheless find no implicit waiver, for Nigeria itself has never implicitly accepted the jurisdiction of American courts. The Congressional history cited by the plaintiff is not dispositive of this issue, indeed, it is at most ambiguous. The comment in the Congressional report, previously mentioned, that the courts had found an implicit waiver "where a foreign state has agreed to arbitration in another country or . . . agreed that the law of a particular country" would apply does not necessarily constitute an endorsement of that result.[145] More importantly, it is by no means clear that Congress intended, in referring to "another country" or "a particular country," to include a third-party country the adoption of whose law or forum by a foreign state as one of the contracting parties would operate as a waiver thereby subjecting the foreign state to jurisdiction in this country. It may be reasonable to suggest that a sovereign state which agrees to be governed by the laws of the United States — which is both "another country" and "a particular country" — has implicitly waived its ability to assert the defense of sovereign immunity when sued in an American court. But it is quite another matter to suggest, as did the Court in *Ipitrade*,[146] that a sovereign state which agrees to be governed by the laws of a third-party country — such as the Netherlands — is thereby precluded asserting its immunity in an American court.

Although both of these interpretations may be consistent with the literal language of the single paragraph of legislative history that addresses implicit waivers, there are strong reasons to reject the latter view. By its peculiar mixture of substantive and procedural provisions, the FSIA confers personal jurisdiction over all foreign states not entitled to immunity (assuming that valid service has been effectuated). Proof of an implicit waiver

---

and sharply constricts the scope of review of arbitral awards. Id. §207. By signing the treaty Nigeria had explicitly waived its objection to such enforcement actions.

144. See Uniform Customs and Practice for Documentary Credits (1962 Rev.); General Provisions and Definitions §(c) ("Credits, by their nature, are separate transactions from the sales or other contracts on which they may be based and banks are in no way concerned with or bound by such contracts.").

145. [House Report No. 1487, 94th Cong., 2d Sess. 18, *reprinted in* 1976 U.S. Code Cong. & Admin. News at 6617.] There is no indication as to which cases the legislators were referring, or even whether they were cases decided under American law by American courts.

146. *Ipitrade International, SA v. Federal Republic of Nigeria*, 465 F. Supp. 824 (D.D.C. 1978).

absolutely defeats the assertion of sovereign immunity. If the language of the Act is applied literally, the result is that a foreign sovereign which has waived its immunity can be subjected to the personal jurisdiction of United States courts regardless of the nature or quality of its contacts with this country.[147]

Plaintiff's view, if adopted, would presage a vast increase in the jurisdiction of federal courts in matters involving sensitive foreign relations: whenever a foreign sovereign had contracted with a private party anywhere in the world, and chose to be governed by the laws or answer in the forum of any country other than its own, it would expose itself to personal liability in the courts of the United States. Verlinden and Nigeria could scarcely have foreseen this untoward result when they signed the contract; and it is unlikely that Congress could have intended it.

Because the Act's waiver provision is written as broadly as it is, it is incumbent upon the Court to narrow that provision's scope. We need not now decide whether the Court would have personal jurisdiction over a foreign state whose only contact with this country occurs by virtue of a private agreement in which it adopts American law or an American forum. We only hold that when a foreign state agrees to submit its disputes with another, non-American private party to the laws of a third country, or to answer in the tribunals of such country, it does not implicitly waive its immunity to the jurisdiction of the courts of the United States. Because Nigeria has not waived the defense of sovereign immunity in the American courts, it necessarily follows that Central Bank has not either.

In sum, we find that none of the exceptions to the Act is applicable here. The motion of the defendant to dismiss the complaint for lack of personal jurisdiction under the FSIA is granted.

CARGILL INT'L, SA v. M/T PAVEL DYBENKO
991 F.2d 1012 (2d Cir. 1993)

OAKES, CIRCUIT JUDGE. [The case arose when Cargill, BV ("CBV") purchased 7,000 tons of soybean oil from Cargill International SA ("CISA"). CISA entered into a charter party with Novorossiysk, an entity owned by the former Soviet Union, to ship the oil from Argentina to the Netherlands on board Novorossiysk's vessel, the M/T Pavel Dybenko. When it arrived, the oil was contaminated. Pursuant to an arbitration clause in the charter party, CISA commenced arbitration in London against Novorossiysk. Simultaneously, CISA and CBV brought an action against Novorossiysk, seeking to compel it to arbitrate against both of them. Although CBV was not a signatory to the charter party, it claimed third-party beneficiary status thereunder. The district court dismissed the action, holding inter alia that neither §1605(a)(1) nor §1605(a)(6) granted it jurisdiction.]

The waiver exception permits federal courts to assert jurisdiction over any foreign sovereign that waives its immunity "either explicitly or by implication." [§1605(a)(1).] The House Report which accompanied the FSIA listed three examples of implicit waivers: when (1) a foreign state has agreed to arbitrate in another country; (2) a foreign state has agreed that the law of a particular country shall govern; or (3) a foreign state has filed a responsive pleading but has failed to raise the defense of sovereign immunity.

---

147. There is reason to believe that Congress did not anticipate this problem at all. On the one hand, the legislative history indicates that Congress intended the courts to exercise personal jurisdiction only over foreign states having sufficient contacts with the United States. See [House Report No. 1487, 94th Cong., 2d Sess. 13-14, reprinted in 1976 U.S. Code Cong. & Admin. News at 6612.] On the other hand, the statute it wrote permits the assertion of jurisdiction either when there are sufficient contacts (i.e., when one of the commercial activity exceptions has been met) or when there has been a waiver.

[H.R. Rep. No. 1487, 94th Cong., 2d Sess. 18, *reprinted in* 1976 U.S. Code Cong. & Admin. News at 6617.]

In *Zernicek v. Petroleos Mexicanos,* 614 F. Supp. 407, 411 (S.D. Tex. 1985), *aff'd,* 826 F.2d 415 (5th Cir. 1987), the court noted that courts have interpreted the waiver provision narrowly: "most courts have refused to find an implicit waiver of immunity to suit in American courts from a contract clause providing for arbitration in a country other than the United States." Moreover, it is rare for a court to find that a country's waiver of immunity extends to third parties not privy to the contract. When the case involves an implied waiver, we think that a court should be even more hesitant to extend the waiver in favor of third parties. We agree with these courts that such a waiver will not be implied absent strong evidence of the sovereign's intent. In *Maritime Ventures Int'l, Inc. v. Caribbean Trading & Fidelity, Ltd.,* 689 F. Supp. 1340, 1351 (S.D.N.Y. 1988), the court warned that a broader interpretation "would result in a vast increase in the jurisdiction of the federal courts over matters involving sensitive foreign relations." Because of these concerns, an agreement to arbitrate in a foreign country, without more, ought not to operate as a waiver of sovereign immunity in United States courts, especially in favor of a non-party to the agreement. Thus, CBV may not depend on Novorossiysk's agreement to arbitrate with CISA in London to show that the Soviet entity had impliedly waived its immunity to jurisdiction in the United States [under §1605(a)(1)].

Section 1605(a)(6)(B) of the FSIA provides an exception to sovereign immunity in cases where a foreign state has agreed to arbitrate and the arbitration agreement is or may be governed by a treaty signed by the United States calling for the recognition and enforcement of arbitral awards. CBV argues that it may enforce the arbitration clause contained in the Charter Party against Novorossiysk as a third party beneficiary to the Charter Party, and that this clause is governed by the Convention on the Recognition and Enforcement of Foreign Arbitral Awards, 21 U.S.T. 2517 (the "Convention"). As stated by Senator Mathias, the main sponsor of the bill to amend the FSIA to provide for this exception, "unless the arbitration agreement is enforceable, the arbitration is meaningless. . . . This amendment will reassure businesses that the international arbitration process will work. It does so by amending the FSIA to say that an agreement to arbitrate constitutes a waiver of immunity in an action to enforce that agreement or the resultant award." 131 Cong. Rec. S5369 (daily ed. May 3, 1985) (Statement of Sen. Mathias). . . .

As the Supreme Court observed in *Scherk v. Alberto-Culver Co.,* 417 U.S. 506, 520 n.15 (1974),

> [t]he goal of the Convention, and the principal purpose underlying the American adoption and implementation of it, was to encourage recognition and enforcement of commercial arbitration agreements in international contracts and to unify the standards by which agreements to arbitrate are observed and arbitral awards are enforced in the signatory countries.

Thus, the Convention should be broadly interpreted to effectuate the goals of the legislation. Moreover, when the Convention is read together with the FSIA's arbitration exception, which gives jurisdiction if an arbitration agreement "is or *may be* governed" by a treaty, [§1605(a)(6)(B)] (emphasis added), it evinces a strong legislative intent to provide enforcement for such agreements. We agree with CBV that the Convention is exactly the sort of treaty Congress intended to include in the arbitration exception. If the alleged arbitration agreement exists, it satisfies the requirements for subject matter jurisdiction under the Convention and FSIA.

We believe the district court in this case erred in deciding that it could not assess CBV's third party beneficiary argument because it did not have jurisdiction to make this initial determination. Rather than considering the allegations to see if they gave the court subject matter jurisdiction, the court stated that "regardless of the merits," the contractual arguments could not be addressed. According to the court, it lacked subject matter jurisdiction because there was no arbitration agreement. We find, however, that the district court was required to weigh the contractual arguments before it could determine that no arbitration agreement existed.

"'Jurisdiction to determine jurisdiction' refers to the power of a court to determine whether it has jurisdiction over the parties to and the subject matter of a suit. . . ." As the Supreme Court noted in *Verlinden,* 461 U.S. at 493-94 "[t]he statute must be applied by the district courts in every action against a foreign sovereign, since subject-matter jurisdiction in any such action depends on the existence of one of the specified exceptions to foreign sovereign immunity. . . . At the threshold of every action in a district court against a foreign state, therefore, the court must satisfy itself that one of the exceptions applies — and in doing so it must apply the detailed federal law standards set forth in the Act." Thus, the district court must look at the substance of the allegations to determine jurisdiction. . . .

CBV alleges that CISA and Novorossiysk intended to make CBV a third party beneficiary of the Charter Party and in particular of its arbitration clause. Thus, to determine whether subject matter jurisdiction existed, the district court ought to have determined whether, if the facts as alleged by CBV are true, the arbitration agreement in the Charter Party was intended to benefit CBV. . . . We note that if CBV is found to be a third party beneficiary to the Charter Party, it may be proper for the district court to enforce the arbitration agreement against Novorossiysk.

Notes *on* Verlinden *and* Cargill

1. *Construction of implied waivers of sovereign immunity.* As *Verlinden* and *Cargill* illustrate, most courts have reasoned that waivers of immunity are disfavored and not lightly to be inferred. *E.g., Carpenter v. Republic of Chile,* 610 F.3d 776, 779 (2d Cir. 2010); *Calzadilla v. Banco Latino Internacional,* 413 F.3d 1285, 1287 (11th Cir. 2005); *In re Republic of Philippines,* 309 F.3d 1143, 1151 (9th Cir. 2002); *Gates v. Victor Fine Foods,* 54 F.3d 1457 (9th Cir. 1995) ("the waiver exception must be narrowly construed"); *Frolova v. USSR,* 761 F.2d 370, 377 (7th Cir. 1985) (courts "have been reluctant to stray beyond" examples of waivers in FSIA's legislative history and have "narrowly construed" purported waivers); *Castro v. Saudi Arabia,* 510 F. Supp. 309, 312 (W.D. Tex. 1980) ("There must be an intentional and knowing relinquishment of the legal right."); *In re China Oil and Gas Pipeline Bureau,* 94 S.W.3d 50, 58-59 (Tex. App. 2002) (implicit waivers under FSIA must be "narrowly construed"). In contrast, a few other courts have adopted expansive views of asserted waivers of sovereign immunity. *E.g., Proyecfin de Venezuela, SA v. Banco Industrial de Venezuela, SA,* 760 F.2d 390, 392 (2d Cir. 1985) ("broad reading of implicit waivers").

Which approach to the interpretation of purported waivers is more sensible? Is it necessary to adopt any general rule of construction? How should one interpret the fairly broad language about waivers in the FSIA's legislative history? *See* H.R. Rep. No. 1487, 94th Cong., 2d Sess. 18, *reprinted in* 1976 U.S. Code Cong. & Admin. News at 6617.

Note that the U.N. State Immunities Convention does not have a general waiver provision, and instead addresses the subject in Articles 8 and 9 (participation in litigation; counterclaims) and 17 (arbitration agreements). Is this wise? Why shouldn't there be express recognition of a foreign state's ability to waive its immunity?

2. Verlinden — *a U.S. "nexus" requirement for waivers?* Foreign states waive their immunity every day, for all sorts of purposes. They waive their immunity from the jurisdiction of different national courts (or arbitral tribunals) in particular contracts or legislation; they submit to the exclusive or nonexclusive jurisdiction of different courts or tribunals; and they agree to be bound by different national laws in various connections.

Read literally, §1605(a)(1) says that a "waiver" of immunity by a foreign state confers personal and subject matter jurisdiction on U.S. courts. *Verlinden* reasoned that, if the FSIA's waiver provision is "applied literally, the result is that a foreign sovereign which has waived its immunity can be subjected to the personal jurisdiction of United States courts regardless of the nature or quality of its contacts with this country." Consequently, the court reasoned, "it is incumbent upon the Court to narrow [§1605(a)(1)'s] scope." Is §1605(a)(1) in fact so open-ended? When it refers to "waivers" of immunity, what sorts of waivers of immunity must §1605(a)(1) have in mind — waivers of immunity from the jurisdiction of U.S. courts, or waivers of something else? If a foreign state impliedly waives its immunity by consenting to the jurisdiction of some foreign court (*e.g.*, Dutch), is that a waiver of immunity from the jurisdiction of U.S. courts? Is this not a fairly straightforward way of making sense out of §1605(a)(1)'s waiver exception? What if the state waives "immunity to suit in any court"? *See Capital Ventures Int'l v. Republic of Argentina*, 552 F.3d 289 (2d Cir. 2009).

3. *Due process limitations on §1605(a)(1)'s waiver exception.* *Verlinden* said that §1605(a)(1)'s scope needed to be restricted, but it did not expressly provide a general formula for doing so. Nonetheless, Judge Weinfeld's opinion suggests limiting waivers to those relating to activities by foreign states that would, putting aside the waiver, have "minimum contacts" with the United States for due process purposes. Is that persuasive? Does the minimum contacts test even apply to foreign sovereigns? *See infra* pp. 352, 355, 359. Is it not more sensible to look at the terms of the foreign state's waiver to determine whether or not the foreign state has waived its immunity from U.S. courts' jurisdiction?

Verlinden suggested that personal jurisdiction might be lacking "over a foreign state whose only contact with this country occurs by virtue of a private agreement in which it adopts American law or an American forum." Is this correct? Note that Judge Weinfeld expressed doubt as to both choice of law and choice of forum clauses. Why should a foreign state's agreement submitting to U.S. courts' jurisdiction not constitute a valid waiver, even absent any other U.S. contacts? Judge Weinfeld's suggestion is squarely contrary to the rationale of *Marlowe v. Argentine Naval Commission*, 604 F. Supp. 703 (D.D.C. 1985), which found an effective waiver of immunity in a foreign sovereign's consent to a choice of U.S. law. The court reasoned that this waiver of immunity in U.S. courts was effective even "in the absence of the normally required minimum contacts." 604 F. Supp. at 710.

Consider Judge Weinfeld's suggestion in *Verlinden* that some additional showing of U.S. contacts is necessary for personal jurisdiction over a foreign state-related entity that expressly consents to U.S. jurisdiction. *Cf. Verlinden BV v. Central Bank of Nigeria*, 461 U.S. 480, 490 n.15 (1983) ("Section 1605(a)(1), which provides that sovereign immunity shall not apply if waived, may be seen as an exception to the normal pattern of the Act, which generally requires some form of contact with the United States. We need not decide whether, by waiving its immunity, a foreign state could consent to suit based on activities wholly unrelated to the United States."). Is Judge Weinfeld's view consistent with due process precedents, which generally treat such submissions to jurisdiction as establishing "minimum contacts" with the chosen forum? *National Equip. Rental, Ltd. v. Szukhent*, 375 U.S. 311, 324-330 (1964). *See supra* pp. 114-115. *See also infra* pp. 345-346 (agreement to arbitrate in the United States held waiver of immunity from action to enforce arbitration agreement in U.S. courts). Would due process analysis be any different for a choice of law clause selecting U.S. law? *See infra* pp. 345-346.

4. *Agreement by foreign state submitting to jurisdiction of national courts as waiver.* Foreign states frequently agree to forum selection clauses, by which they agree to litigate disputes relating to a contract in a specified forum, either exclusively or nonexclusively. *See infra* pp. 462-464. If a foreign state agrees to such a clause, it will often be held to have waived its immunity with respect to *some* types of proceedings in *some* court, but it will be less clear that the foreign state's waiver extends to a particular action on the merits in *U.S.* courts (as opposed to some foreign state's courts).

(a) Agreement by foreign state submitting to jurisdiction of U.S. courts. The agreement of a foreign state to a forum selection clause designating U.S. courts as the contractual forum would appear to constitute a waiver of sovereign immunity in an action on the merits in U.S. courts for purposes of §1605(a)(1). Is this result inevitable? Could a party merely be undertaking to appear in U.S. courts for the purpose of asserting its sovereign immunity (which, after all, can be expressly waived)?

(b) Agreement by foreign state submitting to jurisdiction of a third state's courts. The effect under §1605(a)(1) of a choice of forum clause selecting the courts of a third country is less clear. For example, suppose a Russian state-owned company and a U.S. company enter into a contract with a forum selection clause designating English courts. Several lower courts have indicated that agreement to such a clause will not constitute a waiver of immunity in an action on the merits in U.S. courts. *E.g., Ohntrup v. Firearms Center,* 516 F. Supp. 1281, 1285 (E.D. Pa. 1981), *aff'd,* 760 F.2d 259 (3d Cir. 1985) ("a waiver of immunity by a state as to one jurisdiction cannot be interpreted as a waiver as to all jurisdictions"); *Chicago Bridge & Iron Co. v. Islamic Republic of Iran,* 506 F. Supp. 981, 987 (N.D. Ill. 1980) ("the presence of third-party choice of law and forum clauses does not in any sense implicitly consent to jurisdiction" of U.S. courts).

These decisions are at least arguably supported by the Supreme Court's comment in *Argentine Republic v. Amerada Hess Shipping Corp.,* 488 U.S. 428, 442-443 (1989) that "we [do not] see how a foreign state can waive its immunity under §1605(a)(1) by signing an international agreement that contains no mention of a waiver of immunity to suit in United States courts or even the availability of a cause of action in the United States."

Are the above decisions the only plausible view of forum selection clauses that choose non-U.S. courts? There is a distinction, discussed *infra* pp. 462-464, between exclusive and nonexclusive forum selection clauses. Should a nonexclusive choice of forum clause permitting (but not requiring) suit in a designated third-country foreign forum constitute a general waiver of sovereign immunity, including immunity for purposes of U.S. litigation on the merits? Doesn't a foreign state's agreement to litigation in foreign courts (even if the chosen courts are not U.S. courts) indicate that the state is engaged in nonimmune activities and that the private party expects objective, judicial enforcement?

Consider Judge Weinfeld's concern that this view of §1605(a)(1) would allow suits in U.S. courts against foreign parties "anywhere in the world" where the contract contained a forum selection clause. *See also Maritime Ventures Int'l, Inc. v. Caribbean Trading & Fidelity Ltd.,* 689 F. Supp. 1340, 1351 (S.D.N.Y. 1988). Assuming that this is correct, wouldn't this concern be met by Judge Weinfeld's (and the Due Process Clause's) requirement of a nexus between the defendant's cause of action and the United States?

Note that an exclusive choice of forum clause selecting a non-U.S. forum would generally provide an independent basis for dismissing a U.S. action—since the parties' agreement to litigate in a non-U.S. forum would ordinarily be enforceable. *See infra* pp. 464-472. What about a foreign state's immunity in an action in U.S. courts to enforce a foreign judgment resulting from foreign litigation pursuant to the forum selection clause? What about a foreign state's immunity from an action on the merits in U.S. courts if the foreign state refuses to honor its forum selection agreement?

(c) Agreement by foreign state submitting to jurisdiction of foreign state's own courts. A foreign state's agreement to submit contractual disputes to its own judicial system has generally not been deemed a waiver of immunity in an action on the merits in U.S. courts. *Corzo v. Banco Cent. de Reserva del Peru,* 243 F.3d 519, 522-524 (9th Cir. 2001); *Atlantic Tele-Network, Inc. v. Inter-American Development Bank,* 251 F. Supp. 2d 126, 133-134 (D.D.C. 2003); *Perez v. The Bahamas,* 482 F. Supp. 1208 (D.D.C. 1980), *aff'd,* 652 F.2d 186 (D.C. Cir. 1981). Is this result necessarily correct? As already suggested, does a foreign state's agreement to have a dispute resolved by judicial processes not show that its contractual rights are the subject of judicial resolution — reflective of a quintessentially private, commercial status? Does this constitute a waiver of immunity or is it evidence of a commercial activity?

(d) Defective forum selection agreements. As discussed in Chapter 5 at *infra* pp. 464-472, 456-528, U.S. law imposes a variety of restrictions on private parties' acceptance of forum selection clauses. These cases generally require submissions to jurisdiction to be "reasonable" and to be free of unconscionability. Are there circumstances in which a foreign state could avail itself of these requirements by arguing that its waiver of immunity was defective? *Cf.* Kahale & Vega, *Immunity and Jurisdiction: Toward a Uniform Body of Law in Actions Against Foreign States,* 18 Colum. J. Transnat'l L. 211, 231-235 (1979) (arguing that waiver agreed to by officials lacking authority under foreign law to bind foreign state is defective).

Could a private party argue that an exclusive forum selection clause, choosing a non-U.S. forum, constituted a waiver of immunity, but was not enforceable as to the selected foreign forum, relying on generally applicable defenses to forum selection agreements (*see infra* pp. 486-528)?

5. Agreement by foreign state selecting national law to govern contract as waiver. Foreign states also frequently agree to choice of law clauses, selecting a specific national law to govern a contract to which they also agree. *See infra* pp. 756-773. These clauses are specifically referred to in the FSIA's legislative history (albeit in general terms). H.R. Rep. No. 1487, 94th Cong., 2d Sess. 18, *reprinted in* 1976 U.S. Code Cong. & Admin. News at 6617. Should such choice-of-law clauses be treated like forum selection clauses, which have often been held to constitute waivers of sovereign immunity (at least as to the specific forum)?

(a) Agreement by foreign state selecting U.S. law as waiver. Most U.S. courts have held that a foreign state's agreement to a choice of law clause selecting U.S. law constitutes a waiver of sovereign immunity in an action on the merits in U.S. courts. *E.g., Eckert Int'l, Inc. v. Government of Fiji,* 32 F.3d 77 (4th Cir. 1994); *Transamerican SS Corp. v. Somali Democratic Republic,* 767 F.2d 998, 1005 (D.C. Cir. 1985) (Wald, J., concurring); *Farhang v. Indian Institute of Tech.,* 2010 U.S. Dist. LEXIS 5781 (N.D. Cal. 2010); *Ghawanmeh v. Islamic Saudi Academy,* 672 F. Supp. 2d 3 (D.D.C. 2009); *Lafarge Canada, Inc. v. Bank of China,* 2000 WL 1457012 (S.D.N.Y. 2000); *Berkakin v. Consulado de la Republica de El Salvador,* 912 F. Supp. 458 (C.D. Cal. 1995) (lease selecting California law held to waive immunity); *Marlowe v. Argentine Naval Comm'n,* 604 F. Supp. 703 (D.D.C. 1985); *Ohntrup v. Firearms Center,* 516 F. Supp. 1281 (E.D. Pa. 1981), *aff'd,* 760 F.2d 259 (3d Cir. 1985). There is fairly strong support in the FSIA's legislative history for this view. H.R. Rep. No. 1487, 94th Cong., 2d Sess. 18, *reprinted in* 1976 U.S. Code Cong. & Admin. News at 6617. *Compare Gates v. Victor Fine Foods,* 54 F.3d 1457 (9th Cir. 1995) (choice of law clause in one contract does not waive immunity from claims under separate agreement).

Is it inevitable that a foreign sovereign's agreement to be bound by U.S. law is a submission to the jurisdiction of the U.S. courts? One judge has argued that "[i]n the House Report, Congress declared that a foreign government may not assume duties generally under United States law, only to disclaim them by invoking immunity in United States court when a controversy arises." *Transamerican SS Corp. v. Somali Democratic Republic,* 767 F.2d 998, 1006 (D.C. Cir. 1985) (Wald, J., concurring). Doesn't this confuse applicable law and jurisdiction: there is no reason to suppose that parties choosing one law to apply could not have intended the courts in another country to apply that law. *Cf. Burger King Corp. v. Rudzewicz,* 471 U.S. 462 (1985) (choice of forum's law is relevant to, but does not independently confer, personal jurisdiction); *supra* pp. 172-173.

In the absence of an express waiver of sovereign immunity, why not assume that the foreign state chose U.S. law including the usual sovereign immunity standards? Why is it more sensible to assume that, if U.S. law is selected, then that choice includes all U.S. law *absent those standards*?

Recall that Judge Weinfeld expressed doubt in *Verlinden* that a U.S. choice of law clause would constitute a waiver in the absence of other U.S. contacts. Is that more plausible than his similar doubt about a U.S. choice of forum clause? Note that agreement to the application of a particular law is not the same as submission to the jurisdiction of the courts of that place. *See infra* p. 464. Is a "minimum contacts" test more appropriate in this context? Is the real question whether the parties' choice of law clause was intended to permit U.S. jurisdiction?

(b) Agreement selecting foreign law as waiver. Most U.S. courts have concluded, like *Verlinden,* that a foreign state's choice of its own law or the law of a third country does not constitute a waiver of sovereign immunity in an action on the merits in U.S. courts. *E.g., Af-Cap, Inc. v. Republic of Congo,* 462 F.3d 417 (5th Cir. 2006); *Eaglet Corp. v. Banco Central de Nicaragua,* 839 F. Supp. 232 (S.D.N.Y. 1993), *aff'd,* 23 F.3d 641 (2d Cir. 1994); *Maritime Int'l Nominees Establishment v. Republic of Guinea,* 693 F.2d 1094, 1102 n.13 (D.C. Cir. 1982); *Ohntrup v. Firearms Center,* 516 F. Supp. 1281, 1284 (E.D. Pa. 1981), *aff'd,* 760 F.2d 259 (3d Cir. 1985). *See also* H. Smit, N. Galston & S. Levitsky, *International Contracts* 259-260 (1981) ("a persuasive argument can be made that the choice of a particular law is at most a reference to the foreign sovereign immunity rules of the law chosen and does not constitute an absolute waiver of immunity. In any event . . . the implied waiver should reasonably not be construed to be consent to the competence of a court other than that sitting in the State whose law has been chosen.").

Is the view set forth above persuasive? Why shouldn't any choice of law clause be regarded as a waiver of immunity (since it contemplates the application of objective standards, presumably by a neutral tribunal), thus leaving only the question whether the defendant had sufficient contacts with the United States to permit the exercise of personal jurisdiction by U.S. courts consistent with the Due Process Clause? As *Verlinden* acknowledges, this is the approach suggested by the FSIA's legislative history. H.R. Rep. No. 1487, 94th Cong., 2d Sess. 18, *reprinted in* 1976 U.S. Code Cong. & Admin. News, at 6617.

6. Agreement to arbitrate as waiver of immunity in action to enforce arbitral agreement or award. An agreement to arbitrate is a quintessential instance of a waiver of rights — of access to national courts and otherwise. *See infra* pp. 1157-1160, 1163-1165. Arbitration agreements are commonly found in international contracts and are an essential element of international trade. They are particularly important to commercial dealings with foreign states: they ensure that there can be a neutral, objective means of resolving the parties' disputes. *See* G. Born, *International Commercial Arbitration* 64-71 (3d ed. 2009).

Consistent with the basic purposes of international arbitration agreements, the legislative history of the FSIA makes it clear that §1605(a)(1) was intended to include actions to enforce agreements by foreign states to arbitrate in another country. H.R. Rep. No. 1487, 94th Cong., 2d Sess. 18, *reprinted in* 1976 U.S. Code Cong. & Admin. News, at 6617. Despite this, lower courts have struggled with the application of §1605(a)(1) to arbitration agreements, reaching decisions that frequently precluded effective enforcement of such undertakings. Accordingly, in 1988, the FSIA was amended, by adding §1605(a)(6), in order to deny foreign states immunity in actions brought to enforce either an arbitration agreement or an arbitral award, provided that the relevant agreement had specified (and minimal) contacts with the United States. Nonetheless, lower courts continue to demonstrate considerable reluctance, even under §1605(a)(6), to take steps to enforce international arbitration agreements against foreign states.

(a) Agreement to arbitrate in the United States. Decisions under §1605(a)(1) make it relatively clear that a foreign state's agreement to arbitrate in the United States constitutes a waiver of immunity from actions in U.S. courts to compel arbitration or to confirm the resulting arbitral award. *E.g., Maritime Int'l Nominees Establishment v. Republic of Guinea,* 693 F.2d 1094 (D.C. Cir. 1982) (dicta); *Birch Shipping Corp. v. United Republic of Tanzania,* 507 F. Supp. 311 (D.D.C. 1980). Consider §1605(a)(6)(A), which confirms these decisions.

(b) Agreement to arbitrate outside the United States, but within a New York Convention member state. As discussed below, approximately 145 countries around the world have ratified the New York Convention, committing themselves to recognize and enforce international arbitration agreements and awards. *See infra* pp. 1160-1161. Suppose that a foreign state agrees to arbitrate outside the United States (and outside its territory), but in the territory of a New York Convention member state; has the foreign state waived its immunity to jurisdiction in an action to enforce the agreement in the United States?

As *Cargill* illustrates, considering only the terms of §1605(a)(1), a number of lower courts declined to find a waiver in these circumstances. *See Zernicek v. Petroleos Mexicanos,* 614 F. Supp. 407, 411 (S.D. Tex. 1985), *aff'd,* 826 F.2d 415 (5th Cir. 1987) ("most courts have refused to find an implicit waiver of immunity to suit in American courts from a contract clause providing for arbitration in a country other than the United States"); *Maritime Ventures Int'l, Inc. v. Caribbean Trading & Fidelity, Ltd.,* 689 F. Supp. 1340, 1351 (S.D.N.Y. 1988). *Compare Seetransport Wiking Trader v. Navimpex Centrala Navala,* 989 F.2d 572, 577-578 (2d Cir. 1993) (finding waiver under §1605(a)(1) where agency of New York Convention member state agreed to arbitrate in another New York Convention member state); *Ipitrade Int'l, SA v. Federal Republic of Nigeria,* 465 F. Supp. 824 (D.D.C. 1978) (same).

Are these decisions well considered? Suppose that a foreign state agrees with a U.S. company to arbitrate the parties' disputes in a neutral third country, and then refuses to honor that commitment. If the arbitration agreement is subject to the New York Convention, pursuant to which the foreign state has undertaken to honor its arbitration agreements, why should the foreign state be immune from the jurisdiction of U.S. courts to enforce such an arbitration agreement?

Consider how §1605(a)(6)(B) applies to this scenario. As the *Cargill* decision illustrates, §1605(a)(6) effectively supersedes the results that were reached in these circumstances under §1605(a)(1). Other lower courts have reached similar conclusions under §1605(a)(6). *S & Davis Int'l, Inc. v. Republic of Yemen,* 218 F.3d 1292, 1302 (11th Cir. 2000); *Creighton Ltd. v. Government of Qatar,* 181 F.3d 118, 123-124 (D.C. Cir. 1999); *Continental Transfert Technique Ltd. v. Fed. Gov't of Nigeria,* 697 F. Supp. 2d 46 (D.D.C. 2010); *G.E. Transp. S.p.A. v. Republic of Albania,* 693 F. Supp. 2d 132 (D.D.C. 2010). Is this wise? Suppose that the Russian Federation enters into a contract with an Indian company, having nothing at all to do with the United States in any way, but containing an arbitration clause. (Russia and India are both parties to the New York Convention.) If Russia subsequently dishonors the arbitration agreement, does §1605(a)(6) permit the Indian company to seek to enforce the agreement in U.S. courts? Why would Congress want to do this?

Suppose that a state which has not ratified the New York Convention agrees to arbitrate in a New York Convention member state (other than the United States), and then dishonors that promise. Is the foreign state subject to U.S. jurisdiction in an action to enforce the arbitration agreement? Lower courts have (rightly) rejected this argument. *See S & Davis Int'l, Inc. v. Republic of Yemen*, 218 F.3d 1292, 1301 (11th Cir. 2000); *Creighton Ltd. v. Government of the State of Qatar*, 181 F.3d 118, 123 (D.C. Cir. 1999).

   (c) Agreement to arbitrate outside any New York Convention member state. Suppose that a foreign state agrees to arbitrate in one of the relatively few states that have not ratified the New York Convention. Does it thereby waive immunity from actions to enforce the arbitration agreement in U.S. courts? Most courts have declined to find an implied waiver from an international arbitration agreement where the arbitration is to occur in a state that is not a party to the New York Convention. *See S & Davis Int'l, Inc. v. Republic of Yemen*, 218 F.3d 1292, 1301 (11th Cir. 2000); *Creighton Ltd. v. Government of the State of Qatar*, 181 F.3d 118, 123 (D.C. Cir. 1999).

Given the interpretation that most lower courts have adopted of §1605(a)(1), that provision typically is of no use in such circumstances. Likewise, §1605(a)(6)(B) would be inapplicable. Suppose that a U.S. company agreed to arbitrate with a foreign state in a neutral third country, which was not party to the New York Convention, and the foreign state reneged. Why should §1605(a)(6)(B) *not* permit jurisdiction over an action by the U.S. company to enforce the arbitration agreement, when it would permit jurisdiction in an action by the Indian company in the preceding note?

   (d) Agreement to arbitrate that does not specify an arbitral situs. Several lower court decisions under §1605(a)(1) suggested that an open-ended agreement to arbitrate, without designation of a particular situs, constitutes a waiver of immunity in U.S. courts for actions to compel arbitration or confirm arbitral awards. *E.g., Birch Shipping Corp. v. United Republic of Tanzania*, 507 F. Supp. 311 (D.D.C. 1980); *Libyan American Oil Co. v. Socialist People's Libyan Arab Jamahirya*, 482 F. Supp. 1175 (D.D.C. 1980), *vacated*, 684 F.2d 1032 (D.C. Cir. 1981). What is the rationale for these decisions? Note that, under the arbitration rules of most leading international arbitral institutions, either the arbitral institution or arbitral tribunal is granted the power to select the arbitral seat where the parties have not reached agreement on a seat.

   (e) Agreements with U.S. nexus. Consider §1605(a)(6)(C). When would it permit jurisdiction? Would it partially alleviate the anomalous treatment of the U.S. and Indian companies in Notes 6(b) and (c) above?

   (f) Arbitration agreements under U.N. State Immunities Convention. Consider how the U.N. State Immunities Convention addresses immunity in the context of arbitration agreements. Is this preferable to §1605(a)(6)? Note that enforcement against a foreign state's assets falls under Article 19, not Article 17.

   7. *Waiver of immunity from action to confirm arbitral award.* Suppose that a private party arbitrates against a foreign state and obtains an arbitral award, which the foreign state refuses to honor. Has the foreign state waived its immunity in actions to confirm the award? To *enforce* the award against the foreign state's assets?

   A few U.S. courts have ruled that an agreement to arbitrate in a New York Convention member state constitutes a waiver of a foreign state's immunity if, following the arbitration, the prevailing private parties seek to confirm the foreign arbitral award in the United States. *E.g., Seetransport Wiking Trader etc. v. Navimpex Centrala Navala*, 989 F.2d 572, 577-578 (2d Cir. 1993); *M.B.L. Int'l Contractors, Inc. v. Republic of Trinidad & Tobago*, 725 F. Supp. 52 (D.D.C. 1989). *Compare* H. Smit et al., *International Contracts* 259 (1981) ("[i]t may well not be an effective waiver . . . when suit is brought on the arbitral award in a place other than that of the arbitration") *and Restatement (Third) Foreign*

Relations Law §456(2)(b) (1987) (treating arbitration agreement for any fora as waiver for purposes of enforcement and compelling arbitration in U.S. courts).

In contrast, if the arbitral award is not made in a state which has ratified the New York Convention, it is doubtful that the FSIA will deny the foreign state immunity in U.S. courts in an action to confirm the award. *See S & Davis Int'l, Inc. v. The Republic of Yemen*, 218 F.3d 1292, 1301 (11th Cir. 2000); *Creighton Ltd. v. Government of the State of Qatar*, 181 F.3d 118, 123 (D.C. Cir. 1999). Other courts have declined to find an implied waiver where the action is not to enforce the award but, rather, a related foreign judgment. *See, e.g., Transatlantic Shiffahrtskontor GmbH v. Shanghai Foreign Trade Corp.*, 204 F.3d 384, 391 (2d Cir. 2000).

8. ***Enforcement of arbitral award against foreign state assets.*** Note that the enforcement of awards (and judgments) against foreign state assets are dealt with separately by §1610, including §1610(a)(6). Importantly, the mere waiver of immunity against claims, including in an arbitration, does not waive immunity from enforcement against a foreign state's assets. Note the similar approach of Articles 17 and 19 of the U.N. State Immunities Convention.

9. ***Waiver of immunity by actions taken in U.S. litigation.*** The FSIA's legislative history specifically contemplated that foreign states could waive their sovereign immunity through actions taken in U.S. courts. H.R. Rep. No. 1487, 94th Cong., 2d Sess. 18, *reprinted in* 1976 U.S. Code Cong. & Admin. News, at 6617 ("an implicit waiver would . . . include a situation where a foreign state has filed a responsive pleading in an action without raising the defense of sovereign immunity"). This is consistent with well-settled approaches to personal jurisdiction defenses in other contexts, which are capable of waiver by steps taken during the litigation process. *See* Fed. R. Civ. P. 12(h) (waiver of personal jurisdiction).

Lower courts have considered a variety of cases involving alleged waivers during the course of U.S. litigation. Most courts have insisted on "construing the implied waiver provision narrowly" (*Foremost Mckesson, Inc. v. Islamic Republic of Iran*, 905 F.2d 438 (D.C. Cir. 1990)) and demonstrated "a reticence to find a waiver from the nature of a foreign state's participation in litigation" (*Frolova v. USSR*, 761 F.2d 370, 378 (7th Cir. 1985)). For examples of such reticence, *see, e.g., Calzadilla v. Banco Latino Internacional*, 413 F.3d 1285 (11th Cir. 2005) (sovereign's prosecution of civil action held not to constitute waiver as to subsequent malicious prosecution claim); *Blaxland v. Commonwealth Director of Public Prosecutions*, 323 F.3d 1198 (9th Cir. 2003) (invocation of extradition treaty rights held not to constitute waiver); *Haven v. Polska*, 215 F.3d 727 (7th Cir. 2000) (filing of letter with court held not to constitute waiver); *UNC Lear Services, Inc. v. Kingdom of Saudi Arabia*, 720 F. Supp. 2d 800 (W.D. Tex. 2010) (assertion of counterclaim held not to waive sovereign immunity); *Inversora Murten v. Energoprojeckt Holding Co.*, 671 F. Supp. 2d 152 (D.D.C. 2009) (filing answers to interrogatory not construed as waiver); *Gutch v. Federal Republic of Germany*, 444 F. Supp. 2d 1 (D.D.C. 2006) (filing motion to dismiss and entry of appearance held not to constitute waiver); *Atlantic Tele-Network, Inc. v. Inter-American Kombinat*, 244 F. Supp. 2d 1130, 1139-1140 (D. Colo. 2002) (maintenance of unrelated litigation held not to waive immunity); *Lord Day & Lord v. Socialist Republic of Vietnam*, 134 F. Supp. 2d 549, 559 (S.D.N.Y. 2001) (appearance in interpleader action waives immunity to extent necessary to determine ownership of *res*); *Hirsh v. State of Israel*, 962 F. Supp. 377, 380 (S.D.N.Y. 1997) (submission of letter to court held not to waive immunity); *Castro v. Saudi Arabia*, 510 F. Supp. 309, 311-312 (W.D. Tex. 1980) (failure to file timely answer not a waiver).

Compare the approach of Article 8 of the U.N. State Immunities Convention. Is it preferable to the FSIA's approach?

10. *Decisions requiring that implied waivers be "unambiguous."* A few lower courts have held that waivers under §1605(a)(1) must be "unmistakable" or "unambiguous." *Carpenter v. Republic of Chile*, 610 F.3d 776, 779 (2d Cir. 2010); *World Wide Minerals, Ltd. v. Republic of Kazakhstan*, 296 F.3d 1154, 1162 (D.C. Cir. 2002); *In re Tamimi*, 176 F.3d 274, 279 (4th Cir. 1999). Is this consistent with §1605(a)(1)'s provision that immunity will not exist if a foreign state has "waived its immunity either explicitly *or by implication*"?

11. *Decisions requiring showing of foreign state's intent to waive immunity.* A number of lower court decisions hold that there will be no waiver under §1605(a)(1) unless the foreign state makes a "conscious decision" to waive its immunity. *E.g., Phoenix Consulting Inc. v. Republic of Angola*, 216 F.3d 36, 39 (D.C. Cir. 2000); *In re Tamimi*, 176 F.3d 274, 279 (4th Cir. 1999); *Cabiri v. Government of Republic of Ghana*, 165 F.3d 193, 201-203 (2d Cir. 1999); *Pere v. Nuovo Pignone, Inc.*, 150 F.3d 477, 482 (5th Cir. 1998); *Frolova v. USSR*, 761 F.2d 370, 378 (7th Cir. 1985) (requiring "strong evidence that this [waiver of immunity] is what the foreign state intended"); *Estates of Ungar v. Palestinian Authority*, 315 F. Supp. 2d 164, 173 (D.R.I. 2004).

Is this requirement that the foreign state have intended or consciously chosen to waive its immunity consistent with the FSIA's legislative history, which identifies specifically the possibility of waiver by failure to raise immunity in a responsive pleading (*see supra* p. 350) or through agreement to a forum selection or arbitration clause (*see supra* pp. 343-349)? Do these forms of waivers admit of a requirement that the foreign state intended *to waive its immunity*—as opposed to intending to enter into a forum selection agreement or not to raise immunity in an answer? Isn't it nonsense to suggest that an agreement to litigate in U.S. courts would not be a waiver because of some subjective ideas on the part of some foreign functionary?

Note that §1605(a)(1) contemplates waivers "by implication"? Does the intentionality requirement effectively read the term "by implication" out of the statute? Note that, in determining whether a foreign state's actions fall within the FSIA's exception for "commercial activity," *Republic of Argentina v. Weltover*, 504 U.S. 607, 614 (1992) holds that the "nature" of the conduct, and not its "purpose" or intention, is decisive. *See supra* pp. 284-286. Why should intention be treated differently with regard to waiver?

12. *Waivers of immunity by treaty.* It is possible for a foreign state to waive its immunity in bilateral or multilateral treaties. Such waivers, however, are generally fairly specific and apply only to particular categories of claims or waive immunity only in specific forums. In *Argentine Republic v. Amerada Hess Shipping Corp.*, 488 U.S. 428, 442-443 (1989), the Supreme Court rejected the argument that a sovereign waived its immunity from U.S. courts by virtue of signing treaties that "set forth substantive rules of conduct and state that compensation shall be paid for certain wrongs," but that did not mention "a waiver of immunity to suit in United States courts or even the availability of a cause of action in the United States." *Id.* at 442-443. Plaintiffs often seek to expand these waivers to encompass submissions to U.S. jurisdiction. Relying on *Amerada Hess*, most lower courts have refused to expand waivers beyond the language of the relevant treaty. *E.g., Haven v. Rzeczpospolita Polska*, 215 F.3d 727 (7th Cir. 2000) (WWII claims settlement convention does not contemplate actions in U.S. courts); *Reers v. Deutsche Bahn AG*, 320 F. Supp. 2d 140, 147-148 (S.D.N.Y. 2004) (Germany's ratification of convention waiving sovereign immunity for damage claims brought in courts of foreign countries where injuries from German railway transportation activities allegedly occurred did not waive immunity generally in the United States); *Carpenter v. Republic of Chile*, 610 F.3d 776, 779 (2d Cir. 2010) (no waiver when Chile signed treaty committing it to observe human rights norms); *Anderman v. Federal Republic of Austria*, 256 F. Supp. 2d 1098, 1105-1106 (C.D. Cal. 2003) (Austrian WWII claims settlement convention does not contemplate actions in U.S. courts);

Greenpeace v. France, 946 F. Supp. 773 (C.D. Cal. 1996) (United Nations Convention on the Law of the Sea does not contemplate actions in U.S. courts).

13. *Waivers of immunity by violations of international law.* Can a state implicitly waive its immunity under the FSIA by violating some fundamental principle of international law? Courts consistently have rejected this suggestion. *E.g., Carpenter v. Republic of Chile*, 610 F.3d 776, 779 (2d Cir. 2010); *Sampson v. Federal Republic of Germany*, 250 F.3d 1145, 1149-1150 (7th Cir. 2001); *Princz v. Federal Republic of Germany*, 26 F.3d 1166, 1173 (D.C. Cir. 1994); *Siderman de Blake v. Republic of Argentina*, 965 F.2d 699, 714 (9th Cir. 1992). As these courts have held,

> We think that something more nearly express [than the FSIA implied waiver provision] is wanted before we impute to the Congress an intention that the federal courts assume jurisdiction over the countless human rights cases that might well be brought by the victims of all the ruthless military juntas, presidents-for-life, and murderous dictators of the world, from Idi Amin to Mao Zedong. Such an expansive reading of §1605(a)(1) would likely place an enormous strain not only upon our courts but, more to the immediate point, upon our country's diplomatic relations with any number of foreign nations. In many if not most cases the outlaw regime would no longer even be in power and our Government could have normal relations with the government of the day—unless disrupted by our courts, that is. *Sampson v. Federal Republic of Germany*, 250 F.3d 1145, 1152 (7th Cir. 2001) (quoting *Princz v. Federal Republic of Germany*, 26 F.3d 1166, 1174 n.1 (D.C. Cir. 1994)).

Nonetheless, other provisions of the FSIA such as the noncommercial tort exception and the terrorism exception, both discussed below, may supply a basis for stripping the sovereign of its immunity for such conduct.

5. Terrorism-Related Activities

In 1996, Congress amended the FSIA to add another important exception to foreign states' immunity from the jurisdiction of U.S. courts.[148] Among other things, the 1996 amendments stripped certain, specifically identified countries of sovereign immunity, based upon their involvement in acts of terrorism, regardless of whether those acts had a nexus with the United States.[149] That enactment triggered a wave of litigation against nations like Iran where the action did not otherwise fall under one of the other exceptions of the FSIA, such as the noncommercial tort exception.[150] In 2008, the original anti-terrorism exception was repealed and replaced with a broadly similar exception.[151] In its current form, codified at 28 U.S.C. §1605A, the exception provides that

> [a] foreign state shall not be immune from the jurisdiction of courts of the United States or of the States in any case not otherwise covered by this chapter in which money damages are

148. *See* §221(a) of the Antiterrorism and Effective Death Penalty Act of 1996, Pub. L. No. 104-132, 110 Stat. 1214, 1241-1242 (Apr. 24, 1996); H.R. Rep. No. 383, 104th Cong., 1st Sess. 1995 (legislative history).

149. For commentary on the original 1996 amendments to the FSIA, *see* Strauss, *Enlisting the U.S. Courts in a New Front: Dismantling the International Business Holdings of Terrorist Groups Through Federal Statutory and Common Law Suits*, 38 Vand. L.J. Transnat'l L. 679 (2005); Caplan, *The Constitution and Jurisdiction over Foreign States: The 1996 Amendments to the Foreign Sovereign Immunities Act in Perspective*, 41 Va. J. Int'l L. 369, 406-408 (2001); Glannon & Atik, *Politics and Personal Jurisdiction: Suing State Sponsors of Terrorism Under the 1996 Amendments to the Foreign Sovereign Immunities Act*, 87 Geo. L.J. 675 (1999).

150. Virtually all suits brought under this exception have been litigated in the federal courts of the District of Columbia, causing this court to develop a special expertise in this area.

151. *See* The National Defense Authorization Act for Fiscal Year 2008 §1083(a), 122 Stat. 3. *See Republic of Iraq v. Beatty*, 129 S. Ct. 2183 (2009). For a survey of the terrorism exception, from its original enactment in 1996 to the 2008 revisions, *see In re Islamic Republic of Iran Terrorism Litig.*, 659 F. Supp. 2d 31 (D.D.C. 2009).

sought against a foreign state for personal injury or death that was caused by an act of torture, extrajudicial killing, aircraft sabotage, hostage taking, or the provision of material support or resources for such an act if such act or provision of material support or resources is engaged in by an official, employee, or agent of such foreign state while acting within the scope of his or her office, employment, or agency.[152]

Like the 1996 version of the exception, §1605A reflects several noteworthy changes in sovereign immunity law in the United States.[153] First, the provision applies only to states designated by the Secretary of State as state sponsors of terrorism.[154] In this respect, the anti-terrorism provision differs from other exceptions under the FSIA, such as the commercial activity and noncommercial tort exceptions, which apply regardless of whether the Executive Branch has determined that the sovereign defendant is amenable to suit.

Second, §1605A extends to an act of international terrorism, regardless of where it occurs. In this respect, it differs from other exceptions that impose requirements for some *nexus* to the United States.[155] Due to the absence of any such requirement of a connection with the United States, the anti-terrorism exception tests the constitutional limits of Congress's power to subject foreign states to suit irrespective of whether the exercise of personal jurisdiction over those foreign sovereigns would comport with the limits of the Fifth Amendment's Due Process Clause.[156] This feature of the anti-terrorism exception has prompted some commentators to question the constitutionality of the exception.[157]

Third, in cases where the act occurred in the foreign state, §1605A requires that, under certain circumstances, the foreign state be afforded a reasonable opportunity to arbitrate the claim before a United States court may exercise jurisdiction.[158] In this respect, the anti-terrorism exception differs from other exceptions that do not grant the sovereign a preliminary right to arbitrate in lieu of litigation.

Fourth, §1605A ordinarily requires that the claimant or the victim be a national of the United States.[159] This aspect of the anti-terrorism exception differs from other exceptions that do not expressly connect the availability of jurisdiction with the plaintiff's (or victim's) nationality.

Finally, §1605A creates a cause of action against designated defendants. The cause of action extends liability to a

> foreign state that is or was a state sponsor of terrorism . . . and any official, employee, or agent of that foreign state while acting within the scope of his or her office, employment, or agency . . . for personal injury or death caused by acts [described in the jurisdictional grant

---

152. 28 U.S.C. §1605A(1).

153. Although §1605(a)(7) formally has been repealed, §1605A retains many of its essential qualities. Consequently, caselaw interpreting the former version of the exception undoubtedly will continue to influence interpretation of §1605A.

154. 28 U.S.C. §1605A(2)(a)(1)(I)-(II).

155. *See supra* pp. 276-277, 287-308, 308-314, 331-332, 342-343.

156. Similar questions arise under the Fourteenth Amendment. Recall that the FSIA applies in state courts and that state courts have concurrent jurisdiction over cases arising under the FSIA. Consequently, under the anti-terrorism exception, a state court could have jurisdiction over a foreign sovereign irrespective of whether the sovereign had minimum contacts with the forum state. *Cf. In re Estate of Weinstein*, 712 N.Y.S.2d 300 (Sup. Ct. 2000) (holding that FSIA supplied jurisdiction over claim against Syria for its alleged involvement in terrorist act committed in Israel).

157. *See, e.g.*, Paust, *The History, Nature, and Reach of the Alien Tort Claims Act*, 16 Fla. J. Int'l L. 249 (2004).

158. 28 U.S.C. §1605A(iii).

159. *Id.* §1605A(ii). Alternatively, the claimant or victim must be a member of the armed forces, an employee of the U.S. Government or an employee of a government contractor.

above] . . . . In any such action, damages may include economic damages, solatium, pain and suffering, and punitive damages. In any such action, a foreign state shall be vicariously liable for the acts of its officials, employees, or agents.[160]

By contrast, other sections of the FSIA do not create causes of action.

As you consider these distinctive features of the anti-terrorism exception, compare them to other provisions of the FSIA. Are these novel features wise? *Price v. Socialist People's Libyan Arab Jamahiriya*, excerpted below, addresses some of the novel issues raised by the anti-terrorism exception. The case involves the statutory predecessor to §1605A, 28 U.S.C. §1605(a)(7), and a defendant state that is no longer on the list of designated state sponsors of terrorism.[161] Yet its analysis of the important issues remains entirely valid.

PRICE v. SOCIALIST PEOPLE'S LIBYAN ARAB JAMAHIRIYA
294 F.3d 82 (D.C. Cir. 2002)

EDWARDS, CIRCUIT JUDGE. [Two American citizens, living in Libya and working for a Libyan company, were arrested for taking photographs of the country. Incarcerated for several months, they alleged that they endured unsanitary conditions, were deprived food and medical care, and were physically abused. Many years following their release (and after enactment of the anti-terrorism exception), they sued Libya (which had been designated by the Secretary of State as a state sponsor of terrorism). Libya, claiming sovereign immunity and lack of personal jurisdiction moved to dismiss. The district court denied Libya's motion, relying on §1605(a)(7).]

Before we address the issues arising under the FSIA and the Due Process Clause, we first want to make it clear that our decision today does not address or decide whether the plaintiffs have stated a cause of action against Libya. The parties appear to assume that a substantive claim against Libya arises under the FSIA, but this is far from clear. The FSIA is undoubtedly a jurisdictional statute which, in specified cases, eliminates foreign sovereign immunity and opens the door to subject matter jurisdiction in the federal courts. There is a question, however, whether the FSIA creates a federal cause of action for torture and hostage taking against foreign states. *See Roeder v. Islamic Republic of Iran*, 195 F. Supp. 2d 140, 171-73 (D.D.C. 2002).

The "Flatow Amendment" to the FSIA confers a right of action for torture and hostage taking against an "official, employee, or agent of a foreign state," 28 U.S.C. §1605 (note); *see Flatow v. Islamic Republic of Iran*, 999 F. Supp. 1, 12-13 (D.D.C. 1998), but the amendment does not list "foreign states" among the parties against whom such an action may be brought. While it is possible that such an action could be brought under the "international terrorism" statute, 18 U.S.C. §2333(a), no such claim has been raised in this case. . . .

. . .

The original FSIA was not intended as human rights legislation. Thus, no matter how allegedly egregious a foreign state's conduct, suits that did not fit into one of the statute's

---

160. This cause of action effectively supplants the Flatow Amendment, which provided a more limited cause of action against officers, employees, agencies of instrumentalities of foreign states (but not foreign states proper). *See infra* p. 358.

161. For a discussion of Libya's removal from the state sponsor of terrorism list, the creation of a claims settlement mechanism, and the effect on pending suits against Libya, *see Certain Underwriters at Lloyds London v. Great Socialist People's Libyan Arab Jamahiriya*, 677 F. Supp. 2d 270 (D.D.C. 2010); *Harris v. Socialist People's Libyan Arab Jamahiriya*, 620 F. Supp. 2d 1 (D.D.C. 2009).

discrete and limited exceptions invariably were rejected. . . . Under the original FSIA, therefore, terrorism, torture, and hostage taking committed abroad were immunized forms of state activity. *See* H.R. Rep. No. 103-702, at 4 (1994) ("[T]he FSIA does not currently allow U.S. citizens to sue for gross human rights violations committed by a foreign sovereign on its own soil."). Indeed, in [*Saudi Arabia v. Nelson*, 507 U.S. 349 (1993)] [excerpted at pp. 289-296, *supra*] the Supreme Court recognized that conduct of the sort alleged in the present case — "wrongful arrest, imprisonment, and torture" — amounted to abuses of police power, and "however monstrous such abuse undoubtedly may be, a foreign state's exercise of the power of its police has long been understood for purpose of the restrictive theory as peculiarly sovereign in nature." 507 U.S. at 361 . . .

The mounting concern over decisions such as these eventually spurred the political branches into action. *See* Murphy, *Civil Liability for the Commission of International Crimes as an Alternative to Criminal Prosecution,* 12 Harv. Hum. Rts. J. 1, 34 (1999). In 1996, as part of the comprehensive Antiterrorism and Effective Death Penalty Act ("AEDPA"), Congress amended the FSIA to add a new class of claims [in §1605(a)(7)] for which certain foreign states would be precluded from asserting sovereign immunity. In enacting this provision, Congress sought to create a judicial forum for compensating the victims of terrorism, and in so doing to punish foreign states who have committed or sponsored such acts and deter them from doing so in the future.

While such legislation had long been sought by victims' groups, it had been consistently resisted by the executive branch. *See* Alan Gerson & Jerry Adler, *The Price of Terror* 212-26 (2001); H.R. Rep. No. 102-900, at 3-4, 11 (1992). Executive branch officials feared that the proposed amendment to FSIA might cause other nations to respond in kind, thus potentially subjecting the American government to suits in foreign countries for actions taken in the United States. Although these reservations did not prevent the amendment from passing, they nevertheless left their mark in the final version of the bill.

Section 1605(a)(7) has some notable features which reveal the delicate legislative compromise out of which it was born. First, not all foreign states may be sued. Instead, only a defendant that has been specifically designated by the State Department as a "state sponsor of terrorism" is subject to the loss of its sovereign immunity. Second, even a foreign state listed as a sponsor of terrorism retains its immunity unless (a) it is afforded a reasonable opportunity to arbitrate any claim based on acts that occurred in that state, and (b) either the victim or the claimant was a U.S. national at the time that those acts took place. In the present case, Libya has been designated as a sponsor of terrorism. *See* 31 C.F.R. §596.201 (2001). Moreover, both plaintiffs are American citizens, and Libya does not contend that it has been denied a chance to arbitrate their claims.

If service of process has been made under §1608, personal jurisdiction over a foreign state exists for every claim over which the court has subject matter jurisdiction. *See* 28 U.S.C. §1330(b). In turn, the statute automatically confers subject matter jurisdiction whenever the state loses its immunity pursuant to §1605(a)(7). . . .

Under the original FSIA, however, it was generally understood that in order for immunity to be lost, there had to be some tangible connection between the conduct of the foreign defendant and the territory of the United States. *See Verlinden BV v. Cent. Bank of Nigeria,* 461 U.S. 480, 490 & n.15 (1983); *cf. McKeel v. Islamic Republic of Iran,* 722 F.2d 582, 588 (9th Cir. 1983) ("[N]othing in the legislative history [of the 1976 Act] suggests that Congress intended to assert jurisdiction over foreign states for events occurring wholly within their own territory. Such an intent would not be consistent with the prevailing practice in international law."). In this way, the original statute's immunity exceptions "prescribe[d] the necessary contacts which must exist before our courts can exercise personal jurisdiction." H.R. Rep. No. 94-1487, at 13. . . .

When Congress passed the original FSIA, it was assumed that the exercise of personal jurisdiction over foreign states under the statute always would satisfy the demands of the Constitution. This assumption proved accurate. . . . Indeed, as some courts have noted, the nexus requirements imposed by the original FSIA sometimes exceeded the constitutional standard.

The antiterrorism amendments changed this statutory framework. Under §1605(a)(7), the only required link between the defendant nation and the territory of the United States is the nationality of the claimant. Thus, §1605(a)(7) now allows personal jurisdiction to be maintained over defendants in circumstances that do not appear to satisfy the "minimum contacts" requirement of the Due Process Clause. The Due Process Clause requires that if the defendant "be not present within the territory of the forum, he have certain minimum contacts with it such that the maintenance of the suit does not offend 'traditional notions of fair play and substantial justice.'" In the absence of such contacts, the liberty interest protected by the Due Process Clause shields the defendant from the burden of litigating in that forum. Libya argues that foreign states, no less than private individuals and corporations, are protected by these constitutional strictures. In the present case, it is undisputed that Libya has no connection with the District of Columbia or with the United States, except for the alleged fact that it tortured two American citizens in Libya. This would be insufficient to satisfy the usual "minimum contacts" requirement.

Implicit in Libya's argument is the claim that a foreign state is a "person" within the meaning of the Due Process Clause. *See* U.S. Const. amend. V ("nor shall any person . . . be deprived of life, liberty, or property, without due process of law"). . . . [W]e hold that foreign states are not "persons" protected by the Fifth Amendment. Our conclusion is based on a number of considerations. [First], it is highly significant that in *South Carolina v. Katzenbach*, 383 U.S. 301, 323-24 (1066), the Court was unequivocal in holding that "the word 'person' in the context of the Due Process Clause of the Fifth Amendment cannot, by any reasonable mode of interpretation, be expanded to encompass the States of the Union." Therefore, absent some compelling reason to treat foreign sovereigns more favorably than "States of the Union," it would make no sense to view foreign states as "persons" under the Due Process Clause.

Indeed, we think it would be highly incongruous to afford greater Fifth Amendment rights to foreign nations, who are entirely alien to our constitutional system, than are afforded to the states, who help make up the very fabric of that system. The States are integral and active participants in the Constitution's infrastructure, and they both derive important benefits and must abide by significant limitations as a consequence of their participation. However, a "foreign State lies outside the structure of the Union." *Principality of Monaco v. Mississippi*, 292 U.S. 313, 330 (1934). Given this fundamental dichotomy between the constitutional status of foreign states and States within the United States, we cannot perceive why the former should be permitted to avail themselves of the fundamental safeguards of the Due Process Clause if the latter may not. . . .

In addition to text and structure, history and tradition support our conclusion. Never has the Supreme Court suggested that foreign nations enjoy rights derived from the Constitution, or that they can use such rights to shield themselves from adverse actions taken by the United States. This is not surprising. Relations between nations in the international community are seldom governed by the domestic law of one state or the other. *See* Damrosch, *Foreign States and the Constitution*, 73 Va. L. Rev. 483, 520 (1987) ("The most a foreign state can demand is that other states observe international law, not that they enforce provisions of domestic law."). And legal disputes between the United States and foreign governments are not mediated through the Constitution.

Rather, the federal judiciary has relied on principles of comity and international law to protect foreign governments in the American legal system. This approach recognizes the reality that foreign nations are external to the constitutional compact, and it preserves the flexibility and discretion of the political branches in conducting this country's relations with other nations. . . .

[T]he "core of the concept" of due process is "to secure the individual from the arbitrary exercise of the powers of government, unrestrained by the established principles of private right and distributive justice." *County of Sacramento v. Lewis*, 523 U.S. 833, 845-46 (1998). It is thus quite clear that the constitutional law of personal jurisdiction secures interests quite different from those at stake when a sovereign nation such as Libya seeks to defend itself against the prerogatives of a rival government. It therefore follows that foreign states stand on a fundamentally different footing than do private litigants who are compelled to defend themselves in American courts.

Unlike private entities, foreign nations are the juridical equals of the government that seeks to assert jurisdiction over them. If they believe that they have suffered harm by virtue of being haled into court in the United States, foreign states have available to them a panoply of mechanisms in the international arena through which to seek vindication or redress. These mechanisms, not the Constitution, set the terms by which sovereigns relate to one another. We would break with the norms of international law and the structure of domestic law were we to extend a constitutional rule meant to protect individual liberty so as to frustrate the United States government's clear statutory command that Libya be subject to the jurisdiction of the federal courts in the circumstances of this case. The constitutional limits that have been placed on the exercise of personal jurisdiction do not limit the prerogative of our nation to authorize legal action against another sovereign. Conferring on Libya the due process trump that it seeks against the authority of the United States is thus not only textually and structurally unsound, but it would distort the very notion of "liberty" that underlies the Due Process Clause.

Finally, it is worth noting that serious practical problems might arise were we to hold that foreign states may cloak themselves in the protections of the Due Process Clause. For example, the power of Congress and the President to freeze the assets of foreign nations, or to impose economic sanctions on them, could be challenged as deprivations of property without due process of law. The courts would be called upon to adjudicate these sensitive questions, which in turn could tie the hands of the other branches as they sought to respond to foreign policy crises. . . .

In sum, we hold that the Fifth Amendment poses no obstacle to the decision of the United States government to subject Libya to personal jurisdiction in the federal courts. Our decision on this point reaches only an actual foreign government; we express no view as to whether other entities that fall within the FSIA's definition of "foreign state" — including corporations in which a foreign state owns a majority interest, *see* 28 U.S.C. §1603(b) — could yet be considered persons under the Due Process Clause. We also note that the unavailability of constitutional due process protections will not render foreign states helpless when sued in the United States, for the doctrine of *forum non conveniens* remains fully applicable in FSIA cases.

Notes on Price

1. *Section 1605A's application to designated foreign states.* Like §1605(a)(7) before it, §1605A's terrorism exception applies only where the State Department has designated the foreign sovereign defendant as a state sponsor of terrorism. Currently, four

countries — Iran, Syria, Cuba, and Sudan — have received this designation from the State Department and, consequently, are potentially amenable to suit under this provision. Courts have consistently held that this exception does not supply a basis for jurisdiction against states not designated by the State Department as a state sponsor of terrorism. *Carpenter v. Republic of Chile*, 610 F.3d 776, 779 (2d Cir. 2010); *Mwani v. bin Ladin*, 417 F.3d 1, 15 n.15 (D.C. Cir. 2005).

Generally, the designation can be satisfied in two ways. First, the foreign sovereign can be a designated state sponsor at the time that the prohibited act occurs. *See, e.g., Daliberti v. Republic of Iraq*, 97 F. Supp. 2d 38, 44 (D.D.C. 2000). Second, even if not designated at the time of the act, the foreign sovereign can still qualify under the exception if it is subsequently designated *as a result of the act* forming the basis for the plaintiff's claim. Plaintiffs relying on this second theory face an added evidentiary challenge of proving that a subsequent designation resulted from the act forming the basis for the suit. *See Roeder v. Islamic Republic of Iran*, 195 F. Supp. 2d 140, 159-161 (D.D.C. 2002).

Is this aspect of §1605A not extraordinary? Does it not smack of indefensible double standards? If torture, murder, or blowing up a civilian aircraft by a Libyan official is so heinous as to result in a loss of immunity, why not by a Russian, Chinese, or French official? Recall the Rainbow Warrior incident, in which French intelligence operatives blew up an environmental group's protest vessel in New Zealand, killing one of the group's members. If Libya can be sued for maltreating Mr. Price, why should not the survivors of the French espionage not also be able to sue the Republic of France? What does the unwillingness of Congress to authorize suits for such activities say about the underlying substantive standards (prohibiting torture, extrajudicial killing, and the like)?

How does §1605A interact with the FSIA's other exceptions, specifically the noncommercial tort exception? If a foreign state, not designated as a state sponsor of terrorism, allegedly engages in an act that this section would prohibit but also satisfies the requirements of the noncommercial tort exception, is jurisdiction available under the FSIA? *See In re Terrorist Attacks on September 11, 2001*, 538 F.3d 71, 88-90 (2d Cir. 2008).

Is this aspect of §1605A constitutional — assuming that foreign states have any constitutional rights? Does not the creation of a special legal regime for designated "rogue" states raise questions of equal protection? Of due process? *See Daliberti v. Republic of Iraq*, 97 F. Supp. 2d 38 (D.D.C. 2000). Does this aspect of §1605A unconstitutionally delegate to the Executive Branch the power to control (by means of the designation) the jurisdiction of the federal courts? *See Owens v. Republic of Sudan*, 531 F.3d 884 (D.C. Cir. 2008). Is this power any different from the Executive Branch's power to control the definition of "foreign state" by its choices about what nations to recognize?

2. *Section 1605A's requirement of terrorism-related acts.* Section 1605A's terrorism exception creates jurisdiction over designated states only for specified acts of torture, extrajudicial killing, aircraft sabotage, hostage taking, or the provision of material support or resources for such acts by an employee or agent acting within his scope of authority. As the facts of *Price* illustrate, claimants frequently attempt to characterize their mistreatment by foreign authorities as "torture" or "hostage taking." *Compare Simpson v. Socialist People's Libyan Arab Jamahiriya*, 326 F.3d 230, 235 (D.C. Cir. 2003) (holding that plaintiff's allegations did not satisfy statutory requirement for hostage-taking) *with Simpson v. Socialist People's Libyan Arab Jamahiriya*, 470 F.3d 356 (D.C. Cir. 2006) (finding allegations of hostage-taking sufficient). What standards should be used to define torture and hostage-taking? If the standards are those of international law, does §1605A raise the same questions as the ATS? *See supra* pp. 49-50.

3. *Section 1605A's requirement of "material support."* The inclusion of "material support" for terrorism-related actions in §1605A means that the foreign sovereign need not itself engage in the prohibited act. What exactly does "material support" mean? The statute defines it by reference to the federal Antiterrorism Act; that Act defines material support to include

> currency or monetary instruments or financial securities, financial services, lodging, training, expert advice or assistance, safehouses, false documentation or identification, communications equipment, facilities, weapons, lethal substances, explosives, personnel, transportation, and other physical assets, except medicine or religious materials. 18 U.S.C. §2339A(b)(1).

This definition potentially sweeps quite broadly. *See Holder v. Humanitarian Law Project*, 130 S. Ct. 2705 (2010) (rejecting constitutional challenge to material support provisions of Anti-terrorism Act); *Boim v. Quranic Literacy Inst. & Holy Land Found. for Relief & Dev.*, 291 F.3d 1000 (7th Cir. 2002) (interpreting material support language in Anti-terrorism Act); *Owens v. Republic of Sudan*, 531 F.3d 884 (D.C. Cir. 2008); *Rux v. Republic of Sudan*, 461 F.3d 461 (4th Cir. 2006).

   4. *Section 1605A's causation requirement.* Note that the prohibited act under §1605A must "cause" injury or death. *See Owens v. Republic of Sudan*, 531 F.3d 884, 895 (D.C. Cir. 2008) (finding allegations of causation sufficient); *Kilburn v. Socialist People's Libyan Arab Jamahiriya*, 376 F.3d 1123, 1127-1130 (D.C. Cir. 2004) (adopting a proximate cause standard).

   5. *Jurisdiction versus cause of action under §1605A.* Recall that the FSIA generally merely provides a basis for establishing jurisdiction and does not supply a liability rule or a cause of action. Following the enactment of the 1996 version of the terrorism exception, a separate statute, known as the Flatow Amendment, provided a limited cause of action against agents or employees of state sponsors of terrorism. *See* 28 U.S.C. §1605 note; *Flatow v. Islamic Republic of Iran*, 999 F. Supp. 1, 12-13 (D.D.C. 1998) (discussing history of Flatow Amendment). While the Flatow Amendment supplied a cause of action against agents or instrumentalities of foreign states, lower courts held that it did not supply a cause of action against the foreign state itself. *See Cicippio-Puleo v. Islamic Republic of Iran*, 353 F.3d 1024, 1033 (D.C. Cir. 2004). This required plaintiffs suing a foreign state to turn to another source such as state law to provide a cause of action and raised difficult choice-of-law questions. *See, e.g., Oveissi v. Islamic Republic of Iran*, 573 F.3d 835, 840-844 (D.C. Cir. 2009); *Estate of Botvin ex rel. Ellis v. Islamic Republic of Iran*, 684 F. Supp. 2d 34, 39-42 (D.D.C. 2010).

   The new §1605A unambiguously creates a federal cause of action—against both foreign states and their agencies and instrumentalities—for supporting acts of international terrorism. Not only does this eliminate questions over the existence of the cause of action, it also eliminates the choice-of-law uncertainty. *See In re Islamic Republic of Iran Terrorism Litig.*, 659 F. Supp. 2d 31, 59 (2009). Are there any differences between §1605A's jurisdictional grant and the section's cause of action? If the elements of the jurisdictional grant are proven, does it automatically follow that the plaintiff also has established liability? *See Calderon-Cardona v. Democratic People's Republic of Korea*, 723 F. Supp. 2d 441 (D.P.R. 2010).

   6. *Opportunity to arbitrate under §1605A.* Section 1605A provides that, where a terrorism-related act occurred in the territory of the relevant foreign state, a court shall decline to exercise jurisdiction if the foreign sovereign has not been provided a reasonable opportunity to arbitrate the claim. This requirement, however, does not apply where the prohibited act occurred in another state. *Oveissi v. Islamic Republic of Iran*, 573 F.3d 835, 840 (D.C. Cir. 2009). Why do you think Congress adopted this provision? What purposes does it serve? For judicial gloss on the arbitration requirement, *see Simpson v. Socialist People's Libyan Arab Jamahiriya*, 326 F.3d 230, 233-234 (D.C. Cir. 2003).

7. *No nexus requirement under §1605A.* As *Price* explains, one of the most important novel features of the terrorism exception was to eliminate any requirement of nexus between the United States and the terrorist act other than the nationality of the victim; minimum contacts between the foreign state and the United States are irrelevant. *Rein v. Socialist People's Libyan Arab Jamahiriya,* 162 F.3d 748, 761 (2d Cir. 1998). Indeed, for acts of terrorism within the United States, the noncommercial tort exception generally would already strip the foreign sovereign of its immunity. *See Flatow v. Islamic Republic of Iran,* 999 F. Supp. 1, 15-16 (D.D.C. 1998).

Was it a wise legislative choice to extend U.S. jurisdiction to any acts, anywhere in the world, regardless of their nexus to the United States? What if other countries do the same? Does the U.S. exercise of jurisdiction acknowledge the existence of essentially universal jurisdiction over claims based on alleged violations of prohibitions against torture, hostage-taking, and the like?

What if European Union states permit suits against U.S. Government officials, and the United States, based on their judgments about the legality of actions in Afghanistan, Iraq, or Guantanamo Bay? Note that Iran has enacted legislation authorizing such suits. *See* An Act Conferring Jurisdiction on the Iranian Judiciary to Adjudicate Civil Claims Against Foreign Governments (Nov. 10, 1999) ("According to this Act, Iranian nationals are authorized to file claims with the Judiciary in Teheran, arising out of the following actions of the foreign states which have removed the judicial immunity of the Government of the Islamic Republic of Iran or its officials. The court shall adjudicate the claim on the basis of reciprocity [using a list prepared by the Ministry of Foreign Affairs]. 1. Damages arising out of any actions and activities of the foreign Governments in violation of international law including interference with the internal affairs of Iran resulting in death, physical and mental injuries or financial damages to persons. 2. Damages arising out of acts or activities of persons or terrorist groups, who are supported by the foreign Government. . . ."). In light of §1605A, would the United States have any legal grounds for protesting such legislation? Is there one set of international law rules for rogue states and another for other states? Will other countries let the Secretary of State pick what states go in each category?

8. *Nationality of claimant or victim under §1605A.* Section 1605A generally requires that the claimant (or the victim) be a U.S. national (or be serving the U.S. Government). In practice, the application of this requirement is straightforward. *E.g., Oveissi v. Islamic Republic of Iran,* 573 F. 3d 835, 840-844 (D.C. Cir. 2009) (claimant's nationality); *Stethem v. Islamic Republic of Iran,* 291 F. Supp. 2d 78, 86 n.13 (D.D.C. 2002) (victim's nationality suffices even where claimant is nonnational). *But see Baumel v. Syrian Arab Republic,* 667 F. Supp. 2d 39 (D.D.C. 2009) (act does not cover U.S. citizen captured while serving Israeli Defense Forces during wartime).

Is nationality a sensible limitation? If jurisdiction otherwise would be proper, why should the nationality of the plaintiff matter? Compare this regime with those under the Alien Tort Statute — where jurisdiction is limited to claims by aliens. Does the nationality requirement address some of the potentially exorbitant aspects of §1605A? Does it not at least limit the reach of U.S. jurisdiction to cases involving protection of its own nationals? Recall the U.S. protests against, and the Brussels Convention's prohibition of, jurisdiction under Article 14 of the French Civil Code based on the nationality of the plaintiff. *See supra* pp. 96, 105-106. Is analysis affected by the fact that universal jurisdiction is assertedly limited to a category of outrages against international law?

On the other hand, if the limitation of §1605A to claims by U.S. nationals is sensible, why should it be limited to the terrorism exception? Why not extend this to the other exceptions under §1605A? Why should the courts of the United States *ever* concern themselves with claims against a foreign sovereign brought by nonnationals? Recall your thoughts on similar issues in the study of subject matter jurisdiction, particularly alienage jurisdiction, *supra* pp. 26-27, 50-51.

9. *Due process limits on jurisdiction over foreign states — revisited.* Consider the analysis in *Price* of the applicability of the Due Process Clause to suits against foreign states. Is this analysis persuasive?

First, recall the origins of due process limitations on judicial jurisdiction in *Pennoyer v. Neff* — the territorial restrictions imposed by international law. Is the Court's analysis in *Price* — that foreign states have no rights under the Due Process Clause — consistent with this? Recall also the concerns expressed in *Asahi* about foreign state's sovereignty when U.S. jurisdiction is exercised over their nationals. *See supra* pp. 150-151. Is the Court's analysis in *Price* consistent with this?

Second, recall the contemporary bases for due process protections in *World-Wide Volkswagen, Burger King,* and *Burnham. See supra* pp. 85-90, 101-105. Are the "liberty" interests of the parties the sole factors in contemporary due process analysis? Do not the Supreme Court's recent decisions expressly consider the separate sovereignty interests of states and foreign countries? Is the Court's analysis in *Price* consistent with this?

Third, the Court's analysis in *Price* focuses on the fact that the Due Process Clause protects "persons" which, it reasons, does not include "foreign states." Note that the basic rationale of the FSIA (and Tate Letter) is that when a state functions in the manner of a private person, then the restrictive theory of immunity denies it the immunities that apply when it functions as a sovereign. *See supra* pp. 240-241, 247-248. If the law treats a foreign sovereign as if it were a private person, because of the activities it engages in, then would it not be anomalous to say in these circumstances that the foreign sovereign is not entitled to the protections granted to private persons, because it is a sovereign? Are there textual arguments that a domestic U.S. state would not be a person but a foreign state would be? What are they?

Fourth, note the Court's argument in *Price* that foreign states have other mechanisms available to them to pursue their objections to U.S. jurisdiction. Doesn't that miss the point? Don't foreign nationals always have other mechanisms available to them in objecting to U.S. jurisdiction — specifically, refusing to honor a U.S. judgment and resisting enforcement of that judgment abroad? This does not deprive foreign parties of their due process rights, does it? Is the logic of *Price* limited to foreign states? If *Price* is correct, couldn't an argument be constructed that aliens located outside the United States generally are not entitled to due process protections? *Frontera Resources Azerbaijan Corp. v. State Oil Co. of the Azerbaijani Republic,* 582 F.3d 393 (2d Cir. 2009) (holding that minimum contacts test does not apply to agencies or instrumentalities of foreign state); *TMR Energy Ltd. v. State Property Fund of Ukraine,* 411 F.3d 296, 302 n.* (D.C. Cir. 2005) ("[A]lthough courts often assume the minimum contacts test applies in suits against foreign 'persons,' that assumption appears never to have been challenged.").

Finally, recall the origins of foreign sovereign immunity in *Schooner Exchange. See supra* pp. 236-238, 246-247. Note that contemporary international law imposes jurisdictional limitations on state assertions of jurisdiction over other states. *See Restatement (Third) of Foreign Relations Law* §403(2) (1987) (stating that international law has long recognized limitations on the authority of states to exercise jurisdiction over other states). Should Congress be entirely free to disregard these limitations? What would Chief Justice Marshall have said?

10. *Enforcement of judgments under §1605A.* The countries designated as state sponsors of terror are not exactly regular trading partners with, much less allies of, the United States. Consequently, a party bringing a suit under this exception faces a potentially uphill

battle in collecting on any judgment. Often, they do not enter an appearance in the case, requiring plaintiffs to prove up their case in order to obtain a default judgment. *E.g., Alejandre v. Republic of Cuba,* 996 F. Supp. 1239 (S.D. Fla. 1997). *But see Estate of Botvin ex rel. Ellis v. Islamic Republic of Iran,* 604 F. Supp. 2d 22 (D.D.C. 2009) (finding allegations insufficient to support default judgment).

Congressional legislation enacted shortly after the first anti-terrorism exception seeks to ameliorate this problem. The Victims of Trafficking and Violence Protection Act of 2000 ("VTVPA"), Pub. L. No. 106-386, §2002, 114 Stat. 1464, 1541 (2000), allows prevailing plaintiffs to collect proceeds from the U.S. Department of Treasury in exchange for some of the rights to collect from the foreign sovereign. The Terrorism Risk Insurance Act ("TRIA"), Pub. L. No. 107-297, §201(a), 116 Stat. 2322 (2002) allows prevailing plaintiffs to execute their judgments against certain assets of the foreign sovereign. *See generally Ministry of Defense and Support for the Armed Forces of the Islamic Republic of Iran v. Elahi,* 129 S. Ct. 1732 (2009) (discussing relationship between TRIA and VTVPA); *Weinstein v. Islamic Republic of Iran,* 609 F.3d 43 (2d Cir. 2010) (describing relationship between FSIA and TRIA); *Hegna v. Islamic Republic of Iran,* 376 F.3d 485, 487 (5th Cir. 2004) (describing relationship between the FSIA's terrorism exception, the VTVPA and the TRIA); *Hegna v. Islamic Republic of Iran,* 376 F.3d 226, 230-232 (4th Cir. 2004) (same).

Are these provisions wise? Should similar provisions apply generally to all judgments against foreign states under the FSIA? Why or why not?

11. *Section 1605A's paradigm.* Consider again the basic structure and paradigm of §1605A. Is it appropriate to prescribe one set of jurisdictional/immunity rules for some states and a different set for other states? How different is this from entering into treaties with some states (*e.g.,* BITs or Friendship, Commerce, and Navigation treaties)?

If the §1605A paradigm is appropriate, should it also apply to other exceptions? For example, should the Secretary of State be required to make a designation before a foreign sovereign may be sued under the expropriation or noncommercial tort exception? For example, could not stricter protections against expropriation be imposed on states that do not enter into BITs with the United States? Or could the Secretary of State be permitted to designate certain countries as unfair traders, against whom more expansive jurisdiction could be granted in respect of commercial activities? What would be wrong, if anything, with these approaches?

12. *Terrorism-related activities under the U.N. State Immunities Convention.* Is there any "terrorism" exception in the U.N. State Immunities Convention? Does this affect interpretation of §1605A? Does this affect the legislative wisdom of adopting §1605A? What risks does it pose for the United States?

13. *Section 1605A, Belgium's war crimes law, and the Alien Tort Statute.* Recall the Belgium war crimes law discussed *supra* at 61-62. Like §1605A, that law originally authorized jurisdiction regardless of the nexus between the international law violation and the forum. Unlike §1605A, the original Belgian law did not limit the identity of range of states (or government officials) who could be named as defendants, a key source of international protest against the law. Which model provides a superior method for policing international law violations? A civil law where private plaintiffs bring suit against a list of foreign state defendants maintained by the State Department? Or a criminal law where the state authorities serve as filters for complaints but where the potential foreign state defendants are not limited? Does §1605A also provide a model for the Alien Tort Statute? *See supra* pp. 33-62. What if federal courts had jurisdiction over civil actions by aliens for torts violating "law of nations" but only in cases involving aliens from certain approved countries or torts involving conduct in certain approved countries?

Part Two

Choice of Forum

As the materials set forth in Part One illustrate, many international disputes will be subject to the judicial jurisdiction of two or more different states. That is a consequence of the expansive character of contemporary rules of judicial jurisdiction.[1] Where two or more states may exercise judicial jurisdiction, choice of forum issues arise: which of the states that could adjudicate a particular dispute will do so? Will both states seek to do so? If so, will parallel litigations ensue, or are there means of confining the dispute to a single forum? Selecting the forum where a dispute will be decided has critical practical importance in international disputes, particularly where one potential forum is the United States. The significant differences between substantive and procedural rules, decision-makers, and damage awards produce dramatically different resolutions of the same dispute in different forums. Recall the discussion of these factors in the Introduction to Part One above,[2] as well as in the materials contained in Part One. Under both U.S. federal and state law, several related devices permit litigants to influence the choice of which one, of several competing forums possessing judicial jurisdiction, should adjudicate a dispute. These devices are: (a) the *forum non conveniens* doctrine; (b) forum selection agreements; (c) *lis pendens* stays; and (d) antisuit injunctions. Part Two considers the application of each of these choices of forum devices in U.S. international litigation. Chapter 4 examines the *forum non conveniens* doctrine, pursuant to which a U.S. court may dismiss an action (otherwise within its jurisdiction) in favor of a substantially more convenient and appropriate foreign forum. Chapter 5 explores the enforceability of forum selection clauses, pursuant to which parties can permit or require litigation of disputes in a particular contractually specified forum. Chapter 6 considers the *lis alibi pendens* doctrine, permitting U.S. courts to stay their own proceedings in deference to parallel foreign litigation; it also considers antisuit injunctions, which enjoin parties from participating in foreign parallel litigation. All three chapters also contain comparative materials, which illustrate the manner in which forum selection problems are addressed in selected foreign jurisdictions. Additionally, Chapter 5 addresses the proposed, and as-yet-unratified, Hague Convention on Choice of Court Agreements, which could have the potential to significantly alter existing U.S. approaches to international forum selection agreements.

1. *See supra* pp. 99-101, 105-108.
2. *See supra* pp. 1-4.

4

Forum Non Conveniens in International Litigation[1]

Forum non conveniens is a common law doctrine that permits a court to decline to exercise judicial jurisdiction if an alternative forum would be substantially more convenient or appropriate. Although it has no direct federal statutory or constitutional foundation, the *forum non conveniens* doctrine has been repeatedly applied by U.S. courts in multiple contexts.[2] This chapter examines the application of the *forum non conveniens* doctrine by U.S. courts in international cases.

---

1. Commentary on the *forum non conveniens* doctrine includes, *e.g.*, Barrett, *The Doctrine of Forum Non Conveniens*, 35 Cal. L. Rev. 380, 386 (1947); S. Baumgartner, *The Proposed Hague Convention on Jurisdiction and Foreign Judgments: Trans-Atlantic Lawmaking for Transnational Litigation* (2003); Bell, *Forum Shopping and Venue in Transnational Litigation* (2003); Bickel, *The Doctrine of Forum Non Conveniens as Applied in the Federal Courts in Matters of Admiralty*, 35 Cornell L.Q. 12 (1949); Blair, *The Doctrine of Forum Non Conveniens in Anglo-American Law*, 29 Colum. L. Rev. 1 (1929); Braucher, *The Inconvenient Federal Forum*, 60 Harv. L. Rev. 908 (1947); R. Brand & S. Jablonski, *Forum Non Conveniens: History, Global Practice, and Future Under the Hague Convention on Choice of Court Agreements* (2007); Brand, *Comparative Forum Non Conveniens and the Hague Convention on Jurisdiction and Judgments*, 37 Tex. Int'l L.J. 467 (2002); Burbank, *Jurisdictional Conflict and Jurisdictional Equilibration: Paths to a Via Media*, 26 Hous. J. Int'l L. 385 (2004); Davies, *Time to Change the Federal Forum Nonconveniens Analysis*, 77 Tulane L. Rev. 309 (2002); Dunham & Gladbach, *Forum Non Conveniens and Foreign Plaintiffs in the 1990s*, 24 Brook. J. Int'l L. 665 (1999); Fawcett, *Declining Jurisdiction in Private International Law* (P.B. Carter ed. 1995); Goldsmith, *International Dispute Resolution: The Regulation of Forum Selection* (Fourteenth Sokol Colloquium 1997); Heiser, Forum Non Conveniens and Retaliatory Legislation: The Impact on the Available Alternative Forum Inquiry and on the Desirability of Forum Non Conveniens *as a Defense Tactic*, 56 U. Kan. L. Rev. 609 (2008); Jurianto, Forum Non Conveniens: *Another Look at Conditional Dismissals*, 83 U. Det.-Mercy L. Rev. 369 (2006); Karayanni, *Forum Nonconveniens in the Modern Age* (2004); Lowenfeld, *Forum Shopping, Antisuit Injunctions, Negative Declarations, and Related Tools of International Litigation*, 91 Am. J. Int'l L. 314 (1997); Lear, *National Interests, Foreign Injuries, and Federal* Forum Non Conveniens, 41 U.C. Davis L. Rev. 559 (2007); Lear, *Congress, The Federal Courts, and* Forum Non Conveniens: *Friction on the Frontier of the Inherent Power*, 91 Iowa L. Rev. 1147 (2006); Reus, *Judicial Discretion: A Comparative View of the Doctrine of Forum Non Conveniens in the United States, the United Kingdom, and Germany*, 16 Loy. L.A. Int'l & Comp. L.J. 455 (1994); Reynolds, *The Proper Forum for a Suit: Transnational Forum Non Conveniens and Counter-Suit Injunctions in the Federal Courts*, 70 Tex. L. Rev. 1663 (1992); Samuels, *When Is an Alternative Forum Available? Rethinking the* Forum Non Conveniens *Analysis*, 85 Ind. L.J. 1059 (2010); Silberman, *Developments in Jurisdiction and Forum Non Conveniens in International Litigation: Thoughts on Reform and a Proposal for a Uniform Standard*, 28 Tex. Int'l L.J. 501 (1993); Stein, *Forum Non Conveniens and the Redundancy of Court-Access Doctrine*, 133 U. Pa. L. Rev. 781 (1985); Stuckelberg, *Lis Pendens and Forum Non Conveniens at the Hague Conference*, 26 Brook. J. Int'l L. 949 (2001).

2. *E.g., Piper Aircraft Co. v. Reyno*, 454 U.S. 235 (1981); *Gulf Oil Corp. v. Gilbert*, 330 U.S. 501 (1947); *Koster v. (American) Lumbermens Mutual Casualty Co.*, 330 U.S. 518 (1947); *infra* pp. 372-378.

A.   Introduction and Background

1.   Common Law Origins of *Forum Non Conveniens* Doctrine

The historical origins of the *forum non conveniens* doctrine are fairly described as "obscure" and "murky."[3] The Supreme Court has said on several occasions that the "doctrine of *forum non conveniens* has a long history."[4] In fact, the *forum non conveniens* defense appears to be of relatively recent origin. Despite its Latin name, most commentators have said that there was no evidence in Roman law, or in continental civil practice, of a *forum non conveniens* doctrine.[5] Instead, the doctrine is generally traced to Scottish common law decisions.[6]

Even in Scotland, it was not until the late nineteenth century that the phrase "*forum non conveniens*" was used. The term was apparently a neo-Latin translation of the English phrase "inconvenient forum." This term was coined to distinguish discretionary dismissals based upon convenience and comity from dismissals based upon a lack of judicial jurisdiction (which were termed "*forum non competens*").[7] In the United States, the *forum non conveniens* doctrine was not adopted — at least under that name — until well into the twentieth century.[8]

It was long settled that neither foreign citizens nor foreign residents were barred from access to U.S. courts, including in actions arising abroad under foreign law. This rule rested on principles of international law, and was uniformly acknowledged by commentators.[9]

Nevertheless, throughout the nineteenth century, U.S. courts dismissed actions based on reasoning that closely resembles the contemporary *forum non conveniens* doctrine. These courts relied upon notions of international law, comity, convenience, judicial administration, and relation to the forum, in dismissing actions that were concededly within their jurisdiction. The clearest examples were in federal admiralty actions. Although the name "*forum non conveniens*" was not used, admiralty courts dismissed actions within their jurisdiction from the beginning of the nineteenth century, citing justifications similar to those under the contemporary *forum non conveniens* doctrine.[10] As an 1801 decision explained:

> It has been my general rule not to take cognizance of disputes between the masters and crews of foreign ships. . . . Reciprocal policy, and the justice due from one friendly nation to another, calls for such conduct in the courts of either country.[11]

3. Barrett, *The Doctrine of Forum Non Conveniens*, 35 Cal. L. Rev. 380, 386 (1947); *American Dredging Co. v. Miller*, 510 U.S. 443, 449 (1994) ("origins of the doctrine in Anglo-American law are murky").

4. *Piper Aircraft Co. v. Reyno*, 454 U.S. 235, 248 n.13 (1981).

5. Beale, *The Jurisdiction of Courts Over Foreigners*, 26 Harv. L. Rev. 193, 283 (1913); Pillet, *Jurisdiction in Actions Between Foreigners*, 18 Harv. L. Rev. 325 (1905). One commentator has suggested, however, that the Scottish courts must have borrowed the doctrine from continental sources before its appearance in Scotland in the mid-nineteenth century. Dainow, *The Inappropriate Forum*, 29 Ill. L. Rev. 867, 881-886 & 1.58 (1935); Dicey & Morris, *The Conflict of Laws* 398 (12th ed. 1993).

6. *Piper Aircraft Co. v. Reyno*, 454 U.S. 235, 248 n.13 (1981); *Gulf Oil Corp. v. Gilbert*, 330 U.S. 501, 507 & n.6 (1947).

7. Braucher, *The Inconvenient Federal Forum*, 60 Harv. L. Rev. 908, 909 (1947). Two Scottish decisions — *Logan v. Bank of Scotland* (No. 2), [1906] 1 K.B. 141, and *La Societe du Gaz v. La Societe Anonyme de Navigation "Les Armateurs Francais,"* 1926 Sess. Cas. 13 — are frequently cited as the first modern statements of the *forum non conveniens* doctrine.

8. As discussed below, the Supreme Court first applied the *forum non conveniens* doctrine in diversity actions in *Gulf Oil Co. v. Gilbert*, 330 U.S. 501 (1947) and *Koster v. American Lumbermens Mutual Casualty Co.*, 330 U.S. 518 (1947).

9. J. Story, *Commentaries on the Conflict of Laws* §565 (2d ed. 1841); H. Wheaton, *Elements of International Law* §140-1 (8th ed. 1866); Martens, *Law of Nations* 102 (Cobbett trans. 4th ed. 1829); Wilson, *Access-to-Court Provisions in United States Commercial Treaties*, 47 Am. J. Int'l L. 20 (1953); 3 G. Hackworth, *Digest of International Law* 562 (1941); 4 J. Moore, *Digest of International Law* 2 (1906).

10. *See* Bickel, *The Doctrine of Forum Non Conveniens as Applied in the Federal Courts in Matters of Admiralty*, 35 Cornell L.Q. 12, 13 (1949); A. Ehrenzweig, *The Conflict of Laws* 123 (1962) ("Admiralty courts have administered what in effect has been a doctrine of *forum non conveniens* much longer than land courts.").

11. *Willendson v. Forsoket*, 29 F.Cas. 1283 (No. 17,682) (Pa. 1801).

The Supreme Court repeatedly affirmed this discretionary power of admiralty courts to abstain from deciding sufficiently foreign matters.[12]

U.S. courts also developed rules of abstention, similar to *forum non conveniens*, outside the admiralty context. This was most evident in cases involving the internal affairs of foreign corporations[13] and suits between aliens asserting foreign causes of action.[14] Although these rules were broadly similar to *forum non conveniens*, the doctrine was not invoked by that name.[15]

New York was the leading example of a jurisdiction that apparently permitted *forum non conveniens* dismissals under other names. As early as 1817, a New York court asserted the discretion to dismiss an action otherwise within its jurisdiction for reasons of convenience and comity.[16] Later in the nineteenth century, New York courts repeatedly declined jurisdiction in cases where one foreigner asserted tort claims against another foreigner based on acts committed outside of New York. In 1890, a New York court could declare:

> It is the well-settled rule of this state that, unless special reasons are shown to exist which make it necessary or proper to do so, the courts will not retain jurisdiction of and determine actions between parties residing in another state for personal injuries received in that state. . . . The reason of the rule is obvious, — because the courts of this state should not be vexed with litigations between non-residents over causes of action arising outside of our own territorial limits. Our courts are not supported by the people for any such purpose.[17]

In contrast, New York courts did not recognize any discretionary power to decline contract and other commercial actions where only nonresidents were involved as parties.[18]

With this nineteenth-century background, U.S. commentators during the 1920s proposed adopting the Scottish *forum non conveniens* doctrine.[19] The author most widely

---

12. *Mason v. Ship Blaireau*, 6 U.S. 240, 263 (1804) (referring to "the idea, that upon principles of general policy, this court ought not to take cognizance of a case entirely between foreigners," even absent "any positive incapacity to do so"); *The Maggie Hammond*, 76 U.S. 435, 457 (1869) (U.S. admiralty court may decline jurisdiction in case involving "the citizens or subjects of a foreign country, whose courts are not clothed with the power to give the same remedy in similar controversies to the citizens of the United States"); *The Belgenland*, 114 U.S. 355, 362-369 (1885).

13. *E.g., Williams v. Green Bay & W.R. Co.*, 326 U.S. 549 (1946); *Rogers v. Guaranty Trust Co.*, 288 U.S. 123 (1933); *Burnrite Coal Briquette Co. v. Riggs*, 274 U.S. 208 (1927).

14. *E.g., Great Western Ry. Co. v. Miller*, 19 Mich. 305 (1869); *Gardner v. Thomas*, 14 Johns. 134 (N.Y. 1817); *Johnson v. Dalton*, 1 Cow. 543 (N.Y. 1923); *Avery v. Holland*, 2 Tenn. 71 (1806).

15. One commentator, urging adoption of the *forum non conveniens* doctrine in 1929, could cite only three or four precedents in the United States that had used the term. Blair, *The Doctrine of Forum Non Conveniens in Anglo-American Law*, 29 Colum. L. Rev. 1, 2 & n.4 (1929).

16. *Gardner v. Thomas*, 14 Johns. 134 (N.Y. 1817).

17. *Ferguson v. Neilson*, 11 N.Y.S. 524 (1890). *See also Hoes v. New York, N.H. & H.R.R. Co.*, 66 N.E. 119 (N.Y. 1903); *Collard v. Beach*, 87 N.Y.S. 884 (N.Y. 1904); *Gainer v. Donner*, 251 N.Y.S. 713 (1931).

18. *Wertheim v. Clergue*, 65 N.Y.S. 750 (App. Div. 1900) ("we know of no reason founded in public policy, and certainly nothing resting in precedent, which will close the courts of this State to non-resident suitors who invoke their aid against other non-residents sojourning within our borders for the enforcement of causes of action arising out of commercial transactions and affecting property or property rights. . . . [We] certainly do not intend to establish a precedent which would shut our courts to great numbers of foreign merchants, non-residents of the State, who may find their non-resident debtors, fraudulent or honest, temporarily within our jurisdiction"); *Rodger v. Bliss*, 223 N.Y.S. 401 (1927). That limitation was abandoned by New York courts during the early decades of the twentieth century. *Wedemann v. United States Trust Co.*, 179 N.E. 712 (N.Y. 1932); *Bata v. Bata*, 105 N.E.2d 623, 625-626 (N.Y. 1952) ("it was thought, or held, at one time that only tort cases felt the doctrine's impact").

19. Blair, *The Doctrine of Forum Non Conveniens in Anglo-American Law*, 29 Colum. L. Rev. 1 (1929); Dainow, *The Inappropriate Forum*, 29 Ill. Rev. 867 (1935).

credited with popularizing the doctrine in the United States was Paxton Blair — an associate at a New York law firm with an imperious writing style and brilliant timing.[20] In 1929, he published an article in the Columbia Law Review entitled *The Doctrine of Forum Non Conveniens in Anglo-American Law.* The article began with the observation that, of all the problems of the U.S. bar, "calendar congestion in the trial courts is easily foremost."[21] Blair then offered the following relief:

> in response to th[is] challenge we tender some observations directed toward the possibility of relieving court congestion by partially diverting at its source the flood of litigation by which our courts are being overwhelmed, it being our conviction that an additional effective method of dealing with the problem lies in the wider dissemination of the doctrine, and increased use of the plea, of *forum non conveniens* which deals with the discretionary power of a court to decline to exercise a possessed jurisdiction whenever it appears that the cause before it may be more appropriately tried elsewhere.[22]

Blair supported this argument with a measure of historical authority. He pointed to admiralty and other precedents (described above), which were characterized as having applied the *forum non conveniens* doctrine without realizing that this was what they were doing. In Blair's memorable metaphor, U.S. courts were like "Moliere's M. Jourdain, who found he had been speaking prose all his life without knowing it."[23]

The next 20 years witnessed an extraordinary acceptance of the *forum non conveniens* doctrine by both state and federal courts in the United States. In 1932, the Supreme Court considered in *Canada Malting Co. v. Paterson SS Ltd.*,[24] whether a U.S. district court had the power to dismiss an admiralty action between two Canadian shipowners involved in a dispute occurring on the U.S. side of the international boundary line in Lake Superior. Writing for a unanimous Court, Justice Brandeis dismissed the argument that district judges had no discretion to decline jurisdiction that Congress had granted:

> Obviously, the proposition that a court having jurisdiction must exercise it, is not universally true; else the admiralty court could never decline jurisdiction on the ground that the litigation is between foreigners. Nor is it true of courts administering other systems of our law.[25]

The Court upheld dismissal of the suit, relying on the fact that both parties were Canadian, both vessels were Canadian-registered, all of the witnesses were in Canada, and both vessels were on voyages from one Canadian port to another.[26] The Court's opinion did not mention the phrase "*forum non conveniens*," except by way of citation to Paxton

---

20. *See* Stein, *Forum Non Conveniens and the Redundancy of Court-Access Doctrine,* 133 U. Pa. L. Rev. 781, 811-812 (1985); *Alfaro v. Dow Chemical Co.,* 786 S.W.2d 674, 676 (Tex. 1990) (referring to *forum non conveniens* as the creation of a "Wall Street lawyer").
21. 29 Colum. L. Rev. 1, 1 (1929).
22. 29 Colum. L. Rev. 1, 1 (1929).
23. Blair, *The Doctrine of Forum Non Conveniens in Anglo-American Law,* 29 Colum. L. Rev. 1, 21-22 (1929). Blair's efforts to identify cases that applied a *forum non conveniens* doctrine sub silentio have been criticized. A. Ehrenzweig, *The Conflict of Laws* 125 (1962).
24. 285 U.S. 413 (1932).
25. 285 U.S. at 422.
26. 285 U.S. at 422-423.

Blair's law review article on the subject.[27] Nevertheless, it went out of its way to indicate that courts enjoyed discretion to decline jurisdiction outside the admiralty context:

> Courts of equity and of law also occasionally decline, in the interest of justice, to exercise jurisdiction, where the suit is between aliens or nonresidents, or where for kindred reasons the litigation can more appropriately be conducted in a foreign tribunal.[28]

The Supreme Court soon thereafter went further, again in dicta, remarking that a state court "may in appropriate cases apply the doctrine of *forum non conveniens*."[29] With this background, Justice Frankfurter was comfortable referring in a 1941 dissent to "the familiar doctrine of *forum non conveniens*," which was "firmly imbedded in our law."[30] His comments elicited no objection from the remainder of the Court.

The Supreme Court did not, however, actually apply the *forum non conveniens* doctrine until two 1947 decisions in *Gulf Oil Corp. v. Gilbert*[31] and *Koster v. Lumbermens Mutual Casualty Co.*[32] In these cases, the Court for the first time expressly applied the "doctrine of *forum non conveniens*."[33] The principle has remained an important feature of U.S. civil procedure ever since.

In *Gulf Oil*, Justice Jackson asserted that the *forum non conveniens* doctrine "did not originate in federal but in state courts."[34] That does not appear to be correct. There is no evidence that U.S. state courts applied the *forum non conveniens* doctrine by name prior to 1947, save in a handful of twentieth-century decisions.[35] Indeed, one respected commentator could assert in 1947 that, at that time, the *forum non conveniens* doctrine "can be said to be in operation in barely half a dozen states."[36] In most U.S. states, the *forum non conveniens* doctrine was adopted only after *Gulf Oil* and *Koster;* in many cases, the Supreme Court's *Gulf Oil* and *Koster* decisions were the principal authority cited in support of the doctrine.[37]

2. *Gulf Oil Co. v. Gilbert* and *Koster v. American Lumbermens Mutual Casualty Co.*

Gulf Oil was a diversity action brought in the U.S. District Court for the Southern District of New York. The plaintiff was a Virginian, resident in Virginia; the defendant was a Pennsylvania corporation registered to do business (and subject to personal jurisdiction) in both Virginia and New York. The plaintiff sought damages resulting from the defendant's alleged negligence, resulting in a fire which damaged plaintiff's property. All of the relevant conduct and damage were in Virginia.

---

27. 285 U.S. at 423 n.6 (citing Blair, *The Doctrine of Forum Non Conveniens in Anglo-American Law*, 29 Colum. L. Rev. 1 (1929)).
28. 285 U.S. at 423.
29. *Broderick v. Rosner*, 294 U.S. 629, 643 (1935). It has been observed, however, that "[n]ot until 1948 was the doctrine [of *forum non conveniens*] accepted for general application in the federal courts, and it received little or no attention in the state courts until after the federal adoption." Stein, *Forum Non Conveniens and the Redundancy of Court-Access Doctrine*, 133 U. Pa. L. Rev. 781, 796 (1985).
30. *Baltimore & Ohio R.R. v. Kepner*, 314 U.S. 44, 55-56 (1941) (Frankfurter, J., dissenting).
31. 330 U.S. 501 (1947).
32. 330 U.S. 518 (1947).
33. 330 U.S. at 506-509; 330 U.S. at 522, 525-526.
34. 330 U.S. at 505 n.4.
35. *See supra* pp. 366-369.
36. Barrett, *The Doctrine of Forum Non Conveniens*, 35 Cal. L. Rev. 380, 388-389 (1947). Barrett cited decisions from Florida, Louisiana, Massachusetts, New Hampshire, New Jersey, and New York. *Id.* at 389 n.41.
37. *E.g., Bergquist v. Medtronic, Inc.*, 379 N.W.2d 508 (Minn. 1986); *Union Carbide Corp. v. Aetna Casualty & Surety Co.*, 562 A.2d 15 (Conn. 1989).

The district court dismissed the action on *forum non conveniens* grounds.[38] The Supreme Court affirmed.[39] Expressly relying on the *forum non conveniens* doctrine, the Court reasoned that, even where a district court has personal jurisdiction over the defendant, the court has discretion to decline jurisdiction:

> This Court, in one form of words or another, has repeatedly recognized the existence of the power to decline jurisdiction in exceptional circumstances. . . . The principle of *forum non conveniens* is simply that a court may resist imposition upon its jurisdiction even when jurisdiction is authorized by the letter of a general venue statute.

Gulf Oil declined to "catalogue the circumstances" where a *forum non conveniens* dismissal would be proper. It instead identified two sets of factors bearing on the doctrine's application: "the private interest of the litigants" and "[f]actors of public interest."[40] The Court set forth a detailed list of these factors. The "private interest" factors include:

> the relative ease of access to sources of proof; availability of compulsory process for attendance of unwilling, and the cost of obtaining attendance of willing, witnesses; possibility of view of premises, if view would be appropriate to the action[;] . . . all other practical problems . . . [;] the enforceability of judgment . . . [; and whether] the plaintiff [has sought to] vex, harass or oppress the defendant.[41]

The Court explained the "public interest" factors as follows:

> Administrative difficulties follow for courts when litigation is piled up in congested centers. . . . Jury duty is a burden that ought not to be imposed upon the people of a community which has no relation to the litigation. In cases which touch the affairs of many persons, there is a reason for holding the trial in their view. . . . There is a local interest in having localized controversies decided at home.[42]

The Court made clear that a strong showing of private and public inconvenience was necessary to justify a *forum non conveniens* dismissal: "unless the balance is strongly in favor of the defendant, the plaintiff's choice of forum should rarely be disturbed."[43] The Court also held, however, that the decision whether to grant a *forum non conveniens* dismissal rested largely with the trial judge's discretion: "[t]he doctrine leaves much to the discretion of the court to which the plaintiff resorts."[44]

Applying these standards, *Gulf Oil* upheld the district court's *forum non conveniens* dismissal of the action. It noted that the plaintiff resided in Virginia, and had advanced no plausible reason for why New York was a convenient forum; similarly, it remarked that the evidence in the case was almost all in Virginia, and that Virginia law would likely govern the dispute. Hence, the Court was "convinced that the District Court did not

---

38. The Court cited the fact that all of the conduct giving rise to the litigation occurred in Virginia, the plaintiff's residence was in Virginia, the plaintiff and the defendant did business in Virginia, and most of the witnesses and evidence were in Virginia.
39. 330 U.S. 501 (1947).
40. 330 U.S. at 508.
41. 330 U.S. at 508.
42. 330 U.S. at 508-509.
43. 330 U.S. at 508.
44. 330 U.S. at 508.

exceed its powers or the bounds of its discretion in dismissing plaintiff's complaint."[45] The Court also made it clear that the doctrine applied only where an adequate alternative forum existed: "In all cases in which the doctrine of *forum non conveniens* comes into play, it presupposes at least two forums in which the defendant is amenable to process; the doctrine furnishes criteria for choice between them."[46]

Justice Black dissented in *Gulf Oil*. He concluded that, where Congress had granted federal courts jurisdiction to decide a dispute, they had no discretion to decline to exercise their jurisdiction.[47] He invoked the principle that " 'the courts of the United States are bound to proceed to judgment, and to afford redress to suitors before them, in every case to which their jurisdiction extends. They cannot abdicate their authority or duty in any case in favor of another jurisdiction.' "[48] Justice Black's dissent also warned that

> The broad and indefinite discretion left to federal courts to decide the question of convenience from the welter of factors which are relevant to such a judgment, will inevitably produce a complex of close and indistinguishable decisions from which accurate prediction of the proper forum will become difficult, if not impossible.[49]

Koster v. American Lumbermens Mutual Casualty Co.[50] was a companion case to *Gulf Oil*. It involved a shareholders' derivative action, brought in the Eastern District of New York by a New York resident against three Illinois defendants. The Court reasoned:

> When there are only two parties to a dispute, there is a good reason why it should be tried in the plaintiff's home forum if that has been his choice. He should not be deprived of the presumed advantages of his home jurisdiction except upon a clear showing of facts which either (1) establish such oppressiveness and vexation to a defendant as to be out of all proportion to plaintiff's convenience, which may be shown to be slight or nonexistent, or (2) make trial in the chosen forum inappropriate because of considerations affecting the court's own administrative and legal problems.[51]

Like *Gulf Oil*, *Koster* upheld dismissal.[52]

3. Section 1404(a) — Domestic *Forum Non Conveniens* Statute

In 1948, Congress enacted 28 U.S.C. §1404(a), which codified the *forum non conveniens* doctrine for transfers among federal district courts. Section 1404(a) provides:

> For the convenience of parties and witnesses, in the interest of justice, a district court may transfer any civil action to any other district or division where it might have been brought.

---

45. 330 U.S. at 512.
46. 330 U.S. at 506-507.
47. 330 U.S. at 512 (Black, J., dissenting). *See* Redish, *Abstention, Separation of Powers, and the Limits of the Judicial Function*, 94 Yale L.J. 71 (1984); *W.S. Kirkpatrick & Co. v. Environmental Tectonics Corp.*, 493 U.S. 400 (1990) ("Courts in the United States have the power, and ordinarily the obligation, to decide cases and controversies properly presented to them.").
48. *Gulf Oil Corp.*, 330 U.S. at 513 (quoting *Hyde v. Stone*, 61 U.S. 170, 175 (1858)).
49. 330 U.S. at 516.
50. 330 U.S. at 518.
51. 330 U.S. at 524.
52. Lower courts have consistently held that *Gulf Oil* and *Koster* stated the same principles. *In re Air Crash Disaster Near New Orleans*, 821 F.2d 1147, 1163 n.24 (5th Cir. 1987); *Pain v. United Technologies Corp.*, 637 F.2d 775, 783 (D.C. Cir. 1980); *Alcoa SS Co. v. M/V Nordic Regent*, 654 F.2d 147, 154-158 (2d Cir. 1980).

The legislative history accompanying the section explained that it "was drafted in accordance with the doctrine of *forum non conveniens,* permitting transfer to a more convenient forum, even though the venue is proper."[53]

Section 1404(a) does not play a central role in international litigation, because it applies only to transfers between different federal courts. It does not apply to dismissals in favor of foreign forums, which continue to be governed by the common law doctrine of *forum non conveniens.*[54] In general, §1404(a) has been interpreted as requiring an analysis similar to that applicable under the *forum non conveniens* doctrine.[55]

B.   The Modern *Forum Non Conveniens* Doctrine: Basic Principles

For 34 years following *Gulf Oil* and *Koster,* the Court did not revisit the subject of *forum non conveniens.* During the interim, the doctrine won substantial (but not universal) following in state courts,[56] and was the subject of considerable case law in the federal courts. In 1981, the Supreme Court decided *Piper Aircraft Co. v. Reyno.*[57] Its opinion, which is excerpted below, is the leading contemporary statement of the *forum non conveniens* doctrine.

Virtually all U.S. states have adopted some variation of the *forum non conveniens* doctrine.[58] Some states have adopted it by statute. A typical statute, based on the former Uniform Interstate and International Procedure Act (since withdrawn), provided:

> When the court finds that in the interest of substantial justice the action should be heard in another forum, the court may stay or dismiss the action in whole or in part on any conditions that may be just.[59]

Most states have, by common law decision, recognized the *forum non conveniens* doctrine in some fashion.[60] These decisions have generally done so as a matter of state law — not in express deference to any principle of federal common law.[61] Nevertheless, they have virtually unanimously cited *Gulf Oil* or *Piper Aircraft* as persuasive authority. In some cases, these state decisions rely only on federal case law. In other cases, states purport to apply a more rigorous standard than the federal one.[62] At present, only one state (Montana) refuses to recognize the *forum non conveniens* doctrine, while two others

---

53. 28 U.S.C. §1404(a) annotation (1982) (Historical and Revision Notes). The legislative history's suggestion that §1404 codified a well-established common law doctrine of *forum non conveniens* was not entirely accurate. In fact, the provision had been proposed well before the Supreme Court's decisions in *Gulf Oil* and *Koster.*

54. *See infra* pp. 529-531.

55. *Van Dusen v. Barrack,* 376 U.S. 612 (1964). *See also infra* pp. 529-531.

56. *See infra* p. 372, note 58.

57. 454 U.S. 235 (1981) (excerpted below at pp. 373-378).

58. *See generally* McMahon, Annotation, *Forum Non Conveniens Doctrine in State Court as Affected by Availability of Alternative Forum,* 57 A.L.R. 4th 973 (1987 & Supp. 2010).

59. Uniform Interstate and International Procedure Act, Section 1.05 (withdrawn).

60. *See AT & T Corp. v. Sigala,* 549 S.E.2d 373 (Ga. 2001) (discussing history of doctrine in states); Davies, *Time to Change the Federal* Forum Non Conveniens *Doctrine,* 77 Tul. L. Rev. 309, 315 (2002) (noting that 43 states formally or effectively apply the federal test). For an example of a recent state-court decision where the governing standards differ in a potentially outcome-determinative way from the federal standard, *see In re Pirelli Tires, L.L.C.,* 247 S.W.3d 670 (Tex. 2007).

61. *E.g., Kinney Sys. Inc. v. Continental Ins. Co.,* 674 So. 2d 86, 92 (Fla. 1996); *Satkowiak v. Chesapeake & Ohio Ry.,* 478 N.E.2d 370 (Ill. 1985). For a thorough recent survey of state approaches, *see Kedy v. A.W. Chesterton Co.,* 946 A.2d 1171 (R.I. 2008) (adopting the doctrine of *forum non conveniens*).

62. *See, e.g., Candlewood Timber Group, LLC v. Pan American Energy, LLC,* 859 A.2d 989 (Del. 2004) (requiring "overwhelming hardship"); *Mar-Land Indus. Contractors, Inc. v. Caribbean,* 777 A.2d 774 (Del. 2001).

(Idaho and Oregon) have not formally adopted the doctrine either by statute or an authoritative decision of the state's highest court.[63]

Selected materials illustrating the basic principles of the *forum non conveniens* doctrine are excerpted below. The Supreme Court's opinion in *Piper Aircraft Co. v. Reyno,* excerpted below, remains the leading contemporary statement of the doctrine. The Texas Supreme Court's opinions in *Dow Chemical Co. v. Castro Alfaro* reflect the controversy that the *forum non conveniens* doctrine has generated.

PIPER AIRCRAFT CO. v. REYNO
454 U.S. 235 (1981)

Justice Marshall delivered the opinion of the Court. . . . In July 1976, a small commercial aircraft crashed in the Scottish highlands during the course of a charter flight from Blackpool to Perth. The pilot and five passengers were killed instantly. The decedents were all Scottish subjects and residents, as are their heirs and next of kin. There were no eyewitnesses to the accident. At the time of the crash the plane was subject to Scottish air traffic control. The aircraft, a twin-engine Piper Aztec, was manufactured in Pennsylvania by petitioner Piper Aircraft Co. ("Piper"). The propellers were manufactured in Ohio by petitioner Hartzell Propeller, Inc. ("Hartzell"). At the time of the crash the aircraft was registered in Great Britain and was owned and maintained by Air Navigation and Trading Co., Ltd. ("Air Navigation"). It was operated by McDonald Aviation, Ltd. ("McDonald"), a Scottish air taxi service. Both Air Navigation and McDonald were organized in the United Kingdom. The wreckage of the plane is now in a hangar in Farnborough, England.

The British Department of Trade investigated the accident shortly after it occurred. A preliminary report found that the plane crashed after developing a spin, and suggested that mechanical failure in the plane or the propeller was responsible. At Hartzell's request, this report was reviewed by a three-member Review Board, which held a 9-day adversary hearing attended by all interested parties. The Review Board found no evidence of defective equipment and indicated that pilot error may have contributed to the accident. . . .

In July 1977, a California probate court appointed respondent Gaynell Reyno administratrix of the estates of the five passengers. Reyno is not related to and does not know any of the decedents or other survivors; she was a legal secretary to the attorney who filed this lawsuit. Several days after her appointment, Reyno commenced separate wrongful-death actions against Piper and Hartzell in the Superior Court of California, claiming negligence and strict liability. . . . Reyno candidly admits that the action against Piper and Hartzell was filed in the United States because its laws regarding liability, capacity to sue and damages are more favorable to her position than are those of Scotland. Scottish law does not recognize strict liability in tort. Moreover, it permits wrongful-death actions only when brought by a decedent's relatives. The relatives may sue only for "loss of support and society."

[Following removal to a federal district court in California and transfer under 28 U.S.C. §1404(a) to a federal district court in Pennsylvania, the district judge applied *Gilbert* and *Koster* and dismissed the action on *forum non conveniens* grounds. On appeal, the Third

---

63. *See Rule v. Burlington Northern and Santa Fe Ry. Co.,* 106 P.3d 533, 536 (Mont. 2005) (no *forum non conveniens* doctrine in Montana); *Maricich v. Lacoss,* 129 P.3d 193, 195 n.1 (Or. App. 2006) (assuming that *forum non conveniens* doctrine can be applied in Oregon courts).

Circuit reversed, apparently holding that (1) the district court abused its discretion in its application of *Gilbert* and (2) a *forum non conveniens* dismissal is never appropriate where the law of the alternative forum is less favorable to the plaintiff.]

The Court of Appeals erred in holding that plaintiffs may defeat a motion to dismiss on the ground of *forum non conveniens* merely by showing that the substantive law that would be applied in the alternative forum is less favorable to the plaintiffs than that of the present forum. The possibility of a change in substantive law should ordinarily not be given conclusive or even substantial weight in the *forum non conveniens* inquiry.

We expressly rejected the position adopted by the Court of Appeals in our decision in *Canada Malting Co. v. Paterson Steamships, Ltd.*, 285 U.S. 413 (1932). The District Court dismissed [the Canadian plaintiffs' claims] on grounds of *forum non conveniens*. The plaintiffs argued that dismissal was inappropriate because Canadian laws were less favorable to them. This Court nonetheless affirmed:

> We have no occasion to enquire by what law the rights of the parties are governed, as we are of the opinion that, under any view of that question, it lay within the discretion of the District Court to decline to assume jurisdiction over the controversy. . . . "[T]he court will not take cognizance of the case if justice would be as well done by remitting the parties to their home forum." . . .

It is true that *Canada Malting* was decided before *Gilbert*, and that the doctrine of *forum non conveniens* was not fully crystallized until our decision in that case.[64] However, *Gilbert* in no way affects the validity of *Canada Malting*. Indeed, by holding that the central focus of the *forum non conveniens* inquiry is convenience, *Gilbert* implicitly recognized that dismissal may not be barred solely because of the possibility of an unfavorable change in law. Under *Gilbert*, dismissal will ordinarily be appropriate where trial in the plaintiff's chosen forum imposes a heavy burden on the defendant or the court, and where the plaintiff is unable to offer any specific reasons of convenience supporting his choice.[65] If substantial weight were given to the possibility of an unfavorable change in law, however, dismissal might be barred even where trial in the chosen forum was plainly inconvenient.

The Court of Appeals' decision is inconsistent with this Court's earlier *forum non conveniens* decisions in another respect. Those decisions have repeatedly emphasized the need to retain flexibility. . . . If central emphasis were placed on any one factor, the *forum non conveniens* doctrine would lose much of the very flexibility that makes it so valuable. In fact, if conclusive or substantial weight were given to the possibility of a change in law, the *forum non conveniens* doctrine would become virtually useless. Jurisdiction and venue requirements are often easily satisfied. As a result, many plaintiffs are able to choose from among several forums. Ordinarily, these plaintiffs will select that forum whose choice-of-law rules are most advantageous. Thus, if the possibility of an unfavorable

64. The doctrine of *forum non conveniens* originated in Scotland, *see* Braucher, *The Inconvenient Federal Forum*, 60 Harv. L. Rev. 908, 909-911 (1947), and became part of the common law of many States, *see id.* at 911-912; Blair, *The Doctrine of Forum Non Conveniens in Anglo-American Law*, 29 Colum. L. Rev. 1 (1929). The doctrine was also frequently applied in federal admiralty actions. *See, e.g., Canada Malting Co. v. Paterson Steamships, Ltd.* . . . In previous *forum non conveniens* decisions, the Court has left unresolved the question whether under *Erie R.R. v. Tompkins*, 304 U.S. 64 (1938), state or federal law of *forum non conveniens* applies in diversity cases. The Court did not decide this issue because the same result would have been reached in each case under federal or state law. The lower courts in these cases reached the same conclusion: Pennsylvania and California law on *forum non conveniens* dismissals are virtually identical to federal law. Thus, here also, we need not resolve the *Erie* question.

65. In other words, *Gilbert* held that dismissal may be warranted where a plaintiff chooses a particular forum, not because it is convenient, but solely in order to harass the defendant or take advantage of favorable law. This is precisely the situation in which the Court of Appeals' rule would bar dismissal.

change in substantive law is given substantial weight in the *forum non conveniens* inquiry, dismissal would rarely be proper. . . .

The Court of Appeals' approach is not only inconsistent with the purpose of the *forum non conveniens* doctrine, but also poses substantial practical problems. If the possibility of a change in law were given substantial weight, deciding motions to dismiss on the ground of *forum non conveniens* would become quite difficult. Choice-of-law analysis would become extremely important, and the court would frequently be required to interpret the law of foreign jurisdictions. . . . The doctrine of *forum non conveniens*, however, is designed in part to help courts avoid conducting complex exercises in comparative law. As we stated in *Gilbert*, the public interest factors point towards dismissal where the court would be required to "untangle problems in conflict of laws, and in law foreign to itself."

Upholding the decision of the Court of Appeals would result in other practical problems. At least where the foreign plaintiff named an American manufacturer as defendant,[66] a court could not dismiss the case on grounds of *forum non conveniens* where dismissal might lead to an unfavorable change in law. The American courts, which are already extremely attractive to foreign plaintiffs,[67] would become even more attractive. The flow of litigation into the United States would increase and further congest already crowded courts. . . .

We do not hold that the possibility of an unfavorable change in law should *never* be a relevant consideration in a *forum non conveniens* inquiry. Of course, if the remedy provided by the alternative forum is so clearly inadequate or unsatisfactory that it is no remedy at all, the unfavorable change in law may be given substantial weight; the district court may conclude that dismissal would not be in the interest of justice.[68] In these cases, however, the remedies that would be provided by the Scottish courts do not fall within this category. Although the relatives of the decedents may not be able to rely on a strict liability theory, and although their potential damages award may be smaller, there is no danger that they will be deprived of any remedy or treated unfairly

---

66. In fact, the defendant might not even have to be American. A foreign plaintiff seeking damages for an accident [that] had occurred abroad might be able to obtain service of process on a foreign defendant who does business in the United States. Under the Court of Appeals' holding, dismissal would be barred if the law in the alternative forum were less favorable to the plaintiff — even though none of the parties are American, and even though there is absolutely no nexus between the subject matter of the litigation and the United States.

67. First, all but 6 of the 50 American States — Delaware, Massachusetts, Michigan, North Carolina, Virginia, and Wyoming — offer strict liability. 1 CCH Prod. Liability Rep. §4016 (1981). Rules roughly equivalent to American strict liability are effective in France, Belgium, and Luxembourg. West Germany and Japan have a strict liability statute for pharmaceuticals. However, strict liability remains primarily an American innovation. Second, the tort plaintiff may choose, at least potentially, from among 50 jurisdictions if he decides to file suit in the United States. Each of these jurisdictions applies its own set of malleable choice-of-law rules. Third, jury trials are almost always available in the United States, while they are never provided in civil law jurisdictions. G. Gloss, *Comparative Law* 12 (1979); J. Merryman, *The Civil Law Tradition* 121 (1969). Even in the United Kingdom, most civil actions are not tried before a jury. 1 G. Keeton, *The United Kingdom: The Development of Its Laws and Constitutions* 309 (1955). Fourth, unlike most foreign jurisdictions, American courts allow contingent attorney's fees, and do not tax losing parties with their opponents' attorney's fees. R. Schlesinger, *Comparative Law: Cases, Text, Materials* 275-277 (3d ed. 1970); Orban, *Product Liability: A Comparative Legal Restatement — Foreign National Law and the EEC Directive*, 8 Ga. J. Int'l & Comp. L. 342, 393 (1978). Fifth, discovery is more extensive in American than in foreign courts. R. Schlesinger, *supra*, at 307, 310 and n.33.

68. At the outset of any *forum non conveniens* inquiry, the court must determine whether there exists an alternative forum. Ordinarily, this requirement will be satisfied when the defendant is "amenable to process" in the other jurisdiction. In rare circumstances, however, where the remedy offered by the other forum is clearly unsatisfactory, the other forum may not be an adequate alternative, and the initial requirements may not be satisfied. Thus, for example, dismissal would not be appropriate where the alternative forum does not permit litigation of the subject matter of the dispute. *Cf. Phoenix Canada Oil Co. Ltd. v. Texaco Inc.*, 78 F.R.D. 445 (D. Del. 1978) (court refuses to dismiss, where alternative forum is Ecuador, it is unclear whether Ecuadorean tribunal will hear the case, and there is no generally codified Ecuadorean legal remedy for the unjust enrichment and tort claims asserted).

The Court of Appeals also erred in rejecting the District Court's *Gilbert* analysis. The Court of Appeals stated that more weight should have been given to the plaintiff's choice of forum, and criticized the District Court's analysis of the private and public interests. However, the District Court's decision regarding the deference due plaintiff's choice of forum was appropriate. Furthermore, we do not believe that the District Court abused its discretion in weighing the private and public interests.

The District Court acknowledged that there is ordinarily a strong presumption in favor of the plaintiff's choice of forum, which may be overcome only when the private and public interest factors clearly point towards trial in the alternative forum. It held, however, that the presumption applies with less force when the plaintiff or real parties in interest are foreign. The District Court's distinction between resident or citizen plaintiffs and foreign plaintiffs is fully justified. In *Koster*, the Court indicated that a plaintiff's choice of forum is entitled to greater deference when the plaintiff has chosen the home forum. 330 U.S. at 524.[69] When the home forum has been chosen, it is reasonable to assume that this choice is convenient. When the plaintiff is foreign, however, this assumption is much less reasonable. Because the central purpose of any *forum non conveniens* inquiry is to ensure that the trial is convenient, a foreign plaintiff's choice deserves less deference.

The *forum non conveniens* determination is committed to the sound discretion of the trial court. It may be reversed only where there has been a clear abuse of discretion; where the court has considered all relevant public and private interest factors, and where its balancing of these factors is reasonable, its decision deserves substantial deference. Here, the Court of Appeals expressly acknowledged that the standard of review was one of abuse of discretion. In examining the District Court's analysis of the public and private interests, however, the Court of Appeals seems to have lost sight of this rule, and substituted its own judgment for that of the District Court.

In analyzing the private interest factors, the District Court stated that the connections with Scotland are "overwhelming." This characterization may be somewhat exaggerated. Particularly with respect to the question of relative ease of access to sources of proof, the private interests point in both directions. As respondent emphasized, records concerning the design, manufacture, and testing of the propeller and plane are located in the United States. She would have greater access to sources of proof relevant to her strict liability and negligence theories if trial were held here.[70] However, the District Court did not act unreasonably in concluding that fewer evidentiary problems would be posed if the trial were held in Scotland. A large proportion of the relevant evidence is located in Great Britain.

The Court of Appeals found that the problems of proof could not be given any weight because Piper and Hartzell failed to describe with specificity the evidence they would not be able to obtain if trial were held in the United States. It suggested that defendants seeking *forum non conveniens* dismissal must submit affidavits identifying the witnesses they would call and the testimony these witnesses would provide if the trial were held in the alternative forum. Such detail is not necessary. Piper and Hartzell have moved for dismissal precisely because many crucial witnesses are located beyond the reach of compulsory process, and thus are difficult to identify or interview. Requiring extensive

---

69. In *Koster*, we stated that "[i]n any balancing of conveniences, a real showing of convenience by a plaintiff who had sued in his home forum will normally outweigh the inconvenience the defendant may have shown." 330 U.S. at 524. *See also Swift & Co. Packers v. Compania Colombiana del Caribe*, 339 U.S. 684, 697 (1950) ("suit by a United States citizen against a foreign respondent brings into force considerations very different from those in suits between foreigners"); *Canada Malting Co. v. Paterson Steamships, Ltd.*, 285 U.S. at 421 ("[t]he rule recognizing an unqualified discretion to decline jurisdiction in suits in admiralty between foreigners appears to be supported by an unbroken line of decisions in the lower federal courts"). . . .

70. In the future, where similar problems are presented, district courts might dismiss subject to the condition that defendant corporations agree to provide the records relevant to the plaintiff's claims.

B.   *The Modern* **Forum Non Conveniens** *Doctrine: Basic Principles*   **377**

investigation would defeat the purpose of their motion. Of course, defendants must provide enough information to enable the District Court to balance the parties' interests. Our examination of the record convinces us that sufficient information was provided here. Both Piper and Hartzell submitted affidavits describing the evidentiary problems they would face if the trial were held in the United States.

The District Court correctly concluded that the problems posed by the inability to implead potential third-party defendants clearly supported holding the trial in Scotland. Joinder of the pilot's estate, Air Navigation, and McDonald is crucial to the presentation of petitioners' defense. If Piper and Hartzell can show that the accident was caused not by a design defect, but rather by the negligence of the pilot, the plane's owners, or the charter company, they will be relieved of all liability. It is true, of course, that if Hartzell and Piper were found liable after a trial in the United States, they could institute an action for indemnity or contribution against these parties in Scotland. It would be far more convenient, however, to resolve all claims in one trial. The Court of Appeals rejected this argument. Forcing petitioners to rely on actions for indemnity or contribution would be "burdensome" but not "unfair." Finding that trial in the plaintiff's chosen forum would be burdensome, however, is sufficient to support dismissal on grounds of *forum non conveniens.*

The District Court's review of the factors relating to the public interest was also reasonable. On the basis of its choice-of-law analysis, it concluded that if the case were tried in the Middle District of Pennsylvania, Pennsylvania law would apply to Piper and Scottish law to Hartzell. It stated that a trial involving two sets of laws would be confusing to the jury. It also noted its own lack of familiarity with Scottish law. Consideration of these problems was clearly appropriate under *Gilbert;* in that case we explicitly held that the need to apply foreign law pointed towards dismissal.[71] The Court of Appeals found that the District Court's choice-of-law analysis was incorrect, and that American law would apply to both Hartzell and Piper. Thus, lack of familiarity with foreign law would not be a problem. Even if the Court of Appeals' conclusion is correct, however, all other public interest factors favored trial in Scotland.

Scotland has a very strong interest in this litigation. The accident occurred in its airspace. All of the decedents were Scottish. Apart from Piper and Hartzell, all potential plaintiffs and defendants are either Scottish or English. As we stated in *Gilbert,* there is "a local interest in having localized controversies decided at home." Respondent argues that American citizens have an interest in ensuring that American manufacturers are deterred from producing defective products, and that additional deterrence might be obtained if Piper and Hartzell were tried in the United States, where they could be sued on the basis of both negligence and strict liability. However, the incremental deterrence that would be gained if this trial were held in an American court is likely to be insignificant. The American interest in this accident is simply not sufficient to justify the enormous commitment of judicial time and resources that would inevitably be required if the case were to be tried here.

The Court of Appeals erred in holding that the possibility of an unfavorable change in law bars dismissal on the ground of *forum non conveniens.* It also erred in rejecting the District Court's *Gilbert* analysis. The District Court properly decided that the presumption in favor of the respondent's forum choice applied with less than maximum force because the real parties in interest are foreign. It did not act unreasonably in deciding that the

---

71. Many *forum non conveniens* decisions have held that the need to apply foreign law favors dismissal. . . . Of course, this factor alone is not sufficient to warrant dismissal when a balancing of all relevant factors shows that the plaintiff's chosen forum is appropriate. . . .

private interests pointed towards trial in Scotland. Nor did it act unreasonably in deciding that the public interests favored trial in Scotland. Thus, the judgment of the Court of Appeals is reversed.

DOW CHEMICAL COMPANY v. CASTRO ALFARO

786 S.W.2d 674 (Tex. 1990), abrogated by statute Tex. Civ. Prac. & Rem. Code Ann. §71.051(i)

RAY, JUSTICE. At issue in this cause is whether the statutory right to enforce a personal injury or wrongful death claim in the Texas courts precludes a trial court from dismissing the claim on the ground of *forum non conveniens*. . . . [W]e conclude that the legislature has statutorily abolished the doctrine of *forum non conveniens* in suits brought under §71.031 of the Texas Civil Practice and Remedies Code. . . .

Domingo Castro Alfaro, a Costa Rican resident and employee of the Standard Fruit Company ("Standard Fruit"), and eighty-one other Costa Rican employees and their wives brought suit against Dow Chemical Company ("Dow") and Shell Oil Company ("Shell"). The employees claim that they suffered personal injuries as a result of exposure to dibromochloropropane ("DBCP"), a pesticide manufactured by Dow and Shell, which was allegedly furnished to Standard Fruit. [The Environmental Protection Agency issued . . . an order suspending registrations of pesticides containing DBCP on November 3, 1977. Before and after the E.P.A.'s ban of DBCP in the United States, Shell and Dow allegedly shipped several hundred thousand gallons of the pesticide to Costa Rica for use by Standard Fruit.] The employees exposed to DBCP allegedly suffered several medical problems, including sterility.

Alfaro sued Dow and Shell in Harris County district court in April 1984. The amended petition alleged that the court had jurisdiction under article 4678 of the Revised Statutes. Following an unsuccessful attempt to remove the suit to federal court, Dow and Shell contested the jurisdiction of the trial court . . . and contended in the alternative that the case should be dismissed under the doctrine of *forum non conveniens*. . . . [T]he trial court dismissed the case on the ground of *forum non conveniens*.

Section 71.031 of the [Texas] Civil Practice and Remedies Code provides:

> (a) An action for damages for the death or personal injury of a citizen of this state, of the United States, or of a foreign country may be enforced in the courts of this state, although the wrongful act, neglect, or default causing the death or injury takes place in a foreign state or country, if: (1) a law of the foreign state or country or of this state gives a right to maintain an action for damages for the death or injury; (2) the action is begun in this state within the time provided by the laws of this state for beginning the action; and (3) in the case of a citizen of a foreign country, the country has equal treaty rights with the United States on behalf of its citizens.[72] . . . Tex. Civ. Prac. & Rem. Code Ann. §71.031 (Vernon 1986).

---

72. The United States and Costa Rica agreed to the following:

> The citizens of the high contracting parties shall reciprocally receive and enjoy full and perfect protection for their persons and property, and shall have free and open access to the courts of justice in the said countries respectively, for the prosecution and defense of their just rights; and they shall be at liberty to employ, in all cases, the advocates, attorneys, or agents of whatever description, whom they may think proper, and they shall enjoy in this respect the same rights and privileges therein as native citizens. Treaty of Friendship, Commerce, and Navigation, July 10, 1851 United States-Costa Rica, Art. VII, para. 2, 10 Stat. 916, 920, T.S. No. 621.

Subsection (a)(3) requires the existence of similar treaty provisions before an action by a citizen of a foreign country may be maintained under §71.031.

At issue is whether the language "may be enforced in the courts of this state" of §71.031(a) permits a trial court to relinquish jurisdiction under the doctrine of *forum non conveniens*.

The statutory predecessors of §71.031 have existed since 1913. . . . Texas courts applied the doctrine of *forum non conveniens* in several cases prior to the enactment of article 4678 in 1913. In 1890, this court in dicta recognized the power of a court to refuse to exercise jurisdiction on grounds essentially the same as those of *forum non conveniens*. *See Morris v. Missouri Pac. Ry.*, 14 S.W. 228, 230 (1890). In *Morris*, we stated:

> We do not think the facts alleged show the action to be transitory. But, if so, it has been held in such actions, where the parties were non-residents and the cause of action originated beyond the limits of the state, these facts would justify the court in refusing to entertain jurisdiction. Jurisdiction is entertained in such cases only upon principles of comity, and not as a matter of right. . . .

We . . . must determine whether the legislature in 1913 statutorily abolished the doctrine of *forum non conveniens* in suits brought under article 4678 [now §71.031]. Our interpretation of §71.031 is controlled by this court's refusal of writ of error in *Allen v. Bass*, 47 S.W.2d 426 (Tex. Civ. App. 1932). In *Allen* the Court of Civil Appeals held that old article 4678 conferred an absolute right to maintain a properly brought suit in Texas courts. The suit in *Allen* involved a New Mexico plaintiff and defendant arising out of an accident occurring in New Mexico. The court of appeals reversed a dismissal granted by the trial court on grounds similar to those of *forum non conveniens*, holding that "article 4678 opens the courts of this state to citizens of a neighboring state and gives to them an *absolute right* to maintain a transitory action of the present nature and to try their cases in the courts of this state" (emphasis added). . . . [Like the court in *Allen*,] we conclude that the legislature has statutorily abolished the doctrine of *forum non conveniens* in suits brought under §71.031. . . .

DOGGETT, JUSTICE, concurring. . . . I write separately . . . to respond to the dissenters. . . . In their zeal to implement their own preferred social policy that Texas corporations not be held responsible at home for harm caused abroad, these dissenters refuse to be restrained by either express statutory language or the compelling precedent . . . holding that *forum non conveniens* does not apply in Texas. To accomplish the desired social engineering, they must invoke yet another legal fiction with a fancy name to shield alleged wrongdoers, the so-called doctrine of *forum non conveniens*. . . .

The dissenters are insistent that a jury of Texans be denied the opportunity to evaluate the conduct of a Texas corporation concerning decisions it made in Texas because the only ones allegedly hurt are foreigners. Fortunately Texans are not so provincial and narrow-minded as these dissenters presume. Our citizenry recognizes that a wrong does not fade away because its immediate consequences are first felt far away rather than close to home. Never have we been required to forfeit our membership in the human race in order to maintain our proud heritage as citizens of Texas.

The dissenters argue that it is inconvenient and unfair for farmworkers allegedly suffering permanent physical and mental injuries, including irreversible sterility, to seek redress by suing a multinational corporation in a court three blocks away from its world headquarters and another corporation, which operates in Texas this country's largest chemical plant. Because the "doctrine" they advocate has nothing to do with fairness and convenience and everything to do with immunizing multinational corporations from accountability for their alleged torts causing injury abroad, I write separately. . . .

Shell is a multinational corporation with its world headquarters in Houston, Texas. Dow, though headquartered in Midland, Michigan, conducts extensive operations from its Dow Chemical USA building located in Houston. Dow operates this country's largest chemical manufacturing plant within 60 miles of Houston in Freeport, Texas. The district court where this lawsuit was filed is three blocks away from Shell's world headquarters, One Shell Plaza in downtown Houston. . . .

The banana plantation workers allegedly injured by DBCP were employed by an American company on American-owned land and grew Dole bananas for export solely to American tables. The chemical allegedly rendering the workers sterile was researched, formulated, tested, manufactured, labeled and shipped by an American company in the United States to another American company. The decision to manufacture DBCP for distribution and use in the third world was made by these two American companies in their corporate offices in the United States. Yet now Shell and Dow argue that the one part of this equation that should not be American is the legal consequences of their actions.

. . . Both as a matter of law and of public policy, the doctrine of *forum non conveniens* is without justification. The proffered foundations for it are "considerations of fundamental fairness and sensible and effective judicial administration." In fact, the doctrine is favored by multinational defendants because a *forum non conveniens* dismissal is often outcome-determinative, effectively defeating the claim and denying the plaintiff recovery. . . . A *forum non conveniens* dismissal is often, in reality, a complete victory for the defendant. . . . Empirical data available demonstrate that less than four percent of cases dismissed under the doctrine of *forum non conveniens* ever reach trial in a foreign court.[73] A *forum non conveniens* dismissal usually will end the litigation altogether, effectively excusing any liability of the defendant. The plaintiffs leave the courtroom without having had their case resolved on the merits.[74] . . .

Advances in transportation and communications technology have rendered the private [*Gulf Oil*] factors largely irrelevant: A forum is not necessarily inconvenient because of its distance from pertinent parties or places if it is readily accessible in a few hours of air travel. It will often be quicker and less expensive to transfer a witness or a document than to transfer a lawsuit. Jet travel and satellite communications have significantly altered the meaning of "non conveniens." . . . In sum, the private factors are no longer a predominant consideration — fairness and convenience to the parties have been thrust out of the *forum non conveniens* equation. As the "doctrine" is now applied, the term "*forum non conveniens*" has clearly become a misnomer. . . .

[In addressing the public interest factors, the] dissenting members of the court falsely attempt to paint a picture of Texas becoming an "irresistible forum for all mass disaster

---

73. Professor David Robertson of the University of Texas School of Law attempted to discover the subsequent history of each reported transnational case dismissed under *forum non conveniens* from *Gulf Oil v. Gilbert*, to the end of 1984. Data was received on 55 personal injury cases and 30 commercial cases. Of the 55 personal injury cases, only one was actually tried in a foreign court. Only two of the 30 commercial cases reached trial.

74. Such a result in the name of "convenience" would undoubtedly follow a dismissal under *forum non conveniens* in the case at bar. The plaintiffs, who earn approximately one dollar per hour working at the banana plantation, clearly cannot compete financially with Shell and Dow in carrying on the litigation. More importantly, the cost of just one trip to Houston to review the documents produced by Shell would exceed the estimated maximum possible recovery in Costa Rica. In an unchallenged affidavit, a senior Costa Rican labor judge stated that the maximum possible recovery in Costa Rica would approximate 100,000 colones, just over $1,080 at current exchange rates. . . . Further, Costa Rica permits neither jury trials nor depositions of nonparty witnesses. Attempting to depose a Dow representative concerning the company's knowledge of DBCP hazards will prove to be an impossible task as Dow is not required to produce that person in Costa Rica. It is not unlikely that Shell and Dow seek a *forum non conveniens* dismissal not in pursuit of fairness and convenience, but rather as a shield against the litigation itself. If successful, Shell and Dow, like many American multinational corporations before them, would have secured a largely impenetrable shield against meaningful lawsuits for their alleged torts causing injury abroad.

lawsuits," and for "personal injury cases from around the world." They suggest that our citizens will be forced to hear cases in which "[t]he interest of Texas in these disputes is likely to be . . . slight." Although these suppositions undoubtedly will serve to stir public debate, they have little basis in fact. . . . [A] state's power to assert its jurisdiction is limited by the due process clause of the U.S. Constitution. . . . The personal jurisdiction–due process analysis will ensure that Texas has a sufficient interest in each case entertained in our state's courts.[75] . . .

As stated previously, this suit has been filed against Shell, a corporation with its world headquarters in Texas, doing extensive business in Texas and manufacturing chemicals in Texas. The suit arose out of alleged acts occurring in Texas and alleged decisions made in Texas. The suit also has been filed against Dow, a corporation with its headquarters in Michigan, but apparently having substantial contacts with Texas. Dow operates the country's largest chemical plant in Texas, manufacturing chemicals within sixty miles of the largest population center in Texas, where millions of Texans reside. Shell and Dow cannot now seek to avoid the Texas civil justice system and a jury of Texans.

The next justification offered by the dissenters for invoking the legal fiction of "inconvenience" is that judges will be overworked. Not only will foreigners take our jobs, as we are told in the popular press; now they will have our courts. The xenophobic suggestion that foreigners will take over our courts "forcing our residents to wait in the corridors of our courthouses while foreign causes of action are tried," is both misleading and false. It is the height of deception to suggest that docket backlogs in our state's urban centers are caused by so-called "foreign litigation." . . . Ten states, including Texas, have not recognized the [*forum non conveniens*] doctrine. Within these states, there is no evidence that the docket congestion predicted by the dissenters has actually occurred. . . .

Comity — deference shown to the interests of the foreign forum — is a consideration best achieved by rejecting *forum non conveniens.* Comity is not achieved when the United States allows its multinational corporations to adhere to a double standard when operating abroad and subsequently refuses to hold them accountable for those actions. . . .

The abolition of *forum non conveniens* will further important public policy considerations by providing a check on the conduct of multinational corporations. The misconduct of even a few multinational corporations can affect untold millions around the world. For example, after the United States imposed a domestic ban on the sale of cancer-producing TRIS-treated children's sleepwear, American companies exported approximately 2.4 million pieces to Africa, Asia and South America. A similar pattern occurred when a ban was proposed for baby pacifiers that had been linked to choking deaths in infants. These examples of indifference by some corporations towards children abroad are not unusual. . . .

Some U.S. multinational corporations will undoubtedly continue to endanger human life and the environment with such activities until the economic consequences of these actions are such that it becomes unprofitable to operate in this manner. At present, the tort laws of many third world countries are not yet developed. . . . When a court dismisses a case against a United States multinational corporation, it often removes the most effective restraint on corporate misconduct.

The doctrine of *forum non conveniens* is obsolete in a world in which markets are global and in which ecologists have documented the delicate balance of all life on this planet.

---

75. Justice Cook seems to suggest that it may violate due process for Shell to be sued in Houston. It is an extremely novel holding, unprecedented in American constitutional law, that a corporation could be denied due process by being sued in its hometown. . . .

The parochial perspective embodied in the doctrine of *forum non conveniens* enables corporations to evade legal control merely because they are transnational. This perspective ignores the reality that actions of our corporations affecting those abroad will also affect Texans. Although DBCP is banned from use within the United States, it and other similarly banned chemicals have been consumed by Texans eating foods imported from Costa Rica and elsewhere. In the absence of meaningful tort liability in the United States for their actions, some multinational corporations will continue to operate without adequate regard for the human and environmental costs of their actions. This result cannot be allowed to repeat itself for decades to come.

GONZALEZ, JUSTICE, dissenting. . . . This decision makes us one of the few states in the Union without . . . a procedural tool [like *forum non conveniens*], and if the legislature fails to reinstate this doctrine, Texas will become an irresistible forum for all mass disaster lawsuits. "Bhopal"-type litigation, with little or no connection to Texas will add to our already crowded dockets, forcing our residents to wait in the corridors of our courthouses while foreign causes of action are tried.[76] . . .

COOK, JUSTICE, dissenting. Like turn-of-the-century wildcatters, the plaintiffs in this case searched all across the nation for a place to make their claims. Through three courts they moved, filing their lawsuits on one coast and then on the other. By each of those courts the plaintiffs were rejected, and so they continued their search for a more willing forum. Their efforts are finally rewarded. Today they hit pay dirt in Texas.

No reason exists, in law or in policy, to support their presence in this state. The legislature adopted within the statute the phrase "may be enforced" to permit plaintiffs to sue in Texas, irrespective of where they live or where the cause of action arose. The legislature did not adopt this statute, however, to remove from our courts all discretion to dismiss. To use the statute to sweep away, completely and finally, a common law doctrine painstakingly developed over the years is to infuse the statute with a power not contained in the words. Properly read, the statute is asymmetrical. Although it confers upon the plaintiffs an absolute right to bring claims in our courts, it does not impose upon our courts an absolute responsibility to entertain those claims.

Even if the statute supported the court's interpretation, however, I would remain unwilling to join in the opinion. The decision places too great a burden on defendants who are citizens of our state because, by abolishing *forum non conveniens*, the decision exposes our citizens to the claims of any plaintiff, no matter how distant from Texas is that plaintiff's home or cause of action. The interest of Texas in these disputes is likely to be as slight as the relationship of the plaintiffs to Texas. The interest of other nations, on the other hand, is likely to be substantial. For these reasons, I fear the decision allows assertions of jurisdiction by Texas courts that are so unfair and unreasonable as to violate the due process clause of the federal constitution. . . .

. . . [W]e are inviting into our courts disputes that may involve more substantial connections to foreign countries than to our own. Should we not stop to consider, as the *Asahi* court did, the possible effects of extending our laws beyond the shores of the United States? *See generally* Born, *Reflections on Judicial Jurisdiction in International Cases,* 17 Ga. J. Int'l & Comp. L. 1 (1987). . . . There are in this case unresolved choice of law questions that, once resolved, may diminish the interest of this state in this

---

76. For example, in July 1988, there was an oil rig disaster in Scotland. A Texas lawyer went to Scotland, held a press conference, and wrote letters to victims or their families. He advised them that they had a good chance of trying their cases in Texas where awards would be much higher than elsewhere. Houston Post, July 18, 1988, at 13A, col. 1; The Times (London), July 18, 1988, at 20A, col. 1; Texas Lawyer, Sept. 26, 1988 at 3.

litigation. . . . There is a strong possibility that a choice of law analysis will result in the application of Costa Rican law. If so, what then is Texas' interest in adjudicating a foreign claim by foreign plaintiffs? . . .

HECHT, JUSTICE, dissenting. Today the Court decrees that citizens of a foreign nation, Costa Rica, who claim to have been injured in their own country have an absolute right to sue for money damages in Texas courts. . . . [This] inflicts a blow upon the people of Texas, its employers and taxpayers, that is contrary to sound policy.

The United States does not give aliens unlimited access to its courts. Indeed, one federal district court in California and two in Florida have already dismissed essentially this same lawsuit which the Court now welcomes to Texas. No state has ever given aliens such unlimited admission to its courts. The U.S. Supreme Court, the District of Columbia, and forty states have all recognized what has come to be called the rule of *forum non conveniens*. . . . Until now, no state has ever rejected this rule. . . .

The dearth of authority for the Court's unprecedented holding is disturbing. Far more disconcerting, however, is the Court's silence as to why the rule of *forum non conveniens* should be abolished in personal injury and death cases, either by the Legislature or by the Court. . . . The benefit to the plaintiffs in suing in Texas should be obvious: more money, as counsel was candid enough to admit in oral argument.[77] . . . But what purpose beneficial to the people of Texas is served by clogging the already burdened dockets of the state's courts with cases which arose around the world and which have nothing to do with this state except that the defendant can be served with citation here? Why, most of all, should Texas be the only state in the country, perhaps the only jurisdiction on earth, possibly the only one in history, to offer to try personal injury cases from around the world? Do Texas taxpayers want to pay extra for judges and clerks and courthouses and personnel to handle foreign litigation? If they do not mind the expense, do they not care that these foreign cases will delay their own cases being heard? As the courthouse for the world, will Texas entice employers to move here, or people to do business here, or even anyone to visit? . . . Who gains? A few lawyers, obviously. But who else? If the Court has good answers to these questions, why does it not say so in its opinion? If there are no good answers, then what the Court does today is very pernicious for the state.[78]

---

77. It is equally plain to me that defendants want to be sued in Costa Rica rather than Texas because they expect that their exposure will be less there than here. However, it also seems plain to me that the Legislature would want to protect the citizens of this state, its constituents, from greater exposure to liability than they would face in the country in which the alleged wrong was committed. This would be incentive for the Legislature not to abolish the rule of *forum non conveniens*.

78. Justice Doggett's concurring opinion undertakes to answer these questions that the Court ignores. It suggests that there are essentially two policy reasons to abolish the rule of forum non conveniens: to assure that injured plaintiffs can recover fully, and to assure that American corporations will be fully punished for their misdeeds abroad. Neither reason is sufficient. If the defendants in this case were Costa Rican corporations which plaintiffs could sue only in Costa Rica, plaintiffs would be limited to whatever recovery they could obtain in Costa Rican courts. The concurring opinion has not explained why Costa Rican plaintiffs who claim to have been injured by American corporations are unjustly treated if they are required to sue in their own country where they could only sue if they had been injured by Costa Rican corporations. In other words, why are Costa Ricans injured by an American defendant entitled to any greater recovery than Costa Ricans injured by a Costa Rican defendant, or a Libyan defendant, or an Iranian defendant? Moreover, the concurring opinion does not explain why the American justice system should undertake to punish American corporations more severely for their actions in a foreign country than that country does. If the alleged conduct of the defendants in this case is so egregious, why has Costa Rica not chosen to afford its own citizens the recovery they seek in Texas? One wonders how receptive Costa Rican courts would be to the pleas of American plaintiffs against Costa Rican citizens for recovery of all the damages that might be available in Texas, or anywhere else for that matter.

Notes on Piper and Castro Alfaro

1. *Judicial authority to adopt the* **forum non conveniens** *doctrine.* The district court in *Piper* was granted personal jurisdiction over the defendants by Rule 4 of the Federal Rules of Civil Procedure and a borrowed state long-arm statute. Similarly, statutory venue requirements were satisfied. Nonetheless, the Supreme Court held that the *forum non conveniens* doctrine permitted the trial court to decline jurisdiction on the grounds that it would have been an unduly "inconvenient" forum. *Piper* cited no statutory or constitutional basis for the *forum non conveniens* doctrine.

Is *Piper*'s judicial abstention appropriate? Justice Black, dissenting in *Gulf Oil*, challenged what he characterized as an "abdication" of jurisdiction as violating the obligation of U.S. courts to exercise jurisdiction that Congress confers on them: "the courts of the United States are bound to proceed to judgment . . . in every case to which their jurisdiction extends. They cannot abdicate their authority or duty in any case in favor of another jurisdiction." *Gulf Oil Corp. v. Gilbert*, 330 U.S. 501, 515 (1947) (citing *Hyde v. Stone*, 61 U.S. 170, 175 (1858)). The *Gulf Oil* majority responded that "[o]bviously, the proposition that a court having jurisdiction must exercise it, is not universally true; else the admiralty court could never decline jurisdiction on the ground that the litigation is between foreigners. . . . Courts of equity and law also occasionally decline, in the interest of justice, to exercise jurisdiction, where the suit is between aliens or non-residents or where for kindred reasons the litigation can more appropriately be conducted in a foreign tribunal." 330 U.S. at 504 (quoting *Canada Malting Co. v. Paterson Steamships, Ltd.*, 285 U.S. 413, 422-423 (1932)). *See also Oceanic Sun Line Special Shipping Co. v. Fay*, (1988) 165 C.L.R. 197, 252 (Australian High Court) ("It is a basic tenet of our jurisprudence that, where jurisdiction exists, access to the courts is a right. It is not a privilege which can be withdrawn otherwise than in clearly-defined circumstances.").

Is it appropriate for federal courts to abstain from exercising jurisdiction that Congress has granted them? From where is the authority to do so derived? Should federal courts have inherent power to control their dockets, notwithstanding Congress's jurisdictional statutes? Consider the Court's remarks in *Quackenbush v. Allstate Ins. Co.*, 517 U.S. 706, 716 (1996), where it limited the use of abstention doctrines in the state-federal context, holding that "federal courts have the power to dismiss or remand cases based on abstention principles only where the relief being sought is equitable or otherwise discretionary." At the same time, the Court also declared:

> [W]e have recognized that federal courts have discretion to dismiss damages actions, in certain narrow circumstances, under the common-law doctrine of *forum non conveniens*. . . . The fact that we have applied the *forum non conveniens* doctrine in this manner does not change our analysis in this case. . . . To be sure, the abstention doctrines and the doctrine of *forum non conveniens* proceed from a similar premise: In rare circumstances, federal courts can relinquish their jurisdiction in favor of another forum. But our abstention doctrine is of a distinct historical pedigree, and the traditional considerations behind dismissal for *forum non conveniens* differ markedly from those informing the decision to abstain. Federal courts abstain out of deference to the paramount interests of another sovereign, and the concern is with principles of comity and federalism. Dismissal for *forum non conveniens*, by contrast, has historically reflected a far broader range of considerations, *see Piper* (describing the interests which bear on *forum non conveniens* decision), most notably the convenience to the parties and the practical difficulties that can attend the adjudication of a dispute in a certain locality.

Is this analysis persuasive? Why is it that reasons of convenience and trial management are more important, in terms of justifying abstention, than considerations of federalism and federal-state comity? Is the *forum non conveniens* doctrine only concerned with trial management and convenience, or does it not also concern matters of comity and respect for foreign regulatory interests? *See infra* pp. 408-426. Does legislative inaction following *Piper* and *Gilbert* suggest Congress's acquiescence in the doctrine? Note that the Texas legislature did not hesitate to overrule *Alfaro* by statute when it disagreed with the holding in that case.

2. *Rationale for* forum non conveniens *doctrine*. What reasons are advanced in *Piper* to justify dismissal of a plaintiff's claims, wholly without legislative authorization? What values are served by the *forum non conveniens* doctrine?

(a) Local judicial convenience. Consider the following excerpt from an early decision foreshadowing the *forum non conveniens* doctrine:

> if it appears upon the face of the pleadings that both of the litigant parties are foreigners and a foreign contract, we ought not to interpose. By the nature of all governments, courts were constituted to administer justice in relation to their own citizens; and not to do the business of citizens or subjects of other states. The judges of their own state are employed, and paid for that purpose. To encourage the resort of foreigners to our courts would be doing injustice to our own citizens who have business here to be attended to. *Avery v. Holland*, 2 Tenn. 71 (1806).

Similarly:

> To hold that two foreigners may import, bodily, a cause of action, and insist, as a matter of right, that taxpayers, citizens, and residents shall await the lagging steps of justice in the anteroom while the court hears and decides the foreign controversy, seems, on the face of it, to be unreasonable, if not absurd. *Disconto-Gesellschaft v. Umbreit*, 106 N.W. 821, 823 (Wis. 1906), *aff'd*, 208 U.S. 570 (1908).

Are these legitimate concerns, or mere xenophobia? Do not foreigners have a right of access to U.S. courts? *See supra* pp. 77-78. Even if they are legitimate concerns, are these adequate justifications for the *forum non conveniens* doctrine? What would Justice Doggett say?

(b) Handling private litigation efficiently. To what extent does the *forum non conveniens* doctrine concern issues of convenience and trial management? Note Justice Marshall's statement in *Piper* that "the central purpose of any *forum non conveniens* inquiry is to ensure that the trial is convenient." Consider the discussion in *Piper* of the "private interest" factors, such as the location of documents and witnesses, the availability of compulsory process, and the location of related litigation. Even if these factors indicate that the plaintiff's chosen forum is significantly less convenient than an alternative forum, is this a valid justification for a *forum non conveniens* dismissal? Note Justice Doggett's argument that modern communications and transport have made it easy and cheap to bring foreign evidence to the forum. *See also infra* pp. 391, 414-416. Moreover, why should considerations of private convenience be permitted to override a plaintiff's substantive legal rights in a U.S. forum? Could a federal court, for example, decline to hear Title VII or antitrust claims on the grounds that the parties' disputes could be more expeditiously resolved in state court?

(c) Foreign regulatory interests and public policies. Can the *forum non conveniens* doctrine be justified as a way to prevent U.S. courts from interfering with foreign states' sovereignty and regulatory regimes? Recall that nineteenth-century admiralty courts invoked considerations of international comity and respect for foreign sovereignty in declining to decide certain types of disputes. *See supra* pp. 366-368. Consider *Piper's* discussion of the relative "public interests" of the United States and the United Kingdom. According to Justice Marshall, what were the respective U.S. and U.K. interests? Note Justice Doggett's views about the usefulness of the *forum non conveniens* doctrine in preventing interference with foreign

sovereignty. Are his views persuasive? How do you think the U.K. government would have wanted *Piper* to have been decided? How would Costa Rica have wanted *Alfaro* decided? Recall *Sequihua v. Texaco, Inc.*, excerpted *supra* pp. 63-65. What was Ecuador's position there?

(d) Treating U.S. defendants fairly. Does the *forum non conveniens* doctrine reflect concerns over the unjustified imposition of tort liability on American companies that do business abroad? Consider the Court's concern in *Piper* that, if the Third Circuit's analysis had been accepted, "where the foreign plaintiff named an American manufacturer as defendant, a court could not dismiss the case on grounds of *forum non conveniens* where dismissal might lead to an unfavorable change in law." Justice Hecht's dissent in *Alfaro* is more direct: "[W]hy [should] the American justice system . . . undertake to punish American corporations more severely for their actions in a foreign country than that country does?" "[W]hy are Costa Ricans injured by an American defendant entitled to any greater recovery than Costa Ricans injured by a Costa Rican defendant, or a Libyan defendant, or an Iranian defendant?" What are the answers? Can the *forum non conveniens* doctrine be justified as a device for fostering more equal treatment — from an international perspective — of like cases? Why should Mr. Alfaro (and his Texas lawyers) recover one hundred times more from Dow and Shell than Mr. Alfaro's neighbors could recover from a Costa Rican or Japanese company, guilty of exactly the same conduct as their U.S. counterparts? What would Justice Doggett say?

3. *Wisdom of* **forum non conveniens** *doctrine.* Was the Supreme Court wise in *Gulf Oil* and *Piper* to adopt the *forum non conveniens* doctrine? Consider the scathing remarks by Justice Doggett in *Alfaro,* and the equally vigorous comments by Justices Gonzalez and Hecht. Rhetoric aside, does the *forum non conveniens* doctrine serve useful objectives? What are they?

4. *Relationship between judicial jurisdiction and* **forum non conveniens.** The historical development of the *forum non conveniens* doctrine between 1925 and 1985 was closely related to the evolution of concepts of judicial jurisdiction. As described above, the Due Process Clause was interpreted as imposing strict territorial restrictions on the judicial jurisdiction of U.S. courts during the nineteenth and early twentieth centuries. *See supra* pp. 83-84; *Pennoyer v. Neff,* 95 U.S. 714 (1878). During this era, the *forum non conveniens* doctrine was primarily confined in the United States to admiralty cases — where the attachment of foreign vessels provided jurisdiction over foreign defendants and disputes that generally did not exist in nonadmiralty cases. *See supra* pp. 366-368. Aside from anything else, the existence of strict territorial limits on judicial jurisdiction made principles of *forum non conveniens* largely irrelevant, because foreign defendants and disputes would generally not find their ways into local courts.

Pennoyer's territorial limits were gradually eroded during this century. *See supra* pp. 86-90. This culminated in the Supreme Court's 1945 formulation of the "minimum contacts" test in *International Shoe Co. See supra* pp. 86-87. Under *International Shoe,* plaintiffs enjoyed a new and substantially wider choice of courts in which to commence litigation. This was especially true as to general jurisdiction, which granted U.S. courts personal jurisdiction over defendants with respect to claims that had no connection with the forum. *See supra* p. 90. Inevitably, the new jurisdictional regime meant that courts could adjudicate cases even if they were disproportionately burdensome to the defendant or would have very unusual or favorable choice of law and substantive rules. On occasion, plaintiffs would select a forum to commence litigation precisely because it had these attributes — engaging in "forum-shopping" for a court that would provide it with the maximum practical and legal advantages. U.S. judicial acceptance of the doctrine of *forum non conveniens* occurred at precisely the same time that U.S. principles of judicial jurisdiction were being transformed. As *Pennoyer's* strict territoriality rules were eroded during the 1920s and 1930s, academic commentary such as Paxton Blair's influential 1929 article suggested the *forum non conveniens* doctrine and other devices specifically to moderate newly expanded jurisdictional powers. *See supra* pp. 365-369. Likewise, *Gulf Oil* expressly adopted the *forum non conveniens* doctrine in 1946 — one year after the minimum contacts formula was articulated in *International Shoe*. And *Piper Aircraft* was decided in 1981, around the time the Court was struggling over whether to expand the reach of U.S. jurisdiction under the "stream of commerce" theory and other theories. *See supra* pp. 89-90.

Is the *forum non conveniens* doctrine an appropriate means of moderating the expansion of contemporary judicial jurisdiction? Would it be wiser to articulate more precise jurisdictional rules?

5.   *What does* forum non conveniens *really mean?* Perhaps because it is a catchy neo-Latin phrase, the *forum non conveniens* doctrine appears deceptively easy to comprehend. It is, surely, just a common sense question of determining whether the forum is inconvenient, isn't it? Consider:

> The general inference to be drawn from the Latin phrase is that jurisdiction should be declined when the forum is inconvenient. But inconvenient to whom? The court? The plaintiff? The defendant? Even if we have the answers to these questions, is it enough that the scale is weighted more heavily on the side of inconvenience to the defendant when the plaintiff has acted in good faith? In other words, must there be an element of abuse of court process before jurisdiction is declined? Perhaps, the search should be a broader one for that forum in which the ends of justice will best be served. Obviously, these questions must be answered before we know anything of the meaning of the doctrine of *forum non conveniens*. Barrett, *The Doctrine of Forum Non Conveniens*, 35 Cal. L. Rev. 380, 404 (1947).

In addition to these questions, which concern only issues of "convenience," the *forum non conveniens* doctrine also involves "public interest" factors and allocations of regulatory competence. *See supra* pp. 365-424. What precisely is the legal rule established by the *forum non conveniens* doctrine? What objectives does the doctrine really serve?

6.   *Unexamined substantive assumptions of* forum non conveniens *doctrine.* Although it purports to concern "convenience," the *forum non conveniens* doctrine rests on unarticulated and unexamined substantive assumptions. Compare the excerpt from *Piper,* expressing concern about subjecting U.S. manufacturers to "liberal" U.S. substantive and procedural rules, with Justice Doggett's condemnation of perfidious multinationals engaged in world-wide depredations of the environment and developing nations. Who is correct — Justice Marshall or Justice Doggett? *Compare* the differing views in *Castro Alfaro* concerning international comity and foreign sovereignty. Is there any principled basis for a court to decide between these views without legislative guidance?

7.   *Effect of unfavorable change in law on forum non conveniens analysis under* Piper. *Piper* held that the possibility of an unfavorable change in substantive law for the plaintiff is not to be "given conclusive or even substantial weight" in federal *forum non conveniens* analysis. Given the broad range of public and private interest factors that are relevant to *forum non conveniens* analysis, why should the vitally important question of substantive law changes be disregarded?

In answering this question, *Piper* emphasizes the central role of "convenience" in *forum non conveniens* analysis. Is this persuasive? The "public interest" factors relevant to *forum non conveniens* analysis have little to do with convenience. Moreover, defendants seldom seek *forum non conveniens* dismissals to obtain a more convenient forum; instead, they often want to avoid the substantive, procedural, and other characteristics of the original forum — for exactly the reasons that the plaintiff chose the forum. *See Bewers v. American Home Prods. Corp.*, 459 N.Y.S.2d 666, 668 (Sup. Ct. 1982) ("Plaintiff's choice of forum is being vigorously contested, probably not so much because defendants are unaccustomed to international travel, but because as both sides know, the outcome of this procedural motion may well be dispositive of plaintiffs' claims."). Given the strong substantive character of *forum non conveniens* analysis, is it appropriate to ignore changes in substantive law? In answering this question, what weight should be given to the fact that "changes" in substantive law result from the plaintiff's ability unilaterally to select the forum for its claims? *See also* Heiser, *Forum Non Conveniens and Choice of Law: The Impact of Applying Foreign Law in Transnational Tort Actions,* 51 Wayne L. Rev. 1161 (2005).

   8. *Foreign forum that provides "no remedy at all."* Under *Piper,* are unfavorable changes of law entitled to *any* weight? *Piper* held that "the unfavorable change of law may be given substantial weight," if the "remedy provided by the alternative forum is so clearly inadequate or unsatisfactory that it is no remedy at all." Why must such drastic, all-or-nothing consequences be established before a trial court can take changes in substantive law into account? If it is appropriate for a U.S. court to consider the fact that a plaintiff may not be able to assert a $15,000 claim, why is it apparently inappropriate to consider the fact that a plaintiff's $15 million claim is reduced to $15,000? If other factors are not dispositive, can a court then give weight (including decisive weight) to unfavorable changes in law?

   Note that even where a plaintiff would have "no remedy at all" abroad, *Piper* apparently suggests that a trial court "may" give this factor "substantial weight." "Must" the trial court do so? Even if it must, what other factors might counterbalance the "substantial weight" accorded to the unfavorable change in law? Notwithstanding the Court's language in *Piper,* lower courts generally have held that the lack of any adequate remedy abroad precludes *forum non conveniens* dismissal. *See infra* pp. 427, 437-443.

   9. *Presumptive validity of U.S. plaintiff's choice of U.S. forum under* Piper. *Piper* reaffirmed *Gulf Oil's* holding that a U.S. plaintiff's choice of forum should rarely be disturbed. The Court also said that U.S. citizens do not have any absolute right to protection from dismissal of their claims on *forum non conveniens* grounds. Given the wide range of fora that existing rules of personal jurisdiction allow plaintiffs—and the practical advantages this entails—should the forum selections of U.S. plaintiffs generally receive an automatic presumption of validity? What justifies this deference? Why should people be rewarded for suing first? Recall that, for purposes of due process limitations on judicial jurisdiction, the *plaintiff's* contacts with the forum are relatively unimportant. *See supra* p. 103.

   10. *Reduced deference to a foreign plaintiff's choice of U.S. forum under* Piper. *Piper* also held that a *foreign* plaintiff's choice of a U.S. forum will not receive the "strong presumption" of validity that courts accord to a U.S. plaintiff's choice of a U.S. forum. As *Piper* noted, there are powerful reasons (such as favorable substantive laws, large jury verdicts, contingency fee arrangements, discovery opportunities, and the minimal chance of attorneys' fees being awarded against the losing side) that may entice foreign plaintiffs into U.S. courts without regard to convenience. *See supra* pp. 1-4, 408. The Court justified differential treatment of U.S. and foreign plaintiffs on the grounds that it can be assumed that a U.S. plaintiff will choose a U.S. forum because it is convenient. The Court did not think that this assumption applied to a foreign plaintiff's choice of a U.S. forum, reasoning that foreigners were likely attracted by U.S. damage awards. *Smith Kline & French Labs. v. Bloch* [1983] 2 All E.R. 72, 74 ("[a]s a moth is drawn to the light, so is a litigant drawn to the United States"). Is a plaintiff's U.S. nationality a reasonable proxy for the convenience of a U.S. forum? Does a party's nationality have any real relation to the convenience of different forum for a particular dispute? Won't many foreigners sue in U.S. courts because they are convenient?

   11. *Degree of inconvenience required to warrant* forum non conveniens *dismissal.* *Piper* reaffirmed the demanding *Gulf Oil* standard for a *forum non conveniens* dismissal. If "trial in the chosen forum would 'establish . . . oppressiveness and vexation to a defendant . . . out of all proportion to plaintiff's convenience,' or when the 'chosen forum [is] inappropriate because of considerations affecting the court's own administrative and legal problems,' " then dismissal is permissible. Moreover, "dismissal will ordinarily be appropriate where trial in the plaintiff's chosen forum imposes a heavy burden on the defendant or the court, and where the plaintiff is unable to offer any specific reasons of convenience supporting his choice." Why is this the appropriate standard of proof? Why should it be necessary to show inconvenience to the defendant "out of all proportion" to the plaintiff's convenience? Why ought it not be enough to show "materially greater inconvenience" to the defendant, or simply that, on balance, another forum would permit a somewhat cheaper proceeding?

12. *Wisdom of* Piper *and* Alfaro. Was *Piper* correctly decided? Is it a desirable result? Compare the result in *Alfaro* to that in *Sequihua v. Texaco, Inc.*, 847 F. Supp. 61 (S.D. Tex. 1994) (excerpted above at pp. 63-65). Which result is wiser? Is the defendant's desire in *Sequihua* to be in federal court more comprehensible in the light of *Alfaro*?

13. *Unpredictability of* forum non conveniens *decisions*. Recall Justice Black's warning in *Gulf Oil* that the "broad and indefinite discretion" granted by the *forum non conveniens* doctrine "will inevitably produce a complex of close and indistinguishable decisions from which accurate prediction of the proper forum will become difficult, if not impossible." *See supra* pp. 370-371. 330 U.S. at 516. That may well be correct. *See infra* pp. 389-390. But suppose there were no *forum non conveniens* doctrine. Would it be any easier to make an "accurate prediction" of the "proper forum"? Wouldn't there be inevitable races to the courthouse and parallel proceedings in multiple forums? *See infra* pp. 547-588. Isn't the uncertainty that Justice Black derides a result of expansive rules of judicial jurisdiction, and not the *forum non conveniens* doctrine?

14. *Criticism of* forum non conveniens *standard of review*. Some commentators have vigorously criticized *Piper's* deferential standard of review for *forum non conveniens* decisions. One writer has remarked that it has produced a "crazy quilt of ad hoc, capricious, and inconsistent decisions." Stein, *Forum Non Conveniens and the Redundancy of Court-Access Doctrine*, 133 U. Pa. L. Rev. 781, 785 (1985). Another has said that the *forum non conveniens* doctrine is "notoriously complex and uncertain," Currie, *Change of Venue and the Conflict of Laws*, 22 U. Chi. L. Rev. 405, 416 (1955), while a third has referred to the "chaos of *forum non conveniens*." A. Ehrenzweig, *The Conflict of Laws* 150 (1959). The late Judge Henry Friendly devoted an article — *Indiscretion About Discretion* — to criticizing *Piper's* reliance on trial courts' discretion. Friendly, *Indiscretion About Discretion*, 31 Emory L.J. 747 (1982).

15. *Appellate decisions seeking greater predictability in* forum non conveniens *decisions*. Several courts of appeals have shown greater attention to the predictability of *forum non conveniens* decisions than the Supreme Court. These courts have emphasized that a trial court's discretion in deciding *forum non conveniens* motions is not unlimited. *Forum non conveniens* determinations "represent exercises of structured discretion by trial judges appraising the practical inconveniences posed to the litigants and to the court should a particular action be litigated in one forum rather than another." *Pain v. United Technologies Corp.*, 637 F.2d 775, 781 (D.C. Cir. 1980). In order to permit meaningful analysis and appellate review, these courts have insisted that trial judges consider and evaluate each of the relevant *Gulf Oil* factors and articulate the basis for their decisions. *E.g., Synugy, Inc. v. ZS Assocs., Inc.*, 2009 WL 1532117 (3d Cir. June 1, 2009); *Wilson v. Island Seas Investments, Ltd.*, 590 F.3d 1264 (11th Cir. 2009); *Ito v. Tokio Marine & Fire Ins. Co.*, 2006 WL 204412 (9th Cir. 2006); *McLennan v. American Eurocopter Corp.*, 245 F.3d 403, 424 (5th Cir. 2001); *Boosey & Hawkes Music Publishers, Ltd. v. Walt Disney Co.*, 145 F.3d 481, 491 (2d Cir. 1998). Is this wise? Is it consistent with *Piper*?

16. Forum non conveniens *doctrine in other common law jurisdictions.* As noted above, the *forum non conveniens* doctrine has also been applied in England and other common law jurisdictions. The doctrine's contemporary formulation by English courts was summarized in *Lubbe v. Cape plc* [2000] 1 W.L.R. 1545 (House of Lords):

> Where a plaintiff sues a defendant as of right in the English court and the defendant applies to stay the proceedings on grounds of forum non conveniens, the principles to be applied by the English court in deciding that application in any case not governed by article 2 of the Brussels Convention are not in doubt. They derive from the judgment of Lord Kinnear in *Sim v. Robinow* (1892) 19 R. 665, 668 where he said:
>
> > "the plea can never be sustained unless the court is satisfied that there is some other tribunal, having competent jurisdiction, in which the case may be tried more suitably for the interests of all the parties and for the ends of justice."
>
> Thus it is the interest of all the parties, not those of the plaintiff only or the defendant only, and the ends of justice as judged by the court on all the facts of the case before it, which must control the decision of the court. In the *Spiliada* case [1987] A.C. 460, 476 it was stated:
>
> > "The basic principle is that a stay will only be granted on the ground of forum non conveniens where the court is satisfied that there is some other available forum, having competent jurisdiction, which is the appropriate forum for the trial of the action, i.e. in which the case may be tried more suitably for the interests of all the parties and the ends of justice."
>
> In applying this principle the court's first task is to consider whether the defendant who seeks a stay is able to discharge the burden resting upon him not just to show that England is not the natural or appropriate forum for the trial but to establish that there is another available forum which is clearly or distinctly more appropriate than the English forum. In this way, proper regard is had to the fact that jurisdiction has been founded in England as of right: see [*Spiliada Maritime Corp. v. Cansulex Ltd.* [1987] A.C. 460, 477 (House of Lords)]. At this first stage of the inquiry the court will consider what factors there are which point in the direction of another forum . . . . If the court concludes at that stage that there is no other available forum which is clearly more appropriate for the trial of the action, that is likely to be the end of the matter. But if the court concludes at that stage that there is some other available forum which prima facie is more appropriate for the trial of the action it will ordinarily grant a stay unless the plaintiff can show that there are circumstances by reason of which justice requires that a stay should nevertheless not be granted. In this second stage the court will concentrate its attention not only on factors connecting the proceedings with the foreign or the English forum but on whether the plaintiff will obtain justice in the foreign jurisdiction. The plaintiff will not ordinarily discharge the burden lying upon him by showing that he will enjoy procedural advantages, or a higher scale of damages or more generous rules of limitation if he sues in England; generally speaking, the plaintiff must take a foreign forum as he finds it, even if it is in some respects less advantageous to him than the English forum. It is only if the plaintiff can establish that substantial justice will not be done in the appropriate forum that a stay will be refused.

Importantly, this standard applied where the defendant was located (or served) within England. In other cases, where a defendant had to be served abroad (outside of England), a different standard applied. In particular, in these circumstances, the burden was on the plaintiff to show that England was the "appropriate" forum. *Spiliada*, [1987] A.C. 460, 478. Although the same general factors are relevant in determining whether a particular forum is appropriate and convenient, the burden shifts between the parties depending upon whether the defendant can be served within the jurisdiction.

Compare the English standard to that in *Piper Aircraft.* How do the two standards differ? How are they similar? *See also* Morse, *Not in the Public Interest? Lubbe v. Cape plc*, 37 Tex. J. Int'l L. 541 (2002). Which standard is preferable? Why?

Canadian and Australian courts have generally followed English authorities in this context, but have declined to adopt a rule shifting the burden of proving convenience to the plaintiff in cases involving service abroad. *See, e.g., Voth v. Manildra Flour Mills Pty. Ltd.,* [1990] 65 A.L.J.R. 83 (Australian High Ct.); *Amchem Products Inc. v. British Columbia Worker's Compensation Board,* [1993] 1 S.C.R. 897 (Can. S. Ct.).

17. *No* forum non conveniens *doctrine under Regulation 44/2001*. Recall the rules governing judicial jurisdiction in EU member states under EU Council Regulation 44/2001. *See supra* pp. 105-107. Under Article 2 of the Regulation, persons domiciled in an EU member state (regardless of their nationality) may be sued in that member state's courts (*supra* p. 105; excerpted at Appendix E); in addition, EU domiciliaries may also be sued in other EU member states, specified in Articles 5 and 6 of the Regulation (*supra* p. 105; excerpted at Appendix E). Regulation 44/2001's rules provide a comprehensive legal regime for judicial jurisdictions, which has been interpreted as leaving no room for the *forum non conveniens* doctrine or other devices for discretionarily abstaining from the exercise of jurisdiction. Thus, EU Council Regulation 44/2001 has been interpreted as forbidding application of the *forum non conveniens* doctrine by EU member states, even in cases involving non-EU alternative forums. *Owusu v. Jackson,* Case C-281/02, 1 March 2005. *See also Canales Martinez v. Dow Chemical Co.,* 219 F. Supp. 2d 719, 730-731 (E.D. La. 2002). Suppose that Regulation 44/2001 permits an action to be filed against an EU domiciliary in its EU domicile, but that litigation in that EU member state would be grossly inconvenient (because of language, location of witnesses, and physical evidence, etc.). Suppose further that litigation would be substantially more efficient in either (a) another EU member state, or (b) a non-EU state (*e.g.,* the United States of Mexico). The European Court of Justice has interpreted Regulation 44/2001 as not permitting courts of EU member states to dismiss actions in these circumstances. Consider:

> It must be observed, first, that Article 2 of the Brussels Convention is mandatory in nature and that, according to its terms, there can be no derogation from the principle it lays down except in the cases expressly provided for by the Convention (see, as regards the compulsory system of jurisdiction set up by the Brussels Convention. It is common ground that no exception on the basis of the *forum non conveniens* doctrine was provided for by the authors of the Convention, although the question was discussed when the Convention of 9 October 1978 on the Accession of Denmark, Ireland and the United Kingdom was drawn up. . . . Respect for the principle of legal certainty, which is one of the objectives of the Brussels Convention, would not be fully guaranteed if the court having jurisdiction under the Convention had to be allowed to apply the *forum non conveniens* doctrine. According to its preamble, the Brussels Convention is intended to strengthen in the Community the legal protection of persons established therein, by laying down common rules on jurisdiction to guarantee certainty as to the allocation of jurisdiction among the various national courts before which proceedings in a particular case may be brought. The [ECJ] has thus held that the principle of legal certainty requires, in particular, that the jurisdictional rules which derogate from the general rule laid down in Article 2 of the Brussels Convention should be interpreted in such a way as to enable a normally well-informed defendant reasonably to foresee before which courts, other than those of the State in which he is domiciled, he may be sued. Application of the *forum non conveniens* doctrine, which allows the court seised a wide discretion as regards the question whether a foreign court would be a more appropriate forum for the trial of an action, is liable to undermine the predictability of the rules of jurisdiction laid down by the Brussels Convention, in particular that of Article 2, and consequently to undermine the principle of legal certainty, which is the basis of the Convention.
>
> The legal protection of persons established in the Community would also be undermined. First, a defendant, who is generally better placed to conduct his defence before the courts of his domicile, would not be able, in circumstances such as those of the main proceedings,

reasonably to foresee before which other court he may be sued. Second, where a plea is raised on the basis that a foreign court is a more appropriate forum to try the action, it is for the claimant to establish that he will not be able to obtain justice before that foreign court or, if the court seised decides to allow the plea, that the foreign court has in fact no jurisdiction to try the action or that the claimant does not, in practice, have access to effective justice before that court, irrespective of the cost entailed by the bringing of a fresh action before a court of another State and the prolongation of the procedural time-limits. Moreover, allowing *forum non conveniens* in the context of the Brussels Convention would be likely to affect the uniform application of the rules of jurisdiction contained therein in so far as that doctrine is recognised only in a limited number of Contracting States, whereas the objective of the Brussels Convention is precisely to lay down common rules to the exclusion of derogating national rules. *Owusu v. N.B. Jackson,* Case C-281/02. [2005] ECR I-1383 (E.C.J.)

Should the continental European approach influence U.S. courts' views on the subject of *forum non conveniens*? In what way? Does the European view suggest that the *forum non conveniens* doctrine is ill advised? Does the absence of any such doctrine in European courts suggest that European companies should not be able to invoke the doctrine? Or is European practice irrelevant?

18. Forum non conveniens *in abortive Hague jurisdiction/judgment convention negotiations.* Despite the absence of a *forum non conveniens* doctrine from most civil law systems, the abortive Hague negotiations on a jurisdiction/judgments treaty reached at least tentative agreement on a *forum non conveniens* provision of sorts. Article 22 of the June 2001 Interim Text provided:

(1) In exceptional circumstances, when the jurisdiction of the court seised is not founded on an exclusive choice of court agreement [or on provisions concerning consumers, employee relations or specified bases for exclusive jurisdiction (*e.g.,* real estate)], the court may, on application by a party, suspend its proceedings if in that case it is clearly inappropriate for that court to exercise jurisdiction and if a court of another State has jurisdiction and is clearly more appropriate to resolve the dispute. . . .

(2) The court shall take into account, in particular — (a) any inconvenience to the parties in view of their habitual residence; (b) the nature and location of the evidence, including documents and witnesses, and the procedures for obtaining such evidence; (c) applicable limitation or prescription periods; (d) the possibility of obtaining recognition and enforcement of any decision on the merits.

(3) In deciding whether to suspend the proceedings, a court shall not discriminate on the basis of the nationality or habitual residence of the parties. . . .

How does this standard compare with that in *Piper*? What are the problems with this standard? The advantages? Consider proposed Article 22(3). Is that wiser than the *Piper* approach?

19. *International law and due process limits on judicial competence.* As discussed above, international law arguably imposes limits on the competence of a nation's courts to adjudicate disputes having no connection to the forum — even when judicial jurisdiction exists and restrictions on legislative jurisdiction are observed. *See supra* p. 30. Consider Justice Cook's dissent, arguing that due process imposes limits on a state court's power to adjudicate certain claims against "our citizens" — *e.g.,* Texas corporations or other entities ordinarily subject to general jurisdiction. In Justice Cook's view, the Due Process Clause should not "expose[] our citizens to the claims of any plaintiff, no matter how distant from Texas is that plaintiff's home or cause of action." Is this view consistent with orthodox understandings of general jurisdiction? *See supra* pp. 90, 108-137. Consider Justice Doggett's response to it. Why *shouldn't* (or don't) international law and due process restrict a state court's power to hear claims that have *nothing* to do with it? Consider again the arguments advanced for general jurisdiction.

20. *Effect of modern technology on* **forum non conveniens** *doctrine.* Modern communications and transportation have eliminated much of the "inconvenience" that the *forum non conveniens* doctrine sought to prevent. Documents can be faxed or couriered around the world in seconds; telephone and video conferences are easy and cheap; witnesses and lawyers can travel easily for hearings. In *Fitzgerald v. Texaco, Inc.*, 521 F.2d 448, 456 (2d Cir. 1975) Judge Oakes (in dissent) urged that "the entire doctrine of *forum non conveniens* should be reexamined in the light of the transportation revolution that has occurred" in the last 40 years and the "dispersion of corporate authority . . . by the use of multinational subsidiaries to conduct international business." Judge Oakes went on to suggest abandoning the doctrine in favor of general acceptance of a plaintiff's choice of forum. Is this a sensible course to take? What effect do modern technological developments have on the *forum non conveniens* doctrine? *See Frink America, Inc. v. Champion Road Machinery Ltd.*, 961 F. Supp. 398, 403 (N.D.N.Y. 1997) ("[C]onsiderations of practical convenience must be evaluated 'in light of the increased speed of travel and communication which makes . . . no forum as inconvenient [today] as it was in 1947.'").

21. Forum non conveniens *and institutional competence.* Note that, in the federal system, the *forum non conveniens* doctrine emerged as a result of judicially created federal common law. By contrast, in Texas, the state supreme court judicially abandoned such a doctrine (only to have its decision later overridden by the Texas legislature). Regardless of how one balances the above-described advantages and drawbacks of the *forum non conveniens* doctrine, which governmental institution is in the best position to weigh those considerations? The legislature, by virtue of its traditional function to control the jurisdiction of its courts? Or courts, by virtue of their inherent authority to control their docket? Consider the recent arguments made before the Supreme Court of Rhode Island in a case where the Court considered whether to adopt the doctrine:

> The plaintiffs contend that *forum non conveniens* has not existed in Rhode Island for more than two centuries, and that it is not part of the common law of this state. They allege that *forum non conveniens* is a flawed doctrine that has led to confusion and inconsistency in federal and state courts. They further argue that the General Assembly is the appropriate body to adopt the doctrine, and they point out that it has not enacted the doctrine in any form, except for child-custody cases. The plaintiffs allege that if *forum non conveniens* is an inherent part of Rhode Island's common law, there would have been no need to specifically enumerate the doctrine in [child-custody cases]. The defendants argue that *forum non conveniens* is a doctrine developed at common law that is recognized by [federal and state courts]. The defendants allege that the common law encompasses the inherent judicial power to "protect defendants and the public from injurious and unnecessary forum choices by plaintiffs." They dispute plaintiffs' contention that the *forum non conveniens* doctrine lacks uniformity throughout the states, contending that there are only minor variations among the states and at the federal level. Kedy v. A.W. Chesterton Co., 946 A.2d 1171, 1179 (R.I. 2008).

If you were a justice on the Rhode Island Supreme Court, how would you decide? (In the actual case, the Rhode Island Supreme Court unanimously decided to adopt the doctrine.) Assuming you agree that the doctrine should be adopted, what standards should apply? Should the state simply parrot the federal standards? What would be the implications of that approach? What would be the implications of deliberately adopting different standards? *See infra* at 453-458 (discussing relationship between *forum non conveniens* and *Erie*).

22. *Acceptance of* **forum non conveniens** *by state courts and legislatures.* Despite these criticisms of the *forum non conveniens* doctrine, states have not abandoned, but have instead increasingly embraced, the rule. *See supra* p. 372, notes 58-62. Why is that?

One important point is that the differences between federal and state laws regarding the availability of *forum non conveniens* doctrine would give rise to potential forum shopping concerns. For example, consider a lawsuit involving a foreign accident. Assuming that subject matter and personal jurisdiction exist, a plaintiff might choose to file his suit in a jurisdiction that either lacks a *forum non conveniens* doctrine or, alternatively has a limited one. Such concerns over forum shopping, and the concomitant burden on the courts' dockets, have led some state courts to abandon their traditional limitations on the doctrine. *Kinney Systems, Inc. v. Continental Ins. Co.*, 674 So. 2d 86 (Fla. 1996).

C. Deference to the Plaintiff's Choice of Forum

Piper stressed that the deference to the plaintiff's choice of forum depended on the plaintiff's identity. Sometimes, this principle seems simple. On one end of the spectrum, a high level of deference would apply to a U.S. individual plaintiff, who lived and worked in the United States, suing in his local federal court. On the other end of the spectrum, a relatively lower level of deference would apply to a foreign plaintiff, with few U.S. contacts, suing a foreign defendant in federal court.

But these simple applications mask deeper complexities in the meaning of *Piper*'s principle that the plaintiff's choice of forum is entitled to substantial deference. What level of deference applies in cases to a U.S. citizen-plaintiff who resides in a district other than the one in which the suit is filed? Or who resides abroad? How much deference is due to a resident U.S. plaintiff filing in a representative capacity? What level of deference applies in suits brought by multinational companies, incorporated in the United States but active partly or principally abroad? What level of deference applies when a foreign national, who resides in the United States, sues in the district where he (or she) lives? What is necessary to overcome the high level of deference to the local plaintiff's choice?

U.S. courts have struggled with these various scenarios, reaching a variety of divergent results. The Court of Appeals' decision in *Iragorri v. United Technologies Corp.* reflects one effort to resolve these questions in a systematic way.

IRAGORRI v. UNITED TECHNOLOGIES CORP.
274 F.3d 65 (2d Cir. 2001) (en banc)

LEVAL and CABRANES, CIRCUIT JUDGES. . . . [W]e convene to answer the question . . . "what degree of deference should the district court accord to a United States plaintiff's choice of a United States forum where that forum is different from the one in which the plaintiff resides."[79]

---

79. [In response to an invitation from the Court, the United States Department of Justice ("DOJ") filed a letter making three points]: First, the DOJ noted that "the Supreme Court has already made clear that the fact that the plaintiff is a citizen or resident of the United States is relevant but not dispositive in a *forum non conveniens* analysis." . . . Second, the DOJ observed that "any right to court access afforded to a foreign national plaintiff by treaty will generally be only a right to the same access that would be accorded to a U.S. national plaintiff who is otherwise similarly situated." . . . Third, the DOJ posited that "even if citizenship or nationality per se were held to be dispositive in otherwise evenly balanced cases, and even if national treatment provisions were interpreted under some circumstances to require that the same tie-breaking rule be applied in favor of those non-national plaintiffs who are entitled to the benefit of treaties that include such provisions, . . . it is not obvious that applying such provisions in that way would necessarily be either unworkable or inappropriate." Though the instant case does not implicate any treaty obligations, the *forum non conveniens* analysis that we articulate here is mindful of those considerations.

On October 3, 1992, Mauricio Iragorri — a domiciliary of Florida since 1981 and a naturalized United States citizen since 1989 — fell five floors to his death down an open elevator shaft in the apartment building where his mother resided in Cali, Colombia. Mauricio left behind his widow, Haidee, and their two teenaged children, Patricia and Maurice, all of whom are the plaintiffs in this action. The plaintiffs have been domiciliaries of Florida since 1981. At the time of the accident, however, Haidee and the two children were living temporarily in Bogota, Colombia, because the children were attending a Bogota school as part of an educational exchange program sponsored by their Florida high school.

The Iragorris brought suit in the United States District Court for the District of Connecticut on September 30, 1994. The named defendants were Otis Elevator Company ("Otis"), a New Jersey corporation with its principal place of business in Connecticut; United Technologies Corporation ("United") — the parent of Otis — a Delaware corporation whose principal place of business is also in Connecticut; and International Elevator, Inc. ("International"), a Maine corporation, which since 1988 had done business solely in South America. It is alleged that prior to the accident, an employee of International had negligently wedged open the elevator door with a screwdriver to perform service on the elevator, thereby leaving the shaft exposed and unprotected. The complaint alleged two theories of liability against defendants Otis and United: that (a) International acted as an agent for Otis and United so that the negligent acts of its employee should be imputed to them, and (b) Otis and United were liable under Connecticut's products liability statute for the defective design and manufacture of the elevator which was sold and installed by their affiliate, Otis of Brazil. [The district court dismissed the case on grounds of *forum non conveniens* on the condition that defendants Otis and United agreed to appear in the courts of Cali, Colombia. A panel of the Second Circuit vacated, then the full court decided to hear the case *en banc*.]

The United States Supreme Court authorities establish various general propositions about *forum non conveniens*. We are told that courts should give deference to a plaintiff's choice of forum. "[U]nless the balance is strongly in favor of the defendant, the plaintiff's choice of forum should rarely be disturbed." *Gulf Oil Corp. v. Gilbert*, 330 U.S. 501, 508 (1947). We understand this to mean that a court reviewing a motion to dismiss for *forum non conveniens* should begin with the assumption that the plaintiff's choice of forum will stand unless the defendant meets the burden of demonstrating the points outlined below. At the same time, we are led to understand that this deference is not dispositive and that it may be overcome. Notwithstanding the deference, "dismissal should not be automatically barred when a plaintiff has filed suit in his home forum. As always, if the balance of conveniences suggests that trial in the chosen forum would be unnecessarily burdensome for the defendant or the court, dismissal is proper." *Piper Aircraft Co. v. Reyno, supra*, 454 U.S. at 256 n.23.

We are instructed that the degree of deference given to a plaintiff's forum choice varies with the circumstances. We are told that plaintiff's choice of forum is generally entitled to great deference when the plaintiff has sued in the plaintiff's home forum. *Koster v. (Am.) Lumbermen's Mut. Cas. Co., supra; see also Piper*, 454 U.S. at 255-56, 256 n.23. But we are also instructed that the choice of a United States forum by a foreign plaintiff is entitled to less deference. *Piper*, 454 U.S. at 255-56 ("The District Court's distinction between resident or citizen plaintiffs and foreign plaintiffs is fully justified. . . . When the plaintiff is foreign, . . . [the] assumption [favoring the plaintiff's choice of forum] is much less reasonable."). In our recent cases on the subject of *forum non conveniens*, our Court has faced situations involving a fact pattern not directly addressed by the Supreme Court: a United States resident plaintiff's suit in a U.S. district other than that in which the plaintiff resides. As a full court, we now undertake to apply to this general fact pattern the principles that we find implicit in Supreme Court precedents.

We regard the Supreme Court's instructions that (1) a plaintiff's choice of her home forum should be given great deference, while (2) a foreign resident's choice of a U.S. forum should receive less consideration, as representing consistent applications of a broader principle under which the degree of deference to be given to a plaintiff's choice of forum moves on a sliding scale depending on several relevant considerations. The Supreme Court explained in *Piper* that the reason we give deference to a plaintiff's choice of her home forum is because it is presumed to be convenient. In contrast, when a foreign plaintiff chooses a U.S. forum, it "is much less reasonable" to presume that the choice was made for convenience. In such circumstances, a plausible likelihood exists that the selection was made for forum-shopping reasons, such as the perception that United States courts award higher damages than are common in other countries. Even if the U.S. district was not chosen for such forum-shopping reasons, there is nonetheless little reason to assume that it is convenient for a foreign plaintiff.

Based on the Supreme Court's guidance, our understanding of how courts should address the degree of deference to be given to a plaintiff's choice of a U.S. forum is essentially as follows: The more it appears that a domestic or foreign plaintiff's choice of forum has been dictated by reasons that the law recognizes as valid, the greater the deference that will be given to the plaintiff's forum choice. Stated differently, the greater the plaintiff's or the lawsuit's bona fide connection to the United States and to the forum of choice and the more it appears that considerations of convenience favor the conduct of the lawsuit in the United States, the more difficult it will be for the defendant to gain dismissal for *forum non conveniens*. Thus, factors that argue against *forum non conveniens* dismissal include the convenience of the plaintiff's residence in relation to the chosen forum, the availability of witnesses or evidence to the forum district, the defendant's amenability to suit in the forum district, the availability of appropriate legal assistance, and other reasons relating to convenience or expense. On the other hand, the more it appears that the plaintiff's choice of a U.S. forum was motivated by forum-shopping reasons — such as attempts to win a tactical advantage resulting from local laws that favor the plaintiff's case, the habitual generosity of juries in the United States or in the forum district, the plaintiff's popularity or the defendant's unpopularity in the region, or the inconvenience and expense to the defendant resulting from litigation in that forum — the less deference the plaintiff's choice commands and, consequently, the easier it becomes for the defendant to succeed on a *forum non conveniens* motion by showing that convenience would be better served by litigating in another country's courts. . . .

One of the factors that necessarily affects a plaintiff's choice of forum is the need to sue in a place where the defendant is amenable to suit. Consider for example a hypothetical plaintiff residing in New Jersey, who brought suit in the Southern District of New York, barely an hour's drive from the plaintiff's residence, because the defendant was amenable to suit in the Southern District but not in New Jersey. It would make little sense to withhold deference for the plaintiff's choice merely because she did not sue in her home district. Where a U.S. resident leaves her home district to sue the defendant where the defendant has established itself and is thus amenable to suit, this would not ordinarily indicate a choice motivated by desire to impose tactical disadvantage on the defendant. This is all the more true where the defendant's amenability to suit in the plaintiff's home district is unclear. A plaintiff should not be compelled to mount a suit in a district where she cannot be sure of perfecting jurisdiction over the defendant, if by moving to another district, she can be confident of bringing the defendant before the court. In many circumstances, it will be far more convenient for a U.S. resident plaintiff to sue in a U.S. court than in a foreign country, even though it is not the district in which the plaintiff resides. It is not a correct understanding of the rule to accord deference only when the suit is brought in the plaintiff's home district. Rather, the court must consider a plaintiff's likely motivations in light of all the relevant indications. We thus understand the Supreme Court's teachings on the deference due to plaintiff's forum choice as instructing that we give greater deference to a plaintiff's forum choice to the extent that it was motivated by legitimate reasons, including the plaintiff's convenience and the ability of a U.S. resident plaintiff to obtain jurisdiction over the defendant, and diminishing deference to a plaintiff's forum choice to the extent that it was motivated by tactical advantage. . . . [W]hile plaintiff's citizenship and residence can serve as a proxy for, or indication of, convenience, neither the plaintiff's citizenship nor residence, nor the degree of deference given to her choice of forum, necessarily controls the outcome. There is no "rigid rule of decision protecting U.S. citizen or resident plaintiffs from dismissal for *forum non conveniens.*"

As is implicit in the meaning of "deference," the greater the degree of deference to which the plaintiff's choice of forum is entitled, the stronger a showing of inconvenience the defendant must make to prevail in securing *forum non conveniens* dismissal. At the same time, a lesser degree of deference to the plaintiff's choice bolsters the defendant's case but does not guarantee dismissal. A defendant does not carry the day simply by showing the existence of an adequate alternative forum. The action should be dismissed only if the chosen forum is shown to be genuinely inconvenient and the selected forum significantly preferable. In considering this point, the court furthermore must balance the greater convenience to the defendant of litigating in its preferred forum against any greater inconvenience to the plaintiff if the plaintiff is required to institute the suit in the defendant's preferred foreign jurisdiction.

Courts should be mindful that, just as plaintiffs sometimes choose a forum for forum-shopping reasons, defendants also may move for dismissal under the doctrine of *forum non conveniens* not because of genuine concern with convenience but because of similar forum-shopping reasons. District courts should therefore arm themselves with an appropriate degree of skepticism in assessing whether the defendant has demonstrated genuine inconvenience and a clear preferability of the foreign forum. And the greater the degree to which the plaintiff has chosen a forum where the defendant's witnesses and evidence are to be found, the harder it should be for the defendant to demonstrate inconvenience. [The court then remanded the case to the district court for application of the principles announced in its decision.]

Notes on Iragorri

1. Should a U.S. plaintiff's action in a U.S. court ever be subject to dismissal on forum non conveniens grounds? U.S. citizens pay for the operation of U.S. courts. The Constitution grants U.S. citizens broad rights of access to those courts. Why should the *forum non conveniens* doctrine *ever* permit a U.S. court to dismiss an action brought by a U.S. plaintiff?

(a) Historic rule against forum non conveniens *dismissals of U.S. plaintiffs' claims in U.S. courts.* The law did not always recognize the power of U.S. courts to dismiss U.S. plaintiffs' claims on *forum non conveniens* grounds. For example, in *United States Merchants' & Shippers' Ins. Co. v. A/S Den Norske Afrika Og Australie Line,* 65 F.2d 392, 392 (2d Cir. 1933), Judge Learned Hand wrote:

the libellant is a [U.S.] citizen and asserts its absolute privilege of resort to its own courts, independently of any inconvenience to the respondent. . . . Courts are maintained to give redress primarily to their own citizens; it is enough if these conform to the conditions set upon their jurisdiction.

Other authorities were to the same effect. *Mobil Tankers, Co. v. Mene Grande Oil Co.*, 363 F.2d 611 (3d Cir. 1966). Given the *forum non conveniens* doctrine's concern with imposing upon the forum's *courts*, should the doctrine not similarly reflect concern for imposing on the forum's *plaintiffs?*

(b) Contemporary extension of forum non conveniens *doctrine to U.S. plaintiffs' claims.* Around the time of *Piper*, U.S. courts began to broaden the *forum non conveniens* doctrine to permit dismissal of U.S. plaintiffs' claims, provided there was a sufficient showing of inconvenience: "United States citizens do not have an absolute right to sue in American courts." *Allstate Life Ins. Co. v. Linter Group Ltd.*, 1992 U.S. Dist. Lexis 19617 (S.D.N.Y. 1992). *See also Duha v. Agrium, Inc.*, 340 F. Supp. 2d 787, 792 (E.D. Mich. 2004) ("[D]ismissal is not "automatically barred" when a plaintiff brings suit in his home forum. . . . Courts have dismissed cases brought by American plaintiffs against domestic defendants over contracts to be performed in foreign countries when the balance of conveniences overcomes the deference due and favors the foreign forum."). This is a fundamentally different approach from the historic rule that U.S. plaintiffs had a basic right of access to U.S. courts. The shift was sometimes explained as a natural aspect of the "flexibility" of the *forum non conveniens* doctrine:

> Although such residence [of the plaintiff in the forum] is, of course, an important factor to be considered, *forum non conveniens* relief should be granted when it plainly appears that New York is an inconvenient forum and that another is available which will best serve the ends of justice and the convenience of the parties. The great advantage of the doctrine — its flexibility based on the facts and circumstances of a particular case — is severely, if not completely, undercut when our courts are prevented from applying it solely because one of the parties is a New York resident or corporation. *Silver v. Great American Insurance Co.*, 328 N.Y.S.2d 398, 402-403 (N.Y. 1972).

Others reasoned that insulating U.S. plaintiffs' from *forum non conveniens* dismissals was a "primitive rule," redolent of parochial xenophobia. N.Y. Civ. Pract. Law Rule 327 (McLaughlin, Practice Commentary) (McKinney 1979 Supp.). Consider:

> The plaintiff falls back on its United States citizenship as the sole and only possible basis for suing these defendants in a court of the United States. This is not enough. In an era of increasing international commerce, parties who choose to engage in international transactions should know that when their foreign operations lead to litigation they cannot expect always to bring their foreign opponents into a U.S. forum when every reasonable consideration leads to the conclusion that the site of the litigation should be elsewhere. *Mizokami Bros. of Arizona v. Baychem Corp.*, 556 F.2d 975, 978 (9th Cir. 1977).

Relying on such reasoning, courts have dismissed the claims of U.S. plaintiffs in many cases. *E.g., Loya v. Starwood Hotels & Resorts Worldwide, Inc.*, 583 F.3d 656, 665 (9th Cir. 2009); *Alcoa Steamship Co. v. M/V Nordic Regent*, 654 F.2d 147 (2d Cir. 1980) (dismissing suit by U.S. corporation; "American citizenship alone is not a barrier to dismissal on the ground of *forum non conveniens*").

(c) Wisdom of extending forum non conveniens *doctrine to U.S. plaintiffs' claims.* Which approach to the *forum non conveniens* doctrine is wiser — the historic guarantee of access for U.S. citizens or the "flexible" modern balancing test? Where a U.S. plaintiff seeks relief in his hometown courts, from a court paid for by his taxes, and where Congress or a

state legislature has vested the court with jurisdiction to hear the plaintiff's claims, why should the court have "discretion" to dismiss those claims because of the "convenience" of local judges and jurors?

(d) Considerations of reciprocity. In deciding whether a U.S. plaintiff's claims against a foreign defendant should be subject to *forum non conveniens* dismissal, is it relevant to consider what the courts of the defendant's home nation would do? Suppose that the defendant is from France, and that French courts recognize an absolute right of access to French citizens in international disputes, without regard to issues of convenience. Should U.S. courts nonetheless order a U.S. plaintiff to France to litigate against its French adversary?

2. ***How much deference should be afforded a U.S. plaintiff's choice of a U.S. forum?*** *Piper* did not define with precision what level of deference was due a U.S. plaintiff's choice of a U.S. forum. It said generally that citizens deserve "somewhat more deference than foreign plaintiffs." How much "deference" should trial courts give to a U.S. plaintiff's choice of a U.S. forum? How does one specify an appropriate general standard of deference?

3. ***Should foreign plaintiffs have any right of access to U.S. forum?*** Why should foreign nationals ever be able to sue in United States courts? U.S. taxpayers pay for U.S. courts, and foreign taxpayers do not. Why let foreigners get a free ride by using U.S. courts, usually to pursue suits against U.S. defendants? *See Scotts Co. v. Hacienda Loma Linda*, 2 So. 2d 1013, 1016 (Fla. App. 2008) ("Florida simply cannot become a courthouse for the entire world, our taxpayers should not pay for the resolution of lawsuits that are utterly connected to this state's interests. . . . "); *Tjontveit v. Den Norske Bank ASA*, 997 F. Supp. 799, 807 (S.D. Tex. 1998) ("The United States is not required to be courthouse or law maker for the world."). What if foreign courts denied access to U.S. nationals?

(a) International law and comity. As noted above, international law is widely understood as requiring states to grant foreigners access to their courts. *See supra* pp. 76-77. U.S. courts have generally not imposed any per se bar denying access to foreign plaintiffs. "Ordinarily, nonresidents are permitted to enter New York courts to litigate their disputes as a matter of comity." *Islamic Republic of Iran v. Pahlavi*, 62 N.Y.2d 474, 478 (1984). Is this a wise rule? Why not charge foreigners a special tax for access to the public justice system? What if a foreign state imposes such a tax on U.S. plaintiffs?

(b) Friendship, commerce, and navigation treaties guaranteeing access to courts. The United States has bilateral friendship, commerce, and navigation treaties with a number of countries. Among other things, these treaties usually contain provisions ensuring that citizens of each signatory state receive "national treatment with respect to . . . access to the courts of justice" of the other signatory state. *E.g.,* Treaty of Friendship, Commerce and Navigation between the United States and Ireland, Art. VI, 1 U.S.T. 785, 790-791. Treaties of this character exist with, among other countries, Belgium, China, Denmark, Egypt, Finland, France, Germany, Italy, Ireland, Uruguay, Colombia, Greece, Israel, Switzerland, and the United Kingdom.

(c) Reciprocity. Note that bilateral friendship, commerce, and navigation (FCN) treaties involve a *reciprocal* arrangement in which nationals from each signatory state are granted access to the other signatory's courts on the same terms as its nationals. Compare the legislation at issue in *Dow Chemical Co. v. Alfaro*, which granted foreign nationals an absolute right of access to Texas courts, provided that their home state had entered into an access to courts treaty. Is the Texas statute constitutional? Does it interfere with the federal government's conduct of U.S. foreign relations? *Compare Zschernig v. Miller*, 389 U.S. 429 (1968) (discussed *supra* pp. 12-13 & *infra* pp. 631-632) (holding that Oregon probate statute unconstitutionally interfered with federal forum relations, *inter alia,* because it required reciprocity from foreign states). Is the Texas statute required by FCN treaties?

Would a reciprocity requirement be desirable under common law? Why should foreign nationals be afforded access to U.S. courts if their home state does not afford court access to U.S. citizens? Taking the argument further, why should U.S. courts provide remedies to foreign plaintiffs except when foreign courts provide equivalent remedies (in likely range of recovery) for U.S. plaintiffs? Consider: a U.S. admiralty court may decline jurisdiction in cases involving "the citizens or subjects of a foreign country, whose courts are not clothed with the power to give the same remedy in similar controversies to the citizens of the United States." *The Maggie Hammond,* 76 U.S. 435, 457 (1869).

(d) Bilateral investment treaties guaranteeing nondiscriminatory treatment to foreign nationals. As discussed above, the United States has entered into BITs with some 45 nations around the world. *See supra* pp. 328-329. Articles 3(1) and 5(1) and 5(2)(a) of the model U.S. BIT provide:

> 3(1) Each party shall accord to investors of the other Party treatment no less favorable than that it accords, in like circumstances, to its own investors with respect to the establishment, acquisition, expansion, management, conduct, operation and sale or other disposition of investments in its territory.

and

> 5(1) Each party shall accord to covered investments treatment in accordance with customary international law, including fair and equitable treatment and full protection and security. . . .
> 5(2)(a) fair and equitable treatment includes the obligation not to deny justice in criminal, civil and administrative adjudicatory proceedings in accordance with the principle of due process embodied in the principal legal systems of the world. 2004 U.S. Model Bilateral Investment Treaty, arts. 3(1) & 5(1), available at http://ustr.gov/Trade_Sectors/Investment/ Model_ BIT/Section_Index.html.

Would these provisions permit U.S. courts to deny foreigner investors access to U.S. courts?

(e) Application of friendship, commerce, and navigation treaties in forum non conveniens *context.* Several lower courts have considered whether provisions in FCN treaties guaranteeing national treatment in access to courts affect *forum non conveniens* analysis. In particular, some U.S. courts have held that foreign plaintiffs must be treated as if they were U.S. citizens for purposes of *forum non conveniens* analysis if they are nationals of countries that have entered into such treaties. *See Blanco v. Banco Industrial de Venezuela, SA,* 997 F.2d 974, 981 (2d Cir. 1993); *Irish National Ins. Co. v. Aer Lingus Teoranta,* 739 F.2d 90 (2d Cir. 1984); *Alcoa Steamship Co. v. M/V Nordic Regent,* 654 F.2d 147, 152 (2d Cir. 1978) (*en banc*); *Mendes Junior Int'l Co. v. Banco do Brasil, SA,* 15 F. Supp. 2d 332, 337 (S.D.N.Y. 1998).

Other courts, however, are more skeptical that the general language in most FCN treaties overrides the reduced deference specified in the Supreme Court's decisions. *See Bonzel v. Pfizer, Inc.,* 439 F.3d 1358, 1365 (Fed. Cir. 2006); *Morales v. Ford Motor Co.,* 313 F. Supp. 2d 672, 686-688 (S.D. Tex. 2004). In all events, close attention to the language of the treaty is critical: treaties that merely provide "freedom of access" as opposed to "equal access" may not entitle foreign nationals to the deference ordinarily accorded domestic plaintiffs. *See King v. Cessna Aircraft Co.,* 562 F.3d 1374, 1383 (11th Cir. 2009); *Pollux Holding Ltd. v. Chase Manhattan Bank,* 329 F.3d 64, 72-74 (2d Cir. 2003). Consider the following explanation from the Second Circuit's decision in *Pollux*:

> Even assuming that, by treaty, plaintiffs were entitled to access American courts on the same terms as American citizens . . . , our case law does not support plaintiffs' assertion that such a

treaty would require that their choice of forum be afforded the same deference afforded to a U.S. citizen bringing suit in his or her home forum. Such a proposition impermissibly conflates citizenship and convenience. . . . A court considering a motion for dismissal on the grounds of *forum non conveniens* does not assign "talismanic significance to the citizenship or residence of the parties," . . . and there is no inflexible rule that protects U.S. citizen or resident plaintiffs from having their causes dismissed for forum non conveniens. . . . [A]ppellants cannot successfully lay claim to the deference owed an American citizen or resident suing in her home forum. Plaintiffs are only entitled, at best, to the lesser deference afforded a U.S. citizen living abroad who sues in a U.S. forum. 329 F.3d at 73.

Is this distinction between "access" and "deference" persuasive? Is it consistent with the idea underpinning FCN treaties to treat a foreign citizen as a U.S. citizen living abroad? *Compare Abad v. Bayer Corp.*, 563 F.3d 663 (7th Cir. 2009) (interpreting FCN treaty to require U.S. court to treat foreign citizen as resident of a state other than forum state).

Other treaties raise similar issues but contain different language. How should a court treat language in the International Covenant on Civil and Political Rights, which provides "[a]ll persons shall be equal before the courts and tribunals." *See Gonzalez v. Ford Motor Co.*, 2010 WL 1576831, at *5 (S.D. Ind. Apr. 19, 2010) (collecting cases). What about the Montreal Convention, which identifies certain "convenient" jurisdictions for the purpose of adjudicating air carrier liability? *See Pierre-Louis v. Newvac Corp.*, 584 F.3d 1052, 1058 (11th Cir. 2009).

Are these applications of "national treatment" provisions to *forum non conveniens* presumptions persuasive? *Piper* concluded that the plaintiff's citizenship was an accurate proxy for the convenience of a U.S. forum for litigation. Would foreign plaintiffs receive "national treatment" if U.S. courts considered the inconvenience of a U.S. forum for such plaintiffs on a case-by-case basis? Does the use of an apparently rebuttable presumption require a different conclusion?

4. *Foreign plaintiffs' choice of U.S. forum is entitled to lesser degree of deference.* As discussed above, *Piper* held that a *non-U.S.* plaintiff's choice of a U.S. forum was not entitled to the same deference as a *U.S.* plaintiff's choice of a U.S. forum. *See supra* p. 388; *Sinochem Int'l, Ltd. v. Malaysia Int'l Shipping Corp.*, 549 U.S. 422, 430 (2007) ("When the plaintiff's choice is not its home forum, however, the presumption in the plaintiff's favor applies with less force, for the assumption that the chosen forum is appropriate is in such cases less reasonable."); *Abad v. Bayer Corp.*, 563 F.3d 663 (7th Cir. 2009); *Vivendi SA v. T-Mobile USA, Inc.*, 586 F.3d 689, 693 (9th Cir. 2009); *Duha v. Agrium, Inc.*, 448 F.3d 867, 874 (6th Cir. 2006); *Gross v. British Broadcasting Corp.*, 386 F.3d 224 (2d Cir. 2004).

(a) Reasons for lesser degree of deference for foreign plaintiffs' choice of U.S. forum. In explaining why a foreign plaintiff's choice of a U.S. forum was entitled to less deference than a U.S. plaintiff's choice, *Piper* reasoned: "When the plaintiff is foreign . . . this assumption [that it has selected the forum for reasons of convenience] is much less reasonable. Because the central purpose of any *forum non conveniens* inquiry is to ensure that the trial is convenient, a foreign plaintiff's choice deserves less deference." Does this rationale make sense? First, is it in fact true that the "central purpose" of *forum non conveniens* is to ensure that "the trial is convenient"? If so, what are the "public interest" factors? Considering only the *public* interest factors, would a distinction between U.S. and foreign plaintiffs be warranted?

Second, assuming that convenience *is* the true objective of the *forum non conveniens* analysis, then why adopt a presumption that sometimes may — and sometimes may not — have anything to do with convenience? U.S. plaintiffs can live or have their operations abroad; their documents and witnesses in a particular case can likewise be abroad; and they can select a particular U.S. forum solely to inconvenience and harass the defendant. Conversely, foreign plaintiffs can sue in the United States for reasons solely of convenience. Does the *Piper* distinction between U.S. and foreign plaintiffs in fact reflect considerations of convenience, or is it simply a gesture toward the historic rule that U.S. plaintiffs' claims in U.S. courts were not subject to *forum non conveniens* dismissals?

(b) Criticism of Piper*'s distinction between U.S. and foreign plaintiffs.* In the light of what we have seen about the *forum non conveniens* doctrine, is it appropriate for a foreign plaintiff's choice of a U.S. forum to be treated with less respect and deference than a U.S. plaintiff's choice? Some states have rejected this approach, reasoning instead that the residence of the plaintiff should influence the public and private interest factors but not the level of deference. *See Warburg, Pincus Ventures, LP v. Schrapper*, 774 A.2d 264, 268-269 (Del. 2001). Moreover, some commentators have criticized the differential treatment of U.S. and foreign plaintiffs on the grounds that "citizenship [does not] serve as an adequate proxy for other factors that legitimately weigh against dismissal on grounds of *forum non conveniens*. In particular cases in which the plaintiff's American residence touches upon some other factors — the plaintiff's convenience, for example, or possible bias in the alternative forum — such factors can be dealt with adequately on their merits, case by case." Note, *Forum Non Conveniens and American Plaintiffs in the Federal Courts*, 47 U. Chi. L. Rev. 373 (1980). Consider the following excerpt from an opinion of the Washington Supreme Court, refusing to adopt *Piper*'s analysis:

> The Court's logic [in *Piper*] does not withstand scrutiny. The Court is comparing apples and oranges. Foreigners, by definition, can never choose the United States as their home forum. The Court purports to be giving lesser deference to the foreign plaintiffs' choice of forum when, in reality, it is giving lesser deference to *foreign plaintiffs*, based solely on their status as foreigners. More importantly, it is not necessarily less reasonable to assume that a foreign plaintiff's choice of forum is convenient. Why is it less reasonable to assume that a plaintiff from British Columbia, who brings suit in Washington, has chosen a less convenient forum than a plaintiff from Florida bringing the same suit? To take it one step further, why is it less reasonable to assume that a plaintiff, who is a Japanese citizen residing in Wenatchee, who brings suit in Washington, has chosen a less convenient forum than a plaintiff from Florida bringing the same suit? The Court's reference to the attractiveness of United States courts to foreigners, combined with a holding that, in application, gives less deference to foreign plaintiffs based on their status as foreigners, raises concerns about xenophobia. This alone should put us on guard. *Myers v. Boeing Co.*, 794 P.2d 1272, 1281 (Wash. 1990).

Is that persuasive? Recall also the terms of Article 22(3) of the June 2001 Interim Text in the Hague Conference negotiations. *See supra* p. 390. For a hard-nosed reply, consider:

> The Jehas [Saudi Arabian plaintiffs] have argued that it is un-American to deny them the world's best forum and American rights because they happen to be foreigners. . . . We do not hold as an ideal or practice that America shall be obliged to furnish its public services to anyone in the world who may choose to prefer them to their own country's services. This case, to be candid, has nothing to do with America's commitment to justice or to the plaintiff's legal complaint; it is an attempt to convert America's fragile resource of public civil law into an open buffet for plaintiffs and their lawyers. Money, not justice, is the magnet for cases like this. *Jeha v. Arabian American Oil Co.*, 1990 U.S. Dist. LEXIS 15680 (S.D. Tex. 1990).

Is that persuasive?

(c) Alternative rationale for distinction between U.S. and foreign plaintiffs. Is there a more fundamental logic to the lack of deference accorded foreign plaintiffs' choice of a U.S.

forum? As described above, U.S. verdicts often exceed foreign damage awards by orders of magnitude. *See supra* pp. 1-4, 388. This may be in part due to the absence, in the United States, of the social welfare guarantees that exist in some other countries, to differing costs of living, and to other similar factors. If that is correct, then permitting foreign plaintiffs to proceed in U.S. courts may produce unfair windfalls. Even if this is correct, is *forum non conveniens* an appropriate way to preclude such results? Why not take such factors into account in awarding damages?

(d) Should a foreign plaintiff's choice of a U.S. forum receive more, less, or the same deference as a U.S. plaintiff's choice of a U.S. forum? Piper did not say precisely how much "less deference" a foreign plaintiff's choice of a U.S. forum should receive. It suggested in a footnote that "somewhat more deference" is applicable to U.S. plaintiffs' choices of U.S. fora, 454 U.S. at 256 n.23, and it remarked at the end of its opinion that the presumption in favor of a plaintiff's choice of forum applied "with less than maximum force" because the plaintiff was foreign.

Lower courts have usually concluded that it is error to accord *no* deference to a foreign plaintiff's choice of forum: "reduced deference 'is "not an invitation to accord a foreign plaintiff's selection of an American forum no deference since dismissal for *forum non conveniens* is the exception rather than the rule."'" *Lony v. E.I. Du Pont de Nemours & Co.*, 886 F.2d 628, 633 (3d Cir. 1991) (quoting *Lacey v. Cessna Aircraft Co.*, 862 F.2d 38, 45-46 (3d Cir. 1989) (quoting *In re Air Crash Disaster*, 821 F.2d 1147, 1164 n.26 (5th Cir. 1987))); *see also Bigio v. Coca Cola Co.*, 448 F.3d 176, 179 (2d Cir. 2006); *Ravelo Monegro v. Rosa*, 211 F.3d 509, 514 (9th Cir. 2000).

Even these courts, however, have not provided any specific guidance as to just how much "deference" a foreign plaintiff's choice of a U.S. forum warrants. *Lacey v. Cessna Aircraft Co.*, 1990 U.S. Dist. LEXIS 5489 (W.D. Pa. 1990) ("the Court of Appeals . . . has indicated that, because [the foreign plaintiff] is forced to choose between two inconvenient foreign fora, his choice is due 'at least some weight.' Of course, this provides little direction and is impossible to quantify."). Most decisions merely say that a foreign plaintiff's choice of a U.S. forum is entitled to "some," "less," or "reduced" deference.

What should lower courts and parties do with these various remarks? How much "less deference" should a foreign plaintiff's choice of forum be accorded?

(e) Overcoming the reduced deference to a foreign plaintiff's choice of a U.S. forum. There are, of course, many cases in which a foreign plaintiff brings suit in the United States for reasons of convenience. Whatever the specific standard of deference, most lower courts have permitted foreign plaintiffs to demonstrate that they selected the forum for reasons of convenience, and not to oppress the defendant; such a showing is sometimes held to invest their choice of a U.S. forum with the same deference that U.S. plaintiffs are entitled to. *E.g., Lony v. E.I. Du Pont de Nemours & Co.*, 886 F.2d 628, 634 (3d Cir. 1989) (foreign plaintiff on "the same footing as a domestic plaintiff"); *Banco Nominees Ltd. v. Iroquois Brands, Ltd.*, 1990 WL 161031 (D. Del. 1990) ("If a foreign plaintiff can make a strong showing that the forum is convenient, the foreign plaintiff should be accorded the same deference that a domestic plaintiff would receive.") The Third Circuit has explained:

> Because the reason for giving a foreign plaintiff's choice [of a U.S. forum] less deference is not xenophobia, but merely a reluctance to assume that the choice is a convenient one, that reluctance can readily be overcome by a strong showing of convenience. *Lony v. E.I. Du Pont de Nemours & Co.*, 886 F.2d 628, 634 (3d Cir. 1989).

5. ***Specifying the degree of deference afforded to the choice of a U.S. forum by different categories of U.S. and foreign plaintiffs.*** Following *Piper,* U.S. courts have considered a wide range of factual scenarios where it has been difficult to apply the supposedly simple rule that "U.S. plaintiffs" will be granted greater deference than "foreign plaintiffs" in their choice of a U.S. forum. These scenarios have involved plaintiffs who are not readily characterized as entirely "U.S." or "foreign," or whose selection of a U.S. forum is subject to particular suspicion.

(a) *U.S. plaintiffs with limited U.S. connections.* How should courts deal with a plaintiff who, while nominally U.S. in some respects, has strong (or stronger) connections to a foreign country? A number of decisions hold that the choice of a U.S. forum by a merely nominal U.S. plaintiff, with limited U.S. connections, is entitled to reduced deference. *See Pain v. United Technologies Corp.*, 637 F.2d 775, 797-798 (D.C. Cir. 1980) (choice of U.S. forum by a "nominally American plaintiff," defined as subrogees, assignees, or representatives of foreign companies, is generally not given special deference); *Fitzgerald v. Westland Marine Corp.*, 369 F.2d 499, 502 (6th Cir. 1966); *Cavlam Business Ltd. v. Certain Underwriters at Lloyd's, London, No. 08 Civ. 2225 (JGK)*, 2009 WL 667272, at *4 (S.D.N.Y. Mar. 16, 2009) ("American nationals residing abroad are given little deference with respect to their choice of a forum in the United States."). *Compare Duha v. Agrium, Inc.*, 448 F.3d 867, 875 (6th Cir. 2006) (reversing *forum non conveniens* dismissal partly on ground that district court failed to accord adequate deference to U.S. plaintiff's choice of forum and distinguishing prior circuit precedent on the ground that plaintiff in prior case had "attenuated" connection with United States).

What if the domestic plaintiff is the assignee of a claim of a foreign company? *See VictoriaTea.com, Inc. v. Cott Beverages, Canada*, 239 F. Supp. 2d 377, 381 (S.D.N.Y. 2003). Would either fact affect its nationality for purposes of *forum non conveniens* analysis?

(b) *U.S. plaintiffs engaged in international business.* A number of decisions have suggested that the choice of a U.S. forum by U.S. plaintiffs who have chosen to engage in international business abroad will be entitled to less deference than a similar choice by a purely local plaintiff. *See Carey v. Bayerische Hypo- und Vereinsbank AG*, 370 F.3d 234 (2d Cir. 2004) (plaintiff entered into transaction in Germany, while residing in Germany: "Such transactions in Germany reasonably give rise to the expectation on all sides that any litigation arising from them will be conducted in Germany"); *Guidi v. Inter-Continental Hotels Corp.*, 224 F.3d 142, 147 (2d Cir. 2000) ("Plaintiffs . . . are ordinary American citizens for whom litigating in Egypt presents an obvious and significant inconvenience. . . . This is not a case where the plaintiff is a corporation doing business abroad and can expect to litigate in foreign courts").

Reduced deference is particularly likely where the plaintiff is a corporation, rather than an individual. *Reid-Walen v. Hansen*, 933 F.2d 1390, 1395 (8th Cir. 1991) ("A corporate plaintiff's citizenship or residence may not correlate with its real convenience because of the nature of the corporate entity, while an individual's residence more often will correlate with his or her convenience.").

(c) *U.S. plaintiffs who do not reside in the forum.* Should a U.S. citizen who does not reside in the forum jurisdiction receive the same level of deference as a forum resident? What is the "forum" for these purposes? Consider the following discussion by the First Circuit, after a district court held that New York and Florida plaintiffs who had sued in Massachusetts were not entitled to *Piper's* deference for forum residents:

> In the present case, the choice facing the district court was between two countries — the United States and Turkey. Seen in this light, the district court erred in concluding that the Merciers' non-Massachusetts citizenship and residence favored dismissing the case. Rather, the Merciers' United States citizenship and residence — plus Sheraton International's similar citizenship and residence — are factors that make this a controversy local to

the United States, if not necessarily to Massachusetts. In turn, conducting the case in the United States would serve the substantial public interest of providing a convenient United States forum for an action in which all parties are United States citizens and residents. *Mercier v. Sheraton International, Inc.*, 935 F.2d 419 (1st Cir. 1991).

See also Interpane Coatings, Inc. v. Australia and New Zealand Banking Group Ltd., 732 F. Supp. 909 (N.D. Ill. 1990) ("in *forum non conveniens* cases involving a potential reference to a foreign court the relevant distinction is whether or not the plaintiff who has selected the federal forum is an American citizen, not whether he reside in the particular district where the case was brought"); *Ionescu v. E.F. Hutton & Co.*, 465 F. Supp. 139, 145 (S.D.N.Y. 1979).

Other courts suggest, to the contrary, that citizens who do not reside in the forum are entitled to less deference than resident plaintiffs (though more deference than foreign plaintiffs). *Boston Telecommunications Group, Inc. v. Wood*, 588 F.3d 1201, 1207 (9th Cir. 2009); *Gemini Capital Group, Inc. v. Yap Fishing Corp.*, 150 F.3d 1088, 1091 (9th Cir. 1998). Are these views consistent with *Iragorri?* Recall the similar issues in the context of personal jurisdiction and a "national contacts" test. *See supra* pp. 209-214, 225. Does the answer depend on whether state or federal law governs the *forum non conveniens* doctrine? *See infra* pp. 453-459.

(d) Foreign plaintiffs who reside in the United States. A number of lower courts have held that the choice of a U.S. forum by a foreign national who resides in the United States is entitled to substantial deference. *See Tuazon v. R.J. Reynolds Tobacco Co.*, 433 F.3d 1163, 1177 n.6 (9th Cir. 2006); *Wiwa v. Royal Dutch Petroleum Co.*, 226 F.3d 88, 103 (2d Cir. 2000) (in case involving Nigerian émigrés, "We have never accorded less deference to a foreign plaintiff's choice of a United States forum where that plaintiff was a U.S. resident"); *Varnelo v. Eastwind Transport, Ltd.*, 2003 WL 230741, at *12 n.26 (S.D.N.Y. 2003) ("[B]ecause the touchstone of *forum non conveniens* is the plaintiff's residence (and thus convenience) rather than citizenship, foreign nationals residing in the U.S. receive the same heightened deference as U.S. resident citizens."). *Compare Dattner v. Conagra Foods, Inc.*, 2003 WL 1740448 (S.D.N.Y. 2003) (plaintiff did not reside or pay taxes in United States and was in United States on temporary visa; "the Court applies a relatively weak presumption in favor of Plaintiff's choice of forum").

(e) U.S. plaintiffs in a representative capacity. Suppose that, in a class action, the class representative is a U.S. citizen (or permanent resident) but most other class members are foreign citizens. Should that reduce the level of deference to the plaintiffs' choice of forum? Several courts suggest that this is appropriate. *See, e.g., Lasker v. UBS Securities LLC*, 614 F. Supp. 2d 345, 358 (S.D.N.Y. 2008) ("Plaintiff resides within the forum. Nevertheless, because he is a plaintiff in class action, his choice of forum is given less weight than if he were an individual plaintiff."); *Harper v. American Airlines, Inc.*, 2009 WL 1605800, at *3 (N.D. Ala. May 18, 2009) (collecting cases). This line of reasoning finds support in the Supreme Court's decision in *Koster.* That case involved a *forum non conveniens* dismissal in favor of another domestic forum (prior to Congress's enactment of the transfer statute) and relied partly on the plaintiff's appearance in a representative capacity. Does *Koster's* reasoning apply when the alternative forum is outside the United States?

(f) Foreign plaintiffs suing resident defendants. Suppose that a foreign plaintiff wishes to sue a resident defendant, and the resident defendant requests a *forum non conveniens* dismissal to the foreign plaintiff's own courts. Under those circumstances, isn't the *forum non conveniens* analysis really just a comparative judgment about which party should be allowed to shop for a preferred forum? Consider the following comments from Judge Posner:

When the plaintiff wants to sue on the defendant's home turf, and the defendant want to be sued on the plaintiff's home turf, all really that the court is left to weigh is the relative advantages and disadvantages of the alternative forums. In such a case, there is no *prima facie* reason to think a plaintiff discriminated against by being sent to his home court or a defendant discriminated against by being forced to stay and defend in *his* home court. . . . Where application of the doctrine would send the plaintiffs to their home court, the presumption in favor of giving plaintiffs their choice of court is little more than a tie breaker. And so our focus in these cases must be on particularized circumstances that lean in favor of U.S. courts or foreign courts.

Abad v. Bayer Corp., 563 F.3d 663, 667 (7th Cir. 2009). Does this approach suggest a clearer analytical roadmap in such cases? Or does it completely override the notion of deference to the plaintiff's choice of forum?

6. Iragorri's *approach to the level of deference to the plaintiff's choice of forum.* What was the plaintiff's nationality in *Iragorri?* How much deference did the *Iragorri* plaintiff receive?

(a) Role of plaintiff's nationality and residence in Iragorri. What standards does the *Iragorri* court articulate for defining the appropriate level of deference? What role, if any, does nationality play in the *Iragorri* standards? How does *Iragorri* deal with the traditional deference afforded by *Piper* to a U.S. national's choice of a U.S. forum? Is *Iragorri* consistent with *Piper?* Why should an American citizen be forced to go to a foreign country to litigate claims that are admittedly subject to the jurisdiction of U.S. courts?

(b) Standard for determining deference in Iragorri. What exactly is the standard for determining how much deference will be accorded a plaintiff's choice of forum after *Iragorri?* Consider the following excerpt from the *Iragorri* opinion again:

> We thus understand the Supreme Court's teachings on the deference due to plaintiff's forum choice as instructing that we give greater deference to a plaintiff's forum choice to the extent that it was motivated by legitimate reasons, including the plaintiff's convenience and the ability of a U.S. resident plaintiff to obtain jurisdiction over the defendant, and diminishing deference to a plaintiff's forum choice to the extent that it was motivated by tactical advantage.

What does the *Iragorri* Court mean by a forum selection motivated by "legitimate reasons," as opposed to by "tactical advantage"? *See Bigio v. Coca Cola Co.*, 448 F.3d 176, 179 (2d Cir. 2006) (finding that foreign plaintiff had "legitimate and substantial reasons" for choosing U.S. forum after efforts to seek relief in foreign forum failed). How does one tell the difference between these things?

(c) Wisdom of Iragorri *analysis.* What do you make of the analysis in Iragorri? Does it provide a comprehensive explanation for how and why different plaintiff's choices of U.S. forums will receive different degrees of deference? Or does it further reduce the *forum non conveniens* doctrine to pure, unpredictable discretion?

7. *Wisdom of condemning forum shopping.* Is *Iragorri's* condemnation of forum shopping wise? Should courts even be in the business of policing forum shopping? Consider one judge's spirited opposition to this role:

> Forum-shopping is sanctioned by our judicial system. It is as American as the Constitution, peremptory challenges to jurors, and our dual system of state and federal courts. The extension in Article III of federal judicial power to "controversies between citizens of different states," implemented by statute continuously since 1789, permits a plaintiff who might sue in a state court to select a federal forum for the claim. The statutory provision for removal to federal courts of such diversity cases filed in state court permits the defendant to opt for a federal forum. Virtually all causes of action created by federal law may be asserted in either a state or a federal court. Many claims that may be asserted in the courts of one state may also be asserted in the courts of another. Not only may a litigant frequently select among several

jurisdictions, he may, within a jurisdiction, lay venue in more than one court. The existence of these choices not only permits but indeed invites counsel in an adversary system, seeking to serve his client's interests, to select the forum that he considers most receptive to his cause. The motive of the suitor in making this choice is ordinarily of no moment: a court may be selected because its docket moves rapidly, its discovery procedures are liberal, its jurors are generous, the rules of law applied are more favorable, or the judge who presides in that forum is thought more likely to rule in the litigant's favor. . . .

In a perfect judicial system forum-shopping would be paradoxical. The same results would obtain in every forum and after every type of trial. But the actual litigation process is not a laboratory in which the same result is obtained after every test. In some situations, such as when a statute of limitations is involved, the choice of forum may determine the rule of law that will be applied. Even when legal rules are identical, justice can be obtained only through human beings, and neither judges nor jurors are fungible. In recognition both of this and of the nature of the adversary, client-serving process, we tolerate a certain amount of manipulation without inquiry into motive. Thus, despite defendants' insinuation that plaintiffs' effort to secure the most favorable forum is somehow unscrupulous or unsporting, the Court finds instead that it is consistent with the usual workings of our adversary system. *Perusahaan Umum Listrik Negara Pusat v. M/V Tel Aviv*, 711 F.2d 1231, 1238 (5th Cir. 1983).

Do you agree? Would the *Iragorri* Court?

8. *Practical risk of* **forum non conveniens** *dismissal of U.S. plaintiff's claims.* At least prior to decisions such as *Iragorri*, it remained unusual for U.S. claimants to be subject to *forum non conveniens* dismissals, notwithstanding abandonment of the historic right of U.S. citizens of access to U.S. courts. This result rests upon *Piper's* requirement that substantial deference be accorded a U.S. plaintiff's choice of a U.S. forum. *See supra* p. 388. Note that "[d]espite frequent statements that an American citizen has no constitutional right of access to American courts and that unusually extreme circumstances might bring about a dismissal on *forum non conveniens* grounds, the American plaintiff is almost assured that his case will be heard in this country notwithstanding the inconvenience to defendant. . . . [I]n fact, this writer has found no case in which a bona fide American plaintiff has been sent abroad solely on forum non conveniens grounds." Note, *The Convenient Forum Abroad*, 20 Stan. L. Rev. 57, 67-68, 74 (1967). Although this is an overstatement, U.S. plaintiffs' claims have in practice seldom been dismissed. *See Duha v. Agrium, Inc.*, 340 F. Supp. 2d 787 (E.D. Mich. 2004) (citing cases where American plaintiffs' claims were dismissed on *forum non conveniens* grounds). Could *Iragorri*'s rule alter this?

9. *Availability of* **forum non conveniens** *doctrine where defendant resides in forum.* A number of courts have considered whether the *forum non conveniens* doctrine is available when the defendant resides, operates, or is incorporated in the forum. It has been argued that the doctrine should never apply in such circumstances, because it can be presumed that the forum has been chosen for reasons of convenience and because the forum will in fact be convenient (particularly to the defendant). Consider the remarks on this subject in comment f to §84 of the *Restatement (Second) Conflict of Laws* (1971).

Some state courts have held that the *forum non conveniens* doctrine simply does not apply where the defendant resides in the forum. *E.g., Murdoch v. A.P. Green Industries, Inc.*, 603 So. 2d 655 (Fla. Dist. Ct. App. 1992) ("It is established Florida law that 'a case may be dismissed from the Florida courts in favor of a more convenient forum in another state only where none of the parties involved in the suit are residents of this state'"); *Piper Aircraft Corp. v. Schwendemann*, 578 So. 2d 319 (Fla. Dist. Ct. App. 1991). However, the trend is to abandon such absolute rules. *Silver v. Great American Ins. Co.*, 328 N.Y.S.2d 398 (1972) (overturning rule that no *forum non conveniens* dismissal is available if either party is New York resident).

Nevertheless, defendants who argue that it would be inconvenient for them to litigate in a court located only blocks away from their headquarters often encounter skeptical reactions: "It is, as Alice said, 'curiouser and curiouser.' " *Lony v. E.I. Du Pont de Nemours & Co.*, 935 F.2d 604, 608 (3d Cir. 1991) (noting that "Du Pont, which is headquartered in Wilmington, Delaware, and is the largest employer in that state, seeks to move the action against it to a forum more than 3,000 miles away"). Lower courts have thus generally concluded that a significant factor weighing against *forum non conveniens* dismissals is the defendant's domicile in the forum. *See Galustian v. Peter*, 591 F.3d 724, 732 (4th Cir. 2010); *Geschwind v. Cessna Aircraft Co.*, 161 F.3d 602, 609 (10th Cir. 1998). As the Second Circuit has succinctly put it: "We begin by noting that plaintiff[, a Swiss attorney,] chose this forum and defendant resides here. This weighs heavily against dismissal." *Schertenleib v. Traum*, 589 F.2d 1156, 1164 (2d Cir. 1978). *See also Ellis v. AAR Parts Trading Inc.*, 828 N.E.2d 726, 743 (Ill. App. 2005) ("[I]t is incredulous for two Illinois resident corporations to argue that their home state is inconvenient to them to litigate this matter.") (quoting trial court). That skepticism may be tempered, though, in case of a major multinational defendant whose "home forum" may only represent a fraction of its worldwide operations. *Pollux Holding Ltd. v. Chase Manhattan Bank*, 329 F.3d 64, 73-74 (2d Cir. 2003).

10. *Representative fact patterns.* Can general rules based upon nationality be articulated to structure the *forum non conveniens* analysis? Suppose that there is evidence in both the United States and a foreign state, that the conduct principally occurred abroad with incidental U.S. activities, and that foreign law will probably govern. How should a *forum non conveniens* motion presumptively be handled if: (a) both parties are U.S. nationals; (b) the plaintiff is U.S., but the defendant is foreign; (c) the plaintiff is foreign, but the defendant is U.S.; (d) both parties are foreign nationals? Is this insufficient information to make a generalization? Would generalizations like those set forth above be useful?

D. The "Private and Public Interest" Factors

Central to *Piper* and other formulations of the *forum non conveniens* doctrine is a "weighing" of "private" and "public" interest factors. These factors were first detailed in *Gulf Oil*, and are repeated in *Piper* and subsequent authorities.[80]

Excerpted below are materials that illustrate application of the private and public interest factors referred to in *Gulf Oil* and *Piper*. First, reread *Piper*, and consider how it applied the public and private interest factors. Next, consider the decision in *Howe v. Goldcorp Investments, Ltd.*, which explores the role of the parties' nationalities and the location of evidence in *forum non conveniens* analysis against a backdrop of federal statutory rights. Finally, read the decision in *Harrison v. Wyeth Laboratories*, which illustrates the application *Gulf Oil*'s private and public interest factors in the context of state law claims.

PIPER AIRCRAFT CO. v. REYNO

454 U.S. 235 (1981) [excerpted above at pp. 373-378]

HOWE v. GOLDCORP INVESTMENTS, LTD.

946 F.2d 944 (1st Cir. 1991)

BREYER, CHIEF JUDGE. . . . The plaintiff in this case, Reginald Howe, an American shareholder of Goldcorp, claims that defendants Goldcorp, its officers, its investment advisors,

---

80. 454 U.S. at 241, 257-260; 330 U.S. at 508-509; *Restatement (Second) Conflict of Laws* §84 comment c (1971).

and its lawyers, all of whom are Canadians, violated securities statutes, primarily by failing to disclose adequately their intentions, plans, objectives and other circumstances related to their efforts to take over two other Canadian companies called Dickenson and Kam-Kotia. He claims that, in these same circumstances, some of these defendants violated their fiduciary duties to Goldcorp or to its shareholders, and some, or all, of the defendants violated other statutes as well. The district court dismissed all of Mr. Howe's claims on grounds of *forum non conveniens*. [We affirm.] . . .

The record indicates that Goldcorp's significant contacts with the United States are limited: First, Goldcorp is a Canadian corporation. Its shares trade on Canadian stock exchanges where anyone can buy them. Goldcorp sells its shares to residents of the United States only if they (or their agents) buy those shares in Canada. Goldcorp shares do not trade on stock exchanges (nor are they sold over the counter) in the United States. Second, Goldcorp sends annual reports, proxy statements and similar material to shareholders in whatever country they live [including the U.S.] . . . as part of general, worldwide mailings. Third, Goldcorp sends regular dividends to shareholders in whatever country they live [including the U.S.] . . . as part of a general distribution to all shareholders. . . . Fourth, Goldcorp employees have answered, by mail or by phone, specific questions addressed to them by Goldcorp's shareholders in the United States. Goldcorp employees have, from time to time, sent annual reports and similar written material to investment advisors or stock brokers in the United States, always at the request of those advisors or brokers, who themselves (or who have clients who) were already Goldcorp shareholders. . . . Fifth, in 1989 Goldcorp acquired two Canadian companies (called Dickenson and Kam-Kotia) which owned some assets in the United States and had some American shareholders. In doing so, it had to comply—and did comply—with various U.S. Securities and Exchange Commission requirements. Sixth, Goldcorp's American shareholders, including Mr. Howe, own about one-third of Goldcorp's shares.

Mr. Howe's allegations grow out of the following events: 1. Before 1987 Goldcorp was a company that owned gold and held other diverse, gold-related investments. Its articles of incorporation forbid it to own more than 10 percent of the assets of any other single company or to invest more than 10 percent of its own assets in the shares of any other single company. Thus, investment in Goldcorp amounted to an investment approximately as safe as gold itself; for Goldcorp could itself own only (1) gold and (2) a small or diverse portfolio of other gold-related companies. 2. In 1987 Goldcorp asked its shareholders to approve changes in its articles of incorporation that would permit it to own more than 10 percent of other individual companies and to invest more than 10 percent of its own assets in a single company's shares. The stockholders gave their approval. 3. In January 1989 a Canadian company called Corona tried to take over two other Canadian goldmining companies (Dickenson and Kam-Kotia). Goldcorp, appearing . . . as a "white knight," thwarted Corona's bid by taking over these two companies itself. . . . 4. As a result of the takeovers of Dickenson and Kam-Kotia, the value of Goldcorp's shares declined dramatically.

Mr. Howe's complaint claims that [these] facts . . . reveal several kinds of unlawful activity. First, he says that Goldcorp "defrauded" its shareholders, primarily by failing to explain adequately that the changes in its articles of incorporation meant a radical change in its investment policy. In particular, alleges Mr. Howe, Goldcorp failed to explain that the corporation would no longer invest its assets safely in gold and in a diversified portfolio, but, instead, would invest heavily in the shares of one or two companies, thereby greatly increasing the risks to investors in Goldcorp. This "misrepresentation" or "fraud," the complaint says, violates the federal securities laws, *see* 15 U.S.C. §§78j(b), 77q(a), Massachusetts consumer protection law, *see* Mass. Gen. L. ch. 93A, and the common law of fraud and misrepresentation. Second, the complaint claims another instance of "misrepresentation" or "fraud." It states that Goldcorp failed to disclose to the SEC (as part of its 1989 effort to buy shares of Dickenson and Kam-Kotia from United States shareholders) the existence of legal problems surrounding the 1987 amendment of its articles of incorporation. Third, the complaint says that officers of Goldcorp and Goldcorp's investment managers, when organizing the takeover of Dickenson and Kam-Kotia, tried to help themselves rather than to benefit Goldcorp. It says, for example, that, by improperly looking to their own financial gain, they violated fiduciary duties owed to the company — duties imposed by common law, Canadian law, securities statutes and the American Investment Company Act of 1940. Fourth, the complaint says that these same misrepresentations and violations of fiduciary duty violated various federal criminal statutes, such as the anti-racketeering laws. . . . The district court . . . dismissed Mr. Howe's complaint on grounds of *forum non conveniens.* Mr. Howe appeals this dismissal.

The doctrine of *forum non conveniens* . . . permits a court to dismiss a case because the chosen forum (despite the presence of jurisdiction and venue) is so inconvenient that it would be unfair to conduct the litigation in that place. . . . Appellant, first and most importantly, argues that . . . special legal circumstances here deprive the district court of the legal power to employ the *forum non conveniens* doctrine at all. Supported by the SEC's amicus brief, he says that, no matter what the circumstances, no matter what the unfairness, a federal court (with jurisdiction and proper venue) lacks the power to invoke *forum non conveniens* if Congress has passed an applicable "special" venue statute, a statute that broadens the plaintiff's choice of forum beyond the choices that federal law's "general" venue statute otherwise would provide. [The federal securities laws contain such a "special" venue statute, 15 U.S.C. §78aa, as do the antitrust laws. *See supra* pp. 214-215.] . . .

[I]n the international context one can ask, "What is so special about a special venue statute?" If a general venue statute opening federal court doors (say, in New York) is compatible with an international *forum non conveniens* transfer (say, to Italy), why does a special venue statute which simply opens another court's doors (say, in California) suddenly make the same international transfer unlawful? Both kinds of statutes open otherwise closed court doors. Neither kind of statute, explicitly or (absent some special legislative intent) implicitly, prohibits an international transfer. . . .

[W]e can find no good policy reason for reading the special venue provisions as if someone in Congress really intended them to remove the courts' legal power to invoke the doctrine of *forum non conveniens* in an otherwise appropriate case. The growing interdependence of formerly separate national economies, the increased extent to which commerce is international, and the greater likelihood that an act performed in one country will affect citizens of another, all argue for expanded efforts to help the world's legal systems work together, in harmony, rather than at cross purposes. To insist that American courts hear cases where the balance of convenience and the interests of justice require that they be brought elsewhere will simply encourage an international forum-shopping that would increase the likelihood that decisions made in one country will cause (through lack of awareness or understanding) adverse effects in another, eroding uniformity or thwarting the aims of law and policy. And, to deprive American courts of their transfer power when, but only when, one of more than three hundred special venue statutes applies, would create a hodge-podge, that would, or would not, bring about American adjudication of an essentially foreign controversy, depending upon the pure happenstance of whether Congress — at some perhaps distant period and likely out of a desire to widen plaintiffs' venue choices in typical domestic cases — enacted a "special venue" provision. Such a result would seem thoroughly unsound.

We turn now to the appellant's second argument, also supported by the SEC — that the district court misapplied the doctrine of *forum non conveniens* in the present case. We consider this argument in light of several well-established legal principles. First, *forum non conveniens* is a flexible, practical doctrine designed to avoid trials in places so "inconvenient" that transfer is needed to avoid serious unfairness. Second, although *forum non conveniens* is not "rigid," and "[e]ach case turns on its facts," the Supreme Court has provided an illustrative list of relevant considerations. Third, the *forum non conveniens* determination is committed to the sound discretion of the trial court. . . .

We can find no "clear abuse" of the district court's powers in this case. For one thing, the balance of conveniences seems to favor, with unusual strength, the Canadian defendants. The relevant events surrounding both plaintiff's "misrepresentation" and "breach of fiduciary duty" claims took place in Canada, not in the United States. The Canadian directors of Goldcorp, its officers, its investment advisors, and its lawyers, meeting, speaking, planning, and acting in Canada, took (or failed to take) the actions that allegedly amounted to a failure to remain properly loyal to Goldcorp and its shareholders. Canadian individuals also decided, in Canada, precisely what statements they or the corporation should make, or should not make, in public descriptions of changes in Goldcorp's articles of incorporation, of changes in Goldcorp's investment policies, and of circumstances surrounding the takeover of Dickenson and Kam-Kotia. They presumably arranged to have printed in Canada most of the documents embodying most of those statements (though they then disseminated many of these documents to shareholders throughout the world). Thus, the relevant actions, statements and omissions that underlie the plaintiff's claims of "misrepresentation" or "fraud" originated in Canada. Most of the background facts that might show those statements or omissions to be materially false or misleading occurred in Canada.

Given these facts, it is not surprising that most of the evidence is in Canada and most of the witnesses are in Canada. Indeed, an undisputed affidavit by Goldcorp's President says that, except for Mr. Howe, no resident of the United States "has knowledge relevant to the matters alleged in the amended complaint." And, only Canadian courts, not courts within the United States, have the legal power to compel the testimony of twelve Canadian potential witnesses who are not under the control of any party. . . . Compulsory process would seem especially important where, as here, fraud and subjective intent are elements of the claim, making the live testimony of witnesses for the purposes of presenting demeanor evidence essential to a fair trial. . . . At the same time, trial in Canada will not deprive the plaintiff of relevant legal advantages. Canadian courts will either apply American law, see *Restatement (Second) of Conflict of Laws* §6; or they will apply Canadian laws that offer shareholders somewhat similar protections by forbidding misrepresentation and fraud and imposing fiduciary obligations. We concede there may be some differences between Canadian and American law on these matters. Controlling precedent makes clear, however, that small differences in standards and procedural differences (such as greater difficulty in meeting class action requirements or less generous rules for recovering attorney's fees) are beside the point. . . .

Further, this case, except for the presence of an American shareholder, has little to do with Massachusetts or any other jurisdiction in the United States. Goldcorp's contacts with the United States consist of those listed earlier: (1) sending reports and statements to American shareholders among others, (2) answering questions sent by Americans about, how, for example, they might buy shares in Canada, (3) providing explanations of corporate policies and activities to American shareholders, such as Mr. Howe, who requested them, and (4) filing takeover information with the SEC so that Goldcorp could buy shares that Americans might hold in two Canadian companies (Dickenson and Kam-Kotia). In respect to Massachusetts, Goldcorp's activities apparently come down to keeping a mailing list of eight shareholders, sending those shareholders ordinary information, and answering requests for information from one firm of investment advisors (Shearson Lehman, to which Goldcorp sent ten annual, and ten interim, reports) and seven individuals.

Finally, this case has a great deal to do with Canada. The underlying circumstances involve actions of a Canadian corporation, its directors, officers and advisors. And the plaintiff's claims implicate duties the defendants owed to the corporation and its shareholders under Canadian law. Thus, at least some significant portion of the adjudication of Mr. Howe's case will involve tasks most easily and appropriately handled by a Canadian court: interpreting primarily Canadian law and applying it to matters principally of concern to Canada. . . . Of course, as we said, Goldcorp has a significant number of American shareholders; Mr. Howe claims to represent a class of 2,500 American shareholders; and federal securities laws are designed to protect American investors from misrepresentation and fraud. But, neither Mr. Howe nor the SEC has provided us with any reason to believe those laws seek so strongly to protect Americans who bought their shares abroad from misrepresentations (or violations of fiduciary duty) primarily taking place abroad that a court may not require an American shareholder to bring his case abroad in a nation that offers its shareholders roughly equivalent legal protections. To hold the contrary here would, in effect, remove the court's *forum non conveniens* power in securities cases, raising the practical concerns we mentioned earlier. That is to say, we believe that a holding barring transfer would increase the risk that national legal systems will work to frustrate one another and would hinder efforts to promote greater coordination and harmony among them.

In sum, in respect to Mr. Howe's basic claims involving misrepresentation and violations of fiduciary duties, these factors substantially outweigh Mr. Howe's suggestion in his affidavit that he would find it financially difficult to litigate in Canada. We cannot say that the district court was clearly wrong in finding that the balance of conveniences favors suit in Canada and that litigation in Mr. Howe's chosen forum would likely prove both unfair and oppressive.

HARRISON v. WYETH LABORATORIES DIVISION OF AMERICAN HOME PRODUCTS CORPORATION
510 F. Supp. 1 (E.D. Pa. 1980)

WEINER, DISTRICT JUDGE. Plaintiffs in these actions are all citizens and residents of the United Kingdom. They each allege that they purchased oral contraceptives within the United Kingdom, used them in accordance with the directions and instructions, and as a direct and proximate result of such usage suffered injury, damages, and/or death. . . . Plaintiffs allege that defendant has its principal place of business in Pennsylvania, and is engaged in the development, testing, manufacture, production, sale, marketing, promotion and advertising of the oral contraceptives Ovram-30, Ovram and Ovranette. Plaintiffs allege that defendant caused the marketing, sale and distribution of the drugs in the United Kingdom and either actually produced and manufactured the drugs marketed in the United Kingdom themselves, or did so through others by agency, license, or otherwise. Plaintiffs allege that defendant was negligent in its conduct of these activities, and in its failure to give reasonable or adequate warning concerning the serious risk of which it had knowledge associated with the use of these drugs.

Defendant has submitted the affidavit of David Gibbens, the Secretary of John Wyeth & Brothers Limited ("JWB"), incorporated under the laws of the United Kingdom, a wholly owned subsidiary of American Home Products Corporation ("AHPC"). According to the affidavit, JWB is a sub-licensee of AHPC and pays royalties to AHPC for use of synthetic progestrogens, for which APHC holds the exclusive license, in the contraceptives it manufactures, including Ovram-30, Ovram and Ovranette. The affidavit states that all three of the drugs are manufactured, packaged and labelled in the United Kingdom by, or on behalf of, JWB for distribution in the United Kingdom and Ireland. The affidavit further states that JWB received product licenses under the laws of the United Kingdom authorizing distribution and marketing of the drugs. Defendant argues that the litigation could and should more conveniently and appropriately be brought in the United Kingdom, as that country is the domicile of the plaintiffs, and the situs of the licensing, manufacture, packaging, prescription, purchase, and ingestion of the drugs. Defendant contends that the activities complained of did not occur in Pennsylvania, and Pennsylvania has no legitimate interest in regulating the conduct of its citizens beyond its borders. Defendant reasons that the marketing decisions were made in light of British regulation and law, and should be judged by the standards of the community affected by the allegedly tortious activity. . . .

Plaintiffs argue that while it may well be true that the particular drugs which caused the injury in these cases were actually manufactured and sold in the United Kingdom, such facts are not dispositive of its claim. Plaintiffs contend that the alleged tortious conduct consisted of marketing the drugs and placing them in the stream of commerce with knowledge that the warning accompanying the drugs was inadequate, thus creating an unreasonable risk of harm, irrespective of where the drugs were sold. Plaintiffs claim that the fundamental manufacturing and marketing decision, conceiving the formula for the drugs, the knowledge of the risk involved, the alleged withholding of adequate warning, and distribution of the drugs, all were made by defendant in Pennsylvania. Plaintiffs argue that the alleged tortious acts occurred in Pennsylvania, and that Pennsylvania has an interest in and direct concern with the safety of products which emanate from its borders and with conduct which occurs within Pennsylvania which may cause harm to others, regardless of where that harm may have occurred. . . .

The local interest in having this localized issue decided at home is strong. A Court versed in the law that must govern the case and familiar with the people and the community in which the law is to govern, is better able to establish the appropriate legal standards and apply them to the facts of the case. After careful consideration we have decided that these cases would be more conveniently and appropriately heard in the courts of the United Kingdom. Even assuming arguendo that all production and marketing decisions were made by defendant in Pennsylvania and not by JWB in the United Kingdom, Pennsylvania's interest in the regulation of the *conduct* of drug manufacturers and the safety of drugs produced and distributed *within* its borders does not extend so far as to include such regulation of conduct on drugs produced or distributed in foreign countries. Questions as to the *safety* of drugs marketed in a foreign country are properly the concern of that country; the courts of the United States are ill-equipped to set a standard of product safety for drugs sold in other countries. The issues raised here concern the knowledge, if any, of an allegedly unreasonable risk, and the sufficiency of the warning of that risk to users of the product. Both the British and the American governments have established requirements as to the standards of safety for drugs and the adequacy of any warnings to be given in connection with its use. Each government must weigh the merits of permitting the drug's use and the necessity of requiring a warning. Each makes its own determination as to the standards of degree of safety and duty of care. This balancing of the overall benefits to be derived from a product's use with the risk of harm associated with that use is peculiarly suited to a forum of the country in which the product is to be used. Each country has its own legitimate concerns and its own unique needs which must be factored into its process of weighing the drug's merits, and which will tip the balance for it one way or the other. The United States should not impose its own view of the safety, warning, and duty of care required of drugs sold in the United States upon a foreign country when those same drugs are sold in that country. Here, that foreign country is the United Kingdom, a society in some aspects similar to our own in a standard of living, beliefs, and values. At issue here is, among other things, the delivery of medical care and drugs, oral contraceptives, a category of drugs long considered controversial in the United States for reasons of health and morals. It is therefore tempting for us to believe that our standards of product safety and care, if more stringent than their own, ought to apply to the British in order to afford the British people a higher degree of protection from possibly harmful products.

The impropriety of such an approach would be even more clearly seen if the foreign country involved was, for example, India, a country with a vastly different standard of living, wealth, resources, level of health care and services, values, morals and beliefs than our own. Most significantly, our two societies must deal with entirely different and highly complex problems of population growth and control. Faced with different needs, problems and resources in our example India may, in balancing the pros and cons of a drug's use, give different weight to various factors than would our society, and more easily conclude that any risks associated with the use of a particular oral contraceptive are far outweighed by its overall benefits to India and its people. Should we impose our standards upon them in spite of such differences? We think not.

Furthermore, *fairness to the defendant* mandates that defendant's conduct be judged by the standards of the community affected by its actions. In addition, defendant claims to have complied by the dictates of the British government's requirements as to drug safety and warning standards. While it may be true in most states in this country that compliance with the minimum government requirements does not necessarily constitute compliance with the duty of care which a manufacturer owes users of its products, it is manifestly unfair to the defendant, as well as an inappropriate usurpation of a foreign court's proper authority to decide a matter of local interest, for a court in this country to set a higher standard of care than is required by the government of the country in which the product is sold and used.

Finally, under Pennsylvania choice of law rules, it is clear that the applicable law here is that of the United Kingdom. A federal court sitting in a diversity case must apply the choice of law rules of the forum state. *Klaxon Co. v. Stentor Electric Manufacturing Co.*, 313 U.S. 487 (1941) [*see also infra* pp. 791-796]. Pennsylvania has adopted the "most significant relationship" test for determining which law to apply. This flexible approach permits analysis of the policies and interests underlying the particular issue before the court, and gives the place having the most interest in the problem paramount control over the legal issues arising out of a particular factual context and thereby allows the forum to apply the policy of the jurisdiction most intimately concerned with the outcome of the particular litigation. We have already shown that the United Kingdom, and not Pennsylvania, has the greater interest in the control of drugs distributed and consumed in the United Kingdom. Hence, it is the jurisdiction most intimately concerned with the outcome of this litigation and its law would be applied even if these cases were to be heard in this forum. . . .

Notes on **Piper,** Howe, *and* **Wyeth**

1. Piper*'s "private interest" factors.* Consider again the "private interest" factors set out in *Piper*. On a quick reading, these factors seem sensible: they portray a meticulous assessment of the efficiencies of trial in the competing forums. But do the factors really make sense in today's world?

(a) *Location of evidence.* A crucial factor in many *forum non conveniens* cases is the location of documents, witnesses, and other evidence. *See Piper*, 454 U.S. at 257-258 ("relative ease of access to sources of proof"); *Duha v. Agrium, Inc.*, 448 F.3d 867, 876 (6th Cir. 2006); *Blanco v. Banco Industrial de Venezuela, SA*, 997 F.2d 974, 982-983 (2d Cir. 1993); *Lacey v. Cessna Aircraft Co.*, 932 F.2d 170 (3d Cir. 1991).

Why does it matter where documents or witnesses are located? Can't persons be put on a plane or telephone and can't documents be sent by courier or fax? How do these expenses compare to the costs of preparation for a new set of lawyers? Consider: "The time and expense of obtaining the presence or testimony of foreign witnesses is greatly reduced by commonplace modes of communication and travel." *Reid-Walen v. Hansen*, 933 F.2d 1390, 1396 (8th Cir. 1991). And, "[i]t will often be quicker and less expensive to transfer a witness or a document than to transfer a lawsuit." *Calavo Growers of California v. Belgium*, 632 F.2d 963, 969 (2d Cir. 1980) (Newman, J., concurring); *Overseas Nat'l Airways, Inc. v. Cargolux Airlines Int'l, SA*, 712 F.2d 11, 14 (2d Cir. 1983) (Oakes, J., concurring) ("The entire doctrine of *forum non conveniens* should be reexamined in light of the transportation revolution.").

In an age of transatlantic flights, Internet, faxes, and FedEx, isn't this right? *See also In re Livent, Inc. Securities Litig.*, 78 F. Supp. 2d 194, 211 (S.D.N.Y. 1999) ("current computer technology, in which documents can be scanned and placed on a secure website for viewing by counsel for the parties and by the court, makes the documentary evidence factor far less important than it might have been in the past."); *Itoba Ltd. v. LEP Group PLC*, 930 F. Supp. 36, 44 (D. Conn. 1996) ("to the extent documents exist in England, advances in transportation and communication accord this issue less weight").

Further, as in *Piper*, evidence is often located in both of the competing jurisdictions (as well as other places). Then, either forum will impose some inconvenience on one party or the other:

> the inconveniences in this case run both ways. The fact that maintaining plaintiff's suit in this American forum will necessitate the production of Swedish documents and witnesses is entirely inconclusive; if the case were tried in defendant's preferred alternate forum, Sweden, witnesses and extensive amounts of evidence would have to be transported from the United States to Sweden. *Carlenstolpe v. Merck & Co.*, 638 F. Supp. 901, 907 (S.D.N.Y. 1986).

As one court aptly put it: in international disputes, "much of the 'inconvenience' is not local, but inherent in the situation out of which the lawsuit arises." *Bata v. Bata*, 105 N.E.2d 623, 626 (N.Y. 1952). That was the case in *Wyeth*. What does this suggest about the utility of this factor in deciding *forum non conveniens* issues?

As noted elsewhere, *infra* pp. 969-977, some countries have enacted blocking statutes that prohibit the removal of certain documents and evidence from within the territory of the country. Such statutes could have a significant effect on the availability of evidence in the case. *Ilusorio v. Ilusorio-Bildner*, 103 F. Supp. 2d 672, 679 (S.D.N.Y. 2000). On the other hand, United States courts routinely order parties to comply with their discovery orders regardless of the existence of a foreign blocking statute, *infra* pp. 1000-1024. How much weight, therefore, should a United States court accord the foreign blocking statute when considering with a *forum non conveniens* motion?

(b) *Witnesses subject to compulsory process.* Nonparty witnesses often have material evidence. *Piper* reasons that, where such witnesses are beyond one of the competing forum's compulsory process, this factor should play an important role in *forum non conveniens* analysis. Lower courts have routinely considered the availability of compulsory process over material witnesses. *Interface Partners Int'l, Ltd. v. Hananel,* 575 F.3d 97, 105 (1st Cir. 2009); *Duha v. Agrium, Inc.,* 448 F.3d 867, 877 (6th Cir. 2006); *Kempe v. Ocean Drilling & Exploration Co.,* 876 F.2d 1138, 1146 (5th Cir. 1989); *Schertenleib v. Traum,* 589 F.2d 1156, 1164 (2d Cir. 1978); *Fitzgerald v. Texaco, Inc.,* 521 F.2d 448, 451-452 (2d Cir. 1975). *See generally Kurzke v. Nissan Motor Corporation in U.S.A.,* 320 N.J. Super. 386, 398 n.3 (N.J. Super. A.D. 1999) (surveying federal cases).

But witnesses will often be willing to testify voluntarily (thus not requiring compulsory process); if they will not, parties often choose not to rely upon hostile witnesses. Moreover, as discussed below, the Hague Evidence Convention provides U.S. courts with a workable mechanism for compelling the testimony of foreign nonparty witnesses. *See infra* pp. 1026-1032, 1088. Even where the Convention is not available, customary letters rogatory provide a means that can often provide testimony. *See infra* pp. 1024-1026. *See also Boston Telecommunications Group, Inc. v. Wood,* 588 F.3d 1201, 1208 (9th Cir. 2009); *DiRienzo v. Philip Services Corp.,* 294 F.3d 21, 30 (2d Cir. 2002); *Overseas Programming Companies, Ltd. v. Cinematographische Commerz-Anstalt,* 684 F.2d, 232, 235 (2d Cir. 1982). Given this, why should the reach of compulsory process be particularly important in *forum non conveniens* analysis?

On the other hand, some courts have questioned the efficacy of customary letters rogatory (while indicating that such doubts do not exist with regard to discovery from states party to the Hague Evidence Convention). *Vivendi SA v. T-Mobile USA, Inc.,* 586 F.3d 689, 696 (9th Cir. 2009); *Auxer v. Alcoa, Inc.,* 2010 WL 1337725 (W.D. Pa. Mar. 29, 2010); *Usha (India), Ltd. v. Honeywell Int'l, Inc.,* 2004 WL 540441 (S.D.N.Y. 2004); *Ilusorio v. Ilusori-Bildner,* 103 F. Supp. 2d 672 (S.D.N.Y. 2000). Such doubts are particularly salient where the foreign forum has made a reservation under Article 23 of the Hague Evidence Convention whereunder it can refuse to execute letters of request seeking pretrial discovery of documents. *See Estate of Thomson ex rel. Estate of Rakestraw v. Toyota Motor Corp. Worldwide,* 545 F.3d 357, 366 (6th Cir. 2008).

As discussed below, 28 U.S.C. §1782 entitles parties in a foreign court to seek evidence located in the United States in support of that "foreign proceeding." *See infra* pp. 1033-1076. By contrast, many foreign countries lack an explicit statutory mechanism of that sort. Some courts have reasoned that the availability of §1782 discovery can counsel in favor of dismissal under the *forum non conveniens* doctrine, because evidentiary materials located in the United States will still be capable of being discovered. *See, e.g., Proyectos Orchimex de Costa Rica, SA v. E.I. du Pont de Nemours & Co.,* 896 F. Supp. 1197, 1202-1203 (M.D. Fla. 1995); *Ciba-Geigy Ltd. v. Fish Peddler, Inc.,* 691 So. 2d 1111, 1119 (Fla. App. 1997).

(c) Defendant's amenability to jurisdiction. Recall the discussion in *Iragorri* concerning cases where a plaintiff sues the defendant in its home jurisdiction because it is impossible (or difficult) to obtain jurisdiction over the defendant in the plaintiff's home jurisdiction. *See supra* p. 397. Other courts have also attached substantial weight to a plaintiff's interest in a viable jurisdictional basis for proceeding against the defendant. *Odyssey Re (London) Ltd. v. Stirling Cooke Brown Holdings Ltd.,* 85 F. Supp. 2d 282 (S.D.N.Y. 2000); *Fiacco v. United Technologies Corp.,* 524 F. Supp. 858 (S.D.N.Y. 1981) ("If plaintiffs had commenced this action against defendant in Norway, defendant could have resisted, probably successfully, on the basis that defendant was not subject to jurisdiction in Norway. . . . [The plaintiffs] could not have proceeded against defendant in Norway absent defendant's consent to submit to jurisdiction there. . . . A plaintiff, who jurisdictionally has the right to proceed in one jurisdiction, should not, in my judgment, be required to proceed if at all only in another jurisdiction where jurisdiction will exist not as a matter of law but as a matter of conscious choice on the part of the party against whom he seeks recovery.").

What if jurisdiction would lie, but the plaintiff can point to an adverse decision of the foreign forum's highest court on the subject matter of the litigation? *See DRFP L.L.C. v. Republica Bolivariana de Venezuela*, 2009 WL 414581, at *12 (S.D. Ohio Feb. 13, 2009).

(d) Plaintiff's motive in bringing suit in the forum. As *Piper* remarked, "dismissal may be warranted where a plaintiff chooses a particular forum, not because it is convenient, but solely in order to harass the defendant or to take advantage of favorable law." Why is it relevant to consider the plaintiff's motive in choosing to sue in the forum? Few contemporary cases involve a plaintiff whose motive was held to be "oppressing" or "harassing" the defendant. There are sanctions for such conduct under U.S. law, as well as tactical arguments against it. Less clear is how courts will, and should, regard forum selection based upon favorable substantive or procedural laws, rather than inflicting cost or inconvenience upon the defendant. Most contemporary cases involve a plaintiff whose motive was to obtain a favorable substantive or procedural regime. *Alfaro, Piper,* and *Howe* all illustrate this. And the reason that almost every defendant seeks *forum non conveniens* dismissal is to obtain the same advantages for itself in a foreign forum. Save in the most unusual cases, does it make sense to consider the plaintiff's desire to improve its chances of recovery?

The Supreme Court has, in the personal jurisdiction context, held that the plaintiff's deliberate effort to obtain favorable substantive rules are both permissible and predictable. In *Keeton v. Hustler Magazine, Inc.*, 465 U.S. 770, 779 (1984), the Court rejected a due process challenge to a suit in New Hampshire, by a non-New Hampshire resident, where the sole reason for suing in New Hampshire was the fact that every other state's statute of limitations had already run: "litigation strategy of countless plaintiffs who seek a forum with favorable substantive or procedural rules or sympathetic local populations." On the other hand, *Piper* and other *forum non conveniens* decisions have discussed such efforts in terms that imply disapproval. *See, e.g., Concat LP v. Unilever, plc,* 350 F. Supp. 2d 796, 809 (N.D. Cal. 2004) (dicta that "courts should disregard a plaintiff's forum choice where the suit is a result of forum-shopping"). In few cases, however, do the plaintiff's efforts to obtain favorable substantive or procedural rules appear to have played a significant role in *forum non conveniens* analysis. Consider how the *Iragorri* decision dealt with the "forum-shopping" factor. *See supra* pp. 397-398.

(e) Enforceability of judgment. Why should questions about the enforceability of any judgment factor into the *forum non conveniens* analysis? For example, a plaintiff sues a defendant in the United States to exploit some procedural or substantive advantage, yet the defendant's assets are in a third country. May a court rely on the location of the defendant's assets or speculate about collection matters in ruling on a *forum non conveniens* motion? *See ISI International, Inc. v. Borden Ladner Gervais LLP,* 316 F.3d 731, 732-733 (7th Cir. 2003); *North America Promotions, Ltd. v. Ficodesa (Magefesa Group),* 2003 WL 22532810, at *3 (N.D. Ill. 2003). Doesn't this unduly disrespect the plaintiff's choice? Does it matter that the United States is not (presently) a party to any convention for the enforcement of foreign judgments, *see infra* pp. 1165-1166? And why would a defendant *ever* want to dismiss a case from a forum where it has no assets to one where its assets are located? Might it depend on its assessment of the relative favorability of the substantive and procedural law in the two forums? Can't a court simply circumvent this problem by conditioning the dismissal on the defendant's willingness to satisfy any adverse judgment rendered in the foreign forum?

(f) Private interest factors and the parties' economic strength. Should the private interest factors depend on the relative economic strengths of the parties? Suppose that a foreign plaintiff sues a multinational corporation in a U.S. court for acts that allegedly took place abroad. May a court take into consideration the relative ease with which the foreign

plaintiff could refile and maintain the litigation in the foreign forum? *Compare Presbyterian Church of Sudan v. Talisman Energy, Inc.*, 244 F. Supp. 2d 289, 341 (S.D.N.Y. 2003) (considering such factors) *and In re Ski Train Fire in Kaprun, Austria on Nov. 11, 2000*, 230 F. Supp. 2d 376, 389 (S.D.N.Y. 2002) ("[Defendant], the parent company to a multinational conglomerate, has vast resources and can therefore easily transport witnesses and evidence to this forum, a major city that is a direct flight from any major city in the world. In contrast, the named plaintiffs have only modest means and would suffer hardship if forced to litigate in Austria.") *with Duha v. Agrium, Inc.*, 340 F. Supp. 2d 787, 798 (E.D. Mich. 2004) (holding such factors to be irrelevant) *and Reers v. Deutsche Bank AG*, 320 F. Supp. 2d 140, 162 (S.D.N.Y. 2004) ("The fact that defendants are corporations does not automatically mean that they should bear the significant costs of transporting every document, every piece of physical evidence (which would likely include the train car in question), and every witness relevant to the factual issues in dispute in this case.").

(g) *Miscellaneous other private interest factors.* Many of *Piper*'s other private interest factors are almost always extraneous. Few cases require a "view" of a physical location, and if they do, modern technology offers adequate alternatives. Translating documents or testimony can create problems, but they are almost never insurmountable. Judgments may need to be enforced abroad, but that is potentially true in all international cases.

2. *The irrelevant bottom line.* Lawsuits are about money. They are filed to recover money, and they are defended to save money. The one thing that the parties and their lawyers care about, in almost every case, is how much money they will win or lose.

It hardly seems necessary to say all that. But consider the Court's analysis in *Piper*. It requires trial judges to draw up long lists of witnesses, evaluating where they live, how important they are to the case, what language they speak, how much their air fares to the forum for trial would cost, and the like; similarly, the trial court must consider whether its docket is more congested or less congested than some foreign court (that may not even have a docket). Yet, note the Court's refusal to pay any attention to the bottom line — the amount of money that the plaintiff would likely recover in the alternative forums.

Is this all not a little like teenagers on their first date, conscientiously talking about everything except what is on their minds? Why shouldn't courts try to assess the likely recovery of the plaintiff in the two alternative fora? What could a court do with this information? Suppose it is clear that the plaintiff would recover in both fora; that in the U.S. it would likely recover $600,000, while in the foreign court it would likely recover $300,000; that it would cost $400,000 in combined legal fees (split equally between the parties) to litigate in the United States, and only $50,000 to litigate in the foreign court. Suppose the likely U.S. recovery was $1.6 million or $16 million.

Can courts *really* ignore the bottom line; don't they just peek a bit at it in deciding *forum non conveniens* cases? Consider then Judge Breyer's remark in *Howe* that Canadian law offers shareholders "somewhat similar protection" and "roughly equivalent legal protections." Suppose that *Howe* had involved Liberian companies, or that the *Piper* crash occurred in Sudan, and the alternative forum were Liberia and Sudan. Conversely, note *Piper*'s concern about subjecting U.S. companies to significant tort liability. Won't courts inevitably consider the likely outcome in such forums in deciding whether to dismiss on *forum non conveniens* grounds?

3. *Do the private interest factors serve any meaningful purpose?* If *Piper*'s private interest factors: (i) are mostly concerned with relatively minor logistical issues, which can be overcome by modern communications; and (ii) ignore the vastly more important effects that *forum non conveniens* dismissals have on the substantive outcome of a litigation, then what is the purpose of these factors? Consider cases like *Piper* and *Wyeth*, where U.S. defendants argue that it is more "convenient" to litigate 4,000 miles away, instead of in their hometowns, while foreigners insist that it makes perfect sense to sue an equal distance from where their accidents occurred. Given this, do the private interest factors listed by *Piper* serve any meaningful purpose? Would other private interests — not identified in *Piper* — be more useful to *forum non conveniens* analysis? What about the defendant's interest in having a dispute decided by a court with a reasonable, predictable connection to the parties' conduct? Consider the following comments by Judge Posner in an opinion involving two cases between Argentinean plaintiffs (who seek to litigate in the United States) and U.S. companies (who seek dismissal to Argentina):

> [The *Gilbert* factors] give a party free rein to suggest *any* reason that occurs to him for why the case should be litigated in one court rather than another. But because there *is* a list, and a list sponsored by the Supreme Court, albeit in a case more than a half century old, parties find it difficult to resist trying to make their case correspond to the items in the list, however violent a dislocation of reality results. And so the plaintiffs in our cases argue that the United States has a greater interest in the litigation than Argentina because the defendants are American companies, while the defendants argue that Argentina has a greater interest than the United States because the plaintiffs are Argentines. The reality is that neither country appears to have any interest in having the litigation tried in its courts rather than in the courts of the other country — certainly no one in the government in either country has expressed to us a desire to have these lawsuits in its courts. For this is ordinary private tort litigation that "implicates," as some judges like to say, no national interest. *Abad v. Bayer Corp.*, 563 F.3d 63, 667 (7th Cir. 2009).

Do the *Gilbert* factors really give parties "free rein" to suggest any reason for the appropriate forum? Why should it matter that the seminal case on the public and private interest factors is "more than a half century old"? Yet isn't Judge Posner absolutely right that, at the end of the day, the *Gilbert* factors provide remarkably little guidance to parties and to courts about whether a case should be dismissed?

In contrast to the skepticism expressed in Judge Posner's opinion, some courts place very substantial weight on the private interest factors. According to this line of authority, a court need not even consider the public interest factors provided that the defendant demonstrates the existence of an adequate available forum and that the private interest factors favor dismissal. *See Alpine View Co. Ltd. v. Atlas Copco AB*, 205 F.3d 208, 222 n.9 (5th Cir. 2000); *Morales v. Ford Motor Co.*, 313 F. Supp. 2d 672, 674-675 (S.D. Tex. 2004). Is this view consistent with *Piper*?

4. Piper's "public interest" factors. As discussed above, *Piper* also set forth a variety of "public interest" factors. Like the private interest factors, these initially seem unexceptionable. But again, a closer examination is useful.

(a) Public "private interests." Most of *Gulf Oil's* "public interest" factors bear upon the "convenience" of the forum court. This includes congestion in the forum, the need for a jury trial, the complexity and length of trial, and the need to apply foreign law. For the most part, these factors are simply the "public" side of private inconveniences, looking at the extent to which the local court and jury pool will be imposed upon by a trial.

It is unclear what significance factors such as docket congestion and the burden of jury duty should have. Considered only from the forum's perspective, both factors will always point toward *forum non conveniens* dismissal — because this will reduce docket congestion and the burdens of jury duty. *See Ernst v. Ernst*, 722 F. Supp. 61, 65 n.4 (S.D.N.Y. 1989); *Barrantes Cabalceta v. Standard Fruit Co.*, 667 F. Supp. 833, 838-839 (S.D. Fla. 1986); *Cuevas v. Reading & Bates Corp.*, 577 F. Supp. 462 (S.D. Tex. 1983). Moreover, complaints of docket congestion quickly become self-fulfilling prophecies — once one judge states that a court's docket is overcrowded, subsequent judges can seize upon that language in future cases to support dismissal. *E.g., Gallegos v. Garcia*, 2010 WL 2354585, at * 5 (S.D. Cal. June 9,

2010) ("[T]he Southern District of California remains one of the busiest in the United States. . . . "); *Rivas ex rel. Estate of Gutierrez v. Ford Motor Co.*, 2004 WL 1247018, at *12 (M.D. Fla. 2004) ("The Middle District of Florida is renowned as one of the most congested Federal Court dockets in the nation."); *Gambra v. International Lease Finance Corp.*, 377 F. Supp. 2d 810, 824 (C.D. Cal. 2005) (Central District of California "is one of the busiest districts in the country."); *PT United Can Co. Ltd. v. Crown Cork & Seal Co.*, 1997 WL 31194, at *9 (S.D.N.Y. Jan. 28, 1997) (Southern District of New York is "one of the congested centers of litigation.").

Judge Newman accurately reflected appellate skepticism as to the weight of docket congestion as a public interest factor when he wrote:

> There is an understandable temptation in a busy district like the Southern District of New York to transfer cases that can as appropriately be tried elsewhere. That temptation must be resisted. The plaintiff's choice of forum should normally be respected. *Calavo Growers of Cal. v. Generali Belgium*, 632 F.2d 963, 969 (2d Cir. 1980).

A few courts have said that the relative docket congestion in U.S. and foreign forums must be compared. *Lony v. E.I. Du Pont de Nemours & Co.*, 935 F.2d 604 (3d Cir. 1991); *Mercier v. Sheraton Int'l, Inc.*, 935 F.2d 419 (1st Cir. 1991). But comparing docket congestion and the costs of trial (including jury costs) in different countries is a difficult exercise. In general, the forum's docket has not played a decisive role in *forum non conveniens* analysis. *See, e.g., Miller v. Calotychos*, 303 F. Supp. 2d 420, 429 (S.D.N.Y. 2004) ("The Court is not prepared to make subjective or conclusory comparative assessments of docket congestion here as opposed to London, or of the relative speed with which the matter may be resolved in either venue. Suffice it to say that, with the parties' cooperation and good will, the Court can schedule a trial on the merits within a reasonable period following the completion of all discovery or rulings on any dispositive motions."); *Ellis v. AAR Parts Trading, Inc.*, 828 N.E.2d 726, 748 (Ill. App. 2005) (docket congestion is "relatively insignificant" consideration).

From another perspective, when foreigners come to the United States to litigate, they have to pay U.S. lawyers, reporting services, hotels, experts, and the like. In the context of international arbitration, nations around the world have aggressively sought to *attract* foreign companies to use their territory as an arbitral situs—in large part because of the benefits that accrue to the local legal community from such international business. *See* G. Born, *International Commercial Arbitration* 113-115 (2009). Should U.S. courts take into account the benefits to the local bar that accrue from such foreign cases? Was that a consideration in *Castro Alfaro*?

(b) Need to apply foreign law. Following *Piper*, a number of lower courts have accorded substantial weight to the fact that a U.S. court would be required to apply foreign law (and vice versa). *E.g., Stroitelstvo Bulgaria Ltd. v. Bulgarian-American Enterprise Fund*, 589 F.3d 417, 426 (7th Cir. 2009); *Yavuz v. 61 MM, Ltd.*, 576 F.3d 1166, 1181 (10th Cir. 2009); *Scottish Air Int'l, Inc. v. British Caledonian Group, PLC*, 81 F.3d 1224, 1234-1235 (2d Cir. 1996); *Conte v. Flota Mercante del Estado*, 277 F.2d 664, 667 (2d Cir. 1960) ("[T]ry as we may to apply the foreign law as it comes to us through the lips of the experts, there is an inevitable hazard that, in those areas, perhaps interstitial but far from inconsequential, where we have no clear guides, our labors, moulded by our own habits of mind as they necessarily must be, may produce a result whose conformity with that of the foreign court may be greater in theory than it is in fact.") (Friendly, J.).

Nevertheless, other courts have made clear that this factor is not conclusive. *Reid-Walen v. Hansen*, 933 F.2d 1390, 1396 (8th Cir. 1991); *Hoffman v. Goberman*, 420 F.2d 423, 427 (3d Cir. 1970) ("the mere fact that the court is called upon to determine and apply foreign law does not present a legal problem of the sort which would justify the dismissal of a case otherwise properly before the court."); *In re Air Crash Off Long Island, N.Y., on July 17, 1996*, 65 F. Supp. 2d 207, 218 (S.D.N.Y. 1999).

Shouldn't the weight of this factor depend on whether the applicable principles of foreign law are settled or not? *See In re Air Cargo Shipping Services Antitrust Litig.*, 2008 WL 5858061, at *29 (E.D.N.Y. Sept. 26, 2008) (collecting cases).

(c) The central role of balancing governmental interests and substantive fairness. The principal factor, in most lower court analyses of *Gulf Oil*'s "public interest" factors, has been the two competing forums' "interests" in the dispute. That was true in *Piper*, where the private interest factors tipped at most only modestly toward dismissal; it was the Court's view that there was no "American interest" in the dispute, and that there was a strong Scottish interest, that justified the trial court's decision to dismiss. Similarly, the principal bases for the *Wyeth* decision were that: (a) a U.S. court "should not impose its own view of the safety, warning, and duty of care required of drugs sold in the United States upon a foreign country when those same drugs are sold in that country"; (b) "the United Kingdom, and not Pennsylvania, has the greater interest in the control of drugs distributed and consumed in the United Kingdom"; and (c) "fairness to the defendant mandates that defendant's conduct be judged by the standards of the community affected by its actions."

(d) Defining national "interests" for forum non conveniens *purposes.* In order to "balance" the public interests of competing forums, it is first necessary to define what those interests are. Where did *Piper* and *Wyeth* find the U.S. and U.K. interests that were decisive to their decisions? What federal (or state) statute supports the views, adopted in *Piper* and *Wyeth*, that (i) there is no (or only a minimal) U.S. interest in regulating the export of defective products from the United States; and (ii) there is a strong foreign interest in exclusively regulating the sales of defective U.S. products within the foreign state? Are these propositions so self-evident that they require no legal basis?

Not surprisingly, different judges have reached different conclusions in identifying U.S. and foreign interests in particular cases. Like *Wyeth*, some courts have considered the forum's interest in not burdening local manufacturers with "lawsuits involving extraterritorial injuries." *Doe v. Hyland Therapeutics Division*, 807 F. Supp. 1117 (S.D.N.Y. 1992) (rejecting view that "[w]here the flow of defective products into the stream of world commerce springs from the United States, an American court is deemed aptly interested, and ably situated, to regulate the imprudent conduct . . ."; "While imposing our presumably more stringent standards to deter tortious conduct within our borders could afford a higher degree of protection to the world community, such an approach would also ignore the unique significance of the foreign forum's interest in implementing its own risk benefit analysis, informed by its knowledge of its community's competing needs, values and concerns"); *Jones v. Searles Laboratories*, 444 N.E.2d 157, 162 n.1 (Ill. 1982) (noting amicus briefs by Illinois Attorney General and Illinois corporations warning that "businesses [may be] hesitant to incorporate in this State if they are required to defend 'foreign suits.'"). *Piper* noted this consideration, indicating concern about "American manufacturer[s]" facing suits by foreign plaintiffs seeking the benefits of U.S. laws that are "extremely attractive to foreign plaintiffs."

In contrast, other courts have found the mirror-image interest:

> An American forum has a significant or equal interest to that of a foreign forum in litigation involving foreign plaintiffs and defendant American pharmaceutical corporations . . . where an allegedly defective drug has been developed, tested and manufactured in the United States, and is being distributed to, and presumably used by American citizens. *Carlenstolpe v. Merck*, 638 F. Supp. 901, 909 (S.D.N.Y. 1986).

See also Carijano v. Occidental Petroleum Corp., 626 F.3d 1137, 1154 (9th Cir. 2010) (noting that forum state has a significant interest in providing a forum for those harmed by the actions of its corporate citizens and "in deciding actions against resident corporations whose conduct in this state causes injury to persons in other jurisdictions"); *Penge v. Hillenbrand Industries, Inc.*, 228 F. Supp. 2d 929, 936 (S.D. Ind. 2002) ("if this case turns on the products liability claim, we agree . . . that Indiana has a real stake in seeing that one of its resident corporations produces and markets goods that satisfy a high standard of performance."). Consider Justice Doggett's concurring opinion, excerpted above at *supra* pp. 379-382, in *Alfaro*. What does he think about the relevant public interests when a U.S. company manufactures products that cause injury abroad? Consider again:

> The doctrine of *forum non conveniens* is obsolete in a world in which markets are global and in which ecologists have documented the delicate balance of all life on this planet. The parochial perspective embodied in the doctrine of *forum non conveniens* enables corporations to evade legal control merely because they are transnational. This perspective ignores the reality that actions of our corporations affecting those abroad will also affect Texans. Although DBCP is banned from use within the United States, it and other similarly banned chemicals have been consumed by Texans eating foods imported from Costa Rica and elsewhere. In the absence of meaningful tort liability in the United States for their actions, some multinational corporations will continue to operate without adequate regard for the human and environmental costs of their actions. This result cannot be allowed to repeat itself for decades to come.

How does one decide whether Justice Doggett's views, or those of Judge Weiner in *Wyeth*, are correct? Or are they a wash? *See Adamu v. Pfizer, Inc.*, 399 F. Supp. 2d 495, 505 (S.D.N.Y. 2005). Note that neither judge cites any legal basis for his definition of "interests." What guides a judge in deciding which "interests" he should balance? Is his decision about those interests subject to review only on an abuse of discretion standard?

As discussed below, courts sometimes consider "public policy" as a reason not to dismiss a case on *forum non conveniens* grounds. *See infra* p. 426-428. What is the relationship between "public policy" and the "public interest" factor looking at the respective sovereign interests? Is it possible that "public policy" counsels against dismissal yet the "public interests" collectively favor it? Or it is illogical to conclude that dismissal is appropriate despite a strong public policy favoring retention of the suit in the United States?

(e) Irrelevance of "interest-balancing" to "convenience." *Piper* said that "the central purpose of any *forum non conveniens* inquiry is to ensure that the trial is convenient." Does the balancing of governmental interests and consideration of substantive fairness to the defendant in *Piper* and *Wyeth* have anything to do with the *convenience* of a particular forum? Does Justice Doggett's vehement attack on the *forum non conveniens* doctrine have anything to do with convenience? In each case, haven't the judges adopted substantive principles regarding the allocation of territorial jurisdiction and regulatory competence? Don't these principles reflect questions of choice of law and competence identifying the sovereign state that should have the power to create and apply rules of law to particular disputes?

As discussed below, contemporary American choice-of-law rules are influenced significantly by "interest analysis," which attempts to identify the respective interests of all states having any connection to particular conduct. Consider the summary of interest analysis set forth below. *See infra* pp. 738-756. How does interest analysis in the choice-of-law context compare with interest analysis in the *forum non conveniens* context? Note the pro-forum bias of interest analysis in the choice-of-law context, reflected in rules protecting forum domiciliaries. *See infra* pp. 753-754. Does this suggest any basis for choosing between the interest analyses in *Wyeth* and *Castro Alfaro*?

Doesn't the discussion about "public" interests mask the parties' true incentives for filing in a forum (or seeking dismissal from it)? Consider the following skepticism of one judge dismissing a case on *forum non conveniens* grounds:

> In today's climate of worldwide economies and the internet, there are few companies that have no connection with the United States. However, such a connection alone is insufficient to justify the United States' becoming the Court for all tort disputes in the world. In this case, the major connection to the United States is the law practice of Plaintiff's attorneys. *Bautista v. Cruise Ships Catering and Service Int'l, NV*, 350 F. Supp. 2d 987, 991 (S.D. Fla. 2003).

(f) Appropriateness of engaging in "interest-balancing" in forum non conveniens *analysis.* Is it appropriate to use the *forum non conveniens* doctrine to balance competing national interests and determine what is substantively "fair" to defendants? Doesn't this convert a purportedly procedural, docket control device into a substantive interest balancing doctrine similar to state choice-of-law rules?

(g) Propriety of federal interest balancing rules under Erie *doctrine.* What gives a federal court the power, in a diversity case, to adopt substantive rules regarding the appropriate scope of state regulation of local industries engaged in international commerce? As discussed below, *see infra* pp. 791-796, federal diversity courts are bound under the *Erie* doctrine to apply state choice-of-law rules, which define when state law can regulate conduct abroad. *Klaxon Co. v. Stentor Elec. Mfg. Co.*, 313 U.S. 487 (1941). Is it consistent with *Erie*, and its application in *Klaxon*, for federal diversity courts to determine when a U.S. state has enough of an "interest" in a dispute, as balanced against a foreign state's interest, to be able to litigate it? *See Wong v. PartyGaming, Ltd.*, 589 F.3d 821, 832 (6th Cir. 2009). Recall that the federal diversity court that performs this analysis will be authorized by the U.S. state's long-arm statute to exercise jurisdiction.

(h) Relationship between choice-of-law issues and forum non conveniens. Even if it is appropriate for a federal court to consider U.S. and foreign public interests, could the United Kingdom's supposedly superior interests in *Piper* and *Wyeth* have been accommodated if a U.S. court applied English law to the case? Note that many of the reasons that U.S. courts are favored by plaintiffs arise from procedural rules — contingent fees, jury trials, discovery, and punitive damages — that will almost always be governed by the forum's law. Do concerns about local autonomy and regulatory interests extend beyond what the law is, to who applies the law? Recall the discussion above regarding international law limits on the competence of courts to exercise subject matter jurisdiction over disputes having little connection to the form. *See supra* p. 30.

5. Balancing the private and public interest factors. *Piper* requires the trial court to "balance" private and public interest factors to determine whether to dismiss the case. How is a trial court supposed to do this? And how are litigants supposed to have any idea how trial courts will decide such balancing exercises?

6. Striking the balance: what must the Piper factors show? It is well settled that the burden of proof in *forum non conveniens* analysis is on the party seeking dismissal. Less clear is the level of inconvenience needed to justify dismissal. There is tension in Supreme Court pronouncements concerning this issue. Some remarks suggest that a fairly low showing of inconvenience is necessary: "[T]he ultimate inquiry is where trial will best serve the convenience of the parties and the ends of justice." *Koster v. American Lumbermen's Mutual Casualty Co.*, 330 U.S. 518, 527 (1947).

In general, however, the Court has indicated that a strong showing of substantial inconvenience and inappropriateness is necessary to sustain a *forum non conveniens* dismissal. *Piper* said that "dismissal will ordinarily be appropriate where trial in the plaintiff's chosen forum imposes a heavy burden on the defendant or the court, and where the plaintiff is unable to offer any specific reasons of convenience supporting his choice." Elsewhere, *Piper* remarked that "when trial in the chosen forum would 'establish . . . oppressiveness and vexation to a defendant . . . out of all proportion to plaintiff's convenience,' or 'when the chosen forum [is] inappropriate because of considerations affecting the court's own administrative and legal problems,' the court may, in the exercise of its sound discretion, dismiss the case."

Most lower courts apply some variation of the foregoing standards. *E.g., SME Racks, Inc. v. Sistemas Mecanicos Para Electronica*, 382 F.3d 1097, 1102 (11th Cir. 2004) (dismissal of case by U.S. plaintiff appropriate only where there is "positive evidence of extremely unusual circumstances" and where court is "thoroughly convinced that material injustice is manifest"); *Howe v. Goldcorp Inv., Ltd.*, 946 F.2d 944 (1st Cir. 1991) ("the chosen forum . . . is so inconvenient that it would be unfair to conduct the litigation in that place"); *Cheng v. Boeing Co.*, 708 F.2d 1406, 1410 (9th Cir. 1983) ("[T]he standard to be applied [to a motion to dismiss on *forum non conveniens* grounds] is whether . . . defendants have made a clear showing of facts which . . . establish such oppression and vexation of a defendant as to be out of proportion to plaintiff's convenience, which may be shown to be slight or nonexistent").

How strongly should courts require the public and private interest factors weigh in favor of dismissal in order to justify dismissal on *forum non conveniens* grounds? For whom ought the forum be inconvenient — the plaintiff or the defendant? How much inconvenience was there in *Piper, Alfaro,* and *Wyeth* — where the suits were in the U.S. defendant's hometown? To whom? How much inconvenience was there in *Howe*? To whom?

Consider again the Court's analysis in *Iragorri*. What standard does it articulate for weighing up the various public and private interest factors? What does the following quote mean?

> the greater the plaintiff's or the lawsuit's bona fide connection to the United States and to the forum of choice and the more it appears that considerations of convenience favor the conduct of the lawsuit in the United States, the more difficult it will be for the defendant to gain dismissal for *forum non conveniens*. . . . On the other hand, the more it appears that the plaintiff's choice of a U.S. forum was motivated by forum-shopping reasons — such as attempts to win a tactical advantage resulting from local laws that favor the plaintiff's case, the habitual generosity of juries in the United States or in the forum district, the plaintiff's popularity or the defendant's unpopularity in the region, or the inconvenience and expense to the defendant resulting from litigation in that forum — the less deference the plaintiff's choice commands and, consequently, the easier it becomes for the defendant to succeed on a *forum non conveniens* motion by showing that convenience would be better served by litigating in another country's courts . . . .

Is this "sliding scale" of deference consistent with *Piper*'s requirement that the party seeking dismissal on *forum non conveniens* grounds demonstrate very substantial inconvenience, equivalent to oppressiveness or vexatiousness?

7. ***Relevance of timing of the* forum non conveniens *motion filed.*** What role does the timing of the defendant's *forum non conveniens* motion play in analysis? Suppose that the defendant files the motion months after the case has been filed and when discovery is underway. May the dilatory filing and its consequences count against the defendant's motion? *Compare Genpharm Inc. v. Pliva-Lachema AS*, 361 F. Supp. 2d 49, 61 (E.D.N.Y. 2005) (declining to dismiss case and relying in part on delay); *Krepps v. Insead*, 2004 WL 2066598, at *2 (S.D.N.Y. 2004) (same) *and Prevision Integral de Servicios Funerarios, SA v. Kraft*, 94 F. Supp. 2d 771, 779-780 (W.D. Tex. 2000) (same) *with Chateau des Charmes*

Wines Ltd. v. Sabate USA, Inc., 2003 U.S. Dist. LEXIS 20337, at *1 (N.D. Cal. 2003) (dismissing case despite delay). Note that some state rules actually require that a *forum non conveniens* motion be filed by a certain deadline (such as within a certain number of days following filing of the complaint). *See Ellis v. AAR Parts Trading, Inc.*, 828 N.E.2d 726, 735-741 (Ill. App. 2005) (discussing Illinois Supreme Court Rule requiring *forum non conveniens* motions to be filed within 90 days after last day allowed for filing answer).

On the other hand, sometimes plaintiffs argue (and courts hold) that a *forum non conveniens* argument is premature. Under this line of reasoning, a court can only rule on such an argument after discovery has progressed, and the court can fully ascertain the availability of witnesses and ease of obtaining evidence. *See Kurzke v. Nissan Motor Corp. in U.S.A.*, 752 A.2d 708, 712-713 (N.J. 2000) (holding that lower court ruling on *forum non conveniens* motion was premature and collecting cases on the proper time for filing such motions); *El-Fadl v. Central Bank of Jordan*, 75 F.3d 668 (D.C. Cir. 1996) (remanding for further findings about whether Jordan is adequate alternative forum). But if a defendant waits too long, then it risks a finding against dismissal on the ground that the court already has invested time and energy into the case. *Compare Cromer Finance Ltd. v. Berger*, 158 F. Supp. 2d 347, 355 (S.D.N.Y. 2001) (declining to dismiss where court "already has digested a lengthy and complicated record . . . [held] a multitude of telephone and court conferences on discovery and other issues . . . [and where] [d]ocument discovery is essentially complete") *with Khan v. Delta Airlines, Inc.*, 2010 WL 3210717 (E.D.N.Y. Aug. 12, 2010) (dismissing in part because it was occurring "at such an early stage in the litigation").

8. *Effect of international agreements, to which the United States is not party, on* **forum non conveniens** *analysis.* As discussed above, a number of foreign states have concluded international agreements regulating the jurisdiction of national courts over nationals of other signatories. For example, the Council Regulation 44/2001 specifies the national forums within the EU that may exercise jurisdiction over EU domiciliaries. *See supra* pp. 105-106. Suppose that one EU domiciliary sues another EU domiciliary in U.S. courts. Does Regulation 44/2001 either prevent this or bear upon a *forum non conveniens* analysis? Consider the following excerpt which addresses the relevance of the Brussels Convention, which largely governed such issues prior to the adoption of Regulation 44/2001:

> The defendant argues that plaintiff's choice of this forum violates the European Economic Community's Brussels Convention. . . . Italy and France, the home countries of Carbotrade and B.V., are signatories to the Brussels Convention, which provides that citizens of member countries shall be sued in their place of domicile or, in matters of tort, where the harmful event occurred. The United States is not, however, a signatory to this Convention. "An international agreement does not create either obligations or rights for a third state without its consent." *Restatement (Third) of the Foreign Relations Law of the United States* 324(1) (1987). The defendant has presented no authority for the proposition that a United States Court should give the Brussels Convention determinative weight in deciding a motion to dismiss based on *forum non conveniens. Carbotrade SpA v. Bureau Veritas*, 1992 U.S. Dist. Lexis 17689 (S.D.N.Y. 1992).

Is this persuasive? *Compare Exeter Shipping Ltd. v. Kilakos*, 310 F. Supp. 2d 1301, 1321-1322 (N.D. Ga. 2004) (relying on Council Regulation 44/2001 to support conclusion that England supplied adequate alternative forum). If laws such as the Brussels Convention or Council Regulation 44/2001 were intended to forbid EU domiciliaries from suing in foreign courts in certain cases, shouldn't U.S. courts respect that prohibition as a prudential matter even if they are not legally bound to do so?

9. *Effect of forum selection clause on* **forum non conveniens** *doctrine.* Suppose that the parties have agreed to an exclusive forum selection clause, providing that all litigation must take place exclusively in the U.S. forum where the plaintiff has commenced suit. *See infra* pp. 461-462 for a discussion of exclusive forum selection clauses. If the defendant moves to dismiss in these circumstances, what role, if any, does the *forum non conveniens* doctrine play? Suppose that public interest factors point powerfully toward litigation in a foreign forum. Suppose that the parties' forum selection clause is nonexclusive, providing that litigation may take place in the plaintiff's chosen forum (but not excluding litigation elsewhere). *See infra* pp. 461-462 for a discussion of nonexclusive forum selection clauses. What role, if any, does the *forum non conveniens* doctrine play in these circumstances? Both issues are discussed below. *See infra* pp. 504-507, 510-511.

E.   The Adequate Alternative Forum Requirement and Public Policy Restrictions

1.   Adequate Alternative Forum Requirement

A vital part of any *forum non conveniens* analysis is the so-called "adequate alternative forum" requirement. *Piper* said that "[a]t the outset of any *forum non conveniens* inquiry, the court must determine whether there exists an alternative forum."[81] Similarly, *Gulf Oil* held that the *forum non conveniens* doctrine "presupposes at least two forums in which the defendant is amenable to process."[82] Other authorities concur.[83]

There is no precise definition in *Piper*, or elsewhere, of an "inadequate" foreign forum. U.S. courts have considered a number of arguments that particular foreign courts would provide inadequate forums. In summary, these include cases where: (a) the foreign forum would lack jurisdiction over the subject matter of the dispute; (b) the plaintiff would not enjoy access to the foreign forum; (c) the defendant would not be subject to personal jurisdiction in the foreign forum; (d) the foreign forum would be biased or corrupt; or (e) the foreign forum would apply unfavorable substantive or procedural rules.

Most U.S. courts have required that the party seeking a *forum non conveniens* dismissal bear the burden of proving that none of these circumstances render the proposed alternative forum inadequate.[84] In general, U.S. courts are disinclined to hold that foreign courts are inadequate forums. *Piper* said "[o]rdinarily, th[e] adequate alternative forum requirement will be satisfied when the defendant is 'amenable to process' in the other jurisdiction."[85] Nevertheless, as discussed below, U.S. courts have denied *forum non conveniens* dismissals in a number of cases based upon failure to satisfy the adequate alternative forum requirement.

2.   Public Policy as a Basis for Denying *Forum Non Conveniens* Dismissals

Related to the adequate alternative forum requirement is the less-common argument that the forum's public policy forbids *forum non conveniens* dismissal of certain claims. Neither *Piper* nor the *Restatement (Second) of Conflict of Laws* alludes to the existence of a

---

81. 454 U.S. at 254 n.22.

82. 330 U.S. at 507.

83. *Restatement (Second) Conflict of Laws* §84 (1971); *Mercier v. Sheraton Int'l, Inc.*, 935 F.2d 419 (1st Cir. 1991); *In re Air Crash Disaster Near New Orleans*, 821 F.2d 1147, 1165 (5th Cir. 1987).

84. *King v. Cessna Aircraft Co.*, 562 F.3d 1374, 1382 (11th Cir. 2009); *Adelson v. Hananel*, 510 F.3d 43 (1st Cir. 2007); *Lueck v. Sundstrand Corp.*, 236 F.3d 1137, 1143 (9th Cir. 2001); *Mercier v. Sheraton Int'l, Inc.*, 935 F.2d 419 (1st Cir. 1991) ("it remains the moving defendant's burden to establish that an adequate alternative forum exists"); *Lacey v. Cessna Aircraft Co.*, 862 F.2d 38, 43-44 (3d Cir. 1988); *In re Air Crash Disaster Near New Orleans*, 821 F.2d 1147, 1164 (5th Cir. 1987); *Schertenleib v. Traum*, 589 F.2d 1156, 1160 (2d Cir. 1978).

85. 454 U.S. at 254-255 n.22.

public policy defense to a *forum non conveniens* motion. It is clear, however, from both principle and lower court precedent that such a defense exists.

In most jurisdictions, the *forum non conveniens* doctrine is a common law principle of judicial abstention, or a generalized statutory codification of this principle.[86] Although seldom discussed in these terms, this general *forum non conveniens* principle must give way to specific forum public policies in particular cases. This result is analogous to public policy rules applicable to forum selection agreements, choice-of-law clauses, choice-of-law doctrine, and foreign judgments.[87]

As in other contexts, the public policy inquiry in the *forum non conveniens* context is an uncertain and unpredictable one.[88] The most clear-cut example is where a forum statute forbids *forum non conveniens* dismissals in particular kinds of cases, or requires that particular types of claims be litigated only in the forum.[89] In few cases, however, do U.S. statutes expressly address the applicability of the *forum non conveniens* doctrine,[90] and U.S. courts have rejected most arguments that particular statutes impliedly forbid *forum non conveniens* dismissals.[91]

Absent statutory guidance, the existence of a public policy precluding *forum non conveniens* dismissals must generally be implied from statutory and common law evidence that does not directly address the point. These arguments are most common where a plaintiff asserts claims under a regulatory statute in the forum state — such as antitrust, securities regulation, environmental, or employment laws. More recently, some authority suggests that *forum non conveniens* motions are disfavored under the Alien Tort Statute and the Torture Victim Protection Act.[92]

A few U.S. courts have refused to apply the *forum non conveniens* defense to particular U.S. statutory claims.[93] Most notably, some lower courts have concluded that *forum non conveniens* is not available in federal antitrust actions.[94] In contrast, courts have almost

---

86. *See supra* pp. 369-372.

87. *See infra* pp. 511-528, 736-737, 1133-1146.

88. *See ibid.*

89. *E.g., Dow Chemical Co. v. Castro Alfaro*, 786 S.W.2d 674 (Tex. 1990) (relying on Tex. Civ. Prac. & Rem. Code §71.031).

90. For example, the Antiterrorism Act provides that a district court "shall not dismiss any action brought under section 2333 of this title on the grounds of the inconvenience or inappropriateness of the forum chosen, unless(1) the action may be maintained in a foreign court that has jurisdiction over the subject matter and over all the defendants; (2) that foreign court is significantly more convenient and appropriate; and (3) that foreign court offers a remedy which is substantially the same as the one available in the courts of the United States." 18 U.S.C. §2334(d). For analysis of the relationship between this section and the *forum non conveniens* doctrine, *see Goldberg v. UBS AG*, 690 F. Supp. 2d 92 (E.D.N.Y. 2010).

91. *E.g., Loya v. Starwood Hotels & Resorts Worldwide, Inc.*, 583 F.3d 656 (9th Cir. 2009) (rejecting argument that remedial provisions of Death on High Seas Act preclude application of *forum non conveniens* doctrine); *Howe v. Goldcorp Investments, Ltd.*, 946 F.2d 944 (1st Cir. 1991) (rejecting argument that "special venue" provision of federal securities laws forbids *forum non conveniens* dismissals); *Allstate Life Ins. Co. v. Linter Group, Ltd.*, 994 F.2d 996, 1002 (2d Cir. 1993) ("United States courts have an interest in enforcing United States securities laws, [but] this alone does not prohibit them from dismissing a securities action on the ground of *forum non conveniens*").

92. *See Wiwa v. Royal Dutch Petroleum Co.*, 226 F.3d 88, 103-106 (2d Cir. 2000).

93. *E.g., Zipfel v. Halliburton Co.*, 832 F.2d 1477, 1486 (9th Cir. 1987) (Jones Act); *Needham v. Phillips Petroleum Co. of Norway*, 719 F.2d 1481, 1483 (10th Cir. 1983) (Jones Act); *Cruz v. Maritime Co.*, 702 F.2d 47, 48 (2d Cir. 1983) (Jones Act); *Szumlicz v. Norwegian American Line*, 698 F.2d 1192, 1195 (11th Cir. 1983) (Jones Act); *Priyanto v. M/S Amsterdam*, 2007 WL 4811854, at *5 (C.D. Cal. Sept. 10, 2007) (collecting cases holding that Wage Act claims not subject to *forum non conveniens* dismissal); *Lawford v. New York Life Ins. Co.*, 739 F. Supp. 906 (S.D.N.Y. 1990) (ERISA); *Galon v. M/V Hira II*, 1990 A.M.C. 342 (W.D. Wash. Oct. 27, 1989) (46 U.S.C. §10313); *First Pacific Corp. v. Sociedade de Empreendimentos e Construcoes, Ltda.*, 566 So. 2d 3 (Fla. App. 1990) (Florida statutes).

94. *Compare Industrial Inv. Dev. Corp. v. Mitsui & Co.*, 671 F.2d 876, 890 (5th Cir.), *vacated on other grounds*, 460 U.S. 1007 (1983) *and Laker Airways v. Pan American World Airways*, 568 F. Supp. 811, 817-818 (D.D.C. 1983) *with Capital Currency Exchange, NV v. National Westminster Bank plc*, 155 F.3d 603, 607-609 (2d Cir. 1998). *See generally National Hockey League Players' Ass'n v. Plymouth Whalers Hockey Club*, 166 F. Supp. 2d 1155, 1160-1163 (E.D. Mich. 2001) (summarizing split).

always concluded that most other federal statutory claims are subject to *forum non conveniens* dismissals. Claims under both the Carriage of Goods by Sea Act and the Jones Act have generally been held subject to *forum non conveniens* dismissal.[95] Similarly, lower courts have held that federal securities, RICO, copyright, and ERISA claims are subject to *forum non conveniens* dismissal.[96] While permitting *forum non conveniens* dismissals in such cases, some courts conduct a choice-of-law analysis to determine whether such statutes would apply and, if they do, factor that consideration into their decision whether to dismiss the case.[97]

3.   Conditions on Dismissals

Conditions are frequently imposed as a requirement for granting *forum non conveniens* dismissals. These conditions are typically imposed in order to meet a plaintiff's contentions that a proffered foreign alternative forum would be inadequate. It is particularly common to condition *forum non conveniens* dismissal on: (1) the defendant's consent to suit and service of process in the alternative forum; (2) the defendant's agreement to produce documents or witnesses in the plaintiff's foreign action; (3) the defendant's waiver of any statute of limitation defense in the foreign action; and (4) the defendant's consent to pay any foreign judgment obtained by plaintiffs. If the defendant fails to abide by the U.S. court's conditions or if the foreign court refuses to exercise jurisdiction, the U.S. action may be restored to the trial court's docket.[98]

4.   Selected Materials on Adequate Alternative Forums, Public Policy, and Conditions

Excerpted below are various materials on the alternative forum requirement and the imposition of conditions on *forum non conveniens* dismissals. The *Bhopal* decision considers the significance of differences in procedural rules. The opinions in *Howe, Laker and Wiwa* explore the role of public policy limits on application of the *forum non conveniens* doctrine. Finally, both the *Wyeth* and *Bhopal* decisions illustrate the role of conditions on *forum non conveniens* dismissals. Finally, the provision of Ecuadorian law excerpted below exemplifies the efforts by some foreign countries to discourage *forum non conveniens* dismissals of suits filed by local nationals in United States courts.

---

95. *E.g., Contact Lumber Co. v. P.T. Moges Shipping Co.*, 918 F.2d 1446 (9th Cir. 1990) (COGSA, with court indicating that foreign court might apply COGSA); *BBC Chartering & Logistic GmbH & Co. K.G. v. Siemens Wind Power A/S*, 546 F. Supp. 2d 437 (S.D. Tex. 2008) (same); *Ikospentakis v. Thalassic Steamship Agency*, 915 F.2d 176 (5th Cir. 1990) (Jones Act and maritime claims).

96. *E.g., Vivendi SA v. T-Mobile USA, Inc.*, 586 F.3d 689 (9th Cir. 2009) (RICO); *Yavus v. 61 MM, Ltd.*, 576 F.3d 1166 (10th Cir. 2009) (RICO); *Windt v. Qwest Communications Inter., Inc.*, 529 F.3d 183 (3d Cir. 2008) (collecting cases); *Alfadda v. Fenn*, 159 F.3d 41 (2d Cir. 1998) (RICO and securities claims); *Creative Technology, Ltd. v. Aztech System Pte., Ltd.*, 61 F.3d 696 (9th Cir. 1995) (Copyright Act) *Daley v. NHL*, 987 F.2d 172 (3d Cir. 1993) (ERISA).

97. *Loya v. Starwood Hotels & Resorts Worldwide, Inc.*, 584 F.3d 656 (9th Cir. 2009); *Lueck v. Sundstrand Corp.*, 236 F.3d 1137, 1148 (9th Cir. 2001); *In re Banco Santander Securities-Optimal Litig.*, 2010 WL 3036990, at *5 (S.D. Fla. July 30, 2010). *See generally* Thomas, Annotation, *Validity and Propriety of Conditions Imposed upon Proceeding in Foreign Forum by Federal Court in Dismissing Action under Forum Non Conveniens*, 89 A.L.R. Fed. 238 (1988 & Supp. 2010).

98. *See, e.g., In re Bridgestone/Firestone, Inc.*, 420 F.3d 702 (7th Cir. 2005) (vacating dismissal order where foreign court declined to exercise jurisdiction); *Ford v. Brown*, 319 F.3d 1302, 1310-1311 (11th Cir. 2003) (court may reassert jurisdiction if foreign court refuses to exercise it). *See also* Jurianto, *Forum Non Conveniens: Another Look at Conditional Dismissals*, 83 U. Det.-Mercy L. Rev. 369 (2005).

IN RE UNION CARBIDE CORPORATION GAS PLANT DISASTER AT BHOPAL, INDIA IN DECEMBER, 1984

634 F. Supp. 842 (S.D.N.Y. 1986), aff'd, 809 F.2d 195 (2d Cir. 1987)

KEENAN, DISTRICT JUDGE. On the night of December 2-3, 1984 the most tragic industrial disaster in history occurred in the city of Bhopal, state of Madhya Pradesh, Union of India. Located there was a chemical plant owned and operated by Union Carbide India Limited ("UCIL"). . . . UCIL manufactured the pesticides Sevin and Temik at the Bhopal plant at the request of, and with the approval of, the Government of India. UCIL was incorporated under Indian law in 1934, 50.9% of its stock is owned by the defendant, Union Carbide Corporation, a New York corporation. Methyl isocanate ("MIC"), a highly toxic gas, is an ingredient in the production of both Sevin and Temik. On the night of the tragedy MIC leaked from the plant in substantial quantities for reasons not yet determined. The prevailing winds . . . blew the deadly gas into the overpopulated hutments adjacent to the plant and into the most densely occupied parts of the city. The results were horrendous. Estimates of deaths directly attributable to the leak range as high as 2,100. No one is sure exactly how many perished. Over 200,000 people suffered injuries . . .

On December 7, 1984 the first lawsuit was filed by American lawyers in the United States on behalf of thousands of Indians. Since then 144 additional actions have been commenced in federal courts in the United States. . . . The Indian Government on March 29, 1985 enacted legislation, the Bhopal Gas Leak Disaster (Processing of Claims) Act (21 of 1985) ("Bhopal Act"), providing that the Government of India has the exclusive right to represent Indian plaintiffs in India and elsewhere in connection with the tragedy. Pursuant to the Bhopal Act, the Union of India, on April 8, 1985, filed a complaint with this Court setting forth claims for relief similar to those in the consolidated complaint of June 28, 1985. By order of April 25, 1985 this Court establishes a Plaintiffs' Executive Committee, comprised of [lawyers], who represent individual plaintiffs and [lawyers who represent] the Union of India. . . .

Before this Court is a motion by the defendant Union Carbide Corporation ("Union Carbide") to dismiss the consolidated action on the grounds of *forum non conveniens*. . . . "At the outset of any *forum non conveniens* inquiry, the court must determine whether there exists an alternative forum." *Piper* [454 U.S.], at 254, n.22. . . . [T]he *Piper* Court delved into the relevance of the substantive and procedural difference in law which would be applied in the event a case was transferred on the grounds of *forum non conveniens*. The *Piper* Court determined that it was theoretically inconsistent with the underlying doctrine of *forum non conveniens*, as well as grossly impractical, to consider the impact of the putative transfer forum's law on the plaintiff in this decision on a *forum non conveniens* motion: "[I]f conclusive or substantial weight were given to the possibility of a change in law, the *forum non conveniens* doctrine would become virtually useless." . . .

[T]he plaintiffs in this case argue that Indian courts do not offer an adequate forum for this litigation by virtue of the relative "procedural and discovery deficiencies [which] would thwart the victims' quest for" justice. . . . Plaintiffs' preliminary concern, regarding defendant's amenability to process in the alternative forum, is more than sufficiently met in the instant case. Union Carbide has unequivocally acknowledged that it is subject to the jurisdiction of the courts of India. . . . Beyond this initial test, plaintiffs . . . argue that the Indian legal system is inadequate to handle the Bhopal litigation. [Plaintiffs submitted expert witness testimony on the Indian legal system from a U.S. law professor, not admitted to practice in India; defendants submitted testimony from two senior members of the Indian bar.] . . . According to [plaintiff's expert], India's legal system "was imposed on it" during the period of colonial rule. [He] argues that "Indian legal institutions still reflect their colonial origins," in terms of the lack of broad based legislative activity, inaccessibility of legal information and legal services, burdensome court filing fees and limited innovativeness with reference to legal practice and education. . . . Mr. Palkhivala responds with numerous examples of novel treatment of complex legal issues by the Indian Judiciary. . . . The examples cited by defendant's experts suggest a developed and independent judiciary. . . .

[Plaintiff's expert] discusses the problems of delay and backlog in Indian courts. Indeed, it appears that India has approximately one-tenth the number of judges, per citizen, as the United States and that postponements and high caseloads are widespread. [Plaintiff's expert] urges that the backlog is a result of Indian procedural law, which allows for adjournments in mid-hearing, and for multiple interlocutory and final appeals. . . . This Court acknowledges that delays and backlog exist in Indian courts, but United States courts are subject to delays and backlog, too. . . .

Plaintiffs contend that the Indian legal system lacks the wherewithal to allow it "to deal effectively and expeditiously" with the issues raised in this lawsuit. Plaintiffs urge that Indian practitioners emphasize oral skills rather than written briefs. They allegedly lack specialization, practical investigative techniques and coordination into partnership. These factors, it is argued, limit the Indian bar's ability to handle the Bhopal litigation. . . . While Indian attorneys may not customarily join into large law firms, and as Mr. Palkhivala states, are limited by present Indian law to partnerships of no more than twenty, this . . . does not establish the inadequacy of the Indian legal system. . . . [T]his court is not convinced that the size of a law firm has that much to do with the quality of legal service provided. . . . Many small firms in this country perform work at least on a par with the largest firms. Bigger is not necessarily better. . . .

[Plaintiff's expert] asserts that India lacks codified tort law [and] has little reported case law in the tort field. . . . Mr. Dadachanji responds that tort law is sparsely reported in India due to frequent settlement of such cases, lack of appeal to higher courts, and the publication of tort cases in specialized journals other than the All-India Reports. In addition, tort law has been codified in numerous Indian statutes. . . .

Plaintiffs next assert that India lacks certain procedural devices which are essential to the adjudication of complex cases, the absence of which prevent India from providing an adequate alternative forum. They urge that Indian pre-trial discovery is inadequate alternative forum. [Plaintiff's expert] states that the only forms of discovery available in India are written interrogatories, inspection of documents, and requests for admissions. Parties alone are subject to discovery. Third-party witnesses need not submit to discovery. Discovery may be directed to admissible evidence only, not material likely to lead to relevant or admissible material, as in the courts of the United States. . . . These limits on discovery are adopted from the British system. Similar discovery tools are used in Great Britain today. This Court finds that their application would perhaps, however, limit the victims' access to sources of proof. Therefore, pursuant to its equitable powers, the Court directs that the defendant consent to submit to the broad discovery afforded by the United States Federal Rules of Civil Procedure if or when an Indian court sits in judgment or presides over pretrial proceedings in the Bhopal litigation. . . .

Final points regarding the asserted inadequacies of Indian procedure involve unavailability of juries or contingent fee arrangements in India. . . . They are easily disposed of. The absence of juries in civil cases is a feature of many civil law jurisdictions, and of the United Kingdom. Furthermore, contingency fees are not found in most foreign jurisdictions. In any event, the lack of contingency fees is not an insurmountable barrier to filing claims in India, as demonstrated by the fact that more than 4,000 suits have been filed by victims of the Bhopal gas leak in India already. . . .

Plaintiffs' final contention [is that they would have difficulty enforcing an Indian judgment]. The possibility of non-enforcement of a foreign judgment by courts of either country leads this Court to conclude that issue must be addressed at this time. Since it is defendant Union Carbide which, perhaps ironically, argues for the sophistication of the Indian legal system in seeking a dismissal on grounds of forum non conveniens, and plaintiffs, including the Indian Government, which state a strong preference for the American legal system, it would appear that both parties have indicated a willingness to abide by a judgment of the foreign nation whose forum each seeks to visit. Thus, this Court conditions the grand of a dismissal on forum non conveniens grounds on Union Carbide's agreement to be bound by the judgment of its preferred tribunal, located in India, and to satisfy any judgment rendered by the Indian court, and affirmed on appeal in India. . . .

HOWE v. GOLDCORP INVESTMENTS, LTD.

946 F.2d 944 (1st Cir. 1991) [excerpted above at pp. 408-412]

LAKER AIRWAYS LTD. v. PAN AMERICAN WORLD AIRWAYS

568 F. Supp. 811 (D.D.C. 1983)

HAROLD H. GREENE, District Judge. . . . [The plaintiff, Laker Airways Limited, was a budget air carrier based in the United Kingdom, that provided cheap transatlantic passenger air service between the United States and Europe (principally the United Kingdom). The defendants were Pan American World Airways and TWA (both U.S. air carriers), McDonnell Douglas Corporation, and British Airways, British Caledonia Airways, Lufthansa, Swissair, KLM, and Sabena (all European air carriers).] Briefly, the complaint alleges that the defendants, who in the main are American and foreign air carriers, engaged in a scheme to destroy plaintiff's low cost air service on the transatlantic routes between the United States and Europe. The scheme was allegedly perfected in part through the medium of the International Air Transport Association ("IATA"), including through IATA meetings in Florida and in Switzerland.

When a court considers the issue of *forum non conveniens*, the plaintiff's choice of forum is, of course, given significant weight and should rarely be disturbed.[99] In view of that general principle, the burden is on those who challenge plaintiff's choice to demonstrate that some other forum is more convenient. . . . [T]he defendants contend that, since most of the defendants are airlines anchored in Europe,[100] it may be assumed that the convenience of the witnesses would be served and the documents would more easily be available if the Court were to defer to [an English court, before which was pending actions brought against Laker Airways by various of the defendants seeking antisuit injunctions to halt the U.S. action].

Defendants' argument based on the convenience of witnesses has little validity when advanced in the context of a lawsuit involving transatlantic air passenger carriers. The

---

99. Although that weight is somewhat less when the plaintiff is a foreign resident this does not mean, and the *Piper Aircraft* Court did not say in that case, that plaintiff's choice is not at least presumptively valid. It should also be noted that in *Piper Aircraft*, unlike here, the relationship of the action to the United States was minimal, and that the Supreme Court there did not overturn but upheld a district court's exercise of discretion.

100. Four defendants (Pan American, TWA, McDonnell Douglas Corporation, and McDonnell Douglas Finance Corporation) are American, two defendants (British Airways and British Caledonian Airways) are British, and four defendants (Swissair, Lufthansa, KLM, and Sabena) are incorporated on the European continent. . . .

Court takes judicial notice of the fact that these carriers provide frequent flights between the continents; that the time involved and the expense of transporting witnesses would be minimal; and that all the defendants maintain extensive business establishments in the United States. . . . Beyond that, there is the key fact of the configuration of the alleged conspiracy. If there was a conspiracy, the United States was its hub and the various countries in Europe were its spokes. Insofar as transatlantic traffic is concerned — the focus of the complaint — each of the non-American air carriers provides service between a particular European country and the United States. On that basis, a court in the United States is a far more logical forum than a tribunal elsewhere, for it is here that all the strands, or spokes, come together.[101]

These considerations have direct applicability to the controversy regarding the appropriateness of this Court as a forum versus that of the British tribunal. In the final analysis, what reason is there to ascribe to a British court the responsibility to hear and decide this matter? Only two of the ten defendants are British. Two of the American defendants (the two McDonnell Douglas companies) are firmly located in the United States. The airlines anchored on the European continent (KLM, Sabena, Lufthansa, and Swissair) operate for purposes of this case between the United States and the Netherlands, Belgium, West Germany, and Switzerland, bypassing Great Britain. . . .

For these reasons, absent specific and persuasive evidence to the contrary, a court in the United States must be deemed to be a more convenient forum than a British court or any tribunal in the individual "spoke" countries. To be sure, a trial here will require the movement of witnesses and documents, but certainly the "hub" of the alleged conspiracy is a far more logical place even in that respect, for wherever the trial will be held witnesses and documents will have to be transported. . . . When, finally, to these considerations is added the fact that two of the air carrier defendants and the only two non-air carrier defendants are U.S. corporations based in the United States, the logic of a trial in this country, when compared to any other place that has been suggested, appears overwhelming. . . .

Justice is blind; but courts nevertheless do see what there is clearly to be seen. What is apparent is that the defendants, secure in the knowledge that no liability attaches to their activities under the laws of Great Britain, are seeking to have the matter decided in the British tribunal rather than in an American court.[102] But a United States court, bound to enforce the Sherman Act with respect to those who are resident in or are doing business in the United States, would not be justified in regarding defendants' desire to litigate in Britain — because they expect there to be exonerated — as a search for a more convenient forum. That is not what the doctrine of *forum non conveniens* is all about. . . .

In *Piper*, the Supreme Court . . . reject[ed] the court of appeals' view that a plaintiff may defeat a motion to dismiss on *forum non conveniens* grounds merely by showing that the substantive law which would be applied in the alternative forum is less favorable to him than that of the present forum. Such a rule, said the Court, would render *forum non conveniens* decisions unduly difficult of application for they would require the courts to engage preliminarily in complex exercises in comparative law. The Court then went on to

---

101. We are not concerned here with [air] service between Switzerland and Great Britain, or between Belgium and Germany, or between the Netherlands and Switzerland; we are concerned with [air] service between these countries, on the one hand, and the United States, on the other.

102. Laker, too, may well have considered the effects of the American antitrust laws. It is nevertheless true that for perfectly neutral reasons the United States represents a more legitimate forum for the plaintiff than any other place, for it is doubtful that some of the participants in the alleged conspiracy could have been reached anywhere but in the United States. Moreover, had plaintiff not brought its action in the conspiracy's "hub," it would no doubt have been met with challenges to its choice far more serious and substantive than those which are being raised here.

state, however, that "if the remedy provided by the alternative forum is so clearly inadequate or unsatisfactory that it is no remedy at all, the unfavorable change in law may be given substantial weight; the district court may conclude that dismissal would not be in the interests of justice." . . . [T]hat is precisely the situation in this case. British courts could not and would not[103] enforce the American antitrust laws. As for British substantive law, it fails entirely, for a number of reasons, to recognize liability for the acts which the defendants are alleged to have committed. That being so, this case is precisely within that group of cases which the Supreme Court in *Piper* said should not be dismissed.

It is difficult to see how it could be otherwise. It would be a cruel hoax on the plaintiff to oust it from a court where its allegations, if proved, would entitle it to recovery, and to relegate it instead, in the name of "convenience," to a tribunal which, on the facts alleged, would not be justified under its own laws in entering judgment in plaintiff's favor. Moreover, what is involved here in not an obscure, technical law in the enforcement of which the American courts could be said to have no significant interest. What is in jeopardy is the enforcement of the Sherman Act with respect to a market — travel between the United States and Europe — in which this nation has the highest interest.[104] The Sherman Act, as has often been observed, is our charter of economic liberty, comparable to the importance of the Bill of Rights with respect to personal freedom, and there is thus the highest kind of public interest in preventing the Act from being emasculated in this important area by use of an essentially logistical rule.[105]

In view of these considerations, it is not surprising that it has flatly been held that the doctrine of *forum non conveniens* does not apply to antitrust actions. *See Industrial Investment Development Corp. v. Mitsui & Co.*, 671 F.2d 876 (5th Cir. 1982), where the Court of Appeals for the Fifth Circuit, confronted with an appeal from a decision that Indonesia was a more convenient forum, held that in view of the venue provisions of the antitrust laws (15 U.S.C. §22) and the fact that the Sherman Act is a quasi-penal statute, an antitrust action may never be dismissed on *forum non conveniens* grounds. . . . The Court fully agrees with *Mitsui.*

Antitrust cases are unlike litigation involving contracts, torts, or other matters recognized in some form in every nation. A plaintiff who seeks relief by means of one of these types of actions may appropriately be sent to the courts of another nation where presumably he will be granted, at least approximately, what he is due. But the antitrust laws of the United States embody a specific congressional purpose to encourage the bringing of private claims in the American courts in order that the national policy against monopoly may be vindicated. To relegate a plaintiff to the courts of a nation which does not recognize the antitrust principles would be to defeat this congressional direction by means of a wholly inappropriate procedural device. That is an action which the Court cannot and will not take.

---

103. *See, e.g., British Nylon Spinners Ltd. v. Imperial Chemical Industries, Inc.*, [1953] 1 Ch. 19 (Court of Appeal 1952).

104. Although it is difficult to quantify such matters, it would appear that the United States has an economic and social interest in travel from this country to all of Europe outweighing the interest of any individual European nation in travel from it to the United States.

105. For that reason, too, it is hardly fair to condemn these United States courts which insist upon application of the Sherman Act to those doing business in this country as being engaged in "social jingoism" [citing Respondents' pleadings]. If the jingoism label is to be used at all, it would seem more appropriately to fit those who maintain that fair results may be achieved only under British procedure, and that American courts cannot be trusted, under American law, to do justice.

HARRISON v. WYETH LABORATORIES

510 F. Supp. 1 (E.D. Pa. 1980) [also partially excerpted at pp. 412-414 above]

WEINER, DISTRICT JUDGE. [As described in the excerpt of this opinion at *supra* pp. 412-414, United Kingdom residents who had used oral contraceptives in the United Kingdom brought suit against the defendant American Home Products Corporation ("AHPC"), a Pennsylvania corporation, in U.S. district court in Pennsylvania. The suit alleged negligence in connection with the production and marketing of the contraceptives, which were sold in the United Kingdom by John Wyeth & Brothers Limited ("JWB"), an English company that was wholly owned by AHPC.]

We turn now to consideration of the availability of an alternative forum, and to practical questions of process, expense, production of witnesses and evidence, and enforceability of judgment. Defendant argues that the alternative forum prerequisite is met by the availability of an action in the United Kingdom against AHPC's subsidiary, JWB, and that even if defendant is not subject to United Kingdom jurisdiction, the availability of JWB makes it unnecessary for plaintiffs to include defendant in any action against JWB. We do not agree. We are not sure if a suit against the subsidiary, JWB, is sufficient to constitute an adequate alternative forum for this suit, brought by plaintiffs against this defendant. As we have explained, this action is more appropriately heard and decided by a British court. But in dismissing this action as a matter of convenience, we should not insulate this defendant from judicial determination of its alleged liability and from the consequences of its actions by placing it beyond the reach of the plaintiffs and of the courts of this or any other jurisdiction. An action against JWB may or may not fully protect plaintiffs as regards their claims against defendant for the alleged tortious conduct of defendant.

Defendant itself recognizes the need for the availability of an alternative forum before there may be a dismissal on *forum non conveniens* grounds. Indeed, defendant advances the argument that an alleged lack of foreign jurisdiction over the defendant is not an obstacle to dismissal because courts may deal with the alternative forum prerequisite to a *forum non conveniens* dismissal by conditioning such dismissal upon the defendant's consent to foreign jurisdiction. . . . Defendant has also brought to our attention the case of *Dahl v. United Technologies Corp.*, 472 F. Supp. 696 (D. Del. 1979). In dismissing on the ground of *forum non conveniens*, Chief Judge Latchum conditioned his order on: (1) Defendant's consent to suit and to accept process in a foreign jurisdiction (Norway) in any civil actions instituted by plaintiffs on their claims before the applicable statute of limitations; (2) Defendant's agreement to make available, at its own expense, any documents or witnesses within its control that are needed for fair adjudication of any action brought in Norway by the plaintiffs on their claims; (3) Defendant's consent to pay any judgment, if any, which may be rendered against it in Norway in any civil action brought by plaintiffs on their claims.

In order to preclude the possibility that defendant would be effectively insulated from plaintiff's claims if we dismiss this case on grounds of *forum non conveniens*, we will condition such dismissal on defendant's consent to similar requirements. As we have noted, defendant has itself raised the prospect of so conditioning our dismissal. Accordingly, defendant must agree to submit to the jurisdiction of the courts of the United Kingdom in any civil action timely instituted there against JWB on the claims alleged herein. In addition, important evidence, both documents and witnesses, may be located in Pennsylvania and under the control of defendant. This evidence must be available to plaintiffs and to the courts in any action brought on these claims in the United Kingdom if the courts of the United Kingdom are to constitute an alternative forum in which plaintiffs can receive a fair adjudication. Accordingly, defendant must agree to make available, at its own expense, any documents, witnesses or other evidence under its control that are needed for fair adjudication of any actions brought in the United Kingdom by plaintiffs on their claims. Finally, so that any judgment rendered against defendant in the United Kingdom on plaintiffs' claims will have effect, defendant must agree to pay any judgment so rendered.

WIWA v. ROYAL DUTCH SHELL PETROLEUM CO.
226 F.3d 88 (2d Cir. 2000) [also partially excerpted above at pp. 194-198]

LEVAL, JUDGE. [As excerpted above, Nigerian émigrés to the United States brought claims under the Alien Tort Statute ("ATS") and Torture Victim Protection Act ("TVPA") against Royal Dutch Shell Petroleum Company ("Royal Dutch"), Shell Transport and Trading Company plc ("Shell Transport") and various of their affiliates. The plaintiffs claimed that the defendants had participated in allegedly grave human rights abuses by the Nigerian Government, which damaged them and their families. The Second Circuit denied the defendants' motions to dismiss on personal jurisdiction grounds (in an opinion excerpted above). The Court next considered the defendants' motion to dismiss on *forum non conveniens* grounds.]

The plaintiffs also argue that the ATCA, as supplemented by the Torture Victim Prevention Act ("TVPA"), in 1991, reflects a United States policy interest in providing a forum for the adjudication of international human rights abuses, and that this policy interest should have a role in the balancing of the *Gilbert* factors. . . . In passing the TVPA, in 1991, Congress expressly ratified our holding in *Filartiga* that the United States courts have jurisdiction over suits by aliens alleging torture under color of law of a foreign nation, and carried it significantly further. While the 1789 Act expressed itself in terms of a grant of jurisdiction to the district courts, the 1991 Act (a) makes clear that it creates *liability under U.S. law* where under "color of law, of any foreign nation" an individual is subject to torture or "extra judicial killing," and (b) extends its remedy not only to aliens but to any "individual," thus covering citizens of the United States as well. The TVPA thus recognizes explicitly what was perhaps implicit in the Act of 1789 — that the law of nations is incorporated into the law of the United States and that a violation of the international law of human rights is (at least with regard to torture) *ipso facto* a violation of U.S. domestic law.

Whatever may have been the case prior to passage of the TVPA, we believe plaintiffs make a strong argument in contending that the present law, in addition to merely permitting U.S. District Courts to entertain suits alleging violation of the law of nations, expresses a policy favoring receptivity by our courts to such suits. Two changes of statutory wording seem to indicate such an intention. First is the change from addressing the courts' "jurisdiction" to addressing substantive rights; second is the change from the ATCA's description of the claim as one for "tort . . . committed in violation of the law of nations . . ." to the new Act's assertion of the substantive right to damages under U.S. law. This evolution of statutory language seems to represent a more direct recognition that the interests of the United States are involved in the eradication of torture committed under color of law in foreign nations.

In *Jota v. Texaco, Inc.*, 157 F.3d 153, 159 (2d Cir. 1998), we recognized the plaintiff's argument that "to dismiss . . . [a claim pursuant to the ATCA under *forum non conveniens*] would frustrate Congress's intent to provide a federal forum for aliens suing domestic entities for violation of the law of nations." We expressed "no view" on the question but directed the District Court to consider the issue on remand. In this case, the issue is again advanced (in slightly different form, as *Jota* did not involve torture and the defendants in this case are not domestic entities).

Dismissal on grounds of *forum non conveniens* can represent a huge setback in a plaintiff's efforts to seek reparations for acts of torture. Although a *forum non conveniens* dismissal by definition presupposes the existence of another forum where the suit may be brought dismissal nonetheless requires the plaintiff to start over in the courts of another nation, which will generally at least require the plaintiff to obtain new counsel, as well as perhaps a new residence.

One of the difficulties that confront victims of torture under color of a nation's law is the enormous difficulty of bringing suits to vindicate such abuses. Most likely, the victims cannot sue in the place where the torture occurred. Indeed, in many instances, the victim would be endangered merely by returning to that place. It is not easy to bring such suits in the courts of another nation. Courts are often inhospitable. Such suits are generally time consuming, burdensome, and difficult to administer. In addition, because they assert outrageous conduct on the part of another nation, such suits may embarrass the government of the nation in whose courts they are brought. Finally, because characteristically neither the plaintiffs nor the defendants are ostensibly either protected or governed by the domestic law of the forum nation, courts often regard such suits as "not our business."

The new formulations of the TVPA convey the message that torture committed under color of law of a foreign nation in violation of international law is "our business," as such conduct not only violates the standards of international law but also as a consequence violates our domestic law. In the legislative history of the TVPA, Congress noted that universal condemnation of human rights abuses "provide[s] scant comfort" to the numerous victims of gross violations if they are without a forum to remedy the wrong. H.R. Rep. No. 102-367, at 3, 1992 U.S.C.C.A.N. at 85. This passage supports plaintiffs' contention that in passing the TVPA, Congress has expressed a policy of U.S. law favoring the adjudication of such suits in U.S. courts. If in cases of torture in violation of international law our courts exercise their jurisdiction conferred by the 1789 Act only for as long as it takes to dismiss the case for *forum non conveniens*, we will have done little to enforce the standards of the law of nations.

This is not to suggest that the TVPA has nullified, or even significantly diminished, the doctrine of *forum non conveniens*. The statute has, however, communicated a policy that such suits should not be facilely dismissed on the assumption that the ostensibly foreign controversy is not our business. The TVPA in our view expresses a policy favoring our courts' exercise of the jurisdiction conferred by the ATCA in cases of torture unless the defendant has fully met the burden of showing that the *Gilbert* factors "tilt[] strongly in favor of trial in the foreign forum." [The Second Circuit remanded the case to the trial court to reconsider the defendants' *forum non conveniens* motion in light of its opinion.]

ECUADORIAN LEY 55

Should the lawsuit be filed outside Ecuadorian territory, this will definitely terminate national competency as well as any jurisdiction of Ecuadorian judges over the matter.

MODEL BLOCKING STATUTE ADOPTED BY PARLATINO[106]

National and international jurisdiction. The petition that is validly filed, according to both legal systems, in the defendant's domiciliary court, extinguishes national

---

106. PARLATINO is an intergovernmental organization established by a number of Latin American states.

jurisdiction. The latter is only reborn if the plaintiff desists of his foreign petition and files a new petition in the country, in a completely free and spontaneous way.

Notes on **Bhopal, Howe, Laker, Wyeth, Wiwa,** *and Legislative Materials*

1. *The alternative forum requirement.* *Piper* said that "[a]t the outset of any forum non conveniens inquiry, the court must determine whether there exists an alternative forum." Why is that the case? Recall that a *forum non conveniens* dismissal requires a compelling showing of oppression and inconvenience, coupled with a lack of any public interest in the forum. If the plaintiff's chosen forum is really so inappropriate, why does it matter whether another forum can be shown to exist?

2. *Is an alternative forum required in all cases?* Is the adequate alternative forum requirement really a "requirement," or is the existence of an alternative forum instead an important factor in the balance of public and private interest factors? A few older decisions adopted the latter view, holding that in some cases a *forum non conveniens* dismissal may be granted even if no alternative forum exists. *See Veba-Chemie AG v. M/V Getafix*, 711 F.2d 1243, 1248 n.10 (5th Cir. 1983) ("[p]erhaps if the plaintiff's plight is of his own making — for instance, if the alternative forum was no longer available at the time of dismissal as a result of the deliberate choice of an inconvenient forum — the court would be permitted to disregard [the lack of alternative forum] and dismiss"); *Pietraroia v. New Jersey & Hudson River Ry. & Ferry Co.*, 91 N.E. 120 (N.Y. 1910).

The weight of authority is to the contrary, and imposes an absolute requirement that an adequate alternative forum exist. *E.g., In re Air Crash Disaster Near New Orleans*, 821 F.2d 1147, 1165-1166 (5th Cir. 1987); *Restatement (Second) Conflict of Laws* §84 comment c (1971) ("the action will not be dismissed unless a suitable alternative forum is available to the plaintiff," and "the suit will be entertained, no matter how inappropriate the forum may be, if the defendant cannot be subjected to jurisdiction in other states").

Which of these two positions is wiser?

3. *Reformulating the adequacy analysis.* Given the judicial confusion over how to apply the "adequacy" analysis and its relationship to the public/private interest factors, did the *Piper* Court err in its design of the inquiry? One recent study surveyed every published federal *forum non conveniens* decision and reached the following conclusion:

> [F]ar too often courts conflate the two prongs — treating both as discretionary, bypassing the first prong altogether, or considering [adequate alternative forum] without meaningful review and analysis. Lower courts struggle to apply the two-part *Piper* inquiry. However, by its very nature, that second prong is *ad hoc* and not susceptible to closer scrutiny. This capricious process is unfair to plaintiffs and defendants alike and undermines the authority of the judiciary — at least when ruling on *forum non conveniens* motions. Samuels, *When Is an Alternative Forum Available? Rethinking The* Forum Non Conveniens *Analysis*, 85 Ind. L.J. 1059, 1061 (2010).

Is this a fair criticism of the doctrine? Is this not an inevitable consequence of multi-factor, multi-step discretionary tests? Would not a less discretionary test simply be subject to the flipside criticisms? That it is too rigid and fails to take into account the nuances of particular cases? Compare your answer to the questions raised here with similar questions raised in the context of stays *lis alibi pendens* and antisuit injunctions. *See infra* at 552-566.

In lieu of the *Piper* test, Professor Samuels proposes the following alternative:

> The analysis of an [adequate alternative forum] should be centered on the basic but simple question: is forum two (F2) truly available to the plaintiff(s) in this case for this (or these)

cause(s) of action? . . . [In answering this question,] [t]he factors courts should consider are (1) whether all defendants are subject to the jurisdiction of F2 according to the law of F2; (2) whether F2 provides a meaningful remedy; (3) whether the plaintiff will be treated fairly in F2; (4) whether all plaintiffs have practical access to the courts of F2; (5) whether F2 provides procedural due process; and (6) whether F2 is a stable forum.

How does this test differ from the test in *Piper?* Is it superior? Does it do any better a job at addressing Professor Samuels' criticisms of the current doctrine? Are terms like "meaningful remedy," "treated fairly," "practical access," and "stable forum" any clearer than the terms in the *Piper* test? Does this test offer any better guidance over how to balance these factors? Isn't it inevitable that the meaning of "adequacy" will unfold on a case-by-case basis through the development of caselaw? Isn't that precisely the purpose of a set of common law rules?

4. *Factors relevant to existence of adequate alternative forum.* There is no precise definition in *Piper* or elsewhere of an "inadequate" foreign forum. U.S. courts have identified a variety of circumstances in which a foreign forum will be regarded as an inadequate alternative.

(a) Effect of foreign forum's lack of subject matter jurisdiction. The one example cited by *Piper* of an inadequate alternative forum was "where the alternative forum does not permit litigation of the subject matter of the dispute." Does this exception apply only when foreign law precludes "litigation of the subject matter of the dispute," and not when it merely limits the types of legal claims that can be successfully asserted in connection with the subject matter of the parties' dispute (as with plaintiffs' strict liability claims in *Piper* and *Wyeth*)?

Courts have frequently permitted *forum non conveniens* dismissals even where the proffered alternative forum would not permit litigation of certain of the plaintiff's legal claims. *E.g., Dowling v. Richardson-Merrell, Inc.,* 727 F.2d 608, 615 (6th Cir. 1984) (the fact that "certain theories of tort recovery are not recognized" in alternative forum does not make the "remedy provided by the alternative forum . . . clearly inadequate or unsatisfactory"); *Mercier v. Sheraton Int'l, Inc.,* 935 F.2d 419 (1st Cir. 1991) ("a meaningful cause of action available in the proposed alternative forum"). Is it clear that this requirement was satisfied in *Piper?* In *Howe?* In *Laker?*

How certain must a U.S. court be about the foreign court's subject matter jurisdiction before dismissing the case? *See Bank of Credit and Commerce Int'l (Overseas) Ltd. v. State Bank of Pakistan,* 273 F.3d 241, 247-248 (2d Cir. 2001). In light of the increased use of conditional dismissals, does the subject matter limitation have value anymore? *See Leon v. Million Air, Inc.,* 251 F.3d 1305, 1313 (11th Cir. 2001) (holding that even if Ecuadorian law prohibited exercise of subject matter jurisdiction by local court over case originally filed in United States, *forum non conveniens* defense could still be available because "the District Court would presumably reassert jurisdiction over the case in the event that jurisdiction in the Ecuadorian courts is declined").

(b) Effect of plaintiff's lack of access to foreign forum. Plaintiffs sometimes lack effective access to a putative alternative forum. Obstacles to access can include (i) visa or immigration restrictions that the plaintiff cannot satisfy, (ii) outstanding criminal investigations or prosecutions of the plaintiff, (iii) the risk of being subject to service of process in other, unrelated civil actions, (iv) the costs of travel and foreign counsel, and (v) risks to the plaintiff's safety if he is forced to litigate in a foreign forum. How should each of these asserted obstacles be weighed? *E.g., Licea v. Curaçao Drydock Co., Inc.,* 587 F. Supp. 2d 1270 (S.D. Fla. 2008) (plaintiff received political asylum after escaping foreign forum); *Mujica v. Occidental Petroleum Corp.,* 381 F. Supp. 2d 1134, 1142-1148 (C.D. Cal. 2005) (plaintiff

faced risk of personal harm if forced to litigate in Colombia); *Mercier v. Sheraton Int'l, Inc.,* 744 F. Supp. 380 (D. Mass. 1990) (U.S. plaintiff unable to enter Turkey because of pending criminal charges), *rev'd on other grounds,* 935 F.2d 419 (1st Cir. 1991); *Fiorenza v. U.S. Steel Int'l Ltd.,* 311 F. Supp. 117 (S.D.N.Y. 1969) (plaintiff denied entry to Bahamas for purposes of pursuing his suit). *But see Niv v. Hilton Hotels Corp.,* 2008 WL 4849334 (S.D.N.Y. Nov. 10, 2008) (discussing whether Egypt provides adequate foreign forum for Jewish victims of terrorism taking place in Middle East); *Duha v. Agrium, Inc.,* 340 F. Supp. 2d 787, 794 (E.D. Mich. 2004) ("A plaintiff's fear for his own personal safety, however, does not render a forum inadequate when the fear arises from an unsubstantiated assertion that his safety would be jeopardized by pursuing a claim, especially when the source of the threat is unrelated to the forum's political or legal system.").

(c) Effect of foreign forum's lack of jurisdiction over defendants. As *Piper* noted, the alternative forum requirement will "ordinarily" be satisfied "when the defendant is 'amenable to process' in the other jurisdiction." If the defendant is not subject to the alternative forum's personal jurisdiction, it will not be an adequate alternative. In practice, this requirement is seldom important; defendants seeking a *forum non conveniens* dismissal will usually agree to submit to the jurisdiction of the alternative forum as a condition of obtaining dismissal (as in *Bhopal*). *See infra* p. 449. Suppose that the foreign jurisdiction arguably will not base personal jurisdiction upon consent. What should the U.S. court do if it believes that *forum non conveniens* dismissal is desirable? *See infra* pp. 449-450.

(d) Effect of foreign forum's bias. U.S. courts have generally been skeptical of claims that foreign judicial systems are corrupt or biased, saying that such arguments do "not enjoy a particularly impressive track record" and that there is "substantial temerity to the claim that the forum where a party has chosen to transact business . . . is inadequate." *Eastman Kodak Co. v. Kavlin,* 978 F. Supp. 1078, 1084-1085 (S.D. Fla. 1997). Generalized claims of bias are routinely rejected. *E.g., Stroitelstvo Bulgaria Ltd. v. Bulgarian-American Enterprise Fund,* 589 F.3d 417 (7th Cir. 2009) (collecting cases); *Tang v. Synutra Intern., Inc.,* 2010 WL 1375373, at *9 (D. Md. Mar. 29, 2010) (same).

Nonetheless, in appropriate cases, U.S. courts have held that particular foreign courts would be inadequate forums because of bias, corruption, or incompetence. *E.g., Eastman Kodak Co. v. Kavlin,* 978 F. Supp. 1078, 1084-1085 (S.D. Fla. 1997) ("compelling" evidence of corruption in Bolivian judicial system); *Rasoulzadeh v. Associated Press,* 574 F. Supp. 854 (S.D.N.Y. 1983), *aff'd,* 767 F.2d 908 (2d Cir. 1985); *Canadian Overseas Ores Ltd. v. Compania de Acero del Pacifico, SA,* 528 F. Supp. 1337, 1342-1343 (S.D.N.Y. 1982) (plaintiff "has raised serious questions about the independence of the Chilean judiciary vis a vis the military junta currently in power [and] . . . a significant doubt remains whether [plaintiff] could be assured of a fair trial in the Chilean courts in view of the fact that [defendant] is a state owned corporation"), *aff'd on other grounds,* 727 F.2d 1274 (2d Cir. 1984). In one lower court's formulation, no dismissal will be granted if the plaintiff shows that "conditions in the foreign forum . . . plainly demonstrate that the plaintiffs are highly unlikely to obtain basic justice therein." *Vaz Borralho v. Keydril Co.,* 696 F.2d 379, 393-394 (5th Cir. 1983).

Query whether it is appropriate for U.S. courts to "pass judgment" upon the adequacy of foreign judicial systems. *Carijano v. Occidental Petroleum Corp.,* 548 F. Supp. 2d 823, 832 (C.D. Cal. 2008); "It is not the business of our courts to assume the responsibility for supervising the integrity of the judicial system of another sovereign nation." *Chesley v. Union Carbide Corp.,* 927 F.2d 60, 66 (2d Cir. 1991) (quoting *Jhirad v. Ferrandina,* 536 F.2d 478, 484-485 (2d Cir. 1976)); *see also Leon v. Million Air, Inc.,* 251 F.3d 1305, 1312 (11th Cir. 2001) ("Considerations of comity preclude a court from adversely judging the quality of a foreign justice system absent a showing of inadequate procedural safeguards."); *Moscovits v. Magyar Cukor Rt.,* 2001 WL 767004, at *4 (S.D.N.Y. 2001) ("[F]or this Court generally to pronounce judgment on the adequacy of justice of a particular foreign state would under-mine any efforts those legal systems may be undergoing to reform and to foster domestic and international confidence in the country's laws."); *Warter v. Boston Securities, SA*, 380 F. Supp. 2d 1299, 1310 (S.D. Fla. 2004); *Gonzales v. P.T. Pelangi Niagra Mitra Int'l*, 196 F. Supp. 2d 482, 489 (S.D. Tex. 2002).

How would India have reacted if U.S. courts had concluded that the *Bhopal* case was too complex or sensitive for the Indian judicial system? On the other hand, if a U.S. court is (without statutory basis) to decline to exercise its statutory jurisdiction, must it not ensure that the alternative forum will obey basic standards of fairness? Is this a due process requirement? Note that U.S. courts also sometimes have to evaluate the fairness of a foreign forum in deciding whether to enforce a judgment rendered in that forum, *see infra* pp. 1146-1156. Should the reluctance of U.S. courts to evaluate the fairness of foreign forums vary with whether the analysis occurs at the prejudgment as opposed to the postjudgment stage? Are considerations of comity more dominant in one of these settings?

(e) Effect of differences between U.S. and foreign procedures. As discussed elsewhere, U.S. civil procedure differs dramatically from that in foreign legal systems. Aspects of American procedure such as jury trials, a robust adversary system, cross-examination, broad party-directed discovery, contingent fees, no fee-shifting, and pro-plaintiff substantive laws are unusual in the international context. *See supra* pp. 1-4. *Bhopal* notes a number of these differences (even with a common law jurisdiction such as India), but concludes that they did not render India an inadequate alternative forum. Was *Bhopal* correct? Is not a jury trial, with cross-examination, a constitutional right? Should a discretionary rule of absten-tion be able to deny plaintiffs their constitutional rights?

U.S. courts are generally reluctant to deny dismissal merely because foreign proce-dures differ from those in the United States. *E.g., Tuazon v. R.J. Reynolds Tobacco Co.*, 433 F.3d 1163, 1179-1180 (9th Cir. 2006) (unsubstantiated allegations of delay in foreign forum held inadequate); *Satz v. McDonnell Douglas Corp.*, 244 F.3d 1279, 1283 (11th Cir. 2001) ("The plaintiffs' concerns about Argentine filing fees, the lack of discovery in Argentine courts, and their fear of delays in the Argentine courts do not render Argentina an inadequate forum"); *Lockman Found. v. Evangelical Alliance Mission*, 930 F.2d 764, 768 (9th Cir. 1991) (lack of jury trial does not render Japan inadequate forum); *Stroitelstvo Bulgaria, Ltd. v. Bulgarian-American Enterprise Fund*, 598 F. Supp. 2d 875, 883-884 (N.D. Ill. 2009) (collecting cases for the proposition that filing fees in for-eign forum do not render it inadequate).

Nevertheless, significant procedural differences are occasionally central factors in deci-sions holding foreign forums inadequate. *Bhatnagar v. Surrendra Overseas Ltd.*, 52 F.3d 1220, 1228 (3d Cir. 1995) (delay in litigating case to judgment rendered forum inade-quate); *Mobil Tankers Co. v. Mene Grande Oil Co.*, 363 F.2d 611, 614 (3d Cir. 1966) (limited discovery rules and restrictions on expert witness testimony render foreign forum inad-equate); *Henderson v. Metropolitan Bank & Trust Co.*, 502 F. Supp. 2d 72 (S.D.N.Y. 2007) (excessive filing fees in foreign forum); *Sacks v. Four Seasons Hotel, Ltd.*, 2006 WL 783441 (E.D. Tex. 2006) (lack of discovery, unavailability of contingency fee, delays, and limited damages remedy collectively render foreign forum inadequate); *In re Lernout & Hauspie Securities Litig.*, 208 F. Supp. 2d 74, 92 (D. Mass. 2002) ("When combined with the lack of a fraud-on-the-market theory, however, the lack of a class action mechanism creates virtu-ally insurmountable concerns regarding the adequacy of the foreign forum."). Are these decisions consistent with *Piper*? *Compare In re Banco Santander Securities-Optimal Litig.*, 732 F. Supp. 2d 1305, 1334 (S.D. Fla. 2010) ("The availability of a class action procedure goes to the issue of convenience, not adequacy.").

(f) Unavailability of contingent fees. An especially ripe area for disagreement is whether the lack of contingent fee arrangements in a foreign country renders that forum unavailable for a plaintiff. Lower courts are divided over this issue. The majority rule appears to be that the unavailability of contingent fees arrangements are one factor in the analysis but are not dispositive. *See Murray v. British Broadcasting Corp.*, 81 F.3d 287, 292 (2d Cir. 1996) (collecting cases); *Coakes v. Arabian American Oil Co.*, 831 F.2d 572, 576 (5th Cir. 1987) (ban against contingency fees in England should not "significantly influence the forum non conveniens determination"); *Deirmenjian v. Deutsche Bank A.G.*, 2006 WL 4749756 (C.D. Cal. Sept. 25, 2006) (same); *Stewart v. Adidas AG*, 1997 WL 218431, at *8 (S.D.N.Y. 1997) ("the Second Circuit has specifically noted that the unavailability of contingency fee arrangements in an alternative forum may not be sufficient to preclude dismissal on forum non conveniens grounds"); *Kristoff v. Otis Elevator Co.*, 1997 WL 67797, at *2 (E.D. Pa. 1997) ("The majority of courts reviewing plaintiff's ability to litigate in the foreign forum consider the absence of a contingency fee arrangement one of the balancing factors in a forum non conveniens analysis, not an argument against availability of an alternative forum").

Assuming that the foreign forum's rules on contingency fees are relevant to the *forum non conveniens* inquiry, are they more appropriately part of the "adequate alternative forum" analysis or the public/private factors analysis? Why might the answer be important?

(g) Statutory limit on recovery in foreign forum. Suppose that foreign law imposes a flat limit on the amount recoverable by the plaintiff, but that U.S. law does not. Does such a limit render the foreign forum inadequate? Does the answer depend on the amount of the limit? *See Gonzalez v. Chrysler Corp.*, 301 F.3d 377, 382-383 (5th Cir. 2002) (rejecting argument based on recovery cap under foreign law). Consider *Castro Alfaro*, excerpted *supra* pp. 379-383, and especially *supra* p. 380, n. 77. Suppose that each plaintiff could recover no more than $1,080.00 in Costa Rican courts for serious long-term medical complaints allegedly caused by defendants' use of hazardous chemicals. Would Costa Rican courts satisfy the adequate alternative forum requirement?

(h) Effect of foreign forum's highly unfavorable laws. As discussed above, *Piper* held that adverse changes in applicable law were ordinarily irrelevant to *forum non conveniens* analysis. However, *Piper* also concluded that adverse changes in applicable laws *would* be significant "if the remedy provided by the alternative forum is so clearly inadequate or unsatisfactory that it is no remedy at all."

When will an adverse change in applicable law be so substantial that the plaintiff will have "no remedy at all" in the foreign forum? *See Galustian v. Peter*, 591 F.3d 724 (4th Cir. 2010) (holding Iraqi forum inadequate where defendant failed to make sufficient showing that defamation remedy available); *Agudas Chasidei Chabad of United States v. Russian Fed'n*, 528 F.3d 934 (D.C. Cir. 2008) (holding Russian forum inadequate where law governing return of expropriated goods would not provide adequate relief); *In re XE Servs. Alien Tort Litig.*, 665 F. Supp. 2d 569 (E.D. Va. 2009) (holding Iraqi forum not adequate where defense contractor would be entitled to immunity there); *Cortec Corp. v. Erste Bank der Oesterricischen Sparkasse AG*, 535 F. Supp. 2d 403, 410 (S.D.N.Y. 2008) (collecting cases where differences in substantive law rendered foreign forum inadequate). What if the plaintiff were limited to an administrative remedy in the foreign forum? *EDAPS Consortium v. Kiyanichenko*, 2005 WL 2000940, at *2 (N.D. Cal. 2005) (holding Ukrainian forum inadequate where plaintiff's only remedy would be administrative fine payable to Ukrainian government); *National Hockey League Players' Ass'n v. Plymouth Whalers Hockey Club*, 166 F. Supp. 2d 1155, 1163-1165 (E.D. Mich. 2001) (holding foreign forum inadequate where plaintiff unable to obtain injunctive relief and may be limited to administrative remedy). What about a private commission established to adjudicate claims? *See Nemariam v. Federal Democratic Republic of Ethiopia*, 315 F.3d 390 (D.C. Cir. 2003) (Ethiopia/Eritrea Claims Commission not adequate forum); *In re Assicurazioni Generali SpA Holocaust Ins. Litig.*, 228 F. Supp. 2d 348, 355-358 (S.D.N.Y. 2002) (holding private nongovernmental forum for paying claims to Holocaust victims inadequate).

What if the plaintiff's claims are virtually certain to fail in the foreign court (although they would have good prospects of success in the U.S.)? What if the plaintiff's claims are substantially less likely to succeed? What if the likely amount of a recovery by the plaintiff is much less (say, 10 percent) than in the U.S. forum? Where on this spectrum of adverse changes in law does any "remedy at all" cease to exist?

Consider Judge Greene's opinion in *Laker Airways*. Is it faithful to *Piper*'s rule that adverse changes in law must be ignored? Consider the following passage:

> As for British substantive law, it fails entirely, for a number of reasons, to recognize liability for the acts which the defendants are alleged to have committed. That being so, this case is precisely within that group of cases which the Supreme Court in *Piper Aircraft* said should not be dismissed. It is difficult to see how it could be otherwise. It would be a cruel hoax on the plaintiff to oust it from a court where its allegations, if proved, would entitle it to recovery, and to relegate it instead, in the name of "convenience," to a tribunal which, on the facts alleged, would not be justified under its own laws in entering judgment in plaintiff's favor.

Was it not, under this reasoning, also a "cruel hoax" to dismiss the claims in *Piper* and *Wyeth*? Is a foreign state an inadequate forum merely because the plaintiff is very likely to lose?

How should one go about evaluating whether a foreign forum is "so clearly inadequate or unsatisfactory that it is no remedy at all"? Does "no remedy at all" mean that the plaintiff must have 0 percent chances of recovery? If not, can a percentage likelihood of success be identified that constitutes "no remedy" — say, 20 percent? 10 percent? Does it make sense to speak in black-and-white terms of "adequate alternative forums" and ignoring "changes in substantive laws"? Is it more accurate to view a plaintiff as having greater or lesser probabilities of recovering greater or lesser amounts of money in two or more alternative forums? Should efforts be made to compare the plaintiff's likelihood of success or discounted recovery in its chosen forum and in the alternative forum? Would it not be sensible to do this, and then to compare those numbers with the estimated savings to each party from a *forum non conveniens* dismissal?

(i) Lengthy delays in foreign courts. The existence of long delays before a case can be heard in foreign courts will, in extreme cases, be grounds for concluding that a proposed alternative forum is inadequate. *See Bhatnagar v. Surrendra Overseas Ltd.*, 52 F.3d 1220, 1228 (3d Cir. 1995) (delay in litigating case to judgment, of up to 25 years, rendered Indian forum inadequate); *Sablic v. Armada Shipping Aps.*, 973 F. Supp. 745, 748 (S.D. Tex. 1997). *Compare In re Air Crash Near Pelzoto de Azeveda, Brazil on September 29, 2006*, 574 F. Supp. 2d 272 (E.D.N.Y. 2008) (finding allegations of delay in Brazil insufficient to establish inadequacy); *Usha (India), Ltd. v. Honeywell Int'l, Inc.*, 2004 WL 540441 (S.D.N.Y. 2004) (concluding that delays in Indian courts had been reduced).

(j) Statute of limitations bars foreign suit. Generally, if the limitations period has run on claims in the foreign forum, that fact can render the forum inadequate. *See Bank of Credit & Commerce International (Overseas) v. State Bank of Pakistan*, 273 F.3d 241, 246 (2d Cir. 2001). To avoid this outcome, defendants may agree not to raise a limitations defense in the foreign forum. *See infra* p. 450. In rare cases, there may be evidence that the plaintiff deliberately has timed commencement of the litigation so that the claims would be

untimely in the foreign forum but not the U.S. court. In those rare cases, a U.S. court can dismiss the suit even if the foreign forum is unavailable. *See Chang v. Baxter Healthcare Corp.*, 599 F.3d 728, 736 (7th Cir. 2010); *Compania Naviera Joanna SA v. Koninklijke Boskalis Westminster NV*, 569 F.3d 189, 202-203 (4th Cir. 2009).

5. *Evolving jurisprudence on the adequacy of a foreign forum.* When a court concludes that a foreign forum is adequate (or inadequate), what is the nature of that conclusion? Is it a factual finding relevant only to the case before the court? Or is it a legal conclusion with implications for other cases involving motions to dismiss to the same foreign forum?

The correct answer to this question is critical. It will influence how a defendant constructs its motion to dismiss (and how a plaintiff constructs its opposition), including the extent to which the parties should rely on expert affidavits. Moreover, over time, opinions will develop over the adequacy of a particular foreign forum. Sometimes, those opinions will reach common conclusions. Sometimes, those opinions will reach conflicting conclusions. Indeed, both plaintiffs and defendants who repeatedly litigate such issues have an incentive to develop a jurisprudence about the adequacy (or inadequacy) of a particular foreign forum. Such issues also arise in other contexts, such as the enforceability of forum selection clauses and the enforceability of foreign judgments. *See infra* at pp. 461-546 and 548-567.

For a recent opinion wrestling with this question in the context of a motion to dismiss a suit so it can be refiled in Mexico (and also wrestling with conflicting judicial opinions over Mexico's adequacy), *see Hernandez v. Ford Motor Co.*, 760 N.W.2d 751 (Mich. App. 2008).

6. *Relevance of parties' nationality to adequate alternative forum analysis.* Suppose that in *Bhopal* the parties' positions on the *forum non conveniens* issue had been reversed. That is, suppose that Union Carbide had brought suit in the United States seeking a declaration that it was not liable for the disaster, and the Indian government (and Indian plaintiffs) had moved for *forum non conveniens* dismissal to India. Would the district court's analysis set forth above have been any less applicable? Would you be willing to force Union Carbide to litigate in India—given the limits described above on Indian discovery, jury trials, substantive law, and the like?

Is it not an ironic position, for a U.S. party to extol the benefits of a foreign legal system, while foreign plaintiffs attack it? Although not strictly applicable, does this not raise considerations of waiver and estoppel? Absent some specific bias directed at a foreign entity by its own courts, should it have standing to criticize the adequacy of those courts? Suppose that the plaintiffs in *Bhopal* had been U.S. nationals, working at the ill-fated plant, when the disaster struck. Suppose further that they sued Union Carbide in the United States. Would the same adequate alternative forum analysis apply to them? What would be the relevance of the Indian restrictions on discovery, jury trials, contingent fee arrangements, and the like?

7. *Public policy objections to* **forum non conveniens** *dismissals of statutory claims.* In many aspects of international litigation, general rules are subject to public policy exceptions. Examples include the enforceability of forum selection clauses (*infra* pp. 511-528); arbitration agreements (*infra* pp. 1185-1194); choice of law (*infra* pp. 736-737, 756, 771-773); and foreign judgments (*infra* pp. 1133-1146). Should the *forum non conveniens* doctrine similarly be subject to a public policy exception, where compelling forum interests override generally applicable rules? Do you think that Congress intended for federal antitrust, securities, and RICO claims to be capable of dismissal to foreign courts on grounds of "convenience"? Would refusals to apply the *forum non conveniens* doctrine to statutory claims be consistent with *Piper*'s holding that changes in substantive law are ordinarily irrelevant to *forum non conveniens* analysis?

8. *Refusal of courts to apply foreign "penal" and "revenue" laws—an initial view.* Note the remark in *Laker* that English courts "could not and would not enforce the American antitrust laws." As discussed in greater detail below, it has often been said that one nation's courts will not apply the penal or revenue laws of another nation. *See infra* pp. 737, 1102-1114; *Holman v. Johnson*, 98 Eng. Rep. 1120, 1121 (1775) ("no country ever takes notice of the revenue laws of another"); *Banco Nacional de Cuba v. Sabbatino*, 376 U.S. 398, 413-414 (1964) ("a court need not give effect to the penal or revenue law of foreign countries"). Why is that? England, like the United States and most other countries, has choice-of-law rules that frequently lead to the application of foreign law by English courts. Why wouldn't these rules require application of the U.S. antitrust laws?

What if the U.S. court were to conclude that the foreign court, under its own conflicts principles, would apply substantive federal (or state) law of the United States? Would a *forum non conveniens* dismissal be appropriate? *See Remirez de Arellano v. Starwood Hotels & Resorts Worldwide, Inc.*, 448 F. Supp. 2d 520, 527-528 (S.D.N.Y. 2006).

9. *Applicability of* **forum non conveniens** *doctrine to federal antitrust claims.* As noted above, *supra* p. 444, federal courts disagree over whether the *forum non conveniens* doctrine applies to antitrust claims. Why is it, according to *Laker*, that antitrust claims cannot be subject to *forum non conveniens* dismissals? Note the court's characterization of the Sherman Act as "our charter of economic liberty," and its view that "[a]ntitrust cases are unlike litigation involving contracts, torts, and other matters recognized in some form in every nation."

(*a*) *Absence of any specific statutory prohibition on forum non conveniens.* Does anything in text of the antitrust laws forbid *forum non conveniens* dismissals? Does *Laker* rely on any specific statutory provision to justify its result? Consider the argument that was unsuccessfully made in *Howe*—the "special venue" provisions in the federal securities laws indicate that Congress wished to guarantee plaintiffs the right to pursue their actions in particular "special" forums without risk of transfer or *forum non conveniens* dismissal. *Howe* rejects that argument. Does *Laker* rely on the venue provisions of the antitrust laws?

(*b*) *Relevance of U.S. legislation's "importance."* As noted above, *Laker* referred to the U.S. antitrust laws as a charter of economic liberty, comparable to the Bill of Rights. Does this mean that only claims under "extraordinary" congressional enactments will be immune from *forum non conveniens* dismissal? Is there any principled way to distinguish federal statutes in terms of importance? Can one distinguish between statutes in any way that is relevant to *forum non conveniens* analysis?

(*c*) *Relevance of parallel foreign remedies.* As noted above, *Laker* emphasized that English courts would not apply the antitrust laws, and that applicable English law would "fail" to grant the plaintiff a successful claim. Suppose the defendant in a U.S. antitrust action could show that the proffered foreign alternative forum would apply federal antitrust statutes. For example, suppose there was evidence in *Laker* that the English courts would have applied U.S. antitrust laws. Should Judge Greene still have refused to dismiss the suit? Suppose that English courts would not have applied U.S. antitrust laws, but they would have applied English or European laws that were broadly similar. Would the *Laker* analysis still apply? Note that this was the situation in *Howe*—Canadian courts would have applied Canadian law that was broadly similar to the federal securities laws. Is *Howe* correctly decided? Should not a U.S. court refuse to dismiss unless the foreign court will apply U.S. statutory law (and not some foreign imitation)?

(*d*) *Analogy to forum selection clauses.* Consider the analysis in *Mitsubishi Motors Corp. v. Soler Chrysler-Plymouth Inc.*, 473 U.S. 614 (1987), and in *Richards v. Lloyd's of London*, 135 F.3d 1289 (9th Cir. 1998) (*en banc*), excerpted below at *infra* pp. 515-520. There, the courts held that arbitration agreements and forum selection clauses would be enforced, *provided* that federal statutory claims (or a reasonable foreign analogue) would be considered abroad. Is this a sensible way to approach public policy issues in the *forum non conveniens* context? Should it be easier or harder to get *forum non conveniens* dismissal of an antitrust claim than to enforce a foreign forum clause as to such claim?

(e) Relevance of choice-of-law analysis to public policy analysis. Most of the disputed conduct in *Howe* occurred in Canada. Is it clear that the federal securities laws would have actually applied to that conduct? This is an issue that is examined in detail below. *See infra* pp. 709-723. For present purposes, it is enough to say that there would have been doubts that U.S. securities laws applied to the challenged conduct, because it lacked substantial contacts with the United States. Contrast *Laker*, where it was substantially clearer that the U.S. antitrust laws applied to the defendants' conduct (because it occurred in part in Florida and because it affected air service to and from the United States).

Are these choice-of-law considerations relevant to the *forum non conveniens* analysis? Although neither *Howe* nor *Laker* expressly considered them, note that both courts went to some lengths to describe where the disputed conduct occurred. Note also the discussion of U.S. and foreign interests in regulating the allegedly wrongful conduct. Both the location of the disputed conduct and the competing national interests are key considerations in contemporary U.S. choice-of-law standards. *See infra* pp. 645-796.

Suppose that, in *Howe*, the two target companies had been in the United States. Further, suppose that Goldcorp had conducted two meetings in New York with representatives of the U.S. shareholders to explain its acquisition plans, and that allegedly fraudulent statements were made at these meetings. That conduct would have provided a much more substantial basis for application of the federal securities laws. Under Judge (now Justice) Breyer's analysis, would the case have been decided any differently? Should it have? Suppose that, in *Laker*, Laker had flown on London-Mexico City routes, but not on routes to the United States, and that no allegedly wrongful conduct had occurred within the United States. Would that have affected Judge Greene's analysis? Should it have?

Suppose that U.S. choice-of-law rules would lead to the application of U.S. law to a U.S. plaintiff's claims against a foreign defendant. Suppose that foreign choice-of-law rules would lead to the application of foreign law, and that this law was less favorable to the U.S. plaintiff. In these circumstances, is the adverse change in applicable law relevant? What does *Piper* say? What if the foreign forum would apply its own law in circumstances that would violate U.S. due process limits on legislative jurisdiction? *See infra* pp. 605-644.

10. *Applicability of* **forum non conveniens** *to federal securities and RICO claims.* In contrast to *Laker*'s treatment of antitrust claims, lower courts have unanimously held that federal securities and RICO claims are capable of dismissal on *forum non conveniens* grounds. *See supra* pp. 426-427. *Howe* is one example of such a decision. Why should the *forum non conveniens* doctrine apply in a different way to antitrust claims than to securities claims? Is it because, as *Howe* suggests, foreign courts are more likely to apply either federal securities laws or some closely similar foreign law, than they are to apply the federal antitrust laws or some foreign analogue? If so, does this affect analysis? (Note that the court's generalization about antitrust and securities laws is not accurate: many foreign states (including the European Union, Germany, Japan, and England) have competition laws that are at least as well-developed as their securities law. Of course, these laws may not always produce the same results as the U.S. antitrust laws, but under *Piper* this should not matter.)

11. *Applicability of* **forum non conveniens** *doctrine when federal copyright or trademark claims are involved.* Do claims arising under federal intellectual property laws raise special considerations that countenance against *forum non conveniens* dismissals? Pursuant to the Berne Convention and World Intellectual Property Organization Copyright Treaty, most intellectual property rights are territorial: they are granted by individual nations with regard to national territory. Accordingly, the United States grants copyrights, trademarks, and patents with regard to U.S. territory (and not elsewhere), while foreign states do so with regard to their territory. Given this, how should claims under federal intellectual property statutes be treated under the *forum non conveniens* doctrine? As noted above, lower courts have generally held that federal copyright and trademark claims may be subject to *forum non conveniens* dismissals. *See supra* p. 428.

Is it appropriate to dismiss U.S. copyright claims to a foreign forum? Consider the following dissent:

> I must admit that I am astounded when I read that it is not convenient to try an American copyright case in an American court for copyright infringement that takes place solely in America. . . . Here, the applicable law is the United States Copyright Act and the situs of the alleged infringement is the United States. . . . [T]he district court's error was compounded by its failure to account both for the unique significance of copyright law in American society and federal court jurisprudence and for the enormous complexity of American copyright law, particularly as it pertains to the protection of computer software. . . . Stated simply, the United States courts are the most well-suited forum for adjudicating the rights bestowed by United States copyrights. . . . A copyright may not be as important as the Congressional Medal of Honor, but the district court and the majority have completely disregarded the fact that an American copyright is a valued benefit granted by the United States government for the primary purpose of benefiting the general public good; therefore, a copyright infringement claim must not be treated as a mere private cause of action like a tort or breach of contract. . . . *Creative Technology, Ltd. v. Aztech System Pte, Ltd.*, 61 F.3d 696 (9th Cir. 1995) (Ferguson, J., dissenting).

Is there anything wrong with this analysis?

12. *Applicability of* **forum non conveniens** *doctrine in human rights litigation.* As discussed above, the Alien Tort Statute, the Torture Victim Protection Act, and similar legislation grants federal courts jurisdiction over various categories of human rights claims. *See supra* pp. 48, 59. Is the *forum non conveniens* doctrine applicable to human rights claims under such legislation? What are the arguments for and against application of the *forum non conveniens* doctrine?

Consider the *Wiwa* Court's discussion of the application of the *forum non conveniens* doctrine under the TVPA and ATS. Is the *forum non conveniens* doctrine available as a defense? How much of a defense? What do you make of the Second Circuit's discussion of the role of *forum non conveniens* in human rights litigation?

Compare the Second Circuit's apparent enthusiasm for human rights litigation in U.S. courts with the Supreme Court's repeated emphasis on the need for "great caution" and "vigilant door-keeping" in *Sosa. See supra* pp. 42-47. Is it in fact appropriate to prescribe *forum non conveniens* rules that encourage human rights litigation in U.S. courts? Is that not what the *Wiwa* Court has done?

Note that the TVPA provides, in §2(b), that "A court shall decline to hear a claim under this section if the claimant has not exhausted adequate and available remedies in the place in which the conduct giving rise to the claim occurred." The TVPA's legislative history explains that

> [t]his requirement ensures that U.S. courts will not intrude into cases more appropriately handled by courts where the alleged torture or killing occurred. It will also avoid exposing U.S. courts to unnecessary burdens, and can be expected to encourage the development of meaningful remedies in other countries.

Does this provision weaken, or strengthen, the case for *forum non conveniens* dismissals in TVPA cases? Does it even leave room for application of the doctrine? Consider the following exchange on the Senate floor during deliberations on the TVPA: "Mr. GRASSLEY. Will courts retain their discretion to decline jurisdiction over lawsuits under this bill? Will they be able to dismiss such suits in favor of a more convenient forum in another country? Mr. SPECTER. The answer to both questions is yes. Nothing in this legislation is intended to or does affect the doctrine of *forum non conveniens*, which remains applicable to any lawsuit brought under this act." 138 Cong. Rec. S2667-04, at 2668.

13. *Applicability of the* **forum non conveniens** *doctrine and the FSIA.* The Supreme Court has suggested (albeit in dictum) that the *forum non conveniens* doctrine remains applicable, under the FSIA. *Verlinden BV v. Central Bank of Nigeria*, 461 U.S. 480, 490 n.15 (1983) ("the [FSIA] does not appear to affect the traditional doctrine of *forum non conveniens*"). Lower courts have thus permitted defendants to raise the defense of *forum non conveniens* in actions against foreign states under the FSIA. *E.g., UNC Lear Services, Inc v. Kingdom of Saudi Arabia*, 581 F.3d 210, 221 (5th Cir. 2009); *Agudas Casidei Chabad of United States v. Russian Fed'n*, 528 F.3d 934, 935 (D.C. Cir. 2008); *Gould, Inc. v. Pechiney Ugine Kuhlmann*, 853 F.2d 445 (6th Cir. 1988); *Proyecfin de Venezuela SA v. Banco Industrial de Venezuela SA*, 760 F.2d 390, 394 (2d Cir. 1985). Does the fact that the defendant is a foreign state entity affect the *forum non conveniens* analysis? Does it affect the question whether an adequate alternative forum exists?

14. Forum non conveniens *and extraterritoriality. Laker, Howe*, and *Wiwa* all concern the extent to which dismissal on *forum non conveniens* grounds is appropriate in cases arising under federal statutes or federal common law. The common refrain in these cases is the argument that the existence of a federal cause of action signifies a strong federal interest in ensuring that those claims are heard in a U.S. court. In many cases, those claims will be predicated on conduct that took place partly or entirely in a foreign country.

As discussed in greater detail in Chapter 8, the Court's views on the extraterritorial application of federal law have evolved. In a recent decision, the Court set a high bar, requiring a rather clear indication of congressional intent to give a statute extraterritorial effect. How is this standard likely to affect motions to dismiss cases on grounds of *forum non conveniens*? On the one hand, it may reduce the need for such dismissals because the alleged overseas conduct will not state a claim under federal law. On the other hand, where the necessary evidence of congressional intent is clear, does that not significantly weaken the argument for a *forum non conveniens* dismissal? Or do cases like *Howe* still suggest that such dismissals may be appropriate even where Congress has made clear its intent to give extraterritorial effect to the statute? What about cases like *Wiwa*?

15. *The public interest factors and federal statutory claims.* Even assuming that the doctrine of *forum non conveniens* did "apply" in antitrust, securities, and similar cases, might not courts generally conclude that the public interest factors weighed against dismissal of such claims? How would a *forum non conveniens* analysis apply to federal statutory claims? How would public interest considerations be dealt with? For representative decisions, *see DiRienzo v. Philip Servs. Corp.*, 294 F.3d 21, 32 (2d Cir. 2002); *Creative Technology Ltd. v. Aztech System Pte, Ltd.*, 61 F.3d 696 (9th Cir. 1995).

Does *Howe* afford special weight to federal statutory claims? Would it be better, under the "flexible" *Piper* analysis, to weigh the existence of federal statutory rights in the overall "public interest" inquiry? How would *Laker* have been decided if a *forum non conveniens* analysis had been applied?

16. *Latin American legislation discouraging* **forum non conveniens** *dismissals.* Several Latin American states have enacted legislation designed to discourage the *forum non conveniens* dismissal of suits by local nationals from U.S. courts. *See generally* Heiser, Forum Non

Conveniens *and Retaliatory Legislation: The Impact on the Available Alternative Forum Inquiry and on the Desirability of* Forum Non Conveniens *as a Defense Tactic,* 56 U. Kan. L. Rev. 609 (2008); Figueroa, *Conflicts of Jurisdiction Between the United States and Latin America in the Context of Forum Non Conveniens Dismissal,* 37 U. Miami Inter.-Am. L. Rev. 119 (2005); Symeonides, *Choice of Law in American Courts in 2008: Twenty-Second Annual Survey,* 57 Am. J. Comp. L. 269, 295 (2009). Ecuador's Ley 55 was an early example. While Ecuador's Constitutional Court has declared the law unconstitutional, *see Agiunda v. Texaco, Inc.,* 303 F.3d 470, 477 (2d Cir. 2002), it illustrates that such legislation takes the somewhat unlikely form of purported prohibitions of national court jurisdiction once a U.S. litigation has been commenced in a particular dispute. *See* Decreto Numero 34-97 (Guatemala); Ley de Defensa de Derechos Procesalas de Nacionales y Residentes (Honduras); Ley 55 (Ecuador); Statute of Private International Law, Art. 40 (Venezuela). This legislation is designed to render the local courts inadequate alternative forums, and thereby preclude *forum non conveniens* dismissals, by denying local courts jurisdiction.

U.S. courts generally have been skeptical about the impact of such legislation. *See Paulownia Plantations de Panama Corp. v. Rajamannan,* 2009 WL 3644186 (D. Minn. Nov. 5, 2009) (noting that Panamanian legislation likely would not apply retroactively and, in all events, would not cover plaintiff's case); *Polanco v. H.B. Fuller Co.,* 941 F. Supp. 1512 (D. Minn. 1996) (dismissing, while leaving plaintiff free to refile "in the event that the highest court of any foreign country finally affirms the dismissal for lack of jurisdiction"); *Delgado v. Shell Oil,* 890 F. Supp. 1324 (S.D. Tex. 1995); *Aguinda v. Texaco, Inc.,* 142 F. Supp. 2d 534, 546 (S.D.N.Y. 2001), *aff'd as modified,* 303 F.3d 470 (2d Cir. 2002) (questioning whether Ley 55 would be applied even after *forum non conveniens* dismissal of U.S. litigation). *But see In re Bridgestone/Firestone Inc.,* 190 F. Supp. 2d 1125, 1125-1132 (S.D. Ind. 2002) (finding Venezuela unavailable forum due to statute).

What weight, if any, should such legislation have in U.S. *forum non conveniens* litigation? Can it be permissible for foreign states to essentially control U.S. courts' management of their dockets? Why can't foreign states make judgments about where their nationals should sue? What if the foreign "door-closing statutes" were more nuanced? Suppose that they denied local courts jurisdiction in any case against a company that was amenable to suit in its place of incorporation or business, if the events in question involved conduct or decisions made in that place? What about a statute that did not block jurisdiction but simply made litigation extremely onerous for the defendant (for example, by imposing a bond requirement or simplifying proof of liability)? *See* Nicaragua's Special Law No. 364, La. Gac. 12, 17 de Enero de 2001 (Nicar. 2001). Does this simplify the *forum non conveniens* dismissal if the defendant is willing to be subjected to the more plaintiff-friendly regime? What if the features of this law reduce the likelihood that a U.S. court would enforce the judgment? *See Osorio v. Dole Food Co.,* 665 F. Supp. 2d 1307 (S.D. Fla. 2009) (refusing to enforce judgment rendered pursuant to Special Law No. 364).

Other countries have adopted legislation that requires their courts to apply the liability law and damages rules of the country in which the suit originally was filed. *See generally* Heiser, Forum Non Conveniens *and Retaliatory Legislation: The Impact on the Available Alternative Forum Inquiry and on the Desirability of* Forum Non Conveniens *as a Defense Tactic,* 56 U. Kan. L. Rev. 609 (2008). What effect does such legislation have on the *forum non conveniens* analysis? Unlike statutes like Ley 55, laws of this sort do not strip their courts of jurisdiction. Does that mean these courts are available? Are they adequate? Even if they are adequate, does this cast doubt on the fairness and integrity of the proceeding? Does it jeopardize the enforceability of any judgment rendered by the foreign forum?

Suppose that a foreign plaintiff raises the prospect of a blocking statute as a reason not to dismiss, but the U.S. court is unsure whether the statute applies. So the court conditionally dismisses the action, subject to the foreign court's determination of the blocking statute's application. During the foreign litigation, the foreign plaintiff undertakes "intentional efforts" to obtain dismissal of the litigation in the foreign forum. If the foreign court dismisses the suit in reliance on the blocking statute, what implications do such "intentional efforts" have on the foreign plaintiff's ability to refile in the United States? Despite a blocking statute, does the foreign plaintiff have some good faith effort to attempt to establish jurisdiction in the foreign forum? *See Scotts Co. v. Hacienda Loma Linda*, 2 So. 3d 1013 (Fla. App. 2008) (holding that, under such circumstances, foreign plaintiff was not entitled to refile in United States).

17. *Conditions on* **forum non conveniens** *dismissals.* In both *Wyeth* and *Bhopal*, the courts conditioned their grants of *forum non conveniens* dismissals on the defendant's acceptance of certain "conditions." This is a common practice. *See supra* p. 428. It is designed to ensure that an adequate alternative forum exists, by removing obstacles such as lack of personal jurisdiction, statutes of limitations, and the like.

Indeed, some jurisdictions actually automatically deem a *forum non conveniens* motion to include stipulated conditions such as these. *See Kinney Sys. Inc. v. Continental Ins. Co.*, 674 So. 2d 86, 92 (Fla. 1996). Others hold that, in a dismissal order, a district court must include a "return jurisdiction" clause (one providing for the return of the case to the U.S. court if the defendant subsequently obstructs commencement of the suit in the foreign forum). *Compare Robinson v. TCI/US West Communications Inc.*, 117 F.3d 900, 907-908 (5th Cir. 1997) (district court's failure to include return jurisdiction clause constitutes reversible error) *with Leetsch v. Freedman*, 260 F.3d 1100, 1104 (9th Cir. 2001) (rejecting *per se* rule requiring return jurisdiction clause in any *forum non conveniens* dismissal).

Is the *forum non conveniens* analysis fairly conducted if a U.S. court in effect alters the legal standards that will apply in the foreign forum? Is it not comparing apples and oranges? Moreover, does the practice of imposing conditions interfere with the sovereignty of foreign states? Should plaintiffs be permitted to offer "conditions" on their U.S. trial tactics—such as limiting discovery, waiving punitive damages, and the like? On the other hand, should the availability and adequacy of the foreign forum "be made to depend merely upon the will or grace of a defendant"? *Varo v. Owens-Illinois, Inc.*, 948 A.2d 673, 681 (N.J. App. Div. 2008).

(a) Requirement that defendants consent to personal jurisdiction in foreign forum. *Wyeth* and *Bhopal* required that the defendants submit to the personal jurisdiction of the foreign forum at issue. *See also Jota v. Texaco, Inc.*, 157 F.3d 153, 159 (2d Cir. 1998); *Ilusorio v. Ilusorio-Bildner*, 103 F. Supp. 2d 672, 682 (S.D.N.Y. 2000). In general, this requirement seems unobjectionable. The trial court must, of course, satisfy itself that the defendant's consent will be a sufficient basis for the proffered foreign court to assert jurisdiction, and should not dismiss if this is not the case. *Schertenleib v. Traum*, 589 F.2d 1156, 1163 (2d Cir. 1978) ("the district court should not dismiss . . . unless it justifiably believes that the alternative forum will take jurisdiction, if the defendant consents").

A few courts have conditioned dismissal on the foreign forum actually taking jurisdiction over the plaintiff's substitute action, or provided mechanisms for the plaintiffs to refile in the U.S. forum if the foreign court does not assume jurisdiction. *Mercier v. Sheraton Int'l, Inc.*, 935 F.2d 419 (1st Cir. 1991); *Dowling v. Hyland Therapeutics Division*, 767 F. Supp. 57, 60 (S.D.N.Y. 1991). If a foreign court nonetheless declines jurisdiction, the plaintiff's U.S. action could be refiled (unless the plaintiff meanwhile has sabotaged the foreign litigation in an effort to return the case to the United States). *See MBI Group, Inc. v. Credit Foncier du Cameroun*, 616 F.3d 568 (D.C. Cir. 2010); *Macedo v. Boeing Co.*, 693 F.2d 683, 687 (7th Cir. 1982). How would this affect statutory limitations periods?

Of course, even if the foreign court accepts jurisdiction, there is a risk that the litigation in the foreign forum may take so long as to effectively deprive the plaintiff of any relief. In anticipation of such problems, some courts have designed creative conditions, such as requiring litigation for a period of time in the foreign forum with the possibility of return in the United States if the foreign court does not vigorously pursue the litigation. *See USHA (India), Ltd. v. Honeywell Int'l, Inc.*, 421 F.3d 129, 136 (2d Cir. 2005).

(b) Jurisdiction over U.S. parent. In both *Bhopal* and *Wyeth*, a U.S. parent company was sought to be sued in a dispute occurring in a foreign nation that arose almost entirely from the acts of a foreign subsidiary of the U.S. parent. Is it appropriate for U.S. courts to require U.S. parent companies, in these circumstances, to submit themselves to foreign nations' jurisdiction — where those foreign states might well not otherwise have judicial jurisdiction over the U.S. company? If a foreign state chooses to structure its regulatory and judicial systems in such a fashion that local subsidiaries are regulated and subject to civil actions — but their foreign shareholders are not — why should U.S. courts interfere? As long as the subsidiary is adequately capitalized, why should the plaintiff be provided with a claim against the U.S. parent? If the *forum non conveniens* doctrine permits a plaintiff to be denied some of its claims, why should it not also allow the plaintiff to be denied some of its defendants — especially where those which it cannot pursue are ones that U.S. law says it has no right to pursue?

(c) Requirement that defendant waive statute of limitations defense. As in *Wyeth* and *Bhopal*, courts have frequently required that defendants waive statute of limitations defenses in the alternative foreign forum. *See Chang v. Baxter Healthcare Corp.*, 599 F.3d 728, 736 (7th Cir. 2010) (collecting cases). Is this an appropriate condition? The plaintiffs could have filed suit in what was clearly the convenient forum, but chose not to. Moreover, the plaintiffs generally could have made a protective filing in the alternative forum to safeguard their position, but did not. If it is appropriate to require waivers of statutes of limitations defenses, why shouldn't U.S. courts also require waivers of "reasonable care" defenses, so as to create a strict liability regime in the foreign forum? If this is inappropriate, how is a statute of limitations waiver different?

(d) Requirement that defendant consent to U.S.-style discovery. Following *Piper*'s suggestion, *Wyeth* and *Bhopal* required that the defendant consent to providing the same documents and witnesses in the foreign litigation as would have been required in a U.S. litigation. *See De Melo v. Lederle Laboratories*, 801 F.2d 1058 (8th Cir. 1986); *Ali v. Offshore Co.*, 753 F.2d 1327 (5th Cir. 1985). Is this condition consistent with the rationale for the *forum non conveniens* doctrine? Is it consistent with the respect for foreign regulatory and judicial systems referred to in *Piper* and in *Wyeth*? Did the court in either case require the plaintiff also to give U.S.-style discovery to the defendant? Is it appropriate to have one-sided discovery? The district court's discovery condition was reversed by the Second Circuit in *Union Carbide*, 809 F.2d 195 (2d Cir. 1987), because of its one-sided character. *See also Doe v. Hyland Therapeutics Division*, 807 F. Supp. 1117 (S.D.N.Y. 1992).

There is also the risk that plaintiffs will file suit in inconvenient U.S. forums, in part with the expectation of obtaining a U.S.-style discovery condition even if their actions are dismissed on *forum non conveniens* grounds: as one court has observed, "we share defendants' concern that this District not become a way-station for plaintiffs world-wide, who choose to stop at Foley Square just long enough to obtain a grant of federal discovery with their *forum non conveniens* dismissal." *Doe v. Hyland Therapeutics Division*, 807 F. Supp. 1117 (S.D.N.Y. 1992). Note, however, that *Piper* appeared to bless U.S.-style discovery conditions. *See supra* p. 358, note 70.

(e) Requirement that defendant pay any foreign judgment. Both *Wyeth* and *Bhopal* required the defendant to agree to satisfy any foreign judgment that might be rendered in the

alternative forum. Is it appropriate to condition a *forum non conveniens* dismissal on the defendant's commitment to pay any foreign judgment? Could a court require a defendant to stipulate that the foreign judgment is "entitled to full faith and credit in the courts of the United States"? *See Punyee ex rel. Doe #1 v. Bredimus*, 2004 WL 251144, at *9 (N.D. Tex. 2004). Note that there are ample opportunities for enforcing foreign judgments in U.S. courts. *See* Chapter 12. What if the foreign proceedings turn out to be conducted in a way that is blatantly biased against the defendant? For example, press articles reported that the initial Indian trial judge in *Bhopal* had secretly filed a claim for damages against Union Carbide in the case over which he was presiding. A subsequent judge ordered Union Carbide to make a $190 million payment to Bhopal victims, before deciding whether Union Carbide was liable; the company condemned the action as "a judgment and decree without trial." *The Wall Street Journal*, May 18, 1988, at 33.

(f) Miscellaneous other conditions. Miscellaneous other conditions have been fashioned to meet the needs of particular cases. For example, conditions have been imposed requiring an undertaking from foreign governmental officials not to detain the plaintiff if he prosecuted his action in that nation, *Sussman v. Bank of Israel*, 990 F.2d 71, 71 (2d Cir. 1993); requiring that the foreign forum act within a specified time period on the plaintiff's request for provisional measures, *Borden, Inc. v. Meiji Milk Products Co.*, 919 F.2d 822, 829 (2d Cir. 1990); requiring acceptance of service of process, *Constructora Spilimerg, CA v. Mitsubishi Aircraft Co.*, 700 F.2d 225, 226 (5th Cir. 1983); requiring that the defendants bear the costs of translation, *In re Air Crash Over Taiwan Straits on May 25, 2002*, 331 F. Supp. 2d 1176, 1213 (C.D. Cal. 2004); requiring that the defendant post security, *Aracruz Trading Ltd. v. Japaul Oil and Maritime Services, PLC*, 2009 WL 667298 (S.D.N.Y. Mar. 16, 2009); requiring that a suit be brought in a court near the plaintiff's residence, *Huang v. Advanced Battery Tech., Inc.*, 2010 WL 2143669 (S.D.N.Y. May 26, 2010); requiring that the defendant stipulate to certain facts, *Khan v. Delta Airlines, Inc.*, 2010 WL 3210717 (E.D.N.Y. Aug. 12, 2010); requiring a defendant to use good faith efforts to secure permission from bank account depositors in order to avoid running afoul of foreign bank secrecy laws, *Henderson v. Metropolitan Bank & Trust Co.*, 502 F. Supp. 2d 372, 375 n.12 (S.D.N.Y. 2007); and requiring that a defendant not object to the admissibility of certain evidence, *In re Factor VIII or IX Concentration Blood Products Liability Litig.*, 408 F. Supp. 2d 569, 591 (N.D. Ill. 2006). What sort of a showing should a plaintiff have to make before a district court may impose these sorts of conditions?

(g) No conditions requiring foreign court to entertain particular claims. U.S. courts have thus far *not* conditioned *forum non conveniens* dismissals on the alternative forum's willingness to entertain a particular cause of action. *See, e.g., Goldberg v. UBS AG*, 690 F. Supp. 2d 92 (E.D.N.Y. 2010). It would be possible, at least in principle, for a U.S. court to condition dismissal upon a foreign court's application of U.S. strict products liability standards or U.S. antitrust law. U.S. courts have occasionally imposed such conditions upon orders compelling parties to international arbitration. *E.g., PPG Industries, Inc. v. Pilkington, plc*, 825 F. Supp. 1465 (D. Ariz. 1993) ("the Court directs that any damages determination, or arbitral award, made by the arbitrators shall be determined according to U.S. antitrust law irrespective of any conflict that may exist between those laws and the laws of England [the arbitral situs]"); G. Born, *International Commercial Arbitration* 836-837, 1781-1782 (2009). Where foreign courts, rather than arbitral tribunals, are involved, U.S. legislation might well not be enforced. *See supra* pp. 444-447 & *infra* pp. 1102-1110. Moreover, a U.S. court-ordered condition addressing the law applicable in a foreign court would be perceived as interference with the foreign court's functioning. Are these sufficient reasons not to protect a plaintiff's statutory rights?

(h) Limits on conditions. Can a court impose unlimited conditions on a defendant before dismissing a case for *forum non conveniens*? What if the conditions begin to intrude on the institutional prerogatives of the foreign judicial system? Could a court require that the trial in the foreign forum shall be by jury? *See In re Vioxx Prods. Liability Litig.,* 2009 WL 1636244 (E.D. La. Feb. 10, 2009) *aff'd sub nom. Adams v. Merck & Co., Inc.,* 2009 WL 1636244 (5th Cir. Nov. 30, 2009). Consider the following observations, in dicta, from an opinion reversing a district court's order that had conditioned dismissal on the parties' waiving their rights to contingent fees and fee shifting for the prevailing party:

> There is a point at which conditions cease to be a limitation on the defendant and become instead an unwarranted intrusion on the transferee forum's policies governing its judicial system. By applying conditions that implicate the British legal system's rules on fee-shifting and the availability of contingent fees, the district court effectively stepped into the middle of Britain's policy debate on those issues. Principles of comity demand that we respect those policies. We urge the district courts to be cognizant of the prudential choices made by foreign nations and not to impose conditions on parties that may be viewed as having the effect of undermining the considered policies of the transferee forum. *Gross v. British Broadcasting Corp.,* 386 F.3d 224, 234 (2d Cir. 2004).

Do you agree? Why doesn't the logic of this argument also apply to more traditional conditions such as waivers of jurisdiction or limitations defenses? Must a court first establish its own jurisdiction over the case and the defendants before it can condition dismissal on the defendant's assent to certain terms? *See Sinochem Int'l Co., Ltd. v. Malaysia Int'l Shipping Co.,* 549 U.S. 422, 435 (2007) (reserving the question). *See generally* Rutledge, *Decisional Sequencing,* 62 Ala. L. Rev. 7 (2010) (articulating a theory for the order in which courts should rule on matters like jurisdiction and *forum non conveniens* with a special emphasis on international disputes).

(i) The bottom line. At the end of the day, who benefits from conditional dismissals? The conventional account has been that such dismissals typically benefit defendants. They have successfully deprived plaintiffs of their chosen forum. As long as the burden of the conditions (whether offered or imposed) does not outweigh the benefits of the foreign forum, the defendant comes out ahead. This is particularly true where, as a result of *Piper,* the foreign forum entitles the plaintiff to lower damages or fewer remedies than would be available in U.S. courts.

Is the conventional account correct? According to one recent critique, conditional dismissals benefit plaintiffs far more than observers realize. *See* Jurianto, Forum Non Conveniens: *Another Look at Conditional Dismissals,* 83 U. Det.-Mercy L. Rev. 369 (2006). Consider two sets of plaintiffs who have identical cases. One immediately commences suit in a foreign forum; the other commences suit in the United States but anticipates a strong *forum non conveniens* defense. As a result of conditional dismissals, isn't the latter plaintiff unquestionably better off? Litigation in the United States, even if ultimately dismissed, may enable the plaintiff to avoid certain defenses that otherwise might be available in the foreign litigation, might grant the plaintiff access to documents that might otherwise be unavailable, and might enhance the likelihood of immediate satisfaction of the judgment.

Is this account persuasive? Or does it exaggerate the effect of conditional dismissals? If there is some plausibility to the account, what (if anything) should U.S. courts do about it? Should the availability of the condition be tied to the strength of the plaintiff's claim to jurisdiction in the United States? Should a court investigate whether the case is being filed in the United States in an effort to extract some favorable conditions for foreign litigation? *Compare supra* pp. 394-408 (discussing the deference analysis). Or should a court simply tolerate such tactics as typical of the sort of jockeying that is inevitable in any litigation?

F. The Contemporary *Forum Non Conveniens* Doctrine: Applicable Law and the *Erie* Doctrine

As discussed elsewhere, the *Erie* doctrine generally requires federal courts sitting in diversity actions to apply the substantive law of the states where they sit, except where a valid federal statute, regulation, or other law applies.[107] No federal *"forum non conveniens"* statute exists,[108] and it is therefore at least arguable that *forum non conveniens* issues should be governed by state law in federal diversity actions (and in state courts). Even if no federal statute or regulation is applicable, the *Erie* doctrine permits federal courts to fashion federal law governing various "procedural" issues;[109] these rules are applicable only in federal courts, and not in state courts.[110] In limited circumstances, federal courts also have the power to fashion substantive federal common law, which preempts inconsistent state law; these rules are applicable in both federal and state courts.[111]

Applying these general principles, there are three basic possibilities for defining the character of the *forum non conveniens* doctrine under *Erie:* (1) state substantive law, applicable in both state and federal courts; (2) federal procedural law, applicable in federal courts, and state law, applicable in state courts; and (3) substantive federal common law, applicable in both federal and state courts. We explore each possibility below.[112]

The character of the *forum non conveniens* doctrine can have substantial practical significance. A number of states have adopted approaches to the *forum non conveniens* doctrine that differ from the *Piper* analysis.[113] In a small number of states, no *forum non conveniens* doctrine is recognized; in others, the doctrine is subject to different basic rules (such as the weight to be accorded a U.S. or foreign plaintiff's choice of forum).[114] Although application of the *forum non conveniens* doctrine involves substantial discretion, the differences between particular state versions of the doctrine and *Piper* can be outcome-determinative.

The Supreme Court has thus far avoided directly deciding the status of the *forum non conveniens* doctrine under the *Erie* doctrine, although it recently provided an arguable indication as to its likely conclusion. In both *Piper* and *Gilbert*, the Court specifically declined to decide whether state or federal law provided the applicable *forum non conveniens* principles in a federal diversity case.[115] In each case, the Court concluded that the relevant state law was identical to the result that it reached as a matter of federal law.[116]

In 1994, however, the Court decided *American Dredging Company v. Miller.*[117] There, it arguably suggested that the *forum non conveniens* doctrine is a rule of federal procedural law, applicable in federal (but not state) courts. The Court's holding was directed at, and apparently limited to, domestic cases. Nevertheless, its rationale may apply in international cases.

---

107. *Erie R.R. Co. v. Tompkins*, 304 U.S. 64 (1938); *Stewart Organization, Inc. v. Ricoh Corp.*, 487 U.S. 22 (1988); *supra* pp. 10-11.

108. 28 U.S.C. §1404(a) applies only to transfers between federal districts (and not to dismissals in favor of foreign forums). *See infra* pp. 530-531.

109. *See supra* pp. 10-11; *Stewart Organization, Inc. v. Ricoh Corp.*, 487 U.S. 22 (1988).

110. *See supra* pp. 10-13.

111. *See supra* pp. 11-13; *Boyle v. United Technologies Corp.*, 487 U.S. 500, 504 (1988).

112. *See infra* pp. 454-457.

113. *See supra* p. 372.

114. *See supra* p. 372.

115. *See Piper Aircraft Co. v. Reyno*, 454 U.S. at 248 n.13; *Gulf Oil Corp. v. Gilbert*, 330 U.S. at 509. In one subsequent decision the Court also avoided passing directly on the subject. *Chick Kam Choo v. Exxon Corp.*, 486 U.S. 140 (1988).

116. In each case, the Court had to strain to find that the relevant state law was identical to federal law. Braucher, *The Inconvenient Federal Forum*, 60 Harv. L. Rev. 908, 928 (1947) (noting that lower courts in *Koster* had concluded that state law was different and that in *Gilbert* directly relevant state precedents were contrary).

117. 510 U.S. 443 (1994).

In *American Dredging*, the Court considered whether a state court was bound to apply the federal doctrine of *forum non conveniens* in a domestic admiralty action. The Court acknowledged that in the admiralty context, federal maritime law preempted state law in ways not true (after *Erie*) in diversity actions: general federal admiralty law preempts state laws that "work material prejudice to the characteristic features of the general maritime law or interferes with the proper harmony and uniformity of that law in its international and interstate relations."[118] The Court nevertheless concluded that there was no basis for fashioning a substantive federal doctrine of *forum non conveniens* in state court domestic admiralty actions, reasoning that *forum non conveniens* was not a peculiarly maritime doctrine and that there was no pressing need for domestic uniformity.[119]

American Dredging appears to leave state courts generally free to ignore federal *forum non conveniens* principles and apply state law in domestic admiralty actions. Moreover, the Court also suggested that federal courts were free to continue to apply a federal *forum non conveniens* doctrine; the rationale was that the doctrine was a "procedural" rule. In Justice Scalia's words: "[*Forum non conveniens*] is procedural rather than substantive."[120] He continued, reasoning that, "[a]t bottom, the doctrine of *forum non conveniens* is nothing more or less than a supervening venue provision, permitting displacement of the ordinary rules of venue when, in light of certain conditions, the trial court thinks that jurisdiction ought to be declined. But venue is a matter that goes to process rather than substantive rights — determining which among various competent courts will decide the case."[121]

In the last paragraph of its opinion, the Court observed that *American Dredging* only involved domestic entities, and that the preferred alternative forum was in the United States. Nevertheless, the Court declined the Solicitor General's request to limit its holding to cases involving domestic entities: "We think it unnecessary to do that. Since the parties to this suit are domestic entities it is quite impossible for our holding to be any broader."[122]

After *American Dredging*, it can be argued that the *forum non conveniens* doctrine will be regarded by the Court as a rule of federal procedural law in international cases. On the other hand, it is also arguable that federal interests in foreign commerce and foreign relations provide the basis for a substantive federal common law rule of *forum non conveniens*.[123] But, if federal interests in uniform domestic admiralty rules were an insufficient basis for rules of federal common law, reaching a different result in international cases will require attributing substantial weight to federal interests in foreign relations and foreign commerce. Reread *Sequihua v. Texaco Oil, Inc.*, which is excerpted above, in considering these issues.

SEQUIHUA v. TEXACO, INC.
847 F. Supp. 61 (S.D. Tex. 1994) [excerpted supra pp. 63-65]

Notes on Sequihua

1. Forum non conveniens *as a rule of substantive state law.* A few federal court decisions (usually older ones) have held that, under *Erie*, the *forum non conveniens* doctrine should

---

118. 510 U.S. at 447 (quoting *Southern Pacific Co. v. Jensen*, 244 U.S. 205, 216 (1917)).
119. 510 U.S. at 450-457.
120. 510 U.S. at 452.
121. 510 U.S. at 453.
122. 510 U.S. at 457.
123. *See infra* pp. 457-458.

be governed by state substantive law. *E.g., Weiss v. Routh,* 149 F.2d 193 (2d Cir. 1945) (L. Hand, J.); *Mizokami Bros. v. Mobay Chem. Corp.,* 483 F. Supp. 201 (W.D. Mo. 1980), *aff'd,* 660 F.2d 712 (8th Cir. 1981). Consider Learned Hand's argument for why state substantive law should govern *forum non conveniens* issues in federal court:

> It might well be argued that those considerations which will set a court in motion are peculiar and personal to itself, and that it does not follow that what is enough to move a state court to act, should be enough to move a federal; or vice versa. Such a doctrine would, however, imply that the decision to accept jurisdiction is not controlled by any principle and may be at the judge's whim; and that would certainly be too strong a statement. Here, as elsewhere, although judicial discretion does indeed imply that the limits are not rigidly fixed, it does not mean that there are none; and in dealing with the questions at bar, we are to remember the purpose of conformity in "diversity cases." It is that the accident of citizenship shall not change the outcome: a purpose which extends as much to determining whether the court shall act at all, as to how it shall decide, if it does. For this reason it seems to us that we should follow the New York decisions. *Weiss v. Routh,* 149 F.2d 193, 194-195 (2d Cir. 1945).

Is this persuasive? Given the vital bearing of the *forum non conveniens* doctrine on many international disputes, don't the objectives of the *Erie* doctrine require application of local state law?

2. Forum non conveniens *as a rule of federal procedural law.* Most courts have concluded that in federal courts the *forum non conveniens* doctrine is defined by federal procedural law. *See Esfeld v. Costa Crociere, S.P.A.,* 289 F.3d 1300, 1306-1315 (11th Cir. 2002); *Ravelo Monegro v. Rosa,* 211 F.3d 509, 511-512 (9th Cir. 2000); *Sibaja v. Dow Chemical Co.,* 757 F.2d 1215 (11th Cir. 1985). Moreover, as noted above, the Supreme Court has suggested, in *American Dredging Co. v. Miller,* 510 U.S. 443 (1994), that *forum non conveniens* is a procedural issue in domestic actions, governed in state courts by state law, and in federal courts by federal procedural law.

3. *Should* **forum non conveniens** *be regarded as a rule of federal procedural law?* Why is it that federal courts should apply a federal rule of *forum non conveniens*? Recall that issues of forum selection are often outcome-determinative; parties devote enormous resources to influencing forum selection and, in many cases, the forum in which a dispute is heard has a decisive effect on its resolution. *See supra* pp. 1-4. Recall also that, in at least some states, a local citizen enjoys a fundamental right of access to the local courts. In these circumstances, is it persuasive to permit judge-made notions of judicial administration to override state law?

(a) Argument in American Dredging *that* forum non conveniens *is "procedural."* *American Dredging Co.* reasoned that:

> [*Forum non conveniens*] is procedural rather than substantive, and it is most unlikely to produce uniform results. . . . At bottom, the doctrine of *forum non conveniens* is nothing more or less than a supervening venue provision, permitting displacement of the ordinary rules of venue when, in light of certain conditions, the trial court thinks that jurisdiction ought to be declined. But venue is a matter that goes to process rather than substantive rights—determining which among various competent courts will decide the case. . . . [T]o tell the truth, *forum non conveniens* cannot really be *relied* upon in making decisions about secondary conduct—in deciding, for example, where to sue or where one is subject to being sued. The discretionary nature of the doctrine, combined with the multifariousness of the factors relevant to its application . . . make uniformity and predictability of outcome almost impossible. 510 U.S. 443, 452-455 (1994).

Is this persuasive? Does it explain satisfactorily why issues of *forum non conveniens* are to be decided differently in federal courts than in state courts? Does anything in *American Dredging* meet Learned Hand's argument, excerpted above? Consider the following:

> Matters of "substance" and matters of "procedure" are much talked about in the books as though they defined a great divide cutting across the domain of law. But, of course, "substance" and "procedure" are the same key-words to very different problems. . . . [We should] put[] to one side abstractions regarding "substance" and "procedure." . . . [The *Erie*] policy [is] so important to our federalism [that it] must be kept free from entanglements with analytical or terminological niceties. *Guaranty Trust Co. v. York*, 326 U.S. 99, 108-110 (1945) (Frankfurter, J.).

(b) Erie's "twin aims"—state-federal forum shopping and inequitable administration of law. The Supreme Court has in recent decades generally emphasized the "twin aims" of *Erie*: "discouragement of forum-shopping and avoidance of the inequitable administration of the laws." *Hanna v. Plumer*, 380 U.S. 460, 468 (1965); *supra* pp. 10-11. Consider how the analysis in *American Dredging* affects these twin objectives. Is it likely that plaintiffs will forum shop for state courts that do not have *forum non conveniens* doctrines, or that have different *forum non conveniens* doctrines than federal courts? The answer is unequivocally yes: state-federal forum shopping will occur with a vengeance. That is why the plaintiffs in *Piper, Sequihua*, and *Alfaro* all brought suit initially in state courts.

Is it likely that defendants will seek to remove actions brought in state court to federal court, where state *forum non conveniens* doctrines do not exist or are less favorable than *Piper*? Again, the answer is plainly yes. That is what happened in *Piper* and *Sequihua*. Where diversity, alienage, or federal question jurisdiction exists, removal will generally be possible. *See supra* p. 9. Consequently, identical cases will be decided differently depending upon a party's citizenship; compare *Alfaro* with *Sequihua*, where federal and state courts reached opposite results with respect to identical claims. Indeed, if one accepts the view that many claims dismissed on *forum non conveniens* grounds are simply dropped, *see supra* p. 380, note 73, some claims will never even be heard, while identical ones receive substantial U.S. jury awards.

(c) Federal interests in federal judicial administration. A good appellate analysis of the *Erie* issues raised by the *forum non conveniens* doctrine was *In re Air Crash Disaster Near New Orleans*, 821 F.2d 1147 (5th Cir. 1987), where the Court of Appeals concluded that the doctrine was governed by federal procedural law. The Court acknowledged that this result would produce "a tremendous disparity of result between the two court systems [*i.e.*, state and federal]: One case will proceed to judgment and the other will be dismissed to a foreign land." 821 F.2d at 1157. Nevertheless, the Court reasoned that "the interests of the federal forum in self-regulation, in administrative independence, and in self-management are more important than the disruption of uniformity created by applying federal *forum non conveniens* in diversity cases." 821 F.2d at 1159. Is this reasoning satisfactory? Recall that the *forum non conveniens* doctrine is, in federal courts, a judge-made creature that involves a court's refusal to exercise jurisdiction that Congress has granted it. Is it proper that a party, upon whom Congress has conferred a right of action in federal court, be denied that right because of a judicial rule of "self-management"?

Recall also the *forum non conveniens* doctrine as enunciated in *Piper*. In particular, note that the doctrine contains specific rules regarding the deference owed to a U.S. plaintiff's choice of forum and the need to balance local versus foreign regulatory interests. *See supra* pp. 419-423. Are these really attributes of a rule of "self-management"? Are they in fact not rules of choice of law and jurisdictional competence?

(d) State-state forum shopping. Suppose that Judge Learned Hand's rationale, quoted above from *Weiss v. Routh,* is accepted and state substantive law is held to govern *forum non conveniens* issues in both state and federal actions. Will not forum shopping still occur? Will not plaintiffs seek out states like Montana that do not permit, or that only permit restrictive versions of, the *forum non conveniens* doctrine? Is this state-state forum shopping not an even greater evil than state-federal forum shopping? Even if that is correct, will not state-state forum shopping exist even under *American Dredging,* where plaintiffs expect to be able to avoid removal?

4. *Applicability of* **American Dredging** *in international cases.* As described above, *American Dredging* held that state courts were free to apply state *forum non conveniens* rules in domestic admiralty actions. The Court suggested that federal courts were similarly free to apply a federal *forum non conveniens* doctrine. The essential basis for the Court's holding was that the *forum non conveniens* doctrine is "procedural rather than substantive" and "nothing more or less than a supervening venue provision, permitting displacement of the ordinary rules of venue." Does this reasoning apply in international cases, where the putative alternative forum is not a U.S. court? Venue implies selecting the proper locality within a single national judicial system. It does *not* imply a nation's courts abstaining entirely from jurisdiction. Moreover, *see supra* pp. 419-423, in international cases, *Piper* requires consideration of national regulatory competence and interests — factors that do not exist in domestic cases. Given this, is *American Dredging* relevant to international cases like *Piper*?

5. *Substantive federal common law basis for* **forum non conveniens** *defense.* Should state courts be obliged to follow the *federal* rule of *forum non conveniens* in international cases? Is there any basis for federal courts to articulate a rule of substantive federal common law in international cases, requiring state courts to dismiss claims by foreign plaintiffs that impose undue inconvenience on U.S. courts and parties or that implicate sufficiently substantial foreign sovereign interests?

As discussed above, in order to sustain a federal common law rule, it would generally be necessary to demonstrate that *forum non conveniens* decisions arise in a "uniquely federal" field and that disregarding federal standards would significantly conflict with important federal policies. *See Boyle v. United Technologies Corp.,* 487 U.S. 500 (1988); *supra* pp. 11-13. Are these standards satisfied by the *forum non conveniens* doctrine in international cases? Consider the analysis in *Sequihua.* Does it support a general federal common law rule of *forum non conveniens,* or is its rationale limited to cases where unusual effects on foreign state interests are involved?

Recall *Piper*'s concern that U.S. multinationals will become the targets of tort litigants from around the world, seeking application of U.S. legal standards and procedures to non-U.S. conduct. Does this sufficiently implicate federal interests in U.S. foreign commerce to warrant a federal *forum non conveniens* rule? Recall the governmental interest-balancing and concern for foreign regulatory structures reflected in *Wyeth.* Does this demonstrate that *forum non conveniens* decisions arise in a "uniquely federal" field of foreign relations?

Assuming that the *forum non conveniens* doctrine did arise in a uniquely federal field, would a state court's refusal to apply *Piper*'s formulation of the doctrine "significantly conflict" with federal policies? Does the answer depend on the character of the divergence from *Piper*?

6. Forum non conveniens *dismissals in actions removed to federal court.* Note that in *Sequihua,* the plaintiffs had commenced their actions in state court, but the defendants had removed to federal court. In these circumstances, is it appropriate to dismiss the action to foreign fora? If a state forum stands ready to hear the dispute, then why should a federal court dismiss to a foreign forum? Or should the federal court merely remand to the state court? *See* Burbank, *Jurisdictional Conflict and Jurisdictional Equilibration: Paths to a Via Media,* 26 Hous. J. Int'l L. 385 (2004).

G.   Venue in International Litigation in U.S. Courts

U.S. courts will not adjudicate a case unless applicable U.S. venue requirements, specifying the proper location for the lawsuit, are satisfied. Venue and jurisdiction are often said to be distinguishable: jurisdiction refers to the power of a court to adjudicate a dispute, while venue refers to the place where jurisdiction may be exercised.[124] Venue provisions are designed principally to protect litigants, particularly defendants, from suits in inconvenient forums.[125]

The provisions of federal venue statutes specify the judicial district in which an action may be brought (assuming that personal and subject matter jurisdiction requirements are satisfied). Thus, in domestic diversity cases, venue generally lies in the district where a defendant resides (if all defendants reside in the same state) or where the claim arose.[126] In nondiversity actions, the venue rules are the same as for diversity cases except that venue also will lie where any defendant "may be found" if no district would otherwise be available,[127] or as provided for in specialized venue provisions of particular federal statutes.[128]

Venue in suits against alien defendants is usually not a significant issue in international litigation in federal court. The so-called Alien Venue Statute provides that "[a]n alien may be sued in any district."[129] This enables a plaintiff to initiate an action against an alien in virtually any district in the United States that the plaintiff chooses. It is clear that the statute applies to corporate defendants, as well as to individual defendants.[130] It also appears that the Alien Venue Statute applies in cases involving both alien and U.S. defendants: The lower courts have suggested that, in these circumstances, the residence of the U.S. defendant is the sole relevant criteria for venue purposes.[131]

In general, the expansive Alien Venue Statute has been interpreted to override the more restrictive venue provisions of specific federal statutes.[132] In the Supreme Court's words: "§1391(d) is properly regarded, not as a venue restriction at all, but rather as a declaration of the long-established rule that suits against aliens are wholly outside the

---

124. Clermont, *Restating Territorial Jurisdiction and Venue for State and Federal Courts,* 66 Cornell L. Rev. 411 (1981); *Lindahl v. Office of Personnel Management,* 105 S. Ct. 1620, 1634 n.30 (1985).

125. *See Brunette Machine Works v. Kockum Indus., Inc.,* 406 U.S. 706 (1972); *Leroy v. Great Western United Corp.,* 443 U.S. 173 (1979) ("In most instances, the purpose of a statutorily specified venue is to protect the *defendant* against the risk that a plaintiff will select an unfair or inconvenient place of trial."); C. Wright et al., *Federal Practice and Procedure* §§3801-3829 (2007 & Supp. 2010).

126. 28 U.S.C. §1391(a).

127. 28 U.S.C. §1391(b).

128. *E.g.,* 28 U.S.C. §1400(b) (patent); 15 U.S.C. §15 (antitrust); 15 U.S.C. §22 (antitrust); 28 U.S.C. §1400(a) (copyright).

129. 28 U.S.C. §1391(d). *See* Leff, *The Alien Venue Statute: An Historical Analysis of Federal Venue Provisions and Alien Rights,* 3 N.Y.L. Sch. J. Int'l & Comp. L. 307 (1982).

130. *Brunette Machine Works, Ltd. v. Kockum Indus., Inc.,* 406 U.S. 706 (1972); *Ohio Reinsurance Corp. v. British Nat'l Ins. Co.,* 587 F. Supp. 710 (S.D.N.Y. 1984); *Brunswick Corp. v. Suzuki Motor Co., Ltd.,* 575 F. Supp. 1412 (E.D. Wis. 1983); *Mowrey v. Johnson & Johnson,* 524 F. Supp. 771 (W.D. Pa. 1981); *Holt v. Klosters Rederi A/S,* 355 F. Supp. 354 (W.D. Mich. 1973).

131. *Mowrey v. Johnson & Johnson,* 524 F. Supp. 771 (W.D. Pa. 1981); *Japan Gas Lighters Ass'n v. Ronson Corp.,* 257 F. Supp. 219 (D.N.J. 1966); C. Wright et al., *Federal Practice and Procedure* §3810 (2007 & Supp. 2010).

132. *Brunette Machine Works v. Kockum Indus., Inc.,* 406 U.S. 706 (1972) (Alien Venue Statute overrides venue provisions of patent statute). *See Go-Video, Inc. v. Akai Elec. Co.,* 885 F.2d 1406 (9th Cir. 1989) (Alien Venue Statute supplements venue provisions of Clayton Act); *In re Automotive Refinishing Paint Antitrust Litig.,* 2002 WL 31261330, at *7 (E.D. Pa. 2002), *aff'd,* 358 F.3d 288 (3d Cir. 2004) (same).

operation of all the federal venue laws, general and special."[133] The rationale for this result is that many federal venue provisions rely on the defendants' residence. Because aliens usually lack any U.S. residence, affording them protection under ordinary venue statutes would often make venue in *any* U.S. district improper. Courts have understandably rejected such a result.[134]

One important exception to the general applicability of the Alien Venue Statute arises under the Foreign Sovereign Immunities Act ("FSIA").[135] The FSIA addressed the issue of venue with respect to foreign state defendants by adding a new subsection to the general federal venue statute. That provision, reproduced in the document supplement, states generally that a foreign state may be sued in any district in which a substantial part of the events occurred or a substantial part of the property at issue is situated (it also contains special provisions for cases involving (1) foreign vessels or cargo; (2) agencies or instrumentalities licensed to do business in a jurisdiction; and (3) actions against foreign states or political subdivisions).

The legislative history of the FSIA makes it clear that Congress intended that the specific venue provisions applicable to foreign sovereigns should substitute for the Alien Venue Statute insofar as foreign sovereigns (including their agencies or instrumentalities) are involved.[136] Lower federal courts have routinely assumed that the specific provisions of §1391(f), rather than the general provisions of §1391(d), apply when suits are brought against foreign sovereigns.[137]

Finally, alien *plaintiffs* in U.S. courts often encounter more significant venue obstacles than domestic plaintiffs. There is no federal venue statute, comparable to the Alien Venue Statute, dealing with venue for alien plaintiffs. As a result, alien plaintiffs must rely on generally applicable venue provisions. However, aliens typically have no U.S. residence and, consequently, cannot rely on venue provisions permitting suit at the plaintiff's residence.[138] Instead, they ordinarily can bring suit only in districts where all defendants reside or where the plaintiff's claim arose.[139]

---

133. *Brunette Mach. Works, Ltd. v. Kockum Indus., Inc.*, 406 U.S. 706, 714 (1972).

134. One student commentator has suggested that the Alien Venue Statute unconstitutionally discriminates against aliens in violation of the Fifth Amendment. Note, *The Alien Venue Statute: An Historical Analysis of Federal Venue Provisions and Alien Rights*, 3 N.Y.L. Sch. J. Int'l & Comp. L. 307 (1982). No court appears to have adopted this suggestion.

135. The FSIA and the doctrine of foreign sovereign immunity are discussed in detail in Chapter 3 *supra*.

136. *See* H.R. Rep. No. 94-1487 at 31, *reprinted in* 1976 U.S. Code and Admin. News at 6630.

137. *See, e.g., Proyecfin de Venezuela, SA v. Banco Industrial de Venezuela, SA*, 760 F.2d 390, 395 n.4 (2d Cir. 1985); *Wye Oak Technology, Inc. v. Republic of Iraq*, 2010 WL 2613323 (E.D. Va. June 29, 2010); *Falcoal, Inc. v. Turkiye Komur Isletmeleri Kurumi*, 660 F. Supp. 1536 (S.D Tex. 1987); *Acosta v. Grammer*, 402 F. Supp. 736 (E.D. Mo. 1975).

138. *See Galveston v. H. & S.A. Ry. Co v. Gonzales*, 151 U.S. 496 (1894); *Arevalo-Franco v. INS*, 889 F.2d 589, 590 (5th Cir. 1990); *Williams v. United States*, 704 F.2d 1222, 1226 (11th Cir. 1983).

139. *See, e.g., Fleifel v. Vessa*, 503 F. Supp. 129 (W.D. Va. 1980); *Akbar v. New York Magazine*, 490 F. Supp. 60 (D.D.C. 1980); *Acosta v. Grammer*, 402 F. Supp. 736 (E.D. Mo. 1975).

5

International Forum Selection Agreements[1]

In both domestic and international commercial matters, parties frequently "stipulate in advance to submit their controversies for resolution within a particular jurisdiction."[2] Contractual provisions selecting a particular judicial forum for the adjudication of disputes are typically referred to as "forum selection," "jurisdiction," or "choice of forum" clauses. This chapter discusses forum selection agreements in international litigation.

An important and closely related category of contractual provisions concerns international arbitration agreements, which are examined in Chapter 13. Both international choice of court and international arbitration clauses involve consensual agreements whereby the parties undertake to submit some or all of their disputes for resolution in a specified contractual forum—either a national court or an arbitral tribunal.[3] Both categories of agreements are widely used in international business transactions and serve important commercial purposes. At the same time, both types of clause give rise to significant legal issues and (on occasion) uncertainties.

---

1. Commentary on forum selection clauses includes, *e.g.,* A. Bell, *Forum Shopping and Venue in Transnational Litigation* (2003); Buxbaum, *Forum Selection in International Contract Litigation: The Role of Judicial Discretion,* 12 Willamette J. Int'l L. & Disp. Res. 185 (2004); Gilbert, *Choice of Forum Clauses in International and Interstate Contracts,* 65 Ky. L.J. 1 (1976); Gruson, *Forum-Selection Clauses in International and Interstate Commercial Agreements,* 1982 U. Ill. L. Rev. 133; Heiser, *Forum Selection Clauses in State Courts: Limitations on Enforcement After* Stewart *and* Carnival Cruise, 45 Fla. L. Rev. 361 (1993); A. Lowenfeld, *International Litigation and the Quest for Reasonableness* 199-220 (1996); Mullenix, *Another Choice of Forum, Another Choice of Law: Consensual Adjudicatory Procedure in Federal Courts,* 57 Fordham L. Rev. 291 (1988); Nadelmann, *Choice-of-Court Clauses in the United States: The Road to* Zapata, 21 Am. J. Comp. L. 124 (1973); Panek, *Forum Selection Clauses in Diversity Actions,* 36 J. Marshall L. Rev. 941 (2003); Park, *Bridging the Gap in Forum Selection: Harmonizing Arbitration and Court Selection,* 8 Transnat'l L. & Contemp. Probs. 19 (1998); Perillo, *Selected Forum Agreements in Western Europe,* 13 Am. J. Comp. L. 162 (1964); Sturley, *Strengthening the Presumption of Validity for Choice of Forum Clauses,* 23 J. Mar. L. & Com. 131 (1992); Shantar, *Forum Selection Clauses: Damages in Lieu of Dismissal,* 82 B.U. L. Rev. 1063 (2002); W. Park, *International Forum Selection* (Kluwer 1995); Solimine, *Forum-Selection Clauses and the Privatization of Procedure,* 25 Cornell Int'l L.J. 51 (1992); Taylor, *The Forum Selection Clause: A Tale of Two Concepts,* 66 Temp. L. Rev. 785 (1993); Yackee, *Choice of Law Considerations in the Validity and Enforcement of International Forum Selection Agreements: Whose Law Applies?,* 9 UCLA J. Int'l L. & Foreign Aff. 43 (2004); Hague Conference on Private International Law, *Choice of Court Agreements in International Litigation: Their Use and Legal Problems to Which They Give Rise in the Context of the Interim Text,* Preliminary Document No. 18 (www.hcch.net/e/workprog/jdgm.html).

2. *Burger King Corp. v. Rudzewicz,* 471 U.S. 462, 472 n.14 (1985).

3. For a discussion of the differences and similarities between arbitration and forum selection agreements, *see* G. Born, *International Arbitration and Forum Selection Agreements: Drafting and Enforcing* (3d ed. 2010).

A. Introduction and Historical Background

1. Exclusive and Nonexclusive Forum Selection Agreements

There is a fundamental distinction between *exclusive* and *nonexclusive* forum selection agreements. An exclusive (or mandatory) forum clause requires that any litigation takes place only in the specified forum, and nowhere else.[4] In contrast, a nonexclusive forum selection agreement permits litigation of disputes in a particular forum but does not preclude the parties from pursuing litigation in other courts if those courts also have jurisdiction.[5]

A nonexclusive forum selection clause (also called a "prorogation agreement" or a "permissive" forum clause) involves promises by one or both parties to submit to the jurisdiction of a specified court, without any undertaking to forgo litigation elsewhere. In many cases, a nonexclusive forum clause will expressly submit a party to the personal jurisdiction of the contractual forum; where no express submission is present, such submission is virtually always implicit.[6] As discussed in Chapter 2, U.S. courts have typically enforced prorogation agreements, under applicable local law and the Due Process Clause, absent proof of fraud or coercion.[7]

Determining whether a forum clause is exclusive or nonexclusive is in part an issue of interpretation, dependent largely on the wording of the provision. Nevertheless, different jurisdictions have adopted different presumptions concerning the interpretation of forum selection agreements.

U.S. courts have long been reluctant to hold that a forum clause is exclusive, and often do so only if a provision includes language specifically excluding litigation in courts other than the chosen forum.[8] Thus, several lower U.S. courts have discerned the following "general rule": "When only jurisdiction is specified the clause will generally not be enforced without some further language indicating the parties' intent to make jurisdiction exclusive."[9] As Judge Weinfeld has explained, "the normal construction of the jurisdiction rules includes a presumption that, where jurisdiction exists, it cannot be ousted or waived absent a clear indication of such a purpose."[10]

---

4. Forum selection clauses may also be exclusive as to one party, while leaving the other party free to initiate litigation in courts other than the selected forum. *E.g., Heller Financial, Inc. v. Midwhey Powder Co.,* 883 F.2d 1286 (7th Cir. 1989); *Product Components Inc. v. Regency Door & Hardware Inc.,* 568 F. Supp. 651, 652 (S.D. Ind. 1983) ("The parties agree that all controversies arising hereunder may, at Seller's option, be determined in Indiana and Buyer hereby expressly consents to the jurisdiction of Indiana courts.").

5. *See infra* pp. 467, 485.

6. *E.g., Northwestern Nat'l Life Ins. Co. v. Donovan,* 916 F.2d 372, 376-377 (7th Cir. 1990); *Luce v. Edelstein,* 802 F.2d 49, 57 (2d Cir. 1986); *Merrill Lynch, Pierce, Fenner & Smith Inc. v. Lecopulos,* 553 F.2d 842, 844 (2d Cir. 1977); *Paribas Corp. v. Shelton Ranch Corp.,* 742 F. Supp. 86, 90 (S.D.N.Y. 1990) ("Forum selection clauses are valid and enforceable consents to jurisdiction in the New York courts").

7. *See supra* pp. 115-116.

8. A number of lower courts have held that particular forum selection clauses are nonexclusive. *E.g., McDonnell Douglas Corp. v. Islamic Republic of Iran,* 758 F.2d 341, 343 (8th Cir. 1985) ("[a]ny difference . . . should be settled through Iranian courts"); *Citro Florida v. Citrovale, SA,* 760 F.2d 1231, 1232 (11th Cir. 1985) ("[p]lace of jurisdiction is São Paulo/Brazil"); *Keaty v. Freeport Indonesia,* 503 F.2d 955, 956 (5th Cir. 1974) (per curiam) ("the parties submit to the jurisdiction of the courts of New York"); *Caldas & Sons, Inc. v. Willingham,* 791 F. Supp. 614 (N.D. Miss. 1992) ("the laws and courts of Zurich are applicable").

9. *John Boutari and Son, Wines and Spirits, SA v. Attiki Importers and Distributors Inc.,* 22 F.3d 51 (2d Cir. 1994) (quoting *Docksider, Ltd. v. Sea Technology, Ltd.,* 875 F.2d 762, 764 (9th Cir. 1987)). *See also K & V Scientific Co. v. Bayerische Motoren Werke AG,* 314 F.3d 494, 498-499 (10th Cir. 2002); *IntraComm, Inc. v. Bajaj,* 492 F.3d 285, 290 (4th Cir. 2007).

10. *City of New York v. Pullman, Inc.,* 477 F. Supp. 438, 442 n.11 (S.D.N.Y. 1979). For a comparative perspective, *see* Lenhoff, *The Parties' Choice of Forum: "Prorogation Agreements,"* 15 Rutgers L. Rev. 414 (1961).

Other lower U.S. courts have not demanded such unequivocal evidence of exclusivity. Thus, a number of decisions hold that various combinations of the terms "shall" and "any" are sufficient to render a forum selection agreement exclusive.[11] A few courts have been less demanding and construed forum clauses as exclusive even when no language clearly indicated this result.[12] Some U.S. courts have also applied non-U.S. law to the question whether or not a forum selection clause is exclusive, including when foreign law would produce a different result from U.S. law.[13]

In contrast to these U.S. approaches, civil law jurisdictions have generally treated forum selection clauses as presumptively exclusive. Article 23(1) of EU Council Regulation 44/2001 provides that a forum selection clause selecting an EU Member State court presumptively grants exclusive jurisdiction to that court (requiring other EU Member State courts to decline jurisdiction); this presumption may be overcome by express agreement upon a nonexclusive forum selection agreement, but in the absence of such agreement, any forum selection clause will be exclusive.[14] Other civil law legislation is similar,[15] as is the proposed Hague Convention on Choice of Court Agreements (discussed below).[16]

2. Reasons for Entering into Forum Selection Agreements

Forum selection clauses are widely regarded as essential to international business transactions; they can provide one or both parties to an agreement with very important benefits. As a consequence, many international commercial contracts include either a forum selection or an arbitration agreement.[17]

In some circumstances, bargaining power or negotiating ability may allow a party to obtain an exclusive choice of forum clause selecting the forum it finds most convenient or advantageous. Parties to international agreements typically seek to have disputes resolved

---

11. *E.g., American Soda, LLP v. U.S. Filter Wastewater Group, Inc.*, 428 F.3d 921, 927 (10th Cir. 2005) (finding exclusivity); *Seward v. Devine*, 888 F.2d 957, 962 (2d Cir. 1989) ("the New York State Supreme Court . . . shall have jurisdiction over all litigation which shall arise out of any disputes . . ."); *Sterling Forest Ass'n, Ltd. v. Barnett-Range Corp.*, 840 F.2d 249 (4th Cir. 1988) ("The parties agree that in any dispute jurisdiction and venue shall be in California" held exclusive; contrary district court interpretation reversed as "patently erroneous" and "evidence of a continuing hostility to forum selection clauses"); *Milk 'n' More, Inc. v. Beavert*, 963 F.2d 1342 (10th Cir. 1992) ("venue shall be proper under this agreement in Johnson County" held exclusive); *Kirk v. NCI Leasing, Inc.*, 2005 WL 3115859, at *3 (D. Kan. 2005) ("the clause is mandatory and requires that all disputes arising out of or related to the Agreement be brought and litigated in Seward County, Kansas").

12. *E.g., Frietsch v. Refco, Inc.*, 56 F.3d 825, 827 (7th Cir. 1995) ("[P]lace of jurisdiction is the registered office of the trustee [in Germany], to the extent permissible under the law."); *General Electric Co. v. G. Siempelkamp GmbH*, 29 F.3d 1095 (6th Cir. 1994) ("Place of jurisdiction for all disputes arising in connection with the contract shall be at the principal place of business of the supplier."); *Paper Exp., Ltd. v. Pfankuch Maschinen GmbH*, 972 F.2d 753, 755 (7th Cir. 1992) ("In all disputes arising out of the contractual relationship, the action shall be filed in the court which has jurisdiction for the principal place of business of the supplier. . . . The supplier also has the right to commence an action against the purchaser at the purchaser's principal place of business."); *Commerce Consultants Int'l, Inc. v. Vetrerie Riunite, SpA*, 867 F.2d 697 (D.C. Cir. 1989) ("The validity, enforceability and interpretation of this agreement shall be determined and governed by the appropriate court of Verona, Italy.").

13. *E.g., TH Agriculture & Nutrition, LLC v. ACE European Group Ltd.*, 416 F. Supp. 2d 1054 (D. Kan. 2006) (applying Netherlands law and EU Council Regulation 44/2001 to hold ambiguous forum selection clause exclusive); *Albemarle Corp. v. Astra Zeneca UK Ltd*, 628 F.3d 643 (4th Cir. 2010) (same).

14. EU Council Regulation 44/2001, Art. 23.

15. Lugano Convention, Art. 17; Swiss Law on Private International Law, Art. 5 ("unless the agreement provides otherwise, the agreed court has exclusive jurisdiction").

16. Hague Choice of Court Agreements Convention, June 30, 2005, 44 I.L.M. 1294, Art. 3. *See infra* p. 468.

17. *See* G. Born, *International Arbitration and Forum Selection Agreements: Drafting and Enforcing* 1-4 (3d ed. 2010).

in the courts of their own "home" jurisdiction.[18] Doing so provides a party with a convenient, familiar forum where there may also be perceptions (or the reality) of a "home-court" advantage over foreign litigants.

Even if it is not possible to have disputes resolved in one party's home forum, selection of a neutral forum and avoidance of courts that are highly undesirable to one or both parties is also attractive. In those circumstances, a choice of forum clause provides private parties with a measure of certainty and predictability, and permits parties to avoid forums that are inexperienced, corrupt, or subject to inordinate delays. Particularly when coupled with a choice of law agreement,[19] a forum selection clause removes uncertainties about jurisdiction, procedural rules, and other matters. In the words of the Supreme Court, "[a] contractual provision specifying in advance the forum in which disputes shall be litigated and the law to be applied is . . . an almost indispensable precondition to achievement of the orderliness and predictability essential to any international business transaction."[20]

Forum clauses can also reduce expense and delay in litigation. A forum selection agreement may reduce the likelihood of protracted disputes over jurisdiction, permitting the parties more promptly to focus on the merits of the case without expensive procedural distractions. Moreover, a forum selection agreement makes it more likely that a given dispute will be resolved in a single forum, thus reducing the risk of costly parallel litigation in two or more courts.[21]

It is obvious, but nonetheless occasionally forgotten, that a choice of forum clause is not a choice of law clause, nor is a choice of law clause a forum selection clause. A number of lower courts have held that a choice of forum clause does not constitute the parties' agreement that the chosen forum's law should also govern their relations. Conversely, an agreement as to governing law does not, under either state law or the Due Process Clause, necessarily provide a submission to the jurisdiction of the courts of the chosen state.[22] Agreement on a forum's governing law does, however, sometimes provide at least a measure of evidence that litigation in that forum was foreseeable, for purposes of due process "minimum contacts" analysis.[23] And, agreement on a contractual forum is sometimes held to constitute an implied choice of law.[24]

3. Historical Development of Enforceability of Forum Selection Agreements

The rules governing enforceability of forum clauses have evolved significantly over the past century. Moreover, depending upon applicable law, these rules continue to vary within the United States and internationally. Some states historically regarded, and a very few continue to regard, forum selection clauses as per se unenforceable, while other states apply varying standards of enforceability.[25] In addition, the enforceability of forum clauses in federal courts raises complex questions under the *Erie* doctrine.[26]

---

18. *The Bremen v. Zapata Off-Shore Co.*, 407 U.S. 1, 11-12 (1972) ("Not surprisingly, foreign businessmen prefer, as do we, to have disputes resolved in their own courts, but if that choice is not available, then in a neutral forum with expertise in the subject matter.").

19. Choice-of-law agreements are discussed at *infra* pp. 758-776.

20. *Scherk v. Alberto-Culver Co.*, 417 U.S. 506, 516 (1974).

21. *See* G. Born, *International Arbitration and Forum Selection Agreements: Drafting and Enforcing* 3-4 (3d ed. 2010).

22. *See supra* pp. 108-109.

23. *Burger King Corp. v. Rudzewizc*, 471 U.S. 462, 472 (1985); *supra* pp. 172-173.

24. *See infra* pp. 762-763.

25. *See infra* pp. 465-471.

26. *See infra* pp. 528-546.

a. Historic U.S. Common Law Rule That Forum Selection Agreements Are Unenforceable. U.S. courts were historically hostile to forum clauses, both in international and domestic disputes.[27] Until fairly recently, both exclusive and nonexclusive forum selection agreements were almost uniformly held per se unenforceable in the United States.[28] This paralleled judicial hostility toward arbitration agreements, which were also generally unenforceable during this period.[29]

Until the middle of the twentieth century, the rule against enforcement of forum selection clauses was almost unanimously followed, by state and federal courts, in both domestic and international cases. Courts remarked that "[n]othing is better settled than that agreements of this character are void,"[30] and cited the "universally accepted rule that agreements in advance of controversy whose object is to oust the jurisdiction of the courts are contrary to public policy and will not be enforced."[31] Indeed, in writing the original version of his treatise on Contracts, Professor Corbin thought the subject sufficiently settled to dispose of it by rhetorically asking, "[h]ow can two individuals by private agreement limit or otherwise alter the 'jurisdiction' of the great courts of state or nation!"[32]

b. Rejection of the Historic Rule That Forum Selection Agreements Are Unenforceable. Starting in the late 1940s, U.S. courts began to abandon the traditional rule that forum selection agreements were per se unenforceable. Lower courts[33] and commentators[34] increasingly questioned the rationale of the rule. In 1955, *Wm. H. Muller & Co. v. Swedish American Line Ltd.* expressly rejected the historic prohibition on forum clauses. In a case involving an exclusive forum selection agreement designating Swedish courts as the contractual forum, the Second Circuit held:

> In each case the enforceability of such an agreement depends upon its reasonableness. . . .
> [I]f in the proper exercise of its jurisdiction . . . the court finds that the agreement is not

---

27. *See Bremen v. Zapata Off-Shore Co.*, 407 U.S. 1, 9 (1972) ("Forum-selection clauses have historically not been favored by American courts. Many courts, federal and state, have declined to enforce such clauses on the ground that they were 'contrary to public policy,' or that their effect was to 'oust the jurisdiction' of the court."); Gilbert, *Choice of Forum Clauses in International and Interstate Contracts*, 65 Ky. L.J. 1, 11-19 (1976); Reese, *The Contractual Forum: Situation in the United States*, 13 Am. J. Comp. L. 187 (1964).

28. An extensive compilation of decisions holding forum selection agreements unenforceable is found in Dougherty, *Validity of Contractual Provision Limiting Place or Court in Which Action May Be Brought*, 31 A.L.R.4th 404, 409-411; Tellier, *Validity of Contractual Provision Authorizing Venue of Action in Particular Place, Court, or County*, 69 A.L.R.2d 1324 (1960 & Supp. 1978); Annotation, *Validity of Contractual Provision Limiting Place or Court in Which Action May Be Brought*, 56 A.L.R.2d 300 (1957).

29. *See infra* pp. 1164-1165; G. Born, *International Commercial Arbitration* 39-49 (2009).

30. *Benson v. Eastern Bldg. & Loan Ass'n*, 174 N.Y. 83, 86 (1903).

31. *Carbon Black Export, Inc. v. The S.S. Monrosa*, 254 F.2d 297 (5th Cir. 1958). *See also The Ciano*, 58 F. Supp. 65 (E.D. Pa. 1944); *Mutual Reserve Fund Life Ass'n v. Cleveland Woolen Mills*, 82 F. 508, 510 (6th Cir. 1897); *Nashua River Paper Co. v. Hammermill Paper Co.*, 111 N.E. 678, 681 (Mass. 1916) ("The same rule . . . prevails generally in all states where the question has arisen."); *Kuhnhold v. Compagnie Generale Transatlantique*, 251 F. 387 (S.D.N.Y. 1918); *Gough v. Hamburg Amerikanische Packetfahrt Aktiengesellschaft*, 158 F. 174 (S.D.N.Y. 1907); *Slocum v. Western Assur. Co.*, 42 F. 235 (S.D.N.Y. 1890); *Prince Steam-Shipping Co. v. Lehman*, 39 F. 704 (S.D.N.Y. 1889).

32. 6A A. Corbin, *Corbin on Contracts* §1431, at 381-382 (1962).

33. *See Krenger v. Pennsylvania R.R.*, 174 F.2d 556, 561 (2d Cir. 1949) (L. Hand, J., concurring) ("be the original reasons good or bad, courts have for long looked with strong disfavor upon contracts by which a party surrenders resort to any forum which was lawfully open to him. . . . In truth, I do not believe that, today at least, there is an absolute taboo against such contracts at all; in the words of the Restatement, they are invalid only when unreasonable. . . . What remains of the doctrine is apparently no more than a general hostility, which can be overcome, but which nonetheless does persist"); *Gilbert v. Burnstine*, 174 N.E. 706 (N.Y. 1931); *Kelvin Engineering Co. v. Blanco*, 210 N.Y.S. 10 (Sup. Ct. 1925).

34. Nadelmann, *Choice-of-Court Clauses in the United States: The Road to Zapata*, 21 Am. J. Comp. L. 124, 127-134 (1973); Reese, *The Contractual Forum: Situation in the United States*, 13 Am. J. Comp. L. 187, 189 (1964); A. Ehrenzweig, *Conflict of Laws* 149 (1962) ("Neither history nor rationale thus bear out the much-repeated axiom that parties may not 'oust' the courts from their jurisdiction.").

unreasonable in the setting of a particular case, it may properly decline jurisdiction and relegate a litigant to the forum to which he assented.[35]

In the following years, a number of other lower federal courts refused to hold forum clauses per se unreasonable; such agreements could be enforced, in the trial court's discretion, if they were "reasonable."[36] Some state courts followed suit.[37] Observing this rapid erosion of the traditional rule against forum clauses, one commentator remarked that "[i]t is somewhat difficult to understand how that which was so well settled in 1930 could become unsettled in the space of nineteen years."[38] This trend paralleled (albeit several decades later) the similar evolution in judicial attitudes toward arbitration agreements, where historic doctrines of unenforceability were replaced by the Federal Arbitration Act in 1925 and subsequent judicial decisions upholding the validity and enforceability of international and domestic arbitration agreements.[39]

The rule that forum selection clauses are unenforceable came to be identified with the indefensible adage that private parties cannot "oust" courts of their jurisdiction. According to one court, "[p]erhaps the true explanation [for the rule] is the power of the hypnotic phrase 'oust the jurisdiction.' Give a bad dogma a good name and its bite may become as bad as its bark."[40] Critics increasingly branded this slogan a misleading mischaracterization: the real issue is not whether a court is deprived of its jurisdiction, but "whether, in a proper case, a court should refrain from exercising such jurisdiction as it admittedly possesses in order to give effect to the parties' intentions as expressed in a choice of forum clause."[41] The answer to this question came, almost invariably, to be in the affirmative.

In 1964, the U.S. Supreme Court took what came to be a significant step toward abandoning the traditional prohibition on forum selection agreements in *National Equipment Rental, Ltd. v. Szukhent.*[42] On its facts, *Szukhent* involved an interpretation of Rule 4 of the Federal Rules of Civil Procedure, and particularly the question whether Rule 4 permitted service on an agent designated in advance by contractual agreement.[43] In answering in the affirmative, however, the Court more broadly declared that "it is settled . . . that parties to a contract may agree in advance to submit to the jurisdiction of a

---

35. 224 F.2d 806 (2d Cir. 1955), *overruled on other grounds, Indussa Corp. v. S.S. Ranborg,* 377 F.2d 200 (2d Cir. 1967).

36. *E.g., Furbee v. Vantage Press, Inc.,* 464 F.2d 835 (D.C. Cir. 1972); *Central Contracting Co. v. Maryland Cas. Co.,* 367 F.2d 341 (3d Cir. 1966); *Anastasiadis v. S.S. Little John,* 346 F.2d 281 (5th Cir. 1965). *See also* Bergman, *Contractual Restrictions on the Forum,* 48 Calif. L. Rev. 438, 438-447 (1960); Gilbert, *Choice of Forum Clauses in International and Interstate Contracts,* 65 Ky. L.J. 1, 11-20 (1976).

37. *E.g., Export Insurance Co. v. Mitsui SS Co.,* 274 N.Y.S.2d 977 (1st Dep't 1966); *Central Contracting Co. v. Youngdahl & Co.,* 209 A.2d 810, 816 (Pa. 1965); *Schwartz v. Zim Israel Navigation Co.,* 181 N.Y.S.2d 283 (Sup. Ct. 1958).

38. Bergman, *Contractual Restrictions on the Forum,* 48 Calif. L. Rev. 438, 440 (1960). Some courts resisted the trend toward enforcement of forum clauses. *E.g., Carbon Black Export v. The SS Monrosa,* 254 F.2d 297 (5th Cir. 1958); *United Fuel Gas Co. v. Columbian Fuel,* 165 F.2d 746, 749 (4th Cir. 1948).

39. *See infra* pp. 1164-1166; G. Born, *International Commercial Arbitration* 47-49, 132-144 (2009).

40. *Kulukundis Shipping Co. v. Amtorg Trading Corp.,* 126 F.2d 978, 984 (2d Cir. 1942).

41. Reese, *The Supreme Court Supports Enforcement of Choice-of-Forum Clauses,* 7 Int'l Law. 530, 534 (1973). *See also* Aballi, *Comparative Developments in the Law of Choice of Forum,* 1 N.Y.U. J. Int'l L. & Pol. 178, 179 (1968) ("When a party contracts that it will not bring any future disputes in courts other than that stipulated, it is surrendering a right to bring them before a court which the law has invested with jurisdiction to hear that controversy. The agreement as such does not 'oust' or 'confer' jurisdiction, but is legally effective because the courts will recognize it.").

42. 375 U.S. 311 (1964).

43. According to the Court, "the only question now before us is whether the person upon whom the summons and complaint was served was 'an agent authorized by appointment' to receive the same, so as to subject the respondents to the jurisdiction of the federal court in New York." 375 U.S. at 313.

given court, to permit notice to be served by the opposing party, or even to waive notice altogether."[44]

In 1968, the National Conference of Commissioners on Uniform State Laws approved the Model Choice of Forum Act (which is reproduced in Appendix H).[45] The Act provided for the enforceability of both nonexclusive submissions to jurisdiction and exclusive forum selection clauses. Section 2 of the Act provided that written agreements "that an action on a controversy may be brought in this state," will be enforced if the contractual forum is "reasonably convenient" and if the agreement was not "obtained by misrepresentation, duress, the abuse of economic power, or other unconscionable means." Similarly, §3 provided that, if the parties enter into a written agreement that "an action on a controversy shall be brought only in another state," the forum court shall dismiss or stay the action, unless one of specified exceptions is satisfied.[46]

c. *Restatement (Second) Conflict of Laws.* These developments were the basis in 1971 for a new provision in the *Restatement (Second) Conflict of Laws* (which has no parallel in the *First Restatement*). New §80 provided, for the first time, that forum selection clauses were enforceable, at least in some circumstances.[47] Section 80 of the *Restatement* provided:

> The parties' agreement as to the place of the action [cannot oust a state of judicial jurisdiction, but such an agreement] will be given effect unless it is unfair or unreasonable.[48]

Section 80 was subsequently amended, in 1986, to delete the language appearing in brackets above.

During the same period, traditional restrictions on parties' freedom to choose the law applicable to their contracts were eroded.[49] As discussed elsewhere, §1-105 of the Uniform Commercial Code and §187 of the *Restatement (Second) Conflict of Laws* were significant steps in this development, culminating in the recognition of a significant measure of party autonomy in the choice of law context.[50] The erosion of prohibitions against forum selection agreements was also facilitated by legislative and judicial acceptance of arbitration agreements. As discussed elsewhere, the Federal Arbitration Act was enacted in 1925, making certain arbitration agreements valid and enforceable; judicial

---

44. 375 U.S. at 315-316. As discussed elsewhere, the Supreme Court had long permitted private parties to consent to a forum's personal jurisdiction *after* an action had been commenced there. *See supra* pp. 115-116; *Adam v. Saenger*, 303 U.S. 59 (1938).

45. The Act has been adopted, in varying forms, in the following state statutes: Neb. Rev. Stat. §25-415 (1989); N.H. Rev. Stat. Ann. §508-A (1983); N.Y. Gen. Oblig. Law §5-1402 (McKinney 1989 & Supp. 1994); N.D. Cent. Code §28-04.1 (1991); Ohio Rev. Code §2307.39 (Anderson Supp. 1992). The Act was presaged by the draft Hague Convention on Choice of Court, adopted at the 10th Session of the Hague Conference on Private International Law in 1964. 4 Int'l Legal Mat. 348-349 (1965). The Convention was broadly similar to the Model Act. Only Israel ratified the Convention. Gilbert, *Choice of Forum Clauses in International and Interstate Contracts*, 65 Ky. L.J. 1, 29-30 (1976).

46. The exceptions are discussed in detail below. *See infra* pp. 487-528.

47. For a discussion of the process of adopting §80, *see* Nadelmann, *Choice-of-Court Clauses in the United States: The Road to Zapata*, 21 Am. J. Comp. L. 124, 130-133 (1973).

48. In a remarkably disingenuous exercise in selective citation, the *Restatement*'s drafters acknowledged in the Reporter's Note to §80, that courts "have shown themselves reluctant" to dismiss actions brought in violation of forum selection clauses (without citation to any of the numerous decisions almost uniformly demonstrating not just "reluctance," but absolute refusal), but went on to assert that "actions have been dismissed, however, in situations where the contractual provision was deemed reasonable and serving the convenience of the parties" (citing all of the relatively few decisions then in existence which enforced forum selection agreements on any basis).

49. Prebble, *Choice of Law to Determine the Validity and Effects of Contracts: A Comparison of the English and American Approaches to the Conflict of Laws*, 58 Cornell L. Rev. 433, 442-444 (1973); Gruson, *Governing Law Clauses in Commercial Agreements — New York's Approach*, 18 Colum. J. Transnat'l L. 323, 323 (1980).

50. *See infra* pp. 758-763.

enforcement of the Act was enthusiastic,[51] and inevitably affected judicial attitudes toward forum selection clauses.

One year after §80 of the *Restatement (Second) Conflict of Laws* was adopted, the Supreme Court decided what would become the leading contemporary U.S. case on the enforceability of forum clauses. In *The Bremen v. Zapata Off-Shore Co.*,[52] the Court held that, in federal admiralty suits, forum clauses "are prima facie valid and should be enforced unless enforcement is shown by the resisting party to be 'unreasonable' under the circumstances."[53]

Following *Bremen,* most lower courts abandoned the historic prohibition against forum selection clauses in both domestic and international cases.[54] In 1986, §80 was amended to further emphasize the enforceability of such clauses.[55] Similarly, the Supreme Court's 1991 decision in *Carnival Cruise Lines v. Shute* firmly endorsed the enforceability of forum agreements and emphasized the narrow character to the exceptions to this general rule.[56]

d. Hague Convention on Choice of Court Agreements.   Most recently, in June 2005, the Hague Conference on Private International Law adopted the Hague Convention on Choice of Court Agreements ("Hague Choice of Court Agreements Convention").[57] The Convention is excerpted at Appendix I. The Convention's basic terms provide for the recognition and enforcement of exclusive forum selection clauses in international commercial transactions;[58] the Convention also provides for the recognition of forum selection clauses as a valid jurisdictional base in proceedings to recognize and enforce foreign judgments.[59] The Convention also creates a mechanism whereby states may declare their willingness to enforce nonexclusive forum selection agreements.[60]

The Hague Choice of Courts Convention has thus far been ratified only by Mexico; although the United States and European Union have both signed the Convention, neither has ratified or implemented it. If it is adopted by substantial numbers of states, the Convention would enhance the enforceability of forum selection clauses internationally. In this respect, it would to some extent parallel the effects of the New York Convention on international arbitration agreements (although the international arbitral process would continue to differ materially from national court litigations).[61] It remains unclear, however, whether the Convention will in fact attract substantial support.[62]

B. Contemporary Approaches to Forum Selection Agreements in International Cases

Although *Bremen* and other authorities have abandoned the historic prohibition against forum selection clauses, this has produced less certainty than might be expected concerning the new rules of enforceability. In part because of the discursive character

51. *See infra* pp. 1165-1166; G. Born, *International Commercial Arbitration* 132-144 (2009).
52. 407 U.S. 1 (1972).
53. 407 U.S. at 10.
54. *See* cases cited at *infra* p. 470-471.
55. *See supra* p. 467-468.
56. 499 U.S. 585 (1991).
57. *See* Hague Choice of Court Agreements Convention, June 30, 2005, 44 I.L.M. 1294; www.hcch.net.
58. Hague Choice of Court Agreements Convention, Arts. 5 and 6.
59. Hague Choice of Court Agreements Convention, Arts. 8 and 9.
60. Hague Choice of Court Agreements Convention, Art. 22.
61. *See infra* pp. 1167-1168.
62. For commentary on the Convention, *see* Note, *Recent International Agreement,* 119 Harv. L. Rev. 931 (2006); *United States Plays Leading Role in Negotiating New Convention on Choice of Court Agreements,* 99 Am. J. Int'l L. 921 (2005); Brand, *Introductory Note to the 2005 Hague Convention on Choice of Court Agreements,* 44 I.L.M. 1291 (2005).

of the *Bremen* opinion, and in part because of residual unease with choice of forum agreements, courts in different U.S. jurisdictions have adopted different approaches to the presumptive validity and weight to be accorded to such clauses.

1. Contemporary Approaches to Enforceability of Forum Selection Agreements

The enforceability of forum selection agreements is not as unsettled today as it was in 1964, when Willis Reese remarked: "One thing can be said with certainty. In the United States the effect of a choice of forum clause dealing with future controversies is uncertain."[63] Nevertheless, the standards for enforcement of a choice of forum clause in the United States continue to vary significantly in different jurisdictions. Five general approaches to the issue can be identified in contemporary decisions, ranging from historic per se unenforceability to virtually per se enforceability. Each approach is discussed below.

Despite the legal uncertainties arising from those multiple approaches, international forum selection agreements in commercial contracts are in contemporary practice very often enforced by U.S. courts, regardless of the precise standard that is applied. According to one commentator, "one is hard-pressed to find a recent case which refuses to enforce such clauses."[64] Although this is an overstatement,[65] it reflects the general predisposition of contemporary U.S. courts toward forum clauses.

a. Forum Selection Agreements Per Se Unenforceable. Notwithstanding *Bremen* and the *Restatement (Second) Conflict of Laws,* a few U.S. jurisdictions continue to hold forum agreements unenforceable. Although counts vary, it appears that the law in at least three states—Iowa, Montana, and Idaho—continue to hold that forum clauses choosing an out-of-state forum are per se unenforceable, at least in the domestic U.S. context.[66]

In Montana and Idaho, local statutes render (or have been interpreted to render) forum selection clauses unenforceable.[67] In other states, courts have declared forum clauses unenforceable relying solely on historic, common law notions of public policy. Typical is a 1980 decision in *Redwing Carriers, Inc. v. Foster,* where the Supreme Court of Alabama held that Alabama state public policy forbade enforcement of an exclusive forum clause, designating Florida courts, in a contract between an Alabama purchaser and a Florida seller.[68] The Court declared that "[w]e consider contract provisions which attempt to limit the jurisdiction of the courts of this state to be invalid and unenforceable as being contrary to public policy."[69]

In many such states (including Alabama), recent decisions have rejected older authorities and held that forum selection clauses are presumptively enforceable as a matter of common law.[70] Indeed, it appears that only Iowa courts have recently held that forum

---

63. Reese, *The Contractual Forum: Situation in the United States,* 13 Am. J. Comp. L. 187 (1964) (Proceedings).

64. Solimine, *Forum-Selection Clauses and the Privatization of Procedure,* 25 Cornell Int'l L.J. 51, 51 (1992).

65. *See infra* pp. 487-528.

66. *Cerami-Kote, Inc. v. Energywave Corp.,* 773 P.2d 1143 (Idaho 1989) (relying on public policy expressed by Idaho Code §29-110); *Polaris Indus., Inc. v. District Court,* 695 P.2d 471 (Mont. 1985) (relying on public policy expressed by Montana §28-2-708).

67. *See* Montana Code §28-2-708; Idaho Code §29-110.

68. 382 So. 2d 554 (Ala. 1980), *overruled, Kenco Signs & Awning Div. Inc. v. CDC of Dothan, LLC,* 2001 Ala. Civ. App. LEXIS 5 (Ala. Civ. App. 2001).

69. 383 So. 2d at 556.

70. *See Professional Ins. Corp. v. Sutherland,* 700 So. 2d 347 (Ala. 1997), overruling *White-Spunner Constr. v. Cliff,* 588 So. 2d 865 (Ala. 1991); *Keelean v. Central Bank of the South,* 544 So. 2d 153 (Ala. 1989) *and Redwing Carriers, Inc. v. Foster,* 382 So. 2d 554 (Ala. 1980).

selection clauses are not enforceable.[71] A number of other states — including Arkansas, Connecticut, Florida, Georgia, Illinois, Maine, Massachusetts, North Carolina, Rhode Island, and West Virginia — appear not to have definitively resolved whether forum selection agreements are enforceable. In each state at least some local precedent suggests unenforceability, although in most instances more recent authority lends support for a contrary result.[72]

b.   *Forum Non Conveniens* **Analysis.**   A number of lower courts treat forum clauses as merely one factor in a more generalized *forum non conveniens* analysis. Under this approach, a forum selection agreement is not enforced as a contract; rather, it is merely an indication of the parties' intentions at one time, which is to be weighed together with considerations of convenience, fairness, judicial economy and competence, and other factors.[73] As one lower court described it, a choice of forum clause will be judged under "the totality of the circumstances measured in the interests of justice."[74] In the words of another decision, which is slightly more deferential to the parties' agreement, courts are not "*bound* by forum selection clauses if the interests of the witnesses and of the public strongly favor jurisdiction in a forum other than the one consented to in the contract."[75]

Some lower federal courts continue to follow this approach today,[76] as do a number of state courts (typically based upon domestic precedent).[77] Moreover, as discussed below, the Supreme Court has adopted a *forum non conveniens* analysis in those cases to which 28 U.S.C. §1404(a) is applicable.[78]

c.   **Forum Selection Agreement Enforced If "Reasonable."**   A third general approach to the enforceability of forum selection clauses is reflected by *Bremen,* the *Restatement (Second) Conflict of Laws,* and the Uniform Law Commissioners' Model Choice of Forum Act. With some variations, all of these authorities treat forum clauses as presumptively valid contractual undertakings, provided that they are reasonable.

The rule adopted by all of these authorities accords significantly greater weight to forum selection agreements than a pure *forum non conveniens* analysis. Under this approach, a valid forum clause is not simply one of a number of relevant factors. It is

---

71. *Davenport Mach. & Foundry Co., A Division of Middle States Corp. v. Adolph Coors Co.,* 314 N.W.2d 432 (Iowa 1982).

72. *See* W. Park, *International Forum Selection* 19-20 (1995).

73. *See* the cases compiled in Dougherty, *Validity of Contractual Provision Limiting Place or Court in Which Action May Be Brought,* 31 A.L.R. 4th 404, 415-418 (1984 & Supp. 2006); Lederman, *Viva* Zapata!: *Toward a Rational System of Forum-Selection Clause Enforcement in Diversity Cases,* 66 N.Y.U. L. Rev. 422, (1991) ("Perhaps the best way to understand forum-selection clauses is as a request that the court exercise its discretion to decline to hear the case where there is a more appropriate forum elsewhere, a request resembling the invocation of *forum non conveniens.*").

74. *D'Antuono v. CCH Computax Systems,* 570 F. Supp. 708, 712 (D.R.I. 1983) (setting forth nine factors relevant to this inquiry).

75. *Greenwood v. Tillamook Country Smoker, Inc.,* 857 S.W.2d 654 (Tex. App. 1993).

76. *E.g., Forsythe v. Saudi Arabian Airlines Corp.,* 885 F.2d 285 (5th Cir. 1989) (applying *forum non conveniens* doctrine without analysis even though "the parties had agreed in their contract to bring all disputes before" the Labor and Settlement of Disputes Committee in Saudi Arabia); *Furbee v. Vantage Press, Inc.,* 464 F.2d 835, 837 (D.C. Cir. 1972); *Neo Sack, Ltd. v. Vinmar Impex, Ltd.,* 1993 U.S. Dist. LEXIS 377 (S.D. Tex. 1993). Some of these decisions fail to consider whether or not the forum selection agreement is an exclusive one.

77. *Exum v. Vantage Press, Inc.,* 563 P.2d 1314 (Wash. Ct. App. 1977) (holding, in domestic case, that trial court has discretion not to enforce forum clause); *Eads v. Woodmen of the World Life Ins. Society,* 785 P.2d 328 (Okla. Ct. App. 1989) ("a court in its discretion may refuse to exercise jurisdiction by necessarily respecting the intent of the contracting parties").

78. *See infra* pp. 530-531.

presumptively enforceable, absent an affirmative showing that other factors make enforcement unreasonable.[79]

Nevertheless, the *Restatement* and Model Act analysis often falls short of requiring the enforcement of a choice of forum agreements in the same fashion that other contracts are enforced. The analysis can permit after-the-fact judicial inquiry into the "convenience," "reasonableness," and "fairness" of a particular forum provision — a degree of judicial scrutiny that most other contractual undertakings avoid. Some lower courts have followed this approach, occasionally declining to enforce forum agreements even absent substantial showings of inconvenience, unfairness, or unreasonableness.[80] Most courts, however, have scrutinized forum selection agreements for "reasonableness," but denied enforcement only in unusual circumstances.[81]

d. Forum Selection Agreements Enforced as Contracts. A fourth general approach has been to treat forum selection clauses as contractual obligations, like other contracts, and to enforce them in accordance with their terms. Emphasizing the significant interests in enforcing private agreements,[82] some of the lower courts have adopted this analysis. Decisions adopting this approach vary, with some arguably applying a version of "reasonableness" analysis that is highly deferential to the parties' agreement and that only rarely displaces their choice. The Supreme Court's decision in *Carnival Cruise Lines, Inc. v. Shute* is a leading example of such an approach,[83] as is the proposed Hague Choice of Court Agreements Convention.

e. New York General Obligation Law §5-1402. A fifth general approach is that taken to submissions to New York jurisdiction in §5-1402 of the New York General Obligations Law.[84] The section provides that "[a]ny person may maintain an action or proceeding against a foreign corporation" arising out of a contractual obligation for more than $1 million, where the parties' agreement "contains a provision . . . whereby such foreign corporation . . . agrees to submit to the jurisdiction of the courts of this state." The provision was expressly designed to eliminate uncertainty in the enforcement of forum selection agreements resulting from *forum non conveniens* and reasonableness analysis.[85]

---

79. *Hoes of America, Inc. v. Hoes,* 493 F. Supp. 1205, 1208 (C.D. Ill. 1979) (*Bremen* "rejected the application of the traditional *forum non conveniens* doctrine"). *But see* Gruson, *Forum-Selection Clauses in International and Interstate Commercial Agreements,* 1982 U. Ill. L. Rev. 133, 157 ("Some decisions make a distinction between passing on the reasonableness of a forum-selection clause and the exercise of discretion under the doctrine of *forum non conveniens;* however, the factors to be considered in deciding both motions are the same.").

80. *See infra* pp. 499-502.

81. *See infra* pp. 499-502.

82. *E.g., Stewart Org. Inc. v. Ricoh Corp.,* 810 F.2d 1066, 1075 (11th Cir. 1987) (en banc) (Tjoflat, J., concurring) ("The law of contracts presumes that Ricoh has already compensated Stewart, through lowered costs or some other method, for any inconvenience that Stewart or its witnesses might suffer by trying the case in New York."), *rev'd on other grounds,* 487 U.S. 22 (1988); *Cerro De Pasco Copper Corp. v. Knut Knutsen, O.A.S.,* 187 F.2d 990 (2d Cir. 1951) (Clark, J., concurring) ("I prefer to place my concurrence upon the validity, under the circumstances here disclosed, of the contract requiring all claims to be settled in Norway. The apparently wider discretion granted in the opinion to the district judge to pass upon the appropriateness of the forum may, perhaps, raise more extensive questions which we need not now face.").

83. Solimine, *Forum Selection Clauses and the Privatization of Procedure,* 25 Cornell Int'l L.J. 51, 78 (1992) ("*Carnival* seems to lay to rest the notion that *The Bremen* authorized a free-wheeling balancing-of-interests test to govern the enforceability of choice-of-forum clauses.").

84. *See* Appendix W.

85. Friedler, *Party Autonomy Revisited: A Statutory Solution to a Choice of Law Problem,* 37 U. Kan. L. Rev. 471 (1989); Rashkover, *Title 14, New York Choice of Law Rule for Contractual Disputes: Avoiding the Unreasonable Results,* 71 Cornell L. Rev. 227 (1985).

2. Forum Selection Agreements Involving Consumers and Insureds

An important theme in the contemporary treatment of forum selection clauses involves agreements with consumers, insureds, and similarly situated parties. In many jurisdictions, forum selection clauses involving such parties are either not enforceable or are subject to special limitations. EU Council Regulation 44/2001 expressly excludes forum selection agreements involving consumers and insureds from the Regulation's general provisions permitting the enforcement of choice of forum clauses,[86] as does the proposed Hague Choice of Court Agreements Convention.[87] Similarly, as already noted, §5-1402 of the New York General Obligations Law applies only in actions involving amounts in excess of $1 million, which largely excludes consumer transactions.

3. Selected Materials on Approaches to the Enforceability of International Forum Selection Agreements

Excerpted below are cases and statutory materials that illustrate various approaches to the enforceability of forum clauses. The Oregon Supreme Court's 1928 decision in *Kahn v. Tazwell*[88] refused to enforce an agreement designating Karlsruhe, Germany as the exclusive contractual forum. The Court reasoned that traditional public policy prohibitions prevailed over the parties' agreement (and Karlsruhe's historic setting). Reflecting the same attitude, §28-2-708 of the Montana Code invalidates contractual restraints on a plaintiff's choice of forum (both domestic and foreign). Also excerpted below are the Model Choice of Forum Act, and *Bremen v. Zapata Off-Shore Co.*, the Supreme Court's landmark decision recognizing the enforceability of forum clauses. In contrast, the California Supreme Court's opinion, *Smith, Valentino, & Smith, Inc. v. Superior Court,*[89] illustrates the *forum non conveniens* approach of some contemporary decisions to the enforceability of forum clauses. Finally, §5-1402 of the New York General Obligations Law, EU Council Regulation 44/2001, and the Hague Choice of Court Agreements Convention illustrate a more contemporary, "contractual" approach.

KAHN v. TAZWELL
266 P. 238 (Oregon Supreme Court 1928)

BEAN, JUDGE. This is [a] proceeding . . . to require the defendant, Hon. George Tazwell, judge of the circuit court for Multnomah County, to entertain jurisdiction of an action commenced by the relator, Adolf Kahn, against the New York Life Insurance Company, a New York corporation, on an insurance policy. . . . The application for the policy was made by the plaintiff in Germany, signed by the president and secretary of the New York Life Insurance Company at its main office, New York City, and was signed by the general secretary of the company for Europe at the [New York Life] office in Paris, France.

[New York Life] is authorized to conduct life insurance business anywhere. Prior to the declaration by the United States of war against Germany, this corporation was transacting

---

86. EU Council Regulation 44/2001, Arts. 13, 15-17. *See also id.,* Art. 18-21 (employment contracts).
87. Hague Choice of Court Agreements Convention, Art. 2(1).
88. 266 P. 238 (Or. 1928).
89. 551 P.2d 1206 (Cal. 1976).

life insurance business in Germany. This company, as one of the requirements essential to the right to transact its business in the state of Oregon, on February 16, 1923, executed and filed with the insurance commission, as required by §6327, Or. L., a power of attorney appointing R. A. Durham, a citizen of Oregon, residing at Portland, its attorney in fact, upon whom "lawful and valid service may be made of all writs, processes and summons in any case, suit or proceeding commenced by or against any such company or association in any court mentioned in this section and necessary to give such court complete jurisdiction thereof."

The action mentioned was commenced October 3, 1927, and summons and complaint was served by delivery to the said R. A. Durham, as such attorney in fact. The defendant appeared specially and filed a motion to quash the service of the summons, for the reason that the service was not authorized by law; and that the court could not obtain jurisdiction over the person of the defendant [New York Life] in that plaintiff was and is a resident and citizen of the republic, formerly empire, of Germany, and has not been a resident, inhabitant, or citizen of the state of Oregon, and was not at the time of the commencement of the action, and is not now, within the state of Oregon, as shown by affidavit. . . . [The defendant also relied upon the following forum selection clause, contained in the insurance policy that it issued to Mr. Kahn:]

> For the fulfillment of this contract only the courts of Karlsruhe are competent; as the legal domicile of the company is agreed upon its office at Karlsruhe and for the insured or his legal successor the place mentioned in the application of insurance. . . .

The further question arises whether the court has jurisdiction of a cause of action and of the parties. . . . A corporation which goes into a foreign jurisdiction and there prosecutes its corporate affairs impliedly consents to be sued there. . . . Under this theory, it has been held that process may be served on an actual agent or upon an agent designated by statute. . . . The great weight of authority [holds that] the mere fact that the cause of action arose, or the transaction giving rise to it occurred, beyond the territorial limits of the state of suit, does not prevent effective service of process upon an actual agent of a foreign corporation, if the conditions of service are otherwise satisfied. [New York Life] qualified to do business in this state, and voluntarily, in a formal manner, appointed an agent upon whom service of process might be served in an action against the corporation. . . . The court obtained jurisdiction of the corporation . . . notwithstanding the fact that the contract of insurance was executed outside the state, and notwithstanding the fact that the plaintiff is a nonresident of the state of Oregon.

It is contended by the company that the clause in the policy, quoted above, in regard to domicile, restricts the jurisdiction, and limits the jurisdiction to enforce the conditions of the policy to the "courts of Karlsruhe." In *Sudbury v. Ambi Verwaltung, etc.*, 210 N.Y.S. 164, 166, the court stated: "The federal rule is well settled that contracts by which parties attempt to confer exclusive jurisdiction upon a particular court, foreign or domestic, are contrary to public policy and void." The stipulation of the parties contained in the contract of insurance is contrary to public policy and void. The law prescribes the jurisdiction of our courts, and it cannot be diminished or increased by the convention of the parties. The stipulation is in effect a legal opinion of the parties that only "the courts of Karlsruhe" are competent for the fulfillment of the contracts. In *Kent v. Universal Film Manufacturing Co.*, 193 N.Y.S. 838, Mr. Justice Laughlin said: "The federal court regards contracts by which parties attempt to confer exclusive jurisdiction over a particular court, foreign or domestic, as contrary to public policy and void." . . .

MONTANA CODE ANNOTATED

§28-2-708

Restraints upon legal proceedings void. Every stipulation or condition in a contract by which any party thereto is restricted from enforcing his rights under the contract by the usual proceedings in the ordinary tribunals or which limits the time within which he may thus enforce his rights is void.

THE BREMEN v. ZAPATA OFF-SHORE CO.

407 U.S. 1 (1972)

CHIEF JUSTICE BURGER. We granted certiorari to review a judgment of the United States Court of Appeals for the Fifth Circuit declining to enforce a forum-selection clause governing disputes arising under an international towage contract between petitioners and respondent. . . . For the reasons stated hereafter, we vacate the judgment of the Court of Appeals.

In November 1967, respondent Zapata, a Houston-based American corporation, contracted with petitioner Unterweser, a German corporation, to tow Zapata's ocean-going, self-elevating drilling rig *Chaparral* from Louisiana to a point off Ravenna, Italy, in the Adriatic Sea, where Zapata had agreed to drill certain wells. . . . The contract submitted by Unterweser contained the following provision, which is at issue in this case: "Any dispute arising must be treated before the London Court of Justice." In addition, the contract contained two clauses purporting to exculpate Unterweser from liability for damages to the towed barge.

After reviewing the contract and making several changes, but without any alteration in the forum-selection or exculpatory clauses, a Zapata vice president executed the contract and forwarded it to Unterweser in Germany, where Unterweser accepted the changes, and the contract became effective. . . . Unterweser's deep sea tug *Bremen* departed Venice, Louisiana, with the *Chaparral* in tow bound for Italy. . . . [W]hile the flotilla was in international waters in the middle of the Gulf of Mexico, a severe storm arose, [seriously damaging the *Chaparral*]. In this emergency situation Zapata instructed the *Bremen* to tow its damaged rig to Tampa, Florida, the nearest port of refuge.

On January 12, Zapata, ignoring its contract promise to litigate "any dispute arising" in the English courts, commenced a suit in admiralty in the United States District Court at Tampa, seeking $3,500,000 damages against Unterweser *in personam* and the *Bremen in rem*, alleging negligent towage and breach of contract. Unterweser responded by invoking the forum clause of the towage contract, and moved to dismiss for lack of jurisdiction or on *forum non conveniens* grounds, or in the alternative to stay the action pending submission of the dispute to the "London Court of Justice." Shortly thereafter, in February, before the District Court had ruled on its motion to stay or dismiss the United States action, Unterweser commenced an action against Zapata seeking damages for breach of the towage contract in the High Court of Justice in London, as the contract provided. Zapata appeared in that court to contest jurisdiction, but its challenge was rejected, the English courts holding that the contractual forum provision conferred jurisdiction. . . .

[T]he District Court denied Unterweser's January motion to dismiss or stay Zapata's initial action . . . reiterating the traditional view of many American courts that "agreements in advance of controversy whose object is to oust the jurisdiction of the courts are contrary to public policy and will not be enforced." . . . [T]he District Court gave the forum-selection clause little, if any, weight. Instead, the court treated the motion to dismiss under normal *forum non conveniens* doctrine. . . . Under that doctrine "unless the balance is strongly in favor of the defendant, the plaintiff's choice of forum should rarely be disturbed." . . . The District Court concluded: "The balance of conveniences here is not strongly in favor of [Unterweser] and [Zapata's] choice of forum should not be disturbed."

[The Court of Appeals affirmed.] It noted that (1) the flotilla never "escaped the Fifth Circuit's mare nostrum, and the casualty occurred in close proximity to the district court"; (2) a considerable number of potential witnesses, including Zapata crewmen, resided in the Gulf Coast area; (3) preparation for the voyage and inspection and repair work had been performed in the Gulf area; (4) the testimony of the *Bremen* crew was available by way of deposition; (5) England had no interest in or contact with the controversy other than the forum-selection clause. The Court of Appeals majority further noted that Zapata was a United States citizen and "[t]he discretion of the district court to remand the case to a foreign forum was consequently limited" — especially since it appeared likely that the English courts would enforce the exculpatory clauses. In the Court of Appeals' view, enforcement of such clauses would be contrary to public policy in American courts under *Bisso v. Inland Waterways Corp.*, 349 U.S. 85 (1955). . . . Therefore, "[t]he district court was entitled to consider that remanding Zapata to a foreign forum, with no practical contact with the controversy, could raise a bar to recovery by a United States citizen which its own convenient courts would not countenance."

We hold . . . that far too little weight and effect were given to the forum clause in resolving this controversy. For at least two decades we have witnessed an expansion of overseas commercial activities by business enterprises based in the United States. The barrier of distance that once tended to confine a business concern to a modest territory no longer does so. Here we see an American company with special expertise contracting with a foreign company to tow a complex machine thousands of miles across seas and oceans. The expansion of American business and industry will hardly be encouraged if, notwithstanding solemn contracts, we insist on a parochial concept that all disputes must be resolved under our laws and in our courts. Absent a contract forum, the considerations relied on by the Court of Appeals would be persuasive reasons for holding an American forum convenient in the traditional sense, but in an era of expanding world trade and commerce, the absolute aspects of the doctrine [followed by the Court of Appeals] have little place and would be a heavy hand indeed on the future development of international commercial dealings by Americans. We cannot have trade and commerce in world markets and international waters exclusively on our terms, governed by our laws, and resolved in our courts.

Forum-selection clauses have historically not been favored by American courts. Many courts, federal and state, have declined to enforce such clauses on the ground that they were "contrary to public policy," or that their effect was to "oust the jurisdiction" of the court. Although this view apparently still has considerable acceptance, other courts are tending to adopt a more hospitable attitude toward forum-selection clauses. This view, advanced in the well-reasoned dissenting opinion in the instant case, is that such clauses are prima facie valid and should be enforced unless enforcement is shown by the resisting party to be "unreasonable" under the circumstances. We believe this is the correct doctrine to be followed by federal district courts sitting in admiralty. It is merely the other side of the proposition recognized by this Court in *National Equipment Rental, Ltd. v. Szukhent*, holding that in federal courts a party may validly consent to be sued in a jurisdiction where he cannot be found for service of process through contractual designation of an "agent" for receipt of process in that jurisdiction. In so holding, the Court stated: "[I]t is settled . . . that parties to a contract may agree in advance to submit to the jurisdiction of a given court, to permit notice to be served by the opposing party, or even to waive notice altogether." . . .

This approach is substantially that followed in other common-law countries including England. It is the view advanced by noted scholars and that adopted by the *Restatement [(Second)] Conflict of Laws*. It accords with ancient concepts of freedom of contract and reflects an appreciation of the expanding horizons of American contractors who seek business in all parts of the world. Not surprisingly, foreign businessmen prefer, as do we, to have disputes resolved in their own courts, but if that choice is not available, then in a neutral forum with expertise in the subject matter. Plainly, the courts of England meet the standards of neutrality and long experience in admiralty litigation. The choice of that forum was made in an arm's-length negotiation by experienced and sophisticated businessmen, and absent some compelling and countervailing reason it should be honored by the parties and enforced by the courts. . . .

There are compelling reasons why a freely negotiated private international agreement, unaffected by fraud, undue influence, or overweening bargaining power, such as that involved here, should be given full effect. In this case, for example, we are concerned with a far from routine transaction between companies of two different nations contemplating the tow of an extremely costly piece of equipment from Louisiana across the Gulf of Mexico and the Atlantic Ocean, through the Mediterranean Sea to its final destination in the Adriatic Sea. In the course of its voyage, it was to traverse the waters of many jurisdictions. The *Chaparral* could have been damaged at any point along the route, and there were countless possible ports of refuge. That the accident occurred in the Gulf of Mexico and the barge was towed to Tampa in an emergency were mere fortuities. It cannot be doubted for a moment that the parties sought to provide for a neutral forum for the resolution of any disputes arising during the tow. Manifestly much uncertainty and possibly great inconvenience to both parties could arise if a suit could be maintained in any jurisdiction in which an accident might occur or if jurisdiction were left to any place where the Bremen or Unterweser might happen to be found. The elimination of all such uncertainties by agreeing in advance on a forum acceptable to both parties is an indispensable element in international trade, commerce, and contracting. There is strong evidence that the forum clause was a vital part of the [Zapata/Unterweser] agreement, and it would be unrealistic to think that the parties did not conduct their negotiations, including fixing the monetary terms, with the consequences of the forum clause figuring prominently in their calculations. . . .

Thus, in the light of present-day commercial realities and expanding international trade we conclude that the forum clause should control absent a strong showing that it should be set aside. Although their opinions are not altogether explicit, it seems reasonably clear that the District Court and the Court of Appeals placed the burden on Unterweser to show that London would be a more convenient forum than Tampa, although the contract expressly resolved that issue. The correct approach would have been to enforce the forum clause specifically unless Zapata could clearly show that enforcement would be unreasonable and unjust, or that the clause was invalid for such reasons as fraud or overreaching. Accordingly, the case must be remanded for reconsideration.

We note, however, that there is nothing in the record presently before us that would support a refusal to enforce the forum clause. [The Court discussed and rejected an argument that enforcement of the forum selection clause would violate a U.S. public policy against certain types of contractual exculpatory clauses.] Courts have . . . suggested that a forum clause, even though it is freely bargained for and contravenes no important public policy of the forum, may nevertheless be "unreasonable" and unenforceable if the chosen forum is *seriously* inconvenient for the trial of the action. Of course, where it can be said with reasonable assurance that at the time they entered the contract, the parties to a freely negotiated private international commercial agreement contemplated the claimed inconvenience, it is difficult to see why any such claim of inconvenience should be heard to render the forum clause unenforceable. We are not here dealing with an agreement between two Americans to resolve their essentially local disputes in a remote alien forum. In such a case, the serious inconvenience of the contractual forum to one or both of the parties might carry greater weight in determining the reasonableness of the forum clause. The remoteness of the forum might suggest that the agreement was an adhesive one, or that the parties did not have the particular controversy in mind when they made their agreement; yet even there the party claiming should bear a heavy burden of proof.[90] Similarly, selection of a remote forum to apply differing foreign law to an essentially American controversy might contravene an important public policy of the forum. For example, so long as *Bisso* governs American courts with respect to the towage business in American waters, it would quite arguably be improper to permit an American tower to avoid that policy by providing a foreign forum for resolution of his disputes with an American towee.

This case, however, involves a freely negotiated international commercial transaction between a German and an American corporation for towage of a vessel from the Gulf of Mexico to the Adriatic Sea. As noted, selection of a London forum was clearly a reasonable effort to bring vital certainty to this international transaction and to provide a neutral forum experienced and capable in the resolution of admiralty litigation. Whatever "inconvenience" Zapata would suffer by being forced to litigate in the contractual forum as it agreed to do was clearly foreseeable at the time of contracting. In such circumstances it should be incumbent on the party seeking to escape his contract to show that trial in the contractual forum will be so gravely difficult and inconvenient that he will for all practical purposes be deprived of his day in court. Absent that, there is no basis for concluding that it would be unfair, unjust, or unreasonable to hold that party to his bargain.

In the course of its ruling on Unterweser's second motion to stay the proceedings in Tampa, the District Court did make a conclusory finding that the balance of convenience was "strongly" in favor of litigation in Tampa. However, as previously noted, in making that finding the court erroneously placed the burden of proof on Unterweser to show that the balance of convenience was strongly in its favor. Moreover, the finding falls far short of a conclusion that Zapata would be effectively deprived of its day in court should it be forced to litigate in London. Indeed, it cannot even be assumed that it would be placed to the expense of transporting its witnesses to London. It is not unusual for important issues in international admiralty cases to be dealt with by deposition. Both the District Court and the Court of Appeals majority appeared satisfied that Unterweser could receive a fair hearing in Tampa by using deposition testimony of its witnesses from distant places, and there is no reason to conclude that Zapata could not use deposition testimony to equal advantage if forced to litigate in London as it bound itself to do. Nevertheless, to allow Zapata an opportunity to carry its heavy burden of showing not only that the balance of convenience is strongly in favor of trial in Tampa (that is, that it will be far more

---

90. *See, e.g.,* Model Choice of Forum Act §3(3), comment: "On rare occasions, the state of the forum may be a substantially more convenient place for the trial of a particular controversy than the chosen state. If so, the present clause would permit the action to proceed. This result will presumably be in accord with the desires of the parties. It can be assumed that they did not have the particular controversy in mind when they made the choice-of-forum agreement since they would not consciously have agreed to have the action brought in an inconvenient place."

inconvenient for Zapata to litigate in London than it will be for Unterweser to litigate in Tampa), but also that a London trial will be so manifestly and gravely inconvenient to Zapata that it will be effectively deprived of a meaningful day in court, we remand for further proceedings.

SMITH, VALENTINO & SMITH, INC. v. SUPERIOR COURT
551 P.2d 1206 (Cal. 1976)

RICHARDSON, JUSTICE. . . . [W]e consider the extent to which California courts in breach of contract actions may give effect to a contractual forum selection clause providing for trial of the action in another state. Relying on such a clause, the trial court herein found that the Pennsylvania forum specified in the contract was the proper forum for trial . . . and consequently issued an order staying proceeding in this state. We conclude that the trial court acted within its discretion in doing so.

Petitioner Smith, Valentino & Smith, Inc. ("Smith") is a California corporation. Real party in interest Life Assurance Company of Pennsylvania ("Assurance") is a Pennsylvania corporation doing business in California. In March 1973, the two corporations entered into a contract by which Smith was appointed the "managing general agent" to represent Assurance in soliciting group insurance policies in California and other western states. The contract included a reciprocal forum selection clause whereunder Smith agreed to bring all actions arising out of the agency agreement only in Philadelphia, and Assurance in turn agreed to bring all such actions only in Los Angeles. Despite the provisions of this clause, in November 1974 Smith filed [suit] in the Los Angeles Superior Court against . . . Assurance. Assurance moved for dismissal on the basis of the forum selection clause and Code of Civil Procedure §410.30(a), which provides:

> When a court upon motion of a party or its own motion finds that in the interest of substantial justice an action should be heard in a forum outside this state, the court shall stay or dismiss the action in whole or in part on any conditions that may be just.

Smith opposed this motion on the basis that Smith's intended witnesses were all residents of California and that Smith was financially unable to bear the extra cost incident to the prosecution of the action in Philadelphia. The trial court denied Assurance's motion to dismiss but stayed all proceedings until further order, finding that the proper forum for trial . . . was Philadelphia. Smith [appeals], contending that the forum selection clause is either void per se or unenforceable on the facts of this case. We disagree.

Preliminarily we note that the clause in question, in addition to designating the proper forum for litigation, also provides that Pennsylvania law is to govern disputes concerning the contract. Such choice of law provisions are usually respected by California courts. *Windsor Mills, Inc. v. Collins & Aikman Corp.*, 25 Cal. App. 3d 987, 995 n.6 (1972); *Restatement (Second) Conflict of Laws* §187 [excerpted in Appendix Y]. Assuming that Pennsylvania law applies, we observe that the courts of that state have held that forum selection clauses will be given effect unless the party assailing the clause establishes that its enforcement would be unreasonable, *i.e.*, that the forum selected would be unavailable or unable to accomplish substantial justice. *Central Contracting Co. v. C. E. Youngdahl & Co.*, 209 A.2d 810 (Pa. 1965). . . .

Nonetheless, Smith contends that the subject clause is void and unenforceable as violative of California's declared public policy. In support, Smith cites *General Acceptance Corp. v. Robinson*, 277 P. 1039 (Cal. 1929) . . . [and other decisions]. These cases do recite the general rule that the parties may not, by private agreement, "oust" the jurisdiction of the courts by preventing a court from hearing a cause otherwise within its jurisdiction. In the *General Acceptance* case, for example, the parties had attempted to specify the county in which contract disputes would be tried. We held the contractual provision void since it would contravene general statutory provisions which designate the proper counties in which actions may be tried. Forum selection clauses, in contrast, violate no such carefully conceived statutory patterns.

The assertion that forum selection clauses are void per se as constituting attempts to oust the courts of their jurisdiction has been challenged as "hardly more than a vestigial legal fiction" which "reflects something of a provincial attitude regarding the fairness of other tribunals." *The Bremen v. Zapata Off-Shore Co., supra.* While it is true that the parties may not deprive courts of their jurisdiction over causes by private agreement, it is readily apparent that courts possess discretion to decline to exercise jurisdiction in recognition of the parties' free and voluntary choice of a different forum. Moreover, although we have acknowledged a policy favoring access to California courts by resident plaintiffs, we likewise conclude that the policy is satisfied in those cases where, as here, a plaintiff has freely and voluntarily negotiated away his right to a California forum. In so holding we are in accord with the modern trend which favors enforceability of such forum selection clauses. . . .

No satisfying reason of public policy has been suggested why enforcement should be denied a forum selection clause appearing in a contract entered into freely and voluntarily by parties who have negotiated at arm's length. For the foregoing reasons, we conclude that forum selection clauses are valid and may be given effect, in the court's discretion and in the absence of a showing that enforcement of such a clause would be unreasonable. While *General Acceptance Corp. v. Robinson,* 277 P. 1039, is factually distinguishable and, accordingly, may be said to rest upon policy considerations not involved in the present action, nevertheless to the extent that the rationale of *General Acceptance* is inconsistent with our opinion, we decline to follow it.

We turn to the question whether Smith has carried its burden of establishing that enforcement of the present clause would be unreasonable. Although Smith relies upon the factors of inconvenience and expense of a Pennsylvania forum, both Smith and Assurance reasonably can be held to have contemplated in negotiating their agreement the additional expense and inconvenience attendant on the litigation of their respective claims in a distant forum; such matters are inherent in a reciprocal clause of this type. As stated in *Central Contracting Co. v. C. E. Youngdahl & Co.,* "Mere inconvenience or additional expense is not the test of unreasonableness since it may be assumed that the plaintiff received under the contract consideration for these things." Moreover, although Smith's witnesses may reside in California, no reason appears why their testimony might not be obtained by deposition or at trial, at Smith's expense. Finally, since the trial court stayed the present action rather than dismissing it, the court has retained continuing jurisdiction over the cause. Should the Pennsylvania courts become unavailable for some unforeseeable reason, Smith may seek to reinstate its California action. . . .

Finally, Smith contends that the clause is limited in its application to breach of contract actions and should not apply to the tort counts in Smith's complaint. These counts (unfair competition and intentional interference with advantageous business relationships) arose directly out of Smith's contractual relationship with Assurance and reasonably may be interpreted as falling within the clause which provides for a Pennsylvania forum to litigate "Any actions or proceedings instituted by . . . [Smith] under this Agreement with respect to any matters arising under *or growing out of this agreement.* . . ." (Italics added.)

Mosk, Justice, dissenting. I dissent. Any analysis of this problem should begin with recognition of three basic precepts. First, while the private interests of litigants may be considered, the public interest is paramount. Second, unless a balance is strongly in favor of the defendant, the plaintiff's choice of forum should rarely be disturbed. Third, California has an overriding public policy favoring access to its courts by resident litigants.

Petitioner asserts the forum selection clause of the contract involved herein is void and unenforceable. Its contention is supported by ample authority. It is significant that the majority cite no California cases upholding this type of forum shopping by prearrangement. And without citation of authority from any source they attempt to carve a finely honed dichotomy between a court deprived of jurisdiction by agreement and a court declining to exercise jurisdiction because of an agreement. To a plaintiff denied an opportunity to be heard in the courts of his home state such a gossamer thin distinction is of dubious comfort.

The rule was well stated by the court in *Beirut Universal Bank* [*v. Superior Court*, 74 Cal. Rptr. 333 (Cal. 1969)], citing Corbin: " 'It is a generally accepted rule in the United States that an express provision in a contract that no suit shall be maintained thereon, except in a particular court or in the courts of a particular county, state, or nation, is not effective to deprive any court of jurisdiction that it otherwise could have over litigation based on that contract.'" 6A *Corbin on Contracts* §1445, p. 477 (1962). . . . The majority rely on *The Bremen v. Zapata Off-Shore Co.* But they overlook Chief Justice Burger's observation in that case that "[f]orum-selection clauses have historically not been favored by American courts." Nevertheless the Court concluded that such clauses are enforceable "by federal district courts sitting in *admiralty*." The Court did not direct that admiralty law is to be adapted to state courts in determining their jurisdiction. . . .

NEW YORK GENERAL OBLIGATIONS LAW §§5-1401, 1402
[excerpted in Appendix W]

EUROPEAN UNION COUNCIL REGULATION 44/2001, ART. 23
[excerpted in Appendix E]

HAGUE CONVENTION ON CHOICE OF COURT AGREEMENTS
44 Int'l Legal Mats. 1294 (2005) [excerpted in Appendix I]

Notes on Tazwell, Bremen, Smith, *and Legislative Materials*

1. *Rationale for historic unenforceability of forum selection agreements.* What were the reasons for the historic unenforceability of forum selection agreements? What arguments are advanced in *Tazwell* and in Justice Mosk's dissent in *Smith*?

(a) *"Ousting" courts of jurisdiction.* *Tazwell* invoked the dogma that "agreements in advance to oust the courts of the jurisdiction conferred by law are illegal and void." *Home Insurance Co. v. Morse*, 87 U.S. 445, 451 (1874). The notion that private parties cannot "oust" courts of their jurisdiction paralleled the dogma that "private parties cannot legislate," which was invoked by U.S. courts at the same time to invalidate choice of law agreements. Beale, *The Conflict of Laws, 1886-1936*, 50 Harv. L. Rev. 887 (1936); *Meacham v. Jamestown, Franklin & Clearfield R.R. Co.*, 211 N.Y. 346, 354 (1914) (Cardozo, J., concurring) ("If jurisdiction is to be ousted by contract, we [the judges] must submit to the failure of justice that may result"). What does it mean to "oust" a court of jurisdiction?

Does a forum clause really "oust" a court of its jurisdiction? Is that label necessary to the position that forum agreements should be unenforceable?

Would there by anything wrong with a forum clause requiring that all disputes be litigated before a specifically identified U.S. district judge? Why? What about a clause forbidding a specific judge — for example, Justice Doggett — from deciding the case? Why is either such provision different in principle from a standard exclusive forum selection clause? Do not both even further enhance certainty and predictability? Note the reliance (referred to in *Smith*) in *General Acceptance* on a state venue statute to invalidate a clause designating a specific California court in an intra-state dispute. How is this different from a forum selection clause?

(b) Private agreements regarding public remedies. Consider the remark in *Tazwell* that a forum clause should not be enforced because it is "in effect a legal opinion of the parties that only [specified courts] are competent." *See also Nute v. Hamilton Ins. Co.,* 72 Mass. (6 Gray) 174 (1856) (right to sue is a "remedy" and "the remedy does not depend on contract, but upon law, generally the *lex fori,* regardless of the lex loci contractus, which regulates the construction and legal effect of the contract").

Compare the public policy reflected in §28-2-708 of the Montana Code Annotated. Is there anything disquieting about a private agreement, based ordinarily upon bargaining power, on an issue as open-ended and outcome determinative as the decision-maker that will settle all the parties' disputes? To what extent should it be permissible for private parties to barter over access to public courts and judicial relief?

If there are particular claims or disputes that should not be capable of disposition by private agreement, is it necessary to invalidate all forum selection clauses in order to address this concern? Consider Article 2(2) of the Hague Choice of Court Agreements Convention. What are the benefits of such an approach? What are the costs?

(c) Protecting local residents' access to justice. Forum selection clauses were traditionally disfavored because they were held to burden a citizen's right of access to the courts:

> Every citizen is entitled to resort to all the courts of the country, and to invoke the protection which all the laws or all those courts may afford him. A man may not barter away his life or his freedom, or his substantial rights. *Home Insurance Co. v. Morse,* 87 U.S. 445, 451 (1874).

This rationale was most strongly advanced in cases where consumers or other individuals were involved, particularly when they sought access to their own local courts. Consider Justice Mosk's dissent in *Smith,* and particularly his conclusion that "California has an overriding public policy favoring access to its courts by resident litigants." Compare §28-2-708 of the Montana Code Annotated. Is this an improper legislative purpose? Is the welfare of local residents furthered by refusals to enforce forum selection clauses?

How were local interests implicated in *Tazwell?* Who was the plaintiff? The defendant? Where did the cause of action arise? If ever there was a case calling for *forum non conveniens* dismissal, was it not *Tazwell?*

(d) Protecting consumers and individuals. Some courts reasoned that forum selection clauses would force local residents to litigate in distant, unfavorable forums. *Reichard v. Manhattan Life Ins. Co.,* 31 Mo. 518, 521 (1862) (out-of-state insurance companies would "be licensed to defraud our citizens out of their just dues"). Who was the party resisting the forum clause in *Tazwell?* In *Bremen* and *Smith?* What role did the negotiating power of the parties have in the cases?

Is there any reason to treat forum clauses differently from other provisions in form contracts? Are forum selection agreements the same as most other contractual provisions, such as price, performance, liability, damages, and the like? To what extent is it likely that parties really know what the practical consequences of their agreement on a particular forum will mean when they enter into the agreement?

If there are particular concerns about consumers or similarly vulnerable parties, can these be addressed without invalidating all forum selection clauses? Consider Article 2(1) of the Hague Choice of Court Agreements Convention. How does it deal with such issues? Compare Article 23 of EU Council Regulation 44/2001, together with Articles 8-14, 15-17, and 18-21 of the Regulation.

(e) Preventing forum shopping. It was sometimes also suggested that forum selection clauses were an improper effort to shop for favorable judges or juries, which the law should not countenance. *Nute v. Hamilton Mutual Ins. Co.,* 72 Mass (6 Gray) 174, 184 (1856) (enforcing forum selection clause would permit shopping for partial judges and "disturb the symmetry of the law").

2. *Practical importance of forum selection clauses.* Recall the comments, cited above, regarding the practical importance of forum selection clauses. *See supra* pp. 463-464. A forum clause can oblige a party to litigate in a distant court (imposing expense and inconvenience), where its adversary is on "home ground," subject to unfavorable procedural and substantive law. Note the comparable practical consequences of the *forum non conveniens* doctrine. *See supra* pp. 414-419. Does justice permit private parties to bargain over such matters as their practical ability to litigate effectively and forum bias? Does it not compromise the judicial process to permit parties to agree, in effect, that one party shall be required to present its case less effectively because of distance, cost, and familiarity?

3. *Criticisms of historic rule against forum selection agreements.* How persuasive were the criticisms, launched in the 1950s, of the historic rule against forum clauses? Consider:

> The reasons stated by the courts for denying effect to choice of forum clauses are unconvincing. By and large, the courts have contented themselves with saying either (1) that the parties cannot by their agreement oust a court of jurisdiction, or (2) that to allow the parties to change the rules relating to the place where suit may be brought would "disturb the symmetry of the law" and lead to inconvenience, or (3) simply that choice of forum provisions are against public policy. The last of these reasons does no more than state a conclusion without attempt at explanation. The second — that the parties should not be permitted to tamper with rules relating to the place of suit — also falls wide of the mark. There are in fact no rules, other than those concerned with jurisdiction, which determine whether suit should be brought in one state rather than in another. As to the first reason, it is, of course, true that the parties cannot by their agreement oust a court of jurisdiction. But a court is not always required to exercise such jurisdiction as it may possess. Courts often refuse to hear a case because of *forum non conveniens* considerations. Why cannot they likewise dismiss a suit on the ground that it was not brought in a forum selected by the parties? Reese, *The Contractual Forum,* 13 Am. J. Comp. L. 187, 188 (1964).

Professor Reese's views formed the intellectual justification for the *Second Restatement* (for which he was the Reporter) and *Bremen.* Does Reese really confront the fundamental objections to forum selection clauses? Does he explain why legislative rules conferring jurisdiction on a local court can be ignored? Does he address the concerns that forum clauses will deny local residents the protections of public court systems, for which they have paid, based solely on privately negotiated contracts specifying where public justice may be obtained? Consider Justice Mosk's remark in *Smith* that "a finely honed dichotomy between a court deprived of jurisdiction . . . and a court declining to exercise jurisdiction" would be regarded as a "gossamer thin distinction . . . of dubious comfort" to most plaintiffs.

4. *Results in* Bremen *and* Smith. Was *Bremen* correctly decided? Should the Court have forced Zapata—an American employer, tax-payer, and company—to a far-off foreign court to enforce its tort claims? Why? Consider the facts in *Bremen*; is it not inconceivable that the law should prevent the parties from doing anything to limit the multitude of fora that were potentially available? On the other hand, if U.S. (and German) companies engage in business in many different countries, should they not accept that they will end up in court in those places? Why would that be such a "heavy hand" on international commerce?

Compare the result in *Bremen* with that in *Smith*. Was *Smith* correctly decided? What about Justice Mosk's dissenting views? Suppose that *Smith* had involved a German company and German contractual forum (instead of a Pennsylvania party and forum clause). Should (and would) the California court reach the same result? Are the arguments for enforceability stronger or weaker in this hypothetical than in *Smith*?

5. *Rationales for general enforceability of forum selection agreements.* What are the rationales underlying the general approval of forum agreements in *Bremen*, the Model Choice of Forum Act, the *Restatement (Second)*, EU Council Regulation 44/2001, and the proposed Hague Choice of Court Agreements Convention? Are these rationales persuasive?

(a) "Ancient concepts of freedom of contract." Is it plausible for the Court to cite "ancient freedoms" to contract in support of the *Bremen* rule? Recall the historic status of forum selection agreements at common law. *See supra* pp. 464-465.

(b) "Heavy hand" on international commerce. Will the wheels of international commerce grind to a halt if parties cannot enforce forum selection clauses? What happened before 1972? How exactly is it that forum selection clauses assist international businessmen? Would the Hague Conference have devoted a significant international effort to enhancing the enforcement regime for forum selection clauses if they were unimportant? Or was the Conference desperate to do something (anything) because negotiations on the proposed Judgments Convention collapsed? *See supra* pp. 107-108.

(c) "Elimination of all such uncertainties." Do forum clauses really eliminate the uncertainties that are endemic in international litigation? How? Consider the numerous cases cited in this chapter dealing with the enforceability and interpretation of forum selection clauses. Would there not be greater certainty if forum selection clauses were per se unenforceable? On the other hand, do parties not obtain significantly enhanced (if not perfect) certainty if they know what court will ultimately resolve their disputes? Why is "certainty" so important in commercial matters? Aren't countless uncertainties inherent in any contract? Doesn't that argue for trying to reduce them, in order to encourage parties to enter into mutually beneficial commercial relations?

Consider the numerous exceptions in the proposed Hague Choice of Court Agreements Convention. Do they provide much certainty about the enforceability of forum selection clauses? Is that a criticism of enforcing forum selection agreements or a criticism of the particular terms of the proposed Convention?

6. *Special need for forum selection clauses in international transactions.* Is there any greater need for forum agreements in international contracts than in domestic ones? What does *Bremen* suggest? Suppose that *Bremen* had involved a contract to be performed in a dozen different U.S. states, or that *Smith* had involved a contract with a Canadian company, selecting a Canadian forum. Would the need for a forum clause have been any different? *See* G. Born, *International Arbitration and Forum Selection Agreements: Drafting and Enforcing* 1-4 (3d ed. 2010) for a practically oriented discussion of the commercial benefits of forum selection clauses.

Consider the court's remarks in *General Engineering Corp. v. Martin Marietta Alumina, Inc.,* 783 F.2d 352, 358 n.6 (3d Cir. 1986), that "[in] a private international contract . . . the question of forum selection is considerably more important than it would be in a purely domestic contract." *See In re Oil Spill by the Amoco Cadiz,* 659 F.2d 789, 795 (7th Cir. 1981) ("special deference owed to forum-selection clauses in international contracts"). Do you agree with the suggestion that barriers to the enforcement of forum clauses should be particularly low in international disputes?

   7. *Different contemporary standards of enforceability of forum selection clauses.* Compare the standards of enforceability in *Restatement (Second) Conflict of Laws* §80 (1971), *Bremen, Smith,* and the proposed Hague Choice of Court Agreements Convention. What are the differences in these approaches? Which approach is most likely to result in enforcement of a forum agreement?

   (a) Restatement (Second) Conflict of Laws §80. What is the rule of enforceability set forth in §80? How is that rule influenced by comment a? How is enforcement of a forum selection clause under §80 different from a pure *forum non conveniens* analysis? How is enforcement of a forum selection agreement under §80 different from ordinary enforcement of a contract?

   (b) Bremen. What is the rule of enforceability set forth in *Bremen?* Are forum selection clauses treated in precisely the same fashion as other contracts? Do courts ordinarily scrutinize privately negotiated contracts for "reasonableness" and "fairness"? What, if anything, makes forum selection agreements different? If there are significant differences between forum selection agreements and other contracts, why enforce the former anyway?

   (c) Smith. What is the rule of enforceability set forth in *Smith?* How does the *Smith* rule differ from a pure *forum non conveniens* analysis? Are forum selection clauses entitled to any weight under *Smith?* If so, what weight? Recall the comment in *Bremen* that "it would be unrealistic to think that the parties did not conduct their negotiations, including fixing the monetary terms, with the consequences of the forum clause figuring prominently in their calculations." If that is correct, does the *Smith* approach deny one party of the financial exchange it made to obtain a forum clause of its choosing?

   (d) New York General Obligations Law §5-1402. What is the rule of enforceability for forum selection agreements in §5-1402 of the New York General Obligations Law? How does this differ from *Bremen* and *Smith?* Is it significant from a policy perspective that one of the leading commercial and financial centers in the world enacted this legislation? For a discussion of related aspects of the New York legislation, dealing with the enforceability of choice of law agreements, *see infra* pp. 769-770.

   (e) EU Council Regulation 44/2001. What is the basic rule of enforceability of forum selection clauses in Article 23 of Regulation 44/2001? Is it any different from that in *Bremen?* In §5-1402 of the New York General Obligations Law?

   8. *Appropriate approach to enforcing forum selection clauses.* Assuming that forum clauses are not *per se* unenforceable, which of the foregoing approaches is the *right* one? Is it more appropriate to (a) maintain a pure rule of *forum non conveniens,* in which a forum clause is one of numerous, equally significant factors bearing on the ultimate question of selecting a convenient forum; or (b) enforce forum selection clauses in full accordance with their terms like other contracts; or (c) enforce forum clauses when they are "reasonable" and not "unfair"? Do the differences between forum selection clauses and other contracts require different rules of enforceability? If so, what rules? How would *Tazwell, Bremen,* and *Smith* be decided under each of the foregoing rules?

   Compare these various approaches to the enforceability of forum selection agreements with the treatment of arbitration clauses under the Federal Arbitration Act and New York Convention. As discussed below, the FAA provides that arbitration agreements "shall be valid, irrevocable and enforceable, save upon such grounds as exist at law or in equity for the revocation of any contract." 9 U.S.C. §2. *See also* New York Convention, Art. II(1) & II(3); Appendix R, *infra* pp. 1167-1168. Why shouldn't this same rule of contractual enforceability apply to choice of forum agreements? Is it not odd that agreements to send disputes to private arbitrators (without meaningful judicial review) should be materially more binding and enforceable than choice of court agreements?

9. *Exclusive versus nonexclusive forum selection agreements.* Consider the language of the forum selection clauses at issue in *Tazwell* and in *Bremen*. Is there any doubt that those clauses were "exclusive," in that they required that all disputes be resolved solely in the contractual forum? *See supra* pp. 462-463. How water-tight is the *Bremen* clause in this regard?

Suppose that the clause in *Tazwell* had said "For the fulfillment of this contract the courts of Karlsruhe are competent." Suppose that the *Bremen* clause had said: "Any dispute arising may be treated before the London Court of Justice." Would either clause have been exclusive?

(a) Presumption under U.S. law of nonexclusivity. Note that, under most U.S. jurisdictions' laws, "When only jurisdiction is specified the clause will generally not be enforced without some further language indicating the parties' intent to make jurisdiction exclusive." *John Boutari and Son, Wines and Spirits, SA v. Attiki Importers and Distributors Inc.,* 22 F.3d 51 (2d Cir. 1994) (quoting *Docksider, Ltd. v. Sea Technology, Ltd.,* 875 F.2d 762, 764 (9th Cir. 1987)). As Judge Weinfeld has explained, "the normal construction of the jurisdiction rules includes a presumption that, where jurisdiction exists, it cannot be ousted or waived absent a clear indication of such a purpose." *City of New York v. Pullman, Inc.,* 477 F. Supp. 438, 442 n.11 (S.D.N.Y. 1979). Is this presumption of permissiveness sensible? Why? Is it driven by the concerns that also arise in relation to the enforceability of forum selection clauses?

(b) Presumption in most civil law jurisdictions of exclusivity. Consider Article 23 of EU Council Regulation 44/2001. What presumption does Article 23 adopt with regard to forum selection clauses? *Compare* Swiss Law on Private International Law, Art. 5 ("Unless the agreement provides otherwise, the agreed court has exclusive jurisdiction"). Is this approach wiser than that of U.S. courts? Why or why not?

(c) Exclusivity of forum selection clauses under proposed Hague Choice of Court Agreements Convention. Consider Articles 5 and 6 of the proposed Hague Choice of Court Agreements Convention. What forum selection clauses do Articles 5 and 6 render enforceable? Consider Article 22 of the Convention. Why is it that the Convention renders exclusive forum selection agreements enforceable, while only creating a possible framework for reciprocal agreements rendering nonexclusive forum selection clauses enforceable? From a U.S. perspective, isn't this backwards? Or at least wrong-headed?

Consider Articles 3(a) and 3(b) of the proposed Convention. What do they mean? Does not Article 3(b) adopt the same presumption as Article 23 of EU Council Regulation 44/2001? Why did the U.S. negotiators agree to this? Are not the policies underlying a presumption of nonexclusivity well founded?

(d) Choice of law governing exclusivity of forum selection agreement. Suppose a forum selection clause provides for litigation in a foreign forum and is accompanied by a choice-of-law clause providing for application of the law of that state. If litigation is commenced in U.S. courts, is the exclusivity of the forum selection clause governed by foreign or U.S. law? For one answer, *see TH Agriculture & Nutrition, LLC v. ACE European Group Ltd.,* 416 F. Supp. 2d 1054 (D. Kan. 2006).

10. *Enforceability of forum selection clauses under proposed Hague Choice of Court Agreements Convention.* What is the rule of enforceability for exclusive forum selection agreements in the proposed Hague Choice of Courts Agreements Convention? What about nonexclusive forum selection agreements? Why are these two types of choice of forum clauses treated differently, insofar as enforceability is concerned, by the Convention? Is it peculiar for an exclusive forum selection clause to be *more* enforceable than a nonexclusive one? What rationale might support this?

Putting aside the differing treatment of exclusive and nonexclusive choice of forum clauses, what standard of enforceability does the proposed Hague Convention prescribe for exclusive forum selection agreements? Is it more similar to *Bremen*, to *Smith*, or to N.Y. General Obligations Law §5-1402? Consider Article 19 of the Convention. Compare EU Council Regulation 44/2001.

11. *Wisdom of U.S. ratification of proposed Hague Choice of Court Agreements Convention.* Should the United States ratify the proposed Hague Choice of Court Agreements Convention? Why or why not? What would ratification accomplish?

12. *Application of forum selection clauses to noncontractual claims.* Note that *Smith* involved a California plaintiff's tort claims. Should the standards of enforceability for forum clauses differ because tort, instead of contract, claims were involved? Do tort claims implicate different, more "public" interests, than contract claims? Suppose *Smith* had involved claims based on California state or federal statutory protections. Should forum clauses be enforced in these circumstances? Should the same standards of enforceability apply? How does the proposed Hague Choice of Court Agreements Convention apply to noncontractual claims?

13. *Choice of law governing enforceability of forum selection clauses — an initial view.* What law governed the enforceability of the forum selection clauses in each of *Tazwell, Bremen,* and *Smith*? Did the courts apply the law of the contractual forums (*e.g.,* Germany, England) or the law of the enforcement forums (the United States)? If the law of the contractual forum would enforce the forum selection clause, does that end inquiry?

Suppose that the parties have agreed that the law of the contractual forum will govern their relations. This was the case in both *Bremen* and *Smith*. What role, if any, did English and Pennsylvania law have in each case?

14. *Appropriate remedy for breach of exclusive forum selection clause.* Assuming that exclusive forum selection clauses are valid and enforceable, what relief should be granted if one party brings a suit outside the contractual forum? Is it a foregone conclusion that the forum selection clause should be recognized and enforced, by dismissing any suit by either party outside the contractual forum? Why would not damages be a sufficient remedy? What would the damages for breach of a forum selection clause be? *See* Shantar, *Forum Selection Clauses: Damages in Lieu of Dismissal?*, 82 B.U. L. Rev. 1063 (2002); Tan, *Damages for Breach of Forum Selection Clauses, Principled Remedies, and Control of International Civil Litigation,* 40 Tex. Int'l L.J. 623 (2005); Tan & Yeo, *Breaking Promises to Litigate in a Particular Forum: Are Damages an Appropriate Remedy?*, [2003] 4 LMCLQ 435.

C.   Grounds for Resisting Enforcement of Forum Selection Agreement

1.   Introduction

As described above, *Bremen* declared that forum selection clauses are presumptively enforceable. *The Restatement (Second) Conflict of Laws,* the Model Act, EU Council Regulation 44/2001, the proposed Hague Choice of Court Agreements Convention and other authorities have adopted similar approaches. All of these authorities make it clear, however, that the presumptive enforceability of forum clauses is subject to exceptions. In summary, the following grounds are generally available in U.S. courts for resisting enforcement of forum agreements: (1) defects in the formation or validity of the forum selection agreement and other contractual defenses, such as fraud, duress, unconscionability, and lack of assent; (2) unreasonableness; and (3) public policy. The first category of defenses are based on contract law doctrines, and go to the question whether or not a valid contract providing a choice of forum exists; the latter two categories concern the question whether, assuming a valid choice of forum agreement exists, the agreement will be enforced.[91]

2. Defects in Formation and Other Contract Law Defenses as Grounds for Resisting Enforcement of Forum Selection Agreements

Like other agreements, the enforceability of a forum selection clause can be resisted by challenging the manner in which it has been entered into. These challenges are broadly similar to the defenses that are raised to the enforceability of arbitration agreements.[92] Although relatively few decisions have addressed this, a forum selection agreement would be unenforceable if it did not satisfy general contract law principles for the formation and validity of any contract.

Several specific defects in formation are invoked with particular frequency, all generally relating to unconscionability. *Bremen* said that a choice of forum clause would not be enforced if it was procured by fraud, "undue influence," "overweening bargaining power," or "overreaching."[93] The same exceptions are contemplated by the Model Choice of Forum Act, and the comments to §80 of the *Restatement (Second) Conflict of Laws*.[94]

The *Colonial Leasing* case, excerpted below, illustrates a fairly expansive application of *Zapata*'s exceptions for unconscionability, "overreaching," and "overweening bargaining power." After reading that decision, consider the excerpt, set forth thereafter, from the Supreme Court's decision in *Carnival Cruise Lines, Inc. v. Shute*. As discussed above, *Carnival Cruise* adopts a narrow view of unconscionability exceptions.

COLONIAL LEASING CO. OF NEW ENGLAND v.
PUGH BROTHERS GARAGE

735 F.2d 380 (9th Cir. 1984)

FERGUSON, CIRCUIT JUDGE. Colonial Leasing Company of New England, Inc. (Colonial) filed a complaint for breach of a leasing agreement against . . . Pugh Brothers Garage. Colonial asserted personal jurisdiction over the defendant on the basis of a forum selection clause which was part of Colonial's standard form lease agreement. The district court dismissed for lack of personal jurisdiction on the ground that it would be unfair and unreasonable to enforce the forum selection clause. . . . We affirm.

---

91. Woodward, *Finding the Contract in Contracts for Law, Forum and Arbitration,* 2 Hastings Bus. L.J. 1 (2006).

92. *See infra* p. 1165; G. Born, *International Commercial Arbitration* 563-580 (2009).

93. 407 U.S. at 12, 15. Conversely, the Court repeatedly observed that the parties' forum selection clause had been "freely negotiated" in an "arm's-length negotiation by experienced and sophisticated businessmen." 407 U.S. at 12, 17. The Court also emphasized that "it would be unrealistic to think that the parties did not conduct their negotiations . . . with the consequences of the forum selection clause figuring prominently in their calculations." *Id.* at 14.

94. *Restatement (Second) Conflict of Laws* §80 comment a (1971 & 1986 Revisions) contemplates nonenforcement where a provision is the result of "overreaching" or "the unfair use of unequal bargaining power."

Colonial is a Massachusetts corporation having its principal place of business in Oregon. Colonial purchases equipment from manufacturers and vendors and leases it to businesses in Oregon and other states. The defendants Pugh Brothers Garage, Eugene Pugh and John Pugh (Pugh Bros.) are citizens of Georgia who operate an auto repair business in Georgia. In 1980, Pugh Bros. contacted Major Muffler, Inc., a New York corporation, through Major Muffler's Atlanta, Georgia representative, to obtain a pipe-bending machine and other equipment. At Major Muffler's request, Pugh Bros. filled out a financial statement which Major Muffler submitted to Colonial. Colonial approved the lease application, and agreed to purchase the equipment from Major Muffler and lease it to Pugh Bros. Major Muffler informed Pugh Bros. that the leasing company had approved the application. Major Muffler shipped the pipe-bending machine to Pugh Bros. from Alabama. Colonial then sent Pugh Bros. the lease agreement and began billing Pugh Bros. monthly from Oregon. Pugh Bros. thought that they were dealing with Major Muffler, a New York corporation, and had no idea Colonial was involved. The standard form lease which they signed included in small print on the back a clause which provided:

> 22. CHOICE OF LAW. . . . This Lease shall be considered to have been made in the State of Oregon, and shall be interpreted, and the rights and liabilities of the parties hereto determined, in accordance with the constitution, statutes, judicial decisions, and administrative regulations of the State of Oregon. Lessees waive all right to a trial by jury in any litigation relating to any transaction under this agreement.
>
> Lessee hereby designates as its agent for the purpose of accepting service of process within the State of Oregon and further agrees to arrange for any transmissions of notice of such service of process from said agent to Lessee as Lessee deems necessary or desirable. Lessee consents to Oregon jurisdiction in any action, suit or proceeding arising out of the Lease, and concedes that it, and each of them, transacted business in the State of Oregon in entry into this Lease. In the event of suit enforcing this Lease, Lessee agrees that venue may be laid in the country of Lessor's address below.

This clause was not negotiated nor discussed by the parties. No agent was designated for service of process. Pugh Bros. did not know that they could be sued in Oregon as a result of that clause. . . . [T]he defendants eventually defaulted under the lease agreement. On March 24, 1982, Colonial filed a complaint against Pugh Bros. for breach of the equipment lease contract. Pugh Bros. moved to dismiss for lack of jurisdiction; the district court granted the motion. . . .

Under Oregon law, a choice-of-forum clause will be given effect unless it would be unfair or unreasonable to do so. *The Bremen v. Zapata Off-Shore Co., supra.* We agree with the district court's analysis that the standard of "unfair or unreasonable" is designed to invalidate clauses such as those in question here. The evidence disclosed in each case that there was in fact no bargaining on the clause in question. It was contained in a form contract in fine print at the bottom of a page. . . . [T]his sort of take-it-or-leave-it clause will be disregarded.

CARNIVAL CRUISE LINES, INC. v. SHUTE
499 U.S. 585 (1991)

Justice Blackmun. In this admiralty case we primarily consider whether the United States Court of Appeals for the Ninth Circuit correctly refused to enforce a forum-selection clause contained in tickets issued by petitioner Carnival Cruise Lines, Inc., to respondents Eulala and Russel Shute. The Shutes, through an Arlington, Washington, travel agent, purchased passage for a 7-day cruise on petitioner's ship, the TROPICALE. Respondents paid the fare to the agent who forwarded the payment to petitioner's headquarters in Miami, Florida. Petitioner then prepared the tickets and sent them to respondents [at their home] in the State of Washington. The face of each ticket, at its left-hand lower corner, contained this admonition:

> SUBJECT TO CONDITIONS OF CONTRACT ON LAST PAGES **IMPORTANT!** PLEASE READ CONTRACT—ON LAST PAGES 1,2,3

The following appeared on "contract page 1" of each ticket:

TERMS AND CONDITIONS OF PASSAGE CONTRACT TICKET

> 3.(a)   The acceptance of this ticket by the person or persons named hereon as passengers shall be deemed to be an acceptance and agreement by each of them of all of the terms and conditions of this Passage Contract Ticket.
> 8.   It is agreed by and between the passenger and the Carrier that all disputes and matters whatsoever arising under, in connection with or incident to this Contract shall be litigated, if at all, in and before a Court located in the State of Florida, U.S.A., to the exclusion of the Courts of any other state or country. . . .

Respondents boarded the TROPICALE in Los Angeles, California. The ship sailed to Puerto Vallarta, Mexico, and then returned to Los Angeles. While the ship was in international waters off the Mexican coast, respondent Eulala Shute was injured when she slipped on a deck mat during a guided tour of the ship's galley. Respondents filed suit against petitioner in the United States District Court for the Western District of Washington, claiming that Mrs. Shute's injuries had been caused by the negligence of Carnival Cruise Lines and its employees.

Petitioner moved for summary judgment, contending that the forum clause in respondents' tickets required the Shutes to bring their suit . . . in the State of Florida. . . . [On appeal, the] Court of Appeals acknowledged that a court concerned with the enforceability of such a clause must begin its analysis with *Bremen v. Zapata Off-Shore Co.,* [but] concluded that the forum clause should not be enforced because it "was not freely bargained for." As an "independent justification" for refusing to enforce the clause, the Court of Appeals noted that there was evidence in the record to indicate that "the Shutes are physically and financially incapable of pursuing this litigation in Florida" and that the enforcement of the clause would operate to deprive them of their day in court. . . .

We begin by noting the boundaries of our inquiry. First, this is a case in admiralty, and federal law governs the enforceability of the forum-selection clause we scrutinize. Second, we do not address the question whether respondents had sufficient notice of the forum clause before entering the contract for passage. Respondents essentially have conceded that they had notice of the forum-selection provision. . . . Within this context, respondents urge that the forum clause should not be enforced because, contrary to . . . *Bremen,* the clause was not the product of negotiation, and enforcement effectively would deprive respondents of their day in court. . . .

[In *Bremen,* this Court held that, in general, "freely negotiated private international agreement[s]," should be given full effect, except where doing so would be "unreasonable."] The Court did not define precisely the circumstances that would make it unreasonable for a court to enforce a forum clause. Instead, the Court discussed a number of factors that made it reasonable to enforce the clause at issue in *Bremen* and that, presumably, would be pertinent in any determination whether to enforce a similar clause. . . . In applying *Bremen,* the Court of Appeals in the present litigation took note of the foregoing "reasonableness" factors and rather automatically decided that the forum-selection clause was unenforceable because, unlike the parties in *Bremen,* respondents are not business persons and did not negotiate the terms of the clause with petitioner. Alternatively, the Court of Appeals ruled that the clause should not be enforced because enforcement effectively would deprive respondents of an opportunity to litigate their claim against petitioner.

    Bremen concerned a "far from routine transaction between companies of two different nations contemplating the tow of an extremely costly piece of equipment from Louisiana across the Gulf of Mexico and the Atlantic Ocean, through the Mediterranean Sea to its final destination in the Adriatic Sea." These facts suggest that, even apart from the evidence of negotiation regarding the forum clause, it was entirely reasonable for the Court in *Bremen* to have expected Unterweser and Zapata to have negotiated with care in selecting a forum for the resolution of disputes arising from their special towing contract. In contrast, respondents' passage contract was purely routine and doubtless nearly identical to every commercial passage contract issued by petitioner and most other cruise lines. In this context, it would be entirely unreasonable for us to assume that respondents — or any other cruise passenger — would negotiate with petitioner the terms of a forum-selection clause in an ordinary commercial cruise ticket. Common sense dictates that a ticket of this kind will be a form contract the terms of which are not subject to negotiation, and that an individual purchasing the ticket will not have bargaining parity with the cruise line. But by ignoring the crucial differences in the business contexts in which the respective contracts were executed, the Court of Appeals' analysis seems to us to have distorted somewhat this Court's holding in *Bremen.*

    In evaluating the reasonableness of the forum clause at issue in this case, we must refine the analysis of *Bremen* to account for the realities of form passage contracts. As an initial matter, we do not adopt the Court of Appeals' determination that a non negotiated forum-selection clause in a form ticket contract is never enforceable simply because it is not the subject of bargaining. Including a reasonable forum clause in a form contract of this kind well may be permissible for several reasons: First, a cruise line has a special interest in limiting the fora in which it potentially could be subject to suit. Because a cruise ship typically carries passengers from many locales, it is not unlikely that a mishap on a cruise could subject the cruise line to litigation in several different fora. Additionally, a clause establishing ex ante the forum for dispute resolution has the salutary effect of dispelling any confusion about where suits arising from the contract must be brought and defended, sparing litigants the time and expense of pretrial motions to determine the correct forum, and conserving judicial resources that otherwise would be devoted to deciding those motions. Finally, it stands to reason that passengers who purchase tickets containing a forum clause like that at issue in this case benefit in the form of reduced fares reflecting the savings that the cruise line enjoys by limiting the fora in which it may be sued.

    We also do not accept the Court of Appeals' independent justification for its conclusion that *Bremen* dictates that the clause should not be enforced because "[t]here is evidence in the record to indicate that the Shutes are physically and financially incapable of pursuing this litigation in Florida." We do not defer to the Court of Appeals' findings of fact. . . . [T]he District Court made no finding regarding the physical and financial impediments to the Shutes' pursuing their case in Florida. The Court of Appeals' conclusory reference to the record provides no basis for this Court to validate the finding of inconvenience. Furthermore, the Court of Appeals did not place in proper context this Court's statement in *Bremen* that "the serious inconvenience of the contractual forum to one or both of the parties might carry greater weight in determining the reasonableness of the forum clause." The Court made this statement in evaluating a hypothetical "agreement between two Americans to resolve their essentially local disputes in a remote alien forum." In the present case, Florida is not a "remote alien forum," nor — given the fact that Mrs. Shute's accident occurred off the coast of Mexico — is this dispute an essentially local one inherently more suited to resolution in the State of Washington than in Florida. In light of these distinctions, and because respondents do not claim lack of notice of the forum clause, we conclude that they have not satisfied the "heavy burden of proof," required to set aside the clause on grounds of inconvenience.

It bears emphasis that forum-selection clauses contained in form passage contracts are subject to judicial scrutiny for fundamental fairness. In this case, there is no indication that petitioner set Florida as the forum in which disputes were to be resolved as a means of discouraging cruise passengers from pursuing legitimate claims. Any suggestion of such a bad-faith motive is belied by two facts: petitioner has its principal place of business in Florida, and many of its cruises depart from and return to Florida ports. Similarly, there is no evidence that petitioner obtained respondents' accession to the forum clause by fraud or overreaching. Finally, respondents have conceded that they were given notice of the forum provision and, therefore, presumably retained the option of rejecting the contract with impunity. In the case before us, therefore, we conclude that the Court of Appeals erred in refusing to enforce the forum-selection clause. . . .

JUSTICE STEVENS, with whom JUSTICE MARSHALL joins, dissenting. . . . I begin my dissent by noting that only the most meticulous passenger is likely to become aware of the forum selection provision. . . . [Indeed, even a] careful reader [would] find the forum-selection clause [only] in the eighth of the twenty-five numbered paragraphs. Of course, many passengers, like the respondents in this case, will not have an opportunity to read paragraph 8 until they have actually purchased their tickets. By this point, the passengers will already have accepted the condition set forth in paragraph 16(a), which provides that "[t]he Carrier shall not be liable to make any refund to passengers in respect of . . . tickets wholly or partly not used by a passenger." Not knowing whether or not that provision is legally enforceable, I assume that the average passenger would accept the risk of having to file suit in Florida in the event of an injury, rather than canceling — without a refund — a planned vacation at the last minute. The fact that the cruise line can reduce its litigation costs, and therefore its liability insurance premiums, by forcing this choice on its passengers does not, in my opinion, suffice to render the provision reasonable. . . .

Forum-selection clauses in passenger tickets involve the intersection of two strands of traditional contract law that qualify the general rule that courts will enforce the terms of a contract as written. Pursuant to the first strand, courts traditionally have reviewed with heightened scrutiny the terms of contracts of adhesion, form contracts offered on a take-or-leave basis by a party with stronger bargaining power to a party with weaker power. . . . The second doctrinal principle implicated by forum-selection clauses is the traditional rule that "contractual provisions which seek to limit the place or court in which an action may . . . be brought, are invalid as contrary to public policy." . . . Although adherence to this general rule has declined in recent years, particularly following our decision in [*Bremen*], the prevailing rule is still that forum-selection clauses are not enforceable if they were not freely bargained for, create additional expense for one party, or deny one party a remedy. . . .

EUROPEAN UNION COUNCIL REGULATION 44/2001,
ARTS. 8-14, 15-17, 18-21 & 23
[excerpted in Appendix E]

HAGUE CONVENTION ON CHOICE OF
COURT AGREEMENTS, ARTS. 2, 3, 5 & 6
44 Int'l Legal Mats. 1294 (2005) [excerpted in Appendix I]

Notes *on* Colonial Leasing, Carnival Cruise, *and Legislative Materials*

1. *Separability of the forum selection agreement.* A preliminary issue is whether a forum selection agreement is "separable" from the underlying contract in which it is contained. In the related context of arbitration, governed by the Federal Arbitration Act, the Supreme Court has said that an arbitration agreement is generally a separate, independent agreement from the contract to which it relates. *Prima Paint Corp. v. Flood & Conklin Manufacturing Co.,* 388 U.S. 395 (1967); *infra* p. 1167; G. Born, *International Commercial Arbitration* 328-332 (2009). As a consequence, challenges to the validity, existence, and legality of the underlying contract do not necessarily call into question the "separate" arbitration agreement; this separate arbitration agreement is therefore capable of surviving defects in the underlying contract's formation, termination, invalidity, or illegality. *See infra* p. 1167.

The separability doctrine should be equally applicable to forum clauses. The Supreme Court has remarked that "an agreement to arbitrate before a specialized tribunal [is], in effect, a specialized kind of forum-selection clause." *Scherk v. Alberto-Culver Co.,* 417 U.S. 506, 519 (1974). The rationale for the separability doctrine — an exchange of promises to resolve disputes in a particular manner — thus applies to forum clauses with the same force as arbitration agreements. As noted below, most courts have adopted this analysis, although a few have apparently not.

Consider Article 3(d) of the proposed Hague Choice of Court Agreements Convention, which provides

> An exclusive choice of court agreement that forms part of a contract shall be treated as an agreement independent of the other terms of the contract. The validity of the exclusive choice of court agreement cannot be contested solely on the ground that the contract is not valid.

What is the practical importance of the separability doctrine?

2. *Wisdom of decision in* Carnival Cruise. Was *Carnival Cruise* correctly decided? Compare the opinions by Justice Blackmun and Justice Stevens. Which is a more persuasive reading of *Bremen*? Which result in *Carnival Cruise* is more persuasive from a policy perspective? Consider the following observation about in *Carnival Cruise*: "the Supreme Court not only reaffirmed the presumption favoring enforcement but also narrowed the circumstances in which a choice of forum clause will be held unreasonable." Sturley, *Strengthening the Presumption of Validity for Choice of Forum Clauses,* 23 J. Mar. L. & Com. 131 (1992). Is this accurate? If so, was the Court's action wise? Consider also:

> *Carnival Cruise Lines* was an easy case. It was based on the humblest, most uncomplicated, garden-variety slip-and-fall tort ever to grace the federal courts. It involved a pure, paradigmatic adhesive consumer contract, complete with non-negotiable, tiny, boilerplate print. Nonetheless, in spite of the utter simplicity of its facts, seven Justices managed to get *Carnival*

Cruise Lines wrong. *Carnival Cruise Lines* made bad law. In holding that particular forum-selection clause enforceable, the Supreme Court gave its broad stamp of approval for forum-selection clauses generally as a method for establishing jurisdiction. However, in spite of their persistently touted virtues, forum-selection clauses can be unfair and insidious. The result in *Carnival Cruise Lines* was unfair because under existing precedent, and as a matter of pure contract law, courts should not enforce adhesive consumer forum-selection clauses. Yet, this is precisely what the Supreme Court did.

Furthermore, at both the practical and theoretical levels, adhesive forum-selection clauses are anathema to long-standing jurisdictional principles that defer to a plaintiff's choice of forum balanced against a defendant's due process rights. As a practical matter, these clauses cause unwitting plaintiffs to forfeit legitimate legal claims due to the plaintiff's frequent inability to mount a case in a distant, inconvenient courtroom. As a theoretical matter, engrafting contract principles onto forum-access rules tips the procedural balance in favor of well-heeled, savvy defendants; thus, what repels us as a matter of contract law should repel us as a matter of jurisdictional theory. Mullenix, *Another Easy Case, Some More Bad Law: Carnival Cruise Lines and Contractual Personal Jurisdiction*, 27 Tex. Int'l L.J. 323, 325-326 (1992).

Is Professor Mullenix right?

How would the proposed Hague Convention have applied to the forum selection clause in *Carnival Cruise*? Consider Articles 2(1)(a), 2(2)(f) and 2(2)(j). *Compare* EU Council Regulation 44/2001, Arts. 13, 15-18.

3. *The* Carnival Cruise *forum selection clause.* What was the most troubling feature of the forum clause in *Carnival Cruise*? Note Justice Stevens' discussion of the clause. Consider also the following remarks by Judge Richard Posner concerning the *Carnival Cruise* facts: the forum clause "plainly is neither intended nor likely to be read," and "[i]f ever there was a case for stretching the concept of fraud in the name of unconscionability, it was *Shute,* and perhaps no stretch was necessary." *Northwestern National Insurance Co. v. Donovan,* 916 F.2d 372, 376 (7th Cir. 1990). Judge Posner is not reputed for paternalism or sentimentality. Is his characterization correct? Should, as Judge Posner suggests, the *Carnival Cruise* clause have been invalidated? On what ground? Is this a ground that was before the Supreme Court in *Carnival Cruise*? If the clause in *Carnival Cruise* is not enforceable, would *any* forum selection clause in a standardized form contract ever be enforceable? When?

4. *Forum selection agreements with consumers, insureds, employees, and similar parties.* Note that *Carnival Cruise* involved a consumer. Should that affect the analysis? Consider Articles 8-14, 15-17, and 18-21 of EU Council Regulation; compare Article 2 of the Hague Choice of Court Agreements Convention. Are these legislative provisions wise? Why or why not?

5. *Fraud or duress as bases for resisting enforcement of international forum selection agreements.* *Bremen, Carnival Cruise,* and other authorities recognize exceptions to the enforceability of forum selection clauses obtained by fraud, duress, or undue influence. Compare Article 5(1) of the Hague Choice of Court Agreements Convention.

(a) Lower court authorities finding fraud in formation of forum selection clause. A few courts have found either fraud or duress in the procurement of a forum agreement. *Weidner Communications, Inc. v. H.R.H. Prince Baudar Al Faisal,* 859 F.2d 1302 (7th Cir. 1988) (holding foreign forum selection clause unenforceable because of unequal bargaining power and physical intimidation of party's representative); *Farmland Industries, Inc. v. Frazier-Parrott Commodities, Inc.,* 806 F.2d 848 (8th Cir. 1986) ("in a situation where a fiduciary relationship . . . is created by a contract tainted by fraud, the person defrauded can not be held to the contractual forum selection clause"); *Preferred Capital, Inc. v. Sarasota Kennel Club,* 2005 WL 1799900, at *3 (N.D. Ohio 2005) (holding nonspecific

forum clause unenforceable due to plaintiff's failure to disclose consequences of clause language to defendant); *Armco Inc. v. North Atlantic Ins. Co.,* 68 F. Supp. 2d 330, 340 (S.D.N.Y. 1999) (holding forum clause unenforceable due to collusion by counsel to modify clause without party's knowledge); *Crowson v. Sealaska Corp.,* 705 P.2d 905 (Alaska 1985) (bribery of contracting party's representatives would vitiate forum selection clause).

(b) Most lower courts reject fraud challenges to forum selection agreements. The fraud and duress exceptions have not, however, frequently been invoked. According to one commentator, "[s]ince outright fraud never forms the basis for a forum-selection clause, it is virtually impossible to challenge a clearly drafted provision." Mullenix, *Another Easy Case, Some More Bad Law:* Carnival Cruise Lines *and Contractual Personal Jurisdiction,* 27 Tex. Int'l L.J. 323, 363 (1992). Lower courts have almost uniformly rejected fraud and duress claims on their facts. *Murphy v. Schneider Nat'l, Inc.,* 362 F.3d 1133, 1141 (9th Cir. 2004); *Marano Enterprises of Kansas v. Z-Teca Restaurants, LP,* 254 F.3d 753, 757 (8th Cir. 2001); *Silva v. Encyclopedia Brittanica Inc.,* 239 F.3d 385, 389 (1st Cir. 2001); *Lipcon v. Underwriters at Lloyd's, London,* 148 F.3d 1285, 1296-1297 (11th Cir. 1998); *Afram Carriers, Inc. v. Moeykens,* 145 F.3d 298, 301-302 (5th Cir. 1998); *MacPhail v. Oceaneering Int'l, Inc.,* 170 F. Supp. 2d 718, 725 (S.D. Tex. 2001); *Marra v. Papandreou,* 59 F. Supp. 2d 65, 70-71 nn.3-4 (D.D.C. 1999); *Frietsch v. Refco, Inc.,* 1994 WL 494945 (N.D. Ill. 1994); *Juels v. Deutsche Bank AG,* 1993 U.S. Dist. LEXIS 1914 (N.D.N.Y. 1993); *Envirolite Enterprises, Inc. v. Glastechnische Industrie Peter Lisec GmbH,* 53 B.R. 1007 (S.D.N.Y. 1985).

Recently, some courts have invalidated so-called "floating" forum selection clauses under the fraud exception. *See Secure Financial Service, Inc. v. Popular Leasing USA, Inc.,* 892 A.2d 571, 578 (Md. 2006) (collecting cases). A "floating" clause does not specify the forum where the dispute will be resolved but ties that determination to some fact or agreement extrinsic to the contract containing the forum selection clause. While the fact patterns vary, one situation that courts have found problematic is where the choice of forum is tied to another agreement that specifies the forum but is not disclosed to one of the contracting parties when it enters into the contract containing the "floating" forum selection clause. *See, e.g., Preferred Capital, Inc. v. Aetna Maintenance, Inc.,* 2005 WL 1398549 (N.D. Ohio 2005).

(c) Application of separability doctrine to fraud defense. If the separability doctrine is applied, only fraud or duress relating to the *inclusion of the forum selection clause itself* in the parties' agreement should be relevant. As the Supreme Court explained, in broad language, in a post-*Bremen* decision in the arbitration context:

> [The fraud exception] does not mean that anytime a dispute arising out of a transaction is based upon an allegation of fraud . . . the "forum selection" clause is unenforceable. Rather, it means that . . . [a] forum selection clause in a contract is not enforceable if the *inclusion of that clause in the contract* was the product of fraud or coercion. *Scherk v. Alberto-Culver Co.,* 417 U.S. 506, 519 n.14 (1974) (emphasis in original).

See Marano Enterprises of Kansas v. Z-Teca Restaurants, LP, 254 F.3d 753, 757 (8th Cir. 2001); *Lipcon v. Underwriters at Lloyd's, London,* 148 F.3d 1285, 1296-1297 (11th Cir. 1998); *Afram Carriers, Inc. v. Moeykens,* 145 F.3d 298, 301-302 (5th Cir. 1998); *AVC Nederland BV v. Atrium Inv. Partnership,* 740 F.2d 148, 158 (2d Cir. 1984).

Despite this, some lower courts have held forum clauses unenforceable because the parties' underlying contract was procured by fraud or duress, without specifically considering whether the contract's forum clause was itself allegedly induced by fraud or similar misconduct. *E.g., J.B. Hoffman v. Minuteman Press Int'l Inc.,* 747 F. Supp. 552

(W.D. Mo. 1990) (expressly refusing to apply separability doctrine in domestic context); *Gaskin v. Stumm Handel GmbH,* 390 F. Supp. 361 (S.D.N.Y. 1975).

Nonetheless, most lower courts have adhered fairly closely to the rule that fraud in procuring the parties' underlying contract does not affect a forum clause within that agreement. *See, e.g., Afram Carriers, Inc. v. Moeykens,* 145 F.3d 298, 301-302 (5th Cir. 1998) ("Were we to judge the soundness of the forum-selection clause by what we believe to be the merits of the underlying contract, we would subvert the aforementioned comity concerns by making a merits inquiry that the Supreme Court has determined is best left to the forum selected by the parties. Only when we can discern that *the clause itself* was obtained in contravention of the law will the federal courts disregard it and proceed to judge the merits."); *Stamm v. Barclays Bank of New York,* 960 F. Supp. 724, 729-730 (S.D.N.Y. 1997) ("[T]o overcome the presumed validity of the [forum selection] and [choice of law] clauses, plaintiffs must plead specific fraudulent acts or statements by which defendants induced their consent to these clauses.").

Suppose that Zapata had alleged in *Bremen* that Unterweser had fraudulently induced it into making the towage contract by deliberately misrepresenting its technical expertise and experience. Should such a claim provide a basis for ignoring the forum selection clause? Suppose that Zapata argues that the entire towage contract is void because of Unterweser's fraud.

6. *Unconscionability as basis for resisting enforcement of forum selection agreements.* Several related bases for challenging the formation of a forum clause are broadly comparable to the fraud exception; these are "overweening bargaining power," "the abuse of economic power," and "unconscionability." All of these grounds relate to the relative bargaining power of the parties, the extent and character of bargaining between them, and the exercise of undue commercial or other leverage.

(a) Inequality in bargaining power as basis for nonenforcement of forum selection clause. Challenges to the enforceability of forum selection clauses have frequently relied upon alleged inequalities in bargaining power between the parties. Even before *Carnival Cruise,* mere differences in economic strength would not, without more, require nonenforcement of forum selection clauses. Thus, the *Restatement*'s comment to §80 referred to the "*unfair use* of unequal bargaining power," and §3(4) of the Model Act provided for nonenforcement where a forum selection agreement was obtained by "*the abuse* of economic power." Similarly, lower courts generally did not accord independent significance to disparities in bargaining power. *E.g., Hodes v. S.N.C. Achille Lauro ed Altri-Gestione,* 858 F.2d 905, 913 (3d Cir. 1988) ("while the appellants certainly enjoyed a superior bargaining position, they did not take unfair advantage of that position to 'overween' the Hodes").

Does a disparity of bargaining power have any relevance to the enforceability of forum clauses after *Carnival Cruise?* Given the obvious disparities in bargaining power between Carnival Cruise and the Shutes, how can inequalities in bargaining power be an independent basis for resisting forum agreements in the future? Nevertheless, do inequalities in bargaining power have some relevance to the enforceability of forum selection clauses? If so, what? Note Justice Stevens' remark that "courts traditionally have reviewed with heightened scrutiny the terms of contracts of adhesion, form contracts offered on a take-it-or-leave basis by a party with stronger bargaining power to a party with weaker power."

(b) Absence of bargaining as basis for nonenforcement of forum selection clause. Bremen emphasized that the forum clause at issue was a "vital part" of the parties' agreement, which had been "freely negotiated" in an "arm's-length negotiation by experienced and sophisticated businessmen." *Colonial Leasing* refused to enforce the forum selection clause,

largely on the grounds that "there was in fact no bargaining on the clause," which "was contained in a form contract in fine print at the bottom of a page."

Even before *Carnival Cruise,* however, most courts refused to accord significant weight to the absence of bargaining, with the vast majority of lower court decisions refusing to deny enforcement based on the absence of negotiations over the forum selection clause. *E.g., Lien Ho Hsing Steel Enter. Co. v. Weihtag,* 738 F.2d 1455 (9th Cir. 1984); *Medoil Corp. v. Citicorp,* 729 F. Supp. 1456 (S.D.N.Y. 1990). Characteristic of these decisions was one lower court that declared that the "fact that a particular contractual provision may not have been specifically discussed does not preclude it from being enforceable." *Samson Plastic Conduit & Pipe Corp. v. Battenfeld Extrusionstechnik GmbH,* 718 F. Supp. 886 (M.D. Ala. 1989).

Nevertheless, a few courts refused to give effect to forum clauses based in part on the lack of negotiation or discussion of the provision. *Preferred Capital, Inc. v. Sarasota Kennel Club,* 2005 WL 1799900, at *3 (N.D. Ohio 2005) (forum selection clause was unenforceable where "the selection of Ohio courts as the forum, though known to . . . the Plaintiff, was not timely disclosed to the Defendants . . . [and] Ohio [wa]s not a reasonably anticipated forum from the terms of [the] Agreement."); *Union Ins. Soc'y of Canton v. SS Elikon,* 642 F.2d 721 (4th Cir. 1981) (refusing enforcement in part because of lack of "hard bargaining"); *Corna v. American Hawaii Cruises, Inc.,* 794 F. Supp. 1005 (D. Haw. 1992); *Couch v. First Guaranty, Ltd.,* 578 F. Supp. 331 (N.D. Tex. 1984) ("not knowingly bargained for"; "obscure clause in a form contract").

Carnival Cruise makes it even less likely that the absence of bargaining will independently prevent enforcement of a forum clause. The Court held that the absence of negotiations over the forum clause was not of substantial weight: "Common sense dictates that a ticket of this kind will be a form contract the terms of which are not subject to negotiation, and that an individual purchasing the ticket will not have bargaining parity with the cruise line." Nonetheless, the Court upheld the forum clause, emphasizing the legitimate interests (of Carnival Cruise Lines and of the judicial system) in the certainty and efficiency provided by such clauses.

Should the lack of actual negotiation over a forum clause result in nonenforcement? Should it even be relevant to nonenforcement? Did the facts in *Colonial Leasing* warrant nonenforcement under the *Bremen* standard? How would *Bremen* have been resolved if there had been no negotiation of the towage contract? Do decisions refusing to enforce forum selection clauses principally because they were not individually negotiated survive *Carnival Cruise?* How would *Colonial Leasing* be decided under *Carnival Cruise?*

Under general principles of contract law, there is no rule requiring that the parties either negotiate or be shown to have read every term of their agreement. What rationale supported the apparent willingness of *Colonial Leasing* and other courts to impose particularly high standards of negotiation on forum clauses as compared to other contractual provisions — such as price or warranties? Is there some particular need to ensure that parties focus on and understand forum provisions? Is there a greater risk that this will not occur than with respect to other provisions?

7. *Lack of notice or assent as basis for resisting enforcement of forum selection agreement.* In deciding whether to enforce forum selection clauses, a number of lower courts have considered whether both parties had adequate notice of them. Although *Carnival Cruise* did not consider whether the Shutes had received notice of the forum selection clause, the Court made it clear that inadequate notice would provide a basis for resisting enforcement of such an agreement. 499 U.S. at 590, 595.

It is well settled that a party's failure to read a forum selection provision does not prevent that clause from forming part of the parties' agreement. Especially where businessmen are involved, courts have generally had little sympathy for claimed igno-rance of a forum selection clause. In the words of one court, "no one deterred him from getting his glasses and reading the contract." *Hoffman v. National Equip. Rental,* 643 F.2d 987 (4th Cir. 1981). With this basic attitude, efforts to claim lack of notice or compre-hension of a forum clause have generally failed. *Heller Fin., Inc. v. Midwhey Power Co.,* 883 F.2d 1286, 1292 (7th Cir. 1989); *Paribas Corp. v. Shelton Ranch Corp.,* 742 F. Supp. 86, 92 (S.D.N.Y. 1990) ("a sophisticated business person with practice in contractual negotiation cannot escape the effect of a forum selection clause by claiming lack of focus"); *Karlberg European Tanspa, Inc. v. JK-Josef Kratz Vertriebsgesellschaft mbH,* 618 F. Supp. 344, 347 (N.D. Ill. 1985) ("basic contract law establishes a duty to read the contract").

A few courts have even concluded that parties were obliged to read contracts in a language that they did not understand. *Gaskin v. Stumm Handel GmbH,* 390 F. Supp. 361, 365-367 (S.D.N.Y. 1975) (enforcing forum clause against U.S. party where contract was written in German); *Corna v. American Hawaii Cruises, Inc.,* 794 F. Supp. 1005 (D. Haw. 1992) (enforcing English language form forum clause against native Dutch speaker).

Nevertheless, courts have occasionally refused to enforce forum selection clauses that were buried in pages of finely printed boilerplate or on the back of form contracts—particularly in consumer cases. *Chasser v. Achille Lauro Lines,* 844 F.2d 50, 52 (2d Cir. 1988) ("in tiny type"), *aff'd,* 490 U.S. 495 (1989); *Couch v. First Guaranty Ltd.,* 578 F. Supp. 331, 333 (N.D. Tex. 1984) ("that the provision is knowingly inserted in the contract seems to be the underpinning of the *Bremen* decision"). Courts have also held that, where other circumstances are present such as a material difference in bargaining power, "a forum selection clause should not be enforced where a consumer is told by a corporate agent to ignore boilerplate contract language containing a forum selection clause." *Yoder v. Heinold Commodities, Inc.,* 630 F. Supp. 756, 760 (E.D. Va. 1986). Where a party can demonstrate that a forum clause was not communicated to it in a reasonable fashion, challenges to enforcement continue to be possible.

Should the plaintiffs' counsel in *Carnival Cruise* have conceded that the forum clause was "reasonably communicated" to the Shutes? What standards should be applied to determine whether a party did not receive notice of a forum clause? It cannot be dispos-itive, can it, that the plaintiff did not read the clause? If not, then what must be done to make it sufficiently easy for the plaintiff to read the clause? Would it be sensible to require, in every form contract, that the forum clause be in all capital letters? Note that some state statutes require that arbitration clauses must either be conspicuously printed, contained in a separate agreement, or noted on the first page of the contract. G. Born, *International Commercial Arbitration* 622-623 (2009). Should the law require this for forum clauses? Should courts fashion such a rule? For consumers?

8. Lack of "fundamental fairness" as basis for nonenforcement of forum selection agreement. In *Carnival Cruise,* the Court said that it would not enforce a fundamentally unfair forum selection clause. What does this mean? The Court emphasized that *Carnival Cruise Lines'* forum clause did not designate "a remote alien forum," that there was no suggestion that Florida had been chosen to disadvantage or inconvenience consumers, and that a cruise line had legitimate interests in avoiding litigation in numerous different fora.

Suppose that the circumstances that attend cruise lines—passengers from multiple places on cruises to multiple destinations—are not present. Would the same deferential approach to forum clauses as that adopted in *Carnival Cruise* apply? What would render a forum clause "fundamentally unfair"? What if Carnival Cruise had chosen Panama as the contractual forum? What if Carnival Cruise was incorporated there? What if its vessels called there? What if Panama law drastically limited tort remedies generally? Consider:

After bringing consumer form contracts within *The Bremen's* rule, and then lowering the applicable standard of reasonableness, *Carnival Cruise* proceeds to ensure that few forum-selection clauses will be voided on equitable grounds, . . . [by] adopt[ing] a minimalist idea of what constitutes "fundamental fairness." Purcell, *Geography as a Litigation Weapon: Consumers, Forum-Selection Clauses, and the Rehnquist Court*, 40 UCLA L. Rev. 423, 432-433 (1992).

Is that accurate? Is it desirable?

What is relevant to determining the unconscionability of a forum clause? Suppose that the clause's drafter shows that, in other respects, the parties' underlying agreement was highly favorable to the other party? Suppose that a cruise line agreed to extremely discounted prices because of oversupply in the cruise market and slack consumer demand? What is the relevance of the separability doctrine?

9. *Termination of the underlying contract as a basis for nonenforcement of the forum selection agreement.* A few courts have held that termination of a contract containing a forum clause also terminates the forum selection provision. *Certified Commodities Group, Inc. v. Roccaforte*, 441 So. 2d 264 (La. Ct. App. 1983). *Compare Int'l Longshoremen's Ass'n, AFL-CIO, v. West Gulf Maritime Ass'n*, 605 F. Supp. 723 (S.D.N.Y. 1985). This is inconsistent with the separability doctrine, which would treat the forum clause as a separate agreement, capable of surviving the underlying contract (at least with respect to disputes occurring during the term of the underlying contract). *See supra* p. 492. Suppose that the Shutes had *not* gone on their ill-fated voyage, and had instead terminated their contract with Carnival Cruise on the grounds that the *Tropicale* was allegedly unfit for human habitation. Would claims by the Shutes for return of their payments or deposits, and by Carnival Cruise for breach of contract, have been subject to the forum agreement? How could they be if the underlying contract had been terminated?

10. *Relevance of distinction between exclusive and nonexclusive forum selection agreements.* Note that *Colonial Leasing* involved a nonexclusive, prorogation agreement, unlike the exclusive forum selection clause in *Bremen*. How should this affect the agreement's enforceability? Should it have been easier to enforce a submission to jurisdiction than it would be to enforce an exclusive forum selection clause? Why? *See supra* pp. 462-463.

11. *Choice of law governing forum selection agreement — a closer look.* What law governs the validity and enforceability of a forum selection clause? Is it the law selected by the parties, the law of the forum selected by the parties' choice of forum clause or the law of the judicial forum in which the clause is invoked? Do different bodies of laws apply to different issues — for example, to contractual issues of validity and to issues of enforceability?

As discussed below, most U.S. states (and federal common law) accord substantial deference to party autonomy in the selection of the law governing their contractual relations. *See supra* p. 492. If the parties select the law governing their forum selection clause, then that law should, with rare exceptions (for public policy), govern the parties' clause. Recall the separability doctrine, discussed above. *See supra* p. _____. If the parties' underlying contract includes a choice of law clause, should this be assumed to extend to the "separable" forum selection clause?

If the parties have not agreed to a choice of law clause, or if that clause is interpreted as inapplicable to the separable choice of forum clause, what law should apply to the forum selection agreement? U.S. courts tend to apply the law of the place where the clause is sought to be invoked (and whose courts' jurisdiction would be "excluded"). *See, e.g., Deere Credit, Inc. v. Grupo Granjas Marinas, SA de CV*, 2004 WL 729123, at *3 (S.D. Iowa 2004);

Tri-State Foundation Repair & Waterproofing, Inc. v. Permacrete Sys., Ltd., 2000 WL 245824 (W.D. Mo. 2000).

Consider Articles 5(1) and 6 of the proposed Hague Choice of Court Agreements Convention. How do these provisions deal with the choice of law governing the validity of a forum selection clause? Do these provisions override the parties' choice of law? Note that, under Article 6(a), a U.S. court, considering claims that a choice of forum clause was unconscionable or fraudulently procured, would be required to apply the law of the designated foreign forum. Is that appropriate?

3. Unreasonableness as a Ground for Resisting Enforcement of Exclusive and Nonexclusive Forum Selection Agreements

Unreasonableness or inconvenience can be invoked as grounds for resisting enforcement of both exclusive and nonexclusive choice of forum clauses in many U.S. jurisdictions. The analyses differ depending on the nature of the clause (exclusive vs. nonexclusive). They also differ depending on the jurisdiction in which the question arises, because of substantial disagreements among lower U.S. courts about the appropriate role of *forum non conveniens* and similar considerations in cases involving forum selection agreements: "there seems to be no clear rule as to whether *forum non conveniens* analysis is required in a case where an express forum selection clause exists."[95]

a. Unreasonableness or Inconvenience as Grounds for Resisting Enforcement of Exclusive Forum Selection Agreement. In many U.S. jurisdictions, the enforcement of an exclusive forum selection agreement may be resisted on grounds of "unreasonableness" even if there is no basis for challenging the clause's formation on the basis of fraud, duress, unconscionability, lack of notice, and the like.[96] This exception was recognized in *Bremen,*[97] where the Court said that forum selection agreements will not be enforced if doing so would be "unreasonable and unjust,"[98] or "unreasonable under the circumstances."[99] The unreasonableness defense was also at issue in *Carnival Cruise,* where the Court considered "the circumstances that would make it unreasonable for a court to enforce a forum clause."[100]

An unreasonableness defense to exclusive forum selection agreements is also reflected in the Model Choice of Forum Act. The Act contains specific defenses to enforceability for several of the factors identified in *Bremen* as bearing on unreasonableness, including (a) inability of plaintiff to obtain "effective relief" in the contractual forum; and (b) the fact that the contractual forum would be "a substantially less convenient place for the trial of the action."[101] In addition, the Act also contains a catch-all exception that applies where "it would for some other reason be unfair or unreasonable to enforce the agreement."[102]

Finally, the *Restatement (Second) Conflict of Laws* permits nonenforcement of exclusive forum clauses if they are "unfair or unreasonable."[103] Section 80 does not

---

95. *Paradis Enterprises Ltd. v. Sapir,* 811 A.2d 516, 521-522 (N.J. Super. A.D. 2002).
96. *Mercier v. Sheraton Int'l,* 935 F.2d 419 (1st Cir. 1991); *Apotex Corp. v. Istituto Biologico Chemioterapico S.p.A.,* 2003 WL 21780965 (N.D. Ill. 2003); *Paradis Enterprises Ltd. v. Sapir,* 811 A.2d 516 (N.J. Super. A.D. 2002).
97. 407 U.S. at 10 & 15.
98. 407 U.S. at 15.
99. 407 U.S. at 10.
100. 499 U.S. at 590-594.
101. Uniform Law Commissioners' Model Choice of Forum Act §3(2) & 3(3).
102. Uniform Law Commissioners' Model Choice of Forum Act §3(5).
103. *Restatement (Second) Conflict of Laws* §80 (1971).

itself further define "unreasonableness," but the accompanying comments provide some explanation.[104] Among other things, comment c to §80 says that factors suggesting unreasonableness include the fact that: (a) the "courts of the chosen state would be closed"; and (b) "the chosen state would be so seriously an inconvenient forum" as to be "unjust."

Under almost all analyses, the unreasonableness defense is very difficult to satisfy. The Model Act makes it clear that the burden of proof is on the party resisting enforcement. *Bremen* emphasized that a party must "clearly show" unreasonableness and that it bears of "heavy burden" in so doing.[105] *Carnival Cruise* repeated this formulation, and relied upon it in upholding the parties' forum selection clause.[106] Lower courts have frequently invoked this burden of proof.[107]

A central concern of the "reasonableness" analysis under the foregoing authorities is "convenience." Both *Bremen* and other sources hold that, if an exclusive forum selection clause designates a forum that is *sufficiently* inconvenient, enforcement may be denied.

It is difficult to establish that a foreign forum is sufficiently inconvenient to warrant nonenforcement of an exclusive forum selection clause. To be sure, a few lower court decisions have found the *Bremen* "inconvenience" standard satisfied.[108] Most courts, however, have enforced exclusive forum clauses in the face of inconvenience defenses. A number have done so notwithstanding evidence of considerable inconvenience, including when the resisting party is a U.S. national.[109]

Related to "inconvenience" as a ground for denying enforcement of an exclusive forum selection clause is the plaintiff's inability to obtain effective relief in the contractual forum. Section 3(2) of the Model Choice of Forum Act provides for nonenforcement where "the plaintiff cannot secure effective relief in the other state, for reasons other than delay in bringing the action." *Bremen* acknowledged, albeit in its discussion of

---

104. *Restatement (Second) Conflict of Laws* §80 comment c (1986 Revisions).

105. 407 U.S. at 17.

106. 499 U.S. at 594-595.

107. *E.g., Afram Carriers, Inc. v. Moeykens,* 145 F.3d 298, 301 (5th Cir. 1998) (burden of proving unreasonableness of forum selection clause is a heavy one); *New Moon Shipping Co., Ltd. v. MAN B & W Diesel AG,* 121 F.3d 24, 32 (2d Cir. 1997) ("heavy burden"); *Mitsui & Co. (USA), Inc. v. Mira M/V,* 111 F.3d 33, 35 (5th Cir. 1997) ("burden of proving unreasonableness is a heavy one"); *Interamerican Trade Corp. v. Companhia Fabricadora de Pecas,* 973 F.2d 487 (6th Cir. 1992); *In re Diaz Contracting, Inc.* 817 F.2d 1047 (3d Cir. 1987) ("heavy burden"); *General Engineering Corp. v. Martin Marietta Alumina, Inc.,* 783 F.2d 352, 356 (3d Cir. 1986) ("strict standard"); *Modius, Inc. v. Psinaptic, Inc.,* 2006 WL 1156390, at *5 (N.D. Cal. 2006); *Seecomm Network Services v. Colt Telecommunications,* 2004 WL 1960174, at *9 (N.D. Cal. 2004) ("heavy burden of proof"); *Eisenmann Corp. v. Tek-Mor, Inc.,* 2004 WL 547253, at *2 (N.D. Ill. 2004) ("heavy burden of proof").

108. *E.g., Murphy v. Schneider Nat'l, Inc.,* 362 F.3d 1133, 1141-1143 (9th Cir. 2004) (remanding to district court because forum selection clause would deny plaintiff his day in court under *Bremen* if the plaintiff's allegations about his physical and financial limitations were true); *Cabreras v. Esharis Shipping & Trading Co.,* 1997 WL 698020, at *2 (E.D. La. 1997) ("The forum selection clause therefore poses a grave inconvenience to [plaintiff] and is thus unenforceable"); *Effron v. Sun Line Cruises, Inc.,* 158 F.R.D. 39 (S.D.N.Y. 1994); *Vignolo v. Chandris, Inc.,* 1989 WL 160986 (D. Mass. 1990).

109. *E.g., Argueta v. Banco Mexicano, SA,* 87 F.3d 320, 324 (9th Cir. 1996); ("Appellants had not met their burden of showing that enforcement of the forum selection clause would be unreasonable"); *Spradlin v. Lear Siegler Mgt. Serv. Co.,* 926 F.2d 865, 869 (9th Cir. 1990) ("Although we are troubled by Lear Siegler's standard inclusion of a Saudi Arabian forum selection clause in employment contracts when it is highly foreseeable that terminated American employees will be required to return to the United States and will thus face considerable obstacles in bringing wrongful termination actions, we cannot find that the district court abused its discretion in enforcing the forum selection clause based on the scant and conclusory information presented by Spradlin."); *In re Diaz Contracting,* 817 F.2d 1047, 1051 (3d Cir. 1987) (enforcing forum selection clause notwithstanding district court's finding that bankrupt company would face "financial difficulty" litigating in selected forum); *Modius, Inc. v. Psinaptic, Inc.,* 2006 WL 1156390, at *6 (N.D. Cal. 2006); *Marra v. Papandreou,* 59 F. Supp. 2d 65 (D.D.C. 1999) (upholding enforcement of a forum selection clause against an American plaintiff despite the plaintiff's objection that the foreign forum's discovery procedures were inadequate).

"inconvenience," the possibility of nonenforcement where the plaintiff "will for all practical purposes be deprived of his day in court."[110]

Lower courts have almost always rejected claims that the parties' contractual forum cannot provide effective relief (just as they have usually rejected similar arguments under the *forum non conveniens* doctrine).[111] It is clear that something more is required than differences in substantive law that disadvantage the plaintiff. This is illustrated by *Bremen*'s enforcement of the parties' exclusive forum selection clause even though it was clear that English courts would apply different substantive rules than American courts would.[112] Similarly, claims that foreign forums are unreasonable because of differences between U.S. and foreign procedural rules have also usually failed.[113]

In unusual cases, contractual forums may be found unreasonable because of the qualities of their courts. Where the courts in the contractual forum are biased or corrupt, enforcement may be denied. Similarly, a forum clause will be found unreasonable[114] "if jurisdiction would be lacking in the chosen state."[115] A forum selection agreement might also not be enforced "where the period of the statute of limitations applicable to the particular claim was unusually short [in the contractual forum] and had already expired."[116]

Finally, enforcement will ordinarily be denied "if no court of that state would be competent to hear the suit."[117] More difficult are cases in which the contractual forum will hear a suit, but will not permit assertion of particular causes of action. As discussed above, the fact that unfavorable substantive law will be applied in the contractual forum is generally not grounds for denying enforcement of a forum agreement.[118] The complete absence of any viable legal claim has generally not been considered by lower courts (except in the context of public policy, which is discussed below).[119]

b. Unreasonableness or Inconvenience as Grounds for Resisting Enforcement of Nonexclusive Forum Selection Agreement. Lower courts are divided over the extent to

---

110. 407 U.S. at 18. The comments to §80 of the *Second Restatement* explain: "A court will likewise entertain the action if it finds that for some reason the courts of the chosen state would be closed to the suit or would not handle it effectively or fairly." *Restatement (Second) Conflict of Laws* §80 comment c (1986 Revisions).

111. *See supra* pp. 440-442.

112. Lower courts have generally rejected challenges to forum selection clauses based solely on the fact that the foreign forum's laws were less favorable than U.S. laws. *E.g., Richards v. Lloyd's of London*, 135 F.3d 1289, 1296 (9th Cir. 1998) (*en banc*); *Hugel v. Corporation of Lloyd's*, 999 F.2d 206 (7th Cir. 1993); *Medoil Corp. v. Citicorp*, 729 F. Supp. 1456 (S.D.N.Y. 1990); *Raskin SA v. Datasonic Corp.*, 1987 WL 8180 (N.D. Ill. 1987); *Karlberg European Tanspa, Inc. v. JK-Josef Kratz Vertriebsgesellschaft mbH*, 618 F. Supp. 344 (N.D. Ill. 1985).

113. *E.g., Commerce Consultants Int'l, Inc. v. Vetrerie Riunite, SpA*, 867 F.2d 697 (D.C. Cir. 1989) (in accepting Italian forum selection clause, party "also necessarily accepted the procedures that those courts follow, including different discovery procedures"); *Marra v. Papandreou*, 59 F. Supp.2d 65, 73-74 (D.D.C. 1999) (upholding enforcement of forum selection clause against U.S. plaintiff despite the objection that the foreign forum's discovery procedures were inadequate); *Breindel & Ferstendig v. Willis Faber & Dumas Ltd.*, 1996 WL 413727, at *3 (S.D.N.Y. 1996) ("procedures in foreign forum need not be identical to those in United States to be adequate, so long as they are not 'wholly devoid of due process'"); *Carnival Cruise Lines, Inc. v. Oy Wartsila AB*, 159 B.R. 984, 991 (S.D. Fla. 1993) (Finland's restrictive discovery procedures do not render Finland inadequate forum); *Karlberg European Tanspa, Inc. v. JK-Josef Kratz Vertriebsgesellschaft mbH*, 618 F. Supp. 344, 348 (N.D. Ill. 1985) ("it is not this court's role to guarantee KETS the same probability of success on all its claims").

114. The *Bremen v. Zapata Off-Shore Co.*, 407 U.S. 1, 12 (1972) (emphasizing neutrality and competence of English courts); Gruson, *Forum-Selection Clauses in International and Interstate Commercial Agreements*, 1982 U. Ill. L. Rev. 133, 167-169.

115. *Restatement (Second) Conflict of Laws* §80 comment c (1986 Revisions). This parallels the alternative forum requirement under the *forum non conveniens* doctrine, where lack of subject matter jurisdiction in the asserted alternative forum is grounds for denying dismissal. *See supra* p. 438.

116. *Restatement (Second) Conflict of Laws* §80 comment c (1986 Revisions).

117. *Restatement (Second) Conflict of Laws* §80 comment c (1986 Revisions).

118. *See supra* p. 471.

119. *See infra* pp. 511-528.

which the *forum non conveniens* doctrine may be invoked in a contractual forum specified by a nonexclusive forum selection clause. Some courts hold that the *forum non conveniens* doctrine continues to apply as if there were no forum selection agreement.[120] Other courts appear to hold that no *forum non conveniens* analysis at all is appropriate in the contractual forum selected by a nonexclusive clause.[121] Finally, other courts have held that *forum non conveniens* dismissals are available under a nonexclusive forum selection agreement, but that the *forum non conveniens* doctrine's "private interest" factors will not apply[122] or that the forum selection clause will be given weight in the *forum non conveniens* analysis as an indication of convenience.[123]

c. Selected Materials Relating to Unreasonableness and Inconvenience. The following decision, *Copperweld Steel Co. v. Demag-Mannesmann-Boehler*, considers unreasonableness and inconvenience as defenses to enforcement of an exclusive forum selection clause.

COPPERWELD STEEL CO. v. DEMAG-MANNESMANN-BOEHLER
578 F.2d 953 (3d Cir. 1978)

ROSENN, CIRCUIT JUDGE. [The case arose from the sale by Demag-Mannesmann-Boehler (Demag), a German company, to Copperweld Steel Company (Copperweld), a U.S. company, of a "continuous casting machine." The machine failed to perform to Copperweld's requirements, and the U.S. company brought a diversity action in federal district court alleging: (1) breach of contract; (2) negligent design and manufacture; and (3) negligent and fraudulent misrepresentation. The district judge directed a verdict against Copperweld's fraud claim and, after a jury trial, entered judgment on the jury's verdict against Copperweld on its remaining claims. The district judge also denied Demag's motion, based on a forum selection clause, to dismiss the action. Copperweld appealed from the adverse verdict and Demag cross-appealed from the denial of its motion to dismiss, arguing that Copperweld's breach of an enforceable forum selection clause entitled Demag to damages. The Court of Appeals first affirmed the verdict on the merits against Copperweld and continued as follows.]

Demag has raised a single but interesting question in its cross-appeal — whether the district court erred in accepting jurisdiction in this case. Demag claims that the district court did err and that this error entitles it to a trial on the question of damages suffered because of the district court's failure to enforce the contract. We find no error in the retention of jurisdiction and therefore affirm the district court's disposition of Demag's claim.

120. *Blanco v. Banco Industrial de Venezuela, SA*, 997 F.2d 974, 980 (2d Cir. 1993) (in case involving nonexclusive clause, holding that it was appropriate "to address the *forum non conveniens* issue in terms of the generally applicable standards, rather than the heightened scrutiny required by Bremen for mandatory forum selection clauses"); *Magellan Real Estate Inv. Trust v. Losch*, 109 F. Supp. 2d 1144 (D. Ariz. 2000).

121. *Evolution Online Systems, Inc. v. Koninklijke PTT Nederland NV*, 145 F.3d 505 (2d Cir. 1998); *Von Graffenreid v. Craig*, 246 F. Supp. 2d 553, 563 (N.D. Tex. 2003); *AAR Int'l, Inc. v. Nimelias Enters., SA*, 250 F.3d 510 (7th Cir. 2001); *La Union Francaise v. La Costena*, 818 So.2d 657 (Fla. Dist. Ct. App. 2002); *Sempra Energy Trading Corp. v. Algoma Steel, Inc.*, 2001 WL 282684, at *4 (S.D.N.Y. 2001).

122. *Overseas Partners, Inc. v. PROGEN Musavirlik ve Yonetim Hizmetleri, Ltd. Sikerti*, 15 F. Supp. 2d 47 (D.D.C. 1998).

123. *Royal Bed & Spring Co. v. Famossul Industria e Comercio de Moveis Ltda.*, 906 F.2d 45, 51 (1st Cir. 1990); *Mobil Sales & Supply Corp. v. Republic of Lithuania*, 1998 WL 196194, at *11 (S.D.N.Y. 1998).

During negotiations Demag sent Copperweld a standard form with its conditions for export contracts. Among these conditions was one requiring that "[a]ny disputes arising out of the terms of the contract" would have to be brought before a German court unless Demag chose to bring the action in the United States.[124] This condition expressly applied to any *export contract* negotiated by Demag. Prior to the final agreement on the sale of the caster, however, Demag and Copperweld concluded that the machine, originally to be built in and exported from Germany, would be manufactured in the United States. From this Copperweld reasons that the agreement ceased to be an export contract, that Demag's forum selection clause did not become part of the new contract, and that therefore the district court correctly retained jurisdiction over the case.

The district court indicated some agreement with Copperweld's assertion, concluding that had the parties not amended their contract to provide for construction of the caster in the United States, it would have been inclined to enforce the forum clause. We need not decide whether the clause in fact became part of the contract, however, for there is an alternative reason that leads us to affirm the district court's assumption of jurisdiction over the case. The district court also reasoned and concluded that enforcement of the forum selection clause would be unreasonable. We see no error in that conclusion.

During pre-trial motions, the district court held that it had jurisdiction over Copperweld's complaint and that the forum selection clause did not deprive it of this jurisdiction. Judge McCune concluded that enforcement of the forum selection clause would be "unreasonable under the facts of this case" and refused to enforce the clause.[125]

Subsequent to this pre-trial decision, in *The Bremen v. Zapata Off-Shore Co.,* an admiralty case, the Supreme Court held that a forum selection clause in a contract between the parties is "prima facie valid and should be enforced unless enforcement is shown by the resisting party to be 'unreasonable' under the circumstances." The Court further stated that such a clause should not be set aside "absent a strong showing" such as that enforcement "would be unreasonable and unjust, or that the clause was invalid for such reasons as fraud or overreaching."

Demag contends that the district court's pre-trial decision that enforcement would be unreasonable must be reversed because it was based, at least in part, upon standards enunciated in the *Central Contracting Company* cases, [*Central Contracting Co. v. Maryland Casualty Co.,* 367 F.2d 341 (3d Cir. 1966)] . . . decided prior to *The Bremen.* Demag also made this argument to Judge McCune, who in two separate opinions reiterated his initial reaction and held that the enforcement of the clause would be unreasonable. . . . The district court's reliance on the *Central Contracting Company* cases is not reversible error. Both cases held that a court should generally enforce a forum selection clause unless the

124. The clause provided as follows: "Any disputes arising out of the terms of the contract shall be brought before the court of justice having jurisdiction in the area where the supplier has its main offices." 54 F.R.D. 539 (W.D. Pa. 1972).

125. The district court gave the following reasons for its decisions not to enforce the forum selection clause: (1) that the facility which was the subject of the action was located in Warren, Ohio, and was likely to become the object of an intensive inspection during the trial; (2) that the facility was fabricated by Birdsboro Corporation, a Pennsylvania contractor, in this country; (3) that all of the records concerning operation of the plant were in this country; (4) that all of Copperweld's personnel who operated the plant were in this country; (5) that all of Copperweld's personnel who negotiated the contract were in this country; (6) that certain of Demag's personnel involved in the sale were in this country and that Demag was doing business in the United States and maintained offices in Pittsburgh, Pennsylvania; (7) that practically all of the activities undertaken in connection with the contract took place in the English language; (8) that almost all of the witnesses were English speaking; and (9) that conducting the litigation in Germany would have required translation with inherent inaccuracies. Furthermore, all of the plant's customers were in this country and if their testimony were necessary, the district court envisioned difficulties in compelling their attendance in a German forum.

enforcement would be unreasonable at the time of the litigation, and that mere inconvenience would not show unreasonability. *Id.* The courts instead suggested that the test is whether enforcement "will put one of the parties to an unreasonable disadvantage and thereby subvert the interests of justice." Although *Bremen* has language somewhat different than that relied upon by the district court, *compare Bremen,* 407 U.S. at 18 (deny enforcement of the clause if resisting party will be effectively denied his day in court) *with Maryland Casualty Co.* (deny enforcement if interest of justice is subverted), the district court captured the essence of the Supreme Court's opinion — the resisting party must prove unreasonability [*sic*] — and in fact held that Copperweld might well have been prevented from receiving "a fair and complete hearing" had the forum clause been enforced. We therefore find no material difference between the standards applied by the district court and those requested by Demag and affirm the district court's retention of jurisdiction.

NEW YORK GENERAL OBLIGATIONS LAW §5-1402
[excerpted in Appendix W]

EUROPEAN UNION COUNCIL REGULATION 44/2001, ART. 23
[excerpted in Appendix E]

HAGUE CONVENTION ON CHOICE OF COURT AGREEMENTS
44 Int'l Legal Mats. 1294 (2005) [excerpted in Appendix I]

Notes on Copperweld *and Legislative Materials*

1. *Unreasonableness as defense to enforcement of exclusive choice of forum agreement.* As *Copperweld* illustrates, and as discussed above, the "unreasonableness" of an exclusive forum selection clause is, in many U.S. jurisdictions, a defense to enforcement of the provision. *Morgan Trailer Mfg. Co. v. Hydraroll, Ltd.,* 759 A.2d 926 (Pa. Super. 2000) (holding contractual forum unreasonable because witnesses and evidence were elsewhere). Consider again whether this defense is wise. What justifies subjecting exclusive forum selection agreements — in contrast to other contractual terms — to a reasonableness test? Does anything?

Compare the text of EU Council Regulation 44/2001 and the Hague Choice of Court Agreements Convention. Does anything in either instrument provide the basis for an "unreasonableness" defense? Consider Article 6(c) of the Convention. Note that no similar defense exists to international arbitration agreements. *See* G. Born, *International Commercial Arbitration* 764-765, 1723-1728 (2009).

2. *Structure of reasonableness analysis.* Is each of the various exceptions to enforceability set out in *Bremen* — such as fraud, unconscionability, inconvenience, forum bias, and the like — an independent and separate base for overcoming an exclusive forum selection clause? Alternatively, are all the factors collectively relevant to a single reasonableness inquiry that permits nonenforcement of "unreasonable" forum selection clauses?

A number of authorities have adopted the latter approach. *E.g., Restatement (Second) Conflict of Laws* §80 (1971); *Blanco v. Banco Industrial de Venezuela, SA,* 997 F.2d 974, 986 (2d Cir. 1993) (Oakes, J., dissenting); *Russo v. Ballard Med. Prods.,* 352 F. Supp. 2d 177, 181 (D.R.I. 2005); *Lyon Fin. Servs., Inc. v. Nowobilska Med. Ctr., Ltd.,* 2005 WL 3526682, at *4 (D. Minn. 2005); *Nisselson v. Lernout,* 2004 WL 1630492, at *2 (D. Mass. 2004); *Doe v. Seacamp Ass'n, Inc.,* 276 F. Supp. 2d 222, 225 (D. Mass. 2003); *Capelouto v. Société de Banque*

Suisse, 1991 WL 60387, at *2 (S.D.N.Y. 1991); *Page Constr. Co. v. Perini Constr.,* 712 F. Supp. 9, 12 (D.R.I. 1989).

Is this a sensible approach? Is it appropriate to mush the various *Bremen* factors together into an undisciplined reasonableness inquiry? How is this analysis different from *forum non conveniens* analysis?

3. Grave or serious inconvenience as a basis for denying enforcement of exclusive forum selection agreement based upon inconvenience. As *Bremen* and *Copperweld* illustrate, one basis for resisting enforcement of a forum selection clause in many U.S. jurisdictions is grave or serious inconvenience. Compare again the language of EU Council Regulation 44/2001 and the Hague Choice of Court Agreements Convention.

(a) Rigorous standard for inconvenience. A compelling showing must be made to establish that the parties' chosen forum is so seriously inconvenient that nonenforcement is warranted. *Bremen* adopted the following standard: An exclusive forum selection clause will be enforced unless the resisting party shows "that trial in the contractual forum will be so gravely difficult and inconvenient that he will for all practical purposes be deprived of his day in court." An inconvenient contractual forum would not be grounds for denying enforcement of a forum selection clause merely because "the balance of convenience is strongly in favor" of some place other than the contractual forum. The Court reiterated this in *Carnival Cruise,* where it reversed a Court of Appeals' decision that Miami was an inconvenient forum for two elderly Washington residents. According to the Court, "conclusory" findings of inconvenience do not satisfy the "heavy burden of proof" required to warrant nonenforcement.

In the same fashion, the comments to *Restatement (Second)* §80 also declare:

> It should be emphasized that entertainment of the action in such a situation could not be justified on the simple ground that trial in the state of the forum would be more convenient than in the chosen state. Entertainment of the action could only be justified in the rare situation where the chosen state would be a seriously inconvenient place for the trial and the state of the forum would be far more convenient.

Section 3(3) of the Model Choice of Forum Act requires that the contractual forum be "substantially less convenient."

(b) Copperweld's *standard of inconvenience.* In *Copperweld,* why did the court rule that the forum selection clause was "unreasonable"? Did the Court rely principally (or entirely) on considerations of convenience? Is the *Copperweld* result correct? Is it consistent with *Bremen?* Consider how *Copperweld* compares the *Bremen* standard of inconvenience with that in *Central Contracting.* Which approach to inconvenience is wiser — that in *Central Contracting* or that in *Bremen?*

Consider some of the following decisions, involving findings of grave inconvenience. *Sudduth v. Occidental Peruana, Inc.,* 70 F. Supp. 2d 691, 695 (E.D. Tex. 1999) (U.S. employee "would, in all probability, be unable to afford to travel back to Peru for purposes of litigation"); *James C. Greene Co. v. Great American E&S Ins. Co.,* 321 F. Supp. 2d 717, 721-722 (E.D.N.C. 2004).

(c) Wisdom of Bremen's *rigorous standard for inconvenience.* Why do *Bremen* and other authorities require such an extreme showing of inconvenience before they will deny enforcement? Why is it not enough, to demonstrate "grave inconvenience," to show that it would be significantly more expensive for the plaintiff to litigate in the contractual forum? For example, why shouldn't unreasonableness have been found in *Carnival Cruise?* Recall that the elderly Shutes would have had to travel to Miami to attend relevant hearings.

What if the *overall* costs of litigating in the contractual forum would be higher, both for each party and for both parties together? Does it make sense to enforce a forum clause in these circumstances? How is anyone benefited? Why would it not be enough to show that one party would have its ability to litigate significantly impaired (for example, because of lack of compulsory process, limited discovery, and other procedural matters)? Is it "reasonable" to enforce forum selection agreements in these circumstances? Does it matter whether these impairments could have been foreseen at the time of contracting?

What sorts of showings should satisfy *Bremen*'s requirement that the contractual forum will "for all practical purposes . . . deprive [the party] of his day in court"? The fact that the contractual forum will not entertain the case? A statute of limitations will bar the action in the contractual forum? Indispensable parties could not be joined in the contractual forum (*compare* Model Choice of Forum Act §3(2))? Serious financial burden relative to the resisting party's resources? Did the inconvenience of a German forum in *Copperweld* rise to the level required by *Bremen*?

(d) *Relevance of postcontracting inconveniences.* It is not clear that inconveniences arising *after* the parties made their forum agreement would need to satisfy *Bremen*'s elevated standard of proof. *Bremen* expressly linked the fact that particular inconveniences were "clearly foreseeable at the time of contracting" with the requirement that, "[i]n these circumstances," the plaintiff must show he will be "deprived of his day in court." Few cases have involved changed circumstances, but, as discussed below, it would appear sound to attach greater weight to unforeseen inconveniences than to others.

(e) *Relevance of inconvenience that existed, or could have been foreseen, at time of contracting.* In *Copperweld,* the parties presumably could have foreseen the foreign forum's inconvenience when they agreed to the forum selection clause. What relevance should this fact have? How would *Bremen* treat inconvenience that could have been foreseen at the time the contract was made? Which approach is more persuasive? Why?

Most U.S. authorities that permit a reasonableness defense have concluded that "inconvenience" is ordinarily relevant only if it arises from factors that became apparent *after* the forum selection agreement was entered into. Thus, *Bremen* suggested that inconveniences that were foreseeable at the time of contracting should play little, if any, role in deciding the enforceability of a forum selection clause: "Of course, where it can be said with reasonable assurance that at the time they entered into the contract, the parties to a freely negotiated private international commercial agreement contemplated the claimed inconvenience, it is difficult to see why any such claim of inconvenience should be heard."

Applying this reasoning, lower courts have generally refused to accord substantial weight to factors that existed, or could have been foreseen, at the time the forum clause was entered into. *E.g., Interamerican Trade Corp. v. Companhia Fabricadora de Pecas,* 973 F.2d 487 (6th Cir. 1992) ("This is simply not a case in which a change of circumstances has occurred in Brazilian litigation that would justify a court in relieving ITC of its contractual commitment."); *Kotan v. Pizza Outlet, Inc.,* 400 F. Supp. 2d 44, 50 (D.D.C. 2005); *Price v. Leasecomm Corp.,* 2004 WL 727028, at *4 (M.D.N.C. 2004) ("[Plaintiff] as a reasonable businesswoman could have read the forum selection clause and foreseen the possibility of travel to Massachusetts."); *WHW Machinery, Inc. v. Werkzeugmaschinenhandel GmbH im Aufbau,* 960 F. Supp. 734, 748 (S.D.N.Y. 1997) ("[A]ny inconvenience suffered by being forced to litigate in the contracted forum was clearly foreseeable."); *Deolalikar v. Murlas Commodities, Inc.,* 602 F. Supp. 12, 15 (E.D. Pa. 1984) (" 'Mere inconvenience or additional expense is not the test of unreasonableness, since it may be assumed that the plaintiff received under the contract consideration for these things.' "). *But see Mylar Pharmaceuticals, Inc. v. American Safety Razor Co.,* 265 F. Supp. 2d 635, 638-639 (N.D. W. Va. 2002) (finding forum selection clause unreasonable despite foreseeable consequences at formation where dismissal to contractual forum would be inefficient in multi-party litigation).

Are some levels of inconvenience so extreme that they will justify nonenforcement even if they were foreseeable at the time of contracting? For example, if inconveniences foreseeable at the time of contracting deny a party a meaningful opportunity to present its case, does *Bremen* say that those inconveniences should be ignored? Conversely, if inconveniences were *not* foreseeable at the time of contracting, should a forum selection clause be enforced if it imposes significant inconveniences on one party? As to unforeseen inconveniences, should a pure *forum non conveniens* analysis be adopted?

(f) Effect of Carnival Cruise *on "inconvenience" exception.* In *Carnival Cruise,* the Supreme Court rejected the Court of Appeals' conclusion that Florida was an unreasonable forum; the Supreme Court relied in part on the lack of evidence that Florida would have been inconvenient for the parties. Among other things, the Court flatly dismissed the Court of Appeals' unexplained assertion that "the Shutes are physically and financially incapable of pursuing" their suit in Florida. Was this appropriate?

4. Forum selection agreement's selection of biased or corrupt forum as basis for resisting enforcement. The enforcement of a forum selection agreement can be resisted on the several grounds that relate to the particular situs selected as the contractual forum. Bias or corruption are two such bases.

(a) Biased or corrupt foreign tribunal as basis for nonenforcement of forum selection clause. If a forum selection agreement chooses a forum that is biased or corrupt, U.S. courts will refuse to enforce the clause. The rule was frequently invoked in litigation during the 1980s involving Iranian entities. *E.g., McDonnell Douglas Corp. v. Islamic Republic of Iran,* 758 F.2d 341 (8th Cir. 1985) (Iranian judicial system held inadequate); *Harris Corp. v. National Iranian Radio & Television,* 691 F.2d 1344, 1357 (11th Cir. 1982) ("effective access to Iranian courts unlikely"); *Rasoulzadeh v. Associated Press,* 574 F. Supp. 854, 861 (S.D.N.Y. 1983), *aff'd,* 767 F.2d 908 (2d Cir. 1985) ("courts administered by Iranian mullahs" held inadequate).

(b) Standard for establishing bias or corruption. As with the "unconscionability" exception, U.S. courts have been reluctant to deny enforcement based upon bias or corruption. Outside the Iranian context, U.S. courts have seldom relied on the bias of a foreign forum to deny enforcement to a forum clause. *E.g., Skins Trading Corp. v. SS Punta del Este,* 180 F. Supp. 609 (S.D.N.Y. 1960); *Sociedade Brasileira etc. v. SS Punta del Este,* 135 F. Supp. 394 (D.N.J. 1955). *See also Eastman Kodak Co. v. Kavlin,* 978 F. Supp. 1078, 1084 (S.D. Fla. 1997) (collecting cases relating to Venezuela, Turkey, Peru, and the Dominican Republic).

In the majority of cases, particularly involving developed legal systems, U.S. courts have rejected claims that a foreign forum will be biased. *E.g., Roby v. Corporation of Lloyd's,* 996 F.2d 1353, 1363 (2d Cir. 1993); *Blanco v. Blanco Indus. de Venezuela, SA,* 997 F.2d 974, 981-982 (2d Cir. 1993); *Hodes v. S.N.C. Achille Lauro,* 858 F.2d 905 (3d Cir. 1988) ("The choice of Italian venue for disputes arising out of a cruise on an Italian vessel, departing from and returning to Italy was a sensible and fair choice."); *Hamakua Sugar Co. Inc. v. Fiji Sugar Corp. Ltd.,* 778 F. Supp. 503 (D. Haw. 1991) ("possible community bias" arising from one party's status as major local employer not a "reason sufficient to ignore" the forum clause). This has been true even where the foreign party is a member of a dominant political elite in the foreign forum. *E.g., Forsythe v. Saudi Arabian Airlines Corp.,* 885 F.2d 285, 287-288 n.2 (5th Cir. 1989); *Weidner Communications Inc. v. Al Faisal,* 671 F. Supp. 531 (N.D. Ill. 1987) ("no showing here that the fact of defendants' association with the Saudi royal family will cause Saudi courts to treat plaintiff unfairly"), *rev'd on other grounds,* 859 F.2d 1302 (7th Cir. 1988).

(c) Wisdom of current approach to foreign bias and corruption. Is it appropriate for U.S. courts to sit in judgment on the fairness of foreign tribunals? Won't this have an adverse effect on U.S. foreign relations? Is there any alternative? Compare the treatment of similar issues in the *forum non conveniens* and enforcement of foreign judgments contexts, *see supra* p. 393 & *infra* pp. 1146-1155.

Why shouldn't a party that consents to what it can foresee will be an unfair forum be held to its bargain, at least absent coercion, fraud, or the like? Courts in some countries cannot honestly be described as neutral, unbiased, and regular judicial bodies; sometimes the opposite is true. Is it not fundamentally unjust for a party to be forced to litigate in such a place — even if it has agreed? Does the Due Process Clause permit a U.S. court to compel a party to proceed with its claims in a forum that — whether or not the party could have foreseen it — will be biased?

Would it be acceptable to enforce an arbitration clause selecting an obviously biased arbitrator to finally decide a dispute? *See* G. Born, *International Commercial Arbitration* 1461-1552, 2611-2618, 2803-2813 (2009) (describing arbitrators' obligations of independence and nonrecognition of awards by biased arbitrators). Why should a biased foreign court be different?

(d) Grounds for establishing that foreign forum is biased. How can a party establish that a foreign forum is biased? Is it relevant that a foreign state-entity has selected its own home courts? Can the judges in such courts fairly decide cases involving the state that pays their salaries and decides on their career advancement (and other matters, as well)?

5. *Forum selection agreement designating one party's domicile as contractual forum.* Forum selection clauses frequently designate one party's domicile as the contractual forum. As the Supreme Court remarked in *Bremen,* businessmen "prefer . . . to have disputes resolved in their own courts." Should the fact that a forum selection clause chooses the courts of one party's home state be relevant in the *Bremen* analysis? If so, should it be dispositive?

U.S. courts have almost always rejected enforceability challenges resting solely on the ground that one party, and not the other, is "at home" in the contractual forum. *Forsythe v. Saudi Arabian Airlines Corp,* 885 F.2d 285, 287-288 n.2 (5th Cir. 1989); *Crown Beverage Co. v. Cerveceria Moctezuma, SA,* 663 F.2d 886 (9th Cir. 1981); *Republic Int'l Corp. v. Amco Eng'rs, Inc.,* 516 F.2d 161 (9th Cir. 1975); *Gaskin v. Stumm Handel GmbH,* 390 F. Supp. 361 (S.D.N.Y. 1975). *Cf. Long v. Dart Int'l, Inc.,* 173 F. Supp. 2d 774, 778 (W.D. Tenn. 2001) ("[T]he existence of the forum selection clause demonstrates that the parties clearly contemplated this expense when they entered into the contract. The terms of this contract suggest that the parties intended to shift the burden of travel on Plaintiff. It also may be assumed that Plaintiff received consideration in exchange for its assumption of this expense."). Indeed, one of the affirmative justifications that Justice Blackmun advanced in *Carnival Cruise* for a nonnegotiated forum selection clause was the fact that it designated the defendant's place of business as the contractual forum: "Any suggestion of . . . a bad-faith motive is belied by [the fact that] petitioner has its principal place of business in Florida." Shouldn't the agreement's selection of one party's domicile be a cause for concern, not reassurance?

A few U.S. courts have commented (usually in passing) that selection of one party's domicile as the contractual forum is "suspect," and have considered it as a factor arguing for unenforceability. *Union Ins. Society of Canton, Ltd. v. SS Elikon,* 642 F.2d 721 (4th Cir. 1981) (choice of Bremen as forum "becomes more suspect in view of [the defendant's] headquarter in Bremen"); *Copperweld Steel Co. v. Demag-Mannesmann-Boehler,* 54 F.R.D. 539 (W.D. Pa. 1972), *aff'd,* 578 F.2d 953 (3d Cir. 1978); *Swain v. Auto Service, Inc.,* 128 S.W.3d 103, 108 (Mo. App. E.D. 2003) (declining to enforce forum selection clause in part because only one party had place of business in forum); *Mayeux A/C & Heating, Inc. v. Famous Constr. Corp.,* 1997 WL 567955, at *4 (E.D. La. 1997) (same). *Cf. Sudduth v. Occidental Peruana, Inc.,* 70 F. Supp. 2d 691, 695 (E.D. Tex. 1999) (distinguishing *Bremen* and holding forum selection clause unenforceable where choice of forum was not "neutral" — defendant had contacts with forum and subsidiary regularly conducted business there).

6. *"One-sided" or "asymmetrical" forum selection agreements.* Forum clauses can be "one-sided," or "asymmetrical," requiring one party to sue in a particular place, while leaving the other party free to commence litigation in any forum that it chooses. The clause at issue in *Copperweld* gave Demag the option of suing in either Germany or the United States, while requiring Copperweld to sue in Germany. Does this sort of "one-sided" forum clause further the various policies that *Bremen* and *Carnival Cruise* held were advanced by forum agreements? What purpose(s) underlie such "one-sided" forum clauses? Should U.S. courts enforce such clauses? Against U.S. parties? Most lower U.S. courts have enforced such clauses. *E.g., Medoil Corp. v. Citicorp,* 729 F. Supp. 1456 (S.D.N.Y. 1990); *Karl Koch Erecting Co. v. N.Y. Convention Ctr. Dev. Corp.,* 656 F. Supp. 464, 467 (S.D.N.Y. 1987). *See also Sablosky v. Edward S. Gordon Co.,* 538 N.Y.S.2d 513, 516 (Ct. App. 1989) ("Mutuality of remedy is not required in arbitration contracts."). Similar issues can arise where forum selection provisions allow one party to decide whether a dispute will be resolved by arbitration or, alternatively, litigation in a specified forum. *See* G. Born, *International Commercial Arbitration* 732-736 (2009).

7. *Forum selection agreements selecting the defendant's place of business.* Some forum selection clauses do not choose a particular geographic location, but instead require that disputes be resolved in the place where the defendant (whichever contracting party that may be) has its principal place of business. These clauses require that a party wishing to initiate litigation do so in the courts of its potential adversary. Most U.S. courts have been willing to presumptively enforce such clauses. *E.g., Warner & Swasey Co. v. Salvagnini Transferica SpA,* 633 F. Supp. 1209 (W.D.N.Y. 1986) (approving clause that was "clearly designed by the parties to place the burden of travel on the party who initiated the lawsuit"); *High Life Sales Co. v. Brown-Forman Corp.,* 823 S.W.2d 493 (Mo. 1992) ("Not only does the reciprocal nature of this clause favor its enforcement, but public policy also should favor such a clause because it discourages hasty litigation."); *Burke v. Goodman,* 114 S.W.3d 276, 280 (Mo. App. E.D. 2003) (following *High Life Sales*). Would you advise a party to agree to such a provision? What if your counterparty's courts were unreliable or corrupt?

8. *Forum's lack of connection to the parties' dispute as a basis for resisting enforcement of exclusive forum selection agreement.* Suppose that the parties choose a forum that has no connection whatsoever to their contract or dispute. Does that render the forum clause "unreasonable"? Note, as discussed elsewhere, that a choice of law agreement may not be enforced if it lacks a "reasonable relationship" to the parties' dispute. *See infra* p. 773. Should the same requirement be imposed on forum clauses?

What connection did England have to the parties and their dispute in *Bremen?* Note that *Bremen* emphasized that the parties' chosen forum should be respected precisely because it was "neutral": "[n]ot surprisingly, foreign businessmen prefer, as do we, to have disputes resolved in their own courts, but if that choice is not available then in a neutral forum with expertise in the subject matter." Suppose the towage contract had only involved two territories — Mexico and the United States. Would the selection of a London forum still have been reasonable?

Lower courts have generally rejected arguments that forum selection clauses are unenforceable simply because they designate a forum that has no factual connection to the parties or their dispute. *E.g., Interamerican Trade Corp. v. Companhia Fabricadora de Pecas,* 973 F.2d 487, 489 (6th Cir. 1992). Nevertheless, a forum's factual connection to the parties and their dispute can be relevant to its enforceability. *Bremen* emphasized:

> We are not here dealing with an agreement between two Americans to resolve their essentially local disputes in a remote alien forum. In such a case, the serious inconvenience of the contractual forum to one or both of the parties might carry greater weight in determining the reasonableness of the forum clause. The remoteness of the forum might suggest that the agreement was an adhesive one, or that the parties did not have the particular controversy in mind when they made their agreement; yet even there the party claiming should bear a heavy burden of proof.

If there is no indication that an unrelated forum was selected for its neutrality and expertise, nor that there was a need for a single contractual forum to dispel concerns about multiple possible fora, the selection of a "remote alien" forum to resolve "essentially local disputes" might well be unreasonable. *E.g., Berman v. Cunard Line,* 771 F. Supp. 1175 (S.D. Fla. 1991) (New York forum selection clause denied enforcement on grounds of lack of connection to dispute and inconvenience); *Tisdale v. Shell Oil Co.,* 723 F. Supp. 653 (M.D. Ala. 1987) ("agreement between two Americans to resolve their essentially local dispute in a remote forum . . . would be highly suspect").

9. *Relevance of parties' nationality.* Should it matter, in deciding whether to send a dispute to an arguably biased, inconvenient, or otherwise unreasonable foreign forum, what the nationalities of the parties are? In particular, should U.S. courts exercise any special scrutiny when they are asked to send a U.S. plaintiff to a foreign forum? Recall the presumption, under the *forum non conveniens* doctrine, in favor of a U.S. (but not a foreign) plaintiff's choice of a U.S. forum. *See supra* pp. 397-403. Should the same rationale be applicable to forum clauses — exercising particular scrutiny if they deny a U.S. plaintiff its choice of a U.S. forum?

10. *"Unreasonableness" as defense to enforcement of exclusive forum selection clause under the proposed Hague Choice of Court Agreements Convention.* Consider the enforceability of exclusive forum selection clauses under the proposed Hague Choice of Court Agreements Convention. If the United States ratified the Convention, would the "unreasonableness" defense still be available in U.S. courts where a forum selection clause chose the courts of another Contracting State? Suppose that nation's law did not contain a reasonableness defense. Would not Article 6(a) of the Convention apply? What effect would Article 6(c) have? What does the Convention mean by "manifest injustice"? Is that similar to "unreasonableness"? Is it a wiser standard? In what circumstances might it apply?

Conversely, could parties who challenged forum selection clauses, choosing U.S. courts, in foreign judicial proceedings rely on the U.S. "unreasonableness" defense? Consider Articles 6(a) and 6(c) again.

Suppose that a forum selection clause chose a U.S. court. If the United States ratifies the Convention, could the U.S. court refuse to enforce the clause on the basis of unreasonableness or inconvenience? Consider Article 19 of the proposed Convention.

11. *Inconvenience as grounds for resisting enforcement of nonexclusive forum selection agreement.* Suppose that the forum selection clause in *Copperweld* had merely been permissive, or nonexclusive, and that it had selected U.S. courts, rather than German courts (*e.g.,* "Any disputes arising out of the terms of the contract may be brought before the court of justice having jurisdiction in the area where the purchaser has its main offices."). In that case, what role would (or should) considerations of unreasonableness and inconvenience have played in deciding the German supplier's motion to dismiss a suit in U.S. courts by the U.S. purchaser? As discussed above, U.S. courts have reached widely divergent conclusions on the availability of the *forum non conveniens* doctrine in cases involving nonexclusive forum selection agreements. *See supra* p. 470.

Some courts have held that the *forum non conveniens* doctrine applies as if there were no forum selection clause at all. *See Magellan Real Estate Inv. Trust v. Losch,* 109 F. Supp. 2d 1144 (D. Ariz. 2000) ("The standard approach to the issue of *forum non conveniens* is employed when a forum selection clause is merely permissive, rather than mandatory. Therefore, the permissive forum selection clause is not entitled to weight as a factor."). *See also Blanco v. Banco Industrial de Venezuela, SA,* 997 F.2d 974, 980 (2d Cir. 1993).

Other courts have held that no *forum non conveniens* analysis is appropriate in the contractual forum selected by a nonexclusive clause. *Sempra Energy Trading Corp. v. Algoma Steel, Inc.,* 2001 WL 282684, at *4 (S.D.N.Y. 2001) ("parties to a contract have the right to agree on a forum for settling disputes, and, at least in litigation between sophisticated business entities, a valid forum selection clause will trump the usual considerations governing *forum non conveniens.*"). Finally, some courts have held that *forum non conveniens* dismissals are available under a nonexclusive forum selection agreement, but that the *forum non conveniens* doctrine's "private interest" factors will not apply or that the forum selection clause will be given weight in the *forum non conveniens* analysis as an indication of convenience. *See supra* p. 470.

Which of these various approaches in appropriate? If the parties have agreed that disputes may be litigated in a particular forum, is it consistent with that agreement for a party subsequently to claim that the forum is unreasonable or inconsistent? What does the forum selection agreement mean if parties are free to object to jurisdiction in the contractual forum? Recall the concerns about the legitimacy of the judicially created *forum non conveniens* doctrine, as outlined above. *See supra* pp. 384-385. Given these concerns, is it not rather extraordinary to say, not only that courts have "discretion" to refuse to exercise legislatively conferred jurisdiction, but also to do so even where the parties have made a binding contract to litigate in a particular forum? What gives courts power to ignore legislative grants of jurisdiction and to ignore (or rewrite) private contractual agreements?

12. *Nonexclusive forum selection agreements under New York General Obligations Law §5-1402.* Consider again §5-1402 of the New York General Obligations Law. How would it deal with claims of unreasonableness or inconvenience in the context of a nonexclusive forum selection agreement?

4.   Public Policy as a Ground for Resisting Enforcement of Forum Selection Agreement

a.   Introduction.   A third general reason that U.S. courts may refuse to enforce international forum clauses is "public policy." According to *Bremen,* "[a] contractual choice-of-forum clause should be held unenforceable if enforcement would contravene a strong public policy of the forum in which suit is brought, whether declared by statute or judicial decision."[126] Elsewhere, the Court remarked that "selection of a remote forum to apply differing foreign law to an essentially American controversy might contravene an important public policy of the forum."[127] Other authorities have also acknowledged a public policy defense.[128]

---

126. 407 U.S. at 15.
127. 407 U.S. at 17.
128. Model Choice of Forum Act §3(1); Hague Choice of Court Agreements Convention, Art. 6(c). *Cf. Restatement (Second) Conflict of Laws* §80, comments a-c (1986 Revisions) (not discussing public policy).

b.   Sources of Public Policy.   The public policy defense parallels related defenses to the enforcement of arbitration agreements, choice of law agreements, and foreign judgments.[129] It is settled under U.S. federal and state law that arbitration agreements, choice of law clauses, foreign judgments, and arbitral awards need not be enforced if they are sufficiently contrary to the enforcing forum's law or public policy. Public policy defenses are notoriously difficult to define with precision, in any context.[130] It is clear, however, that *Bremen*'s public policy exception, like public policy rules in related contexts, is relatively narrow.[131]

First, the Court has said that public policies cannot be derived from "general considerations of supposed public interest," but must be based upon explicit and clearly defined "laws and legal precedents."[132] The Court's observation in *Bremen* that public policy must be "declared by statute or judicial decision" suggests comparable limits.[133]

Second, the public policy exception requires something more than a showing that the substantive laws of the chosen forum and the U.S. forum are different.[134] As discussed above, this is illustrated by *Bremen* and confirmed by lower court authority.[135]

Going beyond these generalizations, however, and determining exactly when the public policy exception applies, is less clear. Judge Wisdom remarked:

> [i]n cases of bankruptcy, divorce, successions, real rights and regulation of public authorities, for example, courts cannot remit the dispute to a foreign forum lest a foreign court render a decree conflicting with our ordering of these affairs. And in cases where objectionable activity within our jurisdiction would be encouraged by the foreign court's decree, we would reach a similar result.[136]

The strongest case of a public policy forbidding enforcement of a forum selection clause is a statute in the forum expressly invalidating such agreements with respect to certain substantive causes of action. The *Second Restatement*,[137] the Model Choice of Forum Act,[138] and other authorities[139] expressly recognize that statutory prohibitions of this character provide defenses to the enforcement of forum clauses.

In practice, however, few U.S. statutes (either federal or state) expressly address the enforceability of forum clauses. The Federal Employer's Liability Act is one example of a statutory prohibition against forum selection clauses. The Act permits actions under it to be brought "in the district of the residence of the defendant, or in which the cause of action arose, or in which the defendant shall be doing business," and invalidates any "contract" intended to "enable any common carrier to exempt itself from any liability created by this Act."[140] Another federal example is (or was) 46 U.S.C. App. §183c, which makes (or made) it unlawful for shipowners transporting passengers to or from any U.S.

---

129. *See infra* pp. 760-761, 1133-1146, 1179.

130. *See infra* p. 513.

131. Public policy exceptions are interpreted narrowly, in other circumstances, including recognition of foreign judgments, *see infra* pp. 1133-1146; choice-of-law agreements, *see infra* pp. 760-761; and enforcement of arbitration agreements and awards, *see infra* p. 1179.

132. *W.R. Grace & Co. v. Local Union 759, etc.,* 461 U.S. 757 (1983). *See also United Paperworkers Int'l Union v. Misco, Inc.,* 484 U.S. 29 (1987).

133. 407 U.S. at 17.

134. 407 U.S. at 14-16. *Compare Piper Aircraft Co. v. Reyno,* 454 U.S. 235 (1981) (change in substantive law not grounds for denying *forum non conveniens* dismissal); *supra* pp. 426-428.

135. *See infra* pp. 520-528.

136. *In re Unterweser Reederei, GmbH,* 428 F.2d 888, 906 (5th Cir. 1970) (Wisdom, J., dissenting).

137. *Restatement (Second) Conflict of Laws* §80 comment b (1986 Revisions).

138. Model Choice of Forum Act §3(1).

139. *Bremen,* 407 U.S. at 15.

140. *Boyd v. Grand Trunk W. R.R.,* 338 U.S. 263 (1949) (applying 45 U.S.C. §45).

port to insert in any contract provisions purporting to "lessen, weaken, or avoid the right of *any* claimant to a trial by any court of competent jurisdiction on the question of liability" for loss.[141]

State statutory restrictions on the enforceability of forum selection clauses are also rare. Such prohibitions most frequently occur in legislation designed to protect particular classes — such as distributors[142] and franchisees.[143] These statutory restrictions are analogous to state statutes purporting to limit the enforceability of arbitration agreements in particular cases.[144]

Less explicit statutory statements of public policy are also invoked to justify nonenforcement of forum selection clauses. As discussed above, many federal and state statutes both establish substantive rules of law and specifically grant designated courts jurisdiction to adjudicate claims based on violations of these rules, but do not expressly exclude foreign courts (or arbitral tribunals) from adjudicating such claims. Statutes dealing with antitrust, securities, trademarks, patents, and RICO are leading examples of this on the federal level. Lower courts have occasionally held that particular federal or state statutory claims are not subject to foreign forum clauses.[145]

A number of lower courts have taken a different approach. Applying *Bremen*, these courts have dismissed federal and state statutory claims pursuant to forum selection agreements.[146] These decisions typically reject vigorous arguments that private forum clauses should not be permitted to undercut federal statutory guarantees and regulatory structures.[147]

Even more difficult to define are public policies based upon wholly common law rules. The public policy at issue in *Bremen* was in this category — a common law prohibition on contractual exculpation for negligent or reckless misconduct.[148] A limited additional number of such common law public policies exist, varying between jurisdictions. Representative examples include restraints of trade, bribes and other corrupt

---

141. The word "any," italicized in text, was added to §183c in 1992 to overrule *Carnival Cruise*'s holding that §183c did not invalidate foreign forum selection clauses. Pub. L. No. 102-587, 106 Stat. 5068. The word "any" was deleted, a year later, in 1993, Pub. L. No. 103-206, but legislative history accompanying the deletion purported to explain that it was not intended as a return to *Carnival Cruise*. 139 Cong. Rec. H10928, H10939 (daily ed. Nov. 22, 1993). Subsequent legislative history expressly disclaimed this explanation. 140 Cong. Rec. S1847 (daily ed. Feb. 24, 1994) (statement of Sen. Breaux) (1993 amendment "reinstates the Supreme Court decision in the *Shute* case as the applicable law for interpreting forum selection clauses"). Several lower courts have concluded that the various amendments have left *Carnival Cruise* intact. *Valenti v. Norwegian Cruise Line*, 2005 WL 927167, at *4 (S.D.N.Y. 2005); *Lunday v. Carnival Corp.*, 2004 WL 3753263, at *4 (S.D. Tex. 2004); *Pant v. Princess Cruises, Inc.*, 1994 WL 539277 (S.D. Ohio 1994); *Compagno v. Commodore Cruise Line, Ltd.*, 1994 WL 462997 (E.D. La. 1994).

142. *See Caribbean Wholesales & Service Corp. v. U.S. JVC Corp.*, 855 F. Supp. 627 (S.D.N.Y. 1994) (Puerto Rico Law 75 prohibits enforcement of clauses in distribution agreements selecting foreign forums).

143. *See EEC Computer Centers, Inc. v. Entre Computer Centers, Inc.*, 597 F. Supp. 1182 (N.D. Ill. 1984) (Illinois Franchise Disclosure Act prohibits enforcement of clauses selecting forum outside Illinois).

144. *See infra* pp. 1165-1166.

145. *E.g.*, *Karlberg European Tanspa, Inc. v. JK-Josef Kratz Vertriebsgesellschaft mbH*, 699 F. Supp. 669 (N.D. Ill. 1988); *Red Bull Assocs. v. Best Western Int'l*, 686 F. Supp. 447 (S.D.N.Y. 1988), *aff'd*, 862 F.2d 963 (2d Cir. 1988); *Volkswagen Interamericana, SA v. Rohlsen*, 360 F.2d 437 (1st Cir. 1966) (Automobile Dealers' Day in Court Act); *Cutter v. Scott & Fetzer Co.*, 510 F. Supp. 905 (E.D. Wis. 1981); *High Life Sales Co. v. Brown-Forman Corp.*, 823 S.W.2d 493 (Mo. 1992) (Missouri liquor law).

146. *E.g.*, *Omron Healthcare, Inc. v. Maclaren Exports Ltd.*, 28 F.3d 600 (7th Cir. 1994) (trademark infringement); *Royal Bed & Spring Co. v. Famossul Industria e Comercio de Moveis Ltda.*, 906 F.2d 45 (1st Cir. 1990) (Law 75 of Puerto Rico, protecting distributors); *AVC Nederland BV*, 740 F.2d 148 (federal securities laws); *Coastal Steel Corp. v. Tilghman Wheelabrator, Ltd.*, 709 F.2d 190, 202 (3d Cir. 1983) (claims by debtor in bankruptcy); *Bense v. Interstate Battery Sys. of America, Inc.*, 683 F.2d 718 (2d Cir. 1982) (antitrust); *Medoil Corp. v. Citicorp*, 729 F. Supp. 1456 (S.D.N.Y. 1990) (RICO and federal securities laws).

147. *E.g.*, *AVC Nederland BV*, 740 F.2d at 156-160 (private contractual expectations and foreign regulatory interests outweigh federal regulatory interests). *Cf. Mitsubishi Motors Corp. v. Soler Chrysler-Plymouth, Inc.*, 473 U.S. 614, 637 n.19 (1985).

148. *See* 407 U.S. at 15-16; *Bisso v. Inland Waterways Corp.*, 349 U.S. 85 (1955).

agreements, usury, agreements to commit unlawful acts, and agreements to provide indemnification or exculpation for negligent or reckless misconduct.

Over the past several decades, U.S. courts have progressively narrowed the circumstances in which public policy will permit nonenforcement of a forum selection clause. This development has been strongly supported by parallel decisions in the contexts of international (and domestic) arbitration agreements, where U.S. courts have repeatedly held that various federal and state statutory rights may be the subject of arbitration in foreign states.[149] Similarly, in the forum selection clause context, U.S. courts have held that statutory claims under the federal securities laws may be dismissed for litigation in a foreign forum, even where the foreign court may not give effect to U.S. law and may not apply identical foreign legal protections.[150] Comparable results apply with regard to claims under the Carriage of Goods by Sea Act ("COGSA").[151]

    c. Selected Materials on Public Policy.   Excerpted below are selected materials illustrating the application of public policy defenses to the enforcement of forum selection agreements. A concluding portion of *Bremen* is excerpted, illustrating the narrowness of the contemporary public policy exception, as well as the choice of "law" issues raised by public policies. The Ninth Circuit's decision in *Richards v. Lloyd's of London* is also excerpted, illustrating how federal courts have been increasingly willing to enforce forum selection clauses when applied to federal statutory claims.

THE BREMEN v. ZAPATA OFF-SHORE CO.

407 U.S. 1 (1972) [excerpted above at pp. 474-478]

BURGER, CHIEF JUSTICE. [After concluding, as discussed and excerpted above, that the parties' forum selection clause was presumptively enforceable, the Court went on to consider whether enforcement should be denied on the grounds of some specific public policy. In particular, the Court considered the fact that the parties' agreement contained "two clauses purporting to exculpate Unterweser from liability for damages to the towed barge." The clauses provided: "[Unterweser], their masters and crews are not responsible for defaults and/or errors in the navigation of the tow" and "Damages suffered by the towed object are in any case for account of its Owners." 428 F.2d at 895 n.39. Zapata submitted uncontested expert testimony that English courts would enforce the exculpatory clause. Under U.S. admiralty law, however, contractual exculpations of liability of this character are unenforceable because of their perceived tendency to remove disincentives to negligent conduct and because of the likelihood that they are the product of unequal bargaining power. *Bisso v. Inland Waterways Corp.*, 349 U.S. 85 (1955).]

---

149. *See infra* pp. 1185-1186; *Scherk v. Alberto-Culver Co.*, 417 U.S. 506 (1974) (claims under Securities Exchange Act arbitrable in foreign forum); *Mitsubishi Motors Corp. v. Soler Chrysler-Plymouth, Inc.*, 473 U.S. 614 (1985) (antitrust claims under Sherman Act arbitrable in foreign forum); *Shearson/American Express, Inc. v. McMahon*, 482 U.S. 220 (1987) (securities and RICO claims arbitrable in domestic arbitration).

150. *Riley v. Kingsley Underwriting Agencies, Ltd.*, 969 F.2d 953 (10th Cir. 1992); *Roby v. Corporation of Lloyd's*, 996 F.2d 1353 (2d Cir. 1993); *Bonny v. Society of Lloyd's*, 3 F.3d 156 (7th Cir. 1993); *Shell v. R.W. Sturge, Ltd.*, 55 F.3d 1227 (6th Cir. 1995); *Allen v. Lloyd's of London*, 94 F.3d 923 (4th Cir. 1996); *Haynsworth v. Lloyd's of London*, 121 F.3d 956 (5th Cir. 1997); *Lipcon v. Underwriters at Lloyd's*, 148 F.3d 1285 (11th Cir. 1998).

151. *Fireman's Fund Ins. Co. v. M/V DSR Atlantic*, 131 F.3d 1336 (9th Cir. 1997); *Union Steel America, Inc. v. M/V Sanko Spruce*, 14 F. Supp. 2d 682 (D.N.J. 1998); *Raztory v. Croatia Line*, 918 F. Supp. 961 (E.D. Va. 1996); *Jewel Seafoods, Ltd. v. M/V Peace River*, 39 F. Supp. 2d 628 (D.S.C. 1999). *Compare In re Rationis Enterprises, Inc. of Panama*, 1999 A.M.C. 889 (S.D.N.Y. 1999).

The Court of Appeals suggested that enforcement [of the parties' forum selection clause] would be contrary to the public policy of the forum under *Bisso,* because of the prospect that the English courts would enforce the clauses of the towage contract purporting to exculpate Unterweser from liability for damages to the *Chaparral.* A contractual choice-of-forum clause should be held unenforceable if enforcement would contravene a strong public policy of the forum in which suit is brought, whether declared by statute or by judicial decision. *See, e.g., Boyd v. Grand Trunk W.R.R. Co.,* 338 U.S. 263 (1949). It is clear, however, that whatever the proper scope of the policy expressed in *Bisso,* it does not reach this case. *Bisso* rested on considerations with respect to the towage business strictly in American waters, and those considerations are not controlling in an international commercial agreement. Speaking for the dissenting judges in the Court of Appeals, Judge Wisdom pointed out: "... we should not invalidate the forum-selection clause here unless we are firmly convinced that we would thereby significantly encourage negligent conduct within the boundaries of the United States."

RICHARDS v. LLOYD'S OF LONDON
135 F.3d 1289 (9th Cir. 1998) (en banc)

GOODWIN, CIRCUIT JUDGE. Appellants, all citizens or residents of the United States, are more than 600 "Names" who entered into underwriting agreements. The Names sued four defendants: the Corporation of Lloyd's, the Society of Lloyd's, the Council of Lloyd's, (collectively, "Lloyd's") and Lloyd's of London, (the "unincorporated association").

Lloyd's is a market in which more than three hundred Underwriting Agencies compete for underwriting business. Pursuant to the [United Kingdom] Lloyd's Act of 1871-1982, Lloyd's oversees and regulates the competition for underwriting business in the Lloyd's market. The market does not accept premiums or insure risks. Rather, Underwriting Agencies, or syndicates, compete for the insurance business. Each Underwriting Agency is controlled by a Managing Agent who is responsible for the financial status of its agency. The Managing Agent must attract not only underwriting business from brokers but also the capital with which to insure the risks underwritten.

The Names provide the underwriting capital. The Names become Members of the Society of Lloyd's through a series of agreements, proof of financial means, and the deposit of an irrevocable letter of credit in favor of Lloyd's. To become a Name, one must travel to England to acknowledge the attendant risks of participating in a syndicate and sign a General Undertaking. The General Undertaking is a two page document containing choice of forum and choice of law clauses (collectively the "choice clauses"), which form the basis for this dispute. The choice clauses read:

> 2.1 The rights and obligations of the parties arising out of or relating to the Member's membership of, and/or underwriting of insurance business at, Lloyd's and any other matter referred to in this Undertaking shall be governed by and construed in accordance with the laws of England.

> 2.2 Each party hereto irrevocably agrees that the courts of England shall have exclusive jurisdiction to settle any dispute and/or controversy of whatsoever nature arising out of or relating to the Member's membership of, and/or underwriting of insurance business at, Lloyd's. ...

By becoming a Member, the Names obtain the right to participate in the Lloyd's Underwriting Agencies. The Names, however, do not deal directly with Lloyd's or with the

Managing Agents. Instead, the Names are represented by Members' Agents who, pursuant to agreement, stand in a fiduciary relationship with their Names. Upon becoming a Name, an individual selects the syndicates in which he wishes to participate. In making this decision, the individual must rely to a great extent on the advice of his Members' Agent. The Names generally join more than one underwriting agency in order to spread their risks across different types of insurance. When a Name undertakes an underwriting obligation, that Name is responsible only for his share of an agency's losses; however, his liability is unlimited for that share.

In this case, the risk of heavy losses has materialized[, thereby imposing significant financial losses on various U.S. Names,] and the Names now seek shelter under United States securities laws and the Racketeer Influenced and Corrupt Organizations Act ("RICO"), 18 U.S.C. §1961 *et seq.* The Names claim that Lloyd's actively sought the investment of U.S. residents to fill an urgent need to build up capital. According to the Names, Lloyd's concealed information regarding the possible consequences of the risks undertaken and deliberately and disproportionately exposed the Names to massive liabilities for which sufficient underwriting capital or reinsurance was unavailable. . . . [Among other things, the Names contended that the choice of law and choice of forum clauses were void under the "antiwaiver" provisions of federal securities laws and offended public policy. Lloyd's relied, of course, on *Bremen*].

We analyze the validity of the choice clause under [*Bremen*] where the Supreme Court stated that courts should enforce choice of law and choice of forum clauses in cases of "freely negotiated private international agreement[s]." 407 U.S. at 12-13.[152]

A. The Names . . . contend that *Bremen* does not apply to cases where Congress has spoken directly to the immediate issue — as they claim the antiwaiver provisions do here. The Securities Act of 1933 (the "'33 Act") provides that: "Any condition, stipulation, or provision binding any person acquiring any security to waive compliance with any provision of this subchapter or of the rules and regulations of the Commission shall be void." 15 U.S.C. §77n. The 1934 Securities Exchange Act (the "'34 Act") contains a substantially similar provision. 15 U.S.C. §78cc(a). The Names seize on these provisions and claim that they void the choice clauses in their agreement with Lloyd's. Certainly the antiwaiver provisions are worded broadly enough to reach this case. They cover "any condition, stipulation, or provision binding any person acquiring any security to waive compliance with any provision of this subchapter." Indeed, this language is broad enough to reach any offer or sale of anything that could be alleged to be a security, no matter where the transaction occurs.

Nevertheless, this attempt to distinguish *Bremen* fails. In *Bremen* itself, the Supreme Court contemplated that a forum selection clause may conflict with relevant statutes. *Bremen,* 407 U.S. at 15 ("A contractual choice-of-forum clause should be held unenforceable if enforcement would contravene a strong public policy of the forum in which suit is brought, *whether declared by statute* or by judicial decision.") (emphasis added). Moreover, in *Scherk v. Alberto-Culver Co., supra,* the Supreme Court explicitly relied on *Bremen* in a case involving a securities transaction. Echoing the language of *Bremen,* the Court found that "[a] contractual provision specifying in advance the forum in which disputes shall be litigated and the law to be applied is . . . an almost indispensable precondition to

---

152. While the contract in *Bremen* did not contain a choice of law clause, the Supreme Court explicitly recognized that the forum selection clause also acted as a choice of law clause. *Id.* at 13 n.15 ("[W]hile the contract here did not specifically provide that the substantive law of England should be applied, it is the general rule in English courts that the parties are assumed, absent a contrary indication, to have designated the forum with the view that it should apply its own law. . . . It is therefore reasonable to conclude that the forum clause was also an effort to obtain certainty as to the applicable substantive law.").

achievement of the orderliness and predictability essential to any international business transaction." *Scherk*, 417 U.S. at 516. This passage should leave little doubt as to the applicability of *Bremen* to the case at hand.

Indeed, were we to find that *Bremen* did not apply, the reach of United States securities laws would be unbounded. The Names simply prove too much when they assert that "*Bremen*'s judicially-created policy analysis under federal common law is not controlling when Congress has expressed its will in a statute." This assertion, if true, expands the reach of federal securities law to any and all such transactions, no matter how remote from the United States. We agree with the Fifth Circuit that "we must tread cautiously before expanding the operation of U.S. securities law in the international arena." *Haynsworth v. The Corporation*, 121 F.3d 956, 966 (5th Cir. 1997). . . .

II. We now apply *Bremen* to this case. *Bremen* emphasized that "in the light of present-day commercial realities and expanding international trade we conclude that the forum clause should control absent a strong showing that it should be set aside." The Court reasoned that "[t]he elimination of all [] uncertainties [regarding the forum] by agreeing in advance . . . is an indispensable element in international trade, commerce, and contracting." Thus, "absent some compelling and countervailing reason [a forum selection clause] should be honored by the parties and enforced by the courts." *Bremen*, 407 U.S. at 15. The party seeking to avoid the forum selection clause bears "a heavy burden of proof." The Supreme Court has identified three grounds for repudiating a forum selection clause: first, if the inclusion of the clause in the agreement was the product of fraud or overreaching; second, if the party wishing to repudiate the clause would effectively be deprived of his day in court were the clause enforced; and third, "if enforcement would contravene a strong public policy of the forum in which suit is brought." . . .

A. The Names' strongest argument for escaping their agreement to litigate their claims in England is that the choice clauses contravene a strong public policy embodied in federal and state securities law and RICO. . . . [However, we] follow our six sister circuits that have ruled to enforce the choice clauses. We do so because we apply *Scherk* and because English law provides the Names with sufficient protection.

In *Scherk*, the Supreme Court was confronted with a contract that specified that all disputes would be resolved in arbitration before the International Chamber of Commerce in Paris, France. The arbitrator was to apply the law of the state of Illinois. The Court enforced the forum selection clause despite then hostile precedent. *See Wilko v. Swan*, 346 U.S. 427 (1953), *overruled by Rodriguez de Quijas v. Shearson/American Express, Inc.*, 490 U.S. 477, 485 (1989). The Court's treatment of *Wilko* leaves little doubt that the choice clauses in this case are enforceable. In *Wilko*, the Supreme Court ruled that "the right to select the judicial forum is the kind of 'provision' that cannot be waived under §14 of the Securities Act." *Wilko*, 346 U.S. at 435. In *Scherk*, the Court had before it a case where both the District Court and the Seventh Circuit found a forum selection clause invalid on the strength of *Wilko*. *Scherk*, 417 U.S. at 510.

In distinguishing *Wilko*, the Supreme Court stated that there were "significant and, we find, crucial differences between the agreement involved in *Wilko* and the one signed by the parties here." *Scherk*, 417 U.S. at 515. The first and primary difference that the Court relied upon was that "Alberto-Culver's contract . . . was a truly international agreement." The Court reasoned that such a contract needs, as "an almost indispensable precondition," a "provision specifying in advance the forum in which disputes shall be litigated *and the law to be applied*." *Id.* at 516 (emphasis added).

Moreover, the Supreme Court has explained that, in the context of an international agreement, there is "no basis for a judgment that only United States laws and United States courts should determine this controversy in the face of a solemn agreement between the parties that such controversies be resolved elsewhere." *Id.* at 517 n.11. To require that " 'American standards of fairness' must . . . govern the controversy demeans the standards of justice elsewhere in the world, and unnecessarily exalts the primacy of United States law over the laws of other countries." *Id.* These passages from *Scherk,* we think, resolve the question whether public policy reasons allow the Names to escape their "solemn agreement" to adjudicate their claims in England under English law. *Scherk* involved a securities transaction. The Court rejected *Wilko*'s holding that the antiwaiver provision of the '34 Act prohibited choice clauses. . . .

Relying on *Mitsubishi Motors Corp. v. Soler Chrysler-Plymouth,* Inc., 473 U.S. 614, 634 (1985), the Names argue that federal and state securities laws are of "fundamental importance to American democratic capitalism." They claim that enforcement of the choice clauses will deprive them of important remedies provided by our securities laws. The Supreme Court disapproved of such an outcome, the Names contend, when it stated that "in the event the choice-of-forum and choice-of-law clauses operated in tandem as a prospective waiver of a party's right to pursue statutory remedies for antitrust violations, we would have little hesitation in condemning the agreement as against public policy." *Id.* at 637 n.19.

Without question this case would be easier to decide if this footnote in *Mitsubishi* had not been inserted. Nevertheless, we do not believe dictum in a footnote regarding antitrust law outweighs the extended discussion and holding in *Scherk* on the validity of clauses specifying the forum and applicable law. The Supreme Court repeatedly recognized in *Scherk* that parties to an international securities transaction may choose law other than that of the United States, *Scherk,* 417 U.S. at 516, 517 n.11, 519 n.13, yet it never suggested that this affected the validity of a forum selection clause. . . .

B. Of course, were English law so deficient that the Names would be deprived of any reasonable recourse, we would have to subject the choice clauses to another level of scrutiny. *See Carnival Cruise Lines, Inc. v. Shute,* 499 U.S. 585, 595 (1991) ("It bears emphasis that forum-selection clauses contained in form passage contracts are subject to judicial scrutiny for fundamental fairness."). In this case, however, there is no such danger.

We disagree with the dramatic assertion that "[t]he available English remedies are not adequate substitutes for the firm shields and finely honed swords provided by American securities law." *Richards v. Lloyd's of London,* 107 F.3d 1422, 1430 (9th Cir. 1997). The Names have recourse against both the Member and Managing Agents for fraud, breach of fiduciary duty, or negligent misrepresentation. Indeed, English courts have already awarded substantial judgments to some of the other Names.

While it is true that the Lloyd's Act immunizes Lloyd's from many actions possible under our securities laws, Lloyd's is not immune from the consequences of actions committed in bad faith, including fraud. Lloyd's Act of 1982, Ch. 14(3)(e)(i). The Names contend that entities using the Lloyd's trade name willfully and fraudulently concealed massive long tail liabilities in order to induce them to join syndicates. If so, we have been cited to no authority that Lloyd's partial immunity would bar recovery. . . .

THOMAS, CIRCUIT JUDGE, with whom JUDGES PREGERSON and HAWKINS join, dissenting. The majority espouses a reasonable foreign policy, but one which emanates from the wrong branch of government. Congress has already explicitly resolved the question at hand. In the Securities Act of 1933 and the Securities Exchange Act of 1934 (the "Acts"), Congress expressly provided that investors cannot contractually agree to disregard United States securities law. Thus, in applying the "reasonableness" policy-weighing approach of *M/S Bremen v. Zapata Off-Shore Co., supra,* the majority displaces Congress' specific statutory directive. Furthermore, even assuming that the Bremen analysis applies here, the circumstances surrounding this dispute compel the conclusion that enforcement of the choice clauses would be unreasonable. Accordingly, I respectfully dissent.

I. [T]he Acts do not merely declare "a strong public policy" against the waiver of compliance with United States securities laws. Rather, the Acts explicitly and unconditionally prohibit such a waiver[:]

> Any condition, stipulation, or provision binding any person acquiring any security to waive compliance with any provision of this subchapter or of the rules and regulations of the Commission shall be void. 15 U.S.C. §77n.

The Securities Exchange Act of 1934 contains a similar restriction. See 15 U.S.C. §78cc(a).

Absent these anti-waiver provisions, courts could appropriately examine choice-of-forum clauses in investment contracts under a *Bremen* analysis to determine whether they violated the strong public policy of the United States as embodied in our securities law. However, the Acts' anti-waiver provisions decisively alter this inquiry. With adoption of those sections, Congress announced a per se rule that American laws cannot be ignored in this context.

The majority's fears notwithstanding, it is unnecessary to displace Congress' reasoned judgment in order to contract the "boundless" reach of United States securities laws. First, because plaintiffs alleging securities fraud will at some point have to establish that the disputed transactions involved "securities," as defined under United States law, plaintiffs cannot gain unfettered access to the protection of the securities laws simply by alleging that they have purchased securities. Second, the plaintiffs here do not seek to invoke the Acts' substantive remedies in the context of transactions that enjoy only an incidental nexus with the United States. Lloyd's recruited the plaintiffs, residents of the United States, in the United States, often using United States brokerage firms and recruiters, and availed itself of the United States mails to disseminate information about becoming a Name. . . . To penalize the plaintiffs in this case based upon a hypothetical scenario that differs dramatically from the circumstances at issue here would work an unjust deprivation of the plaintiffs' rights under the Acts.

The majority argues that the Supreme Court's reliance on *Bremen* in *Scherk v. Alberto-Culver Co., supra,* should control here. However, the majority overlooks the crucial differences between the instant dispute and the facts underlying *Scherk. Scherk* involved a contract that contained an agreement to arbitrate any disputes arising out of the contract in Paris, France. This contract specified that "[t]he laws of the State of Illinois, U.S.A. shall apply to and govern this agreement, its interpretation and performance." 417 U.S. at 508. In contrast, the choice clauses here not only select the forum — the courts of England — but mandate that English law shall govern any controversy. Thus, the reasoning and conclusions of *Scherk* should not extend to this case. . . .

Furthermore, the Lloyd's underwriting agreements had substantial connections with the United States, in contrast with the sparse contacts between the United States and the contract in *Scherk.* In *Scherk,* an American company made an initial contact with Scherk, a German citizen, in Germany, pursued negotiations with Scherk in both Europe and the United States, and finally executed a contract in Vienna, Austria, providing for the transfer of the ownership of Scherk's enterprises. The closing of this transaction occurred in Geneva, Switzerland. In comparison, the sole component of Lloyd's campaign to recruit American Names that took place in England was the committee meeting that new Names attended in London. Otherwise, every aspect of the solicitation occurred in the United States. To characterize this extensive and multifaceted recruitment campaign as the mere receipt of "solicitations," as does the majority, is to understate the impact of Lloyd's activities in the United States. . . .

II. In addition to violating the Acts' express antiwaiver provisions, the choice [of law and forum] clauses are unenforceable because they are " 'unreasonable' under the circumstances." *Bremen*, 407 U.S. at 10. Initially, the Supreme Court has twice stated that the type of clauses at issue here are invalid when they prospectively disable parties from pursuing statutory remedies. *See Mitsubishi Motors Corp. v. Soler Chrysler-Plymouth, Inc., supra*, 473 U.S. at 637 n.19, *quoted in Vimar Seguros y Reaseguros, SA v. M/V Sky Reefer*, 515 U.S. 528, 540 (1995). . . .

As applied here, the logic of *Mitsubishi* and *Vimar* militates against enforcing the choice clauses. Not only do the choice clauses preclude the plaintiffs from seeking the substantive remedies the Acts offer, but the protections they provide under English law are markedly inferior to the Acts'. For instance, English law recognizes no remedy for the failure to register securities as required by §12(1) of the Securities Act of 1933. Nor is there any English remedy against Lloyd's for negligent misrepresentation as provided by §12(2) of the Securities Act of 1933, because the 1982 Lloyd's Act expressly immunizes Lloyd's from any claim for "negligence or other tort" unless bad faith was involved. Third, no "controlling person" liability exists in England, whereas §15 of the Securities Act of 1933 and §20(a) of the 1934 Securities Exchange Act impose such liability. Thus, the choice clauses should not be enforced, because they afford a level of protection far lower than the remedies the Acts provide. . . .

Enforcing the choice clauses gravely disadvantages American businesses, because foreign businesses, like Lloyd's, can recruit investors without expending the time and money involved in fulfilling the requirements of the Acts — a burden that American businesses cannot legally evade. Invalidating the choice clauses therefore eliminates any artificial advantage that Lloyd's may have enjoyed in competing in the American insurance market. In addition, the Acts furnish a necessary regulatory check upon an otherwise virtually autonomous organization. . . .

The majority . . . assails footnote 19 in *Mitsubishi* as mere dictum which cannot "outweig[h] the extended discussion and holding in *Scherk* on the validity of clauses specifying the forum and applicable law." . . . [W]hile footnote 19 in *Mitsubishi* was not incorporated into the Court's actual holding, the Court left no doubt about its position on this issue by reiterating it in the entirely different setting of *Vimar*. Hence, the Court implicitly indicated that its concerns about a potential deprivation of plaintiffs' access to statutory remedies were limited to neither the antitrust nor the COGSA context. . . .

When Congress voided waiver clauses, it meant what it said. The antiwaiver provisions of the Acts, whether as clear statutory directives or as embodiments of public policy, render the choice clauses unenforceable. The district court's dismissal of the plaintiffs' claims under the Acts should be reversed. Hence, I respectfully dissent.

Notes on **Bremen** *and* **Richards**

1. *Public policy and noncontractual claims.* Why should forum selection agreements *ever* be enforceable as to noncontractual claims? Do not "ordinary" tort claims rest upon the forum's public policy determinations about what types of conduct is wrongful or economically unacceptable? Should private parties be permitted to delegate these determinations to alien forums?

Are forum selection clauses enforceable as to noncontractual claims under the proposed Hague Choice of Court Agreements Convention? Which kinds of noncontractual claims are covered by the Convention. Consider Articles 2(2)(h), (j) and (k). What sort of practical difficulties do these exceptions create? How hard is it for a party to plead such claims in most business disputes?

2. *Public policy as basis for nonenforcement of forum selection agreements.* As *Bremen* and *Richards* illustrate, there are a variety of related grounds on which enforcement of a forum agreement can be resisted under the public policy exception.

(a) Express statutory prohibition as source of public policy. The most clear-cut example of a public policy basis for resisting enforcement of a forum clause is a statute in the enforcing forum forbidding enforcement. Consider the provisions of the federal securities laws at issue in *Richards* — 15 U.S.C. §§77n and 78cc(a) — invalidating any contractual waiver of compliance with statutory requirements. Why don't these provisions forbid enforcement of any forum selection clause designating non-U.S. courts? *See Wilko v. Swan,* 346 U.S. 427 (1953) (holding that anti-waiver provision forbids enforcement of arbitration clause), *overruled, Rodriquez de Quijas v. Shearson/American Express,* 490 U.S. 477, 484 (1989).

Consider *Richards,* which did not merely enforce a forum clause, but enforced a clause that would, in conjunction with an English choice of law clause, exclude *any* application of the U.S. securities laws. Is this result consistent with the anti-waiver provisions of §§77n and 78cc(a)? As the dissenting opinions explain, isn't it obvious that the Lloyd's choice of forum and choice of law clauses "waive compliance with" *every* provision of the U.S. securities laws? How is it consistent with §§77n and 78cc(a) to permit dismissal of federal securities claims to a forum that will not apply the federal securities laws? What is the majority's response in *Richards?*

(b) Implied statutory prohibition as source of public policy. Very few U.S. federal or state statutes expressly forbid enforcement of a forum selection clause. If no such express prohibition exists, what ought to qualify as "public policies"? Many federal and state statutes provide substantive rules of law and statutory protections, often coupled with jurisdictional grants and procedural rules. The federal antitrust, securities, trademark, patent, and employment discrimination laws are examples of this. Although these statutory regimes may not contain express prohibitions against forum clauses, it is often argued that such prohibitions should be implied, to ensure fulfillment of the regulatory objectives of the legislation. *See infra* pp. 523-524.

Put aside the specific anti-waiver provisions of the federal securities laws, and consider whether the regulatory framework of the federal securities laws permits foreign forum clauses. Was *Richards* right to dismiss a U.S. plaintiff's U.S. securities law claims? The court in *Richards* clearly recognizes that U.S. law would provide the Names with greater protections, and prospects of success, as well as treble damages, which English law would not permit. Given these differences between a U.S. and an English forum, how can one say that enforcing the forum clause will not undercut the purposes of the federal securities laws?

Is *Richards* correctly decided? Why or why not? Consider the reasoning in the dissenting opinion.

Why do claims under the federal securities laws raise any questions of public policy? Aren't securities claims just like other causes of action — like contract and tort claims? Do not the antitrust and securities laws represent fundamentally important U.S. public policies, which will be undermined if foreign courts are permitted to decide statutory claims arising under those statutes? How could a foreign judge, untrained in U.S. law and unfamiliar with U.S. conditions, apply the Sherman Act? Under *Richards'* analysis would a foreign judge even be expected to apply U.S. statutory protections? Is it appropriate, as most lower courts have held, to permit private parties to contract out of the substantive protections of fundamentally important federal regulatory statutes, like the antitrust and securities laws?

(c) Common law as source of public policy. What was the source of the public policy in *Bremen* that allegedly forbade enforcement of the parties' English forum clause? Note that there are a considerable variety of common law public policies that might arguably restrain enforcement of forum clauses; these include prohibitions against bribery, anti-competitive restrictions, usery, and the like. Is it appropriate for these public policies to preclude the enforcement of international forum clauses? Did *Bremen* accept that a U.S. public policy against exculpation for gross negligence might potentially preclude enforcement of a forum clause?

(d) Hypothetical applications of U.S. public policy. Consider whether U.S. "public policy" would preclude enforcement of a forum clause in the following hypotheticals:

In *Bremen,* the accident had occurred within U.S. territorial waters, at the beginning of the oil rig's voyage to the Adriatic Sea.

In a dispute arising out of a U.S. employer's termination of an employment contract, for alleged malfeasance by the employee, the employee brings claims for both wrongful termination and libel (based upon the employer's derogatory public statements alleging that the employee had engaged in wrongful conduct). The employment contract contains a provision selecting English courts as the contractual forum for both the wrongful termination and libel claims. English courts would permit recovery on the libel claim upon a significantly more liberal basis than the First Amendment would permit in the United States. The employer seeks to have the dispute resolved in U.S. courts, arguing that public policies derived from the First Amendment forbade enforcement of the forum selection agreement.

In the foregoing dispute, the employee instead brings race discrimination claims under Title VII — the federal employment discrimination statute — in a U.S. court in violation of the forum clause. The employer seeks to dismiss the case in favor of the English contractual forum.

In a dispute involving military technology, the export of which is prohibited by U.S. law absent an export license, the parties' agreement contains a forum clause specifying Russian courts. The parties are a U.S. seller of products based upon the military technology and a Russian purchaser. The U.S. party brings suit in the United States asserting that the forum clause violates U.S. public policy because it would require disclosure of the technology to unauthorized foreign parties.

(e) Public policy under the proposed Hague Choice of Court Agreements Convention. Consider how Article 6(c) of the proposed Hague Convention deals with public policy defenses to enforcement of a forum selection clause. What does it mean to be "manifestly contrary to the public policy of the State of the court seised"? Is this different from U.S. common law standards?

(f) Relevance of foreign courts' willingness to decide U.S. statutory or other claim. In deciding whether to enforce a forum selection clause as applied to U.S. statutory (or other) claims, is it relevant that a foreign court will or will not apply the U.S. statutory provisions and hear such claims? Where violations of the antitrust and securities law occur within U.S. territory, perpetrated against U.S. nationals, with adverse consequences for U.S. markets and third parties, should U.S. courts enforce a forum clause granting exclusive jurisdiction to the courts of the wrongdoer's home country? How does *Richards* resolve the foregoing questions? Is the content of English law relevant to the *Richards* outcome? If so, is this consistent with the basic premise, set forth in *Bremen,* that changes in substantive law are not relevant to the enforceability of forum clauses?

(g) Prohibition against application of foreign penal and revenue laws — revisited. Why was it that the English courts in *Richards* would not apply the U.S. federal securities laws? Recall the historic rule, discussed above, that one nation's courts will not apply the penal or revenue laws of another nation. *See supra* p. 444 & *infra* pp. 1102-1110. If English and U.S. law were in fact so similar, why should English courts refuse to apply U.S. law?

3. *Forum selection agreements and federal statutory claims.* U.S. courts have considered the application of forum selection agreements to a variety of federal statutory claims. Particularly in recent years, courts have generally held that such claims can properly be subject to a forum selection agreement.

(a) Forum selection agreements and federal securities law claims. As discussed above, and as *Richards* illustrates, most federal courts have held that a forum selection clause must be enforced even as applied to federal securities law claims. *See supra* p. 512. Is that result persuasive? What response is there to the dissent's argument in *Richards* that "[t]he antiwaiver provisions of the Acts, whether as clear statutory directives or as embodiments of public policy, render the choice clauses unenforceable."

(b) Forum selection agreements and federal trademark claims. Can a forum selection agreement validly apply to federal trademark claims? In *Omron Healthcare Inc. v. MacLaren Exports Ltd.,* the Seventh Circuit considered the claim that U.S. public policy forbid enforcement of a forum clause in a case under federal trademark legislation. 28 F.3d 600 (7th Cir. 1994). According to the Court, the U.S. plaintiff "tells us that the 'policies' in question favor sending disputes to courts that have the expertise to resolve them, and ensuring that courts with the interest of Americans at heart interpret laws designed for the protection of American consumers." 28 F.3d at 603.

Judge Easterbrook summarily dismissed the argument. Observing that "neither of these policies has a secure footing in any statute," he held that foreign courts were capable of interpreting federal trademark statutes. 28 F.3d at 603. If a contrary view were accepted, "then *Scherk, Mitsubishi,* and many other cases are wrongly decided, for they depend on the belief that foreign tribunals will interpret U.S. law honestly, just as the federal courts of the United States routinely interpret the laws of the states and other nations." 28 F.3d at 603-604.

(c) Forum selection agreements and the Carriage of Goods by Sea Act. Among other things, COGSA provides: "Any clause, covenant, or agreement in a contract of carriage relieving the carrier or the ship from liability for loss or damage to or in connection with the goods, arising from negligence, fault, or failure in the duties and obligations provided in this section, or lessening such liability otherwise than as provided in this chapter shall be null and void and of no effect." 46 U.S.C. §1303(8). For decades, U.S. courts concluded that this provision invalidated forum selection and arbitration clauses selecting non-U.S. forums. *Carbon Black Export, Inc. v. The SS Monrosa,* 254 F.2d 297 (5th Cir. 1958); *Indusa Corp. v. SS Ranborg,* 377 F.2d 200 (2d Cir. 1967). The principal rationale was that foreign courts would (or might) give effect to liability limitations or exculpatory clauses, thereby relieving shippers of liability or "lessening" such liability, contrary to the protective purposes of 46 U.S.C. §1303(8).

As the *Richards* opinion indicates, however, the Supreme Court rejected the foregoing conclusion in *Vimar Seguros y Reaseguros, SA v. M/V Sky Reefer,* 515 U.S. 528 (1995). The Court reasoned:

> It would also be out of keeping with the objects of the [New York] Convention for the courts of this country to interpret COGSA to disparage the authority or competence of international forums for dispute resolution. Petitioner's skepticism over the ability of foreign arbitrators to apply COGSA or the Hague Rules [*i.e.,* international treaty provisions paralleling COGSA],

524 Chapter 5. International Forum Selection Agreements

and its reliance on this aspect of *Indussa* must give way to contemporary principles of international comity and commercial practice. As the Court observed in *Bremen,* when it enforced a foreign forum selection clause, the historical judicial resistance to foreign forum selection clauses "has little place in an era when businesses once essentially local now operate in world markets." "The expansion of American business and industry will hardly be encouraged," we explained, "if, notwithstanding solemn contracts, we insist on a parochial concept that all disputes must be resolved under our laws and in our courts."

Does the Supreme Court's analysis give due regard to the language of COGSA? If a COGSA claim is dismissed to a foreign forum, which may enforce liability limitations or exculpatory clauses, does this not violate 46 U.S.C. §1303(8)? Although *Sky Reefer* involved a foreign arbitration clause, lower courts have had little difficulty applying the Court's holding to forum selection clauses as well. *Fireman's Fund Ins. Co. v. M/V DSR Atlantic,* 131 F.3d 1336 (9th Cir. 1997); *Union Steel America, Inc. v. M/V Sanko Spruce,* 14 F. Supp. 2d 682 (D.N.J. 1998); *Pasztory v. Croatia Line,* 918 F. Supp. 961 (E.D. Va. 1996); *Jewel Seafoods, Ltd. v. M/V Peace River,* 39 F. Supp. 2d 628 (D.S.C. 1999). *Compare In re Rationis Enterprises, Inc. of Panama,* 1999 A.M.C. 889 (S.D.N.Y. 1999).

(d) Forum selection agreements and antitrust claims. Suppose the plaintiff asserts antitrust claims under the Sherman Act, and the defendant seeks dismissal of the action based on a forum selection agreement. What result under *Richards, Scherk,* and *Mitsubishi? See, e.g., Caribe BMW, Inc. v. Bayerische Motoren Werke Aktiengesellschaft,* 821 F. Supp. 802, 817-821 (D.P.R. 1993), *vacated on other grounds,* 19 F.3d 745 (1st Cir. 1994).

4. Relevance of foreign courts' willingness to decide U.S. statutory or other claim — revisited. Why is it again that public policy permits the dismissal of a federal statutory claim to a foreign court that will refuse to hear the claim? Consider the following passage from footnote 19 of *Mitsubishi Motors Corp. v. Soler Chrysler-Plymouth, Inc.,* 473 U.S. 614 (1985), discussed in *Richards* and also excerpted below, *infra* pp. 1186-1191, which held that federal antitrust claims could be arbitrated outside the United States:

> [C]ounsel for Mitsubishi conceded that American law applied to the antitrust claims and represented that the claims had been submitted to the arbitration panel in Japan on that basis. The record confirms that . . . the arbitral panel had taken these claims under submission. We therefore have no occasion to speculate [on the tribunal's willingness to apply U.S. antitrust laws, rather than Swiss law as contemplated by the parties' choice of law agreement] at this stage in proceedings, when Mitsubishi seeks to enforce the agreement to arbitrate, not to enforce an award. Nor need we consider now the effect of an arbitral tribunal's failure to take cognizance of the statutory cause of action on the claimant's capacity to reinitiate suit in federal court. We merely note that in the event the choice-of-forum and choice-of-law clauses operated in tandem as a prospective waiver of a party's right to pursue statutory remedies for antitrust violations, we would have little hesitation in condemning the agreement as against public policy.

Does the foregoing language mean that a U.S. court would *not* compel arbitration of federal antitrust claims, pursuant to an otherwise valid arbitration agreement, if it was clear that the foreign arbitral tribunal would not apply the U.S. antitrust laws? If so, should a forum clause be treated differently from (and more favorably than) an arbitration agreement?

Is *Richards* consistent with the foregoing language from footnote 19 in *Mitsubishi?* How does the majority explain its result in light of this footnote? How does the dissent respond? Which is more persuasive?

5. Effect of parties' choice of law on U.S. public policy analysis. What state's "law" (or public policy) applies to determine whether a forum selection clause is enforceable or not? The law of the parties' chosen forum? Of the forum where the plaintiff sues (and the forum selection clause is invoked)? Or some other state's law? What state's public policy was applied in *Bremen* and *Richards*?

Why is the public policy of the forum where enforcement of a forum selection clause is sought the applicable public policy under *Bremen* and other authorities? If the parties have agreed that their contract is governed by a law other than that of the enforcement forum, why should not that foreign law be applied? Suppose, in each of the hypotheticals set forth above, that the parties' agreement contained a forum clause selecting the law of the contractual forum, and not U.S. law. Would that choice of law provision make U.S. public policies irrelevant? Would the parties' choice of law agreement be relevant to the U.S. public policy? Was it relevant in *Richards*? Suppose that the facts were identical, except that, while there were no English choice of law clauses, English courts would nevertheless refuse to apply the U.S. securities laws.

What "law" applies to the public policy defense under Article 6(c) of the proposed Hague Convention? Does the Convention permit any public policy, other than that of the place where the clause is invoked, to be applied?

6. *Effect of U.S. state public policies on enforceability of forum selection agreements.* The public policies at issue in *Bremen* and *Richards* were U.S. federal policies (derived respectively from federal admiralty and federal securities laws). What if a U.S. *state* public policy forbids enforcement of an international forum selection clause? Is there anything in federal law — constitutional, statutory, or common law — that forbids application of a state public policy to deny enforcement to an otherwise enforceable international forum clause?

For example, Law 75 in Puerto Rico forbids the enforcement of agreements selecting foreign forums in actions involving Puerto Rico distributors. Other states have comparable public policies that expressly or impliedly forbid enforcement of forum clauses in particular contexts. Examples include franchise agreements and automobile dealership agreements. *See supra* p. 513. May a *state* public policy preclude enforcement of an international forum clause?

As discussed below, most lower courts have held that federal procedural law governs the enforceability of international forum selection clauses in federal courts. *See infra* pp. 540-541. Some courts have concluded, as a consequence, that state public policies are irrelevant to the enforceability of forum clauses in federal courts. *E.g., Royal Bed and Spring Co. v. Famossul,* 906 F.2d 45 (1st Cir. 1990) (holding that "there is no need to consider" Puerto Rico's law 75, forbidding forum clauses, because federal law governs enforceability of forum selection clauses in federal court); *Manetti-Farrow, Inc. v. Gucci America, Inc.,* 858 F.2d 509, 513 (9th Cir. 1988); *Outek Caribbean Distributors, Inc. v. Echo, Inc.,* 206 F. Supp. 2d 263, 270 (D.P.R. 2002); *Stereo Gema, Inc. v. Magnadyne Corp.,* 941 F. Supp. 271, 274-275 (D.P.R. 1996). Other courts have taken the opposite view, permitting state public policies to deny enforcement to foreign forum selection agreements. *E.g., Farmland Indus., Inc. v. Frazier-Parrott Commodities, Inc.,* 806 F.2d 848, 850-852 (8th Cir. 1986) ("Because of the close relationship between substance and procedure in this case we believe that consideration should have been given to the public policy of Missouri."); *National Micrographics Sys., Inc. v. Canon U.S.A., Inc.,* 825 F. Supp. 671, 676 n.9 (D.N.J. 1993); *Snider v. Lone Star Art Trading Co.,* 672 F. Supp. 977, 981-982 (E.D. Mich. 1987).

Which is the correct approach? Should parochial state public policies be permitted to frustrate the enforcement of forum clauses in international cases? Wouldn't this have serious effects on U.S. foreign relations and commerce? Is there any basis for arguing that these state public policies are preempted by federal law of some sort? State public policies regarding forum clauses generally do not contravene any particular federal statute (and if they do, they are preempted). Is there a basis for fashioning federal common law rules that would preempt state public policies rendering foreign forum clauses unenforceable? How would the enforcement of such clauses interfere with federal interests? Does it matter what the content of the state public policy is?

7. *Application of U.S. public policy when conduct occurs outside the United States.* Why did *Bremen* refuse to apply the public policy, set forth in *Bisso,* against exculpatory clauses?

(a) Bremen*'s territoriality limitation.* What was the Court's justification for not giving effect to what was admittedly a strong U.S. public policy against exculpation for negligence? Is it fair to distill from *Bremen* a "territoriality" limitation on U.S. public policies? What would be the source of such a "territoriality" restriction on public policies? Note that U.S. courts have applied a "territoriality" presumption in other contexts, including judicial jurisdiction, *supra* pp. 84-86; service, *infra* pp. 881-882; extraterritorial application of national laws, *infra* pp. 646-651; and choice of law, *infra* pp. 724-725.

(b) Wisdom of territoriality limitation. Why is United States "territory" the correct definition of the limits of U.S. public policy? Recall that the injured plaintiff in *Bremen* was a U.S. company. Why did the relevant U.S. public policy against exculpation clauses not extend to the protection of U.S. citizens from negligence—wherever that negligence might occur? Alternatively, note that the parties' contract in *Bremen* was made in the United States and that the towage would occur at least partially in U.S. waters. Why did the relevant U.S. public policy not apply to performance of the entire contract, where it had this level of U.S. contacts?

(c) Possible application of nationality principle. Recall, as discussed above, that nationality is an accepted base for asserting general personal jurisdiction. *See supra* pp. 109-113. Is that relevant? *See infra* pp. 601-602 for a discussion of the passive personality principle under international law and the treatment of the plaintiff's nationality under contemporary U.S. choice of law rules. Suppose that the defendant in *Bremen* had also been a U.S. company. Would the U.S. public policy against exculpatory clauses have extended to conduct—by a U.S. defendant directed against a U.S. plaintiff outside the United States—in these circumstances?

(d) Possible application of effects doctrine. What if substantial effects of Unterweser's alleged negligence were felt in the United States? For example, suppose that 1,000 U.S. workers lost their jobs when Zapata—bankrupted by the uncompensated loss of its rig—could not continue operations. Suppose that Unterweser's negligence in towing the rig through the Gulf of Mexico caused severe environmental damage that affected U.S. waters and shores. Suppose that the negligence posed a threat to shipping in the area—principally U.S. vessels with U.S. crews, passengers, and cargo. Why, in these circumstances, should U.S. public policies forbidding exculpation for negligence not be applicable? *Compare infra* pp. 760-761 (choice of law).

Suppose that the conduct underlying a federal securities or antitrust claim occurred largely outside the United States, but had significant effects in the United States. In many circumstances, U.S. statutes apply extraterritorially to foreign conduct, *see infra* pp. 665-723, and would likely do so in this hypothetical. In these circumstances, why should the foreign situs of the parties' dispute affect the willingness of a U.S. court to enforce a forum clause applicable to claims arising from the dispute? Compare the public policy analysis under *Howe v. Goldcorp* and *Laker Airways, supra* pp. 408-412, 431-433, in context of the *forum non conveniens* doctrine.

(e) Conflict of laws analysis. Is it desirable, as suggested in *Bremen,* to adopt rigid territorial limits governing the public policy exception? Or is it instead necessary to

consider the situs of the conduct, the nationalities of the parties, and the precise character of the relevant U.S. and foreign regulatory interests before deciding public policy arguments? Would it be better for courts to apply a "conflict of public policies" analysis like that used in the choice of law context? *See infra* pp. 738-742.

Consider how the majority and dissenting opinions in *Richards* dealt with the question of where the disputed conduct occurred. Note the majority's emphasis on the execution of the parties' agreements in England, and the dissent's emphasis on the selling activities in the United States. From the perspective of the securities laws, which category of conduct is likely decisive?

8. *Application of foreign public policies.* If U.S. public policies may generally invalidate forum clauses in cases involving conduct in the United States, then what relevance do *foreign* public policies have in cases involving conduct in a *foreign* country. Suppose that two U.S. companies have entered into a contract, with a U.S. forum clause, involving actions occurring in Europe that implicate strong European public policies; should a U.S. court enforce the clause even if doing so would result in the application of U.S. substantive law and the violation of European public policies? Suppose that a forum selection clause provides for exclusive jurisdiction over a foreign party in a U.S. court, in violation of Articles 13 or 15-18 of EU Council Regulation 44/2001. Should the U.S. court give effect to the forum selection clause? Or to the provisions of Regulation 44/2001?

How would this issue be decided under Article 6(c) of the Hague Choice of Court Agreements Convention? Note that Article 6(c) refers to the public policy of the "seised" court (*i.e.,* in the above hypothetical, the U.S. Court). Does that forbid a U.S. court from taking into account a non-U.S. public policy?

9. *Conflicts between national public policies.* Suppose that a foreign state's public policies are antithetical to U.S. public policies—for example, discriminating against U.S. nationals or on the basis of race or religion. Should U.S. courts apply such foreign public policies in order to invalidate a U.S. forum selection clause? Suppose a U.S. court is asked to enforce a forum selection clause choosing Japanese courts, in a case where wrongful conduct occurred in Europe and where Japanese courts would disregard a fundamental European public policy. Note that in most such cases, European courts could be expected to vindicate their own local public policies and U.S. courts would ordinarily refuse to hear the case on the merits, *supra* p. 492.

10. *Contractual forum's likely application of law of state not connected to parties' dispute.* As discussed elsewhere, the Due Process Clause forbids U.S. courts from applying their substantive law to disputes that lack any reasonable connection to the forum state. *See infra* pp. 619-620. Suppose that a forum clause designates a contractual forum whose courts will apply a substantive law lacking any connection to the parties' dispute. Is this a basis for denying enforcement of the forum clause? Does the Due Process Clause require a U.S. court to deny enforcement in such circumstances?

11. *Showing required to establish violation of public policy.* What must be shown to demonstrate that a foreign court's disposition of a case would be contrary to a U.S. public policy? It is commonly said that something more must be shown than the fact that foreign law provides a different result than U.S. law would. *See Tahan v. Hodgson,* 662 F.2d 862, 864 (D.C. Cir. 1981) (foreign judgment must be "repugnant to fundamental notions of what is decent and just" in the forum); *Loucks v. Standard Oil Co.,* 224 N.Y. 99, 110 (N.Y. 1918) ("We are not so provincial as to say that every solution of a problem is wrong because we deal with it otherwise at home"). Does this standard support the analysis in *Richards,* which emphasized the limited differences between U.S. and English law?

Consider the standard required to demonstrate unenforceability of a forum selection clause under Article 6(c) of the proposed Hague Choice of Court Agreements Convention—"manifestly contrary to the public policy of the State of the court seised." How does this compare to the traditional common law standard in the United States?

D.   Enforceability of Forum Selection Agreements: Applicable Law in U.S. Courts

1.   Introduction

As discussed above, there are significantly differing approaches in various U.S. jurisdictions to the enforceability of forum selection clauses. Foreign courts also take varying approaches to the issue. As a consequence, great practical importance attaches to the law applicable to enforceability of forum selection agreements. This section examines the different approaches that U.S. courts have taken to selecting the law governing the enforceability of forum clauses.

Several basic points are important at the outset. First, under most states' laws (and federal common law), parties are in principle free to mutually agree upon the law governing their contracts, including their forum selection clauses. As noted above, however, the law that governs the validity of a forum agreement is not necessarily the same as the law applicable to the underlying contract (in which the forum selection clause appears).[153] That is because forum clause is generally "separable" from the underlying contract, therefore capable of being governed by a different applicable law and not necessarily encompassed by a choice of law clause applicable to the underlying contract.[154] At the same time, parties seldom specifically select the law governing their forum selection clauses, typically resulting in the question being governed by default choice of law rules.

Second, some U.S. courts have concluded or assumed that the validity and enforceability of forum clauses is governed by the law of the forum.[155] Courts have typically applied the forum's law without detailed consideration of other possibilities.

Third, as also discussed above, the law that governs the *validity* of a forum selection clause is not necessarily the same as that governing questions of *public policy* raised by the clause.[156] Even if the parties have selected the law of another state, or if choice-of-law rules select such laws, the forum's public policies (or the public policies of a third state) might apply to the enforceability of the forum selection clause.[157]

Fourth, the law that governs the *validity* of a forum selection agreement is not necessarily the same as that governing the *capacity* of the parties. A party's capacity is ordinarily governed by the law of its domicile or place of incorporation,[158] which may or may not be the same as the law chosen by the parties or the law of the chosen forum.

Fifth, the law that governs the *validity* of a choice of forum agreement is not necessarily the same as that governing *interpretation* of the agreement. A number of courts have either

---

153. *See supra* p. 492.
154. *See supra* p. 492.
155. *See supra* pp. 498-499.
156. *See id.*
157. *See id.*
158. *Restatement (Second) Conflict of Laws* §§188, 198 (1986 Revisions).

expressly acknowledged this possibility, or assumed that two different laws can apply.[159] Other courts have disagreed, albeit without considered analysis.[160]

Finally, in U.S. courts the enforceability of forum clauses raises peculiarly complex questions under the *Erie* doctrine concerning the applicability of state or federal law.[161] In federal courts, judges must determine which of the following laws governs the enforceability of a forum selection agreement: (a) federal procedural law, based either on 28 U.S.C. §1404(a) or judge-made common law; (b) substantive federal common law, binding on both federal and state courts; (c) substantive state law, chosen by the parties to govern their agreement; or (d) the substantive state law of the forum where the choice of court clause is sought to be enforced. Similar choice-of-law questions arise in state courts, where the alternatives are generally: (e) the substantive state law of the forum where the choice of court clause is sought to be enforced; (f) substantive state law, chosen by the parties to govern their agreement; or (g) federal common law.

2. Approaches to Selecting Law Applicable to Enforceability of Forum Selection Agreements

a. *Bremen*: A Federal Common Law Rule Governing Enforceability of Forum Selection Agreements in Admiralty Cases. The specific holding in *Bremen* concerned forum clauses in international *admiralty* contracts.[162] There is unanimity that federal courts have the power, under their admiralty jurisdiction, to establish rules of federal common law governing the enforceability of forum selection agreements in admiralty cases.[163] Lower federal courts have uniformly applied *Bremen*'s standards for the enforceability of forum selection clauses in admiralty actions.[164]

The Supreme Court has indicated that, by its own terms, *Bremen* applies only in admiralty actions.[165] Nevertheless, the Court has also said that *Bremen* is "instructive" in

159. *E.g., Northwestern Nat'l Ins. Co. v. Donovan,* 916 F.2d 372, 374 (7th Cir. 1990) ("Validity and interpretation are separate issues, and it can be argued that as the rest of the contract in which a forum selection clause is found will be interpreted under the principles of interpretation followed by the state whose law governs the contract, so should that clause be."); *Polar Mfg. Corp. v. Michael Weinig, Inc.,* 994 F. Supp. 1012, 1014 (E.D. Wis. 1998) (applying federal common law to question of validity even though North Carolina law determines the contract's terms).

160. *E.g., Manetti-Farrow, Inc. v. Gucci America, Inc.,* 858 F.2d 509, 513 (9th Cir. 1988) ("because enforcement of a forum clause necessarily entails interpretation of the clause before it can be enforced, federal law [which was held to govern enforcement] also applies to interpretation of forum selection clauses"); *Androutsakos v. M/V PSARA,* 2004 WL 1305802, at *7 (D. Or. 2004) (applying *Manetti-Farrow* standard and holding that "because enforcement of a forum selection clause necessarily entails interpretation of the clause before it can be enforced, federal law also applies to interpretation of forum selection clauses. Thus, contrary to defendants' assertions, this court does need to engage in contract interpretation.").

161. *See* Mullenix, *Another Choice of Forum, Another Choice of Law: Consensual Adjudicatory Procedure in Federal Court,* 57 Fordham L. Rev. 291, 332 (1988) ("Beyond doubt, the most perplexing issue raised by forum-selection clauses for lower federal courts was the *Erie* issue presented by diversity jurisdiction."); Heiser, *Forum Selection Clauses in Federal Courts: Limitations on Enforcement After Stewart and Carnival Cruise,* 45 Fla. L. Rev. 553, 553 (1993) ("One of the ironies in the evolution of forum selection clauses is that their enforcement is now less certain in federal courts than in state courts"); Lee, *Forum Selection Clauses: Problems of Enforcement in Diversity Cases and State Courts,* 35 Colum. J. Transnat'l L. 663 (1997).

162. 407 U.S. at 10.

163. *Offshore Logistics, Inc. v. Tallentire,* 477 U.S. 207, 222-223 (1986).

164. *E.g., Hodes v. S.N.C. Achille Lauro ed Altri-Gestion,* 858 F.2d 905 (3d Cir. 1988); *Marek v. Marpan Two, Inc.,* 817 F.2d 242 (3d Cir. 1987); *Sun World Lines, Ltd. v. March Shipping Corp.,* 801 F.2d 1066 (8th Cir. 1986); *Marco Forwarding Co. v. Continental Casualty Co.,* 2005 WL 3629286, at *2 (S.D. Fla. 2005) (citing *Bremen* and holding that "a forum selection clause in an admiralty case may be overcome only by a clear showing that the clause is unreasonable under the circumstances"); *Intermetals Corp. v. Hanover Int'l Aktiengesellschaft für Industrieversicherungen,* 188 F. Supp. 2d 454, 458 (D.N.J. 2001); *K.K.D. Imports, Inc. v. Karl Heinz Dietrich GmbH & Co. Int'l Spedition,* 36 F. Supp. 2d 200, 202 (S.D.N.Y. 1999).

165. *Stewart Organization, Inc. v. Ricoh Corp.,* 487 U.S. 22, 28 n.7, 33 (1988); *Carnival Cruise Lines v. Shute,* 499 U.S. 585 (1991) ("this is a case in admiralty, and federal law governs the enforceability of the forum-selection clause").

determining the enforceability of forum clauses even where it does not apply.[166] More-over, as discussed below, many lower federal and state courts and commentators have extended the reasoning and rule in *Bremen* beyond the admiralty context, particularly in international cases.[167] They have done so variously on the grounds that *Bremen* states a binding rule of federal law and on the grounds that its rationale is persuasive, even if not binding.

b. Section 1404(a) Governs Enforceability in Federal Courts of Forum Selection Agreements Selecting Other Federal Forums.   The domestic transfer of cases from one federal district court to another federal district court is generally governed by 28 U.S.C. §1404(a).[168] Section 1404(a) provides:

> For the convenience of parties and witnesses, in the interest of justice, a district court may transfer any civil action to any other district or division where it might have been brought.

Under §1404(a), federal district courts are granted broad discretion to decide motions to transfer. The trial court's exercise of discretion is guided by an open-ended list of considerations relating to convenience, fairness, and judicial economy; according to the Supreme Court, the discretion is exercised according to an "individualized, case-by-case consideration of convenience and fairness."[169]

By its terms, §1404(a) would appear to have nothing to do with the enforceability of forum selection agreements; it deals with noncontractual transfers where generalized considerations of convenience and judicial administration come into play. Nevertheless, the Supreme Court held in *Stewart Organization, Inc. v. Ricoh Corp.*[170] that §1404(a) provides a rule of federal law, both in federal question and diversity cases, that governs the enforceability in federal courts of forum selection clauses that designate a U.S. forum (other than a state court). The Court reasoned, over a dissent by Justice Scalia, that:

> Section 1404(a) is intended to place discretion in the district court to adjudicate motions for transfer according to an "individualized, case-by-case consideration of convenience and fairness." [*Van Dusen v. Barrack,* 376 U.S. 612, 622 (1964).] A motion to transfer under §1404(a) thus calls on the district court to weigh in the balance a number of case-specific factors. The presence of a forum selection clause such as the parties entered into in this case will be a significant factor that figures centrally in the district court's calculus. In its resolution of the §1404(a) motion in this case, for example, the District Court will be called on to address such issues as the convenience of a Manhattan forum given the parties' expressed preference for that venue, and the fairness of transfer in light of the forum selection clause and the parties' relative bargaining power. The flexible and individualized analysis Congress prescribed in §1404(a) thus encompasses consideration of the parties' private expression of their venue preferences.[171]

Section 1404(a) clearly applies to purely domestic cases in federal courts. It is, for example, applicable where two U.S. parties have agreed to resolve their disputes in

---

166. *Stewart Organization, Inc. v. Ricoh Corp.,* 487 U.S. 22, 28 n.7, 33 (1988).
167. *See infra* pp. 539-543.
168. As discussed below, transfers between federal districts are also sometimes sought under 28 U.S.C. §1406(a), under Rule 12(b) of the Federal Rules of Civil Procedure, under Rule 56 of the Federal Rules, and under the *forum non conveniens* doctrine. *See infra* p. 538.
169. 487 U.S. at 29 (quoting *Van Dusen v. Barrack,* 376 U.S. 612, 622 (1964)).
170. 487 U.S. 22.
171. 487 U.S. at 29-30.

Kansas, but one party later brings suit in Nebraska federal district court: if the other party seeks to transfer the action to Kansas, §1404(a) and *Ricoh* govern. Conversely, §1404(a) does not by its terms apply to cases in which a foreign forum is specified in the parties' forum selection agreement. In such cases, no transfer to "any other district or division" of the federal judicial system is sought; rather, a dismissal or stay is sought so that a foreign court can hear the action.[172]

A more difficult category of cases arises in international contracts when a *foreign* party and a U.S. party agree that their disputes shall be resolved exclusively in a specific U.S. forum, and thereafter one party initiates litigation in a different U.S. district court (or seeks to transfer litigation to a different U.S. district court). In such cases, the literal terms of §1404(a) would appear to apply — since a transfer to another district is sought. But a substantial argument could be made that in international cases of this kind *Bremen*'s rule of presumptive enforceability should apply, by virtue of a federal common law analysis.

c. *Erie* Problems: Does State or Federal Law Govern Enforceability of Forum Selection Agreements in Federal Diversity Actions?

The Supreme Court has not directly addressed the question whether federal or state law applies to the enforceability of forum clauses in diversity cases (when §1404(a) does not govern). As in the *forum non conveniens* context, the question raises unsettled issues under the *Erie* doctrine. As discussed below, substantial arguments can be made for several possible conclusions, and lower courts have reached divergent results.[173]

A number of lower courts have declined to decide whether federal or state law governs the enforceability of a forum clause, generally concluding or assuming that there is no substantial difference between the two.[174] When the issue has been expressly considered, lower federal diversity courts have reached divided results. As discussed below, some lower

---

172. *See Malaysia Int'l Shipping Corp. v. Sinochem Int'l Co. Ltd.*, 436 F.3d 349, 358 n.19 (3d Cir. 2006) ("We note that *forum non conveniens* is a limited doctrine, typically applying when the alternative forum is in a foreign country or a state court. . . . This is because 28 U.S.C. §1404(a) covers inconvenient forum issues within the federal court system") *rev'd on other grounds*, 549 U.S. 422 (2007); *Vasquez v. Bridgestone/Firestone, Inc.*, 325 F.3d 665 (5th Cir. 2003); *Hosaka v. United Airlines, Inc.*, 305 F.3d 989, 1003 (9th Cir. 2002) ("The reach of our decision is limited to the application of *forum non conveniens* to dismiss a case in favor of a forum in another country. Our decision does not affect whether a particular United States court has subject matter jurisdiction over a case; nor does it alter a federal court's power to transfer a case within the United States pursuant to 28 U.S.C. §1404(a)"); *Hyatt Int'l Corp. v. Coco*, 302 F.3d 707, 717-719 (7th Cir. 2002) ("While, with respect to cases wholly within the system of U.S. federal courts, the [*forum non conveniens*] doctrine has been largely replaced by the transfer of venue statute, 28 U.S.C. §1404(a), it remains available as a ground for dismissal when a foreign court provides a more convenient forum."); *Royal Bed & Spring Co. v. Famossul Indus.*, 906 F.2d 45, 51 (1st Cir. 1990); *Jones v. Weibrecht*, 901 F.2d 17, 19 (2d Cir. 1990); *Instrumentation Assocs., Inc. v. Madsen Electric (Canada), Inc.*, 859 F.2d 4, 6 n.4 (3d Cir. 1988) ("The forum selection clause before us calls for a Canadian forum which, by definition, is outside the limits of any 'district or division' to which . . . §1404(a) permits transfer"). *But see Ritchie v. Carvel Corp.*, 714 F. Supp. 700, 702 n.1 (S.D.N.Y. 1989); *Page Constr. Co. v. Perini Constr.*, 712 F. Supp. 9, 11-12 (D.R.I. 1989).

173. *E.g., Northwestern Nat'l Ins. Co. v. Donovan*, 916 F.2d 372, 374 (7th Cir. 1990)(noting lower court disagreements); Panek, *Forum Selection Clauses in Diversity Actions*, 36 J. Marshall L. Rev. 941, 945 (2003); *Excell, Inc. v. Sterling Boiler & Mech., Inc.*, 106 F.3d 318, 320-321 (10th Cir. 1997) (declining to resolve issue).

174. *E.g., Muzumdar v. Wellness Int'l Network, Ltd.*, 438 F.3d 759, 761 (7th Cir. 2006) ("The clauses certainly seem clear enough, especially because under either federal or Illinois law, forum selection clauses are valid and enforceable."); *IFC Credit Corp. v. Aliano Bros. General Contractors, Inc.*, 437 F.3d 606, 609-610 (7th Cir. 2006) ("Under either federal or Illinois law, forum selection clause in contract for lease of telecommunications equipment was enforceable."); *Silva v. Encyclopedia Britannica Inc.*, 239 F.3d 385, 387 n.1 (1st Cir. 2001); *General Electric Co. v. G. Siempelkamp GmbH & Co.*, 29 F.3d 1095, 1098 n.3 (6th Cir. 1994); *Lambert v. Kysar*, 983 F.2d 1110, 1116 (1st Cir. 1993); *Interamerican Trade Corp. v. Companhia Fabricadora de Pecas*, 973 F.2d 487 (6th Cir. 1992); *Weidner Communications, Inc. v. H.R.H. Prince Baudar Al Faisal*, 859 F.2d 1302 (7th Cir. 1988); *Instrumentation Assoc., Inc. v. Madsen Elec. (Canada) Ltd.*, 859 F.2d 4, 7 (3d Cir. 1988);*Crescent Int'l, Inc. v. Avatar Communities, Inc.*, 857 F.2d 943 (3d Cir. 1988).

federal courts have applied state law.[175] More often, lower federal courts have applied federal law in diversity cases.[176]

d.   Choice-of-Law Rules Applicable to Select Law Governing Enforceability of Forum Selection Agreements.   The *Erie* issues that arise in connection with the enforceability of forum selection clauses are further complicated by the possible applicability of either the law chosen by the parties to govern their contract or the law applicable to their contract under choice of laws rules. The logical possibilities that these lines of analysis pose have repelled most courts, who have simply ignored the issues. Indeed, one commentator has dismissed the possibility as "idle speculation [that] leads courts into predictable conflict-of-laws contortions."[177]

If a forum clause is contained in a contract that is, by operation of a choice-of-law clause, governed by the law of a foreign state, then U.S. courts in principle should apply the laws of that foreign state to the validity of the choice of forum agreement.[178] Under this analysis, foreign law would not override the enforcing forum's public policy,[179] but it would otherwise govern the validity of the forum agreement. Alternatively, a forum agreement could be required to satisfy both the parties' chosen law and the enforcing forum's law.[180]

e.   Choice of Law Under Proposed Hague Choice of Court Agreements Convention. As noted above, it is unclear whether the United States (or other states) will ratify the Hague Choice of Court Agreements Convention. If so, however, the Convention would materially change the choice of law rules applicable to international forum selection clauses in U.S. courts. Specifically, Articles 5 and 6 of the proposed Hague Convention contain choice-of-law provisions, providing generally that the law of the parties' chosen forum will govern the validity of the forum selection clause, that the law of the enforcement forum will govern the parties' capacity and issues of public policy, and that there is

---

175. *E.g., Alexander Proudfoot Co. v. Thayer,* 877 F.2d 912 (11th Cir. 1989); *In re Diaz Contracting, Inc.* 817 F.2d 1047, 1050 (3d Cir. 1987); *Rindal v. Seckler Co.,* 786 F. Supp. 890 (D. Mont. 1992).

176. *E.g., Heller Financial, Inc. v. Midwhey Powder Co.,* 883 F.2d 1286 (7th Cir. 1989) (applying *Bremen* in domestic diversity case, without discussing possible applicability of state law); *Commerce Consultants Int'l, Inc. v. Vetrerie Riunite SpA,* 867 F.2d 697 (D.C. Cir. 1989) (applying *Bremen* without discussion in international diversity case); *Bryant Elec. Co. v. City of Fredericksburg,* 762 F.2d 1192 (4th Cir. 1985) (apply *Bremen* without analysis in domestic diversity case); *Bense v. Interstate Battery Sys. of Am.,* 683 F.2d 718, 721 (2d Cir. 1982); *In re Fireman's Fund Ins. Cos.,* 588 F.2d 93, 95 (5th Cir. 1979); *Crown Beverage Co. v. Cerveceria Moctezuma SA,* 663 F.2d 886, 888 (9th Cir. 1981) (applying *Bremen* without discussion in international case).

177. Mullenix, *Another Choice of Forum, Another Choice of Law: Consensual Adjudicatory Procedure in Federal Court,* 57 Fordham L. Rev. 291, 347 (1988).

178. *See TH Agriculture & Nutrition, LLC v. Ace European Group,* 416 F. Supp. 2d 1054, 1076-1079 (D. Kan. 2006) (applying Dutch law to determine validity of forum clause because choice-of-law clause selected law of Netherlands); *General Electric Co. v. G. Siempelkamp GmbH & Co.,* 809 F. Supp. 1306, 1313-1315 (S.D. Ohio 1993) (applying German law to determine validity of forum clause because choice-of-law clause selected German law); *Hoes of America, Inc. v. Hoes,* 493 F. Supp. 1205 (C.D. Ill. 1979) (requiring that forum clause satisfy German law (where parties agreed German law governed their contract)); *Goff v. AAMCO Automatic Transmissions, Inc.,* 313 F. Supp. 667 (D. Md. 1970) (requiring that forum clause satisfy Pennsylvania law (where parties agreed Pennsylvania law governed their contract)).

179. *See infra* p. 544. *Restatement (Second) Conflict of Laws* §187 (1971).

180. *See Karlberg European Tanspa, Inc. v. JK-Josef Kratz Vertriebsgesellschaft mbH,* 618 F. Supp. 344 (N.D. Ill. 1985) (apparently required that forum clause satisfy both *Bremer* and German law (where parties agreed German law governed their contract)); *Hoffman v. National Equipment Rental, Ltd.,* 643 F.2d 987 (4th Cir. 1981) (apparently requiring that forum clause satisfy New York law (where parties agreed New York law governed their contract) and arguably federal law); *Wellmore Coal Corp. v. Gates Learjet Corp.,* 475 F. Supp. 1140 (W.D. Va. 1979) (apparently requiring that forum clause satisfy Arizona law (where forum's conflicts rules selected Arizona law) and federal law).

an international standard of "manifest injustice" which would permit nonenforcement of the clause.[181]

3. Selected Materials on Law Applicable to Enforceability of Forum Selection Agreements

Excerpted below are cases that illustrate the approaches to choosing the law applicable to the enforceability of forum agreements. The First Circuit's opinion in *Royal Bed & Spring Co. v. Famossul Industria e Comercio de Moveis Ltda,* illustrates the complex *Erie* questions that can arise in enforcing of foreign forum clauses. The Third Circuit's opinion in *Instrumentation Assoc., Inc. v. Madsen Electronics (Canada) Ltd.,* provides an illustration of the choice of law issues that arise in disputes over the enforceability of forum agreements.

ROYAL BED & SPRING CO. v. FAMOSSUL
INDUSTRIA E COMERCIO DE MOVEIS LTDA
906 F.2d 45 (1st Cir. 1990)

Re, Chief Judge. In this diversity action, plaintiff-appellant, Royal Bed and Spring Co., Inc. ("Royal Bed"), sued defendant-appellee, Famossul Industria e Comercio de Moveis Ltda ("Famossul"), . . . for breach of contract in violation of the Puerto Rico Dealer's Contract Act. Royal Bed appeals from the judgment of the district court which granted Famossul's motion to dismiss on the grounds of *forum non conveniens.* . . .

Royal Bed, a corporation organized and existing under the laws of Puerto Rico, distributes furniture products in Puerto Rico. Famossul, a Brazilian corporation, is a manufacturer of furniture products in Brazil. . . . On January 26, 1984, Royal Bed and Famossul signed, in Brazil, an agreement entitled "Letter Of Exclusive Distributorship Appointment." This agreement, written in Portuguese, granted Royal Bed the exclusive distributorship of "products, both furniture and other products, which might be made or introduced into [Famossul's] manufacturing line, for the market in Puerto Rico and adjacent islands." The agreement contained a provision which designated "the judicial district of Curitiba, State of Parana, Brazil, as competent to settle any disputes or interpretations derived from this letter," and that the Brazilian Civil Code would apply "[i]n the case of any violation." . . .

Royal Bed alleges that, during 1986, Famossul terminated the exclusive distributorship and suspended the shipment of goods without just cause[, and claimed damages exceeding $1 million. Famossul replied that Royal Bed had breached the contract. Royal Bed eventually filed a diversity suit in the U.S. District Court for the District of Puerto Rico.] Claiming that the court lacked jurisdiction, based on the doctrine[] of *forum non conveniens* . . . , Famossul filed [a] motion[] to dismiss with the U.S. District Court. . . . The district court acknowledged that, in adjudicating a motion for *forum non conveniens,* the court must conduct a case-by-case analysis of convenience and fairness. The court also recognized that Royal Bed had specifically asserted "that Puerto Rico law refuses to enforce forum-selection clauses providing for out-of-state or foreign venues as a matter of public policy." P.R. Laws Ann. Tit. 10, §278b-2 (Supp. 1987) ("Law 75"). The court noted that, given Law 75, the forum-selection clause in the parties' agreement must be integrated into the balancing of considerations. The court noted that the forum-selection

---

181. Hague Choice of Court Agreements Convention, Art. 6(a), (b), and (c).

clause "should not receive dispositive consideration . . . but should rather be considered a significant factor that will figure centrally in our balancing of factors." The court concluded that "the convenience of a Brazil forum, given the parties' expressed preference for that venue, the fairness of transfer in light of the forum-selection clause and the parties' relative bargaining power, as well as their familiarity with the procedure and laws of that forum," made Brazil the most convenient forum. . . .

According to Royal Bed, since Puerto Rico "has the most significant contacts relating to the . . . alleged termination without just cause of [the] contract[,]" the case should be tried in Puerto Rico under Puerto Rican law. Royal Bed asserts that, under the law of Puerto Rico, its rights and obligations under the agreement were protected by the Distributor's Law ("Law 75"). Pursuant to §278b-2 of this law, "[a]ny stipulation that obligates a dealer to . . . litigate any controversy that comes up regarding his dealer's contract outside of Puerto Rico, or under foreign law or rule of law, shall be . . . considered as violating . . . public policy . . . and is therefore null and void." P.R. Laws Ann. Tit. 10, §278b-2 (Supp. 1987). Hence, Royal Bed concludes that "any action that would imply mere intention of placing a dealers' contract outside the scope of this statute is null and void, as is the provision of this . . . contract. . . ."

Famossul contends that "Law 75 was never mentioned nor contemplated" in the agreement, and, if the forum-selection clause is rendered unenforceable by Law 75, "then . . . all the rest of the contract might be unenforceable as well." Famossul states that it is not requesting that Law 75 be declared unconstitutional, "but rather tha[t] the parties be bound by their own acts."

In the seminal case of *The Bremen*, the Supreme Court upheld the validity of forum-selection clauses between parties of equal bargaining power. . . . As a practical matter, therefore, it follows from the holding in *Bremen* that the burden is upon the party resisting the forum-selection clause to "show that enforcement [of the clause] would be unreasonable and unjust, or that the clause was invalid for such reasons as fraud or overreaching." . . .

The question that has not been resolved, however, is whether the holding of *Bremen*, that is, "applying federal judge-made law to the issue of a forum selection clause's validity in admiralty cases, should be extended to diversity cases." *Instrumentation Assocs., Inc. v. Madsen Elecs. (Canada) Ltd.*, 859 F.2d 4, 7 n.5 (3d Cir. 1988). More than half a century ago, the Supreme Court established what is known as the *Erie* doctrine, pursuant to which the federal courts in diversity cases may not promulgate substantive rules of law that control the controversy. Nonetheless, it is also fundamental that "[f]ederal courts are able to create federal common law . . . in those areas where Congress or the Constitution has given the courts the authority to develop substantive law . . . or where strong federal interests are involved. . . ." *General Eng'g Corp. v. Martin Marietta Alumina, Inc.*, 783 F.2d 352, 356 (3d Cir. 1986).

In *Bremen*, for example, federal law applied to the forum-selection clause because, since the case was in admiralty, the Constitution had vested original jurisdiction in the federal courts. . . . In *Sun World Lines, Ltd. v. March Shipping Corp.*, 801 F.2d 1066 (8th Cir. 1986), the Court of Appeals for the Eighth Circuit held that in diversity cases, federal law controlled the enforceability of a forum-selection clause. The *Sun World Lines* case "held that the enforceability of a forum clause . . . is clearly a federal procedural issue and that federal law controls." The court noted that, in deciding that enforceability of the clause "is a procedural matter, we support a policy of uniformity of venue rules within the federal system, as well as the policies underlying *The Bremen*."

It has been noted that *forum non conveniens* "is a rule of venue, not a rule of decision." *Sibaja* [*v. Dow Chemical Co.*], 757 F.2d at 1219. The court in *Sibaja* explained that: "[t]he doctrine derives from the court's inherent power, under article III of the Constitution, to control the administration of the litigation before it and to prevent its process from becoming an instrument of abuse, injustice and oppression." . . . It follows, therefore, that state *forum non conveniens* laws "ought not to be" binding on federal courts in diversity cases. Since we adopt this view, we decide this case on federal principles and considerations of *forum non conveniens*.

It would also seem clear that, had the transferee forum been a U.S. District Court, the applicable standard would be found in 28 U.S.C. §1404(a) (1988). . . . In *Stewart Org., Inc. v. Ricoh Corp.,* the Supreme Court . . . reasoned that "[a] motion to transfer under §1404(a) . . . calls on the District Court to weigh in the balance a number of case-specific factors. The presence of a forum-selection clause . . . will be a significant factor that figures centrally in the District Court's calculus." . . . As for the Alabama policy which did not favor forum-selection clauses, the Court noted that §1404(a) made "it unnecessary to address the contours of state law." The Court deemed that inquiry unnecessary since "Congress has directed that multiple considerations govern transfer within the federal court system, and a state policy focusing on a single concern or a subset of the factors identified in §1404(a) would defeat that command." . . . *Stewart,* therefore, teaches that, after considering and balancing all of the private and public interest factors, a district court in a particular case may "in the interest of justice" still "refuse to transfer a case notwithstanding the counterweight of a forum-selection clause, . . ."

In this case, since we are dealing with a forum-selection clause that refers to a forum outside of the United States, and not within the scope of the statute, §1404(a) does not apply. Nonetheless, even though a foreign jurisdiction was chosen by the parties, that fact should not preclude the application of the sound principles of *forum non conveniens* enunciated in *Stewart* and similar cases. By their consideration and application, the forum-selection provision in the "Letter of Exclusive Distributorship Appointment" is not given dispositive effect. Rather, it is simply one of the factors that should be considered and balanced by the courts in the exercise of sound discretion. Furthermore, in this case, there is no need to consider the constitutionality of Law 75. . . . Hence, the application of Law 75 is not affected in the courts of the Commonwealth of Puerto Rico. The total relevant factors analysis set forth in *Stewart* permits a "flexible and individualized analysis" which considers "the parties' private expression of their venue preferences" as well as "public-interest factors of systemic integrity and fairness."

In *Piper Aircraft,* the Supreme Court stated "that there is ordinarily a strong presumption in favor of the plaintiff's choice of forum. . . ." . . . [T]he Supreme Court added that the choice of a home forum "may be overcome only when the private and public interest factors clearly point towards trial in the alternative forum." . . . In this case, Royal Bed states that "all the equipment sold by . . . Royal Bed on behalf of . . . Famossul took place in Puerto Rico . . . to Puerto Rican accounts and for use in Puerto Rico. . . ." Hence, Royal Bed contends that, since "Puerto Rico . . . has the most significant contacts[,]" the balance of private and public interest factors makes Puerto Rico the applicable forum.

Although the district court acknowledged that Royal Bed's choice of a forum was entitled to great deference since it chose a home forum, it nonetheless determined that "we must also take into consideration the convenience of a Brazil forum given the parties' expressed preference for that venue. . . ." Hence, the district court also took into consideration that: "[the] contract [was] signed in Brazil[,] [and] . . . drafted in Portuguese. All the furniture provided by [Famossul] and sold by [Royal Bed] in Puerto Rico was manufactured in Brazil. It also appears that [Royal Bed] is no stranger to the judicial system of Brazil since it has previously litigated its disputes in the courts of Brazil and obtained favorable results. Moreover, the contract . . . contains a forum-selection clause providing that any legal action arising out of the contract would be brought in Brazil and Brazilian law would apply."

In giving effect to the validity of the forum-selection clause in *Bremen,* the Supreme Court noted that there was strong evidence "that the forum clause was a vital part of the agreement, and it would be unrealistic to think that the parties did not conduct their negotiations, including fixing the monetary terms, with the consequences of the forum clause figuring prominently in their calculations." The holding and *ratio decidendi* of that case place the burden squarely on the party seeking to avoid the forum-selection clause to show that its enforcement "would be unreasonable and unjust, or that the clause was invalid for such reasons as fraud or overreaching." . . . In this case, there is neither over-reaching nor factors that would counsel against the application of the forum selected by the parties in their agreement. . . . Since the district court considered and balanced all of the relevant factors and did not abuse its discretion, its conclusion that Brazil is the most convenient forum should not be disturbed. Therefore, the judgment of the district court granting Famossul's motion to dismiss on the grounds of *forum non conveniens* is affirmed.

INSTRUMENTATION ASSOCIATES, INC. v. MADSEN ELECTRONICS (CANADA) LTD.
859 F.2d 4 (3d Cir. 1988)

HUTCHINSON, CIRCUIT JUDGE. Madsen Electronics (Canada) Ltd. ("Madsen") appeals from an order of the United States District Court for the Eastern District of Pennsylvania denying its motion to dismiss appellee Instrumentation Associates, Inc.'s ("Instrumentation's") action asserting wrongful termination of a distributorship agreement. Madsen's motion to dismiss was premised on a forum selection clause in the distributorship agreement. . . . The enforceability of a forum selection clause is an issue of law, and our scope of review is plenary.[182] . . .

Instrumentation is a Pennsylvania corporation with a place of business in Upper Darby, Pennsylvania. . . . In August, 1984 it entered into a written agreement with Madsen, a Canadian audiological supply company with a place of business in Oakville, Ontario, Canada. The agreement gave Instrumentation an exclusive right to distribute Madsen products in Delaware, New Jersey, Pennsylvania and parts of New York and West Virginia. The agreement was for an initial one year term from August, 1984 until July, 1985 and provided for automatic annual renewal unless each party gave "at least three months written notice" of termination. On December 23, 1986 Madsen sent Instrumentation a written termination notice giving Instrumentation ninety days to settle outstanding accounts. On April 29, 1987, after unsuccessful attempts to resolve the dispute, Instrumentation filed this action for breach of the agreement in the district court. Madsen filed a motion to dismiss the case based on the agreement's forum selection clause, which provided: "Matters of dispute in connection with this Agreement shall be settled by a Canadian Court of Justice in accordance with the laws of Canada." In denying Madsen's motion to dismiss, the district court reasoned that the forum selection clause's reference to the "laws of Canada" was too ambiguous to enforce because the "laws of Canada" varied widely from province to province. Madsen alleged in its submissions that the

---

182. Other courts of appeals review the district court's decision for abuse of discretion. *See, e.g., Pelleport Investors, Inc. v. Budco Quality Theatres, Inc.,* 741 F.2d 273, 280 n.4 (9th Cir. 1984). The difference is immaterial in this case. Under either standard the forum selection clause must be enforced on this record. As shown *infra,* no exceptional circumstance or strong policy against its enforcement is present in any jurisdiction whose law might apply. Accordingly, a refusal to enforce it would be an abuse of discretion.

"general rule of Canada" required the forum selection clause to be enforced. However, because Madsen offered no evidence of a uniformly recognized "general rule of Canada," the district court held that the entire clause, including its choice of forum, was unenforceable. The agreement, however, purports not only to provide a choice of law, but also a choice of forum. The district court should have resolved the preliminary issue of whether the parties' forum selection clause is enforceable before reaching the issue of whether the contract provision is ambiguous. This conflicts issue, in turn, requires a determination of what law is applicable.

In choosing what law to apply to the issue of whether the parties' forum selection clause is enforceable, a district court sitting in diversity must first determine whether the issue is encompassed by a federal statute or Rule. *See Stewart Organization, Inc. v. Ricoh Corp., supra.*[183] If there is no applicable federal statute or Rule, the district court must next determine whether to apply federal judge-made law or state law. In doing so, the district court must evaluate whether application of federal judge-made law would discourage forum shopping and avoid inequitable administration of the law.

This Court has not yet decided what law a district court sitting in diversity must apply in deciding whether a forum selection clause is enforceable. . . . Fortunately, we need not resolve this unanswered question of whether federal law, the law of the forum state, the law of Canada, or one of its provinces applies.[184] All of these jurisdictions look favorably on forum selection clauses. Thus, even assuming paragraph 21 of the contract is ambiguous as to choice of a particular jurisdiction, the judge-made law of all involved

---

183. We are in agreement with the parties that *Ricoh* does not govern this case. *Ricoh* involved the application of a federal procedural statute, 28 U.S.C. §1404(a). In *Ricoh,* the Supreme Court held that §1404(a) governs a federal court's determination of whether to give effect to a forum selection clause and transfer a case to a different federal court. The Court did not address whether §1404(a) applies when a forum selection clause calls for a forum beyond the geographical scope of that statute. In our case, no §1404(a) application was filed and the motion to dismiss was premised on Fed. R. Civ. P. 12(b)(6). The forum selection clause here calls for a Canadian forum which, by definition, is outside the limits of any "district or division" to which 28 U.S.C. §1404(a) permits transfer. The parties do not contend that any other federal statute controls, such as 28 U.S.C. §1406 permitting retention of venue in the court in which the action is pending in the "interest of justice," nor do they raise the common law doctrine of "forum non conveniens" to which §1404(a) is related, as a bar to a Canadian forum.

184. *Ricoh* leaves open the question of whether the holding in *The Bremen v. Zapata Off-Shore Co.,* 407 U.S. 1 (1972), applying federal judge-made law to the issue of a forum selection clause's validity in admiralty cases, should be extended to diversity cases. Justice Marshall, writing for the Court, states:

Although we agree with the Court of Appeals that the *Bremen* case may prove "instructive" in resolving the parties' dispute, [*Stewart Organization v. Ricoh Corp.,*] 810 F.2d at 1069; . . . we disagree with the court's articulation of the relevant inquiry as "whether the forum selection clause in this case is unenforceable under the standards set forth in *The Bremen.*" 810 F.2d, at 1069. Rather, the *first question* for consideration should have been whether §1404(a) itself controls. . . . *Ricoh,* 108 S. Ct. at 2243 (emphasis added).

Justice Scalia, dissenting, argues that the validity of a forum selection clause is a question of substantive law and accordingly the application of either §1404(a) or federal judge-made law conflicts with *Erie's* twin purposes of discouraging state-federal forum shopping and avoiding inequitable administration of the laws. In *Martin Marietta,* we rejected the idea that courts are bound as a matter of federal common law to apply *The Bremen* standard to forum selection clauses:

"The construction of contracts is usually a matter of state, not federal, common law. Federal courts are able to create federal common law only in those areas where Congress or the Constitution has given the courts the authority to develop substantive law, as in labor and admiralty, or where strong federal interests are involved, as in cases concerning the rights and obligations of the United States. . . . As the Court in *Miree v. DeKalb County, Georgia,* 433 U.S. 25 (1977), observed, in a suit between private parties where federal common law is sought to be applied, 'normally the guiding principle is that a *significant conflict between some federal policy or interest and the use of state law [exists].*'" *Martin Marietta,* 783 F.2d at 356 (emphasis added by *Miree* Court).

jurisdictions would honor the parties' choice of a Canadian forum for resolution of their disputes in connection with this distributorship agreement. . . .

EUROPEAN UNION COUNCIL REGULATION 44/2001, ART. 23
[excerpted in Appendix E]

Notes *on* Royal Bed *and* Madsen Electronics

1. *Application of §1404(a) to international forum selection agreements.* To what categories of forum selection agreements is the rule in §1404(a) and *Ricoh* applicable? Consider the following: (a) a California resident and a French national enter into a forum selection agreement selecting Paris as the exclusive contractual forum, and the California party brings suit in California; and (b) a New York resident and a Mexican national enter into a forum selection agreement selecting New York as the exclusive contractual forum, and the Mexican party brings suit in Arizona.

Does §1404(a) apply to example (a) above if the French party invokes the forum clause? How did *Royal Bed* resolve this question? Is there any doubt about the correctness of this result?

Does §1404(a) apply to example (b) above if the New York party invokes the forum agreement? What does the literal language of §1404(a) suggest? Should the rules governing the enforceability of forum clauses in examples (a) and (b) be different? Why?

Is *Ricoh*'s "interest of justice" standard limited to cases in which a party relies expressly on §1404 in a motion to transfer? Suppose, in example (b) in the preceding note, that the New York party does not seek a transfer under §1404, but instead moves to dismiss under Rule 12 of the Federal Rules of Civil Procedure?

If the United States ratifies the Hague Choice of Court Agreements Convention, how would example (b) above be decided? Consider Article 5(3)(b) of the Convention. Does this mean that a forum selection clause selecting California would merely be one factor in a general §1404 analysis if the plaintiff sues in Arizona? If the United States ratifies the Convention, how would example (a) above be decided?

2. *Authorities holding that state law should govern enforceability of international forum selection agreements where §1404 does not.* If §1404 is not applicable, state law would presumptively appear to govern the enforcement of forum agreements, both in federal diversity actions and state courts. At least until the Hague Choice of Court Agreements Convention is ratified by the United States, no federal treaty or statute governs the enforceability of international forum clauses in diversity suits. A forum agreement is a contractual obligation, the enforceability of which ought presumptively to be subject to substantive rules of contract law. The enforceability of contractual obligations is generally governed by state law—because of the absence of any general federal contract law. Absent some basis for preempting state law with federal common law, *Erie* should therefore require the application of state law to the enforceability of forum clauses. In one court's words:

We must correct the assumption that federal courts are bound as a matter of federal common law to apply *The Bremen* standard to forum selection clauses [in diversity cases]. The construction of contracts is usually a matter of state, not federal, common law. Federal courts are able to create federal common law only in those areas where Congress and the Constitution has given the courts the authority to develop substantive law, as in labor or admiralty, or where strong federal interests are involved, as in cases concerning the rights and obligations of the

> United States. . . . The interpretation of forum selection clauses in commercial contracts is not an area of law that ordinarily requires federal courts to create substantive law. *General Eng'g Corp. v. Martin Marietta Alumina, Inc.*, 783 F.2d 352, 356-57 (3d Cir. 1986).

The Court has emphasized "twin aims of the *Erie* rule: discouragement of forum shopping [between state and federal courts] and avoidance of inequitable administration of the laws." *Hanna v. Plumer,* 380 U.S. 460, 468 (1965); *supra* pp. 10-11. Application of federal procedural law to the enforceability of forum clauses in federal courts, but not in state courts, would lead both to intra-state forum shopping and races to the courthouse. *Stewart Organization, Inc. v. Ricoh Corp.,* 487 U.S. 22, 34-35 (1988) (Scalia, J., dissenting). This would, in turn, produce inequitable administration of the laws, as identically situated parties were treated differently in state and federal court.

Applying the foregoing analysis, a number of federal courts have held that state substantive law governs the enforceability of forum clauses in diversity actions (albeit generally in domestic settings). *E.g., Dunne v. Libbra,* 330 F.3d 1062, 1063-1064 (8th Cir. 2003); *Lambert v. Kysar,* 983 F.2d 1110, 1118 (1st Cir. 1993); *Alexander Proudfoot Co. v. Thayer,* 877 F.2d 912 (11th Cir. 1989); *Diaz Contracting, Inc. v. Nanco Contracting Corp.,* 817 F.2d 1047, 1050 (3d Cir. 1987) ("the law of the state or other jurisdictions whose law governs the construction of the contract generally applies to the enforceability determination unless 'a significant conflict between some federal policy or interest and the use of state law [exists].' "); *Farmland Indus., Inc. v. Frazier-Parrott Commodities, Inc.,* 806 F.2d 848, 850-852 (8th Cir. 1986) ("Because of the close relationship between substance and procedure in this case we believe that consideration should have been given to the public policy of Missouri."); Yackee, *Choice of Law Considerations in the Validity & Enforcement of International Forum Selection Agreements: Whose Law Applies?,* 9 UCLA J. Int'l L. & Foreign Aff. 43, 46 (2004).

Does *Ricoh* suggest that state substantive law should govern the enforceability of forum clauses in diversity cases? Does this include international forum agreements? State law generally applies to most "international" contract disputes. *See supra* p. 7. Why should forum clauses be different from questions of contract validity, force majeure, performance, and damages?

3. *Authorities holding that federal law should govern the enforceability of international forum agreements when §1404(a) does not.* A number of lower federal courts have applied federal law to the enforceability of forum agreements in diversity cases, often without appearing to consider the basis for doing so. *E.g., Wong v. PartyGaming Ltd.,* 589 F.3d 821, 827 (6th Cir. 2009) ("enforceability of a forum selection clause implicates federal procedure and should therefore be governed by federal law"); *Heller Financial, Inc. v. Midwhey Powder Co.,* 883 F.2d 1286 (7th Cir. 1989) (applying *Bremen* in domestic diversity case, without discussing possible applicability of state law); *Commerce Consultants Int'l, Inc. v. Vetrerie Riunite SpA,* 867 F.2d 697 (D.C. Cir. 1989) (applying *Bremen* without discussion in international diversity case); *Bryant Elec. Co. v. City of Fredericksburg,* 762 F.2d 1192, 1196-1197 (4th Cir. 1985); *Pelleport Investors v. Budco Quality Theatres,* 741 F.2d 273, 279 (9th Cir. 1984) ("[w]e see no reason why the principles announced in *Bremen* are not equally applicable to the domestic context. Courts addressing the issue uniformly apply *Bremen* to cases involving domestic forum selection questions"); *Cairo, Inc. v. Crossmedia Servs. Inc.,* 2005 WL 756610, at *4 (N.D. Cal. 2005); *First Interstate Leasing Serv. v. Sagge,* 697 F. Supp. 744, 746 n.3 (S.D.N.Y. 1988).

As discussed in greater detail below, two inconsistent rationales have been invoked to support the application of a federal rule of enforceability of forum clauses in federal courts (assuming that §1404(a) is not applicable). The first would regard this issue as one of federal "procedural" law, properly governed by judge-made federal rules applicable only in the forum (that is, in federal courts). The second rationale would treat the enforceability of forum clauses as a substantive federal common law issue, governed by judge-made federal rules that apply in both state and federal courts.

4. Federal procedural law governs the enforceability of international forum agreements when §1404(a) does not. The most common basis for applying federal law to the enforcement of forum clauses is that their enforcement implicate "procedure," "venue," and judicial docket control issues.

(a) Lower courts applying federal procedural law to enforceability of forum clauses. Most lower courts have held that the enforceability of forum selection clauses is a procedural issue subject to federal procedural law. In the words of one lower court, forum clauses are contracts, but "[i]n a larger sense . . . this issue concerns the proper venue in the federal court system. Venue is clearly a matter of procedure, and, as such, governed by federal law." *Dick Proctor Imports, Inc. v. Sumitomo Corp.,* 486 F. Supp. 815, 818 (E.D. Mo. 1980). *See also Manetti-Farrow, Inc. v. Gucci America, Inc.,* 858 F.2d 509, 512-513 (9th Cir. 1988) ("[i]f venue were to be governed by the law of the state in which the forum court sat, the federal venue statute would be nugatory"); *Jones v. Weibrecht,* 901 F.2d 17 (2d Cir. 1990) ("Questions of venue and the enforcement of forum selection clauses are essentially procedural, rather than substantive in nature.").

The Supreme Court arguably adopted this view in *Stewart Organization v. Ricoh,* where it apparently treated the enforceability of forum selection clauses as a procedural matter. 487 U.S. at 32 ("Section 1404(a) is doubtless capable of classification as a procedural rule . . .").

(b) Criticism of application of federal procedural law to enforceability of forum clauses. Some authorities have criticized the rule that federal procedural law governs the enforceability of forum clauses. The rule rests principally on labelling issues of forum selection as "venue" or "procedural," and does not address the equally clear "substantive" attributes of forum selection clauses, which are contractual undertakings that are bargained for and that significantly affect the parties' economic interests. Justice Scalia's dissent in *Stewart Organization, Inc. v. Ricoh Corp.,* 487 U.S. 22, 39-40 (1988), succinctly captured the extent to which the enforcement of forum clauses implicates "substantive" issues: "Venue is often a vitally important matter, as is shown by the frequency with which parties contractually provide for and litigate the issue. Suit might well not be pursued, or might not be as successful, in a significantly less convenient forum." *See also* Freer, *Erie's Mid-Life Crisis,* 63 Tul. L. Rev. 1087, 1109-1110 (1989) ("Each of these characterizations—contract and venue—is partly correct.").

Is the issue of where an action is litigated a procedural question of venue, that ought to be subject to the forum's law? Consider the analysis in *Royal Bed.* Aren't the considerations of convenience, docket control, and "justice" that §1404 expresses equally applicable outside the section's scope? If this is all correct, then is it not clear—as *Royal Bed* concluded—that federal procedural law should govern the enforceability of forum clauses in federal courts?

(c) Inapplicability of federal procedural law in state courts. Suppose that federal procedural law does govern the enforceability of forum selection clauses in federal courts. What law governs the same clauses in state courts? Under *Erie,* federal procedural law only applies in federal courts, and not in state courts. Would it be appropriate for different laws—state and federal—to apply to the same forum selection clause, depending upon whether the litigation was in state or federal court? Does *Erie* permit federal courts to fashion rules of federal procedural law governing the enforceability of forum clauses? What considerations are relevant to the question? Recall the "twin aims of the *Erie* rule: discouragement

of forum-shopping and avoidance of inequitable administration of the laws." *Hanna,* 380 U.S. at 468. How are these twin aims affected by the application of federal procedural law to the enforceability of forum selection clauses in federal courts? How would international commerce be affected? Under the analysis in *Royal Bed,* what law would govern the enforceability of forum selection clauses in Puerto Rico's courts? What effect does *Royal Bed* indicate would be given to Law 75 in Puerto Rico's courts? Why won't this lead to forum shopping?

5. *Substantive federal common law governs the enforceability of international forum agreements where §1404 does not.* Some lower federal courts have said that *Bremen* states a rule of substantive federal common law that is applicable both in federal and state court actions. *E.g., General Eng'g Corp. v. Martin Marietta Alumina, Inc.,* 783 F.2d 352, 356-357 (3d Cir. 1986) (dicta that federal common law would apply in international cases); *Taylor v. Titan Midwest Constr. Corp.,* 474 F. Supp. 145, 147-148 (N.D. Tex. 1979) ("Resort to state law would balkanize venue rules when a uniform rule is patently preferable").

(a) Authorities holding that substantive federal common law applies in domestic cases. A few decisions appear to conclude that substantive federal common law rules apply even in entirely domestic diversity actions, involving state law claims. There is little reasoned justification for this view, which would presumably rest upon some sort of generalized federal interest in facilitating interstate commerce by ensuring enforceability of private choice of forum agreements. Heiser, *Forum Selection Clauses in Federal Courts: Limitations on Enforcement After* Stewart *and* Carnival Cruise, 45 Fla. L. Rev. 553, 559 (1993) ("Quite clearly, no uniquely federal interest exists when a federal court sitting in diversity determines the enforceability of a forum selection clause in a contract between private parties."). As discussed below, lower courts have applied federal law more frequently in actions involving substantive federal law claims, or in international cases. In both contexts, stronger arguments support the formulation of substantive federal common law rules regarding the enforceability of forum clauses than in simple diversity actions.

(b) Authorities applying federal common law to enforceability of forum clauses in international cases. The Supreme Court has not considered whether there is any basis for substantive federal common law rules governing the enforceability of forum selection agreements in "international" cases. Some lower federal courts have resolved this question affirmatively, even in actions involving substantive state law claims. *E.g., Lipcon v. Underwriters at Lloyd's, London,* 148 F.3d 1285, 1293 (11th Cir. 1998) (quoting *Scherk,* 417 U.S. at 516: "a choice-of-forum clause is 'an almost indispensable precondition to achievement of the orderliness and predictability essential to any international business transaction'"); *Evolution Online Sys., Inc. v. Koninklijke PTT Nederland NV,* 145 F.3d 505, 509 & n.10 (2d Cir. 1998); *TAAG Linhas Aereas de Angola v. Transamerica Airlines, Inc.,* 915 F.2d 1351 (9th Cir. 1990) (in international case under FSIA, "federal law governs the validity of a forum selection clause"); *Appell v. George Philip and Son, Ltd.,* 760 F. Supp. 167, 168 (D. Nev. 1991) ("With respect to international contracts containing forum selection clauses we are governed by" *Bremen*); *Tisdale v. Shell Oil Co.,* 723 F. Supp. 653 (M.D. Ala. 1987). Are these lower courts' decisions consistent with *Erie?* Does *Erie* permit federal courts to fashion rules of federal common law governing the enforceability of forum selection agreements in either international cases or federal question cases?

(c) Do international forum selection agreements arise in a "uniquely federal" field? Is the enforceability of international forum selection clauses a subject involving "uniquely federal interests" that justifies formation of a rule of federal common law? *Boyle v. United Technologies Corp.,* 487 U.S. 500, 504 (1988); *supra* pp. 11-13. As discussed elsewhere, the role of the individual states of the Union in matters involving foreign policy is narrowly limited, and federal foreign affairs powers are commensurately broad. *See infra*

pp. 630-633. Federal authority over U.S. foreign commerce is also broad, and there are significant national interests in U.S. international trade. *See supra* pp. 11-13 & *infra* pp. 630-633; *Japan Line Ltd. v. County of Los Angeles,* 441 U.S. 434 (1979).

Broad federal powers over U.S. foreign affairs and commerce are said to sustain the formation of federal common law standards for the enforcement of forum clauses in international cases. The theory is that there is a substantial federal interest in the encouragement of international commerce, and that the effective enforcement of forum selection clauses in international cases is important to achieving this interest. In the words of the Supreme Court in *Bremen,* "[a] contractual provision specifying in advance the forum in which disputes shall be litigated and the law to be applied is . . . an almost indispensable precondition to achievement of the orderliness and predictability essential to any international business transaction." Moreover, U.S. refusals to enforce forum selection clauses designating foreign forums would provoke foreign diplomatic responses and possible reciprocal refusals to enforce U.S. forum clauses; conversely, U.S. refusals to enforce forum clauses selecting U.S. forums would relegate U.S. citizens to foreign forums that they specifically bargained to avoid. In all these cases, parochial state law prohibitions on forum selection clauses would conflict with broader national interests in facilitating foreign commerce and structuring U.S. relations with foreign sovereigns.

Is this theory persuasive? Would U.S. foreign commerce really be hindered by parochial refusals by U.S. courts to enforce international forum clauses? *Cf. Bremen v. Zapata Off-Shore Co.,* 407 U.S. 1, 9 (1972) (refusal to enforce forum selection clauses "would be a heavy hand indeed on the future development of international commercial dealings by Americans"). Is the following persuasive?

> It is clear from the opinion in *Zapata* that the validity of forum selection clauses in international contracts is viewed by the Supreme Court as a matter affecting important national interests. The federal interest in the effective conduct of foreign commerce is self-evident, and the perceptions of the importance of foreign commerce and the relationship of the forum-selection clause to the effectiveness of its conduct is a principal emphasis of the *Zapata* opinion. Maier, *The Three Faces of Zapata: Maritime Law, Federal Common Law, Federal Courts Law,* 6 Vand. J. Transnat'l L. 387, 396 (1973).

(d) Is there a "significant conflict" between state and federal rules governing enforceability of forum clauses? Federal common law rules will ordinarily not be adopted unless there is a "significant conflict" between state (or foreign) law and asserted federal policies. *Boyle v. United Technologies Corp.,* 487 U.S. 500, 507 (1988). Suppose that a state law (or judicial decision) flatly denies *any* effect to forum selection clauses choosing out-of-state forums? This is the rule in Alabama and a few other states as well. *See supra* p. 469. Suppose that state law denies any effect to clauses choosing any non-U.S. forum? To clauses choosing specific non-U.S. forums, such as nonmarket economy states, nondemocratic states, states with substantial trade surpluses with the United States (or an individual state), or states that practice prison slave labor for commercial products? Are any of these types of state laws in significant conflict with federal policies?

Suppose that a state law imposes more rigorous limits on the enforceability of international forum clauses than does *Bremen;* for example, by reversing the burden of proof and requiring the proponent of the clause to establish the chosen forum's convenience or fairness. Or by requiring the opponent of the clause to have received clear notice of the clause. Or by adopting a *forum non conveniens* analysis in which a forum selection agreement is only one factor relevant to an overall "interest of justice" analysis.

Which of these rules would significantly conflict with the federal policies reflected in *Zapata* (or elsewhere)?

(e) Does federal common law govern the enforceability of forum clauses as applied to federal question claims? *Ricoh* expressly declined to consider whether federal law should govern the enforceability of forum clauses in federal question cases: "Our conclusion that federal law governs the transfer of this case [under §1404(a)] . . . makes this issue academic . . . because the presence of a federal question could cut only in favor of the application of federal law. We therefore are not called on to decide, nor do we decide, whether the existence of federal question as well as diversity jurisdiction necessarily alters a District Court's analysis of applicable law." Almost always without analysis, a number of lower courts have applied federal law, derived from *Bremen,* in such cases. *In re Diaz Contracting, Inc.,* 817 F.2d 1047 (3d Cir. 1987) (bankruptcy); *AVC Nederland BV v. Atrium Inv. Partnership,* 740 F.2d 148 (2d Cir. 1984) (federal securities claims); *Bense v. Interstate Battery Sys. of America, Inc.,* 683 F.2d 718, 720-721 (2d Cir. 1982) (federal antitrust claims). What rationale supports these results?

6. Bremen *in state courts.* Where the federal courts enjoy authority to develop rules of substantive federal common law, the need to avoid forum shopping between state and federal courts has had a "reverse-*Erie*" effect under which substantive federal common law preempts state law even in state court. *See Offshore Logistics, Inc. v. Tallentire,* 477 U.S. 207, 222-223 (1986); *Banco Nacional de Cuba v. Sabbatino,* 376 U.S. 398 (1964). If *Bremen* states a rule of federal common law applicable in federal courts in international cases otherwise governed by state law, should this rule be binding on state courts under the "reverse-*Erie*" doctrine? Wouldn't this prevent the intra-state forum shopping that *Erie* is concerned with?

7. *Choice of law under Hague Choice of Court Agreements Convention.* Consider the various choice-of-law rules contained in Article 6 of the Convention. Are they wise? The same as U.S. choice-of-law rules? Does it make sense to evaluate the validity of the forum selection agreement under the law of the chosen court? Would it make more sense to impose an international standard? Does it make sense to look to the law of the "court seised" on matters of capacity? What if the party in question is domiciled and operating solely in the law of another state?

8. *Effect of choice-of-law clause on forum selection agreement.* Suppose a forum clause selects a foreign forum to resolve claims arising out of an international agreement that contains a choice of law provision selecting foreign law. These were the basic facts in *Madsen.* Should a U.S. court apply the U.S. standards set forth in *Bremen* to enforce the forum selection clause, or should it apply the parties' chosen law? In practice, a number of courts (including *Bremen*) have applied U.S. law, although there is some support for applying the parties' chosen law (or the law otherwise applicable to the agreement). *See supra* pp. 531-532 What was the approach of *Madsen?* What is the appropriate course?

9. *Intended effect of choice-of-law clause on forum selection agreement.* What is the ordinary scope of a choice-of-law clause in a private commercial contract? Does such a clause, by its terms, purport to apply to the parties' choice of forum clause? Note that choice-of-law clauses are typically not construed to extend to "procedural" matters. *See infra* pp. 762-763. Is the enforceability of a forum selection clause within this procedural category? As discussed above, forum selection clauses are also often regarded as "separable" from the parties' underlying agreement. *See supra* p. 492. Does a choice-of-law clause in the parties' underlying agreement apply to the separable forum selection provision?

Consider the court's resolution of these issues in *Madsen.* In considering whether to enforce the forum clause, what weight did *Madsen* give to the parties' agreement that the "laws of Canada" applied? Reread *Smith,* excerpted above at *supra* pp. 478-480. What interpretation of the choice-of-law clause did *Smith* adopt?

10. *Need to satisfy enforcement standards of enforcing forum.* Even assuming that the parties' choice-of-law clause applies to their forum selection agreement, and selects a non-U.S. law, what consequences should that have for a U.S. court asked to dispatch a U.S. litigant to a foreign forum? Is it enough that the law of the foreign contractual forum be satisfied? Suppose that, under the standards of "unreasonableness" and "unfairness" articulated in *Bremen, Restatement* §80, and the Model Act, the clause in *Madsen* had been unenforceable — but that under both Ontario and "Canadian" law, enforcement was required. Should the clause be enforced by a U.S. court under foreign law? What answer do you think *Madsen* would have reached? Consider again the analysis in *Smith, supra* pp. 478-480. Did the California court look solely to the law selected by the parties' choice-of-law clause, or did it also consider California law? What is the relevance of the enforcing forum's law in such cases?

A number of such courts appear to have required that a forum clause satisfy the requirements for enforceability of *both* the forum and the parties' chosen law. *See Karlberg European Tanspa, Inc. v. JK-Josef Kratz Vertriebsgesellschaft mbH,* 618 F. Supp. 344 (N.D. Ill. 1985) (apparently required that forum selection clause satisfy both *Zapata* and German law (where parties agreed that German law governed their contract)).

Other courts have applied only the law selected by the parties to govern their contract. *See also Albemarle Corp. v. AstraZeneca UK Ltd.,* 628 F.3d 643 (4th Cir. 2010) (applying both U.S. and English law to determine exclusivity of forum selection clause choosing English courts); *In re Diaz Contracting, Inc.,* 817 F.2d 1047, 1050 (3d Cir. 1987) (applying New York law pursuant to choice-of-law clause); *General Eng'g Corp. v. Martin Marietta Alumina, Inc.,* 783 F.2d 352, 357 (3d Cir. 1986) (applying Maryland law pursuant to choice-of-law clause: "In this case, the parties specified that the contract was to be governed by the law of Maryland. Therefore the enforceability of the forum selection clause in this case is governed by Maryland law."); *TH Agriculture & Nutrition, L.L.C. v. Ace European Group,* 416 F. Supp. 2d 1054, 1076-1079 (D. Kan 2006) (applying Dutch law to determine the validity of the forum selection clause because the parties' choice-of-law clause provided that the laws of the Netherlands apply); *General Electric Co. v. G. Siempelkamp GmbH & Co.,* 809 F. Supp. 1306, 1313-1315 (S.D. Ohio 1993) (applying German law to determine the validity of the foreign selection agreement because the parties' choice-of-law clause called for the application of German law); *Hoes of Am., Inc. v. Hoes,* 493 F. Supp. 1205, 1207-1208 (C.D. Ill. 1979) (applying German law pursuant to choice-of-law clause).

11. *Possible need to satisfy standards of law chosen by parties' choice-of-law clause.* Suppose that foreign law would not permit the forum selection clause to be enforced; for example, because foreign law has a per se rule against forum selection agreements (as was historically the case in the United States). Should the clause be denied enforcement by a U.S. court, even if the clause would be enforceable under U.S. standards? Suppose, for example, that "Canadian" law would have invalidated the forum selection clause in *Madsen,* but that *Bremen* required enforcement. What should the court do? Alternatively, suppose that foreign contract law requirements are not satisfied, and that the parties' forum clause is invalid under foreign law. Should a U.S. court enforce the clause?

E.   Scope of Forum Selection Agreements

An important and recurrent issue arising in the interpretation of forum selection clauses is the definition of the classes of disputes that are covered by a particular forum clause. This is largely a question of interpretation, turning on what categories of claims or disputes the parties intended to bring within the scope of their agreement.[185] Nevertheless, it can also involve (either explicitly or otherwise) more general presumptions and under-standings of the purposes and desirability of forum selection clauses.

At one extreme, some forum selection clauses cover only specified and limited classes of disputes under an agreement, such as provisions regarding payment.[186] More broadly, forum clauses may cover all disputes arising under the contract, but do not also reach disputes under tort, antitrust, or similar noncontractual theories of recovery. At the other extreme are forum clauses that purport to cover any dispute relating to the parties' contractual relationship, regardless whether tort or other public law claims are involved.[187] Indeed, it is possible, at least as a drafting matter, for parties to agree to settle *all* their future disputes, regardless of connection to a particular agreement, in a designated forum.

There are few general rules that can be derived from decisions interpreting the scope of forum selection clauses. Some courts have, however, suggested that the interpretation of phrases in forum clauses—such as "arising from"—should be the same as interpretation of the same phrases in arbitration agreements. Virtually all lower courts have held or assumed that forum clauses may be drafted to encompass both contract claims or disputes and noncontractual claims or disputes (such as tort or statutory claims).[188] This parallels the treatment of arbitration agreements, which have uniformly been held capable of encompassing noncontractual claims and disputes.[189]

In interpreting the scope of arbitration clauses, U.S. courts have applied a strong "pro-arbitration" policy, resolving all ambiguities in favor of the inclusion of claims with the scope of the arbitration clause.[190] This presumption derives from the statutory provisions of the FAA and has not generally been applied to the interpretation of forum clauses. No similar statutory presumption applies to forum selection agreements. Nor have most courts fashioned any parallel rule of construction regarding the scope of forum clauses.[191] Nevertheless, many lower courts have indicated reluctance to parse forum clauses finely in order to exclude claims.[192] They have generally done so on the grounds

185. *Manetti-Farrow, Inc. v. Gucci America, Inc.*, 858 F.2d 509, 514 (9th Cir. 1988).

186. *Cf. Mitsubishi Motors Corp. v. Soler Chrysler-Plymouth, Inc.*, 473 U.S. 614, 617 (1985) ("[a]ll disputes, controversies, or differences which may arise between [the parties] out of or in relation to Articles I-B through V of this Agreement or for the breach thereof, shall be finally settled by arbitration . . .").

187. *E.g., Pascalities v. Irwin Yacht Sales North, Inc.*, 118 F.R.D. 298 (D.R.I. 1988); *Ronar, Inc. v. Wallace*, 649 F. Supp. 310 (S.D.N.Y. 1986); *Hoes of America, Inc. v. Hoes*, 493 F. Supp. 1205, 1208 (C.D. Ill. 1979) (clause extends to "business torts arising out of the relationship between the parties").

188. *Manetti-Farrow, Inc. v. Gucci America, Inc.*, 858 F.2d 509, 514 (9th Cir. 1988) ("forum selection clauses can be equally applicable to contractual and tort causes of action"); *Coastal Steel Corp. v. Tilghman Wheelabrator Ltd.*, 709 F.2d 190, 203 (3d Cir. 1983); *Clinton v. Janger*, 583 F. Supp. 284, 287-288 (N.D. Ill. 1984).

189. G. Born, *International Commercial Arbitration* 1099-1104 (2009).

190. *See infra* pp. 1194-1195; G. Born, *International Commercial Arbitration* 1067-1076, 1081-1083 (2009).

191. *Manetti-Farrow, Inc. v. Gucci America, Inc.*, 858 F.2d 509, 514 n.4 (9th Cir. 1988); *Omron Healthcare, Inc. v. MacLaren Exports Ltd.*, 28 F.3d 600, 603 (7th Cir. 1994) ("We cannot imagine why the scope of that phrase," *i.e.*, "arise out of" would be different for purposes of a forum selection clause than an arbitration agreement).

192. *American Patriot Ins. Agency, Inc. v. Mutual Risk Management, Ltd.*, 364 F.3d 884, 889 (7th Cir. 2004) ("It is that the existence of multiple remedies for wrongs arising out of a contractual relationship does not obliterate the contractual setting, does not make the dispute any less one arising under or out of or concerning the contract, and does not point to a better forum for adjudicating the parties' dispute than the one they had selected to resolve their contractual disputes."); *Terra Int'l, Inc. v. Mississippi Chemical Corp.*, 119 F.3d 688, 695 (8th Cir. 1997) ("Terra's tort claims arise under the license agreement, and therefore, the forum selection clause applies to Terra's claims."); *Lambert v. Kysar*, 983 F.2d 1110, 1121 (1st Cir. 1993) ("contract-related tort claims involving the same operative facts as a parallel claim for breach of contract should be heard in the forum selected by the contracting parties"); *Interamerican Trade Corp. v. Companhia Fabricadora de Pecas*, 973 F.2d 487 (6th Cir. 1992); *Stewart Organization, Inc. v. Ricoh Corp.*, 810 F.2d 1066, 1070 (11th Cir. 1987), *aff'd on other grounds*, 487 U.S. 22 (1988) ("promotes a more orderly and efficient disposition of the case in accordance with the parties' intent.").

that hearing all disputes in a single forum "promotes a more orderly and efficient disposition of the case in accordance with the parties' intent."[193]

A recurrent issue is whether a forum clause encompasses noncontractual claims (as well as contractual ones). Most courts have reasoned that "pleading alternate non-contractual theories is not alone enough to avoid a forum selection clause if the claims asserted arise out of the contractual relation and implicate the contract's terms."[194] In contrast, a few courts appear to have taken the opposite view, reading forum clauses narrowly and refusing to apply them except where they encompass the parties' entire dispute.[195] It has been held that forum selection clauses will generally not be interpreted as applying to claims based upon intentional torts.[196]

Two common formulations for forum clauses are "all disputes arising under this Agreement" and "all disputes relating to this Agreement." Although these formulations appear similar, courts have sometimes concluded that the phrase "*arising under* this Agreement" is less expansive than the phrase "*relating to* this Agreement."[197] Thus, according to one court, a clause covering all actions "commenced under this agreement" did not include a suit for fraud in inducing the contract.[198] Courts have generally not taken this approach.[199]

193. *Stewart Organization, Inc. v. Ricoh Corp.,* 810 F.2d 1066, 1070 (11th Cir. 1987).

194. *Roby v. Corporation of Lloyd's,* 996 F.2d 1353 (2d Cir. 1993) ("It defies reason to suggest that a plaintiff may circumvent forum selection and arbitration clauses merely by stating claims under laws not recognized by the forum selected in the agreement"); *Hugel v. Corporation of Lloyd's,* 999 F.2d 206 (7th Cir. 1993); *Crescent International, Inc. v. Avatar Communities, Inc.,* 857 F.2d 943 (3d Cir. 1988); *Bowmont Corp. v. Krombacher Brauerei Bernhard GmbH,* 2003 WL 22205615, at *4 (D. Conn. 2003) ("Allowing a party to avoid a forum selection clause by pleading related statutory and/or tort claims would violate the public policy supporting forum selection clauses."); *see also Coastal Steel Corp. v. Tilghman,* 709 F.2d 190, 203 (3d Cir. 1983) ("public policy requires that [forum selection clauses] not be defeated by artful pleading of claims"); *Tisdale v. Shell Oil Co.,* 723 F. Supp. 653 (M.D. Ala. 1987).

195. *Farmland Industries, Inc. v. Frazier-Parrott Commodities, Inc.,* 806 F.2d 848, 852 (8th Cir. 1986) ("we see no reason to require piecemeal resolution of this case"); *J.B. Hoffman v. Minuteman Press International Inc.,* 747 F. Supp. 552, 558 (W.D. Mo. 1990). *But see REO Sales, Inc. v. Prudential Ins. Co. of Am.,* 925 F. Supp. 1491, 1493 (D. Colo. 1996).

196. *Berrett v. Life Ins. Co. of the Southwest,* 623 F. Supp. 946 (D. Utah 1985).

197. *See Medtronic AVE Inc. v. Cordis Corp.,* 100 Fed. Appx. 865, 868 (3d Cir. 2004) ("We give an expansive interpretation to 'arising from.' As we explained in *Battaglia v. McKendry,* 233 F.3d 720, 727 (3d Cir. 2000), 'when phrases such as 'arising under' and 'arising out of' appear in arbitration provisions, they are normally given broad construction.' "); *ACE Capital Re Overseas Ltd. v. Central United Life Ins. Co.,* 307 F.3d 24 (2d Cir. 2002) ("In *Michele Amoruso,* the district court held that an arbitration clause referring to disputes 'arising out of this Agreement' was not broad, because it did not include any reference to disputes 'relating to' the agreement."); *AVC Nederland BV v. Atrium Inv. Partnership,* 740 F.2d 148, 155-156 (2d Cir. 1984) ("arising under" is less inclusive than "relating to"); *In re Kinoshita & Co.,* 287 F.2d 951 (2d Cir. 1961); *General Environmental Science Corp. v. Horsfall,* 753 F. Supp. 664 (N.D. Ohio 1990) (RICO and fraud claims not covered by following clause: "This Agreement shall be governed by the laws of Switzerland and the place of court is Rolle, Switzerland in case of claims by [plaintiff].").

198. *Hodom v. Stearns,* 301 N.Y.S.2d 146 (1969). *See also J.B. Hoffman v. Minuteman Press Int'l Inc.,* 747 F. Supp. 552 (W.D. Mo. 1990); *Fantis Foods, Inc. v. Standard Importing,* 406 N.Y.S.2d 763 (App. Div. 1978), *rev'd on other grounds,* 425 N.Y.S.2d 783 (1980).

199. *See Crowson v. Sealaska Corp.,* 705 P.2d 905 (Alaska 1985) ("arising under this lease" includes claim that lease was fraudulently induced).

6

Parallel Proceedings: *Lis Alibi Pendens* and Antisuit Injunctions[1]

Expansive contemporary principles of jurisdiction often make it possible for the courts of more than one nation to adjudicate the same international dispute. As discussed above, legal and other differences between available forums give private parties strong incentives to litigate in one country rather than another. In some cases, these incentives will lead parties to an international civil litigation to go forward simultaneously in the courts of two or more countries — with each party seeking resolution of the dispute in what it perceives to be the most favorable forum. This chapter examines how U.S. courts have dealt with such parallel proceedings in international cases.

---

1. Commentary on antisuit injunctions and the *lis alibi pendens* doctrine includes, *e.g.,* A. Bell, *Forum Shopping and Venue in Transnational Litigation* (2003); Bermann, *The Use of Antisuit Injunctions in International Litigation,* 28 Colum. J. Transnat'l L. 589 (1990); de Coale, *Stay, Dismiss, Enjoin, or Abstain? A Survey of Foreign Parallel Litigation in the Federal Courts of the United States,* 17 B.U. Int'l L.J. 79 (1999); George, *International Parallel Litigation — A Survey of Current Conventions and Model Laws,* 37 Tex. J. Int'l L. 499 (2002); Hartley, *Comity and the Use of Antisuit Injunctions in International Litigation,* 35 Am. J. Comp. L. 487 (1987); International Law Association, Committee on International Civil and Commercial Litigation, *Third Interim Report: Declining and Deferring Jurisdiction in International Litigation* (McLachlan, Ed./Rapporteur 2000); Lenenbach, *Antisuit Injunctions in England, Germany and the United States: Their Treatment Under European Civil Procedure and the Hague Convention,* 20 Loy. L.A. Int'l & Comp. L.J. 257 (1998); Lowenfeld, *Forum Shopping, Antisuit Injunctions, Negative Declarations and Related Tools of International Litigation,* 91 Am. J. Int'l L. 314 (1997); Miller, Annotation, *Propriety of Federal Court Injunction Against Suit in Foreign Country,* 78 A.L.R. Fed. 831 (1986 & Supp. 2009); Parrish, *Duplicative Foreign Litigation,* 78 Geo. Wash. L. Rev. 237 (2010); Robertson, *Comity Be Damned: The Use of Anti-Suit Injunctions Against the Courts of a Foreign Nation,* 147 U. Pa. L. Rev. 409 (1998); Stueckelberg, *Lis Pendens and Forum Nonconveniens at the Hague Conference,* 26 Brooklyn J. Int'l L. 949 (2001); Swanson, *The Vexatiousness of a Vexation Rule: International Comity and Antisuit Injunctions,* 30 Geo. Wash. J. Int'l L. & Econ. 1 (1996); Tan, *Anti-Suit Injunctions and the Vexing Problem of Comity,* 45 Va. J. Int'l L. 283 (2005); Tan, *Damages for Breach of Forum Selection Clauses, Principled Remedies and Control of International Civil Litigation,* 40 Tex. Int'l L.J. 623 (2005); Teitz, *Both Sides of the Coin: A Decade of Parallel Proceedings and Enforcement of Foreign Judgments in Transnational Litigation,* 10 Roger Williams U. L. Rev. 1 (2004); Teitz, *Taking Multiple Bites of the Apple: A Proposal to Resolve Conflicts of Jurisdiction and Multiple Proceedings,* 26 Int'l L. 21 (1992); Vartanian, Annotation, *Stay of Civil Proceedings Pending Determination of Action in Another State or Country,* 19 A.L.R.2d 301 (1951 & Supp. 2005); Westbrook, *International Judicial Negotiation,* 38 Tex. Int'l L.J. 567 (2003); Kerwin, *A Choice of Law Approach for International Antisuit Injunctions,* 81 Tex. L. Rev. 927 (2003); Comment, *Killing One Bird with One Stone: How the United States Federal Courts Should Issue Antisuit Injunctions in the Information Age,* 8 U. Miami Bus. L. Rev. 123 (1999); Nicolas, *The Use of Preclusion Doctrine, Antisuit Injunctions, and Forum Non Conveniens Dismissals in Transnational Intellectual Property Litigation,* 40 Va. J. Int'l L. 331 (1999); Raushenbush, *Antisuit Injunctions and International Comity,* 71 Va. L. Rev. 1039 (1985); Editorial, *Enjoining Suits in Foreign Jurisdictions,* 17 Colum. L. Rev. 328 (1917); Baer, *Injunctions Against the Prosecution of Litigation Abroad: Towards a Transnational Approach,* 37 Stan. L. Rev. 155 (1984).

A.   Introduction to Parallel Proceedings

There is no federal statutory or constitutional provision governing parallel proceedings in U.S. and foreign courts. Similarly, state legislation generally does not address the subject of parallel proceedings. In the absence of statutory direction, U.S. courts have fashioned several common law devices for dealing with parallel proceedings. These devices are often derived from approaches taken in domestic U.S. parallel proceedings, usually modified for international cases.

One mechanism for dealing with parallel proceedings is the *forum non conveniens* doctrine, considered in detail above, which permits a U.S. court to dismiss an action in favor of a foreign forum.[2] Although the *forum non conveniens* doctrine often applies in the absence of any related foreign litigation, U.S. courts have occasionally applied the doctrine in cases involving parallel foreign litigation.[3]

A second mechanism for dealing with parallel proceedings is the *lis alibi pendens* doctrine.[4] The doctrine is related to *forum non conveniens*, and permits a U.S. court to stay an action before it in deference to pending foreign litigation. It has been most extensively developed in domestic U.S. cases (involving both state-federal and federal-federal proceedings), but is also applicable in international cases.

A third mechanism for dealing with parallel proceedings is an antisuit injunction, which permits a U.S. court to enjoin a litigant from commencing or continuing litigation in a foreign forum.[5] U.S. lower courts have long asserted the power to issue antisuit injunctions, in a variety of circumstances, but the standards for issuing such injunctions remain unclear.

A fourth approach to parallel proceedings is simply to do nothing, and to allow the two (or more) actions to proceed at their own pace to judgment. The first final judgment is ordinarily then available to be pleaded as res judicata in the second forum.[6] As discussed below, this is the generally preferred approach in many U.S. jurisdictions.

B.   The *Lis Alibi Pendens* Doctrine

1.   Introduction

The *lis pendens* doctrine allows a U.S. court to stay proceedings before it in favor of an action in another court that involves similar parties and matters. When a *lis pendens* stay is issued, the foreign court is free to proceed to judgment. That judgment may then be pleaded in the U.S. forum, where it may be entitled to recognition under generally applicable rules for the enforcement of foreign judgments.[7] If the foreign litigation does not proceed, the U.S. action may be revived. The *lis pendens* doctrine is closely related to the *forum non conveniens* doctrine although it permits a stay of U.S. proceedings rather than outright dismissal.[8]

---

2. *See supra* pp. 365-459.

3. *E.g., Blanco v. Banco Industrial de Venezuela, SA,* 997 F.2d 974 (2d Cir. 1993); *Contact Lumber Co. v. P.T. Moges Shipping Co.,* 918 F.2d 1446 (9th Cir. 1990); *Brinco Mining Ltd. v. Federal Ins. Co.,* 552 F. Supp. 1233 (D.D.C. 1982).

4. *See infra* pp. 548-567.

5. *See infra* pp. 567-588.

6. *Laker Airways v. Sabena,* 731 F.2d 909, 928 (D.C. Cir. 1984); *Restatement (Second) Conflict of Laws* §86 (1971) ("A State may entertain an action even though an action on the same claim is pending in another state"); *infra* p. 1078.

7. These rules are discussed in Chapter 12 *infra.*

8. Some authorities treat the *lis pendens* doctrine as a subset of the *forum non conveniens* doctrine, differing only with respect to relief. *Restatement (Second) Conflict of Laws* §84 comment e (1971).

In federal and most state courts *lis pendens* is a common law rule not based upon any statutory or constitutional provision: "[T]he power to stay proceedings is incidental to the power inherent in every court to control the disposition of the causes on its docket with economy of time and effort for itself, for counsel, and for litigants."[9] Although it has occasionally been suggested that the *lis pendens* doctrine is not available in international cases,[10] the doctrine has frequently been invoked to stay domestic actions in favor of parallel proceedings in non-U.S. courts.[11]

There is no direct federal statutory or constitutional guidance for U.S. courts considering requests for stays in deference to foreign litigation, and virtually no state legislative direction.[12] The subject is instead governed almost entirely by common law precedent. Moreover, the Supreme Court has not considered the question in the international context, and few lower court decisions consider the subject in any depth. The content of U.S. law relating to the *lis pendens* doctrine is therefore often uncertain and difficult to discern.

Lower courts have adopted two distinctly different approaches to motions for a stay of a U.S. action in deference to foreign proceedings. As outlined below, one line of authority (derived from the U.S. Supreme Court's decision in *Colorado River* and *Quackenbush*) emphasizes the obligation of U.S. courts to exercise legislatively conferred jurisdiction, and narrowly limits the availability of *lis pendens* stays; the other line of precedent (derived from a Supreme Court decision in *Landis v. North American Co.*) stresses the waste inherent in parallel proceedings, and permits much more liberal grants of *lis pendens* stays.[13] Most lower federal courts agree that, under either approach, the standards for issuing a *lis alibi pendens* stay are governed by federal law.[14] State courts generally appear to apply state law to *lis pendens* issues.[15]

2. *Colorado River*: "Unflagging Obligation" to Exercise Jurisdiction

A substantial body of lower court decisions applying the *lis alibi pendens* doctrine in international cases has adopted the analysis contained in *Colorado River Water Conservation*

---

9. *Landis v. North American Co.*, 299 U.S. 248, 254 (1936). *See I.J.A., Inc. v. Marine Holdings, Ltd.*, 524 F. Supp. 197, 198 (E.D. Penn. 1981).

10. *See* Bermann, *The Use of Antisuit Injunctions in International Litigation*, 28 Colum. J. Transnat'l L. 589, 610 & nn.84-85 (1990) (doctrine not applicable in international context).

11. *E.g., Turner Entertainment Co. v. Aegeto Film GmbH*, 25 F.3d 1512 (11th Cir. 1994) (staying U.S. action pending appeal of German parallel suit); *Saemann v. Everest & Jennings Int'l*, 343 F. Supp. 457, 461 (N.D. Ill. 1972) (staying domestic action pending outcome of parallel English court action where English case had been proceeding for more than three years before filing of U.S. action and hence parallel action would be "inequitable as well as wasteful of judicial resources"); *Barclays Bank, SA v. Tsakos*, 543 A.2d 802, 806-808 (D.C. App. 1988) (staying U.S. action, in lieu of granting *forum non conveniens* motion, pending outcome of parallel proceedings by French plaintiff against Greek debtor in courts of France and Switzerland); *Robinson v. Royal Bank of Canada*, 462 So. 2d 101, 102 (Fla. Dist. Ct. App. 1985) (*per curiam*) (ordering stay of Florida action on grounds of comity pending outcome of Canadian action on similar claim); *Bentil v. Bentil*, 456 N.Y.S.2d 25, 26 (App. Div. 1982) (granting stay of New York divorce action in favor of previously filed action in Ghana).

12. The recently adopted Hague Convention on Choice of Court Agreements, *see supra* p. 468 and Appendix I (which the United States has signed but not yet ratified) contains some direction regarding stays of litigation in parallel proceedings. For cases falling under the agreement (generally speaking, those subject to choice-of-forum clauses), a court other than the court specified in the choice-of-forum clause "shall suspend or dismiss proceedings to which an exclusive choice-of-court agreement applies" unless certain exceptions apply. Those exceptions, detailed in Article 6, include, among others, where the agreement is null and void, where a party lacked capacity to enter into the agreement, and where the giving effect to the agreement would be manifestly contrary to public policy.

13. *See infra* p. 551.

14. *Turner Entertainment Co. v. Degeto Film GmbH*, 25 F.3d 1512, 1518 (11th Cir. 1994); *Ingersoll Milling Machine Co. v. Granger*, 833 F.2d 680, 685 n.1 (7th Cir. 1987); *Faherty v. Fender*, 572 F. Supp. 142, 144 (S.D.N.Y. 1983).

15. *E.g., Hurst v. General Dynamics Corp.*, 583 A.2d 1334 (Del. Ch. 1990) (applying Delaware law to grant stay).

District v. United States.[16] *Colorado River* was a domestic U.S. case involving a dispute over water rights to the Colorado River between two Indian tribes and a state instrumentality. The issue before the Supreme Court was whether a U.S. district court had properly abstained from considering the action because of a pending state court proceeding.[17] The Court reversed the trial judge, holding that the federal action should have proceeded notwithstanding the state court action.

Colorado River emphasized that federal courts are generally obliged to exercise jurisdiction that Congress has granted them. The Court referred to the "duty of a District Court to adjudicate a controversy properly before it,"[18] and the "virtually unflagging obligation of the federal courts to exercise the jurisdiction given them."[19] The Court distinguished between parallel proceedings in two different federal courts, and those in federal court and state court. In the former, the "general principle is to avoid duplicative litigation," while in the latter "the pendency of an action in the state court is no bar to proceedings concerning the same matter in the Federal court having jurisdiction."[20]

Colorado River held that, in a case involving state-federal parallel proceedings, jurisdiction can be declined by a federal court only in "exceptional circumstances."[21] The Court identified a number of "general" principles that guide decision whether such exceptional circumstances are present:[22]

> In assessing the appropriateness of dismissal in the event of an exercise of concurrent juris-diction, a federal court may . . . consider such factors as the inconvenience of the federal forum, *cf. Gulf Oil Corp. v. Gilbert*; the desirability of avoiding piecemeal litigation; and the order in which jurisdiction was obtained by the concurrent forums, *Pacific Live Stock Co. v. Oregon Water Bd.*, 241 U.S. 440, 447 (1916). No one factor is necessarily determinative; a carefully considered judgment taking into account both the obligation to exercise jurisdic-tion and the combination of factors counselling against that exercise is required.

The Court emphasized that "[o]nly the clearest of justifications will warrant dismissal." It found no such exceptional circumstances in *Colorado River*, and reversed the district court's dismissal.

A number of lower federal courts have applied *Colorado River*'s analysis to cases involving foreign parallel proceedings. These courts have generally emphasized the obligation of federal courts to exercise jurisdiction conferred upon them by Congress. They have also analogized foreign courts to U.S. state courts, holding that a foreign proceeding is entitled to no greater (and perhaps less) deference than a state court proceeding.[23]

---

16. 424 U.S. 800 (1976). For cases following the *Colorado River* analysis, *see Royal & Sun Alliance Ins. Co. of Canada v. Century Int'l Arms, Inc.*, 466 F.3d 88 (2d Cir. 2006); *AAR Int'l, Inc. v. Nimelias Enterprises SA*, 250 F.3d 510, 517-518 (7th Cir. 2001); *Neuchatel Swiss General Ins. Co. v. Lufthansa Airlines*, 925 F.2d 1193 (9th Cir. 1991); *Johns Hopkins Health System Corp. v. Al Reem General Trading & Company's Rep.*, 374 F. Supp. 2d 465 (D. Md. 2005); *Szabo v. CGU Int'l Ins., plc*, 199 F. Supp. 2d 715, 718-719 (S.D. Ohio 2002); *Abdullah Sayid Rajab Al-Rifai & Sons WLL v. McDonnell Douglas Foreign Sales Corp.*, 988 F. Supp. 1285, 1289 (E.D. Mo. 1997); *General Motors Corp. v. Ignacio Lopez de Arriortua*, 948 F. Supp. 656, 669 (E.D. Mich. 1996); *Advantage International Management, Inc. v. Martinez*, 1994 WL 482114 (S.D.N.Y. 1994).

17. Although *Colorado River* is routinely applied in cases involving the *lis alibi pendens* doctrine, it in fact involved a district court's dismissal of the plaintiff's action, and not a stay of proceedings. 424 U.S. at 806.

18. 424 U.S. at 813 (quoting *County of Allegheny v. Frank Mashuda Co.*, 360 U.S. 185, 188-189 (1959)).

19. 424 U.S. at 817.

20. 424 U.S. at 817 (quoting *McClellan v. Carland*, 217 U.S. 268, 282 (1910)).

21. 424 U.S. at 818.

22. 424 U.S. at 817. The Court said that these principles "rest on considerations of '[w]ise judicial admin-istration, giving regard to conservation of judicial resources and comprehensive disposition of litigation.'" *Id.*

23. *E.g.*, Neuchatel Swiss General Ins. Co. v. Lufthansa Airlines, 925 F.2d 1193, 1195 (9th Cir. 1991) ("the fact that the parallel proceedings are pending in a foreign jurisdiction is immaterial. We reject the notion that a

3. *Landis*: Stays Within the District Court's "Sound Discretion"

Some lower courts have not followed the *Colorado River* analysis. Rather than analogizing parallel U.S.-foreign proceedings to the state-federal proceedings in *Colorado River*, these decisions have looked to *Landis v. North American Co.*,[24] a case involving parallel proceedings in two different federal courts. There, the Supreme Court upheld a stay on the grounds that it was within the district court's "discretion." In marked contrast to *Colorado River*, *Landis* did not condition the grant of a stay on a showing of exceptional circumstances.

Following *Landis*, a second body of decisions has reasoned that, in international cases, "[a] court's ability to stay an action is 'incidental' to its 'inherent power.' "[25] This line of precedent has often concluded that requests to stay U.S. proceedings in deference to foreign proceedings are within the trial court's "discretion."[26] Relevant to the exercise of this discretion are a variety of factors:

> courts consider numerous factors, including principles of comity, the adequacy of relief available in the alternative forum, promotion of judicial efficiency, the identity of the parties and issues in the two actions, the likelihood of prompt disposition in the alternative forum, the convenience of the parties, counsel and witnesses, and the possibility of prejudice if the stay is granted.[27]

These factors are broadly similar to those identified in *Colorado River*, but with a materially lower standard of proof required to justify a stay.[28]

4. *Quackenbush*: "Unflagging Obligation" Reaffirmed

In 1996, the Supreme Court rendered another decision on the role of judicial abstention in domestic matters. In *Quackenbush v. Allstate Ins. Co.*, the Court held that "federal courts have the power to dismiss or remand cases based on abstention principles only

---

federal court owes greater deference to foreign courts than to our own state courts."). *Compare Ingersoll Milling Machine Co. v. Granger*, 833 F.2d 680 (7th Cir. 1987) ("Here, the alternate forum is not the tribunal of a state of the federal union to which, under our Constitution, we owe a special obligation of comity.") *with Finova Capital Corp. v. Ryan Helicopters U.S.A., Inc.*, 180 F.3d 896, 898 (7th Cir. 1999) (acknowledging language from *Ingersoll* but proceeding to grant stay under "same general principles" used in *Colorado River* abstention).

24. 299 U.S. 248 (1936).

25. *See Itel Corp. v. M/S Victoria U*, 710 F.2d 199 (5th Cir. 1983); *Televisa, SA de CV v. Koch Lorber Films*, 382 F. Supp. 2d 631, 634 (S.D.N.Y. 2005); *Northstar Diamonds, Inc. v. Azran*, 2004 WL 2757910, at *3 (D. Minn. 2004); *Master Card Int'l Inc. v. Argencard Sociedad Anonima*, 2002 WL 432379, at *8 (S.D.N.Y. 2002); *800537 Ontario, Inc. v. World Imports U.S.A. Inc.*, 145 F. Supp. 2d 288, 290-291 (W.D.N.Y. 2001); *Efco Corp. v. Aluma Systems USA, Inc.*, 983 F. Supp. 816, 824 (S.D. Iowa 1997).

26. *Itel Corp. v. M/S Victoria U*, 710 F.2d 199 (5th Cir. 1983) ("abuse of discretion" standard); *Ensign-Bickford Co. v. ICI Explosives USA, Inc.*, 817 F. Supp. 1018 (D. Conn. 1993); *Ronar, Inc. v. Wallace*, 649 F. Supp. 310, 318-319 (S.D.N.Y. 1986).

27. *I.J.A., Inc. v. Marine Holdings, Ltd.*, 524 F. Supp. 197 (E.D. Pa. 1981). *See also Hayes Lemmerz Int'l- Georgia, Inc. v. Punch Prop. Int'l NV*, 2010 U.S. Dist. LEXIS 5613 (N.D. Ga. 2010) (placing great weight on convenience to parties); *Ronar, Inc. v. Wallace*, 649 F. Supp. 310, 318 (S.D.N.Y. 1986) ("Numerous factors bear on the propriety of staying litigation while a foreign proceeding is pending. They include pragmatic concerns such as the promotion of judicial efficiency and the related issues of whether the two actions have parties and issues in common and whether the alternative forum is likely to render a prompt disposition. Also relevant are considerations of fairness to all parties or possible prejudice to any of them. A third group relates to comity between nations.").

28. In light of this similarity, several recent courts are beginning to blur the traditionally fine distinction between the "*Colorado River*" approach and the "*Landis*" approach. Instead, they cite principles from both decisions and announce a set of factors drawing on both lines of authority. *See, e.g., National Union Fire Ins. Co. v. Kozeny*, 115 F. Supp. 2d 1243, 1246-1247 (D. Colo. 2000); *Goldhammer v. Dunkin Donuts, Inc.*, 59 F. Supp. 2d 248, 251-253 (D. Mass. 1999).

where the relief being sought is equitable or otherwise discretionary."[29] In other cases (for example, for damages), "federal courts have a strict duty to exercise the jurisdiction that is conferred upon them by Congress."[30] The Court's opinion reaffirmed the federal courts' "unflagging obligation" to decide domestic cases falling within their jurisdiction, save for in equitable or otherwise discretionary matters.

It is unclear whether, and to what extent, the holdings in *Quackenbush, Colorado River,* and *Landis* apply in the context of international litigation. In each case, the Supreme Court considered purely domestic issues, where the parallel proceedings were in state or other federal courts. A number of lower courts have concluded that, while *Quackenbush* (and *Colorado River*) or *Landis* provide some guidance, they are not decisive in international matters.[31] Other courts have found *Quackenbush* applicable, at least to requests to dismiss a U.S. litigation (as opposed to staying it) in deference to pending foreign proceedings.[32]

5.   Selected Materials on *Lis Alibi Pendens*

Excerpted below are two federal court decisions considering requests for *lis pendens* stays. The first, *Ingersoll Milling Machine Co. v. Granger,* follows *Colorado River:* it considers whether a U.S. action should be stayed in deference to a pending foreign proceeding, both prior to and following the entry of a foreign judgment. The second, *Continental Time Corp. v. Swiss Credit Bank,* follows *Landis,* and dismisses a U.S. action in deference to pending foreign proceedings. Finally, review the recent Hague Convention on Choice of Court Agreements, and the ALI's proposed federal legislation on recognition of foreign judgments, both of which contain provisions relevant to stays of parallel proceedings.

INGERSOLL MILLING MACHINE CO. v. GRANGER
833 F.2d 680 (7th Cir. 1987)

RIPPLE, CIRCUIT JUDGE. Appellant, Ingersoll Milling Machine Co. ("Ingersoll") appeals from a judgment enforcing a money judgment rendered by the Cour de Cassation of Belgium, that country's court of last resort, in favor of appellee, John P. Granger. Ingersoll argues [among other things, that the district court erred in staying a U.S. action that it had brought paralleling the Belgian proceedings]. . . . [W]e affirm. . . .

[Between 1963 and 1971, Mr. Granger worked for Ingersoll at its office in Rockford, Illinois. In 1971, Mr. Granger began working for an Ingersoll subsidiary, Ingersoll Manufacturing Consultants (the "Belgian Company"), in Brussels, Belgium. At the time of his transfer, Mr. Granger negotiated an agreement with Ingersoll governing his transfer. This agreement provided, among other things, for the payment of Mr. Granger's salary, insurance, and expenses, and set forth how these matters would be affected by his move from Illinois to Belgium. In 1975, Mr. Granger was placed on the payroll of the Belgian Company and declared by the Belgian Company for tax purposes in Belgium. In 1977, Mr. Granger's employment with the Belgian Company was terminated.]

---

29. 517 U.S. 706, 707 (1996).
30. 517 U.S. at 716.
31. *Posner v. Essex Ins. Co.,* 178 F.3d 1209, 1223 (11th Cir. 1999); *Goldhammer v. Dunkin' Donuts, Inc.,* 59 F. Supp. 2d 248, 252 (D. Mass. 1999).
32. *BP Chems., Ltd. v. Jiangsu Sopo Corp. Ltd.,* 429 F. Supp. 2d 1179 (E.D. Mo. 2006); *Exxon Research & Eng'g Co. v. Indus. Risk Insurers,* 775 A.2d 601 (N.J. Super. A.D. 2001); *Abdullah Sayid Rajab Al-Rifai & Sons WLL v. McDonnell Douglas Foreign Sales Corp.,* 988 F. Supp. 1285, 1291 (E.D. Mo. 1997).

On April 27, 1978, Mr. Granger brought suit against Ingersoll and the Belgian Company in the Brussels' labor court. [He alleged] that, because he had been employed in Belgium from 1971 through 1977, he was entitled, under Belgian law, to certain compensation and termination benefits from both Ingersoll and the Belgian Company. Both defendants appeared and answered Mr. Granger's complaint. The Belgian Company claimed that Mr. Granger was an employee of Ingersoll only, and that, therefore, he could obtain no relief against the Belgian Company. Ingersoll claimed that, because of the agreement executed by Mr. Granger and Ingersoll prior to Mr. Granger's transfer to Brussels, the employment relationship was governed by Illinois law. . . .

In August 1979, Ingersoll brought suit in the Winnebago County (Illinois) Circuit Court against Mr. Granger. Ingersoll sought a declaratory judgment that Mr. Granger was entitled to no further benefits from Ingersoll [and] the return of funds advanced to Mr. Granger. Finally, Ingersoll sought to enjoin Mr. Granger from proceeding with the Belgian suit. Mr. Granger removed the Illinois suit to the U.S. District Court for the Northern District of Illinois. He also sought to dismiss the case on the ground that an action regarding the same dispute was then pending in Belgium and on the ground of *forum non conveniens.* The district court denied Mr. Granger's motion. The district court held that the pendency of the Belgian action did not deprive it of jurisdiction. Moreover, the court found that . . . Illinois might be a more convenient forum than Belgium. . . .

On March 20, 1980, the Belgian trial court found for Mr. Granger on his complaint and for Ingersoll and the Belgian Company on the counterclaims. The award for Mr. Granger on his complaint was against Ingersoll and the Belgian Company jointly. . . . On appeal, the Belgian Labour Court of Appeal affirmed the holding of the trial court. . . . The Belgian Cour de Cassation affirmed the appellate court's decision on June 3, 1985. . . .

After the Belgian trial court had rendered its judgment, Mr. Granger filed a second motion to dismiss Ingersoll's suit in the district court . . . based on . . . res judicata. Ingersoll opposed Mr. Granger's motion, filed a motion to compel discovery, and sought leave to add another count to its complaint seeking the return of certain funds advanced to Mr. Granger. . . . The district court . . . stayed further proceedings pending the outcome of the Belgian appellate process. After the Labour Court of Appeal issued its decision, Mr. Granger filed a counterclaim in the Illinois suit seeking enforcement of the Belgian judgment. Before the district court made any ruling, however, Ingersoll appealed the Belgian decision to the Cour de Cassation. On March 24, 1986, the district court ruled against Ingersoll on its complaint and granted summary judgment to Mr. Granger on his counterclaim. In so ruling, the court found that the Belgian judgment met the requirements of the Illinois Uniform Foreign Money-Judgments Recognition Act (the Act or the Uniform Act).

On appeal, Ingersoll . . . challenges . . . the district court's March 24, 1986 order [on the grounds, inter alia,] that the court improperly stayed the action in the district court because of the pendency of the Belgian action. . . . Relying on *Colorado River* and *Moses H. Cone Memorial Hosp. v. Mercury Constr. Corp.,* 460 U.S. 1, 16 (1983), Ingersoll argues that it was error for the district court to stay the proceedings simply on the basis that a parallel suit was proceeding in the Belgian courts.

In evaluating this argument, it is important, at the outset, to state the procedural posture of the case at the time a stay was granted with somewhat more precision than does Ingersoll. When Mr. Granger initially sought to dismiss or stay the action before the district court, the court denied Mr. Granger's motion because it recognized that it ought to exercise its jurisdiction over the subject matter concurrently with the Belgian courts. *See Laker Airways Ltd. v. Sabena,* 731 F.2d 909, 926-27 (D.C. Cir. 1984) (federal trial court should usually exercise jurisdiction concurrently with foreign trial court); *Colorado River, supra* (federal court has obligation to exercise concurrent jurisdiction with state court absent exceptional circumstances). It was only after the Belgian trial court had rendered its judgment that the district court decided to stay further proceedings pending the outcome of the Belgian appeal. Therefore, the precise issue before us is whether it was appropriate for the district court to stay its proceedings at this point in the parallel progression of the litigation in the United States and in Belgium.[33]

In *Colorado River* and *Moses H. Cone*, the Supreme Court enumerated the considerations that a federal district court should consider in determining whether it should exercise jurisdiction concurrently with state courts. In *Moses H. Cone*, 460 U.S. at 15-16, describing its earlier decision in *Colorado River*, the Court summarized those factors as follows:

> We declined to prescribe a hard-and-fast rule for dismissals of this type, but instead described some of the factors relevant to the decision.
>
> > "It has been held, for example, that the court first assuming jurisdiction over property may exercise that jurisdiction to the exclusion of other courts. . . . In assessing the appropriateness of dismissal in the event of an exercise of concurrent jurisdiction, a federal court may also consider such factors as the inconvenience of the federal forum; the desirability of avoiding piecemeal litigation; and the order in which jurisdiction was obtained by the concurrent forums. No one factor is necessarily determinative; a carefully considered judgment taking into account both the obligation to exercise jurisdiction and the combination of factors counselling against that exercise is required. Only the clearest of justifications will warrant dismissal." [*Colorado River*, 424 U.S.] at 818-819. . . .

Here the alternate forum is not the tribunal of a state of the federal union to which, under our Constitution, we owe a special obligation of comity. Nevertheless, the factors enunciated in those cases, when applied with this difference in mind, can serve as a helpful guide in our evaluation. When the determination of the district court is reviewed in light of the *Colorado River-Moses H. Cone* factors, it is manifestly clear that the district court did not abuse its discretion in staying proceedings after the rendition of the Belgian trial court's judgment. First of all, there is no particularly strong federal interest in ensuring that this dispute be adjudicated in a federal district court or, indeed, in any American court. This case involves an employment relationship that spanned international boundaries. While the American interest can hardly be termed insubstantial, the Belgian interest also must be recognized as very significant. International judicial comity is an interest not only of Belgium but also of the United States. We certainly cannot fault the district court—informed that the Belgian trial court had rendered a verdict which, unless overturned on appeal, would resolve the dispute—for rejecting the "parochial concept that all disputes must be resolved under our laws and in our courts." *The Bremen, supra.*

Moreover, considerations of judicial economy, especially the need to avoid piecemeal litigation, strongly favored staying the district court proceedings. The Belgian suit, which had begun before the American action was filed, had been brought to a conclusion in the trial court. Absent reversal on appeal, that judgment would adjudicate the rights of the parties. At that point, unless there was a barrier to the recognition of that judgment in the United States, and, as we discuss below, there was little chance of that contingency, there would be no need for further proceedings in the district court. Avoiding such duplication of effort and the possibility of piecemeal litigation is hardly an abuse of discretion. Attention to such "pragmatic concerns," [*Ronar Inc. v. Wallace*, 649 F. Supp. 310

---

33. This question is a matter of federal law. *See Faherty v. Fender*, 572 F. Supp. 142, 144 (S.D.N.Y. 1983).

(S.D.N.Y 1986)], is precisely the sort of "careful balancing of factors," *Moses H. Cone*, 460 U.S. at 16, that must be undertaken in such a situation.

Moreover, it is not insignificant—indeed, it is very significant—that the district court's action in this case was a decidedly measured one. The court did not dismiss the action; it simply stayed further proceedings until the Belgian appeals were concluded. This approach protects the substantial rights of the parties while permitting the district court to manage its time effectively. Such a common sense approach is clearly within the sound discretion of the trial court. *See Landis v. North American Co.*, 299 U.S. 248, 254 (1936). . . .

CONTINENTAL TIME CORP. v. SWISS CREDIT BANK
543 F. Supp. 408 (S.D.N.Y. 1982)

LASKER, DISTRICT JUDGE. Continental Time Corp. ("Continental") sues to recover damages allegedly arising out of Credit Suisse's ("Swiss Credit") wrongful refusal to honor its obligations under an irrevocable letter of credit. The letter of credit was issued on January 10, 1980, in favor of Continental. On January 21, 1980, Continental assigned its entire interest in the letter of credit to S. Frederick & Company ("Frederick") and to Arlington Distributing Co., Inc. ("Arlington"). On January 29, 1980, Swiss Credit advised Merchants Bank, where Frederick held his account, that the air waybill did not conform to the requirements of the letter of credit. The expiration date on the letter of credit subsequently passed with no payment made. On May 28, 1980, Frederick and Arlington separately instituted suit in Switzerland for recovery of their assigned portions of the letter of credit. The Swiss court consolidated the actions and granted Swiss Credit's application to join Georges Bloch, the person who had originally requested the issuance of the letter of credit, in the action. The suit in Switzerland is currently pending.

Continental instituted this suit in 1981. Swiss Credit now moves to dismiss the complaint or stay the action on the grounds that Continental is not the real party in interest and that the precise issues are being litigated in the Swiss action. On March 18, 1982, Continental and Frederick settled related litigation between themselves. As part of the settlement, Frederick assigned back to Continental 75% of its interest in the letter of credit, agreed to attempt to intervene in this suit, and agreed to consent to a stay of the Swiss action. . . .

Swiss Credit contends that, despite Frederick's reassignment of most of its interest in the letter of credit to Continental, the court should exercise its discretionary power to dismiss suits involving the same parties where, as is claimed here, the earlier initiated litigation will resolve the issues in the present suit. Swiss Credit argues that it would be prejudiced by the continuation of this suit through the assignment of claim from Frederick to Continental because it must continue to litigate the same issues in two fora, here and in Switzerland. In this regard, Swiss Credit notes that the assignment was only partial, that there has been no unconditional promise by Frederick to agree to a stay of the Swiss action, and that Frederick has yet to intervene here. Swiss Credit also maintains that Continental's maneuvers with Frederick amount to a method of forum shopping and that Continental has failed to join Arlington, a necessary party, in this suit. Swiss Credit contends that Switzerland is the appropriate forum for the litigation of the letter of credit claims because the Swiss action was filed first, Continental Time may "intervene" in the Swiss action, and all the relevant parties for the letter of credit claim are involved in the Swiss action.

Continental responds that Frederick's assignment to it renders Continental a real party in interest in this suit and that Arlington, as a minority assignee, is not an indispensable party under Fed. R. Civ. Pr. 19(b). Continental contends that this action should not be dismissed or stayed in favor of the Swiss action because the actions may proceed simultaneously, it is pressing claims against defendants other than Swiss Credit here, and Continental is not a party to the Swiss action. Continental emphasizes that this case, in contrast to the Swiss action, will involve all parties having an interest in the proceeds of the letter of credit. Continental also maintains that this action has proceeded to a further stage of litigation than the Swiss action, since discovery is nearly complete in this action and little activity has occurred in the Swiss action.

Swiss Credit's motion for dismissal of the claims against it is granted. The court has the inherent power to dismiss or stay this action in favor of the Swiss litigation presenting the same claims and issues. *See Landis v. North American Co.* The relevant factors in determining whether to grant a stay or a dismissal because of litigation pending in another forum include the adequacy of relief available in the alternative forum, the promotion of judicial efficiency, the identity of the parties and the issues in the two actions, the likelihood of prompt resolution in the alternative forum, the convenience of parties, counsel and witnesses, the possibility of prejudice to any party, and the temporal sequence of filing for each action. Weighing these factors . . . , we conclude that this action should be dismissed. The suit was instituted some six months later than the Swiss action by a party who, at that time, had no cognizable interest in the letter of credit proceeds. Moreover, it appears that the Swiss action will proceed in any event since there is no indication that Arlington, to whom Continental assigned a significant share of its interest in the letter of credit, intends to join this action. In those circumstances, Swiss Credit would be faced with having to defend its actions in two fora with the attendant risk of inconsistent decisions. Moreover, Continental has not challenged Swiss Credit's assertion Continental has the right to join the Swiss action. It thus appears that the Swiss suit has the potential of including all parties necessary for the resolution of the claims relating to the letter of credit transaction.

Finally, while, as Continental asserts, this action may be more convenient for various parties and witnesses, it is also true that it was the choice of Continental's predecessor in interest, Frederick, to sue in Switzerland rather than in the United States. In this regard, the fact that Continental and Frederick appear to have engaged in a type of forum-shopping as a by-product of the resolution of the claims between them militates in favor of Swiss Credit's position on this motion. Swiss Credit should not be required to defend against the letter of credit claims here when it is already engaged in litigation in Switzerland with parties who, at the time that litigation was commenced, represented the entire interests in the proceeds of the letter of credit. Frederick's decision to assign a portion of its interest back to Continental after it had already instituted litigation on the letter of credit should not be permitted to result in Swiss Credit's having to litigate the identical issue in two fora on either side of the Atlantic Ocean.

It is true that this action includes other parties and claims than those in the suit in Switzerland, relating to the purchase and sale of merchandise underlying the letter of credit transaction. However, this factor does not support Continental's contention that only this action can fully resolve the relevant issues, for it is settled that a letter of credit agreement constitutes an independent transaction between the issuer and the beneficiary, to be resolved without reference to underlying contracts or transactions. *Venizelos, SA v. Chase Manhattan Bank,* 425 F.2d 461 (2d Cir. 1970). Swiss Credit's motion to dismiss the action as to it is granted on condition that it not oppose Continental's becoming a party to the Swiss litigation.

HAGUE CHOICE OF COURT AGREEMENTS CONVENTION
[reprinted in Appendix I]

ALI'S PROPOSED FEDERAL FOREIGN JUDGMENTS RECOGNITION
AND ENFORCEMENT ACT §11
[reprinted in Appendix Q]

Notes on Ingersoll, Continental Time, *and Legislative Materials*

1. *Judicial abstention authority in international* lis pendens *cases: analogies to* **Colorado River, Landis,** *and* **Quackenbush.** *Ingersoll* and *Continental Time* look to different Supreme Court precedents to establish the guidelines for *lis alibi pendens* analysis in international cases. *Ingersoll* relied principally on *Colorado River* —a case involving parallel proceedings in state and federal court—while *Continental Time* followed *Landis*—a case involving parallel proceedings in two different federal courts. Which analogy is more appropriate? If a federal court defers to a state court, then no federal court hears the action; the same is true when a federal court defers to a foreign court (and, indeed, no U.S. court hears the action). Does this mean that *Colorado River* is the appropriate analogy?

Do considerations of "international comity" counsel toward greater, or lesser, willingness of federal courts to defer to foreign courts than to state courts? Are "federalism" concerns more, or less, weighty than "international comity" concerns? *See Neuchatel Swiss General Ins. Co. v. Lufthansa Airlines*, 925 F.2d 1193, 1195 (9th Cir. 1991) ("the fact that the parallel proceedings are pending in a foreign jurisdiction is immaterial. We reject the notion that a federal court owes greater deference to foreign courts than to our own state courts.").

How does *Ingersoll* deal with the suggestion that foreign courts are entitled to greater deference than U.S. state courts? Does a federal court have a "virtually unflagging obligation" to exercise jurisdiction over international cases, when the courts of other nations can also resolve the dispute? Note the remark in *Ingersoll* which, while applying *Colorado River*, said: "there is no particularly strong federal interest in ensuring that this dispute be adjudicated in a federal district court or, indeed, in any American court." Is that correct? Does it matter what law—state or federal—governs the underlying substantive claims? Does it matter that both parties were U.S. nationals?

As noted above, some lower courts have been unwilling to extend *Quackenbush*'s analysis of abstention doctrines to international cases. *See Posner v. Essex Ins. Co.*, 178 F.3d 1209, 1223 (11th Cir. 1999) ("the Supreme Court's admonition [in *Quackenbush*] that courts generally must exercise their nondiscretionary authority in cases over which Congress has granted them jurisdiction can apply only to those abstention doctrines addressing the unique concerns of federalism"); *Goldhammer v. Dunkin' Donuts, Inc.*, 59 F. Supp. 2d 248, 252 (D. Mass. 1999) ("*Quackenbush* does not crisply govern in the area of international abstention because the considerations involved in deferring to state court proceedings are different from those involved in deferring to foreign proceedings."). *Compare Abdullah Sayid Rajab Al-Rifai & Sons WLL v. McDonnell Douglas Foreign Sales Corp.*, 988 F. Supp. 1285, 1291 (E.D. Mo. 1997) ("The Court finds that an outright dismissal of the instant action at law is improper in light of *Quackenbush*").

If there are limits on a federal court's power to refrain from hearing claims within legislatively conferred jurisdiction, in deference to state court proceedings, what would make those limits less important when foreign court proceedings are involved? Is not the issue the power of a federal court to abstain from exercising legislatively conferred jurisdiction, not the nature of the parallel proceeding?

2. *Relief in* **lis pendens** *case — dismissal versus stay.* Is the *forum non conveniens* doctrine not a rule of abstention? Would *Quackenbush* preclude its application? Given the well-settled nature of the *forum non conveniens* doctrine, is it not clear that *Quackenbush* cannot extend to the international context? What justifies this?

Compare the relief granted in *Ingersoll* with that in *Continental Time.* Is an outright dismissal less defensible, under *Quackenbush* or otherwise, than a stay? Note that some lower courts have held that *Quackenbush* forbids dismissals, but not stays. *BP Chems., Ltd. v. Jiangsu Sopo Corp. Ltd.,* 429 F.Supp.2d 1179 (E.D. Mo. 2006); *Abdullah Sayid Rajab Al-Rifai & Sons WLL v. McDonnell Douglas Foreign Sales Corp.,* 988 F. Supp. 1285, 1291 (E.D. Mo. 1997); *Exxon Research & Eng'g Co. v. Indus. Risk Insurers,* 775 A.2d 601 (App. Div. 2001). Is this a principled distinction? *See Royal & Sun Alliance Ins. Co. of Canada v. Century Int'l Arms, Inc.,* 466 F.3d 88, 96 (2d Cir. 2006) (discussing relationship between stay and dismissal)

3. **Lis pendens** *compared to* **forum non conveniens.** Beyond the availability of different remedies, what are the similarities and differences between the *lis pendens* and *forum non conveniens* doctrines? Note that the *forum non conveniens* doctrine applies even in the absence of any pending foreign proceeding. *See supra* pp. 431-433. Compare the doubts concerning the legitimacy of *lis pendens* stays to the relatively established and legitimate role of *forum non conveniens* dismissals. What justifies this difference?

Continental Time dismissed a U.S. action in deference to a foreign proceeding. Why is the *forum non conveniens* doctrine not applicable when dismissal of an action is requested? How do the two standards applied in *Ingersoll* and *Continental Time* compare to the *forum non conveniens* doctrine articulated in *Piper Aircraft? See Taub v. Marchesi Di Barolo S.p.A.,* 2009 U.S. Dist. LEXIS 115565 (E.D.N.Y. 2009 (discussing relationship between *forum non conveniens* and *lis pendens* standards). Under which of these standards is it easier to obtain a stay or dismissal?

4. *Relevance of attitude toward parallel proceedings to* **lis pendens** *standard.* The standards that should govern *lis pendens* stays are influenced significantly by one's attitude toward parallel proceedings. Are parallel proceedings an inherently undesirable occurrence? Or are parallel proceedings a natural feature of a multi-state environment, where the same dispute will often fall within the jurisdiction of two or more forums? If the former, then *lis pendens* stays will be more readily granted than in the latter.

Most U.S. courts have taken the view that there is nothing inherently inappropriate in parallel proceedings concerning the same dispute. One court has reasoned that concurrent jurisdiction by two or more national courts is inevitable in international disputes, and that the "fundamental corollary" to concurrent jurisdiction is parallel proceedings: "parallel proceedings on the same in personam claim should ordinarily be allowed to proceed simultaneously, at least until a judgment is reached in one which can be pled as *res judicata* in the other." *Laker Airways Ltd. v. Sabena,* 731 F.2d at 909, 926-927 (D.C. Cir. 1984). Indeed, a number of U.S. lower courts have acknowledged a "rule permitting parallel proceedings in concurrent in personam actions," thus allowing both U.S. and foreign proceedings to go forward to judgment. *Laker Airways,* 731 F.2d at 928. *E.g., BP Chems., Ltd. v. Jiangsu Sopo Corp. Ltd.,* 429 F. Supp. 2d 1179 (E.D. Mo. 2006); *American Cyanamid Co. v. Picaso-Anstalt,* 741 F. Supp. 1150, 1159 (D.N.J. 1990) ("the preferred course of action is to permit each sovereign to reach judgment and apply the findings of one to the other under principles of *res judicata*"); *In the Matter of the Complaint of Maritima Aragua, SA,* 1990 WL 180135, at *1-2 (S.D.N.Y. 1990) (declining to enjoin parallel action where "there is no strong public policy of the United States that is threatened by the continuation of the action in Venezuela" but likewise refusing to grant Venezuelan plaintiffs' motion to dismiss U.S. action because "[n]o reason has been presented as to why claimants, having voluntarily subjected themselves to the jurisdiction of this Court, should not be required to remain in this proceeding while pursuing their claims in Venezuela"); *Black & Decker Corp. v. Sanyei America Corp.*, 650 F. Supp. 406, 408-410 (N.D. Ill. 1986).

Is it in fact sensible to permit parallel proceedings? What are the costs of such an approach? Does it not condemn the parties to two sets of legal proceedings, with duplicate costs, distraction, and risks — as well as the serious possibility of inconsistent results? Why should this be tolerated? Why should courts not attempt, from the outset, to identify which forum is the appropriate one for resolving a dispute, with the appropriate forum then enjoining litigation elsewhere and/or the inappropriate forum staying litigation in its courts?

5. *Standards governing* lis pendens *stays.* Compare the standards adopted by *Ingersoll* and *Continental Time* for the grant of a *lis pendens* stay. What are the differences between them? Should *lis pendens* stays be easy or hard to obtain in international cases?

(a) "Exceptional circumstances." *Ingersoll* held that *lis pendens* stays would be granted only in "exceptional circumstances." This clearly did not include the mere expense of duplicative litigation, as illustrated by the U.S. trial court's refusal to stay its proceedings before any Belgian judgment had been rendered. The majority of other lower court decisions have adopted this view. *E.g., Answers in Genesis of Ky., Inc. v. Creation Ministries Int'l, Ltd.*, 556 F.3d 459 (6th Cir. 2009); *AAR Int'l, Inc. v. Nimelias Enterprises SA*, 250 F.3d 510, 517-518 (7th Cir. 2001); *Neuchatel Swiss General Ins. Co. v. Lufthansa Airlines*, 925 F.2d 1193 (9th Cir. 1991); *Brinco Mining Ltd. v. Federal Ins. Co.*, 552 F. Supp. 1233 (D.D.C. 1982); *Advantage Int'l Management, Inc. v. Martinez*, 1994 WL 482114 (S.D.N.Y. 1994); *supra* p. 550. Is this an appropriate standard? Why should U.S. proceedings be stayed only in extreme circumstances? Why should not the rule be that duplicative U.S. proceedings will be stayed, *absent* exceptional circumstances?

What precisely does the "exceptional circumstances" test mean? The relevant factors are those identified in *Colorado River*, which in turn drew on the *forum non conveniens* analysis of *Gulf Oil.* Were there exceptional circumstances in *Continental Time?*

There are two points in *Ingersoll* where a *lis pendens* stay was arguably appropriate: (i) immediately after filing of the U.S. action, and before any Belgian court decision; and (ii) after the Belgian trial court's decision. What did the U.S. trial judge do at each point? Were there *not* exceptional circumstances to support Mr. Granger's original request for a stay in *Ingersoll* (which the trial judge denied)? Should a stay have been granted before the Belgian decision was rendered? Were there exceptional circumstances supporting the trial court's initial grant of a stay in *Ingersoll* after the first Belgian decision? What were they? Were there exceptional circumstances for granting a stay in *Continental Time?* What were they?

(b) "Sound discretion." *Continental Time* held that the grant of a *lis alibi pendens* stay was within the discretion of the trial court, applying the same factors as those used under *Colorado River* and the *forum non conveniens* doctrine. Is it appropriate to give a trial court "discretion" to make the fundamentally important, and often outcome-determinative, decision whether an action may proceed in the United States? Under the *Continental Time* analysis, would a stay have been granted in *Ingersoll?* Before the Belgian judgment had been rendered? Should such a stay have been entered? A recent decision of the Second Circuit, while not discussing *Continental Time*, adopts a contrary analysis. *See Royal & Sun Alliance Ins. Co. of Canada v. Century Int'l Arms, Inc.*, 463 F.3d 88 (2d Cir. 2006).

(c) Multi-factor balancing. More recently, the Eleventh Circuit has adopted a multi-factor balancing approach to *lis pendens* stays. In *Turner Entertainment Co. v. Degeto Film GmbH,*

25 F.3d 1512, 1518 (11th Cir. 1994), the court granted a stay after applying the following standards:

> [C]ourts have sought to fashion principles that will provide three readily identifiable goals in the area of concurrent international jurisdiction: (1) a proper level of respect for the acts of our fellow sovereign nations — a rather vague concept referred to in American jurisprudence as international comity; (2) fairness to litigants; and (3) efficient use of scarce judicial resources.

Compare this standard with those in *Colorado River* and *Landis.* Does the Eleventh Circuit's standard provide meaningful guidance? *See also Belize Telecom, Ltd. v. Gov't of Belize,* 528 F.3d 1298 (11th Cir. 2008) (applying *Turner* standards to support stay); *Posner v. Essex Ins. Co., Ltd.,* 178 F.3d 1209, 1223-1225 (11th Cir. 1999) (same). An alternative list of factors is set out in the Second Circuit's decision in *Royal & Sun Alliance Ins. Co. of Canada v. Century Int'l Arms, Inc.,* 466 F.3d 88 (2d Cir. 2006):

> In the context of parallel proceedings in a foreign court, a district court should be guided by the principles upon which international comity is based: the proper respect for litigation in and the courts of a sovereign nation, fairness to litigants, and judicial efficiency. Proper consideration of these principles will no doubt require an evaluation of various factors, such as the similarity of the parties, the similarity of the issues, the order in which the actions were filed, the adequacy of the alternate forum, the potential prejudice to either party, the convenience of the parties, the connection between the litigation and the United States, and the connection between the litigation and the foreign jurisdiction. This list is not exhaustive, and a district court should examine the totality of the circumstances to determine whether the specific facts before it are sufficiently exceptional to justify abstention.

Which list of factors is preferable? Why?

Does a multi-factor test make sense in this context? Is such an approach necessary to take into account the salient factual differences between cases? Or does it undermine any predictability or certainty for parties (or courts) in determining whether parallel proceedings may go forward? Are predictability and certainty desirable values in this area of the law? *See supra* pp. 549-550 (alternative approach grounded in the desire for predictability and certainty). Are they more or less important than in other areas such as jurisdiction and choice of law?

(d) Uncertainty regarding lis pendens standards. Ingersoll relies on *Colorado River*'s demanding "exceptional circumstances" standard — until the final paragraph of the opinion. There, the court appears to rely on *Landis'* "discretion" standard. Is this consistent? Is the fact that a Belgian judgment had already issued relevant?

6. Relevance of overlap between parties and issues in the parallel proceedings. One of the most significant issues in any request for a *lis pendens* stay is the extent to which the parties and issues in the U.S. and foreign proceedings are the same. *See supra* pp. 549-550. Consistent with this, *Continental Time* considered whether two parallel proceedings were in fact all that "parallel" — by examining the identities of the parties to, and the similarity of the issues in, the two actions.

Other lower courts have also considered the degree of similarity between pending foreign and U.S. proceedings in deciding whether to grant *lis pendens* stays. *Compare Itel Corp. v. M/S Victoria U,* 710 F.2d 199 (5th Cir. 1983) ("A stay pending adjudication in another tribunal should not be granted unless that tribunal has the power to render an effective judgment on issues that are necessary to the disposition of the stayed action") *with Herbstein v. Bruetman,* 743 F. Supp. 184 (S.D.N.Y. 1990) ("comity requires that the parties and issues in both litigations are the same or sufficiently similar, such that the doctrine of *res judicata* can be asserted"). *See also Seguros Del Estado, SA v. Scientific Games, Inc.*, 262 F.3d 1164, 1170-1171 (11th Cir. 2001) (declining to grant stay where foreign proceedings not sufficiently similar); *AAR Int'l, Inc. v. Nimelias Enterprises SA*, 250 F.3d 510, 519-522 (7th Cir. 2001) (reversing district court stay where foreign proceedings not sufficiently similar); *Finova Capital Corp. v. Ryan Helicopters U.S.A., Inc.*, 180 F.3d 896, 898 (7th Cir. 1999) (parties and issues substantially similar); *Eisenmann Corp. v. Tek-Mor, Inc.*, 2004 WL 547253, at *4 (N.D. Ill. 2004) (declining to stay where foreign proceedings not parallel); *Lexington Ins. Co. v. Forrest*, 263 F. Supp. 2d 986, 1002 (E.D. Pa. 2003) (same); *American Stock Exchange, LLC v. Towergate Consultants Ltd.*, 2003 WL 21692814, at *4 (S.D.N.Y. 2003) (same); *Linear Products, Inc. v. Marotech, Inc.*, 189 F. Supp. 2d 461, 465-468 (W.D. Va. 2002) (same); *General Motors Corp. v. Ignacio Lopez de Arriortua*, 948 F. Supp. 656, 669 (E.D. Mich. 1996) (same).

What degree of similarity or overlap is required before a stay can be granted? *See Royal & Sun Alliance Ins. Co. of Canada v. Century Int'l Arms, Inc.*, 466 F.3d 88, 96 (2d Cir. 2006) ("For two actions to be considered parallel, the parties in the actions need not be the same, but they must be substantially the same, litigating substantially the same issues in both actions."); *Republic of Colombia v. Diageo North America, Inc.*, 531 F. Supp. 2d 365 (E.D.N.Y. 2007) (analysis of overlap and similarity); *Goldhammer v. Dunkin' Donuts, Inc.*, 59 F. Supp. 2d 248, 253 (D. Mass. 1999) (sufficient identity where party in one litigation was majority shareholder of party in second litigation); *800537 Ontario, Inc. v. World Imports U.S.A., Inc.*, 145 F. Supp. 2d 288 (W.D.N.Y. 2001) (similarity of claims more important than similarity of parties). Is there a clear cut answer to this, or are there various gradations of overlap that strengthen or weaken the case for a stay? Is it sufficient that the foreign proceeding will decide *some* (but not all) of the claims in the U.S. suit? Some of the elements of the U.S. claims?

7. *Relevance of foreign forum's procedures and remedies.* Lower courts have also considered the adequacy of the relief available in the parallel foreign proceedings when considering applications for *lis pendens* stays. *Compare Credicom NV v. Colony Credicom LP*, 2000 WL 282968 (S.D.N.Y. 2000) (no indication that party opposing stay would be treated unfairly in foreign forum) *with Dependable Highway Exp., Inc. v. Navigators Ins. Co.*, 498 F.3d 1059 (9th Cir. 2007) (vacating stay where court concerned about prejudice to party's rights and delay in foreign forum). This factor parallels the consideration of similar issues in *forum non conveniens* analysis. *See supra* p. 444.

8. *Relevance of convenience to parties.* As noted above, lower courts also consider the convenience of different forums to the parties. *See supra* p. 560. This involves logistical and language issues (such as location of witnesses and documents, need for translations, and the like).

9. *Relevance of first-filing of complaint to availability of* **lis pendens** *stay.* Note that the *Colorado River* formula takes into account the sequence in which the actions were filed. A number of lower courts including *Continental Time*, have attributed significant weight to the sequence of filings. *E.g., Finova Capital Corp. v. Ryan Helicopters U.S.A., Inc.*, 180 F.3d 896, 899 (7th Cir. 1999); *Northstar Diamonds, Inc. v. Azran*, 2004 WL 2757910, at *6 (D. Minn. 2004); *800537 Ontario, Inc. v. World Imports U.S.A. Inc.*, 145 F. Supp. 2d 288, 291 (W.D.N.Y. 2001) ("[W]hen as here, the foreign action is pending, principles of comity counsel that priority generally goes to the suit first filed."); *National Union Fire Ins. Co. v. Kozeny*, 115 F. Supp. 2d 1243, 1249 (D. Colo. 2000); *Meisel v. Ustaoglu*, 2000 WL 33374486, at *7 (D. Md. 2000); *Ronar, Inc. v. Wallace*, 649 F. Supp. 310, 318 (S.D.N.Y. 1986) ("When . . . the foreign action is pending rather than decided, comity requires that priority generally goes to the suit first filed"; invoking "presumption" in favor of proceeding with first-filed U.S. suit).

Other courts have either given little weight to the order of filing, or greater weight to the relative progress in the litigations. *See Cont'l Cas. Co. v. Axa Global Risks (UK) Ltd.*, 2010 U.S. Dist. LEXIS 32850 (W.D. Mo. 2010); *Palm Bay Int'l, Inc. v. Marchesi Di Barolo S.p.A.*, 659 F. Supp. 2d 407 (E.D.N.Y. 2009); *Televisa, SA de CV v. Koch Lorber Films*, 2005 WL 1017804 (E.D. Pa. 2005); *American Cyanamid Co. v. Picaso-Anstalt*, 741 F. Supp. 1150, 1159 (D.N.J. 1990). Why should it matter whether one party or the other won the race to the courthouse?

Is it not more important whether the foreign proceeding has advanced substantially? Many lower courts have so concluded. *See Kitaru Innovations Inc. v. Chandaria*, 698 F. Supp. 2d 386 (S.D.N.Y. 2010); *Goldhammer v. Dunkin' Donuts, Inc.*, 59 F. Supp. 2d 248, 254 (D. Mass. 1999) (while first-filed status not dispositive, "litigation lethargy" is important consideration); *Loraney Sports Inc. v. Glastic Corp.*, 1997 WL 109473, at *3 (S.D.N.Y. 1997) (noting that "little if any movement has occurred in the [foreign] [a]ction"); *Ludgate Ins. Co. Ltd. v. Becker*, 906 F. Supp. 1233, 1243 (N.D. Ill. 1995) (noting that "although the [foreign] action was brought six months before this one, it has not advanced significantly further than the one before us"). On the other hand, should courts consider whether there are delays in the filing of the second suit—suggestive of an intention to complicate and delay matters? *See also* Rutledge, *Decisional Sequencing*, 62 Ala. L. Rev. 7 (2010).

Consider §11 of the ALI's Proposed Federal Foreign Judgments Recognition Act. How does it treat the issue of first filing? Compare Articles 27 and 28 of EU Council Regulation 44/2001.

10. *First-filing of the complaint and extraterritoriality.* As discussed elsewhere in this book, the traditional territorial limits on the exercise of jurisdiction (both judicial jurisdiction and legislative jurisdiction) have largely broken down. The resulting rise in assertions of jurisdiction over conduct taking place abroad increases the chances of parallel proceedings and, thus, the possible need for a stay. Should the standards for issuance of a stay *lis alibi pendens* take into account this breakdown of the territoriality principle? Consider the following:

> [W]hen courts consider stay requests they must account for the breadth of their increasingly extraterritorial jurisdictional assertions. . . . [C]ourts should do away with references—in the international context—to a court's so-called unflagging obligation to exercise jurisdiction. Courts instead should presumptively find a stay warranted if the moving party can establish that: (1) it filed a parallel foreign action first; and (2) the foreign court would have jurisdiction consistent with U.S. jurisdictional principles. . . . The opposing party can overcome the initial presumption through demonstrating that a manifest injustice would occur if the U.S. litigation fails to proceed. A defendant meets this burden by demonstrating that waiting for the foreign proceedings to conclude would be fundamentally unfair or through establishing that the foreign forum is a *forum non conveniens*. Parrish, *Duplicative Foreign Litigation*, 78 Geo. Wash. L. Rev. 287 (2010).

What exactly does it mean to say that "the foreign court would have jurisdiction consistent with U.S. jurisdiction principles"? Why is this hypothetical inquiry, completely meaningless from the foreign court's perspective, relevant to whether parallel proceedings should be allowed? Consider the author's defense of this novel approach:

> Tethering the initial presumption to U.S. jurisdictional standards . . . would ensure a level of fairness for litigants. . . . [It also] would be easy to apply, lead to greater predictability, and avoid arbitrary results. . . . Lastly, creating symmetry between jurisdiction and international abstention ensures that U.S. interests are accounted for. Parrish, *Duplicative Foreign Litigation*, 78 Geo. Wash. L. Rev. 287 (2010).

Are any of these values presently relevant to the *lis alibi pendens* standards? Should they be? If so, which approach best achieves these values? This one? *Ingersoll Mining*? *Continental Time*? The ALI proposed statute?

11. *Relevance of first court to render judgment.* In *Ingersoll*, the U.S. trial court refused to stay U.S. proceedings before a Belgian judgment was entered. Then, after a Belgian judgment was made, the U.S. court stayed its action. The U.S. appellate court affirmed. *See also Turner Entertainment Co. v. Degeto Film GmbH*, 25 F.3d 1512, 1521 (11th Cir. 1994) ("While courts regularly permit parallel proceedings in an American court and a foreign court, once a judgment on the merits is reached in one of the cases . . . failure to defer to the judgment would have serious implications for the concerns of international comity. For example, the prospect of 'dueling courts,' conflicting judgments, and attempts to enforce conflicting judgments raise major concerns of international comity."); *Laker Airways*, 731 F.2d at 926 ("Parallel proceedings on the same in personam claim should ordinarily be allowed to proceed simultaneously, at least until a judgment is reached in one which can be pled as *res judicata* in the other.").

Is this an appropriate way to proceed? If the U.S. action had sufficient substance to warrant independent prosecution — and was within the U.S. court's jurisdiction — why should the fortuitous fact that the foreign court's docket moved more quickly be the basis for stopping the U.S. action? Does this not encourage races to judgment? More fundamentally, why grant decisive importance to the relative speed of two different judicial systems? It is often thought that fairer, more accurate results require various procedural safeguards — like discovery, cross-examination, and the like. These procedural devices take time. Why should proceedings that move more quickly, presumptively at the expense of procedural safeguards, be permitted to preempt slower, but presumptively more accurate, U.S. proceedings?

In many jurisdictions, a trial court's decision is subject to de novo review on appeal — often including the possibility of submitting new evidence. Should that affect the availability of a stay after a foreign trial court decision?

12. *Relevance of competing forum's jurisdictional claims.* In deciding whether to grant a *lis pendens* stay, should a court consider the respective "strength" of U.S. and foreign jurisdictional claims? If the foreign court lacks a jurisdictional base that would satisfy the Due Process Clause, should a *lis pendens* stay ever be granted? *See Credicom NV v. Colony Credicom LP*, 2000 WL 282968, at *2 (S.D.N.Y. 2000) (deference inappropriate where foreign court may not properly exercise jurisdiction over case). Conversely, if the U.S. court has only a tenuous jurisdictional base, compared to a substantial foreign basis, would this argue for a *lis pendens* stay? *See Ideal Instruments, Inc. v. Rivard Instruments, Inc.*, 434 F. Supp. 2d 640 (N.D. Iowa 2006).

13. *Relevance of enforceability of any foreign judgment.* What is the relevance of the ultimate enforceability of a foreign judgment in the United States to the decision whether to grant a *lis pendens* stay?

Suppose that it is likely that the foreign proceedings will not produce a judgment that can be enforced in the United States, because U.S. standards for the recognition of foreign judgments will not be satisfied. *See infra* pp. 1146-1155. For example, suppose that the foreign court does not possess personal jurisdiction over the defendant under the Due Process Clause; or that the foreign court is hearing claims that are contrary to U.S. public policy. Would it be appropriate — under either *Continental Time* or *Ingersoll* — to grant a stay in these circumstances? *Cf. See Televisa, SA de CV v. Koch Lorber Films*, 2005 WL 1017804, at *11 (E.D. Pa. 2005) ("Comity, therefore, is not extended to foreign proceedings where doing so would be contrary to the public policy of the United States.").

14. ***Relevance of nationality of parties to grant of*** **lis pendens** ***stay.*** Are the parties' nationalities relevant to the grant of a *lis pendens* stay? *See Goldhammer v. Dunkin' Donuts, Inc.,* 59 F. Supp. 2d 248, 254 (D. Mass. 1999) (consideration of parties' nationalities does not favor either party). Recall that the *forum non conveniens* doctrine, in most contemporary formulations, grants U.S. (but not foreign) plaintiffs a strong presumption in favor of their choice of a U.S. forum. *See supra* pp. 394-406. Should the same presumption shield a U.S. plaintiff from a stay of U.S. proceedings in deference to foreign litigation? *See Evergreen Marine Corp. v. Welgrow Int'l Inc.,* 954 F. Supp. 101 (S.D.N.Y. 1997) (forum choice of foreign plaintiff entitled to "less deference"). Note that the plaintiffs in the U.S. proceedings in both *Ingersoll* and *Continental Time* were U.S. nationals.

15. ***Conditional*** **lis pendens** ***stays.*** As *Continental Time* illustrates, some lower courts have granted "conditional" *lis pendens* stays (paralleling the approach in some *forum non conveniens* cases, *see supra* pp. 449-452). *See Evergreen Marine Corp. v. Welgrow Int'l Inc.,* 954 F. Supp. 101 (S.D.N.Y. 1997) (consent to jurisdiction, waiver of statute of limitations defense, acceptance of foreign judgment); *Dragon Capital Partners LP v. Merrill Lynch Capital Services Inc.,* 949 F. Supp. 1123, 1132 (S.D.N.Y. 1997). Is there anything inappropriate about this? Should a U.S. judge, considering such conditions, communicate with his or her foreign counterpart? Why not?

16. ***Stays and second-order parallel proceedings.*** The cases excerpted above all concern parallel proceedings on the merits of the dispute. Sometimes, however, parallel proceedings instead concern the enforceability of the parties' agreement to resolve their dispute in a third jurisdiction. For example, consider a case where two parties enter into a contractual agreement which contains an arbitration clause providing for arbitration in Australia (for more on arbitration clauses, *see* Chapter 13). Despite the arbitration clause, one party commences litigation in the Australian courts and claims that the arbitration clause is unenforceable. The other party brings a motion to compel arbitration in the United States. How do these dynamics affect the *lis pendens* analysis? Does it affect your answer that the United States is a signatory to several important treaties providing for the enforceability of arbitration agreements? *See Answers in Genesis of Ky., Inc. v. Creation Ministries Int'l, Ltd.,* 556 F.3d 459 (6th Cir. 2009). Does it matter if the underlying dispute concerns the existence, as opposed to the enforceability, of the arbitration agreement? *See Dependable Highway Exp., Inc. v. Navigators Ins. Co.,* 498 F.3d 1059 (9th Cir. 2007).

17. ***Does federal law or state law govern*** **lis pendens** ***stays in federal court?*** What law did *Ingersoll* apply to determine the applicable standards for granting a *lis pendens* stay in favor of foreign proceedings — state or federal? What law did *Continental Time* apply?

Why should federal law govern whether a federal court should defer to foreign legal proceedings? In a diversity case, is this not a substantive matter that, under *Erie,* should be governed by state law? Or does the granting of a stay relate either to the jurisdiction of federal courts, or to the procedures and venue of such courts, and thus fall under federal procedural law? Should *lis pendens* stays in international cases be governed by substantive federal common law? Consider the related issues under the *forum non conveniens* doctrine and forum selection agreements. *See supra* pp. 453-458, 528-544.

18. ***Does federal law or state law govern the grant of a*** **lis pendens** ***stay in state court?*** If *Ingersoll* had arisen in state court, what law would have provided the standards for granting a *lis pendens* stay in deference to foreign proceedings? If federal courts apply federal procedural law, then state courts would be free to apply state procedural law. *See supra* pp. 10-11. Why should standards that are derived from federal abstention cases — like *Colorado River* and *Quackenbush* — have anything to do with how a state court responds to foreign proceedings?

Suppose that a state court refuses *ever* to grant a stay in deference to foreign proceedings. What if *Ingersoll* had arisen in a U.S. state court, which refused to stay its proceedings even after the Belgian trial and appellate proceedings? Is there any rule of federal law that precludes such an approach by state courts? Do the federal interests in foreign relations and foreign commerce, discussed above, provide any basis for a federal common law rule? Note that the enforceability of foreign judgments in U.S. courts has generally been governed by state law. *See infra* pp. 1110-1114.

19. Lis pendens *under proposed Hague Choice of Court Agreements Convention.* The proposed Hague Choice of Court Agreements Convention contains provisions which would bear on the availability of *lis pendens* stays in the particular context of forum selection agreements. Article 5 provides that a contracting state's court specified in a forum selection clause "shall not decline to exercise jurisdiction on the ground that the dispute should be decided in a court of another State." In effect, Article 5 would abrogate the doctrine of *lis pendens* in certain parallel proceedings.

In addition, Article 6 provides that a court of a contracting state other than the one specified in the forum selection clause "shall suspend or dismiss proceedings to which an exclusive choice of court agreement applies" unless the case falls under one of five exceptions. These include (a) where the agreement is null and void; (b) where a party lacked the capacity to conclude the agreement; (c) giving effect to the agreement would lead to a manifest injustice or offend public policy; (d) for exceptional reasons, the agreement cannot reasonably be performed; and (e) the court designated in the forum selection agreement has chosen not to hear the case. In effect, Article 6 would mandate application of the doctrine of *lis pendens* in certain parallel proceedings.

20. Lis pendens *under EU Council Regulation 44/2001.* Regulation 44/2001 sets forth a series of rules governing application of the *lis pendens* doctrine. Where parallel proceedings in two Member States involve "the same cause of actions" and the "same parties," all courts other than the one first seised of the action must stay their proceedings until that first court establishes its jurisdiction. Once it does so, all other courts must decline jurisdiction. Art. 27.

Sometimes, jurisdictional disputes may take up several years. How does this rule protect against the possibility that such jurisdictional disputes will tie up a case (and prevent proceedings in a different forum) for years? To address this possibility, a recent proposal by the European Commission would require the first court to establish its jurisdiction within six months. *See* Proposal for a Regulation on Jurisdiction and the Recognition and Enforcement of Judgments in Civil and Commercial Matters (Dec. 14, 2010). Does this proposal address the problem? Doesn't it force a court to make a rushed judgment on jurisdictional matters, which may be quite complex and fact-intensive?

Regulation 44/2001 contains different rules governing "related" actions (as opposed to ones involving the same parties and cause of action). "Related" proceedings are ones "so closely connected that it is expedient to hear and determine them together to avoid the risk of irreconcilable judgments resulting from separate proceedings." Art. 28(3). With respect to such "related" proceedings, any court other than the one first seised of the action *may* stay its proceedings and, if the proceedings are pending at a court of first instance, *may* decline jurisdiction on a party's motion if the court first seised has jurisdiction and can consolidate the cases. Art. 28(1)-(2).

Is this a wise approach for EU litigation? Would it be wise in domestic U.S. litigation? Should Regulation 44/2001 provide a model for U.S. courts confronting parallel foreign litigation?

21. Lis pendens *under ALI's Proposed Federal Foreign Judgments Recognition Act.* Consider §11 of the ALI's proposed legislation on the recognition of foreign judgments. Preliminarily, why is the ALI proposing provisions concerning *lis pendens* stays in legislation on recognizing foreign judgment? What is the relation between recognition of a foreign judgment and staying U.S. litigation based on parallel foreign proceedings?

What is the standard set forth in §11? Is it sensible? Is it appropriate to grant such decisive importance to the subject of first filing? Note that, under §11(a), a *lis pendens* stay is only available where the foreign court is "likely" to enter a judgment entitled to recognition in the United States. Is this an appropriate standard? Can it practicably be applied at an early stage of litigation? Should U.S. courts apply, as a matter of common law, the principles reflected in the ALI's proposed statute?

Note that, as discussed in greater detail below, the ALI's proposed legislation also would include a reciprocity requirement, conditioning recognition of a foreign judgment on the rendering state's recognition of U.S. judgments. *See infra* pp. 1094-1102. As a consequence, *lis pendens* stays would also be subject to this reciprocity requirement. Is that appropriate?

22. *International Law Association Principles on Declining and Deferring Jurisdiction in International Litigation.* In 2000, the International Law Association Committee on International Civil and Commercial Litigation issued a comprehensive comparative report (authored by Professor Campbell McLachlan) on approaches to declining and referring jurisdiction. International Law Association, Committee on International Civil and Commercial Litigation, *Third Interim Report: Declining and Deferring Jurisdiction in International Litigation* (McLachlan, Ed./Rapporteur 2000). The Report also annexes a series of "Principles" designed to capture an international consensus on issues of *lis pendens, forum non conveniens,* and the like. Article 4 of the Principles provides:

The originating court shall decline jurisdiction in the following exceptional circumstances:

Lis Pendens

Where proceedings involving the same parties and the same subject-matter are brought in the courts of more than one state, any court other than the court first seized shall suspend its proceedings until such time as the jurisdiction of the court first seized is established, and not declined under this Principle, and thereafter it shall terminate its proceedings. The court first seized shall apply Principle 4.3. Should that court refer the matter to a court subsequently seized in accordance with Principle 4.3, the latter court will not be obliged to terminate its proceedings.

Related Actions

Where related actions are pending in the courts of more than one state either court may suspend or terminate its proceedings and refer the matter to the alternative court in accordance with the procedures in Principle 5, provided that the actions can be consolidated in the alternative court.

Other Grounds for Referral

An originating court shall decline jurisdiction and refer the matter to an alternative court where it is satisfied that the alternative court is the manifestly more appropriate forum for the determination of the merits of the matter, taking into account the interests of all the parties, without discrimination on the grounds of nationality. In making this decision, the court shall have regard in particular to the following factors:

a. the location and language of the parties, witnesses and evidence;
b. the balance of advantages of each party afforded by the law, procedure and practice of the respective jurisdictions;
c. the law applicable to the merits;

    d. in case under Principle 4.1, the desirability of avoiding multiplicity of proceedings or conflicting judgments having regard to the manner of resort to the respective court's jurisdiction and the substantive progress of the respective actions;

    e. the enforceability of any resulting judgment;

    f. the efficient operation of the judicial system of the respective jurisdictions;

    g. any terms of referral under Principle 5.3 [concerning conditions regarding submission to jurisdiction and waiver of statute of limitations defense].

Consider how the ILA Principles compare to the ALI's work.

C. Antisuit Injunctions

Lis pendens concerns a U.S. court's decision to stay its own proceedings, while *forum non conveniens* concerns a U.S. court's decision to dismiss proceedings before it. In contrast, it is also possible to take the opposite approach, with courts issuing "antisuit injunctions" — orders forbidding a party from initiating or participating in judicial proceedings in foreign forums.[34] An antisuit injunction is sometimes an attractive option in international disputes: it can be sought from a local, convenient, and perhaps sympathetic tribunal as a means of foreclosing litigation in a potentially inconvenient or hostile foreign forum.

Antisuit injunctions are sought in several situations. First, a party to proceedings in a U.S. forum can seek an injunction against litigation by its adversary of the same dispute in a pending or threatened action in a foreign forum.[35] Second, if related but not identical claims are pursued in two forums, an antisuit injunction may be sought to consolidate litigation in the moving party's preferred forum.[36] Third, a party that fears litigation in a foreign forum can initiate litigation in a U.S. court, seeking a declaration of nonliability on the anticipated claims, together with an antisuit injunction against parallel foreign litigation.[37] Fourth, the prevailing party in *completed* U.S. litigation can seek an injunction preventing the unsuccessful party from relitigating the parties' dispute in a foreign forum.[38] Finally, a court may issue a "counter-injunction," or "anti-antisuit injunction," designed to foreclose a party from obtaining an antisuit injunction in a foreign forum against litigation in the issuing court.[39]

---

34. Antisuit injunctions are one example of the power of courts to order persons subject to their personal jurisdiction to perform (or not to perform) specified acts outside of the forum. *E.g., United States v. First Nat'l City Bank*, 379 U.S. 378 (1965); *Restatement (Second) Conflict of Laws* §53 (1971); Messner, *The Jurisdiction of a Court of Equity Over Persons to Compel the Doing of Acts Outside the Territorial Limits of the State*, 14 Minn. L. Rev. 494 (1930). *See also infra* pp. 1012-1024 (extraterritorial discovery orders).

35. *E.g., Quaak v. Klynveld Peat Marwick Goerdeler Bedrijfsrevisoren*, 361 F.3d 11, 16 (1st Cir. 2004); *Stonington Partners, Inc. v. Lernout & Hauspie Speech Products NV*, 310 F.3d 118, 124 (3d Cir. 2002); *In re Rationis Enterprises, Inc. of Panama*, 261 F.3d 264, 266 (2d Cir. 2001); *Kaepa, Inc. v. Achilles Corp.*, 76 F.3d 624, 626 (5th Cir. 1996); *Compagnie des Bauxites de Guinee v. Insurance Co. of N. Am.*, 651 F.2d 877 (3d Cir. 1981), *aff'd on other grounds*, 456 U.S. 644 (1982); *Timberland Co. v. Sanchez*, 129 F.R.D. 382 (D.D.C. 1990); *Cargill, Inc. v. Hartford Accident & Indem. Co.*, 531 F. Supp. 710 (D. Minn. 1982); *Medtronic Inc. v. Catalyst Research Corp.*, 518 F. Supp. 946 (D. Minn. 1981), *aff'd*, 664 F.2d 660 (8th Cir. 1981); *Western Elec. Co. v. Milgo Elec. Corp.*, 450 F. Supp. 835 (S.D. Fla. 1978).

36. *E.g., Seattle Totems Hockey Club v. National Hockey League*, 652 F.2d 852 (9th Cir. 1981).

37. *E.g., Dow Jones & Co. v. Harrods, Ltd.*, 237 F. Supp. 2d 394 (S.D.N.Y. 2002), *aff'd*, 346 F.3d 357 (2d Cir. 2003).

38. *E.g., Princess Lida of Thurn & Taxis v. Thompson*, 305 U.S. 456 (1939); *Wood v. Santa Barbara Chamber of Commerce*, 705 F.2d 1515 (9th Cir. 1983); *Scott v. Hunt Oil Co.*, 398 F.2d 810 (5th Cir. 1968).

39. *E.g., Mutual Services Ins. Co. v. Frit Industries, Inc.*, 358 F.3d 1312, 1324 (11th Cir. 2004); *Karaha Bodas Co., LLC v. Perusahaan Pertambangan Minyak Dan Gas Bumi Negara*, 335 F.3d 357, 362 (5th Cir. 2003); *Teck Metals, Ltd. v. Certain Underwriters at Lloyd's London*, 2009 WL 4716307 (E.D. Wash. Dec. 8, 2009); *Owens-Illinois, Inc. v. Webb*, 809 S.W.2d 899 (Tex. App. 1991); *Laker Airways v. Sabena*, 731 F.2d 909 (D.C. Cir. 1984); *James v. Grand Trunk W. R.R.*, 152 N.E.2d 858 (Ill. 1958).

1.   Standards Governing Foreign Antisuit Injunctions in U.S. Courts

There is no statutory provision in federal law (nor in most state codes) granting courts the power to issue antisuit injunctions. Nevertheless, U.S. courts have long asserted the power to issue antisuit injunctions, regarding such orders as a corollary of a court's general equitable power over parties subject to its jurisdiction.[40] Most federal courts also appear to agree (albeit without analysis) that the standards governing the issuance of an antisuit injunction in federal court are governed by federal law.[41]

There is, however, disagreement over the standards that should govern a U.S. court's grant of an antisuit injunction. Most U.S. courts express caution about the issuance of such orders.[42] This caution arises from the fact that, while antisuit injunctions are not issued directly against foreign tribunals, most courts acknowledge that such orders "effectively restrict the foreign court's ability to exercise its jurisdiction."[43]

Lower courts are divided over the standards that govern the issuance of antisuit injunctions.[44] A number of circuits have adopted extremely stringent standards (only rarely permitting an antisuit injunction), while others have permitted more liberal antisuit orders. These divergent results reflect fundamentally different views regarding the role of international comity in U.S. litigation.

a.   Decisions Applying Stringent Limits on Issuance of Foreign Antisuit Injunctions. The District of Columbia, Third, Sixth, and Eighth Circuits have held that foreign antisuit injunctions should virtually never be issued.[45] The Second Circuit, once a strong proponent of this view, has more recently shown a greater willingness to approve the issuance of such injunctions.[46] The First Circuit has adopted a slightly modified version of this approach.[47] The Eleventh Circuit seems generally supportive of this conservative

---

40. *See* Messner, *The Jurisdiction of a Court of Equity Over Persons to Compel the Doing of Acts Outside the Territorial Limits of the State*, 14 Minn. L. Rev. 494, 495-496 (1930); *Restatement (Second) Conflict of Laws* §84 comment h (1971) ("On occasion, a court may enjoin a person over whom it has personal jurisdiction from bringing suit in what the court deems to be an inappropriate forum."); *Western Elec. Co. v. Milgo Elec. Corp.*, 450 F. Supp. 835, 837 (S.D. Fla. 1978) (a U.S. court "has the power to enjoin a party over whom it has personal jurisdiction from pursuing litigation before a foreign tribunal").

41. *Gau Shan Co. v. Bankers Trust Co.*, 956 F.2d 1349 (6th Cir. 1992); *Sea Containers Ltd. v. Stena AB*, 890 F.2d 1205, 1214 (D.C. Cir. 1989); *China Trade & Dev. Corp. v. MV Choong Yong*, 837 F.2d 33 (2d Cir. 1987); *Laker Airways Ltd. v. Sabena*, 731 F.2d 909 (D.C. Cir. 1984).

42. *See Laker Airways Ltd. v. Sabena*, 731 F.2d 909, 927 (D.C. Cir. 1984) (antisuit injunctions are "rarely issued" and "only in the most compelling circumstances"); *Seattle Totems Hockey Club v. National Hockey League*, 652 F.2d 852, 855 (9th Cir. 1981) (antisuit injunctions should be "used sparingly"); *Philip v. Macri*, 261 F.2d 945, 947 (9th Cir. 1958) (antisuit injunctions "should be used sparingly . . . and 'is not to be lightly exercised' "); *Restatement (Second) Conflict of Laws* §84 comment h (1971) ("injunctions of this sort are only granted in extreme circumstances").

43. *Laker Airways Ltd. v. Sabena*, 731 F.2d 909, 927 (D.C. Cir. 1984). *See Donovan v. Dallas*, 377 U.S. 408, 413 (1964); *Peck v. Jenness*, 48 U.S. 612, 625 (1849); *China Trade and Dev. Corp. v. MV Choong Yong*, 837 F.2d 33, 35-36 (2d Cir. 1987).

44. *Goss Int'l Corp. v. Man Roland Druckmaschinen Aktiengesellschaft*, 491 F.3d 355 (8th Cir. 2007) (summarizing split).

45. *Goss Int'l Corp. v. Man Roland Druckmaschinen Aktiengesellschaft*, 491 F.3d 355 (8th Cir. 2007); *Answers in Genesis of Kentucky, Inc. v. Creation Ministries Int'l, Ltd.*, 556 F.3d 459, 471 (6th Cir. 2009); *LAIF X SPRL v. Axtel, SA de CV*, 390 F.3d 194, 199 (2d Cir. 2004); *Stonington Partners, Inc. v. Lernout & Hauspie Speech Products NV*, 310 F.3d 118, 127 (3d Cir. 2002); *General Elec. Co. v. Deutz AG*, 270 F.3d 144, 161 (3d Cir. 2001); *In re Rationis Enterprises, Inc. of Panama*, 261 F.3d 264, 271 (2d Cir. 2001); *Gau Shan Co. v. Bankers Trust Co.*, 956 F.2d 1349 (6th Cir. 1992); *Sea Containers Ltd. v. Stena AB*, 890 F.2d 1205, 1214 (D.C. Cir. 1989); *Laker Airways Ltd. v. Sabena*, 731 F.2d 909 (D.C. Cir. 1984).

46. *Paramedics Electromedicina Comercial, Ltda v. GE Medical Systems Information Technologies, Inc.*, 369 F.3d 645, 653 (2d Cir. 2004); *China Trade & Dev. Corp. v. MV Choong Yong*, 837 F.2d 33 (2d Cir. 1987).

47. *Quaak v. Klynveld Peat Marwick Goerdeler Bedrijfsrevisoren*, 361 F.3d 11, 17-19 (1st Cir. 2004).

approach but has not expressly adopted it.[48] All of these courts agree that "duplication of parties and issues alone is not sufficient to justify issuance of an antisuit injunction."[49] Rather, a foreign antisuit injunction generally may be issued only to: (a) protect a court's own legitimate jurisdiction (typically by issuing an anti-antisuit injunction); or (b) prevent "litigants' evasion of the forum's important public policies."[50]

The courts adopting this position have relied on notions of international comity and precedent in purely domestic contexts. The leading authority is *Laker Airways,* which placed substantial weight on comity.[51] Other courts have agreed: "Comity dictates that foreign antisuit injunctions be issued sparingly and only in the rarest of cases."[52] *Laker Airways* and other lower courts have also relied upon domestic U.S. precedent, invoking the standards applicable to the issuance by federal courts of injunctions against *state* court proceedings. In particular, they have cited *Colorado River* for the proposition that parallel proceedings in state and federal courts should generally be permitted to proceed.[53]

b. Decisions Applying More Flexible Standards to Issuance of Foreign Antisuit Injunctions. Other lower courts have articulated less demanding standards governing foreign antisuit injunctions. Both the Fifth and Ninth Circuits appear to "hold that a duplication of the parties and issues, alone, is generally sufficient to justify the issuance" of an antisuit injunction.[54] The Seventh Circuit also appears more readily to permit issuance of antisuit injunctions in international cases.[55] In one lower court's statement of this standard, an antisuit "injunction is in order when adjudication of the same issue in two separate actions will result in unnecessary delay, inconvenience, and expense to the parties and witnesses, and where separate adjudications could result in inconsistent rulings or a race to judgment."[56]

2. Selected Materials on Foreign Antisuit Injunctions in U.S. Courts

The excerpts from *China Trade & Development Corp. v. MV Choong Yong* and from the opinions in *Kaepa, Inc. v. Achilles Corp.* illustrate the differing approaches of U.S. courts to issuing antisuit injunctions in international cases. The *China Trade* majority, as well as Judge Garza's dissent in *Kaepa,* adopt a restrictive standard for antisuit injunctions, while the majority in *Kaepa* and the dissenting opinion in *China Trade* apply one of the more flexible standards for issuing such injunctions. As you read these excerpts, consider the rationales underpinning each standard and the results that each is likely to produce.

---

48. *Canon Latin America, Inc. v. Lantech (CR), S.A.,* 508 F.3d 597 (11th Cir. 2007).
49. *Laker Airways,* 731 F.2d at 928-929.
50. *Laker Airways,* 731 F.2d at 927-931; *Gau Shan Co. v. Bankers Trust Co.,* 956 F.2d 1349 (6th Cir. 1992).
51. *Laker Airways,* 731 F.2d at 926-929.
52. *Gau Shan Co. v. Banker Trust Co.,* 956 F.2d 1349, 1354 (6th Cir. 1992).
53. *Laker Airways,* 731 F.2d at 926 (citing *Colorado River* and *Princess Lida of Thurn & Taxis v. Thompson,* 305 U.S. 456, 466 (1939)); *China Trade & Dev. Corp. v. MV Choong Yong,* 837 F.2d 33 (2d Cir. 1987) (citing *Colorado River* and *Donovan v. City of Dallas,* 377 U.S. 408, 412 (1964)). *See also Sea Containers Ltd. v. Stena AB,* 890 F.2d 1205, 1213 (D.C. Cir. 1989) (refusing to follow, in international case, the standards applicable to antisuit injunctions between "two Federal courts [that] entertained jurisdiction over claims arising out of essentially the same facts": "When a second action is brought in a foreign court, however, the possible waste of resources may be outweighed by another concern, international comity.").
54. *Karaha Bodas Co., LLC v. Perusahaan Pertambangan Minyak Dan Gas Bumi Negara,* 335 F.3d 357, 366 (5th Cir. 2003); *Kaepa, Inc. v. Achilles Corp.,* 76 F.3d 624, 627 (5th Cir. 1996); *Seattle Totems Hockey Club v. National Hockey League,* 652 F.2d 852, 856 (9th Cir. 1981).
55. *Allendale Mutual Ins. Co. v. Bull Data Systems, Inc.,* 10 F.3d 425 (7th Cir. 1993) (leaning toward Ninth Circuit's "laxer" test; also requiring "some indication that the issuance of an injunction really would throw a monkey wrench, however small, into the foreign relations of the United States"); *Philips Medical Sys. Int'l BV v. Bruetman,* 8 F.3d 600 (7th Cir. 1993).
56. *Cargill, Inc. v. Hartford Accident & Indemnity Co.,* 531 F. Supp. 710, 715 (D. Minn. 1982).

CHINA TRADE & DEVELOPMENT CORP. v. MV CHOONG YONG
837 F.2d 33 (2d Cir. 1987)

GEORGE C. PRATT, CIRCUIT JUDGE. Following oral argument this court reversed an order of the U.S. District Court for the Southern District of New York and vacated the injunction which had permanently enjoined Ssangyong Shipping Co., Ltd. ("Ssangyong") from proceeding in the courts of Korea with its action against China Trade & Development Corp., Chung Hua Trade & Development Corp. and Soybean Importers Joint Committee of the Republic of China (collectively, "China Trade").

The District Court had granted the injunction because it found that (1) the parties in the Korean action are the same as the parties in this action; (2) the issue of liability raised by Ssangyong in the Korean court is the same as the issue of liability raised here; (3) the Korean litigation would be vexatious to the plaintiffs in the United States action, which was commenced first; and (4) allowing the Korean litigation to proceed would result in a race to judgment. Because no important policy of the forum would be frustrated by allowing the Korean action to proceed, and because the Korean action poses no threat to the jurisdiction of the District Court, we conclude that the interests of comity are not overbalanced by equitable factors favoring an injunction, and we hold that the district court abused its discretion when it enjoined Ssangyong, a Korean corporation, from proceeding in the courts of Korea. . . .

In 1984 China Trade sought to import 25,000 metric tons of soybeans into the Republic of China from the United States. Ssangyong, a Republic of Korea corporation, agreed to transport the soybeans on its ship the MV CHOONG YONG. The vessel ran aground, however, and as China Trade contends, the soybeans, contaminated by seawater, became virtually valueless. The litigation leading to this appeal began in 1985 when attorneys for China Trade attached the MV BOO YONG, another vessel owned by Ssangyong, which was then located in . . . California. To release the vessel, the parties agreed that China Trade would lift the attachment and discontinue the California action and, in exchange, Ssangyong would provide security in the amount of $1,800,000, the approximate value of the attached vessel, and would appear in an action to be commenced by China Trade in the Southern District of New York and waive any right to dismissal of the new action on the ground of forum non conveniens.

China Trade then commenced this action in the Southern District seeking $7,500,000 in damages from Ssangyong for failure to deliver the soybeans. Both parties proceeded to prepare the case for trial through extensive discovery that has included both depositions and document production that required trips to Korea and to the Republic of China. Trial was scheduled to begin in September 1987. On April 22, 1987, while discovery was still progressing, Ssangyong's Korean attorneys filed a pleading in the District Court of Pusan, commencing an action, similar to our declaratory judgment action, which seeks confirmation that Ssangyong is not liable for China Trade's loss. Nearly two months later Ssangyong's New York counsel forwarded a copy of this pleading to counsel for China Trade. Immediately, and before taking any action in the district court of Pusan, China Trade moved by order to show cause in this action for an injunction against further prosecution of the Korean action.

To determine whether to enjoin the foreign litigation, the district court employed a test that has been adopted by some judges in the Southern District. In *American Home Assurance Corp. v. Insurance Corp. of Ireland, Ltd.,* 603 F. Supp. 636, 643 (S.D.N.Y. 1984), the court articulated two threshold requirements for such an injunction: (1) the parties must be the same in both matters, and (2) resolution of the case before the enjoining court must be dispositive of the action to be enjoined.

When these threshold requirements are met, five factors are suggested in determining whether the forgoing action should be enjoined: (1) frustration of a policy in the enjoining forum; (2) the foreign action would be vexatious; (3) a threat to the issuing court's in rem or quasi in rem jurisdiction; (4) the proceedings in the other forum prejudice other equitable considerations; or (5) adjudication of the same issues in separate actions would result in delay, inconvenience, expense, inconsistency, or a race to judgment. *American Home Assurance*, 603 F. Supp. at 643.

Judge Motley found after a hearing that the two threshold requirements were met, since in both actions the parties and the issues of liability are the same. She then considered the additional five factors and found that the Korean litigation in this case would (1) be vexatious to the plaintiffs and (2) result in expense and a race to judgment. Considering these findings sufficient, the District Court permanently enjoined Ssangyong's prosecution of the Korean action. This appeal followed. . . .

The power of federal courts to enjoin foreign suits by persons subject to their jurisdiction is well-established. The fact that the injunction operates only against the parties, and not directly against the foreign court, does not eliminate the need for due regard to principles of international comity, *Peck v. Jenness*, 48 U.S. 612, 625 (1849), because such an order effectively restricts the jurisdiction of the court of a foreign sovereign. Therefore, an anti-foreign-suit injunction should be "used sparingly," and should be granted "only with care and great restraint." *Canadian Filters (Harwich) v. Lear-Siegler*, 412 F.2d 577, 578 (1st Cir. 1969).

Concurrent jurisdiction in two courts does not necessarily result in a conflict. When two sovereigns have concurrent in personam jurisdiction one court will ordinarily not interfere with or try to restrain proceedings before the other. "[P]arallel proceedings on the same in personam claim should ordinarily be allowed to proceed simultaneously, at least until a judgment is reached in one which can be pled as res judicata in the other," *Laker*, 731 F.2d at 926-27, citing *Colorado River*. . . . Since parallel proceedings are ordinarily tolerable, the initiation before a foreign court of a suit concerning the same parties and issues as a suit already pending in a U.S. court does not, without more, justify enjoining a party from proceeding in the foreign forum.

In general, we agree with the approach taken by Judge Motley. She began by inquiring (1) whether the parties to both suits are the same and (2) whether resolution of the case before the enjoining court would be dispositive of the enjoined action. She apparently found that both of these prerequisites were met here. While there is some question as to whether the Korean courts would recognize a judgment of the Southern District, it is not necessary to determine that question of Korean law because the injunction is deficient for another reason. Judge Motley found the necessary additional justification for this injunction in two of the five factors suggested in *American Home Assurance*: "vexatiousness" of the parallel proceeding to China Trade and a "race to judgment" causing additional expense. However, since these factors are likely to be present whenever parallel actions are proceeding concurrently, an anti-suit injunction grounded on these additional factors alone would tend to undermine the policy that allows parallel proceedings to continue and disfavors anti-suit injunctions. Having due regard to the interest of comity, we think that in the circumstances of this case two of the other factors suggested in *American Home Assurance* take on much greater significance in determining whether Ssangyong should be enjoined from proceeding in its Korean action: (a) whether the foreign action threatens the jurisdiction of the enjoining forum, and (b) whether strong public policies of the enjoining forum are threatened by the foreign action.

A long-standing exception to the usual rule tolerating concurrent proceedings has been recognized for proceedings in rem or quasi in rem, because of the threat a second action poses to the first court's basis for jurisdiction. When a proceeding is in rem, and res judicata alone will not protect the jurisdiction of the first court, an anti-suit injunction may be appropriate. Even in personam proceedings, if a foreign court is not merely proceeding in parallel but is attempting to carve out exclusive jurisdiction over the action, an injunction may also be necessary to protect the enjoining court's jurisdiction. In the *Laker* litigation, for example, when the English Court of Appeal enjoined Laker's litigation of its claims against British defendants in a U.S. court under U.S. law, the U.S. district court, in order to protect its own jurisdiction, enjoined other defendants in the *Laker* action from seeking similar injunctions from the English Court of Appeal. *Laker,* 731 F.2d at 917-21. In the present case, however, there does not appear to be any threat to the district court's jurisdiction. While the Korean court may determine the same liability issue as that before the Southern District, the Korean court has not attempted to enjoin the proceedings in New York. Neither the Korean court nor Ssangyong has sought to prevent the Southern District from exercising its jurisdiction over this case.

An anti-suit injunction may also be appropriate when a party seeks to evade important policies of the forum by litigating before a foreign court. While an injunction may be appropriate when a party attempts to evade compliance with a statute of the forum that effectuates important public policies, an injunction is not appropriate merely to prevent a party from seeking "slight advantages in the substantive or procedural law to be applied in a foreign court," *Laker,* 731 F.2d at 931, n.73.

The possibility that a U.S. judgment might be unenforceable in Korea is no more than speculation about the race to judgment that may ensue whenever courts have concurrent jurisdiction. Moreover, we cannot determine at this point whether a judgment of the U.S. court in an amount exceeding the $1.8 million bond would be enforceable in Korea even if the Korean action were now enjoined. Should plaintiffs prevail, enforcement of any excess amount against Ssangyong in Korea may well require relitigation in the Korean courts of the issue of liability. In these circumstances, we are not persuaded that Ssangyong, the party seeking to litigate in the foreign tribunal, is attempting to evade any important policy of this forum. . . .

BRIGHT, SENIOR CIRCUIT JUDGE, dissenting. I dissent. . . . [The District Court found that:]

[t]he defendant agreed to appear in this action in the Southern District of New York and post security in the amount of $1,800,000 in return for the release of the MV BOO YONG. Discovery for the case proceeded and was completed. Trial was scheduled by this court, without objection, for September 21, 1987. Ssangyong, however, some 2 1/2 years after [the accident and 1 1/2 years after] this action was begun, then proceeded to file a suit in Pusan Court of the Republic of Korea, naming the same parties to the action, as well as the same issues. Plaintiffs herein move to enjoin the defendant from proceeding with that action. The court finds as facts that the parties to the two actions are the same and that resolution of the action before this court would be dispositive of the Korean action. The court also finds that the Korean action would be vexatious to plaintiffs, and that the Korean action could potentially frustrate the proceedings before this court.

Those facts receive ample support from the record, and I accept them as true for the purposes of this appeal. . . . It seems to me that in this day of exceedingly high costs of litigation, where no comity principles between nations are at stake in resolving a piece of commercial litigation, courts have an affirmative duty to prevent a litigant from hopping halfway around the world to a foreign court as a means of confusing, obfuscating and complicating litigation already pending for trial in a court in this country. This is especially true when that court has been processing the case for almost two years and has acquired personal jurisdiction over the parties and subject matter jurisdiction over the claim.

KAEPA, INC. v. ACHILLES CORP.
76 F.3d 624 (5th Cir. 1996)

WIENER, CIRCUIT JUDGE. This case arises out of a contractual dispute between two sophisticated, private corporations: Kaepa, an American company which manufactures athletic shoes; and Achilles, a Japanese business enterprise with annual sales that approximate one billion dollars. In April 1993, the two companies entered into a distributorship agreement whereby Achilles obtained exclusive rights to market Kaepa's footwear in Japan. The distributorship agreement expressly provided that Texas law and the English language would govern its interpretation, that it would be enforceable in San Antonio, Texas, and that Achilles consented to the jurisdiction of the Texas courts.[57]

Kaepa grew increasingly dissatisfied with Achilles' performance under the contract. Accordingly, in July of 1994, Kaepa filed suit in Texas state court, alleging (1) fraud and negligent misrepresentation by Achilles to induce Kaepa to enter into the distributorship agreement, and (2) breach of contract by Achilles. Thereafter, Achilles removed the action to federal district court, and the parties began a laborious discovery process which to date has resulted in the production of tens of thousands of documents. In February 1995, after appearing in the Texas action, removing the case to federal court, and engaging in comprehensive discovery, Achilles brought its own action in Japan, alleging mirror-image claims: (1) fraud by Kaepa to induce Achilles to enter into the distributorship agreement, and (2) breach of contract by Kaepa.

Back in Texas, Kaepa promptly filed a motion asking the district court to enjoin Achilles from prosecuting its suit in Japan (motion for an antisuit injunction). Achilles in turn moved to dismiss the federal court action on the ground of *forum non conveniens*. The district court denied Achilles' motion to dismiss and granted Kaepa's motion to enjoin, ordering Achilles to refrain from litigating the Japanese action and to file all of its counterclaims with the district court. Achilles timely appealed the grant of the antisuit injunction. . . .

It is well settled . . . that the federal courts have the power to enjoin persons subject to their jurisdiction from prosecuting foreign suits. The circuits differ, however, on the proper legal standard to employ when determining whether that injunctive power should be exercised. [In prior decisions], we concluded that a district court does not abuse its discretion by issuing an antisuit injunction when it has determined "that allowing simultaneous prosecution of the same action in a foreign forum thousands of miles away would result in 'inequitable hardship' and 'tend to frustrate and delay the speedy and efficient determination of the cause.'" Achilles urges us to give greater deference to comity and apply [a] more restrictive standard. We note preliminarily that, even though the standard espoused in [our prior decisions] focuses on the potentially vexatious nature of foreign litigation, it by no means excludes the consideration of principles of comity. We decline,

---

57. The applicable language of the agreement reads: "This Agreement shall be governed by the laws of the State of Texas, U.S.A., and shall be enforceable in San Antonio, Texas. The English version of this Agreement and the English language shall govern the interpretation and meaning of all words and phrases used herein. Distributor [Achilles] consents to jurisdiction in the State of Texas, U.S.A."

however, to require a district court to genuflect before a vague and omnipotent notion of comity every time that it must decide whether to enjoin a foreign action.

In the instant case, for example, it simply cannot be said that the grant of the antisuit injunction actually threatens relations between the United States and Japan. First, no public international issue is implicated by the case: Achilles is a private party engaged in a contractual dispute with another private party. Second, the dispute has been long and firmly ensconced within the confines of the United States judicial system: Achilles consented to jurisdiction in Texas; stipulated that Texas law and the English language would govern any dispute; appeared in an action brought in Texas; removed that action to a federal court in Texas; engaged in extensive discovery pursuant to the directives of the federal court; and only then, with the federal action moving steadily toward trial, brought identical claims in Japan. Under these circumstances, we cannot conclude that the district court's grant of an antisuit injunction in any way trampled on notions of comity.

On the contrary, the facts detailed above strongly support the conclusion that the prosecution of the Japanese action would entail "an absurd duplication of effort" and would result in unwarranted inconvenience, expense, and vexation. Achilles's belated ploy of filing as putative plaintiff in Japan the very same claims against Kaepa that Kaepa had filed as plaintiff against Achilles smacks of cynicism, harassment, and delay. Accordingly, we hold that the district court did not abuse its discretion by granting Kaepa's motion for an antisuit injunction.

GARZA, CIRCUIT JUDGE, dissenting. International comity represents a principle of paramount importance in our world of ever increasing economic interdependence. Admitting that "comity" may be a somewhat elusive concept does not mean that we can blithely ignore its cautionary dictate. Unless we proceed in each instance with respect for the independent jurisdiction of a sovereign nation's courts, we risk provoking retaliation in turn, with detrimental consequences that may reverberate far beyond the particular dispute and its private litigants. Amicable relations among sovereign nations and their judicial systems depend on our recognition, as federal courts, that we share the international arena with co-equal judicial bodies, and that we therefore act to deprive a foreign court of jurisdiction only in the most extreme circumstances. . . .

I do not quarrel with the well established principle, relied on by the majority, that our courts have the power to control the conduct of persons subject to their jurisdiction, even to the extent of enjoining them from prosecuting in a foreign jurisdiction. I write to emphasize, however, that under concurrent jurisdiction, "parallel proceedings on the same in personam claim should ordinarily be allowed to proceed simultaneously, at least until a judgment is reached in one which can be pled as *res judicata* in the other." *Laker Airways.* . . . In the ordinary case, both forums should be free to proceed to a judgment, unhindered by the concurrent exercise of jurisdiction in another court.

The issuance of an antisuit injunction runs directly counter to this principle of tolerating parallel proceedings. An antisuit injunction "conveys the message . . . that the issuing court has so little confidence in the foreign court's ability to adjudicate a given dispute fairly and efficiently that it is unwilling even to allow the possibility." *Gau Shan Co. v. Bankers Trust Co.*, 956 F.2d 1349, 1355 (6th Cir. 1992). It makes no difference that in formal terms the injunction is only addressed to the parties. The antisuit injunction operates to restrict the foreign court's ability to exercise its jurisdiction as effectively as if it were addressed to the foreign court itself. Enjoining the parties from litigating in a foreign court will necessarily compromise the principles of comity, and may lead to undesirable consequences. For example, the foreign court may react by issuing a similar injunction, thereby preventing any party from obtaining a remedy. The foreign court may also be less inclined to enforce a judgment by our courts. The refusal to enforce a foreign judgment, however, is less offensive than acting to prevent the foreign court from hearing the matter in the first place.

Antisuit injunctions intended to carve out exclusive jurisdiction may also have unintended, widespread effects on international commerce. . . . To operate effectively and efficiently, international markets require a degree of predictability which can only be harmed by antisuit injunctions and the resulting breakdown of cooperation and reciprocity between courts of different nations. The attempt to exercise exclusive jurisdiction over international economic affairs is essentially an intrusion into the realm of international economic policy that should appropriately be left to our legislature and the treaty making process. . . .

The majority appears to require an affirmative showing that the granting of an antisuit injunction in this case would immediately and concretely affect adversely the relations between the United States and Japan. . . . Insisting on evidence of immediate and concrete harm, in the form of a diplomatic protest or otherwise, is both unrealistic and shortsighted. As with most transnational relations, the potential harm to international comity caused by the issuance of a specific antisuit injunction will be as difficult to predict, as it will be to remedy. It is precisely this troubling uncertainty, and the recognition that our courts are ill equipped to weigh these types of international policy considerations, that cautions us to make the respectful deference underlying international comity the rule rather than the exception.

In holding that the district court in this case did not abuse its discretion by enjoining Achilles, a Japanese corporation, from proceeding with its lawsuit filed in the sovereign nation of Japan, the majority appears to rely primarily on the duplicative nature of the Japanese suit and the resulting "unwarranted inconvenience, expense, and vexation." The inconvenience, expense and vexation, however, are factors likely to be present whenever there is an exercise of concurrent jurisdiction by a foreign court. The majority's standard can be understood to hold, therefore, that "a duplication of the parties and issues, alone, is sufficient to justify a foreign antisuit injunction." *Gau Shan Co.*, 956 F.2d at 1353. Under this standard, concurrent jurisdiction involving a foreign tribunal will rarely, if ever, withstand the request for an antisuit injunction.

By focusing on the potential hardship to Kaepa of having to litigate in two forums, the majority applies an analysis that is more appropriately brought to bear in the context of a motion to dismiss for *forum non conveniens*. Considerations that are appropriate in deciding whether to decline jurisdiction are not as persuasive when deciding whether to deprive another court of jurisdiction. "The policies of avoiding hardships to the parties and promoting the economies of consolidated litigation 'do not outweigh the important principles of comity that compel deference and mutual respect for concurrent foreign proceedings. Thus, the better rule is that duplication of parties and issues alone is not sufficient to justify issuance of an antisuit injunction.'" *Gau Shan Co.*, 956 F.2d at 1355 (quoting *Laker Airways*, 731 F.2d at 928). A dismissal on grounds of *forum non conveniens* by either court in this case would satisfy the majority's concern with avoiding hardship to the parties, without harming the interests of international comity. The district court is not in a position, however, to make the *forum non conveniens* determination on behalf of the Japanese court. In light of the important interests of international comity, the decision by a United States court to deprive a foreign court of jurisdiction must be supported by far weightier factors than would otherwise justify that court's decision to decline its own jurisdiction on *forum non conveniens* grounds.

Accordingly, I believe that the standard followed by the Second, Sixth, and D.C. Circuits more satisfactorily respects the principle of concurrent jurisdiction and safeguards the important interests of international comity. Under this stricter standard, a district court should look to only two factors in determining whether to issue an antisuit injunction: (1) whether the foreign action threatens the jurisdiction of the district court; and (2) whether the foreign action was an attempt to evade important public policies of the district court. Neither of these factors are present in this case.

Notes *on* China Trade *and* Kaepa

1. *Power to issue antisuit injunctions.* Neither *Kaepa* nor *China Trade* betrayed any reservations about a U.S. court's *power* to enjoin a party from proceeding with an action in a foreign court: a U.S. court "has the power to enjoin a party over whom it has personal jurisdiction from pursuing litigation before a foreign tribunal." *Western Elec. Co. v. Milgo Elec. Corp.*, 450 F. Supp. 835, 837 (S.D. Fla. 1978); *see also Quaak v. Klynveld Peat Marwick Goerdeler Bedrijfsrevisoren*, 361 F.3d 11, 16 (1st Cir. 2004) (asserting power to issue antisuit injunction).

Where does the power of a U.S. court to issue an antisuit injunction derive from? One of the few commentators to consider the issue has said: "[t]he theory upon which the courts act . . . is that they have authority to control the persons within the territorial limits of the state, and, having jurisdiction of the parties, can render a decree that the parties are bound to respect and obey, even beyond the territorial limits of the state." Messner, *The Jurisdiction of a Court of Equity Over Persons to Compel the Doing of Acts Outside the Territorial Limits of the State*, 14 Minn. L. Rev. 494, 495-496 (1930). Is this persuasive? Is it self-evident that a U.S. court has the authority to order a foreign party, on foreign territory, to refrain from availing itself of avenues of justice provided by a foreign state?

One court has opined that the power to issue antisuit injunctions derives from the inherent equitable power of courts to grant injunctions in suits over which they have jurisdiction. *See Karaha Bodas Co., LLC v. Perusahaan Pertambangan Minyak Dan Gas Bumi Negara*, 335 F.3d 357, 364-365 (5th Cir. 2003). Is this any more persuasive?

What about the All Writs Act? It provides: "The Supreme Court and all courts established by Act of Congress may issue all writs necessary or appropriate in aid of their respective jurisdictions and agreeable to the usages and principles of law." 28 U.S.C. §1651. If it were relevant, what sorts of antisuit injunctions would be permitted under §1651?

Under general principles of remedies, a U.S. court will award equitable relief only where a damages remedy (such as money) is not adequate and where, absent equitable relief, a party will suffer irreparable injury (unless, of course, the parties contractually arrange for equitable relief in advance). *E.g., Morales v. Trans World Airlines, Inc.*, 504 U.S. 374, 381 (1992). In light of this general principle of U.S. remedies law, is an antisuit injunction a necessary remedy to prevent parallel litigation or litigation that undermines a court's jurisdiction? Why wouldn't a damages remedy suffice? Wouldn't it be relatively easy for a court to calculate the costs incurred by a party through parallel litigation (*i.e.,* attorneys' fees, costs, travel, etc.)? *See* Tan, *Damages for Breach of Forum Selection Clauses, Principled Remedies and Control of International Civil Litigation*, 40 Tex. Int'l L.J. 623 (2005); Tan & Yeo, *Breaking Promises to Litigate in a Particular Forum: Are Damages an Appropriate Remedy?*, 2003 Lloyd's Mar. and Com. L.Q. 435.

2. **China Trade** — *stringent standards for issuing antisuit injunctions.* Consider the standards for the issuance of prejudgment antisuit injunctions adopted by the Second Circuit in *China Trade* (as well as by Judge Garza's dissent in *Kaepa*) and the majority of circuits. These courts have concluded that injunctions directed merely against duplicative,

"vexatious" litigation are generally inconsistent with the rule permitting parallel proceedings in concurrent *in personam* actions: "Since parallel proceedings are ordinarily tolerable, the initiation before a foreign court of a suit concerning the same parties and issues as a suit already pending in a U.S. court does not, without more, justify enjoining a party from proceeding in the foreign forum." Under this view, antisuit injunctions are only appropriate to: (a) protect the issuing court's jurisdiction, or (b) prevent evasion of the forum's public policies. *See also Laker Airways,* 731 F.2d 909, for other lower court decisions narrowly limiting antisuit injunctions in international cases.

The stringent standard adopted by *China Trade* makes clear that the exceptions from the general rule against antisuit injunctions are narrow and do not permit injunctions to halt duplicative, wasteful litigation. Is the *China Trade* standard sensible as a matter of policy? Note that the Second Circuit has backed slightly away from some of the strict language in *China Trade*. In more recent decisions, it has held that considerations such as vexatiousness may support issuance of an injunction that is otherwise necessary to protect the court's jurisdiction or to vindicate important forum policies. *See Ibeto Petrochemical Indus. v. M/T Beffen,* 475 F.3d 56 (2d Cir. 2007). Is this a more sensible application of the rule? Is it consistent with the original holding of *China Trade?*

Consider the facts of *China Trade*. As Judge Bright's dissent notes, the case had been pending in U.S. courts for two years; the defendant had agreed to litigate in New York and had waived *forum non conveniens* defenses; discovery had been conducted and largely completed; the trial date scheduled (with the parties' agreement) was only months away; and the Korean lawsuit involved exactly the same issues as that in New York. The district judge, with a front-line perspective on the case, expressly found that the Korean action could be "vexatious." On these facts, does not justice cry out for resolving the dispute in the parties' chosen forum? If the *China Trade* standard forbids an antisuit injunction in these circumstances, is that standard not manifestly wrong?

Consider also the facts in *Kaepa*, where the Japanese defendant had agreed to litigation in Texas and then participated actively in U.S. litigation (including removing to federal court) for nearly a year. Putting aside the rhetoric of the *Kaepa* Court's opinion, does justice again not cry out for resolving the dispute in the parties' chosen forum — especially when the parties have done so, until one of them decided it was unhappy with the course of the litigation? Does not the *Kaepa* result do far more justice than that in *China Trade?* Mustn't standards for antisuit injunctions take such considerations into account?

3. China Trade*'s threshold requirements. China Trade* sets forth two threshold requirements before any antisuit injunction will issue. The parties must be the "same," and resolution of the case by the enjoining court must be "dispositive of the action to be enjoined." What do these terms mean? Why were they met in *China Trade?* Were they met in *Kaepa?*

Recall that the decision whether to issue a stay *lis alibi pendens* raised similar questions of identity. Are the standards the same? Or do the consequences of an antisuit injunction justify a stricter standard for these requirements? Must the parties be identical or does it suffice if they are substantially identical? Must resolution of the case in the enjoining court completely dispose of the action, or is it sufficient if the claims in the two actions are "substantially similar"? Lower courts disagree on the answer. *Compare Canon Latin America Inc. v. Lantech (CR), S.A.,* 508 F.3d 597, 601 & n.8 (11th Cir. 2007) (requiring that proceedings before the enjoining court completely dispose of the parallel action) *with Applied Medical Distribution Corp. v. Surgical Co. BV,* 587 F.3d 909, 916 (9th Cir. 2009) (merely requiring the issues to be "functionally the same").

What if, in *China Trade*, the Korean party filed an action in Korean court that only existed under Korean law and had no counterpart under U.S. law? Under such circumstances, could the second threshold requirement of *China Trade* ever be satisfied? Lower courts disagree on this point as well. *Compare Canon Latin America Inc. v. Lantech (CR), S.A.*, 508 F.3d 597, 601 & n.8 (11th Cir. 2007) *with E. & J. Gallo Winery v. Andina Licores S.A.*, 446 F.3d 984, 991 (9th Cir. 2006). If a uniquely foreign claim suffices to bar issuance of the antisuit injunction, does this create a roadmap for avoiding an antisuit injunction in jurisdictions that employ the *China Trade* test? Does this suggest that the *China Trade* test is too strict? Or is this an appropriate check on the unwarranted issuance of antisuit injunctions?

4. *Rationale for stringent limits on antisuit injunctions.* What rationales would justify a rule permitting the result in *China Trade*?

(a) Parallel proceedings. Citing *Laker Airways*, *China Trade* and Judge Garza's dissent held that concurrent jurisdiction was a frequent occurrence in contemporary international litigation, and that a "fundamental corollary to concurrent jurisdiction" is that "parallel proceedings on the same *in personam* claim should ordinarily be allowed to proceed simultaneously, at least until a judgment is reached in one which can be pled as *res judicata* in the other." *See also Quaak v. Klynveld Peat Marwick Goerdeler Bedrijfsrevisoren*, 361 F.3d 11, 17 (1st Cir. 2004). Is this persuasive?

Note that the same rationale is invoked to deny requests for *lis pendens* stays of U.S. proceedings in deference to foreign litigation. *See supra* pp. 558-559. Does the fact that contemporary jurisdictional rules frequently permit concurrent jurisdiction compel the conclusion that courts are bound to allow parallel proceedings? Doesn't the argument cut the other way: because concurrent jurisdiction makes parallel proceedings so easy to start, courts should be vigilant in limiting the abuses of such proceedings? Recall the discussion above, demonstrating how the *forum non conveniens* doctrine developed to counterbalance the expansion of judicial jurisdiction. *See supra* pp. 386-387.

(b) International comity. *China Trade* and Judge Garza's dissent in *Kaepa* invoked "the need for due regard to principles of international comity" in explaining the standard for antisuit injunctions. Note Judge Garza's concerns about "amicable relations among sovereign nations and their judicial systems" and the risk of "retaliation." *See also Goss International Corp. v. Man Roland Druckmaschinen Aktiengesellschaft*, 491 F.3d 355 (8th Cir. 2007); *Paramedics Electromedicina Comercial, Ltda v. GE Medical Systems Information Technologies, Inc.*, 369 F.3d 645, 652 (2d Cir. 2004); *Quaak v. Klynveld Peat Marwick Goerdeler Bedrijfsrevisoren*, 361 F.3d 11, 16 (1st Cir. 2004); *General Elec. Co. v. Deutz AG*, 270 F.3d 144, 160-162 (3d Cir. 2001). Consider also:

> Comity dictates that foreign antisuit injunctions be issued sparingly and only in the rarest of cases. The days of American hegemony over international economic affairs have long since passed. The United States cannot today impose its economic will on the rest of the world and expect meek compliance, if indeed it ever could. The modern era is one of world economic interdependence, and economic interdependence requires cooperation requires cooperation and comity between nations. . . . Before taking [the] drastic step [of granting an antisuit injunction], this court must consider carefully the implications of such actions under principles of international comity. *Gau Shan Co. v. Bankers Trust Co.*, 956 F.2d 1349, 1354 (6th Cir. 1992).

Is this not patently silly? What do "American hegemony" and "world economic interdependence" have to do with a party's transparent effort to complicate and delay a case that is on the courthouse steps? Does economic interdependence mean that U.S. courts should forsake antisuit injunctions to protect the interests of U.S. litigants under U.S. law?

Consider the implied criticism of the comity doctrine in *Kaepa*. Consider also the explicit criticism of the comity doctrine by other authorities. *See* Maier, *Extraterritorial*

Jurisdiction at a Crossroads: An Intersection Between Public and Private International Law, 76 Am. J. Int'l L. 280, 281 (1982) (international comity is "an amorphous never-never land whose borders are marked by fuzzy lines of politics, courtesy and good faith"); Ramsey, *Escaping "International Comity,"* 83 Iowa L. Rev. 893 (1998); Paul, *Comity in International Law,* 32 Harv. Int'l L.J. 1, 3-4 (1991) (comity supposedly randomly defined as "the basis of international law, a rule of international law, a synonym for private international law, a rule of choice of law, courtesy, politeness, convenience or goodwill between sovereigns, a moral necessity, expediency, reciprocity, or 'consideration of high international politics concerned with maintaining amicable and workable relationships between nations.' "). Is this criticism grounds for more freely granting antisuit injunctions? How would Judge Garza respond?

Note that foreign courts can issue antisuit injunctions to bar the prosecution of litigation in the United States. *See, e.g., Dependable Highway Exp., Inc. v. Navigators Ins. Co.,* 498 F.3d 1059 (9th Cir. 2007); *Doe v. Princess Cruise Lines, Ltd.,* 696 F. Supp. 2d 1282 (S.D. Fla. 2010); *Exteer Shipping Ltd. v. Kilakos,* 310 F. Supp. 2d 1301 (N.D. Ga. 2004). Doesn't that possibility counsel in favor of restraint before a U.S. court issues a similar injunction? Or does it, alternatively, counsel in favor of an analogue to the reciprocity rule, used to evaluate the enforceability of a foreign judgment, *see infra* pp. 1094-1102.

(c) Avoiding preempting foreign proceedings. Related to reliance on principles of international comity, courts often reason that they should not preempt a foreign court's decisions, which may result in dismissal of duplicative actions. For example, note that Judge Garza reasoned:

> A dismissal on grounds of *forum non conveniens* by either court in this case would satisfy the majority's concern with avoiding hardship to the parties, without harming the interests of international comity. The district court is not in a position, however, to make the *forum non conveniens* determination on behalf of the Japanese court.

What if the foreign court does not dismiss a vexatious or oppressive action? Recall the discussion above, that most civil law jurisdictions do not have *forum non conveniens* doctrines and consider the notion of judicial abstention vaguely improper. *See supra* pp. 391-392. What does that do to Judge Garza's argument?

(d) Domestic analogies. Like Judge Garza, some lower courts have also relied upon domestic U.S. precedent, involving the standards applicable to the issuance by federal courts of injunctions against state court proceedings. *See Laker Airways,* 731 F.2d at 926 (citing *Colorado River*); *China Trade,* 837 F.2d 33 (citing *Colorado River* and *Donovan v. City of Dallas*); *supra* pp. 568-569. In particular, they have cited *Colorado River,* which held that parallel proceedings in state and federal courts should generally be permitted to proceed. A similar trend exists in the *lis pendens* context. *See supra* pp. 549-550. Can any inference be drawn from the Anti-Injunction Act, 28 U.S.C. §2283, which severely limits the power of federal courts to issue injunctions against litigation in state courts?

Why might the standards governing federal court injunctions against state court proceedings be relevant to antisuit injunctions against foreign courts in the international context? Recall that state court proceedings are subject to Supreme Court review on federal constitutional and statutory grounds, that U.S. states share a legal heritage, and that the Full Faith and Credit Clause requires recognition and enforcement of judgments among U.S. states. The same is not true in international cases. Is the analogy to federal-state antisuit disputes persuasive?

5. Kaepa — *flexible standards for the issuance of antisuit injunction against "vexatious" or "oppressive" foreign proceedings.* Compare the standards for antisuit injunctions in *Kaepa* to those in *China Trade.* Under this view, a party must satisfy two requirements to obtain an antisuit injunction: (a) there must be parallel foreign and U.S. proceedings involving the same parties and issues; and (b) the foreign proceeding must be vexatious, contrary to U.S. public policy, a threat to the U.S. court's jurisdiction, or otherwise inequitable. *See also supra* pp. 568-569.

6. *Meaning of "vexatious" or "oppressive" foreign proceedings under more liberal antisuit injunction standards.* There is no clear formula defining when a foreign proceeding is "vexatious" or "oppressive" under the standards adopted in *Kaepa* and similar decisions. The Supreme Court has remarked generally that an action is vexatious if it seeks to harass an opponent "by inflicting upon him expense or trouble not necessary to [one's] own right to pursue [one's] remedy." *Gulf Oil Corp. v. Gilbert,* 330 U.S. 501, 508 (1947). *See Paramount Pictures, Inc. v. Blumenthal,* 11 N.Y.S.2d 768 (App. Div. 1939) ("must be shown that [litigation was] instituted maliciously and without probable cause").

In the specific context of foreign antisuit injunctions, lower courts have attempted to apply the "vexatious" or "oppressive" standard in a number of cases. Generally, foreign proceedings will be vexatious if they involved unnecessary delay, substantial inconvenience, and potentially inconsistent rulings. *E.g., Allendale Mutual Ins. Co. v. Bull Data Systems, Inc.,* 10 F.3d 425 (7th Cir. 1993) ("absurd duplication of effort"; parallel French proceeding unable to grant full relief); *Seattle Totems Hockey Club v. National Hockey League,* 652 F.2d 852 (9th Cir. 1981) (location of evidence and witnesses, convenience, and risk of inconsistent results); *Cargill, Inc. v. Hartford Acc. & Indem. Co.,* 531 F. Supp. 710 (D. Minn. 1982) (convenience of parties, location of evidence, risk of inconsistent results). *Compare MacPhail v. Oceaneering Int'l, Inc.,* 302 F.3d 274, 277-278 (5th Cir. 2002) (foreign litigation not duplicative because it involved different issues and relief); *Robinson v. Jardine Ins. Brokers Int'l Ltd.,* 856 F. Supp. 554 (N.D. Cal. 1994) (foreign litigation duplicative, but permitted to continue).

Won't parallel proceedings almost *always* be less convenient, more expensive, and more likely to produce inconsistent results than a single litigation, and therefore "vexatious" under the *Kaepa* analysis? Note Judge Garza's comment in dissent that "concurrent jurisdiction involving a foreign tribunal will rarely, if ever, withstand the request for an antisuit injunction" under the majority's standard in *Kaepa.* Is that exaggerated?

7. *What test should be applied for antisuit injunctions?* Compare the majority and dissenting opinions in *Kaepa* and *China Trade.* Which approach to granting antisuit injunctions do you find wiser? Lower courts are divided in their use of the two approaches illustrated by *Kaepa* and *China Trade,* with some decisions following each approach. *See supra* pp. 568-570. The majority in *Kaepa* harshly criticizes the *China Trade* approach as "genuflect[-ing] before vague and omnipotent notions of comity." In contrast, consider the following critique of the *Kaepa* standard:

> We reject the liberal approach [of *Kaepa*]. We deem international comity an important inte-
> ger in the decisional calculus — and the liberal approach assigns too low a priority to that
> interest. In the bargain, it undermines the age-old presumption in favor of concurrent
> parallel proceedings — a value judgment that leaves us uneasy — and presumes that public
> policy always favors allowing a suit pending in an American court to go forward without any
> substantial impediment. To cinch matters, this approach gives far too easy passage to
> international antisuit injunctions. We understand that the judicial process is a cornerstone
> of the American way of life — but in an area that raises significant separation of powers
> concerns and implicates international relations, we believe that the law calls for a more
> cautious and measured approach.

The conservative approach has more to commend it. First, it recognizes the rebuttable presumption against issuing international antisuit injunctions (and, thus, honors the presumption favoring the maintenance of parallel proceedings). Second, it is more respectful of principles of international comity. Third, it compels an inquiring court to balance competing policy considerations. Last—but far from least—it fits snugly with the logic of *Canadian Filters [(Harwich) v. Lear-Siegler, Inc.*, 412 F.2d 577, 579 (1st Cir. 1969)], in which we said that issuing an international antisuit injunction is a step that should "be taken only with care and great restraint" and with the recognition that international comity is a fundamental principle deserving of substantial deference. *Quaak v. Klynveld Peat Marwick Goerdeler Bedrijfs-revisoren*, 361 F.3d 11, 17-18 (1st Cir. 2004).

See also Kirby v. Norfolk Southern Railway Co., 71 F. Supp. 2d 1363, 1370 (N.D. Ga. 1999) (noting that the liberal approach "too freely allows courts to invade the jurisdiction of sovereign governments" and its underlying justification "reflects an antiquated view of commerce").

Is either approach adequate? Is there a middle ground that would be more desirable? Would it be wise to adopt a rule permitting an antisuit injunction to be issued based on "vexatious" proceedings, but only if extreme vexation is demonstrated?

8. *Issuance of antisuit injunctions for protection of issuing court's jurisdiction.* *China Trade* held that one basis for issuing an antisuit injunction was to protect the issuing court's jurisdiction. This rule is typically invoked, as in *Laker Airways*, when a foreign court threatens to enjoin U.S. proceedings and the U.S. court issues an anti-antisuit injunction. *E.g.*, *Mutual Service Casualty Ins. Co. v. Frit Industries, Inc.*, 805 F. Supp. 919 (M.D. Ala. 1992), *aff'd per curiam*, 3 F.3d 442 (11th Cir. 1993) (granting anti-antisuit injunction); *Owens-Illinois v. Webb*, 809 S.W.2d 899 (Tex. App. 1991) (issuing anti-antisuit injunction against antisuit injunction in Canada).

The exception for protecting U.S. court's jurisdiction also arises when foreign proceedings undermine the integrity of U.S. proceedings. *E.g.*, *Karaha Bodas Co., LLC v. Perusahaan Pertambangan Minyak Dan Gas Bumi Negara*, 500 F.3d 111, 126 (2d Cir. 2007) (Caymans action enjoined to protect U.S. court's judgment confirming and enforcing arbitral award); *Paramedics Electromedicina Comercial, Ltda v. GE Medical Systems Information Technologies, Inc.*, 369 F.3d 645, 654-655 (2d Cir. 2004) (Brazilian action enjoined to protect U.S. court's judgment with respect to arbitrability of claim in U.S.-based arbitration proceeding); *Umbro Int'l, Inc. v. Japan Professional Football League*, 1997 WL 33378853, at *3 (D.S.C. 1997) (issuing antisuit injunction where procedural law in foreign forum did not provide adequate confidentiality protections); *International Fashion Products, BV v. Calvin Klein, Inc.*, 1995 WL 92321, at *2 (S.D.N.Y. 1995) (issuing injunction where foreign court order would prevent award of relief by U.S. court); *Omnium Lyonnais d'Etancheite et Revetement Asphalte v. Dow Chem. Co.*, 441 F. Supp. 1385 (C.D. Cal. 1977) (French proceeding enjoined because French plaintiff based its suit on evidence subject to U.S. confidentiality order).

9. *Antisuit injunction to prevent frustration of U.S. public policy.* *China Trade* also held that an antisuit injunction could be issued to prevent the frustration of the forum's public policy. (Public policy exceptions are discussed in other contexts, *see supra* pp. 426-428 and *infra* pp. 1133-1146.) Some antisuit injunction cases have relied on the public policy rationale. *E.g.*, *Stonington Partners, Inc. v. Lernout & Hauspie Speech Products NV*, 310 F.3d 118, 128 (3d Cir. 2002); *United States v. Davis*, 767 F.2d 1025 (2d Cir. 1985) (enjoining U.S. national from pursuing Cayman Islands action to restrain production of evidence for use in U.S. proceeding); *Software AG, Inc. v. Software Solutions, Inc.*, 2008 WL 563449 (S.D.N.Y. Feb. 21, 2008) (important policy interests reflected in Lanham Act); *Younis Bros. & Co.*,

Inc. v. CIGNA Worldwide Ins. Co., 167 F. Supp. 2d 743, 747 (E.D. Pa. 2001); *Farrell Lines Inc. v. Columbus Cello-Poly Corp.*, 32 F. Supp. 2d 118, 130-131 (S.D.N.Y. 1997) (enjoining foreign suit brought in violation of forum selection clause, on grounds that enforcement of such clauses was important U.S. public policy); *Nagoya Venture Ltd. v. Bacopulos*, 1998 WL 307079, at *5 (S.D.N.Y. 1998).

   10. *Relevance of differences in substantive law to public policy.* Does the public policy exception permit issuance of an antisuit injunction whenever a foreign court would apply foreign law, rather than U.S. law that is more favorable to the U.S. plaintiff? Note the remark in *China Trade* (quoting *Laker*) that an injunction "is not appropriate merely to prevent a party from seeking 'slight advantages in the substantive or procedural law to be applied in a foreign court.' " What if the advantages are not merely "slight"? What if the foreign forum offers a remedy unavailable under U.S. law? *See Canon Latin America, Inc. v. Lantech (CR) S.A.*, 508 F.3d 597 (11th Cir. 2007). Compare the *Piper Aircraft* rule that even significant changes in law are not entitled to "substantial" weight in *forum non conveniens* analysis. *See supra* pp. 441-442.

   Suppose a U.S. libel plaintiff sues a U.S. publisher in a foreign court for damages sustained, principally in the United States, by virtue of misstatements that would not be actionable under the First Amendment. Would the foreign suit constitute an evasion of U.S. public policy? If so, would the public policy exception apply where a foreign court would apply significantly less favorable foreign substantive law to a contractual dispute arising in the United States? What if the libel plaintiff is not a U.S. national? What if the libel occurs principally abroad? Suppose that defendants in a U.S. antitrust action initiate parallel proceedings in a foreign forum seeking a declaration of no liability and favorable factual findings.

   Suppose a U.S. and foreign company enter into a contract, out of which disputes arise. The foreign company sues the U.S. company abroad, where the foreign court will enforce contractual exculpatory provisions benefiting the foreign company. However, those provisions are contrary to U.S. public policy, and U.S. courts would not enforce them with respect to conduct in the United States. Would an antisuit injunction issue against the foreign action, in a case involving conduct in the United States?

   Note *China Trade*'s emphasis on "the litigant's unconscionable evasion of the domestic laws," and its reliance on decisions where "the primary purpose of the foreign action is to avoid the regulatory effect of the domestic forum's statutes." *See also Sea Containers Ltd. v. Stena AB*, 890 F.2d 1205, 1214 (D.C. Cir. 1989) (litigant's decision to seek relief before "a foreign court with a lower standard for preliminary relief . . . allows it to burden its adversary but it does not represent an 'evasion of forum law and policy' that justifies injunctive relief").

   11. *Relevance of federal regulatory legislation to public policy.* Suppose a foreign court will not apply the U.S. antitrust laws to a dispute occurring in the United States and significantly affecting U.S. commerce. Does this provide an adequate basis for issuing an antisuit injunction? *See Seattle Totems Hockey Club v. National Hockey League*, 652 F.2d 852 (9th Cir. 1981) (enjoining foreign proceeding raising same issues as U.S. antitrust action); Hartley, *Comity and the Use of Antisuit Injunctions in International Litigation*, 35 Am. J. Comp. L. 487 (1987) (suggesting that refusal of foreign forum to apply issuing forum's law would provide basis for issuance of antisuit injunction). Recall that many lower courts have held that the *forum non conveniens* doctrine is not applicable in antitrust claims. *See supra* pp. 444-445.

   What if the conduct in question occurred partly in the United States and partly abroad, and that the foreign forum will not apply U.S. law? What if, under U.S. choice-of-law rules, U.S. law would not apply to the claims?

12. *Relevance of nationality of the parties.* What role should nationality play in granting antisuit injunctions? Should a U.S. plaintiff be able to obtain an antisuit injunction more easily than a foreign plaintiff? Should a U.S. defendant be more readily subjected to an antisuit injunction than a foreign defendant? Consider the importance of nationality in the jurisdiction and *forum non conveniens* contexts. *See supra* pp. 397-403. *Laker Airways* considered these points in deciding whether to issue an anti-antisuit injunction against U.S. parties to prevent them from seeking antisuit injunctions in England against an English company. The court held that English courts had no special right to enjoin an English party from commencing U.S. proceedings: "Although a court has power to enjoin its nationals from suing in foreign jurisdictions, it does not follow that the United States courts must recognize an absolute right of the British government to regulate the remedies that the United States may wish to create for British nationals in the United States courts. United States courts must control the access to their forums. No foreign court can supersede the right and obligation of the United States courts to decide whether Congress has created a remedy for those injured by trade practices adversely affecting United States interests." 731 F.2d at 935-936. Is this persuasive? Why shouldn't a national of a country be subject to the orders issued by that country's courts, not to proceed with foreign litigation that violates the country's policies? Why shouldn't U.S. courts respect such orders?

13. *Relevance of reasons for parallel litigation.* Recall that, under the *forum non conveniens* doctrine, the *Irragori* court instructed that courts should consider whether forum shopping factored into the plaintiffs' decision to file in the U.S. forum. Where forum shopping played a considerable role, the court would accord less deference to the plaintiff's choice of forum (and thus be more likely dismiss the suit). Should similar considerations animate the decision whether to issue an antisuit injunction? Can a court distinguish between parallel proceedings that began "as a jurisdictional standoff" and ones that "arose out of [differences between] the legislative policies" of the different forums? *Goss Int'l Corp. v. Man Roland Druckmaschinen Aktiengesellschaft*, 491 F.3d 355, 367 (8th Cir. 2007).

14. *Antisuit injunctions in* **in rem** *matters.* A number of courts—including courts like *China Trade* which adopt a restrictive approach to issuance of antisuit injunctions—have held that antisuit injunctions may be appropriate to protect a court's jurisdiction in cases where the court is exercising *in rem* or *quasi in rem* jurisdiction. *See China Trade*, 837 F.2d at 36; *Kirby v. Norfolk Southern Railway Co.*, 71 F. Supp. 2d 1363, 1371 (N.D. Ga. 1999). *See also Donovan v. City of Dallas*, 377 U.S. 408 (1964). What is the rationale for this exception to the general reluctance to issue antisuit injunctions? Consider the following explanation:

> if the two suits are *in rem*, or *quasi in rem*, so that the court, or its officer, has possession or must have control of the property which is the subject of the litigation in order to proceed with the cause and grant the relief sought the jurisdiction of the one court must yield to that of the other. We have said that the principle applicable to both federal and state courts that the court first assuming jurisdiction over property may maintain and exercise that jurisdiction to the exclusion of the other, is not restricted to cases where property has been actually seized under judicial process before a second suit is instituted, but applies as well where suits are brought to marshal assets, administer trusts, or liquidate estates, and in suits of a similar nature where, to give effect to its jurisdiction, the court must control the property. The doctrine is necessary to the harmonious cooperation of federal and state tribunals.

Does this rationale reflect the notion that U.S. jurisdiction is primary in matters involving property in the United States? Does such a rule not make sense? If that rule is accepted, does its rationale have implications for *in personam* actions?

15. *Relevance of foreign court's jurisdiction (or lack thereof).* Suppose that a parallel proceeding is litigated in a foreign court that lacks personal jurisdiction over the defendant (under U.S. and "international" standards). Should a U.S. court grant an antisuit injunction to prevent litigation abroad in a forum that could not "properly" exercise jurisdiction?

In *Midland Bank plc v. Laker Airways Ltd.* [1986] 1 All E.R. 526, the English Court of Appeal affirmed an English antisuit injunction against Laker Airways barring it from commencing U.S. litigation against Midland Bank, an English financial institution. Midland Bank sought the English antisuit injunction after Laker Airways had threatened to add the bank as a defendant in its U.S. antitrust action, based on Midland's alleged involvement in an airline conspiracy to drive Laker out of business. In granting Midland's request for an antisuit injunction, the English Court of Appeal relied on Midland's lack of any meaningful U.S. presence at the time of the conspiracy against Laker and on the fact that any allegedly unlawful activity by Midland occurred entirely in England. Given this, the court reasoned that the U.S. antitrust laws must be kept "within the territorial jurisdiction of the U.S. in accordance with accepted standards of international law," and that courts should respect the "general principle that 'everyone should be entitled to adjust his conduct to the law of the country in which he acts.'" *Compare Amchem Prods. Inc. v. Workers' Compensation Board*, 75 D.L.R.4th 1 (B.I.C.A. 1990); *reversed*, 102 D.L.R. (4th) 96 (Can. S. Ct. 1993) (enjoining Texas class action in part because of "the tenuous jurisdiction of the Texas courts"); *Hamilton Bank, NA v. Kookmin Bank*, 999 F. Supp. 586 (S.D.N.Y. 1998) (declining to issue antisuit injunction where Korean court's exercise of jurisdiction did not violate American bank's due process rights). Consider also the use of antisuit injunctions against actions brought in violation of forum selection or arbitration clauses. How are such cases different from ones where the foreign court lacks jurisdiction at all?

Is it appropriate for the courts of one nation to sit in judgment on a foreign court's exercise of jurisdiction? Compare the treatment of foreign jurisdiction in the enforcement of judgments context, *infra* pp. 1146-1155.

16. *Wisdom of considering "strength" of competing jurisdictional claims.* Should a U.S. court consider the strength of a foreign forum's jurisdictional claim in deciding whether a foreign proceeding is "vexatious" or "oppressive"? As described above, the reach of national judicial jurisdiction has expanded very substantially in the past century. *See supra* pp. 84-90. As a consequence in many international cases, two or more states will enjoy concurrent jurisdiction over the same dispute. In such cases, why should courts treat both (or all) forums equally, following the *Laker Airways* "rule permitting parallel proceedings in concurrent in personam actions"? Instead, should courts consider the relative strengths of the competing jurisdictional claims? *See, e.g., Athina Investments, Ltd. v. Pinchuk*, 443 F. Supp. 2d 177 (D. Mass. 2006) (declining to issue antisuit injunction where defendants had not yet presented full jurisdictional defenses in U.S. court); *Shell Offshore, Inc. v. Heeremac*, 33 F. Supp. 2d 1111, 1113 (S.D. Tex. 1999) ("While the distinct action in [foreign country] is adjudged to be an unjustified, disingenuous complicating maneuver, an injunction is not now needed. If jurisdiction here has been decided against [foreign plaintiff] and if it persists in [foreign country] and if the [foreign court] does not stay its case, then [the issuance of an antisuit injunction] can be reexamined.").

17. *Antisuit injunctions vs. preliminary injunctions.* Injunctions are extraordinary remedies. They bar a party from pursuing a course of conduct; if a party ignores that injunction, it is subject to sanctions for contempt of court. Ordinarily, therefore, courts require a heavy showing before any injunction will issue; that showing typically requires that a party prove a likelihood of succeeding on the merits.

Should the typical requirements for issuance of a preliminary injunction apply to antisuit injunctions as well? What answer does *China Trade* suggest? What answer does *Kaepa* suggest? If this showing is not necessary, does that mean the standards of even the *China Trade* approach are too weak? Assuming that a party must show some likelihood of success on the merits, what are the "merits" in this context? The merits of the underlying claim? Or merely the merits of its entitlement to a preliminary injunction? Courts that have considered this question generally do not require a party seeking an antisuit injunction to prove the merits of its underlying claim. *See, e.g., E. & J. Gallo Winery v. Andina Licores S.A.*, 446 F.3d 984, 990-991 (9th Cir. 2006); *Karaha Bodas Co., LLC v. Perusahaan Pertambangan Minyak Dan Gas Bumi Negara*, 335 F.3d 357, 364 n.19 (5th Cir. 2003). Is this wise? Given the extraordinary effects of an antisuit injunction, affecting not merely the enjoined party but indirectly at least a foreign court, why shouldn't a court inquire whether the party seeking the injunction has a meritorious claim?

18. *Relevance of first filing of complaint.* To what extent did the Court in *Kaepa* and the dissent in *China Trade* rely on the timing of the filing of the complaints in the respective forums? Should weight ever be attached to the situs of the parties' first filing? What advantages would a first-filed rule have? Is the following persuasive?

> No state is likely to permit the enforcement of its important public policies to rest upon the fortuities of winning the race to the courthouse. A "first-filed" rule would also encourage preemptive resort to litigation. Note, *Antisuit Injunctions and International Comity*, 71 Va. L. Rev. 1039, 1042 n.18 (1985).

Note that even *Laker Airways v. Sabena*, 731 F.2d 909, 929 n.63 (D.C. Cir. 1984), which was one of the early decisions adopting stringent limits on antisuit injunctions, suggested a modified "first-filed" rule that would attach importance to first filing in cases involving lengthy delays between first and second filing.

19. *Antisuit injunctions to enforce arbitration or forum selection clause.* Note that *Kaepa* involved a forum selection clause. Was that clause exclusive or nonexclusive? What role should a nonexclusive forum selection clause, permitting jurisdiction in a U.S. court, have in determining whether to issue an antisuit injunction? Suppose that the forum selection clause in *Kaepa* had been exclusive, providing for litigation solely in Texas. What result should this have had on the decision whether to grant an antisuit injunction?

A number of courts have held that litigation will be deemed vexatious, and subject to an antisuit injunction, where it is designed to avoid an arbitration clause or a forum selection clause. *See Applied Medical Distribution Corp. v. Surgical Co. BV*, 587 F.3d 909 (9th Cir. 2009); *E & J Gallo Winery v. Andina Licores SA*, 446 F.3d 984 (9th Cir. 2006); *LAIF X SPRL v. Axtel SA, de CV*, 390 F.3d 194, 199 (2d Cir. 2004); *Amaprop, Ltd. v. Indiabulls Financial Services, Ltd.*, 2010 WL 1050988 (S.D.N.Y. Mar. 23, 2010); *Indosuez Int'l Finance, BV v. National Reserve Bank*, 304 A.D. 2d 429 (N.Y. App. Div. 2003).

Note that some other jurisdictions also grant antisuit injunctions to ensure performance of exclusive forum selection and arbitration agreements. *Aggeliki Charis Compania Maritima SA v. Pagnan SpA (The Angelic Grace)* [1995] 1 Lloyd's Rep. 87 (granting antisuit injunction to restrain the breach of an arbitration agreement); *Continental Bank NA v. Aeakos Cia Naviera SA* [1994] 1 W.L.R. 588 (granting antisuit injunction to ensure performance of exclusive English forum selection clause); *Through Transport Mutual Insurance Association (Eurasia) Ltd. v. New India Assurance Co. Ltd.*, 2005 1 Lloyd's Rep. 67.

20. *Antisuit injunctions and second-order parallel proceedings.* Recall the hypothetical discussed in the preceding subsection where two parties enter into a contract with an arbitration clause, one party commences litigation (challenging the clause's enforce-ability) and the party commences parallel proceedings to compel arbitration. How do these dynamics affect the antisuit injunction analysis? Does it affect your answer that the United States is a signatory to several important treaties providing for the enforceability of arbitration agreements? Could it ever be appropriate for a U.S. court to enjoin foreign proceedings challenging the enforceability of an arbitration agreement that designates the foreign country as the arbitral forum? *See Answers in Genesis of Ky., Inc. v. Creation Ministries Int'l, Ltd.*, 556 F.3d 459 (6th Cir. 2009). What if, instead, the arbitral forum were in a country other than the one where the foreign parallel proceedings were being brought? *Ibeto Petrochemical Industries Ltd. v. M/T Beffen*, 475 F.3d 56 (2d Cir. 2007).

21. *Distinction between prejudgment and postjudgment injunctions.* *Laker, Ingersoll,* and *China Trade* sharply distinguished between prejudgment and postjudgment antisuit injunctions, setting forth a fairly liberal policy on enjoining foreign proceedings after a U.S. judgment has been reached, but generally denying injunctive relief before U.S. judgment: "The parallel proceeding rule applies only until one court reaches a judgment that may be pled as res judicata in the other."

Other lower courts have adopted the same rule. *See, e.g., Karaha Bodas Co., LLC v. Perusahaan Pertambangan Minyak Dan Gas Bumi Negara*, 500 F.3d 111, 120 (2d Cir. 2007); *Mutual Service Insurance Co. v. Frit Industries, Inc.*, 358 F.3d 1312, 1324-1325 (11th Cir. 2004); *MasterCard Int'l, Inc. v. Federation Internationale de Football Ass'n*, 2007 WL 631312 (S.D.N.Y. Feb. 28, 2007); *Younis Bros. & Co., Inc. v. CIGNA Worldwide Ins. Co.*, 167 F. Supp. 2d 743, 747 (E.D. Pa. 2001). *Cf. Stonington Partners, Inc. v. Lernout & Hauspie Speech Products NV*, 310 F.3d 118, 127 n.7 (3d Cir. 2002) (leaving issue open). Is this consistent with the basic *Laker/China Trade* approach to antisuit injunctions? This approach is premised on the view that concurrent proceedings do not threaten either court's jurisdiction, and therefore should be permitted to proceed. *See supra* pp. 568-569.

How do the principles of these cases apply where a party is attempting to enforce a judgment of a foreign court? *See infra* at 1077-1155 (discussing principles of foreign judgment enforcement). Should a U.S. court *ever* enjoin a party from enforcing a judgment obtained by a foreign tribunal? What if the party seeking the injunction maintains that the foreign judgment is the product of a biased and unfair proceeding? Assuming that the U.S. Court has jurisdiction over the judgment creditor, is that a sufficient reason to support issuance of the injunction? Or would such an injunction amount to overreact-ing by the U.S. Court? *See infra* at 1145-1146 (discussing the Chevron/Ecuador litigation).

22. *Relevance of foreign court's willingness to recognize U.S. judgments.* As described above, the "parallel proceedings" rule rests on the assumption that a final judgment in one proceeding will be recognized in the second proceeding. Suppose that it is clear that a U.S. judgment will not actually be recognized in the foreign forum. Does this affect the appropriateness of the general presumption adopted in cases like *China Trade* against issuing antisuit injunctions against "vexatious" foreign proceedings? If so, how?

In assessing the distinction between pre- and postjudgment injunctions, note that some foreign courts refuse to recognize any U.S. judgments. Two different lines of ana-lysis are possible. First, the fact that foreign courts may not recognize U.S. judgments might argue for more liberal use of prejudgment antisuit injunctions, to help ensure that the outcome of U.S. proceedings is not circumvented. Second, if U.S. judgments are not particularly likely to be recognized abroad, then why should the rendering of a U.S. judgment have such important consequences for antisuit injunctions? Put differently, if comity and respect for foreign regulatory authority preclude issuance of a prejudgment antisuit injunction, don't these same concerns become even greater when a foreign court would invoke its public policy to deny enforcement to a U.S. judgment? Which of these analyses is more persuasive?

23. *No antisuit injunctions under EU Council Regulation 44/2001.* The European Court of Justice has held that Regulation 44/2001 does not permit antisuit injunctions to be issued by a court in one Member State against parties pursuing proceeding in another Member State, even where the proceeding was brought in bad faith and vexatiously, solely for the purpose of oppressing the defendant. *Turner v. Grovit,* Case C-159/02 (ECJ 27 April 2004). For a penetrating critique, *see* Briggs, *The Impact of Recent Judgments of the European Court on English Procedural Law and Practice,* Zeitschrift für Schweizerisches Recht 124 (2005) 11 231-262; Hartley, *The European Union and the Systematic Dismantling of the Common Law of Conflict of Laws,* 54 I.C.L.Q. 813 (2005).

Note that the EU's "no antisuit injunction" rule applies even in the case of a forum selection clause. That is, if a party agrees to an exclusive forum selection clause, selecting an EU forum, and its counterparty brings litigation in another EU state in violation of the forum selection clause, the contractual forum is precluded from issuing injunctive relief to prevent the wrongful litigation. Is that wise? Consider the following comment:

> In view of these cases, businessmen may no longer want to choose the courts of England [or any other European state] as the forum for litigation under international contracts. The European Court has succeeded in making them unattractive. New York might now appear a better alternative, since it is outside the reach of the European Court of Justice. Hartley, *The European Union and the Systematic Dismantling of the Common Law of Conflict of Laws,* 54 I.C.L.Q. 813, 823 (2005).

Is that persuasive? Note that, under the EU's "first-filed" rule of *lis pendens* in Article 27 of Regulation 44/2001, a party can bring litigation in violation of a contractual forum selection clause and its counterparty is then unable to pursue its claims in the contractual forum. *Erich Gusser GmbH v. Misat Srl,* Case C-116/02 (ECJ 9 December 2003).

24. *"Negotiation" or similar interaction between national courts in international litigation.* Consider the extent to which various of the issues addressed by the *forum non conveniens, lis pendens,* and antisuit injunction doctrines might be better resolved with some sort of discussion or coordination between courts (and judges) of the relevant countries. The essential issue in each of these contexts (and to a lesser, more indirect extent in some jurisdictional contexts) is what national court will resolve a particular dispute. Why is it that the involved courts should not directly discuss the specifics of a particular case in an effort to decide this question? For general commentary on the possibility of international judicial "negotiation," *see* Slaughter, *A Global Community of Courts,* 44 Harv. Int'l J.L. 191 (2003); Schlosser, *Direct Interaction of Courts of Different Nations,* 2005 Studio di Diritto Processuale Civile 589; Westbrook, *International Judicial Negotiation,* 38 Tex. Int'l J.L. 567 (2003). Consider the following:

> Using these facts as an example, one can construct a different approach, using communication and negotiation. The New York court might have issued an injunction restraining Ssangyong from further proceeding in the Korean action until it had applied to the Korean court for a stay of that action. It would be required to include in its application a properly translated copy of certain findings by the New York court. These findings would include a recitation of the extensive judicial activity to date in the U.S. court together with a finding by that court that (a) the Korean party had willingly submitted to the jurisdiction of the U.S. courts and had spent years of litigation here before filing in Korea shortly before trial; (b) that China Trade and the U.S. court would be deprived of a substantial investment of time and money if the case were to be resolved in Korea; and (c) that if the stay was refused, the U.S. court would be

assisted by knowing the reasons for refusal of the stay by the Korean court before deciding what, if any, further action to take in the United States. The temporary injunction against Ssangyong would remain in effect until the Korean court ruled. This procedure would give the Korean court an opportunity to acquiesce by staying its action or to assert specific reasons why it would not do so. There is a reasonable chance that this procedure would be less offensive and would end without the need for a permanent injunction, because the Korean court would stay or the U.S. court would decide, after understanding the views of the Korean court, to permit the parallel proceedings to continue. The strict courts [on the limits on antisuit injunctions] might feel this approach is itself too intrusive and the more aggressive courts that it is not aggressive enough, which suggests that it might be just right. Westbrook, *International Judicial Negotiation*, 38 Tex. Int'l J.L. 567, 584-585 (2003).

Is this persuasive? Why? For a case where this sort of communication between trial courts of different nations was directed, *see Stonington Partners, Inc. v. Lernout & Hauspie Speech Prods. NV,* 310 F.3d 118 (3d Cir. 2002) (vacating antisuit injunction and declaring that "[w]e strongly recommend, in a situation such as this, that an actual dialog occur or be attempted between the courts of the different jurisdictions in an effort to reach an agreement on how to proceed or, at the very least, an understanding as to the policy considerations underpinning salient aspects of the foreign laws.").

Part Three

Legislative Jurisdiction and Choice of Law

In addition to resolving issues of judicial jurisdiction and forum selection, courts adjudicating international civil disputes must decide what law governs the resolution of such disputes. This decision involves issues of (a) legislative jurisdiction and (b) choice of law. These issues have historically been at the heart of most "conflict of laws" or "private international law" studies.

Legislative, or prescriptive, jurisdiction is the authority of a state to make its laws applicable to particular conduct, relationships, or status.[1] Put differently, legislative jurisdiction is the power of a state to prescribe substantive rules of conduct regulating private activities and other legal norms.

Restrictions on the legislative jurisdiction of U.S. courts can be imposed by either U.S. constitutional limitations or international law. The principal U.S. constitutional limitations in international matters are imposed by the foreign commerce clause and the Due Process Clause.[2] International law also imposes limitations on the exercise of legislative jurisdiction, although these limits have seldom played a direct role in U.S. courts.[3]

Choice of law involves selection of the law of a particular state to govern a dispute, contract, tort, or issue that has connections to two or more states.[4] Unless a state possesses legislative jurisdiction over the issue in question, its law may not properly be selected by choice of law analysis.[5] Even if a state can properly exercise legislative jurisdiction,

---

1. *See Restatement (Third) Foreign Relations Law* §401 (1987) ("make its law applicable to the activities, relations, or status of persons, or the interests of persons in things, whether by legislation, by executive act or order, by administrative rule or regulation, or by determination of a court"); *Restatement (Second) Conflict of Laws* §9 & comment d (1971); Akehurst, *Jurisdiction in International Law*, 46 Brit. Y.B. Int'l L. 145, 179-212 (1978); Reese, *Legislative Jurisdiction*, 78 Colum. L. Rev. 1587 (1978).

2. *See infra* pp. 606-644.

3. *See infra* pp. 591-605.

4. *See Restatement (Second) Conflict of Laws* §2 & comment a (1971) ("Each state has rules to determine which law (its own local law or the local law of another state) shall be applied by it to determine the rights and liabilities of the parties resulting from an occurrence involving foreign elements."); *Restatement (Third) Foreign Relations Law* §101 comment c (1987).

5. *Restatement (Second) Conflict of Laws* §9 comment b (1971) ("At least two things are implied when the local law of a state is applied to create or affects local interests. The first is that the state has jurisdiction to apply its local law. The second may be either that the state is the state of the applicable law under choice-of-law principles or, when the applicability of a statute of the forum is the point in issue, that a proper construction of the statute leads to its application in the given case."); *Restatement (Third) Foreign Relations Law* §401(a) & comment (b) (1987).

however, it may choose not to do so: a state's substantive laws or choice of law rules may not call for application of its laws, even if they could properly do so.

Choice of law issues are governed primarily by the choice of law rules of the forum state, whose courts decide what law to apply to disputes before them. Different states apply different choice of law rules, which almost necessarily leads to divergent results of choice-of law analyses in different forums. At the same time, both in the United States and elsewhere, choice of law rules have evolved significantly over time. It is often said that the past decades have witnessed an American "conflicts revolution."[6] This revolution has seen the displacement of traditional choice of law rules, based upon strict territorial principles, by more flexible analyses.

Part Three examines U.S. rules governing both legislative jurisdiction and choice of law in international cases. Chapter 7 discusses restrictions on the legislative jurisdiction of U.S. courts, imposed both by the U.S. Constitution and international law. Chapter 8 examines choice of law rules used by U.S. courts. Chapter 9 discusses two specialized choice of law rules — the act of state doctrine and the foreign sovereign compulsion doctrine — that have particular significance in U.S. international civil litigation. Issues of legislative jurisdiction and choice of law have substantial practical importance in international litigation. Different nations have profoundly different legal systems. The variations between different common law jurisdictions (*e.g.,* the United States, England, Canada, Australia) are often significant. These differences are slight, however, when compared with the divergences between common law and civil law, Islamic, or Asian legal systems.

The differences between U.S. substantive laws and the laws of other jurisdictions are often particularly significant. Although basic U.S. rules of contract, agency, property, and the like are often broadly similar to the rules prevailing in many foreign legal systems, other areas of the law are much different. In particular, U.S. approaches to issues of economic and market regulation, product liability, environmental matters, and tort law can be fundamentally different from the laws prevailing in foreign legal systems.

Because of these differences, the same dispute can readily be resolved in dramatically different ways under different nations' laws. As a consequence, the outcome of choice of law analysis is often directly relevant to the outcome of the dispute.

6. *See infra* pp. 738-740.

7

Legislative Jurisdiction[1]

As described above, "legislative" or "prescriptive" jurisdiction involves the authority of a state to make its substantive laws applicable to conduct, relationships, or status. There are two principal constraints on the power of a U.S. legislature to enact laws applicable to international conduct, relationships, or status. First, international law has long been understood as restricting assertions of legislative jurisdiction by states. Second, the U.S. Constitution limits the legislative jurisdiction of both Congress and state legislatures. This chapter explores both sets of limits.

A. International Law Limits on Legislative Jurisdiction

This section examines historic and contemporary views of international law limits on legislative jurisdiction. It does not consider how those limits apply in U.S. courts, or their relationship to U.S. law. These subjects are examined in subsequent sections of this chapter.

1. Introduction and Historical Background

During the nineteenth century, American courts, commentators, and other authorities understood international law as imposing strict territorial limits on national assertions of legislative jurisdiction. Here, as in other contexts,[2] Joseph Story's *Commentaries on the Conflict of Laws* dominated American thinking.

As recounted in greater detail elsewhere, *Story's Commentaries* built upon the work of Continental European jurists, particularly in the Netherlands and France, who had

---

1. Commentary on legislative jurisdiction includes, *e.g.*, Akehurst, *Jurisdiction in International Law*, 46 Brit. Y.B. Int'l L. 145 (1972); Born, *A Reappraisal of the Extraterritorial Reach of U.S. Law*, 24 Law & Pol'y Int'l Bus. 1 (1992); Fruhewald, *Constitutional Constraints on State Choice of Law*, 24 U. Dayton L. Rev. 39 (1998); Gerber, *Beyond Balancing: International Law Restraints on the Reach of National Laws*, 10 Yale J. Int'l L. 185 (1984); Kontorovich, *Beyond the Article I Horizon: Congress's Enumerated Powers and Universal Jurisdiction over Drug Crimes*, 93 Minn. L. Rev. 1191, 1229-1231 (2009); Kontorovich, *The "Define and Punish" Clause and the Limits of Universal Jurisdiction*, 103 Nw. U. L. Rev. 149 (2009); A. Lowenfeld, *International Litigation and the Quest for Reasonableness* 15-45 (1996); A. Lowenfeld, *Public Law in the International Arena: Conflict of Laws, International Law, and Some Suggestions for Their Interaction*, 163 Recueil des Cours 311 (1979); Mann, *The Doctrine of Jurisdiction in International Law*, 111 Recueil des Cours 1 (1964); Mann, *The Doctrine of International Jurisdiction Revisited After Twenty Years*, 1986 Recueil des Cours 9 (1984); Reese, *Legislative Jurisdiction*, 78 Colum. L. Rev. 1587 (1978); Rosen, *Extraterritoriality and Political Heterogeneity in American Federalism*, 150 U. Pa. L. Rev. 855 (2002); Weisburd, *Due Process Limits on Federal Extraterritorial Legislation*, 35 Colum J. Transnat'l L. 379 (1997).

2. *See supra* pp. 84-86 & *infra* pp. 648-649.

argued that international law rested on principles of territorial sovereignty.[3] These commentators emphasized the generally exclusive jurisdiction of a state over events, persons, and property within its territory. Story relied in particular on Ulrich Huber, a seventeenth-century Dutch academic.[4] Huber is best known for his classic work, *De Conflictu Legum*, which articulated three basic principles of international law:

(1) Every state's laws apply within the state's territory, but not beyond.
(2) All persons within a state are subjects of the state.
(3) "Comity" calls on states to recognize and enforce rights created by other states, provided that such recognition does not prejudice the state or its subjects.[5]

Citing Huber and other authorities, Joseph Story formulated several "general maxims of international jurisprudence,"[6] which imposed territorial limits on national sovereignty.

Story began with the premise that "every nation possesses an exclusive sovereignty and jurisdiction within its own territory."[7] Second, he developed the corollary that nations could properly exercise legislative jurisdiction only within their own territory:

> no state or nation can, by its laws, directly affect, or bind property out of its own territory, or bind persons not resident therein . . . for it would be wholly incompatible with the equality and exclusiveness of the sovereignty of all nations, that any one nation should be at liberty to regulate either persons or things not within its own territory.[8]

Story's view of international law was highly influential in nineteenth-century America. Other commentators concurred with his territorial vision of legislative jurisdiction.[9] U.S. courts also agreed. *The Apollon*,[10] decided in 1824, illustrates prevailing U.S. judicial views of international law limits on legislative jurisdiction. The case required an interpretation of federal customs statutes to determine whether they extended to foreign vessels outside U.S. waters. Justice Story wrote that

> [t]he laws of no nation can justly extend beyond its own territory, except so far as regards its own citizens. They can have no force to control the sovereignty or rights of any other nation, within its jurisdiction.[11]

---

3. *See* Davies, *The Influence of Huber's De Conflictu Legum on English Private International Law*, 18 Brit. Y.B. Int'l L. 49 (1937); Nussbaum, *Rise and Decline of the Law-of-Nations Doctrine in the Conflict of Laws*, 42 Colum. L. Rev. 189 (1942); Lorenzen, *Territoriality, Public Policy and the Conflict of Laws*, 33 Yale L.J. 736 (1924); Yntema, *The Comity Doctrine*, 65 Mich. L. Rev. 9, 16-28 (1966).

4. *See supra* p. 85; Lorenzen, *Huber's De Conflictu Legum*, in *Selected Articles on the Conflict of Laws* 136 (1947).

5. *See* Lorenzen, *Huber's De Conflictu Legum*, in *Selected Articles on the Conflict of Laws* 136 (1947). Of Huber's *De Conflictu Legum* it has been said: "In the whole history of law there are probably no five pages which have been so often quoted, and possibly so much read." F. Harrison, *On Jurisprudence and the Conflict of Laws* 116 (1919).

6. J. Story, *Commentaries on the Conflict of Laws*, 19 & Heading to Chapter II (2d ed. 1841).

7. J. Story, *Commentaries on the Conflict of Laws* 19, 21-22 (2d ed. 1841); Mann, *The Doctrine of Jurisdiction in International* Law, 111 Recueil des Cours 1, 33 (1964) ("Although Story's maxims, if properly understood, do have a bearing upon private international law no less than on law in general, they express principles of public international law").

8. J. Story, *Commentaries on the Conflict of Laws* 19, 21-22 (2d ed. 1841).

9. *E.g.*, H. Wheaton, *Elements of International Law* §§77, 111-114, 134-151 (1855) ("Every independent State is entitled to the inclusive power of legislation, in respect to the personal rights and civil state and conditions of its citizens and in respect to all real and personal property situated within its territory, whether belonging to citizens or aliens."); J. Moore, *A Digest of International Law* 236 (1906) ("There is no principle better settled than that the penal laws of a country have no extraterritorial force.").

10. 22 U.S. 362 (1824).

11. 22 U.S. at 370.

Story also observed that the extraterritorial assertion of U.S. jurisdiction would be "at variance with the independence and sovereignty of foreign nations," and that such jurisdictional claims had "never yet been acknowledged by other nations, and would be resisted by none with more pertinacity than by the Americans."[12]

Relying on this territoriality principle, derived from what Story called the "law of nations," the Court in *The Apollon* invoked a presumption of territoriality: "however general and comprehensive the phrases used in our municipal laws may be, *they must always be restricted in construction, to places and persons, upon whom the legislature have authority and jurisdiction.*"[13] As a consequence, Story declined to interpret federal law as authorizing U.S. revenue authorities to seize vessels located in foreign water, concluding: "It would be monstrous to suppose, that our revenue officers were authorized to enter into foreign ports and territories, for the purpose of seizing vessels which had offended against our laws. It cannot be presumed, that Congress would voluntarily justify such a clear violation of the laws of nations."[14] Other early U.S. decisions took the same territorial view of international law.[15]

As Story's opinion in *The Apollon* suggested, the nineteenth-century American understanding of international limits on legislative jurisdiction was related to the United States' resistance to efforts by other nations—particularly Great Britain and other European powers—to apply their criminal laws extraterritorially to conduct occurring on U.S. territory or vessels.[16] As early as 1793, Secretary of State Thomas Jefferson invoked principles of territorial sovereignty and the equality of states when resisting a claim by France of jurisdiction over vessels in U.S. waters:

> Every nation has, of natural right, entirely and exclusively, all the jurisdiction which may be rightfully exercised in the territory it occupies. If it cedes any portion of that jurisdiction to judges appointed by another nation, the limits of their power must depend on the instrument of cession.[17]

Similarly, in the *Cutting Case*, the United States vigorously protested through diplomatic channels against a Mexican judicial proceeding that appeared to apply Mexican libel law to newspaper articles published in El Paso, Texas.[18] Among other things, the United States urged that:

> [t]he assumption of the Mexican tribunal, under the laws of Mexico, to punish a citizen of the United States for an offense wholly committed and consummated in his own country against

---

12. 22 U.S. at 370.

13. 22 U.S. at 370 (emphasis added).

14. 22 U.S. at 370. Similarly, in *United States v. Davis*, 25 Fed. Cas. 786 (C.C.D. Mass. 1837), Story (sitting as a Circuit Judge) concluded that federal criminal legislation did not apply to an American seaman who fired a shot from a U.S. vessel, anchored in non-U.S. waters, which struck and killed a man aboard a non-U.S. vessel. According to Story, "although the gun was fired from the U.S. Ship Rose, the shot took effect and the death happened on board of the Schooner; and the act was, in contemplation of law, done where the shot took effect." 25 Fed. Cas. at 787. "We decide the case wholly on the ground, that the Schooner was a foreign vessel, belonging to foreigners, and at the time under the acknowledged jurisdiction of a foreign government."

15. *E.g.*, *Rose v. Himely*, 8 U.S. 241, 279 (1807); *Schooner Exchange v. McFaddon*, 11 U.S. 116, 135-136 (1812); *United States v. Palmer*, 16 U.S. 610, 631 (1818); *American Banana Co. v. United Fruit Co.*, 213 U.S. 347, 355 (1909); *United States v. Bowman*, 260 U.S. 93, 97-98 (1922).

16. *See* Dumbauld, *John Marshall and the Law of Nations*, 104 U. Pa. L. Rev. 38, 38-44 (1955).

17. American State Papers, Foreign Relations, I, pp. 147-148, 167, 169 (Letter from Mr. Jefferson, Secretary of State, to Mr. Morris, Minister to France, dated Aug. 16, 1793).

18. J. Moore, *Report on Extraterritorial Crime and the Cutting Case* (1887), 1887 U.S. Foreign Relations 757. *See also* 1886 U.S. Foreign Relations viii (Annual Message to Congress by President Cleveland).

its laws was an invasion of the independence of this Government. . . . There is no principle better settled than that the penal laws of a country have no extraterritorial force. Each state may, it is true, provide for the punishment of its own citizens for acts committed by them outside of its territory. . . . *To say, however, that the penal laws of a country can bind foreigners and regulate their conduct, either in their own or in any other foreign country, is to assert a jurisdiction over such countries and impair their independence. . . .*[19]

Successive U.S. governments took similar positions on other occasions in the nineteenth century.[20]

The nineteenth-century American view that international law imposed strict territorial limits on legislative jurisdiction paralleled similar restrictions on judicial jurisdiction. As discussed above, *Story's Commentaries* also viewed international law as imposing strict territorial limits on judicial jurisdiction.[21] Similarly, U.S. decisions like *Rose v. Himely* and *Pennoyer v. Neff* looked to international law as the basis for formulating territorial limitations on the personal jurisdiction of U.S. courts.[22] International law principles of territorial sovereignty and sovereign equality also provided the basis for nineteenth-century American treatment of foreign sovereign immunity.[23]

Even in the nineteenth century, however, the territoriality principle was never quite as absolute as the foregoing might suggest. There was general acknowledgment of "nationality" as a jurisdictional base, both in U.S. judicial opinions[24] and otherwise.[25] Nonetheless, there were very few actual assertions of legislative jurisdiction by the United States based on nationality during the nineteenth century.[26] A few early American state court decisions also embraced very limited versions of what would come to be known as the "effects doctrine," although such decisions appear to have been rare.[27]

19. 1887 U.S. Foreign Relations 751 (emphasis added).

20. Between 1873 and 1875, when British courts entertained civil disputes arising on the high seas between sailors on U.S. vessels, the U.S. Department of State protested, on the grounds that Britain's extraterritorial assertions of both judicial and legislative jurisdiction violated "rules of comity between nations and the principles of international law." Letters from Secretary of State Fish to General Schenck, dated Nov. 8, 1873 and March 12, 1875, *reprinted in Foreign Relations of the United States* 490 (1874) and *id.* at 592, 633 (1875). *See also* Letter from Secretary of State Calhoun to Mr. Everett, dated August 7, 1844, *excerpted in* II J. Moore, *A Digest of International Law* 225 (1906) ("Great Britain can not by her laws make an act committed within the jurisdiction of the United States criminal within her territories, however immoral of itself, and vice versa. The proposition is too clear to require illustration or to be contested."); *Jacob Idler v. Venezuela* (1885), *reprinted in* J. Moore, *International Arbitrations* 3491, 3511-3512 (1898); *Island of Palmas Case* (*Netherlands v. United States*), 2 U.S. Rep. of Int'l Arb. Awards 829, 839 (1928).

21. J. Story, *Commentaries on the Conflicts of Laws* §449-50 (2d ed. 1841). Story wrote: "Considered in an international point of view, jurisdiction, to be rightfully exercised, must be founded either upon the person being within the territory or the thing being within the territory; for otherwise there can be no sovereignty exerted. . . . [N]o sovereignty can extend its process beyond its own territorial limits to subject either persons or property to its judicial decisions."

22. *See supra* pp. 84-86.

23. *See supra* pp. 231-233; *Schooner Exchange v. McFaddon*, 11 U.S. 116 (1812).

24. *E.g., The Apollon*, 22 U.S. 362, 370-371 (1824) ("The laws of no nation can justly extend beyond its own territory, except so far as regards its own citizens"); *Rose v. Himely*, 8 U.S. 241, 279 (1807).

25. J. Story, *Commentaries on the Conflict of Laws* 21-22 (2d ed. 1841).

26. Harvard Research in International Law, *The Law of Nationality*, 23 Am. J. Int'l L. Supp. 11, 80-82 (1929); J. Moore, *Report on Extraterritorial Crime and the Cutting Case*, (1887), *excerpted in* II J. Moore, A Digest of International Law 255 (1906); *Restatement (Third) Foreign Relations Law* §402 Reporters' Note 1 (1987).

27. *Commonwealth v. Smith*, 11 Allen 243 (1865); *Adams v. The People*, Comstock's Rep. (N.Y.) 173, 179; *The People v. Rathbun*, 21 Wend. 509 (N.Y.) (1839); *Barkhamsted v. Parsons*, 3 Conn. 1 (1819); *State v. Grady*, 34 Conn. 118 (1867). *But see People v. Merrill*, 2 Parker's Crim. Rep. 590 (N.Y.) ("It cannot be pretended or assumed that a State has jurisdiction over crimes committed beyond its territorial limits"; declining jurisdiction over non-New York resident for luring black man from New York and selling him as a slave outside New York in violation of New York law). In general, however, even those courts that applied the effects doctrine did so in a fairly narrow category of cases. As John Bassett Moore concluded in 1887, "in no case has an English or an American court assumed jurisdiction, even under statutes couched in the most general language, to try and sentence a foreigner

2.   Contemporary International Law Limits on Legislative Jurisdiction: The "Effects Test" and the Erosion of Territorial Limits

During the early decades of the twentieth century, the United States and other states gradually began to depart from the view that international law imposed strict territorial limits on national assertions of legislative jurisdiction. They increasingly exercised legislative jurisdiction based on the so-called "effects test," the nationality doctrine, and other bases.[28] This trend paralleled developments in other contexts. As discussed elsewhere, *Pennoyer*'s territorial limits on judicial jurisdiction gave way to more flexible rules, while the absolute theory of sovereign immunity was replaced by the restrictive theory during this same period.[29]

Near the turn of the century, John Bassett Moore, a leading U.S. commentator, authored a classic work — *Report on Extraterritorial Crime* — which predicted that the effects doctrine would enjoy growing importance in the future.[30] In his words, "the methods which modern invention has furnished for the performance of criminal acts . . . has made this principle one of constantly growing importance and increasing frequency of application."[31] That prediction was exactly right — with revolutions in transportation and communications making transnational conduct routine and blurring, or arguably blurring, national borders.

"Modern invention" also bred modern regulatory legislation, including antitrust, securities, shipping, employment, and other laws. The application of these statutes to international activities led to further erosion of territorial limits on legislative jurisdiction. In the antitrust field, the so-called "effects doctrine" was frequently invoked by U.S. regulatory authorities in the early twentieth century to justify the extraterritorial application of the Sherman Act.[32] Likewise, various U.S. criminal laws were applied to conduct abroad that had U.S. effects.[33] Congress and other legislatures also began to enact regulatory statutes expressly applicable to foreign conduct by U.S. nationals, such as federal income tax legislation,[34] the Trading With the Enemy Act,[35] and the Walsh Act.[36]

Particularly significant was the 1927 decision of the Permanent Court of International Justice (PCIJ) in *The SS Lotus* (*France v. Turkey*).[37] The PCIJ held in *Lotus* that international law did not forbid Turkey from applying its criminal laws to a French officer's actions on board a French vessel that had collided on the high seas with a Turkish vessel. Several sailors on the Turkish vessel died in the accident and criminal charges were brought

---

for acts done by him abroad, unless they were brought, either by an immediate effect, or by direct and continuance [sic] causal relationship, within the territorial jurisdiction of the court." J. Moore, *Report on Extraterritorial Crime* (1887), *excerpted in* II J. Moore, *A Digest of International Law* 255 (1906).

28. *See infra* pp. 649-672.

29. *See supra* pp. 86-87, 233-234

30. J. Moore, *supra* note 27, at 244.

31. *Id.*

32. *United States v. Bopp*, 237 F. 283 (N.D. Cal. 1916); *United States v. Rintelen*, 233 F. 793 (S.D.N.Y. 1916); *United States v. Pacific and Arctic Railway and Navigation Co.*, 228 U.S. 87 (1913); *United States v. Aluminum Co. of America*, E.Q. 159 (W.D. Tenn. 1912).

33. *E.g., Ford v. United States*, 273 U.S. 593 (1927).

34. Internal Revenue Code §1 (imposing federal income tax on "all citizens of the United States, wherever resident"); *Cook v. Tait*, 265 U.S. 47 (1924).

35. 40 Stat. 415 (1917).

36. 28 U.S.C. §1783. The Walsh Act obliged U.S. nationals residing abroad to return to the United States to provide evidence in certain circumstances. *Blackmer v. United States*, 284 U.S. 421 (1932), upheld the Act against constitutional challenge. *See supra* pp. 109-113.

37. P.C.I.J., Ser. A, No. 10 (1927).

against the French officer in Turkish court; France protested that Turkey could not properly exercise legislative jurisdiction, and the dispute was referred to the PCIJ.

The PCIJ held that Turkey was not barred from exercising legislative jurisdiction over the French officer's conduct. The Court first rejected the argument that international law generally forbid the extraterritorial application of national laws.[38] According to the Court, national regulatory efforts are presumptively valid and states claiming that such efforts violate international law have the burden of persuasion:[39]

> Far from laying down a general prohibition to the effect that states may not extend the application of their laws and the jurisdiction of their courts to persons, property and acts outside their territory, [international law] leaves them in this respect a wide measure of discretion which is only limited in certain cases by prohibitive rules; as regards other cases every state remains free to adopt the principles which it regards as best and most suitable. . . . The territoriality of criminal law, therefore, is not an absolute principle of international law and by no means coincides with territorial sovereignty.[40]

The PCIJ also rejected the argument that international law required states "only to have regard to the place where the author of the offense happens to be at the time of the offense."[41] On the contrary, "the courts of many countries, even of countries which have given their criminal legislation a strictly territorial character, interpret criminal law in the sense that offenses, the authors of which at the moment of commission are in the territory of another state, are nevertheless to be regarded as having been committed in the national territory, if one of the constituent elements of the offense, and more especially its effects, have taken place there."[42] The Court had little difficulty concluding that, under this standard, the defendant's negligence had sufficient effects on the Turkish vessel to sustain Turkish jurisdiction.

The *Lotus* decision aroused considerable controversy, and a variety of interpretations of the decision have been offered.[43] It is clear, however, that the PCIJ's opinion reflects a significant evolution in international law. The PCIJ rejected any strict territorial limit on national legislative jurisdiction and instead recognized an effects doctrine, or "objective territoriality" principle, of some (although disputed) breadth.

The *Lotus* decision's rejection of notions of strict territoriality was rapidly adopted elsewhere. In 1934, the *Restatement (First) Conflict of Laws* was released, adopting the territorial approach to choice of law problems championed by its Reporter, Professor Joseph Beale.[44] Nevertheless, the *First Restatement* contained provisions on legislative

---

38. P.C.I.J., Ser. A, No. 10, at 19 (1927).

39. *Accord* Akehurst, *Jurisdiction in International Law*, 46 Brit. Y.B. Int'l L. 145, 167 (1972); Mann, *The Doctrine of Jurisdiction in International Law*, 111 Recueil des Cours 1, 35 (1964); Berge, *The Case of the S.S. Lotus*, 26 Mich. L. Rev. 361, 377 (1928).

40. P.C.I.J., Ser. A, No. 10, at 19 (1927).

41. P.C.I.J., Ser. A, No. 10, at 23 (1927).

42. P.C.I.J., Ser. A, No. 10, at 23 (1927).

43. *E.g.*, Mann, *The Doctrine of Jurisdiction in International Law*, 111 Recueil des Cours 1, 35 (1964) (suggesting narrow reading of PCIJ's "obiter dictum," but concluding that even "such an approach would considerably undermine the Huber-Storyan canons"); Jennings, *Extraterritorial Jurisdiction and the U.S. Antitrust Laws*, [1957] Brit. Y.B. Int'l L. 152 (PCIJ shifts burden of proving "an ascertained prohibitive rule of international law," but international law forbids use of effects doctrine in criminal context unless a "constituent effect" is involved); Harvard Research in International Law, *Jurisdiction with Respect to Crime*, 29 Am. J. Int'l L. 435, 501 (1935) ("The decision in the S.S. Lotus clearly supports the conclusion that no principle of international law forbids the localization of an offense, consisting of unintended injury caused through negligence, at the place where the negligence takes effect. This conclusion is in harmony with tendencies clearly manifested in modern legislation.").

44. *See infra* pp. 724-725.

jurisdiction which were neither strictly territorial nor as rigid as traditional nineteenth-century views. Section 55 of the *Restatement* stated the traditional territorial limits on national jurisdiction: "A state has jurisdiction over all acts done or events occurring within the territory of a state." In addition, however, §65 provided for an "effects doctrine": "If consequences of an act done in one state occur in another state, each state in which any event in the series of act and consequences occurs may exercise legislative jurisdiction," while §63 recognized the nationality principle.

Similarly, in 1935, the classic Harvard Research in International Law study on *Jurisdiction with Respect to Crime* was published. The study recognized a variety of significant exceptions to a principle of strict territoriality — including the nationality principle[45] and an effects test.[46] More generally, at least in the United States, academic commentators began to recognize the effects doctrine and other extraterritorial jurisdictional bases.[47]

Twentieth-century American courts also began to apply what amounted to an "effects doctrine." In 1911, Justice Holmes reasoned in *Strassheim v. Daily*,[48] a domestic criminal case, that

> the usage of the civilized world would warrant Michigan in punishing [the defendant], although he never had set foot in the state until after the fraud was complete. Acts done outside the jurisdiction, but intended to produce and producing detrimental effects within it, justify a state in punishing the cause of the harm as if he had been present at the effect, if the state should succeed in getting him within its power.

Other U.S. courts followed suit, with increasing frequency as the twentieth century progressed.[49]

More recently, the United States and other countries have adopted increasingly expansive views of national legislative jurisdiction under international law.[50] Following 1945, the United States was often particularly robust in applying its laws extraterritorially, and took a commensurately broad view of international law. These views are reflected in the *Restatement (Second) Foreign Relations Law* and *Restatement (Third) Foreign Relations Law*, excerpted and discussed below. During the same period, foreign states generally took, or purported to take, less expansive views of extraterritorial jurisdiction. As a consequence, post-War assertions of U.S. legislative jurisdiction often aroused diplomatic protests and legal objections from foreign states, which are also examined below.[51] More recently, a number of European states have begun to apply selected national regulatory statutes extraterritorially, with rigor approaching that of

---

45. 29 Am. J. Int'l L. Supp. 435, 519-539 (1935) ("A State has jurisdiction with respect to any crime committed outside its territory, (a) By a natural person who was a national of that State when the crime was committed or who is a national of that State when prosecuted or punished; or (b) By a corporation or other juristic person which had the national character of that State when the crime was committed.").

46. 29 Am. J. Int'l L. Supp. 435, 480-508 (1935). Article 3 of the draft Convention provided: "A State has jurisdiction with respect to any crime committed in whole or in part within its territory. This jurisdiction extends to (a) Any participation outside its territory in a crime committed in whole or in part within its territory; and (b) Any attempt outside its territory to commit a crime in whole or in part within its territory." *Id.* at 480. The commentary to Article 3 made clear that it adopted an effects test. *Id.* at 500-503.

47. *E.g.*, C. Hyde, *International Law* 805 (1945); L. Oppenheim, *International Law* 331-334 (7th ed. 1948) (strict territoriality "is not a view which, consistently with the practice of States and with common sense, can be rigidly adopted in all cases").

48. 221 U.S. 280, 284-285 (1911).

49. *E.g.*, *Ford v. United States*, 273 U.S. 593, 620-621 (1927); *Lamar v. United States*, 240 U.S. 60 (1916); *infra* pp. 666-680.

50. *See Restatement (Third) Foreign Relations Law*, pt. IV, ch. 1, Intro. Note (1987).

51. *See infra* pp. 680-683.

the United States, arousing complaints from both the United States and international businesses.[52]

3. Selected Materials Concerning the Evolution of International Law Limits on Legislative Jurisdiction

Excerpted below are materials that illustrate the evolution of U.S. views regarding international law limitations on legislative jurisdiction. The materials begin with the strict territorial doctrine of Joseph Story's *Commentaries on the Conflict of Laws*. Next, consider the *Restatement (First) of Conflict of Laws*, published in 1934. Finally, examine the successive formulations of increasingly expansive views of legislative jurisdiction reflected in the *Restatement (Second) Foreign Relations Law* (1965), the *Restatement (Second) Conflict of Laws* (1971), and the *Restatement (Third) Foreign Relations Law* (1987).

J. STORY, COMMENTARIES ON THE CONFLICT OF LAWS
§§18, 20 & 23 (2d ed. 1841) [excerpted in Appendix BB]

RESTATEMENT (FIRST) CONFLICT OF LAWS
§§55, 63 & 65 (1934) [excerpted in Appendix X]

RESTATEMENT (SECOND) FOREIGN RELATIONS LAW OF THE UNITED STATES
§§17, 18, 30, 33, 39 & 40 (1965) [excerpted in Appendix Z]

RESTATEMENT (SECOND) CONFLICT OF LAWS
§9 (1971) [excerpted in Appendix Y]

RESTATEMENT (THIRD) FOREIGN RELATIONS LAW OF THE UNITED STATES
§§402, 403 & 441 (1987) [excerpted in Appendix AA]

Notes on Story's Commentaries and Restatements

1. *Nineteenth-century limits on legislative jurisdiction.* Consider the territorial limits on legislative jurisdiction in *Story's Commentaries*. Compare them to the territorial limits imposed by nineteenth-century international law on judicial jurisdiction. *See supra* pp. 84-86. What were the rationales for both sets of limits? What public and private interests are served by international limits on national legislative jurisdiction? Do such limits: (a) protect the sovereignty of other states; (b) protect individuals from unfair, arbitrary, or unforeseeable applications of substantive law; (c) protect international commerce and the international system from unduly burdensome or conflicting national laws; or (d) achieve something else?

Some early U.S. authorities linked territorial limits on legislative jurisdiction to notions of the sovereign equality of States. *The Antelope*, 23 U.S. 66, 122 (1825) ("no principle of general law is more universally acknowledged, than the perfect equality of nations. Russia and Geneva have equal rights. It results from this equality, that no one can rightfully

---

52. *See infra* pp. 680-683.

impose a rule on another."). Are territorial limits on jurisdiction a necessary consequence of sovereign equality? Can't equal states have equally valid powers to apply their laws extraterritorially?

2. *Evolution of U.S. views of international law limits on legislative jurisdiction—1841-1934.* Contrast Story's territorial limits on legislative jurisdiction with the *Restatement (First) Conflict of Laws*, the *Restatement (Second) Foreign Relations Law*, and the *Restatement (Third) Foreign Relations Law.* With the advent of global industries, mass transportation, and international capital and other markets, is there any question that the territorial views of Story, Jefferson, and other nineteenth-century American authorities are now simply unworkable?

Recall that Story and the *Restatements* reflect American conceptions of international law. Were there political, strategic, and commercial reasons for the United States to have different interests in the content of international law in the early nineteenth century — when it was a fledgling state, facing more powerful and expansive European nations — than in the mid-twentieth century — when it had emerged from the Second World War with military and commercial predominance? *See supra* pp. 593-594.

3. *Overview of bases for legislative jurisdiction under contemporary international law.* Contemporary international law recognizes several bases for legislative jurisdiction.

(a) Territoriality. The primary and least controversial jurisdictional base under international law remains the "territoriality principle," which derives from states' sovereignty over national territory. *See Restatement (Third) Foreign Relations Law* §402, comment c (1987) ("[t]he territorial principle is by far the most common basis for the exercise of jurisdiction to prescribe, and it has generally been free from controversy"); *Restatement (Second) Foreign Relations Law* §17 (1965); *Restatement (First) Conflict of Laws* §55 (1934); *Laker Airways v. Sabena,* 731 F.2d 909, 921 (D.C. Cir. 1984) ("the territoriality base of jurisdiction is universally recognized. It is the most pervasive and basic principle underlying the exercise by nations of prescriptive regulatory power."). The territoriality principle permits states to regulate transactions or conduct occurring within national borders, for example, by applying environmental laws to manufacturing activities within the state. In addition, the principle is now understood in the United States as permitting regulation of conduct or transactions occurring partially within and partially outside national territory. *See Restatement (Third) Foreign Relations Law* §402 (1987).

(b) Nationality. International law also recognizes the "nationality principle" as a legitimate base for legislative jurisdiction. The nationality principle permits a state to exercise legislative jurisdiction over its nationals and citizens, even when they are outside national territory. *See Skiriotes v. Florida,* 313 U.S. 69 (1941); *Restatement (Third) Foreign Relations Law* §402(2) & Reporter's Note 1 (1987); *Restatement (Second) Foreign Relations Law* §30 (1965); *Restatement (First) Conflict of Laws* §63 (1934). Under the nationality principle, for example, the United States can generally forbid U.S. citizens from trading with nations hostile to the United States, even if the trading occurs outside U.S. territory.

(c) Effects doctrine. The so-called "effects doctrine" is reflected in the *Restatement (First)* §65, the *Restatement (Second)* §18, and the *Restatement (Third)* §402. The effects doctrine is more controversial than either the territoriality or nationality principle. It permits a state to exercise legislative jurisdiction over conduct occurring outside the state, provided that the conduct has sufficient effects within the state's territory. *Restatement (Third) Foreign Relations Law* §402(1)(c) (1987); *United States v. Aluminum Co. of America,* 148 F.2d 416 (2d Cir. 1945); Harvard Research in International Law, *Jurisdiction with Respect to Crime,* 29 Am. J. Int'l L. Supp. 435, 484-488 (1935).

Unlike the territoriality and nationality principles, many formulations of the "effects doctrine" have been the subject of considerable controversy. *See infra* pp. 680-683. Some authorities still contend that the doctrine can be applied only in very limited categories of cases. Jennings, *Extraterritorial Jurisdiction and the United States Antitrust Laws*, 33 Brit. Y.B. Int'l L. 146 (1957); I. Brownlie, *Principles of Public International Law* 299-303 (4th ed. 1990). In particular, as discussed below, the extraterritorial application of U.S. antitrust laws based on the effects doctrine has provoked considerable controversy. *See infra* pp. 680-683.

(d) Protective principle. The "protective principle" permits the regulation of a narrow range of conduct that threatens national security (such as counterfeiting and espionage). *Restatement (Third) Foreign Relations Law* §402(3) (1987); *Restatement (Second) Foreign Relations Law* §33 (1965). This jurisdictional base is seldom invoked in civil litigation.

(e) Universality principle. The "universality principle," allowing extraterritorial jurisdiction over certain universally condemned crimes (such as piracy). *See Restatement (Third) Foreign Relations Law* §404 (1987). Like the protective principle, international commercial disputes seldom involve the universality principle (although it can be relevant to human rights litigation, *see supra* pp. 50-52).

4. *Evolution of U.S. views of international law limits on legislative jurisdiction — 1934-1971.* Consider the evolution of U.S. views of international law between 1934 and 1971.

(a) Legislative jurisdiction distinguished from choice of law. The *Restatement (First) Conflict of Laws* dealt with both legislative jurisdiction and choice of law, distinguishing carefully between the two subjects. In contrast, *the Restatement (Second) Conflict of Laws* concentrated on choice of law issues and did not deal with issues of legislative jurisdiction in a meaningful way. It instead merely referred readers to the *Restatement (Second) Foreign Relations Law. See Restatement (Second) Conflict of Laws* §9 & comment c (1971) ("As to limitations imposed by international law, *see* Chapters 1 and 2 of the Restatement of the Foreign Relations Law.").

(b) Effects doctrine. Compare the effects doctrine contained in §65 of the *Restatement (First) Conflict of Laws* with that in §18 of the *Restatement (Second) Foreign Relations Law.* Note that §65's effects doctrine is at least nominally more expansive than that in §18. What is the rationale for the limits in §18 of the *Second Restatement?* Consider the following hypotheticals:

> Foreign companies engage in anticompetitive price-fixing outside the United States but directed at U.S. purchasers, and succeed in significantly raising the prices paid by U.S. consumers. The consumers sue in U.S. courts, which apply U.S. antitrust laws.
>
>   U.S. newspapers print articles critical of foreign political and commercial figures, and copies of those newspapers are ultimately disseminated in those figures' home countries. They sue in their home courts, which apply local libel law to the U.S. defendants' U.S. conduct. Suppose the newspapers are distributed only in the United States, but the foreign individuals are damaged at home?

How would the *First Restatement* have resolved these hypotheticals? How would the *Restatement (Second) Conflict of Laws* and the *Restatement (Second) Foreign Relations Law* resolve them?

(c) Nationality principle. Compare the nationality principle contained in §63 of the *Restatement (First) Conflicts of Laws* with that in §§30 and 40 of the *Restatement (Second) Foreign Relations Law.* Note the significant limitation contained in §63, forbidding use of the nationality principle to require conduct in violation of the law or public policy of the state where the conduct occurs. Is this approach preferable to that in §§30 and 40 of the *Restatement (Second) Foreign Relations Law?* What exactly is the latter approach? *See infra* pp. 601-602. Compare the foreign sovereign compulsion doctrine and §441 of the *Third Restatement. See infra* pp. 857-864.

(d) "Reasonableness" limits. Consider the sole reference to limitations on legislative jurisdiction set forth in §9 of the *Restatement (Second) Conflict of Laws*—that the application of a state's law be "reasonable." Compare this limitation to the "reasonableness" standard articulated in the *Restatement (Third) Foreign Relations Law* §403 (1987); Appendix AA. Would it be wise to replace traditional international law limits on legislative jurisdiction with a general "reasonableness" test? What would be the content, in a world of 200 sovereign states, of the "reasonableness" limits? Would "reasonableness" have any meaningful limit on national assertions of legislative jurisdiction? Why is it important for such limits to exist?

5. ***Historic foreign criticisms of U.S. effects doctrine.*** Not all foreign states have agreed with American views of the jurisdictional limits of international law, and some have vigorously and repeatedly protested the extraterritorial applications of U.S. law. The target of much criticism has been the effects doctrine:

> [The effects doctrine, or objective territoriality principle,] is often said to apply where the offense "takes effect" or "produces its effects" in the territory. In relation to elementary cases of direct physical injury, such as homicide, this is unexceptionable, for here the "effect" which is meant is an essential ingredient of the crime. Once we move out of the sphere of direct physical consequences, however, to employ the formula of "effects" is to enter upon a very slippery slope; for here the effects within the territory may be no more than an element of alleged consequential damage which may be more or less remote. . . . [T]o extend the notion of effects, without qualification, from the simple cases of direct physical injury to cases such as defamation, sedition, and the like is to introduce a dangerous ambiguity in to the basis of the doctrine. If indeed it were permissible to found objective territorial jurisdiction upon the territoriality of more or less remote repercussions of an act wholly performed in another territory, then there were virtually no limit to a State's territorial jurisdiction. Jennings, *Extraterritorial Jurisdiction and the United States Antitrust Laws*, [1957] Brit. Y.B. Int'l L. 146, 159.

Are such criticisms persuasive? In today's global economy, doesn't an "effects" doctrine permit almost limitless legislative jurisdiction? Compare the consequences of the effects doctrine on congressional power under the domestic "interstate commerce" clause. *See supra* pp. 5-7. Consider the contemporary acceptance of the effects doctrine by other states in, for example, the antitrust context. *See infra* pp. 673-680.

6. ***Evolution of U.S. views of international law limits on legislative jurisdiction— 1971-2010.*** Contrast the jurisdictional provisions of the *Restatement (Second) Foreign Relations Law* with those of the *Third Restatement*, published in 1987. Note that §402 broadens the "territorial" and "effects" bases for jurisdiction, while substituting a general reasonableness limitation, set forth in §403. Is this desirable? Compare this evolution to the development of principles of judicial jurisdiction. *See supra* pp. 82-90.

7. ***No basis under international law for legislative jurisdiction based on passive personality.*** Section 30(2) of the *Restatement (Second) Foreign Relations Law* provides that international law does not recognize the nationality of the victim of acts committed outside national territory as an independent basis for legislative jurisdiction. That is, if a U.S. national is harmed outside the United States, then the mere fact that the victim was a U.S. national does not permit the United States to apply its law to the harmful conduct. The *Restatement (Third)* affirms this rule, although only in a comment: "The passive personality principle asserts that a state may apply law—particularly criminal law—to an act committed outside its territory by a person not its national where the victim of the act was its national. The principle has not been generally accepted for ordinary torts or crimes, but it is increasingly accepted as applied to terrorist" and similar crimes. *Restatement*

(Third) Foreign Relations Law §402 comment g (1987). Compare the relevance of the plaintiff's nationality to the existence of judicial jurisdiction. *See supra* p. 157.

Is this a wise approach? Why should a nation be forbidden by international law from applying its laws extraterritorially to the misconduct of foreign persons who harm its nationals? In reality, don't nations have a strong and legitimate interest in safeguarding their nationals from mistreatment and injustice, wherever they may be? What is the harm of permitting this? In medieval times, laws were generally "personal," following individuals wherever they might go: "it often happens that five men, each under a different law, may be found walking or sitting together." Letter from St. Agobar, Archbishop of Lyon, to Louis the Pious, dated 817 (quoted in 1 F. von Savigny, *Geschichte des Roemischen Rechts im Mittelalter* 116 (2d ed. 1834)). Is this undesirable? Why? *See Goldberg v. UBS AG*, 690 F. Supp. 2d 92, 110 n.29 (E.D.N.Y. 2010) (discussing views on passive personality principle).

   8. *Concurrent legislative jurisdiction.* Under contemporary international law, two or more states will frequently enjoy legislative jurisdiction over the same conduct. That is expressed in §40 of the *Restatement (Second) Foreign Relations Law* and §403 of the *Restatement (Third) Foreign Relations Law*: "[t]erritoriality and nationality are discrete and independent bases of jurisdiction; the same conduct or activity may provide a basis for exercise of jurisdiction both by the territorial state and by the state of nationality of the actor." *Restatement (Third) Foreign Relations Law* §402 comment b (1987).

   Consider the difficulties that concurrent jurisdiction can produce. Most extreme, one state may require a private party to do something (*e.g.*, perform a contractual obligation), while a second state may forbid it from doing the required act (*e.g.*, not perform the contractual obligations). Conflicting legal obligations of this sort impose obvious unfairness on private parties, as well as chilling international commercial enterprise. Less extreme, if multiple states regulate or tax the same course of conduct, then there is an obvious risk of confiscatory or otherwise crippling results (*e.g.*, taxation in excess of 100 percent of income or property value). Should international law permit concurrent legislative jurisdiction? Is it one thing to abandon territorial limits on national legislative jurisdiction, and another to say that two states can regulate the same conduct? Should international law provide, rather like physics, that two laws cannot occupy the same space?

   9. *Moderation of consequences of concurrent jurisdiction.* Various efforts have been made to moderate the consequences of concurrent jurisdiction.

   (a) Section 63 of the First Restatement. Conflicting legal requirements are imposed when one state requires what another state forbids. Note that conflicting legal requirements were less likely under the *Restatement (First) Conflict of Laws*, which did not permit use of §63's nationality principle to require conduct in violation of the laws of the place of the conduct. *See infra* p. 724. Is this a wise approach? Compare the approach that §65 took to the effects doctrine.

   (b) Section 40 of the Second Restatement. Consider the "obligation" imposed by §40 on states that seek to exercise concurrent jurisdiction in conflicting ways. Does §40 provide a means for deciding which of two states' conflicting laws will apply in particular cases, or does it concern the enforcement of applicable law? Does §40 ever *require* a state refrain from exercising concurrent jurisdiction? Consider the factors that §40 says are relevant to deciding whether a state should decline to enforce its prescriptive jurisdiction. Is it likely that these factors will be useful to courts or private parties?

   (c) Section 403 of the Third Restatement. Compare §403 of the *Third Restatement* to §40 of the *Second Restatement.* Which rule is better? Does §403(1) address legislative or enforcement jurisdiction? Does §403 ever *require* a state not to assert jurisdiction? Does §403 forbid assertions of concurrent jurisdiction where conflicting obligations are imposed?

If you were asked to design a superior rule, for cases of concurrent or conflicting jurisdiction, what would it be?

(d) Foreign sovereign compulsion doctrine. As discussed below, §441 of the *Restatement (Third) Foreign Relations Laws* provides that a state cannot compel acts in other states that are prohibited by the laws of the place of conduct or of the actor's nationality. *See infra* pp. 857-864. Is this a sensible rule? Would any other be imaginable?

10. *Section 403's reasonableness test.* Consider §403's "reasonableness" analysis.

(a) Limits of §403's reasonableness limitation. It is entirely possible for the application of the laws of two or more states to be "reasonable" under §403, even when both (or all) laws are applied to the same conduct. Moreover, §403 does not itself forbid a state from applying its laws extraterritorially, even if this results in the imposition of *conflicting* legal obligations. Instead, in cases involving conflicting legal requirements, §403(3) provides that a state is expected (but not necessarily required) to "defer to the other state if that state's interest is clearly greater." Recall, however, that §441 limits a state's power to compel acts in other states.

(b) Utility of §403 factors. Section 403(2) enumerates a nonexclusive list of "factors" to be considered in determining whether an extraterritorial assertion of prescriptive jurisdiction is reasonable. Do the factors listed in §403 provide meaningful guidance in deciding particular cases? Some critics have argued that §403's balancing approach is unmanageable and unpredictable. For example, how is a U.S. judge to determine "the importance of the regulation to the international political, legal or economic system" or to resolve cases where §403's factors point in different directions? *See Laker Airways Ltd. v. Sabena*, 731 F.2d 909, 948-951 (D.C. Cir. 1984); *In re Uranium Contracts Litig.*, 617 F.2d 1248 (7th Cir. 1980). Could §403's rule of reason be clarified over time as courts build a body of common law precedent?

(c) Doubts about ability of national courts to assess national interests. Some critics of §403's rule of reason have argued that U.S. courts lack the institutional capacities to assess the questions of national interests and foreign relations that the section raises. *See Laker Airways Ltd.*, 731 F.2d at 949 ("[w]e are in no position to adjudicate the relative importance of antitrust regulation or nonregulation to the United States and the United Kingdom"). Is that correct?

(d) Parochial bias of national courts. Other critics of the rule of reason have argued that U.S. courts inevitably resolve interest-balancing tests in favor of U.S. interests. *Laker Airways Ltd.*, 731 F.2d at 948-954 ("courts inherently find it difficult neutrally to balance competing foreign interests"). Is there reason to think that judicial parochialism would be less marked if an interest-balancing analysis were *not* applied in deciding jurisdictional issues? Does §403 cause parochial decisions? Note that, as discussed below, a number of lower courts have applied a comity-based interest analysis to either dismiss U.S. antitrust claims or deny extraterritorial discovery requests. *See infra* pp. 683-691 and 1000-1012.

11. *Comparison between bases for legislative and judicial jurisdiction under international law.* Compare the bases under international law for judicial jurisdiction with those for legislative jurisdiction. Should the two sets of jurisdictional bases be the same, or at least similar? Compare the purposes served by each set of jurisdictional limits.

Recall that international law (and the Due Process Clause) recognized various bases for "general" jurisdiction. General jurisdiction permits jurisdiction over all claims against a defendant, including claims with no connection to the forum state. Bases for general jurisdiction include nationality, domicile, incorporation, tag service, and systematic business presence. *See supra* pp. 108-137. In contrast, specific jurisdiction only permits adjudication of claims arising from the defendant's contacts with the forum. *See supra* p. 90.

The *Restatements* have not drawn any comparable distinction between "general" and "specific" *legislative* jurisdiction. Would such a distinction be useful in deciding questions of legislative jurisdiction? If a state may exercise judicial jurisdiction, should it therefore also be permitted to exercise legislative jurisdiction? Why or why not?

B. International Law Limits on Legislative Jurisdiction in U.S. Courts

International law limits on legislative jurisdiction have a complex relationship to U.S. law. As discussed above, these limits are almost entirely the product of customary international law, not international treaties. It is often said that customary "[i]nternational law is part of our law, and must be ascertained and administered by the courts of justice of appropriate jurisdiction, as often as questions of right depending on it are duly presented for their determination."[53] In fact, as we have seen, the relationship between U.S. and customary international law in U.S. courts is considerably more complex.[54]

1. U.S. Federal Law Prevails over Inconsistent Jurisdictional Limits of Customary International Law in U.S. Courts

If Congress enacts legislation in violation of international law, it is well settled that U.S. courts must disregard international law and apply the domestic statute.[55] This applies to federal statutes that exceed the limits of international law on legislative jurisdiction. Thus, the territorial reach of a federal statute is ultimately an issue of U.S. law — not of foreign or customary international law. "We are concerned only with whether Congress chose to attach liability to the conduct outside the United States. . . . [A]s a court of the United States, we cannot look beyond our own law."[56]

A different result would obtain if a federal statute were superseded by a subsequent self-executing U.S. treaty containing limits on U.S. legislative jurisdiction. That is because, when U.S. self-executing treaties and federal law conflict, U.S. courts will give effect to the "last in time."[57] As a practical matter, however, this is of little importance, because very few U.S. treaties affect U.S. legislative jurisdiction.

A different result also would obtain if a federal statute exceeded U.S. constitutional limits on legislative jurisdiction. We examine this possibility below.[58] A few courts have held that contemporary jurisdictional limits of international law are coextensive with constitutional limits on federal legislative jurisdiction.[59] In general, however, parties have seldom asserted international law objections to U.S. legislative jurisdiction.[60]

---

53. *See supra* pp. 10-11; *The Paquete Habana*, 175 U.S. 677, 700 (1900); *Restatement (Third) Foreign Relations Law* §111(1) (1987).

54. *See supra* pp. 10-11.

55. *See supra* p. 17; *Restatement (Third) Foreign Relations Law* §115(1) & §403, comment g (1987); *Head Money Cases*, 112 U.S. 580, 598-599 (1884); *CFTC v. Nahas*, 738 F.2d 487 (D.C. Cir. 1984). *But see United States v. Daniels*, 2010 WL 2557506, at *6 (N.D. Cal. June 21, 2010) ("[E]ven where Congress expresses its unambiguous intent for a criminal statute to apply extraterritorially, courts must determine whether international law permits the exercise of jurisdiction.").

56. *United States v. Alcoa*, 148 F.2d 416, 443 (2d Cir. 1945).

57. *See supra* p. 16.

58. *See infra* pp. 606-613.

59. *E.g., United States v. Javino*, 960 F.2d 1137 (2d Cir. 1992); *Tamari v. Bache & Co. (Lebanon)*, 730 F.2d 1103, 1107 n.11 (7th Cir. 1984); *United States v. Layton*, 509 F. Supp. 212 (N.D. Cal. 1981).

60. *See* Brilmayer & Norchi, *Federal Extraterritoriality and Fifth Amendment Due Process*, 105 Harv. L. Rev. 1217 (1992).

2.   Presumptions That Congress Has Not Violated International Law and Has Not Extended U.S. Law Extraterritorially

As discussed above, Congress has the power to enact legislation that violates international law. Nevertheless, U.S. courts generally apply the *Charming Betsy* presumption that Congress does not intend to violate international law.[61] Only if a federal statute expressly and plainly requires a result inconsistent with international law will that interpretation be adopted.

Similarly, Congress has the power to enact legislation that applies to conduct outside U.S. territory.[62] However, U.S. courts have long relied upon the related "territoriality presumption": that presumption provides that federal legislation will not be interpreted to apply extraterritorially absent express language requiring this result.[63] In the words of the Supreme Court, "legislation of Congress, unless a contrary intent appears, is meant to apply only within the territorial jurisdiction of the United States."[64] The application of both presumptions is discussed below.[65]

Most recently, the Court has suggested that principles of international comity serve to guide the interpretation of federal statutes that could have extraterritorial effect. In *F. Hoffmann-La Roche, Ltd. v. Empagran, SA*, the Court explained that it "ordinarily construes ambiguous statutes to avoid unreasonable interference with the sovereign authority of other nations."[66] The Court explicitly anchored this interpretive canon in "principles of customary international law" and explained that it "thereby helps the potentially conflicting laws of different nations work together in harmony—a harmony particularly needed in today's highly interdependent commercial world."[67] Its analysis relied heavily on the principles articulated in §§402 and 403 of the *Restatement (Third) Foreign Relations Law*.

3.   Relationship Between U.S. State Law and Jurisdictional Limits of Customary International Law

The relationship between U.S. state (as opposed to federal) law and customary international law is less clear. As discussed above, international law is regarded as federal law; under this view, it is supreme over state law.[68] Thus, at least according to some authorities, state law that is inconsistent with either prior or subsequent rules of customary international law is invalid.[69] There is little precedent reaching such a result.

---

61. *See supra* p. 18 & *infra* pp. 648-650; *Restatement (Third) Foreign Relations Law* §114 (1987); *Murray v. Schooner Charming Betsy*, 6 U.S. 64, 118 (1804).
62. In *EEOC v. Aramco*, 499 U.S. 244 (1991), the Court observed: "Both parties concede, as they must, that Congress has the authority to enforce [sic] its laws beyond the territorial boundaries of the United States." Of course, Congress has no power at all to "enforce its laws"—either inside or outside the United States. U.S. Const. Art. II. The Court meant to refer to Congress's "authority to enact laws applicable to conduct beyond the territorial boundaries of the United States." *See also United States v. Neil*, 312 F.3d 419, 421 (9th Cir. 2002) ("The Constitution does not bar extraterritorial application of United States penal laws.").
63. *Small v. United States*, 544 U.S. 385, 388-389 (2005); *Foley Bros., Inc. v. Filardo*, 336 U.S. 281 (1949); *McCulloch v. Sociedad Nacional de Marineros de Honduras*, 372 U.S. 10, 21-22 (1968).
64. *Foley Bros., Inc. v. Filardo*, 336 U.S. 281, 285 (1949).
65. *See infra* pp. 646-672.
66. 542 U.S. 155, 164 (2004).
67. 542 U.S. at 164-165.
68. *See also Ahmed v. Goldberg*, 2001 WL 1842390, at *7 (D.N. 2001) ("the laws of a state . . . cannot override or preempt international law which is law of the United States and therefore supreme law. . . .").
69. *See supra* pp. 17-18; *Restatement (Third) Foreign Relations Law* §115 comment e (1987).

C. Constitutional Limitations on Legislative Jurisdiction in U.S. Courts

The U.S. Constitution imposes limits on legislative jurisdiction (and, thus, the choice-of-law decisions) in U.S. courts. The principal textual bases for these limits are the Full Faith and Credit Clause and the Due Process Clause.[70] The U.S. Supreme Court has for some time applied both provisions to limit state courts' application of local law to multi-state events.[71] It is well settled that the Full Faith and Credit Clause is not applicable to Congress.[72] The Due Process Clause is, but it has seldom been applied to limit the reach of federal legislation.[73]

1. Constitutional Limits on Federal Legislative Jurisdiction

Early Supreme Court decisions occasionally contained language suggesting that the Constitution forbid Congress from applying federal statutes outside U.S. territory.[74] No decision appears to have held, however, that Congress lacked the constitutional authority to enact extraterritorial legislation.

Nothing in the Constitution expressly or impliedly limits federal legislative power to regulate conduct, persons, or property located on U.S. territory. On the contrary, the Constitution specifically grants Congress broad power to regulate commerce with foreign nations.[75] A fairly natural component of this grant is the power to regulate conduct that occurs outside of U.S. territory. Likewise, the Constitution grants Congress other powers that inevitably call for the extraterritorial application of U.S. legislation.[76] Not surprisingly, early U.S. statutes sometimes reached conduct beyond the territorial boundaries of the United States, particularly activities on the high seas or in so-called Indian territory.[77] As a result, it has long been accepted that federal legislation may constitutionally be applied to conduct outside the United States.[78]

70. The Full Faith and Credit Clause provides: "Full Faith and Credit shall be given in each State to the public Acts, Records and judicial Proceedings of every other State. And the Congress may by general Laws prescribe the Manner in which such Acts, Records and Proceedings shall be proved, and the effect thereof." U.S. Const. Art. IV, §1.

71. *See infra* pp. 613-630.

72. *See infra* p. 627.

73. *See infra* pp. 607-613; Brilmayer & Norchi, *Federal Extraterritoriality and Fifth Amendment Due Process*, 105 Harv. L. Rev. 1217 (1992).

74. *E.g., Rose v. Himely*, 8 U.S. 241, 279 (1807) ("legislation of every country is territorial . . . beyond its own territory, it can only affect its own subjects or citizens"); *United States v. Palmer*, 16 U.S. 610, 641 (1818) (Johnson, J.) ("Congress cannot make that piracy which is not piracy by the law of nations, in order to give jurisdiction to its own courts over such offenses"); *The Apollon*, 22 U.S. 362, 370 (1824) ("The laws of no nation can justly extend beyond its own territory, except so far as regards its own citizens.").

75. Art. I, §8. Indeed, the Framers intended Congress's power to *regulate* foreign commerce to be broader than its authority over interstate commerce. *See supra* p. 19 & *infra* pp. 630-631.

76. Art. I, §8, cl. 9, 11 (granting Congress the power to define offenses on the high seas or against the law of nations and to grant letters of marque and reprisal).

77. An Act for the Punishment of Certain Crimes Against the United States, 1 Stat. 112 (Act of April 30, 1790) (outlawing treason and other crimes on the high seas and other places); An Act More Effectually to Protect the Commerce and Coasts of the United States, 1 Stat. 561 (Act of May 28, 1798) (authorizing U.S. Navy to seize foreign vessels found "hovering on the coasts of the United States"); An Act to Regulate Trade and Intercourse With the Indian Tribes, 1 Stat. 329 (Act of March 1, 1793) (prohibiting various conduct in "Indian country"); An Act to Regulate Trade and Intercourse With the Indian Tribes, and to Preserve Peace on the Frontiers, 1 Stat. 743 (Act of March 3, 1799) (prohibiting various conduct within Indian territory). Nonetheless, there is virtually no early legislation expressly applicable to conduct occurring within the territory of another recognized sovereign state.

78. *EEOC v. Aramco*, 499 U.S. 24 (1991); Born, *A Reappraisal of the Extraterritorial Reach of U.S. Law*, 24 Law & Pol'y Int'l Bus. 1 (1992).

For decades, in many contexts, the Supreme Court has summarily upheld the extra-territorial application of U.S. law against constitutional challenges.[79] Twenty years ago, in 1991, the Court made it clear that the power of Congress to apply U.S. law extraterritorially was no longer open to debate: "Both parties concede, as they must, that Congress has the authority to enforce its laws beyond the territorial boundaries of the United States."[80]

As described above, it is equally well settled that Congress possesses the power under the Constitution to exercise legislative jurisdiction in violation of international law: "Federal courts must give effect to a valid unambiguous congressional mandate, even if such effect would conflict with another nation's laws or violate international law."[81] In short, it is now settled that the Constitution does not categorically forbid Congress from enacting laws applicable to conduct and persons outside of U.S. territory, even where this violates international law.

Nonetheless, the Constitution may forbid the extraterritorial application of U.S. federal law in some circumstances. For example, the Due Process Clause might preclude extension of federal law to conduct abroad that has only *de minimis* contact with or effect upon the United States or its nationals. Despite this theoretical possibility, neither the Due Process Clause nor other constitutional provisions have in fact imposed significant constraints on the extraterritorial reach of U.S. laws: no reported federal court decision has held an extraterritorial application of substantive U.S. law unconstitutional,[82] and only a few lower courts have even alluded to the possibility of such a result.[83] One such decision is *United States v. Davis*, excerpted below.

UNITED STATES v. DAVIS
905 F.2d 245 (9th Cir. 1990)

WIGGINS, CIRCUIT JUDGE. Peter Malcolm Davis appeals his convictions for possession of, and conspiracy to possess, marijuana on a vessel subject to the jurisdiction of the United

79. *E.g.*, *Lauritzen v. Larsen*, 345 U.S. 571, 579 n.7 (1953); *Steele v. Bulova Watch Co.*, 344 U.S. 280, 282-286 (1952) (rejecting constitutional challenge to application of Lanham Act to conduct occurring in Mexico); *Vermilya-Brown Co. v. Connell*, 335 U.S. 377, 381 (1948) (Congress may "regulate the actions of our citizens outside the territorial jurisdiction of the United States whether or not the act punished occurred within the territory of a foreign nation."); *Blackmer v. United States*, 284 U.S. 421, 437 (1932) (rejecting due process challenge to subpoena issued to U.S. citizen residing in France); *United States v. Bowman*, 260 U.S. 94, 97 (1922) (rejecting due process challenge to extraterritorial application of legislation concerning fraud on U.S. Government).

80. *EEOC v. Aramco*, 499 U.S. 24 (1991).

81. *CFTC v. Nahas*, 738 F.2d 487, 495 (D.C. Cir. 1984). Judge Learned Hand said in *United States v. Alcoa* that: "We are concerned only with whether Congress chose to attach liability to the conduct outside the United States. . . . [A]s a court of the United States, we cannot look beyond our own law." *United States v. Alcoa*, 148 F.2d 416, 443 (2d Cir. 1945).

82. In one recent case, the Ninth Circuit did order dismissal of an indictment due to the Government's failure to offer any proof of a nexus between the overseas conduct and the United States. *See United States v. Perlaza*, 439 F.3d 1149 (9th Cir. 2006). Technically, the Court was not finding Congress's assertion of legislative jurisdiction to be unconstitutional but, instead, merely faulted the Government for failing to adduce the necessary proof to satisfy the Ninth Circuit's nexus standard.

83. *E.g.*, *United States v. Clark*, 435 F.3d 1100, 1108 (9th Cir. 2006) ("[T]o comply with the Due Process Clause of the Fifth Amendment, extraterritorial application of federal criminal statutes requires the government to demonstrate a sufficient nexus between the defendant and the United States 'so that such application would not be arbitrary or fundamentally unfair.' "); *United States v. Yousef*, 327 F.3d 56, 111 (2d Cir. 2003) (appearing to adopt nexus requirement); *Tamari v. Bache & Co. (Lebanon)*, 730 F.2d 1103, 1107 n.11 (7th Cir. 1984) ("Were Congress to enact a rule beyond the scope of [the] principles [contained in §§17-18 of the Restatement (Second) Foreign Relations Law], the statute could be challenged as violating the due process clause on the ground that Congress lacked the power to prescribe the rule"); *United States v. Baker*, 609 F.2d 134 (5th Cir. 1980).

States with intent to distribute in violation of the Maritime Drug Law Enforcement Act ["MDLEA"]. . . . [T]he Coast Guard cutter *Cape Romain* encountered the *Myth of Ecurie* ("*Myth*"), approximately 35 miles southwest of Point Reyes, California. The *Myth* is a sailing vessel approximately 58 feet in length. The *Myth* was headed in the direction of San Francisco. The *Cape Romain* approached the *Myth*, and Coast Guard personnel by radio requested permission to board. Peter Davis, the captain of the *Myth*, denied the request. He stated that the Coast Guard had no authority to board his boat because it was of British registry and was sailing on the high seas having departed from Hong Kong. Captain Davis announced his intention to alter his course for the Caribbean by the way of Mexico. The Coast Guard suspected the *Myth* of smuggling contraband. Factors leading to that suspicion were that the El Paso Intelligence Centre had included the *Myth* on a list of vessels suspected of drug smuggling; the *Myth* was sailing in an area in which sailing vessels were infrequently found; and the *Myth* appeared to be carrying cargo.

The Coast Guard then requested permission from the United Kingdom to board the *Myth* in accordance with procedures in a 1981 agreement between the United States and the United Kingdom. . . . By telex message, the United Kingdom gave the Coast Guard permission to board the *Myth* according to the terms of the 1981 Agreement. . . . Crew members from the *Cape Romain* boarded the *Myth*. By that time, the *Myth* had sailed to a location approximately 100 miles west of the California coast. The boarding officer smelled marijuana in the cabin of the *Myth*. . . . Below deck, the boarding officer saw numerous bales of material and smelled marijuana. Davis admitted that the bales were marijuana. The Coast Guard then arrested Davis and his crew and brought the *Myth* to the Coast Guard station on Yerba Buena Island in San Francisco. The Coast Guard there confiscated over 7,000 pounds of marijuana from the *Myth*. Davis is not a citizen of the United States. . . . Davis filed a motion to dismiss for lack of jurisdiction. . . . The district court denied [the motion and later] found Davis guilty . . . Davis timely appealed.

Davis contends that the provisions of the statute under which he was convicted, the [MDLEA], do not apply to persons on foreign vessels outside the territory of the United States. The question of whether the United States may punish Davis' conduct involves three issues: (1) whether Congress has constitutional authority to give extraterritorial effect to the [MDLEA]; if so, (2) whether the Constitution prohibits the United States from punishing Davis' conduct in this instance; and, if not, (3) does the [MDLEA] apply to Davis' conduct?

The [MDLEA], 46 U.S.C. App. §§1903(a) and (j) state:

> (a) It is unlawful for any person on board a vessel of the United States, or on board a vessel subject to the jurisdiction of the United States, to knowingly or intentionally manufacture or distribute, or to possess with intent to manufacture or distribute, a controlled substance.
>
> (j) Any person who attempts or conspires to commit any offense defined in this Act [46 U.S.C. App. §§1904] is punishable by imprisonment or fine, or both, which may not exceed the maximum punishment prescribed for the offense, the commission of which was the object of the attempt of the conspiracy.

The United States Congress sits as a legislature of enumerated and specific powers. *See Marbury v. Madison*, 5 U.S. 137, 176, (1803). The Constitution gives Congress the power to "define and punish piracies and felonies on the high seas. . . ." U.S. Const. Art. 1 §8, cl. 10. The high seas lie seaward of the territorial sea, defined as the three mile belt of sea measured from the low water mark. We therefore find that the Constitution authorized Congress to give extraterritorial effect to the [MDLEA].

We next examine what limitations exist on the United States' power to exercise that authority. Contrary to Davis' assertions, compliance with international law does not determine whether the United States may supply the [MDLEA] to his conduct.[84] Only two restrictions exist on giving extraterritorial effect to Congress' directives. We require Congress make clear its intent to give extraterritorial effect to its statutes. And secondly, as a matter of constitutional law, we require that application of the statute to the acts in question not violate the due process clause of the fifth amendment.

In this case, Congress explicitly stated that it intended the [MDLEA] to apply extraterritorially. 46 U.S.C. App. §1903(h) (Supp. IV 1986) ("This section is intended to reach acts of possession, manufacture, or distribution outside the territorial jurisdiction of the United States"). Therefore, the only issue we must consider is whether application of the [MDLEA] to Davis' conduct would violate due process. In order to apply extraterritorially a federal criminal statute to a defendant consistently with due process, there must be sufficient nexus between the defendant and the United States, *see United States v. Peterson*, 812 F.2d 486, 493 (9th Cir. 1987), so that such application would not be arbitrary or fundamentally unfair.[85] In the instant case, a sufficient nexus exists so that the application of the [MDLEA] to Davis' extraterritorial conduct does not violate the due process clause. "Where an attempted transaction is aimed at causing criminal acts within the United States, there is a sufficient basis for the United States to exercise its jurisdiction." The facts found by the district court in denying Davis' motion to dismiss for lack of jurisdiction support the reasonable conclusion that Davis intended to smuggle contraband into United States territory. At the time of its first detection, the *Myth* was 35 miles away from, and headed for, San Francisco. As the Coast Guard approached, the *Myth* changed its course for the Caribbean by way of Mexico, although the *Myth* was many miles from the Great Circle route from Hong Kong to Acapulco. The *Myth* is on a list of boats suspected of drug smuggling. It is unusual for a 58 foot sailing vessel to have sailed from the *Myth*'s asserted point of departure, Hong Kong. The foregoing evidence is sufficient to establish a nexus between the *Myth* and the United States. We therefore find that the Constitution does not prohibit the application of the [MDLEA] to Davis. . . . [The court then held that the Act applied to Davis' conduct, noting that the United Kingdom had consented to U.S. agents boarding the *Myth*.]

Notes *on* United States v. Davis

1. *Constitutional basis for extraterritorial application of federal legislation.* As discussed above, the Framers granted Congress only limited legislative powers. *See supra* pp. 5-7.

---

84. International law principles, standing on their own, do not create substantive rights or affirmative defenses for litigants in United States courts. *United States v. Thomas*, 893 F.2d 1066, 1068-69 (9th Cir. 1990).

85. Some of our previous decisions have discussed international law jurisdictional principles simultaneously with the constitutionality of Congress' exercise of jurisdiction. *See* [*U.S. v. Petersen*, 812 F.2d 486 (9th Cir. 1987)], (extraterritorial application of statute is justified by protective principle and is constitutional); *Chua Han Mow v. United States*, 730 F.2d 1308, 1312 (9th Cir. 1984) (extraterritorial application of statute is justified by objective territorial and protective principle and is constitutional); *United States v. King*, 552 F.2d 833, 851-52 (9th Cir. 1976) (extraterritorial application of statute is justified by nationality and objective territorial principles and is constitutional); *United States v. Cotten*, 471 F.2d 744, 749 (9th Cir. 1973) (extraterritorial application of statute justified by objective territorial principle); *Rocha v. United States*, 288 F.2d 545, 549 (9th Cir. 1961) (extraterritorial application of statute is justified by protective principle). International law principles may be useful as a rough guide of whether a sufficient nexus exists between the defendant and the United States so that application of the statute in question would not violate due process. *See, e.g., Peterson*, 812 F.2d at 493. However, danger exists that emphasis on international law principles will cause us to lose sight of the ultimate question: would application of the statute to the defendant be arbitrary or fundamentally unfair?

Given that, why is it so clear that Congress can enact legislation applicable outside U.S. territory? What provision of Article I grants Congress such power? Consider the court's analysis in *Davis*. What is it that sustains the Maritime Drug Enforcement Act? *Compare United States v. Suerte*, 291 F.3d 366, 376 (5th Cir. 2002) (relying on the "Piracies and Felonies" Clause in Article I, Section 8, clause 10) *with United States v. Angulo-Hernandez*, 576 F.3d 59 (1st Cir. 2009) (Torruella, J., dissenting from the denial of rehearing *en banc*) (arguing that MDLEA, as applied to non-citizens' overseas acts, exceeds Congress's power under Piracies and Felonies Clause). If the Framers specifically provided Congress with regulatory authority over piracies and felonies "on the high seas," what does that suggest about Congress's extraterritorial regulatory authority in matters not "on the high seas"? Recall the strength of the territoriality doctrine at the time that the Constitution was drafted. *See supra* pp. 84-86.

Does the Foreign Commerce Clause grant Congress affirmative authority to extend federal legislation outside U.S. territory? Note that the clause grants Congress the power to "regulate commerce with foreign nations, and among the several states, and with Indian Tribes." Is it so clear that this confers power to regulate matters beyond U.S. territory? The Supreme Court and commentators have concluded that it is. *See supra* pp. 19-20.

Of course, the foreign commerce power is not without limits. Though the Supreme Court has not recently addressed the outer limits of Congress's power under this clause, some recent jurisprudence hints at those limits. For a recent case where lower court judges divided over whether a congressional enactment exceeded Congress's power under the Foreign Commerce Clause, *see United States v. Clark*, 435 F.3d 1100, 1109-1110 (9th Cir. 2006). Additionally, over the past decade, several Supreme Court decisions have established some outer limits to Congress's power to regulate *interstate* commerce. *See Gonzalez v. Raich*, 545 U.S. 1 (2005); *United States v. Morrison*, 529 U.S. 598 (2000); *United States v. Lopez*, 514 U.S. 549 (1995). The explanatory value of these limits for the Foreign Commerce Clause remains unsettled. In particular, to the extent the limits under the Interstate Commerce Clause rest on federalism principles, they may have limited applicability to setting limits under the foreign commerce clause. *See Clark*, 435 F.3d at 1113 ("Federalism and state sovereignty concerns do not restrict Congress's power over foreign commerce."); *United States v. Martinez*, 599 F. Supp. 2d 784, 805 (W.D. Tex. 2009) ("The *Lopez/Morrison* framework developed in response to the unique federalism concerns that define congressional authority in the interstate context. However, there exists in the realm of foreign commerce the necessity that the nation speak with one voice. Accordingly, any statute that would be granted constitutional deference when it regulates interstate commerce is accorded even greater deference when Congress is regulating foreign commerce.") (citations and internal quotations omitted). To the extent the limits rest on principles of enumerated powers (or limited government), they may have greater explanatory value. *See United States v. Bianchi*, 2010 WL 2650357 (3d Cir. July 2, 2010) (Roth, J., dissenting) ("Although, as the majority notes, Congress's foreign commerce power is broad, it has never been deemed unlimited.") (citation omitted); *Clark*, 435 F.3d at 1117 (Ferguson, J., dissenting) ("[The Foreign Commerce Clause], while giving Congress broad authority over our commercial relations with other nations, is not a grant of international police power.").

Finally, some authority holds that where a statute codifies the United States' obligations under an international treaty, the Necessary and Proper Clause, Art. I §8, cl. 18, supplies an independent constitutional basis for assertions of legislative jurisdiction. *See United States v. Shi*, 525 F.3d 709 (9th Cir. 2008); *Missouri v. Holland*, 252 U.S. 416, 432 (1920) (Necessary and Proper Clause authorizes legislation to implement national government's treaty-making power). According to this line of reasoning, the assertion of extraterritorial jurisdiction was "necessary and proper for carrying into execution" the Treaty powers enumerated elsewhere in the Constitution. *See supra* at 5-7. Is this persuasive? Doesn't this allow constitutional authority to be bootstrapped by whatever the United States agrees to in a treaty? Would the same logic hold if the statute were codifying obligations pursuant to a Sole Executive agreement? *See supra* at 17.

   2. *Due process limits on extraterritorial application of federal legislation.* *Davis* is one of the few U.S. decisions considering due process challenges to federal legislative jurisdiction. Is it correct, in principle, that the Due Process Clause limits the legislative jurisdiction of Congress? Recall the discussion above of the Fifth Amendment's due process limits on federal court judicial jurisdiction. *See supra* pp. 210-213. What is the rationale for due process limits on federal legislative jurisdiction? What is the textual basis?

   Would due process limits on legislative jurisdiction apply to protect foreign nationals outside the United States? Recall the Court's application of due process limits to judicial jurisdiction over non-U.S. defendants. *See supra* p. 104.

   3. *Content of due process limits on extraterritorial application of federal legislation.* Consider the standard adopted in *Davis* for due process limits on the extraterritorial reach of U.S. legislation. What does it mean to require a "sufficient nexus between the defendant and the United States so that . . . application [of U.S. law] would not be arbitrary or fundamentally unfair"? *See United States v. Reumayr*, 530 F. Supp. 2d 1210, 1223 & n.19 (D.N.M. 2008) (collecting cases expressing different views on nexus requirement); *see also United States v. Shi*, 525 F.3d 709, 724 (9th Cir. 2008) (holding that proof of nexus is unnecessary where crime is universally condemned); *United States. v. Moreno-Morillo,* 334 F.3d 819, 828 (9th Cir. 2003) (holding that proof of nexus is unnecessary where Congress is acting pursuant to Piracies and Felonies Clause, as opposed to Foreign Commerce Clause). Was the outcome in *Davis* consistent with this standard? What factors are relevant to deciding whether extraterritorial application of U.S. law is "arbitrary or fundamentally unfair"? Are the factors articulated in the Due Process Clause's "reasonableness" test for judicial jurisdiction relevant? *See United States v. Zakharov,* 468 F.3d 1171, 1177 (9th Cir. 2006) ("Nexus is a constitutional requirement analogous to 'minimum contacts' in personal jurisdiction analysis."). What about the factors set forth in §403 of the *Restatement (Third) Foreign Relations Law*? Does *Davis* consider only the unfairness to private parties, or does it also (or instead) consider foreign nation's sovereignty?

   Note that most of the cases testing the constitutional limits of Congress's assertions of legislative jurisdiction have arisen in the criminal context. Does a less stringent standard apply in civil cases? *See Goldberg v. UBS AG,* 690 F. Supp. 2d 92, 105-106 (E.D.N.Y. 2010).

   4. *Authorities concluding that international law limits on legislative jurisdiction are irrelevant in U.S. courts.* Did extraterritorial application of federal law in *Davis* violate customary international law—as set out in the *Restatement (Third) Foreign Relations Law* §§402 & 403? Assume that it had. What relevance would this illegality have to the outcome of U.S. litigation?

   Consider the comment in *Davis* that "[i]nternational law principles, standing on their own, do not create substantive rights or affirmative defenses for litigants in United States courts." Most lower courts have agreed, *see supra* p. 607. Though the Supreme Court has not squarely confronted the question, its recent *Medellin* decision, discussed *supra* at 16, which held that neither decisions of the International Court of Justice nor non-self-executing treaties create domestically enforceable law, strongly suggests that the Court endorses this view.

   What is the basis for *Davis*'s statement that customary international law is not an independent basis for limits on U.S. legislative jurisdiction? Compare the Supreme Court's statement in *The Paquete Habana*, 175 U.S. 677, 700 (1900): "[i]nternational law is part of our law, and must be ascertained and administered by the courts of justice of appropriate jurisdiction." Under this rule, why don't international law limits on national legislative jurisdiction apply in U.S. courts? If such limits do apply, would a "last-in-time" rule also be applicable, as in the context of treaties?

5. *Authorities concluding that international law limits on legislative jurisdiction are incorporated by the Due Process Clause.* Recall that *Pennoyer* based due process limits on judicial jurisdiction on prevailing principles of international law, drawn principally from Joseph Story's *Commentaries. See supra* pp. 84-86. A broadly similar result applied in the context of legislative jurisdiction. *See supra* pp. 646-649.

Should the Due Process Clause be interpreted to incorporate *contemporary* international law limits on legislative jurisdiction? Consider the Court's willingness to look to contemporary principles of international law in *Sosa. See supra* p. 15 (or full case at pp. 38-47). In contrast to *Davis,* a few courts have suggested that the Due Process Clause does incorporate contemporary international law principles. *United States v. Javino,* 960 F.2d 1137, 1142-1143 (2d Cir. 1992) ("Even had Congress intended all foreign manufacturers of firearms to comply with the requirements set out in [26 U.S.C.] §5822, there is substantial question as to whether it could lawfully have done so. Though Congress may prescribe laws concerning conduct outside the territorial boundaries of the United States 'that has or is intended to have substantial effect' within the United States, *Restatement (Third) Foreign Relations Law* §402(1)(c) (1987) . . . , it may not regulate such conduct 'when the exercise of . . . jurisdiction is unreasonable.' "), *disavowed as dicta by United States v. Yousef,* 327 F.3d 56, 109 n.44 (2d Cir. 2003); *Tamari v. Bache & Co. (Lebanon),* 730 F.2d 1103, 1107 n.11 (7th Cir. 1984) ("[w]ere Congress to enact a rule beyond the scope of [the] principles [contained in §§17-18 of the *Second Restatement*], the statute could be challenged as violating the due process clause"); *Goldberg v. UBS AG,* 690 F. Supp. 2d (E.D.N.Y. 2010) *United States v. Layton,* 509 F. Supp. 212 (N.D. Cal. 1981). Is this an appropriate application of the Due Process Clause?

6. *Authorities concluding that international law limits on legislative jurisdiction are not relevant to due process analysis.* Consider how *Davis* views the suggestion that international law is relevant to due process analysis: "International law principles may be useful as a rough guide of whether a sufficient nexus exists between the defendant and the United States so that application of the statute in question would not violate due process. However, danger exists that emphasis on international law principles will cause us to lose sight of the ultimate question: would application of the statute to the defendant be arbitrary or fundamentally unfair"? Is this a wise approach? Most courts have adopted the *Davis* approach, treating international law as nothing more than background material to what remains a question of fairness under U.S. law. *United States v. Cardales,* 168 F.3d 548, 553 (1st Cir. 1999); *United States v. Caicedo,* 47 F.3d 370, 372 (9th Cir. 1995); *United States v. Juda,* 46 F.3d 961, 967 (9th Cir. 1995); *United States v. Peterson,* 812 F.2d 486 (9th Cir. 1987); *supra* pp. 606-607.

Which approach — that in *Davis* or that in decisions like *Javino* and *Tamari* — is wiser? Which is more consistent with the application of the Due Process Clause to assertions of judicial jurisdiction? Would some other approach be wiser?

7. *Relevance of foreign sovereignty to due process analysis.* Is a violation of a foreign state's sovereignty relevant to due process restrictions on U.S. legislative jurisdiction? The United Kingdom consented to the U.S. conduct in *Davis.* As a consequence, there was no basis for suggesting any infringement on U.K. sovereignty in violation of international law. Does this affect due process analysis? *Compare United States v. Suerte,* 291 F.3d 366, 372 (5th Cir. 2002) (rejecting nexus requirement where flag nation has consented to or waived objection to assertion of jurisdiction) *with United States v. Perlaza,* 439 F.3d 1149,

1169 (9th Cir. 2006) ("The fact that the Government received Colombia's consent to seize the members of the Gran Tauro, remove them to the United States, and prosecute them under United States law in federal court does not eliminate the nexus requirement."). If the United Kingdom consents to the application of U.S. law, does this preclude any due process challenge to assertions of judicial jurisdiction? Or are issues of fairness to private parties still relevant? Given the U.K.'s consent, is the court's focus on "fairness" more defensible?

Suppose that, in *Davis*, the United Kingdom had refused to consent to U.S. agents boarding the *Myth*, and that it had protested the extraterritorial application of U.S. law to *Davis*. Would those factors have been relevant to due process analysis? As discussed above, the Due Process Clause has long been interpreted in the context of judicial jurisdiction as safeguarding the territorial sovereignty of co-equal states. *See supra* pp. 87-90. Recall also the concern in *Asahi Metal* over interference with U.S. foreign relations. *See supra* pp. 140-144. Are not such concerns even greater where legislative jurisdiction is concerned than where judicial jurisdiction is involved?

Alternatively, suppose that the ship in *Davis* were a "stateless" one, that is, one not flying under the flag of a sovereign nation. Would that affect the due process analysis? Some courts, including the Ninth Circuit in post-*Davis* decisions, have held that no due process nexus requirement applies in that context. *See United States v. Juda*, 46 F.3d 961, 966-967 (9th Cir. 1995); *United States v. Caicedo*, 47 F.3d 370, 372-373 (9th Cir. 1995). Why should the constitutional limits on legislative jurisdiction turn on the sovereign connection of the regulated party?

8. *Comparison between due process limits on federal legislation and due process limits on state choice of law.* How should due process limits on federal legislation, like those in *Davis*, compare to due process limits on state legislative jurisdiction, like those in *Dick* and *Allstate* (discussed below, *infra* pp. 613-630)? Should the Due Process Clause impose more stringent limits on federal legislation than on state legislation? Less stringent limits? Or the same limits? Does the answer depend on whether you believe that foreign territorial sovereignty and federal foreign relations concerns are relevant?

2. Constitutional Limits on State Legislative Jurisdiction

a. **Historic Constitutional Limits.** In contrast to the minimal constitutional limits on federal legislative jurisdiction, the Constitution has frequently been invoked as limiting the application of state law to conduct with interstate or international aspects.[86] A leading early decision concerning the Constitution's limits on state choice of law decisions was *New York Life Insurance Company v. Dodge*, decided in 1918.[87] The case arose from an application by

---

86. Indeed, a number of early U.S. state court decisions invoked strict territoriality principles, apparently based on the general common law, to conclude that state legislatures lacked the authority to extend state laws extraterritorially. *E.g., State v. Knight*, 2 Hayw. (N.C.) 109 (1799) (North Carolina "cannot declare that an act done in Virginia by a citizen of Virginia shall be criminal and punishable in this state: our penal laws can only extend to the limits of this state, except as to our own citizens"); *People v. Merrill*, 2 Park. (N.Y.) 590 (1855) ("It cannot be pretended or assumed that a state has jurisdiction over crimes committed beyond its territorial limits"). *See* Beale, *The Jurisdiction of a Sovereign State*, 36 Harv. L. Rev. 241 (1923); George, *Extraterritorial Application of Penal Legislation*, 64 Mich. L. Rev. 609, 621 (1966).

87. 246 U.S. 357 (1918). *See also Western Union Telegraph Co. v. Brown*, 234 U.S. 542, 547 (1914) ("when a person recovers in one jurisdiction for a tort committed in another, he does so on the ground of an obligation incurred at the place of the tort that accompanies the person of the defendant elsewhere, and that is not only the ground but the measure of maximum recovery. The injustice of imposing a greater liability than that created by the law governing the conduct of the parties at the time of the act or omission complained of is obvious; and when a state attempts in this manner to affect conduct outside its jurisdiction, or the consequences of such conduct, and to infringe upon the power of the United States, it must fail.").

Mr. Dodge, a Missouri resident, for life insurance from the New York Life Insurance Company. New York Life was a New York corporation, with its principal place of business in New York. The company accepted Mr. Dodge's application and issued a policy, which gave him the right to apply it to its New York office for loans against the cash surrender value of the policy. Mr. Dodge duly borrowed money from New York Life, sending applications for loans from Missouri to New York, where they were accepted by New York Life.[88]

Disputes arose when Mr. Dodge missed a premium payment. As permitted by New York law, New York Life satisfied Mr. Dodge's outstanding indebtedness by drawing on the cash surrender value of Mr. Dodge's policy, thereby exhausting his funds. As a consequence, New York Life was also entitled to cancel Mr. Dodge's policy, which it did. He died shortly later, and his widow sued in Missouri on his insurance policy. She claimed that New York Life had no right, under Missouri law, to seize the value of Mr. Dodge's policy. The Missouri courts agreed.

The U.S. Supreme Court reversed in a 5-4 opinion by Justice McReynolds. The Court conceded that the life insurance policy was properly governed by Missouri law, because it has been issued in Missouri.[89] However, the Court held that the loans pursuant to the policy were "made" in New York, because that is where New York Life accepted Mr. Dodge's applications. Relying on earlier decisions by the Court (paralleling use of the territoriality doctrine in other contexts), Justice McReynolds reasoned that, for Missouri to apply its law to a New York contract would "transcend[] the power of the state," in violation of the Fourteenth Amendment.[90]

Similarly, in *Home Insurance Company v. Dick*,[91] a 1930 decision, the Supreme Court unanimously restated the continued importance of significant constitutional limits on state choice of law decisions. The Court's opinion in *Dick*, which is excerpted below, involved the application of Texas law to an insurance policy covering a vessel in Mexican waters. The Court reaffirmed its historic territorial focus and held that Texas was forbidden by the Constitution from applying its law to the events in question.

HOME INSURANCE CO. v. DICK
281 U.S. 397 (1930)

BRANDEIS, JUSTICE. Dick, a citizen of Texas, brought this action in a court of that State against Compania General Anglo-Mericana de Seguros SA, a Mexican corporation, to recover on a policy of fire insurance for the total loss of a tug. . . . This suit was not commenced till more than one year after the date of the loss. The policy provided: "It is understood and agreed that no judicial suit or demand shall be entered before any tribunal for the collection of any claim under this policy, unless such suits or demands are filed within one year counted as from the date on which such damage occurs." This provision was in accord with the Mexican law to which the policy was expressly made subject. It was issued by the Mexican company in Mexico to one Bonner, of Tampico, Mexico, and was there duly assigned to Dick prior to the loss. It covered the vessel only in

---

88. 246 U.S. at 365-366.
89. 246 U.S. at 371.
90. 246 U.S. at 377. *Dodge* embraced a strictly territorial view of the Due Process Clause, which appeared to constitutionalize prevailing territorial choice of law rules. The *Dodge* Court followed its earlier decision in *New York Life Ins. Co. v. Head*, 234 U.S. 149 (1914), where the Constitution was held to forbid Missouri from regulating a contract between New Mexico and New York residents: "It would be impossible to permit the statutes of Missouri to operate beyond the jurisdiction of that state and in the state of New York . . . without throwing down the constitutional barrier by which all the states are restricted within the orbits of their lawful authority."
91. 281 U.S. 397 (1930).

certain Mexican waters. The premium was paid in Mexico; and the loss was "payable in the City of Mexico in current funds of the United States of Mexico, or their equivalent elsewhere." At the time the policy was issued, when it was assigned to him, and until after the loss, Dick actually resided in Mexico, although his permanent residence was in Texas. The contracts of reinsurance were effected by correspondence between the Mexican company in Mexico and the New York companies in New York. Nothing thereunder was to be done, or was in fact done, in Texas.

In the trial court, the garnishees contended that since the insurance contract was made and was to be performed in Mexico, and the one year provision was valid by its laws, Dick's failure to sue within one year after accrual of the alleged cause of action was a complete defense to the suit on the policy; that this failure also relieved the garnishees of any obligation as reinsurers. . . . Dick demurred, on the ground that Article 5545 of the Texas Revised Civil Statutes provides: "No person, firm, corporation, association or combination of whatsoever kind shall enter into any stipulation, contract, or agreement, by reason whereof the time in which to sue thereon is limited to a shorter period than two years. And no stipulation, contract, or agreement for any such shorter limitation in which to sue shall ever be valid in this State." . . .

On appeal, both [Texas] courts treated the policy provision as equivalent to a foreign statute of limitation; held that Article 5545 related to the remedy available in Texas courts; [and] concluded that it was validly applicable to the case at bar. . . . The garnishees appealed to this Court on the ground that the statute, as construed and applied, violated their rights under the Federal Constitution. . . .

The Texas statute as here construed and applied deprives the garnishees of property without due process of law. A State may, of course, prohibit and declare invalid the making of certain contracts within its borders. Ordinarily, it may prohibit performance within its borders, even of contracts validly made elsewhere, if they are required to be performed within the State and their performance would violate its laws. But, in the case at bar, nothing in any way relating to the policy sued on, or to the contracts of reinsurance, was ever done or required to be done in Texas. All acts relating to the making of the policy were done in Mexico. All in relation to the making of the contracts of reinsurance were done there or in New York. And, likewise, all things in regard to performance were to be done outside of Texas. Neither the Texas laws nor the Texas courts were invoked for any purpose, except by Dick in the bringing of this suit. The fact that Dick's permanent residence was in Texas is without significance. At all times here material, he was physically present and acting in Mexico. Texas was, therefore, without power to affect the terms of contracts so made. Its attempt to impose a greater obligation than that agreed upon and to seize property in payment of the imposed obligation violates the guaranty against deprivation of property without due process of law. . . .

It is true . . . that a State is not bound to provide remedies and procedure to suit the wishes of individual litigants. It may prescribe the kind of remedies to be available in its courts and dictate the practice and procedure to be followed in pursuing those remedies. Contractual provisions relating to these matters, even if valid where made, are often disregarded by the court of the forum, pursuant to statute or otherwise. But the Texas statute deals neither with the kind of remedy available nor with the mode in which it is to be pursued. It purports to create rights and obligations. It may not validly affect contracts which are neither made nor are to be performed in Texas. . . . Dick urges that Article 5545 of the Texas law is a declaration of its public policy; and that a State may properly refuse to recognize foreign rights which violate its declared policy. . . . [Texas] may not abrogate the rights of parties beyond its borders having no relation to anything done or to be done within them. . . .

Finally, it is urged that the Federal Constitution does not require the States to recognize and protect rights derived from the laws of foreign countries — that as to them the full faith and credit clause has no application. . . . The claims here asserted are not based upon the full faith and credit clause. . . . They rest upon the Fourteenth Amendment. Its protection extends to aliens. . . .

Notes on Dick

1. Historic constitutional limitations on state legislative jurisdiction. Early Supreme Court decisions applied relatively strict constitutional limitations on state legislative jurisdiction. *See New York Life Ins. Co. v. Dodge*, 246 U.S. 357 (1918); *Western Union Telegraph Co. v. Brown*, 234 U.S. 542 (1914); *New York Life Ins. Co. v. Head*, 234 U.S. 149 (1914). What is the Constitution's textual basis for limits on state legislative jurisdiction?

(a) Full Faith and Credit Clause. Consider the language of the Full Faith and Credit Clause: "Full Faith and Credit shall be given in each State to the public Acts, Records and judicial Proceedings of every other State. And the Congress may by general Laws prescribe the Manner in which such Acts, Records and Proceedings shall be proved, and the effect thereof." U.S. Const. Art. IV, §1. Does this provision suggest constitutional limits on the power of a state to make its law applicable to particular conduct? How? Does the Full Faith and Credit Clause apply to the laws of foreign nations?

(b) Due Process Clause. Should the Fourteenth Amendment's Due Process Clause be interpreted to limit the legislative jurisdiction of the several U.S. states? Consider the language of the Due Process Clause: "No state shall . . . deprive any person of life, liberty, or property, without due process of law." Does this suggest constitutional limits on state legislative jurisdiction? If so, would the Fifth Amendment's Due Process Clause impose the same limits on federal legislation?

(c) International law analogy. Recall the strict territorial limits that the Due Process Clause was said to impose on the judicial jurisdiction of state courts in *Rose v. Himely* and *Pennoyer v. Neff. See supra* pp. 84-96. The rationale for those limits was the Court's conclusion that the Due Process Clause, and the federal structure of the Constitution more generally, made prevailing international law limitations on judicial jurisdiction applicable as between the several states. *See supra* pp. 85-96. Recall also the contemporary statement of this view in *World-Wide Volkswagen*, which looked to principles of federalism to limit state judicial jurisdiction:

> [The Due Process Clause] acts to ensure that the States, through their Courts, do not reach out beyond the limits imposed on them by their status as co-equal sovereigns in a federal system. . . . [T]he framers . . . intended that the states retain many essential attributes of sovereignty, including in particular, the sovereign power to try causes in their court. The sovereignty of each state, in turn, implied a limitation on the sovereignty of all its sister states . . . a limitation express or implicit in both the original scheme of the Constitution and the Fourteenth Amendment. 444 U.S. 286, 292 (1980).

Is the same rationale also applicable to international law limitations on legislative jurisdiction?

What were prevailing international law limits on legislative jurisdiction in the nineteenth century? Consider the excerpts from Joseph Story's *Commentaries on the Conflict of Laws*, set forth above, *see* Appendix BB. Consider also decisions like *The Apollon*, 22 U.S. 362 (1824), and *Schooner Exchange v. McFaddon*, 11 U.S. 116 (1812). As discussed above, these decisions reasoned that international law imposed strict territorial limits on national legislative jurisdiction. *See supra* pp. 84-85. Compare the effect of such international law limits on *Home Insurance Co. v. Dick* with the reliance on international law in *Pennoyer*.

(d) Purposes of constitutional limits on state legislative jurisdiction. What interests are served by imposing constitutional limits on state legislative jurisdiction? Do such limits: (a) protect the sovereignty of other states; (b) protect individuals from unfair arbitrary or unforeseeable applications of substantive laws; (c) protect interstate commerce and the interstate system from unduly burdensome or conflicting state regulation; or (d) accomplish something else? Compare the interests that are served by due process limits on judicial jurisdiction. *See supra* pp. 86-90.

2. Constitutional limits on state legislative jurisdiction in Dick. Consider the due process limits on state legislative jurisdiction in *Dick*. According to the Court, the Constitution denies a state the power to affect "the rights of parties beyond its borders having no relation to anything done or to be done within them." In *Dick*, "[a]ll acts relating to the making of the policy were done in Mexico. All in relation to the making of the contracts of reinsurance were done there or in New York. And, likewise, all things in regard to performance were to be done outside of Texas." Because Texas assertedly had no significant connection to Mr. Dick's claim, it was "without power to affect the terms of the contracts" he relied upon. The Court's language, at least, was reflective of territorial limits on state legislative jurisdiction, paralleling *Pennoyer*'s territorial limits on judicial jurisdiction. *See supra* pp. 84-85. Is the result in *Dick* appropriate? Should the Due Process Clause, or other provisions of the Constitution, impose such territorial limits on state legislative jurisdiction?

What precisely is the test in *Dick* for when a state may not constitutionally exercise legislative jurisdiction? On its facts, was *Dick* indeed a case where Texas should have been constitutionally barred from applying its law?

3. Should the Constitution limit the application of state legislation to conduct or persons outside the United States? In *Dick*, Texas courts applied Texas law to conduct in Mexico — and not to conduct in another U.S. state. Is that relevant to due process or full faith and credit analysis? If the focus of constitutional protections is on protecting the sovereignty of other U.S. states, is there any reason to restrict the application of U.S. state laws to conduct in other countries? Conversely, should state infringements of the sovereignty of foreign nations be regarded as more serious than infringement on the sovereignty of other U.S. states? Why?

(a) Full Faith and Credit Clause not applicable to foreign state's laws. The Full Faith and Credit Clause only requires states to accord full faith and credit to the acts of other U.S. states. *Dick* expressly confirms this. Is there any way that the clause can apply in cases involving the laws or judgments of other nations?

(b) Applicability of Due Process Clause in international cases. Does the Due Process Clause have any limitation, like the Full Faith and Credit Clause, to domestic cases? What did the Court hold in *Dick* about the Due Process Clause's applicability to state legislation purporting to extend to conduct in a foreign nation? As discussed above, one rationale for due process limits on state legislative jurisdiction is concern about infringing on the territorial sovereignty of other U.S. states. *See supra* pp. 87-90. This rationale obviously did not apply in *Dick*. What does justify application of the Due Process Clause in such cases? Is it the surprise and unfairness that private parties face when they are subjected to laws lacking any connection to their conduct? Is it the need to avoid infringing on foreign sovereignty?

(c) Content of due process limits in international cases. If the Constitution does impose limits on the application of state legislation to conduct or persons outside the United States, what should those limits be? Is it appropriate to apply the same limits as those applicable to conduct or persons in other U.S. states? Is the sovereignty of foreign states a greater or lesser obstacle than the sovereignty of sister states to the application of U.S. state law to conduct abroad? Recall the similar issues that arise in the context of judicial jurisdiction. *See supra* pp. 139-140. In many cases, foreign law can be expected to be very different from any U.S. state law—while the variations between the substantive laws of different U.S. states are often slight. Does this affect the extent of constitutional limits on the application of U.S. state law to non-U.S. occurrences?

4. *Considerations of reciprocity.* Suppose that, in *Dick*, Mexican courts would readily have applied Mexican law to claims in the reverse circumstances (*i.e.*, cases involving events occurring wholly in Texas and lacking any Mexican nexus). Suppose that a particular foreign nation did not impose any limits at all upon the application of its law to conduct occurring in the United States. Should the Constitution forbid state courts from applying their laws to the conduct of foreign nationals in that country in an equally unrestrained fashion? If a foreign country takes the view that international law does not limit the extraterritorial application of its law, why should U.S. courts take a different view toward that state? Recall the similar issues that arise in the context of judicial jurisdiction. *See supra* p. 105.

5. *Applicability of due process protections to aliens.* One of the defendants in *Dick* was a Mexican company. Why does the Due Process Clause protect non-U.S. parties? What does *Dick* say? Compare the discussion above of due process limits on judicial jurisdiction over non-U.S. defendants. *See supra* p. 109.

6. *Texas's interest in protecting Texan domiciliaries.* Mr. Dick was a permanent resident of Texas. Did this not give Texas an interest in application of its law invalidating contract terms that unfairly treated Texas consumers? Does the Court assign any weight to Mr. Dick's Texas residence? Is that residence a sufficient basis for concluding that the Constitution should not bar application of Texan law? As discussed below, contemporary choice of law theory in the United States sometimes permits application of a state's law based solely on the fact that the injured plaintiff was a forum resident. *See infra* pp. 753-754. Why wasn't a similar analysis followed in *Dick*?

As discussed above, international law does not generally permit legislative jurisdiction based on the "passive personality" principle. This principle would allow a state to apply its laws, outside its territory, to persons or conduct that harm its nationals. *See supra* pp. 601-602. Should due process analysis follow international law in rejecting the passive personality principle? In both domestic and international cases?

7. *Choice of law clause in* **Dick.** Buried in the *Dick* opinion is the passing observation that the parties had agreed that Mexican law would govern their contract. What is the relevance of the Mexican choice of law clause in Mr. Dick's insurance policy to due process analysis? Does it bear upon the Mexican insurer's likely expectations? Should the Due Process Clause make it harder for a state to apply its law to override the parties' choice of law, than to apply its law in the absence of a choice of law agreement?

b.   Contemporary Constitutional Limits on State Legislative Jurisdiction.   As in other jurisdictional contexts, the strict territorial limits of *The Apollon, Dodge,* and *Dick* did not survive for long.[92] The Court made it clear, in a number of decisions during the 1940s and thereafter, that both Congress and the states had the constitutional authority to

---

92. *Compare supra* pp. 86-87.

exercise legislative jurisdiction over persons, property, and conduct beyond their borders.[93]

A 1943 decision in *Hoopeston Canning Company v. Cullen*[94] held that New York could regulate out-of-state reciprocal insurance companies covering New York risks, even where their contracts were made in other states. The territorial limits of *Dick* and earlier decisions were replaced in *Hoopeston* by a flexible attention to "realistic considerations" and state regulatory interests:

> In determining the power of a state to apply its own regulatory laws to insurance business activities, the question in earlier cases became involved by conceptualistic discussion of theories of the place of contracting or of performance. More recently it has been recognized that a state may have substantial interests in the business of insurance of its people or property regardless of these isolated factors. This interest may be measured by highly realistic considerations such as the protection of the citizen insured or the protection of the state from the incidents of loss.[95]

Other decisions evidenced a similarly expansive view of the power of states to apply their own laws to multistate conduct.[96] These decisions broadly paralleled the erosion of territorial limits on judicial jurisdiction, culminating in *International Shoe*'s "minimum contacts" test in 1945.[97]

It is now well settled that "in many situations a state court may be free to apply one of several choices of law."[98] The Court and others have frequently said that the Constitution imposes only "modest restrictions on the application of forum law."[99] In international cases, these restrictions derived principally from: (i) the Due Process Clause, and (ii) the Foreign Commerce Clause and other affirmative grants of authority to the federal government in international matters.[100]

i. Due Process Limitations on State Choice of Law. Although the Court has not addressed the question with any frequency, it has apparently concluded that the Due Process and Full Faith and Credit Clauses impose substantially the same restrictions on state choice of law decisions.[101] As Justice Scalia put it recently, "[t]he nub of the . . . controversy . . . is the scope of constitutionally permissible legislative jurisdiction," and "it matters little whether that is discussed in the context of the Full Faith and Credit Clause . . . or in the context of the Due Process Clause."[102] In contrast, Justice Stevens, as well as some commentators, take the position that the two clauses impose different standards; they reason that the Full Faith and Credit Clause protects the "interests of other sovereign States," while the Due Process Clause ensures "fairness of . . . decision to the litigants."[103]

---

93. *See supra* pp. 596-597 and *infra* pp. 649-651.

94. 318 U.S. 313 (1943).

95. 318 U.S. at 316.

96. *Watson v. Employers Liability Assurance Corp.*, 348 U.S. 66 (1954); *Pacific Employers Ins. Co. v. Industrial Accident Comm'n*, 306 U.S. 493 (1939).

97. *See supra* pp. 86-87.

98. *Phillips Petroleum Co. v. Shutts*, 472 U.S. 797, 823 (1985).

99. 472 U.S. at 818.

100. *See infra* pp. 619-644.

101. 472 U.S. at 818-819.

102. *Sun Oil Co. v. Wortman*, 486 U.S. 717, 730 n.3 (1988). *See also Phillips Petroleum Co. v. Shutts*, 472 U.S. 797, 818 (1985).

103. *Phillips Petroleum Co. v. Shutts*, 472 U.S. 797, 824 (1985) (Stevens, J., concurring); *Allstate Ins. Co. v. Hague*, 449 U.S. 302, 320 (1981) (Stevens, J., concurring).

The basic standard applicable to legislative jurisdiction under the Full Faith and Credit and the Due Process Clauses is broadly similar in language to the Court's constitutional limits on judicial jurisdiction: "'for a State's substantive law to be selected in a constitutionally permissible manner, that State must have a significant contact or significant aggregation of contacts, creating state interests, such that choice of its law is neither arbitrary nor fundamentally unfair.'"[104] In contrast to the judicial jurisdiction context, however, the Court has seldom found state choice of law decisions to violate this standard. The Court's opinion in *Allstate Insurance Co. v. Hague*, excerpted below, is a good illustration of the modest effect of due process limits on contemporary state legislative jurisdiction.

ALLSTATE INSURANCE CO. v. HAGUE
449 U.S. 302 (1981)

JUSTICE BRENNAN announced the judgment of the Court and delivered an opinion, in which JUSTICE WHITE, JUSTICE MARSHALL, and JUSTICE BLACKMUN joined. This Court granted certiorari to determine whether the Due Process Clause of the Fourteenth Amendment or the Full Faith and Credit Clause of Art. IV, §1, of the U.S. Constitution bars the Minnesota Supreme Court's choice of substantive Minnesota law to govern the effect of a provision in an insurance policy issued to respondent's decedent.

I. Respondent's late husband, Ralph Hague, died of injuries suffered when a motorcycle on which he was a passenger was struck from behind by an automobile. The accident occurred in Pierce County, Wisconsin, which is immediately across the Minnesota border from Red Wing, Minnesota. The operators of both vehicles were Wisconsin residents, as was the decedent, who, at the time of the accident, resided with respondent in Hager City, Wisconsin, which is one and one-half miles from Red Wing. Mr. Hague had been employed in Red Wing for the 15 years immediately preceding his death and had commuted daily from Wisconsin to his place of employment. Neither the operator of the motorcycle nor the operator of the automobile carried valid insurance. However, the decedent held a policy issued by petitioner Allstate Insurance Co. covering three automobiles owned by him and containing an uninsured motorist clause insuring him against loss incurred from accidents with uninsured motorists. The uninsured motorist coverage was limited to $15,000 for each automobile.[105]

After the accident, but prior to the initiation of this lawsuit, respondent moved to Red Wing. Subsequently, she married a Minnesota resident and established residence with her new husband in Savage, Minnesota. . . . [She later] brought this action in Minnesota District Court seeking a declaration under Minnesota law that the $15,000 uninsured motorist coverage on each of her late husband's three automobiles could be "stacked" to provide total coverage of $45,000. Petitioner defended on the ground that whether the three uninsured motorist coverages could be stacked should be determined by Wisconsin law, since the insurance policy was delivered in Wisconsin, the accident occurred in Wisconsin, and all persons involved were Wisconsin residents at the time of the accident. The Minnesota District Court disagreed. Interpreting Wisconsin law to disallow stacking, the court concluded that Minnesota's choice-of-law rules required the application of

---

104. 472 U.S. at 818-819 (quoting *Allstate Ins. Co. v. Hague*, 449 U.S. 302, 312-313 (1981)).

105. Ralph Hague paid a separate premium for each automobile including an additional separate premium for each uninsured motorist coverage.

Minnesota law permitting stacking. The court refused to apply Wisconsin law as "inimical to the public policy of Minnesota" and granted summary judgment for respondent.

The Minnesota Supreme Court, sitting en banc, affirmed the District Court. The court, also interpreting Wisconsin law to prohibit stacking, applied Minnesota law after analyzing the relevant Minnesota contacts and interests within the analytical framework developed by Professor Leflar. *See* Leflar, *Choice-Influencing Considerations in Conflicts Law*, 41 N.Y.U. L. Rev. 267 (1966). The state court, therefore, examined the conflict-of-laws issue in terms of (1) predictability of result, (2) maintenance of interstate order, (3) simplification of the judicial task, (4) advancement of the forum's governmental interests, and (5) application of the better rule of law. Although stating that the Minnesota contacts might not be, "in themselves, sufficient to mandate application of [Minnesota] law," under the first four factors, the court concluded that the fifth factor — application of the better rule of law — favored selection of Minnesota law. The court emphasized that a majority of States allow stacking and that legal decisions allowing stacking "are fairly recent and well considered in light of current uses of automobiles." In addition, the court found the Minnesota rule superior to Wisconsin's "because it requires the cost of accidents with uninsured motorists to be spread more broadly through insurance premiums than does the Wisconsin rule." Finally, after rehearing en banc, the court buttressed its initial opinion by indicating "that contracts of insurance on motor vehicles are in a class by themselves" since an insurance company "knows the automobile is a movable item which will be driven from state to state." From this premise the court concluded that application of Minnesota law was "not so arbitrary and unreasonable as to violate due process."

II. It is not for this Court to say whether the choice-of-law analysis suggested by Professor Leflar is to be preferred or whether we would make the same choice-of-law decision if sitting as the Minnesota Supreme Court. Our sole function is to determine whether the Minnesota Supreme Court's choice of its own substantive law in this case exceeded federal constitutional limitations. Implicit in this inquiry is the recognition, long accepted by this Court, that a set of facts giving rise to a lawsuit, or a particular issue within a lawsuit, may justify, in constitutional terms, application of the law of more than one jurisdiction. *See generally Clay v. Sun Insurance Office, Ltd.*, 377 U.S. 179, 181-182 (1964) (hereinafter cited as *Clay II*). As a result, the forum State may have to select one law from among the laws of several jurisdictions having some contact with the controversy.

In deciding constitutional choice-of-law questions, whether under the Due Process Clause or the Full Faith and Credit Clause,[106] this Court has traditionally examined the contacts of the State, whose law was applied, with the parties and with the occurrence or transaction giving rise to the litigation. In order to ensure that the choice of law is neither arbitrary nor fundamentally unfair, the Court has invalidated the choice of law of a State which has had no significant contact or significant aggregation of contacts, creating state interests, with the parties and the occurrence or transaction.[107]

Two instructive examples of such invalidation are *Home Ins. Co. v. Dick* [excerpted above at p. 614], and *John Hancock Mutual Life Ins. Co. v. Yates*, 299 U.S. 178 (1936). In both cases, the selection of forum law rested exclusively on the presence of one

---

106. This Court has taken a similar approach in deciding choice-of-law cases under both the Due Process Clause and the Full Faith and Credit Clause. In each instance, the Court has examined the relevant contacts and resulting interests of the State whose law was applied. *See, e.g., Nevada v. Hall*, 440 U.S. 410, 424 (1979). . . .

107. Prior to the advent of interest analysis in the state courts as the "dominant mode of analysis in modern choice of law theory," Silberman, *Shaffer v. Heitner: The End of an Era*, 53 N.Y.U. L. Rev. 33, 80 n.259 (1978), the prevailing choice-of-law methodology focused on the jurisdiction where a particular event occurred. *See, e.g., Restatement (First) Conflict of Laws* (1934).

nonsignificant forum contact. . . . *Dick and Yates* stand for the proposition that if a State has only an insignificant contact with the parties and the occurrence or transaction, application of its law is unconstitutional. *Dick* concluded that nominal residence — standing alone — was inadequate; *Yates* held that a post-occurrence change of residence to the forum State — standing alone — was insufficient to justify application of forum law. Although instructive as extreme examples of selection of forum law, neither *Dick* nor *Yates* governs this case. For in contrast to those decisions, here the Minnesota contacts with the parties and the occurrence are obviously significant. Thus, this case is like *Alaska Packers Cardillo v. Liberty Mutual Ins. Co.*, 330 U.S. 469 (1947), and *Clay II* — cases where this Court sustained choice-of-law decisions based on the contacts of the State, whose law was applied, with the parties and occurrence.

In *Alaska Packers*, the Court upheld California's application of its Workmen's Compensation Act, where the most significant contact of the worker with California was his execution of an employment contract in California. The worker, a nonresident alien from Mexico, was hired in California for seasonal work in a salmon canning factory in Alaska. As part of the employment contract, the employer, who was doing business in California, agreed to transport the worker to Alaska and to return him to California when the work was completed. Even though the employee contracted to be bound by the Alaska Workmen's Compensation Law and was injured in Alaska, he sought an award under the California Workmen's Compensation Act. The Court held that the choice of California law was not "so arbitrary or unreasonable as to amount to a denial of due process," because "[w]ithout a remedy in California, [he] would be remediless," and because of California's interest that the worker not become a public charge. . . .

Clay II upheld the constitutionality of the application of forum law. There, a policy of insurance had issued in Illinois to an Illinois resident. Subsequently the insured moved to Florida and suffered a property loss in Florida. Relying explicitly on the nationwide coverage of the policy and the presence of the insurance company in Florida and implicitly on the plaintiff's Florida residence and the occurrence of the property loss in Florida, the Court sustained the Florida court's choice of Florida law. The lesson from *Dick* and *Yates*, which found insufficient forum contacts to apply forum law, and from *Alaska Packers*, *Cardillo*, and *Clay II*, which found adequate contacts to sustain the choice of forum law,[108] is that for a State's substantive law to be selected in a constitutionally permissible manner, that State must have a significant contact or significant aggregation of contacts, creating state interests, such that choice of its law is neither arbitrary nor fundamentally unfair. . . .

III. Minnesota has three contacts with the parties and the occurrence giving rise to the litigation. In the aggregate, these contacts permit selection by the Minnesota Supreme Court of Minnesota law allowing the stacking of Mr. Hague's uninsured motorist coverages.

First, and for our purposes a very important contact, Mr. Hague was a member of Minnesota's work force, having been employed by a Red Wing, Minn., enterprise for the 15 years preceding his death. While employment status may implicate a state interest less substantial than does resident status, that interest is nevertheless important. The State of employment has police power responsibilities towards the nonresident employee that are analogous, if somewhat less profound, than towards residents. Thus, such employees use state services and amenities and may call upon state facilities in appropriate circumstances.

108. The Court has upheld choice-of-law decisions challenged on constitutional grounds in numerous other decisions. . . .

In addition, Mr. Hague commuted to work in Minnesota, a contact which was important in *Cardillo v. Liberty Mutual Ins. Co.*, [330 U.S. 469, 475-476 (1947)] (daily commute between residence in District of Columbia and workplace in Virginia), and was presumably covered by his uninsured motorist coverage during the commute. The State's interest in its commuting nonresident employees reflects a state concern for the safety and well-being of its work force and the concomitant effect on Minnesota employers. That Mr. Hague was not killed while commuting to work or while in Minnesota does not dictate a different result. To hold that the Minnesota Supreme Court's choice of Minnesota law violated the Constitution for that reason would require too narrow a view of Minnesota's relationship with the parties and the occurrence giving rise to the litigation. An automobile accident need not occur within a particular jurisdiction for that jurisdiction to be connected to the occurrence.[109] Similarly, the occurrence of a crash fatal to a Minnesota employee in another State is a Minnesota contact. If Mr. Hague had only been injured and missed work for a few weeks the effect on the Minnesota employer would have been palpable and Minnesota's interest in having its employee made whole would be evident. Mr. Hague's death affects Minnesota's interest still more acutely, even though Mr. Hague will not return to the Minnesota work force. Minnesota's work force is surely affected by the level of protection the State extends to it, either directly or indirectly. Vindication of the rights of the estate of a Minnesota employee, therefore, is an important state concern.

Mr. Hague's residence in Wisconsin does not — as Allstate seems to argue — constitutionally mandate application of Wisconsin law to the exclusion of forum law. If, in the instant case, the accident had occurred in Minnesota between Mr. Hague and an uninsured Minnesota motorist, if the insurance contract had been executed in Minnesota covering a Minnesota registered company automobile which Mr. Hague was permitted to drive, and if a Wisconsin court sought to apply Wisconsin law, certainly Mr. Hague's residence in Wisconsin, his commute between Wisconsin and Minnesota, and the insurer's presence in Wisconsin should be adequate to apply Wisconsin's law.[110] Employment status is not a sufficiently less important status than residence, when combined with Mr. Hague's daily commute across state lines and the other Minnesota contacts present, to prohibit the choice-of-law result in this case on constitutional grounds.

Second, Allstate was at all times present and doing business in Minnesota.[111] By virtue of its presence, Allstate can hardly claim unfamiliarity with the laws of the host jurisdiction

109. Numerous cases have applied the law of a jurisdiction other than the situs of the injury where there existed some other link between that jurisdiction and the occurrence. *See, e.g., Cardillo v. Liberty Mutual Ins. Co.; Alaska Packers Assn. v. Industrial Accident Comm'n; Babcock v. Jackson.*

110. Of course, Allstate could not be certain that Wisconsin law would necessarily govern any accident which occurred in Wisconsin, whether brought in the Wisconsin courts or elsewhere. Such an expectation would give controlling significance to the wooden lex loci delicti doctrine. While the place of the accident is a factor to be considered in choice-of-law analysis, to apply blindly the traditional, but now largely abandoned, doctrine would fail to distinguish between the relative importance of various legal issues involved in a lawsuit as well as the relationship of other jurisdictions to the parties and the occurrence or transaction. If, for example, Mr. Hague had been a Wisconsin resident and employee who was injured in Wisconsin and was then taken by ambulance to a hospital in Red Wing, Minn., where he languished for several weeks before dying, Minnesota's interest in ensuring that its medical creditors were paid would be obvious. . . .

111. The Court has recognized that examination of a State's contacts may result in divergent conclusions for jurisdiction and choice-of-law purposes. *See Kulko v. California Superior Court*, 436 U.S. 84, 98 (1978) (no jurisdiction in California but California law "arguably might" apply); *Shaffer v. Heitner*, 433 U.S. at 215 (no jurisdiction in Delaware, although Delaware interest "may support the application of Delaware law"). Nevertheless, "both inquiries 'are often closely related and to a substantial degree depend upon similar considerations.' " *Shaffer*, 433 U.S. at 224-225 (Brennan, J., concurring in part and dissenting in part). Here, of course, jurisdiction in the Minnesota courts is unquestioned, a factor not without significance in assessing the constitutionality of Minnesota's choice of its own substantive law.

and surprise that the state courts might apply forum law to litigation in which the company is involved. "Particularly since the company was licensed to do business in [the forum], it must have known it might be sued there, and that [the forum] courts would feel bound by [forum] law." *Clay v. Sun Ins. Office Ltd.*, 363 U.S. 207, 221 (1960) (Black, J., dissenting).[112] Moreover, Allstate's presence in Minnesota gave Minnesota an interest in regulating the company's insurance obligations insofar as they affected both a Minnesota resident and court-appointed representative — respondent — and a long-standing member of Minnesota's work force — Mr. Hague.

Third, respondent became a Minnesota resident prior to institution of this litigation. The stipulated facts reveal that she first settled in Red Wing, Minn., the town in which her late husband had worked. She subsequently moved to Savage, Minn., after marrying a Minnesota resident who operated an automobile service station in Bloomington, Minn. Her move to Savage occurred "almost concurrently," 289 N.W.2d at 45, with the initiation of the instant case. There is no suggestion that Mrs. Hague moved to Minnesota in anticipation of this litigation or for the purpose of finding a legal climate especially hospitable to her claim.[113] The stipulated facts, sparse as they are, negate any such inference.

While *John Hancock Mutual Life Ins. Co. v. Yates*, 299 U.S. 178 (1936), held that a post-occurrence change of residence to the forum State was insufficient in and of itself to confer power on the forum State to choose its law, that case did not hold that such a change of residence was irrelevant. Here, of course, respondent's bona fide residence in Minnesota was not the sole contact Minnesota had with this litigation. And in connection with her residence in Minnesota, respondent was appointed personal representative of Mr. Hague's estate by the Registrar of Probate for the County of Goodhue, Minn. Respondent's residence and subsequent appointment in Minnesota as personal representative of her late husband's estate constitute a Minnesota contact which gives Minnesota an interest in respondent's recovery, an interest which the court below identified as full compensation for "resident accident victims" to keep them "off welfare rolls" and able "to meet financial obligations."

In sum, Minnesota had a significant aggregation[114] of contacts with the parties and the occurrence, creating state interests, such that application of its law was neither arbitrary nor fundamentally unfair. Accordingly, the choice of Minnesota law by the Minnesota Supreme Court did not violate the Due Process Clause or the Full Faith and Credit Clause.

STEVENS, JUSTICE, concurring. As I view this unusual case — in which neither precedent nor constitutional language provides sure guidance — two separate questions must be answered. First, does the Full Faith and Credit Clause require Minnesota, the forum State, to apply Wisconsin law? Second, does the Due Process Clause of the Fourteenth Amendment prevent Minnesota from applying its own law? The first inquiry implicates the

112. There is no element of unfair surprise or frustration of legitimate expectations as a result of Minnesota's choice of its law. Because Allstate was doing business in Minnesota and was undoubtedly aware that Mr. Hague was a Minnesota employee, it had to have anticipated that Minnesota law might apply to an accident in which Mr. Hague was involved. Indeed, Allstate specifically anticipated that Mr. Hague might suffer an accident either in Minnesota or elsewhere in the United States, outside of Wisconsin, since the policy it issued offered continental coverage. At the same time, Allstate did not seek to control construction of the contract since the policy contained no choice-of-law clause dictating application of Wisconsin law.

113. The dissent [not excerpted here] suggests that considering respondent's post-occurrence change of residence as one of the Minnesota contacts will encourage forum shopping. This overlooks the fact that her change of residence was bona fide and not motivated by litigation considerations.

114. We express no view whether the first two contacts, either together or separately, would have sufficed to sustain the choice of Minnesota law made by the Minnesota Supreme Court.

federal interest in ensuring that Minnesota respect the sovereignty of the State of Wisconsin; the second implicates the litigants' interests in a fair adjudication of their rights. . . .

I. The Full Faith and Credit Clause is one of several provisions in the Federal Constitution designed to transform the several States from independent sovereignties into a single, unified Nation. The Full Faith and Credit Clause implements this design by directing that a State, when acting as the forum for litigation having multistate aspects or implications, respect the legitimate interests of other States and avoid infringement upon their sovereignty. The Clause does not, however, rigidly require the forum State to apply foreign law whenever another State has a valid interest in the litigation. On the contrary, in view of the fact that the forum State is also a sovereign in its own right, in appropriate cases it may attach paramount importance to its own legitimate interests.[115] Accordingly, the fact that a choice-of-law decision may be unsound as a matter of conflicts law does not necessarily implicate the federal concerns embodied in the Full Faith and Credit Clause. Rather in my opinion, the Clause should not invalidate a state court's choice of forum law unless that choice threatens the federal interest in national unity by unjustifiably infringing upon the legitimate interests of another State.

In this case, I think the Minnesota courts' decision to apply Minnesota law was plainly unsound as a matter of normal conflicts law. Both the execution of the insurance contract and the accident giving rise to the litigation took place in Wisconsin. Moreover, when both of those events occurred the plaintiff, the decedent, and the operators of both vehicles were all residents of Wisconsin. Nevertheless, I do not believe that any threat to national unity or Wisconsin's sovereignty ensues from allowing the substantive question presented by this case to be determined by the law of another State. . . .

II. It may be assumed that a choice-of-law decision would violate the Due Process Clause if it were totally arbitrary or if it were fundamentally unfair to either litigant. I question whether a judge's decision to apply the law of his own State could ever be described as wholly irrational. For judges are presumably familiar with their own state law and may find it difficult and time consuming to discover and apply correctly the law of another State. The forum State's interest in the fair and efficient administration of justice is therefore sufficient, in my judgment, to attach a presumption of validity to a forum State's decision to apply its own law to a dispute over which it has jurisdiction.

The forum State's interest in the efficient operation of its judicial system is clearly not sufficient, however, to justify the application of a rule of law that is fundamentally unfair to one of the litigants. . . . Concern about the fairness of the forum's choice of its own rule might arise if that rule favored residents over nonresidents,[116] if it represented a dramatic departure from the rule that obtains in most American jurisdictions, or if the rule itself was unfair on its face or as applied.

The application of an otherwise acceptable rule of law may result in unfairness to the litigants if, in engaging in the activity which is the subject of the litigation, they could not reasonably have anticipated that their actions would later be judged by this rule of law. A choice-of-law decision that frustrates the justifiable expectations of the parties can be fundamentally unfair. This desire to prevent unfair surprise to a litigant has been the

---

115. For example, it is well established that "the Full Faith and Credit Clause does not require a State to apply another State's law in violation of its own legitimate public policy." *Nevada v. Hall*, 440 U.S. 410, 422 (1979).

116. Discrimination against nonresidents would be constitutionally suspect even if the Due Process Clause were not a check upon a State's choice-of-law decisions. Moreover, both discriminatory and substantively unfair rules of law may be detected and remedied without any special choice-of-law analysis; familiar constitutional principles are available to deal with both varieties of unfairness.

central concern in this Court's review of choice-of-law decisions under the Due Process Clause.[117]

Neither the "stacking" rule itself, nor Minnesota's application of that rule to these litigants, raises any serious question of fairness. As the plurality observes, "[s]tacking was the rule in most States at the time the policy was issued." Moreover, the rule is consistent with the economics of a contractual relationship in which the policyholder paid three separate premiums for insurance coverage for three automobiles, including a separate premium for each uninsured motorist coverage. Nor am I persuaded that the decision of the Minnesota courts to apply the "stacking" rule in this case can be said to violate due process because that decision frustrates the reasonable expectations of the contracting parties.

Contracting parties can, of course, make their expectations explicit by providing in their contract either that the law of a particular jurisdiction shall govern questions of contract interpretation, or that a particular substantive rule, for instance "stacking," shall or shall not apply. In the absence of such express provisions, the contract nonetheless may implicitly reveal the expectations of the parties. For example, if a liability insurance policy issued by a resident of a particular State provides coverage only with respect to accidents within that State, it is reasonable to infer that the contracting parties expected that their obligations under the policy would be governed by that State's law.

In this case, no express indication of the parties' expectations is available. The insurance policy provided coverage for accidents throughout the United States; thus, at the time of contracting, the parties certainly could have anticipated that the law of States other than Wisconsin would govern particular claims arising under the policy. By virtue of doing business in Minnesota, Allstate was aware that it could be sued in the Minnesota courts; Allstate also presumably was aware that Minnesota law, as well as the law of most States, permitted "stacking." Nothing in the record requires that a different inference be drawn. Therefore, the decision of the Minnesota courts to apply the law of the forum in this case does not frustrate the reasonable expectations of the contracting parties, and I can find no fundamental unfairness in that decision requiring the attention of this Court.

In terms of fundamental fairness, it seems to me that two factors relied upon by the plurality — the plaintiff's post-accident move to Minnesota and the decedent's Minnesota employment — are either irrelevant to or possibly even tend to undermine the plurality's conclusion. When the expectations of the parties at the time of contracting are the central due process concern, as they are in this case, an unanticipated post-accident occurrence is clearly irrelevant for due process purposes. The fact that the plaintiff became a resident of the forum State after the accident surely cannot justify a ruling in her favor that would not be made if the plaintiff were a nonresident. Similarly, while the fact that the decedent regularly drove into Minnesota might be relevant to the expectations of the contracting parties, the fact that he did so because he was employed in Minnesota adds nothing to the due process analysis. The choice-of-law decision of the Minnesota courts is consistent with due process because it does not result in unfairness to either litigant, not because Minnesota now has an interest in the plaintiff as resident or formerly had an interest in the decedent as employee.

117. Upon careful analysis most of the decisions of this Court that struck down on due process grounds a state court's choice of forum law can be explained as attempts to prevent a State with a minimal contact with the litigation from materially enlarging the contractual obligations of one of the parties where that party had no reason to anticipate the possibility of such enlargement.

Notes on Allstate

1. *Possible differences between Due Process and Full Faith and Credit Clauses.* The Court has generally treated the Full Faith and Credit and Due Process Clauses as imposing substantially the same limits on choice of law decisions. Justice Stevens and others have rejected this approach. Consider:

> [E]ach clause speaks to essentially different considerations. The Due Process Clause addresses issues of the territorial reach of state power and the fairness to individuals in the exercise of that power. Full Faith and Credit, on the other hand, balances conflicting state interests by commanding that the states respect the sovereignty of sister states in a federal context. E. Scoles & P. Hay, *Conflict of Laws* 80 (1982).

Compare Justice Steven's discussion of the difference between the two clauses. Is that persuasive? Consider the application of the Due Process Clause to assertions of judicial jurisdiction. Does it only consider issues of fairness, or does it also consider state territorial sovereignty? As a practical matter, why does the distinction between the Due Process and the Full Faith and Credit Clauses matter? Could the Due Process Clause affirmatively require a state to apply a particular law (rather than merely forbidding it from applying its own law)?

2. *No constitutional bar to application of state law to conduct occurring outside state territory.* It is now clear that there is no general prohibition in the Constitution against a state's application of its substantive laws to conduct occurring outside state territory. *Allstate* said that the "wooden *lex loci delicti* doctrine" had been "largely abandoned" and it emphasized that "[n]umerous cases have applied the law of a jurisdiction other than the situs of the injury." *See Cardillo v. Liberty Mutual Ins. Co.,* 330 U.S. 469 (1947); *Alaska Packers Ass'n v. Industrial Accident Comm'n,* 294 U.S. 532 (1935). *See also Skiriotes v. Florida,* 313 U.S. 69 (1941), discussed below.

3. *State legislative jurisdiction over citizens.* In *Skiriotes v. Florida,* 313 U.S. 69 (1941), the Supreme Court rejected a constitutional challenge to the extraterritorial application of a Florida criminal statute. The statute forbid the use of certain diving apparatus for the purpose of taking commercial sponges from the Gulf of Mexico; a Florida resident was convicted under the statute outside the territorial waters of both the United States and Florida. The Court held that "no question of international law, or of the extent of the authority of the United States in its international relations is presented," because Mr. Skiriotes was a Florida resident and U.S. national. The Court continued: "If the United States may control the conduct of its citizens upon the high seas, we see no reason why the State of Florida may not likewise govern the conduct of its citizens upon the high seas with respect to matters in which the State has a legitimate interest. . . ." Is this persuasive? The Constitution limits the role of the states in international matters. *See supra* pp. 1-13 and *infra* pp. 630-644. Given this, is it persuasive to conclude that a state may exercise legislative jurisdiction simply because Congress may? Does the *Skiriotes* analysis apply where state law is sought to be applied to conduct within the territory of a foreign country? What would be the basis for distinguishing the two instances?

4. *Comparison between constitutional limits on judicial and legislative jurisdiction.* Compare the minimum contacts test for judicial jurisdiction, *see supra* pp. 86-87, with the "significant contacts creating state interests" test for legislative jurisdiction. Are the tests similar?

Which language is more restrictive? In practice, which test has imposed the more rigorous limits on state jurisdiction? Consider:

> [D]iffering treatment of contacts in the jurisdiction and choice-of-law cases turns things on their head. In the typical jurisdiction case, overreaching on the part of the forum state results at worst in inconvenience and greater expense for the defendant. In the typical conflicts case . . . if the plaintiff has chosen his forum wisely, the defendant will lose a case he would otherwise have won, simply because the forum has asserted its legislative jurisdiction. . . . [F]rom the defendant's perspective, it seems irrational to say that due process requires minimum contacts . . . merely to hale him into the forum's courts, while allowing more tenuous contacts to upset the very outcome of the case. Martin, *Personal Jurisdiction and Choice of Law*, 78 Mich. L. Rev. 872, 879-880 (1980).

Is this persuasive? Should due process limits on state legislative jurisdiction be more stringent than *Allstate* concluded? More stringent than limits on judicial jurisdiction?

5. Allstate *plurality — due process standard for state choice-of-law decisions.* What due process limits does the *Allstate* plurality impose on state choice of law decisions? What does the following test mean: "for a State's substantive law to be selected in a constitutionally permissible manner, that State must have a significant contact or significant aggregation of contacts, creating state interests, such that choice of its law is neither arbitrary nor fundamentally unfair"? How does a court determine whether a contact is "significant"? That a contact "creat[es] state interests"? That these contacts prevent a choice of law from being "arbitrary [or] fundamentally unfair"?

(a) Relation between the Allstate contacts. Consider the application of the foregoing standard by the *Allstate* plurality. The Court identified three "contacts" that permitted application of Minnesota law. What is the relation between these contacts? Was it necessary that all three exist, to justify application of Minnesota law?

(b) Decedent's employment in forum. What constitutional weight should be ascribed to the decedent's employment in Minnesota for 15 years? Suppose that the decedent was a *resident* of Minnesota, killed in a Wisconsin accident. Should that have given Minnesota a constitutionally sufficient interest to apply its own law to the question of insurance-stacking? What different weight should be accorded to the fact that the decedent was employed in Minnesota, rather than residing there? Note that Justice Stevens thought that the decedent's employment in Minnesota was "either irrelevant to or possibly even tend[ed] to undermine the plurality's conclusion."

(c) Allstate's doing business in Minnesota. What constitutional weight should be ascribed to the fact that Allstate did business in Minnesota? Suppose a company does business in every state in the Union — as many do. Does that mean that every state may apply its laws to any torts or contracts involving that company, regardless whether they have the slightest connection to the state? What about activities outside the United States?

(d) Survivor's post-accident residence in Minnesota. The *Allstate* plurality relied on the fact that the plaintiff moved to Minnesota after the accident occurred. Why was this relevant? Consider Justice Stevens' criticism.

6. *Justice Stevens' concurrence in* **Allstate.** Compare Justice Stevens' concurring opinion in *Allstate* to the plurality's opinion. Justice Stevens distinguished between analysis under the Full Faith and Credit Clause and the Due Process Clause. He thought that the former required states to "respect the legitimate interests of other states and to avoid infringement upon their sovereignty." Justice Stevens saw no threat to "national unity or Wisconsin's sovereignty" from Minnesota's application of its law to accidents in Wisconsin between Wisconsin residents. Is that correct? Suppose Minnesota courts *always* applied their law to accidents in Wisconsin, and that Minnesota law was significantly more favorable to plaintiffs. Would that affect primary behavior in Wisconsin? Insurance costs? Why isn't that an infringement on Wisconsin's sovereignty?

Justice Stevens reasoned that the Due Process Clause forbids state choice of law decisions that are "totally arbitrary" or "fundamentally unfair." He did not believe that this standard was violated in *Allstate.* Why not? Note Justice Stevens' suggestion that the Due Process Clause would preclude application of laws that a party "could not reasonably have anticipated." Is sovereignty relevant at all to Justice Stevens' due process analysis? Since the Full Faith and Credit Clause does not apply in international cases, how would the Due Process Clause be applied by Justice Stevens in such cases?

7. Correctness of Allstate result. Is *Allstate* correctly decided? Should the Due Process Clause impose greater restrictions on state choice of law decisions? What would be the rationale for such limits?

8. Relevant connecting factors in due process analysis. *Allstate* holds that if there is "no significant contact or significant aggregation of contacts, creating state interests," the Due Process Clause forbids legislative jurisdiction. Under this analysis, what "contacts" are relevant, and how much do they "count" toward establishing a basis for jurisdiction?

(a) Situs of wrongful conduct. Suppose the underlying accident in *Allstate* occurred in Minnesota. Would that have been an independently sufficient basis to permit application of Minnesota law? What does *Dick* suggest? What does *Allstate* suggest?

(b) Situs of injury. Suppose that allegedly wrongful conduct occurs in one state, but causes injury in another state. Examples include the *Sedco* and *Olsen* cases, excerpted above, *supra* pp. 310-313, where negligent conduct allegedly occurred in Mexico, causing injury in the United States. There is little doubt that the Due Process Clause would regard the situs of injury as a significant contact for personal jurisdiction purposes. Would either the Due Process Clause or international law ever forbid the exercise of legislative jurisdiction by a state that was the situs of the injury?

(c) Nationality or domicile of defendant. Suppose that Allstate had been a Minnesota insurance company. Would its nationality or domicile have provided a significant contact, permitting application of Minnesota law? *See Skiriotes v. Florida*, 313 U.S. 69 (1941); *supra* p. 627. Would international law permit the exercise of legislative jurisdiction by a state over its nationals? Should the Due Process Clause permit the application of *any* law to a national's conduct in other states? Presumably, local traffic regulations could not be applied extraterritorially. Why not? Note *Allstate*'s requirement that a "significant contact" must "create state interests."

(d) Defendant's "doing business." One "contact" cited by *Allstate* was the fact that the defendant insurance company did business in Minnesota. Is this a legitimate basis for legislative jurisdiction? Recall that systematic business "presence" in a state provides a basis for general personal jurisdiction under the Due Process Clause. *See supra* pp. 113-114. Should an analogous result follow in the context of legislative jurisdiction? Would contemporary international law permit legislative jurisdiction based on this factor?

(e) Nationality or domicile of plaintiff. Suppose that the decedent and his wife in *Allstate* had been domiciled in Minnesota at the time of the accident in Wisconsin, having moved there after purchasing his insurance policies in Wisconsin. Would the plaintiff's Minnesota domicile have permitted application of Minnesota law to: (a) tort claims against the Wisconsin drivers who caused plaintiff's injuries and (b) the "stacking" issue? *Allstate* made it clear that the plaintiff's domicile or residence is a significant contact for due process. Is that wise? Recall that international law does not permit legislative jurisdiction based on the passive personality principle. *See supra* pp. 601-602. What does this suggest about *Allstate*'s reliance on this factor?

(f) Plaintiff's post-occurrence domicile or residence. Consider: "The post-accident residence of the plaintiff-beneficiary is constitutionally irrelevant to the choice of law question." *Allstate*, 449 U.S. at 337 (Powell, J., dissenting). Justice Stevens also rejected post-accident residence as a relevant connecting factor. Why is that? Why doesn't Minnesota have a significant "interest" in maximizing the recovery of its residents against non-Minnesota defendants? Or at least in insuring that its residents have the right to stack their insurance policies? If the plaintiff's domicile is a significant contact for due process purposes, then why does it matter whether domicile or residence commenced before or after the occurrences giving rise to the parties' dispute? What makes the plaintiff's residence/domicile "significant" for due process purposes? Is it anything more than the forum's interest in protecting its domiciliaries? Isn't that interest applicable regardless of when the plaintiff became domiciled in the forum? What else informs the Court's analysis?

(g) Parties' chosen law. As discussed in detail below, *infra* pp. 758-776, commercial agreements frequently contain choice of law clauses specifying the law applicable to disputes between the parties. The Due Process Clause would virtually always permit application of the parties' chosen law. *See infra* pp. 759-762.

9. *Comparison between due process limits on federal and state legislative jurisdiction.* Compare the due process limits imposed on state laws in *Allstate* with those imposed on federal law in *Davis*. Which standard is more stringent? Should due process limits on state and federal legislative jurisdiction be identical? Neither decision (nor line of decisions) acknowledges or cites the other. Is that sensible?

10. *Relevance of foreign sovereignty to due process analysis.* *Allstate* involved the exercise of legislative jurisdiction that arguably affected the sovereignty of another U.S. state, while *Davis* involved a jurisdictional assertion that affected foreign sovereignty. Suppose *Allstate* had involved an accident killing a Canadian resident on the Canadian side of the Canadian border, and the Canadian widow had subsequently moved to the United States. Would the application of U.S. state rules, permitting the stacking of three Canadian insurance policies, have been permitted — assuming that all of the other facts were identical to *Allstate*? Would international law permit application of U.S. law in this hypothetical? Note that *Dick* was an international choice of law case, while *Allstate* involved a purely domestic dispute. Might that explain differences in the due process standards?

ii. Foreign Commerce and Other Constitutional Limitations on State Legislative Jurisdiction. As discussed above, the Constitution grants Congress and the President broad powers over international matters. The Foreign Commerce Clause grants Congress the power to regulate commerce "with foreign Nations,"[118] while other provisions of Article I grant Congress the power to define offenses against the law of nations, to define and punish piracies, and to declare war.[119] The President is vested with the power to make treaties (with the consent of two-thirds of the Senate), to act as Commander in Chief, and to nominate ambassadors.[120] As discussed above, the Supreme Court has emphasized the breadth of federal powers over foreign commerce and relations.[121]

Broad federal authority over international matters is matched by limited state powers.[122] In particular, the Supreme Court has held that the Constitution imposes

---

118. U.S. Const. Art. I, §8, cl. 3.
119. U.S. Const. Art. I, §8, cl. 10, 11.
120. U.S. Const. Art. II, §2, cl. 1, 2.
121. *See supra* pp. 6-7.
122. *See supra* pp. 6-7; U.S. Const. Art. I, §10 ("No State shall enter into any Treaty, Alliance, or Confederation"; "No State shall, without the Consent of Congress lay any Imports or Duties on Imports or Exports . . . [or] enter into any Agreement or Contract with another State, or with a Foreign Power").

several types of restrictions on state legislative jurisdiction over international commercial matters. Most of these restrictions are based principally on federal common law, derived from the general predominance of federal power in international matters.

First, the Foreign Commerce Clause has been held to restrict state taxation of international commerce and its instrumentalities. In *Japan Line Ltd. v. County of Los Angeles*,[123] the Court held that a local tax on containers used in foreign commerce violated the dormant Foreign Commerce Clause. In reaching its conclusion, the Court reasoned that the Foreign Commerce Clause imposed stricter scrutiny on state taxes than the interstate commerce clause.[124]

Similarly, in *Container Corporation of America v. Franchise Tax Board*,[125] the Court considered challenges to California's corporation franchise tax under the Due Process and Foreign Commerce Clauses. Again emphasizing that taxes on foreign commerce were subject to more exacting scrutiny than interstate taxes,[126] the Court concluded that a state tax on international commerce must satisfy four requirements:[127] (a) the taxed activities must have a substantial nexus to the taxing state; (b) the tax must be fairly apportioned, such that there is a rational relationship between income or property attributed to the state and the intrastate values of the enterprise; (c) the tax must not discriminate against interstate or international commerce; and (d) there must be no substantial risk of international multiple taxation and no interference with the federal government's ability to "speak with one voice"[128] when regulating commercial relations with foreign governments. The Court found all four requirements satisfied on the *Container Corporation* facts.[129]

Second, the Supreme Court recently held a local tax unconstitutional on the ground that it violated the Tonnage Clause. The Tonnage Clause forbids a State "without the Consent of Congress, [to] lay any Duty of Tonnage."[130] In *Polar Tankers v. Miller*, the Court invalidated a local tax that imposes a personal property tax on large ships that travel into and from the city based on the value of cargo that they take on.[131] In reaching its conclusion, the Court explained that the tax at issue singled out a particular category of carriers and was based solely on their tonnage rather than, for example, the actual services provided by the city to the ship while it was in port.

Third, a few Supreme Court decisions have held state laws unconstitutional on the grounds that they unduly affect the federal government's exercise of its constitutional powers to conduct the Nation's foreign relations. The seminal case is *Zschernig v. Miller*,[132] where the Court invalidated an Oregon probate statute on the ground that it "affects international relations in a persistent and subtle way," and must "give way [because it] impair[s] the effective exercise of the Nation's foreign policy."[133] The Oregon law conditioned the rights of foreign nationals to inherit property on their home countries' provision of reciprocal rights to U.S. nationals and the freedom of foreign nationals to

---

123. 441 U.S. 434 (1979).

124. 441 U.S. at 445-450. *See also Container Corp. v. Franchise Tax Board*, 463 U.S. 159 (1983) ("Given that [appellant's business] is international, . . . we must subject this case to the additional scrutiny required by the Foreign Commerce Clause"); *Mobil Oil Corp. v. Comm'r of Taxes*, 445 U.S. 425 (1980); *Antilles Cement Corp. v. Calderon*, 288 F. Supp. 2d 187, 197-202 (D.P.R. 2003).

125. 463 U.S. 159 (1983).

126. 463 U.S. at 170, 184-185.

127. 463 U.S. at 169, 184-185.

128. *See Japan Line, Ltd. v. County of Los Angeles*, 441 U.S. 434 (1979); *Container Corp. v. Franchise Tax Board*, 463 U.S. 159 (1983).

129. 463 U.S. at 180-196.

130. Art. I, §10, cl. 3.

131. 129 S. Ct. 2277 (2009).

132. 389 U.S. 429 (1968).

133. 389 U.S. at 440.

receive the proceeds of Oregon estates "without confiscation." The Court's opinion in *Zschernig* was opaque, but it apparently rested on the view that Oregon (and other) state courts had engaged in detailed (and unflattering) analyses of foreign political and judicial systems.[134]

Justice Stewart filed a concurring opinion in *Zschernig* that was more analytically precise. He reasoned: "We deal here with the basic allocation of power between the States and the Nation. . . . [T]he conduct of our foreign affairs is entrusted under the Constitution to the National Government, not to the probate courts of the several states."[135] According to Justice Stewart's concurrence, each of the conditions imposed by the Oregon probate statute was facially unconstitutional, because "[a]ny realistic attempt to apply any of the three criteria would necessarily involve the Oregon courts in an evaluation, either express or implied, of the administration of foreign law, the credibility of foreign diplomatic statements, and the policies of foreign governments."[136] Justice Harlan concurred, adopting a narrower view of the preemptive effect of federal foreign affairs powers and holding that state laws must only "give way if they impair the effective exercise of the Nation's foreign policy" or conflict with federal policies.[137]

Fourth, the Court has relied on a combination of enumerated powers and the Supremacy Clause to hold that federal law preempts state law that would have the effect of interfering with the conduct of foreign policy. The leading case is the Supreme Court's 2000 decision in *Crosby v. National Foreign Trade Council*.[138] There, Massachusetts enacted a statute that barred state entities from buying or selling goods from anyone doing business with the nation of Burma. Three months later, Congress enacted federal legislation imposing a variety of sanctions on Burma, authorizing the President to impose further sanctions and directing the President to develop a strategy aimed at improving democracy and human rights in Burma. The *Crosby* Court held that the federal statute preempted the Massachusetts law due to conflicts between the two statutory regimes and, notably, because the Massachusetts law interfered with the President's ability to engage in effective diplomacy and to implement the objectives envisioned in the congressional enactment.[139]

Finally, the Court has fashioned rules of federal common law, derived from federal powers over foreign affairs and commerce, governing international matters which have the effect of limiting state choice of law decisions. The classic example is *Banco Nacional de Cuba v. Sabbatino*,[140] which held that U.S. courts could not consider the validity of certain foreign acts of state, notwithstanding contrary rules of U.S. state law.[141] As discussed

134. 389 U.S. at 434-436 ("they radiate some of the attitudes of the 'cold war,' where the search is for the 'democracy quotient' of a foreign regime").
135. 389 U.S. at 443.
136. 389 U.S. at 442. *See also United States v. Belmont*, 301 U.S. 324 (1937); *United States v. Pink*, 315 U.S. 203 (1942); *Deutsch v. Tanner Corp.*, 324 F.3d 692, 708-715 (9th Cir. 2003); *Taiheiyo Cement Corp. v. Superior Court*, 117 Cal. App. 4th 380, 390-391 (Cal. Ct. App. 2004); *Mitsubishi Materials Corp. v. Superior Court*, 113 Cal. App. 4th 55, 66-67 (Cal. Ct. App. 2003); *Miami Light Project v. Miami-Dade County*, 97 F. Supp. 2d 1174, 1180 (S.D. Fla. 2000).
137. 389 U.S. at 440.
138. 530 U.S. 363 (2000).
139. 530 U.S. at 373-374. The Court reasoned: "We see the state Burma law as an obstacle to the accomplishment of Congress's full objectives under the federal Act. We find that the state law undermines the intended purpose and 'natural effect' of at least three provisions of the federal Act, that is, its delegation of effective discretion to the President to control economic sanctions against Burma, its limitation of sanctions solely to United States persons and new investment, and its directive to the President to proceed diplomatically in developing a comprehensive, multilateral strategy towards Burma."
140. 376 U.S. 398 (1964) (excerpted *infra* pp. 801-808).
141. 376 U.S. at 428 ("the Judicial Branch will not examine the validity of a taking of property within its own territory by a foreign sovereign government, extant and recognized by this country at the time of suit, in the absence of a treaty or other unambiguous agreement regarding controlling legal principles, even if the complaint alleges that the taking violates customary international law.").

elsewhere, the federal courts have fashioned other federal common law rules in international matters.[142]

The Supreme Court's recent decision in *American Insurance Association v. Garamendi*, excerpted below, discusses several of the foregoing limits on state legislative jurisdiction in the area of foreign affairs, and particularly the possibility of foreign affairs preemption based on *Zschernig*.

AMERICAN INSURANCE ASSOCIATION v. GARAMENDI
539 U.S. 396 (2003)

SOUTER, JUSTICE. [This case involves claims under life insurance policies issued to Jewish persons during World War II. In some cases, the Nazi Government confiscated those policies. In other cases, following World War II, the insurers refused to honor the policies and cited, among other grounds, failure to pay premiums. At the end of the War, the West German Government paid reparations to victims of the war, but those payments did not reach all claimants.

Following the reunification of Germany, Jewish survivors and their descendents filed class actions for restitution against companies that did business during the Nazi era. To address these lawsuits, the U.S. Government, the German Government, and German companies negotiated various executive agreements, including the "German Foundation Agreement," under which the German Government and the private companies agreed to contribute 10 billion Deutsch marks (roughly $4.5 billion) to settle claims. For insurance claims, the German Foundation would cooperate with an existing insurance claims commission, the "International Commission on Holocaust Era Insurance Claims (ICHEIC)." In exchange, the U.S. Government agreed (1) to file "statements of interest" in any Holocaust-era claim in a U.S. court, urging the court to dismiss the claim in favor of resolution by the Foundation, and (2) to urge state and local governments to use the Foundation as the exclusive dispute resolution mechanism. The Foundation Agreement served as a model for comparable agreements with Austria and France.

In 1999, California enacted the Holocaust Victim Insurance Relief Act ("HVIRA"). The HVIRA required any insurer doing business in California to disclose information about policies sold in Europe between 1920 and 1945 by the company or related entities. Pursuant to the HVIRA, California Insurance officials issued subpoenas to several insurance companies who, at the time, were cooperating with the ICHEIC under the German Foundation Agreement. The insurance companies sought to enjoin application of the HVIRA, arguing that it infringed on federal foreign affairs powers. The procedural history is complex, but, in brief, the district court granted a preliminary injunction, and the appellate court reversed, holding in relevant part that the HVIRA did not unduly intrude on the federal foreign affairs power.]

III. The principal argument for preemption made by petitioners and the United States as *amicus curiae* is that HVIRA interferes with foreign policy of the Executive Branch, as expressed principally in the executive agreements with Germany, Austria, and France. The major premises of the argument, at least, are beyond dispute. There is, of course, no question that at some point an exercise of state power that touches on foreign relations must yield to the National Government's policy, given the "concern for uniformity in this country's dealings with foreign nations" that animated the Constitution's allocation of

---

142. *See supra* pp. 253-265; *First National City Bank v. Bancec*, 462 U.S. 611 (1983) (foreign state agency's corporate status); *Samantha v. Yousof*, 130 S. Ct. 2278 (2010).

the foreign relations power to the National Government in the first place. [*Banco Nacional de Cuba v. Sabbatino*, 376 U.S. 398, 427 n.25 (1964).]

Nor is there any question generally that there is executive authority to decide what that policy should be. Although the source of the President's power to act in foreign affairs does not enjoy any textual detail, the historical gloss on the "executive Power" vested in Article II of the Constitution has recognized the President's "vast share of responsibility for the conduct of our foreign relations." *Youngstown Sheet & Tube Co. v. Sawyer*, 343 U.S. 579, 610-611 (1952) (Frankfurter, J., concurring). While Congress holds express authority to regulate public and private dealings with other nations in its war and foreign commerce powers, in foreign affairs the President has a degree of independent authority to act.

At a more specific level, our cases have recognized that the President has authority to make "executive agreements" with other countries, requiring no ratification by the Senate or approval by Congress, this power having been exercised since the early years of the Republic. . . . Given the fact that the practice goes back over 200 years and has received congressional acquiescence throughout its history, the conclusion "[t]hat the President's control of foreign relations includes the settlement of claims is indisputable." [*United States v. Pink*, 315 U.S. 203, 240 (1942).] The executive agreements at issue here do differ in one respect from those just mentioned insofar as they address claims associated with formerly belligerent states, but against corporations, not the foreign governments. But the distinction does not matter. Historically, wartime claims against even nominally private entities have become issues in international diplomacy, and three of the postwar settlements dealing with reparations implicating private parties were made by the Executive alone. . . . As shown by the history of insurance confiscation mentioned earlier, untangling government policy from private initiative during wartime is often so hard that diplomatic action settling claims against private parties may well be just as essential in the aftermath of hostilities as diplomacy to settle claims against foreign governments. While a sharp line between public and private acts works for many purposes in the domestic law, insisting on the same line in defining the legitimate scope of the Executive's international negotiations would hamstring the President in settling international controversies. . . .

[While] valid executive agreements are fit to preempt state law, just like treaties are, . . . petitioners and the United States as *amicus curiae* both have to acknowledge that the agreements include no preemption clause, and so leave their claim of preemption to rest on asserted interference with the foreign policy those agreements embody. Reliance is placed on our decision in *Zschernig v. Miller*, 389 U.S. 429 (1968). . . . The *Zschernig* majority relied on statements in a number of previous cases open to the reading that state action with more than incidental effect on foreign affairs is preempted, even absent any affirmative federal activity in the subject area of the state law, and hence without any showing of conflict. . . . Likewise, Justice Stewart's concurring opinion viewed the Oregon statute as intruding "into a domain of exclusively federal competence." Justice Harlan, joined substantially by Justice White, disagreed with the *Zschernig* majority on this point, arguing that its implication of preemption of the entire field of foreign affairs was at odds with some other cases suggesting that in the absence of positive federal action "the States may legislate in areas of their traditional competence even though their statutes may have an incidental effect on foreign relations." Thus, for Justice Harlan it was crucial that the challenge to the Oregon statute presented no evidence of a "specific interest of the Federal Government which might be interfered with" by the law. He would, however, have found preemption in a case of "conflicting federal policy," and on this point the majority and Justices Harlan and White basically agreed: state laws "must give way if they impair the effective exercise of the Nation's foreign policy."

It is a fair question whether respect for the executive foreign relations power requires a categorical choice between the contrasting theories of field and conflict preemption evident in the *Zschernig* opinions, but the question requires no answer here. For even on Justice Harlan's view, the likelihood that state legislation will produce something more than incidental effect in conflict with express foreign policy of the National Government would require preemption of the state law. And since on his view it is legislation within "areas of . . . traditional competence" that gives a State any claim to prevail, it would be reasonable to consider the strength of the state interest, judged by standards of traditional practice, when deciding how serious a conflict must be shown before declaring the state law preempted. Judged by these standards, we think petitioners and the Government have demonstrated a sufficiently clear conflict to require finding preemption here.

IV. A. To begin with, resolving Holocaust-era insurance claims that may be held by residents of this country is a matter well within the Executive's responsibility for foreign affairs. Since claims remaining in the aftermath of hostilities may be "sources of friction" acting as an "impediment to resumption of friendly relations" between the countries involved, *Pink, supra,* at 225, there is a "longstanding practice" of the national Executive to settle them in discharging its responsibility to maintain the Nation's relationships with other countries. The issue of restitution for Nazi crimes has in fact been addressed in Executive Branch diplomacy and formalized in treaties and executive agreements over the last half century, and although resolution of private claims was postponed by the Cold War, securing private interests is an express object of diplomacy today, just as it was addressed in agreements soon after the Second World War. Vindicating victims injured by acts and omissions of enemy corporations in wartime is thus within the traditional subject matter of foreign policy in which national, not state, interests are overriding, and which the National Government has addressed.

The exercise of the federal executive authority means that state law must give way where, as here, there is evidence of clear conflict between the policies adopted by the two. . . . [T]he consistent Presidential foreign policy has been to encourage European governments and companies to volunteer settlement funds in preference to litigation or coercive sanctions. . . . This position . . . has also been consistently supported in the high levels of the Executive Branch. . . . The approach taken serves to resolve the several competing matters of national concern apparent in the German Foundation Agreement: the national interest in maintaining amicable relationships with current European allies; survivors' interests in a "fair and prompt" but non-adversarial resolution of their claims so as to "bring some measure of justice . . . in their lifetimes"; and the companies' interest in securing "legal peace" when they settle claims in this fashion. As a way for dealing with insurance claims, moreover, the voluntary scheme protects the companies' ability to abide by their own countries' domestic privacy laws limiting disclosure of policy information.

California has taken a different tack of providing regulatory sanctions to compel disclosure and payment, supplemented by a new cause of action for Holocaust survivors if the other sanctions should fail. . . . [Correspondence between the United States and California officials] show well enough how the portent of further litigation and sanctions has in fact placed the Government at a disadvantage in obtaining practical results from persuading "foreign governments and foreign companies to participate voluntarily in organizations such as ICHEIC." In addition to thwarting the Government's policy of repose for companies that pay through the ICHEIC, California's indiscriminate disclosure provisions place a handicap on the ICHEIC's effectiveness (and raise a further irritant to the European allies) by undercutting European privacy protections. It is true, of course, as it is probably true of all elements of HVIRA, that the disclosure requirement's object of obtaining compensation for Holocaust victims is a goal espoused by the National Government as well. But "[t]he fact of a common end hardly neutralizes conflicting means," [*Crosby, v. National Foreign Trade Council*, 530 U.S. 363, 379 (2000)], and here HVIRA is an obstacle to the success of the National Government's chosen "calibration of force" in dealing with the Europeans using a voluntary approach, 530 U.S. at 380. . . .

C. The basic fact is that California seeks to use an iron fist where the President has consistently chosen kid gloves. We have heard powerful arguments that the iron fist would work better, and it may be that if the matter of compensation were considered in isolation from all other issues involving the European Allies, the iron fist would be the preferable policy. But our thoughts on the efficacy of the one approach versus the other are beside the point, since our business is not to judge the wisdom of the National Government's policy; dissatisfaction should be addressed to the President or, perhaps, Congress. The question relevant to preemption in this case is conflict, and the evidence here is "more than sufficient to demonstrate that the state Act stands in the way of [the President's] diplomatic objectives." *Crosby*, 530 U.S. at 386.

GINSBURG, JUSTICE, dissenting. . . . Despite the absence of express preemption, the Court holds that the HVIRA interferes with foreign policy objectives implicit in the executive agreements. I would not venture down that path.

The Court's analysis draws substantially on *Zschernig v. Miller, supra.* . . . We have not relied on *Zschernig* since it was decided, and I would not resurrect that decision here. The notion of "dormant foreign affairs preemption" with which *Zschernig* is associated resonates most audibly when a state action "reflect[s] a state policy critical of foreign governments and involve[s] 'sitting in judgment' on them." L. Henkin, *Foreign Affairs and the United States Constitution* 164 (2d ed. 1996). The HVIRA entails no such state action or policy. It takes no position on any contemporary foreign government and requires no assessment of any existing foreign regime. It is directed solely at private insurers doing business in California, and it requires them solely to disclose information in their or their affiliates' possession or control. I would not extend *Zschernig* into this dissimilar domain.

Neither would I stretch [prior Supreme Court decisions] to support implied preemption by executive agreement. In each of those cases, the Court gave effect to the express terms of an executive agreement. In [*Dames & Moore v. Regan*, 453 U.S. 654 (1981)], for example, the Court addressed an agreement explicitly extinguishing certain suits in domestic courts. 453 U.S. at 665. Here, however, none of the executive agreements extinguish any underlying claim for relief. The United States has agreed to file precatory statements advising courts that dismissing Holocaust-era claims accords with American foreign policy, but the German Foundation Agreement confirms that such statements have no legally binding effect. It remains uncertain, therefore, whether even litigation on Holocaust-era insurance claims must be abated in deference to the German Foundation Agreement or the parallel agreements with Austria and France. Indeed, ambiguity on this point appears to have been the studied aim of the American negotiating team. If it is uncertain whether insurance litigation may continue given the executive agreements on which the Court relies, it should be abundantly clear that those agreements leave disclosure laws like the HVIRA untouched. . . .

Sustaining the HVIRA would not compromise the President's ability to speak with one voice for the Nation. To the contrary, by declining to invalidate the HVIRA in this case, we would reserve foreign affairs preemption for circumstances where the President, acting under statutory or constitutional authority, has spoken clearly to the issue at hand. "[T]he Framers did not make the judiciary the overseer of our government." *Dames & Moore*, 453

U.S. at 660. And judges should not be the expositors of the Nation's foreign policy, which is the role they play by acting when the President himself has not taken a clear stand. As I see it, courts step out of their proper role when they rely on no legislative or even executive text, but only on inference and implication, to preempt state laws on foreign affairs grounds. In sum, assuming, *arguendo*, that an executive agreement or similarly formal foreign policy statement targeting disclosure could override the HVIRA, there is no such declaration here. Accordingly, I would leave California's enactment in place, and affirm the judgment of the Court of Appeals.

Notes on Garamendi

1. Zschernig — *federal foreign affairs powers as a limit on state legislative jurisdiction.* As discussed in *Garamendi, Zschernig* was an unusual case, involving an Oregon state probate statute which prohibited foreign nationals from inheriting their share of Oregon estates if the country of their nationality either: (a) denied U.S. citizens reciprocal rights to receive inheritances on the same terms as locals; (b) denied U.S. citizens the right to receive inherited sums in the United States; or (c) would confiscate the foreign nationals' inheritances.

(a) Majority opinion in Zschernig. The Court held the statute unconstitutional, on the grounds that it infringed upon federal foreign affairs powers. 389 U.S. 429 (1968). Justice Douglas thought that the law would "affect[] international relations in a persistent and subtle way," while Justice Stewart concluded that each of the three conditions in the statute would "launch the State upon a prohibited voyage into a domain of exclusively federal competence." (The Court in *Garamendi* refers to this as "field" preemption.)

(b) Justice Harlan's concurrence in Zschernig. Justice Harlan concurred in the decision, but based his conclusion entirely on a treaty between the United States and Germany (so-called East Germany being the state whose national was adversely affected in the case). His concurrence went on, however, to reject the reasoning of Justices Douglas and Stewart. Justice Harlan observed that "the States may legislate in areas of their traditional competence even though their statutes may have an incidental effect on foreign relations." 389 U.S. at 459. He pointed out as well that there was no evidence — for example, by way of diplomatic protests — that the state statutes had in fact given offense to foreign governments, and that a U.S. Government amicus brief expressly said that the United States did "not . . . contend that the application of the Oregon escheat statute in the circumstances of this case unduly interferes with the United States' conduct of foreign relations." 389 U.S. at 460. Justice Harlan also observed that state courts routinely inquire into the content of foreign law — for example, when they consider the enforceability of foreign judgments or apply foreign law. He reasoned that, if the Oregon statute was unconstitutional, these state court actions would be as well. (The Court in *Garamendi* refers to this as "conflict" preemption.)

(c) Correctness of Zschernig *majority's rationale.* Which of the views in *Zschernig* is more persuasive? Should the Constitution preempt state legislation that affects the general "field" or "domain" of foreign relations? Doesn't almost any state legislation dealing with international matters have such effects?

Why is it unconstitutional for a state to require reciprocal treatment of its citizens? Note that many states will not enforce foreign judgments against U.S. nationals unless the foreign state's courts will enforce U.S. judgments against foreign nationals. *See infra* pp. 1094-1095. Do not numerous issues in international litigation (such as *forum non conveniens*, choice of law, and extraterritorial discovery) have some nontrivial effect on U.S. foreign relations? Federal law does not forbid or preempt such effects, does it?

(d) Narrower rationale for Zschernig. The Oregon statute would not permit a foreign national to inherit property if his or her home state would confiscate the property. Should a U.S. state be permitted to make legal rights depend on what a foreign government does on foreign territory with respect to its nationals after they inherit U.S. property? Is not the foreign state's conduct, on its own territory, toward its own citizens, a matter that U.S. states cannot properly regulate — both under international law and federal constitutional law? As discussed below, the act of state doctrine provides that federal common law forbids a U.S. court from considering the validity of a foreign state's taking of property within its own territory. *See infra* pp. 801-817. Is *Zschernig* merely an application of this rule?

(e) Zschernig after Garamendi. How do the opinions in *Garamendi* treat *Zschernig*? Does the Court in *Garamendi* indicate whether it accepts *Zschernig*'s theory of "field" preemption? If the Court accepted this theory, would it devote a long opinion to the "conflict" theory of preemption? How does the dissent deal with *Zschernig*? Whose treatment of the *Zschernig* opinion do you find more plausible?

2. Foreign Commerce and Due Process Clause limits on state legislative jurisdiction. Preemption based on the federal foreign affairs power — as occurred in *Zschernig* — is not the only potential constitutional limitation on state legislative jurisdiction. The Foreign Commerce Clause also can limit that jurisdiction. *Japan Line, Ltd. v. County of Los Angeles*, 441 U.S. 434 (1979); *Container Corp. v. Franchise Tax Board*, 463 U.S. 159 (1983); *Kraft General Foods, Inc. v. Iowa Dep't of Revenue and Finance*, 505 U.S. 71, 79 (1992).

Suppose that a U.S. state enacted a statute granting any of its residents the right to sue in state courts, under a state statute forbidding the unauthorized copying of intellectual property belonging to such residents; suppose further that the statute set forth the substantive elements of the offense of copying and was made expressly applicable to conduct anywhere in the world — so long as it injured a resident of the state. Alternatively, suppose a U.S. state statute granted a cause of action under state law for any state resident that was defrauded, in connection with a securities transaction, anywhere in the world. Or suppose a state statute permits any state resident or domiciliary to bring actions for defamatory statements, under local state law, made anywhere in the world.

Would any of these statutes be constitutional? What provision of the Constitution would they violate? Recall the due process limitations, articulated in *Allstate*, on a state court's application of state law to conduct lacking significant contacts with the forum. For a decision parsing the differences between foreign affairs preemption and foreign commerce preemption, *see NFTC v. Giannoulais*, 523 F. Supp. 2d 731 (N.D. Ill. 2007).

3. Japan Lines — *foreign commerce and due process limits on state taxing powers.* Does the fact that a state law is applied to foreign commerce — instead of interstate commerce — result in any stricter constitutional scrutiny? As noted above, the Court has held that the foreign commerce clause imposes stricter scrutiny on state taxes on international commerce than on interstate commerce. *See supra* p. 631; *Container Corp. v. Franchise Tax Board*, 463 U.S. 159 (1983) ("Given that [appellant's business] is international . . . we must subject this case to the additional scrutiny required by the Foreign Commerce Clause").

The Court explained the rationale for this heightened scrutiny in *Japan Lines, Ltd. v. County of Los Angeles*, 441 U.S. 434 (1979). It first observed that in domestic tax matters, it had the power to enforce due process limits on state taxation of interstate activities to ensure that each taxing state's tax was fairly apportioned to the value of the activity or property connected to that jurisdiction. But "neither this Court nor this Nation can ensure full apportionment when one of the taxing entities is a foreign sovereign. If an instrumentality of commerce is domiciled abroad, the country of domicile may have the right, consistently with the custom of nations, to impose a tax on its full value." 441 U.S. at 447. *Japan Line* also observed that state taxes on international commerce or its instrumentalities "may impair federal uniformity in an area where federal uniformity is essential. Foreign commerce is pre-eminently a matter of national concern. . . . [T]he taxation of foreign commerce may necessitate a uniform national rule." State taxes on foreign commerce can give rise to "international disputes over reconciling apportionment formulae" and may provoke retaliation which "of necessity would be directed at American transportation equipment in general, not just that of the taxing State, so that the Nation as a whole would suffer." 441 U.S. at 450.

Do these rationales have application outside the tax context? Should state legislation applicable to foreign (*i.e.*, non-U.S.) commerce be subjected to stricter scrutiny under the Due Process Clause than *Allstate* contemplates for domestic matters?

4. ***The Tonnage Clause—an independent limit?*** As noted above, in *Polar Tankers*, the Supreme Court invalidated a local tax on the value of property of ships anchoring in a city's harbor. The Court resolved the case on the relatively narrow ground that the city's tax discriminated against a particular instrumentality of commerce (large ships) and was based on the value of the cargo that the ship took on (rather than the services provided by the city while the ship was in port).

The implications of *Polar Tankers* for the Tonnage Clause as a distinct limit on state legislative jurisdiction in this field remain unclear. The Court resolved the case solely on grounds of the Tonnage Clause and, consequently, declined to consider the impact of the Foreign Commerce Clause. Moreover, the case involved a domestic-flagged, not foreign-flagged vessel. Finally, part of the decision could not garner a majority opinion, and some Justices were prepared to hold that, under the Tonnage Clause, a State may never impose a property tax on a vessel belonging to a citizen of another State, even if that vessel is taxed in the same manner as other personal property in the taxing state. *See Polar Tankers*, 129 S. Ct. at 2287 (Roberts, C.J., concurring in part and concurring in the judgment).

There have been virtually no reported decisions since *Polar Tankers*, so the scope of the Tonnage Clause remains a fertile area for future litigation.

5. ***Customary international law limits on state legislative jurisdiction.*** Recall the customary international law limits contained in the *Restatement (Third) Foreign Relations Law* §402 and §403. As discussed above, customary international law arguably has the status of federal law and is directly applicable in state courts, notwithstanding inconsistent state law. *See supra* pp. 13-18. Why shouldn't the jurisdictional limits imposed by customary international law be enforceable in the hypotheticals in Note 2 above?

6. ***Foreign affairs "field" preemption in* Garamendi.** On what basis did the Court in *Garamendi* invalidate the HVIRA? Did it rely on field preemption under the Foreign Affairs Clause? Or conflict preemption under the Supremacy Clause?

If the Court in *Garamendi* relied on conflict preemption, what exactly was the federal law, or action, that created the conflict? Did the German Foundation Agreement prohibit litigation over Holocaust-related claims? Did the Agreement prohibit the issuance of subpoenas, seeking information? Did the Agreement purport to preempt state law in any respect?

7. ***Supremacy Clause "conflict" preemption in* Garamendi.** Did the *Garamendi* Court correctly conclude that the German Foundation Agreement preempted the HVIRA? How exactly, according to the majority, did the HVIRA undermine the German Foundation Agreement? Isn't the dissent correct that the relevant state and federal "laws" dealt with

640   *Chapter 7.   Legislative Jurisdiction*

two distinct matters—the German Foundation Agreement covered reparations and the HVIRA dealt with disclosure? Or does this downplay the intrusive effect of the HVIRA on the Agreement's real purposes?

Could the HVIRA be understood as an effort by the State of California to enact consumer protection for its citizens who may not wish to do business with insurance companies subject to exposure from Holocaust-era claims? Although the *Garamendi* Court purports not to apply "field" preemption, does it in fact do so, elevating foreign affairs concerns at the expense of basic federalism principles?

Did the Foundation Agreement in fact prohibit any litigation at all? Was it even clear that the Executive Branch wanted to preclude litigation over Holocaust-era claims? Or did it simply want to preserve the maximum flexibility, through the filing of a statement of interest, discussed *supra* at p. 55, to decide whether a particular piece of litigation interfered with the Executive Branch? If the latter, is Justice Ginsburg correct to conclude, then, that the HVIRA does not interfere with this "flexible" scheme? Or does it force the Executive Branch's hand in ways that may compromise its diplomatic discretion?

To test the scope of *Garamendi*, consider a related problem. It has been the consistent policy of the U.S. Government not to refer to the atrocities committed against Armenians during World War I as "genocide." That policy, however, is not reflected in a federal statute, a treaty or (unlike *Garamendi*) an Executive agreement. Suppose then that a state finds that insurance companies wrongly denied benefits to Armenian victims of that period and, accordingly, extends its statute of limitations to allow them to sue the insurers. Preemption under *Garamendi*? *See Movsesian v. Victoria Versicherung AG*, 2010 WL 5028828 (9th Cir. Dec. 10, 2010).

Alternatively, suppose that a state creates a cause of action for individuals whose art was allegedly looted by the Nazis during World War II. It authorizes actions only against museums and galleries located within the state that possess the allegedly looted art. As far as federal policy, immediately after World War II, the U.S. military set up a program for restitution but wound down that program by the late 1940s. It presently does not have an official mechanism for resolving such claims (unlike *Garamendi*) but continues to pay attention to the issue through incremental legislative and diplomatic activity. Preemption under *Garamendi*? *Von Saher v. Norton Simon Museum of Art at Pasadena*, 592 F.3d 954 (9th Cir. 2010). Should it matter that this case, unlike *Garamendi* or the preceding one, involves the disposition of rights to property located in the state border? Or is the implication of the "field preemption" analysis that the state simply lacks the regulatory authority?

Finally, suppose that in an action to resolve ownership of a piece of art, an heir of an alleged victim of Nazi looting claims ownership of the art. Unlike *Garamendi*, the state has not enacted any special law creating a cause of action or tolling the statute of limitations. Instead, under the generally applicable state statute of limitations, the heir's claim is untimely. The heir, however, argues that the Executive Branch's efforts to assist victims of Nazi looting and various nonbinding declarations establish a federal policy which preempts the unfavorable state statute of limitations. What is the result under *Garamendi*? *See Museum of Fine Arts v. Seger-Thomschitz*, 623 F.3d 1 (1st Cir. 2010); *Dunbar v. Seger-Thomschitz*, 615 F.3d 574 (5th Cir. 2010).

8. *Limiting* Garamendi? In a recent decision discussed elsewhere, *supra* at p. 16 and *infra* at p. 1094, the Supreme Court arguably trimmed back on *Garamendi*'s broad view of foreign affairs preemption. *Medellin v. Texas*, 552 U.S. 491 (2008), concerned the United States' obligations under the Vienna Convention on Consular Relations, specifically its obligation to provide incarcerated nationals of other signatory states access to their consular officials. A group of Mexican nationals on death row in various states of the United States filed an action before the International Court of Justice, arguing that they had been denied their rights under the Vienna Convention. The International Court of Justice found (in a decision known as *Avena*) that 51 of these nationals were entitled to review and reconsideration of their sentence. The problem was, under the applicable state laws, these claims were "defaulted" (or, in slightly less technical jargon, untimely).

Interestingly, the U.S. Government did not summarily reject the ICJ's ruling. While rejecting the proposition that the ICJ's judgment was directly enforceable in the United States, the President issued a memorandum to the Attorney General declaring that "pursuant to the authority vested in me as President by the Constitution and the laws of the United States of America, the United States will discharge its international obligations under the decision of the International Court of Justice in [*Avena*], by having State courts give effect to the decision in accordance with general principles of comity in cases filed by the 51 Mexican nationals addressed in that decision." *Medellin*, 552 U.S. at 503. In essence, the President was asserting that, as part of his foreign affairs power, he could displace state procedural rules that stood in the way of the United States' fulfillment of an obligation under the treaties and protocols to which it was then a party (the United States has subsequently withdrawn from some of the protocols that enabled the ICJ's judgment).

Compared to *Garamendi*, *Medellin* presented a clearer case of conflict between federal policy and state law. Yet when the matter reached the Supreme Court, the Court rejected the Government's view that the President's foreign affairs power enabled him to displace state law in this manner. Dismissing the Government's reliance on *Garamendi*, the Court simply characterized that case as one involving American's claims against foreign governments or foreign citizens. 552 U.S. at 530.

This has caused some scholars to question the continued breadth (and vitality) of *Garamendi*. *See, e.g.*, Weisburd, Medellin, *the President's Foreign Affairs Power and Domestic Law*, 28 Penn. St. Int'l L. Rev. 595 (2010). Courts, while acknowledging the tension, have continued to give *Garamendi* a broad sweep. *See, e.g., Museum of Fine Arts v. Seger-Thomschitz*, 623 F.3d 1, 12 n.12 (1st Cir. 2010); *In re Assicurazioni Generali, S.P.A.*, 592 F.3d 113 (2d Cir. 2010).

9. *Executive Agreements as federal law.* Note that the Foundation Agreement at issue in *Garamendi* was an Executive agreement. Why should an Executive agreement — not approved by Congress, much less two-thirds of the Senate — be entitled to preempt state law? Note that the Court has previously upheld sole Executive agreements (at least in some fields) as sources of federal law. *United States v. Pink*, 315 U.S. 203, 223 (1942); *supra* at p. 17. What is the constitutional basis for this conclusion?

The *Medellin* decision, discussed in the previous note, also casts limits on *Garamendi*'s broad view about the role of Executive agreements. *See* Weisburd, Medellin, *the President's Foreign Affairs Power and Domestic Law*, 28 Penn. St. Int'l L. Rev. 595 (2010). In *Medellin*, the Government relied partly on the preemptive effect historically given to Executive agreements as an analogy supporting the preemptive effect of the President's action in response to the ICJ's judgment. The Court rejected the Government's broad interpretation of these precedents and placed great weight on the fact that those prior precedents involved the President's authority to resolve the claims of American citizens against foreign countries or, possibly, their nationals — a longstanding tradition enjoying congressional support. 552 U.S. at 531-532. By contrast, according to the *Medellin* Court, the action taken by the Executive branch in response to the ICJ's judgment enjoyed neither a longstanding tradition nor congressional complicity. *Id.* Is this a fair reading of the prior precedents? A sensible view of the foreign affairs power? Or a sensible reaction to an error that equated treaties, formally involving the actions of two branches, with Executive agreements, formally involving the actions of only one?

10. *Type of state action that can interfere with federal foreign affairs.* To what extent does the result in *Garamendi* depend on the existence of a new state statute — as opposed to a preexisting state law cause of action? Is there any reason to suppose that an existing cause of action, as opposed to a statute, involves less of an intrusion on the federal foreign affairs power? *Compare Doe v. Exxon Mobil Corp.*, 2006 WL 516744, at *3 (D.D.C. 2006) (no preemption) *with Mujica v. Occidental Petroleum Corp.*, 381 F. Supp. 2d 1164, 1185-1188 (C.D. Cal. 2005) (finding preemption). What if the state merely amended its statute of limitations for a certain cause of action, and the effect of that amendment was to allow certain suits against foreign entities to proceed? *Compare Movsesian v. Victoria Versicherung AG*, 2010 WL 5028828 (9th Cir. Dec. 10, 2010) (finding no preemption of special state statute that extends statute of limitations) *with Dunbar v. Seger-Thomschitz*, 615 F.3d 574 (5th Cir. 2010) (finding no preemption of generally applicable state prescriptive period).

11. *Constitutional limits on state legislative jurisdiction after* **Garamendi.** What constitutional limits apply to state legislative jurisdiction after *Garamendi?* Suppose that claims were asserted under state antitrust laws based upon conduct occurring entirely outside of the United States. Would these claims be preempted by the federal foreign affairs/commerce power (under a theory of "field" preemption)? Suppose that the federal Government was pursuing investigations under the federal antitrust laws into the same conduct. Would the state law claims be preempted by the federal investigation on a theory of "conflict" preemption? What if the federal investigation sought the cooperation of one or more of the defendants in the state litigation?

Relatively few state court decisions have considered foreign affairs preemption claims in a commercial context. *See, e.g., Sun Life Assur. Co. of Canada v. Manna*, 879 N.E.2d 320 (Ill. 2007). One such case was *United Nuclear Corporation v. General Atomic Co.*, 629 P.2d 231 (N.M. 1980), a New Mexico litigation which involved allegations of a worldwide price-fixing cartel, where substantial conduct occurred within New Mexico, but much more occurred elsewhere (and particularly in Canada and other foreign states). The New Mexico Supreme Court considered constitutional challenges (relying on *Zschernig*) to the application of New Mexico law to the defendants' worldwide conduct. The Court rejected the challenges, reasoning that "no pejorative criticism has been directed at Canada or any other foreign government" and "no minute inquiry has been made into the actual administration of foreign law by a foreign government." The court concluded:

> This case involves nothing more than an inquiry into what an American corporation has done in America, a situation which finds no appropriate analogy in *Zschernig* or its exceedingly limited progeny. The states of this country have little interest in how a foreign government treats its own citizens, but they have every conceivable interest in anti-competitive conduct by American corporations occurring within their own borders. Likewise, foreign governments have a legitimate interest in the rights they choose to afford their own citizens: but they have no legitimate interest in whether a state court in this country will lend its judicial processes to the enforcement of contracts entered into in the United States by corporations based in this country for the supply of a resource to be mined and milled in the United States. Our courts have done no more than seek to enforce state laws which are consistent with federal laws, and with actions of the U.S. Congress and U.S. Justice Department concerning [the defendant's] cartel activities. 629 P.2d at 267.

Is it conceivable that the foreign commerce clause might ever forbid a state from applying its law to conduct within its territory? Note that *Japan Line* held that the foreign commerce and due process clauses forbid California localities from applying ad valorem taxes on property located within California (containers used by international shipping companies, which were temporarily present in California). *See supra* pp. 638-639.

Even if New Mexico could apply its law to the allegedly unlawful conduct occurring within its territory, does that mean that it should be constitutionally able to apply its law to the entire course of worldwide conduct engaged in by the various defendants? Suppose different U.S. states conducted parallel proceedings, each applying its own state antitrust law to the same international course of conduct. Is there anything wrong with that? Does anything in the Constitution forbid it? Consider the rationales of *Zschernig* and *Japan Line.* Do these decisions provide support for invalidating application of New Mexico's law to international commerce?

What if New Mexico has sought to apply its antitrust laws to conduct occurring entirely outside the United States, but having effects within the United States (both in New Mexico and elsewhere)? Would anything in the Constitution forbid this?

12. *Federal common law restrictions on state legislative jurisdiction.* In addition to the foreign affairs power the Foreign Commerce Clause, and the Tonnage Clause, federal common law also can bar the exercise of state legislative jurisdiction that touches upon matters of foreign affairs. The Supreme Court's decision in *Sabbatino*, announcing the act of state doctrine and cited in *Garamendi*, supplies one example. But the act of state doctrine is not the only possible exercise of that federal common law making power. *See also Saleh v. Titan Corp.*, 580 F.3d 1 (D.C. Cir. 2009) (relying partly on government contractor defense to preempt state claims). Recall the district court's opinion in *Sequihua v. Texaco Oil, Inc.*, 847 F. Supp. 61 (S.D. Tex. 1994), holding that federal common law governed (and barred) a claim alleging massive environmental abuse in Ecuador by a U.S. company. *See supra* pp. 63-65. Compare the court's analysis in *Sequihua* with that in *United Nuclear*. Are the decisions consistent?

How does *Sosa*'s discussion of the residual common law power of federal courts affect this issue? Do horizontal separation of powers concerns counsel against an expansive view of the federal common law preemption? Or does the need for uniformity require a robust federal common law making power (and the concomitant restriction on state power) in matters touching upon foreign affairs to the extent that the other branches have not spoken? *See supra* pp. 49-50.

13. *Regulatory restrictions on state legislative jurisdiction.* In addition to the constitutional principles and federal common law, federal regulations can preempt state exercises of legislative jurisdiction. *See City of New York v. Permanent Mission of India to the United Nations*, 2010 WL 3221889 (2d Cir. Aug. 17, 2010). In the field of foreign affairs, such preemption typically arises in the context of a conflict between State Department regulations and local law. These cases proceed on the premise that "[f]ederal regulations have no less preemptive effect than federal statutes." *Fidelity Fed. Sav. & Loan Ass'n v. de la Cuesta*, 458 U.S. 141, 153 (1982). Why should this be so? Does the Supremacy Clause put regulations on an equal footing with statutes and treaties? Have they undergone the same vetting by two branches of government? Is it a sufficient answer to these objections to say that the regulations must be a valid interpretation of a statute previously enacted by Congress?

14. *Legislative jurisdiction problem.* In the 2010 election, over 70 percent of Oklahoma voters approved the following to the Oklahoma Constitution (more colorfully known as the "Save Our State" Amendment):

> The Courts of this State when exercising their judicial authority, shall uphold and adhere to the law as provided in the United States Constitution, the Oklahoma Constitution, the United States Code, federal regulations promulgated pursuant thereto, established common law, Oklahoma Statutes and rules promulgated pursuant thereto, and if necessary the law of

another state of the United States provided the law of the other state does not include Sharia Law, in making judicial decisions. The courts shall not look to the legal precepts of other nations or cultures. Specifically, the courts shall not consider international law or Sharia Law. The provisions of this subsection shall apply to all cases before the respective courts including, but not limited to, cases of first impression.

Does the "Save Our State" Amendment run afoul of any of the constitutional limits on state legislative jurisdiction discussed above? *See Awad v. Ziriax,* 2010 WL 4814077 (W.D. Okla. 2010) (granting preliminary injunction). Is it wise policy? What are its implications for choice-of-law clauses? Enforcement of foreign judgments?

8

Choice of Law in International Litigation[1]

International litigation inevitably presents choice-of-law issues, requiring courts to decide what law to apply in cases where two or more states could properly exercise legislative jurisdiction. In the United States, these questions have traditionally been considered under two largely distinct bodies of authority. First, U.S. courts have fashioned canons of construction for determining whether federal legislation applies to international activities, and particularly for determining whether U.S. legislation has extraterritorial reach. Second, U.S. courts have developed choice-of-law rules for deciding whether state law (both statutory and common law) applies to international activities. This chapter examines both subjects.

A. Application of Federal Statutes in International Cases

1. Determining the Territorial Reach of Federal Legislation in International Cases: The Problem of Silent or Ambiguous Statutes[2]

This section examines the applicability of federal statutes in international cases, focusing particularly on the circumstances in which congressional legislation will be applied

---

1. Leading contemporary works dealing with choice of law in the United States include, among others, L. Brilmayer & J. Goldsmith, *Conflict of Laws: Cases and Materials* (5th ed. 2002); B. Currie, *Selected Essays on the Conflict of Laws* (1963); A. Ehrenzweig, *A Treatise on the Conflict of Laws* (1962); A. Lowenfeld, *Conflict of Laws: Federal, State, and International Perspectives* (2d ed. 2002); J. Martin, *Conflict of Laws: Cases and Materials* (2d ed. 1984); L. McDougal et al., *American Conflicts Law* (5th ed. 2001); E. Scoles et al., *Conflict of Laws* (4th ed. 2004); S. Symeonides, *The American Choice-of-Law Revolution in the Courts: Today and Tomorrow*, 298 Recueil des Cours 1 (2003); S. Symeonides et al., *Conflict of Laws: American, Comparative, International* (2d ed. 2003); R. Weintraub, *Commentary on the Conflict of Laws* (6th ed. 2010). For international commentary, *see* L. Collins et al., *Dicey, Morris and Collins on the Conflict of Laws* (14th ed. 2010); E. Gottschalk, R. Michaels, G. Reuhl & J. von Hein, *Conflict of Laws in A Globalized World* (2007); J. Fawcett et al., *Cheshire, North and Fawcett: Private International Law* (2008); F. Juenger, P. Borchers & J. Zekoll (eds.), *International Conflict of Laws for the Third Millennium: Essays in Honor of Friedrich K. Juenger* (2001).

2. Commentary on extraterritoriality includes, for example, Born, *A Reappraisal of the Extraterritorial Reach of U.S. Law*, 24 Law & Pol'y Int'l Bus. 1 (1992); Brilmayer & Norchi, *Federal Extraterritoriality and Fifth Amendment Due Process*, 105 Harv. L. Rev. 1217 (1992); Buxbaum, *Territory, Territoriality and the Resolution of Jurisdictional Conflict*, 57 Am. J. Comp. L. 631 (2009); Dodge, *Understanding the Presumption Against Extraterritoriality*, 16 Berkeley J. Int'l L. 85 (1998); Gerber, *Beyond Balancing: International Law Restraints on the Reach of National Laws*, 10 Yale J. Int'l L. 185 (1984); Griffin, *Extraterritoriality in U.S. and EU Antitrust Enforcement*, 67 Antitrust L.J. 159 (1999); Holbrook, *Extraterritoriality in U.S. Patent Law*, 40 Wm. & Mary L. Rev. 2119 (2008); Kramer, *Vestiges of* Beale: *Extraterritorial Application of American Law*, 1991 Sup. Ct. Rev. 179; Reese, *Legislative Jurisdiction*, 78 Colum. L. Rev.

extraterritorially. As discussed above, it is well-settled that if Congress enacts legislation in violation of international law, U.S. courts must disregard international law and apply the domestic statute.[3] Thus, the extraterritorial reach of federal statutes is ultimately an issue of U.S. law—not foreign or international law. "We are concerned only with whether Congress chose to attach liability to the conduct outside the United States. . . . [A]s a court of the United States, we cannot look beyond our own law."[4]

In most cases, however, Congress's statutes are couched in general terms and provide no meaningful geographic limits. Congress typically legislates by using words of "universal" application.[5] For example, the Sherman Act, one of the principal antitrust statutes in the United States, prohibits "[e]very contract, combination . . . or conspiracy in restraint of trade or commerce . . . with foreign nations." The "literal catholicity"[6] of such language would extend U.S. law to almost all conduct on the globe.[7] As Justice Jackson said of the Jones Act in *Lauritzen v. Larsen*:

> Unless some [limit] is implied, Congress has extended our law and opened our courts to all alien seafaring men injured anywhere in the world in service of watercraft of every foreign nation—a hand on a Chinese junk, never outside Chinese waters, would not be beyond its literal wording.[8]

Rather than adopting this and other implausible results that would follow from a literal reading of most statutes, federal courts have turned to rules of statutory construction to establish the reach of federal law.

2. Historical Introduction: The Territoriality Presumption[9]

The rules of construction applicable to contemporary federal legislation have their origins in the twelfth through sixteenth centuries, when Continental European commentators developed choice-of-law rules. These rules defined when local "statutes," enacted in various city-states or other jurisdictions, applied to conduct or persons having connections to multiple localities. Broadly speaking, the "statutists" divided statutes into categories, and applied different choice-of-laws rules to different categories. Some statutes were said to apply only within the territory of the jurisdiction that promulgated them

---

1587 (1978); Meyer, *Dual Illegality and Geoambiguous Law: A New Rule for Extraterritorial Application of U.S. Law*, 95 Minn. L. Rev. 110 (2010); Parrish, *The Effects Test: Extraterritoriality's Fifth Business*, 61 Vand. L. Rev. 1455 (2008).

3. *See supra* pp. 15-17; *Restatement (Third) Foreign Relations Law* §115(i) & §403, comment g (1987); *Head Money Cases*, 112 U.S. 580, 598-599 (1884); *Whitney v. Robertson*, 124 U.S. 190, 194 (1888); *CFTC v. Nahas*, 738 F.2d 487 (D.C. Cir. 1984).

4. *United States v. Alcoa*, 148 F.2d 416, 443 (2d Cir. 1945).

5. *American Banana Co. v. United Fruit Co.*, 213 U.S. 347, 357 (1909).

6. *Lauritzen v. Larsen*, 345 U.S. 571, 576-77 (1953).

7. Occasionally, Congress clearly specifies that a statute has extraterritorial effect. For example, the Antiterrorism Act of 1991, 18 U.S.C. §2333, provides a civil cause of action for acts of international terrorism, defined in part to include acts "occur[ring] primarily outside the territorial jurisdiction of the United States." 18 U.S.C. §2331. *See Boim v. Holy Land Foundation for Relief and Development*, 549 F.3d 685 (7th Cir. 2008). Conversely, the Federal Tort Claims Act withholds the federal government's waiver of sovereign immunity for claims "arising in a foreign country." 28 U.S.C. §2680(k). The FTCA provision could be treated either as an example of explicit statutory language denying a statute extraterritorial effect (the waiver of sovereign immunity) or an example of a statute expressly given extraterritorial effect (the limit on the waiver). *See Sosa v. Alvarez-Machain*, 542 U.S. 692, 700-701 (2004).

8. *Lauritzen*, 345 U.S. at 577.

9. Choice-of-law theory has a long history, which has frequently been recounted. *See* De Nova, *Historical and Comparative Introduction to Conflict of Laws*, 118 Recueil des Cours 443 (1966); Juenger, *General Course on Private International Law*, 193 Recueil des Cours 119 (1983); Lipstein, *The General Principles of Private International Law*, 135 Recueil des Cours 96 (1972); Yntema, *The Historic Bases of Private International Law*, 2 Am. J. Comp. L. 297 (1953).

(*e.g.,* "real" or "procedural" statutes); other categories were thought to apply elsewhere, typically based upon the nationality of the actor (*e.g.,* "personal" or "substantive" statutes). In order to determine whether a statute was applicable to particular multi-state events, one simply determined what category it fell within.[10]

During the sixteenth and seventeenth centuries, some European writers, particularly in the Netherlands and France, abandoned the "statutist" approach. Instead, they articulated choice-of-law (and other) rules based on principles of territorial sovereignty and international comity.[11] As discussed elsewhere, these analyses emphasized the generally exclusive jurisdiction of a state over events and persons within its territory.[12]

A leading proponent of the territoriality doctrine was Ulrich Huber,[13] whose *De Conflictu Legum* was a landmark in the development of choice-of-law theory. As described above, Huber stated three basic "maxims" of international law.[14] These maxims replaced the statutists' efforts to classify statutes with a strictly territorial approach that affirmed a state's absolute sovereignty within its territory, but no further. Huber's first maxim declared: "Every state's laws apply within the state's territory, but not beyond."[15]

Huber's territorial approach avoided the difficulties inherent in determining how to categorize particular statutes, but it left a difficulty in cases involving conduct or persons located outside the forum. If no law had extraterritorial reach, then the forum's law could not apply to foreign conduct. But the territoriality doctrine also appeared to prevent the forum court from applying foreign law — for this was thought to involve the extraterritorial application of that law.

Huber resolved this perceived dilemma by reference to international comity: "'Comity' calls on states to recognize and enforce rights created by other states, provided that such recognition does not prejudice the state or its subjects."[16] According to Huber, comity was not a precise, binding legal obligation capable of resolving specific cases, but a general principle governing the relations of sovereign states:

> the solution of the [choice-of-law] problem must be derived not exclusively from the civil law, but from convenience and the tacit consent of nations. Although the laws of one nation can have no force directly within another, yet nothing could be more inconvenient to commerce and to international usage than that transactions valid by the law of one place should be rendered of no effect elsewhere on account of a difference in the law.[17]

This general comity doctrine provided the foundation for more precise choice-of-law rules in specific contexts, which Huber developed, permitting courts to apply the laws of foreign jurisdictions.[18]

---

10. Juenger, *General Course on Private International Law,* 193 Recueil des Cours 119, 139-144 (1983). Unfortunately, most statutes could fairly be placed in any category, leading to arbitrary and unpredictable results.

11. *See* Juenger, *General Course on Private International Law,* 193 Recueil des Cours 119, 144-149 (1983); Lorenzen, *Territoriality, Public Policy and the Conflict of Laws,* 33 Yale L.J. 736 (1924); Yntema, *The Comity Doctrine,* 65 Mich. L. Rev. 9, 16-28 (1966).

12. *See supra* pp. 83-86, 231-234.

13. *See supra* pp. 83-86; Davies, *The Influence of Huber's De Conflictu Legum on English Private International Law,* 18 Brit. Y.B. Int'l L. 49 (1937); Nussbaum, *Rise and Decline of the Law-of-Nations Doctrine in the Conflict of Laws,* 42 Colum. L. Rev. 189 (1942); Yntema, *The Comity Doctrine,* 65 Mich. L. Rev. 9 (1966).

14. *See supra* pp. 83-86.

15. *See* U. Huber, *De Conflictu Legum* (in E. Lorenzen, *Selected Articles on the Conflict of Laws* 136 (1947)).

16. *See* U. Huber, *De Conflictu Legum* (in E. Lorenzen, *Selected Articles on the Conflict of Laws* 136 (1947)).

17. U. Huber, *De Conflictu Legum* (in E. Lorenzen, *Selected Articles on the Conflict of Laws* 164-165 (1947)).

18. In one commentator's words, Huber "made it clear beyond a doubt, that the recognition in each state of so-called foreign created rights was a mere concession which such state made on grounds of convenience and utility, and not as the result of a binding obligation or duty. . . . Huber conceived of comity as a political concession which might be granted or withheld arbitrarily by the sovereign." E. Lorenzen, *Selected Articles on the Conflict of Laws* 138-139 (1947).

Huber's conception of international comity had a profound influence on American law.[19] Early American choice-of-law decisions routinely cited Huber's *De Conflictu Legum,* and the Supreme Court took the unusual step in *Emory v. Grenough*[20] of reprinting Huber's maxims in translation as a note to its opinion. But it was Joseph Story—first as a commentator and later as a Supreme Court Justice—who was the most important conduit for bringing Huber's ideas into American law. In particular, Story's monumental treatise— *Commentaries on the Conflict of Laws*—embraced Huber's maxims, and particularly the territoriality doctrine and the use of comity to moderate territorial limits on jurisdiction.[21]

As discussed elsewhere, *Story's Commentaries* began from the premise that "general maxims of international jurisprudence" guaranteed the territorial sovereignty of states.[22] Story's first maxim was that "every nation possesses an exclusive sovereignty and jurisdiction within its own territory."[23] Story went on to declare that nations could properly exercise legislative jurisdiction only within their own territory: his second maxim stated that "no state or nation can, by its laws, directly affect, or bind property out of its own territory, or persons not resident therein."[24]

Finally, Story relied on the doctrine of comity to explain why states would apply foreign law and recognize foreign judgments. Citing Huber's third maxim, Story wrote that "the rules of every empire from comity admit, that the laws of every people, in force within its own limits, ought to have the same force everywhere, so far as they do not prejudice the powers or rights of other governments, or of their citizens."[25] Story, like Huber, saw comity as something less than a binding legal obligation, but more than an invitation to exercise unfettered discretion:

> The true foundation on which the administration of international law must rest is, that the rules which are to govern are those which arise from mutual interest and utility, from a sense of the inconveniences which would result from a contrary doctrine, and from a sort of moral necessity to do justice, in order that justice may be done to us in return.[26]

Relying on the comity doctrine, *Story's Commentaries* formulated a comprehensive set of rules concerning "private" international law topics, including judicial jurisdiction, choice of law, and recognition of foreign judgments.[27]

Story's territorial approach to international law had a significant influence on the application of federal legislation in international cases. As discussed elsewhere, U.S. courts have long presumed that Congress does not intend its enactments to violate international law.[28] Based in significant part on this *Charming Betsy* presumption, and Story's territorial views of international law, U.S. courts began in the early years of the

---

19. *See supra* pp. 83-86.

20. 3 U.S. 369 note a (1797).

21. *See* Lorenzen, *Story's Commentaries on the Conflict of Laws—One Hundred Years After,* 48 Harv. L. Rev. 15 (1934); Nadelmann, *Joseph Story's Contribution to American Conflicts Law: A Comment,* 5 Am. J. Legal Hist. 230 (1961).

22. Story adopted a territorial approach to issues of judicial jurisdiction, recognition of foreign judgments, and related issues. *See supra* pp. 83-86 and *infra* pp. 1082-1083.

23. J. Story, *Commentaries on the Conflict of Laws* 19 (2d ed. 1841).

24. J. Story, *Commentaries on the Conflict of Laws* 19, 21-22 (2d ed. 1841).

25. J. Story, *Commentaries on the Conflict of Laws* 30 (2d ed. 1841).

26. J. Story, *Commentaries on the Conflict of Laws* 32-35 (2d ed. 1841).

27. *See* Lorenzen, *Story's Commentaries on the Conflict of Laws—One Hundred Years After,* 48 Harv. L. Rev. 15 (1934); Nadelmann, *Joseph Story's Contribution to American Conflicts Law: A Comment,* 5 Am. J. Legal Hist. 230 (1961).

28. *See supra* pp. 18, 592-594; *Restatement (Third) Foreign Relations Law* §114 (1987); *Murray v. Schooner Charming Betsy,* 6 U.S. 64, 118 (1804).

Republic to apply a related presumption that Congress did not intend its legislation to apply extraterritorially.[29] As it was later formulated, this "territoriality presumption" provided that "legislation of Congress, unless a contrary intent appears, is meant to apply only within the territorial jurisdiction of the United States."[30]

An early application of the territoriality presumption was *The Apollon,* an 1824 decision discussed above.[31] The case required an interpretation of federal customs statutes to determine whether they extended to foreign vessels outside U.S. waters. Justice Story wrote that "[t]he laws of no nation can justly extend beyond its own territory, except so far as regards its own citizens."[32] He also observed that extraterritorial assertion of U.S. jurisdiction would be "at variance with the independence and sovereignty of foreign nations."[33] Relying on this view of the "law of nations," the Court invoked the following presumption: "however general and comprehensive the phrases used in our municipal laws may be, *they must always be restricted in construction, to places and persons, upon whom the legislature have authority and jurisdiction.*"[34]

The territoriality presumption was invoked by U.S. courts throughout the nineteenth and into the twentieth century.[35] The presumption was reaffirmed in uncompromising terms in the Supreme Court's 1909 decision in *American Banana Company v. United Fruit Company,*[36] excerpted below, which refused to apply the Sherman Act to a U.S. company's actions in Costa Rica. Citing both international law and conflict of laws authorities, Justice Holmes stated "[t]he general and almost universal rule . . . *that the character of an act as lawful or unlawful must be determined wholly by the law of the country where the act is done.*"[37] In the following two decades, the Supreme Court and other U.S. courts repeatedly applied the territoriality presumption.[38]

Despite their historic importance, the territoriality presumption and its rationale eroded over the twentieth century.[39] In place of the territoriality doctrine, U.S. courts adopted an assortment of alternative approaches to determining the reach of federal legislation. A leading example is *Lauritzen v. Larsen,*[40] which is excerpted below. There, the Court considered whether the Jones Act applied to a personal injury claim by a Danish seaman, against a Danish shipowner, for injuries sustained on the defendant's ship while

29. *Rose v. Himely,* 8 U.S. 241 (1807); *United States v. Palmer,* 16 U.S. 610 (1818); *The Apollon,* 22 U.S. 362 (1824).

30. *Foley Bros., Inc. v. Filardo,* 336 U.S. 281, 285 (1949). *See McCulloch v. Sociedad Nacional de Marineros de Honduras,* 372 U.S. 10, 21-22 (1963).

31. 22 U.S. 362 (1824); *supra* pp. 592-594. In 1807, Chief Justice Marshall acknowledged the territoriality presumption in *Rose v. Himely,* where he declared that "[i]t is conceded that the legislation of every country is territorial." 8 U.S. 241, 279 (1807).

32. 22 U.S. at 370.

33. 22 U.S. at 370.

34. 22 U.S. at 370 (emphasis added).

35. *E.g., Rose v. Himely,* 8 U.S. 241, 279 (1807); *United States v. Palmer,* 16 U.S. 610, 631 (1818); *The Apollon,* 22 U.S. 362, 370-371 (1824); *American Banana Co. v. United Fruit Co.,* 213 U.S. 347 (1909); *United States v. Bowman,* 260 U.S. 94 (1922); *New York Central R. Co. v. Chisholm,* 268 U.S. 29 (1925); H. Black, *Handbook on the Construction and Interpretation of the Laws* 90-91 (1896); G. Endlich, *A Commentary on the Interpretation of Statutes* 239-243 (1888).

36. 213 U.S. 347 (1909).

37. 213 U.S. at 356 (emphasis added). The Court supported this formulation with citations to *Slater v. Mexican National R.R. Co.,* 194 U.S. 120, 126 (1904), and *Milliken v. Pratt,* 125 Mass. 374 (1878).

38. *MacLeod v. United States,* 229 U.S. 416, 434 (1913); *Sandberg v. McDonald,* 248 U.S. 185, 195 (1918) ("Legislation is presumptively territorial and confined to limits over which the lawmaking power has jurisdiction."); *United States v. Bowman,* 260 U.S. 94, 98 (1922); *New York Central R. Co. v. Chisholm,* 268 U.S. 29 (1925) (no extraterritorial application of statute that "contains no words which definitely disclose an intention to give it extraterritorial effect, nor do the circumstances require an inference of such purpose").

39. *E.g., Lauritzen v. Larsen,* 345 U.S. 571 (1953); *Romero v. International Terminal Operating Co.,* 358 U.S. 354 (1959); *Benz v. Compania Naviera Hidalgo SA,* 353 U.S. 138 (1957); *McCulloch v. Sociedad Nacional de Marineros,* 372 U.S. 10 (1963); *United States v. Bowman,* 260 U.S. 94 (1922); *Ford v. United States,* 273 U.S. 593 (1927).

40. 345 U.S. 571 (1953).

it was moored in Havana, Cuba.[41] Justice Jackson noted the "literal catholicity of [the Jones Act's] terminology,"[42] and commented that the Act "makes no explicit require-ment that either the seaman, the employment or the injury have the slightest connection with the United States."[43] The Court nevertheless refused to read the Jones Act as afford-ing the plaintiff a cause of action — but in doing so, it rejected the territoriality presumption.

In determining whether the Jones Act applied to particular conduct, *Lauritzen* looked to "prevalent doctrines of international law,"[44] just as *The Apollon* and *American Banana* had. Instead of the historic territoriality doctrine,[45] however, the *Lauritzen* Court under-stood contemporary international law as requiring consideration of a variety of "connect-ing factors."[46] These factors included the place of the wrongful act, the law of the vessel, the plaintiff's nationality or domicile, the defendant's nationality, the place of the parties' contract, and the accessibility of foreign forums.[47] Applying these factors, *Lauritzen* held that the plaintiff's injury was more closely connected to Denmark than to the United States and that the Jones Act therefore did not apply.

Similarly, in 1959, in *Romero v. International Terminal Operating Co.*[48] the Court held that neither the Jones Act nor general maritime law provided a remedy for a foreign seaman, injured on a foreign vessel owned by a foreign shipowner, even though the plaintiff's injury occurred in U.S. territorial waters.[49] After rejecting a "mechanical" *lex loci delicti* test,[50] the Court reasoned:

> In the absence of a contrary congressional direction, we must apply those principles of choice of law that are consonant with the needs of a general federal maritime law and with due recognition of our self-regarding respect for the relevant interest of foreign nations in the regulation of maritime commerce as part of the legitimate concern of the international community.[51]

As in *Lauritzen*, *Romero* concluded that contemporary international maritime law called for a multi-factor analysis which included the place of the wrong, but only as one of many factors.[52]

41. 345 U.S. at 573.

42. 345 U.S. at 573. The Jones Act creates a federal cause of action for seamen, for personal injury suffered in the course of employment. The Act provides: "Any seaman who shall suffer personal injury in the course of his employment may, at his election, maintain an action for damages at law, with the right of trial by jury, and in such action all statutes of the United States modifying or extending the common-law right or remedy in cases of personal injury to railway employees shall apply. . . ." 46 U.S.C. app. §688(a) (1988). In 1982, Congress amended §688 to deny non-resident aliens rights under §688(a) in most cases. 96 Stat. 1954, 1955 (codified at 46 U.S.C. app. §688(b)).

43. 345 U.S. at 576-577.

44. 345 U.S. at 577. Citing *Charming Betsy*, the Court reasoned that international law principles have "the force of law, not from extraterritorial reach of national laws, nor from abdication of its sovereign powers by any nations, but from acceptance by common consent of civilized communities to rules designed to foster amicable and workable commercial relations." 345 U.S. at 581-582.

45. In addition to its nonapplication of the territoriality presumption, *Lauritzen* remarked that "the territorial standard is . . . unfitted to an enterprise conducted many territorial rules."

46. 345 U.S. at 582.

47. 345 U.S. at 583-591.

48. 358 U.S. 354 (1959).

49. 358 U.S. at 384.

50. 358 U.S. at 383.

51. 358 U.S. at 382-383.

52. 358 U.S. at 383-384.

Broadly similar results obtained in other cases involving international shipping. In *Benz v. Compania Naviera Hidalgo, SA,*[53] and *McCulloch v. Sociedad Nacional de Marineros,*[54] the Court held that the Labor Management Relations Act and National Labor Relations Act did not apply to foreign sailors involved in labor disputes aboard foreign vessels, even when they were located within U.S. territorial waters. In each case, the Court cited the territoriality presumption, but then went on to instead consider contemporary international law rules governing jurisdiction over vessels.[55]

These and other developments suggested to many that the territoriality presumption was no longer viable in the mid-twentieth century.[56] Nevertheless, the presumption has been revived, with remarkable vitality, in recent years. This is illustrated by the Supreme Court's decision in *EEOC v. Arabian American Oil Company,* excerpted below. There, the Court reaffirmed the territoriality presumption, holding Title VII's employment discrimination provisions inapplicable to a dispute occurring outside the United States between two U.S. parties.[57]

The materials excerpted below — *American Banana, Lauritzen,* and *Aramco* — illustrate the evolution of the territoriality presumption and the continuing debate over the geographic scope of federal legislation. They also provide a useful parallel to the development of principles of judicial and legislative jurisdiction, discussed in Chapters 2 and 7 above.

AMERICAN BANANA CO. v. UNITED FRUIT CO.
213 U.S. 347 (1909)

HOLMES, JUSTICE. This is an action brought to recover threefold damages under the act to protect trade against monopolies [the Sherman Act].[58] ... The allegations of the complaint may be summed up as follows: The plaintiff is an Alabama corporation, organized in 1904. The defendant is a New Jersey corporation, organized in 1899. Long before the plaintiff was formed, the defendant, with intent to prevent competition

---

53. 353 U.S. 138 (1957).

54. 372 U.S. 10 (1963).

55. *Benz,* 353 U.S. at 146-147; *McCulloch,* 372 U.S. at 21-22.

56. *See* Born, *A Reappraisal of the Extraterritorial Reach of U.S. Law,* 24 Law & Pol'y Int'l Bus. 1 (1992); *supra* pp. 595-598.

57. Several lower courts have relied on *Aramco* in holding that particular federal statutes do not apply extraterritorially. *E.g., Ofori-Tenkorang v. American International Group, Inc.,* 460 F.3d 296 (2d Cir. 2006) (42 U.S.C. §1981 as applied to employee's activities overseas); *Carnero v. Boston Scientific Corp.,* 433 F.3d 1 (1st Cir. 2006) (whistleblower provisions of Sarbanes-Oxley Act as applied to foreign employee working abroad for foreign subsidiary); *ARC Ecology v. U.S. Dep't of Air Force,* 411 F.3d 1092 (9th Cir. 2005) (CERCLA as applied to former U.S. military bases in foreign country); *Asplundh Tree Expert Co. v. N.L.R.B.,* 365 F.3d 168 (3d Cir. 2004) (NLRA as applied to U.S. workers temporarily abroad); *Reyes-Gaona v. North Carolina Growers Ass'n,* 250 F.3d 861 (4th Cir. 2001) (ADEA as applied to foreign plaintiff applying from abroad); *Nieman v. Dryclean U.S.A. Franchise Co., Inc.,* 178 F.3d 1126 (11th Cir. 1999) (FTC's Franchise Rule); *Kollias v. D & G Marine Maintenance,* 29 F.3d 67 (1994) (Longshore and Harbor Workers' Compensation Act); *Subafilms, Ltd. v. MGM-Pathe Communications Co.,* 24 F.3d 1088 (9th Cir. 1994) (*en banc*) (Copyright Act); *Van Blaricom v. Burlington Northern RR Co.,* 17 F.3d 1224 (9th Cir. 1994) (Interstate Commence Act); *United States v. Javino,* 960 F.2d 1137 (2d Cir. 1992) (Firearms Act); *Smith v. United States,* 932 F.2d 791 (9th Cir. 1991) (Federal Tort Claims Act), *aff'd,* 113 S. Ct. 1178 (1993); *Cruz v. Chesapeake Shipping, Inc.,* 932 F.2d 218 (3d Cir. 1991) (Fair Labor Standards Act); *Zheng v. Yahoo! Inc.,* 2009 WL 4430297 (N.D. Cal. Dec. 2, 2009) (Electronic Communications Privacy Act); *Smith v. Raytheon Co.,* 297 F. Supp. 2d 399 (D. Mass. 2004) (FLSA overtime rule); *Maurais v. Snyder,* 2000 WL 1368024 (E.D. Pa. 2000) (ERISA); *Urlic v. American Int'l Group,* 1997 WL 1368024 (S.D.N.Y. 1997) (Diplomatic Relations Act).

58. [Among other things, the Sherman Act forbids "[e]very contract, combination . . . or conspiracy in restraint of trade or commerce . . . with foreign nations."]

and to control and monopolize the banana trade, bought the . . . business of several of its previous competitors, with provision against their resuming the trade, made contracts with others . . . [fixing the price of bananas]. For the same purpose it organized a selling company, of which it held the stock, that by agreement sold at fixed prices all the bananas of the combining parties. . . . [O]ne McConnell, in 1903, started a banana plantation in Panama, then part of the United States of Columbia, and began to build a railway (which would afford his only means of export), both in accordance with the laws of the United States of Columbia. He was notified by the defendant that he must either combine or stop. Two months later, it is believed at the defendant's instigation, the governor of Panama recommended to his national government that Costa Rica be allowed to administer the territory through which the railroad was to run, and this although that territory had been awarded to Colombia under an arbitration agreed to by treaty. The defendant, and afterwards, in September, the government of Costa Rica, it is believed by the inducement of the defendant, interfered with McConnell. In November, 1903, Panama revolted and became an independent republic, declaring its boundary to be that settled by the award. In June, 1904, the plaintiff bought out McConnell and went on with the work, as it had a right to do under the laws of Panama. But in July, Costa Rican soldiers and officials, instigated by the defendant, seized a part of the plantation and a cargo of supplies and have held them ever since, and stopped the construction and operation of the plantation and railway. In August one Astua, by ex parte proceedings, got a judgment from a Costa Rican court, declaring the plantation to be his, although, it is alleged, the proceedings were not within the jurisdiction of Costa Rica, and were contrary to its laws and void. Agents of the defendant then bought the lands from Astua. The plaintiff has tried to induce the government of Costa Rica to withdraw its soldiers, and also has tried to persuade the United States to interfere, but has been thwarted in both by the defendant and has failed. The government of Costa Rica remained in possession down to the bringing of the suit.

As a result of the defendant's acts the plaintiff has been deprived of the use of the plantation, and the railway, the plantation, and supplies have been injured. The defendant also, by outbidding, has driven purchasers out of the market and has compelled producers to come to its terms, and it has prevented the plaintiff from buying for export and sale. This is the substantial damage alleged. . . . It is contended, however, that, even if the main argument fails and the defendant is held not to be answerable for acts depending on the co-operation of the government of Costa Rica for their effect, a wrongful conspiracy resulting in driving the plaintiff out of business is to be gathered from the complaint, and that it was entitled to go to trial upon that.

It is obvious that, however stated, the plaintiff's case depends on several rather startling propositions. In the first place, the acts causing the damage were done, so far as appears, outside the jurisdiction of the United States, and within that of other states. It is surprising to hear it argued that they were governed by the act of Congress.

No doubt in regions subject to no sovereign, like the high seas, or to no law that civilized countries would recognize as adequate, such countries may treat some relations between their citizens as governed by their own law, and keep, to some extent, the old notion of personal sovereignty alive. . . . They go further, at times, and declare that they will punish anyone, subject or not, who shall do certain things, if they can catch him, as in the case of pirates on the high seas. In cases immediately affecting national interests they may go further still and may make, and, if they get the chance, execute, similar threats as to acts done within another recognized jurisdiction. An illustration from our statutes is found with regard to criminal correspondence with foreign governments. Rev. Stat. §5335. . . .

But the general and almost universal rule is that the character of an act as lawful or unlawful must be determined wholly by the law of the country where the act is done.

Slater v. Mexican Nat. R. Co., 194 U.S. 120, 126 (1904). This principle was carried to an extreme in *Milliken v. Pratt,* 125 Mass. 374 (1878) [excerpted below at pp. 777-780]. For another jurisdiction, if it should happen to lay hold of the actor, to treat him according to its own notions rather than those of the place where he did the acts, not only would be unjust, but would be an interference with the authority of another sovereign, contrary to the comity of nations, which the other state concerned justly might resent. *Phillips v. Eyre,* L.R. 4 Q.B. 225, 239; Dicey, [*Conflict of Laws*] 647 (2d ed.). . . .

The foregoing considerations would lead, in case of doubt, to a construction of any statute as intended to be confined in its operation and effect to the territorial limits over which the lawmaker has general and legitimate power. "All legislation is prima facie territorial." *Ex parte Blain,* L. R. 12 Ch. Div. 522, 528. Words having universal scope, such as "every contract in restraint of trade," "every person who shall monopolize," etc., will be taken, as a matter of course, to mean only everyone subject to such legislation, not all that the legislator subsequently may be able to catch. In the case of the present statute, the improbability of the United States attempting to make acts done in Panama or Costa Rica criminal is obvious, yet the law begins by making criminal the acts for which it gives a right to sue. We think it entirely plain that what the defendant did in Panama or Costa Rica is not within the scope of the statute so far as the present suit is concerned. . . .

For again, not only were the acts of the defendant in Panama or Costa Rica not within the Sherman Act, but they were not torts by the law of the place, and therefore were not torts at all, however contrary to the ethical and economic postulates of that statute. The substance of the complaint is that, the plantation being within the de facto jurisdiction of Costa Rica, that state took and keeps possession of it by virtue of its sovereign power. But a seizure by a state is not a thing that can be complained of elsewhere in the courts. *Underhill v. Hernandez,* 168 U.S. 250 (1897). The fact, if it be one, that de jure the estate is in Panama, does not matter in the least; sovereignty is pure fact. The fact has been recognized by the United States, and, by the implications of the bill, is assented to by Panama.

The fundamental reason why persuading a sovereign power to do this or that cannot be a tort is not that the sovereign cannot be joined as a defendant or because it must be assumed to be acting lawfully. . . . The fundamental reason is that it is a contradiction in terms to say that, within its jurisdiction, it is unlawful to persuade a sovereign power to bring about a result that it declares by its conduct to be desirable and proper. It does not, and foreign courts cannot, admit that the influences were improper or the results bad. It makes the persuasion lawful by its own act. The very meaning of sovereignty is that the decree of the sovereign makes law. In the case of private persons, it consistently may assert the freedom of the immediate parties to an injury and yet declare that certain persuasions addressed to them are wrong.

. . . The acts of the soldiers and officials of Costa Rica are not alleged to have been without the consent of the government, and must be taken to have been done by its order. It ratified them, at all events, and adopted and keeps the possession taken by them. The injuries to the plantation and supplies seem to have been the direct effect of the acts of the Costa Rican government, which is holding them under an adverse claim of right. The claim for them must fall with the claim for being deprived of the use and profits of the place. As to the buying at a high price, etc., it is enough to say that we have no ground for supposing that it was unlawful in the countries where the purchases were made. Giving to this complaint every reasonable latitude of interpretation we are of opinion that it alleges no case under the act of Congress, and discloses nothing that we can suppose to have been a tort where it was done. A conspiracy in this country to do acts in another jurisdiction does not draw to itself those acts and make them unlawful, if they are permitted by the local law.

LAURITZEN v. LARSEN
345 U.S. 571 (1953)

JUSTICE JACKSON. The key issue in this case is whether statutes of the United States should be applied to this claim of maritime tort. Larsen, a Danish seaman, while temporarily in New York joined the crew of the *Randa,* a ship of Danish flag and registry, owned by petitioner, a Danish citizen. Larsen signed ship's articles, written in Danish, providing that the rights of crew members would be governed by Danish law and by the employer's contract with the Danish Seamen's Union, of which Larsen was a member. He was negligently injured aboard the *Randa* in the course of employment, while in Havana harbor.

Respondent brought suit under the Jones Act[59] [in] the Southern District of New York and demanded a jury. Petitioner contended that Danish law was applicable and that, under it, respondent had received all of the compensation to which he was entitled. . . . [T]he court ruled that American rather than Danish law applied, and the jury rendered a verdict of $4,267.50. The [Second Circuit] affirmed. . . .

Denmark has enacted a comprehensive code to govern the relations of her shipowners to her seagoing labor which by its terms and intentions controls this claim. Though it is not for us to decide, it is plausibly contended that all obligations of the owner growing out of Danish law have been performed or tendered to this seaman. The shipowner, supported here by the Danish Government, asserts that the Danish law supplies the full measure of his obligation and that maritime usage and international law as accepted by the United States exclude the application of our incompatible statute.

That allowance of an additional remedy under our Jones Act would sharply conflict with the policy and letter of Danish law is plain from a general comparison of the two systems of dealing with shipboard accidents. Both assure the ill or injured seafaring worker the conventional maintenance and cure at the shipowner's cost, regardless of fault or negligence on the part of anyone. But, while we limit this to the period within which maximum possible cure can be effected, the Danish law limits it to a fixed period of twelve weeks, and the monetary measurement is different. The two systems are in sharpest conflict as to treatment of claims for disability, partial or complete, which are permanent, or which outlast the liability for maintenance and cure. . . . Claims for such disability are not made against the owner but against the state's Directorate of Insurance Against the Consequences of Accidents. . . . They are allowed by administrative action, not by litigation, and depend not upon fault or negligence but only on the fact of injury and the extent of disability. Our own law, apart from indemnity for injury caused by the ship's unseaworthiness, makes no such compensation for such disability in the absence of fault or negligence. But, when such fault or negligence is established by litigation, it allows recovery for elements such as pain and suffering not compensated under Danish law and lets the damages be fixed by jury. In this case, since negligence was found, United States law permits a larger recovery than Danish law. If the same injury were sustained but negligence was absent or not provable, the Danish law would appear to provide compensation where ours would not.

Respondent does not deny that Danish law is applicable to his case. The contention as stated in his brief is rather that "A claimant may select whatever forum he desires and receive the benefits resulting from such choice" and "A ship owner is liable under the laws

---

59. "Any seaman who shall suffer personal injury in the course of his employment may, at his election, maintain an action for damages at law, with the right of trial by jury, and in such action all statutes of the United States modifying or extending the common-law right or remedy in cases of personal injury to railway employees shall apply. . . ." 46 U.S.C. §688.

of the forum where he does business as well as in his own country." This contention that the Jones Act provides an optional cumulative remedy is not based on any explicit terms of the Act, which makes no provision for cases in which remedies have been obtained or are obtainable under foreign law. Rather he relies upon the literal catholicity of its terminology. If read literally, Congress has conferred an American right of action which requires nothing more than that plaintiff be "any seaman who shall suffer personal injury in the course of his employment." It makes no explicit requirement that either the seaman, the employment or the injury have the slightest connection with the United States. Unless some relationship of one or more of these to our national interest is implied, Congress has extended our law and opened our courts to all alien seafaring men injured anywhere in the world in service of watercraft of every foreign nation — a hand on a Chinese junk, never outside Chinese waters, would not be beyond its literal wording.

But Congress in 1920 wrote these all-comprehending words, not on a clean slate, but as a postscript to a long series of enactments governing shipping. All were enacted with regard to a seasoned body of maritime law developed by the experience of American courts long accustomed to dealing with admiralty problems in reconciling our own with foreign interests and in accommodating the reach of our own laws to those of other maritime nations.

The shipping laws of the United States . . . comprise a patchwork of separate enactments, some tracing far back in our history and many designed for particular emergencies. While some have been specific in application to foreign shipping and others in being confined to American shipping, many give no evidence that Congress addressed itself to their foreign application and are in general terms which leave their application to be judicially determined from context and circumstance. By usage as old as the Nation, such statutes have been construed to apply only to areas and transactions in which American law would be considered operative under prevalent doctrines of international law. Thus, in *United States v. Palmer,* 16 U.S. 610 (1818), this Court was called upon to interpret a statute of 1790, 1 Stat. 115, punishing certain acts when committed on the high seas by "any person or persons," terms which, as Mr. Chief Justice Marshall observed, are "broad enough to comprehend every human being." But the Court determined that the literal universality of the prohibition "must not only be limited to cases within the jurisdiction of the state, but also to those objects to which the legislature intended to apply them," and therefore would not reach a person performing the proscribed acts aboard the ship of a foreign state on the high seas.

This doctrine of construction is in accord with the long-heeded admonition of Mr. Chief Justice Marshall that "an Act of Congress ought never to be construed to violate the law of nations if any other possible construction remains." *The Charming Betsy,* 6 U.S. 64 (1804). *See The Nereide,* 9 Cranch 388, 389, 423; *MacLeod v. United States,* 229 U.S. 416, 434 (1913); *Sandberg v. McDonald,* 248 U.S. 185, 195 (1918). And it has long been accepted in maritime jurisprudence that "if any construction otherwise be possible, an Act will not be construed as applying to foreigners in respect to acts done by them outside the dominions of the sovereign power enacting. That is a rule based on international law, by which one sovereign power is bound to respect the subjects and the rights of all other sovereign powers outside its own territory." *The Queen v. Jameson* (1896), 2 Q.B. 425, 430. This is not, as sometimes is implied, any impairment of our own sovereignty, or limitation of the power of Congress. "The law of the sea," we have had occasion to observe, "is in a peculiar sense an international law, but application of its specific rules depends upon acceptance by the United States." *Farrell v. United States,* 336 U.S. 511, 517. On the contrary, we are simply dealing with a problem of statutory construction rather commonplace in a federal system by which courts often have to decide whether "any" or "every" reaches to the limits of the enacting authority's usual scope or is to be applied to foreign events or transactions.

. . . In 1920, Congress, under the title "An Act to provide for the promotion and maintenance of the American merchant marine . . ." and other subjects not relevant, provided a plan to aid our mercantile fleet and included the revised provision for injured seamen now before us for construction. 41 Stat. 988, 1007. It did so by reference to the Federal Employers' Liability Act, 45 U.S.C.A. §51 *et seq.,* which we have held not applicable to an American citizen's injury sustained in Canada while in service of an American employer. *New York Central R. Co. v. Chisholm,* 268 U.S. 29 (1925). . . . Congress could not have been unaware of the necessity of construction imposed upon courts by such generality of language and was well warned that in the absence of more definite directions than are contained in the Jones Act it would be applied by the courts to foreign events, foreign ships and foreign seamen only in accordance with the usual doctrine and practices of maritime law.

Respondent places great stress upon the assertion that petitioner's commerce and contacts with the ports of the United States are frequent and regular, as the basis for applying our statutes to incidents aboard his ships. But the virtue and utility of sea-borne commerce lies in its frequent and important contacts with more than one country. If, to serve some immediate interest, the courts of each were to exploit every such contact to the limit of its power, it is not difficult to see that a multiplicity of conflicting and overlapping burdens would blight international carriage by sea. Hence, courts of this and other commercial nations have generally deferred to a non-national or international maritime law of impressive maturity and universality. It has the force of law, not from extraterritorial reach of national laws, nor from abdication of its sovereign powers by any nation, but from acceptance by common consent of civilized communities of rules designed to foster amicable and workable commercial relations.

International or maritime law in such matters as this does not seek uniformity and does not purport to restrict any nation from making and altering its laws to govern its own shipping and territory. However, it aims at stability and order through usages which considerations of comity, reciprocity and long-range interest have developed to define the domain which each nation will claim as its own. Maritime law, like our municipal law, has attempted to avoid or resolve conflicts between competing laws by ascertaining and valuing points of contact between the transaction and the states or governments whose competing laws are involved. The criteria, in general, appear to be arrived at from weighing of the significance of one or more connecting factors between the shipping transaction regulated and the national interest served by the assertion of authority. It would not be candid to claim that our courts have arrived at satisfactory standards or apply those that they profess with perfect consistency. But in dealing with international commerce we cannot be unmindful of the necessity for mutual forbearance if retaliations are to be avoided; nor should we forget that any contact which we hold sufficient to warrant application of our law to a foreign transaction will logically be as strong a warrant for a foreign country to apply its law to an American transaction. . . . We therefore review the several factors which, alone or in combination, are generally conceded to influence choice of law to govern a tort claim, particularly a maritime tort claim, and the weight and significance accorded them.

1. *Place of the Wrongful Act.* — The solution most commonly accepted as to torts in our municipal and in international law is to apply the law of the place where the acts giving rise to the liability occurred, the *lex loci delicti commissi.*[60] This rule of locality, often applied to

---

60. *See Slater v. Mexican National R. Co.,* 194 U.S. 120 (1904); *New York Central R. Co. v. Chisholm,* 268 U.S. 29 (1925); Rheinstein, *The Place of Wrong: A Study in the Method of Case Law,* 19 Tul. L. Rev. 4 (1944). *Cf. Sandberg v. McDonald,* 248 U.S. 185, 195 (1918).

maritime torts, would indicate application of the law of Cuba, in whose domain the actionable wrong took place. The test of location of the wrongful act or omission, however sufficient for torts ashore, is of limited application to shipboard torts, because of the varieties of legal authority over waters she may navigate. . . .

2. *Law of the Flag.* — Perhaps the most venerable and universal rule of maritime law relevant to our problem is that which gives cardinal importance to the law of the flag. Each state under international law may determine for itself the conditions on which it will grant its nationality to a merchant ship, thereby accepting responsibility for it and acquiring authority over it. Nationality is evidenced to the world by the ship's papers and its flag. The United States has firmly and successfully maintained that the regularity and validity of a registration can be questioned only by the registering state.

This Court has said that the law of the flag supersedes the territorial principle, even for purposes of criminal jurisdiction of personnel of a merchant ship, because it "is deemed to be a part of the territory of that sovereignty (whose flag it flies), and not to lose that character when in navigable waters within the territorial limits of another sovereignty." On this principle, we concede a territorial government involved only concurrent jurisdiction of offenses aboard our ships. *United States v. Flores*, 289 U.S. 137, 155-59 (1933). . . .

It is significant to us here that the weight given to the ensign overbears most other connecting events in determining applicable law. As this Court held in *United States v. Flores*, 289 U.S. at 158: "And so by comity it came to be generally understood among civilized nations that all matters of discipline, and all things done on board, which affected only the vessel, or those belonging to her, and did not involve the peace or dignity of the country, or the tranquillity of the port, should be left by the local government to be dealt with by the authorities of the nation to which the vessel belonged as the laws of that nation, or the interests of its commerce should require. . . ." This was but a repetition of settled American doctrine. These considerations are of such weight in favor of Danish and against American law in this case that it must prevail unless some heavy counterweight appears.

3. *Allegiance or Domicile of the Injured.* — Until recent times there was little occasion for conflict between the law of the flag and the law of the state of which the seafarer was a subject, for the long-standing rule, as pronounced by this Court after exhaustive review of authority, was that the nationality of the vessel for jurisdictional purposes was attributed to all her crew. *In re Ross*, 140 U.S. 453, 472. Surely during service under a foreign flag some duty of allegiance is due. But, also, each nation has a legitimate interest that its nationals and permanent inhabitants be not maimed or disabled from self-support. We need not, however, weigh the seaman's nationality against that of the ship, for here the two coincide without resort to fiction. . . .

4. *Allegiance of the Defendant Shipowner.* — A state "is not debarred by any rule of international law from governing the conduct of its own citizens upon the high seas or even in foreign countries when the rights of other nations or their nationals are not infringed." *Skiriotes v. State of Florida*, 313 U.S. 69, 73. Until recent times this factor was not a frequent occasion of conflict, for the nationality of the ship was that of its owners. But it is common knowledge that in recent years a practice has grown, particularly among American shipowners, to avoid stringent shipping laws by seeking foreign registration eagerly offered by some countries. Confronted with such operations, our courts on occasion have pressed beyond the formalities of more or less nominal foreign registration to enforce against American shipowners the obligations which our law places upon them. But here again the utmost liberality in disregard of formality does not support the application of American law in this case, for it appears beyond doubt that this owner is a Dane by nationality and domicile.

5. *Place of Contract.* — Place of contract, which was New York, is the factor on which respondent chiefly relies to invoke American law. It is one which often has significance in choice of law in a contract action. But a Jones Act suit is for tort, in which respect it differs from one to enforce liability for maintenance and cure. . . . But this action does not seek to recover anything due under the contract or damages for its breach.

The place of contracting in this instance, as is usual to such contracts, was fortuitous. A seaman takes his employment, like his fun, where he finds it; a ship takes on crew in any port where it needs them. The practical effect of making the *lex loci contractus* govern all tort claims during the service would be to subject a ship to a multitude of systems of law, to put some of the crew in a more advantageous position than others, and not unlikely in the long run to diminish hirings in ports of countries that take best care of their seamen.

But if contract law is nonetheless to be considered, we face the fact that this contract was explicit that the Danish law and the contract with the Danish union were to control. Except as forbidden by some public policy, the tendency of the law is to apply in contract matters the law which the parties intended to apply. . . . We do not think the place of contract is a substantial influence in the choice between competing laws to govern a maritime tort.

6. *Inaccessibility of Foreign Forum.* — It is argued . . . that justice requires adjudication under American law to save seamen expense and loss of time in returning to a foreign forum. This might be a persuasive argument for exercising a discretionary jurisdiction to adjudge a controversy; but it is not persuasive as to the law by which it shall be judged. . . . [W]e do not find this seaman disadvantaged in obtaining his remedy under Danish law from being in New York instead of Denmark. The Danish compensation system does not necessitate delayed, prolonged, expensive and uncertain litigation. . . .

7. *The Law of the Forum.* — It is urged that, since an American forum has perfected its jurisdiction over the parties and defendant does more or less frequent and regular business within the forum state, it should apply its own law to the controversy between them. The "doing business" which is enough to warrant service of process may fall quite short of the considerations necessary to bring extraterritorial torts to judgment under our law. Under respondent's contention, all that is necessary to bring a foreign transaction between foreigners in foreign ports under American law is to be able to serve American process on the defendant. We have held it a denial of due process of law when a state of the Union attempts to draw into control of its law otherwise foreign controversies, on slight connections, because it is a forum state. *Hartford Accident & Indemnity Co. v. Delta & Pine Land Co.,* 292 U.S. 143 (1934); *Home Insurance Co. v. Dick,* 281 U.S. 397 (1930). The purpose of a conflict-of-laws doctrine is to assure that a case will be treated in the same way under the appropriate law regardless of the fortuitous circumstances which often determine the forum. Jurisdiction of maritime cases in all countries is so wide and the nature of its subject matter so far-flung that there would be no justification for altering the law of a controversy just because local jurisdiction of the parties is obtainable. . . .

This review of the connecting factors which either maritime law or our municipal law of conflicts regards as significant in determining the law applicable to a claim of actionable wrong shows an overwhelming preponderance in favor of Danish law. The parties are both Danish subjects, the events took place on a Danish ship, not within our territorial waters. Against these considerations is only the fact that the defendant was served here with process and that the plaintiff signed on in New York, where the defendant was engaged in our foreign commerce. The latter event is offset by provision of his contract that the law of Denmark should govern. We do not question the power of Congress to condition access to our ports by foreign-owned vessels upon submission to any liabilities it may consider good American policy to exact. But we can find no justification for interpreting the Jones Act to intervene between foreigners and their own law because of acts on a foreign ship not in our waters. . . .

EQUAL EMPLOYMENT OPPORTUNITY COMMISSION v. ARABIAN AMERICAN OIL CO.
499 U.S. 244 (1991)

CHIEF JUSTICE REHNQUIST. These cases present the issue whether Title VII applies extraterritorially to regulate the employment practices of United States employers who employ United States citizens abroad. . . .

Petitioner Boureslan is a naturalized United States citizen who was born in Lebanon. The respondents are two Delaware corporations, Arabian American Oil Company ("Aramco"), and its subsidiary, Aramco Service Company ("ASC"). Aramco's principal place of business is Dhahran, Saudi Arabia, and it is licensed to do business in Texas. ASC's principal place of business is Houston, Texas. In 1979, Boureslan was hired by ASC as a cost engineer in Houston. A year later he was transferred, at his request, to work for Aramco in Saudi Arabia. Boureslan remained with Aramco in Saudi Arabia until he was discharged in 1984.

[Boureslan later filed a complaint alleging, among other things, discrimination on the basis of race, religion, and national origin in violation of Title VII of the Civil Right Act of 1964, 42 U.S.C. §§2000a-2000h-6. The district court found that Title VII's protections do not extend to United States citizens employed abroad by American employers and dismissed the case. The Fifth Circuit affirmed.]

Both parties concede, as they must, that Congress has the authority to enforce its laws beyond the territorial boundaries of the United States. Whether Congress has in fact exercised that authority in this case is a matter of statutory construction. It is our task to determine whether Congress intended the protections of Title VII to apply to U.S. citizens employed by American employers outside of the United States.

It is a long-standing principle of American law "that legislation of Congress, unless a contrary intent appears, is meant to apply only within the territorial jurisdiction of the United States." *Foley Bros.* [*v. Filardo,* 336 U.S. 281, 285 (1949)]. This "canon of construction . . . is a valid approach whereby unexpressed congressional intent may be ascertained." It serves to protect against unintended clashes between our laws and those of other nations which could result in international discord. *See McCulloch v. Sociedad Nacional de Marineros de Honduras,* 372 U.S. 10, 20-22 (1963). In applying this rule of construction, we look to see whether "language in the [relevant act] gives any indication of a congressional purpose to extend its coverage beyond places over which the United States has sovereignty or has some measure of legislative control." *Foley Bros.,* 336 U.S. at 285. We assume that Congress legislates against the backdrop of the presumption against extraterritoriality. Therefore, unless there is "the affirmative intention of the Congress clearly expressed"; *Benz* [*v. Compania Naviera Hidalgo, SA,* 353 U.S. 138], 147, we must presume it "is primarily concerned with domestic conditions." *Foley Bros.,* 336 U.S. at 285.

Boureslan and the EEOC contend that the language of Title VII evinces a clearly expressed intent on behalf of Congress to legislate extraterritorially. . . . First, petitioners argue that the statute's definitions of the jurisdictional terms "employer" and "commerce" are sufficiently broad to include U.S. firms that employ American citizens overseas. Second, they maintain that the statue's "alien exemption" clause, 42 U.S.C. §2000e-1, necessarily implies that Congress intended to protect American citizens from employment discrimination abroad. . . . We conclude that petitioners' evidence, while not totally lacking in probative value, falls short of demonstrating the affirmative congressional intent required to extend the protections of Title VII beyond our territorial borders.

Title VII prohibits various discriminatory employment practices based on an individual's race, color, religion, sex, or national origin. An employer is subject to Title VII if it has employed 15 or more employees for a specified period and is "engaged in an industry affecting commerce." An industry affecting commerce is "any activity, business, or industry in commerce or in which a labor dispute would hinder or obstruct commerce or the free flow of commerce and includes any activity or industry 'affecting commerce' within the meaning of the Labor-Management Reporting and Disclosure Act of 1959 [("LMRDA")] [29 U.S.C. §401 *et seq.*]." §2000e(h). "Commerce," in turn, is defined as "trade, traffic, commerce, transportation, transmission, or communication among the several States; or between a State and any place outside thereof; or within the District of Columbia, or a possession of the United States; or between points in the same State but through a point outside thereof." §2000e(g).

Petitioners argue that by its plain language, Title VII's "broad jurisdictional language" reveals Congress's intent to extend the statute's protections to employment discrimination anywhere in the world by a U.S. employer who affects trade "between a State and any place outside thereof." More precisely, they assert that since Title VII defines "States" to include States, the District of Columbia, and specified territories, the clause "between a State and any place outside thereof" must be referring to areas beyond the territorial limit of the United States.

Respondents offer several alternative explanations for the statute's expansive language. They contend that the "or between a State and any place outside thereof" clause "provide[s] the jurisdictional nexus required to regulate commerce that is not wholly within a single state, presumably as it affects both interstate and foreign commerce" but not to "regulate conduct exclusively within a foreign country." They also argue that since the definitions of the terms "employer," "commerce," and "industry affecting commerce," make no mention of "commerce with foreign nations," Congress cannot be said to have intended that the statute apply overseas. . . .

We need not choose between these competing interpretations as we would be required to do in the absence of the presumption against extraterritorial application discussed above. Each is plausible, but no more persuasive than that. The language relied upon by petitioners — and it is they who must make the affirmative showing — is ambiguous, and does not speak directly to the question presented here. The intent of Congress as to the extraterritorial application of this statute must be deduced by inference from boilerplate language which can be found in any number of congressional acts, none of which have ever been held to apply overseas. *See, e.g.,* Consumer Product Safety Act, 15 U.S.C. §2052(a)(12); Federal Food, Drug, and Cosmetic Act, 21 U.S.C. §321(b); Transportation Safety Act of 1974, 49 U.S.C. App. §1802(1).

Petitioners' reliance on Title VII's jurisdictional provisions also finds no support in our case law; we have repeatedly held that even statutes that contain broad language in their definitions of "commerce" that expressly refer to "foreign commerce," do not apply abroad. For example, in *New York Central R. Co. v. Chisholm,* 268 U.S. 29 (1925), we addressed the extraterritorial application of the Federal Employers Liability Act ("FELA"), 45 U.S.C. §51 *et seq.* FELA provides that common carriers by railroad while engaging in "interstate or foreign commerce" or commerce between "any of the States or territories and any foreign nation or nations" shall be liable in damages to its employees who suffer injuries resulting from their employment. 45 U.S.C. §51. Despite this broad jurisdictional language, we found that the Act "contains no words which definitely disclose an intention to give it extraterritorial effect," *Chisholm,* 268 U.S. at 31, and therefore there was no jurisdiction under FELA for a damages action by a U.S. citizen employed on a U.S. railroad who suffered fatal injuries at a point 30 miles north of the U.S. border into Canada. . . .

The EEOC places great weight on an assertedly similar "broad jurisdictional grant in the Lanham Act" that this Court held applied extraterritorially in *Steele v. Bulova Watch Co.,* [344 U.S. 280, 286 (1952)]. . . . The EEOC's attempt to analogize this case to *Steele* is unpersuasive. The Lanham Act by terms applies to "all commerce which may lawfully be regulated by Congress." The Constitution gives Congress the power "[t]o regulate Commerce with foreign Nations, and among the several States, and with the Indian Tribes." U.S. Const., Art. I, §8, cl. 3. Since the Act expressly stated that it applied to the extent of Congress's power over commerce, the Court in *Steele* concluded that Congress intended that the statute apply abroad. By contrast, Title VII's more limited, boilerplate "commerce" language does not support such an expansive construction of congressional intent. Moreover, unlike the language in the Lanham Act, Title VII's definition of "commerce" was derived expressly from the LMRDA, a statute that this Court had held, prior to the enactment of Title VII, did not apply abroad. *McCulloch,* 372 U.S. at 15.

Thus petitioner's argument based on the jurisdictional language of Title VII fails both as a matter of statutory language and of our previous case law. Many acts of Congress are based on the authority of that body to regulate commerce among the several States, and the parts of these acts setting forth the basis for legislative jurisdiction will obviously refer to such commerce in one way or another. If we were to permit possible, or even plausible interpretations of language such as that involved here to override the presumption against extraterritorial application, there would be little left of the presumption.

Petitioners argue that Title VII's "alien exemption provision," 42 U.S.C. §2000e-1, "clearly manifests an intention" by Congress to protect U.S. citizens with respect to their employment outside of the United States. The alien exemption provision says that the statute "shall not apply to an employer with respect to the employment of aliens outside any State." §2000e-1. Petitioners contend that from this language a negative inference should be drawn that Congress intended Title VII to cover United States citizens working abroad for United States employers. There is "[no] other plausible explanation [that] the alien exemption exists," they argue, because "[i]f Congress believed that the statute did not apply extraterritorially, it would have had no reason to include an exemption for a certain category of individuals employed outside the United States." . . .

Respondents resist petitioners' interpretation of the alien-exemption provision and assert two alternative raisons d'etre for that language. First, they contend that since aliens are included in the statute's definition of employee, and the definition of commerce includes possessions as well as "States," the purpose of the exemption is to provide that employers of aliens in the possessions of the United States are not covered by the statute. Thus, the "outside any State" clause means outside any State, but within the control of the United States [such as leased military bases in foreign lands.] . . .

Second, respondents assert that by negative implication, the exemption "confirm[s] the coverage of aliens in the United States." They contend that this interpretation is consistent with our conclusion in *Espinoza v. Farah Mfg. Co.,* 414 U.S. 86 (1973), that aliens within the United States are protected from discrimination both because Title VII uses the term "individual" rather than "citizen," and because of the alien-exemption provision.

If petitioners are correct that the alien-exemption clause means that the statute applies to employers overseas, we see no way of distinguishing in its application between United States employers and foreign employers. Thus, a French employer of a United States citizen in France would be subject to Title VII—a result at which even petitioners balk. The EEOC assures us that in its view the term "employer" means only "American employer," but there is no such distinction in this statute, and no indication that EEOC in the normal course of its administration had produced a reasoned basis for such a distinction. Without clearer evidence of congressional intent to do so than is contained in the alien-exemption clause, we are unwilling to ascribe to that body a policy which would raise difficult issues of international law by imposing this country's employment-discrimination regime upon foreign corporations operating in foreign commerce.

This conclusion is fortified by the other elements in the statute suggesting a purely domestic focus. The statute as a whole indicates a concern that it not unduly interfere with the sovereignty and laws of the States. *See, e.g.,* 42 U.S.C. §2000h-4 (stating that Title VII should not be construed to exclude the operation of state law or invalidate any state law unless inconsistent with the purposes of the act). . . . While Title VII consistently speaks in terms of "States" and state proceedings, it fails even to mention foreign nations or foreign proceedings.

Similarly, Congress failed to provide any mechanisms for overseas enforcement of Title VII. For instance, the statute's venue provisions, §2000e-5(f)(3), are ill-suited for extraterritorial application as they provide for venue only in a judicial district in the state where certain matters related to the employer occurred or were located. And the limited investigative authority provided for the EEOC, permitting the Commission only to issue subpoenas for witnesses and documents from "any place in the United States or any Territory or possession thereof," §2000e-9, suggests that Congress did not intend for the statute to apply abroad.

It is also reasonable to conclude that had Congress intended Title VII to apply overseas, it would have addressed the subject of conflicts with foreign laws and procedures. In amending the Age Discrimination in Employment Act of 1967, 81 Stat. 602, as amended, 29 U.S.C. §621 *et seq.* ("ADEA"), to apply abroad, Congress specifically addressed potential conflicts with foreign law by providing that it is not unlawful for an employer to take any action prohibited by the ADEA "where such practices involve an employee in a workplace in a foreign country, and compliance with [the ADEA] would cause such employer . . . to violate the laws of the country in which such workplace is located." 29 U.S.C. §623(f)(1). Title VII, by contrast, fails to address conflicts with the laws of other nations. . . .

Our conclusion today is buttressed by the fact that "[w]hen it desires to do so, Congress knows how to place the high seas within the jurisdictional reach of a statute." *Argentine Republic v. Amerada Hess Shipping Corp.,* 488 U.S. 428, 440 (1989). Congress's awareness of the need to make a clear statement that a statute applies overseas is amply demonstrated by the numerous occasions on which it has expressly legislated the extraterritorial application of a statute. . . . Congress, should it wish to do so, may similarly amend Title VII and in doing so will be able to calibrate its provisions in a way that we cannot. . . .

JUSTICE MARSHALL, with whom JUSTICE BLACKMUN and JUSTICE STEVENS join, dissenting. Like any issue of statutory construction, the question whether Title VII protects U.S. citizens from discrimination by U.S. employers abroad turns solely on congressional intent. As the majority recognizes, our inquiry into congressional intent in this setting is informed by the traditional "canon of construction which teaches that legislation of Congress, unless a contrary intent appears, is meant to apply only within the territorial jurisdiction of the United States." *Foley Bros., Inc. v. Filardo.* But contrary to what one would conclude from the majority's analysis, this canon is not a "clear statement" rule, the application of which relieves a court of the duty to give effect to all available indicia of the legislative will. Rather, as our case law applying the presumption against extraterritoriality well illustrates, a court may properly rely on this presumption only after exhausting all of the traditional tools "whereby unexpressed congressional intent may be ascertained." When these tools are brought to bear . . . the conclusion is inescapable that Congress did intend Title VII to protect United States citizens from discrimination by United States employers operating overseas. . . .

Because it supplies the driving force of the majority's analysis, I start with "[t]he canon . . . that legislation of Congress, unless a contrary intent appears, is meant to apply only within the territorial jurisdiction of the United States." The majority recasts this principle as "the need to make a clear statement that a statute applies overseas." . . . In my view, the majority grossly distorts the effect of this rule of construction upon conventional techniques of statutory interpretation. . . .

[For example, in *Foley Brothers,*] the Court . . . engaged in extended analyses of the legislative history of the statute, and of pertinent administrative interpretations. The range of factors that the Court considered in *Foley Brothers* demonstrates that the presumption against extraterritoriality is not a "clear statement" rule. Clear-statement rules operate less to reveal actual congressional intent than to shield important values from an insufficiently strong legislative intent to displace them. When they apply, such rules foreclose inquiry into extrinsic guides to interpretation, and even compel courts to select less plausible candidates from within the range of permissible constructions. The Court's analysis in *Foley Brothers* was by no means so narrowly constrained. Indeed, the Court considered the entire range of conventional sources "whereby *unexpressed* congressional intent may be ascertained," 336 U.S. at 285 (emphasis added), including legislative history, statutory structure, and administrative interpretations. Subsequent applications of the presumption against extraterritoriality confirm that we have not imposed the drastic clear-statement burden upon Congress before giving effect to its intention that a particular enactment apply beyond the national boundaries. *See, e.g., Steele v. Bulova Watch Co.* (relying on "broad jurisdictional grant" to find intention that Lanham Act applies abroad).

The majority also overstates the strength of the presumption by drawing on language from cases involving a wholly independent rule of construction: "that an act of congress ought never to be construed to violate the law of nations if any other possible construction remains. . . ." *McCulloch v. Sociedad Nacional,* quoting *The Charming Betsy; see Benz v. Compania Naviera Hidalgo, SA.* At issue in *Benz* was whether the Labor Management Relations Act of 1947 "applie[d] to a controversy involving damages resulting from the picketing of a foreign ship operated entirely by foreign seamen under foreign articles while the vessel is temporarily in an American port." Construing the statute to apply under such circumstances would have displaced labor regulations that were founded on the law of another nation and that were applicable solely to foreign nationals. In language quoted in the majority's opinion, the Court stated that "there must be present the affirmative intention of the Congress clearly expressed" before it would infer that Congress intended courts to enter "such a delicate field of international relations."

Far from equating *Benz* and *McCulloch*'s clear-statement rule with *Foley*'s presumption against extraterritoriality, the Court has until now recognized that *Benz* and *McCulloch* are reserved for settings in which the extraterritorial application of a statute would "implicat[e] sensitive issues of the authority of the Executive over relations with foreign nations." *NLRB v. Catholic Bishop of Chicago,* 440 U.S. 490, 500 (1979). The strictness of the *McCulloch* and *Benz* presumption permits the Court to avoid, if possible, the separation-of-powers and international-comity questions associated with construing a statute to displace the domestic law of another nation. Nothing nearly so dramatic is at stake when Congress merely seeks to regulate the conduct of U.S. nationals abroad.

Because petitioners advance a construction of Title VII that would extend its extraterritorial reach only to U.S. nationals, it is the weak presumption of *Foley Brothers,* not the strict clear-statement rule of *Benz* and *McCulloch,* that should govern our inquiry here. Confirmation that Congress did in fact expect Title VII's central prohibition to have an extraterritorial reach is supplied by the so-called "alien exemption" provision. The alien-exemption provision states that Title VII "shall not apply to an employer with respect to the employment of aliens *outside any State.*" 42 U.S.C. §2000e-1 (emphasis added). Absent an intention that Title VII apply "outside any State," Congress would have had no reason to craft this extraterritorial exemption. And because only discrimination against aliens is exempted, employers remain accountable for discrimination against United States citizens abroad. . . .

Finally, the majority overstates the importance of Congress' failure expressly to disclaim extraterritorial application of Title VII to foreign employers. As I have discussed, our cases recognize that application of U.S. law to U.S. nationals abroad ordinarily raises considerably less serious questions of international comity than does the application of U.S. law to foreign nationals abroad. *See Steele v. Bulova Watch Co.; Skiriotes v. Florida.* It is the latter situation that typically presents the foreign-policy and conflicts-of-law concerns that underlie the clear-statement rule of *McCulloch* and *Benz.* Because two different rules of construction apply depending on the national identity of the regulated parties, the same statute might be construed to apply extraterritorially to United States nationals but not to foreign nationals.

. . . In the hands of the majority, the presumption against extraterritoriality is transformed from a "valid approach whereby unexpressed congressional intent may be ascertained," *Foley Bros.,* 336 U.S. at 285, into a barrier to any genuine inquiry into the sources that reveal Congress' actual intentions. Because the language, history, and administrative interpretations of the statute all support application of Title VII to U.S. companies employing U.S. citizens abroad, I dissent.

Notes *on* American Banana, Lauritzen, *and* Aramco

1. *The territoriality presumption.* The results and analysis in *American Banana* and *Aramco* rest almost entirely on the so-called "territoriality presumption." According to Justice Holmes in *American Banana,* "in case of doubt," a court should adopt a "construction of any statute as intended to be confined in its operation and effect to the territorial limits over which the lawmaker has general and legitimate power." Similarly, *Aramco* declared that "legislation of Congress, unless a contrary intent appears, is meant to apply only within the territorial jurisdiction of the United States."

(a) *Historical origins of territoriality presumption.* As discussed above the territoriality presumption had its origins in decisions during the early decades of the Republic. *See supra* pp. 646-649; *Rose v. Himely,* 8 U.S. 241, 279 (1808); *The Apollon,* 22 U.S. 362 (1824). It was vigorously restated in *American Banana* and was repeatedly applied during the early decades of the twentieth century. *See supra* pp. 649-650; *Sandberg v. McDonald,* 248 U.S. 185, 195 (1918) ("Legislation is presumptively territorial and confined to limits over which the lawmaking power has jurisdiction."); *United States v. Bowman,* 260 U.S. 94, 98 (1922); *New York Central R. Co. v. Chisholm,* 268 U.S. 29 (1925) (no extraterritorial application of statute that "contains no words which definitely disclose an intention to give it extraterritorial effect, nor do the circumstances require an inference of such purpose").

(b) *Erosion of territoriality presumption.* As *Lauritzen* illustrates, the territoriality presumption was nearly abandoned during the middle decades of the twentieth century. *See supra* pp. 650-651; *United States v. Aluminum Co. of America,* 148 F.2d 416 (2d Cir. 1945); *Romero v. International Terminal Operating Co.,* 358 U.S. 354 (1959); *Steele v. Bulova Watch Co.,* 344 U.S. 280 (1952).

(c) Contemporary resurrection of territoriality presumption. Notwithstanding *Lauritzen* and other decisions abandoning the territoriality presumption, recent Supreme Court precedent has reaffirmed the dominant role of territoriality in interpreting federal statutes. *Aramco* is a leading example of this resurrection of the territoriality presumption. More recent Supreme Court decisions have also applied the territoriality presumption. *See Smith v. United States,* 507 U.S. 197 (1993); *Sale v. Haitian Centers Council, Inc.,* 509 U.S. 155 (1993); *Rasul v. Bush,* 542 U.S. 466, 480 (2004); *Microsoft Corp. v. AT&T Corp.,* 550 U.S. 437, 455-456 (2007); *Morrison v. National Australian Bank Ltd.,* 130 S. Ct. 2869 (2010).

2. *Rationale for territoriality presumption.* What is the rationale for the territoriality presumption?

(a) International law limits on legislative jurisdiction. The territoriality presumption rests in part on international law limits on legislative jurisdiction, explored above. *See supra* pp. 646-648. As *American Banana* said:

> For another jurisdiction . . . to treat [one] according to its own notions rather than those of the place where he did the acts . . . would be an interference with the authority of another sovereign, contrary to the comity of nations, which the other state concerned justly might resent.

Is this a persuasive basis for the territoriality presumption? If international law forbids extraterritorial applications of national law, isn't the territoriality presumption an inevitable corollary of the *Charming Betsy* rule that Congress will not be held to have violated international law unless its legislation expressly commands that result?

(b) Choice-of-law rules. *American Banana* also cited contemporary choice-of-law rules, which provided that "the character of an act as lawful or unlawful must be determined wholly by the law of the country where the act is done" (citing *Slater v. Mexican National R.R. Co.,* 194 U.S. 120 (1904), and *Milliken v. Pratt,* 125 Mass. 374 (Mass. 1878), discussed below, *infra* pp. 777-784). Are choice-of-law rules relevant to determining the extraterritorial reach that Congress intended its statutes to have? On what theory? Did *Aramco* rely on choice-of-law analysis in deciding the reach of Title VII?

(c) Minimizing conflicts between U.S. and foreign laws. Both *American Banana* and *Aramco* reasoned that the territoriality presumption seeks to avoid conflicts between U.S. and foreign law. "It serves to protect against unintended clashes between our laws and those of other nations which could result in international discord." *See also McCulloch v. Sociedad Nacional de Marineros de Honduras,* 372 U.S. 10, 20-22 (1963); *Al-Bihani v. Obama,* 619 F.3d 1, 25 (D.C. Cir. 2010) (Kavanaugh, J., concurring in the denial of rehearing *en banc*). How does the territoriality presumption minimize conflicts with foreign law? Are there not more refined means for avoiding conflicts between U.S. and foreign laws than the territoriality presumption? Note that the Supreme Court has held that the territoriality presumption is applicable even when there is little or no possibility of conflict with foreign law or international discord. *Sale v. Haitian Centers Council,* 509 U.S. 155, 173-174 (1993).

(d) Congress's concern with domestic matters. *Aramco* also reasoned that the territoriality presumption rests on the "assumption that Congress is primarily concerned with domestic conditions." *Foley Bros., Inc. v. Filardo,* 336 U.S. 281, 285 (1949). *See also Smith v. United States,* 507 U.S. 197, 204 n.5 (1993) (even when no "clashes" between U.S. and foreign law exist, "the presumption is rooted in a number of considerations, not the least

of which is the common-sense notion that Congress generally legislates with domestic concerns in mind"). Is that persuasive? Just because Congress is "primarily concerned" with domestic matters, does that mean it does not also intend to address international matters? Recall the interdependence of global markets and the effects of foreign events on U.S. interests. *See supra* pp. 595-598.

(e) Fairness to private parties. American Banana reasoned that it would be "unjust" to judge a private party by the laws of a place other than where he acted. What is the cause of that unfairness? Is it in fact unfair to judge a private party by a law that is applied extraterritorially? Recall the due process limits on legislative jurisdiction in *Dick* and *Allstate. See supra* pp. 613-630.

(f) Separation of powers. Perhaps the presumption against extraterritoriality can be understood as an application of separation of powers principles. *See supra* at _____. It minimizes the risk that courts, in the search for Congress's intended meaning, will impute to Congress a desire to give a statute a broader reach than Congress intended. Put another way, the presumption against extraterritoriality operates as a sort of "default rule" that will both simplify the judicial inquiry and put Congress on clear notice of the need to use specific language if it wishes for statutes to have extraterritorial reach. The clarity afforded by the presumption provides "stable background against which Congress can legislate with predictable effects." *Morrison v. Australia National Bank Ltd.*, 130 S. Ct. at 2881 (footnote omitted).

3. *Criticism of territoriality presumption.* Do the foregoing justifications provide a persuasive basis for the territoriality presumption? What interests does the presumption further? What interests does it frustrate?

(a) International law no longer forbids extraterritorial jurisdiction. As discussed above, international law limits on legislative jurisdiction were one basis for the territoriality presumption. *See supra* pp. 646-649. Note, however, that early decisions, like *The Apollon,* did not in fact articulate a pure territoriality presumption. *See supra* p. 649. Instead, the Court adopted an "international law" presumption that was not strictly territorial: "however general and comprehensive the phrases used in our municipal laws may be, *they must always be restricted in construction, to places and persons, upon whom the legislature have authority and jurisdiction.*" 22 U.S. at 370. Note also that international law recognized both a nationality principle and (less clearly) an effects doctrine in the early twentieth century. *See supra* pp. 595-602. Consider the formulation of both principles in the *Restatement (First) Conflict of Laws,* Appendix X. Would these principles have permitted application of the Sherman Act to the defendant's conduct in *American Banana*? Moreover, this century has seen a substantial erosion of international law limits on legislative jurisdiction. *See supra* pp. 595-604. Thus, the nationality and effects principles are now widely recognized jurisdictional bases. *See supra* pp. 599-600; Kramer, *Vestiges of* Beale: *Extraterritorial Application of American Law,* 1991 Sup. Ct. Rev. 179. What effect does this evolution of international law have on the territoriality presumption?

(b) American choice-of-law analysis no longer rests exclusively on the territoriality doctrine. As discussed below, American conflict of laws underwent what is frequently called a "revolution" during the 1950s and 1960s. *See infra* pp. 738-739. The strict territorial analysis of the *Restatement (First) Conflict of Laws* was replaced by a variety of more flexible analyses. *See infra* pp. 739-742. This evolution is reflected, at least in part, in *Lauritzen.* None of the new analyses of the American conflicts revolution requires application of the law of the place of the tort; they instead look to a broader range of connecting factors and the likely legislative policies of conflicting national laws. These analyses frequently permit application of a state's law to events occurring outside the state's territory. *See infra* pp. 760-761. Should these developments lead to reconsideration of the territoriality presumption?

Should contemporary choice-of-law rules be applied to determine the presumptive reach of federal legislation?

(c) Congress's contemporary concern with international events. Congress is often intensely concerned with events occurring outside the United States. Indeed, because of the interdependent character of the global economy and security environment, it is often difficult to regulate domestic matters meaningfully without taking into account matters abroad. Given that, is it wise to adopt a rule that presumes flatly that Congress cares only about domestic conditions? Why not look more carefully at the particular legislation at issue in a particular case — its language, legislative history, and purposes — to see what sort of territorial or extraterritorial reach Congress likely intended? How would *American Banana* and *Aramco* have been decided under such an approach?

(d) Prevention of conflicts with foreign laws. Is it in fact correct, as *Aramco* said, that the territoriality presumption prevents conflicts between U.S. and foreign law? If so, is that a sufficiently important goal to warrant ignoring other U.S. interests?

First, does the territoriality presumption not undervalue potential U.S. interests? For the reasons noted above, Congress frequently does wish to deal with events and actions outside U.S. territory, and its laws will therefore frequently come into conflict with foreign laws. Doesn't the territoriality presumption automatically resolve all such potential conflicts against U.S. interests? Is that appropriate?

Second, in many cases, an extraterritorial application of U.S. law will not conflict with foreign law. For example, in *American Banana,* the Sherman Act had been applied to the conduct of Costa Rica's courts and militia presumably would have conflicted with Costa Rican law. But would there have been a conflict if the Sherman Act had been applied to the defendant's private price-fixing agreements? In *Aramco,* for example, Saudi law was said to forbid discrimination on the basis of national origin. Does not the territoriality presumption sweep too broadly by preventing "false conflicts" between U.S. and foreign law in cases where both laws would require the same result? As *Lauritzen* suggests, a choice-of-law analysis could specifically inquire into the existence of a conflict between U.S. and foreign law.

Third, does a territoriality presumption perform well in preventing conflicts between U.S. and foreign law? Much modern commercial and other conduct has connections with multiple states, and a "territoriality" rule might permit each state effectively to regulate the entire course of conduct through one connection with its territory. *See Restatement (Third) Foreign Relations Law* §402(1)(a) (1987); Appendix AA.

4. *Correctness* of American Banana. Was *American Banana* correctly decided? The Sherman Act was made applicable to "every contract . . . in restraint of trade or commerce . . . with foreign nations." 26 Stat. 209 (1890). Even accepting the territoriality presumption, doesn't this jurisdictional grant plainly apply to a conspiracy orchestrated from the United States and to contracts by which the defendant allegedly fixed prices of bananas exported to the United States? Doesn't the statutory reference to trade "with foreign nations" apply to sales of Costa Rican bananas to persons in the United States, or to persons intending to distribute the bananas in the United States? Further, why wouldn't the nationality principle or effects doctrine have provided a basis for applying the Sherman Act extraterritorially in *American Banana*?

What would the Sherman Act have had to say to satisfy Justice Holmes? What about: "Every contract, wherever in the world it is made or performed, in restraint of trade or commerce with foreign nations"? Did Costa Rica have any "interest" in the outcome of the *American Banana* dispute? What might that interest have been? How would one go about identifying such an interest? Suppose that the dispute had not involved any acts by purported Costa Rican government authorities, but only private agreements and conduct.

Would Costa Rica have had any interest in the case? What relevance did, and should, Costa Rican interests have to the interpretation of the Sherman Act?

5. *Correctness of* **Aramco.** Was *Aramco* correctly decided? In Chief Justice Rehnquist's view, Title VII did not contain sufficient evidence of Congress's intention to authorize extraterritorial application of U.S. law. Note that there is substantial evidence that Title VII *was* meant to apply extraterritorially. Consider Title VII's jurisdictional grant, which applied the Act to all racial discrimination by any employer "engaged in an industry" affecting commerce "among the several states . . . or between a State and any place outside thereof." Did not Aramco plainly fall within this definition of "employer"? Moreover, the Act's "alien exclusion" provided that "[Title VII] shall not apply to an employer with respect to the employment of aliens outside any State," and the Act's legislative history (not addressed by the Court) explained that "the intent of [this] exemption is to remove conflicts of law which might otherwise exist between the United States and a foreign nation in the employment of aliens outside the United States by an American enterprise." H.R. Rep. No. 570, 88th Cong., 1st Sess. 4 (1963). Doesn't this plainly overcome *any* territoriality "presumption"?

6. *Meaning of territoriality presumption.* What exactly does the territoriality presumption mean? Compare the differing views adopted by the majority and dissenting opinions in *Aramco.* Is the territoriality presumption a "strong" or a "weak" presumption? Must a statute expressly apply outside U.S. territory? Must the statement be in statutory text, or will legislative history suffice? Does *Aramco* hold that a negative implication can never overcome the territoriality presumption? If there *is* to be a territoriality presumption, is Justice Rehnquist's or Justice Marshall's view of the presumption correct? *Compare Benz v. Compania Naviera Hidalgo, SA,* 353 U.S. 138, 147 (1957) ("affirmative intention of the Congress clearly expressed") *with New York Central R. Co. v. Chisholm,* 268 U.S. 29, 31 (1925) ("words which definitely disclose an intention to give [U.S. law] extraterritorial effect").

7. *Relevance of statute's application to "foreign commerce."* As *Aramco* notes, Title VII and many other federal statutes apply to conduct in or affecting "foreign commerce." The Court has sometimes concluded that such statutory language permits the extraterritorial application of the relevant federal law. *E.g., Steele v. Bulova Watch Co.,* 344 U.S. 280 (1952). It has also concluded that such "boilerplate language" does not "speak directly" to the issue of extraterritorial application. *Aramco, supra; New York R. Co. v. Chisholm,* 268 U.S. 29 (1925). When Congress makes federal law applicable to any conduct in, or affecting, U.S. foreign commerce, why *doesn't* this directly address the geographic reach of the legislation?

8. *Alternatives to the territoriality presumption.* Given the erosion of strict notions of territoriality, is *Aramco*'s strict territoriality presumption warranted? Would it be more appropriate for the Court to adopt a principle of statutory construction that replicates contemporary international law limits on the extraterritorial application of U.S. law? For example, would it not be more appropriate to adopt an "international law" presumption, which would call for application of federal law in circumstances where §403 of the *Restatement (Third) Foreign Relations Law* would permit? Alternatively, why should there not be a "choice of law" presumption, which would permit application of federal law in cases where the "most significant relationship" test of the *Restatement (Second) Conflict of Laws* would permit? Or, why not adopt a "constitutional limits" presumption, which would interpret federal statutes as applicable to the limits permitted by the Constitution? Would these alternatives not better serve the asserted purposes of ascertaining congressional intent and fulfilling the goals of the territoriality doctrine? What interests would each presumption further? What interests would each hinder?

9. *Departures from the territoriality presumption*—Lauritzen's "*international law*" *presumption*. Consider the broad language of the Jones Act—its "literal catholicity." Why wasn't the Act applicable to the defendant's conduct in *Lauritzen*? Why shouldn't U.S. courts *always* apply federal law (unless Congress specifically provides otherwise)? Consider *Lauritzen*'s explanation:

> If, to serve some immediate interest, the courts of each were to exploit every such contact to the limit of its power, it is not difficult to see that a multiplicity of conflicting and overlapping burdens would blight international carriage by sea. Hence, courts of this and other commercial nations have generally deferred to a non-national or international maritime law of impressive maturity and universality. It has the force of law, not from extraterritorial reach of national laws, nor from abdication of its sovereign powers by any nation, but from acceptance by common consent of civilized communities of rules designed to foster amicable and workable commercial relations.

Compare this to Joseph Story's explanations for international law limits on national legislative jurisdiction. *See supra* pp. 648-649.

What was the role of the territoriality presumption in *Lauritzen*? Why was the case not resolved simply on the traditional grounds—stated in *American Banana*—that the allegedly wrongful conduct occurred beyond U.S. territory and waters? Instead of applying the territoriality presumption, what canon of statutory construction did *Lauritzen* adopt?

Like *American Banana*, *Lauritzen* looks to principles of international law in defining the reach of federal statutes. What explains the material differences between *American Banana*'s territoriality presumption and *Lauritzen*'s analysis? Consider also the Supreme Court's varying presumptions in the context of the federal antitrust laws, in *Hartford Fire Insurance Co. v. California*, 509 U.S. 764 (1993) and *F. Hoffmann-LaRoche, Ltd. v. Empagran, SA*, 542 U.S. 155 (2004), both excerpted and discussed below, *infra* pp. 691-709.

10. *Departures from the territoriality presumption*—*the effects test*. As described below, *infra* pp. 672-709, the Court subsequently overruled *American Banana* and applied the antitrust laws to conduct occurring outside the United States. *E.g., Continental Ore Co. v. Union Carbide & Carbon Corp.*, 370 U.S. 690, 705 (1962); *W.S. Kirkpatrick v. Environmental Tectonics Corp.*, 493 U.S. 400 (1990). Instead of the historic territoriality doctrine, the antitrust laws were interpreted in light of the "effects test" articulated in *United States v. Alcoa*, 148 F.2d 416 (2d Cir. 1945), excerpted below. And, in *Hartford Fire Insurance Co. v. California*, 509 U.S. 764 (1993), also excerpted below, the Court did not apply a territoriality presumption to the federal antitrust laws—notwithstanding its decision only two years earlier in *Aramco*. Instead, the Court applied *Alcoa*'s effects test, which permitted application of the antitrust laws to "foreign conduct that was meant to produce and did in fact produce some substantial effect in the United States." 509 U.S. at 795, n.21.

11. *Departures from the territoriality presumption*—*a nationality presumption*. Consider the identity of the parties in *American Banana*, *Lauritzen*, and *Aramco*. Two of these cases (*American Banana* and *Aramco*) involved claims by American plaintiffs (citizens or companies) against American companies. The third (*Lauritzen*) involved claims by a Danish plaintiff against a Danish vessel. Putting doctrine to one side, in which set of circumstances do you believe that the U.S. Government has a greater interest?

Recall the discussion in *Blackmer v. United States*, *supra* at 109-113, about a nation's authority to exercise judicial jurisdiction over its citizens even when they are located abroad. Under *Blackmer*'s logic, doesn't the United States also have a compelling interest in setting forth the rules under which those citizens (or companies organized under its laws) will be liable? If companies organized under the laws of the several states can avoid

U.S. legislative jurisdiction with respect to their activities abroad, doesn't that draw a roadmap for them to evade the reach of U.S. law? Perhaps the reason is that a court could not realistically interpret general statutory language to apply to domestic but not foreign defendants. The Court in *Aramco* appeared troubled by the notion that any extraterritorial application of Title VII would extend equally to U.S. *and foreign* employers.

> We see no way of distinguishing in [Title VII's] application between United States employers and foreign employers. . . . Without clearer evidence of congressional intent to do so than is contained in the alien-exemption clause, we are unwilling to ascribe to that body a policy which would raise difficult issues of international law by imposing this country's employment-discrimination regime upon foreign corporations operating in foreign commerce.

Is this assumption correct? Could the Court not apply a "nationality presumption," extending U.S. laws extraterritorially to U.S. parties' conduct?

Consider the consequences of a nationality presumption. U.S. companies operating outside the United States would be subject to two sets of laws — U.S. and foreign. Their foreign competitors would generally not be subject to U.S. law. Would this be a satisfactory state of affairs? Is it likely what Congress intended?

12. Departures from the territoriality presumption — a "constitutional limits" presumption. Why shouldn't U.S. courts assume that Congress intends federal legislation to extend to the full limits permitted by the U.S. Constitution? (Those limits are discussed in detail above, *supra* pp. 606-644.) Recall that, in the personal jurisdiction context, many federal and state long-arm statutes have been interpreted as extending to the limits of the Constitution. *See supra* pp. 82-83. Shouldn't the same result extend to legislative jurisdiction? Note also that many federal grants of legislative jurisdiction expressly extend to "foreign commerce" — just as Article I, §8's grant of legislative power does.

Virtually no courts have adopted any such "constitutional limits" presumption. *But see Arnett v. Thompson*, 433 S.W.2d 109, 113 (Ky. 1968). Commentators have generally rejected the suggestion. *E.g.*, Kramer, *Rethinking Choice of Law*, 90 Colum. L. Rev. 277, 295-296 (1990). What difficulties would arise from a "constitutional limits" presumption? Consider:

> [This approach] would extend U.S. law extraterritorially without regard to conflicts with foreign law or policies and would frequently place the United States in violation of contemporary principles of public international law. The diplomatic protests and other frictions resulting from existing U.S. practice would be multiplied, leading to just the "international complications" that even *Alcoa's* expansive effects doctrine sought to avoid. Moreover, in many cases no real U.S. interests would be served by the attempted regulation of distant activities only tenuously connected to this country. Born, *A Reappraisal of the Extraterritorial Reach of U.S. Law*, 24 Law & Pol'y Int'l Bus. 1, 80 (1992).

Is this persuasive?

13. Choosing between various "presumptions" regarding the extraterritorial application of U.S. statutes. The Supreme Court has not acknowledged that it has adopted the varying "presumptions" regarding the extraterritorial reach of different U.S. statutes in cases like *American Banana, Lauritzen,* and *Aramco.* That is, of course, unsatisfying. The result is confusion for private parties and lower courts. *E.g., In re Simon*, 153 F.3d 991 (9th Cir. 1998) (relying on two competing "presumptions" to override *Aramco* "presumption"); *Kollias v. D & G Marine Maintenance*, 29 F.3d 67 (2d Cir. 1994) (rejecting arguments that *Aramco's* presumption should not apply and that *Lauritzen* presumption should); *Environmental Defense Fund, Inc. v. Massey*, 986 F.2d 528, 531 (D.C. Cir. 1993) (questioning applicability of *Aramco* where there are "adverse effects within the United States"); *Tamari v. Bache & Co. (Lebanon)*, 730 F.2d 1103, 1107 n.11 (7th Cir. 1984) ("Reliance on this [territoriality] presumption is misplaced . . . when the conduct under scrutiny has not occurred wholly outside the United States, or . . . could otherwise affect domestic conditions.").

However, the Supreme Court's recent opinion in *Morrison v. Australia National Bank Ltd.* does contain strong language suggesting that the Court is moving toward universal application of a presumption against extraterritoriality along the lines set forth in *Aramco*:

> The results of judicial-speculation-made law — divining what Congress would have wanted if it had thought of the situation before the Court — demonstrate the wisdom of the presumption against extraterritoriality. Rather than guess anew in each case, *we apply the presumption in all cases*, preserving a stable background against which Congress can legislative with predictable effects. 130 S. Ct. 2069 at para. 8.

While this language is broad, its scope is not entirely clear. The Court made this statement following a reaffirmation of the rule from *Aramco* and an extensive critique of lower court caselaw that had considered the extraterritorial effect of federal securities laws. Thus, it is unclear whether the phrase "in all cases" means "all cases arising under federal securities laws" or instead "all cases arising under federal statutes."

Is the territoriality presumption used for certain types of statutes (*e.g.*, "local" ones), while an international presumption is used for other types? *See* Turley, *"When in Rome": Multinational Misconduct and the Presumption Against Extraterritoriality*, 84 Nw. U. L. Rev. 598 (1990). As discussed below, modern American conflict of law theory focuses on the reasons that a particular statute was enacted. This inquiry requires ascertaining the domestic reasons for a legislature's enactment of a statute, and then determining whether those reasons would apply in a particular multi-state context. *See infra* pp. 749-750. Consider the "purposes" of the Sherman Act, the Jones Act, and Title VII. Do these purposes suggest differing extraterritorial reaches? Are there material differences in the language used to define the jurisdictional reach of the various statutes considered by the Court? Compare the jurisdictional grants in the Sherman Act, Title VII, and the Jones Act.

Should the territoriality presumption be formulated differently with respect to federal criminal laws than civil legislation? *Compare United States v. Corey*, 232 F.3d 1166 (9th Cir. 2000) (applying federal criminal law extraterritorially); *United States v. Felix-Gutierrez*, 940 F.2d 1200 (9th Cir. 1991) (same) *with United States v. Gatlin*, 216 F.3d 207 (2d Cir. 2000) (declining to give extraterritorial effect to federal criminal statute). *Cf. Small v. United States*, 544 U.S. 385 (2005) (relying on *Aramco* by analogy to hold that criminal statute prohibiting felon possession of firearm did not extend to foreign convictions).

If the Supreme Court were squarely to confront the question, should it apply a single analytic framework to all federal statutes or vary the analytic framework with the statute at issue?

14. *Judicial competence to determine extraterritorial reach of federal legislation.* Are courts capable of determining the extraterritorial reach of federal legislation? Consider the comments of Justice Scalia in a recent case concerning the application of U.S. disabilities legislation to foreign-flagged ships operating in U.S. waters: "The fine-tuning of legislation . . . would be better left to Congress. To attempt it through the process of case-by-case adjudication is a recipe for endless litigation and confusion. . . . If Congress desires to impose this time-consuming and intricate process, it is certainly able to do so — though I think it would likely prefer some more manageable solution." *Spector v. Norwegian Cruise Lines Ltd.*, 545 U.S. 119, 158 (2005) (Scalia, J., dissenting). More recently, he has described the process of trying to discern whether Congress intended to give a statute extraterritorial effect as "judicial speculation made law." *Morrison v. Australia National Bank Ltd.*, 130 S. Ct. at 2881. If Congress does not address, or clearly address, the extraterritorial reach of federal legislation, what alternative is there to judicial resolution of the issue? *See* Symeonides, *Cruising in American Waters:* Spector, *Maritime Conflicts and Choice of Law*, 37 J. Mar. L. & Com 491 (2006).

15. *Congressional overruling of* Aramco *result.* Following the Supreme Court's decision, Congress promptly overturned the result in *Aramco*. The Civil Rights Act of 1991, 105 Stat. 1077, added a new §2000e(f), which provided: "With respect to employment in a foreign country, such term [*i.e.*, employee] includes an individual who is a citizen of the United States." In addition, Title VII was amended to include the following provisions:

> (b) It shall not be unlawful under §703 or 704 for an employer (or a corporation controlled by an employer) . . . to take any action otherwise prohibited by such section, with respect to an employee in a workplace in a foreign country if compliance with such section would cause such employer (or such corporation) . . . to violate the law of the foreign country in which such workplace is located.
>
> (c)(1) If an employer controls a corporation whose place of incorporation is a foreign country, any practice prohibited by §703 or 704 engaged in by such corporation shall be presumed to be engaged in by such employer.
>
> (c)(2) Sections 703 and 704 shall not apply with respect to the foreign operations of an employer that is a foreign person not controlled by an American employer.

How do these amendments deal with situations where foreign law requires a U.S. company to discriminate in violation of Title VII? What effect do the amendments have on non-U.S. subsidiaries of U.S. companies? For an illustrative discussion of post-*Aramco* case law, *see Shekoyan v. Sibley Int'l*, 409 F.3d 414 (D.C. Cir. 2005).

16. *Congressional limits on extraterritorial reach of federal legislation.* Despite the "literal catholicity" of many federal statutes, Congress sometimes speaks clearly. For example, recent amendments to the Age Discrimination in Employment Act make clear its extraterritorial reach — to cover U.S. citizens working for American companies abroad but not to cover foreign citizens working abroad. *See, e.g., Reyes-Gaona v. North Carolina Growers Ass'n*, 250 F.3d 861 (4th Cir. 2001); *Denty v. SmithKline Beecham Corp.*, 109 F.3d 147 (3d Cir. 1997); *Hu v. Skadden, Arps, Slate, Meagher & Flom LLP*, 76 F. Supp. 2d 476 (S.D.N.Y. 1999). Similarly, Congress has exempted foreign countries from the application of certain overtime rules of the Fair Labor Standards Act. *See Smith v. Raytheon Co.*, 297 F. Supp. 2d 399 (D. Mass. 2004). To paraphrase Judge Wilkinson, such examples "demonstrate[] that 'when it desires to do so, Congress knows how to' expand 'the jurisdictional reach of a statute.'" *Reyes-Ganoa*, 250 F.3d at 865. What relevance, if any, do such legislative actions have for assessing the territoriality and international law presumptions?

3. Contemporary Approach to Extraterritorial Application of Federal Antitrust Statutes

U.S. courts have considered the extraterritorial reach of a wide range of federal legislation.[61] The extraterritorial reach of the U.S. antitrust laws has received particular

---

61. For a recent discussion of these issues in a case involving extraterritorial application of the Lanham Act, *see McBee v. Delica Co., Ltd.*, 417 F.3d 107 (1st Cir. 2005).

attention, both from U.S. courts and commentators.[62] It has also provoked numerous diplomatic disputes between the United States and foreign states. Because of its practical and academic significance, we examine the subject in detail below.

a. Overview of U.S. Antitrust Laws. Broadly speaking, the U.S. "antitrust laws" include a number of different federal and state laws regulating the methods by which business enterprises compete with one another and deal with their customers, suppliers, and others. These laws range from statutes limiting the circumstances in which sellers can charge different prices for the same products[63] to provisions requiring advance notice to the federal government of certain mergers or acquisitions.[64]

The most commonly invoked provisions of the U.S. antitrust laws are also the provisions that arise most often in the international context. First, §1 of the Sherman Act declares illegal "[e]very contract, combination . . . or conspiracy, in restraint of trade or commerce."[65] Second, §2 of the Sherman Act makes it a felony for any person "to monopolize, or combine or conspire . . . to monopolize any part of the trade or commerce" among the several states or with foreign nations.[66] Section 4 of the Clayton Act authorizes private individuals to bring actions in federal court for treble damages for injuries suffered as a result of violations of Sherman Act §1 or §2,[67] while §16 of the Clayton Act permits private parties to seek injunctive relief.[68] Although provisions of the various antitrust statutes contain language making those laws applicable to foreign commerce,[69] the statutes are generally silent on the specific question of extraterritorial application.[70]

b. From *American Banana*'s Territoriality Presumption to *Alcoa*'s Effects/Intent Test. *American Banana Company v. United Fruit Company*[71] was the Supreme Court's first consideration of the Sherman Act in an international dispute. As described above, *American Banana* presented the question whether the Sherman Act reached allegedly anti-competitive acts performed in Central America by a U.S. company. The Act was, by its terms, applicable to all contracts in restraint of commerce "with foreign nations."[72] Nonetheless, Justice Holmes held that the antitrust laws did not reach beyond U.S. borders, declaring that "in case of doubt as to a construction of any statute [it should be construed] as intended to be confined in its operation and effect to the territorial limits

---

62. *See, e.g.,* S. Waller, *Antitrust and American Business Abroad* (3d ed. 1997 & Cum. Supp.); 1 W. Fugate, *Foreign Commerce and The Antitrust Laws* (5th ed. 1996); Basedow, *International Antitrust: From Extraterritorial Application to Harmonization,* 60 La. L. Rev. 1037 (2000); Buxbaum, *Territory, Territoriality and the Resolution of Jurisdictional Conflict,* 57 Am. J. Comp. L. 631 (2009); Delrahim, *Drawing the Boundaries of the Sherman Act: Recent Developments in the Application of the Antitrust Laws to Foreign Conduct,* 61 N.Y.U. Ann. Surv. Am. L. 415 (2005); Fox, *Extraterritoriality, Antitrust, and the New Restatement: Is "Reasonableness" the Answer?,* 19 N.Y.U. J. Int'l L. & Pol. 565 (1987); Griffin, *Extraterritoriality in U.S. and EU Antitrust Enforcement,* 67 Antitrust L.J. 159 (1999); Connor & Bush, *How to Block Cartel Formation and Price Fixing: Using Extraterritorial Application of the Antitrust Laws as a Deterrence Mechanism,* 112 Penn. St. L. Rev. 813 (2008).

63. Robinson-Patman Anti-Discrimination Act, 15 U.S.C. §13.

64. Hart-Scott-Rodino Antitrust Improvements Act, 15 U.S.C. §§15c-15h, 18a, 66.

65. 15 U.S.C. §1.

66. 15 U.S.C. §2.

67. 15 U.S.C. §15(a).

68. 15 U.S.C. §26.

69. *See, e.g.,* 15 U.S.C. §1 ("[e]very contract, combination . . . or conspiracy in restraint of trade or commerce . . . *with foreign nations*") (emphasis added); 15 U.S.C. §2 ("[e]very person who shall monopolize, or attempt to monopolize . . . any part of trade or commerce . . . *with foreign nations*") (emphasis added).

70. The provision of the antitrust laws that most clearly addresses the subject of extraterritorial application is the Foreign Trade Antitrust Improvements Act, discussed *infra* pp. 697-703.

71. 213 U.S. 347 (1909) (excerpted above at pp. 651-653).

72. 26 Stat. 209 (1890).

over which the lawmaker has general and legitimate power."[73] Although the Sherman Act was couched in broad language, this did not overcome the territoriality presumption.[74]

During the 1920s and 1930s, *American Banana* was eroded in a series of international antitrust decisions that adopted increasingly expansive views of the Sherman Act's jurisdictional reach.[75] This culminated in the 1945 decision in *United States v. Aluminum Co. of America (Alcoa)*,[76] where Judge Learned Hand adopted a fundamentally new approach to the extraterritorial reach of the U.S. antitrust laws. In an opinion excerpted below, he rejected any notion of strict territoriality and instead adopted an expansive formulation of the "effects doctrine."[77]

Alcoa's effects test rapidly gained wide acceptance in the United States.[78] Relying on it, U.S. courts and government agencies frequently applied the U.S. antitrust laws to conduct occurring partially or entirely abroad.[79] Thus, major governmental actions involving the extraterritorial application of the U.S. antitrust laws were brought against the international oil, shipping, paper, synthetic fiber, watch-making, and dyestuff industries.[80]

Although subsequent decisions have reformulated *Alcoa*'s extraterritoriality standards, often very significantly, the decision's basic effects test remains the starting-point for contemporary analysis. *Industrial Investment Development Corp. v. Mitsui & Co.*, excerpted below, illustrates how some U.S. courts have applied *Alcoa*'s effects test.

UNITED STATES v. ALUMINUM COMPANY OF AMERICA ("ALCOA")
148 F.2d 416 (2d Cir. 1945)

LEARNED HAND, CIRCUIT JUDGE. [The U.S. Government filed an antitrust complaint against Alcoa, a U.S. corporation, and Aluminum, Limited ("Limited"), a Canadian company that had acquired Alcoa's properties outside the United States. Limited had been a division of Alcoa in the past and, at the time of the government's suit, continued to be controlled by Alcoa's shareholders. The government's complaint alleged that Alcoa and Limited had unlawfully conspired to restrain both interstate and international production and sale of aluminum ingot. The government's suit sought to prohibit the participation of Alcoa and Limited in an international cartel involving several major European aluminum companies. The district court dismissed on jurisdictional grounds, and the Second Circuit was referred the case (because the Supreme Court could not muster a

73. 213 U.S. at 357. The Court went on to say "'All legislation is prima facie territorial'" (quoting *Ex parte Blain*, 27 N.J. 499; *People v. Merrill*, 2 Parker, Crim. Rep. 590, 596).
74. 213 U.S. at 357. "In the case of the present statute the improbability of the United States attempting to make acts done in Panama or Costa Rica criminal is obvious."
75. *United States v. Pacific & Arctic Railway & Navigation Co.*, 228 U.S. 87 (1913); *Thomsen v. Cayser*, 243 U.S. 66 (1917); *United States v. Sisal Sales Corp.*, 274 U.S. 268 (1927).
76. 148 F.2d 416 (2d Cir. 1945).
77. 148 F.2d at 443-444.
78. *Zenith Radio Corp. v. Hazeltine Research, Inc.*, 395 U.S. 100 (1969); *Continental Ore Co. v. Union Carbide & Carbon Corp.*, 370 U.S. 690 (1962); *Restatement (Second) Foreign Relations Law* §18 (1965) (relying on *Alcoa* to justify effects test as legitimate basis for legislative jurisdiction); U.S. Department of Justice, *Antitrust Guide for International Operations* 6-7 (1977).
79. *E.g., United States v. General Dyestuff Corp.*, 57 F. Supp. 642 (S.D.N.Y. 1944); *United States v. American Bosch Corp.*, 1940-1943 (CCH) Trade Cas. ¶56,253 (S.D.N.Y. 1942); *United States v. Alba Pharmaceutical Co., Inc.*, 1940-1943 (CCH) Trade Cas. ¶56,150 (S.D.N.Y. 1941).
80. *In re Grand Jury Investigation of the Shipping Indus.*, 186 F. Supp. 298 (D.D.C. 1960); *United States v. The Watchmakers of Switzerland Information Center*, 133 F. Supp. 40 (S.D.N.Y. 1955); *United States v. Imperial Chem. Indus.*, 105 F. Supp. 215 (S.D.N.Y. 1952); *In re Investigation of World Arrangements with Relation to the Prod., Ref., Transp. & Distrib. of Petroleum*, 13 F.R.D. 280 (D.D.C. 1952); *United States v. General Elec. Co.*, 80 F. Supp. 989 (S.D.N.Y. 1948); *In re Grand Jury Subpoenas Duces Tecum Addressed to Canadian Int'l Paper Co.*, 72 F. Supp. 1013 (S.D.N.Y. 1947).

quorum). A principal issue on appeal was whether Limited's participation in an "alliance" with a number of foreign aluminum producers was a violation of §1 of the Sherman Act. The Second Circuit held that it was, reasoning as follows:]

Whether Limited itself violated [§1 of the Sherman Act] depends upon the character of the "Alliance." It was a Swiss corporation, created in pursuance of an agreement . . . the signatories of which were a French corporation, two German, one Swiss, a British, and Limited. The original agreement, or "cartel," provided for the formation of a corporation in Switzerland which should issue shares, to be taken up by the signatories. This corporation was from time to time to fix a quota of production for each share, and each shareholder was to be limited to the quantity measured by the number of shares it held, but was free to sell at any price it chose. The corporation fixed a price every year at which it would take off any shareholder's hands any part of its quota which it did not sell. No shareholder was to "buy, borrow, fabricate, or sell" aluminum produced by anyone not a shareholder except with the consent of the board of governors, but that must not be "unreasonably withheld" . . . . [U]ntil 1936, when the new arrangement was made, imports into the United States were not included in the quota.

The agreement of 1936 abandoned the system of unconditional quotas, and substituted a system of royalties. Each shareholder was to have a fixed free quota for every share it held, but as its production exceeded the sum of its quotas, it was to pay a royalty, graduated progressively in proportion to the excess; and these royalties the "Alliance" divided among the shareholders in proportion to their shares. . . . Although this agreement, like its predecessor, was silent as to imports into the United States, when that question arose during its preparation, as it did, all the shareholders agreed that such quotas should be included in the quotas. . . .

Did either the agreement of 1931 or that of 1936 violate §1 of the Act? The answer does not depend upon whether we shall recognize as a source of liability a liability imposed by another state. On the contrary, we are concerned only with whether Congress chose to attach liability to the conduct outside the United States of persons not in allegiance to it. That being so, the only question open is whether Congress intended to impose the liability, and whether our own Constitution permitted it to do so: as a court of the United States, we cannot look beyond our own law. Nevertheless, it is quite true that we are not to read general words, such as those in this Act, without regard to the limitations customarily observed by nations upon the exercise of their powers; limitations which generally correspond to those fixed by the "Conflict of Laws." We should not impute to Congress an intent to punish all whom its courts can catch, for conduct which has no consequences within the United States. *American Banana Co. v. United Fruit Co.,* [excerpted above at pp. 651-653]; *Blackmer v. United States,* [excerpted above at pp. 109-110]. On the other hand, it is settled law — as Limited itself agrees — that any state may impose liabilities, even upon persons not within its allegiance, for conduct outside its borders that has consequences within its borders which the state reprehends; and these liabilities other states will ordinarily recognize. *Stassheim v. Daily,* 221 U.S. 280, 284 (1911); *Lamar v. United States,* 240 U.S. 60, 65 (1916); *Restatement (First) Conflict of Laws* §65 [excerpted in Appendix X; stating effects doctrine as basis for legislative jurisdiction]. It may be argued that this Act extends further. Two situations are possible. There may be agreements made beyond our borders not intended to affect imports, which do affect them, or which affect exports. Almost any limitation of the supply of goods in Europe, for example, or in South America, may have repercussions in the United States if there is trade between the two. Yet when one considers the international complications likely to arise from an effort in this country to treat such agreements as unlawful, it is safe to assume that Congress certainly did not intend the Act to cover them. Such agreements may on the other hand intend to include imports into the

United States, and yet it may appear that they have had no effect upon them. That situation might be thought to fall within the doctrine that intent may be a substitute for performance in the case of a contract made within the United States; or it might be thought to fall within the doctrine that a statute should not be interpreted to cover acts abroad which have no consequence here. We shall not choose between these alternatives; but for argument we shall assume that the Act does not cover agreements, even though intended to affect imports or exports, unless its performance is shown actually to have had some effect upon them. Where both conditions are satisfied, the situation certainly falls within such decisions as *United States v. Pacific & Arctic R. & Nav. Co.,* 228 U.S. 87 (1913); *Thomsen v. Cayser,* 243 U.S. 66 (1917); and *United States v. Sisal Sales Corp.* 274 U.S. 268 (1927). . . . It is true that in those cases the persons held liable had sent agents into the United States to perform part of the agreement; but an agent is merely an animate means of executing his principal's purposes, and, for the purposes of this case, he does not differ from an inanimate means; besides, only human agents can import and sell ingot.

Both agreements would clearly have been unlawful, had they been made within the United States; and it follows from what we have just said that both were unlawful, though made abroad, if they were intended to affect imports and did affect them. [The court held that the 1936 agreement was intended to affect U.S. imports and that, absent rebuttal by Limited, would be presumed to have had such an effect.]

INDUSTRIAL INVESTMENT DEVELOPMENT CORP. v. MITSUI & CO.
671 F.2d 876 (5th Cir. 1982)

REAVLEY, CIRCUIT JUDGE. This is an antitrust suit. [The district court granted summary judgment on the ground] that defendants' conduct is beyond the extraterritorial scope of the antitrust laws. . . . [We reverse.]

The plaintiffs are an American corporation, Industrial Investment Development Corporation ("Industrial Investment"), and its two Hong Kong subsidiaries, Indonesia Industrial Investment Corporation, Ltd. ("Indonesia Industrial") and Forest Products Corporation, Ltd. ("FPC"). The defendants-appellees are a Japanese corporation, Mitsui & Co., Ltd. ("Mitsui-Japan") and its American subsidiary, Mitsui & Co. (U.S.A.), Inc. ("Mitsui-U.S.A."). A third defendant is an Indonesian corporation, P.T. Telaga Mas Kalimantan Company, Ltd. ("Telaga Mas"), which . . . has not appeared. . . .

Plaintiffs claim that the three defendants conspired to keep plaintiffs out of the business of harvesting trees in East Kalimantan (Borneo), Indonesia and exporting logs and lumber from Indonesia to the United States and other countries. Plaintiffs allege that defendants' conspiracy was intended to and did unreasonably restrain and monopolize the foreign commerce of the United States, in violation of §§1 and 2 of the Sherman Act, 15 U.S.C. §§1, 2. . . . A restraint that directly or substantially affects the flow of commerce into or out of the United States is within the scope of the Sherman Act. *See Continental Ore Co. v. Union Carbide & Carbon Corp.* [370 U.S. 690 (1962)]; *United States v. Aluminum Co. of America,* ("*Alcoa*"). A review of the summary judgment submissions and evidence convinces us that defendants have not demonstrated that there is no genuine issue concerning the existence of a direct or substantial effect on United States foreign commerce.

In their briefs prior to the first appeal, defendants' attack on the existence of an effect on United States commerce was only an attack on plaintiffs' pleadings. Defendants placed their own characterization on the complaint and declared that the case involved only the tree-cutting business in Indonesia; thus, they concluded, their conduct had no effect on United States commerce. Plaintiffs had alleged, however, that Mitsui-U.S.A., an American corporation which imports a sizeable amount of lumber or lumber products into the

United States, had conspired to keep them out of the business of harvesting trees and exporting logs and lumber from Indonesia to the United States. There was ample evidence in the record to show that Mitsui-U.S.A. had appropriated much of the business that plaintiffs claim they would have derived from the forestry concession: Mitsui-U.S.A. was purchasing the bulk of the logs from the concession and selling them for export to Mitsui-Japan at a substantial profit.

The competition between two American importers to obtain a source of supply on foreign territory affects the foreign commerce of the United States. *Timberlane Lumber Co. v. Bank of America,* 549 F.2d 597, 604-05, 615 (9th Cir. 1976). Mitsui-Japan was allegedly a co-conspirator in this attempt to restrain competition between two American competitors. Thus, defendants' attack on the pleadings did not make it "appear[] beyond doubt that the plaintiff [could] prove no set of facts in support of his claim which would entitle him to relief." *Conley v. Gibson,* 355 U.S. 41, 45-46 (1957) . . .

After we reversed the district court's first grant of summary judgment, the defendants shifted to a factual attack by arguing that the single, undisputed fact that Mitsui-Japan exported all of the lumber, purchased from Mitsui-U.S.A. in Indonesia, to Japan demonstrated that there was no genuine issue concerning an effect on United States commerce. Mitsui-Japan argued — and this is the argument it advances most strenuously in this court — that when a Japanese business competes with an American business in Indonesia and exports the fruits of that competition solely to Japan, any effect on United States commerce is purely incidental, indirect, and unintentional. Even if defendants' argument is correct — an issue we do not reach — it ignores the allegations in this case. Here, an American corporation with an interest in protection of its import business has allegedly conspired to eliminate a potential American competitor in both the business of purchasing logs in Indonesia and the business of importing lumber and lumber products into the United States.

Defendants' showing did not demonstrate that there was no genuine fact issue for the simple reason that defendants' showing was not responsive to plaintiffs' allegations. That one co-conspirator — Mitsui-Japan — followed a course of business action that, in isolation, might not be considered a violation of the United States antitrust laws does not demonstrate either that the effect of the conspiracy as between the American competitors is not an effect on United States commerce or that the intent of the conspiracy was not to restrain competition between the American competitors. "[S]ummary procedures should be used sparingly in complex antitrust litigation where motive and intent play leading roles [and] the proof is largely in the hands of the alleged conspirators. . . ." *Poller v. CBS,* 368 U.S. 464, 473 (1962). Summary judgment is even less appropriate here, where there is ample evidence of a conspiracy to keep plaintiffs from becoming a competitor, and plaintiffs have not had an opportunity to depose one of the conspirators on the effect and intent of their efforts.

Notes on Alcoa *and* Mitsui

1. Alcoa*'s reliance on international law. In important respects, *Alcoa*'s analysis paralleled that in *American Banana.* In both cases, the courts concluded that the Sherman Act's language did not provide adequate guidance as to the statute's extraterritorial application. In both cases, the courts then looked to international law and choice-of-law principles — or, in Learned Hand's eclectic formulation, to "the limitation customarily observed by nations upon the exercise of their powers . . . 'Conflict of Laws.'" This basic analysis parallels that in *Charming Betsy, Apollon, Blackmer,* and similar decisions. *See supra* pp. 18, 110-113.

2. *Content of international law in* Alcoa. Despite their similar approaches, the international law principles that *Alcoa* relied upon differed significantly from those invoked in *American Banana. American Banana* relied upon the "general and almost universal rule . . . that the character of an act as lawful or unlawful must be determined wholly by the law of the country where the act is done." Three decades later, however, *Alcoa* held that it was "settled law . . . that any state may impose liabilities . . . for conduct outside its borders that has consequences within its borders." Although *Alcoa* cited only *domestic* U.S. decisions, dealing with interstate matters, its holding reflected the development of international law limits on legislative jurisdiction, discussed above, *supra* pp. 589, 603. It also paralleled the evolution in international law limits on personal jurisdiction, and similar developments in American choice-of-law rules. *See supra* pp. 83-90 & *infra* pp. 738-742. In looking to the jurisdictional limits imposed by international law, should courts consider the law prevailing when a statute was enacted (1890, for the Sherman Act) or when the law is applied (1945, in *Alcoa*)?

  3. *Wisdom of **Alcoa**'s effects test.* Is *Alcoa*'s effects test wise? What interests does it advance — and what interests does it hinder? Recall the reasoning in Joseph Story's *Commentaries* and *Lauritzen,* emphasizing the importance of mutual forbearance, uniform results in different forums, and reciprocal tolerance in conflict of laws decisions. *See supra* pp. 648-650.

  Consider the following criticisms of the effects test:

- The effects test provides no meaningful constraint on the exercise of jurisdiction.
- The effects test is a one-way ratchet. Because the assertion is premised on an assumption about legislative intent, courts in a common law system are reluctant to take correct action once they have adopted an expansive interpretation of a statute.
- The effects test creates a slippery slope where increasingly indirect injuries can be analogized to prior cases in an attempt to establish the requisite effects.
- The effects test is inherently undemocratic because it subjects foreign parties to the regulation of laws even though those parties have no meaningful voice in the system regulating them.
- The effects test is diplomatically dangerous for it invites retaliatory assertions of legislative jurisdiction by foreign countries over U.S. companies.
- The effects test is unfair because it fails to provide parties adequate notice of when their conduct will be subject to regulation.
- The effects test is also unfair because it exposes companies to the risk of inconsistent regulation by different sovereigns.

See Parrish, *The Effects Test: Extraterritoriality's Fifth Business,* 61 Vand. L. Rev. 1455 (2008). Which, if any, of these criticisms is valid, in your view? Do those criticisms justify dismantling the effects test, or are they necessary evils outweighed by various benefits that come from greater regulation? If you believe that the effects test should be discarded, what should take its place?

  4. ***Alcoa**'s intent/effects test.* *Alcoa* held that conduct occurring outside the United States would be subject to the Sherman Act if two requirements were satisfied: (a) the conduct was intended to affect U.S. imports; and (b) the conduct actually had such an effect.

  (a) Alcoa's intent prong. There has been disagreement among lower courts about the meaning of *Alcoa*'s "intent" prong. Some courts simply omit the intent requirement, apparently adopting a pure effects test. *E.g., Sabre Shipping Corp. v. American President Lines,* 285 F. Supp. 949 (S.D.N.Y. 1968); *United States v. Imperial Chem. Indus.,* 100 F. Supp. 504 (S.D.N.Y. 1951). Other courts have required only proof of a general intent to affect U.S. commerce, *e.g., Zenith Radio Corp. v. Matsushita Elec. Indus. Co.,* 494 F. Supp. 1161 (E.D. Pa. 1980); *Fleishmann Distilling Corp. v. Distillers Co.,* 395 F. Supp. 221 (S.D.N.Y.

1975), while some courts apparently require a showing of specific intent, *e.g., United States v. General Elec. Co.*, 82 F. Supp. 753, 889-891 (D.N.J. 1949); *United States v. National Lead Co.*, 63 F. Supp. 513, 524-525 (S.D.N.Y. 1945), *aff'd*, 332 U.S. 319 (1947).

What is the purpose of *Alcoa*'s "intent" requirement? How does *Alcoa*'s intent prong compare to the Due Process Clause's "purposeful availment" requirement for judicial jurisdiction? Which of these various "intent" formulations is most desirable?

(b) Alcoa's effects prong—magnitude of effects. Most lower courts agree that extraterritorial application of the antitrust laws is inappropriate when effects within the United States are merely "speculative." *Montreal Trading v. Amax, Inc.*, 661 F.2d 864, 870 (10th Cir. 1981). Nonetheless, U.S. courts have over time applied a wide variety of formulations of the effects prong. *Compare Hartford Fire Insurance Co. v. California*, 509 U.S. 764 (1993) ("some substantial effect in the United States"); *U.S. v. Nippon Paper Industries Co., Ltd.*, 109 F.3d 1, 4 (1st Cir. 1997) ("intended and substantial effect"); *United States v. The Watchmakers of Switzerland Information Center*, 1963 Trade Cas. (CCH) ¶70,600 (S.D.N.Y. 1962) ("substantial and material") *with Dominicus American Bohio v. Gulf & Western Indus.*, 473 F. Supp. 680, 687 (S.D.N.Y. 1979) (any effect that is not "de minimis") *and National Bank of Canada v. Interbank Card Ass'n*, 666 F.2d 6, 9 (2d Cir. 1981) ("appreciable anticompetitive effects") *and United States v. Timken Roller Bearing Co.*, 83 F. Supp. 284, 309 (N.D. Ohio 1949) ("direct and influencing effect"). *See also Dee-K Enterprises, Inc. v. Heveafil Sdn. Bhd*, 299 F.3d 281, 288 (4th Cir. 2002) (describing confusion in formulation of effects test); *Den Norske Stats Oljeselskap AS v. HeereMac Vof*, 241 F.3d 120, 423-424 & n.12 (5th Cir. 2001) (same). Do any of these various verbal formulae provide meaningful or reliable guidance? How likely is it that courts can articulate such guidance?

(c) Alcoa's effects test — character of effects. Only a few lower court decisions have discussed what types of effects — as distinguished from the magnitude of effects — within the United States are necessary to permit extraterritorial application of the antitrust laws. One leading decision held that foreign conduct must have "appreciable *anticompetitive* effects on United States commerce." *National Bank of Canada v. Interbank Card Ass'n*, 666 F.2d 6, 9 (2d Cir. 1981) (emphasis added). Several earlier decisions concluded that restricting imports into the United States, and thereby foreclosing potential competition within this country, sufficiently affected U.S. commerce to sustain antitrust jurisdiction. *See Occidental Petroleum Corp. v. Buttes Gas & Oil Co.*, 331 F. Supp. 92, 102-103 (C.D. Cal. 1971), *aff'd*, 461 F.2d 1261 (9th Cir. 1972); *United States v. General Elec. Co.*, 82 F. Supp. 753, 891 (D.N.J. 1949).

5. *Effect of Aramco's territoriality presumption on Sherman Act.* Section 1 of the Sherman Act prohibits "[e]very contract, combination . . . or conspiracy in restraint of trade or commerce . . . with foreign nations." 15 U.S.C. §1 (1982). Does this language overcome the territoriality presumption articulated in *Aramco* and discussed *supra* pp. 664-670. Does §1's reference to trade "with foreign nations" indicate a more focused congressional intention to extend the antitrust laws extraterritorially than was present in Title VII of the Civil Rights Act? Compare the two statutes' jurisdictional grants. In light of *Aramco*, were *Alcoa* and *Mitsui* correctly decided? If *Aramco*'s territoriality presumption is faithfully applied, isn't it clear that the Sherman Act cannot fairly be applied outside U.S. territory? Notwithstanding this, as discussed in greater detail below, the Supreme Court said in *Hartford Fire Insurance Co. v. California*, 509 U.S. 764 (1993), that "it is well established by now that the Sherman Act applies to foreign conduct that was meant to produce and did in fact produce some substantial effect in the United States."

6. *Mitsui's application of Alcoa's effects test.* Although the allegedly illegal conduct in *Mitsui* occurred entirely outside the United States, the court nonetheless refused to grant summary judgment dismissing the plaintiff's claims on jurisdictional grounds. Instead, *Mitsui* held that the plaintiffs might succeed in showing that the defendants' foreign conduct had sufficiently substantial effects on U.S. commerce to permit application of the antitrust laws. Indeed, *Mitsui* apparently embraced a potentially far-reaching elaboration of the *Alcoa* effects test: "The competition between two American importers to obtain a source of supply on foreign territory affects the foreign commerce in the United States." How might U.S. commerce have actually been affected by the defendants' conduct in *Mitsui*?

7. **Foreign governmental "interests."** Did the Indonesian Government have any "interest" in the outcome of *Mitsui*? If so, what might that interest be? Did such concerns play any role in interpreting the Sherman Act in *Mitsui*? Should they? What about Japanese governmental interests? Are Japanese interests entitled to greater or lesser weight than Indonesian interests? Why? Does *Alcoa* consider either Swiss, Canadian, or any other foreign governmental interests? Should it have?

8. **Relevance of parties' nationality to applicability of antitrust laws.** *Mitsui* went out of its way to identify the nationality of the plaintiffs and defendants; it emphasized that one of the parties suffering the alleged injury and one of the parties allegedly responsible for that injury were U.S. corporations. How are these facts relevant to U.S. antitrust jurisdiction?

(a) Defendant's nationality. As noted above, the actor's nationality provides an accepted basis under international law for the exercise of legislative jurisdiction. *See supra* p. 599. Moreover, the defendant's nationality plays an important role in the personal jurisdiction and choice-of-law contexts. *See supra* pp. 109-113 & *infra* p. 689. Is it appropriate to hold U.S. antitrust defendants to higher standards than foreign companies? Is it likely that Congress would have intended such a result? What role did the defendant's nationality play in *Aramco*?

(b) Plaintiff's nationality. *Mitsui* also emphasized that the plaintiff was a U.S. company. What relevance does this have? Recall that international law does not generally recognize the passive personality principle as a basis for legislative jurisdiction. *See supra* pp. 601-602. Is it appropriate for the antitrust laws to provide greater protection for Americans than for foreigners? Is it something Congress might have intended?

(c) Difficulties in assigning nationality. *Mitsui* also suggests the difficulty in assigning nationality to multinational corporations: in what sense can Mitsui-U.S.A. (one subsidiary of a major Japanese company with worldwide operations) be said to be a U.S. citizen? Does it matter how many U.S. employees it has? How much U.S. business it does? Consider the difficulties of defining nationality for purposes of personal jurisdiction. *See supra* pp. 109-113.

c.   Protests Against the Extraterritorial Application of the U.S. Antitrust Laws.[81]

The extraterritorial application of the U.S. antitrust laws became a frequent occurrence after *Alcoa* was decided.[82] This caused considerable friction between the United States and its trading partners, leading to diplomatic protests, foreign blocking statutes, antisuit injunctions, and other forms of reaction.[83]

Foreign resistance to the extraterritorial application of the U.S. antitrust laws resulted in part from disagreement about the substantive regulatory policies reflected in the

---

81. Commentary on foreign protests to the extraterritorial application of the U.S. antitrust laws includes, for example, C. Olmstead, *Extraterritorial Application of Laws and Responses Thereto* (1984); Griffin, *Foreign Governmental Reactions to U.S. Assertions of Extraterritorial Jurisdiction*, 6 Geo. Mason L. Rev. 505 (1998); Kim, *The Extraterritorial Application of U.S. Antitrust Law and Its Adoption in Korea*, 7 Sing. J. Int'l & Comp. L. 386 (2003); Henry, *The United States Antitrust Laws: A Canadian Viewpoint*, 8 Can. Y.B. Int'l L. 249 (1970); Pengilley, *Extraterritorial Effects of United States Commercial and Antitrust Legislation: A View from "Down Under,"* 16 Vand. J. Transnat'l L. 833 (1983); Shank, *The Justice Department's Recent Antitrust Enforcement Policy: Toward a "Positive Comity" Solution to International Competition Problems*, 29 Vand. J. Transnat'l L. 155 (1996).

82. *See supra* p. 674.

83. The People's Republic of China recently appeared as an *amicus curiae* opposing an extraterritorial application of American antitrust law to the Vitamin C market in China. *See In re Vitamin C Antitrust Litig.*, 584 F. Supp. 2d 546 (E.D.N.Y. 2008).

antitrust laws. Foreign economic and social regulatory policies often did not rely on competition in the same fashion as the United States, and foreign states sometimes saw such competition as a threat to their national economic interests.[84] This perception was complemented by the conviction that the regulation of economic affairs is a vital aspect of national sovereignty and that foreign law, not U.S. law, should govern economic activity occurring on a foreign state's territory. More recently, many foreign states have embraced principles of competition law similar to those embodied in the Sherman Act.[85] Nevertheless, they seldom regard American judges as the appropriate authorities to resolve disputes about international (or foreign) trading practices.

The following remarks, excerpted from debates in the U.K. Parliament, are illustrative of foreign objections to the extraterritorial application of substantive U.S antitrust policies:

> My objective in introducing this Bill is to reassert and reinforce the defenses of the United Kingdom against attempts by other countries to enforce their economic and commercial policies unilaterally on us. From our point of view, the most objectionable method by which this is done is by the extraterritorial application of domestic law. In theory, this is a general problem since many countries have policies which, given the occasion and the inclination, they might seek to enforce on persons located, or engaged in activities, beyond the normal bounds of national jurisdiction as recognized by international law. In effect, however, the practices to which successive United Kingdom Governments have taken exception have arisen in the case of the United States of America.
>
> I must emphasize that we do not dispute the right of the United States or any other nation to pass and enforce what economic laws it likes to govern businesses operating fully in its own country. Our objection arises only at the point when a country attempts to achieve the maximum beneficial regulation of its own economic environment by ensuring that all those having any contact with it abide by its laws and legal principles. In other words, there is an attempt to export economic policy and law to persons domiciled in countries that may have different legal systems and priorities, without recognizing that those countries have the right to lay down the standards to be observed by those trading within their jurisdiction. . . .[86]

Although foreign states' reactions to U.S. antitrust enforcement are often based on differences in substantive regulatory policies, foreign critics have also challenged the procedural framework in which the U.S. antitrust laws are enforced. These protests have focused in part on the provisions of the antitrust laws that permit private plaintiffs to bring actions for treble damages.[87] Even in those foreign nations that have enacted competition laws, enforcement has been largely in governmental hands, and there is resistance abroad to the notion that a private U.S. plaintiff can initiate litigation resulting in an extraterritorial application of the antitrust laws.[88] Moreover, the treble damages

---

84. J. Atwood & K. Brewster, *Antitrust and American Business Abroad* §§1.01-1.14 (2d ed. 1985). Foreign complaints often reflect a suspicion that the United States does not apply the antitrust laws with consistency, and that the enforcement of these laws often seeks to advance the commercial interests of U.S. companies. *E.g., id.* §3.24 ("the assertion is often made that America's less enthusiastic embrace of competition in shipping proves hypocrisy in its espousal of competition in other economic sectors").

85. During the last several decades many foreign states have adopted "competition laws" that are broadly similar to the U.S. antitrust laws. *See* S. Waller, *Antitrust and American Business Abroad* §3:1 *et seq.* (3d ed. 1997 & Cum. Supp.).

86. 973 Parl. Deb., H.C. (5th Ser.) cols. 1533-77 (1979).

87. *E.g., Canadian Government Sponsors Bill to Address Extraterritoriality Issue,* 46 Antitrust & Trade Reg. Rep. (BNA) No. 1168, at 1106 (June 7, 1984) ("[i]t shouldn't be up to private individuals to determine foreign policy considerations for Canada [through U.S. antitrust suits]").

88. *See* Nijenhuis, *Antitrust Suits Involving Foreign Commerce: Suggestions for Procedural Reform,* 135 U. Pa. L. Rev. 1003, 1017-1021 (1987).

available under the U.S. antitrust laws are seen as a draconian penal measure that biases litigation against foreign defendants.[89] Finally, foreign protests about U.S. discovery procedures have special vigor in the antitrust context, where discovery is particularly onerous.[90]

Many foreign protests against the extraterritorial application of U.S. laws have taken the form of diplomatic notes.[91] Such notes typically assert that the extraterritorial application of U.S. law to conduct within the complaining state interferes with its sovereignty and is inconsistent with international law. During the 1970s and 1980s, diplomatic protests of this sort were commonplace:

> almost every bilateral or multilateral meeting between economic officials of the United States and Western Europe has included some objection from the European side to United States antitrust enforcement. It has become almost an automatic agenda item in diplomatic meetings with the Australians and Canadians.[92]

Some foreign states have taken more forceful action than diplomatic notes to resist the extraterritorial application of the U.S. antitrust laws. Most importantly, a number of states have enacted so-called "blocking statutes" designed to impede the application of U.S. antitrust laws to conduct within their territory. As discussed elsewhere, early blocking statutes forbade the production of evidence for use in U.S. antitrust proceedings.[93]

Later statutes sought more directly to prevent the extraterritorial application of the U.S. antitrust laws. The best-known foreign blocking statute is the United Kingdom's Protection of Trading Interests Act ("PTIA").[94] The PTIA deals directly with U.S. antitrust awards by preventing enforcement in the United Kingdom of awards of "multiple damages" and by providing parties in the United Kingdom with a "clawback" remedy by which they can recover in a separate English action two-thirds of any U.S. antitrust award from the U.S. plaintiff. These provisions apparently apply regardless of whether the anticompetitive conduct giving rise to the U.S. antitrust award took place in the United Kingdom, in the United States, or in some third country and regardless whether the party seeking relief is a U.K. national.[95] Australia has also enacted a statute that forbids enforcement of U.S. antitrust judgments.[96]

---

89. Beckett, *Transnational Litigation — Part II: Perspectives from the U.S. and Abroad (United Kingdom)*, 18 Int'l Law. 773, 774 (1984).

90. *See infra* pp. 969-973.

91. 1 S. Waller, *Antitrust and American Business Abroad* §4:14 (3d ed. 1997 & Cum. Supp.).

92. 1 J. Atwood & K. Brewster, *Antitrust and American Business Abroad* §4.15 (2d ed. 1985).

93. *See infra* pp. 972-973.

94. *See supra* pp. 680-681. *See also* Toms, *The French Response to the Extraterritorial Application of United States Antitrust Laws,* 15 Int'l Law. 585 (1981).

95. Lowe, *Blocking Extraterritorial Jurisdiction: The British Protection of Trading Interests Act 1980,* 75 Am. J. Int'l L. 257 (1981); Lowenfeld, *Sovereignty, Jurisdiction and Reasonableness: A Reply to A.V. Lowe,* 75 Am. J. Int'l L. 629 (1981).

96. *See* Pettit & Styles, *The International Response to the Extraterritorial Application of United States Antitrust Laws,* 37 Bus. Law. 697 (1982). With the exception of laws restricting the production of evidence located abroad, there has been relatively little practical experience to date with foreign blocking statutes. (The practical impact of this former class of statutes on U.S. litigation is discussed *infra* pp. 972-973.) Thus, for example, the PTIA's clawback remedy has never been invoked. If it were, its effect on a U.S. plaintiff who successfully obtained an antitrust judgment against an English company is unclear. It is unlikely that a U.S. court would enforce any such judgment and the attitude of other states toward enforcement is uncertain. In addition, it might be possible to obtain a U.S. antisuit injunction against resort to the PTIA. *See* Note, *Enjoining the Application of the British Protection of Trading Interests Act in Private American Antitrust Litigation,* 79 Mich. L. Rev. 1574 (1981).

More recently, the extraterritoriality debate has broadened, to include objections against extraterritorial applications of national competition laws by the EU and other states.[97] In particular, in recent years, the EU competition laws have repeatedly been applied to conduct occurring either predominantly or entirely outside the European Union.[98] U.S. companies and government officials have been among the most vigorous critics of such actions.

d. Moderating the Extraterritorial Application of the U.S. Antitrust Laws: *Timberlane* **and** *Third Restatement §403.*   Opposition to the extraterritorial application of the U.S. antitrust laws prompted various efforts to moderate U.S. jurisdictional claims. Early efforts focused on the enforcement of conflicting legal requirements against private parties. Section 40 of the ALI's *Restatement (Second) Foreign Relations Law,* excerpted in Appendix Z, was an example of this approach. It "balanced" conflicting U.S. and foreign interests in regulating particular conduct, contemplating that a state would decline to enforce its legislative jurisdiction in cases where its "interests" were clearly outweighed by foreign "interests."[99]

Later developments focused directly on the question whether national laws were applicable at all. A number of authorities sought to articulate a "jurisdictional rule of reason" that would limit *Alcoa*'s expansive effects doctrine. The decision in *Timberlane Lumber Co. v. Bank of America,* excerpted below, is the classic statement of this new approach.[100] Other lower court decisions applied *Timberlane*'s approach, both in the antitrust and other contexts.[101]

Section 403 of the *Restatement (Third) Foreign Relations Law,* excerpted in Appendix AA, "codified" the jurisdictional rule of reason. Section 403's rule of reason is closely related to the analysis in *Timberlane.* Section 403 must be read in conjunction with §402 of the *Third Restatement,* which sets out the traditional bases under public international law for jurisdiction to prescribe. As discussed above, even when one of §402's jurisdictional bases is applicable, §403's rule of reason must nonetheless be satisfied.

RESTATEMENT (SECOND) FOREIGN RELATIONS LAW
§40 (1965) [excerpted in Appendix Z]

TIMBERLANE LUMBER CO. v. BANK OF AMERICA N.T. & SA
549 F.2d 597 (9th Cir. 1976)

CHOY, CIRCUIT JUDGE. . . . [This action is] an antitrust suit alleging violations of §§1 and 2 of the Sherman Act. . . . [Timberlane, the principal plaintiff, was a U.S. partnership that

---

97. *See* Griffin, *Extraterritoriality in U.S. and EU Antitrust Enforcement,* 67 Antitrust L.J. 159, 175 (1999); Comment, *The International Language of Convergence: Reviving Antitrust Dialogue Between the United States and the European Union With a Uniform Understanding of "Extraterritoriality,"* 17 U. Pa. J. Int'l Econ. L. 909, 926-927 (1996).

98. *See infra* pp. 689-690.

99. *See* Appendix Z.

100. *Timberlane Lumber Co. v. Bank of America,* 549 F.2d 597 (9th Cir. 1976), *on remand,* 574 F. Supp. 1453 (N.D. Cal. 1983), *aff'd,* 749 F.2d 1378 (9th Cir. 1984). *See* Gill, *Two Cheers for* Timberlane, 10 Swiss Rev. Int'l & Comp. L. 3 (1980); Ongman, *"Be No Longer a Chaos": Constructing a Normative Theory of the Sherman Act's Extraterritorial Jurisdictional Scope,* 71 Nw. U. L. Rev. 733 (1977).

101. *E.g.,* O.N.E. *Shipping Ltd. v. Flota Mercante Grancolombiana,* 830 F.2d 449 (2d Cir. 1987); *Montreal Trading Ltd. v. Amax Inc.,* 661 F.2d 864 (10th Cir. 1981); *Mannington Mills, Inc. v. Congoleum Corp.,* 595 F.2d 1287 (3d Cir. 1979); *Transnor (Bermuda) Ltd. v. BP North America Petroleum,* 1990-1991 Trade Cas. ¶68,997 (S.D.N.Y. 1990); *Dominicus Americana Bohio v. Gulf & Western Indus. Inc.,* 473 F. Supp. 680 (S.D.N.Y. 1979). *See also Star-Kist Foods, Inc. v. P.J. Rhodes & Co.,* 769 F.2d 1393 (9th Cir. 1985) (Lanham Act); *Zenger-Miller, Inc. v. Training Team, GmbH,* 757 F. Supp. 1062 (N.D. Ill. 1991) (same).

imported lumber into the United States from Central America. Bank of America was a U.S.-based bank that financed much of the lumber industry in Honduras. The dispute arose when a Honduran lumber company that the Bank had financed went bankrupt. The company's assets (including a lumber mill and tracts of forest land) passed to the company's creditors, who in turn sold the assets to Timberlane, which had recently decided to begin lumber operations in Honduras. After Timberlane commenced its Honduran lumber operations, the Bank of America allegedly conspired with several other Honduran lumber companies to drive Timberlane out of business. Among other things, the Bank allegedly joined a scheme in which a security interest it held in the property purchased by Timberlane was enforced in the Honduran courts, resulting in a judicial order forbidding Timberlane from using the property. The alleged purpose of the scheme was to drive Timberlane from the Honduran lumber business, so that other companies financed by Bank of America could continue to monopolize that market. The district court dismissed the complaint based on the act of state doctrine and a lack of any direct or substantial effect on U.S. foreign commerce.]

There is no doubt that American antitrust laws extend over some conduct in other nations. There was language in the first Supreme Court case in point, *American Banana*, casting doubt on the extension of the Sherman Act to acts outside United States territory. But subsequent cases have limited *American Banana* to its particular facts, and the Sherman Act—and with it other antitrust laws—has been applied to extraterritorial conduct. *See, e.g., Continental Ore Co. v. Union Carbide & Carbon Corp.; Alcoa.* . . .

That American law covers some conduct beyond this nation's borders does not mean that it embraces all, however. Extraterritorial application is understandably a matter of concern for the other countries involved. Those nations have sometimes resented and protested, as excessive intrusions into their own spheres, broad assertions of authority by American courts. Our courts have recognized this concern and have, at times, responded to it, even if not always enough to satisfy all the foreign critics. In any event, it is evident that at some point the interests of the United States are too weak and the foreign harmony incentive for restraint too strong to justify an extraterritorial assertion of jurisdiction.

What that point is or how it is determined is not defined by international law. . . . Nor does the Sherman Act limit itself. . . . Courts have generally, and logically, fallen back on a narrower construction of congressional intent, such as expressed in Judge Learned Hand's oft-cited opinion in *Alcoa*:

> [I]t is settled law . . . that any state may impose liabilities, even upon persons not within its allegiance, for conduct outside its borders that has consequences within its borders which the state reprehends; and these liabilities other states will ordinarily recognize.

Despite its description as "settled law," *Alcoa*'s assertion has been roundly disputed by many foreign commentators as being in conflict with international law, comity, and good judgment. Nonetheless, American courts have firmly concluded that there is some extraterritorial jurisdiction under the Sherman Act. Even among American courts and commentators, however, there is no consensus on how far the jurisdiction should extend. . . .

The effects test by itself is incomplete because it fails to consider other nations' interests. Nor does it expressly take into account the full nature of the relationship between the actors and this country. Whether the alleged offender is an American citizen, for instance, may make a big difference; applying American laws to American citizens raises fewer problems than application to foreigners. . . . American courts have, in fact, often displayed a regard for comity and the prerogatives of other nations and considered their interests . . . even when professing to apply an effects test. To some degree, the requirement for a "substantial" effect may silently incorporate these additional considerations, with "substantial" as a flexible standard that varies with other factors. The intent requirement suggested by *Alcoa* is one example of an attempt to broaden the court's perspective, as is drawing a distinction between American citizens and non-citizens. The failure to articulate these other elements in addition to the standard effects analysis is costly, however, for it is more likely that they will be overlooked or slighted in interpreting past decisions and reaching new ones. . . .

A tripartite analysis seems to be indicated. As acknowledged above, the antitrust laws require in the first instance that there be *some* effect — actual or intended — on American foreign commerce before the federal courts may legitimately exercise subject matter jurisdiction under those statutes. Second, a greater showing of burden or restraint may be necessary to demonstrate that the effect is sufficiently large to present a cognizable injury to the plaintiffs and, therefore, a civil *violation* of the antitrust laws. Third, there is the additional question which is unique to the international setting of whether the interests of, and links to, the United States — including the magnitude of the effect on American foreign commerce — are sufficiently strong, vis-à-vis those of other nations, to justify an assertion of extraterritorial authority. . . .

The elements to be weighted [in applying this third factor] include the degree of conflict with foreign law or policy, the nationality or allegiance of the parties and the locations or principal places of business of corporations, the extent to which enforcement by either state can be expected to achieve compliance, the relative significance of effects on the United States as compared with those elsewhere, the extent to which there is explicit purpose to harm or affect American commerce, the foreseeability of such effect, and the relative importance to the violations charged of conduct within the United States as compared with conduct abroad. A court evaluating these factors should identify the potential degree of conflict if American authority is asserted. A difference in law or policy is one likely sore spot, though one which may not always be present.[102] Nationality is another; though foreign governments may have some concern for the treatment of American citizens and business residing there, they primarily care about their own nationals.[103] Having assessed the conflict, the court should then determine whether in the face of it the contacts and interests of the United States are sufficient to support the exercise of extraterritorial jurisdiction. . . .

[The Court of Appeals remanded the case to the district court for application of the tripartite test, including its rule of reason. The district court applied the test and concluded that Timberlane's complaint should be dismissed. Timberlane appealed and the Court of Appeals affirmed. 749 F.2d 1378 (9th Cir. 1984).]

RESTATEMENT (THIRD) FOREIGN RELATIONS LAW OF THE UNITED STATES

§§402 & 403 (1987) [excerpted in Appendix AA]

Notes on Second Restatement, Timberlane, *and* Third Restatement

1. Timberlane*'s criticism of* **Alcoa's** *effects test. Timberlane* concluded that *Alcoa*'s effects test was an inadequate formula for determining when the antitrust laws should be applied extraterritorially. In particular, Judge Choy reasoned that *Alcoa* failed to take into account

---

102. Particularly in the field of trade regulation, American laws may not be duplicated by the other nation. That does not necessarily indicate a "conflict," however, since non-prohibition does not always mean affirmative approval. *See* P. Areeda, [*Antitrust Analysis* 127 (1974)].

103. Some argue that a defendant's American citizenship might be enough by itself to support jurisdiction. *See Restatement (Second) Foreign Relations Law* §30 (1965).

the interests of other nations or the relationships between the litigants and the United States. Is *Timberlane*'s criticism of the various formulations of the *Alcoa* "effects doctrine" persuasive? As an exercise in determining Congress's likely intent, which opinion is more persuasive?

2. *Timberlane's reliance on international comity.* Compare *Timberlane* with *American Banana* and *Alcoa*. Does Judge Choy look to international law in interpreting the Sherman Act? What sources does he consult in ascertaining limits on the extraterritorial reach of the antitrust laws? Note *Timberlane*'s reliance on "comity and the prerogatives of other nations" and "international comity and fairness." What does *Timberlane* mean by "international comity"? Is it different from "international law"? What is the source of comity, and how does one ascertain what its limits are? Recall what Huber and Story meant by "comity." *See supra* pp. 647-649. Is "comity" a substitute for the *Charming Betsy* presumption and the territoriality presumption? Is it a wise substitute? Compare the reliance on international comity in other contexts, including *forum non conveniens* (*supra* pp. 385-386); antisuit injunctions (*supra* pp. 578-580); choice of law (*infra* p. 735); extraterritorial discovery (*infra* pp. 1007-1008); and enforcement of foreign judgments (*infra* pp. 1086-1091).

3. *Timberlane's effects test.* The first two of the three prongs of the *Timberlane* analysis are derived from *Alcoa*'s effects test. The first *Timberlane* prong requires only proof that the defendant's conduct had "*some* effect — actual or intended — on American foreign commerce." 549 F.2d at 613 (emphasis in original). Would any significant international economic activity fail to have "some effect" on U.S. commerce?

The second *Timberlane* prong also requires a showing of effects on U.S. commerce. A second Ninth Circuit opinion in *Timberlane* read this prong to require a "direct and substantial anticompetitive effect" on the foreign commerce of the United States. 749 F.2d 1378 (9th Cir. 1984). Nonetheless, the decision confirmed that the second *Timberlane* prong does not require a showing anywhere near as demanding as the traditional "direct, substantial and reasonably foreseeable" test. Some courts that have otherwise followed *Timberlane*'s general approach have refused to adopt an "effects" requirement with the low threshold permitted in *Timberlane*'s first and second prongs. *E.g., Mannington Mills, Inc. v. Congoleum Corp.,* 595 F.2d 1287, 1291-1292 (3d Cir. 1979); *Conservation Council of Western Australia v. Aluminum Co. of Am.,* 518 F. Supp. 270 (W.D. Pa. 1981). *Cf. Zenith Radio Corp. v. Matsushita Elec. Indus. Co.,* 494 F. Supp. 1161, 1177 (E.D. Pa. 1980) (suggesting low threshold for jurisdictional inquiry into effects). *See also Hartford Fire Ins. Co. v. California,* 509 U.S. 764, 817-821 (1993) (Scalia, J., dissenting).

4. *Timberlane's effects test and international law.* Recall the contemporary statements of the effects test under international law. *See supra* p. 600. Is *Timberlane*'s effects test consistent with contemporary international law?

5. *Timberlane's "rule of reason."* The central innovation of *Timberlane* is its third, "interest-balancing" prong: the extraterritorial application of the U.S. antitrust laws requires consideration of "the additional question which is unique to the international setting of whether the interests of, and links to, the United States — including the magnitude of the effect on American foreign commerce — are sufficiently strong, vis-à-vis those of other nations, to justify an assertion of extraterritorial authority." Compare the *Timberlane* interest-balancing test to contemporary rules governing *forum non conveniens, supra* pp. 453-458, choice of law, *infra* pp. 739-740, and extraterritorial discovery, *infra* pp. 1007-1008. *See also Bigio v. Coca-Cola Co.,* 448 F.3d 176 (2d Cir. 2006) (reversing district court for failing to distinguish between *Timberlane* comity analysis and prudential doctrine of international comity).

6. *Basis for* Timberlane *jurisdictional rule of reason.* Timberlane adopted a so-called "jurisdictional rule of reason" in international antitrust cases. However, Judge Choy was not clear about the source of this rule. In particular, the court does not specify whether it was inferring that Congress "intended" such a rule as an implicit limitation on the reach of the U.S. antitrust statutes, whether the rule was a canon of statutory construction, or whether the rule was instead a general principle of international law or international comity that courts may incorporate into U.S. law in the absence of contrary congressional intent.

7. *Factors relevant to the rule of reason.* Timberlane lists a number of factors to be considered in applying the jurisdictional rule of reason, but gives little guidance regarding the weight to be given to any particular factor or the relevance of additional factors. Other authorities that have adopted the *Timberlane* rule of reason have suggested slightly different lists of factors. *See Mannington Mills, Inc. v. Congoleum Corp.*, 595 F.2d 1287 (3d Cir. 1979); *In re CINAR Corp. Securities Litig.*, 186 F. Supp. 2d 279, 293-294 (E.D.N.Y. 2002) (comparing *Timberlane* factors and *Restatement* factors in context of securities case); *Restatement (Third) Foreign Relations Law* §403 (1987). Compare §403's factors to those set out in *Timberlane*. Is either list preferable?

How is a court to decide whether a balancing of the *Timberlane* factors indicates that "the contacts and interests of the United States are sufficient to support the exercise of extraterritorial jurisdiction"? What "weight" should be accorded each factor? What if different factors point strongly in different directions?

8. *Predictability of rule of reason.* Is the rule of reason adopted in *Timberlane* and §403 predictable? Does it not invite entirely subjective, unprincipled decisions? Could §403's rule of reason be clarified over time as courts build on a body of common law precedent?

9. *The* Timberlane/Laker *debate.* Laker Airways Ltd. v. Sabena, 731 F.2d 909, 948-951 (D.C. Cir. 1984), sharply criticized the *Timberlane* rule of reason:

> The suggestion has been made that this court should engage in some form of interest balancing, permitting only a "reasonable" assertion of prescriptive jurisdiction to be implemented. However, this approach is unsuitable when courts are forced to choose between a domestic law which is designed to protect domestic interests, and a foreign law which is calculated to thwart the implementation of the domestic law in order to protect foreign interests allegedly threatened by the objectives of the domestic law. Interest balancing in this context is hobbled by two primary problems: (1) there are substantial limitations on the court's ability to conduct a neutral balancing of the competing interests, and (2) the adoption of interest balancing is unlikely to achieve its goal of promoting international comity. . . .
>
> Those contacts [relevant to the jurisdictional rule of reason] which do purport to provide a basis for distinguishing between competing bases of jurisdiction, and which are thus crucial to the balancing process, generally incorporate purely political factors which the court is neither qualified to evaluate comparatively nor capable of properly balancing. One such proposed consideration is "the degree to which the *desirability of such regulation* [of restrictive practices] is *generally accepted.*" [*Restatement (Revised)* §403(a) (g), (h) (Tentative Draft No. 2).] We doubt whether the legitimacy of an exercise of jurisdiction should be measured by the substantive content of the prescribed law. Moreover, although more and more states are following the United States in regulating restrictive practices, and even exercising jurisdiction based on effects within territory, *the differing English and American assessment of the desirability of antitrust law is at the core of the conflict. An English or American court cannot refuse to enforce law its political branches have already determined is desirable and necessary.* . . .
>
> The "importance of regulation to the state" is another factor on which the court cannot rely to choose between two competing mutually inconsistent legislative policies. We are in no position to adjudicate the relative importance of antitrust regulation or nonregulation to the

United States and the United Kingdom. It is the crucial importance of these policies which has created the conflict. A proclamation by judicial fiat that one interest is less "important" than the other will not erase a real conflict.

Given the inherent limitations of the Judiciary, which must weigh these issues in the limited context of adversarial litigation, we seriously doubt whether we could adequately chart the competing problems and priorities that inevitably define the scope of any nation's interest in a legislated remedy. This court is ill-equipped to "balance the vital national interest of the United States and the [United Kingdom] to determine which interests predominate." [*In re Uranium Antitrust Litig.,* 480 F. Supp. 1138, 1148 (N.D. Ill. 1978).] When one state exercises its jurisdiction and another, in protection of its own interests, attempts to quash the first exercise of jurisdiction "it is simply impossible to judicially 'balance' these totally contradictory and mutually negating actions." *Id. . . .*

We might be more willing to tackle the problems associated with the balancing of competing, mutually inconsistent national interests if we could be assured that our efforts would strengthen the bonds of international comity. However, the usefulness and wisdom of interest balancing to assess the most "reasonable" exercise of prescriptive jurisdiction has not been affirmatively demonstrated. This approach has not gained more than a temporary foothold in domestic law. Courts are increasingly refusing to adopt the approach. Scholarly criticism has intensified. Additionally, there is no evidence that interest balancing represents a rule of international law. Thus, there is no mandatory rule requiring its adoption here, since Congress cannot be said to have implicitly legislated subject to these international constraints.

If promotion of international comity is measured by the number of times U.S. jurisdiction has been declined under the "reasonableness" interest balancing approach, then it has been a failure. Implementation of this analysis has not resulted in a significant number of conflict resolutions favoring a foreign jurisdiction. A pragmatic assessment of those decisions adopting an interest balancing approach indicates *none where U.S. jurisdiction was declined* when there was more than a *de minimis* United States interest. Most cases in which use of the process was advocated arose before a direct conflict occurred when the balancing could be employed without impairing the court's jurisdiction to determine jurisdiction. When push comes to shove, the domestic forum is rarely unseated.

See also Zoelsch v. Arthur Andersen & Co., 824 F.2d 27 (D.C. Cir. 1987); *Reinsurance Co. of Am. v. ADAS,* 902 F.2d 1275 (7th Cir. 1990) (Easterbrook, J., dissenting) (excerpted *infra* pp. 1012-1017). Are *Laker*'s criticisms of the rule of reason persuasive? Putting aside problems with applying the rule of reason, is the Court of Appeals correct in questioning the constitutional and statutory basis for the rule of reason? Recall the similar constitutional questions raised by judicial abstention in the *forum non conveniens* and act of state contexts, discussed *supra* p. 384 and *infra* p. 816. Isn't the rule of reason an illegitimate judicially created limit on the exercise of jurisdiction that Congress did not intend?

10. *No need for conflict between U.S. and foreign law for application of §403(2).* Note that the rule of reason in *Timberlane* and §403(1) and (2) apply even if there is no conflict between U.S. and foreign law. Is this appropriate? If foreign law is not inconsistent with U.S. antitrust laws, should the Sherman Act not presumptively be applicable, or at least require only a *de minimis* connection to the United States? Recall that the rationale for the territoriality presumption was that the extraterritorial application of national law interfered with the sovereignty of foreign states. *See supra* p. 665. If foreign law is not inconsistent with U.S. law, then how is foreign sovereignty interfered with by the application of U.S. law?

11. *Relevance of conflict between U.S. and foreign law under §403(2).* One of the factors listed for consideration by *Timberlane* and §403 is the degree of conflict between U.S. and Honduran laws. After a remand to the district court, the Ninth Circuit considered the application of its "rule of reason" in a second *Timberlane* case. 749 F.2d 1378 (9th Cir.

1984). There, the Court of Appeals found that a conflict between U.S. and Honduran law existed, even though the defendants could not identify any specific Honduran law requiring or even condoning the defendant's allegedly anti-competitive conduct. Instead, *Timberlane II* discerned a conflict between the U.S. antitrust laws and a general effort by the Honduran government to "foster a particular style of business climate." Under this sort of analysis, would there ever *not* be a conflict? *Compare Timberlane I*, 549 F.2d at 614 n.32 ("American laws may not be duplicated by the other nation. That does not necessarily indicate a 'conflict,' however, since non-prohibition does not always mean affirmative approval."). Suppose Honduras had its own antitrust laws, as many industrialized nations have. Would this reduce the conflict with U.S. laws or heighten it?

12. *Relevance of conflict between U.S. and foreign law under §403(3).* Section 403(3) is applicable where U.S. and foreign laws are in conflict. What does it mean for a "conflict" to exist between U.S. and foreign law? Does it require that U.S. law impose a legal obligation requiring a party to do something that foreign law forbids that party from doing? What if foreign law does not require particular conduct, but specifically declines to forbid it? What if foreign law deliberately chooses to leave particular conduct unregulated? The Supreme Court addressed these questions in *Hartford Fire*, discussed below. *See infra* pp. 692-709.

13. *Nationality of parties.* *Timberlane*'s reasonableness analysis accords a significant role to the nationality of the parties: "Whether the alleged offender is an American citizen . . . may make a big difference." This approach rests in part on the nationality principle, which permits a state to regulate the conduct of its nationals abroad, *see supra* p. 599, and on the perception that foreign states will typically be more concerned with actions against their own citizens than with actions against U.S. nationals. *Cf. EEOC v. Aramco*, 499 U.S. 244 (1991).

14. *Applicability of rule of reason to litigation commenced by U.S. Government.* Should the rule of reason be available to dismiss antitrust suits brought by the Department of Justice or by other government agencies? The Justice Department's Antitrust Division has indicated its belief that actions it initiates should not be subject to dismissal on *Timberlane* grounds, on the theory that the Executive Branch takes comity concerns into account in deciding whether to bring suit. U.S. Department of Justice, *Antitrust Enforcement Guidelines for International Operations* 93 n.167 (1988). One lower court has agreed. *United States v. Baker, Hughes, Inc.*, 731 F. Supp. 3 (D.D.C. 1990). Is this an appropriate position? Is the Justice Department necessarily sensitive to the interests of foreign states? Note that discovery requests by U.S. Government agencies are subject to interest-balancing analysis similar to that required by *Timberlane. See infra* pp. 1019-1021.

15. *Effect of choice-of-law clause on extraterritorial reach of U.S. statutes.* International commercial contracts frequently contain choice-of-law clauses. When such a clause selects the laws of a U.S. state, what effect does this have on the extraterritorial application of the U.S. antitrust laws or other federal statutes? In *Zenger-Miller, Inc. v. Training Team, GmbH*, 757 F. Supp. 1062 (N.D. Cal. 1991), the district court refused to apply the Lanham Act to conduct occurring in Europe, notwithstanding a California choice-of-law provision. The court reasoned that "defendants consented to the application of California, not federal law . . . [and] subject matter jurisdiction, unlike personal jurisdiction 'cannot be consented to by the parties. . . . ' " Is this reasoning persuasive? Does such a choice-of-law provision have any relevance to extraterritoriality analysis? *See also Warnaco Inc. v. VF Corp.*, 844 F. Supp. 940, 950 (S.D.N.Y. 1994) (applying Lanham Act extraterritorially despite New York choice-of-law clause).

16. *EU standards for extraterritorial application of antitrust laws.* European Union rules governing the extraterritorial application of EU antitrust laws provide a point of comparison. EU law prohibits certain anti-competitive conduct that may affect trade between member states. While textually not unlike the United States' "effects" test, the European Court of Justice has given the treaty provisions a different gloss. In its seminal decision on the extraterritorial application of EU antitrust laws, the Court of Justice announced the decisive factor to be that "[t]he producers *implemented* their pricing agreement within the common market." *In re Wood Pulp Cartel: A Ahlstrom Oy v. E.C. Commission,* 4 C.M.L.R. 901, 941 (1988) (emphasis added). The "implementation doctrine" announced in *Wood Pulp* arguably resembled something akin to a "territoriality" principle rather than an "effects" test. Nonetheless, in the years since *Wood Pulp,* the European Commission has taken a broad view of the cases that constitute "implementation" of anti-competitive behavior in the European Community. *See* Griffin, *Extraterritoriality in U.S. and EU Antitrust Enforcement,* 67 Antitrust L.J. 159, 175 (1999); Comment, *The International Language of Convergence: Reviving Antitrust Dialogue Between the United States and the European Union with a Uniform Understanding of "Extraterritoriality,"* 17 U. Pa. J. Int'l Econ. L. 909, 926-27 (1996). The Commission's broad interpretation of the "implementation doctrine" prompted a former Assistant Attorney General in charge of the Antitrust Division to comment that the European standard is "very close to, if not indistinguishable from, the so-called effects test as applied by U.S. Courts." Rule, *The Justice Department's Antitrust Enforcement Guidelines for International Operations — A Competition Policy for the 1990s,* Address to the International Trade Section and Antitrust Committee of the D.C. Bar (Nov. 29, 1998). *See also* Basedow, *International Antitrust: From Extraterritorial Application to Harmonization,* 60 La. L. Rev. 1037 (2000). Do you see a substantial difference between *Alcoa*'s effects test versus the EU's implementation doctrine? What about the FTAIA? Would a stricter territoriality principle make sense in antitrust cases?

The EU's standards on comity, like its standards on extraterritorial application, likewise provide an interesting point of comparison. Nominally, the European Commission claims to consider "comity" when deciding whether to exercise its jurisdiction. *See* Sugden, Note, *Global Antitrust and the Evolution of an International Standard,* 35 Vand. J. Transnat'l L. 989, 1013-1015 (2002). It has formally adopted the OECD's Recommendation for extraterritorial application of antitrust laws under which a country should consider "the need [t]o give effect to principles of international law and comity and to use moderation and self-restraint in the interest of cooperation in the field of restrictive business practices." OECD Doc. No. C 86(44) (May 21, 1986).

Nonetheless, the Commission, with the European Court of Justice's blessing, has not hesitated to exercise its jurisdiction even in the face of strong diplomatic objections. *See, e.g., IBM v. EC Commission* (60/81), [1981] E.C.R. 2639; *Gencor v. Comm.,* 1999 ECR II-753. This is particularly true in the area of merger control where legal doctrines on extraterritoriality and parochial protectionist impulses can converge (though in recent years the European Court of Justice has displayed a greater skepticism to overly aggressive merger control by the Commission). *See* Leddy et al., *Transatlantic Merger Control: The Courts and the Agencies,* 43 Cornell Int'l L.J. 25 (2010). In recent years, the Commission has investigated, and in some cases opposed, mergers between U.S. companies even after U.S. regulators have approved the deals. This regulatory activity has led to substantial revisions to the merger in some cases (the Boeing-McDonnell Douglas merger) and to abandonment in others (the GE-Honeywell deal). *See* Griffin, *Extraterritoriality in U.S. and EU Antitrust Enforcement,* 67 Antitrust L.J. 159, 176-177 (1999). How does the EC's formal standard compare to the standard announced in *Timberlane? See* Comment, *A Comparative Analysis of United States and European Union Jurisdiction in Extraterritorial Antitrust Law and the Need for International Standards,* 9 Duq. Bus. L.J. 65 (2007). Reconsider this issue after you read *Hartford Fire* and *Hoffmann-LaRoche,* excerpted below.

17. *Cooperation between national antitrust regulatory authorities.* While many antitrust suits are brought on behalf of private plaintiffs, governmental authorities play an important role as well. Not only do they have the power to bring suits on their own behalf, their investigations of anti-competitive behavior and review of proposed mergers with potential anti-competitive effects play an important role in civil suits. As national and transnational standards for antitrust regulation evolve and countries assert greater authority to regulate foreign transactions, both the need for cooperation and opportunities to cooperate grow as well. In particular, U.S. and European authorities sometimes will cooperate in the conduct of an investigation touching on both the U.S. and European markets. Does such cooperation have the potential to reduce the sort of tensions in antitrust enforcement that characterized litigation in the 1970s and 1980s? *See* Dekeyser et al., *Coordination Among National Antitrust Agencies*, 10 Sedona Conference J. 43 (2009).

e. Contemporary Supreme Court Approach to Extraterritorial Application of U.S. Antitrust Laws: *Hartford Fire* **and** *Hoffmann-LaRoche.* In 1993, the Supreme Court handed down a decision in *Hartford Fire Insurance Company v. California,* excerpted below.[104] *Hartford Fire* sets forth an expansive view of the extraterritorial reach of the U.S. antitrust laws. The decision came barely two years after *EEOC v. Aramco*'s reaffirmation of the territoriality presumption. Nevertheless, neither *Aramco* nor the territoriality presumption was alluded to in the Court's opinion. Instead, over a sharp dissent from Justice Scalia, *Hartford Fire* embraced a relatively expansive effects test, not much different from that in *Alcoa,* which it apparently sought to moderate through a very grudging (mis)reading of §403's rule of reason.

Despite this, in its most recent consideration of the extraterritorial application of federal antitrust legislation, *F. Hoffmann-LaRoche, Ltd. v. Empagran, SA,* also excerpted below, the Supreme Court appeared to reverse course yet again.[105] In *Hoffmann-LaRoche,* the Court interpreted the Foreign Trade Antitrust Improvements Act ("FTAIA") in light of §403 and principles of comity (again without any mention of *Aramco*'s territoriality presumption). Among other things, the Court relied heavily on a dissenting opinion in *Hartford Fire*—barely a decade after that decision was rendered.

As *Aramco, Hartford Fire,* and *Hoffmann-LaRoche* illustrate, the Court's recent approach to the extraterritorial reach of federal legislation leaves much to be desired. With almost haphazard nonchalance, the Court has applied several fundamentally different rules of construction in international cases. One is the traditional *American Banana* rule, revived and applied in *Aramco,* which imposes a strict territoriality presumption on federal legislation. A second is the *Hartford Fire* rule, which looks to the contemporary formulations of *Alcoa*'s effects doctrine. A third is reflected in decisions such as *Lauritzen v. Larsen*[106] and *Steele v. Bulova Watch Co.,*[107] which adopt a multi-factor rule of reason approach, similar to that in *Timberlane,* and which is arguably adopted in *Hoffmann-LaRoche.* Unfortunately, the Court has neither acknowledged the existence of these different approaches, nor provided guidance as to when it will apply one, rather than another. The result is confusion for litigants and lower courts, and arbitrary, unpredictable results.

---

104. 509 U.S. 764 (1993).
105. 542 U.S. 155 (2004).
106. 345 U.S. 571 (1953); *supra* pp. 654-659.
107. 344 U.S. 280 (1952).

HARTFORD FIRE INSURANCE CO. v. CALIFORNIA
509 U.S. 764 (1993)

JUSTICE SOUTER. . . . The Sherman Act makes every contract, combination, or conspiracy in unreasonable restraint of interstate or foreign commerce illegal. 15 U.S.C. §1. These consolidated cases present questions about the application of that Act to the insurance industry . . . abroad. The plaintiffs (respondents here) allege that both domestic and foreign defendants (petitioners here) violated the Sherman Act by engaging in various conspiracies to affect the American insurance market. . . . [The] foreign defendants argue that the principle of international comity requires the District Court to refrain from exercising jurisdiction over certain claims against [them]. We hold that . . . the principle of international comity does not preclude District Court jurisdiction over the foreign conduct alleged.

I. The two petitions before us stem from consolidated litigation comprising the complaints of 19 States and many private plaintiffs alleging that the defendants, members of the insurance industry, conspired in violation of §1 of the Sherman Act to restrict the terms of coverage of commercial general liability ("CGL") insurance available in the United States. . . . According to the complaints, the object of the conspiracies was to force certain primary insurers (insurers who sell insurance directly to consumers) to change the terms of their standard CGL insurance policies to conform with the policies the defendant insurers wanted to sell. . . . [The Fifth Claim for Relief alleges a violation of §1 of the Sherman Act by certain London reinsurers who conspired to coerce primary insurers in the United States to offer CGL coverage on a claims-made basis, thereby making "occurrence CGL coverage . . . unavailable in the State of California for many risks." The Sixth and Eighth Claims were similar.] . . .

The District Court granted the motions to dismiss. It . . . dismissed the three claims that named only certain London-based defendants, invoking international comity and applying the Ninth Circuit's decision in *Timberlane.* . . . The Court of Appeals reversed. . . . [A]s to the three claims brought solely against foreign defendants, the court applied its *Timberlane* analysis, but concluded that the principle of international comity was no bar to exercising Sherman Act jurisdiction. . . .

III. At the outset, we note that the District Court undoubtedly had jurisdiction of these Sherman Act claims, as the London reinsurers apparently concede. *See* [Transcript of Oral Argument] 37 ("Our position is not that the Sherman Act does not apply in the sense that a minimal basis for the exercise of jurisdiction doesn't exist here. Our position is that there are certain circumstances, and that this is one of them, in which the interests of another State are sufficient that the exercise of that jurisdiction should be restrained.").[108] Although the proposition was perhaps not always free from doubt, *see American Banana Co. v. United Fruit Co.,* it is well established by now that the Sherman Act applies to foreign conduct that was meant to produce and did in fact produce some substantial effect in the United States. *See United States v. Alcoa; Restatement (Third) Foreign Relations Law* §415, and Reporters' Note 3 (1987); *cf. Steele v. Bulova Watch Co.*[109] . . . Such

---

108. One of the London reinsurers, Sturge Reinsurance Syndicate Management Limited, argues that the Sherman Act does not apply to its conduct in attending a single meeting at which it allegedly agreed to exclude all pollution coverage from its reinsurance contracts. Sturge may have attended only one meeting, but the allegations, which we are bound to credit, remain that it participated in conduct that was intended to and did in fact produce a substantial effect on the American insurance market.

109. Justice Scalia believes that what is at issue in this case is prescriptive, as opposed to subject-matter, jurisdiction. The parties do not question prescriptive jurisdiction, however, and for good reason: it is well established that Congress has exercised such jurisdiction under the Sherman Act. *See* G. Born & D. Westin,

is the conduct alleged here: that the London reinsurers engaged in unlawful conspiracies to affect the market for insurance in the United States and that their conduct in fact produced substantial effect.[110]

According to the London reinsurers, the District Court should have declined to exercise such jurisdiction under the principle of international comity.[111] The Court of Appeals agreed that courts should look to that principle in deciding whether to exercise jurisdiction under the Sherman Act. This availed the London reinsurers nothing, however. To be sure, the Court of Appeals believed that "application of [American] antitrust laws to the London reinsurance market 'would lead to significant conflict with English law and policy,' " and that "[s]uch a conflict, unless outweighed by other factors, would by itself be reason to decline exercise of jurisdiction." But other factors, in the court's view, including the London reinsurers' express purpose to affect U.S. commerce and the substantial nature of the effect produced, outweighed the supposed conflict and required the exercise of jurisdiction in this litigation.

When it enacted the Foreign Trade Antitrust Improvements Act of 1982 ("FTAIA"), Congress expressed no view on the question whether a court with Sherman Act jurisdiction should ever decline to exercise such jurisdiction on grounds of international comity. *See* H.R. Rep. No. 97-686, p. 13 (1982) ("If a court determines that the requirements for subject matter jurisdiction are met, [the FTAIA] would have no effect on the court['s] ability to employ notions of comity . . . or otherwise to take account of the international character of the transaction") (citing *Timberlane*). We need not decide that question here, however, for even assuming that in a proper case a court may decline to exercise Sherman Act jurisdiction over foreign conduct (or, as Justice Scalia would put it, may conclude by the employment of comity analysis in the first instance that there is no jurisdiction), international comity would not counsel against exercising jurisdiction in the circumstances alleged here.

The only substantial question in this case is whether "there is in fact a true conflict between domestic and foreign law." *Societe Nationale Industrielle Aerospatiale v. District Court*, 482 U.S. 522, 555 (1987) (Blackmun, J., concurring in part and dissenting in part). The London reinsurers contend that applying the Act to their conduct would conflict significantly with British law, and the British Government, appearing before us as amicus curiae, concurs. They assert that Parliament has established a comprehensive regulatory

---

International Civil Litigation in United States Courts 542, n.5 (2d ed. 1992) (Sherman Act is a "prime exampl[e] of the simultaneous exercise of prescriptive jurisdiction and grant of subject matter jurisdiction").

110. Under §402 of the Foreign Trade Antitrust Improvements Act of 1982 ("FTAIA"), 15 U.S.C. §6a, the Sherman Act does not apply to conduct involving foreign trade or commerce, other than import trade or import commerce, unless "such conduct has a direct, substantial, and reasonably foreseeable effect" on domestic or import commerce. 15 U.S.C. §6a(1)(A). The FTAIA was intended to exempt from the Sherman Act export transactions that did not injure the United States economy, *see* H.R. Rep. No. 97-686, pp. 2-3, 9-10 (1982), and it is unclear how it might apply to the conduct alleged here. Also unclear is whether the Act's "direct, substantial, and reasonably foreseeable effect" standard amends existing law or merely codifies it. We need not address these questions here. Assuming that the FTAIA's standard affects this case, and assuming further that that standard differs from the prior law, the conduct alleged plainly meets its requirements.

111. Justice Scalia contends that comity concerns figure into the prior analysis whether jurisdiction exists under the Sherman Act. This contention is inconsistent with the general understanding that the Sherman Act covers foreign conduct producing a substantial intended effect in the United States, and that concerns of comity come into play, if at all, only after a court has determined that the acts complained of are subject to Sherman Act jurisdiction. *See United States v. Aluminum Co. of America*, 148 F.2d 416, 444 (2d Cir. 1945) ("it follows from what we have . . . said that [the agreements at issue] were unlawful [under the Sherman Act], though made abroad, if they were intended to affect imports and did affect them"); *Mannington Mills, Inc. v. Congoleum Corp.*, 595 F.2d 1287, 1294 (3d Cir. 1979) (once court determines that jurisdiction exists under the Sherman Act, question remains whether comity precludes its exercise). *But cf. Timberlane Lumber Co.;* 1 J. Atwood & K. Brewster, *Antitrust and American Business Abroad* 166 (1981). In any event, the parties conceded jurisdiction at oral argument, and we see no need to address this contention here.

regime over the London reinsurance market and that the conduct alleged here was perfectly consistent with British law and policy. But this is not to state a conflict. "[T]he fact that conduct is lawful in the state in which it took place will not, of itself, bar application of the United States antitrust laws," even where the foreign state has a strong policy to permit or encourage such conduct. *Restatement (Third) Foreign Relations Law* §415, Comment j. No conflict exists, for these purposes, "where a person subject to regulation by two states can comply with the laws of both." *Restatement (Third) Foreign Relations Law* §403, Comment e. Since the London reinsurers do not argue that British law requires them to act in some fashion prohibited by the law of the United States, or claim that their compliance with the laws of both countries is otherwise impossible, we see no conflict with British law. *See Restatement (Third) Foreign Relations Law* §403, Comment e, §415, Comment j. We have no need in this case to address other considerations that might inform a decision to refrain from the exercise of jurisdiction on grounds of international comity.

JUSTICE SCALIA delivered a dissenting opinion with respect to Part II, in which JUSTICE O'CONNOR, JUSTICE KENNEDY, and JUSTICE THOMAS have joined. . . . II. The petitioners, various British corporations and other British subjects, argue that certain of the claims against them constitute an inappropriate extraterritorial application of the Sherman Act. It is important to distinguish two distinct questions raised by this petition: whether the District Court had jurisdiction, and whether the Sherman Act reaches the extraterritorial conduct alleged here. On the first question, I believe that the District Court had subject-matter jurisdiction over the Sherman Act claims against all the defendants (personal jurisdiction is not contested). The respondents asserted nonfrivolous claims under the Sherman Act, and 28 U.S.C. §1331 vests district courts with subject-matter jurisdiction over cases "arising under" federal statutes. As precedents such as *Lauritzen v. Larsen,* make clear, that is sufficient to establish the District Court's jurisdiction over these claims. *Lauritzen* involved a Jones Act claim brought by a foreign sailor against a foreign ship-owner. The shipowner contested the District Court's jurisdiction, apparently on the grounds that the Jones Act did not govern the dispute between the foreign parties to the action. Though ultimately agreeing with the shipowner that the Jones Act did not apply, the Court held that the District Court had jurisdiction.

> As frequently happens, a contention that there is some barrier to granting plaintiff's claim is cast in terms of an exception to jurisdiction of subject matter. A cause of action under our law was asserted here, and the court had power to determine whether it was or was not founded in law and in fact. 345 U.S. at 575.

The second question — the extraterritorial reach of the Sherman Act — has nothing to do with the jurisdiction of the courts. It is a question of substantive law turning on whether, in enacting the Sherman Act, Congress asserted regulatory power over the challenged conduct. *See EEOC v. Arabian American Oil Co.* ("*Aramco*") ("It is our task to determine whether Congress intended the protections of Title VII to apply to United States citizens employed by American employers outside of the United States"). If a plaintiff fails to prevail on this issue, the court does not dismiss the claim for want of subject-matter jurisdiction — want of power to adjudicate; rather, it decides the claim, ruling on the merits that the plaintiff has failed to state a cause of action under the relevant statute. . . .

There is, however, a type of "jurisdiction" relevant to determining the extraterritorial reach of a statute; it is known as "legislative jurisdiction," *Aramco,* 499 U.S. at 253; *Restatement (First) Conflict of Laws* §60 (1934), or "jurisdiction to prescribe," *Restatement (Third)*

Foreign Relations Law §235 (1987). This refers to "the authority of a state to make its law applicable to persons or activities," and is quite a separate matter from "jurisdiction to adjudicate," *see id.* at 231. There is no doubt, of course, that Congress possesses legislative jurisdiction over the acts alleged in this complaint: Congress has broad power under Article I, §8, cl. 3 "[t]o regulate Commerce with foreign Nations," and this Court has repeatedly upheld its power to make laws applicable to persons or activities beyond our territorial boundaries where United States interests are affected [citing cases]. But the question in this case is whether, and to what extent, Congress has exercised that undoubted legislative jurisdiction in enacting the Sherman Act.

Two canons of statutory construction are relevant in this inquiry. The first is the "long-standing principle of American law 'that legislation of Congress, unless a contrary intent appears, is meant to apply only within the territorial jurisdiction of the United States.'" *Aramco* (quoting *Foley Bros.*). Applying that canon in *Aramco,* we held that the version of Title VII . . . then in force did not extend outside the territory of the United States even though the statute contained broad provisions extending its prohibitions to, for example, "'any activity, business, or industry in commerce.'" We held such "boilerplate language" to be an insufficient indication to override the presumption against extraterritoriality. The Sherman Act contains similar "boilerplate language," and if the question were not governed by precedent, it would be worth considering whether that presumption controls the outcome here. We have, however, found the presumption to be overcome with respect to our antitrust laws; it is now well established that the Sherman Act applies extraterritorially.

But if the presumption against extraterritoriality has been overcome or is otherwise inapplicable, a second canon of statutory construction becomes relevant: "[A]n act of Congress ought never to be construed to violate the law of nations if any other possible construction remains." *Murray v. The Charming Betsy,* 2 Cranch 64, 118 (1804) (Marshall, C.J.). This canon is "wholly independent" of the presumption against extraterritoriality. It is relevant to determining the substantive reach of a statute because "the law of nations," or customary international law, includes limitations on a nation's exercise of its jurisdiction to prescribe. Though it clearly has constitutional authority to do so, Congress is generally presumed not to have exceeded those customary international-law limits on jurisdiction to prescribe.

Consistent with that presumption, this and other courts have frequently recognized that, even where the presumption against extraterritoriality does not apply, statutes should not be interpreted to regulate foreign persons or conduct if that regulation would conflict with principles of international law. For example, in *Romero v. International Terminal Operating Co.,* the [Court] . . . stated that, "in the absence of contrary congressional direction," it would apply "principles of choice of law that are consonant with the needs of a general federal maritime law and with due recognition of our self-regarding respect for the relevant interests of foreign nations in the regulation of maritime commerce as part of the legitimate concern of the international community." . . .

Romero referred to, and followed, the choice-of-law analysis set forth in *Lauritzen v. Larsen.* As previously mentioned, *Lauritzen* also involved a Jones Act claim brought by a foreign sailor against a foreign employer. The *Lauritzen* Court recognized the basic problem: "If [the Jones Act were] read literally, Congress has conferred an American right of action which requires nothing more than that plaintiff be 'any seaman who shall suffer personal injury in the course of his employment.'" The solution it adopted was to construe the statute "to apply only to areas and transactions in which American law would be considered operative under prevalent doctrines of international law." To support application of international law to limit the facial breadth of the statute, the Court relied upon — of course — Chief Justice Marshall's statement in *The Charming Betsy*. It then set forth "several factors which, alone or in combination, are generally conceded to influence choice of law to govern a tort claim." 345 U.S. at 583 (discussing factors).

Lauritzen, Romero, and *McCulloch* were maritime cases, but we have recognized the principle that the scope of generally worded statutes must be construed in light of international law in other areas as well. More specifically, the principle was expressed in *United States v. Alcoa,* the decision that established the extraterritorial reach of the Sherman Act. In his opinion for the court, Judge Learned Hand cautioned "we are not to read general words, such as those in [the Sherman] Act, without regard to the limitations customarily observed by nations upon the exercise of their powers; limitations which generally correspond to those fixed by the 'Conflict of Laws.' "

More recent lower court precedent has also tempered the extraterritorial application of the Sherman Act with considerations of "international comity." *See Timberlane Lumber Co.; Mannington Mills, Inc.; Montreal Trading Ltd.; Laker Airways* [sic]. The "comity" they refer to is not the comity of courts, whereby judges decline to exercise jurisdiction over matters more appropriately adjudged elsewhere, but rather what might be termed "prescriptive comity": the respect sovereign nations afford each other by limiting the reach of their laws. That comity is exercised by legislatures when they enact laws, and courts assume it has been exercised when they come to interpreting the scope of laws their legislatures have enacted. . . . Comity in this sense includes the choice-of-law principles that, "in the absence of contrary congressional direction," are assumed to be incorporated into our substantive laws having extraterritorial reach. *Romero,* 358 U.S. at 382-83; *Lauritzen,* 345 U.S. at 578-79. Considering comity in this way is just part of determining whether the Sherman Act prohibits the conduct at issue.[112]

In sum, the practice of using international law to limit the extraterritorial reach of statutes is firmly established in our jurisprudence. In proceeding to apply that practice to the present case, I shall rely on the *Restatement (Third) Foreign Relations Law* for the relevant principles of international law. Its standards appear fairly supported in the decisions of this Court construing international choice-of-law principles (*Lauritzen, Romero,* and [another decision]) and in the decisions of other federal courts, especially *Timberlane.* Whether the *Restatement* precisely reflects international law in every detail matters little here, as I believe this case would be resolved the same way under virtually any conceivable test that takes account of foreign regulatory interests.

Under the *Restatement,* a nation having some "basis" for jurisdiction to prescribe law should nonetheless refrain from exercising that jurisdiction "with respect to a person or activity having connections with another state when the exercise of such jurisdiction is unreasonable." *Restatement (Third)* §403(1). The [§403] "reasonableness" inquiry turns on a number of factors [which Justice Scalia quoted]. Rarely would these factors point more clearly against application of U.S. law. The activity relevant to the counts at issue here took place primarily in the United Kingdom, and the defendants in these counts are British corporations and British subjects having their principal place of business or residence outside the United States. Great Britain has established a comprehensive regulatory scheme governing the London reinsurance markets, and clearly has a heavy "interest

---

112. Some antitrust courts, including the Court of Appeals in the present case, have mistaken the comity at issue for the "comity of courts," which has led them to characterize the question presented as one of "abstention," that is, whether they should "exercise or decline jurisdiction." *Mannington Mills, Inc. v. Congoleum Corp.,* 595 F.2d 1287, 1294, 1296 (3d Cir. 1979); *see also In re Insurance Antitrust Litigation,* 938 F.2d 919, 932 (9th Cir. 1991). As I shall discuss, that seems to be the error the Court has fallen into today. Because courts are generally reluctant to refuse the exercise of conferred jurisdiction, confusion on this seemingly theoretical point can have the very practical consequence of greatly expanding the extraterritorial reach of the Sherman Act.

in regulating the activity,"§403(2)(g). . . . Considering these factors, I think it unimaginable that an assertion of legislative jurisdiction by the United States would be considered reasonable, and therefore it is inappropriate to assume, in the absence of statutory indication to the contrary, that Congress has made such an assertion.

It is evident from what I have said that the Court's comity analysis, which proceeds as though the issue is whether the courts should "decline to exercise . . . jurisdiction," rather than whether the Sherman Act covers this conduct, is simply misdirected. I do not at all agree, moreover, with the Court's conclusion that the issue of the substantive scope of the Sherman Act is not in the case. To be sure, the parties did not make a clear distinction between adjudicative jurisdiction and the scope of the statute. Parties often do not, as we have observed (and have declined to punish with procedural default) before. . . . In any event, if one erroneously chooses, as the Court does, to make adjudicative jurisdiction (or, more precisely, abstention) the vehicle for taking account of the needs of prescriptive comity, the Court still gets it wrong. It concludes that no "true conflict" counselling nonapplication of U.S. law (or rather, as it thinks, U.S. judicial jurisdiction) exists unless compliance with U.S. law would constitute a violation of another country's law. That breathtakingly broad proposition, which contradicts the many cases discussed earlier, will bring the Sherman Act and other laws into sharp and unnecessary conflict with the legitimate interests of other countries — particularly our closest trading partners.

In the sense in which the term "conflic[t]" was used in *Lauritzen,* 345 U.S. at 582, and is generally understood in the field of conflicts of laws, there is clearly a conflict in this case. The petitioners here, like the defendant in *Lauritzen,* were not compelled by any foreign law to take their allegedly wrongful actions, but that no more precludes a conflict-of-laws analysis here than it did there. . . . Where applicable foreign and domestic law provide different substantive rules of decision to govern the parties' dispute, a conflict-of-laws analysis is necessary. Literally the only support that the Court adduces for its position is §403 of the *Restatement (Third) Foreign Relations Law*— or more precisely Comment e to that provision, which states: "Subsection (3) [which says that a state should defer to another state if that state's interest is clearly greater] applies only when one state requires what another prohibits, or where compliance with the regulations of two states exercising jurisdiction consistently with this section is otherwise impossible. It does not apply where a person subject to regulation by two states can comply with the laws of both. . . ." The Court has completely misinterpreted this provision. Subsection (3) of §403 (requiring one State to defer to another in the limited circumstances just described) comes into play only after subsection (1) of §403 has been complied with — *i.e.,* after it has been determined that the exercise of jurisdiction by both of the two states is not "unreasonable." That prior question is answered by applying the factors (*inter alia*) set forth in subsection (2) of §403, that is, precisely the factors that I have discussed in text and that the Court rejects.[113]

F. HOFFMANN-LAROCHE, LTD. v. EMPAGRAN, SA

542 U.S. 155 (2004)

Breyer, Justice. The [Foreign Trade Antitrust Improvements Act] excludes from the Sherman Act's reach much anticompetitive conduct that causes only foreign injury.

---

113. The Court skips directly to subsection (3) of §403, apparently on the authority of Comment j to §415 of the *Restatement (Third)*. But the preceding commentary to §415 makes clear that "[a]ny exercise of [legislative] jurisdiction under this section is subject to the requirement of reasonableness" set forth in §403(2). *Restatement (Third)* §415, Comment a. Comment j refers back to the conflict analysis set forth in §403(3) which, as noted above, comes after the reasonableness analysis of §403(2).

It does so by setting forth a general rule stating that the Sherman Act "shall not apply to conduct involving trade or commerce . . . with foreign nations." 96 Stat. 1246, 15 U.S.C. §6a. It then creates exceptions to the general rule, applicable where (roughly speaking) that conduct significantly harms imports, domestic commerce, or American exporters.

We here focus upon anticompetitive price-fixing activity that is in significant part foreign, that causes some domestic antitrust injury, and that independently causes separate foreign injury. We ask two questions about the price-fixing conduct and the foreign injury that it causes. First, does that conduct fall within the FTAIA's general rule excluding the Sherman Act's application? That is to say, does the price-fixing activity constitute "conduct involving trade or commerce . . . with foreign nations"? We conclude that it does.

Second, we ask whether the conduct nonetheless falls within a domestic-injury exception to the general rule, an exception that applies (and makes the Sherman Act nonetheless applicable) where the conduct (1) has a "direct, substantial, and reasonably foreseeable effect" on domestic commerce, and (2) "such effect gives rise to a [Sherman Act] claim." §§6a(1)(A), (2). We conclude that the exception does not apply where the plaintiff's claim rests solely on the independent foreign harm. . . .

In more concrete terms, this case involves vitamin sellers around the world that agreed to fix prices, leading to higher vitamin prices in the United States and independently leading to higher vitamin prices in other countries such as Ecuador. We conclude that, in this scenario, a purchaser in the United States could bring a Sherman Act claim under the FTAIA based on domestic injury, but a purchaser in Ecuador could not bring a Sherman Act claim based on foreign harm.

I. The plaintiffs . . . originally filed a class-action suit on behalf of foreign and domestic purchasers of vitamins under [in relevant part the Sherman and Clayton Acts]. Their complaint alleged that petitioners, foreign and domestic vitamin manufacturers and distributors, had engaged in a price-fixing conspiracy, raising the price of vitamin products to customers in the United States and . . . in foreign countries.

[P]etitioners moved to dismiss the suit as to the foreign purchasers (the respondents here), five foreign vitamin distributors located in Ukraine, Australia, Ecuador, and Panama, each of which bought vitamins from petitioners for delivery outside the United States. [The district court dismissed the foreign purchasers' claims. The foreign purchasers appealed, and the D.C. Circuit reversed, holding that the FTAIA's "domestic injury exception" applied.]

II. The FTAIA seeks to make clear to American exporters (and to firms doing business abroad) that the Sherman Act does not prevent them from entering into business arrangements (say, joint-selling arrangements), however anticompetitive, as long as those arrangements adversely affect only foreign markets. . . . It does so by removing from the Sherman Act's reach, (1) export activities and (2) other commercial activities taking place abroad, unless those activities adversely affect domestic commerce, imports to the United States, or exporting activities of one engaged in such activities within the United States. The FTAIA says:

Sections 1 to 7 of this title [the Sherman Act] shall not apply to conduct involving trade or commerce (other than import trade or import commerce) with foreign nations unless—
   (1) such conduct has a direct, substantial, and reasonably foreseeable effect—(A) on trade or commerce which is not trade or commerce with foreign nations [i.e., domestic trade or commerce], or on import trade or import commerce with foreign nations; or (B) on export trade or export commerce with foreign nations, of a person engaged in such trade or commerce in the United States [i.e., on an American export competitor]; and

(2) such effect gives rise to a claim under the provisions of sections 1 to 7 of this title, other than this section.

If sections 1 to 7 of this title apply to such conduct only because of the operation of paragraph (1)(B), then sections 1 to 7 of this title shall apply to such conduct only for injury to export business in the United States. 15 U.S.C. §6a.

This technical language initially lays down a general rule placing all (non-import) activity involving foreign commerce outside the Sherman Act's reach. It then brings such conduct back within the Sherman Act's reach provided that the conduct both (1) sufficiently affects American commerce, i.e., it has a "direct, substantial, and reasonably foreseeable effect" on American domestic, import, or (certain) export commerce, and (2) has an effect of a kind that antitrust law considers harmful, i.e., the "effect" must "giv[e] rise to a [Sherman Act] claim." §§6a(1), (2). We ask here how this language applies to price-fixing activity that is in significant part foreign, that has the requisite domestic effect, and that also has independent foreign effects giving rise to the plaintiff's claim. [Initially, in an omitted portion of its opinion, the Court held that the FTAIA's application is not limited to exports.]

IV. . . . Because the underlying antitrust action is complex . . . we reemphasize that we base our decision upon the following: The price-fixing conduct significantly and adversely affects both customers outside the United States and customers within the United States, but the adverse foreign effect is independent of any adverse domestic effect. In these circumstances, we find that the FTAIA exception does not apply (and thus the Sherman Act does not apply) for two main reasons.

First, this Court ordinarily construes ambiguous statutes to avoid unreasonable interference with the sovereign authority of other nations. *See, e.g., McCulloch, supra; Romero, supra; Lauritzen v. Larsen, supra.* This rule of construction reflects principles of customary international law that (we must assume) Congress ordinarily seeks to follow. *See Restatement (Third) of Foreign Relations Law* §§403(1), 403(2) (1986); *Hartford Fire Insurance Co.,* 509 U.S. at 817 (Scalia, J., dissenting) (identifying rule of construction as derived from the principle of "prescriptive comity"). This rule of statutory construction cautions courts to assume that legislators take account of the legitimate sovereign interests of other nations when they write American laws. It thereby helps the potentially conflicting laws of different nations work together in harmony—a harmony particularly needed in today's highly interdependent commercial world.

No one denies that America's antitrust laws, when applied to foreign conduct, can interfere with a foreign nation's ability independently to regulate its own commercial affairs. But our courts have long held that application of our antitrust laws to foreign anticompetitive conduct is nonetheless reasonable, and hence consistent with principles of prescriptive comity, insofar as they reflect a legislative effort to redress domestic antitrust injury that foreign anticompetitive conduct has caused. *See United States v. Aluminum Co. of America, supra;* 1 P. Areeda & D. Turner, *Antitrust Law* ¶236 (1978).

But why is it reasonable to apply those laws to foreign conduct insofar as that conduct causes independent foreign harm and that foreign harm alone gives rise to the plaintiff's claim? Like the former case, application of those laws creates a serious risk of interference with a foreign nation's ability independently to regulate its own commercial affairs. But, unlike the former case, the justification for that interference seems insubstantial. *See Restatement* §403(2) (determining reasonableness on basis of such factors as connections with regulating nation, harm to that nation's interests, extent to which other nations regulate, and the potential for conflict). Why should American law supplant, for example, Canada's or Great Britain's or Japan's own determination about how best to protect

Canadian or British or Japanese customers from anticompetitive conduct engaged in significant part by Canadian or British or Japanese or other foreign companies?

We recognize that principles of comity provide Congress greater leeway when it seeks to control through legislation the actions of American companies, *see Restatement* §402; and some of the anticompetitive price-fixing conduct alleged here took place in America. But the higher foreign prices of which the foreign plaintiffs here complain are not the consequence of any domestic anticompetitive conduct that Congress sought to forbid, for Congress did not seek to forbid any such conduct insofar as it is here relevant, i.e., insofar as it is intertwined with foreign conduct that causes independent foreign harm. Rather Congress sought to release domestic (and foreign) anticompetitive conduct from Sherman Act constraints when that conduct causes foreign harm. Congress, of course, did make an exception where that conduct also causes domestic harm. But any independent domestic harm the foreign conduct causes here has, by definition, little or nothing to do with the matter.

We thus repeat the basic question: Why is it reasonable to apply this law to conduct that is significantly foreign insofar as that conduct causes independent foreign harm and that foreign harm alone gives rise to the plaintiff's claim? We can find no good answer to the question. The Areeda and Hovenkamp treatise notes that under the Court of Appeals' interpretation of the statute:

> a Malaysian customer could . . . maintain an action under United States law in a United States court against its own Malaysian supplier, another cartel member, simply by noting that unnamed third parties injured [in the United States] by the American [cartel member's] conduct would also have a cause of action. Effectively, the United States courts would provide worldwide subject matter jurisdiction to any foreign suitor wishing to sue its own local supplier, but unhappy with its own sovereign's provisions for private antitrust enforcement, provided that a different plaintiff had a cause of action against a different firm for injuries that were within U.S. [other-than-import] commerce. It does not seem excessively rigid to infer that Congress would not have intended that result. P. Areeda & H. Hovenkamp, *Antitrust Law* ¶273, pp. 122-123 (Supp. 2006).

We agree with the comment. We can find no convincing justification for the extension of the Sherman Act's scope that it describes.

Respondents reply that many nations have adopted antitrust laws similar to our own, to the point where the practical likelihood of interference with the relevant interests of other nations is minimal. Leaving price fixing to the side, however, this Court has found to the contrary. *See, e.g., Hartford Fire,* 509 U.S. at 797-799 (noting that the alleged conduct in the London reinsurance market, while illegal under United States antitrust laws, was assumed to be perfectly consistent with British law and policy); *see also, e.g.,* 2 W. Fugate, *Foreign Commerce and the Antitrust Laws* §16.6 (5th ed. 1996) (noting differences between European Union and United States law on vertical restraints).

Regardless, even where nations agree about primary conduct, say price fixing, they disagree dramatically about appropriate remedies. The application, for example, of American private treble-damages remedies to anticompetitive conduct taking place abroad has generated considerable controversy. *See, e.g.,* 2 ABA Section of Antitrust Law, Antitrust Law Developments 1208-1209 (5th ed. 2002). And several foreign nations have filed briefs here arguing that to apply our remedies would unjustifiably permit their citizens to bypass their own less generous remedial schemes, thereby upsetting a balance of competing considerations that their own domestic antitrust laws embody. . . . These briefs add that a decision permitting independently injured foreign plaintiffs to pursue private treble-damages remedies would undermine foreign nations' own antitrust enforcement policies by diminishing foreign firms' incentive to cooperate with antitrust authorities in return for prosecutorial amnesty. . . .

Respondents alternatively argue that comity does not demand an interpretation of the FTAIA that would exclude independent foreign injury cases across the board. Rather, courts can take (and sometimes have taken) account of comity considerations case by case, abstaining where comity considerations so dictate. *Cf., e.g., Hartford Fire, supra,* at 797, n.24; *Mannington Mills, Inc. v. Congoleum Corp.,* 595 F.2d 1287, 1294-1295 (3rd Cir. 1979).

In our view, however, this approach is too complex to prove workable. The Sherman Act covers many different kinds of anticompetitive agreements. Courts would have to examine how foreign law, compared with American law, treats not only price fixing but also, say, information-sharing agreements, patent-licensing price conditions, territorial product resale limitations, and various forms of joint venture, in respect to both primary conduct and remedy. The legally and economically technical nature of that enterprise means lengthier proceedings, appeals, and more proceedings — to the point where procedural costs and delays could themselves threaten interference with a foreign nation's ability to maintain the integrity of its own antitrust enforcement system. . . .

We conclude that principles of prescriptive comity counsel against the Court of Appeals' interpretation of the FTAIA. Where foreign anticompetitive conduct plays a significant role and where foreign injury is independent of domestic effects, Congress might have hoped that America's antitrust laws, so fundamental a component of our own economic system, would commend themselves to other nations as well. But, if America's antitrust policies could not win their own way in the international marketplace for such ideas, Congress, we must assume, would not have tried to impose them, in an act of legal imperialism, through legislative fiat.

Second, the FTAIA's language and history suggest that Congress designed the FTAIA to clarify, perhaps to limit, but not to expand in any significant way, the Sherman Act's scope as applied to foreign commerce. *See* House Report 2-3, U.S. Code Cong. & Admin. News 1982, 2487, 2487-2488. And we have found no significant indication that at the time Congress wrote this statute courts would have thought the Sherman Act applicable in these circumstances. . . .

Taken together, these two sets of considerations, the one derived from comity and the other reflecting history, convince us that Congress would not have intended the FTAIA's exception to bring independently caused foreign injury within the Sherman Act's reach. . . .

SCALIA, JUSTICE, with whom JUSTICE THOMAS joins, concurring in the judgment. I concur in the judgment of the Court because the language of the statute is readily susceptible of the interpretation the Court provides and because only that interpretation is consistent with the principle that statutes should be read in accord with the customary deference to the application of foreign countries' laws within their own territories.

Notes *on* Hartford Fire *and* Hoffmann-LaRoche

1. *Scope of FTAIA.* As discussed in *Hartford Fire* and *Hoffmann-LaRoche*, in 1982, Congress enacted the FTAIA, 15 U.S.C. §§6a, 45(a). Among other things, in language excerpted above (*see supra* pp. 697-699), the FTAIA addressed the jurisdictional requirements for the Sherman Act and the Federal Trade Commission Act. Congress enacted the FTAIA in order to improve the competitiveness of U.S. firms in overseas markets, by freeing them from antitrust restraints on activities in "export trade." H.R. Rep. No. 686, 97th Cong., 2d Sess. 10 (1982).

The FTAIA does not apply to "import trade." What exactly does this mean? An early draft of the FTAIA provided that it applied only to "export trade or commerce." A House Committee amended that bill so that it applied to "trade or commerce (other than import trade or commerce)." In *Hoffmann-LaRoche,* the Supreme Court relied on this legislative history to conclude that the FTAIA is not strictly limited to exports. 542 U.S. at 162-163. For recent discussions of the import exception, *see In re TFT-LCD (Flat Panel) Antitrust Litig.,* 2010 WL 2629728 (N.D. Cal. June 29, 2010); *Animal Science Products, Inc. v. China Nat'l Metals & Minerals Import & Export Corp.,* 702 F. Supp. 2d 320 (D.N.J. 2010).

Was the FTAIA applicable in *Hartford Fire?* Is the provision of reinsurance of U.S. insurance risks "import trade"? *Compare In re Insurance Antitrust Litig.,* 723 F. Supp. 464 (N.D. Cal. 1989) (case involved "import trade"), *aff'd,* 938 F.2d 919 (9th Cir. 1991). Does this suggest that the jurisdictional reach of the Sherman Act with respect to import trade is broader or narrower than the FTAIA's formula?

2. *Lower court applications of FTAIA.* A number of courts have relied on the FTAIA to dismiss antitrust actions. *E.g., In re Dynamic Random Access Memory Antitrust Litig.,* 546 F.3d 981 (9th Cir. 2008); *In re Monosodium Glutamate Antitrust Litig.,* 477 F.3d 535 (8th Cir. 2007); *Empagran SA v. F. Hoffmann-LaRoche, Ltd.,* 417 F.3d 1267 (D.C. Cir. 2005); *Sniado v. Bank Austria AG,* 378 F.3d 210 (2d Cir. 2004); *U.S. v. LSL Biotechnologies,* 379 F.3d 672 (9th Cir. 2004); *Turicentro, SA v. American Airlines Inc.,* 303 F.3d 293 (3d Cir. 2002); *Den Norske Stats Oljeselskap AS v. HeereMac Vof,* 241 F.3d 420 (5th Cir. 2001); *McGlinchy v. Shell Chem. Co.,* 845 F.2d 802 (9th Cir. 1988); *Animal Science Products, Inc. v. China Nat'l Metals & Minerals Import & Export Corp.,* 702 F. Supp. 2d 320 (D.N.J. 2010); *Commercial Street Express LLC v. Sara Lee Corp.,* 2008 WL 5377815 (N.D. Ill. Dec. 18, 2008); *Boyd v. AWB, Ltd.,* 544 F. Supp. 2d 236 (S.D.N.Y. 2008); *In re Rubber Chemicals Antitrust Litig.,* 504 F. Supp. 2d 777 (N.D. Cal. 2007). For a recent decision carefully parsing the effect of the FTAIA on claims with both foreign and domestic elements, *see In re Static Random Access Memory (SRAM) Antitrust Litig.,* 2010 WL 5477313 (N.D. Cal. Dec. 31, 2010).

3. *Effects test under FTAIA.* Lower courts have generally concluded that the FTAIA's effects test is more difficult to satisfy than *Alcoa*'s standard. *U.S. v. LSL Biotechnologies,* 379 F.3d 672, 679-683 (9th Cir. 2004); *The 'In' Porters, SA v. Hanes Printables, Inc.,* 663 F. Supp. 494 (M.D.N.C. 1987); *Liamuiga Tours v. Travel Impressions, Ltd.,* 617 F. Supp. 920, 924 (E.D.N.Y. 1985). *But see U.S. v. LSL Biotechnologies,* 379 F.3d 672, 683-701 (9th Cir. 2004) (Aldisert, J. dissenting). *See generally* Link, *Construction and Application of Foreign Trade Antitrust Improvements Act (FTAIA),* 1 A.L.R. Fed. 483 (2005). *Cf. United States v. Anderson,* 326 F.3d 1319, 1330 (11th Cir. 2003); *Papst Motoren GmbH & Co. v. Kanematsu-Goshu (USA), Inc.,* 629 F. Supp. 864 (S.D.N.Y. 1986). *Hartford Fire* declined to consider whether the FTAIA set a different standard from the Sherman Act effects test. Does the Court in *Hoffmann-LaRoche* provide any guidance on this question?

4. *The FTAIA and state law.* While most antitrust claims are brought under federal law, many states have their own competition laws. Are those laws automatically subject to the same limits of comity and reasonableness that temper expansive application of federal antitrust laws? If so, what is the constitutional basis for those limits? The Foreign Commerce Clause? The Supremacy Clause? Do the limitations of the FTAIA apply to antitrust claims brought under state law? Lower federal courts divide on this question. *Compare, e.g., In re Intel Corp. Microprocessor Antitrust Litig.,* 476 F. Supp. 2d 452 (D. Del. 2007) (FTAIA's limits apply to state-law antitrust claims) *with In re Potash Antitrust Litig.,* 667 F. Supp. 2d 907 (N.D. Ill. 2009) (reaching contrary conclusion).

5. The territoriality presumption in Hartford Fire *and* Hoffmann-LaRoche. Two years before it decided *Hartford Fire*, the Supreme Court reaffirmed the territoriality presumption in *Aramco. See supra* pp. 659-664. Why wasn't *Aramco*'s territoriality presumption applicable in *Hartford Fire?* What about in *Hoffmann-LaRoche?* Consider the terms of the Sherman Act, applicable to contracts in restraint of trade "with foreign nations." Recall how *American Banana* interpreted that language in light of the territoriality presumption. How is it that the Court deals with the territoriality presumption in *Hartford Fire?* Note Justice Scalia's comment in dissent that "[t]he Sherman Act contains similar 'boilerplate language' [to that in Title VII], and if the question were not governed by precedent, it would be worth considering whether that presumption controls the outcome here." Consider this view in light of Justice Scalia's plurality opinion in *Burnham*, which forcefully defends the territoriality principle.

Did the territoriality presumption, which Justice Scalia hinted at in *Hartford Fire*, experience a revival in the antitrust context in *Hoffmann-LaRoche?* Justices Scalia and Thomas, concurring in the judgment, surely sought to reassert it. (Note their comment about the "customary deference [owed by courts] to the application of foreign countries' laws within their own territories.")

What about the majority? The central premise of the opinion was that the "Court ordinarily construes ambiguous statutes to avoid unreasonable interferences with the sovereign authority of other states." As part of the authority supporting that proposition, the Court cites Justice Scalia's *dissent* from *Hartford Fire*, which adopted an "international law" presumption of sorts, as well as §403 of the *Restatement (Third)*.

Note also the *Hoffmann-LaRoche* Court's comment that "if America's antitrust policies could not win their own way in the international marketplace for such ideas, Congress, we must assume, would not have tried to impose them, in an act of legal imperialism, through legislative fiat." Compare that to the approach to the effects doctrine taken in *Alcoa* and *Hartford Fire*.

6. Does the FTAIA's language overcome the territoriality presumption? How would the FTAIA be interpreted in light of the territoriality presumption? Can it be said that the FTAIA's language, quoted above, evidences an affirmative congressional intention to apply the Sherman Act extraterritorially? Is it not entirely clear, as a matter of common sense and legislative intent, that the drafters of the FTAIA understood and expected the Sherman Act to apply extraterritorially? Why else would Congress have set forth statutory limits on its extraterritorial application under an effects test? On the other hand, is the FTAIA any different from the alien exemption in Title VII, which *Aramco* found insufficient to overcome the territoriality presumption? With respect to import trade, not covered by the FTAIA, what effect does the territoriality presumption have? Consider Justice Scalia's concurring opinion in *Hoffmann-LaRoche*. What does it suggest about his approach to interpreting the FTAIA?

7. Defendants' concession in Hartford Fire *that jurisdiction existed.* Almost all the defendants in *Hartford Fire* conceded that the Sherman Act applied to their conduct, thereby granting the district court both subject matter and legislative jurisdiction. *See supra* p. 692; *compare supra* pp. 32, 599. Should these defendants have taken the position that they did? In doing so, did the defendants miss the opportunity to argue that either the territoriality presumption or a *Lauritzen/Steele* presumption should apply? Why did they concede jurisdiction? Was it wise to do so? Note Justice Scalia's efforts to disregard this procedural misstep.

8. Role of international comity in Hartford Fire. Although they conceded jurisdiction, the defendants in *Hartford Fire* argued that "the exercise of that jurisdiction should be restrained." Citing *Timberlane* and §403, they relied on "the principle of international comity" to support that contention. The various opinions in *Hartford Fire* treated these arguments in very different ways. In particular, Justices Souter and Scalia disagreed over the relevance of international comity to the existence of jurisdiction under the Sherman Act.

(a) Justice Souter's view that comity is a separate basis for abstention apart from jurisdiction. Justice Souter accepted the defendants' concession that jurisdiction existed, and then proceeded on the assumption that comity provided an additional, discretionary defense. Is this a legitimate mode of analysis? If Congress has applied the antitrust laws to particular conduct, can federal courts abstain from exercising jurisdiction in those cases? Justice Scalia, who usually is skeptical about abstention doctrines, *see W.S. Kirkpatrick & Co. v. Environmental Tectonics Corp.,* 493 U.S. 400 (1990), apparently would have applied an abstention-like doctrine in *Hartford Fire;* he did comment, however, in a footnote, that "courts are generally reluctant to refuse the exercise of conferred jurisdiction."

(b) Propriety of comity or §403 analysis under the FTAIA and other antitrust legislation. Does *Hartford Fire* hold that comity and/or §403 of the *Third Restatement* may be relied upon to decline jurisdiction under the Sherman Act or the FTAIA? Or does Justice Souter leave the question open? How should this question be answered? If Congress *has* granted jurisdiction, and made the antitrust laws applicable, in a particular case, what permits a U.S. court to decline to hear the case on grounds of comity? Consider again the *Timberlane/Laker* debate, *supra* pp. 687-688.

Recall the view that a court has no discretion to decline, on comity grounds, jurisdiction that Congress has conferred. *See supra* p. 692. Is that persuasive? Compare the role of comity in *Hartford Fire* with that in *Timberlane.* Compare also the debate over the legitimacy of the *forum non conveniens* doctrine. *See supra* p. 384.

(c) Justice Scalia's view that comity is relevant to the existence of jurisdiction. Unlike Justice Souter, Justice Scalia thought that considerations of comity were relevant to the jurisdictional reach of the Sherman Act: "That comity is exercised by legislatures when they enact laws, and courts assume that it has been exercised when they come to interpreting the scope of laws that their legislatures have enacted." How does this analysis compare to the approach to interpreting the Sherman Act in *American Banana* and *Alcoa*? Note that, although Justice Scalia refers to "comity," he in fact adopts the "practice of using international *law* to limit the extraterritorial reach of statutes," citing the numerous decisions where the Court has done so (such as *Lauritzen, Romero,* and *McCulloch*).

9. *Justice Souter's §403 analysis in* Hartford Fire. Consider the Court's application of §403 in *Hartford Fire.* Why is it that the Court sees no need to engage in consideration of the various §403(2) factors?

(a) No conflict with English law. Justice Souter concludes that there was no conflict between the U.S. antitrust laws and the English legal regulatory structure for reinsurance. Why is that? Consider Justice Scalia's treatment of the same issue. Which view is correct?

(b) Justice Souter's requirement of a direct conflict between U.S. and foreign law. Justice Souter's opinion is unclear in its discussion of the lack of a conflict between U.S. and foreign law. That discussion arguably required a direct conflict between U.S. and English law, where inconsistent legal requirements are imposed, as a prerequisite to declining jurisdiction on grounds of comity. As Justice Scalia's dissent observes, if this is what Justice Souter was trying to say, it is clearly a misreading of §403 and of *Timberlane.* As discussed above, *see supra* pp. 602-603, §403(2) lists a conflict between U.S. and foreign law as merely *one of many factors* relevant to the exercise of jurisdiction; the same is true of the *Timberlane* analysis, *see supra* p. 687. The absence of a direct conflict—imposing inconsistent legal duties—does *not* make §403 inapplicable. *See also* Lowenfeld, *Conflict, Balancing of Interests, and the Exercise of Jurisdiction to Prescribe: Reflections on the Insurance Antitrust Case,* 89 Am. J. Int'l L. 42, 50 (1995) (comment by Reporter for *Restatement (Third):* "it is clear to me that

Justice Scalia understood, and Justice Souter misunderstood, the approach of the *Restatement*"). Moreover, although §403(3) *does* require a "conflict," this subsection is only applicable if §403(2) has first been satisfied.

Alternatively, Justice Souter might have been trying to say that, once jurisdiction was conceded, then only §403(3) — not §403(2) — is relevant. That would have been reading a great deal into the defendant's concession, although it is most consistent with Justice Souter's opinion.

Finally, Justice Souter might have been saying (albeit opaquely) that a §403(2) comity analysis would only have permitted dismissal if there were a direct conflict. This is perhaps the most sensible position that the Court could have taken, but it is the least consistent with the actual language of Justice Souter's opinion.

10. *Was* Hartford Fire *correctly decided?* How should *Hartford Fire* have been decided? Even if there was a conflict between U.S. and English law, was Justice Scalia right in concluding that the Sherman Act did not apply to the defendants' conduct? Note in particular Justice Scalia's statement that "this case would be resolved the same way under virtually any conceivable test that takes account of foreign regulatory interests." Consider the alleged magnitude of the U.S. effects of the defendants' conduct and the alleged intention of the defendants to affect U.S. conduct. Isn't Justice Scalia wrong about the ultimate outcome in *Hartford Fire?*

11. *Supplemental jurisdiction as a (partial) solution to the problem of conflict.* Recall that under the supplemental jurisdiction statute, 28 U.S.C. §1367, federal courts have the discretion to exercise subject matter jurisdiction over claims that arise out of the same common nucleus of operative facts as claims arising under federal law. Suppose a plaintiff brought a case in federal court alleging violations of both federal antitrust law *and* foreign antitrust law (such as European competition rules). Should a court exercise supplemental jurisdiction over the foreign law claims? Most courts have been reluctant to do so. *See, e.g., In re Urethane Antitrust Litig.*, 683 F. Supp. 2d 1214 (D. Kan. 2010).

Is that reluctance well placed? Would that reduce the risk of conflict because a single adjudicator would resolve all related claims arising under different systems of law in a single proceeding? Do federal courts even have the capacity to evaluate claims arising under foreign law? How does your answer to this question compare to your answer to comparable questions under topics such as *forum non conveniens? See supra* pp. 420-421. If you believe that federal courts lack the necessary capacity, why should we have any more confidence that they possess the necessary capacity to identify a conflict in the first place?

12. *Role of international comity in* Hoffmann-LaRoche. How does *Hoffmann-LaRoche* deal with the question of the proper comity analysis under the antitrust laws? Compare its comity analysis with that in *Lauritzen, Timberlane,* §403, and *Hartford Fire.*

(a) Abstention versus jurisdictional limit. Does the *Hoffmann-LaRoche* Court rely on principles of comity as a basis for abstention or as a basis for interpreting the jurisdictional reach of the FTAIA? Compare Justice Breyer's opinion in *Hoffmann-LaRoche* with Justice Souter's opinion in *Hartford Fire.* Note again that the *Hoffmann-LaRoche* Court relies on Justice Scalia's dissenting opinion in *Hartford Fire.*

(b) Case-by-case analysis versus general rule. Consider how Justice Breyer applies a comity analysis in *Hoffmann-LaRoche.* Note the Court's refusal to consider a case-by-case analysis of particular comity considerations in specific cases. *See supra* p. 701. How does this compare with either the *Timberlane* rule of reason or the §403 analysis? Reread how each source provides for application of the various factors relevant to a comity-based reasonableness analysis. Has the Court's opinion in *Hoffmann-LaRoche* again misunderstood the function of §403 and the rule of reasonableness in a fairly fundamental way? Contrast the

Court's refusal to consider case-by-case comity considerations in *Hoffmann-LaRoche* with its exactly opposite approach in the context of extraterritorial discovery (where it refused to adopt a general rule, on the grounds that comity required a case-by-case analysis). *See infra* pp. 1007-1008. Putting aside its misunderstanding of the rule of reason, did the *Hoffmann-LaRoche* Court nonetheless reach a sensible result? Is it in fact practicable for courts to engage in a case-by-case comity analysis? Is it preferable to try and state a general rule, derived generally from comity-based considerations, but applicable in all cases?

(c) *True conflicts versus policy differences.* Is the Court's approach to comity in *Hoffmann-LaRoche* consistent with Justice Souter's §403 comity analysis in *Hartford Fire?* Was there any "true conflict" in *Hoffmann-LaRoche,* such as that required by Justice Souter in *Hartford Fire?* Note that the Court in *Hoffmann-LaRoche* cites differences between British and American antitrust laws and says that, primary conduct aside, United States and foreign nations differ over the appropriate remedies for anti-competitive behavior. After *Hoffmann-LaRoche,* does Justice Souter's insistence in *Hartford Fire* on inconsistent legal obligations remain valid?

13. Hartford's *effects test and international law.* Recall the contemporary statements of the effects test under international law. *See supra* p. 599. Is the effects test in the FTAIA and *Hartford* consistent with contemporary international law?

14. *Extraterritorial application of antitrust laws based upon foreclosure of U.S. exports.* Suppose that conduct in a foreign country makes it difficult for U.S. companies to export their products to that country. For example, suppose that *Mitsui* had involved efforts by Japanese companies to drive U.S. exporters of U.S. timber out of the Japanese market, by replacing U.S. exports with Indonesian exports. Does this have sufficient effects in the United States to sustain U.S. antitrust jurisdiction?

(a) *Historic approach.* How does Learned Hand answer the question whether the Sherman Act applies to foreign foreclosure of U.S. exports in *Alcoa?* The U.S. Department of Justice's *Antitrust Guide for International Operations* (1977) arguably would have permitted the antitrust laws to apply extraterritorially to the foreclosure of U.S. exports: "the U.S. antitrust laws should be applied to an overseas transaction when there is substantial and foreseeable effect on the United States commerce." Department of Justice, *Antitrust Guide for International Operations,* at E-2 to E-3 (1977). In 1988, however, the Antitrust Division revised the Guide and suggested that it would enforce the antitrust laws only where U.S. *consumers* were harmed. Department of Justice, *Antitrust Guidelines for International Operations,* at 30 n.159.

(b) *Recent developments.* In 1990 the Antitrust Division announced that it "will not tolerate violations of the U.S. antitrust laws where we have jurisdiction, that impair export opportunities for U.S. business." *See also* Department of Justice, Press Release (April 3, 1992); Ohara, *The New U.S. Policy on the Extraterritorial Application of Antitrust Laws and Japan's Response,* 17 World Comp. 49 (1994); Hawk, *The International Application of the Sherman Act in Its Second Century,* 59 Antitrust L.J. 161, 163-164 (1990).

The 1995 version of the *Antitrust Division's International Operations Guide* reasserts the availability of the "export foreclosure" policy but with greater restraint than the 1990 announcement. *See* United States Department of Justice and Federal Trade Commission, *Antitrust Enforcement Guidelines for International Operations* §3.122 (Apr. 1995).

(c) *Appropriate rule.* Which view is a correct interpretation of the Sherman Act? What effect does international law have on these various interpretations? Suppose Japanese or German automobile manufacturers conspire to exclude U.S. car makers from their home markets. Should the U.S. antitrust laws forbid such conduct? Suppose German and Japanese law permits such conduct. Is it more likely that Congress wanted to apply the Sherman Act to imports into America, than to exports from America? Why? Can one say categorically that effects on U.S. imports are more important to the U.S. economy than effects on U.S. exports? What about the effects on foreign economies of applying U.S. antitrust laws?

15. *The requisite nexus between foreign harm and the claim after* Hoffmann-LaRoche. In *Hoffmann,* the Court remanded the case so the foreign plaintiffs could pursue an alternative theory—that the foreign injury was not independent of the domestic effects (in light of the economics of the vitamin market). On remand, the Court of Appeals held that this "nexus" had to be more than "but-for" causation but, instead, something more akin to proximate cause. *Empagran SA v. F. Hoffmann-LaRoche, Ltd.,* 417 F.3d 1267 (D.C. Cir. 2005). *See also In re Dynamic Random Access Memory Antitrust Litig.,* 546 F.3d 981 (9th Cir. 2008); *In re Monosodium Glutamate Antitrust Litig.,* 477 F.3d 535 (8th Cir. 2007); *In re TFT-LCD (Flat Panel) Antitrust Litig.,* 2010 WL 2610641 (N.D. Cal. June 28, 2010); *In re Hydrogen Peroxide Antitrust Litig.,* 702 F. Supp. 2d 548 (E.D. Pa. 2010) (collecting cases). Why do you suppose that these courts require a tighter causal nexus between the foreign and domestic effects? Consider in light of *Hoffmann-LaRoche*'s discussion of comity.

16. *The U.S. Government's position in* Hoffmann-LaRoche. In *Hoffmann-LaRoche,* the U.S. Government, as *amicus curiae,* urged a broader rule than that adopted by the Court. In addition to its textual and historical arguments, the Government cited a variety of policy arguments that merit scrutiny.

First, the Government expressed concern that a more expansive view of extraterritoriality "would open up United States courts to suits that are strikingly localized to foreign countries." Brief for the United States as *Amicus Curiae* in No. 03-724, at 12 (Feb. 2004) ("Government Brief"). Is this necessarily true? Would principles of *forum non conveniens* suffice to filter out these suits? Even in an antitrust case? *See supra* pp. 444-445.

Second, the Government feared that a broader rule on extraterritorial application of U.S. antitrust laws would promote forum shopping:

> It is our understanding that approximately 100 countries now have comprehensive antitrust laws, and [many] allow private lawsuits to recover damages for antitrust violations or provide damages in conjunction with administrative proceedings. . . . At least three of the four home countries of respondents have antitrust laws that prohibit price-fixing and laws that authorize private civil actions by persons who suffer damages from antitrust violations. These countries have enacted the remedies that their governments consider appropriate, and United States law should not promote forum shopping that undermines those sovereign judgments. Government Brief at 24-25.

How valid are the Government's forum shopping concerns? Even if they are valid, what's wrong with forum shopping? *See supra* pp. 406-407. Does the Court in *Hoffmann-LaRoche* credit the Government's forum shopping argument?

What about the Government's comity argument? What exactly are the "sovereign judgments" embodied in foreign nations' antitrust laws? How precisely does the extraterritorial application of U.S. law undermine those judgments? How did the Court in *Hoffmann-LaRoche* treat the Government's comity arguments? How does its treatment compare to its treatment of comity arguments in *Sosa*?

17. *Subject matter versus legislative jurisdiction.* Justices Souter and Scalia disagree over the question whether the jurisdictional issue in *Hartford Fire* was "subject matter" or "legislative" jurisdiction. Citing an earlier edition of this book, Justice Souter said that the case concerned subject matter jurisdiction, because the scope of federal subject matter and legislative jurisdiction was identical under the antitrust laws. G. Born & D. Westin, *International Civil Litigation in U.S. Courts* 542 n.5 (2d ed. 1992). Justice Scalia disagreed, saying that subject matter jurisdiction was broader, and he implied that subject matter jurisdiction might exist even where there was no prescriptive jurisdiction. In his view, the applicability of the Sherman Act to the defendants' conduct "has nothing to do with the jurisdiction of the courts." In fact, earlier editions of this book merely said that the antitrust laws were a simultaneous exercise of prescriptive jurisdiction (*i.e.,* enacting the substantive standards of the Sherman Act) and grant of subject matter jurisdiction (*i.e.,* authorizing federal courts to hear such claims); it was not said that subject matter and prescriptive jurisdiction were co-extensive. G. Born & D. Westin, *International Civil Litigation in United States Courts* 542 & 616 (2d ed. 1991). Nevertheless, which view is correct — Justice Souter or Justice Scalia?

The answer to this question can have substantial practical importance. The extraterritorial application of the antitrust laws can be challenged either in a motion to dismiss for lack of subject matter jurisdiction, under Fed. R. Civ. P. 12(b)(1), or for failure to state a claim, under Fed. R. Civ. P. 12(b)(6). Under Rule 12(b)(6), the allegations of the complaint are assumed to be true, and the complaint is dismissed if, under no set of facts, it could state a claim. In contrast, under Rule 12(b)(1) the trial judge has greater freedom to weigh the evidence and discount the weight of the plaintiff's allegations and evidence.

Prior to *Hartford Fire,* most lower courts had concluded that challenges to the extraterritorial application of the antitrust laws should be treated as attacks on subject matter jurisdiction under Rule 12(b)(1). *E.g., Papst Motoren GmbH & Co. v. Kanematsu-Goshu (U.S.A.), Inc.,* 629 F. Supp. 864, 868 (S.D.N.Y. 1986); *Liamuiga Tours v. Travel Impressions, Ltd.,* 617 F. Supp. 920 (E.D.N.Y. 1985); *Cf. The 'In' Porters, SA v. Hanes Printables, Inc.,* 663 F. Supp. 494, 500 n.5 (M.D.N.C. 1987) ("[t]he better rule appears to be to treat such motions under 12(b)(1), unless the facts central to the merits . . . are intertwined with the jurisdictional facts"). Justice Souter's opinion in *Hartford Fire* similarly treats such challenges as going to subject matter jurisdiction.

18. *The importance of pleading rules.* Apart from different substantive standards, one reason why U.S. law (and U.S. courts) became a favored strategy for antitrust plaintiffs is that, until recently, pleading standards in courts were relatively lax. In contrast to the practice of many other countries (which required plaintiffs to set forth in their complaints a sufficient factual basis for their claims), federal practice generally only required a plaintiff to set forth a short, plain statement of the claim showing why the plaintiff is entitled to relief. This system of "notice pleading" made it far easier for a plaintiff to survive a motion to dismiss and, thereby, take the case to discovery. The plaintiff could then use discovery both to obtain documents incriminating the defendant and as a settlement lever (in light of the defendant's substantial costs of complying with discovery requests, which, generally under U.S. practice, the defendant itself had to bear).

Recent developments in federal pleading law have, however, trimmed this plaintiff-friendly feature of U.S. courts. In *Bell Atlantic v. Twombly,* 550 U.S. 544 (2007), an antitrust conspiracy case, the Court held that, in order to survive a motion to dismiss, the plaintiff must do more than set forth conclusory allegations but must demonstrate in the complaint the "plausibility" of the claim. The Court rested this new "plausibility" standard in part on the heavy costs of complying with discovery in antitrust cases. More recently, in *Ashcroft v. Iqbal,* 129 S. Ct. 1937 (2009), the Court held that *Twombly*'s plausibility standard was not limited to antitrust claims but applied generally to claims brought in federal court.

In light of *Twombly,* can one expect a reduction in conflicts across legal systems? If it becomes relatively more difficult to bring an antitrust claim (or any claim for that matter) in federal court, won't that mean, in the long run, that fewer claims with remote connections to U.S. law will be brought in U.S. courts? If so, is this a salutary development?

19. *Recent legislative proposals to expand extraterritorial application of U.S. antitrust laws.* During the second half of the last decade, the United States experienced a remarkable spike in oil prices. In June 2008, prices reached an all-time high of $145 per barrel.

Political accusations soon followed, and some criticism was directed at the Organization for Petroleum Exporting Countries ("OPEC"). In 2009, members of Congress introduced the "No Oil Producing and Exporting Cartels Act of 2009" (or "NOPEC Act"). The bill, which had been introduced in various forms since 1999, would have amended the Sherman Act to cover price decisions by OPEC member countries and eliminated various defenses (such as sovereign immunity and the act of state doctrine) that had thwarted prior efforts to bring antitrust actions against OPEC and its member states. *See generally* Looper, *NOPEC Goes Bananas: Thwarting Congress's Attempts to Expand U.S. Antitrust Law's Extraterritorial Reach*, 32 Hous. J. Int'l L. 281 (2010). Legislative efforts like the NOPEC Act serve as a telling reminder that questions of extraterritoriality remain squarely on the political agenda and can rise up, particularly in reaction to an economic shock.

4. The Extraterritorial Application of Federal Securities Laws[114]

The federal securities laws contain broad prohibitions against fraudulent conduct in connection with the issuance and trading of securities.[115] As in the antitrust context, U.S. courts struggled to identify the precise circumstances in which federal securities laws will be applied extraterritorially. In many cases, they applied these provisions to conduct occurring partially or entirely abroad.[116] In some respects, however, the guidelines articulated in the securities law context differed from those in antitrust decisions. It is instructive to compare the approach of U.S. courts to the extraterritorial application of the securities laws with the antitrust decisions in *Alcoa, Timberlane, Hartford Fire,* and *Hoffmann-LaRoche*.

The "literal catholicity" of the major federal securities laws (the Securities Act, the Securities Exchange Act, and the Commodities Act) admit of no geographic limitation. Moreover, several courts concluded that the legislative history surrounding the enactment of these statutes suggested that Congress did not consider the matter.[117] Consequently, courts interpreting these laws were confronted with the same interpretive dilemma confronted by the courts in *American Banana, Lauritzen,* and *Aramco*. Lacking (until recently)

---

114. Commentary on the extraterritorial application of the U.S. securities laws includes, for example, Choi & Silberman, *Transnational Litigation and Global Securities Class-Action Lawsuits*, 2009 Wis. L. Rev. 465; Buxbaum, *Multinational Class Actions Under Federal Securities Laws: Managing Jurisdictional Conflict*, 46 Colum. J. Transnat'l L. 14 (2007); Chang, *Multinational Enforcement of U.S. Securities Laws: The Need for the Clear and Restrained Scope of Extraterritorial Subject-Matter Jurisdiction*, 9 Fordham J. Comp. & Fin. L. 89 (2004); Choi & Guzman, *Portable Reciprocity: Rethinking the International Reach of Securities Regulation*, 71 S. Cal. L. Rev. 903 (1998); Sachs, *The International Reach of Rule 10b-5: The Myth of Congressional Silence*, 28 Colum. J. Trans. L. 677 (1990); Thomas, *Extraterritoriality in an Era of Internationalization of the Securities Markets; The Need to Revisit Domestic Policies*, 35 Rutgers L. Rev. 453 (1983); Note, *Defining the Reach of the Securities Exchange Act: Extraterritorial Application of the Antifraud Provisions*, 74 Fordham L. Rev. 213 (2005); Annotation, *Subject Matter Jurisdiction of Securities Fraud Class Action Based on Foreign Transactions Under Securities Exchange Act of 1934*, 56 A.L.R. Fed. 288 (1982 & Cum. Supp.).

115. The three principal antifraud provisions of the federal securities laws are §10(b) of the Securities and Exchange Act of 1934, 15 U.S.C. §78j, and §§12(2) & 17(a) of the Securities Act of 1933, 15 U.S.C. §§77g & 77l(2). In broad outline, all three provisions make it unlawful to engage in fraud in securities transactions.

116. *See, e.g., In re CP Ships Ltd. Securities Litig.*, 57 F.3d 1306 (11th Cir. 2009); *S.E.C. v. Berger*, 322 F.3d 187 (2d Cir. 2003); *Kauthar SDN BHD v. Sternberg*, 149 F.3d 659 (7th Cir. 1998); *Robinson v. TCI/US West Communications Inc.*, 117 F.3d 900 (5th Cir. 1997); *Itoba Ltd. v. Lep Group plc*, 54 F.3d 118 (2d Cir. 1995); *Alfadda v. Fenn*, 935 F.2d 475 (2d Cir. 1991); *Tamari v. Bache & Co. (Lebanon)*, 730 F.2d 1103 (7th Cir. 1984); *Grunenthal GmbH v. Hotz*, 712 F.2d 421, 425 (9th Cir. 1983); *SEC v. Kasser*, 548 F.2d 109 (3d Cir. 1977); *Bersch v. Drexel Firestone, Inc.*, 519 F.2d 974 (2d Cir. 1975); *Leasco Data Processing Equipment Corp. v. Maxwell*, 468 F.2d 1326 (2d Cir. 1972); *Schoenbaum v. Firstbrook*, 405 F.2d 200 (2d Cir. 1968), *rev'd on other grounds*, 405 F.2d 215 (2d Cir. 1968) (*en banc*).

117. *Bersch v. Drexel Firestone, Inc.*, 519 F.2d 974, 993 (2d Cir. 1975) (Friendly, J.) ("We freely acknowledge that if we were asked to point to language in the statutes, or even in the legislative history, that compelled these conclusions, we would be unable to respond."); *Zoelsch v. Arthur Andersen & Co.*, 824 F.2d 27, 29-30 (D.C. Cir. 1987) ("Fifty years ago, Congress did not consider how far American courts should have jurisdiction to decide cases involving predominantly foreign securities transactions with some link to the United States.") (Bork, J.). Some scholarship has called into doubt the validity of this premise. *See* Sachs, *The International Reach of Rule 10b-5: The Myth of Congressional Silence*, 28 Colum. J. Transnat'l L. 677 (1990).

any guidance from the Supreme Court on the precise question of the securities laws' extraterritorial effect, lower federal courts did not follow the path charted by the Supreme Court's precedents in other contexts such as antitrust and employment. Instead, lower courts developed what came to be known as the "conduct" and "effects" tests. A leading early federal appellate opinion concisely captures the dominant analytic framework:

> Finding nothing in the [Commodities Exchange Act ("CEA")] or its legislative history to indicate that Congress did not intend the CEA to apply to foreign agents, but recognizing there also is no direct evidence that Congress intended such application, we believe it is appropriate to rely on the "conduct" and "effects" tests in discerning whether subject matter jurisdiction exists over the dispute. As a matter of foreign relations law, the conduct and effects principles indicate whether the United States has jurisdiction to prescribe a rule that attaches legal consequences to conduct occurring in the United States, or to conduct occurring outside the United States that causes effects within the United States. *See* Restatement (Second) Foreign Relations Law §§17 and 18 (1965). . . . When the question instead is whether Congress intended a statute to have extraterritorial application, the analysis of legislative intent becomes intertwined with these principles of foreign relations law. If extraterritorial application would have no impact on domestic conditions, it is presumed that Congress did not intend the statute to apply outside the territory, unless a contrary intent appears. *Foley Bros., Inc. v. Filardo.* Reliance on this presumption is misplaced, however, when the conduct under scrutiny has not occurred wholly outside the United States, or . . . could otherwise affect domestic conditions. In these cases, courts have looked to the nature of the conduct or effects in the United States to determine whether extraterritorial application would be consistent with the purposes underlying the statute.[118]

This approach on "conduct" and "effects" was inconsistent with the strong territoriality presumption articulated in *Aramco.* Nonetheless, some courts rationalized the differential treatment on the ground that the effect of the foreign conduct on "domestic conditions" necessitated a broader reach for the securities laws.[119]

While most lower federal courts coalesced around the "conduct" and "effects" tests, these generalized categories masked important disagreements over their application. For example, under the conduct test, courts disagreed over how close the "nexus" between the American-based conduct and the resultant harm had to be.[120] Likewise, while courts agreed generally that "merely preparatory" conduct occurring in the United States did not satisfy the "conduct" test, they disagreed over what mixture of conduct was "merely preparatory."[121] Similarly, under the effects test, courts did not chart a particularly clear course about whether generalized economic effects, such as adversely affecting investor confidence in the United States or generalized effects on domestic market liquidity, justified extraterritorial application of federal securities laws.[122] Finally, some courts began to collapse the conduct and effects tests, explaining that an "admixture or

---

118. *Tamari v. Bache & Co. (Lebanon),* 730 F.2d 1103, 1107 & n.11 (7th Cir. 1984).

119. *See, e.g., Sloane Overseas Fund, Ltd. v. Sapiens Int'l Corp., NV,* 941 F. Supp. 1369, 1373-1374 (S.D.N.Y. 1996).

120. *See SDN BHD v. Sternberg,* 149 F.3d 659, 665 (7th Cir. 1998) ("The predominant difference among the circuits, it appears, is the degree to which the American-based conduct must be related causally to the fraud and the resultant harm to justify the application of American securities law.").

121. *See Butte Min. plc v. Smith,* 76 F.3d 287, 291 (9th Cir. 1996) ("We are not to be a haven for scoundrels; nor should we be a host for the world's victims of securities fraud. Vigilant and mature as our securities laws are, they are not to be invoked unless substantial steps in the perpetuation of the fraud were taken here or the criminal conduct engaged in affected our securities markets or American investors.").

122. *See, e.g., Mak v. Wocom Commodities Ltd.,* 112 F.3d 287 (7th Cir. 1997); *Itoba Ltd. v. Lep Group plc,* 54 F.3d 118 (2d Cir. 1995); *In re Alstom SA,* 406 F. Supp. 2d 346, 369 (S.D.N.Y. 2005); *Nikko Asset Mgt. Co., Ltd. v. UBS AG,* 303 F. Supp. 2d 456 (S.D.N.Y. 2004); *Interbrew v. Edperbrascan Corp.,* 23 F. Supp. 2d 425 (S.D.N.Y. 1998); *Pyrenee, Ltd. v. Wocom Commodities, Ltd.,* 984 F. Supp. 1148 (N.D. Ill. 1997); *Kaufman v. Campeau,* 744 F. Supp. 808 (S.D. Ohio 1990).

combination of the two often gives a better picture of whether there is sufficient United States involvement to justify the exercise of jurisdiction by an American court."[123] The confusion was particularly rife among federal courts in New York, home to many of the most important lawsuits under federal securities laws.

In 2010, the Supreme Court finally addressed the subject in *Morrison v. National Australia Bank Ltd.*, excerpted below. In its most recent opinion on the extraterritorial effect of federal law (and its first significant opinion on the extraterritorial application of federal securities laws), the Supreme Court found that lower courts had been charting the wrong course in this area and issued a strong reaffirmation of the *Aramco* principle:

MORRISON v. NATIONAL AUSTRALIA BANK LTD.
130 S. Ct. 2869 (2010)

SCALIA, JUSTICE. [The National Australia Bank ("National") is an Australian-based bank whose ordinary shares are traded on exchanges in Australia and elsewhere but not on any exchange in the United States. However, its American Depositary Receipts ("ADRs") are traded on the New York Stock Exchange. ADRs represent the right to receive a certain number of National's ordinary shares.

National purchased the Florida-based Homeside Lending, Inc., which provides administrative services connected with mortgage payments. For several years following the purchase, both National's annual reports and several of its and Homeside's officers touted Homeside's income stream. Thereafter, the bank was forced to write down the value of Homeside's asserts, causing the value of its shares and ADRs to drop. According to the complaint, Homeside and various executives deliberately manipulated reports of the company's earnings potential in order to inflate artificially the share value.

In relevant part, various Australian citizens who had purchased National's ordinary shares before the write-downs sued National, Homeside, and various executives in United States District Court. They alleged, among other things, violations of Section 10-b of the Securities and Exchange Act of 1934 and Rule 10b-5 of the Securities and Exchange Commission. The district court dismissed the suit, and the Second Circuit affirmed, finding in relevant part that the acts performed in the United States did not "comprise the heart of the alleged fraud."]

[In an omitted part of the opinion, the Court concludes that the challenge to Section 10-b's extraterritorial reach did not raise a question of subject matter jurisdiction but, instead, whether the plaintiffs stated a claim.]

III.A. It is a "longstanding principle of American law 'that legislation of Congress, unless a contrary intent appears, is meant to apply only within the territorial jurisdiction of the United States.'" *EEOC v. Arabian American Oil Co.*, 499 U.S. 244, 248 (1991) (quoting *Foley Bros., Inc. v. Filardo*, 336 U.S. 281, 285 (1949)). This principle represents a canon of construction, or a presumption about a statute's meaning, rather than a limit upon Congress's power to legislate, *see Blackmer v. United States*, 284 U.S. 421, 437 (1932). It rests on the perception that Congress ordinarily legislates with respect to domestic, not foreign matters. Thus, "unless there is the affirmative intention of the Congress clearly expressed" to give a statute extraterritorial effect, "we must presume it is primarily concerned with domestic conditions." *Aramco*, [499 U.S. at] 248. The canon or presumption applies regardless of whether there is a risk of conflict between the American statute

---

123. *Itubo Ltd. v. Lep Group PLC*, 54 F.3d 113, 122 (2d Cir. 1995).

and a foreign law, *see Sale v. Haitian Centers Council, Inc.*, 509 U.S. 155, 173-174 (1993). When a statute gives no clear indication of an extraterritorial application, it has none.

Despite this principle of interpretation, long and often recited in our opinions, the Second Circuit believed that, because the Exchange Act is silent as to the extraterritorial application of §10(b), it was left to the court to "discern" whether Congress would have wanted the statute to apply. This disregard of the presumption against extraterritoriality did not originate with the Court of Appeals panel in this case. It has been repeated over many decades by various courts of appeals in determining the application of the Exchange Act, and §10(b) in particular, to fraudulent schemes that involve conduct and effects abroad. That has produced a collection of tests for divining what Congress would have wanted, complex in formulation and unpredictable in application.

[The Court then traced the development of the conduct and effects tests, discussed in the text preceding this excerpt.] As they developed, these tests were not easy to administer. . . . [The Court then reviewed some of the above-described confusion in the lower courts.] . . .

At least one Court of Appeals has criticized this line of cases and the interpretive assumption that underlies it. In *Zoelsch v. Arthur Andersen & Co.*, 824 F.2d 27, 32 (1987) (Bork, J.), the District of Columbia Circuit observed that rather than courts' "divining what 'Congress would have wished' if it had addressed the problem[, a] more natural inquiry might be what jurisdiction Congress in fact thought about and conferred." Although tempted to apply the presumption against extraterritoriality and be done with it, that court deferred to the Second Circuit because of its "preeminence in the field of securities law," . . .

Commentators have criticized the unpredictable and inconsistent application of §10(b) to transnational cases. Some have challenged the premise underlying the Courts of Appeals' approach, namely that Congress did not consider the extraterritorial application of §10(b) (thereby leaving it open to the courts, supposedly, to determine what Congress would have wanted). Others, more fundamentally, have noted that using congressional silence as a justification for judge-made rules violates the traditional principle that silence means no extraterritorial application.

The criticisms seem to us justified. The results of judicial-speculation-made-law — divining what Congress would have wanted if it had thought of the situation before the court — demonstrate the wisdom of the presumption against extraterritoriality. Rather than guess anew in each case, we apply the presumption in all cases, preserving a stable background against which Congress can legislate with predictable effects.

B. Rule 10b-5, the regulation under which petitioners have brought suit, was promulgated under §10(b), and does not extend beyond conduct encompassed by §10(b)'s prohibition. Therefore, if §10(b) is not extraterritorial, neither is Rule 10b-5.[124]

On its face, §10(b) contains nothing to suggest it applies abroad:

"It shall be unlawful of interstate commerce or of the mails, or of any facility of any national securities exchange . . . [t]o use or employ, in connection with the purchase or sale of any security registered on a national securities exchange or any security not so registered, . . . any manipulative or deceptive device or contrivance in contravention of such rules and regulations as the [Securities and Exchange] Commission may prescribe. . . ." 15 U.S.C. 78j(b), for any person, directly or indirectly, by the use of any means or instrumentality.

---

124. [The part of Rule 10b-5 relevant to this appeal makes it unlawful "for any person, directly or indirectly, by the use of any means or instrumentality of interstate commerce, or of the mails or of any facility of any national securities exchange . . . to make any untrue statement of a material fact or to omit to state a material fact necessary in order to make the statements made, in the light of the circumstances under which they were made, not misleading." — EDS.]

Petitioners and the Solicitor General contend, however, that three things indicate that §10(b) or the Exchange Act in general has at least some extraterritorial application.

First, they point to the definition of "interstate commerce," a term used in §10(b), which includes "trade, commerce, transportation, or communication . . . between any foreign country and any State." 15 U.S.C. §78c(a)(17). But "we have repeatedly held that even statutes that contain broad language in their definitions of 'commerce' that expressly refer to 'foreign commerce' do not apply abroad." *Aramco*, 499 U.S., at 251. The general reference to foreign commerce in the definition of "interstate commerce" does not defeat the presumption against extraterritoriality.

Petitioners and the Solicitor General next point out that Congress, in describing the purposes of the Exchange Act, observed that the "prices established and offered in such transactions are generally disseminated and quoted throughout the United States and foreign countries." 15 U.S.C. §78b(2). The antecedent of "such transactions," however, is found in the first sentence of the section, which declares that "transactions in securities as commonly conducted upon securities exchanges and over-the-counter markets are affected with a national public interest." §78b. Nothing suggests that this national public interest pertains to transactions conducted upon foreign exchanges and markets. The fleeting reference to the dissemination and quotation abroad of the prices of securities traded in domestic exchanges and markets cannot overcome the presumption against extraterritoriality.

Finally, there is §30(b) of the Exchange Act, 15 U.S.C. §78dd(b), which does mention the Act's extraterritorial application: "The provisions of [the Exchange Act] or of any rule or regulation thereunder shall not apply to any person insofar as he transacts a business in securities without the jurisdiction of the United States," unless he does so in violation of regulations promulgated by the Securities and Exchange Commission "to prevent . . . evasion of [the Act]." (The parties have pointed us to no regulation promulgated pursuant to §30(b).) The Solicitor General argues that "[this] exemption would have no function if the Act did not apply in the first instance to securities transactions that occur abroad."

We are not convinced. In the first place, it would be odd for Congress to indicate the extraterritorial application of the whole Exchange Act by means of a provision imposing a condition precedent to its application abroad. And if the whole Act applied abroad, why would the Commission's enabling regulations be limited to those preventing "evasion" of the Act, rather than all those preventing "violation"? The provision seems to us directed at actions abroad that might conceal a domestic violation, or might cause what would otherwise be a domestic violation to escape on a technicality. At most, the Solicitor General's proposed inference is possible; but possible interpretations of statutory language do not override the presumption against extraterritoriality. *See Aramco*, 499 U.S. at 253.

The Solicitor General also fails to account for §30(a), which reads in relevant part as follows:

> "It shall be unlawful for any broker or dealer . . . to make use of the mails or of any means or instrumentality of interstate commerce for the purpose of effecting on an exchange not within or subject to the jurisdiction of the United States, any transaction in any security the issuer of which is a resident of, or is organized under the laws of, or has its principal place of business in, a place within or subject to the jurisdiction of the United States, in contravention of such rules and regulations as the Commission may prescribe. . . ." 15 U.S.C. §78dd(a).

Subsection 30(a) contains what §10(b) lacks: a clear statement of extraterritorial effect. Its explicit provision for a specific extraterritorial application would be quite superfluous if the rest of the Exchange Act already applied to transactions on foreign exchanges — and its limitation of that application to securities of domestic issuers would be inoperative. Even if that were not true, when a statute provides for some extraterritorial application, the presumption against extraterritoriality operates to limit that provision to its terms. *See Microsoft Corp. v. AT & T Corp.*, 550 U.S. 437, 455-456 (2007). No one claims that §30(a) applies here.

The concurrence claims we have impermissibly narrowed the inquiry in evaluating whether a statute applies abroad, citing for that point the dissent in *Aramco.* But we do not say, as the concurrence seems to think, that the presumption against extraterritoriality is a "clear statement rule," if by that is meant a requirement that a statute say "this law applies abroad." Assuredly context can be consulted as well. But whatever sources of statutory meaning one consults to give "the most faithful reading" of the text, there is no clear indication of extraterritoriality here. The concurrence does not even try to refute that conclusion, but merely puts forward the same (at best) uncertain indications relied upon by petitioners and the Solicitor General. As the opinion for the Court in *Aramco* (which we prefer to the dissent) shows, those uncertain indications do not suffice.

In short, there is no affirmative indication in the Exchange Act that §10(b) applies extraterritorially, and we therefore conclude that it does not.

IV. [The Court then turned to the petitioners' contention that the case did not involve extraterritorial application of federal securities laws because the underlying deceptive conduct, namely the manipulation of Homeside's financial strength, occurred in Florida.] This is less an answer to the presumption against extraterritorial application than it is an assertion — a quite valid assertion — that that presumption here (as often) is not self-evidently dispositive, but its application requires further analysis. For it is a rare case of prohibited extraterritorial application that lacks all contact with the territory of the United States. But the presumption against extraterritorial application would be a craven watchdog indeed if it retreated to its kennel whenever some domestic activity is involved in the case. The concurrence seems to imagine just such a timid sentinel, but our cases are to the contrary. In *Aramco*, for example, the Title VII plaintiff had been hired in Houston, and was an American citizen. The Court concluded, however, that neither that territorial event nor that relationship was the "focus" of congressional concern but rather domestic employment.

Applying the same mode of analysis here, we think that the focus of the Exchange Act is not upon the place where the deception originated, but upon purchases and sales of securities in the United States. Section 10(b) does not punish deceptive conduct, but only deceptive conduct "in connection with the purchase or sale of any security registered on a national securities exchange or any security not so registered." 15 U.S.C. §78j(b). Those purchase-and-sale transactions are the objects of the statute's solicitude. It is those transactions that the statute seeks to "regulate," it is parties or prospective parties to those transactions that the statute seeks to "protect." And it is in our view only transactions in securities listed on domestic exchanges, and domestic transactions in other securities, to which §10(b) applies.

[After giving several reasons grounded in the language and structure of the securities laws, the Court gave a final reason for its transactional test]: [As in *Aramco*], [t]he probability of incompatibility with the applicable laws of other countries is so obvious that if Congress intended such foreign application "it would have addressed the subject of conflicts with foreign laws and procedures." Like the United States, foreign countries regulate their domestic securities exchanges and securities transactions occurring within their territorial jurisdiction. And the regulation of other countries often differs from ours as to what constitutes fraud, what disclosures must be made, what damages are recoverable, what discovery is available in litigation, what individual actions may be joined in a single suit, what attorney's fees are recoverable, and many other matters. The Commonwealth of Australia, the United Kingdom of Great Britain and Northern Ireland, and the Republic of France have filed amicus briefs in this case. So have (separately or jointly) such international and foreign organizations as the International Chamber of Commerce, the Swiss Bankers Association, the Federation of German Industries, the French Business Confederation, the Institute of International Bankers, the European Banking Federation, the Australian Bankers' Association, and the Association Francaise des Entreprises Privées. They all complain of the interference with foreign securities regulation that application of §10(b) abroad would produce, and urge the adoption of a clear test that will avoid that consequence. The transactional test we have adopted — whether the purchase or sale is made in the United States, or involves a security listed on a domestic exchange — meets that requirement.

B. [The Court then turned to the Solicitor General's suggestion that the securities laws apply when the "fraud involves significant conduct in the United States that is material to the fraud's success." After noting that the test enjoyed no textual support, the Court articulated several other reasons for rejecting it.]

If, moreover, one is to be attracted by the desirable consequences of the "significant and material conduct" test, one should also be repulsed by its adverse consequences. While there is no reason to believe that the United States has become the Barbary Coast for those perpetrating frauds on foreign securities markets, some fear that it has become the Shangri-La of class-action litigation for lawyers representing those allegedly cheated in foreign securities markets.

As case support for the "significant and material conduct" test, the Solicitor General relies primarily on *Pasquantino v. United States*, 544 U.S. 349 (2005) [*Pasquantino* is discussed in the chapter on enforcement of foreign judgments, *infra* pp. _____. — EDS.] In that case we concluded that the wire-fraud statute, 18 U.S.C. §1343, was violated by defendants who ordered liquor over the phone from a store in Maryland with the intent to smuggle it into Canada and deprive the Canadian Government of revenue. Section 1343 prohibits "any scheme or artifice to defraud," — fraud simpliciter, without any requirement that it be "in connection with" any particular transaction or event. The *Pasquantino* Court said that the petitioners' "offense was complete the moment they executed the scheme inside the United States," and that it was "[t]his domestic element of petitioners' conduct [that] the Government is punishing." Section 10(b), by contrast, punishes not all acts of deception, but only such acts "in connection with the purchase or sale of any security registered on a national securities exchange or any security not so registered." Not deception alone, but deception with respect to certain purchases or sales is necessary for a violation of the statute.

The Solicitor General points out that the "significant and material conduct" test is in accord with prevailing notions of international comity. If so, that proves that if the United States asserted prescriptive jurisdiction pursuant to the "significant and material conduct" test it would not violate customary international law; but it in no way tends to prove that that is what Congress has done. . . .

Section 10(b) reaches the use of a manipulative or deceptive device or contrivance only in connection with the purchase or sale of a security listed on an American stock exchange, and the purchase or sale of any other security in the United States. This case involves no securities listed on a domestic exchange, and all aspects of the purchases complained of by those petitioners who still have live claims occurred outside the United States. Petitioners have therefore failed to state a claim on which relief can be granted. We affirm the dismissal of petitioners' complaint on this ground.

JUSTICE STEVENS, with whom JUSTICE GINSBURG joins, concurring in the judgment. [In an omitted portion of the opinion, Justice Stevens defends the conduct and effects tests developed by the Second Circuit.] The Court's other main critique of the Second Circuit's approach — apart from what the Court views as its excessive reliance on functional considerations and reconstructed congressional intent — is that the Second Circuit has "disregard[ed]" the presumption against extraterritoriality. It is the Court, however, that misapplies the presumption, in two main respects.

First, the Court seeks to transform the presumption from a flexible rule of thumb into something more like a clear statement rule. We have been here before. [*Aramco*]. . . . Yet even *Aramco*—surely the most extreme application of the presumption against extraterritoriality in my time on the Court—contained numerous passages suggesting that the presumption may be overcome without a clear directive. And our cases both before and after *Aramco* make perfectly clear that the Court continues to give effect to "all available evidence about the meaning" of a provision when considering its extraterritorial application, lest we defy Congress' will. Contrary to Justice Scalia's personal view of statutory interpretation, that evidence legitimately encompasses more than the enacted text. Hence, while the Court's dictum that "[w]hen a statute gives no clear indication of an extraterritorial application, it has none," makes for a nice catchphrase, the point is overstated. The presumption against extraterritoriality can be useful as a theory of congressional purpose, a tool for managing international conflict, a background norm, a tiebreaker. It does not relieve courts of their duty to give statutes the most faithful reading possible.

Second, and more fundamentally, the Court errs in suggesting that the presumption against extraterritoriality is fatal to the Second Circuit's test. For even if the presumption really were a clear statement (or "clear indication,") rule, it would have only marginal relevance to this case.

It is true, of course, that "this Court ordinarily construes ambiguous statutes to avoid unreasonable interference with the sovereign authority of other nations," *F. Hoffmann-La Roche Ltd. v. Empagran S.A.*, 542 U.S. 155, 164 (2004), and that, absent contrary evidence, we presume "Congress is primarily concerned with domestic conditions," *Foley Bros., Inc. v. Filardo*, 336 U.S. 281, 285 (1949). Accordingly, the presumption against extraterritoriality "provides a sound basis for concluding that Section 10(b) does not apply when a securities fraud with no effects in the United States is hatched and executed entirely outside this country." But that is just about all it provides a sound basis for concluding. And the conclusion is not very illuminating, because no party to the litigation disputes it. No one contends that §10(b) applies to wholly foreign frauds.

Rather, the real question in this case is how much, and what kinds of, domestic contacts are sufficient to trigger application of §10(b). In developing its conduct-and-effects test, the Second Circuit endeavored to derive a solution from the Exchange Act's text, structure, history, and purpose. Judge Friendly and his colleagues were well aware that United States courts "cannot and should not expend [their] resources resolving cases that do not affect Americans or involve fraud emanating from America."

The question just stated does not admit of an easy answer. The text of the Exchange Act indicates that §10(b) extends to at least some activities with an international component, but, again, it is not pellucid as to which ones. The Second Circuit draws the line as follows: §10(b) extends to transnational frauds "only when substantial acts in furtherance of the fraud were committed within the United States," or when the fraud was "'intended to produce'" and did produce "'detrimental effects within'" the United States.

This approach is consistent with the understanding shared by most scholars that Congress, in passing the Exchange Act, "expected U.S. securities laws to apply to certain international transactions or conduct." It is also consistent with the traditional understanding, regnant in the 1930's as it is now, that the presumption against extraterritoriality does not apply "when the conduct [at issue] occurs within the United States," and has lesser force when "the failure to extend the scope of the statute to a foreign setting will result in adverse effects within the United States." And it strikes a reasonable balance between the goals of "preventing the export of fraud from America," protecting shareholders, enhancing investor confidence, and deterring corporate misconduct, on the one hand, and conserving United States resources and limiting conflict with foreign law, on the other.

Repudiating the Second Circuit's approach in its entirety, the Court establishes a novel rule that will foreclose private parties from bringing §10(b) actions whenever the relevant securities were purchased or sold abroad and are not listed on a domestic exchange.[125] . . . [W]hile the clarity and simplicity of the Court's test may have some salutary consequences, like all bright-line rules it also has drawbacks.

Imagine, for example, an American investor who buys shares in a company listed only on an overseas exchange. That company has a major American subsidiary with executives based in New York City; and it was in New York City that the executives masterminded and implemented a massive deception which artificially inflated the stock price — and which will, upon its disclosure, cause the price to plummet. Or, imagine that those same executives go knocking on doors in Manhattan and convince an unsophisticated retiree, on the basis of material misrepresentations, to invest her life savings in the company's doomed securities. Both of these investors would, under the Court's new test, be barred from seeking relief under §10(b).

The oddity of that result should give pause. For in walling off such individuals from §10(b), the Court narrows the provision's reach to a degree that would surprise and alarm generations of American investors — and, I am convinced, the Congress that passed the Exchange Act. Indeed, the Court's rule turns §10(b) jurisprudence (and the presumption against extraterritoriality) on its head, by withdrawing the statute's application from cases in which there is both substantial wrongful conduct that occurred in the United States and a substantial injurious effect on United States markets and citizens.

Notes on Morrison

1. *The territoriality presumption and* Morrison. How does Justice Scalia articulate the territoriality presumption in *Morrison*? How does his articulation differ from Justice Stevens'? Does it differ from the articulation in *Aramco*? Has Justice Scalia "impermissibly narrowed the inquiry in evaluating whether a statute applies abroad"? Has it "transform[ed] the presumption from a flexible rule of thumb into something more like a clear statement rule"?

Justice Scalia explains that "it is a rare case of prohibited extraterritorial application that lacks all contact with the territory of the United States." Is the proper question, therefore, how much conduct occurred in the United States? Or does it depend instead on the relationship between the conduct and the cause of action? In other words, if the

---

125. The Court's opinion does not, however, foreclose the Commission from bringing enforcement actions in additional circumstances, as no issue concerning the Commission's authority is presented by this case. The Commission's enforcement proceedings not only differ from private §10(b) actions in numerous potentially relevant respects, but they also pose a lesser threat to international comity.

elements of the cause of action are satisfied entirely by the conduct that occurred in the United States (without consideration of extraterritorial conduct), would Justice Scalia then be satisfied that the extraterritoriality presumption did not apply? *See Ofori-Tenkorang v. American Int'l Group, Inc.*, 460 F.3d 296 (2d Cir. 2006); *Quail Cruises Ship Mgmt. Ltd. v. Agencia de Viagens CVC Tur Limitada*, 2010 WL 3119908 (S.D. Fla. Aug. 6, 2010).

Whatever the precise articulation of the presumption, how broadly does *Morrison*'s articulation of the presumption sweep? Justice Scalia indicates that the presumption applies "in all cases." What exactly does this mean? Does it mean all cases arising under the federal securities laws? All cases arising under all federal statutes? If so, what is the fate of decisions like *Lauritzen, Hartford Fire,* and *Empagran*? What about other federal statutes where courts have relied on analogies to the "conduct" or "effects" tests developed in the securities context? *See, e.g., United States v. Philip Morris USA, Inc.*, 566 F.3d 1095 (D.C. Cir. 2009) (employing effects test to conclude that RICO had extraterritorial effect); *Liquidation Comm'n of Banco Intercontinental S.A. v. Renta*, 530 F.3d 1139 (11th Cir. 2008) (same).

Early attempts to apply *Morrison* suggest that this language is likely to sow confusion. *Compare Love v. Associated Newspapers, Ltd.*, 611 F.3d 601 (9th Cir. 2010) (post-*Morrison* decision declining to discard effects test used to determine whether to apply Lanham Act extraterritorially) *and United States v. Finch*, 2010 WL 3938176, at *4 (D. Haw. Sept. 30, 2010) ("*Morrison* does not, however, hold that all federal statutes lacking express language authorizing extraterritorial application must necessarily apply only to acts occurring entirely in the United States.") *with Norex Petroleum Ltd. v. Access Indus., Inc.*, 2010 WL 4968691 (2d Cir. Dec. 8, 2010) (relying partly on *Morrison* to conclude that RICO does not apply to alleged scheme to take over Russian oil industry); *Cede % 25no v. Intech Group, Inc.*, 2010 WL 3359468 (S.D.N.Y. 2010) ("Although *Morrison* does not address the RICO statute, its reasoning is dispositive here.").

What about common law causes of action like those brought under the Alien Tort Statute after *Sosa*? *See supra* at 47-51. Are such causes of action even subject to the presumption against extraterritoriality? If so, how can such a cause of action *ever* satisfy the *Morrison* standard? Given that virtually all cases arising under the Alien Tort Statute involve conduct taking place abroad, does not *Morrison* essentially sound the death knell for such claims? *See Sarei v. Rio Tinto*, 625 F.3d 561 (9th Cir. 2010) (*en banc*) (Kleinfeld, J., dissenting) (quoting *Morrison* and noting that since the ATS "gives no clear indication of an extraterritorial application, it has none."). On the other hand, if common law causes of action are not subject to the *Morrison* standard, does not this create an anomalous result? Why should causes of action created by undemocratic courts have greater extraterritorial effect than those created by the political branches (which as a matter of constitutional law have a greater prerogative over the Nation's foreign affairs)? *See supra* at 18-21.

2. *Rationale for territoriality presumption in* Morrison.

(a) Domestic matters. Justice Scalia anchors the territoriality presumption in the belief that "Congress ordinarily legislates with respect to domestic, not foreign matters." What precisely differentiates a domestic from a foreign matter? Is a foreign company whose shares trade on a U.S. exchange a "domestic" or "foreign" matter? What about an American company whose shares trade on a foreign exchange? Even if a principled distinction between the two can be articulated, does it really make sense in a world where the global economy is increasingly interconnected? Does not an effects test better capture the economic realities of modern-day commercial activity, as Justice Stevens' separate opinion suggests?

(b) Clear rules. Justice Scalia also suggests a new purpose for the territoriality presumption — namely that it "preserv[es] a stable background against which Congress can legislate with predictable effects." How precisely does the presumption provide this necessary

predictability? Compare this with what the Court recently said about the extraterritorial application of the Constitution (in the specific context of the availability of a writ of habeas corpus for detainees at Guantanamo Bay, Cuba): "questions of extraterritoriality turn on objective factors and practical concerns, not formalism," *Boumediene v. Bush*, 553 U.S. 723, 764 (2008). Could Justice Scalia's bright-line test be characterized as precisely the sort of formalism that the Court criticized in *Boumediene*? Is there a greater need for formalism in the statutory, as opposed to constitutional, context? Could not one adopt a different "background" presumption against which Congress could legislate — for example, that Congress intends to legislate to the full extent permitted by the Constitution?

Note that Justice Scalia does not question the ability of Congress to give federal securities laws (or any other federal laws) extraterritorial effect. The presumption does not operate as a "limit on Congress's power to legislate." Rather, he concludes simply that §10(b) lacks the language necessary to give that provision extraterritorial effect. In Justice Scalia's view, how should Congress have drafted §10(b) if it wished to do so? What magic words did §30(a) or the mail fraud statute contain which §10(b) lacked?

Would Congress even need to use specific language in the statute? Justice Scalia denies that the territoriality presumption is a "clear statement rule" and acknowledges that "context can be consulted as well." What "context" precisely does he mean? The statutory structure? Findings in the preamble? Legislative history?

3. *Congressional response* to Morrison. As with *Aramco, supra* pp. 659-664, Congress responded swiftly to the Supreme Court's decision in *Morrison*. As part of major legislation overhauling the financial system in the United States, Congress included the following language:

> The district courts of the United States . . . shall have jurisdiction of an action or proceeding brought or instituted by the Commission or the United States alleging a violation of the antifraud provisions of this title involving . . .
>
> (1) Conduct within the United States that constitutes significant steps in furtherance of the violation, even if the securities transaction occurs outside the United States and involves only foreign investors; or
> (2) Conduct occurring outside the United States that has a foreseeable substantial effect within the United States.

> Dodd-Frank Wall Street Reform and Consumer Protection Act, Title IX, §929P(b); 111th Cong., 2d Sess. (2010).

Effectively, this amendment restores the conduct and effects tests, but only as to actions brought by the Securities and Exchange Commission or the United States Department of Justice. The stricter rule announced in *Morrison* continues to apply to actions brought by private parties.

Is this a wise legislative response? Does it properly balance the desire to regulate overseas conduct having an effect on the United States with the need to remain sensitive to the concerns of foreign countries? What does the promptness of Congress's actions, in overruling *Aramco* and *Morrison*, suggest about the accuracy of the territoriality presumption as a gauge of congressional intent?

4. *Pre-Morrison "conduct" test in the securities law context.* Prior to *Morrison*, many lower courts had held that U.S. law was applicable extraterritorially because foreign transactions were consummated (albeit legally) on a U.S. exchange. For example, in *Zoelsch v. Arthur Andersen & Co.*, 824 F.2d 27, 33 n.4 (D.C. Cir. 1987), Judge Bork made it clear that the securities laws would apply "whenever any individual is defrauded in this country, regardless of whether the offer originates somewhere else, for the actual consummation of securities fraud in the United States in and of itself would constitute domestic conduct that satisfies all the elements of liability." *See also S.E.C. v. Banner Fund Int'l,* 211 F.3d 602, 608-609 (D.C. Cir. 2000); *Europe and Overseas Commodity Traders, SA v. Banque Paribas London,* 147 F.3d 118, 131 n.19 (2d Cir. 1998); *Alfadda v. Fenn,* 935 F.2d 475, 478 (2d Cir. 1991); *Psimenos v. E. F. Hutton & Co.,* 722 F.2d 1041 (2d Cir. 1983); *In re Baan Co. Securities Litig.,* 103 F. Supp. 2d 1, 9 (D.D.C. 2000); *Lobatto v. Berney,* 1999 WL 672994, at *2 (S.D.N.Y. 1999); *Trafton v. Deacon Barclays de Zoete Wedd Ltd.,* 1994 WL 746199, at *10 (N.D. Cal. 1994).

Other pre-*Morrison* decisions upheld application of the securities laws based on U.S. conduct related to trades on securities or commodities exchanges outside the United States. Lower courts adopted differing formulae defining the showing for U.S. jurisdiction under the "conduct test." *E.g., Itoba Ltd. v. Lep Group plc,* 54 F.3d 118 (2d Cir. 1995) (suggesting that an "admixture" of the conduct and the effects test is appropriate); *Zoelsch v. Arthur Andersen & Co.,* 824 F.2d 27 (D.C. Cir. 1987) (fraudulent conduct in the U.S. must "directly cause" harm); *ITT v. Cornfeld,* 619 F.2d 909 (2d Cir. 1980); *Grunenthal GmbH v. Hotz,* 712 F.2d 421 (9th Cir. 1983); *SEC v. Kasser,* 548 F.2d 109 (3d Cir. 1977) ("some activity designed to further a fraudulent scheme occurs in this country"). *See generally Kauthar SDN BHD v. Sternberg,* 149 F.3d 659, 665 (7th Cir. 1998) ("The predominant difference among the circuits, it appears, is the degree to which the American-based conduct must be related causally to the fraud and the resultant harm to justify the application of American securities law."); *Robinson v. TCI/US West Communications Inc.,* 117 F.3d 900, 905-907 (5th Cir. 1997) (same); *In re Cable & Wireless, plc,* 321 F. Supp. 2d 749, 758-759 (E.D. Va. 2004) (collecting cases).

What is the status of these various lines of decisions after *Morrison?* Suppose the fraud concerns securities traded on a foreign exchange?

5. Pre-Morrison "effects test" in the securities law context. Prior to *Morrison,* U.S. courts relied on an "effects" doctrine, similar to that in the antitrust context. For example, the Second Circuit held that the securities laws would apply "if a defendant, even though acting solely abroad, had defrauded investors in the United States by mailing false prospectuses into this country." *Bersch v. Drexel Firestone, Inc.,* 519 F.2d 974, 989 (2d Cir. 1975). *See also Doll v. James Martin Assoc. (Holdings) Ltd.,* 600 F. Supp. 510, 518-520 (E.D. Mich. 1984). Similarly, where tender offer documents are provided by a foreign company to foreign nominees of U.S. shareholders, who are required by foreign law to transmit the documents to the shareholders, and in fact do so, then effects jurisdiction had been upheld. *Consolidated Gold Fields plc v. Minorco, SA,* 871 F.2d 252 (2d Cir. 1989). Greater controversy surrounded the import of more generalized economic effects, such as adversely affecting investor confidence in the United States or generalized effects on domestic market liquidity. *Bersch,* 519 F.2d at 988. *See Mak v. Wocom Commodities Ltd.,* 112 F.3d 287 (7th Cir. 1997); *Itoba Ltd. v. Lep Group plc,* 54 F.3d 118 (2d Cir. 1995); *In re Alstom SA,* 406 F. Supp. 2d 346, 369 (S.D.N.Y. 2005); *Nikko Asset Mgt. Co., Ltd. v. UBS AG,* 303 F. Supp. 2d 456 (S.D.N.Y. 2004); *Interbrew v. Edperbrascan Corp.,* 23 F. Supp. 2d 425 (S.D.N.Y. 1998); *Pyrenee, Ltd. v. Wocom Commodities, Ltd.,* 984 F. Supp. 1148 (N.D. Ill. 1997); *Kaufman v. Campeau,* 744 F. Supp. 808 (S.D. Ohio 1990).

What is the status of these decisions following *Morrison?* Suppose that the securities in question are not traded on a U.S. exchange?

6. The transaction test and the conduct/effects tests compared. As noted above, prior to *Morrison,* lower courts had developed the "conduct" and "effects" tests in order to assess whether to give federal securities laws extraterritorial effect. *Morrison* rejects these tests and favors, instead, a "transactional test." Under that test, "Section 10(b) reaches the use of a manipulative or deceptive device or contrivance only in connection with the purchase or sale of a security listed on an American stock exchange, and the purchase or sale of any other security in the United States."

How exactly does this transactional test differ from the conduct and effects tests? What sorts of cases would have been caught by the conduct or effects tests but, now, fall outside the ambit of the transactional test? Consider the scenarios identified near the end of the excerpt from Justice Stevens' opinion. If an American investor bought shares on a foreign-listed company where the underlying fraudulent scheme was hatched by executives in the offices of a New York subsidiary, would that conduct be subject to §10(b) under the conduct test? The effects test? For recent cases demonstrating the potential bite of *Morrison, see, e.g., Plumbers' Union Local No. 12 Pension Fund v. Swiss Reinsurance Co.,* 2010 WL 3860397 (S.D.N.Y. Oct. 4, 2010); *In re Societe Generale Securities Litig.,* 2010 WL 3910286 (S.D.N.Y. Sept. 29, 2010); *In re Alstom Securities Litig.,* 2010 WL 3718863 (S.D.N.Y. Sept. 14, 2010); *In re Banco Satander Securities Optimal Litig.,* 2001 WL 3036990 (S.D. Fla. July 30, 2010); *Cornwell Credit Suisse Group,* 2010 WL 3069597 (S.D.N.Y. July 27, 2010).

7. Implications of Morrison for "effects" tests under other statutes. As noted above, for several decades, the extraterritorial scope of federal antitrust laws has turned on a type of "effects" test. Under the logic of *Morrison*, does this test remain "good law" for determining whether to give extraterritorial effect to the antitrust statutes? Doesn't the effects test in the antitrust context suffer from all the same uncertainty and unpredictability as its counterpart in the securities context? Can you point to any difference in the language between the two statutes that justifies a different approach to the extraterritorial effect of the antitrust laws? Does the Foreign Trade Antitrust Improvement Act affect your answer?

The majority in *Morrison* explains that the territoriality presumption applies "regardless of whether there is a risk of conflict between the American statute and a foreign law." Is this consistent with *Hartford Fire*? Between this decision and *Hoffman-LaRoche*, has the Court overruled *sub silentio* the "true conflict" analysis of Justice Souter's majority opinion from *Hartford Fire*?

8. Criticism of Morrison.

(a) Roadmap for evasion. While *Morrison* might provide a relatively clear rule in a previously foggy area of the law, does the decision not chart a roadmap for companies to escape the reach of U.S. securities laws? So long as the alleged conduct takes place overseas, a defendant can blatantly defraud investors without having to answer for his conduct under federal securities laws.

Perhaps more important, what effect does *Morrison* have on capital flows? If federal securities laws are relatively more strict than those of other countries, does not a decision like *Morrison* actually enhance the incentive of those companies to solicit investments entirely overseas because now, unlike in the pre-*Morrison* era, they can have relative confidence that they will not be subject to federal securities laws? On the other hand, does not *Morrison* actually facilitate capital flows from U.S. investors in foreign offerings? Prior to *Morrison*, some foreign companies deliberately prohibited U.S. purchasers from participating in foreign offerings for fear that the offeror might become subject to federal securities laws. *See, e.g., MGC, Inc. v. Great Western Energy Corp.,* 896 F.2d 170 (5th Cir. 1990). Does *Morrison* reduce the need for such prophylactic measures?

(b) Unsettled expectations. As noted above, the conduct and effects tests developed as the operative principles in the Second Circuit, where the major financial markets in the United States are located. With one stroke of the pen, the majority in *Morrison* cast away nearly four decades of precedent from that circuit. Was that wise? Should the

Court not have proceeded more cautiously before upending the rules around which securities offerings had been constructed? Was it necessary for the Court to announce such a broad rule in order to resolve the case? Could the Court not simply have held that §10(b) does not cover so-called "foreign-cubed" cases (*i.e.,* cases brought by foreign investors against foreign companies based on securities transactions in foreign countries)? Alternatively, could the Court have held under *Hartford Fire* that, regardless of whether Congress exercised its legislative jurisdiction, considerations of comity counseled against applying federal law in this particular case? *See* Symeonides, *Choice of Law in American Courts in 2010: Twenty-Fourth Annual Survey,* 59 Am. J. Comp. L. 303-393 (forthcoming 2011).

9. ***Territoriality and comity.*** What is the relationship between the territoriality presumption and the principle from *Hoffman-LaRoche,* cited in Justice Stevens' opinion, that "legislators take account of the legitimate sovereign interests of other nations when they write American laws"? *See supra* p. 699. *See also Microsoft v. AT&T Corp.,* 550 U.S. 437, 455-456 (2007). Does this latter principle simply reformulate the territoriality presumption? Does it operate as an independent constraint on the exercise of legislative jurisdiction? Does it potentially replace the territoriality presumption? Does it signal that certain Justices prefer a softer version of the territoriality presumption than that articulated by Justice Scalia's opinion?

10. ***Views of foreign states.*** Justice Scalia places importance on the potential conflict between federal securities laws and foreign laws. In support, he cites a number of briefs filed by foreign governments and foreign financial institutions.

While a number of foreign governments filed briefs *amici curiae* in *Morrison,* that level of interest was exceptional. Until *Morrison,* there had been relatively few cases of foreign governmental objections to the extraterritorial application of the U.S. securities laws. The relative indifference contrasts sharply with the vigorous protests in the antitrust context. *See supra* pp. 680-683. What explains the differences between foreign reactions in the two contexts? Are there fewer substantive differences between U.S. and foreign antifraud protections than between U.S. and foreign competition laws, although this is a matter of degree? *See United Int'l Holdings, Inc. v. Wharf (Holdings) Ltd.,* 210 F.3d 1207, 1223 (10th Cir. 2000) ("A true conflict would exist here only if Hong Kong law *compelled* securities fraud rather than just permitted it."), *aff'd,* 532 U.S. 588 (2001). Did courts implicitly incorporate considerations of comity into their decision whether to exercise subject matter jurisdiction? *See, e.g., Lobatto v. Berney,* 1999 WL 672994, at *3 (S.D.N.Y. 1999). Does this approach minimize the risk of any disruption to foreign relations? Or does it undermine the predictability in the application of securities laws, which may be important to facilitating capital flows? To what extent should the Supreme Court take these consequences into consideration when deciding how to interpret a statute? *See Stoneridge Inv. Partners LLC v. Scientific-Atlanta,* 552 U.S. 148, 164 (2008) (rejecting a proposed interpretation of federal securities laws that might "raise the cost of being a publicly traded company under our law and shift securities offerings away from domestic capital markets").

Whatever the proper weight to be given to these foreign governments' views, is the approach in *Morrison* consistent with *Hartford Fire?* Does Justice Scalia anywhere identify a "true conflict" between the U.S. and foreign systems?

11. ***Hague Securities Convention on Choice of Law.*** Consider also the "Convention on Law Applicable to Certain Rights in Respect of Securities Held with an Intermediary" ("Hague Securities Convention"). The Convention's declared purpose is to "provide legal certainty and predictability as to the law applicable to securities that are now commonly held through clearing and settlement systems or other intermediaries." In general, the Convention supplies a choice-of-law rule for certain issues involving "intermediaries,"

that is persons or entities who maintain securities accounts for others. Art. I.1(c); Art. II.1. It does not, however, determine the applicable law in all matters germane to a securities transaction. For example, the Convention excludes from its scope the applicable law governing the contractual rights and duties of parties to a disposition of securities held with an intermediary. Art. II.3.

For those issues falling within the Convention's scope, Articles IV-VII set forth the applicable choice-of-law rules. Initially, the law of the country specified in the parties' account agreement governs all issues falling within the Convention's scope provided that the intermediary has an office in the specified country and is identified within the agreement by reference to certain information such as account or bank details ("the qualifying office test"). Art. IV.1. If the Article IV requirements are not satisfied, certain fallback rules set forth in Article V take effect. Under those fallback rules, a court first considers whether the agreement "expressly and unambiguously" states that the agreement shall be executed through a particular intermediary's qualifying office. If so, the law of the country where that office is located governs. Art. V.1. If not, a court should consider the country in which the intermediary is incorporated or has its principal place of business. Art. V.2-3. Other articles in the Convention set forth certain factors that courts should disregard in their choice-of-law analysis (Art. VI), rules that govern the applicable law in cases of new legal rules enacted after a securities agreement is executed (Art. VII), rules governing insolvency proceedings (Art. VIII).

At present, only three countries (including the United States) have signed Hague Securities Convention. They have not yet deposited articles of ratification, acceptance, approval, or accession. The Convention takes effect once three countries have deposited such articles. Art. XIX.

B. Choice of Law Applicable to Torts

Largely independently from rules of construction for federal statutes, U.S. courts and commentators have developed choice-of-law rules governing the application of state (and other) tort laws in multi-jurisdictional cases.[126] These rules have traditionally been considered in conflict of law treatises and courses,[127] and in the *First* and *Second Restatement of Conflict of Laws.*

The choice-of-law rules applicable to torts in the United States have undergone very substantial evolution during the past century. As described below, the outcome of that evolution remains uncertain, and different U.S. jurisdictions take significantly differing approaches to determining the law applicable to torts.[128] This section examines these various approaches. It focuses principally on state (as opposed to federal) choice-of-law rules.[129] Because of the uncertainty of prevailing contemporary choice-of-law rules, and

---

126. *See supra* p. 613, n.1.

127. Commentary on the choice of law applicable to torts includes, for example, R. Weintraub, *Commentary on the Conflict of Laws* 346-437 (6th ed. 2010); Heiser, *Forum Non Conveniens and Choice of Law: The Impact of Applying Foreign Law in Transnational Tort Actions,* 51 Wayne L. Rev. 1161 (2005); Juenger, *Choice of Law in Interstate Torts,* 118 U. Pa. L. Rev. 202 (1969); Kuhne, *Choice of Law in Products Liability,* 60 Cal. L. Rev. 1 (1972); Morris, *The Proper Law of a Tort,* 64 Harv. L. Rev. 881 (1951); Reese, *American Trends in Private International Law: Academic and Judicial Manipulation of Choice of Law Rules in Tort Cases,* 33 Vand. L. Rev. 717 (1980); Reed, *The Anglo-American Revolution in Tort Choice of Law Principles: Paradigm Shift or Pandora's Box?,* 18 Ariz. J. Int'l & Comp. L. 867 (2001); Rheinstein, *The Place of Wrong: A Study in the Method of the Case Law,* 19 Tul. L. Rev. 4 (1944); Sedler, *Interest Analysis, "Multistate Policies," and Considerations of Fairness in Conflicts Tort Cases,* 37 Willamette L. Rev. 233 (2001); Symeonides, *The Need for a Third Conflicts Restatement (and a Proposal for Tort Conflicts),* 75 Ind. L.J. 437 (2000).

128. *See infra* pp. 738-742.

129. As discussed below, the *Erie* doctrine generally treats choice-of-law questions as "substantive" issues governed by state law. *See infra* pp. 791-796.

because of the continuing vitality of traditional rules, this section devotes particular attention to historic doctrine and developments.

1.   Traditional Approach: Territoriality and Vested Rights

a.   The Territorial Rule: "Place of the Wrong."   During the nineteenth and early twentieth centuries, the American approach to the choice of law applicable to torts was largely territorial, paralleling approaches to judicial jurisdiction and the extraterritorial application of federal laws.[130] Relying on principles of territorial sovereignty, nineteenth-century American courts and commentators generally looked to the law of the place of the wrong (or *lex loci delicti commissi*).[131] This approach rested in substantial part on Joseph Story's territorial analysis of legislative jurisdiction, which is discussed above.[132]

In the early twentieth century, Story's thinking provided the foundation for another highly influential American choice-of-law treatise — Joseph Beale's *Treatise on the Conflict of Laws*.[133] Beale championed the "vested rights" doctrine, according to which, "[a] right having been created by the appropriate law, the recognition of its existence should follow everywhere. Thus, an act valid where done cannot be called in question anywhere."[134] Beale served as the reporter for the *Restatement (First) Conflict of Laws*, which articulated his vested rights theory.[135] Published in 1934, the *Restatement* included numerous rules based on the traditional nineteenth-century territoriality analysis, including the rule that torts were governed by the law of the "place of the wrong."[136]

The rationale for applying the law of the place of the wrong was based firmly on the territoriality doctrine. The "vested rights" theory rested on the premise that no state's laws could apply outside that state's territory, but that commission of a tort within one state gave rise to a "vested right," that other states would generally recognize.[137] Beale explained the doctrine as follows:

> It is impossible for a plaintiff to recover in tort unless he has been given by some law a cause of action in tort; and this cause of action can be given only by the law of the place where the tort was committed. . . . That is the place where the injurious event occurs, and its law is the law therefore which applies to it.[138]

The *First Restatement*'s rules required determining the "place of the wrong," which Beale defined as the place where the last event necessary to make the tortfeasor liable occurred.[139] Until the second half of this century, most American courts followed the

---

130. *See supra* pp. 83-86, 648-649.

131. *E.g.,* H. Goodrich, *Conflict of Laws* 188 (1927) ("The general rule is that the law governing the creation and extent of tort liability is that of the place where the tort was committed."); *Restatement (First) Conflict of Laws* §377 (1934); *American Banana Co. v. United Fruit Co.,* 213 U.S. 347 (1909); *Slater v. Mexican National R. Co.,* 194 U.S. 120 (1904).

132. *See supra* pp. 648-649.

133. Beale developed the "vested rights" theory of conflict of laws, which rested on principles of territorial sovereignty. *See* J. Beale, *A Selection of Cases on the Conflict of Laws* (1902); J. Beale, *Treatise on the Conflict of Laws* 1289 (1935) ("The existence and nature of a cause of action . . . is governed by the law of the place [of the] wrongful act or omission."); Beale, *The Jurisdiction of a Sovereign State,* 36 Harv. L. Rev. 241 (1923).

134. J. Beale, *Cases on the Conflict of Laws* 517 (1901).

135. *Restatement (First) Conflict of Laws* (1934).

136. *Restatement (First) Conflict of Laws* §§377-378 (1934).

137. *See* 3 J. Beale, *Treatise on the Conflict of Laws* 1964-1965 (1935).

138. 3 J. Beale, *Treatise on the Conflict of Laws* 1964-1965 (1935).

139. *Restatement (First) Conflict of Laws* §378 (1934); *Alabama Great Southern R.R. v. Carroll,* 11 So. 803 (Ala. 1892); H. Goodrich, *Conflict of Laws* 191 (1927) ("The tort, if any, [is] deemed to have been committed where the

First Restatement's "place of the last event" rule in determining the "place of the wrong." Once selected, this law governed virtually all issues relating to a tort, including whether the defendant's conduct was tortious, causation, limitations upon the defendant's liability, vicarious liability, contribution, indemnity, and defenses to liability.[140]

b. Selected Materials on the Traditional "Place of Wrong" Rule. Excerpted below are materials that illustrate the traditional place of wrong rule. Selected passages from Joseph Story's *Commentaries* state the territoriality doctrine that provided the basic foundation for traditional American choice-of-law rules; they also set forth the doctrine of international comity as the explanation for why one state will apply the laws of another state. The *First Restatement*, also excerpted below, provided a comprehensive set of choice-of-law rules based on these territorial principles. Finally, the Alabama Supreme Court's decision in *Alabama Great Southern Railroad Co. v. Carroll* is an example of application of the place of the wrong rule.

J. STORY, COMMENTARIES ON THE CONFLICT OF LAWS
§§18, 20, 23, 29, 32, 33, 35 & 38 (2d ed. 1841) [excerpted in Appendix BB]

RESTATEMENT (FIRST) CONFLICT OF LAWS
§§1, 6, 377 & 378 (1934) [excerpted in Appendix X]

ALABAMA GREAT SOUTHERN RAILROAD CO. v. CARROLL
11 So. 803 (Ala. 1892)

McCLELLAN, JUSTICE. [The plaintiff was an Alabama domiciliary who was hired as a brakeman by the defendant, a railroad incorporated in Alabama. The employment contract was executed in Alabama. Negligence by other employees of the defendant in coupling cars in Alabama, on a train headed for Mississippi, caused the coupling to break. The accident occurred in Mississippi and injured the plaintiff. An Alabama employer's liability act, Alabama Code §2590 (1885), arguably made the defendant liable for the plaintiff's injury. It provided: "When a personal injury is received by a servant . . . in the service . . . of the master . . . the master is liable to answer in damages . . . as if he were a stranger . . . [w]here the injury is caused by reason of the negligence of any person in the service of the master. . . ." In Mississippi, a fellow-servant rule would exculpate the railroad from liability.] . . .

[W]e do not understand appellee's counsel even to deny either the proposition or its application to this case, — that there can be no recovery in one state for injuries to the person sustained in another, unless the infliction of the injuries is actionable under the law of the state in which they were received. Certainly this is the well-established rule of law. . . . The question is as to duty operating effectually at the place where its alleged failure caused harm to result. . . . It is admitted, or at least cannot be denied, that negligence of duty unproductive of damnifying results will not authorize or support a recovery. Up to the time this train passed out of Alabama no injury had resulted. For all that

injury of which the plaintiff complains was inflicted, not where the defendant's acts were done."); Rheinstein, *The Place of Wrong: A Study in the Method of the Case Law,* 19 Tul. L. Rev. 4 (1944).

140. *Restatement (First) Conflict of Laws* §§377, 378, 379, 380, 383, 385, 387 & 388 (1934).

occurred in Alabama, therefore, no cause of action whatever arose. The fact which created the right to sue, — the injury, — without which confessedly no action would lie anywhere, transpired in the state of Mississippi. It was in that state, therefore, necessarily that the cause of action, if any, arose; and whether a cause of action arose and existed at all, or not, must in all reason be determined by the law which obtained at the time and place when and where the fact which is relied on to justify a recovery transpired. Section 2590 of the Code of Alabama had no efficacy beyond the lines of Alabama. It cannot be allowed to operate upon facts occurring in another state, so as to evolve out of them rights and liabilities which do not exist under the law of that state, which is of course paramount in the premises. Where the facts occur in Alabama, and a liability becomes fixed in Alabama, it may be enforced in another state having like enactments, or whose policy is not opposed to the spirit of such enactments; but this is quite a different matter. This is but enforcing the statute upon facts which it is applicable, all of which occurred within the territory for the government of which it was enacted. Section 2590 of the Code, in other words, is to be interpreted in light of universally recognized principles of private, international or interstate law, as if its operation had been expressly limited to this state, and as if its first line read as follows: "When a personal injury is received in Alabama by a servant or employee," etc. The negligent infliction of an injury here, under statutory circumstances, creates a right of action here, which, being transitory, may be enforced in any other state or country the comity of which admits of it; but for an injury inflicted elsewhere than in Alabama our statute gives no right of recovery, and the aggrieved party must look to the local law to ascertain what his rights are. Under that law this plaintiff had no cause of action. . . . [A]n analogy . . . is found in that well-established doctrine of criminal law that where the unlawful act is committed in one . . . state, and takes effect . . . in another . . . state, the crime is deemed to have been committed and is punished in that . . . state in which the result is manifested, and not where the act was committed. . . .

[The plaintiff argued that he had entered into a contract in Alabama with the defendant railroad, providing for employment both in Alabama and elsewhere, and that this Alabama contract should be construed to incorporate the terms of the Alabama legislation, thereby enabling that legislation to be applied outside of Alabama.] [T]he duties and liabilities incident to the relation between the plaintiff and the defendant, . . . are not imposed by, and do not rest in or spring from, the contract between the parties. . . . The whole argument is at fault. The only true doctrine is that each sovereignty, state or nation, has the exclusive power to finally determine and declare what act or omissions in the conduct of one to another . . . shall impose a liability in damages for the consequent injury, and the courts of no other sovereignty can impute a damnifying quality to an act or omission which afforded no cause of action where it transpired. [The court quoted from *Whitford v. Railroad Co.*, 23 N.Y. 465, where a New York court refused to apply New York law to a deceased passenger's claim against a New York railroad, for an accident occurring in New Grenada:]

> Suppose the government of New Grenada to have enacted that the proprietors of a railroad company should not be responsible for the negligence of its servants, provided there was no want of due care in selecting them, it could not be pretended that its will could be set at naught by prosecuting the corporation in the courts of another state, where the law was different. . . . The true theory is that no suit whatever respecting this injury could be sustained in the courts of this state, except pursuant to the law of international comity. By that law, foreign contracts and foreign transactions, out of which liabilities have arisen, may be prosecuted in our tribunals by the implied assent of the government of this state; but in all

such cases we administer the foreign law as from the proofs we find it to be, or as without proofs we presume it to be. . . .

For the error in refusing to instruct the jury to find for the defendant . . . the judgment is reversed. . . .

Notes on Story's Commentaries, First Restatement, *and* Carroll

1. *Choice-of-law rules subject to forum's legislation.* Section 2590 of the Alabama Code was silent about the territory in which conduct had to occur in order for the legislation to apply, and about the domicile or citizenship of persons entitled to claim protection under the law. Thus, courts were left to answer these questions, and *Carroll* interpreted §2590 as if it read: "When a personal injury is received in Alabama by a servant or employee. . . ." Suppose that the actual language of the section had instead read: "When a personal injury is received, anywhere in the world, by a servant or employee of a railroad that does business in Alabama, which servant or employee is domiciled in Alabama and has signed a contract of employment in Alabama. . . ." Putting aside constitutional considerations, would *Carroll* have required any lengthy analysis of choice-of-law precedents or international law? Would the decision have required considering anything beyond the plain language of §2590?

Note Story's caveat that choice-of-law "rules" apply in the "silence of any positive rule, affirming, or denying, or restraining the operation of foreign laws." J. Story, *Commentaries on the Conflict of Laws* §38 (2d ed. 1841). The same is true today. *Restatement (Second) Conflict of Laws* §6(1) (1971). Compare the interpretation of federal statutes. *See supra* pp. 604-605.

2. *Choice-of-law decisions as exercises in statutory construction.* What is the function of choice-of-law rules? Is it something more than an effort to ascertain unexpressed legislative intent (in the case of statutory claims) and the proper reach of judicial rules (in the case of common law rules)? Like many choice-of-law decisions, *Carroll* was ultimately a case concerning the interpretation of §2590. Note the court's statement that §2590 "must be interpreted in light of universally recognized principles of private, international or interstate law." Compare this choice-of-law approach with the role of the territoriality presumption (and other canons of construction like the international law presumption) in interpreting federal statutes. *See supra* pp. 664-670. Is there any difference between the two efforts to decide when American law applies in international cases?

3. *Why should a court ever decline to apply "its" law?* Why should a U.S. court *ever* decline to apply U.S. law? Note Story's observation that it would "annihilate the sovereignty and equality" of states if they were compelled to apply foreign law. In *Carroll*, why shouldn't Alabama courts have applied Alabama law to the claim by Mr. Carroll? What purposes are served when a court refuses to apply the law that the local legislature has enacted? Recall the explanation in *Lauritzen* of international choice-of-law rules in the maritime context and Story's *Commentaries*. *See supra* pp. 648-650. When a U.S. court refuses to apply U.S. law, what law does it apply? What substantive law was applicable in *Carroll*?

4. *Reasons advanced for applying foreign law.* Different explanations have been advanced for why foreign law, instead of the forum's law, should be applied in certain international or interstate cases. These are reasons that courts may, as a general matter, presume to have motivated a legislature.

(a) Territorial sovereignty and international law. Consider the explanation advanced in *Carroll* for the court's refusal to apply the forum's laws. Citing "private international" law, *Carroll* relies on the "only true doctrine," that "each sovereignty, state or nation, has the exclusive power to finally determine and declare what act . . . shall impose a liability in damages for the consequent injury, and the courts of no other sovereignty can impute a damnifying quality to an act or omission which afforded no cause of action where it transpired." Similarly, as described above, Story reasoned that "no state or nation can, by its laws, directly affect, or bind property out of its own territory, or bind persons not resident therein . . . *it would be wholly incompatible with the equality and exclusiveness of the sovereignty of all nations, that any one nation should be at liberty to regulate either persons or things not within its own territory.*" J. Story, *Commentaries on the Conflict of Laws* §§18, 20 (2d ed. 1841) (emphasis added).

Is this a persuasive rationale? Consider Story's first and second maxims. Does the first maxim — territorial sovereignty — in fact dictate the second maxim — that no state's laws may apply within foreign territory? Developing the *Whitford* case, described in *Carroll,* how does it infringe New Grenada's sovereignty for U.S. law to be applied to conduct causing injury in New Grenada? Suppose that a Singapore court applies Singapore libel law to statements made in the *New York Times,* distributed in the United States. Does that infringe U.S. sovereignty?

(b) International comity and reciprocity. Why should U.S. courts care about the sovereignty of New Grenada? Is it not true that U.S. courts are established by the United States, to further U.S. policies for the benefit of U.S. citizens? Why should U.S. courts pay the slightest attention to foreign law or sovereignty? Consider the following observation by Waechter, a prominent nineteenth-century Continental commentator:

> The judge's task is to give effect to the law in case of a dispute and of a resistance. What law shall he effectuate? Certainly only the law laid down or otherwise recognized by the state. This comes from the nature of the positive law and from the relation of the judge to the positive laws whose mere instrument he should be. . . . Waechter, *"On the Collision of Private Laws of Different States," reprinted in* 13 Am. J. Comp. L. 417, 421 (1964) (translation by Nadelmann).

One reason that U.S. courts should respect the sovereignty of foreign states, and international law, is to increase the prospects that foreign states will respect U.S. sovereignty. Simply put, U.S. courts should respect the territorial sovereignty of New Grenada, because it will encourage New Grenada courts to respect U.S. sovereignty. Note the reliance in §35 of Story's *Commentaries* on "mutual interest and utility" and the "moral necessity to do justice, in order that justice may be done to us in return." Compare also the rationale in *Lauritzen, supra* pp. 654-659.

Should U.S. courts only respect the sovereignty of foreign states — and refrain from applying U.S. law to conduct within foreign states — that demonstrate that they will act reciprocally? Is that position not consistent with the rationale that Story articulates? *Compare Restatement (First) Conflict of Laws* §6 (1934).

(c) Predictability. Territorial approaches to choice-of-law issues are also justified as necessary to achieve predictability. Joseph Beale wrote: "International trade could not be carried on as has now become necessary unless the trader could be assured that he would not be placed absolutely at the mercy of the vagaries or unknown requirements of the local law, but would find a well-established body of law to protect his rights." 1 J. Beale, *Treatise on the Conflict of Laws* 4 (1935). Are the *First Restatement*'s choice-of-law rules actually able to produce predictable results? Consider the outcome in *Carroll.* Why is predictability so important? Doesn't predictability depend upon all nations (and states) adopting

identical choice-of-law rules? Would even that provide predictability? Suppose the same substantive rules are applied in different proceedings by a lay jury and a career judge, or by judges with materially different backgrounds and training?

How does the predictability envisioned by the territorial approach in the choice-of-law context compare with the predictability about which Justice Scalia spoke in *Morrison*? Is there a greater need for a predictable background with respect to judge-made rules of tort law as opposed to legislative enactments? Or does the need for predictability decrease because parties anticipate that judges will shape common law rules on a case-by-case basis?

(d) Fairness. Territorial choice-of-law rules were also justified on fairness grounds. Justice Holmes wrote in *American Banana:* "For [a] jurisdiction, if it should happen to lay hold of the actor, to treat him according to its own notions rather than those of the place where he did the acts . . . would be unjust." 213 U.S. at 356. Compare the similar reasoning in due process decisions dealing with judicial and legislative jurisdiction. *See supra* pp. 98-99, 611-612.

If one lives and acts exclusively within one state, and if the consequences of one's acts are confined solely to residents of that state, within that state, it would be surprising to find that another state's laws applied. But few cases involve such hermetically sealed conduct. Where multi-state conduct is involved, do private parties expect that their acts will be subject only to the law of the place they act? Moreover, consider what law the railroad defendant in *Carroll* would have thought applicable to conduct by its employees in Alabama. Is the "last event" rule of *Carroll* and the *First Restatement* consistent with either *American Banana* or the goal of fairness? More fundamentally, aren't expectations merely a reflection of the law? If territorial choice-of-law rules prevail, then parties will expect to be judged according to the law of the place where they act; if other rules prevail, expectations will be different.

(e) Vested rights. The *First Restatement*'s choice-of-law rules purported not to rely directly on international law limits on jurisdiction (which were specifically distinguished, *see infra* p. 731) or on international comity (*see Restatement (First) Conflict of Laws* §6 (1934)). Rather the *Restatement* relied on a theory of "vested rights," which provided for the international recognition of rights that "vested" under the laws of particular sovereignties. In a classic explanation of the vested rights doctrine, Justice Holmes wrote:

> The theory of the foreign suit is that although the act complained of was subject to no law having force in the forum, it gave rise to an obligation, an *obligation* which like other obligations follows the person, and may be enforced wherever the person may be found. But as the only source of this obligation is the law of the place of the act, it follows that that law determines not merely the existence of the obligation, but equally determines the extent. *Slater v. Mexican National RR Co.,* 194 U.S. 120, 126 (1904).

Is this rationale persuasive? Does it make it easier or harder to defend territorial choice-of-law rules?

(f) Uniformity. The *First Restatement*'s rules (like most other choice-of-law rules) seek to ensure that different jurisdictions will apply the same substantive law to the same dispute. This reduces the risk of "forum shopping," and accords with general fairness expectations. How can uniformity be achieved if different nations (and states) apply different choice-of-law rules?

5. *Distinction between international limits on legislative jurisdiction and national choice-of-law rules.* Read §§1 and 65 of the *First Restatement,* together with comment b to §65. *See*

Appendix X. There is a fundamental distinction between: (a) the limits that international law imposes on a nation's exercise of legislative jurisdiction; and (b) the decisions that a nation makes whether to make use of its rights under international law to assert legislative jurisdiction. As comment b to §65 makes clear, international law will frequently permit two (or more) states to assert legislative jurisdiction over the same conduct or transaction. *See supra* pp. 78-79. In these circumstances, national choice-of-law rules determine whether a nation will apply its laws to conduct that it could properly regulate under international law.

6. *What does "territoriality" mean?* Does acceptance of Story's territorial view of national sovereignty, taken alone, solve anything except simple cases where all relevant conduct, effects, and parties are located within one state's territory? Or does accepting the territoriality doctrine merely present the question of what thing or "connecting factors" must be localized within a state's territory? Recall *American Banana,* where it was assumed that "territoriality" meant the application of the laws where the allegedly wrongful conduct occurred. *See supra* pp. 651-653. Compare *Morrison,* where territoriality referred to the locus of the acts necessary to state a cause of action under the statute, or *Pennoyer,* where territoriality meant the service of process within a state's borders. *See supra* pp. 91-93. What connecting factor does *Carroll* use? How are the purposes of the territoriality doctrine advanced by each of the connecting factors described above?

7. *The "place of the wrong" and the "last event" rules of the* **First Restatement.** Do the *First Restatement*'s place of the wrong and last event rules provide constructive clarification of the territoriality doctrine?

(a) The last event rule. Section 377 of the *First Restatement* and *Carroll* provide for application of the tort law of the place where "the last event necessary to make an actor liable for an alleged tort takes place." Consider what this "last event" meant, in practical terms, in *Carroll.* Where did the negligent conduct that killed Mr. Carroll happen — Alabama or Tennessee? Why didn't Alabama law apply?

(b) Does the last event rule protect territorial sovereignty? Consider whether the last event rule furthers the policies — set forth above — supporting a territorial approach to choice-of-law issues. Does the application of Mississippi's law to Mr. Carroll's tort claims protect Mississippi's sovereignty? Does it impair Alabama's sovereignty? If one wanted to discourage negligent operation of railroads, without imposing undue costs upon railroad operators, would one seek to do that in the place where the railroad's allegedly culpable conduct occurs, or where the effects of that conduct occur, or in both places? Suppose that, in *Carroll,* the allegedly negligent conduct by Carroll's co-workers occurred in Mississippi, rather than in Alabama, but he had been killed in Alabama. Would the Alabama legislature have wanted Alabama law to apply to Mr. Carroll's tort claim in that case?

(c) Consistency of last event rule with international law. Carroll and §377 arguably adopt what amounts to an "effects test," granting regulatory authority to the state where harmful effects of conduct occur, rather than the place where the conduct itself occurred. Would this be appropriate? As discussed elsewhere, there is substantial authority providing that it infringes upon a state's territorial sovereignty for a foreign state to regulate conduct occurring within that state based upon effects in the foreign state. *See supra* pp. 601, 648-650; *American Banana, supra.*

(d) Does the last event rule produce predictable results? Is §377's last event test likely to produce predictable and uniform results? Suppose that the negligently coupled trains in *Carroll* had malfunctioned in Georgia, Tennessee, or Florida, instead of in Mississippi.

Then what law would have applied? Suppose that Mr. Carroll had not died until he returned to Alabama. What law would have applied in a suit for wrongful death?

(e) Is the last event rule derived from principles of territorial sovereignty? Is there anything in international law or the doctrine of territorial sovereignty that requires a last event rule? Would a wrongful conduct rule be more consistent with principles of territorial sovereignty— permitting states to regulate conduct within their territory?

8. *Nationality, citizenship, and domicile.* Why do Story and the *First Restatement* focus exclusively on territoriality? Why should not Alabama apply §2590 to any tort claim by an Alabama citizen or domiciliary? That would have permitted Mr. Carroll to take advantage of §2590. Is that desirable? Is it likely to be what the Alabama legislature would have intended had it considered the facts in *Carroll*? Alternatively, why shouldn't §2590 apply to any tort claim against a railroad incorporated or headquartered in Alabama?

9. *Domestic versus international choice-of-law rules.* *Carroll* involved a domestic U.S. choice-of-law question: should Alabama courts apply Alabama or Mississippi law? Contrast both *Whitford* and *American Banana,* which required deciding whether a foreign nation's law should apply, rather than U.S. state or federal law. Should the same choice-of-law rules apply in both domestic and international cases? Why or why not? *See infra* p. 731. Suppose the negligence in Tokyo of an employee of a Japanese trading house tortiously injured a Japanese employee—in New York. Would New York have any interest in regulating the conduct?

c. Characterization, Escape Devices, and Procedural Laws.

Although the *First Restatement* was relentlessly territorial in its formal approach to torts, it also contained a number of significant provisions that called for application of laws other than those of the place of the wrong. These provisions, sometimes referred to as "escape devices," allowed for a forum court to apply its own law to certain issues, or to refuse to apply foreign law in particular circumstances.

First, the *Restatement* distinguished between "substantive" and "procedural" issues. Procedural issues were governed by the law of the forum, without regard to the law governing the substantive aspects of a dispute.[141] Procedural matters included many issues that would not appear capable of influencing the outcome of a dispute, including the form of action, service, evidentiary issues, and mode of trial.[142] Additionally, however, "procedure" could include more "substantive" issues, such as statutes of limitations, contributory negligence, damages, and the like.[143]

Second, like most private international law systems, the *First Restatement* included exceptions to most of its basic rules for "public policy." As discussed elsewhere, tort claims were generally regarded in nineteenth-century America as "transitory," except where they concerned damage to real property.[144] As a consequence, they could be asserted against the defendant—under the law of the place of the wrong—wherever he was subject to personal jurisdiction.[145] Foreign tort law would not be applied, however, where it was contrary to the forum's public policy.[146]

---

141. *Restatement (First) Conflict of Laws* §585 (1934) ("All matters of procedure are governed by the law of the forum.").
142. *Restatement (First) Conflict of Laws* §§586-600 (1934).
143. *Restatement (First) Conflict of Laws* §§601, 603-604 & 606 (1934).
144. *See supra* pp. 724-725.
145. *See supra* pp. 724-725.
146. *Dennick v. RR Co.,* 103 U.S. 11 (1880); *infra* pp. 734-736.

Third, a forum court was not obliged to enforce a foreign tort claim where a foreign penal or revenue claim was involved.[147] Similarly, the *First Restatement* did not require enforcement of foreign tort claims where the forum's legal system was sufficiently dissimilar from the foreign system as to make enforcement inappropriate.[148]

Fourth, the *First Restatement* also depended substantially on issues of "characterization." For example, in order to apply the *Restatement*'s choice-of-law rules for torts, a court first had to determine that the case was in fact a tort case. If the court instead decided that a contract case was involved, different choice-of-law rules—producing different choices of law—were prescribed by the *First Restatement*.[149]

The materials excerpted below introduce these various rules. *Victor v. Sperry* illustrates the application of public policy exceptions, while excerpts from the *Restatement (First) Conflict of Laws* set forth the traditional rules regarding "procedure" and penal or public claims.

VICTOR v. SPERRY

329 P.2d 728 (Cal. Dist. Ct. App. 1958)

MUSSELL, JUSTICE. This is an action for personal injuries sustained by plaintiff in an automobile accident which occurred on the San Quintin highway, approximately 44 kilometers south of Tiajuana, Baja California, Republic of Mexico. At the time of the collision on July 3, 1955, defendant John C. Sperry, with the permission and consent of defendant John M. Sperry, was driving a Mercury automobile northerly on said highway when the Mercury collided with a Chevrolet automobile being driven in a southerly direction on said highway by Defendant Edward Thornton. Plaintiff Rudolph Victor was an occupant of the Thornton vehicle and was severely injured in the collision. Plaintiff and the drivers of both cars were and now are residents and citizens of the State of California. The accident was the result of the negligence (and of the equivalent of negligence under Mexican law) of the drivers of both cars involved in the accident.

Article 1910 of the Civil Code of 1928 for the Federal District and Territories of Mexico, as amended, which had been adopted by the State of Baja California del Norte and which was in effect at the time of the accident, provided as follows: "A person who, acting illicitly or contrary to good customs, causes damages to another, is obligated to repair it, unless it is shown that the damage was produced as a consequence of the guilt or inexcusable negligence of the victim." Neither said code nor the general law of said state or of said Republic distinguished between guests and passengers in motor vehicles nor did they impose any restrictions upon the right of a guest to recover damages from the negligent operator of a motor vehicle in which he was riding.

Prior to the accident plaintiff had been employed as a house mover and his weekly wage was $99. He had not returned to work at the time of the trial and will not be able to engage in the same occupation or any occupation requiring a substantial amount of physical activity. . . . He suffered a paralysis of the left upper and lower extremities and the disability in his left upper extremity is permanent and total. The disability in his lower

---

147. *Restatement (First) Conflict of Laws* §§610 & 611 (1934); *Herrick v. Minneapolis & St. L. Ry. Co.*, 31 Minn. 11 (1883).

148. *Slater v. Mexican National R.R. Co.*, 194 U.S. 120 (1904); *Stewart v. Baltimore & O. R.R. Co.*, 168 U.S. 445 (1897).

149. *See* Appendix X. *E.g., Levy v. Daniels' U-Drive Auto Renting Co.*, 143 A.163 (Conn. 1928).

extremity is permanent and partial. . . . The court further found that plaintiff suffered the following actual damages . . . :

Medical and hospital expenses	$ 2,962.05
Loss of earnings	7,500.00
Impairment of earning capacity	15,000.00
Pain, suffering and mental anguish	15,000.00
	$40,462.05

At the time of the accident the Mexican law in effect imposed restrictions on the recovery of damages for personal injuries regardless of their nature or extent. Under the Mexican law in effect at the time a victim of the negligent conduct of another could recover his medical and hospital expenses. For a temporary total disability he could recover only 75 per cent of his lost wages for a period not to exceed one year. Wages in excess of 25 pesos, or $2 per day, could not be taken into account in computing the amount allowed. If he suffered a permanent and total disability, he could recover lost earnings for only 918 days and, even though he earned more than 25 pesos per day, only that amount could be taken into account in computing the amount of the recovery. Where the disability was permanent but not total, the recovery was scaled down. For a permanent disability of an upper extremity the victim could recover only from 50 to 70 per cent of $2 per day for 918 days, the exact percentage depending upon age, the importance of the disability, and the extent to which the disability prevented the victim from engaging in his occupation. If the injured extremity was the "least useful," the indemnity was reduced by 15 per cent. In addition, "moral damages" up to a maximum of one third of the other recoverable damages might, in the discretion of the court, be awarded. "Moral damages" are defined as "damages suffered by a person in his honor, reputation, personal tranquillity or spiritual integrity of his life, and as damages which are not of a physical nature and not capable of exact monetary evaluation." The trial court concluded that enforcement of these restrictions on the recovery of damages is not contrary to the public policy of this State or to abstract justice or injurious to the welfare of the people of this State and that plaintiff was not entitled to recover his actual damages in the amount of $40,462.05. Judgment was thereupon rendered against defendants John C. Sperry and Edward Thornton in the amount of $6,135.96. The recovery was computed as follows:

Medical and hospital expenses	$ 2,962.05
Temporary total disability (75% of $2.00 for 365 days)	547.50
Permanent partial disability (70% of $2.00 for 918 days less 15%)	1,092.42
Sub-total	$ 4,601.97
Moral damages	1,533.00
Total	$ 6,134.97

Under Article 1913 of the Civil Code of 1928 for the Mexican Federal District and Territories, if a person has the use of mechanisms or instruments which are dangerous per se, by the speed they develop, or otherwise, he is obligated to answer for the damages he causes, even though he does not act illicitly, unless the damage is caused by the guilt or inexcusable negligence of the victim. The Mexican courts hold that an automobile is a dangerous mechanism or instrument within the meaning of this section and that a person injured by a motor vehicle is entitled to recover damages without regard to fault or negligence from both the owner and driver of the automobile. However, if liability exists only under Article 1913 "moral damages" are not recoverable. Since liability under Article 1910 was found to exist on the part of the drivers of both automobiles, it became immaterial whether liability under Article 1913 was found to exist as to them. Plaintiff, however, sought a judgment against John M. Sperry, owner of the [Mercury] automobile, for $4,601.97, under Article 1913. The trial court concluded that this article is contrary to the public policy of this State, is in substantial conflict with the law of this State, and should not be enforced. Judgment was entered in favor of defendant John M. Sperry.

Rudolph Victor appeals from the judgment (a) Insofar as it fails to award damages in excess of $6,134.97 as against defendants John C. Sperry and Edward Thornton; and (b) Insofar as it fails to award any damages against defendant John M. Sperry. . . . [Victor appeals the trial court's] conclusions as to the enforceability of the Mexican law. . . .

In the instant case, since the accident occurred in Mexico, plaintiff's cause of action arose there and the character and measure of his damages are governed by the laws of Mexico. The measure of damages in inseparably connected to the cause of action and cannot be severed therefrom. The limitation upon the amount of damages imposed by the laws of Mexico is not contrary to the public policy of the State of California or injurious to the welfare of the people thereof.

The trial court herein held that the application of Article 1913 . . . , which provides for liability without fault, was in opposition to the public policy of the State of California and refused to enforce that article against John M. Sperry, owner of one of the automobiles involved in the collision. We find no reversible error in this refusal. . . . Since no right of action exists in California for damages for liability without fault under the circumstances set forth herein and in Article 1913 . . . , the trial court herein properly concluded that this article should not be enforced as against John M. Sperry as owner of one of the automobiles involved.

RESTATEMENT (FIRST) CONFLICT OF LAWS
§§384, 585, 610, 611 & 612 (1934) [excerpted in Appendix X]

Notes on Victor and First Restatement

1. ***Characterization and choice of law.*** As discussed below, the *First Restatement* provided that the law governing most contract issues was the law of the state where the contract was made. *See infra* pp. 777. In *Carroll*, Mr. Carroll's contract of employment was made in Alabama — which would have made Alabama law applicable if the case had been characterized as a contract dispute. Why should *Carroll* be viewed as a tort case, rather than a contract case? Does the distinction depend on how the plaintiff pleads the claim?

In time, courts found little difficulty in characterizing claims or elements of claims in whatever manner would achieve their view of justice in particular cases. *See* Cook, *Characterization in the Conflict of Laws,* 51 Yale L.J. 191 (1941); Lorenzen, *The Qualification, Classification and Characterization Problem in Conflict of Laws,* 50 Yale L.J. 743 (1941). The *First Restatement* provided no meaningful restrictions on such exercises in re-characterization. Whatever the merits of individual decisions, the manipulation of choice-of-law rules through characterization significantly detracted from the *First Restatement*'s promise of predictability. The same issue persists under contemporary choice-of-law analysis.

2. ***Enforcement of foreign tort claims.*** Principles of territorial sovereignty and the vested rights doctrine have both a negative and an affirmative aspect. First, as in *Carroll*, they

forbid the application of the forum's law to foreign torts. Second, as in §384 of the *First Restatement,* they permit (indeed, require) a local forum court to apply foreign law to foreign torts.

Even if a state will not apply its law to events occurring outside its territory, why should its courts assist in the enforcement of foreign law by applying a foreign state's laws to foreign torts? Why should U.S. judicial resources be expended in the enforcement of foreign laws? Where does a U.S. court derive the authority to apply foreign law? Consider:

> A party legally liable in New Jersey cannot escape that liability by going to New York. If the liability to pay money was fixed by the law of the State where the transaction occurred, is it to be said it can be enforced nowhere else because it depended upon statute law and not upon common law? It would be a very dangerous doctrine to establish, that in all cases where the several States have substituted the statute for the common law, the liability can be enforced in no other State but that where the statute was enacted and the transaction occurred. *Dennick v. Railroad Co.,* 103 U.S. 11 (1880).

Why should U.S. courts not apply U.S. law to foreign torts? In general, why should not choice of law be determined by personal jurisdiction: if a state can hear a dispute, it should apply its own laws? Recall the reasons for the territoriality doctrine. *See supra* pp. 665-666.

3. Role of comity in choice-of-law analysis. What is the role of "comity" in choice-of-law analysis? Consider again the discussion of comity and reciprocity in Huber's *De Conflictu Legum* and Story's *Commentaries,* particularly §§29 & 33. *See supra* pp. 647-649. What does "comity" mean? For other efforts to describe comity, *see Laker Airways,* 731 F.2d at 937 ("comity serves our international system like the mortar which cements together a brick house. No one would willingly permit the mortar to crumble or be chipped away for fear of compromising the entire structure"); *Republic of the Philippines v. Westinghouse Elec. Corp.,* 43 F.3d 65, 75 (3d Cir. 1995) ("Comity is essentially a version of the golden rule: a 'concept of doing to others as you would have them do to you.' ") (quoting *Lafontant v. Aristide,* 844 F. Supp. 128, 132 (S.D.N.Y. 1994)).

Is there a greater need for comity in cases of judge-made rules as opposed to statutory enactments? Do separation-of-powers considerations counsel greater caution in the case of judge-made law as opposed to legislative enactments? To the extent state law supplies the substantive standard for most tort cases, are not comity concerns especially important to ensure that the Nation "speaks with one voice"? Compare the analysis here with that in cases like *Garamendi* involving exercises of legislative jurisdiction by state governments.

4. Public policy exception to application of foreign tort law. Section 612 of the *First Restatement* provides that a U.S. court will not entertain a claim based upon foreign tort law "which is contrary to the strong public policy of the forum." Compare the similar recognition in §§33, 35, and 38 of Story's *Commentaries* that comity did not require a state to give effect to foreign laws that were contrary to the forum's public policies. What justifies this public policy exception?

How does this exception compare to the Oklahoma "Save Our State" Amendment that provides that Oklahoma courts "shall not look to the legal precepts of other nations or cultures"; "shall not consider international law or Sharia law"; and shall apply the law of another state of the United States only "if necessary" and "provided" that law "does not include Sharia law." *See supra* pp. 643-644. Is the "Save Our State" Amendment simply an extreme, albeit permissible, application of the public policy exception?

5. *Meaning of public policy.* As discussed elsewhere, it is difficult to define the public policy exception. Consider:

> Our own scheme of legislation may be different [from that in a foreign nation.] We may even have no legislation on the subject. That is not enough to show that public policy forbids us to enforce the foreign right. A right of action is property. If a foreign statute gives the right, the mere fact that we do not give a like right is no reason for refusing to help the plaintiff in getting what belongs to him. . . . The misleading word "comity" has been responsible for much of the trouble. It has been fertile in suggesting a discretion unregulated by general principles. . . . The sovereign in its discretion may refuse its aid to the foreign right. From this it has been an easy step to the conclusion that a like freedom of choice has been confided to the courts. But that, of course, is a false view. The courts are not free to refuse to enforce a foreign right at the pleasure of judges, to suit the individual notion of expediency or fairness. They do not close their doors, unless help would violate some fundamental principle of justice, some prevalent conception of good morals, some deep-rooted tradition of the common weal. *Loucks v. Standard Oil Co.,* 224 N.Y. 99, 111 (N.Y. 1918).

Does this provide useful guidance?

6. *Sources of public policy.* What sources should a court consult in ascertaining the existence of a public policy? It is said that public policy is an unruly horse that may carry its rider to unanticipated destinations. Katzenbach, *Conflicts on an Unruly Horse: Reciprocal Claims and Tolerances in Interstate and International Law,* 65 Yale L.J. 1087 (1956). Partially in reaction to this, the Supreme Court has declared that public policy cannot be derived from "general considerations of supposed public interest," but must be based upon explicit and clearly defined "laws and legal precedents." *W. R. Grace & Co. v. Local 759,* 461 U.S. 757 (1983). *See supra* pp. 428-452, 520-528.

7. *Application of public policy exception in* **Victor.** Consider the application of the public policy exception in *Victor.*

(a) Mexican statutory damage limits. Why wasn't the Mexican statutory limit on damages a violation of California public policy? Note that the Mexican statute limited the U.S. plaintiff to $2 per day, which was substantially less than prevailing U.S. wages. Note also that the U.S. plaintiff had returned to California, where his injuries would likely require public assistance. Should California public policy have overridden the Mexican limits? Try to state the California public policy.

Is it relevant to consider what insurance the defendants in *Victor* had? Note that standard automobile insurance policies issued in the United States at the time provided: "This policy applies only to accidents . . . while the automobile is within the United States . . . or Canada. . . . It is agreed that the coverage provided by this policy is extended to apply when the automobile insured is being used for occasional trips into that part of the Republic of Mexico lying not more than 25 miles from the boundary line of the United States of American for a period not exceeding 10 days at any one time." *See* R. Weintraub, *Commentary on the Conflict of Laws* §6.11 at 364 n.76 (4th ed. 2001). Would the standard policy have covered the *Victor* defendants, whose accident occurred 27 miles south of the U.S.-Mexico border? Would Mexican insurance coverage have been based upon Mexican or U.S. damage awards? What about Mexican premiums?

What were the likely legislative policies of the Mexican statutory limits? Were those policies likely to be implicated in a suit between two California residents? Does Mexico have any interest in what damages are awarded for accidents occurring in Mexico? Why does it matter what Mexico's interests are?

(b) Mexican no-fault liability. Victor did apply the public policy exception to deny reliance upon a Mexican no-fault rule of liability for owners of "dangerous mechanisms," such as

automobiles. Why was this rule contrary to California public policy? *Victor* did not mention that §402(a) of the California Code of 1935 provided that the owner of a vehicle was liable for the negligence of "any person using or operating the same with the permission, express or implied, of the owner." Because the defendant driver in *Victor* was negligent, §402(a) would have subjected the defendant owner to liability under California law. Is it sensible to refuse to apply a foreign rule of law, on the grounds that it violates public policy, when it produces the same result on the facts that the forum's law would?

8. Actions based on foreign public rights and foreign penal actions. Sections 610 and 611 of the *First Restatement* provide that a U.S. court will not entertain actions to enforce rights "created by the law of a foreign state as a method of furthering its own governmental interests" or to "recover a penalty" under foreign law. Why were these exceptions not applicable in *Victor?* Would they have been applicable if *American Banana* had involved an effort to persuade a U.S. court to apply a Costa Rican statute identical to the Sherman Act?

9. Rationale for refusal to enforce foreign public rights. Why won't courts enforce foreign penal or public rights? If the application of foreign law rests, in Story's words, on "mutual utility" and reciprocity, shouldn't foreign public claims be the *most* important ones to enforce? Consider:

> While the origin of the exception in the case of penal liabilities does not appear in the books, a sound basis for it exists, in my judgment, which includes liabilities for taxes as well. Even in the case of ordinary municipal liabilities, a court will not recognize those arising in a foreign state, if they run counter to the "settled public policy" of its own. Thus a scrutiny of the liability is necessarily always in reserve, and the possibility that it will be found not to accord with the policy of the domestic state. This is not a troublesome or delicate inquiry when the question arises between private persons, but it takes on quite another face when it concerns the relations between the foreign state and its own citizens or even those who may be temporarily within its borders. To pass upon the provisions for the public order of another state is, or at any rate should be, beyond the powers of a court; it involves the relations between the states themselves, with which courts are incompetent to deal, and which are intrusted to other authorities. It may commit the domestic state to a position which would seriously embarrass its neighbor. Revenue laws fall within the same reasoning; they affect a state in matters as vital to its existence as its criminal laws. No court ought to undertake an inquiry which it cannot prosecute without determining whether those laws are consonant with its own notions of what is proper. *Moore v. Mitchell,* 30 F.2d 600, 604 (2d Cir. 1929) (L. Hand, J., concurring), *aff'd on other grounds,* 281 U.S. 18 (1930).

Is this persuasive? Do not tort laws (and other legal rules) also involve the vital public policies of states? Why is it more "embarrassing" for revenue laws to be scrutinized on public policy grounds than for tort laws to be scrutinized? In any event, why should a state's "embarrassment" dictate the outcome of private litigation?

10. A variation on Victor — Hurtado v. Superior Court. *Hurtado v. Superior Court,* 522 P.2d 666 (Cal. 1974), involved the death of a Mexican resident in California as a result of the tortious acts of a California resident. The victim's survivors, also Mexican residents, filed a wrongful death action in California. Mexican law contained liability limits — like those in *Victor* — that restricted the amount the Mexican plaintiffs could recover. Should the Mexican limits apply in the California action? How would the case be decided under the *First Restatement?* What is the reason for the Mexican limits? What is the reason for the absence of any California limits?

11. Distinction between substantive and procedural laws. Consider §585 of the *First Restatement,* providing that "procedural" matters are governed by the law of the forum. The *First Restatement* defined procedure to include such matters as service of process, time of commencement of an action, form of pleadings, trial procedure, statutes of limitations, damages, and contributory negligence. *Restatement (First) Conflict of Laws* §§585-606 (1934). Why are "procedural" matters governed by the law of the forum? If a tort occurred in a foreign state, and that state's laws are held to govern disputes relating to the tort, why shouldn't that state's procedural rules also apply? Note that some "procedural" rules can have a significant impact on the outcome of the litigation.

12. Statutes of limitations. It was well established at common law that statutes of limitations were generally governed by the law of the forum. Looking to international choice-of-law practice and commentary, early U.S. decisions uniformly held that the forum's statute of limitations applied to foreign claims (even when it was longer than the law of the state whose substantive law governed the merits of the dispute). *McElmoyle v. Cohen*, 13 Pet. 312 (1839); *Nash v. Tupper*, 1 Cai. 402, 412-413 (N.Y. Sup. 1803); *Pearsall v. Dwight*, 2 Mass. 84, 89-90 (1806); *Ruggles v. Keeler*, 3 Johns. 263, 267-268 (N.Y. Sup. 1808). The theory was that statutes of limitations merely affected "remedies," not substantive "rights." *Graves v. Graves's Executors*, 5 Ky. 207, 208-209 (Ky. App. 1810) ("The statute of limitations . . . does not destroy the right but withholds the remedy. It would seem to follow, therefore, that the *lex fori*, and not the *lex loci* was to prevail with respect to the time when the action should be commenced."). Is this persuasive? Why or why not?

2.   Contemporary Approaches to Choice of Law Applicable to Torts

a.   Criticism of Vested Rights Doctrine.
Even as the *First Restatement* was released, criticism of its territorial rules began and progressively intensified. In the field of tort law, critics argued that Beale's territoriality doctrine produced arbitrary results, that it was unpredictable, and that the entire vested rights analysis rested on arbitrary assumptions and question-begging.[150] Moreover, lower courts were thought to have frequently applied various of the *Restatement*'s provisions (such as those concerning public policy and procedure) as escape devices in order to avoid what were perceived to be unacceptable results of the vested rights analysis.[151] Other attacks demonstrated the increasing gulf between notions of territoriality and contemporary regulatory objectives and legislative intent.[152]

Academic commentators also increasingly challenged the propriety of "jurisdiction-selecting" choice-of-law rules, which specified which state's laws should apply without regard to the content or policies of those laws. Rather, commentators suggested that attention be focused on the content and policies of purportedly conflicting laws. "The court is not idly choosing a law; it is determining a controversy. How can it choose wisely without considering how the choice will affect that controversy?"[153] Other commentators suggested that different torts required different choice-of-law rules.[154]

By the 1950s, criticisms of the *First Restatement* had prevailed, at least in academic circles: "the theory of 'vested rights' [was] brutally murdered."[155] Criticism of the *First Restatement* culminated in rejection of the vested rights analysis and the proliferation a

150. *E.g.*, Cook, *The Logical and Legal Bases of the Conflict of Laws*, 33 Yale L.J. 457 (1924); Lorenzen, *Territoriality, Public Policy and the Conflict of Laws*, 33 Yale L.J. 736 (1924); Yntema, *The Hornbook Method and the Conflict of Laws*, 37 Yale L.J. 468 (1928); Cavers, *A Critique of the Choice-of-Law Problem*, 47 Harv. L. Rev. 173 (1933).

151. *E.g.*, *University of Chicago v. Dater*, 270 N.W. 175 (Mich. 1936); *Grant v. McAuliffe*, 264 P.2d 944 (Cal. 1953); *Kilberg v. Northeast Airlines, Inc.*, 211 N.Y.S.2d 133 (N.Y. 1961).

152. *See supra* note 150.

153. Cavers, *A Critique of the Choice-of-Law Problem*, 47 Harv. L. Rev. 173, 189 (1933).

154. Morris, *The Proper Law of a Tort*, 64 Harv. L. Rev. 881 (1951); Cheatam & Reese, *Choice of the Applicable Law*, 52 Colum. L. Rev. 959 (1952).

155. Katzenbach, *Conflicts on an Unruly Horse: Reciprocal Claims and Tolerances in Interstate and International Law*, 65 Yale L.J. 1087, 1087-1088 (1956).

variety of competing alternatives. In place of Beale's territorial vested rights system, an assortment of markedly different approaches to choice of law emerged in a process described as the American "conflicts revolution."[156]

b. Contemporary Approaches: Interest Analysis.   Among the first of the new choice-of-law approaches was Brainerd Currie's "interest analysis."[157] Under Currie's approach, the only real issue in multi-state problems was whether the forum state had an "interest" in the outcome of a particular dispute; if it did, then a forum court had no choice but to apply the forum's law. Indeed, Currie thought that "[w]e would be better off without choice-of-law rules,"[158] because they seduce courts into the application of foreign law (thereby frustrating the forum's policies).[159]

The general approach under Currie's interest analysis was to start by "look[ing] to the law of the forum as the source of the rule of decision."[160] In particular, courts were to determine whether the relevant forum legislation or common law rules were applicable to the parties' dispute, by considering whether "the relationship of the forum state to the case . . . is such as to bring the case within the scope of the state's governmental concern."[161] If so, then Currie would assign the forum state an "interest."

Attention then turned to any arguably interested foreign state, to determine whether those states also had an "interest." In most cases, Currie thought, states other than the forum would not have an interest. In Currie's words, this was a "false conflict," permitting application of the law of the forum.[162] In those cases where a foreign state (as well as the forum state) did have an interest, an "apparent conflict" would exist. Currie's interest analysis then called for "restraint and enlightenment in the determination of what state policy is and where state interests lie."[163] If this moderation of each state's demands eliminated any conflict, analysis would end (with another "false conflict").

If a restrained interpretation does not produce a resolution, there would be a "true conflict," to which Currie would have applied the law of the forum. He reasoned that, if "conflict between the legitimate interests of the two states is unavoidable," then forum law must be applied.[164] Currie expressly said that a court was not to "weigh" the competing interests of its own polity and different states in the case of true conflicts.[165] The result of Currie's "interest analysis" was unreservedly pro-forum: "In contrast to the urbane neutrality of the *First Restatement,* Currie's approach is unabashedly parochial. . . . [H]is governmental interest analysis amounts to little more than a complicated pretext for applying the *lex fori.*"[166]

Following Currie, other academic commentators urged various alternative forms of interest analysis. Many of these approaches expressly required weighing competing state

---

156. For a recent review by the U.S. Supreme Court of the shift from the *lex loci delicti* principle to a more flexible interest analysis, *see Sosa v. Alvarez-Machain,* 542 U.S. 692, 707-710 (2004).

157. *See generally* B. Currie, *Selected Essays on the Conflict of Law* (1963).

158. B. Currie, *Selected Essays on the Conflict of Law* 183 (1963).

159. B. Currie, *Selected Essays on the Conflict of Law* 278 (1963) ("The traditional system of conflict of laws counsels the courts to sacrifice the interests of their own states mechanically and heedlessly, without consideration of the policies and interests involved.").

160. B. Currie, *Selected Essays on the Conflict of Laws* 188 (1963).

161. B. Currie, *Selected Essays on the Conflict of Laws* 188 (1963).

162. B. Currie, *Selected Essays on the Conflict of Laws* 189 (1963).

163. B. Currie, *Selected Essays on the Conflict of Laws* 186 (1963).

164. B. Currie, *Selected Essays on the Conflict of Laws* 357 (1963).

165. B. Currie, *Selected Essays on the Conflict of Laws* 182 (1963). Currie did permit a court to weigh the interests of two foreign states in cases where the forum had no interest. Currie, *The Disinterested Third State,* 28 Law & Contemp. Probs. 754 (1963).

166. Juenger, *General Course on Private International Law,* 193 Recueil des Cours 119, 218 (1982).

interests, even where the forum's interests were at issue.[167] Others required different inquiries, such as which legal rule was the "better law,"[168] or the comparative "impairment" of different states' interests.[169] In many observers' view, there came to be "almost as many approaches as there are legal writers,"[170] inhabiting a landscape littered with "stagnant pools of doctrine, each jealously guarded by its adherents."[171]

More generally, contemporary U.S. choice-of-law doctrines became increasingly arcane and complex, leaving practitioners and judges in confusion. The experience in New York is illustrative. In *Babcock v. Jackson*,[172] the New York Court of Appeals became one of the first U.S. courts to embrace interest analysis. The court considered what New York and Ontario interests were implicated in a tort action arising from an automobile accident in Ontario involving two New York domiciliaries. It expressly rejected the "place of the wrong" test, and instead gave "controlling effect to the law of the jurisdiction which, because of its relationship or contact with the occurrence or the parties has the greatest concern with the specific issues raised in the litigation."[173] Under this standard, the court concluded, New York law should apply to permit recovery, rather than Ontario law (whose guest statute would have denied recovery).

Over the next three decades, however, New York judicial decisions produced a confusing and inconsistent approach to choice of law in tort. New York courts enunciated a variety of differing analyses, emphasizing different factors and governmental interests, in a series of cases involving automobile accidents.[174] "The struggle of the Court with these cases has been awesome to behold—dissents, shifting doctrine, results not easily reconcilable. In short, a law professor's delight but a practitioner's and judge's nightmare."[175] Ultimately, in *Newmeier v. Kuehner*,[176] the Court of Appeals apparently abandoned orthodox interest analysis, and set forth a number of specific rules governing choice of law in automobile tort cases involving guest statutes.[177]

c. **Contemporary Approaches:** *Second Restatement's* **"Most Significant Relationship"** **Standard.**   With this background, the 1971 *Restatement (Second) Conflict of Laws* expressly rejected the *First Restatement's* territorial "vested rights" doctrine. "Instead, the rights and liabilities of the parties in tort are said to be governed by the local law of the state which, with respect to the particular issue, has the most significant relationship to the occurrence and the parties."[178] The *Restatement's* drafters justified their rejection of

---

167. R. Weintraub, *Commentary on the Conflict of Laws* 266, 345-347 (2d ed. 1989); A. von Mehren & D. Trautman, *The Law of Multi-State Problems* 376-378 (1965); R. Leflar, *American Conflicts Law* 193-195 (3d ed. 1977).

168. Leflar, *Conflicts Law: More on Choice Influencing Considerations*, 54 Cal. L. Rev. 1584 (1966).

169. Baxter, *Choice of Law and the Federal System*, 16 Stan. L. Rev. 1 (1963).

170. Juenger, *General Course on Private International Law*, 193 Recueil des Cours 119, 219 (1983).

171. Kay, *The Use of Comparative Impairment to Resolve True Conflicts: An Evaluation of the California Experience*, 68 Calif. L. Rev. 577, 615 (1980) (quoted in Juenger, *General Course on Private International Law*, 193 Recueil des Cours 119, 219 (1983)).

172. 240 N.Y.S.2d 743 (N.Y. 1963).

173. 240 N.Y.S.2d at 749.

174. *Dym v. Gordon*, 262 N.Y.S.2d 463 (N.Y. 1966); *Macey v. Rozbicki*, 274 N.Y.S.2d 591 (N.Y. 1965); *Tooker v. Lopez*, 301 N.Y.S.2d 519 (N.Y. 1969); *Neumeier v. Kuehner*, 335 N.Y.S.2d 64 (N.Y. 1972); *Towley v. King Arthur Rings, Inc.*, 386 N.Y.S.2d 80 (N.Y. 1976).

175. R. Weintraub, *Commentary on the Conflict of Laws* 399 (4th ed. 2001).

176. 335 N.Y.S.2d 64 (N.Y. 1972).

177. Other courts took the same view of the uncertainties and unpredictability of interest analysis. Presented with arguments that they should adopt interest analysis, these courts have refused on the grounds that it is an unadministratable and unpredictable standard. *Abendschein v. Farrell*, 170 N.W.2d 137 (Mich. 1969); *McMillan v. McMillan*, 253 S.E.2d 662 (Va. 1979). Nevertheless, as discussed below, the trend over recent decades has been away from traditional territoriality principles. *See infra* pp. 741-742.

178. *Restatement (Second) Conflict of Laws* 413 (1971).

territoriality principles in the same way that *Pennoyer*'s limits on judicial jurisdiction were abandoned:

> These changes are partly a reflection of a change in our national life. State and national boundaries are of less significance today by reason of the increased mobility of our population and of the increasing tendency of men to conduct their affairs across boundary lines.[179]

Although there was academic consensus that the *First Restatement*'s territoriality principles had to be abandoned, there was little agreement on what should replace it. The *Second Restatement* became an exercise in compromise, seeking to accommodate all of the various factions of the American conflicts revolution. "As a result, the *Second Restatement* became a mixture of discordant approaches."[180]

Section 6 of the *Second Restatement* articulated the basic principles that were said to inform contemporary choice-of-law analysis. Where no legislative choice-of-law directive exists, §6 provides that "the factors relevant to the choice of the applicable rule of law" include: (a) the needs of the international system; (b) the relevant policies of the forum; (c) the relevant policies of other interested states; (d) justified expectations; (e) certainty, predictability, and uniformity; and (f) ease in determining the applicable law. Section 145 of the *Second Restatement* applied this basic analysis to tort claims, producing the following "rule":

> The rights and liabilities of the parties with respect to an issue in tort are determined by the local law of the state which, with respect to that issue, has the most significant relationship to the occurrence and the parties under the principles stated in §6.

Other provisions of the *Second Restatement* further refined the "most significant relationship" standard, setting forth specific rules governing particular torts (*e.g.*, personal injury or defamation)[181] and particular issues (*e.g.*, standard of care or defenses).[182]

d.   Contemporary Lower Court Approaches to Choice of Law Applicable to Tort. Contemporary lower court decisions in the United States concerning the law applicable to torts are almost as diverse as the academic community.[183] A number of states continue to apply the *First Restatement*'s "place of the wrong" rules.[184] The single most substantial group of jurisdictions has adopted the *Second Restatement*'s "most significant relationship" standard.[185] Other jurisdictions follow variations of interest analysis and other contemporary products of the American conflicts revolution.[186]

---

179. *Restatement (Second) Conflict of Laws* 413 (1971).

180. Juenger, *General Course on Private International Law,* 193 Recueil des Cours 119, 220 (1983).

181. *Restatement (Second) Conflict of Laws* §§146-155 (1971).

182. *Restatement (Second) Conflict of Laws* §§156-177 (1971).

183. *See* Westbrook, *A Survey and Evaluation of Competing Choice of Law Methodologies: The Case for Eclecticism,* 40 Mo. L. Rev. 407 (1975); Kozyris & Symeonides, *Choice of Law in the American Courts in 1989: An Overview,* 38 Am. J. Comp. L. 601 (1990); Symeonides, *Choice of Law in the American Courts in 1988,* 37 Am. J. Comp. L. 457 (1989); Symeonides, *The Need for a Third Conflicts Restatement (and a Proposal for Torts Conflicts),* 75 Ind. L.J. 437 (2000).

184. Although estimates vary, approximately 10 states still appear to follow the *First Restatement*. Symeonides, *Choice of Law in American Courts in 2010: Twenty-Fourth Annual Survey,* 59 Am. J. Comp. L. 303 (forthcoming 2011).

185. Although estimates vary, approximately 24 states now appear to follow the *Second Restatement*. Symeonides, *Choice of Law in the American Courts in 2010: Twenty-Fourth Annual Survey,* 59 Am. J. Comp. L. _____ (forthcoming 2011).

186. It appears that about 15 states follow either traditional interest analysis, a "significant contacts" approach, or an interest analysis. Symeonides, *Choice of Law in the American Courts in 2010: Twenty-Fourth Annual Survey,* 59 Am. J. Comp. L. 303 (forthcoming 2011).

In many states, courts have been inconsistent in their approach to choice of law:

> any systematic treatment of the cases will necessarily overstate the differences by making classifications and drawing distinctions when, in reality, the lines tend to be much more fluid. Few courts are entirely consistent in approaching choice of law problems. There are no *purely* "interest-analysis states" or "*Restatement (Second)* states."[187]

Moreover, in some states, courts have encountered serious difficulties in articulating any comprehensible choice-of-law analysis applicable to torts. As described above, New York's choice-of-law rules are said to be in "utter confusion" and "incoherent."[188]

Excerpted below are materials that illustrate the various American conflicts rules in the tort field. Consider the excerpt from Brainerd Currie's *Notes on Methods and Objectives in the Conflict of Laws,* which summarizes traditional interest analysis. Also consider the selected sections of the *Restatement (Second) Conflict of Laws,* setting forth the "most significant relationship" test. Finally, the decision in *Tramontana v. SA Empresa de Viacao Aerea Rio* illustrates a contemporary judicial effort to apply both Currie's interest analysis and the *Second Restatement*'s most significant relationship test.

B. CURRIE, NOTES ON METHODS AND OBJECTIVES IN THE CONFLICT OF LAWS
[1959] Duke L.J. 171
(Reprinted with permission of the Duke Law Journal)

The central problem of conflict of laws may be defined . . . as that of determining the appropriate rule of decision when the interests of two or more states are in conflict—in other words, of determining which interest shall yield. The problem would not exist if this were one world, with an all-powerful central government. It would not exist (though other problems of "conflict of laws" would) if the independent sovereignties in the real world had identical laws. So long, however as we have a diversity of laws, we shall have conflicts of interest among states. Hence, unless something is done, the administration of private law where more than one state is concerned will be affected with disuniformity and uncertainty. To avoid this result by all reasonable means is certainly a laudable objective; but how? Not by establishing a single government; even if such a thing were remotely thinkable as a practical possibility, we attribute positive values to the principle of self-determination for localities and groups. The attainment of uniformity of laws among diverse states is, to put it mildly, a long-range undertaking. . . .

We do not, however, despair. We turn, instead, to the resources of jurisprudence, placing our faith primarily in the judges rather than the lawmakers. The judicial function is not narrowly confined; we indulge the hope that it may even be equal to the ambitious task of bringing uniformity and certainty into a world whose conflicts political action has failed to resolve. At first, of course, the judges will not be so bold (or so frank) as to avow that they are assuming the high political function of passing upon the relative merits of the conflicting policies, or interests, of sovereign states. They will address themselves to metaphysical questions concerning the nature of law and its abstract operation in space—matters remote from mundane policies and conflicts of interest—and will evolve a set of rules for determining which state's law must, in the nature of things, control. If all states can be persuaded to adhere to these rules, the seemingly impossible will have been accomplished:

---

187. E. Scoles & P. Hay, *Conflict of Laws* 551 (1982).
188. Juenger, *General Course on Private International Law,* 193 Recueil des Cours 119, 223 (1983).

there will be uniformity and certainty in the administration of private law from state to state. The fact that this goal will be achieved at the price of sacrificing state interests is not emphasized; rather, it is obscured by the metaphysical apparatus of the method.

The rules so evolved have not worked and cannot be made to work. In our times we have suffered particularly from the jurisprudential theory that has been compounded in order to explain and justify the assumption by the courts of so extraordinary a function. The territorialist conception has been directly responsible for indefensible results and, what is perhaps worse, has therefore driven some of our ablest scholars to consume their energies in purely defensive action against it. But the root of the trouble goes deeper. In attempting to use the rules we encounter difficulties that stem not from the fact that the particular rules are bad, nor from the fact that a particular theoretical explanation is unsound, but rather from the fact that we have such rules at all. . . .

[D]espite the camouflage of discourse, the rules do operate to nullify state interests. The fact that this is often done capriciously, without reference to the merits of the respective policies and even without recognition of their existence, is only incidental. Trouble enough comes from the mere fact that interests are defeated. The courts simply will not remain always oblivious to the true operation of a system that, though speaking the language of metaphysics, strikes down the legitimate application of the policy of a state, especially when that state is the forum. Consequently, the system becomes complicated. It is loaded with escape devices: the concept of "local public policy" as a basis for not applying the "applicable" law; the concept of "fraud on the law"; the device of novel or disingenuous characterization; the device of manipulating the connecting factor; and, not least, the provision of sets of rules that are interchangeable at will. The tensions that are induced by imposing such a system on a setting of conflict introduce a very serious element of uncertainty and unpredictability, even if there is fairly general agreement on the rules themselves. A sensitive and ingenious court can detect an absurd result and avoid it; I am inclined to think that this has been done more often than not and that therein lies a major reason why the system has managed to survive. At the same time, we constantly run the risk that the court may lack sensitivity and ingenuity; we are handicapped in even presenting the issue in its true light; and instances of mechanical application of the rules to produce indefensible results are by no means rare. Whichever of these phenomena is the more common, it is a poor defense of the system to say that the unacceptable results that it will inevitably produce can be averted by disingenuousness if the courts are sufficiently alert. . . .

[W]hen several states have different policies, and also legitimate interests in the application of their policies, a court is in no position to "weigh" the competing interests, or evaluate their relative merits, and choose between them accordingly. This is especially evident when we consider two co-ordinate states, with such decisions being made by the courts of one or the other. A court need never hold the interest of the foreign law inferior; it can simply apply its own law as such. But when the court, in a true conflict situation, holds the foreign law applicable, it is assuming a great deal: it is holding the policy, or interest, of its own state inferior and preferring the policy or interest for the foreign state. . . .

But assessment of the respective values of the competing legitimate interests of two sovereign states, in order to determine which is to prevail, is a political function of a very high order. This is a function that should not be committed to courts in a democracy. It is a function that the courts cannot perform effectively, for they lack the necessary resources. Not even a very ponderous Brandeis brief could marshal the relevant considerations in choosing, for example, between the interest of the state of employment and that of the state of injury in matters concerning workmen's compensation. This is a job for a legislative committee, and determining the policy to be formulated on the basis of the information assembled is a job for a competent legislative body. . . .

We would be better off without the choice-of-law rules. We would be better off if Congress were to give some attention to problems of private law, and were to legislate concerning the choice between conflicting state interests in some of the specific areas in which the need for solutions is serious. In the meantime, we would be better off if we would admit the teachings of sociological jurisprudence into the conceptualistic precincts of conflict of laws. This would imply a basic method along the following lines:

1. Normally, even in cases involving foreign elements, the court should be expected, as a matter of course, to apply the rule of decision found in the law of the forum.

2. When it is suggested that the law of a foreign state should furnish the rule of decision, the court should, first of all, determine the governmental policy expressed in the law of the forum. It should then inquire whether the relation of the forum to the case is such as to provide a legitimate basis for the assertion of an interest in the application of that policy. This process is essentially the familiar one of construction or interpretation. Just as we determine by that process how a statute applies in time, and how it applies to marginal domestic situations, so we may determine how it should be applied to cases involving foreign elements in order to effectuate the legislative purpose.

3. If necessary, the court should similarly determine the policy expressed by the foreign law, and whether the foreign state has an interest in the application of its policy.

4. If the court finds that the forum state has no interest in the application of its policy, but that the foreign state has, it should apply the foreign law.

5. If the court finds that the forum state has an interest in the application of its policy, it should apply the law of the forum, even though the foreign state also has an interest in the application of its contrary policy, and, a fortiori, it should apply the law of the forum if the foreign state has no such interest. . . .

The suggested analysis does not imply the ruthless pursuit of self-interest by the states. . . . There is no need to exclude the possibility of rational altruism: for example, when a state has determined upon the policy of placing upon local industry all the social costs of the enterprise, it may well decide to adhere to this policy regardless of where the harm occurs and who the victim is. There is also room for restraint and enlightenment in the determination of what state policy is and where state interests lie.

I have been told that I give insufficient recognition to governmental policies other than those that are expressed in specific statutes and rules: the policy of promoting a general legal order, that of fostering amicable relations with other states, that of vindicating reasonable expectations, and so on. If this is so, it is not, I hope, because of a provincial lack of appreciation of the worth of those ideals, but because of a felt necessity to emphasize the obstacles that the present system interposes to any intelligent approach to the problem. Let us first clear away the apparatus that creates false problems and obscures the nature of the real ones. Only then can we effectively set about ameliorating the ills that arise from a diversity of laws by bringing to bear all the resources of jurisprudence, politics, and humanism — each in its appropriate way.

RESTATEMENT (SECOND) CONFLICT OF LAWS
§§6, 10, 122, 145, 146, & 156 (1971) [excerpted in Appendix Y]

TRAMONTANA v. SA EMPRESA DE VIAÇÃO AEREA RIO GRANDENSE
350 F.2d 468 (D.C. Cir. 1964)

McGowan, Circuit Judge. This appeal presents an international variant of a recurring domestic conflict of laws problem, namely, the applicability in the forum (the District of

Columbia) of a monetary damage limitation contained in the wrongful death statute of the place of injury (Brazil). . . .

Vincent Tramontana was killed on February 26, 1960, when the U.S. Navy airplane in which he was travelling on naval orders collided over Rio de Janeiro, Brazil, with an airplane owned and operated by a Brazilian airline. At the time of his death, Tramontant was a member of the U.S. Navy Band, which was on an official tour of Latin America. The record does not show his permanent duty station, but he resided with his wife, appellant here, in Hyattsville, Maryland. The Navy plane in which he was travelling when he was killed was en route from Buenos Aires in Argentina to Galeao, Brazil. Appellee Varig Airlines is a Brazilian corporation having its principal place of business in Brazil but carrying on its transportation activities in many parts of the world, including the United States. The Brazilian plane was on a regularly scheduled commercial flight from Campos, Brazil, to Rio de Janeiro when the accident occurred. . . .

[A]ppellant instituted this action in the District Court against Varig and its predecessor, alleging that negligence in the operation of the Brazilian plane had caused her husband's death. She explicitly based her claim for recovery on certain provisions of the Brazilian Code of the Air which provide a cause of action for injury or death resulting from negligent operation of aircraft in Brazil. She claimed damages of $250,000. Service was made on Varig Airlines, which concededly is subject to suit in the District of Columbia. Varig . . . moved for summary judgment dismissing the complaint or, in the alternative, for summary judgement in respect of so much of appellant's claim as exceeded the U.S. dollar equivalent of 100,000 Brazilian cruzeiros. Varig relied on Article 102 of the Brazilian Code, which limits liability for injury or death in aviation accidents to that amount. The District Court, with Varig's consent, entered judgement in favor of appellant in the amount of $170.00, the current dollar value of 100,000 cruzeiros. It awarded judgement in favor of Varig "for all of the plaintiff's claim which exceeds the sum of One Hundred Seventy Dollars ($170.00)." From this latter judgment Mrs. Tramontana appealed.[189]

The only question now before us is whether Brazil's limitation on the damages recoverable for death sustained in airplane accidents occurring there is to be applied in this suit in the District of Columbia. Appellant appears to concede that her cause of action, if any, was created by, and arises under, a provision of Brazilian law enacted coincidentally and in conjunction with the damage limitation. She argues, however, that the forum law regarding damages for wrongful death occurring in the District of Columbia, *i.e.*, unlimited recovery, should govern that aspect of her claim. Initially, she accepts the applicability of the traditional conflict of law rule in personal injury cases that the *lex locus delicti*, the law of the place where the injury occurred, generally governs in a suit brought elsewhere, but she asserts that a court sitting in the District of Columbia should adopt the familiar exception to the effect that the forum will refuse to apply the otherwise applicable foreign law if it is contrary to some strong public policy of the forum. Appellant asserts the existence of a strong policy of the District of Columbia in favor of unlimited recovery for wrongful death, which she claims is evidenced by Congress' repeal in 1948 of the $10,000 maximum until then contained in the local wrongful death statute. She points also the fact that only thirteen states still limit recovery for wrongful death, and that none imposes a ceiling as low as that contained in the Brazilian Air Code. . . . And, finally, she relies on the New York Court of Appeals decision in *Kilberg v. Northeast Airlines, Inc.*, 9 N.Y.2d 34 (1961), as a persuasive precedent for the position she urges us to adopt. . . .

---

189. Seventeen other members of the Navy Band perished in the collision. . . . Of the seventeen other plaintiffs in these two suits, two, and perhaps three, were listed as residents of the District of Columbia, eight as residents of Maryland, and the remainder as residents of other states. . . .

Appellant's essential effort throughout is to urge us to follow the "newer and more realistic judicial approach" to conflict of laws problems exemplified by *Kilberg* and *Babcock v. Jackson,* ... and to reject the assertedly outmoded and discredited teaching of *Slater v. Mexican Nat'l R.R.* ... Under the test we are asked to employ, the choice of law to be applied to each legal issue presented is to be made in light of the jurisdiction which has the "strongest interest in the resolution of that issue." ... A cornerstone of this newer thinking, appellant contends, is the forum's reluctance to subordinate its policies to those of another state when its own interest in the case is real and substantial.

The Supreme Court ... has recognized the inadequacies of the theoretical underpinnings of *Slater* and its progeny. The latter cases have a highly attenuated precedential weight, both in authority and reason. Thus we are free to explore the question presented by this appeal in the light of the newer concepts of conflict laws. ...

The interest underlying the application of Brazilian law seems to us to outweigh any interest of the District of Columbia. Not only is Brazil the scene of the fatal collision, but Varig is a Brazilian corporation which, as a national airline, is an object of concern in terms of national policy. To Brazil, the success of this enterprise is a matter not only of pride and commercial well-being, but perhaps even of national security. The limitation on recovery against airlines operating in Brazil was enacted in the early days of commercial aviation, no doubt with a view toward protecting what was then, and still is, an infant industry of extraordinary public and national importance. The Brazilian limitation in terms applies only to airplane accidents, unlike the Massachusetts provision rejected in *Kilberg,* which was an across-the-board ceiling on recovery for wrongful death in that state. The focus of Brazilian concern could hardly be clearer.

We have seen nothing that would suggest that Brazil's concern for the financial integrity of her local airlines should be deemed to be less genuine now than when Article 102 was enacted, simply because of the depreciation of the cruzeiro. The failure to amend that provision may reflect a conscious desire to avoid enlarging the potential liability of local airlines during a period of general economic difficulty. It may represent an unwillingness to contribute to the inflationary spiral by adjusting "prices" fixed by statute which the government can control. ... [W]e are not persuaded that the fact of inflation itself ... should be deemed to render obsolete Brazil's legitimate interest in limiting recoveries against her airlines.

Appellant relies primarily on *Kilberg* as a precedent for the course she asks us to follow. A close analysis if that court's reasoning reveals that the relationships and interests, which it thought compelled the result reached, do not parallel those here. The decedent in *Kilberg* was both a resident and a domiciliary of New York. He was a paying passenger on the defendant airline, which relationship had originated in New York. As the Court of Appeals pointed out, once on board the plane the place of the injury was merely "fortuitous." New York's long-standing policy in favor of unlimited recovery in actions for wrongful death coalesced in this case with its real and immediate interest in providing full compensation for the death of one of its own citizens. And its interest would have been the same whether the defendant's aircraft had crashed in New York, in Long Island Sound, or, as it did, in Massachusetts.

In the case before us neither appellant, nor children, nor her husband were or are resident or domiciled in the District of Columbia. Vincent Tramontana was not a passenger on appellee's plane, and his "relationship" with appellee commenced and ended in Brazil in one shattering moment. The place of injury, under these circumstances, was clearly not fortuitous, although the accident was something of a freak. Vincent Tramontana could not have been killed by Varig's Campos-to-Rio flight except in Brazil. To suggest that he might have been killed here in the District, or in Maryland, by one of

Varig's international flights is to ignore the facts of this case.[190] It is one thing to say that airlines should not be the beneficiaries, nor their passengers the victims, of the vagaries of weather and faulty equipment that cause an aircraft to crash in one jurisdiction rather than another. It is quite another to say that an American traveller, who is injured in Brazil through the negligence of the operator of a local airline on which he was not a passenger and with which he had no precious connection, is entitled to the benefit of the law of a forum which is not his home, because its successor happens to do business there.[191] The District of Columbia's connection with the occurrence and with the parties and its interest in the resolution of the issue before us, are, if not wholly remote, certainly less than Brazil's. Neither appellant nor her decedent are or were residents of the District of Columbia. Varig Airlines is subject to suit here only because of the international operations in which it is engaged. Whatever negligence it may have been guilty of assuredly did not occur here, nor manifestly, did the decedent's death. If appellant and her children should ever become public charges, the burden will rest not on the District of Columbia but on the citizens of Maryland, where appellant resides.[192]

Although Maryland, the state of the decedent's and appellant's residence, might be thought to have a substantial interest in the amount recoverable for his death, no suggestion has been made that we should apply the law of Maryland to determine the issue before us. But this possibility inevitably suggests itself, and we therefore are inclined to say why we think that, even as between the law of Maryland and the law of Brazil, we are without warrant to look to the former. In striking this balance, the weight to be accorded the interests of Brazil remains unchanged. The question is whether Maryland has a significantly greater claim to the application of its law than the District of Columbia.

Maryland's only relationship with the parties or the transactions is that it is appellant's residence, and was that of the appellant's recovery is not insignificant, for it is on the citizens of Maryland that the burden of her support, if she is unable to support herself, is likely to fall in the first instance.[193] Yet it appears likely that a Maryland court could not have ignored the Brazilian limitation on recovery if this action had been brought there originally. . . . The Maryland Court of Appeals has held that, where both accident and

190. The possible locations of Varig's wrongdoing, if such it was, are irrelevant to the determination of which law should measure appellant's recovery except insofar as they have some other connection with the parties or the accident, or some independent interest in the resolution of this issue. If the mere possibility, however remote, that Vincent Tramontana might have been killed through some negligence of appellee in the District of Columbia were thought to give the District some interest in the application of its law, whatever predictability remains in the conflict of laws of torts would disappear. Concededly, predictability is a depreciated coin in tort law, *see Babcock v. Jackson*, 240 N.Y.S.2d 743, 746-47 (N.Y. 1963), but it still retains some value. Varig's ability to predict and obtain the cost of insurance, for example, may depend to some extent on its ability to estimate its potential liability.

191. . . . The case before us is much the same as if a resident of the State of Maryland, while on a summer vacation trip to Europe and while crossing the street in Amsterdam, were run over and killed by a beer truck making a local delivery. If Holland had a wrongful death act with a limitation on damages, and if the brewing company had a sales office in the District of Columbia, then a suit in the District by the Maryland widow would present us with a problem virtually identical with that we now have. The increasing international mobility of both ordinary citizens and business enterprises suggests that the issue is an important one already and is likely to become more so. There are obvious implications to be considered in respect of the degree of comity which should obtain between sovereign nations unrestrained by a full faith and credit clause in a world constitution.

192. The New York Court of Appeals' dominating concern in *Kilberg* was to ensure "protection for our own State's people against unfair and anachronistic treatment of the lawsuits which result from these [airline] disasters," 211 N.Y.S.2d at 135. The immediate objects of that concern were, of course, the victims and their dependents. The implicit assumption, however, was that if protection were not provided them, the cost of their support might have to be borne by the state and citizens of New York. The District of Columbia may have an altruistic interest in seeing that the survivors of residents of nearby states do not go uncompensated, but it faces no additional burden if compensation is not provided.

193. As noted above, this burden has, by reason of the action of Congress and the Court of Claims, been assumed to some degree by the citizens of the entire United States.

death occurred in another state, the defendant's liability—and thus the plaintiff's right to recover—depends on the law of that state. It has not had an opportunity to consider whether the amount of damages recoverable is an element of that right, but it is speculative in the extreme for us to infer that it would hold it to be otherwise. The amount of damages recoverable for a tort is, in traditional theory, a matter of substantive law. The New York Court of Appeals, shortly after *Kilberg*, abandoned its position in that case that the measure of damages was governed by New York, and not Massachusetts, law because damage limitations are procedural in nature, and not substantive. . . . And if a Maryland court would not disregard Brazilian law for the benefit of one of its own residents in a suit brought there, why should a court sitting in the District of Columbia do so at the expense of substantial and legitimate interests of Brazil? . . .

Our decision is consistent as well with the most recent formulation of the *Restatement (Second) Conflict of Laws.* [The Court quoted a tentative draft of what would become *Restatement (Second) Conflict of Laws* §145 (1971).] This enumeration of significant relationships does not include that of *forum qua forum.*[194] The injury in the case before us occurred in Brazil, as did appellee's negligent conduct, if it was negligent at all. Vincent Tramontana was an American national, domiciled in Maryland, and so are his widow and children. Varig is a Brazilian corporation, which does business throughout the world. The "relationship" between the parties, if it can be called that, existed fleetingly—and in Brazil. By these criteria, the only state, other than Brazil, with a substantial claim to the application of its law is Maryland, which apparently would apply the Brazilian law in a case brought there. Thus it is that the only relationship of the District of Columbia to this claim is that it provides a forum with jurisdiction over appellee. That is hardly a reason for the forum to prefer its own notions of policy to those embodied in the Brazilian law which created the claim appellant is asserting. . . .

A separate facet of appellant's public policy argument is that the Brazilian limitation on recovery for wrongful death should be disregarded entirely because of the recent marked decline in the dollar value of the Brazilian cruzeiro. Brazil's current economic problems are a matter of common knowledge, including the fact that inflation has depreciated the Brazilian currency by more than 600 per cent since the accident occurred in 1960. This development undoubtedly contributes to the appeal of appellant's argument, but it does not, in our view, warrant a result different from that we would reach had the value of the cruzeiro in terms of the dollar remained unchanged.

Brazil's interest in the protection of the financial integrity of its most important means of domestic transportation almost certainly has not been diminished by the decline in the value of its currency. . . . A reluctance to reflect that decline in those prices that are subject to direct government control would be wholly understandable. Moreover, an unpredictable and virtually immeasurable factor would be imported into the decision of international conflict of laws cases if the otherwise applicable law were subject to being displaced because of the recent history of the relative values of the currencies involved. Courts would be called upon in each case to determine at what point a declining rate of exchange of a foreign currency made application of the foreign law intolerable. Should Brazilian law be disregarded if the cruzeiro had depreciated only 300 per cent? Or 50 per cent? . . .

Considerations of comity among sovereign nations certainly have relevance in this context. . . . If the courts of one country make the applicability of the law of another turn on the way the exchange balance happens to be inclined at the moment, a

---

194. *Compare* Currie, *The Constitution and the Choice of Law: Governmental Interests and the Judicial Function*, 26 U. Chi. L. Rev. 9 (1958).

speculative and highly artificial element would be intruded into those considerations normally recognized by civilized nations as germane in the choice of applicable law. And the forum so motivated, whether it knows it or not, wields a two-edged sword.

One further question remains, though it is one not raised by the parties.[195] The District Court converted the 100,000 cruzeiro ceiling in recovery into dollars at the rate of exchange prevailing on October 14, 1963, the date of the entry of its judgment. Although New York, alone among jurisdictions in this country, and England appear to follow a rule that recovery in tort is to be measured in terms of the rate of exchange on the date of the wrong, we think the District Court applied the sounder rule. This "day of judgment" rule has the support of the authors of the *Restatement (Second) Conflict of Laws* §612a (Tent. Draft No. 11, 1965), and is in accord with the Supreme Court's most recent decision on the point, *Die Deutsche Bank Filiale Nurnberg v. Humphrey*, 272 U.S. 517 (1926). . . . The rule provides the plaintiff with the dollar equivalent of the amount he would recover if he had sued in the country whose law determines his right to recover, and it thereby ensures that he neither suffers nor benefits from the fact he chose another forum in which to litigate his claim.

Notes on *Currie*, Second Restatement, *and Tramontana*

1. *Currie's criticism of the* **First** **Restatement.** One of Currie's principal efforts was attacking the traditional approach of the *First Restatement.* "The courts simply will not remain always oblivious to the true operation of a system that, though speaking the language of metaphysics, strikes down the legitimate application of the policy of a state." B. Currie, *Selected Essays on the Conflict of Laws* 181 (1963). Is this correct? Consider how the "place of wrong" rule was applied in *American Banana, Carroll,* and *Victor.* Did the courts apply the rule without consideration of the legislative policies underlying the relevant Alabama and California laws? If so, is this an inevitable result of the *First Restatement*'s rules?

2. *Interest analysis's nominal focus on legislative intent.* What is the rationale for either applying the *First Restatement* rules or engaging in interest analysis? If a court applied interest analysis to the Alabama statute at issue in *Carroll,* to the applicable rules in *Victor,* to the Sherman Act in *American Banana,* or to the Brazilian statute in *Tramontana,* what would justify it in doing so? Is interest analysis anything more than an elaborate way of trying to determine the intended scope of legislative or common law rules (and, if two or more rules overlap, the intended interaction)? Consider the following:

> [If a foreign law is argued, the forum court] should then inquire whether the relation of the forum to the case is such as to provide a legitimate basis for the assertion of an interest in the application of that policy. This process is essentially the familiar one of construction or interpretation. Just as we determine how a statute applies in time, and how it applies to marginal domestic situations, so we may determine how it should be applied to cases involving foreign elements in order to effectuate the legislative purpose. B. Currie, *Selected Essays on the Conflict of Laws* 183-184 (1963).

However, observing that legislative intent is important to choice-of-law analysis only begins debate. In most cases, the legislature will not have specified how statutes ought

---

195. Appellant's argument has been that, because the judgement in dollars reflects a striking weakness if the cruzeiro vis-à-vis the dollar as of the day of its entry, the forum should disregard the Brazilian limitation entirely and apply its own law. It has not asked, even alternatively, that the conversion rate used in the judgement be that either of the date of the accident or of the initial enactment of the Brazilian Air Code.

to apply in multi-state cases. *See supra* pp. 645-646. As a consequence, judges must determine what the legislature intended in a particular multi-state case. The basic purpose of choice-of-law rules is to provide structure and focus in answering this question. That is the purpose of both the *First* and *Second Restatements,* and Currie's choice-of-law analysis.

3. Structure of Currie's interest analysis. State concisely each step in Currie's interest analysis.

(a) Determining a state's "interest" in having its law applicable. How does a court determine whether a state has an "interest" in having its laws apply in a particular case? Why don't states always have *interests* in having their own law applied? What is relevant to deciding whether a state has an interest in applying its laws to certain multi-state conduct? *See* Symeonides, *Accommodative Unilateralism as a Starting Premise in Choice of Law,* in *Balancing of Interests: Liber Americorum Peter Hay,* 417-434 (Rasmussen-Bonne et al. eds., 2005).

(b) Interest defined solely by substantive law. Should a court look solely to the language, legislative history, and purposes of the relevant substantive legislation? That is what Currie suggests, when he argues that choice of law is merely a question of statutory construction and that "we would be better off without choice of law rules." As noted above, however, most substantive statutes (and common law rules) are simply silent regarding their spatial or geographic reach, *see supra* pp. 645-646, and thus provide little guidance in defining a state's interests. What do the policies of the Sherman Act or §2590 of the Alabama Code say about the intended geographic reach of either?

(c) Interest defined by choice-of-law rules. If local legislation will not itself provide guidance regarding the legislature's interest in applying the law in multi-state circumstances, where will a court find such guidance? Some commentators have argued that identifying an "interest" is a choice-of-law decision concerning the applicability of a particular domestic policy in particular multi-state circumstances. Kay, *A Defense of Currie's Governmental Interest Analysis,* 215 Recueil des Cours 13 (1989). Does Currie's outline of interest analysis, excerpted above, provide any guidance for deciding when an interest exists or what choice-of-law rules to use?

(d) Interests as escape devices. As discussed above, a central criticism of the *First Restatement* was that it permitted judges to escape its rules through characterization and other escape devices. The same was later said of Currie's interest analysis. *See supra* pp. 738-740. Consider:

> Studying the vagaries of policy assessment and spatial delimitation, one becomes increasingly suspicious of the premises of interest analysis. As far as the guest statute [*e.g.,* legislation forbidding passengers riding in an automobile as guests from suing their hosts] is concerned, none of the propositions regarding its policies and spatial reach, I submit, can be proved (or disproved) with absolute certainty. An imaginative mind will have little difficulty in selecting and emphasizing the one guest statute rationale that justifies either application or displacement of the rule. de Boer, *Beyond Lex Loci Delicti: Conflicts Methodology and Multistate Torts in American Case Law* 439 (1987).

Is this risk not particularly great in international cases, where U.S. courts seek to determine the purposes of foreign laws, often relying on unfamiliar legislative history in an alien legal, economic, and social environment?

4. "False conflicts." In certain cases, Currie's analysis would indicate that only one of two involved states would have an "interest" in application of its laws to a particular international issue. In these cases, a "false conflict" existed, and there was no need to consider application of any law other than that which was "interested" in the dispute.

Compare the relevance of "conflicts" between U.S. and foreign law in determining the extraterritorial reach of federal legislation under authorities such as *Timberlane,* §403, and *Hartford Fire. See supra* pp. 685-687, 703-704.

Consider *Carroll, Victor,* and *American Banana.* Did any of these cases involve a "false conflict"? How does one go about trying to determine what the Mississippi, Mexican, and Costa Rican interests in each case are? *Compare Curley v. AMR Corp.,* 153 F.3d 5, 5, 13-15 (2d Cir. 1998) (relying on Federal Rule of Civil Procedure 44.1, to determine whether false conflict exists) *with Lou v. Otis Elevator Co.,* 933 N.E.2d 140, 144 (Mass. App. 2010) (noting that, in case involving accident that occurred in China, trial court instructed jury on Massachusetts law, despite China's strong interest, because he was unable confidently to ascertain the content of Chinese tort law). How does one decide what the Alabama, California, and U.S. interests are in each case? Did *Tramontana* involve a false conflict? Where a party has not invoked foreign law, can a court *sua sponte* conclude that a true conflict exists and apply that law? *See Butler v. Stagecoach Group plc,* 900 N.Y.S.2d 541 (App. Div. 2010) (approving trial court's decision to apply Ontario law, which conflicted with New York law, even though defendants did not request its application).

5. *Currie's initial forum bias in "true conflict" cases.* Currie initially concluded that the law of the forum should be applied whenever the forum had an "interest" in its application, notwithstanding the arguable applicability of foreign law and the existence of "stronger" foreign interests in the application of foreign law. *See supra* pp. 739-740. What justifies this preference for forum law? Is it a fair assumption that most legislatures would wish for local law to prevail over foreign law no matter how significant foreign interests might be or how trivial domestic interests might be? Would legislatures consider the international ramifications of such an attitude — including the possibility of reciprocal treatment by foreign states? Recall Story's explanation for the choice-of-law rules in his *Commentaries*: "The true foundation, on which the administration of international law must rest, is, that the rules, which are to govern, are those, which arise from mutual interest and utility, from a sense of the inconveniences, which would result from a contrary doctrine, and from a sort of moral necessity to do justice, in order that justice may be done to us in return." *See supra* pp. 648-649. Would not such considerations affect a legislature's application of its law internationally? Currie subsequently abandoned his suggestion that the forum apply its law in any case where it had an "interest," as discussed below. How would Currie have decided *Tramontana*?

Compare Currie's forum bias with the "territoriality presumption." *See supra* pp. 664-670. How would Currie regard the territoriality presumption? Don't both the forum bias of Currie's interest analysis and the territoriality presumption purport to ascertain unexpressed legislative intent, albeit through extreme (and largely mirror-image) assumptions?

6. *Currie's refusal to balance competing "interests."* Currie expressly rejected any suggestion that the forum court should balance the interests of one forum against another:

> [A]ssessment of the respective values of the competing legitimate interests of two sovereign states, in order to determine which is to prevail, is a political function of a very high order. This is a function that should not be committed to courts in a democracy. B. Currie, *Selected Essays on the Conflict of Laws* 182 (1963).

Is this a satisfactory approach? Is it not likely that a rational legislature would have intended (even if without putting it into words) that its laws apply in international circumstances only where local interests outweighed foreign ones? Recall the balancing of national interests that occurs in certain cases of personal jurisdiction, *supra* pp. 156-160, *forum non conveniens* analysis, *supra* p. 421, as well as in the context of extraterritorial discovery, *infra* pp. 1019-1020, and extraterritorial application of national laws, *supra* pp. 694-697, 697-701. Recall in particular Justice Scalia's application of §403 of the *Third Restatement* in his dissent in *Hartford Fire* and the Court's opinion in *Hoffmann-LaR-oche. See supra* pp. 688, 704-705. Is there really something undemocratic about this mode of analysis, as Currie argues? How would Justice Scalia reply?

   7. *Currie's "restrained" forum.* Currie also suggested at various times that, even where a true conflict was initially apparent, the forum should behave in a restrained and enlightened fashion, and interpret the competing laws with moderation and restraint. B. Currie, *Selected Essays on the Conflict of Laws* 592 (1963). What permits a court to interpret its own state's legislation in a "restrained" manner? Is it not the court's function to simply interpret the law—without special "restraint"? Does Currie's requirement for moderation call for the same sort of interest-balancing (under a different name) that he condemned? Note that, under Currie's analysis, the forum is to apply its own laws if a restrained interpretation indicates that the forum legislature still retains an interest in application.

   8. *Balancing of "interests" in other choice-of-law contexts.* Other commentators and courts rejected Currie's refusal to balance competing interests of different jurisdictions.

   (a) Contemporary choice of law. Some commentators advocate an explicit weighing of national interests. *E.g.,* R. Weintraub, *Commentary on the Conflict of Laws* §7.5 at 480-481 (4th ed. 2001); A. von Mehren & D. Trautman, *The Law of Multi-State Problems* 376-378 (1965); Baxter, *Choice of Law and the Federal System,* 16 Stan. L. Rev. 1 (1963). Consider §§6 and 145 of the *Restatement (Second) Conflict of Laws* (1971). Do they require the weighing of national interests?

   Consider the opinion in *Tramontana.* Did the court balance the interests of the competing jurisdictions? Is it possible for a court to meaningfully balance the interests of two different sovereign states? What provides a court with rules for identifying or assessing the weight of different governmental interests? What permits a U.S. court to decide that foreign interests are more important than U.S. interests?

   (b) Extraterritorial reach of federal legislation. As discussed elsewhere, "interest balancing" analyses have been adopted as a means of determining the extraterritorial reach of federal legislation. Examples include *Hartford Fire, Timberlane,* and §403 of the *Third Restatement.* These analyses explicitly weigh competing national interests. *See supra* pp. 685-687, 703-704. Given these examples, what is your view of Currie's rejection of interest-balancing? Is he correct that courts will never be able to identify, or meaningfully compare, competing national interests? Or that interest-balancing is a "political function of a very high order" that courts should not perform?

   9. *Interest analysis as a guide to statutory interpretation.* At bottom, Currie's interest analysis purported to provide a means of construing statutes or common law rules in multi-state contexts. According to Currie, determining the application of domestic law in international cases is nothing more than the "familiar one of construction or interpretation."

   (a) Utility of interest analysis as guide to statutory interpretation. How useful is interest analysis as a guide to choice-of-law problems? Compare the guidance that interest analysis provides for statutory interpretation to that provided by the *First Restatement* or Story's *Commentaries.* What does interest analysis say should guide a court's construction of a silent statute in international cases? What role does territoriality play? What role do the parties' domiciles or nationality play? What role should other factors (such as place of conduct, place of effects, parties' chosen law, etc.) play in determining legislative intent? Does interest analysis provide any guidance at all in determining how to construe silent legislation?

(b) Omissions of interest analysis. Note that the "familiar" process of statutory construction makes no effort to take into account the basic institutional aspects of multi-state and international problems. These features include the jurisdictional limits of international law; the existence of foreign legal systems with premises and interests that are profoundly different from one another; the possibility of retaliation, reciprocity, and cooperation among states; the desirability of uniform and predictable results; and the special burdens that private parties may encounter in international cases. The rules adopted by Story and the *First Restatement* sought to take these factors into account, as other choice-of-law theories have. Can interest analysis provide a useful guide to international choice-of-law problems without doing the same?

10. *Importance of domicile in interest analysis.* In addition to providing a general statement of interest analysis, Currie also gave examples of its application. Those examples turned significantly on the domiciles of the parties. For example, Currie devoted substantial attention to the classic case of *Milliken v. Pratt*, 125 Mass. 374 (1878) (excerpted below, *infra* pp. 777-780). As discussed below, *Milliken* involved a contract between a seller and a buyer, where the buyer's wife guaranteed his performance. Massachusetts, where the buyer and his wife lived, had a "married woman's contract" statute, that invalidated her guaranty. Maine, where the seller resided and where the contract was deemed made, would have given effect to the guarantee (because it did not have a married woman's contract statute). Currie considered how *Milliken* would have been decided under interest analysis:

> Massachusetts, in common with all other American states and many foreign countries, believes in freedom of contract. . . . It also believes, however, that married women constitute a class requiring special protection. It has therefore subordinated its policy of security of transactions to its policy of protecting married women. More specifically, it has subordinated the interests of creditors to the interests of this particular, favored class of debtors . . . married women. . . . *What* married women? Why, those with whose welfare Massachusetts is concerned, of course — *i.e.*, Massachusetts married women. In 1866 Maine emancipated (its) married women. Is Massachusetts declaring that decision erroneous, attempting to alter its effect? Certainly not. . . . Well, each to his own. Let Maine go feminist and modern; as for Massachusetts, it will stick to the old ways — for Massachusetts woman. B. Currie, *Selected Essays on the Conflict of Law* 85 (1963).

That was the full extent of Currie's analysis. Is this reasoning persuasive? Why is it that Massachusetts is, "of course," concerned with "*Massachusetts* married women"? Why is it not concerned with *any* woman who makes a contract *in* Massachusetts? Why is Massachusetts concerned with what Massachusetts women may do when they go abroad?

Consider the following remarks on Currie's analysis:

> As a general matter, where the laws of the parties' home states differ, each of these laws will either help the party who happens to be a local person or hurt the party who happens to be a local person. If it helps the local person, then the case is a true conflict. The reason is that if forum law helps the local, this means that foreign law hurts the local and therefore helps the foreigner. This gives rise to a forum interest in helping the local but also a foreign interest in helping the foreigner. If, in contrast, forum law hurts the local person, the case will be unprovided-for. The reason is that if forum law hurts the local, then the forum has no interest in applying it. But if forum law hurts the local, then forum law helps the foreigner and foreign law hurts the foreigner. The foreign state therefore has no interest in having its law applied either.
>
> Combining this set of assumptions about when interests exist with the proposed instructions about how to transform interests into case outcomes yields another interesting pattern.

Either the law of the common domicile (if there is one) or forum law applies, and which one applies does not depend on the content of the state's laws. . . . [O]ne can decide which law to apply even before one knows the content of the two competing rules. One need only know the domiciles of the parties, and (where the parties come from different states) whether the two states have identical rules or different ones. An interest analysis based on domiciliary-defined interests and a forum preference is, in other words, jurisdiction selecting like the *First Restatement*. . . . Interest analysis is argued to better effectuate substantive policies than the *[First] Restatement* did because it does a more substantively sensible job of choosing the relevant jurisdiction selecting factors. Its suggested application of either the common domicile law (if there is one) or else forum law is argued to reflect substantive policies better than the vested rights regime did. L. Brilmayer, *Conflict of Laws: Foundations and Future Directions* 59-60 (1991).

Is this an accurate description of interest analysis? If it is, note that interest analysis is fact much like the *First Restatement,* substituting domicile and nationality for territoriality. Which party's (or parties') nationality is important in Currie's interest analysis?

11. *Interest analysis and international law.* Suppose that Professor Brilmayer is correct in the foregoing excerpt and that interest analysis does amount to applying the forum's law to protect forum residents that are injured abroad (where foreign law would limit their recovery) or forum residents that are sued for foreign actions (where foreign law would expand their liability). As discussed above, international law does not generally permit a state to apply its substantive laws to conduct occurring abroad based solely on the nationality or domicile of the plaintiff. *See supra* pp. 601-602. Is that relevant in assessing the wisdom of Currie's interest analysis? Is it relevant to the ability of interest analysis to accurately predict unexpressed legislative intent? Recall the *Charming Betsy* rule that Congress will not be presumed to violate international law. *See supra* p. 18.

12. *Interest analysis in* Tramontana. Consider the application of interest analysis in *Tramontana.* Is the case correctly decided? Did the District of Columbia have *any* interest in the dispute in *Tramontana*? What does *Tramontana* say? Suppose that Mr. Tramontana and his widow had been residents of the District of Columbia at all relevant times. Would, in those circumstances, the District of Columbia have had an interest? How would *Tramontana* have assessed that interest? Would it have balanced the D.C. interest against the Brazilian interest? Or would it have concluded, as Currie would have, that the forum's interest prevailed?

Reconsider *Tramontana's* conclusion that the District of Columbia in fact had no significant interest. The court remarks that the Tramontanas resided in Maryland, and that Maryland (not D.C.) would bear the burden of Tramontana's indigency. Is that persuasive? In an international case? Don't *U.S.* taxpayers contribute to the cost of caring for public charges? In international matters, why should a state court not consider a plaintiff as a *U.S.* resident, rather than as a resident of some particular state of the United States? Recall the similar issue in the context of judicial jurisdiction and *forum non conveniens. See supra* pp. 134-229 & 403-406.

Is it in fact correct, as the court suggests in *Tramontana,* that the case was no different from a case involving a U.S. tourist killed in Amsterdam by a truck? What is the relevance of the fact that Mr. Tramontana was in a U.S. military aircraft on an official mission temporarily passing through Brazil in the course of his employment by the U.S. Navy? Does this affect the D.C. interest? The U.S. interest? What if Mr. Tramontana had been flying over Brazil, without stopping, on his way to Chile? What if the collision with Varig's plane had occurred over Chile, which had similar damage limits?

13. Second Restatement's "most significant relationship" test. Do §§6 and 145 of the *Second Restatement* adopt Currie's interest analysis? Do the two sections consider the underlying policies of the competing laws, or do they look to external jurisdiction-selecting factors like territoriality and domicile? Or do they try to do both?

How would §145 resolve: (a) *Carroll*; (b) *Victor*; (c) *Tramontana*; (d) *American Banana*; and (e) *Hartford Fire*? How certain would you be of the answer in each of these cases? How does §145 compare to (a) the *First Restatement*'s "place of the wrong" rule; and (b) Currie's interest analysis? Which analysis is preferable? Consider:

> [I]t hardly comes as news that the *Second Restatement* is flawed. But one needs to read a lot of opinions in a single sitting fully to appreciate just how badly the *Second Restatement* works in practice. . . . One sees the *Second Restatement* at its worst in [cases applying §6's factors]. Judges try to make sense of the factors listed in §6, but the analysis is predictably question-begging and confusing. The drafters of the *Second Restatement* apparently hoped that courts would eventually sort through the considerations in §6 and construct a more systematic approach to choice of law. But §6 seems to have had exactly the opposite effect — encouraging courts to forego systematic analysis in favor of ad hoc intuition. Kramer, *Choice of Law in the American Courts in 1990: Trends and Developments*, 39 Am. J. Comp. L. 465, 486-487 (1991).

Compare §§145 and 146 of the *Second Restatement*. Is §146 an application of interest analysis? What is the rationale for §146's statement that the "law of the state where the inquiry occurred" generally is the applicable law in personal injury cases? How different is this from the *First Restatement*?

Compare Professor Kramer's reaction to reading a number of choice-of-law opinions in a single sitting to your own reaction after reading *Aramco, Hartford Fire, Hoffmann-LaRoche*, and *Morrison* in succession. *See supra* pp. 651-653, 692-701. What does this suggest about the efficacy of multi-factor reasonableness standards in the conflicts of law context? What alternative is there?

14. *Contemporary choice-of-law theory and legislative purposes.* Post-Currie American choice-of-law theory focuses on the legislative purposes of particular enactments:

> The key insight of the interest analysis . . . was that it depends on the purpose of the law in question. The point is elegantly simple: if — in the interests of comity and mutual accommodation — we presume that a state's law is intended to apply only in cases that are connected to the state in some important way, the significant contacts ought to be those that implicate the reasons the law was enacted for wholly domestic cases. This has two advantages: first, it ensures that the state's laws apply in the cases that are likely to be of greatest concern to the state's law makers; second, it leaves room for the laws of other states in cases that are likely to be of especial concern to those states. Kramer, *Rethinking Choice of Law*, 90 Colum. L. Rev. 277, 298 (1990).

How is this observation applicable in the cases examined above — *Carroll, Victor, American Banana,* and *Tramontana*? What are the purposes of the tort laws at issue in *Carroll* and *American Banana*? Are they not designed to deter undesirable conduct and assist innocent victims to bear the cost of their injury by shifting costs to "wrongdoers"? If so, what classes of "undesirable conduct" and "innocent victims" are covered? Are there any clear (or other) answers to this question in the mere "legislative purpose" of a tort law?

What are the purposes of the liability limits in *Victor* and *Tramontana*? Does a legislative desire to protect defendants from "undue" liability provide any guidance in determining *what* defendants in *which* cases?

15. *Domestic versus international choice-of-law rules.* Consider §10 of the *Second Restatement*. Why might international choice-of-law rules differ from domestic ones? If the accident in *Tramontana* had occurred over Texas, would any different analysis be required? What if *Victor* had involved an accident in Arizona?

16. *Public policy in contemporary choice of law applicable to torts.* As discussed above, public policy remains a basis for a U.S. court to decline to apply foreign law, even under most contemporary choice-of-law principles. As in other contexts, however, defining "public policy" is an unpredictable undertaking. *See supra* pp. 443, 520-523 & *infra* pp. 1133-1146.

Consider the application of the public policy doctrine in *Kilberg* and *Tramontana*. In *Kilberg*, the court held that a damage limitation of a sister state was invalid, as applied to a New York resident killed in the sister state on a flight originating in New York. Is the application of public policy in such cases appropriate? If so, what distinguishes *Kilberg* from *Tramontana*? Recall the discussions above of choice of public policy considerations. *See supra* pp. 520-523.

Courts ordinarily apply the public policy exception narrowly so that it does not swallow conflicts analysis. *E.g.*, *Greenwell v. Davis*, 180 S.W.3d 287, 296-299 (Tex. App. 2005); *Bridas Corp. v. Unocal Corp.*, 16 S.W.3d 893, 900 (Tex. App. 2000); *Cooney v. Osgood Machinery, Inc.*, 612 N.E.2d 277, 284 (N.Y. 1993).

17. *Substance and procedure in contemporary choice-of-law analysis.* Although the *Second Restatement* abandoned many aspects of the *First Restatement*'s approach to choice of law, it did not abandon the general principle that "procedural" matters are governed by the law of the forum. Why? Note, however, that §122 of the *Second Restatement* does not use the "procedural" label, and instead deals with "rules prescribing how litigation shall be conducted." Like its predecessor, the *Second Restatement* provides that the law of the forum governs matters such as form of action, service, rules of pleadings, and conduct of proceedings. *Restatement (Second) Conflict of Laws* §§124, 126 & 127 (1971). However, the *Second Restatement* treats other matters in less clear-cut fashion, providing for example that questions of burden of proof, parties to an action, set-off, and sufficiency of evidence are generally governed by the forum's law, but may be displaced if the otherwise applicable substantive law indicates that such matters are relevant to a decision on the merits. *Restatement (Second) Conflict of Laws* §§125, 128, 133, 134 & 135 (1971).

18. *Statutes of limitations in contemporary U.S. choice-of-law analysis.* Sections 142 and 143 of the *Second Restatement,* which are excerpted above, change the *First Restatement*'s rule regarding statutes of limitations (discussed above at *supra* p. 738). As §142 suggests, many U.S. states have enacted "borrowing statutes," which provide that an action cannot be maintained if the statute of limitations of another state, more closely connected to the dispute, would bar the action. Different borrowing statutes define the state whose limitations period is to be borrowed differently: some refer to the state where the plaintiff's cause of action "arose" or "accrued," while others refer to the state where the defendant was domiciled at the time of the events giving rise to the claim. *See, e.g.,* N.Y.C.P.L.R. §202 ("An action based upon a cause of action accruing without the state cannot be commenced after the expiration of the time limited by the laws of either the state or the place without the state where the cause of action accrued, except that where the cause of action accrued in favor of a resident of the state the time limited by the laws of the state shall apply."). For recent decisions applying a state borrowing statute to a tort action brought by foreign plaintiffs against a U.S. manufacturer, *see Chang v. Baxter Healthcare Corp.*, 599 F.3d 728 (7th Cir. 2010); *Agrofollajes, S.A. v. E.I. Du Pont De Nemours & Co., Inc.*, 2010 WL 4870149 (Fla. App. Dec. 1, 2010).

What does §143 mean? In what circumstances would it apply? In general, a statute of limitations will be held to bar the right, not merely the remedy, only when a statutory claim is involved and when the limitations provision is attached to the substantive right "so specifically as to warrant saying that it qualifie[s] the right." *Davis v. Mills,* 194 U.S. 451, 454 (1904). Is this a sensible distinction?

19. *Statutes of limitations in civil jurisdictions.* Many civil law states treat statutes of limitations as "substantive," and apply the law of the state whose law governs the merits of the parties' dispute. *See* McDonnold, *Limitation of Actions — Conflict of Laws — Lex Fori or Lex Loci?,* 35 Tex. L. Rev. 95 (1957). What arguments speak in favor of this approach? Against it?

20. *The Rome II Regulation.* European law provides a useful point of comparison to the above-described approaches to the law applicable to tort claims. Recently, after several years of thorny negotiations, the Commission completed work on a regulation governing the "Law Applicable to Non-Contractual Obligations" (the "Rome II" Regulation). *See* Regulation No. 864/2007, OJ 2007, L 199/40. While the precise contours of the regulation are complex, several general observations permit some comparison.

First, for torts that fall within the regulation, the general rule governing, among other matters, liability, defenses, and damages (subject to various exceptions set forth elsewhere in the regulation) is *lex loci damni,* namely the law of the country in which the damage occurs (irrespective of whether the underlying conduct giving rise to that damage occurred in the same country). *See* Articles 4, 15. Second, that general principle does not apply where both the plaintiff and defendant have their habitual residence in the same country at the time the damage occurs; in those cases, the law of the place of their residence shall govern. *See* Art. 4(2) Third, the foregoing principles (*lex loci damni* and habitual residence) do not apply when it is clear from all of the circumstances of the case that the tort is manifestly more connected with the law of another country (such as a contractual relationship that is closely related to the tort). *See* Art. 4(3). Fourth, in most cases, the parties are free to designate the law applicable to their noncontractual relationships either by express agreement entered into after the event giving rise to the damage or, in the case of certain commercial undertakings, a freely negotiated express agreement entered into prior to the event giving rise to the damage. *See* Art. 14. This freedom of agreement is subject to certain restrictions where the damage occurred in a country other than that whose law was the parties' selection and where the provisions of that country's law are nonderogable. Finally, the foregoing conflicts rules are all subject to the "mandatory" provisions of the forum's law. *See* Art. 16.

How does this approach compare with the territoriality approach? The most significant relationship approach? Is it wise to allow parties to designate the law governing the non-contractual obligations? How does this differ from the rules governing the scope of choice-of-law clauses? How do the "mandatory" law exceptions differ from the "public policy" requirements discussed above? For exemplary commentary on the Rome II Regulation, *see, e.g.,* Symeonides, *Rome II and Tort Conflicts: A Missed Opportunity,* 56 Am. J. Comp. L. 123 (2008); Michaels, *The New European Choice-of-Law Revolution,* 82 Tul. L. Rev. 1607 (2008).

21. *Method of regulating conflicts.* Note that the decisions in this section all involve conflicts principles developed through judicially crafted rules (rather than legislative enactments). This stands in contrast to the conflicts rules governing contract claims where statutes play a greater role. *See infra* at 758-763. Is this a sensible regime? Does it not severely undermine predictability if the law governing tort claims is subject to common law rules which may evolve (or be discarded entirely) depending on the views of judges? Or is it precisely in the context of tort claims where the greater flexibility offered by a common law system is needed? Doesn't a comprehensive legislative scheme run certain risks, such as setting forth rules that become outmoded or leaving gaps where unanticipated cases arise?

Recently, some state legislatures have begun to wade into this field. In 2009, Oregon became the first state with a common law system to adopt a comprehensive statute governing conflicts analysis in tort cases. *See* An Act on Choice of Law for Torts and Other Non-Contractual Obligations, 2009 Oregon Laws Ch. 451. (Before this enactment, the state of Louisiana (the only civil law system in the United States) was the only state to have a comprehensive statutory scheme governing conflicts analysis in this area.)

C.   Choice of Law Applicable to Contracts

Central features of all choice-of-law systems are rules governing the law applicable to contracts. This was a principal focus of Huber's *De Conflictu Legum* and Story's *Commentaries on the Conflict of Laws,* as well as of the *First* and *Second Restatements.*[196] As with the law applicable to torts, U.S. choice-of-law rules concerning contracts have undergone substantial evolution in the past century, and remain subject to diverse approaches in different U.S. courts. Indeed, it is often said that the choice of law applicable to contracts is "the most complex and confused area of choice-of-law problems."[197] For these reasons, this section devotes particular emphasis to historic rules and developments.

1.   Party Autonomy and Choice-of-Law Clauses[198]

It is common for commercial contracts to include "choice of law" provisions that select the law that the parties agree should govern their disputes. Like forum selection clauses, private parties agree upon choice-of-law clauses in order to increase the predictability of their agreements, to avoid the costs of disputes over applicable law, and to obtain advantages by specifying a favorable body of substantive law.[199] Private parties will often prefer that the law of their own home jurisdiction govern their agreements (although this preference is generally unreflective, and may actually result in the application of unfavorable rules of substantive law). If this cannot be bargained for, international commercial agreements often specify the laws of a neutral, third country with a developed legal system (such as England, New York, or Switzerland).

---

196. *See* J. Story, *Commentaries on the Conflict of Laws* Chapter VIII (2d ed. 1834); *Restatement (First) Conflict of Laws* Chapter 8 (1834); *Restatement (Second) Conflict of Laws* Chapter 8 (1971).

197. R. Weintraub, *Commentary on the Conflict of Laws* 362 (3d ed. 1986).

198. Commentary on choice-of-law agreements includes, for example, Covey & Morris, *The Enforceability of Agreements Providing for Forum and Choice of Law Selection,* 61 Denver L.J. 837 (1984); James, *Effects of the Autonomy of the Parties on the Conflicts of Law Contracts,* 36 Chi.-Kent. L. Rev. 87 (1959); Prebble, *Choice-of-Law to Determine the Validity and Effect of Contracts: A Comparison of English and American Approaches to the Conflict of Laws,* 58 Cornell L. Rev. 433 (1973); Gruson, *Governing Law Clauses in Commercial Agreements — New York's Approach,* 18 Colum. J. Transnat'l L. 323 (1980); James, *Effects of the Autonomy of the Parties on Conflicts of Law,* 36 Chi.-Kent. L. Rev. 87 (1959); O'Hara, *Opting Out of Regulation: A Public Choice Analysis of Contractual Choice of Law,* 53 Vand. L. Rev. 1551 (2000); O'Hara & Ribstein, *From Politics to Efficient in Choice of Law,* 67 U. Chi. L. Rev. 1151 (2000); Weinberger, *Party Autonomy and Choice of Law: The Restatement (Second) Interest Analysis and Search for a Methodological Synthesis,* 4 Hofstra L. Rev. 605 (1976); Yntema, *Contract and Conflict of Laws: "Autonomy" in the Choice of Law in the United States,* 1 N.Y.L.F. 46 (1955).

199. "A contractual provision specifying in advance the forum in which disputes shall be litigated and the law to be applied is . . . an almost indispensable precondition to achievement of the orderliness and predictability essential to any international business transaction." *Scherk v. Alberto-Culver Co.,* 417 U.S. 506, 516 (1974). *See* Lowe, *Choice of Law Clauses in International Contracts: A Practical Approach,* 12 Harv. Int'l L.J. 1 (1971).

When a choice-of-law clause exists, three significant issues arise: (a) is the agreement valid and enforceable; (b) if so, subject to what exceptions; and (c) how is the agreement to be interpreted? Different nations adopt significantly different approaches to all three of these questions; different approaches have prevailed in different historical periods; and different approaches presently prevail in different U.S. jurisdictions.

a.   Traditional U.S. Approach: Choice-of-Law Clauses Not Enforceable.   During the nineteenth and early twentieth century, private choice-of-law agreements were sometimes said to be *per se* unenforceable (much like choice of forum and arbitration agreements).[200] The *Restatement (First) Conflict of Laws* contained no provisions regarding choice-of-law agreements, leaving the question to be governed by generally applicable choice-of-law rules for contracts (which accorded no weight to the parties' intended choice of law). Joseph Beale, the Reporter for the *First Restatement,* made clear that he regarded choice-of-law clauses as unenforceable. Beale characterized the principle of party autonomy in choice of law as "absolutely anomalous," "theoretically indefensible," and "absolutely impracticable."[201] Beale reasoned that enforcement of a choice-of-law clause would mean that "at their will [private parties] can free themselves from the power of the law which would otherwise apply to their acts."[202]

Early U.S. judicial decisions were less doctrinaire and adopted divergent approaches to party autonomy in the choice of law. Some early decisions refused to recognize the concept of party autonomy.[203] But other decisions adopted a different approach, either enforcing express choice-of-law agreements,[204] or inquiring into the substantive law that the parties to a contract likely intended to govern their dealings.[205]

b.   Contemporary Approach: Choice-of-Law Clauses Are Presumptively Enforceable. Historic skepticism about the enforceability of choice-of-law agreements has been substantially eroded in contemporary U.S. courts. As detailed below, such clauses are now generally enforced by U.S. courts, subject to significant exceptions.[206] The *Restatement (Second) Conflict of Laws* states a widely accepted approach, providing in §187(1) that choice-of-law clauses will generally be enforced as to subjects that could have been resolved through an express provision in the parties' agreement (such as the time for performance).[207] Although it does not expressly say so, §187(1) contemplates nonenforcement of agreements in violation of forum public policy (because such agreements

---

200. *See supra* p. 465 & *infra* pp. 1164-1165.

201. 2 J. Beale, *A Treatise on the Conflict of Laws* 1080, 1083, & 1084 (1935).

202. 2 J. Beale, *A Treatise on the Conflict of Laws* 1080 (1935).

203. *E.g., E. Gerli & Co. v. Cunard SS Co.,* 48 F.2d 115, 117 (2d Cir. 1931).

204. *Dolan v. Mutual Reserve Fund Life Ass'n,* 53 N.E. 398 (Mass. 1899); *Griesemer v. Mutual Life Ins. Co. of New York,* 38 P. 1031 (Wash. 1894); *Fonseca v. Cunard SS Co.,* 27 N.E. 665 (Mass. 1891); *Kellogg v. Miller,* 13 Fed. 198 (D. Neb. 1881).

205. *Pritchard v. Norton,* 106 U.S. 124 (1882); *Wayman v. Southard,* 23 U.S. 1, 48 (1825); *Thompson v. Ketcham,* 8 Johns. 189 (N.Y. Sup. 1811).

206. *See Restatement (Second) Conflict of Laws* §187 (1971); Gruson, *Governing Law Clauses in Commercial Agreements — New York's Approach,* 18 Colum. J. Transnat'l L. 323, 324 n.3 (1979) (collecting authorities); Gruson, *Governing-Law Clauses in International and Interstate Loan Agreements — New York's Approach,* 1982 U. Ill. L. Rev. 207.

207. The comments to §187 explain that §187(1) relates to "incorporation by reference and is not a rule of choice of law." In dealing with issues that the parties could have dealt with by explicit agreement, the section contemplates subject that parties ordinarily "spell out . . . in the contract." It extends to "most rules of contract law," which are generally "designed to fill gaps in a contract which the parties could themselves have filled with express provisions." The comment includes within this category "rules relating to construction, to conditions precedent and subsequent, to sufficiency of performance, and to excuse for nonperformance, including questions of frustration and impossibility." "As to all such matters, the forum will apply the provisions of the chosen law." *Restatement (Second) Conflict of Laws* §187 comment c (1971).

would not have been capable of resolution in the manner directed by foreign law even by an express agreement).

Section 187(2) permits enforcement of choice-of-law provisions as to issues that the parties could *not* have expressly dealt with, subject to exceptions.[208] Section 187(2) applies to matters such as capacity, substantive validity, and formalities. The general rule of enforceability is subject to exceptions where there is "no substantial relationship" between the chosen law and the parties or their transaction,[209] or where the chosen law would be contrary to the fundamental public policy of a state with a "materially greater interest."[210] Most contemporary U.S. state and federal courts have adopted approaches that are broadly similar to §187.[211]

The Uniform Commercial Code, widely adopted by states, contains similar restrictions on the enforceability of choice-of-law clauses, though its restrictions have undergone substantial revision over time. Prior to 2001, the Uniform Commercial Code contained both a "reasonable relation" and a public policy restriction.[212] In 2001, the drafters of the Uniform Commercial Code weakened those restrictions. They eliminated the "reasonable restriction" almost entirely (except for consumer contracts) and limited the public policy exception to situations where the parties' chosen law violated a "fundamental policy" of the forum state. [213] These changes encountered significant restrictions in some state legislatures,[214] prompting the commissioners in 2008 to restore the pre-2001 limits.[215] Given the rapid rate of change in this area, it is especially important that practitioners heed the applicable version of the Uniform Commercial Code.

c. Public Policy.   As in other contexts, there is no clear definition of what constitutes a public policy for purposes overriding a choice-of-law agreement,[216] nor of how "strong" a public policy must be before it will override the parties' chosen law.[217] Some courts have considered whether the asserted public policy is derived from statutory prohibitions, which are typically deemed to be more reflective of public policy than common law rules,[218] and if so, whether the statute in question is penal in nature or is specifically applicable in choice-of-law contexts.[219] Public policies that have been found capable of

---

208. Section 187(2) applies "when it is sought to have the chosen law determine issues which the parties could not have determined by explicit agreement directed to the particular issue. Examples of such questions are those involving capacity, formalities and substantial validity. A person cannot vest himself with contractual capacity by stating in the contract that he has such capacity." *Restatement (Second) Conflict of Laws* §187 comment d (1971).

209. *Restatement (Second) Conflict of Laws* §187(2)(a) (1971).

210. *Restatement (Second) Conflict of Laws* §187(2)(b) (1971).

211. *See* Gruson, *Governing Law Clauses in Commercial Agreements — New York's Approach*, 18 Colum. J. Transnat'l L. 323 (1979); Reese, *Power of Parties to Choose Law Governing Their Contract*, 54 Am. Soc'y Int'l L. Proc. 49 (1960).

212. *See* U.C.C. §1-105 (1995 version).

213. *See* U.C.C. §1-301 (2001 version).

214. *See* Nafziger, *The Louisiana and Oregon Codifications of Choice-of-Law Rules in Context*, 2010 Am. J. Comp. L. 165 (2010); Graves, *Party Autonomy in Choice of Commercial Law: The Failure of Revised U.C.C. §1-301 and a Proposal for Broader Reform*, 36 Seton Hall L. Rev. 59 (2005).

215. *See* U.C.C. §1-301 (2008 version).

216. *See Restatement (Second) Conflict of Laws* §187 comment g (1971). For a good overview of the contexts in which public policy arguments have arisen, *see* Symeonides et al., *Conflict of Laws* §18.5 at 966-974 (5th ed. 2010) .

217. *Compare Restatement (Second) Conflict of Laws* §187(2)(b) (1971) ("fundamental policy") *with Intercontinental Hotels Corp. v. Golden*, 254 N.Y.S.2d 527 (N.Y. 1964) ("inherently vicious, wicked or immoral") *with Loucks v. Standard Oil Co. of New York* , 224 N.Y. 99, 110 (1918) ("offend our sense of justice or menace the public welfare").

218. *Restatement (Second) Conflict of Laws* §187 comment g (1971) (by implication).

219. *Reger v. National Assoc. of Bedding Mfrs.*, 372 N.Y.S.2d 97, 116 (N.Y. Sup. 1975); *Big Four Mills, Ltd. v. Commercial Credit Co.*, 211 S.W.2d 831, 836 (Ky. 1948); *MGM Grand Hotel, Inc. v. Imperial Glass Co.*, 65 F.R.D. 624, 632 (D. Nev. 1974), *rev'd on other grounds*, 533 F.2d 486 (9th Cir. 1976).

invalidating a choice-of-law clause have included usury restrictions,[220] labor relations rules (including covenants not to compete),[221] rules concerning governmental corruption,[222] rules concerning set-off,[223] rules protecting dealers or franchisees,[224] rules regarding indemnification,[225] and laws protecting insureds.[226]

As §187(2) indicates, a public policy will not override the parties' chosen law unless it is the public policy of a state (a) whose law would (but for the choice of law clause) apply to the parties' agreement; and (b) which has a "materially greater interest" than the state whose law has been chosen.[227] In general, the closer the relationship between the parties' transaction and the forum state, the more likely that local law will be deemed to constitute a substantial public policy.[228] As §187(2)(b) of the *Second Restatement* suggests, the public policy of states other than the forum may sometimes render the parties' choice-of-law clause unenforceable.[229]

The 2001 version of the Uniform Commercial Code takes a slightly different view from the *Second Restatement*. Unlike the *Second Restatement*, §1-301 of the revised U.C.C. provides that a choice of law will be disregarded where it violates a "fundamental" policy of the state whose law otherwise would govern. Implicitly, therefore, the drafters of the U.C.C. discarded the *Second Restatement*'s other requirement — that the state have a "materially greater interest."[230] It also precluded parties in purely "domestic transactions" from designating a foreign law to govern their relationships.[231] As noted above, the drafters of the U.C.C. removed this requirement in 2008, though it still remains on the books in some states that have not yet adopted the revised version.

d. Reasonable Relationship. Some courts refuse to enforce choice-of-law provisions that select the law of a state that lacks a "reasonable relation" to the parties' transaction. For example, the 1995 and 2008 versions of the Uniform Commercial Code provide that "when a transaction bears a reasonable relationship to this state and also to another state or nation the parties may agree that the law of either this state or of such other state or

---

220. *E.g., Whitaker v. Spiegel, Inc.,* 623 P.2d 1147 (Wash. 1981). The clear weight of authority is that usury restrictions are not sufficiently clear and fundamental to constitute fundamental public policies for choice-of-law purposes. *Seeman v. Philadelphia Warehouse Co.,* 274 U.S. 403 (1927); *Clarkson v. Finance Co.,* 328 F.2d 404 (4th Cir. 1964); *Gamer v. duPont Glore Forgan, Inc.,* 135 Cal. Rptr. 230 (Cal. App. 1976).

221. *De Santis v. Wackenhut Corp.,* 793 S.W.2d 670 (Tex. 1990); *Cherry, Bekaert & Holland v. Brown,* 582 So. 2d 502 (Ala. 1991); *Davis v. Jointless Fire Brick Co.,* 300 F. 1 (9th Cir. 1924); *Blalock v. Perfect Subscription Co.,* 458 F. Supp. 123 (S.D. Ala. 1978).

222. *Triad Financial Establishment v. Tumpane Co.,* 611 F. Supp. 157 (N.D.N.Y. 1985).

223. *Moore v. Subaru of America,* 891 F.2d 1445 (10th Cir. 1989).

224. *Modern Computer Systems, Inc. v. Modern Banking Systems, Inc.,* 858 F.2d 1339 (8th Cir. 1988); *Bush v. National School Studios, Inc.,* 407 N.W.2d 883 (Wis. 1987); *Rutter v. BX of Tri-Cities, Inc.,* 806 P.2d 1266 (Wash. Ct. App. 1991).

225. *Tucker v. R.A. Hanson Co.,* 956 F.2d 215 (10th Cir. 1992); *Donaldson v. Fluor Engineers, Inc.,* 523 N.E.2d 117 (Ill. App. 1st Dist. 1988); *Chrysler Corp. v. Skyline Indus. Services, Inc.,* 502 N.W.2d 715 (Mich. App. 1993) (refusal by Michigan court to enforce contractual indemnification provision that violated laws of Illinois, which was place of relevant conduct, notwithstanding Michigan choice-of-law clause).

226. *New York Life Ins. Co. v. Cravens,* 178 U.S. 389 (1900); *Nelson v. Aetna Life Ins. Co.,* 359 F. Supp. 271, 290-292 (W.D. Mo. 1973).

227. *Restatement (Second) Conflict of Laws* §187(2)(b) (1971).

228. *Restatement (Second) Conflict of Laws* §187 comment f (1971) ("The more closely the state of the chosen law is related to the contract and the parties, the more fundamental must be the policy of the state of the otherwise applicable law to justify denying effect to the choice-of-law provision").

229. *Connecticut General Life Ins. Co. v. Boseman,* 84 F.2d 701, 705 (5th Cir. 1936), *aff'd,* 301 U.S. 196 (1937); *Citizens National Bank v. Waugh,* 78 F.2d 325, 327 (4th Cir. 1935); *Fricke v. Isbrandtsen Co.,* 151 F. Supp. 465, 468 (S.D.N.Y. 1957).

230. Symeonides et al., *Conflict of Laws* §18.4 at 961 (5th ed. 2010).

231. U.C.C. §1-301(a)(1), (c)(1) (2001 version).

nation shall govern their rights and duties."[232] Similarly, §187(2)(a) overrides the party choice where the chosen state "has not substantial relationship to the parties or the transaction and there is no reasonable basis for the parties' choice."

The principal rationale for this requirement appears to be a concern that parties to purely local transactions, relating entirely to one state, not be able to circumvent local laws by choosing a foreign law.[233] Nonetheless, the reasonable relationship requirement is stated more broadly, suggesting that it is applicable to transactions involving relationships with two or more jurisdictions.[234]

e. Interpretation of Choice-of-Law Clauses.

Like other contractual provisions, choice-of-law clauses must be interpreted. This usually turns primarily on the language that the parties used in their agreement. Nevertheless, there are recurrent issues of interpretation, as to which rules of construction have developed.

First, the parties' agreement to a choice-of-forum clause does not necessarily imply agreement that the chosen forum's law should also govern their relations.[235] Conversely, an agreement as to governing law does not, under due process precedents, necessarily provide a submission to the jurisdiction of the courts of the chosen state.[236]

Second, like choice-of-forum clauses, choice-of-law agreements often must be construed to determine their scope — the issues or claims that are subject to the parties' chosen law. As with forum selection agreements, this inquiry turns largely on the particular language of the parties' agreement. Some choice-of-law clauses state only that "[t]his agreement shall be construed in accordance with the laws of State A," which suggests that issues of capacity, contractual validity, formalities, excuses, and damages are not subject to the parties' chosen law. Other choice-of-law clauses state more broadly that "[t]his agreement shall be governed by the laws of State B," or "[t]his agreement and all disputes arising under it shall be subject to the laws of State C." Both formulations suggest that *all* issues of contract law are subject to the parties' chosen law, but that tort or other noncontractual claims that relate to the contract are not.[237] Finally, some choice-of-law clauses are drafted very broadly, attempting to include noncontractual claims (as well as contractual ones):

---

232. U.C.C. §1-301 (2008 version); U.C.C. §1-105 (1995 version). In 2001, the drafters of the Uniform Commercial Code revised this section and eliminated the "reasonable relationship requirement" except in cases involving consumer contracts. That provision proved highly unpopular among states, which largely refused to adopt it. Thereafter, in 2008, the drafters of the Uniform Commercial Code reverted to the original "reasonable relationship" requirement that existed prior to 2001. *See* Nafziger, *The Louisiana and Oregon Codifications of Choice-of-Law Rules in Context,* 58 Am. J. Comp. L. 165, 169-170 (2010).

233. *Dolan v. Mutual Reserve Fund Life Ass'n,* 53 N.E. 398, 399 (Mass. 1899); *New England Mutual Life Ins. Co. v. Olin,* 114 F.2d 131, 136 (7th Cir. 1940).

234. *Restatement (Second) Conflict of Laws* §187(2)(a) (1971); *Seeman v. Philadelphia Warehouse Co.,* 274 U.S. 403 (1927); *Consolidated Jewellers, Inc. v. Standard Financial Corp.,* 325 F.2d 31, 34 (6th Cir. 1963); *First Nat'l Bank of Mitchell v. Daggett,* 497 N.W.2d 358 (Neb. 1993); *Prows v. Pinpoint Retail Systems, Inc.,* 868 P.2d 809 (Utah 1993). For criticism of the reasonable relationship requirement, *see* A. Ehrenzweig, *Conflict of Laws* 469 (1962).

235. Gruson, *Governing-Law Clauses in International and Interstate Loan Agreements — New York's Approach,* 1982 U. Ill. L. Rev. 207 (1982). However, the parties' submission to the jurisdiction of a particular forum can be evidence of an implied selection of applicable law. *E.g., Restatement (Second) Conflict of Laws* §187 comment a (1971); *Lummus v. Commonwealth Oil Refining Co.,* 280 F.2d 915 (1st Cir. 1960); *Kress Corp. v. Levy Co.,* 430 N.E.2d 593 (Ill. 1981). *See also Paper Express Ltd. v. Pfankuch Maschinen GmbH,* 1990 WL 141424 (N.D. Ill. 1990) (acceptance of rules of German trade association included acceptance of jurisdiction of German courts); *Walpex Trading Co. v. Yacimientos Petroliferos Fiscales Bolivianos,* 756 F. Supp. 136 (S.D.N.Y. 1991) (court rejects argument that Bolivian law would have required parties to include forum selection clause in contract, if it had been executed).

236. *See supra* pp. 192-193. It may, however, constitute a significant factor in minimum contacts analysis. *See supra* p. 193.

237. *E.g., T-Bill Option Club v. Brown & Co.,* 1994 WL 201104 (7th Cir. 1994); *Politte v. McDonald's Corp.,* 1994 U.S. App. LEXIS 18027 (10th Cir. 1994); *Union Oil Co. v. John Brown E & C,* 1994 WL 535108 (N.D. Ill. 1994).

"all disputes arising out of or relating to this agreement shall be governed exclusively by the laws of State D."[238]

Third, choice-of-law clauses must be interpreted to determine which aspects of the parties' chosen law are applicable. In particular, does a reference to "the laws of State E" refer to the "whole law" of State E — including its choice-of-law rules — or does it refer only to the "local law" of State E? The *Second Restatement* provides that, absent contrary evidence of intent, the latter interpretation will prevail.[239]

Fourth, will a choice-of-law clause be interpreted to include issues relating to procedure, statutes of limitations, burdens of proof, excuses for nonperformance, or damages?[240] The *Second Restatement* suggests that at least some of these issues will generally *not* be subject to the parties' chosen law, although evidence of contrary intent could produce a different construction.[241]

f. Selected Materials on Party Autonomy. Excerpted below are selected materials on choice-of-law agreements. First, consider §§187 and 204 of the *Restatement (Second) Conflict of Laws,* which adopt a general rule of enforceability for choice-of-law clauses as to specified issues. Then reread the excerpts from *The Bremen v. Zapata Off-Shore Co.* and *Richards v. Lloyd's of London.* Finally, consider N.Y. General Obligations Law §5-1401 and the opinion in *Lehman Brothers Commercial Corp. v. Minmetals International Non-Ferrous Metals Trading Co.*

RESTATEMENT (SECOND) CONFLICT OF LAWS
§§187 & 204 (1971) [excerpted in Appendix Y]

THE BREMEN v. ZAPATA OFF-SHORE COMPANY
407 U.S. 1 (1972) [excerpted above at pp. 474-478]

RICHARDS v. LLOYD'S OF LONDON
135 F.3d 1289 (9th Cir. 1998) (en banc) [excerpted above at pp. 515-520]

N.Y. GENERAL OBLIGATIONS LAW
§5-1401 [excerpted in Appendix W]

LEHMAN BROTHERS COMMERCIAL CORPORATION v. MINMETALS INTERNATIONAL NON-FERROUS METALS TRADING COMPANY
179 F. Supp. 2d 118 (S.D.N.Y. 2000)

KEENAN, DISTRICT JUDGE. [This case arose from purportedly unauthorized foreign exchange ("FX") trading between 1992 and 1994 on behalf of two Chinese state-related entities — China National Metals & Minerals Import & Export Corporation ("Minmetal") and Minmetals International Non-Ferrous Metals Trading Company ("Non-Ferrous") — with Lehman Brothers Commercial Corporation ("LBCC") and Lehman Brothers

---

238. *See* G. Born, *International Arbitration and Forum Selection Agreements: Drafting and Enforcing* 139-140 (3d ed. 2010).

239. *Restatement (Second) Conflict of Laws* §187(3) (1971); *Siegelman v. Cunard White Star Ltd.,* 221 F.2d 189 (2d Cir. 1955); *Fuller Co. v. Compagnie des Bauxites de Guinee,* 421 F. Supp. 938, 946 (W.D. Pa. 1976).

240. *Restatement (Second) Conflict of Laws* §§122-143 (1971).

241. *See* Appendix _____.

Special Financing, Inc. ("LBSF") (together, "Lehman"). Minmetal is the parent of the Minmetals Group, an international trading conglomerate that operates throughout the world. Minmetal is headquartered in Beijing in the People's Republic of China ("China"), is owned by the State, and reports to China's Ministry of Foreign Trade and Economic Cooperation. Non-Ferrous is a wholly owned subsidiary of Minmetal and is located in the same building as Minmetal. Lehman is a world-wide financial services group, based in New York.

The disputed FX trades were entered into by one Hu Xiangdong ("Hu"), an employee of Non-Ferrous, on behalf of Non-Ferrous. Hu executed various documents on behalf of Non-Ferrous, as well as a guarantee by Minmetal which allegedly guaranteed payment of any losses by Non-Ferrous in its FX trading. The transactions began profitably, earning nearly $50 million. In 1994, however, interest rates were significantly raised in the United States, causing substantial losses in Non-Ferrous' FX positions. Non-Ferrous did not pay these losses, leading Lehman to liquidate collateral it held and demand payment from Non-Ferrous. Hu then agreed to a payment schedule under which the margin calls would be met by a series of payments. Lehman received one payment of $5.1 million, but the rest of the plan was not paid. When Lehman demanded payment of the outstanding sums (of more than $50 million), Non-Ferrous and Minmetal responded that Hu's FX trading was unauthorized and refusing to make payment.

Lehman sued Non-Ferrous and Minmetal in New York, asserting breach of contract claims against Non-Ferrous under their FX agreements and against Minmetal under its alleged guarantee. Non-Ferrous and Minmetal defended on multiple grounds, including that the FX contracts were illegal under Chinese law (and unauthorized); they also asserted counterclaims for fraud and breach of fiduciary duties. The defendants moved for summary judgment on their illegality defenses. Lehman responded by relying on a choice-of-law clause in the FX contract between it and Non-Ferrous, providing that the contract was governed by New York law and a similar choice-of-law clause in the guarantee with Minmetal, providing that Delaware law governed the guarantee.]

Although New York has traditionally followed common-law principles in its approach to contractual choice-of-law clauses, it now requires, by statute, that courts enforce the parties' selection of New York law in commercial contracts of $250,000 or more. *See* N.Y. Gen. Oblig. Law §5-1401. . . . Under traditional New York choice-of-law rules, courts looked to common-law principles to determine the law governing a contract, even for a contract containing a choice-of-law clause. Common-law principles limit the effect of a choice-of-law clause where (1) there is no reasonable basis for the parties' choice, or (2) the application of the chosen law would violate a fundamental public policy of another, more-interested jurisdiction. *See Restatement (Second) Conflict of Laws* §187(2).

In 1984, New York modified its common-law approach to choice-of-law clauses and embraced party autonomy by enacting General Obligation Law §5-1401. By doing so, New York sought to secure and augment its reputation as a center of international commerce. Section 5-1401 states that for commercial contracts of at least $250,000, the parties' selection of New York law in the contract is enforceable even if the transaction itself bears no reasonable relation to New York. Despite the apparently broad sweep of §5-1401 the Defendants argue that the statute's effect remains limited by the public-policy principle reported in §187(2) of the *Restatement*. . . .

This proposition that *Restatement* §187(2) limits the effect of §5-1401 was flatly rejected in *Supply & Building Co. v. Estee Lauder International, Inc.*, 2000 WL 223838 (S.D.N.Y. 2000). In *Supply & Building*, Judge Casey stated that "Section 5-1401 is a broad choice of law provision clearly written to leave no doubt that New York substantive law applies when it is provided for in certain contracts." . . . Therefore, because the statute clearly does not include an exception for violations of another jurisdiction's public policy, the court rejected that proposed limitation.

This Court agrees that §5-1401 is not limited by Restatement §187(2)(b). Section 5-1401 is clear on its face, and thus there is no need to look beyond its own provisions to resolve any ambiguity in its meaning. . . . Nevertheless, §5-1401 itself is not without its limits. Although the statute supersedes common-law conflicts principles, it must still remain within constitutional bounds. A court's power to apply its own state's law in a case that affects another U.S. state is limited by both due process and the Full Faith and Credit Clause. *See Allstate Ins. Co. v. Hague, supra.* However, the Supreme Court has indicated that the key inquiry ultimately is whether a court's application of its own state's law is arbitrary or fundamentally unfair. Under this analysis, a court's power to apply its own state's law might be virtually unlimited when done pursuant to the parties' own contractual choice. It remains to be seen, however, whether a state with *no* connection to either the parties or the transactions could apply its own law, consonant with the Full Faith and Credit Clause, when doing so would violate an important public policy of a more-interested state.

The constitutional limits are less clear, but perhaps more controversial, when a state applies its own law to transactions that affect foreign nations. Commentators have surmised that the constitutional limits in those situations are derived from the concept of comity. Comity, essentially, refers to the deference one nation shows to the laws of another nation, "having due regard both to international duty and convenience and to the rights of its own citizens or of other persons who are under the protections of its laws." *See Black's Law Dictionary* (6th ed. 1990). The connection between comity and constitutional obligation is not clearly defined, since the comity concept itself lies somewhere in between an absolute international obligation and a mere courtesy.

The Defendants have not raised any constitutional restrictions upon this Court's ability to enforce the parties' selection of New York law in the contract, as required by §5-1401. Instead, the Defendants stress China's public-policy interest in regulating its foreign exchange. They explain, with the zeal of the newly-converted, the importance of China's licensing requirements to protecting that interest. They therefore urge this Court to respect that policy and to set aside, pursuant to *Restatement* principles, the selection of New York law in Non-Ferrous' agreement with Lehman.

Although the public policy behind China's licensing requirements is no doubt strong, §5-1401 implicates other policies that are vitally important not only to contracting parties but also to New York and to the international community. The Supreme Court has signaled its support for choice-of-law clauses in international contracts because of their importance to international commerce. *See Scherk v. Alberto-Culver Co., supra.* . . . The *Scherk* Court's emphasis on the need to ensure "orderliness and predictability" in international commerce has been echoed by the Ninth Circuit. *See Northrop Corp. v. Triad Int'l Mktg., SA,* 811 F.2d 1265 (9th Cir. 1987). In *Northrop,* a case analogous to this one, the plaintiff agreed to be the defendant's exclusive marketer of military aircraft to Saudi Arabia's air force in return for commissions on all sales. Following a subsequent Saudi decree that prohibited the payment of commissions on arms sales, the defendant refused to pay the commissions it owed the plaintiff under the agreement. Although the parties in *Northrop* had originally selected California law in their contract, the defendant argued, pursuant to *Restatement* §187(2)(b), that an application of California law would violate the Saudi public policy prohibiting commissions on arms sales. The court upheld the parties' original selection of California law, holding that because of the interest stated in *Scherk,* choice-of-law clauses in international contracts "should be enforced absent strong reasons to set them aside."

This Court need not choose from among these various interests, for the New York State Legislature has already done so by enacting §5-1401. This Court, therefore, need only follow §5-1401 and enforce the parties' contractual selection of New York law, absent any constitutional restrictions on that enforcement. As previously noted, the Defendants have not apprised the Court of any such restrictions, nor are any such restrictions apparent in this case. . . .

The fact that New York law governs the parties' contract does not necessarily mean that the contract is enforceable; New York law does not ignore an illegality in China. A contract that is illegal in its place of performance is unenforceable in New York if the parties entered into the contract with a view to violate the laws of that other jurisdiction. *See Rutkin v. Reinfeld,* 229 F.2d 248, 255-56 (2d Cir. 1956). Therefore, even if Lehman's contracts with Non-Ferrous could have been legally performed in New York, they are not enforceable under New York law if Lehman knew that they were illegal under Chinese law or was deliberately ignorant of that fact. *See Rutkin, supra; cf. Restatement (Second) Conflict of Laws* §202 comment c. . . .

The Defendants argue that Lehman entered into the FX and swap contracts with Non-Ferrous with a view to violate Chinese law. [The Court considered detailed evidence on Chinese law and concluded that because "Non-Ferrous entered into [specified] types of transactions without the proper governmental authorization, its agreements with LBCC and LBSF violated this Chinese regulatory scheme and were illegal under Chinese law," but that it could not determine on summary judgment "whether Lehman entered the agreements with a view to violate Chinese law is an issue of fact for trial."] . . .

[The Court next considered Lehman's third claim, that Minmetal breached an agreement to guarantee Non-Ferrous' FX obligations to Lehman (the "Guarantee").] The Defendants move for summary judgment on this claim, arguing, *inter alia,* that Lehman cannot enforce the Guarantee because it was illegal under Chinese law. Lehman responds as it did before with respect to the FX and swap agreements: that any Chinese illegality is irrelevant because the parties selected Delaware law as the governing law of the contract. Unlike before, however, this Court finds that Chinese law governs the Guarantee, thus rendering it illegal and unenforceable. . . . [A]s noted previously, . . . this Court ruled that the selection of New York law was enforceable pursuant to §5-1401. In the Guarantee, however, the parties selected Delaware law as the governing law. Because that choice-of-law selection is not governed by §5-1401, this Court must evaluate that selection pursuant to New York's traditional common-law approach.

Common-law choice-of-law principles generally follow the concept of party autonomy and adhere to contractual choice-of-law provisions. However, the *Restatement* reports that a contractual choice-of-law provision is invalid under the common-law in either of the following situations: (1) where there is no reasonable basis for the parties' choice, or (2) where the application of the chosen law would violate a fundamental public policy of another, more-interested jurisdiction. *See Restatement (Second) Conflict of Laws* §187(2).

The Court finds that enforcement of the choice-of-law provision in the Guarantee would violate a fundamental public policy of China. The Guarantee itself is illegal under Chinese law. Chinese law requires that a state-owned company, such as Minmetal, obtain SAEC approval before entering into any agreement that guarantees debts of foreign currency. Chinese law further requires that such a company register the approved guarantee agreement with the SAEC in return for a Foreign Exchange Guarantee Registration Certificate. State-owned companies undertaking such obligations "must strictly follow" these regulations. China enacted these provisions pursuant to its public policy of strictly regulating its own currency markets as well as the extent to which Chinese companies become indebted in foreign currencies. This public policy plays a fundamental role in China's transition from a command economy to a more market-oriented economy. . . .

This Court also finds that China is a more interested jurisdiction than Delaware with respect to the Guarantee. Virtually all of the significant activity in the underlying FX agreement occurred in China: Lehman went to China to solicit Hu's business;[242] Hu executed the agreements in question in China; Hu placed all of his trades from China; and Lehman regularly called Hu in China to discuss his trading activity and to make recommendations to him. Moreover, Hu executed the Guarantee itself in China, ostensibly to bind his Chinese parent company to Non-Ferrous' trading losses. Delaware, in contrast, has virtually no contacts to this dispute, except for the parties' contractual selection of Delaware law in the Guarantee. LBCC is incorporated in Delaware. LBCC, however, is merely a booking vehicle for Lehman's FX transactions and has no offices or employees of its own. These Delaware contacts are not as significant as China's, and Lehman has not attempted to argue otherwise.

This Court therefore finds that because the choice-of-law provision in the Guarantee violates a fundamental public policy of a more-interested jurisdiction, namely, China, it is invalid under the common-law principles that guide New York's choice-of-law rules. Where there is no valid contractual choice-of-law provision, the common law looks to the law of the jurisdiction with the most significant contacts to the transaction, with particular emphasis on where the contract was negotiated and where it was performed. *See Restatement (Second) Conflict of Laws* §188. . . .

Lehman argues only that New York has more significant contacts to this dispute. Lehman maintained Non-Ferrous' FX account in a New York bank, some money involved in the dispute was transferred into and out of that account, and Non-Ferrous' account statements and confirmations were sent from New York. The vast majority of the trades, however, were executed from Lehman's offices in London and Hong Kong; very few were executed by Lehman's New York office. New York's contacts do not outweigh the contacts China has to the dispute. While it can be debated whether the underlying FX contract was primarily performed in New York, China, or the United Kingdom, this Court finds that the solicitation and negotiation of the FX agreement occurred primarily in China. Moreover, the Guarantee itself was executed by Hu in China. The Court rules, therefore, that Chinese law governs the Guarantee agreement.

Under Chinese law, illegal guarantee agreements such as this one are unenforceable. Contracts that are found to violate the laws of China are invalid, and void *ab initio*. Nevertheless, Chinese law provides a remedy for a party to an illegal contract if the invalidity was due to the fault of the other party to the agreement. Where both parties are at fault, neither party is entitled to a remedy. The issue, therefore, is whether Minmetal, Lehman, or both were at fault under Chinese law in entering the Guarantee agreement. [The Court directed further submissions to decide whether or not Minmetal or Lehman were "at fault" in relation to the Guarantee.]

Notes *on* Second Restatement, Bremen, Richards, *and* Minmetal

1. *Distinction between interpretation, construction, and validity.* Comment a to §204 draws distinctions between: (a) interpretation of a contract; (b) construction of a contract; and (c) validity of a contract.

---

242. This solicitation is an important factor in deciding the forum with the most significant interest. *See Walpex Trading Co. v. Yacimientos Petroliferos Fiscales Bolivianos,* 756 F. Supp. 136, 141 (S.D.N.Y. 1991).

(a) Interpretation of contract not subject to choice-of-law analysis. When a court interprets a contract, it simply looks to the parties' likely intentions. According to the *Second Restatement,* this is not a process requiring the application of legal rules (other than evidentiary rules, which are provided by the forum's procedural law), or the application of choice-of-law rules. It is merely a process of attempting to ascertain what the parties intended.

(b) Construction of contract subject to §§187 and 188. Section 204 distinguishes rules of construction from mere interpretation. If a court cannot satisfactorily ascertain the meaning of a contract by interpreting it, then it must apply the rules of construction of a particular state. Section 204 requires application of the same basic choice-of-law rules as those provided for in §§187 and 188 for determining the rights and duties of parties to a contract. Is this a sensible approach? Aren't rules of construction merely ways of ascertaining the parties' intent? Why shouldn't the forum apply its own, familiar rules to this delicate task?

(c) Validity of contract subject to §§187 and 188. The validity of a contract, as well as issues relating to capacity, performance, and the existence and extent of contractual duties, are issues of law governed principally by §§187 and 188. There was once doubt that the parties could agree upon the law governing the issue of validity, *see Siegelman v. Cunard White Star Ltd.,* 221 F.2d 189 (2d Cir. 1955) ("much doubt"). This doubt has been largely dispelled. *A.S. Rampell, Inc. v. Hyster Co.,* 165 N.Y.S.2d 475 (1957); Weintraub, *Choice of Law in Contract,* 54 Iowa L. Rev. 399, 407 (1968); *supra* pp. 752-759.

2. Basis for traditional rule that choice-of-law clauses are unenforceable. Why is it that private parties should be permitted to select the law that governs their contractual relations? Consider the following remarks by Joseph Beale:

> The fundamental objection . . . is that it involves permission to the parties to do a legislative act. It practically makes a legislative body of any two persons who choose to get together and contract. . . . The meaning of the suggestion, in short, is that since the parties can adopt any foreign law at their pleasure to govern their act, that at their will they can free themselves from the power of the law which would otherwise apply to their acts. So extraordinary a power in the hands of any two individuals is absolutely anomalous. J. Beale, *Treatise on the Conflict of Laws* 1079-1080 (1935).

Is that persuasive? Do parties really "legislate" when they agree on the law to govern certain of their relations with one another?

3. Historic authorities permitting enforcement of choice-of-law clauses. Beale did not express the only traditional view regarding the enforceability of choice-of-law agreements. In *Pritchard v. Norton,* 106 U.S. 124, 136 (1882), the Supreme Court applied Louisiana law to determine the validity of an indemnity bond that had been executed in Louisiana. Under New York law, the bond would have been invalid, for lack of consideration, but under Louisiana law no consideration was required. The Court applied Louisiana law, invoking the "principle that in every forum a contract is governed by the law with a view to which it is made." Other courts upheld express choice of law clauses. *See supra* pp. 758-759.

4. Basis for rule that choice-of-law agreements are enforceable. What is the rationale for enforcing choice-of-law agreements? Is Beale not correct in his observation that choice-of-law agreements are different from other contractual commitments? Consider the following explanation:

> Prime objectives of contract law are to protect the justified expectations of the parties and to make it possible for them to foretell with accuracy what will be their rights under the contract. These objectives may best be attained in multistate transactions by letting the parties choose

the law to govern the validity of the contract and the rights created thereby. In this way, certainty and predictability of result are most likely to be secured. . . . An objection sometimes made in the past was that to give the parties this power of choice would be tantamount to making legislators of them. . . . This view is now obsolete and, in any event, falls wide of the mark. The forum in each case selects the applicable law by application of its own choice-of-law rules. There is nothing to prevent the forum from employing a choice-of-law rule which provides that, subject to stated exceptions, the law of the state chosen by the parties shall be applied to determine the validity of a contract and the rights created thereby. The law of the state chosen by the parties is applied, not because the parties themselves are legislators, but simply because this is the result demanded by the choice-of-law rules of the forum. *Restatement (Second) Conflict of Laws* §187 comment e (1971).

Is this persuasive? Does this not invite sophisticated parties to shop for the most favorable law on the law market and, thereby, evade important regulatory restrictions on their conduct? *See* E. O'Hara & L. Ribstein, *The Law Market* (Oxford 2009). Worse yet, does it not permit particularly powerful companies to lobby lawmakers in a particular country to shape that country's law in a manner favorable to the companies, and, then, subject their relations to that country's law? Suppose, for example, that a U.S.-based international company which provided security services around the world employed the following choice-of-law clause in its employment contracts: "This contract shall be governed by and interpreted under the laws of the Dubai Internet City in the Dubai Technology, Electronic Commerce and Media Free Zone." If one of the company's employees, also a U.S. citizen, is injured while working in Afghanistan, would the employee's claims be subject to the laws of a free trade zone in Dubai? Should they be? *See Deuley v. DynCorp. Int'l, Inc.*, 2010 WL 4970769 (D. Del. Dec. 8, 2010).

5. *Enforceability of choice-of-law clauses under interest analysis.* How do choice-of-law clauses fare under Currie's interest analysis? Consider: "[P]arty autonomy squares no better with interest analysis. If, as that methodology asserts, an important goal of choice of law is to assess the impact of competing choices on governmental duties such as paying welfare and regulating insurance rates within the state, it is doubtful that the parties' private expression of the preferences should be given much weight." Borchers, *Choice of Law in the American Courts in 1992: Observations and Reflections*, 42 Am. J. Comp. L. 125, 134 (1994). Despite this, most states that have adopted Currie's interest analysis presumptively enforce choice-of-law clauses in practice. *E.g., ABF Capital Corp. v. Osley,* 414 F.3d 1061, 1065 (9th Cir. 2005); *Washington Mutual Bank, FA v. Superior Court,* 15 P.3d 1071, 1078-1079 (Cal. 2001); *Lambert v. Kysar,* 983 F.2d 1110, 1118 (1st Cir. 1993); *NedLloyd Lines BV v. Superior Court,* 834 P.2d 1148 (Cal. 1992); *Comdisco Disaster Recovery Services, Inc. v. Money Mgmt. Systems, Inc.,* 789 F. Supp. 48 (D. Mass. 1992).

6. *Standards of enforceability of choice-of-law clauses.* As with forum selection clauses, there are a variety of standards governing the enforceability of choice-of-law clauses in U.S. courts.

(a) Second Restatement §187. What standard for the enforceability of choice-of-law clauses is set forth in §187? Consider how this standard is applied in *Minmetal.* What is the purpose of the *Restatement (Second)* standard? Is this wise?

(b) N.Y. General Obligations Law §5-1401. Compare the standard for enforcing choice-of-law clauses set forth in N.Y. General Obligations Law §5-1401. Note that §5-1401 provides for substantially greater certainty as compared to the *Second Restatement.* Is this wise? What is the scope of application of §5-1401? Consider how this provision was applied in *Minmetal.* For commentary on §5-1401, *see* Ingrim, *Choice-of-Law Clauses: Their Effect on Extraterritorial Analysis—A Scholar's Dream, A Practitioner's Nightmare,* 28 Creighton L.

Rev. 663 (1995); Rashkover, Note, *Title 14, New York Choice of Law Rule for Contractual Disputes: Avoiding the Unreasonable Results*, 71 Cornell L. Rev. 227 (1985); Friedler, *Party Autonomy Revisited: A Statutory Solution to a Choice-of-Law Problem*, 37 Kan. L. Rev. 471 (1989).

(c) Other approaches. Some authorities have adopted less clear-cut rules to the enforceability of choice-of-law provisions, treating them as one factor in a general "center of gravity" or "grouping of contacts" analysis. *E.g., Haag v. Barnes*, 216 N.Y.S.2d 65 (1961). Compare this approach to some decisions concerning the enforceability of forum selection clauses, which hold that the existence of such a clause is merely one factor in a more generalized *forum non conveniens* or "reasonableness" analysis. *See supra* pp. 509-510. Compare this approach to the *Restatement (Second)* and §5-1401. Which of these standards is wiser?

7. Defects in formation of choice-of-law agreement. Choice-of-law agreements, like other agreements, can be defective. Reasons include unconscionability, fraud, illegality, mistake, or lack of consideration. *Restatement (Second) Conflict of Laws* §187 comment b (1971) ("A choice-of-law provision, like any other contractual provision, will not be given effect if the consent of one of the parties to its inclusion in the contract was obtained by improper means, such as by misrepresentation, duress, or undue influence, or by mistake"); *Modern Computer Systems, Inc. v. Modern Banking Systems, Inc.*, 858 F.2d 1339 (8th Cir. 1988). What law should determine whether a choice-of-law clause is invalid? The *Second Restatement* provides that such issues "will be determined by the forum in accordance with its own legal principles." *Restatement (Second) Conflict of Laws* §187 comment b (1971). Why? Why not apply the parties' chosen law? Or the law of the state with the most significant relationship?

8. Separability of choice-of-law agreement. Should choice-of-law clauses be regarded as "separable," as with arbitration and forum selection agreements? *See supra* p. 492 & *infra* p. 1167. What would be the consequences of such a result?

9. Enforceability of contracts where the parties' chosen law invalidates the contract. Suppose that the parties' choice-of-law clause selects a substantive law that invalidates the parties' basic contract. Should the parties' chosen law be applied to nullify the parties' contract? The *Second Restatement* answers in the negative:

> To do so would defeat the expectations of the parties which it is the purpose of the present rule to protect. The parties can be assumed to have intended that the provisions of the contract would be binding upon them. If the parties have chosen a law that would invalidate the contract, it can be assumed that they did so by mistake. If, however, the chosen law is that of the state of the otherwise applicable law under [generally applicable conflict of laws principles in §188], this law will be applied even when it invalidates the contract. *Restatement (Second) Conflict of Laws* §187 comment e (1971).

Is this persuasive? *See Milanovich v. Costa Crociere, SpA*, 954 F.2d 763, 768-769 (D.C. Cir. 1992); *Pisacane v. Italia Societa Per Azione Di Navigazione*, 219 F. Supp. 424 (S.D.N.Y. 1963) (applying chosen Italian law, where Italy was also "center of gravity" of the contract, to find contractual provision presumptively invalid); *Atlas Subsidiaries, Inc. v. O & O, Inc.*, 166 So. 2d 458 (Fla. Dist. Ct. App. 1964) (applying chosen law, where almost all contacts were with that state, to invalidate contractual interest provisions). For a thorough discussion of the issue, *see* Symeonides, *Choice of Law in the American Courts in 2008: Twenty-Second Annual Survey*, 57 Am. J. Comp. L. 269, 303-304 (2009).

10. Forum's public policy as ground for denying enforcement of choice-of-law agreement — Bremen. Section 187(2)(b) provides that a choice-of-law clause will not be given effect if the chosen law "would be contrary to a fundamental policy of a state which has a materially greater interest than the chosen state." This exception parallels public policy exceptions in other contexts. *See supra* pp. 443, 520-523 & *infra* pp. 1133-1146. Compare the analysis in *Bremen,* where a forum selection clause was unsuccessfully challenged on the grounds that it would result in application of English substantive law that violated U.S. public policies. Suppose that *Bremen* had involved an English choice-of-law, rather than a choice-of-forum, clause. How would the case have been decided by a U.S. court? Under §187(2)? Would English law have been applied to determine the validity of the exculpatory clauses in the towage contract?

11. *Forum's public policy as ground for denying enforcement of choice-of-law agreement—* Richards. Reread *Richards,* which involved enforcement of forum selection and choice-of-law clauses. Is the court's decision — permitting the exclusion of U.S. securities laws by means of an English choice-of-law clause — correct?

Do claims under the securities laws raise questions of "public policy"? Why are they different from tort or contract claims? Would *Richards* have been decided the same way if it had only involved a choice-of-law clause (and not a choice-of-forum agreement)? Recall the language excerpted above from footnote 19 of *Mitsubishi Motors Corp. v. Soler Chrysler-Plymouth, Inc.,* 473 U.S. 614 (1985), indicating that the Court would not enforce "a prospective waiver of a party's right to pursue statutory remedies for antitrust violations." *See supra* pp. 517-518.

For a case relying on this language to invalidate a provision of a contract mandating arbitration in the Philippines under Panamanian law (with the effect of depriving a maritime employee of his potential remedies under federal law), *see Thomas v. Carnival Corp.,* 573 F.3d 1109 (11th Cir. 2009). How does this decision square with *Richards*? Is the key fact that the parties to an employment contract, as opposed to commercially sophisticated parties, do not have equal bargaining power? *Compare Cooper v. Meridian Yachts, Ltd.,* 575 F.3d 1151 (11th Cir. 2009) (upholding Dutch choice-of-law clause in shipbuilding contract); *Ambraco, Inc. v. Bosselip B.V.,* 570 F.3d 233 (5th Cir. 2009) (upholding English choice-of-law clause in carriage contract); *APL Co. Pte. Ltd. v. UK Aerosola Ltd.,* 582 F.3d 947 (9th Cir. 2009) (upholding Singapore choice-of-law clause in bill of lading).

12. *Forum's public policy as ground for denying enforcement of choice-of-law agreement— hypotheticals.* What sorts of forum public policies should be capable of rendering a choice of foreign law unenforceable? Consider:

- In *Bremen,* the accident had occurred within U.S. territorial waters, at the beginning of the oil rig's voyage to the Adriatic Sea.
- In an action in U.S. courts, arising out of a U.S. employer's termination of an employment contract, for alleged malfeasance by the employee, the employee brings claims for wrongful termination and libel (based upon the employer's public statements that the employee had engaged in wrongful conduct). The employment contract contains a choice-of-law clause selecting English law, which would permit recovery on libel claims on significantly more liberal basis than the First Amendment would permit. Assume that the employee works (a) solely in the U.S.; (b) solely in England; (c) partially in both the U.S. and England; and (d) solely in France.
- In the foregoing employment dispute, the employee asserts race discrimination claims under Title VII — the federal employment discrimination statute. Assume the same workplaces.
- In *Richards,* suppose that the relevant agreements had been signed in the United States, rather than England.
- A U.S. company licenses its technology to a French company, in an agreement that selects French law and imposes restrictive conditions on competition by the French

company. The conditions violate New York state unfair competition laws and federal antitrust law. In an action in U.S. courts, the French company seeks to invalidate the restrictive conditions under New York and U.S. law. The license territory is: (a) the entire world; (b) Europe; (c) the U.S.; (d) France and New York.

- A U.S. manufacturer of consumer goods (such as cellular phones) includes in its standard customer agreement a choice-of-law clause and a clause prospectively waiving the right to bring a class action. If both are enforceable, individual consumers who may have claims under consumer fraud or other statutes will only have very nominal damages claims and will not have a meaningful incentive to file a suit challenging allegedly unlawful business practices.

13. Erie *issues in enforcing choice-of-law clauses.* What law governs the enforceability of choice-of-law clauses? As discussed below, the Supreme Court has long held that choice-of-law rules are generally provided by state law (for *Erie* purposes). *See infra* pp. 791-796. Is there any reason that the enforceability of choice-of-law agreements would raise different issues? Recall the discussion of *Erie* issues in the context of forum selection agreements. *See supra* pp. 528-544. Is there any basis for a rule of federal common law governing the enforceability of choice-of-law agreements in international cases? Can choice-of-law clauses, like forum selection agreement, be regarded as issues of federal procedural law?

14. *Conspicuous notice requirements for choice-of-law clauses.* Some states require that choice-of-law provisions be "conspicuous." Consider:

> If a contract to which this section applies contains a provision making the contract or any conflict arising under the contract subject to the laws of another state, to litigation in the courts of another state, or to arbitration in another state, the provision must be set out boldfaced print. If the provision is not set conspicuously in print, type, or other form of writing that is bold-faced, capitalized, underlined, or otherwise set out in such a manner that a reasonable person against whom the provision may operate would notice. If the provision is not set out as provided in this subsection, the provision is voidable by a party against whom it is sought to be enforced. Tex. Bus. & Comm. Code Ann. §35.53(b) §§35.53 to 35.591, repealed by Acts 2007, 80th Leg., ch. 885, §2.47(a)(1), eff. Apr. 1, 2009.

Is this provision wise? Is it constitutional? Note that it only applies to the selection of non-Texas law. *See also Merriman v. Convergent Business Systems, Inc.,* 1993 U.S. Dist. LEXIS 10528 (N.D. Fla. 1993) (refusing to apply Texas "conspicuous notice" requirement for choice-of-law clauses).

15. *Foreign public policy as ground for denying enforcement of choice-of-law agreement.* Consider how §187 deals with the possible application of foreign public policies to deny enforcement of a forum selection clause. Was it appropriate in *Minmetal* for the court to decline to enforce the parties' Delaware choice-of-law clause in the Minmetal Guarantee? Why or why not? What exactly did Minmetal need to show to invalidate the choice-of-law clause? How does one demonstrate either a foreign public policy or the existence of a state with a material "greater interest"? Is it appropriate, in an international case where a U.S. national is in dispute with a foreigner, to treat "Delaware" interests is wholly unrelated to "New York" interests?

Contrast the analysis under *Restatement (Second)* §187 with that under N.Y. General Obligations Law §5-1401. Which is the wiser approach, from a policy perspective? Does N.Y. General Obligations Law §5-1401 show inadequate deference to foreign sovereign interests? Could there be instances in which the provision produces results that conflict with federal interests?

Suppose that parties agree on the law of a U.S. state to govern their contract in order to avoid the effect of particular foreign laws? Why should such choice-of-law agreements not be enforced? Suppose that a U.S. company bargains for a U.S. choice-of-law clause specifically to avoid the risk of subsequently enacted foreign legislation that would benefit its contracting partner (*e.g.,* expropriatory regulations benefiting a foreign state entity; provisions entitling foreign licensees or distributors to certain benefits). Why should a U.S. court reject application of the choice-of-law clause, to the detriment of the U.S. company?

16. *"Choice of public policy" problems.* Note that both *Bremen* and *Minmetal* involve a kind of choice-of-law analysis, but that the "laws" that are involved are public policies. Why is it, again, that the U.S. public policy against exculpatory clauses was not applied in *Bremen*? Note the Court's emphasis on the place where the accident occurred. Compare this rationale to (a) §145 of the *Second Restatement;* (b) Currie's interest analysis; and (c) §187(2)(b)'s choice-of-law rules. How should the *Bremen* "choice of public policy" analysis have been resolved under each of these more contemporary methods of choice-of-law analysis? *See Daniel Indus., Inc. v. Barber-Colman Co.,* 1993 U.S. App. LEXIS 24248 (9th Cir. 1993) (refusing under §187 to apply California public policy (requiring reciprocity in contractual attorneys' fee provisions) to override parties' Texas choice-of-law agreement, on grounds that California did not have a "materially greater interest" in the issue).

Consider how the "choice of public policy" analysis was conducted in *Minmetal*. Suppose that New York had not enacted §5-1401 and that the *Second Restatement*'s §187(2)(b) standard had been applied to the underlying Lehman/Non-Ferrous contract to determine whether China had a materially greater interest in the transaction than New York. How should that issue be resolved?

17. *"Reasonable relationship" requirement as ground for denying enforcement of choice-of-law agreement.* Some contemporary authorities permit the enforcement of choice-of-law clauses only if they select a law that has some reasonable relationship to the parties or their transaction. For example, as discussed above, §187(2)(a) of the *Second Restatement* requires a "substantial relationship" between the chosen state and the parties or the transaction. Similarly, the 1995 and 2008 versions of the Uniform Commercial Code required a "reasonable relationship" between the parties' transaction and their chosen law. *See supra* pp. 759-760.

What is the purpose of this "reasonable relationship" requirement? Why should the parties not be free to subject their agreement to whatever law they think best suits their purposes? Note that London was selected as the contractual forum in *Bremen* precisely because it was neutral — not associated with either party or any aspect of the transaction. Also as in *Bremen,* parties frequently agree to a similarly "neutral" governing law; they often choose a jurisdiction with developed commercial laws (like England, Switzerland, or New York). Should such choices be invalid because they lack a reasonable relationship to the parties' agreement? Consider:

> The parties to a multistate contract may have a reasonable basis for choosing a state with which the contract has no substantial relationship. For example, when contracting in countries whose legal systems are strange to them as well as relatively immature, the parties should be able to choose a law on the ground that they know it well and that it is sufficiently developed. For only in this way can they be sure of knowing accurately the extent of their rights and duties under the contract. *Restatement (Second) Conflict of Laws* §187 comment f (1971).

Is this persuasive? What choice-of-law clauses does this rationale protect? Suppose (a) U.S. and Mexican parties doing business in Mexico agree to English law; (b) New York and Florida parties doing business in the U.S. agree to Mexican law; (c) New York parties doing business in New York agree to Swiss law. *See Prows v. Pinpoint Retails Systems, Inc.,* 868 P.2d 809 (Utah 1994) (refusing to enforce New York choice-of-law clause under §187 because "Utah is the only state with an interest in the action").

Note that §5-1401 omits any reasonable relationship requirement. Is that wise? Why? What is the purpose of the requirement? Consider how *Minmetal* treats a lack of reasonable relation as a possible constitutional defect. *See supra* pp. 763-767. Is that persuasive?

18. *Geographic limitations.* Suppose that the parties chose the law of State X to govern their transaction which takes place in State Y. A dispute arises where a statute of State X would apply, except that statute contains language expressly precluding its extraterritorial application. Does this language simply limit the regulatory reach of the statute? Does it affirmatively bar parties from opting into that law? Or does it simply influence the proper interpretation of the choice-of-law clause? Lower courts have reached conflicting conclusions on this point. *Compare Grayquick A/S v. Trimble Navigation Int'l Ltd.,* 323 F.3d 1219 (9th Cir. 2003) ("When a law contains geographic limitations on its application . . . courts will not apply it to parties falling outside those limitations, even if the parties stipulate that the law should apply) *with 1-800-Got Junk LLC v. Superior Court,* 115 Cal. Rptr. 3d 923, 937 (Cal. Ct. App. 2010) ("Irrespective of whether [Washington's franchise statute] otherwise contains territorial restrictions on its application, the parties were free to agree that their franchise relations would be governed by Washington substantive law and they did precisely that by way of a valid choice of law clause.").

19. *Interpreting choice-of-law clauses.* Like other contractual agreements, choice-of-law clauses must be interpreted. For the most part, this is a straightforward question of deciding what the parties meant when they used particular language. A few issues are recurrent, however, and courts appear to follow general approaches to construction.

(a) Whole law versus substantive law. Suppose that a choice-of-law clause chooses the "law of state X." Does that mean that the court should apply the substantive law of state X, or the whole law of state X (including its choice-of-law rules)? Consider §187(3), which provides that only the "local law" of the state of the chosen law should be applied, at least absent indication of contrary intention. Is that a likely statement of the parties' intent? *Restatement (Second) Conflict of Laws* §187 comment h (1971) ("To apply the 'law' of the chosen state would introduce the uncertainties of choice of law into the proceedings and would serve to defeat the basic objectives, namely those of certainty and predictability, which the choice-of-law provision was designed to achieve.").

(b) Substantive versus procedural law. Suppose that the parties choose the "law of state X" to govern all disputes arising from their contract. Does that mean that "procedural" or "judicial administration" issues, dealt with by *Second Restatement* §122, are also governed by the law of state X, even if the case is litigated in state Y? Note that §187 only applies to the law chosen by the parties "to govern their contractual rights and duties." Does this include procedural issues — such as burdens of proof, form of pleadings, evidentiary rules, mode of trial, and statutes of limitations? While lower courts have reached conflicting conclusions, the predominant view is that they do not. *E.g., FDIC v. Wabick,* 335 F.3d 620, 627 (7th Cir. 2003) (choice-of-law clause does not reach statute of limitations); *Trillium USA, Inc. v. Board of County Commissioners of Broward County, Fla.,* 37 P.3d 1093, 1097 & n.2 (Utah 2001) (same, although express choice-of-law clause might reach statute of limitations); *Phelps v. McClellan,* 30 F.3d 658, 662 (6th Cir. 1994) (same rule as *Trillium USA*); *Ekstrom v. Value Health, Inc.,* 68 F.3d 1391, 1395 (D.C. Cir. 1995) (finding limitations period substantive under applicable law); *JKL Components Corp. v. Insul-Reps,*

Inc., 596 N.E.2d 945, 950 (Ind. App. 1992) (choice-of-law clause governs only substantive, not procedural matters); *Gambar Enterprises, Inc. v. Kelly Services Inc.*, 418 N.Y.S.2d 818 (App. Div. 1979) (same); *Cardon v. Cotton Lane Holdings, Inc.*, 841 P.2d 198 (Ariz. 1992) (same); *FDIC v. Petersen*, 770 F.2d 141, 142 (10th Cir. 1985) (same). *But see Hatfield v. Halifax PLC*, 564 F.3d 1177 (9th Cir. 2009) (holding that English choice-of-law clause incorporated English statute of limitations which provided for longer limitations period than comparable statute in forum state).

(c) Applicability of choice-of-law clause to noncontractual claims. Suppose that the parties agree to a choice-of-law clause that extends to "all claims relating to this contract," and that one party asserts a tort claim that is intertwined with the contract. Does the choice-of-law clause reach this claim? Lower courts have generally concluded that there is no *per se* public policy against application of choice-of-law clauses to noncontractual claims. *See Hatfield v. Halifax PLC*, 564 F.3d 1177 (9th Cir. 2009); *Yavuz v. 61 MM, Ltd.*, 576 F.3d 1166 (10th Cir. 2009); *Turtur v. Rothschild Registry Int'l, Inc.*, 26 F.3d 304 (2d Cir. 1994); *Roby v. Corporation of Lloyd's*, 996 F.2d 1353 (2d Cir. 1993). Whether or not a choice-of-law clause reaches a particular tort claim is a matter of interpretation; *Cooper v. Meridian Yachts, Ltd.*, 575 F.3d 1151 (11th Cir. 2009); *Fin. One. Pub. Co. Ltd. v. Lehman Bros. Special Financing, Inc.*, 414 F.3d 325 (2d Cir. 2005); *Jiffy Lube Int'l, Inc. v. Jiffy Lube of Penn.*, 848 F. Supp. 569 (E.D. Pa. 1994) ("contractual choice of law provisions . . . do not govern tort claims between contracting parties unless the fair import of the provision embraces all aspects of the legal relationship"); *Knieriemen v. Bache Halsey Stuart Shields*, 427 N.Y.S.2d 10 (App. Div. 1980) ("This contract shall be governed by the laws of . . . New York" held not applicable to tort claims); *Fustok v. Conticommodity Services, Inc.*, 618 F. Supp. 1082 (S.D.N.Y. 1985) ("This agreement and its enforcement shall be governed by the laws of the State of Illinois" held not applicable to tort claims); *Merriman v. Convergent Business Systems, Inc.*, 1993 U.S. Dist. LEXIS 10528 (N.D. Fla. 1993) ("choice of law provisions in contracts generally will not control the applicable law for tort claims between the contracting parties"). It is not clear whether the forum's rule of construction, or those of the parties' chosen law, should apply to construing the scope of a choice-of-law clause. *NedLloyd Lines BV v. Superior Court*, 834 P.2d 1148 (Cal. 1992).

(d) Choice-of-law clauses versus incorporation (or stabilization) clauses. When parties specify that the law of state [x] shall apply to their contract, do they incorporate the law as it exists at the time the contract becomes executed? Or do they also subject their relationships to changes in the chosen law that postdate the contract's execution? Both forms are possible, and the correct answer often requires a close reading of the choice-of-law clause (as well as an awareness of how the applicable conflicts principles will treat that clause). *See* Symeonides, *Choice of Law in American Courts in 2010: Twenty-Fourth Annual Survey*, 59 Am. J. Comp. L. 303 (forthcoming 2011) (describing the difference between "choice of law" clauses and "incorporation clauses").

20. *Determining the content of the chosen law.* Suppose that a court has concluded that a choice-of-law clause is valid and covers the legal issue in question. If the chosen law differs from the law of the jurisdiction in which the judge sits, how is the judge supposed to go about determining the content of that law? (Recall that similar considerations arise in the *forum non conveniens* analysis when determining the adequacy of the alternative forum.) *See supra* at 438-443. Should the judge rely on his own research of the foreign law? *See Sunstar, Inc. v. Alberto-Culver Co.*, 586 F.3d 487 (7th Cir. 2009) (arguing that "articles, treatises, and judicial opinions" are "superior sources" compared to expert declarations submitted the parties). Is this wise in cases where the chosen law is that of a country where the official language is a language other than English? Does this not force the judge to rely on secondary sources or translations that may be outdated, incomplete, or inaccurate?

In such cases, parties will often submit declarations of experts on the designated law. *See* Fed. R. Civ. P. 44.1. The virtue of experts in such matters, as with experts generally, is that they (hopefully) offer the judge an accurate, current perspective on the foreign law that takes into account sources available only in the foreign language (which the expert presumably speaks). To the extent disagreements exist among the parties' experts, those disagreements help to crystallize the key decision points for the judge.

Yet the "banes of expert testimony" are that the experts are "paid for their testimony and selected on the basis of the convergence of their views with the litigating position of the client or their willingness to fall in with the views urged upon them by the client." *Sunstar*, 486 F.3d at 495-496. Presumably, they have been so chosen because the experts' independent judgment accords with the position that the party wishes to advance. But does this not give rise to the risk (or at least the suspicion) that the expert's viewpoint is somehow shaded to advocate a party's position rather than provide the court with an independent judgment designed to assist with the decision?

For a rich recent discussion between several renowned judges on the virtues of independent research versus reliance on party-appointed experts when determining the content of applicable law, *see Boudin USA, Inc. v. La Cafetiere, Inc.*, 621 F.3d 624 (7th Cir. 2010).

21. *The Rome Convention and the Rome I Regulation.* As with tort law, European law provides a useful point of comparison to the foregoing discussion of the enforceability of contractual choice-of-law clauses. Here, the starting point for any analysis is the 1980 Rome Convention on the Law Applicable to Contractual Obligations. [1998] O.J. C 27/34. Subsequently, the European Commission built upon the Rome Convention to articulate a uniform regulation on choice of law in contractual relationships that largely displaces the Rome Convention in Member States of the European Union. *See* Regulation 593/2008 on the Law Applicable to Contractual Obligations, 2008 O.J. (L. 177) 6 (EC) ("Rome I Regulation"). With respect to contracts that fall within their scope, both the Rome Convention and the Rome I Regulation set forth a general rule favoring parties' autonomy to designate the law applicable to their contractual relations. *See* Rome Convention Art. 3(1); Rome I Regulation Art 3(1). Like the Rome II Regulation governing torts, both documents limit the parties' choice of the applicable law to the extent that it conflicts with the "mandatory rules" of a country more closely connected to the contract. *See* Rome Convention Arts. 3(3), 7; Rome I Regulation Arts. 3(3), 9. Both documents also contain limits on party autonomy with respect to certain types of contracts, such as consumer contracts and employment contracts. *See* Rome Convention Arts. 5, 6; Rome I Regulation Arts. 6, 8. Finally, both documents also permit the court of the forum state to refuse to give effect to the choice-of-law clause where doing so would violate the forum state's public policy. *See* Rome Convention Art. 16; Rome I Regulation Art. 21.

How do these rules compare with the above-described rules governing the enforcement of choice-of-law clauses under American law? Is it sensible to carve out separate rules governing consumer and employment contracts? Couldn't a public policy requirement already do the necessary work? What is the difference between the "mandatory rules" exception and the "public policy" exception? Is there a difference between the *Restatement*'s "reasonable relationship" test and the test regarding "mandatory rules" of the state more closely connected with the contract? For further reading on the European law governing contractual choice-of-law clauses, *see* Ferrari & Leible (eds.), *Rome I Regulation: The Law Applicable to Contractual Obligations in Europe* (2009); M. Giuliano & P. LaGarde, *Report on the Convention of the Law Applicable to Contractual Obligations*, 1980 O.J. (C. 282) (commentary on the Rome Convention by the co-rapporteurs).

2. Traditional Approach to Choice of Law Governing Contracts in the Absence of Choice-of-Law Agreement: Territoriality and Vested Rights

As with choice-of-law rules applicable to torts, traditional approaches to the law applicable to contracts rested on doctrines of territorial sovereignty. Joseph Story, following Huber, emphasized the importance of principles of international law in choosing the law applicable to contracts.[243] For Story, this meant a fairly strict application of the law of the "place of contracting" to determine the validity of contracts, as well as a number of other contract-related issues. The *Restatement (First) Conflict of Laws* followed this approach, providing generally that the law of the place of contracting applied to most issues relating to the contract (while also providing a sub-rule that selected the law of the place of performance for certain performance-related issues).[244]

Nevertheless, to a much lesser extent than with torts, principles of territorial sovereignty did not consistently generate a single choice-of-law rule (such as the "place of the wrong"). Rather, a number of U.S. courts and other authorities adopted different choice-of-law rules. These variously looked to the law of the place of contracting,[245] the law of the place of performance,[246] and the law impliedly chosen by the parties.[247]

The materials excerpted below illustrate the historical approaches of U.S. courts to the choice of law applicable to contracts. Sections 332 and 358 of the *Restatement (First) Conflict of Laws* set forth the basic "place of contracting" and "place of performance" rules. The classic decision in *Milliken v. Pratt*, taught in most conflict of laws courses, applied the place of contracting test. The decision in *Louis-Dreyfus v. Paterson Steamship, Ltd.*, illustrates the "place of performance" test.

RESTATEMENT (FIRST) CONFLICT OF LAWS
§§332 & 358 (1934) [excerpted in Appendix X]

MILLIKEN v. PRATT
125 Mass. 374 (1878)

The plaintiffs are partners doing business in Portland, Maine, under the firm name of Deering, Milliken & Co. The defendant is and has been since 1850, the wife of Daniel Pratt, and both have always resided in Massachusetts. In 1870, Daniel, who was then doing business in Massachusetts, applied to the plaintiffs at Portland for credit, and they required of him, as a condition of granting the same, a guaranty from the defendant to the amount of five hundred dollars, and accordingly he procured from his wife the following instrument:

Portland, January 29, 1870. In consideration of one dollar paid by Deering, Milliken & Co., receipt of which is here by acknowledged, I guarantee the payment to them by Daniel Pratt of the sum of five hundred dollars, from time to time as he may want — this to be continuing guaranty. Sarah A. Pratt.

---

243. *See* J. Story, *Commentaries on the Conflict of Laws* (2d ed. 1841).
244. *Restatement (First) Conflict of Laws* §332 (1934).
245. *Restatement (First) Conflict of Laws* §332 (1934) ("The law of the place of contracting determines the validity and effect of a promise. . . .").
246. *Pritchard v. Norton*, 106 U.S. 124 (1882); *Restatement (First) Conflict of Laws* §358 (1934).
247. *Pritchard v. Norton*, 106 U.S. 124 (1882).

This instrument was executed by the defendant two or three days after its date, at her home in Massachusetts, and there delivered by her to her husband, who sent it by mail from Massachusetts to the plaintiffs in Portland; and the plaintiffs received it from the post office in Portland early in February, 1870.

The plaintiffs subsequently sold and delivered goods to Daniel from time to time until October 7, 1871, and charged the same to him, and, if competent, it may be taken to be true, that in so doing they relied upon the guaranty. Between February, 1870, and September 1, 1871, they sold and delivered goods to him on credit to an amount largely exceeding $500, which were fully settled and paid for by him. This action is brought for goods sold from September 1, 1871, to October 7, 1871, inclusive, amounting to $860.12, upon which he paid $300, leaving a balance due of $560.12. The one dollar mentioned in the guaranty was not paid, and the only consideration moving to the defendant therefore was the giving of credit by the plaintiffs to her husband. Some of the goods were selected personally by Daniel at the plaintiff's store in Portland, others were ordered by letters mailed by Daniel from Massachusetts to the plaintiffs at Portland, and all were sent by the plaintiffs, by express from Portland to Daniel in Massachusetts, who paid all express charges. The parties were cognizant of the facts.

By a statute of Maine, duly enacted and approved in 1866, it is enacted that "the contracts of any married woman, made for any lawful purpose, shall be valid and binding, and may be enforced in the same manner as if she were sole." . . . Payment was duly demanded of the defendant before the date of the writ, and was refused by her. The Superior Court ordered judgment for the defendant; and the plaintiffs appealed to this court.

GRAY, C.J. The general rule is that the validity of a contract is to be determined by the law of the state in which it is made; if it is valid there, it is deemed valid everywhere, and will sustain an action in the courts of a state whose laws do not permit such a contract. Even a contract expressly prohibited by the statutes of the state in which the suit is brought, if not in itself immoral, is not necessarily nor usually deemed so invalid that the comity of the state, as administered by its courts, will refuse to entertain an action on such a contract made by one of its own citizens abroad in a state the laws of which permit it.

If the contract is completed in another state, it makes no difference in principle whether the citizen of this state goes in person, or sends an agent, or writes a letter, across the boundary line between the two states. As was said by Lord Lyndhurst, "If I, residing in England, send down my agent to Scotland, and he makes contracts for me there, it is the same as if I myself went there and made them." *Pattison v. Mills,* 1 Dow & Cl. 342, 363. So if a person residing in this state signs and transmits, either by a messenger or through the post office, to a person in another state, a written contract, which requires no special forms or solemnities in its execution, and no signature of the person to whom it is addressed, and is assented to and acted on by him there, the contract is made there, just as if the writer personally took the executed contract into the other state, or wrote and signed it there; and it is no objection to the maintenance of an action thereon here, that such a contract is prohibited by the law of this Commonwealth.

The guaranty, bearing date of Portland, in the State of Maine, was executed by the defendant, a married woman, having her home in this Commonwealth, as collateral security for the liability of her husband for goods sold by the plaintiffs to him, and was sent by her through him by mail to the plaintiffs at Portland. The sales of the goods ordered by him from the plaintiffs at Portland, and there delivered by them to him in person, or to a carrier for him, were made in the State of Maine. The contract between the defendant and the plaintiffs was complete when the guaranty had been received and acted on by them at Portland, and not before. It must therefore be treated as made and to be performed in the State of Maine.

The law of Maine authorized a married woman to bind herself by any contract as if she were unmarried. The law of Massachusetts, as then existing, did not allow her to enter into a contract as surety or for the accommodation of her husband or of any third person. . . . Since the making of the contract sued on, and before the bringing of this action, the law of this Commonwealth has been changed, so as to enable married women to make such contracts. The question therefore is, whether a contact made in another state by a married woman domiciled here, which a married woman was not at the time capable of making under the law of this Commonwealth, but was then allowed by the law of that state to make, and which she could not lawfully make in this Commonwealth, will sustain an action against her in our courts.

It has been often stated by commentators that the law of the domicil, regulating the capacity of a person, accompanies and governs the person everywhere. But this statement, in modern times at least, is subject to many qualifications; and the opinions of foreign jurists upon the subject the principal of which are collected in the treatises of Mr. Justice Story and of Dr. Francis Wharton on the Conflict of Laws, are too varying and contradictory to control the general current of the English and American authorities in favor of holding that a contract, which by the law of the place is recognized as lawfully made by a capable person, is valid everywhere, although the person would not, under the law of his domicil, be deemed capable of making it. . . .

The principal reasons on which continental jurists have maintained that personal laws of the domicil, affecting the status and capacity of all inhabitants of a particular class, bind them wherever they go, appear to have been that each state has the rightful power to regulating the status and condition of its subjects, and, being best acquainted with the circumstances of climate, race, character, manners and customs, can best judge at what age young persons may begin to act for themselves, and whether and how far married women may act independently of their husbands; that laws limiting the capacity of infants or of married women are intended for their protection, and cannot therefore be dispensed with by their agreement; that all civilized states recognize the incapacity of infants and married women; and that a person, dealing with either, ordinarily has notice, by the apparent age or sex, that the person is likely to be of a class whom the laws protect, and is thus put upon inquiry how far, by the law of the domicil of the person, the protection extends.

On the other hand, it is only by the comity of other states that laws can operate beyond the limit of the state that makes them. In the great majority of cases, especially in this country, where it is so common to travel, or to transact business through agents, or to correspond by letter, from one state to another, it is more just, as well as more convenient, to have regard to the law of the place of the contract, as a uniform rule operating on all contracts of the same kind, and which the contracting parties may be presumed to have in contemplation when making their contracts, than to require them at their peril to know the domicil of those with whom they deal, and to ascertain the law of that domicil, however remote, which in many cases could not be done without such delay as would greatly cripple the power of contracting abroad at all. . . .

It is possible also that in a state where the common law prevailed in full force, by which a married woman was deemed incapable of binding herself by any contract whatever, it might be inferred that such an utter incapacity, lasting throughout the joint lives of husband and wife, must be considered as so fixed by the settled policy of the state, for the protection of its own citizens, that it could not be held by the courts of that state to yield to the law of another state in which she might undertake to contact. But it is not true at the present day that all civilized states recognize the absolute incapacity of married women to make contracts. The tendency of modern legislation is to enlarge their capacity in this respect, and in many states they have nearly or quite the same powers as if unmarried. In Massachusetts, even at the time of the making of the contract in question, a married woman was vested by statute with a very extensive power to carry on business by herself, and to bind herself by contracts with regard to her own property, business and earnings, and, before the bringing of the present action, the power had been extended so as to include the making of all kinds of contracts, with any person but her husband, as if she were unmarried. There is therefore no reason of public policy which should prevent the maintenance of this action.

LOUIS-DREYFUS v. PATERSON STEAMSHIPS, LTD.
43 F.2d 824 (2d Cir. 1930)

L. HAND, CIRCUIT JUDGE. The libellants at Duluth shipped a parcel of wheat upon two ships of the respondent and received in exchange bills of lading, Duluth to Montreal, "with transshipment at Port Colbourne, Ontario." These contained an exception for "dangers of navigation, fire and collision," but nothing further which is here relevant. The respondent exercised its right of reshipment, unloaded the wheat at Port Colbourne, stored it in an elevator, and reloaded thirty-five thousand bushels in another ship, the Advance, belonging to one Webb, chartered by the respondent's agent, the Hall Shipping Company, for that purpose. This ship safely carried her cargo until she reached the entrance to the Cornwall Canal in the St. Lawrence River, where she took the ground, stove in her bottom and sank. The suit is for the resulting damage to the wheat.

The respondent defended on the ground that the strand, not being due to any fault in management, was a danger of navigation. Failing this, it relied upon the Harter Act (46 U.S.C. §§190-195) and the Canadian Water-Carriage of Goods Act (9-10 Edward VII, Chap. 81), which covers among other ships those "carrying goods from any port in Canada to any other port in Canada" (§3). It requires every bill of lading "relating to the carriage of goods from any place in Canada to any place outside Canada" to recite that the shipment is subject to the act (§5), and, like §3 of the Harter Act (46 U.S.C. §192) provides that "if the owner of any ship transporting merchandise or property from any port in Canada exercises due diligence to make the ship in all respects seaworthy and properly manned, equipped and supplied, neither the ship, nor the owner, agent or charterer" shall be liable "for faults or errors in navigation or in the management of the ship" (§6). The respondent tried to prove that the Advance was seaworthy, and was therefore within both statutes. . . .

The important question is whether we should look to Canadian law at all. Here is a contract of carriage, made in Minnesota without any relevant exceptions, to be performed partly in the United States and partly in Canada; the carrier fails in performing that part of it which is to take place in Canada; he does not safely transport the grain from the entrance of the canal to Montreal. The law of the place of that performance excuses him for those faults in navigation which have caused the loss. Does that law control? *Liverpool, etc., Co. v. Phenix Ins. Co.,* 129 U.S. 397, decided that the validity of a provision in a contract of carriage, limiting the carrier's common-law duty, was to be determined by the law of the place where the contract was made, and this is well-settled law, [*Restatement (First) Conflict of Laws* §366 (Tent. Draft No. 4)], even when the parties expressly stipulate that all questions shall be decided according to some foreign law, which would require a different result. *Oceanic Steam Nav. Co. v. Corcoran,* 9 F.2d 724. It is of course only an instance of the usual rule that the law of the place where promises are made determines whether they create a contract (*Restatement (First) Conflict of Laws* §353 (Tent. Draft No. 4)); that law alone attaches any legal consequences to acts within its territory.

On the other hand, it is always said that as to matters of performance the law of the place of performance controls, *Scudder v. Union National Bank*, 91 U.S. 408, though in application the boundaries of this doctrine are not easy to find. . . . An exchange of mutual promises, or whatever other acts may create a contract for future performance, do not put the obligor under any immediate constraint, except so far as the doctrine of anticipatory breach demands. A present obligation arises only in the sense that it is then determined that when the time for performance arrives, his conduct shall not be open to his choice. For the present nothing is required of him; he can commit no fault and incur no liability. When the time comes for him to perform, if he fails, the law requires him to give the equivalent of the neglected performance; that compulsion is the sanction imposed by the state and the measure of the obligation. The default must indeed be at the place of performance, but the promisor need not himself be there, nor may he there have any property to respond. In such cases it is impossible to say that any liability arises under the law of that place where the promisor chanced to be at the time of performance, especially if such a doctrine were extended to all places where he has any property. In the interest of certainty and uniformity there must be some definite place fixed whose law shall control, wherever the suit arises. Whether the place of performance is chosen because of the likelihood that the obligor will be there present at the time of performance, or — what is nearly the same thing — because the agreement presupposes that he shall be, is not important. All we need say here is that the same law which determines what liabilities shall arise upon nonperformance, must determine any excuses for nonperformance, which are no more than exceptions to those liabilities. . . .

In the case at bar, the Canadian law says that performance of the contract of carriage, as respects navigation, shall be excused if the owner uses due care to examine his ship and make her fit for her voyage, to man and victual her and the like. The conduct so specified is thus made an excuse for his failure to carry the goods safely to their destination as he has promised to do. . . . It is indeed possible to say that any excuse for performance is a condition upon the undertaking, written into, and so a part of, the original promise. Courts which have insisted that the parties must be found in some way to have selected foreign law to control their rights, have so reasoned as to the law of the place of performance. We think that the imputation of any such intent is a fiction. [T]he parties cannot select the law which shall control, except as it becomes a term in the agreement, like the by-laws of a private association. When they have said nothing, as here, the local law determines what shall excuse performance *ex proprio vigore;* the parties do nothing about it. An American contract carries with it none of the immunity of the sovereign which created it; Canadian law reaches it and Canadian contracts indifferently. . . .

Notes on First Restatement, Milliken, *and* Louis-Dreyfus

1. *Basis for place of contracting rule for contractual validity.* What was the rationale for §332's "place of contracting" rule? Consider the following excerpt from Story's *Commentaries:*

> Generally speaking, the validity of a contract is to be decided by the law of the place, where it is made. If valid there, it is by the general law of nations, *jure gentium*, held valid everywhere, by the tacit or implied consent of the parties. The rule is founded, not merely in the

convenience, but in the necessities, of nations; for otherwise, it would be impracticable for them to carry on an extensive intercourse and commerce with each other. The whole systems of agencies, of purchases and sales, of mutual credits, and of transfers of negotiable instruments, rests on this foundation; and the nation, which should refuse to acknowledge the common principles, would soon find its whole commercial intercourse reduced to a state, like that, in which it now exists among savage tribes, among the barbarous nations of Sumatra. J. Story, *Commentaries on the Conflict of Laws* §242 (2d ed. 1841).

For a more categorical justification of the "place of contracting" rule, *see* Beale, *What Law Governs the Validity of a Contract?*, 23 Harv. L. Rev. 260, 267 (1909) (to "make the law of the place of performance govern the act of contracting is an attempt to give that law extra-territorial effect").

2. *Does the "place of contracting" rule provide certainty and predictability?* Is it correct, as Story reasoned, that the "place of contracting" rule provides certainty?

(a) Determining the "place of contracting." The place of contracting rule initially requires identifying the state in which a contract was made — which in turn requires reference to the substantive contract law of the forum (or some other state). *Restatement (First) Conflict of Laws* §311 comment d (1934). Of course, different states will have different substantive rules of contract law; that means that the place of contracting rule will produce different results in different forums, because the same course of conduct will result in a contract being formed (or not formed) in different places when different substantive rules of contract law are applied. For example, where negotiations, communications, and conduct occurs in several different states, a contract can easily be found to have be made in each of the different states when different substantive rules of contract law are applied. *See* Cook, *"Contracts" and the Conflict of Laws,* 31 Ill. L. Rev. 143, 158-163 (1936).

What defines the place of contracting? Consider the definition contained in *First Restatement* §311 comment d, looking to "the place of the principal event, if any, which, under the general law of Contracts, would result in a contract." What definition is used in *Milliken?* Note the court's reliance on the place where the contract "was complete."

(b) Distinguishing "performance" from "contracting." The *First Restatement* also provided, in §358, that certain issues of contract would be governed by the place of performance, rather than the place of contracting. This is illustrated by *Louis-Dreyfus.* In particular, the manner, time, sufficiency, and other aspects of performance would generally be governed by the law of the place of performance. Why is this? Note that, whatever its explanation, the sub-rule introduced further uncertainty into the *First Restatement*'s approach to contract choice of law. Consider the following excerpt from comment c to *Restatement (First) Conflict of Laws* §332 (1934):

> A difficult problem is presented in deciding whether a question in a dispute concerning a contract is one involving the creation of an obligation or performance thereof. There is no distinction based on logic alone between determining the creation of the contract and the rights and duties thereunder on the one hand, and its performance on the other. . . . The point at which initiation ceases and performance begins is not a point which can be fixed by any rule of law of universal application in all cases. Like all questions of degree, the solution must depend upon the circumstances of each case and must be governed by the exercise of judgment.

Did the issue in *Louis-Dreyfus* concern performance (under §358) or the validity and effect of the parties' agreement (under §332)? Note §332(f).

3. Milliken v. Pratt — *application of place of contracting rule.* Where was the guaranty contract in *Milliken* signed? Where did *Milliken* say that the guaranty contract was made? Why? Suppose that the case had involved slightly different facts — for example, the seller delivered the goods itself to the buyer in Massachusetts, rather than handing them over to an "express" company. Would that have changed the place of contracting? If so, is the place of contracting rule likely to provide certainty or consistent results?

4. Milliken v. Pratt — *capacity and validity. Milliken* refused to apply Massachusetts law of capacity, instead applying Maine law of contractual validity. Why wasn't Massachusetts law applicable? Consider the Court's reply:

> It is more just, as well as more convenient, to have regard to the law of the place of the contract, as a uniform rule operating on all contracts of the same kind, and which the contracting parties may be presumed to have in contemplation when making their contracts than to require them at their peril to know the domicile of those with whom they deal, and to ascertain the law of that domicile, however remote. . . .

Is this persuasive? Is it easier to consult the law of a party's place of domicile, or to attempt to ascertain the law of the place of contracting? Note the continuing importance of characterization in choice-of-law analysis (as in deciding whether *Milliken* presents a question of validity of capacity).

Suppose that the laws in *Milliken* were reversed: suppose that Massachusetts law had granted Ms. Pratt the capacity to enter into the guarantee, but that Maine had denied her that power. How would *Milliken* have decided that case? What would a straightforward application of the place of contracting test suggest?

5. Milliken v. Pratt — *interest analysis.* How would *Milliken* have been decided under Currie's interest analysis? *See supra* pp. 738-740. How would the hypothetical, discussed in the preceding note where Massachusetts and Maine laws were reversed, be decided?

6. *Law governing capacity to contract.* What law should govern a party's capacity to contract?

(a) Traditional rule. First Restatement §333 provided that "[t]he law of the place of contracting determines the capacity to enter into a contract." What are the justifications for this rule? The advantages?

(b) Contemporary rule. In contrast, as discussed below, contemporary choice-of-law rules generally subject issues of capacity to the contracting party's domicile: "The capacity of a party to contract will usually be upheld if he has such capacity under the local law of the state of his domicile." *Restatement (Second) Conflict of Laws* §198(2) (1971). What is the rationale for §198(2)? What are the advantages?

(c) Choice-of-law clause. Can parties agree upon the law that governs questions of capacity? Why or why not?

7. *The "place of performance" rule. First Restatement* §358 and *Louis-Dreyfus* provide that a party's performance obligations are governed by the "law of the place of performance," rather than the place of contracting. What is the rationale for the rule that the place of performance governs issues relating to the performance of a contract? Is it based upon concerns about interfering with the territorial sovereignty of the place where performance occurred? Note that most issues relating to performance — such as timing, place, manner, and sufficiency — could readily be resolved by private agreement (and often are). Is a state's territorial sovereignty affected when foreign law fills in gaps of this sort in the parties' agreement? Is the place of performance rule based upon the parties' likely expectations?

Consider how the place of performance test was applied in *Minmetal.* Is a contract whose performance would be illegal in the place of performance unenforceable under the *Minmetal* analysis? In all circumstances? What must the party resisting enforcement of the contract prove to succeed?

8. Louis-Dreyfus *and* Minmetal — *choice-of-law clauses and place of performance rule.* Consider the application of the place of performance rule in *Louis-Dreyfus.* Consider how *Louis-Dreyfus* discusses the relationship between choice of law agreements and the place of performance rule. Suppose that the parties had agreed that "all questions shall be decided according to" the laws of some place other than Canada. According to *Louis-Dreyfus,* would the parties' chosen law have displaced Canadian law with respect to excuses for nonperformance? How would *Second Restatement* §187 resolve the foregoing issue?

Was it likely that the parties expected their performance in Canada to be governed by Canadian law, when they entered into a contract in the United States? Suppose that, contrary to U.S. law, Canadian law had imposed the equivalent of strict liability on the vessel owner: reasonable care would not be a defense to nonperformance. Would that affect analysis?

Consider also the interaction between the parties' choice-of-law clause and Chinese law in *Minmetal.* How far can parties go in drafting around problems of illegality in the place of performance? Suppose that the choice-of-law clause in *Minmetal* had explicitly provided that all questions of performance, including illegality, were governed exclusively by New York law.

3.   Contemporary Approach to Choice of Law Governing Contracts in the Absence of Choice-of-Law Agreement: "Most Significant Relationship"

The *First Restatement*'s rules regarding the choice of law applicable to contracts encountered the same sorts of criticism that traditional tort rules met. Indeed, Currie demonstrated the application of interest analysis by means of *Milliken v. Pratt* and hypotheticals derived from married women's contracts.[248]

A number of contemporary U.S. authorities have abandoned the place of contracting rule of the *First Restatement.* A leading example of this trend is the *Second Restatement,* which applies the "most significant relationship" test to contracts. Section 188 of the *Restatement* provides that, in the absence of an effective choice of law by the parties, "the rights and duties of the parties with respect to an issue in contract are determined by the local law of the state which, with respect to that issue, has the *most significant relationship* to the transaction and the parties."

Although there has been considerable erosion of the *First Restatement,* there is little consistency or uniformity among contemporary U.S. choice-of-law decisions involving contracts. That is in part because of "the many different kinds of contracts and of issues involving contracts and by the many relationships a single contract may have to two or more states."[249] In part, however, it is also because lower courts have simply not been able to agree upon any consistent approach to choice-of-law issues relating to contract.

A substantial number of lower U.S. courts — approximately 24 — have followed the most significant relationship analysis of §188 of the *Restatement Second.*[250] Another substantial number of state courts — approximately 11 states — have continued to follow the *First Restatement*'s place of contracting and place of performance standards.[251] According to a leading observer of trends in conflicts jurisprudence, no state applies a pure

---

248. Currie, *Married Women's Contracts: A Study in Conflict-of-Laws Method,* 25 U. Chi. L. Rev. 227 (1958).
249. *Restatement (Second) Conflict of Laws* Chapter 8, Intro. Note (1971) (emphasis added).
250. *See* Symeonides, *Choice of Law in American Courts in 2010: Twenty-Fourth Annual Survey,* 59 Am. J. Comp. L. 303 (forthcoming 2011).
251. *Id.*

"interest analysis," while a handful either appear to be undecided or eclectic in their approach.[252]

These analytical differences are sometimes said to conceal a more fundamental consistency of result. Several commentators have remarked that the trend among contemporary lower U.S. courts is to apply that law which will uphold the parties' agreement. "[T]here is a distinct tendency to apply a law that will uphold the contract provided the parties are not of widely disparate bargaining power and the state of the validating law has substantial contacts with the transaction."[253]

Consider the following materials, which illustrate some of the contemporary approaches to the choice of law applicable to contracts. The approach of the *Second Restatement* is set forth in §188, §202, and §206. Also consider *Lilienthal v. Kaufman*, which applies a version of interest analysis to a contract dispute.

RESTATEMENT (SECOND) CONFLICT OF LAWS
§§188, 198, 202 & 206 (1971) [excerpted in Appendix Y]

LILIENTHAL v. KAUFMAN
395 P.2d 543 (Or. 1964)

DENECKE, JUSTICE. This is an action to collect two promissory notes. The defense is that the defendant maker has previously been declared a spendthrift by an Oregon court and placed under a guardianship and that the guardian has declared the obligations void. The plaintiffs counter is that the notes were executed and delivered in California, that the law of California does not recognize the disability of a spendthrift and that the Oregon court is bound to apply the law of the place of the making of the contract. The trial court rejected plaintiff's argument and held for the defendant.

This same defendant spendthrift was the prevailing party in our recent decision in *Olshen v. Kaufman,* 385 P.2d 161 (Or. 1963). In that case the spendthrift and the plaintiff, an Oregon resident, had gone into a joint venture to purchase binoculars for resale. For this purpose plaintiff had advanced moneys to the spendthrift. The spendthrift had repaid plaintiff by his personal check for the amount advanced and for plaintiff's share of the profits of such venture. The check had not been paid because the spendthrift had had insufficient funds in his account. The action was for the unpaid balance of the check. The evidence in that case showed that the plaintiff had been unaware that Kaufman was under a spendthrift guardianship. The guardian testified that he knew Kaufman was engaging in some business and had bank accounts and that he had admonished him to cease these practices; but he could not control the spendthrift.

The statute applicable in that case and in this one is ORS 126.335:

> After the appointment of a guardian for the spendthrift, all contracts, except for necessaries, and all gifts, sales and transfers of real or personal estate made by such spendthrift thereafter and before the termination of the guardianship are voidable. . . .

We held in that case that the voiding of the contract by the guardian precluded recovery by the plaintiff and that the spendthrift and the guardian were not estopped to deny

252. *Id.*
253. Reese, *American Trends in Private International Law: Academic and Judicial Manipulation of Choice of Law Rules in Tort Cases,* 33 Vand. L. Rev. 717, 737 (1980).

the validity of plaintiff's claim. Plaintiff does not seek to overturn the principle of that decision but contends it has no application because the law of California governs, and under California law the plaintiff's claim is valid.

The facts here are identical to those in *Olshen v. Kaufman,* except for the Californian locale for portions of the transaction. The notes were for the repayment of advances to finance another joint venture to sell binoculars. The plaintiff was unaware that defendant had been declared a spendthrift and placed under guardianship. The guardian, upon demand for payment by the plaintiff declared the notes void. . . .

Before entering the choice-of-law area of the general field of conflict of laws, we must determine whether the laws of the states having a connection with the controversy are in conflict. Defendant did not expressly concede that under the law of California the defendant's obligation would be enforceable, but his counsel did state that if this proceeding were in the courts of California, the plaintiff probably would recover. We agree. . . .

Defendant contends that the law of California should not be applied in this case by the Oregon court because the invalidity of the contract is a matter of remedy, rather than one of substance. Matters of remedy, procedure, are governed by the law of the forum. What is a matter of substance and what is a matter of procedure are sometimes difficult questions to decide. Stumberg states the distinction as follows: "procedural rules should be classified as those which concern methods of presenting to a court the operative facts upon which legal relations depend; substantive rules, those which concern the legal effect of those facts after they have been established." Stumberg, *Principles of Conflict of Laws* 133 (3d ed.). Based upon this conventional statement of the distinction, it is obvious that we are not concerned with a procedural issue, but with a matter of substantive law.

Plaintiff contends that the substantive issue of whether or not an obligation is valid and binding is governed by the law of the place of making, California. This court has repeatedly stated that the law of the place of contract "must govern as to the validity, interpretation, and construction of the contract." *Jamieson v. Potts,* 105 P. 93, 95 (1910). *Restatement (First) Conflict of Laws* §332, so announced and specifically stated that "capacity to make the contract" was to be determined by the law of the place of contract.

This principle, that *lex loci contractus* must govern, however, has been under heavy attack for years. The strongest criticism has been that the place of making frequently is completely fortuitous and that on occasion the state of making has no interest in the parties to the contract or in the performance of the contract. . . . As a result of this long and powerful assault, the principle is no longer a cornerstone of the law of conflicts. There is no need to decide that our previous statements that the law of the place of contract governs were in error. Our purpose is to state that this portion of our decision is not founded upon that principle because of our doubt that it is correct if the only connection of the state whose law would govern is that it was the place of making.

In this case California had more connection with the transaction than being merely the place where the contract was executed. The defendant went to San Francisco to ask the plaintiff, a California resident, for money for the defendant's venture. The money was loaned to defendant in San Francisco, and by terms of the note, it was to be repaid to plaintiff in San Francisco. On these facts, apart from *lex loci contractus,* other accepted principles of conflict of laws lead to the conclusion that the law of California should be applied. . . .

There is another conflict principle calling for the application of California law — . . . the application of the law which upholds the contract. Ehrenzweig calls it the "Rule of Validation." A. Ehrenzweig, *Conflict of Laws* 353 (1962). . . . The "rule" is that, if the contract is valid under the law of any jurisdiction having significant connection with the contract, *i.e.*, place of making, place of performance, etc., the law of that jurisdiction validating the contract will be applied. This would also agree with the intention of the parties, if they had any intentions in this regard. They must have intended their agreement to be valid. . . .

Thus far all signs have pointed to applying the law of California and holding the contract enforceable. There is, however, an obstacle to cross before this end can be logically reached. In *Olshen v. Kaufman,* we decided that the law of Oregon, at least as applied to persons applied domiciled in Oregon contracting in Oregon for performance in Oregon, is that spendthrifts' contracts are voidable. Are the choice-of-law principles of conflict of laws so superior that they overcome this principle of Oregon law?

To answer this question we must determine, upon some basis, whether the interests of Oregon are so basic and important that we should not apply California law despite its several intimate connections with the transaction. The traditional method used by this court and most others is framed in the terminology of "public policy." The court decides whether or not the public policy of the forum is so strong that the law of the forum must prevail although another jurisdiction, with different laws, has more and closer contacts with the transaction. Included in "public policy" we must consider the economic and social interests of Oregon. When these factors are included in a consideration of whether the law of the forum should be applied this traditional approach is very similar to that advocated by many legal scholars. Currie, *Selected Essays on the Conflict of Laws* 64-72 (1963). . . .

The difficulty in deciding what is the fundamental law forming a cornerstone of the forum's jurisprudence and what is not such fundamental law, thus allowing it to give way to foreign law, is caused by the lack of any even remotely objective standards. . . . However, as previously stated, if we include in our search for the public policy of the forum a consideration of the various interests that the forum has in this litigation, we are guided by more definite criteria. In addition to the interests of the forum, we should consider the interests of the other jurisdictions which have some connection with the transaction.

Some of the interests of Oregon in this litigation are set forth in *Olshen v. Kaufman.* The spendthrift's family which is to be protected by the establishment of the guardianship is presumably an Oregon family. The public authority which may be charged with the expense of supporting the spendthrift or his family, if he is permitted to go unrestrained upon his wasteful way, will probably be an Oregon public authority. These, obviously, are interests of some substance. Oregon has other interests and policies regarding this matter which were not necessary to discuss in *Olshen.* As previously stated, Oregon, as well as all other states, has a strong policy favoring the validity and enforceability of contracts. This policy applies whether the contract is made and to be performed in Oregon or elsewhere. The defendant's conduct, — borrowing money with the belief that the repayments of such loan could be avoided — is a species of fraud. Oregon and all other states have a strong policy of protecting innocent persons from fraud. . . . It is in Oregon's commercial interest to encourage citizens of other states to conduct business with Oregonians will be discouraged. If there are Oregon laws, somewhat unique to Oregon, which permit an Oregonian to escape his otherwise binding obligations, persons may well avoid commercial dealing with Oregonians. The substance of these commercial considerations, however, is deflated by the recollection that the Oregon Legislature has determined, despite the weight of these consideration, that a spendthrift's contracts are voidable.

California's most direct interest in this transaction is having its citizen creditor paid. As previously noted, California's policy is that any creditor, in California or otherwise, should be paid even though the debtor is a spendthrift. California probably has another, although more intangible, interest involved. It is presumably to every state's benefit to have the reputation of being a jurisdiction in which contracts can be made and performance be promised with the certain knowledge that such contracts will be enforced. Both of these interests, particularly the former, are also of substance.

We have, then, two jurisdictions, each with several close connections with the transaction, and each with a substantial interest, which will be served or thwarted, depending upon which law is applied. The interests of neither jurisdiction are clearly more important than those of the other. We are of the opinion that in such a case the public policy of Oregon should prevail and the law of Oregon should be applied; we should apply that choice-of-law rule which will "advance the policies or interests of" Oregon. Courts are instruments of state policy. The Oregon Legislature has adopted a policy to avoid possible hardship to an Oregon family of a spendthrift and to avoid possible expenditure of Oregon public funds which might occur if the spendthrift is required to pay his obligations. In litigation Oregon courts are the appropriate instrument to enforce this policy. The mechanical application of choice-of-law rules would be the only apparent reason for an Oregon court advancing the interests of California over the equally valid interests of Oregon. The present principles of conflict of laws are not favorable to such mechanical application. We hold that the spendthrift law of Oregon is applicable and the plaintiff cannot recover.

GOODWIN, JUSTICE. . . . In the case before us, I believe that the policy of both states, Oregon and California, in favor of enforcing contracts, has been lost sight of in favor of a questionable policy in Oregon which gives special privileges to the rare spendthrift for whom a guardian has been appointed. The majority view in the case at bar strikes me as a step backward toward the balkanization of the law of contracts. *Olshen v. Kaufman* held that there was a policy in this state to help keep spendthrifts out of the almshouse. I can see nothing, however, in Oregon's policy toward spendthrifts that warrants its extension to permit the taking of captives from other states down the road to insolvency. I would enforce the contract.

Notes on Second Restatement and Lilienthal

1. *Criticism of traditional place of contracting rule.* *Lilienthal* rejected the *First Restatement*'s place of contracting test. Consider the criticisms of the traditional rule: it can be completely "fortuitous," it ignores the interests of states that are most affected by a transaction, and it gives effect to the law of states with "no interest" in the transaction. Are these persuasive criticisms? Doesn't the place of contracting test provide predictability and certainty, at least in most cases? Can't the real interests of other states be dealt with by the public policy exception?

2. *Rules of alternative reference or validation.* A number of contemporary (and some older) authorities have adopted rules of so-called "alternative reference." These rules permit a court to apply whichever of the laws that are potentially applicable to a contract that will uphold the validity of the parties' agreement. *E.g.*, A. Ehrenzweig, *A Treatise on the Conflict of Laws* 466 (1962) ("Parties entering into a contract upon equal terms intend their agreement to be binding, and the law of conflict of laws will give effect to their intent whenever it can do so under any proper law."); R. Weintraub, *Commentary on the Conflict of Laws* §7.4A at 469 (6th ed. 2010); *Ludwig v. Bottomly and Associates, Inc.*, 1996 WL 426678, at *2 (E.D. La. 1996); *Superior Funding Corp. v. Big Apple Capital Corp.*, 738 F. Supp. 1468, 1471 (S.D.N.Y. 1990); *Cooper v. Cherokee Village Development Co.*, 364 S.W.2d 158 (Ark. 1963) (favors "applying the law of the state that will make the contract valid, rather than void"). *Lilienthal* also cited the "Rule of Validation," although ultimately refusing to

apply it. *See also Frost v. Lotspeich,* 30 P.3d 1185, 1190 (Or. Ct. App. 2001) (reaffirming rule of validation but refusing to apply it due to California's stronger interest in invalidating contract). Consider again the result in *Milliken.* Did it involve considerations of this sort? What is the rationale for a rule of validation?

3. *Legitimacy of rules of validation.* Are rules of alternative reference or validation acceptable in an international context? Virtually all nations now recognize private contracts and will enforce them. But most nations also provide basic limits on the validity and enforceability of contracts; those limits serve important public policies such as the protection of individuals from duress or overreaching, and the protection of the public from anti-competitive, corrupt, or otherwise undesirable agreements. Why is it that a U.S. court should refuse to give effect to such public policies — through the mechanism of applying rules of alternative reference? *See American Equities Group, Inc. v. Ahava Dairy Products Corp.,* 2004 WL 870260, at *8-9 (S.D.N.Y. 2004) (discussing limits on rule of validation). What if the contract in question clearly has closer connections to a foreign state?

Consider a case under §187 of the *Second Restatement,* where foreign public policy is applied to render a choice of domestic law, and the parties' agreement, unenforceable. *See* Appendix Y. Rules of validation would produce the opposite result. Should a U.S. court ignore foreign public policy in order to "validate" as many agreements as it can? What about where a U.S. party bargains for U.S. law to achieve precisely this result?

4. Second Restatement's *"most significant relationship" test.* Consider the choice-of-law rule set forth in §188 of the *Second Restatement.* What does "most significant relationship" mean? In truly international transactions, having multiple contacts with several states, how does one select the most significant relationship? Note that §188 proceeds on an issue by issue basis, with different laws applying to different contractual issues.

A significant number of state courts have adopted some variation of a most significant relationship or "center of gravity" test. *See* Symeonides, *Choice of Law in the American Courts in 2009: Twenty-Fourth Annual Survey,* 59 Am. J. Comp. L. 303 (forthcoming 2011) (listing 23 states as following *Restatement Second* in contracts cases); *supra* pp. 784-785.

5. Lilienthal — *public policy in choice of law governing contracts.* *Lilienthal* invoked Oregon public policy to prevent application of California law. The court acknowledged the "lack of any even remotely objective standards" for defining public policy. Consider the various Oregon public policies that *Lilienthal* identifies, and the court's ultimate conclusion that Oregon's legislature had incorporated these various policies into a spendthrift law. Is the Oregon spendthrift law appropriately characterized as stating public policy? Why is it that Oregon's public policies invalidating contracts by spendthrifts outweigh other *Oregon* public policies?

Consider *Lilienthal's* analysis of competing Oregon and California public policies. How can a court meaningfully weigh one state's policies or interests against those of another state? Is it inevitable that courts will be parochially biased in favor of local public policies? Compare the attention that *Lilienthal* devotes to Oregon's public policies to that devoted to California's policies. Note which policy ultimately prevails.

Compare the *Lilienthal* result to that which would obtain under §333 of the *First Restatement. See* Appendix X.

6. Lilienthal — *application of interest analysis.* The final few paragraphs of *Lilienthal* adopt a form of interest analysis. Indeed, the court ultimately appears to rely on Currie's rule that the forum's interests are to be preferred over foreign interests. Consider the wisdom of *Lilienthal's* application of interest analysis. Compare the result in *Lilienthal* to that in *Milliken;* which case is the wiser result? Which case is more likely to promote a predictable and fair commercial environment? How would *Lilienthal* have been decided under the rules of alternative reference set forth above?

How would *Lilienthal* have been decided under §188 of the *Second Restatement*? Recall §198(2) of the *Second Restatement* and its rules regarding capacity to contract. *See* Appendix Y. Does *Lilienthal* involve an issue of capacity or of invalidity/illegality?

What if the parties had agreed in *Lilienthal* to the application of California law? Would that have changed analysis?

How would Currie have decided *Lilienthal?* Does the case involve a "true conflict"? Would it be possible to adopt a restrained interpretation of Oregon's policies, so as to confine those policies to borrowing within Oregon, thereby revealing a false conflict and permitting application of California's law?

7. ***Criticism of* Lilienthal's *application of interest analysis.*** Consider the dissent's remark in *Lilienthal* that the court's decision is "a step backward toward the balkanization of the law of contracts." What is meant by "balkanization"? How does the *Lilienthal* result affect California's interests? Is *Lilienthal* consistent with §187 of the *Second Restatement?*

8. ***Does* Lilienthal *violate the Constitution?*** Recall contemporary due process and full faith and credit limits on state choice-of-law decisions. Is the application of Oregon law in *Lilienthal* a violation of these constitutional limits? For an affirmative reply, *see* E. Scoles & P. Hay, *Conflict of Laws* 101 (2d ed. 1992). Recall also, however, the treatment of capacity under the *Second Restatement.*

9. ***Procedure versus substance revisited.*** The spendthrift's lawyer in *Lilienthal* argued that the validity of a contract was a matter of "remedy," and therefore a procedural issue subject to the law of the forum. *See supra* pp. 10-11. *Lilienthal* dismissed that suggestion. Was it correct?

10. ***Unpredictability in choice of law governing contracts.*** Consider the various choice-of-law rules that are presently available to select the law governing contracts. Consider also the criticisms made of almost every rule, concerning its unpredictability, and the further uncertainties created by escape devices and characterization. All these factors make it extremely difficult, in any truly international case, to predict with confidence the likely law that a U.S. court will apply to a contract dispute. The possibility that foreign courts will apply different (and also unpredictable) choice-of-law rules makes matters even worse. Is this a satisfactory state of affairs for international businesses? What can be done to improve matters?

11. ***Implicit choices under international agreements.*** Even where parties have not chosen the law applicable to their contracts, sometimes treaties (rather than state conflicts principles) can fill the gap. A familiar treaty is the 1980 United Nations Convention on the International Sale of Goods (which the United States has ratified). Under Article 1 of that treaty, it applies, even absent a choice-of-law clause, where the parties to a contract have their place of business in countries that are signatories to the Convention (unless the parties affirmatively exclude its application). *See American Biophysics Corp. v. Dubois Marine Specialties*, 411 F. Supp. 2d 61 (D.R.I. 2006).

The Convention is not, however, a comprehensive document and leaves many matters to the domestic laws of the signatory states (either explicitly or where the signatory state deposits a reservation). One such example is Article 96 of the Convention, which allows a signatory state to require that a contract be in writing (even though the Convention itself does not contain a writing requirement). Suppose that two parties, both of which hale from states that have signed the Convention, enter into an oral sales contract. One state has adopted the Article 96 reservation; the other has not. If a dispute arises, what law determines whether a contract was validly formed? If the case is brought in federal court, do federal or state conflicts principles apply to the question? For a recent decision wrestling with these issues, *see Forestal Guarani S.A. v. Daros Int'l, Inc.*, 613 F.3d 395 (3d Cir. 2010).

12. *Liability limits absent party choice.* Periodically, parties' contracts will not designate the applicable law but will contain some limits on the available remedies. For example, a carriage contract might cap the carrier's liability to a certain amount. Suppose that a foreign company in Country A retains the services of a U.S.-based carrier to transport cargo from Country A to Country B. The contract contains a per-kilogram liability limit that is enforceable in the United States but not enforceable under the laws of Country A. Under the *Restatement (Second),* what country's laws should determine the enforceability of the liability limit? Would it matter if the United States served as the transshipment point for the cargo? *See Eli Lilly do Brasil Ltda. v. Federal Express Corp.,* 502 F.3d 78 (2d Cir. 2007).

13. *Law applicable to performance.* Consider §§202 and 206 of the *Restatement (Second).* Do these provisions have any application to the facts in *Lilienthal?* Consider again how these provisions were applied in *Minmetal.*

14. *The Rome Convention and the Rome I Regulation (revisited).* As discussed above, *supra* p. 776, the Rome Convention and Rome I Regulation set forth points of contrast for U.S. law governing choice-of-law principles in contract cases. Those instruments also set forth rules governing the law applicable to contract absent party agreement.

Under the Rome Convention, the general approach is to apply the law of the country most closely connected with the contract. *See* Rome Convention Art. 4(1). Subject to certain exceptions, the Convention sets forth a rebuttable presumption that the country most closely connected to the contract generally is the one "where the party who is to effect the performance which is characteristic of the contract has, at the time of the conclusion of the contract, his habitual residence" or in the case of corporations or other legal entities its "central administration." Rome Convention Art. 4(2). *See* Rome Convention Art. 4(2)-(5). The Rome I Regulation is more complex. It sets forth a series of approaches depending on the type of contract. For example, contracts for the sale of goods are presumptively governed by the law of the country where the seller has his habitual residence; by contrast, franchise contracts are presumptively governed by the law of the country where the franchisee has his habitual residence. *See* Rome I Regulation Arts. 4(1)(a), (e). As with contractual choice-of-law clauses, *see supra* pp. 762-763, both documents also permit the court of the forum state to refuse to give effect to the choice-of-law clause where doing so would violate the forum state's public policy. *See* Rome Convention Art. 16; Rome I Regulation Art. 21.

How do these rules compare with the above-described rules for the law governing contractual claims absent a designation by the parties? Is there a meaningful difference between the "closest connection" test and the "most significant relationship" test? Does it make more sense to set forth a general principle (like "most significant relationship") which can then evolve on a case-by-case basis or, instead, to set forth a series of contract-specific rules (as the Rome I Regulation does)? For further reading on the European law governing contractual choice-of-law clauses, *see* Ferrari & Leible (eds.), *Rome I Regulation: The Law Applicable to Contractual Obligations in Europe* (2009); M. Giuliano & P. LaGarde, *Report on the Convention of the Law Applicable to Contractual Obligations,* 1980 O.J. (C. 282).

D.   *Erie* and the Choice-of-Law Rules in Federal Courts

Choice-of-law questions in federal court raise issues under the *Erie* doctrine.[254] In *Klaxon v. Stentor Electric Manufacturing Company,*[255] the Supreme Court held that a federal diversity court must apply the choice-of-law rules of the state in which it sits. The Court

---

254. *See supra* pp. 10-12 for a discussion of *Erie* and its application in international cases.
255. 313 U.S. 487 (1941).

reasoned that application of state conflicts rules was necessary to ensure "equal administration of justice in coordinate state and federal courts sitting side by side."[256] *Klaxon* was extended (without discussion) to international cases in *Day & Zimmerman, Inc. v. Challoner,* which is excerpted below. The Court required a federal district court sitting in Texas to apply Texas choice-of-law rules (based on the *First Restatement*) to an accident occurring in Cambodia.

DAY & ZIMMERMANN, INC. v. CHALLONER
423 U.S. 3 (1975)

PER CURIAM. Respondents sued petitioner in the U.S. District Court for the Eastern District of Texas seeking to recover damages for death and personal injury resulting from the premature explosion of a 105-mm. Howitzer round in Cambodia. Federal jurisdiction was based on diversity of citizenship. The District Court held that the Texas law of strict liability in tort governed and submitted the case to the jury on that theory. The Court of Appeals for the Fifth Circuit affirmed a judgment in favor of respondents.

The Court of Appeals stated that were it to apply Texas choice-of-law rules, the substantive law of Cambodia, the place of injury, would certainly control as to the wrongful death, and perhaps as to the claim for personal injury. It declined nevertheless to apply Texas choice-of-law rules, based in part on an earlier decision in *Lester v. Aetna Life Ins. Co.,* 433 F.2d 884 (5th Cir. 1970), which it summarized as holding that "[w]e refused to look to the Louisiana conflict of law rule, deciding that as a matter of federal choice of law, *we could not apply the law of a jurisdiction that had no interest in the case,* no policy at stake." 512 F.2d at 80 (emphasis in original). The Court of Appeals further supported its decision on the grounds that the rationale for applying the traditional conflicts rule applied by Texas "is not operative under the present facts"; and that it was "a Court of the United States, an instrumentality created to effectuate the laws and policies of the United States."

We believe that the Court of Appeals either misinterpreted our longstanding decision in *Klaxon,* or else determined for itself that it was no longer of controlling force in a case such as this. We are of the opinion that *Klaxon,* is by its terms applicable here and should have been adhered to by the Court of Appeals. In *Klaxon,* this Court said: "The conflict of laws rules to be applied by the federal court in Delaware must conform to those prevailing in Delaware's state courts. Otherwise, the accident of diversity of citizenship would constantly disturb equal administration of justice in coordinate state and federal courts sitting side by side. *See Erie R. Co. v. Tompkins,* 304 U.S. 64, 74-77 (1938)."

By parity of reasoning, the conflict-of-laws rules to be applied by a federal court in Texas must conform to those prevailing in the Texas state courts. A federal court in a diversity case is not free to engraft onto those state rules exceptions or modifications which may commend themselves to the federal court, but which have not commended themselves to the State in which the federal court sits. The Court of Appeals in this case should identify and follow the Texas conflicts rule. What substantive law will govern when Texas' rule is applied is a matter to be determined by the Court of Appeals.

JUSTICE BLACKMUN, concurring. . . . [A]s I read the Court's per curiam opinion, the Court of Appeals on remand is to determine and flatly to apply the conflict of laws

---

256. 313 U.S. at 496.

rules that govern the state courts of Texas. This means to me that the Court of Appeals is not foreclosed from concluding, if it finds it proper so to do under the circumstances of this case, that the Texas state courts themselves would apply the Texas rule of strict liability. If that proves to be the result, I would perceive no violation of any principle of *Klaxon*. I make this observation to assure the Court of Appeals that, at least in my view, today's per curiam opinion does not necessarily compel the determination that it is only the law of Cambodia that is applicable.

LIU v. REPUBLIC OF CHINA
892 F.2d 1419 (9th Cir. 1989) [excerpted above at pp. 320-322]

Notes on Day & Zimmermann *and* Liu

1. Klaxon v. Stentor Electric. *Klaxon* was an early application of *Erie*. It arose from an agreement, executed in New York, which provided for the transfer of a New York corporation's business to a Delaware corporation. Disputes later arose, and the New York seller sued the Delaware purchaser in federal district court in Delaware. After successfully winning a judgment, the plaintiff requested interest under a New York statute. The district court granted the request, without considering what a Delaware state court would have done. The Supreme Court reversed, holding that federal district courts were required to apply Delaware choice-of-law rules: "Otherwise, the accident of diversity of citizenship would constantly disturb equal administration of justice in coordinate state and federal courts, sitting side by side." 313 U.S. at 496.

2. *Is* Klaxon *required by* Erie? The Court's prevailing understanding of *Erie* focuses on the decision's "twin aims": "discouragement of forum-shopping and avoidance of inequitable administration of the laws." *Hanna v. Plumer*, 380 U.S. 460, 468 (1965); *supra* pp. 10-11. Are these twin aims applicable to choice-of-law rules? If federal courts apply one set of conflicts rules and state courts apply another, will parties engage in intrastate forum shopping to obtain the most favorable applicable laws? On the other hand, interstate, as opposed to intrastate, forum shopping will be exacerbated by *Klaxon*. Is that a sufficient reason to reject the *Erie* rule?

3. *The limits of* Klaxon *and* Day & Zimmerman. Are there limits to the *Klaxon* principle? Does *Klaxon* require federal courts sitting in diversity to apply state conflicts principles to matters such as postjudgment interest? Are such matters properly characterized as procedural or substantive? *See FCS Advisors, Inc. v. Fair Finance Co.*, 605 F.3d 144 (2d Cir. 2010) (holding that federal law governs the determination of postjudgment interest). What if the contract contains a choice-of-law clause designating state law? *See id.* (noting that the parties can contract around the federal rate of postjudgment interest but requiring their intent to be "clear, unambiguous and unequivocal").

4. *Should choice-of-law questions in international cases be governed by federal common law?* Unlike *Klaxon, Day & Zimmermann* involved the question of what law a federal court should apply to an accident occurring on the territory of another nation (rather than another U.S. state), and one of the arguably applicable substantive laws was that of a foreign state. In these circumstances, are rules of federal common law appropriate? Did *Day & Zimmermann* suggest that any different *Erie* rule applied to international cases than to domestic ones?

At least one court recently sought, unsuccessfully, to develop analysis in this direction. *Bickel v. Korean Air Lines Co., Ltd.* involved claims that arose after a Russian military jet shot down a KAL passenger jet that had strayed into Russian airspace. U.S. plaintiffs sued KAL (a Korean citizen) and asserted both diversity jurisdiction and federal question jurisdiction (under the Warsaw Convention and a federal statute). Under these circumstances, the Sixth Circuit declined to follow *Klaxon*, but its defense of this holding had broader ramifications for pure diversity cases as well:

> To answer the choice of law question presented by these cases, we apply a federal choice of law rule. In doing so, we are mindful that there is "no federal general common law," *O'Melveny & Myers v. F.D.I.C.*, 512 U.S. 79, 83 (1994) (citing *Erie R.R. v. Tompkins*, 304 U.S. 64, 78 (1938)). The Warsaw Convention, however, embodies a concrete federal policy of uniformity and certainty . . . which would be undermined by the use of state choice of law rules. Consequently, we are of the view that these cases present precisely the type of situation in which it is appropriate to craft a special federal rule which, in these cases, is a choice of law rule. 83 F.3d 127, 130 (6th Cir. 1996), *opinion withdrawn and superseded in part on rehearing*, 96 F.3d 151 (6th Cir. 1996).

For a conflicting view, *see Insurance Co. of North America v. Federal Exp. Co.*, 189 F.3d 914, 919-920 (9th Cir. 1999) (applying *Erie* principles to Warsaw Convention case).

Do questions of the law applicable to conduct outside the United States arise in a "uniquely federal" area? Do such questions sufficiently implicate federal interests in foreign commerce and foreign relations to conclude that they are "uniquely federal"? For affirmative responses, *see* Trautman, *Toward Federalizing Choice of Law*, 70 Tex. L. Rev. 1715, 1735-1736 (1992); Chow, *Limiting* Erie *in a New Age of International Law: Toward a Federal Common Law of International Choice of Law*, 74 Iowa L. Rev. 165 (1988). *See generally* Goldsmith, *Federal Courts, Foreign Affairs, and Federalism*, 83 Va. L. Rev. 1617, 1635 n.80 (1997) (collecting authorities).

Are there federal policies that are violated by the application of state choice-of-law rules in international cases? Can one argue that the United States as a whole has an interest — a federal interest — in the application of a uniform national set of choice-of-law rules that reflect U.S. understandings of international jurisdiction? Wouldn't this be a significant way to avoid parochial state court applications of local law to conduct affecting foreign interests and international commerce, but having no meaningful connection to the United States? Is it necessary to displace all state choice-of-law rules with such an approach, or do the Due Process and Foreign Commerce Clauses accomplish the result? Suppose a state applied Currie's unreservedly pro-forum interest analysis in an international case (like *Tramontana*). *See supra* pp. 744-745 & *infra* pp. 1026-1051. Would the Due Process Clause forbid this? If not, should federal common law choice-of-law principles do so? Recall the general international law prohibition against the passive personality doctrine. *See supra* pp. 601-602.

Recall that issues of judicial jurisdiction are governed largely by the federal Due Process Clause, and that the FSIA provides comprehensive federal jurisdictional and procedural rules governing actions against foreign states. *See supra* pp. 83-91, 234-235. Moreover, as discussed below, the Hague Service Convention and Hague Evidence Convention provide federal rules for other procedural aspects of international disputes. *See infra* pp. 912-917, 1026-1032. Finally, at least in federal courts, issues of *forum non conveniens* and forum selection are generally governed by federal law. *See supra* pp. 453-454, 528-533. Does all this support the argument for federal common law choice-of-law rules?

5. *Federal common law choice-of-law rule under FSIA.* As described above, 28 U.S.C. §1606 requires a federal court with jurisdiction over a foreign state under the FSIA to apply the same rules of liability as those applicable in private actions. Thus, in determining the liability of a foreign state, a court must choose a body of substantive law. *Liu* held that choice-of-law questions under the FSIA were governed by federal common law: "federal common law provides the choice-of-law rule applicable to deciding the merits of an action involving a foreign state." As discussed above, other lower courts have reached the same conclusion. *See supra* pp. 322-324. *Compare Barkanic v. General Administration of Civil Aviation,* 923 F.2d 957 (2d Cir. 1991). These decisions reason that the FSIA provides a uniform federal statutory framework for immunity of foreign states, and that important federal foreign relations interests are served by such uniformity. Moreover, application of local choice-of-law rules would result in disparate substantive laws being applicable in different courts — contrary to the FSIA's goal of uniformity.

6. *Federal common law choice-of-law rules in other federal question contexts.* Federal lower courts have also applied federal common law choice-of-law rules in other contexts where federal question jurisdiction exists (but where no express federal substantive statutory rules apply). For example, in actions arising under the Edge Act (dealing with international banking transactions), appellate courts have held that federal common law choice-of-law rules are applicable. *Corporacion Venezolana de Fomento v. Vintero Sales Corp.,* 629 F.2d 786 (2d Cir. 1980); *Aaron Ferer & Sons Ltd. v. Chase Manhattan Bank,* 731 F.2d 112 (2d Cir. 1984). *See also Johnson v. General American Life Ins. Co.,* 178 F. Supp. 2d 644, 650 (W.D. Va. 2001) (relying on federal common law choice-of-law rules in ERISA case); *Itar-Tass Russian News Agency v. Russian Kurier, Inc.,* 153 F.3d 82, 90 (2d Cir. 1998) (relying on federal common law to develop conflict norms for Copyright Act cases); *Cruz v. United States,* 387 F. Supp. 2d 1057, 1070-1071 (N.D. Cal. 2005) (applying federal common law choice-of-law principles to determine applicable limitations period in FSIA case); *Chrysler Corp. v. Ford Motor Corp.,* 972 F. Supp. 1097, 1101 n.1 (E.D. Mich. 1997) (summarizing conflicting authority over whether to apply federal common law choice-of-law rules in federal question cases). These decisions have generally relied upon the existence of federal question jurisdiction, and federal interests in international matters, to justify this approach. *See also* A. von Mehren & D. Trautman, *The Law of Multistate Problems: Cases and Materials on Conflict of Laws* 1303-1335 (1965).

Is it acceptable to apply federal common law choice-of-law rules in federal question cases? If federal jurisdiction is exclusive, is there any danger of intrastate forum shopping? If federal jurisdiction is not exclusive, then what is the justification for applying federal choice-of-law rules, notwithstanding *Klaxon* and *Day & Zimmermann*?

7. *Content of federal common law choice-of-law rules.* The content of the federal common law choice-of-law rule has generally been determined by reference to the *Restatement (Second) Conflict of Laws* (1971). *See Harris v. Polskie Linie Lotnicze,* 820 F.2d 1000, 1003-1004 (9th Cir. 1987) (applying situs/most significant relationship test of *Restatement (Second) Conflict of Laws* §175 (1971)); *Liu v. Republic of China,* 892 F.2d 1419 (9th Cir. 1989). *But see In re Air Crash over the Taiwan Strait on May 25, 2002,* 331 F. Supp. 2d 1176, 1208-1212 (C.D. Cal. 2004) (declining to decide whether *Lauritzen* test or *Restatement (Second)* test applied to claims arising under Death on High Seas Act).

For an unusual case, where judges on an appellate court disagreed over the choice-of-law rules and applicable substantive law in an international dispute, *see Khulumani v. Barclay Nat'l Bank Ltd.,* 503 F.3d 254 (2d Cir. 2007) (*per curiam*). This case involved claims under the Alien Tort Statute against corporations that allegedly did business in South Africa during the apartheid period. The judges divided over whether international law or federal common law supplied the applicable standard governing the companies' liability under a theory that they "aided and abetted" violations of the law of nations. This case represents an interesting contribution to an ongoing debate over how to perform a conflicts analysis in international tort cases of this sort. *See also Doe I v. Unocal Corp.*, 395 F.3d 932 (9th Cir. 2002), *vacated*, 395 F.3d 978 (9th Cir. 2003) (*en banc*). Subsequently, the Second Circuit resolved the disagreement among the judges in *Khulumani* and opted for an international law standard. *See Presbyterian Church of Sudan v. Talisman Energy, Inc.*, 582 F.3d 244, 259 (2d Cir. 2009).

9

Act of State and Foreign Sovereign Compulsion[1]

The act of state doctrine provides, in broad outline, that U.S. courts will not sit in judgment on the validity of the public acts of foreign sovereigns within their own territory.[2] It is related to the foreign sovereign compulsion doctrine, which provides that otherwise applicable U.S. law will not generally be applied to forbid conduct compelled by a foreign state within its own territory.[3] This chapter examines both the act of state doctrine and the doctrine of foreign sovereign compulsion.

A. Act of State Doctrine: Introduction and Historical Background

The act of state doctrine has a long history.[4] The doctrine is often traced to the 1848 decision of the House of Lords in *Duke of Brunswick v. King of Hanover*.[5] There, the former Duke of Brunswick (a German principality) sued the then Duke of Brunswick (who was

---

1. Commentary on the act of state doctrine includes, *e.g.*, Bazyler, *Abolishing the Act of State Doctrine*, 134 U. Pa. L. Rev. 325 (1986); Bradley & Goldsmith, *Customary International Law as Federal Common Law: A Critique of the Modern Position*, 110 Harv. L. Rev. 815 (1997); Burley, *Law Among Liberal States: Liberal Internationalism and the Act of State Doctrine*, 92 Colum. L. Rev. 1907 (1992); Cane, *Prerogative Acts, Acts of State and Justiciability*, 29 Int'l & Comp. L.Q. 680 (1980); Chow, *Rethinking the Act of State Doctrine: An Analysis in Terms of Jurisdiction to Prescribe*, 62 Wash. L. Rev. 397 (1987); Dellapenna, *Deciphering the Act of State Doctrine*, 35 Vill. L. Rev. 1 (1990); Halberstam, *Sabbatino Resurrected: The Act of State Doctrine in the Revised Restatement of U.S. Foreign Relations Law*, 79 Am. J. Int'l L. 68 (1985); Henkin, *Act of State Today: Recollections in Tranquility*, 6 Colum. J. Trans. L. 175 (1967); Koh, *Is International Law Really State Law?*, 111 Harv. L. Rev. 1824 (1998); Kramer, Annotation, *Modern Status of the Act of State Doctrine*, 12 A.L.R. Fed. 707 (1972 & Supp. 2010); Mathias, *Restructuring the Act of State Doctrine: A Blueprint for Legislative Reform*, 12 Law & Pol'y Int'l Bus. 369 (1980); Patterson, *The Act of State Doctrine Is Alive and Well: Why Critics of the Doctrine Are Wrong*, 15 U.C. Davis J.L. & Int'l Pol'y 111 (2008); Short & Brower, *The Taming of the Shrew: May the Act of State Doctrine and Foreign Sovereign Immunity Eat and Drink as Friends?*, 20 Hamline L. Rev. 723 (1997); Singer, *The Act of State Doctrine of the United Kingdom: An Analysis, with Comparisons to United States Practice*, 75 Am. J. Int'l L. 283 (1981).

2. *See infra* p. 808; *W.S. Kirkpatrick & Co. v. Environmental Tectonics Corp.*, 493 U.S. 400 (1990); *Banco Nacional de Cuba v. Sabbatino*, 376 U.S. 398, 416 (1964).

3. *See infra* p. 857; *Interamerican Ref. Corp. v. Texaco Maracaibo*, 307 F. Supp. 1291, 1298 (D. Del. 1970) ("[W]hen a nation compels a trade practice, firms there have no choice but to obey").

4. *See* Singer, *The Act of State Doctrine of the United Kingdom: An Analysis, with Comparisons to United States Practice*, 75 Am. J. Int'l L. 283 (1981); E. Mooney, *Foreign Seizures* 7-10 (1967) (tracing doctrine to *Blad v. Bamfield*); A. Ehrenzweig, *A Treatise on the Conflict of Laws* §48 n.19 (1962) (tracing doctrine to 1364). A seventeenth-century English decision, *Blad v. Bamfield*, is also cited as the doctrine's common law source. 36 Eng. Rep. 992 (Ch. 1674). In *Blad*, an English court refused to consider a challenge to the validity of a patent granted to a Danish trader by the king of Denmark.

5. (1848) 2 H.L. Cas. 1.

also the King of Hanover), alleging that the defendant had wrongly seized certain funds in Brunswick belonging to the plaintiff. The House of Lords ruled for the defendant, reasoning "that a foreign sovereign . . . cannot be made responsible [in an English court] for an act done in his sovereign character in his own country; . . . the courts of this country cannot sit in judgment upon an act of a sovereign . . . done in the exercise of his authority vested in him as sovereign."[6]

In the United States, the origin of the act of state doctrine is the Supreme Court's 1897 decision in *Underhill v. Hernandez*.[7] *Underhill* arose after a U.S. engineer filed suit in the United States seeking damages from a Venezuelan revolutionary commander for his wrongful imprisonment of the American during a coup in Venezuela. The Supreme Court affirmed dismissal of the claim, adopting (without citation) the *Duke of Brunswick*'s reasoning:

> Every sovereign State is bound to respect the independence of every other sovereign State, *and the courts of one country will not sit in judgment on the acts of the government of another, done within its own territory.*[8]

The rationale in *Underhill* for this "classic American statement"[9] of the act of state doctrine was unclear. On the one hand, the Court suggested that the doctrine was compelled by international law, emphasizing the obligation of national courts "to respect the independence of every other sovereign State."[10] On the other hand, the Court did not clearly say this, and it cited nothing to support its formulation of the act of state doctrine. Moreover, it also referred to the "immunity of individuals from suits," suggesting that principles of sovereign immunity were relevant of the act of state doctrine.[11]

Other early U.S. decisions followed *Underhill* in dismissing suits on act of state grounds. The Court arguably applied the act of state doctrine in *American Banana Company v. United Fruit Company*,[12] where the plaintiff challenged the Costa Rican government's seizure of his banana plantation (allegedly at the defendant's behest). Although dealing principally with the interpretation of the Sherman Act,[13] *American Banana* also cited *Underhill* for the proposition that "a seizure by a state is not a thing that can be complained of elsewhere in the courts."[14]

Unrest in Mexico during the early decades of the twentieth century provided the background for further act of state rulings. In two 1918 cases — *Oetjen v. Central Leather Company* and *Ricaud v. American Metal Company* — U.S. citizens asserted claims against other private parties.[15] In each case, the claims were based upon the allegation that

---

6. (1848) 2 H.L. Cas. at 17 (Lord Cottenham).

7. 168 U.S. 250 (1897). Like *Duke of Brunswick*, *Underhill* might have been resolved on grounds of sovereign immunity over foreign heads of state. *See also The Schooner Exchange v. McFaddon*, 11 U.S. 116, 146 (1812) (raising both act of state and foreign sovereign immunity concerns); *Hatch v. Baez*, 14 N.Y. Sup. Ct. 596 (App. Div. 1876). In *Hatch*, the lower court had held that "the courts of one country are bound to abstain from sitting in judgment on the acts of another government within its territory," citing "universal comity of nations and the established rules of international law." *Id.* at 599. The Appellate Division held that the defendant — the former President of San Domingo — was entitled to continuing sovereign immunity, citing *Schooner Exchange*.

8. 168 U.S. at 252 (emphasis added).

9. *Banco Nacional de Cuba v. Sabbatino*, 376 U.S. 398, 416 (1964).

10. 168 U.S. at 252.

11. 168 U.S. at 253-254.

12. 213 U.S. 347 (1909).

13. *See supra* pp. 651-653.

14. 213 U.S. at 357-358. The Court also said that "[t]he very meaning of sovereignty is that the decree of the sovereign makes law." 213 U.S. at 358. Nevertheless, in *W.S. Kirkpatrick & Co. v. Environmental Tectonics Corp.*, 493 U.S. 400, 407-408 (1990), the Court said that "*American Banana* was not an act of state case."

15. *E.g., Oetjen v. Central Leather Co.*, 246 U.S. 297 (1918); *Ricaud v. American Metal Co.*, 246 U.S. 304 (1918).

the plaintiffs' property had been unlawfully seized by revolutionary forces in Mexico and subsequently transferred to the defendant. The plaintiffs sought return of "their" property, arguing that the defendant could not have obtained good title from the Mexican revolutionary regime, because its seizure of the property had been wrongful.[16] Relying on *Underhill*, both *Oetjen* and *Ricaud* applied the act of state doctrine, and refused to entertain the suits.

Again, however, the precise rationale for the act of state doctrine was unclear. Both *Oetjen* and *Ricaud* contained passages suggesting that the doctrine was derived from principles of international comity. According to *Oetjen*, the act of state doctrine "rests at last upon the highest considerations of international comity and expediency,"[17] reasoning that "[t]o permit the validity of the acts of one sovereign State to be reexamined and perhaps condemned by the courts of another would very certainly imperil the amicable relations between governments and vex the peace of nations."[18] Similarly, in *Ricaud*, the Court referred to the "political nature" of the parties' dispute.[19]

At the same time, however, both *Oetjen* and *Ricaud* also described the act of state doctrine as a choice-of-law rule, selecting the substantive law applicable to the challenged seizure:

> [T]itle to the property in this case must be determined by the result of the action taken by the military authorities of Mexico. . . . [T]he act within its own boundaries of one sovereign State cannot become the subject of reexamination and modification in the courts of another. Such action, when shown to have been taken, becomes . . . a rule of decision for the courts of this country.[20]

Under this view, application of the act of state doctrine was "not a surrender or abandonment of jurisdiction but . . . an exercise of it."[21]

Although these early act of state decisions denied a U.S. judicial remedy, they did not contemplate leaving the plaintiffs with no remedy. Rather, the Court obliged the claimants to seek recovery by requesting the U.S. Government to pursue their claims through diplomatic channels against the foreign state.[22] "The remedy of the former owner . . . must be found in the courts of Mexico or through the diplomatic agencies of the political department of our Government."[23] The U.S. Government frequently agreed to such requests, and the "espousal" of U.S. nationals' claims was a common (and often successful) occurrence in nineteenth-century diplomatic relations.[24]

The Supreme Court's leading contemporary treatment of the act of state doctrine is *Banco Nacional de Cuba v. Sabbatino.*[25] *Sabbatino* arose from a suit by a Cuban state-owned bank seeking recovery of sugar that it had delivered to a U.S. purchaser, but for which it had not received repayment. The U.S. purchaser defended, among other things, on the grounds that Cuba had expropriated the sugar in violation of international law, and thus

---

16. *Oetjen*, 246 U.S. at 299-301; *Ricaud*, 246 U.S. at 305-306.

17. 246 U.S. at 303-304.

18. 246 U.S. at 304.

19. 246 U.S. at 309.

20. 246 U.S. at 309-310. *See also Oetjen*, 246 U.S. at 303.

21. *Oetjen*, 246 U.S. at 309.

22. *Underhill*, 168 U.S. at 252 ("Redress of grievances by reason of such acts must be obtained through the means open to be availed of by sovereign powers between themselves.").

23. *Oetjen*, 246 U.S. at 304.

24. *See Shapleigh v. Mier*, 299 U.S. 468, 469-471 (1937); *Dames & Moore v. Regan*, 453 U.S. 654, 679-684 (1981); *Ozanic v. United States*, 188 F.2d 228 (2d Cir. 1951); *Restatement (Third) Foreign Relations Law* §713, Reporters' Note 9 (1987).

25. 376 U.S. 398 (1964) (excerpted below).

that the Cuban state-owned bank lacked title to the property in question. The bank replied by invoking the act of state doctrine, which, it urged, precluded U.S. judicial inquiry into the validity of Cuba's seizure of the sugar.

In a lengthy opinion, *Sabbatino* both reaffirmed the traditional act of state doctrine and expressed the doctrine's rationale in new terms. According to Justice Harlan, the doctrine has "'constitutional' underpinnings" that reflect "a basic choice regarding the competence and function of the Judiciary and the National Executive in ordering our relationships with other members of the international community."[26] More specifically, the act of state doctrine "expresses the strong sense of the Judicial Branch that its engagement in the task of passing on the validity of foreign acts of state may hinder rather than further this country's pursuit of goals both for itself and for the community of nations."[27] Thus, unlike earlier act of state decisions, which emphasized international law, comity, and choice-of-law principles, *Sabbatino* relied in significant part on domestic separation of powers considerations.

Following *Sabbatino*, lower courts frequently invoked the act of state doctrine to dismiss complaints involving foreign governmental activity.[28] The *Third Restatement*, released in 1987, largely adopted the *Sabbatino* formulation.[29] The doctrine came to play a significant role in international litigation. Disagreement about the character and scope of the doctrine was endemic, however, leading to divergent and unpredictable results: "few doctrines in American law are in such a state of utter confusion as is the act of state doctrine."[30]

In 1990, the Supreme Court decided *W.S. Kirkpatrick & Co. v. Environmental Tectonics Corporation*.[31] The Court's opinion reformulated the act of state doctrine in potentially important respects and offered yet another rationale for the rule. The case arose from competing bids made by two U.S. companies for a Nigerian defense contract. After learning that its U.S. competitor had paid various "commissions" to Nigerian government officials in order to obtain the contract, the losing bidder filed a federal antitrust and RICO action against the successful bidder. The district court dismissed the suit, reasoning that it would require an adjudication of the official motivations for the Nigerian contract award, and that the act of state doctrine forbade such an inquiry.[32]

The Supreme Court rejected the trial court's reasoning and held that the act of state doctrine was simply not applicable. Justice Scalia, writing for a unanimous Court, declared that the act of state doctrine applied only to cases challenging the "validity" of foreign sovereign acts and that "nothing in the present suit required the court to declare invalid, and thus ineffective as 'rule of decision for the courts of this country,' the official act of a foreign sovereign."[33] Specifically overruling several expansive lower court interpretations of *Sabbatino*, the Court concluded that "[a]ct of state issues only arise when a court *must decide*— that is, when the outcome of the case turns upon — the effect of official action by a foreign sovereign."[34] Turning to the rationale for the act of state doctrine, Justice Scalia acknowledged that the doctrine's "jurisprudential foundation . . . has undergone some evolution over the years."[35] Apparently rejecting the notion that the doctrine operated as

26. 376 U.S. at 423, 425.
27. 376 U.S. at 423.
28. *See* Annotation, *Modern Status of the Act of State Doctrine*, 12 A.L.R. Fed. 707 (1972 & Supp. 2010).
29. *Restatement (Third) Foreign Relations Law* §443 (1987). *See infra* p. 808.
30. Dellapenna, *Deciphering the Act of State Doctrine*, 35 Vill. L. Rev. 1, 7 (1990).
31. 493 U.S. 400 (1990) (excerpted below).
32. 659 F. Supp. 1381 (D.N.J. 1987).
33. 493 U.S. at 405.
34. 493 U.S. at 406 (emphasis in original).
35. 493 U.S. at 404.

an international law or separation of powers principle, *Environmental Tectonics* treated the doctrine as a choice-of-law rule: "the act of state doctrine is not some vague doctrine of abstention but a '*principle of decision* binding on federal and state courts alike.' "[36]

The Supreme Court and other authorities have suggested a variety of significant exceptions to the act of state doctrine. Unfortunately, the Court has been unable to produce a majority opinion dealing with any of these exceptions. In *Alfred Dunhill of London v. Republic of Cuba,* four members of the Court embraced an exception to the doctrine encompassing "commercial" acts of foreign states.[37] In *First National City Bank v. Banco Nacional de Cuba,* three members of a badly fractured Court adopted the so-called "*Bernstein*" exception, which provides that the act of state doctrine is inapplicable where the executive branch informs the judiciary that its adjudication of a case will not hinder the nation's foreign policy.[38] Additional exceptions to the act of state doctrine have been formulated by the lower courts[39] and by Congress.[40]

B. Contemporary Formulations of the Act of State Doctrine

1. The *Sabbatino* Decision

Any consideration of the contemporary act of state doctrine must begin with *Banco Nacional de Cuba v. Sabbatino,* excerpted below. The opinion aroused considerable controversy,[41] and shortly after the Supreme Court's decision, Congress enacted legislation to overturn the specific *Sabbatino* holding.[42] Moreover, the Court's subsequent decisions in *Albert Dunhill, First National City Bank,* and *Environmental Tectonics* have eroded *Sabbatino*'s statement of the act of state doctrine. Nonetheless, the Court's rationale remains significant, both in the act of state context and elsewhere.

BANCO NACIONAL DE CUBA v. SABBATINO
376 U.S. 398 (1964)

JUSTICE HARLAN. [In 1960, after Fidel Castro's seizure of power in Cuba, relations between the United States and Cuba grew increasingly strained. In July 1960, in response to a U.S. reduction of Cuba's quota for sugar imports into the United States, Cuba

36. 493 U.S. at 406 (emphasis in original).

37. 425 U.S. 682, 695 (1976). Four other Justices rejected the commercial exception, while Justice Stevens did not expressly state a position. 425 U.S. at 715.

38. 406 U.S. 759, 768 (1972). Four Justices expressly rejected the *Bernstein* exception and two others expressed no clear view. 406 U.S. at 772 (Douglas, J., concurring); 406 U.S. at 775-776 (Powell, J., concurring).

39. See *First Nat'l City Bank v. Banco Nacional de Cuba,* 406 U.S. 759 (1972) (counterclaim exception); *Kalamazoo Spice Extraction Co. v. Provisional Military Gov't of Socialist Ethiopia,* 729 F.2d 422 (6th Cir. 1984) (treaty exception).

40. 22 U.S.C. §2370(e)(2) (1982) (Second Hickenlooper amendment) and 9 U.S.C. §15 (enforcement of certain arbitral awards). See *infra* pp. 856-857.

41. *See, e.g.,* Cardozo, *Congress versus Sabbatino: Constitutional Consideration,* 4 Colum. J. Transnat'l L. 297 (1966); Henkin, *The Foreign Affairs Power of the Federal Courts: Sabbatino,* 64 Colum. L. Rev. 805 (1964); Jennings, *Comments,* in *The Aftermath of Sabbatino* 87 (Tondel ed. 1965); Kline, *An Examination of the Competence of National Courts to Prescribe and Apply International Law: The Sabbatino Case Revisited,* 1 U.S.F. L. Rev. 49 (1966); Mann, *The Legal Consequences of Sabbatino,* 51 Va. L. Rev. 604 (1965); McDougal, *Comments,* in *Panel: Enforcing International Law Against One Country Through Domestic Litigation in Others,* 58 ASIL Proc. 48 (1964); Metzger, *Act-of-State Doctrine Redefined: The Sabbatino Case,* 1964 Sup. Ct. Rev. 223.

42. Second Hickenlooper Amendment, 22 U.S.C. §2370 (e)(1)-(2); *infra* pp. 856-857.

nationalized most property in Cuba belonging to U.S. nationals. In expropriating U.S. property, Castro declared that Cuba must be a "luminous and stimulating example for the sister nations of America and all the underdeveloped countries of the world to follow in their struggle to free themselves from the brutal claws of Imperialism." Among the companies whose property was nationalized was Compania Azucarera Vertientes ("CAV"), which had contracted to sell a shipload of sugar to Farr, Whitlock, a U.S. commodities broker. After nationalization of CAV's sugar, Farr, Whitlock entered into a second contract for the sugar with the Cuban government, which purported to be the new "owner" of the sugar. Farr, Whitlock then shipped the sugar and, after receiving payment from its customers, turned the proceeds over to the receiver for CAV ("Sabbatino"), rather than to Cuba. Banco Nacional de Cuba, which had been assigned the Cuban government's right to payment under Farr, Whitlock's second contract, then filed suit against Farr, Whitlock, and Sabbatino in U.S. courts. The defendants argued that the shipload of sugar never belonged to Cuba, because the Cuban seizure of the sugar violated international law.]

While acknowledging the continuing vitality of the act of state doctrine, the [trial] court believed it inapplicable when the questioned foreign act is in violation of international law. Proceeding on the basis that a taking invalid under international law does not convey good title, the District Court found the Cuban expropriation decree to violate such law in three separate respects: it was motivated by a retaliatory and not a public purpose; it discriminated against American nationals; and it failed to provide adequate compensation. Summary judgment against petitioner was accordingly granted. The Court of Appeals, affirming the decision on similar grounds, relied on two letters (not before the District Court) written by State Department officers which it took as evidence that the Executive Branch had no objection to a judicial testing of the Cuban decree's validity. . . .

The classic American statement of the act of state doctrine . . . is found in *Underhill v. Hernandez,* where Chief Justice Fuller said for a unanimous Court:

> Every sovereign State is bound to respect the independence of every other sovereign State, and the courts of one country will not sit in judgment on the acts of the government of another done within its own territory. Redress of grievances by reason of such acts must be obtained through the means open to be availed of by sovereign powers as between themselves.

Following this precept the Court in that case refused to inquire into acts of Hernandez, a revolutionary Venezuelan military commander whose government had been later recognized by the United States, which were made the basis of a damage action in this country by Underhill, an American citizen, who claimed that he had been unlawfully assaulted, coerced, and detained in Venezuela by Hernandez. None of this Court's subsequent cases in which the act of state doctrine was directly or peripherally involved manifest any retreat from *Underhill. See American Banana Co. v. United Fruit Co.; Oetjen v. Central Leather Co.; Ricaud v. American Metal Co.* On the contrary in two of these cases, *Oetjen* and *Ricaud,* the doctrine as announced in *Underhill* was reaffirmed in unequivocal terms. . . .

In deciding the present case the Court of Appeals relied in part upon an exception to the unqualified teachings of *Underhill, Oetjen,* and *Ricaud* which that court had earlier indicated. In *Bernstein v. Van Heyghen Freres Societe Anonyme,* 163 F.2d 246, suit was brought to recover from an assignee property allegedly taken, in effect, by the Nazi Government because plaintiff was Jewish. Recognizing the odious nature of this act of state, the court, through Judge Learned Hand, nonetheless refused to consider it invalid on that ground. Rather, it looked to see if the Executive had acted in any manner that would indicate that

United States Courts should refuse to give effect to such a foreign decree. Finding no such evidence, the court sustained dismissal of the complaint. In a later case involving similar facts the same court again assumed examination of the German acts improper, *Bernstein v. N.V. Nederlandsche-Amerikaansche Stoomvaart-Maatschappij*, 173 F.2d 71, but, quite evidently following the implications of Judge Hand's opinion in the earlier case, amended its mandate to permit evidence of alleged invalidity, 210 F.2d 375, subsequent to receipt by plaintiff's attorney of a letter from the Acting Legal Adviser to the State Department written for the purpose of relieving the court from any constraint upon the exercise of its jurisdiction to pass on that question. This Court has never had occasion to pass upon the so-called *Bernstein* exception, nor need it do so now. For whatever ambiguity may be thought to exist in the two letters from State Department officials on which the Court of Appeals relied, is now removed by the position which the Executive has taken in this Court on the act of state claim; respondents do not indeed contest the view that these letters were intended to reflect no more than the Department's then wish not to make any statement bearing on this litigation.

The outcome of this case, therefore, turns upon whether any of the contentions urged by respondents against the application of the act of state doctrine in the premises is acceptable: (1) that the doctrine does not apply to acts of state which violate international law, as is claimed to be the case here; (2) that the doctrine is inapplicable unless the Executive specifically interposes it in a particular case; and (3) that, in any event, the doctrine may not be invoked by a foreign government plaintiff in our courts.

Preliminarily, we discuss the foundations on which we deem the act of state doctrine to rest, and more particularly the question of whether state or federal law governs its application in a federal diversity case. We do not believe that this doctrine is compelled either by the inherent nature of sovereign authority, as some of the earlier decisions seem to imply, *see Underhill, supra; American Banana, supra; Oetjen, supra,* or by some principle of international law. If a transaction takes place in one jurisdiction and the forum is in another, the forum does not by dismissing an action or by applying its own law purport to divest the first jurisdiction of its territorial sovereignty; it merely declines to adjudicate or makes applicable its own law to parties or property before it. The refusal of one country to enforce the penal laws of another is a typical example of an instance when a court will not entertain a cause of action arising in another jurisdiction. While historic notions of sovereign authority do bear upon the wisdom of employing the act of state doctrine, they do not dictate its existence.

That international law does not require application of the doctrine is evidenced by the practice of nations. Most of the countries rendering decisions on the subject fail to follow the rule rigidly. No international arbitral or judicial decision suggests that international law prescribes recognition of sovereign acts of governments, and apparently no claim has ever been raised before an international tribunal that failure to apply the act of state doctrine constitutes a breach of international obligation. If international law does not prescribe use of the doctrine, neither does it forbid application of the rule even if it is claimed that the act of state in question violated international law. The traditional view of international law is that it establishes substantive principles for determining whether one country has wronged another. Because of its peculiar nation-to-nation character the usual method for an individual to seek relief is to exhaust local remedies and then repair to the executive authorities of his own state to persuade them to champion his claim in diplomacy or before an international tribunal. Although it is, of course, true that the United States courts apply international law as part of our own in appropriate circumstances, *The Paquete Habana, supra,* the public law of nations can hardly dictate to a country which is in theory wronged how to treat that wrong within its domestic borders.

Despite the broad statement in *Oetjen* that "The conduct of the foreign relations of our Government is committed by the Constitution to the Executive and Legislative . . . Departments," 246 U.S. at 302, it cannot of course be thought that "every case or controversy which touches foreign relations lies beyond judicial cognizance." *Baker v. Carr,* 369 U.S. 186, 211 (1962). . . . The text of the Constitution does not require the act of state doctrine; it does not irrevocably remove from the judiciary the capacity to review the validity of foreign acts of state.

The act of state doctrine does, however, have "constitutional" underpinnings. It arises out of the basic relationships between branches of government in a system of separation of powers. It concerns the competency of dissimilar institutions to make and implement particular kinds of decisions in the area of international relations. The doctrine as formulated in past decisions expresses the strong sense of the Judicial Branch that its engagement in the task of passing on the validity of foreign acts of state may hinder rather than further this country's pursuit of goals both for itself and for the community of nations as a whole in the international sphere. . . . Whatever considerations are thought to predominate, it is plain that the problems involved are uniquely federal in nature. If federal authority, in this instance this Court, orders the field of judicial competence in this area for the federal courts, and the state courts are left free to formulate their own rules, the purposes behind the doctrine could be as effectively undermined as if there had been no federal pronouncement on the subject.

We could perhaps in this diversity action avoid the question of deciding whether federal or state law is applicable to this aspect of the litigation. New York has enunciated the act of state doctrine in terms that echo those of federal decisions decided during the reign of *Swift v. Tyson,* 41 U.S. 1 (1842). In *Hatch v. Baez,* 7 Hun. 596, 599 (N.Y. Sup. Ct.), *Underhill* was foreshadowed by the words, "the courts of one country are bound to abstain from sitting in judgment on the acts of another government done within its own territory." . . . Thus our conclusions might well be the same whether we dealt with this problem as one of state law, *see Erie R. Co. v. Tompkins,* or federal law.

However, we are constrained to make it clear that an issue concerned with a basic choice regarding the competence and function of the Judiciary and the National Executive in ordering our relationships with other members of the international community must be treated exclusively as an aspect of federal law.[43] It seems fair to assume that the Court did not have rules like the act of state doctrine in mind when it decided *Erie R. Co. v. Tompkins.* Soon thereafter, Professor Philip C. Jessup, now a judge of the International Court of Justice, recognized the potential dangers were *Erie* extended to legal problems affecting international relations.[44] He cautioned that the rules of international law should not be left to divergent and perhaps parochial state interpretations. His basic rationale is equally applicable to the act of state doctrine. . . . We conclude that the scope of the act of state doctrine must be determined according to federal law.[45]

If the act of state doctrine is a principle of decision binding on federal and state courts alike but compelled by neither international law nor the Constitution, its continuing vitality depends on its capacity to reflect the proper distribution of functions between

---

43. At least this is true when the Court limits the scope of judicial inquiry. We need not now consider whether a state court might, in certain circumstances, adhere to a more restrictive view concerning the scope of examination of foreign acts than that required by this Court.

44. Jessup, *The Doctrine of* Erie Railroad v. Tompkins *Applied to International Law,* 33 Am. J. Int'l L. 740 (1939).

45. Various constitutional and statutory provisions indirectly support this determination, *see* U.S. Const., Art. I, §8, cls. 3, 10; Art. II, §§2, 3; Art. III, §2; 28 U.S.C. §§1251 (a)(2), (b)(1), (b)(3), 1332 (a)(2), 1333, 1350-1351, by reflecting a concern for uniformity in this country's dealings with foreign nations and indicating a desire to give matters of international significance to the jurisdiction of federal institutions. . . .

the judicial and political branches of the Government on matters bearing upon foreign affairs. It should be apparent that the greater the degree of codification or consensus concerning a particular area of international law, the more appropriate it is for the judiciary to render decisions regarding it, since the courts can then focus on the application of an agreed principle to circumstances of fact rather than on the sensitive task of establishing a principle not inconsistent with the national interest or with international justice. It is also evident that some aspects of international law touch much more sharply on national nerves than do others; the less important the implications of an issue are for our foreign relations, the weaker the justification for exclusivity in the political branches. The balance of relevant considerations may also be shifted if the government which perpetrated the challenged act of state is no longer in existence, as in the *Bernstein* case, for the political interest of this country may, as a result, be measurably altered. Therefore, rather than laying down or reaffirming an inflexible and all-encompassing rule in this case, we decide only that the Judicial Branch will not examine the validity of a taking of property within its own territory by a foreign sovereign government, extant and recognized by this country at the time of suit, in the absence of a treaty or other unambiguous agreement regarding controlling legal principles, even if the complaint alleges that the taking violates customary international law.

There are few if any issues in international law today on which opinion seems to be so divided as the limitations on a state's power to expropriate the property of aliens. There is, of course, authority, in international judicial and arbitral decisions, in the expressions of national governments, and among commentators for the view that a taking is improper under international law if it is not for a public purpose, is discriminatory, or is without provision for prompt, adequate, and effective compensation. However, Communist countries, although they have in fact provided a degree of compensation after diplomatic efforts, commonly recognize no obligation on the part of the taking country. Certain representatives of the newly independent and underdeveloped countries have questioned whether rules of state responsibility toward aliens can bind nations that have not consented to them and it is argued that the traditionally articulated standards governing expropriation of property reflect "imperialist" interests and are inappropriate to the circumstances of emergent states.

The disagreement as to relevant international law standards reflects an even more basic divergence between the national interests of capital importing and capital exporting nations and between the social ideologies of those countries that favor state control of a considerable portion of the means of production and those that adhere to a free enterprise system. It is difficult to imagine the courts of this country embarking on adjudication in an area which touches more sensitively the practical and ideological goals of the various members of the community of nations.[46] . . .

The possible adverse consequences of a conclusion [permitting U.S. courts to characterize foreign expropriations as violations of international law] is highlighted by contrasting the practices of the political branch with the limitations of the judicial process in matters of this kind. Following an expropriation of any significance, the Executive engages in diplomacy aimed to assure that United States citizens who are harmed are compensated fairly. Representing all claimants of this country, it will often be able, either by bilateral or multilateral talks, by submission to the United Nations, or by the employment of economic and political sanctions, to achieve some degree of general redress.

46. There are, of course, areas of international law in which consensus as to standards is greater and which do not represent a battleground for conflicting ideologies. This decision in no way intimates that the courts of this country are broadly foreclosed from considering questions of international law.

Judicial determinations of invalidity of title can, on the other hand, have only an occasional impact, since they depend on the fortuitous circumstance of the property in question being brought into this country.[47] Such decisions would, if the acts involved were declared invalid, often be likely to give offense to the expropriating country; since the concept of territorial sovereignty is so deep seated, any state may resent the refusal of the courts of another sovereign to accord validity to acts within its territorial borders. Piecemeal dispositions of this sort involving the probability of affront to another state could seriously interfere with negotiations being carried on by the Executive Branch and might prevent or render less favorable the terms of an agreement that could otherwise be reached. Relations with third countries which have engaged in similar expropriations would not be immune from effect. The dangers of such adjudication are present regardless of whether the State Department has, as it did in this case, asserted that the relevant act violated international law. If the Executive Branch has undertaken negotiations with an expropriating country, but has refrained from claims of violation of the law of nations, a determination to that effect by a court might be regarded as a serious insult, while a finding of compliance with international law, would greatly strengthen the bargaining hand of the other state with consequent detriment to American interests.

Even if the State Department has proclaimed the impropriety of the expropriation, the stamp of approval of its view by a judicial tribunal, however impartial, might increase any affront and the judicial decision might occur at a time, almost always well after the taking, when such an impact would be contrary to our national interest. Considerably more serious and far-reaching consequences would flow from a judicial finding that international law standards had been met if that determination flew in the face of a State Department proclamation to the contrary. When articulating principles of international law in its relations with other states, the Executive Branch speaks not only as an interpreter of generally accepted and traditional rules, as would the courts, but also as an advocate of standards it believes desirable for the community of nations and protective of national concerns. In short, whatever way the matter is cut, the possibility of conflict between the Judicial and Executive Branches could hardly be avoided. . . .

Another serious consequence of the exception pressed by respondents would be to render uncertain titles in foreign commerce, with the possible consequence of altering the flow of international trade. If the attitude of the United States courts were unclear, one buying expropriated goods would not know if he could safely import them into this country. Even were takings known to be invalid, one would have difficulty determining after goods had changed hands several times whether the particular articles in question were the product of an ineffective state act.

Against the force of such considerations, we find respondents' countervailing arguments quite unpersuasive. Their basic contention is that United States courts could make a significant contribution to the growth of international law, a contribution whose importance, it is said, would be magnified by the relative paucity of decisional law by international bodies. But given the fluidity of present world conditions, the effectiveness of such a patchwork approach toward the formulation of an acceptable body of law concerning state responsibility for expropriations is, to say the least, highly conjectural. Moreover, it rests upon the sanguine presupposition that the decisions of the courts of the world's major capital exporting country and principal exponent of the free enterprise system would be accepted as disinterested expressions of sound legal principle by those adhering to widely different ideologies.

---

47. It is, of course, true that such determinations might influence others not to bring expropriated property into the country, so their indirect impact might extend beyond the actual invalidations of title.

It is contended that regardless of the fortuitous circumstances necessary for United States jurisdiction over a case involving a foreign act of state and the resultant isolated application to any expropriation program taken as a whole, it is the function of the courts to justly decide individual disputes before them. Perhaps the most typical act of state case involves the original owner or his assignee suing one not in association with the expropriating state who has had "title" transferred to him. But it is difficult to regard the claim of the original owner, who otherwise may be recompensed through diplomatic channels, as more demanding of judicial cognizance than the claim of title by the innocent third party purchaser, who, if the property is taken from him, is without any remedy. . . .

It is suggested that if the act of state doctrine is applicable to violations of international law, it should only be so when the Executive Branch expressly stipulates that it does not wish the courts to pass on the question of validity. We should be slow to reject the representations of the Government that such a reversal of the *Bernstein* principle would work serious inroads on the maximum effectiveness of United States diplomacy. Often the State Department will wish to refrain from taking an official position, particularly at a moment that would be dictated by the development of private litigation but might be inopportune diplomatically. . . . We do not now pass on the *Bernstein* exception, but even if it were deemed valid, its suggested extension is unwarranted. However offensive to the public policy of this country and its constituent States an expropriation of this kind may be, we conclude that both the national interest and progress toward the goal of establishing the rule of law among nations are best served by maintaining intact the act of state doctrine in this realm of its application.

Finally, we must determine whether Cuba's status as a plaintiff in this case dictates a result at variance with the conclusions reached above. If the Court were to distinguish between suits brought by sovereign states and those of assignees, the rule would have little effect unless a careful examination were made in each case to determine if the private party suing had taken property in good faith. Such an inquiry would be exceptionally difficult, since the relevant transaction would almost invariably have occurred outside our borders. If such an investigation were deemed irrelevant, a state could always assign its claim. . . . [Moreover,] the distinction proposed would sanction self-help remedies, something hardly conducive to a peaceful international order. . . .

JUSTICE WHITE, dissenting. I am dismayed that the Court has, with one broad stroke, declared the ascertainment and application of international law beyond the competence of the Courts of the United States in a large and important category of cases. I am also disappointed in the Court's declaration that the acts of a sovereign state with regard to the property of aliens within its borders are beyond the reach of international law in the courts of this country. However clearly established that law may be, a sovereign may violate it with impunity, except insofar as the political branches of the government may provide a remedy. This backward-looking doctrine, never before declared in this Court, is carried a disconcerting step further: not only are the courts powerless to question acts of state proscribed by international law but they are likewise powerless to refuse to adjudicate the claim founded upon a foreign law; they must render judgment and thereby validate the lawless act. Since the Court expressly extends its ruling to all acts of state expropriating property, however clearly inconsistent with the international community, all discriminatory expropriations of the property of aliens, as for example the taking of properties of persons belonging to certain races, religions or nationalities, are entitled to automatic validation in the courts of the United States. No other civilized country has found such a rigid rule necessary for the survival of the executive branch of its government; the executive of no other government seems to require such insulation from international

808   Chapter 9.   Act of State and Foreign Sovereign Compulsion

law adjudications in its courts; and no other judiciary is apparently so incompetent to ascertain and apply international law.[48] I do not believe that the act of state doctrine, as judicially fashioned in this Court, and the reasons underlying it, require American courts to decide cases in disregard of international law and the rights of litigants to a full determination on the merits. . . .

Notes on Sabbatino

1. *Elements of act of state doctrine.* As articulated in *Sabbatino,* the act of state doctrine is an invitation to confusion and unmoored expansion. In considering the doctrine, it is essential to distinguish clearly between the legal rule (and the elements of that rule) and the stated rationale for that rule.

What exactly is the legal rule prescribed by the act of state doctrine? What elements must be proven for the act of state doctrine to apply? *Sabbatino* went to some lengths to state only a narrow holding, that U.S. courts "will not examine the validity of a taking of property within its own territory by a foreign sovereign government, extant and recognized by this country at the time of suit, in the absence of a treaty or other unambiguous agreement regarding controlling legal principles, even if the complaint alleges that the taking violates customary international law." The *Third Restatement* proposes the following formulation:

> In the absence of a treaty or other unambiguous agreement regarding controlling legal principles, courts in the United States will generally refrain from examining the validity of a taking by a foreign state of property within its own territory, or from sitting in judgment on other acts of a governmental character done by a foreign state within its own territory and applicable there. *Restatement (Third) Foreign Relations Law* §443 (1987).

The necessary elements of an act of state defense under §443 include: (1) a U.S. court sitting in judgment on, (2) a taking of property or other act of "governmental character," (3) by a "foreign state," (4) within its own territory, (5) that is not governed by any "controlling" statute or international agreement. Are the act of state rules adopted in *Sabbatino* and §443 identical?

2. *Beyond the elements: authorities applying a balancing test to the act of state doctrine.* Most courts continue to apply the act of state doctrine whenever a specified list of elements is satisfied (as apparently contemplated by *Sabbatino* and the *Third Restatement*). In contrast, other courts treat satisfaction of the elements as the beginning, not the end of the analysis. Once determining that a case satisfies the act of state, validity, and situs requirements, they then employ a multi-factor balancing test to determine whether, as a prudential matter, the act of state doctrine should apply. *See United States v. Portrait of Wally*, 663 F. Supp. 2d 232, 248 (S.D.N.Y. 2009) (exemplifying the approach); *Deir menjian v. Deutsche Bank, A.G.*, 2006 WL 4749756 (C.D. Cal. Sept. 25, 2006) (same). Such decisions rest implicitly on the premise that the rationale for the doctrine is a flexible, prudential one—such as abstention or political questions. These factors include, for example, the degree of international consensus about whether an act violated international law,

---

48. The Court does not refer to any country which has applied the act of state doctrine in a case where a substantial international law issue is sought to be raised by an alien whose property has been expropriated. This country and this Court stand alone among the civilized nations of the world in ruling that such an issue is not cognizable in a court of law.

the implications for U.S. foreign policy, whether the sovereign entity still exists, and whether it was acting in the public interest.

Is this balancing approach consistent with the vision of the act of state doctrine articulated in *Sabbatino*? Regardless of its consistency with prior precedent, is a shift toward a multi-factored balancing test a healthy or unhealthy development in this area of law? Doesn't it undermine the value of bright line rules both as a matter of judicial administration and to provide predictability to the executive branch?

In this vein, consider the following comments from a recent decision of the D.C. Circuit. The underlying case involved a claim for recovery of materials that had allegedly been expropriated by the Russian Government under a prior regime. After concluding that the elements of *Sabbatino* had been satisfied with respect to at least part of the claim, the court considered the plaintiff's argument that it had the discretion to decline to apply the doctrine in these circumstances:

> [A]pplication of *Sabbatino*'s invitation to flexibility would here embroil the court in a seemingly rather political evaluation of the character of the regime change itself — in comparison, for example, to de-Nazification and other aspects of Germany's postwar history. It is hard to imagine that we are qualified to make such judgments. Moreover, our plunging into the process would seem likely, at least in the absence of an authoritative lead from the political branches, to entail just the implications for foreign affairs that the doctrine is designed to avert. *Agudas Chasidei Chabad of U.S. v. Russian Fed'n*, 528 F.3d 934, 954 (D.C. Cir. 2008).

Do you agree with the court's suggestion that more rigorous application of the act of state doctrine is called for when the state itself is the defendant? When the current regime opposes the suit? Does a case involving the validity of an act of state entail any more "implications for foreign affairs" than suits against foreign sovereigns generally?

3. *Foreign governmental acts protected by* Sabbatino *— what is an "act of state"*? *Sabbatino*'s specific holding was limited to the taking of property. Does the act of state doctrine also apply to other governmental acts? Are all "public acts," provided that they occur on the foreign state's territory, entitled to protection under the act of state doctrine? How does §443 of the *Third Restatement* resolve this question?

Sabbatino suggests that governmental acts other than expropriations must be independently evaluated, and that relevant considerations to this determination include how sharply a particular issue "touch[es] on national nerves"; the "degree of codification or consensus concerning a particular area of international law"; and the "implications of an issue . . . for our foreign policy." *Compare W.S. Kirkpatrick & Co. v. Environmental Tectonics Corp.*, 493 U.S. 400 (1990) (excerpted below at pp. 824-827 (questioning significance of *Sabbatino* factors)). *See infra* pp. 819-823 for discussion of foreign state actions covered by the act of state doctrine.

4. Sabbatino*'s rationale for act of state doctrine.* There has long been uncertainty about the rationale for the act of state doctrine. In the words of one commentator, "the doctrine resembles the proverbial elephant described by a committee of the blind." Dellapenna, *Deciphering the Act of State Doctrine*, 35 Vill. L. Rev. 1, 7 (1990). Is sovereign immunity the basis for the doctrine? International law? Comity? Separation of powers? Choice-of-law rules? What does *Sabbatino* indicate?

(a) Foreign sovereign immunity. The common law act of state doctrine and U.S. statutory rules governing foreign sovereign immunity address closely related concerns. Broadly speaking, both sets of rules express deference to foreign laws and official acts and seek to minimize international frictions by insulating foreign sovereigns from certain types of legal proceedings in U.S. courts.

Nonetheless, there are significant differences between the act of state and foreign sovereign immunity doctrines. First, the act of state doctrine is limited to a foreign government's conduct that is consummated within its own territory, while foreign sovereign immunity can extend to conduct anywhere in the world. Second, the act of state doctrine can provide a substantive rule of decision that can be used offensively, as in *Sabbatino*, while foreign sovereign immunity merely provides a jurisdictional defense. Third, nongovernmental parties can sometimes avail themselves of protection under the act of state doctrine, while only "foreign states" and their "agencies or instrumentalities" can invoke foreign sovereign immunity, *see supra* pp. 251-253. Finally, the sources of the two sets of rules differ: the act of state doctrine is a common law rule with "constitutional underpinnings," while foreign sovereign immunity presently derives from comprehensive federal legislation. *See also Restatement (Third) Foreign Relations Law* §443, Reporters' Note 11 (1987).

(b) Separation of powers concerns. Many authorities have based the act of state doctrine on constitutional separation of powers concerns. *Sabbatino* declared:

> The act of state doctrine . . . [has]"constitutional" underpinnings. It arises out of the basic relationships between branches of government in a system of separation of powers. It concerns the competency of dissimilar institutions to make and implement particular kinds of decisions in the area of international relations. The doctrine as formulated in past decisions expresses the strong sense of the Judicial Branch that its engagement in the task of passing on the validity of foreign acts of state may hinder rather than further this country's pursuit of goals both for itself and for the community of nations as a whole in the international sphere.

See also First Nat'l City Bank v. Banco Nacional de Cuba, 406 U.S. 759, 765 (1971) (Rehnquist, J., plurality) ("the act of state doctrine justifies its existence primarily on the basis that juridical review of acts of state of a foreign power could embarrass the conduct of foreign relations by the political branches of the government."). Is this concern about judicial interference in foreign policy justified? Haven't the political branches — Congress and the president — expressed their willingness for the courts to adjudicate international cases by vesting them with jurisdiction over those cases? Does *Sabbatino* provide any specific explanation as to how judicial decisions in expropriation cases might frustrate U.S. foreign policy? Consider *Sabbatino*'s discussion of the Executive Branch's role in espousing expropriation claims against foreign states.

(c) Political question doctrine. Other authorities have concluded that the act of state doctrine is an application of the political question doctrine. The political question doctrine is a constitutional limitation on the judicial power of the federal courts, which bars the courts from resolving cases that raise issues more appropriately committed to other branches of government. *See supra* p. 56; *Baker v. Carr*, 369 U.S. 186 (1962); *Goldwater v. Carter*, 444 U.S. 996 (1979). Among the factors relevant to determining whether a case presents a political question are a "textually demonstrable commitment" of an issue to the executive or legislative branches, the lack of "judicially discoverable and manageable standards" for resolving an issue, or the existence of prudential considerations counseling for judicial abstention. 444 U.S. at 997-998 (Powell, J., concurring). Several Justices have taken the position that the act of state doctrine is merely a particular application of the political question doctrine. *E.g., First National City Bank*, 406 U.S. at 785-790 (Brennan, J., dissenting) ("the validity of a foreign act of state in certain circumstances is a 'political question' not cognizable in our courts"); *Alfred Dunhill*, 425 U.S. at 726-728 (Marshall, J., dissenting).

Nonetheless, there are important distinctions between the act of state and the political question doctrines. The latter is a jurisdictional bar that requires abstention, which appears inconsistent with the offensive use of the act of state doctrine in cases like *Sabbatino*. Moreover, notwithstanding its "constitutional underpinnings," the act of state doctrine would appear to be subject to contrary congressional legislation, *see infra* pp. _____; the political question doctrine, in contrast, is an Article III requirement, that is not directly subject to legislative revision.

(d) Abstention. Related to separation of powers concerns and the political question doctrine, other authorities explain the act of state doctrine as a principle of abstention. *Restatement (Third) Foreign Relations Law* §443 comment a (1987) ("doctrine was developed . . . as a principle of judicial restraint, essentially to avoid disrespect for foreign states"). As discussed below, the U.S. Government argued in *Environmental Tectonics* that the act of state doctrine is an "unspecified" principle of abstention. *See infra* pp. 829-830 Given the concerns discussed in *Sabbatino* about judicial interference in U.S. foreign affairs and claims espousal, is abstention the appropriate way of viewing the doctrine? In *Environmental Tectonics*, however, the Court flatly rejected this characterization: "The act of state doctrine is not some vague doctrine of abstention but a 'principle of decision binding on federal and state courts alike.'" 493 U.S. at 405. *See also Republic of Austria v. Altmann*, 541 U.S. 677, 700-701 (2004) (describing the act of state doctrine as a "substantive defense on the merits" even when a court has jurisdiction).

(e) International law. *Sabbatino* held that international law did not require the act of state doctrine. What if the substantive law that U.S. courts would apply to a foreign act of state was U.S. law (rather than international law, as in *Sabbatino*)? Would international law limit the power of a nation to apply its own substantive law to a foreign state's public acts within its own territory? Do any of the international law limits on legislative jurisdiction require the act of state doctrine?

(f) International comity. Recall the rationale most frequently cited in nineteenth-century act of state decisions: "[t]o permit the validity of the acts of one sovereign State to be reexamined and perhaps condemned by the courts of another would very certainly imperil the amicable relations between governments and vex the peace of nations." *Oetjen*, 246 U.S. at 304. Is "comity" a persuasive basis for the act of state doctrine? What is the relationship between comity as a rationale and separation of powers concerns?

(g) Choice-of-law rule. Among other things, *Sabbatino* describes the act of state doctrine as a "principle of decision." This suggests that the doctrine is a choice-of-law rule (permitting a court to exercise jurisdiction, but dictating the applicable substantive law), and not a rule of abstention or an application of the political question doctrine (which would deny jurisdiction). Note also that *Sabbatino* gave affirmative effect to the Cuban government's seizure of sugar; it did *not* refuse to decide the dispute, but instead, in deciding the dispute, gave full effect to the validity of the Cuban government's seizure. A number of authorities have described the act of state doctrine as a choice-of-law rule. *See Alfred Dunhill*, 425 U.S. at 705 n.18 (act of state doctrine can be described in "choice of law terms"); *Ricaud*, 246 U.S. at 309 (act of state doctrine held to select applicable rule of decision, and not to constitute "a surrender or abandonment of jurisdiction but . . . an exercise of it"); *Callejo v. Bancomer, SA*, 764 F.2d 1101, 1114 (5th Cir. 1985) ("super choice of law rule"); *Restatement (Third) Foreign Relations Law* §443, Reporters' Note 1 (1987) ("special rule of conflict of laws"). As discussed below, *Environmental Tectonics* appears to have embraced a choice-of-law explanation of the act of state doctrine. *See infra* p. 829.

If the act of state doctrine is a choice-of-law rule what would its precise content be? Would it provide, in effect, that the validity of acts of state are governed by the law of the state committing the act of state, without regard to the public policies (or other interests) of the forum or other states? *Restatement (Third) Foreign Relations Law* §443, Reporters' Note 1 (1987). *See also American Banana Co. v. United Fruit Co.*, 213 U.S. 347, 358 (1909) ("The very meaning of sovereignty is that the decree of the sovereign makes law").

Consistent with treating the act of state doctrine as a choice-of-law rule, *Sabbatino* applied the doctrine offensively to prevent a U.S. defendant from asserting a defense to a suit brought by a Cuban state-owned bank seeking to recover property that Cuba previously had seized. As a consequence, Cuba's claim of ownership went unchallenged and it obtained affirmative relief. Is this application of the act of state doctrine wise? Even though U.S. courts will not sit in judgment on foreign acts of state, does that mean they should also accept those acts as a basis for affirmatively ordering relief? Does this not make the United States complicit in the foreign state's misconduct? Does it not also inject U.S. courts into U.S. foreign relations — at a time selected by a hostile foreign state — in just the way that the act of state doctrine was meant to prevent? Is it consistent with the Court's asserted affirmation of the well-established principle that U.S. courts will not enforce foreign penal or revenue laws? *See supra* p. 737.

(h) Miscellaneous other explanations. A variety of other explanations have been advanced from time to time for the act of state doctrine. *E.g.*, Dellapenna, *Deciphering the Act of State Doctrine,* 35 Vill. L. Rev. 1, 45-53 (1990) ("a rule of repose"); Chow, *Rethinking the Act of State Doctrine: An Analysis in Terms of Jurisdiction to Prescribe,* 62 Wash. L. Rev. 397, 400-403 (1987) (limit on legislative jurisdiction); Burley, *Law Among Liberal States: Liberal Internationalism and the Act of State Doctrine,* 92 Colum. L. Rev. 1907 (1992) (limit on rule of law in dealing with actions by "nonliberal" states). The act of state doctrine might also be explained as a choice of forum (or remedies) device, providing that certain types of claims must be resolved through diplomatic channels. Alternatively, it might be viewed as a mechanism for applying international law — which is "part of our law" — in U.S. courts, which includes consideration of whether private rights of action are provided by international law and consistent with U.S. policies. Other rationales can also be formulated.

(i) Proper rationale for the act of state doctrine. The importance of a coherent rationale for the act of state doctrine cannot be overstated. To the extent the doctrine operates as a prudential one, that may explain why Congress can abrogate it through legislation. *See infra* pp. 856-857 (Second Hickenlooper Amendment), p. 838 note 72 (Helms-Burton) and pp. 1162-1163 (FAA). But prudential rationales make it difficult to explain why the act of state doctrine could be a substantive rule of decision binding state courts. That is only plausible if the doctrine is a form of substantive federal common law. On the other hand, to the extent that the act of state doctrine rests on constitutional, as opposed to prudential norms, that explains how the doctrine binds the states. But it is harder then to see how Congress can abrogate or alter the doctrine's scope by statute.

The choice of rationale also has other implications. For example, to the extent the doctrine functions as an abstention rule, an appellate court might be more prone to defer to a trial court. To the extent the doctrine functions as a purely legal rule, *de novo* review would seem more appropriate. *See Bigio v. Coca Cola Co.*, 239 F.3d 440, 452 n.7 (2d Cir. 2000). And, as discussed below, the existence and scope of various exceptions to the act of state doctrine depend in substantial part upon the rationale that one accepts for the doctrine.

With that background, which of the foregoing rationales is most persuasive? Which rationale explains the outcome in *Sabbatino*?

5. Comparison between act of state doctrine and rules governing recognition of foreign judgments. As discussed below, U.S. courts have developed rules governing the circumstances in which the judgments of foreign courts will be entitled to recognition in the United States. These rules (which are generally a matter of state law, *see infra* pp. 1110-1114) provide that foreign judgments are presumptively enforceable, but subject to a number of important exceptions. Among other things, a foreign judgment will not be enforced if the foreign court lacked personal jurisdiction over the defendant under U.S. due process requirements, if the judgment is a "penal" or "revenue" judgment, or if the judgment violates the forum's public policy. *See Attorney General of Canada v. R.J. Reynolds Tobacco Holdings, Inc.,* 268 F.3d 103 (2d Cir. 2001) (discussing relation between act of state doctrine and revenue rule). Broadly analogous requirements exist for the recognition of foreign arbitral awards under the New York Convention. *See infra* pp. 1201-1215.

Compare these requirements to the act of state doctrine. Under the act of state doctrine, foreign public acts are given effect (unlike foreign penal or public judgments), even where they violate local public policy or international law (unlike foreign money judgments). Why are foreign acts of state entitled to greater deference in U.S. courts than foreign judgments and arbitral awards? Isn't it anomalous for U.S. courts to accord binding effect to arbitrary foreign expropriations, but not to reasoned judgments following regular court proceedings? Why isn't a foreign court's judgment or a foreign arbitral award an act of state?

6. *Comparison between act of state doctrine and treatment of foreign public laws.* As described above, U.S. courts generally refuse to entertain claims based on foreign penal or revenue laws. *See supra* p. 737. As Justice White observed in dissent in *Sabbatino,* "our courts customarily refuse to enforce the revenue and penal laws of a foreign state, since no country has an obligation to further the governmental interests of a foreign sovereign." Is the act of state doctrine consistent with this rule?

7. *Act of state doctrine is not jurisdictional.* Courts have repeatedly said that the act of state doctrine is a substantive defense on the merits rather than a jurisdictional prerequisite. *See, e.g., Samantar v. Yousuf,* 130 S. Ct. 2278, 2290 (2010). This classification has several important implications. It affects how a motion to dismiss the case is styled and, relatedly, what information can be considered as part of a motion to dismiss. *See In re Potash Antitrust Litig.,* 686 F. Supp. 2d 816 824 (N.D. Ill. 2010). It also affects the sequence in which courts may consider this defense relative to other jurisdictional defenses. *See In re Papandreou,* 139 F.3d 247, 256 (D.C. Cir.1998). Does this characterization shed any light on the theoretical foundations of the doctrine discussed above?

Is the act of state doctrine solely a "defense"? Some courts continue to entertain the possibility that the act of state doctrine can, under certain circumstances, operate as an element of the plaintiff's claim and, thereby, enable the case to qualify for federal subject matter jurisdiction (either as an original matter or in a removal petition). *See generally Restatement (Third) of Foreign Relations* §444, comment i (1986). How does this approach compare with the *Sequiha* decision, discussed *supra* pp. 63-70? Is it correct? Other courts are far more skeptical of the idea that a plaintiff, through creative pleading, can implicate the act of state doctrine in a complaint. *See, e.g., Provincial Gov't of Marinduque v. Placer Dome, Inc.,* 582 F.3d 1083, 1089-1090 (9th Cir. 2008); *Patrickson v. Dole Food Co.,* 251 F.3d 795 (9th Cir. 2001).

Is the act of state doctrine truly "substantive"? Is it any more "substantive" than the various exceptions to sovereign immunity which are unquestionably jurisdictional? *See supra* pp. 276-279. Note that, by contrast, claims of official immunity are considered jurisdictional prerequisites and the *forum non conveniens* doctrine is considered a non-merits defense. Is there a principled reason to treat the act of state doctrine differently? *See* Rutledge, *Decisional Sequencing,* 62 Ala. L. Rev. 7 (2010).

8. *Application of the act of state doctrine to claims based on international law.* The U.S. parties in *Sabbatino* argued not just that Cuba's expropriation of their property violated U.S. law and public policy, but also that the expropriation violated international law. Under prevailing principles of international law, there was substantial support for this argument. *E.g., Restatement (Third) Foreign Relations Law* §712 (1987). Why wouldn't the Court in *Sabbatino* consider international law? Recall that "[i]nternational law is part of our law, and must be ascertained and administered by the courts of justice . . . as often as questions of right depending upon it are duly presented for their determination." *The Paquete Habana,* 175 U.S. 677, 700 (1900); *supra* p. 17. Shouldn't *Sabbatino* have applied international law rules prohibiting expropriations like those Cuba engaged in?

Note that most foreign courts will not apply the act of state doctrine to foreclose claims that international law has been violated. *See Sabbatino,* 376 U.S. at 440 (White, J., dissenting) ("No other civilized country has found such a rigid rule [as *Sabbatino*'s refusal to permit application of international law] necessary for the survival of the executive branch of its government . . . and no other judiciary is apparently so incompetent to ascertain and apply international law").

Sabbatino rejected this argument because of "disagreement as to relevant international law standards" regarding expropriation among different states. Why is the existence of disagreement about international law so important to the act of state doctrine? Doesn't the defendant in most cases disagree about the applicable legal standards? Note that the Court also suggested that a "treaty or other unambiguous agreement regarding controlling legal principles" would permit adjudication by U.S. courts. *See infra* pp. 847-856. Why is an "unambiguous" agreement — rather than, for example, a "reasonably clear" agreement — needed to overcome the act of state doctrine? Why is an international "agreement," rather than customary international law, required? Under almost any standard of international law, the discriminatory, uncompensated seizure of privately owned U.S. property by Cuba was wrongful. *See Restatement (Third) Foreign Relations Law* §712 (1987). Given this, why is it relevant that there might be disagreement about other cases involving less egregious misconduct?

9. Sabbatino *as a rule of federal common law.* *Sabbatino* held that the act of state doctrine is a rule of federal common law, binding on state courts and federal courts in both federal question and diversity cases. The Court reasoned that *Erie R.R. Co. v. Tompkins,* 304 U.S. 64 (1938), did not require application of state law act of state rules because of the federal interest in the Nation's foreign affairs. The Court also indicated that state courts would be required to apply an act of state rule at least as deferential to foreign governmental acts as the federal act of state doctrine. Subsequent state court decisions have done so. *E.g., Roxas v. Marcos,* 969 P.2d 1209, 1248 (Haw. 1998); *Alomang v. Freeport-McMoRan, Inc.,* 718 So. 2d 971, 973 (La. App. 1998); *Republic of Haiti v. Duvalier,* 626 N.Y.S.2d 472, 474 (App. Div. 1995); *Perez v. Chase Manhattan Bank,* 474 N.Y.S.2d 689 (N.Y. 1984); *United Nuclear Corp. v. General Atomic Co.,* 629 P.2d 231 (N.M. 1980); *Hunt v. Coastal States Gas Producing Co.,* 589 S.W.2d 322 (Tex. 1979).

10. *Federal common law basis for act of state doctrine.* What is the constitutional basis for requiring state courts to obey the rule of federal common law enunciated in *Sabbatino?*

(a) Federal common law rules in international litigation. The act of state doctrine is a leading example of federal common law in the international context. Other possible examples of federal common law in international cases include tort claims under international law, *supra* pp. 49-50; aspects of foreign sovereign immunity, *supra* pp. 257-261 and 272-275 (discussing *Bancec* and *Samantar*); forum selection clauses, *supra* p. 543; *forum non conveniens, supra* p. 457; and mandatory resort to the Hague Evidence Convention, *infra* pp. 1041-1044. The basis for the development of a federal

common law rule in each of these contexts is the principle that "a few areas, involving 'uniquely federal interests,' . . . are so committed by the Constitution and laws of the United States to federal control that state law is preempted and replaced, where necessary, by federal law of a content prescribed (absent explicit statutory directive) by the courts — so-called 'federal common law.' " *Boyle v. United Technologies Corp.,* 487 U.S. 500 (1988); *supra* pp. 11-13.

(b) Is a federal common law act of state doctrine appropriate? Is *Sabbatino*'s act of state doctrine an appropriate subject for substantive federal common law? *Sabbatino* declares that "an issue concerned with a basic choice regarding the competence and function of the Judiciary and National Executive in ordering our relationships with other members of the international community must be treated exclusively as an aspect of federal law," because of the federal interests that "the rules of international law should not be left to divergent and perhaps parochial [state court] interpretations" and in ensuring that U.S. judicial proceedings do not "hinder rather than further this country's pursuit of goals . . . in the international sphere." Is this rationale persuasive? Is there a special need for uniform interpretation of international law by U.S. courts? What is it?

Even if there is a need for uniform interpretations of international law, the act of state doctrine can be (and usually is) invoked in cases not involving international law, but instead involving federal or state law. *E.g., Grass v. Credito Mexicana, SA,* 797 F.2d 220 (5th Cir. 1986); *DeRoburt v. Gannett Co.,* 733 F.2d 701 (9th Cir. 1984) (U.S. libel law); *IAM v. OPEC,* 649 F.2d 1354 (9th Cir. 1981) (U.S. antitrust law); *Bandes v. Harlow & Jones, Inc.,* 570 F. Supp. 955 (S.D.N.Y. 1983). Is uniform treatment of any claims involving foreign governmental acts — regardless of applicable law — necessary? Recall that the FSIA dealt with the substantive law applicable to claims against foreign states by leaving the subject to otherwise applicable state (or federal) law. *See supra* pp. 234-235.

The second rationale suggested by *Sabbatino* for a federal act of state rule emphasized the potentially adverse effects on U.S. foreign relations of state court decisions passing upon the validity of foreign acts of state. Is this concern warranted? Will foreign nations really retaliate against the United States because a state court uses one version of the act of state doctrine rather than another? If the act of state doctrine is a choice-of-law rule, why doesn't *Klaxon* require application of state law? *See supra* pp. 791-796.

11. *Power of states to adopt a broader act of state doctrine.* What if a state court wished to adopt an act of state doctrine that was *more deferential* to foreign sovereign acts than the federal rule (*i.e.,* that recognized a broader act of state doctrine than that of the Supreme Court)? *Sabbatino* leaves this question open. Consider the following remark by the late Judge Friendly:

> It would be baffling if a foreign act of state intended to affect property in the United States were ignored on one side of the Hudson but respected on the other. . . . The required uniformity can be secured only by recognizing the expansive reach of the principle . . . that all questions relating to an act of state are questions of federal law. *Republic of Iraq v. First National City Bank,* 353 F.2d 47, 50-51 (2d Cir. 1965).

Is Judge Friendly correct that it would be "baffling" for a foreign act of state to have different effects in different states? As suggested earlier, isn't this an inevitable consequence of a federal system where different states have different laws? What harm could arise from disparate treatment of foreign acts of state by different states?

12. *Criticism of* **Sabbatino.** Many commentators have sharply criticized the *Sabbatino* rule. *E.g.,* Bazyler, *Abolishing the Act of State Doctrine,* 134 U. Pa. L. Rev. 325 (1986); *supra*

p. 797, n. 1. Among other things, critics charge that there is no constitutional basis for the act of state doctrine, that the doctrine is inherently ambiguous and unpredictable, that it undermines important national laws and policies, and that it has precluded the development of international law in U.S. courts:

> the act of state doctrine prompts automatic judicial reflexes that relegate all disputes involving foreign governments and international law to an unspecified—or nonexistent—forum outside the court room. Judicial circumspection . . . as to . . . matters touching on foreign affairs seem[s] to have become synonymous with unquestioning judicial abstention in cases alleging international law violations by foreign governments. Mathias, *Restructuring the Act of State Doctrine: A Blueprint for Legislative Reform*, 12 Law & Pol'y Int'l Bus. 369, 371 (1980).

Does *Sabbatino* provide adequate responses to these charges?

13. ***Act of state doctrine and international law developments concerning state action.*** One of the central themes of international law over the past five decades has been an increasing acceptance in almost all quarters that states are subject to the rule of law in international matters. Recall the development, discussed above, of the restrictive theory of sovereign immunity, culminating in the U.N. Jurisdictional Immunities Convention. *See supra* pp. 232-234. Recall also the development of customary international law prohibitions against genocide, torture, terrorism, and similar offenses, both under the Alien Tort Statute and otherwise. *See supra* pp. 50-52. Note also the development of a pervasive network of bilateral investment treaties, imposing standards of fairness and nondiscrimination on states. *See supra* pp. 328-329.

As a consequence of these developments, states are subject to more extensive legal restraints in their international activities than hitherto. Given this, what legitimacy does the act of state doctrine continue to have? Is the act of state doctrine not based upon a premise that the state is, in principle, beyond legal judgment? Does that premise make sense any longer?

14. ***Act of state doctrine and the Alien Tort Statute.*** As discussed above, the Alien Tort Statute creates federal jurisdiction over certain torts committed against aliens in "violation of the law of nations." 28 U.S.C. §1350; *supra* pp. 33-62. This grant of federal jurisdiction has prompted some courts to conclude that it is a "rare case" where the act of state doctrine will bar a suit under the Alien Tort Statute. *See Kadic v. Karadzic,* 70 F.3d 232, 250 (2d Cir. 1995); *Mujica v. Occidental Petroleum Co.,* 381 F. Supp. 2d 1164, 1189-1190 (C.D. Cal. 2005). Is this a logical analysis? Or does the analysis confuse a jurisdictional grant with a nonjurisdictional doctrine of substantive law or abstention?

Should the answer depend on the norm allegedly violated? What if the plaintiff alleges a violation of a *jus cogens* norm? Consider the following skeptical response by the D.C. Circuit to this argument in the context of a claim that property was expropriated as part of a systematic anti-Semitic campaign:

> The argument is intuitively appealing. But it would require us to embark on a path of ranking violations of international law on a spectrum, dispensing with the act of state doctrine for the vilest. Further, as the Sabbatino Court refused to countenance an exception for violations of international law *simpliciter*, we are unsure what it intended in its references to different degrees of "consensus." While it would be heartening to believe that there is a nearly universal consensus against religious prejudice in general or anti-Semitism in particular, a glance around the world exposes glaring examples to the contrary in areas containing a large fraction of the human population. *Agudas Chasidei Chabad of U.S. v. Russian Fed'n,* 528 F.3d 934, 955 (D.C. Cir. 2008).

What is wrong with "ranking violations of international law on a spectrum"? Does it differ from determining whether a norm has achieved the status of customary international law or *jus cogens*? Does it differ from the standard articulated in *Sosa, supra* at 38-47, to decide whether federal common law recognizes a cause of action redressable through the Alien Tort Statute? If a court were to determine that an international norm satisfies the *Sosa* standard, should a court be especially reluctant to apply the act of state doctrine even if the formal elements are satisfied? To put the matter more strongly, doesn't the "vigilant doorkeeping" mandated by *Sosa* obviate the need for the act of state doctrine in cases under the Alien Tort Statute?

15. *Act of state doctrine and available relief.* Does the availability of the act of state doctrine turn on the type of relief sought? According to one court, it does. In *Doe v. Qi*, a case brought by Falun Gong members alleging human rights violations by government officials, the court held that the act of state doctrine barred claims for damages and injunctive relief *but not* claims for declaratory relief. The court reasoned that declaratory relief was not as "intrusive" as other remedies. 349 F. Supp. 2d 1258, 1301 (C.D. Cal. 2004). Is this approach sensible? Consistent with *Sabbatino*?

2. Elements of the Act of State Doctrine

Sabbatino left a number of uncertainties regarding the elements of the act of state doctrine, which have provoked confusion among both lower courts and in the Supreme Court.[49] In particular, courts grappled with the questions: (a) what constitutes an "act of state"; (b) when does a U.S. court "sit in judgment" on an act of state; and (c) where must an act of state occur? Each of these elements is examined below.

a. Definition of "Act of State." Perennial difficulties have arisen in determining what foreign sovereign acts constitute "acts of state." As discussed above, *Sabbatino* (as well as *Oetjen* and *Ricaud*) involved the expropriation of private property by a foreign state.[50] This is regarded as the quintessential "act of state." Less clear is whether other types of foreign governmental conduct constitute acts of state.

The classic Supreme Court precedent outside the expropriation context is *Underhill v. Hernandez*.[51] There, the Court invoked the act of state doctrine to dismiss a complaint against a foreign head of state arising from the allegedly illegal imprisonment and forced servitude of a U.S. citizen in a foreign country by the foreign revolutionary commander. *Underhill* had no difficulty treating the imprisonment as an act of state.[52]

Relying on *Underhill*, lower courts have frequently applied the act of state doctrine to governmental actions other than expropriations.[53] Nonetheless, some lower court decisions have found the doctrine inapplicable in particular cases to governmental acts other than takings of property.[54] Lower courts continue to struggle with the question whether a particular governmental act is an "act of state," qualifying for protection under the act of state doctrine.[55]

---

49. *See* Dellapenna, *Deciphering the Act of State Doctrine,* 35 Vill. L. Rev. 1 (1990); Bazyler, *Abolishing the Act of State Doctrine,* 134 U. Pa. L. Rev. 325, 365-368 (1986).
50. *See supra* pp. 798-808.
51. 168 U.S. 250 (1897).
52. 168 U.S. at 252-254.
53. *See infra* pp. 819-823.
54. *See infra* pp. 819-823.
55. *See infra* p. 820

The only contemporary Supreme Court precedent considering what constitutes an "act of state" is *Alfred Dunhill of London, Inc. v. Republic of Cuba,*[56] which is excerpted below. *Dunhill* involved the Cuban government's refusal to pay certain invoices rendered to it by the plaintiff. Writing for the Court, Justice White held that the refusal to pay was not an act of state because "[n]o statute, decree, order, or resolution of the Cuban Government itself" was produced.[57]

ALFRED DUNHILL OF LONDON, INC. v. REPUBLIC OF CUBA
425 U.S. 682 (1976)

JUSTICE WHITE. The issue in this case is whether the failure of respondents to return to petitioner Alfred Dunhill of London, Inc. ("Dunhill"), funds mistakenly paid by Dunhill for cigars that had been sold to Dunhill by certain expropriated Cuban cigar businesses was an "act of state" by Cuba precluding an affirmative judgment against respondents.

I. . . . In 1960, the Cuban Government confiscated the business and assets of the five leading manufacturers of Havana cigars. These companies, three corporations and two partnerships, were organized under Cuban law. Virtually all of their owners were Cuban nationals. None were American. These companies sold large quantities of cigars to customers in other countries, including the United States, where the three principal importers were Dunhill, Saks & Co. ("Saks"), and Faber, Coe & Gregg, Inc. ("Faber"). The Cuban Government named "interventors" to take possession of and operate the business of the seized Cuban concerns. Interventors continued to ship cigars to foreign purchasers, including the United States importers. . . .

[It transpired that one U.S. importer (Dunhill) overpaid the Cuban interventors a net amount of approximately $55,000, reflecting the excess of Dunhill's payments for preintervention shipments over its payments in postintervention shipments. In connection with other (protracted) litigation against the interventors, Dunhill demanded repayment of this sum. The District Court dismissed the claim.]

The Court of Appeals agreed that the former owners were entitled to recover from the importers the full amount of preintervention accounts receivable. It also held that the mistaken payments by importers to interventors gave rise to a quasi-contractual obligation to repay these sums. But, contrary to the District Court, the Court of Appeals was of the view that the obligation [of the Cuban cigar exporter] to repay [Dunhill] had a situs in Cuba and had been repudiated in the course of litigation by conduct that was sufficiently official to be deemed an act of state: "[I]n the absence of evidence that the interventors were not acting within the scope of their authority as agents of the Cuban government, their repudiation was an act of state even though not embodied in a formal decree." Although the repudiation of the interventors' obligation was considered an act of state, the Court of Appeals went on to hold that *First Nat'l City Bank v. Banco Nacional de Cuba,* 406 U.S. 759 (1972), entitled importers to recover the sums due them from interventors by way of setoff against the amounts due from them for postintervention shipments. The act of state doctrine was said to bar the affirmative judgment awarded Dunhill to the extent that its claim exceeded its debt. The judgment of the District Court was reversed in this respect, and it is this action which was the subject of the petition for certiorari filed by Dunhill. . . .

56. 425 U.S. 682 (1976).
57. 425 U.S. at 695.

II. The Court of Appeals . . . observed that interventors had "ignored" demands for the return of [money mistakenly paid on preintervention accounts receivable] and had "fail[ed] to honor the importers' demand (which was confirmed by the Cuban government's counsel at trial)." This conduct was considered to be "the Cuban government's repudiation of its obligation to return the funds" and to constitute an act of state not subject to question in our courts. We cannot agree. . . .

In *The "Gul Djemal,"* 264 U.S. 90 (1924), a supplier libeled and caused the arrest of the *Gul Djemal,* a steamship owned and operated for commercial purposes by the Turkish government, in an effort to recover for supplies and services sold to and performed for the ship. The ship's master, "a duly commissioned officer of the Turkish Navy," appeared in court and asserted sovereign immunity, claiming that such an assertion defeated the court's jurisdiction. A direct appeal was taken to this Court, where it was held that the master's assertion of sovereign immunity was insufficient because his mere representation of his government as master of a commercial ship furnished no basis for assuming he was entitled to represent the sovereign in other capacities. Here there is no more reason to suppose that the interventors possess governmental, as opposed to commercial, authority than there was to suppose that the master of the *Gul Djemal* possessed such authority. The master of the *Gul Djemal* claimed the authority to assert sovereign immunity while the interventors' claim that they had the authority to commit an act of state, but the difference is unimportant. In both cases, a party claimed to have had the authority to exercise sovereign power. In both, the only authority shown is commercial authority.

We thus disagree with the Court of Appeals that the mere refusal of the interventors to repay funds followed by a failure to prove that interventors "were not acting within the scope of their authority as agents of the Cuban government" satisfied respondents' burden of establishing their act of state defense. Nor do we consider *Underhill v. Hernandez,* heavily relied upon by the Court of Appeals, to require a contrary conclusion. In that case . . . it was apparently concluded that the facts were sufficient to demonstrate that the conduct in question was the public act of those with authority to exercise sovereign powers and was entitled to respect in our courts. We draw no such conclusion from the facts of the case before us now. As the District Court found, the only evidence of an act of state other than the act of nonpayment by interventors was "a statement by counsel for the interventors, during trial, that the Cuban Government and the interventors denied liability and had refused to make repayment." But this merely restated respondent's original legal position and adds little, if anything, to the proof of an act of state. No statute, decree, order, or resolution of the Cuban Government itself was offered in evidence indicating that Cuba had repudiated its obligations in general or any class thereof or that it had as a sovereign matter determined to confiscate the amounts due three foreign importers. . . . [In a subsequent section of his opinion, excerpted below, Justice White considered whether the act of state doctrine was subject to a "commercial" exception.]

Notes *on* **Alfred Dunhill**

1. *Inquiring whether a foreign act of state exists.* As *Dunhill* illustrates, it is well settled that "[t]he act of state doctrine does not preclude an initial inquiry as to whether a challenged act is in fact an act of state." *Restatement (Third) Foreign Relations Law* §443, comment i (1987). For an apparently contrary view, *see Texaco Maracaibo, infra* pp. 857-859.

2. *Definition of "act of state" in* **Dunhill.** What must be shown to establish an "act of state"? Note that *Dunhill* requires a "public" or "sovereign" act by persons with "authority to exercise sovereign powers." *See also Samantar v. Yousuf,* 130 S. Ct. 2278, 2290 (2010) (explaining that an "official's acts" can be an act of state for purpose of doctrine). The Court in *Dunhill* held that this test was not satisfied and noted the absence of any "statute, decree, order or resolution of the Cuban Government . . . indicating that Cuba had repudiated its obligations in general or any class thereof or that it had as a sovereign matter determined to confiscate the amounts due." A dissenting opinion by Justice Marshall in *Dunhill* reasoned that "an act of state need not be formalized in any particular manner [and] it need not take the form of active, rather than passive, conduct." 425 U.S. at 719-720.

What if the Cuban government in *Dunhill* had promulgated a decree authorizing the interventors to repudiate certain classes of debts, including Dunhill's? How would the plurality in *Dunhill* have resolved the case? The remainder of the Court? How should the case then be resolved?

3. *Lower court definitions of act of state.* Lower courts have reached divergent results in deciding what constitutes an act of state.

(a) "Sovereign" acts by senior officials. Some lower courts have read *Dunhill* to require a fairly unambiguous showing that the case involves "sovereign" conduct by senior government officials. *E.g., Gross v. German Foundation Indus. Initiative,* 456 F.3d 363, 392 (3d Cir. 2006); *Roe v. Unocal Corp.,* 70 F. Supp. 2d 1073, 1079-1080 (C.D. Cal. 1999) (military order was act of state); *Flatow v. Islamic Republic of Iran,* 999 F. Supp. 1, 24 (D.D.C. 1998) (bus bombings not act of state); *Filartiga v. Pena-Irala,* 630 F.2d 876, 889 (2d Cir. 1980) (torture by government officials is not an "act of state" because state did not authorize such conduct); *In re Potash Antitrust Litig.,* 686 F. Supp. 2d 816, 825 (N.D. Ill. 2010); *Bowoto v. Chevron Corp.,* 2007 WL 2349345 (N.D. Cal. Aug. 14, 2007) (test for when acts of lower-level government officials can constitute act of state).

(b) Expansive definitions. Other lower courts have been more willing to apply the act of state doctrine even where the relevant conduct is not the formal, public action of a foreign state. *E.g., Doe v. Qi,* 349 F. Supp. 2d 1258, 1293-1294 (C.D. Cal. 2004) (act of state doctrine applied to official act that contradicted domestic law but was supported unofficially by national government); *Roe v. Unocal Corp.,* 70 F. Supp. 2d 1073 (C.D. Cal. 1999) (actions of military officer constituted act of state); *Hargrove v. Underwriters at Lloyd's, London,* 937 F. Supp. 595 (S.D. Tex. 1996); *DeRoburt v. Gannett Co.,* 733 F.2d 701 (9th Cir. 1984) (act of state doctrine potentially applicable to allegedly illegal loan to foreign head of state); *Hunt v. Mobil Oil Corp.,* 550 F.2d 68, 72-75 (2d Cir. 1977) (act of state doctrine applies to alleged conspiracy involving U.S. oil companies and Libya); *Resco Products, Inc. v. Bosai Minerals Group Co., Ltd.,* 2010 WL 2331069 (W.D. Pa. June 4, 2010) (alleged price manipulation by foreign government working through local chambers of commerce could be act of state).

(c) "Ministerial" exception. Several lower court decisions have recognized a so-called "ministerial exception" to the act of state doctrine, under which routine, ministerial functions (such as the issuance of a patent) are not the kind of governmental action contemplated by the act of state doctrine. *E.g., Mannington Mills, Inc. v. Congoleum Corp.,* 595 F.2d 1287, 1293-1294 (3d Cir. 1979) (issuance of a patent is not an act of state). *Sage Int'l Ltd. v. Cadillac Gage Co.,* 534 F. Supp. 896, 904 (E.D. Mich. 1981) (same); *Forbo-Giubiasco SA v. Congoleum Corp.,* 516 F. Supp. 1210 (S.D.N.Y. 1981) (same). *See Restatement (Third) Foreign Relations Law* §443, Reporters' Note 3 (1987). *But see Voda v. Cordis Corp.,* 476 F.3d 887, 904 (Fed. Cir. 2007) (suggesting that issuance of patent might qualify as act of state).

4. *Is a foreign judgment or arbitral award an "act of state"?* Why isn't a foreign court's judgment or a foreign arbitral award an act of state? *Restatement (Third) Foreign Relations Law* §443, Reporters' Note 10 (1987) ("While the distinction between a foreign judgment and a foreign act of state is not always easy to draw, in general the public judgments doctrine is directed to judicial decisions, whereas the act of state doctrine is directed to acts of general application decided by the executive or legislative branches of the acting state, even if confirmed or applied by courts in that state"). *Compare Restatement (Second) Foreign Relations Law* §41, comment d (1965) ("A judgment of a court may be an act of state. Usually, it is not, because it involves the interests of private litigants or because court adjudication is not the usual way in which the state exercises its jurisdiction to give effect to its public interest."). For cases holding that a foreign judgment constituted an act of state, *see In re Philippine National Bank*, 397 F.3d 768, 772-773 (9th Cir. 2005); *Attorney Grievance Commission v. Shenbein*, 812 A.2d 981 (Md. 2002). Is it appropriate, in ordinary cases, to treat foreign judgments as acts of state? What would that do to the body of U.S. law governing the recognition and enforcement of foreign judgments? To rules requiring that foreign tribunals have been impartial and fair? To rules requiring that foreign judgments not violate U.S. public policy? *See infra* pp. 1133-1146.

   5. *Is foreign legislation an "act of state"?* Is a foreign law an act of state? *Dunhill* emphasized that the existence of an "act of state" depended upon proof of a sovereign decision, as reflected in a "statute, decree, order, or resolution." In *Ricaud* and *Oetjen,* suppose that Mexican authorities had never physically seized the plaintiffs' property, but had enacted a law purporting to transfer title. Would that law have been conclusive, in a subsequent U.S. action, as to ownership of the property? Suppose that the property had been moved out of Mexico to the United States only after enactment of the legislation. *Compare* Zander, *The Act of State Doctrine*, 53 Am. J. Int'l L. 826 (1959) (foreign "act of state" can include legislation); Falk, *Toward a Theory of the International Legal Order: A Critique of* Banco Nacional de Cuba v. Sabbatino, 16 Rutgers L. Rev. 1, 30 (1961) (act of state doctrine applies to "foreign legislation or executive acts"). Similarly, the *Third Restatement* suggests that the act of state doctrine applies to foreign legislation, even without executive implementation. *Restatement (Third) Foreign Relations Law* §443, comment i (1987) ("The act of state doctrine applies to acts such as constitutional amendments, statutes, decrees and proclamations, and in certain circumstances to physical acts, such as occupation of an estate by the state's armed forces in application of state policy"); *see also Society of Lloyd's v. Siemon-Netto,* 457 F.3d 94 (D.C. Cir. 2006) (holding that act of state doctrine barred consideration of whether Lloyd's Act of 1982 represented unlawful delegation under English law).

   Aren't the *Third Restatement,* and the other authorities cited above, wrong? A foreign law can authorize an act of state, but is generally not itself an act of state unless it is implemented. *See Restatement (Second) Foreign Relations Law* §41, comment d (1965) ("In determining whether an act is an act of state, the branch or agency of the government — executive, judicial, or legislative — that performed the act is not as important as is the nature of the action taken."). The unexecuted existence of foreign law presents a traditional choice-of-law issue, not an act of state case.

   6. *Relevance of foreign law to acts of low-ranking officials.* Many act of state decisions involve physical conduct by governmental authorities. When do such actions constitute acts of state? Most courts have concluded that foreign laws are the ultimate source of evidence as to whether particular conduct is a foreign act of state. *E.g., Galu v. Swiss Air Transport Co.,* 873 F.2d 650 (2d Cir. 1989); *Empresa Cubana v. Lamborn & Co.,* 652 F.2d 231, 237 (2d Cir. 1981); *Restatement (Third) Foreign Relations Law* §443, comment i (1987) ("An action or declaration by an official may qualify as an act of state, but only upon a showing (ordinarily by the party raising the issue) that the official had authority to act for and bind the state. . . . An official pronouncement by a foreign government describing a certain act as governmental is ordinarily conclusive evidence of its official character."). *But see In re*

Nakash, 190 B.R. 763 (Bankr. S.D.N.Y. 1996) (holding that conduct of receiver acting for Israeli Ministry of Justice did not constitute act of state).

This approach is in considerable tension with the equally well-settled rule that U.S. courts may not inquire into the validity of a foreign state's official acts under foreign law. *Sabbatino,* 376 U.S. at 415 n.17; *West v. Multibanco Comermex SA,* 807 F.2d 820, 828-829 (9th Cir. 1987); *Banco de Espana v. Federal Reserve Board,* 114 F.2d 438, 444 (2d Cir. 1940); *French v. Banco Nacional de Cuba,* 295 N.Y.S.2d 433, 440-441 (1968).

In *Galu v. Swiss Air Transport Co.,* 873 F.2d 650 (2d Cir. 1989), the Second Circuit considered the significance of foreign law in considerable detail. *Galu* arose from the plaintiff's deportation from Switzerland by Swiss police, who forcibly placed her on a Swissair flight to New York. The plaintiff filed suit against Swissair, seeking damages in tort for Swissair's cooperation in her expulsion. On appeal, the Second Circuit held that, if the Swiss police officers had engaged in acts of state in forcibly expelling the plaintiff, then Swissair would also enjoy act of state protection for participating in those acts. The Court reasoned that conduct by relatively low-ranking officials would constitute an act of state if it was within the general scope of the officials' authority under local law:

> The issue is not whether the police officers may . . . have slightly exceeded their authority in carrying out a decision of their government. The issue is whether the action taken against [the plaintiff] in removing her to the United States was an action that had been ordered in the exercise of the sovereign authority of Switzerland, or whether it was simply an ad hoc decision of local police officers. The burden is on defendant to establish foreign law to the extent necessary to demonstrate its entitlement to the act of state defense. Evidence of foreign law is required not to determine whether the forcible removal of [plaintiff] was lawful but whether it was in fact an act of state. 873 F.2d at 654.

Is this a sensible approach to the definition of acts of state? Does it involve courts in determining the lawfulness of a foreign official's acts under foreign law, one of the inquiries that the act of state doctrine ordinarily forbids? *See Banco de Espana v. Federal Reserve Bank,* 114 F.2d 438, 443 (2d Cir. 1940) ("the courts of this country will not examine the acts of a foreign sovereign within its own borders in order to determine whether or not those acts were legal under the municipal law of the foreign state"). If so, is that dispositive?

7. *"Private" acts of foreign officials.* A number of cases have raised the question whether misconduct of a foreign official, such as receipt of bribes or extortion, can constitute an act of state. In general, lower courts have concluded that a former government official cannot claim the protection of the act of state doctrine for private misconduct while in office. In this context, some lower courts appear to have defined the "public acts" necessary to trigger act of state protection fairly narrowly. *Roxas v. Marcos,* 969 P.2d 1209, 1249-1251 (Haw. 1998); *Republic of Philippines v. Marcos,* 862 F.2d 1355, 1361 (9th Cir. 1988); *Jimenez v. Aristeguieta,* 311 F.2d 547 (5th Cir. 1962) (financial crimes committed in violation of official position are "as far from being an act of state as rape"); *United States v. Noriega,* 1990 U.S. Dist. LEXIS 7653 (S.D. Fla. June 8, 1990) (must show that acts "were taken on behalf of the state and not, as private acts, on behalf of the actor himself"; "The Court fails to see how Noriega's alleged drug trafficking and protection of money launderers could conceivably constitute public action taken on behalf of the Panamanian State"); *Sharon v. Time, Inc.,* 599 F. Supp. 538, 544-545 (S.D.N.Y. 1984).

Other courts have defined "public acts" more broadly, apparently to include misuse of governmental authority for private purposes. *Republic of Philippines v. Marcos,* 818 F.2d 1473, 1484 (9th Cir. 1987) (defining public acts broadly to encompass appropriating public funds by government order), *vacated,* 862 F.2d 1355 (9th Cir. 1988) (*en banc*); *Banco de Espana v. Federal Reserve Bank,* 114 F.2d 438 (2d Cir. 1940).

Should the alleged abuse of official position for private gain constitute an act of state? According to one court, "gain[ing] access to public monies by statute, decree, resolution, order or some other 'governmental act' as president [would be an act of state]. It would greatly weaken the act of state doctrine if parties could put in question the validity of official government acts simply by attacking the motives of the government officials who undertake them." *Republic of Philippines v. Marcos,* 818 F.2d 1473, 1485 (9th Cir. 1987), *vacated,* 862 F.2d 1355 (9th Cir. 1989). Compare the dissenting opinion in the same case: "I cannot adhere to the position that the alleged acts of receiving bribes, plundering the treasury and extortion are [public acts]." 862 F.2d at 1493.

b. "Sitting in Judgment" on an Act of State: Validity vs. Motivations. Lower courts have also reached divergent results in determining whether a particular U.S. litigation would require U.S. courts to "sit in judgment" on a foreign act of state so as to violate the act of state doctrine.[58] In the years after *Sabbatino* was decided, many courts applied the act of state doctrine where the plaintiff's claims would require factual inquiry into the "motivations" for a foreign state's act, as well as where the "validity" or "legality" of the foreign state's conduct was directly challenged.[59] Other courts refused to extend the doctrine to foreign governmental motivations.[60]

The Ninth Circuit's decision in *Clayco Petroleum Corporation v. Occidental Petroleum Corporation*[61] was a leading example of how some lower courts expansively applied the act of state doctrine. *Clayco* involved an antitrust action by one U.S. oil company against a second U.S. oil company. The suit charged the defendant with having made secret payments to an official of Umm Al Qaywayn (treated by all as a foreign state) to obtain an oil concession. The Ninth Circuit dismissed on act of state grounds:

> Appellants also argue that the examination of foreign governmental action which this case requires is not intrusive enough to warrant an act of state defense because the concern here is the motivation behind the sovereign's act, rather than its legal validity. . . . In this case . . . the very existence of plaintiffs' claim depends upon establishing that the motivation for the sovereign act was bribery. Thus, embarrassment would result from adjudication. This circuit's decisions have similarly limited inquiry which would "impugn or question the nobility of a foreign nation's motivation." *Timberlane,* 549 F.2d at 607. In *Buttes,* the trial court, in an opinion adopted by this court, held judicial scrutiny of the motivation for foreign sovereign acts to be precluded by the act of state doctrine, noting that it has traditionally barred antitrust claims based on the defendant's alleged inducement of foreign sovereign action. . . . Appellants thus cannot argue that inquiry into motivation in this case is unprotected.[62]

58. The classic formulations of the act of state doctrine forbid foreign states from "sitting in judgment" on foreign acts of state. *Sabbatino,* 376 U.S. at 416; *Underhill,* 168 U.S. at 252; *Restatement (Third) Foreign Relations Law* §443 (1987).

59. *E.g., O.N.E. Shipping v. Flota Mercante Grancolombiana,* 830 F.2d 449 (2d Cir. 1987); *IAM v. OPEC,* 649 F.2d 1354 (9th Cir. 1981); *Hunt v. Mobil Oil Corp.,* 550 F.2d 68, 73 (2d Cir. 1977); *General Aircraft Corp. v. Air America,* 482 F. Supp. 3, 6 (D.D.C. 1979); *Bokkelen v. Grumman Aerospace Corp.,* 432 F. Supp. 329, 333 (E.D.N.Y. 1977).

60. *E.g., Industrial Inv. Dev. Corp. v. Mitsui & Co.,* 594 F.2d 48, 55 (5th Cir. 1979); *Williams v. Curtiss-Wright Corp.,* 694 F.2d 300, 304 n.5 (3d Cir. 1982); *Sharon v. Time, Inc.,* 599 F. Supp. 538, 548-553 (S.D.N.Y. 1984).

61. 712 F.2d 404 (9th Cir. 1983).

62. 712 F.2d at 407-408. *See also Hunt v. Mobil Oil Corp.,* 550 F.2d 68, 71 (2d Cir. 1977); *IAM v. OPEC,* 649 F.2d 1354, 1358-1361 (9th Cir. 1981) ("act of state doctrine is similar to the political question doctrine in domestic law").

In *W.S. Kirkpatrick & Co. v. Environmental Tectonics Corporation,* however, the Supreme Court disapproved of *Clayco,* and rejected the suggestion that the act of state doctrine was applicable where a U.S. litigation would inquire only into the motivations behind an act of state. The Court instead held that the act of state doctrine applied only to cases where U.S. courts were required to decide the "validity" of foreign acts of state. *Environmental Tectonics* is excerpted below.

W.S. KIRKPATRICK & CO. v. ENVIRONMENTAL TECTONICS CORP.
493 U.S. 400 (1990)

JUSTICE SCALIA. In this case we must decide whether the act of state doctrine bars a court in the United States from entertaining a cause of action that does not rest upon the asserted invalidity of an official act of a foreign sovereign, but that does require imputing to foreign officials an unlawful motivation (the obtaining of bribes) in the performance of such an official act.

I. The facts as alleged in respondent's complaint are as follow: In 1981, Harry Carpenter, who was then Chairman of the Board and Chief Executive Officer of petitioner W.S. Kirkpatrick & Co., Inc. ("Kirkpatrick") learned that the Republic of Nigeria was interested in contracting for the construction and equipment of an aeromedical center at Kaduna Air Force Base in Nigeria. He made arrangements with Benson "Tunde" Akindele, a Nigerian citizen, whereby Akindele would endeavor to secure the contract for Kirkpatrick. It was agreed that, in the event the contract was awarded to Kirkpatrick, Kirkpatrick would pay to two Panamanian entities controlled by Akinele a "commission" equal to 20% of the contract price, which would in turn be given as a bribe to officials of the Nigerian Government. In accordance with this plan, the contract was awarded to petitioner W.S. Kirkpatrick & Co., International ("Kirkpatrick International"), a wholly owned subsidiary of Kirkpatrick; Kirkpatrick paid the promised "commission" to the appointed Panamanian entities; and those funds were disbursed as bribes. All parties agree that Nigerian law prohibits both the payment and the receipt of bribes in connection with the award of a government contract.

Respondent Environmental Tectonics Corporation International, an unsuccessful bidder for the Kaduna contract, learned of the 20% "commission" and brought the matter to the attention of the Nigerian Air Force and the U.S. Embassy in Lagos. Following an investigation by the Federal Bureau of Investigation, the U.S. Attorney for the District of New Jersey brought charges against both Kirkpatrick and Carpenter for violations of the Foreign Corrupt Practices Act of 1977, 15 U.S.C. §78dd-1 *et seq.,* and both pleaded guilty.

Respondent then brought this civil action in the U.S. District Court for the District of New Jersey against Carpenter, Akindele, petitioners, and others, seeking damages under the Racketeer Influenced and Corrupt Organizations Act, the Robinson-Patman Act, and the New Jersey Anti-Racketeering Act. The defendants moved to dismiss the complaint under Rule 12(b)(6) of the Federal Rules of Civil Procedure on the ground that the action was barred by the act of state doctrine.

The District Court, having requested and received a letter expressing the views of the legal advisor to the U.S. Department of State as to the applicability of the act of state doctrine, treated the motion as one for summary judgment . . . and granted the motion. The District Court concluded that the act of state doctrine applies "if the inquiry presented for judicial determination includes the motivation of a sovereign act which would result in embarrassment to the sovereign or constitute interference in the conduct of foreign policy of the United States" [citing *Clayco*]. Applying that principle to the facts at hand, the court held that respondent's suit had to be dismissed because in order to prevail respondents would have to show that "the defendants or certain of them intended to wrongfully influence the decision to award the Nigerian Contract by payment of a bribe, that the Government of Nigeria, its officials or other representatives knew of the offered consideration for awarding the Nigerian Contract to Kirkpatrick, that the bribe was actually received or anticipated and that 'but for' the payment or anticipation of the payment of the bribe, ETC would have been awarded the Nigerian Contract."

The Court of Appeals for the Third Circuit reversed. Although agreeing with the District Court that "the award of a military procurement contract can be, in certain circumstances, a sufficiently formal expression of a government's public interests to trigger application" of the act of state doctrine, it found application of the doctrine unwarranted on the facts of this case. The Court of Appeals found particularly persuasive the letter to the District Court from the legal advisor to the Department of State, which had stated that in the opinion of the Department judicial inquiry into the purpose behind the act of a foreign sovereign would not produce the "unique embarrassment, and the particular interference with the conduct of foreign affairs, that may result from the judicial determination that a foreign sovereign's acts are invalid." The Court of Appeals acknowledged that "the Department's legal conclusions as to the reach of the act of state doctrine are not controlling on the courts," but concluded that "the Department's factual assessment of whether fulfillment of its responsibilities will be prejudiced by the course of civil litigation is entitled to substantial respect." In light of the Department's view that the interests of the Executive Branch would not be harmed by prosecution of the action, the Court of Appeals held that Kirkpatrick had not met its burden of showing that the case should not go forward; accordingly, it reversed the judgment of the District Court and remanded the case for trial.

II. This Court's description of the jurisprudential foundation for the act of state doctrine has undergone some evolution over the years. We once viewed the doctrine as an expression of international law, resting upon "the highest considerations of international comity and expediency," *Oetjen v. Central Leather Co.*, 246 U.S. 297, 303-304 (1918). We have more recently described it, however, as a consequence of domestic separation of powers, reflecting "the strong sense of the Judicial Branch that its engagement in the task of passing on the validity of foreign acts of state may hinder" the conduct of foreign affairs, *Sabbatino*, 376 U.S. at 423. . . . We find it unnecessary [to consider whether any exception to the act of state doctrine is applicable] since the factual predicate for application of the act of state doctrine does not exist. Nothing in the present suit requires the court to declare invalid, and thus ineffective as "a rule of decision for the courts of this country," *Ricaud v. American Metal Co.*, 246 U.S. 304, 310 (1918), the official act of a foreign sovereign.

In every case in which we have held the act of state doctrine applicable, the relief sought or the defense interposed would have required a court in the United States to declare invalid the official act of a foreign sovereign performed within its own territory. In *Underhill*, holding the defendant's detention of the plaintiff to be tortious would have required denying legal effect to "acts of a military commander representing the authority of the revolutionary party as government, which afterwards, succeeded and was recognized by the United States." In *Oetjen v. Central Leather Co.*, and in *Ricaud v. American Metal Co.*, denying title to the party who claimed through purchase from Mexico would have required declaring that government's prior seizure of the property, within its own territory, legally ineffective. In *Sabbatino*, upholding the defendant's claim to the funds would have required a holding that Cuba's expropriation of goods located in Havana was null and void. In the present case, by contrast, neither the claim nor any asserted defense requires a determination that Nigeria's contract with Kirkpatrick International was, or was not, effective.

Petitioners point out, however, that the facts necessary to establish respondent's claim will also establish that the contract was unlawful. Specifically, they note that in order to prevail respondent must prove that petitioner Kirkpatrick made, and Nigerian officials received, payments that violate Nigerian law, which would, they assert, support a finding that the contract is invalid under Nigerian law. Assuming that to be true, it still does not suffice. The act of state doctrine is not some vague doctrine of abstention but a "*principle of decision* binding on federal and state courts alike." *Sabbatino,* 376 U.S. at 427 (emphasis added). As we said in *Ricaud,* "the act within its own boundaries of one sovereign State . . . becomes . . . a rule of decision for the courts of this country." 246 U.S. at 310. Act of state issues only arise when a court must decide — that is, when the outcome of the case turns upon — the effect of official action by a foreign sovereign. When that question is not in the case, neither is the act of state doctrine. That is the situation here. Regardless of what the court's factual findings may suggest as to the legality of the Nigerian contract, its legality is simply not a question to be decided in the present suit, and there is thus no occasion to apply the rule of decision that the act of state doctrine requires. *Cf. Sharon v. Time, Inc.,* 599 F. Supp. 538, 546 (S.D.N.Y. 1984) ("The issue in this litigation is not whether [the alleged] acts are valid, but whether they occurred").

In support of their position that the act of state doctrine bars any factual findings that may cast doubt upon the validity of foreign sovereign acts, petitioners cite Justice Holmes' opinion for the Court in *American Banana Co.* That was a suit under the United States antitrust laws, alleging that Costa Rica's seizure of the plaintiff's property had been induced by an unlawful conspiracy. In the course of a lengthy opinion Justice Holmes observed, citing *Underhill,* that "a seizure by a state is not a thing that can be complained of elsewhere in the courts." The statement is concededly puzzling. *Underhill* does indeed stand for the proposition that a seizure by a state cannot be complained of elsewhere — in the sense of being sought to be declared ineffective elsewhere. The plaintiff in *American Banana,* however, like the plaintiff here, was not trying to undo or disregard the governmental action, but only to obtain damages from private parties who had procured it. Arguably, then, the statement did imply that suit would not lie if a foreign state's actions would be, though not invalidated, impugned.

Whatever Justice Holmes may have had in mind, his statement lends inadequate support to petitioners' position here, for two reasons. First, it was a brief aside, entirely unnecessary to the decision. *American Banana* was squarely decided on the ground (later substantially overruled, *see Continental Ore Co. v. Union Carbide & Carbon Corp.,* 370 U.S. 690, 704-705 (1962)) that the antitrust laws had no extraterritorial application, so that "what the defendant did in Panama or Costa Rica is not within the scope of the statute." Second, whatever support the dictum might provide for petitioners' position is more than overcome by our later holding in *United States v. Sisal Sales Corp.,* 274 U.S. 268 (1927). There we held that, *American Banana* notwithstanding, the defendant's actions in obtaining Mexico's enactment of "discriminating legislation" could form part of the basis for suit under the United States antitrust laws. Simply put, *American Banana* was not an act of state case; and whatever it said by way of dictum that might be relevant to the present case has not survived *Sisal Sales.*

Petitioners insist, however, that the policies underlying our act of state cases — international comity, respect for the sovereignty of foreign nations on their own territory, and the avoidance of embarrassment to the Executive Branch in its conduct of foreign relations — are implicated in the present case because, as the District Court found, a determination that Nigerian officials demanded and accepted a bribe "would impugn or question the nobility of a foreign nation's motivations," and would "result in embarrassment to the sovereign or constitute interference in the conduct of foreign policy of the United States." The United States, as amicus curiae, favors the same approach to the act of state doctrine, though disagreeing with petitioners as to the outcome it produces in the present case. We should not, the United States urges, "attach dispositive significance to the fact that this suit involves only the 'motivation' for, rather than the 'validity' of, a foreign sovereign act," Brief for United States as Amicus Curiae 37, and should eschew "any rigid formula for the resolution of act of state cases generally." In some future case, perhaps, "litigation . . . based on alleged corruption in the award of contracts or other commercially oriented activities of foreign governments could sufficiently touch on 'national nerves' that the act of state doctrine or related principles of abstention would appropriately be found to bar the suit" (quoting *Sabbatino*, 376 U.S. at 428), and we should therefore resolve this case on the narrowest possible ground, *viz.*, that the letter from the legal advisor to the District Court gives sufficient indication that, "in the setting of this case," the act of state doctrine poses no bar to adjudication.[63]

These urgings are deceptively similar to what we said in *Sabbatino*, where we observed that sometimes, even though the validity of the act of a foreign sovereign within its own territory is called into question, the policies underlying the act of state doctrine may not justify its application. We suggested that a sort of balancing approach could be applied — the balance shifting against application of the doctrine, for example, if the government that committed the "challenged act of state" is no longer in existence. But what is appropriate in order to avoid unquestioning judicial acceptance of the acts of foreign sovereigns is not similarly appropriate for the quite opposite purpose of expanding judicial incapacities where such acts are not directly (or even indirectly) involved. It is one thing to suggest, as we have, that the policies underlying the act of state doctrine should be considered in deciding whether, despite the doctrine's technical availability, it should nonetheless not be invoked; it is something quite different to suggest that those underlying policies are a doctrine unto themselves, justifying expansion of the act of state doctrine (or, as the United States puts it, unspecified "related principles of abstention") into new and uncharted fields. The short of the matter is this: Courts in the United States have the power, and ordinarily the obligation, to decide cases and controversies properly presented to them. The act of state doctrine does not establish an exception for cases and controversies that may embarrass foreign governments, but merely requires that, in the process of deciding, the acts of foreign sovereigns taken within their own jurisdictions shall be deemed valid. That doctrine has no application to the present case because the validity of no foreign sovereign act is at issue.

Notes on Environmental Tectonics

1. *Distinction between "validity" and "motivation."* The classic formulation of the act of state doctrine forbids U.S. courts from "sitting in judgment" on foreign acts of state. *See supra* p. 797. According to *Environmental Tectonics*, a U.S. court will not be required to "sit in judgment" on a foreign act of state merely because the plaintiff's claims "impugn

---

63. Even if we agreed with the Government's fundamental approach, we would question its characterization of the legal advisor's letter as reflecting the absence of any policy objection to the adjudication. The letter, which is reprinted as an appendix to the opinion of the Court of Appeals, *see* 847 F.2d 1052, 1067-1069 (3d Cir. 1988), did not purport to say whether the State Department would like the suit to proceed, but rather responded (correctly, as we hold today) to the question whether the act of state doctrine was applicable.

or question the nobility of a foreign nation's motivations" or "may embarrass foreign governments." The Court held that the act of state doctrine does not apply unless "the *validity* of [a] foreign sovereign act is at issue." (Emphasis added.) What exactly does the Court's distinction between the "validity" of foreign acts of state and the "motivations" for those acts mean?

2. *When does a claim challenge the "validity" or "effect" of a foreign act of state?* The defendant urged that plaintiff's claims in *Environmental Tectonics* required proof of facts that would have established a violation of Nigerian law by Nigerian government officials. Nonetheless, the Court held that no challenge to the "validity" of Nigerian act of state was presented. The Court reasoned that "[a]ct of state issues only arise when a court must decide — that is, when the outcome of the case turns upon — the effect of official action by a foreign sovereign." And the Court concluded that "[r]egardless of what the court's factual findings may suggest as to the legality of the Nigerian contract, its legality is simply not a question to be decided in the present suit." Why *didn't Environmental Tectonics* require a decision on the "validity," "effect," or "legality" of the Nigerian contract?

When would a suit challenge the "validity" of a foreign act of state? Would a suit by Environmental Tectonics against Nigeria or Nigerian government officials require decision or the validity on a foreign act of state? What if the action sought specific performance by Nigeria, awarding plaintiff the disputed contract? What if the action sought money damages from Nigeria for failure to award the contract? How would such an action differ from Mr. Underhill's suit? How does either suit differ from the actual suit filed by Environmental Tectonics against W.S. Kirkpatrick? How would either suit differ from *Sabbatino, Oetjen,* or *Ricaud?* Would either action involve any greater U.S. judicial inquiry into the "validity" of a foreign act of state than the actual *Environmental Tectonics* lawsuit?

3. *Possible distinction between "validity" and "legality."* Does *Environmental Tectonics* distinguish between the "validity" of foreign acts of state and their "legality"? Note that in *Sabbatino, Ricaud,* and *Oetjen,* the act of state doctrine was applied in disputes between two U.S. citizens over the title to property — disputes easily characterized as involving the "validity" of one party's asserted ownership interest. In contrast, *Underhill* involved a tort action against a foreign official — a dispute arguably involving only the "legality" of official conduct, and not the "validity" of title derived from a foreign act of state. Did *Environmental Tectonics* hold that the act of state doctrine does not apply to suits challenging the "legality" of foreign acts of state?

When would a case require decision on the "legality" but not the "validity," of a foreign act of state? Suppose that the plaintiff in *Environmental Tectonics* had named either Nigeria or Nigerian officials as defendants? Would this suit have challenged the "legality" or "validity" of the Nigerian government's actions? Note that *Environmental Tectonics* clearly approved the decision in *Underhill,* where the act of state doctrine was held to bar a tort action against a foreign government official for his official acts. On the other hand, consider how Justice Scalia characterized *Underhill:* deciding the U.S. plaintiff's tort claim "would have required denying legal effect to acts of a [foreign state]." That characterization suggests that *Underhill* — like *Sabbatino, Ricaud,* and *Oetjen* — concerned the "validity" of the foreign defendant's acts. Recall, however, that *Underhill* involved a foreign military commander's imprisonment and forced servitude of a U.S. engineer. How would deciding Mr. Underhill's suit against the commander have "required denying legal effect" to foreign acts of state?

4. *Rationale for "validity"/"motivation" distinction.* Is it appropriate to distinguish between the "validity of" and the "motivation for" a foreign act of state? Given the policies underlying the act of state doctrine, is there a more compelling case for judicial abstention in cases like *Ricaud* and *Oetjen* than in cases like *Environmental Tectonics* or *Underhill*? How does Justice Scalia resolve this question?

Consider the following excerpt from *Hunt v. Mobil Oil Corp.*, 550 F.2d 68, 77 (2d Cir. 1977). The case arose from an antitrust action by Nelson Bunker Hunt against seven major oil companies, alleging that the defendants conspired to cut off Hunt's oil supplies from Libya by preventing him from reaching a satisfactory supply agreement with Libya. Barely beneath the surface of Hunt's claims was the fact that, allegedly because of defendants' conspiracy, Libya had nationalized his properties in Libya. The Second Circuit dismissed on act of state grounds, even though Libya was not named as a defendant:

> The United States has officially characterized the motivation of the Libyan government, the very issue which Hunt now seeks to adjudicate here. The attempted transmogrification of Libya from lion to lamb undertaken here [by plaintiff] does not succeed in evading the act of state doctrine because we cannot logically separate Libya's motivation from the validity of its seizure. The American judiciary is being asked to make inquiry into the subtle and delicate issue of the policy of a foreign sovereign, a Serbonian Bog, precluded by the act of state doctrine as well as by the realities of the fact finding competence of the court in an issue of far reaching national concern.

Is this persuasive? More persuasive than Justice Scalia's opinion in *Environmental Tectonics*?

5. *Rationale for act of state doctrine in* Environmental Tectonics. What rationale is advanced for the act of state doctrine in *Environmental Tectonics*? With varying degrees of emphasis, Justice Scalia rejected the suggestions that the act of state doctrine was a "vague doctrine of abstention," "an expression of international law," or a principle of "international comity." If this is what the act of state doctrine is *not*, then what *is* its rationale? *Environmental Tectonics* said at one point that the doctrine rested on separation of powers concerns. Elsewhere, however, Justice Scalia treated the act of state doctrine as a choice-of-law rule, quoting *Ricaud* for the proposition that, "the act within its own boundaries of one sovereign State . . . becomes . . . a rule of decision for the courts of this country." 246 U.S. at 310.

Does this resolve, more clearly than *Sabbatino*, the rationale of the act of state doctrine? Is the doctrine based on both choice-of-law and separation of powers considerations? Are these considerations consistent with one another? What do separation of powers considerations suggest about the correctness of Justice Scalia's distinction between validity and motivations?

6. *U.S. Government position in* Environmental Tectonics. As the Court's opinion indicates, the U.S. Government urged a different approach to the act of state doctrine from that adopted by Justice Scalia. Consider the following excerpt from the Government's *amicus curiae* brief:

> As synthesized in *Sabbatino*, the [act of state] doctrine has evolved from a rather rigid rule based on territorial sovereignty to a more flexible analysis based on international comity and the responsibility of the political Branches for the conduct of foreign relations. . . . Although the Court's prior decisions have appeared to take a rather rigid view of the act of state doctrine, *Sabbatino* expressly declined to lay down or reaffirm any inflexible or all-encompassing rule for application of the doctrine in future cases. Consistent with *Sabbatino*, and in recognition of the widely divergent circumstances in which the issue may arise, we do not urge any rigid formula for the resolution of act of state cases generally. In particular, we do not urge the Court to choose among the expressions in judicial opinions and commentary that have variously sought to explain the act of state doctrine as a rule of judicial abstention, an aspect of the political question doctrine, a choice-of-law rule, a broader conflict-of-laws rule

that incorporates both choice-of-forum and choice-of-law notions or a principle of repose that treats the act of a foreign sovereign as conclusively settling its legality in the courts of the United States. . . . We . . . rest our submission on the identification of a number of factors that, under principles of comity and separation of powers, indicate that application of the act of state doctrine is not required in the circumstances of this case. [In support of this conclusion, the Government's brief cited the facts that: (a) federal law was the basis of the U.S. suit, rather than international or state law; (b) no conflict with Nigerian law was involved; (c) no decision on the validity of the contract was required; (d) the contract was commercial; and (e) the State Department did not believe adjudication of the suit would affect U.S. foreign relations.] Brief for the United States as Amicus Curiae, at 6-10 (October 1989).

Is this a sensible view of the act of state doctrine? Is it more persuasive than that adopted in *Environmental Tectonics*? How does the Government's view differ from the Court's?

7. Correctness of Environmental Tectonics result. Was the result in *Environmental Tectonics* correct, under either the U.S. Government's rationale or that of Justice Scalia? Why should a U.S. court hear the kinds of claims at issue there? Suppose a German or Iranian court were to decide a dispute between two German or Iranian companies that required proof that a U.S. cabinet officer took bribes.

8. Lower court applications of Environmental Tectonics. Following *Environmental Tectonics,* most lower courts have interpreted the act of state doctrine narrowly. *E.g., Provincial Gov't of Marinduque v. Placer Dome, Inc.,* 582 F.3d 1083, 1091-1092 (9th Cir. 2009) (thorough discussion of validity element); *Grupo Protexa v. All American Marine Slip,* 20 F.3d 1224 (3d Cir. 1994) (refusing to apply act of state doctrine to foreclose inquiry into validity of Mexican government decree requiring removal of sunken vessel, in case where private party claimed reimbursement of removal costs from insurer); *Walter Fuller Aircraft Sales, Inc. v. Republic of Philippines,* 965 F.2d 1375 (5th Cir. 1992) (act of state doctrine does not bar contract claim against foreign state, because, even if challenged foreign acts of state were valid, they could breach parties' contract); *Cruz v. United States,* 387 F. Supp. 2d 1057, 1068-1069 (N.D. Cal. 2005); *In re Yukos Oil Co.,* 321 B.R. 396, 409-410 (Bankr. S.D. Tex. 2005). *But see Credit Suisse v. U.S. Dist. Court for the Central District of California,* 130 F.3d 1342, 1347-1348 (9th Cir. 1997) (act of state doctrine barred judicial review of foreign asset freeze order).

9. Foreign corruption suits after Environmental Tectonics. One possible consequence of *Environmental Tectonics* is that lawsuits involving claims of foreign governmental corruption will more readily be maintained in U.S. courts. *See United States v. Labs of Virginia, Inc.,* 272 F. Supp. 2d 764, 772 n.5 (N.D. Ill. 2003) (suggesting existence of a "corruption" exception to the act of state doctrine); *Lamb v. Phillip Morris, Inc.,* 915 F.2d 1024 (6th Cir. 1990). Some pre-*Environmental Tectonics* decisions also permitted actions alleging foreign governmental corruption to go forward. *E.g., Gage Int'l v. Cadillac Gage Co.,* 534 F. Supp. 896, 905 (E.D. Mich. 1981); *Dominicus Americana Bohio v. Gulf & Western Indus.,* 473 F. Supp. 680, 690 (S.D.N.Y. 1979). *See* Note, *Act of State Doctrine: An Emerging Corruption Exception in Antitrust Cases,* 59 Notre Dame L. Rev. 455 (1984). Is it wise for U.S. courts to adjudicate sensitive allegations of foreign sovereign misconduct? Suppose a suit involves claims of corruption, or immoral conduct, by the head of state of a friendly foreign nation, or a hostile and potentially dangerous foreign nation. Note Judge Bork's discussion of separation of powers concerns under the Alien Tort Statute. *See supra* pp. 34, 54. Why are these not equally applicable in the context of corruption actions?

Suits based upon foreign corruption have almost inevitably named U.S. companies as defendants. Is it appropriate for U.S. courts effectively to impose a higher standard of business morality on U.S. companies' foreign operations than that prevailing abroad or imposed upon foreign companies? *See generally* Spahn, *Discovering Secrets: Act of State Defenses to Bribery Cases,* 38 Hofstra L. Rev. 163 (2009).

10. *No requirement regarding presence of foreign state in litigation.* *Environmental Tectonics* considered whether to apply the act of state doctrine at the behest of a private litigant even though the Republic of Nigeria was not a party to the lawsuit. Like *Ricaud* and *Oetjen,* a number of lower court decisions have taken the same course. *E.g., Nocula v. UGS Corp.,* 520 F.3d 719, 727-728 (7th Cir. 2008); *Lamb v. Phillip Morris, Inc.,* 915 F.2d 1024, 1026 n.2 (6th Cir. 1990); *Galu v. Swiss Air Transport Co.,* 873 F.2d 650 (2d Cir. 1989); *O.N.E. Shipping v. Flota Mercanta Grancolombiana,* 830 F.2d 449 (2d Cir. 1987) ("such an inquiry is foreclosed . . . regardless of whether the foreign government is named as a party to the suit . . ."); *Occidental of Umm Al Qaywayn v. A Certain Cargo of Petroleum,* 577 F.2d 1196 (5th Cir. 1978); *Hunt v. Mobil Oil Corp.,* 550 F.2d 68 (2d Cir. 1977). Are the purposes of the act of state doctrine implicated when the foreign state is not a party and has not urged application of the doctrine? To the same extent as when a foreign state is a party?

11. *Application of act of state doctrine in actions brought by the U.S. Government.* Should the act of state doctrine apply to actions brought by the U.S. Government, either against a foreign state itself or against a private party? On the one hand, the "offense" to foreign sovereigns caused by some governmental suits will be greater than that resulting from private suits, particularly where governmental proceedings involve quasi-criminal issues. (Government actions under the Foreign Corrupt Practices Act, 15 U.S.C. §§78dd-1, 78dd-2 (1982), and the antitrust laws are good examples of such proceedings.) On the other hand, when the Executive Branch brings a suit that requires U.S. courts to pass judgment on foreign acts of state, it has presumably concluded that the action will not cause the judiciary to interfere in U.S. foreign relations. As a result, a principal rationale for the act of state doctrine is arguably inapplicable to governmental suits.

The few lower courts that have addressed this issue have generally concluded that the act of state doctrine does not apply to proceedings brought by the U.S. Government. *See Clayco Petroleum Corp. v. Occidental Petroleum Corp.,* 712 F.2d 404, 409 (9th Cir. 1983) ("Executive bodies have discretion in bringing any action. . . . Therefore, any governmental enforcement represents a judgment on the wisdom of bringing a proceeding, in light of the exigencies of foreign affairs. Act of state concerns are thus inapplicable since the purpose of the doctrine is to prevent the judiciary from interfering with the political branch's conduct of foreign policy."); *Jimenez v. Aristeguieta,* 311 F.2d 547, 558 (5th Cir. 1962). A few courts have held, at least implicitly, to the contrary. Under this view, Executive Branch participation in the suit does not categorically foreclose the availability of the act of state doctrine but, nonetheless, tips heavily against its application. *United States v. Lazarenko,* 504 F. Supp. 2d 791, 801-802 (N.D. Cal. 2007); *United States v. Giffen,* 326 F. Supp. 2d 497, 501-502 (S.D.N.Y. 2004); *United States v. Labs of Virginia,* 272 F. Supp. 2d 764, 770-771 (N.D. Ill. 2003); *In re Grand Jury Subpoena Dated August 9, 2000,* 218 F. Supp. 2d 544, 557 (S.D.N.Y. 2002). What if a state government brings a suit? What if a foreign state brings a suit?

12. *Application of act of state doctrine to federal statutory claims.* *Sabbatino* involved application of the act of state doctrine to state law and international law claims. A number of lower courts have held that the act of state doctrine also applies in cases based on federal statutory claims. *E.g., O.N.E. Shipping v. Flota Mercante Grancolombiana,* 830 F.2d 449 (2d Cir. 1987) (antitrust); *IAM v. OPEC,* 649 F.2d 1354 (9th Cir. 1981) (antitrust); *Industrial Inv. Dev. Corp. v. Mitsui & Co.,* 594 F.2d 48 (5th Cir. 1979) (antitrust); *Hunt v. Mobil Oil Corp.,* 550 F.2d 68 (2d Cir. 1977) (antitrust).

Environmental Tectonics involved federal statutory claims and the U.S. Government's *amicus curiae* brief urged the Court to apply the act of state doctrine less readily to bar such claims than claims based on state or foreign law:

> In *Sabbatino* and other cases, the act of the foreign state itself was challenged under the law of that state or international law. Respondent's suit, by contrast, is brought against private parties and arises under provisions of United States law (RICO, the Robinson-Patman Act, and New Jersey law). . . . The interest of the United States in enforcing its laws weighs heavily in the comity analysis. Brief for the United States as Amicus Curiae, at 7.

Is it more difficult to justify application of the act of state doctrine when Congress has prescribed a substantive rule of law and vested the federal courts with jurisdiction over claims based on that rule? Doesn't this sort of federal legislative action embody a determination by the political branches that U.S. foreign policy interests are outweighed by U.S. regulatory interests? If a federal statute is applicable to conduct abroad (for example, under the antitrust laws because the jurisdictional requirements of *Hartford Fire, supra* pp. 629-667, are satisfied), what permits reliance on the common law "choice of law" rule referred in the act of state doctrine to displace U.S. law?

c.   The Situs Requirement.   *Sabbatino,* like previous Supreme Court decisions,[64] was careful to confine the act of state doctrine to acts of a foreign state "within its own territory."[65] Subsequent lower court decisions have emphasized the importance of the "situs requirement," often denying act of state protection to conduct not occurring within the foreign state.[66]

The rationale underlying the situs requirement is not entirely clear. The requirement was first adopted in early act of state decisions that emphasized international law principles and respect for the territorial sovereignty of foreign nations.[67] The apparent erosion of the strict territoriality principle in various jurisdictional contexts[68] and the emphasis on foreign relations concerns as the rationale for the act of state doctrine raises questions about the continued vitality of the situs requirement.[69] Nonetheless, lower courts continue to apply the requirement, saying that "[n]otions of territoriality run deep through the [act of state] doctrine."[70]

The situs requirement has frequently come into issue when foreign governments have attempted to seize property which is physically located outside their territory. U.S. courts have generally refused to afford act of state protection to such attempts.[71] Difficulties have

---

64. *Oetjen,* 246 U.S. at 303-304; *Underhill,* 168 U.S. at 252 ("the courts of one country will not sit in judgment on the acts of the government of another done within its own territory").

65. *Sabbatino,* 376 U.S. at 414-415.

66. *See infra* pp. 833-838.

67. *Underhill v. Hernandez,* 168 U.S. 250 (1987); *Oetjen v. Central Leather Co.,* 246 U.S. 297 (1918); Henkin, *The Foreign Affairs Power of the Federal Courts:* Sabbatino, 64 Colum. L. Rev. 805, 828 (1964); Note, *The Act of State Doctrine: Resolving Debt Situs Confusion,* 86 Colum. L. Rev. 594, 608-610 (1986).

68. *See supra* pp. 86-88 (judicial jurisdiction) and 649-651 (legislative jurisdiction).

69. Comment, *Act of State Doctrine Held Inapplicable to Foreign Seizures of Property When the Property at the Time of the Expropriation Is Located Within the United States,* 9 N.Y.U. J. Int'l L. & Pol'y 515 (1977).

70. *Tchacosh Co. v. Rockwell Int'l Corp.,* 766 F.2d 1333, 1336 (9th Cir. 1985).

71. *See Allied Bank Int'l v. Banco Credito Agricola de Cartago,* 757 F.2d 516 (2d Cir. 1985); *United Bank v. Cosmic Int'l,* 542 F.2d 868, 872 (2d Cir. 1976); *Republic of Iraq v. First Nat'l City Bank,* 353 F.2d 47 (2d Cir. 1965) (foreign decree purporting to expropriate property in the United States); *Libra Bank v. Banco Nacional de Costa Rica,* 570 F. Supp. 870 (S.D.N.Y. 1983); *Compania Ron Bacardi v. Bank of Nova Scotia,* 193 F. Supp. 814 (S.D.N.Y. 1961). *See* Note, *The Territorial Exception to the Act of State Doctrine: Application to French Nationalization,* 6 Fordham Int'l L.J. 121 (1982); Zaitzeff & Kunz, *The Act of State Doctrine and the* Allied Bank *Case,* 40 Bus. Law. 449, 451-458 (1985).

arisen, however, in determining the situs of intangible property, such as debts. These difficulties are illustrated by *Braka v. Bancomer, S.N.C.,* excerpted below.

BRAKA v. BANCOMER, S.N.C.
762 F.2d 222 (2d Cir. 1985)

MESKILL, CIRCUIT JUDGE. This appeal represents our second opportunity in recent months to consider the effect of foreign finance decrees on the investments of United States entities. . . . [W]e agree with the district court that plaintiffs' recovery is barred by the act of state doctrine. . . .

In our previous excursion into the intricacies of the act of state doctrine, *Allied Bank International v. Banco Credito Agricola de Cartago,* 757 F.2d 516 (2d Cir. 1985) (on rehearing), we held that because the situs of the debt was in the United States, the act of state doctrine did not operate to prevent the creditors from recovering for their losses. In the case before us, however, the doctrine does bar relief because the situs of defendant's obligations was in Mexico.

Plaintiffs are a number of United States citizens who purchased peso- and dollar-denominated certificates of deposit ("CDs") from defendant Bancomer, SA ("Bancomer"). When plaintiffs' purchases were made in 1981, Bancomer was a privately run Mexican bank. Plaintiffs arranged for their purchases by telephone with Bancomer's Mexico City office. The purchases were effected either through application of plaintiffs' funds that were on deposit in Mexico or through plaintiffs' delivery of checks drawn on their New York banks payable to Bancomer's New York agency. If the latter method was used, the agency, which was not authorized to accept deposits, transmitted the funds by interbank transfer to the Mexican office. The CDs indicated that Mexico was the place of deposit and the place of payment of principal and interest, although as a convenience such payments were sometimes transmitted to plaintiffs' New York banks. The total value of the CDs was $2,100,000. All of the CDs were scheduled to mature in February 1983, except one, which was to reach maturity in September 1982. The annual interest rates ranged from 14.3 percent to 23.25 percent.

In August 1982, shortly before the first certificate was to reach maturity, the Mexican Ministry of Treasury and Public Credit issued a decree requiring that all domestic obligations be performed by delivery of an equivalent amount in pesos at the prevailing exchange rate. This decree banned the use of foreign currency as legal tender. In September two more decrees were issued. The first nationalized Mexico's banks, including Bancomer. The second mandated a system of exchange controls that was carried out by the subsequent issuance of rules called "General Rules for Exchange Controls." As a result of these and later decrees, plaintiffs received Mexican pesos at the officially prescribed exchange rates, approximately 70-80 pesos per dollar, when they tendered their certificates on the maturity dates. Plaintiffs allege that because they did not receive the then actual market exchange rate of 135-150 pesos per dollar, they lost over $900,000.

Plaintiffs filed suit in federal district court in New York claiming damages for breach of contract and for violation of the federal securities laws. [The district] court held that Bancomer's issuance of CDs was a commercial rather than a sovereign act, and that it therefore fell within the commercial activity exception to the FSIA, 28 U.S.C. §1605(a)(2). . . . However, the court went on to hold that the absence of immunity did not render plaintiffs' claims justiciable. Because the situs of plaintiffs' CDs was in Mexico, the court determined that act of state principles prevented judicial examination of the complaint. In addition . . . the court held that Mexico's issuance of exchange controls was not a commercial activity. Therefore, the court rejected plaintiffs' claims as barred by the act of state doctrine. . . .

[W]e must first determine the situs of the property that was taken by the Mexican exchange controls. As we noted in *Allied,* "the concept of the situs of a debt for act of state purposes differs from the ordinary concept." 757 F.2d at 521. The test we adopted in *Allied* was whether the purported taking was "able to come to complete fruition within the domination of the [Mexican] government." *Tabacalera Severiano Jorge, SA v. Standard Cigar Co.,* 392 F.2d 706, 715-16 (5th Cir. 1968). Here, unlike *Allied,* it is clear that Mexico's actions meet this test.

The property at issue was Bancomer's obligation to pay the contractually mandated return on plaintiffs' investment. Plaintiffs argue that the situs of this obligation was New York. They allege that because they made some purchases by giving checks to Bancomer's New York agency and received some interest payments in New York, they could demand that Bancomer fulfill its obligation by paying them in New York.

The CDs named Mexico City as the place of deposit and of payment of interest and principal. Although some of the CDs were dollar-denominated, Bancomer never agreed to pay them in any location other than Mexico. The fact that plaintiffs' deposits were occasionally accepted and transmitted to Mexico by Bancomer's New York agency does not alter the situs of Bancomer's obligation. It is clear that the accomplishment of interbank transfers, which was the extent of the New York agency's participation, does not change the contractually mandated situs of plaintiffs' property. The CDs were located in Mexico and were therefore subject to the effects of the exchange control regulations. The Mexican government "ha[d] the parties and the res before it and act[ed] in such a manner as to change the relationship between the parties touching the res." *Tabacalera,* 392 F.2d at 715. To intervene to contradict the result of the exchange controls would be an impermissible intrusion into the governmental activities of a foreign sovereign.

Plaintiffs' attempt to equate their case with *Garcia* [*v. Chase Manhattan Bank, NA,* 735 F.2d 645 (2d Cir. 1984),] is unavailing. In *Garcia* we held that the act of state doctrine did not bar recovery because the parties expressly provided for repayment at any Chase branch, anywhere in the world. Here, by contrast, no such wide-ranging agreement exists. Thus, we hold that the situs of defendant's obligation existed wholly within the boundaries of the foreign sovereign, and that the act of state doctrine therefore bars recovery. . . . The act of state doctrine bars consideration of plaintiffs' complaint because the situs of defendant's obligations was in Mexico. . . .

Notes *on* Bancomer

1. ***The situs requirement.*** *Sabbatino* emphasized that its decision was limited to acts of state committed by a foreign state within its own territory. 376 U.S. at 414-445. Lower courts have frequently applied this situs requirement. *E.g. Agudas Chasidei Chabad of U.S. v. Russian Fed'n,* 528 F.3d 934, 952 (D.C. Cir. 2008); *Bandes v. Harlow & Jones, Inc.,* 852 F.2d 661, 666-667 (2d Cir. 1988); *Grass v. Credito Mexicano, SA,* 797 F.2d 220, 222 (5th Cir. 1986); *Tchacosh Co. v. Rockwell Int'l Corp.,* 766 F.2d 1333, 1336 (9th Cir. 1988); *Republic of Iraq v. First National City Bank,* 353 F.2d 47, 51 (2d Cir. 1965).

2. ***Rationale for the situs requirement.*** What is the rationale for the situs requirement's limitation of the act of state doctrine to a foreign state's acts within its own territory?

(a) Territorial limits on national jurisdiction. Territorial limits were included as part of the act of state doctrine by early decisions — like *Underhill* and *Ricaud* — that were decided at a time when legislative and judicial jurisdiction were also subject to strict territorial limits.

See supra pp. 83-86, 646-649. Thus, the situs requirement served as a means of limiting U.S. recognition of acts of state to those acts which a foreign state had jurisdiction to engage in under international law. *See* Chow, *Rethinking the Act of State Doctrine: An Analysis in Terms of Jurisdiction to Prescribe,* 62 Wash. L. Rev. 397, 448-450 (1987).

Chapters 7 and 8 above describe how contemporary international law has increasingly permitted states to extend their legislative jurisdiction extraterritorially in a significant range of cases, and how contemporary choice-of-law rules are no longer territorially defined. Given this evolution in international jurisdictional limits, is a territorial situs requirement still appropriate? Does the answer vary depending on whether the act of state doctrine is a choice-of-law rule or a variation of the political question doctrine?

Was the act of state doctrine based upon a foreign state's exercise of either legislative or judicial jurisdiction? The former permits a state to prescribe laws (recognized by foreign nations pursuant to choice-of-law rules), while the latter permits a state to render judgments (recognized by foreign nations pursuant to rules regarding the enforcement of foreign judgments). In fact, the act of state doctrine involves the exercise of enforcement jurisdiction — a foreign state's executive actions, fulfilling its legislative and judicial jurisdiction. Thus, acts of state include the seizure of property (*Ricaud* and *Oetjen*) or persons (*Underhill*), but generally do not include foreign judgments or legislative enactments. *See supra* pp. 820-821.

International law traditionally limited a nation's exercise of enforcement jurisdiction to acts within its own territory. Moreover, contemporary international law generally continues to impose territorial limits on enforcement jurisdiction. *Restatement (Third) Foreign Relations Law* §432 comment b (1987). What does this suggest about the continued validity of territorial limits on the act of state doctrine?

(b) Impact on U.S. foreign relations. Is the territoriality requirement consistent with rationales for the act of state doctrine which emphasize the need to minimize judicial interference with U.S. foreign policy? Some authorities have reasoned that the situs requirement is based on the expectations of foreign states, which are said to contemplate international scrutiny of their extraterritorial acts, but not of their domestic conduct. Note, *The Act of State Doctrine: Resolving Debt Situs Confusion,* 86 Colum. L. Rev. 594, 608-609 (1986); *Tabacalera Severiano Jorge, SA v. Standard Cigar Co.,* 392 F.2d 706, 715 (5th Cir. 1968).

(c) Choice of law. Is the territoriality requirement consistent with the view that the act of state doctrine is a choice-of-law rule? Recall the American "conflicts revolution" and the erosion of territoriality principles in contemporary choice-of-law thinking.

3. *Acts of state in a third state's territory.* Suppose Mexico's exchange control regulations were, as a matter of Mexican law, applicable to a deposit whose situs was the Guatemalan branch of Bancomer. Would a U.S. court apply the act of state doctrine in a suit by the depositor? Should it? *See Drexel Burnham Lambert Group Inc. v. Galadari,* 777 F.2d 877, 881 (2d Cir. 1985). What if Guatemalan law was in conflict with Mexican exchange controls? Recall one of the early U.S. judicial explanations for the act of state doctrine: "The very meaning of sovereignty is that the decree of the sovereign makes law." *American Banana Co. v. United Fruit Co.,* 213 U.S. 347, 358 (1909). Is a state's conduct outside its territory entitled to this same presumption of absolute legality? *See In re Philippine National Bank,* 397 F.3d 768, 773-774 (9th Cir. 2005) (applying act of state doctrine to federal court review of foreign court order transferring forfeited funds from national bank).

4. *Scope of the situs requirement.* Foreign governmental conduct will usually involve some actions — if only decision-making — within the foreign state's territory. Lower courts have struggled to articulate a general formula for determining when sufficient conduct has occurred outside a foreign state's territory to render the act of state doctrine inapplicable. The standard articulated in *Bancomer* is one of the better-accepted efforts in this context: it inquires "whether the purported taking was 'able to come to complete fruition within the [foreign state's] domination.' " 762 F.2d at 224 (quoting *Tabacalera Severiano Jorge, SA v. Standard Cigar Co.*, 392 F.2d 706, 715-716 (5th Cir. 1968) (also holding that foreign sovereign must be "physically in a position to perform a fait accompli"). *Compare F. & H.R. Farman-Farmaian Consulting Engineers Firm v. Harza Eng'g Co.*, 882 F.2d 281 (7th Cir. 1989) (confiscation must be "complete within the foreign state in the sense that all of the firm's assets and operations were there and the victim is trying to get an American court to undo the confiscation"); *United States v. Giffen*, 326 F. Supp. 2d 497, 503 (S.D.N.Y. 2004) (situs requirement not satisfied because transactions were "dehors the geographic boundaries of [foreign country]"); *Restatement (Third) Foreign Relations Law* §443, Reporters' Note 4 (1987); *Restatement (Second) Foreign Relations Law* §43, comment a (1965) ("Act of state doctrine . . . becomes applicable only when and if the act has been fully executed.").

5. ***The situs of intangibles.*** As *Bancomer* illustrates, the situs requirement has frequently been relevant in cases involving "intangibles," such as debts or causes of action. The situs requirement makes it necessary to determine where debts and other intangibles are "located," because a foreign state's seizure or refusal to pay a debt located within its borders can be deemed an act of state, while refusal to honor a foreign debt will not satisfy the situs requirement. *See* Lowenfeld, *In Search of the Intangible: A Comment on* Shaffer v. Heitner, 53 N.Y.U. L. Rev. 102 (1978); Note, *The Resolution of Act of State Disputes Involving Indefinitely Situated Property*, 25 Va. J. Int'l L. 901, 907-926 (1985).

6. ***The situs of debts.*** In cases involving the "location" of debts, most courts, like *Bancomer,* have concluded that the debt is located at the "contractually mandated" situs for its repayment. Under this analysis, the act of state doctrine is applicable to the repudiation of debts that must be repaid within the foreign state, but not to debts payable only at other locations. *See Allied Bank Int'l v. Banco Credito Agricola de Cartago,* 757 F.2d 516 (2d Cir. 1985); *Weston Banking Corp. v. Turkiye Garanti Bankasi, AS,* 456 N.Y.S.2d 684 (1982) (breach of promise to pay outside foreign state not covered by act of state doctrine). Is this emphasis on private agreement consistent with the notions of territorial sovereignty underlying the situs requirement? Compare the emphasis on the "place of payment" with the historic focus on the "place of contracting" in the *Restatement (First) Conflict of Laws* (1934). *See supra* p. 777. Would it be more appropriate to adopt some variation of the "most significant relation" standard of the *Restatement (Second) Conflict of Laws?* For a discussion of situs in debt cases, *see* Diaz, *The Territoriality Inquiry under the Act of State Doctrine: Continuing the Search for an Appropriate Application of Situs of Debt Rules in International Debt Disputes*, 10 ILSA J Int'l & Comp. L. 525 (2004).

Greater uncertainty surrounds the treatment of debts that are repayable both within the debtor state and elsewhere. Is a foreign state's repudiation of such obligations protected by the act of state doctrine (because the debt is sited, at least in part, in the foreign state) or is it unprotected (because the debt is sited, at least in part, outside the foreign state)? *Compare Garcia v. Chase Manhattan Bank, NA,* 735 F.2d 645 (2d Cir. 1984) (agreement to repay debt anywhere in the world renders act of state doctrine inapplicable) *with Perez v. Chase Manhattan Bank, NA,* 474 N.Y.S.2d 689 (App. Div. 1984) (act of state doctrine applicable to promise to pay anywhere in the world, since promise could have been enforced in Cuba).

7. ***Inferring the situs of intangibles.*** If the parties have not agreed to a place for repayment of a debt, where is the debt's situs? Lower courts have not adopted a consistent approach. *See generally* Courtade, Annotation, *Situs of Debt or Property for Purposes of the Act of State Doctrine*, 77 A.L.R. Fed. 293 (1986 & Supp. 2010).

(a) Location of the debtor. Some courts have looked to the location of the *debtor* in ascertaining the situs of a debt in the absence of clear contractual guidance. *See Harris v. Balk,* 198 U.S. 215, 222 (1904) ("The obligation of the debtor to pay his debt clings to and accompanies him wherever he goes."). Contemporary decisions have modified this analysis by reasoning that a debt is sited wherever the debtor is subject to personal jurisdiction. *See Menendez v. Saks & Co.,* 485 F.2d 1355, 1364-1365 (2d Cir. 1973), *rev'd on other grounds,* 425 U.S. 682 (1976) ("a debt is not 'located' within a foreign state unless that state has the power to enforce or collect it. . . . [T]he power to enforce payment of a debt . . . generally depends on jurisdiction over the person of the debtor."); *United Bank Ltd. v. Cosmic Int'l, Inc.,* 542 F.2d 868 (2d Cir. 1976); *Republic of Iraq v. First Nat'l City Bank,* 353 F.2d 47 (2d Cir. 1965); *Tabacalera Severiano Jorge, SA v. Standard Cigar Co.,* 392 F.2d 706, 715-716 (5th Cir. 1968). As discussed above, contemporary principles of personal jurisdiction generally will permit numerous states to exercise personal jurisdiction over a debtor, and thus to enforce a debt. Does this mean that a debt is sited in numerous places? Would it be consistent with purposes and rationale of the act of state doctrine to treat judgments based on long-arm jurisdiction as acts of state?

(b) Most significant relationship test. Other courts have looked to a wider range of factors to determine whether the relationship between an intangible and the foreign state are "sufficiently close that we will antagonize the foreign government by not recognizing its acts." *Callejo v. Bancomer, SA,* 764 F.2d 1101 (5th Cir. 1985). *See also F. & H.R. Farman-Farmaian Consulting Engineers Firm v. Harza Eng'g Co.,* 882 F.2d 281 (7th Cir. 1989); *Tchacosh Co. v. Rockwell Int'l Corp.,* 766 F.2d 1333 (9th Cir. 1985); *Libra Bank, Ltd. v. Banco Nacional de Costa Rica, SA,* 570 F. Supp. 870, 884 (S.D.N.Y. 1983). *Compare* the *Third Restatement's* view: "it might be preferable to approach the question of the applicability of the act of state doctrine to intangible assets not by searching for an imaginary situs for property that has no real situs, but by determining how the act of the foreign state in the particular circumstances fits within the reasons for the act of state doctrine and for the territorial limitation." *Restatement (Third) Foreign Relations Law* §443, Reporters' Note 4 (1987).

(c) "Complete fruition" test. Some courts have suggested that a debt or other intangible will be sited in a foreign state only if that state "has the parties and the res before it and acts in such a manner as to change the relationship of the parties touching the res." *Tabacalera Severiano Jorge, SA v. Standard Cigar Co.,* 392 F.2d 706, 715 (5th Cir. 1968). *See also Ramirez de Arellano v. Weinberger,* 745 F.2d 1500, 1533-1536 (D.C. Cir. 1984), *vacated,* 471 U.S. 1113 (1985) (presidential expropriation decree is not an "act of state" until property is actually seized); *Allied Bank Int'l v. Banco Credito Agricola de Cartago,* 757 F.2d 516, 521 (2d Cir. 1985); *Universal Trading & Inv. Co. v. Kiritchenko,* 2007 WL 2669841 (N.D. Cal. Sept. 7, 2007); *Wolf v. Federal Republic of Germany,* 1995 WL 263471, at *11-12 (N.D. Ill. 1995).

8. Application of comity doctrine where situs requirement is not satisfied. What are the consequences of *not* satisfying the situs requirement? Lower courts have generally indicated that an action in U.S. courts may be dismissed on "comity" grounds even when a foreign act of state occurs outside the territory of the foreign state (or involves property located outside the foreign state). *Republic of Iraq v. First National City Bank,* 353 F.2d 47, 51 (2d Cir. 1965) ("when property confiscated is within the United States at the time of attempted confiscation, our courts will give effect to acts of state only if they are consistent with the policy and law of the United States"); *Films by Jove, Inc. v. Berov,* 341 F. Supp. 2d 199, 212 (E.D.N.Y. 2004) ("Comity is applied more broadly than the act of state doctrine."). *See* Note, *Informal Foreign Affairs Formalism: The Act of State Doctrine and the Reinterpretation of International Comity,* 43 Va. J. Int'l L. 275 (2002).

Some decisions require some special U.S. policy interest in overriding a foreign act of state notwithstanding the fact that the situs requirement is not satisfied. *Drexel Burnham Lambert Group Inc. v. Galadari*, 777 F.2d 877 (2d Cir. 1985); *Allied Bank Int'l v. Banco Credito Agricola de Cartago*, 757 F.2d 516 (2d Cir. 1985). In most cases, however, the challenged act of state is an expropriation and uncompensated seizures have long been held "contrary to our public policy and shocking to our sense of justice and equity." *Vladikavkazsky Ry. v. New York Trust Co.*, 263 N.Y. 369, 378 (1934). *See Bandes v. Harlow & Jones, Inc.*, 852 F.2d 661, 667 (2d Cir. 1988); *Maltina Corp. v. Cawy Bottling Co.*, 462 F.2d 1021, 1027 (5th Cir. 1972); *Republic of Iraq v. First Nat'l City Bank*, 353 F.2d 47, 51 (2d Cir. 1965); *Castro v. International Telegraph & Telephone Co.*, 1991 Del. Ch. LEXIS 89 (Del. Ch. 1991).

C. Exceptions to the Act of State Doctrine

Various authorities have fashioned significant exceptions to the doctrine. These include, among others, the *Bernstein* exception, an exception for "commercial" acts, an "international law" or treaty exception, and the Second Hickenlooper amendment.[72] The following sections examine each of these exceptions.

Like the basic act of state doctrine itself, considerable uncertainty surrounds most of these exceptions. This uncertainty is due in large part to two sharply divided decisions by the Supreme Court — *Alfred Dunhill* and *First National City Bank* — dealing with the act of state doctrine.[73] Because no Justice's opinion in either case was able to command a majority of the Court, the lower courts have been left largely without guidance in the field. Not surprisingly, their decisions are often inconsistent and sometimes confused.

1. The *Bernstein* Exception

A primary rationale advanced in *Sabbatino* for the act of state doctrine was avoiding judicial interference with the executive branch's conduct of foreign relations.[74] This concern appears to lose much of its force in cases where the Executive Branch states that a judicial decision will not harm U.S. foreign relations. As a result, courts have sometimes declined to apply the act of state doctrine when the Executive Branch formally advises that there is no need to do so. Judicial deference to Executive Branch views regarding the act of state doctrine has been justified under the so-called "*Bernstein* exception."

The term "*Bernstein* exception" derives from the Second Circuit's decisions in *Bernstein v. N.V. Nederlandsche-Amerikaansche Stoomvaart-Maatschappij*.[75] This case involved claims by a Jewish businessman to recover property seized during World War II by the Nazi regime. The Court of Appeals initially dismissed the plaintiff's claims on act of state grounds.[76] Subsequently, the Department of State submitted a letter to the court declaring that the "policy of the Executive . . . is to relieve American courts from any restraint on the exercise of their jurisdiction to pass upon the validity of the acts of Nazi officials." In

---

72. Congress has sometimes excluded application of the act of state doctrine in particular legislation. *See, e.g.,* 9 U.S.C. §15 (arbitration awards); 22 U.S.C. §6082(a)(6) (civil actions under the Helms-Burton Act). *See also Glen v. Club Mediterranee S.A.*, 450 F.3d 1251 (11th Cir. 2006).

73. *See, e.g., Alfred Dunhill of London v. Republic of Cuba*, 425 U.S. 682 (1976); *First Nat'l City Bank v. Banco Nacional de Cuba*, 406 U.S. 759 (1972).

74. *See, e.g., First Nat'l City Bank*, 406 U.S. at 767 (plurality opinion); *Sabbatino*, 376 U.S. at 427-428. As discussed above, *Environmental Tectonics* repeated this separation of powers rationale, while also formulating the act of state doctrine as a choice of law rule. *See supra* p. 824-827.

75. 173 F.2d 71 (2d Cir. 1949) *and* 210 F.2d 375 (2d Cir. 1954).

76. 173 F.2d 71 (2d Cir. 1949).

subsequent proceedings, the Second Circuit expressly relied on the Department of State's letter to reverse its earlier decision. The Court held that the act of state doctrine was inapplicable in the face of an express executive suggestion that U.S. courts exercise jurisdiction, thus giving rise to the so-called "*Bernstein* exception."[77]

The Supreme Court has thus far refused to accept the *Bernstein* exception. In *First National City Bank v. Banco Nacional de Cuba,* Justice Rehnquist delivered the judgment of the Court, and wrote a plurality opinion embracing the *Bernstein* exception.[78] Nevertheless, in the same case, at least five (and perhaps six) Justices rejected the doctrine.[79]

Lower courts have reacted to the Supreme Court's handling of the *Bernstein* exception with confusion. Some courts have applied the exception as it was originally framed in *Bernstein*—when the Executive Branch expressly states that adjudication of a matter will not impair U.S. foreign relations, these courts hold that the act of state doctrine is inapplicable.[80] Other courts have expressly rejected the *Bernstein* exception, and do not appear to give any weight to U.S. Government statements.[81] The largest number of lower courts has adopted a variation of the original *Bernstein* exception, considering the existence of a *Bernstein* letter as a significant—but not dispositive—factor in act of state analysis.[82] In several decisions, the Second Circuit has given effect to *Bernstein* letters, but only where they relate to counterclaims, and where there is no showing that the litigation will interfere with U.S. foreign relations.[83]

W.S. KIRKPATRICK & CO. v. ENVIRONMENTAL TECTONICS CORP.

493 U.S. 400 (1990) [excerpted above at pp. 824-827]

Notes on **Environmental Tectonics**

1. *Application of the* **Bernstein** *exception in* **First National City Bank.** In *First National City Bank,* the Court was not able to agree on a majority opinion. Justice Rehnquist wrote a plurality opinion adopting the *Bernstein* exception, but it was only joined by two other Justices. Five (and perhaps six) of the Justices then on the Court rejected the exception. Justice Rehnquist's plurality opinion offered the following justification for the *Bernstein* exception:

> The line of cases from this Court establishing the act of state doctrine justifies its existence primarily on the basis that juridical review of acts of state of a foreign power could embarrass

---

77. 210 F.2d 375 (2d Cir. 1954).

78. 406 U.S. 759 (1972).

79. 406 U.S. at 770 (Douglas, J., concurring), 772 (Powell, J., concurring), 776 (Brennan, J., dissenting).

80. *See National Coalition Government of the Union of Burma v. Unocal, Inc.,* 176 F.R.D. 329, 354-355 (C.D. Cal. 1997) (dicta); *Williams v. Curtiss-Wright Corp.,* 694 F.2d 300, 303 (3d Cir. 1982) (dicta); *Occidental of Umm Al Qaywayn, Inc. v. A Certain Cargo of Petroleum,* 577 F.2d 1196, 1204 (5th Cir. 1978); *Beck v. Manufacturers Hanover Trust Co.,* 481 N.Y.S.2d 211 (Sup. Ct. 1984) (dicta).

81. *See Braniff Airways v. Civil Aeronautics Board,* 581 F.2d 846, 851 & n.18 (D.C. Cir. 1978) (dicta); *Hunt v. Coastal States Gas Producing Co.,* 570 S.W.2d 503, 507 (Tex. Civ. App. 1978), *aff'd,* 583 S.W.2d 322 (Tex. 1979).

82. *See Environmental Tectonics Corp. v. W.S. Kirkpatrick, & Co.,* 847 F.2d 1052 (3d Cir. 1988), *aff'd on other grounds,* 493 U.S. 400 (1990); *Republic of Philippines v. Marcos,* 806 F.2d 344, 356-360 (2d Cir. 1986); *Allied Bank Int'l v. Banco Credito Agricola de Cartago,* 757 F.2d 516, 521 n.2 (2d Cir. 1985) (act of state analysis "may be guided but not controlled by the position, if any, articulated by the executive as to the applicability *vel non* of the doctrine as to a particular set of facts. Whether to invoke the act of state doctrine is ultimately and always a judicial question."); *Sharon v. Time, Inc.,* 599 F. Supp. 538, 552 (S.D.N.Y. 1984); *Republic of Haiti v. Duvalier,* 1995 WL 279794 (N.Y. App. Div. 1995). This is also how the *Restatement (Third) Foreign Relations Law* §443, Reporters' Note 8 (1987), characterizes the consensus of the lower courts.

83. *E.g., Banco Nacional de Cuba v. Chase Manhattan Bank,* 658 F.2d 875, 884 (2d Cir. 1981).

the conduct of foreign relations by the political branches of the government. . . . We think that [cases such as *Underhill* and *Oetjen* indicate] that this Court has recognized the primacy of the Executive in the conduct of foreign relations quite as emphatically as it has recognized the act of state doctrine. The Court in *Sabbatino* throughout its opinion emphasized the lead role of the Executive in foreign policy, particularly in seeking redress for American nationals who had been the victims of foreign expropriation, and concluded that any exception to the act of state doctrine based on a mere silence or neutrality on the part of the Executive might well lead to a conflict between the Executive and Judicial Branches. Here, however, the Executive Branch has expressly stated that an inflexible application of the act of state doctrine by this Court would not serve the interests of American foreign policy.

   The act of state doctrine is grounded on judicial concern that application of customary principles of law to judge the acts of a foreign sovereign might frustrate the conduct of foreign relations by the political branches of the government. We conclude that where the Executive Branch, charged as it is with primary responsibility for the conduct of foreign affairs, expressly represents to the Court that application of the act of state doctrine would not advance the interests of American foreign policy, that doctrine should not be applied by the courts. In so doing, we of course adopt and approve the so-called *Bernstein* exception to the act of state doctrine. We believe this to be no more than an application of the classical common-law maxim that "[t]he reason of the law ceasing, the law itself also ceases."

Is this persuasive? Note that it depends on Justice Rehnquist's view of the purposes of the act of state doctrine and his view that the President enjoys largely exclusive authority over U.S. foreign relations. Are his views of these two subjects entirely accurate? *See supra* pp. 6-7.

   2. *Criticism of the* Bernstein *exception.* Several concurring or dissenting opinions in *First National City Bank* criticized the *Bernstein* exception. Justice Brennan wrote that adopting the exception would "require us to abdicate our judicial responsibility to define the contours of the act of state doctrine so that the judiciary does not become embroiled in the politics of international relations to the damage not only of the courts and the Executive but of the rule of law." He reasoned:

Sabbatino held that the validity of a foreign act of state in certain circumstances is a "political question" not cognizable in our courts. Only one — and not necessarily the most important — of those circumstances concerned the possible impairment of the Executive's conduct of foreign affairs. Even if this factor were absent in this case because of the Legal Adviser's statement of position, it would hardly follow that the act of state doctrine should not foreclose judicial review of the expropriation of petitioner's properties. To the contrary, the absence of consensus on the applicable international rules, the unavailability of standards from a treaty or other agreement, the existence and recognition of the Cuban government, the sensitivity of the issues to national concerns, and the power of the Executive alone to effect a fair remedy for all U.S. citizens who have been harmed all point toward the existence of a "political question." . . . The Executive Branch, however extensive its powers in the area of foreign affairs, cannot by simple stipulation change a political question into a cognizable claim. . . .

   The task of defining the contours of a political question such as the act of state doctrine is exclusively the function of this Court. The "*Bernstein*" exception relinquishes the function to the Executive by requiring blind adherence to its requests that foreign acts of state be reviewed. Conversely, it politicizes the judiciary. For the Executive's invitation to lift the act of state bar can only be accepted at the expense of supplanting the political branch in its role as a constituent of the international law-making community. The consequence of adopting the "*Bernstein*" approach would only be to bring the rule of law both here at home and in the relations of nations into disrespect. Indeed, the fate of the individual claimant would be subject to the political considerations of the Executive Branch. Since those considerations change as surely as administrations change, similarly situated litigants would not be likely to obtain even-handed treatment.

Justice Douglas also refused to accept the *Bernstein* exception. In his view, it would mean that "the Court [would] become[] a mere errand boy for the Executive Branch which may choose to pick some people's chestnuts from the fire, but not others."

Justice Rehnquist replied:

> Our holding is in no sense an abdication of the judicial function to the Executive Branch. The judicial power of the United States extends to this case, and the jurisdictional standards established by Congress for adjudication by the federal courts have been met by the parties. The only reason for not deciding the case by use of otherwise applicable legal principles would be the fear that legal interpretation by the judiciary of the act of a foreign sovereign within its own territory might frustrate the conduct of this country's foreign relations. But the branch of the government responsible for the conduct of those foreign relations has advised us that such a consequence need not be feared in this case. The judiciary is therefore free to decide the case without the limitations that would otherwise be imposed upon it by the judicially created act of state doctrine.

Which of these views is more persuasive? What is the basis for the act of state doctrine? If its basis is separation of powers concerns about judicial interference in U.S. foreign relations is the *Bernstein* exception sensible? If the basis for the act of state doctrine is choice-of-law considerations, or concerns based on international comity, is the answer different? Does the *Bernstein* exception leave the fate of claimants to the "political considerations of the Executive Branch"? Isn't this charge more accurately leveled against the act of state doctrine itself, which denies plaintiffs judicial relief in favor of Executive Branch espousal of their claims?

3. *Need for formal statement of Executive Branch policy to trigger* Bernstein *exception.* In *Environmental Tectonics,* the Legal Adviser of the U.S. State Department submitted a letter to the lower courts taking the position that the act of state doctrine was not applicable as a matter of law: We do "not believe the Act of State doctrine would bar the Court from adjudicating this dispute." *See* 847 F.2d at 1067-1069 (reprinting Legal Adviser's letter). In their briefs to the Supreme Court, various parties argued that the Legal Adviser's letter did not fall within the *Bernstein* exception, because it merely opined about the legal applicability of the act of state doctrine, and did not formally state the Executive Branch's view that the doctrine should not be applied. Thereafter, the Legal Adviser submitted a new letter, attached to the U.S. Government's *amicus curiae* brief in the Supreme Court, specifically stating the Executive Branch's position that the act of state doctrine should not apply: "Cases could arise which present an unacceptable risk that adjudication would embarrass the Executive Branch in its conduct of U.S. foreign relations, leading the Executive to suggest the desirability of judicial abstention. We do not regard *Environmental Tectonics* as such a case, and we do not see any foreign relations obstacles to its adjudication on the merits."

In his opinion in *Environmental Tectonics,* however, Justice Scalia overlooked the second letter, mistakenly concluding that "we would question [the Government's] characterization of the legal advisor's letter as reflecting the absence of any policy objection to the adjudication. The letter . . . did not purport to say whether the State Department would like to proceed, but rather responded (correctly, as we hold today) to the question whether the act of state doctrine was applicable." The Court then cited to the Legal Adviser's *first* letter, not to the *second* letter submitted to the Supreme Court. *See supra* p. 841. Putting aside the Court's unfortunate confusion about the U.S. Government's position, is the distinction between a legal opinion and a "policy objection" persuasive? What exactly does the *Environmental Tectonics* footnote require a *Bernstein* letter to say? Note also that the second letter submitted by the Legal Adviser in *Environmental Tectonics* went on to say: "We also believe that, in the absence of a representation to the contrary, the courts may properly assume that no unacceptable interference with U.S. foreign relations will occur on account of the adjudication of like cases."

4. *Practical impact of Executive Branch communications in act of state cases.* Although the legal foundation for the *Bernstein* exception is uncertain, an Executive Branch statement on act of state issues continues to be of considerable practical importance. *See Doe I v. Unocal Corp.,* 395 F.3d 932, 959 (9th Cir. 2002); *Republic of Philippines v. Marcos,* 806 F.2d 344, 357 (2d Cir. 1986); *Republic of Philippines v. Marcos,* 818 F.2d 1473 (9th Cir. 1987), *vacated,* 862 F.2d 1355 (9th Cir. 1988) (*en banc*); *Allied Bank Int'l,* 757 F.2d 516 (2d Cir. 1985); *see also Doe v. Qi,* 349 F. Supp. 2d 1258, 1294-1303 (C.D. Cal. 2004) (extensive discussion of importance of Executive Branch's view). *But see Sarei v. Rio Tinto plc,* 456 F.3d 1069 (9th Cir. 2006) (noting that the State Department's "foreign policy concerns are entitled to consideration, but only as one part of [the *Sabbatino*] analysis").

5. *Recent executive power jurisprudence and act of state doctrine.* Reread the Supreme Court's opinions in *Sosa, Altmann, Samantar,* and *Garamendi,* excerpted at *supra* pp. 38-47, 241-244, 261-265, and 633-637. Note the Court's discussion in each of those cases on the Executive Branch's foreign affairs powers and the significance of Executive Branch representations in cases involving foreign states'. What implications do these decisions have for the rationale of the act of state doctrine? For the treatment of *Bernstein* letters, or similar statements, by the State Department? How would the dissent in *Altmann* respond?

2.   The "Commercial" Exception[84]

The United States and most other nations do not accord foreign sovereign immunity to the "commercial" activities of foreign states.[85] As discussed above, this restrictive theory of sovereign immunity developed because the adjudication of claims involving a foreign state's commercial activity was thought less likely to infringe foreign sovereignty or public policy than litigation involving governmental or political acts.[86] In addition, most nations came to agree that it was unjust for a foreign state to enter into commercial relations with private parties and subsequently invoke its sovereignty against claims relating to that activity.[87]

The considerations that generated the commercial exception to foreign sovereign immunity have sometimes been thought applicable in the act of state context.[88] Nonetheless, a "commercial exception" to the act of state doctrine has been slow to develop. Before *Alfred Dunhill,* excerpted below, no lower court had adopted such an exception and, as the Supreme Court's splintered decision indicates, the commercial exception to the act of state doctrine has encountered more resistance than in the sovereign immunity context.

---

84. For commentary on the commercial exception, *see* McCormick, *The Commercial Activity Exception to Foreign Sovereign Immunity and the Act of State Doctrine,* 16 Law & Pol'y Int'l Bus. 477 (1984); Note, *Arguably Commercial, Ergo Adjudicable? The Validity of a Commercial Activity Exception to the Act of State Doctrine,* 18 B.U. Int'l L.J. 139 (2000); Zaitzeff & Kunz, *The Act of State Doctrine and the* Allied Bank *Case,* 40 Bus. Law. 449, 464-469 (1985).

85. *See supra* pp. 277-308.

86. *See supra* pp. 233-234.

87. *See supra* pp. 284-288.

88. *E.g., Alfred Dunhill of London, Inc. v. Republic of Cuba,* 425 U.S. 682 (1976). For a discussion of the commercial exception, *see* Note, *Arguably Commercial, Ergo Adjudicable? The Validity of a Commercial Activity Exception to the Act of State Doctrine,* 18 B.U. Int'l L.J. 139 (2000).

ALFRED DUNHILL OF LONDON, INC. v. REPUBLIC OF CUBA
425 U.S. 682 (1976) [also excerpted above at pp. 818-819]

JUSTICE WHITE.[89] [The facts of the case are excerpted above, *supra* p. 818.] If we assume with the Court of Appeals that the Cuban Government itself had purported to exercise sovereign power to confiscate the mistaken payments belonging to three foreign creditors and to repudiate interventors' adjudicated obligation to return those funds, we are nevertheless persuaded by the arguments of petitioner and by those of the United States that the concept of an act of state should not be extended to include the repudiation of a purely commercial obligation owed by a foreign sovereign or by one of its commercial instrumentalities. . . . Distinguishing between the public and governmental acts of sovereign states on the one hand and their private and commercial acts on the other is not a novel approach [citing *Bank of the United States v. Planters Bank of Georgia,* 9 Wheat. 904, 907 (1824)].

It is the position of the United States, stated in an amicus brief filed by the Solicitor General, that such a line should be drawn in defining the outer limits of the act of state concept and that repudiations by a foreign sovereign of its commercial debts should not be considered to be acts of state beyond legal question in our courts. Attached to the brief of the United States and to this opinion as Appendix I is the letter of November 26, 1975, in which the Department of State, speaking through its Legal Adviser agrees with the brief filed by the Solicitor General and, more specifically, declares that "we do not believe that the *Dunhill* case raises an act of state question because the case involves an act which is commercial, and not public, in nature."

The major underpinning of the act of state doctrine is the policy of foreclosing court adjudications involving the legality of acts of foreign states on their own soil that might embarrass the Executive Branch of our Government in the conduct of our foreign relations. But based on the presently expressed views of those who conduct our relations with foreign countries, we are in no sense compelled to recognize as an act of state the purely commercial conduct of foreign governments in order to avoid embarrassing conflicts with the Executive Branch. On the contrary, for the reasons to which we now turn, we fear that embarrassment and conflict would more likely ensue if we were to require that the repudiation of a foreign government's debts arising from its operation of a purely commercial business be recognized as an act of state and immunized from question in our courts.

Although it had other views in years gone by, in 1952, [in the Tate Letter], the United States abandoned the absolute theory of sovereign immunity and embraced the restrictive view under which immunity in our courts should be granted only with respect to causes of action arising out of a foreign state's public or governmental actions and not with respect to those arising out of its commercial or proprietary actions. This has been the official policy of our Government since that time. . . .

Repudiation of a commercial debt cannot, consistent with this restrictive approach to sovereign immunity, be treated as an act of state; for if it were, foreign governments, by merely repudiating the debt before or after its adjudication, would enjoy an immunity which our Government would not extend them under prevailing sovereign immunity principles in this country. This would undermine the policy supporting the restrictive view of immunity, which is to assure those engaging in commercial transactions with foreign sovereignties that their rights will be determined in the courts whenever possible. . . .

---

89. The following excerpt, contained in Part III of the Dunhill opinion was joined only by the Chief Justice, Justice Powell, and Justice Rehnquist.

Participation by foreign sovereigns in the international commercial market has increased substantially in recent years. The potential injury to private businessmen — and ultimately to international trade itself — from a system in which some of the participants in the international market are not subject to the rule of law has therefore increased correspondingly. As noted above, courts of other countries have also recently adopted the restrictive theory of sovereign immunity. Of equal importance is the fact that subjecting foreign governments to the rule of law in their commercial dealings presents a much smaller risk of affronting their sovereignty than would an attempt to pass on the legality of their governmental acts.[90] In their commercial capacities, foreign governments do not exercise powers peculiar to sovereigns. Instead, they exercise only those powers that can also be exercised by private citizens. Subjecting them in connection with such acts to the same rules of law that apply to private citizens is unlikely to touch very sharply on "national nerves." Moreover, as this Court has noted:

> [T]he greater the degree of codification or consensus concerning a particular area of international law, the more appropriate it is for the judiciary to render decisions regarding it, since the courts can then focus on the application of an agreed principle to circumstances of fact rather than on the sensitive task of establishing a principle not inconsistent with the national interest or with international justice. [*Sabbatino*, 376 U.S. at 428.]

There may be little codification or consensus as to the rules of international law concerning exercises of governmental powers, including military powers and expropriations, within a sovereign state's borders affecting the property or persons of aliens. However, more discernible rules of international law have emerged with regard to the commercial dealings of private parties in the international market. The restrictive approach to sovereign immunity suggests that these established rules should be applied to the commercial transactions of sovereign states.

Of course, sovereign immunity has not been pleaded in this case; but it is beyond cavil that part of the foreign relations law recognized by the United States is that the commercial obligations of a foreign government may be adjudicated in those courts otherwise having jurisdiction to enter such judgments. Nothing in our national policy calls on us to recognize as an act of state a repudiation by Cuba of an obligation adjudicated in our courts and arising out of the operation of a commercial business by one of its instrumentalities. For all the reasons which led the Executive Branch to adopt the restrictive theory of sovereign immunity, we hold that the mere assertion of sovereignty as a defense to a claim arising out of purely commercial acts by a foreign sovereign is no more effective if given the label "Act of State" than if it is given the label "sovereign immunity."[91]

---

90. In *Sabbatino*, 376 U.S. at 428-429, the Court noted in the context of the act of state doctrine: "It is also evident that some aspects of international law touch much more sharply on national nerves than do others; the less important the implications of an issue are for our foreign relations, the weaker the justification for exclusivity in the political branches."

91. The dissent states that the doctrines of sovereign immunity and act of state are distinct — the former conferring on a sovereign "exemption from suit by virtue of its status" and the latter "merely [telling] a court what law to apply to a case." It may be true that the one doctrine has been described in jurisdictional terms and the other in choice-of-law terms; and it may be that the doctrines point to different results in certain cases. It cannot be gainsaid, however, that the proper application of each involves a balancing of the injury to our foreign policy, the conduct of which is committed primarily to the Executive Branch, through judicial affronts to sovereign powers, *compare Mexico v. Hoffman*, 324 U.S. at 35-36 (sovereign immunity), *with Sabbatino*, 376 U.S. at 423, 427-428 (act of state), against the injury to the private party, who is denied through judicial deference to a raw assertion of sovereignty, and a consequent injury to international trade. The State Department has concluded that in the commercial area the need for merchants "to have their rights determined in courts" outweighs any injury to foreign policy. This conclusion was reached in the context of the jurisdictional problem of sovereign immunity. We reach the same one in the choice-of-law context of the act of state doctrine.

In describing the act of state doctrine in the past we have said that it "precludes the courts of this country from inquiring into the validity of the *public* acts of a recognized foreign sovereign power committed within its own territory." *Sabbatino,* 376 U.S. at 401 (emphasis added), and that it applies to "acts done within their own States, in the exercise of *governmental* authority." *Underhill,* 168 U.S. at 252 (emphasis added). We decline to extend the act of state doctrine to acts committed by foreign sovereigns in the course of their purely commercial operations. Because the act relied on by respondents in this case was an act arising out of the conduct by Cuba's agents in the operation of cigar businesses for profit, the act was not an act of state.

Notes *on* Dunhill

1. *Rationale for commercial exception.* What is Justice White's rationale for a "commercial exception" to the act of state doctrine? How does this rationale relate to the commercial exception to foreign sovereign immunity? Is Justice White's analysis persuasive? Does the wisdom of a commercial exception depend upon whether the act of state doctrine is regarded as an abstention doctrine or a choice-of-law rule?

2. *Lower courts' reaction to* Dunhill*'s commercial exception.* The reaction of lower courts to *Dunhill's* "commercial exception" has been mixed. Several courts appear to have adopted some version of the exception. *E.g., Empresa Cubana v. Lamborn & Co.,* 652 F.2d 231, 238 (2d Cir. 1981); *Arango v. Guzman Travel Advisors Corp.,* 621 F.2d 1371, 1380-1381 (5th Cir. 1980); *Animal Science Products, Inc. v. China Nat'l Metals & Minerals Import & Export Corp.,* 702 F. Supp. 2d 320, 421 (D.N.J. 2010); *Lyondell-Citgo Refining LP v. Petroleos de Venezuela SA,* 2003 WL 21878798, at *8-9 (S.D.N.Y. 2003); *United States v. Giffen,* 326 F. Supp. 2d 497, 503 (S.D.N.Y. 2004); *Virtual Defense and Development Int'l, Inc. v. Republic of Moldova,* 133 F. Supp. 2d 1, 8 (D.D.C. 1999); *Egyptian Nav. Co. v. Uiterwyk,* 1988 WL 70047 (M.D. Fla. 1988); *Gage Int'l, Ltd. v. Cadillac Gage Co.,* 534 F. Supp. 896, 899-900 (E.D. Mich. 1981); *Int'l Tin Council v. Amalgamet,* 524 N.Y.S.2d 971 (Sup. Ct. 1988). Other courts have questioned or rejected the commercial exception. *E.g., Honduras Aircraft Registry, Ltd. v. Government of Honduras,* 129 F.3d 543, 550 (11th Cir. 1997) (declining to recognize commercial exception to act of state doctrine); *Kalamazoo Spice Extraction Co. v. Provisional Military Government of Socialist Ethiopia,* 729 F.2d 422, 425 n.3 (6th Cir. 1984); *Callejo v. Bancomer, SA,* 764 F.2d 1101, 1115 n.17 (5th Cir. 1985). Which approach is wiser?

3. *Scope of commercial exception.* Assuming that a commercial exception to the act of state doctrine exists, what types of activity does it cover? The *Dunhill* plurality appeared to limit the exception to "purely" commercial obligations. This formulation appears significantly narrower than the commercial activity exception in the sovereign immunity context, *see supra* pp. 284-288. *See also McKesson Corp. v. Islamic Republic of Iran,* 2009 WL 4250767, at *4 (D.D.C. Nov. 23, 2009) ("an act may be a sovereign act of state even if a court has jurisdiction over the foreign sovereign pursuant to the commercial activity exception to the FSIA."). Assuming that the commercial exception is accepted, should the same standards be used for defining "commerciality" as apply in the sovereign immunity context?

As in the sovereign immunity context, *e.g., MOL, Inc. v. People's Republic of Bangladesh,* 736 F.2d 1326 (9th Cir. 1984), excerpted at *supra* pp. 283-284, the "commercial" exception to the act of state doctrine has been particularly difficult to apply to foreign governmental acts involving the exploitation of natural resources. *See, e.g., Oceanic Exploration Co. v. ConocoPhillips, Inc.,* 2006 WL 2711527 (D.D.C. Sept. 21, 2006) (applying act of state doctrine and stressing role of natural resources in case). For example, in *IAM v. OPEC*, 649 F.2d 1354 (9th Cir. 1981), the Court of Appeals applied the act of state doctrine and dismissed an antitrust suit against OPEC's price-fixing of petroleum. The court reasoned that a U.S. decision against the OPEC member states would amount to "an order from a domestic court instructing a foreign sovereign to alter its chosen means of allocating and profiting from its own valuable natural resources." 649 F.2d at 1361. *See also Callejo v. Bancomer, SA*, 764 F.2d 1101, 1114-1116 (5th Cir. 1985) (foreign state's acts are commercial for FSIA purposes, and noncommercial for act of state purposes); *In re Refined Petroleum Products Antitrust Litig.*, 649 F. Supp. 2d 572, 595-596 (S.D. Tex. 2009) (declining to apply commercial exception to allegations of price-fixing by OPEC member states).

4. ***Mixed commercial/sovereign conduct.*** Foreign states' activities often contain both "sovereign" and "commercial" elements. *See, e.g., Sarei v. Rio Tinto plc*, 221 F. Supp. 2d 1116, 1186 (C.D. Cal. 2002), *aff'd in part, vacated in part, and rev'd in part*, 456 F.3d 1069 (9th Cir. 2006); *Braka v. Bancomer SNC*, 762, F.2d 222 (2d Cir. 1985). In these cases, courts must determine whether the alleged acts of state are commercial or sovereign. In *Braka*, for example, a state-owned Mexican bank failed to repay a certificate of deposit because Mexican foreign exchange controls prohibited repayment. When the certificate holders brought suit in the United States, the Mexican bank resisted on act of state grounds. The Second Circuit rejected the plaintiff's argument that *Dunhill's* commercial activity exception rendered the doctrine inapplicable:

> Even if we decided that the act of state doctrine is not applicable to commercial transactions of foreign governments, the result here would be the same. The activity that implicates act of state concerns here was the issuance by the Mexican government of exchange controls which prevented Bancomer from performing its contractual obligations. This action taken by the Mexican government for the purpose of saving its national economy from the brink of monetary disaster, surely represents the "exercise [of] powers peculiar to sovereigns." *Dunhill*, 425 U.S. at 704 (plurality opinion). Those sovereign powers, unlike acts that could be taken by a private citizen, trigger no commercial exception.
>
> Plaintiffs protest that they seek no intervention into Mexico's sovereign acts; they merely request that we order Bancomer to perform its commercial contractual commitments. However, Bancomer has already paid plaintiffs all that it may under Mexican law. Were we to issue the order they seek, we would find ourselves directing a state-owned entity to violate its own national law with respect to an obligation wholly controlled by Mexican law. This would clearly be an impermissible "inquiry into the legality, validity, and propriety of the acts and motivation of foreign sovereigns acting in their governmental roles within their own boundaries." *Arango v. Guzman Travel Advisors Corp.*, 621 F.2d 1371, 1380 (5th Cir. 1980). Therefore, the action at issue is sovereign rather than commercial. . . .

Like *Dunhill*, *Braka* views the commercial exception to the act of state doctrine more narrowly than the FSIA's commercial exception. *See supra* p. 286 for a discussion of mixed commercial/sovereign conduct in the FSIA context.

5. ***Effects of FSIA.*** What effect does the FSIA's commercial activities exception have on the act of state doctrine? In general, courts have rejected the argument that the FSIA supersedes the doctrine as applied to commercial activities. *E.g., IAM v. OPEC*, 649 F.2d 1354, 1359 (9th Cir. 1981). *Compare Chisholm & Co. v. Bank of Jamaica*, 643 F. Supp. 1393, 1403 n.9 (S.D. Fla. 1986). Commentators are divided, with a substantial number contending that continued application of the act of state doctrine to nonimmune activities would frustrate the FSIA. Bazyler, *Abolishing the Act of State Doctrine*, 134 U. Pa. L. Rev. 325, 377 (1986); Lengel, *The Duty of Federal Courts to Apply International Law: A Polemical Analysis of the Act of State Doctrine*, 1982 BYU L. Rev. 61, 62-63. *Compare* McCormick, *The Commercial*

Activity Exception to Foreign Sovereign Immunity and the Act of State Doctrine, 16 Law & Pol'y Int'l Bus. 477, 519-524 (1984); Dellapenna, *Deciphering the Act of State Doctrine,* 35 Vill. L. Rev. 1, 78-79 (1990). Is this conclusion sensible? Recall the distinctions between sovereign immunity and the act of state doctrine. *See supra* pp. 277-278.

6. *Waiver of act of state doctrine by foreign state.* If one of the bases for the act of state doctrine is a desire to avoid giving offense to foreign states, what is the status of the defense if the foreign state declares that it is willing for litigation to proceed? In general, U.S. courts have not been receptive to arguments that the act of state doctrine can be waived. *See Republic of Philippines v. Marcos,* 818 F.2d 1473, 1485-1487 (9th Cir. 1987), *vacated,* 862 F.2d 1355 (9th Cir. 1988); *Compania de Gas de Nuevo Laredo, SA v. Entex, Inc.,* 686 F.2d 322, 326 (5th Cir. 1982) (declining to find waiver on the facts, and suggesting that even if waiver did exist, it would be only one of several factors relevant to act of state analysis); *Dayton v. Czechoslovak Socialist Republic,* 834 F.2d 203 (D.C. Cir. 1987) (failure to appear in U.S. litigation is not waiver of act of state defense).

One judge has reasoned that "[w]here the country's current government seeks an adjudication . . . there is obviously less of a possibility that our pronouncements will embarrass our relations with that government," *Republic of Philippines,* 818 F.2d at 1486 (J. Kozinski), but that other factors nonetheless will often require abstention, including the fact that "a pronouncement by our courts . . . would have a substantial effect on what may be a delicate political balance abroad" and the fact that "litigation proceeds at its own pace and the [U.S. court's] answer, whatever it may be, may well come at a time most inopportune from the point of view of our foreign policy." *Id.* Nonetheless, some authorities have taken the position that foreign states' waivers of the act of state doctrine are entitled to substantial deference: "insofar as the act of state doctrine is designed to reflect respect for foreign states, indications of consent to adjudication by the courts of another state are highly relevant, though they are not conclusive." *Restatement (Third) Foreign Relations Law* §443, comment e (1987). What bearing, if any, does *Environmental Tectonics*' characterization of the act of state doctrine as a "principle of law," rather than a species of abstention, have on the possibility of waiver of the doctrine?

7. *Use of the act of state doctrine against foreign state.* Should a private defendant be able to invoke the act of state doctrine in a suit by a representative of the foreign government whose act of state is allegedly involved? Lower courts have answered affirmatively. *DeRoburt v. Gannett Co.,* 733 F.2d 701 (9th Cir. 1984); *Sharon v. Time, Inc.,* 599 F. Supp. 538 (S.D.N.Y. 1984). *See* Note, *Private Defendants May Assert the Act of State Defense Against a Resisting Sovereign,* 25 Va. J. Int'l L. 775 (1985). When a foreign state itself initiates suit in U.S. courts in a matter involving a foreign act of state, is the act of state doctrine necessary to prevent interference with U.S. foreign relations? To ensure fairness to private litigants?

3. The "Treaty" Exception[92]

The most widely accepted exception to the act of state doctrine is the so-called "treaty" or "international law" exception. This exception is reflected in the Supreme Court's observation in *Sabbatino* that the act of state doctrine is applicable "in the absence of a treaty or other unambiguous agreement regarding controlling legal principles."[93]

---

92. *See* Note, *Putting Meaning into the Treaty Exception to the Act of State Doctrine,* 17 Case W. Res. J. Int'l L. 107 (1985); Note, A *Treaty Exception to the Act of State Doctrine: A Framework for Judicial Application,* 4 B.U. Int'l L.J. 201 (1986).

93. 376 U.S. at 428.

The apparent rationale for this suggestion is the fact that a treaty provides internationally accepted principles that are binding upon foreign states and that U.S. courts can apply without offending foreign sovereigns or resolving hotly disputed questions of international law. One of the few cases to apply the exception, *Kalamazoo Spice Extraction,* is excerpted below. Compare the Court's analysis with that of the House of Lords in *Kuwait Airways Corp. v. Iraqi Airways Co.,* also excerpted below.

KALAMAZOO SPICE EXTRACTION CO. v. PROVISIONAL MILITARY GOVERNMENT OF SOCIALIST ETHIOPIA
729 F.2d 422 (6th Cir. 1984)

KEITH, CIRCUIT JUDGE. This is an appeal from a district court judgment, which dismissed appellant's counterclaim. The district court held that the act of state doctrine as interpreted by the Supreme Court in *Sabbatino,* precluded judicial inquiry into the validity of an expropriation by the Ethiopian government of shares in an Ethiopian business entity held by an American corporation.

Appellant, Kalamazoo Spice Extraction Company ("Kal-Spice") is an American corporation which, in a joint venture with Ethiopian citizens, established [in 1966] the Ethiopian Spice Extraction Company ("ESESCO"), . . . an Ethiopian based corporation. Kal-Spice owned approximately 80% of the shares of ESESCO. Kal-Spice also contributed capital, built a production facility, and trained ESESCO's staff, which consisted of Ethiopian citizens. Production began in 1970. . . . The Provisional Military Government of Socialist Ethiopia ("PMGSE") came to power in 1974. As part of its program to assure that Ethiopian industries would "be operated according to the philosophy of Ethiopian socialism," the PMGSE announced the seizure of "control of supervision and a majority shareholding" of a number of corporations, including ESESCO, in February 1975. As a result of the expropriation, Kal-Spice's ownership interest in ESESCO was reduced from 80% to approximately 39%.

In December 1975, the PMGSE established a Compensation Commission. The Commission's purpose was to compensate those claimants whose property had been expropriated. Kal-Spice claimed it was entitled to compensation of $11,000,000. In October 1981, the PMGSE offered Kal-Spice the equivalent of $450,000 in Ethiopian currency. Kal-Spice, however, has rejected the PMGSE's offer. The PMGSE contends that Kal-Spice should have accepted the offer because: 1) Kal-Spice retains an interest in ESESCO of approximately 40%; and 2) Kal-Spice carried expropriation insurance based on a total investment in ESESCO of less than $1,000,000.

A few months before the PMGSE's expropriation program, Kal-Spice, placed an order with ESESCO for the purchase of spices to be delivered to Kal-Spice in Michigan between November 1, 1974 and November 5, 1975. ESESCO shipped spices worth more than 1.9 million dollars to Kal-Spice. These shipments occurred in several installments, some before the February 3, 1975 seizure of ESESCO and some after that date. The post-expropriation shipments were drawn from inventories seized on the expropriation date. According to Kal-Spice, it continued to make payments for these shipments for a while after the expropriation until it realized that the PMGSE did not intend to compensate it for the expropriated property. ESESCO, now controlled by the PMGSE, filed a breach of contract action against Kal-Spice, demanding payment for goods received by Kal-Spice. Kal-Spice counter-claimed against ESESCO as the alter ego of the PMGSE, seeking, inter alia, damages for the expropriation of ESESCO. Once the suit reached the District Court of the Western District of Michigan, the court decided that the act of state doctrine precluded adjudication of the claims against the PMGSE based on the expropriation of Kal-Spice's interests. . . .

The act of state doctrine is an exception to the general rule that a court of the United States, where appropriate jurisdictional standards are met, will decide cases before it by choosing the rules appropriate for decision from among various sources of law, including international law. . . . [A]ppellant Kal-Spice, as well as the U.S. Departments of State, Treasury, Justice, and the American Bar Association, as amici curiae, request that this Court recognize a "treaty exception" to the act of state doctrine. According to appellant and amici, the following language in *Sabbatino* provides the basis for a treaty exception:

> [T]he Judicial Branch will not examine the validity of a taking of property within its own territory by a foreign sovereign government, extant and recognized by this country at the time of suit, *in the absence of a treaty or other unambiguous agreement regarding controlling legal principles,* even if the complaint alleges that the taking violates customary international law (emphasis added).

This language and the existence of a treaty between the United States and Ethiopia, asserts appellant and amici, require a "treaty" exception to the rule that a U.S. court will not exercise jurisdiction over a foreign sovereign for an act done by that sovereign within its borders. The treaty in existence between the United States and Ethiopia is the 1953 Treaty of Amity and Economic Relations ("Treaty of Amity"). Article VIII, paragraph two of that treaty provides:

> Property of nationals and companies of either High Contracting Party, including interests in property, shall receive the most constant protection and security within the territories of the other High Contracting Party. *Such property shall not be taken except for a public purpose, nor shall it be taken without prompt payment of just and effective compensation* (emphasis added).

Kal-Spice unsuccessfully argued before the district court that this treaty provision was the type referred to by the Supreme Court in *Sabbatino,* which would allow a court to exercise jurisdiction over a claim of expropriation of property by a foreign sovereign. Specifically, Kal-Spice alleged that the "prompt payment of just and effective compensation" provision of the Treaty of Amity set forth controlling legal principles which was [sic] referred to by the Supreme Court in *Sabbatino.*

The district court . . . agreed with the PMGSE's position that this provision of the treaty calling for the "prompt payment of just and effective compensation" was ambiguous. It found that this provision was "so inherently general, doubtful and susceptible to multiple interpretation that in the absence of an established body of law to clarify their meaning a court cannot reasonably be asked to apply them to a particular set of facts." . . .

We do not agree with the district court's decision that the provision of the treaty requiring payment of prompt, just and effective compensation fails to provide a controlling legal standard. To the contrary, we find that this is a controlling legal standard in the area of international law. As the appellant and amici correctly point out, the term "prompt, just, effective compensation" and similar terms are found in many treaties where the United States and other nations are parties. The Treaty of Amity is one of a series of treaties, also known as the FCN Treaties, between the United States and foreign nations negotiated after World War II. As the legislative history of these treaties indicates, they were adopted to protect American citizens and their interests abroad. Almost all of these treaties contain sections which provide for "prompt, adequate, and effective compensation," "just compensation," or similar language regarding compensation for expropriated property.

The U.S. District Court for the District of Columbia used a treaty to find a "treaty exception" in *American International Group, Inc. v. Islamic Republic of Iran,* 493 F. Supp. 522 (D.D.C. 1980). After examining [a similar treaty provision] the district court determined, *inter alia,* that the act of state doctrine did not preclude it from jurisdiction because the treaty was relevant, unambiguous, and set forth agreed-upon principles of international law, *i.e.,* a standard for compensation for the expropriated property.[94] . . .

Consequently, *American International* provides authoritative guidance to us on the use of the treaty exception. . . . Moreover, the Supreme Court's decision in *Sabbatino* . . . requires a reversal of the district court decision . . . :

> It should be apparent that the greater the degree of codification or consensus concerning a particular area of international law, the more appropriate it is for the judiciary to render decision regarding it, since the courts can then focus on the application of an *agreed principle* to circumstances of fact rather than on the sensitive task of establishing a principle not inconsistent with national interest or with international justice. [376 U.S. at 423.]

Numerous treaties employ the standard of compensation used in the 1953 Treaty of Amity between Ethiopia and the United States. Undoubtedly, the widespread use of this compensation standard is evidence that it is an agreed upon principle in international law. . . . Additionally, there is a great national interest to be served in this case, *i.e.,* the recognition and execution of treaties that we enter into with foreign nations. Article VI of the Constitution provides that treaties made under the authority of the United States shall be the supreme law of the land. Accordingly, the Supreme Court has recognized that treaties, in certain circumstances, have the "force and effect of a legislative enactment." *See, e.g., Whitney v. Robertson,* 124 U.S. 190, 194 (1888). The failure of this court to recognize a properly executed treaty would indeed be an egregious error because of the position that treaties occupy in our body of laws. . . .

KUWAIT AIRWAYS CORP. v. IRAQI AIRWAYS CO.
[2003] 1 CLC 183 (House of Lords)

[The factual summary derives from Lord Nichols's opinion. On 2 August 1990 military forces of Iraq invaded and occupied Kuwait. They completed the occupation in the space of two or three days. The Revolutionary Command Council of Iraq then adopted resolutions proclaiming the sovereignty of Iraq over Kuwait and its annexation to Iraq. Kuwait was designated a "governate" within Iraq.

When the Iraqi forces took over the airport at Kuwait they seized ten commercial aircraft belonging to Kuwait Airways Corporation (KAC). They lost no time in removing these aircraft to Iraq. By 9 August nine of the aircraft had been flown back to Basra, in Iraq. The tenth aircraft, undergoing repair at the time of the invasion, was flown direct to

---

94. The district court also held that the act of state doctrine was inapplicable because the court was not deciding the validity of Iran's expropriation of the plaintiff's interest, but rather it was adjudicating the failure of Iran to provide compensation for the expropriated property in violation of international law. It was also decided that the act of state doctrine did not apply because of the commercial act exception of *Alfred Dunhill.* We decline, however, to reverse the district court on these additional grounds. Our decision to reverse the district court is based only upon the existence of a treaty between the United States and Ethiopia which may provide a basis for Kal-Spice to receive compensation.

Baghdad a fortnight later. On 9 September the Revolutionary Command Council of Iraq adopted a resolution dissolving KAC and transferring all its property worldwide, including the ten aircraft, to the state-owned Iraqi Airways Co (IAC). This resolution, resolution 369, came into force upon publication in the official gazette on 17 September. On the same day IAC's board passed resolutions implementing RCC resolution 369. — EDS.]

[Kuwait Airways later sued Iraq. The case eventually reached the House of Lords, which found that Iraq was immune as to post-invasion conduct but not as to pre-invasion conduct.]

LORD HOPE. There is no doubt as to the general effect of the rule which is known as the act of state rule. It applies to the legislative or other governmental acts of a recognised foreign state or government within the limits of its own territory. The English courts will not adjudicate upon, or call into question, any such acts. They may be pleaded and relied upon by way of defence in this jurisdiction without being subjected to that kind of judicial scrutiny. The rule gives effect to a policy of judicial restraint or abstention. *Buttes Gas and Oil Co v Hammer (No. 3)* [1982] AC 888, 931F-934C per Lord Wilberforce. As the title to moveable property is determined by the lex situs, a transfer of property effected by or under foreign legislation in the country where the property is situated will, as a general rule, be treated as effective by English law for all relevant purposes. It would clearly be possible for a "blue pencil" approach to be taken to Resolution 369, by reading it down so that it applied only to the property of KAC that was situated at the time of the resolution within its own territory. The normal rule is that legislative action applied to property within the territorial jurisdiction will be internationally recognised, despite the fact that it has been combined with action which is unenforceable extraterritorially. If this approach is adopted, that part of Resolution 369 which vested title in the aircraft in IAC will provide IAC with a complete defence to this action. Its legality in international law will not be justiciable in these proceedings.

. . .

It is clear that very narrow limits must be placed on any exception to the act of state rule. As Lord Cross recognised in *Oppenheimer v Cattermole* [1976] AC 249, 277-8, a judge should be slow to refuse to give effect to the legislation of a foreign state in any sphere in which, according to accepted principles of international law, the foreign state has jurisdiction. Among these accepted principles is that which is founded on the comity of nations. This principle normally requires our courts to recognise the jurisdiction of the foreign state over all assets situated within its own territories. A judge should be slow to depart from these principles. He may have an inadequate understanding of the circumstances in which the legislation was passed. His refusal to recognise it may be embarrassing to the executive, whose function is so far as possible to maintain friendly relations with foreign states.

But it does not follow, as . . . IAC has asserted, that the public policy exception can be applied only where there is a grave infringement of human rights. This was the conclusion that was reached on the facts which were before the House in the Oppenheimer case. But Lord Cross based that conclusion on a wider point of principle. This too is founded upon the public policy of this country. It is that our courts should give effect to clearly established principles of international law. . . .

As I see it, the essence of the public policy exception is that it is not so constrained. The golden rule is that care must be taken not to expand its application beyond the true limits of the principle. These limits demand that, where there is any room for doubt, judicial restraint must be exercised. But restraint is what is needed, not abstention. And there is no need for restraint on grounds of public policy where it is plain beyond dispute that a clearly established norm of international law has been violated.

The facts which bear on this issue are quite straightforward. The United Nations Charter and the Security Council Resolutions which were adopted in response to the invasion of Kuwait provide the context. The aims of the Charter as set forth in the Preamble seek to ensure that armed force is not used save in the common interest, and that conditions are established under which justice and respect for the obligations arising from treaties and other sources of international law can be maintained. Membership of the United Nations carries with it the obligation to accept and carry out the decisions of the Security Council, on which members have conferred the primary responsibility for the maintenance of peace and security: Chapter V, articles 24, 25.

Among the resolutions which were adopted by the Security Council after the Iraqi invasion were Resolution 660 on 2 August 1990 which condemned the invasion and demanded that Iraq withdraw from Kuwait immediately and unconditionally, Resolution 661 on 6 August 1990 which called upon all states not to recognise any regime set up by the occupying power, and Resolution 662 on 9 August 1990 which decided that Iraq's annexation of Kuwait under any form and whatever pretext had no legal validity and was considered null and void. Resolution 662 also called upon all states "not to recognise that annexation, and to refrain from any action or dealing that might be interpreted as an indirect recognition of the annexation."

The removal of the aircraft from Kuwait took place on 6-8 August 1990 when nine KAC aircraft were flown from Kuwait to Basra, and 22 August 1990 when the remaining aircraft was flown to Baghdad. These acts were plainly in breach of the Security Council resolutions. So too was RCC Resolution 369, which purported to vest in IAC all the fixed and liquid assets of KAC including all assets of Kuwait Airways offices abroad. Moreover Resolution 369, which was designed to cement that act by depriving KAC permanently of all its assets wherever situated, was of an exorbitant character. Standing the Security Council resolutions, which as a member of the United Nations Iraq (on 5 March 1991 when RCC Resolution 55 was passed) was later to recognise, these were breaches of international law.

It is not disputed that our courts are entitled on grounds of public policy to decline to give effect to clearly established breaches of international law when considering rights in or to property which is located in England. A state lacks international jurisdiction to take property outside its territory, so acts of that kind are necessarily ineffective: Dr F A Mann, *Further Studies in International Law* 175 (1990). There could be no question of Resolution 369 being regarded as effective in the English courts as a transfer to IAC under the lex situs of any of KAC's rights in any property that happened to be situated in this country. IAC could not rely on the act of state doctrine if England was the country of the lex situs at the time when the breaches of international law were committed. But why should effect not also be given here to international law where to do so can be justified on grounds of public policy?

In my search for an answer [to] this question I would take as my guide the observations of Lord Wilberforce in *Blathwayt v Baron Cawley* [1976] AC 397, 426. He said that conceptions of public policy should move with the times and that widely accepted treaties and statutes may point in the direction in which such conceptions, as applied by the courts, ought to move. It would seem therefore to be contrary to principle for our courts to give legal effect to legislative and other acts of foreign states which are in violation of international law as declared under the Charter of the United Nations: see Dr F A Mann, *Further Studies in International Law,* 176. The Security Council has played a key role in recent months, following the events of 11 September 2001, by imposing obligations on all states to suppress terrorist financing and deny terrorists safe havens in which to operate. It is now clear, if it was not before, that the judiciary cannot close their eyes to the need for a concerted, international response to these threats to the rule of law in a democratic society. Their primary role must always be to uphold human rights and civil liberties. But the maintenance of the rule of law is also an important social interest.

Security Council Resolution 662 called upon all states to refrain from any action which might be interpreted as an indirect recognition of the annexation. There is no doubt that the responsibility for answering this call lies in the first instance with the executive arm of government. But, in seeking which direction to take in such matters where decisions must be taken on grounds of public policy, the judges should try to work in harmony with the executive. Furthermore, . . . there is nothing precarious or delicate, and nothing subject to diplomacy, which judicial adjudication might threaten in this case. The taking of KAC's property in breach of Iraq's obligations under the Charter of the United Nations was a clear example of an international wrong to which legal effect should not be given.

There could be no embarrassment to diplomatic relations in our taking this view. In his letter of 7 November 1997, which was written in response to a request by [the trial court] on 24 October 1997, Sir Franklin Berman, then Legal Adviser to the Foreign and Commonwealth Office, informed the court that the conduct of Her Majesty's Government in the United Kingdom has been strictly in conformity with the requirements of the resolutions and all other pertinent decisions of the Security Council relating to the Iraqi invasion and occupation of Kuwait. Nor can it be said that the court needs to defer to the act of the foreign state because it has an inadequate understanding of the circumstances in which Resolution 369 was passed. The arguments for giving effect to international law as declared by the resolutions of the Security Council could hardly be more compelling.

For these reasons I would hold that a legislative act by a foreign state which is in flagrant breach of clearly established rules of international law ought not to be recognised by the courts of this country as forming part of the lex situs of that state.

. . .

The facts are clear, and the declarations by the Security Council were universal and unequivocal. If the court may have regard to grave infringements of human rights law on grounds of public policy, it ought not to decline to take account of the principles of international law when the act amounts — as I would hold that it clearly does in this case — to a flagrant breach of these principles. . . . I would hold that the effectiveness of Resolution 369 as vesting title in IAC to KAC's aircraft is justiciable in these proceedings, and that such a flagrant international wrong should be deemed to be so grave a matter that it would be contrary to the public policy of this country to give effect to it.

Notes *on* Kalamazoo Spice *and* Kuwait Airways

1. *Application of treaty exception.* Only a few lower court decisions have applied the treaty exception to the act of state doctrine. Some lower courts hold that existence of a treaty containing a controlling legal standard renders the act of state doctrine entirely inapplicable. *See Ramirez de Arellano v. Weinberger,* 745 F.2d 1500, 1540 (D.C. Cir. 1984), *vacated,* 471 U.S. 1113 (1985); *Bodner v. Banque Paribas,* 114 F. Supp. 2d 117, 130 n.11 (E.D.N.Y. 2000) (dicta); *Wolf v. Federal Republic of Germany,* 1995 WL 263471, at *13 (N.D. Ill. 1995); *American Int'l Group v. Islamic Republic of Iran,* 493 F. Supp. 522, 525 (D.D.C. 1980), *vacated on other grounds,* 657 F.2d 430 (D.C. Cir. 1981); *Faysound Ltd. v. Walter Fuller Aircraft Sales, Inc.,* 1990 U.S. Dist. LEXIS 14667 (E.D. Ark. 1990).

Other lower courts appear to consider the existence of an applicable treaty as only one factor relevant to a general balancing test to determine whether the act of state doctrine applies. *Callejo v. Bancomer, SA,* 764 F.2d 1101 (5th Cir. 1985); *IAM v. OPEC,* 649 F.2d 1354, 1358-1359 (9th Cir. 1981); *Sharon v. Time, Inc.,* 599 F. Supp. 538 (S.D.N.Y. 1984). Which approach is more consistent with *Sabbatino* and the policies underlying the act of state doctrine? Which approach is more consistent with *Environmental Tectonics* and the apparent status of the act of state doctrine as a choice-of-law rule?

2. Scope of treaty exception. Recall *Sabbatino*'s formulation of the so-called "treaty" exception: the act of state doctrine is applicable "in the absence of a treaty or other unambiguous agreement regarding controlling legal principles." *Kalamazoo Spice* holds that the treaty exception bars application of the act of state doctrine to at least some of Kal-Spice's claims. Does the court reach this conclusion simply because there was an applicable treaty provision providing a "*controlling legal standard*" or instead because there was an applicable treaty provision that contained an "*unambiguous*" legal standard? That is, must a treaty provision be "unambiguous" in order to prevent application of the act of state doctrine? Or is it enough that there simply be a relevant treaty provision — either ambiguous or unambiguous?

Note that the foregoing distinction is potentially critical. Is there any serious argument that Article VIII(2) of the U.S. — Ethiopia Treaty of Amity is "unambiguous"? Consider the final paragraph of the Court's opinion. Does it suggest that Article VIII is clear-cut? One lower court has held that the treaty exception is applicable even if the agreement at issue is ambiguous. *Dayton v. Czechoslovak Socialist Republic,* 834 F.2d 203 (D.C. Cir. 1987). Is this consistent with *Sabbatino*'s refusal to permit U.S. courts to apply disputed issues of international law to foreign acts of state? Note that, in the absence of a treaty, *Sabbatino* clearly required some "other unambiguous agreement regarding controlling legal principles." What would be the rationale for requiring "unambiguous" provisions of international law in the absence of a treaty, but accepting an ambiguous treaty, as grounds for rendering the act of state doctrine inapplicable?

3. Relevance of customary international law. Could customary international law, rather than an "agreement," ever provide the basis for application of the "treaty" exception? Note that in *Sabbatino,* the Court required a "treaty or other unambiguous agreement regarding controlling legal principles." Although in some circumstances customary international law presumably could reflect an unambiguous agreement regarding international law principles, *Sabbatino* appears to have rejected any such possibility. If, as *Kalamazoo Spice* concludes, an ambiguous treaty provision may be applied, why can't an unambiguous rule of customary international law be applied? What answer does Lord Hope suggest in *Kuwait Airways*?

4. Human rights norms. It has been suggested that certain customary international law principles are sufficiently well-established to warrant an exception to the act of the state doctrine. *See* Bazyler, *supra,* 134 U. Pa. L. Rev. at 374 & n.302. The best example of such suggestions occurs in the human rights context. Suppose foreign state officials brutally torture and murder a visiting U.S. citizen. The act of state doctrine articulated in *Sabbatino* would presumptively forbid U.S. courts from sitting in judgment on the foreign state's misconduct. Some authorities have argued, however, that customary international law forbids such human rights abuses, *see Restatement (Third) Foreign Relations Law* §§701-703 (1987), and that this provides an "unambiguous agreement" within the meaning of *Sabbatino.* Thus, comment c to §443 of the *Third Restatement* suggests that the act of state doctrine would not apply in the following circumstances: "A claim arising out of an alleged violation of fundamental human rights . . . would . . . probably not be defeated by the act of state doctrine, since the accepted international law of human rights is well established and contemplates external scrutiny of such acts."

Caselaw is divided on this question. Some cases appear to hold that the act of state doctrine does not apply in cases of certain human rights violations. *E.g., Sarei v. Rio Tinto plc*, 487 F.3d 1198 (9th Cir. 2007) (*en banc*); *Lizarbe v. Rondon*, 642 F. Supp. 2d 473, 488 (D. Md. 2009) ("[T]he acts alleged in the Complaint violate universally agreed upon legal principles, involving, as they do, acts of torture, extrajudicial killing, and crimes against humanity. Such acts, committed in violation of the norms of customary international law, are not deemed official acts for the purposes of the acts of state doctrine."); *Presbyterian Church of Sudan v. Talisman Energy, Inc.*, 244 F. Supp. 2d 289, 345 (S.D.N.Y. 2004). The TVPA's legislative history lends some support to this view. *See* S. Rep. No. 102-249, pt. 4, at 8 (1991) (indicating that torture and similar human rights abuses can never be "public acts" for the purpose of the acts of state doctrine).

Other decisions reject this *per se* rule. *E.g., Doe v. Qi*, 349 F. Supp. 2d 1258, 1292 (N.D. Cal. 2004) ("[T]he act of state doctrine is not rendered inapposite simply because international law or *jus cogens* norms are violated."). These latter courts still give weight to the international law violation and may use that fact to support a conclusion that the act of state doctrine does not apply, typically on the ground that such conduct in violation of international law cannot constitute an "act of state." *E.g., Doe I v. Unocal Corp.*, 395 F.3d 932, 959 (9th Cir. 2002) ("Because *jus cogens* violations are, by definition, internationally denounced, there is a high degree of international consensus against them, which severely undermines" an argument that conduct could constitute an act of state); *Kadic v. Karadzic*, 70 F.3d 232, 250 (2d Cir. 1995) ("[W]e doubt that the acts of even a state official, taken in violation of a nation's fundamental law and wholly unratified by that nation's government, could properly be characterized as an act of state"); *Mujica v. Occidental Petroleum Corp.*, 381 F. Supp. 2d 1164, 1191 (C.D. Cal. 2005) (*jus cogens* violation counsels against application of act of state doctrine).

If the treaty exception was *not* applicable where customary international law is involved, would there be any other way to avoid application of the act of state doctrine in cases involving human rights violations? *See Filartiga v. Pena-Irala*, 630 F.2d 876, 889 (2d Cir. 1980) (official torture not a public act of state). Compare this to the discussion in *Samantar, supra* at 261-265, about whether a foreign official's conduct constitutes an "official act."

5. *A public policy exception?* If treaties and human rights norms supply exceptions to the act of state doctrine, don't these exceptions simply exemplify a broader public policy exception? As explained elsewhere in this book, such exceptions are common in this field of law. *See supra* pp. 446-447 (*forum non conveniens*), 511-528 (forum selection clauses), 770-772 (choice-of-law clauses) and *infra* p. 1142 (foreign judgment enforcement) and 1202-1203 (arbitration awards).

What would be the rationale for a public policy exception in this context? What rationale is suggested by Lord Hope's opinion in *Kuwait Airways*? Are there any pitfalls in describing the exception at a general level (such as public policy) as opposed to a more specific level (such as "treaties")? Is it possible to craft a public policy exception that is compatible with the "very narrow limits [that] must be placed on any exception to the act of state rule"?

Assuming "public policy" does supply an exception to the act of state doctrine, what are its contours? What does Lord Hope suggest in *Kuwait Airways*? Can you articulate precisely what facts were essential to the conclusion that the act of state doctrine did not apply in that case? According to the reasoning in that case, what facts would have been different for the Lords to conclude that the act of state doctrine barred the suit?

6. *Rationale for distinction between treaties and customary international law.* Why are treaties and other international agreements treated so differently from customary international law under the act of state doctrine? Recall that "international law is part of our law." *The Paquete Habana,* 175 U.S. 677, 700 (1900). *See supra* p. 17. Why shouldn't U.S. courts therefore apply customary international law in the same way that they would apply a treaty? If customary international law is too broad a category for an exception to the act of state doctrine, might it make sense to limit the exception to violations of "clearly established principles of international law" (to borrow a phrase from Lord Hope's opinion)? Does an exception crafted along these lines supply the necessary "restraint"? Compare the requirement that a principle be "clearly established" with *Sosa's* requirement that an actionable norm under the Alien Tort Statute have achieved a "definite content and acceptance among civilized nations." *See supra* p. 43.

7. *What agreements satisfy the treaty exception?* Could the "treaty" exception be triggered by a contract between a private party and a foreign state? Suppose that the contract incorporates international law prohibitions against expropriation. What if the contract contains choice of forum or arbitration clauses? *See Restatement (Third) Foreign Relations Law* §443, comment e (1987) ("When a state has expressly subjected certain kinds of obligations to adjudication in the courts of another state, or to international arbitration . . . , it may be said to have acknowledged that its acts with respect to those obligations . . . are subject to international scrutiny; in such cases the justification for applying the act of state doctrine is significantly weaker. A dispute under a mining concession containing a clause calling for commercial arbitration in a neutral state would generally be considered to be arbitrable").

4. The Second Hickenlooper Amendment

The so-called Second Hickenlooper amendment, named after one of its legislative sponsors,[95] forbids any U.S. court from invoking "the federal act of state doctrine" in a case in which (1) "a claim of title or other right to property" (2) within the United States (3) is asserted on the basis of an act of state "in violation of the principles of international law." In addition, the amendment sets out specific principles of international law applicable in expropriation cases and provides that the act of state doctrine *should* apply if the president certifies to U.S. courts that application of the doctrine is required by U.S. foreign policy interests. Although the Hickenlooper amendment appears at first blush substantially to "overrule" *Sabbatino,* its effect has been otherwise.

Most U.S. courts have interpreted the Hickenlooper amendment narrowly and confined its application to a relatively limited class of cases. Courts have generally held that

---

95. 22 U.S.C. §2370(e)(2) provides: "Notwithstanding any other provision of law, no court in the United States shall decline on the ground of the federal act of state doctrine to make a determination on the merits giving effect to the principles of international law in a case in which a claim of title or other right to property is asserted by any party including a foreign state (or party claiming through such state) based upon (or traced through) a confiscation or other taking after January 1, 1959, by an act of that state in violation of the principles of international law, including the principles of compensation and the other standards set out in this subsection: *Provided,* That this subparagraph shall not be applicable (1) in any case in which an act of a foreign state is not contrary to international law or with respect to a claim of title or other right to property acquired pursuant to an irrevocable letter of credit of not more than 180 days duration issued in good faith prior to the time of the confiscation or other taking, or (2) in any case with respect to which the president determines that application of the act of state doctrine is required in that particular case by the foreign policy interests of the United States and a suggestion to this effect is filed on his behalf in that case with the court." Though technically limited to federal courts, at least one state court has relied partly on the Second Hickenlooper amendment to support its rejection of an act of state defense. *See Roxas v. Marcos,* 969 P.2d 1209, 1251 (Haw. 1998).

the amendment applies only if specific property directly involved in the allegedly unlawful foreign act of state is located in the United States.[96] Other courts have held that the amendment does not apply to the expropriation of "contract," as opposed to "property" rights, yet others have held that the amendment does not apply to intangible property.[97]

D. Foreign Sovereign Compulsion Doctrine

The so-called "foreign sovereign compulsion" doctrine provides, in broad terms, that State A generally may not require an individual or company to do an act on the territory of State B that would violate the laws of State B. Applying the doctrine, some U.S. courts have refused to interpret U.S. laws to apply extraterritorially to forbid conduct that was *required* by foreign states.[98]

Relatively few decisions have applied the foreign sovereign compulsion doctrine. One of the best known of these decisions is *Interamerican Refining Corp. v. Texaco Maracaibo, Inc.*, which is excerpted below. Also excerpted below are §441 of the *Restatement (Third) Foreign Relations Law* and §202 of the *Restatement (Second) Conflict of Laws.*

INTERAMERICAN REFINING CORP. v. TEXACO MARACAIBO, INC.
307 F. Supp. 1291 (D. Del. 1970)

WRIGHT, CHIEF JUDGE. This is an action arising under the United States antitrust laws, 15 U.S.C. §§1, 2, 15, commonly known as the Sherman and Clayton Acts. [Plaintiff Interamerican Refining Corp. ("Interamerican") is a company formed by prominent Venezuelan nationals apparently viewed with hostility by the Venezuelan government. Plaintiff sought to purchase crude oil from defendants Texaco Maracaibo, formerly the Superior Oil Co. of Venezuela ("Supven"), Monsanto Co. ("Monsanto"), Monsanto Venezuela ("Monven"), a wholly owned subsidiary of Monsanto, and Amoco Trading Corp. ("Amoco"), now survived by American International Oil Co. Plaintiff intended to export oil purchased from the defendants to the United States, where it was to be refined and reexported without incurring customs or other charges. After a few initial purchases, defendants allegedly refused to sell additional crude oil to plaintiff because the government of Venezuela prohibited such sales. When plaintiff was unable to escape from its lease agreement for a U.S. refinery to be used to process the Venezuelan crude oil, it

---

96. *Fogade v. ENB Revocable Trust,* 263 F.3d 1274, 1294-1296 (11th Cir. 2001); *National Coalition Government of the Union of Burma v. Unocal, Inc.,* 176 F.R.D. 329, 356-357 (C.D. Cal. 1997); *Banco Nacional de Cuba v. Chase Manhattan Bank,* 658 F.2d 875, 882 n.10 (2d Cir. 1981); *Compania de Gas de Nuevo Laredo v. Entex, Inc.,* 696 F.2d 322 (5th Cir. 1982); *United Mexican States v. Ashley,* 556 S.W.2d 784 (Tex. 1977). *Compare Ramirez de Arellano v. Weinberger,* 745 F.2d 1500, 1541-1542 n.180 (D.C. Cir. 1984), *vacated,* 471 U.S. 1113 (1985) ("It may be that a primary purpose of the statute was to prevent invocation of the act of state doctrine when property expropriated in a foreign country subsequently makes its way into the United States, but this was not the *sole* situation in which the amendment was to be activated.").

97. *Hunt v. Coastal States Gas Prods. Co.,* 583 S.W.2d 322 (Tex. 1979). *Compare West v. Multibanco Comermex, SA,* 807 F.2d 820 (9th Cir. 1987); *Najarro de Sanchez v. Banco Central de Nicaragua,* 770 F.2d 1385 (5th Cir. 1985).

98. Several lower courts have apparently approved the doctrine of foreign sovereign compulsion as a defense in antitrust cases. *E.g., Animal Science Products, Inc. v. China Nat'l Metals & Minerals Import & Export Corp.,* 702 F. Supp. 2d 320, 427 (D.N.J. 2010); *In re Vitamin C Antitrust Litig.,* 584 F. Supp. 2d 546, 551 (E.D.N.Y. 2008); *Trugman-Nash, Inc. v. New Zealand Dairy Bd.,* 954 F. Supp. 733, 736 (S.D.N.Y. 1997); *United States v. General Elec. Co.,* 115 F. Supp. 835, 878 (D.N.J. 1953); *United States v. Imperial Chem. Indus.,* 105 F. Supp. 215 (S.D.N.Y. 1952). Additionally, some federal statutes contain language akin to a codification of the foreign sovereign compulsion doctrine. *E.g.,* 29 U.S.C. §623(f)(1) (ADEA); *see Mahoney v. RFE/RL, Inc.,* 47 F.3d 447 (D.C. Cir. 1995).

brought this antitrust action against the defendants, alleging a concerted boycott in violation of the U.S. antitrust laws. The defendants sought summary judgment.]

Plaintiff insists that the evidence [raises] issues of fact requiring trial on the merits. If the evidence, when viewed in the light most favorable to plaintiff, discloses such issues, defendants' motion for summary judgment must be denied. *Continental Ore Co. v. Union Carbide & Carbon Corp.*, 370 U.S. 690 (1962). The Court concludes, however, for reasons hereinafter stated, that the undisputed facts demonstrate that defendants were compelled by regulatory authorities in Venezuela to boycott plaintiff. It also holds that such compulsion is a complete defense to an action under the antitrust laws based on that boycott. . . .

In *Continental Ore Co. v. Union Carbide & Carbon Corp.*, Union Carbide's subsidiary, Electro Met of Canada, had been appointed by the Canadian government to be exclusive wartime purchasing agent for vanadium. That appointment did not immunize a conspiracy with the parent to monopolize vanadium production and sale. "Respondents are afforded no defense from the fact that Electro Met of Canada, in carrying out the bare act of purchasing vanadium from respondents rather than Continental, was acting in a manner permitted by Canadian law." In [*United States v. Sisal Sales Corp.*, 274 U.S. 268 (1927)], defendants secured a monopoly through discriminatory legislation in Mexico and Yucatan. The Court held that inasmuch as the conspiracy was entered into and overt acts performed in this country, jurisdiction existed, and the legislation procured by the conspiracy was beside the point. "True, the conspirators were aided by discriminating legislation, but by their own deliberate acts, here and elsewhere, they brought about forbidden results within the United States."

Nothing in the materials before the Court indicates that defendants either procured the Venezuelan order or that they acted voluntarily pursuant to a delegation of authority to control the oil industry. The narrow question for decision is the availability of genuine compulsion by a foreign sovereign as a defense.

Defendants rely on dicta in *Continental Ore*,[99] and in *United States v. The Watchmakers of Switzerland Information Center, Inc.*, 1963 Trade Cas. 70,600 (S.D.N.Y.)[100] and on language in some consent decrees[101] to establish the defense. Without more, these would be scant authority. It requires no precedent, however, to acknowledge that sovereignty includes the right to regulate commerce within the nation. When a nation compels a trade practice, firms there have no choice but to obey. Acts of business become effectively acts of the sovereign. The Sherman Act does not confer jurisdiction on United States courts over acts of foreign sovereigns. By its terms, it forbids only anticompetitive practices of persons and corporations.[102] . . .

Anticompetitive practices compelled by foreign nations are not restraints of commerce, as commerce is understood in the Sherman Act, because refusal to comply would put an end to commerce. American business abroad does not carry with it the freedom and protection of competition it enjoys here, and our courts cannot impose

99. In *Continental Ore*, the Court pointed out that there was "no indication that the Controller or any other official directed that purchases from Continental be stopped." 370 U.S. at 706.

100. In *Watchmakers*, Judge Cashin held that a collective agreement could form a conspiracy notwithstanding that it was permitted by the laws of Switzerland. He added, "If, of course, the defendants' activities had been required by Swiss law, this Court could indeed do nothing." 1963 Trade Cases ¶70,600, at 77,456.

101. *See* the decrees in *United States v. Gulf Oil Corp.*, 1960 Trade Cases ¶69,851 at 77,349 (S.D.N.Y.); *United States v. Standard Oil Co.*, 1960 Trade Cases ¶69,849, at 77,340 (S.D.N.Y.).

102. This is analogous to the theory stated in *Parker v. Brown*, 317 U.S. 34 (1943), holding that compliance with a state regulatory program does not subject individuals to antitrust liability. The Sherman Act refers only to persons, not to states or nations, and both the Act and the Constitution would be badly misinterpreted to permit liability for acts of a sovereign.

them. Commerce may exist at the will of the government, and to impose liability for obedience to that will would eliminate for many companies the ability to transact business in foreign lands. Were compulsion not a defense, American firms abroad faced with a government order would have to choose one country or the other in which to do business. The Sherman Act does not go so far.

Plaintiff maintains that even if compulsion is a good defense, the acts of compulsion must be valid under Venezuelan laws. It urges the Court to consider the affidavit of a Venezuelan attorney to the effect that the Minister of Mines and Hydrocarbons had no authority to bar sales of crude oil to anyone and that no officer had authority to issue binding orders without putting them in writing and publishing them in the *Gazeta Official.* Since not legal, says plaintiff, the orders were not "compulsive."

This Court may not undertake such an inquiry. In *Sabbatino,* the Supreme Court held that it could not explore the validity under Cuban law of acts of expropriation by the Castro government. The act of state doctrine, based upon proper concepts of sovereignty and separation of powers, commands that conduct of foreign policy reside exclusively in the executive. For our courts to look behind the acts of a foreign government would impinge upon and perhaps impede the executive in that function. Whether or not Venezuelan officials acted within their authority and by legitimate procedures is therefore not relevant to the instant case. . . .

The Court concluded earlier that for it to inquire into the validity of the acts of a foreign state would violate the act of state doctrine. Plaintiff now contends that whether or not action taken by the Ministry was "compulsive" is a question of fact. It urges that it be permitted to show at trial that the order was not binding because oral and without legal authority. For the same reasons as those announced above, whether the act was legal or "compulsive" under the laws of Venezuela is no more a proper inquiry for the jury than it is for the Court. Plaintiff correctly states that whether or not a foreign official "ordered" certain conduct is an evidentiary question. But the factual inquiry is limited to the existence of the officer and the order. Once governmental action is shown, further examination is neither necessary nor proper. . . . The Court must conclude that the evidence relied on by plaintiff presents no issue of material fact and that trial is not necessary to resolve differing versions of the truth.

RESTATEMENT (THIRD) FOREIGN RELATIONS LAW

§441 (1987) [excerpted in Appendix AA]

RESTATEMENT (SECOND) CONFLICT OF LAWS

§202 (1971) [excerpted in Appendix Y]

Notes on Texaco Maracaibo *and* Restatements

1. *Foreign sovereign compulsion doctrine as canon of construction.* The contours of the foreign sovereign compulsion doctrine are relatively unsettled. One commentary recently described this unsettled state of affairs as follows:

> The Supreme Court has not spoken definitively on the parameters and requirements of the foreign sovereign compulsion doctrine. The divergent approaches by lower courts have failed to establish a consistent and predictable standard for application of the defense. The uncertainties about defining the limits of the foreign sovereign compulsion defense have centered around four separate issues. First, courts have been inconsistent about whether compulsion

requires that a foreign law mandated the private party's behavior. Second, courts have been unclear about whether the validity of the private action or government order under foreign law is important to the analysis. Third, there has been disparate treatment of statements submitted by foreign governments acknowledging compulsion. Finally, once compulsion is found, it is unclear what role the foreign sovereign compulsion doctrine plays. Is it a complete bar to liability or simply a separate factor to be considered in an international comity analysis? Note, *Vitamin "C" Is for Compulsion: Delimiting the Foreign Sovereign Compulsion Defense,* 50 Va. J. Int'l L. 757, 765 (2010).

Is the foreign sovereign compulsion doctrine a rule of abstention, a constitutional limit on jurisdiction, or a canon for construing legislation? Suppose that the antitrust laws specifically provided: "The fact that conduct was compelled or required by a foreign state shall not be a defense under this section." If this provision had existed, would *Texaco Maracaibo* have been decided the same way? Is the foreign sovereign compulsion doctrine a rule of statutory construction, like the territoriality presumption?

2. *Foreign sovereign compulsion doctrine as rule of international law.* Is the foreign sovereign compulsion doctrine a rule of international law? The *Third Restatement* indicates that it is. *Restatement (Third) Foreign Relations Laws* §340 (1987) (citing U.S. authorities). If the foreign sovereign compulsion doctrine is a rule of international law, what effect does it have in state courts or on the application of state law? *See supra* pp. 17-18.

3. *Policies underlying foreign sovereign compulsion defense.* Several related policies underlie the foreign sovereign compulsion doctrine. First, the doctrine is rooted in notions that it is unfair to punish private entities that have been subjected to conflicting legal requirements. *See Animal Science Products, Inc. v. China Nat'l Metals & Minerals Import & Export Corp.,* 702 F. Supp. 2d 320, 427 (D.N.J. 2010); *Interamerican Ref. Corp. v. Texaco Maracaibo,* 307 F. Supp. 1291, 1298 (D. Del. 1970) ("[W]hen a nation compels a trade practice, firms there have no choice but to obey"); Competitive Impact Statement for Proposed Consent Judgment in *United States v. Bechtel Corp.,* 42 Fed. Reg. 3716, 3718 (Jan. 10, 1977).

Second, the foreign sovereign compulsion defense rests on principles of international comity akin to those underlying the act of state doctrine and the jurisdictional rule of reason. As one court has remarked, U.S. courts have "no right to condemn the governmental activity of another sovereign nation." *Mannington Mills, Inc. v. Congoleum Corp.,* 595 F.2d 1287, 1292-1294 (3d Cir. 1979). *See Animal Science Products, Inc. v. China Nat'l Metals & Minerals Import & Export Corp.,* 702 F. Supp. 2d 320, 427 (D.N.J. 2010); *In re Vitamin C Antitrust Litig.,* 584 F. Supp. 2d 546, 551 (E.D.N.Y. 2008) ("The defense of foreign sovereign compulsion, on the other hand, focuses on the plight of a defendant who is subject to conflicting legal obligations under two sovereign states. Rather than being concerned with the diplomatic implications of condemning another country's official acts, the foreign sovereign compulsion doctrine recognizes that a defendant trying to do business under conflicting legal regimes may be caught between the proverbial rock and a hard place where compliance with one country's laws results in violation of another's."); *United States v. The Watchmakers of Switzerland Information Center,* 1963 Trade Cases (CCH) ¶70,600, at 77, 456 (S.D.N.Y. 1962) (if "defendant's activities had been required by Swiss law, this court could indeed do nothing. An American court would have under such circumstances no right to condemn the governmental activity of another sovereign nation"), *modified,* 1965 Trade Cases (CCH) ¶71,352 (S.D.N.Y. 1965).

Third, where a foreign state compels conduct on its own territory, choice-of-law considerations argue for application of that state's law to the resulting conduct. *See supra* pp. 811-812.

Fourth, some courts have read the foreign sovereign compulsion doctrine to rest partly on separation of powers grounds. Specifically, it is said that deference to the Executive Branch's primacy in foreign affairs animates the doctrine. *E.g., United States v. Brodie,* 174 F. Supp. 2d 294, 300 (E.D. Pa. 2001), *vacated on other grounds,* 403 F.3d 123 (3d Cir. 2005). To the extent the doctrine rests on this ground, is it available as a defense to a criminal prosecution or a civil action brought by the Government?

Finally, the doctrine also rests on a practical perception that compliance with foreign governmental requirements is a condition to doing business abroad, and that the imposition of antitrust liability for such compliance would generally preclude U.S. companies from operating abroad. Competitive Impact Statement for Proposed Consent Judgment in *United States v. Bechtel Corp.,* 42 Fed. Reg. 3716, 3718 (Jan. 10, 1977); *Interamerican Ref. Corp. v. Texaco Maracaibo,* 307 F. Supp. 1291 (D. Del. 1970).

Why should violations of the antitrust laws or other important public legislation be immunized from liability merely because they were ordered by a foreign state? Aren't government-sponsored cartels or boycotts an even greater threat to the values of free competition protected by the Sherman Act than private cartels? Is this factor outweighed by concerns for fairness to private parties and respect for foreign sovereignty?

4. *Territorial limitations of foreign sovereign compulsion defense.* Suppose it was clear that the Venezuelan government had issued orders regarding petroleum sales or other conduct *within* the United States. Would foreign sovereign compulsion still be a valid defense? Most authorities answer in the negative. *See* U.S. Department of Justice, *Antitrust Enforcement Guidelines for International Operations* §3.32 (1995) ("[A]lthough there can be no strict territorial test for this defense, the defense normally applies only when the foreign government compels conduct which can be accomplished entirely within its own territory."); *Restatement (Third) Foreign Relations Law* §441 & comment b (1987); *Linseman v. World Hockey Ass'n,* 439 F. Supp. 1315, 1324-1325 (D. Conn. 1977); *United Nuclear Corp. v. General Atomic Co.,* 629 P.2d 231, 263 (N.M. 1980). Note that in *Texaco Maracaibo* the defendant's conduct arguably occurred partially in the United States. The Department of Justice Antitrust Division has criticized the case on this ground. U.S. Department of Justice, *Antitrust Guide for International Operations* 51, 55 (1977).

What if State A compels a defendant to engage in anti-competitive conduct in State B? What if conduct compelled by State A within State A has direct and substantial effects on the United States? Should the doctrine of foreign sovereign compulsion apply? Compare the situs requirement of the act of state doctrine. *See supra* pp. 833-838.

5. *"Compulsion" requirement.* What sort of governmental action is required to trigger the foreign sovereign compulsion defense? It is clear that not all forms of governmental involvement with private conduct provide a basis for asserting the defense. A number of decisions have held that particular actions of foreign governments, such as approval of private conduct, did not amount to "compulsion." *See Continental Ore Co. v. Union Carbide & Carbon Corp.,* 370 U.S. 690 (1962); *United States v. Sisal Sales Corp.,* 274 U.S. 268 (1927); *Williams v. Curtiss-Wright Corp.,* 694 F.2d 300, 303 (3d Cir. 1982); *Mannington Mills, Inc. v. Congoleum Corp.,* 595 F.2d 1287, 1293 (3d Cir. 1979) ("One asserting the defense must establish that the foreign decree was basic and fundamental to the alleged antitrust behavior and more than merely peripheral to the overall illegal course of conduct. . . . Where governmental action rises no higher than mere approval, the compulsion defense will not be recognized. It is necessary that the foreign law must have coerced the defendant into violating American antitrust law. . . . The defense is not available if the defendant could have legally refused to accede to the foreign power's wishes."); *Timberlane Lumber Co. v. Bank of America,* 549 F.2d 600 (9th Cir. 1976); *United States v. Brodie,* 174 F. Supp. 2d 294, 301 (E.D. Pa. 2001) (blocking statute), *vacated on other grounds,* 403 F.3d

123 (3d Cir. 2005);*United States v. The Watchmakers of Switzerland Information Center,* 1963 Trade Cases (CCH) ¶70,600, at 77,456-457 (S.D.N.Y. 1962) (Swiss government's approval of cartel not "compulsion").

Other authorities conclude that foreign sovereign compulsion requires the potential imposition of severe sanctions. *Restatement (Third) Foreign Relations Law* §441, comment c & Reporters' Note 4 (1987); U.S. Department of Justice, *Antitrust Enforcement Guidelines for International Operations* §3.32 (1995) ("requiring proof that a 'refusal to comply with the foreign government's command would give rise to the imposition of penal or other severe sanctions' " but recognizing possibility of comity-based defense in wider circumstances); *Texaco Maracaibo,* 307 F. Supp. at 1291.

Is it appropriate to draw this sharp distinction between conduct that is officially compelled and conduct that is merely approved or encouraged by a foreign government? Some commentators have rejected the distinction, on the grounds that nations often "implement important policies without compelling adherence to those policies by legal compulsion." *E.g.,* D. Rosenthal & W. Knighton, *National Laws and International Commerce* 28-29 (1982). In addition, U.S. concepts of governmental authority and compulsion may not accord with foreign cultural and economic realities, where governmental "suggestions" or "encouragement" may in fact be tantamount to binding orders.

The "state action" defense to liability under the domestic antitrust laws provides generally that private conduct will not be subject to antitrust liability if it was "authorized and actively supervised" by a U.S. state government. *Southern Motor Carriers Rate Conference, Inc. v. United States,* 471 U.S. 48, 64-65 (1985). Should the same degree of deference apply to conduct by foreign states? *See* Brief of the Governments of Australia, Canada, France, and the United Kingdom as Amici Curiae, *Matsushita Elec. Indus. Co. v. Zenith Radio Corp.,* 475 U.S. 574 (1986), *reprinted in* 24 Int'l Leg. Mat. 1293 (1985).

6. *Legality of foreign compulsion under foreign law.* *Texaco Maracaibo* refused to consider whether the Venezuelan government's prohibition against sales to Interamerican was lawfully promulgated under Venezuelan law. By contrast, other courts will inquire into the question. *See, e.g., Access Telecom, Inc. v. MCI Telecommunications Corp.,* 197 F.3d 694, 713 (5th Cir. 1999); *Animal Science Products, Inc. v. China Nat'l Metals & Minerals Import & Export Corp.,* 702 F. Supp. 2d 320, 428 (D.N.J. 2010). Compare the treatment of the act of state doctrine, where U.S. courts inquire into the existence of an "act of state." *See supra* pp. 819-823. Suppose alleged foreign sovereign compulsion is the result of action by a low-level official clearly without authority to speak for his government. Compare the discussion below of whether particular conduct by foreign government officials constitutes an act of state, *supra* pp. 821-822.

7. *Legality of foreign compulsion under international law.* What if it is argued that the foreign government's compulsion is a violation of international law? For example, suppose a foreign state requires private parties to engage in conduct that constitutes torture, genocide, or prohibited racial or religious discrimination. Does the foreign sovereign compulsion doctrine shield the private actors from liability in such cases?

8. *Foreign sovereign compulsion as an absolute defense.* *Texaco Maracaibo* apparently assumes that the foreign sovereign compulsion doctrine provides an absolute defense to an antitrust action, rather than merely being one factor that is relevant to antitrust jurisdiction and/or liability. As discussed *infra* pp. 1012-1024, foreign blocking statutes do not provide an absolute defense to failure to comply with U.S. discovery orders. Is there any basis for treating discovery and antitrust differently? Note that the jurisdictional rule of reason would presumably take into account the fact that a foreign government encouraged conduct alleged to violate the antitrust laws. *See supra* pp. 683-689.

9. *Application of foreign sovereign compulsion doctrine in suits by U.S. Government.* The U.S. Government has taken the position that the foreign sovereign compulsion defense does not apply to suits brought by the Government. *Brief of the United States as Amicus Curiae* at 23-24, *Matsushita Elec. Co. v. Zenith Radio Corp.*, No. 83-2004 (U.S. June 1985). What does this suggest about the Government's view of the policy reasons underlying the doctrine? What does the Government's position suggest about the status of the foreign sovereign compulsion doctrine as a rule of international law? Why shouldn't the foreign sovereign compulsion doctrine apply to Government suits?

10. *Comparison between foreign sovereign compulsion and extraterritorial discovery.* As discussed below, *infra* pp. 978-1000, U.S. courts have long ordered parties subject to their personal jurisdiction to give discovery of materials located outside the United States. In some circumstances, foreign law, in the place where evidence is located, forbids compliance with U.S. extraterritorial discovery orders. Nevertheless, U.S. courts have frequently required parties to produce materials in violation of foreign law. *See infra* pp. 1006-1012. Compare this to the foreign sovereign compulsion doctrine. Can the two approaches be reconciled?

11. *Inviting compulsion.* Suppose an antitrust defendant is shown to have requested a foreign government to compel it to take certain actions, in part to gain antitrust immunity. Although there is little direct precedent in the antitrust context, most authorities (including *Texaco Maracaibo*) suggest that the foreign sovereign compulsion defense would not be available in these circumstances. *Telenor Mobile Communications AS v. Storm LLC*, 524 F. Supp. 2d 332, 345-346 (E.D.N.Y. 2007); *United Nuclear Corp. v. General Atomic Co.*, 629 P.2d 231 (N.M. 1980); J. Atwood & K. Brewster, *Antitrust and American Business Abroad* §8.23 (2d ed. 1985 & Cum. Supp.). Compare the significant sanctions that can result from efforts by litigants to procure foreign governmental prohibitions against disclosure of evidence for use in U.S. proceedings. *See infra* pp. 1008-1009.

Is this exception wise? How is a private party's participation in the development of a regulatory rule relevant to "compulsion"? Even if such an exception is sensible as a theoretical matter, what level of participation suffices to trigger the exception? How is a court supposed to evaluate participation as an evidentiary matter? For a skeptical view of the "invited compulsion" exception, *see Animal Science Products, Inc. v. China Nat'l Metals & Minerals Import & Export Corp.*, 702 F. Supp. 2d 320, 425 (D.N.J. 2010) ("[O]ne's participation in coining a legal/regulatory prescript does not render such participant exempt from the compulsion of the law (s)he helped to create. Indeed, had it been otherwise, all the legislators enacting state and federal statutes, agency officials crafting regulations, reporters compiling the Restatements of Law, judges sitting on advisory committees, etc., would be deemed exempt from the reach of laws they helped to create. And, of course, it would be an error to automatically qualify a foreign prescript as non-mandatory on the grounds that a literal translation of a certain term employed in that prescript has non-compulsory connotations to an American ear in light of the socio-political and cultural peculiarities of United States life. Rather, the law of the foreign sovereign has to be examined, with due consideration given to interpretative statements made by that foreign sovereign.").

12. *Applicability of foreign sovereign compulsion doctrine in state courts.* The leading judicial precedent directly relevant to the applicability of the foreign sovereign compulsion doctrine in state courts is *United Nuclear Corp. v. General Atomic Co.*, 629 P.2d 231 (N.M. 1980). *United Nuclear* arose from a suit in New Mexico state court in which a U.S. company sought to be excused from its obligations to perform certain long-term uranium supply contracts on the grounds of fraud and violations of state antitrust laws. The plaintiff claimed that the defendants had participated in an international cartel to fix the prices of uranium on the world market and that this cartel violated New Mexico's unfair competition law. A central element of the defendant's response was that their conduct had been compelled by various foreign sovereigns, and that the act of state and foreign sovereign compulsion doctrines shielded them from liability.

The New Mexico Supreme Court rejected the defendants' claims. Acknowledging that the act of state doctrine "is a matter of federal law which is binding on state courts," the New Mexico court applied prevailing federal decisions and found the doctrine inapplicable. 629 P.2d at 257-259. *United Nuclear* also rejected the defendants' foreign sovereign compulsion argument; it did not specifically hold that the foreign sovereign compulsion defense is a rule of federal law, but it cited only to federal authorities, which it appeared to treat as binding precedents, 629 P.2d at 260-263, and its discussion of the subject was included as a part of its discussion of what it termed "the act of state doctrines." 629 P.2d at 266.

Moreover, *United Nuclear* later went on to consider the argument that "even if the act of state doctrines does not bar an American court from examining [the defendant's] cartel-related actions, the principle of exclusive federal power over the conduct of foreign relations nevertheless precludes an American *state* court from conducting such an examination." 629 P.2d at 266 (emphasis in original). The court rejected the argument that *Zschernig* [discussed *supra* at pp. 631-632, 637-638] precluded a state court from examining a private U.S. defendant's involvement in a cartel that had foreign sovereign involvement. But the court went out of its way to emphasize that it had "done no more than seek to enforce state laws which are consistent with federal laws" and the actions of the federal Executive and Legislative branches. *Id.*

Does the rationale underlying the foreign sovereign compulsion doctrine dictate its character as a rule of federal common law? The impact upon the Nation's foreign relations of disregarding foreign governmental orders relating to conduct within foreign territory is equally great whether a federal or a state court is involved. And the unfairness and disruption to U.S. foreign commerce is also unaffected by the status of the court that is involved. Do these reasons suffice to displace state law? *Compare supra* pp. 11-13. If the foreign sovereign compulsion doctrine is a rule of federal common law, is it merely a rule of statutory construction, or does it have a more binding effect on state law? Suppose that a state statute expressly penalizes or forbids conduct required by foreign law. Does a federal foreign sovereign compulsion doctrine forbid application of this state law?

Recall the discussion above of limits on state statutes that violate customary international law, on the grounds that international law is federal law that preempts state law. *See supra* pp. 814-815. Should the limits of §441 of the *Third Restatement* preempt state legislation that penalizes conduct required by foreign law?

13. *Illegality of contract.* Reread *Restatement (Second) Conflict of Laws* §202 (1971). What is the relation between the foreign sovereign compulsion doctrine and §202? When a U.S. court imposes damages on a party that has not performed its contractual obligations, because the foreign government at the place of performance forbade performance, does this implicate the foreign sovereign compulsion doctrine? Or is it just a question of which party bears the risk that the foreign government will take such action?

Part Four

International Judicial Assistance[1]

International law prohibits a state from engaging in governmental activities within the territory of another state without that state's consent.[2] This principle applies to numerous aspects of international dispute resolution — including the service of process, the taking of evidence, and the enforcement of judgments. As a consequence, courts in one nation often cannot effectively proceed with an international litigation without the assistance of courts in other nations. The aid that the courts of one state lend to courts or litigants of another state is referred to as "international judicial assistance."

International judicial assistance has long occurred even in the absence of treaties or other international agreements. Courts provided judicial assistance for reasons of what they termed comity:

> [The provision of international judicial assistance] appertains to the administration of justice in its best sense, and its exercise is now common and unquestioned among civilized nations. It is true [that] the duty may not be imposed by positive local law, but it rests on national comity, creating a duty that no state could refuse to fulfill without forfeiting its standing among the civilized states of the world.[3]

Thus, U.S. (and other) courts have long been willing to execute foreign "letters rogatory" seeking assistance in serving process or taking evidence, even in the absence of treaty obligations to do so.[4] U.S. and other national courts have also long recognized and enforced at least some judgments of foreign courts, again without requiring any international agreement.[5]

Although international judicial assistance is possible without formal international agreements, the existence of such agreements generally improves cooperation among national courts. Thus, bilateral and multilateral treaties have been entered into by a number of states — including the United States — dealing with particular aspects of international judicial assistance. Most importantly for the United States, the Hague Service Convention and the Hague Evidence Convention deal with the service of process

---

1. Commentary on international judicial assistance includes, *e.g.*, B. Ristau, *International Judicial Assistance* (2000); Jones, *International Judicial Assistance: Procedural Chaos and a Program for Reform*, 62 Yale L.J. 515 (1953); Smit, *International Litigation Under the United States Code*, 65 Colum. L. Rev. 1015 (1965).

2. *Restatement (Third) Foreign Relations Law* §526 (1987).

3. *Oregon v. Bourne*, 27 P. 1048 (Or. 1891) (quoted in B. Ristau, *International Judicial Assistance* 5 (2000)).

4. *See infra* pp. 962-964.

5. *See infra* pp. 1077-1083.

outside the United States and the taking of evidence located in foreign states.[6] Moreover, the United States (together with more than 130 other states) is party to the New York Convention, providing for the recognition and enforcement of foreign arbitral awards.[7] And, for much of the past decade, the United States engaged in detailed, but ultimately unsuccessful, discussions in the Hague Conference on Private International Law[8] aimed at developing an international convention on the mutual recognition and enforcement of foreign judgments.[9]

The materials in Part Four examine the most significant aspects of international judicial assistance in U.S. civil litigation.

Chapter 10 considers the service of process abroad in international disputes involving the United States. It examines the direct service of U.S. process on foreign defendants under Rule 4 of the Federal Rules of Civil Procedure and state counterparts, as well as the service of process abroad under the Hague Service Convention. It also discusses the use of customary letters rogatory as a means of serving process abroad with the assistance of foreign courts.

Chapter 11 examines the taking of evidence abroad and the discovery of materials located outside the United States.[10] It examines the direct discovery of materials located abroad under the Federal Rules of Civil Procedure, as well as the taking of evidence abroad under the Hague Evidence Convention. Chapter 11 also discusses the use of customary letters rogatory as a means of taking evidence abroad with the assistance of foreign courts.

Chapter 12 examines the recognition and enforcement of foreign judgments. This topic is not traditionally included within the category of "judicial assistance."[11] Nevertheless, the enforcement by one state of the judgment of the courts of another state fits squarely within the traditional rubric of international judicial assistance. Chapter 12 considers the standards under U.S. law for recognizing and enforcing judgments rendered by foreign courts.

Finally, Chapter 13 introduces international commercial arbitration, focusing particularly on the assistance that U.S. courts provide to the arbitral process. Again, this topic is also not generally treated as a matter of international judicial assistance, but insofar as the role of national courts is concerned, it can and should be regarded as such. As Chapter 13 illustrates, U.S. (and foreign) courts are required by both international treaty and domestic law to enforce international arbitration agreements and international arbitral awards. In both respects, U.S. courts render judicial assistance to other tribunals — albeit arbitral tribunals — engaged in international dispute resolution.

---

6. *See infra* pp. 909-952 & 1026-1058.

7. *See infra* p. 1161.

8. *See supra* pp. 107-108, 485-486 and *infra* pp. 1083, 1085-1086, for a discussion of the Hague Conference.

9. *See supra* pp. 107-108 and *infra* pp. 1085-1086.

10. The "taking of evidence" often refers only to the formal reception of materials as evidence in a pending trial, while "discovery" is often defined more broadly to include "pre-trial" requests for information that may (and may not) be used as evidence at trial. Collins, *The Hague Evidence Convention and Discovery: A Serious Misunderstanding*, 35 Int'l & Comp. L.Q. 765 (1986).

11. *E.g.*, B. Ristau, *International Judicial Assistance* (2000) (not including recognition of foreign judgments); *Restatement (Third) Foreign Relations Law* Chapters 7 and 8 (1987) (treating international judicial assistance and recognition of foreign judgments as separate topics).

10

Service of U.S. Process on Foreign Persons[1]

Under the laws of most nations, service of process must be effected upon the defendant in order either to commence a civil litigation or to obtain a judgment that will be recognized in other jurisdictions. "Service of process" is the formal transmission of documents to a party involved in litigation, for the purpose of providing it with notice of claims, defenses, decisions, or other important matters. This chapter examines the service of process from U.S. courts on foreign persons.

A. Introduction and Historical Background

In most domestic U.S. cases, the service of process is a fairly routine undertaking; it usually involves nothing more than the delivery of the plaintiff's complaint and summons to the defendant by a private process-server, or the mailing of these documents to the defendant by the plaintiff's lawyers. In contrast, the service of U.S. process in international cases can be difficult, slow, and costly. That is particularly true following the 1993 revisions of Rule 4(f) and 4(h) of the Federal Rules of Civil Procedure, which have introduced substantial uncertainty into what should be a relatively straightforward, inexpensive task. The service of process abroad has therefore been described as "a frequently lengthy, expensive and

---

1. Commentary on the service of process abroad includes, *e.g.,* 1 B. Ristau, *International Judicial Assistance* Pt. IV (rev. ed. 2000); Born & Vollmer, *The Effect of the Revised Federal Rules of Civil Procedure on Personal Jurisdiction, Service and Discovery in International Cases,* 150 F.R.D. 221 (1993); Buhler, *Transnational Service of Process and Discovery in Federal Court Proceedings: An Overview,* 27 Tul. Mar. L.J. 1 (2002); Campbell, *No Sirve: The Invalidity of Service of Process Abroad by Mail or Private Process Server on Parties in Mexico Under the Hague Service Convention,* 19 Minn. J. Int'l L. 107 (2010); Committee on Federal Courts, N.Y. Bar Ass'n, *Service of Process Abroad: A Nuts and Bolts Guide,* 122 F.R.D. 63 (1989); Doyle, *Taking Evidence by Deposition and Letters Rogatory and Obtaining Documents in Foreign Territory,* Proc. A.B.A., Sec. Int'l & Comp. L. 37 (1959); Grossman, *Letters Rogatory: A Symposium Before the Consular Law Society,* Federal Legal Publications, Inc., New York (1956); Hedges, Roshbaum & Losey, *Electronic Service of Process at Home and Abroad: Allowing Domestic Electronic Service of Process in the Federal Courts,* 4 Fed. Cts. L. Rev. 55 (2010); Jacklin, *Annotation, Service of Process by Mail in International Civil Action as Permissible Under Hague Convention,* 18 A.L.R. Fed.2d 241 (1993); Jones, *International Judicial Assistance: Procedural Chaos and a Program for Reform,* 62 Yale L.J. 515 (1953); Raley, *A Comparative Analysis: Notice Requirements in Germany, Japan, Spain, The United Kingdom and The United States,* 10 Ariz. J. Int'l & Comp. L. 301 (1993); Shields, *Annotation: When Is Compliance with Hague Convention on Service Abroad of Judicial and Extrajudicial Documents in Civil and Commercial Matters, Art. 1 et seq., Required,* 1 A.L.R. Fed. 2d 185 (2007); Smit, *International Litigation Under the United States Code,* 65 Colum. L. Rev. 1015 (1965); Smit, *Federalizing International Civil Litigation in the United States: A Modest Proposal,* 8 Transnat'l L. & Contemp. Probs. 57 (1998); Smit, *International Aspects of Federal Civil Procedure,* 61 Colum. L. Rev. 1031 (1961); Stewart & Conley, *Email Service on Foreign Defendants: Time for an International Approach?,* 38 Geo. J. Int'l L. 755 (2007); Tamayo, *Catch Me If You Can: Serving United States Process on an Elusive Defendant Abroad,* 17 Harv. J.L. & Tech. 211 (2003).

twisting process bordered on all sides with fatal pitfalls"[2] and "a tricky proposition."[3] This is an unsatisfactory state of affairs, which would benefit substantially from greater legislative or judicial attention.

1. Choice of Law

Traditional U.S. choice of law rules provide that the manner for effecting service of process is governed by the law of the forum court.[4] Under this analysis, service of process in federal courts is subject to Rules 4 and 4.1 of the Federal Rules of Civil Procedure. In particular, Rules 4(f) and 4(h)(2) of the Federal Rules provide a specialized regime governing the service of process outside U.S. territory.[5] In U.S. state courts, service of process must generally comply with local state law regarding service of process; state law occasionally contains special service mechanisms for service of process abroad, although often only generally applicable mechanisms are available.[6]

Although standard conflict of laws analysis asserts that the forum's law governs the service of process, other jurisdictions' laws are also relevant in international cases. First, where service of process must be made outside U.S. territory, the United States may be party to international agreements that supersede or supplement the Federal Rules of Civil Procedure and state service mechanisms. The Hague Service Convention and the Inter-American Convention on Letters Rogatory are the principal instances of such agreements. As discussed below, under these instruments, the laws of the state where service is effected can apply to the service of U.S. process abroad.[7]

Second, the laws of the place where service is effected can forbid particular service mechanisms, which may be permitted by the forum in which an action is pending. For example, as discussed below, many civil law jurisdictions impose strict limits on the service of foreign process.[8] These restrictions may make service in accordance with the forum's rules impossible as a practical matter. Violation of the laws of the place of service may also render service invalid (under the laws of the forum), or result in criminal or civil liability and/or give rise to issues of professional responsibility.[9]

Third, a foreign judgment will often not be recognized unless service on the defendant was made in accordance with the laws of the state where recognition is sought. Service in accordance with the laws of the forum may not be sufficient to satisfy those requirements.[10]

2. Service of Process in the United States: An Historical Overview

Service of process in the United States has undergone substantial evolution during this century. At common law, the service of civil process was accomplished by a writ of *capias ad respondendum*, which directed the local sheriff to locate the defendant and physically arrest

---

2. Horlick, *A Practical Guide to Service of United States Process Abroad*, 14 Int'l Law. 637, 638 (1980).

3. *Chowaniec v. Heyl Truck Lines*, 1991 U.S. Dist. LEXIS 8138 (N.D. Ill. 1991).

4. *Restatement (Second) Conflict of Laws* §126 (1971) ("The local law of the forum determines the method of serving process and of giving notice of the proceeding to the defendant."); *Restatement (Third) Foreign Relations Law* §471(i) (1986); R. Leflar *et al.*, *American Conflicts Law* §§121-122 (4th ed. 1986).

5. *See infra* pp. 875-879, 909-952.

6. *See infra* p. 879.

7. *See infra* pp. 924-927, 933-939.

8. *See infra* pp. 880-888.

9. *See infra* pp. 884-886, 909.

10. The recognition and enforcement of foreign judgments in the United States is discussed below. *See infra* Chapter 12.

him.[11] Doing so subjected the defendant to the local court's personal jurisdiction. In a very real sense, jurisdiction was based upon physical power.[12]

The use of physical arrest at English common law was gradually abandoned during the eighteenth century. Instead, the sheriff was authorized to "serve" the defendant with documents that "summoned" him to appear in court and defend against the plaintiff's claims.[13] Like physical arrest, personal service within the forum continued to be both necessary and sufficient to confer jurisdiction over the defendant.[14]

U.S. courts in the eighteenth and nineteenth century adopted English common law approaches to service.[15] Service of process in the United States traditionally consisted of hand delivery to the defendant of the plaintiff's complaint, together with a summons.[16] The summons was a document, usually issued by a court official, directing the defendant to answer the complaint. Service on the defendant was generally effected by an official of the forum court, such as a sheriff or marshal.[17] Service of process within the forum's territory continued to be both sufficient and necessary to subject the defendant to personal jurisdiction.[18]

These traditional approaches to the service of process in the United States have significantly evolved in recent decades.[19] First, court officials have ceased to be primarily responsible for service of U.S. process. In 1983, the Federal Rules of Civil Procedure were amended to limit substantially the role of federal marshals in the service of process,[20] and to make the plaintiff responsible for serving its own complaint.[21] Under the Federal Rules, service today is often effected by the plaintiff's attorneys or by private firms specializing in the service of process—not by government officials.[22]

Second, service of process in the United States is no longer dominated by personal delivery to the defendant. The 1983 amendments to the Federal Rules of Civil Procedure permitted service by mail in certain cases. The rules allowed the plaintiff, under some circumstances, to mail the defendant the complaint, summons, a notice of service and acknowledgment form, and a postage pre-paid envelope.[23] In order for mail service to be

---

11. *See* Millar, *Civil Procedure of the Trial Court in Historical Perspective* 76-78 (1952); Dodd, *Jurisdiction in Personal Actions*, 23 Ill. L. Rev. 427, 427-428 (1929); Levy, *Mesne Process in Personal Actions at Common Law and the Power Doctrine*, 78 Yale L.J. 52 (1968).

12. *Cf. McDonald v. Mabee*, 243 U.S. 90, 91 (1917) ("the foundation of jurisdiction is physical power").

13. Dodd, *Jurisdiction in Personal Actions*, 23 Ill. L. Rev. 427, 427-428 (1929); Levy, *Mesne Process in Personal Actions at Common Law and the Power Doctrine*, 78 Yale L.J. 52 (1968).

14. For a more detailed discussion of the jurisdictional consequences of service during the nineteenth and early twentieth centuries, and of the territorial limits on service, *see supra* pp. 83-86, 129-137.

15. Kalo, *Jurisdiction as an Evolutionary Process: The Development of Quasi In Rem and In Personam Principles*, 1978 Duke L.J. 1147, 1150-1153 & nn.31-32; Miller, *Civil Procedure of the Trial Court in Historical Perspective* 76-78 (1952).

16. W. Alderson, *Law of Judicial Writs and Process* 225-226 (1895).

17. For example, until the 1990s the Federal Rules of Civil Procedure provided for service of process from U.S. district courts to be made by federal marshals. *See* Sinclair, *Service of Process: Rethinking the Theory and Procedure of Serving Process Under Federal Rule 4(c)*, 73 Va. L. Rev. 1183, 1190-1191 (1987); *infra* pp. 874-879.

18. *See supra* pp. 83-86, 129-137; *Mississippi Publishing Corp. v. Murphree*, 326 U.S. 438, 44-45 (1946) ("Service of summons is the procedure by which a court having venue and jurisdiction of the subject matter of the suit asserts jurisdiction over the person of the party served.").

19. In addition to service by personal delivery to the defendant, other modes of service were also possible in *in rem* and *quasi in rem* actions, including service by posting and publication. *Pennoyer v. Neff*, 95 U.S. 714 (1878); *supra* pp. 129-137.

20. Sinclair, *Service of Process: Rethinking the Theory and Procedure of Serving Process Under Federal Rule 4(c)*, 73 Va. L. Rev. 1183, 1191 (1987). The amendments were broadly similar to the approach to service in state courts.

21. The Federal Rules now expressly provide that service of the complaint and summons is the responsibility of plaintiff and not the court or any court official. Federal Rules of Civil Procedure, Rule 4(c)(1) ("The plaintiff is responsible for having the summons and complaint served. . . .").

22. Federal Rules of Civil Procedure, Rule 4(c)(2) ("Any person who is at least 18 yeas old and not a party may serve a summons and complaint.").

23. Sinclair, *Service of Process: Rethinking the Theory and Procedure of Serving Process Under Federal Rule 4(c)*, 73 Va. L. Rev. 1183, 1191 (1987).

effective, the defendant was expected (but not required) to execute the acknowledgment form and return it to the plaintiff (or its counsel).

Amendments to the Federal Rules of Civil Procedure in 1993 further departed from the traditional service mechanism of personal delivery. The amendments established a "waiver of service" procedure, discussed below, which permits parties to dispense entirely with formal service of process. Plaintiffs enjoy broad freedom to select a method for transmitting requests for waiver of service of process, including by such mechanisms as mail, courier service, and telecopy transmission.[24]

Third, the jurisdictional consequences of service underwent substantial changes under U.S. law during the twentieth century. As described in Chapter 2, personal service of process on the defendant within the forum's territory was both a necessary and sufficient requirement for personal jurisdiction in the United States for much of the nineteenth century. That is no longer the case. Because state long-arm statutes and the Due Process Clause now permit personal jurisdiction over nonresident defendants based on their contacts with the forum state,[25] personal service within the forum has ceased to be a *necessary* requirement for personal jurisdiction.

Also as discussed in Chapter 2, effecting service of process as a *sufficient* basis for personal jurisdiction has been widely challenged. Thus, although service of process outside the forum's territory has become commonplace in twenty-first-century U.S. litigation, this does not suffice to confer personal jurisdiction.[26] For the time being, the Supreme Court's decision in *Burnham v. Superior Court*[27] has preserved the efficacy of "tag" service within the forum's territory as an independently sufficient jurisdictional base. Nonetheless, the doctrine will likely continue to be challenged by U.S. courts, legislatures, and commentators and will remain subject to broad international criticism.[28]

Finally, a customary means for serving process abroad was by letter rogatory. A letter rogatory is a formal request by the court of one nation to the courts of another country for assistance in performing judicial acts (such as serving process or taking evidence).[29] Federal legislation authorizes the Department of State to transmit letters rogatory from and to foreign courts (while not precluding direct transmittal of letters rogatory between courts).[30] The use of letters rogatory ensured that national sovereignty was not violated by the service of process from a foreign court and that local law regarding service of process was respected; on the other hand, transmission of letters rogatory through multiple layers of bureaucracy often took many months and faced complex formal and administrative requirements.[31]

---

24. *See infra* pp. 878-879.

25. *See supra* pp. 82-83.

26. *See supra* pp. 82-83.

27. 495 U.S. 604 (1990); *C.S.B. Commodities, Inc. v. Urban Trend (HK) Ltd*, 626 F. Supp. 2d 837, 846 (N.D. Ill. 2009) ("Since *Burnham* was decided, there does not appear to be a single published opinion in which a court has found jurisdiction lacking where an individual was served in the forum."); *supra* pp. 129-132.

28. *See supra* pp. 133-135.

29. Jones, *International Judicial Assistance: Procedural Chaos and a Program for Reform*, 62 Yale L.J. 515, 519 (1953); Smit, *International Litigation Under the United States Code*, 65 Colum. L. Rev. 1015, 1019 (1965).

30. 28 U.S.C. §§1696, 1781.

31. Jones, *International Judicial Assistance: Procedural Chaos and a Program for Reform*, 62 Yale L.J. 515, 529-532 (1953).

B. Contemporary U.S. Rules Governing Service of Process on Foreign Defendants

1. Service of Process in Federal Court Proceedings

a. Service of Complaint and Summons Under Rule 4 of the Federal Rules of Civil Procedure. In U.S. civil litigation, the principal classes of "process" that must be "served" are: (i) the summons and complaint, which commence an action;[32] (ii) the subpoena, which demands the giving of testimonial or documentary evidence;[33] and (iii) the notice, for example, of a deposition.[34] Different mechanisms may exist for the service of each of these classes of documents.[35]

At the outset of a civil litigation in U.S. district court, the defendant must ordinarily be served with a complaint and "summons." As discussed in Chapter 2, Federal Rule of Civil Procedure 4 provides that nonresident defendants will be "amenable" to service when applicable state or federal long-arm statutes authorize personal jurisdiction.[36] In addition, Rule 4 also plays a vital role in determining the "manner" or "mechanics" of service of a complaint on those foreign defendants who are amenable to a federal court's personal jurisdiction. Put differently, in addition to defining when a foreign defendant is subject to U.S. judicial jurisdiction, Rule 4 prescribes the mechanical process for notifying the defendant that an action against it has been commenced (*i.e.*, by requiring hand-delivery or sending by registered mail).[37]

Rules 4(a) and 4(b) of the Federal Rules of Civil Procedure prescribe the form and manner of issuance of the summons in federal court.[38] Under contemporary practice, the plaintiff's attorney prepares a summons that: (i) identifies the parties, the court, and the plaintiff's attorney; (ii) specifies the time that the defendant has to reply; and (iii) warns the defendant that, if it does not reply, a default judgment will result.[39] After the complaint in an action is filed, a summons in the action is presented to the clerk of the district court, for signature, and is sealed with the seal of the court.[40] Under Rule 4(c), both a copy of the complaint and the summons must be served upon the defendant (unless service is waived).[41]

b. Service of Summons and Complaint as a Jurisdictional Requirement Under the Federal Rules of Civil Procedure. As described above, service of process often no longer provides a *sufficient* basis for personal jurisdiction, as it did at common law.[42] Nevertheless, service of process generally continues to be described as a jurisdictional *necessity*. Unless the defendant is properly served, or waives service, a U.S. court ordinarily cannot exercise personal jurisdiction over the defendant.[43] In the words of one court: "Personal

---

32. *See* Federal Rules of Civil Procedure, Rule 4.
33. *See* Federal Rules of Civil Procedure, Rule 45.
34. *See* Federal Rules of Civil Procedure, Rules 5, 30(b).
35. *See* Federal Rules of Civil Procedure, Rules 4 and 4.1. *See also* C. Wright & A. Miller, *Federal Practice and Procedure* §1061 *et seq.* (2010).
36. *See supra* pp. 203-229.
37. *See supra* pp. 203-206 for a discussion of the distinction between "amenability" and "manner."
38. The contents of both documents, and the manner of service, is generally prescribed by the applicable procedural rules of the court in which the action is filed: in state courts, local rules of procedure generally apply. *See Restatement (Second) Conflict of Laws* §§126 & 127 (1971).
39. Federal Rules of Civil Procedure, Rule 4(a).
40. Federal Rules of Civil Procedure, Rules 4(a) and 4(b).
41. Federal Rules of Civil Procedure, Rule 4(c)(1).
42. *See supra* pp. 82-91.
43. *Omni Cap. Int'l v. Rudolf Wolff & Co.*, 484 U.S. 97 (1987).

jurisdiction is a composite notion of two separate ideas: amenability to jurisdiction . . . and notice to the defendant through valid service of process."[44]

c. Service of Complaint and Summons as a Means of Notice Under the Federal Rules of Civil Procedure. The principal function of service under the contemporary Federal Rules of Civil Procedure is notification to the defendant. The traditional common law function of service — that is, conferring personal jurisdiction — now exists only in the relatively rare cases of tag service within the forum's territory.[45] In most contemporary cases, the function of service of the complaint is to inform the defendant of the commencement of an action against him and the nature of the plaintiff's claims.[46] "The purpose of the summons is to give notice to the defendant that it has been sued."[47] Likewise, service of the summons provides the defendant with an opportunity to respond to the plaintiff's claims before coercive judicial action is taken.

d. Service as Commencing an Action and Tolling Statutes of Limitations Under the Federal Rules of Civil Procedure. The date of service of process can have important timing consequences. First, it generally provides the basis for calculating the time in which the defendant has to answer the complaint.[48] Second, service can also have important consequences for statute of limitations purposes. In the words of one commentator on Federal Rule of Civil Procedure 4:

> [T]he rule is enmeshed, atomically fused, with the limitations' subject. Indeed, from a practical viewpoint the phenomenon, and perhaps the only one, that gives moment to mistakes made under Rule 4 is the statute of limitations.[49]

Rule 3 of the Federal Rules of Civil Procedure provides: "A civil action is commenced by filing a complaint with the court." The Supreme Court has squarely held that, in federal question cases where a substantive federal claim is asserted, Rule 3 provides a federal rule tolling any applicable statute of limitations by the filing — not the service — of a complaint.[50]

Under the laws of some states, however, the filing of a complaint with a state court does not toll applicable statutes of limitations; in these jurisdictions, only the effective service of the complaint and summons upon the defendant tolls applicable limitation periods. The Supreme Court has held that, in diversity of citizenship cases, where state law claims are asserted and no federal statute of limitations exists, state statutes of limitations and tolling rules apply.[51] Accordingly, the mere filing of a complaint in such diversity cases does not toll applicable statutes of limitations, unless that is what state law provides. "[I]f under forum state law the action is not deemed commenced until, for example, the summons is served on the defendant, the diversity plaintiff must be sure not only to file the complaint

---

44. *Soltex Polymer Corp. v. Fortex Indus., Inc.,* 590 F. Supp. 1453, 1456 (E.D.N.Y. 1984).

45. *See supra* pp. 129-137.

46. *See Volkswagenwerk AG v. Schlunk,* 486 U.S. 694, 700 (1988) ("Service of process refers to a formal delivery of documents that is legally sufficient to charge the defendant with notice of a pending action."); *Mullane v. Central Hanover Bank & Trust Co.,* 339 U.S. 306 (1950); *Milliken v. Meyer,* 311 U.S. 457 (1940).

47. *Grooms v. Greyhound Corp.,* 287 F.2d 95, 97-98 (6th Cir. 1961). As discussed below, the Due Process Clause imposes constitutional requirements of reasonable notice, which service of process must fulfill. *See infra* p. 880.

48. Federal Rules of Civil Procedure, Rule 12(a)(1)(A).

49. D. Siegel, *Supplementary Practice Commentaries,* 28 U.S.C.A., Federal Rules of Civil Procedure, at C4-45 (2007).

50. *West v. Conrail,* 481 U.S. 35 (1987).

51. *Walker v. Armco Steel Corp.,* 446 U.S. 740 (1980).

within the applicable statute of limitations, but also see to it that the summons is actually served on the defendant before the statute expires."[52]

2. Mechanisms for Serving Foreign Defendants with U.S. Process Within the United States

It is often possible to serve a foreign defendant within the United States, rather than in its home jurisdiction. U.S. precedent has long permitted such service, without imposing any requirement that foreign defendants be served at their foreign residence or principal place of business.[53] This is as true under the Hague Service Convention as it is under the Federal Rules.[54] In order to serve a foreign defendant within the United States with process from a U.S. court, applicable U.S. law must provide a mechanism for service that can as a practical matter be used. Both the Federal Rules of Civil Procedure and state law offer a variety of potentially effective service mechanisms.

The most obvious circumstance in which service abroad can be avoided under U.S. law is when an individual foreign defendant is physically present within the forum and can be personally served there.[55] Service by personal delivery within the forum state is permitted under the laws of all the states,[56] and the Federal Rules.[57] It may also be possible, depending upon local law, to effect service upon foreign corporations or other legal persons by serving their officers or directors within the forum.[58]

The need for service of process abroad may also be avoided, at least under U.S. law, if a foreign defendant has appointed an agent to receive service of process within the forum. Rule 4(h)(1) of the Federal Rules of Civil Procedure permits service within the United States upon domestic and foreign corporations either: (a) as authorized by state law (in either the state where the district court is located or in the state where service is effected);[59] or (b) "by delivering a copy of the summons and of the complaint to an officer, a managing or general agent, or any other agent authorized by appointment or by law to receive service of process. . . ." Rule 4(e)(2) also permits service upon individuals within the United States by means of service upon their agents. There is substantial lower court precedent concerning the status of particular persons or entities as agents under Rule 4.[60]

Both federal law and the laws of most states permit service upon foreign (and other) defendants by means of service upon closely affiliated persons or entities. The primary example of this type of service involves service upon a parent company by means of service upon its subsidiary.[61] Typically, such service requires proof of an alter ego or common law

---

52. D. Siegel, *Supplementary Practice Commentaries,* 28 U.S.C.A., Federal Rules of Civil Procedure, at C4-40 (2007).

53. *E.g., Silvious v. Pharaon,* 54 F.3d 697 (11th Cir. 1995) (Rule 4(f) does not require service on foreign defendant outside the United States).

54. *Volkswagenwerk AG v. Schlunk,* 486 U.S. 694 (1988); *infra* pp. 940-946.

55. As discussed above, service within the forum may sometimes confer personal jurisdiction as well as avoid the need for service abroad. That is arguably true under Federal Rule of Civil Procedure 4(k)(2), as well as under state law. *See supra* pp. 228-229.

56. 1 Casad & Richman, *Jurisdiction in Civil Actions* §3-1[1] (3d ed. 1998 & Supp. 2010).

57. Federal Rules of Civil Procedure, Rule 4(f).

58. *See supra* pp. 136-137.

59. Many state laws permit service of process on corporate and individual defendants by means of service upon agents authorized by appointment or by law. *See* 1 Casad & Richman, *Jurisdiction in Civil Actions* §3-1[2] (3d ed. 1998 & Supp. 2010).

60. *See* 1 Casad & Richman, *Jurisdiction in Civil Actions* §3-1[2] (3d ed. 1998 & Supp. 2010); C. Wright & A. Miller, *Federal Practice and Procedure* §§1102-1103 (2010).

61. 1 Casad & Richman, *Jurisdiction in Civil Actions* §3-2[2][b][ix] (3d ed. 1998); C. Wright & A. Miller, *Federal Practice and Procedure* §1069.4 (2010).

agency relationship between the parent and subsidiary.[62] Where such a relationship exists, applicable U.S. law will often permit service upon a foreign parent company by means of service on a local subsidiary.[63]

Individuals may sometimes retain their foreign nationality while acquiring U.S. residences. These individuals can occasionally be served by delivering process to their U.S. residence. Rule 4(e)(2) permits service upon individuals within the United States by "delivering copies [of the complaint and summons] at the individual's dwelling house or usual place of abode with some person of suitable age and discretion then residing therein." Determining whether a foreign defendant's residential property in the United States constitutes a "dwelling house" or "usual place of abode" can raise issues of interpretation.[64]

3.   No Service of U.S. Process Abroad by U.S. Consuls

Before examining what U.S. mechanisms are available for service outside U.S. territory, it is useful to note one conceivable avenue for service abroad that is *not* available. The U.S. Department of State and U.S. embassies virtually never serve process abroad on behalf of private litigants in U.S. courts. Indeed, current U.S. Consular Regulations explicitly prohibit foreign service officers from serving U.S. process abroad unless specifically authorized by the Department of State.[65] U.S. consular officers are precluded by these regulations from serving process even where local foreign law, or a bilateral U.S. treaty, would permit them to.[66]

4.   Service of U.S. Process Abroad Under Old Rule 4(i) of the Federal Rules of Civil Procedure

Until the mid-1990s, the service of process outside U.S. territory was governed in federal courts by Rule 4(i) of the Federal Rules of Civil Procedure. Old Rule 4(i) was added to the Federal Rules in 1963, as part of a comprehensive effort to improve federal law in international procedural matters.[67] The Rule was one of a series of proposals of the Commission on International Rules of Judicial Procedure, a body established by Congress

---

62. The standard that must be satisfied in order to establish an alter ego or agency relationship differs from state to state. *See supra* pp. 175-178, 190-191. In addition, the Due Process Clause imposes restrictions upon both the authority of a state to assert judicial jurisdiction based upon a parent-subsidiary or other corporate affiliation and the use of substituted service to provide the defendant with notice of an action. *See supra* pp. 185-186, 190 and *infra* pp. 946-948.

63. *E.g., Volkswagenwerk AG v. Schlunk,* 486 U.S. 694 (1988).

64. *See, e.g., National Dev. Co. v. Triad Holding Corp.,* 930 F.2d 253 (2d Cir. 1991) (considering whether a Saudi citizen's New York apartment, one of several residences around the world, was a "dwelling house or usual house of abode"). *See also* C. Wright & A. Miller, *Federal Practice and Procedure* §1096 (2010) ("Despite the length of time these words have been a part of federal practice, the judicial decisions do not make clear precisely what they mean and the facts of a particular case often prove to be crucial. Indeed, because of today's environment of global travel, job mobility, and multiple residences, the meaning of the phrase has been blurred even further.").

65. 22 C.F.R. §92.85 provides that "The service of process and legal papers is not normally a Foreign Service function. Except when directed by the Department of State, officers of the Foreign Service are prohibited from serving process or legal papers or appointing other persons to do so." State Department authority is generally granted only in exceptional cases involving governmental litigation.

66. The United States is party to various treaties that would permit U.S. consuls to serve process abroad. *E.g.,* Hague Service Convention, Article 8; *infra* p. 924. U.S. consular regulations do not permit use of the avenues permitted by treaty. *See infra* p. 924.

67. *See* Amram, *The Proposed International Convention on the Service of Documents Abroad,* 51 A.B.A.J. 650, 650-651 (1965); Burbank, *The Reluctant Partner: Making Procedural Law for International Civil Litigation,* 57 Law & Contemp. Probs. 103 (Summer 1994); Kaplan, *Amendments of the Federal Rules of Civil Procedure, 1961-1963 (I),* 77 Harv. L. Rev. 633, 635 (1964).

in 1958 at the President's recommendation.[68] Concluding that "existing means for serving judicial documents abroad [are] cumbersome or insufficient,"[69] Congress directed the new Commission to study international judicial assistance and recommend improvements.[70]

The Commission recommended what became old Rule 4(i) as part of a general effort to liberalize the rules governing the service of process in international cases.[71] Old Rule 4(i) did so by providing plaintiffs with five alternative mechanisms for service abroad, to use as they saw fit:[72] (i) service as provided by local law; (ii) service by personal delivery; (iii) service by letter rogatory; (iv) service by mail, return-receipt requested; and (v) service as directed by court order. These mechanisms supplemented other service mechanisms that might have been available under Rule 4. Rule 4(i) left the plaintiff entirely free to choose whichever mechanism or combination of mechanisms it desired, without imposing any requirements or preferences for particular means of service and without requiring compliance with foreign law.[73] The Rule was reasonably simple to administer and it provoked relatively little litigation (at least prior to enactment of the Hague Service Convention).

5. Service of U.S. Process Abroad on Foreign Defendants Under Rule 4(f) of the Current Federal Rules of Civil Procedure

Rule 4 of the Federal Rules of Civil Procedure was extensively revised in 1993.[74] Rule 4(i)'s provisions regarding service of process abroad were replaced by new Rule 4(f). As discussed in detail below, Rule 4(f) differs substantially from its pre-1993 counterpart, both in terms of its contents and its complexity.[75] New Rule 4(f) is reprinted in Appendix K.

a. Rule 4(f)(1): Service Abroad Pursuant to Hague Service Convention and Other "Internationally Agreed Means."

Rule 4(f)(1) begins by providing that service abroad may be made "by any internationally agreed means of service that is reasonably calculated to give notice, such as those authorized by the Hague Convention on the Service Abroad of Judicial and Extrajudicial Documents." Rule 4(f)(1) had no counterpart in old Rule 4(i), which contained no reference to the Hague Service Convention or other international agreements. The drafters of new Rule 4(f)(1) intended the provision to "call[] attention to the important effect of the Hague Convention and other treaties bearing on service of documents in foreign countries."[76]

Rule 4(f)(1) applies to "internationally agreed means of service." The provision specifically refers to the means authorized by the Hague Service Convention, which is reproduced in Appendix _____ and discussed below.[77] In addition, Rule 4(f)(1) refers more generally to internationally "agreed" means, while the Advisory Committee Notes explain

---

68. *See* Act of Sept. 2, 1958, 72 Stat. 1743, 1744 (1958); S. Rep. No. 2392, 85th Cong., 2d Sess. at 3 (1958), *reprinted in* 1958 U.S. Code Cong. & Admin. News at 5202; Jones, *Commission on International Rules of Judicial Procedure,* 8 Am. J. Comp. L. 341 (1959).

69. S. Rep. No. 85-2392 at 2 (1958).

70. *Id.* at 1-2, *reprinted in* 1958 U.S. Code, Cong. & Admin. News at 5201.

71. Kaplan, *Amendments of the Federal Rules of Civil Procedure, 1961-1963 (I),* 77 Harv. L. Rev. 633, 635 (1964).

72. Federal Rules of Civil Procedure, Rule 4(i), Advisory Committee Notes to the 1963 Amendments.

73. *See* G. Born & D. Westin, *International Civil Litigation in United States Courts* 163-168, 171-179 (2d ed. 1992).

74. *See supra* pp. 203-206, 817-818; Burbank, *The Reluctant Partner: Making Procedural Law for International Civil Litigation,* 57 Law & Contemp. Probs. 103 (Summer 1994).

75. *See infra* pp. 875-879, 898-906.

76. Federal Rules of Civil Procedure, Rule 4, 28 U.S.C.A., Advisory Committee Notes, at 115.

77. *See infra* pp. 909-952.

that the provision applies to "an applicable treaty" or "international agreement." This encompasses the Inter-American Convention on Letters Rogatory, but apparently no other international agreement.[78]

In certain cases, Rule 4(f) *requires* the use of "internationally agreed means" to effect service of process abroad. Rule 4(f)(2) provides that "*if* there is no internationally agreed means, or if an international agreement allows but does not specify other means" of service, then other means may be used.[79] The Advisory Committee Notes to Rule 4 elaborate that internationally agreed means under Rule 4(f)(1) "*shall be* employed if available and if the treaty so requires."[80]

Under Rule 4, it appears that a plaintiff is required to use an "internationally agreed means" of service pursuant to Rule 4(f)(1) if two conditions are satisfied. First, in order for service to be required pursuant to "internationally agreed means" under Rule 4(f)(1), the relevant international method must be "available." That is, there must be an international method, to which both the United States and the relevant foreign country are parties, and which encompasses the plaintiff's action. Second, the relevant international agreement must prescribe the "exclusive" means of service: the agreement must forbid service in ways not specified by its terms.

Where service abroad is concerned, at least some of the provisions of the Hague Service Convention satisfy these requirements. As described below, Article 1 of the Convention provides that the Convention "shall apply" in certain cases, and the Supreme Court has said that "compliance with the Convention is mandatory in all cases to which it applies."[81] Although the Convention allows the use of specified alternative service mechanisms, set forth in the Convention, it does not permit resort to other means not identified in the Convention.[82]

In contrast, federal courts are nearly unanimous that the Inter-American Convention on Letters Rogatory is not exclusive, but merely available as one possible option for service abroad.[83] In such cases, Rule 4(f) does not require that the Inter-American Convention be used (although Rule 4(f)(1) authorizes its use as an option). No other international agreement of the United States appears to provide an exclusive mechanism for service.

As discussed below, significant questions have arisen concerning the scope of Rule 4(f)(1) and the types of service that it authorizes.[84] In particular, it is unclear whether Rule 4(f)(1) authorizes various "alternative" means of service that are contemplated and permitted under the Hague Service Convention — such as service by ordinary

78. Unlike many nations, the United States has not concluded any bilateral service treaties; if it were to do so, Rule 4(f)(1) would appear to encompass them. It is not clear whether "internationally agreed means" include means set forth in contractual provisions in international commercial contracts relating to the service of process. Although a literal reading of Rule 4(f)(1) suggests it could extend to private agreements as well as treaties, there is no evidence in the Rule's legislative history that this was intended.

79. *See infra* pp. 917-924.

80. Federal Rules of Civil Procedure, Rule 4, 28 U.S.C.A., Advisory Committee Notes, at 115 (emphasis added).

81. *Volkswagenwerk AG v. Schlunk*, 486 U.S. 694, 705 (1988); Federal Rules of Civil Procedure, Rule 4, 28 U.S.C.A., Advisory Committee Notes, at 115 ("Use of the Convention procedures, when available, is mandatory if documents must be transmitted broad to effect service."); *infra* pp. 939-952.

82. *See infra* pp. 924-939.

83. *Kreimerman v. CASA VEERKAMP, SA de CV*, 22 F.3d 634, 644 (5th Cir. 1994); *Lyman Morse Boatbuilding Co., Inc. v. Lee*, 2011 WL 52509 (D. Me. 2011); *C & F Sys., LLC v. Limpimax, SA*, 2010 WL 65200 (W.D. Mich. 2010); *Paiz v. Castellanos*, 2006 WL 2578807 (S.D. Fla. 2006); *United States v. Padilla*, 2002 WL 471838 (E.D. Cal. 2002); *Hein v. Cuprum, SA de CV*, 136 F. Supp. 2d 63, 70 (N.D.N.Y. 2001); *Chemical Waste Management, Inc. v. Hernandez*, 1997 WL 47811 (S.D.N.Y. 1997); *Laino v. Cuprum SA de CV*, 663 N.Y.S.2d 275, 278 (App. Div. 1997); *Skanchy v. Calcados Ortope SA*, 952 P.2d 1071, 1075 (Utah 1998). *But see Tucker v. Interarms*, 186 F.R.D. 450 (N.D. Ohio 1999) (declining to decide whether resort to Inter-American Convention is mandatory but requiring plaintiff to obtain letter rogatory in compliance with Brazilian law as a matter of international comity).

84. *See infra* pp. 899-904, 937.

international mail or courier—or whether Rule 4(f)(1) only authorizes those means of service that are affirmatively and specifically provided by the Convention.[85]

b.   Rule 4(f)(2): Alternative Mechanisms of Service Abroad.   If no "internationally agreed means" of service is available (pursuant to Rule 4(f)(1)), or if such a means is nonexclusive, then Rule 4(f)(2) sets out additional alternatives which may be used. Unless these conditions are satisfied, Rule 4(f)(2) cannot be relied upon. Thus, there are several circumstances in which Rule 4(f)(2) will be applicable.

> First, Rule 4(f)(2) applies if service is to be made in a nation that is not a party to the Hague Service Convention. This is true of a majority of foreign states.
>
> Second, Rule 4(f)(2) is applicable if service is to be made in a nation that is a signatory to the Inter-American Convention or another *non-exclusive* service agreement. That is because such international agreements "allow[] but do[] not specify other means of service" than the mechanisms they establish.
>
> Third, Rule 4(f)(2) is applicable in cases which fall outside the scope of the Hague Service Convention.[86] In these cases, there is no applicable "internationally agreed means of service," and service under Rule 4(f)(2) is permitted.
>
> Fourth, Rule 4(f)(2) arguably permits types of service that are not "authorized" by the Hague Service Convention, but that are "allowed" by it (*e.g.*, mail service). This possibility is discussed below.[87]

Where it is applicable, Rule 4(f)(2) sets forth a number of options for service abroad. These are: (i) service in the manner prescribed by foreign law (Rule 4(f)(2)(A)); (ii) service as directed by a foreign authority in response to a letter rogatory (Rule 4(f)(2)(B)); (iii) service by personal delivery to an individual (but not a corporation), unless prohibited by foreign law (Rule 4(f)(2)(C)(i)); and (iv) service by return-receipt mail dispatched by the clerk of the court, unless prohibited by foreign law (Rule 4(f)(2)(C)(ii)). Rule 4(f)(2) imposes no express preferences or hierarchy among these various mechanisms.

All of the options contained in Rule 4(f)(2) expressly or impliedly require compliance with foreign law in the place where the service is effected. In this respect, Rule 4(f)(2) is a departure from former Rule 4(i) of the Federal Rules, which imposed no such requirement.[88] As discussed below, this requirement has provoked substantial uncertainty under Rule 4(f).[89]

c.   Rule 4(f)(3): Service as Directed by District Court.   Rule 4(f)(3) permits service as ordered by the district court. The rule expressly provides that the method of service may not be "prohibited by international agreement," but permits a court to order any method of service "not explicitly authorized by international agreement if not prohibited by the agreement."[90] The literal terms of Rule 4(f)(3) do not forbid a district court from ordering service abroad in violation of foreign law. The Advisory Committee Notes also fairly clearly indicate that courts may order service in violation of foreign law.[91] Rule

85. *See infra* pp. 899-904, 937. For a recent analysis of this question, *see Koss Corp. v. Pilot Air Freight Corp.*, 242 F.R.D. 514, 518 (E.D. Wis. 2007).

86. *See infra* pp. 914-915 for a discussion of the scope of the Hague Service Convention.

87. *See infra* pp. 899-904, 937.

88. *See infra* pp. 899-903.

89. *See infra* pp. 904-905

90. Federal Rules of Civil Procedure, Rule 4, 28 U.S.C.A., Advisory Committee Notes, at 115.

91. Federal Rules of Civil Procedure, Rule 4, 28 U.S.C.A., Advisory Committee Notes, at 115.

4(f)(3) does, however, appear to withhold the power to order service in violation of the Hague Service Convention (or other international agreements).[92]

6. Waivers of Service Under Rule 4(d).

Rule 4(d) of the Federal Rules sets forth "waiver of service" provisions, which were designed to reduce the expense and delay in service of process. The rule permits both domestic and foreign defendants to be asked to waive service. According to the Committee Notes: "The aims of the provision are to eliminate the costs of service of a summons on many parties and to foster cooperation among adversaries and counsel."[93]

Rule 4(d) allows a plaintiff to send a defendant by "first class mail or other reliable means" a complaint, a written request that the defendant waive formal service of process, and specified additional information.[94] Rule 4(d)(5) makes it clear that "waiving service of a summons does not waive any objection to personal jurisdiction or to venue."

This waiver of service procedure contains timing provisions intended to encourage defendants to waive service. Under Rule 4(d)(2), a defendant has "a reasonable time to return the waiver, which shall be at least 30 days from the date on which the request is sent, or 60 days from that date if the defendant is addressed outside any judicial district of the United States."[95] A defendant who "timely" returns a waiver is allowed 60 days from the date when the waiver request was sent to answer the complaint; defendants outside the United States are permitted 90 days from dispatch of the waiver request.[96] In contrast, a defendant that refuses to waive service has only 20 days from the date of service to answer the complaint.[97]

Revised Rule 4(d) creates a "duty to avoid unnecessary expenses of serving the summons."[98] Rule 4(d)(2) authorizes district courts to impose sanctions for a defendant's refusal to waive service. The rule provides: "If a defendant located within the United States fails, without good cause, to sign and return a waiver requested by a plaintiff located in the United States, the court must impose on the defendant . . . the expenses later incurred in making service." Under Rule 4(d)(2), legal fees are not part of recoverable costs except for "the reasonable expenses, including attorney's fees, of any motion required to collect those service expenses."[99]

Rule 4(d)'s waiver mechanism is available for use with foreign defendants. Waivers of service can be sought from any defendant that is subject to service under Rule 4(e), (f), or (h). This includes foreign individuals, corporations, and associations. Indeed, the Committee Notes encourage foreign defendants to agree to waive service.[100]

---

92. *See infra* pp. 900-903

93. 146 F.R.D. 561.

94. Federal Rules of Civil Procedure, Rule 4(d)(1). Rule 4(d)(1) provides: "An individual, corporation, or association that is subject to service under Rule 4(e), (f), or (h) has a duty to avoid unnecessary expenses of serving the summons. The plaintiff may notify such a defendant that an action has been commenced and request that the defendant waive service of a summons." It goes on to prescribe the contents of requests for waivers of service, which are reflected in Form 5, and also requires that the request for waiver, "be sent by first-class mail or other reliable means" and be accompanied by copies of the summons and the complaint. In addition, requests for waivers are to be accompanied by two copies of a waiver form (for example, as provided by Form 6), and a prepaid means for returning the form.

95. Federal Rules of Civil Procedure, Rule 4(d)(1)(F).

96. Federal Rules of Civil Procedure, Rules 4(d)(3), 12(a)(1)(A)(ii).

97. Federal Rules of Civil Procedure, Rule 12(a)(1)(A)(i).

98. Federal Rules of Civil Procedure, Rule 4(d)(1).

99. The Committee Notes allude to the same point. Federal Rules of Civil Procedure, Rule 4, 28 U.S.C.A., Advisory Committee Notes, at 115.

100. *See supra* p. 829.

Versions of Rule 4 that were proposed during the drafting process did not limit Rule 4(d)'s cost-shifting provision to "defendant located within the United States"; they authorized the imposition of service costs on foreign as well as domestic defendants.[101] Foreign states objected, ultimately leading to the inclusion of limits in Rule 4(d). Although the final text of Rule 4 does not explicitly state that service costs may not be imposed on foreign defendants and although *all* defendants have a duty to avoid unnecessary costs of service, Rule 4(d)(2) does not grant district courts discretion to impose service costs on a defendant outside of the United States.[102]

The cost-shifting provision applies only when *both* the plaintiff and defendant are located within the United States. Thus, foreign plaintiffs may not benefit from Rule 4(d)(2)'s cost-shifting rule. If a Swedish plaintiff unsuccessfully requests a Californian defendant to waive service, Rule 4(d)(2)'s cost-shifting provision does not apply. The Committee Notes do not explain this limitation, although it is presumably a "sauce for the gander" reaction to foreign objections to shifting service costs.[103]

7. Service of Process on Foreign Defendants in State Court Proceedings.

Local laws governing the service of process on a foreign defendant in a state court civil action vary from state to state. A number of states have adopted statutes or rules of court that are broadly similar to the pre-1993 version of Rule 4(i) of the Federal Rules of Civil Procedure.[104] Some states have adopted some version of §§2.01 and 2.02 of the (recently withdrawn) Uniform Interstate and International Procedure Act, reproduced in Appendix D.[105] Many other states require that service of process outside the jurisdiction be made "in the same manner as service is made within the state."[106]

In each case, applicable state law provides a variety of options for service abroad, without imposing express requirements or preferences for any particular mechanism. These options generally include service by personal delivery, service by registered mail, service by letter rogatory, service as permitted by foreign law, and service pursuant to court order.[107]

There are two significant exceptions to the general rule that the service of process in state courts is governed by state law. First, service on foreign states or foreign state entities in both federal and state courts is subject to the Foreign Sovereign Immunities Act ("FSIA").[108] Second, service in state court proceedings is subject to the Hague Service Convention if service abroad on a defendant located in another signatory state is required.[109] If either the FSIA or the Hague Service Convention is applicable, service of process must be made in accordance with its terms, even in state court. Service pursuant to inconsistent state law rules is preempted and invalid.[110]

---

101. Born & Vollmer, *The Effect of the Revised Federal Rules of Civil Procedure on Personal Jurisdiction, Service and Discovery in International Cases,* 150 F.R.D. 221, 231-235 (1993).
102. Born & Vollmer, *The Effect of the Revised Federal Rules of Civil Procedure on Personal Jurisdiction, Service and Discovery in International Cases,* 150 F.R.D. 221, 231-233 (1993).
103. The Committee Notes also do not discuss the validity of this provision under either U.S. Friendship, Commerce and Navigation treaties or the Equal Protection Clause.
104. 1 Casad & Richman, *Jurisdiction in Civil Actions* §4-6 (3d ed. 1998 & Supp. 2010).
105. *E.g.,* Ark. Code. §16-4-101; 42 Pa. Cons. St. §5323.
106. *E.g.,* N.Y.C.P.L.R. §313; Conn. G.S. §52-57a; Ga. Code §9-10-94; Fla. Stat. §48.194.
107. For a discussion of old Rule 4(i), *see* G. Born & D. Westin, *International Civil Litigation in United States Courts* 161-166 (2d ed. 1992).
108. *See infra* pp. 953-961.
109. *See infra* pp. 917-924.
110. *See infra* pp. 920-921.

8. Due Process Clause: Reasonable Notice Requirements for Service.

Service of process in both U.S. federal and state courts must comply with the Due Process Clause of the Fifth or Fourteenth Amendments to the U.S. Constitution, as well as with the service requirements imposed by the Federal Rules of Civil Procedure (or their state counterparts). The Due Process Clause requires that service of process be reasonably likely to provide the defendant with notice of the proceedings against it. Specifically, due process demands "notice reasonably calculated under all the circumstances, to apprise interested parties of the pendency of the action and to afford them an opportunity to present their objections. . . . The notice must be of such nature as reasonably to convey the required information."[111]

Personal service upon the defendant will virtually always satisfy the Due Process Clause's "reasonable notice" requirement.[112] Similarly, service by a method of mail requiring some form of signed return receipt will generally satisfy the Due Process Clause.[113]

As international litigation can involve defendants whose whereabouts are difficult to ascertain, parties sometimes resort to less traditional methods of effective service. Along these lines, some courts have approved service of process via email.[114] Likewise, service by publication has become an important method of alternative service in international litigation, although it will ordinarily be permitted only in the case of persons whose location is unknown and cannot reasonably be ascertained.[115]

C. Service of Process in Foreign Legal Systems

1. Rules Governing Service of Process in Foreign Courts

The U.S. approach to the service of process in civil actions differs from that in many foreign nations.[116] In many civil law jurisdictions, the service of process does not provide

---

111. *Mullane v. Central Hanover Bank & Trust Co.*, 339 U.S. 306, 314 (1950). *See also SEC v. Tome*, 833 F.2d 1086 (2d Cir. 1987); *International Controls Corp. v. Vesco*, 593 F.2d 166 (2d Cir. 1979).

112. *Milliken v. Meyer,* 311 U.S. 457 (1940); Federal Rules of Civil Procedure, Rule 4(i)(1)(C), Advisory Committee Note.

113. *Hess v. Pawloski*, 274 U.S. 352 (1927).

114. *E.g., Rio Properties Inc. v. Rio Int'l Interlink*, 284 F.3d 1007, 1016-1017 (9th Cir. 2002); *Craigslist, Inc. v. Meyer*, 2010 WL 2975938 (N.D. Cal. 2010); *Chanel, Inc. v. Zhixian*, 2010 WL 1740695 (S.D. Fla. 2010); *MacLean-Fogg Co. v. Ningbo Fastlink Equip. Co.*, 2008 WL 5100414 (N.D. Ill. 2008); *Phillip Morris USA Inc. v. Veles, Ltd*, 2007 WL 725412 (S.D.N.Y. 2007); *Popular Enters., LLC v. Webcom Media Group, Inc.*, 225 F.R.D. 560 (E.D. Tenn. 2004); *Ryan v. Brunswick Corp.*, 2002 WL 1628933, at *2 (W.D.N.Y. 2002); *Hollow v. Hollow*, 747 N.Y.S.2d 704 (Sup. Ct. 2002); *Greebel v. FTP Software, Inc.*, 939 F. Supp. 57 (D. Mass. 1996).

115. *Mullane v. Central Hanover Bank & Trust Co.*, 339 U.S. 306, 314-315 (1950); *Mwani v. bin Laden*, 417 F.3d 1, 8 (D.C. Cir. 2005); *Moreland v. Dorsey Thornton & Assocs. LLC*, 2010 WL 5463333 (E.D. Wis. 2010); *M & T Bank Corp. v. McGrath*, 2010 WL 3768045 (M.D. Fla. 2010); *Malone v. Highway Star Logistics, Inc.*, 2009 WL 2139857 (D. Colo. 2009); *United States v. Shehyn*, 2008 WL 6150322 (S.D.N.Y. 2008); *BP Prods. North Am., Inc. v. Dagra*, 236 F.R.D. 270 (E.D. Va. 2006); C. Wright & A. Miller, *Federal Practice and Procedure* §1074 (2010). For decisions denying motions for orders authorizing service by publication, *see Gascoigne v. Gascoigne*, 2010 WL 1737581 (D. Utah 2010); *Accu-Tech Corp. v. Network Technologies Group, Inc.*, 2005 WL 1459543, at *2 (E.D. Pa. 2005); *Keefe v. Arthur*, 2003 WL 23109616, at *2 (W.D. Wis. 2003).

116. For descriptions of service of process rules in foreign states, *see* Jones, *International Judicial Assistance: Procedural Chaos and A Program for Reform*, 62 Yale L.J. 515 (1953); Smit, *International Aspects of Federal Civil Procedure*, 61 Colum. L. Rev. 1031 (1961); Miller, *International Cooperation in Litigation Between the United States and Switzerland: Unilateral Procedural Accommodation in a Test Tube*, 49 Minn. L. Rev. 1069 (1965); Schima & Hoyer, *Central European Countries*, Kohl, *Romanist Legal Systems*, and Wengerek, *Socialist Countries*, XVI International Encyclopedia of Comparative Law Ch. 6 (M. Cappelletti ed., 1984) ["Cappelletti"]; Ross *et al.*, *Service of Process in Austria, England, Italy and West Germany*, 9 Int'l Law. 689 (1975); Raley, *A Comparative Analysis: Notice*

an independent basis for judicial jurisdiction. "Normally, regardless of the character of the action, service has a single function — that of providing notice."[117]

Nevertheless, particularly in civil law jurisdictions, the service of process is regarded as a "judicial" or "public" act, that may not be performed by private persons:

> Civil law states generally regard service of judicial process as a sovereign act that may be performed in their territory only by the state's own officials and in accordance with its own law.[118]

In many civil law states, service is effected by an official of the local court, or by specially designated officials subject to the court's control.[119] In France, for example, service is sometimes made by a "*huissier*" — a government official responsible for delivering process to the defendant.[120] In other states, service is effected by mail, dispatched by local court officials, return receipt requested.[121]

2. Restrictions on Service of Foreign Process Within National Territory

Many foreign nations, particularly civil law states, object to the service of process from foreign courts within national territory on local nationals, except where local officials effect the service. Service in a foreign country in violation of that country's law may jeopardize later attempts to enforce a U.S. judgment in that country. Moreover, as described below, local law in some countries makes it a criminal offense to serve or assist in serving foreign process on national territory.

For example, Switzerland has long adhered to the position that Swiss government authorities must serve judicial documents on persons residing in Switzerland, pursuant to properly executed foreign letters rogatory.[122] The Swiss Penal Code forbids the service of foreign process within Switzerland except through Swiss governmental channels.[123]

Requirements in Germany, Japan, Spain, the United Kingdom and the United States, 10 Ariz. J. Int'l & Comp. L. 301 (1993); Kreindler, *Transnational Litigation: A Practitioner's Guide* (rev. ed. 2006).

117. Ginsburg, *The Competent Court in Private International Law: Some Observations on Current Views in the United States,* 20 Rutgers L. Rev. 89, 90 (1965). *See* Dellapenna, *Civil Remedies for International Terrorism,* 12 DePaul Bus. L.J. 169, 225 (1999/2000); Grauper, *Some Recent Aspects of the Recognition and Enforcement of Foreign Judgments in Western Europe,* 12 Int'l & Comp. L.Q. 367, 377 (1963); Kaplan *et al., Phases of German Civil Procedure (I),* 71 Harv. L. Rev. 1193, 1203-1205 (1958); Schlosser, *Lectures on Civil-Law Litigation Systems and American Cooperation with Those Systems,* 45 U. Kan. L. Rev. 9, 19 (1996).

118. *Restatement (Third) Foreign Relations Law* §471, comment b (1987). *See also* Miller, *International Cooperation in Litigation Between the United States and Switzerland: Unilateral Procedural Accommodation in a Test Tube,* 49 Minn. L. Rev. 1069, 1132 (1965); Jones, *International Judicial Assistance: Procedural Chaos and a Program for Reform,* 62 Yale L.J. 515, 537 (1953).

119. *See* Kohl, *Romanist Legal Systems* in XVI Cappelletti Ch. 6, at 72 §92.

120. *See* Kohl, *Romanist Legal Systems* in XVI Cappelletti at Ch. 6, at 72 §92 (describing "huissier" in France); Schlosser, *Lectures on Civil-Law Litigation Systems and American Cooperation with Those Systems,* 45 U. Kan. L. Rev. 9, 19 (1996) (same); Emerson, *The French Huissier as a Model for U.S. Civil Procedure Reform,* 43 U. Mich. J.L. Reform 1043 (2010) (same); U.S. Dep't of State Circular, Judicial Assistance: France, *available at* http://travel.state.gov/law/judicial/judicial_647.html.

121. Miller, *International Cooperation in Litigation Between the United States and Switzerland: Unilateral Procedural Accommodation in a Test Tube,* 49 Minn. L. Rev. 1069, 1083 (1965); T. Hattori & D. Henderson, *Civil Procedure in Japan* §7.01[3] (1985). *See, e.g.,* Retsplejeloven Ch. 17 (Denmark's Administration of Justice Act providing for service via return-receipt mail from court officials). For a country-by-country survey of service of process rules, *see* Kreindler, *Transnational Litigation: A Practitioner's Guide* (rev. ed. 2006).

122. U.S. Department of State, Judicial Assistance: Switzerland, *available at* http://travel.state.gov/law/judicial/judicial_4303.html.

123. Swiss Penal Code, Article 271; *infra* p. 883.

The Swiss government has frequently protested to the United States[124] and other states[125] over the service of foreign process within Switzerland by either private or governmental litigants. These protests have declared that the "service of [judicial] documents by mail constitutes an infringement of Swiss sovereign powers."[126] France, Germany, and other countries have similar objections to the unauthorized service of foreign process within their territory.[127]

Several reasons are advanced for foreign objections to the service of U.S. process within their territory. Such objections rest in part on territorial conceptions of national sovereignty and on concerns about violations of local public policy.[128] In addition, foreign states may seek to ensure that service upon their nationals satisfies local requirements concerning fair notice — such as by requiring translations or summaries. Moreover, foreign states may wish to regulate the manner in which nationals are subjected to the compulsion that attaches to foreign service of process.[129] Finally, there may be a desire to insulate local nationals from liability in foreign proceedings, without regard to principle.[130]

3. Selected Materials on Foreign Service Restrictions and Letters Rogatory

Excerpted below are materials illustrating foreign restrictions on the service of foreign process within national territory and the customary means for addressing such

124. *See* 56 Am. J. Int'l L. 794 (1962) (aide-memoire); Comment, *Service of United States Process in Russian Under Rule 4(f) of the Federal Rules of Civil Procedure,* 10 Pac. Rim L. & Pol'y J. 691, 710 (2001) (describing Russian protests to service by international mail); 1 Ristau, *International Judicial Assistance* §3-1-9 at 92-93 (rev. ed. 2000) (reproducing memorandum from General Counsel of Administrative Office of U.S. Courts describing various countries' diplomatic protests to service by mail and instructing United States District Court clerks to effect future service in those countries by means of letters rogatory); *In re Ski Train Fire in Kaprun, Austria on November 11, 2000,* 2003 WL 1807148, at *7 (S.D.N.Y. 2003) (citing Austrian note verbale); Brief of Republic of Austria as Amicus Curiae in *Prewitt Enters., Inc. v. OPEC,* 2003 WL 23472002, at *2 & n.2 (11th Cir. 2003) (citing Austrian protest to service of process).

125. 33 Annuaire Suisse de Droit International 203-205 (1977) (protest to European Communities Commission for mailing notification to Swiss company of commencement of legal proceedings).

126. *Id.*

127. For case law citing protests, *see In re Ski Train Fire in Kaprun, Austria on November 11, 2000,* 2003 WL 1807148, at *7 (S.D.N.Y. 2003) (citing Austrian note verbale); Brief of Republic of Austria as *Amicus Curiae* in *Prewitt Enters., Inc. v. OPEC,* 2003 WL 23472002, at *2 & n.2 (11th Cir. 2003) (citing Austrian protest to service of process); *Federal Trade Commission v. Compagnie de Saint-Gobain-Pont-a-Mousson,* 636 F.2d 1300, 1306 n.18 (D.C. Cir. 1980) (quoting French diplomatic note); Ettinger, *Service of Process in Austria,* 9 Int'l Law. 693, 694 (1975) (Austria).

For commentary and other secondary material discussing protests, *see* Comment, *Service of United States Process in Russia Under Rule 4(f) of the Federal Rules of Civil Procedure,* 10 Pac. Rim L. & Pol'y J. 691, 710 (2001) (describing Russian protests to service by international mail); Memo of L. Ralph Meacham, Director, Administrative Office of United States Courts, to Clerks of United States District Courts (Nov. 7, 2000) (Russia); Instructions of Administrative Office of U.S. Courts Concerning Mail Service Abroad, Memorandum to All United States District Court Clerks (November 6, 1980) *reprinted in* 1 Bruno A. Ristau, *International Judicial Assistance (Civil and Commercial),* §3-1-9 at 92-93 (rev. ed. 2000) (describing protests from Czechoslovakia, Russia, and Switzerland); Heidenberg, *Service of Process and the Gathering of Information Relative to a Law Suit Brought in West Germany,* 9 Int'l Law. 725, 728-729 (1975) (Germany); Gori-Monanelli & Botwinik, *International Judicial Assistance — Italy,* 9 Int'l Law. 717, 718 (1975) (Italy); Inter-American Juridical Committee, *Report on Uniformity of Legislation on International Cooperation in Judicial Procedures* 20 (1952); *Contemporary Practice of the United States Relating to International Law,* 56 Am. J. Int'l L. 793, 794 (1962) (Swiss diplomatic protest regarding service within Switzerland without use of letters rogatory); Committee on Federal Courts, N.Y. State Bar Ass'n, *Service of Process Abroad: A Nuts and Bolts Guide,* 122 F.R.D. 63, 67 n.22 (1989) (listing German diplomatic protests)

128. Miller, *International Cooperation in Litigation Between the United States and Switzerland: Unilateral Procedural Accommodation in a Test Tube,* 49 Minn. L. Rev. 1069, 1076-1077 (1965). *See generally* C. Wright & A. Miller, *Federal Practice and Procedure* §1133 (2010).

129. Miller, *International Cooperation in Litigation Between the United States and Switzerland: Unilateral Procedural Accommodation in a Test Tube,* 49 Minn. L. Rev. 1069, 1076-1077 (1965).

130. Smit, *International Co-operation in Civil Litigation: Some Observations on the Roles of International Law and Reciprocity,* 9 Netherlands Int'l L. Rev. 137 (1962).

restrictions, being service by letter rogatory. First, consider Article 271 of the Swiss Penal Code, forbidding the performance on Swiss territory of certain governmental or administrative acts. Also excerpted below are two diplomatic notes, from the Republic of France and the Federal Republic of Germany, protesting the service of U.S. process on local territory without the intervention of local government authorities. Finally, consider the U.S. State Department's Circular on the Preparation of Letters Rogatory, whose discussion of the use of letters rogatory to serve process abroad is excerpted in Appendix CC.

SWISS PENAL CODE
Article 271

271. Whoever, without authorization, executes acts on Swiss territory which are attributed to an administrative or government authority, on behalf of a foreign state, and whoever executes such acts on behalf of a foreign state, and whoever executes such acts on behalf of a foreign person or another foreign organization, and whoever encourages or otherwise participates in such acts, will be punished with prison, and in severe cases with penitentiary.

DIPLOMATIC NOTE OF JANUARY 10, 1980 FROM THE EMBASSY OF FRANCE TO THE U.S. DEPARTMENT OF STATE
636 F.2d 1300, 1306 n.18 (D.C. Cir. 1980)

The Embassy of France informs the Department of State that the transmittal by the [Federal Trade Commission] of a subpoena directly by mail to a French company (in this case Saint-Gobain Pont-a-Mousson) is inconsistent with the general principles of international law and constitutes a failure to recognize French sovereignty. Furthermore, the response to certain of the requests from the FTC could subject the directors of Saint-Gobain Pont-a-Mousson to civil and criminal liability and therefore expose them to judicial proceedings in France. Consequently, the Embassy of France would be grateful if the Department of State would make this position known to the various American authorities concerned by informing them that the French Government wishes such steps both in this matter and in any others which may subsequently arise, to be taken solely through diplomatic channels.

DIPLOMATIC NOTE DATED SEPTEMBER 27, 1979 FROM THE EMBASSY OF THE FEDERAL REPUBLIC OF GERMANY TO THE U.S. DEPARTMENT OF STATE

The Embassy of the Federal Republic of Germany presents its compliments to the Department of State and, referring to three recent cases in which German addressees were served judicial documents from the United States by mail, has the honor to inform the Department of State of the German view concerning service by mail of such documents by foreign countries:

Under German legal interpretation, German sovereignty is violated in cases where foreign judicial documents are served directly by mail within the Federal Republic of Germany. By such direct service, an act of sovereignty is conducted without any control by German authorities on the territory of the Federal Republic of Germany. This is not admissible under German laws. Under these laws, the German authorities must be in a position to examine whether the foreign request for service is in compliance with the legal provisions established for this purpose and whether it is in compliance with the ordre public of the Federal Republic of Germany. This is the reason why the Federal Republic of Germany has, when depositing the instrument of ratification to The Hague Convention of November 15, 1965 [*i.e.*, the Hague Service Convention], concerning the service abroad of judicial and extrajudicial documents in civil or commercial matters objected in accordance with Article 21(2)(a) of the Convention to the application of the channels of transmission as stipulated in Article 10 of the Convention. . . . Since the Hague [Service Convention] has gone into effect between the United States of America and the Federal Republic of Germany on June 26, 1979, the Federal Government would appreciate it if service of documents originating from American judicial proceedings to persons within the Federal Republic of Germany would be conducted in compliance with this convention only and if the courts and attorneys involved could be informed accordingly.

UNITED STATES CODE
28 U.S.C. §§1696 & 1781 [excerpted in Appendix A]

U.S. DEPARTMENT OF STATE, CIRCULAR ON PREPARATION OF LETTERS ROGATORY
http://travel.state.gov/law/judicial/judicial_683.html [excerpted in Appendix CC]

Notes on Article 271, Diplomatic Notes, and Letters Rogatory

1. ***Foreign restrictions on service of U.S. process within local territory.*** What does Article 271 provide? Swiss courts have interpreted it to forbid the service of U.S. (and other) process in Switzerland. A leading Swiss judicial decision under Article 271 involved an investigation by German tax authorities of the tax affairs of Germans who owned shares in a Swiss company. The German tax authorities dispatched an accountant (apparently a private practitioner, not a governmental employee) to Switzerland to examine the books and records of the company. After he had done so, he was reported to Swiss police, and arrested. The Swiss Supreme Court held that the accountant had violated Article 271, and that it was irrelevant that he was not shown to be a foreign government official, because he had acted for German government officials. *Kaempfer v. Staatsanwaltschaft Zuerich, Bundesgericht,* March 6, 1939, 65(I), S.B.G. 39.

2. ***Rationale for foreign restrictions on service of U.S. process within local territory.*** What is the rationale of foreign restrictions on service? Note that the French protest relates to the service of a U.S. administrative agency's subpoena, while the German protest relates more broadly to any service of judicial documents (including both civil complaints and subpoenas). What is the rationale underlying Article 271 and French and German protests? Consider:

> The need to examine the contents of foreign documents is . . . defended as an integral element of Swiss sovereignty and essential to the national policies of neutrality and protection of commercial and industrial secrets. The theory appears to be that if requests for service were not channelled through and scrutinized by appropriate Swiss officials, there would be no effective way to insure that the service of the foreign documents was not contrary to Swiss public policy. Miller, *International Cooperation in Litigation Between the United States and*

Switzerland: Unilateral Procedural Accommodation in a Test Tube, 49 Minn. L. Rev. 1069, 1076-1077 (1965).

Is this a legitimate basis for a protest? Compare the reasons stated in the German Note. How are Swiss or German "public policy" really impaired when a piece of paper is mailed to local residents, informing them that legal proceedings have been commenced abroad? What other reasons might a nation have for objecting to service of foreign process within its borders? Are such objections merely pretexts for protecting local companies from liability to foreign claimants, by erecting time-consuming procedural obstacles to foreign legal proceedings? Suppose agents of a foreign state, with a fundamentalist religious regime, were dispatched to serve summonses or judgments of foreign religious tribunals on U.S. citizens. Would there then be a legitimate reason for objection?

3. *Criticism of foreign restrictions on the service of U.S. process within local territory.* Some observers have criticized foreign restrictions on the service of U.S. process within local territory:

> The absence of direct prohibitions under international law of service by . . . private persons is highly desirable since it avoids the creation of unnecessary and improper obstacles to the smooth conduct of litigation with international aspects. . . . Different countries take different views as to how service is to be made . . . and international relations and justice are best served by letting each country conduct its litigation in the way it sees fit. Clearly, a mere local preference for domestic procedures cannot reasonably justify a refusal to let foreign litigants resort to procedures acceptable to foreign courts. It is difficult to ascertain how the domestic order can be disturbed by service by . . . a private person; indeed, even when service is made by . . . an official of the foreign government, the advantage of facilitating litigation with international aspects would ordinarily seem to outweigh by far the disadvantage of having a foreign official act within domestic borders. In a true family of nations, small favors should be readily granted for the benefit of the whole. Smit, *International Co-operation in Civil Litigation: Some Observations on the Roles of International Law and Reciprocity,* 9 Netherlands Int'l L. Rev. 137 (1962).

Is this correct? Are Switzerland, France, and Germany just parochially protectionist in insisting that local officials be involved in serving foreign process on local citizens?

Looked at realistically, why is service of process such a big deal? Countless more important communications — billion dollar or Euro contracts, offers, termination notices, exercises of options — are sent across national borders every day. Massive arbitrations are commenced, with the notice or request for arbitration being "served" by courier or post. Why do countries still treat notice of a foreign litigation with medieval ritualism? Should they? If they do, should U.S. courts humor them? At what cost?

4. *International law restrictions on the service of U.S. process abroad.* Both the French and German diplomatic notes take the position that the service of U.S. process within their territory violates international law. Both notes take this position without reference to specific local legislation — equivalent to Article 271 of the Swiss Penal Code. They rely merely on principles of national sovereignty and international law. Section 471(1) of the *Restatement (Third) Foreign Relations Law* (1987) supports the view that international law forbids one state from effecting service within another state's territory without consent, even absent local legislation restricting foreign service:

> Under international law, a state may determine the conditions for service of process in its territory in aid of litigation in another state, but the state where the litigation is pending may determine the effect of such service.

See id. at 526 ("A state may not conduct official activities in the territory of another state without that state's consent, express or implied. That principle is generally applied as well to the service of judicial documents."). Is the service of U.S. process on a person within a foreign state really the performance of governmental acts within that state? Suppose that the service is effected by a private process-server? By ordinary mail?

5. *Doubts regarding international law restrictions on service of process abroad.* Not all authorities have agreed that international law forbids the service of process abroad without the consent of the destination state:

> In the absence of a treaty, international law does not oblige any country to render assistance in the making of service . . . in connection with litigation conducted abroad. . . . Furthermore, since each country is sovereign within its own territory, it may, without violating international law, enact laws forbidding or regulating the making of service . . . within its territory. However, when internal laws are lacking, such acts are prohibited only if forbidden by international law. When service is made in one country by an official, such as a consul, of another country, the act of the official may be construed as the act of the foreign country. Since under international law one country may forbid another from acting within its borders, it might be argued that such service may be forbidden directly under international law even in the absence of domestic proscriptive legislation. . . . However, this type of argumentation would seem wholly inappropriate when the service is made by . . . a private person. . . . There appears to be no authoritative source of international law specifically supporting the claim that the making of service by, . . . a private person may be forbidden in the absence of prohibitions validly created by domestic law. Nor can the conduct of the private person who makes service . . . possibly qualify as official conduct that may validly be forbidden by direct reference to rules of international law. The making of service by . . . private persons do not in any way involve the exercise of judicial or other official powers. . . . Smit, *International Co-operation in Civil Litigation: Some Observations on the Roles of International Law and Reciprocity,* 9 Netherlands Int'l L. Rev. 137 (1962).

Are these views persuasive? What is Professor Smit's position if local law expressly forbids foreign service? What is his position if local law is silent as to the permissibility of foreign service? Is it persuasive to say that only "internal law" may forbid foreign service? What if German executive officers take the position that, as a matter of German sovereignty and public policy, foreign service must be served through German governmental channels? Does international law require Germany to assert its sovereignty solely through statutory command? If Germany is silent regarding foreign service, is that consent to such service?

Note Professor Smit's assertion that service on foreign territory by a "private" party does not necessarily violate international law, even if service by a government official would. Why exactly is it, in Professor Smit's view, that service by a private party is not a governmental act, not implicating international law? Compare this view with that expressed in the German diplomatic note and in the *Third Restatement.* Which is more persuasive?

6. *Relevance under international law of U.S. nationality of recipients of U.S. process served abroad.* When U.S. process is served abroad, is the nationality of the person on whom the U.S. process is served relevant, for purposes of international law or otherwise? Note that Article 271 of the Swiss Penal Code does not distinguish between Swiss nationals and others. Reread *Blackmer v. United States,* excerpted above at pp. 109-113. In *Blackmer,* a U.S. administrative subpoena was served by a U.S. consul upon a U.S. national residing in France, pursuant to what is now 28 U.S.C. §1783. The Court rejected the suggestion that service could not be effected upon a U.S. national abroad. It reasoned: "The mere giving of such a notice to the citizen in the foreign country of the requirement of his government that he shall return is in no sense an invasion of any right of the foreign government." Is that persuasive? Why is not the delivery to the U.S. national, on foreign territory, of governmental summons, by a U.S. government official, "an invasion of [the] right of the foreign government" to control judicial acts on its own territory? Assuming that the foreign government does not consent, isn't the Supreme Court's statement flatly wrong?

Consider the following excerpt from *SEC v. Briggs*, 234 F. Supp. 618 (N.D. Ohio 1964), where the U.S. Securities and Exchange Commission had served process, allegedly in violation of Canadian law, upon a U.S. citizen residing in Canada:

> We seriously doubt that the defendant, admittedly a citizen of the United States, has standing to complain of an affront to a sovereign which is foreign to her. We need not reach that issue, however, because we perceive of no such invasion of Canada's sovereignty. In *Blackmer v. United States*, the Supreme Court stated: "The mere giving of such a notice to the citizen in the foreign country of the requirement of his government that he shall return is in no sense an invasion of any right of the foreign government." Therefore, we find no principle of comity between nations which precludes this Court from the exercise of jurisdiction over Mrs. Briggs.

What if Mrs. Briggs had been a Canadian? A French national? *Cf.* Hague Service Convention, Art. 8 (permitting receiving state to object to service by consular agents, except with respect to service on nationals of receiving state). What if Canada had protested service of U.S. process in Canada?

7. *Relevance under foreign laws of U.S. nationality of recipients of U.S. process served abroad.* Some states that generally forbid direct service of foreign process within their territory make an exception for service of process upon nationals of the state from which the process emanates. In Switzerland, for example, consular officials may serve process on their nationals, without the intervention of Swiss officials, provided that they do not use "compulsion." Miller, *International Cooperation in Litigation Between the United States and Switzerland: Unilateral Procedural Accommodation in a Test Tube*, 49 Minn. L. Rev. 1069, 1075-1076 (1965). Similarly, as discussed below, Article 8 of the Hague Service Convention permits service upon the nationals of the state making service within the territory of other signatory states. Few states have objected to such service. *See infra* pp. 924-925. Compare this practice to nationality as a basis for judicial and legislative jurisdiction. Are the results in *Blackmer* and *Briggs* explicable on the basis that, where service abroad is made on *U.S.* nationals, the foreign state's consent can be inferred in the absence of an express protest? Does State A have standing to protest unlawful service of State C's process on State B's national while located in State A?

8. *Customary reliance on letters rogatory for service abroad.* Historically, letters rogatory were used to effect service of process abroad. *See* Smit, *International Litigation Under the United States Code*, 65 Colum. L. Rev. 1015, 1019 (1965). Why might letters rogatory have been historically used? Suppose that there had been reliable transportation and telecommunication services in the eighteenth century.

9. *Procedures required for letters rogatory.* Read the State Department Circular's description of the procedures—including the authentication, transmission procedures, fees, and translation—for letters rogatory. Consider how much effort this takes. Try and estimate the costs entailed in such service. What is the object of the service? Is it anything more than providing a party with a copy of the complaint and summons, so that he or she can supply it to his or her counsel? How hard can that be?

10. *Time required for letters rogatory.* Assuming everything goes smoothly, how long will it take for service of process to be effected through a letter rogatory? Note what the State

Department estimates in its Circular. How long would it take to send an email, with PDF attachments of the relevant documents? How long would it take to send a courier? Isn't it absurd that the law would even imagine requiring — much less require — parties to spend six to twelve months waiting for something that could take a couple minutes? What legitimate interests can this possibly serve? How is Swiss or French sovereignty offended by sending a courier package, email, or fax to someone physically present in Switzerland or France?

D.   A Closer Look at Service of U.S. Process Abroad: Selected Issues

1.   Service of U.S. Process Abroad Under New Rule 4(f) and Other Legislative Grants Where Foreign Law Restricts U.S. Service

U.S. courts and legislative bodies have not infrequently been obliged to respond to foreign restrictions on the extraterritorial service of U.S. process like those described above. In particular, U.S. courts and rulemakers have been required to consider whether and when the violation of foreign restrictions should invalidate U.S. service for purposes of U.S. law. U.S. reactions to this question have varied over time, culminating in the current version of the Federal Rule of Civil Procedure 4(f).

a.   Congress May Authorize Service Abroad in Violation of International Law.   A number of lower courts have held that, if Congress specifically authorizes service abroad in violation of foreign law, then that is conclusive for purposes of U.S. law: the fact that the congressionally prescribed mechanism violates foreign law does not affect the mechanism's validity for U.S. purposes. Thus, in *Commodity Futures Trading Commission v. Nahas*,[131] excerpted below, the Court starts from the premise that Congress may authorize service abroad in violation of both foreign and international law: "Federal courts must give effect to a valid, unambiguous congressional mandate, even if such effect would conflict with another nation's laws or violate international law."[132] Similarly, in *Rio Properties, Inc. v. Rio International Interlink*,[133] also excerpted below, the Court held that process could be served abroad in violation of foreign law under Rule 4(f)(3) of the Federal Rules. The decision in *Rio* followed well-settled precedent under former Rule 4(i) of the pre-1993 Federal Rules.[134]

b.   Presumption That Congress Does Not Intend to Authorize Service Abroad in Violation of International Law.   Although Congress has the power to violate international law, this does not dispose of the further question whether U.S. service in violation of foreign or international law has in fact been authorized by Congress. In answering this question, U.S. courts have invoked the familiar presumption that Congress would not choose to violate international law, particularly where the method of service may be particularly intrusive.[135] Thus, in *CFTC v. Nahas*, the D.C. Circuit held that service in Brazil of a subpoena, in violation of Brazilian law, had not been authorized under the

---

131. 738 F.2d 487 (D.C. Cir. 1984).
132. 738 F.2d at 495.
133. 284 F.3d 1007 (9th Cir. 2002).
134. For example, in *Umbenhauer v. Woog*, 969 F.2d 25 (3d Cir. 1992), a decision under old Rule 4 of the Federal Rules of Civil Procedure, the court held that service of a complaint and summons in Switzerland, in violation of Swiss law, was valid for purposes of the old Federal Rules. *See also infra* pp. 898-901.
135. *See supra* pp. 18, 646-651, 664-671 for a discussion of this presumption.

Commodities Future Trading Act.[136] In the absence of an express legislative mandate, the court declined to permit service abroad in violation of international law: "we are unwilling to infer enforcement jurisdiction absent a clearer indication of congressional intent."[137]

c.   Rule 4(f)'s Provisions for Service Abroad in Violation of Foreign Law.   Until 1993, service of federal court process outside the United States was governed by old Rule 4(i) of the Federal Rules of Civil Procedure.[138] Old Rule 4(i) was generally held to permit service abroad even if it violated foreign law.[139] The framers of Rule 4(i) were aware that this might jeopardize the enforcement of resulting U.S. judgments abroad, but thought it best to leave such risks to plaintiff's counsel's assessment: "if enforcement is to be sought in the country of service, the foreign law should be examined before a choice is made among the methods of service allowed by subdivision (i)."[140]

As noted above, since 1993, the revised Rule 4(f) has provided the principal mechanism for service of process abroad in federal civil actions. Rule 4(f) differs from earlier versions of the Federal Rules by *generally* requiring that service of U.S. process abroad comply with foreign law;[141] at the same time, as the *Rio* decision illustrates, service may nonetheless be effected abroad in violation of foreign law, if so ordered by the District Court under Rule 4(f)(3).

In reading *Rio,* consider the list of service mechanisms set forth in Rule 4(f) and whether they facilitate what should be a routine task. In particular, consider whether these mechanisms are arranged in any hierarchy: Are plaintiffs free to use whatever service mechanism listed in Rule 4(f) they desire, or are the mechanisms listed in a mandatory order of preference which parties (and courts) must follow?

COMMODITY FUTURES TRADING COMMISSION v. NAHAS
738 F.2d 487 (D.C. Cir. 1984)

TAMM, CIRCUIT JUDGE. . . . In March 1980, the [Commodity Futures Trading] Commission began investigating whether certain individuals had violated the Commodity

---

136. 738 F.2d 487 (D.C. Cir. 1984); *infra* pp. 889-893.
137. 738 F.2d at 495. *See also FTC v. Compagnie de Saint-Gobain-Pont-a-Mousson,* 636 F.2d 1300, 1327 (D.C. Cir. 1980).
138. Old Rule 4(i) provided:

Manner. When the federal or state law referred to in subdivision (e) of this rule authorizes service upon a party not an inhabitant of or found within the state in which the district court is held, and service is to be effected upon the party in a foreign country, it is also sufficient if service of the summons and complaint is made: (A) in the manner prescribed by the law of the foreign country for service in that country in an action in any of its courts of general jurisdiction; or (B) as directed by the foreign authority in response to a letter rogatory, when service in either case is reasonably calculated to give actual notice; or (C) upon an individual, by delivery to the individual personally, and upon a corporation or partnership or association, by delivery to an officer, a managing or general agent; or (D) by any form of mail, requiring a signed receipt, to be addressed and dispatched by the clerk of the court to the party to be served; or (E) as directed by order of the court. Service under (C) or (E) above may be made by any person who is not a party and is not less than 18 years of age or who is designated by order of the district court or by the foreign court. On request, the clerk shall deliver the summons to the plaintiff for transmission to the person or the foreign court or officer who will make the service.

139. *See supra* p. 888 n. 134 and *infra* pp. 898-900.
140. Kaplan, *Amendments of the Federal Rules of Civil Procedure, 1961-1963(I),* 77 Harv. L. Rev. 633, 635 (1965).
141. Service of federal court process outside the United States was, until 1993, governed by old Rule 4(i) of the Federal Rules of Civil Procedure. Old Rule 4(i) was generally held to permit service abroad even if it was effected in a manner that violated foreign law. *See infra* pp. 899-900.

Exchange Act ("Act"), by manipulating the price of silver and silver futures contracts in 1979 and 1980. In the course of its investigation, the Commission discovered that [Naji Robert] Nahas, a Brazilian citizen and resident, had opened accounts in 1979 with several brokerage houses in the United States. Through these accounts, Nahas had purchased numerous silver futures contracts and approximately ten million ounces of silver bullion. . . .

[T]he Commission issued a subpoena duces tecum pursuant to its investigative power under 7 U.S.C. §15. The subpoena, served by substituted service in São Paulo, Brazil, directed Nahas to appear . . . at the Commission's offices in Washington, D.C. and to produce certain documents.[142] When Nahas failed to comply with the Commission's subpoena, the Commission petitioned the district court for an order directing Nahas to show cause why he should be relieved of compliance. . . . Nahas ignored the show cause order [and the district court issued an order freezing his U.S. assets.]

On November 14, 1983, Nahas formally responded for the first time in this proceeding. . . . Nahas contended that the Commission had exceeded its statutory authority in issuing an investigative subpoena to a foreign citizen in a foreign nation, and that the Commission's method of serving the subpoena was illegal.[143] In support of his contentions, Nahas submitted an affidavit prepared by Professor Irineu Strenger, a Brazilian attorney and a professor of law at the University of São Paulo, stating that the service of the Commission's subpoena violated Brazilian and international law. . . . The district court rejected Nahas' arguments. . . . [On appeal,] Nahas contends that 7 U.S.C. §15 does not empower a district court to enforce an administrative subpoena served on a foreign citizen in a foreign country. He claims the court therefore erred at the contempt proceeding in finding him in contempt and in imposing civil sanctions to compel his compliance. We agree. . . .

A federal court's subject-matter jurisdiction . . . extends only so far as Congress provides by statute. When a federal court reaches beyond its statutory grant of subject-matter jurisdiction, its judgment is void. Similarly, when an enforcement order entered by default is beyond the jurisdictional grant of the issuing court, the order is void. In the instant case, the jurisdiction of the district court to enforce Commission subpoenas arises from 7 U.S.C. §15:

> For the purpose of securing effective enforcement . . . and for the purpose of any investigation or proceeding . . . , any member of the Commission . . . may . . . subpena [sic] witnesses . . . and require the production of any . . . records that the Commission deems relevant. . . . *The attendance of witnesses and the production of any such records may be required from any place in the United States or any State* at any designated place of hearing. In case of . . . refusal to obey a subpena [sic] . . . , the Commission may invoke the aid of any court of the United States within the jurisdiction in which the investigation or proceeding is conducted. . . . *Such court may issue an order requiring such person to appear before the*

---

142. Prior to issuing the subpoena, the Commission consulted the U.S. Department of State concerning the proper method for serving an administrative subpoena on a Brazilian citizen in Brazil. The State Department advised that Brazilian law did not prohibit the service of an administrative subpoena by a Brazilian attorney upon a Brazilian citizen in Brazil. The State Department also provided the Commission with a list of Brazilian attorneys in São Paulo, where Nahas worked and resided, who could act as agents for the Commission in serving a subpoena. The Commission selected a Brazilian attorney from the list to serve the subpoena. The attorney delivered copies of the subpoena on June 14, 1983 to Nahas' office receptionist and to the doormen of Nahas' apartment building.

143. Nahas accompanied his cross-motion with an affidavit in which he averred he was a citizen of Brazil, had resided in Brazil since 1969, had never been a resident or citizen of the United States, had not conducted any business in the United States since May 6, 1983, and had not been personally served with the Commission's subpoena.

> *Commission* ... to produce records ... or to give testimony. ... Any failure to obey such order of the court may be punished by the court as a contempt thereof.

The district court thus has jurisdiction to enforce only those subpoenas issued to "such person[s]" as defined in §15. The plain language of the statute limits "such person[s]" to "witnesses ... from any place in the United States or any State. ..."

Although courts, in some instances, have construed similar language as authorizing enforcement of administrative subpoenas requiring the production of records from outside the United States, those subpoenas were served on individuals within the United States. No court has expressly considered whether Congress intended 7 U.S.C. §15 to authorize judicial enforcement of an investigative subpoena served upon a foreign citizen in a foreign nation. Although the plain language of the statute does not confer such power, the district court in this case nevertheless inferred jurisdiction. ... [W]e believe that sound rules of statutory construction compel a different conclusion.

An important canon of statutory construction teaches that "legislation of Congress, unless a contrary intent appears, is meant to apply only within the territorial jurisdiction of the United States. ..." *Foley Bros., Inc. v. Filardo*, 336 U.S. 281, 285 (1949). The text of 7 U.S.C. §15 does not empower the Commission to serve subpoenas on foreign nationals in foreign countries. Similarly, the legislative history does not indicate that Congress intended to clothe the Commission with the power to serve investigative subpoenas extra-territorially. We are not prepared, in the face of a silent statute and an uninstructive legislative history, to infer the existence of this power: "The service of an investigative subpoena on a foreign national in a foreign country ... [is] a sufficiently significant act as to require that Congress should speak to it clearly." *FTC v. Compagnie de Saint-Gobain-Pont-a-Mousson*, 636 F.2d 1300, 1327 (D.C. Cir. 1980) (McGowan, J., concurring).[144]

We are influenced as well by another canon of statutory construction that requires courts, wherever possible, to construe federal statutes to ensure their application will not violate international law.[145] *Murray v. The Schooner Charming Betsy, supra.* To construe 7 U.S.C. §15 as empowering the district court to enforce an investigative subpoena served on a foreign citizen in a foreign nation would seriously impinge on principles of international law. "When compulsory process is served [on a foreign citizen on foreign soil in the form of an investigative subpoena[146]], ... the act of service itself constitutes an

---

144. The Commission asserts that the court may infer from the language of §15 that Congress intended the Commission to have power to serve its subpoenas extraterritorially. The statute authorizes the Commission to subpoena witnesses and records from "*any* place in the United States or any State. ..." 7 U.S.C. §15 (emphasis added). In support of its assertion, the Commission invites our attention to 7 U.S.C. §3, which discusses transactions in interstate commerce and defines "State" as including foreign nations. The Commission ignores, however, that 7 U.S.C. §3 explicitly limits its definition of "State" to that section. We could as well be influenced by §13a-2, which discusses the jurisdiction of states and defines "State" as "any State of the United States, the District of Columbia, the Commonwealth of Puerto Rico, or any territory or possession of the United States." 7 U.S.C. §13a-2(6). Nevertheless, absent clear evidence of legislative intent, we are unwilling to extend to 7 U.S.C. §15 definitions intended exclusively for other sections. Instead, we are guided by established rules of statutory construction, and we presume that had Congress intended to authorize the Commission to serve subpoenas on foreign citizens in foreign nations, it would unambiguously have expressed that intent.

145. The Constitution commits to the Legislative and Executive Branches, not to the Judicial Branch, the conduct of foreign relations. *Oetjen v. Central Leather Co.*, 246 U.S. 297, 302 (1918). Our rules of statutory construction in the instant case embody concerns for preserving the relationships between the branches of government in a system of separation of powers. Hence, we hesitate to infer from 7 U.S.C. §15, absent clear congressional intent, enforcement jurisdiction that arouses foreign sensibilities and implicates international law concerns.

146. The distinction between service of compulsory process and service of notice is critical under principles of international law due to the difference in judicial enforcement power that accompanies each. When process in the form of a complaint is served extraterritorially, the informational nature of the process renders the act of service relatively benign in terms of infringement on the foreign nation's sovereignty. *See Saint-Gobain*. For

exercise of one nation's sovereignty within the territory of another sovereign. Such an exercise [absent consent by the foreign nation] constitutes a violation of international law." *Saint-Gobain,* 636 F.2d 1313.

The extent of the intrusion on Brazil's sovereignty in this case is reflected in a letter of protest sent by the Brazilian government to the United States Secretary of State. Brazilian law requires that service of process by foreign nations be made pursuant to a letter rogatory or a letter of request transmitted through diplomatic channels. In its letter of protest, Brazil remonstrated that the Commission's method of serving the subpoena "[did] not conform to the [Brazilian laws] governing the handling of . . . material [at the international level]. . . ."[147] Brazil therefore admonished the United States to "ensure compliance, in future cases, with the formalities prescribed by Brazilian law for the execution of legal instruments required by foreign courts."[148] In light of this apparently significant intrusion on Brazilian sovereignty, inferring enforcement jurisdiction under 7 U.S.C. §15 would seriously impact on principles of international law. Because "an act of Congress ought never to be construed to violate the law of nations, if any other possible construction remains," *Charming Betsy,* 6 U.S. at 118, we are unwilling to infer enforcement jurisdiction absent a clearer indication of congressional intent.

We emphasize that this case does not pose a question about the authority of Congress; rather, it poses a question about the congressional intent embodied in 7 U.S.C. §15. Federal courts must give effect to a valid, unambiguous congressional mandate, even if such effect would conflict with another nation's laws or violate international law. A clear congressional mandate authorizing the Commission to serve investigative subpoenas on foreign citizens in foreign nations is lacking in 7 U.S.C. §15, and inferring such a mandate would run contrary to established canons of statutory construction. . . .[149]

---

example, when an agency serves a formal complaint on a foreign citizen in a foreign nation, the recipient simply receives information upon which he may decide whether to negotiate a consent order or proceed to litigation. The result of the litigation may always be appealed before a cease-and-desist order will issue. Not until the cease-and-desist order becomes final can the enforcement power of the courts be invoked. By contrast, when an agency serves compulsory process in the form of an investigative subpoena, it compels the recipient to act. Should the recipient refuse to comply with the subpoena, the enforcement power of the federal courts can be invoked immediately. *See Saint-Gobain,* 636 F.2d at 1311-13. In the instant case, service of the Commission's subpoena on Nahas in Brazil constituted an act of American sovereignty within Brazil, because the subpoena carried with it the full array of American judicial power. Such an intrusion on the sovereignty of another nation impinges on principles of international law and should be avoided unless expressly mandated by Congress.

147. Not only did the Commission fail to observe Brazilian law when serving the subpoena, it ignored guidance by this court in *Saint-Gobain* concerning methods of extraterritorial service that would minimize intrusion on another nation's sovereignty: "[W]herever possible, an agency attempting subpoena service on foreign citizens residing on foreign soil should make initial resort through established diplomatic channels or procedures authorized by international convention." 636 F.2d at 1323. In *Saint-Gobain,* this court discussed the significant international implications of an agency bypassing foreign authorities when serving an investigative subpoena abroad: "Given the compulsory nature of a subpoena, . . . subpoena service by direct mail upon a foreign citizen on foreign soil, without warning to the officials of the local state and without initial request for or prior resort to established channels of international judicial assistance, is perhaps maximally intrusive. Not only does it represent a deliberate bypassing of the official authorities of the local state, it allows the full range of judicial sanctions for noncompliance with an agency subpoena to be triggered merely by a foreign citizen's unwillingness to comply with directives contained in an ordinary registered letter." . . .

148. The intrusion on Brazil's sovereignty is also indicated by a letter from 35 members of the Brazilian Chamber of Deputies, a House in Brazil's bicameral legislature, to the United States Ambassador in Brazil protesting "[t]he proceedings against a citizen not subject to territorial competence (jus loci) of American Justice. . . . [The proceedings] affect personal and family honor of persons foreign to the Sovereignty and Competence of the Government of the United States. . . . We are certain that Your Excellency, due to the international and national importance which the fact represents, will transmit to the honorable authorities of your Country this manifestation and protest."

149. The Commission correctly asserts that agencies generally are granted broad deference in determining the scope of their investigative authority. *CAB v. Deutsche Lufthansa AG,* 591 F.2d 951, 952 (D.C. Cir. 1979).

Finally, our conclusion that Congress did not intend in 7 U.S.C. §15 to empower federal courts to enforce investigative subpoenas served on foreign citizens in foreign nations comports with analogous cases in which courts have construed similar language. For example, in *SEC v. Minas de Artemisa, SA,* 150 F.2d 215 (9th Cir. 1945), the agency was statutorily authorized to subpoena witnesses and documents "from any place in the United States or any Territory. . . ." The Ninth Circuit construed the agency's authority broadly to require the production of documents outside the United States, "provided only that the service of the subpoena is made within the territorial limits of the United States." . . .

Our construction of 7 U.S.C. §15 is further strengthened by the existence of statutes in which Congress explicitly has authorized the extraterritorial service of investigative subpoenas on aliens. For example, Congress has authorized the Department of Justice in its antitrust investigations to serve civil investigative demands on foreign nationals "in such manner as the Federal Rules of Civil Procedure prescribe for service in a foreign country."[150] 15 U.S.C. §1312(d)(2) (1982). Congress also has empowered the Federal Trade Commission to serve its subpoenas on foreign nationals "in such manner as the Federal Rules of Civil Procedure prescribe for service in a foreign nation." *Id.* §57b-1(c)(6)(B). The existence of these statutes "indicates that when Congress intends to authorize extraterritorial service of investigative subpoenas, it will express that intent explicitly." *Saint-Gobain,* 636 F.2d at 1325 n.140. An explicit grant of power is conspicuously absent from 7 U.S.C. §15. Sound rules of statutory construction as well as analogous precedent therefore compel a construction of 7 U.S.C. §15 that does not authorize enforcement jurisdiction in the instant case. . . .

FEDERAL RULES OF CIVIL PROCEDURE, RULE 4(f)
[excerpted at Appendix C]

RIO PROPERTIES, INC. v. RIO INTERNATIONAL INTERLINK
284 F.3d 1007 (9th Cir. 2002)

TROTT, CIRCUIT JUDGE. Las Vegas hotel and casino operator Rio Properties, Inc. ("RIO") sued Rio International Interlink ("RII"), a foreign Internet business entity, asserting various statutory and common law trademark infringement claims. The district court entered default judgment against RII for failing to comply with the court's discovery orders. RII now appeals the sufficiency of the service of process, effected via email and regular mail pursuant to [FRCP 4(f)(3)]. . . .

RIO owns the RIO All Suite Casino Resort, the "Best Hotel Value in the World" according to *Travel and Leisure Magazine,* not to mention the "Best Overall Hotel in Las Vegas," . . . In addition to its elegant hotel, RIO's gambling empire consists of the Rio Race & Sports Book, which allows customers to wager on professional sports. To

---

Because the Commission has construed its jurisdiction under the Act as extending to all market participants regardless of nationality or location, it contends that any ambiguity in 7 U.S.C. §15 should be resolved in favor of promoting its investigative and regulative powers. The Commission fails to recognize, however, that judicial deference to an agency's interpretation of its investigative authority is not justified when the agency's action may have extraterritorial impact. *Saint-Gobain,* 636 F.2d at 1322. . . .

150. [Old] Federal Rule 4(i)(1) provide[d] five alternative methods for service upon a party in a foreign country: in the manner prescribed by the law of the foreign country; as directed by the foreign authority responding to a letter rogatory; by personal service; by any form of mail requiring a signed receipt; or as directed by order of the court where the action is brought.

protect its exclusive rights in the "RIO" name, RIO registered numerous trademarks with the United States Patent and Trademark Office. When RIO sought to expand its presence onto the Internet, it registered the domain name, *www.playrio.com*. At that address, RIO operates a website that informs prospective customers about its hotel and allows those enticed by Lady Luck to make reservations.

RII is a Costa Rican entity that participates in an Internet sports gambling operation, doing business variously as Rio International Sportsbook, Rio Online Sportsbook, or Rio International Sports. RII enables its customers to wager on sporting events online or via a 1-800 telephone number. . . . RII grosses an estimated $3 million annually. RIO became aware of RII's existence by virtue of RII's advertisement in the *Football Betting Guide '98 Preview*. RIO later discovered, in the Nevada edition of the *Daily Racing Form*, another RII advertisement which invited customers to visit RII's website, *www.riosports.com*. RII also ran radio spots in Las Vegas as part of its comprehensive marketing strategy.

Upon learning of RII, RIO fired off an epistle demanding that RII cease and desist from operating the *www.riosports.com* website. Although RII did not formally respond, it promptly disabled the objectionable website. Apparently not ready to cash in its chips, RII soon activated the URL *http://www.betrio.com* to host an identical sports gambling operation. Perturbed, RIO filed the present action alleging various trademark infringement claims and seeking to enjoin RII from the continued use of the name "RIO."

To initiate suit, RIO attempted to locate RII in the United States for service of process. RIO discovered that RII claimed an address in Miami, Florida when it registered the allegedly infringing domain names. As it turned out, however, that address housed only RII's international courier, IEC, which was not authorized to accept service on RII's behalf. Nevertheless, IEC agreed to forward the summons and complaint to RII's Costa Rican courier. After sending a copy of the summons and complaint through IEC, RIO received a telephone call from Los Angeles attorney John Carpenter ("Carpenter") inquiring about the lawsuit. Apparently, RII received the summons and complaint from IEC and subsequently consulted Carpenter about how to respond. Carpenter indicated that RII provided him with a partially illegible copy of the complaint and asked RIO to send him a complete copy. RIO agreed to resend the complaint and, in addition, asked Carpenter to accept service for RII; Carpenter politely declined. Carpenter did, however, request that RIO notify him upon successful completion of service. . . .

Thus thwarted in its attempt to serve RII in the United States, RIO investigated the possibility of serving RII in Costa Rica. Toward this end, RIO searched international directory databases looking for RII's address in Costa Rica. These efforts proved fruitless however; the investigator learned only that RII preferred communication through its email address, *email@betrio.com,* and received snail mail, including payment for its services, at the IEC address in Florida.

Unable to serve RII by conventional means, RIO filed an emergency motion for alternate service of process. RII opted not to respond to RIO's motion. The district court granted RIO's motion, and pursuant to [FRCP] 4(h)(2) and 4(f)(3), ordered service of process on RII through the mail to Carpenter and IEC and via RII's email address, *email@betrio.com*. Court order in hand, RIO served RII by these court-sanctioned methods. RII filed a motion to dismiss for insufficient service of process and lack of personal jurisdiction. The parties fully briefed the issues, and the district court denied RII's motion without a hearing. RII then filed its answer, denying RIO's allegations and asserting twenty-two affirmative defenses.

As the case proceeded, RIO propounded discovery requests and interrogatories on RII. RIO granted RII two informal extensions of time in which to respond. Nonetheless, RII's eventual responses were almost entirely useless, consisting largely of the answer "N/A," ostensibly meaning "Not Applicable." After additional futile attempts to elicit good faith responses from RII, RIO brought a motion to compel discovery. In granting RIO's motion, the district court warned that in the event RII failed to comply, monetary sanctions would be an insufficient remedy and that "preclusive sanctions" would be awarded. When RII failed to comply with the district court's discovery order, RIO moved for terminating sanctions. Although RII belatedly complied, in part, with RIO's discovery request, the district court granted RIO's motion for sanctions and entered default judgment against RII. Citing RII's reprehensible conduct and bad faith, the district court additionally directed RII to pay reasonable attorneys' fees and costs to RIO in the amount of $88,761.50 and $7,859.52 respectively. [RII now appeals the sufficiency of the court-ordered service of process and default judgment.] . . .

[FRCP] 4(h)(2) authorizes service of process on a foreign business entity in the manner prescribed by [FRCP 4(f)] for individuals. The subsection of Rule 4(f) relevant to our decision, Rule 4(f)(3),[151] permits service in a place not within any judicial district of the United States "by . . . means not prohibited by international agreement as may be directed by the court." As obvious from its plain language, service under Rule 4(f)(3) must be (1) directed by the court; and (2) not prohibited by international agreement. No other limitations are evident from the text. In fact, as long as court-directed and not prohibited by an international agreement, service of process ordered under Rule 4(f)(3) may be accomplished in contravention of the laws of the foreign country.

RII argues that Rule 4(f) should be read to create a hierarchy of preferred methods of service of process. RII's interpretation would require that a party attempt service of process by those methods enumerated in Rule 4(f)(2), including by diplomatic channels and letters rogatory, before petitioning the court for alternative relief under Rule 4(f)(3). We find no support for RII's position. No such requirement is found in the Rule's text, implied by its structure, or even hinted at in the advisory committee notes.

By all indications, court-directed service under Rule 4(f)(3) is as favored as service available under Rule 4(f)(1)[152] or Rule 4(f)(2). Indeed, Rule 4(f)(3) is one of three separately numbered subsections in Rule 4(f), and each subsection is separated from the one previous merely by the simple conjunction "or." Rule 4(f)(3) is not subsumed within or in any way dominated by Rule 4(f)'s other subsections; it stands independently, on equal footing. Moreover, no language in Rules 4(f)(1) or 4(f)(2) indicates their primacy, and certainly Rule 4(f)(3) includes no qualifiers or limitations which indicate its availability only after attempting service of process by other means.

The advisory committee notes ("Advisory Notes") bolster our analysis. Beyond stating that service ordered under Rule 4(f)(3) must comport with constitutional notions of due process and must not be prohibited by international agreement, the Advisory Notes indicate the availability of alternate service of process under Rule 4(f)(3) without first attempting service by other means. Specifically, the advisory notes suggest that in cases of "urgency," Rule 4(f)(3) may allow the district court to order a "special method of service," even if other methods of service remain incomplete or unattempted. Thus, examining the language and structure of Rule 4(f) and the accompanying advisory committee notes, we are left with the inevitable conclusion that service of process under Rule 4(f)(3) is . . . merely one means among several which enables service of process on an international defendant.

151. Rule 4(f)(3) was derived from its predecessor, FRCP 4(i)(1)(E), which provided for alternative service of process in a foreign country "by order of the court."

152. A federal court would be prohibited from issuing a Rule 4(f)(3) order in contravention of an international agreement, including the Hague Convention referenced in Rule 4(f)(1). The parties agree, however, that the Hague Convention does not apply in this case because Costa Rica is not a signatory.

RII argues that *Graval v. P.T. Bakrie & Bros.*, 986 F. Supp. 1326, 1330 (C.D. Calif. 1996), requires attempted service by other methods, including through diplomatic channels or letters rogatory, before resort to court-ordered service under Rule 4(f)(3). The court in *Graval* believed that Rule 4(f)(3) was "intended as a last resort, only to be employed when there are no other feasible alternatives." Yet, the court in *Graval* erroneously based this belief on an advisory committee note pertaining solely to Rule 4(f)(2), which simply does not apply to Rule 4(f)(3).[153] . . . Thus, we disapprove of the statements in *Graval* which would require attempted service by all feasible alternatives before service under Rule 4(f)(3) is allowed. Instead, we hold that Rule 4(f)(3) is an equal means of effecting service of process under the Federal Rules of Civil Procedure, and we commit to the sound discretion of the district court the task of determining when the particularities and necessities of a given case require alternate service of process under Rule 4(f)(3).

Applying this proper construction of Rule 4(f)(3) and its predecessor, trial courts have authorized a wide variety of alternative methods of service. . . . *See SEC v. Tome,* 833 F.2d 1086, 1094 (2d Cir. 1987) (condoning service of process by publication in the *Int'l Herald Tribune*); *Smith v. Islamic Emirate,* 2001 WL 1658211, at *2-3 (S.D.N.Y. 2001) (authorizing service of process on terrorism impresario Osama bin Laden and al-Qaeda by publication); *Levin v. Ruby Trading Corp.,* 248 F. Supp. 537, 541-44 (S.D.N.Y. 1965) (employing service by ordinary mail); *Int'l Controls Corp. v. Vesco,* 593 F.2d 166, 176-78 (2d Cir. 1979) (approving service by mail to last known address); *Forum Fin. Group* [*v. President and Fellows of Harvard Coll.*], 199 F.R.D., 23-24 [22], (D. Me. 2001) (authorizing service to defendant's attorney); *New England Merchs. Nat'l Bank v. Iran Power Generation & Transmission Co.,* 485 F. Supp. 73, 80 (S.D.N.Y. 1980) (allowing service by telex for Iranian defendants); *Broadfoot v. Diaz,* 245 B.R. 713, 719-20 (Bankr. N.D. Ga. 2000) (authorizing service via email).

In this case, RIO attempted to serve RII by conventional means in the United States. Although RII claimed an address in Florida, that address housed only IEC, RII's international courier, which refused to accept service of process on RII's behalf. RII's attorney, Carpenter, who was specifically consulted in this matter, also declined to accept service of process. RIO's private investigator subsequently failed to discover RII's whereabouts in Costa Rica. Thus unable to serve RII, RIO brought an emergency motion to effectuate alternative service of process.

Contrary to RII's assertions, RIO need not have attempted every permissible means of service of process before petitioning the court for alternative relief. Instead, RIO needed only to demonstrate that the facts and circumstances of the present case necessitated the district court's intervention. Thus, when RIO presented the district court with its inability to serve an elusive international defendant, striving to evade service of process, the district court properly exercised its discretionary powers to craft alternate means of service. We expressly agree with the district court's handling of this case. . . .

Even if facially permitted by Rule 4(f)(3), a method of service of process must also comport with constitutional notions of due process. To meet this requirement, the method of service crafted by the district court must be "reasonably calculated, under all the circumstances, to apprise interested parties of the pendency of the action and afford them an opportunity to present their objections." *Mullane v. Cent. Hanover Bank & Trust Co.,* 339 U.S. 306, 314 (1950) (Jackson, J.). Without hesitation, we conclude that

---

153. [The Advisory Committee Notes to Rule 4(f)(2) provide that under Rule 4(f)(2), "[s]ervice by methods that would violate foreign law is not generally authorized."] The *Graval* Court did not realize that this advisory committee note speaks only about subparagraphs (A) and (B) of Rule 4(f)(2). The advisory committee notes pertaining to Rule 4(f)(3) suggest no such limitation.

each alternative method of service of process ordered by the district court was constitutionally acceptable. In our view, each method of service was reasonably calculated, under these circumstances, to apprise RII of the pendency of the action and afford it an opportunity to respond. In particular, service through IEC was appropriate because RII listed IEC's address as its own when registering the allegedly infringing domain name. The record also reflects that RII directed its customers to remit payment to IEC's address. Moreover, when RIO sent a copy of the summons and complaint to RII through IEC, RII received it. All told, this evidence indicates that RII relied heavily upon IEC to operate its business in the United States and that IEC could effectively pass information to RII in Costa Rica.

Service upon Carpenter was also appropriate because he had been specifically consulted by RII regarding this lawsuit. He knew of RII's legal positions, and it seems clear that he was in contact with RII in Costa Rica. Accordingly, service to Carpenter was also reasonably calculated in these circumstances to apprise RII of the pendency of the present action.

Finally, we turn to the district court's order authorizing service of process on RII by email at *email@betrio.com*. We acknowledge that we tread upon untrodden ground. The parties cite no authority condoning service of process over the Internet or via email. . . . Despite this dearth of authority, however, we do not labor long in reaching our decision. Considering the facts presented by this case, we conclude not only that service of process by email was proper — that is, reasonably calculated to apprise RII of the pendency of the action and afford it an opportunity to respond — but in this case, it was the method of service most likely to reach RII. . . .

As noted by the court in *New England Merchants,* in granting permission to effect service of process via telex on Iranian defendants: "Courts . . . cannot be blind to changes and advances in technology. No longer do we live in a world where communications are conducted solely by mail carried by fast sailing clipper . . . ships. . . . No longer must process be mailed to a defendant's door when he can receive complete notice at an electronic terminal inside his very office, even when the door is steel and bolted shut." We agree wholeheartedly. Although communication via email and over the Internet is comparatively new, such communication has been zealously embraced within the business community. RII particularly has embraced the modern e-business model and profited immensely from it. In fact, RII structured its business such that it could be contacted *only* via its email address. . . .

If any method of communication is reasonably calculated to provide RII with notice, surely it is email — the method of communication which RII utilizes and prefers. In addition, email was the only court-ordered method of service aimed directly and instantly at RII, as opposed to methods of service effected through intermediaries like IEC and Carpenter. Indeed, when faced with an international e-business scofflaw, playing hide-and-seek with the federal court, email may be the only means of effecting service of process. Certainly in this case, it was a means reasonably calculated to apprise RII of the pendency of the lawsuit, and the Constitution requires nothing more. . . .

Despite our endorsement of service of process by email in this case, we are cognizant of its limitations. In most instances, there is no way to confirm receipt of an email message. Limited use of electronic signatures could present problems in complying with the verification requirements of Rule 4(a) and Rule 11, and system compatibility problems may lead to controversies over whether an exhibit or attachment was actually received. . . . We note, however, that, except for the provisions recently introduced into Rule 5(b), email service is not available absent a Rule 4(f)(3) court decree. Accordingly, we leave it to the discretion of the district court to balance the limitations of email service against its benefits in any particular case. [The Court went on to uphold personal jurisdiction over the defendant and entry of a default judgment as a sanction for noncompliance with discovery obligations.]

Notes on Nahas, Rule 4(f), and Rio

1. *Appropriate U.S. response to foreign restrictions on the service abroad of U.S. process within local territory.* As a matter of policy, how *should* U.S. courts and legislatures approach the question of authorizing service of U.S. process abroad in violation of foreign law? Should such service be treated as valid under U.S. law? Or should U.S. courts hold that service must comply with foreign law? How much should U.S. courts consider the basic purpose of service (providing notice to a defendant) and the technological realities of international communications (where vital communications are made across national borders by email, fax, courier, and other means thousands of times a day)?

2. *Federal statutes authorizing service of process abroad.* A number of federal statutes authorize the service of U.S. process abroad. One example is the Walsh Act, 28 U.S.C. §1783 [reproduced in Appendix A], which specifically authorizes service of subpoenas on U.S. citizens outside the United States.

Other federal statutes, identified in *Nahas,* permit the service of investigative subpoenas abroad. *E.g.,* 15 U.S.C. §1312(d)(2); 15 U.S.C. §576-1(c)(6)(B). Indeed, after *Nahas* was decided, Congress amended 7 U.S.C. §15 to make it clear that the CFTC could serve subpoenas abroad.

3. *U.S. service abroad is valid under U.S. law, notwithstanding violation of foreign law, if federal law specifically permits such service.* If a valid federal statute specifically authorizes a mechanism of service abroad, federal courts generally do not have the power to forbid such service on the grounds that it violates foreign law. That is made clear by the comments in *Nahas* that "this case does not pose a question about authority of Congress; rather, it poses a question about the congressional intent embodied in 7 U.S.C. §15." *Nahas* went on to say that "federal courts must give effect to a valid unambiguous congressional mandate, even if such effect would conflict with another nation's laws or violate international law." Or, as the Court said in *Umbenhauer v. Woog,* 969 F.2d 25 (3d Cir. 1992), "[n]either we, the Department of State, nor the Administrative Office of the United States Courts possess the authority to circumvent, ignore or deviate from the Federal Rules of Civil Procedure." This is, of course, similar to the role of customary international law in other U.S. contexts. *See supra* pp. 18, 646-651, 664-670.

4. *Interpretation of silent or ambiguous federal statutes or rules to determine whether service abroad in violation of foreign law is permitted.* Statutory authorizations for service do not always specifically address the question whether service abroad in violation of foreign law is permitted. In such cases, should U.S. courts interpret a silent or generally worded statute to permit service abroad in violation of foreign law? Recall the *Charming Betsy* presumption that Congress does not intend to violate international law. *See supra* p. 18.

Nahas held that the service of an administrative subpoena in Brazil, in violation of Brazilian law, was not authorized by 7 U.S.C. §15 — notwithstanding the provision's broad language. *Nahas* relied on the "canon of statutory construction that requires courts, wherever possible, to construe federal statutes to ensure their application will not violate international law." 738 F.2d at 493 (citing *Charming Betsy, supra,* 6 U.S. at 118). The same result was reached, with respect to a Federal Trade Commission subpoena served in France, in *Saint-Gobain.* 636 F.2d at 1323 & n.130.

5. *Propriety of presumption against service in violation of foreign law.* Is it appropriate for U.S. courts to adopt a presumption that federal law does not authorize service in violation of foreign, and therefore international, law? Recall the comments by Professor Smit concerning the legitimacy and wisdom of foreign prohibitions on U.S. service. *See supra* p. 886. Is Congress more likely to be mindful of the sentiments underlying these comments, or of the *Charming Betsy* adage against violations of international law? Recall also the debate whether service abroad by private means involves government conduct or implicates international law. *See supra* pp. 884-886.

Suppose that a foreign state simply refuses to permit service of foreign process (or, arguably like Costa Rica in the *Rio* case, service of process in an effective manner). Suppose that it forbids service of various categories of complaints — such as antitrust actions, claims seeking punitive damages, or the like. Should Congress be presumed to defer to such prohibitions? If it voted on the question, what result do you think Congress would reach?

6. *Interpretation of Walsh Act and other federal service statutes.* Reread the Walsh Act and amended 7 U.S.C. §15. Does the text of any of these statutes expressly permit service abroad *in violation of foreign law?* Does an authorization for extraterritorial service necessarily constitute an authorization for service abroad contrary to foreign law? Must such an authorization be implied? Recall the application of the territoriality presumption in *Aramco,* requiring clear and affirmative language to extend U.S. legislation extraterritorially, *see supra* pp. 659-664, 664-668. If an equivalent standard of proof is applied to the Walsh Act and 7 U.S.C. §15, is it satisfied? Under *Nahas,* is it permissible to imply such an authorization?

7. *U.S. governmental responses to foreign diplomatic protests regarding extraterritorial service of U.S. process.* The U.S. Executive Branch has traditionally responded cooperatively to foreign diplomatic protests concerning U.S. service of process within local territory. After Swiss protests during the late 1950s to the service of U.S. administrative subpoenas within Swiss territory, the State Department responded in an aide-memoire expressing regret for the "inadvertent violation of applicable Swiss law" and stating that U.S. agencies would seek to "avoid any future transmittals of such documents in a manner inconsistent with Swiss law." *Contemporary Practice of the United States Relating to International Law,* 56 Am. J. Int'l L. 793, 794 (1962). Is this an appropriate attitude? What would Professor Smit say?

8. *Service abroad under pre-1993 FRCP Rule 4(i).* As described above, old Rule 4(i) set forth five mechanisms for service abroad. *See supra* pp. 874-875 & p. 889 n. 138. Compare this approach to that of current Rule 4(f) and Rule 4(h).

(a) No express prohibition in old Rule 4(i) against service in violation of foreign law. Rule 4(i) contained no express requirement that service under any of these mechanisms be effected consistent with foreign law. The decision on how to serve process was left generally to litigants, without the need to obtain court approval or a court order. Is it appropriate to allow private parties to make decisions whether or not formal process from a U.S. court will be served abroad in violation of foreign law?

(b) Old Rule 4(i) and service of process abroad in violation of foreign law. Lower courts split over whether old Rule 4(i) permitted service abroad in violation of foreign law. Most lower courts rejected the argument that service on the defendant in a foreign state in violation of local foreign law provided a basis for quashing service in U.S. courts and reasoned that, so long as service comported with the Federal Rules, violations of foreign law were simply irrelevant. *See supra* p. 888, n. 139; *Restatement (Third) Foreign Relations Law* §472, Reporters' Note 2 (1987) ("[T]he prevailing view is that, absent a treaty obligation, courts in the United States will give effect to . . . process" served abroad in violation of foreign law.). By contrast, a few U.S. courts refused to permit service of process abroad under old Rule 4 in

violation of foreign law, on the theory that this was not specifically authorized by the Federal Rules. *See, e.g., M.B. Electrostat v. Lectra Trading AG,* 1983 WL 1371 (E.D. Pa. 1983); *Aries Ventures v. AXA Finance SA,* 729 F. Supp. 289 (S.D.N.Y. 1990); *SEC v. Tome,* 833 F.2d 1086, 1091 (2d Cir. 1983).

(c) Administrative Office statement on extraterritorial service of process. Periodically, the Judicial Branch itself has sought to address the potential foreign relations difficulties arising from service abroad in violation of foreign law. During the 1970s, Swiss authorities objected to mail service abroad. In response, the Administrative Office of the United States Court Clerks issued a memorandum, dated November 6, 1980, directing that any service to be effected on Swiss soil be done pursuant to letter rogatory. Among other things, the memorandum requested clerks of U.S. courts to "refrain from sending summonses and complaints by international mail to foreign defendants in those countries which have protested service by international mail." Some courts relied on the Administrative Conference memorandum in requiring service of complaints in Switzerland by letter rogatory under the old Federal Rules; other courts did not give decisive weight to the memorandum. *See also* Memo of L. Ralph Meacham, Director, Administrative Office of United States Courts, to Clerks of United States District Courts (Nov. 7, 2000) (discussing Russian protests to service of process and guiding district court clerks on how to manage foreign service of process so as to avoid such protests).

9. *Service of process abroad under FRCP Rule 4(f).* As discussed above, new Rule 4(f) of the Federal Rules significantly revised the service of U.S. process abroad in civil actions.

(a) Rule 4(f) — "Unless otherwise provided by federal law." The opening line of Rule 4(f) specifies that service may be effected by the manners specified therein "[u]nless federal law provides otherwise." The Advisory Committee Notes to Rule 4(f) explain that the drafters included this language in order to permit service pursuant to federal statutes that set forth special rules for service of process. Courts likewise have interpreted this language to allow service by means specified in a federal statute rather than one of the means detailed in Rules 4(f)(1)-(3). *See generally* C. Wright & A. Miller, *Federal Practice and Procedure* §§1117-18 (2010). For examples of such statutes, *see, e.g.,* 35 U.S.C. §293 (service on nonresident patentees); 15 U.S.C. §1051(e) (service on nonresident trademark holders). When relying on these statutes, counsel should carefully consider whether they extend to private civil actions. *Compare, e.g., Sunshine Distribution, Inc. v. Sports Authority Michigan, Inc.,* 157 F. Supp. 2d 779 (E.D. Mich. 2001) (holding that §1051(e) only applied to proceedings before Patent and Trademark Office) *with V & S Vin & Sprit Aktiebolag v. Cracovia Brands, Inc.,* 212 F. Supp. 2d 852 (N.D. Ill. 2002) (holding that same provision permitted service in private civil action).

(b) FRCP Rule 4(f)(1). Rule 4(f)(1) requires use of any mandatory "internationally agreed means" of service that is reasonably calculated to give notice. This category expressly includes the Hague Service Convention, discussed below. Only "if there is no internationally agreed means [of service], or if an international agreement allows but does not specify other means [of service]," is Rule 4(f)(2) available. *See supra* pp. 875-876.

(c) FRCP Rule 4(f)(2). Rule 4(f)(2), which permits three other types of service, was drafted to require compliance with the laws of the place where service is effected. As already noted, Rule 4(f)(2)'s mechanisms can only be used if there is no treaty specifying a different, mandatory means of service. Thus, Rule 4(f)(2)(A) permits service in "as prescribed by the foreign country's law for service in that country in an action in its courts of general jurisdiction." Rule 4(f)(2)(B) authorizes service as directed by a foreign authority "in response to a letter rogatory or letter of request." And Rule 4(f)(2)(C) permits service by either personal delivery or return-receipt mail "unless prohibited by

the foreign country's law." As *Rio* observes, the Advisory Committee Notes to Rule 4(f) explain that "[s]ervice by methods that would violate foreign law is not generally authorized." This comment is consistent with the text of Rule 4(f)(2) and with other courts' conclusions. *See, e.g., Prewitt Enters. v. OPEC,* 353 F.3d 916, 923-925 (11th Cir. 2003) (rejecting argument that Rule 4(f)(2)(A) authorized service on OPEC by international registered mail in state which forbids such service); *S.E.C. v. Alexander,* 248 F.R.D. 108 (E.D.N.Y. 2007).

(d) FRCP Rule 4(f)(3). Finally, Rule 4(f)(3) provides that service may be made "by other means [than those set forth above] not prohibited by international agreement, as the court orders." Thus, while the provisions of U.S. treaties cannot be violated, Rule 4(f)(3) does not expressly forbid courts from ordering means of service that violate foreign law.

10. *Is there any hierarchy of service mechanisms under FRCP Rule 4(f)(2) and 4(f)(3)?* *Rio* considered whether Rule 4(f) required a plaintiff to proceed in any particular order with regard to the service mechanisms it provides in subparagraphs 4(f)(2) and 4(f)(3). That is, must a litigant first attempt to utilize the service mechanisms set forth in Rule 4(f)(2) — and particularly service by letter rogatory — prior to seeking court-ordered service under Rule 4(f)(3)? What do you make of the *Rio* Court's answer? Is there anything in Rule 4(f) that contradicts the *Rio* analysis? For similar decisions, *see Nuance Communications, Inc. v. Abbyy Software House,* 626 F.3d 1222 (Fed. Cir. 2010); *Studio A Entm't, Inc. v. Active Distribs., Inc.,* 2008 WL 162785, at *3 n.1 (N.D. Ohio 2008); *Williams v. Advertising Sex LLC,* 231 F.R.D. 483, 485-486 (N.D. W. Va. 2005); *Ryan v. Brunswick Corp.,* 2002 U.S. Dist. LEXIS 13837, at *7-8 (W.D.N.Y. 2002); *Forum Fin. Group v. President & Fellows of Harvard Coll.,* 199 F.R.D. 22, 23-24 (D. Me. 2001).

Not all courts have agreed with *Rio.* For example, the Court in *Elisan Entertainment, Inc. v. Suazo,* 206 F.R.D. 335, 336 n.2 (D.P.R. 2002) held that Rule 4(f)(3) should be used only "when none of the other methods of service expressly provided for in the rule is satisfactory or likely to be successful." (quoting C. Wright & A. Miller, *Federal Practice and Procedure* §1134, at 333 (3d ed. 2002)). Is that a wise decision? Putting aside the text of the Rule (and the Advisory Committee Note), is it not sensible to first attempt service by letter rogatory, before pursuing mechanisms of service that do or might violate foreign law? Other courts have not gone so far but nonetheless have been hesitant to exercise their power under Rule 4(f)(3). *See SEC v. Lines,* 2009 WL 2431976, at *2 (S.D.N.Y. Aug. 7, 2009) ("To obtain permission for alternative service pursuant to Fed. R. Civ. P. 4(f)(3), a plaintiff must demonstrate why service through the foreign country's Central Authority under the Hague Service Convention's procedures should not be required."); *SEC v. Shehyn,* 2008 WL 6150322, at *3 (S.D.N.Y. Nov. 26, 2008) (appearing to require plaintiff to wait six months from initial application to foreign authority before requesting service pursuant to Rule 4(f)(3)). What would be the down-side of requiring an effort to serve by letter rogatory? Note that, as discussed below, service by letter rogatory can take a number of months. *See supra* pp. 887-888.

Would it have been possible as a factual matter to seek service by letter rogatory in *Rio?* Why not? If it is futile to attempt service by letter rogatory, should a party be required to do so?

11. *Correctness of interpreting FRCP Rule 4(f)(3) to permit court-ordered service abroad in violation of foreign law.* Consider the Court's analysis of Rule 4(f)(3) in *Rio.* Is it so clear from the text of the revised Federal Rules that service in violation of foreign law is authorized under Rule 4(f)(3)? For different results, *see In re Ski Train Fire in Kaprun, Austria on November 11, 2000,* 2003 WL 21659368 (S.D.N.Y. 2003) ("While Rule 4(f)(3) provides for substitute service 'as may be directed by the court,' any such service must comport with the laws of the foreign country."); *East Cont'l Gems, Inc. v. Yakutiel*, 582 N.Y.S.2d 594, 595-596 (Sup. Ct.), *aff'd*, 591 N.Y.S.2d 778 (App. Div. 1992) (service by registered mail on Swiss corporation invalid although it complied with New York law because "under the doctrine of comity of nations, such service to be valid must not violate the sovereignty of a foreign country"). *Compare Export-Import Bank of the United States v. Asia Pulp & Paper Co., Ltd.*, 2005 WL 1123755, at *5 (S.D.N.Y. 2005) (permitting service by international registered mail and courier under Rule 4(f)(3) "even if it is technically in violation of Indonesian service requirements" and noting that "any offense to that country's sovereignty is minimal").

What impact do the *Charming Betsy* and *Nahas* presumptions have on the interpretation of Rule 4(f)(3)? Does Rule 4(f)(3) expressly permit service in violation of foreign law? Note that Rule 4(f)(3) merely authorizes court-ordered service that does not violate a U.S. treaty. Does this "silence" authorize service in violation of foreign law? *Compare EEOC v. Arabian American Oil Company*, 499 U.S. 244 (1991), excerpted above, holding that a negative implication is insufficient to overcome the presumption that federal statutes apply only to conduct within U.S. territory. *See supra* pp. 875-876.

Is it clear that service by email would have violated Costa Rican law? Suppose that there had been clear evidence that serving RII by email would have violated Costa Rican legislation and public policy. Would it still have been appropriate for U.S. courts to have authorized this mode of service?

12. *Wisdom of generally forbidding service abroad in violation of foreign law under FRCP Rule 4(f)*. Is the approach of new Rule 4(f)(2) sensible from a policy perspective? Should service in violation of foreign law be generally prohibited? Consider:

> Prohibiting U.S. methods of service that violate foreign law . . . could lead to undesirable costs. . . . The costs would stem from the anticipated distracting disputes over whether the method of service used by a plaintiff in a particular case conformed with or infringed foreign law. In the right circumstances, defendants can be expected to challenge service on exactly that ground, and such disputes will be especially burdensome because they will require a U.S. court to determine foreign law on a subject particularly sensitive to some foreign countries. Born & Vollmer, *The Effect of the Revised Federal Rules of Civil Procedure on Personal Jurisdiction, Service and Discovery in International Cases*, 150 F.R.D. 221, 239-240 (1993).

Are these costs important? Is it not more important to avoid giving offense to foreign states? What would Professor Smit, whose views were excerpted above, say? *See* Smit, *Recent Developments in International Litigation*, 35 S. Tex. L. Rev. 215, 224 (1994). Was it error to replace the flexible old Rule 4(i) with more restrictive new Rule 4(f)?

13. *Trial court's "discretion" to order service in violation of foreign law under FRCP Rule 4(f)(3)*. Is it wise for Rule 4(f)(3) to permit district judges to order service abroad in violation of foreign law? Note that the Court in *Rio* holds that service abroad in violation of foreign law is within the trial court's "discretion." Is that appropriate? Does this standard place sufficient weight on avoiding violations of foreign law (and international law)?

The result in *Rio* is obviously right. But did the Court need to approve *all* of the mechanisms of service at issue? Note that the Court upheld service on RII *in the United States* via (a) its courier company (IEC); and (b) its lawyer (Carpenter). Neither service mechanism involved any actions in Costa Rica nor any violation of Costa Rican law. Given this, was there any need to also authorize service via email on RII "in Costa Rica"? Would it have been appropriate to order service by personal delivery in Costa Rica (if an address for RII in Costa Rica could have been found), even if Costa Rican law forbid that?

Try to put aside the unattractive facts in *Rio*. As a matter of principle, what standards should courts apply in deciding whether to order service abroad and what forms of service they should authorize? As a matter of prudence, would it make sense that, absent particular needs, service abroad should be first attempted by letter rogatory? How long would this take?

What if the plaintiffs in *Rio* had attempted service by email and other means *before* obtaining the court order? Could a court enter an order retroactively authorizing such service pursuant to Rule 4(f)(3)? Courts are divided on the question. *See, e.g., Marks v. Alfa Group*, 615 F. Supp. 2d 375, 380 (E.D. Pa. 2009) (approving *nunc pro tunc* alternative service pursuant to Rule 4(f)(3) even though service occurred before party sought court order); *Kaplan v. Hezbollah*, 715 F. Supp. 2d 165, 167 (D.D.C. 2010) (discussing split). How is the concept of retroactive approval consistent with Rule 4(f)(3)'s requirement that service take place "as the court *orders*"? *See United States v. Machat*, 2009 WL 3029303 (S.D.N.Y. Sept. 21, 2009).

14. *FRCP Rule 4(f)(2)(A)'s authorization for service as "prescribed" by foreign law.* As noted above, Rule 4(f)(2)(A) authorizes the service of process "as prescribed by the foreign country's [where service is effected] law for service in that country in an action in its courts of general jurisdiction." Rule 4(f)(2)(A) is an unhappily drafted provision that has produced, and can be expected to continue to produce, confusion.

(a) What foreign service law must be satisfied? An initial question is what foreign service law applies to determine the validity of service under Rule 4(f)(2)(A). Suppose that a foreign state: (a) permits litigants in its local courts to effect service by ordinary mail, but (b) requires that foreign service be made in some other fashion. Does Rule 4(f)(2)(A) authorize service by ordinary mail, notwithstanding the violation of foreign law regarding service from foreign courts? More generally, does Rule 4(f)(2)(A) permit service as prescribed by local law for actions in *local* courts, or does it require reference to local law regarding service from *foreign* courts? Does the text of Rule 4(f)(2)(A) clearly resolve the question? Most courts have held that the relevant law is that governing foreign (not domestic) service. *See, e.g., Brockmeyer v. May*, 383 F.3d 798, 806 (9th Cir. 2004) (local laws governing domestic actions do not control sufficiency of international service under Rule 4(f)(2)(A)); *Prewitt Enters. Inc. v. OPEC*, 353 F.3d 916, 925 (11th Cir. 2003) (same). Doesn't the language of Rule 4(f)(2)(A) suggest that the relevant rules are those concerning service in *local* courts? For cases suggesting this approach, *see, e.g., Retractable Technologies, Inc. v. Occupational & Medical Innovations, Ltd.*, 253 F.R.D. 404, 405-406 (E.D. Tex. 2008); *Mitchell v. Theriault*, 516 F. Supp. 2d 450, 457 (M.D. Pa. 2007).

This issue was considered, under similarly worded language contained in old Rule 4(i)(A), in *Grand Entertainment Group, Ltd. v. Star Media Sales, Inc.*, 988 F.2d 476, 487-488 (3d Cir. 1993). The court concluded that compliance with local law regarding service of *foreign* (not domestic) process was required. The Rule's purpose:

> would be frustrated, and it would be an affront to national sovereignty, if a U.S. court applied Spain's procedures for service in cases brought in a Spanish court against parties found in Spain if Spain has enacted special provisions governing service of process issued out of the courts of other nations on behalf of foreign plaintiffs against persons found in the receiving jurisdiction. It seems to us that Rule 4(i) permits a foreign jurisdiction to refuse to subject its residents or nationals to service of process issued by a foreign court in the same manner as it does for domestic plaintiffs suing in a Spanish court. Spain, or indeed any other foreign jurisdiction, could rationally decide to impose special burdens on foreign process because service of process issued by a foreign court may require residents of the receiving state to defend themselves in distant and inconvenient places against laws that impose duties that

nationals or residents of the receiving state have not foreseen or are unaccustomed to taking into account. . . . It could do so out of a desire to impress on its residents the need to take action, and not to ignore the foreign process simply because the court issuing it is remote, a kind of cavalier attitude that is less likely in the face of domestic process.

Is that persuasive?

(b) Decisions limiting FRCP Rule 4(f)(2)(A) to personal service. Are there any limitations on the types of service that are permitted under Rule 4(f)(2)(A)? Does Rule 4(f)(2)(A)'s authorization of service extend, for example, to mail or email service? In *Brockmeyer v. May,* 383 F.3d 798 (9th Cir. 2004), the Court apparently held that Rule 4(f)(2)(A) only authorized personal service, and not mail service; notwithstanding the fact that English law permitted service by mail in domestic actions, the Court quashed service based on international mail. Among other things, the Court held:

> [T]he common understanding of Rule 4(f)(2)(A) is that it is limited to personal service. . . . Another reason to read Rule 4(f)(2)(A) not to authorize service by international mail is the explicit mention of international registered mail in Rule 4(f)(2)(C)(ii), considered above, and the absence of any such mention in Rule 4(f)(2)(A).

Is this persuasive? Is there anything in the text of Rule 4(f)(2)(A) that so limits the provision? With respect to the Court's second argument, note that Rule 4(f)(2)(C)(i) expressly refers to personal service. What approach *should* courts take to interpreting Rule 4(f)(2)(A)? If a foreign court permits mail service in local litigations, why shouldn't foreign courts be permitted to also use mail service?

(c) The meaning of "as prescribed by the foreign country's law" under Rule 4(f)(2)(A). Regardless of the proper interpretation of Rule 4(f)(2)(A), note that the rule authorizes service by a method "as prescribed by the foreign country's law." What precisely does this formulation mean? For example, suppose a foreign country's law authorizes service by mail but requires the service to be effected by a court clerk or other government official. Does the manner "as prescribed by" foreign law merely include the method (*i.e.*, mail) or does it also include the entity specified by foreign law? Generally, courts interpret this language to include not merely the method but also any limits on the persons authorized to effect the method. *See, e.g., Smallwood v. Allied Pickfords, Inc.,* 2009 WL 3247180 (S.D. Cal. Sept. 29, 2009).

15. FRCP Rule 4(f)(2)(C)'s authorization for service by mail or personal delivery "unless prohibited by the foreign country's law." As noted above, Rule 4(f)(2)(C) permits either personal delivery (Rule 4(f)(2)(C)(i)) or mail (return receipt required) (Rule 4(f)(2)(C)(ii)), save where foreign law forbids such means of service. There is uncertainty as to what it means for foreign law to "prohibit" a particular means of service. Some courts have held that Rule 4(f)(2)(C) permits all types of service except those that are expressly prohibited by the foreign country's law; other courts have held that Rule 4(f)(2)(C) bars any service that is not expressly authorized by foreign law. *Compare Emery v. Wood Industries, Inc.,* 2001 WL 274747, at *2 (D.N.H. 2001) (requiring foreign law expressly to permit manner of service); *Graval v. P.T. Bakrie & Bros.,* 986 F. Supp. 1326, 1329 n.4 (C.D. Cal. 1996) ("Plaintiff attempts to distinguish between the fact that service by mail is not permitted under Indonesian law from the fact that it is not explicitly prohibited under Indonesian law. In light of the fact that these rules regarding overseas service of process are meant to minimize offense to foreign law, the Court finds this distinction without merit.") *with Gannon International, Ltd. v. Blocker,* 2011 WL 111885 (E.D. Mo. Jan. 13, 2011) (requiring express prohibition); *Polargrid LLC v. Videsh Sanchar Nigam Ltd,* 2006 WL

903184, at *2-3 (S.D.N.Y. 2006) (same) *and SEC v. Alexander*, 248 F.R.D. 108, 111 (E.D.N.Y. 2007) (same). *See generally Fireman's Fund Ins. Co. v. Fuji Elec. Systems Co.*, 2005 WL 628034 (N.D. Cal. 2005) (summarizing split).

Consider the following analysis under Rule 4(f)(2)(C)(ii):

> [d]efendants contend that [plaintiff's] failure to comply with the laws of effective service in Indonesia or Malaysia precludes the availability of subsection (C), which only applies where return receipt mail service is not "prohibited." In response, [plaintiff] contends that "prohibited," as used in subsection (f)(2)(C)(ii), refers to forms of service that are a violation of Indonesian or Malaysian law. . . . [T]he plain language of (f)(2)(C)(ii) permits service via any form of return receipt mail that is not "forbid[den] by authority or command." A form of service is not "forbidden by authority" merely because it is not a form explicitly "prescribed" by the laws of a foreign country. It follows that the plain language of (f)(2)(c) merely limits the availability of this section to forms of service that do not violate the law of the country where service is attempted.
>
> This interpretation of (f)(2)(C) is supported by a consideration of the other provisions of subsection (f). Significantly, were subsection (f)(2)(C) inapplicable where a form of return receipt mail is simply not prescribed by the laws of a foreign country, this subsection would be superfluous to subsection (f)(2)(A), which allows service in a foreign country in any manner "prescribed" by the law of that country. In other words, if all forms of service not "prescribed" are "prohibited," then the failure to satisfy subsection (f)(2)(A) would preclude the availability of subsection (f)(2)(C) and the latter subsection would have no effect; it would be useless. A construction of "prohibit" that leads to this result should be avoided for it is well-established that courts should be "reluctant to interpret statutory provisions so as to render superfluous other provisions within the same enactment." *Dee-K Enter., Inc. v. Heveafil Sdn Bhd*, 174 F.R.D. 376, 379-380 (E.D. Va. 1997) (quoting *United States v. Ivester*, 75 F.3d 182 (4th Cir. 1996)).

Is that persuasive? Is there any better way to read Rule 4(f)(2)(C)(ii)?

Suppose that the clerk had sent the summons and complaint by private courier service rather than mail. Would that comply with Rule 4(f)(2)(C)(ii)? Courts are divided on the question. *See, e.g., Alu, Inc. v. Kupo Co., Inc.*, 2007 WL 177836, at *4 (M.D. Fla. Jan. 19, 2007).

16. *FRCP Rule 4(f)(2)(C)(ii)'s requirement of service by the clerk.* Unlike most other service rules, Rule 4(f)(2)(C)(ii) specifies that the "clerk" must "address[] and send[]" the summons and complaint to the individual. Consequently, even where service by mail is otherwise entirely proper, a party cannot rely on Rule 4(f)(2)(C)(ii) if the clerk did not physically mail the papers. *See, e.g., Ansell Healthcare, Inc. v. Maersk Line*, 545 F. Supp. 2d 339, 342 (S.D.N.Y. 2008). What explains the special need for the clerk's involvement as to this form of service? If service is not prohibited by foreign law, who cares whether the service is effected by the party or the clerk? Does not this requirement needlessly inject another party into an already cumbersome and complicated process? As noted above and noted throughout this chapter, service can be effected by parties directly through a variety of means, mail or otherwise. In light of these developments, is not the requirement of service by the clerk a vestige of a bygone era? Or is there some modern-day justification for the clerk to serve as the intermediary in such cases?

17. *Service by email under FRCP Rule 4(f)(3).* Is it appropriate to permit court-ordered service by email (even assuming that this does not violate foreign law)? Are there any risks from this approach? Note that emails are routinely used for the most important corporate communications.

18. *Service on third parties under Rule 4(f)(3).* As discussed below, courts sometimes find that service on a defendant will be proper when it has been effected on an alter ego or agent of the defendant within the United States. *See infra* pp. 947-948. Such cases typically then turn on whether the entity served satisfies the definition of alter ego or agent and on whether service is deemed "complete" under the applicable law.

Suppose, however, that a court pursuant to Rule 4(f)(3) orders service on a domestic entity that would not otherwise satisfy the applicable standards for service upon an agent or alter ego. For example, what if a court ordered service upon a U.S.-based sister corporation of a foreign corporate defendant? Would Rule 4(f)(3) authorize such a result? Is this service "not within any judicial district within the United States"? *See Kuklachev v. Gelfman,* 2008 WL 5068860 (E.D.N.Y. Nov. 24, 2008). Does *Rio* suggest an answer? Does this result seem right as a matter of policy? Note that, even in such cases, the service must satisfy the Due Process Clause. *See Nuance Communications, Inc. v. Abbyy Software House,* 2010 WL 4539396, at *13-14 (Fed. Cir. Nov. 12, 2010).

19. *Due process limitations on means of service of process.* As *Rio* illustrates, the Due Process Clause imposes limitations on the service of process abroad. In general, due process requires that notice be "reasonably calculated, under all the circumstances, to apprise interested parties of the pendency of the action and afford them an opportunity to present their objections." *Mullane v. Cent. Hanover Bank & Trust Co.,* 339 U.S. 306, 314 (1950). As described in *Rio,* this standard has permitted a wide range of innovative service mechanisms, including service by publication and service by delivery to a place frequented by the defendant. *See supra* p. 880; *Chanel, Inc. v. Zhixian,* 2010 WL 1740695 (S.D. Fla. Apr. 29, 2010) (email and public announcement in China); *Marlabs, Inc. v. Jakher,* 2010 WL 1644041 (D.N.J. Apr. 22, 2010) (service on attorney); *Studio A Entertainment, Inc. v. Active Distributors, Inc.,* 2008 WL 162785, at *4 (N.D. Ohio Jan. 15, 2008) (facsimile). *But see Hu v. Lee,* 2009 WL 4823915 (N.D. Cal. Dec. 10, 2009) (refusing to order service by email pursuant to Rule 4(f)(3) until plaintiff provides precise email address and necessary assurances that service on that address can and will reach defendants); *Nabulsi v. H.H. Sheikh Issa Bin Zayed Al Nahyan,* 2007 WL 2964817, at *6-9 (S.D. Tex. Oct. 9, 2007) (reaching similar conclusion); *Blumedia Inc. v. Sordid Ones BV,* 2011 WL 42296 (D. Colo. Jan. 6, 2011) (magistrate judge) (same); *Lyman Morse Boatbuilding Co., Inc. v. Lee,* 2011 WL 52509 (D. Me. Jan. 6, 2011) (magistrate judge) (same). *See generally The Knit With v. Knitting Fever, Inc.,* 2010 WL 4977944 (E.D. Pa. Dec. 7, 2010) (collecting cases analyzing due process issue).

(a) Service on foreign party's U.S. lawyer. In recent years, an especially popular method of court-ordered service is service on the defendant's U.S.-based attorney. Numerous courts have ordered this form of service. *See, e.g., Ehrenfeld v. Salim a Bin Mahfouz,* 2005 WL 696769 (S.D.N.Y. 2005); *FMAC Loan Receivables v. Dagra,* 228 F.R.D. 531 (E.D. Va. 2005); *Forum Fin. Group v. President & Fellows of Harvard Coll.,* 199 F.R.D. 22, 23-24 (D. Me. 2001). By contrast, some courts have relied on due process limitations to reject service on attorneys where doubts exist about whether the attorney presently represents or has regularly communicated with the foreign defendant. *See 1st Technology LLC v. Digital Gaming Solutions, S.A.,* 2008 WL 4790347 (E.D. Mo. Oct. 31, 2008).

Even assuming that counsel does currently represent a foreign defendant, is it an appropriate exercise of a court's Rule 4(f)(3) power to order service on that counsel? Does that not put foreign defendants in a quandary when they face the prospect of a lawsuit? They can retain a U.S. attorney (and risk that individual becoming an agent for acceptance of service of process) or they can deliberately *not* retain a U.S. lawyer (and thereby handicap their ability to obtain legal advice on the merits and resolution of the lawsuit). *See In re TFT-LCD (Flat Panel) Antitrust Litig.,* 2008 WL 4963035 (N.D. Cal. Nov. 19, 2008). Is it fair to place foreign defendants in that position? On the other hand, if service on a party's attorney were categorically precluded, would this not frustrate plaintiffs' efforts to obtain judicial relief and reward recalcitrant defendants who seek to avoid accountability for their conduct?

(b) Service by publication. A Second Circuit decision illustrates the application of due process notice requirements in the international context, where locating and effecting service on defendants can be particularly difficult. In *SEC v. Tome*, 833 F.2d 1086 (2d Cir. 1987), the Securities and Exchange Commission sought and obtained a district court order under Rule 4(i)(1)(E) of the old Federal Rules, authorizing service on the various unknown defendants by means of publication of notice of the suit in the "International Herald Tribune." According to the Second Circuit, "[t]he *International Herald Tribune* is an English language paper which is widely read by the international financial community in Europe." 833 F.2d at 1091. The Second Circuit rejected the defendant's due process challenge to this method of service. Although there was no direct evidence that the defendants had read the published notices, the court concluded that "[p]ublication of the complaint and summons in the *International Herald Tribune* was 'reasonably calculated' to notify the unidentified purchasers . . . [including the defendants] of the suit against them." 833 F.2d at 1093. The court reasoned:

> Where the plaintiff can show that deliberate avoidance and obstruction by the defendants have made the giving of notice impossible, statutes and case law have allowed substitute notice by mail and by publication in media of general and wide circulation. Thus, as business dealings have become increasingly interstate and international, the means of giving notice have been extended to meet these situations, so that parties may be held accountable in our courts of justice. 833 F.2d at 1092.

The court went on to observe that the defendants also were aware of the SEC's suit and that they were intended defendants, but that although they realized this, the SEC did not know their identities. In these circumstances, the court held, service by publication was proper. The court indicated that the Due Process Clause would *not* have been satisfied if "a defendant's name and address are known or may be obtained with reasonable diligence. . . ." 833 F.2d at 1094.

Is this persuasive? If a foreign defendant cannot easily be found, how likely is it that the foreign defendant is going to see the publication of the lawsuit? Especially where the publication is occurring in the English language, and the defendant resides in (or is a citizen of) a non-English-speaking country? Moved by such arguments, some courts have been more reluctant to order service by publication. *See Hinsey v. Better Built Dry Kilns, Inc.*, 2009 WL 176683, at *3-5 (N.D. Ind. June 22, 2009); *Chanel, Inc. v. Lin*, 2009 WL 1034627 (S.D. Fla. Apr. 16, 2009).

(c) Translations. An occasional issue in international cases involves the sufficiency of service upon foreign defendants who cannot read English. Although few decisions have addressed this question, the Due Process Clause probably requires a plaintiff to make reasonable efforts to provide notice of suit in a language the defendant can comprehend. *E.g., Lyman Steel Corp. v. Ferrostaal Metals Corp.*, 747 F. Supp. 389 (N.D. Ohio 1990) (due process obstacle to service of untranslated pleadings on German defendants although recipients were known to be fluent in English); *Lafarge Corp. v. M/V Maced. Hellas*, 2000 WL 687708, at *12 (D. La. 2000) (in some instances "the failure to provide a translation of the document into the recipient's native language might be unconstitutional"); *Teknekron Mgt., Inc. v. Quante Fernmeldetechnik*, 115 F.R.D. 175 (D. Neb. 1987) (failure to translate contract attached to complaint rendered service defective).

It is unlikely, however, that U.S. courts will require U.S. process to be translated into the native language of a foreign defendant where the defendant is capable of reading English. *See Mario Valente Collezioni, Ltd. v. Confezioni Semeraro Paolo, S.R.L.*, 115 F. Supp. 2d 367, 372 (S.D.N.Y. 2000) (due process did not require Italian translation of summons and complaint where defendant brought documents to English-speaking

Italian lawyer); *Heredia v. Transport SAS, Inc.*, 101 F. Supp. 2d 158, 162 (S.D.N.Y. 2000) (rejecting due process challenge given defendant's demonstrated English competency and fact that defendant signed return receipt that accompanied complaint); *Taft v. Moreau*, 177 F.R.D. 201, 204 (D. Vt. 1997) (rejecting due process challenge where parties did not claim an inability to understand the complaint); *Julen v. Larson*, 101 Cal. Rptr. 796 (App. Ct. 1972) (not requiring translation of Swiss complaint against U.S. defendant, but requiring English summary of nature of action, date for any response and consequences of not responding).

20. ***Diligent pursuit of service.*** Absent good cause or a court-ordered extension, Rule 4 requires a plaintiff to effect service within 120 days of filing the complaint. *See* Fed. R. Civ. P. 4(m). This deadline does not, however, apply to service pursuant to Rule 4(f). (Technically, the exception does not mention Rule 4(h), governing corporations, but courts have interpreted the exception to cover foreign corporations by virtue of Rule 4(h)'s reference to Rule 4(f).) Nonetheless, in cases where the time limit does not apply, courts have dismissed cases where plaintiffs have not been reasonably diligent in pursuing service against a foreign defendant. *See Mapping Your Future, Inc. v. Mapping Your Future Services, Ltd.*, 266 F.R.D. 305, 308-309 (D.S.D. 2009) (collecting cases). Additionally, there appears to be a division in authority on the question whether a plaintiff is required to *attempt* service within 120 days of filing the complaint. *See 3M Co. v. Darlet-Marchante Technologie SA*, 2009 WL 1228245 (D. Minn. May 5, 2009); *In re Vivendi Securities Litig.*, 2009 WL 691920 (S.D.N.Y. Mar. 17, 2009); *Allstate Ins. Co. v. Funai Corp.*, 249 F.R.D. 157, 161-162 (M.D. Pa. 2008) (discussing cases and dismissing case against foreign defendant due to plaintiffs' untimely effort to effect service). Finally, some courts simply state that, notwithstanding the inapplicability of Rule 4(m), service must be effected on the foreign defendant within a reasonable time, or the action is subject to dismissal. *See Nabulsi v. Nahyan*, 2008 WL 1924235 (N.D. Tex. Apr. 29, 2008).

While these various requirements might make good sense for policy reasons, what precisely is the source of a court's authority to articulate them? Consider *Umbenhauer v. Woog*, 929 F.2d 25, 31 (3d Cir. 1992) (stating that a time limit would be too burdensome on plaintiffs given the vagaries of foreign service).

21. ***Distinction between service of a civil complaint and service of a subpoena.*** In Note 146 above, *Nahas* drew a sharp distinction between service of a complaint—which it characterized as merely giving "notice"—and service of a subpoena—which it characterized as exerting "compulsion." The court thought that "[w]hen process in the form of a complaint is served extraterritorially, the informational nature of the process renders the act of service relatively benign in terms of infringement on the foreign nation's sovereignty." *See also FTC v. Compagnie de Saint-Gobain-Pont-a-Mousson*, 636 F.2d 1300, 1323 & n.130 (D.C. Cir. 1980).

Is the distinction between "notice" and "compulsory" process satisfying? Failure to comply with a subpoena may result in civil (or in some cases criminal) penalties. For the most part, however, these will be fairly modest—at least when compared with the potentially huge default judgments that can be triggered by proper service of mere "notice" pleadings such as civil complaints. Moreover, why should U.S. distinctions between a complaint and a subpoena determine the permissibility of service in a foreign nation that regards both types of service as unlawful? Does international law recognize a distinction between complaints and subpoenas?

If the notice/compulsion distinction is abandoned, is it possible to square *Nahas* with cases like *Umbenhauer* or *St. Gobain*—where the court apparently made no effort to reconcile the U.S. service provisions with either Swiss or international law? If U.S. service would violate foreign law, and international law, then shouldn't a specific authorization for such a result be required? Note that *Nahas* involved service of a document issued by a U.S. government agency. Is this relevant to the international law concerns underlying *Nahas*? Recall Professor Smit's efforts to distinguish "public" service from "private" service.

22. *Consequences of service abroad in violation of foreign law.* The plaintiff in *Rio* was permitted to proceed with its U.S. lawsuit, notwithstanding the fact that its service would likely be defective under Costa Rican law. Would you counsel a client to ignore the law of the defendant's home state in serving process in that country?

(a) Liability resulting from service abroad in violation of foreign law. One possible consequence of service abroad in violation of foreign law is criminal or civil sanctions against the process server. Recall the difficulties of the German accountant, noted above, who violated Article 271 of the Swiss Penal Code. Several nations have imposed sanctions against U.S. process-servers for attempting to personally deliver U.S. complaints and summonses to foreign defendants. *See, e.g.,* U.S. Department of Justice Memorandum No. 386 at 20 (1977), *reprinted in* 16 Int'l Leg. Mat. 1331, 1338 (1977) (U.S. Government attorneys sued for trespass for serving a subpoena in the Bahamas; U.S. Government attorney indicted for serving subpoena in France). Civil liability is also a possibility.

(b) Unenforceability of U.S. judgment based on service abroad in violation of foreign law. Perhaps most importantly for private plaintiffs, service abroad in violation of foreign law can jeopardize the enforceability of any U.S. judgment that the plaintiff obtains. "The enforcement of a judgment in the foreign country in which the service was made may be embarrassed or prevented if the service did not comport with the law of that country." Federal Rules of Civil Procedure, Rule 4(i) Advisory Committee Notes. *See, e.g.,* Code of Civil Procedure (Federal Republic of Germany) §328 ("A judgment of a foreign court shall not be recognized . . . if a defendant who has not entered an appearance on the merits was not properly served."); *Daiei K.K. v. Blagojevic,* 22 Japanese Annual of Int'l Law 160 (Tokyo Dist. Ct. 1978) (refusing to enforce French judgment because of defective mail service of untranslated complaint and summons). *See also infra* pp. 1084-1085, 1115-1120.

2. Service of Process Abroad Pursuant to the Hague Service Convention[154]

The United States has ratified two multilateral conventions that institutionalize and improve the basic letter rogatory approach to service of process: the Hague Convention on Service Abroad of Judicial and Extrajudicial Documents in Civil and Commercial

---

154. Commentary on the Hague Service Convention includes, *e.g.,* Campbell, *No Sirve: The Invalidity of Service of Process Abroad by Mail or Private Process Server on Parties in Mexico Under the Hague Service Convention,* 19 Minn. J. Int'l L. 107 (2010); Hawkins, *Dysfunctional Equivalence: The New Approach to Defining "Postal Channels" Under the Hague Service Convention,* 55 UCLA L. Rev. 205 (2007); Committee on Federal Courts, N.Y. State Bar Ass'n, *Service of Process Abroad: A Nuts and Bolts Guide,* 122 F.R.D. 63 (1989); Amram, *The Convention on Service Abroad of Judicial and Extrajudicial Documents in Civil and Commercial Matters,* 59 Am. J. Int'l L. 90 (1965); Amram, *The Proposed International Convention on the Service of Documents Abroad,* 51 A.B.A.J. 650 (1965); Hamilton, *An Interpretation of the Hague Convention on the Service of Process Abroad of Judicial and Extrajudicial Documents Concerning Personal Service in Japan,* 6 Loy. L.A. Int'l & Comp. L.J. 143 (1983); Jacklin, *Service of Process by Mail in International Civil Action as Permissible Under Hague Convention,* 112 A.L.R. Fed. 241 (2004); Kim & Sisneros, *Comparative Overview of Service of Process: United States, Japan, and Attempts at International Unity,* 23 Vand. J. Trans. L. 299 (1990); 1 B. Ristau, *International Judicial Assistance* Pt. IV (rev. ed. 2000). *See generally* Permanent Bureau of the Hague Conference on Private International Law, *Practical Handbook on the Operation of the Hague Service Convention* (rev. ed. 2006).

Matters (the Hague Service Convention)[155] and the Inter-American Letters Rogatory Convention.[156] As described below, the Hague Service Convention and the Inter-American Letters Rogatory Convention adopt broadly similar approaches to the service of process abroad. The two conventions' service mechanisms are referred to and incorporated by Rule 4(f)(1).

a. The Hague Service Convention Is Not a Basis for Personal Jurisdiction. The Hague Service Convention does not provide a basis for personal jurisdiction in federal court. Rather, personal jurisdiction must be established through some substantive grant contained in Rule 4 of the Federal Rules of Civil Procedure, or the state and federal long-arm statutes that it incorporates. This result is evident from the language and purposes of the Convention, which dealt only with the giving of notice, and not the granting of jurisdiction. In one court's words:

> We believe that the purpose and nature of the [Hague Service Convention] demonstrates that it does not provide independent authorization for service of process in a foreign country. The treaty merely provides a mechanism by which a plaintiff authorized to serve process under the laws of its country can effect service that will give appropriate notice to the party being served. . . . We believe that the treaty merely serves as an important adjunct to state long-arm rules, and that it specifies a valid method of effecting service abroad only if the state long-arm rule authorizes service abroad. . . . Nor do we read the treaty as the equivalent of a federal statute authorizing service in a foreign country. Instead, we believe that the treaty is similar to Rule 4(i) in that it provides a "manner" of service to be used by a litigant with the requisite authority to serve process. Were we to hold otherwise, we would attribute to the Senate that ratified the treaty the intent to authorize the equivalent of "world-wide" service of process in all federal-question, admiralty, and diversity cases while at the same time not authorizing nationwide service of process for those same claims.[157]

Other lower federal courts uniformly agree,[158] and the same result generally applies in state courts.[159]

b. Historical Background of the Hague Service Convention. The Hague Service Convention was drafted under the auspices of the Hague Conference on Private International Law.[160] The Convention was based upon, and intended to modernize,

155. 20 U.S.T. 361-373, T.I.A.S. No. 6638, 658 U.N.T.S. 163. The Hague Service Convention is reprinted in Appendix K.

156. Inter-American Convention on Letters Rogatory, signed in Panama on January 30, 1975, *reprinted in* 14 Int'l Leg. Mat. 339 (1975) and Additional Protocol to the Inter-American Convention on Letters Rogatory, signed in Montevideo, Uruguay on May 8, 1979, *reprinted in*, 18 Int'l Leg. Mat. 1238 (1979). For commentary on the Convention, *see* Low, *International Judicial Assistance among the American States — The Inter-American Conventions*, 18 Int'l Law. 705 (1984).

157. *DeJames v. Magnificence Carriers, Inc.*, 654 F.2d 280, 288 (3d Cir. 1981). The Court of Appeals remarked that it did "not believe that the treaty in any way affect[ed] a state's chosen limits on the jurisdictional reach of its courts."

158. *See Richardson v. Volkswagenwerk AG*, 552 F. Supp. 73 (W.D. Mo. 1982); *Lana Mora, Inc. v. SS Woermann Ulanga*, 672 F. Supp. 125, 128 (S.D.N.Y. 1987). The Federal Rules of Civil Procedure are in accord. The language of Rules 4(f) and 4(k), which specifically distinguish between the service of process and a basis for personal jurisdiction, also suggest that the Convention was not understood to provide a basis for personal jurisdiction in federal courts.

159. *Re v. Breezy Point Lumber Co.*, 460 N.Y.S.2d 264, 266 (Sup. Ct. 1983).

160. The Hague Conference, organized in 1893, acts as an international forum for representatives of member states to discuss and propose multilateral accords for the unification and harmonization of private international law. *See* Pfund, *International Unification of Private Law: A Report on United States Participation, 1985-86*, 20 Int'l Law. 623 (1986); Pfund, *United States Participation in International Unification of Private Law*, 19 Int'l Law. 505 (1985);

the Hague Convention on Civil Procedure of 1954 and the earlier 1905 Hague Convention on Civil Procedure.[161] Chapter I of both conventions dealt with service of process abroad.

Historically, the United States did not participate in the work of the Hague Conference, citing constitutional limitations arising from the U.S. federal system.[162] As U.S. international commerce expanded following 1945, however, U.S. interest in international judicial assistance increased. At the same time, U.S. federalism doctrines had evolved dramatically, and objections to federal involvement in international litigation reforms were muted. In 1956, the United States sent an observing delegation to the Hague Conference for the first time.[163]

In 1958, Congress established the Commission on International Rules of Judicial Procedure to study methods of international assistance and recommend improvements in federal law.[164] The Commission ultimately recommended a series of proposals, which significantly liberalized both the mechanisms for serving U.S. process abroad and assisting foreign courts in serving process in the United States.[165] On December 30, 1963, President Johnson signed a resolution authorizing U.S. participation in the Hague Conference,[166] and the United States attended the Tenth Session of the Hague Conference. Soon thereafter, the President signed into law the proposals of the Commission on International Rules of Judicial Procedure.[167] The new legislation was denominated as Public Law 88-619, later codified as 28 U.S.C. §§1696, 1781, 1782, and 1783.

The United States actively participated in the Tenth Session of the Hague Conference. The Tenth Session concerned a draft of the Hague Service Convention. Although the United States was not involved in the early drafting of the Convention, the proposed agreement complemented the parallel U.S. efforts to provide foreign nations with more extensive judicial assistance. The U.S. delegates urged that the Convention establish a liberal international regime for the transnational service of process. These delegates subsequently reported their perception that U.S. views were influential in shaping the Convention.[168]

The United States was an early signatory of the new Hague Service Convention in 1967.[169] It ratified the Convention in 1969. As of October, 2010, some 60 nations had

---

Amram, *Report on the Tenth Session of the Hague Conference on Private International Law,* 59 Am. J. Int'l L. 87 (1965); Graveson, *The Tenth Session of the Hague Conference of Private International Law,* 14 Int'l & Comp. L.Q. 528 (1965).

161. Amram, *Report on the Tenth Session of the Hague Conference on Private International Law,* 59 Am. J. Int'l L. 87 (1965); Graveson, *The Tenth Session of the Hague Conference of Private International Law,* 14 Int'l & Comp. L.Q. 528 (1965).

162. Nadelmann, *The United States Joins the Hague Conference on Private International Law (A History with Comments),* 30 Law & Contemp. Probs. 291 (1965); Pfund, *United States Participation in International Unification of Private Law,* 19 Int'l Law. 505 (1985).

163. *See* Pfund, *United States Participation in International Unification of Private Law,* 19 Int'l Law. 505 (1985); Note, *The Effect of the Hague Convention on Service Abroad of Judicial and Extrajudicial Documents in Civil or Commercial Matters,* 2 Cornell Int'l L.J. 125, 126 (1969).

164. *See supra* pp. 874-875; S. Rep. No. 2392, 85th Cong., 2d Sess. 3 (1958).

165. Pub. L. 88-619, 78 Stat. 996 (1964). The Act's legislative history is at H.R. Rep. No. 1052, 88th Cong., 1st Sess. (1963); S. Rep. No. 1580, 88th Cong., 2d Sess. (1964). The proposals included what became Rule 4(i) of the Federal Rules of Civil Procedure, and statutory proposals that would be codified as 28 U.S.C. §§1696, 1781, 1782, and 1783.

166. Pub. L. No. 88-244, 77 Stat. 775 (1963).

167. Pub. L. No. 88-619, 78 Stat. 995 (1964).

168. Amram, *The Proposed International Convention on the Service of Documents Abroad,* 51 A.B.A.J. 650, 652 (1965).

169. *See* Note, *The Effect of the Hague Convention on Service Abroad of Judicial and Extrajudicial Documents in Civil or Commercial Matters,* 2 Cornell Int'l L.J. 125, 127-128 (1969).

ratified or acceded to the Convention.[170] The Convention remains open for accession by any state.[171]

3.   Overview of the Hague Service Convention

The Hague Service Convention consists of 31 articles, which must be read in conjunction with the designations, declarations, and reservations made by individual member states in acceding to the Convention.[172] The Convention is expressed in equally authoritative English and French versions.[173] The Convention's drafting history has been collected, and is useful in interpreting the agreement.[174]

The centerpiece of the Hague Service Convention is the "Central Authority" mechanism for service abroad, set forth in Articles 2 through 7. The Convention requires each contracting state to establish a Central Authority within its governmental administration.[175] In ratifying or acceding to the Convention, contracting states must identify their Central Authority.[176] The Central Authority is responsible for receiving foreign requests for service of process ("letters of request"); serving or arranging for the service of documents on local residents; and returning or arranging for return of proof of service to the requesting state.[177] This mechanism is available to litigants in virtually all civil or commercial cases where process is served from one contracting state into another contracting state.

The Convention establishes uniform requirements regarding the form and authentication of requests for service via the Central Authority mechanism.[178] A model letter of request is attached to the Convention, as is a model certificate of proof of service.[179] These forms must be used. The Convention also establishes requirements concerning the languages to be used in letters of request and the translation of documents accompanying letters of request.[180]

With very limited exceptions, a Central Authority is obliged by the Convention to execute incoming requests for service from other signatory States; it has no discretion to decline to effect service. Only if a letter of request does not comply with the Convention's

---

170. As of October 2005, parties to the Hague Service Convention included, among others, Australia, Canada, China, Czech Republic, Denmark, Egypt, Finland, France, Germany, India, Italy, Japan, Mexico, Netherlands, Poland, Russia, Spain, Sweden, Turkey, the United Kingdom, and the United States. Complete lists of all parties to the Convention are included in the United States Code Annotated sections following Federal Rules of Civil Procedure 4. They also are available at the Hague Conference's website: http://www.hcch.net/index_en.php?act=conventions.status&cid=17.

171. Hague Service Convention, Article 28.

172. Counsel should be sure to identify the *official* instrument of the reservation and be mindful of the official language in which it has been deposited. For example, in recent years, litigation has arisen over the scope of Mexico's reservation, much of which is attributable both to misunderstandings about the scope of Mexico's reservations and error in the "courtesy" translation of those reservations. *Compare, e.g., Griffin v. Mark Travel Co.,* 724 N.W.2d 900 (Wis. App. 2006) *with Cardona v. Kreamer,* 235 P.3d 1026 (Ariz. 2010) *(en banc) and OGM, Inc. v. Televisa, S.A. de C.V.,* 2009 WL 1025971 (C.D. Cal. Apr. 15, 2009).

173. Hague Service Convention, Final Clause.

174. Conference de la Haye de Droit International Privé, *Actes et Documents de la Dixième Session* (1964) (hereinafter "*Actes et Documents*").

175. Hague Service Convention, Article 2.

176. Hague Service Convention, Articles 2 and 21.

177. Hague Service Convention, Articles 5 and 6.

178. Hague Service Convention, Article 7.

179. Hague Service Convention, Articles 3 and 6.

180. Hague Service Convention, Articles 5 and 7.

formal requirements[181] or if it infringes the receiving state's "sovereignty or security" may the request be denied.[182]

In addition to the Central Authority mechanism, the Convention also provides the possibility of service in alternative ways. In particular, Articles 8 and 9 of the Convention permit service through the requesting state's diplomatic or consular agents; Article 10(b) and (c) permit service by "judicial officers or other competent persons"; Article 10(a) permits "sending" of documents by mail; and Article 19 permits service pursuant to the "internal law of a contracting State" where service is to be effected. Importantly, all of these alternative mechanisms are available only if the receiving state permits their use. In ratifying or acceding to the Convention, a state may declare which of these alternative mechanisms of service it will not permit.[183] As discussed below, many contracting states have objected to the use of one or more of these mechanisms.[184]

Finally, the Convention limits the circumstances in which default judgments can be made. Article 15 of the Convention provides that, where service abroad has been made under the Convention, a default judgment cannot be entered unless it is shown either that: (a) service was in accordance with local law in the place where service was effected, or (b) service was actually delivered to the defendant or his residence pursuant to a method permitted by the Convention.[185] The Convention also requires a showing that the defendant received service in sufficient time to respond.

4. Purposes of the Hague Service Convention

The Hague Service Convention was intended to fulfill several related objectives. First, the Convention sought to provide a simple, expeditious procedure for service of process abroad.[186] The Convention's preamble states that its purpose is "to improve the organization of mutual judicial assistance . . . by simplifying and expediting the procedure." The Convention attempts to accomplish this by means of the "Central Authority" mechanism and the introduction of mandatory forms of letters of request and proof of service. At the same time, the Convention also permits alternative forms of service — subject to objection by the state of destination — that are more flexible.

Second, the United States and other nations were concerned about service mechanisms in certain civil law states that did not afford defendants adequate notice.[187] The principal example was *"notification au parquet,"* whereby service was effected by depositing documents with a local government official.[188] The Convention sought to address concerns about service that failed to provide reasonable notice[189] by creating "appropriate means to ensure that judicial and extra-judicial documents to be served abroad shall be

---

181. Hague Service Convention, Article 4.

182. Hague Service Convention, Article 13.

183. Hague Service Convention, Article 21.

184. *See infra* pp. 924-927.

185. *See infra* p. 952.

186. S. Rep. No. 2397, 85th Cong., 2d Sess. at 7 (1958), *reprinted in* 1958 U.S. Code, Cong. & Admin. News at 5206; *Volkswagenwerk AG v. Schlunk,* 486 U.S. 694, 698 (1988).

187. S. Exec. Rep. No. 6, 90th Congress, 1st Sess. 6 (1967) ("Given the continually increasing volume of American travel abroad, especially in Europe, of international business transactions, of United States investment abroad, the subject of insuring that United States citizens who were sued in foreign courts received notice . . . is a matter of substantial importance to this country."); Note, *Service Abroad Under the Hague Convention,* 71 Marq. L. Rev. 649, 650-657 (1988); *Volkswagenwerk AG v. Schlunk,* 486 U.S. 694, 702-705 (1988).

188. *See Volkswagenwerk AG v. Schlunk,* 486 U.S. 694 (1988).

189. Amram, *The Proposed International Convention on the Service of Documents Abroad,* 51 A.B.A.J. 650, 652 (1965); Hague Conference on Private International Law, Practical Handbook on the Operation of the Hague Convention of 15 November 1965 on the Service Abroad of Judicial and Extrajudicial Documents in Civil or Commercial Matters, at 28 (1983) [hereafter "Practical Handbook"]; Report of the Senate Committee

brought to the notice of the addressee in sufficient time."[190] The Convention does so by establishing service mechanisms likely to provide actual notice and by limiting default judgments in cases where proper notice was not given.

Third, some civil law countries were concerned that reliance on "unofficial" means of service in the United States might interfere with their nationals' ability to effect "official" service, as required by foreign law, on U.S. residents in connection with civil law proceedings.[191] By establishing the Central Authority mechanism, the Convention provided a way that service could be effected in the United States (and other nations) by the actions of government agents.

Finally, the Convention was intended to remove obstacles to demonstrating that service had been effected abroad. Article 6 provides a uniform mechanism and form of certificate for attesting that service has been effected. This reduces difficulties in proving that service was actually made on a foreign defendant.

5.   Scope of Hague Service Convention: "Civil or Commercial"

The Hague Service Convention applies in "all cases, in civil or commercial matters, where there is occasion to transmit a judicial or extrajudicial document for service abroad."[192] There is uncertainty as to the meaning of the phrase "civil or commercial matters." The phrase is not defined in the Convention, and there is little guidance in the Convention's negotiating history as to its intended meaning. Ironically, the drafters of the Convention concluded that the phrase "civil or commercial" should be used "to avoid any ambiguity," since earlier international judicial assistance agreements employed the phrase.[193] Unfortunately, neither the text of earlier conventions, nor their negotiating histories, clearly defines the term "civil or commercial."[194]

Disputes about the scope of the Hague Service Convention can arise for U.S. litigants that attempt to serve complaints asserting claims for multiple or punitive damages, or asserting claims based upon "public law" protections (like the antitrust laws). In Germany, the Central Authority for Bavaria refused to serve complaints in U.S. civil actions seeking punitive damages, on the theory that such complaints were penal in character.[195] The Court of Appeals for Munich later overturned the Bavarian Central Authority's action, holding that U.S. civil complaints seeking punitive damages can come within the scope of the Convention.[196] Appellate courts in Frankfurt and Düsseldorf reached the same conclusion, as has the Federal Supreme Court.[197] Despite these decisions, other foreign

---

on Foreign Relations on the Convention on the Service Abroad of Judicial and Extrajudicial Documents, S. Exec. Rep. No. 6, 90th Cong., 1st Sess. 11-12 (Statement of Philip W. Amram) (1967).

190. Hague Service Convention, Preamble.

191. *See* Note, *The Effect of the Hague Convention on Service Abroad of Judicial and Extrajudicial Documents in Civil or Commercial Matters,* 2 Cornell Int'l L.J. 125, 128-129 (1969).

192. Hague Service Convention, Article 1.

193. III Conference de la Haye de Droit International Privé, *Actes et Documents de la Dixième Session* 79 (1964).

194. The "civil or commercial" phase was used in the 1905 and 1954 Hague Civil Procedure Conventions. *See* 1 B. Ristau, *International Judicial Assistance* 148 (rev. ed. 2000). For a decision suggesting that "civil" is defined by reference to state law, *see In re Alyssa F.,* 6 Cal. Rptr. 3d 1, 4 (Cal. Ct. App. 2003).

195. *See* Riesenfeld, *Service of United States Process Abroad: A Practical Guide to Service Under the Hague Service Convention and the Federal Rules of Civil Procedure,* 24 Int'l Law. 55 (1990) (recounting refusals to serve antitrust and RICO complaints seeking treble damages).

196. Decision of May 9, 1989, Docket No. VA 3/89, 29 Int'l Legal Materials 1571 (1989) and 10 Praxis des Internationalen Privat-und Verfahrensrechts [IPRax] 175 (1990); Decision of July 15, 1992, 13 Zeitschrift fuer Wirtschaftsrecht [ZIP] 1271 (1992).

197. Decision of March 21, 1991, 37 RIW 417 (Frankfurt Court of Appeals 1991); Decision of February 19, 1992, 38 RIW 846 (1992) (Düsseldorf Court of Appeal 1992).

authorities have reportedly refused to serve U.S. complaints asserting antitrust claims and other actions that foreign states might regard as "public" or "penal."[198]

6. Service of Process by Central Authorities Under Article 5 of the Hague Service Convention

Although other avenues for service exist under the Hague Service Convention, the "Central Authority" mechanism is the centerpiece of the Convention. The Central Authority mechanism is set out in Articles 2 through 7.

Each state that becomes a party to the Hague Service Convention is *required* by Article 2 of the Convention to designate a "Central Authority" to "receive requests for service coming from other contracting States," and to serve or arrange for the service of complying documents.[199] Additionally, contracting states may, at their option, assign their Central Authorities the responsibility of sending requests for service to other contracting states. The Central Authority in each contracting state is set forth in the notifications of accession to the Convention, some of which are excerpted in Appendix _____.

In the United States, the Central Authority is the Office of International Judicial Assistance (also called the Office of Foreign Litigation) of the Civil Division of the Department of Justice.[200] With respect to service of foreign process in the United States, the Justice Department recently delegated these duties to a private contractor, who is "the only private process server company authorized to act on behalf of the United States to receive requests for service, proceed to serve the documents, and complete the certificate of service."[201]

Service must be made by the receiving Central Authority under Article 5 in one of three ways: (1) under Article 5(a) in the manner used for service of process in domestic actions; (2) under Article 5(b) in any manner specified by the applicant (provided it is not incompatible with the laws of the receiving state); and (3) under the "second paragraph" of Article 5, the defendant may be permitted voluntarily to accept service.

a. Service Under Article 5(a) in the Manner Used for Service in Domestic Actions. Article 5(a) of the Convention provides for service through a Central Authority "by the method prescribed by its internal law for the service of documents in domestic actions upon persons who are within its territory." Unless the applicant requests a particular means of service under Article 5(b), Article 5(a) leaves it to the Central Authority of the receiving state to determine the mechanism of service to be used (at least where local law provides alternative means of service). Once service has been completed, the Central Authority provides a certification to that effect. That certification, according to several decisions, provides *prima facie* evidence of sufficient service even if a defendant later complains that service was defective.[202]

198. *E.g., U.S. ex rel. Bunk v. Birkart Globistics GmbH & Co.*, 2010 WL 423247 (E.D. Va. Feb. 4, 2010); *Railway Express Agency, Inc. v. E.P. Lehmann Co.*, 1989 U.S. Dist. LEXIS 9951 (S.D.N.Y. 1989). In those cases, substitute methods of service such as those available under Rule 4(f)(3) remain available to the plaintiff.

199. Hague Service Convention, Article 5.

200. The U.S. Central Authority's address is: Office of International Judicial Assistance, Civil Division, Department of Justice, 1100 L Street, NW, Room 11006, Washington, D.C. 20530, U.S.A. Its telephone number is (202) 514 7455. In 2005, the Office handled approximately 6,000 requests under the Hague Convention, a slight decrease from the approximately 6,500 that it handled in 2004.

201. Further information on the contracting out of this function can be found at the Hague Conference's website. http://www.hcch.net/index_en.php?act=authorities.details&aid=279. The private contractor, Process Forwarding International, is located in Seattle, Washington and can be reached at (206) 521-2979.

202. *See Northrup King Co. v. Compania Productora Semillas Algodoneras Selectas, SA*, 51 F.3d 1383, 1390 (8th Cir. 1995); *American Medical Sys., Inc. v. Biolitec, Inc.*, 604 F. Supp. 2d 325, 331 (D. Mass. 2009); *Herman Miller Inc. v.*

If Article 5(a) service is made through the Central Authority mechanism in the manner used in domestic actions, the receiving state may insist that the requesting party provide translations of the documents that are to be served into the official language of the receiving state.[203] The translation requirement does not expressly apply to the letter of request,[204] but it does apply to the complaint and summons.[205] At least one lower court has required translations of all documents to be served, including exhibits.[206] This can impose substantial expense on plaintiffs. Some courts have suggested that failure to comply strictly with any translation requirement is not fatal so long as the Central Authority issued the certification of service and the plaintiff later cured any defects in service of the required translations.[207]

A number of foreign contracting states, including Germany and Japan, require that translations of all documents accompany any letter of request. The requirements of contracting states regarding translations can sometimes — but not always — be ascertained from the notifications of such foreign states of their instruments of ratification or accession to the Convention. In other cases, a *Practical Handbook on the Operation of the Hague Convention of 15 November 1965 on the Service Abroad of Judicial and Extrajudicial Documents in Civil or Commercial Matters,* published by the Hague Conference, lists the positions of contracting states regarding translations.

b. Service by Central Authority Pursuant to Article 5(b).   Article 5(b) permits the requesting party to ask that the receiving foreign Central Authority make service in a particular fashion. Article 5(b) was included in the Convention because of concerns that Article 5(a) service might not always permit a manner of service that would satisfy the due process and notice requirements of the requesting state.[208] Examples of service requested under Article 5(b) include service by hand delivery to a specific individual, service with a written receipt acknowledging delivery, and service where the process server attests that service was made on a person shown in a photograph. Article 5(b) does not require a Central Authority to make service in a way that is incompatible with the internal law of the receiving state.

By its terms, Article 5(b) does not expressly give receiving states the right to demand translations if service is made in the method requested by the applicant. U.S. courts have generally not required translations where service is made via an alternative to

---

Alphaville Design Inc., 2009 WL 3429739, at *5 (N.D. Cal. 2009); *Marine Geotechnics, LLC v. Williams,* 2009 WL 2144278 (S.D. Tex. 2009); *United National Retirement Fund v. Ariela, Inc.,* 642 F. Supp. 2d 328, 334-335 (S.D.N.Y. 2008); *Garg v. Winterthur,* 525 F. Supp. 2d 315, 322 (E.D.N.Y. 2007).

203. *See* Hague Service Convention, Article 5 ("If the document is to be served *under the first paragraph above,* the Central Authority may require the document to be written in, or translated into, the official language or one of the official languages of the State addressed.").

204. Hague Service Convention, Article 5 ("the Central Authority may require *the document* to be written in, or translated into. . . .").

205. *LG Electronics, Inc. v. ASKO Appliances, Inc.,* 2009 WL 1811098, at *4 (D. Del. June 23, 2009); *Taylor v. Uniden Corp.,* 622 F. Supp. 1011, 1016 (E.D. Mo. 1985); *Teknekron Mgt, Inc. v. Quante Fernmeldetechnik GmbH,* 115 F.R.D. 175, 177 (D. Nev. 1987); *Froland v. Yamaha Motor Co., Ltd.,* 296 F. Supp. 2d 1004, 1008 (D. Minn. 2003); *Johnson v. Pfizer, Inc.,* 32 Conn. L. Rptr. 207, 2002 WL 1041984 (Conn. Super. Ct. 2002). *But see Northrup King Co. v. Compania Productora Semillas Algodoneras Selectas, SA,* 51 F.3d 1383 (8th Cir. 1995) (service not insufficient for failure to serve a translation of the summons, given no objection by Central Authority and no indication that Spain required translation of the summons).

206. *Teknekron Mgt., Inc. v. Quante Fernmeldetechnik,* 115 F.R.D. 175 (D. Nev. 1987).

207. *Garg v. Winterthur,* 525 F. Supp. 2d 315, 322-323 (E.D.N.Y. 2007).

208. Amram, *Report on the Tenth Session of the Hague Conference on Private International Law,* 59 Am. J. Int'l L. 87, 90 (1957).

Article 5(a),[209] although they have sometimes relied upon the absence of any foreign declaration requiring translations in these circumstances.[210] The U.S. Department of State advises that requests for service under Article 5(b) be accompanied by translations.[211] Similarly, some U.S. courts have suggested that translation of a summary of the complaint and a description of the proceedings is required.[212]

c. Service by the Central Authority Pursuant to Article 5's "Second Paragraph." Article 5's "second paragraph" permits service of process on parties who voluntarily accept service (sometimes referred to in continental Europe as "*remise simple*"), provided that such service is consistent with local law. Voluntary service is not uncommon in Western Europe, notably France, Belgium, Netherlands, and Sweden. It typically involves delivery of documents to a local police station, which then requests the defendant to pick up the documents. The request is ordinarily accompanied by a statement that the defendant is free not to accept the documents.

No translations are expressly required by the Convention when service is made pursuant to Article 5's final paragraph. One U.S. court has held that, where a plaintiff's letter of request (not accompanied by translations), seeks service under Article 5 without specifying a subsection, and the foreign Central Authority makes service notwithstanding its usual practice of requiring translations, then the service will be deemed "voluntary" under Article 5's final paragraph and the absence of translations will not affect its validity.[213]

It is not clear whether Article 5's final paragraph was intended to permit the "private" modes of service commonly used in the United States (*i.e.*, hand-delivery by a private attorney), or whether it only applies to service by a Central Authority.[214] Given the structure of the Convention, and Article 5 in particular, the latter would appear to be the better view. Presumably, even if such private service is permitted, the defendant could refuse service and render it ineffective.

7. "Exclusivity" of the Hague Service Convention

It is important to define clearly the relationship between the Convention and other U.S. mechanisms for extraterritorial service within contracting states. Two issues

---

209. *Hunt v. Mobil Oil Corp.*, 410 F. Supp. 4 (S.D.N.Y. 1975); *Weight v. Kawasaki Heavy Industries, Ltd.*, 597 F. Supp. 1082, 1086 (D.C. Va. 1984); *Sandoval v. Honda Motor Co., Ltd.*, 527 A.2d 564, 567 (Pa. Super. 1987); *Shoei Kako Co. v. Superior Court*, 33 Cal. App. 3d 808 (1973). *But see Lobo v. Celebrity Cruises, Inc.*, 667 F. Supp. 2d 1324, 1338-1339 (S.D. Fla. 2009) ("Several districts have held that only Article 5 service through a central authority requires translation of the documents, and Article 10(a) has no such requirement."); *Weight v. Kawasaki Heavy Indus.*, 597 F. Supp. 1082, 1086 (E.D. Va. 1984).

210. *Vazquez v. Sund Emba AB*, 548 N.Y.S.2d 728 (App. Div. 1989) (where Sweden had not specifically declared that translations were required for alternatives to Article 5(a), no such requirement would be inferred; leaving open question whether Sweden could, consistent with the Convention, demand such translations).

211. U.S. Department of State Publication, Hague Convention on the Service Abroad of Judicial and Extra-Judicial Documents in Civil and Commercial Matters, *available at* http://travel.state.gov/law/judicial/judicial_685.html.

212. *Julen v. Larson*, 25 Cal. App. 3d 325, 328 (1972). *Compare Vazquez v. Sund Emba AB*, 548 N.Y.S.2d 728, 733 (App. Div. 1989); *Hunt v. Mobil Oil Corp.*, 410 F. Supp. 4 (S.D.N.Y. 1975); *Shoei Kako Co. v. Superior Court*, 33 Cal. App. 3d 808 (1973). *See also* 1 B. Ristau, *International Judicial Assistance* §4-3-1(2) at 198 (rev. ed. 2000).

213. *Greenfield v. Suzuki Motor Co.*, 776 F. Supp. 698 (E.D.N.Y. 1991).

214. *See Casa De Cambio Delgado, Inc. v. Casa de Cambio Puebla, SA de CV*, 763 N.Y.S.2d 434, 437-439 (N.Y. Super. 2003); *Tax Lease Underwriters v. Blackwell Green*, 106 F.R.D. 595 (E.D. Mo. 1985); *Tamari v. Bache & Co. (Lebanon)*, 431 F. Supp. 1226, 1229 (N.D. Ill. 1977); *Shoei Kako Co. v. Superior Court*, 411 (Cal. App. 1973); Report of U.S. Delegation, *reprinted in* 17 Int'l Leg. Mat. 312, 316 (1978).

must be distinguished. First, *must* the Convention's mechanisms for service be used, even if U.S. law provides different mechanisms? Second, *can* the Convention's mechanisms for service be used, even if domestic U.S. law does not authorize the use of such mechanisms?

a. The Hague Service Convention Preempts Service Mechanisms Under Local Law.   Most U.S. courts have concluded that, if service is to be made in the territory of a contracting state, and if the Hague Service Convention is available for such service, then the Convention *must* be complied with. According to these courts, traditional mechanisms for U.S. extraterritorial service — including Federal Rule of Civil Procedure 4 and its state counterparts — are preempted by the Convention when service must be made within a contracting state.[215]

In *Volkswagenwerk AG v. Schlunk,*[216] the Supreme Court endorsed this position, opining in dicta that the Hague Service Convention provides the exclusive means for service abroad in those cases where it applies: "By virtue of the Supremacy Clause, U.S. Const. Art. VI, the Convention pre-empts inconsistent methods of service prescribed by state law in all cases to which it applies."[217] This result applies without regard to whether state law makes any reference to the Convention. Even if state law specifically provided that service could be made in particular means *in addition* to the Convention mechanisms, *Schlunk* holds that such state rules are preempted.

The reasoning of those U.S. courts that have required resort to the Convention's service mechanisms is straightforward, at least on its face. Article 1 of the Convention provides that the Convention "*shall* apply in all cases, in civil or commercial matters, where there is occasion to transmit a judicial or extrajudicial document for service abroad." The use of apparently mandatory language — "shall" and "all cases" — has been interpreted to require use of the Convention for service abroad in preference to any other means of service provided for in federal or state law. This is illustrated by the decision in *Kadota v. Hosogai,*[218] excerpted below.

b. The Hague Service Convention Provides Service Mechanisms Supplementing Domestic Law.   It is less clear whether the Convention's service mechanisms independently supplement the service mechanisms available under domestic U.S. law. If domestic law expressly or impliedly authorizes use of the Convention's mechanisms, then those mechanisms will be available. If domestic law does not expressly or impliedly authorize use of the Convention, then the question arises whether the Convention, of its own force, makes its mechanisms available to U.S. litigants. This issue is considered in the notes following *Kadota.*

---

215. *E.g., Darko, Inc. v. MegaBloks, Inc.,* 2006 WL 2945954 (N.D. Ohio 2006); *In re Estate of Grad Droste Zu Vischering,* 782 N.W.2d 141, 146 (Iowa 2010); *Weber v. Zurich Financial Services Group,* 2004 WL 3091635, at *2 (Mass. Super. 2004); *Bakala v. Bakala,* 576 S.E.2d 156, 163 (S.C. 2003); *Bowers v. Wurzburg,* 519 S.E.2d 148, 159 (W. Va. 1999); *Aspinall's Club Ltd. v. Aryeh,* 450 N.Y.S.2d 199, 202 (App. Div. 1982); *Cipolla v. Picard Porsche Audi,* 496 A.2d 130 (R.I. 1985); *Kadota v. Hosogai,* 608 P.2d 68 (Ariz. App. 1980); *Sheets v. Yamaha Motors Corp., U.S.A.,* 891 F.2d 533, 536 (5th Cir. 1990). A few lower courts reached contrary conclusions, but these decisions almost certainly do not survive *Volkswagenwerk AG v. Schlunk,* 486 U.S. 694 (1988). *See International Controls Corp. v. Vesco,* 593 F.2d 166, 179-180 (2d Cir. 1979) (dictum); *Barefield v. Sund Emba, AB,* 1985 WL 4280 (E.D. Pa. 1985) (dictum).

216. 486 U.S. 694 (1988).

217. 486 U.S. at 699.

218. 608 P.2d 68 (Ariz. App. 1980).

KADOTA v. HOSOGAI

608 P.2d 68 (Ariz. App. 1980)

HAIRE, PRESIDING JUDGE. The sole issue on appeal is whether the trial court had personal jurisdiction over the appellant, Hiroshi Kadota, a resident of Japan. The appellant argues that appellee's various attempts to serve process on him were insufficient. . . . This action is based upon an automobile accident that occurred in Arizona. As a result of the accident, appellee's husband, who was a passenger in the automobile driven by Mr. Kadota, died and appellant Kadota suffered severe brain damage. After a stay in a hospital in Arizona, the appellant returned to Japan to live with his family. The appellee, Michiko Hosogai, filed suit alleging that appellant's negligence had caused her husband's death.

The appellee has attempted to achieve valid service of process upon Mr. Kadota at least three times. On April 5, 1976, the appellee filed an affidavit of a private process server stating that he had served the superintendent of motor vehicles pursuant to the [Arizona] non-resident motorists statute. . . . On May 5, 1976, appellee filed an affidavit of a Japanese attorney which stated that he was over 18 years old, not a party to the action and that he had personally served a copy of the summons with a Japanese translation on Mr. Kadota on April 25, 1976 in Japan. . . . The third attempt to serve process upon the appellant involved service on appellant's guardian ad litem on July 7, 1976. . . .

[After the trial court rejected appellant's objections to these methods of service,] the matter proceeded to trial and a jury verdict of $225,000 was awarded in favor of the appellee and against the appellant. . . . On appeal, the appellant argues that all three methods of service were defective, thus depriving the trial court of jurisdiction over him. The three main contentions of the appellant are: (1) that the purported service pursuant to Rule 4(e)(6)(iii), Arizona Rules of Civil Procedure, by the Japanese attorney was invalid inasmuch as it was contrary to a treaty between the United States and Japan; (2) . . . that compliance with [the nonresident motorists statute,] A.R.S. §28-503A(2), was ineffective because that statute is contrary to the treaty between the United States and Japan; and (3) that service upon Mr. Kadota's guardian ad litem by itself was ineffective to confer jurisdiction upon the trial court. . . .

One method of service that appellee relied upon is the personal service by a Japanese attorney on the appellant in Japan. Appellee argues that this service was in compliance with Rule 4(e)(6)(iii), Arizona Rules of Civil Procedure. The appellant contends that, even if the appellee complied with the rule, a treaty between Japan and the United States [(the Hague Service Convention)] prohibits this type of service. . . . The appellant argues that the [Hague Service Convention] provides the exclusive means by which service may be accomplished in Japan, while the appellee contends that the treaty is merely a supplement to the existing methods of service of process provided for in the Arizona Rules of Civil Procedure. . . .

The second clause of Article VI of the United States Constitution provides that: . . . "all Treaties made, or which shall be made, under the Authority of the United States, shall be the supreme Law of the Land. . . ." This provision of the Constitution has always been interpreted to mean that a treaty entered into by the United States shall be superior to and prevail over any conflicting laws of the individual states. Therefore, the State of Arizona cannot attempt to exercise jurisdiction under a rule promulgated by its courts if that rule would violate an international treaty. *United States v. Pink,* 315 U.S. 203 (1942).

Furthermore, Article I of the Treaty in this case expressly provides:

The present Convention shall apply in all cases, in civil or commercial matters, where there is occasion to transmit a judicial or extrajudicial document for service abroad.

. . . "The Convention, through the Supremacy Clause, supersedes all state and federal methods of service abroad, but specifically allows certain prior methods to remain in force." Downs, *The Effect of the Hague Convention on Service Abroad of Judicial and Extrajudicial Documents in Civil or Commercial Matters,* 2 Cornell Int'l L.J. 125, 131 (1969). Therefore, to the extent that the Convention is inconsistent with the Arizona Rules of Civil Procedure, the Convention controls. This being so, an inquiry into the relationship between the methods of service allowed by the Convention and those methods provided for in the Arizona Rules of Civil Procedure is necessary in order to determine to what extent, if any, the corresponding provisions are inconsistent. . . .

[T]he key provision of the Convention in this case is Article 10 which states:

> Provided the State of destination does not object, the present Convention shall not interfere with —
>
> (a) the freedom to send judicial documents, by postal channels, directly to persons abroad,
>
> (b) the freedom of judicial officers, officials or other competent persons of the State of origin to effect service of judicial documents directly through the judicial officers, officials or other competent persons of the State of destination,
>
> (c) the freedom of any person interested in a judicial proceeding to effect service of judicial documents directly through the judicial officers, officials or other competent persons of the State of destination.

Japan signed the Convention, but has objected to Article 10(b) and (c). The complete Convention (including Article 10(b) and (c)) appears to authorize all of the methods of service provided for in the Arizona Rules of Civil Procedure plus some additional methods. Article 19 and Rule 4(e)(6)(i) permit service in a manner prescribed by the law of the foreign country. Article 9 and Rule 4(e)(6)(ii) provide for service of letters rogatory. Rule 4(e)(6)(iii) and Article 10(b) and (c) allow for personal service by competent persons in the foreign country. Therefore, the Convention as a whole does not appear to contravene the Rules of Civil Procedure.

However, Japan has stated "It is declared that the Government of Japan objects to the use of the methods of service referred to in subparagraphs (b) and (c) of Article 10." As a result of this objection, the treaty between Japan and the United States is inconsistent with the Arizona Rules of Civil Procedure to the extent that personal service pursuant to Rule 4(e)(6)(iii) and Article 10(c) is objected to by Japan. If the court were to agree with the appellee that the Convention was supplementary to the rules, Japan's objections would be meaningless in light of the inconsistency between Rule 4(e)(6)(iii) and Japan's objections to Article 10(b) and (c). Therefore, appellee's argument that her compliance with Rule 4(e)(6)(iii) was sufficient service of process on the appellant fails. The treaty between the United States and Japan specifically prohibits this method of service, although the Arizona rules allow for it. The law is clear that state statutes are abrogated to the extent that they are inconsistent with a treaty. Therefore, personal service by a Japanese attorney in Japan is ineffective service of process under the Convention.

Notes on **Kadota**

1. *Hague Service Convention supersedes state law and Federal Rules of Civil Procedure as to service abroad in contracting states. Kadota, Schlunk,* and other federal court decisions have almost unanimously held that the Convention supersedes state service of process rules and old Rule 4(i). *See supra* pp. 917-918. As a consequence, service mechanisms authorized

by state law and old Rule 4(i) could not be used for service in a contracting state unless permitted by the Convention: the Convention was held to be mandatory and to preclude reliance on mechanisms of service other than those which it provided.

2. Hague Service Convention is "self-executing." Critical to the foregoing result is the conclusion that the Convention is "self-executing" — that is, it requires no implementing legislation in order for its terms to be enforced in U.S. courts. *United States v. Belmont,* 301 U.S. 324 (1937); *Restatement (Third) Foreign Relations Law* §111 (1987); *supra* pp. 15-17. Lower courts have uniformly concluded that the Hague Service Convention is "self-executing." *E.g., Vorhees v. Fischer & Krecke,* 697 F.2d 574, 575 (4th Cir. 1983); *Xyrous Commc'ns, LLC v. Bulgarian Telecomms. Co. AD,* 2009 WL 2877084, at *10 (E.D. Va. 2009); *United States S.E.C. v. Int'l Fiduciary Corp., SA,* 2007 WL 7212109, at *2 (E.D. Va. 2007); *Pochop v. Toyota Motor Co.,* 111 F.R.D. 464, 465 (S.D. Miss. 1986). What justifies this conclusion?

3. Are Schlunk and Kadota correctly decided? Is the result in *Kadota,* which was later embraced in *Schlunk,* persuasive? Does the language of the Convention support the conclusion that it was meant independently to supersede all inconsistent state mechanisms for serving process abroad? Consider the precise language of Article 1. It says that the Convention "shall apply" when there is occasion to serve process abroad. Assuming that the Convention does "apply," what makes it exclusive? Note that there is no provision in the Convention that forbids a state from using service mechanisms not identified in the Convention. If the Convention "appl[ies]," does this imply that other service mechanisms do not also apply? Do the purposes of the Convention require holding that it is exclusive? Would the Convention's purposes not be achieved by merely recognizing the Central Authority mechanism as an available (but not exclusive) alternative? It has been said that "the American delegate to the Hague Conference . . . had not even imagined that the Convention might be given exclusive effect." Smit, *Recent Developments in International Litigation,* 35 S. Tex. L. Rev. 215, 222-223 (1994).

4. Hague Service Convention implemented by FRCP Rule 4(f). Unlike old Rule 4(i), Rule 4(f) of the Federal Rules of Civil Procedure expressly incorporates the Hague Service Convention. *See supra* pp. 875-876, 900. Like pre-1993 precedent, Rule 4(f)(1) requires use of the means "authorized" by the Convention. *See supra* pp. 875-876, 917-918. Thus, in federal courts, even if the Convention were not self-executing, it is made applicable in federal courts by Rule 4(f).

5. Service under Hague Service Convention pursuant to FRCP Rule 4(f). Unfortunately, the scope of Rule 4(f)'s authorization for service of process pursuant to the Hague Service Convention is uncertain. Like other aspects of Rule 4(f), the language of Rule 4(f)(1) is poorly drafted and must be examined carefully to determine what particular mechanisms of service are permitted. Even so, substantial uncertainties exist regarding what forms of service are and are not permitted.

(a) What mechanisms of service are available under FRCP Rule 4(f)(1)? Note that, under Rule 4(f)'s express terms, only mechanisms of service that are "agreed" or "authorized" by an applicable international convention may be invoked under Rule 4(f)(1). As described above, the Hague Service Convention contains a variety of provisions regarding the service of process abroad, including: (i) the Central Authority mechanism; (ii) service through diplomatic or consular agents; (iii) service through consular or diplomatic channels designated by the receiving state; (iv) sending of documents by postal channels under Article 10(a); (v) service through the judicial officers or other competent persons of the receiving state; and (vi) Article 19's authorization to use any method of service permitted by the internal law of the country of destination. Which of the Convention's mechanisms are "agreed" or "authorized" by the Convention and therefore available under Rule 4(f)(1)?

(b) FRCP Rule 4(f)(1) authorizes service by Central Authority mechanism. At a minimum, it is clear that the Central Authority mechanism of the Convention is available under Rule 4(f)(1). This mechanism is plainly both "authorized" and "agreed" within the meaning of Rule 4(f)(1). Thus, a U.S. litigant seeking to serve a defendant located in a Convention signatory in a federal court action can effect service by using the Central Authority mechanism.

(c) Does FRCP Rule 4(f)(1) also authorize use of alternative mechanisms? Are all of the Convention's alternative mechanisms for service set forth in Articles 8, 9, 10, and 19 also available under Rule 4(f)(1)? Put differently, are these alternative mechanisms for service either "internationally agreed means of service" or "authorized by the Hague [Service] Convention," and thus within the scope of Rule 4(f)(1)? An affirmative answer to the foregoing question would have an important consequence. It would mean that all of the alternative mechanisms available under the Convention may be used under Rule 4(f)(1), *without regard to whether or not a particular mechanism is also identified in Rule 4(f)(2)*. These mechanisms could be used because they would be "agreed" in the Convention, and could therefore affirmatively be incorporated by Rule 4(f)(1).

It is possible to read Rule 4(f)(1) more narrowly, as encompassing only service mechanisms that are specifically and affirmatively authorized under the Convention — that is, the Central Authority mechanism — and not as authorizing use of the alternative mechanisms under the Convention. That interpretation would rest on the fact that Articles 8, 9, 10, and 19 provide that the Convention leaves states "free" to effect service in alternative ways, or does "not interfere" with such alternatives. Thus, service pursuant to these alternatives is arguably not "internationally agreed," but is instead not internationally forbidden. *See Brockmeyer v. May,* 383 F.3d 798, 804 (9th Cir. 2004) ("The Hague Convention affirmatively authorizes service of process through the Central Authority of a receiving state. Rule 4(f)(1), by incorporating the Convention, in turn affirmatively authorizes use of a Central Authority. However, Rule 4(f)(1) does not go beyond means of service affirmatively authorized by international agreements. It is undisputed that Brockmeyer did not use either the Central Authority under the Hague Convention or any other internationally agreed means for accomplishing service."); *Ballard v. Tyco Int'l, Ltd.,* 2005 WL 1863492, at *4 (D.N.H. 2005) (same).

Under this reading, the alternative mechanisms referred to above could only be used pursuant to Rule 4(f)(2), and not Rule 4(f)(1). This interpretation would rest on the conclusion that the Convention does not affirmatively "authorize" use of alternative mechanisms, but merely leaves the availability of those mechanisms undisturbed. This view would also have important consequences. Under it, the mechanisms of service permitted under Rule 4(f)(2) would be available if they were also authorized by the Hague Service Convention. Importantly, however, other means of service permitted by the Convention, but not listed in Rule 4(f)(2), would not be available. What are some examples of such mechanisms? The most significant example is service by international courier or other form of mail, discussed in detail below. *See infra* pp. 924-939. Which of the foregoing interpretations of Rule 4(f) is most consistent with the purposes of the Rule and the U.S. ratification of the Convention?

(d) Must FRCP Rule 4(f)(1) authorize use of the Convention's alternative mechanisms? Even if Rule 4(f)(1) only authorizes use of the Central Authority mechanism, and even if no other provision in Rule 4 permitted use of a particular service mechanism under the Convention, the Convention itself arguably provides an independent, self-executing means of serving process abroad. Pre-1993 precedent held exactly this. *Ackermann v. Levine,* 788 F.2d 830, 840 (2d Cir. 1986) ("the Convention 'supplements' — and manifestly is not limited by — Rule 4"); *Loral Fairchild Corp. v. Matsushita Electric*

Industrial Co., 805 F. Supp. 3 (E.D.N.Y. 1992) ("service pursuant to the Hague Convention need not meet the requirements of Rule 4"); there is authority to the same effect under Rule 4(f). *See infra* pp. 936-939. Under this view, parties would be free to effect service in accordance with means provided by the Convention, even if not separately authorized by U.S. law.

   6. *Service under Convention in manner not specifically authorized by U.S. state law.* Nothing in Arizona's Rules of Civil Procedure, at least at the time of *Kadota,* authorized use of the Convention's Central Authority mechanism. *See Cardona v. Kreamer,* 235 P.3d 1026 (Ariz. 2010) (*en banc*) (describing Arizona Rule 4.2(i)-(k), which authorize service pursuant to an internationally agreed means). Is the service nevertheless valid, on the grounds that the Convention's mechanisms automatically supplement state service mechanisms without the need for legislative implementation? Until recently, state procedural rules generally did not specifically incorporate the Convention in the manner that Rule 4(f)(1) does. *See, e.g.,* Ariz. R. Civ. P. 4.2(i)-(k) (authorizing service pursuant to an internationally agreed means). Where a state rule is silent, does the Convention nonetheless permit a litigant in state court to ignore state procedural rules and serve process in a manner that the state's legislative body has refused to authorize? Most authorities have answered in the affirmative. "[B]y virtue of the Supremacy Clause, service made by a Central Authority pursuant to the Convention is valid in a state court even if, absent the Convention, the service would be defective." Committee on Federal Courts of the New York State Bar Association, *Service of Process Abroad: A Nuts and Bolts Guide,* 122 F.R.D. 63, 75 (1989); *Restatement (Third) Foreign Relations Law* §472, comment c & Reporters' Note 5 (1986); *In re Estate of Graf Droste zu Versicherung,* 782 N.W.2d 141, 146 (Iowa 2010); *Morgenthau v. Avion Resources Ltd.,* 11 N.Y.3d 383, 390 (2008); *MacIvor v. Volvo Penta of America, Inc.,* 471 So. 2d 187 (Fla. Ct. App. 1985).

   This conclusion does not appear to have been thoroughly analyzed. As we have seen, it appears that the Convention is "self-executing" under U.S. law. *See supra* pp. 917-918, 920-921. Thus, the Convention itself preempts inconsistent state service mechanisms, without the need for implementing legislation. *See supra* pp. 917-918. Suppose, however, that a U.S. state legislature wished to permit only specific service mechanisms in state courts, not all the mechanisms allowed by the Convention. Could a state forbid litigants in state courts from using particular Convention mechanisms? Although the Convention is the "supreme law of the land," and is "self-executing," does this necessarily mean that the Convention was intended to *require* states to use *all* of its alternatives? Is it plausible to suggest that it would be inconsistent with the Convention for a state to decline to make use of one of the Convention's mechanisms?

   On the other hand, the U.S. view of the Convention has long been that it was intended to liberalize service abroad. *See supra* pp. 913-914. The United States (as a whole) at least in theory gave various concessions to obtain the liberal service mechanisms permitted by the Convention. Would not these federal purposes be undercut if individual states could prevent U.S. nationals from making use of the Convention's mechanisms?

   A similar issue arises with respect to federal restrictions on foreign service that pre-date the Convention. Recall that Articles 8 and 9 of the Convention permit service via consular channels. *See supra* pp. 912-913 & *infra* pp. 924-925. As described above, however, U.S. consular regulations have long forbid U.S. litigants from effecting service abroad through consular channels. *See supra* p. 874. Do the foregoing authorities suggest that the U.S. consular regulations are preempted by the Convention?

   7. *Treatment of FRCP Rule 4(d)'s waiver of service mechanism under Convention.* As discussed above, *see supra* pp. 878-879, Rule 4 includes a waiver of service mechanism. Plaintiffs are permitted to send a copy of their complaint to the defendant, together with a request that it waive formal service. Suppose this waiver provision is used as to defendants residing in countries that are signatories to the Hague Service Convention. Does the Convention permit this? If not, would new Rule 4 override the previously adopted Convention? Could it? *See* Burbank, *The World in Our Courts,* 89 Mich. L. Rev. 1456, 1485-1489 (1991).

8. *Effect of good faith compliance with Convention.* Suppose a party attempts to effect service under the Convention but fails to do so. May a court hold that good faith efforts to comply with the Convention are sufficient? *See Burda Media, Inc. v. Viertel,* 417 F.3d 292, 301 (2d Cir. 2005) (where service was attempted in good faith and no prejudice would result, service was not rendered ineffective by defects that were not the fault of plaintiff); *CytoSport, Inc. v. Cytogenix Sports Laboratories, SRL,* 2010 WL 5418883 (E.D. Cal. Dec. 23, 2010) (same); *Seiko Epson Corp. v. Glory South Software Mfg., Inc.,* 2007 WL 219944 (D. Or. Jan. 24, 2007) (holding that service was effective based on good faith efforts and actual notice provided to defendant despite unsuccessful attempt to comply with Hague Convention); *Overseas Food Trading, Ltd. v. Agro Aceitunera S.A.,* 2007 WL 77337 (D.N.J. Jan. 8, 2007) (reaching same result where court was uncertain whether receiving state objected to alternative service pursuant to Article 10(a)).

Does your answer depend on the receiving state's receptivity to the request? For example, several federal courts have noted recently that, since 2003, Russia has not considered the Hague Service Convention to be in effect between Russia and the United States. *See Nuance Communications, Inc. v. Abbyy Software House,* 2010 WL 4539336 (Fed. Cir. Nov. 12, 2010). According to a circular produced by the State Department's Bureau of Consular Affairs, "requests sent [via diplomatic channels or] directly by litigants to the Russian Central Authority under the Hague Service Convention are returned unexecuted." *Id.* If a plaintiff seeks to effect service in Russia, what should it do under these circumstances? Does Rule 4(f) provide an answer? *See* 1993 Advisory Committee Notes to Fed. R. Civ. P. 4(f) (noting that court-ordered service pursuant to Rule 4(f)(3) is particularly appropriate where the receiving state has "refused to cooperate for substantive reasons"). Do these fallback strategies create any risks for the plaintiff? What should a plaintiff do if a court refuses to acknowledge the difficulties in service via the Central Authority in a foreign country? *See, e.g., Nuance Communications, Inc. v. Abbyy Software House,* 2009 WL 2707390, at *2 (N.D. Cal. Aug. 25, 2009) (refusing to accept plaintiff's argument that Russia unilaterally has suspended judicial cooperation in civil matters with the United States).

What if the foreign state has not completely renounced its obligation to effect service but merely refuses in a particular case on the ground that the underlying lawsuit violates its sovereignty and security? *See In re South African Apartheid Litig.,* 643 F. Supp. 2d 423, 437-438 (S.D.N.Y. 2009). In those cases, must a federal court take into consideration the "sovereignty" and "security" concerns of the foreign state in deciding whether to order service pursuant to Rule 4(f)(3)?

8. Alternative Mechanisms for Service Under Articles 8, 10, and 19 of the Hague Service Convention

In addition to establishing the basic Central Authority mechanism of service under Article 5, the Hague Service Convention also permits other means of extraterritorial service. These alternatives are: (i) service through the requesting state's diplomatic or consular agents pursuant to Articles 8 and 9; (ii) service through the receiving state's "judicial officers or other competent persons" pursuant to Article 10(b) and (c); (iii) sending of documents by mail pursuant to Article 10(a); and (iv) service in accordance with the "internal law" of the receiving state pursuant to Article 19. One of the key purposes of the Convention was to ensure the flexibility that these various alternatives offered.

The Convention generally only permits use of one of these alternative mechanisms where the receiving state has not objected to that mechanism.[219] Many of the Convention's contracting states have objected to some or all of the alternatives. Before attempting service under the Convention's alternatives, counsel must consult the declaration of the relevant member state.[220]

a. Direct Service by Consular and Diplomatic Channels Under Article 8. Article 8 provides that "[e]ach contracting State shall be free to effect service of judicial documents upon persons abroad, without application of any compulsion, directly through its diplomatic or consular agents." Service through consular agents is common in many jurisdictions. Given the general refusal of the State Department to assist in serving process abroad, however, Article 8 is of little practical importance to litigants in U.S. courts.[221]

b. Indirect Service by Consular and Diplomatic Channels Under Article 9. Article 9 provides that signatory states "shall be free . . . to use consular channels to forward documents, for the purpose of service, to those authorities of another contracting State which are designated by the latter for this purpose." In "exceptional cases," diplomatic channels may be used for the same purpose. There is no specific provision in Article 9 permitting receiving states to object to such indirect service via consular or diplomatic channels, but service cannot be effected unless the receiving state has designated appropriate authorities for receipt of such service. Again, U.S. State Department regulations preclude effective use by U.S. litigants of this service mechanism.

c. Alternative Service Mechanisms Under Article 10. Article 10 of the Convention provides for three alternative forms of service. Like service under Article 8, the Convention permits member states to object to alternative forms of service under Article 10. Service by an alternative means under Article 10 is permitted only if the receiving state has not objected.

i. Article 10(a): "Sending" Judicial Documents by Mail. Article 10(a) permits the "sending" of judicial documents by postal service directly to the defendant. It reads:

> Provided the State of destination does not object, the present Convention shall not interfere with — (a) the freedom to send judicial documents, by postal channels, directly to persons abroad. . . .

A number of foreign states — including China, Germany, Norway, Turkey, and Egypt — have objected to use of Article 10(a).[222] Other nations — including the United States, Japan, France, and the United Kingdom — have made no objection.

---

219. Under Article 8, contracting states are free (notwithstanding the objections of the receiving state) to effect service on the requesting state's own nationals through consular agents.

220. Selected declarations are excerpted in Appendix L. All such declarations are reproduced in the United States Code Annotated for Federal Rule of Civil Procedure 4.

221. *See supra* p. 874.

222. *See* Memo of L. Ralph Meacham, Director, Administrative Office of United States Courts, to Clerks of United States District Courts (Nov. 7, 2000) (describing states that have objected to use of Article 10(a)).

Like other aspects of Rule 4(f) and the Hague Service Convention, Article 10(a) has engendered substantial litigation in the United States. The litigation has arisen because of attempts by U.S. plaintiffs to serve process on foreign defendants by ordinary mail or international courier under Article 10(a). U.S. lower courts are sharply divided over the validity of such "service."[223]

A number of lower U.S. courts have held that Article 10(a) permits service by registered mail, addressed directly to the foreign defendant, provided that the country in which service is effected has not objected to the use of Article 10(a).[224] In contrast, a number of other lower courts have concluded that Article 10(a) only permits a plaintiff to "send" judicial documents, and not to "serve" them: these courts have held that "service" cannot be effected in a contracting state by mail under Article 10(a), even if that state has not objected to the use of Article 10(a).[225]

One reason that U.S. plaintiffs have sought to use Article 10(a) is its speed and efficiency. Postal service can be completed in a matter of days; Central Authority service takes two or more months, and sometimes substantially longer. In addition, there is no express requirement that translations be provided if service can be made by mail under Article 10(a). Several of the U.S. lower courts that permit Article 10(a) mail service have affirmed this reading of the Convention's translation requirements, though recently a split has emerged on this issue.[226] Nonetheless, failure to provide translations could raise due process questions.[227]

ii.   Articles 10(b) and 10(c): Service by "Competent Persons."   Articles 10(b) and 10(c) permit the sending of letters of request directly to the "judicial officers, officials or other competent persons" of the receiving state. There is uncertainty as to the identity of the "competent persons" who can be requested to make service abroad and as to the law for determining competency (*i.e.*, requesting state law or receiving state law). For example, U.S. law might be said to recognize private process-servers as "competent persons" for the service of process; if so, personal service abroad by a private foreign attorney might be permissible, absent an objection by the foreign state under Article 10(c). Some foreign states permit service under Article 10(c) by local lawyers or process-servers.

d.   Article 19's Savings Provision.   Article 19 of the Convention indicates that neither the Central Authority mechanism, nor the Article 10 alternatives, overrides more liberal

---

223. *See infra* p. 926, notes 224-226; *Williams v. LeBrun*, 2010 WL 3341482 (Conn. Super. July 30, 2010) (summarizing split); *The Knit With v. Knitting Fever, Inc.*, 2010 WL 2788203 (E.D. Pa. July 13, 2010) (same).

224. *E.g.*, *Brockmeyer v. May*, 383 F.3d 798, 802 (9th Cir. 2004); *Research Sys. Corp. v. IPSOS Publicite*, 276 F.3d 914, 926 (7th Cir. 2002); *Ackermann v. Levine*, 788 F.2d 830, 839-840 (2d Cir. 1986). *See generally Willis v. Magic Power Co., Ltd.*, 2011 WL 66017 (E.D. Pa. Jan. 7, 2011) (discussing competing interpretations).

225. *E.g.*, *Nuovo Pignone, SpA v. STORMAN ASIA M/V*, 310 F.3d 374, 383-385 (5th Cir. 2002); *Bankston v. Toyota Motor Corp.*, 889 F.2d 172 (8th Cir. 1989); *Intelsat Corp. v. Multivision TV LLC*, 2010 WL 3368655, at *7 (S.D. Fla. 2010); *Uppendahl v. American Honda Motor Co.*, 291 F. Supp. 2d 531, 533-534 (W.D. Ky. 2003); *Sardanis v. Sumitomo Corp.*, 718 N.Y.S.2d 66, 68 (App. Div. 2001) *Cooper v. Makita U.S.A., Inc.*, 117 F.R.D. 16, 17 (D. Me. 1987); *Melia v. Les Grandes Chais de France*, 135 F.R.D. 28, 38-39 (D.R.I. 1991).

226. For cases holding that Article 10(a) does not impose a translation requirement, *see, e.g., Girafa.com, Inc. v. Smartdevil Inc.*, 2010 WL 3034432 (D. Del. Aug. 4, 2010); *Heredia v. Transport SAS, Inc.*, 101 F. Supp. 2d 158, 161-162 (S.D.N.Y. 2000); *Lemme v. Wine of Japan Import, Inc.*, 631 F. Supp. 456, 464 (E.D.N.Y. 1986); *Weight v. Kawasaki Heavy Indus.*, 597 F. Supp. 1082, 1086 (E.D. Va. 1984); *Miltenberg & Samton, Inc. v. Assicurazioni Generali, SpA*, 2000 WL 33711043, at *9 (Pa. Com. Pl. 2000); *Wright v. American Home Products Corp.*, 768 A.2d 518, 526 (Del. Super. 2000). For a recent discussion of the split on the issue, *see Lobo v. Celebrity Cruises, Inc.*, 667 F. Supp. 2d 1234, 1338-1339 (S.D. Fla. 2009).

227. *See supra* p. 880; *Heredia v. Transport SAS, Inc.*, 101 F. Supp. 2d 158, 161-162 (S.D.N.Y. 2000); *Julen v. Larson*, 101 Cal. Rptr. 796 (App. Ct. 1972).

provisions of law in signatory nations concerning the service of foreign process within their territory. Article 19 provides:

> To the extent that the internal law of a contracting State permits methods of transmission, other than those provided for in the preceding Articles, of documents coming from abroad, for service in its territory, the present Convention shall not affect such provisions.

Article 19 was included in the Convention at the request of the United States to make clear that the Convention would not interfere with more liberal U.S. rules concerning service of process within the United States.[228] Several lower U.S. courts have held that service of process abroad in a Convention signatory state, in compliance with that state's internal law, is valid notwithstanding non-utilization of the procedures specifically identified in the Convention.[229]

It is not clear, under Article 19, when a foreign state's internal law permits a service mechanism. Article 19 could be narrowly construed as only allowing "use of alternative service methods which foreign law *specifically* authorizes" for service from abroad.[230] Alternatively, Article 19 could be interpreted as permitting the use of any service mechanism that foreign law does not expressly forbid.[231]

e. Selected Materials Concerning Alternative Service Mechanisms Under the Hague Service Convention.   A number of U.S. courts have considered when the alternative service mechanisms available under Articles 10 and 19 can be utilized. As described above, lower U.S. courts are divided in their interpretations of Article 10(a), with some permitting the service of process by mail in states that have not formally objected to Article 10(a), and others holding that Article 10(a) does not permit "service" by mail. The decision excerpted below in *Honda Motor* summarizes the support for the various views and adopts the former one. Lower U.S. courts have also disagreed over the availability of service mechanisms other than mail service under Article 10. Also excerpted below is the decision in *Vasquez v. Sund Emba AB*, where the court considers the effect of Articles 10(b) and 10(c) of the Convention on service by personal delivery in Sweden.

HONDA MOTOR CO. v. SUPERIOR COURT
12 Cal. Rptr. 2d 861 (Cal. Ct. App. 1992)

ELIA, ASSOCIATE JUSTICE. . . . The issue presented, as to which the authorities conflict, is whether a California resident may obtain valid service on a Japanese national by a private mail service. We shall hold that such a service is invalid under the Hague Convention. . . .

The dispositive facts are not in controversy. Plaintiff Stephen G. Opperwall served defendant Honda Motor Co., Ltd. ("Honda") by sending the summons, complaint and other documents to Honda's office in Japan by certified mail, return receipt

---

228. 113 Cong. Rec. 9404 (April 17, 1967).

229. *DeJames v. Magnificence Carriers, Inc.*, 654 F.2d 280, 288 (3d Cir. 1981); *Lemme v. Wine of Japan Import, Inc.*, 631 F. Supp. 456, 464 (E.D.N.Y. 1986); *Vasquez v. Sund Emba AB*, 548 N.Y.S.2d 728 (App. Div. 1989).

230. Comment, *Service of Process Abroad Under the Hague Convention*, 71 Marq. L. Rev. 649, 682 (1988) (emphasis in original). *See* Downs, *The Effect of the Hague Convention on Service Abroad of Judicial and Extrajudicial Documents in Civil or Commercial Matters*, 2 Cornell Int'l L.J. 125, 132 (1969). *See also infra* pp. 938-939.

231. These possibilities are discussed below. *See infra* pp. 938-939.

requested. The papers were unaccompanied by any Japanese translation. Honda admitted receipt of the papers. Honda's acknowledgement stamp of receipt on the documents was in English. The superior court denied Honda's motion to quash this service, and this petition followed.

The issue is one of statutory construction and depends on whether Article 10(a) of the Convention allows service of process upon a Japanese corporation by registered mail. . . . The Convention provides specific procedures to accomplish service of process. Authorized modes of service are service through a central authority in each country; service through diplomatic channels; and service by any method permitted by the internal law of the country where the service is made. Each signatory nation may ratify, or object to, each of the articles of the Treaty. . . . In addition to the specifically authorized modes of service, the Treaty also includes Article 10, the crucial provision which we must interpret here. . . . Japan has objected to subparagraphs (b) and (c), but not to (a). It is on subparagraph (a) that plaintiff relies as permitting a mail service on a Japanese corporation.

There are two published California appellate decisions in point, which conflict. [*Compare Shoei Kako Co. v. Superior Court*, 33 Cal. App. 3d 808 (Cal. Ct. App. 1973) *with Suzuki Motor Co. v. Superior Court*, 200 Cal. App. 3d 1476 (Cal. Ct. App. 1988).] The Federal decisions also reach conflicting results, and also differ as to who has the weight of authority. [*Compare*] *Ackermann v. Levine*, 788 F.2d 830 (2d Cir. 1986) *with Bankston v. Toyota Motor Corp.*, 889 F.2d 172 (8th Cir. 1989). However, of the decisions since 1989 . . . a clear majority have agreed with *Suzuki* that the mail service on a Japanese corporation violates the Treaty.

An important observation is that in Article 10 of the Treaty, the two subparagraphs which Japan has objected to — subparagraphs (b) and (c) — both refer to "service" of judicial documents, but subparagraph (a), which Japan has accepted, refers to the freedom to "send" such documents. The cases which have invalidated a mail service on a Japanese corporation have relied heavily on this distinction. They have observed that the difference in wording is significant, not only because of the time honored statutory rule of construction that use of particular language in one part of a statute but not in another is deemed to be purposeful and meaningful, but also because it is not plausible to assume that Japan would reject the relatively formal methods of service provided in subparagraphs (b) and (c), yet would accept the less regulated and more informal method of subparagraph (a), a mail service by a private individual with no official involvement. It is more plausible to assume that Japan did not regard subparagraph (a) as authorizing any service. Rather, it is most likely that the drafters of the Convention intended, and that Japan understood them to intend, that subparagraph (a) merely authorized the mailing of judicial documents other than the summons, but that "service" required more rigorous control.

This interpretation is consistent with the fact that in Japan a private mail service is not authorized, and that service of process in that country cannot be effectuated by either attorneys or lay people, but only through the official action required by the court clerk and also by the mail carrier's implied-in-law acceptance of the role of a special officer of the court when he delivers the service which has been stamped by the clerk. It seems highly unlikely that Japan, which does not allow its own nationals to serve process by mail, would accept such a service by foreign nationals, and it is even more unlikely that Japan, having rejected mail service by its own nationals and also mail service under subparagraphs (b) and (c) of Article 10, of the Treaty would accept an informal mail service under subparagraph (a). Plainly the meaning of the word "send" was taken by that state to be something other than "service." . . .

The authorities which have held otherwise have observed that interpreting Article 10(a) as not applying to service renders it superfluous, in that all it then provides is a "'freedom to send judicial documents'" which presumably has always existed, the mails being open to everyone. This point has some validity, although subparagraph (a) is not entirely superfluous even if it does not authorize original service, since it presumably does permit mailing of judicial documents other than process directly to litigants, a procedure which may not otherwise be available in a foreign state. But the persuasive value of the "superfluity" argument pales beside the reasons to adopt a contrary position, not only supported by canons of statutory construction, but also avoiding a glaring inconsistency with the internal procedural law of Japan. As the *Suzuki* court found, and later decisions have agreed, given that service of process by registered mail is not allowed in Japan, it is "extremely unlikely that Japan's failure to object to Article 10(a) was intended to authorize the use of registered mail as an effective mode of service of process, particularly in light of the fact that Japan specifically objected to the much more formal modes of service by Japanese officials which were available in Article 10(b) and (c)." *See Suzuki,* 200 Cal. App. 3d at 1481.

Also of importance is that the opinion of the court in *Shoei Kako,* is flawed by its misunderstanding of Japanese law. The decision noted that the record before the court did not demonstrate that service by mail with evidence of delivery was not a permissible method for service of documents in domestic Japanese actions. This mistake of Japanese law seriously undermines the persuasive value of *Shoei Kako.* . . .

Plaintiff below . . . emphasized here that there was actual service, the documents were received, and there was also evidence that the papers were understood, even though not translated into Japanese, because the acknowledgement of receipt was in English and the documents were quickly delivered to Honda's American attorneys. However, these arguments share a common fallacy; they assume that in California, actual notice of the documents or receipt of them will cure a defective service. That may be true in some jurisdictions, but California is a jurisdiction where the original service of process, which confers jurisdiction, must conform to statutory requirements or all that follows is void. Specifically, plaintiffs must comply with statutes prescribing the method of service on foreign corporations.

Plaintiff argues that it is ridiculous, wasteful and time consuming to reverse the trial court just to force plaintiff to go through the motions of a service under the Convention, when there is no question but that Honda has notice of the action, its attorneys stand ready to defend it, and no practical aim can be accomplished by quashing the service. However, plaintiff cites no authority permitting a California court to authorize an action to go forward upon an invalid service of process. . . .

STATEMENT BY JAPANESE DELEGATION TO HAGUE CONFERENCE ON PRIVATE INTERNATIONAL LAW
28 Int'l Legal Mats. 1556, 1561 (1989)

Japan has not declared that it objects to the sending of judicial documents, by postal channels, directly to persons abroad. In this connection, Japan has made it clear that no objection to the use of postal channels for sending judicial documents to persons in Japan does not necessarily imply that the sending by such method is considered valid service in Japan; it merely indicates that Japan does not consider it as infringement of its sovereign power.

U.S. DEPARTMENT OF STATE, LEGAL ADVISOR'S OPINION
30 Int'l Legal Mats. 260 (1991)

I am writing with reference to the interpretation of United States treaty obligations in the recent [*Bankston v. Toyota Motor Corp.*, 889 F.2d 172 (8th Cir. 1989) decision, holding that "service" could not be effected by mail in Japan under Article 10(a)]. As you are aware, while courts in the United States have final authority to interpret international treaties for the purposes of their application as law in the United States, they give great weight to treaty interpretations made by the Executive Branch.

The U.S. Government did not have an opportunity to express its views on the issues before the 8th Circuit Court in *Bankston*. The November 28 issue of the U.S. Law Week first brought the November 13, 1989 decision of the Court of Appeals in *Bankston* to the attention of the Office of the Legal Adviser in the Department of State and the Office of Foreign Litigation in the Justice Department, which serves as the U.S. Central Authority under the Hague [Service] Convention. The Circuit Court in *Bankston,* examining Toyota's motion to dismiss for improper service on the defendant in Japan by registered mail rather than under procedures set out in the Hague Service Convention (to which both the United States and Japan are parties), concluded that service of summons and complaint by registered mail to a defendant in a foreign country (Japan) is not a method of service of process permitted by the Hague Convention.

We understand from appellant's/plaintiff's counsel that the time period for filing a petition for a rehearing in *Bankston* has elapsed. We understand further that neither the plaintiff nor the Court of Appeals was aware of a statement made by the delegate of Japan in April, 1989 at a meeting of representatives of countries that have joined the Hague Service Convention that appears to be relevant to the basic question addressed in the *Bankston* case. The Japanese statement in question was the result of efforts by the Departments of State and Justice to encourage the Government of Japan to clarify its position with regard to the service of process in Japan by mail from another country party to the Hague Service Convention. . . .

We consider that the Japanese statement represents the official view of the Japanese Government that Japan does not consider service of process by mail in Japan to violate Japanese judicial sovereignty and that Japan does not claim that such service would be inconsistent with the obligations of any other country party to the Hague Service Convention vis-à-vis Japan. The Japanese statement suggests, however, that it is possible, and even likely, that service in Japan by mail, which may be considered valid service by courts in the United States, would *not* be considered valid service in Japan for the purposes of Japanese law. Thus, a judgment by a court in the United States based on service on the defendant in Japan by mail, while capable of recognition and enforcement throughout the United States, may well not be capable of recognition and enforcement in Japan by the courts of that country. We therefore believe that the decision of the Court of Appeals in *Bankston* is incorrect to the extent that it suggests that the Hague Convention does not permit as a method of service of process the sending of a copy of a summons and complaint by registered mail to a defendant in a foreign country. . . .

VASQUEZ v. SUND EMBA AB
548 N.Y.S.2d 728 (N.Y. App. Div. 1989)

ROSENBLATT, JUSTICE. The case comes to us by virtue of the motion of the defendant Sund Emba AB ([a Swedish company,] hereinafter the appellant) to dismiss the complaint . . . for lack of in personam jurisdiction. The validity of the service of process and, hence, personal jurisdiction depends, for reasons which will follow, on whether service was effectuated in accordance with the Hague Convention. The Supreme Court denied the appellant's motion to dismiss, holding that pursuant to Article 10(c) of the Convention, the "plaintiff's personal service of the summons and complaint on appellant was sufficient service to give this court jurisdiction of the present dispute." We agree.

In his complaint, the plaintiff alleges that he was injured during the course of his employment in Farmingdale, New York, when his hand became caught in a corrugated box folding machine, allegedly manufactured by the appellant. . . . The plaintiff's summons and complaint, written in English, was served by Anders Sandberg, a Swedish notary public, personally upon the appellant's managing director Erik Sjunnesson at the appellant's facility in Orebro, Sweden.

Suits involving parties in different countries present special problems relating to procedure under international law. The means by which a party may be subjected to the jurisdiction of the courts of another country goes to the very heart of national sovereignty and international political sensibilities. In this arena, one of the most vexing problems has involved the acquisition of jurisdiction, in the context of service or delivery of process, and the underlying issues of notice and fairness. . . .

On February 10, 1969, the Hague Convention became effective with respect to the United States. For Sweden it became effective on October 1, 1969. . . . It is noteworthy that while the member states contemplated a uniform procedure by conceiving of a Central Authority within each state, they also determined that the states should be free to consent to additional methods of service within their borders, consonant with their own laws (Articles 8 through 11, 19). . . . In ratifying the Convention, most states, including Sweden, made various declarations reflective of their own sense of sovereignty,[232] in which they set forth objections or requirements with respect to certain methods of service. Sweden signed the Convention with the following declaration:

> (a) The Ministry of Foreign Affairs . . . has been designated Central Authority. (b) The Central Authority (the Ministry for Foreign Affairs) has been designated to receive documents transmitted through consular channels, pursuant to Art. 9. (c) *Swedish authorities are not obliged to assist in serving documents transmitted by using any of the methods referred to in sub-paragraphs (b) and (c) of Art. 10.* By virtue of the third paragraph of Art. 5 of the Convention the Central Authority requires that any document to be served under the first paragraph of the same article must be written in or translated into Swedish. (emphasis supplied).

The appellant argues that the method of service used by the plaintiff is incompatible with this declaration. Specifically, the appellant claims that Sweden's declaration italicized above must be interpreted as that State's objection to personal service of foreign documents except by the Central Authority. The appellant further contends that, in any event, service was improper because a Swedish translation of the summons and complaint was not provided.

Initially, the parties acknowledge, as do we, that compliance with the Convention is mandatory in all cases to which it applies, and that the law of the judicial forum (here, New York) determines whether or not service of process abroad is necessary. *Volkswagenwerk*

---

232. For example, the only form of service from abroad permitted by Switzerland is the use of letters rogatory. "The Swiss position is based on an extreme view of the nature of sovereignty, whereby any act touching Switzerland, including mailing of service *into* Switzerland from the United States, is viewed by Switzerland as a judicial act by the United States *within* Switzerland, thereby invading Swiss Sovereignty." Horlick, *A Practical Guide to Service of United States Process Abroad*, 14 Int'l Law. 637, 641 (emphasis in original).

AG v. Schlunk. . . . Here, although the plaintiff alleged that the appellant was doing business in New York at all relevant times, neither party argues that service in this country was, or could have been, made. The parties therefore implicitly concede that service abroad, pursuant to the Convention, was the only proper means of service.

We hold that Sweden plainly contemplated service pursuant to the methods referred to in Article 10(b) and (c) (*i.e.,* personal service) and that the restrictive language in subdivision (c) of its declaration simply means that Swedish authorities are not constrained to aid in such service. Had Sweden been opposed to any method of service pursuant to Article 10, it could have, and we infer, would have expressly objected, as did, for example, Norway and Denmark, as well as Botswana, Germany, Japan, and Turkey.

This interpretation is consistent with Sweden's pre-Convention policies regarding service of foreign documents. Prior to the 1965 Convention, a Swedish decree based on the 1905 Hague Convention, to which Sweden was a signatory, permitted various modes of service ("delgivning"), including personal service of documents ("personlig delgivning") by authorized process servers ("stamningsmannadelgivning"), in response to requests by foreign authorities. Ginsburg, *Civil Procedure in Sweden,* 230, 231, 234 (1965). The decree, however, only regulated the assistance made available when Swedish authorities were involved, thereby leaving a party free to lawfully effectuate personal service, if possible, without the help of Swedish authorities. . . .

The plaintiff draws our attention to a publication of the United States Department of State. It is a "general guideline" and advises that service of process in Sweden may be accomplished by sending the documents and appropriate forms to the Swedish Central Authority, but that such procedure "need not be used" and that "[a]ny private person may serve process in Sweden. An agent or a Swedish attorney could also be hired to do so." Although the State Department guideline lacks the force of law . . . , we recognize it to the extent that it reflects the State Department's advice to practitioners, based on an interpretation of Swedish law, furnished primarily by the Swedish Ministries of Foreign Affairs and Justice in 1981 to the American Embassy in Stockholm. As the appellant does not claim that Anders Sandberg, the Swedish notary public who served the summons and complaint upon it, was otherwise not qualified under Swedish law to make such service, we conclude that the summons and complaint were delivered personally to the appellant's agent in accordance with the Hague Convention and Sweden's declarations.

The appellant argues that even if the method of service used by the plaintiff was proper, the failure to translate the summons and complaint into Swedish violates Sweden's translation requirement under the Hague Convention. The appellant's contention with respect to Sweden's translation requirement is implausible. Initially, we note that translation is not a necessary element of all methods of service pursuant to the Convention. Article 5 states that "If the document is to be served under the first paragraph above [subparagraph (a)] the Central Authority may require the document to be written in, or translated into, the official language or one of the official languages of the State addressed." It therefore gives the Central Authorities of the signatory nations the right to require translations with respect to service pursuant to Article 5(a). As previously noted, Sweden, in its declaration stated:

> By virtue of the third paragraph of art. 5 of the Convention the Central Authority requires that any document to be served under the first paragraph of the same article must be written in or translated into Swedish.

However, the Convention provides no right to require translation of a document where service is made by the Central Authority "by a particular method requested by the applicant" pursuant to Article 5(b). Moreover, where, as here, the Central Authority is not involved in the service of a particular document, the translation requirement is not triggered at all.

Sweden's declaration clearly imposes no translation requirement where its Central Authority is not involved in the service. . . .[233] [A]lthough we conclude that the requirements of service pursuant to the Convention are satisfied, one more point, while not raised by the appellant, is worth mentioning. Even though the Convention has been strictly followed, our own standards of due process require that the method of service be reasonably calculated, as a matter of fair play, to give actual notice to a prospective party abroad. Failure to provide a translation may, in some instances, constitute a denial of due process. However, in this case, in support of its motion to dismiss, the appellant submitted two affidavits of its Service Manager, Gosta Muhlbach. Those affidavits, which were on the appellant's letterhead containing preprinted English words, were written in English, and notarized in English. United States courts have refused to invalidate service where the defendant is a multinational corporation whose representatives have demonstrated an ability to deal in English, and the defendant is attempting to invalidate service on the grounds that the documents served should have been translated into the language of the country where served.

We conclude that the failure to serve the appellant with a Swedish translation of the summons and complaint violates neither Sweden's own declaration nor the intent of the Convention, and does not offend concepts of fairness in the service of process upon it.

Notes on Honda, U.S. and Japanese Statements, and Vasquez

1. Division in U.S. authority over availability of Article 10(a) for "service." U.S. courts are divided over whether Article 10(a) permits "service" of process in states that have not objected to the section. Like *Honda,* a number of courts have parsed the language of Article 10(a) finely, noting that it refers only to the ability to "send" judicial documents rather than to the right to "effect service," as paragraphs (b) and (c) of Article 10 provide. From this, these courts have inferred that Article 10(a) was not meant to include service of a summons and complaint, but rather was limited to transmittal of routine documents once litigation had begun. Contrary to *Honda,* a number of other courts have held that Japan's failure to object to sending documents under Article 10(a) permits service of process by mail. *See supra* pp. 925-926. (Note that, while this problem still persists with respect to several nations, more recent statements by Japan suggest that it permits service of process by mail under Article 10(a). *See Rojas v. Hitachi Koki Co., Ltd.,* 2009 WL 3924762 (Mass. Super. Sept. 29, 2009).)

2. How should Article 10(a) be interpreted? Which view of the Convention is more persuasive? In almost all articles in the Convention, including Articles 10(b) and 10(c), the word "serve" is used; only in Article 10(a) is the word "send" used. In the equally authoritative French language version of the Convention, the same pattern is followed: only in Article 10(a) is a different word used than in Articles 5, 8, 9, 10(b), 10(c), and 19. That usage suggests that some distinction was intended when different words were used.

On the other hand, some courts and commentators have suggested that a drafting "slip" occurred, and that "send" was supposed to be "serve." *Ackermann, supra,* 788 F.2d

---

233. We need not and do not decide whether Sweden, compatibly with the Convention, could have required translation of documents served by means independent of the Central Authority, such as by personal service by notary public, as was effectuated here.

at 839 ("inescapable" conclusion that use of "send" rather than the otherwise consistently used "service" must be attributed to careless drafting); 1 B. Ristau, *International Judicial Assistance* §4-3-5(2) at 204 (rev. ed. 2000). These authorities note that the negotiating history of the Convention suggests that Article 10(a) was intended to permit "service" of process as well as "sending" of documents. III Conference de la Haye de Droit International Privé, *Actes et Documents de la Dixième Session* 90 (1964) ("The Commission did not accept the proposal that postal channels be limited to registered mail.").

Likewise, in 2003, the Special Commission of the Hague Convention, which was tasked with reviewing the practical operation of the Convention and was attended by most member states, expressly adopted this position, stating that "[t]he [Special Commission] reaffirmed its clear understanding that the term 'send' in Article 10(a) is to be understood as meaning 'service' through postal channels." Conclusions and Recommendations of the Special Commission on the Practical Operation of the Hague Apostille, Evidence and Service Conventions," *available at* http://www.hcch.net/upload/wop/lse_concl_e.pdf, ¶55 (Oct. 28 to Nov. 4, 2003). Similarly, the Practical Handbook on the Convention, prepared by the Permanent Bureau of the Hague Conference on Private International Law contains the following:

> The majority of States do not oppose the forwarding of judicial documents originating in other Contracting States directly by mail to persons on their territory. For these States a distinction can be made between use of the postal channel as the sole method of service and service through the postal channel which is complementary to another means of effecting service. In this latter case, in the opinion of the experts who met in 1977, postal transmission of the judicial document should not be considered as being an infringement on the sovereignty of the State addressed: it should, therefore, be permitted notwithstanding an opposition made under Article 10(a). But of course it was desirable then to take into account only the date of the formal service, particularly where the operation of Article 15 was concerned.

Compare id., at 15 ("Japan has not declared that it objects to service through postal channels."). Which view is more persuasive? Does the inapplicability of any translation requirement to documents "served" under Article 10(a) affect your analysis? If Article 10(a) does not provide for "service," then what is its purpose? Could it be intended merely to clarify that certain actions would not be deemed violations of a state's sovereignty, without classifying them as service? Whatever one's view of the issue, however, it is clear that more definitive judicial or legislative guidance would be very useful for U.S. courts and litigants. Substantial resources are being expended on unnecessary litigation over an issue which the Supreme Court could readily clarify.

3. *Relevance of foreign state's positions to interpretation of Article 10(a).* Despite the split in U.S. authority, foreign courts are generally consistent in holding that Article 10(a) permits service of process by mail. *See, e.g.,* Case C-412/97, *E.D. Srl v. Italo Fenocchio,* [2000] C.M.L.R. 855 (Court of Justice of the European Communities) ("Article 10(a) of [the Hague Convention] allows service by post."); *Integral Energy & Environ. Eng'g Ltd. v. Schenker of Canada Ltd.,* (2001) 295 A.R. 233, 2001 WL 454163 (Alberta Queens Bench) ("Article 10(a) of the Hague Convention provides that if the state of destination does not object, judicial documents may be served by postal channels"), *rev'd on other grounds,* (2001) 293 A.R. 327; *R. v. Re Recognition of an Italian Judgment,* [2002] I.L. Pr. 15, 2000 WL 33541696 (Thessaloniki Court of Appeal, Greece) ("It should be noted that the possibility of serving judicial documents in civil and commercial cases through postal channels . . . is envisaged in Article 10(a) of the Hague Convention.").

To what extent should U.S. courts take into account foreign states' interpretations of the Convention (or other treaties)? Although the Convention is U.S. law, it is also foreign law (and, indeed, analogous to a contract between the two states); given that, are not a foreign state's views concerning the meaning of a treaty at least relevant to its interpretation? Does this apply only to foreign states' executive branches? Or also to foreign courts? Consider the following:

> We can, and should, look to decisions of other signatories when we interpret treaty provisions. Foreign constructions are evidence of the original shared understanding of the contracting parties. Moreover, it is reasonable to impute to the parties an intent that their respective courts strive to interpret the treaty consistently. . . . [E]ven if we disagree, we surely owe the conclusions reached by appellate courts of other signatories the courtesy of respectful consideration. *Olympic Airways v. Husain,* 540 U.S. 644, 660, 661 (2004) (Scalia, J. dissenting).

See also Air France v. Saks, 470 U.S. 392, 404 (1985) (stating that foreign courts' interpretation of treaties are entitled to "considerable weight").

What steps can a foreign state take if it disagrees with a reading of Article 10 that permits mail "service"? Consider the rationale in *Patty v. Toyota Motor Corp.,* 1991 U.S. Dist. LEXIS 16561 (N.D. Ga. 1991):

> given the number of courts which have upheld service of process by direct mail, this Court must assume that the Japanese Government is aware of the interpretation given the Hague Convention in this country. The fact that no efforts to amend the Convention have been undertaken by the Japanese Government can only indicate tacit agreement.

Is that persuasive? *See Lyman Steel Corp. v. Ferrostaal Metals Corp.,* 747 F. Supp. 389 (N.D. Ohio 1990) (service on German defendant by registered mail quashed because of German objection to Article 10(a)). Consider the statement of the Japanese delegation concerning Article 10(a), which is excerpted above. Why does the U.S. Department of State think that it is important? What does the Department of State think the Japanese statement means?

4. *Relevance of domestic service rules under Article 10(a).* The court remarks in *Honda* that Japanese law does not provide for service by mail in domestic Japanese actions. Is that relevant to analyzing Article 10(a)? Would *Honda* have been decided differently if service by mail *were* permitted in domestic actions in Japanese courts? Neither *Honda* nor the Japanese government's statement say that Japanese law forbids mail service in Japan from foreign courts. If Japanese law *permitted* such service, then why isn't mail service available under Article 19 of the Convention?

Even if Japanese internal law *forbids* foreign service by mail, does the Japanese failure to object to Article 10(a) render such service effective under the Convention? If so, both U.S. and Japanese courts would be *required* by the Convention to give effect to mail service. If a Japanese court refused to enforce a U.S. judgment based upon the use of mail service, would the action violate the Convention?

5. *No "service" or "sending" of documents under Article 10(a) if foreign state has objected to Article 10(a).* As noted above, a number of foreign states *have* objected to the use of Article 10(a) to transmit documents to their nationals. *See supra* pp. 925-926. In these cases, no service by mail is permitted, even by those courts that permit Article 10(a) service in the absence of an objection. *See, e.g., Cardona v. Kreamer,* 235 P.3d 1026 (Ariz. 2010) (*en banc*); *Estate of Ungar v. Palestinian Authority,* 412 F. Supp. 2d 328, 335 (S.D.N.Y. 2006); *Pittsburgh Nat'l Bank v. Kassir,* 153 F.R.D. 580, 584 (W.D. Pa. 1994); *Lyman Steel Corp. v. Ferrostaal Metals Corp.,* 747 F. Supp. 389 (N.D. Ohio 1990).

Questions may occasionally arise over whether, how, and to what extent the state has objected to alternative methods of service under Article 10. For a discussion of this issue, *see Mones v. Commercial Bank of Kuwait, S.A.K.*, 502 F. Supp. 2d 363, 370-371 (S.D.N.Y. 2007).

6. *Advantages of alternative service.* Why would a plaintiff choose to effect service by an alternative mechanism if a foreign country permits it? One reason might be speed. Service via the Central Authority often can be slow and cumbersome. This does not simply have consequences for the plaintiff's ability to advance his case; it also can affect the plaintiff's ability to maintain his claim at all. As noted above, *supra* pp. 872-873, under some state statutes of limitations (which will govern in state court and in certain federal cases arising under diversity jurisdiction), the limitations period will not be tolled after the plaintiff has sent papers to the Central Authority. *See, e.g., Thach v. Tiger Corp.*, 609 F.3d 955 (8th Cir. 2010). Does this result seem sensible? Should a reasonably diligent plaintiff be punished due to a foreign bureaucracy's failure to discharge its treaty obligations expeditiously?

7. *Practical reasons not to attempt mail service under Article 10(a).* Even if a U.S. court will permit service by mail under Article 10(a), there are sound reasons for a U.S. plaintiff not to take this avenue.

(a) Need for the defendant to return receipt attached to service by mail under Article 10(a). First, if the foreign defendant does not return the receipt attached to the mail package containing the process, then service may be ineffective because the plaintiff may not be able to prove receipt. *See Lampe v. Xouth, Inc.*, 952 F.2d 697, 701 (3d Cir. 1991) (where plaintiff could not prove that return receipt was signed by defendant or its agent, no effective mail service); *Tinsley v. ING Group*, 2006 WL 533375, at *2 (D. Del. 2006) (service insufficient where plaintiff failed to produce return receipt); *G.A. Modefine, SA v. Burlington Coat Factory Warehouse Corp.*, 164 F.R.D. 24, 26 (S.D.N.Y. 1995) (plaintiffs did not make "proper showing" of service where they failed to produce return receipt); *Chowaniec v. Heyl Truck Lines*, 1991 U.S. Dist. LEXIS 8138 (N.D. Ill. 1991). *But see Randolph v. Hendry*, 50 F. Supp. 2d 572, 578 (S.D. W. Va. 1999) ("There is no requirement within the Hague Convention that service of process be effected by use of registered mail and certainly no requirement that a return receipt be obtained. . . . [W]hether a return receipt is required is a question wholly determined with reference to the applicable law of the forum seeking to obtain jurisdiction over the defendant and the overarching requirements of procedural due process.").

(b) Enforceability of judgments obtained following mail service under Article 10(a). Even if a U.S. court upholds the validity of service under Article 10(a), a U.S. litigant may well encounter difficulty enforcing any subsequent judgment in the defendant's home jurisdiction. *Schlunk* and other authorities have emphasized this risk. *See infra* pp. 943-951.

8. *Possibility of direct service by receiving state's "competent persons" under Article 10(b).* Article 10(b) preserves the "freedom" of a requesting state's "judicial officers, officials, or other competent persons" directly to request the "judicial officers, officials, or other competent persons" of the receiving state to serve process. Like Article 10(a), Article 10(b) can only be used if the receiving state has not objected. Many states have objected, making it important to consult the instrument of accession of a state before attempting Article 10(b) service there. Moreover, Article 10(b) presents a choice of law question: is a person's "competence" under the section to serve process determined by the law of the requesting or the receiving state?

(a) Authorities permitting direct service under Article 10(b) in accordance with foreign law. *Vasquez* upholds service of process effected in Sweden by personal delivery from a Swedish attorney, relying on Article 10(b) and on its view of Swedish law. For other decisions under Article 10(b) permitting service in a foreign state under foreign service rules, *see Koehler v.*

Dodwell, 152 F.3d 304, 307 (4th Cir. 1998) (upholding service via private process server in Bermuda); *Dimensional Communications, Inc. v. Oz Optics Ltd.,* 218 F. Supp. 2d 653, 655-659 (D.N.J. 2002) (upholding service via private process server in Canada; service in any manner permitted under Article 10(b) was authorized under Rules 4(h)(2) and 4(f)); *Tax Lease Underwriters, Inc. v. Blackwall Green, Ltd.,* 106 F.R.D. 595 (E.D. Mo. 1985) (upholding service in England by personal delivery to defendant by English solicitor; service is permitted by Articles 10(b) and (c)); *Balcom v. Hiller,* 46 Cal. App. 4th 1758 (1996) (upholding service effected in England by personal delivery); *White v. Ratcliffe,* 674 N.E.2d 906 (Ill. App. 1996); *Supreme Merchandising Co. v. Iwahori Kinzoku Co.,* 503 N.Y.S.2d 18, 19-20 (App. Div. 1986) ("record does not exclude the possibility that the personal service by a Japanese lawyer, presumably familiar with the requirements of his country's laws, was in pursuance of a procedure authorized by Japanese law, nor does it clearly demonstrate that Japan would not have recognized the service as lawful").

Compare the result in *Vasquez* (permitting personal service by a Swedish attorney) with that in *Kadota* (among other things, not permitting personal service of a Japanese attorney). What explains the different outcomes? Is the *Vasquez* analysis persuasive? Does it undercut the basic structure of the Convention to permit parties to make service in contracting states in whatever way local law allows? Or is this just the kind of flexibility that the Convention was meant to preserve?

(b) Authorities apparently refusing to permit service under Article 10(b) pursuant to foreign law. A few courts have suggested, usually in passing, that only the specific mechanisms of service provided for in the Convention may be used. These decisions suggest that service mechanisms, permitted in the contracting state where service is effected, cannot be used pursuant to Article 10(b) to supplement the Convention. *E.g., Teknekron Mgmt. v. Quante Fernmeldetechnik,* 115 F.R.D. 175, 176 (D. Nev. 1987) ("service must be effected strictly according to the procedures set forth in" Hague Service Convention).

(c) Is authorization under FRCP Rule 4 (or state law) required for service pursuant to Article 10 of the Convention? Recall the question, discussed above, whether Rule 4(f) or Rule 4(h)(2) must authorize a particular means of service (*e.g.,* personal delivery) in order for that means of service to be utilized under Article 10(b) of the Hague Service Convention. *See supra* pp. 877, 903-906. For example, suppose that foreign law permits (as Swedish law did in *Vasquez*) service on a foreign corporation by personal delivery to its officers. Assuming that Article 10(b) of the Convention provides for this mechanism of service, then would such service be permitted under Rule 4? Does anything in Rule 4(f) authorize personal service on the officers or directors of a corporation outside the United States? Note that Rule 4(h)(2) authorizes service abroad on corporations "in any manner prescribed for individuals by subdivision (f) *except personal delivery as provided in paragraph (f)(2)(C)(i) thereof.*"

Does Rule 4(f)(1) authorize service in a manner permitted by Article 10(b) of the Convention and foreign law? Recall that, as discussed above, most courts have held that Rule 4(f)(1) only permits service via the Central Authority mechanism specifically authorized by the Convention, and not by the Article 10 mechanisms (with which the Convention does "not interfere"). *See supra* pp. 921-923; *Brockmeyer v. May,* 383 F.3d 798 (9th Cir. 2004).

Despite this a number of courts have upheld service where permitted by Article 10(b) and foreign law, even if not specifically authorized by Rule 4. *Dimensional Communications, Inc. v. Oz Optics Ltd.,* 218 F. Supp. 2d 653, 655-659 (D.N.J. 2002); *Tax Lease Underwriters, Inc. v. Blackwall Green, Ltd.,* 106 F.R.D. 595 (E.D. Mo. 1985).

Alternatively, does Federal Rule 4(f)(2) authorize service in the manner contemplated by Rule 10(b)? Note that Rule 4(f)(2) provides that the methods detailed therein are available only if "an international agreement allows but does not specify other means." Does Article 10(b) "allow but not specify other means" of service? Or does it "specify" them? What would be the implications of the latter interpretation?

9. Service pursuant to the internal law of the receiving state under Article 19. Recall that Article 19 provides that, where "the internal law of a contracting State permits methods of transmission, other than those provided for in the preceding articles, of documents coming from abroad, for service within its territory," the Convention does not affect those methods.

(a) When does internal law "permit" service? Assuming that service abroad is authorized by Article 19, as its language suggests, in what circumstances does it do so? Few U.S. courts have specifically addressed this question. Those that have considered it reach conflicting interpretations. *Compare, e.g., In re Mak Petroleum, Inc.,* 424 B.R. 912, 920 (Bankr. M.D. Fla. 2010) (holding that Article 19 only encompasses service methods expressly permitted by internal law of foreign state); *Humble v. Gill,* 2009 WL 151668, at *2-3 (W.D. Ky. 2009) (same); *GMA Accessories, Inc. v. BOP, LLC,* 2009 WL 2856230 (S.D.N.Y. Aug. 28, 2009) (same) *with Banco Latino, SACA v. Gomez Lopez,* 53 F. Supp. 2d 1273, 1279-1280 (S.D. Fla. 1999) (holding service under Article 19 valid so long as foreign state does not explicitly prohibit service method).

(b) Authorities concluding that Article 19 permits any service mechanism not forbidden by foreign law. Some commentators have concluded that service may be deemed proper under Article 19 as long as the receiving state's laws do not affirmatively prohibit the mechanism used; if foreign law is silent, then Article 19 allows such service:

> In short, although compliance with the Convention is "mandatory," that compliance encompasses not only methods of service that the Convention or the internal law of the foreign state expressly permit *but also those methods that neither the Convention nor the internal law of the foreign state prohibit.* Committee on Federal Courts, N.Y. State Bar Ass'n, *Service of Process Abroad: A Nuts and Bolts Guide,* 122 F.R.D. 63, 76 (1989) (emphasis added).

Cf. Siegel, Supplementary Practice Commentaries, 28 U.S.C.A. Federal Rules of Civil Procedure, Rule 4, C4-24 (2007) ("We should be able to read the word 'permits' in Article 19 to mean 'does not prohibit.' In order to use one of the methods Rule 4(f) authorizes in paragraph (2), for example, one should not have to show that the method has a precise counterpart (and just how precise?) in the foreign nation's internal law. It should suffice that there is nothing in the foreign law, either explicitly or by compelling implication, to suggest that the method of service violates some deep-rooted policy of the nation involved."). For cases adopting this view, *see e.g., Banco Latino, SACA v. Gomez Lopez,* 53 F. Supp. 2d 1273, 1279-1280 (S.D. Fla. 1999).

(c) Authorities concluding that Article 19 only permits service mechanisms specifically authorized by foreign law. Article 19 can also be interpreted to permit only "use of alternative service methods which foreign law *specifically authorizes.*" Comment, *Service of Process Abroad Under the Hague Convention,* 71 Marq. L. Rev. 649, 682 (1988) (emphasis in original). For cases adopting this view, *see Humble v. Gill,* 2009 WL 151668, at *2-3 (W.D. Ky. Jan. 22, 2009); *Eplus Tech., Inc. v. Aboud,* 155 F. Supp. 2d 692, 697-699 (E.D. Va. 2001); *Dahya v. Second Judicial Dist. Court ex rel. County of Washoe,* 19 P.3d 239, 243 (Nev. 2001).

(d) How should Article 19 be interpreted? Which of the foregoing interpretations of Article 19 is more sensible? What harm results from permitting service abroad in any manner specifically authorized by the receiving state's law? Any manner not prohibited by the receiving state's law? If Swedish law ordinarily permits service by hand-delivery, outside the Convention, does the Convention forbid this?

What effect does the foreign state's position have on interpreting Article 19 in particular cases? If Sweden formally stated that it did not object to service under Article 19 in the manners permitted by Swedish law, does the Convention impose additional requirements? Conversely, if a receiving state does not like service to be made from abroad outside the Central Authority mechanism, why can't it say so?

(e) Is authorization under FRCP Rule 4 or state law required for service under Article 19 of the Convention? Recall the discussion above about the extent to which Rule 4(f) authorizes service abroad pursuant to the Hague Service Convention's alternative means of service (*e.g.*, under Articles 10 and 19). *See supra* pp. 877, 903-906, 921, 923. Suppose that a foreign state has not objected to a means of service which is permitted by Articles 10 and 19 of the Convention, but not specifically authorized by Rule 4(f)(2) (*e.g.*, international mail or courier; hand delivery by a local process-server to a corporate secretary). Can this means of service be utilized? Why shouldn't the answer be "Of course"? What does Rule 4(f)(2) say? *See supra* pp. 903-906.

10. *Service by mail under FRCP Rule 4(f)(2)(A) and 4(f)(2)(C)(ii).* Suppose that the result in *Honda* is accepted, and one concludes that the Hague Service Convention does not authorize service by international mail — even in a state (like Japan or England) that has not objected to such service. Why cannot service nonetheless be effected by mail under either Rule 4(f)(2)(A) or Rule 4(f)(2)(C)(ii)? *See supra* pp. 903-906. Note that in some Hague signatory states (such as England) service by mail is permitted in domestic civil actions. In that case, why would not Rule 4(f)(2)(A) permit service by mail, on the theory that service by mail is "prescribed" by English law? For a negative answer, *see Brockmeyer v. May*, 383 F.3d 798 (9th Cir. 2004) (service by first class mail in England not authorized by Rule 4(f)(2)(A)).

Even if Rule 4(f)(2)(A) does not apply, why would Rule 4(f)(2)(C)(ii) not permit service by mail — at least if dispatched by the clerk of the Court with a receipt requested? *See, e.g., Res. Ventures, Inc. v. Res. Mgmt. Int'l,* 42 F. Supp. 2d 423, 430 (D. Del. 1999) (service by international registered mail to Indonesia is authorized by Rule 4(f)(2)(C)(ii) because Indonesian law did not forbid such service); *Dee-K Enters. v. Heveafil Sdn Bhd,* 174 F.R.D. 376, 378-379 (E.D. Va. 1997) (same); *Napp Technologies, L.L.C. v. Kiel Laboratories, Inc.,* 2008 WL 5233708 (D.N.J. Dec. 12, 2008) (same result regarding service by return-receipt mail in India).

9. Scope of the Hague Service Convention: When Is "Service Abroad" Required and When Can Service Be Effected Within the United States on Foreign Defendants?

As we have seen, the Hague Service Convention provides a variety of mechanisms for use by U.S. litigants when service must be made "abroad" — that is, within the territory of another Contracting States. U.S. courts have held, however, that service need not be made "abroad" when a foreign defendant can be found and served within the United States under U.S. law. As a result, these courts have concluded, the Convention simply has no application when process is served in accordance with U.S. procedural rules on a foreign defendant within the United States.[234]

---

234. *See Yamaha Motor Corp., Ltd. v. Super Ct.*, 174 Cal. App. 4th 264 (Cal. Ct. App. 2009); *Sheets v. Yamaha Motors Corp.*, 891 F.2d 533, 537 (5th Cir. 1990); *Gallagher v. Mazda Motor of America, Inc.*, 1992 U.S. Dist. LEXIS 97 (E.D. Pa. 1992); *Zisman v. Sieger*, 106 F.R.D. 194, 200 (N.D. Ill. 1985); *Ex parte Volkswagenwerk AG*, 443 So. 2d 880, 881 (Ala. 1983); *Luciano v. Garvey Volkswagen, Inc.*, 521 N.Y.S.2d 119, 120-121 (App. Div. 1987).

The Supreme Court expressly endorsed this conclusion in *Volkswagenwerk AG v. Schlunk,* which is excerpted below.[235] It held that the question "whether there is service abroad must be determined by reference to the law of the forum state," because it is not addressed by the Convention itself.[236] Applying the *Schlunk* rationale, lower U.S. courts have considered numerous claims that local service within the United States on a foreign defendant or its U.S. representative obviated the need to serve process abroad under the Convention. This issue has frequently arisen when U.S. plaintiffs effect "indirect" or "substituted" service on foreign companies by serving their U.S. subsidiaries.[237] It also arises, as the notes following *Schlunk* illustrate, in other contexts, including service upon statutory agents and U.S. addresses of foreign defendants.

VOLKSWAGENWERK AG v. SCHLUNK
486 U.S. 694 (1988)

Justice O'Connor. This case involves an attempt to serve process on a foreign corporation by serving its domestic subsidiary which, under state law, is the foreign corporation's involuntary agent for service of process. We must decide whether such service is compatible with the [Hague Service] Convention. . . . [The case was a product liability action, filed in Illinois state court, alleging that Volkswagen of America, Inc. ("VwoA") and Volkswagen Aktiengesellschaft ("VWAG") had designed and sold a defective automobile. VWAG, a German company with its principal place of business in Germany, wholly owns VWoA, a [] corporation. The plaintiff served VWAG by serving VWoA as its agent. The Illinois courts concluded that service on VWoA was effective service on VWAG, because "VWoA is a wholly owned subsidiary of VWAG, . . . a majority of the members of the board of VWoA are members of the board of VWAG, and . . . VWoA is by contract the exclusive importer and distributor of VWAG products sold in the United States."] . . .

The primary innovation of the Convention is that it requires each state to establish a central authority to receive requests for service of documents from other countries. . . . Once a central authority receives a request in the proper form, it must serve the documents by a method prescribed by the internal law of the receiving state or by a method designated by the requester and compatible with that law. Article 5. The central authority must then provide a certificate of service that conforms to a specified model. Article 6. A state also may consent to methods of service within its boundaries other than a request to its central authority. Articles 8-11, 19. The remaining provisions of the Convention that are relevant here limit the circumstances in which a default judgment may be entered against a defendant who had to be served abroad and did not appear, and provide some means for relief from such a judgment. Articles 15, 16.

Article 1 defines the scope of the Convention, which is the subject of controversy in this case. It says: "The present Convention shall apply in all cases, in civil or commercial matters, where there is occasion to transmit a judicial or extrajudicial document for service abroad." The equally authentic French version says, "La presente Convention est applicable, en matiere civile ou commerciale, dans tous les cas ou un acte judiciaire

---

235. 486 U.S. 694 (1988).
236. *Schlunk,* 486 U.S. at 701.
237. In some circumstances, both state and federal law permit the service of process on a foreign corporation by service upon an affiliated corporation within the United States. In general, indirect service of this character is permitted if the U.S. party can show a sufficiently close connection between the foreign parent and the domestic subsidiary to justify treating the subsidiary as the agent or alter ego of the parent. 1 Casad & Richman, *Jurisdiction in Civil Actions* §4-3[5][a]-[b] (3d ed. 1998).

ou extrajudiciaire doit être transmis a l'etranger pour y être signifié ou notifié." This language is mandatory, as we acknowledged last Term in *Societe Nationale Industrielle Aerospatiale, supra,* 482 U.S. at 534 n.15. By virtue of the Supremacy Clause, U.S. Const., Article VI, the Convention pre-empts inconsistent methods of service prescribed by state law in all cases to which it applies. Schlunk does not purport to have served his complaint on VWAG in accordance with the Convention. Therefore, if service of process in this case falls within Article 1 of the Convention, the trial court should have granted VWAG's motion to quash.

When interpreting a treaty, we "begin 'with the text of the treaty and the context in which the written words are used.' " *Societe Nationale,* 482 U.S. at 534 (quoting *Air France v. Saks,* 470 U.S. 392, 397 (1985)). Other general rules of construction may be brought to bear on difficult or ambiguous passages. "'Treaties are construed more liberally than private agreements, and to ascertain their meaning we may look beyond the written words to the history of the treaty, the negotiations, and the practical construction adopted by the parties.'"

The Convention does not specify the circumstances in which there is "occasion to transmit" a complaint "for service abroad." But at least the term "service of process" has a well-established technical meaning. Service of process refers to a formal delivery of documents that is legally sufficient to charge the defendant with notice of a pending action. The legal sufficiency of a formal delivery of documents must be measured against some standard. The Convention does not prescribe a standard, so we almost necessarily must refer to the internal law of the forum state. If the internal law of the forum state defines the applicable method of serving process as requiring the transmittal of documents abroad, then the Hague Service Convention applies.

The negotiating history supports our view that Article 1 refers to service of process in the technical sense. The committee that prepared the preliminary draft deliberately used a form of the term "notification" (formal notice), instead of the more neutral term "remise" (delivery), when it drafted Article 1. Then, in the course of the debates, the negotiators made the language even more exact. The preliminary draft of Article 1 said that the present Convention shall apply in all cases in which there are grounds to transmit or to give formal notice of a judicial or extrajudicial document in a civil or commercial matter to a person staying abroad. . . . To be more precise, the delegates decided to add a form of the juridical term "signification" (service), which has a narrower meaning than "notification" in some countries, such as France, and the identical meaning in others, such as the United States. The delegates also criticized the language of the preliminary draft because it suggested that the Convention could apply to transmissions abroad that do not culminate in service. The final text of Article 1, eliminates this possibility and applies only to documents transmitted for service abroad. The final report (Rapport Explicatif) confirms that the Convention does not use more general terms, such as delivery or transmission, to define its scope because it applies only when there is both transmission of a document from the requesting state to the receiving state, and service upon the person for whom it is intended.

The negotiating history of the Convention also indicates that whether there is service abroad must be determined by reference to the law of the forum state. The preliminary draft said that the Convention would apply "where there are grounds" to transmit a judicial document to a person staying abroad. The committee that prepared the preliminary draft realized that this implied that the forum's internal law would govern whether service implicated the Convention. The reporter expressed regret about this solution because it would decrease the obligatory force of the Convention. Nevertheless, the delegates did not change the meaning of Article 1 in this respect.

VWAG protests that it is inconsistent with the purpose of the Convention to interpret it as applying only when the internal law of the forum requires service abroad. One of the two stated objectives of the Convention is "to create appropriate means to ensure that judicial and extrajudicial documents to be served abroad shall be brought to the notice of the addressee in sufficient time." The Convention cannot assure adequate notice, VWAG argues, if the forum's internal law determines whether it applies. VWAG warns that countries could circumvent the Convention by defining methods of service of process that do not require transmission of documents abroad. Indeed, VWAG contends that one such method of service already exists and that it troubled the Conference: notification au parquet.

Notification au parquet permits service of process on a foreign defendant by the deposit of documents with a designated local official. Although the official generally is supposed to transmit the documents abroad to the defendant, the statute of limitations begins to run from the time that the official receives the documents, and there allegedly is no sanction for failure to transmit them. At the time of the 10th Conference, France, the Netherlands, Greece, Belgium, and Italy utilized some type of notification au parquet. There is no question but that the Conference wanted to eliminate notification au parquet. It included in the Convention two provisions that address the problem. Article 15 says that a judgment may not be entered unless a foreign defendant received adequate and timely notice of the lawsuit. Article 16 provides means whereby a defendant who did not receive such notice may seek relief from a judgment that has become final. Like Article 1, however, Articles 15 and 16 apply only when documents must be transmitted abroad for the purpose of service. VWAG argues that, if this determination is made according to the internal law of the forum state, the Convention will fail to eliminate variants of notification au parquet that do not expressly require transmittal of documents to foreign defendants. Yet such methods of service of process are the least likely to provide a defendant with actual notice.

The parties make conflicting representations about whether foreign laws authorizing notification au parquet command the transmittal of documents for service abroad within the meaning of the Convention. The final report is itself somewhat equivocal. It says that, although the strict language of Article 1 might raise a question as to whether the Convention regulates notification au parquet, the understanding of the drafting Commission, based on the debates, is that the Convention would apply. Although this statement might affect our decision as to whether the Convention applies to notification au parquet, an issue we do not resolve today, there is no comparable evidence in the negotiating history that the Convention was meant to apply to substituted service on a subsidiary like VWoA, which clearly does not require service abroad under the forum's internal law. Hence neither the language of the Convention nor the negotiating history contradicts our interpretation of the Convention, according to which the internal law of the forum is presumed to determine whether there is occasion for service abroad.

Nor are we persuaded that the general purposes of the Convention require a different conclusion. One important objective of the Convention is to provide means to facilitate service of process abroad. Thus the first stated purpose of the Convention is "to create" appropriate means for service abroad, and the second stated purpose is "to improve the organization of mutual judicial assistance for that purpose by simplifying and expediting the procedure." By requiring each state to establish a central authority to assist in the service of process, the Convention implements this enabling function. Nothing in our decision today interferes with this requirement.

VWAG correctly maintains that the Convention also aims to ensure that there will be adequate notice in cases in which there is occasion to serve process abroad. Thus compliance with the Convention is mandatory in all cases to which it applies, and Articles 15 and 16 provide an indirect sanction against those who ignore it. Our interpretation of the Convention does not necessarily advance this particular objective, inasmuch as it makes recourse to the Convention's means of service dependent on the forum's internal law. But we do not think that this country, or any other country, will draft its internal laws deliberately so as to circumvent the Convention in cases in which it would be appropriate to transmit judicial documents for service abroad. For example, there has been no question in this country of excepting foreign nationals from the protection of our Due Process Clause. Under that Clause, foreign nationals are assured of either personal service, which typically will require service abroad and trigger the Convention, or substituted service that provides "notice reasonably calculated, under all the circumstances, to apprise interested parties of the pendency of the action and afford them an opportunity to present their objections." *Mullane v. Central Hanover Bank & Trust Co.,* 339 U.S. 306, 314 (1950).[238]

Furthermore, nothing that we say today prevents compliance with the Convention even when the internal law of the forum does not so require. The Convention provides simple and certain means by which to serve process on a foreign national. Those who eschew its procedures risk discovering that the forum's internal law required transmittal of documents for service abroad, and that the Convention therefore provided the exclusive means of valid service. In addition, parties that comply with the Convention ultimately may find it easier to enforce their judgments abroad. For these reasons, we anticipate that parties may resort to the Convention voluntarily, even in cases that fall outside the scope of its mandatory application.

In this case, the Illinois long-arm statute authorized Schlunk to serve VWAG by substituted service on VWoA, without sending documents to Germany. VWAG has not petitioned for review of the Illinois Appellate Court's holding that service was proper as a matter of Illinois law. VWAG contends, however, that service on VWAG was not complete until VWoA transmitted the complaint to VWAG in Germany. According to VWAG, this transmission constituted service abroad under the Hague Service Convention.

VWAG explains that, as a practical matter, VWoA was certain to transmit the complaint to Germany to notify VWAG of the litigation. Indeed, as a legal matter, the Due Process Clause requires every method of service to provide "notice reasonably calculated, under all the circumstances, to apprise interested parties of the pendency of the action and afford them an opportunity to present their objections." *Mullane v. Central Hanover Bank & Trust Co.* VWAG argues that, because of this notice requirement, every case involving service on a foreign national will present an "occasion to transmit a judicial . . . document for service abroad" within the meaning of Article 1. VWAG emphasizes that in this case,

---

238. The concurrence believes that our interpretation does not adequately guarantee timely notice, which it denominates the "primary" purpose of the Convention, albeit without authority. The concurrence instead proposes to impute a substantive standard to the words, "service abroad." Evidently, a method of service would not be deemed to be "service abroad" within the meaning of Article 1 unless it provides notice to the recipient "in due time." This due process notion cannot be squared with the plain meaning of the words, "service abroad." The contours of the concurrence's substantive standard are not defined, and we note that it would create some uncertainty even on the facts of this case. If the substantive standard tracks the Due Process Clause of the Fourteenth Amendment, it is not self-evident that substituted service on a subsidiary is sufficient with respect to the parent. In the only cases in which it has considered the question, this Court held that the activities of a subsidiary are not necessarily enough to render a parent subject to a court's jurisdiction, for service of process or otherwise. *Cannon Mfg. Co. v. Cudahy Packing Co.,* 267 U.S. 333, 336-337 (1925); *Consolidated Textile Corp. v. Gregory,* 289 U.S. 85, 88 (1933). Although the particular relationship between VWAG and VWoA might have made substituted service valid in this case, a question that we do not decide, the fact-bound character of the necessary inquiry makes us doubt whether the standard suggested by the concurrence would in fact be "remarkably easy" to apply.

the Appellate Court upheld service only after determining that "the relationship between VWAG and VWoA is so close that it is certain that VWAG 'was fully apprised of the pendency of the action' by delivery of the summons to VWoA."

We reject this argument. Where service on a domestic agent is valid and complete under both state law and the Due Process Clause, our inquiry ends and the Convention has no further implications. Whatever internal, private communications take place between the agent and a foreign principal are beyond the concerns of this case. The only transmittal to which the Convention applies is a transmittal abroad that is required as a necessary part of service. And, contrary to VWAG's assertion, the Due Process Clause does not require an official transmittal of documents abroad every time there is service on a foreign national. Applying this analysis, we conclude that this case does not present an occasion to transmit a judicial document for service abroad within the meaning of Article 1. Therefore the Hague Service Convention does not apply, and service was proper.

JUSTICE BRENNAN, concurring. We acknowledged last Term, and the Court reiterates today, that the terms of the [Hague Service] Convention are "mandatory," not "optional" with respect to any transmission that Article 1 covers. *Aerospatiale,* 482 U.S. at 534, and n.15. Even so, the Court holds, and I agree, that a litigant may, consistent with the Convention, serve process on a foreign corporation by serving its wholly owned domestic subsidiary, because such process is not "service abroad" within the meaning of Article 1. The Court reaches that conclusion, however, by depriving the Convention of any mandatory effect, for in the Court's view the "forum's internal law" defines conclusively whether a particular process is "service abroad," which is covered by the Convention, or domestic service, which is not. I do not join the Court's opinion because I find it implausible that the Convention's framers intended to leave each contracting nation, and each of the 50 States within our Nation, free to decide for itself under what circumstances, if any, the Convention would control. Rather, in my view, the words "service abroad," read in light of the negotiating history, embody a substantive standard that limits a forum's latitude to deem service complete domestically.

The first of two objectives enumerated in the Convention's preamble is "to create appropriate means to ensure that judicial . . . documents to be served abroad shall be brought to the notice of the addressee in sufficient time. . . ." Until the Convention was implemented, the contracting nations followed widely divergent practices for serving judicial documents across international borders, some of which did not ensure any notice, much less timely notice, and therefore often produced unfair default judgments. Particularly controversial was a procedure, common among civil-law countries, called "notification au parquet," which permitted delivery of process to a local official who was then ordinarily supposed to transmit the document abroad through diplomatic or other channels. Typically, service was deemed complete upon delivery of the document to the official whether or not the official succeeded in transmitting it to the defendant and whether or not the defendant otherwise received notice of the pending lawsuit.[239]

239. The head of the United States delegation to the Convention described notification au parquet as follows: "This is a system which permits the entry of judgments in personam by default against a nonresident defendant without requiring adequate notice. . . . Under this system of service, the process-server simply delivers a copy of the writ to a public official's office. The time for answer begins to run immediately. Some effort is supposed to be made through the Foreign Office and through diplomatic channels to give the defendant notice, but failure to do this has no effect on the validity of the service. . . . There are no . . . limitations and protections [comparable to due process or personal jurisdiction] under the notification au parquet system. Here jurisdiction lies merely if the plaintiff is a local national; nothing more is needed." S. Exec. Rep. No. 6, at 11-12 (statement by Philip W. Amram).

The United States delegation to the Convention objected to notification au parquet as inconsistent with "the requirements of 'due process of law' under the Federal Constitution." The head of the delegation has derided its " '[i]njustice, extravagance, [and] absurdity . . . .' " . . . The Convention's official reporter noted similar " 'spirited criticisms of the system' . . . which we wish to see eliminated."

In response to this and other concerns, the Convention prescribes the exclusive means for service of process emanating from one contracting nation and culminating in another. As the Court observes, the Convention applies only when the document is to be "transmit[ted] . . . for service abroad"; it covers not every transmission of judicial documents abroad, but only those transmissions abroad that constitute formal "service." It is common ground that the Convention governs when the procedure prescribed by the internal law of the forum nation or state provides that service is not complete until the document is transmitted abroad. That is not to say, however, as does the Court, that the forum nation may designate any type of service "domestic" and thereby avoid application of the Convention.

Admittedly, as the Court points out, the Convention's language does not prescribe a precise standard to distinguish between "domestic" service and "service abroad." But the Court's solution leaves contracting nations free to ignore its terms entirely, converting its command into exhortation. Under the Court's analysis, for example, a forum nation could prescribe direct mail service to any foreigner and deem service effective upon deposit in the mailbox, or could arbitrarily designate a domestic agent for any foreign defendant and deem service complete upon receipt domestically by the agent even though there is little likelihood that service would ever reach the defendant. In fact, so far as I can tell, the Court's interpretation permits any contracting nation to revive notification au parquet so long as the nation's internal law deems service complete domestically, even though, as the Court concedes, "such methods of service are the least likely to provide a defendant with actual notice," and even though "[t]here is no question but that the Conference wanted to eliminate notification au parquet." . . .

The negotiating history and the uniform interpretation announced by our own negotiators confirm that the Convention limits a forum's ability to deem service "domestic," thereby avoiding the Convention's terms. Admittedly, the Convention does not precisely define the contours. But that imprecision does not absolve us of our responsibility to apply the Convention mandatorily, any more than imprecision permits us to discard the words "due process of law." And however difficult it might be in some circumstances to discern the Convention's precise limits, it is remarkably easy to conclude that the Convention does not prohibit the type of service at issue here. Service on a wholly owned, closely controlled subsidiary is reasonably calculated to reach the parent "in due time" as the Convention requires. That is, in fact, what our own Due Process Clause requires, *see Mullane v. Central Hanover Bank & Trust Co.,* 339 U.S. 306, 314-315 (1950), and since long before the Convention's implementation our law has permitted such service, *see, e.g., Perkins v. Benguet Consolidated Mining Co.,* 342 U.S. 437, 444-445 (1952). This is significant because our own negotiators made clear to the Senate their understanding that the Convention would require no major changes in federal or state service-of-process rules. Thus, it is unsurprising that nothing in the negotiating history suggests that the contracting nations were dissatisfied with the practice at issue here, which they were surely aware, much less that they intended to abolish it like they intended to abolish notification au parquet. And since notice served on a wholly owned domestic subsidiary is infinitely more likely to reach the foreign parent's attention than was notice served au parquet (or by any other procedure that the negotiators singled out for criticism) there is no reason to interpret the Convention to bar it.

My difference with the Court does not affect the outcome of this case, and, given that any process emanating from our courts must comply with due process, it may have little practical consequence in future cases that come before us. *But cf.* S. Exec. Rep. No. 6, at 15 (statement by Philip W. Amram suggesting that Convention may require "a minor change in the practice of some of our States in long-arm and automobile accident cases" where "service on the appropriate official need be accompanied only by a minimum effort to notify the defendant"). Our Constitution does not, however, bind other nations haling our citizens into their courts. Our citizens rely instead primarily on the forum nation's compliance with the Convention, which the Senate believed would "provide increased protection (due process) for American Citizens who are involved in litigation abroad." And while other nations are not bound by the Court's pronouncement that the Convention lacks obligatory force, after today's decision their courts will surely sympathize little with any United States national pleading that a judgment violates the Convention because (notwithstanding any local characterization) service was "abroad."

It is perhaps heartening to "think that [no] countr[y] will draft its internal laws deliberately so as to circumvent the Convention in cases in which it would be appropriate to transmit judicial documents for service abroad," although from the defendant's perspective "circumvention" (which, according to the Court, entails no more than exercising a prerogative not to be bound) is equally painful whether deliberate or not. The fact remains, however, that had we been content to rely on foreign notions of fair play and substantial justice, we would have found it unnecessary, in the first place, to participate in a Convention "to ensure that judicial . . . documents to be served abroad [would] be brought to the notice of the addressee in sufficient time."

Notes on Volkswagenwerk v. Schlunk

1. *Service on a foreign defendant within the United States as an alternative to service "abroad" under the Convention.* *Schlunk* held that the Convention need not be used to serve process abroad if the law of the forum permits service on the defendant within the forum. The Court reasoned that the Convention only applies when, under Article 1 of the Convention, there is occasion to make "service abroad." If U.S. law provides that service is effected locally, within the United States, then the Convention simply does not apply.

2. *Was* Schlunk *correctly decided?* Is *Schlunk* correct? Consider the arguments advanced in Justice Brennan's concurrence. If a central objective of the Convention was to eliminate *notification au parquet* and other forms of service that failed to provide adequate notice, would contracting states have been left free to define when service "abroad" was necessary? Conversely, if the Convention meant to define when service abroad was necessary, would it not have said so expressly?

Note the Court's statement that, because the Convention does not directly address the issue, "we almost necessarily must" apply the forum's local laws to decide whether service must be made abroad. What other law might apply to determine the validity of domestic service upon a foreign corporation? Why could the Convention itself not set implied limits on domestic service? Are such limits not "almost necessarily" required to protect the integrity of the Convention and effectuate its basic purposes of ensuring that defendants in international disputes receive fair notice when sued abroad? Consider the limits derived by Justice Brennan, based on the Due Process Clause, for when service must be made abroad under the Convention. Is this reading sensible? Is it a plausible reading of the Convention?

Consider VWAG's argument that service on *it* necessarily entailed VWOA's transmission of the complaint to Germany—in order to satisfy both the Due Process Clause and state law—and that this transmission amounted to "service abroad" regulated by the Convention. How does the Court reply? Is that persuasive? How would Justice Brennan respond to this argument?

How difficult is it as a practical matter for plaintiffs to comply with the Convention? What unfairness will noncompliance cause foreign defendants if service is consistent with the Due Process Clause? What effect will the Court's interpretation of the Convention have on U.S. defendants subject to suit in foreign countries that do not have a Due Process Clause?

3. *Limits under* Schlunk *to use of domestic service mechanisms.* If the *Schlunk* conclusion is accepted, is there any limit to how the Convention might be circumvented by domestic laws permitting substituted service? Suppose a state law authorizes service on a foreign franchisor, by serving its entirely independent U.S. franchisee. Suppose that a state law authorizes service within the United States by service on *any* U.S. subsidiary or affiliate of a foreign parent corporation. Suppose, in Justice Brennan's words, a state "prescribe[s] direct mail service to any foreigner and deem[s] service effective upon deposit in the mailbox." Are any of these service mechanisms consistent with the intent of the framers of the Convention? Are any of these mechanisms prohibited by the analysis of the Convention in *Schlunk*? Note that the *Schlunk* analysis leaves foreign states free under the Convention to permit service in the various ways upon U.S. defendants. Would not Justice Brennan's analysis have been more protective of U.S. defendants? Of the efficacy of the Convention?

4. *Standards applicable to determining whether domestic service on defendant, or a representative, is permitted under Convention.* *Schlunk* holds that local law governs the question whether domestic service within the forum, rather than service "abroad" under the Convention, is permitted. In most cases, the applicable law in U.S. Courts will be state law, because service will be effected pursuant to state long-arm statutes. *See supra* pp. 204-205. Where federal law provides the basis for jurisdiction, it will generally provide the applicable law. Under *Schlunk*, only the Due Process Clause constrains the application of substituted service theories under state or federal law. The Due Process Clause leaves the individual U.S. states broad discretion in serving process on nonresident defendants. *See supra* pp. 879-881.

5. *Possible "international comity" or federal common law limits on domestic service as a means of avoiding service abroad under Convention.* What role, if any, could the principle of "international comity" have in providing a basis for requiring U.S. plaintiffs to utilize the Convention's procedures? As discussed in detail below, the Supreme Court held in *Société Nationale Industrielle Aerospatiale v. U.S. District Court*, 482 U.S. 522 (1987), that international comity requires use of the Hague Evidence Convention in certain circumstances in order to minimize infringements on the sovereignty of foreign nations that objected to direct U.S. discovery. *See infra* pp. 1040-1044. Although it was not argued in *Schlunk*, the same comity rationale would appear applicable to service under the Hague Service Convention, arguably requiring resort to the Convention in cases where foreign states object to substituted service.

6. *Service within the forum on domestic "alter ego" of foreign corporation under Convention.* *Schlunk* affirmed a lower court decision, applying Illinois law, that permitted service within Illinois on the local subsidiary of a foreign corporation. Like Illinois, most states permit indirect service on nonresident defendants through service within the state on either an "alter ego," an agent, or other representative of the foreign company. Federal law is similar. The standards for alter ego, agency, and other statuses vary from jurisdiction to jurisdiction. In general, indirect service on a local subsidiary is permitted only if the subsidiary is closely affiliated with its foreign parent. *See generally* 1 Casad & Richman, *Jurisdiction in Civil Actions* §4-3[5] at 496-504 (3d ed. 1998).

A number of lower courts have reached the same result as *Schlunk,* also applying state law, to permit service on an alter ego of a foreign parent if state alter ego standards are met. *See, e.g., Dewey v. Volkswagen AG,* 558 F. Supp. 2d 505, 513-515 (D.N.J. 2008) (holding that, under New Jersey law, the subsidiary acted as an agent of the foreign parent for purposes of service, but the subsidiary was not an agent for foreign parent's other subsidiaries); *C3 Media & Marketing Group, LLC v. Firstgate Internet, Inc.,* 419 F. Supp. 2d 419 (S.D.N.Y. 2005) (applying New York law and holding that service on subsidiary was effective); *Acapalon Corp. v. Ralston Purina Co.,* 1991 Mo. App. LEXIS 1322 (Mo. Ct. App. 1991) (service on U.S. parent effective as service on foreign subsidiary without need for recourse to Hague Service Convention). Many courts have also acknowledged that service upon an alter ego of a foreign defendant can substitute for service abroad, but have concluded that alter ego standards were not satisfied. *Delta Constructors, Inc. v. Roediger Vacuum, GmbH,* 259 F.R.D. 245, 249-253 (S.D. Miss. 2009); *Kwon v. Yun,* 2006 WL 416375, at *2-5 (S.D.N.Y. 2006); *Vega Glen v. Club Mediterranee, SA,* 359 F. Supp. 2d 1352, 1356-1357 (S.D. Fla. 2005); *Fleming v. Yamaha Motor Corp., U.S.A.,* 774 F. Supp. 992 (W.D. Va. 1991); *Wasden v. Yamaha Motor Co.,* 131 F.R.D. 206 (M.D. Fla. 1990).

7. Service within the forum on domestic "agent" of foreign corporation under Convention. Under the analysis in *Schlunk,* service abroad can presumably be avoided by serving an agent of the defendant within the forum. Moreover, local law and the Due Process Clause presumably provide the sole standards for determining when such service upon a U.S. agent is permitted. State law definitions of the types of agency relationships that will permit substituted service vary. *See* 1 Casad & Richman, *Jurisdiction in Civil Actions* §4-3 (3d ed. 1998 & Supp. 2010); *supra* pp. 190-203.

A number of lower court decisions have permitted service on foreign defendants, based in Convention signatory states, to be effected by serving their U.S. agents within the United States. *See Halo Electronics, Inc. v. Bel Fuse Inc.,* 2010 WL 2605195 (N.D. Cal. June 28, 2010); *In re Cathode Ray Tube (CRT) Antitrust Litig.,* 2008 WL 4104341, at *1 (N.D. Cal. 2008); *Gray v. Mazda Motor America, Inc.,* 560 F. Supp. 2d 928, 932 (C.D. Cal. 2008); *Heffernan v. Robeco Inv. Mgmt., Inc.,* 2007 WL 3244422 (Mass. Super. Oct. 25, 2007); *Actrade Financial Technologies Ltd. v. Aharoni,* 2003 WL 22389891, at *5 (Del. Ch. 2003); *Sankaran v. Club Mediterranee, SA,* 1998 WL 433780, at *5-6 (S.D.N.Y. 1998). *Contra Trask v. Service Merchandise Co.,* 135 F.R.D. 17, 21 (D. Mass. 1991) (alternative holding, without reasoning, that domestic service upon foreign defendant's U.S. lawyers did not avoid need to serve abroad under Convention). Other lower courts have acknowledged that service within the forum on a domestic agent of a foreign corporation is not precluded by the Convention, but have found that local standards regarding agency relationships were not satisfied. *Jerge v. Potter,* 2000 WL 1160459, at *2 (W.D.N.Y. 2000); *Sieng v. Muller GmbH Maschinenfabrik,* 1993 WL 337839 (E.D. Pa. 1993).

8. Service within the forum on foreign corporation's address or mail box under Convention. Some lower courts have suggested that, if a foreign corporation owns an office or a post office box, or operates at an address, within the United States, service can be effected "on" that mail box or address without requiring resort to the Convention. *Pittsburgh Nat'l Bank v. Kassir,* 153 F.R.D. 580, 583-584 (W.D. Pa. 1994); *Gallagher v. Mazda Motor of America, Inc.,* 781 F. Supp. 1079, 1082-1083 (E.D. Pa. 1992); *Jordan v. Global Natural Resources, Inc.,* 564 F. Supp. 59, 69-70 (S.D. Ohio 1983).

9. Service and appearance by the defendant. Defendants "appear" in a civil action in various ways. Generally, when contesting personal jurisdiction or service of process, they enter a "special appearance," confined to litigating those preliminary issues. Occasionally (sometimes mistakenly), defendants enter a "general" appearance in which they contest all issues. Under several states' laws, a party's general appearance is treated as the equivalent of personal service of the summons within the state. *See, e.g., Kern County Dep't of Human Servs. v. Super. Ct.*, 187 Cal. App. 4th 302, 311 (Cal. Ct. App. 2010); *In re Vanessa Q.*, 187 Cal. App. 4th 128, 135 (Cal. Ct. App. 2010). In those circumstances, has service has been effected in the forum state (at least by operation of state law), making resort to the Hague Convention unnecessary?

Would this be a sensible result? How is an unsophisticated foreign defendant, unfamiliar with the nuances of the U.S. legal system, supposed to appreciate the difference between general and special appearances? Or is it appropriate to place this burden on the foreign defendant in the expectation that it will retain local counsel familiar with such rules?

10. *Service by contractually agreed means.* Suppose that two parties enter into a contract which provides, in part, that service of process can be effected by email on either party. Suppose further that those parties come from states which are signatories to the Hague Service Convention and that no other alternative method of service is possible under the law of the defendant's state. Would service pursuant to the contract be sufficient? *See Alfred E. Mann Living Trust v. ETIRC Aviation S.a.r.l.*, 910 N.Y.S.2d 418 (App. Div. 2010); *Camphor Tech., Inc. v. Biofer, S.P.A.*, 916 A.2d 142 (Conn. Super. 2007). Can parties "opt out" of the requirements of the Hague Convention? How is this different from a choice-of-law clause where parties attempt to "opt out" of the otherwise applicable substantive law? Or from a choice-of-forum or arbitration clause where parties attempt to "opt out" of an otherwise competent court? How is it different from prospectively entering a general appearance, discussed in the preceding note? Does the Hague Service Convention simply serve to protect the rights of individual defendants or does it serve some broader non-waivable purpose? What implications would such a contractual waiver have for postjudgment defenses in an enforcement proceeding? *See infra* at 1143-1144.

11. *Service on state officials and other statutory agents of foreign defendants under Convention.* Does the holding in *Schlunk* extend to cases where a foreign company is served within the United States by delivery of service to a state official appointed by law to accept service? Should it?

(a) Lower courts permitting service on statutory agents as substitute for service abroad under Convention. Relying on *Schlunk*, a few courts have upheld service on state officials, such as the Secretary of State or State Insurance Commissioner, appointed by law as statutory service agent for unregistered foreign companies doing business in the state. *See Crescent Towing & Salvage Co., Inc. v. M/V CHIOS BEAUTY*, 2008 WL 3850481, at *12 (E.D. La. Aug. 14, 2008); *Amazon.com, Inc. v. Underwriters, Lloyd's of London*, 2005 WL 1172432, at *3 (W.D. Wash. 2005); *E. & J. Gallo Winery v. Cantine Rallo, S.p.A.*, 430 F. Supp. 2d 1064 (E.D. Cal. 2005) (holding that use of Hague Service Convention not necessary where service effected on nonresident trademark holder's designated agent under Lanham Act); *Daewoo Motor America, Inc. v. Dongbu Fire Ins. Co., Ltd.*, 289 F. Supp. 2d 1127, 1130-1131 (C.D. Cal. 2001) ("Just as VwoA was the agent of VWAG under the internal law of the forum state in [*Schlunk*], . . . the California Insurance Commissioner is the agent (albeit involuntary) of Dongbu under California law. Therefore, the internal law of the forum state does not require service abroad because service is properly effected on DMA's agent."); *Melia v. Les Grands Cahais de France*, 135 F.R.D. 28, 32 (D.R.I. 1991).

(b) Lower courts forbidding service on statutory agents as substitute for service abroad under Convention. Most lower courts have held that *Schlunk* does not extend to domestic service upon statutorily appointed agents, such as a state Secretary of State. *Lobo v. Celebrity*

Cruises, Inc., 667 F. Supp. 2d 1324, 1338 (S.D. Fla. 2009); *Collins v. Westfreight Sys., Inc.,* 2009 WL 1036381, at *2 (E.D. Ky. 2009); *Alternative Delivery Solutions, Inc. v. R.R. Donnelley & Sons Co.,* 2005 WL 1862631, at *2 (W.D. Tex. 2005); *Cupp v. Alberto-Culver USA, Inc.,* 308 F. Supp. 2d 873, 879-880 (W.D. Tenn. 2004); *Davies v. Jobs & Adverts Online, GmbH,* 94 F. Supp. 2d 719 (E.D. Va. 2000) (service on German company via Clerk of the State Corporation Commission subject to Hague Service Convention because Virginia service statute provided for Clerk to forward process via mail to defendant); *Fleming v. Yamaha Motor Corp., USA,* 774 F. Supp. 992, 994-995 (E.D. Va. 1991); *Froland v. Yamaha Motor Co., Ltd.,* 296 F. Supp. 2d 1004, 1007-1008 (D. Minn. 2003) (same result under Minnesota law). The result in this case appears to depend on whether, under state law, service is deemed complete upon delivery to the Secretary of State or, instead, the Secretary of State must also send the document to the foreign nonresident before service is complete. *See Collins v. Westfreight Sys., Inc.,* 2009 WL 1036381 (E.D. Ky. Apr. 17, 2009). Is this a sensible result?

(c) Authorities suggesting that local law regarding service on statutory agents is dispositive under Convention. Some authorities have suggested that *Schlunk* permits local service on a statutory agent, rather than service abroad under the Convention, if local law deems service complete when the statutory agent receives process, but not if service is incomplete until the agent transmits the process abroad to the foreign defendant. *See Amazon.com, Inc. v. Underwriters, Lloyd's of London,* 2005 WL 1172432 (W.D. Wash. 2005); *Daewoo Motor America, Inc. v. Dongbu Fire Ins. Co.,* 289 F. Supp. 2d 1127, 1130-1131 (C.D. Cal. 2001); *Int'l Space Brokers, Inc. v. Redier,* 2000 WL 1052808, at *2 (Va. Cir. Ct. 2000); *Paradigm Entertainment, Inc. v. Video System Co.,* 2000 WL 251731, at *4 (N.D. Tex. 2000); *Bowers v. Wurzburg,* 519 S.E.2d 148, 159-164 (W. Va. 1999); *Bayoil Supply and Trading of Bahamas v. Jorgen Jahre Shipping,* 54 F. Supp. 2d 691 (S.D. Tex. 1999); *Quinn v. Keinicke,* 700 A.2d 147, 154 (Del. Super. 1996); *Sang Young Kim v. Frank Mohn A/S,* 909 F. Supp. 474, 479 (S.D. Tex. 1995).

Note, in this regard, *Schlunk*'s comment that "[w]here service on a domestic agent is *valid and complete* under both state law and the Due Process Clause, our inquiry ends and the Convention has no further implications. . . . The only transmittal to which the Convention applies is a transmittal abroad that is *required as a necessary part of service.*" (Emphasis added.) Consider the following analysis by the Committee on Federal Courts, N.Y. State Bar Ass'n, *Service of Process Abroad: A Nuts and Bolts Guide,* 122 F.R.D. 63, 73-74 (1989):

> Section 306 [New York B.C.L.] provides that one may serve New York corporations, and foreign corporations *licensed* to do business in New York, by delivering two copies of the process to the Secretary of State as agent for the corporation. "Service of process on such corporation shall be complete when the secretary of state is so served."[N.Y. B.C.L. §306(b)] The Secretary of State then sends one of the copies to the corporation. "The jurisdictional act is the delivery of the two copies to the Secretary. The latter's failure to forward one to the corporation does not void the service." A fortiori, if the Secretary transmits the process to the foreign corporation abroad in some manner that violates the Convention, personal jurisdiction over the defendant would still exist.
>
> Under N.Y. B.C.L. §307, one may serve *unlicensed* foreign corporations that are subject to jurisdiction in New York under article 3 of the C.P.L.R. by delivering one copy of the process to the Secretary of State as agent for the corporation and then personally delivering, or mailing, notice of that service, with a copy of the process, to the corporation. Failure to deliver or send a copy of the process to the foreign corporation is a fatal jurisdictional defect [under New York law]. Accordingly, as at least four New York courts have now held, jurisdiction is not obtained under B.C.L. §307 when a copy of the process is transmitted to the corporation abroad in a manner that violates the Convention.

See Vasquez v. Sund Emba AB, 548 N.Y.S.2d 728, 731 n.4 (App. Div. 1989). Is this a persuasive distinction? Is it what *Schlunk* envisaged? Could New York amend N.Y. B.C.L. §307 to make service complete upon delivery to the Secretary of State?

Suppose, instead, that New York law provided that service was only complete after the Secretary of State mailed the served documents to the foreign company at its headquarters abroad. Suppose further that the foreign company is based in a country that has not objected to service by mail under Article 10 of the Hague Service Convention. Can a plaintiff successfully effect service by serving the documents on the local Secretary of State and then having that official mail the documents to the foreign company abroad? *See Conax Florida Corp. v. Astrium, Ltd.,* 499 F. Supp. 2d 1287, 1292-1293 (M.D. Fla. 2007).

12. *Statutory agent must be authorized under local law to accept service in private actions.* Some state and federal statutes require foreign companies to appoint local agents for particular purposes. The National Traffic and Motor Vehicle Safety Act of 1966 is one example of such a statute. Most lower courts have held that service on an agent appointed for a limited statutory purpose is invalid for other, nonstatutory purposes such as a private civil law suit. In such cases, service on the statutory agent is not sufficient service on the defendant under local law. *E.g., Lamb v. Volkswagen,* 104 F.R.D. 95 (S.D. Fla. 1985); *Richardson v. Volkswagenwerk AG,* 552 F. Supp. 73, 77-79 (W.D. Mo. 1982).

13. *Service by publication under Convention.* Some courts have extended the reasoning of *Schlunk* to hold that service by publication does not amount to service "abroad" and, consequently, does not implicate the Convention. *See, e.g., Eto v. Murankana,* 57 P.3d 413 (Hawaii 2002); *People v. Mendocino County Assessor's Parcel No. 056-500-09,* 58 Cal. App. 4th 120, 124-125 (Cal. Ct. App. 1997). *See also BP Products North Am., Inc. v. Dagra,* 236 F.R.D. 270 (E.D. Va. 2006). Are decisions excusing service by publication from the requirements of the Convention consistent with *Schlunk*? Can service by publication be distinguished analytically from service on a foreign defendant's domestic agent, subsidiary or alter ego? If notice of a lawsuit is published in a foreign newspaper, how is the intrusion on sovereignty any different than use of mails or a private process server?

14. *Service outside the forum state, but within the United States, on domestic alter ego of foreign corporation under Convention.* Some courts have extended *Schlunk* to permit service within the United States pursuant to a state long-arm statute on the out-of-state U.S. subsidiary of a foreign parent located in a Convention signatory state. *E.g., Blades v. Illinois Central R. Co.,* 2003 WL 1193662, at *2-3 (E.D. La. 2003) (acknowledging theory but rejecting it on the facts); *Hickory Travel Systems, Inc. v. TUI AG,* 213 F.R.D. 547, 554 (N.D. Cal. 2003) (same); *McHugh v. International Components Corp.,* 461 N.Y.S.2d 166 (Sup. Ct. 1983). Is this extension of *Schlunk* permitted by the Convention?

15. *Practical reasons for using Convention's procedures, instead of effecting service within the United States.* Note that *Schlunk* merely *permits* U.S. plaintiffs to circumvent the Convention, by serving the U.S. agents of foreign defendants. The Court also commented, however, that this course of action may well make it difficult to enforce any resulting U.S. judgment abroad. Foreign courts may not follow *Schlunk*'s interpretation of the Convention: as one lower court remarked, "this court cannot render an interpretation of the treaty which will bind the courts of [a foreign state] in the event plaintiff, if he obtains a judgment against [the foreign defendant], seeks to enforce it through the courts in that nation." *Shoei Kako Co. v. Superior Court,* 33 Cal. App. 2d 808, 822 (1973). Unless practical reasons counsel otherwise, U.S. plaintiffs are generally well advised to comply with the Convention notwithstanding *Schlunk*.

16. *Does Rule 4(f) overrule* Schlunk? It has been suggested that "there would appear to be a distinct danger that the relevant provisions [of new Rule 4(f)] will be construed to require service pursuant to the Hague Convention even when service can be made on an agent in the United States." Smit, *Recent Developments in International Litigation,* 35 S. Tex. L. Rev. 215, 224 (1994). Is this really a danger? What part of Rule 4(f) suggests such a result? Note that the Advisory Committee Rules cite *Schlunk* with approval:

> Use of the Convention procedures, when available, is mandatory if documents must be transmitted abroad to effect service. *See Volkswagenwerk AG v. Schlunk,* 486 U.S. 694 (1988) (noting that voluntary use of these procedures may be desirable even when service could constitutionally be effected in another manner).

Parties have raised the argument that Rule 4(f) overruled *Schlunk,* but courts, relying on the Commentary, have rejected it. *See, e.g., Silvious v. Pharaon,* 54 F.3d 697, 701-702 (11th Cir. 1995) (*per curiam*).

10. Default Judgments Under Article 15 of the Hague Service Convention

In addition to regulating the service of process abroad, the Hague Service Convention also imposes restrictions on the power of national courts to enter default judgments on defendants that were served (or should have been served) pursuant to the Convention. The United States has availed itself of the opportunity, pursuant to the second paragraph of Article 15, to permit U.S. courts to enter default judgments if (i) process was actually transmitted pursuant to one of the Convention's mechanisms, (ii) no report has been made on the attempted service after a period (not less than six months), which the judge considers adequate, and (iii) the plaintiff has made "every reasonable effort" to secure a report on service or an Article 6 certificate.[240] A number of other contracting states have also issued similar declarations.[241]

Article 15 has not frequently been considered in U.S. litigation. Those courts which have dealt with the provision have generally addressed whether the requirements of Article 15 are satisfied, including whether the defendant failed to "appear."[242]

E. Service of Process Abroad Pursuant to the Inter-American Convention on Letters Rogatory

The Inter-American Convention on Letters Rogatory grew out of the first Inter-American Specialized Conference on Private International Law, held in Panama City in 1975.[243] The United States subsequently proposed a Protocol to the Convention at the Second Inter-American Specialized Conference on Private International Law in Montevideo in 1979.[244] The Protocol was adopted with some amendments, thus largely conforming the Letters

---

240. *See* 28 U.S.C.A. Federal Rules of Civil Procedure, Rule 4 (U.S. declaration); Appendix L.

241. *See* 28 U.S.C.A. Federal Rules of Civil Procedure, Rule 4 (Declarations of Canada, China, Germany, and the United Kingdom).

242. *See e360 Insight v. The Spamhaus Project,* 500 F.3d 594 (7th Cir. 2007); *John Galliano, S.A. v. Stallion, Inc.,* 15 N.Y.S. 3d 75 (2010); *Marcus Food Co. v. Dipanfilo,* 2010 WL 3946314 (D. Kan. Oct. 5, 2010); *Malone v. Holder,* 2009 WL 3158159 (D. Colo. Sept. 28, 2009); *Xyrous Commc'n v. Bulgarian Telecomm. Co. AD,* 2009 WL 2877084 (E.D. Va. 2009); *Daly v. Llanes,* 1999 WL 1067876 (S.D.N.Y. 1999); *Thomas v. Biocine Sclavo, SpA,* 1998 WL 51861 (N.D.N.Y. 1998).

243. The Conference is a regional alternative to the Hague Conference on Private International Law. *See* Kearney, *Developments in Private International Law,* 81 Am. J. Int'l L. 724, 735 (1987); Kim, Note, *The Inter-American Convention and Additional Protocol on Letters Rogatory: The Hague Service Convention's "Country Cousins?,"* 36 Colum J. Transnat'l L. 687 (1998).

244. Kearney, *supra,* 81 Am. J. Int'l L. at 737.

Rogatory Convention to the Hague Service Convention and leading to U.S. ratification in October 1986.[245]

Unlike the Hague Service Convention, the Inter-American Letters Rogatory Convention is not "exclusive."[246] The Convention's service mechanisms (which are broadly similar to those under the Hague Service Convention) are incorporated by Rule 4(f)(1) of the Federal Rules of Civil Procedure.[247] Where enforcement of a U.S. judgment abroad may be necessary, the Convention should generally be used.[248] If the Convention is not used, then Rule 4(f)(2) and 4(f)(3) are available.

F. Service of U.S. Process on Foreign States

The foregoing sections of this chapter dealt with state and federal rules regarding service of process on *private* parties outside the United States. An entirely different set of rules apply to the service of U.S. process on foreign states and their agencies and instrumentalities.

1. FSIA's Regime for Service on Foreign States

Service on foreign sovereigns and their agencies and instrumentalities is governed primarily by the Foreign Sovereign Immunities Act ("FSIA"), which establishes a distinct and specialized regime for the service of process.[249] Unlike most other service provisions, the FSIA's rules are uniform throughout all courts in the United States. The FSIA applies without regard to whether the action is in state or federal court and without regard to the character of the plaintiff's cause of action; the statute's service rules also apply both to service within and outside the United States. These aspects of the statute were adopted with the express purposes of promoting uniformity.[250]

The FSIA's general provisions on service of process are contained in §1608. In federal courts, the FSIA's service provisions are incorporated by Rule 4(j)(1) of the Federal Rules of Civil Procedure. It provides that "[s]ervice upon a foreign state or a political subdivision, agency, or instrumentality thereof shall be effected pursuant to 28 U.S.C. §1608."

---

245. Signatories to the Letters Rogatory Convention include, among others, Argentina, Brazil, Chile, Mexico, the United States, and Venezuela. Spain also has acceded to the treaty.

246. *See supra* pp. 875-877.

247. *See supra* pp. 875-877. For decisions under the Inter-American Convention, *see Morgenthau v. Avion Resources, Ltd.*, 11 N.Y.S. 3d 383 (2008); *Southwest Livestock & Trucking Co., Inc. v. Ramon*, 169 F.3d 317, 323 n.5 (5th Cir. 1999); *Kreimerman v. Casa Veerkamp, S.A. de C.V.*, 22 F.3d 634 (5th Cir. 1994); *Malone v. Holder*, 2009 WL 3158159 (D. Colo. Sept. 28, 2009); *Dominion Exploration & Prod., Inc. v. Delmar Sys., Inc.*, 2008 WL 4809453 (E.D. La. 2008); *Paiz v. Castellanos*, 2006 WL 2578807 (S.D. Fla. Aug. 28, 2006); *In re Letter Rogatory*, 2002 WL 257822 (E.D.N.Y. 2002); *Lord v. Living Bridges*, 1999 WL 528833 (E.D. Pa. 1999); *Osario v. Harza Engineering Co.*, 890 F. Supp. 750, 752-753 (N.D. Ill. 1995). For information on procedures under the Convention, *see* U.S. State Department Circular, *Inter-American Convention on Letters Rogatory and Additional Protocol (Inter-American Service Convention)*, *available at* http://travel.state.gov/law/info/judicial/judicial_687.html.

248. *See C & F Systems, LLC v. Limpimax, S.A.*, 2010 WL 65200, at *1 (W.D. Mich. 2010) ("Since both Peru and the United States have seen fit to agree upon a method of service acceptable to both countries, principles of international comity would counsel in favor of at least attempting to comply with the requirements of the Convention, even if they are not the exclusive allowable means of service in a strict sense."); *Lake Charles Cane LaCassine Mill, LLC v. SMAR Int'l Corp.*, 2007 WL 1695722 (W.D. La. June 8, 2007) (relying on comity principles to require plaintiff to attempt to effect service by Inter-American Convention before utilizing other methods).

249. 28 U.S.C. §§1602-1611 (1982). The FSIA is examined in detail in Chapter 3. Rules governing service in certain admiralty proceedings are treated separately by 28 U.S.C. §1605(b).

250. *See* H.R. Rep. No. 1487, 94th Cong., 2d Sess. 24-25, *reprinted in* 1976 U.S. Code Cong. & Admin. News 6604, 6623. *See also Gibbons v. Republic of Ireland*, 532 F. Supp. 668 (D.D.C. 1982).

In state courts, §1608 is directly applicable; it must be complied with, notwithstanding inconsistent state law rules.[251]

2. Alternative Mechanisms for Service Prescribed for "Foreign States Proper" and for Foreign State "Agencies and Instrumentalities"

Section 1608 sets out two separate lists of alternative means for service. The list contained in §1608(a) applies to service on the foreign state or its "political subdivisions"; §1608(b)'s list applies to service on "an agency or instrumentality" of the foreign state.[252] The alternatives listed in §1608(a) are different from those in §1608(b).

In effecting service on a foreign state-related entity, it is important to identify whether a proposed defendant is a "foreign state" or an "agency or instrumentality." That is because service that is appropriate for one category will not necessarily be adequate under the FSIA's provisions for the other.[253] It is also important to distinguish carefully between the foreign state and its agencies, and between different foreign state-related entities. Service upon the foreign state, or one of its agencies, will not necessarily constitute service upon other agencies or instrumentalities of the foreign state.

Although their specific alternatives for service are different, §1608(a) and §1608(b) are similar in that their listings of alternatives are ranked in decreasing order of preference.[254] Plaintiffs are required to follow the statutory order of preference and may only attempt to serve process by less-preferred means if a more-preferred means is not available.[255] As discussed in the excerpt below, lower courts have adopted different approaches over how strictly a party must comply with §1608's service requirements.

---

251. *See Robinson v. Government of Malaysia,* 664 N.Y.S.2d 907, 909 (Sup. Ct. 1997); *2 Tudor Place Associates v. Libya,* 470 N.Y.S.2d 301, 303-304 (Civ. Ct. 1983). Some case law holds that a foreign state can contractually waive the FSIA's service of process requirements. *See Stahl 3 DAG LLC v. Permanent Mission of Chile to the United Nations,* 2005 WL 2219483, at *1 (N.Y. Civ. Ct. 2005); *International Road Federation v. Embassy of the Democratic Republic of the Congo,* 131 F. Supp. 2d 248, 250-252 (D.D.C. 2001). *Compare Berdakin v. Consulado de la Republica de El Salvador,* 912 F. Supp. 458, 466 (C.D. Cal. 1995) (holding that contractual provision not expressly waiving FSIA service rules did not constitute special arrangement); *Underwood v. United Republic of Tanzania,* 1995 WL 46383, at *2 (D.D.C. 1995) (same).

252. Section 1608(b) of the FSIA defines "agency or instrumentality of a foreign state" to be any "separate legal person, corporate or otherwise" that is not a citizen of the United States or created under the laws of any third country and that is either an "organ of a foreign state or political subdivision thereof, or a majority of whose shares or other ownership interest is owned by a foreign state or political subdivision thereof." *See supra* pp. 250-275.

253. *See Bolkiah v. Superior Court,* 74 Cal. App. 4th 984, 993-994 (Cal. Ct. App. 1999); *Transaero, Inc. v. La Fuerza Aerea Boliviana,* 30 F.3d 148 (D.C. Cir. 1994); *Segni v. Commercial Office of Spain,* 650 F. Supp. 1040 (N.D. Ill. 1986), *aff'd,* 835 F.2d 160 (7th Cir. 1987); *Box v. Dallas Mexican Consulate General,* 2010 WL 5437246 (N.D. Tex. 2010); *Lee v. Taipei Econ. and Cultural Representative Office,* 2010 WL 2710661 (S.D. Tex. 2010); *Gates v. Syrian Arab Republic,* 580 F. Supp. 2d 53 (D.D.C. 2008); *Hilaturas Miel, S.L. v. Republic of Iraq,* 573 F. Supp. 2d 781 (S.D.N.Y. 2008); *Nikbin v. Islamic Republic of Iran,* 471 F. Supp. 2d 53 (D.D.C. 2007); *Cosmos Trading Corp. of Panama v. Banco Nacional de Cuba,* 2006 WL 4515304 (E.D. La. 2006); *Resource Dynamic Int'l v. General People's Committee,* 593 F. Supp. 572 (N.D. Ga. 1984); *Unidyne Corp. v. Aerolineas Argentinas,* 590 F. Supp. 398 (E.D. Va. 1984). The distinction between foreign states proper, and their agencies and instrumentalities, is discussed above. *See supra* pp. 262-269.

254. *See* H.R. Rep. No. 1487, 94th Cong., 2d Sess. 24, *reprinted in* 1976 U.S. Code Cong. & Admin. News 6604, 6623.

255. *Magness v. Russian Federation,* 247 F.3d 609, 613 (5th Cir. 2001); *Smith v. Gnassignbe,* 2009 WL 3300037, at *1 (D. Minn. 2009); *Sabbithi v. Al Saleh,* 623 F. Supp. 2d 93, 98 (D.D.C. 2009); *Rubin v. Islamic Republic of Iran,* 2008 WL 2501996 (N.D. Ill. 2008); *Rux v. Republic of Sudan,* 2005 WL 2086202, at *16 (E.D. Va. 2005); *Bybee v. Oper der Stadt Bonn,* 899 F. Supp. 1217, 1221-1222 (S.D.N.Y. 1995); *Filus v. LOT Polish Airlines,* 819 F. Supp. 232 (E.D.N.Y. 1993).

3. Selected Materials on Service Under the Foreign Sovereign Immunities Act

As noted above, the service requirements under §1608(a) and §1608(b), which are excerpted below, differ in important respects. These differences are not confined merely to the statutory text but have also emerged in the case law. One of the emerging differences is the extent to which parties must strictly comply (as opposed to "substantially" comply) with §1608's service requirements. The decision in *Magness v. Russian Federation*, excerpted below, explores these issues and demonstrates some of the difficulties in effecting service on a foreign sovereign or its agencies.

FOREIGN SOVEREIGN IMMUNITIES ACT
28 U.S.C. §1608 [excerpted in Appendix F]

MAGNESS v. RUSSIAN FEDERATION
247 F.3d 609 (5th Cir. 2001)

JOLLY, CIRCUIT JUDGE. [The Magness family alleged that, during the Bolshevik Revolution, the Soviet government expropriated its ancestors' property. Following unsuccessful negotiations with the Russian government, they sued the Russian Federation, the Russian Ministry of Culture, the State Diamond Fund (an agency of the Russian federation) and others seeking damages for the expropriation. They also sought a temporary restraining order (TRO) to prevent some of the Romanov family jewels, which were on tour, from leaving the jurisdiction (a request that the district court denied but which is relevant to the service issues in the case).] . . .

[I]n August 1998 the district court ordered the Magness descendants to serve the summons and complaint on the defendants, and to do so before September 1, 1998. They attempted to serve the defendants in several ways. They first served the attorneys who represented the Russian Federation at the TRO hearing. In addition, they served the Texas Secretary of State, with instructions that the Secretary forward the summons and complaint to "the Russian Federation c/o Boris Yeltsin and the Russian Ministry of Culture/Russian State Diamond Fund c/o Deputy Minister of Culture Mikhail Schvidkoy." The Magness descendants also forwarded the summons and complaint to the Director of Special Consular Affairs at the State Department, with instructions to serve all defendants through diplomatic channels.[256] Finally, the Magness descendants purported to serve process by sending the summons and complaint directly to the Russian Deputy Minister of Culture in Moscow.[257] On November 13, 1998, the State Department informed the Magness descendants that it could not serve the defendants because of several procedural errors.

[The Magness descendants then filed a motion for a default judgment. The district court, finding that the defendants had been properly served, entered a default judgment. Defendants then retained U.S. counsel in an effort to vacate the default judgment. The

---

256. While the Magness descendants recognize that service was never completed through the State Department, they allege that the defendants received service through the Texas Secretary of State and otherwise had actual notice of the suit.

257. The record shows that some persons signed for these mailed documents. However, there is no indication of who specifically signed for the documents. Nor is there any evidence of who in the Russian government may have seen the documents.

district court rejected this motion, holding that descendants had "substantially complied" with the FSIA's service requirements. Defendants appealed.]

The FSIA outlines specific provisions for service of process upon foreign governments and agencies in 28 U.S.C. §1608. The Magness descendants acknowledge that they failed strictly to comply with the service provisions of the FSIA.[258] The provisions for service under §1608 are hierarchical, such that a plaintiff must attempt the methods of service in the order they are laid out in the statute. Regarding the Russian Federation and the Russian Ministry of Culture under §1608(a), they must first be served in accordance with any special arrangement between the parties or in accordance with an applicable international convention. 28 U.S.C. §1608(a)(1-2). Given that there was no special arrangement or international convention governing service here, the Magness descendants are required to have attempted service on the head of the Russian Ministry of Foreign Affairs. 28 U.S.C. §1608(a)(3). Finally, if service could not be made through the Ministry of Foreign Affairs within thirty days, they could resort to service through the State Department. 28 U.S.C. §1608(a)(4). Instead of asking the clerk of the district court to send the summons and notice of suit by return receipt mail to the head of the Russian foreign ministry under §1608(a)(3), the Magness descendants sent their complaint to the Texas Secretary of State for forwarding to Boris Yeltsin, and sent the complaint directly to the Russian Deputy Minister of Culture. Thus, the FSIA was not strictly complied with as to the Russian Federation and Ministry of Culture.

As to the Russian State Diamond Fund, §1608(b) (applicable to instrumentalities of a foreign state) was similarly not strictly followed. A plaintiff must first attempt service in accordance with any special arrangement between the parties. 28 U.S.C. §1608(b)(1). Next, a plaintiff may serve through an authorized agent in the United States or according to an applicable international convention. 28 U.S.C. §1608(b)(2). If no such agent or convention exists, as was the case here, a plaintiff may serve papers via a letter rogatory, through the clerk of the court, or as directed by the court, if these methods are "reasonably calculated to give actual notice." 28 U.S.C. §1608(b)(3). Instead of following the statute, the Magness descendants forwarded a copy of their papers to the State Department and the Texas Secretary of State for service upon the Fund. Thus, the requirements of §1608(b) were not strictly followed as to the Russian State Diamond Fund.

The question before this court, therefore, is whether strict compliance is required for service of process under §1608(a), for a foreign state, and under §1608(b), for an instrumentality of a foreign state. The Magness descendants contend that, even if their attempts at service of process upon the defendants did not strictly comply with §1608, they substantially complied with the FSIA, and that the defendants had actual notice of the suit. . . . The defendants, however, argue that the FSIA makes no provision for anything other than strict compliance with its service of process requirements, and that actual notice cannot substitute for proper service under either §1608(a) or (b). In addition, the appellants and the United States, as amici, contend that, in any event, the Magness descendants failed to even substantially comply with §1608(a) or (b). Because service was never effectuated, the district court had no personal jurisdiction over the defendants, they claim, and thus the default judgment should be vacated pursuant to Rule 60(b)(4).

We conclude that the provisions for service of process upon a foreign state or political subdivision of a foreign state outlined in §1608(a) can only be satisfied by strict compliance. The express language of the statute requires that service "shall" be made upon a

---

258. All parties agree that service upon the Russian Federation (as a foreign state) and the Russian Ministry of Culture (as a political subdivision) is dictated by §1608(a), while service upon the Russian State Diamond Fund (as an instrumentality of Russia) is governed by §1608(b).

foreign state in the manner prescribed. Moreover, the committee report on the FSIA states that "section 1608(a) sets forth the *exclusive* procedures for service on a foreign state." H.R. Rep. No. 94-1487, at 24 (1976), U.S. Code Cong. & Admin. News at 6604, 6623 (emphasis added).[259] This language simply does not support a finding that anything less than strict compliance will suffice under the law. This interpretation is in accord with decisions of the Second, Seventh, and D.C. Circuits.[260] . . .

Based on these decisions, the express language of section 1608(a), and the United States' interest in ensuring that the proper officials of a foreign state are notified when a suit is instituted, we hold that plaintiffs must strictly comply with the statutory service of process provisions when suing a foreign state or political subdivision under §1608(a).[261] [Since plaintiffs had not strictly complied with §1608(a)'s requirements for service on the Russian Federation and the Russian Ministry of Culture, the court concluded that service as to these defendants was inadequate.]

The statutory language and case law concerning §1608(b) present a different question. As such, we are convinced that substantial compliance with the provisions of service upon an agency or instrumentality of a foreign state — that is, service that gives actual notice of the suit and the consequences thereof to the proper individuals within the agency or instrumentality — is sufficient to effectuate service under §1608(b). Perhaps most significant to this determination is the express statement in §1608(b)(3) that delivery under that subsection is authorized "if reasonably calculated to give actual notice." . . . This reference to actual notice is absent from §1608(a). Our holding as to §1608(b) is in accord with the Third, Sixth, Ninth, Eleventh, and D.C. Circuits, all of which have determined that substantial compliance with §1608(b) is sufficient so long as the defendants have actual notice of the suit.[262] . . .

The cases authorizing substantial compliance with the service of process provisions under §1608(b) note that it is actual notice by the defendant that substantiates the compliance. The Magness descendants assert that the defendants all had actual notice of the suit, while the defendants deny having such notice. As to the Russian State Diamond Fund, the defendants contend that the mailing of process to Boris Yeltsin and the Russian State Diamond Fund "c/o Deputy Minister of Culture Mikhail Schvidkoy" was not substantial compliance with §1608(b), which permitted service via a letter rogatory, through the clerk of the court, or as directed by the court. 28 U.S.C. §1608(b)(3). The Magness descendants, in turn, assert that they substantially complied with §1608(b)(3)(B), which authorizes service upon an instrumentality of a foreign state by any form of mail requiring a signed receipt. They point out that they sent service papers to the Texas Secretary of State with a request that those documents be forwarded to the "Russian Ministry of Culture/Russian State Diamond Fund." Finally, the Magness descendants contend that all defendants had

---

259. Incidentally, this "exclusive procedures" language is missing in the discussion of §1608(b) in the legislative history.

260. Although the Ninth Circuit appears to have adopted a blanket "substantial compliance" test for §1608 in *Straub v. Green, Inc.,* 38 F.3d 448, 453 (9th Cir. 1994), that decision dealt only with service under §1608(b), and the court's decision in *Gerritsen v. Consulado General de Mexico,* 989 F.2d 340, 345 (9th Cir. 1993), suggests that plaintiffs must strictly comply with the service provisions on a foreign state under §1608(a).

261. We leave open the possibility that, under extraordinary circumstances not present in this case, when service of process according to the express provisions of §1608(a) is a manifest impossibility, other methods of service that fully satisfy the goals of section 1608(a) might be sufficient. . . .

262. We recognize that not all federal courts have found substantial compliance sufficient under §1608(b). *See, e.g., LeDonne v. Gulf Air, Inc.,* 700 F. Supp. 1400 (E.D. Va. 1988) (requiring strict compliance under 1608(b)); *Lippus v. Dahlgren Mfg. Co.,* 644 F. Supp. 1473, 1479 (E.D.N.Y. 1986) (requiring that certain "exigencies" be present before excusing non-strict compliance with §1608(b)); *Unidyne Corp. v. Aerolineas Argentinas,* 590 F. Supp. 391, 395 (E.D. Va. 1984) (noting that "this Court is directed to strictly interpret the requirements set forth in §1608(b).").

actual notice of the suit, as evidenced by the Russian Federation's appearance at the TRO hearing and the confirmation received by the Texas Secretary of State showing that the return receipt for the service documents had been signed by somebody at the "Russian Ministry of Culture/Russian State Diamond Fund."

As the United States notes, there is no evidence that the Magness descendants included a "notice of suit" in the service documents that allegedly were served. The notice of suit is an integral part of the service requirements upon foreign states, and is "designed to provide a foreign state with an introductory explanation of the lawsuit, together with an explanation of the legal significance of the summons, complaint, and service." H.R. Rep. No. 94-1487, at 11, U.S. Code Cong. & Admin. News at 6609. Most importantly, there is no evidence to establish that the defendants had actual notice of the suit. The Magness descendants bear the burden of proving that the defendants had actual notice. . . . Under the FSIA, proving "actual notice" requires more than a mere showing that somebody in the foreign state knew of the claim. Because the plaintiffs have not established that they provided the Russian State Diamond Fund actual notice of the suit, substantial compliance with §1608(b) was lacking. . . .

The government has emphasized the weighty diplomatic considerations underlying this case, noting that the United States has fought jurisdiction in instances where foreign attorneys have attempted to serve the United States via non-authorized government employees. In its amici brief the United States suggests that it would not consider itself to have been properly served under the attempts utilized by the Magness descendants in this case.[263] In this light, and for the reasons we have explained, we conclude that the default judgment should be vacated, that the case must be remanded, and that the Magness descendants should be allowed a reasonable time to perfect service upon the defendants.

Notes on FSIA and Magness

1. **Service under the FSIA.** *Magness* illustrates two basic features of service on foreign states that are established by the FSIA's text: (a) different rules govern service of states and service of their agencies and instrumentalities; and (b) a hierarchy governs each set of service rules. Consider the overall structure established by §1608. Is this a sensible means for serving foreign states and their agencies or instrumentalities? Compare the FSIA's structure to that of Rule 4(f) and 4(h). Which structure is clearer? Provides better guidance to litigants and courts?

2. **Strict compliance required for service under §1608(a).** *Magness* illustrates the prevailing view among lower courts that parties must strictly comply with the service requirements of §1608(a). *See also Gray v. Permanent Mission of People's Republic of Congo*, 443 F. Supp. 816, 821 (S.D.N.Y.), *aff'd*, 580 F.2d 1044 (2d Cir. 1978); *Alberti v. Empresa Nicaraguense de la Carne*, 705 F.2d 250, 253 (7th Cir. 1983); *Transaero, Inc. v. La Fuerza Aerea Boliviana*, 30 F.3d 148, 154 (D.C. Cir. 1994); *Box v. Dallas Mexican Consulate Gen.*, 2010 WL 5437246, at *5 (N.D. Tex. 2010); *Fly Brazil Grp., Inc. v. The Gov't of Gabon, Africa*, 709 F. Supp. 2d 1274, 1280 (S.D. Fla. 2010) (collecting cases); *Hilaturas Miel, S.L. v. Republic of Iraq*, 573 F. Supp. 2d 781, 796-797 (S.D.N.Y. 2008). *Compare Straub v. Green, Inc.*, 38 F.3d 448, 453 (9th Cir. 1994) (dicta that substantial compliance is sufficient in all cases under §1608).

---

263. That is, the delivery of a package addressed to "George W. Bush, the White House" to a random federal agency that lacks the responsibility for foreign relations would not provide adequate notice of suit to the United States.

Note, however, that *Magness* leaves open the possibility of relaxing the requirement in "extraordinary circumstances." What sorts of circumstances might satisfy this exception? *See Wye Oak Technology, Inc. v. Republic of Iraq,* 2010 WL 2613323 (E.D. Va. June 29, 2010).

3. Substantial compliance required for service under §1608(b). *Magness* also reflects the prevailing view among federal courts that a plaintiff only must "substantially comply" with §1608(b)'s service requirements. Under this view, substantial compliance coupled with "actual notice" of the lawsuit supplies adequate service. *See, e.g., Smith v. Ghana Commercial Bank,* 2009 WL 3327206 (D. Minn. 2009); *In re Perry H. Koplik & Sons, Inc.,* 357 B.R. 231, 249-250 (Bankr. S.D.N.Y. 2006); *Pradhan v. Al-Sabah,* 299 F. Supp. 2d 493, 499-500 (D. Md. 2004); *Lewis & Kennedy, Inc. v. Permanent Mission of The Republic of Botswana to the United Nations,* 2005 WL 1621342, at *3 (S.D.N.Y. 2005) (explaining distinction between "strict compliance" and "substantial compliance"); *BPA Int'l, Inc. v. Kingdom of Sweden,* 281 F. Supp. 2d 73, 84 (D.D.C. 2003); *Trans Commodities, Inc. v. Kazakstan Trading House,* 1997 WL 811474, at *4 (S.D.N.Y. 1997). A few courts appear to reject the substantial compliance doctrine even under §1608(b). *See, e.g., Daly v. Castro Llanes,* 30 F. Supp. 2d 407, 415-417 (S.D.N.Y. 1998).

4. Correctness of differing requirements under §1608(a) and §1608(b). Is the distinction between "strict compliance" under §1608(a) and "substantial compliance" under §1608(b) correct? As *Magness* illustrates, proponents of a strict compliance requirement for service under §1608(a) rely on the text of §1608(a) providing that service "shall" be made upon a foreign state in the manner prescribed. But doesn't §1608(b) use precisely the same term ("shall") in its opening sentence? In light of this identical language, why isn't strict compliance with §1608(b) also required?

Proponents of the distinction also point to the fact that the legislative history suggests that §1608(a) sets forth the "exclusive procedures" for service and that comparable language is missing under §1608(b). But is it correct to infer a "strict compliance" requirement from the term "exclusive procedures" in the legislative history? Conversely, is it correct to infer a lesser "substantial compliance' requirement from the absence of the term "exclusive procedures" in the legislative history underpinning §1608(b)? More fundamentally, is it appropriate for the courts to rely on legislative history in this context? Doesn't the use of the word "shall" in both sections impose a "strict compliance" requirement? *See Connecticut National Bank v. St. Germain,* 503 U.S. 249, 254 (1992) ("When the words of a statute are unambiguous, then, this first canon is also the last: 'judicial inquiry is complete' ").

Alternatively, does the statutory specification of service mechanisms leave for judicial development the question of how strictly the mechanisms must be complied with? Is there anything in the text of §1608 that indicates that different standards of compliance should apply under subparagraphs (a) and (b)? Are there policy reasons for making this distinction? What exactly are those reasons?

Finally, should the standard of strictness be tied to the personal jurisdiction analysis? Recall that the court in *Price, supra* pp. 353-356, held that foreign states are not subject to the minimum contacts test of the Due Process Clause. The court left open whether the same rule applied to agencies or instrumentalities. Could the difference in service rules be justified by the fact that agencies or instrumentalities, but not foreign states, are entitled to greater protections against excessive assertions of personal jurisdiction? If so, does this suggest that cases which have extended the *Price* rule to agencies or instrumentalities of foreign states are wrongly decided? For a discussion of the relationship between the FSIA's service of process rules and the minimum contacts test, *see Murphy v. Islamic Republic of Iran,* 740 F.Supp.2d 51 (D.D.C. 2010).

5. *Section 1608 and Rule 4(f) compared.* Recall from the *Rio* decision the discussion whether the modes of service set forth in Rule 4(f) are hierarchical. *See supra* pp. 893-898. There the court concluded that a plaintiff was not obligated to follow the order of service methods listed in the rule. Does this same flexibility attach to the modes of service set forth in §1608(a)? §1608(b)? Does the text of the statute supply a clear answer? *See Fly Brazil Group, Inc. v. Gabon*, 709 F. Supp. 2d 1274, 1281 (S.D. Fla. 2010); *Sabbithi v. Al Saleh*, 623 F. Supp. 2d 93 (D.D.C. 2009). Do policy considerations support the approach suggested by the text?

6. *Role of the U.S. Government in FSIA cases.* Note that the U.S. Government appeared as *amicus curiae* in support of the Russian Federation in *Magness*. What position did the Government take on the strict compliance/substantial compliance issue? How important should the Government's views on statutory construction be?

At the end of its opinion, the *Magness* Court cites the U.S. Government's view that the type of service made on the Russian Federation would not suffice had it been effected on the United States itself in a foreign court. What weight does the *Magness* Court appear to give to this? Of course, the United States is not subject to service under the FSIA and foreign governmental actions have no bearing on the statutory text of the FSIA. So why did the Government and the Court place emphasis on this fact? Recall the role of reciprocity in various aspects of international litigation. Is it appropriate to consider notions of reciprocity in interpreting the FSIA?

7. *Service of process in practice.* In garden variety civil litigation, a defendant can waive an objection based on inadequate service of process or lack of personal jurisdiction by failing to raise these defenses in a motion to dismiss or in its first responsive pleading. Fed. R. Civ. P. 12(h). How do these waiver rules interact with the doctrine of strict compliance under the FSIA? Can a foreign state waive its service of process defense by failing to raise it promptly? Or does the doctrine of strict compliance necessitate a stricter standard before a court will find waiver? *See Democratic Republic of Congo v. FG Hemisphere Associates, LLC*, 508 F.3d 1062 (D.C. Cir. 2007); *Capital Ventures Int'l v. Republic of Argentina*, 2010 WL 1257611 (S.D.N.Y. Mar. 31, 2010).

As noted above, *supra* p. 933, courts differentiate between service of the complaint and service of other documents (such as discovery requests or post-complaint motions). Literally, §1608 does not address the method of service for those documents. In those cases, do the garden variety rules of federal service apply? Or does the special nature of a suit against the sovereign counsel in favor of a stricter rule? What if the plaintiff served the original complaint in accordance with §1608 and now wishes to serve an amended complaint? *See Belkin v. Islamic Republic of Iran*, 667 F. Supp. 2d 8, 19-20 (D.D.C. 2009). What if a plaintiff filed a motion to hold the sovereign in contempt of court? *See Autotech Technologies LP v. Integral Research & Development Corp.*, 499 F.3d 737 (7th Cir. 2007).

8. *Remedies for imperfect service under the FSIA.* The Fifth Circuit vacated the default judgment in *Magness* and remanded the case in order to allow plaintiffs "a reasonable time to perfect service upon the defendants." Was this an appropriate disposition? Since the plaintiffs had not perfected service, why wasn't the proper remedy to vacate the judgment and remand with instructions to dismiss the case?

Courts differ over whether the proper remedy, in cases of inadequate service, is quashing service with an opportunity to reserve or, instead, dismissal. *Compare ClubCom, Inc. v. Captive Media, Inc.*, 2009 WL 249446 (W.D. Pa. Jan. 31, 2009) (dismissing action) *and Seramur v. Saudi Arabian Airlines*, 934 F. Supp. 48 (E.D.N.Y. 1996) (same) *with Moberg v. 33T LLC*, 666 F. Supp. 2d 415, 425-426 (D. Del. 2009) (quashing service with opportunity to reserve) *and Brown v. Austrian Airlines*, 1997 WL 913334, at *4 (E.D.N.Y. 1997) (granting time to perfect service). *See generally Koss Corp. v. Pilot Air Freight Corp.*, 242 F.R.D. 514, 518

(E.D. Wis. 2007) (collecting cases). Doesn't Federal Rule of Civil Procedure 12 specifically discuss "dismissal" as a remedy for improper service? If so, what is the legal authority for courts to award the more modest remedy of quashing the service? Do any policy reasons support that approach?

9. Service on present and former government officials. Suppose that the plaintiffs in *Magness* had sued individual officials in the Russian Government. What rules would govern the adequacy of service of process on such defendants? Until recently, it was the dominant view among lower courts that the FSIA's provisions governed such service. *See, e.g., Baumel v. Syrian Arab Republic*, 550 F. Supp. 2d 110 (D.D.C. 2008); *Nibkin v. Islamic Republic of Iran*, 517 F. Supp. 2d 416 (D.D.C. 2007). Some individual defendants (like heads of state) were treated as "foreign states" (subject to §1608(a)) while other defendants (like mid-level officials) were treated as "agencies or instrumentalities" (subject to §1608(b)).

The Supreme Court's recent decision in *Samantar* almost certainly calls this view into doubt. Recall that, after *Samantar*, the FSIA does not govern the immunity of foreign government officials. *See supra* pp. 248-249, 272-275. In its decision, the Court noted that the methods of service identified in §1608 "are at best very roundabout ways of serving an individual official." 130 S. Ct. at 2288. The Court also noted that "a plaintiff seeking to sue a foreign official will not be able to rely on the Act's service of process . . . provisions." *Id.* at 2292 n.20. Does this complicate a plaintiff's ability to effect service (because the mere act of effecting service and fitting within does not automatically establish personal jurisdiction)? Or does it simplify a plaintiff's task (because the plaintiff is not bound to observe the service methods set forth in §1608)? Could a court order service of process on the government official by publication pursuant to Rule 4(f)(3)? If so, does this undercut the purpose of the FSIA's service requirements?

G. Service of Foreign Process in the United States

The preceding sections of this chapter discussed the service of U.S. process on foreign defendants. International litigation also involves the service of foreign process on U.S. defendants in the United States.

1. No Direct U.S. Legal Restrictions on Service of Foreign Process in the United States

Unlike many foreign countries, the United States ordinarily imposes no significant direct restrictions on the service of foreign process on U.S. territory.[264] There is no federal law that forbids or criminalizes the service of process from foreign courts in the United States, nor that requires the participation of U.S. Government officials in such service. In general, state laws simply do not address the service of process from foreign courts within state territory.

The result is that, subject to general tort and criminal laws, litigants in foreign courts are free to use whatever service mechanisms may be available under foreign law for serving process in the United States. Section 1696(b) of Title 28 reflects the general freedom of foreign litigants to serve process in the United States without the assistance of U.S. courts or government authorities. As discussed below, §1696(a) permits U.S. district courts to

---

264. *Restatement (Third) Foreign Relations Law* §472(2) (1987); Comment, *Revitalization of the International Judicial Assistance Procedures of the United States: Service of Documents and Taking of Testimony*, 62 Mich. L. Rev. 1375 (1964). As discussed above, many civil law states regard the service of process as a judicial act requiring local governmental participation. *See supra* pp. 880-888.

order the service of foreign process on persons within their districts. Section 1696(b) goes on to provide that "[t]his section does not preclude service of such a document without an order of court." The section's legislative history remarks that the provision "reaffirms preexisting freedom in making service within the United States without the assistance of U.S. courts."[265] This is also acknowledged by the Official Commentary to §2.04 of the former Uniform Interstate and International Procedure Act, which describes the "existing freedom to make service within a state of the United States on behalf of litigation pending elsewhere as long as the particular manner employed does not constitute a disturbance of peace or other violation of law."[266]

2. Absence of Direct U.S. Legal Restrictions on Foreign Service of Process Mechanisms Does Not Imply That U.S. Courts Will Recognize Resulting Foreign Judgments

The absence of direct U.S. restrictions on the service of foreign process does *not* imply that U.S. courts will accept particular foreign service mechanisms in actions to enforce resulting foreign judgments in U.S. courts. U.S. requirements for the enforcement of foreign judgments are discussed in Chapter 12 below, and generally require that foreign service comply with the Due Process Clause's notice requirements.[267] It is important to note that, merely because U.S. law does not forbid a particular form of service, does not mean that such service provides reasonable notice to the defendant.

The foregoing is made express in 28 U.S.C. §1696 (as well as §2.04 of the former Uniform Interstate and International Procedure Act). Section 1696 provides that "[s]ervice pursuant to this subsection does not, of itself, require the recognition or enforcement in the United States of a judgment, decree, or order rendered by a foreign or international tribunal."[268]

3. U.S. Judicial Assistance in Serving Foreign Process in the United States

a. Section 1696.   Foreign litigants sometimes seek the assistance of U.S. judicial authorities in serving process within the United States.[269] Both federal and state statutes contemplate such assistance. Section 1696 of Title 28 expressly authorizes federal district courts to honor foreign requests for judicial assistance in effecting service:

> The district court of the district in which a person resides or is found may order service upon him of any document issued in connection with a proceeding in a foreign or international

---

265. H.R. Rep. No. 1052, 88th Cong., 1st Sess. (1963), *reprinted in* [1964] U.S. Code Cong. & Admin. News 3782, 3785-3786.

266. *See* 13 U.L.A. 484 (1980) & Appendix D; *Restatement (Third) Foreign Relations Law* §472(2) ("Service of any document issued in connection with a proceeding in a foreign court may be made in the United States (a) in any manner permitted by the law of the state of origin of the document; or (b) pursuant to the order of a United States district court in the district where the person to be served resides or is found."); McCusker, *Some United States Practices in International Judicial Assistance,* 37 Dep't of State Bull. 808 (1957). The Uniform Interstate and International Procedure Act has been enacted in Arkansas, the District of Columbia, Massachusetts, Michigan, Oklahoma, and Pennsylvania.

267. *See infra* pp. 1115-1120.

268. Likewise, §2.04(c) provided: "[s]ervice under this Section does not, of itself, require the recognition or enforcement of an order, judgment, or decree rendered outside this state."

269. In some foreign states, service of process abroad must be effected through official governmental channels in order to be valid under local law. *In re Letters Rogatory Out of First Civil Court of City of Mexico,* 261 F. 652 (S.D.N.Y. 1919); Jones, *International Judicial Assistance, Procedural Chaos and a Program for Reform,* 62 Yale L.J. 515, 543-545 (1953).

tribunal. The order may be made pursuant to a letter rogatory issued, or request made, by a foreign or international tribunal or upon application of any interested person and shall direct the manner of service. Service pursuant to this subsection does not, of itself, require the recognition or enforcement in the United States of a judgment, decree, or order rendered by a foreign or international tribunal.

Section 1696 was enacted in 1964 for the purpose of permitting "desirable cooperation with foreign countries in the making of service within the United States."[270] It was intended to overturn the reluctance that U.S. courts had traditionally displayed toward executing foreign letters rogatory issued by foreign courts.[271] By its terms, the authority under §1696 is not limited to service of process but extends to service of "any document."[272]

Section 1696 grants a district judge the power to order service of foreign process, but does not expressly require the judge to do so. Requests for service under §1696 can be made by either a "foreign or international tribunal" or by "any interested person." These categories would appear to permit district courts to execute requests by foreign judges, foreign clerks of court, litigants in foreign judicial proceedings (or their attorneys), and foreign consular officers or commissioners appointed by foreign courts.[273] As a practical matter, however, service of foreign process ordinarily should be made to the district court in the form of a petition by local U.S. counsel for the interested foreign litigant (or court). The final sentence of §1696 makes it clear that the execution of a letter rogatory by a U.S. court does not require U.S. recognition of any subsequent foreign judgment.[274]

b.   Section 1781.   In addition to direct presentation of requests for service to U.S. district courts under §1696, 28 U.S.C. §1781 authorizes the U.S. Department of State to receive requests for judicial assistance from foreign courts and to deliver such requests to the appropriate U.S. agency or court.[275] When the Department of State receives a request for service under §1781, its practice is to refer the request to the Department of Justice, which in turn ordinarily will transmit it to the U.S. Marshal's Service for service. The U.S.

270. H.R. Rep. No. 1052, 88th Cong., 1st Sess. (1963), *reprinted in* [1964] U.S. Code, Cong. & Admin. News 3782, 3785-3786.
271. H.R. Rep. No. 1052, 88th Cong., 1st Sess. (1963), *reprinted in* [1964] U.S. Code, Cong. & Admin. News 3782, 3785-3786. For example, in two frequently cited decisions, both state and federal courts in New York refused to effect service as requested by foreign letters rogatory. *In re Letters Rogatory Out of First Civil Court of City of Mexico*, 261 F. 652 (S.D.N.Y. 1919); *In re Romero*, 107 N.Y.S. 621 (Sup. Ct. 1907). In both cases, the courts reasoned that:

it is apparently possible through the aid of this court to render the person sought to be served subject to a personal judgment in Mexico, because the contract sued upon was to be performed there. Such a result is contrary to our system of jurisprudence, which treats the legal jurisdiction of a court as limited to persons within its territorial jurisdiction. . . . I should hardly feel inclined to assume such a novel jurisdiction as is proposed without statutory authority. 261 F. at 653.

272. *See Intel Corp. v. Advanced Micro Devices, Inc.*, 542 U.S. 241, 257 n.10 (2004). *See, e.g., In re Letter Rogatory*, 2002 WL 257822 (E.D.N.Y. 2002) (relying on §1696 to serve foreign judgment).
273. Some courts have suggested that foreign consular officials may transmit letters rogatory directly to a U.S. court. *See In re Civil Rogatory Letters Filed by the Consulate of the United States of Mexico*, 640 F. Supp. 243 (S.D. Tex. 1986).
274. *Sprague & Rhodes Commodity Corp. v. Instituto Mexicana del Cafe*, 566 F.2d 861 (2d Cir. 1977); *In re Letters Rogatory from the City of Haugesund, Norway*, 497 F.2d 378 (9th Cir. 1978). Section 1696's legislative history goes further, stating that "judicial assistance under this subjection shall not, as a matter of Federal law, add any weight to the claim that the judgment, decree, or order rendered abroad is entitled to recognition in the United States." H.R. Rep. No. 1052, 88th Cong., 1st Sess. 6-7 (1963).
275. Section 1781 is reproduced in Appendix A. For a discussion of procedures under §1781, *see Osario v. Harza Engineering Co.*, 890 F. Supp. 750, 753 (N.D. Ill. 1995).

Marshal's Service will not serve foreign process that is directly transmitted to it by a foreign litigant or court.[276]

4. Ensuring That Foreign Process Is Served in a Manner That Will Permit U.S. Recognition of a Foreign Judgment

Foreign litigants will sometimes wish to ensure that any foreign judgment they obtain against a U.S. defendant will be enforceable in U.S. courts. If this is the case, it is vital for service of foreign process on the U.S. defendant to satisfy U.S. rules governing the recognition of foreign judgments. These rules are discussed in detail below.[277] As noted above, the fact that service has been effected with the assistance of a U.S. court under 28 U.S.C. §1696 does not require U.S. recognition of a resulting judgment.[278]

---

276. 28 U.S.C. §569(b).
277. *See infra* pp. 1114-1120.
278. *See supra* p. 963.

11

Extraterritorial Discovery and Taking Evidence Abroad[1]

International litigation often requires access to materials or witnesses located outside the forum state. In order to obtain evidence located abroad, U.S. litigants and courts usually have two basic alternatives. First, U.S. discovery rules can be unilaterally applied to obtain extraterritorial discovery. Second, U.S. courts can seek judicial assistance from foreign courts. This chapter explores both alternatives, as well as the assistance that U.S. courts will provide to foreign courts and litigants seeking to obtain evidence in the United States.

A. Overview of U.S. Discovery of Materials Located Abroad

A basic premise of U.S. civil litigation is that fair, effective dispute resolution requires giving litigants the legal power to obtain largely unhindered access to all information that could be relevant to the resolution of their dispute. In the Supreme Court's words,

---

1. Commentary on extraterritorial discovery and obtaining evidence from abroad includes, *e.g.*, Born & Hoing, *Comity and the Lower Courts: Post-*Aerospatiale *Applications of the Hague Evidence Convention*, 24 Int'l Law. 393 (1990); Buxbaum, *Assessing Sovereign Interests in Cross-Border Discovery Disputes: Lessons from* Aerospatiale, 38 Tex. Int'l L.J. 87 (2003); Collins, *The Hague Evidence Convention and Discovery: A Serious Misunderstanding?*, 35 Int'l & Comp. L.Q. 765 (1986); Davies, *Bypassing the Hague Evidence Convention: Private International Law Implications of the Use of Video and Audio Conference Technology in Transnational Litigation*, 55 Am. J. Comp. L. 205 (2007); Feagle, *Extraterritorial Discovery: A Social Contract Perspective*, 7 Duke J. Comp. & Int'l L. 297 (1996); Gerber, *Beyond Balancing: International Law Restraints on the Reach of National Laws*, 10 Yale J. Int'l L. 185, (1984); Griffin, *Foreign Government Reactions to U.S. Assertions of Extraterritorial Jurisdiction*, 6 Geo. Mason L. Rev. 505, (1998); Mann *et al.*, *International Agreements and Understandings for the Production of Information and Other Mutual Assistance*, 29 Int'l Law. 780 (1995); Lowenfeld, *Some Reflections on Transnational Discovery*, 8 J. Comp. Bus. & Cap. Mkt. L. 419 (1986); Maier, *Extraterritorial Discovery: Cooperation, Coercion and the Hague Evidence Convention*, 19 Vand. J. Transnat'l L. 239 (1986); Mullenix, *Lessons From Abroad: Complexity and Convergence*, 46 Vill. L. Rev. 1 (2001); O'Brien, *Compelling the Production of Evidence by Nonparties in England under the Hague Convention*, 24 Syracuse J. Int'l L. & Com. 77 (1997); Oxman, *The Choice Between Direct Discovery and Other Means of Obtaining Evidence Abroad: The Impact of the Hague Evidence Convention*, 37 U. Miami L. Rev. 733 (1983); Prescott & Alley, *Effective Evidence-Taking Under the Hague Convention*, 22 Int'l Law. 939 (1988); Rau, *Evidence and Discovery in American Arbitration: The Problem of "Third Parties"*, 19 Am. Rev. Int'l Arb. 1 (2008); B. Ristau, *International Judicial Assistance* (rev. ed. 2000); Subrin, *Discovery in Global Perspective: Are We Nuts?*, 52 DePaul L. Rev. 299 (2002); von Mehren, *Discovery Abroad: The Perspective of the U.S. Private Practitioner*, 16 N.Y.U. J. Int'l L. & Pol. 985 (1984); Wallace, *"Extraterritorial" Discovery and U.S. Judicial Assistance: Promoting Reciprocity or Exacerbating Judiciary Overload?*, 37 Int'l Law. 1055 (2003); Wallace, *"Extraterritorial" Discovery: Ongoing Challenges for Antitrust Litigation in an Environment of Global Investment*, 5 J. Int'l Econ. L. 353 (2002); Weis, *The Federal Rules and the Hague Conventions: Concerns of Conformity and Comity*, 50 U. Pitt L. Rev. 903 (1989).

"[m]odern instruments of discovery . . . make a trial less a game of blind man's bluff and more a fair contest with the basic issues and the facts disclosed to the fullest practicable extent."[2] The purposes of broad U.S. pretrial discovery are variously described, but they include (a) narrowing disputed issues in order to focus trial on matters of real controversy; (b) permitting the parties wide access to information that they may wish to use as evidence at trial; and (c) obtaining information that will lead to, or facilitate the introduction of, evidence at trial.[3]

Consistent with these premises, U.S. law grants litigants relatively broad powers to obtain discovery from both other parties and nonparties. Thus, Rule 26 of the Federal Rules of Civil Procedure grants the parties to a civil action in federal court authority to "obtain discovery regarding any matter, not privileged, that is relevant to the claim or defense of any party, including the existence, description, nature, custody, condition, and location of any books, documents, or other tangible things and the identity and location of persons having knowledge of any discoverable matter."[4] Rule 26 goes on to provide that, "[f]or good cause, the court may order discovery of any matter relevant to the subject matter involved in the action." The Rule underscores the relatively broad scope of discoverable materials by further providing that "[r]elevant information need not be admissible at the trial if the discovery appears reasonably calculated to lead to the discovery of admissible evidence."[5]

The current text of Rule 26 reflects amendments, adopted over the last two decades, that materially narrowed the scope of discovery (which previously extended automatically to any unprivileged matter that was "relevant to the subject matter" of the action).[6] Additionally, the Federal Rules impose presumptive limitations on the extent of discovery (e.g., by limiting the number and length of depositions and the number of interrogatories).[7] 2006 Amendments to the Federal Rules also attempt to control the increasingly complicated (and potentially quite expensive) issue of discovery of electronically stored information such as emails, word-processing documents, and computer back-up tapes.[8] These various limitations have reduced the scope and intrusiveness of pretrial discovery under the Federal Rules, but litigants in U.S. courts continue to enjoy relatively expansive discovery rights.

In addition to permitting discovery of a wide range of information, the Federal Rules provide U.S. litigants with numerous methods for obtaining discoverable materials. The most frequently used methods of discovery are depositions upon oral examination,

---

2. *United States v. Procter & Gamble Co.*, 356 U.S. 677, 682-683 (1958).

3. *See Hickman v. Taylor*, 329 U.S. 495, 500 (1947) ("civil trials in the federal courts no longer need be carried on in the dark. Under the Federal Rules of Civil Procedure, the way is now clear, consistent with recognized privileges, for the parties to obtain the fullest possible knowledge of the issues and facts before trial.").

4. Fed. R. Civ. P. 26(b). Federal Rules of Civil Procedure 26, 30, 32, 34, and 45 are reprinted in Appendix C. *See* C. Wright *et al., Federal Practice and Procedure* §§2001-2070 (2010); *Oppenheimer Fund v. Sanders*, 437 U.S. 340 (1978); *United States v. Procter & Gamble Co.*, 356 U.S. 677, 682 (1958); *Hickman v. Taylor*, 329 U.S. 495, 507 (1947) ("[n]o longer can the time-honored cry of 'fishing expedition' serve to preclude a party from inquiring into the facts underlying his opponent's case"). The discovery rules in many states are similar to the Federal Rules.

5. Fed. R. Civ. P. 26(b)(1).

6. *See* C. Wright *et al., Federal Practice & Procedure* §2003.1 (2010); 6 *Moore's Federal Practice* §26 App. 01 (Cum. Supp. 2007).

7. Fed. R. Civ. P. 30, 31 & 33.

8. Fed. R. Civ. P. 26. For decisions addressing the intersection of international discovery and electronic discovery, *see Accessdata Corp. v. Alste Technologies GmbH*, 2010 WL 318477 (D. Utah Jan. 21, 2010); *Calixto v. Watson Bowman Acme Corp.*, 2009 WL 3823390 (S.D. Fla. Nov. 16, 2009) (magistrate judge); *Columbia Pictures Indus. v. Bunnell*, 2007 WL 2080419 (C.D. Cal. May 29, 2007).

requests for the production of documents, and written interrogatories to parties.[9] In addition, several other forms of discovery—including depositions on written interrogatories, requests for permission to enter and inspect land and other property, physical and mental examinations, and requests for admissions—are also available, although most of these methods are relatively infrequently used. In addition, Rule 26(a) provides for mandatory disclosures (without the need for a discovery request), both initially and during the course of a litigation.[10]

All forms of discovery provided for by the Federal Rules of Civil Procedure are available to obtain evidence from parties to an action. With respect to evidence from uncooperative nonparties, who refuse voluntarily to provide requested evidence, the court where the nonparty is found generally must issue a subpoena to obtain evidence by either deposition or production of documents. Written interrogatories, as well as some of the other less-frequently used forms of the U.S. discovery, are generally not available with respect to nonparties.[11]

U.S. discovery is initiated and largely conducted by the litigants themselves, with little direct judicial supervision.[12] Parties enjoy considerable freedom to make any combination of discovery requests without prior court approval.[13] In many cases, the extent of compliance with those requests is determined through private negotiations between the parties.[14] In the words of one commentator, "[m]odern discovery . . . has removed most of the decisive play from the scrutiny of the court. Because so many civil cases are settled before trial and because the conduct of attorneys is subject only to fitful and superficial judicial review during the discovery stage, much of the decisive gamesmanship of modern litigation takes place in private settings."[15] Judicial intervention in the discovery process typically occurs only after negotiations have failed and the parties have filed either motions to compel or for protective orders against further discovery.[16]

The character of U.S. discovery is often affected by the underlying substantive claims for which discovery is sought. Antitrust, patent, securities fraud, product liability, and similar cases often result in sweeping demands for discovery, particularly of business records and other documents (including electronic resources). Discovery in these

---

9. *See* Fed. R. Civ. P. 28, 30 & 32 (depositions); 34 & 35 (documents requests and subpoenas); 33 (written interrogatories). *See* Appendix C.

10. Fed. R. Civ. P. 26(a)(1), (2) & (3).

11. Fed. R. Civ. P. 31, 34-36. *See* Appendix C.

12. Brazil, *The Adversary Character of Civil Discovery: A Critique and Proposal for Change*, 31 Vand. L. Rev. 1295 (1978); Carter, *Existing Rules and Procedures*, 13 Int'l Law. 5, 6-7 (1979); Cloud, *The 2002 Amendments to the Federal Discovery Rules and the Future of Adversarial Pretrial Litigation*, 74 Temple L. Rev. 27 (2001).

13. Local rules of court in some jurisdictions impose restrictions on some aspects of discovery—such as the number of witnesses that may be deposed, without prior court approval.

14. Brazil, *The Adversary Character of Civil Discovery: A Critique and Proposal for Change*, 31 Vand. L. Rev. 1295, 1304 (1978). In many jurisdictions, local rules of court require litigants to attempt to resolve discovery disputes by negotiation before bringing the matter to the trial judge. In practice, litigants tend to make initial discovery requests containing sweeping demands for all information—and then some—that might bear upon the parties' dispute. The party from whom discovery is sought invariably refuses to comply with substantial portions of such demands, citing various privileges, Rule 26(b)'s relevancy requirement, burdensomeness, and particular practical obstacles. Negotiations then ensue between the parties to narrow their respective discovery requests and, in some cases, negotiated compromises are reached. When negotiations break down, resolution of remaining issues by the trial judge or a magistrate is required.

15. Brazil, *The Adversary Character of Civil Discovery: A Critique and Proposal for Change*, 31 Vand. L. Rev. 1295, 1304 (1978).

16. C. Wright *et al.*, *Federal Practice and Procedure* §§2035-2044 (2010). *See, e.g.*, *Valois of America, Inc. v. Risdon Corp.*, 183 F.R.D. 344 (D. Conn. 1997) (magistrate judge) (declining to require resort to Hague Evidence Convention but requiring parties to meet and confer in effort to reach compromise on document requests served on French company).

cases can result in the production of tens of millions of documents relating to many aspects of a company's operations over a substantial period of time; discovery of electronic materials (emails, drafts of documents) adds further complexity.[17] These demands are fundamentally different from discovery in more straightforward U.S. cases involving routine contract or tort disputes.

Many U.S. judges, commentators, and practitioners have criticized the broad, party-directed character of U.S. pretrial discovery.[18] In particular, the expense and intrusions into personal and business secrets associated with broad pretrial discovery has generated significant concerns. In addition, others have argued that pretrial discovery in fact does not promote definition of disputed issues or early settlement: "instead of concluding [from discovery] that the adversary's position is just and strong, each side may think that it can gain victory from the new information. Consequently, trials do not seem to diminish in number, become more orderly, or become shorter."[19] In recent years, the Supreme Court appears to have grown increasingly attentive of these criticisms; it has largely responded by tightening pleading standards yet, so far, has not narrowly interpreted the discovery entitlements under the Federal Rules.[20]

Finally, as discussed in detail below, U.S. courts are often willing to order the discovery of evidence located abroad unilaterally. Although U.S. courts can seek to obtain evidence located abroad by requesting the assistance of foreign judicial authorities,[21] the uncertainties and delays that were traditionally associated with such requests have led U.S. courts to prefer unilateral U.S. discovery efforts.[22] Thus, U.S. courts have frequently issued discovery orders under the Federal Rules of Civil Procedure (or state procedural rules) requiring both litigants and nonlitigants who are subject to U.S. jurisdiction to bring documents or persons located abroad to the United States for inspection or oral examination.[23] Failures to comply with extraterritorial U.S. discovery orders typically result in the imposition of sanctions under Federal Rule of Civil Procedure 37 and 45.[24]

Although compelled discovery is of fundamental importance, much discovery in U.S. litigation occurs voluntarily and court-ordered coercion is unnecessary. In these circumstances, if the foreign litigant or witness is willing to come to the United States, or send documents there, discovery may proceed in the same way that domestic U.S. discovery would. If the witness or litigant is not able to come to the United States, then discovery can generally be taken abroad, subject to local law restrictions.[25]

---

17. For discussions of electronic discovery, *see, e.g.,* Redish, *Electronic Discovery and the Litigation Matrix,* 51 Duke L.J. 561 (2004); Scheindlin & Rabkin, *Electronic Discovery in Federal Civil Litigation: Is Rule 34 Up to the Task?,* 41 B.C. L. Rev. 327 (2000).

18. 1980 Amendments to the Federal Rules of Civil Procedure, 85 F.R.D. 521 (1980) (Powell, J., dissenting); *Blue Chip Stamps v. Manor Drug Stores,* 421 U.S. 723, 741 (1975) (Rehnquist, J., dissenting); Chase, *American "Exceptionalism" and Comparative Procedure,* 50 Am. J. Comp. L. 277, 295-296 (2002); Rutledge, *The Proportionality Principle and the (Amount in) Controversy,* in *American Illness* (F. Buckley ed., forthcoming 2011).

19. Glaser, *Pretrial Discovery and the Adversary System* 234 (1968).

20. *See Bell Atlantic Corp. v. Twombly,* 550 U.S. 544, 558-560 (2007); *Ashcroft v. Iqbal,* 129 S. Ct. 1937, 1953 (2009).

21. Foreign judicial assistance was customarily sought by means of a letter rogatory, *see infra* pp. 1024-1026, although the Hague Evidence Convention now usually provides a preferable alternative where Member States are concerned. *See infra* pp. 1026-1058.

22. *See infra* pp. 1012-1024.

23. *See infra* pp. 1051-1053; *Société Nationale Industrielle Aérospatiale v. U.S. District Court,* 482 U.S. 522, 552-553 (1987) (Blackmun, J., concurring and dissenting).

24. As discussed below, sanctions range from monetary fines to dismissal of the plaintiffs' complaint to the assumption that facts alleged by the adverse party are true. *See infra* pp. 1008-1009.

25. *See infra* pp. 1051-1053.

B.   Foreign Reactions to Unilateral Extraterritorial U.S. Discovery

1.   Foreign "Discovery" Systems

The broad, party-controlled character of U.S. pretrial discovery contrasts sharply with methods for obtaining evidence in many foreign countries. First, the "discovery" of evidence in most civil law countries is controlled principally by the trial judge, rather than by the litigants.[26] As one commentator described the German "discovery" system, "the court rather than the parties' lawyers takes the main responsibility for gathering and sifting evidence, although the lawyers exercise a watchful eye over the court's work. . . . It should be emphasized . . . that neither plaintiff's nor defendant's lawyer will have conducted any significant search for witnesses or for other evidence unknown to his client. Digging for facts is primarily the work of the judge."[27]

Second, many nations do not permit "private" evidence-taking, in connection with either domestic or foreign judicial proceedings. Civil law nations historically regarded the taking of evidence as a judicial function, requiring the supervision of local judges in order to safeguard nationals and others against undue coercion and to ensure the observance of relevant privileges. In these states, discovery without local judicial supervision was regarded as an infringement of national judicial sovereignty.[28] In recent years, there have been steps in some civil law jurisdictions, to permit a measure of party-initiated discovery.[29] Nonetheless, there remain very significant differences between the approach toward discovery in the United States and in most civil law jurisdictions.

---

26. *See, e.g.,* American College of Trial Lawyers Task Force on Discovery and the Institute for the Advancement of the American Legal System, Final Report App. A at 1 (Mar. 11, 2009); Borel & Boyd, *Opportunities for and Obstacles to Obtaining Evidence in France for Use in Litigation in the United States,* 13 Int'l Law. 35 (1979); Dodson, *The Challenge of Comparative Civil Procedure: Civil Litigation in Comparative Context,* 60 Ala. L. Rev. 133 (2008); Hazard, *Discovery and the Role of the Judge in Civil Law Jurisdictions,* 73 Notre Dame L. Rev. 1017 (1998); Hazard, *From Whom No Secrets Are Hid,* 76 Tex. L. Rev. 1665 (1998); Langbein, *The German Advantage in Civil Procedure,* 52 U. Chi. L. Rev. 823 (1985); Lowenfeld, *Some Reflections on Transnational Discovery,* 8 J. Comp. Bus. & Cap. Mkt. L. 419, 422-423 (1986); Marcus, *Putting American Procedural Exceptionalism into a Globalized Context,* 53 Am. J. Comp. L. 709, 719 (2005); Miller, *The Legal-Economic Analysis of Comparative Civil Procedure,* 45 Am. J. Comp. L. 905 (1997).

27. Langbein, *The German Advantage in Civil Procedure,* 52 U. Chi. L. Rev. 823, 826-827 (1985). Similarly, Japan allows only judicial officers to question witnesses before trial. *See In re Honda Motor Co., Inc. Dealer Relations Litig.,* 168 F.R.D. 535, 538 (D. Md. 1996).

28. Brief for the Federal Republic of Germany as Amicus Curiae at 6-7, *Anschuetz & Co., GmbH v. Mississippi River Bridge Authority,* 474 U.S. 812 (1985) (No. 85-98) ("The Federal Republic of Germany likewise considers it a violation of its sovereignty when a foreign court forces, under the threat of sanctions, a person under the jurisdiction of German courts to remove documents located in Germany to the United States for the purpose of pre-trial discovery, or orders a person, under the threat of sanctions, to leave the Federal Republic of Germany and travel to the United States to be available for oral depositions. The taking of evidence is a judicial function exclusively reserved to the courts of the Federal Republic of Germany."); Note of the Federal Republic of Germany to the U.S. Department of State (April 8, 1986). *Id.* at Exhibit A; Brief of Government of Switzerland as Amicus Curiae in Support of Petitioners at 3, 8 *Aérospatiale* (No. 85-1695) ("If a U.S. court unilaterally attempts to coerce the production of evidence located in Switzerland, without requesting governmental assistance, the U.S. court intrudes upon the judicial sovereignty of Switzerland."); Brief for the Republic of France as Amicus Curiae in Support of Petitioners at 12-15, *Aérospatiale* (No. 85-1695); *Ward-THG, Inc. v. Swiss Reinsurance Co.,* 1997 WL 83294 (S.D.N.Y. 1997) (describing Swiss law barring deposition absent prior permission from Swiss Government).

29. In 2002, Germany broadened the scope of disclosure in civil litigation by vesting courts with discretionary power to order the production of documents in the possession of adverse or third parties, provided that one of the parties has referred to such documents (§142 of the German Code of Civil Procedure). *See, e.g.,* Sachs, *Use of Documents and Document Discovery: "Fishing Expeditions" Versus Transparency and Burden of Proof,"* Schieds VZ 2003, 193, 198; Zekoll & Bolt, *Die Pflicht zur Vorlage von Urkunden im Zivilprozess—Amerikanische Verhältnisse in Deutschland?,* NJW 2002, 3129.

Third, the scope of discovery in most foreign countries is much more limited than pretrial U.S. discovery, which most foreigners regard as permitting unrestrained "fishing expeditions." That is true, for example, in Germany,[30] France,[31] England,[32] and Switzerland.[33] In one commentator's words, the broad "pretrial procedures presently permitted by many American courts is so completely alien to the procedure in most other jurisdictions that an attitude of suspicion and hostility is created, which sometimes causes discovery which would be considered proper, even narrow, in this country to be regarded as a fishing expedition elsewhere."[34] The restrictive scope of foreign "discovery" (or the absence of any discovery at all) generally reflects foreign public policies, including protection against unreasonable intrusion into personal and business privacy.[35]

Fourth, most foreign countries are less willing than the United States to recognize the legitimacy of unilateral extraterritorial discovery under international law. Civil law nations generally regard the discovery of evidence located within their territory as a formal, judicial act that must be conducted or approved by local officials. Unilateral foreign discovery efforts, without the supervision of local authorities, is regarded as a violation of national judicial sovereignty.[36] Indeed, even other common law nations often regard unilateral extraterritorial discovery by foreign courts of materials located within their territory as a violation of their sovereignty. In the words of a 1965 report of the International Law Association:

> It is difficult to find any authority under international law for the issuance of orders compelling the production of documents from abroad. The documents are admittedly located in the territory of another state. To assume jurisdiction over documents located abroad in advance of a finding of effect upon commerce raises the greatest doubts among non-Americans as to the validity of such order.[37]

For all these reasons, unilateral extraterritorial U.S. discovery orders have frequently aroused substantial foreign opposition. In the words of the *Restatement (Third) of Foreign*

30. Gerber, *Extraterritorial Discovery and the Conflict of Procedural Systems: Germany and the United States*, 34 Am. J. Comp. L. 745 (1986); Kaplan *et al.*, *Phases of German Civil Procedure*, 71 Harv. L. Rev. 1193 (1958).

31. Borel & Boyd, *Opportunities for and Obstacles to Obtaining Evidence in France for Use in Litigation in the United States*, 13 Int'l Law. 35 (1979); Herzog, *The 1980 French Law on Documents and Information*, 75 Am. J. Int'l L. 382 (1981); Toms, *The French Response to the Extraterritorial Application of United States Antitrust Laws*, 15 Int'l Law. 585 (1981).

32. English Civil Procedure Rule, Part 31; P. Matthews & H. Malek, *Disclosure* 12-13 and 91-114 (2d ed. 2001).

33. Comment, *The Supreme Court's Impact on Swiss Banking Secrecy:* Société Nationale Industrielle Aérospatiale v. U.S. District Court, 37 Am. U. L. Rev. 827 (1988).

34. Carter, *Existing Rules and Procedures*, 13 Int'l Law. 5 (1979). *See* Lowenfeld, *Some Reflections on Transnational Discovery*, 8 J. Comp. Bus. & Mktg. L. 419, 419-420 (1986) ("[t]he rest of the world . . . thinks U.S. lawyers, agencies and prosecutors start lawsuits or investigations on minimal bases, and rely on their adversaries or targets to build their cases for them").

35. Heck, *Federal Republic of Germany and the EEC*, 18 Int'l Law. 793, 794 (1984). In addition, many foreign states permit prevailing parties to recover their attorneys' fees, including any discovery costs, from losing parties. The inability of foreign defendants to do so in U.S. litigation aggravates displeasure about intrusive and expensive U.S.-style discovery.

36. *See* Brief for Anschuetz & Co. GmbH and Messerschmitt-Boelkow-Blohm GmbH as Amici Curiae in Support of Petitioners, *Aérospatiale*, 482 U.S. 522 (1987); Brief of Amicus Curiae the Republic of France in Support of Petitioners, *Aérospatiale*, 482 U.S. 522 (1987); Oxman, *The Choice Between Direct Discovery and Other Means of Obtaining Evidence Abroad: The Impact of the Hague Evidence Convention*, 37 U. Miami L. Rev. 733 (1983).

37. International Law Association, Report of the Fifty-First Conference 407 (1964). *See* Onkelinx, *Conflict of International Jurisdiction: Ordering the Production of Documents in Violation of the Law of the Situs*, 64 Nw. U.L. Rev. 487 (1969); April & Fried, *Compelling Discovery and Disclosure in Transnational Criminal Litigation — A Canadian View*, 16 N.Y.U. J. Int'l & Pol. 961, 964-965 (1984); Note, *Fishing for the Smoking Gun: The Need for British Courts to Grant American Style Extraterritorial Discovery Requests in U.S. Industry-Wide Tort Actions*, 33 Vand. J. Transnat'l L. 1223, 1250-1251 (2000); Note, *A Comparative Study of U.S. and British Approaches to Discovery Conflicts: Achieving a Uniform System of Extraterritorial Discovery*, 18 Fordham Int'l L.J. 1340, 1377-1399 (1995).

Relations Law "[n]o aspect of the extension of the American legal system beyond the territorial frontier of the United States has given rise to so much friction as the request for documents in investigation and litigation in the United States."[38]

2. Foreign Diplomatic Objections to U.S. Discovery

Unilateral U.S. discovery of materials located abroad has frequently provoked vigorous foreign resistance. The earliest manifestations of resistance to U.S. discovery took the form of diplomatic notes from foreign nations to the United States protesting particular U.S. discovery orders.[39] There is a long history of such protests.

In 1874, for example, several German diplomatic notes protested the conduct of U.S. lawyers who sought to take sworn testimony within Germany from German nationals for use in U.S. judicial proceedings.[40] The United States replied that the evidence was taken by U.S. court-appointed commissioners, in accordance with U.S. procedural rules, and that all nations had an interest in facilitating transnational evidence-taking. Germany rejoined that where the U.S. "system for taking testimony is to be put in force in a foreign country . . . then, according to international law, it can only take place with such limitations and under such restrictions . . . as is provided by the existing law-forms of the respective foreign countries."[41] Germany assured the United States, however, that German courts would comply "very cheerfully" with a letter rogatory, which it characterized as "the proper means to harmonize with our institutions and laws any necessity of American courts . . . for the taking of testimony in Germany."[42] The United States did not appear to press the point any further.

More recently, diplomatic notes involving discovery disputes have generally been reserved for cases of broad significance, usually concerning vital foreign industries or major foreign corporations. Thus, a flurry of foreign diplomatic notes was generated by each of the U.S. Government's major antitrust investigations of international cartels during the 1950s and 1960s.[43] Foreign governmental protests have been less common in smaller-scale private disputes.

Despite the fairly limited circumstances in which diplomatic notes are ordinarily delivered, protests against extraterritorial U.S. discovery have been impressive both in number and vigor. According to one observer, "[t]he orders by American courts to oblige enterprises before the court to go abroad and gather documentary evidence have elicited so many protests from foreign governments that no one could seriously contend that such

---

38. *Restatement (Third) Foreign Relations Law* §442, Reporters' Note 1 (1987).

39. A diplomatic note is a formal communication from the government of one nation to that of another nation, and can deal with almost any conceivable issue of governmental concern. Diplomatic notes are drafted by the foreign ministry of the government lodging the protest and are typically transmitted through the foreign country's U.S. embassy to the U.S. Department of State.

40. Letter from Mr. von Bülow to George Bancroft (June 24, 1874), in *Papers Relating to the Foreign Relations of the United States* 446 (1874). One note described a visit by a U.S. vice-consul and an Assistant U.S. Attorney to a German company in Germany seeking sworn testimony; when this was refused, the U.S. officials threatened that U.S. compulsory process would be issued and that the German company's U.S. business would suffer. The German note described this as a "trespass irreconcilable with the lawful rights and duties of the German authorities." Letter from Nicholas Fish to Hamilton Fish (July 27, 1874) and Letter from Mr. von Bülow to Nicolas Fish (July 25, 1874), *in id.* at 453-454.

41. Letter from Mr. von Bülow to Mr. Schlüzer (Oct. 12, 1874), *in id.* at 463.

42. Letter from Mr. von Bülow to Mr. Schlüzer (Oct. 12, 1874), *in id.* at 463.

43. *See* International Law Association, Report of the Fifty-First Conference 565-92 (1964) (excerpting protests concerning U.S. antitrust investigations of petroleum, shipping, paper, and electric lamp industries).

orders have been considered in conformity with international law by the majority of civilized countries."[44]

Foreign diplomatic notes protesting extraterritorial U.S. discovery typically follow the same general pattern. Foreign governments assert their sovereign right to control documents, witnesses, and other evidence located within their territory and characterize unilateral U.S. efforts to compel the production of such evidence in U.S. proceedings as infringements on their sovereign prerogatives and territorial integrity. These arguments are bolstered by references to local legislation forbidding foreign evidence-taking (discussed below) and by statements emphasizing the importance of the industry under investigation to the foreign economy.

3. Foreign Blocking Statutes[45]

Despite their vigor, foreign protests seldom persuade U.S. courts to abandon unilateral U.S. extraterritorial discovery efforts. As a result, a number of foreign states have taken more vigorous steps to thwart U.S. discovery, at least in some cases, adopting so-called "blocking statutes." The basic effect of these statutes is to prohibit, as a matter of foreign law, compliance with U.S. discovery orders for the production of evidence located within the blocking state's territory. Foreign blocking statutes generally carry some sort of penal sanction for violations of prohibitions against disclosure.

Foreign blocking statutes take a variety of forms. Some nations have long-standing laws prohibiting disclosure of particular information for any reason. Although these statutes prohibit compliance with foreign discovery orders, they were originally designed for other, broader purposes. A classic example of these older blocking statutes is the Swiss bank secrecy law, enacted in 1934 to foreclose German and other governmental enquiries into Swiss commercial affairs.[46] In general, however, most foreign blocking statutes are comparatively recent enactments that were precipitated by unilateral U.S. extraterritorial discovery efforts.

Recently enacted foreign blocking statutes fall into several general categories. First, some foreign blocking statutes prohibit any disclosure of documents or other information in connection with foreign discovery orders, unless the orders are passed through appropriate foreign governmental channels. For example, French blocking legislation contains this sort of blanket prohibition against compliance with foreign discovery orders.[47]

Second, a number of foreign blocking statutes grant discretionary authority to government agencies to forbid compliance with specific foreign discovery orders. For example,

---

44. *Id.* at 403 (1964). *See id.* at 565-592 (reproducing extracts of diplomatic notes and other communications protesting extraterritorial U.S. discovery orders); Note (No. 196) of British Embassy to United States Department of State, July 27, 1978, Brit. Y.B. Int'l L. 390; Copithorne, *Canadian Practice in International Law during 1978 as Reflected Mainly in Public Correspondence and Statements of the Department of External Affairs*, 17 Can. Y.B. Int'l L. 334, 336 (1979).

45. Commentary on foreign blocking statutes includes, *e.g.*, Cira, *The Challenge of Foreign Laws to Block American Antitrust Actions*, 18 Stan. J. Int'l L. 247 (1982); A. Lowe, *Blocking Extraterritorial Jurisdiction: The British Protection of Trading Interests Act*, 75 Am. J. Int'l L. 257 (1981); Pettit & Styles, *The International Response to the Extraterritorial Application of United States Antitrust Laws*, 37 Bus. Law. 697 (1982).

46. Swiss Penal Code, Art. 273 (1971); Switzerland, Law on Banks and Savings Associations, Art. 47, dated Nov. 8, 1934. *See* Miller, *International Cooperation in Litigation Between the United States and Switzerland: Unilateral Accommodation in a Test-Tube*, 49 Minn. L. Rev. 1069 (1965); Note, *Obtaining Evidence in Switzerland for Use in Foreign Courts*, 3 Am. J. Comp. L. 412 (1954).

47. Law No. 80-538, [1980] Journal Officiel 1799, dated July 16, 1980. *See Bodner v. Paribas*, 202 F.R.D. 370, 375-377 (E.D.N.Y. 2000) (describing French blocking statutes); Borel & Boyd, *Opportunities for and Obstacles to Obtaining Evidence in France for Use in Litigation in the United States*, 13 Int'l Law. 35 (1979); Toms, *The French Response to the Extraterritorial Application of the United States Antitrust Laws*, 15 Int'l Law. 585 (1981).

the U.K. Protection of Trading Interests Act authorizes the Secretary of State to prohibit compliance with any foreign discovery order that would infringe the sovereignty or security of the United Kingdom.[48] Australia and Canada have adopted similar legislation.[49]

Finally, the largest number of foreign blocking statutes contain either automatic prohibitions against disclosure of information regarding particular industries, or grants of administrative discretion to prohibit such disclosures. Representative examples include bank secrecy laws,[50] statutes enacted to prohibit disclosure of information regarding uranium production,[51] and laws forbidding disclosure of information concerning the shipping industry.[52] In almost all cases, these statutes were enacted in response to specific U.S. discovery efforts or investigations that were perceived abroad as threatening a particular foreign industry.[53]

4. Selected Materials on Foreign Diplomatic Notes and Blocking Statutes

The text of a representative diplomatic protest—a Canadian note protesting U.S. discovery orders in connection with uranium antitrust litigation in the 1970s—is excerpted below. Also excerpted below are several foreign blocking statutes: (a) a French statute, enacted during the 1980s, which forbids the taking of evidence in France for

48. *See* Protection of Trading Interests Act, 1980, 27 Eliz. 2, ch. 11, *reprinted in* 21 Int'l Leg. Mat. 834 (1982); A. Lowe, *Blocking Extraterritorial Jurisdiction: The British Protection of Trading Interests Act*, 1980, 75 Am. J. Int'l L. 257 (1981); Lowenfeld, *International Litigation and the Quest for Reasonableness* 152-153 (1996); Lowenfeld, *Sovereignty, Jurisdiction, and Reasonableness: A Reply to A.V. Lowe*, 75 Am. J. Int'l L. 629 (1981); O'Brien, *Compelling the Production of Evidence by Nonparties in England under the Hague Convention*, 24 Syracuse J. Int'l L. & Comm. 77 (1997); Note, *A Comparative Study of U.S. and British Approaches to Discovery Conflicts: Achieving a Uniform System of Extraterritorial Discovery*, 18 Fordham Int'l L.J. 1340, 1377-1399 (1995).

49. Ontario Business Protection Act, R.S.O. chap. 56, §2(1) (1980); Foreign Extraterritorial Measures Act, R.S.C., *reprinted in*, 24 Int'l Leg. Mats. (1985) (granting Attorney-General of Canada authority to issue specific orders prohibiting disclosure of materials located within Canada), amended by ch. 28, 1996 S.C. (Can.); Foreign Proceedings (Prohibition of Certain Evidence) Act, 1976, Australian Acts No. 121, amended by both Foreign Proceedings (Prohibition of Certain Evidence) Amendment Act, 1976, Australia Acts No. 202 and Foreign Judgments Act No. 112 (1991); Foreign Evidence Act 1994 Act. No. 59 of 1994, as amended (granting Attorney-General of Australia authority to issue specific orders prohibiting disclosure of materials located within Australia). *See also* Griffin, *Foreign Government Reactions to U.S. Assertions of Extraterritorial Jurisdiction*, 6 Geo. Mason L. Rev. 505, 505-506 (1998); Calvani, *Conflict, Cooperation and Convergence in International Competition*, 72 Antitrust L.J. 1127 (2004-2005); Schmidt, *Keeping U.S. Courts Open to Foreign Antitrust Plaintiffs: A Hybrid Approach to the Effective Deterrence of International Cartels*, 31 Yale J. Int'l L. 211, 221 (2006).

50. *See* Australia, 1979 Banking Statute of Australia §23; Bahamas, Banks and Trust Companies Regulation Act of 1965, §10, 1965 Bah. Act No. 64, as amended by the Banks and Trust Companies Regulation (Amendment) Act 1980, 1980 Bah. Act. No. 3; Bermuda, Evidence Act, 1905 §59; Cayman Islands, The Confidential Relationships (Preservation) (Amendment) Law, 1979; Liechtenstein, Banks and Savings Law of December 21, 1960; Panama, Banking Law of Panama, Rep. of Panama; Singapore, Banking Act, §42.

51. Canada, Uranium Information Security Regulations, Can. Stat. O. & Reg. 76-644 (P.C. 1976-2368, Sept. 21, 1976); South Africa, Atomic Energy Act, §30, 15 Stat. Repub. So. Afr. 1045 (1978). *See also* Philippine Presidential Decree No. 1718 (excerpted at Appendix DD); *Ilusorio v. Ilusorio-Bildner*, 103 F. Supp. 2d 672, 679 (S.D.N.Y. 2000) (describing statute prohibiting removal from Philippines of documents from companies engaged in economic development programs or export promotion).

52. United Kingdom, Shipping Contracts and Commercial Documents Act 1964; Federal Republic of Germany, Law on the Responsibilities of the Federation in the Field of Shipping, dated May 24, 1965 [BGB 2, 835].

53. For example, the Ontario Business Records Protection Act, 1947 Ont. Rev. Stat. c.54, was adopted after U.S. courts ordered the production of documents stored in Canada for use in an antitrust grand jury investigation of the paper industry. Baker, *Antitrust Conflicts Between Friends: Canada and the United States in the Mid-1970's* 11 Cornell Int'l L.J. 165 (1978). Similarly, blocking legislation applicable to the ocean shipping industry was enacted in the United Kingdom, the Federal Republic of Germany, France, and Norway after the U.S. Federal Maritime Commission ordered the production of evidence from a number of foreign states in connection with its investigation in the 1960s of anti-competitive practices in the shipping industry. *See* Batista, *Confronting Foreign "Blocking" Legislation: A Guide to Securing Disclosure from Non-Resident Parties to American Litigation*, 17 Int'l Law. 61 (1983); Pettit & Styles, *The International Response to the Extraterritorial Application of United States Antitrust Laws*, 37 Bus. Law. 697 (1982).

foreign judicial proceedings without French Government approval; (b) a Swiss statute, enacted in 1934 which forbids unauthorized disclosures to foreign government authorities; and (c) a Philippine decree, enacted to forbid compliance with foreign discovery orders.

DIPLOMATIC NOTE FROM THE SECRETARY OF STATE FOR EXTERNAL AFFAIRS OF CANADA TO THE AMBASSADOR OF THE UNITED STATES
17 Can. Y.B. Int'l L. 334, 336 (1979)

I have the honor to refer to civil proceedings relating to international uranium marketing arrangements, now before the courts in various jurisdictions within the United States. In certain of these proceedings U.S. courts have ordered the production of documents located in Canada or the disclosure of information contained in such documents. Persons or corporations to whom such orders have been directed, some of whom are Canadian nationals, have not produced some or all of the documents or information in question and have stated the reason for their inability to do so is that such documents or information are within the terms of the Uranium Information Security Regulations . . . and their disclosure is prohibited by those Regulations. Because the documents and information in question have not been produced in response to the direction of the courts, the persons and corporations directed to produce them may face default judgments, negative inferences of fact, severe pecuniary liability and other sanctions.

A situation in which courts of the United States imposed sanctions for failure to produce documents or information located in Canada where such production would violate Canadian laws and regulations would be a matter of serious concern to the Government of Canada because it would subordinate to the procedures of U.S. courts the authority of the Government of Canada to prohibit the disclosure of certain information in Canada relating to the production and marketing of Canadian uranium. Such a failure on the part of courts in the United States to recognize the authority of the Canadian Government to prohibit such disclosure would be contrary to generally accepted principles of international law and would have an adverse impact on relations between the U.S.A. and Canada. . . .

[T]he participation of all Canadian uranium producers in certain uranium marketing arrangements was a matter of Canadian Government policy. . . . [T]he policy was adopted following action by the United States Government which effectively closed the large U.S. market to Canadian and other foreign uranium producers, with severe adverse consequences for the Canadian uranium mining industry. The Canadian Government . . . was convinced that preservation of a viable uranium producing industry was essential to the Canadian national interest. . . .

The Government of Canada wishes to state its serious objection to the imposition of any sanction by the judicial branch of the United States Government for failure to produce documents or to disclose information located in Canada where such production or disclosure would require a person or corporation in Canada to perform an act or omission in Canada which is prohibited by the Uranium Information Security Regulations or any other law of Canada. The threat or imposition of any such sanction would have the appearance of an attempt to induce the performance in Canada of acts which are prohibited in Canada and of attaching liability for acts performed in Canada in accordance with Canadian law and the publicly declared policy of the Canadian Government. Such procedure would be inconsistent with generally accepted principles of international law, with the manner in which the Governments of Canada and the United States carry on their mutual relations and with the spirit of those relations. I should be grateful if you would convey the foregoing to your Government with the request that these views and concerns be transmitted to those courts in the United States where trials related to this matter are in progress.

FRENCH PENAL CODE LAW NO. 80-538
Articles 1A & 2

1A. Subject to treaties or international agreements and applicable laws and regulations, it is prohibited for any person to request, to investigate or to disclose, in writing, orally or by any other means, economic, commercial, industrial, financial or technical matters leading to the constitution of evidence with a view to foreign judicial or administrative proceedings or as a part of such proceedings. . . .

2. The parties mentioned in [Article 1A] shall forthwith inform the competent minister if they receive any request concerning such disclosures.

SWISS PENAL CODE
Article 273

273. *Supply of economic information.* Anyone who obtains by investigation a secret relating to a manufacturing process or a business in order to render it accessible to an authority abroad, a foreign organization or a private company or to one of its agents, anyone who renders a secret relating to a manufacturing process or a business accessible to an authority abroad, a foreign organization or a private company or to one of its agents, shall be punished by imprisonment, in severe cases by penal servitude. The person receiving a custodial sentence may also be fined.

PHILIPPINE PRESIDENTIAL DECREE
No. 1718
[excerpted in Appendix DD]

Notes on Objections to U.S. Discovery and Blocking Statutes

1. *Basis for foreign objections to U.S. discovery.* Why is it that foreign states object to unilateral extraterritorial U.S. discovery of evidence located on their territory? Is it simply because they want to protect local companies and nationals from liability to foreign plaintiffs? Note the references of local commercial interests in the Canadian note and the Philippine decree. If so, is this not naked parochialism that frustrates the fair and expeditious resolution of civil disputes? Or is there a principled basis for their objections? Is the concept of "judicial sovereignty" a legitimate one? Why should, for example, French courts or government authorities have a right to supervise a French national's disclosures of evidence to a foreign court that possesses personal jurisdiction over the French national?

2. Challenges to the propriety of unilateral extraterritorial discovery under international law. Are unilateral U.S. discovery orders, like that in *In re Uranium Antitrust Litigation, infra* pp. 982-983, consistent with principles of international law? Is it not clear that documents and other matters located within the territory of a foreign state are subject to its jurisdiction under international law? Consider the following excerpts from various amicus curiae briefs on behalf of foreign states or entities in U.S. litigation:

> The Federal Republic of Germany likewise considers it a violation of its sovereignty when a foreign court forces, under the threat of sanctions, a person under the jurisdiction of German courts to remove documents located in Germany to the United States for the purpose of pretrial discovery, or orders a person, under the threat of sanctions, to leave the Federal Republic of Germany and travel to the United States to be available for oral depositions. The taking of evidence is a judicial function exclusively reserved to the courts of the Federal Republic of Germany. Brief for the Federal Republic of Germany as Amicus Curiae at 6-7, *Anschuetz & Co., GmbH v. Mississippi River Bridge Authority*, 474 U.S. 812 (1985).

> The act of taking evidence in a common-law country from a willing witness, without compulsion and without a breach of the peace, in aid of a foreign proceeding, is a purely private matter, in which the host country has no interest and in which its judicial authorities have normally no wish to participate. To the contrary, the same act in a civil-law country may be a public matter, and may constitute the performance of a public judicial act by an unauthorized foreign person. It may violate the "judicial sovereignty" of the host country, unless its authorities participate or give their consent. Brief for the French-American Chamber of Commerce as Amicus Curiae at 13, *American Home Assurance Co. v. Société Commerciale Toutelectric*, 128 Cal. Rptr. 430 (Cal. Ct. App. 2002).

What is the answer to these assertions of territorial sovereignty? Why don't direct U.S. discovery orders violate international law?

One of the basic attributes of national sovereignty — discussed elsewhere in various contexts, *see supra* pp. 83-86, 592-594, 642-649 — is control over national territory and borders. When a U.S. court orders a foreign national to bring materials located in foreign territory to the United States, does it not infringe on the foreign state's territorial sovereignty? Is a state's sovereignty over documents located on its territory necessarily exclusive? How does ordering a foreign defendant to produce documents located abroad differ from ordering it to pay money? Or perform a contract?

3. U.S. Government defense of unilateral extraterritorial discovery under international law. What is the legal basis under international law for unilateral extraterritorial discovery? Consider the following summary of the U.S. position:

> Foreign parties have typically objected to American discovery methods on the ground that such devices violate their home country's "judicial sovereignty." But such assertions often have an abstract quality and do little, in and of themselves, to elucidate the substantive foreign interests at stake. . . . [A]ssertions of "judicial sovereignty" often incorporate legitimate notions of territorial integrity — a reluctance to permit foreign litigants to invade one's borders, literally or figuratively, for the purpose of seizing evidence. . . . [A]ssertions of "judicial sovereignty" [also] may reflect an understandable reluctance to forfeit the moderating effects of judicial supervision and to expose one's citizens to unpredictable and potentially abusive evidentiary demands. On the other hand, assertions of "judicial sovereignty" may simply illustrate a foreign nation's desire to protect its nationals from liability, or reflect a preference for its own mode of dispute resolution instead of our.

In our view, assertions of foreign "judicial sovereignty" must be evaluated in light of the established American principle that a United States court may order a foreign national, properly subject to the court's jurisdiction, to produce evidence located abroad. As a general matter, it is not unreasonable in principle for this Nation's courts to subject foreign corporations doing business here to the same judicial procedures that are applied to domestic corporations. . . . [A]n abstract claim of "judicial sovereignty" cannot equate to a right—indeed, it would be an extraordinary privilege—to have all of the benefits of access to American markets, yet to be free from the burdens that American judicial procedures generally impose. Brief for the United States and the Securities and Exchange Commission as Amici Curiae, at 22-23, *Société Nationale Industrielle Aérospatiale v. U.S. District Court*, 482 U.S. 522 (1987).

What exactly is the U.S. rationale for unilateral extraterritorial discovery? Is this a satisfactory response to the objections set forth above?

4. *Importance of blocking statutes in international law analysis.* Suppose that one foreign state has enacted legislation forbidding compliance with foreign discovery efforts, while a second foreign state has not enacted such legislation. Is extraterritorial foreign discovery in these two states subject to different analyses under international law? *See In re Automotive Refinishing Paint Antitrust Litig.*, 358 F.3d 288, 303-304 (3d Cir. 2004) (ordering extraterritorial discovery from German defendants and noting that Germany does not have a blocking statute); *Madanes v. Madanes*, 199 F.R.D. 135, 141 (S.D.N.Y. 2001) (drawing same distinction with respect to Argentine defendants); *In re Honda Motor Co., Inc. Dealer Relations Litig.*, 168 F.R.D. 535, 538 n.2 (D. Md. 1996) (same distinction with respect to Japanese defendants). Compare the discussion above concerning the service of foreign process. *See supra* pp. 243-248.

5. *Effect of foreign diplomatic notes in U.S. litigation.* It is difficult to assess the value of foreign diplomatic notes in U.S. litigation. On the one hand, U.S. courts frequently allude to the submission and contents of diplomatic notes and generally appear to take such submissions very seriously. *See Société Nationale Industrielle Aérospatiale v. U.S. District Court*, 482 U.S. 522 (1987); *CFTC v. Nahas*, 738 F.2d 487 (D.C. Cir. 1984); *FTC v. Compagnie de Saint-Gobain-Pont-a-Mousson*, 636 F.2d 1300, 1306 (D.C. Cir. 1980); *Minpeco, SA v. Conticommodity Services, Inc.*, 116 F.R.D. 517, 524 (S.D.N.Y. 1987); *In re Grand Jury Investigation of the Shipping Indus.*, 186 F. Supp. 298, 318 (D.D.C. 1960). Moreover, the absence of a diplomatic note may sometimes lead U.S. courts to conclude that foreign governmental interests either do not exist or are unimportant. *E.g., United States v. First National City Bank*, 396 F.2d 898, 904 (2d Cir. 1968) ("[i]t is noteworthy that neither the Department of State nor the German Government has expressed any view on this case or indicated that, under the circumstances present here, enforcement of the subpoena would violate German public policy or embarrass German-American relations"); *United States v. Davis*, 767 F.2d 1025, 1035 (2d Cir. 1985) ("absence of any objection by the Cayman government . . . is significant"); *SEC v. Banca Della Svizzera Italiana*, 92 F.R.D. 111, 117 (S.D.N.Y. 1981). *See also Minpeco, SA v. Conticommodity Services, Inc.*, 116 F.R.D. 517, 525 (S.D.N.Y. 1987) ("a foreign government's failure to express a view in [a transboundary discovery dispute] militates against a finding that strong national interests of the foreign country are at stake").

Nonetheless, U.S. courts are by no means bound by foreign diplomatic notes. *In re Grand Jury Subpoena dated August 9, 2000*, 218 F. Supp. 2d 544, 563 (S.D.N.Y. 2002) (giving weight to foreign country's objections to government subpoena in criminal investigation but still enforcing subpoena).

C.   Direct U.S. Discovery of Materials Located Abroad: Judicial Power

1.   Direct Extraterritorial Discovery of Documents from Parties to U.S. Litigation

Federal Rule of Civil Procedure 34 authorizes litigants in a civil action to request parties to the action to produce all documents within their "possession, custody or control" that are relevant to the claims asserted in the action, whether or not the documents are within the territorial jurisdiction of the court.[54] U.S. lawyers generally view the discovery of documents from adverse parties and witnesses as fundamental to a fair adjudication. "[T]he heart of any United States antitrust case is the discovery of business documents. Without them there is virtually no case."[55] The same is true in many other types of business litigation.

In practical terms, the direct discovery of foreign documents from a litigant can proceed much like the discovery of U.S. documents. Unlike witnesses or property, documents can readily be transported to the United States for production to the requesting party in the same manner that U.S. documents are produced. In addition, U.S. courts have long asserted and repeatedly exercised the power under Rule 34 to order litigants to produce documents located abroad for use in U.S. proceedings — even though this obviously requires substantial activity on foreign territory.[56] A litigant's failure to comply with such discovery orders is punishable by the imposition of sanctions pursuant to Rule 37.[57]

2.   Direct Extraterritorial Discovery from Parties by Deposition upon Oral Examination

As with the production of foreign documents, U.S. litigants can attempt to obtain depositions of foreign deponents either by a unilateral order of a U.S. court under the Federal Rules of Civil Procedure or by requesting assistance from a foreign court. Because of the uncertainties associated with judicial assistance, U.S. courts have preferred the former alternative.

In general, the same principles govern the power of U.S. courts to compel depositions as govern the production of documents. If the proposed deponent is a party, or is otherwise subject to the U.S. court's personal jurisdiction and to subpoena service, the court can require compliance with a deposition notice or subpoena on pain of sanctions under Rule 37 or Rule 45.[58] If, however, the proposed deponent is not subject to the U.S. court's personal jurisdiction, or (in the case of nonparties) to subpoena service, then

---

54. *See* Fed. R. Civ. P. 34(a); C. Wright *et al., Federal Practice and Procedures* §2210 (2010). Similar procedures are often available with respect to nonparties under the subpoena provisions of Rule 45. *See infra* pp. 993-1000.

55. *In re Uranium Antitrust Litig.*, 480 F. Supp. 1138, 1155 (N.D. Ill. 1979). *See also B-S Steel of Kansas, Inc. v. Texas Indus., Inc.*, 2003 WL 21939019, at *3 (D. Kan. 2003); *Callahan v. A.E.V., Inc.*, 947 F. Supp. 175, 179 (W.D. Pa. 1996).

56. *E.g., Wyle v. R.J. Reynolds Indus.*, 709 F.2d 585 (9th Cir. 1983); *Arthur Andersen & Co. v. Finesilver*, 546 F.2d 338 (10th Cir. 1976); *In re Lernout & Hauspie Securities Litig.*, 218 F.R.D. 348 (D. Mass. 2003); *In re Air Crash at Taipei, Taiwan on Oct. 31, 2000*, 211 F.R.D. 374 (C.D. Cal. 2002); *SEC v. Renert*, 2002 WL 32503671 (D. Conn. 2002); *In re Vitamins Antitrust Litig.*, 2001 WL 1049433 (D.D.C. 2001); *White v. Kenneth Warren & Son Ltd.*, 203 F.R.D. 369 (N.D. Ill. 2001).

57. *See infra* pp. 1008-1009.

58. *See* Fed. R. Civ. P. 37; C. Wright *et al., Federal Practice and Procedure* §2083 (2010). Rules 37 and 45 are reproduced in Appendix C.

there will ordinarily be no basis for directly compelling a deposition.[59] In that event, the assistance of a foreign court will be needed to obtain compulsory process.[60]

a. Standards for Ordering Depositions of Foreign Persons. If a proposed foreign deponent is a party to a litigation and subject to a U.S. court's personal jurisdiction, the method most attractive to U.S. litigants for obtaining the person's deposition is to arrange for the deponent to travel to the United States for examination. This obviates the need for compliance with foreign law in taking the deposition and eliminates a number of practical obstacles that frequently arise when depositions are conducted abroad.[61] If the proposed deponent is a party, a notice of deposition pursuant to Rule 30 is sufficient to require attendance.[62] If the deponent is a nonparty witness, attendance can be required only by subpoena pursuant to Rule 45 (subject to the territorial and other restrictions discussed above).[63] In order to resist a deposition that has been noticed or subpoenaed, the proposed deponent must obtain a protective order from the court.

If the parties are unable to agree upon a deposition situs for a foreign deponent, the trial court enjoys broad discretion in selecting a location that is convenient.[64] Despite the attractions of summoning foreign deponents to the United States, U.S. courts are understandably somewhat more hesitant to order persons physically to come to the United States than to require documents to be brought here. Nonetheless, a number of U.S. courts have required foreign litigants and nonparty witnesses subject to their personal jurisdiction to travel to the United States for depositions.[65]

Lower courts have been particularly willing to require foreign parties who commence actions in U.S. courts as plaintiffs to attend U.S. depositions.[66] In the words of one court:

---

59. If the proposed deponent is a U.S. national, the U.S. court may have statutory authority to subpoena attendance at a deposition. *See* 28 U.S.C. §1783, discussed at *infra* pp. 990-1000. This authority has not frequently been invoked. For cases in which a party successfully relied on §1783, *see Estate of Ungar v. Palestinian Authority*, 412 F. Supp. 2d 328 (S.D.N.Y. 2006); *Klesch & Co. Ltd. v. Liberty Media Corp.*, 217 F.R.D. 517 (D. Colo. 2003). *See also Gateway Bank v. GMG Brokerage Services, Inc.*, 2002 WL 32002677, at *1 (D. Conn. 2002).

60. The methods for obtaining such assistance are discussed below, *see infra* pp. 1024-1026.

61. These difficulties include scheduling difficulties and logistical problems such as obtaining a suitable court reporter and interpreter.

62. C. Wright *et al.*, *Federal Practice and Procedure* §2112 (2010); *McKesson Corp. v. Islamic Republic of Iran*, 185 F.R.D. 70, 79-81 (D.D.C. 1999).

63. C. Wright et al., *Federal Practice and Procedure* §2107 (2010); *Cleveland v. Palmby*, 75 F.R.D. 654 (W.D. Okla. 1977). *See infra* pp. 993-1000.

64. *Continental Bank & Trust Co. of Chicago v. Charles N. Wooten, Ltd.*, 890 F.2d 1312 (5th Cir. 1989); *Republic of the Philippines v. Marcos*, 888 F.2d 954 (2d Cir. 1989); *Asea, Inc. v. Southern Pac. Transp. Co.*, 669 F.2d 1242, 1248 (9th Cir. 1981); *Estate of Ungar v. Palestinian Authority*, 412 F. Supp. 2d 328 (S.D.N.Y. 2006); *Klesch & Co. Ltd. v. Liberty Media Corp.*, 217 F.R.D. 517, 524 (D. Colo. 2003). The Federal Rules have been interpreted as contemplating selection of a situs for depositions that is most convenient for the parties and the court. The Seventh Circuit, in one of the few appellate decisions on the situs of depositions of persons located abroad, affirmed the trial court's refusal to order a Greek deponent's deposition in Greece and its decision to order the deposition in the United States. *Afram Export Corp. v. Metallurgiki Halyps, SA*, 772 F.2d 1358, 1365-1366 (7th Cir. 1985). In addition to balancing the relative burdens to the litigants, the court reasoned, "[t]he absence of a federal judge or magistrate in Greece, which would make it difficult — though in an age of excellent international telephony not impossible — to rule on objections, was a factor tilting the balance of convenience."

65. *See, e.g., Dubai Islamic Bank v. Citibank NA*, 2002 WL 1159699, *13-15 (S.D.N.Y. 2002); *McKesson Corp. v. Islamic Republic of Iran*, 185 F.R.D. 70, 79-81 (D.D.C. 1999); *Roberts v. Heim*, 1990 WL 32,553 (N.D. Cal. 1990); *Financial General Bankshares, Inc. v. Lance*, 80 F.R.D. 22 (D.D.C. 1978); *Seuthe v. Renwal Prods.*, 38 F.R.D. 323 (S.D.N.Y. 1965). Indeed, foreign plaintiffs are frequently required to pay their own expenses even when attending depositions noticed by the defendant in the United States. *See Sykes Int'l v. Pilch's Poultry Breeding Farms*, 55 F.R.D. 138 (D. Conn. 1972); *Grotrian, Helfferich, Schultz, Th. Steinweg Nachf. v. Steinway & Sons*, 54 F.R.D. 280 (S.D.N.Y. 1971).

66. *E.g., MCI Worldcom Servs. v. Atlas Excavating, Inc.*, 2004 WL 755786, at *2 (N.D. Ill. 2004); *In re SciMed Life Securities Litig.*, 1992 WL 413867, at *2 (D. Minn. 1992); *Clem v. Allied Van Lines Int'l Corp.*, 102 F.R.D. 938 (S.D.N.Y. 1984); *Sykes Int'l v. Pilch's Poultry Breeding Farm*, 55 F.R.D. 138 (D. Conn. 1972). *See also In re Global Power Equipment Group Inc.*, 418 B.R. 833 (Bankr. D. Del. 2009) (issuing direct discovery order, rather than requiring resort to

"[I]t is well settled that a plaintiff is ordinarily required to make him or herself available for a deposition in the jurisdiction in which the action is brought."[67] Other courts have concluded that, in particular circumstances, requiring foreign deponents (especially defendants) to travel to the United States would be unreasonably burdensome.[68]

U.S. courts generally treat the officers, directors, and managing agents of foreign corporations as part of the corporation, thus permitting these individuals to be required to attend depositions upon notice.[69] In contrast, other corporate employees will usually be treated as third-party witnesses and their attendance at a deposition can be compelled only by subpoena or if a request for foreign judicial assistance is granted.[70] Depositions of corporate officers, directors, or managing agents are frequently ordered at the corporation's principal place of business or, in the case of corporate plaintiffs, in the forum state.[71]

There are many circumstances in which the deponent will be examined abroad.[72] As a general rule, however, depositions can be conducted abroad only if the law of the foreign situs permits the deposition. Many foreign countries prohibit or restrict U.S. depositions on their territory.[73] Where this is the case, foreign judicial assistance will generally be needed to conduct a deposition.[74] Alternatively, a cooperative deponent can travel to a nearby country that does not restrict U.S. depositions,[75] or a telephone or video-link deposition may be possible (again, if local law permits).[76]

Hague Convention, in case involving foreign claimant in U.S. bankruptcy proceeding). *See generally* Kinsler, *The Proper Location of Party-Depositions Under the Federal Rules of Civil Procedure*, 23 Memphis St. U. L. Rev. 763, 765 (1993).

67. *A.I.A Holdings, SA v. Lehman Bros., Inc.*, 2002 WL 1041356, at *1 (S.D.N.Y. 2002). *See also Daly v. Delta Airlines, Inc.*, 1991 WL 33392, at *1 (S.D.N.Y. 1991) (absent showing of substantial hardship, and "in view of the fact that plaintiff chose to file his lawsuit here rather than in Ireland, it is hardly unreasonable to expect that he make himself available in the district where he is litigating his million dollar claim"); *Clem v. Allied Int'l*, 102 F.R.D. 938, 939-940 (S.D.N.Y. 1984) (nonresident plaintiff who sues in district must appear for deposition there absent compelling circumstances); *Grotrian, Helfferich, Schulz, Th. Steinweg Nachf. v. Steinway and Sons*, 54 F.R.D. 280, 281 (S.D.N.Y. 1971) ("Since plaintiff has chosen this forum, it cannot impose upon defendant the extraordinary expense and burden of traveling to a foreign country to conduct a deposition except on a showing of burden and hardship to the plaintiff."); Silberberg, *Civil Practice in the Southern District of New York* §17.11 (2d ed. 2000).

68. For cases involving foreign defendants, *see In re Vivendi Universal Sec. Litig.*, 2004 WL 3019766 (S.D.N.Y. 2004); *Six West Retail Acquisition, Inc. v. Sony Theatre Mgt Corp.*, 203 F.R.D. 98 (S.D.N.Y. 2001); *Work v. Bier*, 107 F.R.D. 789 (D.D.C. 1985). *See generally* Kinsler, *The Proper Location of Party-Depositions Under the Federal Rules of Civil Procedure*, 23 Memphis St. U. L. Rev. 763, 765 (1993). For a decision involving claims that travel to the United States was dangerous after September 11, *see In re Vitamins Antitrust Litig.*, Misc. No. 99-197, MDL No. 1285, Memorandum Opinion re: Deposition Locations, at 11 (D.D.C. Nov. 30, 2001) (in response to claim that September 11 events made travel to U.S. unsafe, "world events do not change the obligations of the foreign defendants with respect to this litigation").

69. C. Wright et al., *Federal Practice and Procedure* §2103 (2010); Annotation, *Who Is a Managing Agent of a Corporate Party (to Civil Litigation) Whose Discovery-Deposition May Be Taken under Federal Rules of Civil Procedure or State Counterparts*, 98 A.L.R.2d 622 (2010). *See In re Honda American Motor Co., Inc. Dealership Relations Litig.*, 168 F.R.D. 535 (D. Md. 1996) (applying managing agent test to permit deposition of one employee but not another).

70. *See Tietz v. Textron*, 94 F.R.D. 638 (E.D. Wis. 1982); *Sykes Int'l v. Pilch's Poultry Breeding Farms*, 55 F.R.D. 138 (D. Conn. 1972); *Haviland & Co. v. Montgomery Ward & Co.*, 31 F.R.D. 578, 580 (S.D.N.Y. 1962); *Reliable Volkswagen Sales & Serv. Co. v. World-Wide Auto. Corp.*, 26 F.R.D. 592, 594 (D.N.J. 1960).

71. C. Wright *et al.*, *Federal Practice and Procedure* §2112 (1994 & Supp. 2005); *infra* p. 991-992.

72. *E.g., Asea, Inc. v. Southern Pac. Transp. Co.*, 669 F.2d 1242, 1248 (9th Cir. 1981) (nonparty witness).

73. *See* U.S. Department of State Circular, "Obtaining Evidence Abroad," *available at* http://travel.state.gov/law/judicial/judicial_688.html; B. Ristau, *International Judicial Assistance* §§3-2-1 through 3-2-8 (rev. ed. 2000).

74. *See infra* pp. 1024-1026.

75. *E.g., The Signe*, 37 F. Supp. 819, 822 (E.D. La. 1941).

76. *Compare McKesson Corp. v. Islamic Republic of Iran*, 185 F.R.D. 70, 81 (D.D.C. 1999) (permitting option of telephonic deposition) *with Dubai Islamic Bank v. Citibank NA*, 2002 WL 1159699, at *13-15 (S.D.N.Y. 2002) (rejecting telephonic deposition) *and Arrocha v. McAuliffe*, 109 F.R.D. 397 (D.D.C. 1986) (refusing to order telephone deposition); *Daly v. Delta Airlines*, 1991 WL 33392, at *1 (live deposition is ordinarily preferable). *See generally* Davies, *Bypassing the Hague Evidence Convention: Private International Law Implications of the Use of Video and Audio Conference Technology in Transnational Litigation*, 55 Am. J. Comp. L. 205 (2007).

Importantly, even foreign states that usually allow depositions on their territory generally object to involuntary depositions.[77] In these circumstances, U.S. courts will generally not order the depositions of a recalcitrant deponent to be conducted abroad. In those foreign states that do not restrict the holding of voluntary U.S. depositions upon their territory,[78] U.S. litigants can proceed with depositions in much the same manner that would be followed domestically.

b. An Introduction to the Mechanics of Conducting Foreign Depositions. If a deposition is to be conducted abroad, Rules 28(b) and 29 of the Federal Rules of Civil Procedure provide five alternative mechanisms for proceeding: (i) pursuant to any applicable treaty or convention; (ii) pursuant to a letter of request; (iii) by notice; (iv) by commission; and (v) by stipulation.[79]

The first two alternatives for taking depositions abroad under Rule 28(b) are by letter of request (or letter rogatory) or pursuant to treaty. Letters rogatory are typically used when foreign law forbids other forms of deposition discovery or when the deponent is uncooperative. The use of letters rogatory to obtain evidence located abroad is discussed below.[80] Also discussed below are treaty mechanisms for taking depositions abroad, including the Hague Evidence Convention.[81]

The three remaining alternatives for depositions under Rule 28(b) do not necessarily require the assistance of foreign authorities. Depositions by notice or stipulation can proceed in the same mechanical fashion (subject to foreign law, discussed below) as depositions in the United States.[82] Rule 28(b) also permits depositions by commission, which require an order from the district court designating a particular individual as a "commissioner."[83]

When a deposition is to be taken outside the United States, by notice, commission, or stipulation under Rule 28(b), principles of U.S. law are overlaid by foreign law. Some foreign states regard the taking of depositions on their territory as judicial acts that infringe their judicial sovereignty if conducted without the supervision of local courts or officials.[84] Moreover, virtually all foreign states permit only "voluntary" depositions on their territory, which excludes examinations compelled by U.S. courts. Conducting a deposition abroad in violation of foreign law may subject counsel to foreign criminal or civil penalties. Information about foreign restrictions on U.S. depositions before consular officers must be obtained on a country-by-country basis from the U.S. Department of State, the appropriate U.S. embassy abroad, or foreign counsel.[85]

---

77. *See* B. Ristau, *International Judicial Assistance* §3-2-3 (2000 Rev.).

78. *See* U.S. Department of State Circular, "Obtaining Evidence Abroad," *available at* http://travel.state.gov/law/judicial/judicial_688.html.

79. Rule 28(b), excerpted in Appendix C, sets forth the procedural alternatives for conducting depositions abroad.

80. *See infra* pp. 1024-1026.

81. *See infra* pp. 1026-1051.

82. *See* C. Wright *et al.*, *Federal Practice and Procedure* §§2131-2133 (2010).

83. The commission will authorize its bearer to administer oaths and take testimony. *See* 4 J. Moore & L. Frumer, 4 *Moore's Manual: Federal Practice Forms*, Forms No. 15A:30-34 (2010); Note, *Taking Evidence Outside of the United States*, 55 B.U. L. Rev. 368, 371 (1975).

84. *See supra* pp. 971-977.

85. For a list of those countries that forbid depositions before U.S. consular officers, *see* U.S. Department of State Circular, dated Apr. 13, 1987, "Obtaining Evidence Abroad," *available at* http://travel.state.gov/law/judicial/judicial_688.html. In addition, the U.S. Department of State's Office of American Citizens Services and Crisis Management provides country summaries for most foreign states, setting out basic rules regarding taking depositions in those countries. *See* U.S. Department of State Circular, "Judicial Assistance: Country Specific Information," *available at* http://travel.state.gov/law/judicial/judicial_2510.html.

Some foreign states that forbid depositions before U.S. court officers or consular officers may permit depositions before foreign officials — an alternative that is specifically permitted by Rule 28(b)(3). As noted above, information about the possibility of depositions before a foreign official must be obtained on a country-by-country basis. If a foreign official is to preside over a deposition, it is important for U.S. counsel carefully to schedule the deposition and describe in advance the character of the deposition, the underlying action, and the officer's responsibilities.[86]

3.   Selected Materials on Direct Extraterritorial Discovery from Parties

The materials excerpted below illustrate the power of U.S. courts to order direct extraterritorial discovery from parties to litigations in U.S. courts. The decision in *In re Uranium Antitrust Litigation*,[87] which is excerpted below, illustrates how most U.S. courts have approached the question whether they have the power to order parties to produce documents located abroad for use in U.S. litigation. Similarly, the decision in *Dubai Islamic Bank v. Citibank, NA*, illustrates how U.S. courts have dealt with orders for depositions of parties located outside the United States. Neither of the excerpts deals with the exercise of the power to order direct extraterritorial discovery from a foreign party where U.S. discovery is contrary to foreign laws; that subject is examined later in this chapter.[88]

IN RE URANIUM ANTITRUST LITIGATION
480 F. Supp. 1138 (N.D. Ill. 1979)

MARSHALL, DISTRICT JUDGE. [The *Uranium Antitrust Litigation* arose from long-term contracts between Westinghouse, on the one hand, and numerous electrical utilities, on the other. The contracts obligated Westinghouse to sell uranium to the utilities at fixed prices for specified terms. When uranium prices dramatically escalated in the 1970s, Westinghouse refused to fulfill its agreements. In addition to claims that its obligations to the utilities were excused by impracticability, Westinghouse filed an antitrust suit against a number of uranium producers, alleging that they had unlawfully conspired to monopolize the market for uranium. In that litigation, Westinghouse sought discovery of documents in the possession of foreign uranium producers. Most foreign uranium producers refused to comply with Westinghouse's requests, and Westinghouse then sought orders compelling production by the defendants.]

At the outset, we should identify the type of jurisdiction exercised by a court in issuing an order to produce foreign documents. In the field of foreign relations law, two types of jurisdiction have been defined. Prescriptive jurisdiction refers to the capacity of a state under international law to make a rule of law. It is exemplified by the enactment of the Federal Rules of Civil Procedure, *e.g.*, Rule 37. Enforcement jurisdiction, on the other hand, refers to the capacity of a state under international law to enforce a rule of law. When a court enters an order compelling production of documents under Rule 37, it exercises its enforcement jurisdiction. *Restatement (Second) Foreign Relations Law* §6 (1965). The jurisdiction of American courts is unquestioned when they order their own nationals to produce documents located within this country. But jurisdiction is less certain when

---

86. It is preferable to have a U.S. consular official preside over U.S. depositions, rather than a foreign official. U.S. officials tend to be more familiar with U.S. practices and laws and can therefore be expected to ensure that the deposition proceeds more smoothly and expeditiously.

87. 480 F. Supp. 1138 (N.D. Ill. 1979).

88. *See infra* pp. 1000-1024.

American courts order a defendant to produce documents located abroad, especially when the country in which the documents are situated prohibits their disclosure.

As a general rule, a court has the power to order a person subject to its jurisdiction to perform an act in another state. *Restatement (Second) Conflict of Laws* §53 (1971). There are two preconditions for the exercise of this power. First, the court must have personal jurisdiction over the person. Second, the person must have control over the documents. The location of the documents is irrelevant.

On the issue of control, there are certain corollary principles which apply to multinational corporations. The test for determining whether an American court can order an American parent corporation to produce the documents of its foreign subsidiary was stated in *In re Investigation of World Arrangements*, 13 F.R.D. 280, 285 (D.D.C. 1952): "[I]f a corporation has power, either directly or indirectly, through another corporation or series of corporations, to elect a majority of the directors of another corporation, such corporation may be deemed a parent corporation and in control of the corporation whose directors it has the power to elect to officer." Thus, for example, if the parent owns more than 50 percent of the foreign subsidiary's stock, it possesses the necessary control.

The test is less clear in situations where an order is directed to the American subsidiary of a foreign corporation to produce documents from its head office located abroad. One court has held that a subpoena duces tecum was enforceable if it was served on the subsidiary's offices in the United States, even though the corporation's board of directors had passed a resolution prohibiting the removal of the requested records from Canada and even though all the board members were residents of Canada. *In re Grand Jury Subpoenas Duces Tecum*, 72 F. Supp. at 1020. The court's reasoning as to how the American officers had control over the withheld documents seems to rest on the theory that it was sufficient that the documents were in possession of the corporation and that a subpoena had been served on some of its officers. More helpful guidance can be drawn from *Société Internationale v. McGranery*, 111 F. Supp. 435, 440-42 (D.D.C. 1953), in which the court held that plaintiff, a Swiss corporation, had control over the papers of its Swiss-based bank, H. Sturzenegger & Cie. The court attached significance to the fact that Sturzenegger was a director and officer of plaintiff and was "perhaps" a dominant personality in plaintiff's affairs. After an extensive examination of the corporate affiliations of the two partners, the court concluded that "[t]hrough the interlocked web of corporate organization, management and finance there runs the thread of a fundamental identity of individuals in the pattern of control." Thus, the issue of control is more a question of fact than of law, and it rests on a determination of whether the defendant has practical and actual managerial control over, or shares such control with, its affiliate, regardless of the formalities of corporate organization. Once personal jurisdiction over the person and control over the documents by the person are present, a United States court has power to order production of the documents. [The Court went on to consider and reject arguments for excusing discovery because of certain foreign blocking statutes.]

DUBAI ISLAMIC BANK v. CITIBANK, NA
2002 WL 1159699 (S.D.N.Y. May 31, 2002)

KATZ, MAGISTRATE, Judge. . . . Plaintiff Dubai Islamic Bank ("DIB") and Defendant Citibank entered an agreement in 1975 that included, *inter alia,* the establishment of a correspondent account by DIB in Citibank's New York office. Plaintiff alleges that Citibank had a duty to safeguard DIB's correspondent account by adhering to anti-money laundering procedures and so-called "know your customer" rules. Citibank's alleged dereliction of these and other obligations, DIB claims, led to the unauthorized transfer of more than $151,000,000 from DIB's correspondent account. These fraudulent transfers were, it is alleged, the handiwork of a group of international financial terrorists led by one Foutanga Dit Babani Sissoko, to whose accounts the stolen money was credited. Because Citibank allegedly "slept," as counsel for DIB has put it, the fraud proceeded unchecked for over two years, from late 1995 to early 1998.

... In defending the case, Citibank has emphasized the complicity of various high-ranking DIB officers in the alleged scheme to defraud. Citibank points out that criminal investigations in Dubai, conducted by Dubai law enforcement agencies with the assistance of KPMG, which performed an independent audit, led to the convictions of a number of officers and other DIB employees for their active roles in the fraud. Apparently, authorizations for many, if not all, of the fraudulent transfers out of DIB's account were issued by DIB's own executives.

Presently before the Court is the application of Citibank for an order directing Plaintiff to produce certain witnesses for deposition, and the corresponding application of DIB for a protective order regarding those witnesses. Citibank seeks to depose, in New York, each of ten employees of DIB, whom it contends may be compelled to appear for deposition by virtue of their status as officers, directors, or managing agents of DIB.[89] DIB contends that none of the ten employees, all of whom live and work in Dubai, may be compelled to appear for deposition under the Federal Rules of Civil Procedure. ... DIB therefore requests that Citibank be required to take discovery of certain witnesses in Dubai, through letters rogatory or otherwise; that Citibank take depositions of certain other witnesses in Dubai or London (the latter at Citibank's expense, and only "if DIB is able to convince" the witnesses to travel to London); and that Citibank be barred altogether from deposing certain other witnesses.

Under Rule 30(b)(1) of the [FRCP], a specific officer, director, or managing agent of a corporate party may be compelled to give testimony pursuant to a notice of deposition. A corporate employee or agent who does not qualify as an officer, director, or managing agent is not subject to deposition by notice. *See, e.g., United States v. Afram Lines (USA), Ltd.,* 159 F.R.D. 408, 413 (S.D.N.Y. 1994). Such an employee is treated as any other non-party witness, and must be subpoenaed pursuant to Rule 45 of the [FRCP]; or, if the witness is overseas, the procedures of the Hague Convention or other applicable treaty must be utilized.

"The test for a managing agent is not formulaic." *Boss Mfg. Co. v. Hugo Boss AG,* 1999 WL 20828, at *3 (S.D.N.Y. 1999). Rather, the question of whether a person is a managing agent, and therefore subject to a notice of deposition, is answered pragmatically and on a fact-specific basis. "The term 'managing agent' should not be given too literal an interpretation," *Tomingas v. Douglas Aircraft Co.,* 45 F.R.D. 94, 96 (S.D.N.Y. 1968), and "[a]s in all matters appertaining to discovery, it is the ends of justice that are to be served." With these principles in mind, courts in this district have generally considered five factors in determining whether an individual is a managing agent: 1) whether the individual is invested with general powers allowing him to exercise judgment and discretion in corporate matters; 2) whether the individual can be relied upon to give testimony, at his employer's request, in response to the demands of the examining party; 3) whether any

---

89. Citibank has issued letters rogatory to depose in Dubai some of these witnesses, as well as other witnesses living in Dubai who are not the subject of the instant motions. Citibank maintains, and the Court agrees, that these letters do not prejudice its right to seek depositions by the more conventional means available under the Federal Rules of Civil Procedure.

person or persons are employed by the corporate employer in positions of higher authority than the individual designated in the area regarding which the information is sought by the examination; 4) the general responsibilities of the individual respecting the matters involved in the litigation; and 5) whether the individual can be expected to identify with the interests of the corporation.

Although typically a corporation cannot be required to produce a former officer or agent for deposition, this rule is not woodenly applied. Rather, courts within and without this district have adopted a "practical" approach "that focuses not only on the formal connection between the witness and the party at the time of the deposition, but also on their functional relationships." Summarizing this pragmatic approach, the D.C. Circuit has observed, "Courts have accorded managing agent status to individuals who no longer exercised authority over the actions in question (and even to individuals who no longer held any position of authority in a corporation), so long as those individuals retained some role in the corporation or at least maintained interests consonant with rather than adverse to its interests." . . . [T]he examining party satisfies its burden when it produces "enough evidence to show that there is at least a close question whether the proposed deponent is the managing agent." This approach permits discovery to proceed, while deferring until trial the ultimate question of whether the witness's testimony is binding on the corporation. The witness's deposition testimony itself may well provide the best evidence of his or her status.

Keeping the above principles in mind, the Court will now address *seriatim* the status of the employees Citibank is seeking to depose. [With regard to Mr. Valiyakatt Ahmed Khalid,] his status as a managing agent regarding the events relevant to this litigation is not seriously in doubt. Numerous documents, including DIB's own personnel file, indicate that Mr. Khalid was Head of the Foreign Department during the time period relevant to this litigation. DIB disputes that this was his title, but concedes that he was "the person responsible for interbank transfers (foreign exchange) in the foreign section." As such, he was seemingly vested with significant enough responsibility and discretion to be considered a managing agent, even if he did not hold the specific title of head of the department. In any event, Citibank has produced more than enough information to make his status as department head, much less his substantial responsibilities "respecting the matters involved in the litigation," a close question that should be resolved in favor of Mr. Khalid's deposition taking place. . . .

[The Court noted that Mr. Khalid was convicted in Dubai of fraud against DIB, but that DIB then waived its civil fraud claims against him, and] maintained him in its employ. . . . Moreover, in addition to retaining Mr. Khalid as an employee, DIB continues to pay him the same salary and to maintain him at the same grade. . . . The Court is persuaded that Mr. Khalid may be considered a managing agent for the purpose of noticing his deposition. The evidence strongly suggests that Mr. Khalid is greatly indebted to DIB, and thus remains subject to its control. . . .

[With regard to Mr. Sayed Najamul Hassan, like Mr. Khalid, he] was convicted [in Dubai] for his apparently significant personal involvement in the fraud, exonerated on appeal after being given a release of liability by DIB, and retained as an employee of DIB. Unlike Khalid . . . , however, Mr. Hassan was a mere clerk in the Foreign Department at the time of the events in question (and remains one now). Citibank does not contest this fact, but contends that Mr. Hassan's "role in the fraud transcended that of a clerk because he was actively involved in forging hundreds of fraudulent documents directly related to the transfers at issue in this case." The Court agrees that Mr. Hassan's importance to the events in question appears supported by the record; unfortunately for Citibank, however, this is not the test for managing agent. There is no evidence that Mr. Hassan's position gave him any independent discretion, and even his role in the fraud appears to be that of a facilitator and subordinate. Accordingly, Mr. Hassan is not an officer, director, or managing agent, and thereby is not subject to deposition by notice.

[With regard to one Mr. Mohammad Sadiq Mohammad Ali, DIB claimed he was a minor functionary, while Citibank claimed he was an important officer with significant responsibility for the underlying fraud. The Court accepted DIB's characterization, but continued:] However, the Court notes that if Citibank remains committed to taking discovery from Mr. Sadiq, he apparently remains on good terms with DIB and thus, most likely, is amenable to DIB's directions. DIB has in fact offered to try to persuade Mr. Sadiq to appear for deposition (albeit in London). The Court therefore suggests that, in the interest of compromise, DIB try to make Mr. Sadiq available for deposition in Dubai, in the event counsel for Citibank travels there. . . .

For each proposed deponent, DIB has raised various equitable reasons why it believes he should not be required to appear in New York for a deposition. Citibank insists that any other solution but requiring these deponents to come to New York is both unfair and impracticable. The Court has considered the equities and the practicalities of the situation regarding each proposed witness, and, in its discretion, concludes that DIB has not overcome the presumption that a plaintiff who brings suit in a particular forum should be prepared to send its agents to be deposed there.

As a general rule, a plaintiff who brings suit in a particular forum may not avoid appearing for examination in that forum. In the end, the decision as to the location of the deposition lies within the discretion of the court. DIB attempts to avoid the normal rule on several grounds. . . . DIB claims that many of the managing agents in question do not want to travel to the United States in general, and New York City in particular, in light of the perceived dangers related to the aftermath of events on September 11, 2001. Citibank contends that the risk for foreign travelers in New York is minimal, and in any event pales in comparison with the threat posed to Americans traveling in the Middle East. The Court agrees with Citibank that the dangers to each party are not completely symmetrical. There is no evidence that foreign visitors to New York face any threat — or at least any threat greater than that to New Yorkers in general. On the other hand, the State Department has issued warnings to Americans traveling abroad in general, and to the Middle East in particular. More importantly, the Court agrees with those courts that have concluded that whatever the increased dangers both in the United States and throughout the world, the U.S. judicial system remains open for business, and its normal operations cannot be upset by mere invocation of the tragedy of September 11. *See also American Int'l Tel., Inc. v. Mony Travel Servs., Inc.*, 203 F.R.D. 153, 155 (S.D.N.Y. 2001) ("The Court can perceive no reason why Duran's alleged fear of flying should require someone else to take to the skies."). . . .

DIB also claims that many of its witnesses cannot come to New York because of family obligations. In particular, many of its witnesses are fathers of "traditional Muslim famil[ies]" that depend on them not only financially, but also for such services as driving, something most of their wives cannot do. While not unsympathetic to the disruption to daily family life that foreign travel may cause, the Court nonetheless cannot allow the simple fact that the proposed deponents are Muslims with dependent families to overcome DIB's discovery obligations. Permitting such an excuse would effectively insulate an entire segment of the global population from the ordinary rules of discovery, regardless of having availed itself of the U.S. court system. . . .

In his Declaration, Mr. Ellison asserts that several of the proposed deponents have medical problems that make their traveling to New York unadvisable. Mr. Khalid has asthma; Mr. Rahman has "slightly raised blood pressure" and also risks "deep vein thrombosis" if subjected to long-distance air travel; Mr. Fawzi Lootah has recently had eye surgery, and "says that he cannot fly anywhere"; and Mr. Karim has "a blood pressure problem, which he controls by medication." None of these conditions, except for Mr. Lootah's, is supported by any documentation, and even Mr. Lootah's medical records conspicuously do not contain a doctor's note prohibiting air travel. Indeed, Mr. Lootah's eye surgery took place in India, not Dubai, and thus presumably required his traveling by air. . . .

Finally, DIB notes that many of the proposed witnesses have miscellaneous personal obligations, such as the administration of a father's estate or the preparation for a daughter's wedding, that allegedly make travel to the United States undesirable or unfeasible. However, none of these objections appear to this Court to involve a substantial hardship or other compelling grounds for setting aside the normal rule regarding the location of depositions, and none presents an insurmountable practical difficulty. Moreover, Citibank has indicated its willingness to work with DIB to accommodate these personal concerns. . . . Whatever hardship and practical difficulties may attend the appearance in New York of the seven managing agents herein discussed would be multiplied by requiring the taking of discovery in Dubai or elsewhere. Requiring depositions to take place in Dubai, or even London, would entail both sides to send abroad, for a far longer period than any one witness would be required to travel to New York, an entourage of lawyers, reporters, and translators, not to mention countless boxes of relevant documentary materials. . . . As for DIB's suggestion that Citibank conduct telephonic or videotaped depositions, this is not a case where financial hardship or other good cause exists for departing from ordinary discovery procedures. Moreover, because of the language barriers and the need for interpreters, telephone depositions would not be practical. . . .

Notes on Uranium Antitrust *and* Dubai Islamic Bank

1. *Discovery under FRCP Rule 34 of documents located outside the United States.* The relevant documents in *Uranium Antitrust* were located outside the United States. *Uranium Antitrust* conceded that U.S. "jurisdiction is less certain when American courts order a defendant to produce documents located abroad." Why is that? Is it not clear that the defendant still "controls" the documents within the meaning of Rule 34(a)? Note the comment in *Uranium Antitrust* that, notwithstanding the court's doubts, "[t]he location of the documents is irrelevant" to the court's power to order discovery. Why is this the case?

Does Rule 34(a) clearly extend to the discovery of documents located outside the United States, within the territory of another sovereign state? Recall the territoriality presumption, discussed above in the context of legislative jurisdiction. *See supra* pp. 592-594, 648-649. Absent express language subjecting documents held abroad to U.S. discovery, should such authority be presumed? Consider also the reasoning in *Nahas* and the *Charming Betsy* presumption that Congress does not intend to violate international law. *See supra* p. 18. Is it relevant, in interpreting Rule 34, to consider whether international law permits U.S. courts to order extraterritorial discovery? Should *Uranium Antitrust* have done so?

2. *Control required to order document production under FRCP Rule 34.* Rule 34(a) permits discovery requests for any documents in the "possession, custody or control" of other parties to a civil action. Corporations and other business entities are presumed to "control" all corporate documents and business records. *See Kestrel Coal Pty Ltd. v. Joy Global, Inc.*, 362 F.3d 401, 405 (7th Cir. 2004); *Alcan Int'l Ltd. v. SA Day Mfg. Co.*, 176 F.R.D. 75, 78-79 (W.D.N.Y. 1996); *Cooper Indus., Inc. v. British Aerospace, Inc.*, 102 F.R.D.

918, 919-920 (S.D.N.Y. 1984); *Elder-Beerman Stores Corp. v. Federated Dep't Stores*, 45 F.R.D. 515 (S.D.N.Y. 1968). *See generally* C. Wright & A. Miller, *Federal Practice and Procedure* §2456 at 31 (2007 & Supp. 2010). Consider application of this rule in international cases. Are there any reasons to think that a company has less control over documents that are located in foreign countries than those in the United States? Note that the Rule 34 test is phrased in the disjunctive, so if a party has "possession" of the document, questions of "control" are not decisive. *See Devon Robotics v. DeViedma*, 2010 WL 3985877 (E.D. Pa. Oct. 8, 2010).

3. *Discovery under FRCP Rule 34 of documents located abroad in violation of foreign law — an initial view.* *Uranium Antitrust* expressed particular concern about its jurisdiction to order discovery of documents located abroad when foreign law forbade disclosure. What is the relevance of the existence — or nonexistence — of foreign law prohibiting extraterritorial discovery? Compare the similar issues that arise in the context of service abroad. *See supra* pp. 883-884. Is the *absence* of a foreign law forbidding discovery equivalent to foreign consent to U.S. extraterritorial discovery? If a foreign law forbidding discovery does exist, should Rule 34(a) nonetheless be interpreted to require discovery? Consider again the *Nahas* rationale. *See supra* pp. 889-893.

Ascertaining the "location" of documents can be problematic in case of discovery of electronic materials. Electronic materials unquestionably fall within the ambit of Rule 34, and courts have routinely ordered parties to turn over electronic materials in discovery. *E.g., Adams v. Unione Mediterranea di Sicurta*, 2002 WL 472252, at *6 (E.D. La. 2002). Suppose that a company maintains an office in the United States, and computers in that office can access servers located in foreign countries. Are all materials on the foreign servers "located" in the United States since they are accessible through the computer that is physically here? What answer makes sense in light of the purposes underpinning Rule 34? Commentary on the issue is sparse. *See* Marcus, *Retooling American Discovery for the Twenty-First Century: Toward a New World Order?*, 7 Tul. J. Int'l & Comp. L. 153, 180-181 (1999).

4. *Lower court decisions ordering discovery from foreign subsidiary of U.S. litigant.* Difficulties in applying Rule 34's "control" test frequently arise where information is held by persons closely related to an entity over which the U.S. court has personal jurisdiction. A recurrent issue in international discovery disputes is whether a U.S. court may order a U.S. parent corporation to produce documents held by a foreign subsidiary that is not itself subject to the personal jurisdiction of the U.S. court. As *In re Uranium Antitrust Litigation* illustrates, lower courts have generally ordered the production of documents held by foreign subsidiaries of domestic corporate litigants, provided that the parent effectively controls the subsidiary. A typical formulation of the control standard was stated in *In re Investigation of World Arrangements*, 13 F.R.D. 280, 285 (D.D.C. 1952), where the court held that "control" would be found if a corporation possesses the power "either directly or indirectly, through another corporation or series of corporations, to elect a majority of the directors of another corporation." Other lower courts have adopted similar tests. *E.g., United States v. Vetco, Inc.*, 691 F.2d 1281 (9th Cir. 1981); *Garpeg Ltd. v. United States*, 583 F. Supp. 789 (S.D.N.Y. 1984); *In re Uranium Antitrust Litig.*, 480 F. Supp. 1138, 1144-1145 (N.D. Ill. 1979).

5. *Wisdom of decisions ordering document discovery from foreign subsidiaries of U.S. parents.* Are decisions ordering discovery from foreign subsidiaries of U.S. parents sound? As discussed above, it is a basic principle of corporate law in the United States and elsewhere that a corporation is a separate and distinct legal entity from both its parent and its subsidiaries. *See supra* pp. 176-177. In general, a subsidiary is neither liable for its parent's obligations nor subject to personal jurisdiction because of its parent's contacts with the forum, even if the parent "controls" the subsidiary. *See supra* pp. 176-203. Given this, why

should the documents of a subsidiary be subject to discovery orders directed to the subsidiary's parent?

Note that in many cases the subsidiary is not a party to the U.S. litigation, and may well not be subject to U.S. personal jurisdiction. Does it not violate basic principles of due process and corporate law to require one company to provide documents held by a different company, not subject to the forum court's jurisdiction? Recall the relatively demanding showing required for alter ego (or agency) jurisdiction based on a parent-subsidiary relationship. *See supra* pp. 176-203. Why shouldn't that same standard apply in determining whether a U.S. parent should be required to produce documents in a U.S. litigation from its foreign subsidiary's files? Why might a less demanding standard apply to discovery than to jurisdiction or liability?

On the other hand, assuming that "control" is the appropriate standard, is it realistic to focus only on parent company's formal power to elect its subsidiary's directors?

6. *Document discovery from foreign parent company of U.S. litigant.* Another recurrent issue under Rule 34 is the power of U.S. courts to order a U.S. subsidiary to produce documents held abroad by its foreign parent. Although the U.S. subsidiary will ordinarily not control the selection of its parent's board of directors, there may nonetheless be circumstances in which an "upstream" control relationship will be found. For example, in *In re Electric & Musical Industries*, 155 F. Supp. 892, 895 (S.D.N.Y. 1957), *appeal dismissed*, 249 F.2d 308 (2d Cir. 1957), the court refused to quash an antitrust grand jury subpoena directed to the English parent of an American subsidiary that was subject to the issuing court's personal jurisdiction. The court relied on the fact that the English company, a multinational record manufacturer and distributor, and its American subsidiaries were "reciprocating partners" in a common enterprise.

The same analysis was applied in *Société Internationale v. McGranery*, 111 F. Supp. 435 (D.D.C. 1953), where the court found that a company controlled a superficially unrelated bank because the same individuals held ownership and management power over both entities. *See also In re Marc Rich & Co. AG*, 707 F.2d 663 (2d Cir. 1983); *Addamax Corp. v. Open Software Foundation, Inc.*, 148 F.R.D. 462, 465 (D. Mass. 1993); *M.L.C. Inc. v. North Am. Philips Corp.*, 109 F.R.D. 134 (S.D.N.Y. 1986); *Cooper Industries, Inc. v. British Aerospace*, 102 F.R.D. 918 (S.D.N.Y. 1984). *See generally Gerling Int'l Ins. Co. v. Commissioner*, 839 F.2d 131, 140-141 (3d Cir. 1988) (collecting cases).

Findings of control in these types of cases typically turn on highly fact-specific circumstances and provide little basis for broad generalizations. Under the logic of these decisions, could a company be compelled to produce documents in possession of a sister corporation? *See Ex parte BASF Corp.*, 957 So. 2d 1104 (Ala. 2006) (applying state procedural rules and holding that domestic subsidiary lacked "possession, custody and control" of documents in foreign parent's possession); *SEC v. Credit Bancorp, Ltd.*, 194 F.R.D. 469, 473 (S.D.N.Y. 2000) (rejecting, on the facts, claim that corporation exercised control over foreign sister corporation); *Uniden America Corp. v. Ericsson Inc.*, 181 F.R.D. 302, 306-308 (M.D.N.C. 1998) (magistrate judge) (ordering discovery from sister corporation); *In re Global Power Equipment Group, Inc.*, 418 B.R. 833 (Bankr. D. Del. 2009) (ordering discovery from sister corporation of foreign bankruptcy claimant on ground that sister corporation was "agent" of party); *Alcan Int'l Ltd. v. SA Day Mfg. Co.*, 176 F.R.D. 75 (W.D.N.Y. 1996) (magistrate judge) (requiring production by foreign affiliate). *See generally Davis v. Gamesa Tech. Corp.*, 2009 WL 3473391 (E.D. Pa. Oct. 20, 2009) (magistrate judge) (collecting cases). What about a corporation that shares a "commonality of interest" with a party?

7. *Documents in the possession of party's agents.* Some decisions have extended the principle of control to external agents of the company. Some courts have ordered parties to produce documents in the possession of their outside counsel, even if the attorneys are not subject to the court's jurisdiction. *E.g.*, *Avery Dennison Corp. v. UCB Films plc*, 1998 WL 293002 (N.D. Ill. 1998). These decisions proceed on the theory that the attorney is the "agent" for the client. Consequently, documents pertaining to the party in the attorney's possession are deemed to be in the party's control (subject to privilege claims). What if the documents are in the possession of a foreign law firm? Does that change matters?

8. *Discovery under FRCP Rule 30(b) by oral deposition of persons located abroad.* Rule 30(b) of the FRCP permits parties to notice depositions of other parties to a litigation, as well as nonparties. The same rule also permits courts to order that parties (individual or corporate) attend such depositions and submit to questioning (under oath). As *Dubai Islamic Bank* illustrates, U.S. courts not infrequently order foreign parties to provide deposition testimony.

Is there anything in Rule 30(b) that suggests that a foreign party can be required to give extraterritorial discovery by way of oral depositions? Suppose that a U.S. company sues a foreign defendant in U.S. courts. What is it that authorizes the court to order the foreign company to give deposition testimony? What if the foreign company disputes the U.S. court's jurisdiction?

9. *Depositions under FRCP Rule 30(b) of managing agents, officers, and directors.* In general, managing agents, directors, and officers of corporations are treated as part of the corporation itself, thus bringing any information in their possession within the effective control of the corporation. As a result, party discovery is frequently ordered of information held by managing agents, directors, and officers of corporate litigants who are not themselves otherwise subject to the U.S. court's personal jurisdiction. *See* C. Wright *et al.*, *Federal Practice and Procedure* §2103 (2010).

10. *No depositions under FRCP Rule 30(b) of ordinary employees/agents.* As *Dubai Islamic Bank* illustrates, however, a court can *only* order depositions, under Rule 30(b), of parties and their "officers, directors or managing agents." It cannot order depositions under Rule 30(b) of other, lower-level employees. *See United States v. Afram Lines (USA), Ltd.*, 159 F.R.D. 408, 413 (S.D.N.Y. 1994); *In re Honda Am. Motor Co.*, 168 F.R.D. 535, 540 (D. Md. 1996). Information held by present or former employees who are not managing agents or officers of the corporate party can be obtained only by a subpoena based on the court's personal jurisdiction over the individual holding the information or via letters rogatory or a request under the Hague Evidence Convention (*see infra* pp. 1026-1044). *See, e.g., Herbert Ltd. Partnership v. Electronic Arts Inc.*, 325 F. Supp. 2d 282, 290 (S.D.N.Y. 2004) (collecting cases).

Where in Rule 30(b) does it say that a court can only order depositions of officers, directors, and managing agents? Suppose that a foreign employee—albeit of low seniority—is a critical witness. Why shouldn't deposition discovery be possible from the employee? Note that the FRCP permit direct document discovery of all documents in the control of a party; why are not depositions possible from all employees of a foreign party (who are presumably under the foreign party's control)?

11. *Test for "managing agents" and "officers" under FRCP Rule 30.* As *Dubai Islamic Bank* indicates, courts consider various factors in determining whether an individual is a managing agent: (a) the extent to which someone is granted general powers allowing the exercise of judgment and discretion in corporate matters; (b) the extent to which someone can be expected to give testimony when requested by his employer; (c) the corporate rank or seniority of the individual in question in relation to the relevant field; (d) the general responsibilities of the individual in question; and (e) the extent to which someone can be expected to identify with the interests of the corporation. *Dubai Islamic Bank v. Citibank, NA*, 2002 WL 1159699, at *3 (S.D.N.Y. May 31, 2002); *Sugarhill Records Ltd. v. Motown Record Corp.*, 105 F.R.D. 166, 170 (S.D.N.Y. 1985).

The standard for who qualifies as a managing agent or officer is flexible and pragmatic. *See Founding Church of Scientology of Washington, D.C., Inc. v. Webster*, 802 F.2d 1448, 1452 (D.C. Cir. 1986); *In re Auction Houses Antitrust Litig.*, 196 F.R.D. 444 (S.D.N.Y. 2000) (ordering company to provide information in possession of its former chief executive); *Boss Mfg. Co. v. Hugo Boss AG*, 1999 WL 20828, at *3 (S.D.N.Y. 1999); *Independent Prods. Corp. v. Loew's, Inc.*, 24 F.R.D. 19, 26 (S.D.N.Y. 1959) (party's former officers still managing directors because of willingness to "serve plaintiffs"); *Libbey Glass, Inc. v. Oneida, Ltd.*, 197 F.R.D. 342, 351 (N.D. Ohio 1999) ("it is clear that the deponent need not have a formal association with the corporation to be deemed its managing agent. . . . Likewise, the deponent need not be associated with the corporation at the time of his deposition."). Moreover, as *Dubai Islamic Bank* shows, the burden of proving an individual's status is modest. *See United States v. Afram Lines (USA), Ltd.*, 159 F.R.D. 408, 413 (S.D.N.Y. 1994); *Boss Mfg. Co. v. Hugo Boss AG*, 1999 WL 20828, at *4 (S.D.N.Y. 1999).

12. *Former "managing agents."* As *Dubai Islamic Bank* indicates, courts are willing to order the deposition of "managing agents" even when they no longer work for the party-corporation (thereby sparing the requesting party the need to serve the former managing agent with a subpoena or, otherwise, seek international judicial assistance by means of a letter of request). The court talks about a "pragmatic approach" to such situations. What precisely does this mean? Does it affect the "managing agent" analysis? Or does it affect the conditions under which the deposition will take place (*i.e.*, requiring the witness to travel to the United States as opposed to requiring the deposition to take place in a location more convenient for the witness)? *See Calixto v. Watson Bowman Acme Corp.*, 2008 WL 4487679 (S.D. Fla. Sept. 29, 2008) (ordering deposition of former managing agent but requiring it to occur in foreign country). *See also In re Flag Telecom Holdings, Ltd. Securities Litig.*, 236 F.R.D. 177 (S.D.N.Y. 2006) (ordering production of corporate documents from former executive).

13. *Depositions and administrative proceedings.* While this section primarily has concerned discovery disputes in civil proceedings before courts, students and practitioners should be aware that some specialized administrative proceedings raise similar issues. For example, in contested matters before the United States Patent and Trademark Office ("PTO"), federal district courts have the authority to issue subpoenas "for any witness residing in or being within such district" to provide testimony "for use in any contested case" before the PTO. 35 U.S.C. §24. Some courts have interpreted §24 to authorize subpoenas requiring foreign applicants for U.S. trademarks to provide deposition testimony in connection with their application even where the applicant otherwise lacks contacts with the United States. *See Rosenruist-Gestao e Servicos LDA v. Virgin Enters. Ltd.*, 511 F.3d 437 (4th Cir. 2007).

Is this view correct as a matter of statutory interpretation? Is a foreign company "residing in" a district simply by virtue of its application for a U.S. trademark? Why doesn't the canon against giving statutes extraterritorial reach control this question? *See id.* at 454 (Wilkinson, J., dissenting). Even if the statute is properly read to have extraterritorial effect, why don't comity considerations counsel against the deposition in these circumstances? *See id.* at 454-457 (Wilkinson, J., dissenting). Or is a foreign applicant for a U.S. trademark more akin to a plaintiff in a civil proceeding who reasonably assumes the risk of discovery orders by virtue of seeking the assistance of U.S. judicial or administrative authorities?

14. *Location of depositions of parties and their managing agents, officers, and directors under FRCP Rule 30(b).* Assuming that the court may order the deposition of a party, or a party's managing agents/officers, where will that deposition be conducted? As *Dubai Islamic Bank* illustrates, U.S. courts have long exercised the power to order foreign parties (and managing agents/officers residing abroad) to travel to the United States and attend a deposition there. *See supra* note 65. Compare the power of U.S. courts to order foreign parties to bring documents from abroad to the United States for production. *See supra* p. 978. What is it that justified a U.S. court forcing someone to travel thousands of miles to the United States to answer hostile questions?

As discussed above, and illustrated by *Dubai Islamic Bank*, U.S. courts are very likely to order foreign plaintiffs to attend depositions in the United States (specifically, in the judicial district where they commenced litigation). *See also supra* pp. 978-982. Nonetheless, U.S. courts have declined to order depositions in the United States in cases involving substantial hardship or other particular reasons. *See supra* pp. 979-980. Consider the various reasons proffered in *Dubai Islamic Bank* for not conducting depositions in New York. What do you make of the Court's resolution of these reasons? Why was the foreign party so anxious to avoid depositions in New York?

Suppose that a deposition in the United States is noticed of a foreign defendant (rather than plaintiff, as in *Dubai Islamic Bank*). Should a U.S. court order a foreign party (or its managing agents/officers) to travel to the United States in those circumstances? Is this a question of jurisdiction or of discretion?

15. *Depositions conducted outside the United States.* Could the Court in *Dubai Islamic Bank* have ordered depositions to be conducted in Dubai, rather than New York? Assuming it could, why did the Court not do so?

In many countries, local law may prohibit compelled foreign evidence-taking on local territory. *See supra* pp. 980-981 In such instances, ordering depositions abroad is worse than pointless. As discussed above, there have been instances where U.S. lawyers conducting depositions in foreign states have been subjected to criminal charges and/or sanctions. *See supra* pp. 973-977.

16. *Telephonic depositions.* The Court in *Dubai Islamic Bank* considered the possibility of ordering a telephonic deposition. Would it not be more efficient to conduct questioning over the telephone? What do you make of the reasons given in *Dubai Islamic Bank* for not doing so? Consider the following:

> Generally it may be assumed that most deposing counsel would prefer to see the witness whom they are deposing. First, the witness's demeanor may be a significant consideration in assessing how effective a witness he will be at trial. Second, the witness's demeanor can also guide an attorney in probing for areas in which the witness may be less confident or sure of himself. Third, although an attorney preparing for a deposition will presumably segregate and identify for himself in advance the documents that he intends to use at the deposition, there will inevitably be occasions on which he decides on the spot to use additional documents as deposition exhibits. This procedure may be somewhat constrained by the use of a telephone deposition since the deposition exhibits must be forwarded to the witness in advance. Moreover, the use of a telephone deposition lessens the ability of the examining attorney to obtain a spontaneous reaction from the witness, since he will presumably have access to the documents before he is questioned about them. *Daly v. Delta Airlines, Inc.*, 1991 WL 33392, at *2 (S.D.N.Y. 1991). *See also Phy v. Thill*, 2007 WL 2681106 (D. Kan. Sept. 7, 2007) (magistrate judge) (denying request for telephonic deposition due to importance of verifying deponent's identity and reliability).

Compare Normande v. Grippo, 2002 WL 59427, at *2 (S.D.N.Y. 2002) (permitting telephonic deposition of Brazilian plaintiff where plaintiff had limited resources and would have been forced to travel to New York with her infant child; case was not complex).

17. *Parties seeking discovery abroad may pursue parallel avenues.* The *Dubai Islamic Bank* Court notes that Citibank was simultaneously pursuing both Rule 30(b) depositions from the individuals involved, as well as letters rogatory issued to the Dubai courts. (The mechanisms for seeking discovery of information located abroad via letters rogatory are discussed below. *See infra* pp. 1024-1026.) The *Dubai Islamic Bank* Court expressly holds that parallel paths may be pursued to obtain the same materials. Is there any reason that this should not be the case?

4. Direct Extraterritorial Discovery from Nonparty Witnesses

The authority of U.S. courts to compel nonparties — persons not named in the lawsuit — to produce documents located abroad raises more complicated issues than party discovery. If a nonparty witness voluntarily complies with a party's request for information, then "discovery" can proceed without difficulty; the witness may provide information informally (either orally or documents) or may agree to testify formally as a witness.[90] This frequently occurs and may obviate the need for a subpoena, formal discovery request, or court order.

Nonetheless, there are many circumstances in which nonparty witnesses will not cooperate voluntarily, and a subpoena must be issued. Rule 45(a) of the Federal Rules permits the attorney for a party to issue subpoenas (and serve them) commanding either attendance at trial, attendance at a deposition, or production of documents or other evidence. In general, a nonparty can be compelled to produce nonprivileged documents and other materials — including materials located outside the United States — if it: (a) can be served with a *subpoena duces tecum* pursuant to the territorial limits of Rule 45; (b) is subject to the personal jurisdiction of a U.S. court; and (c) prudential considerations do not lead to quashing of the subpoena.[91] Failure of a nonparty to comply with a subpoena is punishable by the imposition of sanctions pursuant to Rule 45(e) as a contempt of court.

Excerpted below are Rule 45 of the Federal Rules of Civil Procedure and 28 U.S.C. §1783, both of which permit extraterritorial subpoena discovery. The decision excerpted below in *Laker Airways Ltd. v. Pan American World Airways* illustrates how U.S. courts have exercised the power under Rule 45 to order extraterritorial discovery.

FEDERAL RULES OF CIVIL PROCEDURE
Rule 45 [excerpted in Appendix C]

28 U.S.C. §§1783 & 1784
[excerpted in Appendix A]

LAKER AIRWAYS LIMITED v. PAN AMERICAN WORLD AIRWAYS
607 F. Supp. 324 (S.D.N.Y. 1985)

BRIEANT, DISTRICT JUDGE. By separate motions argued together and fully submitted on March 12, 1985, Midland Bank plc ("Midland") and Samuel Montagu & Co. Ltd. ("Montagu") moved for orders pursuant to Rule 45(b) quashing deposition subpoenas duces tecum, which were served respectively in this district on the Midland Bank's New York

---

90. Foreign law may restrict the availability, scope, and manner of voluntary disclosure, particularly if discovery occurs on foreign territory. *See infra* pp. 1024-1026.

91. *In re Citric Acid Litig.*, 191 F.3d 1090, 1107 (9th Cir. 1999); *In re Sealed Case*, 832 F.2d 1268 (D.C. Cir. 1987); *In re Westinghouse Elec. Corp. Uranium Contracts Litig.*, 563 F.2d 992 (10th Cir. 1977); *Laker Airways v. Pan American World Airways*, 607 F. Supp. 324 (S.D.N.Y. 1985).

branch office, and upon Montagu's New York Representative Office, or agency, . . . by plaintiff. The subpoenas seek information and documents from movant non-party witnesses in the above entitled action, which is now pending in the U.S. District Court for the District of Columbia. . . .

We describe briefly the underlying action. It is a private civil action seeking treble damages for federal antitrust violations alleged to have resulted in injury to Laker Airways Limited ("Laker") at one time a well-known British passenger airline of which Sir Freddie Laker was the founder and chief executive officer. On February 5, 1982, Laker ceased doing business due to insolvency, and on February 17, 1982 an individual residing in the United Kingdom was appointed Liquidator. The action filed November 24, 1982 and thereafter consolidated with companion cases thereafter filed, alleges that plaintiff, described as a "foreign corporation in liquidation," exists under the laws of the Island of Jersey in the Channel Islands having its principal office in London, England. Plaintiff is represented to this Court to be insolvent allegedly as a result of the tortious and conspiratorial misconduct of various defendant American, British, Swiss, German, Dutch and Belgian airlines, the British Airways Board, an American aircraft manufacturer, and its finance subsidiary. The thrust of the two-pronged complaint is, first, that "the airline defendants agreed to a predatory scheme to destroy Trans Atlantic Charters and Laker's scheduled Skytrain [passenger] service by offering, among other things, high cost service, at prices below the costs of those services." After alleging other wrongful competition, which need not concern us here, the complaint also alleged as a second factual basis, that "Laker realized in May of 1981 that it might be unable to meet its aircraft loan repayment requirements in January 1982 and explained the situation to its lenders." . . .

[T]he Complaint alleges that "by Christmas Eve 1981 Laker was advised that all of the lenders had agreed to provide the necessary finance" to reschedule Laker's debts. It is then alleged that certain named airline defendants "pressured Laker's lenders" to deny Laker the necessary finance so as to force Laker out of business, that the lender defendants continued to mislead Laker into believing that the financing was being provided as agreed, that Laker relied on this misrepresentation to its detriment and did not seek other sources of financing. The non-party witnesses Midland and Montagu are not sued in the District of Columbia at this time. Implicit, however, is the suggestion that they are among the "lenders" believed by plaintiff to have colluded with Laker's competitors to deny financing to Laker.

. . . At present [Midland and Montagu] are no more than non-party witnesses, entitled to have their pending motion adjudicated in accordance with the present state of the litigation. Should either or both movants become parties defendant in the future, then any necessary pre-trial discovery may be obtained directly through the exercise of the powers of the district court in which the above entitled action is pending. . . .

This Court concludes that the subpoenas must be vacated for a number of reasons. Foremost among them is the fact that all of Midland's activities in connection with this matter took place solely in the United Kingdom, and Midland's New York branch office had no involvement whatsoever with Laker. This point is not disputed at the hearing. The fact is that the New York branch of Midland did not open until April 1983, long after the alleged antitrust violations sued on in the District of Columbia. Similarly Montagu does not have a branch office in this District; it has a "representative office" which conducts no banking operations in New York. Here again there are no files or documents in the New York Representative Office of Montagu concerning Laker and no person at that office has any knowledge of the matters concerning Laker. That office also was not opened in New York until long after the events complained of by Laker in the District of Columbia action.

Essentially then the deposition subpoenas duces tecum seek to require Midland and Montagu, by officers having custody in the United Kingdom to produce in New York for use in the District of Columbia litigation, documents and records regularly maintained at their home offices in London. This is inappropriate. *See generally Ings v. Ferguson*, 282 F.2d 149 (2d Cir. 1960); *First National City Bank of New York v. Internal Revenue Service*, 271 F.2d 616 (2d Cir. 1959); *Cates v. LTV Aerospace Corp.*, 480 F.2d 620 (5th Cir. 1973), which continue to reflect the law applicable to non-parties.

As a second reason to vacate, this Court finds that the service of the subpoenas in New York is a transparent attempt to circumvent the Hague Convention on the Taking of Evidence Abroad in Civil or Commercial Matters, codified at 28 U.S.C. §1781 (hereinafter the "Hague Convention"), which sets forth agreed international procedures for seeking evidence in this Court from non-parties abroad. The failure to use the Hague Convention is more than a mere technicality.

The extraterritorial jurisdiction asserted over foreign interests by the American antitrust laws has long been a sore point with many foreign governments, including that of the United Kingdom. The English Protection of Trading Interests Act of 1980 ("PTIA") authorizes and empowers the Secretary of State for Trade and Industry to interpose the official power of the British Government so as to prevent persons conducting business in the United Kingdom from complying with foreign judicial or regulatory provisions designated by the Secretary of State as intrusive upon the sovereignty of that nation. With respect to the District of Columbia *Laker* action, the Secretary has already issued one directive that "no person or persons in the United Kingdom shall comply, or cause or permit compliance, whether by themselves, their officers, servants or agents, with any requirement to produce or furnish to the district court any commercial document in the United Kingdom or any commercial information. . . ."

[T]he very real problems presented by the PTIA are cited to demonstrate that the attempt to effect the subpoena duces tecum in this District is in effect an end run, not only around the Hague Convention, but also an end run on the PTIA. In effect, this Court is being asked to aid the plaintiff in the District of Columbia in obtaining an order from this Court which would cause the Midland branch in New York and the Montagu agency to compel their principals in London to violate British law by disgorging in London and transferring to their New York offices, documents which plaintiff would like to see, none of which are now nor ever were located in New York. This is clearly an improper abuse of the subpoena power of this Court, and should not be permitted. . . .

Notes on Rule 45, Pan American World Airways, *and §§1783 and 1784*

1. *Territorial limits on service of subpoenas under FRCP Rule 45.* Rule 45 only permits a federal district court to issue a subpoena for service upon witnesses located within the judicial district of the court (or within 100 miles of the place of trial, deposition or production). *See* Fed. R. Civ. P. 45(b)(2) ("Subject to the provisions of clause (ii) of subparagraph (c)(3)(A) of this rule, a subpoena may be served at any place within the district of the court by which it is issued, or at any place without the district that is within 100 miles of the place of the deposition, hearing, trial, production, or inspection specified in the subpoena. . . ."). *See also* Note, *Minimum Contacts, No Dog: Evaluating Personal Jurisdiction for Nonparty Discovery*, 88 Minn. L. Rev. 968 (2004); Wasserman, *The Subpoena Power: Pennoyer's Last Vestige*, 74 Minn. L. Rev. 37 (1989); Carlisle, *Nonparty Document Discovery from Corporations and Governmental Entities Under the Federal Rules of Civil Procedure*, 32 N.Y.L. Sch. L. Rev. 9 (1988).

Thus, a witness located in California cannot ordinarily be subjected to the subpoena power of the U.S. District Court for the Southern District of New York (unless the witness can be served in the Southern District). Instead, a litigant in an action in the Southern District is required by Rule 45(a)(2) to obtain service of a subpoena from a U.S. district court in the appropriate judicial district in California upon the Californian witness. Fed. R. Civ. P. 45(a)(2) ("A subpoena . . . for attendance at a deposition [must issue] from the court from the court for the district where the deposition is to be taken. . . ."). Such subpoenas are routinely issued and discovery can usually proceed readily in domestic cases. The subpoena at issue in *Pan American* was issued from the Southern District of New York, even though the underlying litigation was pending in the U.S. District Court for the District of Columbia, because Midland and Montagu were located in New York, not the District of Columbia.

2. *Territorial limitations on service of subpoenas in international cases.* In the international context, these territorial limitations on the subpoena power make nonparty discovery substantially more difficult. When discovery is sought from a *foreign* nonparty witness, located in a foreign state, there is no local U.S. district court from which a litigant may obtain subpoena service. The limitation of subpoena service to the territorial jurisdiction of the district court can have important practical consequences. If foreign witnesses cannot be served in any U.S. judicial district, they will be beyond the reach of direct U.S. discovery. *E.g., In re Sealed Case*, 832 F.2d 1268 (D.C. Cir. 1987) (quashing subpoena because it was not served on witness, or acceptable representative, in the district); *Astrazeneca Pharmaceuticals LP v. Mayne Pharma (USA) Inc.*, 2005 WL 2864666, at *28 n.20 (S.D.N.Y. 2005) (witness resident in Great Britain beyond court's subpoena power); *In re Air Crash Over Taiwan Straits on May 25, 2002*, 331 F. Supp. 2d 1176, 1198 & n.89 (C.D. Cal. 2004) (nonparty witnesses located in China cannot be compelled to provide testimony in U.S. court); *Price Waterhouse LLP v. First American Corp.*, 182 F.R.D. 56, 63 (S.D.N.Y. 1998); *United States v. Des Marteau*, 162 F.R.D. 364, 368 (M.D. Fla. 1995); *Orlich v. Heim Brothers, Inc.*, 560 N.Y.S.2d 10 (App. Div. 1990). Suppose, for example, that Midland Bank had never opened a New York office, and could not be served in New York. Would any question of Rule 45 subpoena discovery ever have arisen?

3. *Possibilities for serving subpoenas on foreign nonparty witnesses within U.S. territory under FRCP 45.* Not all nonparty foreign companies and individuals will be beyond the service of a subpoena under Rule 45.

(a) FRCP Rule 45 subpoena service on foreign party's U.S. branch. If a foreign company has a branch office or other significant presence within the forum, then subpoena service on that office would be possible and might provide effective U.S. discovery. *E.g., In re Sealed Case*, 832 F.2d 1268 (D.C. Cir. 1987); *Ssangyong Corp. v. Vida Shoes Int'l, Inc.*, 2004 WL 1125659, at *2-5 (S.D.N.Y. 2004). That was the case in *Laker*, where both Midland and Montagu had New York offices. *Compare Linde v. Arab Bank PLC*, 262 F.R.D. 136 (E.D.N.Y. 2009) (magistrate judge) (declining to order production from foreign parent based on service of subpoena on wholly owned U.S. subsidiary).

The U.S. Government has curtailed this approach in its own use of the subpoena power. In 1987, it entered into a memorandum of understanding with Switzerland in connection with the two countries' Mutual Legal Assistance Treaty, *infra* p. _____. Under the MOU, the United States agreed to refrain from serving subpoenas on U.S. branches of Swiss banks in order to obtain evidence located abroad. *See In re Grand Jury Subpoenas*, 2002 WL 31040322, at *7 n.2 (S.D.N.Y. 2002). *See also In re Grand Jury Subpoenas Dated March 19, 2002 and August 2, 2002*, 318 F.3d 379, 382-383 (2d Cir. 2003). What weight, if any, should this have in civil litigation not involving the United States?

(b) FRCP Rule 45 subpoena service on foreign party's officers, partners, or agents in U.S. Some courts may permit subpoena service upon a foreign company by means of service of the subpoena on an officer, partner, or agent of the company who is physically present within the forum. 1 Casad & Richman, *Jurisdiction in Civil Actions* §3-7 at 377 (3d ed. 1998 & Supp. 2010); C. Wright *et al.*, *Federal Practice and Procedure* §§2454, 2460-2462 (2007 & Supp. 2010); *First American Corp. v. Price Waterhouse LLP*, 154 F.3d 16, 19 (2d Cir. 1998) (upholding subpoena on foreign partnership where served on partner while present in jurisdiction); *In re Marc Rich & Co., AG*, 707 F.2d 663 (2d Cir. 1983) (where minimum contacts existed, "service of a subpoena upon appellant's officers within the territorial boundaries of the United States would be sufficient to warrant judicial enforcement of the grand jury's subpoena"); *In re Sealed Case*, 832 F.2d 1268 (D.C. Cir. 1987); *In re Automotive Refinishing Paint Litig.*, 2005 WL 1791978, at *3-11 (E.D. Pa. 2005); *Application of Johnson and Johnson*, 59 F.R.D. 174 (D. Del. 1973). Even if service is made upon the corporate agent of a witness, however, personal jurisdiction over the corporation must be established. *See supra* pp. 190-191.

(c) FRCP Rule 45 subpoena service on foreign individual temporarily present in U.S. A Rule 45 subpoena can also be served upon a foreign nonparty witness who is temporarily present in the United States. *Cf. In re Edelman*, 295 F.3d 171 (2d Cir. 2002) (person served with subpoena under §1782 held to be "found" in judicial district where subpoena was served).

4. *Personal jurisdiction over nonparty witness required to enforce FRCP Rule 45 subpoena.* Even if Rule 45's territorial limits on subpoena service are satisfied, a nonparty witness can only be compelled to produce documents if it is subject to the court's personal jurisdiction. *See First Am. Corp. v. Price Waterhouse LLP*, 154 F.3d 16, 20 (2d Cir. 1998); *In re Application to Enforce Admin. Subpoenas Duces Tecum of the S.E.C. v. Knowles*, 87 F.3d 413, 418 (10th Cir. 1996); *United States v. First National Bank of Chicago*, 699 F.2d 341 (7th Cir. 1983); *United States v. Bank of Nova Scotia*, 691 F.2d 1384 (11th Cir. 1982); *In re Sealed Case*, 832 F.2d 1268, 1272-1274 (D.C. Cir. 1987). What role, if any, should the fact of service of the subpoena within the jurisdiction have for purposes of personal jurisdiction? Recall the affirmation of tag service as a basis for general jurisdiction in *Burnham*. *See First American Corp. v. Price Waterhouse LLP*, 154 F.3d 16, 20 (2d Cir. 1998) (applying *Burnham* to evaluate personal jurisdiction over defendant personally served with subpoena).

What level of contacts with the forum should be required in order to establish personal jurisdiction for purposes of compelling discovery? The consequences of a discovery order are generally less serious than those of litigation on the merits: the witness is required to provide information (subject to applicable privileges), while a civil defendant may be subjected to significant liability. On the other hand, witnesses often have no personal stake in the underlying litigation, and may suffer considerable harm from compelled disclosures. Lower courts have generally (although without discussion) applied the same due process standard for discovery from witnesses as those applicable to civil litigation. *E.g., In re Application to Enforce Admin. Subpoenas Duces Tecum of the S.E.C. v. Knowles*, 87 F.3d 413, 418-419 (10th Cir. 1996) (applying minimum contacts analysis); *In re Sealed Case*, 832 F.2d 1268, 1273-1274 (D.C. Cir. 1987) (same); *In re Marc Rich & Co.*, 707 F.2d 663 (2d Cir. 1983) (applying "minimum contacts" test based on national contacts); *In re Automotive Refinishing Paint Litig.*, 229 F.R.D. 482, 487-490 (E.D. Pa. 2005) (same). Is this appropriate? Are there reasons that the two standards should differ? Consider the analysis in *Pan American.* Did the court rely on a lack of jurisdiction over Midland and Montagu? Could it have?

5. *Subpoenas served on governmental entities.* Rule 45 commands each "person" to which a subpoena is directed to supply the required testimony or documents. Is an agency of the

U.S. government a "person" for purposes of Rule 45? *See Yousuf v. Samantar*, 451 F.3d 248 (D.C. Cir. 2006) (concluding that it is). What about a foreign agency whose head happens to be temporarily present in the United States? How do the answers to these questions compare with comparable questions arising in the context of whether a foreign state is a "person" for purposes of the due process limits on the exercise of personal jurisdiction? *See supra* pp. 71-72 (FSIA). As discussed below, in addition to Rule 45, another provision of federal law, 28 U.S.C. §1782, authorizes the issuance of subpoenas by U.S. courts to "persons" residing or found in the court's district. *See infra* pp. 1059-1060. Are arms of the U.S. government "persons" for this purpose as well? *See Al Fayed v. CIA*, 229 F.3d 272 (D.C. Cir. 2000) (holding that the United States is not a "person" under §1782).

6. *Territorial limits on materials subject to subpoena power under FRCP Rule 45.* Even where Rule 45's territorial limits on the service of subpoenas are satisfied, and where personal jurisdiction over the witness exists, courts have shown reluctance to exercise subpoena power over foreign nonparty witnesses. For example, *Pan American* refused to order an English bank to produce records located in England even though the bank had a branch office in New York and therefore was presumably subject to the court's personal jurisdiction. What was the principal basis for the court's decision? Was it that the materials sought were located outside the United States and the Southern District? If so, is this a sound basis for decision? *See also In re Application for Order Quashing Deposition Subpoenas*, 2002 WL 1870084, at *3-7 (S.D.N.Y. 2002) (upholding validity of subpoena served on foreign officer while physically present in issuing jurisdiction but declining to order officer's attendance at deposition).

Does it matter that the materials sought by the subpoena in *Pan American* were not located within the territory of the Southern District? Does Rule 45 extend to materials located outside the district of the court from which the subpoena issues? Note Rule 45(a)(2) and the Advisory Committee Note accompanying the Rule:

> Paragraph (a)(2) makes clear that the persons subject to the subpoena is required to produce materials in that person's control whether or not the materials are located within the district or within the territory within which the subpoena can be served. The non-party witness is subject to the same scope of discovery under this rule as that person would be as a party to whom a request is addressed pursuant to Rule 34.

Doesn't this require rejecting at least part of the court's rationale in *Pan American?* Suppose that the documents in *Pan American* had been located in Midland's Los Angeles office. Is there some reason to treat materials located outside the *United States* differently from the broader class of materials located outside the relevant *judicial district?* What would justify the different treatment of documents located outside the United States? Recall the territoriality presumption and the *Nahas* rationale, *see supra* pp. 648-649, 889-893. Would this affect the interpretation of Rule 45? *Compare In re Automotive Refinishing Paint Antitrust Litig.*, 2005 WL 1791978, at *12 (E.D. Pa. 2005) (rejecting argument that subpoena requiring production of documents in District of Columbia did not reach documents located in Belgium).

7. *Prudential limitations on FRCP Rule 45's subpoena power.* Putting aside the territorial limitation on Rule 45 apparently embraced in *Pan American*, the court still probably would not have enforced the subpoena. It cited "foreign policy" concerns, the arguable applicability of English legislation forbidding production of the requested materials, and the fact that Midland's New York office commenced operations after the *Pan American* dispute occurred. Are these legitimate considerations in deciding whether to enforce a Rule 45 subpoena? Suppose that (a) there had been no order under the PTIA forbidding discovery; or (b) Midland's New York office had existed well before the *Pan American* dispute

began, but had no connection to the parties' conduct. Would either (or both) affect the result in *Pan American?*

8. *Mitigation of burden resulting from subpoena for foreign materials.* Even if a court declines to quash a subpoena, it may nonetheless enter an order designed to limit the burden on the party responding to the subpoena. For example, the court may limit the subpoena's scope and/or order the party seeking the documents to compensate the subpoena recipient for the costs of production. *See In re Automotive Refinishing Paint Antitrust Litig.*, 2005 WL 1791978, at *13-14 (E.D. Pa. 2005).

9. *Alternatives for obtaining discovery if FRCP Rule 45 subpoena cannot issue — letters rogatory and Hague Evidence Convention.* If a nonparty cannot be served or is not subject to the personal jurisdiction of the forum court, then the court will lack the power to compel compliance with a subpoena under Rule 45. *See, e.g., United States v. Bank of Nova Scotia*, 691 F.2d 1384 (11th Cir. 1982); *United States v. First Nat'l City Bank*, 396 F.2d 897 (2d Cir. 1968); *In re Urethane Antitrust Litig.*, 267 F.R.D. 361, 364 n.11 (D. Kan. 2010) (magistrate judge) (collecting cases). In this event, obtaining foreign judicial assistance is the only alternative for seeking the requested materials. The two principal alternatives for obtaining foreign judicial assistance — customary letters rogatory and the Hague Evidence Convention — are discussed in detail below. Note that *Pan American* was of the view that the Rule 45 subpoena was in fact a backdoor effort to circumvent the Hague Evidence Convention. We return to this issue below. *See infra* pp. 1032-1044.

10. *Subpoenas ordering testimony by telecommunications links.* Several lower courts have ordered nonparty witnesses to testify via telecommunications links at trial. For example, in one case, the district court ordered nonparty employees of several corporate defendants to testify via satellite television links from their residences (which were outside the trial court's judicial district). *In re San Juan Dupont Plaza Hotel Fire Litig.*, 129 F.R.D. 424 (D.P.R. 1989). Although Rule 45(e)(1) only granted district courts the power to compel attendance of witnesses at trial who are within 100 miles of the place of trial, the court held that this did not "expressly prohibit" coerced testimony by telecommunications: according to the court, the Rule simply "restricts the reach of subpoenas to prevent inconvenience to witnesses, not to confer advantages on parties." In a potentially analogous context, several courts have permitted witnesses located abroad to testify at trial by means of telecommunications links, and 1996 Amendments to the Federal Rule of Civil Procedure 43(a) now permit such testimony "for good cause shown in compelling circumstances and upon appropriate safeguards." *See, e.g., Dagen v. CFC Group Holdings, Ltd.*, 2003 WL 22533425, at *1 (S.D.N.Y. 2003) (permitting telephonic testimony from employees located in Hong Kong); *F.T.C. v. Swedish Match North America, Inc.*, 197 F.R.D. 1 (D.D.C. 2000) (approving testimony via live video transmission); *Official Airline Guides, Inc. v. Churchfield Publications, Inc.*, 756 F. Supp. 1393, 1398 n.2 (D. Or. 1990) (telephonic testimony of witness in United Kingdom); *Harrell v. State*, 689 So.2d 400, 405 (Fla. App. 1997) (testimony of witness in Argentina via live satellite transmission; articulating "satellite testimony protocol"). *But see Murphy v. Tivioli Enters.*, 953 F.2d 354, 359 (8th Cir. 1992) ("We know of no exception in either acts of Congress, the Rules of Civil Procedure, or the Rules of Evidence which permits telephone testimony."). *See generally* Fed. R. Civ. P. 43 Advisory Committee Notes (describing circumstances where contemporaneous transmission of testimony from location other than court will be permitted). *Compare* the discussion of telephonic depositions of parties, *supra* p. 992. *See generally* Davies, *Bypassing the Hague Evidence Convention: Private International Law Implications of the Use of Video and Audio Conference Technology in Transnational Litigation*, 55 Am. J. Comp. L. 205 (2007).

Is telephonic or televised testimony pursuant to a subpoena consistent with the language of Rule 45? If it is permitted, then what would prevent a court from ordering a foreign nonparty witness, subject to its jurisdiction but not to territorial service of a subpoena, to send documents by mail or courier to the United States? Would this be a desirable result?

11. *Subpoena service under 28 U.S.C. §1783 on U.S. citizens or residents located abroad.* Rule 45 also extends the subpoena power of the district courts to cases where evidence is sought from U.S. citizens or residents who are located abroad. Rule 45(b)(2) permits the issuance of subpoenas to persons in foreign countries pursuant to 28 U.S.C. §1783. Section 1783, in turn, authorizes U.S. courts to order the issuance of subpoenas to "a national or resident of the United States who is in a foreign country . . . if the court finds that particular testimony or the production of [documents] . . . is necessary in the interests of justice, and, in other than a criminal action or proceeding, if the court finds, in addition, that it is not possible to obtain his testimony . . . in any other manner." The Supreme Court has upheld §1783 against due process and international law challenges. *See Blackmer v. United States*, 284 U.S. 421 (1932), excerpted above at *supra* pp. 109-110. Why are U.S. citizens or residents treated differently from foreign nationals by Rule 45 and §1783? Is this wise from a policy perspective? In *Pan American*, suppose that the relevant documents had been sought from a U.S. bank's London office, rather than from Midland's head office. Should U.S. banks be subject to different rules than Midland?

Does the U.S. citizenship of the subpoena's target affect the mechanics of a subpoena? In other words, is it more appropriate for a court to order a U.S. citizen to appear in the United States for a deposition than a foreign citizen who is, on some basis, subject to the personal jurisdiction of the U.S. court? Does either §1783 or *Blackmer* supply an answer? *See S.E.C. v. Sabhlok*, 2009 WL 3561523 (N.D. Cal. Oct. 30, 2009) (magistrate judge).

D. Direct U.S. Discovery of Materials Located Abroad: Resolving Conflicts Between U.S. Discovery Orders and Foreign Law

As described above, U.S. courts have traditionally favored direct discovery under the Federal Rules of Civil Procedure (or state equivalents) as a means of obtaining extraterritorial discovery. These direct U.S. discovery orders for evidence located abroad sometimes conflict with foreign blocking statutes. If U.S. courts order discovery in violation of foreign law, they may subject an innocent private party to either U.S. discovery sanctions or foreign criminal penalties. On the other hand, if U.S. courts defer to foreign blocking statutes, the scope of U.S. discovery is placed in the hands of foreign states. As discussed below, each alternative has disadvantages.

1. Extraterritorial Discovery in Violation of Foreign Law: Historical Introduction and Judicial Power

a. Historical Introduction. For some decades, U.S. courts generally declined to order discovery abroad in violation of the laws of the place where the evidence was located. The *Restatement (First) Conflict of Laws* required this result, providing that U.S. courts lacked the power to order acts abroad in violation of the law of the place where the acts would be performed.[92] The few lower court opinions to consider the issue generally

---

92. *Restatement (First) Conflict of Laws* §94 (1934) (excerpted in Appendix X). Lower courts did, however, uphold their power to order discovery of materials outside the forum's territory where this would not entail violations of foreign law. *SEC v. Minas de Artemisa, SA*, 150 F.2d 215 (9th Cir. 1945).

declined to order discovery in violation of foreign law.[93] These decisions reasoned that "[u]pon fundamental principles of international comity, our courts dedicated to the enforcement of our laws should not take such action as may cause a violation of the laws of a friendly neighbor or, at the least, an unnecessary circumvention of its procedures."[94]

By the 1950s, however, U.S. courts abandoned traditional reluctance to order discovery abroad in violation of foreign law, and instead now generally follow a two-step analysis.[95] First, they begin from the premise that a court has the power to order discovery abroad, even where its order conflicts with foreign law, and then consider whether or not to exercise this power.[96] Second, if discovery is ordered, but not provided, U.S. courts then consider what sanctions are appropriate for noncompliance. This two-step analysis derives from the Supreme Court's decision in *Société Internationale pour Participations Industrielles et Commerciales v. Rogers.*[97]

b. *Société Internationale v. Rogers.* *Société Internationale* arose when a U.S. Government agency — the "Alien Property Custodian" — seized assets during World War II pursuant to the Trading with the Enemy Act,[98] which authorized the confiscation of "enemy" assets. The basis for the seizure was the Custodian's conclusion that the assets (cash and shares in a Delaware corporation) were "owned by or held for the benefit of" I.G. Farbenindustrie, a German firm (and then an enemy national). After WWII concluded, a Swiss company named I.G. Chemie brought suit in the United States against the Alien Property Custodian's successors. The suit alleged that the confiscated property had belonged to I.G. Chemie — assertedly not an "enemy" national — rather than to I.G. Farbenindustrie.

The U.S. Government defended by challenging I.G. Chemie's claim that it was a Swiss neutral, alleging that it was owned and dominated by I.G. Farbenindustrie. The Government sought discovery under Rule 34 of the Federal Rules of Civil Procedure of "a large number of the banking records of Sturzenegger & Cie," a Swiss company allegedly controlled by I.G. Chemie.[99] The documents were said to be relevant to the Government's defense. I.G. Chemie did not challenge the documents' relevance, but argued that producing them would violate Swiss penal law.[100] The district court ordered production, which I.G. Chemie partially made; after further proceedings, it supplemented its discovery, but still did not fully comply. At the Government's request, the district court then sanctioned I.G. Chemie under Rule 37 by dismissing its complaint.[101]

On appeal, the Supreme Court adopted a two-step approach, upholding the district court's discovery order but reversing its dismissal of the plaintiff's claims. The Court

---

93. *Ings v. Ferguson*, 282 F.2d 149 (2d Cir. 1960); *SEC v. Minas de Artemisa, SA*, 150 F.2d 215 (9th Cir. 1945).

94. *Ings v. Ferguson*, 282 F.2d 149, 152 (2d Cir. 1960). *See SEC v. Minas de Artemisa, SA*, 150 F.2d 215 (9th Cir. 1945) (ordering discovery of documents located in Mexico after concluding that it would not violate Mexican law); *First Nat'l City Bank v. IRS*, 271 F.2d 616, 618 (2d Cir. 1960).

95. *See Restatement (Third) Foreign Relations Law* §442, comment f (1987); *Société Internationale v. Rogers*, 357 U.S. 197 (1958). *But see SEC v. Banca della Svizzera Italiana*, 92 F.R.D. 111, 117 n.3 (S.D.N.Y. 1981) (suggesting that the Second Circuit, unlike other circuits, does not distinguish the analysis used for deciding to issue an order compelling discovery from that used for imposing sanctions).

96. *See Société Internationale v. Rogers*, 357 U.S. 197 (1958); *Restatement (Third) Foreign Relations Law* §442 (1987).

97. 357 U.S. 197 (1958).

98. 40 Stat. 415, 50 U.S.C. App. §5(b). The Act permitted the Custodian, during periods of war, to seize "any property or interest of any foreign country or national."

99. 357 U.S. at 200.

100. 357 U.S. at 200.

101. 357 U.S. at 200-202.

first rejected the contention that "the interdictions of Swiss law bar a conclusion that petitioner had 'control' of these documents within the meaning of Rule 34."[102] The Court relied on three factors: (a) the policies underlying the Trading with the Enemy Act;[103] (b) the fact that the requested documents "might have a vital influence upon this litigation;"[104] and (c) the fact that I.G. Chemie "is in a most advantageous position to plead with its own sovereign for relaxation of penal laws."[105] The Court refused to issue any broad interpretation of Rule 34's application in international cases: "The propriety of the use to which [Rule 34] is put depends on the circumstances of a given case, and we hold only that accommodation of the Rule in this instance to the policies underlying the Trading with the Enemy Act justified" the district court's discovery order.[106]

Second, *Société Internationale* went on to reverse the district court's dismissal of I.G. Chemie's claims under Rule 37. The Court recited the district court's findings that "petitioner had not been in collusion with the Swiss authorities to block discovery, and had in good faith made diligent efforts to execute the production order."[107] The Court reasoned that "fear of criminal prosecution constitutes a weighty excuse for nonproduction, and this excuse is not weakened because the laws preventing compliance are those of a foreign sovereign."[108] With this background, the Court construed Rule 37 as not permitting dismissal of a complaint where failure to comply with a discovery order "has been due to inability, and not to willfulness, bad faith, or any fault of petitioner."[109] The Court also held, however, that the district court retained "wide discretion" to deal with I.G. Chemie's violation of its order, including by drawing adverse inferences or concluding that petitioner failed to meet its burden of proof.

Notwithstanding the narrow limits on the *Société Internationale* holding, lower courts have adopted its basic two-step approach to extraterritorial discovery. Lower courts have struggled, however, to refine both prongs of *Société Internationale*'s analysis. The Second Circuit's opinion in *United States v. First National City Bank*,[110] which is excerpted below, is an early example of such efforts.

The *City Bank* decision also illustrates how U.S. courts have approached extraterritorial discovery that would require a party to violate foreign public policies or civil laws, rather than penal legislation. As discussed below, U.S. courts have acknowledged that penal blocking statutes are neither the only way of expressing a foreign state's interests in nondisclosure nor the only source of hardship for parties subject to extraterritorial U.S. discovery orders.[111] Moreover, lower courts have sometimes moderated extraterritorial U.S. discovery to accommodate the interests of foreign governments and private litigants even where no foreign blocking statute is involved.[112]

102. 357 U.S. at 204.
103. 357 U.S. at 204-205. The Court observed that the Act sought "to reach enemy interests which masqueraded under . . . innocent fronts." *Clark v. Uebersee Finanz-Korp.*, 332 U.S. 480, 485 (1947).
104. 357 U.S. at 205.
105. 357 U.S. at 205.
106. 357 U.S. at 206.
107. 357 U.S. at 208.
108. 357 U.S. at 211.
109. 357 U.S. at 212.
110. 396 F.2d 897 (2d Cir. 1968).
111. *See, e.g., Société Nationale Industrielle Aérospatiale v. U.S. District Court*, 482 U.S. 522 (1987).
112. *See* cases cited *infra* pp. 1007-1008.

RESTATEMENT (FIRST) CONFLICT OF LAWS
§94 (1934) [excerpted in Appendix X]

RESTATEMENT (SECOND) FOREIGN RELATIONS LAW
§§39 & 40 (1965) [excerpted in Appendix Y]

UNITED STATES v. FIRST NATIONAL CITY BANK
396 F.2d 897 (2d Cir. 1968)

KAUFMAN, CIRCUIT JUDGE. [A federal antitrust grand jury served First National City Bank of New York ("Citibank") with a subpoena *duces tecum* requiring the production of documents held in Citibank's Frankfurt offices. The requested documents related to transactions involving two of the bank's customers, C.F. Boehringer & Soehne, GmbH and Boehringer Mannheim Corporation (collectively, "Boehringer"). After Citibank refused to supply the documents, the trial judge conducted a hearing concerning the validity of the order and the propriety of sanctions. Citibank produced expert witnesses who testified that German law created a bank secrecy privilege for bank customers' records and that breach of this privilege would subject Citibank to potential civil liability in an action by Boehringer. The government produced an expert witness who testified that Citibank's production of the documents would not subject it to criminal liability and that the bank might well be able to raise valid defenses in any civil suit by Boehringer. The trial court found Citibank in civil contempt and fined it $2,000 per day until it produced the requested documents; the court also sentenced the Citibank officer responsible for the bank's noncompliance to up to sixty days' imprisonment. The defendants appealed.]

The basic legal question confronting us is not a total stranger to this Court. With the growing interdependence of world trade and the increased mobility of persons and companies, the need arises not infrequently, whether related to civil or criminal proceedings, for the production of evidence located in foreign jurisdictions. It is no longer open to doubt that a federal court has the power to require the production of documents located in foreign countries if the court has *in personam* jurisdiction of the person in possession or control of the material. *See, e.g., First National City Bank of New York v. Internal Revenue Service etc.*, 271 F.2d 616 (2d Cir. 1959). [Citibank does not contend that records located in its Frankfurt branch are not within the possession, custody, and control of the head office.] Thus, the task before us, as Citibank concedes, is not one of defining power but of developing rules governing the proper exercise of power. The difficulty arises, of course, when the country in which the documents are located has its own rules and policies dealing with the production and disclosure of business information — a circumstance not uncommon. This problem is particularly acute where the documents are sought by an arm of a foreign government. The complexities of the world being what they are, it is not surprising to discover nations having diametrically opposed positions with respect to the disclosure of a wide range of information. It is not too difficult, therefore, to empathize with the party or witness subject to the jurisdiction of two sovereigns and confronted with conflicting commands. . . .

In any event, under the principles of international law, "A state having jurisdiction to prescribe or enforce a rule of law is not precluded from exercising its jurisdiction solely because such exercise requires a person to engage in conduct subjecting him to liability under the law of another state having jurisdiction with respect to that conduct." *Restatement (Second) Foreign Relations Law* §39(1) (1965). It is not asking too much, however, to expect that each nation should make an effort to minimize the potential conflict flowing from their joint concern with the prescribed behavior. *Id.* at §39(2). Where, as here, the burden of resolution ultimately falls upon the federal courts, the difficulties are manifold because the courts must take care not to impinge upon the prerogatives and responsibilities of the political branches of the government in the extremely sensitive and delicate area of foreign affairs. Mechanical or overbroad rules of thumb are of little value; what is required is a careful balancing of the interests involved and a precise understanding of the facts and circumstances of the particular case.

With these principles in mind, we turn to the specific issues presented by this appeal. Citibank concedes, as it must, that compliance with the subpoena does not require the violation of the criminal law of a foreign power, as in *Société Internationale etc. v. Rogers*, *supra* (discovery under the Federal Rules of Civil Procedure); *Ings v. Ferguson*, 282 F.2d 149, 152 (2d Cir. 1960), or risk the imposition of sanctions that are the substantial equivalent of criminal penalties, as in *Application of Chase Manhattan Bank*, 297 F.2d 611, 613 (2d Cir. 1962), or even conflict with the public policy of a foreign state as expressed in legislation. Instead, all that remains, as we see it, is a possible prospective civil liability flowing from an implied contractual obligation between Citibank and its customers that, we are informed, is considered implicit in the bank's license to do business in Germany.

But the government urges vigorously that to be excused from compliance with an order of a federal court, a witness, such as Citibank, must show that following compliance it will suffer criminal liability in the foreign country. We would be reluctant to hold, however, that the mere absence of criminal sanctions abroad necessarily mandates obedience to a subpoena. Such a rule would show scant respect for international comity; and, if this principle is valid, a court of one country should make an effort to minimize possible conflict between its orders and the law of a foreign state affected by its decision. The vital national interests of a foreign nation, especially in matters relating to economic affairs, can be expressed in ways other than through the criminal law. For example, it could not be questioned that, insofar as a court of the United States is concerned, a statement or directive by the Bundesbank (the central bank of Germany) or some other organ of government, expresses the public policy of Germany and should be given appropriate weight. Equally important is the fact that a sharp dichotomy between criminal and civil penalties is an imprecise means of measuring the hardship for requiring compliance with a subpoena. . . .

In evaluating Citibank's contention that compliance should be excused because of the alleged conflict between the order of the court below and German law, we are aided materially by the rationale of the recent *Restatement (Second) Foreign Relations Law* §40 (1965) [excerpted at Appendix Z]. . . . In the instant case, the obvious, albeit troublesome, requirement for us is to balance the national interests of the United States and Germany and to give appropriate weight to the hardship, if any, Citibank will suffer.

The important interest of the United States in the enforcement of the subpoena warrants little discussion. The federal Grand Jury before which Citibank was summoned is conducting a criminal investigation of alleged violations of the antitrust laws. These laws have long been considered cornerstones of this nation's economic policies, have been vigorously enforced and the subject of frequent interpretation by our Supreme Court. We would have great reluctance, therefore, to countenance any device that would place relevant information beyond the reach of this duly impaneled Grand Jury or impede or delay its proceedings. Judge Learned Hand put the issue in perspective many years ago: "The suppression of truth is a grievous necessity at best, more especially where as here the inquiry concerns the public interest; it can be justified at all only where the opposing private interest is supreme." *McMann v. SEC*, 87 F.2d 377, 378 (2d Cir. 1937).

We examine the importance of bank secrecy within the framework of German public policy with full recognition that it is often a subtle and difficult undertaking to determine the nature and scope of the law of a foreign jurisdiction. There is little merit, however, in Citibank's suggestion that the mere existence of a bank secrecy doctrine requires us to accept on its face the bank's assertion that compliance with the subpoena would violate an important public policy of Germany. While we certainly do not intend to deprecate the importance of bank secrecy in the German scheme of things neither can we blind ourselves to the doctrine's severe limitations as disclosed by the expert testimony. We have already made the assumption that the absence of criminal sanctions is not the whole answer to or finally determinative of the problem. But, it is surely of considerable significance that Germany considers bank secrecy simply a privilege that can be waived by the customer and is content to leave the matter of enforcement to the vagaries of private litigation. Indeed, bank secrecy is not even required by statute. *See Restatement (Second)* §40, comment c: "A state will be less likely to refrain from exercising its jurisdiction when the consequence of obedience to its order will be a civil liability abroad."

[Moreover,] it is not of little significance that a German court has noted, "The fact that bank secrecy has not been included in the penal protection of §300 of the Criminal Code must lead to the conclusion that the legislature did not value the public interest in bank secrecy as highly as it did the duty of secrecy of doctors and attorneys." . . . In addition, it is noteworthy that neither the Department of State nor the German Government has expressed any view on this case or indicated that, under the circumstances present here, enforcement of the subpoena would violate German public policy or embarrass German-American relations. The Supreme Court commented on this aspect in other litigation involving Citibank: "[If] the litigation might in time be embarrassing to United States diplomacy, the District Court remains open to the Executive Branch, which, it must be remembered, is the moving party in the present proceeding." *United States v. First National City Bank,* 379 U.S. 378, 384-385 (1965). We are fully aware that when foreign governments, including Germany, have considered their vital national interests threatened, they have not hesitated to make known their objections to the enforcement of a subpoena to the issuing court. So far as appears, both the United States and German governments have voiced no opposition to Citibank's production of the subpoenaed records.

We turn now to the nature and extent of the alleged hardships to which Citibank would be subjected if it complied with the subpoena. It advances two grounds on which it will suffer injury. First, it states that it will be subjected to economic reprisals by Boehringer and will lose foreign business that will harm it and the economic interests of the United States. . . . A partial answer is that the protection of the foreign economic interests of the United States must be left to the appropriate departments of our government, especially since the government is the moving litigant in these proceedings. . . . Second, Citibank complains that it will be subject to civil liability in a suit by Boehringer. . . . Judge Pollack concluded that risk of civil damages was slight and speculative, and we agree.[113] The chance that Boehringer will suffer compensable damages is quite remote and Citibank appears to have a number of valid defenses if it is sued, both under the terms of the contract and principles of German civil law.

---

113. Judge Pollack based his finding of lack of good faith on the fact that Citibank, as noted above, had failed to even make a simple inquiry into the nature or extent of the records available at the Frankfurt branch. In addition, the expert testimony was clear that the bank secrecy doctrine applied only to material entrusted to a bank within the framework of any confidential relationship of bank and customer but not to records that were the bank's own work product. Citibank failed to produce any documents reflecting its own work product that were within the terms of the subpoena or to indicate that none existed.

Notes *on* Restatements *and* City Bank

1. *Historic refusal of U.S. courts to order discovery in violation of foreign law.* U.S. courts historically showed greater deference than *Société Internationale* to the laws of the place where discovery was to be ordered. That is reflected in *Restatement (First) Conflict of Laws* §94 (1934), which did not permit courts to order conduct abroad that was "*contrary to the law of the state in which it is to be performed.*" U.S. courts adhered to this rule until surprisingly late. *See Ings v. Ferguson*, 282 F.2d 149 (2d Cir. 1960) (refusing to order production of documents located in Canada because this would arguably violate Quebec law); *SEC v. Minas de Artemisa, SA*, 150 F.2d 215 (9th Cir. 1945) (indicating court would refuse to enforce subpoena for documents located in Mexico when this would violate Mexican law).

2. *Contemporary willingness of U.S. courts to order discovery in violation of foreign law.* Compare §§39 and 40 of the *Restatement (Second) Foreign Relations Law*, and the *City Bank* decision, with §94 of the *Restatement (First) Conflict of Laws.* Note the significant change in the treatment of orders requiring conduct outside the forum state in violation of the laws of the place of the conduct. The comments to §39 offer little explanation: "The rule stated in this Section is based upon the fact that international law, in most situations, does not provide for choosing among competing bases of jurisdiction to prescribe rules of conduct." *Restatement (Second) Foreign Relations Law* §39, comment b (1965). Is this a satisfactory explanation? What justifies a court in one country ordering a party to violate another country's laws on that state's own territory?

3. *Source of authority to order discovery of evidence located abroad in violation of foreign law.* As *Société Internationale* indicates, U.S. courts have had little difficulty ordering production of documents located abroad, even if production would violate foreign law. What is the basis under U.S. law for a U.S. court's power to order extraterritorial discovery? Does any provision of the Federal Rules of Civil Procedure grant such authority?

Consider the present language of Rules 34 and 45. Does anything in these Rules permit U.S. courts to order discovery in violation of foreign law? Recall *Schooner Exchange* and *Nahas*, and the presumption that Congress does not intend to violate international law. *See supra* pp. 18, 889-893. In the light of this presumption, and the historic refusal of U.S. courts to order discovery abroad in violation of foreign law, should Rule 34 and 45 be construed to permit extraterritorial discovery in violation of foreign law? Compare the broader deference currently afforded to foreign laws under the act of state doctrine, *see supra* pp. 801-817, and the doctrine of foreign sovereign compulsion, *see supra* pp. 857-864. Why should blocking statutes be treated differently? Should U.S. courts be permitted to order the discovery of evidence located abroad in violation of foreign law?

4. **Société Internationale'*s two-step analysis in extraterritorial discovery disputes.*** As discussed above, *Societe Internationale* distinguished between two issues: (1) the propriety of an order under Rule 34 for the production of foreign documents in violation of foreign law, and (2) the propriety of sanctions under Rule 37 for failure to comply with a discovery order. *City Bank* and most other lower courts have followed this basic two-step analysis in extraterritorial discovery disputes. *E.g., Ohio v. Arthur Andersen & Co.*, 570 F.2d 1370 (10th Cir. 1978); *Trade Dev. Bank v. Continental Ins. Co.*, 469 F.2d 35 (2d Cir. 1972); *In re Uranium Antitrust Litig.*, 480 F. Supp. 1138 (N.D. Ill. 1979).

5. *Rationale for bifurcating decision to order discovery from imposition of sanctions.* One reason that U.S. courts bifurcate the decision to order discovery from the decision to sanction noncompliance is to place pressure upon the party from whom discovery is sought, who must take steps to comply (typically by obtaining a waiver of foreign blocking statutes) or face sanctions. Is it fair to hold private parties "hostage" to the decisions of foreign governments?

Using the threat of sanctions to coerce production reflects the often unstated suspicion of U.S. courts and litigants that foreign nondisclosure laws or policies are little more than efforts to assist foreign litigants in resisting discovery and that sanctions will never actually be imposed pursuant to foreign blocking statutes. *See Compagnie Française d'Assurance pour le Commerce Exterieur v. Phillips Petroleum Co.,* 105 F.R.D. 16, 30 (S.D.N.Y. 1984) ("never expected nor intended to be enforced against French subjects but was intended rather to provide them with tactical weapons and bargaining chips in foreign courts"); *Graco, Inc. v. Kremlin, Inc.,* 101 F.R.D. 503, 514 (N.D. Ill. 1984). This suspicion is reinforced by the legislative history of at least some foreign blocking statutes, which indicate that the laws were not intended actually to be enforced, but were instead designed to be used as bargaining chips by foreign companies to resist U.S. discovery. For example, the legislative history of the French blocking statutes says:

> [It] is necessary not to misunderstand the actual scope of these penalties, which does not clearly appear on the simple reading of the [statute]. . . . [T]hese penalties are applied only on the improvable assumption that the companies would refuse to make use of the protective provisions offered to them. In all other cases, those potential fines will assure foreign judges of the judicial basis for the legal excuse which the companies will not fail to make use of.

Report Made in the Name of the Commission of Production and Exchanges on the Law Project Adopted by the Senate Relating to the Communication of Documents and Information of Economic, Commercial or Technical Nature to Foreign Physical Persons or Companies, No. 1814, at 63-64 (quoted in Note, *Strict Enforcement of Extraterritorial Discovery,* 38 Stan. L. Rev. 841, 863-865 (1986)).

6. *Lower court applications of* **Société Internationale***'s standard for ordering extraterritorial discovery in violation of foreign law.* Lower courts have reached divergent results in deciding whether to order discovery under *Société Internationale.* This uncertainty is partially attributable to the limited reach of the holding in *Societe Internationale* and to the Court's refusal to articulate any generally applicable analytical approach. 357 U.S. at 205-206 ("depends upon the circumstances of a given case"; "[w]e do not say that this ruling would apply to every situation where a party is restricted by law from producing documents").

In approving the district court's discovery order, *Société Internationale* considered three factors: (1) the policies underlying the Trading with the Enemy Act; (2) the "vital influence" that the requested materials might have on the lawsuit; and (3) the fact that *Societe Internationale* was a Swiss national and therefore was best-suited to seek relief from the Swiss blocking statute. Some courts have rigorously applied *Société Internationale,* considering only the three factors specifically identified by the Supreme Court in deciding whether to order discovery. *E.g., Trade Dev. Bank v. Continental Ins. Co.,* 469 F.2d 35 (2d Cir. 1972); *In re Uranium Antitrust Litig.,* 480 F. Supp. 1138, 1148 (N.D. Ill. 1979).

Other lower courts have adopted an expanded version of *Société Internationale*'s three-factor test in deciding whether to order discovery. These courts have considered additional factors derived from *Restatement (Second) Foreign Relations Law* §40 (1965) — including a balancing of both U.S. and foreign national public policies and the hardships likely to be suffered by the private party. *E.g., Cochran Consulting, Inc. v. Uwatec USA, Inc.,* 102 F.3d 1224, 1226-1227 (Fed. Cir. 1996); *United States v. First National Bank of Chicago,* 699 F.2d 341, 345 (7th Cir. 1983); *United States v. First Nat'l City Bank,* 396 F.2d 897, 902 (2d Cir. 1968). A few other lower courts have looked to an even broader range of factors than those contemplated by Restatement §40 in deciding whether to order discovery, considering in addition the good faith of the party from whom discovery would be ordered. *E.g., United States v. Vetco, Inc.*, 691 F.2d 1281, 1288 (9th Cir. 1981); *In re Westinghouse Elec. Corp. Uranium Contracts Litig.*, 563 F.2d 992, 998 (10th Cir. 1977); *In re Grand Jury Subpoena dated August 9, 2000*, 218 F. Supp. 2d 544, 554 (S.D.N.Y. 2002). Finally, some lower courts have interpreted *Société Internationale* as reserving all questions relating to foreign blocking statutes and U.S. governmental interests to the sanctions stage. *E.g., Civil Aeronautics Board v. Deutsche Lufthansa AG*, 591 F.2d 951, 953 (D.C. Cir. 1979); *Arthur Andersen & Co. v. Finesilver*, 546 F.2d 338, 341 (10th Cir. 1976) ("consideration of foreign law problems in a discovery context is required in dealing with sanctions . . . and not in deciding whether the discovery order should issue").

Which of these various approaches to extraterritorial discovery is preferable? Does the existence of a foreign blocking statute have any relevance to the question whether a party "controls" documents? How did *Société Internationale* answer this question?

7. *Dismissal as a sanction for failure to comply with U.S. discovery order under FRCP Rule 37.* Federal Rule of Civil Procedure 37, set forth in Appendix C, provides trial courts with broad discretion to impose sanctions upon a party for failure to produce discovery as ordered. *Societe Internationale* considered whether it was appropriate to impose the drastic sanction of dismissal under Rule 37 for failure to comply with the district court's discovery order. The Court relied principally on the fact that Societe Internationale's failure to comply was "due to inability, and not to willfulness, bad faith, or any fault of petitioner." Because Societe Internationale had not acted in bad faith the Court held that the sanction of dismissal was unduly severe. *See also National Hockey League v. Metropolitan Hockey Club, Inc.*, 427 U.S. 639, 643 (1976). Nonetheless, where bad faith or "conscious disregard" for the discovery process is present, even the extraordinary remedy of dismissal is permitted. *Sexton v. Uniroyal Chemical Co.*, 62 Fed. Appx. 615 (6th Cir. 2003) (relying on Rule 41); *United States v. Reyes*, 307 F.3d 451 (6th Cir. 2002); *Republic of the Philippines v. Marcos*, 888 F.2d 954 (2d Cir. 1989); *Founding Church of Scientology Inc. v. Webster*, 802 F.2d 1448, 1458 (D.C. Cir. 1986).

8. *Trial court's discretion to impose sanctions for failure to comply with discovery order.* Even if the ultimate sanction of dismissal is not imposed, *Société Internationale* and *City Bank* illustrate that U.S. courts retain significant discretion to sanction failure to comply with their extraterritorial discovery orders (including where the failure was required by foreign law). *Restatement (Third) Foreign Relations Law* §442(2)(c) (1987) (excerpted at Appendix AA). Even if a litigant acts in good faith and avoids dismissal or other similar sanctions, it may nevertheless be subjected to evidentiary rulings (such as adverse inferences, or exclusion of particular evidence). Is it appropriate for a U.S. court to adopt adverse inferences against a party that acts in good faith but cannot lawfully disclose requested discovery materials?

Another possible type of sanction for violation of discovery orders or subpoenas is a monetary fine. Where nonparties refuse to produce requested information, fines may be the only means for punishing noncompliance (since evidentiary sanctions or default judgments will not concern a nonparty). *See In re Grand Jury Proceedings*, 280 F.3d 1103 (7th Cir. 2002) ($1,500 fine per day and imprisonment for failure to comply with grand jury subpoena); *United States v. Bank of Nova Scotia*, 740 F.2d 817 (11th Cir. 1984) ($25,000 fine per day); *United States v. First Nat'l City Bank*, 396 F.2d 897 (2d Cir. 1968) ($2,000 fine per day plus 60 days imprisonment); *Diamant v. GMS Diamonds Corp.*, 2004 WL 2710028, at *2 (S.D.N.Y. 2004) ($1,000 fine per day); *Vanguard Int'l Mfg. v. United States*, 588 F. Supp. 1229 (S.D.N.Y. 1984) ($10,000 fine per day). Although fines are also imposed outside the nonparty witness context, this is less common. *In re Marc Rich & Co. AG*, 707 F.2d 663 (2d Cir. 1983); *Remington Prods. v. North Am. Philips Corp. NV*, 107 F.R.D. 643 (D. Conn. 1985).

9. *Relevance of good faith to imposition of sanctions.* The likelihood that a foreign party will be subject to sanctions, and the severity of those sanctions, depends in significant part on the good faith efforts of the party to comply fully with the discovery process. *See, e.g., Cochran Consulting, Inc. v. Uwatec USA, Inc.*, 102 F.3d 1224 (Fed. Cir. 1996); *United States v. Bank of Nova Scotia*, 691 F.2d 1384 (11th Cir. 1982) (failure to seek customer's waiver of nondisclosure law is bad faith); *Ohio v. Arthur Andersen & Co.*, 570 F.2d 1370 (10th Cir. 1978) (failure to investigate effect of foreign nondisclosure law on defendant's documents is bad faith); *United States v. First Nat'l City Bank*, 396 F.2d 897 (2d Cir. 1968) (failure to ascertain precise effect of foreign nondisclosure law is bad faith).

It is settled that a party's actions "inviting" foreign prohibitions against U.S. discovery will be regarded as bad faith. *Restatement (Third) Foreign Relations Law* §442, comment b (1987) ("Evidence that parties or targets have actively sought a prohibition against disclosure, or that the information was deliberately moved to a state with blocking legislation, may be regarded as evidence of bad faith."). In addition, some courts have concluded that actions taken well before U.S. litigation is initiated evidence bad faith. In *General Atomic Co. v. Exxon Nuclear Co.*, 90 F.R.D. 290 (S.D. Cal. 1981), for example, the court did not hesitate to find bad faith on the part of a Canadian company for taking various actions before the U.S. litigation began, including keeping particular documents in Canada, destroying copies of these documents in the United States, and postponing discovery in other litigation. *See also SEC v. Banca della Svizzera Italiana*, 92 F.R.D. 111 (S.D.N.Y. 1981) (deliberately structuring a transaction so that it will fall within foreign nondisclosure law is bad faith). *Compare Restatement (Third) Foreign Relations Law* §442, comment h (1987) ("Merely notifying the authorities of another state or consulting with them about a request for discovery is not evidence of bad faith.").

In general, few U.S. courts have found that a party who failed to comply with a valid U.S. discovery order acted in sufficient good faith to escape sanctions. The leading post-*Societe Internationale* cases on the issue suggest that affirmative conduct by the party from whom discovery is sought — including vigorous efforts to secure a waiver from foreign authorities or customers — will be necessary to a finding of good faith. *See In re Westinghouse Elec. Corp. Uranium Contracts Litig.*, 563 F.2d 992 (10th Cir. 1977) (formal letter to Canadian Government, coupled with other efforts, to obtain waiver of nondisclosure law constitute good faith). *Compare Cochran Consulting, Inc. v. Uwatec USA, Inc.*, 102 F.3d 1224, 1228-1230 (Fed. Cir. 1996) (citing defendant's "good faith" efforts through commencing foreign litigation against contract partner in order to secure documents subject to federal court discovery order) *with United States v. Bank of Nova Scotia*, 691 F.2d 1384 (11th Cir. 1982) (failure to seek waiver from customer is bad faith); *CFTC v. Lake Shore Asset Mgmt., Ltd.*, 2007 WL 2915647 (N.D. Ill. Oct. 4, 2007) (same).

10. *Need to take U.S. discovery orders seriously.* U.S. courts typically have little patience with foreign companies that seek to justify noncompliance with discovery orders by reference to their unfamiliarity with the U.S. discovery process. For example, in *Phibro Energy v. Empresa de Polimeros*, 720 F. Supp. 312 (S.D.N.Y. 1989), the magistrate ordered a foreign defendant to pay attorneys' fees incurred by the plaintiff in a discovery dispute. The magistrate rejected the argument that the defendant's "lack of familiarity with the American Litigation System" and its "good faith" justified an inadequate production of documents. It is important for U.S. counsel to work particularly closely with non-U.S. litigants in ensuring adequate compliance with discovery requests; failure to do so will often leave foreign employees with the difficult task of complying with unfamiliar requests. *See also King v. Perry & Sylvia Machinery Co.*, 1991 U.S. Dist. LEXIS 7901 (N.D. Ill. 1991) (construing untranslated Japanese interrogatory answers against Japanese litigant).

11. *Application of interest-balancing outside the blocking statute context.* *City Bank* determined whether or not to require extraterritorial discovery by balancing a variety of factors, including U.S. and German governmental interests and private hardships. As noted above, *supra* pp. 1007-1008, this approach represents an extension of *Société Internationale* from situations where foreign law *affirmatively prohibits* U.S. discovery to cases where foreign public policy merely disfavors U.S.-style discovery. Is this extension warranted? Why should U.S. courts concern themselves with foreign public policy in these circumstances? Is this a "false conflict," in choice of law terms? *See also supra* pp. 738-739.

12. *Effect of* **Hartford Fire** *on* **City Bank** *interest balancing.* Recall that *Hartford Fire Insurance v. California* (mistakenly) held that the doctrine of international comity, and §403 of the *Restatement (Third) Foreign Relations Law,* did not apply except where U.S. and foreign substantive laws imposed conflicting obligations. *See supra* pp. 704-705. Does this holding undermine *City Bank*'s application of §40's balancing analysis even in the absence of conflicting legal obligations?

13. *Balancing U.S. and foreign governmental interests.* A central feature of the *City Bank* and *Restatement* §40 analysis is the weighing of U.S. and foreign governmental interests. Application of this approach in deciding whether to order discovery is a departure from *Société Internationale* which, as noted earlier, considered only U.S. interests, the importance of the requested documents, and the defendant's nationality in deciding whether to order discovery. A number of other lower courts have followed *City Bank* and §40 in balancing *both* U.S. and foreign governmental interests in deciding whether to order discovery. *See supra* pp. 1007-1008.

Nonetheless, U.S. courts appear to be divided over the usefulness of attempting to balance U.S. interests against foreign interests in resolving extraterritorial discovery disputes. Unlike the decisions cited above, some courts have sharply criticized the *City Bank* interest-balancing approach. These decisions argue that U.S. judges are ill-equipped to balance competing national policies and, in any event, that U.S. judges invariably conclude that U.S. interests should prevail. *See Arthur Andersen & Co. v. Finesilver,* 546 F.2d 338 (10th Cir. 1976); *In re Uranium Antitrust Litig.,* 480 F. Supp. 1138, 1148 (N.D. Ill. 1979) ("Aside from the fact that the judiciary has little expertise, or perhaps even authority, to evaluate the economic and social policies of a foreign country, such a balancing test is inherently unworkable in this case. The competing interests here display an irreconcilable conflict on precisely the same plane of national policy"). In addition, commentators have argued that balancing national interests is a political, not legal task, and is inconsistent with policies underlying the act of state and political question doctrines. *E.g.,* Gerber, *Beyond Balancing: International Law Restraints on the Reach of National Laws,* 10 Yale J. Int'l L. 185, 205 (1984). Compare the similar arguments made in the choice of law context. *See supra* p. 752.

Which approach is wiser? Should U.S. courts attempt to assess and "balance" conflicting U.S. and foreign governmental interests? Do *City Bank* and §40 actually require "evaluat[ing] economic and social policies of a foreign country"? Is there any realistic alternative to examining foreign laws and public policies, and seeking to reconcile those authorities with U.S. law?

14. *Is a foreign blocking statute or nondisclosure policy applicable?* *City Bank* considered the scope of the asserted German interest in bank secrecy, concluding that various exceptions limited the importance of the interest and made the possibility that German sanctions would be imposed speculative. Other courts have also examined particular foreign blocking statutes and concluded that they are not applicable to the facts of the proposed discovery and, thus, that foreign sovereign interests are not implicated. *E.g., Roberts v. Heim,* 1990 WL 32,553 (N.D. Cal. 1990).

Can U.S. courts reliably determine the meaning of foreign blocking statutes? Consider the following judge's response to disagreement among litigants over whether a Philippine blocking statute (excerpted in Appendix DD) prohibited the production of certain documents:

> This Court lacks familiarity with Philippine law and believes that the uncertain task of addressing questions of Philippine substantive and procedural law is better left with the Philippine courts. In reaching this conclusion, the Court is mindful of Judge Friendly's observation: "[T]ry as we may to apply the foreign law as it comes to us through the lips of the experts, there is an inevitable hazard that, in those areas, perhaps interstitial but far from inconsequential, where we have no clear guides, our labors, moulded by our own habits of mind as they necessarily must be, may produce a result whose conformity with that of the foreign court may be greater in theory than it is in fact." *Ilusorio v. Ilusorio-Bildner*, 103 F. Supp. 2d 672, 679-680 (S.D.N.Y. 2000) (quoting *Conte v. Flota Mercante Del Estado*, 277 F.2d 664, 667 (2d Cir. 1960)).

Is this any different from application of foreign law in other contexts by U.S. courts?

15. *Evaluating the "strength" of foreign governmental interests.* As noted earlier, *City Bank* relied on the German Government's failure to express any concern about the requested U.S. discovery in concluding that German interests were not particularly great. *See supra* pp. 1003-1005. How does a court decide how "strong" a legislative policy is, particularly a policy of a foreign nation? Is it not just mumbo-jumbo to talk about the "strength" of particular foreign "interests"? Alternatively, could a court at least sensibly consider how a single legislature that enacted two conflicting laws would have wanted them to interact? Does that analysis work where the laws are broad discovery rules and blocking statutes?

In addition, in evaluating the "strength" of the German governmental interests opposed to U.S. discovery, *City Bank* considered the legal form in which the German interests were expressed, apparently envisaging a continuum of methods of expressing foreign public policy running from criminal statutes, to draconian civil sanctions, to public policy expressed in legislation, to public policy expressed in judicial decisions. Although the court emphasized that a nation need not enact criminal laws to express its public policies, the absence of such a law (or an equivalently severe civil sanction) appears to have caused *City Bank* to conclude that German sovereign interests were not particularly strong. Other authorities have also considered the legal form in which foreign interests are manifested in assessing the weight of those interests. *See Restatement (Third) Foreign Relations Law* §442, comment c (1987).

16. *Nationality and residence of person from whom discovery is sought.* What role does the nationality of the party from whom discovery is sought play in extraterritorial discovery analysis? *See Restatement (Second) Foreign Relations Law* §40(d) (1965) (listing nationality as relevant factor); *Société Internationale v. Rogers*, 357 U.S. 197 (1958) (relying on Swiss nationality in ordering discovery since Swiss company was best situated to deal with Swiss government). *Compare Restatement (Third) Foreign Relations Law* §442(1)(c) (1987) (not specifically including nationality of party from whom discovery is sought as relevant factor). The party from whom discovery was sought in *City Bank* was, of course, a U.S. business. Should this be relevant to the outcome of the case?

In *United States v. Rubin*, 836 F.2d 1096 (8th Cir. 1988), a U.S. national appealed his conviction for securities fraud, arguing among other things that the district court had erred by quashing a *subpoena duces tecum* that sought allegedly exculpatory documents located in the Cayman Islands. The court of appeals held that the district court had properly quashed the defendant's subpoena. It observed initially that Cayman Islands bank secrecy laws forbid disclosure of the records in question. Moreover, the court emphasized, the defendant "is attempting to obtain records of Cayman Island residents who are neither the target of a United States criminal proceeding nor subject to the laws of the United States." *Id.* at 1002. *Rubin* contrasted this to cases in which "the government was seeking the bank records of United States citizens who are the target of a United States criminal proceeding" and in which U.S. courts concluded that "the Cayman interest in preserving the privacy of its banking customers is substantially diminished when the privacy interest is that of an American citizen (or entity) subject to American laws." *Id.* (citing *United States v. Field*, 532 F.2d 404, 408-409 (5th Cir. 1976)).

Is it appropriate for U.S. courts to order extraterritorial discovery more readily from U.S. companies than from foreign entities? Although extraterritorial discovery from U.S. nationals might not offend foreign states, is it wise to establish a double standard that treats U.S. companies less favorably than their foreign competitors?

2. Extraterritorial Discovery in Violation of Foreign Law: Contemporary Approaches

The *Restatement (Third) Foreign Relations Law* adopted a specific provision for moderating extraterritorial U.S. discovery, based on the interest-balancing analysis of *City Bank* and similar lower court decisions. The formulation, which is contained in §442 (excerpted in Appendix AA), was adopted only after considerable debate, and continues to be controversial.[114] Nonetheless, many courts have applied variations of §442's interest-balancing analysis.[115] Examples include the Seventh Circuit's opinion in *Reinsurance Co. of America, Inc. v. Administratia Asigurarilor de Stat*, and the decision in *In re Air Cargo Shipping Services Antitrust Litigation*, both excerpted below.

FOREIGN RELATIONS LAW OF THE UNITED STATES RESTATEMENT (THIRD)
§442 (1987) [excerpted in Appendix AA]

REINSURANCE CO. OF AMERICA, INC. v. ADMINISTRATIA ASIGURARILOR DE STAT
902 F.2d 1275 (7th Cir. 1990)

BAUER, CHIEF JUDGE. Plaintiff-appellee Reinsurance Company of America ("RCA"), an Illinois corporation engaged in the reinsurance business, [cross-appeals] asserting that the district court's denial of its request for post-judgment interrogatories [directed to defendant-appellant Administratia Asigurarilor de Stat ("ADAS")], was . . . an abuse of discretion. We find no abuse of discretion by the district court . . . and therefore affirm. . . .

114. *E.g.*, Houck, *Restatement of the Foreign Relations Law of the United States (Revised): Issues and Resolutions*, 20 Int'l Law. 1361 (1986); Robinson, *Compelling Discovery and Evidence in International Litigation*, 18 Int'l Law. 533 (1984). In preliminary drafts, §442 was numbered as §437, and early judicial decisions refer to §437.

115. For some of the cases relying on §442, *see Société National Industrielle Aérospatiale v. U.S. District Court*, 482 U.S. 522 (1987); *Reinsurance Co. of America, Inc. v. Administratia Asigurarilor de Stat*, 902 F.2d 1275 (7th Cir. 1990) ("new §442 provides a modified balancing test substantially similar to that of . . . §40"); *United States v. First Nat'l Bank of Chicago*, 699 F.2d 341, 346 (7th Cir. 1983); *In re Baycol Prods. Litig.*, 2003 WL 22023449 (D. Minn. 2003) (magistrate judge); *In re Air Crash at Taipei, Taiwan on Oct. 31, 2000*, 211 F.R.D. 374, 377-379 (C.D. Cal. 2002); *McKesson Corp. v. Islamic Republic of Iran*, 1991 U.S. Dist. LEXIS 10226 (D.D.C. 1991). *Cf. United States v. Davis*, 767 F.2d 1025, 1034 n.16 (2d Cir. 1985) (noting existence of §437, but following Restatement (Second) §40); *Garpeg Ltd. v. United States*, 583 F. Supp. 789 (S.D.N.Y. 1984).

Plaintiff and defendant entered into two Quota Share Retrocession Agreements, effective October 1, 1977, and January 1, 1980, respectively. Under the terms of the contract, ADAS agreed to participate as a retrocessionaire for risks which were reinsured by RCA. The contract was executed by representatives of RCA and CJV Associates ("CJV") which acted as agents for ADAS. On January 19, 1983, RCA sued ADAS for breach of these retrocession agreements. ADAS removed the case to federal court. . . . [The district court eventually granted summary judgment against ADAS on liability and] awarded damages in the amount of $337,597.00. [RCA then sought to compel ADAS to answer certain postjudgment interrogatories designed to assist it in enforcing the judgment in its favor.] ADAS . . . objected to RCA's inquiries as violating Rumanian law prohibiting disclosure of state secrets. RCA then sought a motion to compel responses. . . . [T]he district court denied RCA's motion to compel indicating that the balance of the interests weighed in favor of Romania's laws protecting national secrecy.

RCA contends that the district court abused its discretion by denying its request for post-judgment interrogatories. . . . Each of the interrogatories in controversy asked ADAS to provide information regarding insurance contracts with firms in the United States, Canada and the United Kingdom.[116] In explaining this refusal to furnish a response, ADAS claimed that Rumanian law forbade disclosure of the requested information.[117]

When the laws of the United States and those of a foreign country are in conflict, as they are here, this circuit, along with several others, has employed a balancing test derived

116. Specifically, ADAS objected to interrogatories 2, 6, and 9. These interrogatories provided:

2. For each and every person, partnership or corporation maintaining a residence or which is domiciled in the United States, which is insured or reinsured by ADAS and which has exposures in the United States, Canada and/or the United Kingdom, identify the following: (a) The name and address of the insured or reinsured; (b) The policy treaty or facultative certificates which provide the coverage; and (c) The policy limit for each coverage in U.S. dollars.

6. State whether ADAS has in force any reinsurance agreements with any ceding companies located in the United States, Canada and/or the United Kingdom, pursuant to which funds held by such ceding companies earn interest which is ultimately payable to ADAS, and if so, identify for each: (a) The name of the ceding company; (b) The business address of the ceding company; (c) The date on which each agreement was entered into; and (d) The termination date, if any, for each agreement.

9. State whether ADAS has accepted reinsurance submissions from brokers or agents located in the United Kingdom who ADAS knows or believes receives business offerings from reinsurance brokers located in the United States and/or Canada, and if so, state: (a) Whether the United Kingdom brokers or agents issue cover-notes or other formal evidence of coverage on behalf of ADAS; (b) Whether the United Kingdom brokers or agents collect premiums which are ultimately due to ADAS, and if so; (c) Identify the brokers, agents or companies located in the United States and Canada who remit such premiums, and provide their business addresses.

117. ADAS particularly raises two points of Rumanian law defining "state secrets" and "service secrets." A rough translation of the relevant law . . . provides:

Art. 2. It is considered State secret according to the stipulations of the Penal Code, any information, data and documents which evidently show this character as well as those declared and qualified as such by a Council of Ministers decision.

The transmission or divulging of information data and documents which constitute State secrets, loss, detained outside Service duties, destruction [sic] alteration or taking away of documents with such character negligence which led to one of these facts or which enabled other persons to take possession of information data or documents which might endanger the economic, technical-scientific, military or political interests of the State as well as other infringement of the norms regarding the protection of the State secret, constitute unusually grave facts and are punished by penal law.

Art. 4. The information, data and documents which according to the present law do not constitute State secrets but are not destined to publicity are Service secrets and cannot be divulged.

Art. 251. The divulgement of the State secret, if this does not constitute infringement of art. 169, and also the divulgement of data or information which, although it does not constitute State secrets are not destined to publicity, if the act is of the nature to affect public interest, are punished by imprisonment from 6 months to 5 years.

from §40, *Restatement (Second) Foreign Relations Law* (1965) ("§40"). Applying [the §40] test, [the district court] determined that because Rumanian law considered the requested information a "service secret" and punished disclosure with criminal sanctions, and the law was apparently vigorously enforced, the balance favored ADAS's refusal to respond to the interrogatories over RCA's right to such responses. As the following discussion of the §40 factors demonstrates, [this] conclusion is correct.

Initially, we must balance the "vital national interests" of both the United States and Romania. We approach this task with some misgivings. As Judge Marshall of the Northern District of Illinois noted, "the judiciary has little expertise, or perhaps even authority to evaluate the economic and social policies of a foreign country." *In re Uranium Antitrust Litigation*, 480 F. Supp. 1138 (N.D. Ill. 1979). Moreover, when allegedly considering only "vital national interests," we are left with the rather ridiculous assignment of determining which competing national interest is the more vital. Whatever the semantic difficulties of our test, the courts of the United States undoubtedly have a vital interest in providing a forum for the final resolution of disputes and for enforcing these judgments. This rather general interest, however, is not as compelling as those interests implicated in other §40 cases cited by RCA. For instance, in *Graco, Inc. v. Kremlin, Inc.*, the court held that the United States had a compelling interest in ensuring that its patent laws were not undermined by a French blocking statute. Similarly, vital interests are involved when a commercial dispute implicates the integrity of American antitrust laws. *In re Uranium Antitrust Litigation, supra.* When the United States itself is a party in the litigation, the national interest involved may become compelling. Thus, enforcement of the tax laws, *United States v. Vetco, supra*, and the securities laws, *SEC v. Banca della Svizzera Italiana*, have been considered compelling national interest. In the case at hand, though, we are presented with a private dispute between two reinsurance corporations. The disputed materials are the subject of a post-judgment interrogatory request and not vital to the case-in-chief. While there is unquestionably a vital national interest in protecting the finality of judgments and meaningfully enforcing these decisions, this interest alone does not rise to the level of those found in these earlier cases.

Against this, we must weigh on the opposing side of the balance the Rumanian interest in protecting its state and so-called "service" secrets. Given the scope of its protective laws and the strict penalties it imposes for any violation, Romania places a high price on this secrecy. Unlike a blocking statute, Romania's law appears to be directed at domestic affairs rather than merely protecting Rumanian corporations from foreign discovery request. *Cf. Compagnie Française d'Assurance v. Phillips Petroleum Co.*, 105 F.R.D. 16, 30 (S.D.N.Y. 1984) (French blocking statute "never expected nor intended to be enforced against French subjects but was intended rather to provide them with tactical weapons and bargaining chips in foreign courts."). Given this choice between the relative interests of Romania in its national secrecy and the American interest in enforcing its judicial decisions, we have determined that Romania's, at least on the facts before us, appears to be the more immediate and compelling.[118]

The remaining factors are far less problematic. In evaluating the extent and nature of the hardship imposed upon ADAS by inconsistent enforcement actions, §40(b), our sole

---

118. We pause to note that between the argument of this case and this decision, there has been a profound and much celebrated change in the political structure of Romania. The high priority which national secrecy enjoyed under the old regime is presumably no longer in vogue. Neither plaintiff nor defendant, however, has brought supplemental information to this court regarding this matter. Thus we must decide this case on the facts before us. Should the parties believe that new facts have materially altered the foundation of our judgment, they are free to resubmit their claims. We note, however, that relevant changes in the law must be presented to the court rather than illusory changes in the political climate which provide little basis for re-evaluating this decision.

reference is the affidavit provided by Mr. Dumitriu, a Rumanian attorney. Mr. Dumitriu states that the officers of ADAS would face criminal sanctions for revealing "service" secrets as classified by the Rumanian government. Moreover, Dumitriu's affidavit states that the law protecting state and "service" secrets is vigorously enforced, thus, satisfying the factor under §40(e). RCA contends that §40(c), [which concerns] the extent to which the required conduct is to take place in the territory of the foreign state, was mismeasured by the district court. We disagree. All the information which plaintiff sought through these interrogatories is located within Romania. The offices of ADAS are located within Romania as well. Any responses to RCA's interrogatories would have to be prepared in Romania using this information. Obviously, ADAS could deliver this material to a site in the United States and prepare some of the responses there, as plaintiff contends. Yet, this does not affect the very real threat faced by officials at ADAS who would have to remove this information from Romania. Finally, it is undisputed that §40(d), the consideration of the nationality of the person in question, weighs in favor of ADAS. This is a Rumanian corporation whose offices are located only within that country. Those persons forced to comply with this discovery order would be Rumanian citizens subject to the criminal sanctions of the law protecting state secrets. Thus, considering all five factors provided under §40 — the competing national interests involved, the hardship to ADAS of compliance, the place of compliance, the nationality of ADAS and the likelihood of enforcement of the criminal sanctions — we conclude that on balance the district court correctly denied RCA's motion to compel responses to the interrogatories.

Complicating our determination, however, is the recent publication of the *Restatement (Third) Foreign Relations Law*. . . . [T]he new §442 follows the path announced by this court in *First National Bank of Chicago* that "[t]he fact that foreign law may subject a person to criminal sanctions in the foreign country if he produces certain information does not automatically bar a domestic court from compelling production." 699 F.2d 341, 345 (7th Cir. 1983). The new §442 provides a modified balancing test substantially similar to that of *First National Bank of Chicago* and §40. Although there are certain differences in emphasis, the factors to be considered remain largely synonymous and do not alter our determination that the district court's judgment was reasonable and correct.

Section 442, however, does make one significant change to the old standard by introducing an element of good faith to be included at the court's discretion. . . . Similarly, in *United States v. First National Bank of Chicago*, this court remanded a case to the Northern District of Illinois in order to determine whether First Chicago must make a good faith effort to receive permission from the Greek authorities to produce bank information located in Greece but unavailable due to the bank secrecy provisions of Greek law. . . . Our earlier case is easily distinguishable from the one at hand. In *First National Bank of Chicago*, the Greek law at issue appeared to provide a limited exception for furnishing certain information. Thus, it was unclear whether compliance would have resulted in criminal sanctions. Moreover, a treaty existed between the United States and Greece for the purposes of diplomatically resolving such banking disputes. Given this welter of uncertainty, there appeared at least the possibility of obtaining permission from the Greek authorities if First Chicago made a good faith effort.

By contrast, here the law is apparently strictly applied. There are no exceptions to Romania's secrecy law. There exists no treaty between these governments to diplomatically resolve such problems. Unlike . . . *First National Bank of Chicago* . . . there would be little purpose to requiring a good faith effort to comply with the discovery request. Therefore, the district court's decision not to impose a requirement of a good faith effort upon ADAS was reasonable. The denial of RCA's motion to compel responses was consistent with our prior holdings as well as the new standard under *Restatement (Third)* §442 and not an abuse of discretion. [The Court left RCA free, however, to renew its discovery request in light of new legislation in Romania.]

EASTERBROOK, CIRCUIT JUDGE, concurring. Events have overtaken this case. Romania adopted a strict code of secrecy out of fear that sunlight would jeopardize the regime. Under Romanian law, anything that is not a "State secret" is a "Service secret" — in other words, everything is a secret. The regime fell nonetheless, and not because of loose lips. Revolution in Romania means that yesterday's secrecy laws are of little moment. . . .

We have not heard from Romania's lawyer, perhaps because he has no idea who speaks for his client. I therefore join the court's opinion, which observes that the plaintiff may return to the district court for a fresh decision under contemporary law. The court applies a balancing approach that the parties agree is apt. Given this agreement, we have no occasion to decide whether to follow the *Restatement (Third) Foreign Relations Law* §442 (1987), to the extent we may create a federal common law of privileges. If we were free of the parties' agreement, I would be most reluctant to accept an approach that calls on the district judge to throw a heap of factors on a table and then slice and dice to taste. Although it is easy to identify many relevant considerations, as the ALI's Restatement does, a court's job is to reach judgments on the basis of rules of law, rather than to use a different recipe for each meal.

Two sources of law dominate here. The first is Federal Rule of Evidence 501, which says that when state law supplies the rule of decision (as Illinois law does in this case), it also supplies the law with respect to privileges. Federal Rule of Civil Procedure 69, which governs this enforcement action, also directs the court to follow state law. Does (would?) Illinois follow the *Restatement (Third) Foreign Relations* in deciding whether documents held abroad are privileged? The parties do not discuss the question.

The other rules come from the Foreign Sovereign Immunities Act, 28 U.S.C. §§1602-11. Defendant in this case ("AAS"), an arm of the Rumanian government, is open to suit under §1605(a)(2) because the claim is based on its commercial activity within the United States. With a default judgment in hand, plaintiff seeks to discover AAS's assets. AAS invokes Romania's secrecy laws, which forbid it to disclose any information in its hands, even information about assets located outside Romania. Their effect is that no judgment against Romania may be collected. I doubt that general interest-balancing principles of the sort discussed in the *Restatement* may countermand the decision of Congress that courts of the United States may impose liability. The FSIA provides that a prevailing party may execute against the foreign government's assets except to the extent the statute creates exceptions, *see* §§1609-11. This catalog of what is, and is not, available to satisfy a judgment eclipses any attempt by the foreign defendant to create its preferred list by using its domestic secrecy law. If we allow foreign states to exempt themselves after the fashion of (the old) Romania, we might as well forget about the FSIA.

Even the *Restatement* is no longer as favorable to foreign defendants as it once was. The catalog of relevant interests in §442(1)(c) of the *Third Restatement* is not to be used generally to assess demands for information. It is designed to inform the discretionary decision whether to impose one of the sanctions mentioned in Fed. R. Civ. P. 37 and §442(1)(b), such as contempt of court of a default judgment. As a rule, parties are entitled to seek information and, without regard to balancing national interests, the foreign party must make a good faith effort to secure its release, §442(2)(a) and (b). If release is not forthcoming, then

> a court or agency may, in appropriate cases, make findings of fact adverse to a party that has failed to comply with the order for production, even if that party has made a good faith effort

to secure permission from the foreign authorities to make the information available and that effort has been unsuccessful.

Section 442(2)(c). In other words, the party seeking the information obtains its equivalent despite foreign secrecy rules. The balancing approach of §442(1)(c) in conjunction with the adverse inference under §442(2)(c) means that the party caught between inconsistent obligations to two nations with equal sovereign authority is not subject to extra penalty, such as imprisonment or fines exceeding the stakes of the case. A party may lose no more than the case — and then only if the law favors the adverse party once the facts have been deemed admitted under §442(2)(c). Such an approach is a careful accommodation of the legitimate interests of the parties and the nations alike, all without authorizing unconfined "balancing" of the "importance" of the nations' policies.

If I thought we had to do such balancing, I would be at sea. If I knew how to balance incommensurables, I would be hard pressed to agree with courts saying (as the district judge did) that a suit by the government is "more important" than private litigation. In a capitalist economy enforcement of contracts is a subject of the first magnitude. The gravity of the nation's interest is no less when it decides to enforce vital rules through private initiative. A court would need to know the "importance" of the substantive rule, which is not well correlated with the enforcement mechanism. (The antitrust laws are "more important" than the littering laws although the former are largely enforced by private suits and the latter by public prosecutions.)

Section 442(2)(c) breaks down in a case such as this one in which the judgment has been rendered and the prevailing party seeks to discover assets. This problem, which the Restatement does not discuss, is closer in principle to the rule of §442(2)(c) than to that of §442(1). Ascertaining assets under Rule 69 is not a "sanction" for misconduct. A prevailing party is entitled to relief; so much has been determined by the judgment. At this point resort to secrecy laws does nothing to nullify the rendering nation's substantive law. Because the FSIA does not contemplate such a step, foreign secrecy laws are not sufficient to block disclosures under Rule 69.

IN RE AIR CARGO SHIPPING SERVICES ANTITRUST LITIGATION
2010 WL 2976220 (E.D.N.Y. July 23, 2010)

POHORELSKY, MAGISTRATE JUDGE. The plaintiffs have moved to compel the defendant South African Airways, Ltd. ("SAA") to produce certain transaction and cost information and to respond to their First Set of Interrogatories.[119] The defendant has withheld the requested information on the ground that disclosure is prohibited by South African law, specifically, the Protection of Businesses Act No. 99 of 1978 (hereinafter the "Act"). That Act absolutely prohibits anyone from, among other things, furnishing "any information as to any business whether carried on in or outside the Republic" in response to any request or interrogatory "emanating from outside the Republic in connection with any civil proceedings," "except with the permission of the Minister of Economic Affairs." Protection of Businesses Act 99 of 1978 §1(b) (S. Afr.).

. . .

---

119. [S]tated generally, the terms ["transaction information" and "cost information"] cover information about the pricing of each shipment for which SAA provided services, and the costs incurred in providing those services. The Interrogatories seek information about meetings and participants in communications concerning the imposition of various surcharges and related pricing matters, as well as information about the surcharges actually imposed by SAA.

[W]hen deciding whether to compel the production of information located abroad, the court should consider the following factors: (1) the importance to the litigation of the information requested; (2) the degree of specificity of the requests; (3) whether the information originated in the United States; (4) the availability of alternative means of securing the information; (5) the extent to which noncompliance with the request would undermine important interests of the United States, or compliance with the request would undermine important interests of the state where the information is located; (6) the hardship that compliance would impose on the party from whom the information is sought; and (7) the good faith of the party resisting production [citing *Restatement* §442].

The above considerations weigh heavily in favor of the plaintiffs' motion. There is no serious dispute that the requested information is highly relevant to the case. Since this is a price-fixing case, the transaction and cost information sought by the plaintiffs is essential to the proof of their claims against SAA. It is the principal way — perhaps the only way — that the plaintiffs will be able to establish the prices charged and the costs incurred by SAA for its air cargo services, and thus be able to prove whether SAA engaged in unlawful price-fixing. The interrogatories seek information about, among other things, communications directly related to the price-fixing allegations in the complaint, communications which would be central to the plaintiffs' proof of SAA's participation in a price-fixing conspiracy. The defendant argues that the information is not crucial because it relates to only a relatively minor player in the conspiracy, but that does not render the information any less essential to the proof of the plaintiffs' claims against SAA.

Nor is there any serious dispute about the specificity of the plaintiffs' requests, which provide ample detail about precisely what information is sought. Although the requests for transaction and cost data may result in the production of large volumes of data, the requests themselves are highly detailed and there is no attempt to show that production would be burdensome. Similarly, the interrogatories are specific about the meetings and communications to which they are directed, and the surcharge information they seek.

Comparing the national interests at stake, the United States interest in enforcing antitrust laws through private civil actions is one of fundamental importance to this country's effort to encourage and maintain a competitive economy. The South African interest in enforcing the blocking statute at issue here, on the other hand, is entitled to less deference since it is not a substantive rule of law at variance with the law of the United States, but rather one whose primary purpose is to protect its citizens from discovery obligations in foreign courts.

The possibility that SAA will suffer hardship in complying with a discovery order is speculative at best. Although the defendant cites the prospect of criminal sanctions if it violates the blocking statute, it has cited no instance in which such sanctions have ever been imposed. Any such prospect is further diminished by SAA's contention that it is itself an organ of the government.

The defendant's principal argument in opposition to a compulsion order is that the plaintiffs have not established that the information they seek is otherwise unavailable. SAA points out that approval for disclosure is possible under the blocking statute if authorized by the [Ministry] from whom the defendant "has sought official guidance." At oral argument, however, the defendant conceded that the matter has been under consideration by the Ministry since the beginning of this year, without any indication when a decision will be made. Nor has the defendant made any showing about how or under what standards the Ministry treats such requests for "official guidance." Given the passage of time and the absence of any indication that the Ministry will soon act on the defendant's request for guidance, it is fair to conclude that this "alternative" for obtaining the requested information has not proved to be viable. Nor is there any other avenue to obtain disclosure. Regardless of how a request for disclosure is made, the South African statute does not permit disclosure absent approval by the Ministry. Thus, for example, in contrast to the French blocking statute that was the subject of the previous opinion by this court, the South African statute does not even permit a response via the Hague Convention or letters rogatory absent ultimate approval by the Ministry.

Of the remaining two considerations, only one clearly favors the defendant, the fact that most if not all of the information apparently did not originate in the United States, but rather elsewhere. The question of the defendant's good faith in resisting disclosure cannot be resolved on the basis of the information in the present record.

Having weighed the above considerations, the court is convinced that the plaintiffs' motion should be granted. Accordingly, SAA is directed to produce the requested transaction and cost data and to respond fully to the plaintiffs' interrogatories. Supplemental responses to the interrogatories that provide the information requested are to be served within thirty days. As to the transaction and cost data, the defendant shall meet and confer with the plaintiffs' counsel within fourteen days in an effort to reach agreement on a reasonable schedule for production of that data.

Notes on Restatement §442, Reinsurance Company *and* Air Cargo

1. *Section 442's heightened standard of materiality.* The comments to §442 state that extraterritorial discovery ordinarily should be ordered only of materials that are "necessary to the action — typically, evidence not otherwise readily obtainable — and directly relevant and material." *Id.* comment a. This standard is considerably more rigorous than the usually broad scope of discoverable material under domestic U.S. discovery rules. *See* Fed. R. Civ. P. 26(b)(1) ("any matter, not privileged, that is relevant to the claim or defense of any party"); *Hickman v. Taylor,* 329 U.S. 495, 507 (1947); *supra* p. 966.

In applying an interest-balancing analysis, some lower courts appear to have adopted §442's heightened standard of materiality for extraterritorial discovery and to either have refused to order discovery of documents whose importance was not apparent or to have limited the scope of discovery. *See, e.g., Trade Dev. Bank v. Continental Ins. Co.,* 469 F.2d 35, 40-41 (2d Cir. 1972); *In re Baycol Prods. Litig.,* 2003 WL 22023449, at *6 (D. Minn. 2003); *Minpeco, SA v. Conticommodity Services Inc.,* 116 F.R.D. 517 (S.D.N.Y. 1987); *Graco, Inc. v. Kremlin, Inc.,* 101 F.R.D. 503, 515-516 (N.D. Ill. 1984). *See also White v. Kenneth Warren & Son, Ltd.,* 203 F.R.D. 369, 375 (N.D. Ill. 2001) ("Where evidence sought is, 'directly relevant,' to issues in litigation, this factor weighs in favor of production."). Is this requirement of heightened materiality appropriate? Will a U.S. party, litigating against a foreign party, also be entitled to a heightened standard of materiality with respect to discovery of its U.S. materials? Is it appropriate to order discovery in an asymmetrical fashion?

2. *Section 442's interest-balancing analysis.* Section 442(1)(a)'s general rule permitting direct extraterritorial discovery is elaborated upon by subsection (1)(c), which calls on U.S. courts to take into account a variety of different factors. Several lower courts have adopted interest-balancing analyses that are similar to that proposed by §442(1)(c). *See United States v. Davis,* 767 F.2d 1025 (2d Cir. 1985); *Dexia Credit Local v. Rogan,* 231 F.R.D. 538, 540, 542-543 (N.D. Ill. 2004); *In re Grand Jury Subpoena dated August 9, 2000,* 218 F. Supp. 2d 544, 554, 562-564 (S.D.N.Y. 2002); *In re Air Crash at Taipei, Taiwan on Oct. 31, 2000,* 211 F.R.D. 374, 377 (C.D. Cal. 2002). *See also Société Nationale Industrielle Aérospatiale v. U.S. District Court,* 482 U.S. 522 (1987).

3. *The strength of the sovereign interests.* Like multi-factor balancing tests elsewhere, a key issue in the context of §442 analysis is which factors ultimately drive a court's analysis of the proper outcome. According to some courts, "[t]he extent to which noncompliance with the request would undermine important interests of the United States or compliance with the request would undermine the important interests of the state where the information is located, *is the most important of the five factors* [set forth in §442]." *Strauss v. Credit Lyonnais, S.A.*, 242 F.R.D. 199, 214 (E.D.N.Y. 2007) (magistrate judge) (emphasis added). Is this view consistent with §442? Is it a sensible approach?

To the extent this approach is correct, it underscores the importance of carefully balancing the competing interests of two or more sovereign governments. Are there some U.S. interests that are so compelling as to outweigh any countervailing foreign interest? What about combating international terrorism in the context of civil suits against banks that are alleged to have facilitated terrorist attacks? *See, e.g., Strauss v. Credit Lyonnais, S.A.*, 249 F.R.D. 429 (E.D.N.Y. 2008) (magistrate judge); *Weiss v. National Westminster Bank, PLC*, 242 F.R.D. 33 (E.D.N.Y. 2007) (magistrate judge). Conversely, are there foreign interests that are so compelling as to outweigh countervailing U.S. interests? What about a foreign government's interest in conducting an ongoing investigation (in a case where the requesting party seeks information that its opponent has provided the foreign government on a confidential basis during the course of the investigation)? *Compare In re Rubber Chemicals Antitrust Litig.*, 486 F. Supp. 2d 1078 (N.D. Cal. 2007) (magistrate judge) (holding that principles of comity outweighed need for documents produced to European Commission in the course of competition law investigation) *with In re Vivendi Universal, S.A. Securities Litig.*, 618 F. Supp. 2d 335 (S.D.N.Y. 2009) (ordering production of documents produced at request of foreign company's statutory auditors); *Emerson Elec. Co. v. Le Carbone Lorraine, S.A.*, 2008 WL 4126602 (D.N.J. Aug. 27, 2008) (ordering production of documents previously supplied to American and European authorities in course of investigation). *See generally In re Payment Card Interchange Fee and Merchant Discount Antitrust Litig.*, 2010 WL 3420517 (E.D.N.Y. Aug. 27, 2010) (collecting cases that reach conflicting conclusions on this question).

   4. *Section 442 and injunctions.* Suppose that, instead of a foreign blocking statute impeding the discovery, a foreign court had entered an injunction precluding the foreign party from disclosing the information sought in the U.S. proceeding. Is a foreign court injunction entitled to more or less weight than a foreign blocking statute under §442? *See Export-Import Bank of U.S. v. Asia Pulp & Paper Co., Ltd.*, 2009 WL 1055673 (S.D.N.Y. Apr. 17, 2009) (ordering discovery even on the assumption that foreign court's injunction prohibited disclosure); *Abiola v. Abubakar*, 2007 WL 2875493 (N.D. Ill. Sept. 28, 2007) (ordering discovery despite foreign court's injunction). How do considerations of comity in the context of "anti-discovery" injunctions compare to those in the context of antisuit injunctions? *See supra* pp. 578-579.

   5. *Continued application of* Société Internationale'*s two-step analysis under §442.* Section 442 continues to use the two-step approach to issuing discovery orders and imposing sanctions that the Supreme Court adopted in *Société Internationale*. Does §442(2) alter the traditional rules governing the imposition of sanctions or the determination of good faith noncompliance with discovery orders?

   6. *Comparison between discovery under §442 and foreign sovereign compulsion doctrine.* Compare §442(2) with the foreign sovereign compulsion doctrine, particularly as set out in §441 of the *Third Restatement* (excerpted in Appendix AA), which generally forbids states from requiring conduct abroad in violation of the law of the place of the conduct. What explains the different approaches? Consider:

   [Section] 441 is concerned with conflicts in substantive law between two or more states . . . in situations where both states have jurisdiction to prescribe; [§442], in contrast, deals with the litigation process, and in particular with pretrial procedures, in situations where the forum state by definition has jurisdiction over the parties and the proceedings, and foreign substantive law would not ordinarily be involved. Accordingly, somewhat less deference to the law of the other state may be called for. *Restatement (Third) Foreign Relations Law* §442, comment e (1987).

Is this persuasive? Are there better explanations for the different treatment?

   7. *Power to impose sanctions under §442.* Note that §442(2)(c) preserves the authority of U.S. courts to make findings of fact adverse to a party who fails to provide requested discovery, even where the party has unsuccessfully made good faith efforts to obtain waivers of foreign blocking statutes. In addition, however, note that §442(2)(b) restricts the circumstances in which sanctions of contempt, dismissal, or default are imposed. *See Shcherbakovskiy v. Da Capo Al Fine, Ltd.*, 490 F.3d 130 (2d Cir. 2007) (holding that district court abused discretion in dismissing claims and entering default judgment based on foreign litigant's failure to produce documents). For a rare instance in which a court orders "that the allegations in [the plaintiffs' complaint] relevant to [the defendant's] liability are taken as established," *see Abiola v. Abubakar*, 2007 WL 2875493, at *20 (N.D. Ill. Sept. 28, 2007).

   8. *Distinction between private and governmental litigation.* Both *Société Internationale* and *City Bank* were cases involving the U.S. Government, while *Reinsurance Company* involved only a private U.S. plaintiff. What weight should the U.S. Government's role in litigation have in the interest-balancing envisioned by §40 and *City Bank*? Note that *City Bank* relied on the U.S. Government's involvement in emphasizing the strength of U.S. interests, while *Reinsurance Company* emphasized that only "private litigation" was involved. *See also United States v. Vetco, Inc.*, 691 F.2d 1281, 1288 (9th Cir. 1981) ("[T]he instant case turns upon an IRS summons issued pursuant to an investigation of potentially criminal conduct. Such summonses appear to serve a more pressing national function than civil discovery."); *United States v. Toyota Motor Corp.*, 569 F. Supp. 1158, 1162-1163 (C.D. Cal. 1983) ("[T]he fact that this action was brought by the government, rather than a private litigant, weighs heavily towards finding a strong American interest in obtaining the information sought"). Note Judge Easterbrook's criticism of this distinction between private and governmental litigation. Is his criticism persuasive?

   Some commentators have suggested that the interest-balancing test is a misnomer in cases involving the U.S. Government. In their view, "the balance of the interests test is virtually no test at all. In any case where the U.S. government asserts an interest in enforcing its laws overseas, America's interests will be held paramount by an American court." Razzano, *Conflicts of Interest Between American & Foreign Law: Does the "Balance of Interest" Test Always Equal America's Interest?*, 37 Int'l Law. 61, 67 (2003). Is this right? What about in civil cases where the U.S. Government is not a party? What does this suggest about the balancing test?

   9. *Federal common law character of §442 analysis.* Judge Easterbrook's concurrence suggests substantial doubt that "a federal common law of privilege" governs conflicts between extraterritorial U.S. discovery orders and foreign blocking statutes. Is this skepticism warranted? Consider the federal common law rules that have been recognized in other international litigation contexts. *See supra* pp. 257-275 (attribution of liability among foreign state entities); pp. 557-560 (comity as basis for dismissing suit); pp. 567-588 (antisuit injunctions); pp. 801-817 (act of state); and pp. 683-689 (extraterritoriality). Does extraterritorial discovery in violation of foreign law implicate sufficiently weighty federal interests in foreign policy and commerce to justify a rule of federal common law?

   10. *Basis for* **Reinsurance Company** *decision.* What were the decisive considerations underlying the decision in *Reinsurance Company*? The supposedly "vigorous" enforcement of Romanian secrecy laws? The fact that these laws were neutrally applied in domestic affairs, not just in cases involving U.S. discovery? The nationality of ADAS? The supposedly attenuated U.S. interests? Which of these factors is most significant? Which could be ignored?

Did *Reinsurance Company* reach the correct result? What result would Judge Easterbrook have reached? What weight should be assigned to the fact that the requested information related principally to contracts involving U.S. companies?

11. *Criticism of §442's interest-balancing.* The *Reinsurance Company* Court characterizes the interest-balancing test as "rather ridiculous," while Judge Easterbrook's concurrence says: "If I thought we had to do such balancing, I would be at sea." Does §442 provide any meaningful guidance for courts and litigants? Do judicial decisions interpreting §442 (and its predecessors) do so? Compare the debate about interest-balancing in the context of legislative jurisdiction and choice of law, *supra* pp. 685-687, 703-704, 752.

12. *Significance of foreign privileges in U.S. discovery.* Rule 26 does not require the disclosure of documents or information to the extent they are subject to an applicable privilege. What law determines the "applicable privilege"? According to Federal Rule of Evidence 501, questions of privilege are "governed by the principles of common law." These "principles of common law" include choice-of-law principles. *See Astra Aktiebolag v. Andrx Pharm., Inc.*, 208 F.R.D. 92, 97 (S.D.N.Y. 2002). Consequently, as in other areas explored in this book, discovery disputes raise difficult questions regarding what law governs an asserted privilege.

Most countries recognize various privileges against compelled disclosure of information. Examples include the attorney-client privilege and marital privileges.

Traditionally, the forum's law governed procedural matters, which were generally understood as including questions of privilege. *See Restatement (Second) Conflict of Laws* §§122, 127 (1971); *Société Internationale v. Brownell*, 225 F.2d 532 (D.C. Cir. 1955), *rev'd on other grounds*, 357 U.S. 197 (1958).

More recently, several courts have taken a more flexible view and appear not to rigidly apply the forum's law, and to view claims of privilege with substantially greater favor than claims based upon blocking statutes. *E.g., Linde v. Arab Bank PLC*, 262 F.R.D. 136 (E.D.N.Y. 2009) (magistrate judge) (taking Israeli privilege law into account in §442 analysis); *In re Lernout & Hauspie Securities Litig.*, 218 F.R.D. 348, 353 n.10 (D. Mass. 2003) (taking Belgian discovery procedures into account in light of privilege claim); *Tulip Computers Int'l BV v. Dell Computer Corp.*, 210 F.R.D. 100, 104 (D. Del. 2002) ("communications that relate to activity in a foreign country are governed by that country's privilege law, while communications that 'touch base' with the United States are controlled by United States privilege law."); *Aktiebolag v. Andrx Pharmaceuticals, Inc.*, 208 F.R.D. 92, 97-102 (S.D.N.Y. 2002) (detailed privilege analysis applying three different countries' laws to different documents depending on nature of document, whether it "touched base" in United States and relationship between foreign and American law); *Renfield Corp. v. Remy Martin SA*, 98 F.R.D. 442 (D. Del. 1982) (applying choice of law principles to determine that U.S., not French, attorney-client privilege should govern); *Duplan Corp. v. Deering Milliken, Inc.*, 397 F. Supp. 1146, 1169-1171 (D.S.C. 1974) ("any communications touching base with the United States will be governed by the federal discovery rules while any communications related to matters solely involving France or Great Britain will be governed by the applicable foreign statute"). *See generally 2M Asset Management, LLC v. Netmass, Inc.*, 2007 WL 666987 (E.D. Tex. Feb. 28, 2007) (magistrate judge) (summarizing different approaches). Why do foreign privileges appear to warrant different treatment than blocking statutes? Is there a principled basis for a distinction? *See also supra* pp. 972-973.

In addressing the choice-of-law question, some courts apply the "touch base" approach. *See, e.g., Golden Trade S.r.L. v. Lee Apparel Co.*, 143 F.R.D. 514, 522 (S.D.N.Y.

1992). The contours of this approach are not entirely well defined, but the analysis appears to hinge on which jurisdiction has the predominant interest in the privilege (or non-privileged status) of the communications. For example, if an Italian company seeks advice from its in-house counsel in connection with its intellectual property rights in Italy, Italian law would govern the privilege claim *even in litigation in the United States.* By contrast, communications generated in connection with legal rights or proceedings in the United States will be governed by U.S. law *even if they are generated by the same individual.*

Of course, a great deal turns on determining which country has the predominant interest in the privilege claim. Under the "touch base" approach, factors relevant to this determination include, among other things, the law that is the subject of the communication and the location of any present or prospective proceedings that are the subject of the communication. Considerations of comity and public policy also may factor into the analysis. *See Gucci America, Inc. v. Guess? Inc.*, 271 F.R.D. 58 (S.D.N.Y. Sept. 23, 2010) (magistrate judge).

Does this approach make sense? Does it even begin to provide the sort of predictability to which conflicts principles often aspire? Even if a degree of flexibility is necessary in conflicts principles, does the "touch base" approach provide any predictability at all? Why should considerations of comity factor into the choice-of-law determination governing privilege claims when they already factor into the question whether to order discovery? On the other hand, what would be wrong with a rule that provided privilege claims are subject to the law of the forum? Or the law of the country in which the document was generated or the communication occurred? Or, in the case of claims of attorney-client privilege, the law of the country of the attorney? Don't these alternatives raise similar problems of overinclusiveness, underinclusiveness, and lack of sensitivity to the competing policy concerns? In that respect, isn't the "touch base" approach perhaps the best one can hope for in this area?

13. *Discovery from foreign sovereign entities.* Private parties often seek to take discovery from the foreign sovereign entities, just as they would do in the case of private litigants. In general, U.S. courts have been willing to order discovery from foreign sovereigns in actions under the FSIA. *E.g., First City, Texas Houston, NA v. Rafidain Bank*, 281 F.3d 48 (2d Cir. 2002) (postjudgment discovery); *McKesson Corp. v. Islamic Republic of Iran*, 185 F.R.D. 70 (D.D.C. 1999); *McKesson Corp. v. Islamic Republic of Iran*, 138 F.R.D. 1 (D.D.C. 1991); *United States v. Crawford Enterprises, Inc.*, 643 F. Supp. 370 (S.D. Tex. 1986). This willingness extends to "jurisdictional" discovery, as well as discovery on the merits. *E.g., In re Bedford Computer Corp.*, 114 B.R. 2 (D.N.H. 1990); *In the Matter of SEDCO, Inc.*, 543 F. Supp. 561, 569 (S.D. Tex. 1982). *See generally* Comment, *Jurisdictional Discovery Under the Foreign Sovereign Immunities Act*, 66 U. Chi. L. Rev. 1029 (1999). Indeed, U.S. courts appear to be less receptive to efforts of foreign states to rely on their own blocking statutes than they are to the efforts of private litigants. *See Laker Airways v. Pan American World Airways*, 103 F.R.D. 42, 47 (D.D.C. 1984) ("the [defendant's] argument is really a claim that it should not have to comply with discovery because its owner — the German government — has decided . . . not to comply with such discovery. Such a claim of *de facto* immunity is fallacious, and is rejected"); *Aérospatiale*, 482 U.S. at 544 n.29 ("It would be particularly incongruous to recognize such a preference [against direct U.S. discovery] for corporations that are wholly owned by the enacting nation.").

Nonetheless, some U.S. courts have also required careful consideration of foreign governmental interests before ordering discovery from foreign sovereign entities, and have suggested that discovery concerning the acts of foreign government officials raises especially sensitive issues. *E.g., Environmental Tectonics v. W.S. Kirkpatrick, Inc.*, 847 F.2d 1052, 1062 n.11 (3d Cir. 1988), *rev'd on other grounds*, 484 U.S. 852 (1990).

14. *Discovery and the act of state doctrine.* As discussed *supra* pp. 801-817, the act of state doctrine precludes U.S. courts from reviewing the validity of certain actions of foreign nations. Most lower courts have rejected the argument that the act of state doctrine forbids ordering extraterritorial discovery that will violate foreign blocking statutes. These courts reason that their discovery orders do not require passing on the validity of the foreign statutes — they merely require foreign nationals to disregard those foreign statutes. *See United States v. Bank of Nova Scotia,* 740 F.2d 817, 831-832 (11th Cir. 1985); *Associated Container Transp. (Australia) v. United States,* 705 F.2d 53, 60-62 (2d Cir. 1983); *In re Payment Card Interchange Fee and Merchant Discount Antitrust Litig.,* 2010 WL 3420517, at *5 n.10 (E.D.N.Y. Aug. 27, 2010). *But see Credit Suisse v. U.S. Dist. Ct.,* 130 F.3d 1342 (9th Cir. 1997) (granting Swiss bank's petition for writ of mandamus, dismissing action for injunctive and declaratory relief on act of state grounds and justifying mandamus partly on ground that "compelling the Banks to respond to the discovery requests therefore places the Banks in the position of having to choose between being in contempt of court for failing to comply with the district court's order, or violating Swiss banking secrecy and penal laws by complying with the order").

E.   Discovery Pursuant to Customary International Judicial Assistance

As described previously, U.S. courts have traditionally favored the use of direct discovery orders under the Federal Rules of Civil Procedure to obtain evidence located abroad. In some circumstances, however, persons who refuse to provide information voluntarily may not be subject to the personal jurisdiction or subpoena power of U.S. courts.[120] In these cases, U.S. courts are unable to order discovery directly and litigants must seek the assistance of foreign courts.

The historic method of obtaining foreign judicial assistance in taking evidence abroad was by letter rogatory. As described previously, a letter rogatory is a formal request by the court of one nation to the courts of another country for assistance in performing judicial acts.[121] Federal legislation specifically authorizes the Department of State to receive and transmit letters rogatory from and to foreign courts (while not precluding direct transmittal of letters rogatory between courts).[122]

The Federal Rules clearly contemplate the use of letters rogatory and most federal courts have also concluded that they possess inherent authority to issue letters rogatory.[123] The Department of State has prepared a guide to the preparation and

120. *See supra* pp. 990-998.
121. *See supra* pp. 912-913. For cases where letters rogatory were used to obtain evidence located abroad, *see Ethypharm S.A. France v. Abbott Laboratories,* 271 F.R.D. 82 (D. Del. 2010) (magistrate judge); *Pronova BioPharma Norge AS v. Teva Pharmaceuticals USA, Inc.,* 708 F. Supp. 2d 450 (D. Del. 2010) (magistrate judge); *Brake Parts, Inc. v. Lewis,* 2009 WL 1939039 (E.D. Ky. July 6, 2009); *In re Baycol Prods. Litig.,* 348 F. Supp. 2d 1058 (D. Minn. 2004); *Abbott Laboratories v. Impax Laboratories, Inc.,* 2004 WL 1622223 (D. Del. 2004); *Tulip Computers Intern. BV v. Dell Computer Corp.,* 254 F. Supp. 2d 469 (D. Del. 2003). *Compare Seoul Semiconductor, Ltd. v. Nokia Corp.,* 590 F. Supp. 2d 832 (E.D. Tex. 2008) (denying letter of request directed at French Government). A variety of forms exist for letters rogatory requesting assistance in the taking of evidence. *See, e.g.,* 22 C.F.R. §§92.54-92.66 (2006); 4 J. Moore, *Moore's Federal Practice* §§28.01, 28.10, 28.12 (2007); 3 J. Moore & L. Frumer, 4 *Moore's Manual: Federal Practice Forms,* Forms No. 15A:50-52 (2010); B. Ristau, *International Judicial Assistance* §§3-3-1 through 3-3-5 (rev. ed. 2000).
122. 28 U.S.C. §1781.
123. *United States v. Reagan,* 453 F.2d 165, 171-173 (6th Cir. 1971); *Zassenhaus v. Evening Star Newspaper Co.,* 404 F.2d 1361 (D.C. Cir. 1968); *United States v. Staples,* 256 F.2d 290 (9th Cir. 1958); *Evanston Ins. Co. v. OEA, Inc.,* 2006 WL 1652315, at *1 (E.D. Cal. 2006); *United States v. Strong,* 608 F. Supp. 188, 194 (E.D. Pa. 1985); *B & L Drilling Electronics v. Totco,* 87 F.R.D. 543, 545 (W.D. Okla. 1978); *De Villeneuve v. Morning Journal Ass'n,* 206 F. 70 (S.D.N.Y.

transmission of letters rogatory, which sets forth an appropriate format and provides guidance on necessary elements.[124] In the discovery context, a U.S. letter rogatory will typically request the foreign court receiving the letter to compel a person within the foreign court's jurisdiction to provide specified testimony or documents to the foreign court, which will in turn forward the evidence to the requesting court.

When letters rogatory are executed as requested, they can serve important purposes. Most obviously, if the person from whom discovery is sought is not subject to U.S. jurisdiction or subpoena power, then proceeding by letter rogatory may be the only avenue for compelling discovery from a recalcitrant foreign witness. Moreover, taking evidence abroad by letter rogatory will not offend foreign sovereignty, since the foreign state may decide whether to grant its assistance and a foreign judge will preside over the evidence-taking process.[125] Finally, in countries that forbid U.S. depositions within their borders, letters rogatory may provide the only method for obtaining evidence from cooperative witnesses who do not wish to travel to the United States.

Despite their potential importance, letters rogatory have historically had significant disadvantages as a means of obtaining extraterritorial discovery. First, foreign courts are under no obligation to execute letters rogatory. Foreign courts have frequently refused to execute U.S. letters of request—including because of poor diplomatic relations, because the underlying dispute involves claims that conflict with foreign public policy, or simply because of bureaucratic inertia.[126] Moreover, even when foreign courts agree to execute letters rogatory, they often prove to be unwilling to require the full extent of discovery sought by U.S. letters of request; the precise limits that foreign courts will place on U.S. discovery requests vary from country to country.[127] Finally, in at least some nations, courts object to (or misunderstand) "pretrial discovery" and will honor only requests for materials to be used as evidence at trial.[128]

When foreign courts provide judicial assistance to U.S. litigants, they ordinarily will do so according to their own judicial procedures. In the case of oral testimony, this can often mean that no oath is administered to the deponent, no transcript is made, and questioning is conducted by the judge (without participation by counsel).[129] Although U.S. procedural rules have been modified to ensure that evidence produced according to foreign procedures of this sort is admissible,[130] the value of the evidence-taking exercise may nonetheless be substantially diminished. Similarly, foreign courts will seldom enforce broad U.S.-style document requests to which U.S. lawyers are accustomed.[131]

1913); *Gross v. Palmer*, 105 F. 833 (C.C. Ill. 1900); *In re Urethane Antitrust Litig.*, 267 F.R.D. 361, 364 (D. Kan. 2010) (magistrate judge).

124. U.S. Department of State, Preparation of Letters Rogatory, *available at* http://travel.state.gov/law/judicial/judicial_683.html; U.S. Department of State, Obtaining Evidence Abroad, *available at* http://travel.state.gov/law/judicial/judicial_688.html.

125. Note, *Taking Evidence Outside of the United States*, 55 B.U. L. Rev. 368, 374 (1975).

126. *See, e.g.*, Jones, *International Judicial Assistance: Procedural Chaos and a Program for Reform*, 62 Yale L.J. 515, 529-534 (1953).

127. *E.g., Rio Tinto Zinc Corp. v. Westinghouse Elec. Corp.*[1978] 1 All E.R. 434 (H.L. 1977); *In re Raychem Corp. v. Canusa Coating Sys., Inc.* [1970] 14 D.L.R.3d 684; *In re Radio Corp. of America v. Rauland Corp.* [1956] 5 D.L.R.2d 424.

128. *Cf. Court of Appeals (Munich), Petition for Review of an Administrative Ruling under Secs. 23 et seq.*, EGGVG, Docket Nos. 9 VA 4/80, 9 VA 3/80, *reprinted in* 20 Int'l Leg. Mats. 1025 & 1049 (1981) (decision of West German appellate court under Hague Evidence Convention).

129. Jones, *International Judicial Assistance: Procedural Chaos and a Program for Reform*, 62 Yale L.J. 515, 529-532 (1953); Note, *Taking Evidence Outside of the United States*, 55 B.U. L. Rev. 368, 372-374 (1975).

130. Fed. R. Civ. P. 28(b) provides "Evidence obtained in response to a letter rogatory need not be excluded merely for the reason that it is not a verbatim transcript, or because the testimony was not taken under oath, or that the testimony was not taken under oath or for any similar departure from the requirements for depositions taken within the United States under these rules."

131. *See supra* pp. 969-971.

Finally, letters rogatory must be transmitted to the appropriate foreign court through diplomatic channels.[132] This usually requires sending the letter to the U.S. Department of State, which will forward the letter to the receiving state's ministry of foreign affairs, which will in turn transmit the letter to the foreign court.[133] This process can be slow and unpredictable; it often requires a minimum of three months for completion and delays of more than a year are not uncommon.[134] Some countries permit direct transmittal of letters rogatory from the requesting U.S. court to the receiving foreign courts; where this alternative is available it should be used because it reduces somewhat the risk of bureaucratic delays.

F.   Discovery Abroad Under the Hague Evidence Convention

1.   Overview of the Hague Evidence Convention[135]

The difficulties that traditionally arose in the execution of U.S. letters rogatory led the United States to undertake efforts to facilitate the transnational taking of evidence. The principal U.S. initiative occurred in the Hague Conference on Private International Law.[136] At the urging of the United States, the Hague Conference negotiated and drafted the Hague Convention on the Taking of Evidence Abroad in Civil or Commercial Matters ("Hague Evidence Convention"),[137] in a comparatively short period of time, between 1967 and 1968. The United States became a party to the Convention in 1972. There are now more than 50 parties to the Convention, including most European nations.[138]

The avowed objective of the Convention was "to improve mutual judicial cooperation in civil or commercial matters."[139] This required drafting an agreement providing "methods to reconcile the differing legal philosophies of the Civil Law, Common Law, and other

---

132. *See* 22 C.F.R. §92.66 (2011) ; B. Ristau, *International Judicial Assistance* §3-3-3 (rev. ed. 2000).

133. As noted above, 28 U.S.C. §1781(a)(2) authorizes the transmittal of letters rogatory to foreign authorities by the Department of State.

134. *See* U.S. Department of State Circular on "Obtaining Evidence Abroad," *available at* http://travel.state.gov/law/judicial/judicial_688.html; Note, *Taking Evidence Outside of the United States*, 55 B.U. L. Rev. 368, 374 n.38 (1975).

135. Commentary on the Hague Evidence Convention includes Borchers, *The Incredible Shrinking Hague Evidence Convention*, 38 Tex. Int'l L.J. 73 (2003); Collins, *The Hague Evidence Convention and Discovery: A Serious Misunderstanding?*, 35 Int'l & Comp. L.Q. 765 (1986); Davies, *Bypassing the Hague Evidence Convention: Private International Law Implications of the Use of Video and Audio Conference Technology in Transnational Litigation*, 55 Am. J. Comp. L. 205 (2007); Iontcheva, *Sovereignty on Our Terms*, 110 Yale L.J. 885 (2001); Nafziger, *Another Look at the Hague Evidence Convention after* Aerospatiale, 38 Tex. Int'l L.J. 103 (2003); Oxman, *The Choice Between Direct Discovery and Other Means of Obtaining Evidence Abroad: The Impact of the Hague Evidence Convention*, 37 U. Miami L. Rev. 733 (1983); Prescott & Alley, *Effective Evidence-Taking Under the Hague Convention*, 22 Int'l Law. 939 (1988); Rogers, *On the Exclusivity of the Hague Evidence Convention*, 21 Tex. Int'l L.J. 441 (1986); B. Ristau, *International Judicial Assistance* §5-1-1 through 5-3-3 (rev. ed. 2000); Weis, *The Federal Rules and the Hague Conventions: Concerns of Conformity and Comity*, 50 U. Pitt L. Rev. 903 (1989).

136. The Hague Conference on Private International Law is described *supra* pp. 910-912. In addition, the United States also is a party to the Inter-American Convention Regarding Letters Rogatory, a regional designed to facilitate inter-state requests for judicial assistance in civil matters. *See In re Clerici*, 481 F.3d 1324 (11th Cir. 2008).

137. Hague Convention on the Taking of Evidence Abroad in Civil or Commercial Matters, Mar. 18, 1970; entered into force for the United States October 7, 1972, 23 U.S.T. 2555, T.I.A.S. No. 7444 [hereinafter Hague Evidence Convention]. The Hague Convention is reproduced in Appendix M.

138. Parties include, among others, Argentina, Australia, China (Hong Kong), France, Germany, India, Mexico, Russia, Singapore, South Africa, Sweden, the United Kingdom, and the United States. For a complete list, *see* http://www.hcch.net/index_en.php?act=conventions.status&cid=82.

139. Hague Evidence Convention, Preamble.

systems," as well as "methods to satisfy doctrines of judicial sovereignty."[140] In broad outline, the Convention's drafters sought to accomplish these goals by establishing a "Central Authority" mechanism.

States that ratify the Convention are obliged to designate a "Central Authority." When a court in one Member State seeks evidence located in another Member State, it sends a "letter of request" to the Central Authority for the second state. With limited exceptions, the receiving Central Authority is obliged by the Convention to execute the foreign letters of request that it receives. The receiving Central Authority forwards such letters to the appropriate local court for execution, including by coercive means, and the evidence obtained thereunder is then returned to the requesting court.

a. Scope of the Convention. The Convention is subject to a number of significant limitations. First, the Convention is applicable only to the taking of evidence in "civil or commercial" matters. As with the Hague Service Convention, this phrase is not defined in either the Convention or its negotiating history and Member States have expressed differing views about the phrase's scope. Thus, the United States and United Kingdom exclude criminal matters from the Convention's coverage, but regard fiscal, administrative, and "public law" proceedings as "civil or commercial."[141] In contrast, most civil law states do not regard fiscal proceedings as within the Convention's scope, and probably have the same view with respect to administrative matters.[142] It is not yet clear how foreign countries will respond to letters of request in cases involving only treble damage claims under the antitrust laws.[143]

Second, the Convention is limited to requests for assistance made by "judicial authorities."[144] Some commentators have suggested that this formulation excludes administrative agencies and executive bodies, as well as requests by courts in aid of such entities.[145] The status of other proceedings, such as bankruptcy and arbitration, is unclear.[146]

---

140. Rapport de la Commission Speciale, 4 *Conference de La Haye de droit international privé: Actes et documents de la Onzieme session* 55 (1970) [hereinafter cited as Hague Evidence Convention Negotiating History]. The Hague Evidence Convention Negotiating History is a compilation of reports, questionnaires, drafts, and other communications regarding the Convention, as well as a transcript of certain negotiating sessions.

141. Report of U.S. Delegation to the Special Commission on the Operation of the Convention of 18 March 1970 on the Taking of Evidence Abroad in Civil or Commercial Matters, The Hague, The Netherlands, 12-15 June, 1978, 17 Int'l Leg. Mat. 1417 (1978) [hereafter "U.S. Delegation Report"]; *In re State of Norway*, 28 Int'l Leg. Mat. 693 (House of Lords 1989) (tax assessment proceeding is "civil" matter under both U.K. and Norwegian law); Report on the Work of the Special Commission of April 1989 on the Operation of the Hague Convention of 15 November 1965 on the Service Abroad of Judicial and Extrajudicial Documents in Civil or Commercial Matters and of 18 March 1970 on the Taking of Evidence Abroad in Civil or Commercial Matters [hereinafter "1989 Report on Hague Conventions"], 28 Int'l Leg. Mat. 1556, 1563-1565 (1989). Criminal matters often are the subject of Mutual Legal Assistance Treaties between the United States and other countries. For a good discussion of the relationship between such treaties and the Hague Convention, *see United Kingdom v. United States*, 228 F.3d 1312, 1316-1317 (11th Cir. 2001).

142. *See* U.S. Delegation Report; 1989 Report on Hague Conventions. The 1989 Report on Hague Conventions observed that "a number of experts" would leave it to the requesting State to characterize actions as "civil or commercial." 1989 Report on Hague Conventions at 1559.

143. *See Court of Appeals (Munich) Petition for Review of an Administrative Ruling under Secs. 23 et seq.*, EGGVG, Docket Nos. 9 VA 4/80, 9 VA 3180, *reprinted in* 20 Int'l Leg. Mats. 1025 & 1049 (1981) (rejecting claim that antitrust suit is not "civil or commercial" because U.S. action involved other claims not seeking treble damages). *Compare* the reactions in the past of some foreign Central Authorities to U.S. requests under the Hague Service Convention in cases seeking punitive damages, *supra* pp. 914-915.

144. Hague Evidence Convention, Article 16.

145. B. Ristau, *International Judicial Assistance* §5-1-4 (rev. ed. 2000).

146. Report on the Second Meeting of the Special Commission on the Operation of the Hague Convention of 18 March 1970 on the Taking of Evidence Abroad in Civil or Commercial Matters, The Hague, The Netherlands July 1985, *reprinted in* 24 Int'l Leg. Mats. 1668, 1676 (1985) [hereinafter cited as "Second U.S. Delegation Report"]. *See* 1989 Report on Hague Conventions, 28 Int'l Leg. Mats. 1556, 1563 (1989).

Finally, the Convention is limited to requests "to obtain evidence" or to perform "other judicial act[s]."[147] These phrases are not defined, although the Convention's negotiating history makes it clear that they include oral depositions, the production of documents, and the inspection of property.[148] Moreover, Article 1 of the Convention makes it clear that the Convention applies to requests for assistance even with respect to proceedings that have not commenced.[149] The Convention's coverage of other quasi-judicial acts — such as appointing receivers or conducting conciliation — is unclear.[150]

b. Central Authority Mechanism. The principal means of taking evidence under the Convention is through the "letter of request" procedure provided by Articles 1 through 14. The Convention establishes the framework for this procedure by requiring each Member State to designate a "Central Authority."[151] The purpose of the Central Authority is to receive letters of request from courts in other nations and to transmit the foreign requests to the appropriate domestic authorities for execution.[152] Unlike letters rogatory, Member States are generally *required* by the Convention to execute properly completed letters of request.

Two features of the obligation to execute letters of request are important. First, Member States are required to obtain requested evidence by applying the "appropriate measures of compulsion" available under internal law.[153] Thus, the Convention enables U.S. litigants to obtain evidence even if the foreign witness is uncooperative. Second, Article 9 of the Convention provides that letters of request "shall be executed expeditiously." At least in theory, the lengthy delays that letters rogatory encounter should be avoided.[154]

The general obligation of Member States to execute letters of request under the Convention is subject to a number of important exceptions. Article 5 of the Convention allows Central Authorities to object to letters of request that do not "comply with the provisions" of the Convention. The objecting state is required to notify the requesting state promptly of its objections. Among the grounds for objection are failure of a letter of request to fall within the scope of Article 1 of the Convention or failure of a letter of request to satisfy the language or information requirements of Articles 3 and 4.[155]

Article 12 of the Convention permits a receiving state to refuse to execute requests seeking the performance of nonjudicial functions or that the receiving state considers would prejudice its "sovereignty or security." Although other international agreements

---

147. Hague Evidence Convention, Article 1. It is clear, however, that the Convention does not apply to requests for the service of process or recognition of judgments, which are the subject of a specific exclusion in Article 1.

148. Hague Evidence Convention Negotiating History 57, 203.

149. Hague Evidence Convention, Article 1 ("judicial proceedings, commenced *or contemplated*") (emphasis added).

150. Hague Evidence Convention Negotiating History at 203.

151. Hague Evidence Convention, Article 2.

152. Article I of the Convention authorizes "a judicial authority of a Contracting State . . . in accordance with the provisions of the law of that State" to request evidence-taking by means of a letter of request. After some uncertainty, foreign Central Authorities have generally accepted the proposition that U.S. law authorizes attorneys to act as "judicial authorities" in preparing letters of request.

153. Hague Evidence Convention, Article 10. The requested state is only obliged to apply the same degree of compulsion in responding to letters of request as is available in domestic actions. Thus, if compulsory process would not be available in purely domestic proceedings, then the receiving court need not use compulsion in attempting to execute a letter of request under the Convention.

154. Practical experience under the Convention suggests that between four and ten months are generally required for the execution of letters of request, and that longer delays are entirely possible.

155. "Any difficulties which may arise between Contracting States in connection with the operation of the Convention shall be settled through diplomatic channels." Hague Evidence Convention, Article 36.

have used the "sovereignty or security" formula,[156] there has been little experience with the exception. The leading decision was in 1978, when the House of Lords concluded that the phrase could be properly invoked by the United Kingdom to refuse execution of a U.S. request for information in the Westinghouse uranium antitrust litigation. The House of Lords reasoned that "[i]t is axiomatic that in antitrust matters the policy of one state may be to defend what it is the policy of another state to attack."[157]

c. **Article 23's Exception for Pretrial Document Requests.** One of the Convention's exceptions to the obligation to execute letters of request is of special importance to U.S. litigants. Under Article 23, Member States are given the option to declare that they "will not execute Letters of Request issued for the purpose of obtaining pretrial discovery of documents as known in Common Law countries." With the exception of the Czech Republic and Slovakia, Israel, and the United States, all Member States to the Convention have entered Article 23 declarations. A number of these declarations flatly provide that the declaring State will execute no letter of request seeking pretrial discovery.[158] Several other Member States have made more limited Article 23 declarations, which refuse execution of requests for "pretrial discovery" except as to requests for specified documents or classes of documents.[159]

Article 23 severely limits the value of the Convention to U.S. litigants by permitting Member States to refuse to execute a large category of U.S. requests for the production of documents. The drafters of the Convention included Article 23 at the United Kingdom's suggestion. Although the Convention's negotiating history contains little discussion of the provision,[160] subsequent events indicate the reasoning underlying Article 23.

In adopting Article 23, the United Kingdom and at least some other countries wished to ensure that they would not be obliged to assist U.S. "fishing expeditions" into the files of local companies. Moreover, it appears that civil law states, at least in part, misunderstood the purposes of U.S. discovery. Subsequent discussions among the Convention's Member States suggested that most civil law states believed that U.S. pretrial discovery is permitted before initiation of any legal proceedings and can be used to build a case that subsequently may be filed. Clarifications of the role of pretrial discovery by U.S. authorities have alleviated some, but not all, civil law concerns. As a consequence, several foreign states have limited the scope of their Article 23 reservations.[161]

Article 23 allows refusals to execute letters of request only for "pretrial discovery of documents." Thus, Article 23 does not purport to affect methods of discovery other than requests for document production (*i.e.*, depositions or interrogatories) or the examination of documents for purposes other than pretrial discovery (*i.e.*, for production as

---

156. *E.g.*, 1 Am. J. Comp. L. 282 (1952) (1954 Hague Civil Procedure Convention); Hague Service Convention; *supra* pp. 914-915.

157. *Rio Tinto Zinc Corp. v. Westinghouse Elec. Corp.* [1978] 1 All E.R. 434, 448. Several members of the House of Lords also emphasized that the U.S. antitrust investigation involved the extraterritorial application of U.S. law to conduct in the United Kingdom. Article 12 provides that execution cannot be refused solely because a receiving state does not recognize a particular cause of action or claims exclusive subject matter jurisdiction over the subject matter of the action. The interplay of this provision with Article 12's "sovereignty or security" exception is not entirely clear, particularly in the light of the House of Lords' decision in *Westinghouse*.

158. These states currently include, among others, Australia, China (Hong Kong), France, Germany, Italy, Luxembourg, Norway, Portugal, South Africa, and Spain.

159. Nations with comparatively limited Article 23 declarations include, among others, the United Kingdom, Denmark, Finland, India, Mexico, Sweden, Switzerland, Singapore, and Venezuela. The United Kingdom's Article 23 declaration provides that no letter of request seeking pretrial discovery will be executed if the request requires a person to (1) state what documents relevant to the foreign proceeding are in his control; or (2) produce any document other than particular documents specified in the letter of request.

160. Hague Evidence Convention Negotiating History at 204.

161. *See Aérospatiale*, 482 U.S. at 536-537, 563-564.

evidence at trial). Nonetheless, as a practical matter, foreign law and practice determine the extent to which foreign courts will execute U.S. letters of request.[162] Because of the considerable differences between U.S. and civil law discovery, U.S. litigants not infrequently encounter foreign resistance to their letters of request.[163]

Even in England, where common law discovery rules are not dissimilar to U.S. procedures, Article 23 significantly restricts the value of the Convention to U.S. litigants. In *In re Asbestos Insurance*,[164] the House of Lords held that the United Kingdom's Article 23 reservation and the Evidence (Procedure in Other Jurisdictions) Act 1975 imposed strict limits on the assistance that English courts would provide under the Hague Evidence Convention. First, the House of Lords emphasized that "mere 'fishing' expeditions" would not be permitted.[165] Second, only "separately described" documents could be obtained: "an order for production of the respondent's 'monthly bank statements for the year 1984 relating to his current account' with a named bank would satisfy the requirements. . . . But a general request for 'all the respondent's bank statements for 1984' would in my view refer to a class of documents and would not be admissible."[166] Third, the documents requested "must be actual documents, about which there is evidence which has satisfied the judge that they exist, or at least that they did exist. . . ."[167]

Limitations on the scope of discovery in civil law states can be even more restrictive.[168] Most civil law jurisdictions have made declarations under Article 23 that narrowly limit the scope of documentary[169] disclosure, and practical experience has done little to erode these limits.

d. Alternative Methods of Taking Evidence Pursuant to the Hague Evidence Convention. In negotiating the Hague Evidence Convention, the United States was anxious to maximize the flexibility for taking evidence abroad. The Convention was drafted to include provisions permitting specified alternative methods of taking evidence which go beyond the basic Central Authority mechanism.[170] Unlike the Central Authority mechanism, however, these alternatives cannot be used without the approval (or acquiescence) of the receiving state and they do not ordinarily permit the use of compulsion to obtain evidence. In order to determine whether these alternatives are available in particular cases, counsel must consult the accessions of individual Member States to the Convention.[171]

Article 15 authorizes consuls (*i.e.*, certain diplomatic representatives of one nation stationed in a second country) to take evidence from nationals of the consul's home state. This right is subject to three important limitations: (1) the consul cannot use compulsion to require the giving of evidence; (2) each Member State may declare that consuls may take evidence only after obtaining permission to do so from the appropriate local

---

162. Hague Evidence Convention, Article 9 (discussed *infra* at p. 1032).
163. *See Rio Tinto Zinc Corp. v. Westinghouse Elec. Corp.* [1978] 1 All E.R. 434, (H.L. 1977), *reprinted in* 17 Int'l Leg. Mats. 38 (1978); *Appeal of ITT (Opinion and Judgment of October 31, 1980, Docket No. 9 VA 3/80), reprinted in* 20 Int'l Leg. Mat. 1049 (1981) (Germany); *Appeal of Siemens Siecor and Individual Corporate Officers (Opinion and Judgment of November 27, 1980), reprinted in* 20 Int'l Leg. Mats. 1025 (1981) (Germany).
164. [1985] 1 W.L.R. 331 (House of Lords).
165. [1985] 1 W.L.R. at 337.
166. [1985] 1 W.L.R. at 337-338.
167. [1985] 1 W.L.R. at 338.
168. *See supra* pp. 969-971.
169. *See supra* pp. 1029-1030.
170. Hague Evidence Convention, Articles 15-17.
171. Excerpted accessions of some Hague Evidence Convention parties are contained in Appendix M. The complete accessions of all Convention parties are contained at 28 U.S.C.A. §1781 (note).

authorities;[172] and (3) the consul may take evidence only for use in proceedings actually "commenced" (as opposed to merely "contemplated," *cf.* Article 1) in his or her home state.

Article 16 authorizes consuls to take evidence from nationals of the state where the consuls are stationed. Evidence-taking under Article 16 is subject to somewhat stricter limits than those under Article 15: (1) no compulsion may be used; (2) evidence can be taken only for proceedings that are actually commenced in the consul's home state; and (3) prior approval of the appropriate local authorities must be obtained in individual cases, unless the host state has affirmatively filed a declaration generally permitting Article 16 evidence-taking.[173]

Article 17 authorizes "commissioners" to take evidence within the receiving state,[174] but only subject to limitations equivalent to those imposed by Article 16: (1) no compulsion may be used; (2) evidence may be taken only for use in proceedings actually commenced in the courts of a member state; and (3) prior approval of the appropriate local authorities must be obtained in individual cases, unless the host state has filed a declaration generally permitting Article 17 evidence-taking. Commissioners must be appointed by a judicial authority of the requesting state, and not by a private body or executive authority (*e.g.*, an arbitral institution or a consul).

Persons taking evidence under Article 15, 16, or 17 are specifically authorized to administer oaths and to take any form of evidence that is not "incompatible with the law of the State where the evidence is taken or contrary to any permission granted" to the person taking the evidence.[175] Article 21 also establishes various procedural requirements for evidence-taking under Articles 15, 16, and 17. These include a requirement that persons from whom evidence is taken (except for nationals of the requesting state) be provided with a request in the language of the host state and that the request inform the recipient that he or she is entitled to legal representation and is not under any compulsion to appear. In addition, persons giving evidence under Articles 15 through 17 are entitled to invoke the same privileges and immunities as those authorized by Article 11 in connection with letters of request. The accessions of a number of signatories to the Convention provide important elaboration on these conditions.[176]

Although evidence-taking pursuant to Articles 15, 16, and 17 must ordinarily be conducted without compulsion, Article 18 permits Member States to declare that foreign consuls and commissioners may seek coercive orders from local authorities to compel the giving of evidence.[177] Finally, any Member State making a declaration under Article 15, 16, or 17, or granting a specific permission under these provisions, may attach whatever conditions it deems fit to the declaration or permission.[178]

---

172. Australia, Denmark, Iceland, Norway, Portugal, and Sweden have filed declarations requiring foreign consuls to obtain prior approval of evidence-taking under Article 15.

173. The United States, Finland and Norway have permitted Article 16 evidence-taking without prior approval. The United Kingdom, the Czech Republic, and Slovakia permit evidence-taking under Article 16 without prior approval only on the basis of reciprocity.

174. Commissioners are persons authorized by court order to preside over the taking of evidence in specified circumstances. The practice of appointing commissioners is a familiar procedure for taking depositions abroad under Fed. R. Civ. P. 28(b). *See supra* p. 981. At least in common law countries, commissioners are ordinarily entitled to exercise compulsion to require the giving of discovery. Article 17 of the Convention precludes the use of compulsion by commissioners.

175. Hague Evidence Convention, Article 21(a).

176. *See* Appendix M & *supra* note 171.

177. Only the United States and Italy filed an unconditional declaration under Article 18, although the United Kingdom, Cyprus, the Czech Republic, Switzerland, and Slovakia have declared that they will permit requests for compulsion on a reciprocal basis.

178. Hague Evidence Convention, Article 19.

e. Execution of Letters of Request.   The execution of letters of request under the Convention ordinarily occurs according to the judicial procedures of the receiving state. Article 9 states this general principle: "The judicial authority which executes a Letter of Request shall apply its own law as to the methods and procedures to be followed." The use of local judicial procedures in executing letters of request obviously has important practical consequences.

As described above, judicial procedures in civil law nations differ significantly from those in the United States.[179] In many states, the judge (and not counsel) conducts the examination of witnesses. In some states, counsel may attend the examination and suggest questions; in others, examinations may be closed to counsel. In addition, "counsel" in some countries refers only to local counsel; U.S. counsel may be unable to participate in, or sometimes even attend, evidence-taking sessions. Moreover, in many civil law countries the examination of witnesses is not under oath and is recorded in a summary prepared by the judge rather than in a verbatim transcript.

Because of differences among methods of evidence-taking, Article 9 requires receiving states to follow a "special method or procedure" for evidence-taking if requested by the applicant. Under this provision, U.S. attorneys can request permission to take verbatim transcripts of witnesses' testimony, to participate in questioning, to allow cross-examination, and the like.[180] The requirement that "special" methods be used is subject to two important exceptions: receiving states' judicial authorities need not follow a procedure that (1) "is incompatible with the internal law of the state of execution"; or (2) "is impossible of performance by reason of its internal practice and procedure or by reason of practical difficulties." In practice foreign authorities appear generally to have accommodated most requests by U.S. counsel.[181]

Article 10 governs the use of compulsion against witnesses who refuse to provide evidence sought by a proper letter of request. As noted earlier, receiving states are obligated in these circumstances to use coercive process to obtain the requested evidence. This obligation is subject to two limitations. First, any compulsion must be "appropriate." Second, the receiving state is only required to use the type of compulsion (if any) that its domestic law provides for analogous internal proceedings.

2. "Exclusivity" of the Hague Evidence Convention: *Aérospatiale*

The Hague Evidence Convention has been the subject of frequent litigation in the United States, most often over the extent to which U.S. litigants are required to use the Convention's procedures exclusively instead of resorting to the more customary route of direct U.S. discovery of information located abroad. Lower courts initially reached divergent conclusions as to the Convention's exclusivity.

Some courts concluded that Convention procedures had to be used in the first instance when a U.S. litigant sought to compel a party to produce documents, answer interrogatories, or make witnesses available from abroad.[182] Other courts ruled that the Convention was optional, at least where the U.S. court ordered that the formal

---

179. *See supra* pp. 969-971.

180. For descriptions of how these provisions operate in practice, *see* Collins, *Opportunities for and Obstacles to Obtaining Evidence in England for Use in Litigation in the United States*, 17 Int'l Law. 27 (1983); Platto, *Taking Evidence Abroad for Use in Civil Cases in the United States — A Practical Guide*, 16 Int'l Law. 575 (1982).

181. 1989 Report on Hague Conventions, 28 Int'l Leg. Mats. 1562 (1989); Second U.S. Delegation Report, 24 Int'l Leg. Mats. 1668, 1674-1675 (1985); U.S. Delegation Report, 17 Int'l Leg. Mats. 1425, 1431 (1978).

182. *See, e.g., Gebr. Eickhoff Maschinenfabrik und Eisengießerei Mott v. Starcher*, 328 S.E.2d 492 (W. Va. 1985); *Th. Goldschmidt AG v. Smith*, 676 S.W.2d 443 (Tex. Ct. App. 1984); *Vincent v. Ateliers de la Motobecane, SA*, 475 A.2d 686 (N.J. Super. 1984); *Pierburg GmbH & Co. KG v. Superior Court*, 186 Cal. Rptr. 876 (Cal. Ct. App. 1982).

production of the requested information take place on U.S. soil (*i.e.*, the deposition in the United States of a deponent who has traveled to this country or the production in the United States of documents transported here from abroad).[183] Finally, at least one court ruled that the Convention provided the exclusive means for obtaining evidence located in signatory countries; according to this decision, U.S. courts could not directly order discovery from signatory countries even if Convention procedures proved unavailing.[184] This conflict was resolved by the Supreme Court in its decision in *Aérospatiale*, excerpted below.

SOCIÉTÉ NATIONALE INDUSTRIELLE AÉROSPATIALE v. U.S. DISTRICT COURT
482 U.S. 522 (1987)

JUSTICE STEVENS. The United States, the Republic of France, and 15 other Nations have acceded to the Hague [Evidence] Convention. This Convention . . . prescribes certain procedures by which a judicial authority in one contracting State may request evidence located in another contracting State. The question presented in this case concerns the extent to which a Federal District Court must employ the procedures set forth in the Convention when litigants seek answers to interrogatories, the production of documents, and admissions from a French adversary over whom the court has personal jurisdiction.

The two petitioners are corporations owned by the Republic of France.[185] They are engaged in the business of designing, manufacturing, and marketing aircraft. One of their planes, the "Rallye," was allegedly advertised in American aviation publications as "the World's safest and most economical STOL plane." On August 19, 1980, a Rallye crashed in Iowa, injuring the pilot and a passenger. Dennis Jones, John George, and Rosa George brought separate suits based upon this accident in the United States District Court for the Southern District of Iowa, alleging that petitioners had manufactured and sold a defective plane and that they were guilty of negligence and breach of warranty. Petitioners answered the complaints, apparently without questioning the jurisdiction of the District Court. . . .

[After initially complying with plaintiffs' discovery requests, defendants subsequently resisted production. Among other things, defendants argued that the French "blocking statute"[186] forbade compliance with the U.S. discovery requests and that the Convention provided the exclusive means of obtaining discovery of evidence located in France. The trial court rejected both arguments and defendants appealed. The Court of Appeals for the Eighth Circuit held that "when the district court has jurisdiction over a foreign litigant the Hague Convention does not apply to the production of evidence in that litigant's possession, even though the documents and information sought may physically be located within the territory of a foreign signatory to the Convention."]

Petitioners correctly assert that both the discovery rules set forth in the Federal Rules of Civil Procedure and the Hague Convention are the law of the United States. This observation, however, does not dispose of the question before us; we must analyze the

183. *See, e.g., In re Messerschmitt Bolkow Blohm, GmbH*, 757 F.2d 729 (5th Cir. 1985), *vacated*, 483 U.S. 1002 (1987); *In re Anschuetz & Co., GmbH*, 754 F.2d 602 (5th Cir. 1985), *vacated*, 483 U.S. 1002 (1987); *International Society for Krishna Consciousness v. Lee*, 105 F.R.D. 435 (S.D.N.Y. 1984); *Cooper Indus. v. British Aerospace*, 102 F.R.D. 918 (S.D.N.Y. 1984).

184. *See Cuisinarts v. Robot Coupe, SA*, No. CV 80 0050083C (Conn. Super. Ct. July 22, 1982).

185. Petitioner Société Nationale Industrielle Aérospatiale is wholly owned by the Government of France. Petitioner Société de Construction d'Avions de Tourism is a wholly-owned subsidiary of Société Nationale Industrielle Aérospatiale.

186. [The French blocking statute is excerpted above at p. 975.]

interaction between these two bodies of federal law. Initially, we note that at least four different interpretations of the relationship between the federal discovery rules and the Hague Convention are possible. Two of these interpretations assume that the Hague Convention by its terms dictates the extent to which it supplants normal discovery rules. First, the Hague Convention might be read as requiring its use to the exclusion of any other discovery procedures whenever evidence located abroad is sought for use in an American court. Second, the Hague Convention might be interpreted to require first, but not exclusive, use of its procedures. Two other interpretations assume that international comity, rather than the obligations created by the treaty, should guide judicial resort to the Hague Convention. Third, then, the Convention might be viewed as establishing a supplemental set of discovery procedures, strictly optional under treaty law, to which concerns of comity nevertheless require first resort by American courts in all cases. Fourth, the treaty may be viewed as an undertaking among sovereigns to facilitate discovery to which an American court should resort when it deems that course of action appropriate, after considering the situations of the parties before it as well as the interests of the concerned foreign state. . . .

We reject the first two of the possible interpretations as inconsistent with the language and negotiating history of the Hague Convention. The Preamble of the Convention specifies its purpose "to facilitate the transmission and execution of Letters of Request" and to "improve mutual judicial cooperation in civil or commercial matters." The Preamble does not speak in mandatory terms which would purport to describe the procedures for all permissible transnational discovery and exclude all other existing practices.[187] The text of the Evidence Convention itself does not modify the law of any contracting State, require any contracting State to use the Convention procedures, either in requesting evidence or in responding to such requests, or compel any contracting State to change its own evidence-gathering procedures.

The Convention contains three chapters. Chapter I, entitled "Letters of Requests," and Chapter II, entitled "Taking of Evidence by Diplomatic Officers, Consular Agents and Commissioners," both use permissive rather than mandatory language. Thus, Article 1 provides that a judicial authority in one contracting State "may" forward a letter of request to the competent authority in another contracting State for the purpose of obtaining evidence. Similarly, Articles 15, 16, and 17 provide that diplomatic officers, consular agents, and commissioners "may . . . without compulsion," take evidence under certain conditions. The absence of any command that a contracting State must use Convention procedures when they are not needed is conspicuous.

[In addition,] Article 23 expressly authorizes a contracting State to declare that it will not execute any letter of request in aid of pretrial discovery in a common law country. Surely, if the Convention had been intended to replace completely the broad discovery powers that the common law courts in the United States previously exercised over foreign litigants subject to their jurisdiction, it would have been most anomalous for the common law contracting Parties to agree to Article 23, which enables a contracting Party to revoke its consent to the treaty's procedures for pretrial discovery. In the absence of explicit textual support, we are unable to accept the hypothesis that the common law contracting States abjured recourse to all preexisting discovery procedures at the same time that they accepted the possibility that a contracting Party could unilaterally abrogate even the Convention's procedures. Moreover, Article 27 plainly states that the Convention does

---

187. The Hague Conference on Private International Law's omission of mandatory language in the preamble is particularly significant in light of the same body's use of mandatory language in the Preamble to the Hague Service Convention.

not prevent a contracting State from using more liberal methods of rendering evidence than those authorized by the Convention. Thus, the text of the Evidence Convention, as well as the history of its proposal and ratification by the United States, unambiguously supports the conclusion that it was intended to establish optional procedures that would facilitate the taking of evidence abroad. . . . We conclude accordingly that the Hague Convention did not deprive the District Court of the jurisdiction it otherwise possessed to order a foreign national party before it to produce evidence physically located within a signatory nation.[188]

While the Hague Convention does not divest the District Court of jurisdiction to order discovery under the Federal Rules of Civil Procedure, the optional character of the Convention procedures sheds light on one aspect of the Court of Appeals' opinion that we consider erroneous. That court concluded that the Convention simply "does not apply" to discovery sought from a foreign litigant that is subject to the jurisdiction of an American court. Plaintiffs argue that this conclusion is supported by two considerations. First, the Federal Rules of Civil Procedure provide ample means for obtaining discovery from parties who are subject to the court's jurisdiction, while before the Convention was ratified it was often extremely difficult, if not impossible, to obtain evidence from non-party witnesses abroad. Plaintiffs contend that it is appropriate to construe the Convention as applying only in the area in which improvement was badly needed. Second, when a litigant is subject to the jurisdiction of the District Court, arguably the evidence it is required to produce is not "abroad" within the meaning of the Convention, even though it is in fact located in a foreign country at the time of the discovery request and even though it will have to be gathered or otherwise prepared abroad.

Nevertheless, the text of the Convention draws no distinction between evidence obtained from third parties and that obtained from the litigants themselves; nor does it purport to draw any sharp line between evidence that is "abroad" and evidence that is within the control of a party subject to the jurisdiction of the requesting court. Thus, it appears clear to us that the optional Convention procedures are available whenever they will facilitate the gathering of evidence by the means authorized in the Convention. Although these procedures are not mandatory, the Hague Convention does "apply" to the production of evidence in a litigant's possession in the sense that it is one method of seeking evidence that a court may elect to employ.

Petitioners contend that even if the Hague Convention's procedures are not mandatory, this Court should adopt a rule requiring that American litigants first resort to those procedures before initiating any discovery pursuant to the normal methods of the Federal Rules of Civil Procedure. The Court of Appeals rejected this argument

---

188. The opposite conclusion of exclusivity would create three unacceptable asymmetries. First, within any lawsuit between a national of the United States and a national of another contracting Party, the foreign party could obtain discovery under the Federal Rules of Civil Procedure, while the domestic party would be required to resort first to the procedures of the Hague Convention. This imbalance would run counter to the fundamental maxim of discovery that "[m]utual knowledge of all the relevant facts gathered by both parties is essential to proper litigation." *Hickman v. Taylor*, 329 U.S. 495, 507 (1947). Second, a rule of exclusivity would enable a company which is a citizen of another contracting State to compete with a domestic company on uneven terms, since the foreign company would be subject to less extensive discovery procedures in the event that both companies were sued in an American court. Petitioners made a voluntary decision to market their products in the United States. They are entitled to compete on equal terms with other companies operating in this market. But since the District Court unquestionably has personal jurisdiction over petitioners, they are subject to the same legal constraints, including the burdens associated with American juridical procedures, as their American competitors. A general rule according foreign nationals a preferred position in pretrial proceedings in our courts would conflict with the principle of equal opportunity that governs the market they elected to enter. Third, since a rule of first use of the Hague Convention would apply to cases in which a foreign party is a national of a contracting State, but not to cases in which a foreign party is a national of any other foreign state, the rule would confer an unwarranted advantage on some domestic litigants over others similarly situated.

because it was convinced that an American court's order ultimately requiring discovery that a foreign court had refused under Convention procedures would constitute "the greatest insult" to the sovereignty of that tribunal. We disagree with the Court of Appeals' view. It is well known that the scope of American discovery is often significantly broader than is permitted in other jurisdictions, and we are satisfied that foreign tribunals will recognize that the final decision on the evidence to be used in litigation conducted in American courts must be made by those courts. We therefore do not believe that an American court should refuse to make use of Convention procedures because of a concern that it may ultimately find it necessary to order the production of evidence that a foreign tribunal permitted a party to withhold.

Nevertheless, we cannot accept petitioners' invitation to announce a new rule of law that would require first resort to Convention procedures whenever discovery is sought from a foreign litigant. Assuming, without deciding, that we have the lawmaking power to do so, we are convinced that such a general rule would be unwise. In many situations the Letter of Request procedure authorized by the Convention would be unduly time consuming and expensive, as well as less certain to produce needed evidence than direct use of the Federal Rules.[189] A rule of first resort in all cases would therefore be inconsistent with the overriding interest in the "just, speedy, and inexpensive determination" of litigation in our courts. *See* Fed. Rule Civ. Proc. 1.

Petitioners argue that a rule of first resort is necessary to accord respect to the sovereignty of states in which evidence is located. It is true that the process of obtaining evidence in a civil law jurisdiction is normally conducted by a judicial officer rather than by private attorneys. Petitioners contend that if performed on French soil, for example, by an unauthorized person, such evidence-gathering might violate the "judicial sovereignty" of the host nation. Because it is only through the Convention that civil law nations have given their consent to evidence-gathering activities within their borders, petitioners argue, we have a duty to employ those procedures whenever they are available. We find that argument unpersuasive. If such a duty were to be inferred from the adoption of the Convention itself, we believe it would have been described in the text of that document. Moreover, the concept of international comity[190] requires in this context a more particularized analysis of the respective interests of the foreign nation and the requesting nation than petitioners' proposed general rule would generate.[191] We therefore decline to hold as a blanket matter that comity requires resort to Hague Evidence

---

189. We observe, however, that in other instances a litigant's first use of the Hague Convention procedures can be expected to yield more evidence abroad more promptly than use of the normal procedures governing pretrial civil discovery. In those instances, the calculations of the litigant will naturally lead to a first-use strategy.

190. Comity refers to the spirit of cooperation in which a domestic tribunal approaches the resolution of cases touching the laws and interests of over sovereign states. This Court referred to the doctrine of comity among nations in *Emory v. Grenough*, 3 Dall. 369, 370 n. (1797) (dismissing appeal from judgment for failure to plead diversity of citizenship, but setting forth an extract from a treatise by Ulrich Huber (1636-1694), a Dutch jurist):

> By the courtesy of nations, whatever laws are carried into execution, within the limits of any government, are considered as having the same effect everywhere, so far as they do not occasion a prejudice to the rights of the other governments, or their citizens . . . [n]othing would be more inconvenient in the promiscuous intercourse and practice of mankind, than that what was valid by the laws of one place, should be rendered of no effect elsewhere, by a diversity of law. . . . [*Id.*, at 370 n. (quoting 2 Huberus, B.I., Tit. 3, p. 26).

See also Hilton v. Guyot, 159 U.S. 113, 163-164 (1895). . . .

191. The nature of the concerns that guide a comity analysis are suggested by the *Restatement of Foreign Relations Law (Revised)* §437(1)(c) (Tent. Draft No. 7, 1986) (approved May 14, 1986). [This section is numbered §442 in the final draft of the *Restatement.*] While we recognize that §437 of the *Restatement* may not represent a consensus of international views on the scope of the District Court's power to order foreign discovery in the face of objections of foreign states, these factors are relevant to any comity analysis. . . .

Convention procedures without prior scrutiny in each case of the particular facts, sovereign interests, and likelihood that resort to those procedures will prove effective.[192]

Some discovery procedures are much more "intrusive" than others. In this case, for example, an interrogatory asking petitioners to identify the pilots who flew flight tests in the Rallye before it was certified for flight by the Federal Aviation Administration, or a request to admit that petitioners authorized certain advertising in a particular magazine, is certainly less intrusive than a request to produce all of the "design specifications, line drawings and engineering plans and all engineering change orders and plans and all drawings concerning the leading edge slats for the Rallye type aircraft manufactured by the Defendants." Even if a court might be persuaded that a particular document request was too burdensome or too "intrusive" to be granted in full, with or without an appropriate protective order, it might well refuse to insist upon the use of Convention procedures before requiring responses to simple interrogatories or requests for admissions. The exact line between reasonableness and unreasonableness in each case must be drawn by the trial court, based on its knowledge of the case and of the claims and interests of the parties and the governments whose statutes and policies they invoke.

American courts, in supervising pretrial proceedings, should exercise special vigilance to protect foreign litigants from the danger that unnecessary, or unduly burdensome, discovery may place them in a disadvantageous position. Judicial supervision of discovery should always seek to minimize its costs and inconvenience and to prevent improper uses of discovery requests. When it is necessary to seek evidence abroad, however, the District Court must supervise pretrial proceedings particularly closely to prevent discovery abuses. For example, the additional cost of transportation of documents or witnesses to or from foreign locations may increase the danger that discovery may be sought for the improper purpose of motivating settlement, rather than finding relevant and probative evidence. Objections to "abusive" discovery that foreign litigants advance should therefore receive the most careful consideration. In addition, we have long recognized the demands of comity in suits involving foreign states, either as parties or as sovereigns with a coordinate interest in the litigation. *See Hilton v. Guyot*, 159 U.S. 113 (1895). American courts should therefore take care to demonstrate due respect for any special problem confronted by the foreign litigant on account of its nationality or the location of its operations, and for any sovereign interest expressed by a foreign state. We do not articulate specific rules to guide this delicate task of adjudication.

In the case before us, the Magistrate and the Court of Appeals correctly refused to grant the broad protective order that petitioners requested. The Court of Appeals erred, however, in stating that the Evidence Convention does not apply to the pending

---

192. The French "blocking statute" does not alter our conclusion. It is well-settled that such statutes do not deprive an American court of the power to order a party subject to its jurisdiction to produce evidence even though the act of production may violate that statute. *See Société Internationale supra* note 97, at 204-206. Nor can the enactment of such a statute by a foreign nation require American courts to engraft a rule of first resort onto the Hague Convention, or otherwise to provide the nationals of such a country with a preferred status in our courts. It is clear that American courts are not required to adhere blindly to the directives of such a statute. Indeed, the language of the statute, if taken literally, would appear to represent an extraordinary exercise of legislative jurisdiction by the Republic of France over a United States District Judge, forbidding him or her from ordering any discovery from a party of French nationality, even simple requests for admissions or interrogatories that the party could respond to on the basis of personal knowledge. It would be particularly incongruous to recognize such a preference for corporations that are wholly owned by the enacting nation. Extraterritorial assertions of jurisdiction are not one-sided. While the District Court's discovery orders arguably have some impact in France, the French blocking statute asserts similar authority over acts to take place in this country. The lesson of comity is that neither the discovery order nor the blocking statute can have the same omnipresent effect that it would have in a world of only one sovereign. The blocking statute thus is relevant to the court's particularized comity analysis only to the extent that its terms and its enforcement identify the nature of the sovereign interests in nondisclosure of specific kinds of material.

1038   Chapter 11.   Extraterritorial Discovery and Taking Evidence Abroad

discovery demands. This holding may be read as indicating that the Convention procedures are not even an option that is open to the District Court. It must be recalled, however, that the Convention's specification of duties in executing States creates corresponding rights in requesting States; holding that the Convention does not apply in this situation would deprive domestic litigants of access to evidence through treaty procedures to which the contracting States have assented. Moreover, such a rule would deny the foreign litigant a full and fair opportunity to demonstrate appropriate reasons for employing Convention procedures in the first instance, for some aspects of discovery process.

JUSTICE BLACKMUN, with whom JUSTICE BRENNAN, JUSTICE MARSHALL, and JUSTICE O'CONNOR join, concurring in part and dissenting in part. Some might well regard the Court's decision in this case as an affront to the nations that have joined the United States in ratifying the Hague Convention. . . . The Court ignores the importance of the Convention by relegating it to an "optional" status, without acknowledging the significant achievement in accommodating divergent interests that the Convention represents. Experience to date indicates that there is a large risk that the case-by-case comity analysis now to be permitted by the Court will be performed inadequately and that the somewhat unfamiliar procedures of the Convention will be invoked infrequently. I fear the Court's decision means that courts will resort unnecessarily to issuing discovery orders under the Federal Rules of Civil Procedure in a raw exercise of their jurisdictional power to the detriment of the United States' national and international interests. The Court's view of this country's international obligations is particularly unfortunate in a world in which regular commercial and legal channels loom ever more crucial.

I do agree with the Court's repudiation of the positions at both extremes of the spectrum with regard to the use of the Convention. Its rejection of the view that the Convention is not "applicable" at all to this case is surely correct: the Convention clearly applies to litigants as well as to third parties, and to requests for evidence located abroad, no matter where that evidence is actually "produced." The Court also correctly rejects the far opposite position that the Convention provides the exclusive means for discovery involving signatory countries. I dissent, however, because I cannot endorse the Court's case-by-case inquiry for determining whether to use Convention procedures and its failure to provide lower courts with any meaningful guidance for carrying out that inquiry. In my view, the Convention provides effective discovery procedures that largely eliminate the conflicts between United States and foreign law on evidence gathering. I therefore would apply a general presumption that, in most cases, courts should resort first to the Convention procedures. An individualized analysis of the circumstances of a particular case is appropriate only when it appears that it would be futile to employ the Convention or when its procedures prove to be unhelpful. . . .

By viewing the Convention as merely optional and leaving the decision whether to apply it to the court in each individual case, the majority ignores the policies established by the political branches when they negotiated and ratified the treaty. The result will be a duplicative analysis for which courts are not well designed. The discovery process usually concerns discrete interests that a court is well equipped to accommodate — the interests of the parties before the court coupled with the interest of the judicial system in resolving the conflict on the basis of the best available information. When a lawsuit requires discovery of materials located in a foreign nation, however, foreign legal systems and foreign interests are implicated as well. The presence of these interests creates a tension between the broad discretion our courts normally exercise in managing pretrial discovery and the discretion usually allotted to the Executive in foreign matters. . . .

Not only is the question of foreign discovery more appropriately considered by the Executive and Congress, but in addition, courts are generally ill equipped to assume the role of balancing the interests of foreign nations with that of our own. Although transnational litigation is increasing, relatively few judges are experienced in the area and the procedures of foreign legal systems are often poorly understood. As this Court recently stated, it has "little competence in determining precisely when foreign nations will be offended by particular acts." *Container Corp. v. Franchise Tax Bd.* 463 U.S. 159, 194 (1983). A pro-forum bias is likely to creep into the supposedly neutral balancing process and courts not surprisingly often will turn to the more familiar procedures established by their local rules. . . . Exacerbating these shortcomings is the limited appellate review of interlocutory discovery decisions, which prevents any effective case-by-case correction of erroneous discovery decisions.

The principle of comity leads to more definite rules than the ad hoc approach endorsed by the majority. . . . Comity is not just a vague political concern favoring international cooperation when it is in our interest to do so. Rather it is a principle under which judicial decisions reflect the systemic value of reciprocal tolerance and goodwill. As in the choice-of-law analysis, which from the very beginning has been linked to international comity, the threshold question in a comity analysis is whether there is in fact a true conflict between domestic and foreign law. When there is a conflict, a court should seek a reasonable accommodation that reconciles the central concerns of both sets of laws. In doing so, it should perform a tripartite analysis that considers the foreign interests, the interests of the United States, and the mutual interests of all nations in a smoothly functioning international legal regime. [Under this analysis, U.S. courts should ordinarily require first use of the Convention.] . . .

There are, however, some situations in which there is legitimate concern that certain documents cannot be made available under Convention procedures. Thirteen nations have made official declarations pursuant to Article 23 of the Convention, which permits a contracting state to limit its obligation to produce documents in response to a letter of request. These reservations may pose problems that would require a comity analysis in an individual case, but they are not so all-encompassing as the majority implies — they certainly do not mean that a "contracting Party could unilaterally abrogate the Convention's procedures." First, the reservations can apply only to letters of request for documents. Thus, an Article 23 reservation affects neither the most commonly used informal Convention procedures for taking of evidence by a consul or a commissioner nor formal requests for depositions or interrogatories. Second, although Article 23 refers broadly to "pretrial discovery," the intended meaning of the term appears to have been much narrower than the normal United States usage. The contracting parties for the most part have modified the declarations made pursuant to Article 23 to limit their reach. Indeed, the emerging view of this exception to discovery is that it applies only to "requests that lack sufficient specificity or that have not been reviewed for relevancy by the requesting court." Thus, in practice, a reservation is not the significant obstacle to discovery under the Convention that the broad wording of Article 23 would suggest. . . .

The second major United States interest is in fair and equal treatment of litigants. The Court cites several fairness concerns in support of its conclusion that the Convention is not exclusive and apparently fears that a broad endorsement of the use of the Convention would lead to the same "unacceptable asymmetries." Courts can protect against the first two concerns noted by the majority — that a foreign party to a lawsuit would have a discovery advantage over a domestic litigant because it could obtain the advantages of the Federal Rules of Civil Procedure, and that a foreign company would have an economic competitive advantage because it would be subject to less extensive discovery — by exercising their discretionary powers to control discovery in order to ensure fairness to both parties. A court may "make any order which justice requires" to limit discovery, including an order permitting discovery only on specified terms and conditions, by a particular discovery method, or with limitation in scope to certain matters. Fed. Rule Civ. Proc. 26(c). If, for instance, resort to the Convention procedures would put one party at a disadvantage, any possible unfairness could be prevented by postponing that party's obligation to respond to discovery requests until completion of the foreign discovery. Moreover, the Court's arguments focus on the nationality of the parties, while it is actually the locus of the evidence that is relevant to use of the Convention: a foreign litigant trying to secure evidence from a foreign branch of an American litigant might also be required to resort to the Convention.

When resort to the Convention would be futile, a court has no choice but to resort to a traditional comity analysis. But even then, an attempt to use the Convention will often be the best way to discover if it will be successful, particularly in the present state of general inexperience with the implementation of its procedures by the various contracting states. An attempt to use the Convention will open a dialogue with the authorities in the foreign state and in that way a United States court can obtain an authoritative answer as to the limits on what it can achieve with a discovery request in a particular contracting state.

Notes *on* Aérospatiale

1. *Mandatory use of the Convention for discovery conducted "on" foreign territory.* Suppose a U.S. litigant wishes to conduct the deposition of a foreign person within a Member State's territory or to inspect a factory or other site at a foreign location. Must the Hague Evidence Convention be used? *Aérospatiale* did not address this question. Most authorities have concluded that the Convention must be used when the physical act of discovery formally occurs on foreign territory (e.g., a deposition). *See Belmont Textile Machinery Co. v. Superba, SA,* 48 F. Supp. 2d 521, 524 (W.D.N.C. 1999); *Scotch Whiskey Ass'n v. Majestic Distilling Co.,* 1988 WL 1091943 (D. Md. 1988); *Jenco v. Martech Int'l Inc.,* 1988 U.S. Dist. LEXIS 4727 (E.D. La. 1988); *Work v. Bier,* 106 F.R.D. 45, 48 (D.D.C. 1985); *McLaughlin v. Fellows Gear Shaper Co.,* 102 F.R.D. 956, 957 (E.D. Pa. 1984); *Graco, Inc. v. Kremlin, Inc.,* 101 F.R.D. 503, 524 (N.D. Ill. 1984). *See also* Department of State, *Obtaining Evidence Abroad,* http://travel.state.gov/law/info/judicial/judicial_688.html ("When evidence sought is in a foreign country, it is necessary to observe not only applicable state or federal rules, but also the laws and regulations of the foreign country where the evidence is located. Procedures may vary in civil, criminal and administrative cases. Some countries view the taking of any form of evidence, even voluntary depositions, as an infringement on their judicial sovereignty. This applies to party and non-party witnesses. . . . This proviso also applies to depositions or other proceedings conducted at U.S. embassies/consulates abroad. . . .").

Based on *Aérospatiale*'s reading of the Convention, could the Convention *itself* forbid direct U.S. discovery occurring abroad? If not, then what would permit U.S. courts to require resort to the Convention in such cases? How is discovery "in" foreign territory different from discovery "from" foreign territory? What differences could justify different treatment of the two types of discovery by U.S. courts? Recall the diplomatic protests that Germany made to the United States in the nineteenth century over the efforts by U.S. commissioners to take depositions on German territory. *See supra* pp. 971-972. Do such efforts constitute a greater infringement of foreign sovereignty than discovery "from" foreign territory? Recall the *Charming Betsy* presumption that Congress will not be assumed to have violated international law. *See supra* p. 18.

2. *Optional use of the Convention for discovery conducted in the United States.* *Aérospatiale* squarely rejected the position of some lower courts that the Hague Evidence Convention simply had no application if the formal act of "producing" the requested information was to take place in the United States (*i.e.*, a deposition conducted in the United States or documents that are copied abroad and brought to the United States where they are then "produced"). *See, e.g., In re Anschuetz & Co.*, 754 F.2d 602 (5th Cir. 1985), *vacated*, 483 U.S. 1002 (1987). In this respect, the Court ruled that the Convention applied to taking evidence "from" a foreign country as well as to taking it "in" the foreign country.

Nonetheless, *Aerospatiale* emphasized that the Convention is not the *only* mechanism available for obtaining discovery from a foreign state. *Aérospatiale* held that the Convention does not by its terms supplant the use of direct discovery orders by U.S. courts: "the Hague Convention did not deprive the District Court of the jurisdiction it otherwise possessed to order a foreign national party before it to produce evidence physically located within a signatory nation."

3. *Aérospatiale's reliance on international comity.* According to *Aérospatiale*, when information is to be produced "from" (but not "in") a Convention signatory, by a party over whom the court has personal jurisdiction, two alternative discovery procedures are available: direct discovery under the Federal Rules of Civil Procedure or a letter of request through the Convention. *Aerospatiale* also holds that the U.S. court's choice between these two alternatives must be informed by principles of "international comity," rather than dictated by the Convention itself: "The concept of international comity requires in this context a more particularized analysis of the respective interests of the foreign nation and the requesting nation." Compare the use of the comity doctrine in other areas of U.S. litigation, including choice of law (*supra* pp. 683-691), enforcement of foreign judgments (*see infra* pp. 1084-1091), choice of forum (*supra* pp. 385-386), act of state doctrine (*supra* p. 811), antisuit injunctions (*supra* pp. 578-579), and personal jurisdiction (*supra* pp. 159-160).

4. *Meaning of* Aérospatiale's *comity analysis.* Unfortunately, the application of comity in individual discovery cases is left unclear after *Aérospatiale*. At one point, the majority refers to the factors set out in §442 of the *Third Restatement* (reproduced in Appendix ____) as "relevant to any comity analysis." Nonetheless, at other points in its opinion, the Court sets forth other descriptions of the comity analysis, requiring "prior scrutiny in each case of the particular facts, sovereign interests, and likelihood that resort to those procedures will prove effective" and "more particularized analysis of the respective interests of the foreign nation and the requesting nation." Elsewhere, the Court said, the "exact line . . . must be drawn by the trial court, based on its knowledge of the case and of the claims and interests of the parties and the governments whose statutes and policies they invoke." How is a court to apply these various standards? Do they all mean the same thing?

5. *Source of judicial authority to require resort to Convention.* *Aérospatiale* held that the Hague Evidence Convention does not by its terms require use of the Convention's procedures rather than use of direct discovery under the Federal Rules. Nonetheless, the Court also held that in some cases international comity required litigants to resort to the Convention's procedures. From where is this "comity" requirement derived? What gives federal courts the power to deny litigants access to the discovery rights that are provided in the Federal Rules? *See supra* pp. 76-86, 591-594, 646-648, discussing historical foundations of comity. What is the relation of comity to the Convention and to the Federal Rules? Why doesn't the *Aérospatiale* opinion discuss international law limits on extraterritorial discovery? *See supra* pp. 969-977. If these limits forbid compelled discovery "on" foreign territory, why should courts not also consider whether they forbid compelled discovery "from" foreign territory?

6. ***Justice Blackmun's*** **Aérospatiale** *opinion.* Justice Blackmun's concurring and dissenting opinion in *Aérospatiale* also applied a comity analysis but, unlike the majority, concluded that lower courts should follow a rule ordinarily requiring exhaustion of Hague Evidence Convention procedures before direct discovery under the Federal Rules is sought. What exactly are the differences between the approach of the four concurring and dissenting Justices and the majority? Which approach to use of the Convention is preferable? Why?

7. *Appellate review and uniformity.* The lack of certainty in the majority's comity approach in *Aerospatiale* may be exacerbated by the nature of the disputes to be reviewed. The essence of the majority's opinion is that judgments must be made in individual discovery cases based on a wide variety of factors. In the normal case this will call for deference to the trial court's discretion. *See In re Anschuetz & Co. GmbH*, 838 F.2d 1362, 1363 (5th Cir. 1988); *Sandsend Fin. Consultants, Ltd. v. Wood*, 743 S.W.2d 364 (Tex. App. 1988). Interlocutory appeals are sometimes possible, *see, e.g., In re Automotive Refinishing Paint Antitrust Litig.*, 358 F.3d 288 (3d Cir. 2004), but discovery disputes involving parties generally are *not* reviewable at the interlocutory stage. (*Aérospatiale* itself reached the Supreme Court by way of an extraordinary writ of mandamus, something that is not to be anticipated except in unusual circumstances.) As a practical matter therefore, it seems unlikely that the courts of appeals will have much opportunity to review and ensure uniformity in the application of the *Aérospatiale* decision. Given the involvement of foreign governmental interests, is it appropriate to defer so extensively to single district judges?

8. *Possibility of parochial bias in applying* **Aérospatiale** *balancing test.* To what extent will trial courts — as opposed to Courts of Appeals or the Supreme Court — be likely to focus primarily on managing individual cases expeditiously and therefore tend to disregard "comity"? How likely is it that trial judges will be familiar with foreign public policies? Compare the similar concerns about parochial bias in the context of legislative jurisdiction and choice of law. *See supra* pp. 563-565.

9. *Balancing U.S. and foreign interests.* The *Aérospatiale* majority did not hesitate to adopt a comity analysis requiring lower courts to "balance" U.S. and foreign interests. In contrast, Justice Blackmun cautioned that "courts are generally ill equipped to assume the role of balancing the interests of foreign nations with that of our own." *See also supra* pp. 646-648. Are Justice Blackmun's concerns justified? Compare the criticisms that have been made of ad hoc balancing analyses in other international civil litigation contexts. *See supra* pp. 386-387 (*forum non conveniens*) & pp. 683-691 (extraterritoriality).

10. *Exhaustiveness of* **Aérospatiale** *factors.* Are the factors listed by *Aérospatiale* designed to be exclusive? Or are they merely illustrative, thereby preserving the possibility for courts to consider additional factors in the analysis? Some courts have considered, in addition to the factors explicitly listed in *Aérospatiale*, factors such as the hardship of compliance and the party's good faith efforts to comply with the request. *See Milliken & Co. v. Bank of China*, 758 F. Supp. 2d 238 (S.D.N.Y. 2010); *Gucci America, Inc. v. Curveal Fashion*, 2010 WL 808639 (S.D.N.Y. Mar. 8, 2010) (magistrate judge); *In re Air Cargo Shipping Services Antitrust Litig.*, 2010 WL 1189341 (E.D.N.Y. Mar. 29, 2010). Is this approach faithful to *Aérospatiale*? Is it wise? Does it undermine the predictability of an already fuzzy test? How does the multi-factor approach here compare to the approach taken in other areas explored in this book? *See supra* at 81-91 (reasonableness of exercise of personal jurisdiction), pp. 408-426 (*forum non conveniens*), 559-560 (*lis alibi pendens*) and 576-578 (antisuit injunctions).

11. *Effect of foreign litigant's use of U.S. discovery rules.* Suppose that a foreign litigant avails itself of the benefits of full discovery from adverse parties under the Federal Rules of Civil Procedure. Should the foreign litigant be able to require that discovery from it be conducted only under the Convention? In *Aerospatiale*, both Justice Stevens and Justice Blackmun disapproved such a result. *See Great Lakes Dredge & Dock Co. v. Harnischfeger Corp.*, 1990 U.S. Dist. LEXIS 12843 (N.D. Ill. 1990) (refusing to permit German litigant to "have the best of all worlds"). *Cf. In re Automotive Refinishing Paint Antitrust Litig.*, 358 F.3d 288, 303 (3d Cir. 2004) (declining to mandate resort to Convention for jurisdictional discovery where defendant made use of Federal Rules of Civil Procedure to file dispositive motion and seek preliminary hearing); *Fishel v. BASF Group*, 175 F.R.D. 525, 529 (S.D. Iowa 1997) (same).

12. *Application of Aérospatiale to state courts.* As noted above, *Aérospatiale* involved an interpretation of the Convention itself. In particular, the Court decided that the Convention by its terms need not be used, but is available even where production of information is to take place on U.S. soil. As a treaty of the United States, the Convention is the supreme law of the land and therefore these interpretations by the Supreme Court bind the state courts, as well as lower federal courts. *See supra* pp. 15-17; *Restatement (Third) Foreign Relations Law* §115(2) (1987); *Volkswagenwerk AG v. Schlunk*, 486 U.S. 694 (1988).

Aérospatiale also rested in part on international comity; the effect of this holding on state courts is less clear. Is *Aérospatiale's* comity analysis a rule of federal law that state courts are obliged to follow? *See Buttitta v. Allied Signal, Inc.*, 2006 WL 2355200 (N.J. App. Div. Aug. 16, 2006) (*per curiam*) (reversing trial court's ruling on discovery dispute for failure to conduct analysis under *Aerospatiale* comity factors); *American Home Assurance Co. v. Société Commerciale Toutelectric*, 104 Cal. App. 4th 406, 421-426 (Cal. Ct. App. 2002) (*Aérospatiale* "superseded rule of first resort" developed in prior state court decision; declining to adopt different rule as a matter of state law); *Sandsend Financial Consultants, Ltd. v. Wood*, 734 S.W.2d 364 (Tex. Ct. App. 1988) (applying *Aérospatiale* comity analysis: "this Court is duty-bound to follow Supreme Court precedent"); *Bank of Tokyo-Mitsubishi, Ltd. v. Kvaerner*, 671 N.Y.S.2d 902 (Sup. Ct. 1998); *Scarminach v. Goldwell GmbH*, 531 N.Y.S.2d 188, 190 (Sup. Ct. 1988) ("the preemption argument . . . would require that the Convention procedures provide the exclusive, rather than an optional, method to obtain evidence abroad, a conclusion expressly rejected by the Supreme Court" in *Aérospatiale*). Recall the discussions above of the status of international law as federal law. *See supra* pp. 17-18.

On the one hand, state courts should arguably be bound to be at least as deferential to foreign sovereign interests as federal courts are. The Supreme Court's concerns about infringing foreign sovereignty apply as fully to state courts as to federal courts. On the other hand, from where would federal courts derive the authority to invoke international comity to regulate state court discovery practice? Similar issues arise with respect to the applicability of federal common law rules of *forum non conveniens*, forum selection, the act of state doctrine, the extraterritorial application of national laws, and the enforcement of foreign judgments. *See supra* pp. 453-458, 528-544, 568-569, 702-704 and *infra* pp. 1110-1114.

A related issue concerns the power of state courts to go beyond the minimum standard of deference to foreign interests established by *Aérospatiale*. For example, could a state court conclude that international comity requires first use of the Convention in all cases? Could this reading of comity harm U.S. interests? How? What if the state court based its first-use rule on concerns about local judicial administration? *See* Westin & Born, *Applying the Aérospatiale Decision to State Court Proceedings*, 26 Colum. J. Transnat'l L. 901 (1988). *Compare American Home Assurance Co. v. Société Commerciale Toutelectric*, 104 Cal. App. 4th 406, 421-426 (Cal. Ct. App. 2002).

13. *Effect of Article 23 reservations on Convention's efficacy.* One of the issues which drove the Court's analysis in *Aérospatiale* was the extent to which U.S. litigants could obtain meaningful discovery through Convention procedures. The large number of broad

Article 23 declarations make this issue particularly important for U.S. litigants, and no doubt led to the Supreme Court's conclusion that "[i]n many situations the Letter of Request procedure authorized by the Convention would be unduly time-consuming and expensive, as well as less certain to produce needed evidence than direct use of the Federal Rules." Several states, including major trading partners of the United States, have adopted this reservation. *See supra* pp. 1029-1030. How important should the existence of Article 23 reservations have been in deciding *Aérospatiale?*

The effectiveness of the Convention continues to be an important issue in disputes about use of the Convention. This derives from the role played in the Court's comity analysis of the "likelihood that resort to [the Convention's] procedures will prove effective." 482 U.S. at 544. *See supra* pp. 1033-1038. What relevance should the existence of an Article 23 reservation, and the likelihood of effective discovery from a particular country pursuant to the Convention, have in deciding whether to require first-use of the Convention? This question is addressed in greater detail below, *see supra* pp. 683-690.

14. *Applicability of Convention to "discovery."* *Aérospatiale* and virtually every other U.S. authority assumes that the Hague Evidence Convention applies to "discovery." Note, however, that the Convention applies to "taking of evidence." Does that mean that pretrial discovery is not covered by the Convention? For an argument that the Convention was narrowly limited to taking "evidence," and does not apply to mere "discovery," *see* Collins, *The Hague Evidence Convention and Discovery: A Serious Misunderstanding?*, 35 Int'l & Comp. L.Q. 765 (1986). What does Article 23 suggest? What about Article 1, permitting the use of letters of request "to obtain evidence, or to *perform some other judicial act*," but not to "obtain evidence which is not intended for use in judicial proceedings, commenced or contemplated."

3.   "Exclusivity" of the Hague Evidence Convention: Post-*Aérospatiale* Experience

U.S. trial courts have had frequent occasion to apply the Supreme Court's analysis in *Aérospatiale.*[193] Many district judges have found the *Aérospatiale* comity standard of dubious assistance. First, read the Article 23 reservations by selected parties to the Convention. Next, read the opinions in *Benton Graphics v. Uddeholm Corp.* and *In re Vitamins Antitrust Litigation,* which are illustrative of trial court efforts to apply the *Aerospatiale* comity analysis. Finally, reread the U.S. Department of State Circular on the Preparation of Letters Rogatory.

ARTICLE 23 RESERVATIONS OF FRANCE, GERMANY, AND SWEDEN
[excerpted in Appendix N]

BENTON GRAPHICS v. UDDEHOLM CORP.
118 F.R.D. 386 (D.N.J. 1987)

FREDA L. WOLFSON, MAGISTRATE. This litigation involves allegations of fraud and breach of contract against several defendants, including two Swedish companies, Uddeholms,

---

193. For commentary on *Aérospatiale, see* Baumgartner, *Is Transnational Litigation Different?*, 25 U. Pa. J. Int'l Econ. L. 1297, 1327-1338 (2004); Buxbaum, *Assessing Sovereign Interests in Cross-Border Discovery Disputes: Lessons from* Aérospatiale, 38 Tex. Int'l L.J. 87 (2003); Kutac, Note, *Reallocating the Burden of Persuasion Under the* Aérospatiale *Approach to Transnational Discovery*, 24 Rev. Lit. 173 (2004); Iontcheva, *Sovereignty on Our Terms*, 110 Yale L.J. 885 (2001).

A.B. and Uddeholm Strip Steel, A.B. The plaintiff, Benton Graphics, Inc., originally brought the instant motion on for an order compelling responses to interrogatories and the production of documents. The defendants opposed this motion claiming that the principles of comity required that discovery must first be sought under the applicable Hague Convention procedures. . . .

In the instant motion, a major dispute is whether either party carries the burden in determining whether the Federal Rules or Convention procedures should be followed. . . . [T]he plaintiff argues that parties seeking to invoke the Convention are required "to demonstrate appropriate reasons for employing the Convention" in lieu of the Federal Rules. On the other hand . . . defendants argue that a party seeking discovery outside the Convention should be required to show by clear and convincing evidence that the Convention's procedures would be inefficient or unnecessarily burdensome. Anything less, according to the defendants, would derogate from the United States' obligations under the Convention and violate the judicial sovereignty of Sweden. . . . While the majority opinion [in *Aérospatiale*] is not crystal clear on the issue of who bears the burden of establishing which discovery procedure to utilize, I agree with the plaintiff that the party seeking to utilize Convention procedures must demonstrate appropriate reasons. *But see Hudson v. Hermann Pfauter GmbH & Co.*, 117 F.R.D. 33 (N.D.N.Y. 1987).[194] This is consistent with the policy expressed by the Court in *Aérospatiale* that foreign competitors voluntarily marketing their product in the United States should be subject to the same judicial burdens as their domestic counterparts. . . . Therefore, foreign litigants attempting to supplant the federal rules with Convention procedures must demonstrate why the particular facts and sovereign interests support using the Convention. They must also demonstrate that resort to these procedures will prove effective. . . .

Plaintiff, Benton Graphics, Inc., is a New Jersey corporation in the business of manufacturing and distributing doctor blades for use in the gravure printing industry. Defendant, Uddeholm Strip Steel, A.B. is a Swedish corporation which manufactures and distributes steel products, including carbon steel for use in manufacturing doctor blades. Between 1979 and 1985, Benton Graphics entered into a series of contracts with defendants to purchase doctor blades. Prior to 1980, defendants manufactured and sold doctor blades under the designation UHB-20R steel. After 1980, defendants manufactured and sold to Benton a different grade carbon steel under the designation UHB-18CR. Benton claims that defendant Knudsen represented on numerous occasions that the steel delivered to Benton since 1980 was UHB-20R. In February 1986, Benton brought this action against defendants alleging breach of contract, breach of warranty, fraud and RICO violations based on the theory that defendants conspired to misrepresent the grade of steel sold to Benton between 1980 and 1985. Benton claims that there is a material difference between UHB-20R and UHB-18CR steel and that defendants intentionally withheld this information from Benton. . . .

In the instant motion, defendants have made no attempt to relate the "particular facts" of this case to the discovery sought. Defendants only argue that the interrogatories and requests for documents are overbroad and burdensome. I note that the defendants have not identified the specific interrogatories or document requests that are overbroad or burdensome. They have not alleged that the discovery is unduly expensive or that the discovery is being sought for the "improper purpose of motivating settlement rather than

---

194. In *Hudson*, the court found that the burden should be placed on the party opposing the use of Convention procedures to demonstrate that those procedures would be ineffective. In reaching this decision the district court relied upon Justice Blackmun's concurring and dissenting opinion in *Aérospatiale*. . . . While Justice Blackmun's opinion certainly is thoughtful and well reasoned, it is not the opinion of the majority of the members on the Supreme Court. . . .

finding relevant and probative evidence." Moreover, defendants have failed to allege any special problems because of their nationality or the location of their operations.

Because defendants have largely failed to specifically identify their objections it is impossible for me to determine which, if any, requests are overbroad and burdensome. However, having reviewed the interrogatories, I believe that a number of the requests are not "simple" and may require streamlining if we are to proceed under the federal rules. For example, a number of questions seek information held by "any employee of Uddeholm Strip Steel"; these appear too encompassing. I believe these questions can be limited to a defined group of individuals from Uddeholm who were involved in the manufacture of and the decision to sell UHR-18CR grade steel in place of UHB-20R steel products. . . . [T]hese questions, as phrased, include even clerical employees. Identification of such persons, while being of little or no moment, would, however, involve substantial investigation by the foreign litigants. This type of expansive discovery without concomitant relevance is not what the Court envisioned when it handed down the *Aérospatiale* decision: "Some discovery procedures are much more 'intrusive' than others."

Thus, the parties shall have 10 days to confer in an effort to limit and resolve the scope of the discovery requests to ensure that they are reasonable and not overly burdensome, keeping in mind that discovery requests that are too "intrusive" may be limited by this court. After making such good faith effort to reach accommodation, I will permit the defendants to address any specific objections to interrogatories or document requests within ten days thereafter. Defendants are cautioned that they must explain why specific discovery sought is overbroad or burdensome. . . .

Notwithstanding defendants' blanket objections to all discovery, I do not find that the "particular facts" of this case require resort to Convention procedures. The discovery sought in this case largely relates to the composition, qualities and testing of defendants' steel. Several of the defendants and all relevant tests are located in Sweden. . . . It is essential that plaintiff and its experts have access to the tests if this litigation is to proceed to any semblance of a timely fashion. The foreign defendants have identified no special problem with responding to the requested discovery because of their nationality. Since discovery of these tests and other relevant information can be accomplished efficiently under the federal rules the "particular facts" of this case do not necessitate resort to the Convention.

The second factor which must be analyzed before ordering use of the Convention is the sovereign interest involved. Defendants argue that "critical sovereign interests of Sweden" support utilizing Convention procedures. They have submitted the duly authenticated Declaration of Wanja Tornberg, Assistant Under-Secretary of the Swedish Ministry for Foreign Affairs (the "Tornberg Declaration"). According to Tornberg, use of the Hague Convention serves a number of important Swedish interests including:

(a) It serves as an essential link and an effective mechanism for cooperation between different legal systems.

(b) It minimizes conflicts between the legal requirements of different states.

(c) It satisfies the urging of the United States for Sweden and other civil law nations to provide a means for complying with requests for pretrial discovery of documentary evidence in a manner which is consistent with the laws of Sweden.

(d) It discourages "fishing expedition" methods of obtaining unspecified evidence, which are regarded as unacceptable in Sweden and in other civil law nations.

(e) It effectively balances the divergent interests promoted by the United States' and Sweden's conflicting rules on who bears the costs associated with compliance. The rule in Sweden, as in most civil law countries, is that the losing party reimburses the winner for litigation expenses. Unlike the general rule in the United States, the Swedish rule forces plaintiffs to evaluate carefully the merits of a case before bringing it.

(f) It enables Swedish courts to limit discovery in sensitive and protected areas under Swedish law such as trade secrets and national security.

These "critical sovereign interests" are merely general reasons why Sweden prefers civil law discovery procedures to the more liberal discovery permitted under the federal rules. Defendants cite no reasons how the specific discovery sought by Benton implicates any specific sovereign interest of Sweden. . . . In short, because defendant has not explained, and I do not see why Benton's discovery requests in their entirety or any particular request, violate any special sovereign interests of Sweden, resort to the Hague Convention is not required.

Lastly, I must consider whether Convention procedures in this case will prove effective. Here, I find that they will not. The Tornberg Declaration states that the defendants' letter of request should be processed by the Swedish authorities in approximately two months. That is an approximation based upon past history; there are certainly no guarantees. This case has already endured numerous delays and discovery should proceed apace. . . . Therefore, in light of the lengthy history of discovery in this case and the potential for additional delays, I do not find that Convention procedures will prove effective. . . .

IN RE VITAMINS ANTITRUST LITIGATION
120 F. Supp. 2d 45 (D.D.C. 2000)

JUDGE HOGAN. [Various purchasers and sellers of vitamins commenced class action lawsuits in the United States against various foreign businesses claiming that they had engaged in price fixing in the vitamins market. The foreign defendants, who were based in both Hague-signatory and nonsignatory countries, claimed that the court lacked personal jurisdiction. Plaintiffs sought jurisdictional discovery, and the defendants argued, *inter alia,* that the Hague Evidence Convention had to be used when seeking jurisdictional discovery. The case was referred to a Special Master. The following excerpts come from the district court's opinion reviewing the Special Master's report.]

The first question to be answered is whether the Court must always require first-resort to Hague procedures for jurisdictional discovery or whether the three-prong test established by the Supreme Court in *Aerospatiale* governs even in cases where personal jurisdiction has not yet been conclusively established. Defendants argue that, since *Aérospatiale* makes repeated references to the presence of personal jurisdiction in that case, the Supreme Court did not intend for its holding to apply to actions in which personal jurisdiction is still at issue. . . .

[I]mportantly, the question decided by the Eighth Circuit and certified by the Supreme Court for review in *Aerospatiale* was whether "when the district court has jurisdiction over a foreign litigant the Hague Convention . . . appl[ies] to the production of evidence in that litigant's possession, even though the documents and information sought may physically be located within the territory of a foreign signatory to the Convention." Therefore, it is clear that the Supreme Court in *Aerospatiale* never addressed the issue of what procedures to follow in cases of jurisdictional discovery; that issue was never before the Court and certainly was not resolved by the holding of *Aerospatiale.*

Since *Aerospatiale* does not answer the question at issue here, this Court must consider whether there are legal or policy reasons for requiring first use of [the Convention] for jurisdictional discovery of foreign defendants despite the Supreme Court's clear rejection of this first-resort rule in cases where jurisdiction has been established. Defendants maintain that a rule of first-resort is more important for jurisdictional discovery than for merits discovery because the comity interests of the foreign nations are higher before defendants are conclusively found to be subject to the Court's jurisdiction. This Court disagrees. It is well-established that a trial court has jurisdiction to determine its jurisdiction. Since the Court has jurisdiction over these foreign defendants to the extent necessary to determine whether or not they are subject to personal jurisdiction in this forum, the Court sees no legal barrier to exercising the discretion given to trial courts by *Aerospatiale* in cases of jurisdictional discovery. . . .

[T]his is not a case of speculative jurisdiction. All six of the defendants from signatory countries have already admitted their involvement in this antitrust price-fixing conspiracy. In addition, although the Court denied defendants' motions to dismiss without prejudice and ordered plaintiffs to undertake further jurisdictional discovery, the Court did find plaintiffs' allegations to show strong potential for findings of jurisdiction. Therefore, although this Court agrees that plaintiffs have not yet alleged facts sufficient to give this Court conclusive jurisdiction over these defendants, it believes that plaintiffs' allegations amount to more than mere blanket fishing expeditions. In fact, the Court agreed to allow plaintiffs jurisdictional discovery solely because it felt that they had essentially established a prima-facie basis for jurisdiction; therefore, the allegations in plaintiffs' complaints are not the type of bare-boned allegations that potentially could lead to the fishing expeditions of obvious concern to the signatory countries.

[T]he Court [also] finds that the Special Master has sufficiently revised plaintiffs' jurisdictional discovery requests so as to make them narrowly tailored to issues relating to the jurisdictional questions at issue rather than to the defendants' general liability. Accordingly, the Court does not believe that the sovereign interests of these foreign signatory nations would be any more offended by this narrowed jurisdictional discovery than they would be by the broader, merits-related discovery allowed by *Aerospatiale*. In conclusion, . . . this Court agrees with the Special Master that the first-resort rule, explicitly rejected by the Supreme Court in *Aerospatiale*, would not be any more applicable in this case than it was in *Aerospatiale*. . . .

The three-prong test of *Aerospatiale* dictates that in determining whether to proceed with discovery under [the Convention] or the Federal Rules, the court should consider "the particular facts, the sovereign interests, and likelihood that resort to [Convention] procedures will prove effective." *Aerospatiale* did not specifically rule on the burden of proof for these factors, but most courts have placed this burden on the party seeking to require first-use of the Convention. The Court agrees with the Special Master that the cases placing the burden of proof on the proponents of [the Hague Evidence Convention] are more persuasive. . . .

Under the *Aerospatiale* analysis, the first factor for the Court to consider are the particular facts of this case. . . . Defendants argue that the burdens imposed by the plaintiffs' discovery requests require use of Hague procedures. However, as discussed above, this Court finds plaintiffs' discovery requests, as refined by the Special Master, to be narrowly tailored to the issue of personal jurisdiction and thus highly relevant and not nearly as intrusive as merits discovery. While this Court recognizes that plaintiffs' discovery requests extend far beyond the ten interrogatories sought in *Rich* [*v. KIS California, Inc.*, 121 F.R.D. 254 (M.D.N.C. 1988)], the pertinent question is whether the requests are narrowly tailored, material to the issues in question, and as unintrusive as possible under the circumstances. . . . The sheer number of requests must be measured against the size and magnitude of the case at hand; given the unprecedented size and complexity of this price-fixing action, this Court cannot find that plaintiffs are bound to follow the Hague

Convention based solely on the number of their discovery requests. Considering the nature of this case, plaintiffs' requests, as refined by plaintiffs themselves and then again by the Special Master,[195] are as narrowly tailored and unintrusive as possible. Furthermore, these requests are highly relevant and crucial to the resolution of the jurisdictional questions pending before this Court. Therefore, the Court rejects defendants' argument that the burdens imposed by plaintiffs' discovery requests necessitates use of Hague procedures. . . .

The second factor to consider under *Aerospatiale* are the sovereign interests at stake. The Court agrees with the signatory defendants that their respective nations have significant sovereign interests in proceeding with discovery according to the Hague Convention procedures. In fact, the Court finds that most of the lower courts which have considered the issue of whether to proceed under Hague or the Federal Rules appear to have given considerably less deference to the foreign nations' sovereign interests than this Court believes is warranted. Clearly, these signatory nations have a strong interest in protecting their citizens from what they may perceive as unduly burdensome discovery under evidence laws foreign to and incompatible with their own procedures. The Court agrees with the Special Master that whether plaintiffs are correct that foreign nations have no sovereign interests in protecting admitted antitrust violators is irrelevant, since those nations retain a separate and important sovereign interest in ensuring that discovery involving their citizens be taken in accord with their traditions and accepted practices. . . .

However, the Court agrees with the Special Master that the second prong of *Aerospatiale* requires not only an analysis of the sovereign interests of the signatory nations but also of those of the United States. In fact, the Supreme Court specifically listed as a factor in the comity analysis "the extent to which noncompliance with the request would undermine important interests of the United States, or compliance with the request would undermine important interests of the state where the information is located." As previously discussed, the Court finds that plaintiffs' revised discovery requests are narrowly tailored to the jurisdictional question and that the information sought is crucial to resolution of this issue and thus to the prompt conclusion of this antitrust action. . . .

The third prong of *Aerospatiale* requires the Court to decide in each case whether resort to Hague procedures would likely prove effective. The question is whether proceeding with jurisdictional discovery under Hague would allow these plaintiffs to obtain the necessary testimony, documents, and written answers called for by their revised discovery requests in a timely and effective manner. . . . After reviewing the Special Master's findings and conclusions as well as the entire record in this case and the Court's own experience with the Hague procedures, the Court finds that the Special Master's conclusions are accurate and that [the Convention] would be extremely unlikely to provide efficient and effective discovery in this case. Given the need for prompt resolution of these jurisdictional questions and the time and cost to both sides in dragging out this process any longer than is necessary, the Court finds that jurisdictional discovery under the Federal Rules is appropriate in this case. . . .

As noted above, the protective orders of defendants ECL [a Japanese company] and UCB SA [a Belgian company] must be analyzed separately because Japan and Belgium, these defendants' respective countries, are not signatories to the Hague [Evidence] Convention. The Court does not agree with the Special Master's recommendation that the

---

195. As discussed in the Special Master's Report, plaintiffs significantly narrowed their own discovery requests in response to specific objections raised by defendants. The Special Master further refined these requests in the Appendix to his Report and Recommendation. The Court finds these revised requests to be reasonably tailored to ascertain jurisdictional facts and as unintrusive as possible given the size and complexity of this case.

situation of these non-signatory defendants be analyzed under the *Aerospatiale* test. Since *Aerospatiale* is concerned exclusively with the question of whether to apply the Federal Rules or the Hague Convention to discovery being sought from a signatory country, the Supreme Court's holding in that case is clearly limited to countries that have adopted the Hague Convention procedures for the taking of evidence. . . .

Unfortunately, after finding that *Aerospatiale* is inapplicable to defendants ECL and UCB SA, the Court is left with little guidance as to what analysis it should employ in order to determine whether to proceed under the Federal Rules or the laws of these non-signatory countries for jurisdictional discovery in this case. When asked by these defendants at the hearing what test should be applied to their situation, their response was simply: the general principles of comity and territorial preferences as expressed in international treaties and laws. In the absence of any other prescribed analysis, the Court will defer to these two defendants and analyze their situation under principles of comity, affording special attention to the international territorial preference which favors discovery procedures governed by the law of the territory where discovery is sought in the absence of any conflict between the Federal Rules and the laws of that territory. Therefore, the Court will first consider whether there is in fact any conflict between the evidence laws of Japan and Belgium and the United States; and second, in the event that there is a conflict, the Court will analyze the principles of comity in order to determine whether these principles require use of the nonsignatories' laws in this case.

The record shows that Japan did not join the Hague Convention apparently out of fear of American-type discovery procedures; that under Japanese law "the scope of witness examination and document discovery is narrowly tailored to the allegations"; and that when the one-hundred-year-old Code of Civil Procedure Law was revised in 1996, "the Japanese legislature refused to adopt the American-type discovery system (particularly, the out-of-court deposition and document-request procedure) as excessively intrusive and therefore undesirable in the non-litigious Japanese society." Although limited pretrial discovery of witnesses and documents is allowed under the laws of Japan, document requests must identify specifically the documents sought, and various documentary and testimonial privileges would prevent the taking of much evidence even if the specificity requirements were met. . . .

Apparently recognizing the conflicts between the Japanese system and the Federal Rules, ECL asserts that its offer to voluntarily, upon proper service, make one deponent available to testify in Tokyo "provided that the plaintiffs narrow the topics to be covered" and to produce documents "provided that the plaintiffs narrow the scope of their request" will permit plaintiffs to obtain "reasonable discovery" under the laws of Japan. The Court agrees with the Special Master's finding that plaintiffs will not likely be able to obtain the necessary pretrial testimony and documentary evidence found to be proper by the Special Master and through adoption by this Court under the Laws of Japan. First, the Court is not satisfied with ECL's quite reserved and contingent offer for voluntary discovery; the Court has now decided that plaintiffs' revised requests, the very ones ECL says must be further revised, are narrowly tailored and should be answered. Second, the Court is convinced, considering Japan's antipathy to even the Hague procedures, that plaintiffs' discovery requests would not be sufficiently specific to meet the requirements of the Japanese Civil Code. Therefore, despite the Court's respect for the principles of comity and Japan's sovereign interests in protecting its citizens from unduly burdensome discovery, this Court cannot find that these concerns outweigh the need for prompt and efficient resolution of the jurisdictional questions in this case. Accordingly, the Court will adopt the Special Master's recommendation that jurisdictional discovery against ECL proceed under the Federal Rules.

UCB SA's own expert [Dr. Heinemann] stated that Belgium generally disfavors pretrial discovery in civil litigation. In fact, Belgian scholars cited by Dr. Heinemann say that pretrial discovery in Belgium is "tantamount to a private house search of the opposing party" and these scholars note that "if Belgium were to ratify the Hague Evidence Convention it would make a reservation under article 23 of the Convention in order to avoid inquisitorial acts which are not meant to gather specific evidentiary materials pertaining to a pending procedure, or consist in fact of 'fishing expeditions.'" Dr. Heinemann does say that "a foreign litigant is able to obtain specified documents and deposition testimony" and that under Belgium law, Belgian courts are required to execute letters rogatory properly issued "so long as the discovery sought by such letters rogatory is specific and narrow and does not breach fundamental rules of Belgium." However, there is no indication that plaintiffs' requests would meet this criteria.

After considering the entire record in this case, the Court disagrees with UCB SA that Belgian law affords "a reasonable and effective method of obtaining jurisdictional discovery" in this case. The Court finds that the Letters of Request procedure available under Belgian law is unlikely to secure for plaintiffs the jurisdictional discovery approved by this Court. Document and deposition discovery would most likely be thwarted by the stringent requirements for specificity. Therefore, despite the strong interest in comity and the respect that this Court has for Belgium's sovereign interests,[196] the Court will adopt the Special Master's recommendation that jurisdictional discovery involving UCB SA proceed under the Federal Rules. . . .

U.S. DEPARTMENT OF STATE, CIRCULAR ON PREPARATION OF LETTERS ROGATORY

[excerpted in Appendix CC]

Notes on Article 23 Reservations, Uddeholm, In re Vitamins, and Department of State Circular

1.   *Foreign courts' willingness to execute Hague letters of request from U.S. courts.* Consider the Article 23 reservations to the Hague Evidence Convention by France, Germany, and Sweden. How much scope do these reservations leave for ordinary "U.S.-style" document discovery under the Convention? What exactly is it that a French or German court would permit under their countries' respective Article 23 reservations?

English courts, applying a common law approach to document discovery, are often said to be more receptive than most national courts to U.S. requests under the Hague Evidence Convention. Nonetheless, it is well settled that English courts will only order discovery of "particular" documents or narrow, specifically defined categories of documents, that were already known to exist, that were intended to be used as evidence, and that are directly relevant to disputed issues. *See Genira Trade & Finance Inc. v. Refco Capital Markets Ltd.* [2001] EWCA Civ. 1733. In one recent case, an English court denied a Hague

---

196. The Court notes that Belgium's sovereign interests are particularly strong since this defendant has not pled guilty or entered into any agreement and therefore has admitted no involvement in this price-fixing conspiracy. For this reason, the Court was particularly concerned with UCB SA's situation and afforded them individual consideration; however, after reviewing the entire record in this case, the Court finds that Belgium's sovereign interests will not be unduly offended by this jurisdictional discovery and that the unlikelihood of effective discovery under Belgian procedures and the need for a rapid and effective resolution of the jurisdictional questions in this case necessitate a finding in favor of the Federal Rules in this case.

letter of request, declaring: "This was in reality a typical United States style discovery deposition which was being requested and that is an exercise which the English Statute simply does not allow." *Ibid.* Is it not clear that there is an enormous gulf between U.S. and English — not to mention civil law — expectations about pretrial discovery and evidence-taking under the Hague Evidence Convention?

2. U.S. perceptions of efficacy of Hague Evidence Convention procedures. One important factor in the *Aerospatiale* comity analysis is the perceived efficacy and speed of discovery under the Hague Evidence Convention. Consider the court's conclusion in *In re Vitamins Antitrust Litigation* that, based on its prior experience, "the Hague [Evidence Convention] would be extremely unlikely to provide efficient and effective discovery in this case." *See also Lechoslaw v. Bank of America, N.A.*, 618 F.3d 49, 57 (1st Cir. 2010) ("The procedures of the Hague [Evidence] Convention do not come without a significant time cost."); *In re Air Cargo Shipping Services Antitrust Litig.*, 2010 WL 1189341 (E.D.N.Y. Mar. 29, 2010) ("The outcome of a request pursuant to the Convention is by no means certain, and making the request will undeniably result in delays of unknown, and perhaps considerable, duration."); *Manoir-Electroalloys Corp. v. Amalloy Corp.*, No. 88-4707 (D.N.J. July 24, 1989) (Transcript: "Court: Are you seriously suggesting that the Hague Convention is a speedy process?"). Parties wishing to require use of the Convention must, therefore, be prepared to provide evidence that the Convention has worked well in the past in a particular nation and that they will cooperate in ensuring full and expeditious discovery in the pending matter. *See generally* Baker, *Obtaining Evidence: International Discovery Techniques — The Taking of Evidence Abroad for Use in American Courts* 688 PLI/Lit 173, 187 (2003). Consider whether these views are well founded.

3. Reluctance of U.S. trial courts to require first-use of Convention. Justice Blackmun's opinion in *Aérospatiale* warned: "I fear the Court's decision means that courts will resort unnecessarily to issuing discovery orders under the Federal Rules of Civil Procedure in a raw exercise of their jurisdictional power." The first post-*Aérospatiale* decision by a lower court seemed to belie Justice Blackmun's concern. The Court in *Hudson v. Pfauter,* 117 F.R.D. 33 (N.D.N.Y. 1987) held:

> It appears that the major obstacle to the effective use of Convention procedures by litigants and the courts is the fact that we are less familiar with those procedures than with the discovery provisions of the Federal Rules. Consequently, use of Convention procedures will, at least initially, result in greater expenditures of time and money for attorneys pursuing causes of action against foreign parties on behalf of their clients and could require an increased commitment of judicial resources. Nonetheless, these inconveniences alone do not outweigh the important purposes served by the Hague Convention. Further, as judges and lawyers become more familiar with the discovery rules of the Convention, it is quite possible that its procedures will prove just as effective and cost-efficient as those of the Federal Rules. To assume that the "American" rules are superior to those procedures agreed upon by the signatories of the Hague Convention without first seeing how effective Convention procedures will be in practice would reflect the same parochial biases that the Convention was designed to overcome.

Is that persuasive? What about the numerous reservations under Article 23 and the very different attitude toward "discovery" in non-U.S. jurisdictions? Whatever the case, *Uddeholm* and *In re Vitamins* were unwilling to require first-use of the Convention. Most other lower courts have reached the same conclusion. *See Loops LLC v. Phoenix Trading, Inc.*, 2010 WL 786030 (W.D. Wash. Mar. 4, 2010); *Schindler Elevator Corp. v. Otis Elevator Co.*, 657 F. Supp. 2d 525 (D.N.J. 2009) (magistrate judge); *In re Aspartame Antitrust Litig.*, 2008 WL 2275531 (E.D. Pa. May 13, 2008); *Madanes v. Madanes*, 199 F.R.D. 135 (S.D.N.Y. 2001);

Bodner v. Paribas, 202 F.R.D. 370 (E.D.N.Y. 2000); *In re Aircrash Disaster Near Roselawn, Ind, Oct. 31, 1994*, 172 F.R.D. 295 (N.D. Ill. 1997).

A few lower courts have reached contrary decisions, requiring first use of the Convention's procedures under *Aérospatiale. See AstraZeneca v. Ranbaxy Pharmaceuticals, Inc.*, 2008 WL 314627 (D.N.J. Jan. 29, 2008) (magistrate judge); *In re Perrier Bottled Water Litig.*, 138 F.R.D. 348 (D. Conn. 1991) ("all three prongs of the test set forth in *Societe* suggest utilization of Convention procedures"); *Hudson v. Hermann Pfauter GmbH & Co.*, 117 F.R.D. 33 (N.D.N.Y. 1987); *Husa v. Laboratories Servier SA*, 740 A.2d 1092, 1096-1097 (App. Div. 1999) (holding that Convention "should be utilized unless it is demonstrated that its use will substantially impair the search for truth, which is at the heart of all litigation, or will cause unduly prejudicial delay"). Is this trend against requiring resort to the Convention undesirable? Consistent with the Convention?

Consider the following:

> [T]he Hague Convention has been given short shrift since the Supreme Court's decision in [*Aérospatiale*]. . . . In *Aerospatiale*, the Hague Convention was referred to as a "permissive supplement" and an "optional procedure." However the Hague Convention is only as "optional" as deciding to use the Federal Rules is "optional" in such a case. . . . Unfortunately, I believe the language used in *Aerospatiale* has unintentionally compounded the problem inherent with the Convention: that "relatively few judges are experienced in the area [of international law] and the procedures of foreign legal systems are often poorly understood." *Aérospatiale*, 482 U.S. at 552 (Blackmun, J., dissenting). Many times, rather than wade through the mire of a complex set of foreign statutes and case law, judges marginalize the Convention as an unnecessary "option." I believe the *Aérospatiale* decision should be reexamined to ensure that lower courts are in fact exercising "special vigilance to protect foreign litigants" and demonstrating respect "for any sovereign interest expressed by the foreign state." *In re Automotive Refinishing Paint Antitrust Litig.*, 358 F.3d 288, 306 (3d Cir. 2004) (Roth, concurring).

Is Judge Roth correct in suggesting that the Supreme Court reconsider the decision altogether? Does that view take adequate account of Article 23 and foreign attitudes towards U.S. discovery?

4. *Burden of proof that Convention procedures should be used.* What party had the burden of proof in *Uddeholm* and *In re Vitamins* on the question whether first-use of the Convention was required? Other lower courts have reached divergent results on this issue. *Compare In re Automotive Refinishing Paint Antitrust Litig.*, 358 F.3d 288, 305 (3d Cir. 2004) (collecting cases and holding that party resisting discovery must demonstrate need to use Convention); *American Home Assurance Co. v. Société Commerciale Toutelectric*, 104 Cal. App. 4th 406, 427 (Cal. Ct. App. 2002) (same) *with Hudson v. Hermann Pfauter GmbH & Co.*, 117 F.R.D. 33 (N.D.N.Y. 1987) (contra). Which party should bear the burden of proof? Which party do you think the *Aerospatiale* majority intended to bear the burden of proof?

5. *Waiver and first resort.* As noted above, parties objecting to discovery have the option of requesting a protective order from a trial court. *See supra* p. 976. Suppose that discovery has been underway in a case for nearly a half-year and suddenly the foreign party requests a protective order requiring its opponent to obtain further discovery by resort to the Hague Evidence Convention. Under these circumstances, has the moving party waived its opportunity to require resort to the Convention? *See Milliken & Co. v. Bank of China*, 758 F. Supp. 2d 238 (S.D.N.Y. 2010) (finding no waiver). Even if the party has not waived the right to make the request, does the delay factor into the *Aérospatiale* analysis? Should it?

Parties should be especially sensitive about demanding resort to the Hague Evidence Convention after a discovery schedule, such as a deposition, has been agreed upon. Under such circumstances, eleventh-hour requests that the party seeking information resort to the Convention may result in the imposition of severe sanctions. *See Société Civile Succession Richard Guiono v. Besder Inc.*, 2007 WL 3238703 (D. Ariz. 2007) (awarding party a significant percentage of costs and fees associated with deposition where opponent demanded compliance with Convention on eve of deposition).

6. *Waiver and the letter of request.* Alternatively, sometimes parties realize in the middle of litigation that they may require discovery from abroad. In such circumstances, courts occasionally have denied the letter of request where it would delay the conclusion of discovery. *See, e.g., Seoul Semiconductor Co., Ltd. v. Nichia Corp.*, 590 F. Supp. 2d 832 (E.D. Tex. 2008); *Jovanovic v. Northrop Grumman Corp.*, 2008 WL 4950064 (D.N.J. Nov. 18, 2008) (magistrate judge).

7. *Foreign sovereign interests in* Aérospatiale *analysis.* Note the *Uddeholm* court's discussion of the sovereign interests of Sweden in this case, and in particular its refusal to accord any weight to the "general" interests identified by the Swedish Government. Other courts have taken the same approach. *In re Automotive Refinishing Paint Antitrust Litig.*, 358 F.3d 288, 304 & n.20 (3d Cir. 2004); *Rich v. KIS Cal., Inc.*, 121 F.R.D. 254, 258 (M.D.N.C. 1988) (foreign sovereign interests are "overly broad and vague" and do not "warrant" much deference); *MeadWestvaco Corp. v. Rexam PLC*, 2010 WL 5574325 (E.D. Va. Dec. 14, 2010) (magistrate judge) (same); *Milliken & Co. v. Bank of China*, 758 F. Supp. 2d 238 (S.D.N.Y. 2010) (finding foreign sovereign interest not compelling due to lack of objection to discovery in particular case). *See Aérospatiale*, 482 U.S. at 544 n.29 ("identify the nature of the sovereign interests in the nondisclosure of specific types of material"). These courts have instead demanded a showing of some "specific" interest that protects the sought-after information. Parties seeking to require resort to the Convention must therefore apparently come forward with evidence of narrowly tailored foreign nondisclosure laws aimed at particular subjects.

Compare the approach of the Court in *In re Vitamins* to foreign sovereign interests. Note that the Court's rhetoric, at least, gives substantial weight and deference to foreign state interests. Does the Court in fact give any weight to these interests in its decision? Compare how the Court discusses U.S. interests in *In re Vitamins*.

8. *Tailoring discovery under* Aérospatiale *analysis.* The magistrate in *Uddeholm* and the Court in *In re Vitamins* refused to fully enforce the plaintiff's discovery requests. Instead, relying on *Aérospatiale*, the courts narrowed the scope of those requests. Other lower courts have taken much the same approach. *See In re Automotive Refinishing Paint Litig.*, 229 F.R.D. 482, 495-496 (E.D. Pa. 2005); *Bodner v. Paribas,* 202 F.R.D. 370 (E.D.N.Y. 2000); *Valois of America, Inc. v. Risdon Corp.*, 183 F.R.D. 344, 349 (D. Conn. 1997); *Fishel v. BASF Group,* 175 F.R.D. 525, 529-531 (S.D. Iowa 1997); *Rich v. KIS Cal., Inc.*, 121 F.R.D. 254, 260 (M.D.N.C. 1988); *Scarminach v. Goldwell GmbH,* 531 N.Y.S. 2d 188, 191 (Sup. Ct. 1988); *In re Bedford Computer Corp.*, 114 B.R. 2 (Bankr. D.N.H. 1990). Is the general approach of these courts—foregoing first-use of the Convention but narrowing the breadth of direct U.S. discovery—a fair and sensible compromise? Consider the following:

At least in principle, this analysis would provide a mechanism for compromising extraterritorial discovery disputes by carefully identifying what U.S. and foreign sovereign interests actually are at stake in particular cases and by carefully tailoring U.S.-style discovery to avoid compromising relevant foreign interests. In practical terms, the lower courts' heightened scrutiny of sovereign interests would mean that extraterritorial discovery would be conducted pursuant to U.S. procedural rules, but would be more limited than occurs in the purely domestic context; direct U.S. discovery would also apparently be subject to a requirement of first use of the Convention where specific and clearly articulated foreign nondisclosure laws exist. There is undeniably an attractive element of rough justice and reciprocity about this proposal.

Ultimately, however, this approach is premised on a faulty view of foreign and U.S. sovereign interests. Specific foreign nondisclosure laws are generally relevant to the ultimate substantive question whether particular evidence can ever be produced, not to the procedures governing how such evidence can ever be produced. Foreign bank secrecy laws and privileges for confidential relationships do not reflect a desire that discovery into these matters occur pursuant to the Convention—instead, these laws generally reflect a prohibition against any discovery of protected materials. Similarly, in considering U.S. interests, the lower courts have typically inquired whether particular evidence is really needed by the U.S. litigant and how intrusive such discovery would be. Again, these questions are not relevant to the procedure for taking discovery into a particular matter, but instead go to the ultimate issue of whether particular materials should be discoverable at all.

All of this suggests that the lower courts that have attempted conscientiously to apply the *Aerospatiale* comity analysis have considered the wrong types of sovereign interests. These courts should be examining the U.S. interest in obtaining broad discovery very promptly (rather than somewhat less broadly and less quickly pursuant to the Convention), not the more generalized question whether discovery of certain subjects is needed. Conversely, lower courts should inquire whether the foreign State has expressed a specific interest that particular types of inquiries be conducted pursuant to the Convention, not whether the foreign State has indicated that inquiries in a particular field are simply forbidden. Only by evaluating U.S. and foreign sovereign interests for and against use of the Convention can U.S. courts determine intelligently whether or not use of the Convention is required by comity. Evaluating other interests simply does not bear on the desirability of requiring resort to the Convention. Born & Hoing, *Comity and the Lower Courts: Post-Aérospatiale Applications of the Hague Evidence Convention*, 24 Int'l Law. 393, 404-405 (1990).

Is this persuasive?

9. *Aérospatiale* and disclosure. Amendments to the Federal Rules of Civil Procedure adopted since ratification of the Hague Evidence Convention require parties to make certain disclosures without awaiting a discovery request. Among other things, each party must disclose to the other party "[a] copy—or description by category and location—of all documents, electronically stored information, and tangible things that the disclosing party has in its possession, custody or control and may use to support its claims or defenses, unless the use would be solely for impeachment." Fed. R. Civ. P. 26(a)(1)(A)(ii).

Under *Aérospatiale*, should a party ever be obligated to utilize the Hague Evidence Convention to obtain information falling under another party's disclosure obligations? No, according to one judge:

Relegating a party to the Convention in the context of initial disclosure is unwarranted for two reasons. First, the comity interests embodied in the Convention and recognized by *Aerospatiale* are attenuated in this situation. . . . Second there are equitable considerations at issue in disclosure that are not always in play in discovery. It is one thing to require a party bringing a claim to resort to Convention procedures in order to obtain evidence from another entity necessary to support that claim. It is entirely a different matter to permit a party to decline to disclose, except pursuant to Convention, protocols information that it expects to use to support the claims or defenses that it has affirmatively asserted. *Milliken & Co. v. Bank of China,* 758 F. Supp. 2d 238 (S.D.N.Y. 2010).

Is this persuasive? Why precisely are comity interests any more "attenuated" in the context of disclosure, as opposed to discovery, obligations? In both cases, isn't a foreign party being obligated to engage in acts potentially on another country's soil that the foreign country might not support? Moreover, what are the "equitable considerations" that warrant a different rule for disclosure? Those might make sense in the case of a foreign plaintiff, but why do they make sense in the case of a foreign defendant who is being unwillingly dragged into the U.S. forum? Depending on the scope of a party's disclosure obligation, does not the logic of this decision drive a huge hole through the Hague Evidence Convention?

10. *Jurisdictional discovery under Federal Rules.* U.S. courts can unilaterally compel discovery only from persons subject to their personal jurisdiction. This is true for both litigants and nonparty witnesses. *See supra* pp. 920-923.

Although personal jurisdiction is a requirement for court-ordered discovery, it is also settled that "jurisdictional discovery" can be compelled from a foreign entity in order to determine whether it is subject to a U.S. court's jurisdiction. *See Insurance Corp. of Ireland, Ltd. v. Compagnie des Bauxites de Guinee,* 456 U.S. 694 (1982); *In re Automotive Refinishing Paint Antitrust Litig.,* 358 F.3d 288, 302 (3d Cir. 2004); *Fishel v. BASF Group,* 175 F.R.D. 525, 528 (S.D.N.Y. 1997); *In re Bedford Computer Corp.,* 114 B.R. 2, 5 (Bankr. D.N.H. 1990).

Jurisdictional discovery is an important litigation tactic. Carefully crafted jurisdictional discovery may enable a plaintiff to obtain information related to its case on the merits even before the judge has ruled on motions to dismiss. Moreover, discovery can be expensive, so a plaintiff who successfully obtains a jurisdictional discovery order strengthens its bargaining position in extracting an early settlement from the defendant, who may prefer to settle a case rather than disclose large numbers of internal documents or incur the expense of doing so.

11. *Standards for jurisdictional discovery under FRCP.* The decision whether or not to permit jurisdictional discovery lies in part within the discretion of the trial judge. *Platten v. HG Bermuda Exempted Ltd.,* 437 F.3d 118, 139 (1st Cir. 2006); *Beecham v. Socialist People's Libyan Arab Jamahiriya,* 424 F.3d 1109, 1112 (D.C. Cir. 2005); *Fielding v. Hubert Burda Media, Inc.,* 415 F.3d 419, 428-429 (5th Cir. 2005); *United States v. Swiss Am. Bank, Ltd.,* 274 F.3d 610 (1st Cir. 2001); *Data Disc Inc. v. Systems Tech. Assocs.,* 557 F.2d 1280, 1285 n.1 (9th Cir. 1977). Trial judges can abuse their discretion if they decline to permit jurisdictional discovery despite a *prima facie* case by the plaintiffs. *Lakin v. Prudential Securities, Inc.,* 348 F.3d 704, 713 (8th Cir. 2003); *Harris Rutsky & Co. Ins. Services, Inc. v. Bell & Clements Ltd.,* 328 F.3d 1122, 1135 (9th Cir. 2003).

In order to obtain jurisdictional discovery, the moving party must ordinarily demonstrate "a reasonable probability that ultimately it will succeed in establishing the facts necessary for the exercise of jurisdiction." *In re Marc Rich & Co. AG,* 707 F.2d 663, 670 (2d Cir. 1983); *In re Sealed Case,* 832 F.2d 1268, 1274 (D.C. Cir. 1987). *Compare Data Disc Inc. v. Systems Tech. Assocs.,* 557 F.2d 1280, 1285 n.1 (9th Cir. 1977) (jurisdictional discovery appropriate "where pertinent facts bearing on the question of jurisdiction are controverted or where a more satisfactory showing of the facts is necessary"). Courts will also consider factors such as whether jurisdictional facts are peculiarly within the control of the defendant, whether the defendant has presented competent evidence demonstrating an absence of jurisdiction, and other equitable factors. *Kamen v. American Tel. & Tel. Co.,* 791 F.2d 1006 (2d Cir. 1986); *John Briley, Trevone Prods., Inc. v. Blackford,* 1990 U.S. Dist. LEXIS 10967 (S.D.N.Y. 1990). Jurisdictional discovery may be directed only to the issue of jurisdiction, not the merits of the parties' dispute. *Compagnie des Bauxites de Guinee v. L'Union,* 723 F.2d 357, 363 (3d Cir. 1983); *In re Chocolate Confectionary Antitrust Litig.,* 602 F. Supp. 2d 538 (M.D. Pa. 2009). *See generally* Strong, *Jurisdictional Discovery in United States Federal Courts,* 67 Wash. & Lee L. Rev. 489 (2010).

In international cases, is it appropriate to order jurisdictional discovery? What permits a U.S. court to order persons who may not be subject to U.S. jurisdiction to produce documents in the United States? Consider again the *Nahas* rationale. *See supra* pp. 889-893.

12. *Interplay between opportunity for jurisdictional discovery and showing required to establish jurisdiction.* If the plaintiff is not permitted jurisdictional discovery, then it may be difficult as a practical matter to satisfy the minimum contacts test and other jurisdictional requirements. Consequently, most courts have applied a less demanding burden of proof on jurisdictional issues when no jurisdictional discovery has been available. According to some lower courts, if jurisdictional discovery and a hearing on jurisdiction are conducted, then the plaintiff must generally carry the burden of establishing jurisdiction by a preponderance of the evidence. 2 Casad & Richman, *Jurisdiction in Civil Actions* §6-1[3][b] at 11 (1998). If jurisdictional discovery is not permitted, however, the plaintiff, according to this line of authority, generally need only make a "*prima facie* showing of jurisdictional facts." *In re Magnetic Audiotape Antitrust Litig.*, 334 F.3d 204, 206 (2d Cir. 2003); *Jazini v. Nissan Motor Co.*, 148 F.3d 181, 184 (2d Cir. 1998); *In re Parmalat Securities Litig.*, 381 F. Supp. 2d 283, 287 (S.D.N.Y. 2005). According to a conflicting line of authority, a plaintiff merely must have a "good faith belief" that jurisdictional discovery will supplement its allegations. *See, e.g., Burnett v. Al Baraka Inv. & Dev. Corp.*, 274 F. Supp. 2d 86, 97 (D.D.C. 2003); *Diamond Chemical Co., Inc. v. Atofina Chemicals, Inc.*, 268 F. Supp. 2d 1, 15 (D.D.C. 2003); *In re Vitamins Antitrust Litig.*, 94 F. Supp. 2d 26, 35 (D.D.C. 2000).

13. *Jurisdictional discovery under Hague Evidence Convention.* If jurisdictional facts are located in a Convention signatory state, is first-use or exclusive use of the Convention required? As the court in *In re Vitamins* noted, *Aérospatiale* emphasized that the French defendants were concededly subject to the District Court's jurisdiction. What does this indicate about the availability of jurisdictional discovery under the Federal Rules? Is the analysis in *In re Vitamins* persuasive? Why?

Lower courts are divided on the question whether jurisdictional discovery must proceed under the Convention. *See In re Automotive Refinishing Paint Antitrust Litig.*, 358 F.3d 288, 301-305 (3d Cir. 2004) (summarizing split and declining to mandate resort to Convention for jurisdictional discovery); *Synthes (U.S.A.) v. G.M. dos Reis Jr. Ind. Com. de Equip. Medico*, 2008 WL 81111 (S.D. Cal. Jan. 8, 2008) (same); *In re Vitamins Antitrust Litig.*, 120 F. Supp. 2d 45, 48 (D.D.C. 2000) (same); *Fishel v. BASF Group*, 175 F.R.D. 525, 529 (S.D. Iowa 1997) (same); *Rich v. KIS California, Inc.*, 121 F.R.D. 254 (M.D.N.C. 1988) (same); *Geo-Culture, Inc. v. Siam Inv. Mgmt. SA*, 936 P.2d 1063, 1067 (Or. App. 1997) (requiring resort to Convention where plaintiff failed to make prima facie showing of personal jurisdiction). *Compare Jenco v. Martech, Int'l, Inc.*, 1988 WL 54733 (E.D. La. 1988); *Knight v. Ford Motor Co.*, 615 A.2d 297, 301 n.11 (N.J. L. Div. 1992).

Even if use of the Convention is not *per se* required, does *Aérospatiale*'s *ad hoc* comity analysis take into account the fact that jurisdiction has not yet been established? If so, what weight should this factor have? What weight, if any, did the Court give to the fact that jurisdictional discovery was involved in *In re Vitamins*? Does the *Aérospatiale* analysis depend on the form of jurisdictional discovery sought by a party? In other words, should courts be more inclined to order resort to the Convention when a party requests deposition testimony as opposed to document production? *See Schindler Elevator Corp. v. Otis Elevator Co.*, 657 F. Supp. 2d 525 (D.N.J. 2009) (declining to order resort to Convention where party sought deposition of opponent's employee during jurisdictional discovery).

14. *Application of* Aérospatiale *comity analysis to require use of letters rogatory not subject to Hague Evidence Convention.* To what extent does *Aérospatiale*'s comity analysis apply outside the context of the Hague Evidence Convention, and in particular, to require a party initially to seek discovery through customary letters rogatory? That is, does the *Aérospatiale* analysis require that trial courts weigh the scope of and need for U.S. extraterritorial discovery against foreign sovereign interests in deciding whether to order direct extraterritorial discovery from foreign countries that are not party to the Convention?

Portions of the Court's opinion in *Aerospatiale* are arguably not tied to the Convention, but apply equally to all transnational discovery. Indeed, the language the Court quotes from §442 of the *Third Restatement* does not pertain specifically to the Convention, but concerns extraterritorial U.S. discovery generally. Are there circumstances where a court should refuse to order discovery from a foreign litigant, under the Federal Rules, and instead require that any discovery efforts proceed through "first-use" of customary letters rogatory? *Compare supra* pp. 1051-1053 (discussion of lower court decisions requiring use of letters rogatory to serve process abroad). In answering this question consider the materials excerpted above concerning the preparation and use of letters rogatory. *See supra* pp. 1024-1026. Also consider the following cautionary advice from the U.S. Department of State's *Circular on Obtaining Evidence Abroad,* excerpted in Appendix CC ("Letters rogatory are a cumbersome, time consuming mechanism which should not be used unless there is no other alternative.").

Consider how the Court resolves this issue in *In re Vitamins.* Are you persuaded? Does the Court take adequate account of §442 and its role in *Aérospatiale?*

If the *Aérospatiale* formula *is* generally applicable outside the Convention context, how does this alter the analysis of decisions like *City Bank,* excerpted above? Even if the *Aérospatiale* analysis is not directly applicable outside the context of Convention procedures, is the §442 interest-balancing analysis that *Aérospatiale* adopts nonetheless applicable? How did the Court in *In re Vitamins* resolve this question? How different was its analysis from that applicable directly under *Aérospatiale?*

15. *Necessity of using Convention or letters rogatory to obtain discovery from nonparty witnesses. Aerospatiale* involved discovery from foreign companies that were parties to the U.S. litigation and concededly subject to the U.S. court's personal jurisdiction. Discovery from nonparty witnesses, however, will often require obtaining materials from persons or entities that are not subject to U.S. personal jurisdiction or to effective subpoena service. *See supra* pp. 990-998. In these circumstances, direct U.S. discovery is not available and the Hague Evidence Convention (or customary letters rogatory) must be used. *See In re Urethane Antitrust Litig.,* 267 F.R.D. 361 (D. Kan. 2010) (magistrate judge); *Linde v. Arab Bank PLC,* 262 F.R.D. 136 (E.D.N.Y. 2009) (magistrate judge); *In re Baycol Products Litig.,* 348 F. Supp. 2d 1058, 1060 (D. Minn. 2004) (resort to Convention was "only means available to obtain the requested discovery" sought by nonparty not otherwise subject to court's jurisdiction); *Abbott Laboratories v. Impax Laboratories, Inc.,* 2004 WL 1622223, at *2 (E.D. La. 2004); *Tulip Computers Int'l BV v. Dell Computer Corp.,* 254 F. Supp. 2d 469, 474 (D. Del. 2003); *Elliott Assocs. v. Republic of Peru,* 1997 WL 436493, at *2 (S.D.N.Y. 1997); *Intercontinental Credit Corp. v. Roth,* 595 N.Y.S.2d 602 (Sup. Ct. 1991) ("When discovery is sought from a nonparty in a foreign jurisdiction, application of the Hague Convention . . . which encompasses principles of international comity, is virtually compulsory"); *Orlich v. Helm Bros., Inc.,* 560 N.Y.S.2d 10 (App. Div. 1990) ("When discovery is sought from a nonparty in a foreign jurisdiction, application of the Hague Evidence Convention . . . is virtually compulsory."). The only exception to this is where a nonparty witness is subject to subpoena service and personal jurisdiction; in this case, resort to the Convention is not necessarily required. *See First American Corp. v. Price Waterhouse LLP,* 154 F.3d 16 (2d Cir. 1998); *supra* pp. 995-997.

G. Taking of Evidence in the United States in Aid of Foreign Proceedings

Litigants in foreign proceedings often require the taking of evidence located in the United States, just as U.S. litigants require evidence located abroad. This section examines the treatment of such evidence-taking under U.S. law.

1. Taking of Evidence in the United States Without Court Assistance

Unlike some civil law jurisdictions, the United States imposes no general prohibition against the taking of evidence on U.S. territory for use in foreign judicial proceedings. The legislative history to 28 U.S.C. §1782(b) refers to the "pre-existing freedom of persons within the United States voluntarily to give statements or produce tangible evidence in connection with foreign or international proceedings or investigations."[197] This general freedom is subject, of course, to restrictions such as export control laws, privileges, confidentiality duties, and the like.

2. Taking of Evidence in the United States with Court Assistance

U.S. courts will assist foreign courts and litigants in the taking of evidence located in the United States. As early as 1855, Congress enacted legislation authorizing federal courts to assist foreign courts in obtaining evidence.[198] Unfortunately, the statute was miscatalogued, and apparently never used.[199] In 1863, Congress enacted another statute providing for U.S. judicial assistance, but only in a narrow range of cases — specifically, where a foreign state itself, with which the United States was at peace, sought recovery of money or property.[200] Given the restrictive character of this authorization, it was seldom successfully invoked.[201]

Following 1945, Congress and the Executive Branch anticipated increased international commerce and litigation. As a consequence, the existing letter rogatory

---

197. S. Rep. No. 1580, 88th Cong., 1st Sess. (1963), *reprinted in* [1964] U.S. Code Cong. & Admin. News 3782, 3789-3790. Section 1782(a) is discussed below. *See infra* pp. 1066-1076. Section 1782(b) itself provides: "This chapter does not preclude a person within the United States from voluntarily giving his testimony or statement, or producing a document or other thing, for use in a proceeding in a foreign or international tribunal before any person and in any manner acceptable to him." 28 U.S.C. §1782. The former Uniform Interstate and International Procedure Act provides that "[a] person within this state may voluntarily give his testimony or statement or produce documents or other things for use in a proceeding before a tribunal outside this state in any manner acceptable to him." Uniform Interstate and International Procedure Act §302(b), *excerpted in* Appendix D. The Commentary to this provision explains: "Sub-section (b) re-affirms the existing freedom of persons within the United States voluntarily to give testimony or produce evidence for use in proceedings or investigations elsewhere. The explicit reaffirmation is desirable in order to stress the large degree of freedom existing in this area." 13 U.L.A. 492 (1980).

198. 10 Stat. 630, ch. 140 §2 (March 2, 1855) ("Where letters rogatory shall have [been] addressed, from any court of a foreign country to any circuit court of the United States, and a United States commissioner designated by said circuit court to make the examination of witnesses in said letters mentioned, said commissioner shall be empowered to compel the witnesses to appear and depose in the same manner as to appear and testify in court."). The statute was enacted because the U.S. Department of State and Attorney General had concluded that a U.S. court lacked the power to execute a French letter rogatory. Jones, *International Judicial Assistance: Procedural Chaos and a Program for Reform*, 62 Yale L.J. 515, 540 (1953).

199. Jones, *International Judicial Assistance: Procedural Chaos and a Program for Reform*, 62 Yale L.J. 515, 540 n.77 (1953).

200. 12 Stat. 769, 769-770, ch. 95 (March 3, 1863).

201. *Janssen v. Belding-Corticelli, Ltd.*, 84 F.2d 577 (3d Cir. 1936); *In re Letters Rogatory from Examining Magistrate of Tribunal of Versailles, France*, 26 F. Supp. 852 (D. Md. 1939); *In re Letters Rogatory From the First District Judge of Vera Cruz*, 36 F. 306 (S.D.N.Y. 1888).

legislation was amended, in both 1948 and 1949.[202] Both amendments broadened the availability of U.S. judicial assistance, eliminating the requirement that a foreign state be a party to foreign proceedings and expanding the statute to assistance in aid of any pending foreign judicial proceeding.

As discussed above,[203] the Commission and Advisory Committee on International Rules of Judicial Procedure was established in 1958 to study the general subject of international judicial assistance.[204] Among other things, the Commission recommended, and Congress adopted in 1964, amendments to the existing letters rogatory statute.[205] As amended, §1782 provides:

> The district court of the district in which a person resides or is found may order him to give his testimony or statement or to produce a document or other thing for use in a proceeding in a foreign or international tribunal, including criminal investigations conducted before formal accusation. The order may be made pursuant to a letter rogatory issued, or request made, by a foreign or international tribunal or upon the application of any interested person. . . .[206]

Section 1782 has been invoked with increasing frequency in international civil litigation during the past two decades. Parties to foreign judicial, arbitral, and investigative proceedings have frequently sought to take discovery under §1782 of materials located in the United States. These efforts gave rise to a number of questions about the interpretation of §1782.

The Supreme Court's decision in *Intel Corporation v. Advanced Micro Devices, Inc.,* which is excerpted below, resolved several questions about the meaning of §1782. At the same time, the Court's opinion created the potential for future litigation over the scope of §1782.

INTEL CORPORATION v. ADVANCED MICRO DEVICES, INC.
542 U.S. 241 (2004)

GINSBURG, JUSTICE. This case concerns the authority of federal district courts to assist in the production of evidence for use in a foreign or international tribunal. . . .

[Respondent Advanced Micro Devices, Inc. ("AMD") and petitioner Intel Corporation ("Intel")] are worldwide competitors in the microprocessor industry. . . . In October 2000, AMD filed an antitrust complaint with the Directorate-General for Competition ("DG-Competition") of the Commission of the European Communities ("European Commission" or "Commission"). . . . The European Commission is the executive and administrative organ of the European Communities. . . . AMD's complaint alleged that Intel, in violation of European competition law, had abused its dominant position in the European market through loyalty rebates [and other practices]. AMD recommended that the DG-Competition seek discovery of documents Intel had produced in a private antitrust suit. . . . After the DG-Competition declined to seek judicial assistance in the United States, AMD, pursuant to §1782(a), petitioned the District Court for the Northern District of California[207] for an order directing Intel to produce documents discovered in the

---

202. Pub. L. No. 80-773, 62 Stat. 869, 949 (June 25, 1948); Pub. L. No. 81-72, 63 Stat. 89, 103 (May 24, 1949).
203. *See supra* pp. 874-875.
204. *See supra* p. 875.
205. Pub. L. No. 88-619, 78 Stat. 995, 997 §9 (Oct. 3, 1964).
206. 28 U.S.C. §1782(a). *See* Appendix A. Congress amended the statute in 1996 to include criminal investigations among the "proceedings" to which §1782 applies.
207. Both Intel and AMD are headquartered in the Northern District of California.

[private antitrust suit]. AMD asserted that it sought the materials in connection with the complaint it had filed with the European Commission. [The District Court dismissed AMD's request. The Court of Appeals reversed, holding that §1782 applied to nonjudicial matters such as the DG-Competition's investigation and that §1782 imposed no discoverability requirement.]

The DG-Competition's overriding responsibility is to conduct investigations into alleged violations of the European Union's competition prescriptions. On receipt of a complaint or *sua sponte*, the DG-Competition conducts a preliminary investigation. In that investigation, the DG-Competition may take into account information provided by a complainant, and it may seek information directly from the target of the complaint. Ultimately, DG Competition's preliminary investigation results in a formal written decision whether to pursue the complaint. If [the DG-Competition] declines to proceed, that decision is subject to judicial review by the Court of First Instance and, ultimately, by the court of last resort for European Union matters, the Court of Justice for the European Communities (European Court of Justice).

If the DG-Competition decides to pursue the complaint, it typically serves the target of the investigation with a formal "statement of objections" and advises the target of its intention to recommend a decision finding that the target has violated European competition law. The target is entitled to a hearing before an independent officer, who provides a report to the DG-Competition. Once the DG-Competition has made its recommendation, the European Commission may dismiss the complaint, or issue a decision finding infringement and imposing penalties. The Commission's final action dismissing the complaint or holding the target liable is subject to review in the Court of First Instance and the European Court of Justice. Although lacking formal "party" or "litigant" status in Commission proceedings, the complainant has significant procedural rights. Most prominently, the complainant may submit to the DG-Competition information in support of its allegations, and may seek judicial review of the Commission's disposition of a complaint. . . .

We turn first to Intel's contention that the catalog of "interested person[s]" authorized to apply for judicial assistance under §1782(a) includes only "litigants, foreign sovereigns, and the designated agents of those sovereigns," and excludes AMD, a mere complainant before the Commission, accorded only "limited rights." Highlighting §1782's caption, "[a]ssistance to foreign and international tribunals and to litigants before such tribunals," Intel urges that the statutory phrase "any interested person" should be read, correspondingly, to reach only "litigants."

The caption of a statute . . . cannot undo or limit that which the [statute's] text makes plain. The text of §1782(a), "upon the application of any interested person," plainly reaches beyond the universe of persons designated "litigant." No doubt litigants are included among, and may be the most common example of, the "interested person[s]" who may invoke §1782; we read §1782's caption to convey no more. . . .

The complainant who triggers a European Commission investigation has a significant role in the process. As earlier observed, in addition to prompting an investigation, the complainant has the right to submit information for the DG-Competition's consideration, and may proceed to court if the Commission discontinues the investigation or dismisses the complaint. Given these participation rights, a complainant "possess[es] a reasonable interest in obtaining [judicial] assistance," and therefore qualifies as an "interested person" within any fair construction of that term.

We next consider whether the assistance in obtaining documents here sought by an "interested person" meets the specification "for use in a foreign or international tribunal." Beyond question, the reviewing authorities, both the Court of First Instance and the

European Court of Justice, qualify as tribunals. But those courts are not proof-taking instances. Their review is limited to the record before the Commission. Hence, AMD could "use" evidence in the reviewing courts only by submitting it to the Commission in the current, investigative stage.

Moreover, when Congress established the Commission on International Rules of Judicial Procedure in 1958, it instructed the Rules Commission to recommend procedural revisions "for the rendering of assistance to foreign courts and quasi-judicial agencies." Section 1782 had previously referred to "any judicial proceeding." The Rules Commission's draft, which Congress adopted, replaced that term with "a proceeding in a foreign or international tribunal." Congress understood that change to "provid[e] the possibility of U.S. judicial assistance in connection with [administrative and quasi-judicial proceedings abroad]." S. Rep. No. 1580, at 7-8. . . . We have no warrant to exclude the European Commission, to the extent that it acts as a first-instance decision-maker, from §1782(a)'s ambit.

Intel also urges that AMD's complaint has not progressed beyond the investigative stage; therefore, no adjudicative action is currently or even imminently on the Commission's agenda. Section 1782(a) does not limit the provision of judicial assistance to "pending" adjudicative proceedings. In 1964, when Congress eliminated the requirement that a proceeding be "judicial," Congress also deleted the requirement that a proceeding be "pending." The legislative history of the 1964 revision is in sync; it reflects Congress' recognition that judicial assistance would be available "whether the foreign or international proceeding or investigation is of a criminal, civil, administrative, or other nature." S. Rep. No. 1580, at 9. In 1996, Congress amended §1782(a) to clarify that the statute covers "criminal investigations conducted before formal accusation." *See* §1342(b), 110 Stat. 486. Nothing suggests that this amendment was an endeavor to rein in, rather than to confirm, by way of example, the broad range of discovery authorized in 1964.

In short, we reject the view . . . that §1782 comes into play only when adjudicative proceedings are "pending" or "imminent." Instead, we hold that §1782(a) requires only that a dispositive ruling by the Commission, reviewable by the European courts, be within reasonable contemplation.

We take up next the foreign-discoverability rule on which lower courts have divided: Does §1782(a) categorically bar a district court from ordering production of documents when the foreign tribunal or the "interested person" would not be able to obtain the documents if they were located in the foreign jurisdiction?

We note at the outset, and count it significant, that §1782(a) expressly shields privileged material: "A person may not be compelled to give his testimony or statement or to produce a document or other thing in violation of any legally applicable privilege." Beyond shielding material safeguarded by an applicable privilege, however, nothing in the text of §1782 limits a district court's production-order authority to materials that could be discovered in the foreign jurisdiction if the materials were located there. "If Congress had intended to impose such a sweeping restriction on the district court's discretion, at a time when it was enacting liberalizing amendments to the statute, it would have included statutory language to that effect." *In re Application of Gianoli Aldunate,* 3 F.3d 54, 59 (2d Cir. 1993).

Nor does §1782(a)'s legislative history suggest that Congress intended to impose a blanket foreign-discoverability rule on the provision of assistance under §1782(a). The Senate Report observes in this regard that §1782(a) "leaves the issuance of an appropriate order to the discretion of the court which, in proper cases, may refuse to issue an order or may impose conditions it deems desirable." S. Rep. No. 1580, at 7.

Intel raises two policy concerns in support of a foreign-discoverability limitation on §1782(a) aid — avoiding offense to foreign governments, and maintaining parity between litigants. While comity and parity concerns may be important as touchstones for a district court's exercise of discretion in particular cases, they do not permit our insertion of a generally applicable foreign-discoverability rule into the text of §1782(a).

We question whether foreign governments would in fact be offended by a domestic prescription permitting, but not requiring, judicial assistance. A foreign nation may limit discovery within its domain for reasons peculiar to its own legal practices, culture, or traditions — reasons that do not necessarily signal objection to aid from United States federal courts.[208] A foreign tribunal's reluctance to order production of materials present in the United States similarly may signal no resistance to the receipt of evidence gathered pursuant to §1782(a). *See South Carolina Ins. Co. v. Assurantie Maatschappij "De Zeven Provincien" NV,* [1987] 1 App. Cas. 24 (House of Lords ruled that nondiscoverability under English law did not stand in the way of a litigant in English proceedings seeking assistance in the United States under §1782). When the foreign tribunal would readily accept relevant information discovered in the United States, application of a foreign-discoverability rule would be senseless. The rule in that situation would serve only to thwart §1782(a)'s objective to assist foreign tribunals in obtaining relevant information that the tribunals may find useful but, for reasons having no bearing on international comity, they cannot obtain under their own laws.

Concerns about maintaining parity among adversaries in litigation likewise do not provide a sound basis for a cross-the-board foreign-discoverability rule. When information is sought by an "interested person," a district court could condition relief upon that person's reciprocal exchange of information. Moreover, the foreign tribunal can place conditions on its acceptance of the information to maintain whatever measure of parity it concludes is appropriate.[209]

We also reject Intel's suggestion that a §1782(a) applicant must show that United States law would allow discovery in domestic litigation analogous to the foreign proceeding. Section 1782 is a provision for assistance to tribunals abroad. It does not direct United States courts to engage in comparative analysis to determine whether analogous proceedings exist here. Comparisons of that order can be fraught with danger.[210] For example, we have in the United States no close analogue to the European Commission regime under which AMD is not free to mount its own case in the Court of First Instance or the European Court of Justice, but can participate only as complainant, an "interested person," in Commission-steered proceedings.

As earlier emphasized, a district court is not required to grant a §1782(a) discovery application simply because it has the authority to do so. We note below factors that bear consideration in ruling on a §1782(a) request.

First, when the person from whom discovery is sought is a participant in the foreign proceeding (as Intel is here), the need for §1782(a) aid generally is not as apparent as it ordinarily is when evidence is sought from a non-participant in the matter arising abroad.

---

208. Most civil-law systems lack procedures analogous to the pretrial discovery regime operative under the Federal Rules of Civil Procedure.

209. A civil-law court, furthermore, might attend to litigant-parity concerns in its merits determination: "In civil law countries, documentary evidence is generally submitted as an attachment to the pleadings or as part of a report by an expert. . . . A civil law court generally rules upon the question of whether particular documentary evidence may be relied upon only in its decision on the merits." Smit, Recent Developments 235-236, n.94.

210. Among its proposed rules, the dissent would exclude from §1782(a)'s reach discovery not available "under foreign law" and "under domestic law in analogous circumstances." Because comparison of systems is slippery business, the dissent's rule is infinitely easier to state than to apply. As the dissent's examples tellingly reveal, a foreign proceeding may have no direct analogue in our legal system. In light of the variety of foreign proceedings resistant to ready classification in domestic terms, Congress left unbounded by categorical rules the determination whether a matter is proceeding "in a foreign or international tribunal." While we reject the rules the dissent would inject into the statute, we do suggest guides for the exercise of district-court discretion.

A foreign tribunal has jurisdiction over those appearing before it, and can itself order them to produce evidence. In contrast, non-participants in the foreign proceeding may be outside the foreign tribunal's jurisdictional reach; hence, their evidence, available in the United States, may be unobtainable absent §1782(a) aid.

Second, as the 1964 Senate Report suggests, a court presented with a §1782(a) request may take into account the nature of the foreign tribunal, the character of the proceedings underway abroad, and the receptivity of the foreign government or the court or agency abroad to U.S. federal-court judicial assistance. *See* S. Rep. No. 1580, at 7. Further, the grounds Intel urged for categorical limitations on §1782(a)'s scope may be relevant in determining whether a discovery order should be granted in a particular case. Specifically, a district court could consider whether the §1782(a) request conceals an attempt to circumvent foreign proof-gathering restrictions or other policies of a foreign country or the United States. Also, unduly intrusive or burdensome requests may be rejected or trimmed.

Intel maintains that, if we do not accept the categorical limitations it proposes, then, at least, we should exercise our supervisory authority to adopt rules barring §1782(a) discovery here. We decline, at this juncture, to adopt supervisory rules. Any such endeavor at least should await further experience with §1782(a) applications in the lower courts.[211]

The European Commission has stated in *amicus curiae* briefs to this Court that it does not need or want the District Court's assistance. It is not altogether clear, however, whether the Commission, which may itself invoke §1782(a) aid, means to say "never" or "hardly ever" to judicial assistance from United States courts. Nor do we know whether the European Commission's views on §1782(a)'s utility are widely shared in the international community by entities with similarly blended adjudicative and prosecutorial functions.

Several facets of this case remain largely unexplored. Intel and its *amici* have expressed concerns that AMD's application, if granted in any part, may yield disclosure of confidential information, encourage "fishing expeditions," and undermine the European Commission's Leniency Program.[212] Yet no one has suggested that AMD's complaint to the Commission is pretextual. Nor has it been shown that §1782(a)'s preservation of legally applicable privileges, and the controls on discovery available to the District Court, *see, e.g.,* Fed. Rule Civ. Proc. 26(b)(2) and (c), would be ineffective to prevent discovery of Intel's business secrets and other confidential information. On the merits, this case bears closer scrutiny than it has received to date. Having held that §1782(a) authorizes, but does not require, discovery assistance, we leave it to the courts below to assure an airing adequate to determine what, if any, assistance is appropriate.[213]

BREYER, JUSTICE, dissenting. The Court reads the scope of §1782 to extend beyond what I believe Congress might reasonably have intended. Some countries allow a private citizen to ask a court to review a criminal prosecutor's decision not to prosecute. On the

---

211. The dissent sees a need for "categorical limits" to ward off "expensive, time-consuming battles about discovery." That concern seems more imaginary than real. There is no evidence whatsoever, in the 40 years since §1782(a)'s adoption, of the costs, delays, and forced settlements the dissent hypothesizes. The Commission, we note, is not obliged to respond to a discovery request of the kind AMD has made. The party targeted in the complaint and in the §1782(a) application would no doubt wield the laboring oar in opposing discovery, as Intel did here. Not only was there no "need for the Commission to respond," the Commission in fact made no submission at all in the instant matter before it reached this Court.

212. The European Commission's "Leniency Program" allows "cartel participants [to] confess their own wrongdoing" in return for prosecutorial leniency.

213. The District Court might also consider the significance of the protective order entered by the [court where the private antitrust proceeding occurred].

majority's reading, that foreign private citizen could ask an American court to help the citizen obtain information, even if the foreign prosecutor were indifferent or unreceptive. Many countries allow court review of decisions made by any of a wide variety of nonprosecutorial, nonadjudicative bodies. On the majority's reading, a British developer, hoping to persuade the British Housing Corporation to grant it funding to build a low-income housing development, could ask an American court to demand that an American firm produce information designed to help the developer obtain the British grant. This case itself suggests that an American firm, hoping to obtain information from a competitor, might file an antitrust complaint with the European antitrust authorities, thereby opening up the possibility of broad American discovery—contrary to the antitrust authorities' desires.

One might ask why it is wrong to read the statute as permitting the use of America's court processes to obtain information in such circumstances. One might also ask why American courts should not deal case by case with any problems of the sort mentioned. The answer to both of these questions is that discovery and discovery-related judicial proceedings take time, they are expensive, and cost and delay, or threats of cost and delay, can themselves force parties to settle underlying disputes. To the extent that expensive, time-consuming battles about discovery proliferate, they deflect the attention of foreign authorities from other matters those authorities consider more important; they can lead to results contrary to those that foreign authorities desire; and they can promote disharmony among national and international authorities, rather than the harmony that §1782 seeks to achieve. They also use up domestic judicial resources and crowd our dockets. That is why I believe the statute, while granting district courts broad authority to order discovery, nonetheless must be read as subject to some categorical limits, at least at the outer bounds—a matter that today's decision makes even more important. Those limits should rule out instances in which it is virtually certain that discovery (if considered case by case) would prove unjustified. . . .

First, when a foreign entity possesses few tribunal-like characteristics, so that the applicability of the statute's word "tribunal" is in serious doubt, then a court should pay close attention to the foreign entity's own view of its "tribunal"-like or non-"tribunal"-like status. By paying particular attention to the views of the very foreign nations that Congress sought to help, courts would better achieve Congress' basic cooperative objectives in enacting the statute.

Second, a court should not permit discovery where both of the following are true: (1) A private person seeking discovery would not be entitled to that discovery under foreign law, and (2) the discovery would not be available under domestic law in analogous circumstances. The Federal Rules of Civil Procedure, for example, make only limited provisions for nonlitigants to obtain certain discovery. *See* Fed. Rule Civ. Proc. 27. The limitations contained in the Rules help to avoid discovery battles launched by firms simply seeking information from competitors. Where there is benefit in permitting such discovery, and the benefit outweighs the cost of allowing it, one would expect either domestic law or foreign law to authorize it. If, notwithstanding the fact that it would not be allowed under either domestic or foreign law, there is some special need for the discovery in a particular instance, one would expect to find foreign governmental or intergovernmental authorities making the case for that need. Where none of these circumstances is present, what benefit could offset the obvious costs to the competitor and to our courts? I cannot think of any. . . .

What is the legal source of these limiting principles? In my view, they, and perhaps others, are implicit in the statute itself, given its purpose and use of the terms "tribunal" and "interested person." But even if they are not, this Court's "supervisory powers . . . permit, at the least, the promulgation of procedural rules governing the management of litigation." . . . *Thomas v. Arn,* 474 U.S. 140, 146-147 (1985). Intel Corp. has asked us to exercise those powers in this case. We should do so along the lines that I suggest. . . .

Notes on Intel

1. ***Parties entitled to utilize §1782.*** Recall that the classic form of international judicial assistance, via letters rogatory, was from one court to another court. *See supra* pp. 1024-1026. Letters rogatory were not customarily served merely by litigants in particular proceedings, but rather by the court in which the proceeding was pending.

What persons are entitled to utilize §1782? Note that §1782 authorizes a U.S. court to order discovery "pursuant to a letter rogatory issued, or request made, by a foreign or international tribunal or upon the application of any interested person."

(a) *"Interested persons" under §1782.* It is clear that the parties to a foreign litigation can be "interested persons." *See* S. Rep. No. 1580, 88th Cong., 2d Sess. (1964), *reprinted in* U.S. Code, Cong. & Admin. News 3782, 3789 ("interested person" includes "person designated by or under foreign law, or a party to the foreign or international litigation"). Who else qualifies as an "interested person"? *See In re Application of Esses,* 101 F.3d 873 (2d Cir. 1996); *Lancaster Factoring Co. v. Mangone,* 90 F.3d 98 (2d Cir. 1996). Why was AMD deemed to be an "interested person" in *Intel?* Where does the Supreme Court's definition stop? Does *Intel* hold that *all* complainants to a foreign investigatory body qualify as "interested persons"? *Lazaridis v. Int'l Centre for Missing and Exploited Children,* 2011 WL 180033 (D.D.C. Jan. 20, 2011). Would another competitor of Intel, not involved in the European Commission proceeding, also have been an "interested person" in *Intel?*

What is the rationale for permitting "interested persons" in foreign litigation — including private parties — to obtain the assistance of U.S. courts directly, without the permission of the foreign court presiding over the foreign litigation? As already noted, this is a dramatic departure from traditional notions of international judicial assistance, which involved the aid of one court for another court. Is it wise for §1782 to provide judicial assistance at the request of foreign litigants? What policies does it advance? What risks does it involve? Note that, in general, §1782 will permit foreign parties to obtain discovery of U.S.-located materials in the possession of U.S. parties, in circumstances in which the U.S. party will not voluntarily produce them. Note further that the party seeking §1782 discovery is likely to be a foreign (not U.S.) entity, which has chosen to avail itself of local courts against a U.S. adversary. Why in the world would Congress have authorized U.S. courts to order discovery in these circumstances — at the expense of the U.S. taxpayer?

(b) *U.S. Government as "interested person" under §1782.* Sometimes the U.S. Government can be an "interested person" under §1782. For example, the Government may sometimes receive discovery requests sent from a foreign court via a letter rogatory. In response, the Government may then file a §1782 petition requesting that a local federal prosecutor be appointed a "commissioner" for purposes of obtaining the evidence requested by the foreign court pursuant to the letter rogatory. Federal courts have approved of this practice. *See In re Clerici,* 481 F.3d 1324 (11th Cir. 2008); *In re Letter of Request,* 2010 WL 1655823 (S.D. Fla. Apr. 23, 2010); *In re Wilhelm,* 470 F. Supp. 2d 409 (S.D.N.Y. 2007). Is this approach correct? While §1782 authorizes assistance pursuant to a letter rogatory, what provision of the statute entitles the U.S. Government to request relief under §1782? Does the Government's desire to honor a treaty obligation supply the necessary interest? Are there any pitfalls in the method of appointing a local federal prosecutor to obtain the information? Doesn't this essentially allow a foreign court to co-opt the criminal justice mechanism of the United States and compel an individual located in the United States to give sworn testimony, thereby risking criminal sanctions?

Additionally, the Government also may seek discovery under §1782 when it receives a request from foreign law enforcement authorities pursuant to a Mutual Legal Assistance Treaties. Under such treaties, a signatory country may request the assistance from law enforcement authorities in another signatory country as part of a criminal investigation. Though such treaties only cover criminal matters, civil litigants should be aware of them, particularly in matters that often have overlapping civil and criminal components such as antitrust or securities. For a discussion of the relationship between Mutual Legal Assistance Treaties and §1782, *see In re Commissioner's Subpoena*, 325 F.3d 1287 (11th Cir. 2003).

(c) Complainants in foreign criminal proceedings as "interested person." Can a complainant in a foreign criminal proceeding be an "interested person"? Does the answer depend on whether a Mutual Legal Assistance Treaty exists between the United States and the foreign country where the proceeding is taking place? If such a treaty does exist, why should private parties be able to circumvent the framework of those treaties (through which governments request assistance from each other)? Does *Intel* supply an answer? Instead of influencing the interpretation of "interested person," does the existence of a Mutual Legal Assistance Treaty influence the factors guiding a district court's discretion under *Intel? See Lazaridis v. Int'l Centre for Missing and Exploited Children*, 2011 WL 180033, at *4 (D.D.C. Jan. 20, 2011).

(d) Defendants in foreign criminal proceedings as "interested person." Suppose that an individual is a defendant in a foreign criminal proceeding. That individual believes that a company located in the United States possesses information that may assist in the individual's defense. May he seek that information through a §1782 proceeding? Would the existence of a Mutual Legal Assistance Treaty, discussed in the preceding subsections, foreclose the defendant's entitlement to that information? Note that Mutual Legal Assistance Treaties typically set forth obligations between Contracting States and therefore typically involve requests from one state's prosecutor to another state's prosecutor. Does the existence of such a prosecutorial assistance regime foreclose efforts by criminal defendants to obtain assistance by means of a §1782 petition? *See Weber v. Finker*, 554 F.3d 1379, 1383-1384 (11th Cir. 2009).

2. "Foreign or international tribunal." Section 1782 also authorizes courts to order discovery pursuant to a request by "a foreign or international tribunal." What is a "foreign or international tribunal?" A court? An administrative agency? *In re Application of Wilander*, 1996 WL 421938 (E.D. Pa. 1996) (sports appeal committee not a tribunal). A prosecutorial agency? An investigative agency? All of the above? *See* Annotation, *What Is a Foreign Tribunal Within 28 U.S.C. §1782?*, 46 A.L.R. Fed. 956 (2004).

Was it not important in *Intel* to consider whether the European Commission deemed itself to be a tribunal? Consider the following excerpts from the dissent in *Intel:* "the Commission has told this Court that it is not a 'tribunal' under the Act. It has added that, should it be considered, against its will, a 'tribunal,' its 'ability to carry out its governmental responsibilities' will be seriously threatened." How much weight did the *Intel* Court give the Commission's views? Should the Court have given more weight to the European Commission's characterization of itself? Or is this just a matter of construing a U.S. statute? Does this question implicate principles of comity?

Why did the Court conclude that the Commission's proceedings were before a foreign "tribunal"? Suppose that the European Court of First Instance's review were not limited to the record created during the Commission's investigation. Would that difference in any way alter an "interested person's" ability to "use" that information in post-Commission proceedings?

One interpretive question that has provoked litigation is whether an arbitral tribunal constitutes a "foreign or international tribunal" under §1782. *See generally* Rau, *Evidence and Discovery in American Arbitration: The Problem of "Third Parties"*, 19 Am. Rev. Int'l Arb. 1 (2008). Prior to *Intel*, several courts had held that it did not. *See Republic of Kazakhstan v. Biedermann Int'l*, 168 F.3d 880 (5th Cir. 1999) (holding that arbitral tribunal established pursuant to parties' commercial contract was not a foreign tribunal); *National Broadcasting Co., Inc. v. Bear & Stearns, Inc.*, 165 F.3d 184 (2d Cir. 1999) (same). After *Intel*, courts issued conflicting rulings, often holding that an arbitral tribunal did constitute a foreign tribunal (thereby allowing a party to a commercial arbitration to obtain discovery in the United States). *Compare, e.g., In re Roz Trading*, 469 F. Supp. 2d 1221 (N.D. Ga. 2006) (holding that §1782 applied to commercial arbitral tribunals) *and In re Application of Oxus Gold*, 2007 WL 1037387 (D.N.J. Apr. 2, 2007) (holding that §1782 applied to investment tribunal) *with, e.g., La Comision Ejecutiva Hidroelectrica del Rio Lempa v. El Paso Corp.*, 617 F. Supp. 2d 481 (S.D. Tex. 2008), *aff'd*, 341 Fed. Appx. 31 (5th Cir. 2009) (holding that §1782 did not apply to commercial arbitral tribunal) *and Norfolk So. Corp. v. Gen. Sec. Ins. Co.*, 626 F. Supp. 2d 882, 885 (N.D. Ill. 2009) (holding that §1782 applied to state-sponsored arbitral bodies but not private ones); *In re Application of Winning (HK) Shipping Co., Ltd.*, 2010 WL 1796579 (S.D. Fla. Apr. 30, 2010) (magistrate judge) (same).

Many decisions rely on a line in the majority opinion of *Intel* where the Court quoted a law review article stating that "the term 'tribunal' . . . includes investigating magistrates, administrative and arbitral tribunals, and quasi-judicial agencies as well as conventional civil, commercial, criminal and administrative courts." *Intel*, 542 U.S. at 258 (quoting Smit, *International Litigation Under the United States Code*, 65 Colum. L. Rev. 1015, 1026-1027 & nn.71, 73 (1965)). Of course, that line is technically dicta. Nonetheless, does the reasoning behind *Intel* support this decision? Even if the result does not follow logically from *Intel*, does such a conclusion make sense as a policy matter?

Are there any countervailing considerations why an arbitral tribunal, as opposed to a foreign court, should not be considered a "foreign or international tribunal"? *See In re Application of Caratube Int'l Oil Col., LLC*, 730 F. Supp. 2d 101 (D.D.C. 2010) (denying §1782 petition and noting that, by opting into arbitration, parties bargained for a discretionary process of discovery guided largely by their mutual agreement and, barring that, the tribunal's discretion). Does the use of §1782 in support of an arbitral tribunal risk turning what was designed to be an extrajudicial arbitral proceeding into a judicially managed one where a court in the United States becomes involved in the intricacies of the foreign proceeding? *See In re Application of Michael Wilson & Partners*, 2009 WL 1193874 (D. Colo. Apr. 30, 2009) (addressing, among other things, Rule 30(b)(6) deposition, adequacy of search for documents, contents of privilege log, and bond to cover costs in §1782 proceeding related to foreign arbitration). Could reliance on §1782, where the parties have not agreed on the applicable procedural law in the arbitration, jeopardize the enforceability of an award? *See* Martinez-Fraga, *The Future of 28 U.S.C. §1782: The Continued Advance of American-Style Discovery in International Commercial Arbitration*, 64 U. Miami L. Rev. 89 (2009).

3. *"Proceedings" in a foreign or international tribunal.* Section 1782 also only permits evidence-taking for use in "a proceeding in a foreign or international tribunal." What was the relevant "proceeding" in *Intel*?

Suppose that it was clear that the European Commission was a politically motivated institution, biased against a U.S. litigant (or all U.S. litigants). Should U.S. courts really provide judicial assistance? What would make §1782 inapplicable?

4. *No requirement that foreign "proceeding" be pending.* Prior to *Intel*, some courts had held that an adjudicative proceeding must be "pending" or "imminent" for §1782 to be available. *See, e.g., In re Isihara Chemical Co.*, 251 F.3d 120 (2d Cir. 2001). *Intel* rejects this, noting legislative history that removed the requirement that a proceeding be "pending" from the statutory language. Instead, the Court requires only that "a dispositive ruling by the Commission, reviewable by the European courts, be within reasonable contemplation."

According to this definition, what is the "proceeding" that is relevant for purpose of §1782 in *Intel*—the Commission ruling or the action in the European courts? Does reviewability in the European courts matter? The Court apparently requires only that a Commission decision "be within reasonable contemplation." What exactly does that mean? Must the European Commission even complete its investigation in order for an "interested party" to invoke §1782?

What effect might the Court's interpretation of "proceeding" have on investigations such as the Commission's? What effect might it have on the Commission's willingness to cooperate with private actors in the future?

5. *Foreign discoverability.* An important issue under §1782 has been the extent to which the requested materials would be "discoverable" under foreign law (assuming that they were within its jurisdiction).

(a) Lower court authority imposing "foreign discoverability" requirement. Section 1782 does not contain any language expressly requiring that the materials sought be discoverable in a foreign proceeding. Nonetheless, prior to *Intel*, several courts imposed such a requirement. *See, e.g., In re Application of Asta Medica, SA,* 981 F.2d 1, 7 (1st Cir. 1992); *In re Request From Crown Prosecution Service of United Kingdom*, 870 F.2d 686, 692-693 & n.7 (D.C. Cir. 1989); *John Deere Ltd. v. Sperry Corp.*, 754 F.2d 132, 136 (3d Cir. 1985). These decisions have found a discoverability requirement to be "implicitly required by §1782, based upon its history, rationale, and . . . policy considerations." *Asta Medica*, 981 F.2d at 7. These policies were (a) maintaining equality between the parties in respect of discovery opportunities; (b) preventing circumvention of foreign limitations on discovery in local judicial proceedings; and (c) avoiding offense to foreign courts.

(b) No absolute discoverability requirement after Intel. *Intel* rejects an absolute foreign discoverability requirement (instead merely including foreign discoverability among several factors in its analysis, discussed below). Was the Court's rejection of an absolute requirement wise? Did the majority adequately address the policy concerns identified above?

(c) Foreign discoverability relevant to decision of trial court whether to order discovery under §1782. Under the *Intel* majority's view, foreign discoverability clearly is relevant to the §1782 inquiry even if it is not dispositive: "While comity and parity concerns may be important as touchstones for a district court's exercise of discretion in particular cases, they do not permit our insertion of a generally applicable foreign-discoverability rule into the text of §1782(a)." How exactly are courts supposed to take into account foreign discoverability? *See Minatec Finance S.A.R.L. v. SI Group, Inc.,* 2008 WL 3884374 (N.D.N.Y. Aug. 18, 2008) ("Little can be gleaned from conflicting and bias[ed] interpretation of the law which becomes a consuming and inherently unreliable method of deciding Section 1782 requests. . . .") (citation and internal quotations omitted). What exactly is the "discretion" of the trial court?

(d) Meaning of foreign discoverability requirement. What must be established to show that the materials requested under §1782 are "discoverable" in the foreign jurisdiction? In one case, the First Circuit required a "showing that the information would be discoverable in the foreign jurisdiction if located there." *Application of Asta Medica*, 981 F.2d 1, 6 (1st Cir. 1992). Why does the *Asta Medica* analysis "move" the sought-after evidence to the

foreign jurisdiction in considering whether it is "discoverable"? If evidence is not discoverable in a foreign proceeding, because it is located in the United States, why is that not an end of matters? Does not §1782 discovery of such evidence intrude upon the foreign jurisdiction's decision not to permit unilateral party-directed extraterritorial discovery? If the foreign court wants the evidence, can it not issue a letter rogatory?

6. *U.S. discoverability requirement.* Intel argued that §1782 should be unavailable where U.S. law would not allow discovery in an analogous domestic proceeding. Justice Breyer relied partly on this argument to support his limiting principles, but the Court squarely rejected it. The Court opined that Intel's position would require U.S. courts to "to engage in comparative analysis to determine whether analogous proceedings exist here," an undertaking that the majority found could be "fraught with danger." What exactly is the "danger" feared by the Court? Is it really so unusual for a court to explore the differences between a foreign proceeding and its own? How does your view on this issue compare with your view about the "adequate alternate forum" requirement under the *forum non conveniens* doctrine? Is the Court's approach, which relies on a detailed analysis of the inner workings of the European Commission, any less "fraught with danger"?

7. *Factors guiding court's discretion under §1782.* Section 1782 provides that a court "may" order discovery under certain circumstances. Relying upon the use of this discretionary language, *Intel* identifies a series of factors that should guide a district court's decision whether to order discovery. What are those factors? Did the Court identify the right ones?

Does the *Intel* Court supply sufficient guidance about how a court should balance the factors where they cut in different directions? If you were the district judge in *Intel,* how would you apply the Court's factors once the case was remanded to you? *See Advanced Micro Devices v. Intel Corp.,* 2004 WL 2282320 (N.D. Cal. 2004) (denying AMD's amended discovery requests in their entirety).

Consider the interplay of the discretionary factors against *Intel*'s interpretation of §1782's requirements. In several respects, *Intel* interpreted §1782's requirements to impose relatively few limits. Consequently, much litigation under §1782 will involve application of the Court's unquestionably fuzzy multi-factor test guiding the district court's discretion to issue the subpoena. When, in your view, would these factors counsel against a subpoena? *See, e.g., Aventis Pharma v. Wyeth,* 2009 WL 3754191 (S.D.N.Y. Nov. 9, 2009) (denying §1782 petition where matter had been pending in foreign court for five years, ordering discovery might delay foreign proceedings, and compliance with electronic discovery request would be burdensome); *In re Application of OOO Promnefstory for an Order to Conduct Discovery for Use in a Foreign Proceeding,* 2009 WL 335608 (S.D.N.Y. Oct. 15, 2009) (denying request where three of four *Intel* factors counseled against discovery); *In re Apotex Inc.,* 2009 WL 618243 (S.D.N.Y. Mar. 9, 2009) (denying discovery primarily on grounds of burdensomeness); *In re Marano,* 2009 WL 482649 (N.D. Cal. 2009) (same); *In re Babcock Borsig AG,* 583 F. Supp. 2d 233 (D. Mass. 2008) (denying discovery until party produces evidence demonstrating private arbitral tribunal's receptivity to requested materials); *In re Degitechnic,* 2007 WL 1367697 (W.D. Wash. May 8, 2008) (denying discovery where *Intel* factors weighed against it). When, in your view, would a district court abuse its discretion in granting one? Notably, in the last five years, only a single appellate court has reversed a district court's order on a §1782 subpoena (and that reversal was based on changes in circumstances since the district court issued the order). *See Kulzer v. Esschem, Inc.* 390 Fed. Appx. 88 (3d Cir. 2010).

8. *Legitimacy of* Intel *standards under §1782.* The Court in *Intel* was unwilling to exercise its supervisory powers to impose limits on the availability of discovery under §1782. What

would be the authority for judicial creation of an absolute foreign discoverability requirement? On what authority did Justice Breyer rely in supporting a modified foreign discoverability requirement in his dissent? Do you find his justification persuasive? Do you see any dangers in it?

What was the basis for the Court's "standards" to guide a court's exercise of discretion whether to order discovery under §1782? Is the Court's formulation of these "standards" any more legitimate than Justice Breyer's articulation of his two limiting principles? Shouldn't this be a matter for Congress? Or should it depend on the litigating position of the Executive Branch in a particular case? What if the U.S. Government opposed disclosure of the documents on national security grounds? *See Al Fayed v. United States,* 210 F.3d 421 (4th Cir. 2000).

9. *Parties from whom §1782 discovery may be obtained.* Section 1782 authorizes orders by district courts in districts "in which a person resides or is found." What (or who) is a "person" under §1782? Can a government be a person? *See Al Fayed v. CIA,* 229 F.3d 272 (D.C. Cir. 2000) (holding that the United States is not a "person" under §1782). Recall that, under Rule 45, an agency of the U.S. Government may be a "person" for purposes of a subpoena in connection with litigation in the United States. *See supra* pp. 997-998. Is there a principled reason to distinguish between subpoenas in support of domestic proceedings and those in support of foreign proceedings?

Regardless of the meaning of "person," where does a person "reside"? Is the meaning the same as for other purposes for which residence matters (*e.g.,* personal jurisdiction, diversity jurisdiction)? What about where a person is "found"? Where is a business "found"? *See In re Godfrey,* 526 F. Supp. 2d 417 (S.D.N.Y. 2007). Is a business found wherever its agents reside? *See In re Microsoft Corp.,* 428 F. Supp. 2d 188 (S.D.N.Y. 2006). Wherever it maintains its principal place of business? *See In re Application of Nokia Corp.,* 2007 WL 1729664 (W.D. Mich. June 13, 2007). Again, should the meaning be the same as in the jurisdictional context?

What if a foreign individual is served with a §1782 request while passing through the United States? Is that person "found" in the United States? *See In re Edelman,* 295 F.3d 171 (2d Cir. 2002) (holding that §1782 subpoena served via tag service on foreign citizen traveling in United States could be valid but remanding for consideration of whether Rule 45 requires quashing or whether district court should exercise discretion not to order discovery); *In re Application of Grabski Inwestycje Finansowe Sp. z.o.o.,* 2004 WL 1234046 (S.D.N.Y. 2004). Suppose that the target of the §1782 request argues that the foreign tribunal lacks jurisdiction over him. Does that argument cut against granting the request until the jurisdictional challenge is resolved? Does it counsel in favor of the request because, until the jurisdiction challenge is resolved, the information likely is unavailable in the foreign proceeding? *See In re Request for Judicial Assistance from the Dist. Court in Svitavy, Czech Republic,* 748 F. Supp. 2d 522 (E.D. Va. 2010). Or does it simply mean that the first discretionary *Intel* factor favors neither party? *See Cryolife, Inc. v. Tenaxis Medical, Inc.,* 2009 WL 88348 (N.D. Cal. Jan. 13, 2009) (magistrate judge). Would it matter whether the information sought goes to establishing the court's jurisdiction over the defendant as opposed to the merits of the claim?

10. *Discovery "in accordance with" the Federal Rules of Civil Procedure.* Note that §1782 provides that, to the extent that the court's order does not prescribe otherwise, "the testimony or statement shall be taken and the document or other thing produced, in accordance with the Federal Rules of Civil Procedure." What precisely does the phrase "in accordance with" mean? Does this simply incorporate the *method* of obtaining the information? *See In re Clerici,* 481 F.3d 1324 (11th Cir. 2007) (holding that reference to Federal Rules only refers to manner of obtaining information); *Weber v. Finker,* 2007 WL 4285362

(M.D. Fla. 2007) (same). Or does it also incorporate additional defenses to the production of information set forth in the Federal Rules? *See In re Application Pursuant to 28 U.S.C. Section 1782*, 249 F.R.D. 96, 106 (S.D.N.Y. 2008) ("The proper scope of discovery sought under section 1782, like all federal discovery, is governed by Federal Rule 26(b)."); *In re Application of Eli Lilly & Co.*, 2010 WL 2509133 (D. Conn. June 15, 2010) (same). The Federal Rules contemplate protective orders in cases where the discovery entails "annoyance, embarrassment, oppression, or undue burden or expense." Fed. R. Civ. P. 26(c). Accordingly, some courts, even after granting §1782 discovery, have imposed protective orders limiting the scope of that discovery. *See, e.g., In re Application of Time, Inc.*, 1999 WL 1059744 (E.D. La. 1999); *In re Application of Noboa*, 1995 WL 581713 (S.D.N.Y. 1995). Other courts have applied provisions of Rule 26 regarding the sharing of information with experts to rule on claims of privilege. *See, e.g., Chevron Corp. v. Camp*, 2010 WL 3418394 (W.D.N.C. Aug. 30, 2010).

Section 1782's reference to the Federal Rules has sparked a dizzying array of legal questions. For example, if a third party is served with a subpoena pursuant to §1782, do the requirements of Rule 45 (such as the service requirements and the geographic limitations), *see supra* pp. 995-1000, apply even where (1) the requirements of *Intel* are satisfied and (2) a district court concludes that the discretionary factors under *Intel* favor enforcement of the request? *See In re Edelman*, 295 F.3d 171 (2d Cir. 2002); *In re Application of Inversiones y Gasolinera Petroleos Venezuela, S. de R.L.*, 2011 WL 181311 (S.D. Fla. Jan. 19, 2011) (magistrate judge).

Similarly, if a party seeks to take depositions in the United States pursuant to §1782, do the limits on depositions set forth in Rule 30 apply? *See Chevron Corp. v. Shefftz*, 754 F. Supp. 2d 254 (D. Mass. 2010).

Finally, Rule 27 sets forth rules governing depositions to preserve testimony, including in situations before an action is filed. Do these rules govern an analogous petition to preserve testimony for use in a foreign proceeding where there is reason to believe that the documents or witness will soon no longer be "found" in the United States? *Compare In re Raffles Shipping Int'l Pte. LTD*, 2010 WL 819820 (E.D. La. Mar. 4, 2010) (magistrate judge) (ordering preservation of documents and production of witness pursuant to Rule 27) *with In re Petition of Graf Tech Switzerland S.A. to Perpetuate Testimony of Certain Crewmembers and Documentary Evidence*, 2010 WL 2342580 (W.D. La. June 8, 2010) (denying application to perpetuate testimony due to failure to comply with service requirements of Federal Rules).

11. *Tactics in §1782 proceedings.* Managing §1782 proceedings requires sensitive tactical decisions, both by the party requesting the information and by the party from whom the information is requested. The requesting party may naturally be inclined to seek the information from multiple sources (including the foreign proceeding), but the availability of those multiple sources might undermine any claim that the requesting party has demonstrated a "substantial need" for assistance under §1782. On the other hand, the target of the request may naturally be inclined to offer a portion of the information sought in order to avoid a court order to produce it, but such offers run the risk that a court will conclude that the burden on the target is not "substantial." *See Chubb Ins. Co. of Europe SE v. Zurich American Ins. Co.*, 2010 WL 411323 (N.D. Ohio Jan. 28, 2010) (denying objection to §1782 request and noting, in response to burdensomeness objection, that party had been able to assemble the requested information quickly). For a decision considering these sorts of tactical choices made by both parties, *see Kulzer v. Esschem, Inc.*, 390 Fed. Appx. 88 (3d Cir. 2010).

12. *What materials are discoverable under §1782?* Most §1782 motions concern the production of documents or a request for a deposition. But the language of §1782 potentially sweeps more broadly. Section 1782 authorizes courts to order "testimony," a "statement," a "document," or an "other thing." For decisions holding that the scope of a court's authority is not limited to ordering document production or a deposition, *see In re Letter of Request*, 2010 WL 1655823 (S.D. Fla. Apr. 23, 2010) (ordering DNA sample); *In re Letter of Request from Dist. Court stara Lubovna*, 2009 WL 3711924 (M.D. Fla. Nov. 5, 2009) (same); *In re Letter Rogatory from Nedenes County Dist. Court, Norway*, 216 F.R.D. 277 (S.D.N.Y. 2003) (ordering blood sample); *In re Letters Rogatory from Local Court (Amtsgericht) of Plon, Germany*, 29 F. Supp. 2d 776 (E.D. Mich. 1998) (same).

13. *Section 1782 and corporate structures.* Recall the discussion about documents in the "possession, custody or control" of a corporate entity that is a party to litigation in the United States. *See supra* pp. 1055-1056. This issue raised significant complications in the context of service on corporate entities, particularly where those entities arguably exercised control over subsidiary or related corporations. Do similar principles of "possession, custody and control" apply when the U.S. company is served as a target of a §1782 subpoena? What answer does the text of §1782 suggest? Would such production be "in accordance with the Federal Rules of Civil Procedure"? Would the obligation extend to documents in the possession of a foreign subsidiary? What if the subsidiary were located in the country where the foreign proceeding was taking place? *See In re Application for an Order for Judicial Assistance in a Foreign Proceeding in the Labor Court of Brazil*, 244 F.R.D. 434 (N.D. Ill. 2007) (magistrate judge); *In re Application for an Order for Judicial Assistance in a Foreign Proceeding in the Labor Court of Brazil*, 466. F. Supp. 2d 1020 (N.D. Ill. 2006) (magistrate judge).

14. *Section 1782 and parallel litigation.* As noted *supra* pp. 1071-1072, litigation in U.S. courts sometimes results in the imposition of protective orders on the use of information. For example, a protective order may specify documents are "attorneys' eyes only": or may bar parties from sharing the information with third parties. Suppose that, during the course of litigation in the United States, a party receives information pursuant to discovery and later seeks to use that information in a foreign proceeding. What standards govern the modification of the protection order? Section 1782? Or something else? Most courts conclude that, in such circumstances, §1782 drops out, and the ordinary standards governing modification of the protective order apply. *See, e.g., In re Jenoptik AG*, 109 F.3d 721, 723 (Fed. Cir. 1997); *Oracle Corp. v. SAP AG*, 2010 WL 545842 (N.D. Cal. Feb. 12, 2010) (magistrate judge).

15. *What §1782 does not require.* *Intel* focused on a number of requirements under §1782. It is important to note that §1782 does *not* contain certain requirements traditionally associated with invoking judicial assistance in various other contexts.

(a) No reciprocity requirement under §1782. Prior to *Intel*, U.S. courts repeatedly held that §1782 imposes no reciprocity requirement. That is, if a national of State A is litigating against a U.S. party in State A courts (or State B courts), §1782 permits the State A national to obtain U.S.–style discovery from the U.S. party even if State A (or State B) would not provide similar assistance to a U.S. party. *In re Malev Hungarian Airlines*, 964 F.2d 97, 100-101 (2d Cir. 1992); *John Deere Ltd. v. Sperry Corp.*, 754 F.2d 132, 135 (3d Cir. 1985) (§1782 "does not require reciprocity as a predicate to the grant of a discovery order"); *In re Letter Rogatory From the Justice Court, District of Montreal, Canada*, 523 F.2d 562, 565 (6th Cir. 1975); *In re Request for Judicial Assistance From Seoul, Korea*, 428 F. Supp. 109, 112 (N.D. Cal. 1977), *aff'd*, 555 F.2d 720 (9th Cir. 1977).

Why should the United States provide assistance to foreign litigants, whose courts will not provide similar aid to U.S. courts and litigants? Recall who are the most likely parties to have evidence located in the United States and who are the most likely parties to request that evidence under §1782. Compare the discussion of reciprocity in other contexts, *e.g.,* pp. 83-86 (personal jurisdiction), pp. 482-484 (forum selection clauses), p. 563 (*lis pendens*), and pp. 1094-1102 (foreign judgments).

Consider the following rationale for §1782's lack of any reciprocity requirement:

> Enactment of the bill into law will constitute a major step in bringing the United States to the forefront of nations adjusting their procedures to those of sister nations and thereby providing equitable and efficacious procedures for the benefit of tribunals and litigants involved in litigation with international aspects. *It is hoped that the initiative taken by the United States in improving its procedures will invite foreign countries similarly to adjust their procedures.* S. Rep. No. 1580, 88th Cong. 2d Sess. (1964), *reprinted in* U.S. Code, Cong., & Admin. News 3782, 3783.

Is this a desirable goal? Is the enactment of §1782 a plausible basis for achieving the goal? Does it matter that, since 1964, not a single foreign state has granted reciprocal treatment? Or that the EU's attitude in *Intel* toward §1782 was one of ill-concealed hostility? Given foreign attitudes toward discovery, do you think it is conceivable that any foreign state will ever grant reciprocal treatment? Recall the question above asking why Congress would provide for unilateral U.S. discovery of evidence from U.S. companies, for use against them in foreign proceedings by foreign companies. Is that not bizarre?

What if a religious tribunal in Iran, or a prosecutor in North Korea, seeks evidence located in the United States? What warrants denial of such a request? Suppose the request seeks information identical to that requested by an English court. Should the requests be treated the same?

Intel suggests that reciprocity might be a factor guiding a district court's discretion to order discovery. This approach finds some support in earlier letters rogatory practice. *See supra* pp. 1024-1026; *The Signe,* 37 F. Supp. 819, 821 (E.D. La. 1941); Stahr, *Discovery Under 28 U.S.C. §1782 for Foreign and International Proceedings,* 30 Va. J. Int'l L. 597 (1990). How important should reciprocity be in order discovery under §1782?

(b) No exhaustion requirement under §1782. When a litigant in a foreign proceeding seeks discovery under §1782, is there any requirement that it first have attempted to obtain discovery in the foreign proceeding? Is there any such requirement in the statute's text? Should such a requirement be implied? U.S. courts have refused to impose any exhaustion requirement under §1782. *In re Malev Hungarian Airlines,* 964 F.2d 97, 100 (2d Cir. 1992); *Eco Swiss China Time Ltd. v. Timex Corp.,* 944 F. Supp. 134, 138 (D. Conn. 1996).

(c) No admissibility requirement under §1782. Lower U.S. courts have uniformly held that §1782 does not impose any requirement that the requested information be admissible as evidence under foreign law. *See John Deere Ltd. v. Sperry Corp.,* 754 F.2d 132, 132 (3d Cir. 1985); *In re Letter of Request from Supreme Court of Hong Kong,* 821 F. Supp. 204, 211 (S.D.N.Y. 1993).

16. *Conditioning discovery under §1782 on reciprocal exchange.* Allowing unilateral discovery under §1782 gives one party an advantage — specifically, broad U.S.-style discovery — that the other party does not enjoy. Is this a legitimate concern? If so, how should a court address this problem? Some courts have required reciprocal discovery. *See, e.g., In re Application of Esses,* 101 F.3d 873 (2d Cir. 1996).

How does the *Intel* Court address the problem of asymmetrical discovery? Note the Court's statement that

> When information is sought by an "interested person," a district court could condition relief upon that person's reciprocal exchange of information. Moreover, the foreign tribunal can place conditions on its acceptance of the information to maintain whatever measure of parity it concludes is appropriate.

Do such conditions not amount to a U.S. court assuming responsibility for managing discovery in a foreign proceeding — where discovery procedures do not even exist? Why should U.S. courts do this? Is it not meddling — to the expense of (generally) U.S. parties and (always) U.S. taxpayers? Should not the *Intel* Court have held: "Section 1782 is an obscure statutory provision, whose legislative assumptions concerning foreign states' actions have proven wrong. It should be used in only exceptional cases, where justice absolutely requires, and only on conditions that guarantee equal treatment of the parties"?

17. *Requiring submission of all materials obtained in §1782 discovery to foreign court.* Some courts have suggested that §1782 orders might require parties to submit all materials obtained in U.S. discovery to the foreign court. *See Euromepa SA v. R. Esmerian, Inc.,* 51 F.3d 1095 (2d Cir. 1995). Is this a sensible suggestion? Would such U.S. orders interfere with foreign judicial administration? What about *Intel*'s suggestion that "the foreign tribunal can place conditions on its acceptance of the information to maintain whatever measure of parity it concludes is appropriate"? What if the European Commission had announced, in advance, that it would not consider any information obtained through AMD's §1782 motion? Would a district court properly exercise its discretion if it ordered discovery in that case?

18. *Privilege and other limits on discovery under §1782.* Section 1782 provides that "[a] person may not be compelled to give his testimony or statement or to produce a document or other thing in violation of any legally applicable privilege." What privileges can be invoked under this exception? *See, e.g., Chevron Corp. v. Berlinger,* 629 F.3d 297 (2d Cir. 2011) (journalist's privilege); *United Kingdom v. United States,* 238 F.3d 1312, 1320-1324 (11th Cir. 2001) (grand jury and work product privileges). What law determines the scope of the privilege? *See McKevitt v. Pallasch,* 339 F.3d 530, 533 (7th Cir. 2003) ("State-law privileges are not 'legally applicable' in federal-question cases like, this one."); *United Kingdom v. United States,* 238 F.3d 1312, 1320-1324 (11th Cir. 2001) (applying federal law); *In re Veiga,* 746 F. Supp. 2d 27 (D.D.C. 2010) ("Because the jurisdictional basis for this [§1782] action rests on a federal statute, federal common law governs any assertions of privilege.").

Can foreign law ever govern the privilege claim? Since §1782 petitions entail requests for information for use in a "foreign proceeding," doesn't it logically follow that foreign law can (and sometimes should) supply the relevant law for privilege claims? Consider the following comments from one skeptical court:

> [T]he legislative history of §1782(a) suggests that parties may rely on foreign privileges to shield information from discovery in the United States. In our view, however, to avoid speculative forays into legal territories unfamiliar to federal judges, parties must provide authoritative proof that a foreign tribunal would reject evidence because of a violation of an alleged foreign privilege. *Ecuadorian Plaintiffs v. Chevron Corp.,* 619 F.3d 373, 378 (5th Cir. 2010). *See also In re Veiga,* 746 F. Supp. 2d 27 (D.D.C. 2010).

Is this persuasive? Why should legislative history matter if the text of §1782 is silent on the law governing the privilege? Even if the legislative history is dispositive on the question, what exactly are the "speculative forays" about which the court in *Chevron* complains? Are these "speculative forays" any different from the sorts of inquiries into foreign law that U.S. courts must undertake in other contexts, such as resolving international discovery disputes or *forum non conveniens* claims? *See supra* pp. 387-388, 419-424, 1000-1024. Assuming the *Chevron* court announces the proper standard, what sorts of evidence would supply the "authoritative proof" demanded by the court? Would expert affidavits suffice?

Judicial or legislative declarations? How does this compare with Judge Posner's discussion regarding the manner of proof with respect to the content of foreign law? *See infra* pp. 1146-1148. *Compare Chubb Ins. Co. of Europe SE v. Zurich American Ins. Co.,* 2010 WL 411323 n.5 (N.D. Ohio Jan. 28, 2010) (faulting parties for failing to provide expert affidavits on the content of Swiss law).

12

Recognition and Enforcement of Foreign Judgments[1]

International litigation, like domestic litigation, does not necessarily come to an end when one party succeeds in obtaining a favorable judgment. An unsuccessful defendant may refuse voluntarily to pay a judgment rendered against it, while a disappointed plaintiff may seek to relitigate its claim in a different forum. This chapter deals with the principal mechanisms — the recognition and enforcement of foreign judgments — that prevailing parties in international litigation can use in U.S. courts to compel compliance with favorable foreign judgments that they have obtained.[2]

A. Introduction

In most circumstances, the judgment of a court has no independent force outside the forum's territory. Thus, most courts will enforce their own money judgments only against assets within their territorial jurisdiction;[3] likewise, most courts will only infrequently attempt to preclude relitigation in foreign forums of claims already decided in a domestic

---

1. Commentary on recognizing foreign judgments includes Baumgartner, *How Well Do U.S. Judgments Fare in Europe?*, 40 Geo. Wash. Int'l L. Rev. 173 (2008); Briggs, *Which Foreign Judgments Should We Recognise Today?*, 36 Int'l & Comp. L.Q. 240 (1987); Chao & Neuhoff, *Enforcement and Recognition of Foreign Judgments in United States Courts: A Practical Perspective*, 29 Pepp. L. Rev. 147 (2001); R. Lutz, *A Lawyer's Handbook for Enforcing Foreign Judgments in the United States and Abroad* (2007); Miller, *Playground Politics: Assessing the Wisdom of Writing a Reciprocity Requirement into U.S. International Recognition and Enforcement Laws*, 35 Geo. J. Int'l L. 239 (2004); Monestier, *Foreign Judgments at Common Law: Rethinking the Enforcement Rules*, 28 Dalhousie L.J. 163 (2005); Peterson, *Foreign Country Judgments and the Second Restatement of Conflict of Laws*, 72 Colum. L. Rev. 220 (1972); Perez, *The International Recognition of Judgments: The Debate Between Private and Public Law Solutions*, 19 Berkeley J. Int'l L. 44 (2001); Reese, *The Status in This Country of Judgments Rendered Abroad*, 50 Colum. L. Rev. 783 (1950); Rosen, *Should Un-American Foreign Judgments Be Enforced?*, 88 Minn. L. Rev. 783 (2004); Silberman & Lowenfeld, *A Different Challenge for the ALI: Herein of Foreign Country Judgments, an International Treaty and an American Statute*, 75 Ind. L.J. 635 (2000); Smit, *International Res Judicata and Collateral Estoppel in the United States*, 9 UCLA L. Rev. 44 (1962); Trooboff, *Proposed Principles for United States Implementation of the New Hague Convention on Choice of Court Agreements*, 42 N.Y.U. J. Int'l L. & Pol. 237 (2009); von Mehren, *Recognition and Enforcement of Sister-State Judgments: Reflections on General Theory and Current Practice in the European Economic Community and the United States*, 81 Colum. L. Rev. 1044 (1981); von Mehren, *Enforcement of Foreign Judgments in the United States*, 17 Va. J. Int'l L. 401 (1977); von Mehren & Trautman, *Recognition of Foreign Adjudications: A Survey and a Suggested Approach*, 81 Harv. L. Rev. 1601 (1968); *A Global Law of Jurisdiction and Judgments: Lessons from the Hague* (John J. Barcelo III & Kevin M. Clermont eds., 2002).

2. The enforcement of foreign (and domestic) judgments against foreign states, and their agencies and instrumentalities, is comprehensively dealt with by the FSIA, 28 U.S.C. §§1602-1611 (1982). *See supra* pp. 234-235.

3. *E.g., FTC v. Compagnie Saint-Gobain-Pont-a-Mousson*, 636 F.2d 1300, 1316 (D.C. Cir. 1980).

proceeding.[4] As a general rule, therefore, a judgment will operate in foreign states only if the courts of those states are willing to provide assistance by recognizing or enforcing the judgment: "[a]s an act of government [a judgment's] effects are limited to the territory of the sovereign whose court rendered the judgment, unless some other state is bound by treaty to give the judgment effect in its territory, or unless some other state is willing, for reasons of its own, to give the judgment effect."[5]

1.   Recognition and Enforcement Distinguished

"Recognition" and "enforcement" of foreign judgments are related but distinct concepts. The recognition of a foreign judgment occurs when a U.S. court relies upon a judicial ruling to preclude litigation of a claim, or issue, on the ground that it has been previously litigated abroad.[6] Recognition is akin to the domestic U.S. doctrines of res judicata and collateral estoppel.[7] In contrast, the enforcement of a foreign judgment occurs when a court uses its coercive powers to compel a defendant ("judgment debtor") to satisfy a judgment rendered abroad.[8] The enforcement of foreign judgments is typically sought by a plaintiff ("judgment creditor") who has obtained a money judgment in foreign proceedings that the judgment debtor refuses to satisfy.

2.   Recognition and Enforcement of Sister State Judgments Under the U.S. Full Faith and Credit Clause

Before examining the recognition and enforcement of "foreign" judgments, it is useful to consider the treatment of this issue in domestic U.S. litigation, where the judgments of one state's courts are routinely enforced in sister states.[9] As discussed above, Article IV, §1 of the U.S. Constitution requires that "Full Faith and Credit shall be given in each State to the public Acts, Records, and Judicial Proceedings of every other State."[10] The Full Faith and Credit Clause *requires* state courts, as a matter of federal law, to recognize any valid final judgment rendered in another state of the Union.[11]

The enforceability of state court judgments under the Full Faith and Credit Clause is subject to limited exceptions. These permit nonenforcement only where a judgment was

---

4. Although U.S. courts will sometimes issue antisuit injunctions seeking to preclude relitigation of disputes in foreign courts, this is not a common occurrence. *See supra* pp. 540-560.

5. Casad, *Issue Preclusion and Foreign Country Judgments: Whose Law?*, 70 Iowa L. Rev. 53, 58 (1984).

6. *Restatement (Second) Conflict of Laws*, Chap. 5, Topic 2, Introductory Note & §§93-98 (1971); *Restatement (Third) Foreign Relations Law* §481, comments a & b (1987); ALI, *The Foreign Judgments Recognition and Enforcement Act*, at p. 8 (2005).

7. *Res judicata* (or "claim preclusion") prevents parties or their privies that have litigated the merits of a claim from relitigating the same claim against the parties to the prior proceeding. *Cromwell v. County of Sac*, 94 U.S. 351 (1877). Collateral estoppel (or "issue preclusion") precludes relitigation of issues that were decided in a prior action. *Restatement (Second) Judgments* §§18-19 (1980). *See also* ALI, *The Foreign Judgments Recognition and Enforcement Act*, at p. 10 (2005).

8. *Restatement (Second) Conflict of Laws*, Chap. 5, Topic 2, Introductory Note & §§99-102 (1971); *Restatement (Third) Foreign Relations Law* §481, comments a & b (1987); ALI, *The Foreign Judgments Recognition and Enforcement Act*, at p. 19 (2005).

9. Judgments rendered in a foreign nation are generally referred to as "foreign judgments" or "foreign country judgments." Judgments rendered in a different U.S. state than the state where recognition or enforcement is sought are referred to as "state judgments" or "sister state judgments." Judgments rendered within the state where recognition or enforcement is sought are referred to as "domestic judgments."

10. Congress has implemented the Full Faith and Credit Clause by statutory enactment, providing that judicial proceedings "shall have the same full faith and credit in every court within the United States . . . as they have by law or usage in the courts of such State . . . from which they are taken." 28 U.S.C. §1738 (1982).

11. *Restatement (Second) Conflict of Laws* §93 (1971).

rendered by a court without personal or subject matter jurisdiction,[12] where the defendant did not receive adequate notice or an opportunity to be heard,[13] or where the judgment was obtained by fraud.[14] Moreover, if the rendering court has considered and rejected defenses based on lack of jurisdiction or inadequate notice, the court where recognition is sought is precluded from relitigating these issues.[15] Under the Full Faith and Credit Clause, recognition of a sister state judgment is required even where the underlying claim is contrary to the public policy of the state where enforcement is sought.[16] According to the U.S. Supreme Court, "our decisions support no roving 'public policy exception' to the full faith and credit due judgments."[17]

The Full Faith and Credit Clause reflects fundamental national policies. The clause rests on the belief that national unity will be promoted by requiring individual states to give effect to the judicial decisions of other states:

> The very purpose of the full faith and credit clause was to alter the status of the several states as independent foreign sovereignties, each free to ignore obligations created under the laws or by the judicial proceedings of the others, and to make them integral parts of a single nation throughout which a remedy upon a just obligation might be demanded as of right irrespective of the state of its origin.[18]

The clause also reflects the public interest in judicial finality.[19] In the Supreme Court's words, "[t]o preclude parties from contesting matters that they have had a full and fair opportunity to litigate protects their adversaries from the expense and vexation attending multiple lawsuits, conserves judicial resources, and fosters reliance on judicial action by minimizing the possibility of inconsistent decision."[20]

B. Recognition and Enforcement of Foreign Judgments by U.S. Courts

1. No Express Federal Law Governing Recognition and Enforcement of Foreign Judgments

There is presently no federal standard governing the enforcement by U.S. courts of judgments rendered by foreign courts.[21] Unlike state judgments, foreign judgments are not governed by the Full Faith and Credit Clause.[22] Likewise, although legislative

---

12. *Restatement (Second) Conflict of Laws* §§104, 105 (1971); *Adam v. Saenger*, 303 U.S. 59 (1938).

13. *Mullane v. Central Hanover Bank & Trust Co.*, 339 U.S. 306 (1950); *Restatement (Second) Conflict of Laws* §104 (1971).

14. *Christopher v. Christopher*, 31 S.E.2d 818 (Ga. 1944); *Restatement (Second) Judgments* §70 (1972).

15. *American Surety Co. v. Baldwin*, 287 U.S. 156 (1932); *Baldwin v. Iowa State Traveling Men's Ass'n*, 283 U.S. 522 (1931); *Restatement (Second) Conflict of Laws* §§96-97 (1971).

16. *Fauntleroy v. Lum*, 210 U.S. 230 (1908); *Restatement (Second) Conflict of Laws* §117 (1971).

17. *Baker by Thomas v. General Motors Corp.*, 522 U.S. 222, 233 (2002).

18. *Milwaukee County v. M. E. White Co.*, 296 U.S. 268, 276-277 (1935). *See Baker by Thomas v. General Motors Corp.*, 522 U.S. 222, 233 (2002); *Industrial Comm'n v. McCartin*, 330 U.S. 622 (1947).

19. *See Allen v. McCurry*, 449 U.S. 90 (1980); *Restatement (Second) Conflict of Laws* §98, comment b (1971).

20. *Montana v. United States*, 440 U.S. 147, 153-154 (1979). *See also Baldwin v. Iowa State Traveling Men's Ass'n*, 283 U.S. 522, 525 (1931).

21. *See infra* pp. 1110-1114; ALI, *The Foreign Judgments Recognition and Enforcement Act*, at p. 8 (2005). This distinguishes the recognition and enforcement of foreign court judgments from the enforcement of international arbitral awards, where most issues are governed by federal statute (the Federal Arbitration Act) or by treaty (the New York Convention). *See infra* pp. 1160-1163.

22. *Hilton v. Guyot*, 159 U.S. 113 (1895); *Restatement (Second) Conflict of Laws* §§98, 102, comment g (1971).

proposals have been tabled,[23] there is no federal statute generally applicable to the enforcement of foreign judgments in U.S. courts.

Unlike many foreign states, the United States is not a party to any international agreement regarding the recognition of judgments.[24] (In contrast, the United States is a party to the New York Convention, dealing among other things with the recognition of foreign arbitral awards.[25]) Indeed, the United States has made few attempts to conclude treaties with other countries on the reciprocal recognition and enforcement of judgments, and when it has, those attempts have failed.

In the 1970s, the United States and the United Kingdom unsuccessfully sought to conclude a bilateral agreement on mutual recognition of judgments.[26] Similarly, at the initiative of the United States, the Hague Conference on Private International Law made efforts to produce an acceptable text of a multilateral judgments convention between 1992 and 2001.[27] These negotiations eventually failed and the Hague Conference instead turned its attention to the much more limited proposed Convention on Choice of Court Agreements.[28]

As discussed above,[29] the Hague Choice of Court Agreements Convention would apply to judgments entered by courts that had been specified in a forum selection clause between the parties.[30] In general, the Convention would require a court in a signatory state to enforce such a judgment rendered by a court of another signatory state unless an enumerated exception applied.[31] At present, the United States (like most other nations) has not ratified the proposed Convention.

Thus, for the present, there is no direct source of federal law governing the recognition of foreign judgments. According to most authorities, the recognition of foreign judgments in the United States is therefore governed by the laws of the several states.[32] In some states, the recognition and enforcement of foreign judgments continues to be governed by state common law. A majority of states, however, have adopted the Uniform Foreign Money Judgments Recognition Act (the "UFMJRA"), which codifies and alters common law principles.[33] Further, although it has been urged that federal common law

---

23. As discussed below, the American Law Institute has approved a proposed federal statute governing the recognition and enforcement of foreign judgments. *See* ALI, *The Foreign Judgments Recognition and Enforcement Act* (2005). The ALI's proposed Foreign Judgments Recognition and Enforcement Act is excerpted in Appendix Q. This proposal has not been enacted and it is unclear whether Congress will take steps to do so in the foreseeable future.

24. A few lower courts have interpreted standard friendship, commerce, and navigation treaties as covering the recognition and enforcement of foreign judgments, but this is a minority view. *See infra* p. 1114.

25. *See infra* p. 1161.

26. The agreement was tentatively titled the United Kingdom-United States Convention on the Reciprocal Recognition and Enforcement of Judgments in Civil Matters. *See* North, *The Draft U.K./U.S. Judgments Convention: A British Viewpoint*, 1 Nw. J. Int'l L. & Bus. 219 (1979). The agreement foundered on differences over the size and punitive nature of some U.S. civil judgments and the reach of U.S. judicial jurisdiction. Smit, *The Proposed United States-United Kingdom Convention on Recognition and Enforcement of Judgments: A Prototype for the Future?*, 17 Va. J. Int'l L. 443 (1977).

27. von Mehren, *Recognition and Enforcement of Foreign Judgments: A New Approach for the Hague Conference?*, 57 Law & Contemp. Probs. 271 (1994); Lowenfeld, *Thoughts About a Multinational Judgments Convention: A Reaction to the von Mehren Report*, 57 Law & Contemp. Probs. 289 (1994).

28. Convention on Choice of Court Agreements, June 30, 2005, 44 I.L.M. 1294. For discussions of the history behind the new Convention on Choice of Court Agreements, *see supra* pp. 107-108. For a discussion of a roadmap for implementation of the Convention, *see* Trooboff, *Proposed Principles for United States Implementation of the New Hague Convention on Choice of Court Agreements*, 42 N.Y.U. J. Int'l L. & Pol. 237 (2009).

29. *See supra* pp. 107-108.

30. Hague Convention on Choice of Court Agreements, Art. 8.

31. Hague Convention on Choice of Court Agreements, Art. 9.

32. *See infra* pp. 1110-1113.

33. *See infra* pp. 1082-1083. A few authorities have instead claimed a role for federal common law standards in the field. *See infra* pp. 1112-1113. The suggestion remains controversial.

standards may properly be developed to govern the recognition of foreign judgments, few courts have done so.[34]

2.   Contemporary Approaches to Recognition of Foreign Judgments in the United States

Although the United States lacks a uniform nationwide standard for enforcing foreign judgments, there are surprisingly few fundamental differences in the approaches taken by the various states. In approximately 18 states, the recognition of foreign judgments is governed by state common law, derived from the Supreme Court's 1895 decision in *Hilton v. Guyot*.[35] Thirty-two other states (plus the District of Columbia) have adopted the UFMJRA, modeled largely on *Hilton*'s standards.[36]

a.   *Hilton v. Guyot*: International Comity and the Presumptive Recognition of Foreign Judgments.   Most state courts have adopted the basic approach to foreign judgments taken almost a century ago in *Hilton v. Guyot*.[37] There, a French citizen sought to enforce in the United States a judgment of a French court against two New York residents arising out of the New Yorkers' business in France. The Supreme Court reviewed a New York federal court's enforcement of the judgment.

Writing for the Court, Justice Gray began by suggesting that the enforceability of a foreign judgment required looking to international law, citing the *Paquete Habana* rule that international law "is part of our law, and must be ascertained and administered by the courts of justice, as often as such questions are presented in litigation."[38] With this explanation, Justice Gray turned to prevailing territorial limits on national jurisdiction as a ground for denying the French judgment any independent effect in the United States: "No law has any effect, of its own force, beyond the limits of the sovereignty from which its authority is derived."[39]

The Court went on to consider what rationale would justify a U.S. court in giving effect to a foreign judgment. It reasoned that international comity was the source of authority:

> The extent to which the law of one nation, as put in force within its territory, whether by executive order, by legislative act, or by judicial decree, shall be allowed to operate within the dominion of another nation, depends upon what our greatest jurists have been content to call "the comity of nations." Although the phrase has been often criticized, no satisfactory substitute has been suggested. "Comity," in the legal sense, is neither a matter of absolute obligation, on the one hand, nor of mere courtesy and good will, upon the other. But it is the recognition which one nation allows within its territory to the legislative, executive or judicial acts of another nation, having due regard both to international duty and convenience, and to the rights of its own citizens or of other persons who are under the protection of its laws.[40]

---

34. *See infra* pp. 1112-1113.
35. 159 U.S. 113 (1895).
36. *See infra* pp. 1082-1083.
37. 159 U.S. 113 (1895).
38. 159 U.S. at 163. He referred to "[i]nternational law in its widest and most comprehensive sense," which included "not only questions of right between nations, governed by what has appropriately called the law of nations," but also questions "concerning the rights of persons within the territory and dominion of one nation, by reason of acts, private or public, done within the dominions of another nation" — so-called "private international law, or the conflict of laws." 159 U.S. at 163.
39. 159 U.S. at 163.
40. 159 U.S. at 163-164.

Based upon this principle of comity,[41] *Hilton* fashioned a rule of general common law governing when U.S. federal courts should enforce foreign judgments:

> [W]here there has been opportunity for a full and fair trial abroad before a court of competent jurisdiction, conducting the trial upon regular proceedings, after due citation or voluntary appearance of the defendant, and under a system of jurisprudence likely to secure an impartial administration of justice between the citizens of its own country and those of other countries, and there is nothing to show either prejudice in the court, or in the system of laws under which it was sitting, or fraud in procuring the judgment, or any other special reason why the comity of this nation should not allow it full effect, the merits of the case should not, in an action brought in this country upon the judgment, be tried afresh, as on a new trial or an appeal, upon the mere assertion of the party that the judgment was erroneous in law or in fact.[42]

The Court rejected earlier U.S. (and other) authorities which had concluded that foreign judgments were only prima facie evidence of the defendant's liability and were subject to rebuttal in the court where recognition was sought.[43] On the facts in *Hilton,* the Court found that the French decree satisfied the above requirements, but nonetheless refused to enforce the judgment, citing a "reciprocity requirement." In a 5-4 decision, Justice Gray reasoned that comity did not require enforcement of the French judgment because French courts would not reciprocally enforce a U.S. judgment in reverse circumstances.[44]

Hilton's basic rule continued to be followed in the United States, with various modifications, for the next century. Over time, however, various rationales other than international comity were suggested to justify the presumptive enforceability of foreign judgments. Relying on Joseph Beale's "vested rights" doctrine, the *Restatement (First) Conflict of Laws* adopted the theory that a foreign judgment creates a "vested right" or "legal obligation" that is entitled to enforcement wherever the judgment debtor or his property can be found.[45]

The *Restatement (Second) Conflict of Laws* adopted the same basic rules regarding the enforceability of foreign judgments as those set forth in *Hilton* and the *First Restatement.*[46] In justifying this approach, the *Second Restatement* emphasized that the recognition of foreign judgments rests on the fact that "the public interest requires that there be an end of litigation."[47]

b. Statutory Mechanisms for the Recognition of Foreign Judgments: Uniform Foreign Money Judgments Recognition Act and Uniform Foreign-Country Money Judgments Recognition Act.   Although a significant number of states continue to follow

41. *See also* Casad, *Issue Preclusion and Foreign Country Judgments: Whose Law?,* 70 Iowa L. Rev. 53, 58 (1984); Peterson, *Foreign Country Judgments and the Second Restatement of Conflict of Laws,* 72 Colum. L. Rev. 220, 239-248 (1972); Barry, *Comity,* 12 Va. L. Rev. 353 (1926); Yntema, *The Enforcement of Foreign Judgments in Anglo American Law,* 33 Mich. L. Rev. 1129, 1142 (1935).

42. 159 U.S. at 202-203.

43. *E.g., Williams v. Preston,* 3 J.J. Marsh. 600 (Ky. 1830); *Buttrick v. Allen,* 8 Mass. 273 (1811); *Smith v. Lewis,* 3 Johns. 157 (N.Y. 1808). *Compare Dunstan v. Higgins,* 138 N.Y. 70 (1893) (giving conclusive effect to foreign judgment); *Lazier v. Wescott,* 26 N.Y. 146 (1862) (same).

44. 159 U.S. at 227-228. In *Ritchie v. McMullen,* 159 U.S. 235 (1895), decided the same day as *Hilton,* a Canadian judgment was recognized because Canadian courts gave conclusive effect to U.S. judgments.

45. *See Restatement (First) Conflict of Laws* §§429, 430 & 434 (1934). *Johnston v. Compagnie Generale Transatlantique,* 152 N.E. 121 (N.Y. 1926).

46. *See Restatement (Second) Conflict of Laws* §98 (1971) in Appendix Y.

47. *Restatement (Second) Conflict of Laws* §98, comment b (1971). *See also* Reese, *The Status in This Country of Judgments Rendered Abroad,* 50 Colum. L. Rev. 783, 784 (1950); Smit, *International Res Judicata and Collateral Estoppel in the United States,* 9 UCLA L. Rev. 44 (1962).

Hilton's common law approach, slightly over 30 states have instead enacted statutes setting forth the circumstances in which their courts will enforce foreign money judgments.[48] Each of these states has adopted some form of the UFMJRA, which was developed in 1962 by the National Conference of Commissioners on Uniform State Laws and the American Bar Association.[49] The Act was based closely on common law principles derived from *Hilton v. Guyot.* Thus, the Uniform Act includes provisions on finality (§2); fairness and impartiality of foreign court (§4(a)(1)); personal jurisdiction of foreign court (§4(a)(2)); subject matter jurisdiction of foreign court (§4(a)(3)); notice to judgment debtor of foreign proceedings (§4(b)(1)); fraud (§4(b)(2)); and public policy (§4(b)(3)).

As with the common law, foreign judgments are presumptively entitled to recognition under the UFMJRA if they are "final and conclusive and enforceable where rendered even though an appeal therefrom is pending or it is subject to an appeal."[50] If a foreign judgment does satisfy this standard, then it is "conclusive between the parties to the extent that it grants or denies recovery of a sum of money."[51] Again like *Hilton,* however, the Act sets forth a number of exceptions to the general enforceability of foreign money judgments.[52]

Section 4 of the Act established two types of grounds for nonenforcement of foreign judgments. Section 4(a) sets forth three grounds — unfair foreign courts, lack of personal jurisdiction, and lack of subject matter jurisdiction — which *forbid* a state court from enforcing a judgment. Section 4(b) sets forth six other grounds that *permit,* but do not require, a U.S. court to deny recognition. These grounds include lack of notice, fraud, public policy, existence of an inconsistent judgment, violation of forum selection clause, and inconvenient forum.

In 2005, the National Conference of Commissioners on Uniform State Laws approved the Uniform Foreign-Country Money Judgments Recognition Act ("UFCMJRA"). The purpose of the UFCMJRA was "to update the [UFMJRA], to clarify its provisions and to correct problems created by the interpretation of the provisions of [the UFMJRA] since its promulgation."[53] Fourteen states have adopted the UFCMJRA, while 18 others (plus the District of Columbia) continue to use the UFMJRA.[54]

---

48. Alaska, California, Colorado, Connecticut, Delaware, Florida, Georgia, Hawaii, Idaho, Illinois, Iowa, Maine, Maryland, Massachusetts, Michigan, Minnesota, Missouri, Montana, New Jersey, New Mexico, New York, North Carolina, North Dakota, Ohio, Oklahoma, Oregon, Pennsylvania, Texas, Virginia, and Washington. Washington, D.C. and the U.S. Virgin Islands also have adopted the Act. *See* http://www.nccusl.org/Update/uniformact_factsheets/uniformacts-fs-ufmjra.asp.

49. *See* 13 Unif. Laws Annot. 263 (1980 & 1991 Supp.). *See also* Brand, *Enforcement of Foreign Money-Judgments in the United States: In Search of Uniformity and International Acceptance,* 67 Notre Dame L. Rev. 253 (1991); Kulzer, *Recognition of Foreign Country Judgments in New York: The Uniform Foreign Money-Judgments Recognition Act,* 18 Buffalo L. Rev. 1 (1968); Scoles & Aarnas, *The Recognition and Enforcement of Foreign Nation Judgments: California, Oregon, and Washington,* 57 Or. L. Rev. 377 (1978); Sorkowitz, *Enforcing Judgments under the Uniform Foreign Money-Judgments Recognition Act,* 37 Prac. Law. 57 (1991); Annotation, *Construction and Application of Uniform Foreign Money Judgments Recognition Act,* 88 A.L.R.5th 545 (2001 & Supp. 2010).

50. UFMJRA, §2.

51. UFMJRA, §3.

52. *See infra* pp. 1114-1115.

53. UFCMJRA, 13 U.L.A. 5 (Supp. 2006). For commentary on the UFCMJRA, *see* Silberman & Lowenfeld, *A Different Challenge for the ALI: Herein of Foreign Country Judgments, an International Treaty and an American Statute,* 75 Ind. L.J. 635 (2000); Teitz, *Both Sides of the Coin: A Decade of Parallel Proceedings and Enforcement of Foreign Judgments in Transnational Litigation,* 10 Roger Williams U. L. Rev. 1 (2004). The UFCMJRA is excerpted in Appendix P.

54. For up-to-date information on the status of state enactment of uniform laws like the UFMJRA and the UFCMJRA, *see* the website of the National Commission on Uniform State Laws, http://www.nccusl.org. Status tables on the UFMJRA and UFCMJRA can be found at http://www.nccusl.org/nccusl/uniformact_factsheets/uniformacts-fs-ufmjra.asp and http://www.nccusl.org/Update/uniformact_factsheets/uniformacts-fs-ufcmjra.asp.

3.   Foreign Approaches to the Recognition of U.S. and Other Judgments

There is no uniform practice among foreign states regarding the recognition of foreign judgments.[55] In many states (particularly civil law jurisdictions), the recognition of foreign judgments has been dealt with by bilateral or multilateral international agreements. Where no international agreement exists (as is the case where U.S. judgments are concerned), recognition of foreign judgments is often difficult.[56]

This difficulty can be particularly acute with regard to U.S. judgments, because of the complexity of U.S. litigation procedures, the size of damage awards, and the nature of U.S. jurisdictional claims. Thus, the drafters of the UFCMJRA recently commented that "recognition of U.S. judgments continues to be problematic in a number of countries."[57] Or, in the words of a leading European commentator, who was intimately involved in negotiations for the abortive Hague judgments convention, "everybody fears to be obliged to enforce what they consider to be excessive judgments coming out of U.S. courts."[58]

In Germany, for example, the recognition of foreign judgments is governed by §328 of the German Code of Civil Procedure. Section 328 provides:

> Recognition of a judgment of a foreign court shall not be permitted:
>
> 1.   if the courts of the relevant foreign state would not have jurisdiction pursuant to German law;
> 2.   if the defendant, who did not appear in the proceeding and objects on that basis, was not properly served or served in sufficient time to allow him to defend himself;
> 3.   if the judgment is inconsistent with a German judgment or with a prior foreign judgment whose recognition is sought or with a pending proceeding concerning the same facts;
> 4.   if recognition of the judgment would manifestly lead to a result which is incompatible with fundamental principles of German law (ordre public), particularly, if recognition would be incompatible with constitutional principles;
> 5.   if reciprocity is not assured. . . .

In England, the recognition of foreign judgments is, in the absence of an international agreement, subject to common law standards, which can be summarized as follows:

> The basic rule under English law is that any foreign judgment for a debt or definite sum of money (not being a sum payable in respect of taxes, or other charges of a like nature, a fine or other penalty) which is final and conclusive on the merits, may be enforced at Common Law in the absence of fraud or some other overriding consideration of public policy provided that the foreign court had jurisdiction over the defendant in accordance with conflict of law principles.[59]

---

55. *Restatement (Third) Foreign Relations Law* §481, Reporters' Note 6 (1987); ALI, *The Foreign Judgments Recognition and Enforcement Act* §7, Reporters' Note 7 (2005); Committee on Foreign and Comparative Law, Ass'n of Bar, City of New York, Survey on Foreign Recognition of U.S. Money Judgments (July 2001); Baumgartner, *How Well Do U.S. Judgments Fare in Europe?*, 40 Geo. Wash. Int'l L. Rev. 173, 185-190 (2008) (surveying foreign approaches).

56. *See* Baumgartner, *How Well Do U.S. Judgments Fare in Europe?*, 40 Geo. Wash. Int'l L. Rev. 173 (2008) ("[O]n average, U.S. judgments face more obstacles in Europe than do European judgments in the United States. Nonetheless, much depends on the country, the subject matter involved, the person of the defendant, and the connection of the dispute to the recognition state, among other things.").

57. UFCMJRA, Prefatory Note (Final Draft July 2005).

58. Kessedjian, *Remarks, Proceedings of the 76th Annual Meeting of the American Law Institute,* 76 A.L.I. Proc. 457 (1999).

59. D. Campbell & S. Rodriguez, *International Execution Against Judgment Debtors* (1998).

In cases involving default judgments, English law imposes strict jurisdictional limits. In particular, a foreign court will be found to have properly exercised jurisdiction only if the defendant was physically present in the foreign state at the time of the action,[60] if the defendant voluntarily appeared in the action, or if the defendant contractually submitted to the jurisdiction of the foreign court.[61]

Other jurisdictions impose different requirements, which frequently can lead to difficulties in recognition of U.S. (or other foreign) judgments. These difficulties were summarized in a study by the Association of the Bar of the City of New York:

> The relevant substantive and procedural laws themselves, or more precisely the variances found in them between the United States and the [foreign] states surveyed, constitute significant hurdles to efficient recognition. While at first glance, many of the differences may appear minimal, in the actual reality of daily practice they constitute significant obstacles to the efficient recognition of foreign judgments. These substantive and procedural differences result from both historic and cultural factors and from conscious domestic policy choices, and while their existence is understandable, their impact on international commercial activity is indisputable.[62]

Anecdotally, experienced international practitioners confirm the significant obstacles that attend efforts to enforce U.S. (and other) judgments outside the country of origin.[63]

4.   Abortive Hague Jurisdiction and Judgments Convention and ALI's Proposed Judgments Legislation

As discussed in detail above, the United States initiated negotiations in 1992 under the auspices of the Hague Conference on Private International Law on a multilateral jurisdiction and judgments convention.[64] These negotiations aimed at a convention that would have regulated the jurisdiction of contracting states' courts, as well as requiring mutual recognition of contracting states' judgments.[65] Ultimately, in 2001, the negotiations were suspended, following disagreements (principally between the United States and civil law states in Europe) over the scope of judicial jurisdiction.[66]

---

60. *Adams v. Cape Industries plc*, [1990] Ch. 433 (suggesting that, in case of corporate defendant, English law would require the carrying on the defendant's own business for more than a minimal time in the foreign state through agents or representatives at a fixed place of business); *State Bank of India v. Murjani*, (transcript of March 27, 1991) (dicta that principal residence of defendant in foreign state was sufficient even without physical presence at time of action).

61. *Emanuel v. Symon* [1908] 1 K.B. 302, 308-309.

62. Committee on Foreign and Comparative Law, Association of the Bar of the City of New York, *Survey on Foreign Recognition of U.S. Money Judgments*, at pp. 1-2 (2001).

63. *See* Trooboff, *Ten (and Probably More) Difficulties in Negotiating a Worldwide Convention on the Enforcement of Judgments: Some Initial Lessons in a Global Law of Jurisdiction and Judgments: Lessons from the Hague* 263 (John J. Barcelo & Kevin M. Clermont eds., 2002); Wurmnest, *Recognition and Enforcement of U.S. Money Judgments in Germany*, 23 Berkley J. Int'l L. 175, 176 (2005); Zhang, *International Civil Litigation in China: A Practical Analysis of the Chinese Judicial System*, 25 B.C. Int'l & Comp. L. Rev. 59, 90-92 (2002).

64. *See supra* pp. 107-108. *See also* Miller, *Playground Politics: The Wisdom of Writing a Reciprocity Requirement into U.S. International Recognition and Enforcement Laws*, 35 Geo. J. Int'l L. 239 (2004); Lowenfeld & Silberman, *A Different Challenge for the ALI: Herein of Foreign Country Judgments, an International Treaty and an American Statute*, 75 Ind. L.J. 635 (2000); Pfund, *Intergovernmental Efforts to Prepare a Convention on Jurisdiction and the Enforcement of Judgments*, 76 A.L.I. Proc. 927 (1999).

65. See *supra* pp. 107-108.

66. At the same time, European negotiators were concerned about obligations to enforce U.S. judgments. Miller, *Playground Politics: Assessing the Wisdom of Writing Reciprocity Requirement into U.S. International Recognition and Enforcement Law*, 35 Geo. J. Int'l L. 239, 261 (2004).

In conjunction with the Hague negotiations, and with the encouragement of the U.S. State Department, the American Law Institute ("ALI") undertook a study on the advisability of federal legislation concerning the recognition of foreign judgments (commencing in May 1999).[67] A key aspect of the ALI project was to explore possibilities for federal legislation concerning the recognition of foreign judgments even if the Hague negotiations foundered. Among other things, in a departure from the ALI's usual approach toward "restating" the law, the project considered ways in which the U.S. bargaining position in the Hague negotiations might be improved.[68]

In May 2005, the ALI proposed draft federal legislation concerning the recognition of foreign judgments ("ALI's Proposed Judgments Legislation").[69] As discussed below, the ALI's proposal is broadly similar to the UFCMJRA, but is proposed for enactment at the federal level. Moreover, the ALI's Proposed Judgments Legislation also contains a form of reciprocity requirement, designed to encourage foreign states either to reform their laws (to afford better recognition of foreign judgments) or negotiate international agreements with the United States.[70]

5. Selected Materials on the Presumptive Recognition of Foreign Judgments

The following materials explore the basis for presumptively recognizing foreign judgments. Consider first the excerpts from *Hilton v. Guyot*. Then consider the excerpts from the *Restatement (Second) Conflict of Laws* and the UFMJRA. Finally, compare these approaches with that under the EU Council Regulation 44/2001 (which superseded the Brussels Convention) and the ALI's Proposed Judgments Legislation.

HILTON v. GUYOT
159 U.S. 113 (1895)

JUSTICE GRAY. [Gustave Guyot was the French liquidator of a French firm named Charles Fortin & Co. Henry Hilton and William Libbey were U.S. nationals, residing in New York, who ran a business that operated in New York, Paris, and elsewhere under the name A.T. Stewart & Co. Guyot sued A.T. Stewart & Co., Hilton, and Libbey in French courts, for obligations they allegedly owed to Charles Fortin & Co. The defendants appeared and defended on the merits, but unsuccessfully. The French court of first instance entered a substantial judgment against Hilton and Libbey, who appealed, but again unsuccessfully.

During the pendency of the French litigation, Hilton and Libbey removed their assets from France. When their French appeals were rejected, the U.S. defendants refused to pay the French judgment. Mr. Guyot then sought to enforce the judgment against them in the United States. A New York federal court permitted enforcement, and the Supreme Court reversed.] . . .

International law in its widest and most comprehensive sense — including not only questions of right between nations, governed by what has been appropriately called the law of nations; but also questions arising under what is usually called private international law, or of persons within the territory and dominion of one nation, by reason of acts,

---

67. Foreword to ALI, *International Jurisdiction and Judgments Project*, at xi (Discussion Draft, Mar. 29, 2002).
68. Sean D. Murphy (ed.), *Contemporary Practice of the United States Relating to International Law,* 95 Am. J. Int'l L. 387, 420 (2001).
69. ALI, *The Foreign Judgments Recognition and Enforcement Act* (May 2005). *See* Appendix Q.
70. *See infra* pp. 1094-1102.

private or public, done within the dominions of another nation — is part of our law, and must be ascertained and administered by the courts of justice, as often as such questions are presented in litigation between man and man, duly submitted to their determination. The most certain guide, no doubt, for the decision of such questions is a treaty or a statute of this country. But when, as is the case here, there is no written law upon the subject, the duty still rests upon the judicial tribunals of ascertaining and declaring what the law is, whenever it becomes necessary to do so in order to determine the rights of parties to suits regularly brought before them. In doing this, the courts must obtain such aid as they can from judicial decisions, from the works of jurists and commentators, and from the acts and usages of civilized nations.

No law has any effect, of its own force, beyond the limits of the sovereignty from which its authority is derived. The extent to which the law of one nation, as put in force within its territory, whether by executive order, by legislative act, or by judicial decree, shall be allowed to operate within the dominion of another nation, depends upon what our greatest jurists have been content to call "the comity of nations." Although the phrase has been often criticized, no satisfactory substitute has been suggested. "Comity," in the legal sense, is neither a matter of absolute obligation on the one hand, nor of mere courtesy and good will upon the other. But it is the recognition which one nation allows within its territory to the legislative, executive, or judicial acts of another nations, having due regard both the international duty and convenience, and to the rights of its own citizens or of other persons who are under the protection of its laws. [The Court then quoted at length from Joseph Story's *Commentaries on the Conflict of Laws,* particularly §§23 through 28, excerpted in Appendix BB.]

Mr. Wheaton[, author of a leading treatise on international law,] says: . . . "No sovereign is bound, unless by special compact, to execute within his dominions a judgment rendered by the tribunals of another state; and if execution be sought by suit upon the judgment, or otherwise, the tribunal in which the suit is brought . . . is on principle, at liberty to examine into the merits of such judgment, and to give effect to it or not, as may be found just and equitable. The general comity, utility, and convenience of nations have, however, established a usage among most civilized states, by which the final judgments of foreign courts of competent jurisdiction are reciprocally carried into execution, under certain regulations and restrictions, which differ in different countries." [H. Wheaton, *International Law* §147 (8th ed. 1866).] . . .

A judgment *in rem*, adjudicating the title to a ship or other movable property within the custody of the court, is treated as valid everywhere. . . . A judgment affecting the status of persons, such as a decree confirming or dissolving a marriage, is recognized as valid in every country, unless contrary to the policy of its own law. . . . Other foreign judgments which have been held conclusive of the matter adjudged were judgments discharging obligations contracted in the foreign country between citizens or residents thereof. . . .

The extraterritorial effect of judgments *in personam*, at law or in equity, may differ according to the parties to the cause. A judgment of that kind between two citizens or residents of the country, and thereby subject to the jurisdiction in which it is rendered, may be held conclusive as between them everywhere. So, if a foreigner invokes the jurisdiction by bringing an action against a citizen, both may be held bound by a judgment in favor of either. And if a citizen sues a foreigner, and judgment is rendered in favor of the latter, both may be held equally bound. The effect to which a judgment purely executory, rendered in favor of a citizen or resident of the country, in a suit there brought by him against a foreigner, may be entitled in an action thereon against the latter in his own country, — as is the case now before us, — presents a more difficult question, upon which there has been some diversity of opinion. . . .

What was English law, being then our own law, before the Declaration of Independence? They demonstrate that by that law, . . . a judgment recovered in a foreign country for a sum of money, when sued upon in England, was only prima facie evidence of the demand and was subject to be examined and impeached. . . . It was because of that condition of the law as between the American colonies and states, that the United States, at the very beginning of their existence as a nation, ordained that full faith and credit should be given to the judgments of one of the states of the Union in the courts of another of those states. . . . The decisions of this court have clearly recognized that judgments of a foreign state are prima facie evidence only, and that, but for these constitutional and legislative provisions, judgments of a state of the Union, when sued upon in another state, would have no greater effect. . . . But [in no case] has this Court hitherto been called upon to determine how far foreign judgments may be reexamined upon their merits, or be impeached for fraud in obtaining them. In the courts of the several states, it was long recognized and assumed as undoubted and indisputable, that by our law, as by the law of England, foreign judgments for debts were not conclusive, but only prima facie, evidence of the matter adjudged. . . .

[The Court quoted from Joseph Story's *Commentaries on the Conflict of Laws*:] "It is, indeed, very difficult to perceive what could be done . . . [if a rule were adopted] to the full extent of opening all the evidence and merits of the cause anew on a suit upon the foreign judgment. Some of the witnesses may be since dead; some of the vouchers may be lost or destroyed. The merits of the cause, as formerly before the court upon the whole evidence, may have been decidedly in favor of the judgment; upon a partial possession of the original evidence, they may now appear otherwise. . . . [T]he rule that the judgment is to be prima facie evidence for the plaintiff would be a mere delusion, if the defendant might still question it by opening all or any of the original merits on his side; for under such circumstances it would be equivalent to granting a new trial. . . ." [*Id.* §607.] [The Court again quoted Story:] "It is difficult to ascertain what the prevailing rule is in regard to foreign judgments in some of the other nations of continental Europe; whether they are deemed conclusive evidence, or only prima facie evidence. Holland seems, at all times, upon the general principle of reciprocity, to have given great weight to foreign judgments, and in many cases, if not in all cases, to have given to them a weight equal to that given to domestic judgments, wherever the like rule of reciprocity with regard to Dutch judgments has been adopted by the foreign country whose judgment is brought under review. This is certainly a very reasonable rule, and may perhaps hereafter work itself firmly into the structure of international jurisprudence." [*Id.* §618.] . . . [I]n *Bradstreet v. Neptune Ins. Co.*, (1839), in the circuit court of the United States for the district of Massachusetts, Mr. Justice Story said: "If a civilized nation seeks to have the sentences of its own courts held of any validity elsewhere, they ought to have a just regard to the rights and usages of other civilized nations, and the principles of public and national law in the administration of justice." 2 Sumn. 600, 608-9.

[The Court then reviewed more recent English and U.S. authorities, and concluded:] In view of all the authorities upon the subject, and of the trend of judicial opinion in this country and in England following the lead of Kent and Story, we are satisfied that where there has been opportunity for a full and fair trial abroad before a court of competent jurisdiction, conducting the trial upon regular proceedings, after due citation or voluntary appearance of the defendant, and under a system of jurisprudence likely to secure an impartial administration of justice between the citizens of its own country and those of other countries, and there is nothing to show either prejudice in the court or in the system of laws under which it was sitting, or fraud in procuring the judgment, or any other special reason why the comity of this nation should not allow it full effect, the merits of the case should not, in an action brought in this country upon the judgment, be tried afresh, as on a new trial or an appeal, upon the mere assertion of the party that the judgment was erroneous in law or in fact. . . .

[The Court then considered detailed evidence of foreign practice, leading it to conclude that:] It appears, therefore, that there is hardly a civilized nation on either continent, which, by its general law, allows conclusive effect to an executory foreign judgment for the recovery of money. In France and in a few smaller States . . . the merits of the controversy are reviewed, as of course, allowing to the foreign judgment, at the most, no more effect than of being prima facie evidence of the justice of the claim. In the great majority of the countries on the continent of Europe . . . and in a great part of South America, the judgment rendered in a foreign country is allowed the same effect only as the courts of that country allow to the judgments of the country in which the judgment in question is sought to be executed. The prediction of Mr. Justice Story (in §618 of his *Commentaries on the Conflict of Laws,* already cited) has thus been fulfilled, and the rule of reciprocity has worked itself firmly into the structure of international jurisprudence. The reasonable, if not the necessary conclusion appears to us to be that judgments rendered in France or in any other foreign country by the laws of which our own judgments are reviewable upon the merits, are not entitled to full credit and conclusive effect when sued upon in this country, but are prima facie evidence only of the justice of the plaintiff's claim. In holding such a judgment, for want of reciprocity, not to be conclusive evidence of the merits of the claim, we do not proceed upon any theory of retaliation upon one person by reason of injustice does to another, but upon the broad ground that international law is founded upon mutuality and reciprocity, and that by the principles of international law recognized in most civilized nations, and by the comity of our own country, the judgment is not entitled to be considered conclusive. . . . [The Court therefore refused to enforce the French judgment.]

CHIEF JUSTICE FULLER, dissenting. . . . [This case] I regard as one to be determined by the ordinary and settled rule in respect of allowing a party, who has had an opportunity to prove his case in a competent court, to retry it on the merits, and it seems to me that the doctrine of res judicata applicable to domestic judgments should be applied to foreign judgments as well, and rests on the same general ground of public policy that there should be an end of litigation. This application of the doctrine is in accordance with our own jurisprudence, and it is not necessary that we should hold it to be required by some rule of international law. . . .

[I]t is difficult to see why rights acquired under foreign judgments do not belong to the category of private rights acquired under foreign laws. Now the rule is universal in this country that private rights acquired under the laws of foreign states will be respected and enforced in our courts unless contrary to the policy or prejudicial to the interests of the state where this is sought to be done; and although the source of this rule may have been the comity characterizing the intercourse between nations, it prevails today by its own strength, and the right to the application of the law to which the particular transaction is subject to a juridical right. . . . I cannot yield my assent to the proposition that because by legislation and judicial decision in France [recognition] is not there given to judgments recovered in this country which, according to our jurisprudence, we think should be given to judgments wherever recovered, (subject, of course, to the recognized exception,) therefore we should pursue the same line of conduct as respects the judgments of French courts. The application of the doctrine of res judicata does not rest in discretion; and it is for the government, and not for its courts, to adopt the principle of retorsion, if deemed under any circumstances desirable or necessary. . . .

RESTATEMENT (SECOND) CONFLICT OF LAWS
§§92 & 98 (1971) [excerpted in Appendix Y]

UNIFORM FOREIGN MONEY JUDGMENTS RECOGNITION ACT
13 Uniform Laws Ann. 269 (1980) [excerpted as Appendix O]

EUROPEAN UNION COUNCIL REGULATION (EC) NO. 44/2001 OF 22 DECEMBER 2000 ON JURISDICTION AND THE RECOGNITION AND ENFORCEMENT OF JUDGMENTS IN CIVIL AND COMMERCIAL MATTERS
[excerpted at Appendix E]

AMERICAN LAW INSTITUTE PROPOSED FOREIGN JUDGMENTS LEGISLATION
[excerpted in Appendix Q]

Notes on Hilton, Second Restatement, *and Legislative Materials*

1. *Rationale for enforceability of foreign judgments in* **Hilton.** Consider the Court's rationale for presumptively enforcing foreign judgments in *Hilton.* Why is it that a U.S. court should *ever* give effect to the judgment of a foreign court?

(a) Finality. The *Second Restatement* reasoned that the recognition of foreign judgments rests on the fact that "the public interest requires that there be an end of litigation." *Restatement (Second) Conflict of Laws* §98, comment b (1971). *See also* Reese, *The Status in This Country of Judgments Rendered Abroad,* 50 Colum. L. Rev. 783, 784 (1950); Smit, *International Res Judicata and Collateral Estoppel in the United States,* 9 UCLA L. Rev. 44 (1962). Is this a satisfactory explanation for the *Hilton* and *Second Restatement* rules?

What interests are served by finality? To the extent that finality is justified as conserving judicial resources, does this rationale apply to foreign judgments (where no prior U.S. judicial resources have been expended)? Consider the discussion in Chief Justice Fuller's dissent in *Hilton* of the reasons for recognizing foreign judgments, and compare his reasoning to Justice Gray's. Is Chief Justice Fuller correct that *Hilton* can be decided without reference to international law, based simply on principles of res judicata? Is the identity and character of the foreign tribunal entirely irrelevant?

If finality supplies the primary rationale for giving effect to foreign judgments, should recognition actions and enforcement actions be subject to the same standards? On this rationale, recognition advances finality interests by preventing a disappointed litigant from reopening a proceeding. By contrast, what is the precise relationship between finality and *enforcement?* Enforcement, as noted above, involves an attempt to invoke the coercive power of one state to seize property in satisfaction of a judgment rendered by a foreign state. *See supra* pp. 1077-1078. Does such a proceeding implicate finality? Or are other values at stake in enforcement proceedings?

(b) International law. Does international law require U.S. courts to enforce foreign judgments, subject to the exceptions set forth in *Hilton?* Note the opening paragraphs of the Court's opinion, and its discussion of the practices of other states. Does *Hilton* conclude that state practice creates a rule of international law — sharing both public and private characteristics — that *requires* U.S. courts to recognize certain foreign judgments? Should international law impose any such obligation? What sources would support such a rule? Consider: "There is no uniformity of practice among foreign states in regard to recognition

of judgments of other states." *Restatement (Third) Foreign Relations Law* §481, Reporters' Note 6 (1987). *See also* Golumb, *Recognition of Foreign Money Judgments: A Goal-Oriented Approach,* 43 St. John's L. Rev. 604, 610 (1969) ("Clearly, there is no internationally acknowledged customary rule of international law that a state must recognize any judgment.").

(c) "International comity." Consider the role of international comity in *Hilton.* What precisely is international comity? How does it differ from international law? Why does "comity" argue for recognition of foreign judgments? Is it to ensure that private parties are treated fairly, to further the public policies of sovereign states, to strengthen the international legal system, or something else? What public policies does the recognition of foreign judgments further? Compare the role of international comity in *Hilton* with its role in other contexts, particularly choice of law (*supra* pp. 683-689), *forum non conveniens* (*supra* pp. 385-386), antisuit injunctions (*supra* pp. 578-579), and taking evidence abroad (*supra* pp. 1007-1008).

Does comity subsume concerns about international relationships among sovereign states—just as the Full Faith and Credit Clause reflects domestic policies concerning the relationships among sister states? *See supra* pp. 1078-1079. It has been said that international comity reflects the notion that standards governing the recognition of foreign judgments should reflect the "interest in fostering stability and unity in an international order in which many aspects of life are not confined to any single jurisdiction." von Mehren & Trautman, *Recognition of Foreign Adjudications: A Survey and a Suggested Approach,* 81 Harv. L. Rev. 1601, 1604 (1968). Put differently, liberal enforcement of foreign judgments facilitates international commercial and other relationships by making such relationships more stable and predictable. *See* Peterson, *Res Judicata and Foreign Country Judgments,* 24 Ohio St. L.J. 291, 307 & n.83 (1963). Is that persuasive? For criticism, *see* Smit, *International Res Judicata and Collateral Estoppel in the United States,* 9 UCLA L. Rev. 44, 54 (1962) (comity "says in fact only that recognition will be given when it will be given"); Ramsey, *Escaping "International Comity,"* 83 Iowa L. Rev. 893 (1999).

2. *Wisdom of recognizing foreign judgments.* Is the rule of presumptive recognition adopted in *Hilton* and the UFMJRA wise? Why should U.S. courts *ever* recognize foreign judgments? Does the practice of doing so advance or hinder U.S. public policies and interests? In deciding whether U.S. courts should enforce foreign judgments, should U.S. public interests be considered? Should foreign public interests be considered? Should the private interests of the parties, and, if so, which parties, be considered? Is it relevant to know whether, as an empirical matter, U.S. companies are more likely to enforce U.S. judgments abroad, or have foreign judgments enforced against them in the United States? Is it relevant to know what the practice of foreign states is?

3. *Comparison between* Hilton *and UFMJRA or UFCMJRA.* Compare the basic approach to the recognition of foreign judgments in *Hilton* with that in the UFMJRA (or UFCMJRA). How does each source deal with the basic enforceability of foreign judgments? Consider §3 of the UFMJRA. What exceptions does each source recognize to the presumptive enforceability of foreign judgments? How are those exceptions implemented? Note the distinction between the exceptions in §4(a) and those in §4(b) of the UFMJRA (or those in §4(b) and §4(c) of the UFCMJRA).

4. *Comparison between* Hilton *and Full Faith and Credit Clause.* As *Hilton* notes, the Full Faith and Credit Clause of the U.S. Constitution requires U.S. state courts to recognize and enforce the judgments of other U.S. states, subject only to limited exceptions. *See supra* pp. 1078-1079. Compare the approach to foreign judgments in *Hilton* and the UFMJRA with that in the Full Faith and Credit Clause. Why should a different rule apply to foreign judgments than to state judgments? Why did the Framers confine the Full Faith and Credit Clause to U.S. state judgments?

5. *Comparison between* Hilton *and EU Council Regulation 44/2001.* With minor exceptions, Regulation 44/2001 supersedes the Brussels Convention, which previously governed the enforcement of foreign judgments among members of the European Community. Regulation 44/2001 is subject to jurisdictional limits, set forth primarily in Article 1, and are discussed above. *See supra* pp. 105-106. In addition, the Convention also requires mutual recognition of the judgments of member state courts — in some ways like the Full Faith and Credit Clause. Regulation 44/2001, Art. 33.

Council Regulation 44/2001 begins from the premise that "[i]n no circumstances may a foreign judgment be reviewed as to its substance," and that in general "[a] judgment given in a Contracting State shall be recognized in the other Contracting States." Arts. 33, 36. To these general rules, the Regulation makes several exceptions, including for (a) public policy; (b) default judgments in the absence of proper service and opportunity to defend; (c) conflicts with earlier final judgments of the Contracting State where recognition is sought; (d) inconsistency with certain jurisdictional principles laid down in the Regulation; and (e) judgments falling outside its scope such as those involving status, marital status, capacity, or succession.

Consider Articles 34 and 35 of Regulation 44/2001. Compare the grounds for denying enforcement to foreign judgments under (a) Regulation 44/2001; (b) the Full Faith and Credit Clause; and (c) the UFMJRA. Consider how each source treats the following:

* presumptive enforceability of foreign judgments;
* challenges to judicial jurisdiction of rendering court;
* challenges based on violation of the public policy of the forum (or another state);
* challenges based on the fairness of the rendering court and its procedures;
* challenges based on errors in foreign judgments;
* challenges based on rendering court's choice-of-law decisions.

Note that, unlike the Full Faith and Credit Clause, Regulation 44/2001 permits nonrecognition based on public policy.

6. *Comparison between* Hilton *and ALI's Proposed Judgments Legislation.* Compare *Hilton* and the ALI's Proposed Judgments Legislation. What are the principal differences between the ALI proposal and *Hilton?* Would it be wise to have a federal standard for the recognition of foreign judgments, with review by the Supreme Court? Compare the approach under Regulation 44/2001. What are the benefits of this?

7. *Requirement of "final" foreign judgment.* U.S. courts uniformly require that a foreign judgment be final and binding in the country where it was rendered before it will be recognized in the United States. *See* UFMJRA §2; *Restatement (Second) Conflict of Laws* §92, comment c, §98, comment a, & §107 (1971); *Seetransport Wiking etc. v. Navimpex Centrala Navala,* 29 F.3d 79 (2d Cir. 1994); ALI, *The Foreign Judgments Recognition and Enforcement Act* §1(b) (2005). The fact that a foreign judgment is on appeal in the rendering forum does not prevent it from being "final." UFMJRA, §2 ("This Act applies to any foreign judgment that is final and conclusive and enforceable where rendered even though an appeal therefrom is pending or it is subject to appeal."); *Manco Contracting Co. (W.L.L.) v. Bezdikian,* 195 P.3d 604 (Cal. 2008); *S.C Chimexim SA v. Velco Enterprises Ltd.,* 36 F. Supp. 2d 206 (S.D.N.Y. 1999); ALI, *The Foreign Judgments Recognition and Enforcement Act* §1(b) (2005). Nevertheless, the U.S. court where enforcement is sought may stay its proceedings pending the foreign appeal. UFMJRA, §6.

The possibility that a judgment may be modified by the foreign court in the future is not necessarily inconsistent with U.S. enforcement. *See Alberta Securities Comm'n v. Ryckman,* 30 P.3d 121 (Ariz. Ct. App. 2001); *Dart v. Dart,* 568 N.W.2d 353, 357 (Mich. App. 1997), *aff'd*, 597 N.W.2d 82 (1999); *S.C. Chimexim SA v. Velco-Enterprises Ltd.*, 36 F. Supp. 2d 206 (S.D.N.Y. 1999); *Restatement (Third) Foreign Relations Law* §481, comment e (1987); *Restatement (Second) Conflict of Laws* §109, comment d (1971). For a U.S. decision refusing to reconsider a U.S. court's recognition of an English judgment, even though an English court had vacated the original English judgment, *see DSQ Property Co. v. DeLorean*, 745 F. Supp. 1234 (E.D. Mich. 1990).

8. *Burden of proof of finality of foreign judgment.* Who bears the burden of proving that the judgment is final, conclusive, and enforceable? The UFMJRA is silent on this matter. Case law interpreting the UFMJRA generally has placed the burden on the party seeking recognition. *Bridgeway Corp. v Citibank*, 132 F. Supp. 2d 279, 285 (S.D.N.Y. 1999); *Mayekawa Mfg. Co., Ltd. v. Sasaki*, 888 P.2d 183, 189 (Wash. App. 1995). *But see Hernandez v. Seventh Day Adventist Corp., Ltd.*, 54 S.W.3d 335, 337 (Tex. App. 2001) (placing initial burden on judgment debtor to show that judgment is "facially" not final then shifting it to judgment creditor to prove that judgment is final).

9. *Default judgments.* The fact that a foreign judgment was issued by default does not mean that U.S. courts will not enforce it. *See Bank of Montreal v. Kough*, 612 F.2d 467 (9th Cir. 1980) (enforcing Canadian default judgment); *John Sanderson & Co. (Wool) v. Ludlow Jute Co.*, 569 F.2d 696 (1st Cir. 1978) (enforcing Australian default judgment); *Restatement (Third) Foreign Relations Law* §481, Reporters' Note 4 (1987); ALI, *The Foreign Judgments Recognition and Enforcement Act* §3(b) (2005).

Not all foreign states take a similar approach to foreign default judgments — even if they take an otherwise liberal approach to the enforcement of foreign judgments. In England, for example, foreign default judgments will not in general be recognized at common law unless the defendant was present in the foreign forum at the time the litigation was initiated or submitted to the foreign court's jurisdiction. *Adams v. Cape Industries plc* [1990] Ch. 433, 517-518 (C.A.); Dicey & Morris, *The Conflict of Laws*, 487-499 (L. Collins ed., 13th ed. 2000). Is this a more sensible approach than that in the United States? Why or why not?

10. *Residual applicability of* Hilton*'s principles of comity in UFMJRA jurisdictions.* Are the principles of comity in *Hilton* and the statutory provisions of the UFMJRA mutually exclusive? In other words, does the inapplicability of the UFMJRA in a state that has adopted the Act preclude a court from enforcing a foreign judgment under principles of comity? *Compare Roxas v. Marcos*, 969 P.2d 1209, 1261 (Haw. 1998) (analyzing foreign judgment under comity principles where state UFMJRA did not apply); *Dart v. Dart*, 568 N.W.2d 353, 358 (Mich. App. 1997) (relying on comity to enforce portion of foreign judgment not covered by UFMJRA) *and Nahar v. Nahar*, 656 So. 2d 225, 228-230 (Fla. App. 1995) *with Mayekawa Manufacturing Co. v. Sasaki*, 888 P.2d 183, 188 (Wash. App. 1995) (absent "compelling reasons" comity does not require enforcement of judgment not enforceable under UFMJRA) *and Bianichi v. Savino Del Bene Int'l Freight*, 770 N.E.2d 684, 701 (Ill. App. 2002) (same). Of course, the grounds for denying recognition of a foreign judgment under the Act may be compelling grounds for denying recognition under *Hilton* as well.

11. *Effect of nonenforcement.* The refusal of a U.S. court to enforce a foreign court's judgment does not preclude the judgment creditor from obtaining relief in U.S. courts. The judgment creditor can continue to pursue its claim on the merits in U.S. courts. *Restatement (Second) Conflict of Laws* §95, comment c(1) (1971). *But see* Peterson, *Foreign Country Judgments and the Second Restatement of Conflict of Laws*, 72 Colum. L. Rev. 220, 230-232 (1972). Indeed, in some circumstances, the judgment creditor may be able to make some evidentiary use in its action on the merits of its foreign judgment.

12. *Enforcement of foreign injunctions and other decrees.* The UFMJRA is, by its terms, applicable only to "money judgments," defined to include most judgments "granting or denying a sum of money." This definition does not include injunctive or similar non-monetary relief. Nonetheless, this scope limitation does not bar enforcement of the equitable decree. Under the Act's savings clause, §7, courts remain free to rely on principles of comity or some other source of law permitting the enforcement of foreign awards. *See* UFCMJRA, §3(a)(1) & Comment 2 and *id.* §10 (revised Act only applicable to money judgments; savings clause).

The law concerning U.S. recognition of foreign injunctions or other decrees concerning status or ordering that specified action be taken is not well developed. *See Clarkson Co. v. Shaheen*, 544 F.2d 624 (2d Cir. 1976) (recognizing Canadian bankruptcy order concerning preservation of documents); *Nicor Int'l Corp. v. El Paso Corp.*, 292 F. Supp. 2d 1357, 1365 (S.D. Fla. 2003); *Pilkington Bros. v. AFG Indus.*, 518 F. Supp. 1039 (D. Del. 1984) (declining to issue injunction tracking language of English injunction because enforcement could be inconsistent with comity); *Bianchi v. Savino Del Bene Int'l Freight*, 770 N.E.2d 684, 697-698 (Ill. App. 2002) (UFMJRA did not apply to foreign judgment awarding damages but not specifying amount); *Cantrade Privatbank AG Zurich v. Bangkok Bank Public Co. Ltd.*, 681 N.Y.S.2d 21 (App. Div. 1998); *Farrow Mortg. Svcs. Pty. Ltd. v. Singh*, 1995 WL 809561 (Mass. Super. Ct. 1995), *aff'd*, 675 N.E.2d 445 (Mass. App. 1997) (denying enforcement to foreign judgment that determined liability but not amount of damages). *See Restatement (Second) Conflict of Laws* §102 (1971); Note, *U.S. Recognition and Enforcement of Foreign Country Injunctive and Specific Performance Decrees*, 20 Cal. W. Int'l L.J. 91 (1990).

Compare the approach of the ALI's Proposed Judgments Legislation, providing that a foreign judgment includes "any final judgment or final order of the court of a foreign state granting or denying a sum of money or determining a legal controversy." ALI, *The Foreign Judgments Recognition and Enforcement Act* §1(b) (2005).

Recently, the Supreme Court suggested that "judgments of foreign courts awarding injunctive relief, even as to private parties . . . , are not generally entitled to enforcement." *Medellin v. Texas*, 552 U.S. 491, 522 (2008). The Court made the observations in an unusual setting—addressing the effect of an order by the International Court of Justice issued to the United States—so the Court did not have before it the precise situation of an injunction issued by a foreign state's court against a private party. Nonetheless, its language has the potential to apply broadly.

Should foreign judgments granting injunctive relief or similar decrees be subject to recognition in U.S. courts? *Cf. Baker v. General Motors Corp.*, 522 U.S. 222 (1998) (in full faith and credit case, "there is no reason why the preclusive effects of an adjudication on parties . . . should differ depending solely on the type of relief sought in a civil action"). Is that correct? Would it not take judicial resources to monitor compliance with an injunction and to consider when and whether it should be lifted or modified? If the U.S. court did grant the injunction, could it fulfill these functions properly? What is the alternative?

6.   The Reciprocity Requirement

As discussed above, *Hilton* enunciated a "reciprocity" requirement for the enforceability of foreign judgments. Justice Gray reasoned that, in most nations, "the judgment rendered in a foreign country is allowed the same effect only as the courts of that country allow to the judgments of the country in which the judgment in question is sought to be executed."[71] *Hilton* adopted this reciprocity requirement, applying it to deny recognition to the French judgment obtained by Mr. Guyot.

71. 159 U.S. at 227.

Many authorities have criticized the reciprocity requirement.[72] The UFMJRA did not include a reciprocity requirement, and a number of states have adopted versions of the UFMJRA that also omit the requirement.[73] Similarly, the *Restatement (Third) Foreign Relations Law* does not contain any reciprocity requirement.[74] Most recently, the National Conference of Commissioners on Uniform State Laws considered, but rejected, a reciprocity requirement in the UFCMJRA.[75]

This criticism is not uniformly accepted and the reciprocity requirement has recently enjoyed at least a modest resurgence. Some states, such as Ohio and Texas, include a reciprocity requirement as a discretionary ground for denying enforcement to a foreign judgment, while others, such as Georgia and Massachusetts, mandate reciprocal treatment for recognition of foreign judgments.[76] Moreover, as discussed above, the ALI's Proposed Judgments Legislation contains a modified reciprocity requirement.[77] The requirement was intended, in part, as a response to the failure of negotiations on the Hague judgments convention.[78]

The materials excerpted below illustrate historic and contemporary U.S. approaches to the reciprocity requirement. *Hilton* adopts the reciprocity requirement, after concluding that it "has worked itself firmly into the structure of international jurisprudence."[79] In contrast, *Somportex, Ltd. v. Philadelphia Chewing Gum Corp.* abandons the requirement. Finally, the excerpt from *Reading & Bates Constr. Co. v. Baker Energy Resources Corp.* illustrates application of the reciprocity requirement.

HILTON v. GUYOT
159 U.S. 113 (1895) [excerpted above at pp. 1086-1089]

SOMPORTEX, LTD. v. PHILADELPHIA CHEWING GUM CORP.
318 F. Supp. 161 (E.D. Pa. 1970)

LORD, CHIEF JUDGE. [Somportex, Ltd., an English company, obtained a default judgment from an English court against Philadelphia Chewing Gum Corp., a company doing business in Pennsylvania. Somportex then brought suit in the United States to enforce the judgment. After concluding that none of *Hilton*'s specific exceptions were applicable, the district court considered the reciprocity requirement.] . . .

[D]efendant argues that the English judgment should not be recognized and enforced by this Court because an English court would not enforce an American judgment under

---

72. *See infra* p. 1099.

73. *See* Appendix O.

74. *Restatement (Third) Foreign Relations Law* §481 & Reporters' Note 1 (1987).

75. *See* Silberman, *Enforcement and Recognition of Foreign Country Judgments in the United States*, 688 PLI/Lit. 451, 458-459 (2003); Adler, *If We Build It, Will They Come? — The Need for a Multilateral Convention on the Recognition and Enforcement of Civil Monetary Judgments*, 26 Law & Pol'y Int'l Bus. 79 (1994); Borchers, *A Few Little Issues for the Hague Judgments Negotiations*, 24 Brook. J. Int'l L. 157 (1998).

76. *See* ALI, *The Foreign Judgments Recognition and Enforcement Act* (May 2005). Unlike the reciprocity requirement in *Hilton*, the ALI's proposal specifies that a foreign court's refusal to recognize a judgment for punitive damages does not bar reciprocal enforcement of a judgment from that foreign court. It also authorizes the Secretary of State to negotiate reciprocal practice agreements with foreign states. For comment opposing the reintroduction of the reciprocity requirement, *see* Miller, *Playground Politics: The Wisdom of Writing a Reciprocity Requirement into U.S. International Recognition and Enforcement Laws*, 35 Geo. J. Int'l L. 239 (2004).

77. *Compare* National Conference of Commissioners on Uniform State Laws, Uniform Foreign-Country Money Judgments Recognition Act, Tent. Draft Nov. 2004 *with* Uniform Foreign Country Money-Judgments Recognition Act (final draft July 2005).

78. *See supra* pp. 107-108 & 1085-1086.

79. 159 U.S. at 227.

similar circumstances. The position that reciprocity is an essential element in determining whether or not to enforce a foreign judgment was first enunciated in 1895 by the Supreme Court in the *Hilton* case. In that case, the Court found all of the requisite conditions for enforcement of the French judgment had been met except that a French court, sitting *mutatis mutandis,* would not enforce the American judgment. Therefore the Court refused to give conclusive effect to the French judgment. However, we do not find the teaching of *Hilton* on reciprocity to be controlling in this case. The *Hilton* decision was a pre-*Erie R.R. Co. v. Tompkins* case and it has never been suggested that it was constitutionally dictated and therefore binding on the states. It is clear . . . that the law governing the enforceability of foreign judgments by a federal court is the law of the state where the court is located. Therefore, the issue, as this Court perceives it, is whether the courts of Pennsylvania would hold that reciprocity is a necessary precondition to the enforcement of foreign judgments. The issue of the enforceability of foreign judgments has not frequently been litigated in Pennsylvania, and the Court has not been cited to . . . any Pennsylvania cases which even intimate that a finding of reciprocity is an essential precondition to their enforcing a foreign judgment.

Since its beginning in *Hilton,* the concept of reciprocity has not found favor in the United States. It has often been the subject of criticism by commentators[80] and most courts have refused to follow *Hilton* on this issue. The concept has been expressly rejected by the courts of New York,[81] and has been rejected by statute in California.[82] . . . The primary reason which has been advanced is that our legal system has adopted a policy that calls for an end to litigation. Whether or not a foreign court would recognize an American judgment is not relevant to this policy. However, it is in furtherance of that objective if litigation which was begun in a foreign court and which is presently before an American tribunal, is brought to an end. The Court finds that the concept of reciprocity is a provincial one, one which fosters decisions that do violence to the legitimate goals of comity between foreign nations. Therefore, absent a positive showing that Pennsylvania would follow the *Hilton* decision with respect to reciprocity, this Court will not presume that [the Pennsylvania courts] would adhere to such an undermined concept. . . .

READING & BATES CONSTR. CO. v. BAKER ENERGY RESOURCES CORP.
976 S.W.2d 702 (Tex. App. 1998)

JUSTICE HEDGES. [Reading & Bates Construction Co. ("Reading & Bates") sued Baker Energy Resources Corporation ("Baker Energy") in Canadian courts alleging that processes and techniques used by Baker Energy infringed two Canadian patents held by Reading & Bates. In March 1986, the Federal Court of Canada, Ottawa, Ontario, declared one of the Canadian patents valid and found that Baker Energy had infringed it. On July 6, 1992, the Federal Court entered a judgment reciting that "[Baker Energy] earned profits of $2,934,205 (Canadian) in the installation of a pipeline under the St. Lawrence River." . . .

Reading & Bates sought to enforce the Canadian judgment in Texas. Baker Energy resisted on the ground, among others, that Canada did not provide the reciprocal respect

80. *E.g.,* 2 J. Beale, *Conflict of Laws* 1385-89 (1935); Goodrich, *Conflict of Laws* 605-08 (3d ed. 1949); Reese, *The Status in This Country of Judgments Rendered Abroad,* 50 Colum. L. Rev. 783, 790-93 (1950).

81. *Cowens v. Ticonderoga Pulp & Paper Co.,* 219 N.Y.S. 284, *aff'd,* 246 N.Y. 603 (1927); *Johnston v. Compagnie Generale Transatlantique,* 242 N.Y. 381 (Ct. Apps. 1926).

82. Cal. Code Civ. P. §1713(3)-(4).

to Texas judgments required under Texas's foreign money judgment recognition act. The trial court agreed, holding that "based on my reading of Canadian law it appears to me that Canada will not recognize a judgment wherein the measure of damages in the American court was not recognized by it."]

Under the UFMJRA, Texas may deny recognition to a foreign country judgment if "it is established that the foreign country in which the judgment was rendered does not recognize judgments rendered in this state that, but for the fact that they are rendered in this state, conform to the definition of 'foreign country judgment.'" We must first decide what is meant by "reciprocity." More specifically, we must divine what is meant by the words, "it is established that the foreign country in which the judgment was rendered does not recognize judgments rendered in this state that, but for the fact that they are rendered in this state, conform to the definition of 'foreign country judgment.'"

Several federal court cases have affirmatively stated that Canada will give effect to judgments from the United States. As early as 1895, the United States Supreme Court noted that where a United States citizen had appeared through attorneys and answered a petition against him filed in an Ontario court: "By the law of England, prevailing in Canada, a judgment rendered by an American court under like circumstances would be allowed full and conclusive effect." *Ritchie v. McMullen*, 159 U.S. 235, 242 (1895). . . . *See also Norkan Lodge Co. v. Gillum*, 587 F. Supp. at 1458 ("The Court can find no instance of a Texas court refusing to enforce a Canadian judgment against a party who has made a general appearance and then refused to appear for trial. Neither has the Court found an instance where a Canadian court refused to enforce a Texas judgment entered under similar circumstances. Thus, the Court holds that it has not been established that Canada fails to recognize similar judgments rendered in Texas."). . . .

We hold that the language in §36.005(b)(7) [of the Texas UFMJRA] means that the foreign country (like Canada) will not enforce a Texas judgment to the same extent that it would a judgment rendered within its own borders. We believe that whether Canada (or Ontario) would recognize and enforce a (hypothetical) Texas judgment similar to the Canadian judgment before us and rendered under similar circumstances depends upon two issues: (1) did the (hypothetical) Texas court have jurisdiction over the defendant and (2) did the (hypothetical) Texas proceedings offend some Canadian notion of "natural justice."

Canada will enforce a foreign country's judgment if the defendant was present at the time of the action or agreed to the foreign court's exercise of jurisdiction. *Morguard Invs. Ltd. v. De Savoye*, 76 D.L.R.(4th) 256, 262, 265 (Can. 1990). *Morguard* explained that historically Canadian courts had recognized five instances in which a foreign country's judgment would be enforced in Canada, one of which was when the defendant had voluntarily appeared in the foreign country court[, which Baker Energy concededly did.]. . . .

Baker Energy notes that the Canadian judgment awarded Reading & Bates an amount in excess of ten to twenty times the damages available (allegedly) in an American court under the same facts. It argues that if a Texas judgment sought to be enforced in Canada had differed from the Canadian's measure of damages to the same extent that the Canadian judgment differs from the Texas damages' standard, a Canadian court would review the Texas judgment to determine if enforcement of it would be consistent with Canadian public policy. . . . Based on our review of Canadian authority, we find no reason to believe that a Canadian court would automatically refuse to enforce a foreign country judgment on the sole basis that the damages were excessive compared to Canadian standards. We hold that the district court erred if it concluded as a matter of law that recognition of the Canadian judgment should be denied based on lack of reciprocity under the UFMJRA. . . .

Notes on Hilton, Somportex, and Baker Energy

1. The Hilton *reciprocity requirement.* *Hilton* concluded that foreign judgment would not be recognized unless the foreign country would "give like effect to our own judgments." Simply put, if a U.S. court had rendered the judgment at issue in *Hilton* against a French citizen, would a French court enforce that judgment? If not, then a U.S. court would not enforce the French judgment. The New York Court of Appeals has described Justice Gray's discussion of the reciprocity requirement as "magnificent dictum," on the theory that *Hilton* could in fact have been decided on one of Justice Gray's specific exceptions (*i.e.,* that for fraud). *Johnston v. Compagnie Generale Transatlantique,* 242 N.Y. 381 (Ct. App. 1926). Compare the more representative view of *Hilton* in *Somportex.*

2. *Scope of reciprocity requirement.* What exactly does the *Hilton* reciprocity requirement mean? Is it limited to suits where a foreign national obtains a judgment against a *U.S.* citizen in the foreign national's home courts? That is, suppose that Mr. Hilton had sued Mr. Guyot in France, and obtained a judgment, which he sought to enforce against assets of Mr. Guyot in the United States. Would the refusal of French courts to enforce U.S. judgments prevent the U.S. judgment creditor from enforcing the French judgment against a French defendant? Or is the reciprocity requirement available generally, without regard to the nationality of the parties?

Consider the discussion at the outset of the *Hilton* opinion, regarding the scope of the issue before the Court, which excludes from consideration suits between foreign parties, suits between U.S. parties, suits by U.S. nationals against foreign parties, and suits where a U.S. national prevails. On the other hand, consider the broader formulations at the conclusion of Justice Gray's opinion. Some authorities have concluded that the reciprocity exception will not apply in suits involving only foreign nationals, where a U.S. national seeks to enforce a foreign judgment against a foreign national, or where the rendering court is not in the foreign national's home state. *See Bata v. Bata,* 163 A.2d 493, 504 (Del. 1960) (reciprocity requirement "limited to cases in which it is invoked by an American citizen"). Is that appropriate?

3. *Rationale of reciprocity requirement.* What is the rationale underlying the reciprocity rule? Is it that foreign courts and states will have no incentive to recognize U.S. judgments if U.S. courts indiscriminately recognize foreign judgments? Perez, *The International Recognition of Judgments: The Debate Between the Private and Public Law Solution,* 19 Berkeley J. Int'l L. 44, 60 (2001); Moore, *Federalism and Foreign Relations,* 1965 Duke L.J. 248, 254-255. Does the reciprocity requirement reflect a sense that it is unfair to enforce a foreign judgment against a U.S. litigant who could not have obtained enforcement of a U.S. judgment against its foreign adversary in its home country? If a U.S. litigant cannot effectively proceed in U.S. courts against a foreign defendant, doesn't enforcement of a foreign court's judgment by U.S. courts amount to acquiescence in a forum selection imposed by foreign law on the U.S. party? *See* Ghei, *The Role of Reciprocity in International Law,* 36 Cornell Int'l L.J. 93 (2003).

What rationale does *Hilton* rely on for the reciprocity requirement? Consider the Court's reasoning, particularly:

> It is not to be supposed that, if any statute or treaty had been or should be made, it would recognize as conclusive the judgments of any country which did not give like effect to our own

judgments. In the absence of statute or treaty, it appears to us equally unwarrantable to assume that the comity of the United States requires anything more.

Is this persuasive? Note the Court's attempt to determine what comity requires, by predicting what the terms of a U.S. treaty would be negotiated to provide. Is that a sensible approach?

4. *Proving or disproving reciprocity.* Assuming that some version of the reciprocity requirement does apply, how does a litigant go about proving that a foreign court would (or would not) enforce a comparable judgment by a U.S. court? What sources did the parties in *Baker Energy* cite in their attempts to prove the existence or nonexistence of reciprocity? At what level of generality should a court define "comparable" judgment? Must it involve the same legal claims? The same jurisdictional bases? How do *Hilton* and *Baker Energy* answer these questions? *See Alfadaa v. Fenn*, 966 F. Supp. 1317, 1326 (S.D.N.Y. 1997); *Chabert v. Bacquie*, 694 So.2d 805, 814-815 (Fla. App. 1997). What if there is no authority involving U.S. parties in the foreign jurisdiction?

5. *Comparison between* **Hilton** *and* **New York Convention.** As discussed elsewhere, the United States is a party to the New York Convention, providing for the recognition of foreign arbitral awards. *See infra* p. 1161. Among other things, the Convention permits signatory states to declare that they will enforce foreign awards on the basis of reciprocity—only enforcing awards made in states that have ratified the Convention. G. Born, *International Commercial Arbitration* 2389-2396 (2009). The United States has declared that it will enforce the Convention only on the basis of reciprocity. *Id.* What relevance does this have to determining the wisdom of *Hilton*'s reciprocity exception?

6. *Majority rule rejecting reciprocity requirement.* As *Somportex* illustrates, the majority U.S. rule presently disfavors any reciprocity requirement. *See Phillips USA, Inc. v. Allflex USA, Inc.*, 77 F.3d 354, 359 n.6 (10th Cir. 1996); *Bank of Montreal v. Kough*, 612 F.2d 467, 471 (9th Cir. 1980); *Dow Jones & Co, Inc. v. Harrods, Ltd.*, 237 F. Supp. 2d 394, 429 n.136 (S.D.N.Y. 2002); *Biggela v. Wagner*, 978 F. Supp. 848, 859 n.12 (N.D. Ind. 1997); *De La Mata v. American Life Insurance Co.*, 1991 U.S. Dist. LEXIS 11274 (D. Del. 1991); *Hunt v. BP Exploration Co. (Libya)*, 492 F. Supp. 885, 898-899 (N.D. Tex. 1980); *Hilkmann v. Hilkmann*, 858 A.2d 58, 66 (Pa. 2004); *Johnston v. Compagnie Generale Transatlantique*, 152 N.E. 121 (N.Y. 1926); *Restatement (Second) Conflict of Laws* §98, comment e (1971); *Restatement (Third) Foreign Relations Law* §481, comment d & Reporters' Note 1 (1987).

California was one of the first states to abandon the reciprocity requirement. In 1907, after German courts refused to recognize California judgments against a German insurer, Cal. Code Civil Procedure §1915 was enacted, which overturned the reciprocity requirement. The legislation's purpose was to improve the prospects of enforcing Californian judgments abroad (in foreign states following a reciprocity rule) by making it clear that foreign judgments would be recognized in California.

7. *Foreign states' reciprocity requirements.* A number of foreign states continue to impose a reciprocity requirement. *E.g.*, German Code of Civil Procedure Article 328. *See also Genunjo Lok Beteiligungs GmbH v. Zorn*, 943 A.2d 573 (Me. 2008) (discussing German law); *Dow Jones & Co., Inc. v. Harrods, Ltd.*, 237 F. Supp. 2d 394, 429 n.136 (S.D.N.Y. 2002) (discussing foreign reciprocity requirements generally). *See generally* Baumgartner, *How Well Do U.S. Judgments Fare in Europe?*, 40 Geo. Wash. Int'l L. Rev. 173, 191-193 (2008) (discussing foreign reciprocity requirements). When they are applied as to the United States, are foreign reciprocity requirements satisfied by state—as opposed to federal—law? If state law is relevant, which state's laws? Suppose that a court in a U.S. state that has not enacted the UFMJRA, and that has not recently applied *Hilton*, renders a judgment. Is that judgment entitled to enforcement in a foreign country that requires reciprocity?

Suppose that a U.S. judgment is rendered in State A; is it relevant for reciprocity purposes what the law with regard to the recognition of foreign judgments in State B is? *See* ALI, *The Foreign Judgments Recognition and Enforcement Act* §7, Reporters' Note 7 (2005).

Most discussions of reciprocity rest on the premise that the foreign courts sometimes will not enforce or recognize a judgment rendered by a U.S. court. What happens in the converse situation? Suppose that a U.S. court has received satisfactory proof that a foreign court would respect a U.S. court's judgment. Under those circumstances, does that conclusion influence the U.S. court's application of the other exceptions to the recognition and enforcement of the foreign court's judgment? What answer does *Hilton* supply? The UFMJRA? The ALI statute? Consider the following statement: "Where the foreign jurisdiction gives full and conclusive effect to a judgment rendered by an American court, comity generally requires that the American doctrine of *res judicata* be applied to the foreign judgment." *Belmont Partners, LLC v. Mina Mar Group, Inc.*, 741 F. Supp. 2d 743 (W.D. Va. 2010). Is this an accurate statement of the law? Does it reflect a sensible view as a matter of policy?

8. *Rationale for rejection of reciprocity requirement.* The rationale underlying rejection of the reciprocity rule urges that private rights in U.S. courts are not ordinarily dependent on the laws of foreign states, that it is unfair and arbitrary to penalize foreign judgment creditors for the positions of their home states (or, in some cases, other nations), and that the reciprocity rule cannot be predictably or efficiently applied. Comment, *The Reciprocity Rule and Enforcement of Foreign Judgments,* 16 Colum. J. Transnat'l L. 327, 346-348 (1977); Reese, *The Status in this Country of Judgments Rendered Abroad,* 50 Colum. L. Rev. 783, 793 (1950) ("the creditor is not to blame for the fact that the state of rendition does not accord conclusive effect to American judgments"). Moreover, some authorities have questioned whether U.S. *courts* should concern themselves with influencing the attitude of foreign states toward U.S. judgments. As the dissenting opinion in *Hilton v. Guyot* reasoned, "the doctrine of *res judicata* does not rest on discretion; and it is for the government, and not for its courts, to adopt the principle of retorsion, if deemed under any circumstances desirable or necessary." 159 U.S. at 234 (Fuller, C.J., dissenting). For judicial criticism, consider:

> *Hilton* has been severely and consistently criticized by commentators and courts. Three significant criticisms have been advanced. First, *Hilton* mandates a misplaced retaliation against judgment creditors for the acts of foreign states irrelevant to their case and over which they had no control. Second, judgments are enforced to bring an end to litigation so that the rights of the parties might finally be determined and judicial energies might be conserved. These considerations are thwarted by the reciprocity requirement. . . . Third, there is serious doubt that *Hilton* achieves either of its two probable goals: (1) protecting Americans abroad; and (2) encouraging foreign nations to enforce United States judgments. If protecting United States interests abroad was a goal of *Hilton,* it is clear that reciprocity does not achieve that goal because it does not look to the fairness or persuasiveness of the foreign judgments. *Nicol v. Tanner,* 256 N.W.2d 796 (Minn. 1976).

Is this persuasive? Does it adequately consider the national interest in encouraging recognition of U.S. judgments?

9. *No reciprocity requirement under the UFMJRA or UFCMJRA.* The UFMJRA did not contemplate a reciprocity exception to the enforcement of foreign judgments. One reason the UFMJRA was adopted was to promote enforcement of U.S. judgments in countries that employ reciprocity requirements. *See* Prefatory Note, UFMJRA §4, 13 U.L.A. 40 pt. II (1962). Prior to its adoption, foreign courts applying their reciprocity requirements were less likely to enforce U.S. judgments. This was partly due to the fact that the U.S. lacked statutory standards for enforcement of foreign judgments and, consequently, the foreign court could not assess whether a U.S. court would respect a foreign judgment. The UFMJRA sought to provide foreign courts the predictability necessary for them to enforce the judgment of a U.S. court. *See In re Transamerica Airlines, Inc. v. Akande,* 2007 WL 1555734 (Del. Ch. 2007); *Pure Fishing, Inc. v. Silver Star Co., Ltd.,* 202 F. Supp. 2d 905, 911-912 (N.D. Iowa 2002); *Electrolines, Inc. v. Prudential Assurance Co.,* 677 N.W.2d 874, 880-881 (Mich. App. 2003); *Kam-Tech Systems, Ltd. v. Yardeni,* 774 A.2d 644, 648 (N.J. Super. 2001).

Note also that the UFCMJRA declined to add a reciprocity requirement. Uniform Foreign Country Money-Judgments Recognition Act (Final Draft July 2005). The drafters concluded that "there was insufficient evidence to establish that a reciprocity requirement would have a greater effect on encouraging foreign recognition of U.S. judgments than does the approach taken by the Act." *Id.* Prefatory Note. Moreover, they reasoned that "the certainty and uniformity provided by the [Uniform Act's rejection of a reciprocity requirement] . . . creates a stability in this area that facilitates international transactions." *Id.* Is that wise?

10. *Continued legislative acceptance of reciprocity requirement.* Despite the UFMJRA/UFCMJRA's omission of any reciprocity requirement, several states have adopted provisions excusing their courts from recognizing judgments of foreign courts that would not enforce U.S. judgments in similar circumstances. *See* Ga. Code Ann. §9-12-114(10) (2002) (reciprocity is mandatory condition of recognition); Mass. Gen. Laws Ann. ch. 235, §23A (Law Coop 2002) (same); Fla. Stat. ch. 55.605(2)(g) (2000) (lack of reciprocity is discretionary basis for nonrecognition); Me. Rev. Stat. Ann. Tit. 14, §8505(2)(g) (2001) (same); Ohio Rev. Code Ann. §2329.92 (Anderson 2002) (same); Tex. Civ. Prac. & Rem. Code Ann. §36.005(b)(7) (2002) (same); N.H. Rev. Stat. Ann. §524.11 (1974) (with respect to Canadian judgments). If reciprocity is relevant to recognition decisions, should it be a mandatory or a discretionary basis for denying recognition?

Does the failure to prove reciprocity under the UFMJRA preclude recognition of a foreign judgment in states retaining a reciprocity requirement? For a decision holding that comity principles can support recognition of a foreign judgment even where lack of reciprocity precluded recognition under the then-operative (now superseded) statute, *see Milhoux v. Linder,* 902 P.2d 856, 860-862 (Colo. App. 1995).

11. *Continued judicial acceptance of reciprocity requirement.* It is often said that the *Hilton* reciprocity requirement "is no longer followed in the great majority of State and federal courts in the United States." *Restatement (Third) Foreign Relations Law* §481, comment d (1987). Nevertheless, a number of common law decisions have refused to abandon the reciprocity requirement. *Banque Libanaise pour Le Commerce v. Khreich,* 915 F.2d 1000, 1004-1006 (5th Cir. 1990); *Corporacion Salvadorena de Calzado, SA v. Injection Footwear Corp.,* 533 F. Supp. 290 (S.D. Fla. 1982); *Medical Arts Bldg. v. Eralp,* 290 N.W.2d 241 (N.D. 1980).

12. *ALI's proposed reciprocity requirement.* As discussed above, the drafters of the ALI's Proposed Judgments Legislation included a reciprocity requirement. *See supra* pp. 1085-1086. Consider the terms of the requirement, set forth in §7(a):

> A foreign judgment shall not be recognized or enforced in a court in the United States if the court finds that comparable judgments of courts in the United States would not be recognized or enforced in the courts of the state of origin.

Consider also the terms of §7(e) authorizing the Secretary of State to negotiate agreements with foreign states setting forth reciprocal relations.

13. *Future of reciprocity requirement.* Why have numerous U.S. and foreign authorities refused to abandon the reciprocity requirement? Did the gradual abandonment of *Hilton*'s reciprocity requirement promote or hinder the foreign relations of the United States? Consider the fact that European countries already enjoy a multilateral regime for the enforcement of foreign judgments; they also often subject U.S. judgments to a reciprocity requirement and are often unwilling to enforce U.S. judgments. By contrast, the United States is not a party to any multilateral or bilateral enforcement regime and, with the exception of a relatively limited number of states, does not require reciprocity as a condition of enforcement. How does this state of affairs influence the United States' ability to encourage enforcement of its judgments? Consider the ALI's explanation:

> The purpose of the reciprocity provision in this Act is not to make it more difficult to secure recognition and enforcement of foreign judgments but rather to create an incentive to foreign countries to commit to recognition and enforcement of judgments rendered in the United States. American Law Institute, *Proposed Foreign Judgments Recognition and Enforcement Act* §7, comment (b).

See also Note, *Commanding International Judicial Respect: Reciprocity and the Recognition and Enforcement of Foreign Judgments,* 26 Hastings Int'l & Comp. L. Rev. 115 (2002). Is this persuasive? Would you vote for the ALI's Proposed Judgments Legislation if you were a member of Congress? Do you think that the legislation is likely to have any impact on the future willingness of foreign states to enter into recognition of judgments treaties with the United States?

7.   The Revenue Rule

Notwithstanding the general presumption of enforceability of foreign judgments articulated in *Hilton,* U.S. courts have long refused to recognize foreign penal or revenue judgments.[83] As discussed below, this rule is grounded in common law doctrine. This doctrine rests in part on concerns that U.S. enforcement of foreign judgments necessarily requires a degree of U.S. judicial scrutiny of foreign proceedings; where those proceedings involve sensitive foreign governmental interests, U.S. judicial scrutiny might offend foreign states.[84] Related to this concern are separation of power principles — the notion that other branches of government, particularly the executive branch, should be making judgments potentially affecting foreign policy. Another justification offered for the revenue rule is that courts are ill equipped to examine the validity and meaning of foreign tax laws.

To address these concerns, U.S. law has traditionally held that foreign penal and revenue judgments are not enforceable in the United States. Although the revenue rule has frequently been criticized,[85] the following decision, *Her Majesty the Queen v. Gilbertson,* illustrates the continuing vitality of the doctrine.

---

83. *See Johansson v. United States,* 336 F.2d 809 (5th Cir. 1964); *In re Bliss' Trust,* 208 N.Y.S.2d 725 (1960); *Restatement (Second) Conflict of Laws* §120 (1971); Leflar, *Extrastate Enforcement of Penal and Governmental Claims,* 46 Harv. L. Rev. 193 (1932); Stoel, *The Enforcement of Non-Criminal Penal and Revenue Judgments in England and the United States,* 16 Int'l & Comp. L.Q. 663 (1967).
84. *Moore v. Mitchell,* 30 F.2d 600 (2d Cir. 1929) (L. Hand, J., concurring); Leflar, *Extrastate Enforcement of Penal and Governmental Claims,* 46 Harv. L. Rev. 193 (1932); *infra* pp. 1106-1107.
85. *See infra* pp. 1107-1108.

HER MAJESTY THE QUEEN IN RIGHT OF THE PROVINCE OF BRITISH COLUMBIA v. GILBERTSON
597 F.2d 1161 (9th Cir. 1979)

J. Blaine Anderson, Circuit Judge. The plaintiff, the Canadian Province of British Columbia, filed this diversity action . . . in the U.S. District Court for the District of Oregon. . . . The defendants are all citizens of Oregon who received income from logging operations in British Columbia. This income was apparently subject to taxation under the British Columbia Logging Tax Act. British Columbia originally assessed an amount of $210,600.00 for the logging tax against the defendants. . . . British Columbia then served a "Notice of Intention to Enforce Payment" on the defendants in the United States, and filed a certificate of assessment in the Vancouver Registry of the Supreme Court of British Columbia. . . . [U]nder the laws of British Columbia [the] filing [of the certificate] gave it the same effect as a judgment of the court. British Columbia then instituted the present action in the United States. It was dismissed because the court below concluded that the Oregon Courts would follow the "revenue rule." Stated simply, the revenue rule merely provides that the courts of one jurisdiction do not recognize the revenue laws of another jurisdiction. . . .

In a diversity action, a federal district court applies the law of the forum state. Not only the substantive law, but also the conflicts of law rules of the forum are applied in diversity actions. *Klaxon Co. v. Stentor Electric Mfg. Co., supra.* Normally, this would automatically limit our analysis to the law of Oregon since it is the forum state in the present case. However, the question presented here carries foreign relations overtones which may create an inference that this should not be decided merely by reference to Oregon law. Nevertheless, we do not need to decide whether federal or state law should control, since the conclusion we reach would be the same under either Oregon or federal law.

Generally, judgments from a foreign country are recognized by the courts of this country when the general principles of comity are satisfied. Two often-stated exceptions to comity occur when the judgment is based on either the tax (the revenue rule) or penal laws of the foreign country. . . . Lord Mansfield is generally credited as being the first to express the revenue rule. In 1775, while deciding a contract action, he said that ". . . no country ever takes notice of the revenue laws of another." *Holman v. Johnson*, 98 Eng. Rep. 1120, 1121 (1775). A few years later, Lord Mansfield . . . said: "One nation does not take notice of the revenue laws of another." *Planche v. Fletcher*, 99 Eng. Rep. 164, 165 (1779). . . . [S]ince its inception [the revenue rule] has become so well recognized that this appears to be the first time that a foreign nation has sought to enforce a tax judgment in the courts of the United States.

Judge Learned Hand best expressed the purpose behind the revenue rule:

> While the origin of the exception in the case of penal liabilities does not appear in the books, a sound basis for it exists, in my judgment, which includes liabilities for taxes as well. Even in the case of ordinary municipal liabilities, a court will not recognize those arising in a foreign state, if they run counter to the "settled public policy" of its own. Thus a scrutiny of the liability is necessarily always in reserve, and the possibility that it will be found not to accord with the policy of the domestic state. This is not a troublesome or delicate inquiry when the question arises between private persons, but it takes on quite another face when it concerns the relations between the foreign state and its own citizens or even those who may be temporarily within its borders. To pass upon the provisions for the public order of another state is, or at any rate should be, beyond the powers of a court; it involves the relations between the

states themselves, with which courts are incompetent to deal, and which are entrusted to other authorities. It may commit the domestic state to a position which would seriously embarrass its neighbor. Revenue laws fall within the same reasoning; they affect a state in matters as vital to its existence as its criminal laws. No court ought to undertake an inquiry which it cannot prosecute without determining whether those laws are consonant with its own notions of what is proper. *Moore v. Mitchell,* 30 F.2d 600, 604 (2d Cir. 1929) (L. Hand, J., concurring), *aff'd on other grounds,* 281 U.S. 18 (1930).

While this reasoning no longer prevents a state from enforcing its tax judgment in the courts of a sister state because of the full faith and credit clause, this same rationale has continued validity in the international context. Additionally, if the court below was compelled to recognize the tax judgment from a foreign nation, it would have the effect of furthering the governmental interests of a foreign country, something which our courts customarily refuse to do.

Although the Supreme Court has never had occasion to address the ... revenue rule ... the indications are strong that the Court would reach the same result as we reach in the present case. Both the majority and the dissenting opinion in *Banco Nacional de Cuba v. Sabbatino* discussed the rule in a spirit which indicates a continued recognition of the revenue rule in the international sphere.

There is no Oregon case law on point. The only inference which can be drawn from Oregon statutory law supports our conclusion. In 1977, Oregon adopted the [UFMJRA]. This provides that judgments from a foreign country for a sum of money which meet certain requirements are enforceable in the Oregon courts. However, the Act defines the judgments to which it applies as "(a)ny judgment of a foreign state granting or denying recovery to a sum of money, *other than a judgment for taxes.* . . ." (emphasis added) 1977 Or. Laws, S.B. 28 §1(2). The only conclusion which can be drawn from this specific exclusion is that the Oregon legislature continues to recognize the revenue rule.

The political branches of the U.S. Government have entered into two tax treaties with the Canadian Government. . . . These treaties are quite extensive. . . . One section provides for the exchange of information between the two countries for the purpose of preventing international tax evasion. This is as close as the treaties come to providing for enforcement powers. Even though the political branches of the two countries could have abolished the revenue rule between themselves at the time they entered into the treaties, they did not. . . . The revenue rule has been with us for centuries and as such has become firmly embedded in the law. There were sound reasons which supported its original adoption, and there remain sound reasons supporting its continued validity. When and if the rule is changed, it is a more proper function of the policy-making branches of our government to make such a change.

Notes on **Her Majesty**

1. *General refusal of U.S. courts to enforce foreign tax judgments.* As *Her Majesty* indicates, the general rule is that foreign tax judgments will not be enforced by U.S. courts. *See supra* p. 737. *Compare Restatement (Third) Foreign Relations Law* §483 (1987) ("Courts in the United States are not required to recognize or to enforce judgments for the collection of taxes, fines, or penalties rendered by the courts of other states."). What is the difference between the *Third Restatement* position and the historic revenue rule as articulated in *Her Majesty*? Note that the *Restatement* leaves U.S. courts free to recognize foreign revenue judgments.

What precisely does it mean to enforce a foreign revenue judgment or rule? Isn't it necessary to differentiate between judicial acts? Consider the following:

> There is a continuum along which a claim will require a court to consider or "pass on" a foreign tax law. At the least problematic end of the continuum is the mere recognition of a foreign tax law. At the next point along the continuum, a court must apply such a foreign law. Next, a claim might require a court to rule on the validity of a foreign tax law. Finally, a claim might require a court to explicitly enforce a foreign revenue law. *Republic of Colombia v. Diageo N. Am., Inc.*, 531 F. Supp. 2d 365, 388 (E.D.N.Y. 2007).

Is this "continuum" helpful? Do some of the acts along it even implicate the revenue rule as described by *Her Majesty*? The *Restatement*?

2. Treatment of revenue rule in UFMJRA and UFCMJRA. As *Her Majesty* illustrates, the UFMJRA does not apply to foreign revenue judgments. *See* UFMJRA §1(2) (" 'foreign judgment' means any judgment of a foreign state granting or denying recovery of a sum of money, *other than a judgment for taxes, a fine or other penalty* . . ."). The UFCMJRA provides in Article 3(b)(1) that the revised Act does not apply to a "judgment for taxes." *Compare* ALI, *The Foreign Judgments Recognition and Enforcement Act* §2(b)(i) (2005) (judgments for "taxes, fines and penalties may, but need not, be recognized and enforced"). Is there a difference between these provisions and the historic revenue rule?

3. Revenue rule in Pasquantino. The U.S. Supreme Court considered the revenue rule in *Pasquantino v. United States*, 544 U.S. 349 (2005). The case arose from a prosecution under a federal wire fraud statute, 18 U.S.C. §1343, making it a crime to use interstate wires to effect "any scheme or artifice to defraud, or for obtaining money or property by means of false or fraudulent pretenses, representations or promises." The Pasquantinos were prosecuted under §1343 for smuggling liquor from Canada into the United States without paying taxes imposed by Canada (which was said to constitute a fraudulent scheme). The defendants argued that the revenue rule barred the prosecution because it required a U.S. court to assess their possible violations of Canada's revenue laws; they reasoned that Congress could not have intended such a result.

The Supreme Court rejected the defendants' arguments, over a dissent by Justice Ginsburg. The Court first acknowledged the historic origins of the revenue rule:

> Since the late 19th and early 20th century, courts have treated the common-law revenue rule as a corollary of the rule that, as Chief Justice Marshall put it, "[t]he Courts of no country execute the penal laws of another." *The Antelope*, 10 Wheat. 66, 123 (1825). The rule against the enforcement of foreign penal statutes, in turn, tracked the common-law principle that crimes could only be prosecuted in the country in which they were committed. *See, e.g.,* J. Story, *Commentaries on the Conflict of Laws* §620, p. 840 (M. Bigelow ed. 8th ed. 1883). The basis for inferring the revenue rule from the rule against foreign penal enforcement was an analogy between foreign revenue laws and penal laws.

The Court concluded, however, that the case was "not a suit that recovers a foreign tax liability, like a suit to enforce a judgment," but instead "a criminal prosecution brought by the United States in its sovereign capacity to punish domestic criminal conduct." The Court reasoned that "A prohibition on the enforcement of foreign penal law does not plainly prevent the Government from enforcing a domestic criminal law. Such an extension, to our knowledge, is unprecedented in the long history of either the revenue rule or the rule against enforcement of penal laws." Justice Ginsburg dissented, arguing that the U.S. Government prosecution implicated the enforcement of Canadian tax laws, which should be left to the Canadian authorities.

4. *Origins of revenue and penal exceptions.* As *Her Majesty* indicates, the revenue and penal exceptions have lengthy pedigrees. Both rules appear to date to a 1775 opinion by Lord Mansfield, ruling that a French seller of tea could recover damages from an English purchaser notwithstanding the fact that the tea sale violated French penal and revenue laws. In explaining that the lawfulness of the plaintiff's conduct in France would not be challenged, Lord Mansfield said broadly that "no country ever takes notice of the revenue laws of another." *Holman v. Johnson,* 98 Eng. Rep. 1120 (K.B. 1775). This dicta was subsequently invoked to justify the refusal of English (and U.S.) courts to enforce foreign judgments based on tax or penal claims. *E.g., Government of India v. Taylor* [1955] A.C. 491 (H.L.(E.)); *Her Majesty the Queen v. Gilbertson,* 597 F.2d 1161 (9th Cir. 1979). This result is closely related to the choice of law rule that a state will not hear claims based on the penal or revenue laws of other nations. *Restatement (Second) Conflict of Laws* §89 (1971); *supra* p. 737. For a general discussion of the history of the revenue rule, *see* Mallinak, *The Revenue Rule: A Common Law Doctrine for the Twenty-First Century,* 16 Duke J. Comp. & Int'l L. 79 (2006).

5. *Rationale for penal and revenue rule.* Why do courts generally refuse to enforce penal and revenue judgments? A number of related rationales are typically cited.

(a) Avoiding offense to foreign states. If U.S. courts were to hold out the possibility of recognizing foreign revenue judgments, they would be obliged to consider all of the various requirements that *Hilton* prescribed for enforcement. It is often argued that doing so might gravely offend foreign states. "The rule appears to reflect a reluctance of courts to subject foreign public law to judicial scrutiny." *Restatement (Third) Foreign Relations Law* §483, Reporters' Note 2 (1988). Consider Learned Hand's reasoning in *Moore v. Mitchell,* 30 F.2d 600, 601 (2d Cir. 1929), *aff'd on other grounds,* 281 U.S. 18 (1930):

> when it concerns the relations between the foreign state and its own citizens . . . to pass upon the provisions for the public order of another state is, or at any rate should be, beyond the powers of a court; it involves the relations between the states themselves, with which courts are incompetent to deal, and which are entrusted to other authorities.

How are revenue or penal judgments different from other judgments? Is it because they are based on proceedings by foreign governments against private litigants? Why should this be important? Suppose a foreign state agency recovers on an ordinary contract claim in "its" own courts and seeks to enforce judgment in U.S. courts. Should such a judgment be recognized? Does it give less offense to foreign states to simply refuse ever to enforce their judgments, than to consider whether they were fairly rendered?

Alternatively, are revenue and penal judgments different because they are based on laws whose substantive content is different from "ordinary" judgments? If so, what would be the status of antitrust or securities law judgments obtained by private litigants, which are based on regulatory statutes reflecting public policy objectives? Recall that some foreign nations have enacted legislation denying recognition or enforcement to U.S. antitrust judgments. *See supra* pp. 680-683. What about judgments based on product liability claims?

(b) Public policy concerns. A second explanation for the revenue and penal exceptions may be "a reluctance to enforce laws that may conflict with the public policy of the forum state." *Restatement (Third) Foreign Relations Law* §483, Reporters' Note 2 (1988). Would the United States be willing to enforce Russian penal and revenue judgments? Iranian? Venezuelan? To the extent that foreign penal and revenue laws violate U.S. public policy, then wouldn't the public policy exception provide the appropriate response?

(c) Separation of powers. A third rationale for the revenue rule is separation of powers. *See Pasquantino v. United States,* 544 U.S. at 368-370 (citing "the principal evil against which

the revenue rule was traditionally thought to guard: judicial evaluation of the policy-laden enactments of other sovereigns"). Under this analysis, the Executive Branch should be the primary institution making sensitive foreign policy determinations regarding the validity and meaning of foreign tax judgments. Is this a persuasive basis for the revenue rule? Cannot Congress and the President take steps to avoid judicial interference with U.S. foreign policy? How much will judicial refusal to enforce a foreign tax judgment really affect U.S. foreign relations?

Some bilateral tax treaties between the United States and foreign countries contain provisions under which the signatory nations would assist each other in the collection of revenue obligations. *See* Mallinak, *The Revenue Rule: A Common Law Doctrine for the Twenty-First Century*, 16 Duke J. Comp. & Int'l L. 79 (2006). What effect should such treaties have on the revenue rule? Do they bar its application entirely? Or would the rule continue to apply in cases where a foreign sovereign attempts to avail itself of a civil litigation remedy as in *Her Majesty*?

(d) Judicial competence. A fourth possible rationale for the revenue rule is that U.S. courts may lack the ability to understand foreign tax schemes. In *Pasquantino*, the Court cited "the concern that courts lack the competence to examine the validity of unfamiliar foreign tax schemes." The Court responded, however, that Federal Rule of Criminal Procedure 26.1, which allows judges to consider any relevant material (including testimony) pertinent to foreign law, "gives courts a sufficient means to resolve the incidental foreign law issues they may encounter in a wire fraud prosecution." The Federal Rules of Civil Procedure contain an analogous provision allowing a judge to consider a variety of sources in discerning the meaning of foreign law. *See* Fed. R. Civ. P. 44.1. Will expert testimony and written material really enable a judge to understand the intricacies of foreign tax or penal law?

On the other hand, U.S. courts must evaluate foreign law frequently, such as under the *forum non conveniens* doctrine or when applying foreign law. One could respond that foreign tax laws are a special case — that they are especially complex and susceptible to judicial misunderstanding. Aren't foreign antitrust and securities laws also complex? Are all tax law issues complicated? Does this rationale provide a principled basis for according special treatment to revenue (and penal) judgments?

(e) Individual rights and fairness. Concerns about individual rights and possible abuse of taxing power are also implicated by the revenue rule. Note that a foreign revenue judgment will be the result of litigation in a foreign court between the foreign government and a private party. Is there particular reason to be hesitant to accept a foreign court's judgment in favor of its "own" government? Suppose that a Syrian or Chinese court renders a tax judgment in favor of the Government, against a local? Against a U.S. company? What about a Russian or a French court? Should U.S. courts afford such judgments the presumptive validity of other foreign judgments? Does not this rationale extend beyond tax and revenue judgments?

6. *General refusal of U.S. courts to enforce foreign penal judgments.* The general rule in the United States is that foreign "penal" judgments will not be enforced by U.S. courts. *See Restatement (Third) Foreign Relations Law* §483 (1987); UFMJRA §1(2) (" 'foreign judgment' means any judgment of a foreign state granting or denying recovery of a sum of money, *other than a judgment for taxes, a fine or other penalty* . . ."). The rationale for the penal exception is similar to that for the revenue rule, and the two doctrines are frequently considered together. Are the reasons advanced for the revenue rule (*see supra* pp. 1106-1107) more compelling when applied to penal judgments?

7. *Criticism of revenue rule.* The revenue rule has been subjected to considerable criticism (while the penal exception has not been criticized similarly). *See Restatement (Third)*

Foreign Relations Law §483, Reporters' Note 2 (1987) (permitting, but not requiring, nonrecognition of foreign tax and penal judgments and expressing doubts as to continued wisdom of revenue rule); *United States v. Trapilo,* 130 F.3d 547, 550 n.4 (2d Cir. 1997); Briggs, *The Revenue Rule in the Conflict of Laws: Time for a Makeover,* 2001 Sing. J. Legal Studies 280; Kovatch, *Recognizing Foreign Tax Judgments: An Argument for Revocation of the Revenue Rule,* 22 Hous. J. Int'l L. 265 (2000).

Consider, however, a recent spirited defense of the rule:

> The revenue rule fills, in the twenty-first century, a role necessary to protect the judiciary from making decisions better left to the other branches of government and immersing itself in the intricate and sensitive area of tax enforcement for other nations. In a world with far more international contact and far greater reliance on international trade than Lord Mansfield could imagine when he first attempted to protect British trade and British courts from the vagaries of foreign revenue laws, the revenue rule stands on firm ground and should not be abandoned or modified so that courts must deal with matters best left to others. Mallinak, *The Revenue Rule: A Common Law Doctrine for the Twenty-First Century,* 16 Duke J. Comp. & Int'l L. 79, 124 (2006).

Are these considerations valid? Or do they simply represent a desperate attempt to preserve an archaic rule that has outlived its usefulness in a world where money flows easily across borders and virtually all sovereigns collect revenue?

> Although the rule as commonly stated treats tax and penal judgments alike, the considerations concerning foreign tax judgments are different from those for penal judgments. In an age when virtually all states impose and collect taxes and when instantaneous transfer of assets can be easily arranged, the rationale for not recognizing or enforcing tax judgments is largely obsolete. *Restatement (Third) Foreign Relations Law* §483, Reporters' Note 1 (1987).

Is that correct? What is the difference between "tax" and "penal" judgments? Is there a clear distinction?

Recall that in *Sabbatino,* the act of state doctrine effectively required U.S. courts to give effect to a Cuban expropriation. *See supra* pp. 801-808. Why wasn't the Canadian judgment in *Her Majesty* an act of state? If U.S. courts will act to uphold a Cuban expropriation decree, why not the Canadian tax judgment in *Her Majesty*? In truth, would it not be more appropriate for U.S. courts to inquire into the international legality of both the Cuban decree and the Canadian judgment in deciding what effect to give to them?

8. *What is a tax or revenue judgment?* There is little authority on what constitutes a "tax" or "revenue" judgment. The *Third Restatement* concludes that a revenue judgment is "a judgment in favor of a foreign state . . . based on a claim for an assessment of a tax, whether imposed in respect of income, property, transfer of wealth, or transactions in the taxing state." *Restatement (Third) Foreign Relations Law* §483, comment c (1987). The commentary to the UFCMJRA explains that "A judgment for taxes is a judgment in favor of a foreign country or one of its subdivisions based on a claim for an assessment of a tax." UFCMJRA, §3(b), comment 4.

What if a foreign judgment awarded not only forgone tax revenue but forgone profits (because state-owned entities participated in the market)? Would the revenue rule bar enforcement of that latter portion of the judgment? Consider one recent case's holding that the revenue rule does not bar the latter remedy:

> [T]ax laws are problematic not because they raise revenue for the government and the government may use such revenues for a controversial purpose, but because the laws, in

and of themselves, embody policy choices that are infused with moral and political judgments. As a result . . . the [revenue] rule is not triggered by every foreign law that causes a foreign sovereign to generate revenue; rather, the rule is targeted to those revenue-generating statutes that involve moral and political judgments.

A sovereign's commercial activities do not involve the kind of moral and political judgments that the tax or revenue laws typically involve. A sovereign engages in commercial activity for the same reason a private individual or corporation participates in such activity — to turn a profit. A sovereign's decision to drill for oil, manufacture airplanes, or provide postal services is not infused with the kinds of moral and political judgments necessarily involved in taxing cigarettes or providing a tax credit for higher education spending.

To read the revenue rule to prohibit sovereigns from bringing damages claims irrespective of the nature of the damages claim would have extremely troubling consequences. . . . Such an interpretation of the revenue rule would (1) make it very difficult for sovereigns to participate in commercial activities and (2) provide strong disincentives for foreign sovereigns to do business with United States corporations. Such a reading of the revenue rule would cause these problems while achieving absolutely no public policy purpose: prohibiting sovereigns from bringing claims arising out of purely commercial activities would in no way serve the separation of powers or extraterritoriality concerns that currently motivate federal courts to recognize the revenue rule.

Further, if the revenue rule barred suits by foreign sovereigns suing in their commercial capacity, foreign sovereigns would find themselves at a unique disadvantage in federal courts. Under the Foreign Sovereign Immunities Act ("FSIA"), a foreign sovereign is subject to jurisdiction in federal courts with respect to actions arising out of a commercial activity carried on by the foreign state, provided that there is some connection between the commercial activity and the United States. Thus, under Defendants' reading of the revenue rule, a private plaintiff could sue a foreign sovereign in United States courts for claims arising out of commercial activity but the foreign sovereign could not bring a counterclaim arising out of that same course of conduct. Such an outcome would be manifestly unjust. *Republic of Colombia v. Diageo N. Am., Inc.,* 531 F. Supp. 2d 365, 385-386 (E.D.N.Y. 2007).

Is this persuasive? Is there a valid distinction between revenue-generating and profit-making activities by a foreign sovereign? Recall the treatment of "commercial activities" in the foreign sovereign immunity context. *See supra* pp. 277-279. How likely is the parade of horribles predicted by the court in *Diageo?* Does the FSIA support the distinction? Is the court in *Diageo* correct that a sovereign defendant could not bring a counterclaim arising out of its commercial conduct?

9. *What is a penal judgment?* There is also uncertainty about what constitutes a penal judgment. In *Huntingdon v. Attrill,* 146 U.S. 657, 673-674 (1892), the Supreme Court said, "whether a statute of one State . . . is a penal law in the international sense, so that it cannot be enforced in the courts of another State, depends upon the question whether its purpose is to punish an offence against the public justice of the State, or to afford a private remedy to a person injured by the wrongful act." The *Third Restatement* defines a penal judgment as "a judgment in favor of a foreign state . . . and primarily punitive rather than compensatory in character." *Restatement (Third) Foreign Relations Law* §483, comment b (1987). *See Java Oil Ltd. v. Sullivan,* 168 Cal. App. 4th 1178 (Cal. Ct. App. 2008) (assessing whether foreign judgment was penal by reference to sister state judgments and principles of comity); *Desjardins Ducharme v. Hunnewell,* 1992 Mass. LEXIS 28 (1992) (award of attorney fees against unsuccessful plaintiff not a fine, even where amount was based upon percentage of damages claimed); *Chase Manhattan Bank, NA v. Hoffman,* 665 F. Supp. 73, 75-76 (D. Mass. 1987) ("the judgment was remedial . . . [and] accrued in its particulars to the private party plaintiff").

Is an award of punitive damage a penal judgment? *See S.A. Consortium General Textiles v. Sun & Sand Agencies* [1978] Q.B. 279, 299-300 ("nothing contrary to English public policy in enforcing a claim for exemplary damages").

10. *Recognition and enforcement of administrative decisions.* In many countries, a wide range of private disputes are resolved by administrative agencies and other quasi-judicial bodies. There is relatively little precedent concerning the recognition of "judgments" rendered by administrative agencies in the U.S. courts. *E.g., Apostolou v. Merrill Lynch & Co.,* 2007 U.S. Dist. LEXIS 74682 (E.D.N.Y. 2007) (holding that deference to foreign judgments extends to administrative forums but reserving judgment on specific question whether foreign agency's dismissal of employee was entitled to deference); *Petition of Wayne Breau,* 565 A.2d 1044 (N.H. 1989) (giving collateral estoppel effect to decision of Canadian administrative agency); *Regierungspraesident Land Nordrhein-Westfalen v. Rosenthal,* 232 N.Y.S.2d 963 (App. Div. 1962) (recognizing decision of German administrative agency); *Restatement (Third) Foreign Relations Law* §481, Reporters' Note 5 (1987). Is it sensible to attempt to fashion a per se rule either that foreign administrative decisions are, or are not, enforceable in U.S. courts? Or does the status of such decisions vary depending upon the character of the administrative agency, its process, and the type of dispute it has resolved?

Does the UFMJRA apply to administrative decisions? Note that the Act applies only to "judgments." Is it clear whether a disposition of an administrative tribunal is a "judgment"? Compare the UFCMJRA, which provides in §2(2) that the revised Act applies to the judgment of "a court" of a foreign state. The revised Act's comments refer to an "adjudicative body."

8.   Applicable Law and the *Erie* Doctrine

As in other international litigation contexts, the recognition of foreign judgments in U.S. courts raises questions under the *Erie* doctrine. For the most part, U.S. courts have held that state law governs the enforceability of foreign judgments.[86] Nevertheless, a few courts have suggested (typically in dicta) that federal common law rules may play a role in enforcing foreign judgments.[87] Reread *Somportex* and *Her Majesty,* excerpted above, which illustrate both approaches.

SOMPORTEX, LTD. v. PHILADELPHIA CHEWING GUM CORP.
318 F. Supp. 161 (E.D. Pa. 1970) [excerpted above at pp. 1095-1096]

HER MAJESTY THE QUEEN IN RIGHT OF THE PROVINCE OF BRITISH COLUMBIA v. GILBERTSON
597 F.2d 1161 (9th Cir. 1979) [excerpted above at pp. 1103-1104]

Notes on Somportex *and* Her Majesty

1. *Source of law governing recognition of foreign judgments in diversity actions.* What law provided the rule in *Hilton?* Was it state, federal, or international? Reread the first few paragraphs of *Hilton. See supra* pp. 1086-1087.

---

86. *See infra* p. 1111.
87. *See infra* pp. 1111-1112.

2. *Application of state law to recognition of foreign judgments.* What law did *Somportex* hold governed the recognition of foreign judgments in the United States? Relying on *Erie* and *Klaxon, supra* pp. 10-11 & 791-796, most lower federal courts have assumed or held that, in diversity actions, they are required to apply state law. *See, e.g., Phillips USA, Inc. v. Allflex USA, Inc.,* 77 F.3d 354, 359 (10th Cir. 1996); *Choi v. Kim,* 50 F.3d 244, 248 n.7 (3d Cir. 1995); *Seetransport Wiking v. Navimpex Centrala Navala,* 989 F.2d 572, 582 (2d Cir. 1993); *Success Motivation Institute of Japan, Ltd. v. Success Motivation Institute Inc.,* 966 F.2d 1007, 1009-1010 (5th Cir. 1992) ("*Erie* applies even though some courts have found that these suits necessarily involve relations between the U.S. and foreign governments, and even though some commentators have argued that the enforceability of these judgments . . . - should be governed by reference to a general rule of federal law."); *V.F. Jeanswear Ltd. v. Molina,* 320 F. Supp. 2d 412, 417 (M.D.N.C. 2004); *Pure Fishing, Inc. v. Silver Star Co.,* 202 F. Supp. 2d 905, 909 (N.D. Iowa 2002); *Biggelaar v. Wagner,* 978 F. Supp. 848, 853 (N.D. Ind. 1997); *Svenska Handelsbanken v. Carlson,* 258 F. Supp. 448 (D. Mass. 1966).

State courts have also generally concluded that they are free to disregard *Hilton* and to develop their own rules governing foreign judgments. *E.g., Monks Own, Ltd. v. Monastery of Christ in the Desert,* 168 P.3d 121 (N.M. 2007); *Hilkmann v. Hilkmann,* 858 A.2d 58, 66 (Pa. 2004); *Bonfils v. Gillespie,* 139 P. 1054 (Colo. 1914); *Restatement (Third) Foreign Relations Law* §481, comment a (1987) ("State courts, and federal courts applying State law, recognize and enforce foreign country judgments without reference to federal rules"). A leading decision in this regard was *Johnston v. Compagnie Generale Transatlantique,* 152 N.E. 121 (N.Y. 1926), where the Court held that the recognition of foreign judgments was a matter of "private rather than public international law, of private right rather than public relations," on which state law was controlling.

Nonetheless, many state courts incorporate the *Hilton* principles into their own common law. *Kwongyuen Hangkee Co. v. Starr Fireworks, Inc.,* 634 N.W.2d 95, 97 (S.D. 2001); *Mori v. Mori,* 931 P.2d 854, 856 (Utah 1997); *Milhoux v. Linder,* 902 P.2d 856, 860-861 (Colo. App. 1995).

3. *Possible applicability of federal common law to recognition of foreign judgments.* Is reliance on state law appropriate in enforcing *foreign* judgments? Some commentators have suggested that the recognition of foreign judgments should be governed by a uniform federal rule. *E.g.,* Casad, *Issue Preclusion and Foreign Country Judgments: Whose Law?,* 70 Iowa L. Rev. 53, 77-80 (1984); Moore, *Federalism and Foreign Relations,* 1965 Duke L.J. 248, 261-268, 285-286; Scoles, *Interstate and International Distinctions in Conflict of Laws in the United States,* 54 Calif. L. Rev. 1599 (1966); Comment, *Recognition and Enforcement of Foreign Judgments in the United States: The Need for Federal Legislation,* 37 John Marshall L. Rev. 229 (2003). For a recent discussion of these authorities, *see Evans Cabinet Corp. v. Kitchen Intern., Inc.,* 593 F.3d 135, 141 nn.6-7 (1st Cir. 2010).

What national interests would be served by a uniform federal approach to the enforcement of foreign judgments? Recall that some foreign nations refuse to enforce U.S. judgments. Could a uniform federal approach help remedy this state of affairs? Recall the discussions of this issue in the context of the reciprocity rule. Does the existence of multiple state law rules governing enforcement confuse foreigners or give foreign courts a reason for refusing to enforce U.S. judgments? *See supra* pp. 1101-1102. If so, are these grounds sufficient for adopting a federal common law rule? Are these not arguments that Congress should enact the ALI's Proposed Judgments Legislation, rather than that courts should fashion rules of federal common law?

4. *Lower court authorities suggesting that federal common law affects recognition of foreign judgments.* Contrary to the *Third Restatement,* several courts have suggested that state law is not the exclusive source for the rules governing the recognition and enforcement of foreign judgments. *See Her Majesty v. Gilbertson,* 597 F.2d 1161 (9th Cir. 1979) (because of "foreign relations overtones" this matter "should not be decided merely by reference to Oregon law"); *Pony Express Records, Inc. v. Springsteen,* 163 F. Supp. 2d 465, 472 (D.N.J. 2001); *Alfadaa v. Fenn,* 966 F. Supp. 1317, 1325 (S.D.N.Y. 1997) (federal law governs enforcement of foreign judgment "[i]n cases involving federal questions"); *Toronto-Dominion Bank v. Hall,* 367 F. Supp. 1009, 1011 (E.D. Ark. 1975) ("suits of this kind necessarily involve to some extent the relations between the United States and foreign governments and for that reason perhaps should be governed by a single uniform rule"); *Hunt v. BP Exploration Co. (Libya),* 492 F. Supp. 885 (N.D. Tex. 1980) (because of the unsettled nature of Texas law on recognition of foreign judgments, "coupled with the realization that recognition of foreign judgments is an element of United States foreign policy, the law of Texas is not the sole referent"). As yet, however, no lower court has actually formulated a rule of federal common law governing the enforcement of foreign judgments.

5. *Power of federal courts to apply federal common law to recognition of foreign judgments.* Questions about the authority of federal courts to fashion federal common law arise in other international contexts. *See supra* pp. 49-50 (causes of action under the Alien Tort Statute); pp. 453-458 (foreign sovereign immunity and official immunity); pp. 528-544 (forum selection clauses); p. 270 (*forum non conveniens*); p. 1043 (discovery); and pp. 808-814 (act of state); pp. 564-565 (*lis alibi pendens* stays and antisuit injunctions). The same issue arises in the recognition context: would federal courts have the authority to establish a rule of federal common law governing the recognition of foreign judgments?

As discussed elsewhere, development of a federal common law rule regarding the recognition of foreign judgments would require demonstrating that this issue was "uniquely federal" and that state rules in the field undercut federal policies. *See supra* pp. 11-13. A rule of federal common law would presumably be derived from extensive federal constitutional authority over foreign commerce and foreign relations, and from the "uniquely federal" character of this field. *See Banco Nacional de Cuba v. Sabbatino,* 376 U.S. 398 (1964); *Zschernig v. Miller,* 389 U.S. 429 (1968); *supra* pp. 18-20, 637-638. On the other hand, there is substantial historical support for treating the recognition of judgments as a matter of state law. *Cf. Zschernig v. Miller,* 389 U.S. 429, 443 (1968) (Harlan, J., concurring).

Assuming that the enforcement of foreign judgments is a uniquely federal issue, are any federal policies undercut by independent state policies? Consider the following:

> If *Hilton* was erroneously decided, then the solution is to change the federal rule, not to encourage a hodgepodge of independent state rules. In any event, the independent state positions regarding [the recognition and enforcement of foreign judgments], although perhaps more enlightened on the merits, have failed to achieve the foreign relations goal sought, namely the recognition of United States judgments abroad by reciprocity among nations. Thus, the lesson of *Hilton* reaffirms that the voice of foreign relations must be a federal voice. Moore, *Federalism and Foreign Relations,* 1965 Duke L.J. 248, 265.

Suppose that a state (a) refuses ever to recognize or enforce any foreign judgment; (b) refuses to recognize or enforce any foreign judgment against a U.S. national; (c) rejects the reciprocity requirement; (d) imposes much stricter scrutiny of foreign courts' jurisdiction than that contemplated by *Hilton* and the UFMJRA; or (e) only recognizes and enforces judgments of English-speaking countries. Would any of these state positions interfere with federal policies?

Consider the following statements in conjunction with the ALI's Proposed Judgments Legislation:

> A priori, it would strike anyone as strange to learn that a judgment of an English or German or Japanese court might be recognized or enforced in Texas but not in Arkansas. . . . The present [ALI] project rejects the view of the New York Court of Appeals [in *Johnston v. Compagnie Generale Transatlantique*, 152 N.E. 121, 123 (N.Y. 1926)] and takes as its point of departure the view that recognition and enforcement of foreign judgments is and ought to be a matter of national concern. . . . ALI, *Recognition and Enforcement of Foreign Judgments: Analysis and Proposed Federal Statute*, at 3 (April 2005).

Why, "a priori," is it so odd that two jurisdictions—Texas and Arkansas, in the ALI's example—might treat legal issues differently? Is it not equally "strange" that Texas and Arkansas have different rules regarding choice of law? Regarding personal jurisdiction over foreign companies? Regarding enforceability of forum selection agreements? In fact, is it not at least as "strange" to think that Congress is asked to legislate in a field of private rights governed for at least the past century by state law?

6. *Role of international law.* Recall *Hilton*'s treatment of the recognition of foreign judgments as a subject governed by international law, *see supra* pp. 1090-1091, and the status of international law as federal law, *see supra* pp. 17-18. Compare the reasoning of the New York Court of Appeals:

> To what extent is this court bound by *Hilton v. Guyot?* It is argued with some force that questions of international relations and the comity of nations are to be determined by the Supreme Court of the United States. . . . But the question is one of private rather than public international law, of private right rather than public relations. . . . *Johnston v. Compagnie Generale Transatlantique*, 152 N.E. 121, 123 (N.Y. 1926).

Is that persuasive? Note that federal common law arises in many areas affecting "private" rights, and that such matters can affect federal interests just as readily as "public" issues.

7. *Grounds for denying recognition distinguished from preclusive effect.* When answering the *Erie* questions involved in the context of recognition proceedings, is it necessary to differentiate between the law governing the *grounds* for refusing to recognize the foreign judgment and the law governing the *preclusive effect* of the foreign judgment? Even assuming that state (or conceivably federal) law supplies the grounds for denying recognition, should foreign law apply to the question of the preclusive effect of that judgment? According to one recent decision:

> Cases addressing *res judicata* choice of law questions as they relate to foreign judgments, however, are in considerable conflict. Some courts apply the law of the rendering jurisdiction in determining what preclusive effect should be afforded to the judgment. Others employ domestic rules of *res judicata* giving the same effect to a foreign judgment as would be given to domestic or sister state judgments. *King v. Cessna Aircraft Co.*, 2010 WL 5253526 (S.D. Fla. 2010) (magistrate judge). *See also Seale & Associates, Inc. v. Vector Aerospace Corp.*, 2010 WL 5186410 (E.D. Va. Dec. 7, 2010) (collecting cases).

Courts sometimes can avoid resolving this thorny issue by determining that the preclusive effect would be the same under applicable law (*i.e.*, a false conflict). *See, e.g., King v. Cessna Aircraft Co.*, 2010 WL 5253526 (S.D. Fla. 2010) (magistrate judge). Could a U.S. court give a foreign judgment *more* preclusive effect than it would be entitled to under the law of the rendering court? Would that advance, or undermine, principles of comity?

   8. **Comparison with act of state doctrine.** Recall that the act of state doctrine is a rule of federal common law, requiring U.S. courts to give effect to foreign acts of state. *See supra* pp. 814-815. Why does not the same rationale support federal common law rules governing the effect of foreign judgments? The Court's opinion in *Pasquantino* relied heavily on the act of state doctrine and separation of powers concerns as justifying the revenue rule. 544 U.S. at 368-370. How does this affect the question whether the recognition of foreign judgments should be governed by federal common law standards?

   9. **Comparison with foreign arbitral awards.** As discussed below, foreign arbitral awards are generally subject to enforcement under the New York Convention and Federal Arbitration Act. *See infra* pp. 1161-1163. Does this have any relevance to the argument that federal common law rules should govern the enforceability of foreign judgments?

   10. **Role of friendship, commerce, and navigation treaties in enforcing foreign judgments.** As described above, the United States is party to numerous friendship, commerce, and navigation ("FCN") treaties. These treaties typically include a so-called "national treatment" provision, along the following lines:

> Nationals and companies of either [nation] shall be accorded national treatment and most-favored-nation treatment with respect to access to the courts of justice and to administrative tribunals and agencies within the territories of the other [nation], in all degrees of jurisdiction, both in pursuit and in defense of their rights. Treaty of Friendship, Commerce, and Navigation Between the United States of America and the Republic of Korea, 8 U.S.T. 2217, Article V.

Several lower courts have held that such "national treatment" provisions "elevat[e] a [foreign] judgment to the status of a sister state judgment." *Choi v. Kim*, 50 F.3d 244, 248 (3d Cir. 1995). *See also Vagenas v. Continental Gin Co.*, 988 F.2d 104, 106 (11th Cir. 1993); *Otos Tech Co., Ltd. v. OGK America, Inc.*, 2010 WL 5239235 (D.N.J. Dec. 16, 2010). In one court's words:

> the Court is precluded from applying comity principles established under New Jersey law, and must instead utilize those New Jersey standards that govern the enforcement of sister state judgments. In other words, the Friendship Treaty is effectively analogous to the Full Faith and Credit Clause because it obligates "the states to afford a [Korean] national the same treatment that any United States citizen would receive in an action to enforce a judgment." *Song v. Kim*, 1993 WL 526340, *aff'd in relevant part sub nom. Choi v. Kim*, 50 F.3d 244 (3d Cir. 1995).

Is this correct? Suppose a U.S. national holds a foreign judgment. What law ordinarily governs efforts to enforce the judgment in the United States? Suppose a foreign national holds a U.S. state judgment. What law governs the foreign national's efforts to enforce the judgment in the United States?

C. Exceptions to the Presumptive Recognition of Foreign Judgments in U.S. Courts

The presumptive recognition of foreign judgments in U.S. courts under both common law standards and the UFMJRA (and UFCMJRA) is subject to important exceptions. As described below, there are many circumstances in which U.S. courts will *not* enforce foreign judgments. In some circumstances, foreign judgments can be resisted on the same grounds as are available for challenging domestic judgments. In other cases, U.S. courts will not enforce a foreign judgment, even though they might enforce a comparable state judgment.

According to *Hilton*, a foreign judgment would not be enforced where:

1. There was no "due citation or voluntary appearance of the defendant" in the foreign judicial proceedings.
2. The foreign court lacked personal jurisdiction over the defendant.
3. The foreign court lacked subject matter jurisdiction over the dispute.
4. There was a showing of fraud or other irregularity in the foreign proceedings.
5. The foreign cause of action on judgment violates U.S. public policy.
6. The foreign proceedings were biased or unfair.[88]

The UFMJRA establishes similar exceptions (as would the UFCMJRA). Section 4 of the Act established two types of grounds for nonrecognition of foreign judgments. Section 4(a) sets forth three grounds — unfair foreign courts, lack of personal jurisdiction, and lack of subject matter jurisdiction — which *forbid* a U.S. court from enforcing a foreign judgment. Section 4(b) sets forth six other grounds that *permit*, but do not require, a U.S. court to deny recognition. These grounds include lack of notice, fraud, public policy, an inconsistent judgment, violation of a forum selection clause, and inconvenient forum.[89]

The UFCMJRA sets forth both mandatory and discretionary exceptions that are almost identical to those in the UFMJRA. Unlike its predecessor, however, the new Act would expressly address the burden of proof with regard to the two sets of exceptions. Section 4(d) provides that the party resisting recognition has the burden of proving the existence of either the mandatory or the discretionary grounds for nonrecognition.[90]

1. Adequate Notice and Proper Service

One exception to the principle favoring recognition of foreign judgments concerns adequate notice. According to *Hilton*, foreign judgments will not be recognized if they were not based upon "the due citation or voluntary appearance of the defendant."[91] In contrast, the UFMJRA permits nonrecognition of a judgment if "the defendant in the proceedings in the foreign court did not receive notice of the proceedings in sufficient time to enable him to defend."[92] These two formulations identify two related, but distinguishable, requirements: (a) adequate notice; and (b) service of process in accordance with formal requirements (either international or national). The decision in *Ackermann v. Levine* illustrates these requirements.

ACKERMANN v. LEVINE
788 F.2d 830 (2d Cir. 1986) [also excerpted below at pp. 1115-1117]

PIERCE, CIRCUIT JUDGE. [Mr. Ackermann, a German lawyer, sued Mr. Levine, a U.S. businessman, in German courts. Mr. Levine defaulted and Mr. Ackermann obtained a judgment which he sought to enforce in the United States. Among other things, Mr.

---

88. *See supra* pp. 1086-1089.
89. *Compare* the generally similar approach of the *Restatement (Third) Foreign Relations Law* §482 (1987).
90. UFCMJRA, §4(d).
91. 159 U.S. at 163.
92. UFMJRA §4(b)(1). *See also Restatement (Second) Conflict of Laws* §92(b) (1971) ("a reasonable method of notification is employed and a reasonable opportunity to be heard is afforded to persons affected"); *Restatement (Third) Foreign Relations Law* §482(2)(b) (1987) ("defendant did not receive notice of the proceedings in sufficient time to enable him to defend"); UFCMJRA, §4(c)(1).

Levine challenged the judgment on the grounds that he had not received adequate notice.] . . . We [next address] the question of whether service of the summons and complaint by registered mail provided Levine with adequate notice of the action.

Service of process must satisfy both the statute under which service is effectuated and constitutional due process.[93] The statutory prong is governed principally by the Hague [Service] Convention. The service of process by registered mail did not violate the Hague Convention. Plaintiffs declined to follow the service route allowed under Article 5 of the Convention, which permits service via a "Central Authority" of the country in which service is to be made. Instead, plaintiffs chose to follow the equally acceptable route allowed under Articles 8 and 10. Article 8 permits each contracting state "to effect service of judicial documents upon persons abroad . . . directly through its diplomatic or consular agents." The Regional Court of Berlin availed itself of this method by first sending the summons and complaint to the German Consulate in New York. As to the forwarding of those documents by registered mail from the Consulate to Levine's residence, the method of service was appropriate under Article 10(a), [which permits parties to "send judicial documents, by postal channels, directly to persons abroad."] Since the United States has made no objection to the use of "postal channels" under Article 10(a), service of process by registered mail remains an appropriate method of service in this country under the Convention. . . .

Nor was service ineffective because it did not satisfy the Federal Rules of Civil Procedure. The old Federal Rule 4 was superseded by the Hague Convention and thus presumptively should not limit application of the Convention. . . . The district court correctly notes that [old] Rule 4(c)(2)(C)(ii), permitting mail service conforming to certain technical requirements, did not exist when Ackermann's summons and complaint were served. In any event, whether Ackermann's service satisfied Rule 4 as it then existed or as it now exists is irrelevant because the United States has made no declaration or limitation to its ratification of the Convention. . . . Thus, the Convention "supplements" — and is manifestly *not* limited by — Rule 4.

The district court erred in holding that service under the Convention must satisfy both federal and state law. The court improperly cited *Aspinall's Club v. Aryeh,* 450 N.Y.S.2d 199 (App. Div. 1982), for the proposition. *Aspinall's Club* expressly held quite the opposite — that service of process under the Convention must satisfy federal *but not state* law. *See Aspinall's Club,* 450 N.Y.S.2d at 202 (service on an adult at defendant's residence must satisfy Federal Rule 4 but not the more stringent requirements under N.Y. C.P.L.R. §308(2)). Indeed, it seems to us that the only reason that service had to satisfy even Federal Rule 4 in *Aspinall's Club* was that the Convention is silent as to service on persons other than the defendant. Thus, some external law was needed to fill the interstices of the Convention, and the court in *Aspinall's Club,* though a state court, noted that "the Federal laws and treaties" are supreme to state law on this point, and that it would be "untenab[le]" to "promot[e] New York law over the Convention and the Federal Rule." In sum, where the Convention provides a rule of decision, that rule is dispositive, barring any contrary declaration by the United States; where the Convention is silent, federal law should govern where possible.

To construe the Convention otherwise would unduly burden foreign judgment holders with the procedural intricacies of fifty states. *Cf.* 18 C. Wright, A. Miller & E. Cooper, *Federal Practice and Procedure* §4473 at 743 (1981) ("It is intrinsically awkward

---

93. Defendant-appellee also argues that service violated service of process laws of West Germany, [citing] *Appel v. Scheuler,* 78 Civ. 582 (E.D.N.Y. 1979). . . . [T]his court, upon review [finds] that, under the evidence presented herein, service did not violate current German law.

to confront foreign judgments with the potentially divergent law of fifty states and federal courts, and recognition of foreign judgments at least touches concerns of foreign relations in which the national government has paramount interests."). While we could not similarly subordinate New York's interests in the *public policy* implications of the subject foreign judgment, as discussed *infra,* New York's rules regarding service are undoubtedly less compelling. *See Hanna v. Plumer,* 380 U.S. 460, 469 (1965) (state service rules not "substantial" enough to override federal rule). . . .

It is of no moment that an employee of appellee Levine's apartment building received and signed for the service of process. First, as to this issue on which the Convention is silent, Federal Rule 4 requires merely that service be made on one of suitable age and discretion at the defendant's residence. *See Aspinall's Club,* 450 N.Y.S.2d at 202. Second, contrary to dicta in *Aspinall's Club* as to the more stringent requirements of the C.P.L.R., even New York law may permit service upon one of suitable age and discretion who accepts process for residents of an apartment building.

Finally, service by registered mail does not violate constitutional due process. *See Mullane v. Central Hanover Bank & Trust Co.,* 339 U.S. 306, 314 (1950) (due process permits service of process by mail so long as such service provides "notice reasonably calculated . . . to provide interested parties notice of the pendency of the action"). . . .

Notes *on* Ackermann

1. *Foreign service must comply with requirements of adequate notice or "due citation."* One of the *Hilton* requirements for the enforcement of foreign judgments is that of "proceedings following due citation or voluntary appearance of adversary parties." 159 U.S. at 202-203. The "due citation" requirement focuses on whether service from the foreign proceedings was properly effected on the defendant in time for him to respond adequately. Compare §4(b)(1) of the UFMJRA ("the defendant in the proceedings in the foreign court did not receive notice of the proceedings in sufficient time to enable him to defend"); *Restatement (Third) Foreign Relations Law* §482(2)(b) (1987) ("the defendant did not receive notice of the proceedings in sufficient time to enable him to defend"). *Compare Restatement (Second) Conflict of Laws* §92(b) (1971) ("a reasonable method of notification is employed and a reasonable opportunity to be heard is afforded to persons affected") *and* ALI, *The Foreign Judgments Recognition and Enforcement Act* §5(a)(iv) (2005) ("the judgment was rendered without notice reasonably calculated to inform the defendant of the pendency of the proceedings in a timely manner"). In these latter authorities the inquiry is directed toward whether a reasonable method of notification was attempted, not whether the defendant actually received notice in a particular instance.

Which basic approach — actual notice or reasonable efforts to provide notice — is preferable? In both cases, note that the inquiry is directed toward general considerations of fairness and opportunity to defend, not toward technical compliance (or noncompliance) with prescribed formal requirements for service of process.

What exactly do the "adequate notice" and "due citation" standards require? What role should formal service of process requirements, as distinct from lack of substantive notice or opportunity to defend, play in the recognition of foreign judgments? More specifically, should U.S. courts refuse to enforce foreign judgments if they involved service of foreign process within the United States in a manner that violates: (a) the Due Process Clause; (b) the Hague Service Convention; (c) Federal Rule of Civil Procedure 4; (d) state rules regarding the service of process; or (e) foreign law regarding the service of process? How does *Ackermann* answer this question?

2. *Foreign service must comply with Due Process Clause's adequate notice requirement.* As *Ackermann* illustrates, U.S. courts universally require that the judgment debtor have been given adequate notice and opportunity to appear in the foreign proceeding from which the judgment arose. The standard for adequacy of notice has been defined by reference to the Due Process Clause. Thus, in *Ackermann,* the Court of Appeals inquired whether the German court's use of registered mail for service satisfied the Due Process Clause. *See also Ma v. Continental Bank, NA,* 905 F.2d 1073, 1076 (7th Cir. 1990); *Tahan v. Hodgson,* 662 F.2d 862, 864 (D.C. Cir. 1981); *Somportex Ltd. v. Philadelphia Chewing Gum Corp.,* 453 F.2d 435, 443 (3d Cir. 1971) ("The polestar is whether a reasonable method of notification is employed and reasonable opportunity to be heard is afforded to the person affected"); *Bank of Montreal v. Kough,* 430 F. Supp. 1243, 1248 (N.D. Cal. 1977), *aff'd,* 612 F.2d 467 (9th Cir. 1980); *Roy v. Buckley,* 698 A.2d 497, 502-503 (Me. 1997); *In re Estate of Klein,* 609 N.Y.S.2d 375 (App. Div. 1994).

For decisions where foreign service was found inadequate under the Due Process Clause, *see International Transactions Ltd. v. Embotelladora Agral Regiomontana,* 347 F.3d 589, 594 (5th Cir. 2003) (declining to recognize Mexican bankruptcy court order under principles of comity where no showing that party had adequate notice); *Choi v. Kim,* 50 F.3d 244, 249-250 (3d Cir. 1995) (declining to recognize Korean judgment where judgment debtor did not receive notice of entry of order of execution); *Thorteinsson v. M/V Brangur,* 891 F.2d 1547 (11th Cir. 1990); *De La Mata v. American Life Ins. Co.,* 771 F. Supp. 1375, 1386-1388 (D. Del. 1991) (service upon former agent does not satisfy Due Process Clause); *Rotary Club v. Chaprales Ramos de Pena,* 773 P.2d 467 (Ariz. App. 1989) (Mexican judgment based on substituted service not enforceable); *Julen v. Larson,* 25 Cal. App. 3d 325 (1972) (service of process in German without U.S. translation did not provide U.S. defendant with adequate notice and resulting German judgment would therefore not be enforced).

Note that the UFMJRA (and the UFCMJRA) treat the lack of "notice" as a discretionary basis for nonrecognition under §4(b). Would a U.S. court be constitutionally permitted to enforce a foreign judgment based on service that did not satisfy the Due Process Clause?

3. *Must foreign service comply with the Hague Service Convention?* Apart from requiring adequate notice under due process standards, *Ackermann* also required the German court's service of process on the judgment debtor to have satisfied what it called the "statute under which service is effectuated" — a requirement that the Court equated with the Hague Service Convention. *See also Aspinall's Club v. Aryeh,* 450 N.Y.S.2d 199 (App. Div. 1982) (requiring compliance with Hague Service Convention). Is this an appropriate requirement? Why shouldn't *only* the Due Process Clause be relevant? *Cf. Volkswagenwerk AG v. Schlunk,* 486 U.S. 694 (1988) (suggesting that foreign courts will not honor U.S. judgments that are based on service that does not comply with the Hague Service Convention).

Suppose that foreign service of process satisfies the Due Process Clause, but does not comply with the Hague Service Convention. Should a resulting foreign judgment be denied enforcement? Why or why not? Recall that the United States has long had a liberal policy regarding the service of foreign process within U.S. territory, and that the Hague Service Convention was not intended to limit this freedom. *See supra* pp. 939-952.

Note that in *Ackermann* the German plaintiff (or, more accurately, the German court) did not use Article 5's Central Authority mechanism. Recall also that the Hague Service Convention permits numerous alternative mechanisms of service, and that the United States has not objected to these alternatives. What theory justified the service in *Ackermann? See supra* pp. 924-927.

Suppose that the Central Authority mechanism *had* been used in *Ackermann,* and that the U.S. Central Authority had forwarded the documents to a U.S. Marshal who served them on a purported agent of Levine. Would Levine have been able to challenge compliance with the Convention? *See Galliano S.A. v. Stallion, Inc.,* 930 N.E.2d 756, 759 (N.Y. 2010) (rejecting claim of noncompliance based on service of papers in foreign language and observing that "as long as we do not find the [service] procedure used to be fundamentally unfair, the propriety of the service under the Hague Convention was an issue for the [foreign] court."). Suppose that the "agent" that accepted the process was not in fact an agent permitted by Rule 4's formula ("an officer, a managing or general agent, or . . . any other agent authorized by appointment or by law to receive service of process") to receive service. Does this render notice inadequate? Under *Ackermann*'s analysis? Under the UFMJRA?

Suppose that service is not consistent with the Hague Service Convention but the defendant nevertheless receives actual notice. *Compare Aspinall's Club v. Aryeh,* 450 N.Y.S.2d 199 (App. Div. 1982) (apparently requiring that Rule 4 be satisfied where service was made through Article 5 of Hague Service Convention and U.S. Marshal's Service: "The [receiving state's] Central Authority is to see that the papers in question are served 'by a method prescribed by its internal law for the service of documents in domestic actions upon persons who are within its territory.' The provisions of the Convention were duly observed in the instant matter. We thus conclude that the service on Aryeh met the standards of Rule 4 of the Federal Rules of Civil Procedure and thus satisfied the provisions of the Convention.").

4. *Must foreign service comply with FRCP Rule 4?* Citing *Aspinall's Club, Ackermann* arguably held that a foreign court's service of process on a U.S. defendant in the United States would be required to comply in at least some respects with the service provisions of the Federal Rules of Civil Procedure before the resulting foreign judgment would be recognized. The rationale for this requirement would apparently be that the Hague Service Convention does not always address particular aspects of service and that, where the Convention is silent, federal law should "fill the interstices of the Convention." Is compliance with the Federal Rules an appropriate requirement for recognition of foreign judgments? Why is not the Due Process Clause alone an adequate safeguard? Read the final paragraphs of *Ackermann* carefully. Does the court require compliance with Rule 4, and, if so, when? Does the court adopt *Aspinall's* view of Rule 4, or does it merely require compliance with the Convention and the Due Process Clause? Reconsider the hypothetical in the preceding note.

Ackermann did not require compliance with Rule 4's requirements concerning service by mail. Why not? Is it because Article 10 of the Convention permits specified types of mail service and the judgment creditor complied with these requirements?

Suppose that a foreign judgment is rendered by the court of a nation that is *not* a party to the Hague Service Convention. Would the foreign court's service on a defendant within the United States be required to satisfy the Federal Rules of Civil Procedure, as well as the Due Process Clause? For one decision answering in the affirmative, *see Corporacion Salvadorena de Calzado, SA v. Injection Footwear Corp.,* 533 F. Supp. 290, 296-297 (S.D. Fla. 1982) ("service must nevertheless comport with Fed. R. Civ. P. 4. The relevant provisions of Rule 4 require that service on a corporation be made upon 'an officer, a managing or general agent or any other agent authorized by appointment or by law to receive service of process,' or alternatively, in accordance with subsection (i), Alternative Provisions for Service in a Foreign Country.").

Is this wise? Did the drafters of Rule 4 have any intention that it should govern the service of process from foreign courts? *Compare International Transactions Ltd. v. Embotelladora Agral Regiomontana,* 347 F.3d 589, 595-596 (5th Cir. 2003) ("While there is no requirement that Mexican law be identical to U.S. bankruptcy law, the notice requirements in our law give us some guidance as to what notice would satisfy our concept of due process") *with Tahan v. Hodgson,* 662 F.2d 862, 864 (D.C. Cir. 1981) ("It would be unrealistic for the United States to require all foreign judicial systems to adhere to the Federal Rules of Civil Procedure"; case involved service outside the United States). Is it not odd that U.S. law is entirely unclear on basic issues such as the service requirements applicable for recognition of a foreign judgment?

5. ***Must foreign service comply with state service requirements?*** In addition to requiring compliance with the Federal Rules of Civil Procedure, *Ackermann* refused to require that foreign service of process satisfy *state* rules regarding the service of process. *See also Aspinall's Club v. Aryeh,* 450 N.Y.S.2d 199, 202 (App. Div. 1982) (same). *But see DSQ Property Co. v. DeLorean,* 891 F.2d 128 (6th Cir. 1989) (apparently applying state service rules). What was the basis for this conclusion? The Hague Service Convention? Or "concerns of foreign relations" referred to in the quotation from Wright and Miller?

Suppose the case had involved the judgment of a court in a country that is *not* party to the Hague Service Convention. Would state requirements regarding the service of process upon persons within the state be applicable? Having regard to the fact that state law governs the recognition of foreign judgments, *supra* pp. 1110-1114, what would provide the basis for a federal law rule governing service?

6. ***Significance of actual notice.*** Suppose that the defendant receives actual notice of the foreign proceeding, in a manner that does not satisfy the Due Process Clause. Some lower U.S. courts have suggested that the fact of actual notice is not sufficient, and that the failure to utilize service mechanisms that satisfy the Due Process Clause results in nonrecognition. *See Boivin v. Talcott,* 102 F. Supp. 979 (N.D. Ohio 1951). Other lower courts have apparently regarded the defendant's actual notice as sufficient evidence of service. *The Standard SS Owners' Protection and Indemnity Ass'n (Bermuda) Ltd. v. C & G Marine Services, Inc.,* 1992 WL 111186 (E.D. La. 1992); *Knothe v. Rose,* 392 S.E.2d 570, 573 (Ga. App. 1990).

7. ***Service of foreign process outside the United States.*** Many U.S. enforcement decisions involve U.S. judgment debtors who were, or should have been, served with foreign process in the United States. Some cases, however, involve non-U.S. defendants who were, or should have been, served with foreign process outside the United States. *E.g., Thomas and Agnes Carvel Foundation v. Carvel,* 736 F. Supp. 2d 730 (S.D.N.Y. 2010); *Tahan v. Hodgson,* 662 F.2d 862 (D.C. Cir. 1981); *National Fire Ins. Co. v. People's Republic of Congo,* 727 F. Supp. 936 (S.D.N.Y. 1989). What standards should apply to such service of process? Suppose the service rules of both the foreign issuing court and the foreign defendant's state permit service that is inconsistent with the Due Process Clause?

8. ***Compliance with service requirements of issuing court.*** Some U.S. courts have inquired whether service of process from a foreign court complied with the service of process rules of the foreign jurisdiction. *E.g., K & R Robinson Enterprises Ltd. v. Asian Export,* 178 F.R.D. 332, 342 (D. Mass. 1998) (assessing sufficiency of service under U.S. and British Columbian law); *De La Mata v. American Life Ins. Co.,* 771 F. Supp. 1375, 1385-1386 (D. Del. 1991) ("Analysis begins by examining the law governing service in Bolivia and determining whether the Bolivian court adhered to Bolivian laws"); *Royal Bank of Canada v. Trentham Corp.,* 491 F. Supp. 404 (S.D. Tex. 1980); *Bank of Montreal v. Kough,* 430 F. Supp. 1243, 1249-1250 (N.D. Cal. 1977), *aff'd,* 612 F.2d 467 (9th Cir. 1980). Is this a sensible requirement? Is it consistent with the act of state doctrine? How does *Ackermann* deal with this issue?

2. Personal and Subject Matter Jurisdiction of Rendering Court

U.S. courts will not enforce a foreign judgment unless the court rendering the judgment possessed both personal and subject matter jurisdiction. Thus, *Hilton* required that a judgment be rendered by "a court of competent jurisdiction . . . after due citation or voluntary appearance of the defendant."[94] Similarly, the UFMJRA deals with the subject of jurisdiction in §§4 and 5.[95] The opinions in the following cases, *Mercandino v. Devoe & Raynolds, Inc.*, and *S.C. Chimexim SA v. Velco Enterprises Ltd.*, illustrate application of the jurisdiction requirements.

MERCANDINO v. DEVOE & RAYNOLDS, INC.
436 A.2d 942 (N.J. Super. 1981)

PER CURIAM. Plaintiff Franco Mercandino filed suit in the Hudson County District Court to enforce a default judgment which he had obtained against defendant Devoe and Raynolds, Inc., in Italy. Trial resulted in the entry of a judgment in plaintiff's favor, and defendant appeals, contending the Italian judgment should not have been enforced because . . . the Italian court was without jurisdiction. . . . We . . . affirm.

A judgment issued by a court of a foreign nation will be recognized in the United States courts on the basis of comity, providing the court rendering the judgment had subject matter and personal jurisdiction over the defendant and provided further that recognition will not offend the policies of the enforcing State. *Hilton v. Guyot, supra.* It is well established that the issue of jurisdiction underlying such a judgment is always open to inquiry, provided that it has not been actually and fully litigated. In determining whether the Italian court had jurisdiction we deem it appropriate to apply the minimum contacts test. Under this test sufficient contacts are established when a nonresident seeking to avail himself of some benefit within a state affirmatively acts in a manner which he knows or should know will result in a significant impact within the forum state. Although this test was developed to determine whether a judgment of a sister state is entitled to full faith and credit, it is equally applicable where a court of a foreign nation has exercised long-arm jurisdiction. In either instance, the minimum contacts standard provides assurance that the exercise of jurisdiction "does not offend traditional notions of fair play and substantial justice." *International Shoe Co. v. Washington.* . . .

The record before us establishes that the defendant had a European representative, headquartered in Rotterdam, who went to Genoa and conducted talks with a representative of plaintiff. They reached an oral agreement, corroborated by correspondence whereby plaintiff was to attempt to find marketing opportunities for defendant's products in Italy. Pursuant to that agreement plaintiff performed a variety of activities which, however, were unsuccessful. Plaintiff instituted this suit to recover for its expenditure of time and money on defendant's behalf. Though defendant had notice of this suit pending in Italy, it decided not to appear there but rather to take its chances fighting in the American courts. Plaintiff obtained a default judgment in Genoa which it seeks to enforce in this pending action.

[The Court analyzed the judgment debtor's action and concluded that it] is clear that defendant acted in a manner which it knew or should have known would result in a significant impact within the jurisdiction of the Italian court, and the minimum contacts test is satisfied. . . .

---

94. 159 U.S. at 163-164.
95. The proposed UFCMJRA addresses jurisdictional issues in §§4(b) and 5.

S.C. CHIMEXIM SA v. VELCO ENTERPRISES LTD.
36 F. Supp. 2d 206 (S.D.N.Y. 1999)

CHIN, DISTRICT JUDGE. [S.C. Chimexim SA ("Chimexim") is a Romanian corporation with principal offices located in Bucharest Romania. Velco Enterprises Ltd. ("Velco") is a Connecticut corporation with its principal place of business in New York. In addition, at relevant times to this suit, Velco had a "Representative Office" in Romania, which was authorized by the Ministry of Foreign Trade Organization Department to do business in Romania. The Authorization states that Velco's principal place of business is New York and that the scope of activity of the Representative Office is "to support the trading activity of Velco[] in Romania concerning the import and export of chemical products." The Representative Office was staffed by an office manager, two secretaries, and a messenger, and it was open approximately 40 hours a week.

Chimexim and Velco had various business dealings, including a transaction in 1991 involving the sale of polyvinylchloride ("PVC") to a Brazilian customer, which defaulted. That transaction resulted in a 1991 settlement agreement between Chimexim and Velco, which provided for Velco to make specified payments to Chimexim. Although Velco made some of the specified payments, further disputes arose between the parties, resulting in Chimexim demanding payment and, subsequently, bringing suit against Velco before the Bucharest Tribunal, Commercial Section ("Tribunal") in Bucharest, Romania. Chimexim served Velco with a summons, but Velco did not appear in proceedings before the Tribunal. The Tribunal entered judgment in favor of Chimexim (for $201,087) against Velco, reciting that Velco had been served and that it was liable under the parties' agreement ("Bucharest Judgment").

Velco then appeared and appealed the Bucharest Judgment on multiple grounds, including (a) failure of Chimexim's initial pleading to comply with Romanian law, (b) inadequate service, (c) lack of personal jurisdiction, and (d) the Tribunal's failure to investigate the merits and its disregard for the terms of the parties' 1991 settlement agreement. A three-judge Court of Appeal rejected Velco's appeal as "groundless." With regard to Velco's personal jurisdiction argument, the Court of Appeal held that the Tribunal possessed jurisdiction over the Representative Office "as long as the representative have legal personality and represents the interests of the parent company on the Romanian Territory." Velco appealed to the Romanian Supreme Judicial Court, while Chimexim sought to enforce the Bucharest Judgment in New York.]

New York has codified the principles of comity by statute as the UFMJRA, N.Y. C.P.L.R. ("CPLR") Article 53. Article 53 provides that "a foreign country judgment . . . is conclusive between the parties to the extent that it grants or denies recovery of a sum of money." C.P.L.R. §5303. The article applies to "any foreign country judgment which is final, conclusive and enforceable where rendered even though an appeal therefrom is pending or it is subject to appeal." A foreign country judgment is "not conclusive" if . . . "the foreign court did not have personal jurisdiction over the defendant." C.P.L.R. §5304(a). [This basis] of non-recognition preclude[s] courts from recognizing the foreign judgment as a matter of law. . . . A foreign country judgment "need not be recognized," however, if: (1) the foreign court did not have subject matter jurisdiction. . . . C.P.L.R. §5404(b). [This basis] of non-recognition [is] discretionary. A foreign country judgment "shall not be refused recognition for lack of personal jurisdiction" if, *inter alia:* (1) defendant was served in person in the foreign state; (2) defendant voluntarily appeared in the proceedings, other than for the purpose of protecting property seized; (3) defendant had its principal place of business, was incorporated, or had otherwise acquired corporate status in the foreign state; or (4) defendant had a business office in the foreign state and the proceedings in the foreign court involved a cause of action arising out of business done by defendant in the foreign state. C.P.L.R. §5305. . . . [I]t would appear that plaintiff has the burden of proving that no mandatory basis for non-recognition pursuant to C.P.L.R. §5304(a) exists, and that defendant has the burden of proving that a discretionary basis for non-recognition pursuant to C.P.L.R. §5304(b) applies. . . .

Chimexim . . . contends that the Bucharest Judgment is entitled to recognition because the Bucharest courts had personal jurisdiction over Velco. I agree. Pursuant to C.P.L.R. §5305(a), at least three separate bases existed for the Tribunal to exercise jurisdiction over Velco in Romania.

First, Velco voluntarily appeared in the proceedings, other than for the purpose of protecting property seized or protesting jurisdiction. C.P.L.R. §5305(a)(2). Velco contends that its appeal from the Bucharest Judgment does not constitute a voluntary appearance. Velco is mistaken. One of Velco's arguments on appeal concerned the merits of the underlying dispute. Velco argued that the Tribunal "mistakenly settled the case, without actually investigating the merits of the dispute and by breaching [certain provisions of Romania's] Civil Code." Because it appeared in the Romanian proceedings in part to attack the Bucharest Judgment on the merits, Velco cannot now complain that the Romanian courts did not have personal jurisdiction over it. "If the judgment debtor did any more than [it] had to do . . . to preserve [a] jurisdictional objection in the foreign court, [it] would thereby have submitted voluntarily to its jurisdiction and forfeited the right to claim an exception." Siegel Commentaries at 556. On this basis alone, Chimexim has met its burden of proving that the Romanian courts had personal jurisdiction over Velco. . . .

Even were I to conclude that Velco did not voluntarily appear, I would still find that personal jurisdiction was proper because: (1) Velco's Representative Office had acquired a corporate status in Romania (C.P.L.R. §5304(a)(4)); and (2) Velco had a business office in Romania and the underlying dispute "involved a cause of action arising out of business done by [Velco] through that office" in Romania. C.P.L.R. §5305(a). It is undisputed that Velco's Representative Office was authorized to do business in Romania by Romania's Ministry of Foreign Trade Organization Department. Thus, Velco acquired a "corporate status" in Romania, even though its principal place of business was New York and it was incorporated in Connecticut. Velco's Representative Office was registered in Romania and was authorized to "to support the trading activity of Velco[] in Romania concerning the import and export of chemical products." In addition, Chimexim's claim against Velco arose out of business done by Velco *through* its foreign office. The purchase orders for the PVC transaction state that they were "conveyed through Velco Bucharest." . . . Accordingly, the Romanian courts had at least three valid bases for exercising personal jurisdiction over Velco. . . .

Velco [also] contends that this Court should exercise its discretion to deny enforcement of the Bucharest judgment because: (a) the Romanian courts did not have subject matter jurisdiction. . . . The Romanian courts had subject matter jurisdiction over the underlying case, and Velco offers no valid argument or evidence to the contrary. . . .

Notes *on* Mercandino *and* S.C. Chimexim

1. *Subject matter jurisdiction or competence.* As *Chimexim* indicates, it is well settled that U.S. courts will not enforce foreign judgments unless the foreign court possessed "competence" or subject matter jurisdiction under *foreign* law. *See Hilton,* 159 U.S. at 202 (foreign court must be one "of competent jurisdiction"); *Restatement (Second) Conflict of Laws* §92, comment i, §98, comment c, §105 (1971) (for a foreign judgment to be enforced, it must be "valid," which requires that the foreign court be competent to render judgment under local law); *Restatement (Third) Foreign Relations Law* §482(2)(a) (1987); *Hunt v. BP Exploration Co. (Libya)*, 492 F. Supp. 885 (N.D. Tex. 1980); UFMJRA §4(a)(3) (lack of subject matter jurisdiction is mandatory basis for nonrecognition); UFCMJRA, §4(b)(3); ALI, *The Foreign Judgments Recognition and Enforcement Act* §5(c)(i) (2005) ("the state of origin of the court that issued the foreign judgment did not have jurisdiction to prescribe, or the foreign court was not competent to adjudicate, with respect to the subject matter of the controversy").

Note that the *Chimexim* Court appeared to consider whether the Bucharest Tribunal possessed subject matter jurisdiction under Romanian law. Is it appropriate for U.S. courts to consider whether a foreign court properly exercised jurisdiction under *foreign law*? Is this consistent with the act of state doctrine? Should not foreign courts be presumed to have acted within their rightful subject matter jurisdiction under foreign law? *See The Standard SS Owners' Protection and Indemnity Ass'n (Bermuda) Ltd. v. C & G Marine Services, Inc.*, 1992 WL 111186 (E.D. La. 1992) ("Louisiana law presumes a rendering court has subject matter jurisdiction, and the burden rests with the judgment debtor to prove otherwise."); *Restatement (Third) Foreign Relations Law* §482, comment a (1987).

Does the subject matter jurisdiction requirement extend beyond the question whether foreign law granted jurisdiction? Suppose that foreign law grants a foreign court subject matter jurisdiction over a dispute that is entirely unrelated to the foreign state. Moreover, suppose that the foreign state prescribes a substantive rule of law that applies extraterritorially. If the foreign court grants a judgment in these circumstances, should the subject matter jurisdiction of the foreign court be open to challenge under U.S. (or international) standards? *Cf. Osorio v. Dole Food Co.*, 665 F. Supp. 2d 1307 (S.D. Fla. 2009) (finding that foreign court lacked subject matter jurisdiction under foreign law even though foreign trial court had concluded that relevant statute was not jurisdictional); *Barry E. (Anonymous) v. Ingraham*, 400 N.Y.S.2d 772 (1977) (New York court refuses to recognize Mexican adoption where the child, the natural parents, and the adoptive parents were New York residents); *Restatement (Third) Foreign Relations Law* §482, comment d (1987) ("While jurisdiction of the foreign court over the subject matter of the action is normally presumed . . . an order of a foreign court affecting rights in land in the United States or rights in a United States patent, trademark, or copyright is not entitled to that presumption.").

Does (or should) the subject matter jurisdiction requirement impose external limits on the subjects that a foreign judgment may dispose of, if it is to be recognized in U.S. courts? What would be the source of these limits? International law? Due process limits? Public policy?

2. *Requirement that issuing court had personal jurisdiction.* As *Ackermann, Mercandino,* and *Chimexim* illustrate, a basic prerequisite for the enforcement of a foreign judgment is that the foreign court have possessed personal jurisdiction over the defendant. In one court's words, the rendering court must have had "in the international sense, jurisdiction over the defendant." *Somportex Ltd. v. Philadelphia Chewing Gum Corp.*, 318 F. Supp. 161, 165 (E.D. Pa. 1970), *aff'd*, 453 F.2d 435 (3d Cir. 1971). *See also Restatement (Third) Foreign Relations Law* §482(1)(b) (1987); *Restatement (Second) Conflict of Laws* §104 (1971); UFMJRA §§4(a)(2) & 5; ALI, *The Foreign Judgments Recognition and Enforcement Act* §§5(a)(iii) & 6 (2005).

An illustration classically (but perhaps imperfectly) cited for the personal jurisdiction requirement was *Buchanan v. Rucker,* 9 East. 192 (K.B. 1808). There, a judgment made in

Tobago against a foreign (non-Tobagoan) defendant was sought to be enforced in English courts. Enforcement was resisted on the grounds that service had been effected by nailing a notice to the courthouse door. The English courts denied recognition: "Can the island of Tobago pass a law to bind the rights of the whole world?" Recall that the jurisdictional limits in *Pennoyer v. Neff, supra,* were developed in the context of an action to enforce a foreign judgment. *See supra* pp. 91-93. Recall also the central role of jurisdiction in negotiations concerning the recognition of foreign judgments in the abortive Hague judgments convention. *See supra* pp. 107-108.

3. Applicable law for determining foreign court's personal jurisdiction. What law should provide the standards for personal jurisdiction in the recognition context—U.S. law, the rendering court's law, or international law? As one court recently recognized, "there is a division of authority on this question." *Evans Cabinet Corp. v. Kitchen Int'l, Inc.,* 593 F.3d 135, 142 & n.10 (1st Cir. 2010) (collecting cases).

(a) U.S. authorities requiring that foreign court's jurisdiction satisfy U.S. jurisdictional standards. Most U.S. courts have reviewed the personal jurisdiction of foreign courts according to U.S. jurisdictional standards, rather than by using the standards applicable under foreign law. *See Genujo Lok Beteiligungs GmbH v. Zorn,* 943 A.2d 573 (Me. 2008); *Cunard SS Co. v. Salen Reefer Services, AB,* 773 F.2d 452, 457 (2d Cir. 1985); *Koster v. Automark Indus.,* 640 F.2d 77, 78 (7th Cir. 1981); *Pure Fishing, Inc. v. Silver Star Co., Ltd.,* 202 F. Supp. 2d 905, 914-917 (N.D. Iowa 2002); *Pony Express Records, Inc. v. Springsteen,* 163 F. Supp. 2d 465, 472-473 & n.3 (D.N.J. 2001); *Oman Int'l Finance, Ltd. v. Hoiyang Gems Corp.,* 616 F. Supp. 351 (D.R.I. 1985); *Hunt v. BP Exploration Co. (Libya),* 492 F. Supp. 885, 895 (N.D. Tex. 1980). *See also* Reese, *The Status in This Country of Judgments Rendered Abroad,* 50 Colum. L. Rev. 783, 789 (1950).

In the absence of statutory guidance, what U.S. jurisdictional standard should apply to recognition of a foreign judgment? Should foreign courts be required to satisfy the Due Process Clause? Or the relevant state long-arm statute? If a state's long-arm statute does not extend to the limits of the Due Process Clause, must a foreign court's judgment satisfy the more restrictive requirements of the state long-arm statute?

What jurisdictional standard did *Mercandino* apply? Was it the same standard as that in *Chimexim?* For other decisions applying a due process/minimum contacts standard in the recognition context, *see Koster v. Automark Indus.,* 640 F.2d 77, 78 (7th Cir. 1981) ("the company must pass a threshold of minimum contacts with the forum state so that it is fair to subject it to the jurisdiction of that state's courts"); *Pure Fishing, Inc. v. Silver Star Co., Ltd.,* 202 F. Supp. 2d 905, 914-917 (N.D. Iowa 2002) ("the court will consider whether the Australian court's personal jurisdiction over Silver Star met the requirements of traditional notions of fair play and substantial justice under the due process clause of the United States Constitution"); *Biggelaar v. Wagner,* 978 F. Supp. 848, 855 (N.D. Ind. 1997) (due process and "minimum contacts" govern jurisdictional issue); *de la Mata v. American Life Ins. Co.,* 771 F. Supp. 1375, 1383-1385 (D. Del. 1991) ("federal courts have held that the issue of whether a foreign court had jurisdiction over a United States national should be determined by our own standards of judicial power as promulgated by the Supreme Court under the due process clause of the Fourteenth Amendment"); *In re Transamerica Airlines, Inc.,* 2007 WL 1555734 (Del. Ch. May 25, 2007) ("In certain circumstances that plainly would satisfy a minimum contacts jurisdictional requirement, the UFMJRA authorizes recognition of foreign judgments even if the foreign court technically may have lacked personal jurisdiction over the defendant according to its own law.") (footnote omitted). Would the facts in *Mercandino* have satisfied the *Chimexim* (and N.Y.C.P.L.R.) standard for personal jurisdiction?

(b) UFMJRA approach to personal jurisdiction. The UFMJRA goes beyond existing common law in providing standards by which U.S. courts should judge the sufficiency

of foreign courts' personal jurisdiction over judgment debtors. (The N.Y.C.P.L.R. is similar, as the decision in *Chimexim* illustrates.) Under §5 of the UFMJRA, a foreign court's personal jurisdiction is to be upheld if it is based on personal service within the foreign state, voluntary appearance (other than to protect property or to contest jurisdiction), prior agreement to submit to the jurisdiction of the foreign court, domicile or principal place of business in the foreign country, business office in the foreign country (or the action arose out of business done through that office), or operation of a motor vehicle or airplane in the foreign country (if the action arose out of such operation). These sections of the Act, unlike some common law decisions, *see supra* pp. 1110-1114, clearly contemplate application of U.S. standards of personal jurisdiction in deciding whether to enforce foreign judgments. The new UFCMJRA adopts the same approach, in §§4(b)(2) and 5 of the Act.

Note that the jurisdictional bases enumerated in the UFMJRA (and UFCMJRA) are fairly limited (and not as expansive as due process limits). Suppose a U.S. manufacturer aggressively markets its goods in a foreign country through a network of unrelated distributors. The goods malfunction, causing serious injuries to foreign purchasers, who successfully obtain personal jurisdiction over the nonresident U.S. manufacturer in foreign courts on theories analogous to those endorsed in *Asahi* and *International Shoe, see supra* pp. 86-90, 140-144. Does the Act require recognition of resulting foreign judgments? Why not?

Note that §5(b) of the Act permits, but does not require, U.S. courts to recognize bases of jurisdiction other than those enumerated in §5(a). What additional bases of personal jurisdiction should U.S. courts recognize? How should a U.S. court exercise its authority under §5(b) of the Act if confronted by the hypothetical in the previous paragraph? Some courts have relied on §5(b) to extend the permitted bases for foreign court jurisdiction to the same reach as the enforcing court's jurisdiction. *See Porisini v. Petricca,* 456 N.Y.S.2d 888, 890 (App. Div. 1982) (New York's version of the UFMJRA "permits the court to recognize other bases of jurisdiction and New York may, and appropriately should, recognize a foreign judgment predicated on any jurisdictional basis it recognizes in its internal law"); *Pure Fishing, Inc. v. Silver Star Co., Ltd.,* 202 F. Supp. 2d 905, 914-917 (N.D. Iowa 2002).

Note also that §5(a)(1) approves tag service within the foreign state as a jurisdictional base. Recall the discussion above on the objections to tag service as a jurisdictional base in international cases. *See supra* pp. 129-137.

(c) U.S. authorities applying foreign jurisdictional requirements. A few U.S. courts have apparently considered only whether the foreign court had personal jurisdiction according to foreign law. *E.g., Manches & Co v. Gilbey,* 646 N.E.2d 86, 87 (Mass. 1995); *Hager v. Hager,* 274 N.E.2d 157, 160-161 (Ill. 1971).

(d) U.S. authorities applying both U.S. and foreign jurisdictional requirements. Some authorities take the position that the rendering court must have had jurisdiction under *both* U.S. and foreign law. *E.g., EOS Transp., Inc. v. Agri-Source Fuels LLC,* 37 So. 3d 349 (Fla. Dist. Ct. App.-1st Dist. 2010); *Monks Own, Ltd. v. Monastery of Christ in the Desert,* 168 P.3d 121 (N.M. 2007); *Canadian Imperial Bank of Commerce v. Saxony Carpet Co.,* 899 F. Supp. 1248, 1253-1254 (S.D.N.Y. 1995); *Falcon Mfg. (Scarborough) v. Ames,* 278 N.Y.S.2d 684, 686 (N.Y. Civ. Ct. 1967).

(e) U.S. authorities applying "international" standards. The *Restatement (Third) Foreign Relations Law* §482(1)(b) (1987) provides that a judgment may not be recognized if "the court that rendered the judgment did not have jurisdiction over the defendant in accordance with the law of the rendering state and with the rules set forth in §421." Section 421, excerpted in Appendix AA, purports to state international law limitations on judicial jurisdiction. Is this more or less expansive than the UMFJRA approach?

(f) Appropriate approach to rendering court's jurisdiction. Which of the foregoing approaches to the personal jurisdiction requirement is preferable?

The *Restatement (Second) Conflict of Laws* §98, comment d (1971), suggests that a U.S. court may impose more rigorous personal jurisdiction requirements on foreign courts than apply to the U.S. court itself when it exercises jurisdiction over foreign defendants in civil actions:

> The foreign court must have had jurisdiction under the rules relating to the recognition of foreign nation judgments of the State where recognition of the judgment is sought. It is possible that a given basis of jurisdiction, such as the doing of an act or the causing of consequences in a state (*see* §§36-37), might not meet the requirements of a particular State of the United States for the recognition of a foreign nation judgment even though the given basis did meet the requirements of due process (*see* §24) and under the rules of competence of the particular State (*see* §24, Comment f) would authorize an assumption of jurisdiction in a similar case by the courts of that State.

What would justify imposing a higher jurisdictional standard on foreign courts, as a condition for recognizing their judgments, than on domestic courts, as a condition for issuing a judgment? Would this be consistent with the "national treatment" guarantees of U.S. FCN treaties (*see supra* p. 1114)? Would it be consistent with how the United States would wish for its own judgments to be treated?

Should the standards for exercising U.S. jurisdiction and for enforcing foreign judgments be identical (*e.g.,* if a U.S. court could exercise jurisdiction in analogous circumstances, then the foreign court's jurisdictional exercise would be upheld)? Is there an argument that more rigorous jurisdictional standards should be applied? Recall how the Brussels Convention (now EU Regulation 44/2001) and the abortive Hague judgments convention both involved so-called "double conventions," where the same jurisdictional requirements applied to both the exercise of jurisdiction and the recognition of foreign judgments. *See supra* pp. 103-107.

(g) ALI's Proposed Judgments Legislation. Read §6 of the ALI's Proposed Judgments Legislation. How much guidance does §6 provide about permissible jurisdictional bases? Does §6 improve on the treatment of personal jurisdiction in the UFMJRA and UFCMJRA? Or does it actually make resolution of such questions more difficult?

4. *Judgment debtor's right to challenge jurisdiction in U.S. enforcement proceeding.* As discussed previously, if a judgment debtor did not appear to contest (and did not waive) the foreign court's personal and subject matter jurisdiction in the foreign proceedings, it can resist recognition on jurisdictional grounds. *Monks Own, Ltd. v. Monastery of Christ in the Desert,* 168 P.3d 121 (N.M. 2007); *Ackermann v. Levine,* 788 F.2d 830 (2d Cir. 1986); *Somportex, Ltd. v. Philadelphia Chewing Gum Corp.,* 318 F. Supp. 161 (E.D. Pa. 1970); *Restatement (Third) Foreign Relations Law* §482, Reporters' Note 3 (1987) ("if jurisdiction of the foreign court was not contested or waived, the judgment debtor may challenge the jurisdiction of the rendering court in resisting enforcement in the United States").

5. *Effect of appearance in foreign proceeding on personal jurisdiction challenge in U.S. recognition action.* A defendant may choose *not* to default in the foreign proceedings. As discussed below, the treatment of the jurisdiction requirement in cases where the judgment debtor did appear in foreign proceedings is difficult. Consider the first ground on which the *Chimexim* Court upheld the Bucharest Tribunal's jurisdiction. How exactly did Velco appear in the foreign proceedings?

(a) Litigation on the merits without challenging jurisdiction. Most authorities indicate that a party that litigates in a foreign forum on the merits without raising a jurisdictional defense

cannot subsequently challenge the jurisdiction of the foreign court. *Restatement (Third) Foreign Relations Law* §482, Reporters' Note 3 (1987) ("If the defendant . . . defended on the merits without challenging the [foreign] court's jurisdiction, a . . . challenge to the jurisdiction of the rendering court is generally precluded"); *Norkan Lodge Co. v. Gillum,* 587 F. Supp. 1457 (N.D. Tex. 1984); *Dart v. Balaam,* 953 S.W.2d 478, 481 (Tex. App. 1997); UFMJRA, §5(a)(2) (jurisdiction established if "the defendant voluntarily appeared in the proceedings, other than for the purpose of protecting property seized or threatened with seizure in the proceedings or of contesting the jurisdiction of the court over him"); ALI, *The Foreign Judgments Recognition and Enforcement Act* §6(c) (2005).

As a noted English jurist has reasoned, the defendant "cannot be allowed, at one and the same time, to say that he will accept the decision on the merits if it is favorable to him and will not submit to it if it is unfavorable." *In re Dulles' Settlement* [1951] Ch. 842, 850, *quoted in* von Mehren & Trautman, *Recognition of Foreign Adjudications: A Survey and Suggested Approach,* 81 Harv. L. Rev. 1601, 1669 (1968). Is this a sensible approach? Is it just to require a defendant to accept a default judgment as a price of being able to contest jurisdiction under the enforcement forum's jurisdictional requirements? Is there any necessary logical connection between a defendant's jurisdictional objections and its substantive defenses?

(b) Litigation on the merits after unsuccessfully challenging jurisdiction. Like *Chimexim,* some U.S. courts also hold that a defendant who unsuccessfully litigates the issue of personal jurisdiction in a foreign court *and* subsequently defends on the merits has waived any right to challenge jurisdiction in the United States. *E.g., Genujo Lok Beteiligungs GmbH v. Zorn,* 943 A.2d 573 (Me. 2008); *Nippon Emo-Trans. Co. v. Emo-Trans. Co.,* 744 F. Supp. 1215 (E.D.N.Y. 1990); *South Carolina National Bank v. Westpac Banking Corp.,* 678 F. Supp. 596, 598-599 (D.S.C. 1987); *Cherun v. Frishman,* 236 F. Supp. 292, 295-296 (D.D.C. 1964); *Restatement (Third) Foreign Relations Law* §482, Reporters' Note 3 (1987); *Restatement (Second) Conflict of Laws* §33, comment d ("[a] general appearance is one where the defendant either enters an appearance in an action without limiting the purpose for which he appears or where he asks for relief which the court may give only if it has jurisdiction over him"; this includes where a defendant "makes a motion raising a question as to the merits of the plaintiff's claim even though the defendant shows that he does not intend thereby to submit himself to the jurisdiction of the court").

This approach requires defendants to choose between having a U.S. court resolve jurisdictional challenges and having an opportunity to defend against the plaintiff's claims on the merits. Query whether this approach is warranted. Note that the standards for determining when a party has gone beyond objecting to jurisdiction can be uncertain. For example, in *CIBC Mellon Trust Co. v. Mora Hotel Corp. NV,* 100 N.Y.2d 215, 223-226 (2003), the judgment debtors (unsuccessfully) resisted claims against them in an English litigation on jurisdictional grounds, while defaulting on the merits and refusing to comply with interim freezing orders issued by the English courts. Thereafter, the judgment creditor obtained a $330 million default judgment and successfully obtained an order from a New York trial court recognizing the English judgment. In response, the judgment debtors sought leave (unsuccessfully) to set aside the English default judgments and defend on the merits. On appeal in New York, the Court of Appeals held that, when the "defendants applied to the High Court to set aside the English judgments and to defend on the merits, they did more than they had to do to preserve a jurisdictional objection . . . and so they voluntarily appeared in the foreign proceeding." *Id.* at 226. What would you have done in the judgment debtors' position?

(c) Unsuccessfully challenging jurisdiction in the foreign proceeding. It is unclear what preclusive effect results from a defendant's unsuccessful challenge in a foreign proceeding to

the foreign court's jurisdiction, followed by a default on the merits. Under the Full Faith and Credit Clause (and Regulation 44/2001) the foreign court's jurisdictional ruling is preclusive. *Baldwin v. Iowa State Traveling Men's Ass'n,* 283 U.S. 522 (1931). What result should follow in international cases? Suppose that foreign jurisdictional standards are different from — and more expansive than — U.S. ones. Can it be correct that litigation in a foreign court about foreign jurisdictional rules, which do not satisfy the Due Process Clause, can preclude a due process defense in the United States? Would the Constitution permit this? *See Hunt v. BP Exploration Co. (Libya),* 492 F. Supp. 885, 895 (N.D. Tex. 1980) ("Litigating on the merits after loss on a jurisdictional challenge is thus not considered to be consent to jurisdiction.").

Nonetheless, some authorities suggest that res judicata effect will generally be afforded to contested foreign jurisdictional decisions. *Somportex, Ltd. v. Philadelphia Chewing Gum Corp.,* 454 F.2d 435 (3d Cir. 1971); *Sprague & Rhodes Commodity Corp. v. Instituto Mexicano del Cafe,* 566 F.2d 861, 863 (2d Cir. 1977); *Fairchild, Arabatzis & Smith, Inc. v. Prometco (Produce & Metals) Co.,* 470 F. Supp. 610, 615 (S.D.N.Y. 1979) ("by litigating and losing the issue of personal jurisdiction in Britain, [the defendant] has no right to contest the jurisdiction of that court in a collateral action").

In contrast, other U.S. courts have permitted personal jurisdiction challenges even though the judgment debtor litigated and lost a jurisdictional defense in the foreign proceeding. *See, e.g., CIBC Mellon Trust Co. v. Mora Hotel Corp. NV,* 743 N.Y.S.2d 408, 418 (App. Div. 2002), *aff'd,* 100 N.Y.2d 215, 223-226 (2003) ("Since the statute provides that recognition is *not* required where a defendant appeared in the proceedings solely for the purpose of contesting the jurisdiction of the court over him, logic informs us that the propriety of the personal jurisdiction exercised by the foreign court is not absolutely established as a fact following that appearance and unsuccessful challenge. If the contrary were true, then any time a defendant appeared in a foreign jurisdiction for the limited purpose of challenging jurisdiction, once the foreign court rejected that challenge and issued a money judgment, no further challenge here would be permissible. Since a foreign court's determination that it has personal jurisdiction does not necessarily comport with the prerequisites of this country's Constitution for such a finding, an assertion of jurisdiction by a foreign court should not preclude a challenge here."); *Hunt v. BP Exploration Co. (Libya),* 492 F. Supp. 885, 895-896 (N.D. Tex. 1980).

Consider the following excerpt from the *Restatement (Third) Foreign Relations Law* §482, comment c (1987):

[A] court in the United States asked to recognize a foreign judgment should scrutinize the basis for asserting jurisdiction in the light of international concepts of jurisdiction to adjudicate. *See* §421. Since all the bases for jurisdiction to adjudicate listed in §421 satisfy the requirements of due process in the United States, any foreign judgment rendered on one of those bases will be entitled to recognition, provided the facts support the assertion of jurisdiction. . . . If the defendant appeared in the foreign court to challenge the jurisdiction of the court and failed to prevail it is not clear whether such determination will be considered *res judicata* by a court in the United States asked to recognize the resulting judgment. If the determination of jurisdiction depended on a finding of fact to support an otherwise unobjectionable basis of jurisdiction — for example, whether X was an agent through whom the defendant did business in the forum state — the determination after contest ordinarily will be respected. *See* §481, Reporters' Note 3. If the determination depended on a question of law or a mixed law/fact question — for example, whether a nonresident corporation is present in the forum state by virtue of having an "alter ego" subsidiary there — the court asked to recognize the resulting judgment will scrutinize the jurisdictional determination on its merits. *See* Reporters' Note 3. If the judgment of the foreign court is founded on a basis of jurisdiction not meeting the standards of §421 — for instance, the plaintiff's nationality under Article 14 of the French Civil Code — but another basis of jurisdiction would have supported the action — for instance, that the action grew out of an activity of the defendant conducted in the territory of the forum, §421(i) — a court in the United States may recognize and enforce the judgment.

Is this a sensible approach? *See also Nippon Emo-Trans. Co. v. Emo-Trans. Co.*, 744 F. Supp. 1215 (E.D.N.Y. 1990) ("[a] defendant who appears solely for purposes of contesting jurisdiction will not, by such appearance, waive any jurisdictional objection in a subsequent suit to enforce the foreign judgment"; however, even though the jurisdictional theory relied upon by Japanese court was not consistent with U.S. due process clause, Japanese judgment will be enforced because facts found by Japanese court will be accepted and because they supported a jurisdictional predicate recognized in U.S.).

6. *"Acquired a corporate status."* The *Chimexim* Court also relied on the fact that Velco's Representative Office in Romania had "acquired a corporate status," for purposes of N.Y.C.P.L.R. §5304(1)(4). Why was that? What if Velco had incorporated a local subsidiary? Would that have subjected Velco itself (as distinct from the subsidiary) to jurisdiction in Romania? Recall the limits on alter ego and agency theories of jurisdiction. *See supra* pp. 175-203. What if Velco merely registered to do business in Romania?

7. *Effect of default judgment on scrutiny of foreign court's jurisdiction.* As discussed above, U.S. courts will in principle enforce foreign default judgments. At the same time, U.S. courts often take a hard look at the foreign court's jurisdiction, procedural protections, and the like before enforcing a default judgment. *Cf. EOS Transp., Inc. v. Agri-Source Fuels LLC,* 37 So. 3d 349 (Fla. Dist. Ct. App.-1st Dist. 2010) (declining to enforce Canadian default judgment); *Electrolines, Inc. v. Prudential Assurance Co.,* 677 N.W.2d 874, 879-889 (Mich. App. 2004) (declining to enforce Liberian default judgment); *Attorney General of Canada v. Gorman,* 769 N.Y.S.2d 369, 372-374 (N.Y. Sup. 2003) (refusing enforcement of Canadian default judgment); *Falcon Mfg. (Scarborough) v. Ames,* 278 N.Y.S.2d 684, 687 (Civ. Ct. 1967) ("Since the judgment under consideration is a default judgment based upon personal service of the writ of summons outside of the jurisdiction of the rendering court it is *ipso facto* not as persuasive as it might have been were it rendered after a trial on the merits."); *Restatement (Second) Conflict of Laws* §98, comment e (1971).

8. *Inconvenient foreign forum under the UFMJRA and UFCMJRA.* Section 4(b)(6) of the UFMJRA permits U.S. courts to deny recognition to foreign judgments rendered in forums that were seriously inconvenient to the judgment debtor, but only where the foreign court's jurisdiction was based solely on personal service. Section 4(c)(6) of the UFCMJRA is identical. *Compare Restatement (Third) Foreign Relations Law* §482(2) (1987), which contains an inconvenient forum defense but omits the personal service limitation, and ALI, *The Foreign Judgments Recognition and Enforcement Act* §5(c)(iv) (2005).

Suppose a U.S. court upholds a foreign court's personal jurisdiction based on the stream of commerce theory. *See supra* at 150-155. Why shouldn't an inconvenient forum defense be permitted? *See Ingersoll Milling Machine Co. v. Granger,* 833 F.2d 680, 689 (7th Cir. 1987); *Bank of Montreal v. Kough,* 430 F. Supp. 1243 (N.D. Cal. 1980), *aff'd,* 612 F.2d 467 (9th Cir. 1980); *Southern Bell Tel. & Tel. Co. v. Woodstock, Inc.,* 339 N.E.2d 423 (Ill. 1975). What if the foreign court would have permitted assertion of a *forum non conveniens* defense?

9. *Violation of forum selection clause under the UFMJRA.* Section 4(b)(5) of the Act permits U.S. courts to deny recognition to foreign judgments that are entered in violation of a forum selection agreement. *See also* UFCMJRA, §4(c)(5) (same); ALI, *The Foreign*

Judgments Recognition and Enforcement Act §5(b) (2005). Recall the rule, derived from the Supreme Court's decision in *Bremen,* that forum selection clauses in international contracts are enforceable except in limited circumstances. *See supra* pp. 474-478. The *Restatement (Third) Foreign Relations Law* §482(2)(f) & Reporters' Note 5 (1987) ("the proceeding in the foreign court was contrary to an agreement between the parties to submit the controversy on which the judgment is based to another forum"), adopts a rule that is similar to that in §4(b)(5).

Suppose the foreign court considers the parties' forum selection clause, but concludes that it is unenforceable (for example, because of duress or lack of notice). Suppose that the foreign court concludes that the forum selection clause violates local public policy and should not be enforced. Should a U.S. court enforce a resulting foreign judgment? Does your answer depend upon the particular defense or public policy invoked by the foreign court?

Failure to invoke the forum selection clause during the foreign proceeding may waive a subsequent challenge to the judgment on this ground. *See Biggelaar v. Wagner,* 978 F. Supp. 848, 856 (N.D. Ind. 1997); *Dart. v. Balaam,* 953 S.W.2d 478, 482 (Tex. App. 1997); ALI, *The Foreign Judgments Recognition and Enforcement Act* §5(b)(ii) (2005). Suppose a defendant unsuccessfully resists the jurisdiction of a foreign court on the ground that a forum selection clause calls for litigation in U.S. courts, and then defends on the merits, again unsuccessfully. Can the judgment debtor resist enforcement by invoking the forum selection clause? *See id.,* comment h ("participation by the judgment debtor in an action other than the one previously selected effectively waives the contractual choice of forum").

10. *Statutes of limitations.* Suppose a judgment creditor obtains a favorable judgment from a Brazilian court and wishes to enforce it in California. Is the enforcement action subject to any limitations period? The limitations period governing the claim? The limitations period governing the enforcement action? If so, what law governs these issues? According to one court, "decisions reached by various jurisdictions with regard to application of statutes of limitations have produced a marvel of diversity and non-uniform results." *Le Credit Lyonnais, S.A. v. Nadd,* 741 So. 2d 1165 (Fla. Dist. Ct. App. 1999).

Section 9 of the UFCMJRA sets forth a limitation period tied to the date when the judgment becomes effective (the earlier of the period during which the judgment is effective in the foreign country or 15 years from its effective date). Neither *Hilton* nor the UFMJRA contains a rule on this issue. In those circumstances, some courts have suggested that an action will be time-barred if it is untimely under the foreign court's limitations period governing actions to enforce a judgment. *E.g., Nadd v. Le Credit Lyonnais, S.A.,* 804 So. 2d 1226 (Fla. 2001); *In re Transamerica Airlines, Inc. v. Akande,* 2007 WL 1555734 (Del. Ch. 2007). These view invokes the language in the UFMJRA providing that the foreign judgment must be "enforceable where rendered." Is this a reasonable interpretation of the quoted language? If so, does the logic of the argument stop with limitations arguments? Doesn't it potentially open the floodgates to enforceability challenges whenever there is a question about "enforceability" of the judgment on the basis of the rendering court's law?

States also may have a separate limitations period that may govern the enforcement petition itself. Some state courts have applied their statutes of limitations governing the enforcement of sister state judgments. *See, e.g., Manco Contracting Co. (W.L.L.) v. Bezdikian,* 195 P.3d 604 (Cal. 2008); *Nadd v. Le Credit Lyonnais, S.A.,* 804 So. 2d 1226, 1233 (Fla. 2001); *La Société Anonyme Goro v. Conveyor Accessories, Inc.,* 677 N.E.2d 30 (Ill. Ct. App. 1997). A few have argued against this view and have suggested, instead, that the state's catchall limitations period (which may be shorter) should govern the question. *See In re Transamerica Airlines, Inc. v. Akande,* 2007 WL 1555734 (Del. Ch. 2007) (declining to apply shorter limitations periods set forth in state statutes and, instead, applying longer common law presumption); *Attorney General of Canada v. Tysowski,* 800 P.3d 133 (Idaho App. 1990) (applying catchall in pre-UFMJRA case); *Manco,* 195 P.3d at 215-217 (Kennard, J. dissenting) (arguing against application of the limitations period governing sister state judgments and, instead, in favor of shorter catchall limitations period). Yet other courts interpret the absence of a limitations period to mean that none applies. *See Pinilla v. Harza Engineering Co.,* 755 N.E.2d 23 (Ill. Ct. App. 2001). On this point, it is important to pay close attention to the precise statutory scheme adopted by the state legislature — some state legislatures may have different statutes governing recognition and enforcement of the foreign judgment, which may be subject to different limitations periods. *Compare La Société Anonyme Goro v. Conveyor Accessories, Inc.,* 677 N.E.2d 30 (Ill. Ct. App. 1997) (applying limitations period from Illinois enforcement statute) *with Pinilla v. Harza Engineering Co.,* 755 N.E.2d 23 (Ill. Ct. App. 2001) (finding no limitations period in Illinois recognition statute).

11. *Personal jurisdiction of enforcing court.* Most personal jurisdiction questions in the recognition context concern the jurisdiction of the foreign rendering court. Fewer courts have addressed the requisite connection between the court enforcing the foreign judgment and the judgment debtor. Must a plaintiff seeking recognition of a foreign judgment prove that the enforcement court has personal jurisdiction over the judgment debtor? The UFMJRA is silent, while courts are divided. Some courts conclude that personal jurisdiction over the judgment debtor is not a precondition to recognition. *See Pure Fishing, Inc. v. Silver Star Co., Ltd.,* 202 F. Supp. 2d 905, 909-910 (N.D. Iowa 2002); *Lenchyshyn v. Pelko Electric, Inc.,* 723 N.Y.S.2d 285 (App. Div. 2001). Rather, the presence of property of the judgment debtor within the jurisdiction of a U.S. court ordinarily creates a sufficient nexus to permit enforcement of a foreign judgment against that property. *See Shaffer v. Heitner,* 433 U.S. 186, 210-211 n.36 (1977); *Haaksman v. Diamond Offshore (Bermuda), Ltd.,* 260 S.W.3d 476 (Tex. App. 2008); *Pure Fishing, Inc. v. Silver Star Co.,* 202 F. Supp. 2d 905, 909-910 (N.D. Iowa 2002); *Lenchyshyn v. Pelko Electric, Inc.,* 723 N.Y.S.2d 285 (App. Div. 2001); *Biel v. Boehm,* 406 N.Y.S.2d 231 (Sup. Ct. 1978); *Restatement (Third) Foreign Relations Law* §481, comment h (1987).

Other courts, by contrast, require the enforcement forum to have personal jurisdiction over the judgment debtor. *Electrolines, Inc. v. Prudential Assurance Co.,* 677 N.W.2d 874, 886-889 (Mich. App. 2004); *Jiminez v. Mobil Oil Co.,* 1991 U.S. Dist. LEXIS 4996 (S.D.N.Y. 1991).

12. *Burden of proving exception to obligation to recognize foreign judgment.* Consider how *Chimexim* addresses the allocation of the burden of proof of an exception to the obligation to recognize foreign judgments. What party was required to demonstrate that the Bucharest Tribunal had jurisdiction over Velco? Why? Consider the text of the UFMRJA. How does it allocate the burden of proof, if at all? *Compare Bridgway Corp. v. Citibank NA,* 45 F. Supp. 2d 276, 285 (S.D.N.Y. 1999) (plaintiff has burden for mandatory exceptions, defendant has burden for nonmandatory exceptions) *with The Courage Co. LLC v. The ChemShare Corp.,* 93 S.W.3d 323, 331 (Tex. App. 2002) (defendant has burden for all exceptions). *See generally Kam-Tech Systems Ltd. v. Yardeni,* 774 A.2d 644, 650 & n.4 (N.J. Super. Ct. 2001) (collecting cases). As noted above, §4(d) of the newly proposed UFCMJRA would impose the burden of proving any exception on the judgment debtor.

3. Public Policy

It is well established that a U.S. court need not recognize a foreign judgment that is contrary to the enforcement forum's "public policy." This exception parallels analogous public policy rules in other international contexts.[96]

Although *Hilton* did not expressly adopt a public policy exception, the Court's opinion clearly provided the basis for one to develop. Justice Gray remarked that a foreign judgment was presumptively enforceable, except where "the comity of this nation should not allow it full effect."[97] Elsewhere, *Hilton* invoked Joseph Story's description of comity's limits:

> comity . . . must necessarily depend on a variety of circumstances which cannot be reduced to any certain rule; . . . *no nation will suffer the laws of another to interfere with her own to the injury of her citizens;* . . . [and] whether they do or not must depend on the condition of the country in which the foreign law is sought to be enforced, the particular nature of her legislation, her policy, and the character of her institutions. . . .[98]

Subsequent decisions expressly accepted a public policy exception to *Hilton*'s basic rule.[99] The UFMJRA also contains a public policy exception, with §4(b) permitting, but not requiring, nonrecognition of a foreign judgment if "the [cause of action][claim for relief] on which the judgment is based is repugnant to the public policy of this state."[100] The UFCMJRA is similar, although drafted somewhat more broadly.[101]

As in other international contexts,[102] application of the public policy exception has been difficult.[103] The decisions excerpted below illustrate this. First, consider *Ackermann v. Levine,* where the court invokes the public policy exception to deny partial recognition to a German judgment based on a statutory claim for attorneys' fees. Then, consider *Telnikoff v. Matusevitch* where the court denies recognition to an English libel judgment.[104] Finally, consider *Southwest Livestock and Trucking Co. v. Ramon,* where the

---

96. *Compare supra* p. 443 (forum selection clauses); *supra* pp. 520-523 (*forum non conveniens*); *supra* pp. 770-771 (choice of law); and *infra* pp. 1211-1212 (arbitral awards).

97. 159 U.S. at 202-203 (emphasis added).

98. 159 U.S. at 164-165 (quoting J. Story, *Commentaries on the Conflict of Laws* §28).

99. *Neporany v. Kir,* 173 N.Y.S.2d 146 (App. Div. 1958); *Spann v. Compania Mexicana Radiodifusora Fromteriza,* 41 F. Supp. 907 (N.D. Tex. 1941), *aff'd,* 131 F.2d 609 (5th Cir. 1942).

100. UFMJRA, 13 U.L.A. 39 (1962). *See also Restatement (Third) Foreign Relations Law* §482(2)(d) (1987) ("the cause of action on which the judgment was based, or the judgment itself, is repugnant to the public policy of the United States or of the State where recognition is sought"); *Restatement (Second) Conflict of Laws* §117, comment c (1971).

101. UFCMJRA, §4(c)(3) ("the judgment or the [cause of action] [claim for relief] on which the judgment is based is repugnant to the public policy of this state or of the United States").

102. *See supra* p. 443 (forum selection clauses), pp. 520-523 (*forum non conveniens*), and pp. 581-582 (antisuit injunction), and pp. 770-771 (choice of law).

103. *See* Minehan, *The Public Policy Exception to the Enforcement of Foreign Judgments: Necessary or Nemesis?,* 18 Loy. L.A. Int'l & Comp. L.J. 795 (1996).

104. In addition to *Telnikoff,* a number of lower U.S. courts have considered whether the First Amendment precludes recognition of foreign judgments in the United States. *See, e.g., Sarl Louis Feraud Int'l v. Viewfinder, Inc.,* 489 F.3d 474 (2d Cir. 2007); *Bachchan v. India Abroad Publications, Inc.,* 585 N.Y.S.2d 661 (Sup. Ct. 1992) (refusing to enforce English libel judgment on grounds similar to *Telnikoff*); *Yahoo, Inc. v. La Ligue Contre le Racisme et l'Antisemitisme,* 169 F. Supp. 2d 1181 (N.D. Cal. 2001), *rev'd,* 433 F.3d 1199 (9th Cir. 2006) (*en banc*) (granting injunction, reversed on appeal, against private French parties forbidding enforcement of French order requiring Yahoo to remove materials from website accessible in United States); *Abdullah v. Sheridan Square Press, Inc.,* 1994 WL 419847 (S.D.N.Y. May 4, 1994); *Dow Jones & Co. v. Harrods Ltd.,* 237 F. Supp. 2d 394 (S.D.N.Y. 2002), *aff'd,* 346 F.3d 357 (2d Cir. 2003). *See* Kyu Ho Youm, *Suing American Media in Foreign Courts: Doing an End-Run Around U.S. Libel Law,* 16 Hastings Comm. & Enter. L.J. 235 (1994); Stern, *Foreign Judgments and the Freedom of Speech: Looks Who's Talking,* 60 Brook. L. Rev. 999 (1994).

court gave a close reading to the text of the UFMJRA to reject a public policy argument, notwithstanding a compelling state public policy.

ACKERMANN v. LEVINE
788 F.2d 830 (2d Cir. 1986) [also excerpted above at pp. 1115-1117]

PIERCE, CIRCUIT JUDGE. [Ackermann was a German lawyer and Levine was a U.S. real estate developer. In 1979, Levine visited Germany to interest local investors in participating in one of his developments. During his visit, Levine sought German legal advice and was referred to Ackermann. Ackermann and Levine met for a disputed period (between 20 and 90 minutes) to discuss Levine's proposed transactions. They did not discuss attorneys' fees. In a subsequent letter and telephone conversation, Levine authorized Ackermann to act on his behalf in connection with the transactions. Ackermann obtained documents relating to the transaction from a mutual friend of both Ackermann and Levine; Levine stated that he did not know that Ackermann had received or reviewed the file. For various reasons, the transactions were never consummated. Ackermann subsequently claimed to have spent 20 days working full-time on Levine's project, although he was unable to produce any written materials reflecting his efforts. In late 1979 Ackermann billed Levine for his services, computed pursuant to the German legal fee statute (Bundesrechtsanwaltsgebuehrenordnung or BRAGO), which totalled 190,827 Deutsche Marks (approximately $100,000). The fee comprised two basic elements: (1) discussions with prospective German investors and (2) study of Levine's proposed transaction. Levine did not respond to the bill and Ackermann filed suit in German court. Process was served on Levine by registered mail, but he ignored the suit. Ackermann obtained a default judgment and sought recognition in the U.S. District Court for the Southern District of New York. The court refused to enforce the German judgment because enforcement would violate a "New York public policy" that attorneys seeking recovery of fees "bear the burden of proving that a compensation arrangement is fair, reasonable and fully comprehended by the client." Ackermann appealed.] . . .

II. The district court held that, based on the undisputed fact that Ackermann never discussed fees with Levine, the German judgment was rendered unenforceable as violative of New York's public policy that "the attorney, not the client, must ensure the fairness, reasonableness and full comprehension by the client of their compensation agreement." On that basis, the district court declined enforcement of the entire award of approximately $100,000.

A judgment is unenforceable as against public policy to the extent that it is "repugnant to fundamental notions of what is decent and just in the State where enforcement is sought." *Tahan v. Hodgson,* 662 F.2d 862, 864 (D.C. Cir. 1981). . . . The standard is high, and infrequently met. As one court wrote, "[o]nly in clear-cut cases ought it to avail defendant." *Tahan,* 662 F.2d at 866 n.17. . . . In the classic formulation, a judgment that "tends clearly" to undermine the public interest, the public confidence in the administration of the law, or security for individual rights of personal liberty or of private property is against public policy.

The narrowness of the public policy exception to enforcement would seem to reflect an axiom fundamental to the goals of comity and res judicata that underlie the doctrine of recognition and enforcement of foreign judgments. As Judge Cardozo so lucidly observed: "We are not so provincial as to say that every solution of a problem is wrong because we deal with it otherwise at home." *Loucks v. Standard Oil Co.,* 120 N.E. 198 (N.Y. 1918). Further, the narrowness of the public policy exception indicates a jurisprudential compromise between two guiding but sometimes conflicting principles in the law of recognition and enforcement of foreign judgments: (1) res judicata and (2) . . . fairness regarding the underlying transaction.

Since a foreign default judgment is not more or less conclusive but "*as* conclusive an adjudication" as a contested judgment, *Somportex,* 453 F.2d at 442-43 & n.13 (emphasis added), the district court quite properly afforded Levine the same opportunity to contest the enforceability of the German judgment in light of the public policy issue. We disagree with dicta in *Tahan,* 662 F.2d at 867, suggesting that a defendant may not raise a public policy defense once he has defaulted in the foreign adjudication. By defaulting, a defendant ensures that a judgment will be entered against him, and assumes the risk that an irrevocable mistake of law or fact may underlie that judgment. . . . However, we believe that the district court erred in holding that the failure of German law regarding attorneys' fees to meet our more rigorous principles of fiduciary duties sufficiently offended local public policy as to justify nonenforcement of the entire judgment. . . .

The narrow public policy exception to enforcement is not met merely because Ackermann did not inform Levine of the BRAGO billing statute. *See Compania Mexicana Rediodifusora Franteriza v. Spann,* 41 F. Supp. 907 (N.D. Tex. 1941), *aff'd,* 131 F.2d 609 (5th Cir. 1942) (exception not met where a foreign attorney had failed to apprise his American client of Mexico's rule that a losing plaintiff's liability for costs is proportionate to the amount of relief originally sought). Nor is the exception met in the event that Ackermann's bill should exceed the amount which American lawyers might reasonably have charged. *See Somportex,* 453 F.2d at 443 (exception not met where a British default judgment of $94,000 against an American defendant to a contract action included in substantial part damages for loss of good will and for attorneys' fees and other costs, none of which would be awarded by Pennsylvania, the state in which enforcement was granted). Certainly it is not enough merely that Germany provides a billing scheme by statute rather than by contractual arrangements subject to an attorney's fiduciary duties. We note that even New York policy permits statute-based billing systems in certain instances. . . . Nor can we say that the German judgment is unenforceable because the attorney-client relationship herein was not structured commensurate with the New York policy favoring, though not requiring, written retainer agreements. It is not enough merely that a foreign judgment fails to fulfill domestic practice or policy. . . . Thus, we think that the district court erred in holding the judgment unenforceable as offensive to New York's public policy that lawyers discharge their fiduciary duty to ensure fair and reasonable fees, fully disclosed to and understood by their clients. However, that this broad, fiduciary-based public policy does not render the judgment unenforceable does not preclude the possibility that a narrower, evidentiary-based public policy might render the judgment unenforceable.

We hold that the applicable theory of public policy requires that recovery of attorneys' fees be predicated on evidence of, at a minimum, (1) the existence of some authorization by the client for the attorney to perform the work allegedly performed; and (2) the very existence of that work. These evidentiary predicates, we hold, constitute the *sine qua non* of a client's liability for legal fees. Without these predicates, there is a grave risk that American courts could become the means of enforcing unconscionable attorney fee awards, thereby endangering "public confidence" in the administration of the law and a "sense of security for individual rights . . . of private property." *Somportex,* 453 F.2d at 443. Further, to forsake this fundamental public policy would impose upon American citizens doing business abroad an undue risk in dealing with foreign counsel — a result that, ironically, could undermine the very processes of transnational legal relations that the doctrines of comity and res judicata seek to promote. . . . In applying this evidentiary-based public policy, we note that courts are not limited to recognizing a judgment entirely or not at all. Where a foreign judgment contains discrete components, the enforcing court should endeavor to discern the appropriate "extent of recognition," *cf.* 18 C. Wright & A. Miller, *Federal Practice and Procedure* §4473, at 745 (1981), with reference to applicable public policy concerns.

Ackermann has laid the predicate in support of his bill for "detailed discussions with prospective buyers" and for the related travel and office expenses, but he has not done so for the "basic fee for the study of the project files, [and] discussion with client and his counsel." . . . Recognition of the foreign judgment to this extent is consonant with the evidence that Levine engaged Ackermann's services and benefited therefrom. . . . Levine clearly would have benefited from German law had his work with Ackermann proved fruitful. . . . He thus "finds himself in the quite unenviable position of trying to take the good without the bad, the sweet without the bitter." As to the fifteen to twenty days of work that comprise the bulk of the "basic fee for study of the project files," the record reflects no evidence of an authorization to do such work or of the existence of any work product. The mere fact that Ackermann possessed the project files is inconsequential since Levine did not know that [a friend of Ackermann] had given those files to Ackermann. Nor do we find authorization in the office visit [between Levine and Ackermann], of late May or early June, since the district court found that visit had accomplished only the creation of a misunderstanding. Even if there had been an authorization, there was not a scintilla of evidence of work product. Ackermann offered no client memoranda, no memoranda to his files, no handwritten notes, no markings on the papers that [Ackermann's friend] had given him, and no other indicia of actual performance. . . . We do not challenge the district court's finding as to Ackermann's character. However, we need not say that an attorney acted fraudulently or dishonestly to hold, as we do here, that the failure to adduce any evidence of work product requires disallowance of claimed legal fees. . . .

The increasing internationalization of commerce requires "that American courts recognize and respect the judgments entered by foreign courts to the greatest extent consistent with our own ideals of justice and fair play." *Tahan,* 662 F.2d at 868. In light of that important imperative, we hold the Germany judgment to be enforceable in all respects except for the first item of DM 89.347,50 for the "[b]asic fee for the study of project files, discussion with client and his counsel." . . .

TELNIKOFF v. MATUSEVITCH
702 A.2d 230 (Md. 1997)

ELDRIGE, JUDGE. [Mr. Telnikoff was an English citizen, born and raised in the former Soviet Union; he later moved to England and was a former freelance writer and broadcaster for the British Broadcasting Corporation ("BBC"). Mr. Matusevitch was a U.S. citizen of Jewish descent who had lived for a period in the former Soviet Union. In February 1984, Telnikoff published an article in a London newspaper criticizing BBC's Russian Service. Subsequently, the same newspaper published a letter written by Matusevitch. In it, Matusevitch criticized Telnikoff for allegedly requiring a "blood test" for the BBC's Russian Service and accuses him of spreading "racialist" and anti-Semitic views. Telnikoff wrote a reply and later filed a libel action against Matusevitch in English courts.

Following extensive proceedings that reached the House of Lords, an English jury awarded Telnikoff 240,000 pounds (roughly $400,000 at the time). After Telnikoff sought to enforce the English judgment in the United States, Matusevitch filed an action in U.S.

District Court in Maryland, seeking a declaration that the judgment was "repugnant" to, among other things, the First Amendment to the Constitution. Following the case's transfer to the District of Columbia, the district court agreed and, applying Maryland's [UFMJRA,] found that the judgment would offend the public policy of Maryland and the United States. On appeal, the U.S. Court of Appeals for the District of Columbia Circuit certified to Maryland's highest state court the question whether the English judgment would violate Maryland public policy.]

The question before us is whether Telnikoff's English libel judgment is based upon principles which are so contrary to Maryland's public policy concerning freedom of the press and defamation actions that recognition of the judgment should be denied. While we shall rest our decision in this case upon the non-constitutional ground of Maryland public policy, . . . it is appropriate to examine and rely upon the history, policies, and requirements of the First Amendment and Article 40 of the [Maryland] Declaration of Rights. [The Court then examined a wide range of historical sources to conclude that] "American and Maryland history reflects a public policy in favor of a much broader and more protective freedom of the press than ever provided for under English law."

The contrast between English standards governing defamation actions and the present Maryland standards is striking. For the most part, English defamation actions are governed by principles which are unchanged from the earlier common law period. . . . Thus, under English defamation law, it is unnecessary for the plaintiff to establish fault, either in the form of conscious wrongdoing or negligence. . . . Moreover, under English law, defamatory statements are presumed to be false unless a defendant proves them to be true. . . . In England, a qualified privilege can be overcome without establishing that the defendant actually knew that the publication was false or acted with reckless disregard of whether it was false or not. It can be overcome by proof of "spite or ill-will or some other wrong or improper motive." Peter F. Carter-Ruck, *Libel and Slander,* 137 (1973). English law authorizes punitive or exemplary damages under numerous circumstances in defamation actions; unlike Maryland law, they are not limited to cases in which there was actual knowledge of the falsehood or reckless disregard as to truth or falsity. . . . English defamation law presumes that a statement is one of fact, and the burden is on the defendant to prove "fair comment." Finally, English defamation law flatly rejects the principles set forth in *New York Times Co. v. Sullivan,* [376 U.S. 254 (1964)], and *Gertz v. Robert Welch, Inc.,* [418 U.S. 323 (1974)]. The basic rules are the same regardless of whether the plaintiff is a public official, public figure, or a private person, regardless of whether the alleged defamatory statement involves a matter of public concern, and regardless of the defendant's status.

A comparison of English and present Maryland defamation law does not simply disclose a difference in one or two legal principles. Instead, present Maryland defamation law is totally different from English defamation law in virtually every significant respect. Moreover, the differences are rooted in historic and fundamental public policy differences concerning freedom of the press and speech.

The stark contrast between English and Maryland law is clearly illustrated by the underlying litigation between Telnikoff and Matusevitch. Telnikoff . . . was undisputably a public official or public figure. In this country, he would have had to prove, by clear and convincing evidence, that Matusevitch's letter contained false statements of fact and that Matusevitch acted maliciously in the sense that he knew of the falsity or acted with reckless disregard of whether the statements were false or not. The English courts, however, held that there was no evidence supporting Telnikoff's allegations that Matusevitch acted with actual malice, either under the *New York Times Co. v. Sullivan* definition or in the sense of ill-will, spite or intent to injure. Despite the absence of actual malice under any definition, Telnikoff was allowed to recover. He was not even required to prove negligence, which is the minimum a purely private defamation plaintiff must establish to recover under Maryland law. In addition, Telnikoff was not required to prove that Matusevitch's letter contained a false statement of fact, which would have been required under present Maryland law. Instead, falsity was presumed, and the defendant had the risky choice of whether to attempt to prove truth. Furthermore, Telnikoff did not have to establish that the alleged defamation even contained defamatory statements of fact; the burden was upon the defendant to establish that the alleged defamatory language amounted to comment and not statements of fact.

Finally, contrary to the decisions of the Supreme Court and this Court, Matusevitch's letter was not examined in context but in isolation. It must be remembered that Telnikoff began the public debate with his published article, and Matusevitch's letter constituted his rebuttal. Undoubtedly, in this country, . . . Matusevitch's alleged defamatory language would, as a matter of law, be treated as "rhetorical hyperbole" in the course of rebuttal during a vigorous public debate. An apt description of what would have happened in Maryland to Telnikoff's libel suit was set forth by this Court ninety-five years ago (*Shepherd v. Baer,* 53 A. 790, 791, 792 (Md. 1902)): " 'A man who commences a newspaper war cannot subsequently come to the Court to complain that he has had the worst of it.' . . . [T]he article [in response] does not exceed the bounds of legitimate self-defense."

The principles governing defamation actions under English law, which were applied to Telnikoff's libel suit, are so contrary to Maryland defamation law, and to the policy of freedom of the press underlying Maryland law, that Telnikoff's judgment should be denied recognition under principles of comity. In the language of the [UFMJRA] §10-704(b)(2), Telnikoff's English "cause of action on which the judgment is based is repugnant to the public policy of the State. . . ."

CHASANOW, JUDGE, dissenting. . . . The [Maryland UFMJRA] gives our courts discretion to subordinate our State's public policy. Our interest in international good will, comity, and res judicata fostered by recognition of foreign judgments must be weighed against our minimal interest in giving the benefits of our local libel public policy to residents of another country who defame foreign public figures in foreign publications and who have no reasonable expectation that they will be protected by the Maryland Constitution. Unless there is some United States interest that should be protected, there is no good reason to offend a friendly nation like England by refusing to recognize a purely local libel judgment for a purely local defamation. . . . Public policy should not require us to give First Amendment protection or Article 40 protection to English residents who defame other English residents in publications distributed only in England. Failure to make our constitutional provisions relating to defamation applicable to wholly internal English defamation would not seem to violate fundamental notions of what is decent and just and should not undermine public confidence in the administration of law. The Court does little or no analysis of the global public policy considerations and seems inclined to make Maryland libel law applicable to the rest of the world by providing a safe haven for foreign libel judgment debtors.

SOUTHWEST LIVESTOCK & TRUCKING CO., INC. v. RAMON
169 F.3d 317 (5th Cir. 1999)

GARZA, CIRCUIT JUDGE. . . . Darrel and Mary Jane Hargrove (the "Hargroves") are citizens of the United States and officers of Southwest Livestock & Trucking Co., Inc. ("Southwest Livestock"), a Texas corporation involved in the buying and selling of livestock. In 1990, Southwest Livestock entered into a loan arrangement with Reginaldo Ramón ("Ramón"), a citizen of the Republic of Mexico. Southwest Livestock borrowed $400,000 from Ramón. To accomplish the loan, Southwest Livestock executed a "pagaré"—a Mexican promissory note—payable to Ramón with interest within thirty days. Each month, Southwest Livestock executed a new pagaré to cover the outstanding principal and paid the accrued interest. Over a period of four years, Southwest Livestock made payments towards the principal, but also borrowed additional money from Ramón. In October of 1994, Southwest Livestock defaulted on the loan. With the exception of the last pagaré executed by Southwest Livestock, none of the pagarés contained a stated interest rate. Ramón, however, charged Southwest Livestock interest at a rate of approximately fifty-two percent. The last pagaré stated an interest rate of forty-eight percent, and under its terms, interest continues to accrue until Southwest Livestock pays the outstanding balance in full.

After Southwest Livestock defaulted, Ramón filed a lawsuit in Mexico to collect on the last pagaré. The Mexican court granted judgment in favor of Ramón, and ordered Southwest Livestock to satisfy its debt and to pay interest at forty-eight percent. Southwest Livestock appealed, claiming that Ramón had failed to effect proper service of process. . . . The Mexican appellate court rejected this argument and affirmed the judgment in favor of Ramón.

After Ramón filed suit in Mexico, but prior to the entry of the Mexican judgment, Southwest Livestock brought suit in United States District Court, alleging that the loan arrangement violated Texas usury laws. Southwest Livestock then filed a motion for partial summary judgment, claiming that the undisputed facts established that Ramón charged, received and collected usurious interest in violation of Texas law. . . . By then the Mexican court had entered its judgment, and Ramón sought recognition of that judgment. He claimed that, under principles of collateral estoppel and res judicata, the Mexican judgment barred Southwest Livestock's suit. . . .

Under Texas law, Ramon indisputably charged usurious interest. [Accordingly, the district judge granted Southwest Livestock's motion for summary judgment. It held that the Mexican judgment violated Texas public policy against usury.]

Under the Texas Recognition Act, a court must recognize a foreign country judgment assessing money damages unless the judgment debtor establishes one of ten specific grounds for nonrecognition. Southwest Livestock . . . notes that the Texas Constitution places a six percent interest rate limit on contracts that do not contain a stated interest rate. *See* Tex. Const. art. XVI, §11. It also points to a Texas statute that states that usury is against Texas public policy. *See* Vernon's Tex. Civ. Stat., Art. 5069-1C.001 ("All contracts for usury are contrary to public policy"). Thus, according to Southwest Livestock, the Mexican judgment violates Texas public policy. . . .

[W]e note that the level of contravention of Texas law has "to be high before recognition [can] be denied on public policy grounds." *Hunt v. BP Exploration Co. (Libya) Ltd.*, 492 F. Supp. 885, 900 (N.D. Tex. 1980). . . . To decide whether the district court erred in refusing to recognize the Mexican judgment on public policy grounds, we consider the plain language of the Texas Recognition Act. . . . Section 36.005(b)(3) of the Texas Recognition Act permits the district court not to recognize a foreign country judgment if "the *cause of action on which the judgment is based* is repugnant to the public policy" of Texas. This subsection of the Texas Recognition Act does not refer to the judgment itself, but specifically to the "cause of action on which the judgment is based." Thus, the fact that a judgment offends Texas public policy does not, in and of itself, permit the district court to refuse recognition of that judgment. *See Norkan Lodge Co. v. Gillum*, 587 F. Supp. 1457, 1461 (N.D. Tex. 1984) (a "judgment may only be attacked in the event that 'the cause of action [on] which the judgment is based is repugnant to the public policy of this state,' not the judgment itself").

In this case, the Mexican judgment was based on an action for collection of a promissory note. This cause of action is not repugnant to Texas public policy. *See, e.g., Akin v. Dahl,* 661 S.W.2d 914 (Tex. 1983) (enforcing a suit for the collection of a promissory note). Under the Texas Recognition Act, it is irrelevant that the Mexican judgment itself contravened Texas's public policy against usury. . . .

[The court then analyzed several prior decisions supporting its view that "although Texas has a strong public policy against usury, this policy is not inviolable." The court emphasized that Texas public policy accorded importance to fulfilling contractual obligations; it also reasoned that "the purpose behind Texas usury laws is to protect unsophisticated borrowers from unscrupulous lenders," and that "Southwest Livestock is managed by sophisticated and knowledgeable people with experience in business," who "negotiated the loan in good faith and at arms length."] Accordingly, in light of the plain language of the Texas Recognition Act, and after consideration of our [prior decisions] and the purpose behind Texas public policy against usury, we hold that Texas's public policy does not justify withholding recognition of the Mexican judgment. . . .

Notes on Ackermann, Telnikoff, *and* Southwest Livestock

1. *Rationale for public policy exception.* Unlike the enforcement of state judgments under the Full Faith and Credit Clause, U.S. courts will not recognize foreign judgments that violate important public policies of the enforcement forum. *See Restatement (Second) Conflict of Laws* §117, comment c (1971); *Restatement (Third) Foreign Relations Law* §482(2)(d) (1987); UFMJRA, §4(b)(3); UFCMJRA, §4(c)(3).

Why is there a public policy exception to the enforcement of foreign, but not domestic, judgments? Note that, in contrast to the Full Faith and Credit Clause, the EU's Council Regulation 44/2001 provides for a public policy exception to the general obligation to enforce foreign judgments. *See* Appendix E.

As discussed above, there are exceptions to the general enforcement requirement for foreign judgments for lack of jurisdiction, unfair foreign proceedings, fraud, lack of notice, and so forth. Given these exceptions, what purpose does the public policy exception serve? *Cf.* Scoles, *Interstate and International Distinctions in Conflict of Laws in the United States,* 54 Cal. L. Rev. 1599, 1606 n.33 (1966) ("in the great bulk of cases any reasonably cognizable defense of public policy can be accommodated under the [other] limitations" on the enforcement of foreign judgment); Peterson, *Foreign Country Judgments and the Second Restatement of Conflict of Laws,* 72 Colum. L. Rev. 220, 253 (1972) ("the policies involved [in the public policy exception] are potentially so numerous and variable, perhaps it is not feasible to provide the courts with . . . specific guidance"). For a recent decision analyzing the relationship between the "fraud" and "public policy" exceptions, *see Thomas & Agnes Carvel Foundation v. Carvel,* 736 F. Supp. 2d 730 (S.D.N.Y. 2010).

2. *Scope of public policy exception.* It is often said that the mere fact that the enforcing forum's law would not have permitted the foreign plaintiff to recover in an original action in that forum is not sufficient to warrant nonrecognition of a foreign judgment on public policy grounds. *See Pariente v. Scott Meredith Literary Agency,* 771 F. Supp. 609 (S.D.N.Y. 1991); *Hunt v. BP Exploration Co. (Libya),* 492 F. Supp. 885, 901 (N.D. Tex. 1980); *Toronto-Dominion Bank v. Hall,* 367 F. Supp. 1009 (E.D. Ark. 1973); *Knothe v. Rose,* 392 S.E.2d 570, 572-573 (Ga. App. 1990). *Compare* ALI, *The Foreign Judgments Recognition and Enforcement Act* §5(a)(vi) (2005).

Rather, for the public policy exception to apply, the foreign judgment (or the claim on which that judgment was based) must run directly contrary to some fundamental policy of the forum where enforcement is sought. In the words of *Ackermann,* the public policy exception applies only where enforcement of a foreign judgment (or the claim on which that judgment was based) would "undermine the public interest, the public confidence in the administration of the law or security for individual rights." 788 F.2d at 844. For example, lower courts have found the public policy exception applicable where a foreign judgment undermines First Amendment protections for free speech (*see supra* note 104); state law protections for bail recovery agents (*see Jaffe v. Snow,* 610 So. 2d 482 (Fla. Ct. App. 5th Dist. 1992)); federal policies disfavoring irrebuttable presumptions on tort causation (*Osorio v. Dole Food Co.,* 665 F. Supp. 2d 1307 (S.D. Fla. 2009)); federal policy concerning priority of IRS claims in bankruptcy (*see Overseas Inns SA v. United States,* 911 F.2d 1146 (5th Cir. 1990)); federal policy favoring arbitration of international disputes (*see South Ionian Shipping Co. v. Hugo Neu & Sons Int'l Sales Corp.,* 545 F. Supp. 323 (S.D.N.Y. 1982)); state policy prohibiting the entry of judgments against deceased persons (*see In re Davis' Will,* 219 N.Y.S.2d 533 (Sur. Ct. 1961), *aff'd mem.,* 227 N.Y.S.2d 894 (1962)); state policy relieving divorced husbands from alimony obligations subsequent to the divorced wife's remarriage (*see Pentz v. Kuppinger,* 107 Cal. Rptr. 540 (1973)); state policies against expropriation of property (*Films by Jove, Inc. v. Barov,* 341 F. Supp. 2d 199, 213 (E.D.N.Y. 2004)); state public policies encouraging whistleblowers (*Aguerre v. Schering-Plough Corp.,* 393 N.J. Super. 459 (App. Div. 2007)); or state policies governing the enforcement of letters of credit according to their terms (*see Cantrade Privatbank AG Zurich v. Bangkok Bank Public Co.,* 681 N.Y.S.2d 21, 22-23 (App. Div. 1998) and *In re Perry H. Koplik & Sons, Inc.,* 357 B.R. 231 (Bankr. S.D.N.Y. 2006)). Compare the similar difficulties that courts have encountered in defining and applying public policy exceptions in the forum selection clause (*supra* pp. 520-523), antisuit injunction (*supra* pp. 581-582), and choice of law (*supra* p. 715) contexts.

3. *Application of public policy exception in* Ackermann. *Ackermann* held that the public policy exception was applicable, notwithstanding the court's assertions about the exception's narrow scope. The Court of Appeals discerned a "narrow[], evidentiary-based public policy" that required foreign attorneys to establish the client's authorization of their services and their actual performance of services before a judgment rendered abroad would be enforced. This requirement applies without regard to the existence of comparable requirements under the foreign law on which the foreign judgment was based.

What was the basis for the public policy rule cited in *Ackermann*? Was the rule a product of federal law or New York law? Was the public policy constitutional, statutory, or common law? Did the public policy standard adopted in *Ackermann* reflect truly fundamental policies?

Recall that a fundamental purpose of the recognition of foreign judgments is avoiding the need to relitigate the merits of disputes that have been fairly resolved abroad. *See supra* pp. 1078-1085. Did *Ackermann* apply the public policy exception in a manner that permitted it *sub silentio* to readjudicate the merits of the plaintiff's underlying claim? If so, is this appropriate?

Suppose that a more "narrow, evidentiary-based" public policy standard had been applied in *Southwest Livestock,* as in *Ackermann.* Would the result have been different?

4. *Application of public policy exception in* Telnikoff. What was the source of the public policy rule in *Telnikoff*? What exactly does this rule provide? Was the *Telnikoff* rule compelled by the sources cited by the Court? How does the *Telnikoff* public policy analysis differ from that in *Ackermann*? Is *Telnikoff* an appropriate application of the public policy exception?

   5. *Application of the public policy exception in* **Southwest Livestock.** *Southwest Livestock* holds that a family business can be required to pay 48 percent annual interest, notwithstanding (a) a Texas constitutional and statutory prohibition against usury, and (b) acknowledgment that "under Texas law, Ramón undisputably [sic] charged usurious interest." Why exactly did the Court nonetheless recognize the Mexican judgment? Note the Court's reliance on the "plain language" of UFMJRA, §4(b)(3), and its asserted requirement that the "cause of action on which the judgment is based" violate local public policy. Consider the Court's reasoning that "the Mexican judgment was based on an action for collection of a promissory note," which is recognized in Texas law. Is that persuasive? Is it even serious? What about a promissory note providing 1,000 percent interest? When would *any* cause of action, in the abstract, violate U.S. public policy?

   For other decisions relying on a narrow reading of UFMJRA, §4(b)(3), *see Society of Lloyd's v. Reinhart*, 402 F.3d 982, 995 (10th Cir. 2005); *Society of Lloyd's v. Turner*, 303 F.3d 325 (5th Cir. 2002); *Guinness plc v. Ward*, 955 F.3d 875 (4th Cir. 1992). Are you persuaded by the distinction between a judgment contrary to public policy and a judgment based on a cause of action contrary to public policy?

   The UFCMJRA includes provisions that reject the rationale in *Southwest Livestock*. Section 4(c)(3) of the UFCMJRA permits nonrecognition where "the judgment or the [cause of action][claim for relief] on which the judgment is based is repugnant to the public policy of this state or of the United States." The comments on this provision explain "Subsection 4(c)(3) rejects this narrow focus [citing *Southwest Livestock*] by providing that the forum court may deny recognition if either the cause of action or the judgment itself violates public policy." *See also* ALI, *The Foreign Judgments Recognition and Enforcement Act* §5(a)(vi) (2005) ("the judgment or the claim on which the judgment is based is repugnant to the public policy of the United States, or to the public policy of a particular State of the United States when the relevant legal interest, right or policy is regulated by state law.").

   Is the public policy analysis in *Southwest Livestock* consistent with that in *Telnikoff*? With that in *Ackermann*? In *Telnikoff,* isn't it true that a cause of action for libel would not violate U.S. public policy? In *Ackermann,* isn't it true that a cause of action for unpaid attorneys' fees would not violate U.S. public policy? Contrast the "narrow, evidentiary-based public policy" analysis in *Ackermann* with the analysis of the UFMJRA in *Southwest Livestock*.

   6. *Source of public policy: state or federal law?* What were the bases for the public policy rules cited in *Ackermann, Telnikoff,* and *Southwest Livestock*? Whose laws and policies should be consulted to establish a public policy defense to a foreign judgment? Those of the United States, those of the individual state where enforcement is sought, or some international standard?

   As *Ackermann* suggests, state law is generally regarded as the source of public policies. 788 F.2d at 840 ("we could not . . . subordinate New York's interests in the *public policy* implications of the subject foreign judgment"). *See also Society of Lloyd's v. Siemon-Netto,* 457 F.3d 94, 100 (D.C. Cir. 2006) ("Accordingly, the dispositive question is whether the core principles of English contract law are repugnant to the public policy of the District of Columbia."). The same is true in *Southwest Livestock.* Note, however, the First Amendment basis for the *Telnikoff* decision.

   7. *Federal limitations on state public policy.* Would it be appropriate for U.S. courts to refuse to enforce foreign judgments based on parochial state policies disfavoring foreign tribunals? What if a state refused to enforce any foreign judgment from a totalitarian state? Any judgment from a theocratic state? Any foreign judgment from a state that practices unfair trading or commits human rights violations? *Cf. Zschernig v. Miller,* 389 U.S. 429 (1968); *supra* pp. 637-638.

8. *"Choice of public policy" considerations.* Assume that U.S. (or U.S. state) law does contain each of the public policy rules cited in *Ackermann, Telnikoff,* and *Southwest Livestock* Why would those public policies be applicable on the facts of each case?

(a) Ackermann. Note that *all* of the relevant conduct in *Ackermann* occurred in Germany. Suppose that Mr. Levine had been a German businessman (rather than a U.S. citizen), who dealt with Mr. Ackermann solely in Berlin, and later moved to the United States for unrelated reasons. Would the asserted New York public policy still apply to forbid enforcement of the German judgment? Recall the Supreme Court's treatment of U.S. public policy in *Bremen, supra* pp. 474-478. Why would New York public policy concern itself with dealings between two Germans in Germany in connection with a German real estate venture? If New York public policy would not apply to this hypothetical, what makes the actual *Ackermann* case any different? Is it relevant that Mr. Ackermann was an American? Recall both the role of nationality (or domicile) in contemporary interest analysis and the rejection of the passive personality principle under international law. *See supra* pp. 109-113, 599-600. Compare the situation of the U.S. judgment debtor in *Southwest Livestock.*

(b) Telnikoff. Where did the allegedly wrongful conduct in *Telnikoff* occur? Where did the allegedly false publications circulate? What were the nationalities and domiciles of the parties? Note the dissenting opinion's declaration that: "Public policy should not require us to give First Amendment protection . . . to English residents who defame other English residents in publications distributed only in England." Is there not substantial force to this?

Suppose that *Telnikoff* had involved an international newspaper, with both U.S. and U.K. offices, and that the allegedly wrongful conduct had occurred in London. Suppose further that all allegedly false statements were circulated in Europe (not the United States). Would an English judgment be enforceable in U.S. courts? Why would the First Amendment apply in this example? How is the actual *Telnikoff* case different from this hypothetical?

Suppose that a European court imposes damages for statements by a U.S. national, resident in the United States, intended principally for U.S. audiences? Accessible principally by U.S. audiences? Does it matter if the damages are proportionate to the publication's circulation in the European state? What if China, Iran, and Venezuela imposed similar damages? What if European states recognized such damage awards by China, Iran, or Venezuela?

(c) Southwest Livestock. Again, note the location of the conduct in *Southwest Livestock.* Where were the borrowers in the loan transaction located? What was the currency of the loan? Where would the effects of the usury be manifested? What sorts of persons was the Texas usury statute likely intended to protect? Would there be anything unusual if, under Texas choice-of-law principles, the Texas constitutional and statutory provisions applied to the Southwest Livestock loan? Suppose that the loan payments were payable in Texas. Would that have affected the result in *Southwest Livestock?* Suppose that the loan agreements had been, by the terms of a choice-of-law clause, governed by Texas law. Would that have affected the result?

9. *Waivability of public policy and other defenses.* As discussed elsewhere, parties in international transactions routinely will enter into contracts containing forum selection clauses that designate an exclusive forum for their dispute. *See supra* p. 461. Those clauses sometimes will also contain language committing the parties "agree to be bound" by any judgment rendered by the designated forum. What effect, if any, does such language have on the scope of the public policy defense and other defenses? Can parties prospectively waive their defenses to the enforceability of a judgment? What if the contract expressly contained language in which the parties "agree to waive any defense in this country or another country"? Would a court in the enforcement forum be obligated to give effect to that language? What if a court in the designated forum found that the language was enforceable? Would a court in the enforcement forum be obligated to give preclusive effect to *that* determination? How, if at all, do considerations of prospective waiver in the judgment enforcement context differ from those in other contexts (like the enforceability of a forum selection clause or an arbitration clause)?

10. ***Hypotheticals involving public policy exception to recognition of foreign judgments.*** When will the public policy exception apply in the following hypotheticals?

Suppose foreign laws that invidiously discriminate on religious, ethnic, or racial grounds are fairly applied in foreign judicial proceedings, producing a judgment against a U.S. national. Does it matter that the parties' dispute — for example, employment — took place entirely outside the United States? Suppose that the judgment debtor is a foreign national. Does that change matters?

Following *Bremen, supra* pp. 474-478, suppose that an English court rendered a judgment against Zapata Off-Shore, giving effect to contractual exculpatory provisions, which excused Unterweser for grossly negligent conduct. Would it matter if the conduct occurred in U.S. waters?

Following *Telnikoff,* suppose that the judgment debtor had been a U.K. national, living in England, who had a bank account in the United States.

11. ***Declaratory relief against foreign judgments.*** Note that in *Southwest Livestock,* the U.S. company did not merely resist enforcement of a Mexican judgment, but also sought damages (for past, usurious interest, which it had paid). In other cases, parties have sought declaratory relief from a U.S. court, declaring that a foreign judgment is unenforceable (typically on public policy grounds) in the forum. *See Yahoo, Inc. v. La Ligue Contre le Racisme et l'Antisemitisme,* 169 F. Supp. 2d 1181 (N.D. Cal. 2001), *rev'd,* 433 F.3d 1199 (9th Cir. 2006) (*en banc*); *Dow Jones & Co. v. Harrods Ltd.,* 237 F. Supp. 2d 394 (S.D.N.Y. 2002), *aff'd,* 346 F.3d 357 (2d Cir. 2003). Is there a difference between efforts to preclude recognition of a foreign judgment and to resist such recognition? Why should there be?

In *Yahoo, Inc.,* the U.S. Internet service provider sought declaratory relief in U.S. courts. Specifically, Yahoo sought a declaration that French groups could not enforce, in the United States, a French judgment imposing penalties against it for failing to block access by French nationals to Nazi-related materials on Yahoo.com's auction site. The district court granted the declaration, reasoning:

> The French order's content and viewpoint-based regulation of the web pages and auction site on Yahoo.com, while entitled to great deference as an articulation of French law, clearly would be inconsistent with the First Amendment if mandated by a court in the United States. What makes this case uniquely challenging is that the Internet in effect allows one to speak in more than one place at the same time. Although France has the sovereign right to regulate what speech is permissible in France, this Court may not enforce a foreign order that violates the protections of the United States Constitution by chilling protected speech that occurs simultaneously within our borders. . . .

The district court went on to issue declaratory relief, that the French judgments could not be enforced in the United States. 169 F. Supp. 2d 1181. The order was subsequent reversed by a badly splintered *en banc* Court of Appeal. 433 F.3d 1199. Among other things, the Court of Appeal (or members thereof) held that the French judgment creditors were not subject to personal jurisdiction (because they had only threatened to enforce the French judgments in the United States) and that the dispute was not ripe (because no effort to enforce might ever be made).

Is there any reason that declaratory relief should not be available to preclude enforcement of foreign judgments? Suppose that the judgment is fraudulent? Issued by a corrupt judiciary? Otherwise defective? Why should a U.S. defendant be obliged to wait until the foreign judgment creditor chooses to proceed?

12. *Developing nations and judgments against multinational corporations.*

The discussion of the Alien Tort Statute, *supra* pp. 33-36, illustrated how plaintiffs sometimes employ unique features of the U.S. legal system as part of an effort to hold multinational corporations accountable for their alleged conduct in foreign countries. In recent years, particularly since the Supreme Court's decision in *Sosa* trimmed the ATS, plaintiffs are now turning to foreign courts, often with the assistance of the foreign states themselves.

One recent example of this tactic has been a lawsuit brought in Ecuador against Chevron/Texaco ("Chevron"), a major U.S. oil company. The basic claim was that the oil exploration activities of Chevron's predecessors in interest caused massive damage in the country's Oriente region. Those activities, according to the plaintiffs, both devastated parts of Ecuador's environment and harmed tens of thousands of indigenous residents of the affected regions. Chevron, which no longer has assets in Ecuador, maintains that its predecessors cleaned up the affected sites before turning them over to Petroecuador, a state-run oil company.

Initially, the plaintiffs sought relief in the U.S. courts under the Alien Tort Statute. Following protracted pretrial proceedings, the case was eventually dismissed after Chevron agreed to consent to the jurisdiction of the Ecuadoran courts and agreed to waive certain limitations defenses. *See Aguinda v. Texaco, Inc.*, 303 F.3d 470 (2d Cir. 2002) (affirming conditional *forum non conveniens* dismissal); *see generally* Lambert, *At the Crossroads of Environmental and Human Rights Standards*, 10 Transnat'l L. & Pol'y 109 (2000) (providing background).

The case then shifted to Ecuador where it became a highly politicized cause. Human rights activists claimed that Chevron, having successfully avoided jurisdiction in the United States, was now seeking entirely to avoid responsibility for its alleged conduct. Chevron responded with claims that the plaintiffs' lawyers were fabricating evidence and paying witnesses to make outrageous allegations against the company. Chevron also went on the offensive, commencing arbitration against Ecuador under a bilateral investment treaty, and filing a host of §1782 petitions to prove its claims of fabricated evidence, *see supra* pp. 1059-1076.

In February 2011, the judge in the Lago Agrio Court in Ecuador entered a $8.6 billion dollar judgment against the company. More than half of that amount was dedicated to restore polluted soil. The remainder covered matters such as creating a health system for the affected communities, restoring the habitats of native species, and providing potable water for the area. The victorious plaintiffs have argued that they will seek to enforce the judgment around the world. Chevron has decried the judgment as "illegitimate and unenforceable" and "contrary to the legitimate scientific evidence." Chevron also brought a civil racketeering lawsuit against various parties involved in the Lago Agrio litigation and obtained orders from both a U.S. court and an international arbitral tribunal to prevent enforcement of the Lago Agrio judgment.

If plaintiffs sought to enforce the Lago Agrio judgment in the United States, could Chevron successfully invoke the public policy exception to block its enforcement? In what respect precisely would the judgment contravene public policy under the UFMJRA or the *Hilton* standards? If public policy were unavailable as a defense, what other defenses might

Chevron invoke? For more on this remarkable case, see Dhooge, Aguinda v. Chevron/ Texaco: *Discretionary Grounds for the Nonrecognition of Foreign Judgments for Environmental Injury in the United States,* 28 Va. Envt'l L. J. 241 (2010).

4.   Fairness of Foreign Judicial System

Another exception to the general principle calling for enforcement of foreign judgments is the requirement that the judgment be rendered under a fair judicial system. According to *Hilton,* judgments will not be recognized where there has not been "the full and fair opportunity for a trial abroad before a court of competent jurisdiction, conducting the trial upon regular proceedings . . . and under a system of jurisprudence likely to secure an impartial administration of justice between the citizens of its own county and those of other countries."[105] Similarly, the UFMJRA denies recognition to a judgment where it "was rendered under a system which does not provide impartial tribunals or procedures compatible with the requirements of due process of law."[106] This exception rests on the premise that U.S. courts should not give effect to foreign judgments unless they result from proceedings that satisfy basic standards of fairness.

The decisions excerpted below illustrate the application of the fairness exception. Initially, consider *Society of Lloyd's v. Ashenden,* where the court applies the UFMJRA to reject a fairness challenge to the English judicial system. Then consider *Bridgeway Corp. v. Citibank,* where a U.S. court holds that a foreign judicial system is incapable of rendering fair results.

SOCIETY OF LLOYD'S v. ASHENDEN
233 F.3d 473 (7th Cir. 2000)

POSNER, CIRCUIT JUDGE. These are diversity suits brought in the federal district court in Chicago by Lloyd's, a foreign corporation, against American members ("names") of insurance syndicates that Lloyd's manages. Lloyd's wanted to use the Illinois UFMJRA, to collect money judgments, each for several hundred thousand dollars, that it had obtained against the defendants in an English court. . . . Lloyd's filed the judgments in the district court and then issued "citations" pursuant to the Illinois procedure for executing a judgment. . . . The filing of the judgments inaugurated this federal-court proceeding to collect them. . . .

The defendants . . . argued that [the English] judgments had denied them due process of law and therefore were not enforceable under the [UFMJRA], which makes a judgment rendered by a court outside the United States unenforceable in Illinois if "the judgment was rendered under a *system* which does not provide impartial tribunals or procedures compatible with the requirements of due process of law." 735 ILCS 5/12-621 (emphasis added). . . . We have italicized the word that defeats the defendants' argument. . . . Any suggestion that [the English] system of courts "does not provide impartial tribunals or procedures compatible with the requirements of due process of law" borders on the risible. "[T]he courts of England are fair and neutral forums." *Riley v. Kingsley Underwriting Agencies, Ltd.,* 969 F.2d 953, 958 (10th Cir. 1992). . . . Not that the English concept of fair procedure is identical to ours; but we cannot believe that the Illinois statute is intended to bar the enforcement of all judgments of any foreign legal system that does

---

105. 159 U.S. at 163.
106. UFMJRA, §4(a)(1).

not conform its procedural doctrines to the latest twist and turn of our courts. . . . It is a fair guess that no foreign nation has decided to incorporate our due process doctrines into its own procedural law; and so we interpret "due process" in the Illinois statute (which, remember, is a uniform act, not one intended to reflect the idiosyncratic jurisprudence of a particular state) to refer to a concept of fair procedure simple and basic enough to describe the judicial processes of civilized nations, our peers. . . .

We'll call this the "international concept of due process" to distinguish it from the complex concept that has emerged from American case law. We note that it is even less demanding than the test the courts use to determine whether to enforce a foreign arbitral award under the New York Convention. . . .

We need not consider what kind of evidence would suffice to show that a foreign legal system "does not provide impartial tribunals or procedures compatible with the requirements of due process of law" if the challenged judgment had been rendered by Cuba, North Korea, Iran, Iraq, Congo, or some other nation whose adherence to the rule of law and commitment to the norm of due process are open to serious question, as England's are not. It is anyway not a question of fact. It is not, strictly speaking, a question of law either, but it is a question about the law of a foreign nation, and in answering such questions a federal court is not limited to the consideration of evidence that would be admissible under the Federal Rules of Evidence; any relevant material or source may be consulted.

Rather than trying to impugn the English legal system *en grosse*, the defendants argue that the Illinois statute requires us to determine whether the particular judgments that they are challenging were issued in proceedings that conform to the requirements of due process of law . . . as it has come to be understood in the case law of Illinois and other American jurisdictions. The [UFMJRA], with its reference to "system," does not support such a retail approach, which would moreover be inconsistent with providing a streamlined, expeditious method for collecting money judgments rendered by courts in other jurisdictions — which would in effect give the judgment creditor a further appeal on the merits. The process of collecting a judgment is not meant to require a second lawsuit, thus converting every successful multinational suit for damages into two suits. . . .

Even if the retail approach is valid — and we want to emphasize our belief that it is not — it cannot possibly avail the defendants here unless they are right that the approach requires subjecting the foreign proceeding to the specifics of the American doctrine of due process. They are not right. . . . In a case decided by a foreign court system that has not adopted every jot and tittle of American due process (and no foreign court system has, to our knowledge, done that), it will be sheer accident that a particular proceeding happened to conform in every particular to our complex understanding of due process. So even the retail approach, in order to get within miles of being reasonable, would have to content itself with requiring foreign conformity to the international concept of due process. And now let us for the sake of completeness apply that concept to the particulars of these judgments. . . .

In the English court the defendants opposed Lloyd's suit on the basis of two clauses which they contend would, if enforced, deny them due process of law; and they renew the contention here. The first clause, the "pay now sue later" clause as the parties call it, forbids names, in suits (such as the ones before us) by Lloyd's to collect the assessment, to set off against the claim by Lloyd's any claim the names might have against Lloyd's, such as a claim that the contract had been induced by fraud. . . . The second clause, the "conclusive evidence" clause, makes Lloyd's determination of the amount of the assessment "conclusive" "in the absence of manifest error." The defendants claim that the High Court refused to order Lloyd's to provide them with enough information about how the assessment had been calculated to enable them to prove manifest error. . . .

The pay now sue later clause was designed to enable [Lloyd's to implement an important financial restructuring.] That would work to the benefit of the names by giving them surer, earlier, and fuller reinsurance. In exchange it was reasonable to ask them to postpone the enforcement of any claims they might have against Lloyd's. . . . In these circumstances the clause did not violate international due process or, we add unnecessarily, domestic due process. . . . [T]his procedure ("pay now, dispute later,") has survived due process challenge. *See, e.g., Debreceni v. Merchants Terminal Corp.*, 889 F.2d 1, 3-4 (1st Cir. 1989). Anyway the question is not whether Lloyd's accorded due process to the names, but whether the English courts did. All they did was enforce the clause, and they did so on the basis of an interpretation of a provision of the original contract between the names and Lloyd's. . . . Stated differently, the courts held that the names had waived their procedural rights in advance, thus bringing the case within the rule of *D.H. Overmyer Co. v. Frick Co.*, 405 U.S. 174 (1972). That case upheld against a due process challenge similar to that mounted by the names in this case the enforcement of a cognovit note, by which a debtor consents in advance to the creditor's obtaining a judgment against him on the note without notice or hearing, and possibly even — to make the analogy to the present case even closer — with the appearance on the debtor's behalf, to confess judgment, of an attorney designated by the creditor. . . .

[T]he conclusive-evidence . . . clause does more than postpone claims by the names; it extinguishes them by shrinking the names' entitlement to a right to the rectification of only those errors that leap out from the assessment figure itself with no right to pretrial discovery to search out possible errors in the actuarial or other assumptions that generated the figure. This extinction of rights could raise a question if what we are calling international due process had a substantive component. But the defendants do not argue that it does. Though we cannot find a case on the point, the cases that deal with international due process talk only of procedural rights. . . .

[A] one-sided contract is a substantive, not a procedural, offense. . . . The [names'] real objection to the exclusive-evidence clause, moreover, is that it curtails pretrial discovery, and the right to pretrial discovery is not a part of the U.S. concept of due process, let alone of international due process. *See, e.g.,* Hague Convention, art. 23; *Panama Processes, SA v. Cities Service Co.*, 500 F. Supp. 787, 800 (S.D.N.Y. 1981), *aff'd*, 650 F.2d 408 (2d Cir. 1981); Born, *International Civil Litigation in United States Courts* 843-55 (1996). . . . We conclude that the judgments are enforceable under the foreign money-judgments statute. . . .

BRIDGEWAY CORP. v. CITIBANK
45 F. Supp. 2d 276 (S.D.N.Y. 1999), aff'd, 201 F.3d 134 (2d Cir. 2000)

CHIN, DISTRICT JUDGE. In this case, plaintiff Bridgeway Corporation ("Bridgeway") seeks to enforce a $189,376.66 judgment rendered in its favor by the Supreme Court of Liberia in Monrovia, Liberia (the "Liberian Judgment") against defendant Citibank d/b/a Citicorp, NA ("Citibank"). . . . Bridgeway is a Liberian corporation with a principal place of business in Monrovia, Liberia. Citibank is a national banking association incorporated under the laws of the United States with a principal place of business in New York, New York. Bridgeway maintained funds at Citibank Liberia, located in Monrovia.

In November of 1991, the decision was made to close Citibank Liberia because Liberia was undergoing a violent civil war. Thereafter, Citibank Liberia formulated a plan of liquidation that was ultimately approved by the National Bank of Liberia (the "National Bank"), the government agency that regulates the commercial banking industry in

Liberia. Under the liquidation plan, Citibank Liberia remitted funds to the National Bank. The National Bank, in turn, remitted funds to Meridien Bank Liberia Limited ("Meridien"), an entity appointed by the National Bank to pay all deposit liabilities on behalf of Citibank Liberia. Pursuant to Liberian law, implementation of the liquidation plan had to be completed within three years. Accordingly, the liquidation period for Citibank Liberia began on February 1, 1992 and ended on January 31, 1995. At the end of the three-year period, all deposit liabilities of Citibank Liberia that had not been settled by Meridien were identified, and title to the funds remitted to Meridien passed back to the National Bank, also as required by Liberian law. . . .

Bridgeway had opened an account at Citibank Liberia on June 7, 1982 by depositing an amount of funds in U.S. dollars. The . . . passbook issued by Citibank Liberia to Bridgeway contained the following statement: "Withdrawals from an account may be made only at the Bank and only upon the presentation of the pass-book and withdrawal orders satisfactory as to form and signature to the Bank. Payment may be made by the Bank in any money lawfully circulating in Liberia at the time of withdrawal."

In 1992, Bridgeway had a balance of L$189,376.66 in its account at Citibank Liberia. Concerned about the security of its deposits in light of the civil war and the liquidation of Citibank Liberia, Bridgeway demanded repayment of its funds from Citibank Liberia in U.S. dollars. Citibank Liberia refused to repay the funds in U.S. dollars. Citibank Liberia did, however, remit funds in Liberian dollars to the National Bank to cover Citibank Liberia's deposit liability to Bridgeway. . . .

On November 21, 1992, Bridgeway commenced a declaratory judgment action against Citibank in the Liberian courts claiming that it was entitled to be repaid its deposited funds in U.S. dollars. The trial court rendered judgment in favor of Citibank and against Bridgeway in August of 1993, holding that the relevant banking laws permitted Citibank to repay deposits in U.S. dollars or in Liberian dollars, at its option, and that, in any event, the two currencies have the same par value. Bridgeway appealed, and on July 28, 1995, the Supreme Court of Liberia reversed the judgment of the trial court and entered judgment for Bridgeway, holding that Citibank must repay Bridgeway's deposited funds in U.S. dollars. Unhappy with the decision of the Supreme Court, Citibank prepared a petition for reargument on August 1, 1995. The justices unanimously refused to approve the petition, however. Faced with the prospect of paying twice for the same deposit liability, Citibank made several requests of the National Bank to satisfy the judgment in U.S. dollars out of certain reserve funds that Citibank was required to maintain with the National Bank, or out of the [Liberian currency] that Citibank Liberia had previously deposited with the National Bank to satisfy its deposit liability to Bridgeway under the liquidation plan. The National Bank refused these requests. . . .

In this case, Bridgeway seeks enforcement of the Liberian Judgment. Citibank, on the other hand, asserts . . . that, under New York C.P.L.R. Art. 53, the judgment is unenforceable as a matter of law because the judgment was "rendered under a system which does not provide impartial tribunals or procedures compatible with the requirements of due process of law." *See* N.Y.C.P.L.R. §5304(a)(1) (McKinney 1997). . . . Article 53 provides that "a foreign country judgment . . . is conclusive between the parties to the extent that it grants or denies recovery of a sum of money." C.P.L.R. §5303. . . . A foreign country judgment is "not conclusive," however, if . . . "the judgment was rendered under a system which does not provide impartial tribunals or procedures compatible with the requirements of due process of law." Id. §5304(a). . . .

In this case, . . . Citibank challenges enforcement of the Liberian Judgment on the ground that Bridgeway has failed to offer any evidence that the Liberian Supreme Court was impartial or that its procedures were compatible with due process of law, at the time the Liberian Judgment was rendered. On the record before the Court, a reasonable factfinder could only conclude that, at the time the judgment at issue here was rendered, the Liberian judicial system was not fair and impartial and did not comport with the requirements of due process. . . .

First, the record demonstrates that, throughout the period during which the Liberian action was pending, the country was embroiled in a civil war.[107] The country was in a state of chaos, as the various factions fought. The Liberian Constitution was ignored. Some 200,000 Liberian citizens were killed, more than one million more were left homeless, and approximately 750,000 fled Liberia to seek refuge in other countries. It is difficult to imagine any judicial system functioning properly in these circumstances.

Second, the record shows that the regular procedures governing the selection of justices and judges had not been followed since the suspension of the 1986 Constitution. As a result, justices and judges served at the will of the leaders of the warring factions, and judicial officers were subject to political and social influence. The Liberian judicial system simply did not provide for impartial tribunals.

Third, the courts that did exist were barely functioning. The due process rights of litigants were often ignored, as corruption and incompetent handling of cases were prevalent. Although the Liberian judicial system might have been modeled on our own, it did not comport with the requirements of due process during the period of civil war.

Bridgeway offers the following as evidence that the Liberian judicial system is a system of jurisprudence likely to secure an impartial administration of justice: (1) a statement in the certification of James E. Pierre, Esq., a member of the Liberian Bar and the attorney who represented Bridgeway in the Liberian action, that the procedural rules of Liberia's courts are modeled on those of the New York State courts; (2) H. Varney G. Sherman's statement in his First Sworn Statement that, "[i]n essence, the Liberian Government is patterned after state governments of the United States of America"; and (3) a statement in the certification of N. Oswald Tweh, former Vice President of the Liberian National Bar Association and also counsel to Bridgeway, that "Liberia's judicial system was and is structured and administered to afford party-litigants therein impartial justice."

The evidence presented by Bridgeway does not create a genuine issue of fact requiring a trial. . . . First, that the Liberian judicial system was modeled after judicial systems in the United States does not mean, of course, that the Liberian system was actually implemented in a manner consistent with procedures used in the American courts. Second, the statement that "Liberia's judicial system was and is structured and administered to afford party-litigants therein impartial justice" is purely conclusory. . . . On the record before the Court, a reasonable factfinder could only conclude that the Liberian Judgment was rendered by a system that does not provide impartial tribunals or procedures compatible with the requirements of due process. Accordingly, the Liberian Judgment will not be enforced.

Notes on Ashenden *and* Bridgeway

1. *The "fairness" exception to the enforceability of foreign judgments.* As *Ashenden* and *Bridgeway* illustrate, one of the mandatory exceptions to the general obligation to enforce

---

107. Pursuant to Fed. R. Evid. 201(b)(1), I am permitted to take judicial notice of adjudicative facts "generally known" within the territorial jurisdiction of this Court, including facts pertaining to matters of history and politics. . . . Accordingly, I take judicial notice of the facts contained in these sources for purposes of resolution of this dispute.

foreign money judgments is where the judgment was rendered by a court that was not impartial or in accordance with procedures that were fundamentally unfair. As provided by UFMJRA, §4(b)(1), a judgment shall not be recognized if it was "rendered under a system which does not provide impartial tribunals or procedures incompatible with the requirements of due process of law." *See also* ALI, *The Foreign Judgments Recognition and Enforcement Act* §5(a)(i) and (ii) (2005). In Judge Posner's pithy summary, a foreign judgment must comply with "international due process."

The fairness exception has been the subject of substantial litigation in recent years. As *Bridgeway* illustrates, this has resulted from increasingly frequent efforts by courts and legislatures around the world to impose substantial judgments against companies perceived to have the wherewithal to pay them. *See, e.g., CBS Corp. v. WAK Orient Power & Light Ltd.,* CA 99-2996 (E.D. Pa. April 2001) ($1.4 billion Pakistani default judgment, plus Pakistani order to provide $11.5 billion letter of credit). The existence of such "judgments" poses a significant threat to the basic premises for enforcing foreign judgments with minimal scrutiny. Indeed, the notion of according "comity" to a corrupt judgment or to a kangaroo court (rather than an impartial tribunal) is worse than nonsensical; it causes enormous damage to innocent parties, while making U.S. (and other) courts parties to genuine wrong-doing.

At the same time, as *Ashenden* illustrates, the "fairness" exception should not, in an ideal world, be grounds for relitigating every material procedural decision in a foreign action. Doing so would frustrate the recognition and enforcement of legitimate foreign judgments, and also work substantial unfairness on innocent parties. Striking a workable balance between these two extremes is essential.

2. *Meaning of the fairness exception — "due process."* What does the UFMJRA mean when it refers to a "system which does not provide . . . procedures compatible with the requirements of due process of law"? And what does *Hilton* mean when it refers to a "system of jurisprudence likely to secure an impartial administration of justice"?

(a) U.S. due process standards. The UFMJRA explicitly refers to "due process" and arguably incorporates U.S. standards of that concept. Many courts have referred to U.S. due process standards, at least as a starting point for considering the fairness of foreign judicial procedures. *See Allstate Life Ins. Co. v. Linter Group Ltd.,* 994 F.2d 996, 999 (2d Cir. 1993).

On the other hand, as Judge Posner's opinion in *Ashenden* makes clear, there is no requirement that the foreign judicial system afford all of the procedural rights required under the Due Process Clause. *See Hilton v. Guyot,* 159 U.S. 113, 202-205 (1895); *Genujo Lok Beteiligungs GmbH v. Zorn,* 943 A.2d 573 (Me. 2008); *Wilson v. Marchington,* 127 F.3d 805, 811 (9th Cir. 1997); *Society of Lloyd's v. Tanner,* 303 F.3d 325, 330 (5th Cir. 2002) (foreign legal system must merely provide procedures "compatible" with requirements of due process but "need not comply with the traditional rigors of American due process"); *Ingersoll Milling Machine Co. v. Granger,* 833 F.2d 680, 687-688 (7th Cir. 1987) ("the Uniform Act does not require that the procedures employed by the foreign tribunal be identical to those employed in American courts"); UFMJRA §4, comment ("[A] mere difference in the procedural system is not a sufficient basis for non-recognition. A case of serious injustice must be involved."). Is it appropriate to give effect to judgments rendered in fundamentally alien procedural systems? How can U.S. courts conclude that the results of such procedures are fair?

(b) Procedural versus substantive due process. Note Judge Posner's distinction between procedural and substantive due process rights. Is that persuasive? Does that mean that a foreign statute could dictate grossly arbitrary results, or employ discriminatory categorizations, without any unfairness? Are these examples better addressed by the public policy exception?

(c) Judicial due process versus arbitral due process. Note Judge Posner's comment that a foreign court is held to a lower standard of due process than a foreign arbitral tribunal (under the New York Convention). Why should that be? Is it because a foreign judge is subject to appellate review (unlike a foreign arbitral tribunal), to professional discipline (different from a foreign arbitral tribunal), and to public scrutiny (unlike a foreign arbitral tribunal)? Do these distinctions apply in all countries? Note Judge Posner's list of countries whose judgments he would be uncomfortable with. Is that an unduly provocative thing to say? Is it not right?

3. *Meaning of fairness exception— "impartial tribunals."* Section 4(b)(1) of the UFMJRA provides that a judgment shall not be recognized if it was "rendered under a system which does not provide impartial tribunals." Many foreign governmental systems face pervasive, serious challenges from corruption. *See* U.S. Department of State, *Battling International Bribery* (2004). This can drastically affect the fairness of legal proceedings. How can a U.S. court assess the existence or nonexistence of corruption? Is there a realistic way of discovering that bribery, political influence, or similar factors have affected the outcome of a foreign decision? Would U.S. standards for judicial impartiality be applicable (if only as guidelines)? Would standards for the impartiality of foreign arbitral tribunals be applicable (again, if only as guidelines)?

Note that the UFCMJRA introduces a new exception, not present in the UFMJRA, applicable in cases of corruption. Section 4(c)(7) provides for nonrecognition if a judgment was rendered "in circumstances that raise substantial doubt about the integrity of the rendering court with respect to the judgment." *See also* ALI, *The Foreign Judgments Recognition and Enforcement Act* §5(a)(ii) (2005) ("substantial and justifiable doubt about the integrity of the rendering court with respect to the judgment in question"). Is this an improvement over the UFMJRA? Does it permit nonrecognition even without proof of corruption? Is that desirable?

4. *Procedural unfairness of foreign judicial "system" under the UFMJRA.* How does *Hilton* frame the "fairness" inquiry? Recall that its holding required "the full and fair opportunity for a trial abroad before a court of competent jurisdiction, conducting the trial upon regular proceedings . . . and under a system of jurisprudence likely to secure and impartial administration of justice between the citizens of its own county and those of other countries." Note that the inquiry was directed to both the foreign judicial system and the particular trial involving the parties.

Compare §4(b)(1) of the UFMJRA, particularly as interpreted in *Ashenden.* As Judge Posner observed, UFMJRA, §4(b)(1) refers only to "a system" that does not provide impartial judges or due process. Are these differences between the *Hilton* and UFMJRA formulations important? How?

In addition to *Ashenden,* a number of other courts have concluded that UFMJRA, §4(b)(1) requires a showing that the entire foreign legal system — rather than a particular trial or proceeding — is unfair. *See Society of Lloyd's v. Reinhart,* 402 F.3d 982 (10th Cir. 2005) ("Although the New Mexico Name would prefer to have us focus on this particular *judgment,* rather than the English *system,* at this stage of these matters, we are not permitted to do so").

Why does the UFMJRA's fairness analysis focus on an entire foreign judicial or legal system? Cannot one have a basically fair foreign legal system, within which a particular fundamentally unfair proceeding takes place? Cannot one judge be incompetent (or corrupt) or make a fundamentally unfair decision, even if the overall legal system is fair? Isn't U.S. judicial inquiry into the fairness of an entire foreign legal system more likely to raise comity and separation of powers concerns than inquiry into the fairness of a particular legal proceeding? Isn't a judicial body better equipped to judge the fairness of a particular proceeding (as appellate courts frequently do) than the fairness of an entire legal system?

5. *Procedural fairness under UFCMJRA.* The UFCMJRA amends the UFMJRA's language dealing with procedural fairness. In addition to retaining former §4(b)(1), the UFCMJRA introduces a new §4(c)(8), which provides that a judgment need not be recognized if "the specific proceeding in the foreign court leading to the judgment was not compatible with the requirements of due process of law." Note that the focus of this provision is not on the foreign judicial system, but the particular proceeding that produced the foreign judgment. Is this an appropriate change?

6. *Rationale for the fairness exception.* Why do U.S. courts review the foreign judicial system that rendered a judgment for fairness? Is it to protect the judgment debtor? What if the judgment debtor is a foreign citizen? Is it to protect the U.S. court from participating in an act of injustice? Or some other purpose?

7. *Wisdom of the fairness exception.* Consider the *Bridgeway* and *Ashenden* opinions. Is it sensible for U.S. courts to engage in a review of the "fairness" of a foreign judicial system at all? Doesn't this simply invite the court to engage in sweeping moral or political judgments about the acceptability or unacceptability of the foreign judicial system? Is it simply because of the factual record that the English system was found impeccable and the Liberian system was found impossible? Or is it because of cultural bias? Would Nigerian, Chinese, Russian, German, or Venezuelan courts agree with the analyses in *Ashenden* and *Bridgeway*? Is that the test? Is it relevant? Are there some basic principles of fairness that a U.S. court can legitimately identify and apply? Is it conceivable that a U.S. (or any) court would simply enforce a foreign judgment without any inquiry into its fairness? Would that be justice?

What implications does a U.S. court's review of a foreign judicial system have for U.S. foreign relations? Is this the same undertaking as analyzing an act of state or applying foreign law? Or does it involve an even more political inquiry? Wouldn't it be more consistent with comity for a court not to engage in such an inquiry? Or if it does so, only to do so pursuant to standards articulated by the other branches of government?

8. *Evidence of unfairness of foreign judicial system.* As an evidentiary matter, how can a court actually assess the fairness of a foreign judicial "system"? What evidence do the courts in *Ashenden* and *Bridgeway* rely on?

Consider the affidavits that were relied on in *Bridgeway*. How useful are such materials? How likely is it that there will not be two completely contradictory affidavits from local lawyers? Note that the U.S. Department of State publishes reports on human rights in different countries, which include discussions of the judicial systems. *See, e.g.,* U.S. Department of State, *Country Reports on Human Rights Practices* (2005), *available at* http://www.state.gov/g/drl/rls/hrrpt/2005/index.htm.

9. *Foreign judicial system need not mirror U.S. procedures.* As Judge Posner notes, foreign courts are not required to provide the same procedural opportunities as available in U.S. courts. *See also Tonga Air Services Ltd. v. Fowler*, 826 P.2d 204 (Wash. 1992) (lack of verbatim transcript not violative of due process); *Panama Processes v. Cities Service Co.*, 796 P.2d 276, 285 (Okla. 1990) (differences between U.S. and foreign procedures not a basis for non-recognition even where "in Brazil (1) no witnesses of any party may be subpoenaed, (2) testimony of corporate employees is inadmissible, (3) there is no available process for requiring testimony of indispensable U.S. witnesses, (4) there is no right of cross-examination, and (5) the parties may neither conduct pre-trial discovery nor subpoena documents"). How should the treatment of foreign tribunals' fairness in the enforcement context compare to the approaches by U.S. courts to the fairness of foreign legal systems in the context of forum selection clauses or *forum non conveniens*? *See supra* pp. 437-447.

10. ***General tendency of U.S. courts to find foreign legal systems fair.*** In general, U.S. courts are hesitant to deny the fairness of other countries' judicial systems. *See British Midland Airways v. International Travel*, 497 F.2d 869, 871 (9th Cir. 1974) ("unless a foreign country's judgments are the result of outrageous departure"); *Kam-Tech Systems Ltd. v. Yardeni*, 774 A.2d 644, 649-652 (N.J. Super. 2001) (finding no basis for concluding that Israeli civil justice system violated notions of fundamental fairness).

As *Ashenden* illustrates, U.S. courts appear especially willing to enforce Western European judgments (and particularly English judgments). *See, e.g., Somportex, Ltd. v. Philadelphia Chewing Gum Corp.*, 453 F.2d 435, 440 (3d Cir. 1971) (the English legal system "is the very fount from which our system has developed") *and Hunt v. BP Exploration Co. (Libya)*, 492 F. Supp. 885, 906 (N.D. Tex. 1980) ("In sum, a litigant is entitled to no more than one clean bite of one clean apple C at least at the table of our British brethren."). *See generally Society of Lloyd's v. Siemon-Netto*, 457 F.3d 94, 105 n.12 (D.C. Cir. 2006) (collecting cases).

For cases holding that a foreign country's judicial system was so fundamentally unfair as to bar recognition under the UFMJRA, *see Bank Melli Iran v. Pahlavi*, 58 F.3d 1406, 1410-1413 (9th Cir. 1995) (Iran); *Choi v. Kim*, 50 F.3d 244, 249-250 (3d Cir. 1995); *Maersk, Inc. v. Neewra, Inc.*, 2010 U.S. Dist. LEXIS 69863 (S.D.N.Y. 2010) (Kuwait); *Osorio v. Dole Food Co.*, 665 F. Supp. 2d 1307 (S.D. Fla. 2009) (Nicaragua); *Banco Minero v. Ross*, 172 S.W. 711, 714-715 (Tex. 1915).

11. ***Proving the fairness or unfairness of a foreign judicial system.*** Which party bears the burden of proving the fairness (or unfairness) of the foreign judicial system or proceeding? How did the Court in *Bridgeway* answer that question? If you represented the judgment debtor attacking the fairness of the foreign country's judicial system, how would you go about proving your case in the enforcement forum? How did the judgment debtors in *Bridgeway* do so? Would you raise the challenge already in the foreign country during the initial litigation? Are there risks in raising such an argument? In not doing so? For a decision assessing the sources of proof offered by a party challenging a foreign legal system, *see Fox v. Bank Mandiri (In re Perry H. Koplik & Sons, Inc.)*, 357 B.R. 231 (Bankr. S.D.N.Y. 2007).

12. ***Fair forums and multinational corporations.*** Recall the litigation against Chevron/ Texaco for its activities in Ecuador, *supra* pp. 1145-1146. As noted above, the case resulted in an $8.6 billion judgment against the company. Chevron's reaction to the judgment included claims that it was the product of fraud (including claims that witnesses had been bribed to provide evidence against the company) and was completely contrary to the legitimate scientific evidence of what had occurred in the country. Relying on these claims, could Chevron successfully prevent enforcement of the Ecuadoran court judgment on the ground that the Ecuadoran judicial system was fundamentally unfair? In an earlier stage of the proceedings, the plaintiffs had sought to bring claims in the United States under the Alien Tort Statute, and Chevron successfully persuaded a court to dismiss the case on grounds of *forum non conveniens*. One precondition for *forum non conveniens* dismissal is a finding that the foreign forum is "adequate." How (if at all) should this earlier finding affect a U.S. court's view of the fairness of the Ecuadoran judicial system in enforcement proceedings? Does Chevron's prior position on its *forum non conveniens* motion affect its ability now to claim that the Ecuadoran judicial system is fundamentally unfair?

13. ***Differing treatment of sister state and foreign country judgments.*** The foregoing materials illustrate that the enforcement of foreign country judgments is a significantly more difficult undertaking than the enforcement of sister state judgments under the Full Faith and Credit Clause. The public policy defense, the treatment of jurisdictional requirements, and the reciprocity rule all contribute to this result. Why should it be more difficult to enforce foreign judgments than domestic judgments? Does this merely reflect parochialism or unspoken distrust of foreign legal systems? Or are there valid reasons for each of the various defenses to the enforcement of foreign country judgments?

Recall that foreign jurisdictional rules, service mechanisms, standards of procedural fairness, and substantive laws often differ substantially from their U.S. counterparts. Moreover, U.S. courts may be less concerned about the waste of judicial resources when an earlier litigation occurred abroad and thus did not involve U.S. judicial resources. Consider the following:

> Many of the reasons for recognition and enforcement of foreign country judgments are the same as for giving conclusive effect to domestic judgments: prevention of harassment of the successful party, elimination of duplicative judicial proceedings, and providing some measure of settled expectations to the parties. In a domestic context, the benefits of preclusion are palpable. In our Union, since courts in each state are subject to due process limitations, are subject to the same overlap of federal laws and the Constitution, are sharing to a large extent the same body of court precedents and socio-economic ideas and are presumptively fair and competent, the benefits of giving conclusive effect are not balanced by any recognizable costs. Giving an automatically conclusive effect — full faith and credit — to sister state judgments could be fully justified on the grounds of fairness to litigants and judicial economy; there is no reason for a second trial — the rendering forum had at least the constitutionally requisite contacts with the litigant, there is little possibility of an error in the rendering forum and the substantive policies given effect by that forum are likely fully acceptable in the recognizing forum.
>
> The benefit-cost calculation for giving an automatically conclusive effect to foreign country judgments is far less favorable. There is less expectation that the courts of a foreign country will follow procedures which would comport with our notions of due process and jurisdiction and that they will apply substantively tolerable laws. Moreover, especially if the loser in the initial litigation is American, there will be suspicions here of unfairness or fraud. The modern versions of the *Hilton v. Guyot* rule — neither pretending that the initial litigation never occurred, nor giving it an automatic conclusive effect — is a natural and tempered response to the tension between the benefits and costs of giving effect to foreign country judgments. By going to the halfway house, courts can deny effect to foreign country judgments when the rendering court has acted in ways intolerable by our country's then felt ideal of fundamental fairness. *Hunt v. BP Exploration Co. (Libya)*, 492 F. Supp. 885, 905-906 (N.D. Tex. 1980).

Are you persuaded?

14. *Wisdom of U.S. approach to recognition of foreign judgments.* Consider the current U.S. approach to the recognition of foreign judgments, and the results it produces. In general, U.S. courts are fairly willing to enforce foreign judgments, but "our judgments are treated shabbily in other nations." Golumb, *Recognition of Foreign Money Judgments: A Goal-Oriented Approach*, 43 St. John's L. Rev. 604, 635 (1969). What is the cause of this imbalance? How should U.S. policy-makers respond to the foregoing state of affairs? Should the ALI's Proposed Judgments Legislation be adopted? What else should be considered?

13

International Commercial Arbitration and U.S. Courts: An Overview[1]

Over the past several decades, "international arbitration" has become a preferred means of resolving commercial disputes among international businesses. This chapter briefly describes the international arbitral process and explores the role of U.S. courts in this process. It focuses in particular on the enforcement of international arbitration agreements and arbitral awards by U.S. courts.

A. Overview of International Arbitration

1. Introduction

International arbitration is a means by which a dispute can be definitively resolved, pursuant to the parties' voluntary agreement, by a disinterested, nongovernmental decision-maker that applies adjudicatory procedures affording the parties an opportunity to present their cases. In the words of the U.S. Supreme Court, "an agreement to arbitrate before a specified tribunal [is], in effect, a specialized kind of forum-selection clause that posits not only the situs of suit but also the procedure to be used in resolving the dispute."[2] A substantial proportion of international commercial, financial, and investment agreements contain arbitration clauses, providing that disputes relating to the parties' contract will be submitted to arbitration. In the words of one commentator, "in th[e] realm of international commercial transactions, arbitration has become the preferred method of dispute resolution."[3]

International commercial arbitration has several defining characteristics. First, arbitration is almost always *consensual*—the parties must agree to resolve their differences by

---

1. Commentary on international commercial arbitration includes, *e.g.*, G. Born, *International Commercial Arbitration* (2009); E. Gaillard *et al.*, *Fouchard Gaillard Goldman on International Commercial Arbitration* (1999); A. Redfern & M. Hunter, *Law and Practice of International Commercial Arbitration* (4th ed. 2004); W. Craig *et al.*, *International Chamber of Commerce Arbitration* (3d ed. 2000).

2. *Scherk v. Alberto-Culver Co.*, 417 U.S. 506, 519 (1974). *See also* G. Born, *International Commercial Arbitration* 217 (2009) ("a process by which parties consensually submit a dispute to a non-governmental decision-maker, selected by or for the parties, to render a binding decision resolving the dispute in accordance with neutral, adjudicatory procedures affording the parties an opportunity to be heard"); A. Redfern & M. Hunter, *Law and Practice of International Commercial Arbitration* 3 (4th ed. 2004) ("two or more parties, faced with a dispute which they cannot resolve for themselves, agreeing that some private individual will resolve it for them and if the arbitration runs its full course . . . it will not be settled by a compromise, but by a decision.").

3. Buchanan, *Public Policy and International Commercial Arbitration*, 26 Am. Bus. L.J. 511, 512 (1988).

arbitration.[4] Most arbitration agreements are included as clauses in commercial contracts and provide for the arbitration of any dispute that may arise in the future between the parties within a defined category. It is also possible, although much less common, for parties to an *existing* dispute to agree to settle their disagreement through arbitration.

Second, arbitration produces a *definitive and binding award*, which is capable of enforcement through national courts. As discussed below, in most jurisdictions, arbitral awards are generally subject to only very limited judicial review, which can be exercised in either actions to vacate or annul an award (typically in the arbitral seat) or in actions to recognize and enforce such awards (in places other than the arbitral seat).[5] Ordinarily, mistakes of law or fact will not be grounds for denying recognition or enforcement of an award, while a tribunal will enjoy broad discretion with respect to its procedural decisions.[6]

Third, arbitrations are resolved by *nongovernmental decision-makers* — arbitrators are not government agents, but private persons selected by the parties. Arbitrators are often selected because of their experience or competence in a particular area (*e.g.*, construction projects, investment disputes, accounting matters).[7] Additionally, parties often agree to three-person arbitral tribunals, in which each party is entitled to select one arbitrator — giving both litigants a role and measure of confidence in the tribunal's composition.

Although arbitration is common in domestic settings, it is particularly attractive in international matters. Parties to international transactions are often of different nationalities; they choose arbitration in order to obtain a neutral decision-maker (detached from the governmental institutions and cultural biases of either party) who will apply internationally neutral procedural rules (rather than a particular national legal regime). In addition, by designating a single dispute resolution mechanism for the parties' disagreements, arbitration is a means of mitigating some of the peculiar uncertainties of international litigation — which, as discussed above, can include protracted disputes about jurisdiction, *forum non conveniens*, service of process, sovereign immunity, and choice of law, as well as expensive parallel proceedings.[8] Moreover, international arbitration is often seen as a means of obtaining an award that is more readily enforceable than a national court judgment.

International arbitration can be either "institutional" or "*ad hoc.*" A number of organizations, located in different countries, provide institutional arbitration services. The best-known international arbitral institutions are the International Chamber of Commerce ("ICC"), the American Arbitration Association ("AAA"), and the London Court of International Arbitration ("LCIA").[9]

Many arbitral institutions have promulgated procedural rules that apply to arbitrations where parties have agreed to arbitration pursuant to such rules.[10] Among other things, institutional rules set out the basics of a procedural framework for the arbitral process (while leaving implementation and most details to the tribunal). In addition, such rules

---

4. *E.g., United Steelworkers of America v. Warrior & Gulf Navigation Co.*, 363 U.S. 574, 582 (1960) ("arbitration is a matter of contract and a party cannot be required to submit to arbitration any dispute which he has not agreed to so submit"); *infra* pp. 1163-1164. There is an increasingly important category of non-consensual arbitrations, involving bilateral investment treaty disputes, where host states agree generally to arbitrate defined types of investment disputes with foreign investors. *See supra* pp. 328-329.

5. *See infra* pp. 1201-1203.

6. *See infra* pp. 1209-1211.

7. G. Born, *International Commercial Arbitration* 78-81, 83-84 (2009); A. Redfern & M. Hunter, *Law and Practice of International Commercial Arbitration* 186-199 (4th ed. 2004).

8. *See supra* pp. 1209-1211.

9. For descriptions of these and other arbitral institutions, *see* G. Born, *International Commercial Arbitration* 153-169 (2009); Y. Derains & E. Schwartz, *A Guide to the ICC Rules of Arbitration* 7-8 (2005).

10. These include the ICC's Rules of Arbitration, the LCIA Rules, numerous specialized rules of the AAA (such as the Commercial Arbitration Rules and the International Arbitration Rules), and the ICSID Rules.

typically authorize the host arbitral institution to select arbitrators in particular disputes, to resolve challenges to the neutrality of the arbitrators, to designate the place of arbitration, to fix the arbitrators' fees, and (sometimes) to review the arbitrators' awards on formal or other grounds.[11] Arbitral institutions do *not* themselves arbitrate the merits of the parties' dispute. This is the responsibility of the particular individuals selected as arbitrators.

Ad hoc arbitration is not conducted under the supervision of an arbitral institution. Instead, parties simply select an arbitrator (or arbitrators) who resolves the dispute without institutional support. The parties sometimes also select a preexisting set of procedural rules designed for *ad hoc* arbitration. The United Nations Commission on International Trade Law ("UNCITRAL") has published a commonly used set of such rules.[12] Alternatively, the parties' arbitration agreement will set forth the relevant procedural rules or the arbitral tribunal will independently formulate procedural rules, tailored to the specific needs of the parties and their dispute. In either *ad hoc* or institutional arbitration agreements, parties usually will (and certainly should) designate an "appointing authority,"[13] that will select the arbitrator(s) if the parties cannot agree.[14]

It is the procedural conduct of international arbitration proceedings, as much as any other factor, that leads parties to agree to arbitrate their disputes. National courts play little or no role in the arbitration proceedings themselves (at least in the major trading countries where arbitrations are commonly conducted).[15] Rather, the parties and the tribunal enjoy substantial autonomy to fashion an arbitral procedure tailored to their particular needs.

It goes without saying that the procedures used in arbitration proceedings are different from those in judicial proceedings. "As a speedy and informal alternative to litigation, arbitration resolves disputes without confinement to many of the procedural and evidentiary structures that protect the integrity of formal trials."[16] One of the reasons parties choose to arbitrate is their desire to obtain the comparative informality, flexibility, and occasional speed of arbitration. In theory, a party "trades the procedures and opportunity for review of the courtroom for the simplicity, informality, and expedition of arbitration."[17]

Nevertheless, particularly in major matters, the contrast between litigation and arbitration can be exaggerated and the procedures of an arbitration assume a fairly "judicial" cast. "Though litigation is compulsory and arbitration is consensual, both are judicial processes of an adversarial character."[18] Tribunals and parties often conclude that complex cases require considerable issue definition, scheduling, and the like, and it is common in international arbitration to encounter written pleadings, briefs, cross-

11. *See* G. Born, *International Commercial Arbitration* 148-149, 153-154 (2009); E. Gaillard *et al.*, *Fouchard Gaillard Goldman on International Commercial Arbitration* 544-555 (1999).

12. For a discussion of the UNCITRAL Rules, *see* G. Born, *International Commercial Arbitration* 151-153 (2009).

13. Most leading arbitration institutions (including the ICC, the AAA, and the LCIA) will act as an appointing authority, for a fee, in ad hoc arbitrations.

14. If the parties fail to select an appointing authority, then the national arbitration statutes of many nations, including the United States, permit national courts to appoint arbitrators. *See* G. Born, *International Commercial Arbitration* 1417-1431 (2009).

15. These countries include England, Switzerland, France, Belgium, the Netherlands, Sweden, and Singapore. Elsewhere, and particularly in Latin America and the Middle East, local law sometimes still imposes restrictive conditions on international arbitrations and permits interference by local courts in the arbitral process. *See* G. Born, *International Commercial Arbitration* 144-147 (2009). In general, however, the past two decades have witnessed substantially greater acceptance, including in emerging markets, of international arbitration as a means of resolving international commercial and investment disputes.

16. *Forsythe Int'l, SA v. Gibbs Oil Co.*, 915 F.2d 1017, 1022 (5th Cir. 1990).

17. *Mitsubishi Motors Corp. v. Soler Chrysler-Plymouth Inc.*, 473 U.S. 614, 628 (1985).

18. Nariman, *Standards of Behaviour of Arbitrators*, 4 Arb. Int'l 311 (1988).

examination, testimony under oath, verbatim transcripts, and a measure of discovery. Indeed, some argue that arbitration has lost the informality and expedition that once characterized it, and urge a return to less judicial procedures.[19]

One of the most fundamental characteristics of international arbitration is the parties' freedom to agree upon the arbitral procedure. Nevertheless, parties often do not agree in advance on detailed procedural rules for their arbitrations. At most, their arbitration agreement will adopt a set of institutional rules, which supply only a broad procedural framework. Filling in the considerable gaps in this framework will be left to the subsequent agreement of the parties or, if they cannot agree, the arbitral tribunal.

Under U.S. and many other national laws, the tribunal has substantial discretion to establish the arbitral procedures.[20] A tribunal's use of this discretion will often be influenced significantly by the arbitrators' legal training, experience, and personal characteristics. In general, arbitrators with civil law backgrounds can be expected to adopt more "inquisitorial" procedures, with somewhat less scope for adversarial procedures — such as broad, party-initiated discovery, depositions, lengthy oral hearings, counsel-controlled cross-examination, and the like — than is familiar to U.S. lawyers. Arbitrators from U.S. and other common law jurisdictions will be inclined to adopt "adversarial" procedures more broadly similar to those prevailing in common law litigation.

International arbitrations are typically commenced by a "notice of arbitration" or "request for arbitration," which identifies the parties to the proceeding and the claimant's claims (and which is "served" on the respondent by courier).[21] Ordinarily, the respondent then files a "reply" or "answer," within a specified time period, which sets forth its defenses (and any counterclaims). At the same time, the arbitrator(s) will be selected, either by agreement between the parties or by a contractually designated "appointing authority."[22]

Once a tribunal is in place, it will control the subsequent arbitral procedures, which will ordinarily include further written submissions detailing the parties' positions on factual and legal matters and submitting relevant documents, document disclosure (often limited, as compared to U.S. discovery), evidentiary hearings, and issuance of a reasoned written decision ("award").[23] The International Bar Association has issued "Rules on the Taking of Evidence in International Commercial Arbitration" which are often relied upon for guidance in international arbitrations.[24]

2.   Overview of International Legal Framework for Arbitration

The legal framework for international arbitration is markedly different from that for international litigation in the United States. As we have seen, choice-of-forum clauses and foreign judgments are not (for the most part) governed by any U.S. treaty or federal

---

19. Wetter, *The Present Status of the International Court of Arbitration of the ICC: An Appraisal,* 1 Am. Rev. Int'l Arb. 91, 101 (1990); G. Born, *International Commercial Arbitration* 82-86 (2009).

20. *See* G. Born, *International Commercial Arbitration* 82-84, 1758-1764 (2009); E. Gaillard *et al., Fouchard Gaillard Goldman on International Commercial Arbitration* 655-659 (1999).

21. *See* G. Born, *International Commercial Arbitration* 1795-1800 (2009); E. Gaillard *et al., Fouchard Gaillard Goldman on International Commercial Arbitration* 452-460 (1999). Most tribunals consist of either one or three arbitrators. Where there is a three-person tribunal, each party will typically nominate one "co-arbitrator," and the "presiding arbitrator" or "chairman" will be selected either by agreement between the co-arbitrators or by the arbitral institution.

22. ICC, *Taking Evidence in International Arbitral Proceedings* (1990); Marriott, *Evidence in International Arbitration,* 5 Arb. Int'l 280, 283-286 (1989); G. Born, *International Commercial Arbitration* 1363-1431, 1803 (2009).

23. *See* G. Born, *International Commercial Arbitration* 1794-1874 (2009).

24. The IBA Rules are excerpted in Appendix V.

legislation.[25] Rather, in most instances, the enforceability of forum clauses and foreign judgments is governed by state law.

In contrast, the legal regime governing international arbitration agreements and arbitral awards in U.S. courts is almost entirely federal. As discussed below, the United States is party to a number of multilateral treaties dealing with international arbitration, and Congress has enacted federal legislation providing for the enforcement of international arbitration agreements and awards in U.S. courts. For the most part, this federal regime is distinctly more effective and efficient than its state counterparts in the litigation context. (As noted above, there are pending proposals for both ratification of the Hague Choice of Court Agreements Convention and enactment of the ALI's Proposed Judgments Legislation — each of which would "federalize" the law relating to forum selection clauses and foreign judgments.[26])

a. The New York Convention. Although international arbitration is a *consensual* means of dispute resolution, it has binding legal effect by virtue of a complex framework of national and international law. The United Nations Convention on Recognition and Enforcement of Foreign Arbitral Awards (the "New York Convention")[27] has been ratified by some 144 states, including virtually all significant trading states. The Convention, which is reproduced in Appendix R, is by far the most significant contemporary international agreement relating to commercial arbitration.[28]

The Convention was designed to "encourage the recognition and enforcement of commercial arbitration agreements in international contracts and to unify the standards by which agreements to arbitrate are observed and arbitral awards are enforced in the signatory countries."[29] In broad outline, the Convention requires national courts to: (a) recognize and enforce foreign arbitral awards, subject to specified exceptions;[30] (b) recognize the validity of international arbitration agreements, subject to specified exceptions;[31] and (c) to refer parties to arbitration when they have entered into a valid agreement to arbitrate that is subject to the Convention.[32]

b. National Legislation Concerning International Commercial Arbitration. The New York Convention has been implemented in most Contracting States by national arbitration legislation. As discussed below, the relevant implementing legislation in the United States is the second chapter of the Federal Arbitration Act.[33] Different nations have adopted widely differing international arbitration statutes. Among other things, different countries apply varying standards to such matters as the extent of judicial review of arbitration awards made within national territory, the roles of courts and arbitral tribunals in enforcing arbitration agreements, and the availability of judicial support

---

25. As discussed above, there are proposals for federal legislation governing the enforceability of foreign judgments (the ALI's proposed federal legislation, *see supra* pp. 1085-1086) and for U.S. ratification of the Hague Choice of Court Agreements Convention (*see supra* pp. 107-108).

26. *See supra* pp. 107-108 and 1085-1086.

27. *See* 9 U.S.C. §201.

28. The Convention is widely regarded as "the most important Convention in the field of arbitration and . . . the cornerstone of current international commercial arbitration." A. van den Berg, *The New York Arbitration Convention of 1958* 1 (1981). The Convention was signed in 1958 in New York after lengthy negotiations under U.N. auspices. *Id.* at 1-10. *See also* G. Born, *International Commercial Arbitration* 92-101 (2009).

29. *Scherk v. Alberto-Culver Co.*, 417 U.S. 506, 520 n.15 (1974).

30. New York Convention, Articles III and V. *See infra* pp. 1201-1215.

31. New York Convention, Article II(1). *See infra* pp. 1163-1185.

32. New York Convention, Article II(3). *See infra* p. 1168.

33. *See infra* p. 1168; 9 U.S.C. §§201-210.

for the arbitral process (*e.g.*, selection of arbitrators, provisional measures, evidence-taking).[34]

In recent years, there has been a tendency toward uniformity among national arbitration statutes, principally by virtue of the United Nations Commission on International Trade Law's Model Law on International Commercial Arbitration ("UNCITRAL Model Law").[35] Negotiated under U.N. auspices to make the international arbitral process more predictable and efficient, the Model Law consists of some 36 articles, which deal comprehensively with the issues that arise in national courts in connection with international arbitration. Among other things, the Model Law contains provisions concerning the enforcement of arbitration agreements (Articles 7-9), appointment of and challenges to arbitrators (Articles 10-15), jurisdiction of arbitrators (Article 16), provisional measures (Article 17), conduct of arbitral proceedings (including language, seat, and procedures) (Articles 18-26), evidence-taking (Article 27), applicable law (Article 28), setting aside or vacating awards (Article 34), and recognition and enforcement of awards (including bases for nonrecognition) (Articles 35-36). With increasing numbers of states adopting the Model Law, there is a growing body of international precedent interpreting its terms.[36]

  c. U.S. Legislation Concerning International Commercial Arbitration.   The basic source of U.S. law dealing with arbitration, both domestic and international, is the Federal Arbitration Act ("FAA"). The Act was first enacted in 1925, but has been significantly expanded since then.[37] The FAA currently consists of three chapters: (a) the "domestic" FAA, 9 U.S.C. §§1-16, applicable to agreements and awards affecting interstate or foreign commerce; (b) the New York Convention's implementing legislation, 9 U.S.C. §§201-210, applicable to awards and agreements falling within the New York Convention; and (c) the Inter-American Arbitration Convention's implementing legislation, 9 U.S.C. §§301-07.[38]

The FAA applies to arbitration agreements and awards affecting either interstate or foreign commerce — a jurisdictional grant that U.S. courts have interpreted expansively.[39] The FAA is considerably less detailed than arbitration legislation in most other major jurisdictions. At least for the time being, however, calls for legislative reform have gone unheeded.

The centerpiece of the FAA is §2, which provides that arbitration agreements involving interstate and foreign commerce "shall be valid, irrevocable, and enforceable, save upon such grounds as exist at law or in equity for the revocation of any contract."[40] Other

---

  34. G. Born, *International Commercial Arbitration* 109-147 (2009); E. Gaillard *et al.*, *Fouchard Gaillard Goldman on International Commercial Arbitration* 636-637 (1999).

  35. The UNCITRAL Model Law has been enacted by a number of major trading states, including Australia, Austria, Bahrain, Canada, Egypt, England (to an extent), Germany, Hong Kong, India, Mexico, and Russia. The UNCITRAL Model Law, together with amendments adopted by UNCITRAL in 2006, is excerpted in Appendices T and U.

  36. H. Alvarez *et al.*, *Model Law Decisions: Cases Applying the UNCITRAL Model Law on International Commercial Arbitration (1985-2001)* (2003).

  37. Federal Arbitration Act, 43 Stat. 883 (1925), 61 Stat. 669 (1947) (as codified at 9 U.S.C. §§1-16). The FAA is excerpted at Appendix S.

  38. In 1975, the United States and most South American nations negotiated the Inter-American Convention on International Commercial Arbitration, also known as the "Panama Convention." 9 U.S.C.A. §301. The United States ratified the Convention in 1990; other parties include Mexico, Venezuela, Columbia, Chile, Costa Rica, El Salvador, Guatemala, Honduras, Panama, Paraguay, and Uruguay. The Inter-American Convention is similar to the New York Convention in many respects. Among other things, it provides for the general enforceability of arbitration agreements and arbitral awards, subject to specified exceptions similar to those in the New York Convention.

  39. 9 U.S.C. §1. The FAA's focus was principally domestic, although it also expressly applies to "foreign commerce." 9 U.S.C. §1.

  40. 9 U.S.C. §2.

sections of the FAA address, in a fairly skeletal manner, different aspects of the arbitral process. Section 5 grants district courts the power to appoint arbitrators if the parties have neither done so nor agreed upon an appointing authority.[41] Section 7 permits district courts to issue compulsory process to assist arbitral tribunals in taking evidence.[42]

Central to the arbitral process, both internationally and domestically, is the final and binding nature of arbitral awards, which are subject to substantially more limited appellate review than national court judgments. Thus, §§9, 10, and 11 of the FAA provide that an award may be vacated in only limited cases (involving violations of due process, excess of jurisdiction, and fraud). Unless one of these exceptions is satisfied, awards are final and binding, and may be enforced in the same manner as the judgment of a court.[43]

After U.S. ratification of the New York Convention in 1970, Congress enacted amendments to the FAA, in a second chapter to the Act.[44] Like the domestic Act, the FAA's second chapter is remarkably brief and noncomprehensive. It provides that arbitration agreements and awards shall be enforceable (subject to specified exceptions), and contains provisions assisting the arbitral process (particularly selection of arbitrators).[45] In addition, the amendments expand federal subject matter jurisdiction, removal authority, and injunctive powers.[46] Of particular practical importance, §205 provides a broad grant of removal jurisdiction "where the subject matter of an action or proceeding pending in a State court relates to an arbitration agreement or award falling under the Convention."[47]

The New York Convention and the FAA establish substantive federal law, generally ensuring the enforceability of international arbitration agreements and awards, that preempts inconsistent state law.[48] Nonetheless, state law can also be relevant to international arbitration issues in U.S. courts. The Supreme Court has held that the FAA does not "occupy the entire field" relating to arbitration.[49] As a result, state law is applicable to arbitration agreements and awards when — but only when — the Convention and FAA are inapplicable. That may be the case, for example, because the agreement or award does not affect interstate or foreign commerce. State law may also be applicable to ancillary issues bearing on international arbitration that federal statutory and common law do not address.

B.   Enforceability of International Arbitration Agreements Under the New York Convention and the FAA

It is a fundamental principle of U.S. law that "[a]rbitration is a matter of contract and a party cannot be required to submit to arbitration any dispute which he has not agreed to

---

41. 9 U.S.C. §5; G. Born, *International Commercial Arbitration* 1421-1422 (2009).
42. 9 U.S.C. §7; G. Born, *International Commercial Arbitration* 1883-1885, 1926-1937 (2009).
43. 9 U.S.C. §§9-11; G. Born, *International Commercial Arbitration* 2564-2566, 2895-2904 (2009).
44. 9 U.S.C. §§201-210.
45. 9 U.S.C. §§206-207.
46. 9 U.S.C. §§203, 205, 206. *See* G. Born, *International Commercial Arbitration* 136-139 (2009).
47. 9 U.S.C. §205.
48. *Prima Paint Corp. v. Flood & Conklin Mfg. Co.*, 388 U.S. 395, 399-400 (1967); *Moses H. Cone Memorial Hospital v. Mercury Construction Corp.*, 460 U.S. 1, 24-25 (1983) (§2 of the FAA "create[s] a body of federal substantive law of arbitrability, applicable to any arbitration agreement within the coverage of the Act"); *Southland Corp. v. Keating*, 465 U.S. 1, 12 (1984) ("federal substantive law requiring the parties to honor arbitration agreements"). These substantive provisions of federal law are applicable in state as well as federal court. *Southland Corp. v. Keating*, 465 U.S. 1, 12 (1984); *Volt Information Sciences, Inc. v. Board of Trustees*, 489 U.S. 468, 477 n.6 (1989).
49. *See Volt Information Sciences, Inc. v. Board of Trustees*, 489 U.S. 468, 477 (1989) ("The FAA contains no express pre-emptive provision, nor does it reflect a congressional intent to occupy the entire field of arbitration. But even when Congress has not completely displaced state regulation in an area, state law may nonetheless be preempted to the extent that it actually conflicts with federal law."); *Perry v. Thomas*, 482 U.S. 483 (1987). Some state courts have taken a more nuanced view of the FAA's preemptive effect. While acknowledging that Section 2 of the FAA (governing the enforcement of arbitration agreements) displaces contrary state law, these courts hold that the FAA's confirmation and vacatur provisions (Sections 9-11) do not preempt state law. *See, e.g., Cable Connection, Inc. v. DirectTv, Inc.*, 190 P.3d 586, 599 (Cal. 2008).

so submit."[50] Arbitration agreements come in countless forms. As a model of brevity, if not prudence, European commentators cite a clause that provided "English law — arbitration, if any, London according ICC Rules."[51] At the opposite end of the spectrum are multi-paragraph arbitration clauses, recommended by assiduous practitioners for inclusion in major contracts.[52] Falling between these extremes are model clauses promulgated by the ICC, AAA, LCIA, and other institutions.[53]

As with forum selection clauses, disputes can arise as to the validity or scope of arbitration agreements, typically when one party decides that it no longer wishes to arbitrate and would prefer to litigate in its home courts. These disputes have the potential to lead to delays in the enforcement of arbitration agreements and resolution of the parties' dispute — although U.S. and other national courts have sought to minimize such delays.

Disputes regarding international arbitration agreements ordinarily fall into three basic categories. First, the existence, validity, or legality of the arbitration agreement may be challenged. Second, one party may argue that particular claims are by their nature "non-arbitrable," regardless what the parties have agreed. Third, disputes arise over the interpretation of arbitration clauses — particularly over their scope or the classes of disputes that are subject to arbitration. As discussed below, U.S. (and other) courts are frequently called upon to resolve such disputes.

1. Introduction to Enforceability of International Arbitration Agreements

a. Historical Background.   Historically, U.S. courts would not enforce arbitration agreements (just as they would not enforce forum selection agreements).[54] Many courts held that agreements to arbitrate were revocable at will, because they "ousted" courts of jurisdiction contrary to public policy.[55] Even when such agreements were deemed valid, a party could not obtain specific performance ordering its counter-party to arbitrate. Joseph Story made clear the common law hostility to arbitration:

> Now we all know that arbitrators, at the common law, possess no authority whatsoever, even to administer an oath, or to compel the attendance of witnesses. They cannot compel the production of documents and papers and books of account, or insist upon a discovery of facts from the parties under oath. They are not ordinarily well enough acquainted with the

---

50. *United Steelworkers of America v. Warrior & Gulf Navigation Co.*, 363 U.S. 574, 582 (1960). *See First Options of Chicago, Inc. v. Kaplan*, 514 U.S. 938, 944 (1995); *AT&T Technologies, Inc. v. Communications Workers of America*, 475 U.S. 643, 648-649 (1986).

51. *Arab African Energy Corp. Ltd. v. Olieprodukten Nederland BV* [1983] 2 Lloyd's Rep. 419.

52. *See*, for example, the clauses recommended in Ulmer, *Drafting the International Arbitration Clause*, 20 Int'l Law. 1335 (1986).

53. G. Born, *International Commercial Arbitration* 172-180 (2009). For example, model ICC and AAA clauses provide:

> Any disputes arising out of or in connection with the present contract shall be finally settled under the Rules of Arbitration of the International Chamber of Commerce by one or more arbitrators appointed in accordance with the said Rules. Any controversy or claim arising out of or relating to this contract shall be determined by arbitration in accordance with the International Arbitration Rules of the American Arbitration Association.

54. Jones, *Historical Development of Commercial Arbitration in the United States*, 21 Minn. L. Rev. 240 (1927); F. Kellor, *American Arbitration: Its History, Functions and Achievements* (1948); G. Born, *International Commercial Arbitration* 39-47, 133-134 (2009). *See supra* p. 465 for a discussion of the parallel developments with regard to the unenforceability of forum selection agreements.

55. *Home Ins. Co. v. Morse*, 87 U.S. 445, 457-458 (1874) (agreement to arbitrate future disputes illegal and void); *Dickson Mfg. Co. v. American Locomotive Co.*, 119 F. Supp. 488 (M.D. Pa. 1902); G. Born, *International Commercial Arbitration* 39-47 (2009).

principles of law or equity, to administer either effectually, in complicated cases; and hence it has often been said, that the judgment of arbitrators is but *rusticum judicium.* Ought then a court of equity to compel a resort to such a tribunal, by which, however honest and intelligent, it can in no case be clear that the real legal or equitable rights of the parties can be fully ascertained or perfectly protected? . . . [An arbitration agreement is not specifically enforceable because it] is essentially, in its very nature and character, an agreement which must rest in the good faith and honor of the parties, and like an agreement to paint a picture, to carve a statue, or to write a book . . . must be left to the conscience of the parties, or to such remedy in damages for the breach thereof, as the law has provided.[56]

Throughout the nineteenth century, Story's attitude toward specific performance of arbitration agreements generally prevailed in U.S. courts.[57] At the same time, damages were seldom an effective means of enforcement, since proof of injury resulting from a refusal to arbitrate was difficult. Moreover, U.S. courts also refused to stay judicial proceedings where a valid arbitration agreement covered the parties' dispute. As a consequence, the utility of commercial arbitration in the United States was limited until the early decades of the twentieth century.[58]

b. Overview of Enforceability of International Arbitration Agreements Under the FAA.

During the early twentieth century, international businesses and national governments began to seek mechanisms for resolving international disputes more reliably and efficiently. These efforts culminated in two early treaties — the Geneva Protocol of 1923 and the Geneva Convention of 1927 — whose objectives were to require the enforcement of foreign arbitration agreements and arbitral awards. The Geneva treaties were ratified by a dozen major trading nations (but not the United States).[59]

In 1925, prompted by the same concerns about judicial efficiency in resolving business disputes, Congress enacted the FAA. The Act's principal objective purpose was to make interstate and international arbitration agreements (and awards) enforceable.[60] At the heart of the FAA is §2's provision that a written arbitration provision in a contract shall be "valid, irrevocable, and enforceable," subject only to a savings clause permitting non-enforcement on "such grounds as exist at law or in equity for the revocation of any contract."[61] The section's purpose was to "revers[e] centuries of judicial hostility to arbitration agreements . . . by plac[ing] arbitration agreements 'upon the same footing as other contracts.' "[62]

As a result of the FAA, arbitration agreements are a significant exception to the general rule that state law governs the interpretation and enforcement of contracts.[63] The

---

56. *Tobey v. County of Bristol,* 23 F. Cas. 1313, 1321-1323 (C.C.D. Mass. 1845).

57. *See Kulukundis Shipping Co. v. Amtorg Trading Corp.,* 126 F.2d 978 (2d Cir. 1942), for a thorough review of the treatment of arbitration agreements at common law. *See also Red Cross Line v. Atlantic Fruit Co.,* 264 U.S. 109 (1924); *Rowe v. Williams,* 97 Mass. 163 (1887).

58. *See* H.R. Rep. 96, 68th Cong., 1st Sess. 1 (1924); Sayre, *Development of Commercial Arbitration Law,* 37 Yale L.J. 595 (1927); G. Born, *International Commercial Arbitration* 133-134 (2009).

59. Geneva Protocol on Arbitration Clauses of 1923, 27 League of Nations Treaty Series 158 (1924); Convention for the Execution of Foreign Arbitral Awards, signed at Geneva, Switzerland, September 26, 1927, 92 League of Nations Treaty Series 302 (1929-1930); A. van den Berg, *The New York Convention of 1958* 6-7, 113-118 (1981); G. Born, *International Commercial Arbitration* 58-63 (2009).

60. 43 Stat. 883 (1925), *codified* 61 Stat. 669 (1947); G. Born, *International Commercial Arbitration* 133-136 (2009).

61. 9 U.S.C. §2.

62. *Shearson/American Express, Inc. v. McMahon,* 482 U.S. 220, 226 (1987) (quoting *Scherk v. Alberto-Culver Co.,* 417 U.S. 506, 510-511 (1974)).

63. In the United States, most contracts are interpreted according to, and are enforceable under, the laws of the several States. *See supra* pp. 10-11; *United States v. Little Lake Misere Land Co.,* 412 U.S. 580 (1973); *Clearfield Trust Co. v. United States,* 318 U.S. 363 (1943).

Supreme Court has repeatedly held that §2 creates *substantive federal* law. That federal law is binding in both federal and state courts, and it preempts inconsistent state law.[64] Section 2 requires, as a matter of federal law, "courts to enforce privately negotiated agreements to arbitrate, like other contracts, in accordance with their terms."[65] Thus:

> Section 2 is a congressional declaration of a liberal federal policy favoring arbitration agreements, notwithstanding any state substantive or procedural policies to the contrary. The effect of the section is to create a *body of federal substantive law of arbitrability,* applicable to any arbitration agreement within the coverage of the Act.[66]

Although it is clear that §2 establishes a basic federal rule that arbitration agreements are valid and enforceable, there has been debate over the precise role that federal law plays under §2's "savings clause." A few older decisions held that federal law governs *all* issues of formation, validity, and interpretation of arbitration agreements (including domestic arbitration agreements).[67] Most other lower courts — and recent Supreme Court precedents — hold that the savings clause preserves otherwise applicable state contract law dealing with issues of formation and validity of domestic arbitration agreements, subject however to a federal preemption of state laws that single out domestic arbitration agreements for special disfavor.[68] With regard to arbitration agreements governed by the New York Convention, lower courts have held that the validity and enforceability of such agreements are subject to uniform international standards established by the Convention.[69]

Notwithstanding §2's basic federal rule of validity, arbitration agreements will be invalid in some circumstances. Relying on §2's "savings clause," U.S. courts have applied generally applicable contract defenses to refuse to enforce arbitration agreements. These grounds include lack of consent, incapacity, fraud, illegality, unconscionability, and waiver.[70] In domestic cases, these defenses have been held by U.S. courts to be governed by generally applicable state contract law;[71] in cases involving agreements governed by the New York Convention, lower courts have typically applied uniform standards of validity derived from the Convention.[72]

---

64. *Southland Corp. v. Keating,* 465 U.S. 1, 11, 15-16 n.9 (1984); *Mitsubishi Motors Corp. v. Soler Chrysler-Plymouth Inc.,* 473 U.S. 614 (1985); *Moses H. Cone Memorial Hospital v. Mercury Construction Corp.,* 460 U.S. 1, 24 (1983); *infra* pp. 1177-1178.

65. *Prima Paint Corp. v. Flood & Conklin Manufacturing Co.,* 388 U.S. 395, 404 n.12 (1967) (Congress intended to "make arbitration agreements as enforceable as other contracts, but not more so.").

66. *Moses H. Cone Memorial Hospital v. Mercury Construction Corp.,* 460 U.S. 1, 24 (1983) (emphasis added).

67. *See Cohen v. Wedbush, Noble, Cooke, Inc.,* 841 F.2d 282, 285 (9th Cir. 1988) ("the availability and validity of defenses against arbitration are therefore to be governed by application of federal standards"); *Genesco, Inc. v. T. Kakiuchi & Co.,* 815 F.2d 840, 845 (2d Cir. 1987); *Johnson Controls, Inc. v. City of Cedar Rapids,* 713 F.2d 370, 376 (8th Cir. 1983) ("federal substantive law preempts state law governing the enforceability of arbitration agreements in interstate contracts").

68. *See infra* pp. 1180-1183; *AT&T Mobility LLC v. Concepcion,* 131 S. Ct. 1740 (2011); *Perry v. Thomas,* 482 U.S. 483 (1987); *Progressive Casualty Ins. Co. v. CA Reaseguvadora Nacional de Venezuela,* 991 F.2d 42 (2d Cir. 1993).

69. *See Doctor's Assocs., Inc. v. Casarotto,* 517 U.S. 681, 686-687 (1996); *Southland Corp. v. Keating,* 465 U.S. 1, 16 (1984); *Jenkins v. First Am. Cash Advance of Ga., LLC,* 400 F.3d 868, 875 (11th Cir. 2005); *Stone v. Doerge,* 328 F.3d 343, 345 (7th Cir. 2003); *Great Earth Cos., Inc. v. Simons,* 288 F.3d 878, 889 (6th Cir. 2002); *Circuit City Stores, Inc. v. Adams,* 279 F.3d 889, 892 (9th Cir. 2002); *Chelsea Square Textiles, Inc. v. Bombay Dyeing & Mfg. Co.,* 189 F.3d 289, 295-296 (2d Cir. 1999); *Harris v. Green Tree Fin. Corp.,* 183 F.3d 173, 179 (3d Cir. 1999); *Gibson v. Neighborhood Health Clinics, Inc.,* 121 F.3d 1126, 1130 (7th Cir. 1997).

70. *See infra* pp. 1180-1181; G. Born, *International Commercial Arbitration* 563-765 (2009).

71. *See infra* pp. 1177-1180.

72. *McDermott Int'l Inc. v. Lloyds Underwriters of London,* 944 F.2d 1199 (5th Cir. 1991); G. Born, *International Commercial Arbitration* 485-496 (2009).

c. Separability of the Arbitration Agreement.[73] Central to analysis of the enforceability of international arbitration agreements is the so-called "separability" doctrine, which provides that an arbitration clause is presumptively separable from the parties' underlying contract.[74] The doctrine plays a vital role in enforcing arbitration agreements in the United States (and elsewhere). It is analogous to the related, but less developed, principle that choice of court clauses are separable from the parties' underlying contract.[75]

The separability doctrine provides that an arbitration agreement, even though included in an underlying contract, is an autonomous agreement. There is "a distinction between the *entire contract* between the parties on the one hand and the *arbitration clause* of the contract on the other."[76] Or, as the Supreme Court said in *Prima Paint*, "*except where the parties otherwise intend* . . . arbitration clauses as a matter of federal law are 'separable' from the contracts in which they are embedded."[77] More recently, the Court reaffirmed the separability doctrine in *Buckeye Check Cashing Inc. v. Cardegna*, holding that: "as a matter of substantive federal arbitration law, an arbitration provision is severable from the remainder of the contract."[78]

The separability doctrine has highly important consequences for the arbitral process: "Acceptance of [the] autonomy of the international arbitration clause is a conceptual cornerstone of international arbitration."[79] Among other things, the separability doctrine provides a basis for the survival of arbitration clauses notwithstanding the expiration, termination, or invalidity of the parties' underlying contract.[80] Additionally, as discussed below, the Supreme Court has relied on the separability doctrine to declare that, "unless [a] challenge is to the arbitration clause itself, the issue of the contract's validity is considered by the arbitrator in the first instance."[81]

d. Enforceability of International Arbitration Agreements in U.S. Courts Under the New York Convention. A primary objective of the New York Convention was to render international arbitration agreements enforceable.[82] The Convention contains a number of jurisdictional requirements, three of which warrant mention.[83] First, the Convention is applicable in U.S. courts only to differences arising out of "commercial" relationships. Second, the Convention is applicable in U.S. courts only on the basis of reciprocity (*i.e.*, vis-à-vis other nations that also have ratified the Convention). Third, the parties' agreement must provide for arbitration of "differences which have arisen or which may arise . . . in respect of a defined legal relationship, whether contractual or not."[84]

If these jurisdictional requirements are satisfied, then Article II of the Convention imposes a general obligation on Contracting States to "recognize" valid arbitration

---

73. For commentary on the separability doctrine, *see* G. Born, *International Commercial Arbitration* 311-408 (2009); A. Redfern & M. Hunter, *Law and Practice of International Commercial Arbitration* 154-156 (3d ed. 1999); Nussbaum, *The Separability Doctrine in American and Foreign Arbitration*, 17 N.Y.U. L.Q. Rev. 609 (1940); S. Schwebel, *The Severability of the Arbitration Agreement*, in *International Arbitration: Three Salient Problems* 1 (1987).

74. *See* G. Born, *International Commercial Arbitration* 410-411 (2009); E. Gaillard *et al.*, *Fouchard Gaillard Goldman on International Commercial Arbitration* 198-199 (1999).

75. *See supra* p. 492.

76. *Robert Lawrence Co. v. Devonshire Fabrics, Inc.*, 271 F.2d 402, 409 (2d Cir. 1959) (emphasis added).

77. *Prima Paint Corp. v. Flood & Conklin Mfg. Co.*, 388 U.S. 395, 402 (1967) (emphasis in original).

78. *Buckeye Check Cashing, Inc. v. Cardegna*, 546 U.S. 440, 445 (2006).

79. *See* W. Craig, W. Park & J. Paulsson, *International Chamber of Commerce Arbitration* §5.04 (3d ed. 2000).

80. *See infra* pp. 1177-1178.

81. *Buckeye Check Cashing Inc. v. Cardegna*, 546 U.S. 440, 445-46 (2009).

82. *See* G. Born, *International Commercial Arbitration* 96, 203-205 (2009).

83. These jurisdictional requirements are discussed in greater detail elsewhere. *See* G. Born, *International Commercial Arbitration* 208-211, 211-305 (2009).

84. New York Convention, Art. II(1).

agreements,[85] provided that they satisfy the Convention's requirement of written form,[86] and "refer the parties to arbitration."[87] Article II sets forth the Convention's basic rules of validity and enforceability, as well as limited exceptions to that rule:

> 1. Each Contracting State shall recognize an agreement in writing under which the parties undertake to submit to arbitration all or any differences which have arisen or which may arise between them in respect of a defined relationship, whether contractual or not, concerning a subject matter capable of settlement by arbitration. . . .
> 3. The court of a Contracting State, when seized of an action in a matter in respect of which the parties have made an agreement within the meaning of this article, shall, at the request of one of the parties, refer the parties to arbitration, unless it finds that the said agreement is null and void, inoperative or incapable of being performed.

U.S. courts have interpreted Article II in an avowedly "pro-enforcement" fashion:

> [t]he goal of the Convention, and the principal purpose underlying American adoption and implementation of it, was to encourage the recognition and enforcement of commercial arbitration agreements in international contracts and to unify the standards by which agreements to arbitrate are observed. . . .[88]

U.S. courts have frequently said that the judicial role in determining whether to enforce an arbitration agreement under the Convention is very limited. Assuming that jurisdiction, venue, and similar requirements are satisfied, U.S. courts have emphasized that Article II(3) requires that national courts "shall" refer parties to arbitration, save where the arbitration agreement is "null and void, inoperative or incapable of being performed."[89] As noted above, U.S. courts have generally held that the validity and legality of arbitration agreements subject to the Convention is governed by federal law, derived from the Convention's uniform rules.[90]

The FAA provides mechanisms to implement the substantive provisions of §2 of the FAA and Article II of the Convention. Sections 3 and 4 of the FAA provide the principal mechanism for enforcing the general rule that arbitration agreements are valid: §3 requires "any court of the United States" to stay proceedings before it, if they involve issues that are "referable to arbitration," while §4 requires "United States district court[s]" to issue orders compelling arbitration of such issues.[91] Similarly, §206 of the FAA grants federal courts the power to compel arbitration in accordance with agreements subject to the Convention,[92] while §208 incorporates §3's stay provision.[93]

e. Who Decides Challenges to Arbitral Jurisdiction: Competence-Competence and *First Options v. Kaplan.*

Closely related to the separability doctrine is the allocation of authority between arbitrators and national courts to resolve disputes over the interpretation and enforceability of the parties' arbitration agreement. The Supreme Court has

---

85. G. Born, *International Commercial Arbitration* 203-205, 567-569, 709-712 (2009).
86. New York Convention, Art. II(1), II(2); G. Born, *International Commercial Arbitration* 580-624 (2009).
87. New York Convention, Art. II(3).
88. *Scherk v. Alberto-Culver Co.*, 417 U.S. 506, 517 n.10 (1974). *See also Mitsubishi Motors Corp. v. Soler Chrysler-Plymouth Inc.*, 473 U.S. 614, 626-627 (1985); *Rhone Mediterranee etc. v. Achille Lauro*, 712 F.2d 50 (3d Cir. 1983) ("Signatory nations have effectively declared a joint policy that presumes the enforceability of agreements to arbitrate").
89. *See McCreary Tire & Rubber Co. v. CEAT*, 501 F.2d 1032 (3d Cir. 1974); *Cooper v. Ateliers de la Motobecane, SA*, 442 N.E.2d 1239 (N.Y. 1982).
90. *See supra* pp. 1162-1163; G. Born, *International Commercial Arbitration* 485-496 (2009).
91. 9 U.S.C. §§3-4.
92. 9 U.S.C. §206.
93. 9 U.S.C. §208.

referred to this as the "Who decides?" question (as in, "Who decides challenges to an arbitral tribunal's jurisdiction?").[94] Many institutional arbitration rules, and some national laws, expressly provide that arbitral tribunals have jurisdiction to determine their own jurisdiction.[95] This principle — permitting arbitral tribunals to consider and decide challenges to their own jurisdiction — is frequently referred to as the doctrine of "competence-competence" or "Kompetenz-Kompetenz."[96]

The competence-competence doctrine can have significant effects on the resolution of disputes over the interpretation and enforcement of arbitration clauses. At a minimum, the doctrine means that arbitrators *can* determine their own jurisdiction: if one party asserts that the arbitrators lack jurisdiction, the arbitrators may generally consider the challenge themselves (subject to eventual judicial review), and do not need to halt the arbitral proceedings pending a judicial decision. More broadly, the competence-competence doctrine could *require* parties to initially submit their jurisdictional challenges to the tribunal, subject to eventual *de novo* judicial review, rather than seeking an immediate judicial determination. Most broadly, the doctrine might vest arbitrators with sole jurisdiction to determine their own jurisdiction, subject only to minimal subsequent judicial review (of the same nature applicable to the merits of the parties' dispute) or to no review at all.

The leading U.S. decision is *First Options of Chicago, Inc. v. Kaplan*, where the Supreme Court considered the question: "who — court or arbitrator — has the primary authority to decide whether a party has agreed to arbitrate."[97] In answering, the Court declared:

> Just as the arbitrability of the merits of a dispute depends upon whether the parties agreed to arbitrate that dispute, . . . so the question "who has the primary power to decide arbitrability" turns upon what the parties agreed about that matter. Did the parties agree to submit the arbitrability question itself to arbitration?[98]

Related to this holding, the *First Options* Court also set forth two presumptions for determining whether an agreement to arbitrate what it termed "arbitrability questions" exists: (a) the existence of an agreement to arbitrate disputes about an arbitral tribunal's jurisdiction requires "clear and unmistakable" evidence; and (b) the scope of an existent arbitration agreement should be interpreted broadly, in favor of arbitrability. In the Court's words:

> Courts should not assume that the parties agreed to arbitrate arbitrability unless there is "clea[r] and unmistakabl[e]" evidence that they did so. In this manner the law treats silence or ambiguity about the question "***who*** (primarily) should decide arbitrability" differently from the way it treats silence or ambiguity about the question "***whether*** a particular merits-related dispute is arbitrable because it is within the scope of a valid arbitration agreement" — for in respect to this latter question the law reverses the presumption.[99]

94. *First Options of Chicago, Inc. v. Kaplan*, 514 U.S. 938, 942 (1995). *See also Howsam v. Reynolds*, 537 U.S. 79, 82 (2002).

95. G. Born, *International Commercial Arbitration* 855-871 (2009).

96. G. Born, *International Commercial Arbitration* 853-855, 877-985 (2009).

97. 514 U.S. 938, 942 (1995). More recently, the Supreme Court expanded the *First Options* allocation principle. In *Rent-A-Center v. Jackson*, 130 S. Ct. 2772 (2010), the Court held (in the context of a domestic arbitration) that where the parties have by agreement delegated to the arbitrator the power to rule on challenges to the arbitration agreement, the only residual role for the Court is to rule on challenges specifically directed at the delegation agreement.

98. 514 U.S. at 943.

99. *First Options of Chicago v. Kaplan*, 514 U.S. at 944-945. The Court reasoned that "the latter question arises when the parties have a contract that provides for arbitration of some issues. And, given the law's permissive policies in respect to arbitration, one can understand why the law would insist upon clarity before concluding that the parties did *not* want to arbitrate a related matter." It continued: "On the other hand, the former question — the 'who (primarily) should decide arbitrability question' — is rather arcane. A party often might not focus upon

Put differently, *First Options* held that parties would be presumed not to have agreed to arbitrate jurisdictional disputes, and that clear evidence would be required to overcome this presumption.[100] The Court went on to review the parties' agreements, and subsequent conduct, concluding that the parties had not agreed to submit jurisdictional issues to the arbitral tribunal.[101]

Lower courts have applied *First Options'* analysis in a variety of different settings.[102] Although the decision arose in a domestic context, the Court's decision concerning an arbitral tribunal's jurisdiction to decide issues concerning its own jurisdiction applies equally in international cases.[103]

2. Selected Materials on Enforcement of International Arbitration Agreements in U.S. Courts

The materials excerpted below illustrate the enforcement of international arbitration agreements in U.S. courts. The FAA sets forth the statutory framework for the enforcement of arbitration clauses — domestic as well as international — in U.S. courts, while the UNCITRAL Model Law sets forth a commonly used international alternative. *Rhone Mediterranee* illustrates the approach of U.S. courts to Articles II(1) and II(3) of the New York Convention, while *Republic of Nicaragua v. Standard Fruit Co.* provides an example — albeit a controversial one — of a U.S. court's handling of a challenge to the existence of an arbitration agreement and the roles of the courts and arbitrators. Finally, compare the approach of the Swiss court to similar questions in *Nokia Maillefer SA v. Mazzer* and consider how a U.S. court would have addressed the issue presented there.

FEDERAL ARBITRATION ACT
9 U.S.C. §§1-16, 201-210, §§301-307 [excerpted in Appendix S]

UNCITRAL MODEL LAW
[excerpted in Appendices T and U]

RHONE MEDITERRANEE COMPAGNIA FRANCESE DI ASSICURAZIONI E RIASSICURAZIONI v. ACHILLE LAURO
712 F.2d 50 (3d Cir. 1983)

GIBBONS, CIRCUIT JUDGE. . . . The action results from a fire loss which occurred when the vessel Angelina Lauro burned at the dock of the East Indian Co. Ltd. in Charlotte Amalie,

---

that question or upon the significance of having arbitrators decide that scope of their own powers. And, given the principle that a party can be forced to arbitrate only those issues it specifically has agreed to submit to arbitration, one can understand why courts might hesitate to interpret silence or ambiguity on the 'who should decide arbitrability' point as giving the arbitrators that power, for doing so might too often force unwilling parties to arbitrate a matter they reasonably would have thought a judge, not an arbitrator, would decide."

100. If there is a challenge to the existence or validity of the arbitration clause itself, or if a party denies being party to the relevant arbitration agreement, then *First Options* would arguably require judicial determination whether any valid arbitration agreement exists, as a necessary issue preliminary to deciding whether an agreement to arbitrate jurisdictional issues exists. *See Coady v. Ashcraft & Gerel*, 223 F.3d 1, 8 (1st Cir. 2000); *Menorah Ins. Co. v. INX Reinsurance Corp.*, 72 F.3d 218, 222 (1st Cir. 1995).

101. 514 U.S. at 947.

102. *See Coady*, 223 F.3d at 8 (domestic dispute between an attorney and his former employer); *Sarhank Group v. Oracle Corp.*, 404 F.3d 657, 661 (2d Cir. 2005) (international contract dispute between an Egyptian and Delaware corporation).

103. *Sarhank*, 404 F.3d at 661; *Menorah*, 72 F.3d at 222.

St. Thomas. At the time of the fire the vessel was under time charter to Costa Armatori SpA ("Costa"), an Italian Corporation. [Rhone Mediterranee Compagnia Francese di Assicurazioni e Riassicurazioni ("Rhone")] insured Costa, and reimbursed it for property and fuel losses totalling over one million dollars. Rhone, as subrogee of Costa, sued the owner of the vessel, Achille Lauro ("Lauro") . . . alleging breach of the Lauro-Costa time charter, unseaworthiness, and negligence of the crew. The district court granted defendants' motion for a stay of the action pending arbitration, and Rhone appeals.

As subrogee, Rhone stands in place of its insured, the time charterer Costa. In the time charter contract there is a clause:

> 23. Arbitration. Any dispute arising under the Charter to be referred to arbitration in London (or such other place as may be agreed according to box 24) one arbitrator to be nominated by the Owners and the other by the Charterers, and in case the Arbitrators shall not agree then to the decision of an Umpire to be appointed by them, the award of the Arbitrators or the Umpire to be final and binding upon both parties.
>
> Box 24
>
> Place of arbitration (only to be filled in if place other than London agreed (cl. 23) NAPOLI. . . .

The [FAA,] 9 U.S.C. §§201-208 (1976), implements the United States' accession on September 1, 1970 to the Convention by providing that it "shall be enforced in United States courts in accordance with this chapter." 9 U.S.C. §201. [Rhone does not dispute that the Convention is applicable.] What Rhone does contend is that under the terms of the Convention the arbitration clause in issue is unenforceable. Rhone's argument proceeds from a somewhat ambiguous provision in Article II(3) of the Convention:

> The court of a Contracting State, when seized of an action in a matter in respect of which the parties have made an agreement within the meaning of this article, shall, at the request of one of the parties, refer the parties to arbitration, unless it finds that the said agreement is null and void, inoperative or incapable of being performed.

Ambiguity occurs from the fact that no reference appears in II(3) to what law determines whether "said agreement . . . is null and void, inoperative or incapable of being performed." Rhone contends that when the arbitration clause refers to a place of arbitration, here Naples, Italy, the law of that place is determinative. It then relies on the affidavit of an expert on Italian law which states that in Italy an arbitration clause calling for an even number of arbitrators is null and void, even if, as in this case there is a provision for their designation of a tie breaker.

The ambiguity in Article II(3) of the Convention with respect to governing law contrasts with Article V, dealing with enforcement of awards. Article V(1)(a) permits refusal of recognition and enforcement of an award if the "agreement is not valid under the law to which the parties have subjected it or, failing any indication thereon, under the law of the country where the award was made." . . . Thus Article V unambiguously refers the forum in which enforcement of an award is sought to the law chosen by the parties, or the law of the place of the award.

Rhone and the defendants suggest different conclusions that should be drawn from the differences between Article II and Article V. Rhone suggests that the choice of law rule of Article V should be read into Article II. The defendants urge that in the absence of a specific reference Article II should be read so as to permit the forum, when asked to refer a dispute to arbitration, to apply its own law respecting validity of the arbitration clause. . . .

[W]e conclude that the meaning of Article II(3) which is most consistent with the overall purposes of the Convention is that an agreement to arbitrate is "null and void" only (1) when it is subject to an internationally recognized defense such as duress, mistake, fraud, or waiver, *see Ledee v. Ceramiche Ragno,* 684 F.2d 184 (1st Cir. 1982), or (2) when it contravenes fundamental policies of the forum state. The "null and void" language must be read narrowly, for the signatory nations have jointly declared a general policy of enforceability of agreements to arbitrate. . . .

Signatory nations have effectively declared a joint policy that presumes the enforceability of agreements to arbitrate. Neither the parochial interests of the forum state, nor those of states having more significant relationships with the dispute, should be permitted to supersede that presumption. The policy of the Convention is best served by an approach which leads to upholding agreements to arbitrate. The rule of one state as to the required number of arbitrators does not implicate the fundamental concerns of either the international system or forum, and hence the agreement is not void.

Rhone urges that this rule may result in a Neapolitan arbitration award which, because of Italy's odd number of arbitrators rule, the Italian courts would not enforce. . . . Rhone's objection does not compel the conclusion that we should read Article II(3) as it suggests. . . . Rhone is not faced with an Italian public policy disfavoring arbitration, but only with an Italian procedural rule of arbitration which may have been overlooked by the drafters of the time charter agreement. Certainly the parties are free to structure the arbitration so as to comply with the Italian procedural rule by having the designated arbitrators select a third member before rather than after impasse. Even if that is not accomplished an award may still result, which can be enforced outside Italy.

Rhone urges that Article V(1)(d) prohibits such enforcement outside Italy, because it refers a non-Italian forum to the law of Italy. We disagree. Section 1 says only that "enforcement of an award may be refused" on the basis of the law of the country where it was made. Where, as here, the law of such a country generally favors enforcement of arbitration awards, and the defect is at best one of a procedural nature, Article V(1) certainly permits another forum to disregard the defect and enforce. That is especially the case when defendants come before the court and, relying on Article II, seek a stay of the action in favor of arbitration. They will hardly be in a position to rely on Italy's odd number of arbitrators rule if Rhone seeks to enforce an award in the District Court of the Virgin Islands.[104]

The forum law implicitly referenced by Article II(3) is the law of the United States, not the local law of the Virgin Islands or of a state. That law favors enforcement of arbitration clauses. *Scherk v. Alberto-Culver Co.,* 417 U.S. 506 (1974); *Becker Autoradio USA Inc. v. Becker Autoradiowerk GmbH,* 585 F.2d 39 (3d Cir. 1978). . . . Since no federal law imposes an odd number of arbitrators rule — the only defect relied upon by Rhone — the district court did not err in staying the suit for breach of the time charter agreement pending arbitration. . . .

REPUBLIC OF NICARAGUA v. STANDARD FRUIT CO.
937 F.2d 469 (9th Cir. 1991)

FERGUSON, JUDGE. The Republic of Nicaragua appeals from two orders of the district court which denied its motion to compel international arbitration . . . (Count I) and

---

104. Had Rhone so requested it would have been proper for the district court to condition its stay order on the defendants' agreement to reform the arbitration clause so as to satisfy Italy's procedural requirement. Since no such request was made we do not consider whether, had it been made, we would remand for such a modification.

granted summary judgment to Standard Fruit Company ("SFC") and its two parent companies, Standard Fruit and Steamship Company ("Steamship") and Castle & Cooke, Inc. ("C&C"),[105] on Nicaragua's breach of contract claim (Count II). Nicaragua . . . argues [on appeal] that the questions of whether a document entitled "Memorandum of Intent" was a valid contract and whether Standard Fruit Company was bound by that contract should have been referred to arbitration in the first instance, not decided by the district court. . . . We hold that although it was the court's responsibility to determine the threshold question of arbitrability, the district court improperly looked to the validity of the contract as a whole and erroneously determined that the parties had not agreed to arbitrate this dispute. Instead, it should have considered only the validity and scope of the arbitration clause itself. In addition, the district court ignored strong evidence in the record that both parties intended to be bound by the arbitration clause. As all doubts over the scope of an arbitration clause must be resolved in favor of arbitration, and in light of the strong federal policy favoring arbitration in international commercial disputes, Nicaragua's motion to compel arbitration should have been granted. Whether the Memorandum was binding, whether it covered banana purchases, and whether Standard Fruit Company was bound by it are all questions properly left to the arbitrators. . . .

Since 1970, defendant Standard Fruit Company has been involved in the production and purchase of bananas in western Nicaragua. . . . In 1979, the Sandinistas overthrew the Somoza government in Nicaragua, forming a new "Government of National Reconstruction," led by a three-person junta. . . . [After threats and unsuccessful negotiations,] Nicaragua promulgated "Decree No. 608," which declared that the banana industry was to become a state monopoly, that all plantation leases would be transferred to a new government agency, and that all preexisting lease, partnership, and fruit purchase contracts were nullified. SFC interpreted this decree as an expropriation of its business, and immediately ceased all operations in Nicaragua. As a result, Nicaragua requested a "summit meeting" at which SFC and its two parent companies, Steamship and C&C, could sort out their differences with the Sandinistas and come back to the country. . . .

The meeting commenced in San Francisco on Friday, January 9, 1981, and continued for three days of intense negotiations, led by C&C Vice-President and General Counsel Robert Moore (principal draftsman of the Memorandum) and Norton Tennille, Nicaragua's legal counsel. On Sunday, January 11, a document entitled "Memorandum of Intent" was executed by two officers of C&C, two officers of Steamship, and two Ministers of Trade and a member of the ruling junta of Nicaragua. . . .

The Memorandum, termed an "agreement in principle," contained an arbitration provision, and envisioned the renegotiation and replacement of four operating contracts between SFC and "the competent Nicaraguan national entity." These were to include a detailed fruit purchase contract, a technical assistance contract, the transfer of SFC's shares in the production societies, and Nicaragua's purchase of SFC's assets in the country. The Memorandum also established the essential elements of the fruit purchase contract [including price and duration]. . . . Additional provisions rescinded the terms of Decree 608 for five years, reinstated SFC's favored tax status, and clarified the financing arrangements for Nicaragua's banana industry.

Within a week after the Memorandum was signed, SFC returned to Nicaragua and resumed its operations there. In addition, it began negotiating with Nicaraguan officials regarding the technical assistance and fruit purchase contracts referred to in the Memorandum, as well as the share transfers and asset buy-outs. Many subsequent drafts of these

105. The three companies are herein referred to collectively as "Standard."

four documents were exchanged, some similar to the Memorandum and some not, although none were ever finalized and executed. . . . Although SFC, Steamship, C&C, and Nicaragua all acted as though the Memorandum was binding for almost two years, the implementing contracts were never finalized, and SFC left Nicaragua for good on October 25, 1982.

The arbitration clause [contained in the Memorandum] states that:

> Any and all disputes arising under the arrangements contemplated hereunder . . . will be referred to mutually agreed mechanisms or procedures of international arbitration, such as the rules of the London Arbitration Association.

Nicaragua . . . introduced a letter written by Robert Moore, principal draftsman of the Memorandum, to explain [this provision]. The letter . . . explained that, during the negotiations themselves, neither side could remember the name of the arbitration body in London, and stated: "What resulted was an agreement for providing for arbitration but without finally fixing the forum or an automatic method of transmitting disputes." Moore suggested "we would be better off agreeing in advance that Paragraph IV was to be read and interpreted to provide for arbitration by [a certain] agency," and concluded "I am sure you will agree that it is best done in the infancy of *the agreement* and at a time that negotiations of the implementing agreements are being worked out." (Emphasis added).[106] Although this letter seems to suggest both that C&C intended the clause to be binding and that the parties intentionally left it vague because they could not remember the name of the London arbitration agency, the district court disregarded this evidence. . . .

Nicaragua contends that the district court erred in denying its motion to compel international arbitration of its breach of contract claim and to stay judicial proceedings pending arbitration. . . . Both parties agree that federal substantive law governs the question of arbitrability. . . . Section 2 [of the FAA] . . . embodies a clear federal policy of requiring arbitration unless the agreement to arbitrate is . . . is revocable "upon such grounds as exist at law or in equity for the revocation of any contract." . . . The standard for demonstrating arbitrability is not a high one. . . . The Supreme Court has emphasized that the Act leaves no place for the exercise of discretion by a district court, but instead mandates that district courts shall direct the parties to proceed to arbitration on issues as to which an arbitration agreement has been signed. *Dean Witter Reynolds Inc. v. Byrd*, 470 U.S. 213, 218 (1985). . . . Therefore, the only issue properly before the district court was whether the parties had entered into a contract . . . committing both sides to arbitrate the issue of the contract's validity. . . .

Prima Paint demands that arbitration clauses be treated as severable from the documents in which they appear unless there is clear intent to the contrary. An arbitration clause may thus be enforced even though the rest of the contract is later held invalid by the arbitrator. . . . [I]n *Prima Paint* the Supreme Court did not rule on whether the contract was valid or enforceable — just that it existed. The Court rejected *Prima Paint*'s argument that it could not be forced into arbitration because its entire contract (including the arbitration clause at issue) was fraudulently induced and therefore void. The Court held that because the fraud did not go to the making of the arbitration clause itself, the clause was severable and enforceable. It therefore ordered the parties to

---

106. Attached to the letter was a very explicit page-long "substitute arbitration clause," providing for arbitration in London pursuant to the Arbitration Act of Great Britain.

proceed to arbitration of all disputed issues, including the question of fraud in the inducement and the entire contract's validity.

In the instant case, the district court made a preliminary "Factual Conclusion" that the Memorandum "was not intended as a binding contract," in direct opposition to the *Prima Paint* rule.[107] . . . [T]his conclusion is . . . the basis for the [district court's] holdings that no agreement to arbitrate existed, and that the present dispute lay outside the scope of the clause. . . . [We repeat] *Prima Paint*'s clear directive that courts disregard surrounding contract language and "consider only issues relating to the making and performance of the agreement to arbitrate." 388 U.S. at 404. The correct analysis is set forth in *Sauer-Getriebe KG v. White Hydraulics, Inc.*, 715 F.2d 348, 350 (7th Cir. 1983):

> White argues that if there is no contract to buy and sell motors there is no agreement to arbitrate. The conclusion does not follow its premise. The agreement to arbitrate and the agreement to buy and sell motors are separate. Sauer's promise to arbitrate was given in exchange for White's promise to arbitrate and each promise was sufficient consideration for the other. . . .

Thus, in the absence of any evidence that Paragraph IV of the Memorandum was intended as non-severable, we must strictly enforce any agreement to arbitrate, regardless of where it is found. Under *Prima Paint . . . ,* we hold that the district court erred in considering the contract as a whole to determine the threshold question of whether Nicaragua may enforce the arbitration agreement contained in Paragraph IV. . . .

The next question is whether Paragraph IV in fact constitutes an agreement to arbitrate, and whether it encompasses the dispute at hand. The district court stated that the parties had not made any present agreement to submit all disputes under the Memorandum to arbitration, but merely agreed to include such clauses in future contracts. . . . However, because of the presumption of arbitrability established by the Supreme Court, courts must be careful not to overreach and decide the merits of an arbitrable claim. Our role is strictly limited to determining arbitrability and enforcing agreements to arbitrate, leaving the merits of the claim and any defenses to the arbitrator. Here, the district court disregarded "the emphatic federal policy in favor of arbitral dispute resolution [which] applies with special force in the field of international commerce." *Mitsubishi Motors Corp. v. Soler Chrysler-Plymouth, Inc.*, 473 U.S. 614, 631 (1985). . . .

The district court also found that the clause's "lack of specificity" mitigated against its enforcement. However, the clear weight of authority holds that the most minimal indication of the parties' intent to arbitrate must be given full effect, especially in international disputes. *See, e.g., Bauhinia Corp. v. China Nat'l Machinery and Equip. Co.*, 819 F.2d 247 (9th Cir. 1987) (arbitration ordered where contract contained two incomplete and contradictory arbitration clauses). Under this analysis, Paragraph IV here was not too vague to be given effect, especially when considered in light of Robert Moore's letter explaining the ambiguity. . . . Nicaragua's motion to compel arbitration is granted, and the case remanded to determine the appropriate arbitral agency.

---

107. The district court reasoned that an arbitrator can derive his or her power only from a contract, so that when there is a challenge to the existence of the contract itself, the court must first decide whether there is a valid contract between the parties. Although this appears logical, it goes beyond the requirements of the statute and violates the clear directive of *Prima Paint*, 388 U.S. at 404. . . .

NOKIA MAILLEFER SA v. MAZZER

(Vaud Cantonal Court of Appeals 1993)
XXI Y.B. Comm. Arb. 687 (1996)

[On 30 March 1988, Nokia-Maillefer SA ("Nokia"), a Swiss company, sent one Mr. Mazzer, an Italian businessman, a confirmation of an order which he had placed. The confirmation referred to Nokia's enclosed conditions of sale, which contained a forum clause choosing Swiss courts. On 31 March 1988, Leasindustria, an Italian company, replied to Nokia by sending a purchase order to which its conditions of purchase were annexed. Article 10 of the conditions included a forum selection clause providing for the jurisdiction of the Milan courts. Two months later, Nokia returned the purchase order, replacing the word "Milan" in Article 10 with "International Chamber of Commerce, Paris." By a telex to Leasindustria, Mr. Mazzer accepted the modification. When a dispute arose, the Italian buyer commenced court proceedings before a Swiss court in Canton Vaud, where Nokia was headquartered. Nokia requested the Court to refer the dispute to arbitration.]

The dispute is whether Article 10 of the purchase order, as modified, is a valid arbitration clause. The autonomy of the arbitration clause as to the contract in which it is contained or to which it refers is unanimously recognized. Hence, [with] the exception of cases where a ground for nullity of the contract also affects the clause, the validity of the arbitration clause must be examined separately. An arbitration clause can only be validly concluded where there is a common intention of the parties to refer a possible dispute to arbitration. The existence of such an agreement must be ascertained according to the general principles of the Code of Obligations, in particular Art. 2.[108] Considering the important consequences of an arbitration agreement, the court shall beware of finding too easily that such an agreement has been concluded.

In the present case, . . . [the parties' treatment of] the question of the authority having jurisdiction to decide on a possible dispute has not been provided for straightaway in a clear and indisputable manner. In this evolutionary and uncertain context, there is no common intent on arbitration unless the "final" arbitration clause, that is, Article 10 as modified, has a manifest and certain meaning. . . . Considering the clause, it is not possible to ascertain the common intent of the parties, in particular as to the arbitration agreement. Initially, the clause at issue provides under "forum" for the jurisdiction of the (State) courts of Milan. Only the term "Milan" has been replaced by "International Chamber of Commerce, Paris," with no mention of the fact that the jurisdiction of the courts is excluded and replaced by private arbitration. . . . Appellant must bear the consequences of the ambiguity and obscurity of the alleged clause, which it modified with the intention of transforming a *prorogatio fori* into an arbitration clause functioning also as arbitration agreement. In a context in which it should not be held too easily that an agreement has been concluded, we cannot accept an unclear clause as proof of an agreement having an uncertain subject matter. Hence, we must hold that the parties did not conclude a valid arbitration agreement nor an arbitral clause. . . .

---

108. [Article 2 of the Swiss Code of Obligations reads:

When the parties have agreed with regard to all essential points, it is presumed that a reservation of ancillary points is not meant to affect the binding nature of the contract. Where agreement with regard to such ancillary points so reserved is not reached, the judge shall determine them in accordance with the nature of the transaction. The foregoing shall not affect the provisions regarding the form of contracts (Arts. 9-16).]

Notes on Statutory Materials, Rhone, Standard Fruit, *and* Nokia

1. *Historic unenforceability of arbitration agreements.* As *Standard Fruit, Rhone,* and *Nokia* illustrate, parties not infrequently decide after disputes have arisen that they no longer wish to abide by their arbitration agreements. Why might parties do so?

Recall that arbitration agreements were unenforceable at common law in the United States. Compare this to the unenforceability of forum selection clauses at common law. *See supra* p. 465. Were the historic approaches wise? What were the reasons for these historic approaches? Compare the different ways in which the common law approach to each type of agreement was abandoned.

2. *Contemporary international arbitration legislation.* Review the FAA (particularly the second chapter thereof) and the UNCITRAL Model Law. Which statute is preferable? Why? How much guidance does each statute provide with regard to questions concerning the enforcement of international arbitration agreements and awards? Other aspects of the arbitral process?

3. *Scope of FAA and UNCITRAL Model Law.* What arbitration agreements and awards are governed by the FAA and by the Model Law? With respect to international arbitration agreements, compare §§1, 2, and 202 and Articles 1 and 8 of the UNCITRAL Model Law. With regard to international arbitral awards, compare §§1, 9-11, 202, and 207 and Articles 1 and 34-36 of the UNCITRAL Model Law. *See also* G. Born, *International Commercial Arbitration* 208-211, 255-310 (2009); E. Gaillard *et al., Fouchard Gaillard Goldman on International Arbitration* 82-101, 1028-1029 (1999). Note that under both the FAA and the UNCITRAL Model Law, different legal regimes apply to "domestic" and to "international" arbitration agreements and arbitral awards. Is that sensible? Is it not an inevitable consequence of the New York Convention and similar international treaties?

4. *The separability presumption*—**Prima Paint.** As discussed above, U.S. (and foreign) courts have generally held that an arbitration agreement is "separable" from the underlying contract in which it appears. The leading Supreme Court decision on the subject is *Prima Paint Corp. v. Flood & Conklin Mfg. Co.,* 388 U.S. 395 (1967), relied on in *Standard Fruit.* In *Prima Paint,* the Court considered whether the FAA required arbitration of a claim that a contract, containing an arbitration clause, had been fraudulently induced. The Court held that the fraudulent inducement claim was arbitrable. In particular, the Court relied on §4, which authorizes the issuance of orders compelling arbitration where "the making of *the agreement for arbitration* . . . is not in issue":

> Under §4, with respect to a matter within the jurisdiction of the federal courts save for the existence of an arbitration clause, the federal court is instructed to order arbitration to proceed once it is satisfied that "the making of the agreement for arbitration or the failure to comply [with the arbitration agreement] is not in issue." Accordingly, *if the claim is fraud in the inducement of the arbitration clause itself—an issue which goes to the "making" of the agreement to arbitrate—the federal court may proceed to adjudicate it.* But the statutory language *does not permit the federal court to consider claims of fraud in the inducement of the contract generally.*

Concluding that "no claim has been advanced by [plaintiff] that [defendant] fraudulently induced it to enter into the agreement to arbitrate," the Court affirmed a stay of federal court proceedings pending arbitration.

Is the result in *Prima Paint* sensible? If a party challenges the validity of the parties' underlying contract—for example, on grounds of fraud—why shouldn't that challenge necessarily include a challenge to the arbitration clause contained within the contract? What if a party challenges the validity of the parties' underlying contract on the grounds that it never consented to that document (for example, by never executing the agreement or by an unauthorized agent executing the agreement)? *See Buckeye Check Cashing Inc. v. Cardegna*, 546 U.S. 440, 445-446 (2006).

Compare the approach to the separability doctrine in *Prima Paint* with that which would apply under the UNCITRAL Model Law (particularly Article 16). Are there any apparent differences? Compare the approach in *Nokia*.

5. *Separability presumption and law applicable to validity of international arbitration agreement.* One consequence of the separability presumption is that the separable arbitration agreement may be governed by a different law than the underlying contract. *See* G. Born, *International Commercial Arbitration* 354-355, 411-424 (2009). Consider the circumstances in which this might occur. Suppose that the parties' underlying contract involves conduct occurring solely in the United States and India, but that the arbitral seat is Singapore. What laws might govern the underlying contract? The arbitration agreement?

6. *Federal substantive law applies to validity of international arbitration agreements in U.S. courts.* What law will U.S. courts apply to determine the validity of an arbitration agreement? As discussed above, §2 of the FAA provides that arbitration agreements are valid and enforceable, "save upon such grounds as exist at law or in equity for the revocation of any contract." Section 2's rule of enforceability is incorporated into the second chapter of the FAA by §208. It is paralleled by Article II of the New York Convention, which requires recognition of arbitration agreements unless they are "null and void, inoperative or incapable of being performed." As *Standard Fruit* and *Rhone* illustrate, federal law therefore plays a significant role in enforcing international arbitration agreements in U.S. courts.

Compare this approach to the law governing the enforceability of forum clauses. Recall that forum clauses have generally been held to be governed by federal procedural law in federal courts and by state law in state courts. *See supra* pp. 528-544. Which allocation of state and federal competence is more desirable — that governing international forum agreements or that governing international arbitration clauses?

7. *Presumptive validity and enforceability of contemporary international arbitration agreements.* Compare the enforceability of international arbitration agreements under the New York Convention (Article II), the FAA (§2), and the Model Law (Article 8) to that of international forum selection clauses under existing U.S. common law standards. *See supra* pp. 528-544. Which type of agreement is more readily and predictably enforceable? Is there any exception to the enforceability of arbitration clauses that are "unreasonable" or that provide for "inconvenient" situs? Should there be?

8. *"Pro-enforcement" bias of Article II of the New York Convention.* *Rhone* interprets Article II of the Convention as establishing a strong presumption favoring the enforceability of arbitration agreements. Other lower U.S. courts have endorsed the same pro-enforcement bias. *E.g., Riley v. Kingsley Underwriting Agencies, Ltd.*, 969 F.2d 953, 960 (10th Cir. 1992) (" 'null and void' exception . . . is to be narrowly construed"); *I.T.A.D. Associates, Inc. v. Podar Brothers*, 636 F.2d 75 (4th Cir. 1981); *Technetronics, Inc. v. Leybold-Geaeus GmbH*, 1993 U.S. Dist. LEXIS 7683 (E.D. Pa. 1993). There is also precedent reasoning that "the liberal federal arbitration policy 'applies with special force in the field of international commerce.' " *David L. Threlkeld & Co. v. Metallgesellschaft Ltd.*, 923 F.2d 245, 248 (2d Cir. 1991) (quoting *Mitsubishi Motors*, 473 U.S. at 631).

Why should federal law encourage enforcement of international arbitration agreements? Enforcing an arbitration agreement usually means depriving parties of basic rights such as a jury trial, broad discovery, appellate review, and other procedural safeguards. Is it wise to affirmatively encourage the enforcement of such agreements? Is this a different approach from that taken toward forum clauses in *Bremen*?

9. *Content of Article II(3).* What is the content of substantive federal law governing the validity of international arbitration agreements under Article II(3) of the Convention?

(a) Article II(3)'s "null and void" exception. Article II(3) contains an exception, similar to §2's savings clause, for arbitration agreements which are "null and void, inoperative or incapable of being performed." Like §2 of the FAA, Article II(3) does not expressly set forth standards of nullity or voidness; instead, it arguably looks to some national (or other) law to govern issues of nullity and validity. Sanders, *A Twenty Years' Review of the Convention on Foreign Arbitral Awards*, 13 Int'l L. 269 (1979) (Article II(3) refers to conflict of laws); Contini, *International Commercial Arbitration*, 8 Am. J. Comp. L. 283, 296 (1959) (since Article II(3) is silent, courts may make determination on basis of forum law, including forum choice-of-law rules).

A variety of laws are potentially applicable under Article II(3) to determine the validity of an arbitration agreement. These include: (i) the law which the parties have selected to govern their arbitration agreement; (ii) the law of the forum (where judicial action is brought to enforce the arbitration agreement); (iii) the law of the arbitral seat; (iv) the law of the place where an arbitral award would be enforced; and (v) international law, either derived from the New York Convention or other sources. Based on what you have read thus far, which of these laws should be selected to govern the enforceability of international arbitration agreements under Article II(3)? Why?

(b) Article II(3)—"internationally neutral" defenses. Rhone holds that Article II(3)'s exception for "null and void" agreements applies to defenses that can be applied "neutrally on an international scale." The *Rhone* formulation appears to exclude state and foreign laws—that single out arbitration agreements for special disfavor. *See Riley v. Kingsley Underwriting Agencies, Ltd.*, 969 F.2d 953, 960 (10th Cir. 1992); *I.T.A.D. Associates, Inc. v. Podar Brothers*, 636 F.2d 75 (4th Cir. 1981); *Chloe Z Fishing Co. v. Odyssey Re (London)*, 109 F. Supp. 2d 1236, 1259-1260 (S.D. Cal. 2000); *Meadows Indemnity Co. v. Baccala & Shoop Ins. Serv., Inc.*, 760 F. Supp. 1036, 1043 (E.D.N.Y. 1991). *See also* G. Born, *International Commercial Arbitration* 485-496, 506-507 (2009).

What kinds of legal rules does *Rhone*'s "internationally neutral" requirement permit to be invoked? Note the court's reference to defenses "such as fraud, mistake, duress, and waiver." What defines the content of "international neutral" defenses like fraud, mistake, duress, and waiver? Does *Rhone* contemplate uniform international standards of fraud or waiver that each nation must apply? What would determine the content of such an international standard? Alternatively, does *Rhone* regard the requirement of international neutrality as essentially negative, preempting parochial defenses otherwise available under domestic law, but leaving it to national law (such as §2 of the FAA) to define the details of internationally neutral defenses? If so, what choice-of-law rules should be applied to select the appropriate national law?

(c) Article II(3)—forum's public policy. Rhone also holds that an arbitration agreement is null and void if it contravenes a fundamental public policy of the forum. What sorts of laws (on public policies) would this exception cover? What about U.S. export control legislation? How, if at all, would export controls apply to the separable arbitration agreement?

(d) Articles II(3) and V(1)(a)—law of arbitral seat. In *Rhone*, the court refused to apply Italian law, which appeared to render the parties' arbitration agreement invalid (because it called for an even number of arbitrators). Note that the arbitral seat in *Rhone* was Italy. Consider Article V(1)(a). What does it provide with regard to the law governing the arbitration agreement? Other U.S. courts have also refused to apply foreign law to determine the validity of arbitration agreements in actions under the New York Convention. *See I.T.A.D. Associates, Inc. v. Podar Brothers*, 636 F.2d 75 (4th Cir. 1981); *Ferrara SpA v. United*

Grain Growers, Ltd., 441 F. Supp. 778, 781 n.2 (S.D.N.Y. 1977). These decisions have reasoned:

> For example, consider the case where a contract containing an arbitration clause provides that the law of state X shall govern the agreement. Assume that the law of state X will not enforce, or gives very limited effect to arbitration clauses, such that under X law the dispute would not be submitted to arbitration. If one party sues on the contract in federal court, and the contract involves "commerce," the federal district court . . . would look to federal law in determining the scope of the arbitration clause. *Becker Autoradio USA, Inc. v. Becker Autoradio-werk GmbH*, 585 F.2d 39, 43 n.8 (3d Cir. 1978).

Compare again the rules of alternative reference discussed above.

Assume that the law of the parties' chosen arbitral seat rendered the arbitration agreement illegal or, at a minimum, incapable of performance. Why should a U.S. court order arbitration in those circumstances? What is the harm in doing so? What would be the harm in concluding incorrectly that foreign law prohibits arbitration and permitting U.S. litigation to go forward?

10. *Substantive grounds for challenging international arbitration agreements.* What substantive grounds are available under Article II of the Convention and Articles 7 and 8 of the UNCITRAL Model Law for challenging the validity of an arbitration agreement? As discussed above, all these provisions refer to other bodies of substantive law—either state or foreign—subject to the preemption of discriminatory legislation discussed above. In general terms, those bodies of substantive law recognize generally applicable contract law defenses similar to those under U.S. law: (i) lack of consent by the parties; (ii) formal defects; (iii) lack of capacity; (iv) illegality under national law (such as the antitrust or securities laws); (v) fraud in the factum (*e.g.*, forgery) or fraudulent inducement; (vi) waiver; or (vii) unconscionability. G. Born, *International Commercial Arbitration* 563-840 (2009). What defenses were raised in *Rhone*? In *Standard Fruit* and *Nokia*?

11. *Allocation of competence to decide challenges to the parties' underlying contract.* If the existence or validity of an arbitration agreement is challenged, who decides the jurisdictional dispute — the arbitral tribunal or a national court? The allocation of competence to decide challenges to the existence or validity of an arbitration agreement in U.S. courts is affected by the separability presumption (discussed *supra* pp. 1177-1178), providing that an agreement to arbitrate is presumptively separable from the underlying contract. In many circumstances, U.S. courts have held that challenges to the parties' underlying contract do not impeach the validity of the parties' associated arbitration agreement and are therefore for the arbitrators (not the courts) to decide. Nonetheless, in limited circumstances, U.S. courts have suggested that some types of challenges to the underlying contract may require judicial resolution.

(a) Fraudulent inducement of the underlying contract. Following *Prima Paint*, courts have almost always refused to hear claims that the underlying contract containing the parties' arbitration agreement was procured by fraud, instead requiring these arguments to be submitted to the arbitrators. *E.g., In re Oil Spill by Amoco Cadiz*, 659 F.2d 789 (7th Cir. 1981); *Al-Salamah Arabian Agencies Co. v. Reece*, 673 F. Supp. 748 (M.D.N.C. 1987); *Brener v. Becker Paribas, Inc.*, 628 F. Supp. 442, 446 (S.D.N.Y. 1985); G. Born, *International Commercial Arbitration* 714-721 (2009). Is this wise? If one party fraudulently induces another to enter into a contract with it, should the victim be required to forgo judicial remedies and limit itself to "contractual" dispute resolution mechanisms? Is this likely what it intended when entering into the contract?

(b) Unconscionability of underlying contract. Suppose that one party claims that the underlying contract, containing an arbitration clause, is grossly unfair and unconscionable. Is that claim subject to resolution by a court or by the arbitrators? U.S. courts have almost always referred such unconscionability claims to arbitration. *See* G. Born, *International Commercial Arbitration* 724-732 (2009). Is that appropriate? Why or why not?

(c) Illegality of the underlying contract. U.S. courts have also held that most disputes about the legality of the parties' underlying agreement must initially be arbitrated. *See, e.g., Buckeye Check Cashing Inc. v. Cardegna*, 546 U.S. 440, 446 (2006) (claim that agreement violated lending and consumer protection laws was arbitrable); *Lawrence v. Comprehensive Business Services Co.*, 833 F.2d 1159 (5th Cir. 1987) (claim that underlying contract violated Texas Public Accountancy Act must be arbitrated); *Island Territory of Curacao v. Solitron Devices, Inc.*, 489 F.2d 1313 (2d Cir. 1973); *Rubin v. Sona Int'l Corp.*, 2006 WL 525658, at *3 (S.D.N.Y. 2006).

Nonetheless, some lower courts have held that courts must resolve at least some claims that the parties' underlying agreement is illegal. *E.g., Durst v. Abrash*, 253 N.Y.S.2d 351 (App. Div. 1964), *aff'd*, 266 N.Y.S.2d 806 (1966) ("If usurious agreements could be made enforceable by the simple device of employing arbitration clauses the courts would be surrendering their control over public policy."); *Kramer & Uchitelle, Inc. v. Eddington Fabrics Corp.*, 43 N.E.2d 493 (N.Y. 1942). Most of these decisions do not appear to survive *Buckeye Check Cashing Inc. v. Cardegna*, 546 U.S. 440 (2006). *See* G. Born, *International Commercial Arbitration* 755-764 (2009).

Which approach is wiser? Is it in fact defensible to require arbitration of claims that the parties' agreement is illegal? Suppose that an arbitration clause is included in a contract for payment of unlawful bribes or sale of unlawful weapons. Should a court require arbitration of claims arising from that unlawful agreement?

(d) Nonexistence of underlying contract. Standard Fruit holds that the arbitral tribunal — rather than a court — must initially decide whether the Memorandum (containing the alleged arbitration clause) is in fact a contract at all. Is that holding correct?

Some U.S. courts have concluded that disputes about the *existence* of the parties' underlying contract (as distinguished from the separable arbitration agreement) must be arbitrated. *Burden v. Check Into Cash of Kentucky, LLC*, 267 F.3d 483, 491-492 (6th Cir. 2001); *R.M. Perez & Assoc., Inc. v. Welch*, 960 F.2d 534 (5th Cir. 1992); *Teledyne, Inc. v. Kone Corp.*, 892 F.2d 1404, 1410 (9th Cir. 1990) (only issue for court is "whether there are grounds for an *independent* challenge to the arbitration clause, rather than a challenge to the arbitration clause which must rise or fall with a challenge to the contract as a whole"); *Hall v. Shearson Lehman Hutton, Inc.*, 708 F. Supp. 711 (D. Md. 1989) (arbitrator to resolve whether one party forged signature on agreement containing arbitration clause).

In contrast, other courts have held that challenges to the very existence of any underlying agreement must be decided by the court. *E.g., Microchip Tech. Inc. v. U.S. Philips Corp.*, 367 F.3d 1350, 1358 (Fed. Cir. 2004) ("[c]ontrary to the Ninth Circuit's decision in *Teledyne*, the responsibility of the judiciary to resolve the gateway dispute of whether an agreement to arbitrate exists is not limited to situations in which there is an independent challenge to the arbitration clause"); *Will-Drill Resources, Inc. v. Samson Resources Co.*, 353 F.3d 211, 219 (5th Cir. 2003) ("where a party attacks the very existence of an agreement, as opposed to its continued validity or enforcement, the courts must first resolve that dispute"); *Sandvik AB v. Advent Int'l Corp.*, 220 F.3d 99, 110-112 (3d Cir. 2000); *Interocean Shipping Co. v. National Shipping & Trading Corp.*, 462 F.2d 673, 676 (2d Cir. 1972); *In re Kinoshita & Co.*, 287 F.2d 951, 953 (2d Cir. 1961) ("if it were claimed that . . . there had at no time existed as between the parties any contractual relation whatever, . . . a trial of this issue would be required"); *Donato v. Merrill Lynch, Pierce, Fenner & Smith, Inc.*, 663 F. Supp. 669 (N.D. Ill. 1987) (§4 trial on claim that signature on contract containing arbitration clause was forged). *See also* G. Born, *International Commercial Arbitration* 643, 911-948 (2009).

Which line of authority is correct? If the parties simply never entered into a contract at all, how can they be said to have agreed to arbitrate? Why is this not unanswerable? What would be the response of the author of *Standard Fruit?*

Although the Supreme Court has not definitively resolved the question, its recent decisions lend support to the latter view. *Buckeye Check Cashing Inc. v. Cardegna*, 546 U.S. 440, 444 n.1 (2006), while holding that a challenge to the legality of the parties' underlying contract was arbitrable, obserevd that "[t]he issue of the contracts' validity is different from the issue of whether any agreement between the alleged obligor and obligee was ever concluded." More recently, *Granite Rock Co. v. International Brotherhood of Teamsters*, 130 S. Ct. 2847 (2010), addressed this question (at least in part) in a domestic labor setting. *Granite Rock* involved a dispute between a company and an employee union. Following a strike, the company and the union entered into a collective bargaining agreement containing an arbitration clause. A dispute arose over the date when the collective bargaining agreement was "formed" and whether that question was properly decided by a court or an arbitrator. The Supreme Court held that a court should resolve the formation dispute and, in its opinion, stated that where a dispute "concerns contract formation, the dispute is generally for courts to decide." *Id.* at 2855-2856. The Court also made clear that its conclusion applied equally under the FAA, at least in domestic cases; although international arbitration disputes, under the second and third chapters of the FAA, are arguably distinguishable, it is difficult to see how the same conclusion would not apply.

12. *Arbitrability of challenges to the arbitration agreement itself.* In some cases, one party will not merely challenge the existence, validity, or legality of the parties' underlying contract, but will challenge the arbitration agreement itself. Should such disputes be resolved by the arbitrators, or, if one party insists, must a court consider them? Compare the approaches in *Standard Fruit* and *Nokia.* What role, if any, does the separability doctrine play in resolving such questions?

(a) Relevance of parties' arbitration agreement. The jurisdiction of an arbitrator to decide at least some issues of arbitrability can depend on the parties' arbitration agreement. As discussed above, the Supreme Court held in *First Options of Chicago, Inc. v. Kaplan*, 514 U.S. 938 (1995), that parties may grant an arbitrator jurisdiction to determine issues of arbitrability. *See supra* pp. 1169-1170. The Court reasoned that "when deciding whether the parties agreed to arbitrate a certain matter (including arbitrability), courts generally . . . should apply ordinary state-law principles that govern the formation of contracts." The Court then declared that courts "should not assume that the parties agreed to arbitrate arbitrability unless there is 'clea[r] and unmistakabl[e]' evidence that they did so."

How far does this reasoning extend? Suppose that one party challenges the scope of a concededly existing and valid arbitration agreement, or the validity or legality of an arbitration agreement that one party concededly executed. On the other hand, suppose that one party denies that it ever executed or otherwise committed itself to a purported arbitration agreement. Can the parties' arbitration agreement grant the arbitrators power to decide each of these types of disputes? Do all of the disputes involve the same issues? How does Article 16 of the UNCITRAL Model Law deal with this issue? How does the *Nokia* decision deal with the issue?

(b) Disputes about the existence of the arbitration agreement. As we have seen, §4 provides for orders compelling arbitration except where "the making of the agreement for

arbitration . . . is not in issue." Where the "making of the agreement for arbitration" *is* "in issue" then §4 arguably requires a trial on that question. Note the Court's distinction between validity/legality and existence in *Buckeye Check Cashing. See supra* p. 1181; G. Born, *International Commercial Arbitration* 938-947 (2009).

A number of lower courts have concluded that §4's language requires judicial resolution of claims that no arbitration agreement exists. *E.g., Moseley v. Electronic & Missile Facilities, Inc.,* 374 U.S. 167, 172 (1963) ("fraud in the procurement of an arbitration contract . . . makes it void and unenforceable and . . . this question of fraud is a judicial one, which must be determined by a court") (Black, J., concurring); *David L. Threlkeld & Co. v. Metallgesellschaft Ltd.,* 923 F.2d 245 (2d Cir. 1991); *Becker Autoradio v. Becker Autoradiowerk GmbH,* 585 F.2d 39, 44 & n.10 (3d Cir. 1978); *Interbras Cayman Co. v. Orient Victory Shipping Co.,* 663 F.2d 4, 7 (2d Cir. 1981) (ordering trial under §4 because of "genuine issue of fact" as to existence of arbitration agreement). How can an arbitration agreement—no matter how broadly drafted—confer jurisdiction on arbitrators with respect to a party that denies that agreement's existence? Compare Article 16 of the UNCITRAL Model Law and the *Nokia* decision.

(c) Disputes concerning interpretation of arbitration agreement. As discussed below, a number of lower courts have held that disputes about the *scope* of an arbitration agreement that concededly *exists* are presumptively for resolution by the arbitrators. *See infra* p. 1182; *Apollo Computer, Inc. v. Berg,* 886 F.2d 469 (1st Cir. 1989); *Matter of Arbitration No. AAA13-161-0511-85,* 867 F.2d 130, 133 (2d Cir. 1989); *Societe Generale etc. v. Raytheon European Mgt. and Systems Co.,* 643 F.2d 863, 869 (1st Cir. 1981); G. Born, *International Commercial Arbitration* 1080-1081, 1087-1091 (2009). Why should questions regarding the scope of a concededly valid arbitration agreement be treated differently from questions regarding the existence or validity of an alleged arbitration agreement?

(d) Parties' submission of dispute to arbitrators. Even if the parties' arbitration agreement does not grant the arbitrators power to decide issues of arbitrability, the parties may through their subsequent conduct submit such issues to the arbitrators. *See First Options of Chicago, Inc. v. Kaplan,* 514 U.S. 938 (1995) (claim that entity's participation in arbitration, for purpose of challenging jurisdiction of tribunal, was not submission of jurisdictional objection to arbitration).

13. *The* Standard Fruit *decision.* Is it sensible to conclude, as *Standard Fruit* does, that the parties' arbitration agreement is binding even if the underlying Memorandum of Intent is not? How could that be? Suppose that Standard Fruit argued that the Memorandum of Intent was a forgery—that it had never discussed, much less signed, any such document. Would this really be irrelevant to Nicaragua's motion to compel arbitration? *See supra* pp. 1180-1181. If the Memorandum is *not* a binding contract, then how can its arbitration provision contained within it be binding?

The standard answer to the foregoing, of course, is that the arbitration agreement is separable and therefore that it is supported by separate consideration (the exchange of promises to arbitrate) and separate evidence as to its existence (for example, the parties' subsequent correspondence). *See supra* p. 1167. Is that answer persuasive in cases involving claims that *no* underlying agreement exists? If the very existence of *any* contract is challenged, is that not necessarily relevant to the existence of an agreement to arbitrate? In concrete terms, if Standard Fruit and Nicaragua had no intention to be bound by the Memorandum of Intent, would they have intended to be bound by the Memorandum's arbitration clause? Consider Mr. Moore's letter regarding the alleged arbitration provision. Might the parties have agreed to the terms of an arbitration agreement before agreeing to their underlying contract? How plausible is that?

Even assuming that the binding character of the Memorandum is irrelevant, Standard Fruit *also* challenged the existence of the arbitration "agreement" itself. In particular, it argued that the arbitration clause was only a statement of intention to attempt to agree on an arbitration mechanism in the future. How did *Standard Fruit* resolve this? Consider the terms of the alleged arbitration "agreement." Was the provision relied upon by Nicaragua an agreement to arbitrate? Did the Ninth Circuit decide that it was?

Note that the *Standard Fruit* Court relied on an "emphatic federal policy in favor of arbitral dispute resolution [which] applies with special force in the field of international commerce." What is the basis for this policy? Note that, as discussed below, the relevant policy in fact concerns broad interpretation of admittedly existent arbitration agreements. *See infra* p. 1200. In deciding whether an arbitration agreement *exists*, is it satisfactory to rely on the federal policy favoring broad *interpretation* of arbitration agreements? What might justify a federal policy making it easier, rather than harder, to establish the existence of an arbitration agreement?

What are the limits of the *Standard Fruit* rationale? Suppose that the Memorandum of Intent had not been signed, but that Nicaragua argued it had been orally agreed to. Suppose the arbitration clause was contained in a draft prepared by Nicaragua, but not included in the unsigned Memorandum of Intent?

14. *The* **Nokia** *decision.* Compare the approach in *Nokia* to that in *Standard Fruit*. Note the Swiss court's statement that "Considering the important consequences of an arbitration agreement, the court shall beware of finding too easily that such an agreement has been concluded." Is this a sort of "anti-arbitration" presumption? What is its rationale? Compare this to the "emphatic" policy in favor of arbitration in *Standard Fruit*. Which approach is preferable? How would the *Nokia* Court have decided *Standard Fruit*? How would the *Standard Fruit* Court have decided *Nokia*?

15. *Judicial review of arbitrator's jurisdictional rulings.* Suppose a court requires the parties to arbitrate disputes concerning arbitrability. How should the arbitrator's jurisdictional ruling be reviewed?

(a) Interlocutory review of jurisdictional rulings. Some foreign arbitration statutes permit interlocutory judicial review of arbitrators' jurisdictional rulings. G. Born, *International Commercial Arbitration* 894-898, 900-904 (2009). Consider how Article 16 of the UNCITRAL Model Law deals with this issue. In contrast, U.S. courts have not frequently considered interlocutory appeals from arbitrators' jurisdictional rulings. *See* G. Born, *International Commercial Arbitration* 951 (2009); *Transportacion Maritima Mexicana, SA v. Companhia de Navegaçao Lloyd Brasileiro*, 636 F. Supp. 474 (S.D.N.Y. 1983).

Is the U.S. approach a sensible one? Why shouldn't courts entertain challenges to interim jurisdictional awards? Consider the wasted resources if the tribunal incorrectly upholds its own jurisdiction. On the other hand, consider the delays that can result from preliminary litigation of arbitrability disputes. Which approach — that under Article 16 of the UNCITRAL Model Law or that under the FAA — is preferable?

(b) Limited scope of judicial review of jurisdictional rulings under U.S. law. As discussed in detail below, *infra* pp. 1201-1215, judicial review of the merits of most arbitral awards in U.S. courts is extremely limited. Should the same standard apply to jurisdictional rulings? For a discussion of the treatment of this issue by U.S. courts, *see infra* pp. 1213-1215.

16. *Differences between New York Convention and Hague Choice of Court Agreements Convention.* Compare the enforceability of arbitration clauses under the New York Convention with the enforceability of choice of court agreements under the Hague Convention. How broad is the scope of each Convention? On what grounds may an arbitration agreement and a forum clause be resisted? What law governs the enforceability of arbitration agreements and of choice of forum clauses? Which Convention

provides the more predictable and secure enforcement terms? Which Convention is wiser public policy?

3. The Non-Arbitrability Doctrine in U.S. Courts

a. Introduction. Virtually all nations treat some categories of claims as incapable of resolution by arbitration. Claims are ordinarily deemed "non-arbitrable" because of their perceived public importance or a felt need for formal judicial procedures in resolving such claims. The types of claims that are non-arbitrable are defined, at least in the first instance, by national law and differ from nation to nation. Among other things, various nations refuse to permit arbitration of domestic disputes concerning consumer and labor grievances; intellectual property; antitrust claims; real estate; and franchise relations.[109]

Broadly similar exceptions exist in international matters. Article II(1) of the New York Convention does not require Contracting States to recognize agreements providing for the arbitration of disputes that are not "capable of settlement by arbitration." Similarly, Article V(2)(a) provides that an arbitral award need not be recognized if "[t]he subject matter of the difference is not capable of settlement by arbitration under the law" of the country where recognition is sought. Together, these provisions permit the assertion of non-arbitrability defenses to the enforcement of international arbitration agreements and awards.

Both U.S. federal law and state have, at various times, treated various claims as non-arbitrable.[110] Nevertheless, the FAA itself contains no provisions dealing expressly with the subject of non-arbitrability. Prohibitions on the arbitrability of claims under U.S. law are based, therefore, on other statutes or public policies. As discussed below, U.S. statutes have seldom dealt expressly with the subject of non-arbitrability, thus leaving development of the doctrine largely to the courts.

The Supreme Court's first treatment of the non-arbitrability doctrine was *Wilko v. Swan*.[111] There, an investor brought an action in district court against his brokers under the federal Securities Act of 1933, seeking damages for alleged misrepresentations. The defendants sought to stay the plaintiff's action, relying on an arbitration provision in the parties' margin agreement.

The Supreme Court rejected the defendants' motion for a stay, reasoning that, while Congress wished to encourage arbitration generally, "it has enacted the Securities Act to protect the rights of investors and has forbidden a waiver of any of those rights."[112] The Court relied principally on §14 of the Securities Act, which provides:

> Any condition, stipulation, or provision binding any person acquiring any security to waive compliance with any provision of this subchapter or of the rules and regulations of the Commission shall be void.[113]

The Court concluded that "[r]ecognizing the advantages that prior agreements for arbitration may provide for the solution of commercial controversies, we decide that the

---

109. *See* G. Born, *International Commercial Arbitration* 767-840 (2009).

110. *E.g., Wilko v. Swan*, 346 U.S. 427 (1953) (Securities Act of 1933); *Alexander v. Gardner-Denver Co.*, 415 U.S. 36 (1974) (Title VII); Ark. Stat. Ann. §§34-511 (Supp. 1985) (not permitting enforcement of arbitration agreements as to personal injury, tort, employer-employee, or insurance contract claims); Iowa Code §679A.1(2) (1985) (same as to adhesion contracts, employer-employee contracts, and tort claims (unless covered by a separate writing)).

111. 346 U.S. 427 (1953).

112. 346 U.S. at 438.

113. 15 U.S.C. §77n.

intention of Congress concerning the sale of securities is better carried out by holding invalid such an agreement for arbitration of issues arising under the Act."[114]

Relying on *Wilko*, lower federal courts subsequently fashioned a variety of non-arbitrability exceptions designed to protect perceived public values or legislative objectives. Thus, patent, federal antitrust, RICO, and COGSA claims were held too important to be left to "private" arbitration.[115] At the same time, the Supreme Court concluded that other categories of federal statutory claims were also non-arbitrable under the FAA.[116]

During the 1980s, the Supreme Court brought the expansion of the non-arbitrability doctrine to a fairly decisive end. Two landmark decisions concluded that federal securities and antitrust claims *could* be arbitrated, at least when they arose from "international" transactions. In *Scherk v. Alberto-Culver Co.*, the Supreme Court distinguished *Wilko* and held that a claim under the Securities Exchange Act of 1934 was arbitrable, provided that it arose from an "international" transaction.[117] And, in *Mitsubishi Motors Corp. v. Soler Chrysler-Plymouth, Inc.*, which is excerpted below, the Court held that federal antitrust claims were also arbitrable, again provided that they arose from an "international" transaction.[118]

More recently, the Supreme Court expressly overruled *Wilko v. Swan*, holding in two decisions that claims — both domestic and international — under the Racketeer Influenced and Corrupt Organizations Act ("RICO") and the Securities Exchange Act are arbitrable.[119] In another decision, after remarking that "[i]t is by now clear that statutory claims may be the subject of an arbitration agreement," the Court held that claims under the Age Discrimination in Employment Act are arbitrable.[120]

b.   Selected Materials on the Non-Arbitrability Doctrine.   Excerpted below is the Supreme Court's opinion in *Mitsubishi Motors Corp. v. Soler Chrysler-Plymouth, Inc.* After considering *Mitsubishi*, reread *Richards v. Lloyd's of London* (excerpted *supra* pp. 515-520).

MITSUBISHI MOTORS CORP. v. SOLER CHRYSLER-PLYMOUTH, INC.

473 U.S. 614 (1985) [also excerpted below at pp. 1186-1191]

JUSTICE BLACKMUN. The principal question presented by these cases is the arbitrability, pursuant to the [FAA] and the [New York] Convention of claims arising under the Sherman Act, 15 U.S.C. §1 *et seq.*, and encompassed within a valid arbitration clause in an agreement embodying an international commercial transaction.

[Mitsubishi Motors Corporation ("Mitsubishi") is a Japanese corporation that manufactures automobiles in Tokyo, Japan. Mitsubishi is a joint venture between Chrysler International ("CISA"), a Swiss corporation owned by Chrysler Corporation, and Mitsubishi Heavy Industries, a Japanese corporation. Soler Chrysler-Plymouth, Inc. ("Soler"),

---

114. 346 U.S. at 438.

115. *See* G. Born, *International Commercial Arbitration* 781-786 (2009).

116. *Alexander v. Gardner-Denver Co.*, 415 U.S. 36 (1974) (Title VII); *Barrentine v. Arkansas-Best Freight System, Inc.*, 450 U.S. 728 (1981) (Fair Labor Standards Act); *Austin v. Owens-Brockway Glass Container, Inc.*, 78 F.3d 875, 883 (4th Cir. 1996); *Tran v. Tran*, 54 F.3d 115, 117-118 (2d Cir. 1995).

117. 417 U.S. 506 (1974).

118. 473 U.S. 614 (1985).

119. *Shearson/American Express, Inc. v. McMahon*, 482 U.S. 220 (1987); *Rodriguez de Quijas v. Shearson/American Express, Inc.*, 490 U.S. 477 (1989) (overruling *Wilko v. Swan*); *In re Piper Funds, Inc.*, 71 F.3d 298, 301 (8th Cir. 1995); *Lehman v. Detray Investment Group*, 2004 WL 1474651, at *3 (N.D. Ohio 2004); *Vitzethum v. Dominick & Dominick Inc.*, 1996 WL 19062, at *4 (S.D.N.Y. 1996).

120. *Gilmer v. Interstate/Johnson Lane Corp.*, 500 U.S. 20, 26 (1991).

is a Puerto Rico corporation. Soler entered into a distributor agreement with CISA that provided for the sale by Soler of Mitsubishi-manufactured vehicles within a designated area. At the same time, CISA, Soler, and Mitsubishi entered into a sales agreement ("sales agreement") that provided for the direct sale of Mitsubishi products to Soler and governed the terms of such sales. Paragraph VI of the Sales Agreement, labeled Arbitration of Certain Matters, provides:

> All disputes, controversies or differences which may arise between [Mitsubishi] and [Soler] out of or in relation to Articles I-B through V of this Agreement or for the breach thereof, shall be finally settled by arbitration in Japan in accordance with the rules and regulations of the Japan Commercial Arbitration Association.

Soler failed to maintain the sales volume specified in its agreements and requested that Mitsubishi delay or cancel shipment of several orders. Mitsubishi and CISA refused, and Mitsubishi later brought an action against Soler in the District of Puerto Rico under the [FAA] and the Convention. Mitsubishi sought an order, pursuant to 9 U.S.C. §4 and §206, to compel arbitration. Shortly after filing the complaint, Mitsubishi filed a request for arbitration before the Japan Commercial Arbitration Association seeking damages from Soler for breach of the sales agreement. Soler denied the allegations and counterclaimed against Mitsubishi and CISA under the Sherman Act; the Puerto Rico competition statute; and the Puerto Rico Dealers' Contract Act. In the counterclaim premised on the Sherman Act, Soler alleged that Mitsubishi and CISA had conspired to divide markets in restraint of trade. The Court of Appeals held that antitrust claims were "non-arbitrable" and permitted Soler's suit to proceed. The Supreme Court initially concluded that the parties' arbitration agreement was broadly enough drafted to encompass Soler's antitrust claims. *See infra* pp. 1186-1191.]

We now turn to consider whether Soler's antitrust claims are non-arbitrable even though it has agreed to arbitrate them. In holding that they are not, the Court of Appeals followed the decision . . . in *American Safety Equipment Corp. v. J.P. Maguire & Co.*, 391 F.2d 821 (1968). Notwithstanding the absence of any explicit support for such an exception in either the Sherman Act or the [FAA], the Second Circuit there reasoned that "the pervasive public interest in enforcement of the antitrust laws, and the nature of the claims that arise in such cases, combine to make . . . antitrust claims . . . inappropriate for arbitration." We find it unnecessary to assess the legitimacy of the *American Safety* doctrine as applied to agreements to arbitrate arising from domestic transactions. As in *Scherk v. Alberto-Culver Co.*, 417 U.S. 506 (1974), we conclude that concerns of international comity, respect for the capacities of foreign and transnational tribunals, and sensitivity to the need of the international commercial system for predictability in the resolution of disputes require that we enforce the parties' agreement, even assuming that a contrary result would be forthcoming in a domestic context.

Even before *Scherk*, this Court had recognized the utility of forum selection clauses in international transactions. [One example is the Court's decision in *The Bremen v. Zapata Off-Shore Co.*, 407 U.S. 1 (1972), which] clearly eschewed a provincial solicitude for the jurisdiction of domestic forums. . . . *The Bremen* and *Scherk* establish a strong presumption in favor of enforcement of freely negotiated contractual choice-of-forum provisions. Here, as in *Scherk*, that presumption is reinforced by the emphatic federal policy in favor of arbitral dispute resolution. And at least since this Nation's accession in 1970 to the Convention . . . that federal policy applies with special force in the field of international commerce. Thus, we must weigh the concerns of *American Safety* against a strong belief in the efficacy of arbitral procedures for the resolution of international commercial disputes and an equal commitment to the enforcement of freely negotiated choice-of-forum clauses.

At the outset, we confess to some skepticism of certain aspects of the *American Safety* doctrine. As distilled by the First Circuit, the doctrine comprises four ingredients[, all of which we find insufficient.] . . . [First, the] mere appearance of an antitrust dispute does not alone warrant invalidation of the selected forum on the undemonstrated assumption that the arbitration clause is tainted. A party resisting arbitration of course may attack directly the validity of the agreement to arbitrate. . . .

[Second,] potential complexity should not suffice to ward off arbitration. We might well have some doubt that even the courts following *American Safety* subscribe fully to the view that antitrust matters are inherently insusceptible to resolution by arbitration, as these same courts have agreed that an undertaking to arbitrate antitrust claims entered into after the dispute arises is acceptable. . . . [A]daptability and access to expertise are hallmarks of arbitration. The anticipated subject matter of the dispute may be taken into account when the arbitrators are appointed, and arbitral rules typically provide for the participation of experts either employed by the parties or appointed by the tribunal. . . .

[Third,] we also reject the proposition that an arbitration panel will pose too great a danger of innate hostility to the constraints on business conduct that antitrust law imposes. International arbitrators frequently are drawn from the legal as well as the business community; where the dispute has an important legal component, the parties and the arbitral body with whose assistance they have agreed to settle their dispute can be expected to select arbitrators accordingly.

We are left, then, with the core of the *American Safety* doctrine — the fundamental importance to American democratic capitalism of the regime of the antitrust laws. Without doubt, the private cause of action plays a central role in enforcing this regime. . . . The importance of the private damages remedy, however, does not compel the conclusion that it may not be sought outside an American court. . . .

There is no reason to assume at the outset of the dispute that international arbitration will not provide an adequate mechanism. To be sure, the international arbitral tribunal owes no prior allegiance to the legal norms of particular states; hence, it has no direct obligation to vindicate their statutory dictates. The tribunal, however, is bound to effectuate the intentions of the parties. Where the parties have agreed that the arbitral body is to decide a defined set of claims which includes, as in these cases, those arising from the application of American antitrust law, the tribunal therefore should be bound to decide that dispute in accord with the national law giving rise to the claim.[121] And so long as the

---

121. In addition to the clause providing for arbitration before the Japan Commercial Arbitration Association, the Sales Agreement includes a choice-of-law clause which reads: "This Agreement is made in, and will be governed by and construed in all respects according to the laws of the Swiss Confederation as if entirely performed therein." The United States raises the possibility that the arbitral panel will read this provision not simply to govern interpretation of the contract terms, but wholly to displace American law even where it otherwise would apply. The International Chamber of Commerce opines that it is "[c]onceivabl[e], although we believe it unlikely, [that] the arbitrators could consider Soler's affirmative claim of anticompetitive conduct by CISA and Mitsubishi to fall within the purview of this choice-of-law provision, with the result that it would be decided under Swiss law rather than the U.S. Sherman Act." At oral argument, however, counsel for Mitsubishi conceded that American law applied to the antitrust claims and represented that the claims had been submitted to the arbitration panel in Japan on that basis. The record confirms that before the decision of the Court of Appeals the arbitral panel had taken these claims under submission. We therefore have no occasion to speculate on this matter at this stage in proceedings, when Mitsubishi seeks to enforce the agreement to arbitrate, not to enforce an award. Nor need we consider now the effect of an arbitral tribunal's failure to take cognizance of the statutory cause of action on the claimant's capacity to reinitiate suit in federal court. We merely note that in the event the choice-of-forum and choice-of-law clauses operated in tandem as a prospective waiver of a party's right to pursue statutory remedies for antitrust violations, we would have little hesitation in condemning the agreement as against public policy.

prospective litigant effectively may vindicate its statutory cause of action in the arbitral forum, the statute will continue to serve both its remedial and deterrent function.

Having permitted the arbitration to go forward, [U.S.] courts will have the opportunity at the award enforcement stage to ensure that the legitimate interest in the enforcement of the antitrust laws has been addressed. The Convention reserves to each signatory country the right to refuse enforcement of an award where the "recognition or enforcement of the award would be contrary to the public policy of that country." Article V(2)(b). While the efficacy of the arbitral process requires that substantive review at the award-enforcement stage remain minimal, it would not require intrusive inquiry to ascertain that the tribunal took cognizance of the antitrust claims and actually decided them.[122]

As international trade has expanded in recent decades, so too has the use of international arbitration to resolve disputes arising in the course of that trade. . . . If [international arbitral institutions] are to take a central place in the international legal order, national courts will need to "shake off the old judicial hostility to arbitration," and also their customary and understandable unwillingness to cede jurisdiction of a claim arising under domestic law to a foreign or transnational tribunal. To this extent, at least, it will be necessary for national courts to subordinate domestic notions of arbitrability to the international policy favoring commercial arbitration.[123] . . .

JUSTICE STEVENS, dissenting. This Court's holding rests almost exclusively on the federal policy favoring arbitration of commercial disputes and vague notions of international comity arising from the fact that the automobiles involved here were manufactured in Japan. I respectfully dissent. . . .

[The] Court has repeatedly held that a decision by Congress to create a special statutory remedy renders a private agreement to arbitrate a federal statutory claim unenforceable. Thus, . . . the express statutory remedy provided in the Ku Klux Act of 1871, the express statutory remedy in the Securities Act of 1933, the express statutory remedy in the Fair Labor Standards Act, and the express statutory remedy in Title VII of the Civil Rights Act of 1964, each provided the Court with convincing evidence that Congress did not intend the protections afforded by the statute to be administered by a private arbitrator. The reasons that motivated those decisions apply with special force to the federal policy that is protected by the antitrust laws. . . . It was Chief Justice Hughes who characterized

---

122. We note, for example that the rules of the Japan Commercial Arbitration Association provide for the taking of a "summary" of each hearing, Rule 28.1; for the stenographic recording of the proceedings where the tribunal so orders or a party requests one, Rule 28.2; and for a statement of reasons for the award unless the parties agree otherwise, Rule 36.1(4).

123. We do not quarrel with the Court of Appeals' conclusion that Article II(1) of the Convention, which requires the recognition of agreements to arbitrate that involve "subject matter capable of settlement by arbitration," contemplates exceptions to arbitrability grounded in domestic law. And it appears that before acceding to the Convention the Senate was advised by a State Department memorandum that the Convention provided for such exceptions. In acceding to the Convention the Senate restricted its applicability to commercial matters, in accord with Article I(3). Yet in implementing the Convention by amendments to the Federal Arbitration Act, Congress did not specify any matters it intended to exclude from its scope. In *Scherk*, this Court recited Article II(1), including the language relied upon by the Court of Appeals, but paid heed to the Convention delegates' "frequent[ly voiced] concern that courts of signatory countries in which an agreement to arbitrate is sought to be enforced should not be permitted to decline enforcement of such agreements on the basis of parochial views of their desirability or in a manner that would diminish the mutually binding nature of the agreements." There, moreover, the Court dealt *arguendo* with an exception to arbitrability grounded in express congressional language; here, in contrast, we face a judicially implied exception. The utility of the Convention in promoting the process of international commercial arbitration depends upon the willingness of national courts to let go of matters they normally would think of as their own. Doubtless, Congress may specify categories of claims it wishes to reserve for decision by our own courts without contravening this Nation's obligations under the Convention. But we decline to subvert the spirit of the United States' accession to the Convention by recognizing subject-matter exceptions where Congress has not expressly directed the courts to do so.

the Sherman Antitrust Act as "a charter of freedom" that may fairly be compared to a constitutional provision. *See Appalachian Coals, Inc. v. United States,* 228 U.S. 344, 359-360 (1933). . . .

In a landmark opinion for the Court of Appeals for the Second Circuit, Judge Feinberg wrote:

> A claim under the antitrust laws is not merely a private matter. The Sherman Act is designed to promote the national interest in a competitive economy; thus, the plaintiff asserting his rights under the Act has been likened to a private attorney-general who protects the public's interest. . . . Antitrust violations can affect hundreds of thousands — perhaps millions — of people and inflict staggering economic damage. . . . We do not believe that Congress intended such claims to be resolved elsewhere than in the courts. . . . [I]t is also proper to ask whether contracts of adhesion between alleged monopolists and their customers should determine the forum for trying antitrust violations. *American Safety Equipment Corp. v. J. P. Maguire & Co.,* 391 F.2d 821, 826-827 (1968). . . .

Arbitration awards are only reviewable for manifest disregard of the law, 9 U.S.C. §§10, 207, and the rudimentary procedures which make arbitration so desirable in the context of a private dispute often mean that the record is so inadequate that the arbitrator's decision is virtually unreviewable.[124] Despotic decision making of this kind is fine for parties who are willing to agree in advance to settle for a best approximation of the correct result in order to resolve quickly and inexpensively any contractual dispute that may arise in an ongoing commercial relationship. Such informality, however, is simply unacceptable when every error may have devastating consequences for important businesses in our national economy and may undermine their ability to compete in world markets. Instead of "muffling a grievance in the cloakroom of arbitration," the public interest in free competitive markets would be better served by having the issues resolved "in the light of impartial public court adjudication."[125]

The Court assumes for the purposes of its decision that the antitrust issues would not be arbitrable if this were a purely domestic dispute, but holds that the international character of the controversy makes it arbitrable. The holding rests on vague concerns for the international implications of its decision and a misguided application of *Scherk.* Before relying on its own notions of what international comity requires, it is surprising that the Court does not determine the specific commitments that the United States has made to enforce private agreements to arbitrate disputes arising under public law. As the Court acknowledges, the only treaty relevant here is the [New York Convention]. . . . However, the United States, as *amicus curiae,* advises the Court that the Convention "clearly contemplates" that signatory nations will enforce domestic laws prohibiting the arbitration of certain subject matters. This interpretation is . . . beyond doubt.

Article II(3) of the Convention . . . [does not apply] (i) if the agreement "is null and void, inoperative or incapable of being performed," Article II(3), or (ii) if the dispute does not concern "a subject matter capable of settlement by arbitration,"

---

124. The arbitration procedure in this case does not provide any right to evidentiary discovery or a written decision, and requires that all proceedings be closed to the public. Moreover, Japanese arbitrators do not have the power of compulsory process to secure witnesses and documents, nor do witnesses who are available testify under oath. *Cf.* 9 U.S.C. §7 (arbitrators may summon witnesses to attend proceedings and seek enforcement in a district court).

125. The Court notes that some courts which have held that agreements to arbitrate antitrust claims generally are unenforceable have nevertheless enforced arbitration agreements to settle an existing antitrust claim. These settlement agreements, made after the parties have had every opportunity to evaluate the strength of their position, are obviously less destructive of the private treble-damages remedy that Congress provided. Thus, it may well be that arbitration as a means of settling disputes is permissible.

Article II(1). . . . The latter clause plainly suggests the possibility that some subject matters are not capable of arbitration under the domestic laws of the signatory nations, and that agreements to arbitrate such disputes need not be enforced. . . . [Moreover, if] an arbitration award is "contrary to the public policy of [a] country" called upon to enforce it, or if it concerns a subject matter which is "not capable of settlement by arbitration under the law of that country," the Convention does not require that it be enforced. Articles V(2)(a) and (b). Thus, reading Articles II and V together, the Convention provides that agreements to arbitrate disputes which are non-arbitrable under domestic law need not be honored, nor awards rendered under them enforced.

It is clear then that the international obligations of the United States permit us to honor Congress' commitment to the exclusive resolution of antitrust disputes in the federal courts. The Court today refuses to do so, offering only vague concerns for comity among nations. The courts of other nations, on the other hand, have applied the exception provided in the Convention, and refused to enforce agreements to arbitrate specific subject matters of concern to them.[126]

[*Scherk v. Alberto-Culver Co.* is not relevant. In *Scherk*, the Court] based its decision on the [fact] that the outcome in *Wilko* was governed entirely by American law whereas in *Scherk* foreign rules of law would control and, if the arbitration clause were not enforced, a host of international conflict-of-laws problems would arise. . . . That distinction fits this case precisely, since I consider it perfectly clear that the rules of American antitrust law must govern the claim of an American automobile dealer that he has been injured by an international conspiracy to restrain trade in the American automobile market. . . . The merits of those claims are controlled entirely by American law. . . .

RICHARDS v. LLOYD'S OF LONDON
135 F.3d 1289 (9th Cir. 1998) [excerpted supra at 515-520]

Notes on Mitsubishi *and* Richards

1. *New York Convention's exception for matters "not capable of settlement by arbitration.*" Could the Supreme Court, consistently with the New York Convention, have held in *Mitsubishi* that federal antitrust claims are *not* arbitrable? Justice Stevens argued and the Court agreed that the Convention does not *require* enforcement of agreements to arbitrate a "subject matter [not] capable of settlement by arbitration." Moreover, the *Mitsubishi* Court was of the view that the Convention would not have prohibited a holding that antitrust claims were non-arbitrable. Is that correct? How might the Convention limit a Contracting State's freedom to declare certain categories of disputes non-arbitrable?

2. *Law governing non-arbitrability under New York Convention.* What law governs the question of non-arbitrability when a U.S. court considers a claim that an international arbitration agreement, subject to the New York Convention, should not be enforced? What law did the Court look to in *Mitsubishi*?

---

126. For example, the Cour de Cassation in Belgium has held that disputes arising under a Belgian statute limiting the unilateral termination of exclusive distributorships are not arbitrable under the Convention in that country, *Audi-NSU Auto Union A.G. v. SA Adelin Petit & Cie* (1979), in 5 Yearbook Commercial Arbitration 257, 259 (1980), and the Corte di Cassazione in Italy has held that labor disputes are not arbitrable under the Convention in that country, *Compagnia Generale Construzioni v. Piersanti*, [1980] Foro Italiano I 190, in 6 Yearbook Commercial Arbitration 229, 230 (1981).

Mitsubishi involved the arbitrability of U.S. statutory claims. What nation's standard would *Mitsubishi* have looked to if *foreign* statutory claims were at issue? Suppose, for example, that a U.S. court was asked to compel arbitration of competition law claims under European Union and German law. Would U.S. law apply? Or would EU and German rules of non-arbitrability apply? Note Article V(2)(a) of the Convention. What choice-of-law rule does it provide?

3. Mitsubishi's *rationale for non-arbitrability doctrine. Mitsubishi* concluded that particular federal statutory claims were arbitrable. If the Convention does not *require* arbitration of antitrust claims, should the Court have done so? Consider the following explanation from *Mitsubishi*:

> The utility of the Convention in promoting the process of international commercial arbitra-tion depends upon the willingness of national courts to let go of matters they normally would think of as their own. . . . [W]e decline to subvert the spirit of the United States' accession to the Convention by recognizing subject matter exceptions where Congress has not expressly directed the courts to do so.

Is that persuasive? Consider the reasons advanced for the *American Safety* doctrine. Do they not strongly support application of the non-arbitrability doctrine to antitrust claims? Recall the treatment of antitrust claims under forum selection clauses and the *forum non conveniens* doctrine. *See supra* pp. 444-446, 523-524. Why should arbitration agree-ments be treated differently?

4. *Potentially different treatment of international and domestic antitrust claims. Mitsubishi* held that an arbitration clause contained in an *international* contract was enforceable, even as to federal antitrust claims. The Court expressly refused to decide whether the same result would apply in a purely *domestic* context, rather than in "an international commercial transaction." The Court based its decision to treat international and domestic transactions differently on the New York Convention's "spirit" and on "con-cerns of international comity, respect for the capacities of foreign and transnational tribunals, and sensitivity to the need of the international commercial system for predict-ability in the resolution of disputes." Is this a persuasive rationale? Is it appropriate for one set of rules to apply to international arbitration agreements and another to domestic ones? Why would one do this? Recall the discussion above about the scope of the UNCI-TRAL Model Law and second chapter of the FAA, both of which are specifically limited to particular international arbitration agreements and awards. *See supra* pp. 1167-1168.

5. *Criticism of* **Mitsubishi.** Although the Court's decision was applauded by international businesses, *Mitsubishi* also provoked criticism:

> if such fundamental issues as antitrust matters (and RICO claims) can be submitted to arbi-tration, what possible limits could there be to the reach of arbitrability in the international . . . context? The confusing and potentially dangerous shift of domestic public law concerns to the enforcement stage is likely to be ineffectual, destined to act as the shadow of a safeguard rather than a genuine means of protection. . . . The Court's rush to eradicate all national legal con-straints not only compromises legitimate national concerns, but also threatens the integrity of international arbitral adjudication itself, frustrating its normal tendency to seek guidance and appropriate limits from external factors. Carbonneau, *The Exuberant Pathway to Quixotic Inter-nationalism: Assessing the Folly of Mitsubishi*, 19 Vand. J. Transnat'l L. 265, 297-298 (1986).

Is this persuasive? Was *Mitsubishi* correctly decided?

6. *Procedural efficacy of arbitration of "public law" claims.* Does the arbitration process allow for adequate presentation and consideration of securities, antitrust, and other public law claims? Note the various aspects of arbitration (much valued by its proponents) which trouble the dissent in *Mitsubishi*—confidentiality, lack of U.S.-style discovery, non-judicial decision-maker, informal rules of evidence, lack of appeal, and (frequently, in the United States) the absence of a reasoned award. Even if these features of arbitration do not amount to what Justice Stevens uncharitably terms "despotic decision-making" in *Mitsubishi,* do they render arbitration inadequate for resolving "public" law claims? If so, is it because arbitrators are more likely than judges to make mistakes in applying public law claims? Is this risk greater for public law claims than private law claims? What are the broader economic and social consequences of errors in each case? For a more recent Supreme Court view of these issues, *see Shearson/American Express, Inc. v. McMahon,* 482 U.S. 220 (1987) ("the mistrust of arbitration that formed the basis for the *Wilko* opinion in 1953 is difficult to square with the assessment of arbitration that has prevailed since that time").

7. *Future versus existing disputes.* The majority in *Mitsubishi* reasons that, if arbitration can satisfactorily resolve an *existing* dispute, then there is no reason that arbitral procedures cannot suffice for *future* disputes. How does Justice Stevens reply to this? Is his answer persuasive?

8. *Showing required for non-arbitrability after* **Mitsubishi.** *Mitsubishi* acknowledged that "[d]oubtless, Congress may specify categories of claims it wishes to reserve for decision by our own Courts without contravening . . . the Convention." Nonetheless, *Mitsubishi* formulated a high standard for holding a statutory claim non-arbitrable: "We must assume that if Congress intended the substantive protection afforded by a given statute to include protection against waiver of the right to a judicial forum, that intention will be deducible from text or legislative history." The Court also said that claims will be deemed arbitrable unless Congress "expressly directed" a contrary result. Why is such a high standard of proof required? Is this standard of proof wise?

9. **Mitsubishi's** *treatment of choice-of-law clause excluding U.S. public policy or statutory claims.* How will a U.S. court asked to enforce an arbitral award dealing with U.S. antitrust claims react if the tribunal refuses to apply U.S. law? In a footnote (originally, footnote 19), *Mitsubishi* suggests that, where antitrust claims are concerned, such an agreement would not be enforced by U.S. courts: "in the event the choice-of-forum and choice-of-law clauses operated in tandem as a prospective waiver of a party's right to pursue statutory remedies for antitrust violations, we would have little hesitation in condemning the agreement as against public policy." Consider the choice-of-law clause in *Mitsubishi.* Why did it not amount to a prospective waiver of U.S. antitrust claims? Compare the public policy exceptions to forum selection and choice-of-law agreements. *See supra* pp. 511-528 and pp. 763-774.

10. *Treatment of public policy and statutory claims under* **Mitsubishi** *and* **Bremen**—*a comparison.* Is *Mitsubishi's* treatment of "prospective waivers" of statutory claims consistent with the result in *Bremen*? In *Bremen,* the Court enforced a forum selection clause where the foreign forum would not apply U.S. law (which included important protections for the plaintiff that were imposed by U.S. public policy). Note, however, that *Bremen* emphasized that the case involved a dispute arising from activities conducted outside the United States. Note also that *Bremen* suggested, and some lower courts have held, that, as to "essentially American" disputes, forum selection clauses that result in a waiver of substantive statutory rights are not enforceable. *See supra* pp. 423-426.

Suppose *Mitsubishi* had involved conduct having little or no relation to the United States—a distributorship termination in Canada or Mexico, for example. Would the Court still refuse to enforce forum selection/choice-of-law clauses that excluded the U.S. antitrust laws? Why should this hypothetical be treated differently from the actual facts in *Mitsubishi*? Suppose *Mitsubishi* had involved conduct with equally substantial connections to both the United States and Japan? How would *Bremen* have treated activities with this sort of U.S. nexus?

11. The Richards *decision — revisited.* Recall the decision in *Richards* (excerpted *supra* pp. 515-520). Was the decision consistent with the rationale in *Mitsubishi* [footnote 121 as reproduced in this chapter]?

(a) Prospective waivers of federal statutory rights. How does the *Richards* decision comport with *Mitsubishi*'s treatment of "prospective waivers" of antitrust rights? Is it possible that securities law claims are simply entitled to less protection under U.S. law than antitrust claims? Note that although the securities laws contain provisions specifically forbidding waivers of their protections, *see Wilko v. Swan, supra*, no analogous provision exists under the antitrust laws.

(b) Importance of comparable foreign remedies. Under the *Richards* analysis, how is a U.S. court to conclude that foreign law and remedies are comparable to U.S. ones? Is it likely that Congress intended such a test for arbitrability? In *Scherk*, Justice Douglas wrote in dissent: "When a foreign corporation undertakes fraudulent action which subjects it to the jurisdiction of our federal securities laws, nothing justifies the conclusion that only a diluted version of those laws protects American investors." Does *Richards* permit such dilution?

(c) Richards' *analysis.* Consider again the analysis in *Richards*, particularly of footnote 19 in *Mitsubishi*. Is it persuasive?

12. *"Second look" doctrine — judicial review of arbitral award's application of U.S. antitrust law.* In requiring arbitration of antitrust claims, *Mitsubishi* relies in significant part on the ability of U.S. courts to take a "second look" at the award: "Having permitted the arbitration to go forward, the national courts of the United States will have the opportunity at the award-enforcement stage to ensure that the legitimate interest in the enforcement of the antitrust laws has been addressed." Moreover, the Court indicated that nonrecognition of an award would be appropriate if the tribunal did not take "cognizance of the antitrust claims and actually decide[] them." *Mitsubishi* also said, however, that a U.S. court reviewing the arbitral awards should engage in only "minimal" "substantive review." This is consistent with U.S. law regarding domestic arbitral awards, which at most only permits nonrecognition for "manifest disregard of law." *See infra* pp. 1209-1211.

On the other hand, is it realistic to expect U.S. courts to defer almost entirely to decisions of private (often foreign) arbitrators on questions involving vital local public policies? Park, *Private Adjudicators and the Public Interest: The Expanding Scope of International Arbitration,* 12 Brook. J. Int'l L. 629, 642 (1986) ("The 'second look' doctrine is a problematic safety valve for ensuring that public law issues receive proper consideration. If it calls for review on the merits, it disrupts the arbitral process. But if it calls only for a mechanical examination of the face of the award, it may not provide an effective check on an arbitrator who mentions the Sherman Act before he proceeds to ignore it."). Is such a second look permitted under Article V of the New York Convention?

4.   Interpretation of International Commercial Arbitration Agreements

Where a valid arbitration agreement concerning arbitrable matters exists, determining whether particular disputes are subject to arbitration is principally a matter of interpreting the relevant contractual provisions. "[T]he first task of a court asked to compel arbitration is to determine whether the parties agreed to arbitrate that dispute."[127]

---

127. *See Mitsubishi Motors Corp. v. Soler Chrysler-Plymouth, Inc.,* 473 U.S. 614, 626 (1985).

Disputes frequently arise concerning the "scope" of the parties' arbitration agreement: that is, what category of disputes or claims have the parties agreed to submit to arbitration? Questions concerning the scope of arbitration agreements raise choice-of-law issues — specifically what national law governs the construction of the arbitration clause? In interpreting international arbitration agreements under the FAA, U.S. courts have generally applied a federal common law rule of contract interpretation that is expressly and vigorously "pro-arbitration." In the Supreme Court's words, "questions of arbitrability must be addressed with a healthy regard for the federal policy favoring arbitration [and] any doubts concerning the scope of arbitrable issues should be resolved in favor of arbitration."[128] Federal courts have generally applied this federal common law of contract interpretation, albeit without considered analysis, even when the parties' agreement selects a foreign or state governing law.[129]

U.S. courts have adopted divergent approaches to the respective roles of the arbitrators and national courts in interpreting arbitration agreements. Some U.S. courts appear to take the view, albeit not consistently or clearly, that the interpretation of the scope of an arbitration agreement is, in the first instance, a matter for the arbitral tribunal, and only thereafter is judicial review appropriate.[130] In contrast, other U.S. courts have held that the resolution of disputes about arbitrability are for the courts, not for the arbitrators: "the question of arbitrability . . . is undeniably an issue for judicial determination."[131] In both cases, the tribunal's jurisdictional decisions are ultimately subject to judicial review in actions to confirm, vacate, or enforce the arbitrators' award, including for excess of authority under Article V(1)(c) of the New York Convention and §10(d) of the domestic FAA.[132]

Excerpted below are materials that illustrate U.S. judicial approaches to the interpretation of arbitration agreements. *Apollo Computer* is an example of judicial deference to jurisdictional rulings of an arbitral tribunal, while *Mitsubishi* suggests a greater judicial role in such matters.

APOLLO COMPUTER, INC. v. BERG
886 F.2d 469 (1st Cir. 1989)

Torruella, Circuit Judge. The plaintiff appeals from a district court order refusing its request for a permanent stay of arbitration proceedings. . . . Apollo Computer, Inc. ("Apollo") and Dicoscan Distributed Computing Scandinavia AB ("Dico") entered into an agreement granting Dico, a Swedish company having its principal place of business in Stockholm, the right to distribute Apollo's computers in four Scandinavian countries. Helge Berg and Lars Arvid Skoog, the defendants in this action, signed the agreement on Dico's behalf in their respective capacities as its chairman and president. The agreement contained a clause stating that all disputes arising out of or in connection with the agreement would be settled in accordance with the Rules of Arbitration of the International Chamber of Commerce ("ICC"), and another clause that stated that the

128. *Moses H. Cone Mem. Hosp. v. Mercury Construction Corp.*, 460 U.S. 1, 24-25 (1983). *See Mitsubishi Motors Corp. v. Soler Chrysler-Plymouth Inc.*, 473 U.S. 614 (1985).

129. *See, e.g.*, *Becker Autoradio USA, Inc. v. Becker Autoradiowerk GmbH*, 585 F.2d 39, 43-44 & n.8 (3d Cir. 1978), discussed at *supra* pp. 1165-1167 and *infra* pp. 1199-1200.

130. *See* cases cited *infra* p. 1199.

131. *AT&T Technologies, Inc. v. Communications Workers of America*, 475 U.S. 643, 649 (1986). *See supra* pp. 1168-1170.

132. For discussion of judicial review of arbitrators' jurisdictional decisions, *see infra* pp. 1201-1215.

agreement was to be governed by Massachusetts law. The agreement also provided that it could not be assigned by Dico without the written consent of Apollo.

In September 1984, after disputes relating to the financing of Dico's purchases, Apollo notified Dico that it intended to terminate the agreement, effective immediately. Dico then filed for protection from its creditors under Swedish bankruptcy law and subsequently entered into liquidation, with its affairs being handled by its trustee in bankruptcy. The trustee assigned Dico's right to bring claims for damages against Apollo to the defendants. In May 1988, the defendants filed a complaint and a request for arbitration with the ICC.

On August 24, 1988, Apollo rejected arbitration, claiming that there was no agreement to arbitrate between it and the defendants, and that assignment of Dico's contractual right to arbitrate was precluded by the agreement's nonassignment clause. The ICC requested both parties to submit briefs on the issue. On December 15, 1988, the ICC's Court of Arbitration decided that pursuant to its rules, the arbitrator should resolve the issue of arbitrability, and directed the parties to commence arbitration proceedings to resolve that issue and, if necessary, the merits.

On January 11, 1989, Apollo filed the instant action in federal district court under diversity of citizenship jurisdiction. It sought a permanent stay of the arbitration . . . on the grounds that there is no arbitration agreement between the parties. . . . Apollo then moved for summary judgment. On May 11, 1989, the district court denied the request to stay arbitration and the motion for summary judgment. . . .

We . . . find that the parties contracted to submit issues of arbitrability to the arbitrator. There is no question that this contract falls under the aegis of the [FAA]. Both parties agree that under the [FAA], the *general* rule is that the arbitrability of a dispute is to be determined by the court. Parties may, however, agree to allow the arbitrator to decide both whether a particular dispute is arbitrable as well as the merits of the dispute.

In this case, the parties agreed that all disputes arising out of or in connection with their contract would be settled by binding arbitration "in accordance with the rules of arbitration of the International Chamber of Commerce." Article 8.3 of the ICC's Rules . . . states:

> Should one of the parties raise one or more pleas concerning the existence or validity of the agreement to arbitrate, and should the [ICC Court of Arbitration] be satisfied of the *prima facie* existence of such an agreement, the [ICC Court of Arbitration] may, without prejudice to the admissibility or merits of the plea or pleas, decide that the arbitration shall proceed. In such a case, any decision as to the arbitrator's jurisdiction shall be taken by the arbitrator himself.

Article 8.4 of the ICC's Rules of Arbitration states:

> Unless otherwise provided, the arbitrator shall not cease to have jurisdiction by reason of any claim that the contract is null and void or allegation that it is inexistent provided that he upholds the validity of the agreement to arbitrate. He shall continue to have jurisdiction, even though the contract itself may be inexistent or null and void, to determine the respective rights of the parties and to adjudicate upon their claims and pleas.

The contract therefore delegates to the arbitrator decisions about the arbitrability of disputes involving the existence and validity of a *prima facie* agreement to arbitrate. Both the ICC's Court of Arbitration and the district court determined that a *prima facie* agreement to arbitrate existed. Therefore, they reasoned, Article 8.3 requires the arbitrator to determine the validity of the arbitration agreement in this specific instance — in other words, decide whether the arbitration agreement applies to disputes between Apollo and the assignees of Dico.

Apollo did not discuss this issue in its brief. At oral argument, it averred that Article 8.3 is inapplicable because no *prima facie* agreement to arbitrate exists between it and the defendants. We are unpersuaded by this argument. The relevant agreement here is the one between Apollo and Dico. The defendants claim that Dico's right to compel arbitration under that agreement has been assigned to them. We find that they have made the *prima facie* showing required by Article 8.3. Whether the right to compel arbitration survives the termination of the agreement, and if so, whether that right was validly assigned to the defendants and whether it can be enforced by them against Apollo are issues relating to the continued existence and validity of the agreement.

Ordinarily, Apollo would be entitled to have these issues resolved by a court. By contracting to have all disputes resolved according to the Rules of the ICC, however, Apollo agreed to be bound by Articles 8.3 and 8.4. These provisions clearly and unmistakably allow the arbitrator to determine her own jurisdiction when, as here, there exists a *prima facie* agreement to arbitrate whose continued existence and validity is being questioned. The arbitrator should decide whether a valid arbitration agreement exists between Apollo and the defendants under the terms of the contract between Apollo and Dico. . . .

MITSUBISHI MOTORS CORP. v. SOLER CHRYSLER-PLYMOUTH, INC.
473 U.S. 614 (1985)

JUSTICE BLACKMUN. [The facts and arbitration clause are set forth above at pp. 1186-1187.][133] . . . [W]e address the contention raised in Soler's cross-petition that the arbitration clause at issue may not be read to encompass the statutory counterclaims stated in its answer to the complaint. In making this argument, Soler does not question the Court of Appeals' application of Paragraph VI of the Sales Agreement to the disputes involved here as a matter of standard contract interpretation.[134] Instead, it argues that as a matter of law a court may not construe an arbitration agreement to encompass claims arising out of statutes designed to protect a class to which the party resisting arbitration belongs "unless [that party] has expressly agreed" to arbitrate those claims, by which Soler presumably means that the arbitration clause must specifically mention the statute giving rise to the claims that a party to the clause seeks to arbitrate. . . .

[T]he first task of a court asked to compel arbitration of a dispute is to determine whether the parties agreed to arbitrate that dispute. The court is to make this determination by applying the "federal substantive law of arbitrability, applicable to any arbitration agreement within the coverage of the Act." And that body of law counsels

---

133. The District Court found that the arbitration clause did not cover the fourth and six counterclaims, which sought damages for defamation, or the allegations in the seventh counterclaim concerning discriminatory treatment and the establishment of minimum-sales volumes. Accordingly, it retained jurisdiction over those portions of the litigation.

134. . . . Soler does suggest that, because the title of the clause referred only to "certain matters," and the clause itself specifically referred only to "Articles I-B through V," it should be read narrowly to exclude the statutory claims. Soler ignores the inclusion within those "certain matters" of "[a]ll disputes, controversies or differences which may arise between [Mitsubishi] and [Soler] out of or in relation to [the specified provisions] or for the breach thereof." Contrary to Soler's suggestion, the exclusion of some areas of possible dispute from the scope of an arbitration clause does not serve to restrict the reach of an otherwise broad clause in the areas in which it was intended to operate. . . .

that questions of arbitrability must be addressed with a healthy regard for the federal policy favoring arbitration. . . . The Arbitration Act establishes that, as a matter of federal law, any doubts concerning the scope of arbitrable issues should be resolved in favor of arbitration, whether the problem at hand is the construction of the contract language itself or an allegation of waiver, delay, or a like defense to arbitrability.

Thus, as with any other contract, the parties' intentions control, but those intentions are generously construed as to issues of arbitrability. There is no reason to depart from these guidelines where a party bound by an arbitration agreement raises claims founded on statutory rights, [*Wilko v. Swan, supra,* and] the Act itself provides no basis for disfavoring agreements to arbitrate statutory claims by skewing the otherwise hospitable inquiry into arbitrability. . . .

JUSTICE STEVENS, dissenting. . . . [First,] as a matter of ordinary contract interpretation, there are at least two reasons why that clause does not apply to Soler's antitrust claim against Chrysler and Mitsubishi. First, the clause only applies to two-party disputes between Soler and Mitsubishi. The antitrust violation alleged in Soler's counterclaim is a three-party dispute. Soler has joined both Chrysler and its associated company, Mitsubishi, as counterdefendants. . . . Only by stretching the language of the arbitration clause far beyond its ordinary meaning could one possibly conclude that it encompasses this three-party dispute.

Second, the clause only applies to disputes "which may arise between MMC and BUYER out of or in relation to Articles I-B through V of this Agreement or the breach thereof. . . ." Thus, disputes relating to only 5 out of a total of 15 Articles in the Sales Procedure Agreement are arbitrable. Those five Articles cover: (1) the terms and conditions of direct sales (matter such as the scheduling of orders, deliveries, and payment); (2) technical and engineering changes; (3) compliance by Mitsubishi with customs laws and regulations, and Soler's obligation to inform Mitsubishi of relevant local laws; (4) trademarks and patent rights; and (5) Mitsubishi's right to cease production of any products. It is immediately obvious that Soler's antitrust claim did not arise out of Articles I-B through V and it is not a claim "for the breach thereof." The question is whether it is a dispute "in relation to" those Articles. . . .

The federal policy favoring arbitration cannot sustain the weight that the Court assigns to it. A clause requiring arbitration of all claims "relating to" a contract surely could not encompass a claim that the arbitration clause was itself part of a contract in restraint of trade. Nor in my judgment should it be read to encompass a claim that relies, not on a failure to perform the contract, but on an independent violation of federal law. The matters asserted by way of defense do not control the character, or the source, of the claim that Soler has asserted. Accordingly, simply as a matter of ordinary contract interpretation, I would hold that Soler's antitrust claim is not arbitrable. . . .

[Second,] until today all of our cases enforcing agreements to arbitrate under the [FAA] have involved contract claims. In one, the party claiming a breach of contractual warranties also claimed that the breach amounted to fraud actionable under §10(b) of the Securities Exchange Act of 1934. *Scherk v. Alberto-Culver Co., supra.* But this is the first time the Court has considered the question whether a standard arbitration clause referring to claims arising out of or relating to a contract should be construed to cover statutory claims that have only an indirect relationship to the contract. In my opinion, neither the Congress that enacted the [FAA], nor the many parties who have agreed to such standard clauses, could have anticipated the Court's answer to that question. . . .

In view of the Court's repeated recognition of the distinction between federal statutory rights and contractual rights, together with the undisputed historical fact that arbitration has functioned almost entirely in either the area of labor disputes or in "ordinary disputes between merchants as to questions of fact," it is reasonable to assume that most lawyers and executives would not expect the language in the standard arbitration clause to cover federal statutory claims. Thus, in my opinion, both a fair respect for the importance of the interests that Congress has identified as worthy of federal statutory protection, and a fair appraisal of the most likely understanding of the parties who sign agreements containing standard arbitration clauses, support a presumption that such clauses do not apply to federal statutory claims. . . .

Notes on Apollo and Mitsubishi

1. *Who decides jurisdictional objections in* Apollo *and* Mitsubishi*?* Compare the respective roles of the court and the arbitral tribunal in interpreting the scope of the arbitration agreement in *Mitsubishi* and *Apollo*. Is it the court or the arbitrator that decides the scope of the parties' arbitration clause in each case? Are the two decisions consistent? Note that the *Mitsubishi* Court itself held that certain claims were outside the scope of the arbitration agreement and could not be arbitrated. Would that result have been possible under the analysis in *Apollo*? Or would issues of interpretation of the scope of the arbitration clause have been submitted in the first instance to the arbitrators? Are there material differences between the arbitration agreements in the two cases which explain the different approaches? What are they?

2. *Lower U.S. court decisions considering allocation of competence to decide disputes over the scope of an arbitration agreement.* How should competence to decide disputes over the scope of international arbitration agreements be allocated? Some lower U.S. courts have held that disputes over the scope of an arbitration agreement are to be resolved by a court. *See Griffin v. Semperit of America, Inc.*, 414 F. Supp. 1384, 1389 (S.D. Tex. 1976); *Pollux Marine Agencies, Inc. v. Louis Dreyfus Corp.*, 455 F. Supp. 211, 218 (S.D.N.Y. 1978) ("Absent an agreement to the contrary, arbitrability is clearly a question for the Court"). One lower court put the issue as follows:

> Imagine a contract for construction of a one room log cabin. The parties agreed that disputes over the glass used in the windows would be subject to arbitration. If the owner were to sue the builder on broad breach of contract and tort causes of action, alleging drafty walls, a leaky roof, and a complete lack of wooden flooring, it would defy logic to force the owner to submit the entire dispute to arbitration, when all he had agreed to arbitrate was disputes over window glass. *Mesquite Lake Associates v. Lurgi Corp.*, 754 F. Supp. 161 (N.D. Cal. 1991).

In contrast, most U.S. lower courts have held that disputes over the scope of an arbitration agreement may be for resolution by the arbitral tribunal. *E.g., Teledyne v. Kone*, 892 F.2d 1404 (9th Cir. 1990); *Sauer-Getriebe KG v. White*, 715 F.2d 348 (7th Cir. 1983). Which approach better accords with the parties' expectations? Which approach better serves the arbitral process?

3. *Role of parties' agreement in allocation of competence to decide disputes over scope of arbitration agreement —* First Options. As discussed above, the Supreme Court held in *First Options of Chicago, Inc. v. Kaplan*, 514 U.S. 938 (1995), that there is a distinction between disputes over the existence of an arbitration agreement and disputes over the scope of an admittedly valid agreement. As to the former, *First Options* said that courts "should not assume that the parties agreed to arbitrate arbitrability unless there is 'clea[r] and unmistakabl[e]' evidence that they did so." 514 U.S. at 939. As to the latter—whether a dispute is within the scope of a valid agreement—the opposite presumption applies: "[A]ny doubts concerning the scope of arbitrable issues should be resolved in favor of arbitration." 514 U.S. at 945. *See supra* pp. 1177-1192. Is this a sensible approach? When might these be "clear and unmistakable evidence" of an agreement to arbitrate disputes over the scope of an arbitration agreement? Consider the agreement to arbitrate, and the provisions of the ICC Rules it incorporates, in *Apollo Computer.* Are Articles 8.3 and 8.4 of the ICC Rules such an agreement? What if the existence or validity of the parties' arbitration agreement had been challenged in *Apollo Computer*?

   4. *"Pro-arbitration" bias of interpretation under the FAA and New York Convention.* If a court does consider issues of arbitrability, *Mitsubishi* held that "any doubts concerning the scope of arbitrable issues should be resolved in favor of arbitration." Or, as the Court put it even more expansively in *United Steelworkers of America v. Warrior & Gulf Navigation Co.,* 363 U.S. 574, 582-583 (1960), arbitration must be compelled unless the court can say with "positive assurance that the arbitration clause is not susceptible to an interpretation that covers the asserted dispute."

   Most lower U.S. courts have followed this vigorously pro-arbitration rule of interpretation of arbitration agreements. *E.g., Pennzoil Exploration and Production Co. v. Ramco Energy Ltd.,* 139 F.3d 1061, 1067 (5th Cir. 1998); *Progressive Casualty Ins. Co. v. CA Reaseguradora Nacional de Venezuela,* 991 F.2d 42 (2d Cir. 1993); *Riley v. Kingsley Underwriting Agencies, Ltd.,* 969 F.2d 953 (10th Cir. 1992); *David L. Threlkeld & Co. v. Metallgesellschaft Ltd.,* 923 F.2d 245, 250-251 (2d Cir. 1991). *See* G. Born, *International Commercial Arbitration* 1067-1072 (2009).

   5. *Rationale for pro-arbitration rule of interpretation.* Does the federal rule interpreting arbitration agreements expansively accord with the likely intent of private parties? Does either the FAA or the New York Convention contain provisions governing the interpretation of arbitration agreements? Are such rules necessary to safeguard the arbitral process?

   6. *Possible applicability of foreign law to the interpretation of arbitration agreements.* In *Mitsubishi,* the parties' underlying agreement was subject to Swiss law. Why isn't interpretation of the parties' arbitration agreement therefore a question of Swiss law, not subject to the FAA? Note that the parties' agreement calls for arbitration in Japan. Arguably, therefore, Japanese law might govern the arbitration agreement. *See* G. Born, *International Commercial Arbitration* 459-515, 1086-1087 (2009). Why was U.S. law applied to the interpretation of the arbitration agreement? Was it appropriate for the Court to apply U.S. law? Or should it have applied Swiss or Japanese law?

   U.S. courts have almost unanimously applied U.S. (federal) law to interpret the scope of arbitration agreements, even where a choice-of-law clause selected foreign law. In addition to *Mitsubishi, see Deprenyl Animal Health, Inc. v. University of Toronto Innovations,* 297 F.3d 1343, 1349 (Fed. Cir. 2002) (applying federal law despite Canadian choice-of-law clause); *General Elec. Co. v. Deutz,* 270 F.3d 144, 154 (3d Cir. 2001) ("[f]ederal law applies to the interpretation of arbitration agreements"); *Morewitz v. West of England Ship Owners Mut. Prot. & Indem. Ass'n,* 62 F.3d 1356, 1364 (11th Cir. 1995); *Becker Autoradio USA, Inc. v. Becker Autoradiowerk GmbH,* 585 F.2d 39, 43-44 & n.8 (3d Cir. 1978) ("[W]hether a particular dispute is within the class of those disputes governed by the arbitration and choice of law clause is a matter of federal law"); *Chloe Z Fishing Co. v. Odyssey Re (London) Ltd.,* 109 F. Supp. 2d 1236, 1254 & n.16 (S.D. Cal. 2000).

There are a few lower court decisions that appear to apply foreign law to the interpretation of the parties' arbitration agreement. *E.g.*, *Motorola Credit Corp. v. Uzan*, 388 F.3d 39 (2d Cir. 2004) (applying Swiss law to determine applicability of arbitration clauses); *In re Oil Spill by Amoco Cadiz etc.*, 659 F.2d 789 (7th Cir. 1981) (apparently relying on English law to interpret scope of arbitration clause, but also relying on FAA's presumption of arbitrability). Is this approach wise? Why or why not?

7. *Application of arbitration agreement to statutory claims. Mitsubishi* held that the parties had intended to arbitrate the antitrust claims asserted by Soler. Is that persuasive? Do parties ordinarily consider the existence and arbitrability of statutory claims — not based on the contract itself — when they include an arbitration provision in their agreement? If not, why is *Mitsubishi* willing to "distort the process of contract interpretation," 473 U.S. at 627, in this context? Or do businessmen not really concern themselves with the precise legal basis for particular claims? Consider Justice Stevens' dissent in *Mitsubishi*. As a matter of contract interpretation, is it persuasive? Should a pro-arbitration bias also apply to statutory claims?

C. Recognition and Enforcement of International Arbitral Awards

The arbitral process generally results in an award which, like the judgment of a national court, disposes of the parties' claims. As a practical matter, many awards do not require judicial enforcement, because they are voluntarily complied with.[135] Nevertheless, the ultimate test of any arbitration proceeding is its ability to render an award which, if necessary, will be enforced in any relevant national court.

An arbitral award is not a judgment of a court.[136] Instead, judicial confirmation and enforcement of an award must be sought in order to invoke coercive state enforcement mechanisms.[137] It is only if an arbitral award can successfully be enforced that a successful claimant can ensure that it will recover damages awarded to it.[138] And it is only if an award will be recognized that a successful respondent can ensure that new litigation on previously arbitrated claims is not commenced against it by a persistent claimant.[139]

In marked contrast to foreign court judgments, whose enforcement in the United States is subject principally to state law,[140] the enforcement of international arbitral awards in the United States is governed primarily by federal law. Two sources of authority are particularly important — the New York Convention and the FAA (specifically, the second chapter of the FAA).[141] This parallels approaches in many foreign states, where

---

135. *See* Lalive, *Enforcing Awards,* in ICC, *60 Years of ICC Arbitration* 317, 319 (1984) (voluntary compliance with ICC awards exceeds 90 percent).

136. A foreign arbitral award "may not itself be treated as a foreign money judgment." *Fotochrome, Inc. v. Copal Co., Ltd.*, 517 F.2d 512 (2d Cir. 1975).

137. *Sentry Life Ins. Co. v. Borad,* 759 F.2d 695, 698 (9th Cir. 1985); *Tamari v. Conrad,* 522 F.2d 778, 781 (7th Cir. 1977) ("An arbitrator's award is not self-executing.").

138. As with money judgments, the "enforcement" of an arbitral award refers to the implementation of coercive measures by national courts or other government authorities to effectuate the award. *See supra* p. 1078; *Fotochrome Inc. v. Copal Co. Ltd.*, 517 F.2d, 519 (2d Cir. 1975).

139. Again like money judgments, the "recognition" or "confirmation" of an arbitral award refers to the decision of a national court (or comparable body) to give preclusive effect to the arbitrator's disposition of the parties' claim. *See supra* p. 1078.

140. *See supra* pp. 1110-1114.

141. In a limited number of cases, other international agreements (such as the Inter-American Convention, bilateral treaties, and the ICSID Convention) are also potentially important. *See* G. Born, *International Commercial Arbitration* 90-108 (2009).

the recognition of foreign arbitral awards is governed by the Convention and national legislation applicable to international arbitration (specifically, in many cases, some version of the UNCITRAL Model Law).[142]

1.   Enforceability of International Arbitral Awards Under the New York Convention

The New York Convention was designed in large measure to facilitate the enforcement of foreign arbitral awards.[143] Article III of the Convention imposes a general requirement that Contracting States recognize arbitral awards made in other countries:

> Each contracting state shall recognize arbitral awards as binding and enforce them in accordance with the rules of procedure of the territory where the award is relied upon, under the conditions laid down in the following articles. There shall not be imposed substantially more onerous conditions or higher fees or charges on the recognition or enforcement of arbitral awards to which the Convention applies than are imposed on the recognition or enforcement of domestic arbitral awards.

Several aspects of the Convention give special force to Article III's requirement and underscore its drafters' goal of facilitating transnational enforcement of arbitral awards. First, the Convention presumes the validity of awards and places the burden of proving invalidity on the party opposing enforcement.[144] Second, awards need not be confirmed in the arbitral seat before enforcement can be sought abroad (*i.e.,* no "double exequatur" requirement).[145] Third, as Article III expressly provides, Contracting States may not impose either conditions or procedural requirements for Convention awards that are more onerous than those applicable to domestic awards.[146]

Finally, Article V of the Convention sets forth a limited set of grounds for nonrecognition of arbitral awards. Article V of the Convention is implemented by §207 of the FAA. Section 207 provides that a court "shall confirm" awards subject to the Convention "unless . . . one of the grounds for refusal" specified in the Convention is present. U.S. courts have generally regarded Article V's exceptions as exclusive, and have emphasized the "general pro-enforcement bias informing the Convention."[147]

---

142. G. Born, *International Commercial Arbitration* 91-145 (2009); E. Gaillard *et al., Fouchard Gaillard Goldman on International Commercial Arbitration* 776 (1999).

143. *See* A. van den Berg, *The New York Convention of 1958* 6-10, 264-274 (1981); *Bergesen v. Joseph Muller Corp.,* 710 F.2d 928, 932 (2d Cir. 1983) ("intended purpose" of Convention is "to encourage the recognition and enforcement of international arbitration awards"); *Parsons & Whittemore Overseas Co. v. Societe Generale de L'Industrie du Papier,* 508 F.2d 969, 973 (2d Cir. 1974).

144. *See* A. van den Berg, *The New York Convention of 1958* 9 (1981) (Geneva Convention required party enforcing award to prove its validity; New York Convention reversed burden of proof); G. Born, *International Commercial Arbitration* 2718-2720 (2009); *Parsons & Whittemore,* 508 F.2d at 973 ("While the Geneva Convention [of 1927] placed the burden of proof on the party seeking enforcement of a foreign arbitral award and did not circumscribe the range of available defenses to those enumerated in the Convention, the 1958 Convention clearly shifted the burden of proof to the party defending against enforcement and limited his defenses to seven set forth in Article V.").

145. G. Born, *International Commercial Arbitration* 2720-2721 (2009).

146. New York Convention, Article III.

147. *Parsons & Whittemore Overseas Co. v. Societe Generale de L'Industrie du Papier,* 508 F.2d 969, 973 (2d Cir. 1974). *See also Management & Technical Consultants SA v. Parson-Jurden Int'l Corp.,* 820 F.2d 1531, 1533 (9th Cir. 1987); *Biotronik etc. v. Medford Medical Instrument Co.,* 415 F. Supp. 133, 136-137 (D.N.J. 1976) ("basic thrust of the Convention was to liberalize the procedures for enforcing foreign arbitral awards"); G. Born, *International Commercial Arbitration* 2721-2722, 2736-2781 (2009).

The presumption of enforceability, established in Article III of the New York Convention, and described above, is subject to eight exceptions, set forth in Articles V and VI. In summary, they are:

1. Article V(1)(a) — The award was rendered pursuant to an arbitration agreement that was invalid because, under the applicable law, the parties lacked capacity to make the agreement or the agreement was itself invalid.
2. Article V(1)(b) — The losing party "was not given proper notice of the appointment of the arbitrator or of the arbitration proceedings or was otherwise unable to present his case."
3. Article V(1)(c) — The arbitral award "deals with a difference not contemplated by or not falling within the terms of the submission to arbitrate."
4. Article V(1)(d) — The composition of the arbitral tribunal or the tribunal's procedures violated either the parties' agreement or, in the absence of any such agreement, the law of the arbitral seat.
5. Article V(1)(e) — The arbitral award is either not yet "binding" or has been set aside or suspended "by a competent authority of the country in which, or under the law of which, that award was made."
6. Article V(2)(a) — The subject matter of the parties' dispute is "not capable of settlement by arbitration" under the law of the enforcing state.
7. Article V(2)(b) — Recognition or enforcement of the arbitral award would be contrary to the public policy of the enforcing state.
8. Article VI — Where an application has been made to a court or other competent authority of the "country in which, or under the law of which, that award was made," then the court where enforcement is sought "may, if it considers it proper, adjourn the decision on the enforcement of the award. . . ."

The Convention is implemented in the United States by the second chapter of the FAA. Among other things, §207 of the Act provides for the confirmation of awards "falling under the [New York] Convention," unless the court "finds one of the grounds for refusal or deferral of recognition or enforcement of the award specified in the [New York] Convention."[148] U.S. courts have generally held that the Convention is self-executing and that its provisions concerning recognition of awards must be applied in federal courts (as well as state courts).[149]

2. Selected Materials on the Enforceability of International Arbitral Awards

The materials excerpted below provide an introduction to the enforceability of international arbitral awards in U.S. courts and elsewhere. First, consider how arbitral awards are dealt with by the UNCITRAL Model Law and the FAA. Next, review *Parsons & Whittemore*, which considers a number of challenges to the enforceability of an arbitral award under the FAA and New York Convention. Finally, *Northern Corp. v. Triad International Marketing SA* addresses a public policy challenge to an award.

---

148. 9 U.S.C. §207.

149. *Chloe Z Fishing Co. v. Odyssey Re (London) Ltd.*, 109 F. Supp. 2d 1236, 1252 (S.D. Cal. 2000); *Hartford Fire Ins. Co. v. Lloyds Syndicate 0056 ASH*, 1997 WL 33491787, at *2 (D. Conn. 1997); *Filanto, SpA v. Chilewich Int'l Corp.*, 789 F. Supp. 1229, 1236 (S.D.N.Y. 1992); *F.A. Richards & Assocs. v. General Marine Catering Co.*, 688 So. 2d 199 (La. App. 1997).

FEDERAL ARBITRATION ACT
9 U.S.C. §§1-16, 201-210, §§301-307 [excerpted in Appendix S]

UNCITRAL MODEL LAW
[excerpted in Appendices T and U]

PARSONS & WHITTEMORE OVERSEAS CO. v. SOCIETE GENERALE DE L'INDUSTRIE DU PAPIER
508 F.2d 969 (2d Cir. 1974)

J. JOSEPH SMITH, CIRCUIT JUDGE. Parsons & Whittemore Overseas Co., Inc. ("Overseas"), an American corporation, appeals from the entry of summary judgment . . . on the counter-claim by Societe Generale de l'Industrie du Papier ("RAKTA"), an Egyptian corporation, to confirm a foreign arbitral award holding Overseas liable to RAKTA for breach of contract. . . . We affirm the district court's confirmation of the foreign award.

In November 1962, Overseas consented by written agreement with RAKTA to construct, start up and, for one year, manage and supervise a paperboard mill in Alexandria, Egypt. The Agency for International Development ("AID") . . . would finance the project by supplying RAKTA with funds with which to purchase letters of credit in Overseas' favor. Among the contract's terms was an arbitration clause which provided a means to settle differences arising in the course of performance, and a "force majeure" clause, which excused delay in performance due to causes beyond Overseas' reasonable capacity to control.

Work proceeded as planned until May 1967. Then, with the Arab-Israeli Six Day War on the horizon, recurrent expressions of Egyptian hostility to Americans — nationals of the principal ally of the Israeli enemy — caused the majority of the Overseas work crew to leave Egypt. On June 6, the Egyptian government broke diplomatic ties with the United States and ordered all Americans expelled from Egypt except those who would apply and qualify for a special visa. Having abandoned the project for the present with the construction phase near completion, Overseas notified RAKTA that it regarded this postponement as excused by the force majeure clause. RAKTA disagreed and sought damages for breach of contract. Overseas refused to settle and RAKTA, already at work on completing the performance promised by Overseas, invoked the arbitration clause. Overseas responded by calling into play the clause's option to bring a dispute directly to a three-man arbitral board governed by the rules of the International Chamber of Commerce. [The tribunal issued a preliminary award, which recognized Overseas' force majeure defense as good only during the period from May 28 to June 30, 1967, and a final award in March, 1973: Overseas was held liable to RAKTA for $312,507.45 in damages for breach of contract and $30,000 for RAKTA's costs; additionally, the arbitrator's compensation was set at $49,000, with Overseas responsible for three-fourths of the sum.] . . .

Article V(2)(b) of the Convention allows the court in which enforcement of a foreign arbitral award is sought to refuse enforcement . . . if "enforcement of the award would be contrary to the public policy of [the forum] country." . . . [Article V(2)(b)'s] precursors in the Geneva Convention and the 1958 Convention's *ad hoc* committee draft extended the public policy exception to, respectively, awards contrary to "principles of the law" and awards violative of "fundamental principles of the law." In one commentator's view, the Convention's failure to include similar language signifies a narrowing of the defense. Contini, [*International Commercial Arbitration,*] 8 Am. J. Comp. L. 283 at 304. . . .

Perhaps more probative, however, are the inferences to be drawn from the history of the Convention as a whole. The general pro-enforcement bias informing the Convention . . . points toward a narrow reading of the public policy defense. An expansive construction of this defense would vitiate the Convention's basic effort to remove preexisting obstacles to enforcement. . . . Additionally, considerations of reciprocity—considerations given express recognition in the Convention itself—counsel courts to invoke the public policy defense with caution lest foreign courts frequently accept it as a defense to enforcement of arbitral awards rendered in the United States. We conclude, therefore, that the Convention's public policy defense should be construed narrowly. Enforcement of foreign arbitral awards may be denied on this basis only where enforcement would violate the forum state's most basic notions of morality and justice. *Cf.* 1 *Restatement (Second) Conflict of Laws* §117, comment c, at 340 (1971); *Loucks v. Standard Oil Co.*, 224 N.Y. 99, 111 (1918).

Under this view of the public policy provision in the Convention, Overseas' public policy defense may easily be dismissed. Overseas argues that various actions by United States officials subsequent to the severance of American-Egyptian relations—most particularly, AID's withdrawal of financial support for the Overseas-RAKTA contract—required Overseas, as a loyal American citizen, to abandon the project. Enforcement of an award predicated on the feasibility of Overseas' returning to work in defiance of these expressions of national policy would therefore allegedly contravene United States public policy. In equating "national" policy with United States "public" policy, the appellant quite plainly misses the mark. To read the public policy defense as a parochial device protective of national political interests would seriously undermine the Convention's utility. This provision was not meant to enshrine the vagaries of international politics under the rubric of "public policy." Rather, a circumscribed public policy doctrine was contemplated by the Convention's framers and every indication is that the United States, in acceding to the Convention, meant to subscribe to this supranational emphasis. To deny enforcement of this award largely because of the United States' falling out with Egypt in recent years would mean converting a defense intended to be of narrow scope into a major loophole in the Convention's mechanism for enforcement. We have little hesitation, therefore, in disallowing Overseas' proposed public policy defense.

Article V(2)(a) authorizes a court to deny enforcement . . . of a foreign arbitral award when "[t]he subject matter of the difference is not capable of settlement by arbitration under the law of that [the forum] country." . . . Overseas' argument, that "United States foreign policy issues can hardly be placed at the mercy of foreign arbitrators 'who are charged with the execution of no public trust' and whose loyalties are to foreign interests," plainly fails to raise [a] substantial . . . issue of arbitrability. The mere fact that an issue of national interest may incidentally figure into the resolution of a breach of contract claim does not make the dispute not arbitrable. Rather, certain *categories* of claims may be non-arbitrable because of the special national interest vested in their resolution. . . .

Under Article V(I)(b) of the Convention, enforcement of a foreign arbitral award may be denied if the defendant can prove that he was "not given proper notice . . . or was otherwise unable to present his case." This provision essentially sanctions the application of the forum state's standards of due process. Overseas seeks relief under this provision for the arbitration court's refusal to delay proceedings in order to accommodate the speaking schedule of one of Overseas' witnesses, David Nes, the United States Charge d'Affaires in Egypt at the time of the Six Day War. This attempt to state a due process claim fails for several reasons. First, inability to produce one's witnesses before an arbitral tribunal is a risk inherent in an agreement to submit to arbitration. By agreeing to submit disputes to arbitration, a party relinquishes his courtroom rights—including that to subpoena witnesses—in favor of arbitration "with all of its well known advantages and drawbacks." *Washington-Baltimore Newspaper Guild, Local 35 v. The Washington Post Co.*, 442 F.2d 1234, 1288 (1971). Secondly, the logistical problems of scheduling hearing dates convenient to parties, counsel and arbitrators scattered about the globe argues against deviating from an initially mutually agreeable time plan unless a scheduling change is truly unavoidable. In this instance, Overseas' allegedly key witness was kept from attending the hearing due to a prior commitment to lecture at an American university—hardly the type of obstacle to his presence which would require the arbitral tribunal to postpone the hearing as a matter of fundamental fairness to Overseas. . . . The arbitration tribunal acted within its discretion in declining to reschedule a hearing for the convenience of an Overseas witness. Overseas' due process rights under American law, rights entitled to full force under the Convention as a defense to enforcement, were in no way infringed by the tribunal's decision. . . .

Both [Article V(1)(c) and FAA §10(d)] basically allow a party to attack an award predicated upon arbitration of a subject matter not within the agreement to submit to arbitration. This defense to enforcement of a foreign award, like the others already discussed, should be construed narrowly. Once again a narrow construction would comport with the enforcement-facilitating thrust of the Convention. In addition, the case law under the similar provision of the [FAA] strongly supports a strict reading.

In making this defense . . . Overseas must therefore overcome a powerful presumption that the arbitral body acted within its powers. Overseas principally directs its challenge at . . . $185,000 awarded for loss of production. Its jurisdictional claim focuses on the provision of the contract reciting that "[n]either party shall have any liability for loss of production." The tribunal cannot properly be charged, however, with simply ignoring this alleged limitation on the subject matter over which its decision-making powers extended. Rather, the arbitration court interpreted the provision not to preclude jurisdiction on this matter. As in *United Steelworkers of America v. Enterprise Wheel & Car Corp.*, 363 U.S. 593 (1960), the court may be satisfied that the arbitrator premised the award on a construction of the contract and that it is "not apparent," 363 U.S. at 598, that the scope of the submission to arbitration has been exceeded.

The appellant's attack on . . . $60,000 awarded for start-up expenses . . . cannot withstand the most cursory scrutiny. In characterizing the $60,000 as "consequential damages" (and thus proscribed by the arbitration agreement), Overseas is again attempting to secure a reconstruction in this court of the contract—an activity wholly inconsistent with the deference due arbitral decisions on law and fact. . . . Although the Convention recognizes that an award may not be enforced where predicated on a subject matter outside the arbitrator's jurisdiction, it does not sanction second-guessing the arbitrator's construction of the parties' agreement. . . .

Both the legislative history of Article V, and the statute enacted to implement the United States' accession to the Convention are strong authority for treating as exclusive the bases set forth in the Convention for vacating an award. On the other hand, the [FAA], specifically 9 U.S.C. §10, has been read to include an implied defense to enforcement where the award is in "manifest disregard" of the law. *Wilko v. Swan*, 346 U.S. 427, 436 (1953). This case does not require us to decide, however, whether this defense stemming from dictum in *Wilko, supra*, obtains in the international arbitration context. For even assuming that the "manifest disregard" defense applies under the Convention, we would have no difficulty rejecting the appellant's contention that such "manifest disregard" is in evidence here. Overseas in effect asks this court to read this defense as a license to review the record of arbitral proceedings for errors of fact or law—a role which we have emphatically declined to assume in the past and reject once again. "[E]xtensive judicial review frustrates the basic purpose of arbitration, which is to dispose of disputes quickly and avoid the expense and delay of extended court proceedings." *Saxis Steamship Co.* [*v. Multifacs Int'l Traders*, 375 F.2d 577, 582 (2d Cir. 1967)]. Insofar as this defense to enforcement of awards in "manifest disregard" of law may be cognizable under the Convention, it, like the other defenses raised by the appellant, fails to provide a sound basis for vacating the foreign arbitral award. . . .

NORTHROP CORP. v. TRIAD INTERNATIONAL MARKETING SA
811 F.2d 1265 (9th Cir. 1987)

BROWNING, JUDGE. In October 1970 Northrop and Triad entered into a "Marketing Agreement," under which Triad became Northrop's exclusive marketing representative [for certain armaments] in return for commissions on sales. Northrop made substantial sales to Saudi Arabia and paid Triad a substantial part of the commissions due under the Marketing Agreement. On September 17, 1975, the Council of Ministers of Saudi Arabia issued Decree No. 1275, prohibiting the payment of commissions in connection with armaments contracts. Northrop ceased paying commissions to Triad [which protested and then sought arbitration under AAA rules].

[The Marketing Agreement contained a choice-of-law clause, which provided: "The validity and construction of this Agreement shall be governed by the laws of the State of California." The arbitrators relied on the choice-of-law clause and rejected Northrop's argument that Saudi Decree No. 1275 rendered the Marketing Agreement unenforceable. Northrop pressed the argument on appeal, and the Ninth Circuit responded as follows.] Northrop also argues that if the Saudi Decree did not excuse performance of the Marketing Agreement under California [law], the choice-of-law clause in the Agreement should be set aside and the Saudi Decree should be applied directly to invalidate the Marketing Agreement under the principle announced in *Restatement (Second) Conflict of Laws* §187(2)(b) (1971). However, choice-of-law and choice-of-forum provisions in international commercial contracts . . . should be enforced absent strong reasons to set them aside. . . . We agree with the arbitrators that the general principle of conflicts Northrop cites is not sufficient standing alone to overcome the strong policy consideration announced in *Scherk* and *Bremen*. . . .

Northrop's argument that the courts should decline to enforce the Marketing Agreement because it conflicts with the public policy Saudi Arabia announced in Decree No. 1275 flies in the face of the parties' agreement that the law of California, and not Saudi Arabia, would determine the validity and construction of the contract. Northrop has cited no California regulation, statute, or court decision demonstrating that enforcement of a contract to pay commissions to a marketing representative is contrary to the public policy of California, whether such commissions are illegal under the law of a foreign state or are not.

Northrop's most substantial argument is that the public policy reflected in Decree No. 1275 was also the policy of the United States Department of Defense. In its opinion the district court said "it is clear [the Department of Defense] wished to conform its policy precisely to that announced by Saudi Arabia." . . . To justify refusal to enforce an arbitration award on grounds of public policy, the policy "must be well defined and dominant." The Saudi Arabian policy the Department of Defense arguably adopted was neither. It is clear the Department wished to accommodate Saudi Arabian interests and sensibilities. It is also clear, however, that the Department was interested in encouraging sales to Saudi Arabia of American manufactured military equipment, and considered the efforts of Triad critical to that end. . . . [The district court concluded that commissions on weapons were flatly prohibited,] but even if we were to agree, we could not say on this record the policy the Department adopted was "well-defined and dominant." The district court's refusal to enforce the arbitrators' decision on the ground that it conflicted with the policy of the Department of Defense was, therefore, unwarranted.

Notes on Statutory Materials, **Parsons & Whittemore,** *and* **Triad**

1. *Distinction between action to vacate (or annul) and action to recognize.* Articles III and V of the New York Convention apply to recognition of awards (specifically, foreign and non-domestic awards). These provisions do not apply to actions to vacate or annul an award in the place where it was made. Rather, the Convention leaves Contracting States free to apply national law to annul awards, including on grounds not specified in Article V of the Convention. *See* G. Born, *International Commercial Arbitration* 2334-2344, 2554-2560 (2009). In contrast, when a party seeks to recognize an arbitral award in a place outside the arbitral seat, then Article III (requiring presumptive recognition of the award) and Article V (specifying exceptions to the recognition obligation) apply.

Compare Articles 34 and 35-36 of the UNCITRAL Model Law. Note how they deal separately with issues of (a) annulling or vacating an arbitral award made in the relevant court's jurisdiction; and (b) recognizing an arbitral award made in another jurisdiction. Although the grounds for annulment and for nonrecognition are very similar under the Model Law, this is not always the case under national arbitration statutes. In particular, some states permit fairly far-reaching judicial review of arbitral awards in actions to vacate or annul. *See* G. Born, *International Commercial Arbitration* 2568-2657 (2009).

2. *Scope of New York Convention's provisions concerning arbitral awards.* Note that the pro-enforcement provisions of the Convention only apply to specified arbitral awards. In particular, the Convention applies only to awards made in "commercial" matters, which are either "foreign" or "non-domestic" awards in the place where they are sought to be enforced, and which are final or binding.

(a) *"Commercial" awards.* As discussed above, the New York Convention generally applies only to "commercial" arbitration agreements and arbitral awards (by reason of reservations entered by many signatory states pursuant to Article 1(3) of the Convention). *See supra* p. 1161. Consider how a party, seeking to avoid application of the Convention's pro-enforcement provisions, might make use of this limitation.

(b) *"Foreign" and "non-domestic" awards.* Article I(1) of the Convention provides that

> This Convention shall apply to the recognition and enforcement of arbitral awards made in the territory of a State other than the State where the recognition and enforcement of such awards are sought. . . . It shall also apply to arbitral awards not considered as domestic awards in the State where their recognition and enforcement are sought.

Consider, from the perspective of recognizing an award in the United States, what arbitral awards fall within this definition. Suppose an award is made in England, in a dispute between French and Italian parties. Is the award a "foreign" award in France? In England?

Suppose that an award is made in London, in a dispute between two U.S. parties. Is the award a "foreign" award in England? In the United States? What if the dispute involves a

U.S. transaction with no foreign connections at all (other than the London arbitral seat)? *See Jones v. Sea Tow Services Freeport NY Inc.*, 30 F.3d 360 (2d Cir. 1994); *Brier v. Northstar Marine, Inc.*, 1992 WL 350292 (D.N.J. 1992) (arbitral award made in England between two U.S. parties not foreign).

When is an award "not considered as domestic" under the Convention? Note that the FAA defines this provision (as permitted by Article I(1), in the following terms:

> An arbitration agreement or arbitral award arising out of a legal relationship, whether contractual or not, which is considered as commercial . . . falls under the Convention. An arbitration agreement or award that arises out of such a relationship which is entirely between United States citizens shall be deemed not to fall under the Convention unless that relationship involves property located abroad, envisages performance or enforcement abroad, or has some other reasonable relation with one or more foreign states.

Note that, under this definition, an award made in the United States may nonetheless be subject to the New York Convention, on the grounds that it is non-domestic. Suppose that French and Italian parties arbitrate a dispute over a European contract in New York; will the resulting award be subject to the New York Convention in New York? *See Industrial Risk Insurers v. M.A.N. Gutehoffnungshutte GmbH*, 141 F.3d 1434 (11th Cir. 1998) (award made in U.S. held non-domestic); *Lander Co v. MMP Investments Inc.*, 107 F.3d 476 (7th Cir. 1997) (same).

What are the consequences of treating an award as non-domestic in a state? Is the award subject to annulment only under the standards set forth in Article V of the New York Convention? *See* G. Born, *International Commercial Arbitration* 2382-2384 (2009).

3. *Presumptive obligation to recognize Convention awards.* Consider Articles III and V of the Convention. What do these provisions require Contracting States to do when a Convention award, made in another Contracting State, is presented for recognition? *See supra* pp. 1202-1203. Consider also Articles 35 and 36 of the UNCITRAL Model Law.

4. *Exclusivity of exceptions enumerated in Article V of the New York Convention.* *Parsons & Whittemore* raises, but does not decide, the question whether the Convention's enumerated defenses are the exclusive grounds for resisting recognition of an arbitral award outside its country of origin. Should U.S. courts recognize additional defenses to enforcement under the Convention? Read Articles III and V of the Convention. Do these provisions require that states recognize foreign arbitral awards subject to the specific exceptions in Articles V and VI of the Convention? Or does the Convention permit states to deny enforcement of foreign awards on the same grounds as those available under domestic law for domestic awards? Does §207 of the FAA permit awards to be denied recognition on grounds not specified in the Convention?

The language of the second chapter of the FAA suggests that *only* the Convention's defenses will be permitted. *See* 9 U.S.C. §207 ("The court *shall* confirm the award *unless* it finds one of the grounds for refusal or deferral of recognition or enforcement of the award specified in the [New York] Convention."). *See also Industrial Risk Insurers v. M.A.N. Gutehoffnungshutte GmbH*, 141 F.3d 1434, 1445 (11th Cir. 1998); *Yusuf Ahmed Alghanim & Sons, WLL v. Toys "R" Us, Inc.*, 126 F.3d 15, 20 (2d Cir. 1997). Note also the approach of Article 36 of the UNCITRAL Model Law.

5. *Availability of "manifest disregard of law" defense under New York Convention.* Under the domestic FAA, U.S. courts have frequently held that domestic awards may be vacated if the arbitrators acted in "manifest disregard of law." *See* G. Born, *International Commercial Arbitration* 2639-2646 (2009).

When the defense is permitted, "manifest disregard of law" has universally been held to require a deliberate and serious refusal to apply applicable law, involving more than just an erroneous statement of applicable law or an erroneous interpretation of the parties' agreement. *See Northrop Corp. v. Triad International Marketing, SA*, 811 F.2d 1265 (9th Cir. 1987); *National Oil Corp. v. Libyan Sun Oil Co.*, 733 F. Supp. 800 (D. Del. 1990) ("A mere error of law would not, however, be sufficient grounds to refuse recognition of the award.").

Different courts have given a range of divergent interpretations to the manifest disregard exception. *Compare San Martine Compagnia de Navegacion v. Saguenay Terminals*, 293 F.2d 796, 801 (9th Cir. 1961) ("manifest disregard of the law must be something beyond and different from a mere error in the law or failure on the part of the arbitrators to understand or apply the law") *with DiRussa v. Dean Witter Reynolds, Inc.*, 121 F.3d 818, 821 (2d Cir. 1997) ("manifest disregard 'clearly means more than error or misunderstanding with respect to the law.' The error must have been obvious and capable of being readily and instantly perceived by the average person qualified to serve as an arbitrator. Moreover, the term 'disregard' implies that the arbitrator appreciates the existence of a clearly governing legal principle but decides to ignore or pay no attention to it").

Regardless of its contours, recent decisions have cast doubt on the continuing vitality of the manifest disregard doctrine. These decisions rely on the Supreme Court's opinion in *Hall Street Assocs., L.L.C. v. Mattel, Inc.* 552 U.S. 576 (2008). *Hall Street* held that the FAA did not permit parties to expand, by contract, the grounds for vacatur of an arbitral award and contained language hinting that the phrase "manifest disregard of the law" might not state an independent ground for vactur but, instead, "merely referred to the §10 grounds collectively." *Id.* at 585. Federal appellate courts have reached conflicting conclusions over whether the "manifest disregard" ground survives *Hall Street. Compare, e.g., Frazier v. CitiFinancial Corp., LLC*, 604 F.3d 1313 (11th Cir. 2010) (manifest disregard does not survive *Hall Street*), *with Comedy Club, Inc. v. Improv West Assocs.* 553 F.3d 1277 (9th Cir. 2009) (reaching opposite conclusion).

The Convention's list of exceptions to enforceability in Article V does not include "manifest disregard." Can such a defense nonetheless be invoked to object to recognition of a foreign arbitral award? What about relying on manifest disregard as grounds for vacating an international arbitral award made in the United States?

Note that *Mitsubishi Motors*, 473 U.S. at 638, reasons that "substantive review at the award-enforcement stage [must] remain minimal," which suggests at least some sort of review of the substance of the arbitrators' ruling. For a few early decisions apparently recognizing the availability of a manifest disregard exception under the Convention, *see, e.g., Office of Supply, Government of the Republic of Korea v. New York Navigation Co.*, 496 F.2d 377, 379-380 (2d Cir. 1972); *Jamaica Commodity Trading Co. v. Connell Rice & Sugar Co.*, 1991 U.S. Dist. LEXIS 8976 (S.D.N.Y. 1991); *American Construction Machinery & Equipment Corp. v. Mechanised Construction of Pakistan Ltd.*, 659 F. Supp. 426 (S.D.N.Y. 1987). *See also Baxter Int'l, Inc. v. Abbott Laboratories*, 315 F.3d 829, 836 n.4 (7th Cir. 2003) (Cudahy, J., dissenting).

Despite the foregoing decisions, lower U.S. courts have repeatedly concluded that the Convention would not permit nonrecognition for manifest disregard of law. *E.g., Yusuf Ahmed Alghanim & Sons, WLL v. Toys "R" Us, Inc.*, 126 F.3d 15, 20 (2d Cir. 1997); *M & C Corp. v. Erwin Behr GmbH & Co.*, 87 F.3d 844, 851 (6th Cir. 1996); *Avraham v. Shigur Express Ltd.*, 1991 U.S. Dist. LEXIS 12267 (S.D.N.Y. 1991).

Which line of precedent is more persuasive? Should U.S. courts recognize and enforce foreign arbitral awards that are not just plainly wrong, but that manifestly ignore applicable law and the facts? Does *Whittemore* recognize the manifest disregard exception? Consider Article 36 of the UNCITRAL Model Law: does it permit anything like a manifest disregard defense?

Recall the treatment of foreign court judgments. *See supra* pp. 1114-1155. Was there a manifest disregard exception to the enforceability of foreign judgments in *Hilton* and the UFMJRA? Should there be?

6. New York Convention's public policy exception. One of the most commonly invoked defense to the New York Convention's requirement for enforcement of arbitral awards involves Article V(2)(b)'s exception for cases where "the recognition or enforcement of the award would be contrary to the public policy of [the country asked to enforce the award]." The Convention's public policy exception derives in part from historic common law treatment of foreign judgments. *See supra* pp. 1133-1146. *See also* UNCITRAL Model Law, Articles 34(2)(b)(ii) & 36(2)(b)(ii).

Like most U.S. decisions, *Parsons & Whittemore* and *Triad* construed Article V(2)(b)'s public policy exception narrowly to apply only where enforcement would violate the forum state's "most basic notions of morality and justice." 508 F.2d at 974. *See also Waterside Ocean Nav. Co. v. International Nav.*, 737 F.2d 150 (2d Cir. 1984) (public policy defense not implicated by claims of false testimony before arbitral tribunal); *Bergesen v. Joseph Muller Corp.*, 710 F.2d 928 (2d Cir. 1983); G. Born, *International Commercial Arbitration* 2827-2862 (2009). Although the weight of authority reaches contrary results, a few U.S. decisions have invoked the public policy exception to deny recognition to a foreign arbitral award. *Laminoirs-Trefileries-Cableries de Lens, SA v. Southwire Co.*, 484 F. Supp. 1063 (N.D. Ga. 1980); *Victrix SS Co. v. Salen Dry Cargo AB*, 825 F.2d 709 (2d Cir. 1987). Should U.S. courts be more forceful in protecting U.S. interests and public policies under the Convention? Compare the treatment of the public policy defense in the contexts of forum selection clauses and the recognition and enforcement of foreign judgments. *See supra* pp. 521-528 and 1133-1146.

7. *Source of public policy standards under Article V(2)(b) — domestic or international?* From where are standards of public policy derived in cases under Article V(b)(2)? Do *Parsons & Whittemore* and *Triad* rely on the same sources of public policy?

(a) "International" public policy. A few U.S. courts appear to have looked at least in part to what they have called "international" public policy, as distinguished from U.S. "domestic" public policy. *See Parsons & Whittemore*, 508 F.2d at 974 (requiring "supranational emphasis" rather than reliance on "national political interests"); *MGM Productions Group, Inc. v. Aeroflot Russian Airlines*, 2003 WL 21108637, at *4 (S.D.N.Y. 2003) (violations of U.S. foreign policy do not satisfy Convention's public policy exception), *aff'd*, 91 Fed. Appx. 716 (2d Cir. 2004); *National Oil Corp. v. Libyan Sun Oil Co.*, 733 F. Supp. 800, 819 (D. Del. 1990) ("'public policy' and 'foreign policy' are not synonymous"). Is this consistent with the text of Article V(2)(b)? How are U.S. courts to ascertain international public policy? What if international public policy permits actions that violate basic U.S. policies and laws, such as policies against racial or religious discrimination? *Cf. Karen Maritime Ltd. v. Omar Int'l, Inc.*, 322 F. Supp. 2d 224, 227-229 (E.D.N.Y. 2004) (rejecting public policy defense to stay pending arbitration where parties' agreement contained provisions requiring boycott of Israel); *Antco Shipping Co. v. & Sidermar, SpA*, 417 F. Supp. 207, 215-217 (S.D.N.Y. 1976) (same).

(b) U.S. decisions adopting "national" public policy. Notwithstanding the references to international public policy in *Parsons & Whittemore*, other U.S. courts have looked to *national* public policy. *See Slaney v. The Int'l Amateur Athletic Federation*, 244 F.3d 580, 594 (7th Cir. 2001) ("United States public policy"); *Industrial Risk Insurers v. M.A.N. Gutehoffnungshutte GmbH*, 141 F.3d 1434, 1445 (11th Cir. 1998) (appearing to equate domestic and international public policy standards); *Victrix SS Co. v. Salen Dry Cargo AB*, 825 F.2d 709 (2d Cir. 1987); *Waterside Ocean Nav. Co. v. International Nav.*, 737 F.2d 150, 152 (2d Cir. 1984) ("public policy of the United States"). Assuming that the public policy

contemplated by Article V(2)(b) is national—not international—public policy, what is the source of that public policy in the United States? Is it state, or federal, public policy?

8. *Effect of foreign public policies on enforceability of awards in U.S. courts.* To what extent should U.S. courts give effect to the public policies of *foreign* states in applying the Convention? Suppose, for example, that an arbitral award orders relief against European companies operating in Europe that violates European Union competition laws? Or that requires or rewards conduct in a foreign state that is unlawful there? Should a U.S. court enforce the award? Would a U.S. court enforce a contract calling for such conduct?

How does *Triad* deal with Saudi Arabian public policy against bribery? Did it reach a sensible result? As *Triad* suggests, even if foreign public policy were demonstrably in conflict with an arbitral award, and even if the concerned foreign jurisdiction has a reasonably close relationship to the parties' dispute, U.S. courts have been reluctant to vacate the award. *E.g., American Construction Machinery & Equipment Corp. v. Mechanised Construction of Pakistan, Ltd.,* 659 F. Supp. 426, 429 (S.D.N.Y. 1987) (rejecting argument that "United States public policy would be offended by confirming an arbitral award in the face of a Pakistani judgment that the arbitration clause and proceeding were void," at least where Pakistan was not arbitral situs).

9. *Procedural fairness and opportunity to present party's case.* The New York Convention's grounds for refusal of enforcement include cases where the "party against whom the award is invoked was not given proper notice of the appointment of the arbitrator or of the arbitration proceedings or was otherwise unable to present his case." Article V(1)(b). Similarly, §10(a)(3) of the FAA permits an award to be vacated "[w]here the arbitrators were guilty of misconduct in refusing to postpone the hearing, upon sufficient cause shown, or in refusing to hear evidence pertinent and material to the controversy; or of any other misbehavior by which the rights of any party have been prejudiced." 9 U.S.C. §10(a)(3). *See also* UNCITRAL Model Law, Articles 34(2)(a)(ii) & 36(2)(a)(ii). Broadly speaking, these exceptions permit challenges for grave procedural defects in the arbitral proceedings.

As with other exceptions under Article V, U.S. courts have been reluctant to deny recognition of an award on the grounds of procedural irregularity. That reluctance is reflected, again, by *Parsons & Whittemore.* Consider the alleged procedural unfairness in *Parsons & Whittemore.* Was it sufficient to warrant nonrecognition? What types of procedural unfairness should permit nonrecognition?

10. *Applicable law for procedural objections under Article V(1)(b).* The New York Convention does not specify what nation's laws, or what international standards, apply in determining whether Article V(1)(b)'s procedural fairness exception is met. *Parsons & Whittemore* held that the law of the forum where enforcement is sought—there, the United States—should be applied to determine whether a party was given "proper" notice or was "unable" to present his case. Other lower U.S. courts have agreed. *Karaha Bodas Co. v. Perusahaan Pertambangan Minyak Dan Gas Bumi Negara,* 364 F.3d 274, 298 (5th Cir. 2004); *Generica Ltd. v. Pharmaceutical Basics, Inc.,* 125 F.3d 1123, 1129-1130 (7th Cir. 1997); *Iran Aircraft Industries v. Avco Corp.,* 980 F.2d 141, 145-146 (2d Cir. 1992). Compare this use of U.S. due process standards to the treatment of adequate notice in the enforcement of foreign court judgments. *See supra* pp. 1115-1120. *See also Society of Lloyd's v. Ashenden,* 233 F.3d 473, 477 (7th Cir. 2000) (comparing due process standards governing enforcement of arbitration award and enforcement of foreign judgment). Is it appropriate to apply national law under Article V(1)(b)? Or should the Convention be interpreted as imposing a uniform international standard of procedural fairness?

When U.S. law applies under Article V(1)(b), what is the source of U.S. standards of procedural fairness? Is it the FAA, state law, or the U.S. Constitution? Lower U.S. courts have generally concluded that arbitral awards falling under the Convention are subject to scrutiny under the "due process" standards of the Fifth and Fourteenth Amendments to the Constitution. *Iran Aircraft Industries v. Avco Corp.*, 980 F.2d 141 (2d Cir. 1992) (" 'the fundamental requirement of due process is the opportunity to be heard at a meaningful time and in a meaningful manner.' "); *Fotochrome, Inc. v. Copal Co.*, 517 F.2d 512 (2d Cir. 1975); *Parsons & Whittemore*, 508 F.2d at 975. U.S. courts generally have not looked to state law procedural rules in applying Article V(1)(b). *But see Employers Ins. of Wausau v. Banco de Seguros del Estado*, 199 F.3d 937, 942 (7th Cir. 1999) ("Absent any agreement to the contrary, Article V(1)(b) [of the Panama Convention, indistinguishable from New York Convention] grants a party the due process rights of the forum state, in this case those of Wisconsin and the United States."). Is that appropriate? Should procedural rules applicable under state arbitration statutes apply under Article V(1)(b)? Why should the FAA or the Convention preempt such rules?

11. *Deference to special character of arbitral process under Article V(1)(b).* Decisions under Article V(1)(b) and the related provisions of §10(a)(3) of the FAA defer to the procedural informality and flexibility of arbitration. "Although arbitration hearings are of a quasi-judicial nature the prime virtue of arbitration is its informality, and it would be inappropriate for courts to mandate rigid compliance with procedural rules." *Transport Workers Union v. Philadelphia Transportation Co.*, 283 F. Supp. 597, 600 (E.D. Pa. 1968). *See also Schoenduve Corp. v. Lucent Technologies, Inc.*, 442 F.3d 727, 730-731 (9th Cir. 2006); *Slaney v. The Int'l Amateur Athletic Federation*, 244 F.3d 580, 592 (7th Cir. 2001); *Generica Ltd. v. Pharmaceutical Basics, Inc.*, 125 F.3d 1123, 1130 (7th Cir. 1997).

Parsons & Whittemore and other authorities make it plain that the enforcing court will not sit in *de novo* review of procedural decisions of the arbitral panel. Rather, U.S. courts generally accord international arbitrators broad discretion in their conduct of proceedings. *See Compagnie des Bauxites de Guinee v. Hammermills, Inc.*, 1992 WL 122712 (D.D.C. 1992); *Laminoirs etc. v. Southwire Co.*, 484 F. Supp. 1063, 1066-1067 (N.D. Ga. 1980) (curtailing cross-examination did not deny petitioner fair hearing). Is this appropriate? Recall Justice Stevens' concerns in *Mitsubishi* about "despotic decision-making."

12. *Excess of authority and no valid arbitration agreement.* As we have seen, international arbitration is consensual: unless the parties agreed to arbitrate a particular issue, the arbitral tribunal lacks authority to resolve it. *See supra* pp. 1157-1158. A corollary of this principle is the unenforceability of awards that are not supported by a valid arbitration agreement.

Article V(1)(a) permits nonrecognition of an award if "the parties to the agreement referred to in Article II were, under the law applicable to them, under some incapacity, or the said agreement is not valid under the law to which the parties have subjected it or, failing any indication thereon, under the law of the country where the award was made." Article V(1)(a)'s requirement for a valid arbitration agreement is closely related to similar provisions in Articles II(1) and II(3). *See supra* pp. 1178-1180. Articles V(1)(c) and Article V(1)(d) impose related requirements, permitting nonenforcement of awards that deal with matters not submitted to the arbitrators or where the procedural and other provisions of the parties' arbitration agreement were not followed. Similarly, §10(a)(4) of the FAA authorizes a U.S. court to vacate an award "[w]here the arbitrators exceeded their powers." *See also* UNCITRAL Model Law, Articles 34(2)(b)(i) and (iii) & 36(2)(b)(i) and (iii).

Lower courts have interpreted the Convention's "excess of authority" exception under Article V(1)(c) narrowly, and seldom found it satisfied. *See Management & Tech.*

Consultants v. Parsons-Jurden Int'l Corp., 820 F.2d 1531 (9th Cir. 1987) ("we construe arbitral authority broadly to comport with the enforcement facilitating thrust of the Convention and the policy favoring arbitration"); *Andros Compania Maritima v. Marc Rich & Co.*, 579 F.2d 691 (2d Cir. 1978); *Avraham v. Shigur Express Ltd.*, 1991 U.S. Dist. LEXIS 12267 (S.D.N.Y. 1991). Did *Parsons & Whittemore* involve a jurisdictional challenge'? Or did it instead involve a claim that the arbitrators' substantive contract interpretation was incorrect?

13. *Excess of authority under Article V(1)(c) by exceeding scope of arbitration agreement.* When a case involves a *true* jurisdictional challenge — for example, to the existence, validity, or scope of an arbitration agreement — what deference should a court give to a ruling by the arbitrators on this issue? Suppose that the arbitrators reject one party's argument that it was not party to the purported arbitration agreement, or that the agreement is invalid. Suppose that the arbitrators reject the argument that the scope of the arbitration agreement does not extend to particular claims or disputes. Is the same deference applicable to each ruling?

As discussed above, in *First Options of Chicago, Inc. v. Kaplan*, 514 U.S. 938 (1995), the Court considered whether an award had validly been made against two individual shareholders of a corporate defendant in an arbitration. The individuals had argued to the arbitrators that they were not party to the arbitration agreement, but the tribunal rejected their argument. The individuals moved to vacate the award, for excess of authority, and the Supreme Court held that independent *de novo* judicial review of the individuals' jurisdiction challenge was required.

First Options initially held that the question "who should have the primary power to decide" the arbitrability of a claim "turns upon what the parties agreed about that matter." If the parties had agreed to have the arbitrator decide arbitrability, then the court's standard for reviewing the arbitrator's decision about that matter should not differ from the highly deferential standard that courts apply when they review any other matter the parties have agreed to arbitrate. On the other hand, if "the parties did not agree to submit the arbitrability question itself to arbitration, then the court should decide the question just as it would decide any other question that the parties did not submit to arbitration, namely independently."

The Court then considered whether the parties had agreed to arbitrate the question whether the individuals were personally bound to arbitrate. The Court reasoned that "when deciding whether the parties agreed to arbitrate a certain matter (including arbitrability), courts generally . . . should apply ordinary state-law principles that govern the formation of contracts." The Court then declared that courts "should not assume that the parties agreed to arbitrate arbitrability unless there is 'clea[r] and unmistakabl[e]' evidence that they did so." The Court distinguished this presumption — about "who" decides arbitrability — from the reverse presumption about "whether" a particular dispute is within the scope of a concededly valid arbitration agreement: "Any doubts concerning the scope of arbitrable issues should be resolved in favor of arbitration." Applying this standard, the Court held that the individuals had not indicated a clear willingness to arbitrate the question whether they were bound by the arbitration agreement, and remanded to the lower courts for a *de novo* decision on that issue.

Is the *First Options* analysis persuasive? Why is there such a sharp distinction between the existence of an arbitration agreement and its scope? Is it appropriate to permit arbitrators to determine their own jurisdiction without meaningful judicial review — even where the parties have granted them this authority? Most jurisdictions permit essentially *de novo* judicial review of arbitrators' jurisdictional determinations (albeit generally without considering arguments that the parties have submitted jurisdictional issues to the tribunal for resolution). *See* E. Gaillard *et al., Fouchard Gaillard Goldman on International Commercial Arbitration* 649 (1999).

14. *Bias or lack of independence of arbitrators.* Suppose that an arbitrator (or an entire arbitral tribunal) is not impartial. The New York Convention does not expressly provide for nonrecognition of an award based upon bias or lack of impartiality or independence. Nonetheless, it is well settled that these provide grounds for denying recognition of an award. G. Born, *International Commercial Arbitration* 2803-2813 (2009); E. Gaillard *et al., Fouchard Gaillard Goldman on International Commercial Arbitration* 566-577 (1999). Consider Articles 9-14 of the UNCITRAL Model Law. What do they provide concerning selection of an arbitral tribunal? Compare §10(a)(1) and (2) of the FAA.

What if the parties' arbitration agreement provides the tribunal with a longer period of time than local law (and the tribunal complies with the contractual time limit)? Does Article V(1)(d) still permit nonrecognition?

15. *Nonrecognition under Article V(1)(d).* Consider the exception to the Convention's obligation to recognize awards in Article V(1)(d). How do the two clauses of Article V(1)(d) relate to one another? What if the parties' arbitration agreement provides for a tribunal of two arbitrators, but that the two arbitrators insist on appointing a third arbitrator? Is the resulting tribunal's award subject to nonrecognition under the first clause of Article V(1)(d)?

Alternatively, suppose the parties' arbitration agreement is silent concerning the duration of the arbitration and the law of the arbitral seat requires that the award be made within 180 days from formation of the tribunal; if the award is not made within this time period, is it subject to nonrecognition under the second clause of Article V(1)(d)?

16. *Limitations on forums for annulment of awards.* Where may an award subject to the Convention be annulled? For example, what nation's courts could annul an award made by the tribunal in *Mitsubishi*, which would be seated in Japan? Could U.S. courts annul the award? Swiss courts? Consider Article V(1)(e). What does it suggest regarding the competent authority to annul a Convention award? *See* G. Born, *International Commercial Arbitration* 2403-2426 (2009).

D. Professional Responsibility in International Arbitration[150]

International arbitration (and litigation) raise issues of attorney conduct and professional responsibility, as well as substantive legal issues. As the materials contained in this book illustrate, international disputes almost inevitably involve conduct by counsel in multiple countries — ranging from meeting with and advising clients, to participation in evidence-taking, to formal participation in arbitral or litigation proceedings. It is therefore critical that a lawyer, whether acting as an adviser, trial counsel, or an arbitrator, understand the

---

150. For commentary on professional responsibility in international arbitration and litigation, *see* Brand, *Professional Responsibility in a Transnational Transactions Practice,* 17 J. L. & Com. 301 (1998); Jarvis, *Cross-Border Legal Practice and Ethics Rule 4-8.5: Why Greater Guidance Is Needed,* 72 Fla. B.J. 59 (1998); Krystinik, *The Complex Web of Conflicting Disciplinary Standards in International Litigation,* 38 Tex. Int'l L.J. 815 (2003); Orlandi, *Ethics for International Arbitrators,* 67 U.M.K.C. L. Rev. 93 (1998); Paulsson, *Standards of Conduct for Counsel in International Arbitration,* 3 Am. Rev. Int'l Arb. 214 (1992); Rogers, *Fit and Function in Legal Ethics: Developing a Code of Conduct for International Arbitration,* 23 Mich. J. Int'l L. 341 (2002); Rogers, *Context and Institutional Structure in Attorney Regulation: Constructing an Enforcement Regime for International Arbitration,* 39 Stan. J. Int'l L. 1 (2003); Rogers, *Lawyers Without Borders,* 30 U. Penn. Int'l L. Rev. 1035 (2009);Thomas, *Disqualifying Lawyers in Arbitrations: Do the Arbitrators Play Any Proper Role?,* 1 Am. Rev. Int'l Arb. 562 (1990); Ulmer, *Ethics and Effectiveness: Doing Well by Doing Good,* in *The Commercial Way to Justice: The 1996 International Conference of the Chartered Institute of Arbitrators* 167 (G. Hartwell ed., 1997); Vagts, *The International Legal Profession A Need for More Governance?,* 90 Am J. Int'l 250 (1996); Vagts, *Professional Responsibility in Transborder Practice,* 13 Geo. J. Legal Ethics 677 (2000); Zimmett, *Ethics in International Commercial Litigation and Arbitration,* 670 PIL/Lit. 475 (2000).

ethical rules governing his or her activities in foreign jurisdictions or other international contexts. That is especially true because the lawyer will often not be fully qualified to practice as a lawyer in all concerned jurisdictions. This section considers these rules, with a particular focus on international arbitral proceedings.

Rules governing attorney conduct in international arbitrations and litigations take several different forms. These rules can affect a number of different aspects of lawyers' conduct, in sometimes unexpected ways.

First, local statutes or judicial decisions can forbid or restrict the participation of foreign lawyers as counsel or arbitrators in legal proceedings conducted on local territory. For example, many foreign jurisdictions have adopted legislation that forbids what U.S. law terms the "unauthorized practice of law" by persons not admitted to the local bar. This sort of legislation almost always precludes foreign lawyers from acting as counsel of record in local litigations in foreign courts (absent special permission),[151] and can prohibit or restrict the participation of foreign lawyers as counsel or arbitrators in local arbitral proceedings. Similarly, some countries impose citizenship requirements on arbitrators with respect to arbitrations taking place in those countries.[152]

Second, local law frequently regulates certain aspects of conduct by participants in local arbitral proceedings. For example, local legislation may forbid arbitrators from administering oaths,[153] or may criminalize false statements to an arbitral tribunal.[154]

Third, local statutes or judicial decisions can prohibit or regulate conduct by foreign attorneys in connection with foreign legal proceedings (*e.g.*, State A regulates actions by State B lawyers within its territory concerning legal proceedings in State B). In particular, some civil law jurisdictions have enacted legislation that forbids or limits the gathering of evidence for use in foreign legal proceedings.[155] Violation of these regulations can result in criminal or other sanctions against the individuals involved.

Fourth, codes of professional responsibility or ethics regulate the activities of members of a jurisdiction's bar, including when they engage in activities outside of that jurisdiction. In some cases, a lawyer's professional or ethical obligations (*e.g.*, to maintain confidentiality or to pursue an issue zealously) may conflict with local law in the place where he or she provides legal services (*e.g.*, to disclose certain information to a tribunal, to government authorities or otherwise; to refrain from advancing arguments or claims in certain circumstances).

Fifth, international disputes almost inevitably involve questions of foreign law (*i.e.*, the law of State A is relevant to proceedings pending in State B). Lawyers qualified in the laws of one jurisdiction (*i.e.*, State B) must therefore take care not to ignore or provide uninformed advice on the laws of other jurisdiction (*i.e.*, State A). Doing so can create risks of legal malpractice, as well as unauthorized practice of law.

The following materials illustrate the application of rules governing attorney conduct in international arbitration and litigation. Consider the excerpt from Michigan's statute forbidding the unauthorized practice of law and the application of similar legislation in *Williamson v. John D. Quinn Construction Corp.* and *Lawler, Matusky & Skeller v. Attorney General of Barbados*; compare these decisions with that in *Bidermann Indus. Licencing, Inc. v. Avmar NV*. Thereafter, read the provisions of the Swiss and French Penal Codes,

---

151. *See, e.g.*, Mich. Comp. Laws §600.916 (1961).

152. *See, e.g.*, Saudi Arabia Statutory Provisions on Arbitration §1, Art. 3 (1985).

153. *See, e.g.*, Swedish Arbitration Act §25 (1999) ("arbitrators may not administer oaths . . . or otherwise use compulsory measures in order to obtain requested evidence"). By contrast, as noted above, the Federal Arbitration Act expressly authorizes arbitrators to issue subpoenas. 9 U.S.C. §7 (2006).

154. *See, e.g.*, Swiss Penal Law Art. 307(1). Article 309 of the Penal Law extends these provisions to arbitration proceedings.

155. Swiss Penal Code, Art. 273 (excerpted *supra* p. 975); French Penal Code Law No. 80-538, Arts. 1A & 2 (excerpted *supra* p. 975).

which impose criminal sanctions on persons who gather materials on local territory for use in foreign legal proceedings, and criminalize false testimony before arbitral tribunals. Finally, consider the excerpts from the ABA Model Rules on Professional Conduct, dealing with international practice.

MICH. COMP. LAWS
§600.916 (1961)

A person shall not practice law or engage in the law business, shall not in any manner whatsoever lead others to believe that he or she is authorized to practice law or to engage in the law business, and shall not in any manner whatsoever represent or designate himself or herself as an attorney and counselor, attorney at law, or lawyer, unless the person is regularly licensed and authorized to practice law in this state. A person who violates this section is guilty of contempt of the supreme court and of the circuit court of the county in which the violation occurred. . . . This section does not apply to a person who is duly licensed and authorized to practice law in another state while temporarily in this state and engaged in a particular matter.

WILLIAMSON v. JOHN D. QUINN CONSTRUCTION CO.
537 F. Supp. 613 (S.D.N.Y. 1982)

EDWARD WEINFELD, DISTRICT JUDGE. [The John D. Quinn Construction Company ("Quinn") was involved in a construction-related arbitration with another company. Initially, a New York law firm represented Quinn. During the arbitration, Quinn allegedly authorized the New York law firm to retain Williamson P.A., a two-member New Jersey law firm with expertise in construction litigation, to assist in the representation. According to the retention agreement, David Williamson, a partner admitted in both New York and New Jersey, would supervise all activities and strategy; Michael Rehill, an associate admitted only in New Jersey, would be responsible for day-to-day services. Following completion of the arbitration, Quinn refused to pay Williamson P.A. and argued, among other things, that neither Williamson P.A. nor Mr. Rehill was authorized to practice in New York.]

There remains Quinn's claim that Williamson P.A. is foreclosed from recovery of any fees because Michael Rehill, who performed the bulk of the services, was not admitted to practice in this State and Williamson P.A. likewise is not authorized to practice in this State. Plaintiff's services were rendered solely in the arbitration proceeding. An arbitration tribunal is not a court of record; its rules of evidence and procedures differ from those of courts of record; its fact finding process is not equivalent to judicial fact finding; it has no provision for the admission pro hac vice of local or out-of-state attorneys. In *Spanos v. Skouras Theatres Corp.*, Judge Friendly held that an attorney not admitted to practice law in New York could recover fees for legal services even though he had not been admitted pro hac vice because "there is not the slightest reason to suppose that if (a motion had been made it) would have been denied." [364 F.2d 161, 168 (2d Cir. 1966).] This observation applies with even greater force with respect to an arbitration proceeding which is of such an informal nature. . . .

[T]he Association of the Bar of The City of New York issued a report stating] "the Committee is of the opinion that representation of a party in an arbitration proceeding by a non-lawyer or a lawyer from another jurisdiction is not the unauthorized practice of law." . . .

LAWLER, MATUSKY & SKELLER v. ATTORNEY GENERAL OF BARBADOS

Civ. Case No. 320 of 1981 (High Court Barbados Aug. 22, 1983)

[An arbitration was to be conducted in Barbados. One party wished to be represented by Mr. Kannry, who was admitted to practice law in jurisdictions other than Barbados, but not in Barbados. The other party objected to the arbitrator, who ruled that Mr. Kannry could participate, provided he was assisted by local Barbados counsel. The opposing party then persuaded the Attorney General of Barbados to file an action in local courts to preclude Mr. Kannry from acting as counsel in the arbitration.] It is submitted on behalf of the Attorney General that if Mr. Kannry were to represent the claimants at the arbitration hearings in Barbados, he would be practising law in breach of section 12(1)(a); and that the arbitrator cannot authorize or permit Mr. Kannry to do any act which would be in contravention of the law of Barbados. My task therefore is to determine whether representation of a party at a hearing in Barbados in a private arbitration constitutes the practice of law within the meaning of the Act. . . .

Far from the Legal Profession Act disclosing in clear and unambiguous terms the intention to reserve exclusively to attorneys-at-law advocacy and like functions, the indications are that it was not Parliament's intention to make such a significant change in the law. In my judgment the Act did not affect the powers of an arbitrator in a private arbitration to regulate its procedure or the common law right of a party, if permitted by the arbitrator, to be represented by someone chosen by him.

The findings of the arbitrator disclose, that, in giving his ruling, he took into account Mr. Kannry's qualifications and references, general as well as in the particular case, his own experience and the possibility of prejudice being caused to the claimants if they were deprived of Mr. Kannry's continued assistance. In my opinion these were all matters which he could properly take into consideration and it cannot be said that he exercised his discretion in any improper manner. I would answer the first question in this way: The Arbitrator had and still has, the power in law to determine and has correctly and validly determined that the applicants are entitled to be represented at hearings in Barbados by Mr. Jack Kannry, a person not registered under the provisions of the Legal Profession Act.

The Arbitration Act . . . governs the proceedings and the High Court of Barbados has jurisdiction under the Act and common law to control them. The Court may set aside an award where the arbitrator misconducts himself or the proceedings or where an arbitration or award has been improperly procured (Section 26). The court may on application give relief where an arbitrator is not impartial or there is a dispute whether a party has been guilty of fraud (Section 27). And at common law the court may intervene if there is a breach of the rules of natural justice. There are good reasons therefore for requiring an attorney-at-law registered in Barbados to be associated with Mr. Kannry. Any applications to the court would be dealt with by someone acquainted with the case. The reasons given by the arbitrator for directing that Mr. Kannry be assisted by a Barbados attorney-at-law at all hearings were to enable Mr. Kannry to be advised on Barbadian law. It seems to me that the considerations I mentioned earlier are more to the point. However that may be, the arbitrator's direction is in my opinion [justifiable]. I would therefore answer the second question by saying that the arbitrator could permit the applicants to be represented by Mr. Kannry and could also permit such representation subject to the proviso that Mr. Kannry be associated with an attorney-at-law registered under the Legal Profession Act.

BIDERMANN INDUS. LICENCING, INC. v. AVMAR NV
570 N.Y.S. 2d 33 (App. Div. 1991)

Petitioner Bidermann Industries, Inc. ("BILI"), makes this application for an order pursuant to CPLR §7503 staying the arbitration demanded by respondents, Avmar N.V. ("Avmar"), Leit Moti, Inc. ("LMI") and Karl Lagerfeld ("Lagerfeld"), as to the issue of whether BILI's counsel, Coudert Brothers, should be disqualified from representing them in the arbitration proceedings pending between BILI and the respondents. The issue presented is one of apparent first impression: May the issue of attorney disqualification be determined in an arbitration, or is it a matter exclusively within the province and jurisdiction of the courts? . . .

Generally, New York favors arbitration. "Those who agree to arbitrate should be made to keep their solemn written promises." *Matter of Grayson-Robinson Stores, Inc.,* 8 N.Y.2d 133, 138 (1960). . . . [A]n arbitration agreement will be enforced by the courts provided it does not transgress a provision or statute or violate public policy. . . . "Public policy, whether derived from, and whether explicit or implicit in statue or decisional law, or in neither, may also restrict the freedom to arbitrate." *Susquehanna Valley Central School Dist. v. Susquehanna Valley Teacher's Ass'n,* 37 N.Y.2d 614, 616-617 (1975). It is for courts to decide whether the enforcement of an agreement to arbitrate would contravene an important public policy.

Where an important interest of public at large is likely to be affected by the resolution of a dispute, decision by arbitration is inappropriate, notwithstanding agreement by parties to the dispute. For example, even if child custody and visitation agreements provide for arbitration as the forum for dispute resolution, the courts have jurisdiction to consider the issues *de novo.* . . . Violations of state antitrust laws are not arbitrable [sic], . . . nor are violations of criminal law . . . and matters involving civil penalties. . . .

Similarly, the regulation of attorneys, and determinations as to whether clients should be deprived of counsel of their choice as a result of professional responsibilities and ethical obligations, implicate fundamental public interests and policies which should be reserved for the courts and should not be subject to arbitration. . . . Among the competing public interests which must be balanced against a client's right to counsel of her choice is "the courts' duty to protect the integrity of the judicial system and preserve the ethical standards of the legal profession." *Matter of Abrams,* 62 N.Y.2d 183, 196 (1984). The general policy favoring arbitration . . . must be balanced against the important policy favoring judicial determination of attorney disqualification. While jurisdiction to discipline an attorney for misconduct is vested exclusively in the Appellate Division, disqualification in a particular matter should be sought in the court in which the motion is pending, or, if no action is pending, at a Special Term of the Supreme Court. . . . The court has the inherent power to disqualify an attorney for a party upon a finding that it is improper for him to represent the litigant or to participate in a proceeding. . . . [Accordingly,] I hold that the issue of attorney disqualification is not appropriate for arbitration.

SWISS PENAL CODE
Articles 271 [excerpted above at p. 975] and 307

307. (1) Whoever testifies in [court] proceedings as a witness of fact, expert witness or translator and gives false testimony as to the facts, provides false expertise or false translation shall be sentenced to the penitentiary for up to five years or imprisoned. . . .

(3) If the false testimony relates to facts, which are irrelevant for the outcome of the decision [of the court], the punishment is up to 6 months imprisonment.

FRENCH PENAL CODE LAW NO. 80-538
[excerpted above at p. 975]

ABA MODEL RULES ON PROFESSIONAL CONDUCT
Rules 5.5(c) & 8.5(b) and Comments
(Reprinted with permission of the American Bar Association)

5.5(c). A lawyer admitted in another United States jurisdiction, and not disbarred or suspended from practice in any jurisdiction, may provide legal services on a temporary basis in this jurisdiction that . . . (1) are undertaken in association with a lawyer who is admitted to practice in this jurisdiction and who actively participates in the matter . . . or (3) are in or reasonably related to a pending or potential arbitration, mediation or other alternative dispute resolution proceeding in this or another jurisdiction, if the services arise out of or are reasonably related to the lawyer's practice in a jurisdiction in which the lawyer is admitted to practice and are not services for which the forum requires pro hac vice admission.

Comment to 5.5(c). Paragraphs (c)(3) and (c)(4) require that the services arise out of or be reasonably related to the lawyer's practice in a jurisdiction in which the lawyer is admitted. A variety of factors evidence such a relationship. The lawyer's client may have been previously represented by the lawyer, or may be resident in or have substantial contacts with the jurisdiction in which the lawyer is admitted. The matter, although involving other jurisdictions, may have a significant connection with that jurisdiction. In other cases, significant aspects of the lawyer's work might be conducted in that jurisdiction or a significant aspect of the matter may involve the law of that jurisdiction. The necessary relationship might arise when the client's activities or the legal issues involve multiple jurisdictions, such as when the officers of a multinational corporation survey potential business sites and seek the services of their lawyer in assessing the relative merits of each. In addition, the services may draw on the lawyer's recognized expertise developed through the regular practice of law on behalf of clients in matters involving a particular body of federal, nationally-uniform, foreign, or international law.

8.5(b). In any exercise of the disciplinary authority of this jurisdiction, the rules of professional conduct to be applied shall be as follows:

(1) for conduct in connection with a matter pending before a tribunal, the rules of the jurisdiction in which the tribunal sits, unless the rules of the tribunal provide otherwise; and

(2) for any other conduct, the rules of the jurisdiction in which the lawyer's conduct occurred, or, if the predominant effect of the conduct is in a different jurisdiction, the rules of that jurisdiction shall be applied to the conduct. A lawyer shall not be subject to discipline if the lawyer's conduct conforms to the rules of a jurisdiction in which the lawyer reasonably believes the predominant effect of the lawyer's conduct will occur.

Comments to 8.5(b). The choice of law provision applies to lawyers engaged in transnational practice, unless international law, treaties or other agreements between competent regulatory authorities in the affected jurisdictions provide otherwise.

Notes on Williamson, Lawler, Bidermann, *and Legislative Materials*

1. *Prohibitions on the unauthorized practice of law.* Consider Mich. Comp. Laws §600.916, which is very similar to statutes in many U.S. jurisdictions and broadly similar to regulations in foreign jurisdictions. What impact does it have on a non-U.S. practitioner appearing in a Michigan proceeding? What is the logic of such prohibitions? Consider the following rationale: "In national legal systems, the goals of ethical regulation are to guide, punish, and deter attorney conduct in an effort to protect client and third parties, and to ensure the proper functioning of the state adjudicatory apparatus." Rogers, *Context and Institutional Structure in Attorney Regulation: Constructing an Enforcement Regime for International Arbitration*, 39 Stan. J. Int'l L. 1, 20 (2003).

If foreigners can provide music, software, cars, or jet aircraft in the United States, why not legal services? If Volkswagen or Société Generale wanted to be represented by their usual European counsel in a U.S. litigation, what would be wrong with that? If Microsoft wanted its U.S. law firm to represent it in a European legal proceeding, why could this not happen? Is it a matter of competence? Or something else?

U.S. courts generally require attorneys appearing before them to be members of the relevant bar. Often, U.S. counsel will secure admission *pro hac vice*, that is admission limited for a particular matter following a formal application to the court. In these situations, counsel must certify that he will observe the rules of the court and, in most cases, appear alongside local counsel who is admitted to the local bar. If this is done, admission is routinely granted. *See, e.g.*, Connecticut Rules of the Superior Court, Regulating Admission to the Bar, §2-16. What purposes does this requirement serve? Is it legitimate?

2. *Representation in international arbitration and the unauthorized practice of law.* Putting aside litigation conducted in national courts, how do unauthorized practice regulations apply to lawyers acting as counsel in international arbitrations? Despite the seemingly broad sweep of such provisions, national courts divide over whether they restrict representation before international arbitral tribunals (sometimes the rules governing appearances in domestic tribunals differ from those governing appearances before international ones).

Both *Williamson* and *Lawler* hold that representation by an attorney in an international arbitration does not constitute the unauthorized practice of law. Other tribunals, both in the United States and abroad, have reached similar conclusions. *See, e.g.*, *Colmar Ltd. v. Fremantlemedia North America, Inc.*, 801 N.E.2d 1017 (Ill. App. 2003); *Am. Auto. Ass'n v. Merrick*, 117 F.2d 23 (D.C. Cir. 1940); New Jersey Supreme Court Committee on Unauthorized Practice, Op. 28 (1994), *available at* 1994 WL 719208.

Why exactly is this so? What is the practice of law? Doesn't it consist of matters like preparing witnesses, drafting pleadings, and examining witnesses? Doesn't it also consist of matters like offering one's opinion on the legal consequences of certain conduct, as occurred in *Williamson*? If so, why does it make a difference that these acts occur in the context of an arbitration (as opposed to ordinary litigation)?

Other courts have refused to graft an "arbitration exception" onto unauthorized practice of law statutes. In one oft-cited case, *Birbrower, Montalbano, Condon & Frank v. Superior Court*, 949 P.2d 1 (Cal. 1998), the California Supreme Court refused to hold that its unauthorized practice of law statute contained a domestic arbitration exception (the statute did contain a narrow international arbitration exception but did not contain a similar exception for domestic arbitration):

> We decline . . . to craft an arbitration exception to [California's] prohibition of the unlicensed practice of law in this state. Any exception for arbitration is best left to the Legislature, which has the authority to determine qualifications for admission to the State Bar and to decide what constitutes the practice of law. Even though the Legislature has spoken with respect to international arbitration and conciliation, it has not enacted a similar rule for private arbitration proceedings. Of course, private arbitration and other alternative dispute resolution practices are important aspects of our justice system. [California's law], however,

articulates a strong public policy favoring the practice of law in California by licensed State Bar members. In the face of the Legislature's silence, we will not create an arbitration exception under the facts presented. 949 P.2d at 9.

This provoked a spirited dissent:

> Representing another in an arbitration proceeding does not invariably present difficult or doubtful legal questions that require a trained legal mind for their resolution. Under California law, arbitrators are "not ordinarily constrained to decide according to the rule of law. . . ." Thus, arbitrators, "unless specifically required to act in conformity with rules of law, may base their decision upon broad principles of justice and equity, and in doing so may expressly or impliedly reject a claim that a party might successfully have asserted in a judicial action." . . . For this reason, "the existence of an error of law apparent on the face of the [arbitration] award that causes substantial injustice does not provide grounds for judicial review." Moreover, an arbitrator in California can award any remedy "arguably based" on "the contract's general subject matter, framework or intent." This means that "an arbitrator in a commercial contract dispute may award an essentially unlimited range of remedies, whether or not a court could award them if it decided the same dispute, so long as it can be said that the relief draws its 'essence' from the contract and not some other source." To summarize . . . arbitration proceedings are not governed or constrained by the rule of law; therefore, representation of another in an arbitration proceeding, including the activities necessary to prepare for the arbitration hearing, does not necessarily require a trained legal mind. *Id.* at 17 (Kennard, J., dissenting).

Following *Birbrower*, the California Legislature abrogated its holding by statute. Why do you suppose the Legislature was so concerned about ensuring that foreign lawyers could appear in arbitrations conducted within the state? Wouldn't one expect a state to be more concerned about protecting its citizens from lawyers, not admitted to the state bar, practicing within its borders (or, more cynically, protecting local lawyers from outside competition) through robust enforcement of its unauthorized practice of law statute?

Putting aside U.S. decisions, a few foreign jurisdictions have adopted legislation (or interpreted existing law) as requiring that the representatives in an international arbitration conducted on national territory be admitted to the practice of local law. *See Builders Federal (Hong Kong) Ltd. v. Turner (East Asia) Pte. Ltd.*, March 30, 1988 (Singapore Legal Profession Act held to preclude representation by New York lawyers in Singapore arbitration; Act subsequently amended to permit joint and, later, sole representation); Ragan, *Arbitration in Japan: Caveat Foreign Drafter and Other Lessons*, 7 Arb. Int'l 93 (1991); Eastman, *Note,* 94 Am. J. Int'l 400 (2000).

What is the rationale for national law requirements that parties be represented in international arbitrations by locally qualified lawyers? Is it naked protectionism or unreconstructed parochialism? Consider one observer's comment that it is important "not only for the international arbitration community, but for the much larger international business community, for international arbitration not to become clogged by the vested interests of a local bar. Only if it fends off or limits the spread of localism will arbitration live up to its promise of assistance and support to the continuing growth of international trade, finance, and investment." Lowenfeld, *Singapore and the Local Bar: Aberration or Ill Omen,* J. Int'l Arb. 71 (1988).

An arbitral award made in a particular nation becomes an expression of that state's sovereignty. The award is recognized under the New York Convention as having been made in that state, is subject to actions to annul in that state (and, generally, not elsewhere), is entitled to recognition in other nations because it was made in that state (depending on membership in the New York Convention and other international treaties), and so forth. Does not a state therefore have a substantial interest in ensuring that the proceedings that produce an award of such consequence are regular, transparent, and fair? Is not the imposition of strict, policeable, ethical requirements, such as through the requirement of admission to the local bar, a good way to accomplish this? Are there less restrictive alternatives?

Who would enforce ethical restrictions on foreign lawyers appearing in local arbitration? The arbitral tribunal? The local bar association or courts? The foreign lawyers' bar association or home courts? Does not a flat requirement of local admission solve all these problems? At what cost?

All leading institutional arbitration rules guarantee parties the right to select their legal representatives in arbitral proceedings. *E.g.*, UNCITRAL Arbitration Rules, Art. 4 ("The parties may be represented or assisted by persons of their choice"); ICC Arbitration Rules, Art. 21(4) (same). These provisions are incorporated into the parties' arbitration agreement when parties agree to arbitrate pursuant to specified institutional rules. What effect, if any, does this have on legislation concerning the unauthorized practice of law? Consider Article II of the New York Convention.

3. *Regulations requiring joint representation with local counsel in international arbitrations.* Consider the result in *Lawler*. What exactly does the Barbados court hold? Is it appropriate for arbitral tribunals to decide such "ethical" issues? Compare the reasoning in *Bidermann*.

What are the arguments in favor of requiring that counsel in arbitral proceedings conducted in a particular state be locally qualified? What damage is done by requiring that a party at least retain co-counsel that is locally qualified if it participates in local proceedings? Suppose that you were in-house counsel for a U.S. company with a dispute, very possibly subject to Singapore substantive law, which was being arbitrated in Singapore. Putting aside what Singapore law compels, would you be content with your usual outside U.S. counsel to run the case alone? Why or why not? What would a Singapore lawyer be able to offer that the New York lawyers could not?

4. *Forum selection and arbitrability questions relating to ethics issues in international arbitration.* Putting aside what substantive standards apply to ethical obligations, what forum should apply these standards? Should the arbitral tribunal do so? Does an arbitral tribunal have the authority to decide issues of professional responsibility?

Suppose that a French partner in a New York law firm, who is based in the firm's London office, represents a French company in an arbitration seated in Stockholm under ICC Rules against a Danish company. Suppose further that the Danish company was a former client of the French lawyer and that it objects to his representation of an adverse party in the Stockholm arbitration. If the lawyer does not withdraw, who should decide whether the objection is merited? The French bar? The New York bar (responsible for regulating the French lawyer's New York partners)? The English Solicitors Regulation Authority (responsible for regulating foreign lawyers practicing in England and Wales)? The Stockholm bar or courts (since Stockholm is the arbitral seat)? New York or Danish courts (in an action brought by the Danish company on contractual or fiduciary duty theories)?

Should a local court or bar association in the place where a lawyer is qualified have competence to decide issues relating to his or her conduct in an international arbitration sited elsewhere? What problems would arise from such a conclusion? Could different legal representatives, on opposing sides of the same international arbitration, be subject to differing ethical rules? Is that a problem? Could one legal representative be subject to multiple ethical regimes?

Consider the result and analysis in *Bidermann*. Is the court's analysis of the arbitrability of ethical issues wise? Why shouldn't conflicts issues be arbitrable? Couldn't arbitral tribunals interpret and apply national ethical rules (just as they interpret and apply national substantive law)? What is there about ethical issues that arguably makes them non-arbitrable?

As a matter of interpretation, would most arbitration agreements extend to issues of conflicts of interest? Suppose that the ICC Rules provided that the ICC would decide ethical issues raised during an arbitration with respect to the parties' legal representatives. Would this be a good idea? Would it be enforceable?

5. *Service as international arbitrator and unauthorized practice of law.* Do individuals who serve as international arbitrators engage in the unauthorized practice of law when they render a decision within a jurisdiction? What about when they render a decision under a particular jurisdiction's substantive law? Does it matter that, in some cases, an arbitrator might not be a lawyer?

6. *Regulations affecting counsel, witnesses, and arbitrators in international arbitral proceedings.* Consider Article 307 of the Swiss Penal Code (which is made applicable in international arbitrations sited in Switzerland by Article 309 of the Code). Many jurisdictions have similar provisions. It is common practice in Switzerland for arbitrators to specifically advise witnesses (and counsel) of these provisions. One authority suggests the following: "Mr. A., you are to testify before this Arbitral Tribunal as a witness. I have to tell you what I tell all witnesses: You must tell the truth, the whole truth and nothing but the truth and, should you not tell the truth — intentionally not tell the truth — this would be punishable under Swiss law by imprisonment up to five years or a fine or both." Schneider, *Actes de la Procédure Arbitrale*, 1993 ASA Bull. 591.

Does Article 307 apply to counsel's statements in argument? What if counsel is making representations about facts that are known to him or her? What should an arbitrator do if he or she becomes aware that a witness or counsel has lied? What must an arbitrator do?

Note that different jurisdictions adopt significantly different approaches to the taking of evidence. *Compare* Swedish Arbitration Act §25 (1999) (prohibiting arbitrators from administering oaths) *with* Malaysian Arbitration Act of 1952 §13(3) (authorizing arbitrator to place witnesses under oath unless the arbitration agreement specifies otherwise).

7. *Regulations affecting serving process, taking of evidence, witness preparation, and similar activities in connection with litigation.* Consider Article 271 of the Swiss Penal Code and Articles 1A and 2 of the French Penal Code Law 80-538. Other civil law countries have other restrictions on the activities of foreign counsel. For example, as discussed above, Germany and other countries forbid the conduct of depositions (including voluntary depositions) on local territory (absent prior approval from competent authorities). *See supra* pp. 972-973.

Foreign counsel who fail to heed these restrictions risk serious sanctions. In one case, Swiss authorities arrested and jailed three Dutch attorneys for obtaining signed interrogatory answers from a Dutch citizen in Switzerland. *See* Jones, *International Judicial Assistance: Procedural Chaos and a Program for Reform*, 62 Yale L.J. 515, 520 (1953). More recently, a U.S. attorney was subject to a civil damages action for malicious trespass when he served a subpoena on a residence in the Bahamas. *See generally* U.S. Department of State, *Service of Legal Documents Abroad*, *available at* http://travel.state.gov/law/info/judicial/judicial_680.html ("It may be prudent to consult local foreign counsel early in the process on this point. American process servers and other agents may not be authorized by the laws of the foreign country to effect service abroad, and such action could result in their arrest and/or deportation."); U.S. Department of Justice Instructions for

Serving Foreign Judicial Documents in the U.S. and Processing Requests for Serving American Judicial Documents Abroad, *reprinted in* 16 Int'l Legal Mat. 1331, 1337 (1977).

How far do these foreign restrictions extend? Suppose that a U.S. lawyer wishes to conduct a formal interview of a witness? Have an informal discussion to consider whether further discussions are appropriate? Collect documents from his client's files for possible use in U.S. litigation? As a practical matter, U.S. counsel must consult with local attorneys (or the U.S. State Department) before proceeding with significant evidence-gathering activities abroad.

Other regulations may also affect evidence-gathering. Many European states have stringent data protection and privacy regulations. This may affect disclosure of particular types of business records (*e.g.*, personnel files, customer information) or steps to obtain information from corporate employees (*e.g.*, email communications). Again, these provisions are enforceable by criminal sanctions and require careful attention from foreign counsel.

8. *Professional responsibility codes and international practice.* The bar associations of every U.S. state (and almost every developed country) have adopted codes of conduct or professional responsibility governing the activities of lawyers admitted to that bar. *See, e.g.,* American Bar Association, Model Rules of Professional Conduct (2004); Council of Bars and Law Societies of the European Union, Code of Conduct for Lawyers in the European Union (2002). *See generally* Toulmin, *A Worldwide Common Code of Professional Ethics?*, 15 Fordham Int'l L. Rev. 673 (1992). These rules generally regulate, among other things: (a) quality of representation ("zealous" representation of client interests; definition of malpractice); (b) conflicts of interest; (c) compensation (disclosure, contingent fee arrangements, rates); (d) confidentiality and privilege; (e) relations with other counsel and courts; (f) publicity and advertising. Inevitably, different jurisdictions take very different approaches to particular issues, including matters such as conflicts of interest, permissibility of particular fee arrangements, contacting and "preparing" witnesses, and privilege. *See* Vagts, *Professional Responsibility in Transborder Practice: Conflict and Resolution*, 13 Geo. J. Legal Ethics 677, 683, 688 (2000).

It is essential for U.S. (and other) counsel involved in foreign litigations or international arbitrations to be familiar with the ethical requirements and expectations of foreign or international tribunals, adversaries and co-counsel. Failure to do so may lead to embarrassment, tainting of evidence, or worse. The following topics are areas of particular sensitivity.

(a) Witness interviews and preparation. It is elementary in U.S. litigation that lawyers will carefully interview potential witnesses and will subsequently prepare them for testimony. Failure to do so could well constitute malpractice and a violation of an attorney's obligation to zealously represent his or her client. D.C. Bar. Op. 79 (1979), *reprinted in* D.C. Bar, Code of Professional Responsibility and Opinions of the D.C. Bar Legal Ethics Comm. 138, 139 (1991); Rogers, *Fit and Function in Legal Ethics: Developing a Code of Conduct for International Arbitration*, 23 Mich. J. Int'l L. 341, 359-362 (2002). In contrast, in some civil law jurisdictions it is unethical or even potentially criminal to attempt to affect a witness's testimony. Damaska, *Presentation of Evidence and Fact-finding Precision*, 123 U. Pa. L. Rev. 1083, 1088-1089 (1975).

(b) Contingent fees. In many jurisdictions outside the United States, contingent fee arrangements are either flatly prohibited or stringently regulated (*e.g.*, to limit the size of any premium or the circumstances in which such arrangements may be used). *See* Vagts, 13 Geo. J. Legal Ethics, 677, 683. In contrast, contingent fee arrangements are not only permitted in most U.S. litigation but are considered an almost essential aspect of a fair

procedure (designed to ensure adequate representation for parties with limited resources). *Id.*

The *Bhopal* case, discussed *supra* pp. 429-431, provides a good example of the pitfalls for counsel handling an international matter. Following the Bhopal disaster, U.S. plaintiffs' attorneys traveled to India and (following relatively common U.S. practice) signed contingent fee agreements with hundreds (or more) potential Indian plaintiffs. As noted above, the U.S. courts eventually dismissed the case on *forum non conveniens* grounds and the defendants settled subsequent Indian litigation for some $470 million. The U.S. plaintiffs' attorneys then filed suit in the United States, seeking an award of fees based on their contingent fee agreements. Not only did the U.S. court reject their claims, but some attorneys were censured by bar authorities in the United States for their *en masse* solicitation of clients in India. *See Chesley v. Union Carbide Corp.*, 927 F.2d 60 (2d Cir. 1991); Mullenix, *Problems in Complex Litigation*, 10 Review of Litigation 213, 220 & n.35 (1991).

(c) Privilege and communications with opposing counsel. The privileged character of attorney-client communications is central to the U.S. legal system. Other jurisdictions also have concepts of privilege, but take very different approaches to the types of communications (and actors) entitled to privilege, the scope of privilege, and the possibility of waiver. *See* Rogers, 23 Mich. J. Int'l L. at 392 n.245. In some jurisdictions, privileges will be substantially narrower than in the United States (*e.g.,* in-house counsel may not enjoy privilege); in other cases, foreign privilege may be broader (*e.g.,* communications between opposing counsel may be inadmissible and confidential as between counsel). *Id.* at 371-372. Again, these differences can lead to significant disputes in multi-jurisdictional disputes. Moreover, as noted above, these issues can give rise to significant confusion over the applicable law, *supra* pp. 1022-1023, 1075-1076.

(d) Settlement communications. In the United States, settlement communications are generally inadmissible (under Federal Rule of Evidence Rule 408 and state counterparts). *See* Fed. R. Evid. 408; N.Y. R. Evid. §4547. Other jurisdictions may also treat settlement communications as confidential or inadmissible, but in ways that differ from the U.S. model. Counsel involved in international disputes, or dealings with foreign counsel, need to be aware of such differences during any settlement discussions.

These sorts of issues can arise when attorneys in some Continental European jurisdictions send correspondence marked "confidential" to other attorneys (including U.S. attorneys). In such jurisdictions (*e.g.,* Italy), that label is presumed to mean that the receiving attorney cannot disclose the document to the adjudicating tribunal and can require that confidentiality be maintained as against the receiving attorney's client. At the same time, such correspondence could very readily contain information that a U.S. attorney would be ethically obliged to convey to a client (for example, if it touches on issues of settlement) or to a tribunal (for example, if it contains concessions).

9. *Professional responsibility codes and international arbitration.* Many professional conduct rules either expressly or impliedly regulate attorney activity in international arbitration proceedings. *See, e.g.,* Council of Bars and Law Societies of the European Union, Code of Conduct for Lawyers in the European Union §4.5 ("The rules governing a lawyer's relations with the courts apply also to his relations with arbitrators. . . ."); N.Y. Judiciary Law (Appendix: Code of Professional Responsibility §1200.1(f)). Where this is the case, counsel remains accountable to his local bar association for his conduct during the arbitration and can be subject to disciplinary sanctions for violating the applicable rules of professional conduct. For example, a Minnesota attorney was suspended from the practice of law for six months after presenting misleading documentation in support of a client's arbitration proceeding in violation of Minnesota Rules of Professional Conduct 3.3(a)(4). *See In re Disciplinary Action Against Zotaley*, 546 N.W.2d 16, 20 (Minn. 1996). On the other hand, in some states, nonlawyers are permitted to conduct arbitration proceedings (including international arbitration proceedings). Brand, *Professional Responsibility in a Transnational Transactions Practice*, 17 J. L. & Com. 301, 334-335 (1998).

State rules of professional conduct also regulate the activities of lawyers serving in the capacity as arbitrators. In addition to the generally applicable rules of professional conduct, some states have enacted specific ethical rules for domestic and international arbitrators. *See, e.g.,* North Carolina Bar Association Dispute Resolution Section & Its Committee on Ethics and Professionalism, North Carolina Canons of Ethics for Arbitrators (1998); Cal. R. Ct., App. Div. VI, Ethics Standards for Neutral Arbitrators in Contractual Arbitration (rev. 2003).

10. *Choice-of-law issues affecting professional responsibility.* The multiplicity of statutes and professional rules that might govern the duties of an international litigator gives rise to complex choice-of-law issues. What conflicts rules determine the applicable professional responsibility norms in international cases? *Compare* ABA Commission on Multijurisdictional Practice, Model Rules of Professional Conduct Rule 8.5 (providing that in a matter before a tribunal, the tribunal's rules presumptively apply and that in other matters the rules of the jurisdiction where the alleged misconduct occurred presumptively apply) *with* EC Directive 98-5 Art. 6 (Feb. 16, 1998) (where lawyers from one Member State are practicing in another Member State, they are subject to the host state's rules of professional conduct for activities occurring there irrespective of the obligations of their home state).

Is it possible for lawyers from different jurisdictions to be subject to different ethical restraints in the same case? *See* ABA Commission on Multijurisdictional Practice, Model Rules of Professional Conduct, Rule 8.5, Comment 7 ("The choice of law provision applies to lawyers engaged in transnational practice, unless international law, treaties or other agreements between competent regulatory authorities in the affected jurisdictions provide otherwise."). If so, wouldn't that favor the attorney from the jurisdiction with more liberal rules regarding attorney activity? For discussions of the relationship between choice-of-law principles and professional responsibility, *see* Rogers, *Lawyers Without Borders*, 30 U. Penn. Int'l L. Rev. 1035 (2009); Moulton, *Federalism and Choice of Law in the Regulation of Legal Ethics*, 82 Minn. L. Rev. 73, 103 (1997); Vagts, 13 Geo. J. Legal Ethics 677.

11. *Attorney malpractice and international arbitration.* In addition to unauthorized practice of law statutes and ethical rules, malpractice lawsuits provide another, albeit indirect, method of regulating attorney conduct during an arbitration. In *Williamson*, the construction company also sued Williamson P.A. for malpractice based on the firm's advice during the arbitration. Do you think malpractice suits serve as a beneficial means of regulating attorney misconduct during the arbitration? Aren't they the ultimate measure of whether the attorney is adequately safeguarding the client's interests?

What about lawsuits against arbitrators? If malpractice suits are one way of deterring misconduct by lawyers, couldn't they also deter misconduct by arbitrators? What if the arbitrator failed to observe his duty of independence and impartiality? What if he failed to heed the arbitral rules chosen by the party? Generally, most nations' laws and most institutional rules provide the arbitrator with immunity from civil liability. *See generally* Rutledge, *Toward a Contractual Approach for Arbitral Immunity*, 39 Ga. L. Rev. 151 (2004). Is this wise policy? Are there differences between arbitrators and counsel that justify immunity in one case but not the other?

12. *Foreign legal consultants.* Countries frequently regulate the extent to which foreign lawyers may establish practices within their territory. For example, can an attorney admitted in one country (*e.g.,* Mexico) maintain an office in a state (*e.g.,* New York) from which he dispenses advice about exclusively Mexican but not New York law? *Compare El Gemayel v. Seaman*, 533 N.E.2d 545 (N.Y. 1988) (holding that Lebanese attorney with office in Washington did not violate unauthorized practice of law statute when dispensing advice about Lebanese law to New York resident), *with In re New York County Lawyers' Ass'n v. Roel*, 144 N.E.2d 24 (N.Y. 1957) (holding that Mexican attorney violated unauthorized practice of law statute when advising public on matters of Mexican law).

Many U.S. jurisdictions permit foreign lawyers to be licensed as foreign legal consultants. *See, e.g.,* New Jersey Foreign Legal Consultant Rules, Rule 1:21-9. As a foreign legal consultant a foreign attorney may dispense advice on legal matters about jurisdictions where he is admitted. He may not, however, engage in all of the activities of an attorney admitted in the local bar or provide consultation on local law. If a foreign attorney advises clients in a U.S. jurisdiction without the foreign legal consultant status, he may be in violation of prohibitions against the unauthorized practice of law. Furthermore, if he associates with local counsel in his informal practice, the local counsel may also be at risk of engaging in the unauthorized practice of law. *See In the Matter of Albert F. Dalena*, 157 N.J. 242 (1999). Currently, 24 jurisdictions in the United States have adopted some form of the foreign legal consultant designation. *See* Silver, *Regulatory Mismatch in the International Market for Legal Services*, 23 Nw. J. Int'l L. & Bus. 487, 510 (2003).

Just as the United States restricts the activities of foreign lawyers, so too do foreign countries restrict (often more severely) the activities of attorneys not admitted to the local bar. For example, some countries only allow citizens to become lawyers whereas others permit (at least theoretically) foreign attorneys to become members of the bar. *Compare, e.g.,* Figueres & Ros, *Notes on the New Chilean Law on International Arbitration*, 20-27 Mealey's Int'l Arb. Rep. 21 (2005) (describing Chile's strict nationality requirement) *with* Kim, *Legal Market Liberalization in South Korea: Preparations for Change*, 15 Pac. Rim. L. & Pol'y J. 199, 205-206 (2006) (describing Korean rules that technically allow admission of foreigners but, in practice, have not led to such admissions). Why do you suppose some foreign countries restrict bar admission to their citizens? Do those reasons counsel in favor of a similar requirement in the United States? *See In re Griffiths*, 413 U.S. 717, 730-731 (1973) (Burger, C.J., dissenting) (advocating the inclusion of attorneys in the occupations subject to citizenship requirements).

Index